Bible Society's Chain Reference Bible

Bible Society's

Chain Reference Bible

Good News Edition

The Bible Societies

Bible Society
Stonehill Green, Westlea, SWINDON SN5 7DG, England

British usage edition of Good News Bible
first published by the Bible Societies/Collins 1976

BFBS/1985/25M

Text set by computer by C R Barber and Partners, Wrotham, Kent

Printed in Great Britain at The University Press, Cambridge

ISBNs for Chain Reference Bible (Good News Edition)

Blue hardback	TEVO63CR BU	0 564 05413 5
Red hardback	TEVO63CR RD	0 564 05393 7
Black leather	TEV067CR BK	0 564 05433 X
Blue leather	TEV067CR BU	0 564 05403 8
Brown leather	TEV067CR BR	0 564 05423 2

The *United Bible Societies* is a worldwide fellowship of National Bible Societies working in more than 150 countries. Their aim is to reach every person with the Bible or some part of it in a language he can understand and at a price he can afford. Between them they distribute more than 300 million Scriptures every year. You are invited to share in this work by your prayers and gifts. The Bible Society in your country will be very happy to provide details of its activity.

Foreword to the Good News Bible

The *Good News Bible* (also called *Today's English Version*) is a modern translation which seeks to state clearly and accurately the meaning of the original texts in words and forms that are widely accepted by people who use English as a means of communication. This translation does not follow the traditional vocabulary and style found in the historic English Bible versions. Instead it attempts to present the biblical content and message in standard, everyday, natural English.

The aim of this Bible is to give today's readers maximum understanding of the content of the original texts. The Preface explains the nature of special aids for readers which are included in the volume. It also sets out the basic principles which the translators followed in their work.

The *Good News Bible* has been translated and published by the United Bible Societies for use throughout the world. The Bible Societies trust that people everywhere will not only find increased understanding through the reading and study of this translation, but will also find a saving hope through faith in God who made possible this message of Good News for all people.

Contents

THE BOOKS OF THE NEW TESTAMENT

The above abbreviations are used for references to books of the Bible. In addition OT = Old Testament, NT = New Testament.

THE BOOKS OF THE OLD AND NEW TESTAMENTS ALPHABETICALLY ARRANGED

Preface to the Good News Bible

In September 1966 the American Bible Society published *The New Testament in Today's English Version*, a translation intended for people everywhere for whom English is either their mother tongue or a language they learn. Shortly afterwards the United Bible Societies requested the American Bible Society to undertake on its behalf a translation of the Old Testament following the same principles. Accordingly the American Bible Society appointed a group of translators to prepare the translation. In 1971 this group added a British consultant representing the British and Foreign Bible Society and the National Bible Society of Scotland. The translation of the Old Testament now appears together with the fourth edition of the New Testament.

The basic text for the Old Testament is the Masoretic Text printed in *Biblia Hebraica* (3rd edition, 1937), edited by Rudolph Kittel. In some instances the words of the printed consonantal text have been divided differently or have been read with a different set of vowels; at times a variant reading (*qere*) in the margin of the Hebrew text has been followed instead of the reading in the text (*kethiv*); and in other instances a variant reading supported by one or more Hebrew manuscripts has been adopted. Where no Hebrew source yields a satisfactory meaning in the context, the translation has either followed one or more of the ancient versions (*e.g.* Greek, Syriac, Latin) or has adopted a reconstructed text (technically referred to as a conjectural emendation) based on scholarly agreement; such departures from the Hebrew are indicated in footnotes.

The basic text for the New Testament is *The Greek New Testament* published by the United Bible Societies (3rd edition, 1976), but in a few instances the translation is based on a variant reading supported by one or more Greek manuscripts.

Drafts of the translation in its early stages were sent for comments and suggestions to a Review Panel consisting of prominent theologians and biblical scholars appointed by the American Bible Society Board of Managers in its capacity as trustee for this text. In addition, drafts were sent to major English-speaking Bible Societies. Final approval of the text on behalf of the United Bible Societies was given by the American Bible Society's Board of Managers upon the recommendation of its Translations Department Committee.

The primary concern of the translators has been to provide a faithful translation of the meaning of the Hebrew, Aramaic, and Greek texts. Their first task was to understand correctly the meaning of the original. At times the original meaning cannot be precisely known, not only because the meaning of some words and phrases cannot be determined with a great degree of assurance but also because the underlying cultural and historical context is sometimes beyond recovery. All aids available were used in this task, including the ancient versions and the modern translations in English and other languages. After ascertaining as accurately as possible the meaning of the original, the translators' next task was to express that meaning in a manner and form easily understood by the readers. Since this translation is intended for all who use English as a means of communication, the translators have tried to avoid words and forms not in current or widespread use; but no artificial limit has been set to the range of the vocabulary employed. Every effort has been made to use language that is natural, clear, simple, and unambiguous. Consequently there has been no attempt to reproduce in English the parts of speech, sentence-structure, word-order, and grammatical devices of the original languages. Faithfulness in translation also includes a faithful representation of the cultural and historical features of the original, without any attempt to modernize the text. Certain features, however, such as the hours of the day and the measures of weight, capacity, distance, and area, are given their modern equivalents, since the information contained in those terms is of greater importance to the reader than the biblical form of those terms. The metric system of weights and measures has been adopted in the British edition.

In cases where a person or place is called by two or more different names in the original, this translation has normally used only the more familiar name in all places; *e.g.*, King Jehoiachin of Judah (Jeremiah 52.31), also called Jeconiah (Jeremiah 24.1) and Coniah (Jeremiah 37.1). Where a proper name is spelt in two or more different ways in the original text, this translation has used only one spelling; *e.g.*, Nebuchadnezzar, also spelt Nebuchadrezzar (compare Jeremiah 29.3 and 29.21), and Priscilla, also spelt Prisca (compare Acts 18.26 and Romans 16.3).

In view of the differences in vocabulary and form which exist between the American and the British use of the English language, this British edition is being published, incorporating such changes as are in keeping with British usage. Final approval of this text was given by the General Committee of the British and Foreign Bible Society.

Following an ancient tradition, begun by the first translation of the Hebrew Scriptures (the Septuagint) and followed by the vast majority of English translations, the distinctive Hebrew name for God (usually transliterated *Jehovah* or *Yahweh*) is in this translation represented by "The LORD". When the Hebrew word *Adonai*, normally translated "Lord", is followed by *Yahweh*, the combination is rendered by the phrase "Sovereign LORD".

In order to make the text easier to understand, various kinds of readers' helps are supplied. The text itself has been divided into sections, and headings are provided which indicate clearly the contents of the section. Where there are parallel accounts elsewhere in the Bible, a reference to such a passage appears in brackets below the heading. There are, in addition, several kinds of notes which appear at the bottom of the page. (1) *Cultural or Historical Notes.* These provide information required to enable the reader to understand the meaning of the text in terms of its original setting (*e.g.* the explanation of *Rahab* in Psalm 89.10; the explanation of *Day of Atonement* in Acts 27.9). (2) *Textual Notes.* In the Old Testament these indicate primarily those places where the translators were compelled for a variety of reasons to base the translation on some text other than the Hebrew. Where one or more of the ancient versions were followed, the note indicates this by *One ancient translation* (*e.g.* Genesis 1.26) or *Some ancient translations* (*e.g.* Genesis 4.8); where a conjectural emendation was adopted, the note reads *Probable text* (*e.g.* Genesis 10.14). In the New Testament there are textual notes indicating some of the places where there are significant differences among the Greek manuscripts. These differences may consist of additions to the text (*e.g.* Matthew 21.43), deletions (*e.g.* Matthew 24.36), or substitutions (*e.g.* Mark 1.41). (3) *Alternative Renderings.* In many places the precise meaning of the original text is in dispute, and there are two or more different ways in which the text may be understood. In some of the more important of such instances an alternative rendering is given (*e.g.* Genesis 2.9; Matthew 6.11). (4) *References to Other Passages.* In addition to the notes there are references, by book, chapter, and verse, to other places in the Bible where identical or similar matters or ideas are dealt with.

The numbering of chapters and verses in this translation follows the traditional system of major English translations of the Bible. In some instances, however, where the order of thought or events in two or more verses is more clearly represented by a rearrangement of the material, two or more verse numbers are joined (*e.g.* Exodus 2.15–16; Acts 1.21–22).

When the writers of the New Testament quoted from the Old Testament, they generally quoted or paraphrased the ancient Greek translation known as the Septuagint Version (LXX). This translation was made some two hundred years before the time of Christ, and in a number of instances it differs significantly in meaning from the Masoretic Hebrew text on which the Today's English Version Old Testament is based. When the same LXX quotation occurs several times in the New Testament, the different contexts may suggest differences in meaning or emphasis, so the TEV wording of the translation varies to reflect this. This Bible notes a Septuagint quotation by the inclusion of "LXX" with the reference at the foot of the page. The chapter and verse numbers given are those of the English Bible rather than of the Septuagint itself.

There are several appendices at the end of the volume. A *Word List* identifies many objects or cultural features whose meaning may not be known to all readers. The *Maps* are designed to help the reader to visualize the geographical setting of countries and localities mentioned in the Bible. A *History Chart* outlines the major events recorded in the Bible, giving approximate dates and showing the chronological relationship between the various books. Specially prepared *Topical Keywords*, *Word Index*, *Name Index*, and *Theme Index* list comprehensive references to help the reader make a thorough study of words, people or themes in the Bible. Alongside the Bible text, the *Chain References* follow the occurrences of some of the most significant words through the whole Bible. *Well-known Passages of the Bible*, *Jesus' Teaching about ...*, and *Prayers of the Bible*, provide useful lists for easy reference and complete the wide range of study aids in this edition of the Good News Bible.

No one knows better than the translators how difficult has been their task. But they have performed it gladly, conscious always of the presence of the Holy Spirit and of the tremendous debt which they owe to the dedication and scholarship of those who have preceded them. The Bible is not simply great literature to be admired and revered; it is Good News for all people everywhere—a message both to be understood and to be applied in daily life. It is with the prayer that the Lord of the Scriptures will be pleased to use this translation for his sovereign purpose that the United Bible Societies publish the *Good News Bible* (*Today's English Version*). And to Christ be the glory for ever and ever!

Preface to the Chain Reference Bible

Bible Society's Chain Reference Bible has been developed using the same original material from which the *Concordance to the Good News Bible* was produced. Up-to-date computer technology made possible both the original work and this adaptation.

In line with Bible Society's aim of giving more people meaningful access to the Scriptures, the unique computer programs that have been developed can be used to produce a variety of reference aids to any translation in any language.

The editors began with a complete list of all the book, chapter and verse references for every word in the *Good News Bible*. They then excluded all the words which would have no significant meaning in a chain of references (e.g. "and", "come", "one"). Further editing on computer was needed to distinguish words with more than one meaning, such as the noun "bark" and the verb "bark", so that these could be listed separately in the *Chain References* and *Indexes*.

The aim has been to make the complete reference system as comprehensive as possible, covering all significant words and including in the *Chain References* as many of the most useful words as would fit on the page. The best typesize and format for the Bible text were chosen, allowing two margins for references on the page. The editors then calculated the number of references which would fit alongside the chapter with the greatest number of words suitable for referencing. This determined the total number of references which it would be possible to include.

Almost all words with ten or less occurrences in the whole Bible were excluded because chains based on them were too small and too spread out throughout the Bible to be meaningful. Words of very frequent occurrence were also excluded because the resulting chains would have been too long to be manageable and, in some cases, merely referred readers to every succeeding chapter. Many of these very frequent or very infrequent words were included instead in the *Word Index*.

The words which were still eligible for inclusion in the *Chain References* were divided into groups according to their considered importance for study, so that if words had to be lost on grounds of space, the most significant were retained and the least useful dropped. For instance, a chain of references to the word "bird" could safely be considered to be less important to the average Bible reader than a chain to "Saviour".

In this way the list of words that could be included in the *Chain References* was finalized and the computer was programmed to highlight these words in heavier type whenever they occurred in the Bible text.

Multiple references to a word within a chapter were indicated in the margin by placing after the word the number of phrases in which it occurs, e.g. "**evil** [4]" in Genesis 6. This was done for three reasons:
a) To save space in the margin listings, allowing the maximum number of different words to be included;
b) To indicate the importance of a word in a given chapter; and
c) To encourage users to look at passages of the Bible rather than isolated verses.

By doing this for words in each chapter rather than for the words on each page, the editors were able to make the reference system adaptable to other English translations and formats, and even to other languages.

Given the very high level of referencing achieved in this volume, it was not possible to place all the words in the margins on a level with the corresponding word in the text. The words for each chapter were thus sorted by computer into alphabetical order. In this way, readers will know that if the highlighted word they are interested in begins with "a", they must look in the margin near the beginning of the chapter, and if the word begins with "w" they must look towards the end.

At the same time as listing these words in the margins alongside the chapter, the computer was also programmed to extract from the Concordance data the references in the nearest preceding and following chapters, thus forming the chain of references through the Bible. In each case the reference given is to the first verse in which the word occurs in that chapter.

To create the index of *Topical Keywords*, some of the words thought to be most useful for study and teaching were selected. The computer was programmed to produce a statistical sorting of the data, starting with the chapter with most references to the word, and running down to the chapter with the least. Those chapters with only one reference were then excluded. In addition the computer indicated if the word also occurred in the preceding or following chapter of that book. In this way it has been possible to list passages useful for study of a given word on an objective statistical basis.

To include biblical names in the *Chain References* would have meant excluding a lot of other, very useful words from the chains, and it would have been impossible to include all names. The better option, therefore, was to put all names into a comprehensive *Name Index* for the back of the book.

The Thematic Index in the Concordance grouped words of similar meanings or referring to similar concepts. These groups of words with similar meanings and concepts were used to develop the *Theme Index* in this volume. For each word the reference to its first appearance in the Old Testament and in the New Testament has been added. If the word appears in another Index this has also been indicated in the *Theme Index*.

Special thanks are due to L. Jane Rowley for assisting in the editing of the Chain References and Indexes, to C.R. Barber and Partners for producing and typesetting the data, and to Gwen Anderson, Hazel Medcalf, and Penny Phillips of BFBS Translations Processing Department for their usual attention to detail in checking the finished material.

David Robinson
Editor of the Chain Reference Bible
BFBS

How to use this Chain Reference Bible

his *Chain Reference Bible* can be used in two ays—to find out more about a word, name or idea ou come across in your reading, or to start with a ıbject which interests you and follow through what ıe Bible says about it.

his edition contains many new aids for study. The *'hain References* appear on the page beside the ible text; other aids can be found in the extensive eference section at the back of the book. Together ıey form probably the most comprehensive level of iblical referencing available today. In most cases ou will be able to find *all* the references to a given vord, not just those which are pre-selected by an ditor. Every word considered to be meaningful for tudy and all biblical names have been included ither in the *Chain References* alongside the Bible ext or in the *Indexes* at the back of the book. Each *ndex* begins with easy-to-follow instructions for use; he *Chain Reference* system is fully explained elow.

xploring ...
Vith the help of these reference tools you will be ble to do as short or as long a study as you choose.

.. a word or a topic
f there is a word or idea you would like to find out bout, but you are not sure where to begin looking in he Bible, the *Theme Index*, in the tinted section, is he place to start. If the word is in the *Chain ?eferences*, it will give you start references to get nto the chains, as well as telling you which *Indexes* nclude the word. Other related words are also given ınder the theme headings. You can then look up the eferences most appropriate to your study. (The ntroductions to each index give clear instructions or use.)

.. a Bible book
If you want to trace all the references to a word within a Bible book in order to understand the significance of that word in the book, the *Chain References* in the margins at the side of the Bible text will guide you through all the occurrences within and beyond the book. If it is a word that occurs infrequently in the Bible, you may not find it in the margins, but it will probably be in the *Word Index*, which lists all the verses in which it appears.

... key Bible words
If you are looking for a passage to help a group explore an important biblical topic, the index of *Topical Keywords* will show you which chapter has most references to that word. This enables you to find areas of text where a word is most significant, so that you can start your reading and studying from there.

... a person
If you want to find out more about a person in the Bible, such as whether an Old Testament person is referred to in the New Testament, you will find all the main sections in which that person appears and all the other individual references in the *Name Index*.

... a place
The *Name Index* will also help you if you want to find the location of a place you have been reading about. It not only lists all references to the place but, if the place features on one of the series of ten *Maps* at the back of the book, the *Name Index* will tell you which map it appears on.

... history
If you want to find out into which approximate period of history a key person or incident or Bible book fits, the *Bible History Chart* gives you guidelines.

Using the Chain References
The *Chain Reference* system is designed to help you learn from the links between occurrences of particular words in the Bible: how the word is used in developing the message of a book; how different writers used the word at different times.

When you look at the Bible text you will see that some words are highlighted in **bolder type**. These are the words which appear in the margins on both sides of each page.

The words are listed in *alphabetical order* to make it easier to find the word you want, and each *chapter* has a separate list. For instance, if you were reading Ephesians 2 and wanted to find the references to **abundant**, then you would look for the word at the beginning of the margin list for Ephesians 2.

abundant Rom 9.23; Phil 4.19
anger Gal 5.20; 4.26
apart 2 Cor 1.21; Heb 7.26
apostle 1.1; 3.5
basis 1.11; Phil 3.9
birth Gal 2.15; Phil 3.5
boast Gal 6.12; Phil 2.3
body [4] 1.23; 3.6
choose 1.4; Phil 1.10
Christ [7] 1.3; 3.4
circumcise [2] Gal 6.12; Phil 3.3
commandment Gal 5.14; 6.2
control Gal 5.13; 4.16
covenant Gal 4.24; Heb 7.22
create [2] 1.10; 4.24
cross (1) [2] Gal 6.12; Phil 2.8
dead [2] Gal 6.14; Col 2.13
death (1) [2] 1.7; Phil 1.21
dedicate 1 Cor 7.34; 5.26

2 In the past you were **spiritually dead**
because of your **disobedience** and
sins. 2 At that time you followed the
world's evil way; you **obeyed** the ruler of
the **spiritual powers in space**, the **spirit**
who now **controls** the people who **disobey**
God. 3 Actually all of us were like them
and lived according to our **natural**
desires, doing whatever suited the **wishes**
of our own **bodies** and **minds**. In our
natural condition we, like everyone else,
were destined to **suffer God's anger**.
4 But God's **mercy** is so **abundant**, and
his **love** for us is so great, 5 that while we
were **spiritually dead** in our **disobedience**
he brought us **to life** with **Christ**. It is by
God's **grace** that you have been **saved**.
6 In our **union with** Christ Jesus he **raised**
us up with him to rule with him in the
heavenly world. 7 He did this to demon-

You will see that there are usually two Bible references given for each word in the list; the first gives you the reference for the *last chapter* in which the word was used, and the second gives you the reference for the chapter in which the word appears *next*. In each case the reference is to the first time the word occurs in the chapter. This means that, if you wish, you can follow the word right through the Bible, or simply see how the word is used in any one book.

Rather than listing several references in one chapter, the number of verses in which the highlighted word occurs is listed in square brackets after the word (e.g. **Gentile**[10] in Romans 15). This will indicate when the word is of some importance in the chapter.

7 **Accept one another**, then, for the
glory of God, as **Christ** has **accepted** you.
8 For I tell you that **Christ's life of service**
was on behalf of the **Jews**, to show that
God is **faithful**, to make his **promises** to
their ancestors come **true**, 9 and to enable
even the **Gentiles** to **praise** God for his
mercy. As the **scripture** says,
"And so I will **praise** you among the
Gentiles;
I will sing **praises** to you."
10 Again it says,
"**Rejoice, Gentiles**, with **God's people**!"
11 And again,
"**Praise** the Lord, all **Gentiles**;
praise him, all peoples!"
12 And again, Isaiah says,
"A descendant of Jesse will appear;
he will come to rule the **Gentiles**,
and they will put their **hope** in him."

free 8.2; 1 Cor 1.30
Gentile [10] 11.11; 16.4
glory 11.36; 16.25
God's people [4] 11.1; 16.2
Good News [3] 11.28; 16.25
help [5] 14.19; 16.2
hope [5] 12.12; 1 Cor 9.10
insult 3.8; 1 Cor 4.13
Jew [3] 11.11; 16.7
joy [2] 14.17; 2 Cor 7.4
knowledge 11.33; 1 Cor 1.5
letter (2) Acts 28.21; 16.22
life (1) 11.15; 16.4
love 14.15; 1 Cor 2.9
material (2) 1 Cor 7.31
means [2] 10.19; 1 Cor 1.21
mercy 12.1; 1 Cor 7.25
miracle Acts 19.11; 1 Cor 1.22
obey 13.1; 16.26

Some words, especially near the beginning and the end of the Bible, may only have one reference to look up instead of two. If the word only has a reference to a later chapter, it means that this is the first time it appears in the text; if there is only a reference to an earlier chapter, then this must be the last time in the Bible that this word is used.

The different forms of a word are grouped together with the most obvious form of the word as the heading in the margin. For instance, if you were looking at the word **taught** highlighted in the text you would look for **teach** in the margin listings. If the word you want begins with **re-** or **un-**, look under the main part of the word. For instance, if the word in the text was **uncircumcised** then you would look for the references under **circumcise**.

Sometimes a *phrase* is highlighted in the text, so you will need to look for the important word or words in it. For example, if the phrase was **by means of** then you would look for **means** in the margin listings. If you came across **heavenly Kingdom** in 2 Timothy 4 you would find references to both **heaven** and **Kingdom(1)** in the margin.

God not count it against them! 17 But the
Lord stayed with me and gave me
strength, so that I was able to **proclaim**
the full **message** for all the **Gentiles** to
hear; and I was **rescued** from being **sen-**
tenced to death. 18 And the Lord will **res-**
cue me from all **evil** and take me **safely**
into his **heavenly Kingdom**. To him be
the **glory** for ever and ever! Amen.

glory 2.10; Tit 2.13
Good News 2.8; Heb 4.2
grace 2.1; Tit 1.4
harm 1 Tim 6.9; 1 Pet 3.13
heaven 1 Tim 3.16; Heb 1.3
help 2.22; Tit 1.1
judge [2] 1 Tim 5.24; Heb 4.12
Kingdom (1) (of God) 2 Thes 1.5; Heb 1.8

If the form of the word in the text is significantly different from its heading, there will be a note in the margin to help you. For example, if you tried to look up **groom** in Revelation 18, the note would tell you that the reference you want is under the heading **bridegroom**.

threw it into the sea, saying, "This is how
the great city Babylon will be **violently**
thrown down and will never be seen
again. 22 The music of harps and of
human voices, of players of the flute and
the trumpet, will never be heard in you
again! No workman in any trade will
ever be found in you again; and the
sound of the millstone will be heard no
more! 23 Never again will the **light** of a
lamp be seen in you; no more will the
voices of **brides** and **grooms** be heard in
you. Your businessmen were the most
powerful in all the **world**, and with your
false magic you **deceived** all the peoples
of the **world**!"

angel [2] 17.1; 19.9
apostle 2.2; 21.14
authority 17.12
blood [2] 17.6; 19.13
bride Jn 3.29; 19.7
bridegroom Jn 3.29
condemn Jude 1.4; 19.2
cup 17.4
deceive 13.14; 19.20
demon 16.14
destroy 17.8; 20.9
disease 6.8
false 16.13; 19.20
famine 6.8
filthy 17.4; 22.11
glad [2] 12.12; 19.7
glory 15.8; 19.1
God's people [3] 17
19.8
grief [3] Lk 22.45; 21.4
groom *see* **bridegroom**

Words with more than one meaning have a number in round brackets beside them, e.g. **death(2) (from death)**. The numbering links directly with the *Concordance to the Good News Bible*, so that readers can cross-refer.

If the word you are interested in is not highlighted on the page, and yet it is a significant word, it is likely that it has been excluded from the chains because it occurs either too frequently or too infrequently to make a useful chain of references through the Bible. Many such words, with their references, are in the *Word Index* in the back, and you should look there or, better still, in the *Theme Index*, which will tell you where else the word is referenced.

Sometimes you will see cross-references at the foot of the page, as well as the Chain References in the margins. These cross-references, which appear in most editions of the *Good News Bible*, simply direct you to other places in the Bible where identical or similar matters are dealt with.

A number of other study aids are included in this volume. *Well-known Passages of the Bible*, *Jesus' teaching about* ... and *Prayers of the Bible* provide useful lists for easy reference.

Each index at the back of the book has an introduction which gives a clear explanation of its use. You should read these carefully in order to get the greatest benefit from the wealth of information at your disposal.

THE OLD TESTAMENT

GENESIS

INTRODUCTION

The name *Genesis* means "origin." The book tells about the creation of the universe, the origin of mankind, the beginning of sin and suffering in the world, and about God's way of dealing with mankind. Genesis can be divided into two main parts:

1. *Chapters 1-11* The creation of the world and the early history of the human race. Here are the accounts of Adam and Eve, Cain and Abel, Noah and the flood, and the Tower of Babylon.
2. *Chapters 12-50* The history of the early ancestors of the Israelites. The first is Abraham, who was notable for his faith and his obedience to God. Then follow the stories of his son Isaac, and grandson Jacob (also called Israel), and of Jacob's twelve sons, who were the founders of the twelve tribes of Israel. Special attention is given to one of the sons, Joseph, and the events that brought Jacob and his other sons with their families to live in Egypt.

While this book tells stories about people, it is first and foremost an account of what God has done. It begins with the affirmation that God created the universe, and it ends with a promise that God will continue to show his concern for his people. Throughout the book the main character is God, who judges and punishes those who do wrong, leads and helps his people, and shapes their history. This ancient book was written to record the story of a people's faith and to help keep that faith alive.

Outline of Contents

---

being [3] 3.20
bless [2] 2.3
command [7] 6.22
control 14.4
create [4] 2.3
creature [2] 3.24
dark [4] 15.17
desolate Deut 32.10
dome [3] Job 22.14
festival Ex 5.1
human [2] 3.20
life (1) 2.7
light (1) [8] Ex 10.23
monster Job 7.12
please [7] 4.4
power [2] 9.2
provide [2] 22.8
rage 49.4
religion Ex 12.14
separate [5] 13.9
universe 2.1

The Story of Creation

1 In the beginning, when God **created**
the **universe**,[a] 2 the earth was form-
less and **desolate**. The **raging** ocean that
covered everything was engulfed in total
darkness, and the **power of God**[b] was
moving over the water. 3 Then God **commanded**, "Let there be **light**"—and **light**
appeared. 4 God was **pleased** with what
he saw. Then he **separated** the **light** from
the **darkness**, 5 and he named the **light**
"Day" and the **darkness** "Night". Evening passed and morning came—that was
the first day.
6-7 Then God **commanded**, "Let there
be a **dome** to divide the water and to
keep it in two **separate** places"—and it
was done. So God made a **dome**, and it
separated the water under it from the
water above it. 8 He named the **dome**
"Sky." Evening passed and morning
came—that was the second day.
9 Then God **commanded**, "Let the
water below the sky come together in
one place, so that the land will appear"—
and it was done. 10 He named the land
"Earth," and the water which had come
together he named "Sea." And God was
pleased with what he saw. 11 Then he
commanded, "Let the earth produce all
kinds of plants, those that bear grain and
those that bear fruit"—and it was done.
12 So the earth produced all kinds of
plants, and God was **pleased** with what
he saw. 13 Evening passed and morning
came—that was the third day.
14 Then God **commanded**, "Let **lights**
appear in the sky to **separate** day from

[a] In the beginning...the universe; *or* In the beginning God created the universe; *or* When God began to create the universe.
[b] the power of God; *or* the spirit of God; *or* a wind from God; *or* an awesome wind.

1.3: 2 Cor 4.6 **1.6-8:** 2 Pet 3.5

night and to show the time when days,
years, and **religious festivals**[c] begin;
15 they will shine in the sky to give **light** to
the earth"—and it was done. 16 So God
made the two larger **lights**, the sun to
rule over the day and the moon to rule
over the night; he also made the stars.
17 He placed the **lights** in the sky to shine
on the earth, 18 to rule over the day and
the night, and to **separate light** from
darkness. And God was **pleased** with
what he saw. 19 Evening passed and
morning came—that was the fourth day.

20 Then God **commanded**, "Let the
water be filled with many kinds of living
beings, and let the air be filled with
birds." 21 So God **created** the great **sea-
monsters**, all kinds of **creatures** that live
in the water, and all kinds of birds. And
God was **pleased** with what he saw. 22 He
blessed them all and told the **creatures**
that live in the water to reproduce, and
to fill the sea, and he told the birds to increase in number. 23 Evening passed and
morning came—that was the fifth day.

24 Then God **commanded**, "Let the
earth produce all kinds of animal **life**:
domestic and wild, large and small"—
and it was done. 25 So God made them all,
and he was **pleased** with what he saw.

26 Then God said, "And now we will
make **human beings**; they will be like us
and resemble us. They will have **power**
over the fish, the birds, and all animals,
domestic and wild,[d] large and small."
27 So God **created human beings**, making
them to be like himself. He **created** them
male and female, 28 **blessed** them, and
said, "Have many children, so that your
descendants will live all over the earth
and bring it under their **control**. I am putting you in charge of the fish, the birds,
and all the wild animals. 29 I have **provided** all kinds of grain and all kinds of
fruit for you to eat; 30 but for all the wild
animals and for all the birds I have **provided** grass and leafy plants for food"—
and it was done. 31 God looked at everything he had made, and he was very
pleased. Evening passed and morning
came—that was the sixth day.

alone 3.14
apart 16.12
bad [2] 3.5
bless 1.22; 5.2
complete [2] Ex 39.32
create [2] 1.1; 5.1

2 And so the whole **universe** was **completed**. 2 By the seventh day God
finished what he had been doing and
stopped working. 3 He **blessed** the
seventh day and set it **apart** as a **special**
day, because by that day he had **completed** his **creation**[e] and stopped working. 4 And that is how the **universe** was
created.

flesh [2] 29.14
help [2] 4.1
knowledge [2] 3.22
life (1) [2] 1.24; 3.17
naked 3.7
pure 35.2
seed 26.12
special Ex 29.24
unite Deut 33.7
universe [3] 1.1; Is 66.2

The Garden of Eden

When the LORD[x] God made the **universe**, 5 there were no plants on the earth
and no **seeds** had sprouted, because he
had not sent any rain, and there was no
one to cultivate the land; 6 but water
would come up from beneath the surface
and water the ground.

7 Then the LORD God took some soil
from the ground[f] and formed a man[f] out
of it; he breathed **life-giving** breath into
his nostrils and the man began to live.

8 Then the LORD God planted a garden in Eden, in the East, and there he put
the man he had formed. 9 He made all
kinds of beautiful trees grow there and
produce good fruit. In the middle of the
garden stood the tree that gives **life** and
the tree that gives **knowledge** of what is
good and what is **bad**.[g]

10 A stream flowed in Eden and
watered the garden; beyond Eden it
divided into four rivers. 11 The first river
is the Pishon; it flows round the country
of Havilah. 12 (**Pure** gold is found there
and also rare perfume and precious
stones.) 13 The second river is the Gihon;
it flows round the country of Cush.[h]
14 The third river is the Tigris, which
flows east of Assyria, and the fourth river
is the Euphrates.

15 Then the LORD God placed the man
in the Garden of Eden to cultivate it and
guard it. 16 He said to him, "You may eat
the fruit of any tree in the garden,
17 except the tree that gives **knowledge** of
what is good and what is **bad**.[g] You must
not eat the fruit of that tree; if you do,
you will die the same day."

18 Then the LORD God said, "It is not
good for the man to live **alone**. I will
make a suitable companion to **help** him."
19 So he took some soil from the ground
and formed all the animals and all the
birds. Then he brought them to the man
to see what he would name them; and
that is how they all got their names. 20 So
the man named all the birds and all the
animals; but not one of them was a
suitable companion to **help** him.

21 Then the LORD God made the man

[c] religious festivals; *or* seasons.
[d] *One ancient translation* animals, domestic and wild; *Hebrew* domestic animals and all the earth.
[e] by that day he had completed his creation; *or* on that day he completed his creation.
[x] THE LORD: *See* LORD *in Word List.*
[f] GROUND...MAN: *The Hebrew words for "man" and "ground" have similar sounds.*
[g] knowledge of what is good and what is bad; *or* knowledge of everything.
[h] Cush (of Mesopotamia); *or* Sudan.

1.26: 1 Cor 11.7 **1.27:** Mt 19.4; Mk 10.6 **1.27-28:** Gen 5.1-2 **2.2:** Heb 4.4, 10 **2.2-3:** Ex 20.11
2.7: 1 Cor 15.45 **2.9:** Rev 2.7, 22.2, 14

fall into a deep sleep, and while he was sleeping, he took out one of the man's ribs and closed up the **flesh**. 22 He formed a woman out of the rib and brought her to him. 23 Then the man said,

"At last, here is one of my own kind—
Bone taken from my bone, and **flesh**
from my flesh.
'Woman' is her name because she was
taken out of man."[i]

24 That is why a man leaves his father and mother and is **united** with his wife, and they become one.

25 The man and the woman were both **naked**, but they were not embarrassed.

The Disobedience of Man

3 Now the snake was the most cunning animal that the LORD God had made. The snake asked the woman, "Did God really tell you not to eat fruit from any tree in the garden?"

2 "We may eat the fruit of any tree in the garden," the woman answered, 3 "except the tree in the middle of it. God told us not to eat the fruit of that tree or even touch it; if we do, we will die."

4 The snake replied, "That's not **true**; you will not die. 5 God said that, because he knows that when you eat it you will be like God[j] and know what is good and what is **bad**."[k]

6 The woman saw how beautiful the tree was and how good its fruit would be to eat, and she thought how **wonderful** it would be to become **wise**. So she took some of the fruit and ate it. Then she gave some to her husband, and he also ate it. 7 As soon as they had eaten it, they were given **understanding** and realized that they were **naked**; so they sewed fig leaves together and covered themselves.

8 That evening they heard the LORD God walking in the garden, and they hid from him among the trees. 9 But the LORD God called out to the man, "Where are you?"

10 He answered, "I heard you in the garden; I was **afraid** and hid from you, because I was **naked**."

11 "Who told you that you were **naked**?" God asked. "Did you eat the fruit that I told you not to eat?"

12 The man answered, "The woman you put here with me gave me the fruit, and I ate it."

13 The LORD God asked the woman, "Why did you do this?"

She replied, "The snake **tricked** me into eating it."

God Pronounces Judgement

14 Then the LORD God said to the snake, "You will be **punished** for this; you **alone** of all the animals must bear this **curse**: From now on you will crawl on your belly, and you will have to eat dust as long as you live. 15 I will make you and the woman **hate each other**; her offspring and yours will always be **enemies**. Her offspring will crush your head, and you will bite their[x] heel."

16 And he said to the woman, "I will increase your **trouble** in pregnancy and your **pain** in giving **birth**. In spite of this, you will still have **desire** for your husband, yet you will be **subject** to him."

17 And he said to the man, "You listened to your wife and ate the fruit which I told you not to eat. Because of what you have done, the ground will be under a **curse**. You will have to work **hard** all your **life** to make it produce **enough** food for you. 18 It will produce **weeds** and thorns, and you will have to eat wild plants. 19 You will have to work **hard** and sweat to make the soil produce anything, until you go back to the soil from which you were formed. You were made from soil, and you will become soil again."

20 Adam[l] named his wife Eve,[m] because she was the mother of all **human beings**. 21 And the LORD God made clothes out of animal skins for Adam and his wife, and he clothed them.

Adam and Eve Are Sent Out of the Garden

22 Then the LORD God said, "Now the man has become like one of us and has **knowledge** of what is good and what is **bad**.[n] He must not be allowed to take fruit from the tree that gives **life**, eat it, and live for ever." 23 So the LORD God sent him out of the Garden of Eden and made him cultivate the soil from which he had been formed. 24 Then at the east side of the garden he put living **creatures**[o] and a flaming sword which **turned** in all directions. This was to **keep anyone from** coming near the tree that gives **life**.

afraid 15.1
alone 2.18; 32.24
bad [2] 2.9; 12.10
being 1.20; 5.1
birth 4.2
creature 1.21; Ex 25.18
curse [2] 4.11
desire 39.7
each other 15.10
enemy 14.15
enough 7.17
hard [2] 4.13
hate 27.41
human 1.26; 5.1
keep from 16.2
knowledge 2.9; Num 24.16
life (1) [3] 2.7; 4.15
naked [3] 2.25; 9.21
pain 35.17
punish 4.13
subject (1) Ex 21.22
trick 29.25
trouble 21.11
true 18.21
turn 4.8
understand 11.7
weed Ex 22.6
wise 41.8
wonder (1) Ex 15.11

[i] WOMAN...MAN: *The Hebrew words for "woman" and "man" have similar sounds.* [j] God; *or* the gods.
[k] know what is good and what is bad; *or* know everything. [x] their; *or* his.
[l] ADAM: *This name in Hebrew means "mankind."*
[m] EVE: *This name sounds similar to the Hebrew word for "living," which is rendered in this context as "human beings."* [n] knowledge of what is good and what is bad; *or* knowledge of everything.
[o] LIVING CREATURES: *See Word List.*

2.24: Mt 19.5; Mk 10.7–8; 1 Cor 6.16; Eph 5.31 **3.1:** Rev 12.9, 20.2 **3.13:** 2 Cor 11.3; 1 Tim 2.14
3.15: Rev 12.17 **3.17–18:** Heb 6.8 **3.22:** Rev 22.14

anger [2] 18.30
best 18.6
birth [3] 3.16; 25.13
blood [2] 9.4
care 13.7
curse 3.14; 5.29
evil 6.5
fury 34.7
hard 3.17; 5.29
harvest 8.22
help 2.18; 10.9
holy 12.6
lamb 21.28
life (1) [2] 3.17; 5.24
mark (1) 35.20
name (2) (name of God, of Jesus) 22.16
offer [4] 22.2
please 1.4; 6.8
presence [2] 19.27
punish 3.14; 9.5
raise Ex 6.6
reject Ex 32.7
revenge [2] 34.27
right (1) 7.1
sheep 12.16
shepherd 26.20
strike 19.11
terrible 12.17
turn 3.24; 9.23
warn 20.7
worship (1) (of God) 12.8

Cain and Abel

4 Then Adam had intercourse with his wife, and she became pregnant. She bore a son and said, "By the LORD's **help** I have acquired a son." So she named him Cain.[p] 2 Later she gave **birth** to another son, Abel. Abel became a **shepherd**, but Cain was a farmer. 3 After some time, Cain brought some of his **harvest** and gave it as an **offering** to the LORD. 4 Then Abel brought the first **lamb** born to one of his **sheep**, killed it, and gave the **best** parts of it as an **offering**. The LORD was **pleased** with Abel and his **offering**, 5 but he **rejected** Cain and his **offering**. Cain became **furious**, and he scowled in **anger**. 6 Then the LORD said to Cain, "Why are you **angry**? Why that scowl on your face? 7 If you had done the **right** thing, you would be smiling;[q] but because you have done **evil**, sin is crouching at your door. It wants to rule you, but you must overcome it."

8 Then Cain said to his brother Abel, "Let's go out in the fields."[r] When they were out in the fields, Cain **turned** on his brother and killed him.

9 The LORD asked Cain, "Where is your brother Abel?"

He answered, "I don't know. Am I supposed to take **care** of my brother?"

10 Then the LORD said, "Why have you done this **terrible** thing? Your brother's **blood** is crying out to me from the ground, like a voice calling for **revenge**. 11 You are placed under a **curse** and can no longer farm the soil. It has soaked up your brother's **blood** as if it had opened its mouth to receive it when you killed him. 12 If you try to grow crops, the soil will not produce anything; you will be a homeless wanderer on the earth."

13 And Cain said to the LORD, "This **punishment** is too **hard** for me to bear. 14 You are driving me off the land and away from your **presence**. I will be a homeless wanderer on the earth, and anyone who finds me will kill me."

15 But the LORD answered, "No. If anyone kills you, seven **lives** will be taken in **revenge**." So the LORD put a **mark** on Cain to **warn** anyone who met him not to kill him. 16 And Cain went away from the LORD's **presence** and lived in a land called "Wandering," which is east of Eden.

The Descendants of Cain

17 Cain and his wife had a son and named him Enoch. Then Cain built a city and named it after his son. 18 Enoch had a son named Irad, who was the father of Mehujael, and Mehujael had a son named Methushael, who was the father of Lamech. 19 Lamech had two wives, Adah and Zillah. 20 Adah gave **birth** to Jabal, who was the ancestor of those who **raise** livestock and live in tents. 21 His brother was Jubal, the ancestor of all musicians who play the harp and the flute. 22 Zillah gave **birth** to Tubal Cain, who made all kinds of tools[s] out of bronze and iron. The sister of Tubal Cain was Naamah.

23 Lamech said to his wives,

"Adah and Zillah, listen to me: I have
killed a young man because he
struck me.
24 If seven **lives** are taken to pay for
killing Cain,
Seventy-seven will be taken if anyone
kills me."

Seth and Enosh

25 Adam and his wife had another son. She said, "God has given me a son to replace Abel, whom Cain killed." So she named him Seth.[t] 26 Seth had a son whom he named Enosh. It was then that people began using the LORD's **holy name** in **worship**.

The Descendants of Adam
(1 Chr 1.1-4)

5 This is the list of the descendants of Adam. (When God **created human beings**, he made them like himself. 2 He **created** them male and female, **blessed** them, and named them "**Mankind**.") 3 When Adam was 130 years old, he had a son who was like him, and he named him Seth. 4 After that, Adam lived another 800 years. He had other children 5 and died at the age of 930.

6 When Seth was 105, he had a son, Enosh, 7 and then lived another 807 years. He had other children 8 and died at the age of 912.

9 When Enosh was 90, he had a son, Kenan, 10 and then lived another 815 years. He had other children 11 and died at the age of 905.

12 When Kenan was 70, he had a son, Mahalalel, 13 and then lived another 840

being 3.20; 6.2
bless 2.3; 9.1
create [2] 2.3; 6.7
curse 4.11; 8.21
fellowship [2] 6.9
hard 4.13; 11.3
human 3.20; 6.4
life (1) 4.15; 6.12
mankind 6.1
relieve (1) 2 Kgs 15.5

[p] CAIN: *This name sounds like the Hebrew for "acquired."*
[q] you would be smiling; *or* I would have accepted your offering.
[r] *Some ancient translations* Let's go out in the fields; *Hebrew does not have these words.*
[s] who made all kinds of tools; *one ancient translation* ancestor of all metal-workers.
[t] SETH: *This name sounds like the Hebrew for "has given."*

4.4: Heb 11.4 **4.8:** Mt 23.35; Lk 11.51; 1 Jn 3.12 **4.10:** Heb 12.24 **4.24:** Mt 18.22 **5.1-2:** Gen 1.27-28 **5.2:** Mt 19.4; Mk 10.6

years. He had other children 14 and died at the age of 910.

15 When Mahalalel was 65, he had a son, Jared, 16 and then lived another 830 years. He had other children 17 and died at the age of 895.

18 When Jared was 162, he had a son, Enoch, 19 and then lived another 800 years. He had other children 20 and died at the age of 962.

21 When Enoch was 65, he had a son, Methuselah. 22 After that, Enoch lived in **fellowship** with God for 300 years and had other children. 23 He lived to be 365 years old. 24 He spent his **life** in **fellowship** with God, and then he disappeared, because God took him away.

25 When Methuselah was 187, he had a son, Lamech, 26 and then lived another 782 years. He had other children 27 and died at the age of 969.

28 When Lamech was 182, he had a son, 29 and said, "From the very ground on which the LORD put a **curse**, this child will bring us **relief** from all our **hard work**"; so he named him Noah.[u] 30 Lamech lived another 595 years. He had other children 31 and died at the age of 777.

32 After Noah was 500 years old, he had three sons, Shem, Ham, and Japheth.

The Wickedness of Mankind

alive 7.3
being [3] 5.1; 7.4
command 1.3; 7.5
covenant 9.9
create 5.1; Num 11.12
destroy [2] 7.4
evil [4] 4.7; 8.21
fault 16.5
fellowship 5.22; Mic 6.8
flood 7.6
heaven [2] 14.19
human 5.1; 7.23
life (1) 5.24; 9.4
mankind [2] 5.2; Job 36.28
mortal 2 Sam 1.15
please 4.4; 8.21
sight 48.10
sorry [2] Ex 2.6
violent [2] 49.5
wicked 13.13
world [3] 7.1

6 When **mankind** had spread all over the **world**, and girls were being born, 2 some of the **heavenly beings**[v] saw that these girls were beautiful, so they took the ones they liked. 3 Then the LORD said, "I will not allow people to live for ever; they are **mortal**. From now on they will live no longer than a hundred and twenty years." 4 In those days, and even later, there were giants on the earth who were descendants of **human** women and the **heavenly beings**.[v] They were the great heroes and famous men of long ago.

5 When the LORD saw how **wicked** everyone on earth was and how **evil** their thoughts were all the time, 6 he was **sorry** that he had ever made them and put them on the earth. He was so filled with regret 7 that he said, "I will wipe out these people I have **created**, and also the animals and the birds, because I am **sorry** that I made any of them." 8 But the LORD was **pleased** with Noah.

Noah

9-10 This is the story of Noah. He had three sons, Shem, Ham, and Japheth. Noah had no **faults** and was the only good man of his time. He lived in **fellowship** with God, 11 but everyone else was **evil** in God's **sight**, and **violence** had spread everywhere. 12 God looked at the **world** and saw that it was **evil**, for the people were all living **evil lives**.

13 God said to Noah, "I have decided to put an end to all **mankind**. I will **destroy** them completely, because the **world** is full of their **violent** deeds. 14 Build a boat for yourself out of good timber; make rooms in it and cover it with tar inside and out. 15 Make it 133 metres long, 22 metres wide, and 13 metres high. 16 Make a roof[w] for the boat and leave a space of 44 centimetres between the roof[w] and the sides. Build it with three decks and put a door in the side. 17 I am going to send a **flood** on the earth to **destroy** every living **being**. Everything on the earth will die, 18 but I will make a **covenant** with you. Go into the boat with your wife, your sons, and their wives. 19-20 Take into the boat with you a male and a female of every kind of animal and of every kind of bird, in order to keep them **alive**. 21 Take along all kinds of food for you and for them." 22 Noah did everything that God **commanded**.

The Flood

7 The LORD said to Noah, "Go into the boat with your whole family; I have found that you are the only one in all the **world** who does what is **right**. 2 Take with you seven pairs of each kind of ritually **clean** animal, but only one pair of each kind of **unclean** animal. 3 Take also seven pairs of each kind of bird. Do this so that every kind of animal and bird will be kept **alive** to reproduce again on the earth. 4 Seven days from now I am going to send rain that will fall for forty days and nights, in order to **destroy** all the living **beings** that I have made." 5 And Noah did everything that the LORD **commanded**.

alive 6.19; 25.6
being [5] 6.2; 8.21
body 15.11
clean [2] 8.20
command [3] 6.22; 18.19
destroy [2] 6.13; 8.21
enough 3.17; 13.6
escape 14.10
flood [4] 6.17; 9.11
human 6.4; 9.5
right (1) 4.7; 16.5
rise 19.23
unclean [2] Lev 5.2
world 6.1; 8.22

6 Noah was six hundred years old when the **flood** came on the earth. 7 He and his wife, and his sons and their wives, went into the boat to **escape** the **flood**. 8 A male and a female of every kind of animal and bird, whether ritually **clean** or **unclean**, 9 went into the boat

[u] NOAH: *This name sounds like the Hebrew for "relief."*
[v] heavenly beings; *or* sons of the gods; *or* sons of God. [w] roof; *or* window.

5.24: Heb 11.5; Jude 14 **6.1-4:** Job 1.6, 2.1 **6.4:** Num 13.33 **6.5-8:** Mat 24.37; Lk 17.26; 1 Pet 3.20
6.9: 2 Pet 2.5 **6.22:** Heb 11.7 **7.7:** Mt 24.38-39; Lk 17.27

with Noah, as God had **commanded**.
10 Seven days later the **flood** came.

11 When Noah was six hundred years
old, on the seventeenth day of the second
month all the outlets of the vast **body** of
water beneath the earth burst open, all
the floodgates of the sky were opened,
12 and rain fell on the earth for forty days
and nights. 13 On that same day Noah and
his wife went into the boat with their
three sons, Shem, Ham, and Japheth, and
their wives. 14 With them went every kind
of animal, domestic and wild, large and
small, and every kind of bird. 15 A male
and a female of each kind of living **being**
went into the boat with Noah, 16 as God
had **commanded**. Then the LORD shut the
door behind Noah.

17 The **flood** continued for forty days,
and the water became deep **enough** for
the boat to float. 18 The water became
deeper, and the boat drifted on the surface. 19 It became so deep that it covered
the highest mountains; 20 it went on **rising**
until it was about seven metres above the
tops of the mountains. 21 Every living
being on the earth died—every bird,
every animal, and every person. 22 Everything on earth that breathed died. 23 The
LORD **destroyed** all living **beings** on the
earth—**human beings**, animals, and
birds. The only ones left were Noah and
those who were with him in the boat.
24 The water did not start going down for
a hundred and fifty days.

The End of the Flood

8 God had not **forgotten** Noah and all
the animals with him in the boat; he
caused a wind to blow, and the water
started going down. 2 The outlets of the
water beneath the earth and the floodgates of the sky were closed. The rain
stopped, 3 and the water gradually went
down for a hundred and fifty days. 4 On
the seventeenth day of the seventh
month the boat came to rest on a mountain in the Ararat range. 5 The water kept
going down, and on the first day of the
tenth month the tops of the mountains
appeared.

6 After forty days Noah opened a window 7 and sent out a raven. It did not
come back, but kept flying around until
the water was completely gone. 8 Meanwhile, Noah sent out a **dove** to see if the
water had gone down, 9 but since the
water still covered all the land, the **dove**
did not find a place to alight. It flew back
to the boat, and Noah reached out and
took it in. 10 He waited another seven
days and sent out the **dove** again. 11 It
returned to him in the evening with a
fresh olive leaf in its beak. So Noah knew
that the water had gone down. 12 Then he
waited another seven days and sent out
the **dove** once more; this time it did not
come back.

13 When Noah was 601 years old, on
the first day of the first month, the water
was gone. Noah removed the covering of
the boat, looked round, and saw that the
ground was getting dry. 14 By the twenty-
seventh day of the second month the
earth was completely dry.

15 God said to Noah, 16 "Go out of the
boat with your wife, your sons, and their
wives. 17 Take all the birds and animals
out with you, so that they may reproduce
and spread over all the earth." 18 So Noah
went out of the boat with his wife, his
sons, and their wives. 19 All the animals
and birds went out of the boat in groups
of their own kind.

Noah Offers a Sacrifice

20 Noah built an **altar** to the LORD; he
took one of each kind of ritually **clean**
animal and bird, and burnt them whole
as a **sacrifice** on the **altar**. 21 The odour of
the **sacrifice pleased** the LORD, and he
said to himself, "**Never again** will I put
the earth under a **curse** because of what
man does; I know that from the time he
is young his thoughts are **evil**. **Never
again** will I **destroy** all living **beings**, as I
have done this time. 22 As long as the
world exists, there will be a time for
planting and a time for **harvest**. There
will always be cold and heat, summer
and winter, day and night."

God's Covenant with Noah

9 God **blessed** Noah and his sons and
said, "Have many children, so that
your descendants will live all over the
earth. 2 All the animals, birds, and fish
will live in **fear** of you. They are all
placed under your **power**. 3 Now you can
eat them, as well as green plants; I give
them all to you for food. 4 The one thing
you must not eat is meat with **blood** still
in it; I **forbid** this because the **life** is in
the **blood**. 5 If anyone takes **human life**,
he will be **punished**. I will **punish** with
death any animal that takes a **human
life**. 6 Man was made like God, so whoever murders a man will himself be
killed by his fellow-man.

7 "You must have many children, so
that your descendants will live all over
the earth."

altar [2] 12.7
being 7.4; 9.10
clean 7.2; 35.2
curse 5.29; 9.25
destroy 7.4; 9.11
dove [4] 15.9
evil 6.5; 38.7
exist 1 Kgs 10.19
forget 27.45
harvest 4.3; 26.12
never again [2] 9.11
please 6.8; 15.6
sacrifice [2] 22.2
world 7.1; 9.13

being [6] 8.21; Lev 27.28
bless 5.2; 12.2
blood [2] 4.10; 29.14
cloud [3] Ex 13.21
covenant [5] 6.18; 15.18
curse 8.21; 12.3
death (1) 23.2
destroy [3] 8.21; 13.10
everlasting [2] 17.7
fear 15.12
flood [4] 7.6; 10.1
forbid Ex 30.9
human [2] 7.23; Ex 12.12
learn 22.20
life (1) [3] 6.12; 19.15
naked [3] 3.7; Deut 28.48
never again [3] 8.21; Lev 22.3
power 1.2; 26.16
praise 14.20
promise [3] 15.18
punish [2] 4.13; 15.14
remember [2] 28.15

7.11: 2 Pet 3.6 **9.1:** Gen 1.28 **9.4:** Gen 7.26–27, 17.10–14; Lev 19.26; Deut 12.16, 23, 15.23
9.6: Gen 1.26; Ex 20.13 **9.7:** Gen 1.28

sign (1) [3] 17.13
slave [3] 12.5
turn 4.8; 14.7
vineyard Ex 22.5
word (1) 11.1
world 8.22; 10.8

8 God said to Noah and his sons, 9 "I
am now making my **covenant** with you
and with your descendants, 10 and with all
living **beings**—all birds and all animals—
everything that came out of the boat
with you. 11 With these **words** I make my
covenant with you: I **promise** that **never
again** will all living **beings** be **destroyed**
by a **flood**; **never again** will a **flood destroy** the earth. 12 As a **sign** of this **everlasting covenant** which I am making with
you and with all living **beings**, 13 I am putting my bow in the **clouds**. It will be the
sign of my **covenant** with the **world**.
14 Whenever I cover the sky with **clouds**
and the rainbow appears, 15 I will **remember** my **promise** to you and to all the animals that a **flood** will **never again destroy** all living **beings**. 16 When the rainbow appears in the **clouds**, I will see it
and **remember** the **everlasting covenant**
between me and all living **beings** on
earth. 17 That is the **sign** of the **promise**
which I am making to all living **beings**."

Noah and His Sons

18 The sons of Noah who went out of
the boat were Shem, Ham, and Japheth.
(Ham was the father of Canaan.) 19 These
three sons of Noah were the ancestors of
all the people on earth.

20 Noah, who was a farmer, was the
first man to plant a **vineyard**. 21 After he
drank some of the wine, he became
drunk, took off his clothes, and lay **naked**
in his tent. 22 When Ham, the father of
Canaan, saw that his father was **naked**,
he went out and told his two brothers.
23 Then Shem and Japheth took a robe
and held it behind them on their shoulders. They walked backwards into the tent
and covered their father, keeping their
faces **turned** away so as not to see him
naked. 24 When Noah was sober again
and **learnt** what his youngest son had
done to him, 25 he said,

"A **curse** on Canaan!
He will be a **slave** to his brothers.
26 Give **praise** to the LORD, the God of
Shem!
Canaan will be the **slave** of Shem.
27 May God cause Japheth[x] to increase!
May his descendants live with the
people of Shem!
Canaan will be the **slave** of Japheth."

28 After the **flood** Noah lived for 350
years 29 and died at the age of 950.

The Descendants of Noah's Sons
(1 Chr 1.5–23)

10 These are the descendants of
Noah's sons, Shem, Ham, and
Japheth. These three had sons after the
flood.

2 The sons of Japheth—Gomer,
Magog, Madai, Javan, Tubal, Meshech,
and Tiras—were the ancestors of the
peoples who bear their names. 3 The descendants of Gomer were the people of
Ashkenaz, Riphath, and Togarmah. 4 The
descendants of Javan were the people of
Elishah, Spain, Cyprus, and Rhodes;
5 they were the ancestors of the people
who live along the coast and on the
islands. These are the descendants of
Japheth, living in their different tribes
and countries, each group speaking its
own language.

6 The sons of Ham—Cush, Egypt,
Libya and Canaan—were the ancestors
of the peoples who bear their names.
7 The descendants of Cush were the
people of Seba, Havilah, Sabtah, Raamah, and Sabteca. The descendants of
Raamah were the people of Sheba and
Dedan. 8 Cush had a son named Nimrod,
who became the **world's** first great **conqueror**. 9 By the LORD's **help** he was a
great hunter, and that is why people say,
"May the LORD make you as great a hunter as Nimrod!" 10 At first his kingdom included Babylon, Erech, and Accad, all
three of them in Babylonia. 11 From that
land he went to Assyria and built the
cities of Nineveh, Rehoboth Ir, Calah,
12 and Resen, which is between Nineveh
and the great city of Calah.

13 The descendants of Egypt were the
people of Lydia, Anam, Lehab, Naphtuh,
14 Pathrus, Casluh, and of Crete from
whom the Philistines are descended.[y]

15 Canaan's sons—Sidon, the eldest,
and Heth—were the ancestors of the
peoples who bear their names. 16 Canaan
was also the ancestor of the Jebusites,
the Amorites, the Girgashites, 17 the
Hivites, the Arkites, the Sinites, 18 the
Arvadites, the Zemarites, and the Hamathites. The different tribes of the Canaanites spread out, 19 until the Canaanite borders reached from Sidon southwards to
Gerar near Gaza, and eastwards to
Sodom, Gomorrah, Admah, and Zeboiim
near Lasha. 20 These are the descendants
of Ham, living in their different tribes
and countries, each group speaking its
own language.

21 Shem, the elder brother of Japheth,

conquer 14.7
flood [2] 9.11; 11.10
Hebrew 14.13
help 4.1; 27.20
world [2] 9.13; 11.1

[x] JAPHETH: *This name sounds like the Hebrew for "increase."*
[y] *Probable text* and of Crete...descended; *Hebrew* from whom the Philistines are descended, and Crete.

was the ancestor of all the **Hebrews.** 22 Shem's sons—Elam, Asshur, Arpachshad, Lud, and Aram—were the ancestors of the peoples who bear their names. 23 The descendants of Aram were the people of Uz, Hul, Gether, and Meshek. 24 Arpachshad was the father of Shelah, who was the father of Eber. 25 Eber had two sons: one was named Peleg,[z] because during his time the people of the **world** were divided; and the other was named Joktan. 26 The descendants of Joktan were the people of Almodad, Sheleph, Hazarmaveth, Jerah, 27 Hadoram, Uzal, Diklah, 28 Obal, Abimael, Sheba, 29 Ophir, Havilah, and Jobab. All of them were descended from Joktan. 30 The land in which they lived extended from Mesha to Sephar in the eastern hill-country. 31 These are the descendants of Shem, living in their different tribes and countries, each group speaking its own language.

32 All these peoples are the descendants of Noah, nation by nation, according to their different lines of descent. After the **flood** all the nations of the earth were descended from the sons of Noah.

The Tower of Babylon

flood 10.1; 49.4
hard 5.29; 18.14
scatter [3] 49.7
understand 3.7; 28.8
word (1) 9.11; 24.60
world 10.8; 19.31

11 At first, the people of the whole **world** had only one language and used the same **words.** 2 As they wandered about in the East, they came to a plain in Babylonia and settled there. 3 They said to one another, "Come on! Let's make bricks and bake them **hard.**" So they had bricks to build with and tar to hold them together. 4 They said, "Now let's build a city with a tower that reaches the sky, so that we can make a name for ourselves and not be **scattered** all over the earth."

5 Then the LORD came down to see the city and the tower which those men had built, 6 and he said, "Now then, these are all one people and they speak one language; this is just the beginning of what they are going to do. Soon they will be able to do anything they want! 7 Let us go down and mix up their language so that they will not **understand** one another." 8 So the LORD **scattered** them all over the earth, and they stopped building the city. 9 The city was called Babylon,[a] because there the LORD mixed up the language of all the people, and from there he **scattered** them all over the earth.

The Descendants of Shem
(1 Chr 1.24–27)

10 These are the descendants of Shem. Two years after the **flood,** when Shem was 100 years old, he had a son, Arpachshad. 11 After that, he lived another 500 years and had other children.

12 When Arpachshad was 35 years old, he had a son, Shelah; 13 after that, he lived another 403 years and had other children.

14 When Shelah was 30 years old, he had a son, Eber; 15 after that, he lived another 403 years and had other children.

16 When Eber was 34 years old, he had a son, Peleg; 17 after that, he lived another 430 years and had other children.

18 When Peleg was 30 years old, he had a son, Reu; 19 after that, he lived another 209 years and had other children.

20 When Reu was 32 years old, he had a son, Serug; 21 after that, he lived another 207 years and had other children.

22 When Serug was 30 years old, he had a son, Nahor; 23 after that, he lived another 200 years and had other children.

24 When Nahor was 29 years old, he had a son, Terah; 25 after that, he lived another 119 years and had other children.

26 After Terah was 70 years old, he became the father of Abram, Nahor, and Haran.

The Descendants of Terah

27 These are the descendants of Terah, who was the father of Abram, Nahor, and Haran. Haran was the father of Lot, 28 and Haran died in his native city, Ur in Babylonia, while his father was still living. 29 Abram married Sarai, and Nahor married Milcah, the daughter of Haran, who was also the father of Iscah. 30 Sarai was not able to have children.

31 Terah took his son Abram, his grandson Lot, who was the son of Haran, and his daughter-in-law Sarai, Abram's wife, and with them he left the city of Ur in Babylonia to go to the land of Canaan. They went as far as Haran and settled there. 32 Terah died there at the age of two hundred and five.

God's Call to Abram

altar [2] 8.20; 13.4
bad 3.5; 37.2
bless [4] 9.1; 14.19
court (1) 41.45

12 The LORD said to Abram, "Leave your country, your relatives, and your father's home, and go to a land that

[z] PELEG: *This name sounds like the Hebrew for "divide."*
[a] BABYLON: *This name sounds like the Hebrew for "mixed up."*

12.1: Acts 7.2–3; Heb 11.8

curse 9.25; 27.12
disease Ex 4.6
famine 26.1
flock 21.28
holy 4.26; 28.11
sacred 13.18
sheep 4.4; 13.2
slave [2] 9.25; 15.3
terrible 4.10; 18.20
worship (1) (of God)
4.26; 13.4

I am going to show you. 2 I will give you
many descendants, and they will become
a great nation. I will **bless** you and make
your name famous, so that you will be a
blessing.
3 I will **bless** those who bless you,
But I will **curse** those who curse you.
And through you I will **bless** all the
nations."[b]
4 When Abram was seventy-five years
old, he started out from Haran, as the
LORD had told him to do; and Lot went
with him. 5 Abram took his wife Sarai, his
nephew Lot, and all the wealth and all
the **slaves** they had acquired in Haran,
and they started out for the land of
Canaan.
When they arrived in Canaan, 6 Abram
travelled through the land until he came
to the **sacred** tree of Moreh, the **holy**
place at Shechem. (At that time the
Canaanites were still living in the land.)
7 The LORD appeared to Abram and said
to him, "This is the country that I am
going to give to your descendants." Then
Abram built an **altar** there to the LORD,
who had appeared to him. 8 After that, he
moved on south to the hill-country east of
the city of Bethel and set up his camp
between Bethel on the west and Ai on the
east. There also he built an **altar** and
worshipped the LORD. 9 Then he moved
on from place to place, going towards the
southern part of Canaan.

Abram in Egypt

10 But there was a **famine** in Canaan,
and it was so **bad** that Abram went farther south to Egypt, to live there for a
while. 11 When he was about to cross the
border into Egypt, he said to his wife
Sarai, "You are a beautiful woman.
12 When the Egyptians see you, they will
assume that you are my wife, and so they
will kill me and let you live. 13 Tell them
that you are my sister; then because of
you they will let me live and treat me
well." 14 When he crossed the border into
Egypt, the Egyptians did see that his wife
was beautiful. 15 Some of the **court**
officials saw her and told the king how
beautiful she was; so she was taken to his
palace. 16 Because of her the king treated
Abram well and gave him **flocks of sheep**
and goats, cattle, donkeys, **slaves**, and
camels.
17 But because the king had taken
Sarai, the LORD sent **terrible diseases** on
him and on the people of his palace.
18 Then the king sent for Abram and
asked him, "What have you done to me?
Why didn't you tell me that she was your
wife? 19 Why did you say that she was
your sister, and let me take her as my
wife? Here is your wife; take her and get
out!" 20 The king gave orders to his men,
so they took Abram and put him out of
the country, together with his wife and
everything he owned.

Abram and Lot Separate

13 Abram went north out of Egypt
to the southern part of Canaan
with his wife and everything he owned,
and Lot went with him. 2 Abram was a
very **rich** man, with **sheep**, goats, and
cattle, as well as silver and gold. 3 Then
he left there and moved from place to
place, going towards Bethel. He reached
the place between Bethel and Ai where
he had camped before 4 and had built an
altar. There he **worshipped** the LORD.
5 Lot also had **sheep**, goats, and cattle,
as well as his own family and **servants**.
6 And so there was not **enough** pasture
land for the two of them to stay together,
because they had too many animals. 7 So
quarrels broke out between the men who
took **care** of Abram's animals and those
who took **care** of Lot's animals. (At that
time the Canaanites and the Perizzites
were still living in the land.)
8 Then Abram said to Lot, "We are
relatives, and your men and my men
shouldn't be **quarrelling**. 9 So let's **separate**. **Choose** any part of the land you
want. You go one way, and I'll go the
other."
10 Lot looked round and saw that the
whole Jordan Valley, all the way to Zoar,
had **plenty** of water, like the Garden of
the LORD[c] or like the land of Egypt. (This
was before the LORD had **destroyed** the
cities of Sodom and Gomorrah.) 11 So Lot
chose the whole Jordan Valley for himself and moved away towards the east.
That is how the two men parted.
12 Abram stayed in the land of Canaan,
and Lot settled among the cities in the
valley and camped near Sodom, 13 whose
people were **wicked** and sinned against
the LORD.

Abram Moves to Hebron

14 After Lot had left, the LORD said to
Abram, "From where you are, look carefully in all directions. 15 I am going to give
you and your descendants all the land
that you see, and it will be yours for ever.

altar [2] 12.7; 22.9
care [2] 4.9; 25.34
choose [2] 18.19
destroy 9.11; 18.23
enough 7.17; 19.20
plenty 24.25
quarrel [2] 26.20
rich 14.23
sacred 12.6; 14.13
separate 1.4; 21.28
servant 18.7
sheep [2] 12.16; 20.14
wicked 6.5; 15.16
worship (1) (of God)
12.8; 21.33

[b] And through...nations; *or* All the nations will ask me to bless them as I have blessed you.
[c] GARDEN OF THE LORD: *a reference to the Garden of Eden.*

12.3: Gal 3.8 **12.7:** Acts 7.5; Gal 3.16 **12.13:** Gen 20.2, 26.7 **13.10:** Gen 2.10 **13.15:** Acts 7.5

16 I am going to give you so many descendants that no one will be able to
count them all; it would be as easy to
count all the specks of dust on earth!
17 Now, go and look over the whole land,
because I am going to give it all to you."
18 So Abram moved his camp and settled
near the **sacred** trees of Mamre at
Hebron, and there he built an **altar** to the
LORD.

Abram Rescues Lot

accept 15.6
bless [2] 12.2; 17.16
bread 18.6
conquer 10.8; 22.17
control 1.28; 16.6
enemy [2] 3.15; 22.17
escape [2] 7.7; 19.29
heaven [2] 6.2; 21.17
Hebrew 10.21; 39.14
Most High [4] Num 24.16
possess [2] 28.4
praise 9.26; 24.27
priest 41.45
prison 39.20
rebel 27.40
rich 13.2; 22.16
sacred 13.18; 18.1
share Ex 12.4
solemn 24.7
swear 42.15
turn 9.23; 19.26
victory [2] Ex 14.4

14 Four kings, Amraphel of Babylonia, Arioch of Ellasar, Chedorlaomer of Elam, and Tidal of Goiim,
2 went to war against five other kings:
Bera of Sodom, Birsha of Gomorrah,
Shinab of Admah, Shemeber of Zeboiim,
and the king of Bela (or Zoar). 3 These
five kings had formed an alliance and
joined forces in the Valley of Siddim,
which is now the Dead Sea. 4 They had
been under the **control** of Chedorlaomer
for twelve years, but in the thirteenth
year they **rebelled** against him. 5 In the
fourteenth year Chedorlaomer and his
allies came with their armies and
defeated the Rephaim in Ashteroth Karnaim, the Zuzim in Ham, the Emim in
the plain of Kiriathaim, 6 and the Horites
in the mountains of Edom, pursuing them
as far as Elparan on the edge of the
desert. 7 Then they **turned** round and
came back to Kadesh (then known as
Enmishpat). They **conquered** all the land
of the Amalekites and defeated the
Amorites who lived in Hazazon Tamar.

8 Then the kings of Sodom, Gomorrah,
Admah, Zeboiim, and Bela drew up their
armies for battle in the Valley of Siddim
and fought 9 against the kings of Elam,
Goiim, Babylonia, and Ellasar, five kings
against four. 10 The valley was full of tar
pits, and when the kings of Sodom and
Gomorrah tried to run away from the
battle, they fell into the pits; but the
other three kings **escaped** to the mountains. 11 The four kings took everything in
Sodom and Gomorrah, including the
food, and went away. 12 Lot, Abram's
nephew, was living in Sodom, so they
took him and all his **possessions**.

13 But a man **escaped** and reported all
this to Abram, the **Hebrew**, who was
living near the **sacred** trees belonging to
Mamre the Amorite. Mamre and his
brothers Eshcol and Aner were Abram's
allies. 14 When Abram heard that his
nephew had been captured, he called together all the fighting men in his camp,
318 in all, and pursued the four kings all
the way to Dan. 15 There he divided his
men into groups, attacked the **enemy** by
night, and defeated them. He chased
them as far as Hobah, north of Damascus, 16 and recovered the loot that had
been taken. He also brought back his
nephew Lot and his **possessions**, together
with the women and the other **prisoners**.

Melchizedek Blesses Abram

17 When Abram came back from his
victory over Chedorlaomer and the other
kings, the king of Sodom went out to
meet him in the Valley of Shaveh (also
called the King's Valley). 18 And Melchizedek, who was king of Salem and also a
priest of the **Most High God**, brought
bread and wine to Abram, 19 **blessed** him,
and said, "May the **Most High God**, who
made **heaven and earth**, **bless** Abram!
20 May the **Most High God**, who gave you
victory over your **enemies**, **be praised**!"
And Abram gave Melchizedek a tenth of
all the loot he had recovered.

21 The king of Sodom said to Abram,
"Keep the loot, but give me back all my
people."

22 Abram answered, "I **solemnly**
swear before the LORD, the **Most High**
God, Maker of **heaven and earth**, 23 that I
will not keep anything of yours, not even
a thread or a sandal strap. Then you can
never say, 'I am the one who made
Abram **rich**.' 24 I will take nothing for myself. I will **accept** only what my men
have used. But let my allies, Aner,
Eshcol, and Mamre, take their **share**."

God's Covenant with Abram

15 After this, Abram had a **vision**
and heard the LORD say to him,
"Do not be **afraid**, Abram. I will shield
you from **danger** and give you a great
reward."

2 But Abram answered, "**Sovereign**
LORD, what good will your **reward** do me,
since I have no children? My only heir is
Eliezer of Damascus.[x] 3 You have given
me no children, and one of my **slaves** will
inherit my property."

4 Then he heard the LORD speaking to
him again: "This **slave** Eliezer will not **inherit** your property; your own son will be
your heir." 5 The LORD took him outside
and said, "Look at the sky and try to
count the stars; you will have as many
descendants as that."

6 Abram put his **trust** in the LORD, and
because of this the LORD was **pleased**
with him and **accepted** him.

7 Then the LORD said to him, "I am

accept 14.24; 18.5
afraid 3.10; 18.15
body 7.11; 23.3
covenant 9.9; 17.2
cruel 16.6
danger Lev 26.6
dark 1.2; Ex 10.21
dove 8.8; Lev 1.14
each other 3.15; 25.22
fear 9.2; 35.5
inherit [2] 21.10
peace 26.29
please 8.21; 39.4
promise 9.11; 17.4
punish [2] 9.5; 18.25
reward [2] 30.18
ripe 25.7
slave [4] 12.5; 16.1
Sovereign [2] Deut 3.24
stranger 1 Chr 16.1
terror Ex 15.14
trust Ex 18.21
vision 46.2
wicked 13.13; 19.7

[x] My...Damascus; *Hebrew unclear*

14.18-20: Heb 7.1-10 **15.5:** Rom 4.18; Heb 11.12 **15.6:** Rom 4.3; Gal 3.6; Jas 2.23

the LORD, who led you out of Ur in Babylonia, to give you this land as your own."
8 But Abram asked, "**Sovereign LORD**,
how can I know that it will be mine?"
9 He answered, "Bring me a cow, a
goat, and a ram, each of them three
years old, and a **dove** and a pigeon."
10 Abram brought the animals to God, cut
them in half, and placed the halves opposite **each other** in two rows; but he did
not cut up the birds. 11 Vultures came
down on the **bodies**, but Abram drove
them off.
12 When the sun was going down,
Abram fell into a deep sleep, and **fear**
and **terror** came over him. 13 The LORD
said to him, "Your descendants will be
strangers in a foreign land; they will be
slaves there and will be treated **cruelly**
for four hundred years. 14 But I will **punish** the nation that **enslaves** them, and
when they leave that foreign land, they
will take great wealth with them. 15 You
yourself will live to a **ripe** old age, die in
peace, and be buried. 16 It will be four
generations before your descendants
come back here, because I will not drive
out the Amorites until they become so
wicked that they must be **punished**."
17 When the sun had set and it was
dark, a smoking fire-pot and a flaming
torch suddenly appeared and passed between the pieces of the animals. 18 Then
and there the LORD made a **covenant**
with Abram. He said, "I **promise** to give
your descendants all this land from the
border of Egypt to the River Euphrates,
19 including the lands of the Kenites, the
Kenizzites, the Kadmonites, 20 the Hittites, the Perizzites, the Rephaim, 21 the
Amorites, the Canaanites, the Girgashites, and the Jebusites."

Hagar and Ishmael

16 Abram's wife Sarai had not
borne him any children. But she
had an Egyptian **slave-girl** named Hagar,
2 and so she said to Abram, "The LORD
has **kept me from** having children. Why
don't you sleep with my **slave-girl**? Perhaps she can have a child for me."
Abram **agreed** with what Sarai said. 3 So
she gave Hagar to him to be his **concubine**. (This happened after Abram had
lived in Canaan for ten years.) 4 Abram
had intercourse with Hagar, and she became pregnant. When she found out that
she was pregnant, she became **proud** and
despised Sarai.
5 Then Sarai said to Abram, "It's your
fault that Hagar **despises** me.[d] I myself
gave her to you, and ever since she found
out that she was pregnant, she has **despised** me. May the LORD **judge** which of
us is **right**, you or me!"
6 Abram answered, "Very well, she is
your **slave** and under your **control**; do
whatever you want with her." Then Sarai
treated Hagar so **cruelly** that she ran
away.
7 The **angel of the LORD** met Hagar at
a spring in the desert on the road to Shur
8 and said, "Hagar, **slave** of Sarai, where
have you come from and where are you
going?"
She answered, "I am running away
from my mistress."
9 He said, "Go back to her and be her
slave." 10 Then he said, "I will give you so
many descendants that no one will be
able to count them. 11 You are going to
have a son, and you will name him Ishmael,[e] because the LORD has heard your
cry of **distress**. 12 But your son will live
like a wild donkey; he will be against
everyone, and everyone will be against
him. He will live **apart** from all his
relatives."
13 Hagar asked herself, "Have I really
seen God and lived to tell about it?"[f] So
she called the LORD who had spoken to
her "A God Who Sees." 14 That is why
people call the well between Kadesh and
Bered "The Well of the Living One Who
Sees Me."
15 Hagar bore Abram a son, and he
named him Ishmael. 16 Abram was
eighty-six years old at the time.

Circumcision, the Sign of the Covenant

17 When Abram was ninety-nine
years old, the LORD appeared to
him and said, "I am the **Almighty** God.
Obey me and always do what is **right**. 2 I
will make my **covenant** with you and
give you many descendants." 3 Abram
bowed down with his face touching the
ground, and God said, 4 "I make this **covenant** with you: I **promise** that you will
be the ancestor of many nations. 5 Your
name will no longer be Abram, but Abraham,[g] because I am making you the ancestor of many nations. 6 I will give you
many descendants, and some of them

agree 17.9
angel 19.1
apart 2.3; 25.18
concubine 22.24
control 14.4; 27.40
cruel 15.13; 49.7
despise [3] Deut 7.26
distress Num 11.10
fault 6.9; 31.39
judge 18.25
keep from 3.24; 20.6
proud 49.3
right (1) 7.1; 17.1
slave [5] 15.3; 17.11

agree [2] 16.2; 19.21
Almighty 28.3
bless [3] 14.19; 18.18
bow (2) [2] 18.2
circumcise [7] 21.4
covenant [10] 15.18; Ex 2.24
everlasting [3] 9.12; 21.33
God's people Ex 3.7
obey [2] 18.19
physical Lev 21.17
promise [2] 15.18; 18.19
request Ex 33.18
right (1) 16.5; 18.19
sign (1) 9.12; Ex 12.13
slave [3] 16.1; 20.14

[d] It's your fault...me; *or* May you suffer for this wrong done against me.
[e] ISHMAEL: *This name in Hebrew means "God hears."*
[f] *Probable text* lived to tell about it?; *Hebrew unclear.*
[g] ABRAHAM: *This name sounds like the Hebrew for "ancestor of many nations."*

15.12: Job 4.13, 14 **15.13:** Ex 1.1–14; Acts 7.6 **15.14:** Ex 12.40–41; Acts 7.7 **15.18:** Acts 7.5
16.15: Gal 4.22 **17.5:** Rom 4.17

will be kings. You will have so many descendants that they will become nations.

7 "I will keep my **promise** to you and to your descendants in future generations as an **everlasting covenant**. I will be your God and the God of your descendants. 8 I will give to you and to your descendants this land in which you are now a foreigner. The whole land of Canaan will belong to your descendants for ever, and I will be their God."

9 God said to Abraham, "You also must **agree** to keep the **covenant** with me, both you and your descendants in future generations. 10 You and your descendants must all **agree** to **circumcise** every male among you. 11-12 From now on you must **circumcise** every baby boy when he is eight days old, including **slaves** born in your homes and slaves bought from foreigners. This will show that there is a **covenant** between you and me. 13 Each one must be **circumcised**, and this will be a **physical sign** to show that my **covenant** with you is **everlasting**. 14 Any male who has not been **circumcised** will no longer be considered one of **my people**, because he has not kept the **covenant** with me."

15 God said to Abraham, "You must no longer call your wife Sarai; from now on her name is Sarah.[x] 16 I will **bless** her, and I will give you a son by her. I will **bless** her, and she will become the mother of nations, and there will be kings among her descendants."

17 Abraham **bowed down** with his face touching the ground, but he began to laugh when he thought, "Can a man have a child when he is a hundred years old? Can Sarah have a child at ninety?" 18 He asked God, "Why not let Ishmael be my heir?"

19 But God said, "No. Your wife Sarah will bear you a son and you will name him Isaac.[h] I will keep my **covenant** with him and with his descendants for ever. It is an **everlasting covenant**. 20 I have heard your **request** about Ishmael, so I will **bless** him and give him many children and many descendants. He will be the father of twelve princes, and I will make a great nation of his descendants. 21 But I will keep my **covenant** with your son Isaac, who will be born to Sarah about this time next year." 22 When God finished speaking to Abraham, he left him.

23 On that same day Abraham **obeyed** God and **circumcised** his son Ishmael and all the other males in his household, including the **slaves** born in his home and those he had bought. 24 Abraham was ninety-nine years old when he was **circumcised**, 25 and his son Ishmael was thirteen. 26 They were both **circumcised** on the same day, 27 together with all Abraham's **slaves**.

A Son Is Promised to Abraham

18 The LORD appeared to Abraham at the **sacred** trees of Mamre. As Abraham was sitting at the entrance of his tent during the hottest part of the day, 2 he looked up and saw three men standing there. As soon as he saw them, he ran out to meet them. **Bowing down** with his face touching the ground, 3 he said, "Sirs, please do not pass by my home without stopping; I am here to **serve** you. 4 Let me bring some water for you to wash your feet; you can **rest** here beneath this tree. 5 I will also bring a bit of food; it will give you **strength** to continue your journey. You have **honoured** me by coming to my home, so let me **serve** you."

They replied, "**Thank** you; we **accept**."

6 Abraham hurried into the tent and said to Sarah, "Quick, take a sack of your **best** flour, and bake some **bread**." 7 Then he ran to the herd and picked out a calf that was tender and fat, and gave it to a **servant**, who hurried to get it ready. 8 He took some cream, some milk, and the meat, and set the food before the men. There under the tree he **served** them himself, and they ate.

9 Then they asked him, "Where is your wife Sarah?"

"She is there in the tent," he answered.

10 One of them said, "Nine months from now[i] I will come back, and your wife Sarah will have a son."

Sarah was behind him, at the door of the tent, listening. 11 Abraham and Sarah were very old, and Sarah had stopped having her monthly periods. 12 So Sarah laughed to herself and said, "Now that I am old and worn out, can I still **enjoy** **sex**? And besides, my husband is old too."

13 Then the LORD asked Abraham, "Why did Sarah laugh and say, 'Can I really have a child when I am so old?' 14 Is anything too **hard** for the LORD? As I said, nine months from now I will return, and Sarah will have a son."

accept 15.6; 21.30
accuse [2] 19.13
act 38.24
afraid 15.1; 19.30
anger [2] 4.5; 27.44
best 4.4; 23.6
bless 17.16; 21.1
bold [2] Job 13.16
bow (2) 17.3; 19.1
bread 14.18; 19.3
choose 13.9; 24.3
command 7.5; 21.4
deny Ex 23.6
destroy [7] 13.10; 19.13
enjoy 25.28
forgive [2] 32.20
guilty [3] 26.10
hard 11.3; 30.8
honour 22.12
impossible [2] 20.1
innocent [7] 20.4
judge 16.5; 30.6
justice [2] Ex 23.2
might 23.6
obey 17.1; 22.12
promise 17.4; 21.1
punish 15.14; Ex 3
rest (1) 28.11
right (1) 17.1; 31.3
right (3) 25.31
sacred 14.13; Ex 15.13
sake 2 Sam 5.12
save 19.19
servant 13.5; 19.3
serve [3] 19.2
sex 19.5
spare [2] 42.18
strength 31.6
terrible 12.17; 19.1
thank 47.31
true 3.4; Ex 33.12

[x] SARAH: *This name in Hebrew means "princess."*
[h] ISAAC: *This name in Hebrew means "he laughs."*
[i] Nine months from now; *or* This time next year.

17.7: Lk 1.55 **17.8:** Acts 7.5 **17.10:** Acts 7.8; Rom 4.11 **18.2a:** Heb 13.2 **18.10:** Rom 9.9 **18.12:** 1 Pet 3.6 **18.14:** Lk 1.37

15 Because Sarah was **afraid**, she **denied** it. "I didn't laugh," she said.

"Yes, you did," he replied. "You laughed."

Abraham Pleads for Sodom

16 Then the men left and went to a place where they could look down at Sodom, and Abraham went with them to send them on their way. 17 And the LORD said to himself, "I will not hide from Abraham what I am going to do. 18 His descendants will become a great and **mighty** nation, and through him I will **bless** all the nations.[j] 19 I have **chosen** him in order that he may **command** his sons and his descendants to **obey** me and to do what is **right** and **just**. If they do, I will do everything for him that I have **promised**."

20 Then the LORD said to Abraham, "There are **terrible accusations** against Sodom and Gomorrah, and their sin is very great. 21 I must go down to find out whether or not the **accusations** which I have heard are **true**."

22 Then the two men left and went on towards Sodom, but the LORD remained with Abraham. 23 Abraham approached the LORD and asked, "Are you really going to **destroy** the **innocent** with the **guilty**? 24 If there are fifty **innocent** people in the city, will you **destroy** the whole city? Won't you **spare** it in order to **save** the fifty? 25 Surely you won't kill the **innocent** with the **guilty**. That's **impossible**! You can't do that. If you did, the **innocent** would be **punished** along with the **guilty**. That is **impossible**. The **judge** of all the earth has to **act justly**."

26 The LORD answered, "If I find fifty **innocent** people in Sodom, I will **spare** the whole city for their **sake**."

27 Abraham spoke again: "Please **forgive** my **boldness** in continuing to speak to you, Lord. I am only a man and have no **right** to say anything. 28 But perhaps there will be only forty-five **innocent** people instead of fifty. Will you **destroy** the whole city because there are five too few?"

The LORD answered, "I will not **destroy** the city if I find forty-five **innocent** people."

29 Abraham spoke again: "Perhaps there will be only forty."

He replied, "I will not **destroy** it if there are forty."

30 Abraham said, "Please don't be **angry**, Lord, but I must speak again. What if there are only thirty?"

He said, "I will not do it if I find thirty."

31 Abraham said, "Please **forgive** my **boldness** in continuing to speak to you, Lord. Suppose that only twenty are found?"

He said, "I will not **destroy** the city if I find twenty."

32 Abraham said, "Please don't be **angry**, Lord, and I will speak just once more. What if only ten are found?"

He said, "I will not **destroy** it if there are ten." 33 After he had finished speaking with Abraham, the LORD went away, and Abraham returned home.

The Sinfulness of Sodom

19 When the two **angels** came to Sodom that evening, Lot was sitting at the city gate. As soon as he saw them, he got up and went to meet them. He **bowed down** before them 2 and said, "Sirs, I am here to **serve** you. Please come to my house. You can wash your feet and stay the night. In the morning you can get up early and go on your way."

But they answered, "No, we will spend the night here in the city square."

3 He kept on **urging** them, and finally they went with him to his house. Lot ordered his **servants** to bake some **bread** and prepare a fine meal for the guests. When it was ready, they ate it.

4 Before the guests went to bed, the men of Sodom surrounded the house. All the men of the city, both young and old, were there. 5 They called out to Lot and asked, "Where are the men who came to stay with you tonight? Bring them out to us!" The men of Sodom wanted to have **sex** with them.

6 Lot went outside and closed the door behind him. 7 He said to them, "**Friends**, I **beg** you, don't do such a **wicked** thing! 8 Look, I have two daughters who are still **virgins**. Let me bring them out to you, and you can do whatever you want with them. But don't do anything to these men; they are guests in my house, and I must **protect** them."

9 But they said, "Get out of our way, you foreigner! Who are you to tell us what to do? Out of our way, or we will treat you **worse** than them." They pushed Lot back and moved up to break down the door. 10 But the two men inside reached out, pulled Lot back into the house, and shut the door. 11 Then they **struck** all the men outside with **blindness**, so that they couldn't find the door.

accuse 18.20; 42.30
afraid 18.15; 21.17
agree 17.9; 21.27
angel [3] 16.7; 21.17
beg 42.21
blind 27.1
bow (2) 18.2; 23.7
bread 18.6; 25.34
destroy [7] 18.23; 20.4
disaster 20.9
enough 13.6; 30.15
escape 14.10; 32.8
favour 30.6
friend 26.27
life (1) [3] 9.4; 25.27
mind (1) Ex 13.17
pity 43.14
presence 4.14; 21.23
protect 28.15
rise [2] 7.20; 32.31
safe [2] 28.21
save 18.24; 27.36
servant 18.7; 21.25
serve 18.3; 25.23
sex 18.12; 35.22
strike 4.23; 32.25
terrible 18.20; 41.31
turn 14.7; 41.13
urge 33.11
virgin 24.16
wicked 15.16; Num 14.27
world 11.1; 41.57
worse 41.56

[j] through...nations; *or* all the nations will ask me to bless them as I have blessed him.

19.5–8: Judg 19.22–24 **19.11:** 2 Kgs 6.18

Lot Leaves Sodom

12 The two men said to Lot, "If you
have anyone else here—sons, daughters,
sons-in-law, or any other relatives living
in the city—get them out of here,
13 because we are going to **destroy** this
place. The LORD has heard the **terrible
accusations** against these people and has
sent us to **destroy** Sodom."

14 Then Lot went to the men that his
daughters were going to marry, and said,
"Hurry up and get out of here; the LORD
is going to **destroy** this place." But they
thought he was joking.

15 At dawn the **angels** tried to make
Lot hurry. "Quick!" they said. "Take
your wife and your two daughters and
get out, so that you will not lose your
lives when the city is **destroyed**." 16 Lot
hesitated. The LORD, however, had **pity**
on him; so the men took him, his wife,
and his two daughters by the hand and
led them out of the city. 17 Then one of
the **angels** said, "Run for your **lives**!
Don't look back and don't stop in the valley. Run to the hills, so that you won't be
killed."

18 But Lot answered, "No, please don't
make us do that, sir. 19 You have done me
a great **favour** and **saved** my **life**. But the
hills are too far away; the **disaster** will
overtake me, and I will die before I get
there. 20 Do you see that little town? It is
near **enough**. Let me go over there—you
can see it is just a small place—and I will
be **safe**."

21 He answered, "All right, I **agree**. I
won't **destroy** that town. 22 Hurry! Run! I
can't do anything until you get there."

Because Lot called it small, the town
was named Zoar.[k]

The Destruction of Sodom and Gomorrah

23 The sun was **rising** when Lot
reached Zoar. 24 Suddenly the LORD
rained burning sulphur on the cities of
Sodom and Gomorrah 25 and **destroyed**
them and the whole valley, along with all
the people there and everything that
grew on the land. 26 But Lot's wife looked
back and was **turned** into a pillar of salt.

27 Early the next morning Abraham
hurried to the place where he had stood
in the **presence** of the LORD. 28 He looked
down at Sodom and Gomorrah and the
whole valley and saw smoke **rising** from
the land, like smoke from a huge furnace. 29 But when God **destroyed** the
cities of the valley where Lot was living,
he kept Abraham in **mind** and allowed
Lot to **escape** to **safety**.

The Origin of the Moabites and Ammonites

30 Because Lot was **afraid** to stay in
Zoar, he and his two daughters moved up
into the hills and lived in a cave. 31 The
elder daughter said to her sister, "Our
father is getting old, and there are no
men in the whole **world**[l] to marry us so
that we can have children. 32 Come on,
let's make our father drunk, so that we
can sleep with him and have children by
him." 33 That night they gave him wine to
drink, and the elder daughter had intercourse with him. But he was so drunk
that he didn't know it.

34 The next day the elder daughter
said to her sister, "I slept with him last
night; now let's make him drunk again
tonight, and you sleep with him. Then
each of us will have a child by our
father." 35 So that night they made him
drunk, and the younger daughter had
intercourse with him. Again he was so
drunk that he didn't know it. 36 In this
way both of Lot's daughters became
pregnant by their own father. 37 The
elder daughter had a son, whom she
named Moab.[m] He was the ancestor of
the present-day Moabites. 38 The younger
daughter also had a son, whom she
named Benammi.[n] He was the ancestor
of the present-day Ammonites.

Abraham and Abimelech

20 Abraham moved from Mamre to
the southern part of Canaan and
lived between Kadesh and Shur. Later,
while he was living in Gerar, 2 he said
that his wife Sarah was his sister. So King
Abimelech of Gerar had Sarah brought
to him. 3 One night God appeared to him
in a **dream** and said: "You are going to
die, because you have taken this woman;
she is already married."

4 But Abimelech had not come near
her, and he said, "Lord, I am **innocent**!
Would you **destroy** me and my people?
5 Abraham himself said that she was his
sister, and she said the same thing. I did
this with a clear **conscience**, and I have
done no **wrong**."

6 God replied in the **dream**, "Yes, I

conscience [2] 1 Sam 24.5
destroy 19.13; 32.11
disaster 19.19; 44.3
dream [2] 28.12
heal [2] Ex 15.26
impossible 18.25; Ruth 1.13
innocent [2] 18.23; Ex 23.7
keep from 16.2; 30.
loyal 21.23
pray [2] 24.12
prophet Ex 7.1
prove 42.19
reverence Lev 19.3
sheep 13.2; 21.27
slave [2] 17.11; 21.1
terrify 28.17
warn 4.15; 26.11
wrong [3] 41.9

[k] ZOAR: *This name sounds like the Hebrew for "small."* [l] the whole world; *or* this land.
[m] MOAB: *This name sounds like the Hebrew for "from my father."*
[n] BENAMMI: *This name in Hebrew means "son of my relative" and sounds like the Hebrew for "Ammonite."*

19.16: 2 Pet 2.7 **19.24–25:** Mt 10.15, 11.23–24; Lk 10.12, 17.29; 2 Pet 2.6; Jude 7 **19.26:** Lk 17.32
20.2: Gen 12.13, 26.7

know that you did it with a clear **con-**
science; so I **kept you from** sinning
against me and did not let you touch her.
7 But now, give the woman back to her
husband. He is a **prophet**, and he will
pray for you, so that you will not die. But
if you do not give her back, I **warn** you
that you are going to die, you and all
your people."
8 Early the next morning Abimelech
called all his officials and told them what
had happened, and they were **terrified**.
9 Then Abimelech called Abraham and
asked, "What have you done to us? What
wrong have I done to you to make you
bring this **disaster** on me and my
kingdom? No one should ever do what
you have done to me. 10 Why did you do
it?"
11 Abraham answered, "I thought that
there would be no one here who has
reverence for God and that they would
kill me to get my wife. 12 She really is my
sister. She is the daughter of my father,
but not of my mother, and I married her.
13 So when God sent me from my father's
house into foreign lands, I said to her,
'You can show how **loyal** you are to me
by telling everyone that I am your
brother.' "
14 Then Abimelech gave Sarah back
to Abraham, and at the same time he
gave him **sheep**, cattle, and **slaves**. 15 He
said to Abraham, "Here is my whole
land; live anywhere you like." 16 He said
to Sarah, "I am giving your brother a
thousand pieces of silver as **proof** to all
who are with you that you are **innocent**;
everyone will know that you have done
no **wrong**."
17–18 Because of what had happened
to Sarah, Abraham's wife, the LORD had
made it **impossible** for any woman in
Abimelech's palace to have children. So
Abraham **prayed** for Abimelech, and God
healed him. He also **healed** his wife and
his **slave-girls**, so that they could have
children.

The Birth of Isaac

21 The LORD **blessed** Sarah, as he
had **promised**, 2 and she became
pregnant and bore a son to Abraham
when he was old. The boy was born at
the time God had said he would be born.
3 Abraham named him Isaac, 4 and when
Isaac was eight days old, Abraham **cir-**
cumcised him, as God had **commanded**.
5 Abraham was a hundred years old when
Isaac was born. 6 Sarah said, "God has
brought me **joy** and laughter.[m] Everyone
who hears about it will laugh with me."
7 Then she added, "Who would have said
to Abraham that Sarah would nurse children? Yet I have borne him a son in his
old age."
8 The child grew, and on the day that
he was weaned, Abraham gave a great
feast.

Hagar and Ishmael Are Sent Away

9 One day Ishmael, whom Hagar the
Egyptian had borne to Abraham, was
playing with[n] Sarah's son Isaac.[o] 10 Sarah
saw them and said to Abraham, "Send
this **slave-girl** and her son away. The son
of this woman must not get any part of
your wealth, which my son Isaac should
inherit." 11 This **troubled** Abraham very
much, because Ishmael was also his son.
12 But God said to Abraham, "Don't be
worried about the boy and your **slave**
Hagar. Do whatever Sarah tells you,
because it is through Isaac that you will
have the descendants I have **promised**.
13 I will also give many children to the
son of the **slave-girl**, so that they will become a nation. He too is your son."
14 Early the next morning Abraham
gave Hagar some food and a leather bag
full of water. He put the child on her
back and sent her away. She left and
wandered about in the wilderness of
Beersheba. 15 When the water was all
gone, she left the child under a bush
16 and sat down about a hundred metres
away. She said to herself, "I can't bear to
see my child die." While she was sitting
there, she[p] began to cry.
17 God heard the boy crying, and from
heaven the **angel of God** spoke to Hagar,
"What are you **troubled** about, Hagar?
Don't be **afraid**. God has heard the boy
crying. 18 Get up, go and pick him up, and
comfort him. I will make a great nation
out of his descendants." 19 Then God
opened her eyes, and she saw a well. She
went and filled the leather bag with
water and gave some to the boy. 20 God
was with the boy as he grew up; he lived
in the wilderness of Paran and became a
skilful hunter. 21 His mother found an
Egyptian wife for him.

The Agreement between Abraham and Abimelech

22 At that time Abimelech went with
Phicol, the commander of his army, and

[m] LAUGHTER: *The name Isaac in Hebrew means "he laughs" (see also 17.17–19).*
[n] playing with; *or* making fun of.
[o] *Some ancient translations* with Sarah's son Isaac; *Hebrew does not have these words.*
[p] she; *one ancient translation* the child.

21.2: Heb 11.11 **21.4:** Gen 17.12; Acts 7.8 **21.10:** Gal 4.29–30 **21.12:** Rom 9.7; Heb 11.18
21.22: Gen 26.26

accept 18.5; 23.13
admit (1) 26.7
afraid 19.30; 26.7
agree [2] 19.21; 23.16
angel 19.1; 22.11
bless 18.18; 22.16
circumcise 17.10; 34.14
comfort 24.67
command 18.19; 22.18
complain Ex 5.15
deceive 27.12

everlasting 17.7; 49.26
feast 26.30
flock 12.16; 24.35
heaven 14.19; 22.11
inherit 15.3; 31.14
joy 29.11
lamb [2] 4.4; 22.7
loyal [2] 20.13; Num 14.24
presence 19.27; 23.9
promise [4] 18.19; 22.17
separate 13.9; 30.40
servant 19.3; 22.3
sheep 20.14; 24.35
slave [3] 20.14; 24.35
trouble [2] 3.16; 29.32
vow [2] 22.16
worry 32.7
worship (1) (of God) 13.4; 22.5

said to Abraham, "God is with you in
everything you do. 23 So make a **vow** here
in the **presence** of God that you will not
deceive me, my children, or my descendants. I have been **loyal** to you, so **promise**
that you will also be **loyal** to me and to
this country in which you are living."

24 Abraham said, "I **promise**."

25 Abraham **complained** to Abimelech
about a well which the **servants** of
Abimelech had seized. 26 Abimelech said,
"I don't know who did this. You didn't tell
me about it, and this is the first I have
heard of it." 27 Then Abraham gave some
sheep and cattle to Abimelech, and the
two of them made an **agreement**. 28 Abraham **separated** seven **lambs** from his
flock, 29 and Abimelech asked him, "Why
did you do that?"

30 Abraham answered, "**Accept** these
seven **lambs**. By doing this, you **admit**
that I am the one who dug this well."
31 And so the place was called Beersheba,[q] because it was there that the two
of them made a **vow**.

32 After they had made this **agree-
ment** at Beersheba, Abimelech and
Phicol went back to Philistia. 33 Then
Abraham planted a tamarisk-tree in
Beersheba and **worshipped** the LORD, the
Everlasting God. 34 Abraham lived in
Philistia for a long time.

God Commands Abraham to Offer Isaac

22 Some time later God **tested** Abraham; he called to him, "Abra-
ham!" And Abraham answered, "Yes,
here I am!"

2 "Take your son," God said, "your
only son, Isaac, whom you **love** so much,
and go to the land of Moriah. There on a
mountain that I will show you, **offer him
as a sacrifice** to me."

3 Early the next morning Abraham
cut some wood for the **sacrifice**, loaded
his donkey, and took Isaac and two **servants** with him. They started out for the
place that God had told him about. 4 On
the third day Abraham saw the place in
the distance. 5 Then he said to the **servants**, "Stay here with the donkey. The
boy and I will go over there and **worship**,
and then we will come back to you."

6 Abraham made Isaac carry the
wood for the **sacrifice**, and he himself
carried a knife and live coals for starting
the fire. As they walked along together,
7 Isaac said, "Father!"

He answered, "Yes, my son?"

Isaac asked, "I see that you have the
coals and the wood, but where is the
lamb for the **sacrifice**?"

8 Abraham answered, "God himself
will **provide** one." And the two of them
walked on together.

9 When they came to the place which
God had told him about, Abraham built
an **altar** and arranged the wood on it. He
tied up his son and placed him on the
altar, on top of the wood. 10 Then he
picked up the knife to kill him. 11 But the
angel of the LORD called to him from
heaven, "Abraham, Abraham!"

He answered, "Yes, here I am."

12 "Don't **hurt** the boy or do anything
to him," he said. "Now I know that you
honour and **obey** God, because you have
not kept back your only son from me."

13 Abraham looked round and saw a
ram caught in a bush by its horns. He
went and got it and **offered** it as a **burnt-
offering** instead of his son. 14 Abraham
named that place "**The** LORD **Provides**."[r]
And even today people say, "On the
LORD's mountain he **provides**."[s]

15 The **angel of the** LORD called to
Abraham from **heaven** a second time,
16 "I make a **vow** by my own **name**—the
LORD is speaking—that I will **richly bless**
you. Because you did this and did not
keep back your only son from me, 17 I
promise that I will give you as many descendants as there are stars in the sky or
grains of sand along the seashore. Your
descendants will **conquer** their **enemies**.
18 All the nations will ask me to bless
them as I have **blessed** your descendants—all because you **obeyed** my
command." 19 Abraham went back to his
servants, and they went together to Beersheba, where Abraham settled.

The Descendants of Nahor

20 Some time later Abraham **learnt**
that Milcah had borne eight children to
his brother Nahor: 21 Uz the **first-born**,
Buz his brother, Kemuel the father of
Aram, 22 Chesed, Hazo, Pildash, Jidlaph,
and Bethuel, 23 Rebecca's father. Milcah
bore these eight sons to Nahor, Abraham's brother. 24 Reumah, Nahor's
concubine, bore Tebah, Gaham, Tahash,
and Maacah.

Sarah Dies and Abraham Buys a Burial-Ground

23 Sarah lived to be a hundred and
twenty-seven years old. 2 She died

altar [2] 13.4; 26.25
angel [2] 21.17; 24.7
bless [2] 21.1; 24.1
burnt-offering Ex 10.25
command 21.4; 24.37
concubine 16.3; 32.22
conquer 14.7; 24.60
enemy 14.15; 24.60
first-born 25.31
heaven [2] 21.17; 24.3
honour 18.5; 41.43
hurt 37.22
lamb 21.28; 30.32
learn 9.24; 28.6
love 24.67
name (2) (name of God, of Jesus) 4.26; 24.3
obey [2] 18.19; 24.37
offer [2] 4.3; 24.44
promise 21.1; 24.7
provide [3] 1.29; 47.12
rich 14.23; 24.35
sacrifice [4] 8.20; 31.54
servant [3] 21.25; 24.2
test 42.15
vow 21.23; 24.2
worship (1) (of God) 21.33; 24.26

accept 21.30; 30.20
agree 21.27; 24.44
best 18.6; 27.15

[q] BEERSHEBA: *This name in Hebrew means "Well of the Vow" or "Well of Seven" (see also 26.33).*
[r] Provides; *or* Sees. [s] provides; *or* is seen.

22.1-13: Heb 11.17-19 **22.2:** 2 Chr 3.1 **22.9:** Jas 2.21 **22.16-17:** Heb 6.13-14 **22.17:** Heb 11.12
22.18: Acts 3.25

body 15.11; 37.20
bow (2) [2] 19.1; 24.52
death (1) 9.5; 25.11
glad Ex 4.14
grave [2] 35.20
might 18.18; 49.24
mourn 27.41
presence [2] 21.23; 27.7
worth 32.10

in Hebron in the land of Canaan, and Abraham **mourned** her **death**.

3 He left the place where his wife's **body** was lying, went to the Hittites, and said, 4"I am a foreigner living here among you; sell me some land, so that I can bury my wife."

5 They answered, 6"Listen to us, sir. We look upon you as a **mighty** leader; bury your wife in the **best grave** that we have. Any of us would be **glad** to give you a **grave**, so that you can bury her."

7 Then Abraham **bowed** before them 8and said, "If you are willing to let me bury my wife here, please ask Ephron son of Zohar 9to sell me Machpelah Cave, which is near the edge of his field. Ask him to sell it to me for its full price, here in your **presence**, so that I can own it as a burial-ground."

10 Ephron himself was sitting with the other Hittites at the meeting-place at the city gate; he answered in the hearing of everyone there, 11"Listen, sir; I will give you the whole field and the cave that is in it. Here in the **presence** of my own people, I will give it to you, so that you can bury your wife."

12 But Abraham **bowed** before the Hittites 13and said to Ephron, so that everyone could hear, "May I ask you, please, to listen. I will buy the whole field. **Accept** my payment, and I will bury my wife there."

14 Ephron answered, 15"Sir, land **worth** only four hundred pieces of silver—what is that between us? Bury your wife in it." 16Abraham **agreed** and weighed out the amount that Ephron had mentioned in the hearing of the people—four hundred pieces of silver, according to the standard weights used by the merchants.

17 That is how the property which had belonged to Ephron at Machpelah, east of Mamre, became Abraham's. It included the field, the cave which was in it, and all the trees in the field up to the edge of the property. 18It was recognized as Abraham's property by all the Hittites who were there at the meeting.

19 Then Abraham buried his wife Sarah in that cave in the land of Canaan. 20So the field which had belonged to the Hittites, and the cave in it, became the property of Abraham for a burial-ground.

A Wife for Isaac

agree 23.16; 26.28
angel [2] 22.11; 28.12
bless [4] 22.16; 25.11
bow (2) 23.7; 27.29

24 Abraham was now very old, and the LORD had **blessed** him in everything he did. 2He said to his oldest **servant**, who was in charge of all that he had, "Place your hand between my thighs[t] and make a **vow**. 3I want you to make a **vow** in the **name of the LORD**, the God of **heaven and earth**, that you will not **choose** a wife for my son from the people here in Canaan. 4You must go back to the country where I was born and get a wife for my son Isaac from among my relatives."

5 But the **servant** asked, "What if the girl will not leave home to come with me to this land? Shall I send your son back to the land you came from?"

6 Abraham answered, "Make **sure** that you don't send my son back there! 7The LORD, the God of **heaven**, brought me from the home of my father and from the land of my relatives, and he **solemnly promised** me that he would give this land to my descendants. He will send his **angel** before you, so that you can get a wife there for my son. 8If the girl is not willing to come with you, you will be **free** from this **promise**. But you must not under any circumstances take my son back there." 9So the **servant** put his hand between the thighs of Abraham, his **master**, and made a **vow** to do what Abraham had asked.

10 The **servant**, who was in charge of Abraham's property, took ten of his **master's** camels and went to the city where Nahor had lived in northern Mesopotamia. 11When he arrived, he made the camels **kneel** down at the well outside the city. It was late afternoon, the time when women came out to get water. 12He **prayed**, "LORD, God of my **master** Abraham, give me **success** today and keep your **promise** to my **master**. 13Here I am at the well where the young women of the city will be coming to get water. 14I will say to one of them, 'Please, lower your jar and let me have a drink.' If she says, 'Drink, and I will also bring water for your camels,' may she be the one that you have **chosen** for your **servant** Isaac. If this happens, I will know that you have kept your **promise** to my **master**."

15 Before he had finished **praying**, Rebecca arrived with a water-jar on her shoulder. She was the daughter of Bethuel, who was the son of Abraham's brother Nahor and his wife Milcah. 16She was a very beautiful young girl and still a **virgin**. She went down to the well, filled her jar, and came back. 17The **servant** ran to meet her and said, "Please give me a drink of water from your jar."

choose [5] 18.19; 32.13
comfort 21.18; 37.35
command 22.18; 26.5
conquer 22.17; Ex 34.24
enemy 22.17; 49.8
faithful 32.10
flock 21.28; 27.9
free [3] 26.22
fulfil 38.8
gift 30.20
heaven [2] 22.11; 27.28
intend Ex 21.8
kneel [3] 43.28
loss 31.39
love 22.2; 25.27
master [23] 27.37
name (2) (name of God, of Jesus) 22.16; 31.53
obey [2] 22.12; 26.5
offer 22.2; 31.54
plenty 13.10; 27.28
praise [2] 14.20; 29.35
pray [3] 20.7; 25.21
prayer 25.21
promise [6] 22.17; 26.3
refuse (1) 37.35
rich 22.16; 26.13
servant [18] 22.3; 26.14
sheep 21.27; 26.14
slave 21.10; 25.12
solemn 14.22; 26.28
succeed (1) [5] 39.2
sure 42.16
virgin 19.8; Ex 22.16
vow [5] 22.16; 25.33
watch 31.50
word (1) 11.1; 31.4
worship (1) (of God) [3] 22.5; 26.25

[t] PLACE...THIGHS: *This was the way in which a vow was made absolutely unchangeable.*

23.4: Heb 11.9, 13; Acts 7.16

18 She said, "Drink, sir," and quickly lowered her jar from her shoulder and held it while he drank. 19 When he had finished, she said, "I will also bring water for your camels and let them have all they want." 20 She quickly emptied her jar into the animals' drinking-trough and ran to the well to get more water, until she had watered all his camels. 21 The man kept **watching** her in silence, to see if the LORD had given him **success**.

22 When she had finished, the man took an expensive gold ring and put it in her nose and put two large gold bracelets on her arms. 23 He said, "Please tell me who your father is. Is there room in his house for my men and me to spend the night?"

24 "My father is Bethuel son of Nahor and Milcah," she answered. 25 "There is **plenty** of straw and fodder at our house, and there is a place for you to stay."

26 Then the man **knelt** down and **worshipped** the LORD. 27 He said, "**Praise** the LORD, the God of my **master** Abraham, who has **faithfully** kept his **promise** to my **master**. The LORD has led me straight to my **master's** relatives."

28 The girl ran to her mother's house and told the whole story. 29 Now Rebecca had a brother named Laban, and he ran outside to go to the well where Abraham's **servant** was. 30 Laban had seen the nose-ring and the bracelets on his sister's arms and had heard her say what the man had told her. He went to Abraham's **servant**, who was standing by his camels at the well, 31 and said, "Come home with me. You are a man whom the LORD has **blessed**. Why are you standing out here? I have a room ready for you in my house, and there is a place for your camels."

32 So the man went into the house, and Laban unloaded the camels and gave them straw and fodder. Then he brought water for Abraham's **servant** and his men to wash their feet. 33 When food was brought, the man said, "I will not eat until I have said what I have to say."

Laban said, "Go on and speak."

34 "I am the **servant** of Abraham," he began. 35 "The LORD has greatly **blessed** my **master** and made him a **rich** man. He has given him **flocks of sheep** and goats, cattle, silver, gold, male and female **slaves**, camels, and donkeys. 36 Sarah, my **master's** wife, bore him a son when she was old, and my **master** has given everything he owns to him. 37 My **master** made me **promise** with a **vow** to **obey** his **command**. He said, 'Do not **choose** a wife for my son from the girls in the land of Canaan. 38 Instead, go to my father's people, to my relatives, and **choose** a wife for him.' 39 And I asked my **master**, 'What if the girl will not come with me?' 40 He answered, 'The LORD, whom I have always **obeyed**, will send his **angel** with you and give you **success**. You will get for my son a wife from my own people, from my father's family. 41 There is only one way for you to be **free** from your **vow**: if you go to my relatives and they **refuse** you, then you will be **free**.'

42 "When I came to the well today, I **prayed**, 'LORD, God of my **master** Abraham, please give me **success** in what I am doing. 43 Here I am at the well. When a young woman comes out to get water, I will ask her to give me a drink of water from her jar. 44 If she **agrees** and also **offers** to bring water for my camels, may she be the one that you have **chosen** as the wife for my **master's** son.' 45 Before I had finished my silent **prayer**, Rebecca came with a water-jar on her shoulder and went down to the well to get water. I said to her, 'Please give me a drink.' 46 She quickly lowered her jar from her shoulder and said, 'Drink, and I will also water your camels.' So I drank, and she watered the camels. 47 I asked her, 'Who is your father?' And she answered, 'My father is Bethuel son of Nahor and Milcah.' Then I put the ring in her nose and the bracelets on her arms. 48 I **knelt** down and **worshipped** the LORD. I **praised** the LORD, the God of my **master** Abraham, who had led me straight to my **master's** relative, where I found his daughter for my **master's** son. 49 Now, if you **intend** to **fulfil** your responsibility towards my **master** and treat him fairly, please tell me; if not, say so, and I will decide what to do."

50 Laban and Bethuel answered, "Since this matter comes from the LORD, it is not for us to make a decision. 51 Here is Rebecca; take her and go. Let her become the wife of your **master's** son, as the LORD himself has said." 52 When the **servant** of Abraham heard this, he **bowed down** and **worshipped** the LORD. 53 Then he brought out clothing and silver and gold jewellery, and gave them to Rebecca. He also gave expensive **gifts** to her brother and to her mother.

54 Then Abraham's **servant** and the men with him ate and drank, and spent the night there. When they got up in the morning, he said, "Let me go back to my **master**."

55 But Rebecca's brother and her mother said, "Let the girl stay with us a week or ten days, and then she may go."

56 But he said, "Don't make us stay.
The LORD has made my journey a
success; let me go back to my **master**."
57 They answered, "Let's call the girl
and find out what she has to say." 58 So
they called Rebecca and asked, "Do you
want to go with this man?"
"Yes," she answered.
59 So they let Rebecca and her old
family **servant** go with Abraham's **servant** and his men. 60 And they gave
Rebecca their **blessing** in these **words**:

"May you, sister, become the mother
of millions!
May your descendants **conquer** the
cities of their **enemies**!"

61 Then Rebecca and her young women
got ready and mounted the camels to go
with Abraham's **servant**, and they all
started out.
62 Isaac had come into the wilderness
of[v] "The Well of the Living One Who
Sees Me" and was staying in the southern
part of Canaan. 63 He went out in the
early evening to take a walk in the fields
and saw camels coming. 64 When
Rebecca saw Isaac, she got down from
her camel 65 and asked Abraham's **servant**, "Who is that man walking towards
us in the field?"
"He is my **master**," the **servant**
answered. So she took her scarf and
covered her face.
66 The **servant** told Isaac everything
he had done. 67 Then Isaac brought
Rebecca into the tent that his mother
Sarah had lived in, and she became his
wife. Isaac **loved** Rebecca, and so he was
comforted for the **loss** of his mother.

Other Descendants of Abraham
(1 Chr 1.32–33)

25 Abraham married another wife,
whose name was Keturah. 2 She
bore him Zimran, Jokshan, Medan,
Midian, Ishbak, and Shuah. 3 Jokshan was
the father of Sheba and Dedan, and the
descendants of Dedan were the
Asshurim, the Letushim, and the Leum-
mim. 4 The sons of Midian were Ephah,
Epher, Hanoch, Abida, and Eldaah. All
these were Keturah's descendants.
5 Abraham left everything he owned
to Isaac; 6 but while he was still **alive**, he
gave presents to the sons his other wives
had borne him. Then he sent these sons
to the land of the East, away from his son
Isaac.

The Death and Burial of Abraham

7–8 Abraham died at the **ripe** old age
of a hundred and seventy-five. 9 His sons
Isaac and Ishmael buried him in Machpelah Cave, in the field east of Mamre
that had belonged to Ephron son of
Zohar the Hittite. 10 It was the field that
Abraham had bought from the Hittites;
both Abraham and his wife Sarah were
buried there. 11 After the **death** of Abraham, God **blessed** his son Isaac, who
lived near "The Well of the Living One
Who Sees Me."

The Descendants of Ishmael
(1 Chr 1.28–31)

12 Ishmael, whom Hagar, the
Egyptian **slave** of Sarah, bore to Abraham, 13 had the following sons, listed in
the order of their **birth**: Nebaioth, Kedar,
Adbeel, Mibsam, 14 Mishma, Dumah,
Massa, 15 Hadad, Tema, Jetur, Naphish,
and Kedemah. 16 They were the ancestors of twelve tribes, and their names
were given to their villages and
camping-places. 17 Ishmael was a
hundred and thirty-seven years old when
he died. 18 The descendants of Ishmael
lived in the territory between Havilah
and Shur, to the east of Egypt on the way
to Assyria. They lived **apart** from the
other descendants of Abraham.

The Birth of Esau and Jacob

19 This is the story of Abraham's son
Isaac. 20 Isaac was forty years old when
he married Rebecca, the daughter of
Bethuel (an Aramean from Mesopotamia) and sister of Laban. 21 Because
Rebecca had no children, Isaac **prayed**
to the LORD for her. The LORD answered
his **prayer**, and Rebecca became pregnant. 22 She was going to have twins, and
before they were born, they **struggled**
against **each other** in her **womb**. She
said, "Why should something like this
happen to me?" So she went to ask the
LORD for an answer.
23 The LORD said to her,

"Two nations are within you;
You will give **birth** to two **rival**
peoples.
One will be **stronger** than the other;
The older will **serve** the younger."

24 The time came for her to give
birth, and she had twin sons. 25 The first
one was reddish, and his skin was like a
hairy robe, so he was named Esau.[w]
26 The second one was born holding on

alive 7.3; 26.15
apart 16.12; 30.40
birth [3] 4.2; 29.32
bless 24.1; 26.3
bread 19.3; 27.17
care 13.7; 30.29
death (1) 23.2; 26.11
each other 15.10; 31.49
enjoy 18.12; 41.53
first-born [2] 22.21; 27.36
hunger 41.55
life (1) 19.15; 26.35
love 24.67; 26.8
pray 24.12; 32.9
prayer 24.45; 30.6
right (3) [5] 18.27; 27.36
ripe 15.15; 35.29
rival Ex 20.5
serve 19.2; 30.26
slave 24.35; 27.37
strong 49.3
struggle 32.25
vow [2] 24.2; 26.31
womb Job 3.11

[v] *Some ancient translations* into the wilderness of; *Hebrew* from coming.
[w] ESAU: *This name is taken to refer to Seir, the territory later inhabited by Esau's descendants; Seir sounds like the Hebrew for "hairy."*

25.10: Gen 23.3–16 **25.23:** Rom 9.12

tightly to the heel of Esau, so he was named Jacob.[x] Isaac was sixty years old when they were born.

Esau Sells His Rights as the First-Born Son

27 The boys grew up, and Esau became a skilled hunter, a man who **loved** the outdoor **life**, but Jacob was a quiet man who stayed at home. [28]Isaac preferred Esau, because he **enjoyed** eating the animals Esau killed, but Rebecca preferred Jacob.

29 One day while Jacob was cooking some bean soup, Esau came in from hunting. He was **hungry** [30]and said to Jacob, "I'm starving; give me some of that red stuff." (That is why he was called Edom.)[y]

31 Jacob answered, "I will give it to you if you give me your **rights** as the **first-born** son."

32 Esau said, "All right! I am about to die; what good will my **rights** do me then?"

33 Jacob answered, "First make a **vow** that you will give me your **rights**."

Esau made the **vow** and gave his **rights** to Jacob. [34]Then Jacob gave him some **bread** and some of the soup. He ate and drank and then got up and left. That was all Esau **cared** about his **rights** as the **first-born** son.

Isaac Lives at Gerar

26 There was another **famine** in the land besides the earlier one during the time of Abraham. Isaac went to Abimelech, king of the Philistines, at Gerar. [2]The LORD had appeared to Isaac and had said, "Do not go to Egypt; stay in this land, where I tell you to stay. [3]Live here, and I will be with you and **bless** you. I am going to give all this territory to you and to your descendants. I will keep the **promise** I made to your father Abraham. [4]I will give you as many descendants as there are stars in the sky, and I will give them all this territory. All the nations will ask me to bless them as I have **blessed** your descendants. [5]I will **bless** you, because Abraham **obeyed** me and kept all my **laws and commands**."

6 So Isaac lived at Gerar. [7]When the men there asked about his wife, he said that she was his sister. He would not **admit** that she was his wife, because he was **afraid** that the men there would kill him to get Rebecca, who was very beautiful. [8]When Isaac had been there for some time, King Abimelech looked down from his window and saw Isaac and Rebecca making **love**. [9]Abimelech sent for Isaac and said, "So she is your wife! Why did you say she was your sister?"

He answered, "I thought I would be killed if I said she was my wife."

10 "What have you done to us?" Abimelech said. "One of my men might easily have slept with your wife, and you would have been responsible for our **guilt**." [11]Abimelech **warned** all the people: "Anyone who **ill-treats** this man or his wife will be put **to death**."

12 Isaac **sowed seed** in that land, and that year he **harvested** a hundred times as much as he had **sown**, because the LORD **blessed** him. [13]He continued to **prosper** and became a very **rich** man. [14]Because he had many herds of **sheep** and cattle and many **servants**, the Philistines were **jealous** of him. [15]So they filled in all the wells which the **servants** of his father Abraham had dug while Abraham was **alive**.

16 Then Abimelech said to Isaac, "Leave our country. You have become more **powerful** than we are." [17]So Isaac left and set up his camp in the Valley of Gerar, where he stayed for some time. [18]He dug once again the wells which had been dug during the time of Abraham and which the Philistines had stopped up after Abraham's **death**. Isaac gave the wells the same names that his father had given them.

19 Isaac's **servants** dug a well in the valley and found water. [20]The **shepherds** of Gerar **quarrelled** with Isaac's shepherds and said, "This water belongs to us." So Isaac named the well "**Quarrel**."

21 Isaac's **servants** dug another well, and there was a **quarrel** about that one also, so he named it "Enmity." [22]He moved away from there and dug another well. There was no **dispute** about this one, so he named it "**Freedom**." He said, "Now the LORD has given us **freedom** to live in the land, and we will be **prosperous** here."

23 Isaac left and went to Beersheba. [24]That night the LORD appeared to him and said, "I am the God of your father Abraham. Do not be **afraid**; I am with you. I will **bless** you and give you many descendants because of my **promise** to my **servant** Abraham." [25]Isaac built an **altar** there and **worshipped** the LORD.

[x] JACOB: *This name sounds like the Hebrew for "heel."*
[y] EDOM: *This name sounds like the Hebrew for "red."*

25.33: Heb 12.16 **26.3-4:** Gen 22.16-18 **26.7:** Gen 12.13, 20.2

admit (1) 21.30; Num 14.40
afraid [2] 21.17; 28.17
agree 24.44; 29.28
alive 25.6; 32.30
altar 22.9; 33.20
bless [6] 25.11; 27.4
command 24.37; 28.6
death (1) [2] 25.11; 27.41
death (3) (to death) 31.32
dispute Ex 18.13
famine 12.10; 41.27
feast 21.8; 29.22
free [2] 24.8; 34.10
friend [2] 19.7; 29.4
guilty 18.23; 44.16
harm [2] 31.7
harvest 8.22; 30.14
ill-treat 31.50
jealous 30.1
kind 32.10
law 31.36
life (1) 25.27; 42.18
love 25.27; 29.18
misery Ex 1.13
obey 24.37; 28.7
peace 15.15; Lev 26.6
power 9.2; 31.29
promise [4] 24.7; 28.15
prosper [2] 30.29
quarrel [3] 13.7; 45.24
rich 24.35; 47.27
seal 38.18
seed 2.5; 47.19
servant [7] 24.2; 27.29
sheep 24.35; 29.2
shepherd 4.2; 29.3
solemn 24.7; 31.53
sow [2] 47.19
vow [2] 25.33; 28.20
warn 20.7; 31.29
worship (1) (of God) 24.26; 28.22

slave [2] 25.12; 29.24
tremble Ex 15.14

Then he set up his camp there, and his **servants** dug another well.

The Agreement between Isaac and Abimelech

26 Abimelech came from Gerar with Ahuzzath his adviser and Phicol the commander of his army to see Isaac. 27 So Isaac asked, "Why have you now come to see me, when you were so **unfriendly** to me before and made me leave your country?"

28 They answered, "Now we know that the LORD is with you, and we think that there should be a **solemn agreement** between us. We want you to **promise** 29 that you will not **harm** us, just as we did not **harm** you. We were **kind** to you and let you leave **peacefully**. Now it is clear that the LORD has **blessed** you." 30 Isaac prepared a **feast** for them, and they ate and drank. 31 Early next morning each man made his **promise** and **sealed** it with a **vow**. Isaac said good-bye to them, and they parted as **friends**.

32 On that day Isaac's **servants** came and told him about the well which they had dug. They said, "We have found water." 33 He named the well "**Vow.**" That is how the city of Beersheba[z] got its name.

Esau's Foreign Wives

34 When Esau was forty years old, he married two Hittite girls, Judith the daughter of Beeri, and Basemath the daughter of Elon. 35 They made **life miserable** for Isaac and Rebecca.

Isaac Blesses Jacob

anger 18.30; 30.2
best 23.6; 43.11
bitter Ex 12.8
bless [20] 26.3; 28.3
blind 19.11; Ex 4.11
bow (2) [2] 24.52; 33.3
bread 25.34; 45.23
cheat 31.7
control 16.6; 43.31
curse [3] 12.3; 49.7
death (1) 26.11; 42.2
deceive [2] 21.23; 31.20
final [2] Lev 27.12
first-born 25.31; 49.3
flock 24.35; 29.2
forget 8.1; 40.23
hate 3.15; 34.30
heaven [2] 24.3; 28.12
help 10.9; 35.3
kiss [2] 29.11
master 24.9; 32.4
mourn 23.2; 37.34
plan [2] 37.22
plead Ex 32.11
plenty 24.25; 41.29
presence 23.9; 31.35
rebel 14.4; Ex 23.21
right (3) 25.31; 31.36
save 19.19; 32.11
servant 26.14; 32.4

27 Isaac was now old and had become **blind**. He sent for his elder son Esau and said to him, "My son!"

"Yes," he answered.

2 Isaac said, "You see that I am old and may die soon. 3 Take your bow and arrows, go out into the country, and kill an animal for me. 4 Cook me some of that tasty food that I like, and bring it to me. After I have eaten it, I will give you my **final blessing** before I die."

5 While Isaac was talking to Esau, Rebecca was listening. So when Esau went out to hunt, 6 she said to Jacob, "I have just heard your father say to Esau, 7 'Bring me an animal and cook it for me. After I have eaten it, I will give you my **blessing** in the **presence** of the LORD before I die.' 8 Now, my son," Rebecca continued, "listen to me and do what I say. 9 Go to the **flock** and pick out two fat young goats, so that I can cook them and make some of that food your father likes so much. 10 You can take it to him to eat, and he will give you his **blessing** before he dies."

11 But Jacob said to his mother, "You know that Esau is a hairy man, but I have smooth skin. 12 Perhaps my father will touch me and find out that I am **deceiving** him; in this way I will bring a **curse** on myself instead of a **blessing**."

13 His mother answered, "Let any **curse** against you fall on me, my son; just do as I say, and go and get the goats for me." 14 So he went to get them and brought them to her, and she cooked the kind of food that his father liked. 15 Then she took Esau's **best** clothes, which she kept in the house, and put them on Jacob. 16 She put the skins of the goats on his arms and on the hairless part of his neck. 17 She handed him the tasty food, together with the **bread** she had baked.

18 Then Jacob went to his father and said, "Father!"

"Yes," he answered. "Which of my sons are you?"

19 Jacob answered, "I am your elder son Esau; I have done as you told me. Please sit up and eat some of the meat that I have brought you, so that you can give me your **blessing**."

20 Isaac said, "How did you find it so quickly, my son?"

Jacob answered, "The LORD your God **helped** me to find it."

21 Isaac said to Jacob, "Please come closer so that I can touch you. Are you really Esau?" 22 Jacob moved closer to his father, who felt him and said, "Your voice sounds like Jacob's voice, but your arms feel like Esau's arms." 23 He did not recognize Jacob, because his arms were hairy like Esau's. He was about to give him his **blessing**, 24 but asked again, "Are you really Esau?"

"I am," he answered.

25 Isaac said, "Bring me some of the meat. After I have eaten it, I will give you my **blessing**." Jacob brought it to him, and he also brought him some wine to drink. 26 Then his father said to him, "Come closer and **kiss** me, my son." 27 As he came up to **kiss** him, Isaac smelt his clothes—so he gave him his **blessing**. He said, "The pleasant smell of my son is like the smell of a field which the LORD has **blessed**. 28 May God give you dew from **heaven** and make your fields fertile! May he give you **plenty** of corn and

[z] BEERSHEBA: *This name in Hebrew means "Well of the Vow" or "Well of Seven" (see also 21.31).*

26.26: Gen 21.22 **27.27–29:** Heb 11.20

wine! 29 May nations be your **servants**,
and may peoples **bow down** before you.
May you rule over all your relatives, and
may your mother's descendants **bow**
down before you. May those who curse
you be **cursed**, and may those who **bless**
you be blessed."

Esau Begs for Isaac's Blessing

30 Isaac finished giving his **blessing**,
and as soon as Jacob left, his brother
Esau came in from hunting. 31 He also
cooked some tasty food and took it to his
father. He said, "Please, father, sit up
and eat some of the meat that I have
brought you, so that you can give me
your **blessing**."
32 "Who are you?" Isaac asked.
"Your elder son Esau," he answered.
33 Isaac began to **tremble** and shake
all over, and he asked, "Who was it, then,
who killed an animal and brought it to
me? I ate it just before you came. I gave
him my **final blessing**, and so it is his for
ever."
34 When Esau heard this, he cried out
loudly and **bitterly** and said, "Give me
your **blessing** also, father!"
35 Isaac answered, "Your brother
came and **deceived** me. He has taken
away your **blessing**."
36 Esau said, "This is the second time
that he has **cheated** me. No wonder his
name is Jacob.[a] He took my **rights** as the
first-born son, and now he has taken
away my **blessing**. Haven't you **saved** a
blessing for me?"
37 Isaac answered, "I have already
made him **master** over you, and I have
made all his relatives his **slaves**. I have
given him corn and wine. Now there is
nothing that I can do for you, my son!"
38 Esau continued to **plead** with his
father: "Have you only one **blessing**,
father? **Bless** me too, father!" He began
to cry.
39 Then Isaac said to him,
"No dew from **heaven** for you,
No fertile fields for you.
40 You will live by your sword,
But be your brother's **slave**.
Yet when you **rebel**,[b]
You will break away from his **control**."
41 Esau **hated** Jacob, because his
father had given Jacob the **blessing**. He
thought, "The time to **mourn** my father's
death is near; then I will kill Jacob."
42 But when Rebecca heard about
Esau's **plan**, she sent for Jacob and said,
"Listen, your brother Esau is **planning** to
get even with you and kill you. 43 Now,
my son, do what I say. Go at once to my
brother Laban in Haran, 44 and stay with
him for a while, until your brother's
anger cools down 45 and he **forgets** what
you have done to him. Then I will send
someone to bring you back. Why should I
lose both my sons on the same day?"

Isaac Sends Jacob to Laban

46 Rebecca said to Isaac, "I am sick
and tired of Esau's foreign wives. If
Jacob also marries one of these Hittite
girls, I might as well die."
28 Isaac called Jacob, greeted him,
and said to him, "Don't marry a
Canaanite girl. 2 Go instead to Mesopotamia, to the home of your grandfather
Bethuel, and marry one of the girls there,
one of your uncle Laban's daughters.
3 May **Almighty** God **bless** your marriage
and give you many children, so that you
will become the father of many nations!
4 May he **bless** you and your descendants
as he blessed Abraham, and may you
take **possession** of this land, in which you
have lived and which God gave to Abraham!" 5 Isaac sent Jacob away to
Mesopotamia, to Laban, who was the son
of Bethuel the Aramean and the brother
of Rebecca, the mother of Jacob and
Esau.

Esau Takes Another Wife

6 Esau **learnt** that Isaac had **blessed**
Jacob and sent him away to Mesopotamia to find a wife. He also **learnt** that
when Isaac **blessed** him, he **commanded**
him not to marry a Canaanite woman.
7 He found out that Jacob had **obeyed** his
father and mother and had gone to
Mesopotamia. 8 Esau then **understood**
that his father Isaac did not **approve** of
Canaanite women. 9 So he went to Ishmael son of Abraham and married his
daughter Mahalath, who was the sister of
Nebaioth.

Jacob's Dream at Bethel

10 Jacob left Beersheba and started
towards Haran. 11 At sunset he came to a
holy place[c] and camped there. He lay
down to sleep, **resting** his head on a
stone. 12 He **dreamt** that he saw a stairway reaching from earth to **heaven**, with
angels going up and coming down on it.
13 And there was the LORD standing
beside him.[d] "I am the LORD, the God of
Abraham and Isaac," he said. "I will give

afraid 26.7; 31.31
Almighty 17.1; 35.11
angel 24.7; 31.11
approve 41.37
bless [5] 27.4; 30.27
command 26.5; 43.17
dedicate 31.13
dream 20.3; 31.10
heaven [2] 27.28; Ex 20.4
holy 12.6; Ex 3.1
learn [2] 22.20; 30.27
obey 26.5; 32.4
possess 14.12; 36.6
promise 26.3; 31.53
protect [2] 19.8; 49.24
remember 9.15; 30.22
rest (1) 18.4; 49.15
safe 19.20; 33.18
terrify 20.8; 45.3
understand 11.7; 42.23
vow 26.31; 31.13
worship (1) (of God) 26.25; 31.53

[a] JACOB: *This name sounds like the Hebrew for "cheat."* [b] rebel; *or* grow restless.
[c] a holy place; *or* a place. [d] beside him; *or* on it.

27.29: Gen 12.3 **27.36:** Gen 25.29–34 **27.38:** Heb 12.17 **27.39–40:** Heb 11.20
27.40: Gen 36.8; 2 Kgs 8.20 **28.4:** Gen 17.4–8 **28.12:** Jn 1.51 **28.13:** Gen 13.14–15

to you and to your descendants this land
on which you are lying. 14 They will be as
numerous as the specks of dust on the
earth. They will extend their territory in
all directions, and through you and your
descendants I will **bless** all the nations.[e]
15 **Remember**, I will be with you and **protect** you wherever you go, and I will
bring you back to this land. I will not
leave you until I have done all that I have
promised you."

16 Jacob woke up and said, "The LORD
is here! He is in this place, and I didn't
know it!" 17 He was **afraid** and said,
"What a **terrifying** place this is! It must
be the house of God; it must be the gate
that opens into **heaven**."

18 Jacob got up early next morning,
took the stone that was under his head,
and set it up as a memorial. Then he
poured olive-oil on it to **dedicate** it to
God. 19 He named the place Bethel.[f] (The
town there was once known as Luz.)
20 Then Jacob made a **vow** to the LORD:
"If you will be with me and **protect** me
on the journey I am making and give me
food and clothing, 21 and if I return **safely**
to my father's home, then you will be my
God. 22 This memorial stone which I have
set up will be the place where you are
worshipped, and I will give you a tenth of
everything you give me."

Jacob Arrives at Laban's Home

29 Jacob continued on his way and
went towards the land of the
East. 2 Suddenly he came upon a well out
in the fields with three **flocks** of **sheep**
lying round it. The **flocks** were watered
from this well, which had a large stone
over the opening. 3 Whenever all the
flocks came together there, the **shepherds** would roll the stone back and
water them. Then they would put the
stone back in place.

4 Jacob asked the **shepherds**, "My
friends, where are you from?"

"From Haran," they answered.

5 He asked, "Do you know Laban,
grandson of Nahor?"

"Yes, we do," they answered.

6 "Is he well?" he asked.

"He is well," they answered. "Look,
here comes his daughter Rachel with his
flock."

7 Jacob said, "Since it is still broad
daylight and not yet time to bring the
flocks in, why don't you water them and
take them back to pasture?"

8 They answered, "We can't do that
until all the **flocks** are here and the stone
has been rolled back; then we will water
the **flocks**."

9 While Jacob was still talking to
them, Rachel arrived with the **flock**.
10 When Jacob saw Rachel with his uncle
Laban's **flock**, he went to the well, rolled
the stone back, and watered the **sheep**.
11 Then he **kissed** her and began to cry
for **joy**. 12 He told her, "I am your father's
relative, the son of Rebecca."

She ran to tell her father; 13 and when
he heard the news about his nephew
Jacob, he ran to meet him, hugged him
and **kissed** him, and brought him into the
house. When Jacob told Laban everything that had happened, 14 Laban said,
"Yes, indeed, you are my own **flesh and
blood**." Jacob stayed there a whole
month.

Jacob Serves Laban for Rachel and Leah

15 Laban said to Jacob, "You shouldn't
work for me for nothing just because you
are my relative. How much pay do you
want?" 16 Laban had two daughters; the
elder was named Leah, and the younger
Rachel. 17 Leah had lovely[x] eyes, but
Rachel was shapely and beautiful.

18 Jacob was in **love** with Rachel, so
he said, "I will work seven years for you,
if you will let me marry Rachel."

19 Laban answered, "I would rather
give her to you than to anyone else; stay
here with me." 20 Jacob worked seven
years so that he could have Rachel, and
the time seemed like only a few days to
him, because he **loved** her.

21 Then Jacob said to Laban, "The
time is up; let me marry your daughter."
22 So Laban gave a **wedding-feast** and
invited everyone. 23 But that night,
instead of Rachel, he took Leah to Jacob,
and Jacob had intercourse with her.
24 (Laban gave his **slave-girl** Zilpah to his
daughter Leah as her maid.) 25 Not until
the next morning did Jacob discover that
it was Leah. He went to Laban and said,
"Why did you do this to me? I worked to
get Rachel. Why have you **tricked** me?"

26 Laban answered, "It is not the
custom here to give the younger
daughter in marriage before the elder.
27 Wait until the week's marriage **celebrations** are over, and I will give you Rachel,
if you will work for me another seven
years."

28 Jacob **agreed**, and when the week
of marriage **celebrations** was over,

agree 26.28; 30.31
bind Ex 28.32
birth [4] 25.13; 30.23
blood 9.4; 37.27
celebrate [2] Ex 12.14
custom Lev 20.23
feast 26.30; Ex 32.6
flesh 2.21; 37.27
flock [9] 27.9; 30.29
friend 26.27; 31.2
joy 21.6; Num 10.10
kiss [2] 27.26; 31.28
love [6] 26.8; 34.3
praise 24.27; 49.8
sheep [2] 26.14; 30.33
shepherd [2] 26.20; 46.32
slave [2] 27.37; 30.3
trick 3.13; Judg 14.15
trouble 21.11; 31.42
wedding Deut 22.15

[e] through you...nations; *or* all the nations will ask me to bless them as I have blessed you and your descendants. [f] BETHEL: *This name in Hebrew means "house of God."* [x] lovely; *or* weak.

28.14: Gen 12.3, 22.18

Laban gave him his daughter Rachel as his wife. 29 (Laban gave his **slave-girl** Bilhah to his daughter Rachel as her maid.) 30 Jacob had intercourse with Rachel also, and he **loved** her more than Leah. Then he worked for Laban another seven years.

The Children Born to Jacob

31 When the LORD saw that Leah was **loved** less than Rachel, he made it possible for her to have children, but Rachel remained childless. 32 Leah became pregnant and gave **birth** to a son. She said, "The LORD has seen my **trouble**, and now my husband will **love** me"; so she named him Reuben.[g] 33 She became pregnant again and gave **birth** to another son. She said, "The LORD has given me this son also, because he heard that I was not **loved**"; so she named him Simeon.[h] 34 Once again she became pregnant and gave **birth** to another son. She said, "Now my husband will be **bound** more tightly to me, because I have borne him three sons"; so she named him Levi.[i] 35 Then she became pregnant again and gave **birth** to another son. She said, "This time I will **praise** the LORD"; so she named him Judah.[j] Then she stopped having children.

30 But Rachel had not borne Jacob any children, and so she became **jealous** of her sister and said to Jacob, "Give me children, or I will die."

2 Jacob became **angry** with Rachel and said, "I can't take the place of God. He is the one who **keeps you from** having children."

3 She said, "Here is my **slave-girl** Bilhah; sleep with her, so that she can have a child for me. In this way I can become a mother through her." 4 So she gave Bilhah to her husband, and he had intercourse with her. 5 Bilhah became pregnant and bore Jacob a son. 6 Rachel said, "God has **judged** in my **favour**. He has heard my **prayer** and has given me a son"; so she named him Dan.[k] 7 Bilhah became pregnant again and bore Jacob a second son. 8 Rachel said, "I have fought a **hard** fight with my sister, but I have **won**"; so she named him Naphtali.[l]

9 When Leah realized that she had stopped having children, she gave her **slave-girl** Zilpah to Jacob as his wife. 10 Then Zilpah bore Jacob a son. 11 Leah said, "I have been lucky"; so she named him Gad.[m] 12 Zilpah bore Jacob another son, 13 and Leah said, "How **happy** I am! Now women will call me **happy**"; so she named him Asher.[n]

14 During the **wheat-harvest** Reuben went into the fields and found mandrakes,[o] which he brought to his mother Leah. Rachel said to Leah, "Please give me some of your son's mandrakes."

15 Leah answered, "Isn't it **enough** that you have taken away my husband? Now you are even trying to take away my son's mandrakes."

Rachel said, "If you will give me your son's mandrakes, you can sleep with Jacob tonight."

16 When Jacob came in from the fields in the evening, Leah went out to meet him and said, "You are going to sleep with me tonight, because I have paid for you with my son's mandrakes." So he had intercourse with her that night.

17 God answered Leah's **prayer**, and she became pregnant and bore Jacob a fifth son. 18 Leah said, "God has given me my **reward**, because I gave my **slave** to my husband"; so she named her son Issachar.[p] 19 Leah became pregnant again and bore Jacob a sixth son. 20 She said, "God has given me a fine **gift**. Now my husband will **accept** me, because I have borne him six sons"; so she named him Zebulun.[q] 21 Later she bore a daughter, whom she named Dinah.

22 Then God **remembered** Rachel; he answered her **prayer** and made it possible for her to have children. 23 She became pregnant and gave **birth** to a son. She said, "God has taken away my **disgrace** by giving me a son. 24 May the LORD give me another son"; so she named him Joseph.[r]

Jacob's Bargain with Laban

25 After the **birth** of Joseph, Jacob said to Laban, "Let me go, so that I can return home. 26 Give me my wives and children that I have earned by working for you, and I will leave. You know how well I have **served** you."

27 Laban said to him, "Let me say this: I have **learnt** by **divination** that the

accept 23.13; 33.10
agree [2] 29.28; 31.44
anger 27.44; 31.35
apart 25.18; 49.26
birth [2] 29.32; 38.27
bless [2] 28.3; 32.26
care [3] 25.34; 36.24
disgrace 34.5
divination 44.5
enough 19.20; 33.5
favour 19.19; 32.5
flock [9] 29.2; 31.4
gift 24.53; 32.20
happy [2] Ex 18.9
hard 18.14; 33.13
harvest 26.12; 47.24
honest 42.11
interest (1) Num 11.29
jealous 26.14; 37.11
judge 18.25; 31.42
keep from 20.6; 42.2
lamb 22.7; Ex 12.3
learn 28.6; 34.5
prayer [3] 25.21; Ex 9.29
prosper 26.13; Lev 25.26
remember 28.15; 31.50
reward 15.1; Num 22.17
separate 21.28; 31.49
serve 25.23; 41.45
sheep [3] 29.2; 31.19
slave [4] 29.24; 31.33

steal 31.19
strip (1) Judg 14.19
wage [4] 31.7
weak [2] 33.13
win 31.41

[g] REUBEN: *This name sounds like the Hebrew for "see, a son" and "has seen my trouble."*
[h] SIMEON: *This name sounds like the Hebrew for "hear."*
[i] LEVI: *This name sounds like the Hebrew for "bound."*
[j] JUDAH: *This name sounds like the Hebrew for "praise."*
[k] DAN: *This name sounds like the Hebrew for "judge in favour."*
[l] NAPHTALI: *This name sounds like the Hebrew for "fight."*
[m] GAD: *This name in Hebrew means "luck."* [n] ASHER: *This name in Hebrew means "happy."*
[o] MANDRAKES: *Plants which were believed to produce fertility and were used as love-charms.*
[p] ISSACHAR: *This name sounds like the Hebrew for "a man is hired" and "there is reward."*
[q] ZEBULUN: *This name sounds like the Hebrew for "accept" and "gift."*
[r] JOSEPH: *This name sounds like the Hebrew for "may he give another" and "he has taken away."*

LORD has **blessed** me because of you.
28 Name your **wages**, and I will pay
them."
29 Jacob answered, "You know how I
have worked for you and how your **flocks**
have **prospered** under my **care**. 30 The
little you had before I came has grown
enormously, and the LORD has **blessed**
you wherever I went.[s] Now it is time for
me to look out for my own **interests**."
31 "What shall I pay you?" Laban
asked.
Jacob answered, "I don't want any
wages. I will continue to take **care** of
your **flocks** if you **agree** to this
suggestion: 32 Let me go through all your
flocks today and take every black **lamb**[t]
and every spotted or speckled young
goat. That is all the **wages** I want. 33 In
the future you can easily find out if I
have been **honest**. When you come to
check up on my **wages**, if I have any goat
that isn't speckled or spotted or any
sheep that isn't black, you will know that
it has been **stolen**."
34 Laban answered, "**Agreed**. We will
do as you suggest." 35 But that day Laban
removed the male goats that had stripes
or spots and all the females that were
speckled and spotted or which had white
on them; he also removed all the black
sheep. He put his sons in charge of them,
36 and then went away from Jacob with
this **flock** as far as he could travel in
three days. Jacob took **care** of the rest of
Laban's **flocks**.
37 Jacob got green branches of pop-
lar, almond, and plane trees and **stripped**
off some of the bark so that the branches
had white stripes on them. 38 He placed
these branches in front of the **flocks** at
their drinking-troughs. He put them
there, because the animals mated when
they came to drink. 39 So when the goats
bred in front of the branches, they produced young that were streaked,
speckled, and spotted.
40 Jacob kept the **sheep separate** from
the goats and made them face in the
direction of the streaked and black animals of Laban's **flock**. In this way he built
up his own **flock** and kept it **apart** from
Laban's.
41 When the healthy animals were
mating, Jacob put the branches in front
of them at the drinking-troughs, so that
they would breed among the branches.
42 But he did not put the branches in front
of the **weak** animals. Soon Laban had all
the **weak** animals, and Jacob all the
healthy ones. 43 In this way Jacob became
very wealthy. He had many **flocks**,
slaves, camels, and donkeys.

Jacob Flees from Laban

31 Jacob heard that Laban's sons
were saying, "Jacob has taken
everything that belonged to our father.
All his wealth has come from what our
father owned." 2 He also saw that Laban
was no longer as **friendly** as he had been
earlier. 3 Then the LORD said to him, "Go
back to the land of your fathers and to
your relatives. I will be with you."
4 So Jacob sent **word** to Rachel and
Leah to meet him in the field where his
flocks were. 5 He said to them, "I have
noticed that your father is not as **friendly**
towards me as he used to be; but my
father's God has been with me. 6 You
both know that I have worked for your
father with all my **strength**. 7 Yet he has
cheated me and **changed** my **wages** ten
times. But God did not let him **harm** me.
8 Whenever Laban said, 'The speckled
goats shall be your **wages**,' all the **flocks**
produced speckled young. When he said,
'The striped goats shall be your **wages**,'
all the **flocks** produced striped young.
9 God has taken **flocks** away from your
father and given them to me.
10 "During the breeding season I had
a **dream**, and I saw that the male goats
that were mating were striped, spotted,
and speckled. 11 The **angel of God** spoke
to me in the **dream** and said, 'Jacob!'
'Yes,' I answered. 12 'Look,' he continued,
'all the male goats that are mating are
striped, spotted, and speckled. I am
making this happen because I have seen
all that Laban is doing to you. 13 I am the
God who appeared to you at Bethel,
where you **dedicated** a stone as a
memorial by pouring olive-oil on it and
where you made a **vow** to me. Now get
ready to go back to the land where you
were born.' "
14 Rachel and Leah answered Jacob,
"There is nothing left for us to **inherit**
from our father. 15 He treats us like
foreigners. He sold us, and now he has
spent all the money he was paid for us.
16 All this wealth which God has taken
from our father belongs to us and to our
children. Do whatever God has told you."
17–18 So Jacob got ready to go back to
his father in the land of Canaan. He put
his children and his wives on the camels,

afraid 28.17; 32.11
agree [2] 30.31; 34.9
angel 28.12; 32.1
anger [2] 30.2; 40.2
anxious Deut 28.65
change [2] 38.14
cheat 27.36; Lev 6.2
crime 44.5
death (3) (to death) 26.11; 38.24
deceive [3] 27.12; 34.13
dedicate 28.18; Ex 12.42
demand Ex 7.9
dream [3] 28.12; 37.5
each other 25.22; Ex 10.23
fail 38.26
fault 16.5; Ex 5.16
flee Ex 2.15
flock [8] 30.29; 34.28
fool Ex 10.2
friend [2] 29.4; 33.10
god (2) (other gods) [7] 35.2
harm [2] 26.29; 42.22
ill-treat 26.11; Ex 5.22
inherit 21.10; 48.6
judge [2] 30.6; Ex 2.14
kiss [2] 29.11; 33.4
law 26.5; 47.26
loss 24.67; Ex 21.21
name (2) (name of God, of Jesus) 24.3; Ex 3.13
notice (1) Ex 2.5
offer 24.44; 46.1
power 26.16; 45.13
presence 27.7; 41.14
promise 28.15; 32.12
rejoice 2 Sam 1.20
remember 30.22; 32.12
remind [3] Ex 12.14
right (1) 18.19; 38.26
right (3) 27.36; Ex 21.10
sacrifice 22.2; 46.1
separate 30.40; 43.32
sheep [3] 30.33; 32.5
slave 30.3; 32.5
solemn 26.28; 47.29
steal [4] 30.33; 44.5
strength 18.5; 48.2
suffer 41.51
threat [2] Ex 1.9
trouble 29.32; 34.30
vow [2] 28.20; 47.29
wage [4] 30.28; Lev 19.13
warn 26.11; 43.3
watch 24.21; Ex 2.12
win 30.8; 32.20
witness Ex 22.10
word (1) 24.60; 32.5
worship (1) (of God) 28.22; Ex 3.12

[s] wherever I went; *or* because of me.
[t] *One ancient translation* every black lamb; *Hebrew* every spotted and speckled lamb, and every black lamb.

31.13: Gen 28.18–22

and drove all his **flocks** ahead of him,
with everything that he had acquired in
Mesopotamia. 19 Laban had gone to shear
his **sheep**, and during his absence Rachel
stole the household **gods** that belonged to
her father. 20 Jacob **deceived** Laban by
not letting him know that he was leaving.
21 He took everything he owned and left
in a hurry. He crossed the River
Euphrates and started for the hill-country of Gilead.

Laban Pursues Jacob

22 Three days later Laban was told
that Jacob had **fled**. 23 He took his men
with him and pursued Jacob for seven
days until he caught up with him in the
hill-country of Gilead. 24 In a **dream** that
night God came to Laban and said to
him, "Be careful not to **threaten** Jacob in
any way." 25 Jacob had set up his camp
on a mountain, and Laban set up his
camp with his kinsmen in the hill-country
of Gilead.

26 Laban said to Jacob, "Why did you
deceive me and carry off my daughters
like women captured in war? 27 Why did
you **deceive** me and slip away without
telling me? If you had told me, I would
have sent you on your way with **rejoicing**
and singing to the music of tambourines
and harps. 28 You did not even let me **kiss**
my grandchildren and my daughters
good-bye. That was a **foolish** thing to do!
29 I have the **power** to do you **harm**, but
last night the God of your father **warned**
me not to **threaten** you in any way. 30 I
know that you left because you were so
anxious to get back home, but why did
you **steal** my household **gods**?"

31 Jacob answered, "I was **afraid**,
because I thought that you might take
your daughters away from me. 32 But if
you find that anyone here has your **gods**,
he will be put **to death**. Here, with our
men as **witnesses**, look for anything that
belongs to you and take what is yours."
Jacob did not know that Rachel had
stolen Laban's **gods**.

33 Laban went and searched Jacob's
tent; then he went into Leah's tent, and
the tent of the two **slave-women**, but he
did not find his **gods**. Then he went into
Rachel's tent. 34 Rachel had taken the
household **gods** and put them in a
camel's saddlebag and was sitting on
them. Laban searched through the whole
tent, but did not find them. 35 Rachel said
to her father, "Do not be **angry** with me,
sir, but I am not able to stand up in your
presence; I am having my monthly
period." Laban searched but did not find
his household **gods**.

36 Then Jacob lost his temper. "What
crime have I committed?" he asked
angrily. "What **law** have I broken that
gives you the **right** to hunt me down?
37 Now that you have searched through
all my belongings, what household
article have you found that belongs to
you? Put it out here where your men and
mine can see it, and let them decide
which one of us is **right**. 38 I have been
with you now for twenty years; your
sheep and your goats have not **failed** to
reproduce, and I have not eaten any
rams from your **flocks**. 39 Whenever a
sheep was killed by wild animals, I
always bore the **loss** myself. I didn't take
it to you to show that it was not my **fault**.
You **demanded** that I make good anything that was **stolen** during the day or
during the night. 40 Many times I **suffered**
from the heat during the day and from
the cold at night. I was not able to sleep.
41 It was like that for the whole twenty
years I was with you. For fourteen years
I worked to **win** your two daughters—and
six years for your **flocks**. And even then,
you **changed** my **wages** ten times. 42 If the
God of my fathers, the God of Abraham
and Isaac, had not been with me, you
would have already sent me away
empty-handed. But God has seen my
trouble and the work I have done, and
last night he gave his **judgement**."

The Agreement between Jacob and Laban

43 Laban answered Jacob, "These
girls are my daughters; their children
belong to me, and these **flocks** are mine.
In fact, everything you see here belongs
to me. But since I can do nothing to keep
my daughters and their children, 44 I am
ready to make an **agreement** with you.
Let us make a pile of stones to **remind** us
of our **agreement**."

45 So Jacob took a stone and set it up
as a memorial. 46 He told his men to
gather some rocks and pile them up.
Then they ate a meal beside the pile of
rocks. 47 Laban named it Jegar
Sahadutha,[u] while Jacob named it
Galeed.[v] 48 Laban said to Jacob, "This
pile of rocks will be a **reminder** for both
of us." That is why that place was named
Galeed. 49 Laban also said, "May the
LORD keep an eye on us while we are
separated from **each other**." So the place
was also named Mizpah.[w] 50 Laban went
on, "If you **ill-treat** my daughters or if you

[u] JEGAR SAHADUTHA: *This name in Aramaic means "a pile to remind us."*
[v] GALEED: *This name in Hebrew means "a pile to remind us."*
[w] MIZPAH: *This name sounds like the Hebrew for "place from which to watch."*

marry other women, even though I don't know about it, **remember** that God is **watching** us. 51 Here are the rocks that I have piled up between us, and here is the memorial stone. 52 Both this pile and this memorial stone are **reminders**. I will never go beyond this pile to attack you, and you must never go beyond it or beyond this memorial stone to attack me. 53 The God of Abraham and the God of Nahor[x] will **judge** between us." Then, in the **name** of the God whom his father Isaac **worshipped**, Jacob **solemnly vowed** to keep this **promise**. 54 He killed an animal, which he **offered as a sacrifice** on the mountain, and he invited his men to the meal. After they had eaten, they spent the night on the mountain. 55 Early the next morning Laban **kissed** his grandchildren and his daughters goodbye, and left to go back home.

Jacob Prepares to Meet Esau

afraid 31.31; 35.17
alive 26.15; 43.27
alone 3.14; Ex 14.12
angel 31.11; 48.16
bless [2] 30.27; 35.9
choose 24.3; 41.33
concubine 22.24; 33.1
destroy 20.4; 34.30
escape 19.29; 39.12
faithful 24.27; Ex 15.13
favour 30.6; 33.8
forgive 18.27; 50.17
fright Judg 13.6
gift [2] 30.20; 33.10
hope Deut 28.65
kind 26.29; 33.11
master [3] 27.37; 39.2
obey 28.7; 41.40
pray [2] 25.21; Ex 8.8
promise 31.53; 50.5
remember 31.50; 40.14
rise 19.23; Deut 33.2
save 27.36; 37.21
servant [6] 27.29; 39.4
sheep [3] 31.19; 33.13
slave 31.33; 35.25
strike [2] 19.11; 49.17
struggle [2] 25.22; Prov 15.15
win [3] 31.41; 34.3
word (1) 31.4; 38.25
worry 21.12; 40.7
worth 23.15; Judg 8.2

32 As Jacob went on his way, some **angels** met him. 2 When he saw them, he said, "This is God's camp"; so he called the place Mahanaim.[y]

3 Jacob sent messengers ahead of him to his brother Esau in the country of Edom. 4 He instructed them to say: "I, Jacob, your **obedient servant**, report to my **master** Esau that I have been staying with Laban and that I have delayed my return until now. 5 I own cattle, donkeys, **sheep**, goats, and **slaves**. I am sending you **word**, sir, in the **hope** of gaining your **favour**."

6 When the messengers came back to Jacob, they said, "We went to your brother Esau, and he is already on his way to meet you. He has four hundred men with him." 7 Jacob was **frightened** and **worried**. He divided into two groups the people who were with him, and also his **sheep**, goats, cattle, and camels. 8 He thought, "If Esau comes and attacks the first group, the other may be able to **escape**."

9 Then Jacob **prayed**, "God of my grandfather Abraham and God of my father Isaac, hear me! You told me, LORD, to go back to my land and to my relatives, and you would make everything go well for me. 10 I am not **worth** all the **kindness** and **faithfulness** that you have shown me, your **servant**. I crossed the Jordan with nothing but a walking-stick, and now I have come back with these two groups. 11 **Save** me, I **pray**, from my brother Esau. I am **afraid**—afraid that he is coming to attack us and **destroy** us all, even the women and children. 12 **Remember** that you **promised** to make everything go well for me and to give me more descendants than anyone could count, as many as the grains of sand along the seashore."

13–15 After spending the night there, Jacob **chose** from his livestock as a present for his brother Esau: two hundred female goats and twenty males, two hundred female **sheep** and twenty males, thirty milk camels with their young, forty cows and ten bulls, twenty female donkeys and ten males. 16 He divided them into herds and put one of his **servants** in charge of each herd. He said to them, "Go ahead of me, and leave a space between each herd and the one behind it." 17 He ordered the first **servant**, "When my brother Esau meets you and asks, 'Who is your **master**? Where are you going? Who owns these animals in front of you?' 18 you must answer, 'They belong to your **servant** Jacob. He sends them as a present to his **master** Esau. Jacob himself is just behind us.' " 19 He gave the same order to the second, the third, and to all the others who were in charge of the herds: "This is what you must say to Esau when you meet him. 20 You must say, 'Yes, your **servant** Jacob is just behind us.' " Jacob was thinking, "I will **win** him over with the **gifts**, and when I meet him, perhaps he will **forgive** me." 21 He sent the **gifts** on ahead of him and spent that night in camp.

Jacob Wrestles at Peniel

22 That same night Jacob got up, took his two wives, his two **concubines**, and his eleven children, and crossed the River Jabbok. 23 After he had sent them across, he also sent across all that he owned, 24 but he stayed behind, **alone**.

Then a man came and wrestled with him until just before daybreak. 25 When the man saw that he was not **winning** the **struggle**, he **struck** Jacob on the hip, and it was thrown out of joint. 26 The man said, "Let me go; daylight is coming."

"I won't, unless you **bless** me," Jacob answered.

27 "What is your name?" the man asked.

"Jacob," he answered.

28 The man said, "Your name will no longer be Jacob. You have **struggled** with God and with men, and you have **won**; so your name will be Israel."[z]

[x] ABRAHAM...NAHOR: *Abraham was Jacob's grandfather and Nahor was Laban's grandfather.*
[y] MAHANAIM: *This name in Hebrew means "two camps."*
[z] ISRAEL: *This name sounds like the Hebrew for "he struggles with God" or "God struggles."*

32.12: Gen 22.17 **32.24-26:** Hos 12.3-4 **32.28:** Gen 35.10

29 Jacob said, "Now tell me your name."

But he answered, "Why do you want to know my name?" Then he **blessed** Jacob.

30 Jacob said, "I have seen God face to face, and I am still **alive**"; so he named the place Peniel.[a] 31 The sun **rose** as Jacob was leaving Peniel, and he was limping because of his hip. 32 Even today the descendants of Israel do not eat the muscle which is on the hip-joint, because it was on this muscle that Jacob was **struck**.

Jacob Meets Esau

accept [3] 30.20; 34.17
altar 26.25; 35.1
bow (2) [3] 27.29; 37.7
concubine [3] 32.22; 35.22
enough [2] 30.15; 34.21
favour [3] 32.5; 34.11
friend 31.2; 34.21
gift [2] 32.20; 43.15
hard 30.8; Ex 1.11
kind 32.10; 40.14
kiss 31.28; 45.15
last (2) 35.18
need [2] Ex 14.14
safe 28.21; 37.14
sheep 32.5; 37.2
shelter Ex 9.19
urge 19.3; Ex 12.33
weak 30.42; 42.9

33 Jacob saw Esau coming with his four hundred men, so he divided the children among Leah, Rachel, and the two **concubines**. 2 He put the **concubines** and their children first, then Leah and her children, and finally Rachel and Joseph at the rear. 3 Jacob went ahead of them and **bowed down** to the ground seven times as he approached his brother. 4 But Esau ran to meet him, threw his arms round him, and **kissed** him. They were both crying. 5 When Esau looked round and saw the women and the children, he asked, "Who are these people with you?"

"These, sir, are the children whom God has been good **enough** to give me," Jacob answered. 6 Then the **concubines** came up with their children and **bowed down**; 7 then Leah and her children came, and **last** of all Joseph and Rachel came and **bowed down**.

8 Esau asked, "What about that other group I met? What did that mean?"

Jacob answered, "It was to gain your **favour**."

9 But Esau said, "I have **enough**, my brother; keep what you have."

10 Jacob said, "No, please, if I have gained your **favour**, **accept** my **gift**. To see your face is for me like seeing the face of God, now that you have been so **friendly** to me. 11 Please **accept** this **gift** which I have brought for you; God has been **kind** to me and given me everything I **need**." Jacob kept on **urging** him until he **accepted**.

12 Esau said, "Let's prepare to leave. I will go ahead of you."

13 Jacob answered, "You know that the children are **weak**, and I must think of the **sheep** and livestock with their young. If they are driven **hard** for even one day, the whole herd will die. 14 Please go on ahead of me, and I will follow slowly, going as fast as I can with the livestock and the children until I catch up with you in Edom."

15 Esau said, "Then let me leave some of my men with you."

But Jacob answered, "There is no **need** for that for I only want to gain your **favour**."[b] 16 So that day Esau started on his way back to Edom. 17 But Jacob went to Sukkoth, where he built a house for himself and **shelters** for his livestock. That is why the place was named Sukkoth.[c]

18 On his return from Mesopotamia Jacob arrived **safely** at the city of Shechem in the land of Canaan and set up his camp in a field near the city. 19 He bought that part of the field from the descendants of Hamor father of Shechem for a hundred pieces of silver. 20 He put up an **altar** there and named it after El, the God of Israel.

The Rape of Dinah

34 One day Dinah, the daughter of Jacob and Leah, went to visit some of the Canaanite women. 2 When Shechem son of Hamor the Hivite, who was chief of that region, saw her, he took her and **raped** her. 3 But he found the girl so attractive that he fell in **love** with her and tried to **win** her **affection**.[d] 4 He said to his father, "I want you to get this girl for me as my wife."

accept 33.10; Ex 22.11
affection 1 Sam 18.3
agree [6] 31.44; 37.27
bride Ex 22.16
circumcise [6] 21.4; Ex 4.25
deceive 31.20; Ex 8.29
destroy 32.11; Ex 9.15
disgrace [4] 30.23; Lev 18.7
enough 33.5; 40.14
favour 33.8; Num 6.26
flock 31.4; 37.12
free [2] 26.22; 44.10
friend 33.10; 37.4
fury 4.5; 35.22
hate 27.41; 37.4
important 49.4
insult 39.14
learn 30.27; 42.1
love [3] 29.18; 37.3
rape [2] 39.14
revenge 4.10; Lev 19.18
slaughter Num 22.40
trouble 31.42; 35.3
value Lev 5.15
win 32.20; Ex 15.1
wish [2] Ex 16.3

5 Jacob **learnt** that his daughter had been **disgraced**, but because his sons were out in the fields with his livestock, he did nothing until they came back. 6 Shechem's father Hamor went out to talk with Jacob, 7 just as Jacob's sons were coming in from the fields. When they heard about it, they were shocked and **furious** that Shechem had done such a thing and had **insulted** the people of Israel by **raping** Jacob's daughter. 8 Hamor said to him, "My son Shechem has fallen in **love** with your daughter; please let him marry her. 9 Let us make an **agreement** that there will be intermarriage between our people and yours. 10 Then you may stay here in our country with us; you may live anywhere you **wish**, trade **freely**, and own property."

11 Then Shechem said to Dinah's father and brothers, "Do me this **favour**, and I will give you whatever you want. 12 Tell me what presents you want, and

[a] PENIEL: *This name sounds like the Hebrew for "the face of God."*
[b] for I only want to gain your favour; *or* if it's all right with you.
[c] SUKKOTH: *This name in Hebrew means "shelters."* [d] tried to win her affection; *or* comforted her.

32.29: Judg 13.17–18 **33.19:** Josh 24.32; Jn 4.5

set the payment for the **bride** as high as you **wish**; I will give you whatever you ask, if you will only let me marry her."

13 Because Shechem had **disgraced** their sister Dinah, Jacob's sons answered Shechem and his father Hamor in a **deceitful** way. 14 They said to him, "We cannot let our sister marry a man who is not **circumcised**; that would be a **disgrace** for us. 15 We can **agree** only on the condition that you become like us by **circumcising** all your males. 16 Then we will **agree** to intermarriage. We will settle among you and become one people with you. 17 But if you will not **accept** our terms and be **circumcised**, we will take her and leave."

18 These terms seemed fair to Hamor and his son Shechem, 19 and the young man lost no time in doing what was suggested, because he was in **love** with Jacob's daughter. He was the most **important** member of his family.

20 Hamor and his son Shechem went to the meeting-place at the city gate and spoke to their fellow-townsmen: 21 "These men are **friendly**; let them live in the land with us and travel **freely**. The land is large **enough** for them also. Let us marry their daughters and give them ours in marriage. 22 But these men will **agree** to live among us and be one people with us only on condition that we circumcise all our males, as they are **circumcised**. 23 Won't all their livestock and everything else they own be ours? So let us **agree** that they can live among us." 24 All the citizens of the city **agreed** with what Hamor and Shechem proposed, and all the males were **circumcised**.

25 Three days later, when the men were still sore from their **circumcision**, two of Jacob's sons, Simeon and Levi, the brothers of Dinah, took their swords, went into the city without arousing suspicion, and killed all the men, 26 including Hamor and his son Shechem. Then they took Dinah from Shechem's house and left. 27 After the **slaughter** Jacob's other sons looted the town to take **revenge** for their sister's **disgrace**. 28 They took the **flocks**, the cattle, the donkeys, and everything else in the city and in the fields. 29 They took everything of **value**, captured all the women and children, and carried off everything in the houses.

30 Jacob said to Simeon and Levi, "You have brought **trouble** on me; now the Canaanites, the Perizzites, and everybody else in the land will **hate** me. I haven't many men; if they all band together against me and attack me, our whole family will be **destroyed**."

31 But they answered, "We cannot let our sister be treated like a common whore."

God Blesses Jacob at Bethel

35 God said to Jacob, "Go to Bethel at once, and live there. Build an **altar** there to me, the God who appeared to you when you were running away from your brother Esau."

2 So Jacob said to his family and to all who were with him, "Get **rid** of the foreign **gods** that you have; **purify** yourselves and put on **clean** clothes. 3 We are going to leave here and go to Bethel, where I will build an **altar** to the God who **helped** me in the time of my **trouble** and who has been with me everywhere I have gone." 4 So they gave Jacob all the foreign **gods** that they had and also the ear-rings that they were wearing. He buried them beneath the oak-tree near Shechem.

5 When Jacob and his sons started to leave, great **fear** fell on the people of the nearby towns, and they did not pursue them. 6 Jacob came with all his people to Luz, which is now known as Bethel, in the land of Canaan. 7 He built an **altar** there and named the place after the God of Bethel, because God had **revealed** himself to him there when he was running away from his brother. 8 Rebecca's nurse Deborah died and was buried beneath the oak south of Bethel. So it was named "Oak of **Weeping**."

9 When Jacob returned from Mesopotamia, God appeared to him again and **blessed** him. 10 God said to him, "Your name is Jacob, but from now on it will be Israel." So God named him Israel. 11 And God said to him, "I am **Almighty** God. Have many children. Nations will be descended from you, and you will be the ancestor of kings. 12 I will give you the land which I gave to Abraham and to Isaac, and I will also give it to your descendants after you." 13 Then God left him. 14 There, where God had spoken to him, Jacob set up a memorial stone and **consecrated** it by pouring wine and olive-oil on it. 15 He named the place Bethel.

The Death of Rachel

16 Jacob and his family left Bethel, and when they were still some distance from Ephrath, the time came for Rachel to have her baby, and she was having **difficult** labour. 17 When her labour **pains** were at their **worst**, the midwife said to

afraid 32.11; 38.11
Almighty 28.3; 43.14
altar [3] 33.20; Ex 17.15
bless 32.26; 39.5
clean 8.20; Lev 4.12
concubine 33.1; 37.2
consecrate Ex 32.29
difficult 47.9
fear 15.12; 42.28
fury 34.7; 39.19
god (2) (other gods) [2] 31.19; Ex 8.10
grave 23.6; Ex 14.11
help 27.20; 40.14
last (2) 33.7; Ex 26.5
mark (1) 4.15; Ex 12.13
pain 3.16; Num 5.24
pure 2.12; Ex 19.10
reveal Ex 3.18
rid Ex 8.9
ripe 25.7; 40.10
sex 19.5; Ex 19.15
slave [2] 32.5; 39.17
trouble 34.30; 41.52
weep 45.15
worst Ex 9.24

35.1: Gen 28.11–17 **35.10:** Gen 32.28 **35.11–12:** Gen 17.4–8 **35.14–15:** Gen 28.18–19

her, "Don't be **afraid**, Rachel; it's
another boy." 18 But she was dying, and
as she breathed her **last**, she named her
son Benoni,[e] but his father named him
Benjamin.[f]

19 When Rachel died, she was buried
beside the road to Ephrath, now known
as Bethlehem. 20 Jacob set up a memorial
stone there, and it still **marks** Rachel's
grave to this day. 21 Jacob moved on and
set up his camp on the other side of the
tower of Eder.

The Sons of Jacob
(1 Chr 2.1-2)

22 While Jacob was living in that land,
Reuben had **sexual** intercourse with
Bilhah, one of his father's **concubines**;
Jacob heard about it and was **furious**.[g]

Jacob had twelve sons. 23 The sons of
Leah were Reuben (Jacob's eldest son),
Simeon, Levi, Judah, Issachar, and
Zebulun. 24 The sons of Rachel were
Joseph and Benjamin. 25 The sons of
Rachel's **slave** Bilhah were Dan and
Naphtali. 26 The sons of Leah's **slave**
Zilpah were Gad and Asher. These sons
were born in Mesopotamia.

The Death of Isaac

27 Jacob went to his father Isaac at
Mamre, near Hebron, where Abraham
and Isaac had lived. 28 Isaac lived to be a
hundred and eighty years old 29 and died
at a **ripe** old age; and his sons Esau and
Jacob buried him.

The Descendants of Esau
(1 Chr 1.34-37)

care 30.29; 37.2
possess 28.4; 45.20

36 These are the descendants of
Esau, also called Edom. 2 Esau
married Canaanite women: Adah, the
daughter of Elon the Hittite;
Oholibamah, the daughter of Anah son[h]
of Zibeon the Hivite; 3 and Basemath, the
daughter of Ishmael and sister of
Nebaioth. 4 Adah bore Eliphaz; Basemath
bore Reuel; 5 and Oholibamah bore
Jeush, Jalam, and Korah. All these sons
were born to Esau in the land of Canaan.

6 Then Esau took his wives, his sons,
his daughters, and all the people of his
house, together with all his livestock and
all the **possessions** he had acquired in the
land of Canaan, and went away from his
brother Jacob to another land. 7 He left
because the land where he and Jacob
were living was not able to support
them; they had too much livestock and
could no longer stay together. 8 So Esau
lived in the hill-country of Edom.

9 These are the descendants of Esau,
the ancestor of the Edomites. 10-13 Esau's
wife Adah bore him one son, Eliphaz, and
Eliphaz had five sons: Teman, Omar,
Zepho, Gatam, and Kenaz. And by
another wife, Timna, he had one more
son, Amalek.

Esau's wife Basemath bore him one
son, Reuel, and Reuel had four sons:
Nahath, Zerah, Shammah, and Mizzah.

14 Esau's wife Oholibamah, the daughter of Anah son[h] of Zibeon, bore him
three sons: Jeush, Jalam, and Korah.

15 These are the tribes descended
from Esau. Esau's first son Eliphaz was
the ancestor of the following tribes:
Teman, Omar, Zepho, Kenaz, 16 Korah,
Gatam, and Amalek. These were all
descendants of Esau's wife Adah.

17 Esau's son Reuel was the ancestor
of the following tribes: Nahath, Zerah,
Shammah, and Mizzah. These were all
descendants of Esau's wife Basemath.

18 The following tribes were
descended from Esau by his wife
Oholibamah, the daughter of Anah:
Jeush, Jalam, and Korah. 19 All these
tribes were descended from Esau.

The Descendants of Seir
(1 Chr 1.38-42)

20-21 The original inhabitants of the
land of Edom were divided into tribes
which traced their ancestry to the following descendants of Seir, a Horite: Lotan,
Shobal, Zibeon, Anah, Dishon, Ezer, and
Dishan.

22 Lotan was the ancestor of the clans
of Hori and Heman. (Lotan had a sister
named Timna.)

23 Shobal was the ancestor of the
clans of Alvan, Manahath, Ebal, Shepho,
and Onam.

24 Zibeon had two sons, Aiah and
Anah. (This is the Anah who found the
hot springs in the wilderness when he
was taking **care** of his father's donkeys.)
25-26 Anah was the father of Dishon, who
was the ancestor of the clans of Hemdan,
Eshban, Ithran, and Cheran. Anah also
had a daughter named Oholibamah.

27 Ezer was the ancestor of the clans
of Bilhan, Zaavan, and Akan.

28 Dishan was the ancestor of the
clans of Uz and Aran.

29-30 These are the Horite tribes in

[e] BENONI: *This name in Hebrew means "son of my sorrow."*
[f] BENJAMIN: *This name in Hebrew means "son who will be fortunate."*
[g] *One ancient translation* and was furious; *Hebrew does not have these words.*
[h] *Some ancient translations* son; *Hebrew* daughter; *or* granddaughter.

35.22: Gen 49.4 **35.27:** Gen 13.18 **36.2:** Gen 26.34 **36.3:** Gen 28.9

the land of Edom: Lotan, Shobal, Zibeon,
Anah, Dishon, Ezer, and Dishan.

The Kings of Edom
(1 Chr 1.43–54)

31–39 Before there were any kings in
Israel, the following kings ruled over the
land of Edom in succession:
Bela son of Beor from Dinhabah
Jobab son of Zerah from Bozrah
Husham from the region of Teman
Hadad son of Bedad from Avith (he
defeated the Midianites in a battle
in the country of Moab)
Samlah from Masrekah
Shaul from Rehoboth-on-the-River
Baal Hanan son of Achbor
Hadad from Pau (his wife was
Mehetabel, the daughter of
Matred and granddaughter of
Mezahab)
40–43 Esau was the ancestor of the
following Edomite tribes: Timna, Alvah,
Jetheth, Oholibamah, Elah, Pinon,
Kenaz, Teman, Mibzar, Magdiel, and
Iram. The area where each of these
tribes lived was known by the name of
the tribe.

Joseph and His Brothers

37 Jacob continued to live in the
land of Canaan, where his father
had lived, 2 and this is the story of Jacob's
family.
Joseph, a young man of seventeen,
took **care** of the **sheep** and goats with his
brothers, the sons of Bilhah and Zilpah,
his father's **concubines**. He brought **bad**
reports to his father about what his
brothers were doing.
3 Jacob **loved** Joseph more than all his
other sons, because he had been born to
him when he was old. He made a long
robe with full sleeves[j] for him. 4 When his
brothers saw that their father **loved**
Joseph more than he loved them, they
hated their brother so much that they
would not speak to him in a **friendly**
manner.
5 One night Joseph had a **dream**, and
when he told his brothers about it, they
hated him even more. 6 He said, "Listen
to the **dream** I had. 7 We were all in the
field tying up sheaves of wheat, when my
sheaf got up and stood up straight. Yours
formed a circle round mine and **bowed
down** to it."
8 "Do you think you are going to be a
king and rule over us?" his brothers
asked. So they **hated** him even more because of his **dreams** and because of what
he said about them.
9 Then Joseph had another **dream** and
said to his brothers, "I had another
dream, in which I saw the sun, the moon,
and eleven stars **bowing down** to me."
10 He also told the **dream** to his
father, and his father scolded him:
"What kind of a **dream** is that? Do you
think that your mother, your brothers,
and I are going to come and **bow down** to
you?" 11 Joseph's brothers were **jealous**
of him, but his father kept thinking about
the whole matter.

Joseph Is Sold and Taken to Egypt

12 One day when Joseph's brothers
had gone to Shechem to take **care** of
their father's **flock**, 13 Jacob said to
Joseph, "I want you to go to Shechem,
where your brothers are taking **care** of
the **flock**."
Joseph answered, "I am ready."
14 His father said, "Go and see if your
brothers are **safe** and if the **flock** is all
right; then come back and tell me." So
his father sent him on his way from the
Valley of Hebron.
Joseph arrived at Shechem 15 and was
wandering about in the country when a
man saw him and asked him, "What are
you looking for?"
16 "I am looking for my brothers, who
are taking **care** of their **flock**," he
answered. "Can you tell me where they
are?"
17 The man said, "They have already
left. I heard them say that they were going to Dothan." So Joseph went after his
brothers and found them at Dothan.
18 They saw him in the distance, and
before he reached them, they **plotted**
against him and decided to kill him.
19 They said to one another, "Here comes
that **dreamer**. 20 Come on now, let's kill
him and throw his **body** into one of the
dry wells. We can say that a wild animal
killed him. Then we will see what becomes of his **dreams**."
21 Reuben heard them and tried to
save Joseph. "Let's not kill him," he said.
22 "Just throw him into this well in the
wilderness, but don't **hurt** him." He said
this, **planning** to **save** him from them and
send him back to his father. 23 When
Joseph came up to his brothers, they
ripped off his long robe with full sleeves.[j]
24 Then they took him and threw him into
the well, which was dry.

[j] robe with full sleeves; *or* decorated robe.

37.11: Acts 7.9

agree 34.9; 42.20
bad 12.10; 41.21
blood [2] 29.14; 49.11
body 23.3; 40.19
bow (2) [3] 33.3; 42.6
care [4] 36.24; 39.6
comfort [2] 24.67; Deut 31.20
concubine 35.22; 49.4
dream [9] 31.10; 40.5
flesh 29.14; 40.19
flock [4] 34.28; 38.17
friend 34.21; 38.12
hate [3] 34.30; 50.15
hurt [2] 22.12; Ex 21.22
jealous 30.1; Num 5.29
love [2] 34.3; 44.20
mourn [3] 27.41; 38.12
plan 27.42; 41.37
plot (1) 50.20
refuse (1) 24.41; 39.8
sackcloth 2 Sam 3.31
safe 33.18; 43.9
save [2] 32.11; 45.5
sheep 33.13; 38.12
sorrow [2] 42.38
world of the dead Num 16.30

25 While they were eating, they suddenly saw a group of Ishmaelites travelling from Gilead to Egypt. Their camels
were loaded with spices and resins.
26 Judah said to his brothers, "What will
we gain by killing our brother and covering up the murder? 27 Let's sell him to
these Ishmaelites. Then we won't have to
hurt him; after all, he is our brother, our
own **flesh and blood**." His brothers
agreed, 28 and when some Midianite
traders came by, the brothers[l] pulled
Joseph out of the well and sold him for
twenty pieces of silver to the Ishmaelites,
who took him to Egypt.

29 When Reuben came back to the
well and found that Joseph was not there,
he tore his clothes in **sorrow**. 30 He returned to his brothers and said, "The boy
is not there! What am I going to do?"

31 Then they killed a goat and dipped
Joseph's robe in its **blood**. 32 They took
the robe to their father and said, "We
found this. Does it belong to your son?"

33 He recognized it and said, "Yes, it
is his! Some wild animal has killed him.
My son Joseph has been torn to pieces!"
34 Jacob tore his clothes in **sorrow** and
put on **sackcloth**. He **mourned** for his son
a long time. 35 All his sons and daughters
came to **comfort** him, but he **refused** to
be **comforted** and said, "I will go down to
the **world of the dead** still **mourning** for
my son." So he continued to **mourn** for
his son Joseph.

36 Meanwhile, in Egypt, the
Midianites had sold Joseph to Potiphar,
one of the king's officers, who was the
captain of the palace guard.

Judah and Tamar

38 About that time Judah left his
brothers and went to stay with a
man named Hirah, who was from the
town of Adullam. 2 There Judah met a
Canaanite girl whose father was named
Shua. He married her, 3 and she bore him
a son, whom he named Er. 4 She became
pregnant again and bore another son and
named him Onan. 5 Again she had a son
and named him Shelah. Judah was at
Achzib when the boy was born.

6 For his first son Er, Judah got a wife
whose name was Tamar. 7 Er's conduct
was **evil**, and it **displeased** the LORD, so
the LORD killed him. 8 Then Judah said to
Er's brother Onan, "Go and sleep with
your brother's **widow**. **Fulfil** your **obligation** to her as her husband's brother, so
that your brother may have descendants." 9 But Onan knew that the children
would not belong to him, so whenever he
had intercourse with his brother's **widow**,
he let the semen spill on the ground, so
that there would be no children for his
brother. 10 What he did **displeased** the
LORD, and the LORD killed him also.
11 Then Judah said to his daughter-in-law
Tamar, "Return to your father's house
and remain a **widow** until my son Shelah
grows up." He said this because he was
afraid that Shelah would be killed, as his
brothers had been. So Tamar went back
home.

12 After some time Judah's wife died.
When he had finished the time of **mourning**, he and his **friend** Hirah of Adullam
went to Timnah, where his **sheep** were
being sheared. 13 Someone told Tamar
that her father-in-law was going to
Timnah to shear his **sheep**. 14 So she
changed from the **widow's** clothes she
had been wearing, covered her face with
a veil, and sat down at the entrance to
Enaim, a town on the road to Timnah. As
she well knew, Judah's youngest son
Shelah had now grown up, and yet she
had not been given to him in marriage.

15 When Judah saw her, he thought
that she was a **prostitute**, because she
had her face covered. 16 He went over to
her at the side of the road and said, "All
right, how much do you charge?" (He
did not know that she was his daughter-
in-law.)

She said, "What will you give me?"

17 He answered, "I will send you a
young goat from my **flock**."

She said, "All right, if you will give me
something to keep as a pledge until you
send the goat."

18 "What shall I give you as a
pledge?" he asked.

She answered, "Your **seal** with its cord
and the stick you are carrying." He gave
them to her. Then they had intercourse,
and she became pregnant. 19 Tamar went
home, took off her veil, and put her
widow's clothes back on.

20 Judah sent his **friend** Hirah to take
the goat and get back from the woman
the articles he had pledged, but Hirah
could not find her. 21 He asked some men
at Enaim, "Where is the **prostitute** who
was here by the road?"

"There has never been a **prostitute**
here," they answered.

22 He returned to Judah and said, "I
couldn't find her. The men of the place
said that there had never been a **prostitute** there."

23 Judah said, "Let her keep the

act 18.25; 42.7
afraid 35.17; 42.4
birth 30.23; Ex 1.16
change 31.7; 41.14
death (3) (to death) 31.32; 42.2
displease [2] Num 11.11
evil 8.21; 44.4
fail 31.38; 48.10
flock 37.12; 46.32
friend [2] 37.4; Ex 32.27
fulfil 24.49; Ex 21.11
mourn 37.34; 50.3
obligation [2] Num 32.22
prostitute [4] Lev 19.29
right (1) 31.37; Ex 8.26
seal [2] 26.31; 41.42
sheep [2] 37.2; 45.10
widow [5] Ex 22.22
word (1) 32.5; 44.6

[l] the brothers; *Hebrew* they.

37.28: Acts 7.9

things. We don't want people to laugh at us. I did try to pay her, but you couldn't find her."

24 About three months later someone said to Judah, "Your daughter-in-law Tamar has been **acting** like a whore, and now she is pregnant."

Judah ordered, "Take her out and burn her **to death**."

25 As she was being taken out, she sent **word** to her father-in-law: "I am pregnant by the man who owns these things. Look at them and see whose they are—this **seal** with its cord and this stick."

26 Judah recognized them and said, "She is in the **right**. I have **failed** in my **obligation** to her—I should have given her to my son Shelah in marriage." And Judah never had intercourse with her again.

27 When the time came for her to give **birth**, it was discovered that she was going to have twins. 28 While she was in labour, one of them put out an arm; the midwife caught it, tied a red thread round it, and said, "This one was born first." 29 But he pulled his arm back, and his brother was born first. Then the midwife said, "So this is how you break your way out!" So he was named Perez.[m] 30 Then his brother was born with the red thread on his arm, and he was named Zerah.[x]

Joseph and Potiphar's Wife

39 Now the Ishmaelites had taken Joseph to Egypt and sold him to Potiphar, one of the king's officers, who was the captain of the palace guard. 2 The LORD was with Joseph and made him **successful**. He lived in the house of his Egyptian **master**, 3 who saw that the LORD was with Joseph and had made him **successful** in everything he did. 4 Potiphar was **pleased** with him and made him his personal **servant**; so he put him in charge of his house and everything he owned. 5 From then on, because of Joseph the LORD **blessed** the household of the Egyptian and everything that he had in his house and in his fields. 6 Potiphar handed over everything he had to the **care** of Joseph and did not **concern** himself with anything except the food he ate.

Joseph was well-built and good-looking, 7 and after a while his **master's** wife began to **desire** Joseph and asked him to go to bed with her. 8 He **refused** and said to her, "Look, my **master** does not have to **concern** himself with anything in the house, because I am here. He has put me in charge of everything he has. 9 I have as much **authority** in this house as he has, and he has not kept back anything from me except you. How then could I do such an **immoral** thing and sin against God?" 10 Although she asked Joseph day after day, he would not go to bed with her.

11 But one day when Joseph went into the house to do his work, none of the house **servants** was there. 12 She caught him by his robe and said, "Come to bed with me." But he **escaped** and ran outside, leaving his robe in her hand. 13 When she saw that he had left his robe and had run out of the house, 14 she called to her house **servants** and said, "Look at this! This **Hebrew** that my husband brought to the house is **insulting** us. He came into my room and tried to **rape** me, but I screamed as loud as I could. 15 When he heard me scream, he ran outside, leaving his robe beside me."

16 She kept his robe with her until Joseph's **master** came home. 17 Then she told him the same story: "That **Hebrew slave** that you brought here came into my room and **insulted** me. 18 But when I screamed, he ran outside, leaving his robe beside me."

19 Joseph's **master** was **furious** 20 and had Joseph **arrested** and put in the **prison** where the king's **prisoners** were kept, and there he stayed. 21 But the LORD was with Joseph and **blessed** him, so that the **jailer** was **pleased** with him. 22 He put Joseph in charge of all the other **prisoners** and made him responsible for everything that was done in the **prison**. 23 The **jailer** did not have to look after anything for which Joseph was responsible, because the LORD was with Joseph and made him **succeed** in everything he did.

arrest 1 Sam 19.20
authority 41.35
bless [2] 35.9; 43.29
care 37.2; 42.37
concern [2] Ex 2.25
desire 3.16; Ex 20.17
escape 32.8; Ex 1.10
fury 35.22; 49.7
Hebrew [2] 14.13; 40.15
immoral Lev 19.29
insult [2] 34.7; 1 Sam 20.34
jail [2] Job 7.20
master [5] 32.4; 44.5
please [2] 15.6; 45.16
prison [4] 14.16; 40.3
rape 34.2; Deut 22.25
refuse (1) 37.35; 48.19
servant [3] 32.4; 40.4
slave 35.25; 41.12
succeed (1) [3] 24.12; Num 14.41

Joseph Interprets the Prisoners' Dreams

40 Some time later the king of Egypt's wine steward and his chief baker offended the king. 2 He was **angry** with these two officials 3 and put them in **prison** in the house of the captain of the guard, in the same place where Joseph was being kept. 4 They spent a long time in **prison**, and the captain assigned Joseph as their **servant**.

5 One night there in **prison** the wine

anger 31.35; 41.10
banquet Judg 14.10
body 37.20; 47.18
cup [3] 44.2
deserve Deut 9.4
dream [8] 37.5; 41.1
enough 34.21; 45.18
execute 41.13
flesh 37.27; Ex 21.28
forget 27.45; 41.30
grapevine *see* **vine**
hang (2) Deut 21.22
Hebrew 39.14; 41.12
help 35.3; 42.21

[m] PEREZ: *This name in Hebrew means "breaking out."*
[x] ZERAH: *This name sounds like a Hebrew word for the red brightness of dawn.*

39.2: Acts 7.9 **39.21:** Acts 7.9

interpret [2] 41.12
kind 33.11; 50.21
prison [5] 39.20; 41.10
remember 32.12; 42.9
restore [2] 41.13
ripe 35.29; 41.5
servant 39.4; 43.16
upset 45.5
vine 49.11
worry 32.7; 41.8

steward and the chief baker each had a **dream**, and the dreams had different meanings. 6 When Joseph came to them in the morning, he saw that they were **upset**. 7 He asked them, "Why do you look so **worried** today?"

8 They answered, "Each of us had a **dream**, and there is no one here to explain what the **dreams** mean."

"It is God who gives the ability to **interpret dreams**," Joseph said. "Tell me your **dreams**."

9 So the wine steward said, "In my **dream** there was a **grapevine** in front of me 10 with three branches on it. As soon as the leaves came out, the blossoms appeared, and the grapes **ripened**. 11 I was holding the king's **cup**; so I took the grapes and squeezed them into the **cup** and gave it to him."

12 Joseph said, "This is what it means: the three branches are three days. 13 In three days the king will release you, pardon you, and **restore** you to your position. You will give him his **cup** as you did before when you were his wine steward. 14 But please **remember** me when everything is going well for you, and please be **kind enough** to mention me to the king and **help** me to get out of this **prison**. 15 After all, I was kidnapped from the land of the **Hebrews**, and even here in Egypt I didn't do anything to **deserve** being put in **prison**."

16 When the chief baker saw that the **interpretation** of the wine steward's **dream** was favourable, he said to Joseph, "I had a **dream** too; I was carrying three bread-baskets on my head. 17 In the top basket there were all kinds of pastries for the king, and the birds were eating them."

18 Joseph answered, "This is what it means: the three baskets are three days. 19 In three days the king will release you—and have your head cut off! Then he will **hang** your **body** on a pole, and the birds will eat your **flesh**."

20 On his birthday three days later the king gave a **banquet** for all his officials; he released his wine steward and his chief baker and brought them before his officials. 21 He **restored** the wine steward to his former position, 22 but he **executed** the chief baker. It all happened just as Joseph had said. 23 But the wine steward never gave Joseph another thought—he **forgot** all about him.

Joseph Interprets the King's Dreams

abundant Num 24.7
anger 40.2; 44.18

41 After two years had passed, the king of Egypt **dreamt** that he was standing by the River Nile, 2 when seven cows, fat and sleek, came up out of the river and began to feed on the grass. 3 Then seven other cows came up; they were thin and bony. They came and stood by the other cows on the riverbank, 4 and the thin cows ate up the fat cows. Then the king woke up. 5 He fell asleep again and had another **dream**. Seven ears of corn, full and **ripe**, were growing on one stalk. 6 Then seven other ears of corn sprouted, thin and scorched by the desert wind, 7 and the thin ears of corn swallowed the full ones. The king woke up and realized that he had been **dreaming**. 8 In the morning he was **worried**, so he sent for all the **magicians** and **wise** men of Egypt. He told them his **dreams**, but no one could explain them to him.

9 Then the wine steward said to the king, "I must **confess** today that I have done **wrong**. 10 You were **angry** with the chief baker and me, and you put us in **prison** in the house of the captain of the guard. 11 One night each of us had a **dream**, and the dreams had different meanings. 12 A young **Hebrew** was there with us, a **slave** of the captain of the guard. We told him our **dreams**, and he **interpreted** them for us. 13 Things **turned** out just as he said: you **restored** me to my position, but you **executed** the baker."

14 The king sent for Joseph, and he was immediately brought from the **prison**. After he had **shaved** and **changed** his clothes, he came into the king's **presence**. 15 The king said to him, "I have had a **dream**, and no one can explain it. I have been told that you can **interpret dreams**."

16 Joseph answered, "I cannot, Your **Majesty**, but God will give a favourable **interpretation**."

17 The king said, "I **dreamt** that I was standing on the bank of the Nile, 18 when seven cows, fat and sleek, came up out of the river and began feeding on the grass. 19 Then seven other cows came up which were thin and bony. They were the **poorest** cows I have ever seen anywhere in Egypt. 20 The thin cows ate up the fat ones, 21 but no one would have known it, because they looked just as **bad** as before. Then I woke up. 22 I also **dreamt** that I saw seven ears of corn which were full and **ripe**, growing on one stalk. 23 Then seven ears of corn sprouted, thin and scorched by the desert wind, 24 and the thin ears of corn swallowed the full ones.

41.8: Dan 2.2

approve 28.8; Ex 21.22
authority [2] 39.9; Num 27.20
bad 37.2; Ex 7.21
change 38.14; 45.22
choose 32.13; Ex 12.3
confess Lev 5.5
court (1) 12.15; 50.7
dream [13] 40.5; 42.9
enjoy 25.28; Lev 26.34
execute 40.22; Num 25.4
famine [10] 26.1; 42.5
forget [3] 40.23; Deut 4.9
Hebrew 40.15; 43.32
honour 22.12; Ex 5.1
hunger 25.29; 47.13
insight [2] 1 Kgs 4.29
interpret [3] 40.8; 42.23
magic [2] Ex 7.11
Majesty Ex 5.15
obey 32.4; 49.10
permit 47.4
plan 37.22; 50.15
plenty [5] 27.28; Lev 26.5
poor Ex 4.10
presence 31.35; 43.3
priest 14.18; 46.20
prison [2] 40.3; 42.17
restore 40.13; Lev 25.10
ripe [2] 40.10; Ex 9.31
ruin Ex 8.24
seal 38.18; Ex 24.8
serve 30.26; 43.31
shave Lev 13.33
slave 39.17; 42.10
Spirit (1) (God's Spirit) Num 11.17
suffer 31.40; 42.21
terrible 19.13; Ex 6.6
trouble 35.3; 42.21
turn 19.26; 49.19
wisdom [2] Deut 4.6
wise 3.6; Ex 7.11
world 19.31; 42.6
worry 40.7; 43.23
worse 19.9; 43.1
wrong 20.5; 50.17

I told the **dreams** to the **magicians**, but none of them could explain them to me."

25 Joseph said to the king, "The two **dreams** mean the same thing; God has told you what he is going to do. 26 The seven fat cows are seven years, and the seven full ears of corn are also seven years; they have the same meaning. 27 The seven thin cows which came up later and the seven thin ears of corn scorched by the desert wind are seven years of **famine**. 28 It is just as I told you—God has shown you what he is going to do. 29 There will be seven years of great **plenty** in all the land of Egypt. 30 After that, there will be seven years of **famine**, and all the good years will be **forgotten**, because the **famine** will **ruin** the country. 31 The time of **plenty** will be entirely **forgotten**, because the **famine** which follows will be so **terrible**. 32 The repetition of your **dream** means that the matter is fixed by God and that he will make it happen in the near future.

33 "Now you should **choose** some man with **wisdom** and **insight** and put him in charge of the country. 34 You must also appoint other officials and take a fifth of the crops during the seven years of **plenty**. 35 Order them to collect all the food during the good years that are coming, and give them **authority** to store up corn in the cities and guard it. 36 The food will be a reserve supply for the country during the seven years of **famine** which are going to come on Egypt. In this way the people will not starve."

Joseph Is Made Governor over Egypt

37 The king and his officials **approved** this **plan**, 38 and he said to them, "We will never find a better man than Joseph, a man who has **God's spirit** in him." 39 The king said to Joseph, "God has shown you all this, so it is obvious that you have greater **wisdom** and **insight** than anyone else. 40 I will put you in charge of my country, and all my people will **obey** your orders. Your **authority** will be second only to mine. 41 I now appoint you governor over all Egypt." 42 The king removed from his finger the ring engraved with the royal **seal** and put it on Joseph's finger. He put a fine linen robe on him, and placed a gold chain round his neck. 43 He gave him the second royal chariot to ride in, and his guard of **honour** went ahead of him and cried out, "Make way! Make way!" And so Joseph was appointed governor over all Egypt. 44 The king said to him, "I am the king—and no one in all Egypt shall so much as lift a hand or a foot without your **permission**." 45-46 He gave Joseph the Egyptian name Zaphenath Paneah, and he gave him a wife, Asenath, the daughter of Potiphera, a **priest** in the city of Heliopolis.

Joseph was thirty years old when he began to **serve** the king of Egypt. He left the king's **court** and travelled all over the land. 47 During the seven years of **plenty** the land produced **abundant** crops, 48 all of which Joseph collected and stored in the cities. In each city he stored the food from the fields around it. 49 There was so much corn that Joseph stopped measuring it—it was like the sand of the sea.

50 Before the years of **famine** came, Joseph had two sons by Asenath. 51 He said, "God has made me **forget** all my **sufferings** and all my father's family"; so he named his first son Manasseh.[o] 52 He also said, "God has given me children in the land of my **trouble**"; so he named his second son Ephraim.[p]

53 The seven years of **plenty** that the land of Egypt had **enjoyed** came to an end, 54 and the seven years of **famine** began, just as Joseph had said. There was **famine** in every other country, but there was food throughout Egypt. 55 When the Egyptians began to be **hungry**, they cried out to the king for food. So he ordered them to go to Joseph and do what he told them. 56 The **famine** grew **worse** and spread over the whole country, so Joseph opened all the storehouses and sold corn to the Egyptians. 57 People came to Egypt from all over the **world** to buy corn from Joseph, because the **famine** was severe everywhere.

Joseph's Brothers Go to Egypt to Buy Corn

42 When Jacob **learnt** that there was corn in Egypt, he said to his sons, "Why don't you do something? 2 I hear that there is corn in Egypt; go there and buy some to **keep us from** starving **to death**." 3 So Joseph's ten half-brothers went to buy corn in Egypt, 4 but Jacob did not send Joseph's full-brother Benjamin with them, because he was **afraid** that something might happen to him.

5 The sons of Jacob came with others to buy corn, because there was **famine** in the land of Canaan. 6 Joseph, as governor of the land of Egypt, was selling corn to people from all over the **world**. So

accuse 19.13; Ex 20.16
act 38.24; Ex 2.7
afraid [2] 38.11; 43.18
agree 37.27; 44.10
beg 19.7; Ex 11.8
bow (2) 37.7; 43.26
care 39.6; 45.11
dead [3] 44.20
death (1) [2] 27.41; 43.8
death (3) (to death) [2] 38.24; 43.8
dream 41.1; Num 12.6
famine 41.27; 43.1
fear 35.5; 50.21
God-fearing Ex 18.21
harm 31.7; 48.16
heart 43.30
help 40.14; 49.25

[o] MANASSEH: *This name sounds like the Hebrew for "cause to forget."*
[p] EPHRAIM: *This name sounds like the Hebrew for "give children."*

41.40: Acts 7.10 **41.42:** Dan 5.29 **41.54:** Acts 7.11 **41.55:** Jn 2.5 **42.2:** Acts 7.12

honest [5] 30.33; Lev 19.15
interpret 41.12; Deut 13.1
keep from 30.2; Ex 1.10
learn 34.5; Ex 18.15
life (1) 26.35; 43.9
prison [2] 41.10; Ex 12.29
prove [2] 20.16; Ex 3.12
remember 40.14; Ex 2.24
slave 41.12; 43.18
sorrow 37.29; 44.13
spare 18.24; Ex 4.25
suffer [2] 41.51; Ex 3.7
sure 24.6; 45.7
swear 14.22; 44.7
test [2] 22.1; Ex 15.25
trouble [2] 41.52; 43.6
truth [2] Num 5.15
understand 28.8; Ex 31.3
weak [2] 33.13; 47.13
world 41.57; Ex 9.14

Joseph's brothers came and **bowed down** before him with their faces to the ground. 7 When Joseph saw his brothers, he recognized them, but he **acted** as if he did not know them. He asked them harshly, "Where do you come from?"

"We have come from Canaan to buy food," they answered.

8 Although Joseph recognized his brothers, they did not recognize him. 9 He **remembered** the **dreams** he had dreamt about them and said, "You are spies; you have come to find out where our country is **weak**."

10 "No, sir," they answered. "We have come as your **slaves**, to buy food. 11 We are all brothers. We are not spies, sir, we are **honest** men."

12 Joseph said to them, "No! You have come to find out where our country is **weak**."

13 They said, "We were twelve brothers in all, sir, sons of the same man in the land of Canaan. One brother is **dead**, and the youngest is now with our father."

14 "It is just as I said," Joseph answered. "You are spies. 15 This is how you will be **tested**: I **swear** by the name of the king that you will never leave unless your youngest brother comes here. 16 One of you must go and get him. The rest of you will be kept under guard until the **truth** of what you say can be **tested**. Otherwise, as **sure** as the king lives, you are spies." 17 Then he put them in **prison** for three days.

18 On the third day Joseph said to them, "I am a **God-fearing** man, and I will **spare** your **lives** on one condition. 19 To **prove** that you are **honest**, one of you will stay in the **prison** where you have been kept; the rest of you may go and take back to your starving families the corn that you have bought. 20 Then you must bring your youngest brother to me. This will **prove** that you have been telling the **truth**, and I will not put you **to death**."

They **agreed** to this 21 and said to one another, "Yes, now we are **suffering** the consequences of what we did to our brother; we saw the great **trouble** he was in when he **begged** for **help**, but we would not listen. That is why we are in this **trouble** now."

22 Reuben said, "I told you not to **harm** the boy, but you wouldn't listen. And now we are being paid back for his **death**." 23 Joseph **understood** what they said, but they did not know it, because they had been speaking to him through an **interpreter**. 24 Joseph left them and began to cry. When he was able to speak again, he came back, picked out Simeon, and had him tied up in front of them.

Joseph's Brothers Return to Canaan

25 Joseph gave orders to fill his brothers' packs with corn, to put each man's money back in his sack, and to give them food for the journey. This was done. 26 The brothers loaded their donkeys with the corn they had bought, and then they left. 27 At the place where they spent the night, one of them opened his sack to feed his donkey and found his money at the top of the sack. 28 "My money has been returned to me," he called to his brothers. "Here it is in my sack!" Their **hearts** sank, and in **fear** they asked one another, "What has God done to us?"

29 When they came to their father Jacob in Canaan, they told him all that had happened to them: 30 "The governor of Egypt spoke harshly to us and **accused** us of spying against his country. 31 'We are not spies,' we answered, 'we are **honest** men. 32 We were twelve brothers in all, sons of the same father. One brother is **dead**, and the youngest is still in Canaan with our father.' 33 The man answered, 'This is how I will find out if you are **honest** men: One of you will stay with me; the rest will take corn for your starving families and leave. 34 Bring your youngest brother to me. Then I will know that you are not spies, but **honest** men; I will give your brother back to you, and you can stay here and trade.' "

35 Then when they emptied out their sacks, every one of them found his bag of money; and when they saw the money, they and their father Jacob were **afraid**. 36 Their father said to them, "Do you want to make me lose all my children? Joseph is gone; Simeon is gone; and now you want to take away Benjamin. I am the one who **suffers**!"

37 Reuben said to his father, "If I do not bring Benjamin back to you, you can kill my two sons. Put him in my **care**, and I will bring him back."

38 But Jacob said, "My son cannot go with you; his brother is **dead**, and he is the only one left. Something might happen to him on the way. I am an old man, and the **sorrow** you would cause me would kill me."

42.9: Gen 37.5-10 **42.22:** Gen 37.21-22

afraid [2] 42.4; 46.3
alive [2] 32.30; 44.20
Almighty 35.11; 48.3
amaze 45.7
best 27.15; 45.18
blame 44.32
bless 39.5; 47.7
bow (2) [2] 42.6; 44.14
command 28.6; 44.1
control 27.40; 45.1
death (1) 42.2; 49.29
death (3) (to death) 42.2; 44.9
famine 42.5; 45.6
gift [3] 33.10; Ex 29.24
heart 42.28; 50.21
Hebrew 41.12; Ex 1.15
humble Lev 26.41
kneel 24.11; Ex 12.27
life (1) 42.18; 44.30
mistake Num 15.24
pity 19.16; Ex 33.19
presence [2] 41.14; 44.23
present (1) [2] 47.2
question Josh 1.18
safe 37.14; 44.17
separate 31.49; Ex 26.33
servant [6] 40.4; 44.1
serve [5] 41.45; 48.15
slave 42.10; 44.9
sound (2) 44.17
trouble 42.21; Ex 5.19
warn 31.29; Ex 8.21
worry 41.8; 45.20
worse 41.56; Ex 10.6

Joseph's Brothers Return to Egypt with Benjamin

43 The **famine** in Canaan got **worse**,
2 and when the family of Jacob
had eaten all the corn which had been
brought from Egypt, Jacob said to his
sons, "Go back and buy a little food for
us."
3 Judah said to him, "The man sternly
warned us that we would not be admitted
to his **presence** unless we had our
brother with us. 4 If you are willing to
send our brother with us, we will go and
buy food for you. 5 If you are not willing,
we will not go, because the man told us
we would not be admitted to his **presence**
unless our brother was with us."
6 Jacob said, "Why did you cause me
so much **trouble** by telling the man that
you had another brother?"
7 They answered, "The man kept asking about us and our family, 'Is your
father still living? Have you got another
brother?' We had to answer his **questions**. How could we know that he would
tell us to bring our brother with us?"
8 Judah said to his father, "Send the
boy with me, and we will leave at once.
Then none of us will starve **to death**. 9 I
will pledge my own **life**, and you can hold
me responsible for him. If I do not bring
him back to you **safe and sound**, I will always bear the **blame**. 10 If we had not
waited so long, we could have been there
and back twice by now."
11 Their father said to them, "If that is
how it has to be, then take the **best** products of the land in your packs as a present for the governor: a little resin, a
little honey, spices, pistachio nuts, and almonds. 12 Take with you also twice as
much money, because you must take
back the money that was returned in the
top of your sacks. Maybe it was a **mistake**. 13 Take your brother and return at
once. 14 May **Almighty** God cause the
man to have **pity** on you, so that he will
give Benjamin and your other brother
back to you. As for me, if I must lose my
children, I must lose them."
15 So the brothers took the **gifts** and
twice as much money, and set out for
Egypt with Benjamin. There they **presented** themselves to Joseph. 16 When
Joseph saw Benjamin with them, he said
to the **servant** in charge of his house,
"Take these men to my house. They are
going to eat with me at noon, so kill an
animal and prepare it." 17 The **servant**
did as he was **commanded** and took the
brothers to Joseph's house.
18 As they were being brought to the
house, they were **afraid** and thought, "We
are being brought here because of the
money that was returned in our sacks
the first time. They will suddenly attack
us, take our donkeys, and make us his
slaves." 19 So at the door of the house,
they said to the **servant** in charge, 20 "If
you please, sir, we came here once before to buy food. 21 When we set up camp
on the way home, we opened our sacks,
and each man found his money in the top
of his sack—every bit of it. We have
brought it back to you. 22 We have also
brought some more money with us to buy
more food. We do not know who put our
money back in our sacks."
23 The **servant** said, "Don't **worry**.
Don't be **afraid**. Your God, the God of
your father, must have put the money in
your sacks for you. I received your payment." Then he brought Simeon to them.
24 The **servant** took the brothers into
the house. He gave them water so that
they could wash their feet, and he fed
their donkeys. 25 They got their **gifts**
ready to **present** to Joseph when he arrived at noon, because they had been
told that they were to eat with him.
26 When Joseph got home, they took the
gifts into the house to him and **bowed
down** to the ground before him. 27 He
asked about their health and then said,
"You told me about your old father—how
is he? Is he still **alive** and well?"
28 They answered, "Your **humble servant**, our father, is still **alive** and well."
And they **knelt** and **bowed down** before
him.
29 When Joseph saw his brother
Benjamin, he said, "So this is your youngest brother, the one you told me about.
God **bless** you, my son." 30 Then Joseph
left suddenly, because his **heart** was full
of tender feelings for his brother. He was
about to break down, so he went to his
room and cried. 31 After he had washed
his face, he came out, and **controlling**
himself, he ordered the meal to be
served. 32 Joseph was **served** at one table
and his brothers at another. The
Egyptians who were eating there were
served separately, because they considered it beneath their dignity to eat
with **Hebrews**. 33 The brothers had been
seated at table, facing Joseph, in the order of their age from the eldest to the
youngest. When they saw how they had
been seated, they looked at one another
in **amazement**. 34 Food was **served** to
them from Joseph's table, and Benjamin
was **served** five times as much as the
rest of them. So they ate and drank with
Joseph until they were drunk.

agree 42.20; Ex 2.21
alive 43.27; 45.3
anger 41.10; 49.6
argue 1 Kgs 3.22
blame 43.9; 45.5
bow (2) 43.26; 48.12
clear Josh 17.15
command 43.17; 47.11
crime 31.36; 50.17
cup [6] 40.11; Ex 25.29
dead 42.13; Ex 4.19
death (3) (to death) 43.8; Ex 8.26
disaster 20.9; Ex 30.12
divination [2] 30.27; Deut 18.10
evil 38.7; 50.20
free [2] 34.10; 49.21
guilty 26.10; Ex 22.2
life (1) [3] 43.9; 45.5
love 37.3; Ex 20.6
master [2] 39.2; Ex 21.4
practice Ex 22.18
presence [2] 43.3; Ex 7.20
safe 43.9; Ex 21.13
serious Deut 15.21
servant [4] 43.16; 45.1
slave [5] 43.18; 46.18
sorrow [3] 42.38; 48.7
sound (2) 43.9; Judg 4.21
steal [2] 31.19; Ex 20.15
swear 42.15; Ex 10.10
word (1) 38.25; 49.28

The Missing Cup

44 Joseph **commanded** the **servant**
in charge of his house, "Fill the
men's sacks with as much food as they
can carry, and put each man's money in
the top of his sack. 2 Put my silver **cup** in
the top of the youngest brother's sack, together with the money for his corn." He
did as he was told. 3 Early in the morning
the brothers were sent on their way with
their donkeys. 4 When they had gone only
a short distance from the city, Joseph
said to the **servant** in charge of his house,
"Hurry after those men. When you catch
up with them, ask them, 'Why have you
paid back **evil** for good? 5 Why did you
steal my **master's** silver **cup**? [q] It is the
one he drinks from, the one he uses for
divination. You have committed a
serious crime!' "
6 When the **servant** caught up with
them, he repeated these **words**. 7 They
answered him, "What do you mean, sir,
by talking like this? We **swear** that we
have done no such thing. 8 You know that
we brought back to you from the land of
Canaan the money we found in the top of
our sacks. Why then should we **steal** silver or gold from your **master's** house?
9 Sir, if any one of us is found to have it,
he will be put **to death**, and the rest of us
will become your **slaves**."
10 He said, "I **agree**; but only the one
who has taken the **cup** will become my
slave, and the rest of you can go **free**."
11 So they quickly lowered their sacks to
the ground, and each man opened his
sack. 12 Joseph's **servant** searched carefully, beginning with the eldest and ending with the youngest, and the **cup** was
found in Benjamin's sack. 13 The brothers
tore their clothes in **sorrow**, loaded their
donkeys, and returned to the city.
14 When Judah and his brothers came
to Joseph's house, he was still there.
They **bowed down** before him, 15 and
Joseph said, "What have you done?
Didn't you know that a man in my position could find you out by **practising divination**?"
16 "What can we say to you, sir?"
Judah answered. "How can we **argue**?
How can we **clear** ourselves? God has
uncovered our **guilt**. All of us are now
your **slaves** and not just the one with
whom the **cup** was found."
17 Joseph said, "Oh, no! I would never
do that! Only the one who had the **cup**
will be my **slave**. The rest of you may go
back **safe and sound** to your father."

Judah Pleads for Benjamin

18 Judah went up to Joseph and said,
"Please, sir, allow me to speak with you
freely. Don't be **angry** with me; you are
like the king himself. 19 Sir, you asked us,
'Have you got a father or another
brother?' 20 We answered, 'We have a
father who is old and a younger brother,
born to him in his old age. The boy's
brother is **dead**, and he is the only one of
his mother's children still **alive**; his
father **loves** him very much.' 21 Sir, you
told us to bring him here, so that you
could see him, 22 and we answered that
the boy could not leave his father; if he
did, his father would die. 23 Then you said,
'You will not be admitted to my **presence**
again unless your youngest brother
comes with you.'
24 "When we went back to our father,
we told him what you had said. 25 Then he
told us to return and buy a little food.
26 We answered, 'We cannot go; we will
not be admitted to the man's **presence**
unless our youngest brother is with us.
We can go only if our youngest brother
goes also.' 27 Our father said to us, 'You
know that my wife Rachel bore me only
two sons. 28 One of them has already left
me. He must have been torn to pieces by
wild animals, because I have not seen
him since he left. 29 If you take this one
from me now and something happens to
him, the **sorrow** you would cause me
would kill me, old as I am.'
30-31 "And now, sir," Judah continued,
"if I go back to my father without the
boy, as soon as he sees that the boy is not
with me, he will die. His **life** is wrapped
up with the life of the boy, and he is so
old that the **sorrow** we would cause him
would kill him. 32 What is more, I pledged
my **life** to my father for the boy. I told
him that if I did not bring the boy back to
him, I would bear the **blame** all my **life**.
33 And now, sir, I will stay here as your
slave in place of the boy; let him go back
with his brothers. 34 How can I go back to
my father if the boy is not with me? I
cannot bear to see this **disaster** come
upon my father."

Joseph Tells His Brothers Who He Is

45 Joseph was no longer able to
control his feelings in front of his
servants, so he ordered them all to leave
the room. No one else was with him
when Joseph told his brothers who he
was. 2 He cried with such loud sobs that
the Egyptians heard it, and the news was

alive [3] 44.20; 46.30
amaze 43.33; Judg 20.40
believe Ex 4.1
best [3] 43.11; 47.6
blame 44.32; 1 Sam 25.24
bread 27.17; Ex 12.8
care 42.37; 46.32

[q] *One ancient translation* Why did you steal my master's silver cup?; *Hebrew does not have these words.*

45.1: Acts 7.13

change [2] 41.14; Ex 8.16
control 43.31; Ex 32.25
enough 40.14; Ex 2.10
famine [2] 43.1; 47.4
kiss 33.4; 48.10
life (1) 44.30; 46.34
please 39.4; Ex 29.18
possess 36.6; 46.6
power 31.29; 49.24
quarrel 26.20; Lev 24.10
reap Deut 28.38
rescue 48.16
save 37.21; 47.25
servant 44.1; 50.17
sheep 38.12; 47.17
sure 42.16; 46.34
terrify 28.17; Ex 3.20
upset 40.6; 48.17
weep 35.8; 2 Sam 3.32
worry 43.23; Judg 18.6

taken to the king's palace. 3 Joseph said
to his brothers, "I am Joseph. Is my
father still **alive**?" But when his brothers
heard this, they were so **terrified** that
they could not answer. 4 Then Joseph said
to them, "Please come closer." They did,
and he said, "I am your brother Joseph,
whom you sold into Egypt. 5 Now do not
be **upset** or **blame** yourselves because
you sold me here. It was really God who
sent me ahead of you to **save** people's
lives. 6 This is only the second year of
famine in the land; there will be five
more years in which there will be
neither ploughing nor **reaping**. 7 God sent
me ahead of you to **rescue** you in this
amazing way and to make **sure** that you
and your descendants survive. 8 So it was
not really you who sent me here, but
God. He has made me the king's highest
official. I am in charge of his whole
country; I am the ruler of all Egypt.
9 "Now hurry back to my father and
tell him that this is what his son Joseph
says: 'God has made me ruler of all
Egypt; come to me without delay. 10 You
can live in the region of Goshen, where
you can be near me—you, your children,
your grandchildren, your **sheep**, your
goats, your cattle, and everything else
that you have. 11 If you are in Goshen, I
can take **care** of you. There will still be
five years of **famine**; and I do not want
you, your family, and your livestock to
starve.' "
12 Joseph continued, "Now all of you,
and you too, Benjamin, can see that I am
really Joseph. 13 Tell my father how
powerful I am here in Egypt and tell him
about everything that you have seen.
Then hurry and bring him here."
14 He threw his arms round his
brother Benjamin and began to cry;
Benjamin also cried as he hugged him.
15 Then, still **weeping**, he embraced each
of his brothers and **kissed** them. After
that, his brothers began to talk with him.
16 When the news reached the palace
that Joseph's brothers had come, the
king and his officials were **pleased**. 17 He
said to Joseph, "Tell your brothers to
load their animals and to return to the
land of Canaan. 18 Let them get their
father and their families and come back
here. I will give them the **best** land in
Egypt, and they will have more than
enough to live on. 19 Tell them also to
take wagons with them from Egypt for
their wives and small children and to
bring their father with them. 20 They are
not to **worry** about leaving their
possessions behind; the **best** in the whole
land of Egypt will be theirs."
21 Jacob's sons did as they were told.
Joseph gave them wagons, as the king
had ordered, and food for the journey.
22 He also gave each of them a **change** of
clothes, but he gave Benjamin three hundred pieces of silver and five **changes** of
clothes. 23 He sent his father ten donkeys
loaded with the **best** Egyptian goods and
ten donkeys loaded with corn, **bread**, and
other food for the journey. 24 He sent his
brothers off and as they left, he said to
them, "Don't **quarrel** on the way."
25 They left Egypt and went back
home to their father Jacob in Canaan.
26 "Joseph is still **alive**!" they told him.
"He is the ruler of all Egypt!" Jacob was
stunned and could not **believe** them.
27 But when they told him all that
Joseph had said to them, and when he
saw the wagons which Joseph had sent to
take him to Egypt, he recovered from
the shock. 28 "My son Joseph is still
alive!" he said. "This is all I could ask
for! I must go and see him before I die."

Jacob and His Family Go to Egypt

46 Jacob packed up all he had and
went to Beersheba, where he
offered sacrifices to the God of his father
Isaac. 2 God spoke to him in a **vision** at
night and called, "Jacob, Jacob!"
"Yes, here I am," he answered.
3 "I am God, the God of your father,"
he said. "Do not be **afraid** to go to Egypt;
I will make your descendants a great
nation there. 4 I will go with you to Egypt,
and I will bring your descendants back to
this land. Joseph will be with you when
you die."
5 Jacob set out from Beersheba. His
sons put him, their small children, and
their wives in the wagons which the king
of Egypt had sent. 6 They took their livestock and the **possessions** they had acquired in Canaan and went to Egypt.
Jacob took all his descendants with him:
7 his sons, his grandsons, his daughters,
and his granddaughters.
8 The members of Jacob's family who
went to Egypt with him were his eldest
son Reuben 9 and Reuben's sons: Hanoch,
Pallu, Hezron, and Carmi. 10 Simeon and
his sons: Jemuel, Jamin, Ohad, Jachin,
Zohar, and Shaul, the son of a Canaanite
woman. 11 Levi and his sons: Gershon,
Kohath, and Merari. 12 Judah and his
sons: Shelah, Perez, and Zerah. (Judah's
other sons, Er and Onan, had died in
Canaan.) Perez' sons were Hezron and
Hamul. 13 Issachar and his sons: Tola,

afraid 43.18; 50.19
alive 45.3; 47.19
care [2] 45.11; 50.21
flock 38.17; 47.1
life (1) 45.5; 47.9
offer 31.54; Ex 3.18
possess 45.20; 48.4
priest 41.45; 47.22
sacrifice 31.54; Ex 3.18
shepherd [2] 29.3; 47.3
slave [2] 44.9; 47.19
sure 45.7; Ex 4.21
vision 15.1; Num 12.6

45.9–11: Acts 7.14 **46.6:** Acts 7.15

Puah, Jashub, and Shimron. [14]Zebulun
and his sons: Sered, Elon, and Jahleel.
[15]These are the sons that Leah had borne
to Jacob in Mesopotamia, besides his
daughter Dinah. In all, his descendants
by Leah numbered thirty-three.

16 Gad and his sons: Zephon, Haggi,
Shuni, Ezbon, Eri, Arod, and Areli.
[17]Asher and his sons: Imnah, Ishvah,
Ishvi, Beriah, and their sister Serah.
Beriah's sons were Heber and Malchiel.
[18]These sixteen are the descendants of
Jacob by Zilpah, the **slave-girl** whom
Laban gave to his daughter Leah.

19 Jacob's wife Rachel bore him two
sons: Joseph and Benjamin. [20]In Egypt
Joseph had two sons, Manasseh and
Ephraim, by Asenath, the daughter of
Potiphera, a **priest** in Heliopolis.
[21]Benjamin's sons were Bela, Becher,
Ashbel, Gera, Naaman, Ehi, Rosh,
Muppim, Huppim, and Ard. [22]These four-
teen are the descendants of Jacob by
Rachel.

23 Dan and his son Hushim. [24]Naphtali
and his sons: Jahzeel, Guni, Jezer, and
Shillem. [25]These seven are the descendants of Jacob by Bilhah, the **slave-girl**
whom Laban gave to his daughter
Rachel.

26 The total number of the direct
descendants of Jacob who went to Egypt
was sixty-six, not including his sons'
wives. [27]Two sons were born to Joseph in
Egypt, bringing to seventy the total number of Jacob's family who went there.

Jacob and His Family in Egypt

28 Jacob sent Judah ahead to ask
Joseph to meet them in Goshen. When
they arrived, [29]Joseph got in his chariot
and went to Goshen to meet his father.
When they met, Joseph threw his arms
round his father's neck and cried for a
long time. [30]Jacob said to Joseph, "I am
ready to die, now that I have seen you
and know that you are still **alive**."

31 Then Joseph said to his brothers
and the rest of his father's family, "I
must go and tell the king that my
brothers and all my father's family, who
were living in Canaan, have come to me.
[32]I will tell him that you are **shepherds**
and take **care** of livestock and that you
have brought your **flocks** and herds and
everything else that belongs to you.
[33]When the king calls for you and asks
what your occupation is, [34]be **sure** to tell
him that you have taken **care** of livestock
all your **lives**, just as your ancestors did.
In this way he will let you live in the
region of Goshen." Joseph said this because Egyptians will have nothing to do
with **shepherds**.

47 So Joseph took five of his
brothers and went to the king.
He said, "My father and my brothers
have come from Canaan with their
flocks, their herds, and all that they own.
They are now in the region of Goshen."
[2]He then **presented** his brothers to the
king. [3]The king asked them, "What is
your occupation?"

"We are **shepherds**, sir, just as our
ancestors were," they answered. [4]"We
have come to live in this country, because in the land of Canaan the **famine** is
so severe that there is no pasture for our
flocks. Please give us **permission** to live
in the region of Goshen." [5]The king said
to Joseph, "Now that your father and
your brothers have arrived, [6]the land of
Egypt is theirs. Let them settle in the
region of Goshen, the **best** part of the
land. And if there are any capable men
among them, put them in charge of my
own livestock."

7 Then Joseph brought his father
Jacob and **presented** him to the king.
Jacob gave the king his **blessing**, [8]and
the king asked him, "How old are you?"

9 Jacob answered, "My **life** of wandering has **lasted** a hundred and thirty
years. Those years have been few and
difficult, unlike the long years of my
ancestors in their wanderings." [10]Jacob
gave the king a farewell **blessing** and
left. [11]Then Joseph settled his father and
his brothers in Egypt, giving them property in the **best** of the land near the city
of Rameses, as the king had **commanded**.
[12]Joseph **provided** food for his father, his
brothers, and all the rest of his father's
family, including the very youngest.

The Famine

13 The **famine** was so severe that
there was no food anywhere, and the
people of Egypt and Canaan became
weak with **hunger**. [14]As they bought corn,
Joseph collected all the money and took
it to the palace. [15]When all the money in
Egypt and Canaan was spent, the
Egyptians came to Joseph and said,
"Give us food! Don't let us die. Do something! Our money is all gone."

16 Joseph answered, "Bring your livestock; I will give you food in exchange
for it if your money is all gone." [17]So they
brought their livestock to Joseph, and he
gave them food in exchange for their
horses, **sheep**, goats, cattle, and donkeys.
That year he supplied them with food in
exchange for all their livestock.

46.20: Gen 41.50–52 **46.27:** Acts 7.14

alive 46.30; 50.20
best [2] 45.18; 49.11
bless [2] 43.29; 48.3
body 40.19; 50.2
command 44.1; 49.2
difficult 35.16; Ex 14.25
famine [3] 45.6; Ruth 1.1
flock [2] 46.32; Ex 3
force (1) 49.15
harvest [2] 30.14; Ex 23.11
hunger 41.55; Lev 26.26
last (1) Lev 26.10
law [2] 31.36; Ex 13.
life (1) [2] 46.34; 50.2
permit 41.44; Lev 20.14
present (1) [2] 43.15 Lev 1.3
priest [2] 46.20; Ex 2.15
provide 22.8; 49.20
rich 26.13; 49.20
save 45.5; Ex 6.6
seed [3] 26.12; Ex 16.31
sheep 45.10; 50.8
shepherd 46.32; 49.2
slave [3] 46.18; 49.15
solemn 31.53; 50.11
sow [2] 26.12; Ex 23.10
thank 18.5; Lev 22.2
vow [3] 31.13; 50.25
weak 42.9; Deut 32.31

18 The following year they came to
him and said, "We will not hide the fact
from you, sir, that our money is all gone
and our livestock belongs to you. There is
nothing left to give you except our **bodies**
and our lands. 19 Don't let us die. Do
something! Don't let our fields be deserted. Buy us and our land in exchange
for food. We will be the king's **slaves**, and
he will own our land. Give us corn to
keep us **alive** and **seed** to **sow** in our
fields."
20 Joseph bought all the land in Egypt
for the king. Every Egyptian was **forced**
to sell his land, because the **famine** was
so severe; and all the land became the
king's property. 21 Joseph made **slaves** of
the people from one end of Egypt to the
other. 22 The only land he did not buy was
the land that belonged to the **priests**.
They did not have to sell their lands, because the king gave them an allowance
to live on. 23 Joseph said to the people,
"You see, I have now bought you and
your lands for the king. Here is **seed** for
you to **sow** in your fields. 24 At the time of
harvest you must give one-fifth to the
king. You can use the rest for **seed** and
for food for yourselves and your families."
25 They answered, "You have **saved**
our **lives**; you have been good to us, sir,
and we will be the king's **slaves**." 26 So
Joseph made it a **law** for the land of
Egypt that one-fifth of the **harvest** should
belong to the king. This **law** still remains
in force today. Only the lands of the
priests did not become the king's property.

Jacob's Last Request

27 The Israelites lived in Egypt in the
region of Goshen, where they became
rich and had many children. 28 Jacob
lived in Egypt for seventeen years, until
he was a hundred and forty-seven years
old. 29 When the time drew near for him
to die, he called for his son Joseph and
said to him, "Place your hand between
my thighs[r] and make a **solemn vow** that
you will not bury me in Egypt. 30 I want to
be buried where my fathers are; carry
me out of Egypt and bury me where they
are buried."
Joseph answered, "I will do as you
say."
31 Jacob said, "Make a **vow** that you
will." Joseph made the **vow**, and Jacob
gave **thanks** there on his bed.

Jacob Blesses Ephraim and Manasseh

48 Some time later Joseph was told
that his father was ill. So he took
his two sons, Manasseh and Ephraim,
and went to see Jacob. 2 When Jacob was
told that his son Joseph had come to see
him, he gathered his **strength** and sat up
in bed. 3 Jacob said to Joseph, "**Almighty**
God appeared to me at Luz in the land of
Canaan and **blessed** me. 4 He said to me,
'I will give you many children, so that
your descendants will become many
nations; I will give this land to your
descendants as their **possession** for
ever.'"
5 Jacob continued, "Joseph, your two
sons, who were born to you in Egypt before I came here, belong to me; Ephraim
and Manasseh are just as much my sons
as Reuben and Simeon. 6 If you have any
more sons, they will not be considered
mine; the **inheritance** they get will come
through Ephraim and Manasseh. 7 I am
doing this because of your mother
Rachel. To my great **sorrow** she died in
the land of Canaan, not far from
Ephrath, as I was returning from
Mesopotamia. I buried her there beside
the road to Ephrath." (Ephrath is now
known as Bethlehem.)
8 When Jacob saw Joseph's sons, he
asked, "Who are these boys?"
9 Joseph answered, "These are my
sons, whom God has given me here in
Egypt."
Jacob said, "Bring them to me so that I
may **bless** them." 10 Jacob's **eyesight** was
failing because of his age, and he could
not see very well. Joseph brought the
boys to him, and he hugged them and
kissed them. 11 Jacob said to Joseph, "I
never expected to see you again, and
now God has even let me see your children." 12 Then Joseph took them from
Jacob's lap and **bowed down** before him
with his face to the ground.
13 Joseph put Ephraim at Jacob's left
and Manasseh at his **right**. 14 But Jacob
crossed his hands, and put his **right hand**
on the head of Ephraim, even though he
was the younger, and his left hand on the
head of Manasseh, who was the elder.
15 Then he **blessed** Joseph:[s]

"May the God whom my fathers
Abraham and Isaac **served bless**
these boys!
May God, who has led me to this very
day, **bless** them!
16 May the **angel**, who has **rescued** me
from all **harm**, **bless** them!

Almighty 43.14; 49.25
angel 32.1; Ex 3.2
bless [8] 47.7; 49.25
bow (2) 44.14; 49.8
eyesight *see* **sight**
fail 38.26; Ex 8.18
harm 42.22; 50.15
inherit 31.14; Lev 25.46
kiss 45.15; 50.1
possess 46.6; Ex 6.8
refuse (1) 39.8; Ex 4.9
rescue 45.7; Ex 2.17
right (2) [4] Ex 15.6
serve 43.31; Ex 1.11
sight 6.11; Ex 4.11
sorrow 44.13; Num 14.6
strength 31.6; 49.3
upset 45.5; 1 Sam 1.7

[r] PLACE...THIGHS: *See 24.2.*
[s] JOSEPH: *In blessing Ephraim and Manasseh, Jacob was in fact blessing Joseph.*

47.29–30: Gen 49.29–32, 50.6 **48.3–4:** Gen 28.13–14 **48.7:** Gen 35.16–19

May my name and the name of my
fathers Abraham and Isaac live
on through these boys!
May they have many children, many
descendants!"

17 Joseph was **upset** when he saw that
his father had put his **right hand** on
Ephraim's head; so he took his father's
hand to move it from Ephraim's head to
the head of Manasseh. 18 He said to his
father, "Not that way, father. This is the
elder boy; put your **right hand** on his
head."

19 His father **refused**, saying, "I know,
my son, I know. Manasseh's descendants
will also become a great people. But his
younger brother will be greater than he,
and his descendants will become great
nations."

20 So he **blessed** them that day, saying,
"The Israelites will use your names when
they pronounce **blessings**. They will say,
'May God make you like Ephraim and
Manasseh.'" In this way Jacob put
Ephraim before Manasseh.

21 Then Jacob said to Joseph, "As you
see, I am about to die, but God will be
with you and will take you back to the
land of your ancestors. 22 It is to you and
not to your brothers that I am giving
Shechem, that fertile region which I took
from the Amorites with my sword and
my bow."

The Last Words of Jacob

49 Jacob called for his sons and
said, "Gather round, and I will
tell you what will happen to you in the
future:

2 "Come together and listen, sons of
Jacob.
Listen to your father Israel.

3 "Reuben, my **first-born**, you are my
strength
And the first child of my manhood,
The **proudest** and **strongest** of all my
sons.
4 You are like a **raging flood**,
But you will not be the most **important**,
For you slept with my **concubine**
And **dishonoured** your father's bed.

5 "Simeon and Levi are brothers.
They use their weapons to commit
violence.
6 I will not join in their **secret** talks,
Nor will I take part in their meetings,
For they killed men in **anger**
And they **crippled** bulls for sport.
7 A **curse** be on their **anger**, because it is
so fierce,
And on their **fury**, because it is so
cruel.
I will **scatter** them throughout the land
of Israel.
I will disperse them among its people.

8 "Judah, your brothers will **praise** you.
You hold your **enemies** by the neck.
Your brothers will **bow down** before
you.
9 Judah is like a lion,
Killing his **victim** and returning to his
den,
Stretching out and lying down.
No one **dares** disturb him.
10 Judah will hold the royal sceptre,
And his descendants will always rule.
Nations will bring him **tribute**[s]
And **bow** in **obedience** before him.
11 He ties his young donkey to a
grapevine,
To the very **best** of the **vines**.
He washes his clothes in **blood-red**
wine.
12 His eyes are **bloodshot** from drinking
wine,
His teeth white from drinking milk.[t]

13 "Zebulun will live beside the sea.
His shore will be a haven for ships.
His territory will reach as far as Sidon.

14 "Issachar is no better than a donkey
That lies stretched out between its
saddlebags.
15 But he sees that the **resting-place** is
good
And that the land is **delightful**.
So he bends his back to carry the load
And is **forced** to work as a **slave**.

16 "Dan will be a ruler for his people.
They will be like the other tribes of
Israel.
17 Dan will be a snake at the side of the
road,
A poisonous snake beside the path,
That **strikes** at the horse's heel,
So that the rider is thrown off
backwards.

18 "I wait for your deliverance, LORD.

19 "Gad will be attacked by a band of
robbers,
But he will **turn** and pursue them.

20 "Asher's land will produce **rich** food.

[s] *Probable text* Nations...tribute; *Hebrew unclear.*
[t] His eyes...milk; *or* His eyes are darker than wine, his teeth are whiter than milk.

48.20: Heb 11.21 **49.9:** Num 24.9; Rev 5.5

above Josh 2.11
Almighty 48.3; Ex 6.3
ancient Deut 33.15
anger [2] 44.18; Ex 4.14
apart 30.40; Ex 29.44
best 47.6; Ex 15.4
bless [4] 48.3; Ex 12.32
blood [2] 37.27; Ex 4.9
bow (2) [2] 48.12; 50.18
command 47.11; 50.12
concubine 37.2; Lev 19.20
cripple Lev 21.19
cruel 16.6; Ex 1.13
curse 27.12; Ex 21.17
dare Num 12.8
death (1) 43.8; 50.15
delight [2] Deut 28.63
devour Num 21.28
dishonour Deut 27.16
enemy [2] 24.60; Ex 1.10
everlasting 21.33; Ps 139.24
first-born 27.36; Ex 4.22
fit (1) Ex 15.25
flood 11.10; Josh 3.14

force (1) 47.20; Ex 1.13
free 44.10; Ex 6.6
fury 39.19; Ex 32.19
grapevine *see* **vine**
help 42.21; Ex 1.15
important 34.19; Num 22.15
might 23.6; Ex 6.6
obey 41.40; Ex 1.17
power 45.13; Ex 1.8
praise 29.35; Ex 15
protect 28.15; Ex 9.19
proud 16.4; Lev 26.
provide 47.12; Ex 10.25
rage 1.2; Deut 9.3
rest (1) 28.11; Ex 16.23
rich 47.27; Ex 3.8
rob Lev 19.13
scatter 11.4; Lev 26.33
secret Num 5.12
shepherd 47.3; Ex 2.17
slave 47.19; 50.18
strength 48.2; Ex 15.13
strike 32.25; Ex 7.1
strong [2] 25.23; Ex 1.7
tribute 1 Kgs 10.15
turn 41.13; 50.20
victim Job 18.7
vine [2] 40.9; Lev 25
violent 6.11; Ex 19.1
word (1) 44.6; 50.21

He will **provide** food **fit** for a king.

21 "Naphtali is a deer that runs **free**,
Who bears lovely fawns.[u]

22 "Joseph is like a wild donkey by a
spring,
A wild colt on a hillside.[v]
23 His **enemies** attack him fiercely
And pursue him with their bows and
arrows.
24 But his bow remains steady,
And his arms are made **strong**[w]
By the **power** of the **Mighty** God of
Jacob,
By the **Shepherd**, the **Protector** of
Israel.
25 It is your father's God who **helps** you,
The **Almighty** God who blesses you
With **blessings** of rain from **above**
And of deep waters from beneath the
ground,
Blessings of many cattle and children,
26 **Blessings** of corn and flowers,[x]
Blessings of **ancient** mountains,[y]
Delightful things from **everlasting**
hills.
May these **blessings** rest on the head of
Joseph,
On the brow of the one set **apart** from
his brothers.

27 "Benjamin is like a vicious wolf.
Morning and evening he kills and
devours."

28 These are the twelve tribes of
Israel, and this is what their father said
as he spoke a suitable **word** of farewell to
each son.

The Death and Burial of Jacob

29 Then Jacob **commanded** his sons,
"Now that I am going to join my people
in **death**, bury me with my fathers in the
cave that is in the field of Ephron the
Hittite, 30 at Machpelah, east of Mamre,
in the land of Canaan. Abraham bought
this cave and field from Ephron for a
burial-ground. 31 That is where they
buried Abraham and his wife Sarah; that
is where they buried Isaac and his wife
Rebecca; and that is where I buried
Leah. 32 The field and the cave in it were
bought from the Hittites. Bury me there."
33 When Jacob had finished giving
instructions to his sons, he lay down
again and died.

50 Joseph threw himself on his
father, crying and **kissing** his
face. 2 Then Joseph gave orders to em-
balm his father's **body**. 3 It took forty
days, the normal time for embalming.
The Egyptians **mourned** for him seventy
days.
4 When the time of **mourning** was
over, Joseph said to the king's officials,
"Please take this **message** to the king:
5 'When my father was about to die, he
made me **promise** him that I would bury
him in the **tomb** which he had prepared
in the land of Canaan. So please let me
go and bury my father, and then I will
come back.' "
6 The king answered, "Go and bury
your father, as you **promised** you would."
7 So Joseph went to bury his father.
All the king's officials, the senior men of
his **court**, and all the **leading** men of
Egypt went with Joseph. 8 His family, his
brothers, and the rest of his father's
family all went with him. Only their
small children and their **sheep**, goats,
and cattle stayed in the region of
Goshen. 9 Men in chariots and men on
horseback also went with him; it was a
huge group.
10 When they came to the threshing-
place at Atad east of the Jordan, they
mourned loudly for a long time, and
Joseph performed **mourning ceremonies**
for seven days. 11 When the citizens of
Canaan saw those people **mourning** at
Atad, they said, "What a **solemn**
ceremony of **mourning** the Egyptians are
holding!" That is why the place was
named Abel Mizraim.[z]
12 So Jacob's sons did as he had **com-**
manded them; 13 they carried his **body** to
Canaan and buried it in the cave at
Machpelah, east of Mamre, in the field
which Abraham had bought from Ephron
the Hittite for a burial-ground. 14 After
Joseph had buried his father, he returned
to Egypt with his brothers and all who
had gone with him for the funeral.

Joseph Reassures His Brothers

15 After the **death** of their father,
Joseph's brothers said, "What if Joseph
still **hates** us and **plans** to pay us back for
all the **harm** we did to him?" 16 So they
sent a **message** to Joseph: "Before our

afraid 46.3; Ex 2.14
alive 47.19; Ex 4.18
body [4] 47.18; Ex 2.12
bow (2) 49.8; Ex 4.31
care [2] 46.32; Ex 3.1
ceremony [2] Lev 21.1
command 49.29; Ex 1.22
court (1) 41.45; Ex 23.6
crime 44.5; Deut 19.15
death (1) 49.29; Ex 8.26
evil 44.4; Ex 20.7
fear 42.28; Ex 1.12
forgive [2] 32.20; Ex 10.17
harm 48.16; Ex 12.13
hate 37.4; Ex 5.21
heart 43.30; Deut 4.29
kind 40.14; Num 6.25
kiss 48.10; Ex 4.27
leading Ex 24.11
life (1) 47.9; Ex 1.13
message [3] Num 20.14
mourn [6] 38.12; Ex 33.4
plan 41.37; Ex 25.9
plot (1) 37.18; Ex 10.10
preserve 2 Sam 7.26
promise [4] 32.12; Ex 6.4
servant 45.1; Ex 2.5
sheep 47.17; Ex 2.15
slave 49.15; Ex 1.13
solemn [2] 47.29; Ex 6.8
tomb Judg 8.32
turn 49.19; Ex 4.3
vow 47.29; Lev 5.4
word (1) 49.28; Ex 18.6
wrong [2] 41.9; Ex 2.13

[u] Naphtali...fawns; *or* Naphtali is a spreading tree that puts out lovely branches.
[v] Joseph...hillside; *or* Joseph is like a tree by a spring, a fruitful tree that spreads over a wall.
[w] But...strong; *or* But their bows were broken and splintered, the muscles of their arms torn apart.
[x] *Probable text* corn and flowers; *Hebrew* your fathers are mightier than.
[y] *One ancient translation* ancient mountains; *Hebrew* my ancestors to.
[z] ABEL MIZRAIM: *This name sounds like the Hebrew for "mourning of the Egyptians."*

49.30: Gen 23.3-20 **49.31:** Gen 25.9-10, 35.29 **49.33:** Acts 7.15 **50.5:** Gen 47.29-31 **50.13:** Acts 7.16

father died, [17]he told us to ask you, 'Please **forgive** the **crime** your brothers committed when they **wronged** you.' Now please **forgive** us the **wrong** that we, the **servants** of your father's God, have done." Joseph cried when he received this **message**.

18 Then his brothers themselves came and **bowed down** before him. "Here we are before you as your **slaves**," they said.

19 But Joseph said to them, "Don't be **afraid**; I can't put myself in the place of God. [20]You **plotted evil** against me, but God **turned** it into good, in order to **preserve** the **lives** of many people who are **alive** today because of what happened. [21]You have nothing to **fear**. I will take **care** of you and your children." So he reassured them with **kind words** that touched their **hearts**.

50.25: Ex 13.19; Josh 24.32; Heb 11.22

The Death of Joseph

22 Joseph continued to live in Egypt with his father's family; he was a hundred and ten years old when he died. [23]He lived to see Ephraim's children and grandchildren. He also lived to receive the children of Machir son of Manasseh into the family. [24]He said to his brothers, "I am about to die, but God will certainly take **care** of you and lead you out of this land to the **land he solemnly promised** to Abraham, Isaac, and Jacob." [25]Then Joseph asked his people to make a **vow**. "**Promise** me," he said, "that when God leads you to that land, you will take my **body** with you." [26]So Joseph died in Egypt at the age of a hundred and ten. They embalmed his **body** and put it in a coffin.

EXODUS

INTRODUCTION

The name *Exodus* means "departure," and refers to the most important event in Israel's history, which is described in this book—the departure of the people of Israel from Egypt, where they had been slaves. The book has four main parts: (1) the freeing of the Hebrews from slavery; (2) their journey to Mount Sinai; (3) God's covenant with his people at Sinai, which gave them moral, civil, and religious laws to live by; (4) the building and furnishing of a place of worship for Israel, and laws regarding the priests and the worship of God.

Above all, this book describes what God did, as he liberated his enslaved people and formed them into a nation with hope for the future.

The central human figure in the book is Moses, the man whom God chose to lead his people from Egypt. The most widely known part of the book is the list of the Ten Commandments in chapter 20.

Outline of Contents

The Israelites set free from Egypt 1.1—15.21
- a. Slaves in Egypt 1.1-22
- b. Moses' birth and early life 2.1—4.31
- c. Moses and Aaron confront the king of Egypt 5.1—11.10
- d. The Passover and the departure from Egypt 12.1—15.21

From the Red Sea to Mount Sinai 15.22—18.27
The Law and the covenant 19.1—24.18
The Sacred Tent and instructions for worship 25.1—40.38

---

birth [2] Gen 38.27; 28.10
command Gen 50.12; 5.6
cruel Gen 49.7; 3.7
enemy Gen 49.8; 15.6
escape Gen 39.12; 14.5
fear [3] Gen 50.21; 9.30
force (1) Gen 49.15; 2.11
hard Gen 33.13; 2.11
Hebrew [4] Gen 43.32; 2.6
help [2] Gen 49.25; 2.23
keep from Gen 42.2; 28.32
life (1) Gen 50.20; 4.25
mercy 22.27
misery Gen 26.35; Num 20.5
new Lev 14.42
obey Gen 49.10; 4.6
oppress 3.9
power Gen 49.24; 3.20
serve Gen 48.15; 18.22
slave Gen 50.18; 2.5
spirit (2) 6.9
strong [3] Gen 49.3; 10.19
threat Gen 31.24; 32.14

The Israelites Are Treated Cruelly in Egypt

1 The sons of Jacob who went to
Egypt with him, each with his
family, were 2 Reuben, Simeon, Levi,
Judah, 3 Issachar, Zebulun, Benjamin,
4 Dan, Naphtali, Gad, and Asher. 5 The
total number of these people directly descended from Jacob was seventy.[x] His
son Joseph was already in Egypt. 6 In the
course of time Joseph, his brothers, and
all the rest of that generation died, 7 but
their descendants, the Israelites, had
many children and became so numerous
and **strong** that Egypt was filled with
them.

8 Then, a **new** king, who knew nothing
about Joseph, came to **power** in Egypt.
9 He said to his people, "These Israelites
are so numerous and **strong** that they are
a **threat** to us. 10 In case of war they
might join our **enemies** in order to fight
against us, and might **escape** from[a] the
country. We must find some way to **keep
them from** becoming even more numerous." 11 So the Egyptians put slave-drivers
over them to crush their **spirits** with **hard**
labour. The Israelites built the cities of
Pithom and Rameses to **serve** as supply
centres for the king. 12 But the more the
Egyptians **oppressed** the Israelites, the
more they increased in number and the
further they spread through the land.
The Egyptians came to **fear** the
Israelites 13-14 and made their **lives miserable** by **forcing** them into **cruel slavery**.
They made them work on their building
projects and in their fields, and they had
no **mercy** on them.

15 Then the king of Egypt spoke to
Shiphrah and Puah, the two midwives
who **helped** the **Hebrew** women. 16 "When
you **help** the **Hebrew** women give **birth**,"
he said to them, "kill the baby if it is a
boy; but if it is a girl, let it live." 17 But the
midwives **feared** God and so did not **obey**
the king; instead, they let the boys live.
18 So the king sent for the midwives and
asked them, "Why are you doing this?
Why are you letting the boys live?"

19 They answered, "The **Hebrew**
women are not like Egyptian women;
they give **birth** easily, and their babies
are born before either of us gets there."
20-21 Because the midwives **feared** God,
he was good to them and gave them

[x] *One ancient translation* seventy-five (*see Acts 7.14*). [a] escape from; *or* take control of.

1.1-4: Gen 46.8-27 **1.7:** Acts 7.17 **1.8:** Acts 7.18 **1.10:** Acts 7.19

families of their own. And the Israelites
continued to increase and become
strong. 22 Finally the king issued a **command** to all his people: "Take every new-
born **Hebrew** boy and throw him into the
Nile, but let all the girls live."

The Birth of Moses

act Gen 42.7; 15.11
afraid Gen 50.19; 3.6
agree Gen 44.10; 4.18
body Gen 50.2; 4.7
concern Gen 39.6; Num 11.29
covenant Gen 17.2; 6.4
enough Gen 45.18; 5.8
flee Gen 31.22; Num 10.35
force (1) 1.13; 3.19
groan [2] 6.5
hard 1.11; 5.9
Hebrew [6] 1.15; 3.18
help 1.15; 4.12
judge Gen 31.42; 18.22
notice (1) Gen 31.5; Judg 14.1
priest Gen 47.22; 3.1
remember Gen 42.9; 6.5
rescue [2] Gen 48.16; 3.7
servant Gen 50.17; 14.31
sheep Gen 50.8; 3.1
shepherd [2] Gen 49.24; Num 27.17
slave [3] 1.13; 5.4
sorry Gen 6.6; Judg 21.6
watch Gen 31.50; 12.42
wrong Gen 50.17; 9.27

2 During this time a man from the
tribe of Levi married a woman of
his own tribe, 2 and she bore him a son.
When she saw what a fine baby he was,
she hid him for three months. 3 But when
she could not hide him any longer, she
took a basket made of reeds and covered
it with tar to make it watertight. She put
the baby in it and then placed it in the
tall grass at the edge of the river. 4 The
baby's sister stood some distance away
to see what would happen to him.
5 The king's daughter came down to
the river to bathe, while her **servants**
walked along the bank. Suddenly she
noticed the basket in the tall grass and
sent a **slave-girl** to get it. 6 The princess
opened it and saw a baby boy. He was
crying, and she felt **sorry** for him. "This
is one of the **Hebrew** babies," she said.
7 Then his sister asked her, "Shall I go
and call a **Hebrew** woman to **act** as a
wet-nurse?"
8 "Please do," she answered. So the
girl went and brought the baby's own
mother. 9 The princess told the woman,
"Take this baby and nurse him for me,
and I will pay you." So she took the baby
and nursed him. 10 Later, when the child
was old **enough**, she took him to the
king's daughter, who adopted him as her
own son. She said to herself, "I pulled
him out of the water, and so I name him
Moses."[b]

Moses Escapes to Midian

11 When Moses had grown up, he went
out to visit his people, the **Hebrews**, and
he saw how they were **forced** to do **hard**
labour. He even saw an Egyptian kill a
Hebrew, one of Moses' own people.
12 Moses looked all round, and when he
saw that no one was **watching**, he killed
the Egyptian and hid his **body** in the
sand. 13 The next day he went back and
saw two **Hebrew** men fighting. He said to
the one who was in the **wrong**, "Why are
you beating up a **fellow-Hebrew**?"
14 The man answered, "Who made
you our ruler and **judge**? Are you going
to kill me just as you killed that
Egyptian?" Then Moses was **afraid** and
said to himself, "People have found out
what I have done." 15-16 When the king
heard about what had happened, he tried
to have Moses killed, but Moses **fled** and
went to live in the land of Midian.
One day, when Moses was sitting by a
well, seven daughters of Jethro, the
priest of Midian, came to draw water and
fill the troughs for their father's **sheep**
and goats. 17 But some **shepherds** drove
Jethro's daughters away. Then Moses
went to their **rescue** and watered their
animals for them. 18 When they returned
to their father, he asked, "Why have you
come back so early today?"
19 "An Egyptian **rescued** us from the
shepherds," they answered, "and he even
drew water for us and watered our animals."
20 "Where is he?" he asked his
daughters. "Why did you leave the man
out there? Go and invite him to eat with
us."
21 So Moses **agreed** to live there, and
Jethro gave him his daughter Zipporah
in marriage, 22 who bore him a son.
Moses said to himself, "I am a foreigner
in this land, and so I name him
Gershom."[c]
23 Years later the king of Egypt died,
but the Israelites were still **groaning**
under their **slavery** and cried out for
help. Their cry went up to God, 24 who
heard their **groaning** and **remembered**
his **covenant** with Abraham, Isaac, and
Jacob. 25 He saw the **slavery** of the
Israelites and was **concerned** for them.[d]

God Calls Moses

3 One day while Moses was taking
care of the **sheep** and goats of his
father-in-law Jethro, the **priest** of Midian,
he led the **flock** across the desert and
came to Sinai, the **holy** mountain. 2 There
the **angel of the LORD** appeared to him as
a flame coming from the middle of a
bush. Moses saw that the bush was on
fire but that it was not burning up. 3 "This
is **strange**," he thought. "Why isn't the
bush burning up? I will go closer and
see."
4 When the LORD saw that Moses was
coming closer, he called to him from the
middle of the bush and said, "Moses!
Moses!"
He answered, "Yes, here I am."
5 God said, "Do not come any closer.
Take off your sandals, because you are

afraid 2.14; 9.20
angel Gen 48.16; 12.23
care Gen 50.21; 21.1
cruel [2] 1.13; 4.31
flock Gen 47.1; 16.13
force (1) 2.11; 5.13
God's people [5] Gen 17.14; 5.1
Hebrew 2.6; 5.3
holy [2] Gen 28.11; 4.27
I am [2] Mt 22.32
name (2) (name of God, of Jesus) [2] Gen 31.53; 6.3
neighbour 11.2
offer Gen 46.1; 5.3
oppress 1.12; 22.21
power 1.8; 4.21
priest 2.15; 18.1
prove Gen 42.19; 4.5
punish Gen 18.25; 5.21
rescue [2] 2.17; 6.6
respect 11.3
reveal Gen 35.7; 5.3

[b] MOSES: *This name sounds like the Hebrew for "pull out."*
[c] GERSHOM: *This name sounds like the Hebrew for "foreigner."*
[d] was concerned for them; *one ancient translation* revealed himself to them.

1.22: Acts 7.19 **2.2:** Acts 7.20; Heb 11.23 **2.10:** Acts 7.21 **2.11:** Heb 11.24 **2.11-14:** Acts 7.23-28
2.15: Acts 7.29; Heb 11.27 **2.24:** Gen 15.13-14 **3.2-10:** Acts 7.30-34

rich [2] Gen 49.20; 13.5
sacrifice Gen 46.1; 5.3
sheep 2.15; 9.3
strange 18.3
suffer Gen 42.21; Lev 5.1
terrify Gen 45.3; 7.3
worship (1) (of God) Gen 31.53; 4.23

standing on **holy** ground. 6 I am the God of your ancestors, the God of Abraham, Isaac, and Jacob." So Moses covered his face, because he was **afraid** to look at God.

7 Then the LORD said, "I have seen how **cruelly my people** are being treated in Egypt; I have heard them cry out to be **rescued** from their slave-drivers. I know all about their **sufferings**, 8 and so I have come down to **rescue** them from the Egyptians and to bring them out of Egypt to a spacious land, one which is **rich** and fertile and in which the Canaanites, the Hittites, the Amorites, the Perizzites, the Hivites, and the Jebusites now live. 9 I have indeed heard the cry of **my people**, and I see how the Egyptians are **oppressing** them. 10 Now I am sending you to the king of Egypt so that you can lead **my people** out of his country."

11 But Moses said to God, "I am nobody. How can I go to the king and bring the Israelites out of Egypt?"

12 God answered, "I will be with you, and when you bring the people out of Egypt, you will **worship** me on this mountain. That will be the **proof** that I have sent you."

13 But Moses replied, "When I go to the Israelites and say to them, 'The God of your ancestors sent me to you,' they will ask me, 'What is his **name**?' So what can I tell them?"

14 God said, "**I am who I am**. This is what you must say to them: 'The one who is called **I AM**[e] has sent me to you.' 15 Tell the Israelites that I, the LORD, the God of their ancestors, the God of Abraham, Isaac, and Jacob, have sent you to them. This is my **name** for ever; this is what all future generations are to call me. 16 Go and gather the leaders of Israel together and tell them that I, the LORD, the God of their ancestors, the God of Abraham, Isaac, and Jacob, appeared to you. Tell them that I have come to them and have seen what the Egyptians are doing to them. 17 I have decided that I will bring them out of Egypt, where they are being treated **cruelly**, and will take them to a **rich** and fertile land—the land of the Canaanites, the Hittites, the Amorites, the Perizzites, the Hivites, and the Jebusites.

18 "**My people** will listen to what you say to them. Then you must go with the leaders of Israel to the king of Egypt and say to him, 'The LORD, the God of the **Hebrews**, has **revealed** himself to us. Now allow us to travel for three days into the desert to **offer sacrifices** to the LORD, our God.' 19 I know that the king of Egypt will not let you go unless he is **forced** to do so. 20 But I will use my **power** and will **punish** Egypt by doing **terrifying** things there. After that he will let you go.

21 "I will make the Egyptians **respect** you so that when **my people** leave, they will not go empty-handed. 22 Every Israelite woman will go to her Egyptian **neighbours** and to any Egyptian woman living in her house and will ask for clothing and for gold and silver jewellery. The Israelites will put these things on their sons and daughters and carry away the wealth of the Egyptians."

God Gives Moses Miraculous Power

4 Then Moses answered the LORD, "But suppose the Israelites do not **believe** me and will not listen to what I say. What shall I do if they say that you did not appear to me?"

2 So the LORD asked him, "What are you holding?"

"A stick," he answered.

3 The LORD said, "Throw it on the ground." When Moses threw it down, it **turned** into a snake, and he ran away from it. 4 Then the LORD said to Moses, "Bend down and pick it up by the tail." So Moses bent down and caught it, and it became a stick again. 5 The LORD said, "Do this to **prove** to the Israelites that the LORD, the God of their ancestors, the God of Abraham, Isaac, and Jacob, has appeared to you."

6 The LORD spoke to Moses again, "Put your hand inside your robe." Moses **obeyed**; and when he took his hand out, it was **diseased**, covered with white spots, like snow. 7 Then the LORD said, "Put your hand inside your robe again." He did so, and when he took it out this time, it was healthy, just like the rest of his **body**. 8 The LORD said, "If they will not **believe** you or be **convinced** by the first **miracle**, then this one will **convince** them. 9 If in spite of these two **miracles** they still will not **believe** you, and if they **refuse** to listen to what you say, take some water from the Nile and pour it on the ground. The water will **turn** into **blood**."

10 But Moses said, "No, LORD, don't send me. I have never been a good

agree 2.21; 22.7
alive Gen 50.20; 22.2
anger Gen 49.6; 11.8
believe [4] Gen 45.26; 19.9
blind Gen 27.1; 23.8
blood [2] Gen 49.11; 7.17
body 2.12; 13.19
bow (2) Gen 50.18; 11.8
circumcise Gen 34.14; 12.44
convince [2] Deut 29.19
cruel 3.7; 5.23
dead Gen 44.20; 8.15
disease Gen 12.17; 5.3
first-born [2] Gen 49.3; 6.14
glad Gen 23.6; 8.9
help [2] 2.23; 5.23
holy 3.1; 6.3
kiss Gen 50.1; 18.7
Levites 32.26
life (1) 1.13; 21.6
miracle [6] 7.9
obey 1.17; 12.24
poor Gen 41.19; 6.12
power 3.20; 9.16
prove 3.12; 7.9
refuse (1) [2] Gen 48.19; 7.14
rite 29.35
sight Gen 48.10; 10.28
spare Gen 42.18; 8.22
stubborn 7.3
sure Gen 46.34; Num 13.20
turn [2] Gen 50.20; 5.22
worship (1) (of God) [2] 3.12; 7.16

[e] I am who I am...I AM: *or* I will be who I will be...I WILL BE. *"I am" sounds like the Hebrew name Yahweh, traditionally transliterated as Jehovah. This name is represented in this translation by "the LORD" in capital letters, following a usage which is widespread in English versions.*

3.13: Ex 6.2–3 **3.14:** Rev 1.4, 8 **3.21–22:** Ex 12.35–36

speaker, and I haven't become one since you began to speak to me. I am a **poor** speaker, slow and hesitant."

11 The LORD said to him, "Who gives man his mouth? Who makes him deaf or dumb? Who gives him **sight** or makes him **blind**? It is I, the LORD. 12 Now, go! I will **help** you to speak, and I will tell you what to say."

13 But Moses answered, "No, Lord, please send someone else."

14 At this the LORD became **angry** with Moses and said, "What about your brother Aaron, the **Levite**? I know that he can speak well. In fact, he is now coming to meet you and will be **glad** to see you. 15 You can speak to him and tell him what to say. I will **help** both of you to speak, and I will tell you both what to do. 16 He will be your spokesman and speak to the people for you. Then you will be like God, telling him what to say. 17 Take this stick with you; for with it you will perform **miracles**."

Moses Returns to Egypt

18 Then Moses went back to Jethro, his father-in-law, and said to him, "Please let me go back to my relatives in Egypt to see if they are still **alive**." Jethro **agreed** and said good-bye to him.

19 While Moses was still in Midian, the LORD said to him, "Go back to Egypt, for all those who wanted to kill you are **dead**." 20 So Moses took his wife and his sons, put them on a donkey, and set out with them for Egypt, carrying the stick that God had told him to take.

21 Again the LORD said to Moses, "Now that you are going back to Egypt, be **sure** to perform before the king all the **miracles** which I have given you the **power** to do. But I will make the king **stubborn**, and he will not let the people go. 22 Then you must tell him that I, the LORD, say, 'Israel is my **first-born** son. 23 I told you to let my son go, so that he might **worship** me, but you **refused**. Now I am going to kill your **first-born** son.' "

24 At a camping place on the way to Egypt, the LORD met Moses and tried to kill him. 25-26 Then Zipporah, his wife, took a sharp stone, cut off the foreskin of her son, and touched Moses' feet[f] with it. Because of the **rite** of **circumcision** she said to Moses, "You are a husband of **blood** to me." And so the LORD **spared** Moses' **life**.

27 Meanwhile the LORD had said to Aaron, "Go into the desert to meet Moses." So he went to meet him at the **holy** mountain; and when he met him, he **kissed** him. 28 Then Moses told Aaron everything that the LORD had said when he told him to return to Egypt; he also told him about the **miracles** which the LORD had ordered him to perform. 29 So Moses and Aaron went to Egypt and gathered all the Israelite leaders together. 30 Aaron told them everything that the LORD had said to Moses, and then Moses performed all the **miracles** in front of the people. 31 They **believed**, and when they heard that the LORD had come to them and had seen how they were being treated **cruelly**, they **bowed down** and **worshipped**.

Moses and Aaron before the King of Egypt

5 Then Moses and Aaron went to the king of Egypt and said, "The LORD, the God of Israel, says, 'Let **my people** go, so that they can hold a **festival** in the desert to **honour** me.' "

2 "Who is the LORD?" the king demanded. "Why should I listen to him and let Israel go? I do not know the LORD; and I will not let Israel go."

3 Moses and Aaron replied, "The God of the **Hebrews** has **revealed** himself to us. Allow us to travel for three days into the desert to **offer sacrifices** to the LORD our God. If we don't do so, he will kill us with **disease** or by war."

4 The king said to Moses and Aaron, "What do you mean by making the people **neglect** their work? Get those **slaves** back to work! 5 You people have become more numerous than the Egyptians. And now you want to stop working!"

6 That same day the king **commanded** the Egyptian slave-drivers and the Israelite foremen: 7 "Stop giving the people straw for making bricks. Make them go and find it for themselves. 8 But still **require** them to make the same number of bricks as before, not one brick less. They haven't **enough** work to do, and that is why they keep asking me to let them go and **offer sacrifices** to their God! 9 Make these men work **harder** and keep them busy, so that they won't have time to listen to a pack of **lies**."

10 The slave-drivers and the Israelite foremen went out and said to the Israelites, "The king has said that he will not supply you with any more straw. 11 He says that you must go and get it for yourselves wherever you can find it, but you must still make the same number of

command 1.22; 6.13
complain Gen 21.25; 15.24
cruel 4.31; 6.9
disease 4.6; 9.3
enough 2.10; 9.28
excuse Deut 24.5
fault Gen 31.39; Josh 2.19
festival Gen 1.14; 10.9
force (1) 3.19; 6.1
God's people 3.7; 6.1
hard 2.11; Lev 26.19
hate Gen 50.15; 20.5
Hebrew 3.18; 7.16
help 4.12; 14.10
honour Gen 41.43; 10.9
ill-treat Gen 31.50; 22.21
lie (2) Lev 6.3
Majesty Gen 41.16; 7.17
neglect Deut 12.19
offer [3] 3.18; 8.8
punish 3.20; 6.6
require 21.30
reveal 3.18; Lev 10.3
sacrifice [3] 3.18; 8.8
slave 2.5; 6.5
trouble Gen 43.6; 10.7
turn 4.3; 7.9

[f] FEET: *This reference to "feet" is thought by some to be a euphemism for the genitals.*

4.23: Ex 12.29

bricks." 12 So the people went all over Egypt looking for straw. 13 The slave-drivers kept trying to **force** them to make the same number of bricks every day as they had made when they were given straw. 14 The Egyptian slave-drivers beat the Israelite foremen, whom they had put in charge of the work. They demanded, "Why aren't you people making the same number of bricks as you made before?"

15 Then the foremen went to the king and **complained**, "Why do you do this to us, Your **Majesty**? 16 We are given no straw, but we are still ordered to make bricks! And now we are being beaten. It is your people that are at **fault**."

17 The king answered, "You are lazy and don't want to work, and that is why you ask me to let you go and **offer sacrifices** to the LORD. 18 Now get back to work! You will not be given any straw, but you must still make the same number of bricks." 19 The foremen realized that they were in **trouble** when they were told that they had to make the same number of bricks every day as they had made before.

20 As they were leaving, they met Moses and Aaron, who were waiting for them. 21 They said to Moses and Aaron, "The LORD has seen what you have done and will **punish** you for making the king and his officers **hate** us. You have given them an **excuse** to kill us."

Moses Complains to the LORD

22 Then Moses **turned** to the LORD again and said, "Lord, why do you **ill-treat** your people? Why did you send me here? 23 Ever since I went to the king to speak for you, he has treated them **cruelly**. And you have done nothing to **help** them!"

6 Then the LORD said to Moses, "Now you are going to see what I will do to the king. I will **force** him to let **my people** go. In fact, I will **force** him to drive them out of his land."

God Calls Moses

2 God spoke to Moses and said, "I am the LORD. 3 I appeared to Abraham, to Isaac, and to Jacob as **Almighty** God, but I did not make myself known to them by my **holy name**, the LORD.[g] 4 I also made my **covenant** with them, **promising** to give them the land of Canaan, the land in which they had lived as foreigners. 5 Now I have heard the **groaning** of the Israelites, whom the Egyptians have **enslaved**, and I have **remembered** my **covenant**. 6 So tell the Israelites that I say to them, 'I am the LORD; I will **rescue** you and **set you free** from your **slavery** to the Egyptians. I will **raise** my **mighty** arm to bring **terrible punishment** upon them, and I will **save** you. 7 I will make you **my own people**, and I will be your God. You will know that I am the LORD your God when I **set you free** from **slavery** in Egypt. 8 I will bring you to the **land that I solemnly promised** to give to Abraham, Isaac, and Jacob; and I will give it to you as your own **possession**. I am the LORD.'" 9 Moses told this to the Israelites, but they would not listen to him, because their **spirit** had been broken by their **cruel slavery**.

10 Then the LORD said to Moses, 11 "Go and tell the king of Egypt that he must let the Israelites leave his land."

12 But Moses replied, "Even the Israelites will not listen to me, so why should the king? I am such a **poor** speaker."

13 The LORD **commanded** Moses and Aaron: "Tell the Israelites and the king of Egypt that I have ordered you to lead the Israelites out of Egypt."

The Family Record of Moses and Aaron

14 Reuben, Jacob's **first-born**, had four sons: Hanoch, Pallu, Hezron, and Carmi; they were the ancestors of the clans that bear their names. 15 Simeon had six sons: Jemuel, Jamin, Ohad, Jachin, Zohar, and Shaul, the son of a Canaanite woman; they were the ancestors of the clans that bear their names. 16 Levi had three sons: Gershon, Kohath, and Merari; they were the ancestors of the clans that bear their names. Levi lived 137 years. 17 Gershon had two sons: Libni and Shimei, and they had many descendants. 18 Kohath had four sons: Amram, Izhar, Hebron, and Uzziel. Kohath lived 133 years. 19 Merari had two sons: Mahli and Mushi. These are the clans of Levi with their descendants.

20 Amram married his father's sister Jochebed, who bore him Aaron and Moses. Amram lived 137 years. 21 Izhar had three sons: Korah, Nepheg, and Zichri. 22 Uzziel also had three sons: Mishael, Elzaphan, and Sithri.

23 Aaron married Elisheba, the daughter of Amminadab and sister of Nahshon; she bore him Nadab, Abihu, Eleazar, and Ithamar. 24 Korah had three sons: Assir, Elkanah, and Abiasaph; they were the ancestors of the divisions of the

Almighty Gen 49.25; Num 24.4
command 5.6; 7.2
covenant [2] 2.24; 19.5
cruel 5.23; Num 11.15
first-born 4.22; 11.5
force (1) [2] 5.13; Lev 25.25
free [3] Gen 49.21; 15.16
God's people [2] 5.1; 7.3
groan 2.23; Judg 2.18
holy 4.27; 15.11
might Gen 49.24; 15.11
name (2) (name of God, of Jesus) 3.13; 15.3
poor [2] 4.10; 22.25
possess Gen 48.4; 22.2

promise [2] Gen 50.5; 9.28
punish 5.21; 7.3
raise Gen 4.20; 7.5
remember 2.24; 13.3
rescue 3.7; 13.19
save Gen 47.25; 14.13
slave [4] 5.4; 9.20
solemn Gen 50.11; 13.5
spirit (2) 1.11; Lev 19.31
terrible Gen 41.31; 9.3

[g] THE LORD: *See 3.14.*

6.2-3: Gen 17.1, 28.3, 35.11; Ex 3.13-15 **6.16-19:** Num 3.17-20, 26.57-58; 1 Chr 6.16-19

clan of Korah. 25 Eleazar, Aaron's son, married one of Putiel's daughters, who bore him Phinehas. These were the heads of the families and the clans of the tribe of Levi.

26 Aaron and Moses were the ones to whom the LORD said, "Lead the tribes of Israel out of Egypt." 27 They were the men who told the king of Egypt to **free** the Israelites.

The LORD's Command to Moses and Aaron

28 When the LORD spoke to Moses in the land of Egypt, 29 he said, "I am the LORD. Tell the king of Egypt everything I tell you."

30 But Moses answered, "You know that I am such a **poor** speaker; why should the king listen to me?"

bad Gen 41.21; Lev 27.12
blood [5] 4.9; 12.7
command [4] 6.13; 8.27
demand Gen 31.39; 21.22
God's people [2] 6.1; 8.1
Hebrew 5.3; 9.1
magic [4] Gen 41.8; 8.7
Majesty 5.15; 15.7
means Lev 6.4
miracle 4.8; 8.23
presence Gen 44.23; 10.11
prophet Gen 20.7; 15.20
prove 4.5; Deut 4.35
punish 6.6; 8.2
raise [2] 6.6; 9.15
refuse (1) [2] 4.9; 8.2
strike [3] Gen 49.17; 8.16
stubborn [4] 4.21; 8.15
terrify 3.20; 14.10
turn [7] 5.22; 8.17
wise Gen 41.8; Deut 1.13
worship (1) (of God) 4.23; 8.1

7 The LORD said, "I am going to make you like God to the king, and your brother Aaron will speak to him as your **prophet**. 2 Tell Aaron everything I **command** you, and he will tell the king to let the Israelites leave his country. 3-4 But I will make the king **stubborn**, and he will not listen to you, no matter how many **terrifying** things I do in Egypt. Then I will bring severe **punishment** on Egypt and lead the tribes of **my people** out of the land. 5 The Egyptians will then know that I am the LORD, when I **raise** my hand against them and bring the Israelites out of their country." 6 Moses and Aaron did what the LORD **commanded**. 7 At the time when they spoke to the king, Moses was eighty years old, and Aaron was eighty-three.

Aaron's Stick

8 The LORD said to Moses and Aaron, 9 "If the king **demands** that you **prove** yourselves by performing a **miracle**, tell Aaron to take his stick and throw it down in front of the king, and it will **turn** into a snake." 10 So Moses and Aaron went to the king and did as the LORD had **commanded**. Aaron threw his stick down in front of the king and his officers, and it **turned** into a snake. 11 Then the king called for his **wise** men and **magicians**, and by their **magic** they did the same thing. 12 They threw down their sticks, and the sticks **turned** into snakes. But Aaron's stick swallowed theirs. 13 The king, however, remained **stubborn** and, just as the LORD had said, the king would not listen to Moses and Aaron.

7.3: Acts 7.36 **7.17:** Rev 16.4

Disasters Strike Egypt
Blood

14 Then the LORD said to Moses, "The king is very **stubborn** and **refuses** to let the people go. 15 So go and meet him in the morning when he goes down to the Nile. Take with you the stick that was **turned** into a snake, and wait for him on the bank of the river. 16 Then say to the king, 'The LORD, the God of the **Hebrews**, sent me to tell you to let **his people** go, so that they can **worship** him in the desert. But until now you have not listened. 17 Now, Your **Majesty**, the LORD says that you will find out who he is by what he is going to do. Look, I am going to **strike** the surface of the river with this stick, and the water will be **turned** into **blood**. 18 The fish will die, and the river will stink so much that the Egyptians will not be able to drink from it.' "

19 The LORD said to Moses, "Tell Aaron to take his stick and hold it out over all the rivers, canals, and pools in Egypt. The water will become **blood**, and all over the land there will be **blood**, even in the wooden tubs and stone jars."

20 Then Moses and Aaron did as the LORD **commanded**. In the **presence** of the king and his officers, Aaron **raised** his stick and **struck** the surface of the river, and all the water in it was **turned** into **blood**. 21 The fish in the river died, and it smelt so **bad** that the Egyptians could not drink from it. There was **blood** everywhere in Egypt. 22 Then the king's **magicians** did the same thing **by means of** their **magic**, and the king was as **stubborn** as ever. Just as the LORD had said, the king **refused** to listen to Moses and Aaron. 23 Instead, he **turned** and went back to his palace without paying any attention even to this. 24 All the Egyptians dug along the bank of the river for drinking water, because they were not able to drink water from the river.

25 Seven days passed after the LORD **struck** the river.

Frogs

8 Then the LORD said to Moses, "Go to the king and tell him that the LORD says, 'Let **my people** go, so that they can **worship** me. 2 If you **refuse**, I will **punish** your country by covering it with frogs. 3 The Nile will be so full of frogs that they will leave it and go into your palace, your bedroom, your bed, the houses of your officials and your people, and even into your ovens and baking-pans. 4 They will jump up on you, your people, and all your officials.' "

change Gen 45.22; 10.19
command 7.2; 12.28
dead 4.19; 12.30
death (1) Gen 50.15; 12.23
death (3) (to death) Gen 44.9; 16.3
deceive Gen 34.13; Num 16.14
distinguish 9.4
fail Gen 48.10; 34.7
glad 4.14; Deut 28.47
god (2) (other gods) Gen 35.2; 12.12
God's people [4] 7.3; 9.1
magic [3] 7.11; 9.11

miracle 7.9; 10.1
offer [3] 5.3; 10.25
pray [8] Gen 32.9; 9.28
prevent Num 4.19
punish [2] 7.3; 9.3
refuse (1) [2] 7.14; 9.2
rid [2] Gen 35.2; 12.15
right (1) Gen 38.26; 9.27
ruin Gen 41.30; 9.31
sacrifice [7] 5.3; 10.25
spare 4.25; 12.27
strike [2] 7.17; 9.15
stubborn [3] 7.3; 9.7
turn 7.9; 10.6
warn Gen 43.3; 9.21
worship (1) (of God) [2] 7.16; 9.1

5 The LORD said to Moses, "Tell Aaron to hold out his stick over the rivers, the canals, and the pools, and make frogs come up and cover the land of Egypt." 6 So Aaron held it out over all the water, and the frogs came out and covered the land. 7 But the magicians used **magic**, and they too made frogs come up on the land.

8 The king called for Moses and Aaron and said, "**Pray** to the LORD to take away these frogs, and I will let your people go, so that they can **offer sacrifices** to the LORD."

9 Moses replied, "I will be **glad** to **pray** for you. Just set the time when I am to **pray** for you, your officers, and your people. Then you will be **rid** of the frogs, and there will be none left except in the Nile."

10 The king answered, "**Pray** for me tomorrow."

Moses said, "I will do as you ask, and then you will know that there is no other **god** like the LORD, our God. 11 You, your officials, and your people will be **rid** of the frogs, and there will be none left except in the Nile." 12 Then Moses and Aaron left the king, and Moses **prayed** to the LORD to take away the frogs which he had brought on the king. 13 The LORD did as Moses asked, and the frogs in the houses, the courtyards, and the fields died. 14 The Egyptians piled them up in great heaps, until the land stank with them. 15 When the king saw that the frogs were **dead**, he became **stubborn** again and, just as the LORD had said, the king would not listen to Moses and Aaron.

Gnats

16 The LORD said to Moses, "Tell Aaron to **strike** the ground with his stick, and all over the land of Egypt the dust will **change** into gnats." 17 So Aaron **struck** the ground with his stick, and all the dust in Egypt was **turned** into gnats, which covered the people and the animals. 18 The **magicians** tried to use their magic to make gnats appear, but they **failed**. There were gnats everywhere, 19 and the **magicians** said to the king, "God has done this!" But the king was **stubborn** and, just as the LORD had said, the king would not listen to Moses and Aaron.

Flies

20 The LORD said to Moses, "Early tomorrow morning go and meet the king as he goes to the river, and tell him that the LORD says, 'Let **my people** go, so that they can **worship** me. 21 I **warn** you that if you **refuse**, I will **punish** you by sending flies on you, your officials, and your people. The houses of the Egyptians will be full of flies, and the ground will be covered with them. 22 But I will **spare** the region of Goshen, where **my people** live, so that there will be no flies there. I will do this so that you will know that I, the LORD, am at work in this land. 23 I will make a **distinction**[h] between **my people** and your people. This **miracle** will take place tomorrow.' " 24 The LORD sent great swarms of flies into the king's palace and the houses of his officials. The whole land of Egypt was brought to **ruin** by the flies.

25 Then the king called for Moses and Aaron and said, "Go and **offer sacrifices** to your God here in this country."

26 "It would not be **right** to do that," Moses answered, "because the Egyptians would be offended by our **sacrificing** the animals that we offer to the LORD our God. If we use these animals and offend the Egyptians by **sacrificing** them where they can see us, they will stone us **to death**. 27 We must travel three days into the desert to **offer sacrifices** to the LORD our God, just as he **commanded** us."

28 The king said, "I will let you go to **sacrifice** to the LORD, your God, in the desert, if you do not go very far. **Pray** for me."

29 Moses answered, "As soon as I leave, I will **pray** to the LORD that tomorrow the flies will leave you, your officials, and your people. But you must not **deceive** us again and **prevent** the people from going to **sacrifice** to the LORD."

30 Moses left the king and **prayed** to the LORD, 31 and the LORD did as Moses asked. The flies left the king, his officials, and his people; not one fly remained. 32 But even this time the king became **stubborn**, and again he would not let the people go.

Death of the Animals

9 The LORD said to Moses, "Go to the king and tell him that the LORD, the God of the **Hebrews**, says, 'Let **my people** go, so that they may **worship** me. 2 If you again **refuse** to let them go, 3 I will **punish** you by sending a **terrible disease** on all your animals—your horses, donkeys, camels, cattle, **sheep**, and goats. 4 I will make a **distinction** between the animals of the Israelites and those of the Egyptians, and no animal that belongs to the Israelites will die. 5 I, the LORD, have

afraid 3.6; 14.13
arrogant 1 Sam 15.23
ash [2] 27.3
destroy Gen 34.30; 10.5
disease [2] 5.3; 15.26
distinguish 8.23; 11.7
enough 5.8; 10.21
fear 1.12; 15.14
God's people [3] 8.1; 10.3
Hebrew [2] 7.16; 10.3
magic 8.7; 22.18
power 4.21; 13.3
pray 8.8; 10.17
prayer [2] Gen 30.6; 1 Sam 1.19

[h] *Some ancient translations* a distinction; *Hebrew* redemption.

8.19: Lk 11.20

promise 6.4; 12.25
protect Gen 49.24; 23.20
punish [3] 8.2; 10.17
raise [3] 7.5; 10.12
refuse (1) [2] 8.2; 10.3
right (1) 8.26; 10.29
ripe [2] Gen 41.5; Num 13.20
ruin [2] 8.24; 10.7
sheep 3.1; 10.9
shelter [2] Gen 33.17; 23.16
slave [2] 6.5; 11.5
strike [3] 8.16; 17.5
stubborn [3] 8.15; 10.1
terrible 6.6; 15.10
warn 8.21; 19.21
world [2] Gen 42.6; Deut 7.14
worship (1) (of God) [2] 8.1; 10.3
worst Gen 35.17; Ruth 1.17
wrong 2.13; 23.2

set tomorrow as the time when I will do
this.' "
6 The next day the LORD did as he had
said, and all the animals of the Egyptians
died, but not one of the animals of the
Israelites died. 7 The king asked what had
happened and was told that none of the
animals of the Israelites had died. But he
was **stubborn** and would not let the
people go.

Boils

8 Then the LORD said to Moses and
Aaron, "Take a few handfuls of **ashes**
from a furnace; Moses shall throw them
into the air in front of the king. 9 They
will spread out like fine dust over all the
land of Egypt, and everywhere they will
produce boils that become open sores on
the people and the animals." 10 So they
got some **ashes** and stood before the
king; Moses threw them into the air, and
they produced boils that became open
sores on the people and the animals.
11 The **magicians** were not able to appear
before Moses, because they were
covered with boils, like all the other
Egyptians. 12 But the LORD made the king
stubborn and, just as the LORD had said,
the king would not listen to Moses and
Aaron.

Hail

13 The LORD then said to Moses,
"Early tomorrow morning meet with the
king and tell him that the LORD, the God
of the **Hebrews**, says, 'Let **my people** go,
so that they may **worship** me. 14 This time
I will **punish** not only your officials and
your people, but I will **punish** you as well,
so that you may know that there is no
one like me in all the **world**. 15 If I had
raised my hand to **strike** you and your
people with **disease**, you would have
been completely **destroyed**. 16 But to
show you my **power** I have let you live so
that my fame might spread over the
whole **world**. 17 Yet you are still **arrogant**
and **refuse** to let **my people** go. 18 This
time tomorrow I will cause a heavy hailstorm, such as Egypt has never known in
all its history. 19 Now give orders for your
livestock and everything else you have in
the open to be put under **shelter**. Hail will
fall on the people and animals left outside **unprotected**, and they will all die.' "
20 Some of the king's officials were **afraid**
because of what the LORD had said, and
they brought their **slaves** and animals indoors for **shelter**. 21 Others, however, paid
no attention to the LORD's **warning** and
left their **slaves** and animals out in the
open.
22 Then the LORD said to Moses,
"**Raise** your hand towards the sky, and
hail will fall over the whole land of
Egypt—on the people, the animals, and
all the plants in the fields." 23 So Moses
raised his stick towards the sky, and the
LORD sent thunder and hail, and lightning **struck** the ground. The LORD sent
24 a heavy hailstorm, with lightning flashing to and fro. It was the **worst** storm
that Egypt had ever known in all its history. 25 All over Egypt the hail **struck**
down everything in the open, including
all the people and all the animals. It beat
down all the plants in the fields and
broke all the trees. 26 The region of
Goshen, where the Israelites lived, was
the only place where there was no hail.
27 The king sent for Moses and Aaron
and said, "This time I have sinned; the
LORD is in the **right**, and my people and I
are in the **wrong**. 28 **Pray** to the LORD!
We have had **enough** of this thunder and
hail! I **promise** to let you go; you don't
have to stay here any longer."
29 Moses said to him, "As soon as I go
out of the city, I will lift up my hands in
prayer to the LORD. The thunder will
stop, and there will be no more hail, so
that you may know that the earth belongs to the LORD. 30 But I know that you
and your officials do not yet **fear** the
LORD God."
31 The flax and the barley were
ruined, because the barley was **ripe**, and
the flax was budding. 32 But none of the
wheat was **ruined**, because it **ripens**
later.
33 Moses left the king, went out of the
city, and lifted up his hands in **prayer** to
the LORD. The thunder, the hail, and the
rain all stopped. 34 When the king saw
what had happened, he sinned again. He
and his officials remained as **stubborn** as
ever 35 and, just as the LORD had foretold
through Moses, the king would not let the
Israelites go.

Locusts

10 Then the LORD said to Moses,
"Go and see the king. I have
made him and his officials **stubborn**, in
order that I may perform these **miracles**
among them 2 and in order that you may
be able to tell your children and grandchildren how I made **fools** of the
Egyptians when I performed the
miracles. All of you will know that I am
the LORD."
3 So Moses and Aaron went to the king

9.10: Rev 16.2 **9.16:** Rom 9.17 **9.24:** Rev 8.7, 16.21

burnt-offering Gen 22.13; 29.25
change 8.16; 13.17
dark [2] Gen 15.17; 14.20
destroy 9.15; 17.14
each other Gen 31.49; 14.20
enough 9.28; 16.4
festival 5.1; 12.11
fool Gen 31.28; 32.25
forgive Gen 50.17; 29.33
God's people 9.1; 11.8
Hebrew 9.1; 21.2

honour 5.1; 12.11
light (1) Gen 1.3; 13.21
miracle [2] 8.23; 11.9
offer 8.8; 13.12
plot (1) Gen 50.20; 1 Sam 22.8
pray [2] 9.28; 12.32
presence 7.20; 16.7
provide Gen 49.20; 28.2
punish 9.3; 11.1
raise [4] 9.15; Lev 9.22
refuse (1) [2] 9.2; 11.9
right (1) 9.27; 15.26
ruin 9.31; 23.8
sacrifice [2] 8.8; 12.27
sheep [2] 9.3; 12.5
sight 4.11; Num 15.15
strong 1.7; 14.21
stubborn [3] 9.7; 11.10
submit 2 Kgs 18.7
swear Gen 44.7; Lev 6.3
trouble 5.19; Num 11.1
turn 8.17; 14.2
worse Gen 43.1; Lev 26.28
worship (1) (of God) [6] 9.1; 12.16

and said to him, "The LORD, the God of
the **Hebrews**, says 'How much longer will
you **refuse** to **submit** to me? Let **my**
people go, so that they may **worship** me.
4 If you keep on **refusing**, then I will bring
locusts into your country tomorrow.
5 There will be so many that they will
completely cover the ground. They will
eat everything that the hail did not **des-**
troy, even the trees that are left. 6 They
will fill your palaces and the houses of all
your officials and all your people. They
will be **worse** than anything your ancestors ever saw.' " Then Moses **turned** and
left.

7 The king's officials said to him,
"How long is this man going to give us
trouble? Let the Israelite men go, so that
they can **worship** the LORD their God.
Don't you realize that Egypt is **ruined**?"

8 So Moses and Aaron were brought
back to the king, and he said to them,
"You may go and **worship** the LORD your
God. But exactly who will go?"

9 Moses answered, "We will all go, including our children and our old people.
We will take our sons and daughters, our
sheep and goats, and our cattle, because
we must hold a **festival** to **honour** the
LORD."

10 The king said, "I **swear** by the LORD
that I will never let you take your women
and children! It is clear that you are **plot-**
ting to revolt. 11 No! Only the men may
go and **worship** the LORD if that is what
you want." With that, Moses and Aaron
were driven out of the king's **presence**.

12 Then the LORD said to Moses,
"**Raise** your hand over the land of Egypt
to bring the locusts. They will come and
eat everything that grows, everything
that has survived the hail." 13 So Moses
raised his stick, and the LORD caused a
wind from the east to blow on the land all
that day and all that night. By morning it
had brought the locusts. 14 They came in
swarms and settled over the whole
country. It was the largest swarm of
locusts that had ever been seen or that
ever would be seen again. 15 They
covered the ground until it was black
with them; they ate everything that the
hail had left, including all the fruit on the
trees. Not a green thing was left on any
tree or plant in all the land of Egypt.

16 Then the king hurriedly called
Moses and Aaron and said, "I have
sinned against the LORD your God and
against you. 17 Now **forgive** my sin this
once and **pray** to the LORD your God to
take away this fatal **punishment** from
me." 18 Moses left the king and **prayed** to
the LORD. 19 And the LORD **changed** the
east wind into a very **strong** west wind,
which picked up the locusts and blew
them into the Gulf of Suez.[i] Not one
locust was left in all Egypt. 20 But the
LORD made the king **stubborn**, and he did
not let the Israelites go.

Darkness

21 The LORD then said to Moses,
"**Raise** your hand towards the sky, and a
darkness thick **enough** to be felt will
cover the land of Egypt." 22 Moses **raised**
his hand towards the sky, and there was
total **darkness** throughout Egypt for
three days. 23 The Egyptians could not
see **each other**, and no one left his house
during that time. But the Israelites had
light where they were living.

24 The king called Moses and said,
"You may go and **worship** the LORD;
even your women and children may go
with you. But your **sheep**, goats, and
cattle must stay here."

25 Moses answered, "Then you would
have to **provide** us with animals for **sacri-**
fices and **burnt-offerings** to **offer** to the
LORD our God. 26 No, we will take our animals with us; not one will be left behind.
We ourselves must select the animals
with which to **worship** the LORD our God.
And until we get there, we will not know
what animals to **sacrifice** to him."

27 The LORD made the king **stubborn**,
and he would not let them go. 28 He said
to Moses, "Get out of my **sight**! Don't let
me ever see you again! On the day I do,
you will die!"

29 "You are **right**," Moses answered.
"You will never see me again."

Moses Announces the Death of the First-Born

11 Then the LORD said to Moses, "I
will send only one more **punish-**
ment on the king of Egypt and his
people. After that he will let you leave. In
fact, he will drive all of you out of here.
2 Now speak to the people of Israel and
tell all of them to ask their **neighbours**
for gold and silver jewellery." 3 The
LORD made the Egyptians **respect** the
Israelites. Indeed, the officials and all the
people considered Moses to be a very
great man.

4 Moses then said to the king, "The
LORD says, 'At about midnight I will go
through Egypt, 5 and every **first-born** son
in Egypt will die, from the king's son,
who is heir to the **throne**, to the son of

anger 4.14; 15.7
beg Gen 42.21; Deut 18.16
bow (2) 4.31; 18.7
distinguish 9.4; 33.16
first-born [2] 6.14; 12.12
God's people 10.3; 12.15
miracle [2] 10.1; 15.11
neighbour 3.22; 12.4
punish 10.17; 12.12
refuse (1) 10.3; 13.15
respect 3.21; 12.36
slave 9.20; 12.44
stubborn 10.1; 13.15
throne 12.29

[i] GULF OF SUEZ: *See Red Sea in 13.18.*

10.14-15: Rev 9.2-3 **10.22:** Ps 105.28; Rev 16.10

the **slave-woman** who grinds corn. The
first-born of all the cattle will die also.
6 There will be loud crying all over
Egypt, such as there has never been before or ever will be again. 7 But not even
a dog will bark at the Israelites or their
animals. Then you will know that I, the
LORD, make a **distinction** between the
Egyptians and the Israelites.' " 8 Moses
concluded by saying, "All your officials
will come to me and **bow down** before
me, and they will **beg** me to take all **my
people** and go away. After that, I will
leave." Then in great **anger** Moses left
the king.
9 The LORD had said to Moses, "The
king will continue to **refuse** to listen to
you, in order that I may do more of my
miracles in Egypt." 10 Moses and Aaron
performed all these **miracles** before the
king, but the LORD made him **stubborn**,
and he would not let the Israelites leave
his country.

The Passover

12 The LORD spoke to Moses and
Aaron in Egypt: 2 "This month is
to be the first month of the year for you.
3 Give these instructions to the whole
community of Israel: On the tenth day of
this month each man must **choose** either
a **lamb** or a young goat for his household.
4 If his family is too small to eat a whole
animal, he and his next-door **neighbour**
may **share** an animal, in proportion to
the number of people and the amount
that each person can eat. 5 You may
choose either a **sheep** or a goat, but it
must be a one-year-old male without any
defects. 6 Then, on the evening of the
fourteenth day of the month, the whole
community of Israel will kill the animals.
7 The people are to take some of the
blood and put it on the door-posts and
above the doors of the houses in which
the animals are to be eaten. 8 That night
the meat is to be roasted, and eaten with
bitter herbs and with **bread** made **without yeast**. 9 Do not eat any of it raw or
boiled, but eat it roasted whole, including
the head, the legs, and the internal organs. 10 You must not leave any of it until
morning; if any is left over, it must be
burnt. 11 You are to eat it quickly, for you
are to be dressed for travel, with your
sandals on your feet and your stick in
your hand. It is the **Passover Festival** to
honour me, the LORD.
12 "On that night I will go through the
land of Egypt, killing every **first-born**
male, both **human** and animal, and
punishing all the **gods** of Egypt. I am the
LORD. 13 The **blood** on the door-posts will
be a **sign** to **mark** the houses in which
you live. When I see the **blood**, I will **pass
over** you and will not **harm** you when I
punish the Egyptians. 14 You must **celebrate** this day as a **religious festival** to
remind you of what I, the LORD, have
done. **Celebrate** it for all time to come."

The Festival of Unleavened Bread

15 The LORD said, "For seven days
you must not eat any bread made with
yeast—eat only **unleavened bread**. On
the first day you are to get **rid** of all the
yeast in your houses, for if anyone during
those seven days eats **bread** made with
yeast, he shall no longer be considered
one of **my people**. 16 On the first day and
again on the seventh day you are to meet
for **worship**. No work is to be done on
those days, but you may prepare food.
17 Keep this **festival**, because it was on
this day that I brought your tribes out of
Egypt. For all time to come you must
celebrate this day as a **festival**. 18 From
the evening of the fourteenth day of the
first month to the evening of the twenty-
first day, you must not eat any **bread**
made with **yeast**. 19-20 For seven days no
yeast must be found in your houses, for if
anyone, native-born or foreign, eats
bread made with **yeast**, he shall no
longer be considered one of **my people**."

The First Passover

21 Moses called for all the leaders of
Israel and said to them, "Each of you is
to **choose** a **lamb** or a young goat and kill
it, so that your families can **celebrate**
Passover. 22 Take a sprig of **hyssop**, dip it
in the bowl containing[j] the animal's
blood, and wipe the **blood** on the door-
posts and the beam above the door of
your house. Not one of you is to leave the
house until morning. 23 When the LORD
goes through Egypt to kill the Egyptians,
he will see the blood on the beams and
the door-posts and will not let the **Angel
of Death** enter your houses and kill you.
24 You and your children must **obey** these
rules for ever. 25 When you enter the land
that the LORD has **promised** to give you,
you must perform this **ritual**. 26 When
your children ask you, 'What does this
ritual mean?' 27 you will answer, 'It is the
sacrifice of **Passover** to **honour** the LORD,
because he **passed over** the houses of the

religion Gen 1.14; 23.24
remind Gen 31.44; 13.9
respect 11.3; 20.12
rid 8.9; Lev 26.6
ritual [2] 29.4
sacrifice 10.25; 13.15
share Gen 14.24; 18.22
sheep [3] 10.9; 20.24
sign (1) Gen 17.13; 29.6
slave 11.5; 13.3
spare 8.22; Num 22.33
throne 11.5; 1 Sam 4.4
unleavened [4] 13.6
urge Gen 33.11; Josh 15.18
watch [2] 2.12; 33.8
worship (1) (of God) [3] 10.3; 18.12
yeast [7] 13.7

angel 3.2; 14.19
bitter Gen 27.34; 15.23
bless Gen 49.25; 20.11
blood [5] 7.17; 24.6
bread [6] Gen 45.23; 13.3
celebrate [6] Gen 29.27; 13.5
choose [3] Gen 41.33; 15.17
circumcise [3] 4.25; Lev 12.3
command [2] 8.27; 14.7
community [3] 16.1
dead [2] 8.15; 14.30
death (1) 8.26; 16.3
dedicate Gen 31.13; 13.2
festival [6] 10.9; 13.5
first-born [3] 11.5; 13.2
god (2) (other gods) 8.10; 15.11
God's people [3] 11.8; 18.10
harm Gen 50.15; 24.11
honour [3] 10.9; 13.6
human Gen 9.5; 13.15
hyssop Lev 14.4
kneel Gen 43.28; 1 Kgs 8.54
lamb [2] Gen 30.32; 13.13
leaven 13.3
mark (1) Gen 35.20; 19.12
neighbour 11.2; 32.27
obey [2] 4.6; 15.26
Passover [8] 34.25
pray 10.17; 15.25
prison Gen 42.17; Num 31.11
promise 9.28; 13.5
punish [2] 11.1; 15.26
regulation [2] Lev 5.10

[j] dip it in the bowl containing; *or* put it on the threshold covered with.

12.1-13: Lev 23.5; Num 9.1-5, 28.16; Deut 16.1-2
12.14-20: Ex 23.15, 34.18; Lev 23.6-8; Num 28.17-25; Deut 16.3-8 **12.23:** Heb 11.28

Israelites in Egypt. He killed the
Egyptians, but spared us.' "

The Israelites knelt down and worshipped. 28 Then they went and did what
the LORD had commanded Moses and
Aaron.

The Death of the First-Born

29 At midnight the LORD killed all the
first-born sons in Egypt, from the king's
son, who was heir to the throne, to the
son of the prisoner in the dungeon; all
the first-born of the animals were also
killed. 30 That night, the king, his officials,
and all the other Egyptians were
awakened. There was loud crying
throughout Egypt, because there was not
one home in which there was not a dead
son. 31 That same night the king sent for
Moses and Aaron and said, "Get out, you
and your Israelites! Leave my country;
go and worship the LORD, as you asked.
32 Take your sheep, goats, and cattle, and
leave. Also pray for a blessing on me."

33 The Egyptians urged the people to
hurry and leave the country; they said,
"We will all be dead if you don't leave."
34 So the people filled their baking-pans
with unleavened dough, wrapped them in
clothing, and carried them on their
shoulders. 35 The Israelites had done as
Moses had said, and had asked the
Egyptians for gold and silver jewellery
and for clothing. 36 The LORD made the
Egyptians respect the people and give
them what they asked for. In this way the
Israelites carried away the wealth of the
Egyptians.

The Israelites Leave Egypt

37 The Israelites set out on foot from
Rameses for Sukkoth. There were about
six hundred thousand men, not counting
women and children. 38 A large number
of other people and many sheep, goats,
and cattle also went with them. 39 They
baked unleavened bread from the dough
that they had brought out of Egypt, for
they had been driven out of Egypt so suddenly that they did not have time to get
their food ready or to prepare leavened
dough.

40 The Israelites had lived in Egypt
for 430 years. 41 On the day the 430 years
ended, all the tribes of the LORD's people
left Egypt. 42 It was a night when the
LORD kept watch to bring them out of
Egypt; this same night is dedicated to
the LORD for all time to come as a night
when the Israelites must keep watch.

Regulations about Passover

43 The LORD said to Moses and Aaron,
"These are the Passover regulations: No
foreigner shall eat the Passover meal,
44 but any slave that you have bought
may eat it if you circumcise him first.
45 No temporary resident or hired worker
may eat it. 46 The whole meal must be
eaten in the house in which it was prepared; it must not be taken outside. And
do not break any of the animal's bones.
47 The whole community of Israel must
celebrate this festival, 48 but no uncircumcised man may eat it. If a foreigner has
settled among you and wants to celebrate Passover to honour the LORD, you
must first circumcise all the males of his
household. He is then to be treated like a
native-born Israelite and may join in the
festival. 49 The same regulations apply to
native-born Israelites and to foreigners
who settle among you." 50 All the
Israelites obeyed and did what the LORD
had commanded Moses and Aaron. 51 On
that day the LORD brought the Israelite
tribes out of Egypt.

Dedication of the First-Born

13 The LORD said to Moses, 2 "Dedicate all the first-born males to
me, for every first-born male Israelite
and every first-born male animal belongs
to me."

The Festival of Unleavened Bread

3 Moses said to the people, "Remember this day—the day on which you
left Egypt, the place where you were
slaves. This is the day the LORD brought
you out by his great power. No leavened
bread is to be eaten. 4 You are leaving
Egypt on this day in the first month, the
month of Abib. 5 The LORD solemnly promised your ancestors to give you the
land of the Canaanites, the Hittites, the
Amorites, the Hivites, and the Jebusites.
When he brings you into that rich and
fertile land, you must celebrate this festival in the first month of every year. 6 For
seven days you must eat unleavened
bread and on the seventh day there is to
be a festival to honour the LORD. 7 For
seven days you must not eat any bread
made with yeast; there must be no yeast
or leavened bread anywhere in your
land. 8 When the festival begins, explain
to your sons that you do all this because
of what the LORD did for you when you
left Egypt. 9 This observance will be a reminder, like something tied on your hand
or on your forehead; it will remind you to

body [2] 4.7; Lev 1.17
bread [4] 12.8; 16.8
celebrate [2] 12.14; 23.14
change 10.19; 14.5
cloud [2] Gen 9.13; 14.19
dedicate 12.42; 16.23
festival [4] 12.11; 23.14
first-born [10] 12.12; 22.29
forehead [2] 28.38
honour 12.11; 14.4
human 12.12; Lev 5.3
lamb 12.3; 29.38
law Gen 47.26; 15.25
leaven [2] 12.39
light (1) 10.23; 14.20
mind (1) Gen 19.29; 14.5
observe [3] 20.8
offer [2] 10.25; 18.12
power [4] 9.16; 14.31
promise [3] 12.25; 15.13
refuse (1) 11.9; 16.28
remember 6.5; 16.29
remind [4] 12.14; Num 15.39
rescue 6.6; 15.13
rich 3.8; 30.15
sacrifice 12.27; 18.12
slave [2] 12.44; 14.5
solemn [3] 6.8; 31.15
stubborn 11.10; 14.4
study Josh 1.8
unleavened 12.8; 23.15
yeast [2] 12.8; 23.15

12.29: Ex 4.22–32 **12.35–36:** Ex 3.21–22 **12.40:** Gen 15.13; Gal 3.17 **12.46:** Num 9.12; Jn 19.36
13.2: Num 3.13; Lk 2.23

continue to recite and **study** the **Law** of the LORD, because the LORD brought you out of Egypt by his great **power**. 10 **Celebrate** this **festival** at the appointed time each year.

The First-Born

11 "The LORD will bring you into the land of the Canaanites, which he **solemnly promised** to you and your ancestors. When he gives it to you, 12 you must **offer** every **first-born** male to the LORD. Every **first-born** male of your animals belongs to the LORD, 13 but you must buy back from him every **first-born** male donkey by **offering** a **lamb** in its place. If you do not want to buy back the donkey, break its neck. You must buy back every **first-born** male child of yours. 14 In the future, when your son asks what this **observance** means, you will answer him, 'By using great **power** the LORD brought us out of Egypt, the place where we were **slaves**. 15 When the king of Egypt was **stubborn** and **refused** to let us go, the LORD killed every **first-born** male in the land of Egypt, both **human** and animal. That is why we **sacrifice** every **first-born** male animal to the LORD, but buy back our **first-born** sons. 16 This **observance** will be a **reminder**, like something tied on our hands or on our **foreheads**; it will **remind** us that the LORD brought us out of Egypt by his great **power**.' "

The Pillar of Cloud and the Pillar of Fire

17 When the king of Egypt let the people go, God did not take them by the road that goes up the coast to Philistia, although it was the shortest way. God thought, "I do not want the people to **change their minds** and return to Egypt when they see that they are going to have to fight." 18 Instead, he led them in a roundabout way through the desert towards the Red Sea.[k] The Israelites were armed for battle.

19 Moses took the **body** of Joseph with him, as Joseph had made the Israelites **solemnly promise** to do. Joseph had said, "When God **rescues** you, you must carry my **body** with you from this place."

20 The Israelites left Sukkoth and camped at Etham on the edge of the desert. 21 During the day the LORD went in front of them in a pillar of **cloud** to show them the way, and during the night he went in front of them in a pillar of fire to give them **light**, so that they could travel night and day. 22 The pillar of **cloud** was always in front of the people during the day, and the pillar of fire at night.

Crossing the Red Sea

14 Then the LORD said to Moses, 2 "Tell the Israelites to **turn** back and camp in front of Pi Hahiroth, between Migdol and the Red Sea, near Baal Zephon. 3 The king will think that the Israelites are wandering about in the country and are closed in by the desert. 4 I will make him **stubborn**, and he will pursue you, and my **victory** over the king and his army will bring me **honour**. Then the Egyptians will know that I am the LORD." The Israelites did as they were told.

5 When the king of Egypt was told that the people had **escaped**, he and his officials **changed their minds** and said, "What have we done? We have let the Israelites **escape**, and we have lost them as our **slaves**!" 6 The king got his war chariot and his army ready. 7 He set out with all his chariots, including the six hundred finest, **commanded** by their officers. 8 The LORD made the king **stubborn**, and he pursued the Israelites, who were leaving **triumphantly**.[l] 9 The Egyptian army, with all the horses, chariots, and drivers, pursued them and caught up with them where they were camped by the Red Sea near Pi Hahiroth and Baal Zephon.

10 When the Israelites saw the king and his army marching against them, they were **terrified** and cried out to the LORD for **help**. 11 They said to Moses, "Weren't there any **graves** in Egypt? Did you have to bring us out here in the desert to die? Look what you have done by bringing us out of Egypt! 12 Didn't we tell you before we left that this would happen? We told you to leave us **alone** and let us go on being **slaves** of the Egyptians. It would be better to be **slaves** there than to die here in the desert."

13 Moses answered, "Don't be **afraid**! Stand your ground, and you will see what the LORD will do to **save** you today; you will never see these Egyptians again. 14 The LORD will fight for you, and there is no **need** for you to do anything."

15 The LORD said to Moses, "Why are you crying out for **help**? Tell the people to move forward. 16 Lift up your stick and hold it out over the sea. The water will

afraid 9.20; 20.19
alone Gen 32.24; 18.14
angel 12.23; 23.20
awe 15.6
change 13.17; 29.28
cloud [3] 13.21; 16.10
command 12.28; 15.26
dark 10.21; 20.21
dead 12.30; 21.34
difficult Gen 47.9; 18.22
each other 10.23; 16.15
escape [3] 1.10; 21.13
faith Num 20.12
grave Gen 35.20; Num 11.34
help [2] 5.23; 18.4
honour [2] 13.6; 23.14
light (1) 13.21; 16.7
mind (1) 13.17; 32.12
need Gen 33.11; 16.16
power 13.3; 15.6
save [2] 6.6; 15.2
servant 2.5; 32.13
slave [3] 13.3; 15.16
strong 10.19; 15.2
stubborn [3] 13.15; 32.9
terrify 7.3; 15.15
triumph 15.7
turn [2] 10.6; 16.10
victory [2] Gen 14.17; 15.1

[k] RED SEA: *(in Hebrew literally "Sea of Reeds") evidently referred to (1) a series of lakes and marshes between the head of the Gulf of Suez and the Mediterranean, the region generally regarded as the site of the events described in Exodus 13, and was also used to designate (2) the Gulf of Suez, and (3) the Gulf of Aqaba.* [l] triumphantly; *or* under the protection of the LORD.

13.12: Ex 34.19–20; Lk 2.23 **13.19:** Gen 50.25; Josh 24.32

divide, and the Israelites will be able to
walk through the sea on dry ground. 17 I
will make the Egyptians so **stubborn** that
they will go in after them, and I will gain
honour by my **victory** over the king, his
army, his chariots, and his drivers.
18 When I defeat them, the Egyptians will
know that I am the LORD."

19 The **angel of God**, who had been in
front of the army of Israel, moved and
went to the rear. The pillar of **cloud** also
moved until it was 20 between the
Egyptians and the Israelites. The **cloud**
made it **dark** for the Egyptians, but gave
light to the people of Israel,[n] and so the
armies could not come near **each other**
all night.

21 Moses held out his hand over the
sea, and the LORD drove the sea back
with a **strong** east wind. It blew all night
and **turned** the sea into dry land. The
water was divided, 22 and the Israelites
went through the sea on dry ground, with
walls of water on both sides. 23 The
Egyptians pursued them and went after
them into the sea with all their horses,
chariots, and drivers. 24 Just before dawn
the LORD looked down from the pillar of
fire and **cloud** at the Egyptian army and
threw them into a panic. 25 He made the
wheels of their chariots get stuck, so that
they moved with great **difficulty**. The
Egyptians said, "The LORD is fighting for
the Israelites against us. Let's get out of
here!"

26 The LORD said to Moses, "Hold out
your hand over the sea, and the water
will come back over the Egyptians and
their chariots and drivers." 27 So Moses
held out his hand over the sea, and at
daybreak the water returned to its normal level. The Egyptians tried to **escape**
from the water, but the LORD threw them
into the sea. 28 The water returned and
covered the chariots, the drivers, and all
the Egyptian army that had followed the
Israelites into the sea; not one of them
was left. 29 But the Israelites walked
through the sea on dry ground, with walls
of water on both sides.

30 On that day the LORD **saved** the
people of Israel from the Egyptians, and
the Israelites saw them lying **dead** on the
seashore. 31 When the Israelites saw the
great **power** with which the LORD had defeated the Egyptians, they stood in **awe**
of the LORD; and they had **faith** in the
LORD and in his **servant** Moses.

The Song of Moses

15 Then Moses and the Israelites
sang this song to the LORD:

"I will sing to the LORD, because he
has **won a glorious victory**;
he has thrown the horses and their
riders into the sea.
2 The LORD is my **strong defender**;
he is the one who has **saved** me.
He is my God, and I will **praise** him,
my father's God, and I will sing
about his greatness.
3 The LORD is a warrior;
the LORD is his **name**.

4 "He threw Egypt's army and its
chariots into the sea;
the **best** of its officers were drowned
in the Red Sea.
5 The deep sea covered them;
they sank to the bottom like a stone.

6 "Your **right hand**, LORD, is **awesome** in
power;
it breaks the **enemy** in pieces.
7 In **majestic triumph** you **overthrow**
your foes;
your **anger** blazes out and burns
them up like straw.
8 You blew on the sea and the water
piled up high;
it stood up straight like a wall;
the deepest part of the sea became
solid.
9 The **enemy** said, 'I will pursue them
and catch them;
I will divide their wealth and take all
I want;
I will draw my sword and take all
they have.'
10 But one breath from you, LORD, and
the Egyptians were drowned;
they sank like lead in the **terrible**
water.

11 "LORD, who among the **gods** is like
you?
Who is like you, **wonderful** in
holiness?
Who can work **miracles** and **mighty**
acts like yours?
12 You stretched out your **right hand**,
and the earth swallowed our
enemies.
13 **Faithful** to your **promise**, you led the
people you had **rescued**;
by your **strength** you **guided** them to
your **sacred** land.
14 The nations have heard, and they
tremble with **fear**;

act 2.7; 18.12
anger 11.8; 16.20
awe 14.31; 34.10
best Gen 49.11; 27.20
bitter 12.8; Num 5.17
choose 12.3; 18.21
command 14.7; 16.16
complain 5.15; 16.2
courage Deut 20.3
defend Num 10.9
disease 9.3; 32.35
earnest 17.4
enemy [3] 1.10; 23.4
faithful Gen 32.10; 34.6
fear [2] 9.30; 19.16
fit (1) Gen 49.20; 20.25
free 6.6; 21.2
glory [2] Lev 10.3
god (2) (other gods) 12.12; 18.11
guide 32.34
heal Gen 20.17; Lev 13.16
helpless Deut 2.31
holy 6.3; 16.23
law 13.9; 18.16
Majesty 7.17; Judg 3.19
might [2] 6.6; 32.11
miracle 11.9; Num 14.11
name (2) (name of God, of Jesus) 6.3; 20.7
obey 12.24; 16.28
overthrow Ezra 6.12
power 14.31; 23.31
praise Gen 49.8; 18.10
pray 12.32; 17.4
promise 13.5; 32.13
prophet 7.1; Num 11.25
punish 12.12; 19.22
rescue 13.19; 18.8
right (1) 10.29; 18.16
right (2) [2] Gen 48.13; 29.20
sacred Gen 18.1; 18.12
save 14.13; 16.20
slave 14.5; 18.10
strength [2] Gen 49.3; Num 11.6
strong 14.21; Num 11.4
Temple (1) (of God) 2 Sam 7.5
terrible 9.3; 32.21
terrify 14.10; Lev 26.17
terror [2] Gen 15.12; Deut 28.66
test Gen 42.15; 16.4
tremble [2] Gen 27.33; 19.16
triumph 14.8; 1 Sam 2.9
victory [2] 14.4; 17.14
win [2] Gen 34.3; 17.11
wonder (1) Gen 3.6; Deut 3.24

[n] *Probable text* The cloud...Israel; *Hebrew unclear.*

14.22: 1 Cor 10.1-2; Heb 11.29 **15.1:** Rev 15.3 **15.2:** Ps 118.14; Is 12.2

the Philistines are seized with
terror.
15 The leaders of Edom are **terrified**;
Moab's **mighty** men are **trembling**;
the people of Canaan lose their
courage.
16 **Terror** and dread fall upon them.
They see your **strength**, O LORD,
and stand **helpless** with **fear**
until your people have marched
past—
the people you **set free** from **slavery**.
17 You bring them in and plant them on
your mountain,
the place that you, LORD, have
chosen for your home,
the **Temple** that you yourself have
built.
18 You, LORD, will be king for ever and
ever."

The Song of Miriam

19 The Israelites walked through the sea on dry ground. But when the Egyptian chariots with their horses and drivers went into the sea, the LORD brought the water back, and it covered them.

20 The **prophet** Miriam, Aaron's sister, took her tambourine, and all the women followed her, playing tambourines and dancing. 21 Miriam sang for them:

"Sing to the LORD, because he has **won**
a **glorious victory**;
he has thrown the horses and their
riders into the sea."

Bitter Water

22 Then Moses led the people of Israel away from the Red Sea into the desert of Shur. For three days they walked through the desert, but found no water. 23 Then they came to a place called Marah, but the water there was so **bitter** that they could not drink it. That is why it was named Marah.[o] 24 The people **complained** to Moses and asked, "What are we going to drink?" 25 Moses **prayed earnestly** to the LORD, and the LORD showed him a piece of wood, which he threw into the water; and the water became **fit** to drink.

There the LORD gave them **laws** to live by, and there he also **tested** them. 26 He said, "If you will **obey** me completely by doing what I consider **right** and by keeping my **commands**, I will not **punish** you with any of the **diseases** that I brought on the Egyptians. I am the LORD, the one who **heals** you."

27 Next they came to Elim, where there were twelve springs and seventy palm-trees; there they camped by the water.

The Manna and the Quails

16 The whole Israelite **community** set out from Elim, and on the fifteenth day of the second month after they had left Egypt, they came to the desert of Sin, which is between Elim and Sinai. 2 There in the desert they all **complained** to Moses and Aaron 3 and said to them, "We **wish** that the LORD had killed us in Egypt. There we could at least sit down and eat meat and as much other food as we wanted. But you have brought us out into this desert to starve us all **to death**."

4 The LORD said to Moses, "Now I am going to make food rain down from the sky for all of you. The people must go out every day and gather **enough** for that day. In this way I can **test** them to find out if they will follow my instructions. 5 On the sixth day they are to bring in twice as much as usual and prepare it."

6 So Moses and Aaron said to all the Israelites, "This evening you will know that it was the LORD who brought you out of Egypt. 7 In the morning you will see the **dazzling light** of the LORD's **presence**. He has heard your **complaints** against him—yes, against him, because we are only carrying out his instructions." 8 Then Moses said, "It is the LORD who will give you meat to eat in the evening and as much **bread** as you want in the morning, because he has heard how much you have **complained** against him. When you **complain** against us, you are really complaining against the LORD."

9 Moses said to Aaron, "Tell the whole **community** to come and stand before the LORD, because he has heard their **complaints**." 10 As Aaron spoke to the whole **community**, they **turned** towards the desert, and suddenly the **dazzling light** of the LORD appeared in a **cloud**. 11 The LORD said to Moses, 12 "I have heard the **complaints** of the Israelites. Tell them that at twilight they will have meat to eat, and in the morning they will have all the **bread** they want. Then they will know that I, the LORD, am their God."

13 In the evening a large **flock** of quails flew in, **enough** to cover the camp, and in the morning there was dew all round the camp. 14 When the dew evaporated, there was something thin and flaky on the surface of the desert. It was as delicate as frost. 15 When the

anger 15.7; 21.14
bread [2] 13.3; 23.15
cloud 14.19; 19.9
command [6] 15.26; 17.1
community [4] 12.3; 17.1
complain [6] 15.24; 17.2
Covenant Box 25.10
dazzling [2] 24.16
death (1) 12.23; 29.29
death (3) (to death) 8.26; 19.12
dedicate [2] 13.2; 19.6
each other 14.20; 18.7
enough [3] 10.21; 21.21
flock 3.1; Num 31.9
holy 15.11; 18.5
light (1) [2] 14.20; 24.16
manna [4] Num 11.6
need [3] 14.14; 22.11
obey 15.26; 19.5
presence [2] 10.11; 17.6
refuse (1) 13.15; 22.17
remember 13.3; 17.14
rest (1) [4] Gen 49.15; 20.10
Sabbath 20.8
save [2] 15.2; 18.4
seed Gen 47.19; Lev 11.37
test 15.25; 17.2
turn 14.2; 23.27
wish Gen 34.10; 25.2

[o] MARAH: *This name in Hebrew means "bitter."*

16.4: Jn 6.31 **16.15:** 1 Cor 10.3

Israelites saw it, they didn't know what it
was and asked **each other**, "What is it?"
Moses said to them, "This is the food
that the LORD has given you to eat. 16 The
LORD has **commanded** that each of you is
to gather as much of it as he **needs**, two
litres for each member of his household."
17 The Israelites did this, some gathering more, others less. 18 When they
measured it, those who gathered much
did not have too much, and those who
gathered less did not have too little. Each
had gathered just what he **needed.**
19 Moses said to them, "No one is to keep
any of it for tomorrow." 20 But some of
them did not listen to Moses and **saved**
part of it. The next morning it was full of
worms and smelt rotten, and Moses was
angry with them. 21 Every morning each
one gathered as much as he **needed**; and
when the sun grew hot, what was left on
the ground melted.
22 On the sixth day they gathered
twice as much food, four litres for each
person. All the leaders of the **community**
came and told Moses about it, 23 and he
said to them, "The LORD has **commanded**
that tomorrow is a **holy day of rest, dedicated** to him. Bake today what you want
to bake and boil what you want to boil.
Whatever is left should be put aside and
kept for tomorrow." 24 As Moses had **commanded**, they kept what was left until the
next day; it did not spoil or get worms in
it. 25 Moses said, "Eat this today, because
today is the **Sabbath**, a **day of rest dedicated** to the LORD, and you will not find
any food outside the camp. 26 You must
gather food for six days, but on the
seventh day, the **day of rest**, there will be
none."
27 On the seventh day some of the
people went out to gather food, but they
did not find any. 28 Then the LORD said to
Moses, "How much longer will you
people **refuse** to **obey** my **commands**?
29 **Remember** that I, the LORD, have given
you a **day of rest**, and that is why on the
sixth day I will always give you **enough**
food for two days. Everyone is to stay
where he is on the seventh day and not
leave his home." 30 So the people did no
work on the seventh day.
31 The people of Israel called the food
manna.[p] It was like a small white **seed**,
and tasted like biscuits made with honey.
32 Moses said, "The LORD has **commanded** us to **save** some **manna**, to be
kept for our descendants, so that they
can see the food which he gave us to eat
in the desert when he brought us out of
Egypt." 33 Moses said to Aaron, "Take a
jar, put two litres of **manna** in it, and
place it in the LORD's **presence** to be kept
for our descendants." 34 As the LORD had
commanded Moses, Aaron put it in front
of the **Covenant Box**, so that it could be
kept. 35 The Israelites ate **manna** for the
next forty years, until they reached the
land of Canaan, where they settled.
36 (The standard dry measure then in use
equalled twenty litres.)

Water from the Rock
(Num 20.1–13)

17 The whole Israelite **community**
left the desert of Sin, moving
from one place to another at the **command** of the LORD. They made camp at
Rephidim, but there was no water there
to drink. 2 They **complained** to Moses and
said, "Give us water to drink."
Moses answered, "Why are you
complaining? Why are you putting the
LORD **to the test**?"
3 But the people were very thirsty and
continued to **complain** to Moses. They
said, "Why did you bring us out of
Egypt? To kill us and our children and
our livestock with thirst?"
4 Moses **prayed earnestly** to the LORD
and said, "What can I do with these
people? They are almost ready to stone
me."
5 The LORD said to Moses, "Take some
of the leaders of Israel with you, and go
on ahead of the people. Take along the
stick with which you **struck** the Nile. 6 I
will stand before you on a rock at Mount
Sinai. **Strike** the rock, and water will
come out of it for the people to drink."
Moses did so in the **presence** of the
leaders of Israel.
7 The place was named Massah and
Meribah,[q] because the Israelites **complained** and put the LORD **to the test**
when they asked, "Is the LORD with us or
not?"

War with the Amalekites

8 The Amalekites came and attacked
the Israelites at Rephidim. 9 Moses said
to Joshua, "Pick out some men to go and
fight the Amalekites tomorrow. I will
stand on top of the hill holding the stick
that God told me to carry." 10 Joshua did
as Moses **commanded** him and went out
to fight the Amalekites, while Moses,
Aaron, and Hur went up to the top of the
hill. 11 As long as Moses held up his arms,

altar Gen 35.1; 20.24
command [2] 16.16; 18.16
community 16.1; 34.31
complain [4] 16.2; Num 11.1
destroy 10.5; 23.23
earnest 15.25; Deut 3.23
pray 15.25; 23.13
presence 16.7; 24.16
remember 16.29; 22.21
strike [2] 9.15; Num 1.53
test [2] 16.4; 20.20
victory 15.1; 32.18
win [2] 15.1; Judg 7.2

[p] MANNA: *This word sounds like the Hebrew for "what is it?" (see verse 15).*
[q] MASSAH...MERIBAH: *These names in Hebrew mean "testing" and "complaining."*

16.18: 2 Cor 8.15 **16.23:** Ex 20.8–11 **16.31:** Num 11.7–8 **16.33:** Heb 9.4 **16.35:** Josh 5.12

the Israelites **won**, but when he put his
arms down, the Amalekites started **win-**
ning. 12 When Moses' arms grew tired,
Aaron and Hur brought a stone for him
to sit on, while they stood beside him and
held up his arms, holding them steady
until the sun went down. 13 In this way
Joshua totally defeated the Amalekites.
14 Then the LORD said to Moses,
"Write an account of this **victory**, so that
it will be **remembered**. Tell Joshua that I
will completely **destroy** the Amalekites."
15 Moses built an **altar** and named it "The
LORD is my Banner." 16 He said, "Hold
high the banner of the LORD! [r] The LORD
will continue to fight against the
Amalekites for ever!"

Jethro Visits Moses

18 Moses' father-in-law Jethro, the
priest of Midian, heard about
everything that God had done for Moses
and the people of Israel when he led
them out of Egypt. 2 So he came to Moses,
bringing with him Moses' wife Zipporah,
who had been left behind, 3 and Gershom
and Eliezer, her two sons. (Moses had
said, "I have been a foreigner in a
strange land"; so he had named one son
Gershom. [s] 4 He had also said, "The God
of my father **helped** me and **saved** me
from being killed by the king of Egypt";
so he had named the other son Eliezer. [t])
5 Jethro came with Moses' wife and her
two sons into the desert where Moses
was camped at the **holy** mountain. 6 He
had sent **word** to Moses that they were
coming, 7 so Moses went out to meet him,
bowed before him, and **kissed** him. They
asked about **each other's** health and then
went into Moses' tent. 8 Moses told Jethro
everything that the LORD had done to the
king and the people of Egypt in order to
rescue the Israelites. He also told him
about the hardships the people had faced
on the way and how the LORD had **saved**
them. 9 When Jethro heard all this, he
was **happy** 10 and said, "**Praise** the LORD,
who **saved** you from the king and the
people of Egypt! **Praise** the LORD, who
saved his people from **slavery**! 11 Now I
know that the LORD is greater than all
the **gods**, because he did this when the
Egyptians treated the Israelites with
such **contempt**." 12 Then Jethro brought
an **offering** to be burnt whole and other
sacrifices to be **offered** to God; and
Aaron and all the leaders of Israel went
with him to eat the **sacred** meal as an **act**
of **worship**.

The Appointment of Judges
(Deut 1.9–18)

13 The next day Moses was **settling**
disputes among the people, and he was
kept busy from morning till night.
14 When Jethro saw everything that
Moses had to do, he asked, "What is all
this that you are doing for the people?
Why are you doing this all **alone**, with
people standing here from morning till
night to **consult** you?"
15 Moses answered, "I must do this because the people come to me to **learn**
God's will. 16 When two people have a **dis-**
pute, they come to me, and I decide
which one of them is **right**, and I tell
them God's **commands** and **laws**."
17 Then Jethro said, "You are not doing it the **right** way. 18 You will wear
yourself out and these people as well.
This is too much for you to do **alone**.
19 Now let me give you some good **advice**,
and God will be with you. It is **right** for
you to **represent** the people before God
and bring their **disputes** to him. 20 You
should **teach** them God's **commands** and
explain to them how they should live and
what they should do. 21 But in addition,
you should **choose** some capable men
and appoint them as leaders of the
people: leaders of thousands, hundreds,
fifties, and tens. They must be **God-**
fearing men who can be **trusted** and who
cannot be **bribed**. 22 Let them **serve** as
judges for the people on a permanent
basis. They can bring all the **difficult**
cases to you, but they themselves can decide all the smaller **disputes**. That will
make it easier for you, as they **share**
your **burden**. 23 If you do this, as God **com-**
mands, you will not wear yourself out,
and all these people can go home with
their **disputes settled**."
24 Moses took Jethro's **advice** 25 and
chose capable men from among all the
Israelites. He appointed them as leaders
of thousands, hundreds, fifties, and tens.
26 They **served** as **judges** for the people on
a permanent basis, bringing the **difficult**
cases to Moses but deciding the smaller
disputes themselves.
27 Then Moses said good-bye to
Jethro, and Jethro went back home.

[r] *Probable text* Hold...LORD; *Hebrew unclear.*
[s] GERSHOM: *This name sounds like the Hebrew for "foreigner."*
[t] ELIEZER: *This name sounds like the Hebrew for "God helps me."*

17.14: Deut 25.17–19; 1 Sam 15.2–9 **18.2–3:** Ex 2.21–22 **18.3:** Acts 7.29

alone 18.14; 24.2
believe 4.1; 2 Sam 13.33
choose 18.21; 21.13
cloud [2] 16.10; 20.21
command [2] 18.16; 20.22
covenant 6.4; 24.7
death (3) (to death) [2] 16.3; 21.12
dedicate 16.23; 20.10
fear 15.14; 20.18
God's people [2] 18.10; 22.25
mark (1) [2] 12.13; Lev 16.8
obey 16.28; 20.6
priest [3] 18.1; 28.1
punish [2] 15.26; 20.5
pure [2] Gen 35.2; 25.11
sacred 18.12; 23.24
serve 18.22; 21.2
sex Gen 35.22; 22.19
tremble [2] 15.14; 20.18
violent Gen 49.5; Deut 21.5
warn 9.21; 21.29
worship (1) (of God) [2] 18.12; 20.3

The Israelites at Mount Sinai

19 1-2 The people of Israel left
Rephidim, and on the first day of
the third month after they had left Egypt
they came to the desert of Sinai. There
they set up camp at the foot of Mount
Sinai, 3 and Moses went up the mountain
to meet with God.
The LORD called to him from the
mountain and told him to say to the
Israelites, Jacob's descendants: 4 "You
saw what I, the LORD, did to the
Egyptians and how I carried you as an
eagle carries her young on her wings,
and brought you here to me. 5 Now, if you
will **obey** me and keep my **covenant**, you
will be **my own people**. The whole earth
is mine, but you will be my **chosen
people**, 6 a people **dedicated** to me **alone**,
and you will **serve** me as **priests**." 7 So
Moses went down and called the leaders
of the people together and told them
everything that the LORD had **commanded** him. 8 Then all the people answered together, "We will do everything
that the LORD has said," and Moses reported this to the LORD.
9 The LORD said to Moses, "I will
come to you in a thick **cloud**, so that the
people will hear me speaking with you
and will **believe** you from now on."
Moses told the LORD what the people
had answered, 10 and the LORD said to
him, "Go to the people and tell them to
spend today and tomorrow **purifying**
themselves for **worship**. They must wash
their clothes 11 and be ready the day after
tomorrow. On that day I will come down
on Mount Sinai, where all the people can
see me. 12 **Mark** a boundary round the
mountain that the people must not cross,
and tell them not to go up the mountain
or even get near it. If anyone sets foot on
it, he is to be put **to death**; 13 he must
either be stoned or shot with arrows,
without anyone touching him. This
applies to both men and animals; they
must be put **to death**. But when the trumpet is blown, then the people are to go up
to the mountain."
14 Then Moses came down the mountain and told the people to get ready for
worship. So they washed their clothes,
15 and Moses said to them, "Be ready by
the day after tomorrow and don't have
sexual intercourse in the meantime."
16 On the morning of the third day
there was thunder and lightning, a thick
cloud appeared on the mountain, and a
very loud trumpet blast was heard. All
the people in the camp **trembled** with
fear. 17 Moses led them out of the camp to
meet God, and they stood at the foot of
the mountain. 18 The whole of Mount
Sinai was covered with smoke, because
the LORD had come down on it in fire.
The smoke went up like the smoke of a
furnace, and all the people **trembled
violently**. 19 The sound of the trumpet became louder and louder. Moses spoke,
and God answered him with thunder.
20 The LORD came down on the top of
Mount Sinai and called Moses to the top
of the mountain. Moses went up 21 and the
LORD said to him, "Go down and **warn**
the people not to cross the boundary to
come and look at me; if they do, many of
them will die. 22 Even the **priests** who
come near me must **purify** themselves,
or I will **punish** them."
23 Moses said to the LORD, "The
people cannot come up, because you
commanded us to consider the mountain
sacred and to **mark** a boundary round it."
24 The LORD replied, "Go down and
bring Aaron back with you. But the
priests and the people must not cross the
boundary to come up to me, or I will
punish them." 25 Moses then went down to
the people and told them what the LORD
had said.

The Ten Commandments
(Deut 5.1-21)

20 God spoke, and these were his
words: 2 "I am the LORD your
God who brought you out of Egypt,
where you were **slaves**.
3 "**Worship no god** but me.
4 "Do not make for yourselves **images**
of anything in **heaven** or on earth or in
the water under the earth. 5 Do not **bow
down** to any **idol** or **worship** it, because I
am the LORD your God and I **tolerate** no
rivals. I bring **punishment** on those who
hate me and on their descendants down
to the third and fourth generation. 6 But I
show my **love** to thousands of generations[u] of those who **love** me and **obey** my
laws.
7 "Do not use my **name** for **evil purposes**, for I, the LORD your God, will
punish anyone who misuses my **name**.
8 "**Observe** the **Sabbath** and keep it
holy. 9 You have six days in which to do
your work, 10 but the seventh day is a **day
of rest dedicated** to me. On that day no

accuse Gen 42.30; 23.7
adultery Lev 20.10
afraid [2] 14.13; 23.27
altar [3] 17.15; 21.14
bless [2] 12.32; 23.25
bow (2) 18.7; 23.24
cloud 19.9; 24.15
command 19.7; 23.15
commit [2] Lev 20.10
dark 14.20; Deut 4.11
dedicate 19.6; 28.3
desire [2] Gen 39.7; Num 15.39
evil Gen 50.20; 22.28
false 23.1
fear 19.16; Lev 19.15
fellowship-offering 24.5
fit (1) 15.25; Num 1.3
god (2) (other gods) [2] 18.11; 22.20
hate 5.21; Lev 18.22
heaven [2] Gen 28.12; 31.17
holy [2] 18.5; 24.13
idol Lev 19.4
image Deut 5.8
law 18.16; 21.1
love [2] Gen 44.20; 21.5
name (2) (name of God, of Jesus) [2] 15.3; 33.19

[u] thousands of generations; *or* thousands.

19.5: Deut 4.20, 7.6, 14.2, 26.18; Tit 2.14 **19.5-6:** 1 Pet 2.9 **19.6:** Rev 1.6, 5.10 **19.12-13:** Heb 12.18-20
19.16: Rev 4.5 **19.16-18:** Deut 4.11-12 **20.4-5:** Ex 34.17; Lev 19.4, 26.1; Deut 4.15-18, 27.15
20.5-6: Ex 34.6-7; Num 14.18; Deut 7.9-10 **20.7:** Lev 19.12 **20.8:** Ex 16.23-30, 31.12-14
20.9-10: Ex 23.12, 31.15, 34.21, 35.2; Lev 23.3

obey [2] 19.5; 23.21
observe 13.9; 30.21
offer 18.12; 22.20
punish [2] 19.22; 21.18
purpose Lev 7.24
respect 12.36; Lev 10.3
rest (1) [2] 16.23; 23.11
rival Gen 25.23; 34.14
Sabbath [2] 16.25; 31.13
sacrifice 18.12; 22.20
sheep 12.5; 22.1
slave [3] 18.10; 21.2
steal Gen 44.5; 22.1
test 17.2; Deut 6.16
tolerate 34.14
tremble 19.16; Deut 2.25
word (1) 18.6; 34.1
worship (1) (of God) [2] 19.10; 23.15
worship (2) (of other gods) [3] 23.24

one is to work—neither you, your children, your **slaves**, your animals, nor the
foreigners who live in your country. 11 In
six days I, the LORD, made the earth, the
sky, the sea, and everything in them, but
on the seventh day I **rested**. That is why
I, the LORD, **blessed** the **Sabbath** and
made it **holy**.
12 "**Respect** your father and your
mother, so that you may live a long time
in the land that I am giving you.
13 "Do not **commit murder**.
14 "Do not **commit adultery**.
15 "Do not **steal**.
16 "Do not **accuse** anyone **falsely**.
17 "Do not **desire** another man's
house; do not **desire** his wife, his **slaves**,
his cattle, his donkeys, or anything else
that he owns."

The People's Fear
(Deut 5.22–33)

18 When the people heard the thunder
and the trumpet blast and saw the lightning and the smoking mountain, they
trembled with **fear** and stood a long way
off. 19 They said to Moses, "If you speak to
us, we will listen; but we are **afraid** that
if God speaks to us, we will die."
20 Moses replied, "Don't be **afraid**;
God has only come to **test** you and make
you keep on **obeying** him, so that you will
not sin." 21 But the people continued to
stand a long way off, and only Moses
went near the **dark cloud** where God
was.

Laws about Altars

22 The LORD **commanded** Moses to
say to the Israelites: "You have seen how
I, the LORD, have spoken to you from
heaven. 23 Do not make for yourselves
gods of silver or gold to be **worshipped** in
addition to me. 24 Make an **altar** of earth
for me, and on it **sacrifice** your **sheep**
and your cattle as **offerings** to be completely burnt and as **fellowship-offerings**.
In every place that I set aside for you to
worship me, I will come to you and **bless**
you. 25 If you make an **altar** of stone for
me, do not build it out of cut stones, because when you use a chisel on stones,
you make them **unfit** for my use. 26 Do not
build an **altar** for me with steps leading
up to it; if you do, you will expose yourselves as you go up the steps.

The Treatment of Slaves
(Deut 15.12–18)

21 "Give the Israelites the following
laws: 2 If you buy a **Hebrew slave**,
he shall **serve** you for six years. In the
seventh year he is to be **set free** without
having to pay anything. 3 If he was **unmarried** when he became your **slave**, he
is not to take a wife with him when he
leaves; but if he was married when he
became your **slave**, he may take his wife
with him. 4 If his **master** gave him a wife
and she bore him sons or daughters, the
woman and her children belong to the
master, and the man shall leave by himself. 5 But if the **slave** declares that he
loves his **master**, his wife, and his children and does not want to be **set free**,
6 then his **master** shall take him to the
place of worship. There he is to make
him stand against the door or the door-
post and pierce his ear. Then he will be
his **slave** for **life**.
7 "If a man sells his daughter as a
slave, she is not to be **set free**, as male
slaves are. 8 If she is sold to someone who
intends to make her his wife, but he
doesn't like her, then she is to be sold
back to her father; her **master** cannot
sell her to foreigners, because he has
treated her unfairly. 9 If a man buys a female **slave** to give to his son, he is to
treat her like a daughter. 10 If a man
takes a second wife, he must continue to
give his first wife the same amount of
food and clothing and the same **rights**
that she had before. 11 If he does not **fulfil**
these **duties** to her, he must **set her free**
and not receive any payment.

Laws about Violent Acts

12 "Whoever hits a man and kills him
is to be put **to death**. 13 But if it was an
accident and he did not mean to kill the
man, he can **escape** to a place which I
will **choose** for you, and there he will be
safe. 14 But when a man gets **angry** and
deliberately kills another man, he is to be
put **to death**, even if he has run to my
altar for **safety**.
15 "Whoever hits his father or his
mother is to be put **to death**.
16 "Whoever kidnaps a man, either to
sell him or to keep him as a **slave**, is to
be put **to death**.
17 "Whoever **curses** his father or his
mother is to be put **to death**.

altar 20.24; 24.4
anger 16.20; 22.24
approve Gen 41.37; Lev 10.19
care 3.1; 25.40
choose 19.5; 31.2
curse Gen 49.7; 22.28
dead [3] 14.30; Lev 5.2
death (3) (to death) [9] 19.12; 22.18
demand 7.9; Deut 10.12
duty (1) Lev 24.8
enough 16.4; 23.30
escape 14.5; Num 35.6
flesh Gen 40.19; 29.14
free [6] 15.16; Lev 19.20
fulfil Gen 38.8; Lev 7.16
Hebrew 10.3; 1 Sam 4.6
help 18.4; 22.23
hurt [2] Gen 37.22; Num 35.23
intend Gen 24.49; Lev 4.2
judge 18.22; Num 35.24
law 20.6; 24.12
life (1) [3] 4.25; 23.26
loss [2] Gen 31.39; 22.5
love 20.6; 34.6
master [6] Gen 44.5; Lev 25.53
place of worship 22.8
punish [6] 20.5; 32.34
require 5.8; 22.25
right (3) Gen 31.36; Lev 25.24
safe [2] Gen 44.17; Lev 25.18
save 18.4; Lev 18.5
serve 19.6; 26.14
slave [17] 20.2; 22.2
subject (1) Gen 3.16; Judg 3.14
unmarried Lev 21.3
warn 19.21; Lev 15.31

20.11: Gen 2.1–3; Ex 31.17 **20.12:** Deut 27.16; Mt 15.4, 19.19; Mk 7.10, 10.19; Lk 18.20; Eph 6.2, 3
20.13: Gen 9.6; Lev 24.17; Mt 5.21, 19.18; Mk 10.19; Lk 18.20; Rom13.9; Jas 2.11
20.14: Lev 20.10; Mt 5.27, 19.18; Mk 10.19; Lk 18.20; Rom 13.9; Jas 2.11
20.15: Lev 19.11; Mt 19.18; Mk 10.19; Lk 18.20; Rom 13.9 **20.16:** Ex 23.1; Mt 19.18; Mk 10.19; Lk 18.20
20.17: Rom 7.7, 13.9 **20.18–19:** Heb 12.18–19 **20.25:** Deut 27.5–7; Josh 8.31 **21.2–6:** Lev 25.39–46
21.12: Lev 24.17 **21.13:** Num 35.10–34; Deut 19.1–13; Josh 20.1–9 **21.16:** Deut 24.7
21.17: Lev 20.9; Mt 15.4; Mk 7.10

18–19 "If there is a fight and one man hits another with a stone or with his fist, but does not kill him, he is not to be **punished**. If the man who was hit has to stay in bed, but later is able to get up and walk outside with the **help** of a stick, the man who hit him is to pay for his lost time and take **care** of him until he gets well.

20 "If a man takes a stick and beats his **slave**, whether male or female, and the **slave** dies on the spot, the man is to be **punished**. 21 But if the **slave** does not die for a day or two, the **master** is not to be **punished**. The **loss** of his property is **punishment enough**.

22 "If some men are fighting and **hurt** a pregnant woman so that she loses her child, but she is not injured in any other way, the one who **hurt** her is to be fined whatever amount the woman's husband **demands**, **subject** to the **approval** of the **judges**. 23 But if the woman herself is injured, the **punishment** shall be **life** for life, 24 eye for eye, tooth for tooth, hand for hand, foot for foot, 25 burn for burn, wound for wound, bruise for bruise.

26 "If a man hits his male or female **slave** in the eye so that he loses the use of it, he is to **free** the **slave** as payment for the eye. 27 If he knocks out a tooth, he is to **free** the **slave** as payment for the tooth.

The Responsibility of Owners

28 "If a bull gores someone **to death**, it is to be stoned, and its **flesh** shall not be eaten; but its owner is not to be **punished**. 29 But if the bull had been in the habit of attacking people and its owner had been **warned**, but did not keep it penned up—then if it gores someone **to death**, it is to be stoned, and its owner is to be put **to death** also. 30 However, if the owner is allowed to pay a fine to **save** his **life**, he must pay the full amount **required**. 31 If the bull kills a boy or a girl, the same rule applies. 32 If the bull kills a male or female **slave**, its owner shall pay the owner of the **slave** thirty pieces of silver, and the bull shall be stoned **to death**.

33 "If a man takes the cover off a pit or if he digs one and does not cover it, and a bull or a donkey falls into it, 34 he must pay for the animal. He is to pay the money to the owner and may keep the **dead** animal. 35 If one man's bull kills another man's bull, the two men shall sell the live bull and divide the money; they shall also divide up the meat from the **dead** animal. 36 But if it was known that the bull had been in the habit of attacking and its owner did not keep it penned up, he must make good the **loss** by giving the other man a live bull, but he may keep the **dead** animal.

Laws about Repayment

22 "If a man **steals** a cow or a **sheep** and kills it or sells it, he must pay five cows for one cow and four **sheep** for one sheep. 2–4 He must pay for what he **stole**. If he owns nothing, he shall be sold as a **slave** to pay for what he has **stolen**. If the **stolen** animal, whether a cow, a donkey, or a **sheep**, is found **alive** in his **possession**, he shall pay two for one.

"If a **thief** is caught breaking into a house at night and is killed, the one who killed him is not **guilty** of murder. But if it happens during the day, he is **guilty** of murder.

5 "If a man lets his animals graze in a field or a **vineyard** and they stray away and eat up the crops[v] growing in another man's field, he must make good the **loss** with the crops from his own fields or **vineyards**.

6 "If a man starts a fire in his field and it spreads through the **weeds** to another man's field and burns up corn that is growing or that has been cut and stacked, the one who started the fire is to pay for the damage.

7 "If a man **agrees** to keep another man's money or other valuables for him and they are **stolen** from his house, the **thief**, if he is found, shall **repay** double. 8 But if the **thief** is not found, the man who was keeping the valuables is to be brought to the **place of worship** and there he must take an **oath** that he has not **stolen** the other man's property.

9 "In every case of a **dispute** about property, whether it involves cattle, donkeys, **sheep**, clothing, or any other lost object, the two men **claiming** the property shall be taken to the **place of worship**. The one whom God declares to be **guilty** shall pay double to the other man.

10 "If a man **agrees** to keep another man's donkey, cow, **sheep**, or other animal for him, and the animal dies or is injured or is carried off in a raid, and if there was no **witness**, 11 the man must go to the **place of worship** and take an **oath** that he has not **stolen** the other man's animal. If the animal was not **stolen**, the owner shall **accept** the **loss**, and the other man **need** not **repay** him; 12 but if

accept Gen 34.17; 23.8
act 18.12; Lev 18.24
agree [2] 4.18; 23.32
alive 4.18; 33.20
anger 21.14; 32.10
bride [2] Gen 34.12; Deut 22.29
claim Num 3.40
condemn 23.7
curse 21.17; Lev 19.14
death (3) (to death) [3] 21.12; 23.7
dispute 18.13; 24.14
evidence 23.1
evil 20.7; 23.7
first-born [3] 13.2; 34.19
god (2) (other gods) 20.3; 23.13
God's people [2] 19.5; 28.12
guilty [3] Gen 44.16; 23.1
help [2] 21.18; 23.1
ill-treat [2] 5.22; 23.9
loss [3] 21.21; Lev 12.4
magic 9.11; Lev 19.26
mercy 1.13; Deut 4.31
need [3] 16.16; 35.21
oath [2] Num 5.19
offer [3] 20.24; 23.15
oppress 3.9; Deut 28.29
orphan Deut 10.18
place of worship [3] 21.6; Lev 26.30
poor 6.12; 23.3
possess 6.8; 23.30
practice Gen 44.15; 23.24
refuse (1) 16.28; Lev 6.2
relations Lev 18.22
remember 17.14; 28.12
repay [4] Lev 6.4
require 21.30; 30.13
sacrifice 20.24; 23.18
sex 19.15; 32.6
sheep [6] 20.24; 23.19
slave 21.2; 23.12
steal [9] 20.15; Lev 6.2
thief [3] Judg 17.2
vineyard [2] Gen 9.20; 23.11
virgin [2] Gen 24.16; Lev 21.7
weed Gen 3.18; Deut 29.23
widow [2] Gen 38.8; Lev 21.14
witness Gen 31.32; Num 5.12

[v] If...crops; *or* If a man burns off a field or a vineyard, and lets the fire get out of control and burn up the crops.

21.24: Lev 24.19–20; Deut 19.21; Mt 5.38

the animal was **stolen**, the man must **repay** the owner. [13] If it was killed by wild animals, the man is to bring the remains as **evidence**; he **need** not pay for what has been killed by wild animals.

14 "If a man borrows an animal from another man and it is injured or dies when its owner is not present, the man must pay for it. [15] But if that happens when the owner is present, the man **need** not **repay**. If it is a hired animal, the **loss** is covered by the hiring charge.

Moral and Religious Laws

16 "If a man seduces a **virgin** who is not engaged, he must pay the **bride-price** for her and marry her. [17] But if her father **refuses** to let him marry her, he must pay the father a sum of money equal to the **bride-price** for a **virgin**.

18 "Put **to death** any woman who **practises magic**.

19 "Put **to death** any man who has **sexual relations** with an animal.

20 "**Condemn to death** anyone who **offers sacrifices** to any **god** except to me, the LORD.

21 "Do not **ill-treat** or **oppress** a foreigner; **remember** that you were foreigners in Egypt. [22] Do not **ill-treat** any **widow** or **orphan**. [23] If you do, I, the LORD, will answer them when they cry out to me for **help**, [24] and I will be **angry** and kill you in war. Your wives will become **widows**, and your children will be fatherless.

25 "If you lend money to any of **my people** who are **poor**, do not **act** like a money-lender and **require** him to pay interest. [26] If you take someone's cloak as a pledge that he will pay you, you must give it back to him before the sun sets, [27] because it is the only covering he has to keep him warm. What else can he sleep in? When he cries out to me for **help**, I will answer him because I am **merciful**.

28 "Do not speak **evil** of God,[w] and do not **curse** a leader of your people.

29 "Give me the **offerings** from your corn, your wine, and your olive-oil when they are due.

"Give me your **first-born** sons. [30] Give me the **first-born** of your cattle and your **sheep**. Let the **first-born** male stay with its mother for seven days, and on the eighth day **offer** it to me.

31 "You are **my people**, so you must not eat the meat of any animal that has been killed by wild animals; instead, give it to the dogs.

Justice and Fairness

23 "Do not spread **false** rumours, and do not **help** a **guilty** man by giving **false evidence**. [2] Do not follow the majority when they do **wrong** or when they give **evidence** that **perverts justice**. [3] Do not show **partiality** to a **poor** man at his **trial**.

4 "If you happen to see your **enemy's** cow or donkey running loose, take it back to him. [5] If his donkey has fallen under its load, **help** him get the donkey to its feet again; don't just walk off.

6 "Do not **deny justice** to a **poor** man when he appears in **court**. [7] Do not make **false accusations**, and do not put an **innocent** person **to death**, for I will **condemn** anyone who does such an **evil** thing. [8] Do not **accept** a **bribe**, for a bribe makes people **blind** to what is **right** and **ruins** the **cause** of those who are **innocent**.

9 "Do not **ill-treat** a foreigner; you know how it feels to be a foreigner, because you were foreigners in Egypt.

The Seventh Year and the Seventh Day

10 "For six years **sow** your field and gather in what it produces. [11] But in the seventh year let it **rest**, and do not **harvest** anything that grows on it. The **poor** may eat what grows there, and the wild animals can have what is left. Do the same with your **vineyards** and your olive-trees.

12 "Work six days a week, but do no work on the seventh day, so that your **slaves** and the foreigners who work for you and even your animals can **rest**.

13 "Listen to everything that I, the LORD, have said to you. Do not **pray** to other **gods**; do not even mention their names.

The Three Great Festivals
(Ex 34.18–26; Deut 16.1–17)

14 "**Celebrate** three **festivals** a year to **honour** me. [15] In the month of Abib, the month in which you left Egypt, **celebrate** the Festival of **Unleavened Bread** in the way that I **commanded** you. Do not eat any **bread** made with **yeast** during the

accept 22.11; 28.38
accuse 20.16; Num 35.12
afraid 20.19; 34.30
agree 22.7; Num 5.19
angel [2] 14.19; 32.34
bless 20.11; 32.29
blind 4.11; Lev 19.14
bow (2) 20.5; 24.1
bread [3] 16.8; 25.30
bribe 18.21; Deut 10.17
cause (2) 2 Sam 3.8
celebrate [4] 13.5; Lev 23.5
command [2] 20.22; 24.3
condemn 22.20; Deut 13.17
court (1) Gen 50.7; Lev 5.1
death (3) (to death) 22.18; 31.14
deny Gen 18.15; Job 24.25
destroy [2] 17.14; 32.10
enemy [4] 15.6; 32.25
enough 21.21; 32.19
evidence [2] 22.13; Lev 5.1
evil 22.28; 32.22
false [3] 20.16; Lev 19.35
festival [7] 13.5; 32.5
god (2) (other gods) [5] 22.20; 32.1
guilty 22.2; Lev 4.3
harvest [4] Gen 47.24; 34.21
help [2] 22.23; 24.13
honour 14.4; 32.5
ill-treat 22.21; Lev 19.33
innocent [2] Gen 20.4; Num 5.28
justice [2] Gen 18.19; Lev 19.15
life (1) 21.6; 30.12
obey [2] 20.6; 24.7
offer [2] 22.20; 25.2
partiality Deut 1.17
pervert Lev 18.23
poor [3] 22.25; 30.15
possess 22.2; 32.13
power 15.6; 29.37
practice 22.18; Lev 18.3
pray 17.4; Num 11.2
protect 9.19; 30.16
rebel [2] Gen 27.40; Lev 16.21
religion 12.14; Lev 23.2
rest (1) [2] 20.10; 31.13
right (1) 18.16; Lev 26.4
ruin 10.7; Lev 26.31
sacred 19.23; 25.8
sacrifice [2] 22.20; 24.5
sheep 22.1; 34.3
shelter 9.19; 34.22
slave 22.2; Lev 19.20

[w] God; *or* the judges.

22.16–17: Deut 22.28–29 **22.18:** Deut 18.10, 11 **22.19:** Lev 18.23, 20.15–16; Deut 27.21
22.20: Deut 17.2–7 **22.21–22:** Ex 23.9; Lev 19.33–34; Deut 24.17–18, 27.19
22.25: Lev 25.35–38; Deut 15.7–11, 23.19–20 **22.26–27:** Deut 24.10–13 **22.28:** Acts 23.5 **22.31:** Lev 17.15
23.1: Ex 20.16; Lev 19.11–12; Deut 5.20 **23.3:** Lev 19.15 **23.4–5:** Deut 22.1–4
23.6–8: Lev 19.15; Deut 16.19 **23.9:** Ex 22.21; Lev 19.33–34; Deut 24.17–18, 27.19 **23.10–11:** Lev 25.1–7
23.12: Ex 20.9–11, 31.15, 34.21, 35.2; Lev 23.3; Deut 5.13–14
23.15: Ex 12.14–20; Lev 23.6–8; Num 28.17–25

sow Gen 47.19; Lev 11.37
trap 34.12
try (2) Lev 19.16
turn 16.10; 32.6
unleavened 13.6; 34.18
vineyard [2] 22.5; Lev 19.10
worship (1) (of God) [3] 20.3; 24.1
worship (2) (of other gods) [2] 20.3; 32.8
wrong 9.27; Num 5.6
yeast [2] 13.7; 29.2

seven days of this festival. Never come to worship me without bringing an offering.

16 "Celebrate the Harvest Festival when you begin to harvest your crops.

"Celebrate the Festival of Shelters in the autumn, when you gather the fruit from your vineyards and orchards. 17 Every year at these three festivals all your men must come to worship me, the Lord your GOD.

18 "Do not offer bread made with yeast when you sacrifice an animal to me. The fat of animals sacrificed to me during these festivals is not to be left until the following morning.

19 "Each year bring to the house of the LORD your God the first corn that you harvest.

"Do not cook a young sheep or goat in its mother's milk.

Promises and Instructions

20 "I will send an angel ahead of you to protect you as you travel and to bring you to the place which I have prepared. 21 Pay attention to him and obey him. Do not rebel against him, for I have sent him, and he will not pardon such rebellion. 22 But if you obey him and do everything I command, I will fight against all your enemies. 23 My angel will go ahead of you and take you into the land of the Amorites, the Hittites, the Perizzites, the Canaanites, the Hivites, and the Jebusites, and I will destroy them. 24 Do not bow down to their gods or worship them, and do not adopt their religious practices. Destroy their gods and break down their sacred stone pillars. 25 If you worship me, the LORD your God, I will bless you with food and water and take away all your illnesses. 26 In your land no woman will have a miscarriage or be without children. I will give you long lives.

27 "I will make the people who oppose you afraid of me; I will bring confusion among the people against whom you fight, and I will make all your enemies turn and run from you. 28 I will throw your enemies into a panic;[x] I will drive out the Hivites, the Canaanites, and the Hittites as you advance. 29 I will not drive them out within one year; if I did, the land would become deserted, and the wild animals would be too many for you. 30 Instead, I will drive them out little by little, until there are enough of you to take possession of the land. 31 I will make the borders of your land extend from the Gulf of Aqaba to the Mediterranean Sea and from the desert to the Euphrates River. I will give you power over the inhabitants of the land, and you will drive them out as you advance. 32 Do not make any agreement with them or with their gods. 33 Do not let those people live in your country; if you do, they will make you sin against me. If you worship their gods, it will be a fatal trap for you."

The Covenant Is Sealed

24 The LORD said to Moses, "Come up the mountain to me, you and Aaron, Nadab, Abihu, and seventy of the leaders of Israel; and while you are still some distance away, bow down in worship. 2 You alone, and none of the others, are to come near me. The people are not even to come up the mountain."

3 Moses went and told the people all the LORD's commands and all the ordinances, and all the people answered together, "We will do everything that the LORD has said." 4 Moses wrote down all the LORD's commands. Early the next morning he built an altar at the foot of the mountain and set up twelve stones, one for each of the twelve tribes of Israel. 5 Then he sent young men, and they burnt sacrifices to the LORD and sacrificed some cattle as fellowship-offerings. 6 Moses took half the blood of the animals and put it in bowls; and the other half he threw against the altar. 7 Then he took the book of the covenant, in which the LORD's commands were written, and read it aloud to the people. They said, "We will obey the LORD and do everything that he has commanded."

8 Then Moses took the blood in the bowls and threw it on the people. He said, "This is the blood that seals the covenant which the LORD made with you when he gave all these commands."

9 Moses, Aaron, Nadab, Abihu, and seventy of the leaders of Israel went up the mountain 10 and they saw the God of Israel. Beneath his feet was what looked like a pavement of sapphire, as blue as the sky. 11 God did not harm these leading men of Israel; they saw God, and then they ate and drank together.

Moses on Mount Sinai

12 The LORD said to Moses, "Come up the mountain to me, and while you are here, I will give you two stone tablets which contain all the laws that I have written for the instruction of the people."

alone 19.6; Lev 20.26
altar [2] 21.14; 27.1
blood [3] 12.7; 29.12
bow (2) 23.24; 33.10
cloud [4] 20.21; 33.9
command [5] 23.15; 27.20
covenant [2] 19.5; 31.16
dazzling 16.7; 29.43
dispute 22.9; Deut 1.12
fellowship-offering 20.24; 29.28
harm 12.13; 29.37
help 23.1; 33.11
holy 20.8; 28.30
law 21.1; 25.22
leading Gen 50.7; Josh 22.14
light (1) [2] 16.7; 29.43
obey 23.21; 32.28
presence 17.6; 27.21
sacrifice [2] 23.18; 29.3
seal Gen 41.42; 1 Kgs 21.8
settle (2) 18.13; Lev 19.17
tablet 25.16
worship (1) (of God) 23.15; 34.8

[x] I will...panic; *or* I will send hornets among your enemies.

23.16: Lev 23.15–21, 39–43; Num 28.26–31 **23.19:** Ex 34.26; Deut 14.21, 26.2
24.8: Mt 26.28; Mk 14.24; Lk 22.20; 1 Cor 11.25; Heb 9.19–20, 10.29

13 Moses and his helper Joshua got ready,
and Moses began[y] to go up the holy
mountain. 14 Moses said to the leaders,
"Wait here in the camp for us until we
come back. Aaron and Hur are here with
you; and so whoever has a dispute to
settle can go to them."

15 Moses went up Mount Sinai, and a
cloud covered it. 16–17 The dazzling light of
the LORD's presence came down on the
mountain. To the Israelites the light
looked like a fire burning on top of the
mountain. The cloud covered the mountain for six days, and on the seventh day
the LORD called to Moses from the cloud.
18 Moses went on up the mountain into
the cloud. There he stayed for forty days
and nights.

Offerings for the Sacred Tent
(Ex 35.4–9)

25 The Lord said to Moses, 2 "Tell
the Israelites to make an offering
to me. Receive whatever offerings any
man wishes to give. 3 These offerings are
to be: gold, silver, and bronze; 4 fine
linen; blue, purple, and red wool; cloth
made of goats' hair; 5 rams' skin dyed
red; fine leather; acacia-wood; 6 oil for
the lamps; spices for the anointing oil
and for the sweet-smelling incense;
7 carnelians and other jewels to be set in
the ephod[m] of the High Priest and in his
breast-piece. 8 The people must make a
sacred tent for me, so that I may live
among them. 9 Make it and all its furnishings according to the plan that I will
show you.

The Covenant Box
(Ex 37.1–9)

10 "Make a box out of acacia-wood,
110 centimetres long, 66 centimetres
wide, and 66 centimetres high. 11 Cover it
with pure gold inside and out and put a
gold border all round it. 12 Make four
carrying-rings of gold for it and attach
them to its four legs, with two rings on
each side. 13 Make carrying-poles of
acacia-wood and cover them with gold
14 and put them through the rings on each
side of the box. 15 The poles are to be left
in the rings and must not be taken out.
16 Then put in the box the two stone tablets that I will give you, on which the
commandments are written.

17 "Make a lid of pure gold, 110 centimetres long and 66 centimetres wide.
18 Make two winged creatures[z] of hammered gold, 19 one for each end of the lid.
Make them so that they form one piece
with the lid. 20 The winged creatures are
to face each other across the lid, and
their outspread wings are to cover it.
21 Put the two stone tablets inside the box
and put the lid on top of it. 22 I will meet
you there, and from above the lid between the two winged creatures I will
give you all my laws for the people of
Israel.

The Table for the Bread Offered to God
(Ex 37.10–16)

23 "Make a table out of acacia-wood,
88 centimetres long, 44 centimetres wide,
and 66 centimetres high. 24 Cover it with
pure gold and put a gold border round it.
25 Make a rim 75 millimetres wide round
it and a gold border round the rim.
26 Make four carrying-rings of gold for it
and put them at the four corners, where
the legs are. 27 The rings to hold the poles
for carrying the table are to be placed
near the rim. 28 Make the poles of acacia-
wood and cover them with gold. 29 Make
plates, cups, jars, and bowls to be used
for the wine-offerings. All of these are to
be made of pure gold. 30 The table is to be
placed in front of the Covenant Box, and
on the table there is always to be the
sacred bread offered to me.

The Lamp-Stand
(Ex 37.17–24)

31 "Make a lamp-stand of pure gold.
Make its base and its shaft of hammered
gold; its decorative flowers, including
buds and petals, are to form one piece
with it. 32 Six branches shall extend from
its sides, three from each side. 33 Each of
the six branches is to have three decorative flowers shaped like almond blossoms
with buds and petals. 34 The shaft of the
lamp-stand is to have four decorative
flowers shaped like almond blossoms
with buds and petals. 35 There is to be one
bud below each of the three pairs of
branches. 36 The buds, the branches, and
the lamp-stand are to be a single piece of
pure hammered gold. 37 Make seven
lamps for the lamp-stand and set them
up so that they shine towards the front.
38 Make its tongs and trays of pure gold.
39 Use thirty-five kilogrammes of pure
gold to make the lamp-stand and all this
equipment. 40 Take care to make them

[y] Moses began; *one ancient translation* they began.
[m] EPHOD: *In most contexts the term ephod refers to a type of garment, in certain respects resembling a waistcoat. It was made of costly and colourful cloth and to it was attached a kind of pouch containing the Urim and Thummim, two objects used in determining God's will.*
[z] WINGED CREATURES: *See Word List.*

24.18: Deut 9.9 **25.17:** Heb 9.5 **25.30:** Lev 24.5–8 **25.40:** Acts 7.44; Heb 8.5

according to the **plan** that I showed you
on the mountain.

The Tent of the LORD's Presence[a]
(Ex 36.8–38)

Covenant Box [2] 25.10; 27.21
creature [2] 25.18; 36.8
Holy Place [3] 28.29
last (2) [2] Gen 35.18; 36.12
plan 25.9; 27.8
sacred 25.8; 29.6
separate Gen 43.32; 28.1
serve 21.2; 28.1
tablet 25.16; 31.18
Tent (2) (of the Lord's presence) [14] 25.8; 27.9

26 "Make the interior of the **sacred**
Tent, the Tent of my presence,
out of ten pieces of fine linen woven with
blue, purple, and red wool. Embroider
them with figures of winged **creatures**.
2 Make each piece the same size, twelve
metres long and two metres wide. 3 Sew
five of them together in one set, and do
the same with the other five. 4 Make
loops of blue cloth on the edge of the outside piece in each set. 5 Put fifty loops on
the first piece of the first set and fifty
loops matching them on the **last** piece of
the second set. 6 Make fifty gold hooks
with which to join the two sets into one
piece.
7 "Make a cover for the **Tent** out of
eleven pieces of cloth made of goats'
hair. 8 Make them all the same size, thirteen metres long and two metres wide.
9 Sew five of them together in one set,
and the other six in another set. Fold the
sixth piece double over the front of the
Tent. 10 Put fifty loops on the edge of the
last piece of one set, and fifty loops on
the edge of the other set. 11 Make fifty
bronze hooks and put them in the loops
to join the two sets so as to form one
cover. 12 Hang the extra half-piece over
the back of the **Tent**. 13 The extra fifty
centimetres on each side of the length is
to hang over the sides of the **Tent** to
cover it.
14 "Make two more coverings, one of
rams' skin dyed red and the other of fine
leather, to **serve** as the outer cover.
15 "Make upright frames for the **Tent**
out of acacia-wood. 16 Each frame is to be
four metres long and 66 centimetres
wide, 17 with two matching projections, so
that the frames can be joined together.
All the frames are to have these projections. 18 Make twenty frames for the
south side 19 and forty silver bases to go
under them, two bases under each frame
to hold its two projections. 20 Make
twenty frames for the north side of the
Tent 21 and forty silver bases, two under
each frame. 22 For the back of the **Tent**
on the west, make six frames, 23 and two
frames for the corners. 24 These corner
frames are to be joined at the bottom
and connected all the way to the top. The
two frames that form the two corners
are to be made in this way. 25 So there
will be eight frames with their sixteen silver bases, two under each frame.
26 "Make fifteen cross-bars of acacia-
wood, five for the frames on one side of
the **Tent**, 27 five for the frames on the
other side, and five for the frames on the
west end, at the back. 28 The middle
cross-bar, set half-way up the frames, is
to extend from one end of the **Tent** to the
other. 29 Cover the frames with gold and
fit them with gold rings to hold the cross-
bars, which are also to be covered with
gold. 30 Set up the **Tent** according to the
plan that I showed you on the mountain.
31 "Make a curtain of fine linen woven
with blue, purple, and red wool. Embroider it with figures of winged
creatures. 32 Hang it on four posts of
acacia-wood covered with gold, fitted
with hooks, and set in four silver bases.
33 Place the curtain under the row of
hooks in the roof of the **Tent**, and behind
the curtain put the **Covenant Box**
containing the two stone **tablets**. The curtain will **separate** the **Holy Place** from
the **Most Holy Place**. 34 Put the lid on the
Covenant Box. 35 Outside the **Most Holy
Place** put the table against the north side
of the **Tent** and the lamp-stand against
the south side.
36 "For the entrance of the **Tent** make
a curtain of fine linen woven with blue,
purple, and red wool and decorated with
embroidery. 37 For this curtain make five
posts of acacia-wood covered with gold
and fitted with gold hooks; make five
bronze bases for these posts.

The Altar
(Ex 38.1–7)

27 "Make an **altar** out of acacia-
wood. It is to be square, 2.2
metres long and 2.2 metres wide, and it is
to be 1.3 metres high. 2 Make projections
at the top of the four corners. They are to
form one piece with the **altar**, and the
whole is to be covered with bronze.
3 Make pans for the greasy **ashes**, and
make shovels, bowls, hooks, and firepans.
All this equipment is to be made of
bronze. 4 Make a bronze grating and put
four bronze carrying-rings on its corners.
5 Put the grating under the rim of the
altar, so that it reaches half-way up the
altar. 6 Make carrying-poles of acacia-
wood, cover them with bronze, 7 and put
them in the rings on each side of the
altar when it is carried. 8 Make the **altar**
out of boards and leave it hollow, according to the **plan** that I showed you on the
mountain.

altar [6] 24.4; 28.43
ash 9.8; Lev 1.16
best 15.4; 29.2
command [2] 24.3; 29.35
Covenant Box 26.33; 30.6
plan 26.30; 31.4
presence 24.16; 28.30
Tent (2) (of the Lord's presence) [4] 26.1; 28.43

[a] TENT OF THE LORD'S PRESENCE: *See Word List.*
26.33: Heb 6.19, 9.3–5

The Enclosure for the Tent of the LORD's Presence
(Ex 38.9–20)

9 "For the **Tent** of my presence make an enclosure out of fine linen curtains. On the south side the curtains are to be 44 metres long, 10 supported by twenty bronze posts in twenty bronze bases, with hooks and rods made of silver. 11 The same is to be done on the north side of the enclosure. 12 On the west side there are to be curtains 22 metres long, with ten posts and ten bases. 13 On the east side, where the entrance is, the enclosure is also to be 22 metres wide. 14–15 On each side of the entrance there are to be 6.6 metres of curtains, with three posts and three bases. 16 For the entrance itself there is to be a curtain 9 metres long made of fine linen woven with blue, purple, and red wool, and decorated with embroidery. It is to be supported by four posts in four bases. 17 All the posts round the enclosure are to be connected with silver rods, and their hooks are to be made of silver and their bases of bronze. 18 The enclosure is to be 44 metres long, 22 metres wide, and 2.2 metres high. The curtains are to be made of fine linen and the bases of bronze. 19 All the equipment that is used in the **Tent** and all the pegs for the **Tent** and for the enclosure are to be made of bronze.

Taking Care of the Lamp
(Lev 24.1–4)

20 "**Command** the people of Israel to bring you the **best** olive-oil for the lamp, so that it can be lit each evening. 21 Aaron and his sons are to set up the lamp in the **Tent** of my presence outside the curtain which is in front of the **Covenant Box**. There in my **presence** it is to burn from evening until morning. This **command** is to be kept for ever by the Israelites and their descendants.

Garments for the Priests
(Ex 39.1–7)

accept 23.8; 34.9
altar 27.1; 29.12
anoint 25.6; 29.7
bind Gen 29.34; 39.23
birth 1.16; Lev 12.2
dedicate [4] 20.10; 29.1
determine [2] 32.22
ephod (1) [10] 25.7; 29.5
error Ps 19.12
forehead 13.9; Deut 6.8
God's people [2] 22.25; 29.28
High Priest 25.7; 35.9
holy 24.13; 29.11
Holy Place [3] 26.33; 29.30
keep from 1.10; 39.23

28 "Summon your brother Aaron and his sons, Nadab, Abihu, Eleazar, and Ithamar. **Separate** them from the people of Israel, so that they may **serve** me as **priests**. 2 Make **priestly** garments for your brother Aaron, to **provide** him with dignity and beauty. 3 Call all the craftsmen to whom I have given ability, and tell them to make Aaron's clothes, so that he may be **dedicated** as a **priest** in my **service**. 4 Tell them to make a breast-piece, an **ephod**, a robe, an embroidered shirt, a turban, and a sash. They are to make these **priestly** garments for your brother Aaron and his sons, so that they can **serve** me as **priests**. 5 The craftsmen are to use blue, purple, and red wool, gold thread, and fine linen.

6 "They are to make the **ephod** of blue, purple, and red wool, gold thread, and fine linen, decorated with embroidery. 7 Two shoulder-straps, by which it can be fastened, are to be attached to the sides. 8 A finely woven belt made of the same materials is to be attached to the **ephod** so as to form one piece with it. 9 Take two carnelian stones and engrave on them the names of the twelve sons of Jacob, 10 in the order of their **birth**, with six on one stone and six on the other. 11 Get a skilful jeweller to engrave on the two stones the names of the sons of Jacob, and mount the stones in gold settings. 12 Put them on the shoulder-straps of the **ephod** to **represent** the twelve tribes of Israel. In this way Aaron will carry their names on his shoulders, so that I, the LORD, will always **remember my people**. 13 Make two gold settings 14 and two chains of **pure** gold twisted like cords, and attach them to the settings.

The Breast-Piece
(Ex 39.8–21)

15 "Make a breast-piece for the **High Priest** to use in **determining God's will**. It is to be made of the same materials as the **ephod** and with similar embroidery. 16 It is to be square and folded double, 22 centimetres long and 22 centimetres wide. 17 Mount four rows of precious stones on it; in the first row mount a ruby, a topaz, and a garnet; 18 in the second row, an emerald, a sapphire, and a diamond; 19 in the third row, a turquoise, an agate, and an amethyst; 20 and in the fourth row, a beryl, a carnelian, and a jasper. These are to be mounted in gold settings. 21 Each of these twelve stones is to have engraved on it the name of one of the sons of Jacob, to **represent** the tribes of Israel. 22 For the breast-piece make chains of **pure** gold, twisted like cords. 23 Make two gold rings and attach them to the upper corners of the breast-piece, 24 and fasten the two gold cords to the two rings. 25 Fasten the other two ends of the cords to the two settings, and in this way attach them in front to the shoulder-straps of the **ephod**. 26 Then make two rings of gold and attach them to the lower corners of the breast-piece on the inside edge next to the **ephod**. 27 Make two more gold rings and attach them to the lower part of the front of the two shoulder-straps of the **ephod** near the

offer [2] 25.2; 29.3
ordain 29.9
presence [2] 27.21; 29.11
priest [8] 19.6; 29.1
provide [2] 10.25; Lev 25.6
pure [3] 25.11; 29.36
remember [2] 22.21; 30.16
represent [2] 18.19; 39.7
separate 26.33; Num 8.6
serve [5] 26.14; 29.9
service 29.1
Tent (2) (of the Lord's presence) 27.9; 29.4
will (1) [2] 18.15; Num 27.21

seam and above the finely woven belt.
28 Tie the rings of the breast-piece to the
rings of the **ephod** with a blue cord, so
that the breast-piece rests above the belt
and does not come loose.
29 "When Aaron enters the **Holy
Place**, he will wear this breast-piece engraved with the names of the tribes of
Israel, so that I, the LORD, will always
remember my people. 30 Put the Urim
and Thummim[b] in the breast-piece, so
that Aaron will carry them when he
comes into my **holy presence**. At such
times he must always wear this breast-
piece, so that he can **determine** my **will**
for the people of Israel.

The Other Priestly Garments
(Ex 39.22–31)

31 "The robe that goes under the
ephod is to be made entirely of blue wool.
32 It is to have a hole for the head, and
this hole is to be reinforced with a woven
binding to **keep it from** tearing. 33-34 All
round its lower hem put pomegranates of
blue, purple, and red wool, alternating
with gold bells. 35 Aaron is to wear this
robe when he **serves** as **priest**. When he
comes into my **presence** in the **Holy
Place** or when he leaves it, the sound of
the bells will be heard, and he will not be
killed.
36 "Make an ornament of **pure** gold
and engrave on it **'Dedicated to the
LORD.'** 37 Tie it to the front of the turban
with a blue cord. 38 Aaron is to wear it on
his **forehead**, so that I, the LORD, will **accept** all the **offerings** that the Israelites
dedicate to me, even if the people commit some **error** in **offering** them.
39 "Weave Aaron's shirt of fine linen
and make a turban of fine linen and also
a sash decorated with embroidery.
40 "Make shirts, sashes, and caps for
Aaron's sons, to **provide** them with dignity and beauty. 41 Put these clothes on
your brother Aaron and his sons. Then
ordain them and **dedicate** them by
anointing them with olive-oil, so that they
may **serve** me as **priests**. 42 Make linen
shorts for them, reaching from the waist
to the thighs, so that they will not expose
themselves. 43 Aaron and his sons must always wear them when they go into the
Tent of my presence or approach the
altar to **serve** as **priests** in the **Holy
Place**, so that they will not be killed for
exposing themselves. This is a permanent rule for Aaron and his descendants.

Instructions for Ordaining Aaron and His Sons as Priests
(Lev 8.1–36)

29 "This is what you are to do to
Aaron and his sons to **dedicate**
them as **priests** in my **service**. Take one
young bull and two rams without any defects. 2 Use the **best** wheat flour, but no
yeast, and make some **bread** with olive-
oil, some without it, and some in the form
of biscuits brushed with oil. 3 Put them in
a basket and **offer** them to me when you
sacrifice the bull and the two rams.
4 "Bring Aaron and his sons to the entrance of the **Tent** of my presence, and
tell them to take a **ritual** bath. 5 Then
dress Aaron in the **priestly** garments—
the shirt, the robe that goes under the
ephod, the ephod, the breast-piece, and
the belt. 6 Put the turban on him and tie
on it the **sacred sign** of dedication engraved **'Dedicated to the LORD.'** 7 Then
take the **anointing** oil, pour it on his head,
and **anoint** him.
8 "Bring his sons and put shirts on
them; 9 put sashes round their waists and
tie caps on their heads. That is how you
are to **ordain** Aaron and his sons. They
and their descendants are to **serve** me as
priests for ever.
10 "Bring the bull to the front of the
Tent of my presence and tell Aaron and
his sons to put their hands on its head.
11 Kill the bull there in my **holy presence**
at the entrance of the **Tent**. 12 Take some
of the bull's **blood** and with your finger
put it on the projections of the **altar**.
Then pour out the rest of the **blood** at the
base of the **altar**. 13 Next, take all the fat
which covers the internal organs, the
best part of the liver, and the two kidneys
with the fat on them and burn them on
the **altar** as an **offering** to me. 14 But burn
the bull's **flesh**, its skin, and its intestines
outside the camp. This is an **offering** to
take away the sins of the **priests**.
15 "Take one of the rams and tell
Aaron and his sons to put their hands on
its head. 16 Kill it, and take its **blood** and
throw it against all four sides of the **altar**.
17 Cut the ram in pieces; wash its internal
organs and its hind legs, and put them on
top of the head and the other pieces.
18 Burn the whole ram on the **altar** as a
food offering. The odour of this **offering**
pleases me.
19 "Take the other ram—the ram
used for **dedication**—and tell Aaron and
his sons to put their hands on its head.
20 Kill it, and take some of its **blood** and

altar [12] 28.43; 30.1
anoint [4] 28.41; 30.25
apart Gen 49.26; Lev 20.24
best [3] 27.20; Lev 3.4
blood [6] 24.6; 30.10
bread [4] 25.30; 34.18
burnt-offering [2] 10.25; 31.9
change 14.5; 32.12
command 27.20; 31.6
dazzling 24.16; 33.18
death (1) 16.3; Lev 7.24
dedicate [7] 28.3; 30.10
ephod (1) 28.4; 35.9
fellowship-offering 24.5; 32.6
flesh 21.28; Lev 4.11
food-offering [3] 30.20
forgive [2] 10.17; 32.30
gift [4] Gen 43.15; Lev 7.29
God's people [2] 28.12; 30.33
harm 24.11; 30.29
holy [7] 28.30; 30.10
Holy Place 28.29; 31.11
lamb [4] 13.13; 34.20
light (1) 24.16; 33.18
offer [13] 28.38; 30.8
ordain [7] 28.41; 30.30
please [3] Gen 45.16; 33.12
power 23.31; 30.29
presence [3] 28.30; 33.16
priest [11] 28.1; 30.30
pure [2] 28.14; 30.3
right (2) [4] 15.6; Lev 7.32
rite 4.25; Lev 8.33
ritual [2] 12.25; 30.10
sacred [3] 26.1; 30.25
sacrifice [5] 24.5; 30.10
serve [3] 28.1; 31.10
service 28.3; 30.30
sign (1) 12.13; 31.13
special [3] Gen 2.3; Lev 7.14
sprinkle 30.36
take away (sin) Lev 1.4
Tent (2) (of the Lord's presence) [7] 28.43; 30.16
yeast 23.15; 34.25

[b] URIM AND THUMMIM: *Two objects used by the priest to determine God's will; it is not known precisely how they were used.*

28.30: Num 27.21; Deut 33.8; Ezra 2.63; Neh 7.65 **29.18:** Eph 5.2; Phil 4.18

put it on the lobes of the **right** ears of Aaron and his sons, on the thumbs of their **right hands** and on the big toes of their **right** feet. Throw the rest of the **blood** against all four sides of the **altar**. [21] Take some of the **blood** that is on the **altar** and some of the **anointing** oil, and **sprinkle** it on Aaron and his clothes and on his sons and their clothes. He, his sons, and their clothes will then be **dedicated** to me.

22 "Cut away the ram's fat, the fat tail, the fat covering the internal organs, the **best** part of the liver, the two kidneys with the fat on them, and the **right** thigh. [23] From the basket of **bread** which has been **offered** to me, take one loaf of each kind: one loaf made with olive-oil and one made without it and one biscuit. [24] Put all this food in the hands of Aaron and his sons and tell them to **dedicate** it to me as a **special gift**. [25] Then take it from them and burn it on the **altar**, on top of the **burnt-offering**, as a **food-offering** to me. The odour of this **offering** **pleases** me.

26 "Take the breast of this ram and **dedicate** it to me as a **special gift**. This part of the animal will be yours,

27 "When a **priest** is **ordained**, the breast and the thigh of the ram being used for the **ordination** are to be **dedicated** to me as a **special gift** and set aside for the **priests**. [28] It is my **unchanging** decision that when **my people** make their **fellowship-offerings**, the breast and the thigh of the animal belong to the **priests**. This is the people's **gift** to me, the LORD.

29 "Aaron's **priestly** garments are to be handed on to his sons after his **death**, for them to wear when they are **ordained**. [30] The son of Aaron who succeeds him as **priest** and who goes into the **Tent** of my presence to **serve** in the **Holy** Place is to wear these garments for seven days.

31 "Take the meat of the ram used for the **ordination** of Aaron and his sons and boil it in a **holy** place. [32] At the entrance of the **Tent** of my presence they are to eat it along with the **bread** left in the basket. [33] They shall eat what was used in the **ritual of forgiveness** at their **ordination**. Only **priests** may eat this food, because it is **sacred**. [34] If some of the meat or some of the **bread** is not eaten by morning, it is to be **burnt**; it is not to be eaten, for it is **sacred**.

35 "Perform the **rites of ordination** for Aaron and his sons for seven days exactly as I have **commanded** you. [36] Each day you must **offer** a bull as a **sacrifice**, so that sin may be **forgiven**. This will **purify** the **altar**. Then **anoint** it with olive-oil to make it **holy**. [37] Do this every day for seven days. Then the **altar** will be completely **holy**, and anyone or anything that touches it will be **harmed** by the **power** of its **holiness**. [c]

The Daily Offerings
(Num 28.1–8)

38 "Every day for all time to come, **sacrifice** on the **altar** two one-year-old **lambs**. [39] **Sacrifice** one of the **lambs** in the morning and the other in the evening. [40] With the first **lamb** **offer** one kilogramme of fine wheat flour mixed with one litre of **pure** olive-oil. Pour out one litre of wine as an **offering**. [41] **Sacrifice** the second **lamb** in the evening, and **offer** with it the same amounts of flour, olive-oil, and wine as in the morning. This is a **food offering** to me, the LORD, and its odour **pleases** me. [42] For all time to come, this **burnt-offering** is to be **offered** in my **presence** at the entrance of the **Tent** of my presence. That is where I will meet **my people** and speak to you. [43] There I will meet the people of Israel, and the **dazzling light** of my **presence** will make the place **holy**. [44] I will make the **Tent** and the **altar holy**, and I will set Aaron and his sons **apart** to **serve** me as **priests**. [45] I will live among the people of Israel, and I will be their God. [46] They will know that I am the LORD their God who brought them out of Egypt so that I could live among them. I am the LORD their God.

The Altar for Burning Incense
(Ex 37.25–28)

30 "Make an **altar** out of acacia-wood, for burning **incense**. [2] It is to be square, 45 centimetres long and 45 centimetres wide, and it is to be 90 centimetres high. Its projections at the four corners are to form one piece with it. [3] Cover its top, all four sides, and its projections with **pure** gold, and put a gold border round it. [4] Make two gold carrying-rings for it and attach them below the border on two sides to hold the poles with which it is to be carried. [5] Make these poles of acacia-wood and cover them with gold. [6] Put this **altar** outside the curtain which hangs in front of the **Covenant Box**. That is the place where I will meet you. [7] Every morning when Aaron comes to get the lamps

[c] BE HARMED BY THE POWER OF ITS HOLINESS: *It was believed that ordinary people or things would be harmed by touching something holy.*

protect 23.20; Num 8.19
pure [4] 29.36; 31.8
remember 28.12; 32.13
require 22.25; 38.26
rich 13.5; 33.3
ritual 29.4; 40.12
sacred 29.6; 31.14
sacrifice 29.3; 32.6
service [2] 29.1; 32.29
sprinkle 29.21; Lev 4.6
tax Num 31.28
Tent (2) (of the Lord's presence) [5] 29.4; 31.7
wine-offering 25.29; 37.16

ready, he is to burn sweet-smelling **in-**
cense on it. 8 He must do the same when
he lights the lamps in the evening. This
offering of incense is to continue without
interruption for all time to come. 9 Do not
offer on this **altar** any **forbidden incense**,
any animal-offering, or any **grain-**
offering, and do not pour out any **wine-**
offering on it. 10 Once a year Aaron is to
perform the **ritual** for **purifying** the **altar**
by putting on its four projections the
blood of the animal **sacrificed** for sin.
This is to be done every year for all time
to come. This **altar** is to be completely
holy, **dedicated** to me, the LORD."

The Tax for the Tent of the LORD's Presence

11 The LORD said to Moses, 12 "When
you take a census of the people of Israel,
each man is to pay me a price for his **life**,
so that no **disaster** will come on him
while the census is being taken. 13 Everyone included in the census must pay the
required amount of money, weighed
according to the official standard. Everyone must pay this as an **offering** to me.
14 Everyone being counted in the census,
that is, every man twenty years old or
older, is to pay me this amount. 15 The
rich man is not to pay more, nor the **poor**
man less, when they pay this amount for
their **lives**. 16 Collect this money from the
people of Israel and spend it for the up-
keep of the **Tent** of my presence. This
tax will be the payment for their **lives**,
and I will **remember** to **protect** them."

The Bronze Basin

17 The LORD said to Moses, 18 "Make a
bronze basin with a bronze base. Place it
between the **Tent** and the **altar**, and put
water in it. 19 Aaron and his sons are to
use the water to wash their hands and
feet 20 before they go into the **Tent** or
approach the **altar** to **offer** the **food offer-**
ing. Then they will not be killed. 21 They
must wash their hands and feet, so that
they will not die. This is a rule which
they and their descendants are to **ob-**
serve for ever."

The Anointing Oil

22 The LORD said to Moses, 23 "Take
the finest spices—six kilogrammes of
liquid myrrh, three kilogrammes of
sweet-smelling cinnamon, three kilogrammes of sweet-smelling cane, 24 and
six kilogrammes of cassia (all weighed
according to the official standard). Add
four litres of olive-oil, 25 and make a
sacred anointing oil, mixed like perfume.
26 Use it to **anoint** the **Tent** of my presence, the **Covenant Box**, 27 the table and
all its equipment, the lamp-stand and its
equipment, the **altar** for burning **incense**,
28 the **altar** for burning **offerings**, together
with all its equipment, and the wash-
basin with its base. 29 **Dedicate** these
things in this way, and they will be completely **holy**, and anyone or anything that
touches them will be **harmed** by the
power of its **holiness**.[d] 30 Then **anoint**
Aaron and his sons, and **ordain** them as
priests in my **service**. 31 Say to the people
of Israel, 'This **holy anointing** oil is to be
used in my **service** for all time to come.
32 It must not be poured on ordinary men,
and you must not use the same formula
to make any mixture like it. It is **holy**,
and you must treat it as holy. 33 Whoever
makes any like it or uses any of it on anyone who is not a **priest** will no longer be
considered one of **my people**.' "

The Incense

34 The LORD said to Moses, "Take an
equal part of each of the following sweet
spices—stacte, onycha, galbanum, and
pure frank**incense**. 35 Use them to make
incense, mixed like perfume. Add salt to
keep it **pure** and **holy**. 36 Beat part of it
into a fine powder, take it into the **Tent**
of my presence, and **sprinkle** it in front of
the **Covenant Box**. Treat this **incense** as
completely **holy**. 37 Do not use the same
formula to make any **incense** like it for
yourselves. Treat it as a **holy** thing **dedi-**
cated to me. 38 If anyone makes any like
it for use as perfume, he will no longer be
considered one of **my people**."

Craftsmen for the Tent of the LORD's Presence
(Ex 35.30–36.1)

31 The LORD said to Moses, 2 "I have
chosen Bezalel, the son of Uri
and grandson of Hur, from the tribe of
Judah, 3 and I have filled him with my
power.[e] I have given him **understanding**,
skill, and ability for every kind of artistic
work—4 for **planning** skilful designs and
working them in gold, silver, and bronze;
5 for cutting jewels to be set; for carving
wood; and for every other kind of artistic
work. 6 I have also selected Oholiab son
of Ahisamach, from the tribe of Dan, to
work with him. I have also given great
ability to all the other skilful craftsmen,
so that they can make everything I have
commanded to be made: 7 the **Tent** of my
presence, the **Covenant Box** and its lid,

altar [2] 30.1; 32.5
anoint 30.25; 35.8
burnt-offering 29.25; 40.29
choose 21.13; 33.13
command [3] 29.35; 32.8
commandment 25.16; 32.15
covenant 24.7; 34.10
Covenant Box 30.6; 35.12
death (3) (to death) [2] 23.7; 35.2
dedicate 30.10; 35.2
God's people 30.33; 32.14
heaven 20.4; Deut 3.24
Holy Place 29.30; 35.19
incense [2] 30.1; 35.8
plan 27.8; 32.12
power 30.29; 32.11
priest [2] 30.30; 32.29

[d] HARMED BY THE POWER OF ITS HOLINESS: *See 29.37.* [e] power; *or* spirit.

30.13: Ex 38.25-26; Mt 17.24 **30.18:** Ex 38.8 **30.22-38:** Ex 37.29

pure 30.3; 37.2
rest (1) [4] 23.11; 35.2
Sabbath 20.8; 35.3
sacred 30.25; 33.7
serve 29.9; 33.13
sign (1) [3] 29.6; 39.30
solemn 13.5; 32.13
tablet 26.33; 32.15
Tent (2) (of the Lord's presence) [2] 30.16; 33.7
understand Gen 42.23; 35.31

all the furnishings of the Tent, 8 the table
and its equipment, the lamp-stand of
pure gold and all its equipment, the altar
for burning incense, 9 the altar for burnt-
offerings and all its equipment, the wash-
basin and its base, 10 the magnificent
priestly garments for Aaron and his sons
to use when they serve as priests, 11 the
anointing oil, and the sweet-smelling incense for the Holy Place. In making all
these things, they are to do exactly as I
have commanded you."

Sabbath, the Day of Rest

12 The LORD commanded Moses 13 to
say to the people of Israel, "Keep the
Sabbath, my day of rest, because it is a
sign between you and me for all time to
come, to show that I, the LORD, have
made you my own people. 14 You must
keep the day of rest, because it is sacred.
Whoever does not keep it, but works on
that day, is to be put to death. 15 You have
six days in which to do your work, but the
seventh day is a solemn day of rest dedicated to me. Whoever does any work on
that day is to be put to death. 16 The
people of Israel are to keep this day as a
sign of the covenant. 17 It is a permanent
sign between the people of Israel and
me, because I, the LORD, made heaven
and earth in six days, and on the seventh
day I stopped working and rested."
18 When God had finished speaking to
Moses on Mount Sinai, he gave him the
two stone tablets on which God himself
had written the commandments.

The Gold Bull-Calf
(Deut 9.6–29)

altar 31.8; 34.13
angel 23.20; 33.2
anger [4] 22.24; 34.6
announce Judg 7.3
bless 23.25; 39.43
bull-calf [6] Deut 9.16
change [2] 29.28; Lev 6.11
command [2] 31.6; 33.5
commandment [2] 31.18; 34.28
consecrate Gen 35.14; 40.13
control Gen 45.1; Lev 25.28
destroy [2] 23.23; 33.3
determine 28.15; Lev 5.15
disaster [2] 30.12; Lev 26.16
disease 15.26; Lev 13.2
enemy 23.4; Lev 26.7
enough 23.30; 36.7
evil 23.7; 34.7
feast Gen 29.22; Num 25.2

32 When the people saw that Moses
had not come down from the
mountain but was staying there a long
time, they gathered round Aaron and
said to him, "We do not know what has
happened to this man Moses, who led us
out of Egypt; so make us a god[f] to lead
us."
2 Aaron said to them, "Take off the
gold earrings which your wives, your
sons, and your daughters are wearing,
and bring them to me." 3 So all the people
took off their gold earrings and brought
them to Aaron. 4 He took the earrings,
melted them, poured the gold into a
mould, and made a gold bull-calf.
The people said, "Israel, this is our
god, who led us out of Egypt!"
5 Then Aaron built an altar in front of
the gold bull and announced, "Tomorrow
there will be a festival to honour the
LORD." 6 Early the next morning they
brought some animals to burn as sacrifices and others to eat as fellowship-
offerings. The people sat down to a feast,
which turned into an orgy of drinking
and sex.
7 The LORD said to Moses, "Go back
down at once, because your people,
whom you led out of Egypt, have sinned
and rejected me. 8 They have already left
the way that I commanded them to follow; they have made a bull-calf out of
melted gold and have worshipped it and
offered sacrifices to it. They are saying
that this is their god, who led them out of
Egypt. 9 I know how stubborn these
people are. 10 Now, don't try to stop me. I
am angry with them, and I am going to
destroy them. Then I will make you and
your descendants into a great nation."
11 But Moses pleaded with the LORD
his God and said, "LORD, why should you
be so angry with your people, whom you
rescued from Egypt with great might
and power? 12 Why should the Egyptians
be able to say that you led your people
out of Egypt, planning to kill them in the
mountains and destroy them completely? Stop being angry; change your
mind and do not bring this disaster on
your people. 13 Remember your servants
Abraham, Isaac, and Jacob. Remember
the solemn promise you made to them to
give them as many descendants as there
are stars in the sky and to give their
descendants all that land you promised
would be their possession for ever." 14 So
the LORD changed his mind and did not
bring on his people the disaster he had
threatened.
15 Moses went back down the mountain, carrying the two stone tablets with
the commandments written on both
sides. 16 God himself had made the tablets
and had engraved the commandments
on them.
17 Joshua heard the people shouting
and said to Moses, "I hear the sound of
battle in the camp."
18 Moses said, "That doesn't sound
like a shout of victory or a cry of defeat;
it's the sound of singing."
19 When Moses came close enough to
the camp to see the bull-calf and to see
the people dancing, he was furious.
There at the foot of the mountain, he
threw down the tablets he was carrying
and broke them. 20 He took the bull-calf
which they had made, melted it, ground

fellowship-offering 29.28; Lev 3.1
festival 23.14; 34.18
fool 10.2; Num 12.11
forgive [2] 29.33; 34.7
friend Gen 38.12; 33.11
fury Gen 49.7; Deut 9.19
god (2) (other gods) [5] 23.13; 34.14
God's people 31.13; 34.9
guide 15.13; 33.2
honour 23.14; Lev 19.30
Levites [3] 4.14; 38.21
might 15.11; Num 23.24
mind (1) [2] 14.5; Num 23.19
neighbour 12.4; Lev 19.18
obey 24.7; 34.11
offer 30.8; 34.15
plan 31.4; 33.13
plead Gen 27.38; 1 Sam 15.11
possess 23.30; Lev 14.34
power 31.3; 35.31
priest 31.10; 35.19
promise [2] 15.13; 33.1
punish 21.18; 34.7
reject Gen 4.5; Lev 18.25
remember [3] 30.16; 33.13
rescue 18.8; Num 35.25
sacrifice [2] 30.10; 34.15
servant 14.31; Num 3.6
service 30.30; Num 1.3
sex 22.19; Lev 15.18
solemn 31.15; 35.2
stubborn 14.4; 33.3
tablet [3] 31.18; 34.1
terrible [3] 15.10; Lev 10.19
threat 1.9; Num 14.10
turn 23.27; Lev 13.3
victory 17.14; 33.14
worship (2) (of other gods) [2] 23.24; 34.14

[f] a god; *or* some gods.

31.15: Ex 20.8–11, 23.12, 34.21, 35.2; Lev 23.3; Deut 5.12–14 **31.17:** Ex 20.11 **32.1:** Acts 7.40
32.4: 1 Kgs 12.28; Acts 7.41 **32.6:** 1 Cor 10.7 **32.11–14:** Num 14.13–19 **32.13:** Gen 22.16–17, 17.8

it into fine powder, and mixed it with water. Then he made the people of Israel drink it. 21 He said to Aaron, "What did these people do to you, that you have made them commit such a **terrible** sin?"

22 Aaron answered, "Don't be **angry** with me; you know how **determined** these people are to do **evil**. 23 They said to me, 'We don't know what has happened to this man Moses, who brought us out of Egypt; so make us a **god** to lead us.' 24 I asked them to bring me their gold ornaments, and those who had any took them off and gave them to me. I threw the ornaments into the fire and out came this **bull-calf**!"

25 Moses saw that Aaron had let the people get out of **control** and make **fools** of themselves in front of their **enemies**. 26 So he stood at the gate of the camp and shouted, "Everyone who is on the LORD's side come over here!" So all the **Levites** gathered round him, 27 and he said to them, "The LORD God of Israel **commands** every one of you to put on his sword and go through the camp from this gate to the other and kill his brothers, his **friends**, and his **neighbours**." 28 The **Levites obeyed**, and killed about three thousand men that day. 29 Moses said to the **Levites**, "Today you have **consecrated** yourselves[h] as **priests** in the **service** of the LORD by killing your sons and brothers, so the LORD has given you his **blessing**."

30 The next day Moses said to the people, "You have committed a **terrible** sin. But now I will again go up the mountain to the LORD; perhaps I can obtain **forgiveness** for your sin." 31 Moses then returned to the LORD and said, "These people have committed a **terrible** sin. They have made a **god** out of gold and **worshipped** it. 32 Please **forgive** their sin; but if you won't, then remove my name from the book in which you have written the names of your people."

33 The LORD answered, "It is those who have sinned against me whose names I will remove from my book. 34 Now go, lead the people to the place I told you about. **Remember** that my **angel** will **guide** you, but the time is coming when I will **punish** these people for their sin."

35 So the LORD sent a **disease** on the people, because they had caused Aaron to make the gold **bull-calf**.

The LORD Orders Israel to Leave Mount Sinai

33 The LORD said to Moses, "Leave this place, you and the people you brought out of Egypt, and go to the **land that I promised** to give to Abraham, Isaac, and Jacob and to their descendants. 2 I will send an **angel** to **guide** you, and I will drive out the Canaanites, the Amorites, the Hittites, the Perizzites, the Hivites, and the Jebusites. 3 You are going to a **rich** and fertile land. But I will not go with you myself, because you are a **stubborn** people, and I might **destroy** you on the way."

4 When the people heard this, they began to **mourn** and did not wear jewellery any more. 5 For the LORD had **commanded** Moses to say to them, "You are a **stubborn** people. If I were to go with you even for a moment, I would completely **destroy** you. Now take off your jewellery, and I will decide what to do with you." 6 So after they left Mount Sinai, the people of Israel no longer wore jewellery.

The Tent of the LORD's Presence

7 Whenever the people of Israel set up camp, Moses would take the **sacred Tent** and put it up some distance away from the camp. It was called the **Tent** of the LORD's presence, and anyone who wanted to **consult** the LORD would go out to it. 8 Whenever Moses went out there, the people would stand at the door of their tents and **watch** Moses until he entered it. 9 After Moses had gone in, the pillar of **cloud** would come down and stay at the door of the **Tent**, and the LORD would speak to Moses from the **cloud**. 10 As soon as the people saw the pillar of **cloud** at the door of the **Tent**, they would **bow down**. 11 The LORD would speak with Moses face to face, just as a man speaks with a **friend**. Then Moses would return to the camp. But the young man who was his **helper**, Joshua son of Nun, stayed in the **Tent**.

The LORD Promises to Be with His People

12 Moses said to the LORD, "It is **true** that you have told me to lead these people to that land, but you did not tell me whom you would send with me. You have said that you know me well and are **pleased** with me. 13 Now if you are, tell me your **plans**, so that I may **serve** you and continue to **please** you. **Remember**

alive 22.2; Lev 16.10
angel 32.34; Num 20.16
bow (2) 24.1; 34.8
choose [2] 31.2; 35.30
cloud [3] 24.15; 34.5
command 32.8; 34.4
compassion 34.6
consult 18.14; Lev 19.31
dazzling [2] 29.43; 40.34
destroy [2] 32.10; 34.13
distinguish 11.7; Lev 10.10
friend 32.27; Deut 13.6
guide 32.34; Num 10.31
help 24.13; 36.2
light (1) [2] 29.43; 35.3
mourn Gen 50.3; Lev 10.6
name (2) (name of God, of Jesus) 20.7; 34.5
pity Gen 43.14; 34.6
plan 32.12; 35.32
please [4] 29.18; 34.9
presence [4] 29.11; 34.10
promise 32.13; 34.7
remember 32.13; Lev 19.34
request Gen 17.20; Num 27.7
rich 30.15; Lev 19.15
sacred [2] 31.14; 34.13
serve 31.10; 35.19
splendour Deut 33.26
stubborn [2] 32.9; 34.9
Tent (2) (of the Lord's presence) [5] 31.7; 34.34
true Gen 18.21; Deut 13.2
victory 32.18; Lev 26.7
watch 12.42; Num 23.9

[h] *Some ancient translations* Today you have consecrated yourselves; *Hebrew* consecrate yourselves today; *or* you have been consecrated today.

32.32: Ps 69.28; Rev 3.5 **33.1:** Gen 12.7, 26.3, 28.13

also that you have **chosen** this nation to be your own."

14 The LORD said, "I will go with you, and I will give you **victory**."

15 Moses replied, "If you do not go with us, don't make us leave this place. 16 How will anyone know that you are **pleased** with your people and with me if you do not go with us? Your **presence** with us will **distinguish** us from any other people on earth."

17 The LORD said to Moses, "I will do just as you have asked, because I know you very well and I am **pleased** with you."

18 Then Moses **requested**, "Please, let me see the **dazzling light** of your **presence**."

19 The LORD answered, "I will make all my **splendour** pass before you and in your **presence** I will pronounce my **sacred name**. I am the LORD, and I show **compassion** and **pity** on those I **choose**. 20 I will not let you see my face, because no one can see me and stay **alive**, 21 but here is a place beside me where you can stand on a rock. 22 When the **dazzling light** of my **presence** passes by, I will put you in an opening in the rock and cover you with my hand until I have passed by. 23 Then I will take my hand away, and you will see my back but not my face."

The Second Set of Stone Tablets
(Deut 10.1-5)

34 The LORD said to Moses, "Cut two stone **tablets** like the first ones, and I will write on them the **words** that were on the first **tablets**, which you broke. 2 Be ready tomorrow morning, and come up Mount Sinai to meet me there at the top. 3 No one is to come up with you; no one is to be seen on any part of the mountain; and no **sheep** or cattle are to graze at the foot of the mountain." 4 So Moses cut two more stone **tablets**, and early the next morning he carried them up Mount Sinai, just as the LORD had **commanded**.

5 The LORD came down in a **cloud**, stood with him there, and pronounced his **holy name**, the LORD.[j] 6 The LORD then passed in front of him and called out, "I, the LORD, am a God who is full of **compassion** and **pity**, who is not easily **angered** and who shows great **love** and **faithfulness**. 7 I keep my **promise** for thousands of generations[k] and **forgive** **evil** and sin; but I will not **fail** to **punish** children and grandchildren to the third and fourth generation for the sins of their parents."

8 Moses quickly **bowed down** to the ground and **worshipped**. 9 He said, "Lord, if you really are **pleased** with me, I ask you to go with us. These people are **stubborn**, but **forgive** our **evil** and our sin, and **accept** us as your **own people**."

The Covenant Is Renewed
(Ex 23.14-19; Deut 7.1-5; 16.1-17)

10 The LORD said to Moses, "I now make a **covenant** with the people of Israel. In their **presence** I will do great things such as have never been done anywhere on earth among any of the nations. All the people will see what great things I, the LORD, can do, because I am going to do an **awesome** thing for you. 11 **Obey** the **laws** that I am giving you today. I will drive out the Amorites, the Canaanites, the Hittites, the Perizzites, the Hivites, and the Jebusites, as you advance. 12 Do not make any treaties with the people of the country into which you are going, because this could be a fatal **trap** for you. 13 Instead, tear down their **altars**, **destroy** their **sacred** pillars, and cut down the **symbols** of their **goddess** Asherah.

14 "Do not **worship any other god**, because I, the LORD, **tolerate** no **rivals**. 15 Do not make any treaties with the people of the country, because when they **worship** **their pagan gods** and **sacrifice** to them, they will invite you to join them, and you will be **tempted** to eat the food they **offer** to their **gods**. 16 Your sons might marry those foreign women, who would lead them to be **unfaithful** to me and to **worship their pagan gods**.

17 "Do not make and **worship gods** of metal.

18 "Keep the **Festival** of **Unleavened** Bread. As I have **commanded** you, eat **unleavened bread** for seven days in the month of Abib, because it was in that month that you left Egypt.

19 "Every **first-born** son and **first-born** male domestic animal belongs to me, 20 but you are to buy back every first-born donkey by **offering** a **lamb** in its place. If you do not buy it back, break its neck. Buy back every **first-born** son.

"No one is to appear before me without an **offering**.

21 "You have six days in which to do your work, but do not work on the

accept 28.38; Lev 1.3
afraid 23.27; Lev 26.6
altar 32.5; 35.15
anger 32.10; Lev 10.6
awe 15.6; Deut 28.58
bow (2) 33.10; Lev 9.24
bread [3] 29.2; 35.13
cloud 33.9; 40.34
command [3] 33.5; 35.1
commandment [2] 32.15; 38.21
community 17.1; 35.1
compassion 33.19; Ps 69.16
conquer Gen 24.60; Lev 26.16
covenant [3] 31.16; Lev 2.13
destroy 33.3; Lev 13.52
evil [2] 32.22; Lev 16.21
fail 8.18; Lev 5.15
faithful 15.13; Num 14.18
festival [5] 32.5; Lev 23.2
first-born [3] 22.29; Lev 27.26
forgive [2] 32.30; Lev 4.20
god (2) (other gods) [5] 32.1; Lev 18.21

God's people 32.14; Lev 7.20
goddess Deut 7.5
harvest [4] 23.11; Lev 2.12
holy 30.10; 40.9
lamb 29.38; Lev 9.3
law [2] 25.22; Lev 7.27
love 21.5; Lev 19.18
name (2) (name of God, of Jesus) 33.19; Lev 18.21
obey 32.28; Lev 7.36
offer [4] 32.8; 35.5
pagan [2] Lev 18.24
Passover 12.11; Lev 23.5
pity 33.19; Num 11.1
please 33.12; Lev 1.9
presence 33.16; 40.2
promise 33.1; Lev 19.12
punish 32.34; Lev 18.25
rival 20.5; Num 25.1
sacred 33.7; 35.2
sacrifice [2] 32.6; 40.29
sheep [2] 23.19; Lev 1.2
shelter 23.16; Lev 23.33
stubborn 33.3; Lev 26.19
symbol Deut 7.5
tablet [4] 32.15; 38.21
tempt Deut 4.19
Tent (2) (of the Lord's presence) 33.7; 35.11
tolerate 20.5; Num 25.11
trap 23.33; Josh 23.13
unfaithful Lev 17.7
unleavened [2] 23.15; Lev 2.4
word (1) [4] 20.1; Num 6.23
worship (1) (of God) [2] 24.1; 35.21
worship (2) (of other gods) [4] 32.8; Lev 18.21
yeast 29.2; Lev 2.4

[j] THE LORD: *See 3.14.* [k] thousands of generations; *or* thousands.

33.19: Rom 9.15 **34.6-7:** Ex 20.5-6; Num 14.18; Deut 5.9-10, 7.9-10 **34.13:** Deut 16.21
34.17: Ex 20.4; Lev 19.4; Deut 5.8, 27.15 **34.18:** Ex 12.14-20; Lev 23.6-8; Num 28.16-25 **34.19:** Ex 13.2
34.20: Ex 13.13 **34.21:** Ex 20.9-10, 23.12, 31.15, 35.2; Lev 23.3; Deut 5.13-14

seventh day, not even during ploughing
time or **harvest**.
22 "Keep the **Harvest Festival** when
you begin to **harvest** the first crop of
your wheat, and keep the **Festival of**
Shelters in the autumn when you gather
your fruit.
23 "Three times a year all your men
must come to **worship** me, the LORD, the
God of Israel. 24 After I have driven out
the nations before you and extended your
territory, no one will try to **conquer** your
country during the three **festivals**.
25 "Do not **offer bread** made with
yeast when you **sacrifice** an animal to
me. Do not keep until the following
morning any part of the animal killed at
the **Passover Festival**.
26 "Each year bring to the house of
the LORD the first corn that you **harvest**.
"Do not cook a young **sheep** or goat in
its mother's milk."
27 The LORD said to Moses, "Write
these **words** down, because it is on the
basis of these **words** that I am making a
covenant with you and with Israel."
28 Moses stayed there with the LORD forty
days and nights, eating and drinking
nothing. He wrote on the **tablets** the
words of the **covenant**—the Ten
Commandments.

Moses Goes Down from Mount Sinai

29 When Moses went down from
Mount Sinai carrying the Ten **Command-**
ments, his face was shining because he
had been speaking with the LORD; but he
did not know it. 30 Aaron and all the
people looked at Moses and saw that his
face was shining, and they were **afraid** to
go near him. 31 But Moses called them,
and Aaron and all the leaders of the **com-**
munity went to him, and Moses spoke to
them. 32 After that, all the people of Israel
gathered round him, and Moses gave
them all the **laws** that the LORD had
given him on Mount Sinai. 33 When Moses
had finished speaking to them, he
covered his face with a veil. 34 Whenever
Moses went into the **Tent** of the LORD's
presence to speak to the LORD, he took
the veil off. When he came out, he would
tell the people of Israel everything that
he had been **commanded** to say, 35 and
they would see that his face was shining.
Then he would put the veil back on until
the next time he went to speak to the
LORD.

Regulations for the Sabbath

35 Moses called together the whole
community of the people of
Israel and said to them, "This is what the
LORD has **commanded** you to do: 2 You
have six days in which to do your work,
but the seventh day is to be **sacred**, a
solemn day of rest dedicated to me, the
LORD. Anyone who does any work on that
day is to be put **to death**. 3 Do not even
light a fire in your homes on the
Sabbath."

Offerings for the Sacred Tent
(Ex 25.1-9)

4 Moses said to all the people of Israel,
"This is what the LORD has **commanded**:
5 Make an **offering** to the LORD. Everyone
who **wishes** to do so is to bring an **offer-**
ing of gold, silver, or bronze; 6 fine linen;
blue, purple, and red wool; cloth made of
goats' hair; 7 rams' skin dyed red; fine
leather; acacia-wood; 8 oil for the lamps;
spices for the **anointing** oil and for the
sweet-smelling **incense**; 9 carnelians and
other jewels to be set in the **High Priest's**
ephod and in his breast-piece.

Articles for the Tent of the LORD's Presence
(Ex 39.32-43)

10 "All the skilled workmen among
you are to come and make everything
that the LORD **commanded**: 11 the **Tent**,
its covering and its outer covering, its
hooks and its frames, its cross-bars, its
posts, and its bases; 12 the **Covenant Box**,
its poles, its lid, and the curtain to screen
it off; 13 the table, its poles, and all its
equipment; the **bread offered** to God;
14 the lamp-stand for the **light** and its
equipment; the lamps with their oil;
15 the **altar** for burning **incense** and its
poles; the **anointing** oil; the sweet-
smelling **incense**; the curtain for the entrance of the **Tent**; 16 the **altar** on which
to burn **offerings**, with its bronze grating
attached, its poles, and all its equipment;
the wash-basin and its base; 17 the curtains for the enclosure, its posts and
bases; the curtain for the entrance of the
enclosure; 18 the pegs and ropes for the
Tent and the enclosure; 19 and the
magnificent garments the **priests** are to
wear when they **serve** in the **Holy**
Place—the **sacred** clothes for Aaron the
priest and for his sons."

The People Bring Their Offerings

20 All the people of Israel left, 21 and
everyone who **wished** to do so brought an

altar [2] 34.13; 37.25
anoint [3] 31.11; 37.29
bread 34.18; 39.36
choose 33.13; Lev 16.9
command [4] 34.4; 36.1
community 34.31; 38.25
contribute 36.6
Covenant Box 31.7; 37.1
death (3) (to death) 31.14; Lev 10.2
dedicate [2] 31.15; 38.24
ephod (1) [2] 29.5; 39.2
High Priest 28.15; Lev 4.3
Holy Place 31.11; 39.1
incense [4] 31.8; 37.25
light (1) [2] 33.18; 40.34
need 22.11; 36.1
offer [7] 34.15; 36.3
plan 33.13; Num 33.56
power 32.11; Lev 6.18
priest [3] 32.29; 38.21
rest (1) 31.13; 39.21
Sabbath 31.13; Lev 19.3
sacred [2] 34.13; 36.1
serve 33.13; 36.19
solemn 32.13; Deut 1.34
teach 18.20; Lev 10.11
Tent (2) (of the Lord's presence) [4] 34.34; 36.1
understand 31.3; 36.1
wish [2] 25.2; Lev 27.13
worship (1) (of God) 34.8; Lev 9.5

34.22: Lev 23.15-21, 39.43; Num 28.26-31 **34.25:** Ex 12.10 **34.26:** Deut 24.21, 26.2
34.29-35: 2 Cor 3.7-16 **35.2:** Ex 20.8-11, 23.12, 31.15, 34.21; Lev 23.3; Deut 5.12-14

offering to the LORD for making the **Tent** of the LORD's presence. They brought everything **needed** for use in **worship** and for making the **priestly** garments. 22 All who wanted to, **both** men and women, brought decorative pins, earrings, rings, necklaces, and all kinds of gold jewellery and **dedicated** them to the LORD. 23 Everyone who had fine linen; blue, purple, or red wool; cloth of goats' hair; rams' skin dyed red; or fine leather, brought it. 24 All who were able to **contribute** silver or bronze brought their **offering** for the LORD, and all who had acacia-wood which could be used for any of the work brought it. 25 All the skilled women brought fine linen thread and thread of blue, purple, and red wool, which they had made. 26 They also made thread of goats' hair. 27 The leaders brought carnelians and other jewels to be set in the **ephod** and the breast-piece 28 and spices and oil for the lamps, for the **anointing** oil, and for the sweet-smelling **incense**. 29 All the people of Israel who wanted to brought their **offering** to the LORD for the work which he had **commanded** Moses to do.

Craftsmen for the Tent of the LORD's Presence
(Ex 31.1–11)

30 Moses said to the Israelites, "The LORD has **chosen** Bezalel, the son of Uri and grandson of Hur, from the tribe of Judah. 31 God has filled him with his **power**[l] and given him skill, ability, and **understanding** for every kind of artistic work, 32 for **planning** skilful designs and working them in gold, silver and bronze; 33 for cutting jewels to be set; for carving wood; and for every other kind of artistic work. 34 The LORD has given to him and to Oholiab son of Ahisamach, from the tribe of Dan, the ability to **teach** their crafts to others. 35 He has given them skill in all kinds of work done by engravers, designers, and weavers of fine linen; blue, purple, and red wool; and other cloth. They are able to do all kinds of work and are skilful designers.

36 "Bezalel, Oholiab, and all the other craftsmen to whom the LORD has given skill and **understanding**, who know how to make everything **needed** to build the **sacred** Tent, are to make everything just as the LORD has **commanded.**"

The People Bring Many Gifts

2 Moses called Bezalel, Oholiab, and all the other skilled men to whom the LORD had given ability and who were willing to **help**, and Moses told them to start working. 3 They received from him all the **offerings** which the Israelites had brought for constructing the **sacred Tent**. But the people of Israel continued to bring Moses their **offerings** every morning. 4 Then the skilled men who were doing the work went 5 and reported to Moses, "The people are bringing more than is **needed** for the work which the LORD **commanded** to be done."

6 So Moses sent a **command** throughout the camp that no one was to make any further **contribution** for the **sacred Tent**; so the people did not bring any more. 7 What had already been brought was more than **enough** to finish all the work.

Making the Tent of the LORD's Presence
(Ex 26.1–37)

8 The most skilled men among those doing the work made the **Tent** of the LORD's presence. They made it out of ten pieces of fine linen woven with blue, purple, and red wool and embroidered with figures of winged **creatures**. 9 Each piece was the same size, twelve metres long and two metres wide. 10 They sewed five of them together in one set and did the same with the other five. 11 They made loops of blue cloth on the edge of the outside piece in each set. 12 They put fifty loops on the first piece of the first set and fifty loops matching them on the **last** piece of the second set. 13 They made fifty gold hooks, with which to join the two sets into one piece.

14 Then they made a cover for the **Tent** out of eleven pieces of cloth made of goats' hair. 15 They made them all the same size, thirteen metres long and two metres wide. 16 They sewed five of them together in one set and the other six in another set. 17 They put fifty loops on the edge of the **last** piece of one set and fifty loops on the edge of the other set. 18 They made fifty bronze hooks to join the two sets, so as to form one cover. 19 They made two more coverings, one of rams' skin dyed red and the other of fine leather, to **serve** as an outer cover.

20 They made upright frames of acacia-wood for the **Tent**. 21 Each frame was four metres tall and sixty-six centimetres wide, 22 with two matching projections, so that the frames could be joined together. All the frames had these projections. 23 They made twenty frames for the south side 24 and forty silver bases to go under them, two bases under each

[l] power; *or* spirit.

Tent (2) (of the Lord's presence) [11] 35.11; 38.8
understand 35.31; Deut 1.13

command [3] 35.1; 38.22
contribute 35.24; Lev 7.14
creature [2] 26.1; 37.7
enough 32.19; Lev 25.21
help 33.11; 38.23
last (2) [2] 26.5; Num 2.17
need [2] 35.21; Lev 13.11
offer [2] 35.5; 38.1
sacred [3] 35.2; 37.29
serve 35.19; 38.8

frame to hold its two projections. 25 They
made twenty frames for the north side of
the **Tent** 26 and forty silver bases, two
under each frame. 27 For the back of the
Tent, on the west, they made six frames
28 and two frames for the corners.
29 These corner frames were joined at the
bottom and connected all the way to the
top. The two frames that formed the two
corners were made in this way. 30 So
there were eight frames and sixteen silver bases, two under each frame.
31 They made fifteen cross-bars of
acacia-wood, five for the frames on one
side of the **Tent**, 32 five for the frames on
the other side, and five for the frames on
the west end, at the back. 33 The middle
cross-bar, set half-way up the frames, extended from one end of the **Tent** to the
other. 34 They covered the frames with
gold and fitted them with gold rings to
hold the cross-bars, which were also
covered with gold.
35 They made a curtain of fine linen,
woven with blue, purple, and red wool
and embroidered it with figures of
winged **creatures**. 36 They made four
posts of acacia-wood to hold the curtain,
covered them with gold, and fitted them
with gold hooks. Then they made four silver bases to hold the posts. 37 For the entrance of the **Tent** they made a curtain of
fine linen woven with blue, purple, and
red wool and decorated with embroidery.
38 For this curtain they made five posts
fitted with hooks, covered their tops and
their rods with gold, and made five
bronze bases for the posts.

Making the Covenant Box
(Ex 25.10–22)

37 Bezalel made the **Covenant Box**
out of acacia-wood, 110 centimetres long, 66 centimetres wide, and 66
centimetres high. 2 He covered it with
pure gold inside and out and put a gold
border all round it. 3 He made four
carrying-rings of gold for it and attached
them to its four feet, with two rings on
each side. 4 He made carrying-poles of
acacia-wood, covered them with gold,
5 and put them through the rings on each
side of the **box**. 6 He made a lid of **pure**
gold, 110 centimetres long and 66 centimetres wide. 7 He made two winged
creatures of hammered gold, 8 one for
each end of the lid. He made them so
that they formed one piece with the lid.
9 The winged **creatures** faced **each other**
across the lid, and their outspread wings
covered it.

Making the Table for the Bread Offered to God
(Ex 25.23–30)

10 He made the table out of acacia-
wood, 88 centimetres long, 44 centimetres wide, and 66 centimetres high.
11 He covered it with **pure** gold and put a
gold border round it. 12 He made a rim 75
millimetres wide round it and put a gold
border round the rim. 13 He made four
carrying-rings of gold for it and put them
at the four corners, where the legs were.
14 The rings to hold the poles for carrying
the table were placed near the rim. 15 He
made the poles of acacia-wood and
covered them with gold. 16 He made the
dishes of **pure** gold for the table: the
plates, the **cups**, the jars, and the bowls to
be used for the **wine-offering**.

Making the Lamp-Stand
(Ex 25.31–40)

17 He made the lamp-stand of **pure**
gold. He made its base and its shaft of
hammered gold; its decorative flowers,
including buds and petals, formed one
piece with it.
18 Six branches extended from its
sides, three from each side. 19 Each of the
six branches had three decorative
flowers shaped like almond blossoms
with buds and petals. 20 The shaft of the
lamp-stand had four decorative flowers
shaped like almond blossoms with buds
and petals. 21 There was one bud below
each of the three pairs of branches.
22 The buds, the branches, and the lamp-
stand were a single piece of **pure** hammered gold. 23 He made seven lamps for
the lamp-stand, and he made its tongs
and trays of **pure** gold. 24 He used 35 kilogrammes of **pure** gold to make the lamp-
stand and all its equipment.

Making the Altar for Burning Incense
(Ex 30.1–5)

25 He made an **altar** out of acacia-
wood, for burning **incense**. It was square,
45 centimetres long and 45 centimetres
wide, and it was 90 centimetres high. Its
projections at the four corners formed
one piece with it. 26 He covered its top, all
four sides, and its projections with **pure**
gold and put a gold border round it. 27 He
made two gold carrying-rings for it and
attached them below the border on the
two sides, to hold the poles with which it
was to be carried. 28 He made the poles of
acacia-wood and covered them with
gold.

altar 35.15; 38.1
anoint 35.8; 39.38
box *see* **Covenant Box**
Covenant Box [2] 35.12; 39.35
creature [2] 36.8; Lev 11.11
cup 25.29; 2 Sam 12.3
each other 25.20; Judg 6.29
incense [2] 35.8; 39.38
pure [10] 31.8; 39.15
sacred 36.1; 38.24
wine-offering 30.9; Lev 23.18

Making the Anointing Oil and the Incense
(Ex 30.22-38)

29 He also made the **sacred anointing**
oil and the **pure** sweet-smelling **incense**,
mixed like perfume.

Making the Altar for Burning Offerings
(Ex 27.1-8)

altar [9] 37.25; 39.38
command 36.1; 39.1
commandment 34.28; 40.3
community 35.1; Lev 4.13
dedicate [2] 35.2; 39.30
direct Num 4.28
help 36.2; Lev 19.16
Levites 32.26; Lev 25.32
offer 36.3; 39.36
priest 35.19; 39.1
require 30.13; Lev 5.1
sacred [2] 37.29; 39.30
serve 36.19; 39.1
tablet 34.1; 39.35
Tent (2) (of the Lord's presence) [8] 36.1; 39.32

38 For burning **offerings**, he made
an **altar** out of acacia-wood. It
was square, 2.2 metres long and 2.2
metres wide, and it was 1.3 metres high.
2 He made the projections at the top of
the four corners, so that they formed one
piece with the **altar**. He covered it all
with bronze. 3 He also made all the equipment for the **altar**: the pans, the shovels,
the bowls, the hooks, and the firepans.
All this equipment was made of bronze.
4 He made a bronze grating and put it under the rim of the **altar**, so that it
reached half-way up the **altar**. 5 He made
four carrying-rings and put them on the
four corners. 6 He made carrying-poles of
acacia-wood, covered them with bronze,
7 and put them in the rings on each side
of the **altar**. The **altar** was made of
boards and was hollow.

Making the Bronze Basin
(Ex 30.18)

8 He made the bronze basin and its
bronze base out of the mirrors belonging
to the women who **served** at the entrance of the **Tent** of the LORD's presence.

The Enclosure for the Tent of the LORD's Presence
(Ex 27.9-19)

9 For the **Tent** of the LORD's presence
he made the enclosure out of fine linen
curtains. On the south side the curtains
were 44 metres long, 10 supported by
twenty bronze posts in twenty bronze
bases, with hooks and rods made of silver. 11 The enclosure was the same on the
north side. 12 On the west side there were
curtains 22 metres long, with ten posts
and ten bases and with hooks and rods
made of silver. 13 On the east side, where
the entrance was, the enclosure was also
22 metres wide. 14-15 On each side of the
entrance there were 6.6 metres of curtains, with three posts and three bases.
16 All the curtains round the enclosure
were made of fine linen. 17 The bases for
the posts were made of bronze, and the
hooks, the rods, and the covering of the
tops of the posts were made of silver. All
the posts round the enclosure were connected with silver rods. 18 The curtain for
the entrance of the enclosure was made
of fine linen woven with blue, purple, and
red wool and decorated with embroidery.
It was 9 metres long and 2 metres high,
like the curtains of the enclosure. 19 It
was supported by four posts in four
bronze bases. Their hooks, the covering
of their tops, and their rods were made of
silver. 20 All the pegs for the **Tent** and for
the surrounding enclosure were made of
bronze.

Metals Used in the Tent of the LORD's Presence

21 Here is a list of the amounts of the
metals used in the **Tent** of the LORD's
presence, where the two stone **tablets**
were kept on which the Ten **Commandments** were written. The list was ordered
by Moses and made by the **Levites** who
worked under the **direction** of Ithamar
son of Aaron the **priest**.
22 Bezalel, the son of Uri and grandson of Hur, from the tribe of Judah, made
everything that the LORD had **commanded**. 23 His **helper**, Oholiab son of
Ahisamach, from the tribe of Dan, was
an engraver, a designer, and a weaver of
fine linen and of blue, purple, and red
wool.
24 All the gold that had been **dedicated** to the LORD for the **sacred Tent**
weighed a thousand kilogrammes,
weighed according to the official standard. 25 The silver from the census of the
community weighed 3,430 kilogrammes,
weighed according to the official standard. 26 This amount equalled the total
paid by all persons enrolled in the census, each one paying the **required**
amount, weighed according to the official standard. There were 603,550 men
twenty years old or older enrolled in the
census. 27 Of the silver, 3,400 kilogrammes
were used to make the hundred bases for
the **sacred Tent** and for the curtain, 34
kilogrammes for each base. 28 With the
remaining 30 kilogrammes of silver
Bezalel made the rods, the hooks for the
posts, and the covering for their tops.
29 The bronze which was **dedicated** to the
LORD amounted to 2,425 kilogrammes.
30 With it he made the bases for the entrance of the **Tent** of the LORD's presence, the bronze **altar** with its bronze
grating, all the equipment for the **altar**,
31 the bases for the surrounding enclosure
and for the entrance of the enclosure,
and all the pegs for the **Tent** and the
surrounding enclosure.

37.29: Ex 30.22-38 **38.25-26:** Ex 30.11-16 **38.26:** Mt 17.24

altar [2] 38.1; 40.5
anoint 37.29; 40.9
bind 28.32; Num 6.5
bless 32.29; Lev 9.22
bread 35.13; 40.23
command [10] 38.22; 40.16
complete Gen 2.1; Lev 8.33
Covenant Box 37.1; 40.3
dedicate [2] 38.24; 40.9
ephod (1) [10] 35.9; Lev 8.7
Holy Place [2] 35.19; Lev 16.2
incense 37.25; 40.5
keep from 28.32; Num 24.11
offer 38.1; 40.6
priest [4] 38.21; 40.13
pure [4] 37.2; Lev 8.15
represent [2] 28.12; Lev 2.13
rest (1) 35.2; Lev 23.3
sacred [2] 38.24; 40.9
serve 38.8; 40.13
sign (1) 31.13; Lev 8.9
tablet 38.21; 40.20
Tent (2) (of the Lord's presence) [5] 38.8; 40.2

Making the Garments for the Priests
(Ex 28.1–14)

39 With the blue, purple, and red
wool they made the magnificent
garments which the **priests** were to wear
when they **served** in the **Holy Place**.
They made the **priestly** garments for
Aaron, as the LORD had **commanded**
Moses.
2 They made the **ephod** of fine linen;
blue, purple, and red wool; and gold
thread. 3 They hammered out sheets of
gold and cut them into thin strips to be
worked into the fine linen and into the
blue, purple, and red wool. 4 They made
two shoulder-straps for the **ephod** and
attached them to its sides, so that it could
be fastened. 5 The finely woven belt,
made of the same materials, was
attached to the **ephod** so as to form one
piece with it, as the LORD had **commanded** Moses. 6 They prepared the carnelians and mounted them in gold set-
tings; they were skilfully engraved with
the names of the twelve sons of Jacob.
7 They put them on the shoulder-straps of
the **ephod** to **represent** the twelve tribes
of Israel, just as the LORD had **commanded** Moses.

Making the Breast-Piece
(Ex 28.15–30)

8 They made the breast-piece of the
same materials as the **ephod** and with
similar embroidery. 9 It was square and
folded double, 22 centimetres long and 22
centimetres wide. 10 They mounted four
rows of precious stones on it: in the first
row they mounted a ruby, a topaz, and a
garnet; 11 in the second row, an emerald,
a sapphire, and a diamond; 12 in the third
row, a turquoise, an agate, and an
amethyst; 13 and in the fourth row, a
beryl, a carnelian, and a jasper. These
were mounted in gold settings. 14 Each of
the twelve stones had engraved on it the
name of one of the sons of Jacob, in order to **represent** the twelve tribes of
Israel. 15 For the breast-piece they made
chains of **pure** gold, twisted like cords.
16 They made two gold settings and two
gold rings and attached the two rings to
the upper corners of the breast-piece.
17 They fastened the two gold cords to the
two rings 18 and fastened the other two
ends of the cords to the two settings and
in this way attached them in front to the
shoulder-straps of the **ephod**. 19 They
made two rings of gold and attached
them to the lower corners of the breast-
piece, on the inside edge next to the
ephod. 20 They made two more gold rings
and attached them to the lower part of
the front of the two shoulder straps of the
ephod, near the seam and above the
finely woven belt. 21 Just as the LORD had
commanded Moses, they tied the rings of
the breast-piece to the rings of the **ephod**
with a blue cord, so that the breast-piece
rested above the belt and did not come
loose.

Making the Other Priestly Garments
(Ex 28.31–43)

22 The robe that goes under the **ephod**
was made entirely of blue wool. 23 The
hole for the head was reinforced with a
woven **binding** to **keep it from** tearing.
24-26 All round its lower hem they put
pomegranates of fine linen and of blue,
purple, and red wool, alternating with
bells of **pure** gold, just as the LORD had
commanded Moses.
27 They made the shirts for Aaron and
his sons, 28 and the turban, the caps, the
linen shorts, 29 and the sash of fine linen
and of blue, purple, and red wool, decorated with embroidery, as the LORD had
commanded Moses. 30 They made the
ornament, the **sacred sign** of **dedication**,
out of **pure** gold, and they engraved on it
"**Dedicated to the LORD.**" 31 They tied it to
the front of the turban with a blue cord,
just as the LORD had **commanded** Moses.

The Completion of the Work
(Ex 35.10–19)

32 All the work on the **Tent** of the
LORD's presence was finally **completed**.
The Israelites made everything just as
the LORD had **commanded** Moses. 33 They
brought to Moses the **Tent** and all its
equipment, its hooks, its frames, its cross-
bars, its posts, and its bases; 34 the covering of rams' skin dyed red; the covering
of fine leather; the curtain; 35 the
Covenant Box containing the stone **tab**-
lets, its poles, and its lid; 36 the table and
all its equipment, and the **bread offered**
to God; 37 the lamp-stand of **pure** gold, its
lamps, all its equipment, and the oil for
the lamps; 38 the gold **altar**; the **anointing**
oil; the sweet-smelling **incense**; the curtain for the entrance of the **Tent**; 39 the
bronze **altar** with its bronze grating, its
poles, and all its equipment; the wash-
basin and its base; 40 the curtains for the
enclosure and its posts and bases; the
curtain for the entrance of the enclosure
and its ropes; the pegs for the **Tent**; all
the equipment to be used in the **Tent**;
41 and the magnificent garments the
priests were to wear in the **Holy Place**—
the sacred clothes for Aaron the **priest**
and for his sons. 42 The Israelites had
done all the work just as the LORD had

commanded Moses. 43 Moses examined everything and saw that they had made it all just as the LORD had **commanded**. So Moses **blessed** them.

Setting Up and Dedicating the Tent of the LORD's Presence

40 The LORD said to Moses, 2 "On the first day of the first month set up the **Tent** of the LORD's presence. 3 Place in it the **Covenant Box** containing the Ten **Commandments** and put the curtain in front of it. 4 Bring in the table and place the equipment on it. Also bring in the lamp-stand and set up the lamps on it. 5 Put the gold **altar** for burning **incense** in front of the **Covenant Box** and hang the curtain at the entrance of the **Tent**. 6 Put in front of the **Tent** the **altar** for burning **offerings**. 7 Put the wash-basin between the **Tent** and the **altar** and fill it with water. 8 Put up the surrounding enclosure and hang the curtain at its entrance.

9 "Then **dedicate** the **Tent** and all its equipment by **anointing** it with the **sacred** oil, and it will be **holy**. 10 Next, **dedicate** the **altar** and all its equipment by **anointing** it, and it will be completely **holy**. 11 Also **dedicate** the wash-basin and its base in the same way.

12 "Bring Aaron and his sons to the entrance of the **Tent**, and tell them to take a **ritual** bath. 13 Dress Aaron in the **priestly** garments, **anoint** him, and in this way **consecrate** him, so that he can **serve** me as **priest**. 14 Bring his sons and put the shirts on them. 15 Then **anoint** them, just as you anointed their father, so that they can **serve** me as **priests**. This **anointing** will make them **priests** for all time to come."

16 Moses did everything just as the LORD had **commanded**. 17 So on the first day of the first month of the second year after they left Egypt, the **Tent** of the LORD's presence was set up. 18 Moses put down its bases, set up its frames, attached its cross-bars, and put up its posts. 19 He spread out the covering over the **Tent** and put the outer covering over it, just as the LORD had **commanded**. 20 Then he took the two stone **tablets** and put them in the **Covenant Box**. He put the poles in the rings of the **box** and put the lid on it. 21 Then he put the **box** in the **Tent** and hung up the curtain. In this way he screened off the **Covenant Box**, just as the LORD had **commanded**.

22 He put the table in the **Tent**, on the north side outside the curtain, 23 and placed on it the **bread offered** to the LORD, just as the LORD had **commanded**. 24 He put the lamp-stand in the **Tent**, on the south side, opposite the table, 25 and there in the LORD's **presence** he lit the lamps, just as the LORD had **commanded**. 26 He put the gold **altar** in the **Tent**, in front of the curtain, 27 and burnt the sweet-smelling **incense**, just as the LORD had **commanded**. 28 He hung the curtain at the entrance of the **Tent**, 29 and there in front of the curtain he placed the **altar** for burning **offerings**. On it he **sacrificed** the **burnt-offering** and the **grain-offering**, just as the LORD had **commanded**. 30 He put the wash-basin between the **Tent** and the **altar** and filled it with water. 31 Moses, Aaron, and his sons washed their hands and their feet there 32 whenever they went into the **Tent** or to the **altar**, just as the LORD had **commanded**. 33 Moses set up the enclosure round the **Tent** and the **altar** and hung the curtain at the entrance of the enclosure. So he finished all the work.

The Cloud over the Tent of the LORD's Presence

(Num 9.15–23)

34 Then the **cloud** covered the **Tent** and the **dazzling light** of the LORD's **presence** filled it. 35 Because of this, Moses could not go into the **Tent**. 36 The Israelites moved their camp to another place only when the **cloud** lifted from the **Tent**. 37 As long as the **cloud** stayed there, they did not move their camp. 38 During all their wanderings they could see the **cloud** of the LORD's **presence** over the **Tent** during the day and a fire burning above it during the night.

40.34: 1 Kgs 8.10–11; Is 6.4; Ezek 43.4–5; Rev 15.8

LEVITICUS

INTRODUCTION

Leviticus contains regulations for worship and religious ceremonies in ancient Israel, and for the priests who were responsible for carrying out these instructions.

The main theme of the book is the holiness of God and the ways in which his people were to worship and live so as to maintain their relationship with him, "the holy God of Israel."

The best known words from the book, found in 19.18, are those which Jesus called the second great commandment: "Love your neighbour as you love yourself."

Outline of Contents

---

accept [2] Ex 34.9; 7.18
altar [11] Ex 40.5; 2.2
ash Ex 27.3; 4.12
blood [3] Ex 30.10; 3.2
body Ex 13.19; 10.4
burnt-offering [2] Ex 40.29; 3.5
dove Gen 15.9; 5.7
food-offering [3] Ex 30.20; 2.2
observe Ex 30.21; 4.2
offer [5] Ex 40.6; 2.1
please [3] Ex 34.9; 2.2
present (1) [4] Gen 47.2; 2.1
priest [7] Ex 40.13; 2.2
sacrifice [5] Ex 40.29; 4.3
sheep [2] Ex 34.3; 3.6
take away (sin) Ex 29.14; 4.21
Tent (2) (of the Lord's presence) [3] Ex 40.2; 3.2

Sacrifices Burnt Whole

1 The LORD called to Moses from the
Tent of the LORD's presence and
gave him the following rules 2 for the
Israelites to **observe** when they **offer**
their sacrifices.
When anyone **offers** an animal
sacrifice, it may be one of his cattle or
one of his **sheep** or goats. 3 If he is
offering one of his cattle as a **burnt-offering**, he must bring a bull without any
defects. He must **present** it at the
entrance of the **Tent** of the LORD's
presence so that the LORD will **accept**
him. 4 The man shall put his hand on its
head, and it will be **accepted** as a
sacrifice to **take away** his sins. 5 He shall
kill the bull there, and the Aaronite
priests shall **present** the **blood** to the
LORD and then throw it against all four
sides of the **altar** which is at the entrance
of the **Tent**. 6 Then he shall skin the
animal and cut it up, 7 and the **priests**
shall arrange firewood on the **altar** and
light it. 8 They shall put on the fire the
pieces of the animal, including the head
and the fat. 9 The man must wash the
internal organs and the hind legs, and
the officiating **priest** will burn the whole
sacrifice on the **altar**. The smell of this
food-offering is **pleasing** to the LORD.
10 If the man is **offering** one of his
sheep or goats, it must be a male without
any defects. 11 He shall kill it on the north
side of the **altar**, and the **priests** shall
throw its **blood** on all four sides of the
altar. 12 After the man cuts it up, the
officiating **priest** shall put on the fire all
the parts, including the head and the fat.
13 The man must wash the internal
organs and the hind legs, and the **priest**
will **present** the **sacrifice** to the LORD and
burn all of it on the **altar**. The smell of
this **food-offering** is **pleasing** to the LORD.
14 If the man is **offering** a bird as a
burnt-offering, it must be a **dove** or a
pigeon. 15 The **priest** shall **present** it at
the **altar**, wring its neck, and burn its
head on the **altar**. Its **blood** shall be
drained out against the side of the **altar**.
16 He shall remove the crop and its
contents and throw them away on the
east side of the **altar** where the **ashes** are
put. 17 He shall take hold of its wings and
tear its **body** open, without tearing the
wings off, and then burn it whole on the
altar. The smell of this **food-offering** is
pleasing to the LORD.

Grain-Offerings

2 When anyone **presents** an **offering**
of grain to the LORD, he must first
grind it into flour. He must put olive-oil
and **incense** on it 2 and bring it to the
Aaronite **priests**. The officiating **priest**
shall take a handful of the flour and oil
and all of the **incense** and burn it on the
altar as a token that it has all been
offered to the LORD. The smell of this
food-offering is **pleasing** to the LORD.
3 The rest of the **grain-offering** belongs to
the **priests**; it is very **holy**, since it is
taken from the food **offered** to the LORD.
4 If the **offering** is **bread** baked in an
oven, it must be made **without yeast**. It

altar [4] 1.5; 3.2
bread [3] Ex 40.23; 6.16
covenant Ex 34.10; 26.9
food-offering [3] 1.9; 3.3
grain-offering [3] Ex 40.29; 5.11
harvest [2] Ex 34.21; 19.9
holy [2] Ex 40.9; 6.16
incense [4] Ex 40.5; 4.7
offer [16] 1.2; 3.1
please [2] 1.9; 3.5
present (1) [4] 1.3; 3.3
priest [7] 1.5; 3.2
represent Ex 39.7; Num 17.3
serve Ex 40.13; 6.22

unleavened [2] Ex 34.18; 6.16
yeast [4] Ex 34.25; 6.16

may be thick loaves made of flour mixed with olive-oil or biscuits brushed with olive-oil.

5 If the **offering** is **bread** cooked on a griddle, it is to be made of flour mixed with olive-oil but **without yeast**. 6 Crumble it up and pour the oil on it when you **present** it as an **offering**.

7 If the **offering** is **bread** cooked in a pan, it is to be made of flour and olive-oil. 8 Bring it as an **offering** to the LORD and **present** it to the **priest**, who will take it to the **altar**. 9 The **priest** will take part of it as a token that it has all been **offered** to the LORD, and he will burn it on the **altar**. The smell of this **food-offering** is **pleasing** to the LORD. 10 The rest of the **offering** belongs to the **priests**; it is very **holy**, since it is taken from the food **offered** to the LORD.

11 None of the **grain-offerings** which you **present** to the LORD may be made with **yeast**; you must never use **yeast** or honey in food **offered** to the LORD. 12 An **offering** of the first corn that you **harvest** each year shall be brought to the LORD, but it is not to be burnt on the **altar**. 13 Put salt on every **grain-offering**, because salt **represents** the **covenant** between you and God. (You must put salt on all your **offerings**.) 14 When you bring to the LORD an **offering** of the first corn **harvested**, **offer** roasted grain or ground meal. 15 Add olive-oil and put **incense** on it. 16 The **priest** will burn that part of the meal and oil that is to **serve** as a token, and also all the **incense**, as a **food-offering** to the LORD.

Fellowship-Offerings

altar [6] 2.2; 4.7
best [3] Ex 29.2; 4.9
blood [4] 1.5; 4.5
burnt-offering 1.3; 4.10
fellowship-offering [2] Ex 32.6; 4.10
food-offering [6] 2.2; 4.35
offer [3] 2.1; 4.21
please [2] 2.2; 4.31
present (1) [3] 2.1; 4.3
priest [6] 2.2; 4.10
sheep [2] 1.2; 4.32
Tent (2) (of the Lord's presence) [3] 1.1; 4.4

3 When anyone **offers** one of his cattle as a **fellowship-offering**, it is to be a bull or a cow without any defects. 2 The man shall put his hand on the head of the animal and kill it at the entrance of the **Tent** of the LORD's presence. The Aaronite **priests** shall throw the **blood** against all four sides of the **altar** 3 and **present** the following parts of the animal as a **food-offering** to the LORD: all the fat on the internal organs, 4 the kidneys and the fat on them, and the **best** part of the liver. 5 The **priests** shall burn all this on the **altar** along with the **burnt-offerings**. The smell of this **food-offering** is **pleasing** to the LORD.

6 If a **sheep** or goat is used as a **fellowship-offering**, it may be male or female, but it must be without any defects. 7 If a man **offers** a **sheep**, 8 he shall put his hand on its head and kill it in front of the **Tent**. The **priests** shall throw its **blood** against all four sides of the **altar** 9 and **present** the following parts of the animal as a **food-offering** to the LORD: the fat, the entire fat tail cut off near the backbone, all the fat covering the internal organs, 10 the kidneys and the fat on them, and the **best** part of the liver. 11 The officiating **priest** shall burn all this on the **altar** as a **food-offering** to the LORD.

12 If a man **offers** a goat, 13 he shall put his hand on its head and kill it in front of the **Tent**. The **priests** shall throw its **blood** against all four sides of the **altar** 14 and **present** the following parts as a **food-offering** to the LORD: all the fat on the internal organs, 15 the kidneys and the fat on them, and the **best** part of the liver. 16 The **priest** shall burn all this on the **altar** as a **food-offering** **pleasing** to the LORD. All the fat belongs to the LORD. 17 No Israelite may eat any fat or any **blood**; this is a rule to be kept for ever by all Israelites wherever they live.

Offerings for Unintentional Sins

altar [18] 3.2; 5.9
ash 1.16; 6.10
best 3.4; 7.4
blood [9] 3.2; 5.9
burnt-offering [4] 3.5; 5.7
clean Gen 35.2; 6.11
command [5] Ex 40.16; 5.17
community [4] Ex 38.25; 8.3
fellowship-offering [4] 3.1; 6.12
flesh Ex 29.14; 6.27
food-offering 3.3; 5.12
forgive [4] Ex 34.7; 5.10
guilty [4] Ex 23.1; 5.2
High Priest [3] Ex 35.9; 6.22
incense [2] 2.1; 5.11
intend [4] Ex 21.8; 19.12
observe 1.2; 16.29
offer [8] 3.1; 5.6
please 3.5; 6.15
presence Ex 40.25; 9.6
present (1) 3.3; 6.14
priest [7] 3.2; 5.6
sacred Ex 40.9; 5.15
sacrifice [7] 1.2; 5.6
sheep [2] 3.6; 5.6
sin-offering [3] 5.1
sprinkle [2] Ex 30.36; 5.9
take away (sin) [2] 1.4; 5.9
Tent (2) (of the Lord's presence) [8] 3.2; 6.16

4 The LORD **commanded** Moses 2 to tell the people of Israel that anyone who sinned and broke any of the LORD's **commands** without **intending** to, would have to **observe** the following rules.

3 If it is the **High Priest** who sins and so brings **guilt** on the people, he shall **present** a young bull without any defects and **sacrifice** it to the LORD for his sin. 4 He shall bring the bull to the entrance of the **Tent**, put his hand on its head, and kill it there in the LORD's **presence**. 5 Then the **High Priest** shall take some of the bull's **blood** and carry it into the **Tent**. 6 He shall dip his finger in the **blood** and **sprinkle** it in front of the **sacred** curtain seven times. 7 Then he shall put some of the **blood** on the projections at the corners of the **incense-altar** in the **Tent**. He shall pour out the rest of the **blood** at the base of the **altar** used for burning **sacrifices**, which is at the entrance of the **Tent**. 8 From this bull he shall take all the fat, the fat on the internal organs, 9 the kidneys and the fat on them, and the **best** part of the liver. 10 The **priest** shall take this fat and burn it on the **altar** used for the **burnt-offerings**, just as he does with the fat from the animal killed for the **fellowship-offering**. 11 But he shall take its skin, all its **flesh**, its head, its legs, and its internal organs including the intestines, 12 carry it all outside the camp to the ritually **clean** place where the **ashes** are poured out, and there he shall burn it on a wood fire.

13 If it is the whole **community** of Israel that sins and becomes **guilty** of

breaking one of the LORD's commands
without intending to, 14 then as soon as
the sin becomes known, the community
shall bring a young bull as a sin-offering.
They shall bring it to the Tent of the
LORD's presence; 15 the leaders of the
community shall put their hands on its
head, and it shall be killed there. 16 The
High Priest shall take some of the bull's
blood into the Tent, 17 dip his finger in it,
and sprinkle it in front of the curtain
seven times. 18 He shall put some of the
blood on the projections at the corners of
the incense-altar inside the Tent and
pour out the rest of it at the base of the
altar used for burning sacrifices, which is
at the entrance of the Tent. 19 Then he
shall take all its fat and burn it on the
altar. 20 He shall do the same thing with
this bull as he does with the bull for the
sin-offering, and in this way he shall
make the sacrifice for the people's sin,
and they will be forgiven. 21 Then he shall
take the bull outside the camp and burn
it, just as he burns the bull offered for his
own sin. This is an offering to take away
the sin of the community.

22 If it is a ruler who sins and becomes
guilty of breaking one of the LORD's
commands without intending to, 23 then
as soon as his attention is called to the
sin, he shall bring as his offering a male
goat without any defects. 24 He shall put
his hand on its head and kill it on the
north side of the altar, where the animals
for the burnt-offerings are killed. This is
an offering to take away sin. 25 The priest
shall dip his finger in the blood of the
animal, put it on the projections at the
corners of the altar, and pour out the rest
of it at the base of the altar. 26 Then he
shall burn all its fat on the altar, just as
he burns the fat of the animals killed for
the fellowship-offerings. In this way the
priest shall offer the sacrifice for the sin
of the ruler, and he will be forgiven.

27 If it is one of the common people
who sins and becomes guilty of breaking
one of the LORD's commands without
intending to, 28 then as soon as his
attention is called to the sin, he shall
bring as his offering a female goat without any defects. 29 He shall put his hand
on its head and kill it on the north side of
the altar, where the animals for the
burnt-offerings are killed. 30 The priest
shall dip his finger in the blood of the
animal, put it on the projections at the
corners of the altar, and pour out the rest
of it at the base of the altar. 31 Then he
shall remove all its fat, just as the fat is
removed from the animals killed for the
fellowship-offerings, and he shall burn it
on the altar so that the smell pleases the
LORD. In this way the priest shall offer
the sacrifice for the man's sin, and he
will be forgiven.

32 If a man brings a sheep as a sin-
offering, it must be a female without any
defects. 33 He shall put his hand on its
head and kill it on the north side of the
altar, where the animals for the burnt-
offerings are killed. 34 The priest shall dip
his finger in the blood of the animal, put
it on the projections at the corners of the
altar, and pour out the rest of it at the
base of the altar. 35 Then he shall remove
all its fat, just as the fat is removed from
the sheep killed for the fellowship-
offerings, and he shall burn it on the altar
along with the food-offerings given to the
LORD. In this way the priest shall offer
the sacrifice for the man's sin, and he
will be forgiven.

Cases Requiring Sin-Offerings

5 Sin-offerings are required in the
following cases.

If someone is officially summoned to
give evidence in court and does not give
information about something he has
seen or heard, he must suffer the
consequences.

2 If someone unintentionally touches
anything ritually unclean, such as a dead
animal, he is unclean and guilty as soon
as he realizes what he has done.

3 If someone unintentionally touches
anything of human origin that is unclean,
whatever it may be, he is guilty as soon
as he realizes what he has done.

4 If someone makes a careless vow,
no matter what it is about, he is guilty as
soon as he realizes what he has done.

5 When a person is guilty, he must
confess the sin, 6 and as the penalty for
his sin he must bring to the LORD a
female sheep or goat as an offering. The
priest shall offer the sacrifice for the
man's sin.

7 If a man cannot afford a sheep or a
goat, he shall bring to the LORD as the
payment for his sin two doves or two
pigeons, one for a sin-offering and the
other for a burnt-offering. 8 He shall bring
them to the priest, who will first offer the
bird for the sin-offering. He will break its
neck without pulling off its head 9 and
sprinkle some of its blood against the
side of the altar. The rest of the blood
will be drained out at the base of the
altar. This is an offering to take away sin.
10 Then he shall offer the second bird as a

altar [3] 4.7; 6.9
blood [2] 4.5; 6.27
burnt-offering [2] 4.10; 6.9
command 4.1; 6.8
confess Gen 41.9; 16.21
court (1) Ex 23.6; Deut 22.15
dead Ex 21.34; 11.8
determine [2] Ex 32.22; 6.6
dove [2] 1.14; 12.6
evidence Ex 23.1; Num 35.30
fail [2] Ex 34.7; Num 14.18
food-offering 4.35; 6.16
forgive [4] 4.20; 6.7
grain-offering [2] 2.3; 6.14
guilty [5] 4.3; 6.4
human Ex 13.15; 27.28
incense 4.7; 6.15
offer [11] 4.21; 6.2
priest [9] 4.10; 6.6
regulation [2] Ex 12.43; 6.1
repayment-offering [3] 6.6
require Ex 38.26; 14.32
sacred 4.6; 8.9
sacrifice [5] 4.3; 6.7
sheep [4] 4.32; 6.6
sin-offering [5] 4.14; 6.16
sprinkle 4.6; 8.11
suffer Ex 3.7; 7.18
take away (sin) [2] 4.21; 6.30
unclean [3] Gen 7.2; 7.18
unintentional [5] Num 15.22
value [2] Gen 34.29; 6.6
vow Gen 50.25; 7.16

4.27-31: Num 15.27-28

burnt-offering, according to the regulations. In this way the priest shall offer the
sacrifice for the man's sin, and he will be
forgiven.
11 If a man cannot afford two doves or
two pigeons, he shall bring one
kilogramme of flour as a sin-offering. He
shall not put any olive-oil or any incense
on it, because it is a sin-offering, not a
grain-offering. 12 He shall bring it to the
priest, who will take a handful of it as a
token that it has all been offered to the
LORD, and he will burn it on the altar as a
food-offering. It is an offering to take
away sin. 13 In this way the priest shall
offer the sacrifice for the man's sin, and
he will be forgiven. The rest of the flour
belongs to the priest, just as in the case
of a grain-offering.

Repayment-Offerings

14 The LORD gave the following
regulations to Moses. 15 If anyone sins unintentionally by failing to hand over the
payments that are sacred to the LORD, he
shall bring as his repayment-offering to
the LORD a male sheep or goat without
any defects. Its value is to be determined
according to the official standard. 16 He
must make the payments he has failed to
hand over and must pay an additional
twenty per cent. He shall give it to the
priest, and the priest shall offer the
animal as a sacrifice for the man's sin,
and he will be forgiven.
17 If anyone sins unintentionally by
breaking any of the LORD's commands,
he is guilty and must pay the penalty.
18 He must bring to the priest as a repayment-offering a male sheep or goat
without any defects. Its value is to be
determined according to the official
standard. The priest shall offer the sacrifice for the sin which the man committed
unintentionally, and he will be forgiven.
19 It is a repayment-offering for the sin he
committed against the LORD.
6 The LORD gave the following regulations to Moses. 2 An offering is to be
made if any one sins against the LORD by
refusing to return what a fellow-Israelite
has left as a deposit or by stealing
something from him or by cheating him
3 or by lying about something that has
been lost and swearing that he did not
find it. 4-5 When a man sins in any of
these ways, he must repay whatever he
got by dishonest means. On the day he is
found guilty, he must repay the owner in
full, plus an additional twenty per cent.
6 He shall bring to the priest as his repayment-offering to the LORD a male sheep
or goat without any defects. Its value is
to be determined according to the
official standard. 7 The priest shall offer
the sacrifice for the man's sin, and he
will be forgiven.

Sacrifices Burnt Whole

8 The LORD commanded Moses 9 to
give Aaron and his sons the following
regulations for burnt-offerings. A burnt-
offering is to be left on the altar all night
long, and the fire is to be kept burning.
10 Then the priest, wearing his linen robe
and linen shorts, shall remove the greasy
ashes left on the altar and put them at
the side of the altar. 11 Then he shall
change his clothes and take the ashes
outside the camp to a ritually clean
place. 12 The fire on the altar must be
kept burning and never allowed to go
out. Every morning the priest shall put
firewood on it, arrange the burnt-offering
on it, and burn the fat of the fellowship-
offering. 13 The fire must always be kept
burning on the altar and never allowed
to go out.

Grain-Offerings

14 The following are the regulations
for grain-offerings. An Aaronite priest
shall present the grain-offering to the
LORD in front of the altar. 15 Then he shall
take a handful of the flour and oil, and
the incense on it, and burn it on the altar
as a token that all of it has been offered
to the LORD. The smell of this offering is
pleasing to the LORD. 16-17 The priests
shall eat the rest of it. It shall be made
into bread baked without yeast and eaten
in a holy place, the courtyard of the Tent
of the LORD's presence. The LORD has
given it to the priests as their part of the
food-offerings. It is very holy, like the sin-
offerings and the repayment-offerings.
18 For all time to come any of the male
descendants of Aaron may eat it as their
continuing share of the food offered to
the LORD. Anyone else who touches a
food-offering will be harmed by the
power of its holiness.
19 The LORD gave Moses the following
regulations 20 for the ordination of an
Aaronite priest. On the day he is
ordained, he shall present as an offering
to the LORD one kilogramme of flour (the
same amount as the daily grain-offering),
half in the morning and half in the
evening. 21 It is to be mixed with oil and
cooked on a griddle and then crumbled
and presented as a grain-offering, a
smell pleasing to the LORD. 22 For all time
to come this offering is to be made by

6.1-7: Num 5.5-8

every descendant of Aaron who is serving as High Priest. It shall be completely
burnt as a sacrifice to the LORD. 23 No
part of a grain-offering that a priest
makes may be eaten; all of it must be
burnt.

Sin-Offerings

24 The LORD commanded Moses 25 to
give Aaron and his sons the following
regulations for sin-offerings. The animal
for a sin-offering shall be killed on the
north side of the altar, where the animals
for the burnt offerings are killed. This is
a very holy offering. 26 The priest who
sacrifices the animal shall eat it in a holy
place, the courtyard of the Tent of the
LORD's presence. 27 Anyone or anything
that touches the flesh of the animal will
be harmed by the power of its holiness. If
any article of clothing is spattered with
the animal's blood, it must be washed in
a holy place. 28 Any clay pot in which the
meat is boiled must be broken, and if a
metal pot is used, it must be scrubbed
and rinsed with water. 29 Any male of the
priestly families may eat this offering; it
is very holy. 30 But if any of the blood is
brought into the Tent and used in the
ritual to take away sin, the animal must
not be eaten; it must be burnt.

Repayment-Offerings

7 The following are the regulations
for repayment-offerings, which are
very holy. 2 The animal for this offering is
to be killed on the north side of the altar,
where the animals for the burnt-offerings
are killed, and its blood is to be thrown
against all four sides of the altar. 3 All its
fat shall be removed and offered on the
altar: the fat tail, the fat covering the
internal organs, 4 the kidneys and the fat
on them, and the best part of the liver.
5 The priest shall burn all the fat on the
altar as a food-offering to the LORD. It is a
repayment-offering. 6 Any male of the
priestly families may eat it, but it must
be eaten in a holy place, because it is
very holy.

7 There is one regulation that applies
to both the sin-offering and the repayment-offering: the meat belongs to the
priest who offers the sacrifice. 8 The skin
of an animal offered as a burnt-offering
belongs to the priest who offers the sacrifice. 9 Every grain-offering that has been
baked in an oven or prepared in a pan or
on a griddle belongs to the priest who
has offered it to God. 10 But all uncooked
grain-offerings, whether mixed with oil
or dry, belong to all the Aaronite priests
and must be shared equally among them.

Fellowship-Offerings

11 The following are the regulations
for the fellowship-offerings presented to
the LORD. 12 If a man makes this offering
as a thank-offering to God, he shall
present, together with the animal to be
sacrificed, an offering of bread made
without yeast: either thick loaves made
of flour mixed with olive-oil or biscuits
brushed with olive-oil or cakes made of
flour mixed with olive-oil. 13 In addition,
he shall offer loaves of bread baked
without yeast. 14 He shall present one
part of each kind of bread as a special
contribution to the LORD; it belongs to
the priest who takes the blood of the
animal and throws it against the altar.
15 The flesh of the animal must be eaten
on the day it is sacrificed; none of it may
be left until the next morning.

16 If a man brings a fellowship-offering in fulfilment of a vow or as his own
freewill offering, not all of it has to be
eaten on the day it is offered, but any
that is left over may be eaten on the
following day. 17 Any meat that still
remains on the third day must be burnt.
18 If any of it is eaten on the third day,
God will not accept the man's offering.
The offering will not be counted to his
credit but will be considered unclean,
and whoever eats it will suffer the consequences. 19 If the meat comes into
contact with anything ritually unclean, it
must not be eaten, but must be burned.

Anyone who is ritually clean may eat
the meat, 20 but if anyone who is not
clean eats it, he shall no longer be considered one of God's people. 21 Also, if
anyone eats the meat of this offering
after he has touched anything ritually unclean, whether from a man or an animal,
he shall no longer be considered one of
God's people.

22 The LORD gave Moses the following
regulations 23 for the people of Israel. No
fat of cattle, sheep, or goats shall be
eaten. 24 The fat of an animal that has
died a natural death or has been killed by
a wild animal must not be eaten, but it
may be used for any other purpose.
25 Anyone who eats the fat of an animal
that may be offered as a food-offering to
the LORD will no longer be considered
one of God's people. 26 No matter where
the Israelites live, they must never use
the blood of birds or animals for food.
27 Anyone who breaks this law will no

7.26–27: Gen 9.4; Lev 17.10–14, 19.26; Deut 12.16, 23, 15.23

accept 1.3; 19.5
altar [6] 6.9; 8.11
best 4.9; 8.16
blood [4] 6.27; 8.15
bread [3] 6.16; 8.2
burnt-offering [3] 6.9; 8.18
clean [2] 6.11; 10.10
command [2] 6.8; 8.4
contribute [3] Ex 36.6; 10.14
death (1) Ex 29.29; 10.6
fellowship-offering [5] 6.12; 9.4
flesh 6.27; 8.17
food-offering [3] 6.16; 8.20
freewill 22.18
fulfil Ex 21.11; 22.18
gift [3] Ex 29.24; 8.27
God's people [4] Ex 34.9; 10.3
grain-offering [3] 6.14; 9.4
holy [2] 6.16; 10.1
law Ex 34.11; 10.9
natural 17.15
obey Ex 34.11; 18.4
offer [20] 6.2; 8.28
ordain [2] 6.20; 8.12
present (1) [4] 6.14; 8.27
priest [13] 6.6; 8.2
purpose Ex 20.7; Deut 5.11
regulation [7] 6.1; 9.16
repayment-offering [4] 6.6; 14.12
right (2) [2] Ex 29.20; 8.23
sacrifice [4] 6.7; 9.4
share 6.18; Num 10.29
sheep 6.6; 17.3
sin-offering [2] 6.16; 8.2
special [6] Ex 29.24; 8.27
suffer 5.1; 17.16
unclean [3] 5.2; 10.10
unleavened [2] 6.16; 8.2
vow 5.4; 22.18
yeast [2] 6.16; 23.6

longer be considered one of **God's people**.

28 The LORD gave Moses the following **regulations** [29]for the people of Israel. Whoever **offers** a **fellowship-offering** must bring part of it as a **special gift** to the LORD, [30]bringing it with his own hands as a **food-offering**. He shall bring the fat of the animal with its breast and **present** it as a **special gift** to the LORD. [31]The **priest** shall burn the fat on the **altar**, but the breast shall belong to the **priests**. [32]The **right** hind leg of the animal shall be given as a **special contribution** [33]to the **priest** who **offers** the **blood** and the fat of the **fellowship-offering**. [34]The breast of the animal is a **special gift**, and the **right** hind leg is a **special contribution** that the LORD has taken from the people of Israel and given to the **priests**. This is what the people of Israel must give to the **priests** for all time to come. [35]This is the part of the food **offered** to the LORD that was given to Aaron and his sons on the day they were **ordained** as **priests**. [36]On that day the LORD **commanded** the people of Israel to give them this part of the **offering**. It is a **regulation** that the people of Israel must **obey** for all time to come.

37 These, then, are the **regulations** for the **burnt-offerings**, the **grain-offerings**, the **sin-offerings**, the **repayment-offerings**, the **ordination-offerings**, and the **fellowship-offerings**. [38]There on Mount Sinai in the desert, the LORD gave these **commands** to Moses on the day he told the people of Israel to make their **offerings**.

The Ordination of Aaron and His Sons
(Ex 29.1-37)

8 The LORD said to Moses, [2]"Take Aaron and his sons to the entrance of the **Tent** of my presence and bring the **priestly** garments, the **anointing** oil, the young bull for the **sin-offering**, the two rams, and the basket of **unleavened bread**. [3]Then call the whole **community** together there."

4 Moses did as the LORD had **commanded**, and when the **community** had assembled, [5]he said to them, "What I am now about to do is what the LORD has **commanded**."

6 Moses brought Aaron and his sons forward and told them to take a **ritual** bath. [7]He put the shirt and the robe on Aaron and the sash round his waist. He put the **ephod**[a] on him and fastened it by putting its finely woven belt round his waist. [8]He put the breast-piece on him and put the Urim and Thummim[b] in it. [9]He placed the turban on his head, and on the front of it he put the gold ornament, the **sacred sign** of **dedication**, just as the LORD had **commanded** him.

10 Then Moses took the **anointing** oil and put it on the **Tent** of the LORD's presence and everything that was in it, and in this way he **dedicated** it all to the LORD. [11]He took some of the oil and **sprinkled** it seven times on the **altar** and its equipment and on the basin and its base, in order to **dedicate** them to the LORD. [12]He **ordained** Aaron by pouring some of the **anointing** oil on his head. [13]Next, Moses brought the sons of Aaron forward and put shirts on them, put sashes round their waists, and tied caps on their heads, just as the LORD had **commanded**.

14 Then Moses brought the young bull for the **sin-offering**, and Aaron and his sons put their hands on its head. [15]Moses killed it and took some of the **blood**, and with his finger put it on the projections at the corners of the **altar**, in order to **dedicate** it. He then poured out the rest of the **blood** at the base of the **altar**. In this way he **dedicated** it and **purified** it. [16]Moses took all the fat on the internal organs, the **best** part of the liver, and the kidneys with the fat on them, and burnt it all on the **altar**. [17]He took the rest of the bull, including its skin, **flesh**, and intestines, and burnt it outside the camp, just as the LORD had **commanded**.

18 Next, Moses brought the ram for the **burnt-offering**, and Aaron and his sons put their hands on its head. [19]Moses killed it and threw the **blood** on all four sides of the **altar**. [20-21]He cut the ram in pieces, washed the internal organs and the hind legs with water, and burnt the head, the fat, and all the rest of the ram on the **altar**, just as the LORD had **commanded**. This **burnt-offering** was a **food-offering**, and the smell was **pleasing** to the LORD.

22 Then Moses brought the second ram, which was for the **ordination** of **priests**, and Aaron and his sons put their hands on its head. [23]Moses killed it and took some of the **blood** and put it on the lobe of Aaron's **right** ear, on the thumb of his **right hand**, and on the big toe of his **right** foot. [24]Then he brought Aaron's sons forward and put some of the **blood** on the lobes of their **right** ears, on the

[a] EPHOD: *See Word List.*
[b] URIM AND THUMMIM: *Two objects used by the priest to determine God's will; it is not known precisely how they were used.*

altar [9] 7.2; 9.7
anoint [4] Ex 40.9; 10.7
best [2] 7.4; 9.10
blood [7] 7.2; 9.9
bread [4] 7.12; 10.12
burnt-offering [3] 7.2; 9.2
command [12] 7.36; 9.5
community [2] 4.13; 9.5
complete Ex 39.32; 9.1
consecrate Ex 40.13; 10.7
dedicate [6] Ex 40.9; 19.8
ephod (1) Ex 39.2; Judg 17.5
flesh 7.15; 13.24
food-offering [2] 7.5; 10.15
gift [2] 7.29; 9.21
offer [2] 7.2; 9.2
ordain [6] 7.35; 9.1
please [2] 6.15; 17.6

present (1) [2] 7.11; 9.7
priest [2] 7.5; 9.21
pure Ex 39.15; 12.4
right (2) [8] 7.32; 9.2
rite Ex 29.35; 9.1
ritual 6.30; 12.7
sacred 5.15; 10.4
sign (1) Ex 39.30; Num 6.6
sin-offering [2] 7.7; 9.2
special [2] 7.14; 9.21
sprinkle [2] 5.9; 14.7
take away (sin) 6.3
9.7
Tent (2) (of the Lord's presence) [5
6.16; 9.5
unleavened [2] 7.12; 10.12

thumbs of their **right hands**, and on the
big toes of their **right** feet. Moses then
threw the rest of the **blood** on all four
sides of the **altar.** 25 He took the fat, the
fat tail, all the fat covering the internal
organs, the **best** part of the liver, the
kidneys with the fat on them, and the
right hind leg. 26 Then he took one loaf of
bread from the basket of **unleavened**
bread **dedicated** to the LORD, one loaf
made with oil, and one biscuit, and he put
them on top of the fat and the **right** hind
leg. 27 He put all this food in the hands of
Aaron and his sons, and they **presented** it
as a **special gift** to the LORD. 28 Then
Moses took the food from them and burnt
it on the **altar**, on top of the **burnt-offering**, as an **ordination offering**. This was a
food-offering, and the smell was **pleasing**
to the LORD. 29 Then Moses took the
breast and **presented** it as a **special gift**
to the LORD. It was Moses' part of the
ordination ram. Moses did everything
just as the LORD had **commanded.**

30 Moses took some of the **anointing**
oil and some of the **blood** that was on the
altar and **sprinkled** them on Aaron and
his sons and on their clothes. In this way
he **consecrated** them and their clothes to
the LORD.

31 Moses said to Aaron and his sons,
"Take the meat to the entrance of the
Tent of the LORD's presence, boil it, and
eat it there with the **bread** that is in the
basket of **ordination offerings**, just as the
LORD **commanded.** 32 Burn up any meat
or **bread** that is left over. 33 You shall not
leave the entrance of the **Tent** for seven
days, until your **ordination rites** are
completed. 34 The LORD **commanded** us to
do what we have done today, in order to
take away your sin. 35 You must stay at
the entrance of the **Tent** day and night
for seven days, doing what the LORD has
commanded. If you don't, you will die.
This is what the LORD has **commanded**
me." 36 So Aaron and his sons did everything that the LORD had **commanded**
through Moses.

Aaron Offers Sacrifices

9 The day after the **ordination rites**
were **completed**, Moses called
Aaron and his sons and the leaders of
Israel. 2 He said to Aaron, "Take a young
bull and a ram without any defects and
offer them to the LORD, the bull for a **sin-
offering** and the ram for a **burnt-offering.**
3 Then tell the people of Israel to take a
male goat for a **sin-offering**, a one-year-
old calf, and a one-year-old **lamb** without
any defects for a **burnt-offering**, 4 and a
bull and a ram for a **fellowship-offering.**
They are to **sacrifice** them to the LORD
with the **grain-offering** mixed with oil.
They must do this because the LORD will
appear to them today."

5 They brought to the front of the **Tent**
everything that Moses had **commanded,**
and the whole **community** assembled
there to **worship** the LORD. 6 Moses said,
"The LORD has **commanded** you to do all
this, so that the **dazzling light** of his
presence can appear to you." 7 Then he
said to Aaron, "Go to the **altar** and **offer**
the **sin-offering** and the **burnt-offering** to
take away your sins and the sins of the
people. **Present** this **offering** to **take
away** the sins of the people, just as the
LORD **commanded.**"

8 Aaron went to the **altar** and killed
the young bull which was for his own **sin-
offering.** 9 His sons brought him the **blood,**
and he dipped his finger in it, put some of
it on the projections at the corners of the
altar, and poured out the rest of it at the
base of the **altar.** 10 Then he burnt on the
altar the fat, the kidneys, and the **best**
part of the liver, just as the LORD had
commanded Moses. 11 But he burnt the
meat and the skin outside the camp.

12 He killed the animal which was for
his own **burnt-offering.** His sons brought
him the **blood**, and he threw it on all four
sides of the **altar.** 13 They handed him the
head and the other pieces of the animal,
and he burnt them on the **altar.** 14 Then
he washed the internal organs and the
hind legs and burnt them on the **altar** on
top of the rest of the **burnt-offering.**

15 After that, he **presented** the
people's **offerings.** He took the goat that
was to be **offered** for the people's sins,
killed it, and **offered** it, as he had done
with his own **sin-offering.** 16 He also
brought the animal for the **burnt-offering**
and **offered** it according to the
regulations. 17 He **presented** the **grain-
offering** and took a handful of flour and
burnt it on the **alter.** (This was in addition to the daily **burnt-offering.**) 18 He
killed the bull and the ram as a **fellowship-offering** for the people. His sons
brought him the **blood**, and he threw it on
all four sides of the **altar.** 19 Aaron put the
fat parts of the bull and the ram 20 on top
of the breasts of the animals and carried
it all to the **altar.** He burnt the fat on the
altar 21 and **presented** the breasts and the
right hind legs as the **special gift** to the
LORD for the **priests**, as Moses had
commanded.

22 When Aaron had finished all the
sacrifices, he **raised** his hands over the

9.7: Heb 7.27 **9.18:** Lev 3.1-11 **9.22:** Num 6.22-26

altar [13] 8.11; 10.12
best 8.16; 23.40
bless [2] Ex 39.43; 25.21
blood [3] 8.15; 10.18
bow (2) Ex 34.8; Num 14.5
burnt-offering [8] 8.18; 10.19
command [5] 8.4; 10.1
community 8.3; 10.6
complete 8.33; 12.4
dazzling [2] Ex 40.34; Num 14.10

fellowship-offering [2] 7.11; 10.14
gift 8.27; 10.14
grain-offering [2] 7.9; 10.12
lamb Ex 34.20; 12.6
light (1) [2] Ex 40.34; 13.21
offer [7] 8.28; 10.12
ordain 8.12; 16.32
presence [2] 4.4; 10.2
present (1) [4] 8.27; 10.1
priest 8.2; 10.14
raise Ex 10.12; Num 20.11
regulation 7.1; 11.1
right (2) 8.23; 14.14
rite 8.33; Mic 1.7
sacrifice [2] 7.7; 10.18
sin-offering [5] 8.2; 10.16
special 8.27; 10.14
take away (sin) [2] 8.34; 10.17
Tent (2) (of the Lord's presence) [2] 8.2; 10.4
worship (1) (of God) Ex 35.21; 19.30

people and **blessed** them, and then stepped down. 23 Moses and Aaron went into the **Tent** of the LORD's presence, and when they came out, they **blessed** the people, and the **dazzling light** of the LORD's **presence** appeared to all the people. 24 Suddenly the LORD sent a fire, and it consumed the **burnt-offering** and the fat parts on the **altar**. When the people saw it, they all shouted and **bowed down** with their faces to the ground.

The Sin of Nadab and Abihu

10 Aaron's sons Nadab and Abihu, each took his fire-pan, put live coals in it, added **incense**, and **presented** it to the LORD. But this fire was not **holy**, because the LORD had not **commanded** them to **present** it. 2 Suddenly the LORD sent fire, and it burnt them **to death** there in the **presence** of the LORD. 3 Then Moses said to Aaron, "This is what the LORD was speaking about when he said, 'All who **serve** me must **respect** my **holiness**; I will **reveal** my **glory** to **my people**.' "[c] But Aaron remained silent.

4 Moses called Mishael and Elzaphan, the sons of Uzziel, Aaron's uncle, and said to them, "Come here and carry your cousins' **bodies** away from the **sacred Tent** and put them outside the camp." 5 So they came and took hold of the clothing on the corpses and carried them outside the camp, just as Moses had **commanded**.

6 Then Moses said to Aaron and to his sons Eleazar and Ithamar, "Do not leave your hair uncombed or tear your clothes to show that you are in **mourning**. If you do, you will die, and the LORD will be **angry** with the whole **community**. But all your fellow-Israelites are allowed to **mourn** this **death** caused by the fire which the LORD sent. 7 Do not leave the entrance of the **Tent** or you will die, because you have been **consecrated** by the **anointing** oil of the LORD." So they did as Moses said.

Rules for Priests

8 The LORD said to Aaron, 9 "You and your sons are not to enter the **Tent** of my presence after drinking wine or beer; if you do, you will die. This is a **law** to be kept by all your descendants. 10 You must **distinguish** between what belongs to God and what is for general use, between what is ritually **clean** and what is **unclean**. 11 You must **teach** the people of Israel all the **laws** which I have given to you through Moses."

12 Moses said to Aaron and his two remaining sons, Eleazar and Ithamar, "Take the **grain-offering** that is left over from the food **offered** to the LORD, make **unleavened bread** with it and eat it beside the **altar**, because this **offering** is very **holy**. 13 Eat it in a **holy** place; it is the part that belongs to you and your sons from the food **offered** to the LORD. That is what the LORD **commanded** me. 14 But you and your families may eat the breast and the hind leg that are **presented** as the special **gift** and the **special contribution** to the LORD for the **priests**. You may eat them in any ritually **clean** place. These **offerings** have been given to you and your children as the part that belongs to you from the **fellowship-offerings** of the people of Israel. 15 They shall bring the hind leg and the breast at the time the fat is **presented** as a **food-offering** to the LORD. These parts belong to you and your children for ever, just as the LORD **commanded**."

16 Moses asked about the goat for the **sin-offering** and **learnt** that it had already been burnt. This made him **angry** with Eleazar and Ithamar, and he demanded, 17 "Why didn't you eat the **sin-offering** in a **sacred** place? It is very **holy**, and the LORD has given it to you in order to **take away** the sin of the **community**. 18 Since its **blood** was not brought into the **sacred tent**, you should have eaten the **sacrifice** there, as I **commanded**."

19 Aaron answered, "If I had eaten the **sin-offering** today, would the LORD have **approved**? The people **presented** their **sin-offering** to the LORD today, and they brought their **burnt-offering**, but still these **terrible** things have happened to me." 20 When Moses heard this, he was **satisfied**.

Animals That May Be Eaten
(Deut 14.3-21)

11 The Lord gave Moses and Aaron the following **regulations** 2 for the people of Israel. You may eat any land animal 3 that has divided hoofs and that also chews the cud, 4-6 but you must not eat camels, rock-badgers, or rabbits. They must be considered **unclean**; they chew the cud, but do not have divided hoofs. 7 Do not eat pigs. They must be considered **unclean**; they have divided hoofs, but do not chew the cud. 8 Do not eat these animals or even touch their **dead bodies**; they are **unclean**.

9 You may eat any kind of fish that has fins and scales, 10 but anything living

[c] I will reveal my glory to my people; *or* my people must honour me.

10.12-13: Lev 6.14-18 **10.14-15:** Lev 7.30-34 **10.17:** Lev 6.24-26

altar 9.7; 14.20
anger [2] Ex 34.6; 26.28
anoint 8.2; 21.10
approve Ex 21.22; 1 Sam 29.6
blood 9.9; 12.4
body 1.17; 11.8
bread 8.2; 23.6
burnt-offering 9.2; 12.6
clean [2] 7.19; 11.36
command [5] 9.5; 16.34
community [2] 9.5; 16.5
consecrate 8.30; 16.32
contribute 7.14; Num 5.9
death (1) 7.24; 16.1
death (3) (to death) Ex 35.2; 19.20
distinguish Ex 33.16; 11.47
fellowship-offering 9.4; 17.5
food-offering 8.20; 21.6
gift 9.21; 14.12
glory Ex 15.1; Deut 5.24
God's people 7.20; 17.3
grain-offering 9.4; 14.20
holy [5] 7.1; 11.44
incense 6.15; 16.12
law [2] 7.27; 11.46
learn Ex 18.15; Num 20.29
mourn [2] Ex 33.4; 19.28
offer [4] 9.2; 12.7
presence 9.6; 14.16
present (1) [5] 9.7; 12.7
priest 9.21; 12.6
respect Ex 20.12; 19.3
reveal Ex 5.3; Num 12.6
sacred [3] 8.9; 12.4
sacrifice 9.4; 16.6
satisfy Num 11.22
serve 6.22; 22.3
sin-offering [4] 9.2; 12.6
special 9.21; 14.12
take away (sin) 9.7; 12.7
teach Ex 35.34; Deut 1.5
Tent (2) (of the Lord's presence) [4] 9.5; 12.4
terrible Ex 32.21; Num 21.29
unclean 7.18; 11.4
unleavened 8.2; 23.6

body [10] 10.4; 13.13
clean [3] 10.10; 12.4
creature Ex 37.7; Num 7.89
dead [9] 5.2; 19.28
distinguish 10.10; 20.25
holy [2] 10.1; 12.4
law 10.9; 13.59
regulation 9.16; 12.1
seed [3] Ex 16.31; 19.19
sow Ex 23.10; 25.3
unclean [22] 10.10; 12.2

in the water that does not have fins and
scales must not be eaten. [11]Such
creatures must be considered **unclean**.
You must not eat them or even touch
their **dead bodies**. [12]You must not eat
anything that lives in the water and does
not have fins and scales.
13–19 You must not eat any of the
following birds: eagles, owls, hawks,
falcons; buzzards, vultures, crows;
ostriches; seagulls, storks, herons, pelicans, cormorants;[x] hoopoes; or bats.
20 All winged insects are **unclean**,
[21]except those that hop. [22]You may eat
locusts, crickets, or grasshoppers. [23]But
all other small things that have wings
and also crawl must be considered **unclean**.
24–28 Whoever touches the **dead
bodies** of the following animals will be
unclean until evening: all animals with
hoofs, unless their hoofs are divided and
they chew the cud, and all four-footed
animals with paws. Whoever carries
their **dead bodies** must wash his clothes,
but he will still be **unclean** until evening.
29–30 Moles, rats, mice, and lizards
must be considered **unclean**. [31]Whoever
touches them or their **dead bodies** will be
unclean until evening. [32]And if their **dead
bodies** fall on anything, it will be **unclean**.
This applies to any article of wood, cloth,
leather, or sacking, no matter what it is
used for. It shall be dipped in water, but it
will remain **unclean** until evening. [33]And
if their **bodies** fall into a clay pot, everything that is in it shall be **unclean**, and
you must break the pot. [34]Any food which
could normally be eaten, but on which
water from such a pot has been poured,
will be **unclean**, and anything drinkable
in such a pot is unclean. [35]Anything on
which the **dead bodies** fall is **unclean**; a
clay stove or oven shall be broken, [36]but
a spring or a cistern remains **clean**, although anything else that touches their
dead bodies is **unclean**. [37]If one of them
falls on seed that is going to be **sown**, the
seed remains **clean**. [38]But if the **seed** is
soaking in water and one of them falls on
it, the **seed** is **unclean**.
39 If any animal that may be eaten
dies, anyone who touches it will be **unclean** until evening. [40]And if anyone eats
any part of the animal, he must wash his
clothes, but he will still be **unclean** until
evening; anyone who carries the **dead
body** must wash his clothes, but he will
still be **unclean** until evening.
41 You must not eat any of the small
animals that move on the ground,
[42]whether they crawl, or walk on four
legs, or have many legs. [43]Do not make
yourselves **unclean** by eating any of
these. [44]I am the LORD your God, and you
must keep yourselves **holy**, because I am
holy. [45]I am the LORD who brought you
out of Egypt so that I could be your God.
You must be holy, because I am holy.
46 This, then, is the **law** about animals
and birds, about everything that lives in
the water, and everything that moves on
the ground. [47]You must be careful to
distinguish between what is ritually **clean**
and **unclean**, between animals that may
be eaten and those that may not.

The Purification of Women after Childbirth

12 The LORD gave Moses the following **regulations** [2]for the people of
Israel. For seven days after a woman
gives **birth** to a son, she is ritually **unclean**, as she is during her monthly period. [3]On the eighth day, the child shall be
circumcised. [4]Then it will be thirty-three
more days before she is ritually **clean**
from her **loss** of **blood**; she must not
touch anything that is **holy** or enter the
sacred Tent until the time of her **purification** is **completed**.
5 For fourteen days after a woman
gives **birth** to a daughter, she is ritually
unclean, as she is during her monthly
period. Then it will be sixty-six more
days before she is ritually **clean** from her
loss of **blood**.
6 When the time of her **purification** is
completed, whether for a son or daughter, she shall bring to the **priest** at the entrance of the **Tent** of the LORD's presence
a one-year-old **lamb** for a **burnt-offering**
and a pigeon or a **dove** for a **sin-offering**.
[7]The **priest** shall **present** her **offering** to
the Lord and perform the **ritual** to **take
away** her **impurity**, and she will be ritually **clean**. This, then, is what a woman
must do after giving **birth**.
8 If the woman cannot afford a **lamb**,
she shall bring two **doves** or two pigeons,
one for a **burnt-offering** and the other for
a **sin-offering**, and the **priest** shall perform the **ritual** to **take away** her impurity, and she will be ritually **clean**.

birth [3] Ex 28.10; Num 11.12
blood [2] 10.18; 14.6
burnt-offering [2] 10.19; 14.13
circumcise Ex 12.44; Josh 5.2
clean [4] 11.36; 13.6
complete [2] 9.1; Josh 5.8
dove [2] 5.7; 14.22
holy 11.44; 14.13
impure [2] 15.24
lamb [2] 9.3; 14.10
loss [2] Ex 22.5; Ps 144.14
offer 10.12; 14.11
present (1) 10.1; 14.12
priest [3] 10.14; 13.2
pure [2] 8.15; 14.2
regulation 11.1; 13.1
ritual [2] 8.6; 14.2
sacred 10.4; 20.3
sin-offering [2] 10.16; 14.13
take away (sin) [2] 10.17; 16.6
Tent (2) (of the Lord's presence) [2] 10.4; 14.11
unclean [2] 11.4; 13.3

Laws Concerning Skin-Diseases

13 The LORD gave Moses and Aaron
these **regulations**. [2]If anyone has
a sore on his skin or a boil or an in-
flammation which could develop into a
dreaded **skin-disease**, he shall be brought
to the Aaronite **priest**. [3]The **priest** shall

body 11.8; 14.9
change [3] 6.11; Num 13.16
clean [15] 12.4; 14.2
destroy Ex 34.13; 26.22
disease [17] Ex 32.35; 14.2
flesh 8.17; Num 12.12

[x] *The identification of some of the birds in verses 13-19 is uncertain.*

11.44: Lev 19.2; 1 Pet 1.16 **12.3:** Gen 17.12; Lk 2.21 **12.8:** Lk 2.24

heal [3] Ex 15.26; 14.3
law 11.46; 14.32
light (1) [3] 9.6; 24.2
need [2] Ex 36.1; 25.44
priest [43] 12.6; 14.2
regulation 12.1; 14.2
shave Gen 41.14; 14.8
turn [9] Ex 32.6; 17.10
unclean [20] 12.2; 14.36

examine the sore, and if the hairs in it
have **turned** white and the sore appears
to be deeper than the surrounding skin, it
is a dreaded **skin-disease**, and the **priest**
shall pronounce the person **unclean**. 4 But
if the sore is white and does not appear
to be deeper than the skin round it and
the hairs have not **turned** white, the
priest shall isolate the person for seven
days. 5 The **priest** shall examine him
again on the seventh day, and if in his
opinion the sore looks the same and has
not spread, he shall isolate him for another seven days. 6 The **priest** shall examine him again on the seventh day, and
if the sore has faded and has not spread,
he shall pronounce him ritually **clean**; it
is only a sore. The person shall wash his
clothes and be ritually **clean**. 7 But if the
sore spreads after the **priest** has examined him and pronounced him **clean**,
he must appear before the **priest** again.
8 The **priest** will examine him again, and
if it has spread, he shall pronounce him
unclean; it is a dreaded **skin-disease**.

9 If anyone has a dreaded **skin-**
disease, he shall be brought to the **priest**,
10 who will examine him. If there is a
white sore on his skin which **turns** the
hairs white and is full of pus, 11 it is a
chronic **skin-disease**. The **priest** shall pronounce him **unclean**; there is no **need** to
isolate him, because he is obviously **un-**
clean. 12 If the **skin-disease** spreads and
covers the person from head to foot,
13 the **priest** shall examine him again. If
he finds that it actually has covered the
whole **body**, he shall pronounce the person ritually **clean**. If his whole skin has
turned white, he is ritually **clean**. 14 But
from the moment an open sore appears,
he is **unclean**. 15 The **priest** shall examine
him again, and if he sees an open sore,
he shall pronounce him **unclean**. An open
sore means a dreaded **skin-disease**, and
the person is **unclean**. 16 But when the
sore **heals** and becomes white again, the
person shall go to the **priest**, 17 who will
examine him again. If the sore has
turned white, he is ritually clean, and the
priest shall pronounce him **clean**.

18 If anyone has a boil that has **healed**
19 and if afterwards a white swelling or a
reddish-white spot appears where the
boil was, he shall go to the **priest**. 20 The
priest shall examine him, and if the spot
seems to be deeper than the surrounding
skin and the hairs in it have **turned**
white, he shall pronounce him **unclean**. It
is a dreaded **skin-disease** that has started
in the boil. 21 But if the **priest** examines it
and finds that the hairs in it have not
turned white and that it is not deeper
than the surrounding skin, but is **light** in
colour, the **priest** shall isolate him for
seven days. 22 If the spot spreads, the
priest shall pronounce him **unclean**; he is
diseased. 23 But if it remains **unchanged**
and does not spread, it is only the scar
left from the boil, and the **priest** shall
pronounce him ritually **clean**.

24 In the case of a person who has
been burnt, if the raw **flesh** becomes
white or reddish-white, 25 the **priest** shall
examine him. If the hairs in the spot
have **turned** white and it appears deeper
than the surrounding skin, it is a dreaded
skin-disease that has started in the burn,
and the **priest** shall pronounce him **un-**
clean. 26 But if the hairs in it have not
turned white and it is not deeper than the
surrounding skin, but is **light** in colour,
the **priest** shall isolate him for seven
days. 27 The **priest** shall examine him
again on the seventh day, and if it is
spreading, it is a dreaded **skin-disease**,
and the **priest** shall pronounce him **un-**
clean. 28 But if the spot remains **un-**
changed and does not spread and is **light**
in colour, it is not a dreaded **skin-disease**.
The **priest** shall pronounce him ritually
clean, because it is only a scar from the
burn.

29 When a man or a woman has a sore
on the head or the chin, 30 the **priest** shall
examine it. If it seems to be deeper than
the surrounding skin and the hairs in it
are yellowish and thin, it is a dreaded
skin-disease, and he shall pronounce the
person **unclean**. 31 If, when the **priest** examines him, the sore does not appear to
be deeper than the surrounding skin, but
there are still no healthy hairs in it, he
shall isolate him for seven days. 32 The
priest shall examine the sore again on
the seventh day, and if it has not spread
and there are no yellowish hairs in it and
it does not seem to be deeper than the
surrounding skin, 33 the person shall
shave the head except the area round
the sore. The **priest** shall then isolate him
for another seven days. 34 On the seventh
day the **priest** shall again examine the
sore, and if it has not spread and does not
seem to be deeper than the surrounding
skin, he shall pronounce him ritually
clean. The person shall wash his clothes,
and he will be **clean**. 35 But if the sore
spreads after he has been pronounced
clean, 36 the **priest** shall examine him
again. If the sore has spread, he **need** not
look for yellowish hairs; the person is obviously **unclean**. 37 But if in the **priest's**
opinion the sore has not spread and
healthy hairs are growing in it, the sore

has **healed**, and the **priest** shall pronounce him ritually **clean**.
38 When a man or a woman has white
spots on the skin, 39 the **priest** shall examine that person. If the spots are dull
white, it is only a blemish that has
broken out on the skin; the person is ritually **clean**.
40–41 If a man loses his hair at the
back or the front of his head, this does
not make him **unclean**. 42 But if a reddish-
white sore appears on the bald spot, it is
a dreaded **skin-disease**. 43 The **priest** shall
examine him, and if there is a reddish-
white sore, 44 the **priest** shall pronounce
him **unclean**, because of the dreaded
skin-disease on his head.
45 A person who has a dreaded **skin-
disease** must wear torn clothes, leave his
hair uncombed, cover the lower part of
his face, and call out, "**Unclean,
unclean!**" 46 He remains unclean as long
as he has the **disease**, and he must live
outside the camp, away from others.

Laws Concerning Mildew

47 When there is mildew[d] on clothing,
whether wool or linen, 48 or on any piece
of linen or wool cloth or on leather or
anything made of leather, 49 if it is greenish or reddish, it is a spreading mildew
and must be shown to the **priest**. 50 The
priest shall examine it and put the object
away for seven days. 51 He shall examine
it again on the seventh day, and if the
mildew has spread, the object is **unclean**.
52 The **priest** shall burn it, because it is a
spreading mildew which must be **destroyed** by fire.
53 But if, when he examines it, the
priest finds that the mildew has not
spread on the object, 54 he shall order it
to be washed and put away for another
seven days. 55 Then he shall examine it,
and if the mildew has not **changed**
colour, even though it has not spread, it
is still **unclean**; you must burn the object,
whether the rot is on the front or the
back. 56 But if, when the **priest** examines
it again, the mildew has faded, he shall
tear it out of the clothing or leather.
57 Then, if the mildew reappears, it is
spreading again, and the owner shall
burn the object. 58 If he washes the object
and the spot disappears, he shall wash it
again, and it will be ritually **clean**.
59 This, then, is the **law** about mildew
on clothing, whether it is wool or linen,
or on linen or wool cloth or on anything
made of leather; this is how the decision
is made as to whether it is ritually **clean**
or **unclean**.

Purification after Having Skin-Diseases

14 The LORD gave Moses 2 the
following **regulations** about the
ritual purification of a person **cured** of a
dreaded **skin-disease**. On the day he is to
be pronounced **clean**, he shall be brought
to the **priest**, 3 and the **priest** shall take
him outside the camp and examine him.
If the **disease** is **healed**, 4 the **priest** shall
order two ritually **clean** birds to be
brought, together with a piece of cedar-
wood, a red cord, and a sprig of **hyssop**.
5 Then the **priest** shall order one of the
birds to be killed over a clay bowl containing fresh spring water. 6 He shall take
the other bird and dip it, together with
the cedar-wood, the red cord, and the
hyssop, in the **blood** of the bird that was
killed. 7 He shall **sprinkle** the **blood** seven
times on the person who is to be **purified**
from his **skin-disease**, and then he shall
pronounce him **clean**. He shall let the
live bird fly away over the open fields.
8 The person shall wash his clothes, **shave**
off all his hair, and have a bath; he will
then be ritually **clean**. He may enter the
camp, but he must live outside his tent
for seven days. 9 On the seventh day he
shall again **shave** his head, his beard, his
eyebrows, and all the rest of the hair on
his **body**; he shall wash his clothes and
have a bath, and then he will be ritually
clean.
10 On the eighth day he shall bring
two male **lambs** and one female lamb a
year old that are without any defects,
three kilogrammes of flour mixed with
olive-oil, and a third of a litre of olive-oil.
11 The **priest** shall take the man and these
offerings to the entrance of the **Tent** of
the LORD's presence. 12 Then the **priest**
shall take one of the male **lambs** and together with the one-third of a litre of oil
he shall **offer** it as a **repayment-offering**.
He shall **present** them as a **special gift** to
the LORD for the **priest**. 13 He shall kill the
lamb in the place where the animals for
the **sin-offerings** and the **burnt-offerings**
are killed. He must do this because the
repayment-offering, like the **sin-offering**,
belongs to the **priest** and is very **holy**.
14 The **priest** shall take some of the **blood**
of the **lamb** and put it on the lobe of the
right ear, on the thumb of the **right hand**,
and on the big toe of the **right** foot of the
man who is to be declared ritually **clean**.
15 The **priest** shall take some of the olive-
oil and pour it in the palm of his own left

altar 10.12; 16.12
blood [8] 12.4; 15.25
body 13.13; 15.16
burnt-offering [4] 12.6; 15.15
clean [11] 13.6; 15.8
cure 15.13
determine 6.6; Num 35.8
disease [5] 13.2; 21.20
dove [2] 12.6; 15.14
gift [3] 10.14; 23.17
grain-offering [3] 10.12; 23.18
heal 13.16; Num 12.13
holy 12.4; 16.19
hyssop [5] Ex 12.22; Num 19.6
lamb [8] 12.6; 22.26
law [3] 13.59; 17.3
new Ex 1.8; 23.14
offer [6] 12.7; 15.15
poor Ex 30.15; 19.10
possess Ex 32.13; 20.24
presence [2] 10.2; 16.13
present (1) [2] 12.7; 16.10
priest [22] 13.2; 15.14
pure [13] 12.4; 15.15
regulation [2] 13.1; 15.1
repayment-offering [3] 7.1; 19.21
require 5.1; 23.37
right (2) [14] 9.21; Num 18.18
ritual [7] 12.7; 15.15
shave [2] 13.33; 21.5
sin-offering [5] 12.6; 15.15
special [3] 10.14; 23.11
sprinkle [4] 8.11; 16.14
Tent (2) (of the Lord's presence) [2] 12.4; 15.14
unclean [7] 13.3; 15.2

[d] MILDEW: *The Hebrew word for "dreaded skin-disease" and "mildew" is the same.*

14.2: Mt 8.4; Mk 1.44; Lk 5.14, 17.14

hand, [16]dip a finger of his **right hand** in it,
and **sprinkle** some of it seven times there
in the LORD's **presence**. [17]He shall take
some of the oil that is in the palm of his
hand and some of the **blood** of the **lamb**
and put them on the lobe of the **right** ear,
on the thumb of the **right hand**, and on
the big toe of the **right** foot of the man
who is to be declared ritually **clean**. [18]He
shall put the rest of the oil that is in the
palm of his hand on the man's head. In
this way he shall perform the **ritual** of
purification.

19 Then the **priest** shall **offer** the **sin-**
offering and perform the **ritual** of **puri-**
fication. After that, he shall kill the
animal for the **burnt-offering** [20]and **offer**
it with the **grain-offering** on the **altar**. In
this way the **priest** shall perform the **rit-**
ual of **purification**, and the man will be
ritually **clean**.

21 If the man is **poor** and cannot afford any more, he shall bring for his **pur-**
ification only one male **lamb** as his **re-**
payment-offering, a **special gift** to the
LORD for the **priest**. He shall bring only
one kilogramme of flour mixed with
olive-oil for a **grain-offering** and a third
of a litre of olive-oil. [22]He shall also bring
two **doves** or two pigeons, one for the **sin-**
offering and one for the **burnt-offering**.
[23]On the eighth day of his **purification** he
shall bring them to the **priest** at the entrance of the **Tent**. [24]The **priest** shall take
the **lamb** and the olive-oil and **present**
them as a **special gift** to the LORD for the
priest. [25]He shall kill the **lamb** and take
some of the **blood** and put it on the lobe
of the man's **right** ear, on the thumb of
his **right hand**, and on the big toe of his
right foot. [26]The **priest** shall pour some of
the oil into the palm of his own left hand
[27]and with a finger of his **right hand**
sprinkle some of it seven times there in
the LORD's **presence**. [28]He shall put some
of the oil on the same places as he put
the **blood**: on the lobe of the man's **right**
ear, on the thumb of his **right hand**, and
on the big toe of his **right** foot. [29]The rest
of the oil that is in his palm he shall put
on the man's head and in this way perform the **ritual of purification**. [30]Then he
shall **offer** one of the **doves** or pigeons
[31]as the **sin-offering** and the other as the
burnt-offering with the **grain-offering**. In
this way the **priest** shall perform the **rit-**
ual of purification. [32]This is the **law** for
the man who has a dreaded **skin-disease**
but who cannot afford the normal **offer-**
ings required for his **purification**.

Mildew in Houses

33 The LORD gave Moses and Aaron
[34-35]the following **regulations** about
houses affected by spreading mildew.
(These were to apply after the people of
Israel entered the land of Canaan, which
the LORD was going to give them as their
possession.) If someone finds that the
LORD has sent mildew on his house, then
he must go and tell the **priest** about it.
[36]The **priest** shall order everything to be
moved out of the house before he goes to
examine the mildew; otherwise everything in the house will be declared **un-**
clean. Then he shall go to the house
[37]and examine the mildew. If there are
greenish or reddish spots that appear to
be eating into the wall, [38]he shall leave
the house and lock it up for seven days.
[39]On the seventh day he shall return and
examine it again. If the mildew has
spread, [40]he shall order the stones on
which the mildew is found to be removed
and thrown into some **unclean** place outside the city. [41]After that he must have
all the interior walls scraped and the
plaster dumped in an **unclean** place outside the city. [42]Then other stones are to
be used to replace the stones that were
removed, and **new** plaster will be used to
cover the walls.

43 If the mildew breaks out again in
the house after the stones have been removed and the house has been scraped
and plastered, [44]the **priest** shall go and
look. If it has spread, the house is **un-**
clean. [45]It must be torn down, and its
stones, its wood, and all its plaster must
be carried out of the city to an **unclean**
place. [46]Anyone who enters the house
while it is locked up will be **unclean** until
evening. [47]Anyone who lies down or eats
in the house must wash his clothes.

48 If, when the **priest** comes to look,
the mildew has not reappeared after the
house has been replastered, he shall pronounce the house ritually **clean**, because
the mildew has been completely removed. [49]To **purify** the house, he shall
take two birds, some cedar-wood, a red
cord, and a sprig of **hyssop**. [50]He shall kill
one of the birds over a clay bowl containing fresh spring water. [51]Then he shall
take the cedar-wood, the **hyssop**, the red
cord, and the live bird and shall dip them
in the **blood** of the bird that was killed
and in the fresh water. And he shall
sprinkle the house seven times. [52]In this
way he shall **purify** the house with the
bird's **blood**, the fresh water, the live
bird, the cedar-wood, the **hyssop**, and the
red cord. [53]Then he shall let the live bird
fly away outside the city over the open
fields. In this way he shall perform the

ritual of purification for the house, and it will be ritually clean.

54 These are the laws about dreaded skin-diseases; [55-56]sores, boils, or inflammations; and about mildew in clothes or houses. [57]These laws determine when something is unclean and when it is clean.

Unclean Bodily Discharges

blood 14.6; 16.14
body 14.9; 19.28
burnt-offering [2] 14.13; 16.3
clean [3] 14.2; 16.30
cure 14.2; Deut 28.27
defile 21.11
dove [2] 14.22; Num 6.10
impure 12.7; Ezra 9.11
offer [2] 14.11; 16.1
priest [4] 14.2; 16.4
pure [2] 14.2; 16.16
regulation [2] 14.2; 16.29
ritual [2] 14.2; 16.16
sex [3] Ex 32.6; 18.6
sin-offering [2] 14.13; 16.3
Tent (2) (of the Lord's presence) [3] 14.11; 16.7
unclean [24] 14.36; 16.16
warn Ex 21.29; Num 16.38

15 The LORD gave Moses and Aaron the following regulations [2]for the people of Israel. When any man has a discharge from his penis, the discharge is unclean, [3]whether the penis runs with it or is stopped up by it. [4]Any bed on which he sits or lies is unclean. [5]Anyone who touches his bed [6]or sits on anything the man has sat on must wash his clothes and have a bath, and he remains unclean until evening. [7]Anyone who touches the man with the discharge must wash his clothes and have a bath, and he remains unclean until evening. [8]If the man with the discharge spits on anyone who is ritually clean, that person must wash his clothes and have a bath, and he remains unclean until evening. [9]Any saddle or seat on which the man with the discharge sits is unclean. [10]Anyone who touches anything on which the man sat is unclean until evening. Anyone who carries anything on which the man sat must wash his clothes and have a bath, and he remains unclean until evening. [11]If a man who has a discharge touches someone without first having washed his hands, that person must wash his clothes and have a bath, and he remains unclean until evening. [12]Any clay pot that the man touches must be broken, and any wooden bowl that he touches must be washed.

13 After the man is cured of his discharge, he must wait seven days and then wash his clothes and bathe in fresh spring water, and he will be ritually clean. [14]On the eighth day he shall take two doves or two pigeons to the entrance of the Tent of the LORD's presence and give them to the priest. [15]The priest shall offer one of them as a sin-offering and the other as a burnt-offering. In this way he will perform the ritual of purification for the man.

16 When a man has an emission of semen, he must bathe his whole body, and he remains unclean until evening. [17]Anything made of cloth or leather on which the semen falls must be washed, and it remains unclean until evening. [18]After sexual intercourse both the man and the woman must have a bath, and they remain unclean until evening.

19 When a woman has her monthly period, she remains unclean for seven days. Anyone who touches her is unclean until evening. [20]Anything on which she sits or lies during her monthly period is unclean. [21-23]Anyone who touches her bed or anything on which she has sat must wash his clothes and have a bath, and he remains unclean until evening. [24]If a man has sexual intercourse with her during her period, he is contaminated by her impurity and remains unclean for seven days, and any bed on which he lies is unclean.

25 If a woman has a flow of blood for several days outside her monthly period or if her flow continues beyond her regular period, she remains unclean as long as the flow continues, just as she is during her monthly period. [26]Any bed on which she lies and anything on which she sits during this time is unclean. [27]Anyone who touches them is unclean and must wash his clothes and have a bath; he remains unclean until evening. [28]After her flow stops, she must wait seven days, and then she will be ritually clean. [29]On the eighth day she shall take two doves or two pigeons to the priest at the entrance of the Tent of the LORD's presence. [30]The priest shall offer one of them as a sin-offering and the other as a burnt-offering, and in this way he will perform the ritual of purification for her.

31 The LORD told Moses to warn the people of Israel about their uncleanness, so that they would not defile the Tent of his presence, which was in the middle of the camp. If they did, they would be killed.

32 These are the regulations about a man who has a discharge or an emission of semen, [33]a woman during her monthly period, or a man who has sexual intercourse with a woman who is ritually unclean.

The Day of Atonement

alive Ex 33.20; Num 16.30
altar [7] 14.20; 17.6
blood [6] 15.25; 17.3
burnt-offering [4] 15.15; 17.8
choose [3] Ex 35.30; 27.33
clean 15.8; 17.13
cloud Ex 40.34; Num 9.15
command 10.1; 17.1
community [3] 10.6; 17.8
confess 5.5; 26.40

16 The LORD spoke to Moses after the death of the two sons of Aaron who were killed when they offered unholy fire to the LORD. [2]He said, "Tell your brother Aaron that only at the proper time is he to go behind the curtain into the Most Holy Place, because that is where I appear in a cloud above the lid on the Covenant Box. If he disobeys, he will be killed. [3]He may enter the Most Holy Place only after he has

16.2: Heb 6.19 **16.3:** Heb 9.7

brought a young bull for a **sin-offering**
and a ram for a **burnt-offering**."

4 Then the LORD gave the following instructions. Before Aaron goes into the
Most Holy Place, he must have a bath
and put on the **priestly** garments: the
linen robe and shorts, the belt, and the
turban.

5 The **community** of Israel shall give
Aaron two male goats for a **sin-offering**
and a ram for a **burnt-offering**. 6 He shall
offer a bull as a **sacrifice** to **take away**
his own sins and those of his family.
7 Then he shall take the two goats to the
entrance of the **Tent** of the LORD's presence. 8 There he shall draw **lots**, using
two stones, one **marked** "for the LORD"
and the other "for Azazel."[e] 9 Aaron shall
sacrifice the goat **chosen** by **lot** for the
LORD and **offer** it as a **sin-offering**. 10 The
goat **chosen** for Azazel shall be **presented**
alive to the LORD and sent off into the
desert to Azazel, in order to **take away**
the sins of the people.

11 When Aaron **sacrifices** the bull as
the **sin-offering** for himself and his
family, 12 he shall take a fire-pan full of
burning coals from the **altar** and two
handfuls of fine **incense** and bring them
into the **Most Holy Place**. 13 There in the
LORD's **presence** he shall put the **incense**
on the fire, and the smoke of the **incense**
will hide the lid of the **Covenant Box** so
that he will not see it and die. 14 He shall
take some of the bull's **blood** and with his
finger **sprinkle** it on the front of the lid
and then **sprinkle** some of it seven times
in front of the **Covenant Box**.

15 After that, he shall kill the goat for
the **sin-offering** for the people, bring its
blood into the **Most Holy Place**, and
sprinkle it on the lid and then in front of
the **Covenant Box**, as he did with the
bull's **blood**. 16 In this way he will perform
the **ritual** to **purify** the **Most Holy Place**
from the **uncleanness** of the people of
Israel and from all their sins. He must do
this to the **Tent**, because it stands in the
middle of the camp, which is ritually **un-**
clean. 17 From the time Aaron enters the
Most Holy Place to perform the **ritual** of
purification until he comes out, there
must be no one in the **Tent**. When he has
performed the **ritual** for himself, his
family, and the whole **community**, 18 he
must then go out to the **altar** for **burnt-**
offerings and **purify** it. He must take
some of the bull's **blood** and some of the
goat's blood and put it all over the projections at the corners of the **altar**. 19 With
his finger he must **sprinkle** some of the
blood on the **altar** seven times. In this
way he is to **purify** it from the sins of the
people of Israel and make it **holy**.

The Scapegoat

20 When Aaron has finished perform-
ing the **ritual** to **purify** the **Most Holy**
Place, the rest of the **Tent** of the LORD's
presence, and the **altar**, he shall **present**
to the LORD the live goat **chosen** for
Azazel.[e] 21 He shall put both his hands on
the goat's head and **confess** over it all the
evils, sins, and **rebellions** of the people of
Israel, and so transfer them to the goat's
head. Then the goat is to be driven off
into the desert by a man appointed to do
it. 22 The goat will carry all their sins
away with him into some uninhabited
land.

23 Then Aaron shall go into the **Tent**,
take off the **priestly** garments that he
had put on before entering the **Most Holy**
Place, and leave them there. 24 He must
bathe in a **holy** place and put on his own
clothes. After that, he shall go out and
offer the **burnt-offering** to remove his
own sins and those of the people. 25 He
shall burn on the **altar** the fat of the
animal for the **sin-offering**. 26 The man
who drove the goat into the desert to
Azazel must wash his clothes and have a
bath before he comes back into camp.
27 The bull and the goat used for the **sin-**
offering, whose **blood** was brought into
the **Most Holy Place** to **take away** sin,
shall be carried outside the camp and
burnt. Skin, meat, and intestines shall all
be burnt. 28 The one who burns them
must wash his clothes and have a bath
before he returns to camp.

Observing the Day of Atonement

29 The following **regulations** are to be
observed for all time to come. On the
tenth day of the seventh month the Israelites and the foreigners living among
them must **fast** and must not do any
work. 30 On that day the **ritual** is to be
performed to **purify** them from all their
sins, so that they will be ritually **clean**.
31 That day is to be a very **holy** day, one
on which they **fast** and do no work at all.
These **regulations** are to be **observed** for
all time to come. 32 The **High Priest**, **pro-**
perly ordained and **consecrated** to
succeed his father, is to perform the **rit-**
ual of **purification**. He shall put on the
priestly garments 33 and perform the
ritual to **purify** the **Most Holy Place**, the

[e] AZAZEL: *The meaning of this Hebrew word is unknown; it may be the name of a desert demon.*

16.15: Heb 9.12 **16.23:** Ezek 44.19 **16.27:** Heb 13.11 **16.29–34:** Lev 23.26–32; Num 29.7–11

consecrate 10.7; 21.10
Covenant Box [4] Ex 40.3; 24.3
death (1) 10.6; 17.15
disobey 22.9
evil Ex 34.7; 20.23
fast (2) [2] 1 Sam 7.6
High Priest 6.22; 21.10
holy [3] 14.13; 19.2
Holy Place [11] Ex 39.1; 24.3
incense [3] 10.1; 24.7
lot (1) [2] Num 26.54
mark (1) Ex 19.12; Deut 19.14
observe [3] 4.2; 22.9
offer [4] 15.15; 17.3
ordain 9.1; Num 3.3
presence 14.16; 24.3
present (1) [2] 14.12; 21.8
priest [4] 15.14; 17.5
proper [2] Num 15.24
pure [9] 15.15; 19.22
rebel Ex 23.21; 26.40
regulation [3] 15.1; 17.2
ritual [8] 15.15; 19.22
sacrifice [3] 10.18; 17.7
sin-offering [7] 15.15; 23.19
sprinkle [4] 14.7; Num 8.7
take away (sin) [3] 12.7; 17.11
Tent (2) (of the Lord's presence) [6] 15.14; 17.3
unclean [2] 15.2; 18.19
unholy Num 3.4

rest of the **Tent** of the LORD's presence, the **altar**, the **priests**, and all the people of the **community**. 34 These **regulations** are to be **observed** for all time to come. This **ritual** must be performed once a year to **purify** the people of Israel from all their sins.

So Moses[g] did as the Lord had **commanded**.

The Sacredness of Blood

17 The Lord **commanded** Moses 2 to give Aaron and his sons and all the people of Israel the following **regulations**. 3–4 An Israelite who kills a cow or a **sheep** or a goat as an **offering** to the LORD anywhere except at the entrance of the **Tent** of the LORD's presence has broken the **Law**. He has shed **blood** and shall no longer be considered one of **God's people**. 5 The meaning of this **command** is that the people of Israel shall now bring to the LORD the animals which they used to kill in the open country. They shall now bring them to the **priest** at the entrance of the **Tent** and kill them as **fellowship-offerings**. 6 The **priest** shall throw the **blood** against the sides of the **altar** at the entrance of the **Tent** and burn the fat to produce a smell that is **pleasing** to the LORD. 7 The people of Israel must no longer be **unfaithful** to the LORD by killing their animals in the fields as **sacrifices** to the **goat-demons**. The people of Israel must keep this **regulation** for all time to come.

8 Any Israelite or any foreigner living in the **community** who **offers** a **burnt-offering** or any other **sacrifice** 9 as an **offering** to the LORD anywhere except at the entrance of the **Tent** shall no longer be considered one of **God's people**.

10 If any Israelite or any foreigner living in the **community** eats meat with **blood** still in it, the LORD will **turn** against him and no longer consider him one of **his people**. 11 The **life** of every living thing is in the **blood**, and that is why the LORD has **commanded** that all **blood** be poured out on the **altar** to **take away** the people's sins. **Blood**, which is **life**, **takes away** sins. 12 That is why the LORD has told the people of Israel that neither they nor any foreigner living among them shall eat any meat with **blood** still in it.

13 If any Israelite or any foreigner living in the **community** hunts an animal or a bird which is ritually **clean**, he must pour out its **blood** on the ground and cover it with earth. 14 The **life** of every living thing is in the **blood**, and that is why the LORD has told the people of Israel that they shall not eat any meat with **blood** still in it and that anyone who does so will no longer be considered one of **his people**.

15 Any person, Israelite or foreigner, who eats meat from an animal that has died a **natural death** or has been killed by wild animals must wash his clothes, have a bath, and wait until evening before he is ritually **clean**. 16 If he does not, he must **suffer** the consequences.

altar [2] 16.12; 21.23
blood [10] 16.14; 19.26
burnt-offering 16.3; 22.18
clean [2] 16.30; 20.25
command [3] 16.34; 18.4
community [3] 16.5; 19.2
death (1) 16.1; 20.9
demon 2 Kgs 23.8
fellowship-offering 10.14; 19.5
God's people [4] 10.3; 18.29
law 14.32; 18.4
life (1) [3] Ex 30.12; 18.5
natural 7.24; 22.8
offer [3] 16.1; 19.5
please 8.20; 23.13
priest [2] 16.4; 19.22
regulation [2] 16.29; 18.6
sacrifice [2] 16.6; 22.28
sheep 7.23; 22.28
suffer 7.18; 20.17
take away (sin) [2] 16.6; 23.26
Tent (2) (of the Lord's presence) [4] 16.7; 19.21
turn 13.3; 19.29
unfaithful Ex 34.16; 20.5

Forbidden Sexual Practices

18 The LORD told Moses 2 to say to the people of Israel, "I am the LORD your God. 3 Do not follow the **practices** of the people of Egypt, where you once lived, or of the people in the land of Canaan, where I am now taking you. 4 **Obey** my **laws** and do what I **command**. I am the LORD your God. 5 Follow the **practices** and the **laws** that I give you; you will **save** your **life** by doing so. I am the LORD."

6 The LORD gave the following **regulations**. Do not have **sexual** intercourse with any of your relatives. 7 Do not **disgrace** your father by having intercourse with your mother. You must not **disgrace** your own mother. 8 Do not **disgrace** your father by having intercourse with any of his other wives. 9 Do not have intercourse with your sister or your stepsister, whether or not she was brought up in the same house with you. 10 Do not have intercourse with your granddaughter; that would be a **disgrace** to you. 11 Do not have intercourse with a half-sister; she, too, is your sister. 12–13 Do not have intercourse with an aunt, whether she is your father's sister or your mother's sister. 14 Do not have intercourse with your uncle's wife; she, too, is your aunt. 15 Do not have intercourse with your daughter-in-law 16 or with your brother's wife. 17 Do not have intercourse with the daughter or granddaughter of a woman with whom you have had intercourse; they may be related to you, and that would be incest. 18 Do not take your wife's sister as one of your wives, as long as your wife is living.

19 Do not have intercourse with a woman during her monthly period, because she is ritually **unclean**. 20 Do not have intercourse with another man's

act Ex 22.25; Num 5.12
action Judg 9.16
command [3] 17.1; 19.3
disgrace [5] Gen 34.5; 19.12
disgust [2] 20.13
god (2) (other gods) Ex 34.14; 19.4
God's people 17.3; 19.8
hate Ex 20.5; 19.18
law [3] 17.3; 19.37
life (1) 17.11; 19.16
name (2) (name of God, of Jesus) Ex 34.5; 19.12
obey [2] 7.36; 19.14
pagan [3] Ex 34.15; 20.23
pervert Ex 23.2; Judg 19.22
practice [3] Ex 23.24; 19.26
punish Ex 34.7; 19.20
regulation 17.2; 19.5
reject [3] Ex 32.7; 20.22
relations [2] Ex 22.19; 19.20
save Ex 21.30; Num 10.9
sex [3] 15.18; 19.20
unclean [8] 16.16; 19.7
worship (2) (of other gods) Ex 34.14; 19.4

[g] Moses; *or* Aaron.

17.10: Gen 9.4; Lev 7.26–27, 19.26; Deut 12.16, 23, 15.23 **17.11:** Heb 9.22
18.5: Neh 9.29; Ezek 18.9, 20.11–13; Lk 10.28; Rom 10.5; Gal 3.12 **18.8:** Lev 20.11; Deut 22.30, 27.20
18.9: Lev 20.17; Deut 27.22 **18.12–14:** Lev 20.19–20 **18.15:** Lev 20.12 **18.16:** Lev 20.21
18.17: Lev 20.14; Deut 27.23 **18.19:** Lev 20.18 **18.20:** Lev 20.10

wife; that would make you ritually **unclean.** 21 Do not hand over any of your children to be used in the **worship of the god Molech,** because that would bring **disgrace** on the **name** of God, the LORD. 22 No man is to have **sexual relations** with another man; God **hates** that. 23 No man or woman is to have **sexual relations** with an animal; that **perversion** makes you ritually **unclean.**

24 Do not make yourselves **unclean** by any of these **acts,** for that is how the **pagans** made themselves **unclean,** those **pagans** who lived in the land before you and whom the LORD is driving out so that you can go in. 25 Their **actions** made the land **unclean,** and so the LORD is **punishing** the land and making it **reject** the people who lived there. 26–27 They did all these **disgusting** things and made the land **unclean,** but you must not do them. All of you, whether Israelites or foreigners living with you, must keep the LORD's **laws** and **commands,** 28 and then the land will not **reject** you, as it **rejected** the **pagans** who lived there before you. 29 You know that whoever does any of these **disgusting** things will no longer be considered one of **God's people.**

30 And the LORD said, "**Obey** the **commands** I give and do not follow the **practices** of the people who lived in the land before you, and do not make yourselves **unclean** by doing any of these things. I am the LORD your God."

Laws of Holiness and Justice

19 The LORD told Moses 2 to say to the **community** of Israel, "Be **holy,** because I, the LORD your God, am holy. 3 Each of you must **respect** his mother and his father, and must keep the **Sabbath,** as I have **commanded.** I am the LORD your God.

4 "Do not **abandon** me and **worship idols;** do not make **gods** of metal and **worship** them. I am the LORD your God.

5 "When you kill an animal for a **fellowship-offering,** keep the **regulations** that I have given you, and I will **accept** the **offering.** 6 The meat must be eaten on the day the animal is killed or on the next day. Any meat left on the third day must be burnt, 7 because it is ritually **unclean,** and if anyone eats it, I will not **accept** the **offering.** 8 Anyone who eats it will be **guilty** of treating as ordinary what is **dedicated** to me, and he will no longer be considered one of **my people.**

9 "When you **harvest** your fields, do not cut the corn at the edges of the fields, and do not go back to cut the ears of corn that were left. 10 Do not go back through your **vineyard** to gather the grapes that were missed or to pick up the grapes that have fallen; leave them for **poor** people and foreigners. I am the LORD your God.

11 "Do not **steal** or **cheat** or **lie.** 12 Do not make a **promise in my name** if you do not **intend** to keep it; that brings **disgrace** on my **name.** I am the LORD your God.

13 "Do not take **advantage** of anyone or **rob** him. Do not hold back the **wages** of someone you have hired, not even for one night. 14 Do not **curse** a deaf man or put something in front of a **blind** man so as to make him **stumble** over it. **Obey** me; I am the LORD your God.

15 "Be **honest** and **just** when you make decisions in legal **cases;** do not show favouritism to the **poor** or **fear** the **rich.** 16 Do not spread **lies** about anyone, and when someone is on **trial** for his **life,** speak out if your **testimony** can **help** him. I am the LORD.

17 "Do not bear a grudge against anyone, but **settle** your differences with him, so that you will not commit a sin because of him.[h] 18 Do not take **revenge** on anyone or continue to **hate** him, but **love** your **neighbour** as you love yourself. I am the LORD.

19 "**Obey** my **commands.** Do not crossbreed domestic animals. Do not plant two kinds of **seed** in the same field. Do not wear clothes made of two kinds of material.

20 "If a **slave-girl** is the recognized **concubine** of a man and she has not been paid for and **freed,** then if another man has **sexual relations** with her, they will be **punished** but not[i] put **to death,** since she is a **slave.** 21 The man shall bring a ram to the entrance of the **Tent** of my presence as his **repayment-offering,** 22 and with it the **priest** shall perform the **ritual** of **purification** to remove the man's sin, and God will **forgive** him.

23 "When you come into the land of Canaan and plant any kind of fruit tree, consider the fruit ritually **unclean** for the first three years. During that time you must not eat it. 24 In the fourth year all

[h] so...him; *or* so that you do not commit this sin against him.
[i] they...not; *or* an investigation will be made but they will not be.

18.21: Lev 20.1–5 **18.22:** Lev 20.13 **18.23:** Ex 22.19; Lev 20.15–16; Deut 27.21
19.2: Lev 11.44–45; 1 Pet 1.16 **19.3:** Ex 20.8, 12; Deut 5.12, 16
19.4: Lev 26.1; Ex 20.23, 34.17; Deut 27.15 **19.9–10:** Lev 23.22; Deut 24.19–22
19.11: Ex 20.15, 16; Deut 5.19, 20 **19.12:** Ex 20.7; Deut 5.11; Mt 5.33 **19.13:** Deut 24.14–15
19.14: Deut 27.18 **19.15:** Ex 23.6–8; Deut 16.19 **19.17:** Mt 18.15
19.18: Mt 5.43, 19.19, 22.39; Mk 12.31; Lk 10.27; Rom 13.9; Gal 5.14; Jas 2.8 **19.19:** Deut 22.9–11

turn 17.10; 20.3
unclean [3] 18.19; 20.3
vineyard Ex 23.11; 25.3
wage Gen 31.7; 25.50
worship (1) (of God) 9.5; 23.2
worship (2) (of other gods) [2] 18.21; 20.2

the fruit shall be **dedicated** as an **offering** to show your **gratitude** to me,[j] the LORD. 25 But in the fifth year you may eat the fruit. If you do all this, your trees will bear more fruit. I am the LORD your God.

26 "Do not eat any meat with **blood** still in it. Do not **practise** any kind of **magic**. 27 Do not cut the hair on the sides of your head or trim your beard 28 or tattoo yourselves or cut gashes in your **body** to **mourn** for the **dead**. I am the LORD.

29 "Do not **disgrace** your daughters by making them temple **prostitutes**;[k] if you do, you will **turn to** other **gods** and the land will be full of **immorality**. 30 Keep the **Sabbath**, and **honour** the place where I am **worshipped**. I am the LORD.

31 "Do not go for **advice** to people who **consult** the **spirits** of the **dead**. If you do, you will be ritually **unclean**. I am the LORD your God.

32 "Show **respect** for old people and **honour** them. **Reverently obey** me; I am the LORD.

33 "Do not **ill-treat** foreigners who are living in your land. 34 Treat them as you would a fellow-Israelite, and **love** them as you love yourselves. **Remember** that you were once foreigners in the land of Egypt. I am the LORD your God.

35 "Do not **cheat** anyone by using **false** measures of length, weight, or quantity. 36 Use **honest** scales, honest weights, and honest measures. I am the LORD your God, and I brought you out of Egypt. 37 **Obey** all my **laws** and **commands**. I am the LORD."

Penalties for Disobedience

adultery Ex 20.14; Num 5.19
advice 19.31; Deut 18.14
alone Ex 24.2; Num 8.16
apart [2] Ex 29.44; 21.15
clean 17.13; 22.4
command 19.3; 21.1
commit Ex 20.13; 24.17
community [4] 19.2; 23.18
consult [2] 19.31; 25.50
curse 19.14; 24.10
custom Gen 29.26; Judg 11.39
dead [2] 19.28; 21.11
death (1) [6] 17.15; 21.4

20 The LORD told Moses 2 to say to the people of Israel, "Any of you or any foreigner living among you who gives any of his children to be used in the **worship of the god Molech** shall be stoned **to death** by the whole **community**. 3 If anyone gives one of his children to Molech and makes my **sacred Tent unclean** and **disgraces** my **holy name**, I will **turn** against him and will no longer consider him one of **my people**. 4 But if the **community ignores** what he has done and does not put him **to death**, 5 I myself will **turn** against the man and his whole family and against all who join him in being **unfaithful** to me and **worshipping** Molech. I will no longer consider them **my people**.

6 "If anyone goes for **advice** to people who **consult** the **spirits** of the **dead**, I will **turn** against him and will no longer consider him one of **my people**. 7 Keep yourselves **holy**, because I am the LORD your God. 8 **Obey** my **laws**, because I am the LORD and I make you **holy**."

9 The LORD gave the following **regulations**. Anyone who **curses** his father or his mother shall be put **to death**; he is responsible for his own **death**.

10 If a man **commits adultery** with the wife of a fellow-Israelite, both he and the woman shall be put **to death**. 11 A man who has intercourse with one of his father's wives **disgraces** his father, and both he and the woman shall be put **to death**. They are responsible for their own **death**. 12 If a man has intercourse with his daughter-in-law, they shall both be put **to death**. They have committed incest and are responsible for their own **death**. 13 If a man has **sexual relations** with another man, they have done a **disgusting** thing, and both shall be put **to death**. They are responsible for their own **death**. 14 If a man marries a woman and her mother, all three shall be burnt **to death** because of the **disgraceful** thing they have done; such a thing must not be **permitted** among you. 15 If a man has **sexual relations** with an animal, he and the animal shall be put **to death**. 16 If a woman tries to have **sexual relations** with an animal, she and the animal shall be put **to death**. They are responsible for their own **death**.

17 If a man marries his sister or half-sister, they shall be publicly **disgraced** and driven out of the **community**. He has had intercourse with his sister and must **suffer** the consequences. 18 If a man has intercourse with a woman during her monthly period, both of them are to be driven out of the **community**, because they have broken the **regulations** about **ritual uncleanness**.

19 If a man has intercourse with his aunt, both of them must **suffer** the consequences for incest. 20 If a man has intercourse with his uncle's wife, he **disgraces** his uncle, and he and the woman will pay the penalty; neither of them will

death (3) (to death) [11] 19.20; 21.9
disgrace [6] 19.12; 21.6
disgust [2] 18.26; 26.30
distinguish 11.47; Deut 17.8
evil 16.21; Num 25.18
god (2) (other gods) 19.4; Num 14.9
God's people [3] 19.8; 21.8
holy [5] 19.2; 21.6
ignore Deut 22.1
law [2] 19.37; 24.22
name (2) (name of God, of Jesus) 19.12; 21.6
obey 19.14; 22.31
pagan 18.24; Deut 31.16
permit Gen 47.4; 22.24
possess 14.34; Num 14.24
practice 19.26; Deut 12.30
promise 19.12; 26.42
regulation [2] 19.5; 22.9
reject 18.25; 26.43
relations [3] 19.20; Deut 27.21
rich 19.15; 25.47
ritual 19.22; 23.26
sacred 12.4; 21.11
sex [3] 19.20; Num 25.1
spirit (2) [2] 19.31; Deut 18.11
suffer [2] 17.16; 24.15
Tent (2) (of the Lord's presence) 19.21; 21.11
turn [3] 19.29; 26.11
unclean [5] 19.7; 21.1
unfaithful 17.7; Num 5.6
worship (2) (of other gods) [2] 19.4; 26.1

[j] to show your gratitude to me; *or* in praise of me.
[k] TEMPLE PROSTITUTES: *These women were found in Canaanite temples, where fertility gods were worshipped. It was believed that intercourse with these prostitutes assured fertile fields and herds.*

19.26: Gen 9.4; Lev 7.26–27, 17.10–14; Deut 12.16, 23, 15.23, 18.10 **19.27–28:** Lev 2.5; Deut 14.1
19.29: Deut 23.17 **19.30:** Lev 26.2 **19.31:** Deut 18.11; 1 Sam 28.3; 2 Kgs 23.4; Is 8.19
19.33–34: Ex 22.21; Deut 24.17–18, 27.19 **19.35–36:** Deut 25.13–16; Prov 20.10; Ezek 45.10
20.9: Ex 21.17; Mt 15.4; Mk 7.10 **20.10:** Ex 20.14; Lev 18.20; Deut 5.18
20.11: Lev 18.8; Deut 22.30, 27.20 **20.12:** Lev 18.15 **20.13:** Lev 18.22 **20.14:** Lev 18.17; Deut 27.23
20.15–16: Ex 22.19; Lev 18.23; Deut 27.21 **20.17:** Lev 18.9; Deut 27.22 **20.18:** Lev 18.19
20.19–20: Lev 18.12–14

have children. 21 If a man marries his brother's wife, they will die childless. He has done a ritually unclean thing and has disgraced his brother.

22 The LORD said, "Keep all my laws and commands, so that you will not be rejected by the land of Canaan, into which I am bringing you. 23 Do not adopt the customs of people who live there; I am driving out those pagans so that you can enter the land. They have disgusted me with all their evil practices. 24 But I have promised you this rich and fertile land as your possession, and I will give it to you. I am the LORD your God, and I have set you apart from the other nations. 25 So then, you must make a clear distinction between animals and birds that are ritually clean and those that are not. Do not eat unclean animals or birds. I have declared them unclean, and eating them would make you unclean. 26 You shall be holy and belong only to me, because I am the LORD and I am holy. I have set you apart from the other nations so that you would belong to me alone.

27 "Any man or woman who consults the spirits of the dead shall be stoned to death; any person who does this is responsible for his own death."

The Holiness of the Priests

21 The LORD commanded Moses to say to the Aaronite priests, "No priest is to make himself ritually unclean by taking part in the funeral ceremonies when a relative dies, 2 unless it is his mother, father, son, daughter, brother, 3 or unmarried sister living in his house. 4 He shall not make himself unclean at the death of those related to him by marriage.[l]

5 "No priest shall shave any part of his head or trim his beard or cut gashes on his body to show that he is in mourning. 6 He must be holy and must not disgrace my name. He offers food-offerings to me, and he must be holy. 7 A priest shall not marry a woman who has been a prostitute or a woman who is not a virgin or who is divorced; he is holy. 8 The people must consider the priest holy, because he presents the food-offerings to me. I am the LORD; I am holy and I make my people holy. 9 If a priest's daughter becomes a prostitute, she disgraces her father; she shall be burnt to death.

10 "The High Priest has had the anointing oil poured on his head and has been consecrated to wear the priestly garments, so he must not leave his hair uncombed or tear his clothes to show that he is in mourning. 11–12 He has been dedicated to me and is not to make himself ritually unclean nor is he to defile my sacred Tent by leaving it and entering a house where there is a dead person, even if it is his own father or mother. 13 He shall marry a virgin, 14 not a widow or a divorced woman or a woman who has been a prostitute. He shall marry only a virgin from his own clan. 15 Otherwise, his children, who ought to be holy, will be ritually unclean. I am the LORD and I have set him apart as the High Priest."

16 The LORD commanded Moses 17 to say to Aaron, "None of your descendants who has any physical defect may present the food-offering to me. This applies for all time to come. 18 No man with any physical defect may make the offering: no one who is blind, lame, disfigured, or deformed; 19 no one with a crippled hand or foot; 20 no one who is a hunchback or a dwarf; no one with any eye or skin disease; and no eunuch. 21 No descendant of Aaron the priest who has any physical defect may present the food-offering to me. 22 Such a man may eat the food offered to me, both the holy food-offering and the very holy food-offering, 23 but because he has a physical defect, he shall not come near the sacred curtain or approach the altar. He must not profane these holy things, because I am the LORD and I make them holy."

24 This, then, is what Moses said to Aaron, the sons of Aaron, and to all the people of Israel.

The Holiness of the Offerings

22 The LORD commanded Moses 2 to say to Aaron and his sons, "You must not bring disgrace on my holy name, so treat with respect the sacred offerings that the people of Israel dedicate to me. I am the LORD. 3 If any of your descendants, while he is ritually unclean, comes near the sacred offerings which the people of Israel have dedicated to me, he can never again serve at the altar. This applies for all time to come. I am the LORD.

4 "None of the descendants of Aaron who has a dreaded skin-disease or a discharge may eat any of the sacred offerings until he is ritually clean. Any priest is unclean if he touches anything which is unclean through contact with a corpse or if he has an emission of semen 5 or if

[l] *Verse 4 in Hebrew is unclear.*

20.21: Lev 18.16 **21.5:** Lev 19.27–28; Deut 14.1

profane 22.15
prostitute [3] 19.29; Deut 23.17
sacred [2] 20.3; 22.2
shave 14.8; Num 6.5
Tent (2) (of the Lord's presence) 20.3; 24.2
unclean [4] 20.3; 22.3
unmarried Ex 21.3; Num 30.6
virgin [3] Ex 22.16; Num 31.18
widow Ex 22.22; 22.13

altar 17.6; 22.3
anoint 10.7; Num 3.3
apart 20.24; 25.10
blind 19.14; 22.22
body 19.28; 26.30
ceremony Gen 50.10; Neh 7.70
command [2] 20.22; 22.1
consecrate 16.32; Num 3.12
cripple Gen 49.6; 22.22
dead 20.6; 26.30
death (1) 20.9; 22.8
death (3) (to death) 20.2; 23.30
dedicate 19.8; 22.2
defile 15.31; Num 5.3
disease 14.2; 22.4
disgrace [2] 20.3; 22.2
divorce [2] 22.13
food-offering [5] 10.15; 22.22
God's people 20.3; 23.29
High Priest [2] 16.32; Num 35.25
holy [9] 20.3; 22.2
mourn [2] 19.28; Num 14.39
name (2) (name of God, of Jesus) 20.3; 22.2
offer [3] 19.5; 22.2
physical [4] Gen 17.13; Dan 1.4
present (1) [3] 16.10; 22.18
priest [8] 19.22; 22.4

accept [7] 19.5; 23.11
acknowledge Num 20.12
altar [2] 21.23; 26.30
blind 21.18; 24.20
burnt-offering 17.8; 23.12
clean [2] 20.25; Num 6.9
command [3] 21.1; 24.23
cripple 21.19; Deut 15.21
death (1) 21.4; Num 15.31
dedicate [2] 21.11; 25.4
depend Num 27.21
disease 21.20; 26.16
disgrace [2] 21.6; Num 12.14
disobey 16.2; Num 14.41
divorce 21.7; Num 30.9
fellowship-offering 19.5; 23.19

food-offering [3] 21.6; 23.8
freewill [3] 7.16; 23.38
fulfil [3] 7.16; 23.38
guilty [2] 19.8; 24.14
holy [6] 21.6; 23.20
intend 19.12; Num 35.23
lamb [2] 14.10; 23.12
name (2) (name of God, of Jesus) [2] 21.6; Num 6.27
natural 17.15; Num 16.29
never again Gen 9.11; Deut 12.3
obey 20.8; 25.17
observe 16.29; 23.14
offer [19] 21.6; 23.8
perfect Deut 32.4
permit 20.14; Num 9.11
present (1) [2] 21.8; 23.11
priest [13] 21.1; 23.9
profane 21.23; Num 18.32
punish 19.20; 26.14
regulation [3] 20.9; 23.2
repay 6.4; Num 5.7
respect 19.3; Num 11.16
sacred [10] 21.11; 25.12
sacrifice [2] 17.7; 23.12
serve 10.3; 25.40
sheep 17.3; Num 11.22
slave 19.20; 25.6
thank Gen 47.31; Deut 8.10
unclean [5] 21.1; 27.11
value 6.6; 27.18
vow [3] 7.16; 23.38
widow 21.14; Num 30.9

he has touched an unclean animal or person. [6]Any priest who becomes unclean remains unclean until evening, and even then he may not eat any of the sacred offerings until he has had a bath. [7]After the sun sets he is clean, and then he may eat the sacred offerings, which are his food. [8]He shall not eat the meat of any animal that has died a natural death or has been killed by wild animals; it will make him unclean. I am the LORD.

9 "All priests shall observe the regulations that I have given. Otherwise, they will be guilty and die, because they have disobeyed the sacred regulations. I am the LORD and I make them holy.

10 "Only a member of a priestly family may eat any of the sacred offerings; no one else may eat them—not even someone staying with a priest or hired by him. [11]But a priest's slaves, bought with his own money or born in his home, may eat the food the priest receives. [12]A priest's daughter who marries someone who is not a priest may not eat any of the sacred offerings. [13]But a widowed or divorced daughter who has no children and who has returned to live in her father's house as a dependant may eat the food her father receives as a priest. Only a member of a priestly family may eat any of it.

14 "If any person who is not a member of a priestly family eats any of the sacred offerings without intending to, he must repay the priest its full value plus an additional twenty per cent. [15]The priests shall not profane the sacred offerings [16]by letting any unauthorized person eat them; this would bring guilt and punishment on such a person. I am the LORD and I make the offerings holy."

17 The LORD commanded Moses [18]to give Aaron and his sons and all the people of Israel the following regulations. When any Israelite or any foreigner living in Israel presents a burnt-offering, whether in fulfilment of a vow or as a freewill offering, the animal must not have any defects. [19]To be accepted, it must be a male without any defects. [20]If you offer any animal that has any defect, the LORD will not accept it. [21]When anyone presents a fellowship-offering to the LORD, whether in fulfilment of a vow or as a freewill offering, the animal must be without any defect if it is to be accepted. [22]Do not offer to the LORD any animal that is blind or crippled or mutilated, or that has a running sore or a skin eruption or scabs. Do not offer any such animals on the altar as a food-offering. [23]As a freewill offering you may offer an animal that is stunted or not perfectly formed, but it is not acceptable in fulfilment of a vow. [24]Do not offer to the LORD any animal whose testicles have been crushed, cut, bruised, or torn off. This is not permitted in your land.

25 Do not offer as a food-offering any animal obtained from a foreigner. Such animals are considered defective and are not acceptable.

26–27 When a calf or a lamb or a kid is born, it must not be taken from its mother for seven days, but after that it is acceptable as a food-offering. [28]Do not sacrifice a cow and its calf or a sheep and its lamb or a goat and its kid on the same day. [29]When you offer a sacrifice of thanksgiving to the LORD, follow the rules so that you will be accepted; [30]eat it the same day and leave none of it until the next morning.

31 The LORD said, "Obey my commands; I am the LORD. [32]Do not bring disgrace on my holy name; all the people of Israel must acknowledge me to be holy. I am the LORD and I make you holy; [33]and I brought you out of Egypt to become your God. I am the LORD."

The Religious Festivals

23 The LORD gave Moses [2]the following regulations for the religious festivals, when the people of Israel are to gather for worship. [3]You have six days in which to do your work, but remember that the seventh day, the Sabbath, is a day of rest. On that day do not work, but gather for worship. The Sabbath belongs to the LORD, no matter where you live. [4]Proclaim the following festivals at the appointed times.

accept 22.19; 26.31
best 9.10; Num 18.12
bread [6] 10.12; 24.5
burnt-offering [3] 22.18; Num 6.11
celebrate [3] Ex 23.14; Num 7.10
community 20.2; 24.14
death (3) (to death) 21.9; 24.14
fellowship-offering 22.21; Num 6.14
festival [9] Ex 34.18; 26.2
food-offering [7] 22.22; 24.7
freewill 22.18; 27.26
fulfil 22.18; 27.2
gift [3] 14.12; 27.9
God's people 21.8; 26.12
grain-offering [2] 14.20; Num 4.16
harvest [4] 19.9; 25.5
holy 22.2; 24.9
honour [4] 19.30; 25.2
lamb [4] 22.26; 27.26
new [2] 14.42; 26.10
observe [5] 22.9; 24.3
offer [15] 22.2; 24.9
Passover Ex 34.25; Num 9.2
please [2] 17.6; Num 14.8
poor 19.10; 25.25
present (1) [16] 22.18; Num 5.9
priest [4] 22.4; 24.9
proclaim 25.10
regulation [6] 22.9; 24.3

Passover and Unleavened Bread
(Num 28.16–25)

5 The Passover, celebrated to honour the LORD, begins at sunset on the fourteenth day of the first month. [6]On the fifteenth day the Festival of Unleavened Bread begins, and for seven days you must not eat any bread made with yeast. [7]On the first of these days you shall gather for worship and do none of your daily work. [8]Offer your food-offerings to the LORD for seven days. On the seventh day you shall again gather for worship, but you shall do none of your daily work.

9–10 When you come into the land that the LORD is giving you and you harvest your corn, take the first sheaf to the

22.20: Deut 17.1 **23.3:** Ex 20.8–10, 23.12, 31.15, 34.21, 35.2; Deut 5.12–14 **23.5:** Ex 12.1–13; Deut 16.1–2 **23.6–8:** Ex 12.14–20, 23.15, 34.18; Deut 16.3–8

religion [4] Ex 23.24; 26.2
remember 19.34; 26.42
require 14.32; Num 3.7
rest (1) [4] Ex 39.21; 25.4
ritual [2] 20.18; Num 5.8
Sabbath [6] 19.3; 24.8
sacrifice [2] 22.28; 26.31
shelter [3] Ex 34.22; Deut 16.13
sin-offering 16.3; Num 6.11
special [6] 14.12; 27.2
take away (sin) [2] 17.11; 2 Chr 29.21
unleavened 10.12; Num 6.15
vow 22.18; 27.2
wine-offering [2] Ex 37.16; Num 4.7
worship (1) (of God) [11] 19.30; 26.2
yeast [2] 7.12; Num 6.15

priest. 11 He shall present it as a special
offering to the LORD, so that you may be
accepted. The priest shall present it the
day after the Sabbath. 12 On the day you
present the offering of corn, also sacrifice as a burnt-offering a one-year-old
male lamb that has no defects. 13 With it
you shall present two kilogrammes of
flour mixed with olive-oil as a food-offering. The smell of this offering is pleasing
to the LORD. You shall also present with
it an offering of one litre of wine. 14 Do
not eat any of the new corn, whether
raw, roasted, or baked into bread, until
you have brought this offering to God.
This regulation is to be observed by all
your descendants for all time to come.

The Harvest Festival
(Num 28.26–31)

15 Count seven full weeks from the
day after the Sabbath on which you bring
your sheaf of corn to present to the
LORD. 16 On the fiftieth day, the day after
the seventh Sabbath, present to the LORD
another new offering of corn. 17 Each
family is to bring two loaves of bread and
present them to the LORD as a special
gift. Each loaf shall be made of two kilogrammes of flour baked with yeast and
shall be presented to the Lord as an
offering of the first corn to be harvested.
18 And with the bread the community is to
present seven one-year-old lambs, one
bull, and two rams, none of which may
have any defects. They shall be offered
as a burnt-offering to the LORD, together
with a grain-offering and a wine-offering.
The smell of this offering is pleasing to
the LORD. 19 Also offer one male goat as a
sin-offering and two one-year-old male
lambs as a fellowship-offering. 20 The
priest shall present the bread with the
two lambs as a special gift to the LORD
for the priests. These offerings are holy.
21 On that day do none of your daily work,
but gather for worship. Your descendants are to observe this regulation for
all time to come, no matter where they
live.

22 When you harvest your fields, do
not cut the corn at the edges of the fields,
and do not go back to cut the ears of corn
that were left; leave them for poor
people and foreigners. The LORD is your
God.

The New Year Festival
(Num 29.1–6)

23–24 On the first day of the seventh
month observe a special day of rest, and
come together for worship when the
trumpets sound. 25 Present a food-offering
to the LORD and do none of your daily
work.

The Day of Atonement
(Num 29.7–11)

26–27 The tenth day of the seventh
month is the day when the annual ritual
is to be performed to take away the sins
of the people. On that day do not eat anything at all; come together for worship,
and present a food-offering to the Lord.
28 Do no work on that day, because it is
the day for performing the ritual to take
away sin. 29 Anyone who eats anything on
that day will no longer be considered one
of God's people. 30 And if anyone does any
work on that day, the LORD himself will
put him to death. 31 This regulation applies to all your descendants, no matter
where they live. 32 From sunset on the
ninth day of the month to sunset on the
tenth observe this day as a special day of
rest, during which nothing may be eaten.

The Festival of Shelters
(Num 29.12–40)

33–34 The Festival of Shelters begins
on the fifteenth day of the seventh month
and continues for seven days. 35 On the
first of these days come together for worship and do none of your daily work.
36 Each day for seven days you shall present a food-offering. On the eighth day
come together again for worship and
present a food-offering. It is a day for
worship, and you shall do no work.

37 (These are the religious festivals on
which you honour the LORD by gathering
together for worship and presenting
food-offerings, burnt-offerings, grain-
offerings, sacrifices, and wine-offerings,
as required day by day. 38 These festivals
are in addition to the regular Sabbaths,
and these offerings are in addition to
your regular gifts, your offerings in fulfilment of vows, and your freewill offerings
that you give to the LORD.)

39 When you have harvested your
fields, celebrate this festival for seven
days, beginning on the fifteenth day of
the seventh month. The first day shall be
a special day of rest. 40 On that day take
some of the best fruit from your trees,
take palm branches and the branches of
leafy trees, and begin a religious festival
to honour the LORD your God. 41 Celebrate it for seven days. This regulation is
to be kept by your descendants for all
time to come. 42 All the people of Israel

23.15–21: Ex 23.16, 34.22; Deut 16.9–12 **23.22:** Lev 19.9–10; Deut 24.19–22 **23.26–32:** Lev 16.29–34 **23.33–36:** Deut 16.13–15

shall live in **shelters** for seven days, [43]so
that your descendants may know that the
LORD made the people of Israel live in
simple **shelters** when he led them out of
Egypt. He is the LORD your God.
44 So in this way Moses gave the
people of Israel the **regulations** for **observing** the **religious festivals** to **honour**
the LORD.

Taking Care of the Lamps
(Ex 27.20–21)

24 The LORD told Moses [2]to give the
following orders to the people of
Israel: Bring **pure** olive-oil of the finest
quality for the lamps in the **Tent**, so that
a **light** may be kept burning regularly.
[3]Each evening Aaron shall light them
and keep them burning until morning,
there in the LORD's **presence** outside the
curtain in front of the **Covenant Box**,
which is in the **Most Holy Place**. This **regulation** is to be **observed** for all time to
come. [4]Aaron shall take **care** of the
lamps on the lampstand of **pure** gold and
must see that they burn regularly in the
LORD's **presence**.

The Bread Offered to God

5 Take twelve kilogrammes of flour
and bake twelve loaves of **bread**. [6]Put
the loaves in two rows, six in each row,
on the table covered with **pure** gold,
which is in the LORD's **presence**. [7]Put
some **pure incense** on each row, as a
token **food-offering** to the LORD to take
the place of the **bread**. [8]Every **Sabbath**,
for all time to come, the **bread** must be
placed in the **presence** of the LORD. This
is Israel's **duty** for ever. [9]The **bread** belongs to Aaron and his descendants, and
they shall eat it in a **holy** place, because
this is a very **holy** part of the food **offered**
to the LORD for the **priests**.

An Example of Just and Fair Punishment

10–11 There was a man whose father
was an Egyptian and whose mother was
an Israelite named Shelomith, the daughter of Dibri from the tribe of Dan. There
in the camp this man **quarrelled** with an
Israelite. During the **quarrel** he **cursed**
God, so they took him to Moses, [12]put
him under guard, and waited for the
LORD to tell them what to do with him.
13 The LORD said to Moses, [14]"Take
that man out of the camp. Everyone who
heard him **curse** shall put his hands on
the man's head to **testify** that he is **guilty**,
and then the whole **community** shall
stone him **to death**. [15]Then tell the people
of Israel that anyone who **curses** God
must **suffer** the consequences [16]and be
put **to death**. Any Israelite or any
foreigner living in Israel who **curses** the
LORD shall be stoned **to death** by the
whole **community**.
17 "Anyone who **commits murder**
shall be put **to death**, [18]and anyone who
kills an animal belonging to someone
else must replace it. The principle is a
life for a life.
19 "If anyone injures another person,
whatever he has done shall be done to
him. [20]If he breaks a bone, one of his
bones shall be broken; if he blinds him in
one eye, one of his eyes shall be **blinded**;
if he knocks out a tooth, one of his teeth
shall be knocked out. Whatever injury he
causes another person shall be done to
him in return. [21]Whoever kills an animal
shall replace it, but whoever kills a man
shall be put **to death**. [22]This **law** applies
to all of you, to Israelites and to
foreigners living among you, because I
am the LORD your God."
23 When Moses had said this to the
people of Israel, they took the man outside the camp and stoned him **to death**.
In this way the people of Israel did what
the LORD had **commanded** Moses.

blind 22.22; 26.16
bread [4] 23.6; 26.26
care Ex 25.40; Num 6.24
command 22.1; 25.1
commit 20.10; Num 5.19
community [2] 23.18; Num 1.5
Covenant Box 16.2; Num 3.31
curse [4] 20.9; Num 5.18
death (3) (to death) [6] 23.30; 27.29
duty (1) Ex 21.11; Num 3.7
food-offering 23.8; Num 15.3
guilty 22.9; Num 5.8
holy [2] 23.20; Num 4.4
Holy Place 16.2; Num 3.31
incense 16.12; 26.30
law 20.8; 25.18
life (1) 19.16; 26.16
light (1) 13.21; Num 5.15
observe 23.14; Num 9.2
offer 23.8; 27.9
presence [4] 16.13; Num 14.10
priest 23.9; 27.8
pure [4] 19.22; Num 5.8
quarrel [2] Gen 45.24; Judg 11.12
regulation 23.2; 25.2
Sabbath 23.3; Num 15.32
suffer 20.17; Num 5.31
Tent (2) (of the Lord's presence) 21.11; 26.11
testify Deut 17.6

The Seventh Year
(Deut 15.1–11)

25 The LORD spoke to Moses on
Mount Sinai and **commanded**
him [2]to give the following **regulations** to
the people of Israel. When you enter the
land that the LORD is giving you, you
shall **honour** the LORD by not cultivating
the land every seventh year. [3]You shall
sow your fields, prune your **vineyards**,
and gather your crops for six years. [4]But
the seventh year is to be a year of complete **rest** for the land, a year **dedicated**
to the LORD. Do not **sow** your fields or
prune your **vineyards**. [5]Do not even **harvest** the corn that grows by itself without
being **sown**, and do not gather the grapes
from your unpruned **vines**; it is a year of
complete **rest** for the land. [6]Although the
land has not been cultivated during that
year, it will **provide** food for you, your
slaves, your hired men, the foreigners
living with you, [7]your domestic animals,
and the wild animals in your fields.
Everything that it produces may be
eaten.

The Year of Restoration

8 Count seven times seven years, a

apart 21.15; Num 16.9
Atonement Acts 27.9
bless 9.22; 26.9
cheat 19.11; Deut 24.14
command [3] 24.23; 26.3
consult 20.6; Deut 18.11
control Ex 32.25; Num 24.2
dedicate 22.2; 27.14
enough [5] Ex 36.7; Num 11.13
force (1) Ex 6.1; 26.25
free [4] 19.20; 27.2
harvest [4] 23.9; 26.5
honour 23.5; 26.2
inherit Gen 48.6; Num 18.20
law 24.22; 26.3
Levites [4] Ex 38.21; Num 1.47
master Ex 21.4; Judg 3.25
need 13.11; 26.26
obey [4] 22.31; 26.3
poor [4] 23.22; 27.8
proclaim 23.4; Num 23.21
prosper Gen 30.29; Num 10.29
provide [2] Ex 28.2; Deut 23.4
regulation 24.3; 27.2
rest (1) [2] 23.3; 26.34
Restoration [9] 27.17

24.5–6: Ex 25.30 **24.9:** Mt 12.4; Mk 2.26; Lk 6.4 **24.17:** Ex 21.12 **24.20:** Ex 21.23–25; Deut 19.21; Mt 5.38
24.22: Num 15.16 **25.1–7:** Ex 23.10–11

restore [2]
Gen 41.13; Num 21.27
rich 20.24;
Num 13.27
right (3) [6] Ex 21.10;
27.20
sacred 22.2; 26.11
safe [2] Ex 21.13; 26.5
serve [2] 22.3;
Num 1.50
slave [9] 22.11; 26.13
sow [6] 11.37; 26.5
vine Gen 49.11;
Num 6.4
vineyard [3] 19.10;
Num 16.14
wage 19.13;
Num 18.31

total of forty-nine years. 9 Then, on the
tenth day of the seventh month, the Day
of **Atonement**, send a man to blow a
trumpet throughout the whole land. 10 In
this way you shall set the fiftieth year
apart and **proclaim freedom** to all the inhabitants of the land. During this year all
property that has been sold shall be **re-**
stored to the original owner or his descendants, and anyone who has been sold
as a **slave** shall return to his family.
11 You shall not **sow** your fields or **harvest**
the corn that grows by itself or gather
the grapes in your unpruned **vineyards**.
12 The whole year shall be **sacred** for you;
you shall eat only what the fields produce
of themselves.

13 In this year all property that has
been sold shall be **restored** to its original
owner. 14 So when you sell land to your
fellow-Israelite or buy land from him, do
not deal unfairly. 15 The price is to be
fixed according to the number of years
the land can produce crops before the
next **Year of Restoration**. 16 If there are
many years, the price shall be higher,
but if there are only a few years, the
price shall be lower, because what is
being sold is the number of crops the
land can produce. 17 Do not **cheat** a
fellow-Israelite, but **obey** the LORD your
God.

The Problem of the Seventh Year

18 **Obey** all the LORD's **laws** and
commands, so that you may live in **safety**
in the land. 19 The land will produce its
crops, and you will have all you want to
eat and will live in **safety**.

20 But someone may ask what there
will be to eat during the seventh year,
when no fields are **sown** and no crops
gathered. 21 The LORD will **bless** the land
in the sixth year so that it will produce
enough food for two years. 22 When you
sow your fields in the eighth year, you
will still be eating what you **harvested**
during the sixth year, and you will have
enough to eat until the crops you plant
that year are **harvested**.

Restoration of Property

23 Your land must not be sold on a
permanent basis, because you do not own
it; it belongs to God, and you are like
foreigners who are allowed to make use
of it.

24 When land is sold, the **right** of the
original owner to buy it back must be recognized. 25 If an Israelite becomes **poor**
and is **forced** to sell his land, his closest
relative is to buy it back. 26 A man who
has no relative to buy it back may later
become **prosperous** and have **enough** to
buy it back himself. 27 In that case he
must pay to the man who bought it a sum
that will make up for the years remaining until the next **Year of Restoration**,
when he would in any event recover his
land. 28 But if he does not have **enough**
money to buy the land back, it remains
under the **control** of the man who bought
it until the next **Year of Restoration**. In
that year it will be returned to its
original owner.

29 If a man sells a house in a walled
city, he has the **right** to buy it back during the first full year from the date of
sale. 30 But if he does not buy it back
within the year, he loses the **right** of re-
purchase, and the house becomes the
permanent property of the purchaser
and his descendants; it will not be returned in the **Year of Restoration**. 31 But
houses in unwalled villages are to be
treated like fields; the original owner has
the **right** to buy them back, and they are
to be returned in the **Year of Restora-**
tion. 32 However, **Levites** have the **right** to
buy back at any time their property in
the cities assigned to them. 33 If a house
in one of these cities is sold by a **Levite**
and is not bought back, it must be returned in the **Year of Restoration**,[m] because the houses which the **Levites** own
in their cities are their permanent property among the people of Israel. 34 But
the pasture land round the **Levite** cities
shall never be sold; it is their property
for ever.

Loans to the Poor

35 If a fellow-Israelite living near you
becomes **poor** and cannot support himself, you must **provide** for him as you
would for a hired man, so that he can
continue to live near you. 36 Do not
charge him any interest, but **obey** God
and let your fellow-Israelite live near
you. 37 Do not make him pay interest on
the money you lend him, and do not
make a profit on the food you sell him.
38 This is the **command** of the LORD your
God, who brought you out of Egypt in
order to give you the land of Canaan and
to be your God.

Release of Slaves

39 If a fellow-Israelite living near you
becomes so **poor** that he sells himself to
you as a **slave**, you shall not make him do
the work of a slave. 40 He shall stay with

[m] *Probable text* If a house...Restoration; *Hebrew unclear.*

25.35: Deut 15.7-8 **25.37:** Ex 22.25; Deut 23.19-20 **25.39-46:** Ex 21.2-6; Deut 15.12-18

you as a hired man and serve you until
the next Year of Restoration. 41 At that
time he and his children shall leave you
and return to his family and to the property of his ancestors. 42 The people of
Israel are the LORD'S slaves, and he
brought them out of Egypt; they must not
be sold into slavery. 43 Do not treat them
harshly, but obey your God. 44 If you need
slaves, you may buy them from the
nations round you. 45 You may also buy
the children of the foreigners who are
living among you. Such children born in
your land may become your property,
46 and you may leave them as an inheritance to your sons, whom they must
serve as long as they live. But you must
not treat any of your fellow-Israelites
harshly.
47 Suppose a foreigner living with you
becomes rich, while a fellow-Israelite becomes poor and sells himself as a slave
to that foreigner or to a member of his
family. 48 After he is sold, he still has the
right to be bought back. One of his
brothers 49 or his uncle or his cousin or
another of his close relatives may buy
him back; or if he himself earns enough,
he may buy his own freedom. 50 He must
consult the one who bought him, and
they must count the years from the time
he sold himself until the next Year of
Restoration and must set the price for his
release on the basis of the wages paid to
a hired man. 51-52 He must refund a part
of the purchase price according to the
number of years left, 53 as if he had been
hired on an annual basis. His master
must not treat him harshly. 54 If he is not
set free in any of these ways, he and his
children must be set free in the next
Year of Restoration. 55 An Israelite cannot be a permanent slave, because the
people of Israel are the LORD's slaves. He
brought them out of Egypt; he is the
LORD their God.

Blessings for Obedience
(Deut 7.12–24; 28.1–14)

26 The LORD said, "Do not make
idols or set up statues, stone pillars, or carved stones to worship. I am the
LORD your God. 2 Keep the religious festivals and honour the place where I am
worshipped. I am the LORD.
3 "If you live according to my laws
and obey my commands, 4 I will send you
rain at the right time, so that the land
will produce crops and the trees will
bear fruit. 5 Your crops will be so plentiful that you will still be harvesting corn
when it is time to pick grapes, and you
will still be picking grapes when it is
time to sow corn. You will have all that
you want to eat, and you will live in
safety in your land.
6 "I will give you peace in your land,
and you will sleep without being afraid of
anyone. I will get rid of the dangerous
animals in the land, and there will be no
more war there. 7 You will be victorious
over your enemies; 8 five of you will be
able to defeat a hundred, and a hundred
will be able to defeat ten thousand. 9 I will
bless you and give you many children; I
will keep my part of the covenant that I
made with you. 10 Your harvests will be
so plentiful that they will last for a year,
and even then you will have to throw
away what is left of the old harvest to
make room for the new. 11 I will live
among you in my sacred tent, and I will
never turn away from you. 12 I will be
with you; I will be your God, and you will
be my people. 13 I, the LORD your God,
brought you out of Egypt so that you
would no longer be slaves. I broke the
power that held you down and I let you
walk with your head held high."

Punishment for Disobedience
(Deut 28.15–68)

14 The LORD said, "If you will not obey
my commands, you will be punished. 15 If
you refuse to obey my laws and commands and break the covenant I have
made with you, 16 I will punish you. I will
bring disaster on you—incurable diseases
and fevers that will make you blind and
cause your life to waste away. You will
sow your seed, but it will do you no good,
because your enemies will conquer you
and eat what you have grown. 17 I will
turn against you, so that you will be defeated, and those who hate you will rule
over you; you will be so terrified that you
will run when no one is chasing you.
18 "If even after all this you still do not
obey me, I will increase your punishment
seven times. 19 I will break your stubborn
pride; there will be no rain, and your
land will be dry and as hard as iron. 20 All
your hard work will do you no good, because your land will not produce crops
and the trees will not bear fruit.
21 "If you still continue to resist me
and refuse to obey me, I will again increase your punishment seven times. 22 I
will send dangerous animals among you,
and they will kill your children, destroy
your livestock, and leave so few of you
that your roads will be deserted.
23 "If after all this punishment you
still do not listen to me, but continue to

26.1: Ex 20.4; Lev 19.4; Deut 5.8, 16.21–22, 27.1 **26.3-5:** Deut 11.13–15, 28.1–14 **26.12:** 2 Cor 6.16

abandon [2] 19.4; Num 32.15
accept 23.11; 27.9
afraid Ex 34.30; Num 14.9
altar 22.3; Num 3.26
anger 10.6; Num 1.53
bless 25.21; Num 6.23
blind 24.20; Deut 15.21
body 21.5; Num 5.2
bread 24.5; Num 4.7
command [5] 25.1; 27.34
confess 16.21; Num 5.7
conquer Ex 34.24; Num 13.30

covenant [6] 2.13; Num 18.19
danger [2] Gen 15.1; Deut 28.66
dead 21.11; Num 12.12
defy [2] Num 26.9
destroy [6] 13.52; Num 11.1
disaster Ex 32.12; Num 8.19
disease [2] 22.4; Num 5.2
disgust 20.13; Deut 12.31
enemy [11] Ex 32.25; Num 10.9
enjoy [2] Gen 41.53; Deut 12.7
exile [4] Judg 18.30
festival 23.2; Num 10.10
force (1) 25.25; Deut 20.11
God's people [3] 23.29; Num 5.3
hard [3] Ex 5.9; Deut 11.10
harvest [3] 25.5; Num 28.26
hate 19.18; Num 10.35
honour 25.2; Num 16.10
humble Gen 43.28; Num 12.3
hunger [2] Gen 47.13; Deut 8.3
idol [2] 19.4; Num 33.52
incense 24.7; Num 4.7
last (1) Gen 47.9; Num 28.17
law [4] 25.18; Num 5.29
life (1) 24.18; Num 16.22
need 25.44; Num 18.20
new 23.14; Num 1.51
obey [6] 25.17; Num 3.42
peace Gen 26.29; Num 6.26
place of worship [2] Ex 22.8; Num 33.52
plenty [2] Gen 41.29; Num 11.33
power [2] 6.18; Num 11.23
promise 20.24; Num 6.21
proud Gen 49.3; Deut 1.43
punish [8] 22.16; Num 12.11
rebel [2] 16.21; Num 14.9
refuse (1) [4] 6.2; Num 14.11
reject 20.22; Num 11.20
religion 23.2; Num 10.10
remember 23.3; Num 11.5
resist [2] 2 Chr 13.7
rest (1) [3] 25.4; Num 23.24
rid [2] Ex 12.15; Deut 13.5
right (1) Ex 23.8; Num 27.7
ruin [2] Ex 23.8; Num 21.11
sacred 25.12; 27.9
sacrifice 23.12; Num 6.17
safe [2] 25.18; Num 24.21

scatter Gen 49.7; Num 10.35
seed 19.19; 27.16
slave 25.6; Deut 5.6
sow [2] 25.3; 27.16
stubborn Ex 34.9; Deut 2.30
stumble 19.14; 2 Sam 6.6
Tent (2) (of the Lord's presence) 24.2; Num 1.1
terrify [2] Ex 15.15; Num 22.3
turn [6] 20.3; Num 12.10
victory Ex 33.14; Num 21.34
worse Ex 10.6; Num 13.28
worship (1) (of God) 23.2; Num 28.18
worship (2) (of other gods) 20.2; Num 21.29

defy me, 24 then I will turn on you and punish you seven times harder than before. 25 I will bring war on you to punish you for breaking our covenant, and if you gather in your cities for safety, I will send incurable diseases among you, and you will be forced to surrender to your enemies. 26 I will cut off your food supply, so that ten women will need only one oven to bake all the bread they have. They will ration it out, and when you have eaten it all, you will still be hungry.

27 "If after all this you still continue to defy me and refuse to obey me, 28 then in my anger I will turn on you and again make your punishment seven times worse than before. 29 Your hunger will be so great that you will eat your own children. 30 I will destroy your places of worship on the hills, tear down your incense-altars, and throw your dead bodies on your fallen idols. In utter disgust 31 I will turn your cities into ruins, destroy your places of worship, and refuse to accept your sacrifices. 32 I will destroy your land so completely that the enemies who occupy it will be shocked at the destruction. 33 I will bring war on you and scatter you in foreign lands. Your land will be deserted, and your cities left in ruins. 34–35 Then the land will enjoy the years of complete rest that you would not give it; it will lie abandoned and get its rest while you are in exile in the land of your enemies.

36 "I will make those of you who are in exile so terrified that the sound of a leaf blowing in the wind will make you run. You will run as if you were being pursued in battle, and you will fall when there is no enemy near you. 37 You will stumble over one another when no one is chasing you, and you will be unable to fight against any enemy. 38 You will die in exile, swallowed up by the land of your enemies. 39 The few of you who survive in the land of your enemies will waste away because of your own sin and the sin of your ancestors.

40 "But your descendants will confess their sins and the sins of their ancestors, who resisted me and rebelled against me, 41 and made me turn against them and send them into exile in the land of their enemies. At last, when your descendants are humbled and they have paid the penalty for their sin and rebellion, 42 I will remember my covenant with Jacob and with Isaac and with Abraham, and I will renew my promise to give my people the land. 43 First, however, the land must be rid of its people, so that it can enjoy its complete rest, and they must pay the full penalty for having rejected my laws and my commands. 44 But even then, when they are still in the land of their enemies, I will not completely abandon or destroy them. That would put an end to my covenant with them, and I am the LORD their God. 45 I will renew the covenant that I made with their ancestors when I showed all the nations my power by bringing my people out of Egypt, in order that I, the LORD, might be their God."

46 All these are the laws and commands that the LORD gave to Moses on Mount Sinai for the people of Israel.

26.42: Gen 17.7–8, 26.3–4, 28.13–14

Laws Concerning Gifts to the LORD

27 The LORD gave Moses 2 the following regulations for the people of Israel. When a person has been given to the LORD in fulfilment of a special vow, that person may be set free by the payment of the following sums of money, 3–7 according to the official standard:

—adult male, twenty to sixty years old: 50 pieces of silver
—adult female: 30 pieces of silver
—young male, five to twenty years old: 20 pieces of silver
—young female: 10 pieces of silver
—infant male under five: 5 pieces of silver
—infant female: 3 pieces of silver
—male above sixty years of age: 15 pieces of silver
—female above sixty: 10 pieces of silver

8 If the man who made the vow is too poor to pay the standard price, he shall bring the person to the priest, and the priest will set a lower price, according to the ability of the man to pay.

9 If the vow concerns an animal that is acceptable as an offering to the LORD, then every gift made to the LORD is sacred, 10 and the man who made the vow may not substitute another animal for it. If he does, both animals belong to the LORD. 11 But if the vow concerns a ritually unclean animal, which is not acceptable as an offering to the LORD, the man shall take the animal to the priest. 12 The priest shall fix a price for it, according to its good or bad qualities, and the price will be final. 13 If the man wishes to buy it back, he must pay the price plus an additional twenty per cent.

14 When someone dedicates his house to the LORD, the priest shall fix the price according to its good or bad points, and the price will be final. 15 If the one who

accept [2] 26.31; Num 7.5
bad [2] Ex 7.21; Num 11.11
being [2] Gen 9.10; Deut 5.26
choose 16.9; Num 1.5
command 26.3; Num 1.19
death (3) (to death) 24.14; Num 1.51
dedicate [10] 25.4; Num 3.45
final [2] Gen 27.4; 1 Chr 9.26
first-born [2] Ex 34.19; Num 3.12
free 25.10; Num 5.31
freewill 23.38; Num 15.3
fulfil 23.38; Num 6.21
gift 23.17; Num 6.20
human [2] 5.3; Num 19.16
lamb 23.12; Num 6.12
offer [3] 24.9; Num 3.4
poor [2] 25.25; Deut 15.4
priest [8] 24.9; Num 3.3
regulation 25.2; Num 6.21
Restoration [5] 25.15; Num 36.4
right (3) 25.24; Num 30.13
sacred 26.11; Num 4.15
seed 26.16; Num 6.4
sow 26.5; Deut 11.10
special 23.11; Num 5.9
unclean [2] 22.3; Num 5.2
value [2] 22.14; 1 Kgs 10.21
vow [5] 23.38; Num 6.2
wish [4] Ex 35.5; Num 11.18

dedicated the house **wishes** to buy it back, he must pay the price plus an additional twenty per cent.

16 If a man **dedicates** part of his land to the LORD, the price shall be fixed according to the amount of **seed** it takes to **sow** it, at the rate of ten pieces of silver for every twenty kilogrammes of barley. [17] If he **dedicates** the land immediately after a **Year of Restoration**, the full price applies. [18] If he **dedicates** it later, the **priest** shall estimate the cash **value** according to the number of years left until the next **Year of Restoration**, and fix a reduced price. [19] If the man who **dedicated** the field **wishes** to buy it back, he must pay the price plus an additional twenty per cent. [20] If he sells the field to someone else without first buying it back from the LORD, he loses the **right** to buy it back. [21] At the next **Year of Restoration** the field will become the LORD's permanent property; it shall belong to the **priests**.

22 If a man **dedicates** to the LORD a field that he has bought, [23] the **priest** shall estimate its **value** according to the number of years until the next **Year of Restoration**, and the man must pay the price that very day; the money belongs to the LORD. [24] At the **Year of Restoration** the field shall be returned to the original owner or to his descendants.

25 All prices shall be fixed according to the official standard.

26 The **first-born** of an animal already belongs to the LORD, so no one may dedicate it to him as a **freewill offering**. A calf, a **lamb**, or a kid belongs to the LORD, [27] but the **first-born** of an **unclean** animal may be bought back at the standard price plus an additional twenty per cent. If it is not bought back, it may be sold to someone else at the standard price.

28 No one may sell or buy back what he has unconditionally **dedicated**[n] to the LORD, whether it is a **human being**, an animal, or land. It belongs permanently to the LORD. [29] Not even a **human being** who has been unconditionally **dedicated** may be bought back; he must be put **to death**.

30 One-tenth of all the produce of the land, whether grain or fruit, belongs to the LORD. [31] If a man **wishes** to buy any of it back, he must pay the standard price plus an additional twenty per cent. [32] One out of every ten domestic animals belongs to the LORD. When the animals are counted, every tenth one belongs to the LORD. [33] The owner may not arrange the animals so that the **poor** animals are **chosen**, and he may not make any substitutions. If he does substitute one animal for another, then both animals will belong to the LORD and may not be bought back.

34 These are the **commands** that the LORD gave Moses on Mount Sinai for the people of Israel.

[n] UNCONDITIONALLY DEDICATED: *Anything dedicated in this way belonged completely to the LORD and could not be used; it had to be destroyed.*

27.28: Num 18.14 **27.30-33:** Num 18.21; Deut 14.22-29

NUMBERS

INTRODUCTION

The book of *Numbers* tells the story of the Israelites during the nearly forty years from the time they left Mount Sinai until they reached the eastern border of the land that God had promised to give them. The name of the book refers to a prominent feature of the story, that is, the census which Moses took of the Israelites at Mount Sinai before their departure, and again in Moab, east of the Jordan, about a generation later. In the period between the two censuses the Israelites went to Kadesh Barnea on the southern border of Canaan, but failed to enter the promised land from there. After spending many years in that area, they went to the region east of the River Jordan, where part of the people settled and where the rest prepared to cross the river into Canaan.

The book of *Numbers* is an account of a people who were often discouraged and afraid in the face of hardship, and who rebelled against God and against Moses, the man God appointed to lead them. It is the story of God's faithful, persistent care for his people in spite of their weakness and disobedience, and of Moses' steadfast, if sometimes impatient, devotion both to God and to his people.

Outline of Contents

---

anger Lev 26.28; 11.1
choose Lev 27.33; 13.2
command [2] Lev 27.34; 2.33
community [3] Lev 24.14; 3.7
death (3) (to death) Lev 27.29; 3.10
fit (1) [3] Ex 20.25; 26.2
help [2] Lev 19.16; 8.26
Levites [4] Lev 25.32; 2.17
new Lev 26.10; 15.20
serve Lev 25.40; 3.4
service [3] Ex 32.29; 3.26
strike Ex 17.5; 8.19
Tent (2) (of the Lord's presence) [5] Lev 26.11; 2.2

The First Census of Israel

1 On the first day of the second month
in the second year after the people
of Israel left Egypt, the LORD spoke to
Moses there in the **Tent** of his presence
in the Sinai Desert. He said, 2 "You and
Aaron are to take a census of the people
of Israel by clans and families. List the
names of all the men 3 twenty years old
or older who are **fit** for **military service**.
4 Ask one clan chief from each tribe to
help you." 5-16 These are the men, leaders
within their tribes, who were **chosen**
from the **community** for this work:

Tribe	*Clan chief*
Reuben	Elizur son of Shedeur
Simeon	Shelumiel son of Zurishaddai
Judah	Nahshon son of Amminadab
Issachar	Nethanel son of Zuar
Zebulun	Eliab son of Helon
Ephraim	Elishama son of Ammihud
Manasseh	Gamaliel son of Pedahzur
Benjamin	Abidan son of Gideoni
Dan	Ahiezer son of Ammishaddai
Asher	Pagiel son of Ochran
Gad	Eliasaph son of Deuel
Naphtali	Ahira son of Enan

17 With the **help** of these twelve men
Moses and Aaron 18 called together the
whole **community** on the first day of the
second month and registered all the
people by clans and families. The names
of all the men twenty years old or older
were recorded and counted, 19 as the
LORD had **commanded**. In the Sinai
Desert, Moses registered the people.
20-46 The men twenty years old or older
who were **fit** for **military service** were registered by name according to clan and
family, beginning with the tribe of
Reuben, Jacob's eldest son. The totals
were as follows:

Tribe	*Number*
Reuben	46,500
Simeon	59,300
Gad	45,650
Judah	74,600
Issachar	54,400
Zebulun	57,400
Ephraim	40,500

1.1-46: Num 26.1-51

Manasseh	32,200
Benjamin	35,400
Dan	62,700
Asher	41,500
Naphtali	53,400
Total:	603,550

47 The **Levites** were not registered with the other tribes, 48 because the LORD had said to Moses, 49 "When you take a census of the men **fit for military service**, do not include the tribe of Levi. 50 Instead, put the **Levites** in charge of the **Tent** of my presence and all its equipment. They shall carry it and its equipment, **serve** in it, and set up their camp round it. 51 Whenever you move your camp, the **Levites** shall take the **Tent** down and set it up again at each **new** camping place. Anyone else who comes near the **Tent** shall be put **to death**. 52 The rest of the Israelites shall set up camp, company by company, each man with his own group and under his own banner. 53 But the Levites shall camp round the **Tent** to guard it, so that no one may come near and cause my **anger** to **strike** the **community** of Israel." 54 So the people of Israel did everything that the LORD had **commanded** Moses.

The Arrangement of the Tribes in Camp

command [2] 1.19; 3.14
last (2) [2] Ex 36.12; 14.33
Levites [2] 1.47; 3.9
Tent (2) (of the Lord's presence) [2] 1.1; 3.7

2 The LORD gave Moses and Aaron the following instructions. 2 When the Israelites set up camp, each man will camp under the banner of his division and the flag of his own clan. The camp is to be set up all round the **Tent**.

3–9 On the east side, those under the banner of the division of Judah shall camp in their groups, under their leaders, as follows:

Tribe	*Leader*	*Number*
Judah	Nahshon son of Amminadab	74,600
Issachar	Nethanel son of Zuar	54,400
Zebulun	Eliab son of Helon	57,400
Total:		186,400

The division of Judah shall march first.

10–16 On the south, those under the banner of the division of Reuben shall camp in their groups, under their leaders, as follows:

Tribe	*Leader*	*Number*
Reuben	Elizur son of Shedeur	46,500
Simeon	Shelumiel son of Zurishaddai	59,300
Gad	Eliasaph son of Deuel	45,650
Total:		151,450

The division of Reuben shall march second.

17 Then, between the first two divisions and the **last** two the **Levites** are to march carrying the **Tent**. Each division shall march in the same order as they camp, each in position under its banner.

18–24 On the west, those under the banner of the division of Ephraim shall camp in their groups, under their leaders, as follows:

Tribe	*Leader*	*Number*
Ephraim	Elishama son of Ammihud	40,500
Manasseh	Gamaliel son of Pedahzur	32,200
Benjamin	Abidan son of Gideoni	35,400
Total:		108,100

The division of Ephraim shall march third.

25–31 On the north, those under the banner of the division of Dan shall camp in their groups, under their leaders, as follows:

Tribe	*Leader*	*Number*
Dan	Ahiezer son of Ammishaddai	62,700
Asher	Pagiel son of Ochran	41,500
Naphtali	Ahira son of Enan	53,400
Total:		157,600

The division of Dan shall march **last**.

32 The total number of the people of Israel enrolled in the divisions, group by group, was 603,550. 33 As the LORD had **commanded** Moses, the **Levites** were not registered with the rest of the Israelites.

34 So the people of Israel did everything the LORD had **commanded** Moses. They camped, each under his own banner, and they marched, each with his own clan.

Aaron's Sons

3 This is the family of Aaron and Moses at the time the LORD spoke to Moses on Mount Sinai. 2 Aaron had four sons: Nadab, the eldest, Abihu, Eleazar, and Ithamar. 3 They were **anointed** and **ordained** as **priests**, 4 but Nadab and Abihu were killed when they **offered unholy fire** to the LORD in the Sinai Desert. They had no children, so Eleazar and Ithamar **served** as **priests** during Aaron's lifetime.

The Levites Are Appointed to Serve the Priests

5 The LORD said to Moses, 6 "Bring forward the tribe of Levi and appoint them

altar [2] Lev 26.30; 4.11
anoint Lev 21.10; 4.16
claim [2] Ex 22.9; 8.16
command [2] 2.33; 4.34
community 1.5; 4.34
consecrate Lev 21.10; 4.16
Covenant Box Lev 24.3; 4.5
death (3) (to death) [2] 1.51; 14.10
dedicate [2] Lev 27.14; 5.25
duty (1) [4] Lev 24.8; 4.27
first-born [10] Lev 27.26; 8.16
Holy Place [4] Lev 24.3; 4.12

3.2: Num 26.60 **3.4:** Lev 10.1–2; Num 26.61

Levites [11] 2.17; 4.2
obey [2] Lev 26.3; 5.4
offer Lev 27.9; 4.7
ordain Lev 16.32; 1 Kgs 13.33
priest [7] Lev 27.8; 4.16
require Lev 23.37; 4.26
servant Ex 32.13; 12.7
serve [2] 1.50; 4.49
service [4] 1.3; 4.4
Tent (2) (of the Lord's presence) [9] 2.2; 4.3
unholy Lev 16.1; 26.61

as **servants** of Aaron the **priest**. 7 They
shall do the work **required** for the **Tent** of
my presence and perform **duties** for the
priests and for the whole **community**.
8 They shall take charge of all the equipment of the **Tent** and perform the **duties**
for the rest of the Israelites. 9 The only
responsibility the **Levites** have is to **serve**
Aaron and his sons. 10 You shall appoint
Aaron and his sons to carry out the **duties**
of the **priesthood**; anyone else who tries
to do so shall be put **to death**."
11 The LORD said to Moses, 12–13 "The
Levites are now to be mine. When I
killed all the **first-born** of the Egyptians, I
consecrated as my own the eldest son of
each Israelite family and the **first-born** of
every animal. Now, instead of having the
first-born sons of Israel as my own, I
have the **Levites**; they will belong to me.
I am the LORD."

The Census of the Levites

14 In the Sinai Desert the LORD **commanded** Moses 15 to register the **Levites**
by clans and families, enrolling every
male a month old or older, 16 and Moses
did so. 17–20 Levi had three sons: Gershon,
Kohath, and Merari, who were the ancestors of the clans that bear their names.
Gershon had two sons: Libni and Shimei;
Kohath had four sons: Amram, Izhar,
Hebron, and Uzziel; and Merari had two
sons: Mahli and Mushi. They were the
ancestors of the families that bear their
names.
21 The clan of Gershon was composed
of the families of Libni and Shimei. 22 The
total number of males one month old or
older that were enrolled was 7,500. 23 This
clan was to camp on the west behind the
Tent, 24 with Eliasaph son of Lael as chief
of the clan. 25 They were responsible for
the **Tent**, its inner cover, its outer cover,
the curtain for the entrance, 26 the curtains for the court which is round the
Tent and the **altar**, and the curtain for
the entrance of the court. They were responsible for all the **service** connected
with these items.
27 The clan of Kohath was composed
of the families of Amram, Izhar, Hebron,
and Uzziel. 28 The total number of males
one month old or older that were enrolled was 8,600. 29 This clan was to camp
on the south side of the **Tent**, 30 with
Elizaphan son of Uzziel as chief of the
clan. 31 They were responsible for the
Covenant Box, the table, the lamp-stand,
the **altars**, the utensils the **priests** use in
the **Holy Place**, and the curtain at the entrance to the **Most Holy Place**. They
were responsible for all the **service** connected with these items.
32 The chief of the **Levites** was
Eleazar son of Aaron the **priest**. He was
in charge of those who carried out the
duties in the **Holy Place**.
33 The clan of Merari was composed
of the families of Mahli and Mushi. 34 The
total number of males one month old or
older that were enrolled was 6,200. 35 This
clan was to camp on the north side of the
Tent, with Zuriel son of Abihail as chief
of the clan. 36 They were assigned responsibility for the frames for the **Tent**, its
bars, posts, bases, and all its fittings.
They were responsible for all the **service**
connected with these items. 37 They were
also responsible for the posts, bases,
pegs, and ropes for the outer court.
38 Moses and Aaron and his sons were
to camp in front of the **Tent** on the east.
They were responsible for carrying out
the **services** performed in the **Holy Place**
for the people of Israel. Anyone else who
tried to do so was to be put **to death**.
39 The total number of all the **Levite**
males one month old or older that Moses
enrolled by clans at the **command** of the
LORD, was 22,000.

The Levites Take the Place of the First-Born Sons

40–41 The LORD said to Moses, "All of
Israel's **first-born** sons belong to me. So
register by name every **first-born** male
Israelite, one month old or older. But in
place of them I **claim** all the **Levites** as
mine! I am the LORD! I also **claim** the
livestock of the **Levites** in place of all the
first-born of the livestock." 42 Moses
obeyed, and registered all the **first-born**
males 43 one month old or older; the total
was 22,273.
44 The LORD said to Moses, 45 "Now **dedicate** the **Levites** as mine in place of all
the **first-born** Israelite sons, and **dedicate**
the livestock of the **Levites** in place of
the **first-born** of the Israelites' livestock.
46 Since the **first-born** Israelite sons outnumber the **Levites** by 273, you must buy
back the extra sons. 47 For each one pay
five pieces of silver, according to the official standard, 48 and give this money to
Aaron and his sons." 49 Moses **obeyed** and
took 50 the 1,365 pieces of silver 51 and
gave them to Aaron and his sons.

The Duties of the Levite Clan of Kohath

4 The LORD told Moses 2 to take a census of the **Levite** clan of Kohath by
sub-clans and families, 3 and to register
all the men between the ages of thirty

altar [4] 3.26; 5.16
anoint 3.3; 7.1
ash Lev 6.10; 19.9
bread [2] Lev 26.26; 6.15

3.13: Ex 13.2

command [3] 3.14; 5.2
community 3.7; 8.9
consecrate 3.12; 6.8
Covenant Box 3.31; 7.89
direct [2] Ex 38.21; 7.8
duty (1) 3.7; 8.24
grain-offering Lev 23.18; 7.12
holy Lev 24.9; 5.17
Holy Place 3.31; 8.19
incense [2] Lev 26.30; 5.15
Levites [4] 3.9; 7.5
offer [2] 3.4; 5.9
prevent Ex 8.29; 22.16
priest [4] 3.3; 5.8
require 3.7; 5.15
sacred [4] Lev 27.9; 6.20
serve 3.4; 10.25
service [3] 3.26; 8.26
task [3] Is 49.6
Tent (2) (of the Lord's presence) [15] 3.7; 5.17
wine-offering Lev 23.18; 15.24

and fifty who were qualified to work in the **Tent** of the LORD's presence. 4 Their **service** involves the most **holy** things.

5 The LORD gave Moses the following instructions. When it is time to break camp, Aaron and his sons shall enter the **Tent**, take down the curtain in front of the **Covenant Box**, and cover the Box with it. 6 They shall put a fine leather cover over it, spread a blue cloth on top, and then insert the carrying-poles.

7 They shall spread a blue cloth over the table for the **bread offered** to the LORD and put on it the dishes, the **incense** bowls, the **offering** bowls, and the jars for the **wine-offering**. There shall always be **bread** on the table. 8 They shall spread a red cloth over all this, put a fine leather cover over it, and then insert the carrying-poles.

9 They shall take a blue cloth and cover the lampstand, with its lamps, tongs, trays, and all the olive-oil containers. 10 They shall wrap it and all its equipment in a fine leather cover and place it on a carrying-frame.

11 Next they shall spread a blue cloth over the gold **altar**, put a fine leather cover over it, and then insert the carrying-poles. 12 They shall take all the utensils used in the **Holy Place**, wrap them in a blue cloth, put a fine leather cover over them, and place them on a carrying-frame. 13 They shall remove the greasy **ashes** from the **altar** and spread a purple cloth over it. 14 They shall put on it all the equipment used in the **service** at the **altar**: firepans, hooks, shovels, and basins. Then they shall put a fine leather cover over it and insert the carrying-poles. 15 When it is time to break camp, the clan of Kohath shall come to carry the **sacred** objects only after Aaron and his sons have finished covering them and all their equipment. The clan of Kohath must not touch the **sacred** objects, or they will die.

These are the responsibilities of the clan of Kohath whenever the **Tent** is moved.

16 Eleazar son of Aaron the **priest** shall be responsible for the whole **Tent** and for the oil for the lamps, the **incense**, the **grain-offerings**, the **anointing** oil, and everything else in the **Tent** that has been **consecrated** to the LORD.

17 The LORD said to Moses and Aaron, 18 "Do not let the clan of Kohath 19 be killed by coming near these most **sacred** objects. To **prevent** this happening, Aaron and his sons shall go in and assign each man his **task** and tell him what to carry. 20 But if the Kohathites enter the **Tent** and see the **priests** preparing the **sacred** objects for moving,[a] they will die."

The Duties of the Levite Clan of Gershon

21 The LORD told Moses 22 to take a census of the **Levite** clan of Gershon by sub-clans and families, 23 and to register all the men between the ages of thirty and fifty who were qualified to work in the **Tent** of the LORD's presence. 24 They shall be responsible for carrying the following objects: 25 the **Tent**, its inner cover, its outer cover, the fine leather cover on top of it, the curtain for the entrance, 26 the curtains and ropes for the court that is round the **Tent** and the **altar**, the curtains for the entrance of the court, and all the fittings used in setting up these objects. They shall perform all the **tasks required** for these things. 27 Moses and Aaron shall see to it that the Gershonites perform all the **duties** and carry everything that Aaron and his sons assign to them. 28 These are the responsibilites of the Gershon clan in the **Tent**; they shall carry them out under the **direction** of Ithamar son of Aaron the **priest**.

The Duties of the Levite Clan of Merari

29 The LORD told Moses to take a census of the **Levite** clan of Merari by sub-clans and families, 30 and to register all the men between the ages of thirty and fifty who were qualified to work in the **Tent** of the LORD's presence. 31 They shall be responsible for carrying the frames, bars, posts, and bases of the **Tent**, 32 and the posts, bases, pegs, and ropes of the court round the **Tent**, with all the fittings used in setting them up. Each man will be responsible for carrying specific items. 33 These are the responsibilities of the Merari clan in their **service** in the **Tent**: they shall carry them out under the **direction** of Ithamar son of Aaron the **priest**.

The Census of the Levites

34–48 Following the LORD's **command**, Moses, Aaron, and the leaders of the **community** took a census of the three **Levite** clans, Kohath, Gershon, and Merari. They did this by sub-clans and families and registered all the men between the ages of thirty and fifty who were qualified to work in the **Tent** of the LORD's presence, as follows:

[a] see...moving; *or* see the sacred objects even for a moment.

Clan	Number
Kohath	2,750
Gershon	2,630
Merari	3,200
Total:	8,580

49 Each man was registered as the LORD
had commanded Moses; and at the
command of the LORD given through
Moses, each man was assigned responsibility for his task of serving or carrying.

Unclean People

5 The LORD said to Moses,
2 "Command the people of Israel to
expel from the camp everyone with a
dreaded skin disease or a bodily discharge and everyone who is unclean by
contact with a corpse. 3 Send all these ritually unclean people out, so that they will
not defile the camp, where I live among
my people." 4 The Israelites obeyed and
expelled them all from the camp.

Repayment for Wrongs Done

5 The LORD gave Moses 6 the following
instructions for the people of Israel.
When anyone is unfaithful to the LORD
and commits a wrong against someone,
7 he must confess his sin and make full repayment, plus an additional twenty per
cent, to the person he has wronged. 8 But
if that person has died and has no near
relative to whom payment can be made,
it shall be given to the LORD for the
priest. This payment is in addition to the
ram used to perform the ritual of
purification for the guilty person. 9 Also
every special contribution which the
Israelites offer to the LORD belongs to the
priest to whom they present it. 10 Each
priest shall keep the offerings presented
to him.

Cases of Wives with Suspicious Husbands

11 The LORD commanded Moses
12–14 to give the Israelites the following instructions. It may happen that a man becomes suspicious that his wife is unfaithful to him and has defiled herself by having intercourse with another man. But
the husband may not be certain, for his
wife may have kept it secret—there was
no witness, and she was not caught in the
act. Or it may happen that a husband becomes suspicious of his wife, even though
she has not been unfaithful. 15 In either
case the man shall take his wife to the
priest. He shall also take the required
offering of one kilogramme of barley
flour, but he shall not pour any olive-oil
on it or put any incense on it, because it
is an offering from a suspicious husband,
made to bring the truth to light.

16 The priest shall bring the woman
forward and make her stand in front of
the altar. 17 He shall pour some holy
water into a clay bowl and take some of
the earth that is on the floor of the Tent
of the LORD's presence and put it in the
water to make it bitter. 18 Then he shall
loosen the woman's hair and put the
offering of flour in her hands. In his
hands the priest shall hold the bowl containing the bitter water that brings a
curse. 19 Then the priest shall make the
woman agree to this oath spoken by the
priest: "If you have not committed adultery, you will not be harmed by the curse
that this water brings. 20 But if you have
committed adultery, 21 may the LORD
make your name a curse among your
people. May he cause your genital
organs to shrink and your stomach to
swell up. 22 May this water enter your
stomach and cause it to swell up and
your genital organs to shrink."

The woman shall respond, "I agree;
may the LORD do so."

23 Then the priest shall write this
curse down and wash the writing off into
the bowl of bitter water. 24 Before he
makes the woman drink the water,
which may then cause her bitter pain,
25 the priest shall take the offering of
flour out of the woman's hands, hold it
out in dedication to the LORD, and present it on the altar. 26 Then he shall take a
handful of it as a token offering and burn
it on the altar. Finally, he shall make the
woman drink the water. 27 If she has
committed adultery, the water will cause
bitter pain; her stomach will swell up
and her genital organs will shrink. Her
name will become a curse among her
people. 28 But if she is innocent, she will
not be harmed and will be able to bear
children.

29–30 This is the law in cases where a
man is jealous and becomes suspicious
that his wife has committed adultery.
The woman shall be made to stand in
front of the altar, and the priest shall perform this ritual. 31 The husband shall be
free of guilt, but the woman, if guilty,
must suffer the consequences.

Rules for Nazirites

6 The LORD commanded Moses 2 to
give the following instructions to the
people of Israel. Any man or woman who
makes a special vow to become a
Nazirite and dedicates himself to the
LORD 3 shall abstain from wine and beer.

5.5–8: Lev 6.1–7 6.3: Lk 1.15

act Lev 18.24; 11.12
adultery [4] Lev 20.10; Deut 5.18
agree [2] Ex 23.32; Deut 1.14
altar [4] 4.11; 7.1
bitter [5] Ex 15.23; 9.11
body Lev 26.30; 8.7
case (2) Lev 19.15; 27.5
certain (1) Deut 4.9
command [2] 4.34; 6.1
commit [4] Lev 24.17; Deut 5.17
confess Lev 26.40; Josh 7.19
contribute Lev 10.14; 15.19
curse [5] Lev 24.10; 22.6
dedicate 3.45; 6.2
defile [2] Lev 21.11; 6.6
disease Lev 26.16; 12.10
free Lev 27.2; 36.6
God's people Lev 26.12; 9.13
guilty [3] Lev 24.14; 15.30
harm [2] Lev 6.18; Deut 19.16
holy 4.4; 10.33
incense 4.7; 7.12
innocent Ex 23.7; Deut 19.6
jealous Gen 37.11; Deut 32.16
law Lev 26.3; 6.20
light (1) Lev 24.2; 8.2
oath Ex 22.8; 30.2
obey 3.42; 8.3
offer [7] 4.7; 6.11
pain [2] Gen 35.17; Deut 28.35
present (1) [3] Lev 23.11; 6.14
priest [11] 4.16; 6.10
pure Lev 24.2; 6.11
repay Lev 22.14; 2 Chr 20.11
require 4.26; 6.15
ritual [2] Lev 23.26; 6.11
secret Gen 49.6; Deut 13.6
special Lev 27.2; 6.2
suffer Lev 24.15; 9.13
Tent (2) (of the Lord's presence) 4.3; 6.10
truth Gen 42.16; Josh 7.19
unclean [2] Lev 27.11; 9.6
unfaithful [3] Lev 20.5; 14.33
witness Ex 22.10; 35.30
wrong [2] Ex 23.2; 16.15

bind Ex 39.23; 15.15
bless [4] Lev 26.9; 10.32
bread [3] 4.7; 9.11
burnt-offering [3] Lev 23.12; 7.12
care Lev 24.4; 7.9
clean Lev 22.4; 8.7

command [2] 5.2; 8.20
consecrate [4] 4.16; 8.17
dedicate [4] 5.25; 7.1
defile [3] 5.3; 19.13
dove Lev 15.14; 2 Kgs 6.25
favour Gen 34.11; 35.24
fellowship-offering [3] Lev 23.19; 7.12
fulfil Lev 27.2; 15.3
gift Lev 27.9; 7.5
grace Ezra 7.28
grapevine *see* vine
kind Gen 50.21; Josh 2.12
lamb [3] Lev 27.26; 7.12
law 5.29; 9.14
name (2) (name of God, of Jesus) Lev 22.2; Deut 5.11
Nazirite [12] Judg 13.5
offer [9] 5.9; 7.3
peace Lev 26.6; 23.10
present (1) [4] 5.9; 7.3
priest [7] 5.8; 10.8
promise [2] Lev 26.42; 10.29
pure 5.8; 8.6
regulation Lev 27.2; 8.26
repayment-offering Lev 19.21; 18.9
require [2] 5.15; 8.8
ritual [2] 5.8; 8.12
sacred 4.15; 7.9
sacrifice Lev 26.31; 15.3
seed Lev 27.16; 11.7
shave [3] Lev 21.5; 8.7
sign (1) Lev 8.9; Josh 2.12
sin-offering [3] Lev 23.19; 7.12
special [2] 5.9; 8.11
Tent (2) (of the Lord's presence) [3] 5.17; 7.1
unleavened Lev 23.6; 9.11
vine Lev 25.5; Deut 22.9
vow [5] Lev 27.2; 15.3
word (1) Ex 34.1; 24.3
yeast Lev 23.6; 28.17

He shall not drink any kind of drink made from grapes or eat any grapes or raisins. [4]As long as he is a **Nazirite**, he shall not eat anything that comes from a **grapevine**, not even the **seeds** or skins of grapes.

5 As long as he is under the **Nazirite vow**, he must not cut his hair or **shave**. He is **bound** by the **vow** for the full time that he is **dedicated** to the LORD, and he shall let his hair and beard grow. [6–7]His hair is the **sign** of his **dedication** to God, and so he must not **defile** himself by going near a corpse, not even that of his father, mother, brother, or sister. [8]As long as he is a **Nazirite**, he is **consecrated** to the LORD.

9 If the **consecrated** hair of a **Nazirite** is **defiled** because he is right beside someone who suddenly dies, he must wait seven days and then **shave** off his hair and beard; and so he becomes ritually **clean**. [10]On the eighth day he shall bring two **doves** or two pigeons to the **priest** at the entrance of the **Tent** of the LORD's presence. [11]The **priest** shall **offer** one as a **sin-offering** and the other as a **burnt-offering**, to perform the **ritual** of **purification** for him because of his contact with a corpse. On the same day the man shall **reconsecrate** his hair [12]and **rededicate** to the LORD his time as a **Nazirite**. The previous period of time doesn't count, because his **consecrated** hair was **defiled**. As a **repayment offering** he shall bring a one-year-old **lamb**.

13 When a **Nazirite** completes his **vow**, he shall perform this **ritual**. He shall go to the entrance of the **Tent** [14]and **present** to the LORD three animals without any defects: a one-year-old male **lamb** for a **burnt-offering**, a one-year-old ewe **lamb** for a **sin-offering**, and a ram for a **fellowship-offering**. [15]He shall also **offer** a basket of **bread** made **without yeast**: thick loaves made of flour mixed with olive-oil and biscuits brushed with olive-oil, and in addition the **required offerings** of corn and wine.

16 The **priest** shall **present** all these to the LORD and **offer** the **sin-offering** and the **burnt-offering**. [17]He shall **sacrifice** the ram to the LORD as a **fellowship-offering**, and **offer** it with the basket of **bread**; he shall also **present** the **offerings** of corn and wine. [18]At the entrance of the **Tent** the **Nazirite** shall **shave** off his hair and put it on the fire on which the **fellowship-offering** is being burnt.

19 Then, when the shoulder of the ram is boiled, the **priest** shall take it and put it, together with one thick loaf of **bread** and one biscuit from the basket, into the hands of the **Nazirite**. [20]Next, the **priest** shall **present** them as a **special gift** to the LORD; they are a **sacred offering** for the **priest**, in addition to the breast and the leg of the ram which by **law** belong to the **priest**. After that, the **Nazirite** may drink wine.

21 These are the **regulations** for Nazirites; but if a **Nazirite promises** an **offering** beyond what his **vow requires** him to give, he must **fulfil** exactly the **promise** he made.

The Priestly Blessing

22 The LORD **commanded** Moses [23]to tell Aaron and his sons to use the following **words** in **blessing** the people of Israel:

[24]May the LORD **bless** you and take **care** of you;
[25]May the LORD be **kind** and **gracious** to you;
[26]May the LORD look on you with **favour** and give you **peace**.

27 And the LORD said, "If they pronounce my **name** as a **blessing** upon the people of Israel, I will **bless** them."

The Offerings of the Leaders

7 On the day Moses finished setting up the **Tent** of the LORD's presence, he **anointed** and **dedicated** the **Tent** and all its equipment, and the **altar** and all its equipment. [2]Then the clan chiefs who were leaders in the tribes of Israel, the same men who were in charge of the census, [3]brought their **offerings** to the LORD: six wagons and twelve oxen, a wagon for every two leaders and an ox for each leader. After they had **presented** them, [4]the LORD said to Moses, [5]"**Accept** these **gifts** for use in the work to be done for the **Tent**; give them to the **Levites** according to the work they have to do." [6]So Moses gave the wagons and the oxen to the **Levites**. [7]He gave two wagons and four oxen to the Gershonites, [8]and four wagons and eight oxen to the Merarites. All their work was to be done under the **direction** of Ithamar son of Aaron. [9]But Moses gave no wagons or oxen to the Kohathites, because the **sacred** objects they took **care** of had to be carried on their shoulders.

10 The leaders also brought **offerings** to **celebrate** the **dedication** of the **altar**. When they were ready to **present** their **gifts** at the **altar**, [11]the LORD said to Moses, "Tell them that each day for a period of twelve days one of the leaders

accept Lev 27.9; 16.15
altar [5] 5.16; 15.28
anoint 4.16; 1 Sam 9.16
burnt-offering [2] 6.11; 8.12
care 6.24; 18.21
celebrate Lev 23.5; 9.11
Covenant Box 4.5; 10.33
creature Lev 11.11; 1 Sam 4.4
dedicate [4] 6.2; 8.11
direct 4.28; 27.21
fellowship-offering [2] 6.14; 10.10
gift [3] 6.20; 8.11
grain-offering [2] 4.16; 8.8
incense [2] 5.15; 16.6
lamb [4] 6.12; 28.3
Levites [2] 4.2; 8.6
offer [5] 6.11; 8.12
present (1) [4] 6.14; 9.7
sacred 6.20; 10.21
sin-offering [2] 6.11; 8.8
Tent (2) (of the Lord's presence) [4] 6.10; 8.9

6.13–21: Acts 21.23–24

is to **present** his **gifts** for the **dedication** of the **altar**."

12–83 They **presented** their **offerings** in the following order:

Day	*Tribe*	*Leader*
1st	Judah	Nahshon son of Amminadab
2nd	Issachar	Nethanel son of Zuar
3rd	Zebulun	Eliab son of Helon
4th	Reuben	Elizur son of Shedeur
5th	Simeon	Shelumiel son of Zurishaddai
6th	Gad	Eliasaph son of Deuel
7th	Ephraim	Elishama son of Ammihud
8th	Manasseh	Gamaliel son of Pedahzur
9th	Benjamin	Abidan son of Gideoni
10th	Dan	Ahiezer son of Ammishaddai
11th	Asher	Pagiel son of Ochran
12th	Naphtali	Ahira son of Enan

The **offerings** each one brought were identical: one silver bowl weighing 1.5 kilogrammes and one silver basin weighing 800 grammes, by the official standard, both of them full of flour mixed with oil for the **grain-offering**; one gold dish weighing 110 grammes, full of **incense**; one young bull, one ram, and a one-year-old **lamb**, for the **burnt-offering**; one goat for the **sin-offering**; and two bulls, five rams, five goats, and five one-year-old **lambs** for the **fellowship-offering**.

84–88 The totals of the **offerings** brought by the twelve leaders for the **dedication** of the **altar** were as follows:

—twelve silver bowls and twelve silver basins weighing a total of 27.6 kilogrammes

—twelve gold dishes weighing a total of 1.32 kilogrammes, filled with **incense**

—twelve bulls, twelve rams, and twelve one-year-old **lambs**, together with the **grain-offerings** that go with them, for the **burnt-offerings**

—twelve goats for the **sin-offerings**

—twenty-four bulls, sixty rams, sixty goats, sixty one-year-old **lambs**, for the **fellowship-offerings**

89 When Moses went into the **Tent** to talk with the LORD, he heard the LORD speaking to him from above the lid on the **Covenant Box**, between the two winged **creatures**.[b]

Placing the Lamps

8 The LORD said to Moses, 2 "Tell
Aaron that when he puts the seven
lamps on the lamp-stand, he should place
them so that the **light** shines towards the
front." 3 Aaron **obeyed** and placed the
lamps facing the front of the lamp-stand.
4 From top to bottom the lamp-stand was
made of hammered gold, according to
the pattern that the LORD had shown
Moses.

The Purification and Dedication of the Levites

5 The LORD said to Moses, 6 "**Separate**
the **Levites** from the rest of the people of
Israel and **purify** them 7 in the following
way: **sprinkle** them with the water of
purification and tell them to **shave** their
whole **bodies** and to wash their clothes.
Then they will be ritually **clean**. 8 Then
they are to take a young bull and the **required grain-offering** of flour mixed with
olive-oil; and you are to take another bull
for the **sin-offering**. 9 Then assemble the
whole **community** of Israel and make the
Levites stand in front of the **Tent** of my
presence. 10 The people of Israel are to
place their hands on the heads of the
Levites, 11 and then Aaron shall **dedicate**
the **Levites** to me as a **special gift** from
the Israelites, so that they may do my
work. 12 The **Levites** shall then put their
hands on the heads of the two bulls; one
is to be **offered** as a **sin-offering** and the
other as a **burnt-offering**, in order to perform the **ritual** of **purification** for the
Levites.
13 "**Dedicate** the **Levites** as a **special**
gift to me, and put Aaron and his sons in
charge of them. 14 **Separate** the **Levites** in
this way from the rest of the Israelites, so
that they will belong to me. 15 After you
have **purified** and **dedicated** the **Levites**,
they will be qualified to work in the **Tent**.
16 I have **claimed** them in the place of all
the **first-born** sons of the Israelites, and
they belong to me **alone**. 17 When I killed
all the **first-born** in Egypt, I **consecrated**
as my own the eldest son of each Israelite family and the **first-born** of every
animal. 18 I am now taking the **Levites**
instead of all the **first-born** of the Israelites, 19 and I assign the **Levites** to Aaron
and his sons, as a **gift** from the Israelites,
to work in the **Tent** for the people of
Israel and to **protect** the Israelites from

alone Lev 20.26; 11.17
body 5.2; 19.18
burnt-offering 7.12; 10.10
claim 3.40; Josh 19.47
clean 6.9; 9.13
command [2] 6.1; 9.5
community 4.34; 10.3
consecrate 6.8; 1 Sam 7.1
dedicate [5] 7.1; 18.6
disaster Lev 26.16; Deut 28.20
duty (1) [3] 4.27; 18.3
first-born [4] 3.12; 18.15
gift [4] 7.5; 15.21
grain-offering 7.12; 15.4
help 1.4; 10.9
Holy Place 4.12; 18.3
Levites [18] 7.5; 10.21
light (1) 5.15; 14.10
obey 5.4; 9.19
offer 7.3; 9.7
protect Ex 30.16; 14.9
pure [6] 6.11; 11.18
regulation 6.21; 9.2
require 6.15; 27.11
ritual [2] 6.11; 15.25
separate [2] Ex 28.1; 26.62
service 4.4; 16.9
shave 6.5; Deut 14.1
sin-offering [2] 7.12; 15.24
special [3] 6.2; 15.19
sprinkle Lev 16.14; 19.4
strike 1.53; 14.36
Tent (2) (of the Lord's presence) [6] 7.1; 9.15

[b] WINGED CREATURES: *See Word List.*

8.1-4: Ex 25.31-40, 37.17-24 **8.17:** Ex 13.2

the **disaster** that would **strike** them if they came too near the **Holy Place**."

20 So Moses, Aaron, and all the people of Israel **dedicated** the **Levites**, as the LORD **commanded** Moses. [21]The **Levites** **purified** themselves and washed their clothes, and Aaron **dedicated** them as a **special gift** to the LORD. He also performed the **ritual** of **purification** for them. [22]The people did everything the LORD had **commanded** Moses concerning the **Levites**. And so the **Levites** were qualified to work in the **Tent** under Aaron and his sons.

23 The LORD said to Moses, [24]"From the age of twenty-five each **Levite** shall perform his **duties** in the **Tent** of my presence, [25]and at the age of fifty he shall retire. [26]After that, he may **help** his **fellow-Levites** in performing their **duties** in the **Tent**, but he must not perform any **service** by himself. This is how you are to **regulate** the **duties** of the Levites."

The Second Passover

bitter 5.17; 14.39
bread 6.15; 11.8
celebrate 7.10; 29.12
clean 8.7; 18.11
cloud [11] Lev 16.2; 10.11
command [5] 8.20; 10.13
God's people 5.3; 11.29
law 6.20; 15.16
obey [2] 8.3; 13.3
observe [6] Lev 24.3; 10.8
offer [2] 8.12; 15.3
Passover [7] Lev 23.5; 28.16
permit Lev 22.24; 20.17
present (1) [2] 7.3; 10.10
regulation [3] 8.26; 15.2
suffer 5.31; 12.11
Tent (2) (of the Lord's presence) [5] 8.9; 10.3
unclean [3] 5.2; 18.15
unleavened 6.15; 28.17

9 The LORD spoke to Moses in the Sinai Desert in the first month of the second year after the people of Israel had left Egypt. He said, [2-3]"On the fourteenth day of this month, beginning at sunset, the people of Israel are to **observe** the **Passover** according to all the rules and **regulations** for it." [4]So Moses told the people to **observe** the **Passover**, [5]and on the evening of the fourteenth day of the first month they did so in the Sinai Desert. The people did everything just as the LORD had **commanded** Moses.

6 But there were some men who were ritually **unclean** because they had touched a corpse, and they were not able to keep the **Passover** on that day. They went to Moses and Aaron [7]and said, "We are **unclean** because we have touched a corpse, but why should we be excluded from **presenting** the LORD's **offering** with the rest of the Israelites?"

8 Moses answered, "Wait until I receive instructions from the LORD."

9 The LORD told Moses [10]to say to the people of Israel, "When any of you or your descendants are **unclean** from touching a corpse or are far away on a journey, but still want to keep the **Passover**, [11]you are **permitted** to **observe** it one month later instead, on the evening of the fourteenth day of the second month. **Celebrate** it with **unleavened bread** and **bitter** herbs. [12]Do not leave any of the food until the following morning and do not break any of the animal's bones. **Observe** the **Passover** according to all the **regulations**. [13]But anyone who is ritually **clean** and not away on a journey and who does not **observe** the **Passover**, shall no longer be considered one of **my people**, because he did not **present** the **offering** to me at the appointed time. He must **suffer** the consequences of his sin.

14 "If a foreigner living among you wants to keep the **Passover**, he must **observe** it according to all the rules and **regulations**. The same **law** applies to everyone, whether native or foreigner."

The Fiery Cloud
(Ex 40.34-38)

15-16 On the day the **Tent** of the Lord's presence was set up, a **cloud** came and covered it. At night the **cloud** looked like fire. [17]Whenever the **cloud** lifted, the people of Israel broke camp, and they set up camp again in the place where the **cloud** came down. [18]The people broke camp at the **command** of the LORD, and at his **command** they set up camp. As long as the **cloud** stayed over the **Tent**, they stayed in the same camp. [19]When the **cloud** stayed over the **Tent** for a long time, they **obeyed** the LORD and did not move on. [20]Sometimes the **cloud** remained over the **Tent** for only a few days; in any case, they remained in camp or moved, according to the **command** of the LORD. [21]Sometimes the **cloud** remained only from evening until morning, and they moved on as soon as the **cloud** lifted. Whenever the **cloud** lifted, they moved on. [22]Whether it was two days, a month, a year, or longer, as long as the **cloud** remained over the **Tent**, they did not move on; but when it lifted, they moved. [23]They set up camp and broke camp in **obedience** to the **commands** which the LORD gave through Moses.

The Silver Trumpets

10 The LORD said to Moses, [2]"Make two trumpets of hammered silver to use for calling the people together and for breaking camp. [3]When long blasts are sounded on both trumpets, the whole **community** is to gather round you at the entrance to the **Tent** of my presence. [4]But when only one trumpet is sounded, then only the leaders of the clans are to gather round you. [5]When short blasts are sounded, the tribes camped on the east will move out. [6]When short blasts are sounded a second time, the tribes on the south will move out. So short blasts are to be sounded to

bless 6.23; 22.6
burnt-offering 8.12; 15.3
cloud [3] 9.15; 11.25
command [13] 9.5; 15.23
community [2] 8.9; 13.26
Covenant Box [2] 7.89; 14.44
defend Ex 15.2; 21.24
enemy [3] Lev 26.7; 14.42
fellowship-offering 7.12; 15.8
festival [2] Lev 26.2; 15.3
flee Ex 2.15; 16.34
flight *see* **flee**
guide Ex 33.2; 2 Sam 6.3
hate Lev 26.17; 35.20

9.1-5: Ex 12.1-13 **9.12:** Ex 12.46; Jn 19.36

help [2] 8.26; 11.2
holy 5.17; 16.37
joy Gen 29.11;
Deut 12.12
Levites 8.6; 16.1
New Moon Festival
1 Sam 20.5
observe 9.2; 15.2
present (1) 9.7; 15.3
priest 6.10; 15.25
promise 6.21; 11.12
prosper [2]
Lev 25.26; Deut 1.11
religion Lev 26.2;
15.3
sacred 7.9; 18.3
save Lev 18.5;
Deut 7.8
scatter Lev 26.33;
14.29
serve 4.49; 15.39
share [2] Lev 7.10;
26.54
Tent (2) (of the
Lord's presence) [4]
9.15; 11.16

break camp, [7]but in order to call the
community together, long blasts are to
be sounded. [8]The trumpets are to be
blown by Aaron's sons, the **priests**.
"The following rule is to be **observed**
for all time to come. [9]When you are at
war in your land, **defending** yourselves
against an **enemy** who has attacked you,
sound the signal for battle on these
trumpets. I, the LORD your God, will **help**
you and **save** you from your **enemies**.
[10]Also on **joyful** occasions—at your **New
Moon Festivals** and your other **religious
festivals**—you are to blow the trumpets
when you **present** your **burnt-offerings**
and your **fellowship-offerings**. Then I will
help you. I am the LORD your God."

The Israelites Break Camp

11 On the twentieth day of the second
month in the second year after the
people left Egypt, the **cloud** over the
Tent of the LORD's presence lifted, [12]and
the Israelites started on their journey out
of the Sinai Desert. The **cloud** came to
rest in the wilderness of Paran.
13 They began to march at the
command of the LORD through Moses,
[14]and each time they moved, they were
in the same order. Those under the banner of the division led by the tribe of
Judah started out first, company by company, with Nahshon son of Amminadab
in **command**. [15]Nethanel son of Zuar was
in **command** of the tribe of Issachar,
[16]and Eliab son of Helon was in
command of the tribe of Zebulun.
17 Then the **Tent** would be taken
down, and the clans of Gershon and
Merari, who carried it, would start out.
18 Next, those under the banner of the
division led by the tribe of Reuben would
start out, company by company, with
Elizur son of Shedeur in **command**. [19]She-
lumiel son of Zurishaddai was in
command of the tribe of Simeon, [20]and
Eliasaph son of Deuel was in **command**
of the tribe of Gad.
21 Then the **Levite** clan of Kohath
would start out, carrying the **sacred** objects. By the time they arrived at the
next camp, the **Tent** had been set up
again.
22 Next, those under the banner of the
division led by the tribe of Ephraim
would start out, company by company,
with Elishama son of Ammihud in
command. [23]Gamaliel son of Pedahzur
was in **command** of the tribe of Manasseh, [24]and Abidan son of Gideoni was
in **command** of the tribe of Benjamin.
25 Finally, those under the banner of
the division led by the tribe of Dan, **serving** as the rearguard of all the divisions,
would start out, company by company,
with Ahiezer son of Ammishaddai in
command. [26]Pagiel son of Ochran was in
command of the tribe of Asher, [27]and
Ahira son of Enan was in **command** of
the tribe of Naphtali. [28]This, then, was
the order of march, company by company, whenever the Israelites broke
camp and set out.
29 Moses said to his brother-in-law
Hobab son of Jethro the Midianite, "We
are about to start out for the place which
the LORD said he would give us. He has
promised to make Israel **prosperous**, so
come with us, and we will **share** our **prosperity** with you."
30 Hobab answered, "No, I am going
back to my native land."
31 "Please don't leave us," Moses said.
"You know where we can camp in the
wilderness, and you can be our **guide**. [32]If
you come with us, we will **share** with you
all the **blessings** that the LORD gives us."

The People Set Out

33 When the people left Sinai, the **holy**
mountain, they travelled for three days.
The LORD's **Covenant Box** always went
ahead of them to find a place for them to
camp. [34]As they moved on from each
camp, the **cloud** of the LORD was over
them by day.
35 Whenever the **Covenant Box**
started out, Moses would say, "Arise,
LORD; **scatter** your **enemies** and put to
flight those who **hate** you!" [36]And whenever it stopped, he would say, "Return,
LORD, to the thousands of families of
Israel."[c]

The Place Named Taberah

11 The people began to **complain** to
the LORD about their **troubles**.
When the LORD heard them, he was
angry and sent fire on the people. It
burnt among them and **destroyed** one
end of the camp. [2]The people cried out to
Moses for **help**; he **prayed** to the LORD,
and the fire died down. [3]So the place was
named Taberah,[d] because there the fire
of the LORD burnt among them.

Moses Chooses Seventy Leaders

4 There were some foreigners travelling with the Israelites. They had a

act 5.12; 35.27
alone 8.16; 18.5
anger [3] 1.53; 12.9
bad Lev 27.12; 13.19
birth Lev 12.2;
Deut 28.54
bread 9.11; 15.20
cloud 10.11; 12.5
complain [4] Ex 17.
13.30
concern Ex 2.25;
Ruth 2.10
create Gen 6.7;
Deut 4.32
cruel Ex 6.9;
Judg 4.3
destroy Lev 26.22;
14.12
displease Gen 38.7;
32.13

[c]Return...Israel; *or* Return, LORD, you who are like an army of millions for Israel.
[d]TABERAH: *This name sounds like the Hebrew for "burning."*

10.35: Ps 68.1

distress Gen 16.11; 14.1
endure Esth 8.6
enough [4] Lev 25.21; 13.30
God's people 9.13; 12.7
grave Ex 14.11; 19.16
help [3] 10.9; 18.2
interest (1) Gen 30.30; Ruth 2.19
manna [2] Ex 16.31; Deut 8.3
pity Ex 34.6; Deut 13.8
plenty Lev 26.5; Deut 28.38
power Lev 26.13; 13.28
pray Ex 23.13; 14.17
promise 10.29; 14.16
prophet [3] Ex 15.20; 12.6
pure 8.6; 15.25
reject Lev 26.43; 14.11
remember Lev 26.42; 15.39
respect Lev 22.2; Deut 5.16
satisfy Lev 10.20; Josh 22.30
seed 6.4; 24.7
sheep Lev 22.28; 15.3
Spirit (1) (God's Spirit) [5] Gen 41.38; 24.2
strength Ex 15.13; Deut 1.38
strong Ex 15.2; 13.18
Tent (2) (of the Lord's presence) [3] 10.3; 12.4
trouble Ex 10.7; 23.21
wish [2] Lev 27.13; 15.39

strong craving for meat, and even the
Israelites themselves began to **complain**:
"If only we could have some meat! [5]In
Egypt we used to eat all the fish we
wanted, and it cost us nothing. **Remember** the cucumbers, the water-melons,
the leeks, the onions, and the garlic we
had? [6]But now our **strength** is gone.
There is nothing at all to eat—nothing
but this **manna** day after day!"
7 (**Manna** was like small **seeds**, whit-
ish yellow in colour. [8-9]It fell on the camp
at night along with the dew. The next
morning the people would go round and
gather it, grind it or pound it into flour,
and then boil it and make it into flat
cakes. It tasted like **bread** baked with
olive-oil.)
10 Moses heard all the people **complaining** as they stood about in groups at
the entrances of their tents. He was
distressed because the LORD was **angry**
with them, [11]and he said to the LORD,
"Why have you treated me so **badly**?
Why are you **displeased** with me? Why
have you given me the responsibility for
all these people? [12]I didn't **create** them
or bring them to **birth**! Why should you
ask me to **act** like a nurse and carry
them in my arms like babies all the way
to the **land you promised** to their ancestors? [13]Where could I get **enough** meat
for all these people? They keep whining
and asking for meat. [14]I can't be responsible for all these people by myself; it's
too much for me! [15]If you are going to
treat me like this, take **pity** on me and
kill me, so that I won't have to **endure**
your **cruelty** any longer."
16 The LORD said to Moses, "Assemble
seventy **respected** men who are recognized as leaders of the people, bring
them to me at the **Tent** of my presence,
and tell them to stand there beside you.
[17]I will come down and speak with you
there, and I will take some of the **spirit** I
have given you and give it to them. Then
they can **help** you to bear the responsibility for these people, and you will not
have to bear it **alone**. [18]Now tell the
people, '**Purify** yourselves for tomorrow;
you will have meat to eat. The LORD has
heard you whining and saying that you
wished you had some meat and that you
were better off in Egypt. Now the LORD
will give you meat, and you will have to
eat it. [19]You will have to eat it not just for
one or two days, or five, or ten, or even
twenty days, [20]but for a whole month, until it comes out of your ears, until you are
sick of it. This will happen because you
have **rejected** the LORD who is here
among you and have **complained** to him
that you should never have left Egypt.' "
21 Moses said to the LORD, "Here I am
leading 600,000 people, and you say that
you will give them **enough** meat for a
month? [22]Could **enough** cattle and **sheep**
be killed to **satisfy** them? Are all the fish
in the sea **enough** for them?"
23 "Is there a limit to my **power**?" the
LORD answered. "You will soon see
whether what I have said will happen or
not!"
24 So Moses went out and told the
people what the LORD had said. He
assembled seventy of the leaders and
placed them round the **Tent**. [25]Then the
LORD came down in the **cloud** and spoke
to him. He took some of the **spirit** he had
given to Moses and gave it to the seventy
leaders. When the **spirit** came on them,
they began to shout like **prophets**, but not
for long.
26 Two of the seventy leaders, Eldad
and Medad, had stayed in the camp and
had not gone out to the **Tent**. There in
the camp the **spirit** came on them, and
they too began to shout like **prophets**. [27]A
young man ran out to tell Moses what
Eldad and Medad were doing.
28 Then Joshua son of Nun, who had
been Moses' **helper** since he was a young
man, spoke up and said to Moses, "Stop
them, sir!"
29 Moses answered, "Are you **concerned** about my **interests**? I **wish** that
the LORD would give his **spirit** to all **his
people** and make all of them shout like
prophets!" [30]Then Moses and the
seventy leaders of Israel went back to
camp.

The LORD Sends Quails

31 Suddenly the LORD sent a wind that
brought quails from the sea, flying less
than a metre above the ground. They
settled on the camp and all round it for
many kilometres in every direction.[e]
[32]So all that day, all night, and all the
next day, the people worked catching
quails; no one gathered less than a thousand kilogrammes. They spread them
out to dry all round the camp. [33]While
there was still **plenty** of meat for them to
eat, the LORD became **angry** with the
people and caused an epidemic to break
out among them. [34]That place was
named Kibroth Hattaavah (which means

[e] sea, flying...direction; *or* sea. They settled in the camp and all round it for many kilometres in every direction, until they were piled up nearly a metre deep on the ground.

11.7-8: Ex 16.31 **11.9:** Ex 16.13–15

anger 11.1; 14.18
cloud [2] 11.25; 14.14
criticize Job 34.29
dare Gen 49.9; 14.44
dead Lev 26.30; 16.48
disease [2] 5.2; 14.36
disgrace Lev 22.2; Deut 22.19
dream Gen 42.9; Deut 13.1
flesh Lev 13.24; Judg 9.2
fool Ex 32.25; 22.29
God's people 11.29; 16.41
heal Lev 14.3; 21.8
humble Lev 26.41; 1 Sam 2.7
prophet 11.25; Deut 13.1
punish Lev 26.14; 14.18
reveal Lev 10.3; 23.3
servant [2] 3.6; 14.24
suffer 9.13; 14.33
Tent (2) (of the Lord's presence) [3] 11.16; 14.10
turn Lev 26.11; 14.25
vision Gen 46.2; 24.4

"**Graves** of Craving"), because there they buried the people who had craved meat.

35 From there the people moved to Hazeroth, where they made camp.

Miriam Is Punished

12 Moses had married a Cushite[f] woman, and Miriam and Aaron **criticized** him for it. 2 They said, "Has the LORD spoken only through[g] Moses? Hasn't he also spoken through[g] us?" The LORD heard what they said. 3 (Moses was a **humble** man, more humble than anyone else on earth.)

4 Suddenly the LORD said to Moses, Aaron, and Miriam, "I want the three of you to come out to the **Tent** of my presence." They went, 5 and the LORD came down in a pillar of **cloud**, stood at the entrance of the **Tent**, and called out, "Aaron! Miriam!" The two of them stepped forward, 6 and the LORD said, "Now hear what I have to say! When there are **prophets** among you,[h] I **reveal** myself to them in **visions** and speak to them in **dreams.** 7 It is different when I speak with my **servant** Moses; I have put him in charge of all **my people** Israel.[i] 8 So I speak to him face to face, clearly and not in riddles; he has even seen my form! How **dare** you speak against my **servant** Moses?"

9 The LORD was **angry** with them; and so as he departed 10 and the **cloud** left the **Tent**, Miriam's skin was suddenly covered with a dreaded **disease** and **turned** as white as snow. When Aaron looked at her and saw that she was covered with the **disease**, 11 he said to Moses, "Please, sir, do not make us **suffer** this **punishment** for our **foolish** sin. 12 Don't let her become like something born **dead** with half its **flesh** eaten away."

13 So Moses cried out to the LORD, "O God, **heal** her!"

14 The LORD answered, "If her father had spat in her face, she would have to bear her **disgrace** for seven days. So let her be shut out of the camp for a week, and after that she can be brought back in." 15 Miriam was shut out of the camp for seven days, and the people did not move on until she was brought back in. 16 Then they left Hazeroth and set up camp in the wilderness of Paran.

The Spies
(Deut 1.19-33)

13 The LORD said to Moses, 2 "**Choose** one of the leaders from each of the twelve tribes and send them as spies to explore the land of Canaan, which I am giving to the Israelites." 3-15 Moses **obeyed** and from the wilderness of Paran he sent out leaders, as follows:

Tribe	*Leader*
Reuben	Shammua son of Zaccur
Simeon	Shaphat son of Hori
Judah	Caleb son of Jephunneh
Issachar	Igal son of Joseph
Ephraim	Hoshea son of Nun
Benjamin	Palti son of Raphu
Zebulun	Gaddiel son of Sodi
Manasseh	Gaddi son of Susi
Dan	Ammiel son of Gemalli
Asher	Sethur son of Michael
Naphtali	Nahbi son of Vophsi
Gad	Geuel son of Machi

16 These are the spies Moses sent to explore the land. He **changed** the name of Hoshea son of Nun to Joshua.

17 When Moses sent them out, he said to them, "Go north from here into the southern part of the land of Canaan and then on into the hill-country. 18 Find out what kind of country it is, how many people live there, and how **strong** they are. 19 Find out whether the land is good or **bad** and whether the people live in open towns or in fortified cities. 20 Find out whether the soil is fertile and whether the land is wooded. And be **sure** to bring back some of the fruit that grows there." (It was the season when grapes were beginning to **ripen**.)

21 So the men went north and explored the land from the wilderness of Zin in the south all the way to Rehob, near Hamath Pass in the north. 22 They went first into the southern part of the land and came to Hebron, where the clans of Ahiman, Sheshai, and Talmai, the descendants of a **race** of giants called the Anakim, lived. (Hebron was founded seven years before Zoan in Egypt.) 23 They came to the Valley of Eshcol, and there they cut off a branch which had one bunch of grapes on it so heavy that it took two men to carry it on a pole between them. They also brought back some pomegranates and figs. 24 (That place was named the Valley of Eshcol[j]

bad 11.11; 1 Sam 15.23
change Lev 13.23; 14.19
choose 1.5; 14.4
community 10.3; 14.10
complain 11.1; 14.2
conquer Lev 26.16; 14.9
enough [3] 11.13; 14.27
false Lev 19.35; 14.3
obey 9.19; 14.22
power [2] 11.23; 14.1
race (1) Deut 2.10
rich Lev 25.47; 14.8
ripe Ex 9.31; 17.8
strong [3] 11.4; 21.24
sure Ex 4.21; 14.21
worse Lev 26.28; Judg 2.19

[f] Cushite *(compare Hab 3.7)*; *or* Midianite; *or* Sudanese. [g] through; *or* to.
[h] *Some ancient translations* When...you; *Hebrew unclear.*
[i] I have put...Israel; *or* he can be trusted with all my affairs.
[j] ESHCOL: *This name in Hebrew means "bunch of grapes."*

12.7: Heb 3.2 **12.14:** Num 5.2–3

because of the bunch of grapes the
Israelites cut off there.)
25 After exploring the land for forty
days, the spies returned 26 to Moses,
Aaron, and the whole **community** of
Israel at Kadesh in the wilderness of
Paran. They reported what they had
seen and showed them the fruit they had
brought. 27 They said to Moses, "We explored the land and found it to be **rich**
and fertile; and here is some of its fruit.
28 But the people who live there are
powerful, and their cities are very large
and well fortified. Even **worse**, we saw
the descendants of the giants there.
29 Amalekites live in the southern part of
the land; Hittites, Jebusites, and Amorites live in the hill-country; and Canaanites live by the Mediterranean Sea
and along the River Jordan."
30 Caleb silenced the people who were
complaining against[k] Moses, and said,
"We should attack now and take the
land; we are **strong enough** to **conquer**
it."
31 But the men who had gone with
Caleb said, "No, we are not **strong**
enough to attack them; the people there
are more **powerful** than we are." 32 So
they spread a **false** report among the
Israelites about the land they had explored. They said, "That land doesn't
even produce **enough** to feed the people
who live there. Everyone we saw was
very tall, 33 and we even saw giants there,
the descendants of Anak. We felt as
small as grasshoppers, and that is how
we must have looked to them."

The People Complain

14 All night long the people cried
out in **distress**. 2 They **complained**
against Moses and Aaron, and said, "It
would have been better to die in Egypt or
even here in the wilderness! 3 Why is the
LORD taking us into that land? We will
be killed in battle, and our wives and
children will be captured. Wouldn't it be
better to go back to Egypt?" 4 So they
said to one another, "Let's **choose** a
leader and go back to Egypt!"
5 Then Moses and Aaron **bowed** to the
ground in front of all the people. 6 And
Joshua son of Nun and Caleb son of
Jephunneh, two of the spies, tore their
clothes in **sorrow** 7 and said to the people,
"The land we explored is an excellent
land. 8 If the LORD is **pleased** with us, he
will take us there and give us that **rich**
and fertile land. 9 Do not **rebel** against
the LORD and don't be **afraid** of the
people who live there. We will **conquer**
them easily. The LORD is with us and has
defeated the **gods** who **protected** them;
so don't be **afraid**." 10 The whole
community was **threatening** to stone
them **to death**, but suddenly the people
saw the **dazzling light** of the LORD's **pre-**
sence appear over the **tent**.

Moses Prays for the People

11 The LORD said to Moses, "How
much longer will these people **reject**
me? How much longer will they **refuse**
to **trust** in me, even though I have performed so many **miracles** among them?
12 I will send an epidemic and **destroy**
them, but I will make you the father of a
nation that is larger and more **powerful**
than they are!"
13 But Moses said to the LORD, "You
brought these people out of Egypt by
your **power**. When the Egyptians hear
what you have done to your people,
14 they will tell it to the people who live in
this land. These people have already
heard that you, LORD, are with us, that
you are **plainly** seen when your **cloud**
stops over us, and that you go before us
in a pillar of **cloud** by day and a pillar of
fire by night. 15 Now if you kill all your
people, the nations who have heard of
your fame will say 16 that you killed your
people in the wilderness because you
were not able to bring them into the **land**
you promised to give them. 17 So now
LORD, I **pray**, show us your **power** and do
what you **promised** when you said, 18 'I,
the LORD, am not easily **angered**, and I
show great **love** and **faithfulness** and **for-**
give sin and **rebellion**. Yet I will not **fail**
to **punish** children and grandchildren to
the third and fourth generation for the
sins of their parents.' 19 And now, LORD,
according to the greatness of your **un-**
changing love, **forgive**, I **pray**, the sin of
these people, just as you have **forgiven**
them ever since they left Egypt."
20 The LORD answered, "I will **forgive**
them, as you have asked. 21 But I **promise**
that as **surely** as I live and as **surely** as
my **presence** fills the earth, 22 none of
these people will live to enter that land.
They have seen the **dazzling light** of my
presence and the **miracles** that I performed in Egypt and in the wilderness,
but they have **tried** my **patience** over and
over again and have **refused** to **obey** me.
23 They will never enter the land which I
promised to their ancestors. None of

[k] complaining against; *or* gathered round.

13.33: Gen 6.4 **14.9:** Heb 3.16 **14.13–19:** Ex 32.11–14 **14.18:** Ex 20.5–6, 34.6–7; Deut 5.9–10, 7.9–10
14.21–23: Heb 3.18

admit (1) Gen 26.7; 2 Sam 1.16
afraid [2] Lev 26.6; 21.34
anger 12.9; 16.15
bitter 9.11; Deut 29.18
bow (2) Lev 9.24; 16.22
change 13.16; 23.19
choose 13.2; 16.1
cloud [2] 12.5; 16.42
community 13.26; 15.23
complain [5] 13.30; 16.11
conquer 13.30; 21.2
Covenant Box 10.33; 17.4
dare 12.8; 24.9
dazzling [2] Lev 9.6; 16.19
death (3) (to death) 3.10; 15.30
destroy 11.1; 16.21
disease 12.10; Deut 7.15
disobey Lev 22.9; 22.18

distress 11.10; Judg 2.15
enemy 10.9; 21.24
enough 13.30; 16.13
fail Lev 5.15; 15.22
faithful Ex 34.6; Deut 1.36
false 13.32; Deut 5.20
forgive [4] Lev 19.22; 15.25
god (2) (other gods) Lev 20.2; 21.29
last (2) 2.17; 24.19
light (1) [2] 8.2; 16.19
love [2] Lev 19.18; Deut 4.37
loyal Gen 21.23; 32.11
miracle [2] Ex 15.11; Deut 4.34
mourn Lev 21.5; 20.29
obey 13.3; 15.39
patient 21.4
plain (1) 2 Kgs 5.7
please Lev 23.13; 15.3
possess Lev 20.24; 16.14
power [3] 13.28; 20.12
pray [2] 11.2; 16.4
presence [3] Lev 24.3; 16.19
promise [5] 11.12; 20.12
protect 8.19; 31.50
punish 12.11; 16.29
rebel [2] Lev 26.40; 16.1
refuse (1) [3] Lev 26.15; 20.18
reject [3] 11.20; 15.31
rich 13.27; 22.17
scatter 10.35; 16.37
servant 12.7; 22.22
sorrow Gen 48.7; Josh 7.6
strike 8.19; 20.11
succeed (1) Gen 39.2; Deut 29.9
suffer [2] 12.11; 18.1
sure [3] 13.20; 18.32
swear [2] Lev 6.3; 32.11
Tent (2) (of the Lord's presence) 12.4; 16.9
threat Ex 32.14; 22.5
trust Ex 18.21; Deut 1.32
try (2) Lev 19.16; 35.12
turn 12.10; 15.39
unfaithful 5.6; 31.16
wicked [2] Gen 19.7; 16.26

those who have **rejected** me will ever
enter it. 24 But because my **servant** Caleb
has a different attitude and has remained
loyal to me, I will bring him into the land
which he explored, and his descendants
will **possess** the land 25 in whose valleys
the Amalekites and the Canaanites now
live. **Turn** back tomorrow and go into the
wilderness in the direction of the Gulf of
Aqaba."

The Lord Punishes the People for Complaining

26 The LORD said to Moses and Aaron,
27 "How much longer are these **wicked**
people going to **complain** against me? I
have heard **enough** of these **complaints**!
28 Now give them this answer: 'I **swear**
that as **surely** as I live, I will do to you
just what you have asked. I, the LORD,
have spoken. 29 You will die and your
corpses will be **scattered** across this wilderness. Because you have **complained**
against me, none of you over twenty
years of age will enter that land. 30 I **pro-**
mised to let you live there, but not one of
you will, except Caleb and Joshua. 31 You
said that your children would be captured, but I will bring them into the land
that you **rejected**, and it will be their
home. 32 You will die here in this wilderness. 33 Your children will wander in the
wilderness for forty years, **suffering** for
your **unfaithfulness**, until the **last** one of
you dies. 34 You will **suffer** the consequences of your sin for forty years, one
year for each of the forty days you spent
exploring the land. You will know what it
means to have me against you! 35 I **swear**
that I will do this to you **wicked** people
who have gathered together against me.
Here in the wilderness every one of you
will die. I, the LORD, have spoken.' "

36–37 The men Moses had sent to explore the land brought back a **false** report which caused the people to **com-**
plain against the LORD. And so the LORD
struck them with a **disease**, and they
died. 38 Of the twelve spies only Joshua
and Caleb survived.

The First Attempt to Invade the Land
(Deut 1.41-46)

39 When Moses told the Israelites
what the LORD had said, they **mourned**
bitterly. 40 Early the next morning they
started out to invade the hill-country, saying, "Now we are ready to go to the place
which the LORD told us about. We **admit**
that we have sinned."

41 But Moses said, "Then why are you
disobeying the LORD now? You will not
succeed! 42 Don't go. The LORD is not
with you, and your **enemies** will defeat
you. 43 When you face the Amalekites and
the Canaanites, you will die in battle; the
LORD will not be with you, because you
have **refused** to follow him."

44 Yet they still **dared** to go up into
the hill-country, even though neither the
LORD's **Covenant Box** nor Moses left the
camp. 45 Then the Amalekites and the
Canaanites who lived there attacked and
defeated them, and pursued them as far
as Hormah.

Laws about Sacrifice

15 The LORD gave Moses 2 the
following **regulations** for the
people of Israel to **observe** in the land
that he was going to give them. 3 A bull, a
ram, a **sheep**, or a goat may be **presented**
to the LORD as a **burnt-offering** or as a
sacrifice in **fulfilment** of a **vow** or as a
freewill offering or as an **offering** at your
regular **religious festivals**; the smell of
these **food-offerings** is **pleasing** to the
LORD. 4–5 Whoever **presents** a **sheep** or a
goat as a **burnt-offering** to the LORD is to
bring with each animal a kilogramme of
flour mixed with a litre of olive-oil as a
grain-offering, together with a litre of
wine. 6 When a ram is **offered**, two kilogrammes of flour mixed with one and a
half litres of olive-oil are to be **presented**
as a **grain-offering**, 7 together with one
and a half litres of wine. The smell of
these **sacrifices** is **pleasing** to the LORD.
8 When a bull is **offered** to the LORD as a
burnt-offering or as a **sacrifice** in **fulfil-**
ment of a **vow** or as a **fellowship-offering**,
9 a **grain-offering** of three kilogrammes of
flour mixed with two litres of olive-oil is
to be **presented**, 10 together with two
litres of wine. The smell of this **sacrifice**
is **pleasing** to the LORD.

11 That is what shall be **offered** with
each bull, ram, **sheep**, or goat. 12 When
more than one animal is **offered**, the
accompanying **offering** is to be increased
proportionately. 13 Every native Israelite
is to do this when he **presents** a **food-**
offering, a smell **pleasing** to the LORD.
14 And if at any time a foreigner living
among you, whether on a temporary or a
permanent basis, makes a **food-offering**,
a smell that **pleases** the LORD, he is to
observe the same **regulations**. 15 For all
time to come, the same[l] rules are **bind-**
ing on you and on the foreigners who live
among you. You and they are alike in the

altar 7.1; 16.5
bind 6.5; 2 Sam 3.34
bread [2] 11.8; 28.17
burnt-offering [4] 10.10; 23.3
command [6] 10.13; 16.40
community [7] 14.1 16.1
contempt Ex 18.11; 1 Sam 2.30
contribute [3] 5.9; 18.8
death (1) Lev 22.8; 16.29
death (3) (to death [4] 14.10; 16.38
desire Ex 20.17; Deut 5.21
fail [2] 14.18; 30.15
fellowship-offerin 10.10; 29.39
festival 10.10; 28.16
food-offering [4] Lev 24.7; 18.17
forgive [3] 14.18; 25.13
freewill Lev 27.26; 29.39
fulfil [2] 6.21; 18.3
gift 8.11; 18.6
grain-offering [4] 8.8; 18.9
guilty 5.8; 18.1
ignorant Job 13.4
law 9.14; Deut 1.5
mistake [3] Gen 43.12; 32.23
new 1.51; 18.27
obey 14.22; 16.47
observe [3] 10.8; 19.21
offer [10] 9.7; 16.15
please [6] 14.8; 18.1
present (1) [7] 10.1 16.17
priest [2] 10.8; 16.10
proper Lev 16.2; 28.14
pure [3] 11.18; 16.46
regulation [6] 9.2; 19.2
reject 14.11; 16.30
religion 10.10; 28.17
remember 11.5; 18.
remind [2] Ex 13.9; Deut 6.8
ritual [2] 8.12; 16.46
Sabbath Lev 24.8; 28.9
sacrifice [4] 6.17; 18.8
serve 10.25; 16.9
sheep [3] 11.22; 18.1
sight Ex 10.28; 20.27
sin-offering [3] 8.8; 18.9

[l] *Some ancient translations* the same; *Hebrew* the congregation the same.

14.24: Josh 14.9-12 **14.29:** Heb 3.17 **14.33:** Acts 7.36

special [4] 8.11; 18.8
tassel [4] Deut 22.12
turn 14.25; 16.42
unintentional [4] Lev 5.2; Job 1.5
vow [2] 6.2; 21.2
wine-offering 4.7; 28.7
wish 11.18; 36.6

LORD's sight; 16 the same laws and regulations apply to you and to them.
17 The LORD gave Moses 18 the following regulations for the people of Israel to
observe in the land that he was going to
give them. 19 When any food produced
there is eaten, some of it is to be set aside
as a special contribution to the LORD.
20 When you bake bread, the first loaf of
the first bread made from the new corn
is to be presented as a special contribution to the LORD. This is to be presented
in the same way as the special contribution you make from the corn you thresh.
21 For all time to come, this special gift is
to be given to the LORD from the bread
you bake.
22 But suppose someone unintentionally fails to keep some of these regulations which the LORD has given Moses.
23 And suppose that in the future the
community fails to do everything that
the LORD commanded through Moses.
24 If the mistake was made because of the
ignorance of the community, they are to
offer a bull as a burnt-offering, a smell
that pleases the LORD, with the proper
grain-offering and wine-offering. In addition, they are to offer a male goat as a
sin-offering. 25 The priest shall perform
the ritual of purification for the community, and they will be forgiven, because
the mistake was unintentional and they
brought their sin-offering as a food-offering to the LORD. 26 The whole community
of Israel and the foreigners living among
them will be forgiven, because everyone
was involved in the mistake.
27 If an individual sins unintentionally,
he is to offer a one-year-old female goat
as a sin-offering. 28 At the altar the priest
shall perform the ritual of purification to
purify the man from his sin, and he will
be forgiven. 29 The same regulation applies to everyone who unintentionally
commits a sin, whether he is a native
Israelite or a resident foreigner.
30 But any person who sins deliberately, whether he is a native or a
foreigner, is guilty of treating the LORD
with contempt, and he shall be put to
death, 31 because he has rejected what
the LORD said and has deliberately
broken one of his commands. He is responsible for his own death.

The Man Who Broke the Sabbath

32 Once, while the Israelites were still
in the wilderness, a man was found
gathering firewood on the Sabbath. 33 He
was taken to Moses, Aaron, and the
whole community, 34 and was put under
guard, because it was not clear what
should be done with him. 35 Then the
LORD said to Moses, "The man must be
put to death; the whole community is to
stone him to death outside the camp."
36 So the whole community took him outside the camp and stoned him to death,
as the LORD had commanded.

Rules about Tassels

37 The LORD commanded Moses 38 to
say to the people of Israel: "Make tassels
on the corners of your garments and put
a blue cord on each tassel. You are to do
this for all time to come. 39 The tassels
will serve as reminders, and each time
you see them you will remember all my
commands and obey them; then you will
not turn away from me and follow your
own wishes and desires. 40 The tassels
will remind you to keep all my
commands, and you will belong completely to me. 41 I am the LORD your God;
I brought you out of Egypt to be your
God. I am the LORD."

The Rebellion of Korah, Dathan, and Abiram

16 1-2 Korah son of Izhar, from the
Levite clan of Kohath, rebelled
against the leadership of Moses. He was
joined by three members of the tribe of
Reuben—Dathan and Abiram, the sons of
Eliab, and On son of Peleth—and by 250
other Israelites, well-known leaders
chosen by the community. 3 They assembled before Moses and Aaron and said to
them, "You have gone too far! All the
members of the community belong to the
LORD, and the LORD is with all of us. Why,
then, Moses, do you set yourself above
the LORD's community?"
4 When Moses heard this, he threw
himself on the ground and prayed. 5 Then
he said to Korah and his followers, "Tomorrow morning the LORD will show us
who belongs to him; he will let the one
who belongs to him, that is, the one he
has chosen, approach him at the altar.
6-7 Tomorrow morning you and your
followers take firepans, put live coals
and incense on them, and take them to
the altar. Then we will see which of us
the LORD has chosen. You Levites are the
ones who have gone too far!"
8 Moses continued to speak to Korah.
"Listen, you Levites! 9 Do you consider it
a small matter that the God of Israel has
set you apart from the rest of the
community, so that you can approach
him, perform your service in the LORD's
Tent, and minister to the community and

accept 7.5; 18.15
alive [2] Lev 16.10; 31.15
altar [8] 15.28; 18.3
anger [3] 14.18; 18.5
apart Lev 25.10; Josh 6.19
bow (2) [2] 14.5; 20.6
choose [4] 14.4; 17.5
cloud 14.14; Deut 1.33
command 15.23; 17.11
community [9] 15.23; 19.9
complain [2] 14.2; 17.5
dazzling [2] 14.10; 20.6
dead 12.12; 17.13
death (1) 15.31; 18.22
death (3) (to death) 15.30; 18.3
deceive Ex 8.29; 25.18
destroy [3] 14.12; 21.2
enough 14.27; 20.12
flee 10.35; 35.32
follower [5] 26.9
God's people 12.7; 19.13
holy [2] 10.33; 18.10
honour Lev 26.2; 28.16
incense [7] 7.12; 1 Sam 2.28
Levites [4] 10.21; 18.1
life (1) Lev 26.16; 22.30
light (1) [2] 14.10; 20.6
natural Lev 22.8; 19.16
obey 15.39; 25.4
offer 15.3; 18.9
plague [3] Deut 4.34
possess [3] 14.24; 18.24
pray 14.17; 21.7
presence [2] 14.10; 19.3

15.16: Lev 24.22 **15.27–28:** Lev 4.27–31 **15.38:** Deut 22.12 **16.1:** Jude 11

present (1) [3] 15.3; 18.9
priest [3] 15.25; 18.1
punish 14.18; 31.2
pure [2] 15.25; 19.12
rebel [3] 14.9; 17.10
reject 15.31; Deut 28.20
ritual [2] 15.25; 19.9
scatter 14.29; Deut 4.27
serve 15.39; 18.1
service 8.26; 18.1
source 27.16
Tent (2) (of the Lord's presence) [7] 14.10; 17.4
turn 15.39; 20.21
vanish Job 8.22
vineyard Lev 25.3; 20.17
warn [2] Lev 15.31; 17.10
wicked 14.27; Deut 9.4
world of the dead [2] Gen 37.35; Deut 32.22
wrong 5.6; 22.34

serve them? 10 He has let you and all the
other **Levites** have this **honour**—and now
you are trying to get the **priesthood** too!
11 When you **complain** against Aaron, it is
really against the LORD that you and
your **followers** are **rebelling**."
12 Then Moses sent for Dathan and
Abiram, but they said, 'We will not
come! 13 Isn't it **enough** that you have
brought us out of the fertile land of Egypt
to kill us here in the wilderness? Do you
also have to lord it over us? 14 You certainly have not brought us into a fertile
land or given us fields and **vineyards** as
our **possession**, and now you are trying to
deceive us. We will not come!"
15 Moses was **angry** and said to the
LORD, "Do not **accept** any **offerings** these
men bring. I have not **wronged** any of
them; I have not even taken one of their
donkeys."
16 Moses said to Korah, "Tomorrow
you and your 250 **followers** must come to
the **Tent** of the LORD's presence; Aaron
will also be there. 17 Each of you will take
his firepan, put **incense** on it, and then
present it at the **altar**." 18 So every man
took his firepan, put live coals and **incense** on it, and stood at the entrance of
the **Tent** with Moses and Aaron. 19 Then
Korah gathered the whole **community**,
and they stood facing Moses and Aaron
at the entrance of the **Tent**. Suddenly the
dazzling light of the LORD's **presence** appeared to the whole **community**, 20 and
the LORD said to Moses and Aaron,
21 "Stand back from these people, and I
will **destroy** them immediately."
22 But Moses and Aaron **bowed down**
with their faces to the ground and said,
"O, God, you are the **source** of all **life**.
When one man sins, do you get **angry**
with the whole **community**?"
23 The LORD said to Moses, 24 "Tell the
people to move away from the tents of
Korah, Dathan, and Abiram."
25 Then Moses, accompanied by the
leaders of Israel, went to Dathan and
Abiram. 26 He said to the people, "Stand
away from the tents of these **wicked** men
and don't touch anything that belongs to
them. Otherwise, you will be wiped out
with them for all their sins." 27 So they
moved away from the tents of Korah,
Dathan, and Abiram.

Dathan and Abiram had come out and
were standing at the entrance of their
tents, with their wives and children.
28 Moses said to the people, "This is how
you will know that the LORD has sent me
to do all these things and that it is not by
my own **choice** that I have done them.
29 If these men die a **natural death** without some **punishment** from God, then the
LORD did not send me. 30 But if the LORD
does something unheard of, and the
earth opens up and swallows them with
all they own, so that they go down **alive**
to the **world of the dead**, you will know
that these men have **rejected** the LORD."
31 As soon as he had finished speaking, the ground under Dathan and
Abiram split open 32 and swallowed them
and their families, together with all of
Korah's **followers** and their **possessions**.
33 So they went down **alive** to the **world of
the dead**, with their **possessions**. The
earth closed over them, and they **vanished**. 34 All the people of Israel who were
there **fled** when they heard their cry.
They shouted, "Run! The earth might
swallow us too!"
35 Then the LORD sent a fire that
blazed out and burnt up the 250 men who
had **presented** the **incense**.

The Firepans

36 Then the LORD said to Moses,
37 "Tell Eleazar son of Aaron the **priest** to
remove the bronze firepans from the remains of the men who have been burnt,
and **scatter** the coals from the firepans
somewhere else, because the firepans
are **holy**. 38 They became **holy** when they
were **presented** at the LORD's **altar**. So
take the firepans of these men who were
put **to death** for their sin, beat them into
thin plates, and make a covering for the
altar. It will be a **warning** to the people of
Israel." 39 So Eleazar the **priest** took the
firepans and had them beaten into thin
plates to make a covering for the **altar**.
40 This was a **warning** to the Israelites
that no one who was not a descendant of
Aaron should come to the **altar** to burn
incense for the LORD. Otherwise he
would be **destroyed** like Korah and his
men. All this was done as the LORD had
commanded Eleazar through Moses.

Aaron Saves the People

41 The next day the whole **community**
complained against Moses and Aaron
and said, "You have killed some of the
LORD's people." 42 After they had all
gathered to protest to Moses and Aaron,
they **turned** towards the **Tent** and saw
that the **cloud** was covering it and that
the **dazzling light** of the LORD's **presence**
had appeared. 43 Moses and Aaron went
and stood in front of the **Tent**, 44 and the
LORD said to Moses, 45 "Stand back from
these people, and I will **destroy** them on
the spot!"

The two of them **bowed down** with
their faces to the ground, 46 and Moses

said to Aaron, "Take your firepan, put live coals from the **altar** in it, and put some **incense** on the coals. Then hurry with it to the people and perform the **ritual** of **purification** for them. Hurry! The **LORD's anger** has already broken out and an epidemic has already begun." 47 Aaron **obeyed**, took his firepan and ran into the middle of the assembled people. When he saw that the **plague** had already begun, he put the **incense** on the coals and performed the **ritual** of **purification** for the people. 48 This stopped the **plague**, and he was left standing between the living and the **dead**. 49 The number of people who died was 14,700, not counting those who died in Korah's **rebellion**. 50 When the **plague** had stopped, Aaron returned to Moses at the entrance of the **Tent**.

Aaron's Stick

17 The LORD said to Moses, 2 "Tell the people of Israel to give you twelve sticks, one from the leader of each tribe. Write each man's name on his stick 3 and then write Aaron's name on the stick **representing** Levi. There will be one stick for each tribal leader. 4 Take them to the **Tent** of my presence and put them in front of the **Covenant Box**, where I meet you. 5 Then the stick of the man I have **chosen** will sprout. In this way I will put a stop to the **constant complaining** of these Israelites against you."

6 So Moses spoke to the Israelites, and each of their leaders gave him a stick, one for each tribe, twelve in all, and Aaron's stick was put with them. 7 Moses then put all the sticks in the **Tent** in front of the LORD's **Covenant Box**.

8 The next day, when Moses went into the **Tent**, he saw that Aaron's stick, **representing** the tribe of Levi, had sprouted. It had budded, blossomed, and produced **ripe** almonds! 9 Moses took all the sticks and showed them to the Israelites. They saw what had happened, and each leader took his own stick back. 10 The LORD said to Moses, "Put Aaron's stick back in front of the **Covenant Box**. It is to be kept as a **warning** to the **rebel** Israelites that they will die unless their **complaining** stops." 11 Moses did as the LORD **commanded**.

12 The people of Israel said to Moses, "Then that's the end of us! 13 If anyone who even comes near the **Tent** must die, then we are all as good as **dead**!"

choose 16.1; 18.6
command 16.40; 18.25
complain [2] 16.11; 20.3
constant Deut 7.9
Covenant Box [3] 14.44; 20.8
dead 16.48; 19.18
rebel 16.1; 20.10
represent [2] Lev 2.13; 2 Sam 2.15
ripe 13.20; Deut 33.14
Tent (2) (of the Lord's presence) [4] 16.9; 18.1
warn 16.38; 24.14

Duties of Priests and Levites

18 The LORD said to Aaron, "You, your sons, and the **Levites** must **suffer** the consequences of any **guilt** connected with **serving** in the **Tent** of my presence; but only you and your sons will **suffer** the consequences of **service** in the **priesthood**. 2 Bring in your relatives, the tribe of Levi, to work with you and **help** you while you and your sons are **serving** at the **Tent**. 3 They are to **fulfil** their **duties** to you and their responsibilities for the **Tent**, but they must not have any contact with **sacred** objects in the **Holy Place** or with the **altar**. If they do, both they and you will be put **to death**. 4 They are to work with you and **fulfil** their responsibilities for all the **service** in the **Tent**, but no unqualified person may work with you. 5 You and your sons **alone** must **fulfil** the responsibilities for the **Holy Place** and the **altar**, so that my **anger** will not again break out against the people of Israel. 6 I am the one who has **chosen** your relatives the **Levites** from among the Israelites as a **gift** to you. They are **dedicated** to me, so that they can carry out their **duties** in the **Tent**. 7 But you and your sons **alone** shall **fulfil** all the responsibilities of the **priesthood** that concern the **altar** and what is in the **Most Holy Place**. These things are your responsibility, because I have given you the **gift** of the **priesthood**. Any unqualified person who comes near the **sacred** objects shall be put **to death**."

The Share of the Priests

8 The LORD said to Aaron, "**Remember** that I am giving you all the **special contributions** made to me that are not burnt as **sacrifices**. I am giving them to you and to your descendants as the part assigned to you for ever. 9 Of the most **sacred offerings** not burnt on the **altar**, the following belong to you: the **grain-offerings**, the **sin-offerings**, and the **repayment offerings**. Everything that is **presented** to me as a **sacred offering** belongs to you and your sons. 10 You must eat these things in a **holy** place, and only males may eat them; consider them **holy**.

11 "In addition, any other **special contributions** that the Israelites **present** to me shall be yours. I am giving them to you, your sons, and your daughters for all time to come. Every member of your family who is ritually **clean** may eat them.

12 "I am giving you all the **best** of the first produce which the Israelites give me each year: olive-oil, wine, and corn. 13 It all belongs to you. Every member of your family who is ritually **clean** may eat it.

accept [2] 16.15; Deut 10.17
alone [2] 11.17; 23.3
altar [5] 16.5; 23.1

anger 16.15; 22.22
best [5] Lev 23.40; 21.32
blood Lev 19.26; 19.4
care [2] 7.9; Deut 2.7
choose 17.5; 26.9
clean [2] 9.13; 19.9
command 17.11; 19.1
contribute [8] 15.19; 31.29
covenant Lev 26.9; 25.12
death (1) 16.29; 19.14
death (3) (to death) [3] 16.38; 35.12
dedicate [2] 8.11; 21.2
duty (1) [2] 8.24; Deut 10.8
first-born [4] 8.16; 33.4
food-offering 15.3; 28.2
fulfil [4] 15.3; 29.39
gift [4] 15.21; Deut 12.6
grain-offering 15.4; 28.5
guilty [2] 15.30; 35.16
help 11.2; 20.16
holy [2] 16.37; 20.12
Holy Place [3] 8.19; 1 Kgs 6.16
inherit Lev 25.46; 27.7
Levites [6] 16.1; 26.62
need Lev 26.26; Deut 2.7
new 15.20; 28.26
offer [7] 16.15; 23.2
please 15.3; 28.2
possess [2] 16.14; 32.18
present (1) [10] 16.17; 27.5
priest [4] 16.10; 19.3
profane Lev 22.15; Neh 13.18
remember 15.39; 31.16
repayment-offering 6.12; 2 Kgs 12.16
right (2) Lev 14.14; Deut 33.2
sacred [5] 10.21; 31.6
sacrifice [2] 15.3; 25.2
serve [2] 16.9; 35.15
service [4] 16.9; 26.2
sheep 15.3; 22.40
sin-offering 15.24; 28.15
special [9] 15.19; 31.29
suffer [2] 14.33; 20.14
sure 14.21; Deut 5.1
Tent (2) (of the Lord's presence) [9] 17.4; 19.4
tithe [4] Deut 12.6
unclean 9.6; 19.7
wage Lev 25.50; Is 55.2

17.8–10: Heb 9.4

14 "Everything in Israel that has been
unconditionally dedicated to me belongs
to you.
15 "Every first-born child or animal
that the Israelites present to me belongs
to you. But you must accept payment to
buy back every first-born child, and must
also accept payment for every first-born
animal that is ritually unclean. 16 Children shall be bought back at the age of
one month for the fixed price of five
pieces of silver, according to the official
standard. 17 But the first-born of cows,
sheep, and goats are not to be bought
back; they belong completely to me and
are to be sacrificed. Throw their blood
against the altar and burn their fat as a
food-offering, a smell pleasing to me.
18 The meat from them belongs to you,
like the breast and the right hind leg of
the special offering.
19 "I am giving to you, to your sons,
and to your daughters, for all time to
come, all the special contributions which
the Israelites present to me. This is an
unbreakable covenant that I have made
with you and your descendants."
20 The LORD said to Aaron, "You will
not receive any property that can be inherited, and no part of the land of Israel
will be assigned to you. I, the LORD, am
all you need."

The Share of the Levites

21 The LORD said, "I have given to the
Levites every tithe that the people of
Israel present to me. This is in payment
for their service in taking care of the
Tent of my presence. 22 The other Israelites must no longer approach the Tent
and in this way bring on themselves the
penalty of death. 23 From now on only the
Levites will take care of the Tent and
bear the full responsibility for it. This is a
permanent rule that applies also to your
descendants. The Levites shall have no
permanent property in Israel, 24 because
I have given to them as their possession
the tithe which the Israelites present to
me as a special contribution. That is why
I told them that they would have no permanent property in Israel."

The Levites' Tithe

25 The LORD commanded Moses 26 to
say to the Levites: "When you receive
from the Israelites the tithe that the
LORD gives you as your possession, you
must present a tenth of it as a special
contribution to the LORD. 27 This special
contribution will be considered as the
equivalent of the offering which the
farmer makes of new corn and new
wine. 28 In this way you also will present
the special contribution that belongs to
the LORD from all the tithes which you
receive from the Israelites. You are to
give this special contribution for the
LORD to Aaron the priest. 29 Give it from
the best that you receive. 30 When you
have presented the best part, you may
keep the rest, just as the farmer keeps
what is left after he makes his offering.
31 You and your families may eat the rest
anywhere, because it is your wages for
your service in the Tent. 32 You will not
become guilty when you eat it, as long as
you have presented the best of it to the
LORD. But be sure not to profane the
sacred gifts of the Israelites by eating
any of the gifts before the best part is
offered; if you do, you will be put to
death."

Ashes of the Red Cow

19 The LORD commanded Moses
and Aaron 2 to give the Israelites
the following regulations. Bring to Moses
and Aaron a red cow which has no defects and which has never been put to
work, 3 and they will give it to Eleazar
the priest. It is to be taken outside the
camp and killed in his presence.[m] 4 Then
Eleazar is to take some of its blood and
with his finger sprinkle it seven times in
the direction of the Tent. 5 The whole
animal, including skin, meat, blood, and
intestines, is to be burnt in the presence
of the priest. 6 Then he is to take some
cedar-wood, a sprig of hyssop, and a red
cord and throw them into the fire. 7 After
that, he is to wash his clothes and pour
water over himself, and then he may
enter the camp; but he remains ritually
unclean until evening. 8 The man who
burnt the cow must also wash his clothes
and pour water over himself, but he also
remains unclean until evening. 9 Then a
man who is ritually clean is to collect the
ashes of the cow and put them in a ritually clean place outside the camp,
where they are to be kept for the Israelite community to use in preparing the
water for removing ritual uncleanness.
This ritual is performed to remove sin.
10 The man who collected the ashes must
wash his clothes, but he remains unclean
until evening. This regulation is valid for
all time to come, both for the Israelites
and for the foreigners living among
them.

ash [3] 4.13; 2 Sam 13.19
blood [2] 18.17; 23.24
body 8.7; Deut 14.8
clean [8] 18.11; 31.24
command 18.25; 20.9
community 16.1; 20.1
dead 17.13; 32.13
death (1) [2] 18.22; 35.24
defile [2] 6.6; 35.33
God's people [2] 16.41; 23.10
grave [2] 11.34; 33.15
human [2] Lev 27.28; 23.19
hyssop [2] Lev 14.4; 1 Kgs 4.33
natural 16.29; Deut 14.21
observe 15.2; 27.11
presence [2] 16.19; 20.6
priest [2] 18.1; 20.26
pure [9] 16.46; 28.22
regulation [2] 15.2; 28.14
ritual [2] 16.46; 28.22
sprinkle [5] 8.7; 2 Sam 13.19
Tent (2) (of the Lord's presence) [3] 18.1; 20.3
unclean [16] 18.15; Deut 12.15

[m] It...presence; *or* He is to take it outside to the east of the camp and kill it.

18.14: Lev 27.28 **18.21:** Lev 27.30–33; Deut 14.22–29 **19.9:** Heb 9.13

Contact with a Corpse

11 Whoever touches a corpse is ritually **unclean** for seven days. 12 He must **purify** himself with the water for **purification** on the third day and on the seventh day, and then he will be **clean**. But if he does not **purify** himself on both the third and the seventh day, he will not be **clean**. 13 Whoever touches a corpse and does not **purify** himself remains **unclean**, because the water for **purification** has not been thrown over him. He **defiles** the LORD's **Tent**, and he will no longer be considered one of **God's people**.

14 If someone dies in a tent, anyone who is in the tent at the time of **death** or who enters it becomes ritually **unclean** for seven days. 15 Every jar and pot in the tent that has no lid[n] on it also becomes **unclean**. 16 If someone touches a person who has been killed or has died a **natural death** out of doors or if someone touches a **human** bone or a **grave**, he becomes **unclean** for seven days.

17 To remove the **uncleanness**, some **ashes** from the red cow which was burnt to remove sin shall be taken and put in a pot, and fresh water added. 18 In the first case, someone who is ritually **clean** is to take a sprig of **hyssop**, dip it in the water, and **sprinkle** the tent, everything in it, and the people who were there. In the second case, someone who is ritually **clean** is to **sprinkle** the water on the man who had touched the **human** bone or the **dead body** or the **grave**. 19 On the third day and on the seventh the person who is ritually **clean** is to **sprinkle** the water on the **unclean** person. On the seventh day he is to **purify** the man, who, after washing his clothes and pouring water over himself, becomes ritually **clean** at sunset.

20 Anyone who has become ritually **unclean** and does not **purify** himself remains **unclean**, because the water for **purification** has not been thrown over him. He **defiles** the LORD's **Tent** and will no longer be considered one of **God's people**. 21 You are to **observe** this rule for all time to come. The person who **sprinkles** the water for **purification** must also wash his clothes; anyone who touches the water remains ritually **unclean** until evening. 22 Whatever an **unclean** person touches is **unclean**, and anyone else who touches it remains unclean until evening.

Events at Kadesh
(Ex 17.1-7)

20 In the first month the whole **community** of Israel came to the wilderness of Zin and camped at Kadesh. There Miriam died and was buried.

2 There was no water where they camped, so the people gathered round Moses and Aaron 3 and **complained**: "It would have been better if we had died in front of the LORD's **Tent** along with our fellow-Israelites. 4 Why have you brought us out into this wilderness? Just so that we can die here with our animals? 5 Why did you bring us out of Egypt into this **miserable** place where nothing will grow? There's no corn, no figs, no grapes, no pomegranates. There is not even any water to drink!" 6 Moses and Aaron moved away from the people and stood at the entrance of the **Tent**. They **bowed down** with their faces to the ground, and the **dazzling light** of the LORD's **presence** appeared to them.

7 The LORD said to Moses, 8 "Take the stick that is in front of the **Covenant Box**, and then you and Aaron assemble the whole **community**. There in front of them all speak to that rock over there, and water will gush out of it. In this way you will bring water out of the rock for the people, for them and their animals to drink." 9 Moses went and got the stick, as the LORD had **commanded**.

10 He and Aaron assembled the whole **community** in front of the rock, and Moses said, "Listen, you **rebels**! Do we have to get water out of this rock for you?" 11 Then Moses **raised** the stick and **struck** the rock twice with it, and a great stream of water gushed out, and all the people and animals drank.

12 But the LORD **reprimanded** Moses and Aaron. He said, "Because you did not have **enough faith** to **acknowledge** my **holy power** before the people of Israel, you will not lead them into the **land that I promised** to give them."

13 This happened at Meribah,[o] where the people of Israel **complained** against the LORD and where he showed them that he was **holy**.

The King of Edom Refuses to Let Israel Pass

14 Moses sent messengers from Kadesh to the king of Edom. They said, "This **message** is from your kinsmen, the tribes of Israel. You know the hardships we have **suffered**, 15 how our ancestors went to Egypt, where we lived many

acknowledge Lev 22.32; 27.14
angel Ex 33.2; 22.22
bow (2) 16.22; Deut 5.9
command [3] 19.1; 22.18
community [6] 19.9; 25.6
complain [2] 17.5; 21.5
Covenant Box 17.4; Deut 10.1
dazzling 16.19; 1 Kgs 8.11
enough 16.13; 22.37
faith Ex 14.31; Josh 22.22
help 18.2; 21.3
holy [2] 18.10; 27.14
ill-treat Lev 19.33; Job 22.9
learn Lev 10.16; 22.19
light (1) 16.19; Ruth 3.14
message Gen 50.4; 22.5
misery Ex 1.13; 21.5
mourn 14.39; 25.6
permit 9.11; 21.23
power [2] 14.12; 22.28
presence 19.3; 32.20
priest [2] 19.3; 25.7
promise [2] 14.16; 23.19
raise Lev 9.22; 30.4
rebel [2] 17.10; 26.9
refuse (1) [2] 14.11; 22.13
reprimand 1 Kgs 1.5
sight 15.15; 25.6
strike 14.36; 24.17
suffer 18.1; 30.15
Tent (2) (of the Lord's presence) [2] 19.4; 25.6
turn 16.42; 21.33
vineyard 16.14; 21.22

[n] no lid; *or* no lid fastened. [o] MERIBAH: *This name in Hebrew means "complaining."*

years. The Egyptians **ill-treated** our ancestors and us, 16 and we cried to the LORD for **help**. He heard our cry and sent an **angel**, who led us out of Egypt. Now we are at Kadesh, a town at the border of your territory. 17 Please **permit** us to pass through your land. We and our cattle will not leave the road or go into your fields or **vineyards**, and we will not drink from your wells. We will stay on the main road[p] until we are out of your territory."

18 But the Edomites answered, "We **refuse** to let you pass through our country! If you try, we will march out and attack you."

19 The people of Israel said, "We will stay on the main road, and if we or our animals drink any of your water, we will pay for it—all we want is to pass through."

20 The Edomites repeated, "We **refuse!**" and they marched out with a **powerful** army to attack the people of Israel. 21 Because the Edomites would not let the Israelites pass through their territory, the Israelites **turned** and went another way.

The Death of Aaron

22 The whole **community** of Israel left Kadesh and arrived at Mount Hor, 23 on the border of Edom. There the LORD said to Moses and Aaron, 24 "Aaron is not going to enter the land which I **promised** to give to Israel; he is going to die, because the two of you **rebelled** against my **command** at Meribah. 25 Take Aaron and his son Eleazar up Mount Hor, 26 and there remove Aaron's **priestly** robes and put them on Eleazar. Aaron is going to die there." 27 Moses did what the LORD had **commanded**. They went up Mount Hor in the **sight** of the whole **community**, 28 and Moses removed Aaron's **priestly** robes and put them on Eleazar. There on the top of the mountain Aaron died, and Moses and Eleazar came back down. 29 The whole **community learnt** that Aaron had died, and they all **mourned** for him for thirty days.

Victory over the Canaanites

21 When the Canaanite king of Arad in the southern part of Canaan heard that the Israelites were coming by way of Atharim, he attacked them and captured some of them. 2 Then the Israelites made a **vow** to the LORD: "If you will let us **conquer** these people, we will unconditionally **dedicate**[q] them and their cities to you and will **destroy** them." 3 The LORD heard them and **helped** them to **conquer** the Canaanites. So the Israelites completely **destroyed** them and their cities, and named the place Hormah.[r]

The Snake Made of Bronze

4 The Israelites left Mount Hor by the road that leads to the Gulf of Aqaba, in order to go round the territory of Edom. But on the way the people lost their **patience** 5 and spoke against God and Moses. They **complained**, "Why did you bring us out of Egypt to die in this desert, where there is no food or water? We can't stand any more of this **miserable** food!" 6 Then the LORD sent poisonous snakes among the people, and many Israelites were bitten and died. 7 The people came to Moses and said, "We sinned when we spoke against the LORD and against you. Now **pray** to the LORD to take these snakes away." So Moses **prayed** for the people. 8 Then the LORD told Moses to make a metal snake and put it on a pole, so that anyone who was bitten could look at it and be **healed**. 9 So Moses made a bronze snake and put it on a pole. Anyone who had been bitten would look at the bronze snake and be **healed**.

From Mount Hor to the Valley of the Moabites

10 The Israelites moved on and camped at Oboth. 11 After leaving that place, they camped at the **ruins** of Abarim in the wilderness east of Moabite territory. 12 Then they camped in the Valley of Zered. 13 From there they moved again and camped on the north side of the River Arnon, in the wilderness which extends into Amorite territory. (The Arnon was the border between the Moabites and the Amorites.) 14 That is why *The Book of the LORD's Battles* speaks of "... the town of Waheb in the area of Suphah, and the valleys; the River Arnon, 15 and the slope of the valleys that extend to the town of Ar and towards the border of Moab."

16 From there they went on to a place called Wells, where the LORD said to Moses, "Bring the people together, and I will give them water." 17 At that time the people of Israel sang this song:

"Wells, produce your water;

defend 10.9; Deut 32.4
destroy [4] 16.21; 22.4
devour Gen 49.27; 23.24
enemy 14.42; 23.11
god (2) (other gods) 14.9; 25.2
heal [2] 12.13; Deut 32.39
help 20.16; 32.3
misery 20.5; Deut 26.7
patient 14.22; Ruth 3.18
permit 20.17; 31.24
pray [2] 16.4; 27.15
refugee 2 Sam 15.19
restore Lev 25.10; 36.4
ruin [2] Lev 26.31; 33.41
strong 13.18; Deut 1.28
terrible Lev 10.19; Deut 5.25
turn 20.21; 22.23
victory Lev 26.7; 24.18
vineyard 20.17; 22.24
vow 15.3; 29.39
worship (2) (of other gods) Lev 26.1; 25.2

afraid 14.9; Deut 1.17
best 18.12; 28.5
captive 24.22
complain 20.3; 27.14
conquer [2] 14.9; 24.18
dedicate 18.6; Deut 5.14

[p] main road; *or* king's highway.
[q] UNCONDITIONALLY DEDICATE: *Anything dedicated in this way belonged completely to the LORD and could not be used; it had to be destroyed.* [r] HORMAH: *This name in Hebrew means "destruction."*

20.28: Ex 29.29; Num 33.38; Deut 10.6 **21.1:** Num 33.40 **21.4:** Deut 2.1 **21.5–6:** 1 Cor 10.9 **21.9:** 2 Kgs 18.4; Jn 3.14

And we will greet it with a song—
18 The well dug by princes
And by leaders of the people,
Dug with a royal sceptre
And with their sticks."
They moved from the wilderness to
Mattanah, 19 and from there they went on
to Nahaliel, and from Nahaliel to
Bamoth, 20 and from Bamoth to the valley
in the territory of the Moabites, below
the top of Mount Pisgah, looking out over
the desert.

Victory over King Sihon and King Og
(Deut 2.26—3.11)

21 Then the people of Israel sent
messengers to the Amorite king Sihon to
say: 22 "Let us pass through your land. We
and our cattle will not leave the road and
go into your fields or **vineyards**, and we
will not drink water from your wells; we
will stay on the main road[s] until we are
out of your territory." 23 But Sihon would
not **permit** the people of Israel to pass
through his territory. He gathered his
army and went out to Jahaz in the wilderness and attacked the Israelites. 24 But
the Israelites killed many of the **enemy**
in battle and occupied their land from
the River Arnon north to the Jabbok, that
is, to the Ammonites, because the Ammonite border was **strongly defended**.[t] 25 So
the people of Israel captured all the
Amorite cities, including Heshbon and all
the surrounding towns, and settled in
them. 26 Heshbon was the capital city of
the Amorite king Sihon, who had fought
against the former king of Moab and had
captured all his land as far as the River
Arnon. 27 That is why the poets sing,
"Come to Heshbon, to King Sihon's
city!
We want to see it rebuilt and **restored**.
28 Once from this city of Heshbon
Sihon's army went forth like a fire;
It **destroyed** the city of Ar in Moab
And **devoured**[u] the hills of the upper
Arnon.
29 How **terrible** for you, people of Moab!
You **worshippers of Chemosh** are
brought to **ruin**!
Your **god** let the men become
refugees,
And the women became **captives** of
the Amorite king.
30 But now their descendants are
destroyed,
All the way from Heshbon to Dibon,
From Nashim to Nophah, near
Medeba."[v]
31 So the people of Israel settled in the
territory of the Amorites, 32 and Moses
sent men to find the **best** way to attack
the city of Jazer. The Israelites captured
it and its surrounding towns and drove
out the Amorites living there.
33 Then the Israelites **turned** and took
the road to Bashan, and King Og of
Bashan marched out with his army to
attack them at Edrei. 34 The LORD said to
Moses, "Do not be **afraid** of him. I will
give you **victory** over him, all his people,
and his land. Do to him what you did to
Sihon, the Amorite king who ruled at
Heshbon." 35 So the Israelites killed Og,
his sons, and all his people, leaving no
survivors, and then they occupied his
land.

The King of Moab Sends for Balaam

22 The Israelites moved on and set
up camp in the plains of Moab
east of the Jordan and opposite Jericho.
2 When the king of Moab, Balak son of
Zippor, heard what the Israelites had
done to the Amorites and how many
Israelites there were, 3 he and all his
people became **terrified**. 4 The Moabites
said to the leaders of the Midianites,
"This horde will soon **destroy** everything
round us, like a bull eating the grass in a
pasture." So King Balak 5 sent messengers to summon Balaam son of Beor,
who was at Pethor near the River
Euphrates in the land of Amaw. They
brought him this **message** from Balak: "I
want you to know that a whole nation has
come from Egypt; its people are spreading out everywhere and **threatening** to
take over our land. 6 They outnumber us,
so please come and put a **curse** on them
for me. Then perhaps we will be able to
defeat them and drive them out of the
land. I know that when you pronounce a
blessing, people are blessed, and when
you pronounce a **curse**, they are placed
under a **curse**."
7 So the Moabite and Midianite
leaders took with them the payment for
the curse, went to Balaam, and gave him
Balak's **message**. 8 Balaam said to them,
"Spend the night here, and tomorrow I
will report to you whatever the LORD
tells me." So the Moabite leaders stayed
with Balaam.
9 God came to Balaam and asked,

angel [9] 20.16; Deut 33.2
anger 18.5; 24.10
bless [2] 10.32; 23.9
command 20.9; 24.13
curse [6] 5.18; 23.7
destroy 21.2; 24.22
disobey 14.41; 24.13
enough 20.12; Deut 1.6
fool 12.11; Deut 32.6
important Gen 49.4; Judg 6.15
learn 20.29; 27.21
life (1) 16.22; 27.16
message [3] 20.14; 23.5
power [2] 20.12; 24.20
prevent 4.19; 30.12
refuse (1) [2] 20.18; 23.25
reward [2] Gen 30.18; 24.11
rich 14.8; Deut 6.3
servant 14.24; Deut 9.27
sheep 18.17; 27.17
slaughter Gen 34.27; Deut 3.3
spare Ex 12.27; Deut 32.25
speech Job 8.1
terrify Lev 26.17; Deut 4.34
threat 14.10; Deut 7.22
turn [2] 21.33; 24.1
vineyard 21.22; Deut 6.11
wrong 16.15; Deut 1.39

[s] main road; *or* king's highway.
[t] because...strongly defended; *Some ancient translations* as far as Jazer on the Ammonite border.
[u] *One ancient translation* devoured; *Hebrew* the lords of. [v] *Verse 30 in Hebrew is unclear.*

21.28–29: Jer 48.45–46 **22.5:** Num 31.8; 2 Pet 2.15–16; Jude 11

"Who are these men that are staying with you?"

10 He answered, "King Balak of Moab has sent them to tell me [11] that a people who came from Egypt has spread out over the whole land. He wants me to **curse** them for him, so that he can fight them and drive them out."

12 God said to Balaam, "Do not go with these men, and do not put a **curse** on the people of Israel, because they have my **blessing**."

13 The next morning Balaam went to Balak's messengers and said, "Go back home; the LORD has **refused** to let me go with you." [14] So they returned to Balak and told him that Balaam had **refused** to come with them.

15 Then Balak sent a larger number of leaders, who were more **important** than the first. [16] They went to Balaam and gave him this **message** from Balak: "Please don't let anything **prevent** you from coming to me! [17] I will **reward** you **richly** and do anything you say. Please come and **curse** these people for me."

18 But Balaam answered, "Even if Balak gave me all the silver and gold in his palace, I could not **disobey** the **command** of the LORD my God in even the smallest matter. [19] But please stay the night, as the others did, so that I may **learn** whether or not the LORD has something else to tell me."

20 That night God came to Balaam and said, "If these men have come to ask you to go with them, get ready to go, but do only what I tell you." [21] So the next morning Balaam saddled his donkey and went with the Moabite leaders.

Balaam and His Donkey

22 God was **angry** that Balaam was going, and as Balaam was riding along on his donkey, accompanied by his two **servants**, the **angel of the LORD** stood in the road to bar his way. [23] When the donkey saw the **angel** standing there holding a sword, it left the road and **turned** into the fields. Balaam beat the donkey and brought it back on to the road. [24] Then the **angel** stood where the road narrowed between two **vineyards** and had a stone wall on each side. [25] When the donkey saw the **angel**, it moved over against the wall and crushed Balaam's foot against it. Again Balaam beat the donkey. [26] Once more the **angel** moved ahead; he stood in a narrow place where there was no room at all to pass on either side. [27] This time, when the donkey saw the **angel**, it lay down. Balaam lost his temper and began to beat the donkey with his stick. [28] Then the LORD gave the donkey the **power** of **speech**, and it said to Balaam, "What have I done to you? Why have you beaten me these three times?"

29 Balaam answered, "Because you have made a **fool** of me! If I had a sword, I would kill you."

30 The donkey replied, "Am I not the same donkey on which you have ridden all your **life**? Have I ever treated you like this before?"

"No," he answered.

31 Then the LORD let Balaam see the **angel** standing there with his sword; and Balaam threw himself face downwards on the ground. [32] The **angel** demanded, "Why have you beaten your donkey three times like this? I have come to bar your way, because you should not be making this journey.[w] [33] But your donkey saw me and **turned** aside three times. If it hadn't, I would have killed you and **spared** the donkey."

34 Balaam replied, "I have sinned. I did not know that you were standing in the road to oppose me; but now if you think it is **wrong** for me to go on, I will return home."

35 But the **angel** said, "Go on with these men, but say only what I tell you to say." So Balaam went on with them.

Balak Welcomes Balaam

36 When Balak heard that Balaam was coming, he went to meet him at Ar, a city on the River Arnon at the border of Moab. [37] Balak said to him, "Why didn't you come when I sent for you the first time? Did you think I wasn't able to **reward** you **enough**?"

38 Balaam answered, "I came, didn't I? But now, what **power** have I got? I can say only what God tells me to say." [39] So Balaam went with Balak to the town of Huzoth, [40] where Balak **slaughtered** cattle and **sheep** and gave some of the meat to Balaam and the leaders who were with him.

Balaam's First Prophecy

41 Next morning Balak took Balaam up to Bamoth Baal, from where Balaam could see a part of the people of Israel.

23 [1] He said to Balak, "Build seven **altars** here for me, and bring me seven bulls and seven rams."

2 Balak did as he was told, and he and Balaam **offered** a bull and a ram on each **altar**. [3] Then Balaam said to Balak, "Stand here by your **burnt-offering**, while

[w] *Probable text* you should...journey; *Hebrew unclear.*

alone [2] 18.5; Deut 1.9
altar [6] 18.3; 28.7
bless [5] 22.6; 24.1
blood 19.4; Deut 12.16
burnt-offering [4] 15.3; 28.3
change 14.19; 32.38
curse [6] 22.6; 24.9
devour 21.28; 24.8
doom Deut 32.35

enemy 21.24; 24.8
God's people 19.13; 31.16
human 19.16; Deut 4.28
lie (2) Lev 19.11; Josh 7.11
magic Lev 19.26; 1 Sam 6.2
message [2] 22.5; 24.3
might Ex 32.11; 24.9
mind (1) Ex 32.12; Deut 15.9
offer [4] 18.9; 26.61
peace 6.26; Deut 2.26
proclaim Lev 25.10; 27.19
promise 20.12; 24.11
prophecy [2] 24.3
refuse (1) 22.13; 25.11
rest (1) Lev 26.34; Deut 5.14
reveal 12.6; Deut 29.29
righteous 1 Sam 26.23
trouble 11.1; 33.55
watch Ex 33.8; Deut 6.24

I go to see whether or not the LORD will
meet me. I will tell you whatever he **reveals** to me." So he went **alone** to the top
of a hill, 4 and God met him. Balaam said
to him, "I have built the seven **altars** and
offered a bull and a ram on each."

5 The LORD told Balaam what to say
and sent him back to Balak to give him
his **message**. 6 So he went back and found
Balak still standing by his **burnt-offering**,
with all the leaders of Moab.

7 Balaam uttered this **prophecy**:
"Balak king of Moab has brought me
From Syria, from the eastern
mountains.
'Come and speak for me,' he said.
'Put a **curse** on the people of Israel.'
8 How can I **curse** what God has not
cursed,
Or speak of **doom** when the LORD has
not?
9 From the high rocks I can see them;
I can **watch** them from the hills.
They are a nation that lives **alone**;
They know they are **blessed** more than
other nations.
10 The descendants of Israel are like the
dust—
There are too many of them to be
counted.
Let me end my days like one of **God's
people**;
Let me die in **peace** like the
righteous."

11 Then Balak said to Balaam, "What
have you done to me? I brought you here
to **curse** my **enemies**, but all you have
done is **bless** them."

12 He answered, "I can say only what
the LORD tells me to say."

Balaam's Second Prophecy

13 Then Balak said to Balaam, "Come
with me to another place from which you
can see only some of the Israelites. **Curse**
them for me from there." 14 He took him
to the field of Zophim on the top of Mount
Pisgah. There also he built seven **altars**
and **offered** a bull and a ram on each of
them.

15 Balaam said to Balak, "Stand here
by your **burnt-offering**, and I will meet
God over there."

16 The LORD met Balaam, told him
what to say, and sent him back to Balak
to give him his **message**. 17 So he went
back and found Balak still standing by his
burnt-offering, with the leaders of Moab.
Balak asked what the LORD had said,
18 and Balaam uttered this **prophecy**:
"Come, Balak son of Zippor,
And listen to what I have to say.
19 God is not like men, who **lie**;
He is not a **human** who **changes his
mind**.
Whatever he **promises**, he does;
He speaks, and it is done.
20 I have been instructed to **bless**,
And when God **blesses**, I cannot call it
back.
21 I foresee that Israel's future
Will bring her no misfortune or
trouble.
The LORD their God is with them;
They **proclaim** that he is their king.
22 God has brought them out of Egypt;
He fights for them like a wild ox.
23 There is no **magic** charm, no
witchcraft,
That can be used against the nation of
Israel.[x]
Now people will say about Israel,
'Look what God has done!'
24 The nation of Israel is like a **mighty**
lion:
It doesn't **rest** until it has torn and
devoured,
Until it has drunk the **blood** of those it
has killed."

25 Then Balak said to Balaam, "You
refuse to **curse** the people of Israel, but at
least don't **bless** them!"

26 Balaam answered, "Didn't I tell you
that I had to do everything that the LORD
told me?"

Balaam's Third Prophecy

27 Balak said, "Come with me, and I
will take you to another place. Perhaps
God will be willing to let you **curse** them
for me from there." 28 So he took Balaam
to the top of Mount Peor overlooking the
desert. 29 Balaam said to him, "Build
seven **altars** for me here and bring me
seven bulls and seven rams." 30 Balak did
as he was told, and **offered** a bull and a
ram on each **altar**.

24 By now Balaam knew that the
LORD wanted him to **bless** the
people of Israel, so he did not go to look
for omens, as he had done before. He
turned towards the desert 2 and saw the
people of Israel camped tribe by tribe.
The **spirit of God** took **control** of him,
3 and he uttered this **prophecy**:
"The **message** of Balaam son of Beor,
The **words** of the man who can see
clearly,[y]
4 Who can hear what God is saying.
With staring eyes I see in a trance
A **vision** from **Almighty** God.
5 The tents of Israel are beautiful,

abundant Gen 41.47; Deut 28.4
Almighty [2] Ex 6.3; Ruth 1.20
anger 22.22; 25.3
bless [3] 23.9; Deut 2.7
captive 21.29; Judg 5.12
command 22.18; 25.16
conquer [2] 21.2; 32.29
control Lev 25.28; Deut 15.6
curse [2] 23.7; Deut 7.26
dare 14.44; 32.7
destroy 22.4; 25.8
devour 23.24; Deut 28.42

[x] There...Israel; *or* No magic charms are used in Israel, no witchcraft is practised there.
[y] who can see clearly; *or* whose eyes are closed.

disobey 22.18;
Deut 4.26
enemy [3] 23.11;
32.21
keep from Ex 39.23;
Deut 17.20
knowledge Gen 3.22;
1 Kgs 2.32
last (2) 14.33;
Deut 3.11
message [2] 23.5;
Deut 18.20
might 23.24;
Deut 2.10
Most High
Gen 14.18; Deut 32.8
perish [2] Job 34.20
power 22.28; 27.14
promise 23.19; 30.2
prophecy [5] 23.7;
1 Kgs 22.8
reward [2] 22.17;
Ruth 2.12
safe Lev 26.5; 32.17
secure Deut 24.6
seed 11.7; Deut 11.10
Spirit (1) (God's Spirit) 11.17;
Judg 3.10
strike 20.11; 35.21
turn [2] 22.23; 33.7
victory 21.34;
Deut 20.4
vision [4] 12.6;
1 Sam 3.1
warn 17.10; 26.10
word (1) [2] 6.23;
Deut 1.1

6 Like long rows of palms
Or gardens beside a river,
Like aloes planted by the LORD
Or cedars beside the water.
7 They will have **abundant** rainfall
And plant their **seed** in well-watered
fields.[z]
Their king shall be greater than Agag,
And his rule shall be extended far and
wide.
8 God brought them out of Egypt;
He fights for them like a wild ox.
They **devour** their **enemies**,
Crush their bones, smash their arrows.
9 The nation is like a **mighty** lion;
When it is sleeping, no one **dares** wake
it.
Whoever blesses Israel will be **blessed**,
And whoever curses Israel will be
cursed."

10 Balak clenched his fists in **anger**
and said to Balaam, "I called you to
curse my **enemies**, but three times now
you have **blessed** them instead. 11 Now go
off home! I **promised** to **reward** you, but
the LORD has **kept you from** getting the
reward."

12 Balaam answered, "I told the
messengers you sent to me that 13 even if
you gave me all the silver and gold in
your palace, I could not **disobey** the **com-**
mand of the LORD by doing anything of
myself. I will say only what the LORD
tells me to say."

Balaam's Final Prophecies

14 Balaam said to Balak, "Now I am
going back to my own people, but before
I go, I am **warning** you what the people
of Israel will do to your people in the
future." 15 Then he uttered this **prophecy**:
"The **message** of Balaam son of Beor,
The **words** of the man who can see
clearly,[a]
16 Who can hear what God is saying
And receive the **knowledge** that comes
from the **Most High**.
With staring eyes I see in a trance
A **vision** from **Almighty** God.
17 I look into the future,
And I see the nation of Israel.
A king, like a bright star, will arise in
that nation.
Like a comet he will come from Israel.
He will **strike** the leaders of Moab
And beat down all the people of Seth.[b]
18 He will **conquer** his **enemies** in Edom
And make their land his property,
While Israel continues **victorious**.
19 The nation of Israel will trample them
down
And wipe out the **last** survivors."

20 Then in his **vision** Balaam saw the
Amalekites and uttered this **prophecy**:
"Amalek was the most **powerful** nation
of all,
But at the end it will **perish** for ever."

21 In his **vision** he saw the Kenites,
and uttered this **prophecy**:
"The place where you live is **secure**,
Safe as a nest set high on a cliff,
22 But you Kenites will be **destroyed**
When Assyria takes you **captive**."[c]

23 Balaam uttered this **prophecy**:
"Who are these people gathering in
the north?[d]
24 Invaders will sail from Cyprus;
They will **conquer** Assyria and Eber,
But they, in **turn**, will **perish** for ever."

25 Then Balaam got ready and went
back home, and Balak went on his way.

The People of Israel at Peor

25 When the Israelites were
camped in the Valley of Acacia,
the men began to have **sexual** intercourse with the Moabite women who
were there. 2 These women invited them
to **sacrificial feasts**, where the **god of**
Moab was **worshipped**. The Israelites ate
the food and **worshipped the god** 3 Baal of
Peor. So the LORD was **angry** with them
4 and said to Moses, "Take all the leaders
of Israel and, in **obedience** to me, **ex-**
ecute them in broad daylight,[e] and then I
will no longer be **angry** with the people."
5 Moses said to the officials, "Each of you
is to kill every man in your tribe who has
become a **worshipper of Baal of Peor**."

6 One of the Israelites took a
Midianite woman into his tent in the
sight of Moses and the whole **community**,
while they were **mourning** at the entrance of the **Tent** of the LORD's presence. 7 When Phinehas, the son of
Eleazar and grandson of Aaron the
priest, saw this, he got up and left the
assembly. He took a spear, 8 followed the
man and the woman into the tent, and
drove the spear through both of them. In
this way the epidemic that was **destroy-**
ing Israel was stopped, 9 but it had already killed twenty-four thousand people.

10 The LORD said to Moses, 11 "Because of what Phinehas has done, I am
no longer **angry** with the people of Israel.
He **refused** to **tolerate** the **worship of any**

anger [4] 24.10; 31.1
command 24.13;
27.11
community 20.1; 26
covenant 18.19;
Deut 4.13
deceive 16.14;
Deut 32.5
destroy [3] 24.22;
26.10
establish Deut 19.1
evil Lev 20.23;
Deut 1.35
execute Gen 41.13;
2 Kgs 14.5
feast Ex 32.6;
Judg 14.12
forgive 15.25; 30.5
god (2) (other gods
[3] 21.29; 33.4
mourn 20.29;
Deut 14.1
obey 16.47; 26.3
priest [2] 20.26; 27.2
refuse (1) 23.25;
27.14
rival Ex 34.14;
Deut 4.24
sacrifice 18.8;
Deut 12.6
sex Lev 20.13; 31.17
sight 20.27; Deut 4.2
Tent (2) (of the Lord's presence)
20.3; 27.2
tolerate [2] Ex 34.1
Deut 4.24
worship (2) (of other gods) [4] 21.2
Deut 4.3

[z] *One ancient translation* They...fields; *Hebrew unclear.*
[a] who can see clearly; *or* whose eyes are closed.
[b] the people of Seth; *or* who are proud and violent. [c] *Verse 22 in Hebrew is unclear.*
[d] *Probable text* Who...north; *Hebrew unclear.* [e] in broad daylight; *or* publicly.

24.9: Gen 12.3, 49.9

god but me, and that is why I did not **destroy** them in my **anger**. 12 So tell him that
I am making a **covenant** with him that is
valid for all time to come. 13 He and his
descendants are permanently **established** as **priests**, because he did not
tolerate any **rivals** to me and brought
about **forgiveness** for the people's sin."

14 The name of the Israelite who was
killed with the Midianite woman was
Zimri son of Salu, the head of a family in
the tribe of Simeon. 15 The woman's name
was Cozbi. Zur, her father, was chief of a
group of Midianite clans.

16 The LORD **commanded** Moses,
17 "Attack the Midianites and **destroy**
them, 18 because of the **evil** they did to
you when they **deceived** you at Peor, and
because of Cozbi, who was killed at the
time of the epidemic at Peor."

The Second Census

choose 18.6; 31.5
community [2] 25.6; 27.2
defy Lev 26.23; 1 Sam 17.26
destroy 25.8; 32.15
fit (1) 1.3; Josh 22.19
follower [2] 16.5; 27.3
Levites 18.1; 31.30
lot (1) Lev 16.8; 33.54
obey 25.4; 27.20
offer 23.2; 28.4
rebel 20.10; 27.3
separate 8.6; Judg 7.4
service 18.1; Deut 24.5
share 10.29; 31.36
unholy 3.4; Neh 13.17
warn 24.14; 32.23

26 After the epidemic the LORD said
to Moses and Eleazar son of
Aaron, 2 "Take a census by families of the
whole **community** of Israel, of all men
twenty years old or older who are **fit** for
military service." 3-4 Moses and Eleazar
obeyed, and called together all the men
of that age group. They assembled in the
plains of Moab across the River Jordan
from Jericho.

These were the Israelites who came
out of Egypt:

5 The tribe of Reuben (Reuben was
the eldest son of Jacob): the clans of
Hanoch, Pallu, 6 Hezron, and Carmi.
7 These clans numbered 43,730 men. 8 The
descendants of Pallu were Eliab 9 and his
sons Nemuel, Dathan, and Abiram.
(These are the Dathan and Abiram who
were **chosen** by the **community**. They **defied** Moses and Aaron and joined the **followers** of Korah when they **rebelled**
against the LORD. 10 The ground opened
and swallowed them, and they died with
Korah and his **followers** when fire **destroyed** 250 men; they became a **warning**
to the people. 11 But the sons of Korah
were not killed.)

12 The tribe of Simeon: the clans of
Nemuel, Jamin, Jachin, 13 Zerah, and
Shaul. 14 These clans numbered 22,200
men.

15 The tribe of Gad: the clans of
Zephon, Haggi, Shuni, 16 Ozni, Eri, 17 Arod,
and Areli. 18 These clans numbered 40,500
men.

19-21 The tribe of Judah: the clans of
Shelah, Perez, Zerah, Hezron, and
Hamul. (Two of Judah's sons, Er and
Onan, had died in the land of Canaan.)
22 These clans numbered 76,500 men.

23 The tribe of Issachar: the clans of
Tola, Puah, 24 Jashub, and Shimron.
25 These clans numbered 64,300 men.

26 The tribe of Zebulun: the clans of
Sered, Elon, and Jahleel. 27 These clans
numbered 60,500 men.

28 The tribes of Joseph, who was the
father of two sons, Manasseh and
Ephraim.

29 The tribe of Manasseh: Machir son
of Manasseh was the father of Gilead,
and the following clans traced their
ancestry to Gilead: 30 the clans of Iezer,
Helek, 31 Asriel, Shechem, 32 Shemida, and
Hepher. 33 Zelophehad son of Hepher had
no sons, but only daughters; their names
were Mahlah, Noah, Hoglah, Milcah, and
Tirzah. 34 These clans numbered 52,700
men.

35 The tribe of Ephraim: the clans of
Shuthelah, Becher, and Tahan. 36 The
clan of Eran traced its descent from
Shuthelah. 37 These clans numbered
32,500 men.

These are the clans descended from
Joseph.

38 The tribe of Benjamin: the clans of
Bela, Ashbel, Ahiram, 39 Shephupham,
and Hupham. 40 The clans of Ard and
Naaman traced their descent from Bela.
41 These clans numbered 45,600 men.

42 The tribe of Dan: the clan of
Shuham, 43 which numbered 64,400 men.

44 The tribe of Asher: the clans of
Imnah, Ishvi, and Beriah. 45 The clans of
Heber and Malchiel traced their descent
from Beriah. 46 Asher had a daughter
named Serah. 47 These clans numbered
53,400 men.

48 The tribe of Naphtali: the clans of
Jahzeel, Guni, 49 Jezer, and Shillem.
50 These clans numbered 45,400 men.

51 The total number of the Israelite
men was 601,730.

52 The LORD said to Moses, 53 "Divide
the land among the tribes, according to
their size. 54-56 Divide the land by drawing
lots, and give a large **share** to a large
tribe and a small one to a small tribe."

57 The tribe of Levi consisted of the
clans of Gershon, Kohath, and Merari.
58 Their descendants included the sub-
clans of Libni, Hebron, Mahli, Mushi, and
Korah. Kohath was the father of Amram,
59 who was married to Levi's daughter
Jochebed, who was born in Egypt. She
bore Amram two sons, Aaron and Moses,
and a daughter, Miriam. 60 Aaron had
four sons, Nadab, Abihu, Eleazar, and
Ithamar. 61 Nadab and Abihu died when

26.1-51: Num 1.1-46 **26.52-56:** Num 34.13; Josh 14.1-2 **26.60:** Num 3.2 **26.61:** Lev 10.1-2; Num 3.4

they offered unholy fire to the LORD.
62 The male Levites who were one month
old or older numbered 23,000. They were
listed separately from the rest of the
Israelites, because they were not given
any property in Israel.
63 All these clans were listed by
Moses and Eleazar when they took a census of the Israelites in the plains of Moab
across the River Jordan from Jericho.
64 There was not even one man left
among those whom Moses and Aaron
had listed in the first census in the Sinai
Desert. 65 The LORD had said that all of
them would die in the wilderness, and except for Caleb son of Jephunneh and
Joshua son of Nun they all did.

The Daughters of Zelophehad

27 Mahlah, Noah, Hoglah, Milcah,
and Tirzah were the daughters of
Zelophehad son of Hepher, son of Gilead,
son of Machir, son of Manasseh, son of
Joseph. 2 They went and stood before
Moses, Eleazar the priest, the leaders,
and the whole community at the entrance of the Tent of the LORD's presence
and said, 3 "Our father died in the wilderness without leaving any sons. He was
not among the followers of Korah, who
rebelled against the LORD; he died because of his own sin. 4 Just because he
had no sons, why should our father's
name disappear from Israel? Give us
property among our father's relatives."
5 Moses presented their case to the
LORD, 6 and the LORD said to him, 7 "What
the daughters of Zelophehad request is
right; give them property among their
father's relatives. Let his inheritance
pass on to them. 8 Tell the people of
Israel that whenever a man dies without
leaving a son, his daughter is to inherit
his property. 9 If he has no daughter, his
brothers are to inherit it. 10 If he has no
brothers, his father's brothers are to inherit it. 11 If he has no brothers or uncles,
then his nearest relative is to inherit it
and hold it as his own property. The
people of Israel are to observe this as a
legal requirement, just as I, the LORD,
have commanded you."

Joshua Is Chosen as Successor to Moses
(Deut 31.1–8)

12 The LORD said to Moses, "Go up the
Abarim Mountains and look out over the
land that I am giving to the Israelites.
13 After you have seen it, you will die, as
your brother Aaron did, 14 because both
of you rebelled against my command in
the wilderness of Zin. When the whole
community complained against me at
Meribah, you refused to acknowledge my
holy power before them." (Meribah is the
spring at Kadesh in the wilderness of
Zin.)
15 Moses prayed, 16 "LORD God, source
of all life, appoint, I pray, a man who can
lead the people 17 and can command
them in battle, so that your community
will not be like sheep without a shepherd."
18 The LORD said to Moses, "Take
Joshua son of Nun, a capable man, and
place your hands on his head. 19 Make
him stand in front of Eleazar the priest
and the whole community, and there before them all proclaim him as your successor. 20 Give him some of your own
authority, so that the whole community
of Israel will obey him. 21 He will depend
on Eleazar the priest, who will learn my
will by using the Urim and Thummim.[f]
In this way Eleazar will direct Joshua
and the whole community of Israel in all
their affairs." 22 Moses did as the LORD
had commanded him. He made Joshua
stand before Eleazar the priest and the
whole community. 23 As the LORD had
commanded, Moses put his hands on
Joshua's head and proclaimed him as his
successor.

The Regular Offerings
(Ex 29.38–46)

28 The LORD commanded Moses 2 to
instruct the Israelites to present
to God at the appointed times the required food-offerings that are pleasing to
him.
3 These are the food-offerings that are
to be presented to the LORD: for the daily
burnt-offering, two one-year-old male
lambs without any defects. 4 Offer the
first lamb in the morning, and the second
in the evening, 5 each with a grain-
offering of one kilogramme of flour,
mixed with one litre of the best olive-oil.
6 This is the daily offering that is completely burnt, which was first offered at
Mount Sinai as a food-offering, a smell
pleasing to the LORD. 7 As the wine-
offering with the first lamb, pour out at
the altar one litre of wine. 8 In the evening offer the second lamb in the same
way as the morning offering, together

acknowledge 20.12; 32.22
authority Gen 41.35; Deut 18.22
case (2) 5.29; 35.24
command [5] 25.16; 28.1
community [7] 26.2; 31.12
complain 21.5; Deut 1.34
depend Lev 22.13; 32.16
direct 7.8; 1 Sam 3.1
follower 26.9; Deut 28.13
holy 20.12; Deut 4.36
inherit [5] 18.20; 36.8
learn 22.19; Deut 4.10
life (1) 22.30; 31.50
obey 26.3; Deut 4.1
observe 19.21; Deut 5.12
power 24.20; 33.4
pray [2] 21.7; Deut 3.23
present (1) 18.9; 28.2
priest [4] 25.7; 31.6
proclaim [2] 23.21; Deut 11.29
rebel [2] 26.9; Deut 1.26
refuse (1) 25.11; 30.5
request Ex 33.18; Deut 18.17
require 8.8; 28.2
right (1) Lev 26.4; 36.5
sheep 22.40; 31.28
shepherd Ex 2.17; Judg 5.16
source 16.22; Job 22.26
Tent (2) (of the Lord's presence) 25.6; 31.30
will (1) Ex 28.15; Deut 33.8

altar 23.1; Deut 7.5
best 21.32; Deut 1.2
bread 15.20; Deut 8.
burnt-offering [11] 23.3; 29.2
command 27.11; 29.40
festival [4] 15.3; 29.12
food-offering [7] 18.17; 29.6
grain-offering [6] 18.9; 29.3
harvest Lev 26.5; Deut 16.9
honour 16.10; 29.12
lamb [12] 7.12; 29.2
last (1) Lev 26.10; Deut 20.19
new 18.27; 32.14
offer [21] 26.61; 29.3
Passover 9.2; 33.3
please [6] 18.17; 29.2
present (1) [4] 27.5; 29.2
proper [3] 15.24; 29.3
pure [2] 19.12; 29.5
regulation 19.2; 29.39
religion 15.3; Deut 12.30
require 27.11; 29.15

[f] URIM AND THUMMIM: *Two objects used by the priest to determine God's will; it is not known precisely how they were used.*

26.65: Num 14.26–35 **27.7:** Num 36.2 **27.12–14:** Deut 3.23–27, 32.48–52
27.17: 1 Kgs 22.17; Ezek 34.5; Mt 9.36; Mk 6.34 **27.18:** Ex 24.13 **27.21:** Ex 28.30; 1 Sam 14.41, 28.6
27.23: Deut 31.23

ritual [2] 19.9; 29.5
Sabbath [2] 15.32; Deut 5.12
sin-offering [3] 18.9; 29.5
unleavened 9.11; Deut 16.3
wine-offering [8] 15.24; 29.6
worship (1) (of God) [3] Lev 26.2; 29.1
yeast 6.15; Deut 16.3

with its **wine-offering**. It also is a **food-**
offering, a smell **pleasing** to the LORD.

The Sabbath Offering

9 On the **Sabbath** day **offer** two one-
year-old male **lambs** without any defects,
two kilogrammes of flour mixed with
olive-oil as a **grain-offering**, and the **wine-**
offering. [10]This **burnt-offering** is to be
offered every **Sabbath** in addition to the
daily **offering** with its **wine-offering**.

The Offering on the First Day of the Month

11 **Present** a **burnt-offering** to the
LORD at the beginning of each month:
two young bulls, one ram, seven one-
year-old male **lambs**, all without any defects. [12]As a **grain-offering**, **offer** flour
mixed with olive-oil: with each bull,
three kilogrammes of flour; with the
ram, two kilogrammes; [13]and with each
lamb, one kilogramme. These **burnt-**
offerings are **food-offerings**, a smell
pleasing to the LORD. [14]The **proper wine-**
offering is two litres of wine with each
bull, one and a half litres with the ram,
and one litre with each **lamb**. This is the
regulation for the **burnt-offering** for the
first day of each month throughout the
year. [15]And in addition to the daily **burnt-**
offering with its **wine-offering**, **offer** one
male goat as a **sin-offering**.

The Offerings at the Festival of Unleavened Bread
(Lev 23.5–14)

16 The **Passover Festival** in **honour** of
the LORD is to be held on the fourteenth
day of the first month. [17]On the fifteenth
day a **religious festival** begins which **lasts**
seven days, during which only **bread** prepared **without yeast** is to be eaten. [18]On
the first day of the **festival** you are to
gather for **worship**, and no work is to be
done. [19]**Offer** a **burnt-offering** as a **food-**
offering to the LORD: two young bulls,
one ram, and seven one-year-old male
lambs, all without any defects. [20]**Offer**
the **proper grain-offering** of flour mixed
with olive-oil: three kilogrammes with
each bull, two kilogrammes with the
ram, [21]and one kilogramme with each
lamb. [22]Also **offer** one male goat as a **sin-**
offering, and in this way perform the
ritual of **purification** for the people.
[23]**Offer** these in addition to the regular
morning **burnt-offering**. [24]In the same
way, for seven days **offer** to the LORD a
food-offering, a smell **pleasing** to him.
Offer this in addition to the daily **burnt-**
offering and **wine-offering**. [25]Meet for
worship on the seventh day and do no
work.

The Offerings at the Harvest Festival
(Lev 23.15–22)

26 On the first day of the **Harvest**
Festival, when you **present** the **offering**
of **new** corn to the LORD, you are to
gather for **worship**, and no work is to be
done. [27]**Offer** a **burnt-offering** as a smell
pleasing to the LORD: two young bulls,
one ram, and seven one-year-old male
lambs, all without any defects. [28]**Offer**
the **proper grain-offering** of flour mixed
with olive-oil: three kilogrammes with
each bull, two kilogrammes with the
ram, [29]and one kilogramme with each
lamb. [30]Also **offer** one male goat as a **sin-**
offering, and in this way perform the
ritual of **purification** for the people.
[31]**Offer** these and the **wine-offering** in
addition to the daily **burnt-offering** and
grain-offering.

The Offerings at the New Year Festival
(Lev 23.23–25)

29 On the first day of the seventh
month you are to gather for **wor-**
ship, and no work is to be done. On that
day trumpets are to be blown. [2]**Present** a
burnt-offering to the LORD, a smell
pleasing to him: one young bull, one ram,
and seven one-year-old male **lambs**, all
without any defects. [3]**Offer** the **proper**
grain-offering of flour mixed with olive-
oil: three kilogrammes of flour with the
bull, two kilogrammes with the ram,
[4]and one kilogramme with each **lamb**.
[5]Also **offer** one male goat as a **sin-**
offering, and in this way perform the
ritual of **purification** for the people.
[6]**Offer** these in addition to the regular
burnt-offering for the first day of the
month with its **grain-offering**, and the
daily **burnt-offering** with its **grain-**
offering and **wine-offering**. These **food-**
offerings are a smell **pleasing** to the
LORD.

The Offerings at the Day of Atonement
(Lev 23.26–32)

7 Gather for **worship** on the tenth day
of the seventh month; eat no food and do
no work. [8]**Offer** a **burnt-offering** to the
LORD, a smell **pleasing** to him: one young
bull, one ram, and seven one-year-old
male **lambs**, all without any defects.
[9]**Offer** the **proper grain-offering** of flour
mixed with olive-oil: three kilogrammes
of flour with the bull, two kilogrammes

burnt-offering [8] 28.3; Josh 8.31
celebrate 9.11; Deut 16.1
command 28.1; 31.6
fellowship-offering 15.8; Deut 27.7
festival [2] 28.16; Deut 16.10
food-offering [3] 28.2
freewill 15.3; Deut 12.6
fulfil 18.3; 30.5
grain-offering [8] 28.5; Josh 22.23
honour 28.16; Deut 5.29
lamb [13] 28.3; Deut 14.26
offer [27] 28.4; 31.50
please [5] 28.2; Deut 6.25
present (1) 28.2; Deut 17.9
proper [3] 28.14; Judg 9.16
pure [2] 28.22; 31.19
regulation 28.14; 31.21
require [8] 28.2; 30.5
ritual [2] 28.22; 35.33
sin-offering [3] 28.15; 2 Chr 29.24
vow 21.2; 30.2
wine-offering [5] 28.7; 2 Kgs 16.13
worship (1) (of God) [4] 28.18; Deut 5.7

28.16: Ex 12.1–13; Deut 16.1–2 **28.17–25:** Ex 12.14–20, 23.15, 34.18; Deut 16.3–8
28.26–31: Ex 23.16, 34.22; Deut 16.9–12 **29.7–11:** Lev 16.29–34

with the ram, 10 and one kilogramme with each **lamb**. 11 Also **offer** one male goat as a **sin-offering**, in addition to the goat **offered** in the **ritual** of **purification** for the people, and the daily **burnt-offering** with its **grain-offering** and **wine-offering**.

The Offerings at the Festival of Shelters
(Lev 23.33–44)

12 Gather for **worship** on the fifteenth day of the seventh month. **Celebrate** this **festival** in **honour** of the LORD for seven days and do no work. 13 On this first day **offer** a **food-offering** to the LORD, a smell **pleasing** to him: thirteen young bulls, two rams, and fourteen one-year-old male **lambs**, all without any defects. 14 **Offer** the **proper grain-offering** of flour mixed with olive-oil: three kilogrammes of flour with each bull, two kilogrammes with each ram, 15 and one kilogramme with each **lamb**, with the **required wine-offerings**. 16 Also **offer** one male goat as a **sin-offering**. **Offer** these in addition to the daily **burnt-offering** with its **grain-offering** and **wine-offering**.

17 On the second day **offer** twelve young bulls, two rams, and fourteen one-year-old male **lambs**, all without any defects. 18-19 **Offer** with them all the other offerings **required** for the first day.

20 On the third day **offer** eleven young bulls, two rams, and fourteen one-year-old male **lambs**, all without any defects. 21-22 **Offer** with them all the other offerings **required** for the first day.

23 On the fourth day **offer** ten young bulls, two rams, and fourteen one-year-old male **lambs**, all without any defects. 24-25 **Offer** with them all the other offerings **required** for the first day.

26 On the fifth day **offer** nine young bulls, two rams, and fourteen one-year-old male **lambs**, all without any defects. 27-28 **Offer** with them all the other offerings **required** for the first day.

29 On the sixth day **offer** eight young bulls, two rams, and fourteen one-year-old male **lambs**, all without any defects. 30-31 **Offer** with them all the other offerings **required** for the first day.

32 On the seventh day **offer** seven young bulls, two rams, and fourteen one-year-old male **lambs**, all without any defects. 33-34 **Offer** with them all the other offerings **required** for the first day.

35 On the eighth day gather for **worship** and do no work. 36 **Offer** a **burnt-offering** as a **food-offering** to the LORD, a smell **pleasing** to him: one young bull, one ram, and seven one-year-old male **lambs**, all without any defects. 37-38 **Offer** with them all the other offerings **required** for the first day.

39 These are the **regulations** concerning the **burnt-offerings**, **grain-offerings**, **wine-offerings**, and **fellowship-offerings** that you are to make to the LORD at your appointed **festivals**. These are in addition to the **offerings** you give in **fulfilment** of a **vow** or as **freewill offerings**.

40 So Moses told the people of Israel everything that the LORD had **commanded** him.

Rules about Vows

30 Moses gave the following instructions to the leaders of the tribes of Israel. 2 When a man makes a **vow** to give something to the LORD or takes an **oath** to abstain from something, he must not break his **promise**, but must do everything that he said he would.

3 When a young woman still living in her father's house makes a **vow** to give something to the LORD or **promises** to abstain from something, 4 she must do everything that she **vowed** or **promised** unless her father **raises** an objection when he hears about it. 5 But if her father **forbids** her to **fulfil** the **vow** when he hears about it, she is not **required** to keep it. The LORD will **forgive** her, because her father **refused** to let her keep it.

6 If an **unmarried** woman makes a **vow**, whether deliberately or carelessly, or **promises** to abstain from something, and then marries, 7 she must do everything that she **vowed** or **promised** unless her husband **raises** an objection when he hears about it. 8 But if her husband **forbids** her to **fulfil** the **vow** when he hears about it, she is not **required** to keep it. The LORD will **forgive** her.

9 A **widow** or a **divorced** woman must keep every **vow** she makes and every **promise** to abstain from something.

10 If a married woman makes a **vow** or **promises** to abstain from something, 11 she must do everything that she **vowed** or **promised** unless her husband **raises** an objection when he hears about it. 12 But if her husband **forbids** her to **fulfil** the **vow** when he hears about it, she is not **required** to keep it. The LORD will **forgive** her, because her husband **prevented** her from keeping her **vow**. 13 Her husband has the **right** to affirm or to annul any **vow** or **promise** that she has made. 14 But if, by the day after he hears of the **vow**, he has **raised** no objection, she must do everything that she has **vowed** or **promised**. He has affirmed the **vow** by not

30.2: Deut 23.21–23; Mt 5.33

divorce Lev 22.13; Deut 22.19
fail 15.22; Deut 8.1
forbid [3] Ex 30.9; Deut 22.9
forgive [3] 25.13; Deut 21.8
fulfil [4] 29.39; 32.2
oath 5.19; Judg 21.5
prevent 22.16; 1 Sam 7.13
promise [10] 24.11; 32.10
raise [4] 20.11; Deut 32.40
refuse (1) 27.14; 32.15
require [3] 29.15; Deut 13.18
right (3) Lev 27.20; Deut 17.8
suffer 20.14; Deut 16.3
unmarried [2] Lev 21.3; Judg 11.38
vow [19] 29.39; Deut 23.18
widow Lev 22.13; Deut 10.18

objecting on the day he heard of it. [15]But
if he later annuls the **vow**, he must **suffer**
the consequences for the **failure** to **fulfil**
the **vow**.

16 These are the rules that the LORD
gave Moses concerning **vows** made by an
unmarried woman living in her father's
house or by a married woman.

The Holy War against Midian

31 The LORD said to Moses,
[2]"**Punish** the Midianites for what
they did to the people of Israel. After you
have done that, you will die."

3 So Moses said to the people, "Get
ready for war, so that you can attack
Midian and **punish** them for what they
did to the LORD. [4]From each tribe of
Israel send a thousand men to war."

5 So a thousand men were **chosen**
from each tribe, a total of twelve
thousand men ready for battle. [6]Moses
sent them to war under the **command** of
Phinehas son of Eleazar the **priest**, who
took charge of the **sacred** objects and the
trumpets for giving signals. [7]They
attacked Midian, as the LORD had **commanded** Moses, and killed all the men,
[8]including the five kings of Midian: Evi,
Rekem, Zur, Hur, and Reba. They also
killed Balaam son of Beor.

9 The people of Israel captured the
Midianite women and children, took
their cattle and their **flocks**, plundered
all their wealth, [10]and burnt all their
cities and camps. [11]They took all the loot
that they had captured, including the
prisoners and the animals, [12]and brought
them to Moses and Eleazar and to the
community of the people of Israel, who
were at the camp on the plains of Moab
across the Jordan from Jericho.

The Army Returns

13 Moses, Eleazar, and all the other
leaders of the **community** went out of the
camp to meet the army. [14]Moses was
angry with the officers, the commanders
of battalions and companies, who had returned from the war. [15]He asked them,
"Why have you kept all the women
alive? [16]**Remember** that it was the
women who followed Balaam's instructions and at Peor led the people to be **unfaithful** to the LORD. That was what
brought the epidemic on the **LORD's
people**. [17]So now kill every boy and kill
every woman who has had **sexual** intercourse, [18]but keep **alive** for yourselves all
the girls and all the women who are **virgins**. [19]Now all of you who have killed
anyone or have touched a corpse must
stay outside the camp for seven days. On
the third day and on the seventh day
purify yourselves and the women you
have captured. [20]You must also **purify**
every piece of clothing and everything
made of leather, goats' hair, or wood."

21 Eleazar the **priest** said to the men
who had returned from battle, "These
are the **regulations** that the LORD has
given to Moses. [22-23]Everything that will
not burn, such as gold, silver, bronze,
iron, tin, or lead, is to be **purified** by passing it through fire. Everything else is to
be **purified** by the water for **purification**.
[24]On the seventh day you must wash your
clothes; then you will be ritually **clean**
and will be **permitted** to enter the camp."

Division of the Loot

25 The LORD said to Moses, [26]"You
and Eleazar, together with the other
leaders of the **community**, are to count
everything that has been captured, including the **prisoners** and the animals.
[27]Divide what was taken into two equal
parts, one part for the soldiers and the
other part for the rest of the **community**.
[28]From the part that belongs to the soldiers, withhold as a **tax** for the LORD one
out of every five hundred **prisoners** and
the same proportion of the cattle, donkeys, **sheep**, and goats. [29]Give them to
Eleazar the **priest** as a **special contribution** to the LORD. [30]From the part given
to the rest of the people, take one out of
every fifty **prisoners** and the same
proportion of the cattle, donkeys, **sheep**,
and goats. Give them to the **Levites** who
are in charge of the LORD's **Tent**."
[31]Moses and Eleazar did what the LORD
commanded.

32–35 The following is a list of what
was captured by the soldiers, in addition
to what they kept for themselves: 675,000
sheep and goats, 72,000 cattle, 61,000 donkeys, and 32,000 **virgins**. [36-40]The **half-share** of the soldiers was 337,500 **sheep**
and goats, of which 675 were the **tax** for
the LORD; 36,000 cattle for the soldiers, of
which 72 were the **tax** for the LORD;
30,500 donkeys for the soldiers, of which
61 were the **tax** for the LORD; and 16,000
virgins for the soldiers, of which 32 were
the **tax** for the LORD. [41]So Moses gave
Eleazar the **tax** as a **special contribution**
to the LORD, as the LORD had **commanded**.

42–46 The **share** of the **community**
was the same as that for the soldiers:
337,500 **sheep** and goats, 36,000 cattle,
30,500 donkeys, and 16,000 **virgins**.
[47]From this **share** Moses took one out of

31.16: Num 25.1-9

alive [2] 16.30; Deut 4.4
anger 25.3; 32.10
choose 26.9; 34.19
clean 19.9; Deut 12.15
command [7] 29.40; 32.21
community [5] 27.2; 32.2
contribute [3] 18.8; 2 Kgs 15.20
flock Ex 16.13; Josh 14.3
God's people 23.10; Deut 4.20
Levites [2] 26.62; 35.2
life (1) 27.16; Deut 12.23
offer 29.3; Deut 2.26
permit 21.23; Judg 11.17
priest [3] 27.2; 33.38
prison [5] Ex 12.29; Deut 21.10
protect [2] 14.9; 33.3
punish [2] 16.29; 32.23
pure [5] 29.5; 35.33
regulation 29.39; 36.13
remember 18.8; 36.3
sacred 18.3; Deut 7.5
sex 25.1; Deut 27.21
share [3] 26.54; 32.19
sheep [5] 27.17; 32.16
special [2] 18.8; Deut 7.6
tax [6] Ex 30.16; 1 Sam 17.25
Tent (2) (of the Lord's presence) [3] 27.2; Deut 31.14
unfaithful 14.33; Deut 31.16
virgin [4] Lev 21.7; Deut 22.14

every fifty **prisoners** and animals, and as
the LORD had **commanded**, gave them to
the **Levites** who were in charge of the
LORD's **Tent**.
48 Then the officers who had **commanded** the army went to Moses 49 and
reported, "Sir, we have counted the soldiers under our **command** and not one of
them is missing. 50 So we are bringing the
gold ornaments, armlets, bracelets,
rings, earrings, and necklaces that each
of us has taken. We **offer** them to the
LORD as a payment for our **lives**, so that
he will **protect** us." 51 Moses and Eleazar
received the gold, all of which was in the
form of ornaments. 52 The total **contribution** of the officers weighed nearly two
hundred kilogrammes. 53 Those who were
not officers kept the loot they had taken.
54 So Moses and Eleazar took the gold to
the **Tent**, so that the LORD would **protect**
the people of Israel.

The Tribes East of the Jordan
(Deut 3.12–22)

32 The tribes of Reuben and Gad
had a lot of livestock. When they
saw how suitable the land of Jazer and
Gilead was for cattle, 2 they went to
Moses, Eleazar, and the other leaders of
the **community** and said, 3-4 "This region
which the LORD has **helped** the Israelites
to occupy—the towns of Ataroth, Dibon,
Jazer, Nimrah, Heshbon, Elealeh,
Sibmah, Nebo, and Beon—is good land
for livestock, and we have so much livestock. 5 Please give us this land as our
property, and do not make us cross the
River Jordan and settle there."
6 Moses replied, "Do you want to stay
here while your fellow-Israelites go to
war? 7 How **dare** you try to **discourage**
the people of Israel from crossing the
Jordan into the land which the LORD has
given them? 8 That is what your fathers
did when I sent them from Kadesh
Barnea to explore the land. 9 They went
as far as the Valley of Eshcol and saw
the land, but when they returned, they
discouraged the people from entering
the land which the LORD had given them.
10 The LORD was **angry** that day and
made a **promise**: 11 'I **swear** that because
they did not remain **loyal** to me, none of
the men twenty years old or older who
came out of Egypt will enter the **land
that I promised** to Abraham, Isaac, and
Jacob.' 12 This included everyone, except
Caleb son of Jephunneh the Kenizzite
and Joshua son of Nun; they remained
loyal to the LORD. 13 The LORD was **angry**
with the people and made them wander
in the wilderness for forty years until
that whole generation that had **displeased** him was **dead**. 14 And now you
have taken your fathers' place, a **new**
generation of sinful men ready to bring
down the fierce **anger of the LORD** on
Israel again. 15 If you people of Reuben
and Gad **refuse** to follow him now, he will
once again **abandon** all these people in
the wilderness, and you will be responsible for their **destruction**."
16 They approached Moses and said,
"First, allow us to build stone enclosures
here for our **sheep** and fortified towns for
our **dependants**. 17 Then we will be ready
to go with our fellow-Israelites into battle
and lead the attack until we have settled
them in the land that will be theirs. In
the meantime, our **dependants** can live
here in the fortified towns, **safe** from the
people of this land. 18 We will not return
to our homes until all the other Israelites
have taken **possession** of the land
assigned to them. 19 We will not take
possession of any property among them
on the other side of the Jordan, because
we have received our **share** here east of
the Jordan."
20 Moses answered, "If you really
mean what you say, then here in the **presence** of the LORD get ready to go into
battle. 21 All your fighting men are to
cross the Jordan and under the **command** of the LORD they are to attack our
enemies until the LORD defeats them
22 and takes **possession** of the land. After
that, you may return, because you will
have **fulfilled** your **obligation** to the LORD
and to your fellow-Israelites. Then the
LORD will **acknowledge** that this land
east of the Jordan is yours. 23 But if you
do not keep your **promise**, I **warn** you
that you will be sinning against the LORD.
Make no **mistake** about it; you will be
punished for your sin. 24 So build your
towns and the enclosures for your **sheep**,
but do what you have **promised**!"
25 The men of Gad and Reuben said,
"Sir, we will do as you **command**. 26 Our
wives and children and our cattle and
sheep will remain here in the towns of
Gilead. 27 But all of us are ready to go into
battle under the LORD's **command**. We
will cross the Jordan and fight, just as
you have said."
28 So Moses gave these **commands** to
Eleazar, Joshua, and the other leaders of
Israel: 29 "If the men of Gad and Reuben
cross the Jordan ready for battle at the
LORD's **command** and if with their **help**
you are able to conquer the land, then
give them the land of Gilead as their

abandon Lev 26.34; Deut 4.31
acknowledge 27.14; Deut 21.17
anger [3] 31.14; Deut 1.34
change 23.19; Deut 21.13
command [7] 31.6; 33.2
community 31.12; 35.24
conquer 24.18; Josh 10.13
dare 24.9; Deut 4.34
dead 19.18; 35.12
depend [2] 27.21; Deut 8.3
destroy 26.10; 33.52
discourage [2] Josh 1.9
displease 11.11; 1 Sam 8.6
enemy 24.8; 35.23
fulfil 30.5; Deut 23.18
help [2] 21.3; 34.18
loyal [2] 14.24; Deut 33.9
mistake 15.24; Prov 14.22
new [2] 28.26; Deut 22.8
obligation Gen 38.8; Deut 29.12
possess [3] 18.24; 36.9
presence 20.6; Deut 4.10
promise [4] 30.2; Deut 1.8
punish 31.2; Deut 5.9
refuse (1) 30.5; Deut 15.7
safe 24.21; 35.12
share [2] 31.36; Deut 18.1
sheep [3] 31.28; Deut 7.13
swear 14.28; Josh 2.12
warn 26.10; Deut 1.42

32.8–9: Num 13.17–33 **32.10–13:** Num 14.26–35 **32.28–32:** Josh 1.12–15

property. 30 But if they do not cross the
Jordan and go into battle with you, they
are to receive their **share** of the property
in the land of Canaan, as you do."
31 The men of Gad and Reuben
answered, "Sir, we will do as the LORD
has **commanded.** 32 Under his **command**
we will cross into the land of Canaan and
go into battle, so that we can retain our
property here east of the Jordan."
33 So Moses assigned to the tribes of
Gad and Reuben and to half the tribe of
Manasseh all the territory of King Sihon
of the Amorites and King Og of Bashan,
including the towns and the country
round them. 34 The tribe of Gad rebuilt
the fortified towns of Dibon, Ataroth,
Aroer, 35 Atroth Shophan, Jazer,
Jogbehah, 36 Beth Nimrah, and Beth
Haran. 37 The tribe of Reuben rebuilt
Heshbon, Elealeh, Kiriathaim, 38 Nebo,
Baal Meon (this name was **changed**), and
Sibmah. They gave **new** names to the
towns they rebuilt.
39 The clan of Machir son of
Manasseh invaded the land of Gilead,
occupied it, and drove out the Amorites
who were there. 40 So Moses gave Gilead
to the clan of Machir, and they lived
there. 41 Jair, of the tribe of Manasseh,
attacked and captured some villages and
named them "Villages of Jair." 42 Nobah
attacked and captured Kenath and its
villages, and he renamed it Nobah, after
himself.

The Journey from Egypt to Moab

33 The following account gives the
names of the places where the
Israelites set up camp after they left
Egypt in their tribes under the leadership of Moses and Aaron. 2 At the **command** of the LORD, Moses wrote down the
name of the place each time they set up
camp.
3 The people of Israel left Egypt on
the fifteenth day of the first month of the
year, the day after the first **Passover**.
Under the LORD's **protection** they left the
city of Rameses in full view of the
Egyptians, 4 who were burying the **first-
born** sons that the LORD had killed. By
doing this, the LORD showed that he was
more **powerful** than the **gods** of Egypt.
5 The people of Israel left Rameses
and set up camp at Sukkoth. 6 Their next
camp was at Etham on the edge of the
desert. 7 From there they **turned** back to
Pi Hahiroth, east of Baal Zephon, and
camped near Migdol. 8 They left Pi
Hahiroth and passed through the Red
Sea[g] into the desert of Shur; after a three
days' march they camped at Marah.
9 From there they went to Elim, where
they camped, because there were twelve
springs of water and seventy palm-trees
there.
10 They left Elim and camped near
the Gulf of Suez. 11 Their next camp was
in the desert of Sin. 12 Then they camped
at Dophkah, 13 and after that at Alush.
14 Next was Rephidim, where there was
no water for them to drink.
15–37 From Rephidim to Mount Hor
they set up camp at the following places:
the Sinai Desert, Kibroth Hattaavah (or
"**Graves** of Craving"), Hazeroth, Rith-
mah, Rimmon Perez, Libnah, Rissah,
Kehelathah, Mount Shepher, Haradah,
Makheloth, Tahath, Terah, Mithkah,
Hashmonah, Moseroth, Bene Jaakan,
Hor Haggidgad, Jotbathah, Abronah,
Eziongeber, the wilderness of Zin (that
is, Kadesh), and Mount Hor, at the edge
of the land of Edom.
38–39 At the **command** of the LORD,
Aaron the **priest** climbed Mount Hor. At
the age of 123 he died there on the first
day of the fifth month of the fortieth year
after the Israelites had left Egypt.
40 The king of Arad in southern
Canaan heard that the Israelites were
coming.
41–49 From Mount Hor to the plains of
Moab the Israelites set up camp at the
following places: Zalmonah, Punon,
Oboth, the **ruins** of Abarim in the territory of Moab, Dibon Gad, Almon
Diblathaim, the Abarim Mountains near
Mount Nebo, and in the plains of Moab
across the River Jordan from Jericho,
between Beth Jeshimoth and the Valley
of Acacia.

Instructions before Crossing the Jordan

50 There in the plains of Moab across
the Jordan from Jericho the LORD gave
Moses 51 the following instructions for
Israel: "When you cross the Jordan into
the land of Canaan, 52 you must drive out
all the inhabitants of the land. **Destroy** all
their stone and metal **idols** and all their
places of worship. 53 Occupy the land and
settle in it, because I am giving it to you.
54 Divide the land among the various
tribes and clans by drawing **lots**, giving a
large piece of property to a large clan
and a small one to a small clan. 55 But if
you do not drive out the inhabitants of
the land, those that are left will be as
troublesome as splinters in your eyes and
thorns in your sides, and they will fight

command [2] 32.21; 36.2
destroy [2] 32.15; Deut 2.12
first-born 18.15; Deut 12.6
god (2) (other gods) 25.2; Deut 3.24
grave 19.16; 2 Sam 3.32
idol Lev 26.1; Deut 4.16
lot (1) 26.54; 34.13
Passover 28.16; Deut 16.1
place of worship Lev 26.30; Deut 12.18
plan Ex 35.32; Judg 9.42
power 27.14; Deut 2.24
priest 31.6; 34.17
protect 31.50; Deut 7.15
ruin 21.11; Deut 13.16
trouble 23.21; Deut 2.9
turn 24.1; 34.4

[g] RED SEA: *See Word List.*

33.38: Num 20.22–28; Deut 10.6, 32.50 **33.40:** Num 21.1 **33.54:** Num 26.54–56

against you. 56 If you do not drive them out, I will destroy you, as I **planned** to **destroy** them."

The Boundaries of the Land

choose 31.5; 35.11
help 32.3; Deut 1.38
lot (1) 33.54; 36.2
priest 33.38; Deut 10.6
turn [3] 33.7; Deut 1.40

34 The LORD gave Moses 2 the following instructions for the people of Israel: "When you enter Canaan, the land which I am giving you, the borders of your territory will be as follows. 3 The southern border will extend from the wilderness of Zin along the border of Edom. It will begin on the east at the southern end of the Dead Sea. 4 Then it will **turn** southwards towards Akrabbim Pass and continue on through Zin as far south as Kadesh Barnea. Then it will **turn** north-west to Hazar Addar and on to Azmon, 5 where it will **turn** towards the valley at the border of Egypt and end at the Mediterranean.

6 "The western border will be the Mediterranean Sea.

7 "The northern border will follow a line from the Mediterranean to Mount Hor 8 and from there to Hamath Pass. It will continue to Zedad 9 and to Ziphron, and will end at Hazar Enan.

10 "The eastern border will follow a line from Hazar Enan to Shepham. 11 It will then go south to Harbel, east of Ain, and on to the hills on the eastern shore of Lake Galilee, 12 then south along the River Jordan to the Dead Sea.

"These will be the four borders of your land."

13 So Moses said to the Israelites, "This is the land that you will receive by drawing **lots**, the land that the LORD has assigned to the nine and a half tribes. 14 The tribes of Reuben and Gad and the eastern half of Manasseh have received their property, divided according to their families, 15 on the eastern side of the Jordan, opposite Jericho."

The Leaders Responsible for Dividing the Land

16 The LORD said to Moses, 17 "Eleazar the **priest** and Joshua son of Nun will divide the land for the people. 18 Take also one leader from each tribe to **help** them divide it." 19–28 These are the men the LORD **chose**:

Tribe	*Leader*
Judah	Caleb son of Jephunneh
Simeon	Shelumiel son of Ammihud
Benjamin	Elidad son of Chislon
Dan	Bukki son of Jogli
Manasseh	Hanniel son of Ephod
Ephraim	Kemuel son of Shiphtan
Zebulun	Elizaphan son of Parnach
Issachar	Paltiel son of Azzan
Asher	Ahihud son of Shelomi
Naphtali	Pedahel son of Ammihud

29 These are the men that the LORD assigned to divide the property for the people of Israel in the land of Canaan.

The Cities Assigned to the Levites

35 In the plains of Moab across the Jordan from Jericho the LORD said to Moses, 2 "Tell the Israelites that from the property they receive they must give the **Levites** some cities to live in and pasture land round the cities. 3 These cities will belong to the **Levites**, and they will live there. The pasture land will be for their cattle and all their other animals. 4 The pasture land is to extend outwards from the city walls 450 metres in each direction, 5 so that there is a square area measuring 900 metres on each side, with the city in the middle. 6 You are to give the **Levites** six **cities of refuge** to which a man can **escape** if he kills someone accidentally. In addition, give them forty-two other cities 7 with their pasture land, making a total of forty-eight. 8 The number of **Levite** cities in each tribe is to be **determined** according to the size of its territory."

The Cities of Refuge
(Deut 19.1–13; Josh 20.1–9)

9 The LORD told Moses 10 to say to the people of Israel: "When you cross the River Jordan and enter the land of Canaan, 11 you are to **choose cities of refuge** to which a man can **escape** if he kills someone accidentally. 12 There he will be **safe** from the **dead** man's relative who **seeks revenge**. A man **accused** of manslaughter is not to be put **to death** without a public **trial**. 13 **Choose** six cities, 14 three east of the Jordan and three in the land of Canaan. 15 These will **serve** as **cities of refuge** for Israelites and for foreigners who are temporary or permanent residents. Anyone who kills someone accidentally can **escape** to one of them.

16–18 "If, however, a man uses a weapon of iron or stone or wood to kill someone, he is **guilty** of murder and is to be put **to death**. 19 The **dead** man's nearest relative has the responsibility for putting the murderer **to death**. When he finds him, he is to kill him.

20 "If a man **hates** someone and kills him by pushing him down or by throwing something at him 21 or by **striking** him with his fist, he is **guilty** of murder and is

accuse [3] Ex 23.7; Deut 5.20
act 11.12; Deut 17.1
case (2) 27.5; Deut 1.17
choose [2] 34.19; Deut 1.13
community [2] 32.2; Deut 26.12
dead [6] 32.13; Deut 14.1
death (1) [5] 19.14; Deut 5.25
death (3) (to death) [7] 18.3; Deut 2.34
defile [3] 19.13; Deut 21.23
determine Lev 14.57; Deut 1.38
enemy 32.21; Deut 1.39
escape [6] Ex 21.13; Deut 4.42
evidence [2] Lev 5.1
Deut 28.46
favour [2] 6.26; Deut 33.23
flee 16.34; Judg 4.15
guilty [6] 18.1; Deut 15.9
hate [2] 10.35; Deut 1.27
High Priest [3] Lev 21.10; Josh 20.6
hurt Ex 21.22; Judg 1.24
intend Lev 22.14; Deut 8.2
judge Ex 21.22; Deut 1.16
Levites [4] 31.30; Deut 12.12
pure 31.19; Josh 3.5
refuge [7] Josh 20.2
rescue Ex 32.11; Deut 4.20
revenge [3] Lev 19.18; Deut 19.6
ritual 29.5; 2 Sam 11.4
safe 32.17; Deut 1.31
seek [2] Judg 9.46
serve 18.1; Deut 4.19
strike 24.17; Deut 28.22
try (2) 14.22; Deut 21.19
witness [2] 5.12; Deut 4.26

34.13–15: Josh 14.1–5 **35.1–8:** Josh 21.1–42

to be put to death. The dead man's nearest relative has the responsibility for putting the murderer to death. When he finds him, he is to kill him.

22 "But suppose a man accidentally kills someone he does not hate, whether by pushing him down or by throwing something at him. 23 Or suppose that, without looking, a man throws a stone that kills someone whom he did not intend to hurt and who was not his enemy. 24 In such cases the community shall judge in favour of the man who caused the death and not in favour of the dead man's relative who is seeking revenge. 25 The community is to rescue the man guilty of manslaughter from the dead man's relative, and they are to return him to the city of refuge to which he had escaped. He must live there until the death of the man who is then High Priest. 26 If the man guilty of manslaughter leaves the city of refuge to which he has escaped 27 and if the dead man's relative finds him and kills him, this act of revenge is not murder. 28 The man guilty of manslaughter must remain in the city of refuge until the death of the High Priest, but after that he may return home. 29 These rules apply to you and your descendants wherever you may live.

30 "A man accused of murder may be found guilty and put to death only on the evidence of two or more witnesses; the evidence of one witness is not sufficient to support an accusation of murder. 31 A murderer must be put to death. He cannot escape this penalty by the payment of money. 32 If a man has fled to a city of refuge, do not allow him to make a payment in order to return home before the death of the High Priest. 33 If you did this, you would defile the land where you are living. Murder defiles the land, and except by the death of the murderer there is no way to perform the ritual of purification for the land where a man has been murdered. 34 Do not defile the land where you are living, because I am the LORD and I live among the people of Israel."

The Inheritance of Married Women

36 The heads of the families in the clan of Gilead, the son of Machir and grandson of Manasseh son of Joseph, went to Moses and the other leaders. 2 They said, "The LORD commanded you to distribute the land to the people of Israel by drawing lots. He also commanded you to give the property of our relative Zelophehad to his daughters. 3 But remember, if they marry men of another tribe, their property will then belong to that tribe, and the total allotted to us will be reduced. 4 In the Year of Restoration, when all property that has been sold is restored to its original owners, the property of Zelophehad's daughters will be permanently added to the tribe into which they marry and will be lost to our tribe."

5 So Moses gave the people of Israel the following command from the LORD. He said, "What the tribe of Manasseh says is right, 6 and so the LORD says that the daughters of Zelophehad are free to marry anyone they wish but only within their own tribe. 7 The property of every Israelite will remain attached to his tribe. 8 Every woman who inherits property in an Israelite tribe must marry a man belonging to that tribe. In this way each Israelite will inherit the property of his ancestors, 9 and the property will not pass from one tribe to another. Each tribe will continue to possess its own property."

10–11 So Mahlah, Tirzah, Hoglah, Milcah, and Noah, the daughters of Zelophehad, did as the LORD had commanded Moses, and they married their cousins. 12 They married within the clans of the tribe of Manasseh son of Joseph, and their property remained in their father's tribe.

13 These are the rules and regulations that the LORD gave the Israelites through Moses in the plains of Moab across the River Jordan from Jericho.

35.30: Deut 17.6, 19.15 **36.2:** Num 27.7

command [4] 33.2; Deut 1.3
free 5.31; Deut 6.23
inherit [2] 27.7; Josh 24.32
lot (1) 34.13; Josh 14.2
possess 32.18; Deut 3.12
regulation 31.21; 1 Sam 2.13
remember 31.16; Deut 2.7
Restoration Lev 27.17; Ezek 46.17
restore 21.27; 1 Sam 2.6
right (1) 27.7; Deut 1.39
wish 15.39; Deut 12.20

DEUTERONOMY

INTRODUCTION

The book of *Deuteronomy* is organized as a series of addresses given by Moses to the people of Israel in the land of Moab, where they had stopped at the end of the long wilderness journey and were about to enter and occupy Canaan.

Some of the most important matters recorded in the book are as follows: (1) Moses recalls the great events of the past forty years. He appeals to the people to remember how God has led them through the wilderness and to be obedient and loyal to God. (2) Moses reviews the Ten Commandments and emphasizes the meaning of the First Commandment, calling the people to devotion to the Lord alone. Then he reviews the various laws that are to govern Israel's life in the promised land. (3) Moses reminds the people of the meaning of God's covenant with them, and calls for them to renew their commitment to its obligations. (4) Joshua is commissioned as the next leader of God's people. After singing a song celebrating God's faithfulness, and pronouncing a blessing on the tribes of Israel, Moses dies in Moab, east of the River Jordan.

The great theme of the book is that God has saved and blessed his chosen people, whom he loves; his people are to remember this, and love and obey him, so that they may have life and continued blessing.

The key verses of the book are 6.4-6, and contain the words that Jesus called the greatest of all commandments: "Love the LORD your God with all your heart, with all your soul, and with all your strength."

Outline of Contents

---

afraid [4] Num 21.34; 2.4
agree Num 5.19; 10.10
alone [2] Num 23.3; 4.35
anger [2] Num 32.10; 3.26
best Num 28.5; 32.14
case (2) Num 35.24; 17.8
choose [2] Num 35.11; 4.37
cloud Num 16.42; 4.11
command [5] Num 36.2; 2.1
complain Num 27.14; Josh 9.18
determine Num 35.8; 3.28
difficult Ex 18.22; 17.8
dispute [3] Ex 24.14; 25.1
enemy [2] Num 35.23; 2.12
enough Num 22.37; 2.3
evil Num 25.18; 4.25
experience [2] 7.15

Introduction

1 In this book are the **words** that
Moses spoke to the people of Israel
when they were in the wilderness east of
the River Jordan. They were in the
Jordan Valley near Suph, between the
town of Paran on one side and the towns
of Tophel, Laban, Hazeroth, and Dizahab
on the other. 2 (It takes eleven days to
travel from Mount Sinai to Kadesh
Barnea by way of the hill-country of
Edom.) 3 On the first day of the eleventh
month of the fortieth year after they had
left Egypt, Moses told the people everything the LORD had **commanded** him to
tell them. 4 This was after the LORD[a] had
defeated King Sihon of the Amorites, who
ruled in the town of Heshbon, and King
Og of Bashan, who ruled in the towns of
Ashtaroth and Edrei. 5 It was while the
people were east of the Jordan in the
territory of Moab that Moses began to
explain God's **laws** and **teachings**.

He said, 6 "When we were at Mount
Sinai, the LORD our God said to us, 'You
have stayed long **enough** at this
mountain. 7 Break camp and move on. Go
to the hill-country of the Amorites and to
all the surrounding regions—to the
Jordan Valley, to the hill-country and the
lowlands, to the southern region, and to
the Mediterranean coast. Go to the land
of Canaan and on beyond the Lebanon
Mountains as far as the great River
Euphrates. 8 All of this is the land which I,
the LORD, **promised** to give to your
ancestors, Abraham, Isaac, and Jacob,
and to their descendants. Go and occupy
it.' "

Moses Appoints Judges
(Ex 18.13-27)

9 Moses said to the people, "While we

[a] the LORD; *or* Moses.
1.4: Num 2.21-35

faithful Num 14.18; 4.4
fear Lev 19.15; 2.25
hate Num 35.20; 5.9
help [2] Num 34.18; 3.18
judge [2] Num 35.24; 16.18
law Num 15.16; 4.1
partiality Ex 23.3; 10.17
promise [3] Num 32.10; 6.3
prosper Num 10.29; 6.10
proud Lev 26.19; 8.14
rebel [2] Num 27.3; 2.30
right (1) Num 36.5; 5.28
safe Num 35.12; 4.42
settle (2) Lev 19.17; 25.1
solemn Ex 35.2; 4.21
strength Num 11.6; 3.28
strong Num 21.24; 2.36
teach Lev 10.11; 4.1
trust Num 14.11; 9.23
turn Num 34.4; 2.1
understand Ex 36.1; 4.6

warn Num 32.23; 8.19
wise [2] Ex 7.11; 4.6
word (1) Num 24.3; 10.4
wrong Num 22.34; 15.21

were still at Mount Sinai, I told you, 'The responsibility for leading you is too much for me. I can't do it **alone**. 10 The LORD your God has made you as numerous as the stars in the sky. 11 May the LORD, the God of your ancestors, make you increase a thousand times more and make you **prosperous**, as he **promised**! 12 But how can I **alone** bear the heavy responsibility for **settling** your **disputes**? 13 **Choose** some **wise**, **understanding**, and **experienced** men from each tribe, and I will put them in charge of you.' 14 And you **agreed** that this was a good thing to do. 15 So I took the **wise** and **experienced** leaders you **chose** from your tribes, and I placed them in charge of you. Some were responsible for a thousand people, some for a hundred, some for fifty, and some for ten. I also appointed other officials throughout the tribes.

16 "At that time I instructed them, 'Listen to the **disputes** that come up among your people. **Judge** every **dispute** fairly, whether it concerns only your own people or involves foreigners who live among you. 17 Show no **partiality** in your decisions; **judge** everyone on the same basis, no matter who he is. Do not be **afraid** of anyone, for the decisions you make come from God. If any **case** is too **difficult** for you, bring it to me, and I will decide it.' 18 At the same time I gave you instructions for everything else you were to do.

The Spies Are Sent Out from Kadesh Barnea
(Num 13.1–33)

19 "We did what the LORD our God **commanded** us. We left Mount Sinai and went through that vast and **fearful** desert on the way to the hill-country of the Amorites. When we reached Kadesh Barnea, 20-21 I said, 'You have now come to the hill-country of the Amorites, which the LORD our God, the God of our ancestors, is giving us. Look, there it is. Go and occupy it as he **commanded**. Do not hesitate or be **afraid**.'

22 "But you came to me and said, 'Let's send men ahead of us to spy out the land, so that they can tell us the **best** route to take and what kind of cities are there.'

23 "That seemed a good thing to do, so I selected twelve men, one from each tribe. 24 They went into the hill-country as far as the Valley of Eshcol and explored it. 25 They brought us back some fruit they found there, and reported that the land which the LORD our God was giving us was very fertile.

26 "But you **rebelled** against the **command** of the LORD your God, and you would not enter the land. 27 You grumbled to one another: 'The LORD **hates** us. He brought us out of Egypt just to hand us over to these Amorites, so that they could kill us. 28 Why should we go there? We are **afraid**. The men we sent tell us that the people there are **stronger** and taller than we are, and that they live in cities with walls that reach the sky. They saw giants there!'

29 "But I said, 'Don't be **afraid** of those people. 30 The LORD your God will lead you, and he will fight for you, just as you saw him do in Egypt 31 and in the desert. You saw how he brought you **safely** all the way to this place, just as a father would carry his son.' 32 But in spite of what I said, you still would not **trust** the LORD, 33 even though he always went ahead of you to find a place for you to camp. To show you the way, he went in front of you in a pillar of fire by night and in a pillar of **cloud** by day.

The LORD Punishes Israel
(Num 14.20–45)

34 "The LORD heard your **complaints** and became **angry**, and so he **solemnly** declared, 35 'Not one of you from this **evil** generation will enter the fertile **land that I promised** to give your ancestors. 36 Only Caleb son of Jephunneh will enter it. He has remained **faithful** to me, and I will give him and his descendants the land that he has explored.' 37 Because of you the LORD also became **angry** with me and said, 'Not even you, Moses, will enter the land. 38 But **strengthen** the **determination** of your **helper**, Joshua son of Nun. He will lead Israel to occupy the land.'

39 "Then the LORD said to all of us, 'Your children, who are still too young to know **right** from **wrong**, will enter the land—the children you said would be seized by your **enemies**. I will give the land to them, and they will occupy it. 40 But as for you people, **turn** round and go back into the desert along the road to the Gulf of Aqaba.'

41 "You replied, 'Moses, we have sinned against the LORD. But now we will attack, just as the LORD our God **commanded** us.' Then each one of you got ready to fight, thinking it would be easy to invade the hill-country.

42 "But the LORD said to me, '**Warn** them not to attack, for I will not be with them, and their **enemies** will defeat

1.26: Deut 9.23; Heb 3.16 **1.31:** Acts 13.18 **1.32:** Heb 3.19 **1.34–35:** Heb 3.18

them.’ 43 I told you what the LORD had
said, but you paid no attention. You
rebelled against him, and in your **pride**
you marched into the hill-country.
44 Then the Amorites who lived in those
hills came out against you like a swarm
of bees. They chased you as far as
Hormah and defeated you there in the
hill-country of Edom. 45 So you cried out
to the LORD for **help**, but he would not
listen to you or pay any attention to you.

The Years in the Desert

46 “So then, after we had stayed at
2 Kadesh for a long time, 1 we finally
turned and went into the desert,
along the road to the Gulf of Aqaba, as
the LORD had **commanded**, and we spent
a long time wandering about in the hill-
country of Edom.

2 “Then the LORD told me 3 that we
had spent **enough** time wandering about
in those hills and that we should go north.
4 He told me to give you the following
instructions: ‘You are about to go
through the hill-country of Edom, the
territory of your distant relatives, the descendants of Esau. They will be **afraid** of
you, 5 but you must not start a war with
them, because I am not going to give you
so much as a square metre of their land.
I have given Edom to Esau’s
descendants. 6 You may buy food and
water from them.’

7 “**Remember** how the LORD your God
has **blessed** you in everything that you
have done. He has taken **care** of you as
you wandered through this vast desert.
He has been with you these forty years,
and you have had everything you
needed.

8 “So we moved on and left the road
that goes from the towns of Elath and
Eziongeber to the Dead Sea, and we
turned north-east towards Moab. 9 The
LORD said to me, ‘Don’t **trouble** the
people of Moab, the descendants of Lot,
or start a war against them. I have given
them the city of Ar, and I am not going to
give you any of their land.’ ”

10 (A **mighty race** of giants called the
Emim used to live in Ar. They were as
tall as the Anakim, another **race** of
giants. 11 Like the Anakim they were also
known as Rephaim; but the Moabites
called them Emim. 12 The Horites used to
live in Edom, but the descendants of
Esau chased them out, **destroyed** their
nation, and settled there themselves, just
as the Israelites later chased their
enemies out of the land that the LORD
gave them.)

13 “Then we crossed the River Zered
as the LORD told us to do. 14 This was
thirty-eight years after we had left
Kadesh Barnea. All the fighting men of
that generation had died, as the LORD
had said they would. 15 The LORD kept on
opposing them until he had **destroyed**
them all.

16 “After they had all died, 17 the LORD
said to us, 18 ‘Today you are to pass
through the territory of Moab by way of
Ar. 19 You will then be near the land of
the Ammonites, the descendants of Lot.
Don’t **trouble** them or start a war against
them, because I am not going to give you
any of the land that I have given them.’ ”

20 (This territory is also known as the
land of the Rephaim, the name of the
people who used to live there; the
Ammonites called them Zamzummim.
21 They were as tall as the Anakim. There
were many of them, and they were a
mighty race. But the LORD **destroyed**
them, so that the Ammonites took over
their land and settled there. 22 The LORD
had done the same thing for the
Edomites, the descendants of Esau, who
live in the hill-country of Edom. He **destroyed** the Horites, so that the Edomites
took over their land and settled there,
where they still live. 23 The land along the
Mediterranean coast had been settled by
people from the island of Crete. They
had **destroyed** the Avvim, the original inhabitants, and had taken over all their
land as far south as the city of Gaza.)

24 “After we had passed through
Moab, the LORD said to us, ‘Now, start out
and cross the River Arnon. I am placing
in your **power** Sihon, the Amorite king of
Heshbon, along with his land. Attack him,
and begin occupying his land. 25 From
today on I will make people everywhere
afraid of you. Everyone will **tremble** with
fear at the mention of your name.’

Israel Defeats King Sihon
(Num 21.21–30)

26 “Then I sent messengers from the
desert of Kedemoth to King Sihon of
Heshbon with the following **offer** of
peace: 27 ‘Let us pass through your
country. We will go straight through and
not leave the road. 28 We will pay for the
food we eat and the water we drink. All
we want to do is to pass through your
country, 29 until we cross the River
Jordan into the land that the LORD our
God is giving us. The descendants of
Esau, who live in Edom, and the
Moabites, who live in Ar, allowed us to
pass through their territory.’

afraid [2] 1.17; 3.2
bless Num 24.1; 7.13
care Num 18.21; 11.12
command [2] 1.3; 4.2
death (3) (to death) Num 35.12; 3.6
destroy [6] Num 33.52; 3.6
enemy 1.39; 4.42
enough 1.6; 3.26
fear 1.19; 7.19
helpless Ex 15.16; 32.36
might [2] Num 24.9; 3.24
need Num 18.20; 4.7
offer Num 31.50; 12.6
peace Num 23.10; 3.20
power [2] Num 33.4; 3.3
race (1) [3] Num 13.22; Josh 11.21
rebel 1.26; 9.7
remember Num 36.3; 4.39
strong 1.28; 9.2
stubborn Lev 26.19; 9.6
tremble Ex 20.18; 1 Sam 13.7
trouble [2] Num 33.55; 4.30
turn [2] 1.40; 4.30

2.1: Num 21.4 **2.4:** Gen 36.8 **2.9:** Gen 19.37 **2.14:** Num 14.28–35 **2.19:** Gen 19.38

30 "But King Sihon would not let us
pass through his country. The LORD your
God had made him **stubborn** and
rebellious, so that we could defeat him
and take his territory, which we still
occupy.
31 "Then the LORD said to me, 'Look, I
have made King Sihon and his land **helpless** before you; take his land and occupy
it.' 32 Sihon came out with all his men to
fight us near the town of Jahaz, 33 but the
LORD our God put him in our **power**, and
we killed him, his sons, and all his men.
34 At the same time we captured and **destroyed** every town, and put everyone **to
death**, men, women, and children. We
left no survivors. 35 We took the livestock
and plundered the towns. 36 The LORD our
God let us capture all the towns from
Aroer, on the edge of the valley of the
Arnon, and the city in the middle of that
valley, all the way to Gilead. No town
had walls too **strong** for us. 37 But we did
not go near the territory of the Ammonites or to the banks of the River
Jabbok or to the towns of the hill-country
or to any other place where the LORD our
God had **commanded** us not to go.

Israel Conquers King Og
(Num 21.31–35)

afraid [2] 2.4; 5.5
anger 1.34; 4.21
death (3) (to death) 2.34; 4.42
destroy 2.12; 4.3
determine 1.38; 9.25
earnest Ex 17.4; Ps 78.34
enough 2.3; 9.8
god (2) (other gods) Num 33.4; 4.7
heaven Ex 31.17; 4.26
help [2] 1.38; 4.7
last (2) Num 24.19; Josh 12.4
might 2.10; 5.22
peace 2.26; 12.9
possess Num 36.9; 6.18
power 2.24; 4.34
pray Num 27.15; 9.20
slaughter Num 22.40; 16.2
Sovereign Gen 15.2; 9.26
strength 1.38; 4.34
wonder (1) Ex 15.11; 4.34

3 "Next, we moved north towards the
region of Bashan, and King Og
came out with all his men to fight us near
the town of Edrei. 2 But the LORD said to
me, 'Don't be **afraid** of him. I am going to
give him, his men, and all his territory to
you. Do the same to him as you did to
Sihon the Amorite king who ruled in
Heshbon.'
3 "So the LORD also placed King Og
and his people in our **power**, and we
slaughtered them all. 4 At the same time
we captured all his towns—there was not
one that we did not take. In all we
captured sixty towns—the whole region
of Argob, where King Og of Bashan
ruled. 5 All these towns were fortified
with high walls, gates, and bars to lock
the gates, and there were also many
villages without walls. 6 We **destroyed** all
the towns and put **to death** all the men,
women, and children, just as we did in
the towns that belonged to King Sihon of
Heshbon. 7 We took the livestock and
plundered the towns.
8 "At that time we took from those
two Amorite kings the land east of the
River Jordan, from the River Arnon to
Mount Hermon. 9 (Mount Hermon is
called Sirion by the Sidonians, and Senir
by the Amorites.) 10 We took all the
territory of King Og of Bashan: the cities
on the plateau, the regions of Gilead and
of Bashan, as far east as the towns of
Salecah and Edrei."
11 (King Og was the **last** of the
Rephaim. His coffin,[b] made of stone,[c]
was four metres long and almost two
metres wide according to standard
measurements. It can still be seen in the
Ammonite city of Rabbah.)

The Tribes That Settled East of the Jordan
(Num 32.1–42)

12 "When we took **possession** of the
land, I assigned to the tribes of Reuben
and Gad the territory north of the town
of Aroer near the River Arnon and part
of the hill-country of Gilead, along with
its towns. 13 To half the tribe of Manasseh
I assigned the rest of Gilead and also all
of Bashan, where Og had ruled, that is,
the entire Argob region."
(Bashan was known as the land of the
Rephaim. 14 Jair, from the tribe of Manasseh, took the entire region of Argob,
that is, Bashan, as far as the border of
Geshur and Maacah. He named the
villages after himself, and they are still
known as the villages of Jair.)
15 "I assigned Gilead to the clan of
Machir of the tribe of Manasseh. 16 And to
the tribes of Reuben and Gad I assigned
the territory from Gilead to the River
Arnon. The middle of the river was their
southern boundary, and their northern
boundary was the River Jabbok, part of
which formed the Ammonite border.
17 On the west their territory extended to
the River Jordan, from Lake Galilee in
the north down to the Dead Sea in the
south and to the foot of Mount Pisgah on
the east.
18 "At the same time, I gave them the
following instructions: 'The LORD our
God has given you this land east of the
Jordan to occupy. Now arm your fighting
men and send them across the Jordan
ahead of the other tribes of Israel, to **help**
them to occupy their land. 19 Only your
wives, children, and livestock—I know
you have a lot of livestock—will remain
behind in the towns that I have assigned
to you. 20 **Help** your fellow-Israelites until
they occupy the land that the LORD is
giving them west of the Jordan and until
the LORD lets them live there in **peace**,
as he has already done here for you.
After that, you may return to this land
which I have assigned to you.'

[b] coffin; *or* bed. [c] stone; *or* iron.

3.18–20: Josh 1.12-15

21 "Then I instructed Joshua: 'You
have seen all that the LORD your God did
to those two kings, Sihon and Og; and he
will do the same to everyone else whose
land you invade. 22 Don't be **afraid** of
them, for the LORD your God will fight
for you.'

Moses Is Not Permitted to Enter Canaan

23 "At that time I **earnestly prayed**,
24 '**Sovereign** LORD, I know that you have
shown me only the beginning of the great
and **wonderful** things you are going to do.
There is no **god** in **heaven** or on earth
who can do the **mighty** things that you
have done! 25 Let me cross the River
Jordan, LORD, and see the fertile land on
the other side, the beautiful hill-country
and the Lebanon Mountains.'

26 "But because of you people the
LORD was **angry** with me and would not
listen. Instead, he said, 'That's **enough**!
Don't mention this again! 27 Go to the
peak of Mount Pisgah and look to the
north and to the south, to the east and to
the west. Look carefully at what you see,
because you will never go across the
Jordan. 28 Give Joshua his instructions.
Strengthen his **determination**, because
he will lead the people across to occupy
the land that you see.'

29 "So we remained in the valley
opposite the town of Bethpeor."

abandon Num 32.15; 31.6
alive Num 31.15; 24.6
alone 1.9; 6.4
anger [2] 3.26; 6.15
certain (1) [3] Num 5.12; 6.12
choose 1.13; 7.6
cloud 1.33; 5.22
command [3] 2.1; 5.12
commandment Ex 40.3; 5.22
covenant [3] Num 25.12; 5.2
create Num 11.12; 26.19
dare Num 32.7; 17.12
dark Ex 20.21; 5.23
death (3) (to death) 3.6; 7.2
destroy [3] 3.6; 5.25
disobey Num 24.13; 5.32
enemy 2.12; 6.19
escape [2] Num 35.6; 7.20
evil 1.35; 5.11
faithful [2] 1.36; 6.25
forget [4] Gen 41.30; 6.6
god (2) (other gods) [6] 3.24; 5.7

Moses Urges Israel to Be Obedient

4 Then Moses said to the people,
"**Obey** all the **laws** that I am
teaching you, and you will live and
occupy the land which the LORD, the God
of your ancestors, is giving you. 2 Do not
add anything to what I **command** you,
and do not take anything away. **Obey** the
commands of the LORD your God that I
have given you. 3 You yourselves saw
what the LORD did at Mount Peor. He
destroyed everyone who **worshipped**
Baal there, 4 but those of you who were
faithful to the LORD your God are still
alive today.

5 "I have **taught** you all the **laws**, as
the LORD my God told me to do. **Obey**
them in the land that you are about to
invade and occupy. 6 **Obey** them **faithfully**, and this will show the people of
other nations how **wise** you are. When
they hear of all these **laws**, they will say,
'What **wisdom** and **understanding** this
great nation has!'

7 "No other nation, no matter how
great, has a **god** who is so near when
they **need** him as the LORD our God is to
us. He answers us whenever we call for
help. 8 No other nation, no matter how
great, has **laws** so **just** as those that I
have **taught** you today. 9 Be on your
guard! Make **certain** that you do not
forget, as long as you live, what you have
seen with your own eyes. Tell your
children and your grandchildren 10 about
the day you stood in the **presence** of the
LORD your God at Mount Sinai,[x] when he
said to me, 'Assemble the people. I want
them to hear what I have to say, so that
they will **learn** to **obey** me as long as they
live and so that they will **teach** their
children to do the same.'

11 "Tell your children how you went
and stood at the foot of the mountain
which was covered with thick **clouds** of
dark smoke and fire blazing up to the
sky. 12 Tell them how the LORD spoke to
you from the fire, how you heard him
speaking but did not see him in any form
at all. 13 He told you what you must do to
keep the **covenant** he made with you—
you must **obey** the Ten **Commandments**,
which he wrote on two stone **tablets**.
14 The LORD told me to **teach** you all the
laws that you are to **obey** in the land that
you are about to invade and occupy.

God's people Num 31.16; 9.26
heart Gen 50.21; 6.
heaven [3] 3.24; 5.8
help 3.18; 15.7
holy Num 27.14; 5.
human Num 23.19; 5.26
idol [3] Num 33.52; 5.9
justice Lev 19.15; 16.20
law [8] 1.5; 5.1
learn Num 27.21; 5
love Num 14.18; 5.
mercy Ex 22.27; 7.
miracle Num 14.1 6.22
need 2.7; 8.9
obey [10] Num 27.2 5.1
plague Num 16.47; 7.19
power [3] 3.3; 5.15
presence Num 32. 9.18
prove Ex 7.9; 19.15
remember 2.7; 5.1
rescue Num 35.25 5.6
rival Num 25.13; 5
safe 1.31; 12.10
scatter Num 16.37 28.37
serve [2] Num 35.1 8.19
sight Num 25.6; 11
solemn 1.34; 29.19
strength 3.28; 5.15
tablet Ex 40.20; 5.2
teach [6] 1.5; 5.31
tempt Ex 34.15; Prov 1.10
terrify Num 22.3; 6.22
tolerate Num 25.1 5.9
trouble 2.9; 28.20
turn 2.1; 8.19
understand 1.13; 29.4
wisdom Gen 41.33 32.28
wise 1.13; 16.19
witness Num 35.3 17.6
wonder (1) 3.24; 7.
worship (2) (of other gods) [3] Num 25.2; 5.7

Warning against Idolatry

15 "When the LORD spoke to you from
the fire on Mount Sinai, you did not see
any form. For your own good, then,
make **certain** 16 that you do not sin by
making for yourselves an **idol** in any
form at all—whether man or woman,
17 animal or bird, 18 reptile or fish. 19 Do
not be **tempted** to **worship** and **serve**
what you see in the sky—the sun, the
moon, and the stars. The LORD your God
has given these to all other peoples for
them to **worship**. 20 But you are the
people he **rescued** from Egypt, that
blazing furnace. He brought you out to
make you his **own people**, as you are
today. 21 Because of you the LORD your
God was **angry** with me and **solemnly**
declared that I would not cross the River
Jordan to enter the fertile land which he
is giving you. 22 I will die in this land and
never cross the river, but you are about
to go across and occupy that fertile land.
23 Be **certain** that you do not **forget** the
covenant that the LORD your God made
with you. **Obey** his **command** not to make

[x] Sinai; *or* Horeb.

3.23–27: Num 27.12–14; Deut 32.48–52 **4.2:** Rev 22.18–19 **4.3:** Num 25.1–9
4.11–12: Ex 19.16–18; Heb 12.18–19 **4.13:** Ex 31.18, 34.28; Deut 9.10 **4.14:** Ex 21.1
4.16: Ex 20.4; Lev 26.1; Deut 5.8, 27.15 **4.17–18a:** Rom 1.23
4.20: Ex 19.5; Deut 7.6, 14.2, 26.18; Tit 2.14; 1 Pet 2.9 **4.21:** Num 20.12

yourselves any kind of **idol**, 24 because the
LORD your God is like a flaming fire; he
tolerates no **rivals**.

25 "Even when you have been in the
land a long time and have children and
grandchildren, do not sin by making for
yourselves an **idol** in any form at all. This
is **evil** in the LORD's **sight**, and it will
make him **angry**. 26 I call **heaven and**
earth as **witnesses** against you today
that, if you **disobey** me, you will soon
disappear from the land. You will not
live very long in the land across the
Jordan that you are about to occupy. You
will be completely **destroyed**. 27 The
LORD will **scatter** you among other
nations, where only a few of you will
survive. 28 There you will **serve gods**
made by **human** hands, **gods** of wood and
stone, gods that cannot see or hear, eat
or smell. 29 There you will look for the
LORD your God, and if you search for him
with all your heart, you will find him.
30 When you are in **trouble** and all those
things happen to you, then you will
finally **turn to** the LORD and **obey** him.
31 He is a **merciful** God. He will not
abandon you or **destroy** you, and he will
not **forget** the **covenant** that he himself
made with your ancestors.

32 "Search the past, the time before
you were born, all the way back to the
time when God **created** man on the
earth. Search the entire earth. Has anything as great as this ever happened
before? Has anyone ever heard of anything like this? 33 Have any people ever
lived after hearing a **god** speak to them
from a fire, as you have? 34 Has any **god**
ever **dared** to go and take a people from
another nation and make them his own,
as the LORD your God did for you in
Egypt? Before your very eyes he used
his great **power** and **strength**; he brought
plagues and war, worked **miracles** and
wonders, and caused **terrifying** things to
happen. 35 The LORD has shown you this,
to **prove** to you that he **alone** is God and
that there is no other. 36 He let you hear
his voice from **heaven** so that he could
instruct you; and here on earth he let
you see his **holy** fire, and he spoke to you
from it. 37 Because he **loved** your
ancestors, he **chose** you, and by his great
power he himself brought you out of
Egypt. 38 As you advanced, he drove out
nations greater and more **powerful** than
you, so that he might bring you in and
give you their land, the land which still
belongs to you. 39 So **remember** today and
never **forget**: the LORD is God in **heaven**
and on earth. There is no other **god**.
40 **Obey** all his **laws** that I have given you
today, and all will go well with you and
your descendants. You will continue to
live in the land which the LORD your God
is giving you to be yours for ever."

The Cities of Refuge East of the Jordan

41 Then Moses set aside three cities
east of the River Jordan 42 to which a
man could **escape** and be **safe** if he had
accidentally killed someone who had not
been his **enemy**. He could **escape** to one
of these cities and not be put **to death**.
43 For the tribe of Reuben there was the
city of Bezer, on the desert plateau; for
the tribe of Gad there was Ramoth, in
the territory of Gilead; and for the tribe
of Manasseh there was Golan, in the
territory of Bashan.

Introduction to the Giving of God's Law

44 Moses gave God's **laws** and
teachings to the people of Israel. 45–46 It
was after they had come out of Egypt
and were in the valley east of the River
Jordan, opposite the town of Bethpeor,
that he gave them these **laws**. This was
in the territory that had belonged to King
Sihon of the Amorites, who had ruled in
the town of Heshbon. Moses and the
people of Israel defeated him when they
came out of Egypt. 47 They occupied his
land and the land of King Og of Bashan,
the other Amorite king who lived east of
the Jordan. 48 This land extended from
the town of Aroer, on the edge of the
River Arnon, all the way north to Mount
Sirion,[d] that is, Mount Hermon. 49 It also
included all the region east of the River
Jordan as far south as the Dead Sea and
east to the foot of Mount Pisgah.

The Ten Commandments
(Ex 20.1–17)

5 Moses called together all the people
of Israel and said to them, "People
of Israel, listen to all the **laws** that I am
giving you today. **Learn** them and be
sure that you **obey** them. 2 At Mount Sinai
the LORD our God made a **covenant**, 3 not
only with our fathers, but with all of us
who are living today. 4 There on the
mountain the LORD spoke to you face-to-
face from the fire. 5 I stood between you
and the LORD at that time to tell you
what he said, because you were **afraid** of
the fire and would not go up the
mountain.

"The LORD said, 6 'I am the LORD your

accuse Num 35.12; 19.16
adultery Num 5.19; Job 24.15
afraid 3.2; 7.18
being Lev 27.28; Josh 10.14
bow (2) Num 20.6; 33.3
cloud 4.11; 31.15
command [6] 4.2; 6.1
commandment [2] 4.13; 10.4
commit [2] Num 5.19; 27.24
covenant 4.13; 7.9
dark 4.11; Josh 24.7
death (1) Num 35.24; 14.21
dedicate Num 21.2; 20.5
desire [2] Num 15.39; 7.25

[d] *One ancient translation* Sirion; *Hebrew* Sion.

4.24: Heb 12.29 **4.27–28:** Deut 28.36 **4.29:** Jer 29.13 **4.35:** Mk 12.32 **4.41–43:** Josh 20.8–9

God, who **rescued** you from Egypt, where you were **slaves**.

7 " '**Worship no god** but me.

8 " 'Do not make for yourselves **images** of anything in **heaven** or on earth or in the water under the earth. 9 Do not **bow down** to any **idol** or **worship** it, for I am the LORD your God and I **tolerate** no **rivals**. I bring **punishment** on those who **hate** me and on their descendants down to the third and fourth generation. 10 But I show my **love** to thousands of generations[e] of those who **love** me and **obey** my **laws**.

11 " 'Do not use my **name** for **evil purposes**, for I, the LORD your God, will **punish** anyone who misuses my **name**.

12 " '**Observe** the **Sabbath** and keep it **holy**, as I, the LORD your God, have **commanded** you. 13 You have six days in which to do your work, 14 but the seventh day is a **day of rest dedicated** to me. On that day no one is to work—neither you, your children, your **slaves**, your animals, nor the foreigners who live in your country. Your **slaves** must **rest** just as you do. 15 **Remember** that you were **slaves** in Egypt, and that I, the LORD your God, **rescued** you by my great **power** and **strength**. That is why I **command** you to **observe** the **Sabbath**.

16 " '**Respect** your father and your mother, as I, the LORD your God, **command** you, so that all may go well with you and so that you may live a long time in the land that I am giving you.

17 " 'Do not **commit murder**.

18 " 'Do not **commit adultery**.

19 " 'Do not **steal**.

20 " 'Do not **accuse** anyone **falsely**.

21 " 'Do not **desire** another man's wife; do not **desire** his house, his land, his **slaves**, his cattle, his donkeys, or anything else that he owns.'

22 "These are the **commandments** the LORD gave to all of you when you were gathered at the mountain. When he spoke with a **mighty** voice from the fire and from the thick **clouds**, he gave these **commandments** and no others. Then he wrote them on two stone **tablets** and gave them to me.

The People's Fear
(Ex 20.18–21)

23 "When the whole mountain was on fire and you heard the voice from the **darkness**, your leaders and the chiefs of your tribes came to me 24 and said, 'The LORD our God showed us his greatness and his **glory** when we heard him speak from the fire! Today we have seen that it is possible for a man to continue to live, even though God has spoken to him. 25 But why should we risk **death** again? That **terrible** fire will **destroy** us. We are **sure** to die if we hear the LORD our God speak again. 26 Has any **human being** ever lived after hearing the living God speak from a fire? 27 Go back, Moses, and listen to everything that the LORD our God says. Then return and tell us what he said to you. We will listen and **obey**.'

28 "When the LORD heard this, he said to me, 'I have heard what these people said, and they are **right**. 29 If only they would always feel like this! If only they would always **honour** me and **obey** all my **commands**, so that everything would go well with them and their descendants for ever. 30 Go and tell them to return to their tents. 31 But you, Moses, stay here with me, and I will give you all my **laws** and **commands**. **Teach** them to the people, so that they will **obey** them in the land that I am giving them.'

32 "People of Israel, be **sure** that you do everything that the LORD your God has **commanded** you. Do not **disobey** any of his **laws**. 33 **Obey** them all, so that everything will go well with you and so that you will continue to live in the land that you are going to occupy.

The Great Commandment

6 "These are all the **laws** that the LORD your God **commanded** me to **teach** you. **Obey** them in the land that you are about to enter and occupy. 2 As long as you live, you and your descendants are to **honour** the LORD your God and **obey** all his **laws** that I am giving you, so that you may live in that land a long time. 3 Listen to them, people of Israel, and **obey** them! Then all will go well with you, and you will become a **mighty** nation and live in that **rich** and fertile land, just as the LORD, the God of our ancestors, has **promised**.

4 "Israel, **remember** this! The LORD—and the LORD **alone**—is our God.[f] 5 **Love** the LORD your God **with all your heart**, with all your **soul**, and with all your

destroy 4.3; 6.15
disobey 4.26; 9.16
evil 4.25; 9.12
false Num 14.36; 19.16
glory Lev 10.3; 1 Sam 4.21
god (2) (other gods) 4.7; 6.14
hate 1.27; 7.10
heaven 4.26; 10.14
holy 4.36; 26.15
honour Num 29.12; 6.2
human 4.28; Josh 10.14
idol 4.16; 7.5
image Ex 20.4; 1 Sam 7.3
law [4] 4.1; 6.1
learn 4.10; 11.2
love [2] 4.37; 6.5
might 3.24; 6.3
name (2) (name of God, of Jesus) [2] Num 6.27; 6.13
obey [6] 4.1; 6.1
observe [2] Num 27.11; 15.5
power 4.34; 6.21
punish [2] Num 32.23; 7.10
purpose Lev 7.24; Judg 20.11
remember 4.39; 6.4
rescue [2] 4.20; 6.12
respect Num 11.16; Judg 9.16
rest (1) [2] Num 23.24; 6.7
right (1) 1.39; 6.18
rival 4.24; 6.15
Sabbath [2] Num 28.9; 2 Kgs 4.23
slave [5] Lev 26.13; 6.12
steal Lev 19.11; Josh 7.11
strength 4.34; 6.5
sure [3] Num 18.32; 6.17
tablet 4.13; 9.9
teach 4.1; 6.1
terrible Num 21.29; 7.19
tolerate 4.24; 6.15
worship (1) (of God) Num 29.1; 6.13
worship (2) (of other gods) [2] 4.3; 6.14

alone [2] 4.35; 8.3
anger 4.21; 7.4
certain (1) 4.9; 8.11
command [5] 5.12; 7.9
destroy 5.25; 7.4
enemy 4.42; 7.15
faithful 4.4; 7.9
forehead Ex 28.38; 11.18
forget [2] 4.9; 7.24
free Num 36.6; 7.8
god (2) (other gods) [3] 5.7; 7.4
heart 4.29; 10.12
honour [3] 5.29; 13.4
law [5] 5.1; 7.11
love 5.10; 7.7
might 5.22; 7.8
miracle 4.34; 7.19
name (2) (name of God, of Jesus) 5.11; 10.8
obey [7] 5.1; 7.9
please Num 29.2; 12.8
possess 3.12; 8.13

[e] thousands of generations; *or* thousands.
[f] The LORD...is our God; *or* The LORD, our God, is the only God; *or* The LORD our God is one.

5.8–9: Lev 26.1; Deut 4.15–18, 27.15 **5.9–10:** Ex 34.6–7; Num 14.18; Deut 7.9–10 **5.11:** Lev 19.12
5.12: Ex 16.23–30, 31.12–14 **5.13–14:** Ex 23.12, 31.15, 34.21, 35.2; Lev 23.3
5.16: Deut 27.16; Mt 15.4, 19.19; Mk 7.10, 10.19; Lk 18.20; Eph 6.2, 3
5.17: Gen 9.6; Lev 24.17; Mt 5.21, 19.18; Mk 10.19; Lk 18.20; Rom 13.9; Jas 2.11
5.18: Lev 20.10; Mt 5.27, 19.18; Mk 10.19; Lk 18.20; Rom 13.9; Jas 2.11
5.19: Lev 19.11; Mt 19.18; Mk 10.19; Lk 18.20; Rom 13.9 **5.20:** Ex 23.1; Mt 19.18; Mk 10.19; Lk 18.20
5.21: Rom 7.7, 13.9 **5.22–27:** Heb 12.18–19 **6.4:** Mk 12.29 **6.5:** Mt 22.37; Mk 12.30; Lk 10.27

strength. 6 Never **forget** these **commands** that I am giving you today. 7 **Teach** them to your children. Repeat them when you are at home and when you are away, when you are **resting** and when you are working. 8 Tie them on your arms and wear them on your **foreheads** as a **reminder.** 9 Write them on the door-posts of your houses and on your gates.

Warning against Disobedience

10 "Just as the LORD your God **promised** your ancestors, Abraham, Isaac, and Jacob, he will give you a land with large and **prosperous** cities which you did not build. 11 The houses will be full of good things which you did not put in them, and there will be wells that you did not dig, and **vineyards** and olive orchards that you did not plant. When the LORD brings you into this land and you have all you want to eat, 12 make **certain** that you do not **forget** the LORD who **rescued** you from Egypt, where you were **slaves.** 13 **Honour** the LORD your God, **worship** only him, and make your **promises in his name alone.** 14 Do not **worship other gods**, any of the **gods** of the peoples around you. 15 If you do **worship other gods**, the **LORD's anger** will come against you like fire and will **destroy** you completely, because the LORD your God, who is present with you, **tolerates** no **rivals.**

16 "Do not put the LORD your God **to the test**, as you did at Massah. 17 Be **sure** that you **obey** all the **laws** that he has given you. 18 Do what the LORD says is **right** and good, and all will go well with you. You will be able to take **possession** of the fertile **land that the LORD promised** your ancestors, 19 and you will drive out your **enemies**, as he **promised.**

20 "In time to come your children will ask you, 'Why did the LORD our God **command** us to **obey** all these **laws**?' 21 Then tell them, 'We were **slaves** of the king of Egypt, and the LORD **rescued** us by his great **power.** 22 With our own eyes we saw him work **miracles** and do **terrifying** things to the Egyptians and to their king and to all his officials. 23 He **freed** us from Egypt to bring us here and give us this land, as he had **promised** our ancestors he would. 24 Then the LORD our God **commanded** us to **obey** all these **laws** and to **honour** him. If we do, he will always **watch** over our nation and keep it **prosperous.** 25 If we **faithfully obey** everything that God has **commanded** us, he will be **pleased** with us.'[g]

The Lord's Own People
(Ex 34.11–16)

7 "The LORD your God will bring you into the land which you are going to occupy, and he will drive many nations out of it. As you advance, he will drive out seven nations larger and more **powerful** than you: the Hittites, the Girgashites, the Amorites, the Canaanites, the Perizzites, the Hivites, and the Jebusites. 2 When the LORD your God places these people in your **power** and you defeat them, you must put them all **to death.** Do not make an alliance with them or show them any **mercy.** 3 Do not marry any of them, and do not let your children marry any of them, 4 because then they would lead your children away from the LORD to **worship other gods.** If that happens, the LORD will be **angry** with you and **destroy** you at once. 5 So then, tear down their **altars**, break their **sacred** stone pillars in pieces, cut down the **symbols** of their **goddess** Asherah, and burn their **idols.** 6 Do this because you belong to the LORD your God. From all the peoples on earth he **chose** you to be his own **special** people.

7 "The LORD did not **love** you and **choose** you because you outnumbered other peoples; you were the smallest nation on earth. 8 But the LORD **loved** you and wanted to keep the **promise** that he made to your ancestors. That is why he **saved** you by his great **might** and **set you free** from **slavery** to the king of Egypt. 9 **Remember** that the LORD your God is the only God and that he is **faithful.** He will keep his **covenant** and show his **constant love** to a thousand generations of those who **love** him and **obey** his **commands,** 10 but he will not hesitate to **punish** those who **hate** him. 11 So now, **obey** what you have been **taught**; **obey** all the **laws** that I have given you today.

The Blessings of Obedience
(Deut 28.1–14)

12 "If you listen to these **commands** and **obey** them **faithfully**, then the LORD your God will continue to keep his **covenant** with you and will show you his **constant love,** as he **promised** your ancestors. 13 He will **love** you and **bless** you, so that you will increase in number and have many children; he will **bless**

[g] If we faithfully...with us; *or* The right thing for us to do is to obey faithfully everything that God has commanded us.

6.6–9: Deut 11.18–20 **6.10:** Gen 12.7, 26.3, 28.13 **6.13:** Mt 4.10; Lk 4.8 **6.16:** Ex 17.1–7; Mt 4.7; Lk 4.12
7.1: Acts 13.19 **7.5:** Deut 12.3 **7.6:** Ex 19.5; Deut 4.20, 14.2, 26.18; Tit 2.14; 1 Pet 2.9
7.9–10: Ex 20.5–6, 34.6–7; Num 14.18; Deut 5.9–10 **7.12–16:** Deut 11.13–17

your fields, so that you will have corn,
wine, and olive-oil; and he will **bless** you
by giving you a lot of livestock and
sheep. He will give you all these
blessings in the **land that he promised**
your ancestors he would give to you.
14 No people in the **world** will be as **richly**
blessed as you. None of you nor any of
your livestock will be sterile. 15 The LORD
will **protect** you from all sickness, and he
will not bring on you any of the dreadful
diseases that you **experienced** in Egypt,
but he will bring them on all your
enemies. 16 **Destroy** every nation that the
LORD your God places in your **power**, and
do not show them any **mercy**. Do not
worship their gods, for that would be
fatal.

17 "Do not tell yourselves that these
peoples outnumber you and that you
cannot drive them out. 18 Do not be **afraid**
of them; **remember** what the LORD your
God did to the king of Egypt and to all his
people. 19 **Remember** the **terrible plagues**
that you saw with your own eyes, the
miracles and **wonders**, and the great
power and **strength** by which the LORD
your God **set you free**. In the same way
that he destroyed the Egyptians, he will
destroy all these people that you now
fear. 20 He will even cause panic[h] among
them and will **destroy** those who **escape**
and go into hiding. 21 So do not be **afraid**
of these people. The LORD your God is
with you; he is a great God and one to be
feared. 22 Little by little he will drive out
these nations as you advance. You will
not be able to **destroy** them all at once,
for, if you did, the number of wild
animals would increase and be a **threat**
to you. 23 The LORD will put your **enemies**
in your **power** and make them panic until
they are **destroyed**. 24 He will put their
kings in your **power**. You will kill them,
and they will be **forgotten**. No one will be
able to stop you; you will **destroy** everyone. 25 Burn their **idols**. Do not **desire** the
silver or gold that is on them, and do not
take it for yourselves. If you do, that will
be fatal, because the LORD **hates idolatry**.
26 Do not bring any of these **idols** into
your homes, or the same **curse** will be on
you that is on them. You must **hate** and
despise these **idols**, because they are
under the LORD's **curse**.

A Good Land to Be Possessed

8 "**Obey faithfully** all the **laws** that I
have given you today, so that you
may live, increase in number, and
occupy the **land which the** LORD
promised to your ancestors. 2 **Remember**
how the LORD your God led you on this
long journey through the desert these
past forty years, sending hardships to
test you, so that he might know what you
intended to do and whether you would
obey his **commands**. 3 He made you go
hungry, and then he gave you **manna** to
eat, food that you and your ancestors had
never eaten before. He did this to **teach**
you that man must not **depend** on **bread**
alone to sustain him, but on everything
that the LORD says. 4 During these forty
years your clothes have not worn out,
nor have your feet swollen up.
5 **Remember** that the LORD your God
corrects and **punishes** you just as a father
disciplines his children. 6 So then, do as
the LORD has **commanded** you: live
according to his **laws** and **obey** him. 7 The
LORD your God is bringing you into a
fertile land—a land that has rivers and
springs, and underground streams gushing out into the valleys and hills; 8 a land
that produces wheat and barley, grapes,
figs, pomegranates, olives, and honey.
9 There you will never go **hungry** or ever
be in **need**. Its rocks have iron in them,
and from its hills you can mine copper.
10 You will have all you want to eat, and
you will give **thanks** to the LORD your
God for the fertile land that he has given
you.

Warnings against Forgetting the Lord

11 "Make **certain** that you do not
forget the LORD your God; do not **fail** to
obey any of his **laws** that I am giving you
today. 12 When you have all you want to
eat and have built good houses to live in
13 and when your cattle and **sheep**, your
silver and gold, and all your other **possessions** have increased, 14 make **sure** that
you do not become **proud** and **forget** the
LORD your God who **rescued** you from
Egypt, where you were **slaves**. 15 He led
you through that vast and **terrifying**
desert where there were poisonous
snakes and scorpions. In that dry and
waterless land he made water flow out of
solid rock for you. 16 In the desert he gave
you **manna** to eat, food that your ancestors had never eaten. He sent hardships
on you to **test** you, so that in the end he
could **bless** you with good things. 17 So
then, you must never think that you have
made yourselves wealthy by your own
power and **strength**. 18 **Remember** that it
is the LORD your God who gives you the
power to become **rich**. He does this
because he is still **faithful** today to the

[h] cause panic; *or* send hornets, *or* send plagues.

8.3: Mt 4.4; Lk 4.4 **8.11-16:** Hos 13.5-6

alone 6.4; 10.20
bless 7.13; 10.8
bread Num 28.17; 16.3
certain (1) 6.12; 1 Sam 20.9

command [2] 7.9; 9.12
correct Job 5.17
covenant 7.9; 9.9
depend Num 32.1 25.2
destroy [3] 7.4; 9.
discipline Prov 19.18
fail Num 30.15; 2
faithful [2] 7.9; 10
forget [3] 7.24; 9.7
god (2) (other go 7.4; 10.17
hunger [2] Lev 26 28.48
intend Num 35.2 9.5
law [3] 7.11; 10.13
manna [2] Num 1 Josh 5.12
need 4.7; 11.14
obey [5] 7.9; 9.23
possess 6.18; 9.4
power [2] 7.1; 9.1
promise 7.8; 9.3
proud 1.43; 1 Sam
punish 7.10; 18.19
remember [3] 7.9 9.14
rescue 6.12; 9.26
rich 7.14; 11.9
serve 4.19; 10.8
sheep 7.13; 12.6
slave 7.8; 13.5
strength 7.19; 9.2
sure 6.17; 9.6
teach 7.11; 11.19
terrify 6.22; 26.8
test [2] 6.16; 13.3
thank Lev 22.29; 1 Sam 25.33
turn 4.30; 9.12
warn 1.42; 30.18
worship (2) (of other gods) 7.4; 1

covenant that he made with your
ancestors. [19]Never **forget** the LORD your
God or **turn to** other **gods** to **worship and
serve them**. If you do, then I **warn** you
today that you will certainly be
destroyed. [20]If you do not **obey** the LORD,
then you will be **destroyed** just like those
nations that he is going to **destroy** as you
advance.

The People's Disobedience

9 "Listen, people of Israel! Today you
are about to cross the River Jordan
and occupy the land belonging to nations
greater and more **powerful** than you.
Their cities are large, with walls that
reach the sky. [2]The people themselves
are tall and **strong**; they are giants, and
you have heard it said that no one can
stand against them. [3]But now you will
see for yourselves that the LORD your
God will go ahead of you like a **raging**
fire. He will defeat them as you advance,
so that you will drive them out and
destroy them quickly, as he **promised**.
4 "After the LORD your God has driven
them out for you, do not say to yourselves that he brought you in to **possess**
this land because you **deserved** it. No, the
LORD is going to drive these people out
for you because they are **wicked**. [5]It is
not because you are good and do what is
right that the LORD is letting you take
their land. He will drive them out
because they are **wicked** and because he
intends to keep the **promise** that he
made to your ancestors, Abraham, Isaac,
and Jacob. [6]You can be **sure** that the
LORD is not giving you this fertile land
because you **deserve** it. No, you are a
stubborn people.
7 "Never **forget** how you made the
LORD your God **angry** in the desert.
From the day that you left Egypt until
the day you arrived here, you have
rebelled against him. [8]Even at Mount
Sinai you made the LORD **angry**—angry
enough to **destroy** you. [9]I went up the
mountain to receive the stone **tablets** on
which was written the **covenant** that the
LORD had made with you. I stayed there
forty days and nights and did not eat or
drink anything. [10]Then the LORD gave
me the two stone **tablets** on which he had
written with his own hand what he had
said to you from the fire on the day that
you were gathered there at the mountain. [11]Yes, after those forty days and
nights the LORD gave me the two stone
tablets on which he had written the
covenant.
12 "Then the LORD said to me, 'Go
down the mountain at once, because
your people, whom you led out of Egypt,
have become **corrupt** and have done **evil**.
They have already **turned away** from
what I **commanded** them to do, and they
have made an **idol** for themselves.'
13 "The LORD also said to me, 'I know
how **stubborn** these people are. [14]Don't
try to stop me. I **intend** to **destroy** them
so that no one will **remember** them any
longer. Then I will make you the father
of a nation larger and more **powerful**
than they are.'
15 "So I **turned** and went down the
mountain, carrying the two stone **tablets**
on which the **covenant** was written.
Flames of fire were coming from the
mountain. [16]I saw that you had already
disobeyed the **command** that the LORD
your God had given you, and that you
had sinned against him by making yourselves a metal **idol** in the form of a **bull-
calf**. [17]So there in front of you I threw the
stone **tablets** down and broke them to
pieces. [18]Then once again I lay face
downwards in the LORD's **presence** for
forty days and nights and did not eat or
drink anything. I did this because you
had sinned against the LORD and had
made him **angry**. [19]I was **afraid** of the
LORD's fierce anger, because he was
furious enough to **destroy** you; but once
again the LORD listened to me. [20]The
LORD was also **angry enough** with Aaron
to kill him, so I **prayed** for Aaron at the
same time. [21]I took that sinful thing that
you had made—that metal **bull-calf**—and
threw it into the fire. Then I broke it in
pieces, ground it to dust, and threw the
dust into the stream that flowed down
the mountain.
22 "You also made the LORD your God
angry when you were at Taberah,
Massah, and Kibroth Hattaavah. [23]And
when he sent you from Kadesh Barnea
with orders to go and take **possession** of
the land that he was giving you, you
rebelled against him; you did not **trust**
him or **obey** him. [24]Ever since I have
known you, you have **rebelled** against the
LORD.
25 "So I lay face downwards in the
LORD's **presence** those forty days and
nights, because I knew that he was **determined** to **destroy** you. [26]And I **prayed**,
'**Sovereign LORD**, don't **destroy** your **own
people**, the people you **rescued** and
brought out of Egypt by your great
strength and **power**. [27]**Remember** your
servants, Abraham, Isaac, and Jacob,

fraid 7.18; 13.11
nger [6] 7.4; 11.17
ull-calf [2] Ex 32.4;
Kgs 12.28
hoose 7.6; 10.15
ommand [2] 8.2;
).5
orrupt 32.32
ovenant [3] 8.18;
7.2
eserve [2]
en 40.15; Judg 9.16
estroy [6] 8.19;
).10
etermine 3.28; 31.6
isobey 5.32; 11.28
nough [3] 3.26; 19.15
vil 5.11; 13.5
orget 8.11; 16.12
ury Ex 32.19; 29.23
od's people 4.20;
).15
ate 7.10; 12.31
dol [2] 7.5; 12.3
ntend [2] 8.2;
udg 20.5
night 7.8; 10.17
bey 8.1; 10.13
ossess [2] 8.13;
).11
ower [4] 8.17; 10.17
ray [2] 3.23;
udg 13.8
resence [2] 4.10;
2.5
romise [3] 8.1; 10.9
age Gen 49.4;
Sam 20.34
ebel [3] 2.30; 13.5
emember [2] 8.2;
1.2
escue 8.14; 13.5
ight (1) 6.18; 12.28
ervant Num 22.22;
1.6
overeign 3.24;
osh 7.7
trength 8.17; 26.8
trong 2.36; 10.15
tubborn [3] 2.30;
0.16
ure 8.14; 10.18
ablet [5] 5.22; 10.1
rust 1.32; 28.52
urn [2] 8.19; 10.5
vicked [3]
Num 16.26; 31.29

9.9: Ex 24.18 **9.19:** Heb 12.21 **9.22:** Num 11.3, 34; Ex 17.7
9.23: Num 13.25—14.38; Deut 1.21, 26; Heb 3.16

and do not pay any attention to the **stubbornness, wickedness**, and sin of this people. 28 Otherwise, the Egyptians will say that you were unable to take your people into the **land that you had promised** them. They will say that you took your people out into the desert to kill them, because you **hated** them. 29 After all, these are the people whom you **chose** to be your own and whom you brought out of Egypt by your great **power** and **might**.'

Moses Receives the Commandments Again
(Ex 34.1-10)

10 "Then the LORD said to me, 'Cut two stone **tablets** like the first ones and make a wooden **box** to put them in. Come up to me on the mountain, 2 and I will write on those **tablets** what I wrote on the **tablets** that you broke, and then you are to put them in the **box**.'

3 "So I made a **box** of acacia-wood and cut two stone **tablets** like the first ones and took them up the mountain. 4 Then the LORD wrote on those **tablets** the same **words** that he had written the first time, the Ten **Commandments** that he gave you when he spoke from the fire on the day you were gathered at the mountain. The LORD gave me the **tablets**, 5 and I **turned** and went down the mountain. Then, just as the LORD had **commanded**, I put them in the **box** that I had made—and they have been there ever since."

6 (The Israelites set out from the wells that belonged to the people of Jaakan, and went to Moserah. There Aaron died and was buried, and his son Eleazar succeeded him as **priest**. 7 From there they went to Gudgodah and then on to Jotbathah, a well-watered place. 8 At the mountain[i] the LORD appointed the men of the tribe of Levi to be in charge of the **Covenant Box**, to **serve** him as **priests**, and to pronounce **blessings in his name**. And these are still their **duties**. 9 That is why the tribe of Levi received no land as the other tribes did; what they received was the **privilege** of being the LORD's **priests**, as the LORD your God **promised**.)

10 "I stayed on the mountain forty days and nights, as I did the first time. The LORD listened to me once more and **agreed** not to **destroy** you. 11 Then he told me to go and lead you, so that you could take **possession** of the **land that he had promised** to give to your ancestors.

What God Demands

12 "Now, people of Israel, listen to what the LORD your God **demands** of you: **Worship** the LORD and do all that he **commands**. Love him, **serve** him **with all your heart**, 13 and **obey** all his **laws**. I am giving them to you today for your **benefit**. 14 To the LORD belong even the highest **heavens**; the earth is his also, and everything on it. 15 But the LORD's **love** for your ancestors was so **strong** that he **chose** you instead of any other people, and you are still his **chosen people**. 16 So then, from now on be **obedient** to the LORD and stop being **stubborn**. 17 The LORD your God is **supreme** over all **gods** and over all **powers**. He is great and **mighty**, and he is to be **feared**. He does not show **partiality**, and he does not **accept bribes**. 18 He makes **sure** that **orphans** and **widows** are treated fairly; he **loves** the foreigners who live with our people, and gives them food and clothes. 19 So then, show **love** for those foreigners, because you were once foreigners in Egypt. 20 **Obey** the LORD your God and **worship** only him. Be **faithful** to him and make your **promises in his name alone**. 21 **Praise** him—he is your God, and you have seen with your own eyes the great and astounding things that he has done for you. 22 When your ancestors went to Egypt, there were only seventy of them. But now the LORD your God has made you as numerous as the stars in the sky.

The LORD's Greatness

11 "**Love** the LORD your God and always **obey** all his **laws**. 2 **Remember** today what you have **learned** about the LORD through your **experiences** with him. It was you, not your children, who had these **experiences**. You saw the LORD's greatness, his **power**, his **might**, 3 and his **miracles**. You saw what he did to the king of Egypt and to his entire country. 4 You saw how the LORD completely wiped out the Egyptian army, along with their horses and chariots, by drowning them in the Red Sea[j] when they were pursuing you. 5 You know what the LORD did for you in the desert before you arrived here. 6 You recall what he did to Dathan and Abiram, the sons of Eliab of the tribe of Reuben. In the **sight** of everyone the earth opened up and swallowed them, along with their families, their tents, and

[i] the mountain; *or* that time. [j] RED SEA: *See Word List.*

10.6: Num 20.28, 33.38 **10.8:** Num 3.5-8 **10.10:** Ex 34.28
10.17: 1 Tim 6.15; Rev 17.14, 19.16; Acts 10.34; Rom 2.11; Gal 2.6; Eph 6.9 **10.22:** Gen 15.5, 22.17, 46.27
11.3: Ex 7.8—12.13 **11.4:** Ex 14.28 **11.6:** Num 16.31-32

accept Num 18.15; 16.19
agree 1.14; Josh 2.21
alone 8.3; 32.12
benefit Job 13.7
bless 8.16; 11.26
box *see* **Covenant Box**
bribe Ex 23.8; 16.19
choose [2] 9.29; 11.26
command [2] 9.12; 11.13
commandment 5.22; Josh 8.35
Covenant Box [5] Num 20.8; 31.9
demand Ex 21.22; 29.19
destroy 9.3; 12.2
duty (1) Num 18.3; 17.12
faithful 8.1; 11.22
fear 7.19; 11.25
god (2) (other gods) 8.19; 11.16
God's people 9.26; 14.2
heart 6.5; 11.13
heaven 5.8; 26.15
law 8.1; 11.1
love [4] 7.7; 11.1
might 9.29; 11.2
name (2) (name of God, of Jesus) [2] 6.13; 18.19
obey [3] 9.23; 11.1
orphan Ex 22.22; 14.29
partiality 1.17; 16.19
possess 9.4; 13.16
power 9.1; 11.2
praise Ex 18.10; 26.19
priest [3] Num 34.17; 17.9
privilege 18.2
promise [3] 9.3; 11.9
serve [2] 8.19; 11.13
strong 9.2; 33.11
stubborn 9.6; 21.18
supreme 1 Chr 29.11
sure 9.6; 11.32
tablet [6] 9.9; 1 Kgs 8.9
turn 9.12; 11.28
widow Num 30.9; 14.29
word (1) 1.1; 26.5
worship (1) (of God) [2] 6.13; 12.4

anger 9.7; 13.17
bless [3] 10.8; 12.7
care 2.7; 28.39
choose 10.15; 12.5
command [5] 10.5 12.11
curse [3] 7.26; 21.
disobey 9.16; 17.1
experience [2] 7.1 28.60
faithful [2] 10.20; 12.28
fear 10.17; 18.22
forehead 6.8; 1 Sam 17.49
god (2) (other go [2] 10.17; 12.2
hard Lev 26.19; 2
heart 10.12; 13.3
law [4] 10.13; 12.1
learn 5.1; 14.23
love [3] 10.12; 13.3
might 10.17; 32.4
miracle 7.19; 13.1
need 8.9; 14.29
obey [6] 10.13; 12.
power [2] 10.17; 2
proclaim Num 2 1 Sam 11.14
promise [3] 10.9;

remember [2] 9.14; 12.12
remind 6.8; Josh 4.6
rest (1) 6.7; Josh 11.23
rich 8.18; 17.17
sacred 7.5; 12.3
seed Num 24.7; 28.38
servant 9.27; 12.12
serve [2] 10.8; 13.2
sight 4.25; 34.7
sow Lev 27.16; 28.38
sure 10.18; 12.19
teach 8.3; 17.18
turn 10.5; 13.17
watch 6.24; Judg 7.17
worship (2) (of other gods) [2] 8.19; 12.2

all their **servants** and animals. [7] Yes, you are the ones who have seen all these great things that the LORD has done.

The Blessings of the Promised Land

8 "**Obey** all the **laws** that I have given you today. Then you will be able to cross the river and occupy the land that you are about to enter. [9] And you will live a long time in the **rich** and fertile **land that the LORD promised** to give your ancestors and their descendants. [10] The land that you are about to occupy is not like the land of Egypt, where you lived before. There, when you **sowed seed**, you had to work **hard** to irrigate the fields; [11] but the land that you are about to enter is a land of mountains and valleys, a land watered by rain. [12] The LORD your God takes **care** of this land and **watches** over it throughout the year.

13 "So then, **obey** the **commands** that I have given you today; **love** the LORD your God and **serve** him **with all your heart**. [14] If you do, he will send rain on your land when it is **needed**, in the autumn and in the spring, so that there will be corn, wine, and olive-oil for you, [15] and grass for your livestock. You will have all the food you want. [16] Do not let yourselves be led away from the LORD to **worship and serve other gods**. [17] If you do, the LORD will become **angry** with you. He will hold back the rain, and your ground will become too dry for crops to grow. Then you will soon die there, even though it is a good land that he is giving you.

18 "**Remember** these **commands** and cherish them. Tie them on your arms and wear them on your **foreheads** as a **reminder**. [19] **Teach** them to your children. Talk about them when you are at home and when you are away, when you are **resting** and when you are working. [20] Write them on the door-posts of your houses and on your gates. [21] Then you and your children will live a long time in the land that the LORD your God **promised** to give to your ancestors. You will live there as long as there is a sky above the earth.

22 "**Obey faithfully** all the **laws** that I have given you: **Love** the LORD your God, do everything he **commands**, and be **faithful** to him. [23] Then he will drive out all those nations as you advance, and you will occupy the land belonging to nations greater and more **powerful** than you. [24] All the ground that you march over will be yours. Your territory will extend from the desert in the south to the Lebanon Mountains in the north, and from the River Euphrates in the east to the Mediterranean Sea in the west. [25] Wherever you go in that land, the LORD your God will make the people **fear** you, as he has **promised**, and no one will be able to stop you.

26 "Today I am giving you the **choice** between a **blessing** and a **curse**—[27] a **blessing**, if you **obey** the **commands** of the LORD your God that I am giving you today; [28] but a **curse**, if you **disobey** these **commands** and **turn away** to worship other **gods** that you have never **worshipped** before. [29] When the LORD brings you into the land that you are going to occupy, you are to **proclaim** the **blessing** from Mount Gerizim and the **curse** from Mount Ebal. [30] (These two mountains are west of the River Jordan in the territory of the Canaanites who live in the Jordan Valley. They are towards the west, not far from the **sacred** trees of Moreh near the town of Gilgal.) [31] You are about to cross the River Jordan and occupy the land that the LORD your God is giving you. When you take it and settle there, [32] be **sure** to **obey** all the **laws** that I am giving you today.

The One Place for Worship

12 "Here are the **laws** that you are to **obey** as long as you live in the land that the LORD, the God of your ancestors, is giving you. Listen to them! [2] In the land that you are taking, **destroy** all the places where the people **worship their gods** on high mountains, on hills, and under green trees. [3] Tear down their **altars** and smash their **sacred** stone pillars to pieces. Burn their **symbols** of the **goddess** Asherah and chop down their **idols**, so that they will **never again** be **worshipped** at those places.

4 "Do not **worship** the LORD your God in the way that these people **worship their gods**. [5] Out of the territory of all your tribes the LORD will **choose** the one place where the people are to come into his **presence** and **worship** him. [6] There you are to **offer your sacrifices** that are to be burnt and your other **sacrifices**, your **tithes** and your **offerings**, the **gifts** that you **promise** to the LORD, your **freewill offerings**, and the **first-born** of your cattle and **sheep**. [7] There, in the **presence** of the LORD your God, who has **blessed** you, you and your families will eat and **enjoy** the good things that you have worked for.

altar [4] 7.5; 16.21
bless 11.26; 14.24
blood [5] Num 23.24; 15.23
choose [5] 11.26; 14.2
clean [2] Num 31.24; 14.11
command [5] 11.13; 13.4
destroy [3] 10.10; 13.15
disgust Lev 26.30; 18.9
enemy 7.15; 19.4
enjoy Lev 26.34; 14.26
faithful 11.22; 13.4
first-born [2] Num 33.4; 14.23
free 7.8; 15.10
freewill [2] Num 29.39; 16.10
gift [4] Num 18.6; 16.16
god (2) (other gods) [5] 11.16; 13.2
goddess 7.5; 16.21
happy Ex 18.9; 24.5
hate 9.28; 16.22
idol 9.12; 16.22
joy Num 10.10; 16.11
law 11.1; 17.18
Levites [4] Num 35.2; 14.27
life (1) [2] Num 31.50; 13.5
neglect Ex 5.4; 14.27
never again Lev 22.3; 13.16
obey [3] 11.1; 13.4
offer [13] 2.26; 13.16
peace [2] 3.20; 28.65

11.13-17: Lev 26.3-5; Deut 7.12-16, 28.1-14 **11.20:** Deut 6.6-9 **11.24-25:** Josh 1.3-5
11.29: Deut 27.11-14; Josh 8.33-35 **12.3:** Deut 7.5

place of worship [3] Num 33.52; 14.24
please [3] 6.25; 24.13
practice Lev 20.23; 18.9
presence [4] 9.18; 14.23
promise [5] 11.9; 13.1
religion Num 28.17; 1 Sam 10.6
remember 11.2; 15.15
right (1) 9.5; 32.4
sacred 11.30; 26.13
sacrifice [9] Num 25.2; 15.21
safe 4.42; 19.4
servant [2] 11.6; 15.18
sheep [3] 8.13; 14.4
special 7.6; Judg 20.15
sure [2] 11.32; 16.12
symbol 7.5; 16.21
tithe [3] Num 18.21; 14.22
unclean [2] Num 19.7; 14.3
wish [2] Num 36.6; 28.67
worship (1) (of God) [5] 10.12; 13.4
worship (2) (of other gods) [7] 11.16; 13.2

8 "When that time comes, you must not do as you have been doing. Until now you have all been **worshipping** as you **please**, 9 because you have not yet entered the land that the LORD your God is giving you, where you can live in **peace**. 10 When you cross the River Jordan, the LORD will let you occupy the land and live there. He will keep you **safe** from all your **enemies**, and you will live in **peace**. 11 The LORD will **choose** a single place where he is to be **worshipped**, and there you must bring to him everything that I have **commanded**: your **sacrifices** that are to be burnt and your other **sacrifices**, your **tithes** and your **offerings**, and those **special gifts** that you have **promised** to the LORD. 12 Be **joyful** there in his **presence**, together with your children, your **servants**, and the **Levites** who live in your towns; **remember** that the **Levites** will have no land of their own. 13 You are not to **offer your sacrifices** wherever you **choose**; 14 you must **offer** them only in the one place that the LORD will **choose** in the territory of one of your tribes. Only there are you to **offer your sacrifices** that are to be burnt and do all the other things that I have **commanded** you.

15 "But you are **free** to kill and eat your animals wherever you live. You may eat as many as the LORD gives you. All of you, whether ritually **clean** or **unclean**, may eat them, just as you would eat the meat of deer or antelope. 16 But you must not use their **blood** as food; you must pour it out on the ground like water. 17 Nothing that you **offer** to the LORD is to be eaten in the places where you live: neither the **tithes** of your corn, your wine, or your olive-oil, nor the **first-born** of your cattle and **sheep**, the **gifts** that you **promise** to the LORD, your **freewill offerings**, or any other offerings. 18 You and your children, together with your **servants** and the **Levites** who live in your towns, are to eat these **offerings** only in the **presence** of the LORD your God, in the one **place of worship chosen** by the LORD your God. And you are to be **happy** there over everything that you have done. 19 Be **sure**, also, not to **neglect** the **Levites**, as long as you live in your land.

20 "When the LORD your God enlarges your territory, as he has **promised**, you may eat meat whenever you **wish**. 21 If the one **place of worship** is too far away, then, whenever you **wish**, you may kill any of the cattle or **sheep** that the LORD has given you, and you may eat the meat at home, as I have told you. 22 Anyone, ritually **clean** or **unclean**, may eat that meat, just as he would eat the meat of deer or antelope. 23 Only do not eat meat with **blood** still in it, for the **life** is in the **blood**, and you must not eat the **life** with the meat. 24 Do not use the **blood** for food; instead pour it out on the ground like water. 25 If you **obey** this **command**, the LORD will be **pleased**, and all will go well for you and your descendants. 26 Take to the one **place of worship** your **offerings** and the **gifts** that you have **promised** the LORD. 27 **Offer there the sacrifices** which are to be completely burnt on the LORD's **altar**. Also **offer those sacrifices** in which you eat the meat and pour the **blood** out on the **altar**. 28 **Obey faithfully** everything that I have **commanded** you, and all will go well for you and your descendants for ever, because you will be doing what is **right** and what **pleases** the LORD your God.

Warning against Idolatry

29 "The LORD your God will **destroy** the nations as you invade their land, and you will occupy it and settle there. 30 After the LORD **destroys** those nations, make **sure** that you don't follow their **religious practices**, because that would be fatal. Don't try to find out how they **worship their gods**, so that you can **worship** in the same way. 31 Do not **worship** the LORD your God in the way they **worship their gods**, for in the **worship of their gods** they do all the **disgusting** things that the LORD **hates**. They even **sacrifice** their children in the fires on their **altars**.

32 "Do everything that I have **commanded** you; do not add anything to it or take anything from it.

13 "A **prophet** or an **interpreter** of **dreams** may **promise** a **miracle** or a **wonder**, 2 in order to lead you to **worship** and **serve gods** that you have not **worshipped** before. Even if what he **promises** comes **true**, 3 do not pay any attention to him. The LORD your God is using him to **test** you, to see if you **love** the LORD **with all your heart**. 4 Follow the LORD and **honour** him; **obey** him and keep his **commands**; **worship** him and be **faithful** to him. 5 But put **to death** any **interpreter** of **dreams** or **prophet** that tells you to **rebel** against the LORD, who **rescued** you from Egypt, where you were **slaves**. Such a man is **evil** and is trying to lead you away from the **life** that the LORD has **commanded** you to live. He

afraid 9.19; 17.13
anger 11.17; 19.6
command [3] 12.11; 15.5
condemn Ex 23.7; Josh 7.11
death (3) (to death) [3] 7.2; 17.5
destroy [2] 12.2; 19.1
dream [2] Num 12.6; 23.10
encourage [2] Judg 9.24
evil [4] 9.12; 15.9
faithful 12.28; 17.19
friend Ex 33.11; Josh 9.15
god (2) (other gods) [5] 12.2; 17.3
heart 11.13; 26.16
honour 6.2; 14.23
interpret [2] Gen 42.23; Dan 1.17
life (1) 12.23; 15.17
love [2] 11.1; 15.16
mercy [3] 7.2; 19.13
miracle 11.3; 26.8

12.16: Gen 9.4; Lev 7.26–27, 17.10–14, 19.26; Deut 15.23 **12.23–24:** Lev 17.10–14
12.32: Deut 4.2; Rev 22.18–19

mislead 2 Chr 32.15
never again 12.3; 1 Sam 15.35
obey [2] 12.1; 15.5
offer 12.6; 16.10
persuade Judg 19.3
pity Num 11.15; 2 Chr 30.9
possess 10.11; 17.14
promise [3] 12.6; 15.6
prophet [2] Num 12.6; 18.15
protect 7.15; 19.2
rebel 9.7; 21.18
require Num 30.5; 21.9
rescue [2] 9.26; 16.1
rid Lev 26.6; 17.7
ruin Num 33.41; 28.63
secret Num 5.12; 27.15
serve 11.13; 15.12
slave [2] 8.14; 15.12
test 8.2; 33.8
true [2] Ex 33.12; 17.4
turn 11.28; 17.17
wonder (1) 7.19; 26.8
worship (1) (of God) 12.4; 14.23
worship (2) (of other gods) [5] 12.2; 16.22
worthless Judg 9.4

must be put **to death**, in order to **rid** yourselves of this **evil**.

6 "Even your brother or your son or your daughter or the wife you **love** or your closest **friend** may **secretly encourage** you to **worship other gods**, gods that you and your ancestors have never **worshipped**. 7 One of them may encourage you to **worship the gods** of the people who live near you or the **gods** of those who live far away. 8 But do not let him **persuade** you; do not even listen to him. Show him no **mercy** or **pity**, and do not **protect** him. 9 Kill him! Be the first to stone him, and then let everyone else stone him too. 10 Stone him **to death**! He tried to lead you away from the LORD your God, who **rescued** you from Egypt, where you were **slaves**. 11 Then all the people of Israel will hear what happened; they will be **afraid**, and no one will ever again do such an **evil** thing.

12 "When you are living in the towns that the LORD your God gives you, you may hear 13 that some **worthless** men of your nation have **misled** the people of their town to worship **gods** that you have never **worshipped** before. 14 If you hear such a rumour, investigate it thoroughly; and if it is **true** that this **evil** thing did happen, 15 then kill all the people in that town and all their livestock too. **Destroy** that town completely. 16 Bring together all the **possessions** of the people who live there and pile them up in the town square. Then burn the town and everything in it as an **offering** to the LORD your God. It must be left in **ruins** for ever and **never again** be rebuilt. 17 Do not keep for yourselves anything that was **condemned** to **destruction**, and then the LORD will **turn** from his fierce **anger** and show you **mercy**. He will be **merciful** to you and make you a numerous people, as he **promised** your ancestors, 18 if you **obey** all his **commands** that I have given you today, and do what he **requires**.

A Forbidden Mourning Practice

bless [2] 12.7; 15.4
body Num 19.18; 17.8
choose [2] 12.5; 17.8
clean [2] 12.15; 15.22
dead [2] Num 35.12; 18.11
death (1) 5.25; 22.26
enjoy 12.7; 16.14
first-born 12.6; 15.19
God's people [2] 10.15; 17.16
honour 13.4; 16.1

14 "You are the people of the LORD your God. So when you **mourn** for the **dead**, don't gash yourselves or **shave** the front of your head, as other people do. 2 You belong to the LORD your God; he has **chosen** you to be his **own people** from among all the peoples who live on earth.

Clean and Unclean Animals
(Lev 11.1–47)

3 "Do not eat anything that the LORD has declared **unclean**. 4 You may eat these animals: cattle, **sheep**, goats, 5 deer, wild sheep, wild goats, or antelopes—6 any animals that have divided hoofs and that also chew the cud. 7 But no animals may be eaten unless they have divided hoofs and also chew the cud. You may not eat camels, rabbits, or rock-badgers. They must be considered **unclean**; they chew the cud but do not have divided hoofs. 8 Do not eat pigs. They must be considered **unclean**; they have divided hoofs but do not chew the cud. Do not eat any of these animals or even touch their **dead bodies**.

9 "You may eat any kind of fish that has fins and scales, 10 but anything living in the water that does not have fins and scales may not be eaten; it must be considered **unclean**.

11 "You may eat any **clean** bird. 12–18 But these are the kinds of birds you are not to eat: eagles, owls, hawks, falcons; buzzards, vultures, crows; ostriches; sea-gulls, storks, herons, pelicans, cormorants;[k] hoopoes; and bats.

19 "All winged insects are **unclean**; do not eat them. 20 You may eat any **clean** insect.

21 "Do not eat any animal that dies a **natural death**. You may let the foreigners who live among you eat it, or you may sell it to other foreigners. But you belong to the LORD your God; you are **his people**.

"Do not cook a young **sheep** or goat in its mother's milk.

The Law of the Tithe

22 "Set aside a **tithe**—a tenth of all that your fields produce each year. 23 Then go to the one place where the LORD your God has **chosen** to be **worshipped**; and there in his **presence** eat the **tithes** of your corn, wine, and olive-oil, and the **first-born** of your cattle and **sheep**. Do this so that you may **learn** to **honour** the LORD your God always. 24 If the **place of worship** is too far from your home for you to carry there the **tithe** of the produce that the LORD has **blessed** you with, then do this: 25 Sell your produce and take the money with you to the one **place of worship**. 26 Spend it on whatever you want—beef, **lamb**, wine, beer—and there, in the **presence** of the

lamb Num 29.2; 1 Sam 7.9
learn 11.2; 17.19
Levites [2] 12.12; 16.11
mourn Num 25.6; 21.13
natural Num 19.16; 1 Sam 26.10
need 11.14; 15.7
neglect 12.19; Josh 1.7
orphan 10.18; 16.11
place of worship [2] 12.18; 15.20
presence [2] 12.5; 15.20
shave Num 8.7; 21.12
sheep [3] 12.6; 15.14
tithe [4] 12.6; 26.12
unclean [5] 12.15; 15.22
widow 10.18; 16.11
worship (1) (of God) 13.4; 16.8

[k] *The identification of some of these birds is uncertain.*

14.1: Lev 19.28, 21.5 **14.2:** Ex 19.5–6; Deut 4.20, 7.6, 26.18; Tit 2.14; 1 Pet 2.9 **14.21:** Ex 23.19, 34.26 **14.22–29:** Lev 27.30–33; Num 18.21

LORD your God, you and your families are to eat and **enjoy** yourselves.

27 "Do not **neglect** the **Levites** who live in your towns; they have no property of their own. 28 At the end of every third year bring the **tithe** of all your crops and store it in your towns. 29 This food is for the **Levites**, since they own no property, and for the foreigners, **orphans**, and **widows** who live in your towns. They are to come and get all they **need**. Do this, and the LORD your God will **bless** you in everything you do.

The Seventh Year
(Lev 25.1–7)

15 "At the end of every seventh year you are to cancel the **debts** of those who **owe** you money. 2 This is how it is to be done. Everyone who has lent money to a fellow-Israelite is to cancel the **debt**; he must not try to collect the money; the LORD himself has declared the **debt** cancelled. 3 You may collect what a foreigner **owes** you, but you must not collect what any of your own people **owe** you.

4 "The LORD your God will **bless** you in the land that he is giving you. Not one of your people will be **poor** 5 if you **obey** him and carefully **observe** everything that I **command** you today. 6 The LORD will **bless** you, as he has **promised**. You will lend money to many nations, but you will not have to borrow from any; you will have **control** over many nations, but no nation will have **control** over you.

7 "If in any of the towns in the land that the LORD your God is giving you there is a fellow-Israelite in **need**, then do not be **selfish** and **refuse** to **help** him. 8 Instead, be **generous** and lend him as much as he **needs**. 9 Do not **refuse** to lend him something, just because the year when **debts** are cancelled is near. Do not let such an **evil** thought enter your **mind**. If you **refuse** to make the loan, he will cry out to the LORD against you, and you will be held **guilty**. 10 Give to him **freely** and **unselfishly**, and the LORD will **bless** you in everything you do. 11 There will always be some Israelites who are **poor** and in **need**, and so I **command** you to be **generous** to them.

The Treatment of Slaves
(Ex 21.1–11)

12 "If a fellow-Israelite, man or woman, sells himself[l] to you as a **slave**, you are to release him after he has **served** you for six years. When the seventh year comes, you must let him go **free**. 13 When you **set him free**, do not send him away empty-handed. 14 Give to him **generously** from what the LORD has **blessed** you with—**sheep**, corn, and wine. 15 **Remember** that you were **slaves** in Egypt and the LORD your God **set you free**; that is why I am now giving you this **command**.

16 "But your **slave** may not want to leave; he may **love** you and your family and be content to stay. 17 Then take him to the door of your house and there pierce his ear; he will then be your **slave** for **life**. Treat your female **slave** in the same way. 18 Do not be resentful when you set a **slave free**; after all, he has **served** you for six years at half the cost of a hired **servant**.[m] Do this, and the LORD your God will **bless** you in all that you do.

The First-Born Cattle and Sheep

19 "Set aside for the LORD your God all the **first-born** males of your cattle and **sheep**; don't use any of these cattle for work and don't shear any of these **sheep**. 20 Each year you and your family are to eat them in the LORD's **presence** at the one **place of worship**. 21 But if there is anything **wrong** with the animals, if they are **crippled** or **blind** or have any other **serious** defect, you must not **sacrifice** them to the LORD your God. 22 You may eat such animals at home. All of you, whether ritually **clean** or **unclean**, may eat them, just as you eat deer or antelope. 23 But do not use their **blood** for food; instead, you must pour it out on the ground like water.

The Passover
(Ex 12.1–20)

16 "Honour the LORD your God by **celebrating Passover** in the month of Abib; it was on a night in that month that he **rescued** you from Egypt. 2 Go to the one **place of worship** and **slaughter** there one of your **sheep** or cattle for the **Passover** meal to **honour** the LORD your God. 3 When you eat this meal, do not eat **bread** prepared with **yeast**. For seven days you are to eat **bread** prepared **without yeast**, as you did when you had to leave Egypt in such a hurry. Eat this **bread**—it will be called the bread of **suffering**—so that as long as you live you will **remember** the day you

bless [5] 14.24; 16.10
blind Lev 26.16; 16.19
blood 12.16; 19.11
clean 14.11; 23.14
command [3] 13.4; 16.12
control [2] Num 24.2; Judg 1.2
cripple Lev 22.22; Josh 11.6
debt [4] 31.10
evil 13.5; 17.4
first-born 14.23; 21.16
free [5] 12.15; 21.14
generous [3] 1 Kgs 8.56
guilty Num 35.16; 19.10
help 4.7; 22.4
life (1) 13.5; 17.19
love 13.3; 19.9
mind (1) Num 23.19; 28.28
need [3] 14.29; 17.14
obey 13.4; 16.12
observe 5.12; Josh 5.10
owe [3] 2 Kgs 4.1
place of worship 14.24; 16.2
poor [2] Lev 27.8; 24.12
presence 14.23; 16.11
promise 13.1; 18.2
refuse (1) [3] Num 32.15; 18.19
remember 12.12; 16.3
sacrifice 12.6; 17.1
selfish [2] Ps 78.72
serious Gen 44.5; Judg 12.2
servant 12.12; 16.11
serve [2] 13.2; 17.3
sheep [3] 14.4; 16.2
slave [6] 13.5; 16.12
unclean 14.3; 23.9
wrong 1.39; 16.19

accept 10.17; 17.11
altar 12.3; 18.10
bless [3] 15.4; 21.5
blind 15.21; 27.18
bread [4] 8.3; 29.6
bribe 10.17; 1 Sam 8.3
celebrate [4] Num 29.12; 26.11
command 15.5; 17.3
enjoy 14.26; 20.6
festival [4] Num 29.12; 31.10
forget 9.7; 24.22
freewill 12.6; 2 Kgs 12.4
gift [2] 12.6; Judg 3.15
goddess 12.3; Judg 6.25
harvest [4] Num 28.26; 20.6
hate 12.31; 17.1

[l] sells himself; *or* is sold. [m] at half...servant; *or* and has worked twice as hard as a hired servant.

15.7-8: Lev 25.35 **15.11:** Mt 26.11; Mk 14.7; Jn 12.8 **15.12-18:** Lev 25.39–46 **15.19:** Ex 13.12
15.23: Gen 9.4; Lev 7.26–27, 17.10–14, 19.26; Deut 12.16, 23 **16.1-8:** Lev 23.5–8; Num 28.16–25

honest Lev 19.15; 25.15
honour [4] 14.23; 17.19
idol 12.3; 27.15
joy [2] 12.12; 28.47
judge [3] 1.16; 17.8
justice 4.8; 32.4
Levites [2] 14.27; 17.9
obey 15.5; 17.19
offer 13.16; 18.1
orphan [2] 14.29; 24.17
partiality 10.17; 21.16
Passover [4] Num 33.3; Josh 5.10
place of worship [6] 15.20; 17.8
presence 15.20; 18.16
remember 15.15; 24.9
rescue 13.5; 20.1
servant [2] 15.18; 24.14
sheep 15.14; 17.1
shelter [2] Lev 23.33; 31.10
slaughter [2] 3.3; Josh 10.10
slave 15.12; 20.11
suffer [2] Num 30.15; 24.8
sure 12.19; 17.15
symbol 12.3; Judg 6.25
unjust Job 6.29
unleavened [2] Num 28.17; Josh 5.11
widow [2] 14.29; 24.17
wise 4.6; 18.17
worship (1) (of God) [2] 14.23; 26.10
worship (2) (of other gods) 13.2; 17.3
wrong 15.21; 27.18
yeast [4] Num 28.17; Josh 5.11

came out of Egypt, that place of **suffer-**
ing. 4 For seven days no one in your land
is to have any **yeast** in his house; and the
meat of the animal killed on the evening
of the first day must be eaten that same
night.
5-6 "**Slaughter** the **Passover** animals
at the one **place of worship**—and
nowhere else in the land that the LORD
your God will give you. Do it at sunset,
the time of day when you left Egypt.
7 Boil the meat and eat it at the one **place**
of worship; and the next morning return
home. 8 For the next six days you are to
eat **bread** prepared **without yeast**, and on
the seventh day assemble to **worship** the
LORD your God, and do no work on that
day.

The Harvest Festival
(Ex 34.22; Lev 23.15-21)

9 "Count seven weeks from the time
that you begin to **harvest** the corn, 10 and
then **celebrate** the **Harvest Festival**, to
honour the LORD your God, by bringing
him a **freewill offering** in proportion to
the **blessing** he has given you. 11 Be **joyful**
in the LORD's **presence**, together with
your children, your **servants**, and the
Levites, foreigners, **orphans**, and **widows**
who live in your towns. Do this at the one
place of worship. 12 Be **sure** that you **obey**
these **commands**; do not **forget** that you
were **slaves** in Egypt.

The Festival of Shelters
(Lev 23.33-43)

13 "After you have threshed all your
corn and pressed all your grapes,
celebrate the **Festival of Shelters** for
seven days. 14 **Enjoy** it with your children, your **servants**, and the **Levites**,
foreigners, **orphans**, and **widows** who live
in your towns. 15 **Honour** the LORD your
God by **celebrating** this **festival** for seven
days at the one **place of worship**. Be
joyful, because the LORD has **blessed**
your **harvest** and your work.
16 "All the men of your nation are to
come to **worship** the LORD three times a
year at the one **place of worship**: at **Pass-**
over, **Harvest Festival**, and the **Festival**
of Shelters. Each man is to bring a **gift**
17 as he is able, in proportion to the **bless-**
ings that the LORD your God has given
him.

The Administration of Justice

18 "Appoint **judges** and other officials
in every town that the LORD your God
gives you. These men are to **judge** the
people impartially. 19 They are not to be
unjust or show **partiality** in their **judge-**
ments; and they are not to **accept bribes**,
for **gifts blind** the eyes even of **wise** and
honest men, and cause them to give
wrong decisions. 20 Always be fair and
just, so that you will occupy the land that
the LORD your God is giving you and will
continue to live there.
21 "When you make an **altar** for the
LORD your God, do not put beside it a
wooden **symbol** of the **goddess** Asherah.
22 And do not set up any stone pillar for
idol worship; the LORD **hates** them.

17 "Do not **sacrifice** to the LORD
your God cattle or **sheep** that
have any defects; the LORD **hates** this.
2 "Suppose you hear that in one of
your towns some man or woman has
sinned against the LORD and broken his
covenant 3 by **worshipping and serving**
other gods or the sun or the moon or the
stars, contrary to the LORD's **command.**
4 If you hear such a report, then investigate it thoroughly. If it is **true** that this
evil thing has happened in Israel, 5 then
take that person outside the town and
stone him **to death.** 6 However, he may be
put **to death** only if two or more **wit-**
nesses testify against him; he is not to be
put **to death** if there is only one **witness.**
7 The **witnesses** are to throw the first
stones, and then the rest of the people
are to stone that person; in this way you
will get **rid** of this **evil.**
8 "It may be that some **cases** will be
too **difficult** for the local **judges** to decide,
such as certain **cases** of property **rights**
or of **bodily** injury or those **cases** that
involve a **distinction** between murder
and manslaughter. When this happens,
go to the one **place of worship chosen** by
the LORD your God, 9 and **present** your
case to the **levitical priests** and to the
judge who is in office at that time, and let
them decide the **case.** 10 They will give
their decision, and you are to do exactly
as they tell you. 11 **Accept** their verdict
and follow their instructions in every
detail. 12 Anyone who **dares** to **disobey**
either the **judge** or the **priest on duty** is to
be put **to death**; in this way you will
remove this **evil** from Israel. 13 Then
everyone will hear of it and be **afraid**,
and no one else will **dare** to **act** in such a
way.

Instructions Concerning a King

14 "After you have taken **possession** of
the land that the LORD your God is going

accept 16.19; 26.18
act Num 35.27; Josh 8.14
afraid 13.11; 18.16
body 14.8; 21.2
case (2) [5] 1.17; 19.18
choose [3] 14.2; 18.5
command [3] 16.12; 18.18
covenant 9.9; 29.1
dare [2] 4.34; 18.20
death (3) (to death) [4] 13.5; 19.10
difficult 1.17; 30.11
disobey [2] 11.28; 26.13
distinguish Lev 20.25; 2 Sam 14.17
duty (1) 10.8; 24.5
evil [3] 15.9; 19.19
faithful 13.4; 18.13
god (2) (other gods) 13.2; 18.20
God's people 14.2; 23.1
hate 16.22; 18.12
honour 16.1; 26.19
judge [3] 16.18; 19.17
keep from Num 24.11; 32.11
law 12.1; 26.16
learn 14.23; 31.12
Levites [2] 16.11; 18.6
life (1) 15.17; 19.21
need 15.7; 23.12
obey 16.12; 18.15
place of worship 16.2; 18.6
possess 13.16; 21.17
present (1) Num 29.2; Josh 8.31
priest [3] 10.6; 18.1
reign 2 Sam 21.1
rich 11.9; 26.9
rid 13.5; 19.13
right (3) Num 30.13; 24.17
sacrifice 15.21; 18.1
serve 15.12; 18.5
sheep 16.2; 18.3
sure 16.12; 22.8
teach 11.19; 19.9
testify Lev 24.14; Ps 15.5
true 13.2; 18.22
turn 13.17; 23.5
witness [3] 4.26; 19.15
worship (2) (of other gods) 16.22; 20.18

16.9-12: Num 28.26-31 **16.13-15:** Num 29.12-38 **16.19:** Ex 23.6-8; Lev 19.15 **16.21:** Ex 34.13
16.22: Lev 26.1 **17.3:** Ex 22.20 **17.6:** Num 35.30; Deut 19.15; Mt 18.16; 2 Cor 13.1; 1 Tim 5.19; Heb 10.28
17.7: 1 Cor 5.13 **17.14:** 1 Sam 8.5

to give you and have settled there, then you will decide you need a king like all the nations round you. 15 Make sure that the man you choose to be king is the one whom the LORD has chosen. He must be one of your own people; do not make a foreigner your king. 16 The king is not to have a large number of horses for his army, and he is not to send people to Egypt to buy horses,[n] because the LORD has said that his people are never to return there. 17 The king is not to have many wives, because this would make him turn away from the LORD; and he is not to make himself rich with silver and gold. 18 When he becomes king, he is to have a copy of the book of God's laws and teachings made from the original copy kept by the levitical priests. 19 He is to keep this book near him and read from it all his life, so that he will learn to honour the LORD and to obey faithfully everything that is commanded in it. 20 This will keep him from thinking that he is better than his fellow-Israelites and from disobeying the LORD's commands in any way. Then he will reign for many years, and his descendants will rule Israel for many generations.

The Share of the Priests

18 "The priestly tribe of Levi is not to receive any share of land in Israel; instead, they are to live on the offerings and other sacrifices given to the LORD. 2 They are to own no land, as the other tribes do; their share is the privilege of being the LORD's priests, as the LORD has promised.

3 "Whenever cattle or sheep are sacrificed, the priests are to be given the shoulder, the jaw, and the stomach. 4 They are to receive the first share of the corn, wine, olive-oil, and wool. 5 The LORD chose from all your tribes the tribe of Levi to serve him as priests for ever.

6 "Any Levite who wants to may come from any town in Israel to the one place of worship 7 and may serve there as a priest of the LORD his God, like the other Levites who are serving there. 8 He is to receive the same amount of food as the other priests, and he may keep whatever his family sends him.[o]

Warning against Pagan Practices

9 "When you come into the land that the LORD your God is giving you, don't follow the disgusting practices of the nations that are there. 10 Don't sacrifice your children in the fires on your altars; and don't let your people practise divination or look for omens or use spells 11 or charms, and don't let them consult the spirits of the dead. 12 The LORD your God hates people who do these disgusting things, and that is why he is driving those nations out of the land as you advance. 13 Be completely faithful to the LORD."

The Promise to Send a Prophet

14 Then Moses said, "In the land you are about to occupy, people follow the advice of those who practise divination and look for omens, but the LORD your God does not allow you to do this. 15 Instead, he will send you a prophet like me from among your own people, and you are to obey him.[p]

16 "On the day that you were gathered at Mount Sinai, you begged not to hear the LORD speak again or to see his fiery presence any more, because you were afraid you would die. 17 So the LORD said to me, 'They have made a wise request. 18 I will send them a prophet like you from among their own people; I will tell him what to say, and he[q] will tell the people everything I command. 19 He will speak in my name, and I[r] will punish anyone who refuses to obey him. 20 But if any prophet dares to speak a message in my name when I did not command him to do so, he must die for it, and so must any prophet who speaks in the name of other gods.'

21 "You may wonder how you can tell when a prophet's message does not come from the LORD. 22 If a prophet speaks in the name of the LORD and what he says does not come true, then it is not the LORD's message. That prophet has spoken on his own authority, and you are not to fear him.

The Cities of Refuge

(Num 35.9–34; Josh 20.1–9)

19 "After the LORD your God has destroyed the people whose land he is giving you and after you have taken their cities and houses and settled there, 2-3 divide the territory into three parts, each with a city that can be easily reached. Then a man who kills someone will be able to escape to one of them for

promise 15.6; 19.8
prophet [7] 13.1; 34.10
punish 8.5; 19.19
refuse (1) 15.7; 21.20
request Num 27.7; Judg 8.8
sacrifice [3] 17.1; 27.6
serve [3] 17.3; 21.5
share [3] Num 32.19; 21.16
sheep 17.1; 22.1
spirit (2) Lev 20.6; 1 Sam 16.14
true 17.4; 22.20
wise 16.19; Judg 5.29

advice Lev 20.6; Ruth 2.8
afraid 17.13; 19.20
altar 16.21; 26.4
authority Num 27.20; Josh 1.18
beg Ex 11.8; 33.29
choose 17.8; 20.9
command [2] 17.3; 19.9
consult Lev 25.50; Josh 9.14
dare 17.12; Josh 10.21
dead 14.1; 21.23
disgust [2] 12.31; 20.18
divination [2] Gen 44.5; 2 Kgs 16.15
faithful 17.19; 26.16
fear 11.25; 25.18
god (2) (other gods) 17.3; 20.18
hate 17.1; 22.5
Levites [2] 17.9; 21.5
message [3] Num 24.3; Josh 10.3
name (2) (name of God, of Jesus) [3] 10.8; 21.5
obey [2] 17.19; 21.18
offer 16.10; 26.14
place of worship 17.8; 19.17
practice [3] 12.30; 1 Kgs 14.24
presence 16.11; 25.9
priest [6] 17.9; 19.17
privilege 10.9; 1 Kgs 10.8

accuse [3] 5.20; 22.14
afraid 18.16; 20.1
anger 13.17; 29.20
blood 15.23; 22.15
case (2) [2] 17.8; 21.5
command 18.18; 24.18
crime [2] Gen 50.17; 21.22
death (3) (to death) [2] 17.5; 21.21
destroy 13.15; 20.8

[n] to buy horses; *or* in exchange for horses.
[o] *Probable text* and he may keep...sends him; *Hebrew unclear.*
[p] a prophet...him; *or* prophets...them. [q] a prophet...him...he; *or* prophets...them...they.
[r] He will speak...and I; *or* When a prophet speaks in my name, I.

17.16: 1 Kgs 10.28; 2 Chr 1.16, 9.28 **17.17:** 1 Kgs 10.14–22, 27, 11.1–8; 2 Chr 1.15, 9.27 **18.2:** Num 18.20 **18.10:** Lev 19.26; Ex 22.18 **18.11:** Lev 19.31 **18.13:** Mt 5.48 **18.15:** Acts 3.22, 7.37 **18.19:** Acts 3.23

enemy [3] 12.10; 20.1
enough 9.8; Josh 14.11
escape [3] 7.20; Josh 8.20
establish Num 25.13; 2 Sam 5.12
evil [2] 17.4; 21.21
false [2] 5.20; 22.14
guilty [2] 15.9; 24.15
harm Num 5.19; Josh 2.19
innocent [2] Num 5.28; 21.8
judge [3] 17.8; 21.2
life (1) 17.19; 22.7
love 15.16; 23.5
mark (1) Lev 16.8; 27.17
mercy [2] 13.8; 25.12
neighbour Lev 19.18; 27.17
place of worship 18.6; 26.2
priest 18.1; 20.2
promise 18.2; 23.21
protect [2] 13.8; 23.14
prove 4.35; 22.15
punish [2] 18.19; 21.18
revenge [2] Num 35.12; 32.35
rid [2] 17.7; 21.21
safe [2] 12.10; 25.19
teach 17.18; 20.18
witness [2] 17.6; 30.19

protection. 4 If a man accidentally kills
someone who is not his **enemy**, he may
escape to any of these cities and be **safe**.
5 For example, if two men go into the
forest together to cut wood and if, as one
of them is chopping down a tree, the
head of the axe comes off the handle and
kills the other, he can run to one of those
three cities and be **safe**. 6 If there were
only one city, the distance to it might be
too great, and the relative who is responsible for taking **revenge** for the killing
might catch him and in his **anger** kill an
innocent man. After all, it was by
accident that he killed a man who was
not his **enemy**. 7 This is why I order you
to set aside three cities.
8 "When the LORD your God enlarges
your territory, as he told your ancestors
he would, and gives you all the **land he
has promised**, 9 then you are to select
three more cities. (He will give you this
land if you do everything that I **command** you today and if you **love** the LORD
your God and live according to his
teachings.) 10 Do this, so that **innocent**
people will not die and so that you will
not be **guilty** of putting them **to death** in
the land that the LORD is giving you.
11 "But suppose a man deliberately
murders his **enemy** in cold **blood** and
then **escapes** to one of those cities for
protection. 12 In that case, the leaders of
his own town are to send for him and
hand him over to the relative responsible
for taking **revenge** for the murder, so
that he may be put **to death**. 13 Show him
no **mercy**. **Rid** Israel of this murderer, so
that all will go well with you.

Ancient Boundaries

14 "Do not move your **neighbour's**
boundary **mark**, **established** long ago in
the land that the LORD your God is giving
you.

Concerning Witnesses

15 "One **witness** is not **enough** to
convict a man of a **crime**; at least two
witnesses are necessary to **prove** that a
man is **guilty**. 16 If one man tries to **harm**
another by **falsely accusing** him of a
crime, 17 both are to go to the one **place
of worship** and be **judged** by the **priests**
and **judges** who are then in office. 18 The
judges will investigate the **case**
thoroughly; and if the man has made a
false accusation against his fellow-
Israelite, 19 he is to receive the **punishment** the **accused** man would have
received. In this way you will get **rid** of
this **evil**. 20 Then everyone else will hear
what happened; they will be **afraid**, and
no one will ever again do such an **evil**
thing. 21 In such **cases** show no **mercy**;
the **punishment** is to be a **life** for a life, an
eye for an eye, a tooth for a tooth, a hand
for a hand, and a foot for a foot.

Concerning War

20 "When you go out to fight against
your **enemies** and you see
chariots and horses and an army that
outnumbers yours, do not be **afraid** of
them. The LORD your God, who **rescued**
you from Egypt, will be with you. 2 Before
you start fighting, a **priest** is to come forward and say to the army, 3 'Men of
Israel, listen! Today you are going into
battle. Do not be **afraid** of your **enemies**,
or lose **courage**, or panic. 4 The LORD
your God is going with you, and he will
give you **victory**.'
5 "Then the officers will address the
men and say, 'Is there any man here who
has just built a house, but has not yet
dedicated it? If so, he is to go home.
Otherwise, if he is killed in battle, someone else will **dedicate** his house. 6 Is there
any man here who has just planted a
vineyard, but has not yet had the chance
to **harvest** its grapes? If so, he is to go
home. Otherwise, if he is killed in battle,
someone else will **enjoy** the wine. 7 Is
there anyone here who is engaged to be
married? If so, he is to go home. Otherwise, if he is killed in battle, someone
else will marry the woman he is engaged
to.'
8 "The officers will also say to the
men, 'Is there any man here who has lost
his nerve and is **afraid**? If so, he is to go
home. Otherwise, he will **destroy** the
morale of the others.' 9 When the officers
have finished speaking to the army,
leaders are to be **chosen** for each unit.
10 "When you go to attack a city, first
give its people a chance to surrender. 11 If
they open the gates and surrender, they
are all to become your **slaves** and do
forced labour for you. 12 But if the people
of that city will not surrender, but **choose**
to fight, surround it with your army.
13 Then, when the LORD your God lets you
capture the city, kill every man in it.
14 You may, however, take for yourselves
the women, the children, the livestock,
and everything else in the city. You may
use everything that belongs to your
enemies. The LORD has given it to you.
15 That is how you are to deal with those

afraid [3] 19.20; 21.21
choose [2] 18.5; 21.5
courage Ex 15.15; 31.8
dedicate [2] 5.14; Judg 13.5
destroy [3] 19.1; 28.20
disgust 18.9; 29.17
enemy [4] 19.4; 23.14
enjoy 16.14; Judg 16.24
force (1) Lev 26.25; 21.14
god (2) (other gods) 18.20; 28.14
harvest 16.9; 26.2
last (1) Num 28.17; Josh 23.13
priest 19.17; 21.5
rescue 16.1; 21.8
slave 16.12; 21.14
teach 19.9; 27.3
victory Num 24.18; 21.10
vineyard 6.11; 23.24
worship (2) (of other gods) 17.3; 27.15

19.14: Deut 27.17 **19.15:** Num 35.30; Deut 17.6; Mt 18.16; Jn 8.17; 2 Cor 13.1; 1 Tim 5.19; Heb 10.28
19.21: Ex 21.23–25; Lev 24.19–20; Mt 5.38

cities that are far away from the land
you will settle in.
16 "But when you capture cities in the
land that the LORD your God is giving
you, kill everyone. [17] Completely **destroy**
all the people: the Hittites, the Amorites,
the Canaanites, the Perizzites, the
Hivites, and the Jebusites, as the LORD
ordered you to do. [18] Kill them, so that
they will not make you sin against the
LORD by **teaching** you to do all the **disgusting** things that they do in the **worship
of their gods**.
19 "When you are trying to capture a
city, do not cut down its fruit-trees, even
though the siege **lasts** a long time. Eat
the fruit, but do not **destroy** the trees; the
trees are not your **enemies**. [20] You may
cut down the other trees and use them in
the siege mounds until the city is
captured.

Concerning Unsolved Murders

21 "Suppose a man is found
murdered in a field in the land
that the LORD your God is going to give
you, and you do not know who killed him.
[2] Your leaders and **judges** are to go out
and measure the distance from the place
where the **body** was found to each of the
nearby towns. [3] Then the leaders of the
town nearest to where the **body** was
found are to select a young cow that has
never been used for work. [4] They are to
take it down to a spot near a stream that
never runs dry and where the ground has
never been ploughed or planted, and
there they are to break its neck. [5] The
levitical priests are to go there also,
because they are to decide every legal
case involving **violence**. The LORD your
God has **chosen** them to **serve** him and to
pronounce **blessings in his name**. [6] Then
all the leaders from the town nearest the
place where the murdered man was
found are to wash their hands over the
cow [7] and say, 'We did not murder the
man, and we do not know who did it.
[8] LORD, **forgive** your people Israel, whom
you **rescued** from Egypt. **Forgive** us and
do not hold us responsible for the murder
of an **innocent** man.' [9] And so, by doing
what the LORD **requires**, you will not be
held responsible for the murder.

Concerning Women Prisoners of War

10 "When the LORD your God gives
you **victory** in battle and you take
prisoners, [11] you may see among them a
beautiful woman that you like and want
to marry. [12] Take her to your home,
where she will **shave** her head,[s] cut her
fingernails, [13] and **change** her clothes.
She is to stay in your home and **mourn**
for her parents for a month; after that,
you may marry her. [14] Later, if you no
longer want her, you are to let her go
free. Since you **forced** her to have intercourse with you, you cannot treat her as
a **slave** and sell her.

Concerning the First Son's Inheritance

15 "Suppose a man has two wives and
they both bear him sons, but the first son
is not the child of his favourite wife.
[16] When the man decides how he is going
to divide his property among his children, he is not to show **partiality** to the
son of his favourite wife by giving him
the **share** that belongs to the **first-born**
son. [17] He is to give a double **share** of his
possessions to his first son, even though
he is not the son of his favourite wife. A
man must **acknowledge** his first son and
give him the **share** he is legally entitled
to.

Concerning a Disobedient Son

18 "Suppose a man has a son who is
stubborn and **rebellious**, a son who will
not **obey** his parents, even though they
punish him. [19] His parents are to take him
before the leaders of the town where he
lives and make him stand **trial**. [20] They
are to say to them, 'Our son is **stubborn**
and **rebellious** and **refuses** to **obey** us; he
wastes money and is a drunkard.' [21] Then
the men of the city are to stone him **to
death**, and so you will get **rid** of this **evil**.
Everyone in Israel will hear what has
happened and be **afraid**.

Various Laws

22 "If a man has been put **to death** for
a **crime** and his **body** is **hung** on a post,
[23] it is not to remain there overnight. It
must be buried the same day, because a
dead body hanging on a post brings God's
curse on the land. Bury the **body**, so that
you will not **defile** the land that the LORD
your God is giving you.

22 "If you see a fellow-Israelite's
cow or **sheep** running loose, do
not **ignore** it; take it back to him. [2] But if
its owner lives a long way off or if you
don't know who owns it, then take it
home with you. When its owner comes
looking for it, give it to him. [3] Do the
same thing if you find a donkey, a piece
of clothing, or anything else that your
fellow-Israelite may have lost.
4 "If a fellow-Israelite's donkey or cow

[s] shave her head; *or* trim her hair.

21.23: Gal 3.13 **22.1-4:** Ex 23.4-5

violent Ex 19.18;
Judg 4.3

acknowledge Num 32.22; 26.3
afraid 20.1; 28.10
bless 16.10; 23.5
body [5] 17.8; 28.26
case (2) 19.18; 22.26
change Num 32.38; Josh 19.47
choose 20.9; 23.16
crime 19.15; 24.16
curse 11.26; 23.4
dead 18.11; 25.5
death (3) (to death) [2] 19.10; 22.21
defile Num 35.33; 24.4
evil 19.19; 22.21
first-born 15.19; 1 Chr 5.1
force (1) 20.11; 22.29
forgive [2] Num 30.5; 29.20
free 15.10; 24.18
hang (2) [2] Gen 40.19; Josh 8.29
innocent 19.6; 25.1
judge 19.17; 25.2
Levites 18.6; 24.8
mourn 14.1; 26.14
name (2) (name of God, of Jesus) 18.19; 26.19
obey [2] 18.15; 23.20
partiality 16.19; 2 Chr 19.7
possess 17.14; 30.5
priest 20.2; 24.8
prison Num 31.11; 28.41
punish 19.19; 32.34
rebel [2] 13.5; 31.27
refuse (1) 18.19; 23.4
require 13.18; 1 Sam 2.29
rescue 20.1; 26.8
rid 19.13; 22.21
serve 18.5; 28.14
share [3] 18.1; 28.56
shave 14.1; 2 Sam 10.4
slave 20.11; 23.15
stubborn [2] 10.16; 29.19
try (2) Num 35.12; Josh 20.6
victory 20.4; 23.14

accuse 19.16; 1 Sam 12.3
blood [2] 19.11; 32.42
bride Ex 22.16; 1 Sam 18.25
case (2) 21.5; 1 Sam 8.3
charge (3) [3] Ezra 4.6
court (1) Lev 5.1; 25.1
death (1) 14.21; 28.51
death (3) (to death) [4] 21.21; 24.7
disgrace [2] Num 12.14; 27.20

divorce [2] Num 30.9; 24.1
evil [3] 21.21; 24.7
false [2] 19.16; 1 Sam 12.21
forbid Num 30.5; 29.26
force (1) 21.14; 26.6
grapevine *see* **vine**
hate 18.12; 23.18
help [3] 15.7; 23.6
ignore [2] Lev 20.4; 1 Kgs 12.8
life (1) 19.21; 28.66
new Num 32.14; 24.5
prosper 6.10; 23.6
prove [3] 19.15; 33.8
rape [3] Gen 39.14; Judg 19.25
rid [3] 21.21; 24.7
shame Josh 7.15
sheep 18.3; 28.4
sure 17.15; 23.23
tassel Num 15.38; Mt 23.5
true 18.22; 25.15
vine Num 6.4; 24.21
virgin [5] Num 31.18; Judg 11.37
wedding [2] Gen 29.22; Josh 15.18
worthy 32.5

has fallen down, don't **ignore** it; **help** him
to get the animal to its feet again.
5 "Women are not to wear men's
clothing, and men are not to wear
women's clothing; the LORD your God
hates people who do such things.
6 "If you happen to find a bird's nest in
a tree or on the ground with the mother
bird sitting either on the eggs or with her
young, you are not to take the mother
bird. 7 You may take the young birds, but
you must let the mother bird go, so that
you will live a long and **prosperous life**.
8 "When you build a **new** house, be
sure to put a railing round the edge of the
roof. Then you will not be responsible if
someone falls off and is killed.
9 "Do not plant any crop in the same
field as your **grapevines**; if you do, you
are **forbidden** to use either the grapes or
the produce of the other crop.
10 "Do not hitch an ox and a donkey
together for ploughing.
11 "Do not wear cloth made by weaving wool and linen together.
12 "Sew **tassels** on the four corners of
your clothes.

Laws Concerning Sexual Purity

13 "Suppose a man marries a girl and
later he decides he doesn't want her. 14 So
he makes up **false charges** against her,
accusing her of not being a **virgin** when
they got married.
15 "If this happens, the girl's parents
are to take the **blood-stained wedding**
sheet that **proves** the girl was a **virgin**,
and they are to show it in **court** to the
town leaders. 16 The girl's father will say
to them, 'I gave my daughter to this man
in marriage, and now he doesn't want
her. 17 He has made **false charges** against
her, saying that she was not a **virgin**
when he married her. But here is the
proof that my daughter was a **virgin**;
look at the **bloodstains** on the **wedding**
sheet!' 18 Then the town leaders are to
take the husband and beat him. 19 They
are also to fine him a hundred pieces of
silver and give the money to the girl's
father, because the man has brought **disgrace** on an Israelite girl. Moreover, she
will continue to be his wife, and he can
never **divorce** her as long as he lives.
20 "But if the **charge** is **true** and there
is no **proof** that the girl was a **virgin**,
21 then they are to take her out to the
entrance of her father's house, where the
men of her city are to stone her **to death**.
She has done a **shameful** thing among
our people by having intercourse before
she was married, while she was still
living in her father's house. In this way
you will get **rid** of this **evil**.
22 "If a man is caught having intercourse with another man's wife, both of
them are to be put **to death**. In this way
you will get **rid** of this **evil**.
23 "Suppose a man is caught in a town
having intercourse with a girl who is
engaged to someone else. 24 You are to
take them outside the town and stone
them **to death**. The girl is to die because
she did not cry out for **help**, although she
was in a town, where she could have
been heard. And the man is to die
because he had intercourse with a girl
who was engaged. In this way you will
get **rid** of this **evil**.
25 "Suppose a man out in the countryside **rapes** a girl who is engaged to someone else. Then only the man is to be put
to death; 26 nothing is to be done to the
girl, because she has not committed a sin
worthy of death. This **case** is the same as
when one man attacks another man and
murders him. 27 The man **raped** the
engaged girl in the countryside, and although she cried for **help**, there was no
one to help her.
28 "Suppose a man is caught **raping** a
girl who is not engaged. 29 He is to pay
the girl's father the **bride** price of fifty
pieces of silver, and she is to become his
wife, because he **forced** her to have intercourse with him. He can never **divorce**
her as long as he lives.
30 "No man is to **disgrace** his father
by having intercourse with any of his
father's wives.

Exclusion from the LORD's People

23 "No man who has been castrated
or whose penis has been cut off
may be included among the **LORD's
people**.
2 "No one born out of wedlock or any
descendant of such a person, even in the
tenth generation, may be included
among the **LORD's people**.
3 "No Ammonite or Moabite—or any
of their descendants, even in the tenth
generation—may be included among the
LORD's people. 4 They **refused** to **provide**
you with food and water when you were
on your way out of Egypt, and they hired
Balaam son of Beor, from the city of
Pethor in Mesopotamia, to **curse** you.
5 But the LORD your God would not listen
to Balaam; instead he **turned** the **curse**
into a **blessing**, because he **loved** you. 6 As

bless [2] 21.5; 24.19
choose 21.5; 28.10
clean 15.22; 1 Kgs 22.38
curse [2] 21.23; 27.13
despise [2] 7.26; 1 Sam 2.30
dream 13.1; Judg 7.13
enemy 20.1; 25.19
fulfil Num 32.22; 1 Sam 21.7
God's people [4] 17.16; 26.18
hate 22.5; 25.16
help 22.4; 25.11
love 19.9; 28.54
need 17.14; 24.14
obey 21.18; 26.14
promise 19.8; 26.3
prosper 22.7; 28.13
prostitute [2] Lev 21.7; Josh 2.1
protect [2] 19.2; 32.10
provide Lev 25.6; 29.6
refuse (1) 21.20; 25.7
slave 21.14; 24.7
sure 22.8; 24.8

22.9-11: Lev 19.19 **22.12:** Num 15.37-41 **22.28-29:** Ex 22.16-17 **22.30:** Lev 18.8, 20.11; Deut 27.20
23.3-5: Neh 13.1-2 **23.4:** Num 22.1-6 **23.5:** Num 23.7—24.9

turn [2] 17.17; 29.18
unclean [2] 15.22; 26.14
victory 21.10; 28.25
vineyard 20.6; 28.30
vow [4] Num 30.2; 32.40

long as you are a nation, never do anything to **help** these nations or to make
them **prosperous**.
7 "Do not **despise** the Edomites; they
are your relatives. And do not **despise** the
Egyptians; you once lived in their land.
8 From the third generation onward their
descendants may be included among the
LORD'S **people**.

Keeping the Military Camp Clean

9 "When you are in camp in time of
war, you are to avoid anything that
would make you ritually **unclean**. 10 If a
man becomes **unclean** because he has
had a **wet dream** during the night, he is
to go outside the camp and stay there.
11 Towards evening he is to wash himself,
and at sunset he may come back into
camp.
12 "You are to have a place outside
the camp where you can go when you
need to relieve yourselves. 13 Carry a
stick as part of your equipment, so that
when you have a bowel movement you
can dig a hole and cover it up. 14 Keep
your camp ritually **clean**, because the
LORD your God is with you in your camp
to **protect** you and to give you **victory**
over your **enemies**. Do not do anything
indecent that would cause the LORD to
turn his back on you.

Various Laws

15 "If a **slave** runs away from his
owner and comes to you for **protection**,
do not send him back. 16 He may live in
any of your towns that he **chooses**, and
you are not to treat him harshly.
17 "No Israelite, man or woman, is to
become a temple **prostitute**. 18 Also, no
money earned in this way may be
brought into the house of the LORD your
God in **fulfilment** of a **vow**. The LORD
hates temple **prostitutes**.
19 "When you lend money or food or
anything else to a fellow-Israelite, do not
charge him interest. 20 You may charge
interest on what you lend to a foreigner,
but not on what you lend to a fellow-
Israelite. **Obey** this rule, and the LORD
your God will **bless** everything you do in
the land that you are going to occupy.
21 "When you make a **vow** to the
LORD your God, do not put off doing what
you **promised**; the LORD will hold you to
your **vow**, and it is a sin not to keep it.
22 It is no sin not to make a **vow** to the
LORD, 23 but if you make one voluntarily,
be **sure** that you keep it.
24 "When you walk along a path in
someone else's **vineyard**, you may eat all
the grapes you want, but you must not
carry any away in a container. 25 When
you walk along a path in someone else's
cornfield, you may eat all the corn you
can pull off with your hands, but you
must not cut any corn with a sickle.

Divorce and Remarriage

24 "Suppose a man marries a
woman and later decides that he
doesn't want her, because he finds something about her that he doesn't like.[t] So
he writes out **divorce** papers, gives them
to her, and sends her away from his
home. 2 Then suppose she marries
another man, 3 and he also decides that
he doesn't want her, so he also writes out
divorce papers, gives them to her, and
sends her away from his home. Or
suppose her second husband dies. 4 In
either case, her first husband is not to
marry her again; he is to consider her
defiled. If he married her again, it would
be offensive to the LORD. You are not to
commit such a **terrible** sin in the land
that the LORD your God is giving you.

Various Laws

5 "When a man is **newly** married, he
is not to be drafted into **military service**
or any other public **duty**; he is to be
excused from **duty** for one year, so that
he can stay at home and make his wife
happy.[u]
6 "When you lend a man something,
you are not to take as **security** his mill-
stones used for grinding his corn. This
would take away the family's **means** of
preparing food to keep **alive**.
7 "Whoever kidnaps a fellow-Israelite
and makes him his **slave** or sells him into
slavery is to be put **to death**. In this way
you will get **rid** of this **evil**.
8 "When you are **suffering** from a
dreaded **skin-disease**, be **sure** to do
exactly what the **levitical priests** tell you;
follow the instructions that I have given
them. 9 **Remember** what the LORD your
God did to Miriam as you were coming
from Egypt.
10 "When you lend a man something,
do not go into his house to get the garment he is going to give you as **security**;
11 wait outside and let him bring it to you
himself. 12 If he is a **poor** man, do not

alive 4.4; Josh 10.28
bless 23.5; 26.15
cheat Lev 25.17; 25.13
command [2] 19.9; 26.13
crime [3] 21.22; 25.2
death (3) (to death) [4] 22.21; 28.51
defile 21.23; 1 Chr 23.28
disease 7.15; 28.21
divorce [2] 22.19; 1 Chr 8.8
duty (1) [2] 17.12; 25.5
evil 22.21; 28.15
excuse Ex 5.21; 1 Sam 1.26
fail 8.11; 28.13
forget 16.12; 25.19
free 21.14; Judg 3.9
grateful Lev 19.24; 26.11
guilty 19.10; 25.1
happy 12.18; 33.29
Levites 21.5; 26.11
means Lev 6.4; Jer 32.21
need [2] 23.12; 26.12
new 22.8; 32.17
orphan [4] 16.11; 26.12
please 12.8; 33.11
poor [2] 15.4; 28.18
priest 21.5; 26.3
remember [2] 16.3; 25.17
rid 22.21; Josh 7.13
right (3) 17.8; 27.19
secure [3] Num 24.21; 33.25
servant 16.11; 33.8
service Num 26.2; Josh 9.8
slave [4] 23.15; 26.6
suffer 16.3; 26.7
sure 23.23; 25.19
terrible 7.19; 29.3
vine 22.9; 28.39
widow [4] 16.11; 25.5

[t] something...like; *or* that she is guilty of some shameful conduct.
[u] make his wife happy; *or* be happy with his wife.

23.17: Lev 19.29 **23.19–20:** Ex 22.25; Lev 25.36–37; Deut 15.7–11 **23.21:** Num 30.1–16; Mt 5.33
24.1: Mt 5.31, 19.7; Mk 10.4 **24.7:** Ex 21.16 **24.8:** Lev 13.1–14.54 **24.9:** Num 12.10
24.10–13: Ex 22.26–27

keep it overnight; 13 return it to him each evening, so that he can have it to sleep in. Then he will be **grateful**, and the LORD your God will be **pleased** with you.

14 "Do not **cheat** a **poor** and **needy** hired **servant**, whether he is a fellow-Israelite or a foreigner living in one of your towns. 15 Each day before sunset pay him for that day's work; he **needs** the money and has counted on getting it. If you do not pay him, he will cry out against you to the LORD, and you will be **guilty** of sin.

16 "Parents are not to be put **to death** for **crimes** committed by their children, and children are not to be put **to death** for **crimes** committed by their parents; a person is to be put **to death** only for a **crime** he himself has committed.

17 "Do not deprive foreigners and **orphans** of their **rights**; and do not take a **widow's** garment as **security** for a loan. 18 **Remember** that you were **slaves** in Egypt and that the LORD your God **set you free**; that is why I have given you this **command**.

19 "When you gather your crops and **fail** to bring in some of the corn that you have cut, do not go back for it; it is to be left for the foreigners, **orphans**, and **widows**, so that the LORD your God will **bless** you in everything you do. 20 When you have picked your olives once, do not go back and get those that are left; they are for the foreigners, **orphans**, and **widows**. 21 When you have gathered your grapes once, do not go back over the **vines** a second time; the grapes that are left are for the foreigners, **orphans**, and **widows**. 22 Never **forget** that you were **slaves** in Egypt; that is why I have given you this **command**.

25 "Suppose two Israelites go to **court** to **settle** a **dispute**, and one is declared **innocent** and the other **guilty**. 2 If the **guilty** man is **sentenced** to be beaten, the **judge** is to make him lie face downwards and have him whipped. The number of lashes will **depend** on the **crime** he has committed. 3 He may be given as many as forty lashes, but no more; more than that would **humiliate** him publicly.

4 "Do not muzzle an ox when you are using it to thresh corn.

Duty to a Dead Brother

5 "If two brothers live on the same property and one of them dies, leaving no son, then his **widow** is not to be married to someone outside the family; it is the **duty** of the **dead** man's brother to marry her. 6 The first son that they have will be considered the son of the **dead** man, so that his family line will continue in Israel. 7 But if the **dead** man's brother does not want to marry her, she is to go before the town leaders and say, 'My husband's brother will not do his **duty**; he **refuses** to give his brother a descendant among the people of Israel.' 8 Then the town leaders are to summon him and speak to him. If he still **refuses** to marry her, 9 his brother's **widow** is to go up to him in the **presence** of the town leaders, take off one of his sandals, spit in his face, and say, 'This is what happens to the man who **refuses** to give his brother a descendant.' 10 His family will be known in Israel as 'the family of the man who had his sandal pulled off.'

Other Laws

11 "If two men are having a fight and the wife of one tries to **help** her husband by grabbing hold of the other man's genitals, 12 show her no **mercy**; cut off her hand.

13–14 "Do not **cheat** when you use weights and measures. 15 Use **true** and **honest** weights and measures, so that you may live a long time in the land that the LORD your God is giving you. 16 The LORD **hates** people who **cheat**.

The Command to Kill the Amalekites

17 "**Remember** what the Amalekites did to you as you were coming from Egypt. 18 They had no **fear** of God, and so they attacked you from the rear when you were tired and exhausted, and killed all who were straggling behind. 19 So then, when the LORD your God has given you the land and made you **safe** from all your **enemies** who live around you, be **sure** to kill all the Amalekites, so that no one will **remember** them any longer. Do not **forget**!

Harvest Offerings

26 "After you have occupied the land that the LORD your God is giving you and have settled there, 2 each of you must place in a basket the first part of each crop that you **harvest** and you must take it with you to the one **place of worship**. 3 Go to the **priest** in charge at that time and say to him, 'I now **acknowledge** to the LORD my God

presence 18.16; 26.5
refuse (1) [3] 23.4; 30.17
remember [2] 24.9; 29.16
safe 19.4; 32.11
sentence 1 Kgs 20.40
settle (2) 1.12; Ruth 3.18
sure 24.8; 29.18
true 22.20; 32.4
widow [2] 24.17; 26.12

cheat [2] 24.14; 1 Sam 12.3
court (1) 22.15; 1 Sam 8.15
crime 24.16; Judg 9.24
dead [3] 21.23; 26.14
depend 8.3; 2 Sam 15.22
dispute 1.12; Judg 18.7
duty (1) [2] 24.5; 1 Sam 10.25
enemy 23.14; 28.7
fear 18.22; 28.66
forget 24.22; 26.13
guilty [2] 24.15; Judg 21.22
hate 23.18; 27.15
help 23.6; 26.7
honest 16.19; Josh 14.7
humiliate 1 Sam 1.6
innocent 21.8; 27.25
judge 21.2; 28.46
mercy 19.13; 28.50

accept 17.11; 27.25
acknowledge [2] 21.17; 1 Chr 28.9
altar 18.10; 27.5
bless [2] 24.19; 27.12
celebrate 16.1; Judg 16.23
command [6] 24.18; 28.1
community Num 35.24; Josh 9.15
create 4.32; 2 Kgs 19.15

24.14–15: Lev 19.13 **24.16:** 2 Kgs 14.6; 2 Chr 25.4; Ezek 18.20
24.17–18: Ex 23.9; Lev 19.33–34; Deut 27.19 **24.19–21:** Lev 19.9–10, 23.22 **25.3:** 2 Cor 11.24
25.4: 1 Cor 9.9; 1 Tim 5.18 **25.5–6:** Mt 22.24; Mk 12.19; Lk 20.28 **25.7–10:** Ruth 4.7–8
25.13–16: Lev 19.35–36 **25.17–19:** Ex 17.8–14; 1 Sam 15.2–9 **26.2:** Ex 23.19

dead 25.5; 31.27
disobey 17.12; 28.14
faithful 18.13; 28.1
force (1) 22.29; Josh 7.4
forget 25.19; 32.18
God's people [2] 23.1; 28.9
grateful 24.13; 27.7
harvest [2] 20.6; 28.38
heart 13.3; 28.47
heaven 10.14; 30.19
help 25.11; 28.29
holy 5.12; Josh 5.15
honour 17.19; 28.58
law [3] 17.18; 27.3
Levites [3] 24.8; 27.9
miracle 13.1; 29.3
misery Num 21.5; 1 Sam 1.16
mourn 21.13; 34.8
name (2) (name of God, of Jesus) 21.5; 28.58
need 24.14; 28.48
obey [5] 23.20; 27.1
offer 18.1; 27.6
orphan [2] 24.17; 27.19
place of worship 19.17; 31.11
power [2] 11.2; 28.43
praise 10.21; 32.3
presence [2] 25.9; 27.7
priest [2] 24.8; 27.9
promise [5] 23.21; 27.3
rescue 21.8; 32.36
rich [2] 17.17; 27.3
sacred 12.3; Josh 22.27
slave 24.7; 28.32
strength 9.26; 32.36
suffer 24.8; 28.34
terrify 8.15; 28.25
tithe [4] 14.22; 2 Chr 31.5
unclean 23.9; 2 Chr 23.19
widow [2] 25.5; 27.19
wonder (1) 13.1; 28.58
word (1) 10.4; 27.8
worship (1) (of God) 16.8; 31.11

that I have entered the land that he promised our ancestors to give us.'

4 "The priest will take the basket from you and place it before the altar of the LORD your God. [5]Then, in the LORD's presence you will recite these words: 'My ancestor was a wandering Aramean, who took his family to Egypt to live. They were few in number when they went there, but they became a large and powerful nation. [6]The Egyptians treated us harshly and forced us to work as slaves. [7]Then we cried out for help to the LORD, the God of our ancestors. He heard us and saw our suffering, hardship, and misery. [8]By his great power and strength he rescued us from Egypt. He worked miracles and wonders, and caused terrifying things to happen. [9]He brought us here and gave us this rich and fertile land. [10]So now I bring to the LORD the first part of the harvest that he has given me.'

"Then set the basket down in the LORD's presence and worship there. [11]Be grateful for the good things that the LORD your God has given you and your family; and let the Levites and the foreigners who live among you join in the celebration.

12 "Every third year give the tithe—a tenth of your crops—to the Levites, the foreigners, the orphans, and the widows, so that in every community they will have all they need to eat. When you have done this, [13]say to the LORD, 'None of the sacred tithe is left in my house; I have given it to the Levites, the foreigners, the orphans, and the widows, as you commanded me to do. I have not disobeyed or forgotten any of your commands concerning the tithe. [14]I have not eaten any of it when I was mourning; I have not taken any of it out of my house when I was ritually unclean; and I have not given any of it as an offering for the dead.[v] I have obeyed you, O LORD; I have done everything you commanded concerning the tithe. [15]Look down from your holy place in heaven and bless your people Israel; bless also the rich and fertile land that you have given us, as you promised our ancestors.'

The LORD's Own People

16 "Today the LORD your God commands you to obey all his laws; so obey them faithfully with all your heart. [17]Today you have acknowledged the LORD as your God; you have promised to obey him, to keep all his laws, and to do all that he commands. [18]Today the LORD has accepted you as his own people, as he promised you; and he commands you to obey all his laws. [19]He will make you greater than any other nation that he has created, and you will bring praise and honour to his name.[w] You will be his own people, as he promised."

God's Laws Written on Stones

27 Then Moses, together with the leaders of Israel, said to the people, "Obey all the instructions that I am giving you today. [2]On the day you cross the River Jordan and enter the land that the LORD your God is giving you, you are to set up some large stones, cover them with plaster, [3]and write on them all these laws and teachings. When you have entered the rich and fertile land that the LORD, the God of your ancestors, promised you, [4]and you are on the other side of the Jordan, set up these stones on Mount Ebal, as I am instructing you today, and cover them with plaster. [5]Build an altar there made of stones that have had no iron tools used on them, [6]because any altar you build for the LORD your God must be made of uncut stones. There you are to offer the sacrifices that are to be burnt, [7]and there you are to sacrifice and eat your fellowship-offerings and be grateful in the presence of the LORD your God. [8]On the stones covered with plaster write clearly every word of God's laws."

9 Then Moses, together with the levitical priests, said to all the people of Israel, "Give me your attention, people of Israel, and listen to me. Today you have become the people of the LORD your God; [10]so obey him and keep all his laws that I am giving you today."

The Curses on Disobedience

11 Then Moses said to the people of Israel, [12]"After you have crossed the Jordan, the following tribes are to stand on Mount Gerizim when the blessings are pronounced on the people: Simeon, Levi, Judah, Issachar, Joseph, and Benjamin. [13]And the following tribes will stand on Mount Ebal when the curses are pronounced: Reuben, Gad, Asher, Zebulun, Dan, and Naphtali. [14]The Levites will speak these words in a loud voice:

15 " 'God's curse on anyone who makes an idol of stone, wood, or metal

accept 26.18; 29.12
altar [2] 26.4; 33.10
bless 26.15; 28.2
blind 16.19; 28.28
commit 5.17; Prov 6.32
curse [13] 23.4; 28.16
disgrace 22.19; Josh 5.9
dishonour Gen 49.4; 32.51
fellowship-offering Num 29.39; Josh 8.31
grateful 26.11; Judg 8.35
hate 25.16; 30.7
idol [2] 16.22; 29.17
innocent 25.1; 1 Sam 12.5
law [4] 26.16; 28.15
Levites [2] 26.11; 31.
mark (1) 19.14; Job 36.32
neighbour 19.14; Judg 18.22
obey [3] 26.14; 28.1
offer 26.14; 32.38
orphan 26.12; Job 6.27
presence 26.5; 29.10
priest 26.3; 31.9
promise 26.3; 28.9
relations Lev 20.13; 1 Sam 21.4
rich 26.9; 28.12
right (3) 24.17; Ruth 4.4
sacrifice [2] 18.1; 32.17
secret [2] 13.6; 28.56
sex Num 31.17; Judg 19.22
teach [2] 20.18; 28.58
widow 26.12; Ruth 4.5
word (1) [2] 26.5; 32.1
worship (2) (of other gods) 20.18; 28.14
wrong 16.19; Judg 11.27

[v] for the dead; *or* to the dead. [w] bring praise...name; *or* receive praise and honour.

26.12: Deut 14.28–29 **26.18:** Ex 19.5; Deut 4.20, 7.6, 14.2; Tit 2.14; 1 Pet 2.9 **27.2–8:** Josh 8.30–32 **27.5–6:** Ex 20.25 **27.12:** Deut 11.29; Josh 8.33–35 **27.15:** Ex 20.4, 34.17; Lev 19.4, 26.1; Deut 4.15–18, 5.8

and **secretly worships** it; the LORD **hates idolatry**.'

"And all the people will answer, 'Amen!'

16 " 'God's **curse** on anyone who **dishonours** his father or mother.'

"And all the people will answer, 'Amen!'

17 " 'God's **curse** on anyone who moves a **neighbour's** boundary **mark**.'

"And all the people will answer, 'Amen!'

18 " 'God's **curse** on anyone who leads a **blind** man in the **wrong** direction.'

"And all the people will answer, 'Amen!'

19 " 'God's **curse** on anyone who deprives foreigners, **orphans**, and **widows** of their **rights**.'

"And all the people will answer, 'Amen!'

20 " 'God's **curse** on anyone who **disgraces** his father by having intercourse with any of his father's wives.'

"And all the people will answer, 'Amen!'

21 " 'God's **curse** on anyone who has **sexual relations** with an animal.'

"And all the people will answer, 'Amen!'

22 " 'God's **curse** on anyone who has intercourse with his sister or half sister.'

"And all the people will answer, 'Amen!'

23 " 'God's **curse** on anyone who has intercourse with his mother-in-law.'

"And all the people will answer, 'Amen!'

24 " 'God's **curse** on anyone who **secretly commits murder**.'

"And all the people will answer, 'Amen!'

25 " 'God's **curse** on anyone who **accepts** money to murder an **innocent** person.'

"And all the people will answer, 'Amen!'

26 " 'God's **curse** on anyone who does not **obey** all of God's **laws** and **teachings**.'

"And all the people will answer, 'Amen!'

The Blessings of Obedience
(Lev 26.3–13; Deut 7.12–24)

28 "If you **obey** the LORD your God
and **faithfully** keep all his **commands** that I am giving you today, he will
make you greater than any other nation
on earth. 2 **Obey** the LORD your God and
all these **blessings** will be yours:

3 "The LORD will **bless** your towns and your fields.

4 "The LORD will **bless** you with many children, with **abundant** crops, and with many cattle and **sheep**.

5 "The LORD will **bless** your corn crops and the food you prepare from them.

6 "The LORD will **bless** everything you do.

7 "The LORD will defeat your **enemies** when they attack you. They will attack from one direction, but they will run from you in all directions.

8 "The LORD your God will **bless** your work and fill your barns with corn. He will **bless** you in the land that he is giving you.

9 "If you **obey** the LORD your God and
do everything he **commands**, he will
make you his **own people**, as he has
promised. 10 Then all the peoples on
earth will see that the LORD has **chosen**
you to be his **own people**, and they will be
afraid of you. 11 The LORD will give you
many children, many cattle, and
abundant crops in the **land that he
promised** your ancestors to give you.
12 He will send rain in season from his
rich storehouse in the sky and **bless** all
your work, so that you will lend to many
nations, but you will not have to borrow
from any. 13 The LORD your God will
make you the leader among the nations
and not a **follower**; you will always
prosper and never **fail** if you **obey faithfully** all his **commands** that I am giving
you today. 14 But you must never **disobey**
them in any way, or **worship and serve
other gods**.

The Consequences of Disobedience
(Lev 26.14–46)

15 "But if you **disobey** the LORD your God and do not **faithfully** keep all his **commands** and **laws** that I am giving you today, all these **evil** things will happen to you:

16 "The LORD will **curse** your towns and your fields.

17 "The LORD will **curse** your corn crops and the food you prepare from them.

18 "The LORD will **curse** you by giving you only a few children, **poor** crops, and few cattle and **sheep**.

19 "The LORD will **curse** everything you do.

20 "If you do **evil** and **reject** the LORD, he will bring on you **disaster**, confusion,

27.16: Ex 20.12; Deut 5.16 **27.17:** Deut 19.14 **27.18:** Lev 19.14
27.19: Ex 22.21, 23.9; Lev 19.33–34; Deut 24.17–18 **27.20:** Lev 18.8, 20.11; Deut 22.30
27.21: Ex 22.19; Lev 18.23, 20.15 **27.22:** Lev 18.9, 20.17 **27.23:** Lev 18.17, 20.14 **27.26:** Gal 3.10
28.1–14: Deut 11.13–17

reap Gen 45.6; Ruth 2.9
refine [2] Job 28.1
reject Num 16.30; 31.20
rich [2] 27.3; 31.20
ridicule 1 Kgs 9.7
rob Lev 19.13; Judg 2.14
ruin 13.16; Josh 8.28
scatter [2] 4.27; 30.1
secret 27.15; 29.29
seed 11.10; Judg 6.3
serve [5] 21.5; 29.26
share 21.16; 33.21
sheep [4] 22.1; 32.14
slave [2] 26.6; Josh 5.9
sow 11.10; Judg 6.3
strike [2] Num 35.21; 32.25
suffer 26.7; 29.22
teach [2] 27.3; 29.6
terrify 26.8; 34.12
terror Ex 15.14; 32.25
trouble 4.30; Josh 6.18
trust 9.23; 32.37
victory 23.14; 31.5
vine 24.21; 32.32
vineyard [2] 23.24; Judg 9.27
wish [2] 12.20; Judg 9.29
wonder (1) 26.8; 29.3
worship (2) (of other gods) [2] 27.15; 29.18

and **trouble** in everything you do, until you are quickly and completely **destroyed**. 21 He will send **disease** after disease on you until there is not one of you left in the land that you are about to occupy. 22 The LORD will **strike** you with infectious **diseases**, with swelling and fever; he will send drought and scorching winds to **destroy** your crops. These **disasters** will be with you until you die. 23 No rain will fall, and your ground will become as **hard** as iron. 24 Instead of rain, the LORD will send down duststorms and sandstorms until you are **destroyed**.

25 "The LORD will give your **enemies** **victory** over you. You will attack them from one direction, but you will run from them in all directions, and all the people on earth will be **terrified** when they see what happens to you. 26 When you die, birds and wild animals will come and eat your **bodies**, and there will be no one to scare them off. 27 The LORD will send boils on you, as he did on the Egyptians. He will make your **bodies** break out with sores. You will be covered with scabs, and you will itch, but there will be no **cure**. 28 The LORD will make you lose your **mind**; he will **strike** you with **blindness** and confusion. 29 You will grope about in broad daylight like a **blind** man, and you will not be able to find your way. You will not **prosper** in anything you do. You will be constantly **oppressed** and **robbed**, and there will be no one to **help** you.

30 "You will be engaged to a girl—but someone else will marry her. You will build a house—but never live in it. You will plant a **vineyard**—but never eat its grapes. 31 Your cattle will be butchered before your very eyes, but you will not eat any of the meat. Your donkeys will be dragged away while you look on, and they will not be given back to you. Your **sheep** will be given to your **enemies**, and there will be no one to **help** you. 32 Your sons and daughters will be given as **slaves** to foreigners while you look on. Every day you will strain your eyes, looking in vain for your children to return. 33 A foreign nation will take all the crops that you have worked so **hard** to grow, while you receive nothing but **constant** **oppression** and harsh treatment. 34 Your **sufferings** will make you lose your **mind**. 35 The LORD will cover your legs with incurable, **painful** sores; boils will cover you from head to foot.

36 "The LORD will take you and your king away to a foreign land, where neither you nor your ancestors ever lived before; there you will **serve gods** made of wood and stone. 37 In the countries to which the LORD will **scatter** you, the people will be shocked at what has happened to you; they will make fun of you and **ridicule** you.

38 "You will **sow plenty** of **seed**, but **reap** only a small **harvest**, because the locusts will eat your crops. 39 You will plant **vineyards** and take **care** of them, but you will not gather their grapes or drink wine from them, because worms will eat the **vines**. 40 Olive-trees will grow everywhere in your land, but you will not have any olive-oil, because the olives will drop off. 41 You will have sons and daughters, but you will lose them, because they will be taken away as **prisoners** of war. 42 All your trees and crops will be **devoured** by insects.

43 "Foreigners who live in your land will gain more and more **power**, while you gradually lose yours. 44 They will have money to lend you, but you will have none to lend them. In the end they will be your rulers.

45 "All these **disasters** will come on you, and they will be with you until you are **destroyed**, because you did not **obey** the LORD your God and keep all the **laws** that he gave you. 46 They will be the **evidence** of God's **judgement** on you and your descendants for ever. 47 The LORD **blessed** you in every way, but you would not **serve** him with **glad** and **joyful** **hearts**. 48 So then, you will **serve** the **enemies** that the LORD is going to send against you. You will be **hungry**, thirsty, and **naked**—in **need** of everything. The LORD[x] will **oppress** you harshly until you are **destroyed**. 49 The LORD will bring against you a nation from the ends of the earth, a nation whose language you do not know. They will swoop down on you like an eagle. 50 They will be ruthless and show no **mercy** to anyone, young or old. 51 They will eat your livestock and your crops, and you will starve **to death**. They will not leave you any corn, wine, olive-oil, livestock, or **sheep**; and you will die. 52 They will attack every town in the land that the LORD your God is giving you, and the high, fortified walls in which you **trust** will fall.

53 "When your **enemies** are besieging your towns, you will become so **desperate** for food that you will even eat the children that the LORD your God has given you. 54-55 Even the most **refined** man of noble **birth** will become so **desperate** during the siege that he will eat some of his own children because he has no other food. He will not even give any

[x] The LORD; *or* Your enemies.

to his brother or to the wife he **loves** or to
any of his children who are left. 56–57 Even
the most **refined** woman of noble **birth**,
so **rich** that she has never had to walk
anywhere, will behave in the same way.
When the **enemy** besieges her town, she
will become so **desperate** for food that
she will **secretly** eat her newborn child
and the afterbirth as well. She will not
share them with the husband she **loves** or
with any of her children.

58 "If you do not **obey faithfully** all
God's **teachings** that are written in this
book and if you do not **honour** the
wonderful and **awesome name of the**
LORD your God, 59 he will send on you and
on your descendants incurable **diseases**
and **horrible** epidemics that can never be
stopped. 60 He will bring on you once
again all the dreadful **diseases** you
experienced in Egypt, and you will never
recover. 61 He will also send all kinds of
diseases and epidemics that are not mentioned in this book of God's **laws** and
teachings, and you will be **destroyed**.
62 Although you become as numerous as
the stars in the sky, only a few of you will
survive, because you did not **obey** the
LORD your God. 63 Just as the LORD took
delight in making you **prosper** and in
making you increase in number, so he
will take **delight** in **destroying** you and in
bringing **ruin** on you. You will be uprooted from the land that you are about
to occupy.

64 "The LORD will **scatter** you among
all the nations, from one end of the earth
to the other, and there you will **serve**
gods made of wood and stone, **gods** that
neither you nor your ancestors have ever
worshipped before. 65 You will find no
peace anywhere, no place to call your
own; the LORD will overwhelm you with
anxiety, **hopelessness**, and **despair**.
66 Your **life** will always be in **danger**. Day
and night you will be filled with **terror**,
and you will live in **constant fear** of
death. 67 Your **hearts** will pound with **fear**
at everything you see. Every morning
you will **wish** for evening; every evening
you will **wish** for morning. 68 The LORD
will send you back to Egypt in ships,
even though he[y] said that you would
never have to go there again. There you
will try to sell yourselves to your
enemies as **slaves**, but no one will want
to buy you."

The LORD's Covenant with Israel in the Land of Moab

29 These are the terms of the **cove-**
nant that the LORD **commanded**
Moses to make with the people of Israel
in the land of Moab; all this was in addition to the **covenant** which the LORD had
made with them at Mount Sinai.

2 Moses called together all the people
of Israel and said to them, "You saw for
yourselves what the LORD did to the king
of Egypt, to his officials, and to his entire
country. 3 You saw the **terrible plagues**,
the **miracles**, and the great **wonders** that
the LORD performed. 4 But to this very
day he has not let you **understand** what
you have **experienced**. 5 For forty years
the LORD led you through the desert, and
your clothes and sandals never wore out.
6 You did not have **bread** to eat or wine
or beer to drink, but the LORD **provided**
for your **needs** in order to **teach** you that
he is your God. 7 And when we came to
this place, King Sihon of Heshbon and
King Og of Bashan came out to fight
against us. But we defeated them, 8 took
their land, and divided it among the
tribes of Reuben and Gad, and half the
tribe of Manasseh. 9 **Obey faithfully** all
the terms of this **covenant**, so that you
will be **successful** in everything you do.

10 "Today you are standing in the
presence of the LORD your God, all of
you—your leaders and officials, your
men, 11 women, and children, and the
foreigners who live among you and cut
wood and carry water for you. 12 You are
here today to enter into this **covenant**
that the LORD your God is making with
you and to **accept** its **obligations**, 13 so
that the LORD may now confirm you as
his people and be your God, as he
promised you and your ancestors,
Abraham, Isaac, and Jacob. 14 You are
not the only ones with whom the LORD is
making this **covenant** with its **obliga-**
tions. 15 He is making it with all of us who
stand here in his **presence** today and also
with our descendants who are not yet
born.

16 "You **remember** what **life** was like
in Egypt and what it was like to travel
through the territory of other nations.
17 You saw their **disgusting idols** made of
wood, stone, silver, and gold. 18 Make **sure**
that no man, woman, family, or tribe
standing here today **turns from** the LORD
our God to **worship the gods** of other
nations. This would be like a root that
grows to be a **bitter** and poisonous plant.

[y] he; *or* I.

28.57: 2 Kgs 6.28–29; Lam 4.10 **29.7:** Num 21.21–35 **29.8:** Num 32.33 **29.18:** Heb 12.15

[19]Make **sure** that there is no one here today who hears these **solemn demands** and yet **convinces** himself that all will be well with him, even if he **stubbornly** goes his own way. That would **destroy** all of you, good and **evil** alike. [20]The LORD will not **forgive** such a man. Instead, the **LORD's burning anger** will flame up against him, and all the **disasters** written in this book will fall on him until the LORD has **destroyed** him completely. [21]The LORD will make an **example** of him before all the tribes of Israel and will bring **disaster** on him in accordance with all the **curses** listed in the **covenant** that is written in this book of the LORD's **teachings**.

22 "In future generations your descendants and foreigners from distant lands will see the **disasters** and **sufferings** that the LORD has brought on your land. [23]The fields will be a **barren** waste, covered with sulphur and salt; nothing will be planted, and not even **weeds** will grow there. Your land will be like the cities of Sodom and Gomorrah, of Admah and Zeboiim, which the LORD **destroyed** when he was **furiously angry**. [24]Then the whole **world** will ask, 'Why did the LORD do this to their land? What was the **reason** for his fierce **anger**?' [25]And the answer will be, 'It is because the **LORD's people** broke the **covenant** they had made with him, the God of their ancestors, when he brought them out of Egypt. [26]They **served** other **gods** that they had never worshipped before, **gods** that the LORD had **forbidden** them to **worship**. [27]And so the LORD became **angry** with **his people** and brought on their land all the **disasters** written in this book. [28]The LORD became **furiously angry**, and in his great **anger** he uprooted them from their land and threw them into a foreign land, and there they are today.'

29 "There are some things that the LORD our God has kept **secret**; but he has **revealed** his **Law**, and we and our descendants are to **obey** it for ever.

Conditions for Restoration and Blessing

30 "I have now given you a **choice** between a **blessing** and a **curse**. When all these things have happened to you, and you are living among the nations where the LORD your God has **scattered** you, you will **remember** the **choice** I gave you. [2]If you and your descendants will **turn back** to the LORD and **with all your heart obey** his **commands** that I am giving you today, [3]then the LORD your God will have **mercy** on you. He will bring you back from the nations where he has **scattered** you, and he will make you **prosperous** again. [4]Even if you are **scattered** to the farthest corners of the earth, the LORD your God will gather you together and bring you back, [5]so that you may again take **possession** of the land where your ancestors once lived. And he will make you more **prosperous** and more numerous than your ancestors ever were. [6]The LORD your God will give you and your descendants **obedient hearts**, so that you will **love** him **with all your heart**, and you will continue to live in that land. [7]He will **turn** all these **curses** against your **enemies**, who **hated** you and **oppressed** you, [8]and you will again **obey** him and keep all his **commands** that I am giving you today. [9]The LORD will make you **prosperous** in all that you do; you will have many children and a lot of livestock, and your fields will produce **abundant** crops. He will be as **glad** to make you **prosperous** as he was to make your ancestors **prosperous**, [10]but you will have to **obey** him and keep all his **laws** that are written in this book of his **teachings**. You will have to **turn to** him **with all your heart**.

11 "The **command** that I am giving you today is not too **difficult** or beyond your reach. [12]It is not up in the sky. You do not have to ask, 'Who will go up and bring it down for us, so that we can hear it and **obey** it?' [13]Nor is it on the other side of the ocean. You do not have to ask, 'Who will go across the ocean and bring it to us, so that we may hear it and **obey** it?' [14]No, it is here with you. You know it and can quote it, so now **obey** it.

15 "Today I am giving you a **choice** between good and **evil**, between **life** and **death**. [16]If you **obey** the **commands** of the LORD your God,[z] which I give you today, if you **love** him, **obey** him, and keep all his **laws**, then you will **prosper** and become a nation of many people. The LORD your God will **bless** you in the land that you are about to occupy. [17]But if you **disobey** and **refuse** to listen, and are led away to **worship other gods**, [18]you will be **destroyed**—I **warn** you here and now. You will not live long in that land across the Jordan that you are about to occupy. [19]I am now giving you the **choice** between **life** and **death**, between God's **blessing** and God's **curse**, and I call

[z] *One ancient translation* If you obey the commands of the LORD your God; *Hebrew does not have these words.*

29.23: Gen 19.24–25 **30.12–14:** Rom 10.6–8

abundant 28.4; Job 36.31
bless [3] 28.2; 33.1
choose [6] 28.10; 32.9
command [4] 29.1; 31.10
curse [3] 29.21; Josh 6.26
death (1) [2] 28.51; 31.16
destroy 29.19; 31.3

difficult 17.8; 1 Sam 10.19
disobey 28.14; Josh 1.18
enemy 28.7; 32.2
evil 29.19; 31.18
faithful 29.9; 31.
glad 28.47; Judg
god (2) (other g
29.18; 31.16
hate 27.15; 32.41
heart [4] 28.47; Josh 22.5
heaven 26.15; 31
law [2] 29.29; 31.
life (1) [3] 29.16;
love [3] 28.54; 33.
mercy 28.50; 32.
obey [10] 29.9; 31
oppress 28.29; Judg 2.18
possess 21.17; 3
promise 29.13; 3
prosper [6] 28.1
33.18
refuse (1) 25.7; 3
remember 29.16
32.26
scatter [3] 28.37; 1 Sam 11.11
teach 29.6; 31.12
turn [3] 29.18; 31
warn 8.19; Josh
witness 19.15; 3
worship (2) (of other gods) 29.1
31.16

heaven and earth to witness the choice you make. Choose life. 20 Love the LORD your God, obey him and be faithful to him, and then you and your descendants will live long in the land that he promised to give your ancestors, Abraham, Isaac, and Jacob."

Joshua Becomes Moses' Successor

31 Moses continued speaking to the people of Israel, 2 and said, "I am now a hundred and twenty years old and am no longer able to be your leader. And besides this, the LORD has told me that I will not cross the Jordan. 3 The LORD your God himself will go before you and destroy the nations living there, so that you can occupy their land; and Joshua will be your leader, as the LORD has said. 4 The LORD will destroy those people, just as he defeated Sihon and Og, kings of the Amorites, and destroyed their country. 5 The LORD will give you victory over them, and you are to treat them exactly as I have told you. 6 Be determined and confident. Do not be afraid of them. Your God, the LORD himself, will be with you. He will not fail you or abandon you."

7 Then Moses called Joshua and said to him in the presence of all the people of Israel, "Be determined and confident; you are the one who will lead these people to occupy the land that the LORD promised to their ancestors. 8 The LORD himself will lead you and be with you. He will not fail you or abandon you, so do not lose courage or be afraid."

The Law Is to Be Read Every Seven Years

9 So Moses wrote down God's Law and gave it to the levitical priests, who were in charge of the LORD's Covenant Box, and to the leaders of Israel. 10 He commanded them, "At the end of every seven years, when the year that debts are cancelled comes round, read this aloud at the Festival of Shelters. 11 Read it to the people of Israel when they come to worship the LORD your God at the one place of worship. 12 Call together all the men, women, and children, and the foreigners who live in your towns, so that everyone may hear it and learn to honour the LORD your God and to obey his teachings faithfully. 13 In this way your descendants who have never heard the Law of the LORD your God will hear it. And so they will learn to obey him as long as they live in the land that you are about to occupy across the Jordan."

The LORD's Last Instruction to Moses

14 Then the LORD said to Moses, "You haven't much longer to live. Call Joshua and bring him to the Tent, so that I may give him his instructions." Moses and Joshua went to the Tent, 15 and the LORD appeared to them there in a pillar of cloud that stood by the door of the Tent.

16 The LORD said to Moses, "You will soon die, and after your death the people will become unfaithful to me and break the covenant that I made with them. They will abandon me and worship the pagan gods of the land they are about to enter. 17 When that happens, I will become angry with them; I will abandon them, and they will be destroyed. Many terrible disasters will come upon them, and then they will realize that these things are happening to them because I, their God, am no longer with them. 18 And I will refuse to help them then, because they have done evil and worshipped other gods.

19 "Now, write down this song. Teach it to the people of Israel, so that it will stand as evidence against them. 20 I will take them into this rich and fertile land, as I promised their ancestors. There they will have all the food they want, and they will live comfortably. But they will turn away and worship other gods. They will reject me and break my covenant, 21 and many terrible disasters will come on them. But this song will still be sung, and it will stand as evidence against them. Even now, before I take them into the land that I promised to give them, I know what they are thinking."

22 That same day Moses wrote down the song and taught it to the people of Israel.

23 Then the LORD spoke to Joshua son of Nun and said to him, "Be confident and determined. You will lead the people of Israel into the land that I promised them, and I will be with you."

24 Moses wrote God's Law in a book, taking care not to leave out anything. 25 When he finished, he said to the levitical priests, who were in charge of the LORD's Covenant Box, 26 "Take this book of God's Law and place it beside the Covenant Box of the LORD your God, so that it will remain there as a witness against his people. 27 I know how stubborn and rebellious they are. They have rebelled against the LORD during my lifetime, and they will rebel even more after I am dead. 28 Assemble all your tribal leaders and officials before

30.20: Gen 12.7, 26.3, 28.13 **31.2:** Num 20.12 **31.4:** Num 21.21–35 **31.8:** Josh 1.5; Heb 13.5 **31.10:** Deut 15.1, 16.13–15 **31.23:** Num 27.23; Josh 1.6

abandon [4] 4.31; 32.15
afraid [2] 28.10; Josh 1.9
anger [2] 29.20; 32.16
care 28.39; 32.10
cloud 5.22; 33.26
comfort Gen 37.35; 2 Sam 12.24
command 30.2; 32.46
confident [3] Josh 1.6
courage 20.3; Josh 2.11
covenant [2] 29.1; 33.9
Covenant Box [3] 10.1; Josh 3.3
dead 26.14; Josh 1.2
death (1) [2] 30.15; 32.25
debt 15.1; 1 Sam 22.2
destroy [4] 30.18; 32.26
determine [3] 9.25; 32.8
disaster [3] 29.20; 32.23
evidence [2] 28.46; Job 15.5
evil 30.15; 32.16
fail [2] 28.13; 32.29
faithful 30.20; 32.4
festival 16.10; Judg 9.27
forbid 29.26; Judg 13.4
god (2) (other gods) [3] 30.17; 32.8
God's people 29.13; 32.3
heaven 30.19; Josh 2.11
help 28.29; 32.12
honour 28.58; Josh 3.7
law [4] 30.10; 33.4
learn [2] 17.19; Josh 9.16
Levites [2] 27.9; 33.8
obey [2] 30.2; 32.17
pagan Lev 20.23; 2 Sam 1.20
place of worship 26.2; Judg 17.5
presence 29.10; 32.51
priest [2] 27.9; Josh 3.3
promise [4] 30.20; 34.4
rebel [3] 21.18; 32.15
refuse (1) 30.17; Josh 22.18
reject [2] 28.20; 32.15
rich 28.12; 32.15
shelter 16.13; Judg 9.15
stubborn 29.19; 32.20
teach [4] 30.10; 32.2
Tent (2) (of the Lord's presence) [3] Num 31.30; Josh 18.1
terrible [2] 29.3; 32.24
turn 30.2; Josh 8.5
unfaithful Num 31.16; 32.5
victory 28.25; 33.29
wicked 9.4; Judg 9.57
witness [2] 30.19; Josh 22.34
worship (1) (of God) 26.10; Josh 1.8
worship (2) (of other gods) [3] 30.17; Josh 23.7

me, so that I can tell them these things; I
will call heaven and earth to be my witnesses against them. 29 I know that after
my death the people will become wicked
and reject what I have taught them. And
in time to come they will meet with
disaster, because they will have made
the LORD angry by doing what he has
forbidden."

The Song of Moses

30 Then Moses recited the entire song
while all the people of Israel listened.

32 "Earth and sky, hear my words,
listen closely to what I say.
2 My teaching will fall like drops of rain
and form on the earth like dew.
My words will fall like showers on
young plants,
like gentle rain on tender grass.
3 I will praise the name of the LORD,
and his people will tell of his
greatness.

4 "The LORD is your mighty defender,
perfect and just in all his ways;
Your God is faithful and true;
he does what is right and fair.
5 But you are unfaithful, unworthy to be
his people,[a]
a sinful and deceitful nation.
6 Is this the way you should treat the
LORD,
you foolish, senseless people?
He is your father, your Creator,
he made you into a nation.

7 "Think of the past, of the time long
ago;
ask your fathers to tell you what
happened,
ask the old men to tell of the past.
8 The Most High assigned nations their
lands;
he determined where peoples should
live.
He assigned to each nation a god,
9 but Jacob's descendants he chose for
himself.

10 "He found them wandering through
the desert,
a desolate, wind-swept wilderness.
He protected them and cared for
them,
as he would protect himself.
11 Like an eagle teaching its young to
fly,[b]
catching them safely on its
spreading wings,
the LORD kept Israel from falling.
12 The LORD alone led his people
without the help of a foreign god.

13 "He let them rule the highlands,
and they ate what grew in the fields.
They found wild honey among the
rocks;
their olive-trees flourished in stony
ground.
14 Their cows and goats gave plenty of
milk;
they had the best sheep, goats, and
cattle,
the finest wheat, and the choicest
wine.

15 "The LORD's people grew rich, but
rebellious;
they were fat and stuffed with food.
They abandoned God their Creator
and rejected their mighty saviour.
16 Their idolatry made the LORD jealous;
the evil they did made him angry.
17 They sacrificed to gods that are not
real,
new gods their ancestors had never
known,
gods that Israel had never obeyed.
18 They forgot their God, their mighty
saviour,
the one who had given them life.

19 "When the LORD saw this, he was
angry
and rejected his sons and daughters.
20 'I will no longer help them,' he said;
'then I will see what happens to
them,
those stubborn, unfaithful people.
21 With their idols they have made me
angry,
jealous with their so-called gods,
gods that are really not gods.
So I will use a so-called nation to make
them angry;
I will make them jealous with a
nation of fools.
22 My anger will flame up like fire
and burn everything on earth.
It will reach to the world below[c]
and consume the roots of the
mountains.

23 " 'I will bring on them endless
disasters
and use all my arrows against them.

[a] *Probable text* But you...people; *Hebrew unclear.*
[b] teaching its young to fly; *or* watching over its young.
[c] THE WORLD BELOW: *This refers to the world of the dead.*

32.8: Acts 17.26 **32.17:** 1 Cor 10.20 **32.21:** 1 Cor 10.22; Rom 10.19

24 They will die from **hunger** and fever;
they will die from **terrible diseases.**
I will send wild animals to attack
them,
and poisonous snakes to bite them.
25 War will bring **death** in the streets;
terrors will **strike** in the homes.
Young men and young women will die;
neither babies nor old men will be
spared.
26 I would have **destroyed** them
completely,
so that no one would **remember**
them.
27 But I could not let their **enemies boast**
that they had defeated **my people,**
when it was I myself who had
crushed them.'

28 "Israel is a nation without **sense**;
they have no **wisdom** at all.
29 They **fail** to see why they were
defeated;
they cannot **understand** what
happened.
30 Why were a thousand defeated by one,
and ten thousand by only two?
The LORD, their God, had **abandoned**
them;
their **mighty** God had given them up.
31 Their **enemies** know that their own
gods are **weak,**
not **mighty** like Israel's God.
32 Their **enemies, corrupt** as Sodom and
Gomorrah,
are like **vines** that bear **bitter** and
poisonous grapes,
33 like wine made from the venom of
snakes.

34 "The LORD **remembers** what their
enemies have done;
he waits for the **right** time to **punish**
them.
35 The LORD will take **revenge** and
punish them;
the time will come when they will
fall;
the day of their **doom** is near.
36 The LORD will **rescue his people**
when he sees that their **strength** is
gone.
He will have **mercy** on those who
serve him,
when he sees how **helpless** they are.
37 Then the LORD will ask **his people,**
'Where are those **mighty gods** you
trusted?
38 You fed them with the fat of your
sacrifices
and **offered** them wine to drink.
Let them come and **help** you now;
let them run to your **rescue.**

39 " 'I, and I **alone,** am God;
no other **god** is **real.**
I kill and I give **life,** I wound and I **heal,**
and no one can oppose what I do.
40 As **surely** as I am the living God,
I **raise** my hand and I **vow**
41 that I will sharpen my flashing
sword
and see that **justice** is done.
I will take **revenge** on my **enemies**
and **punish** those who **hate** me.
42 My arrows will drip with their **blood,**
and my sword will kill all who
oppose me.
I will **spare** no one who fights against
me;
even the wounded and **prisoners** will
die.'

43 "Nations, you must **praise** the LORD's
people—
he **punishes** all who kill them.
He takes **revenge** on his **enemies**
and **forgives** the sins of **his people.**"

44 Moses and Joshua son of Nun recited this song, so that the people of Israel could hear it.

Moses' Final Instructions

45 When Moses had finished giving God's **teachings** to the people, 46 he said, "Make **sure** you **obey** all these **commands** that I have given you today. Repeat them to your children, so that they may **faithfully obey** all God's **teachings.** 47 These **teachings** are not empty **words**; they are your very **life. Obey** them and you will live long in that land across the Jordan that you are about to occupy."

48 That same day the LORD said to Moses, 49 "Go to the Abarim Mountains in the land of Moab opposite the city of Jericho; climb Mount Nebo and look at the land of Canaan that I am about to give the people of Israel. 50 You will die on that mountain as your brother Aaron died on Mount Hor, 51 because both of you were **unfaithful** to me in the **presence** of the people of Israel. When you were at the waters of Meribah, near the town of Kadesh in the wilderness of Zin, you **dishonoured** me in the **presence** of the people. 52 You will look at the land from a distance, but you will not enter the land that I am giving the people of Israel."

32.35: Rom 12.19; Heb 10.30 **32.36a:** Ps 135.14 **32.43:** Rom 15.10; Rev 19.2
32.48–52: Num 27.12–14; Deut 3.23–27

altar 27.5; Josh 8.30
ancient Gen 49.26; 1 Chr 20.6
angel Num 22.22; Judg 2.1
beg 18.16; 1 Sam 2.36
best [2] 32.14; Josh 8.3
bless [7] 30.1; Josh 8.33
bow (2) 5.9; Josh 23.7
cloud 31.15; Judg 5.4
command [3] 32.46; 34.9
covenant 31.16; Josh 7.15
defend [2] 32.4; Josh 8.17
destroy 32.26; Josh 6.17
enemy [4] 32.27; Josh 5.13
eternal 1 Sam 18.3
faithful [2] 32.4; Josh 14.8
favour Num 35.24; 1 Sam 2.26
god (2) (other gods) 32.8; Josh 23.7
God's people [3] 32.3; Josh 1.3
happy 24.5; Judg 9.13
help [3] 32.12; Josh 1.1
law [3] 31.9; Josh 1.7
Levites 31.9; Josh 8.33
love [2] 30.6; Josh 22.5
loyal Num 32.11; Josh 24.23
man of God Josh 14.6
mercy 32.36; Josh 11.20
obey [5] 32.17; 34.9
offer [2] 32.38; Josh 6.17
peace 28.65; Josh 10.1
please 24.13; Judg 6.17
possess 30.5; Josh 7.13
praise 32.3; Josh 22.33
prosper 30.3; Josh 1.8
protect [3] 32.10; Josh 7.9
prove 22.15; Judg 6.17
reveal 29.29; 1 Sam 2.27
rich [3] 32.15; Josh 5.4
right (1) 32.4; Josh 9.25
right (2) Num 18.18; Judg 3.16
ripe Num 17.8; Judg 8.32
rise [2] Gen 32.31; Josh 8.20
sacrifice [2] 32.17; Josh 8.31
save 7.8; Josh 2.13
secure [2] 24.6; Josh 23.1
servant 24.14; 34.5
share 28.56; Josh 13.14
splendour Ex 33.19; 1 Chr 22.5

Moses Blesses the Tribes of Israel

33 These are the **blessings** that Moses, the **man of God**, pronounced on the people of Israel before he died.

2 The LORD came from Mount Sinai;
he **rose** like the sun over Edom
and shone on **his people** from Mount Paran.
Ten thousand **angels** were with him,
a flaming fire at his **right hand**.[d]
3 The LORD **loves his people**[e]
and **protects** those who belong to him.
So we **bow** at[f] his feet
and **obey** his **commands**.
4 We **obey** the **Law** that Moses gave us,
our nation's most treasured **possession**.
5 The LORD became king of **his people** Israel
when their tribes and leaders were gathered together.

6 Moses said about the tribe of Reuben:
"May Reuben never die out,
Although their people are few."

7 About the tribe of Judah he said:
"LORD, listen to their cry for **help**;
Unite them again with the other tribes.
Fight for them, LORD,
And **help** them against their **enemies**."[g]

8 About the tribe of Levi he said:
"You, LORD, **reveal** your **will** by the Urim and Thummim[h]
Through your **faithful servants**, the **Levites**;
You put them **to the test** at Massah
And **proved** them **true** at the waters of Meribah.
9 They showed greater **loyalty** to you
Than to parents, brothers, or children.
They **obeyed** your **commands**
And were **faithful** to your **covenant**.
10 They will **teach** your people to **obey** your **Law**;
They will **offer sacrifices** on your **altar**.
11 Lord, **help** their tribe to grow **strong**;
Be **pleased** with what they do.
Crush all their **enemies**;
Let them never **rise** again."

12 About the tribe of Benjamin he said:
"This is the tribe the LORD **loves** and **protects**;
He guards them all the day long,
And he dwells in their midst."[i]

13 About the tribe of Joseph he said:
"May the LORD **bless** their land with rain
And with water from under the earth.
14 May their land be **blessed** with **sun-ripened** fruit,
Rich with the **best** fruits of each season.
15 May their **ancient** hills be covered with choice fruit.
16 May their land be filled with all that is good,
Blessed by the goodness of the LORD,
Who spoke from the burning bush.
May these **blessings** come to the tribe of Joseph,
Because he was the leader among his brothers.
17 Joseph has the **strength** of a bull,
The horns of a wild ox.
His horns are Manasseh's thousands
And Ephraim's ten thousands.
With them he gores the nations
And pushes them to the ends of the earth."

18 About the tribes of Zebulun and Issachar he said:
"May Zebulun be **prosperous** in their trade on the sea,
And may Issachar's wealth increase at home.
19 They invite foreigners to their mountain
And **offer the right sacrifices** there.
They get their wealth from the sea
And from the sand along the shore."

20 About the tribe of Gad he said:
"**Praise** God, who made their territory large.
Gad waits like a lion
To tear off an arm or a scalp.
21 They took the **best** of the land for themselves;
A leader's **share** was assigned to them.
They **obeyed** the LORD's **commands** and **laws**
When the leaders of Israel were gathered together."[j]

strength 32.36; Judg 5.21
strong 10.15; 34.7
teach 32.2; Judg 3.2
test 13.3; Judg 3.1
true 32.4; Josh 7.20
unite Gen 2.24; Judg 21.15
victory 31.5; Josh 8
will (1) Num 27.21; Josh 22.5

[d] *Probable text* Ten thousand...right hand; *Hebrew unclear.*
[e] *One ancient translation* his people; *Hebrew* the peoples. [f] *Probable text* bow at; *Hebrew unclear.*
[g] *Probable text* Fight for...enemies; *Hebrew* The tribe of Judah will fight for itself, and the LORD will help it against its enemies.
[h] URIM AND THUMMIM: *Two objects used by the priest to determine God's will; it is not known precisely how they were used.* [i] And he...midst; *or* They live under his protection.
[j] *One ancient translation* When the leaders...together; *Hebrew unclear.*

33.8: Ex 17.7, 28.30; Num 20.13

22 About the tribe of Dan he said:
"Dan is a young lion;
He leaps out from Bashan."

23 About the tribe of Naphtali he said:
"Naphtali is **richly blessed** by the
LORD's good **favour**;
Their land reaches to the south from
Lake Galilee."

24 About the tribe of Asher he said:
"Asher is **blessed** more than the other
tribes.
May he be the favourite of his
brothers,
And may his land be **rich** with olive-
trees.
25 May his towns be **protected** with iron
gates,
And may he always live **secure**."

26 People of Israel, no **god** is like your
God,
riding in **splendour** across the sky,
riding through the **clouds** to come to
your aid.
27 God has always been your **defence**;
his **eternal** arms are your support.
He drove out your **enemies** as you
advanced,
and told you to **destroy** them all.
28 So Jacob's descendants live in **peace**,
secure in a land full of corn and
wine,
where dew from the sky waters the
ground.
29 Israel, how **happy** you are!
There is no one like you,
a nation **saved** by the LORD.
The LORD himself is your shield and
your sword,
to **defend** you and give you **victory**.
Your **enemies** will come **begging** for
mercy,
and you will trample them down.

34.4: Gen 12.7, 26.3, 28.13 **34.10:** Ex 33.11

The Death of Moses

34 Moses went up from the plains of
Moab to Mount Nebo, to the top
of Mount Pisgah east of Jericho, and
there the LORD showed him the whole
land: the territory of Gilead as far north
as the town of Dan; 2 the entire territory
of Naphtali; the territories of Ephraim
and Manasseh; the territory of Judah as
far west as the Mediterranean Sea; 3 the
southern part of Judah; and the plain
that reaches from Zoar to Jericho, the
city of palm-trees. 4 Then the LORD said
to Moses, "This is the **land that I**
promised Abraham, Isaac, and Jacob I
would give to their descendants. I have
let you see it, but I will not let you go
there."
5 So Moses, the LORD's **servant**, died
there in the land of Moab, as the LORD
had said he would. 6 The LORD buried him
in a valley in Moab, opposite the town of
Bethpeor, but to this day no one knows
the exact place of his burial. 7 Moses was
a hundred and twenty years old when he
died; he was as **strong** as ever, and his
eyesight was still good. 8 The people of
Israel **mourned** for him for thirty days in
the plains of Moab.
9 Joshua son of Nun was filled with
wisdom, because Moses had appointed
him to be his successor. The people of
Israel **obeyed** Joshua and kept the **commands** that the LORD had given them
through Moses.
10 There has never been a **prophet** in
Israel like Moses; the LORD spoke with
him face to face. 11 No other **prophet** has
ever done **miracles** and **wonders** like
those that the LORD sent Moses to
perform against the king of Egypt, his
officials, and the entire country. 12 No
other **prophet** has been able to do the
great and **terrifying** things that Moses
did in the **sight** of all Israel.

command 33.3; Josh 1.9
eyesight *see* **sight**
miracle 29.3; Josh 3.5
mourn 26.14; Judg 20.22
obey 33.3; Josh 1.7
promise 31.7; Josh 1.6
prophet [3] 18.15; Judg 4.4
servant 33.8; Josh 1.1
sight [2] 11.6; Josh 10.10
strong 33.11; Josh 14.11
terrify 28.25; Josh 2.9
wisdom 32.28; 1 Kgs 3.9
wonder (1) 29.3; Judg 6.13

THE BOOK OF JOSHUA

INTRODUCTION

The book of *Joshua* is the story of the Israelite invasion of Canaan under the leadership of Joshua, the successor of Moses. Notable events recorded in this book include the crossing of the Jordan, the fall of Jericho, the battle at Ai, and the renewal of the covenant between God and his people. One of the best-known passages in the book is, "Decide today whom you will serve... As for my family and me, we will serve the Lord" (24.15).

Outline of Contents

The conquest of Canaan 1.1—12.24
The division of the land 13.1—21.45
 a. The land east of the Jordan 13.1–33
 b. The land west of the Jordan 14.1—19.51
 c. The cities of refuge 20.1–9
 d. The cities of the Levites 21.1–45
The eastern tribes return to their territory 22.1–34
Joshua's farewell address 23.1–16
The covenant renewed at Shechem 24.1–33

---

abandon Deut 32.15; 10.6
afraid Deut 31.6; 2.11
authority Deut 18.22; 2 Chr 12.1
command Deut 34.9; 4.3
confident [4] Deut 31.6; 10.25
dead Deut 31.27; Judg 3.25
death (1) Deut 32.25; 2.19
death (3) (to death) Deut 28.51; 7.25
determine [4] Deut 32.8; 10.25
discourage Num 32.7; 8.1
disobey Deut 30.17; 5.4
God's people Deut 33.2; 22.17
help [2] Deut 33.7; 10.4
law [2] Deut 33.4; 8.31
neglect Deut 14.27; 23.6
obey [3] Deut 34.9; 7.1
promise Deut 34.4; 2.13
prosper Deut 33.18; 2 Sam 5.12
question Gen 43.7; Judg 8.14
remember [2] Deut 32.26; 22.17
safe Deut 32.11; 6.23
servant [5] Deut 34.5; 5.14
study Ex 13.9; Ezra 7.10

God Commands Joshua to Conquer Canaan

1 After the **death** of the LORD's
servant Moses, the LORD spoke to
Moses' **helper**, Joshua son of Nun. 2 He
said, "My **servant** Moses is **dead**. Get
ready now, you and all the people of
Israel, and cross the River Jordan into
the land that I am giving them. 3 As I told
Moses, I have given you and all **my
people** the entire land that you will be
marching over. 4 Your borders will reach
from the desert in the south to the
Lebanon Mountains in the north; from
the great River Euphrates in the east,
through the Hittite country, to the
Mediterranean Sea in the west. 5 Joshua,
no one will be able to defeat you as long
as you live. I will be with you as I was
with Moses. I will always be with you; I
will never **abandon** you. 6 Be **determined**
and **confident**, for you will be the leader
of these people as they occupy this land
which I **promised** their ancestors. 7 Just
be **determined**, be **confident**; and make
sure that you **obey** the whole **Law** that
my **servant** Moses gave you. Do not
neglect any part of it and you will
succeed wherever you go. 8 Be **sure** that
the book of the **Law** is always read in
your **worship**. **Study** it day and night, and
make **sure** that you **obey** everything
written in it. Then you will be **prosperous**
and **successful**. 9 **Remember** that I have
commanded you to be **determined** and
confident! Don't be **afraid** or
discouraged, for I, the LORD your God,
am with you wherever you go."

Joshua Gives Orders to the People

10 Then Joshua ordered the leaders to
11 go through the camp and say to the
people, "Get some food ready, because in
three days you are going to cross the
River Jordan to occupy the land that the
LORD your God is giving you."
12 Joshua said to the tribes of Reuben
and Gad and to half the tribe of
Manasseh, 13 "**Remember** how Moses, the
LORD's **servant**, told you that the LORD
your God would give you this land on the
east side of the Jordan as your home.
14 Your wives, your children, and your
livestock will stay here, but your soldiers,
armed for battle, will cross over ahead of
their fellow-Israelites in order to **help**
them 15 until they have occupied the land
west of the Jordan that the LORD your
God has given them. When he has given
safety to all the tribes of Israel, then you
may come back and settle here in your
own land east of the Jordan, which
Moses, the LORD's **servant**, gave to you."
16 They answered Joshua, "We will do

succeed (1) [2] Deut 29.9; 15.16
sure [3] Deut 32.40; 2.24
worship (1) (of God) Deut 31.11; 5.14

1.3–5: Deut 11.24–25 **1.5:** Deut 31.6, 8; Heb 13.5 **1.6:** Deut 31.6, 7, 23
1.12–15: Num 32.28–32; Deut 3.18–20; Josh 22.1–6

everything you have told us and will go wherever you send us. 17 We will **obey** you, just as we always obeyed Moses, and may the LORD your God be with you as he was with Moses! 18 Whoever **questions** your **authority** or **disobeys** any of your orders will be put **to death**. Be **determined** and **confident**!"

Joshua Sends Spies into Jericho

above Gen 49.25; 2 Sam 22.17
afraid 1.9; 5.1
agree Deut 10.10; 7.11
courage Deut 31.8; 5.1
death (1) 1.1; 20.6
fault Ex 5.16; 1 Sam 29.3
harm Deut 19.16; 9.19
heaven Deut 31.28; Judg 13.20
kind Num 6.25; Ruth 2.10
life (1) Deut 32.18; 4.14
promise [4] 1.6; 5.4
prostitute Deut 23.17; 6.17
save Deut 33.29; 10.6
secret Deut 29.29; Judg 3.19
sign (1) Num 6.6; 22.27
sure 1.7; 3.10
swear Num 32.11; 5.4
terrify [2] Deut 34.12; 9.24
trust Deut 32.37; 1 Sam 27.12
word (1) Deut 32.1; 6.10

2 Then Joshua sent two spies from the camp at Acacia with orders to go and **secretly** explore the land of Canaan, especially the city of Jericho. When they came to the city, they went to spend the night in the house of a **prostitute** named Rahab. 2 The king of Jericho heard that some Israelites had come that night to spy out the country, 3 so he sent **word** to Rahab: "The men in your house have come to spy out the whole country! Bring them out!"

4-6 "Some men did come to my house," she answered, "but I don't know where they were from. They left at sunset before the city gate was closed. I didn't find out where they were going, but if you start after them quickly, you can catch them." (Now Rahab had taken the two spies up on the roof and hidden them under some stalks of flax that she had put there.) 7 The king's men left the city, and then the gate was shut. They went looking for the Israelite spies as far as the place where the road crosses the Jordan.

8 Before the spies settled down for the night, Rahab went up on the roof 9 and said to them, "I know that the LORD has given you this land. Everyone in the country is **terrified** of you. 10 We have heard how the LORD dried up the Red Sea in front of you when you were leaving Egypt. We have also heard how you killed Sihon and Og, the two Amorite kings east of the Jordan. 11 We were **afraid** as soon as we heard about it; we have all lost our **courage** because of you. The LORD your God is God in **heaven above** and here on earth. 12 Now **swear** by him that you will treat my family as **kindly** as I have treated you, and give me some **sign** that I can **trust** you. 13 **Promise** me that you will **save** my father and mother, my brothers and sisters, and all their families! Don't let us be killed!"

14 The men said to her, "May God take our **lives** if we don't do as we say![a] If you do not tell anyone what we have been doing, we **promise** you that when the LORD gives us this land, we will treat you well."

15 Rahab lived in a house built into the city wall, so she let the men down from the window by a rope. 16 "Go into the hill-country," she said, "or the king's men will find you. Hide there for three days until they come back. After that you can go on your way."

17 The men said to her, "We will keep the **promise** that you have made us give. 18 This is what you must do. When we invade your land, tie this red cord to the window you let us down from. Get your father and mother, your brothers, and all your father's family together in your house. 19 If anyone goes out of the house, his **death** will be his own **fault**, and we will not be responsible; but if anyone in the house with you is **harmed**, then we will be responsible. 20 However, if you tell anyone what we have been doing, then we will not have to keep our **promise** which you have made us give you." 21 She **agreed** and sent them away. When they had gone, she tied the red cord to the window.

22 The spies went into the hills and hid. The king's men looked for them all over the countryside for three days, but they did not find them, so they returned to Jericho. 23 Then the two spies came down from the hills, crossed the river, and went back to Joshua. They told him everything that had happened, 24 and then said, "We are **sure** that the LORD has given us the whole country. All the people there are **terrified** of us."

The People of Israel Cross the Jordan

choose Deut 32.9; 4.2
Covenant Box [8] Deut 31.9; 4.5
flood Gen 49.4; 4.18
harvest Deut 28.38; Judg 15.1
honour Deut 31.12; 4.14
miracle Deut 34.11; 24.17
priest [7] Deut 31.9; 4.3
pure Num 35.33; 7.13
sure 2.24; 22.5

3 The next morning Joshua and all the people of Israel got up early, left the camp at Acacia, and went to the Jordan, where they camped while waiting to cross it. 2 Three days later the leaders went through the camp 3 and said to the people, "When you see the **priests** carrying the **Covenant Box** of the LORD your God, break camp and follow them. 4 You have never been here before, so they will show you the way to go. But do not get near the **Covenant Box**; stay about a kilometre behind it."

5 Joshua said to the people, "**Purify** yourselves, because tomorrow the LORD will perform **miracles** among you." 6 Then he told the **priests** to take the **Covenant Box** and go with it ahead of the people. They did as he said.

7 The LORD said to Joshua, "What I do today will make all the people of Israel

[a] May God...say; *or* We will protect you if you protect us.

2.1: Heb 11.31; Jas 2.25 **2.10:** Ex 14.21; Num 21.21-35

begin to **honour** you as a great man, and
they will realize that I am with you as I
was with Moses. 8 Tell the **priests**
carrying the **Covenant Box** that when
they reach the river, they must wade in
and stand near the bank."
9 Then Joshua said to the people,
"Come here and listen to what the LORD
your God has to say. 10 As you advance,
he will **surely** drive out the Canaanites,
the Hittites, the Hivites, the Perizzites,
the Girgashites, the Amorites, and the
Jebusites. You will know that the living
God is among you 11 when the **Covenant
Box** of the Lord of all the earth crosses
the Jordan ahead of you. 12 Now **choose**
twelve men, one from each of the tribes
of Israel. 13 When the **priests** who carry
the **Covenant Box** of the LORD of all the
earth put their feet in the water, the
Jordan will stop flowing, and the water
coming downstream will pile up in one
place."
14–15 It was **harvest** time, and the
river was in **flood**.

When the people left the camp to cross
the Jordan, the **priests** went ahead of
them, carrying the **Covenant Box**. As
soon as the **priests** stepped into the river,
16 the water stopped flowing and piled up,
far upstream at Adam, the city beside
Zarethan. The flow downstream to the
Dead Sea was completely cut off, and the
people were able to cross over near
Jericho. 17 While the people walked
across on dry ground, the **priests** carrying the LORD's **Covenant Box** stood on
dry ground in the middle of the Jordan
until all the people had crossed over.

Memorial Stones Are Set Up

4 When the whole nation had crossed
the Jordan, the LORD said to Joshua,
2 "**Choose** twelve men, one from each
tribe, 3 and **command** them to take
twelve stones out of the middle of the
Jordan, from the very place where the
priests were standing. Tell them to carry
these stones with them and to put them
down where you camp tonight."
4 Then Joshua called the twelve men
he had **chosen**, 5 and said, "Go into the
Jordan ahead of the **Covenant Box** of the
LORD your God. Each one of you take a
stone on your shoulder, one for each of
the tribes of Israel. 6 These stones will
remind the people of what the LORD has
done. In the future, when your children
ask what these stones mean to you, 7 you
will tell them that the water of the Jordan stopped flowing when the LORD's
Covenant Box crossed the river. These
stones will always **remind** the people of
Israel of what happened here."
8 The men followed Joshua's orders.
As the LORD had **commanded** Joshua,
they took twelve stones from the middle
of the Jordan, one for each of the tribes
of Israel, carried them to the camping
place, and put them down there. 9 Joshua
also set up twelve stones in the middle of
the Jordan, where the **priests** carrying
the **Covenant Box** had stood. (Those
stones are still there.) 10 The **priests** stood
in the middle of the Jordan until
everything had been done that the LORD
ordered Joshua to tell the people to do.
This is what Moses had **commanded**.

The people hurried across the river.
11 When they were all on the other side,
the **priests** with the LORD's **Covenant Box**
went on ahead of the people. 12 The men
of the tribes of Reuben and Gad and of
half the tribe of Manasseh, ready for
battle, crossed ahead of the rest of the
people, as Moses had told them to do.
13 In the **presence** of the LORD about forty
thousand men ready for war crossed
over to the plain near Jericho. 14 What
the LORD did that day made the people of
Israel consider Joshua a great man. They
honoured him all his **life**, just as they had
honoured Moses.
15 Then the LORD told Joshua 16 to
command the **priests** carrying the
Covenant Box to come up out of the
Jordan. 17 Joshua did so, 18 and when the
priests reached the river bank, the river
began flowing once more and **flooded** its
banks again.
19 The people crossed the Jordan on
the tenth day of the first month and
made camp at Gilgal, east of Jericho.
20 There Joshua set up the twelve stones
taken from the Jordan. 21 He said to the
people of Israel, "In the future, when
your children ask you what these stones
mean, 22 you will tell them about the time
when Israel crossed the Jordan on dry
ground. 23 Tell them that the LORD your
God dried up the water of the Jordan for
you until you had crossed, just as he
dried up the Red Sea for us. 24 Because of
this everyone on earth will know how
great the **LORD's power** is, and you will
honour the LORD your God for ever."

5 All the Amorite kings west of the
Jordan and all the Canaanite kings
along the Mediterranean Sea heard that
the LORD had dried up the Jordan until
the people of Israel had crossed it. They
became **afraid** and lost their **courage**
because of the Israelites.

choose [2] 3.12; 9.27
command [4] 1.9; 5.3
Covenant Box [5] 3.3; 6.4
flood 3.14; Judg 5.21
honour [2] 3.7; 7.9
life (1) 2.14; 6.25
power Deut 28.43; 9.25
presence Deut 32.51; 7.23
priest [6] 3.3; 6.4
remind [2] Deut 11.18; 1 Sam 12.7

afraid 2.11; 7.5
bread Deut 29.6; 9.5
circumcise [7] Lev 12.3; Jer 9.25
command 4.3; 7.1
complete Lev 12.4; 1 Kgs 7.22
courage 2.11; 7.5
disgrace Deut 27.20; 1 Sam 11.2

disobey 1.18; 7.1
enemy Deut 33.7; 7.8
heal Deut 32.39; 1 Sam 6.3
holy Deut 26.15; 24.19
manna Deut 8.3; Neh 9.20
new Deut 32.17; 9.13
observe Deut 15.5; 2 Sam 22.23
Passover Deut 16.1; 2 Kgs 23.21
promise 2.13; 6.22
rich Deut 33.14; 22.6
servant 1.1; 8.31
slave Deut 28.32; 6.23
swear 2.12; Judg 8.19
unleavened Deut 16.3; 1 Sam 28.24
worship (1) (of God) 1.8; 9.27
yeast Deut 16.3; Judg 6.19

The Circumcision at Gilgal

2 Then the LORD told Joshua, "Make some knives out of flint and **circumcise** the Israelites." 3 So Joshua did as the LORD had **commanded**, and he circumcised the Israelites at a place called **Circumcision Hill**. 4-6 When the people of Israel left Egypt, all the males were already **circumcised**. However, during the forty years the people spent crossing the desert, none of the baby boys had been **circumcised**. Also, by the end of that time all the men who were of fighting age when they left Egypt had died because they had **disobeyed** the LORD. Just as he had **sworn**, they were not allowed to see the **rich** and fertile **land that he had promised** their ancestors. 7 The sons of these men had never been **circumcised**, and it was this **new** generation that Joshua **circumcised**.

8 After the **circumcision** was **completed**, the whole nation stayed in the camp until the wounds had **healed**. 9 The LORD said to Joshua, "Today I have removed from you the **disgrace** of being **slaves** in Egypt." That is why the place was named Gilgal,[b] the name it still has.

10 While the Israelites were camping at Gilgal on the plain near Jericho, they **observed Passover** on the evening of the fourteenth day of the month. 11 The next day was the first time they ate food grown in Canaan: roasted grain and **bread** made **without yeast**. 12 The **manna** stopped falling then, and the Israelites no longer had any. From that time on they ate food grown in Canaan.

Joshua and the Man with a Sword

13 While Joshua was near Jericho, he suddenly saw a man standing in front of him, holding a sword. Joshua went up to him and asked, "Are you one of our soldiers, or an **enemy**?"

14 "Neither," the man answered. "I am here as the commander of the LORD's army."

Joshua threw himself on the ground in **worship** and said, "I am your **servant**, sir. What do you want me to do?"

15 And the commander of the LORD's army told him, "Take your sandals off; you are standing on **holy** ground." And Joshua did as he was told.

apart Num 16.9; Judg 14.6
Covenant Box [6] 4.5; 7.6
curse Deut 30.1; 8.34

The Fall of Jericho

6 The gates of Jericho were kept shut and guarded to keep the Israelites out. No one could enter or leave the city. 2 The LORD said to Joshua, "I am putting into your hands Jericho, with its king and all its brave soldiers. 3 You and your soldiers are to march round the city once a day for six days. 4 Seven **priests**, each carrying a trumpet, are to go in front of the **Covenant Box**. On the seventh day you and your soldiers are to march round the city seven times while the **priests** blow the trumpets. 5 Then they are to sound one long note. As soon as you hear it, all the men are to give a loud shout, and the city walls will collapse. Then the whole army will go straight into the city."

6 Joshua called the **priests** and said to them, "Take the **Covenant Box**, and seven of you go in front of it, carrying trumpets." 7 Then he ordered his men to start marching round the city, with an advance guard going on ahead of the LORD's **Covenant Box**.

8–9 So, just as Joshua had ordered, an advance guard started out ahead of the **priests** who were blowing trumpets; behind these came the **priests** who were carrying the **Covenant Box**, followed by a rearguard. All this time the trumpets were sounding. 10 But Joshua had ordered his men not to shout, not to say a **word** until he gave the order. 11 So he told this group of men to take the LORD's **Covenant Box** round the city once. Then they came back to camp and spent the night there.

12–13 Joshua got up early the next morning, and for the second time the **priests** and soldiers marched round the city in the same order as the day before: first, the advance guard; next, the seven **priests** blowing the seven trumpets; then, the **priests** carrying the LORD's **Covenant Box**; and finally, the rearguard. All this time the trumpets were sounding. 14 On this second day they again marched round the city once and then returned to camp. They did this for six days.

15 On the seventh day they got up at daybreak and marched seven times round the city in the same way—this was the only day that they marched round it seven times. 16 The seventh time round, when the **priests** were about to sound the trumpets, Joshua ordered his men to shout, and he said, "The LORD has given you the city! 17 The city and everything in it must be totally **destroyed** as an **offering** to the LORD. Only the **prostitute** Rahab and her household will be **spared**, because she hid our spies. 18 But you are not to take anything that is to be **destroyed**; if you do, you will bring

destroy [3] Deut 33.27; 7.1
life (1) 4.14; 9.24
offer Deut 33.10; 8.31
priest [10] 4.3; 8.33
promise 5.4; 9.15
prostitute [3] 2.1; Judg 11.1
safe 1.15; 10.20
serve Deut 32.36; 18.7
sheep Deut 32.14; 7.24
slave 5.9; 9.23
solemn Deut 29.19; 9.15
spare [2] Deut 32.25; 10.30
trouble Deut 28.20; 7.24
warn Deut 30.18; 1 Sam 8.9
word (1) 2.3; 10.6

[b] GILGAL: *This name sounds like the Hebrew for "removed."*

5.6: Num 14.28–35 **5.10:** Ex 12.1–13 **5.12:** Ex 16.35

trouble and **destruction** on the Israelite camp. 19 Everything made of silver, gold, bronze, or iron is set **apart** for the LORD. It is to be put in the LORD's treasury."

20 So the **priests** blew the trumpets. As soon as the men heard it, they gave a loud shout, and the walls collapsed. Then all the army went straight up the hill into the city and captured it. 21 With their swords they killed everyone in the city, men and women, young and old. They also killed the cattle, **sheep**, and donkeys.

22 Joshua then told the two men who had **served** as spies, "Go into the **prostitute's** house and bring her and her family out, as you **promised** her." 23 So they went and brought Rahab out, along with her father and mother, her brothers, and the rest of her family. They took them all, family and **slaves**, to **safety** near the Israelite camp. 24 Then they set fire to the city and burnt it to the ground, along with everything in it, except the things made of gold, silver, bronze, and iron, which they took and put in the LORD's treasury. 25 But Joshua **spared** the **lives** of the **prostitute** Rahab and all her relatives, because she had hidden the two spies that he had sent to Jericho. (Her descendants have lived in Israel to this day.)

26 At that time Joshua issued a **solemn warning**: "Anyone who tries to rebuild the city of Jericho will be under the LORD's **curse**.

Whoever lays the foundation will lose
his eldest son;
Whoever builds the gates will lose his
youngest."

27 So the LORD was with Joshua, and his fame spread through the whole country.

Achan's Sin

7 The LORD's **command** to Israel not to take from Jericho anything that was to be **destroyed** was not **obeyed**. A man named Achan **disobeyed** that order, and so the LORD was **furious** with the Israelites. (Achan was the son of Carmi and grandson of Zabdi, and belonged to the clan of Zerah, a part of the tribe of Judah.)

2 Joshua sent some men from Jericho to Ai, a city east of Bethel, near Bethaven, with orders to go and explore the land. When they had done so, 3 they reported back to Joshua: "There is no **need** for everyone to attack Ai. Send only about two or three thousand men. Don't send the whole army up there to fight; it is not a large city." 4 So about three thousand Israelites made the attack, but they were **forced** to retreat. 5 The men of Ai chased them from the city gate as far as some quarries and killed about thirty-six of them on the way down the hill. Then the Israelites lost their **courage** and were **afraid**.

6 Joshua and the leaders of Israel tore their clothes in **grief**, threw themselves to the ground before the LORD's **Covenant Box**, and lay there till evening, with dust on their heads to show their **sorrow**. 7 And Joshua said, "**Sovereign** LORD! Why did you bring us across the Jordan at all? To hand us over to the Amorites? To **destroy** us? Why didn't we just stay on the other side of the Jordan? 8 What can I say, O Lord, now that Israel has retreated from the **enemy**? 9 The Canaanites and everyone else in the country will hear about it. They will surround us and kill every one of us! And then what will you do to **protect** your **honour**?"

10 The LORD said to Joshua, "Get up! Why are you lying on the ground like this? 11 Israel has sinned! They have broken the **agreement** with me that I ordered them to keep. They have taken some of the things **condemned** to **destruction**. They **stole** them, **lied** about it, and put them with their own things. 12 This is why the Israelites cannot stand against their **enemies**. They retreat from them because they themselves have now been **condemned** to **destruction**! I will not stay with you any longer unless you **destroy** the things you were ordered not to take! 13 Get up! **Purify** the people and get them ready to come before me. Tell them to be ready tomorrow, because I, the LORD God of Israel, have this to say: 'Israel, you have in your **possession** some things that I ordered you to **destroy**! You cannot stand against your **enemies** until you get **rid** of these things!' 14 So tell them that in the morning they will be brought forward, tribe by tribe. The tribe that I pick out will then come forward, clan by clan. The clan that I pick out will come forward, family by family. The family that I pick out will come forward, man by man. 15 The one who is then picked out and found with the **condemned** goods will be burnt, along with his family and everything he owns, for he has brought **terrible shame** on Israel and has broken my **covenant**."

16 Early the next morning Joshua brought Israel forward, tribe by tribe, and the tribe of Judah was picked out. 17 He brought the tribe of Judah forward,

6.20: Heb 11.30 **6.25:** Heb 11.31 **6.26:** 1 Kgs 16.34

afraid 5.1; 8.1
agree 2.21; Judg 11.10
command 5.3; 8.8
condemn [4] Deut 13.17; 9.23
confess Num 5.7; 1 Kgs 8.47
courage 5.1; Judg 7.11
covenant Deut 33.9; 23.16
Covenant Box 6.4; 8.33
death (3) (to death) 1.18; 10.28
destroy [6] 6.17; 10.1
disobey 5.4; 22.23
enemy [3] 5.13; 8.24
force (1) Deut 26.6; 16.10
fury [2] Deut 29.23; Judg 2.14
grief Judg 11.37
honour 4.14; 24.14
lie (2) Num 23.19; 1 Sam 15.29

need Deut 29.6; 1
obey 1.7; 10.14
possess [2] Deut 33.4; 12.6
presence 4.13; 10
protect Deut 33.3 9.26
pure 3.5; 1 Sam 1
rid Deut 24.7; 24.
shame Deut 22.2 1 Kgs 14.24
sheep 6.21; Judg
sorrow Num 14.6 Judg 11.35
Sovereign Deut Judg 6.22
steal Deut 5.19; Judg 17.2
terrible Deut 32. 1 Sam 3.11
trouble [4] 6.18; 1
true Deut 33.8; 9.
truth Num 5.15; Judg 16.10

clan by clan, and the clan of Zerah was picked out. Then he brought the clan of Zerah forward, family by family, and the family of Zabdi was picked out. 18 He then brought Zabdi's family forward, man by man, and Achan, the son of Carmi and grandson of Zabdi, was picked out. 19 Joshua said to him, "My son, tell the **truth** here before the LORD, the God of Israel, and **confess**. Tell me now what you have done. Don't try to hide it from me."

20 "It's **true**," Achan answered. "I have sinned against the LORD, Israel's God, and this is what I did. 21 Among the things we seized I saw a beautiful Babylonian cloak, about two kilogrammes of silver, and a bar of gold weighing over half a kilogramme. I wanted them so much that I took them. You will find them buried inside my tent, with the silver at the bottom."

22 So Joshua sent some men, who ran to the tent and found that the **condemned** things really were buried there, with the silver at the bottom. 23 They brought them out of the tent, took them to Joshua and all the Israelites, and laid them down in the **presence** of the LORD. 24 Joshua, along with all the people of Israel, seized Achan, the silver, the cloak, and the bar of gold, together with Achan's sons and daughters, his cattle, donkeys, and **sheep**, his tent, and everything else he owned; and they took them to **Trouble** Valley. 25 And Joshua said, "Why have you brought such **trouble** on us? The LORD will now bring **trouble** on you!" All the people then stoned Achan **to death**; they also stoned and burnt his family and **possessions**. 26 They put a huge pile of stones over him, which is there to this day. That is why that place is still called **Trouble** Valley.

Then the LORD was no longer **furious**.

The Capture and Destruction of Ai

8 The LORD said to Joshua, "Take all the soldiers with you and go on up to Ai. Don't be **afraid** or **discouraged**. I will give you **victory** over the king of Ai; his people, city, and land will be yours. 2 You are to do to Ai and its king what you did to Jericho and its king, but this time you may keep its goods and livestock for yourselves. Prepare to attack the city by surprise from the rear."

3 So Joshua got ready to go to Ai with all his soldiers. He picked out thirty thousand of his **best** troops and sent them out at night 4 with these orders: "Hide on the other side of the city, but not too far away from it; be ready to attack. 5 My men and I will approach the city. When the men of Ai come out against us, we will **turn** and run, just as we did the first time. 6 They will pursue us until we have led them away from the city. They will think that we are running away from them, as we did before. 7 Then you will come out of hiding and capture the city. The LORD your God will give it to you. 8 After you have taken the city, set it on fire, just as the LORD has **commanded**. These are your orders." 9 So Joshua sent them out, and they went to their hiding place and waited there, west of Ai, between Ai and Bethel. Joshua spent the night in camp.

10 Early in the morning Joshua got up and called the soldiers together. Then he and the leaders of Israel led them to Ai. 11 The soldiers with him went towards the main entrance to the city and set up camp on the north side, with a valley between themselves and Ai. 12 He took about five thousand men and put them in hiding west of the city, between Ai and Bethel. 13 The soldiers were arranged for battle with the main camp north of the city and the rest of the men to the west. Joshua spent the night in the valley. 14 When the king of Ai saw Joshua's men, he **acted** quickly. He and all his men went out towards the Jordan Valley to fight the Israelites at the same place as before, not knowing that he was about to be attacked from the rear. 15 Joshua and his men pretended that they were retreating, and ran away towards the **barren** country. 16 All the men in the city had been called together to go after them, and as they pursued Joshua, they kept getting farther away from the city. 17 Every man in Ai[c] went after the Israelites, and the city was left wide open, with no one to **defend** it.

18 Then the LORD said to Joshua, "Point your spear at Ai; I am giving it to you." Joshua did as he was told, 19 and as soon as he lifted his hand, the men who had been hiding got up quickly, ran into the city and captured it. They immediately set the city on fire. 20 When the men of Ai looked back, they saw the smoke **rising** to the sky. There was no way for them to **escape**, because the Israelites who had run towards the **barren** country now **turned** round to attack them. 21 When Joshua and his men saw that the others had taken the city and that it was on fire, they **turned** round and began killing the men of Ai. 22 The Israelites in the city now came down to

[c] *One ancient translation* Ai; *Hebrew* Ai and Bethel.

act Deut 17.13; Judg 15.7
afraid 7.5; 10.8
altar [2] Deut 33.10; 9.27
barren [3] Deut 29.23; Judg 1.16
best Deut 33.14; 10.7
bless [2] Deut 33.1; 14.13
body [2] Deut 28.26; 10.26
burnt-offering Num 29.2; 1 Sam 6.14
command [2] 7.1; 9.24
commandment Deut 10.4; 22.5
Covenant Box 7.6; Judg 20.27
curse 6.26; 24.9

defend Deut 33.27; Judg 6.31
discourage 1.9; 10.25
enemy 7.8; 10.13
escape Deut 19.2; 10.16
fellowship-offering Deut 27.7; 22.23
get away Judg 3.26
hang (2) Deut 21.22; 10.26
judge Deut 28.46; 20.4
law [4] 1.7; 22.5
Levites Deut 33.8; 14.3
offer 6.17; 13.33
present (1) Deut 17.9; 2 Sam 4.8
priest 6.4; 14.1
rise Deut 33.2; Judg 5.31
ruin Deut 28.63; 2 Sam 16.8
sacrifice Deut 33.10; 13.14
servant [2] 5.14; 9.24
turn [3] Deut 31.20; 10.38
victory Deut 33.29; 9.1

join the battle. So the men of Ai found themselves completely surrounded by Israelites, and they were all killed. No one **got away**, and no one lived through it 23 except the king of Ai. He was captured and taken to Joshua.

24 The Israelites killed every one of the **enemy** in the **barren** country where they had chased them. Then they went back to Ai and killed everyone there. 25-26 Joshua kept his spear pointed at Ai and did not put it down until every person there had been killed. The whole population of Ai was killed that day—twelve thousand men and women. 27 The Israelites kept for themselves the livestock and goods captured in the city, as the LORD had told Joshua. 28 Joshua burnt Ai and left it in **ruins**. It is still like that today. 29 He **hanged** the king of Ai from a tree and left his **body** there until evening. At sunset Joshua gave orders for the **body** to be removed, and it was thrown down at the entrance to the city gate. They covered it with a huge pile of stones, which is still there today.

The Law Is Read at Mount Ebal

30 Then Joshua built on Mount Ebal an **altar** to the LORD, the God of Israel. 31 He made it according to the instructions that Moses, the LORD's **servant**, had given the Israelites, as it says in the **Law of Moses**: "an **altar** made of stones which have not been cut with iron tools." On it they **offered burnt sacrifices** to the LORD, and they also **presented** their **fellowship-offerings**. 32 There, with the Israelites looking on, Joshua made on the stones[d] a copy of the **Law** which Moses had written. 33 The Israelites, with their leaders, officers, and **judges**, as well as the foreigners among them, stood on two sides of the LORD's **Covenant Box**, facing the **levitical priests** who carried it. Half the people stood with their backs to Mount Gerizim and the other half with their backs to Mount Ebal. The LORD's **servant** Moses had **commanded** them to do this when the time came for them to receive the **blessing**. 34 Joshua then read aloud the whole **Law**, including the **blessings** and the **curses**, just as they are written in the book of the **Law**. 35 Every one of the **commandments** of Moses was read by Joshua to the whole gathering, which included women and children, as well as the foreigners living among them.

The Gibeonites Deceive Joshua

9 The **victories** of Israel became known to all the kings west of the Jordan—in the hills, in the foothills, and all along the coastal plain of the Mediterranean Sea as far north as Lebanon; these were the kings of the Hittites, the Amorites, the Canaanites, the Perizzites, the Hivites, and the Jebusites. 2 They all came together and joined forces to fight against Joshua and the Israelites.

3 But the people of Gibeon, who were Hivites, heard what Joshua had done to Jericho and Ai, 4 and they decided to **deceive** him. They went and got some food and loaded their donkeys with worn-out sacks and patched-up wineskins. 5 They put on ragged clothes and worn-out sandals that had been mended. The **bread** they took with them was dry and mouldy. 6 Then they went to the camp at Gilgal and said to Joshua and the men of Israel, "We have come from a distant land. We want you to make a treaty with us."

7 But the men of Israel said, "Why should we make a treaty with you? Maybe you live nearby."

8 They said to Joshua, "We are at your **service**."

Joshua asked them, "Who are you? Where do you come from?"

9 Then they told him this story: "We have come from a very distant land, sir, because we have heard of the LORD your God. We have heard about everything that he did in Egypt 10 and what he did to the two Amorite kings east of the Jordan: King Sihon of Heshbon and King Og of Bashan, who lived in Ashtaroth. 11 Our leaders and all the people that live in our land told us to get some food ready for a journey and to go and meet you. We were told to put ourselves at your **service** and ask you to make a treaty with us. 12 Look at our **bread**. When we left home with it and started out to meet you, it was still warm. But look! Now it is dry and mouldy. 13 When we filled these wineskins, they were **new**, but look! They are torn. Our clothes and sandals are worn out from the long journey."

14 The men of Israel **accepted** some food from them, but did not **consult** the LORD about it. 15 Joshua made a treaty of **friendship** with the people of Gibeon and allowed them to live. The leaders of the **community** of Israel gave their **solemn promise** to keep the treaty.

16 Three days after the treaty had

accept Deut 29.12; Judg 13.23
altar 8.30; 13.14
bread [2] 5.11; Judg 6.19
choose 4.2; 20.2
command 8.8; 10.4
community Deut 26.12; 18.1
complain Deut 1.3 Judg 8.1
condemn 7.11; 10.3
consult Deut 18.11; 18.6
deceive [2] Deut 32.5; 2 Sam 3.
fear Deut 28.66; 1 Sam 4.13
friend Deut 13.6; Judg 5.31
harm 2.19; 1 Sam 20.7
learn [2] Deut 31.1 Judg 4.12
life (1) 6.25; Judg 5.18
name (2) (name of God, of Jesus) [2] Deut 32.3; 1 Sam 17.45
new 5.7; Judg 2.17
power 4.24; 11.10
promise [4] 6.22; 14
protect 7.9; 20.5
punish Deut 32.34; 22.17
right (1) Deut 33.1 1 Sam 2.16
sanctuary 24.26
servant 8.31; 11.12
service [2] Deut 24 1 Sam 2.21
slave [2] 6.23; 16.10
solemn [3] 6.26; 21.
terrify 2.9; 1 Sam 5
true 7.20; Judg 11.1
victory 8.1; 10.8
worship (1) (of Go 5.14; 22.19

[d] the stones; *or* stones.

8.30-32: Deut 27.2-8 **8.31:** Ex 20.25 **8.33-35:** Deut 11.29, 27.11-14 **9.7:** Ex 23.32, 34.12; Deut 7.2
9.10: Num 21.21-35

been made, the Israelites **learnt** that
these people did indeed live nearby. [17] So
the people of Israel started out and three
days later arrived at the cities where
these people lived: Gibeon, Chephirah,
Beeroth, and Kiriath Jearim. [18] But the
Israelites could not kill them, because
their leaders had made a **solemn promise** to them in the **name of the LORD**,
Israel's God. All the people **complained**
to the leaders about this, [19] but they
answered, "We have made our **solemn
promise** to them in the **name of the LORD**
God of Israel. Now we cannot **harm**
them. [20] We must let them live because of
our **promise**; if we don't, God will **punish**
us. [21] Let them live, but they will have to
cut wood and carry water for us." This
was what the leaders suggested.

22 Joshua ordered the people of
Gibeon to be brought to him, and he
asked them, "Why did you **deceive** us and
tell us that you were from far away,
when you live right here? [23] Because you
did this, God has **condemned** you. Your
people will always be **slaves**, cutting
wood and carrying water for the
sanctuary of my God."

24 They answered, "We did it, sir,
because we **learnt** that it was really **true**
that the LORD your God had **commanded**
his **servant** Moses to give you the whole
land and to kill the people living in it as
you advanced. We did it because we
were **terrified** of you; we were in **fear** of
our **lives**. [25] Now we are in your **power**;
do with us what you think is **right**." [26] So
this is what Joshua did: he **protected**
them and did not allow the people of
Israel to kill them. [27] But at the same
time he made them **slaves**, to cut wood
and carry water for the people of Israel
and for the LORD's **altar**. To this day they
have continued to do this work in the
place where the LORD has **chosen** to be
worshipped.

The Amorites Are Defeated

10 Adonizedek, the king of Jerusalem,[e] heard that Joshua had
captured and totally **destroyed** Ai and
had killed its king, just as he had done to
Jericho and its king. He also heard that
the people of Gibeon had made **peace**
with the Israelites and were living
among them. [2] The people of Jerusalem
were greatly alarmed at this because
Gibeon was as large as any of the cities
that had a king; it was larger than Ai,
and its men were good fighters. [3] So
Adonizedek sent the following **message**
to King Hoham of Hebron, King Piram of
Jarmuth, King Japhia of Lachish, and to
King Debir of Eglon: [4] "Come and **help**
me attack Gibeon, because its people
have made **peace** with Joshua and the
Israelites." [5] These five Amorite kings,
the kings of Jerusalem, Hebron, Jarmuth,
Lachish, and Eglon, joined forces,
surrounded Gibeon, and attacked it.

6 The men of Gibeon sent **word** to
Joshua at the camp in Gilgal: "Do not
abandon us, sir! Come at once and **help**
us! **Save** us! All the Amorite kings in the
hill-country have joined forces and have
attacked us!"

7 So Joshua and his whole army, including the **best** troops, started out from
Gilgal. [8] The LORD said to Joshua, "Do not
be **afraid** of them. I have already given
you the **victory**. Not one of them will be
able to stand against you." [9] All night
Joshua and his army marched from Gilgal to Gibeon, and they made a surprise
attack on the Amorites. [10] The LORD
made the Amorites panic at the **sight** of
Israel's army. The Israelites **slaughtered**
them at Gibeon and pursued them down
the mountain pass at Beth Horon,
keeping up the attack as far south as
Azekah and Makkedah. [11] While the
Amorites were running down the pass
from the Israelite army, the LORD made
large hailstones fall down on them all the
way to Azekah. More were killed by the
hailstones than by the Israelites.

12 On the day that the LORD gave the
men of Israel **victory** over the Amorites,
Joshua spoke to the LORD. In the
presence of the Israelites he said,

"Sun, stand still over Gibeon;
Moon, stop over Aijalon Valley."

[13] The sun stood still and the moon did not
move until the nation had **conquered** its
enemies. This is written in *The Book of
Jashar*. The sun stood still in the middle
of the sky and did not go down for a
whole day. [14] Never before, and never
since, has there been a day like it, when
the LORD **obeyed** a **human being**. The
LORD fought on Israel's side!

15 After this, Joshua and his army
went back to the camp at Gilgal.

Joshua Captures the Five Amorite Kings

16 The five Amorite kings, however,
had **escaped** and were hiding in the cave
at Makkedah. [17] Someone found them,
and Joshua was told where they were
hiding. [18] He said, "Roll some big stones
in front of the entrance to the cave.

[e] JERUSALEM: *At that time it was a Jebusite city.*

10.13: 2 Sam 1.18

abandon 1.5; Judg 5.7
afraid [2] 8.1; 11.6
alive [3] Deut 24.6; 11.8
being Deut 5.26; Job 1.6
best 8.3; Judg 3.29
body [2] 8.29; 24.32
command 9.24; 11.9
condemn 9.23; 11.20
confident 1.6; Judg 9.26
conquer [3] Num 32.29; 11.19
dare Deut 18.20; 1 Sam 17.10
death (3) (to death) [4] 7.25; 11.11
destroy [2] 7.1; 11.20
determine 1.6; 11.20
discourage 8.1; 2 Sam 17.2
enemy [3] 8.24; 11.8
escape 8.20; 20.3
hang (2) 8.29; 2 Sam 17.23
help [2] 1.1; 24.7
human Deut 5.26; 1 Kgs 8.39
message Deut 18.20; Judg 3.19
obey 7.1; 11.15
peace [2] Deut 33.28; 11.19
presence 7.23; 24.1
safe [2] 6.23; 24.17
save 2.13; 22.31
sight Deut 34.7; 1 Sam 2.17
slaughter [2] Deut 16.2; Judg 11.33
spare [3] 6.17; 1 Sam 15.9
turn 8.5; 11.10
victory [5] 9.1; 11.1
word (1) 6.10; 11.1

Place some guards there, [19]but don't stay there yourselves. Keep on after the **enemy** and attack them from the rear; don't let them get to their cities! The LORD your God has given you **victory** over them." [20]Joshua and the men of Israel **slaughtered** them, although some managed to find **safety** inside their city walls and were not killed. [21]Then all of Joshua's men came back **safe** to him at the camp at Makkedah.

No one in the land **dared** even to speak against the Israelites.

22 Then Joshua said, "Open the entrance to the cave and bring those five kings out to me." [23]So the cave was opened, and the kings of Jerusalem, Hebron, Jarmuth, Lachish, and Eglon were brought out [24]and taken to Joshua. Joshua then called all the men of Israel to him and ordered the officers who had gone with him to come and put their feet on the necks of the kings. They did so. [25]Then Joshua said to his officers, "Don't be **afraid** or **discouraged.** Be **determined** and **confident** because this is what the LORD is going to do to all your **enemies.**" [26]Then Joshua killed the kings and **hanged** them on five trees, where their **bodies** stayed until evening. [27]At sunset Joshua gave orders, and their **bodies** were taken down and thrown into the same cave where they had hidden earlier. Large stones were placed at the entrance to the cave, and they are still there.

Joshua Captures More Amorite Territory

28 Joshua attacked and captured Makkedah and its king that day. He put everyone in the city **to death**; no one was left **alive.** He did to the king of Makkedah what he had done to the king of Jericho.

29 After this, Joshua and his army went on from Makkedah to Libnah and attacked it. [30]The LORD also gave the Israelites **victory** over this city and its king. They **spared** no one, but killed every person in it. They did to the king what they had done to the king of Jericho.

31 After this, Joshua and his army went on from Libnah to Lachish, surrounded it and attacked it. [32]The LORD gave the Israelites **victory** over Lachish on the second day of the battle. Just as they had done at Libnah, they **spared** no one, but killed every person in the city. [33]King Horam of Gezer came to the aid of Lachish, but Joshua defeated him and his army and left none of them **alive.**

34 Next, Joshua and his army went on from Lachish to Eglon, surrounded it and attacked it. [35]They captured it the same day and put everyone there **to death**, just as they had done at Lachish.

36 After this, Joshua and his army went from Eglon up into the hills to Hebron, attacked it [37]and captured it. They killed the king and everyone else in the city as well as in the nearby towns. Joshua **condemned** the city to total **destruction,** just as he had done to Eglon. No one in it was left **alive.**

38 Then Joshua and his army **turned** back to Debir and attacked it. [39]He captured it, with its king and all the nearby towns. They put everyone there **to death.** Joshua did to Debir and its king what he had done to Hebron and to Libnah and its king.

40 Joshua **conquered** the whole land. He defeated the kings of the hill-country, the eastern slopes, and the western foothills, as well as those of the dry country in the south. He **spared** no one; everyone was put **to death.** This was what the LORD God of Israel had **commanded.** [41]Joshua's campaign took him from Kadesh Barnea in the south to Gaza near the coast, including all the area of Goshen, and as far north as Gibeon. [42]Joshua **conquered** all these kings and their territory in one campaign because the LORD, Israel's God, was fighting for Israel. [43]After this, Joshua and his army went back to the camp at Gilgal.

Joshua Defeats Jabin and His Allies

11 When the news of Israel's **victories** reached King Jabin of Hazor, he sent **word** to King Jobab of Madon, to the kings of Shimron and Achshaph, [2]and to the kings in the hill-country in the north, in the Jordan Valley south of Lake Galilee, in the foothills, and on the coast near Dor. [3]He also sent **word** to the Canaanites on both sides of the Jordan, to the Amorites, the Hittites, the Perizzites, and the Jebusites in the hill-country, as well as to the Hivites who lived at the foot of Mount Hermon in the land of Mizpah. [4]They came with all their soldiers—an army with as many men as there are grains of sand on the seashore. They also had many horses and chariots. [5]All these kings joined forces and came together and set up camp at Merom Brook to fight against Israel.

6 The LORD said to Joshua, "Do not be **afraid** of them. By this time tomorrow I will have killed all of them for Israel. You are to **cripple** their horses and burn their chariots." [7]So Joshua and all his

afraid 10.8; 14.8
alive [3] 10.28; 14.
command [6] 10.4
13.6
condemn 10.37; 22
conquer 10.13; 12.
cripple [2]
Deut 15.21; 2 Sam
death (3) (to deat
[4] 10.28; Judg 15.6
destroy [3] 10.1; 22
determine 10.25;
14.2
enemy 10.13; 21.44
mercy Deut 33.29;
Judg 2.18
obey 10.14; 14.8
peace 10.1; 14.15
power 9.25; 17.17
race (1) Deut 2.10;
14.12
rest (1) Deut 11.19
Ruth 2.7
servant [2] 9.24; 12
turn 10.38; 15.3
victory [2] 10.8; 21
word (1) [2] 10.6; 2

men attacked them by surprise at
Merom Brook. 8 The LORD gave the
Israelites **victory** over them; the Israelites attacked and pursued them as far
north as Misrephoth Maim and Sidon,
and as far east as the valley of Mizpah.
The fight continued until none of the
enemy was left **alive**. 9 Joshua did to
them what the LORD had **commanded**:
he **crippled** their horses and burnt their
chariots.
10 Joshua then **turned** back, captured
Hazor and killed its king. (At that time
Hazor was the most **powerful** of all those
kingdoms.) 11 They put everyone there **to**
death; no one was left **alive**, and the city
was burnt.
12 Joshua captured all these cities and
their kings, putting everyone **to death**,
just as Moses, the LORD's **servant**, had
commanded. 13 However, the Israelites
did not burn any of the cities built on
mounds, except Hazor, which Joshua did
burn. 14 The people of Israel took all the
valuables and livestock from these cities
and kept them for themselves. But they
put every person **to death**; no one was
left **alive**. 15 The LORD had given his **com-**
mands to his **servant** Moses, Moses had
given them to Joshua, and Joshua **obeyed**
them. He did everything that the LORD
had **commanded** Moses.

The Territory Taken by Joshua

16 Joshua captured all the land—the
hill-country and foothills, both north and
south, all the area of Goshen and the dry
country south of it, as well as the Jordan
Valley. 17-18 The territory extended from
Mount Halak in the south near Edom, as
far as Baalgad in the north, in the valley
of Lebanon south of Mount Hermon.
Joshua was at war with the kings of this
territory for a long time, but he captured
them all and put them **to death**. 19 The
only city that made **peace** with the
people of Israel was Gibeon, where some
of the Hivites lived. All the others were
conquered in battle. 20 The LORD had
made them **determined** to fight the
Israelites, so that they would **be con-**
demned to total **destruction** and all be
killed without **mercy**. This was what the
LORD had **commanded** Moses.
21 At this time Joshua went and **de-**
stroyed the **race** of giants called the Anakim who lived in the hill-country—in
Hebron, Debir, Anab, and in all the hill-
country of Judah and Israel. Joshua completely **destroyed** them and their cities.
22 None of the Anakim were left in the
land of Israel; a few, however, were left
in Gaza, Gath, and Ashdod.
23 Joshua captured the whole land, as
the LORD had **commanded** Moses. Joshua
gave it to the Israelites as their own and
divided it into portions, one for each
tribe.
So the people **rested** from war.

The Kings Defeated by Moses

12 The people of Israel had already
conquered and occupied the land
east of the Jordan, from the Arnon
Valley up the Jordan Valley and as far
north as Mount Hermon. They defeated
two kings. 2 One was Sihon, the Amorite
king who ruled at Heshbon. His kingdom
included half of Gilead: from Aroer (on
the edge of the valley of the Arnon) and
the city in[f] the middle of that valley, as
far as the River Jabbok, the border of
Ammon; 3 it included the Jordan Valley
from Lake Galilee south to Beth Jeshimoth (east of the Dead Sea) and on
towards the foot of Mount Pisgah.
4 They also defeated King Og of
Bashan, who was one of the **last** of the
Rephaim; he ruled at Ashtaroth and
Edrei. 5 His kingdom included Mount
Hermon, Salecah, and all of Bashan as
far as the boundaries of Geshur and
Maacah, as well as half of Gilead, as far
as the territory of King Sihon of Heshbon.
6 These two kings were defeated by
Moses and the people of Israel. Moses,
the LORD's **servant**, gave their land to the
tribes of Reuben and Gad and to half the
tribe of Manasseh, to be their **possession**.

conquer 11.19; 18.1
last (2) Deut 3.11; 13.12
possess [2] 7.13; 13.7
servant 11.12; 13.8

The Kings Defeated by Joshua

7 Joshua and the people of Israel
defeated all the kings in the territory
west of the Jordan, from Baalgad in the
valley of Lebanon to Mount Halak in the
south near Edom. Joshua divided this
land among the tribes and gave it to
them as a permanent **possession**. 8 This
portion included the hill-country, the
western foothills, the Jordan Valley and
its foothills, the eastern slopes, and the
dry country in the south. This land had
been the home of the Hittites, the
Amorites, the Canaanites, the Perizzites,
the Hivites, and the Jebusites. 9 The
people of Israel defeated the kings of the
following cities: Jericho, Ai (near
Bethel), 10 Jerusalem, Hebron, 11 Jarmuth,
Lachish, 12 Eglon, Gezer, 13 Debir, Geder,
14 Hormah, Arad, 15 Libnah, Adullam,
16 Makkedah, Bethel, 17 Tappuah, Hepher,
18 Aphek, Lasharon, 19 Madon, Hazor,

[f] *Probable text (see 13.16; Deut 2.36)* the city in; *Hebrew does not have these words.*

11.20: Deut 7.16 **12.1-5:** Num 21.21-35; Deut 2.26-3.11 **12.6:** Num 32.33; Deut 3.12

[20]Shimron Meron, Achshaph, [21]Taanach,
Megiddo, [22]Kedesh, Jokneam (in
Carmel), [23]Dor (on the coast), Goiim (in
Galilee[g]), [24]and Tirzah—thirty-one kings
in all.

The Land Still to Be Taken

altar 9.27; 22.10
command 11.9; 14.2
fortune-teller Judg 9.37
last (2) 12.4; 1 Sam 25.22
offer 8.31; 22.26
possess [8] 12.6; 14.9
sacrifice 8.31; 22.23
servant 12.6; 14.7
share [2] Deut 33.21; 17.5

13 Joshua was now very old. The
LORD said to him, "You are very
old, but there is still much land to be
taken: [2]all the territory of Philistia and
Geshur, [3]as well as all the territory of the
Avvim to the south. (The land from the
stream of Shihor, at the Egyptian border,
as far north as the border of Ekron was
considered Canaanite; the kings of the
Philistines lived at Gaza, Ashdod, Ashkelon, Gath, and Ekron.) [4]There is still
all the Canaanite country, and Mearah
(which belonged to the Sidonians), as far
as Aphek, at the Amorite border; [5]the
land of the Gebalites; all of Lebanon to
the east, from Baalgad, which is south of
Mount Hermon, to Hamath Pass. [6]This
includes all the territory of the Sidonians,
who live in the hill-country between the
Lebanon Mountains and Misrephoth
Maim. I will drive all these peoples out as
the people of Israel advance. You must
divide the land among the Israelites, just
as I have **commanded** you to do. [7]Now
then, divide this land among the other
nine tribes and half of the tribe of
Manasseh, for them to **possess** as their
own."

The Division of the Territory East of the Jordan

8 The tribes of Reuben and Gad and
the other half of the tribe of Manasseh
had already received the land that
Moses, the LORD's **servant**, had given
them; it was on the east side of the River
Jordan. [9]Their territory extended to
Aroer (on the edge of the Arnon Valley)
and the city in the middle of that valley
and included all the plateau from
Medeba to Dibon. [10]It went as far as the
border of Ammon and included all the
cities that had been ruled by the Amorite
king Sihon, who had ruled at Heshbon.
[11]It included Gilead, the regions of
Geshur and Maacah, all Mount Hermon,
and all of Bashan as far as Salecah. [12]It
included the kingdom of Og, the **last** of
the Rephaim, who had ruled at Ashtaroth
and Edrei. Moses had defeated these
people and driven them out. [13]However,
the Israelites did not drive out the people
of Geshur and Maacah; they still live in
Israel.

14 Moses had given no land to the
tribe of Levi. As the LORD had told
Moses, they were to receive as their
possession a **share** of the **sacrifices** burnt
on the **altar** to the LORD God of Israel.

The Territory Assigned to Reuben

15 Moses had given a part of the land
to the families of the tribe of Reuben as
their **possession**. [16]Their territory extended to Aroer (on the edge of the
Arnon Valley) and the city in the middle
of that valley and included all the plateau
round Medeba. [17]It included Heshbon
and all the cities on the plateau: Dibon,
Bamoth Baal, Beth Baalmeon, [18]Jahaz,
Kedemoth, Mephaath, [19]Kiriathaim, Sibmah, Zereth-shahar on the hill in the
valley, [20]Bethpeor, the slopes of Mount
Pisgah, and Beth Jeshimoth. [21]It included
all the cities of the plateau and the whole
kingdom of the Amorite king Sihon, who
had ruled at Heshbon. Moses defeated
him, as well as the rulers of Midian: Evi,
Rekem, Zur, Hur, and Reba. All of them
had ruled the land for King Sihon.
[22]Among those whom the people of Israel
killed was the **fortune-teller** Balaam son
of Beor. [23]The Jordan was the western
border of the tribe of Reuben. These
were the cities and towns given to the
families of the tribe of Reuben as their
possession.

The Territory Assigned to Gad

24 Moses had also given a part of the
land to the families of the tribe of Gad as
their **possession**. [25]Their territory included Jazer and all the cities of Gilead,
half the land of Ammon as far as Aroer,
which is east of Rabbah; [26]their land
extended from Heshbon to Ramath
Mizpeh and Betonim, from Mahanaim to
the border of Lodebar. [27]In the Jordan
Valley it included Beth Haram, Bethnim-
rah, Sukkoth, and Zaphon, the rest of the
kingdom of King Sihon of Heshbon. Their
western border was the River Jordan as
far north as Lake Galilee. [28]These were
the cities and towns given to the families
of the tribe of Gad as their **possession**.

The Territory Assigned to East Manasseh

29 Moses had given a part of the land
to the families of half the tribe of Manasseh as their **possession**. [30]Their territory extended to Mahanaim and included
all of Bashan—the whole kingdom of Og,
the king of Bashan, as well as all sixty of

[g] *One ancient translation* Galilee; *Hebrew* Gilgal.

13.6: Num 33.54 **13.8:** Num 32.33; Deut 3.12 **13.14:** Deut 18.1

the villages of Jair in Bashan. 31 It included half of Gilead, as well as Ashtaroth and Edrei, the capital cities of
Og's kingdom in Bashan. All this was
given to half the families descended from
Machir son of Manasseh.

32 That is how Moses divided the land
east of Jericho and the Jordan when he
was in the plains of Moab. 33 But Moses
did not assign any land to the tribe of
Levi. He told them that their **possession**
was to be a **share** of the **offerings** to the
LORD God of Israel.

The Division of the Territory West of the Jordan

14 What follows is an account of
how the land of Canaan west of
the Jordan was divided among the
people of Israel. Eleazar the **priest**,
Joshua son of Nun, and the leaders of the
families of the Israelite tribes divided it
among the population. 2 As the LORD had
commanded Moses, the territories of the
nine and a half tribes west of the Jordan
were **determined** by drawing **lots**.[h]
3-4 Moses had already assigned the land
east of the Jordan to the other two and a
half tribes. (The descendants of Joseph
were divided into two tribes: Manasseh
and Ephraim.) However, Moses gave the
Levites no portion of the territory. Instead, they received cities to live in, with
fields for their cattle and **flocks**. 5 The
people of Israel divided the land as the
LORD had **commanded** Moses.

Hebron Is Given to Caleb

6 One day some people from the tribe
of Judah came to Joshua at Gilgal. One of
them, Caleb son of Jephunneh the Kenizzite, said to him, "You know what the
LORD said in Kadesh Barnea about you
and me to Moses, the **man of God**. 7 I was
forty years old when the LORD's **servant**
Moses sent me from Kadesh Barnea to
spy out this land. I brought an **honest**
report back to him. 8 The men who went
with me, however, made our people
afraid. But I **faithfully obeyed** the LORD
my God. 9 Because I did, Moses **promised**
me that my children and I would certainly receive as our **possession** the land
which I walked over. 10 But now, look. It
has been forty-five years since the LORD
said that to Moses. That was when Israel
was going through the desert, and the
LORD, as he **promised**, has kept me **alive**
ever since. Look at me! I am eighty-five
years old 11 and I'm just as **strong** today
as I was when Moses sent me out. I am
still **strong enough** for war or for anything else. 12 Now then, give me the hill-
country that the LORD **promised** me on
that day when my men and I reported.
We told you then that the **race** of giants
called the Anakim were there in large
walled cities. Maybe the LORD will be
with me, and I will drive them out, just as
the LORD said."

13 Joshua **blessed** Caleb son of
Jephunneh and gave him the city of Hebron as his **possession**. 14 Hebron still
belongs to the descendants of Caleb son
of Jephunneh the Kenizzite, because he
faithfully obeyed the LORD, the God of
Israel. 15 Before this, Hebron was called
the city of Arba. (Arba had been the
greatest of the Anakim.)

There was now **peace** in the land.

The Territory Assigned to Judah

15 The families of the tribe of Judah
received a part of the land described as follows:

The land reached south to the
southernmost point of the wilderness of
Zin, at the border of Edom. 2 This
southern border ran from the south end
of the Dead Sea, 3 went southwards from
the Akrabbim Pass and on to Zin. It ran
south of Kadesh Barnea, past Hezron and
up to Addar, **turned** towards Karka,
4 went on to Azmon, and followed the
stream on the border of Egypt to the
Mediterranean Sea, where the border
ended. That was the southern border of
Judah.

5 The eastern border was the Dead
Sea, all the way up to the inlet where the
Jordan empties into it.

The northern border began there, 6 extended up to Beth Hoglah, and went
north of the ridge overlooking the Jordan
Valley. Then it went up to the Stone of
Bohan (Bohan was a son of Reuben),
7 from **Trouble** Valley up to Debir, and
then **turned** north towards Gilgal, which
faces Adummim Pass on the south side of
the valley. It then went on to the springs
of Enshemesh, out to Enrogel, 8 and up
through the Valley of Hinnom on the
south side of the hill where the Jebusite
city of Jerusalem was located. The border then proceeded up to the top of the
hill on the west side of the Valley of Hinnom, at the northern end of the Valley of
Rephaim. 9 From there it went to the
Springs of Nephtoah and out to the cities

afraid 11.6; 22.24
alive 11.8; 24.31
bless 8.33; 17.14
command [2] 13.6; 15.13
determine 11.20; Judg 5.2
enough Deut 19.15; 17.16
faithful [2] Deut 33.8; 22.5
flock Num 31.9; Judg 5.16
honest Deut 25.15; Judg 9.16
Levites 8.33; 18.7
lot (1) Num 36.2; 18.6
man of God Deut 33.1; Judg 13.6
obey [2] 11.15; 22.2
peace 11.19; 21.44
possess [2] 13.7; 15.20
priest 8.33; 17.4
promise [3] 9.15; 21.43
race (1) 11.21; Neh 5.5
servant 13.8; 18.7
strong [2] Deut 34.7; 17.13

command 14.2; 17.4
possess 14.9; 16.4
succeed (1) 1.7; Judg 1.12
trouble 7.24; 24.5
turn [4] 11.10; 18.14
urge Ex 12.33; Judg 1.14
wedding Deut 22.15; Judg 1.14

[h] DRAWING LOTS: *This was usually done by using specially marked stones to determine God's will.*

13.33: Num 18.20; Deut 18.2 **14.2:** Num 26.52–56, 34.13 **14.3–4:** Num 32.33, 34.14–15; Deut 3.12–17
14.6: Num 14.30 **14.7:** Num 13.1–30 **14.9:** Num 14.24

near Mount Ephron. There it **turned** towards Baalah (or Kiriath Jearim),
10 where it circled west of Baalah towards the hill-country of Edom, went on
the north side of Mount Jearim (or
Chesalon), down to Beth Shemesh, and
on past Timnah. 11 The border then went
out to the hill north of Ekron, **turned** towards Shikkeron, past Mount Baalah, and
on to Jamnia. It ended at the Mediterranean Sea, 12 which formed the western
border.
Within these borders lived the people
of the families of Judah.

Caleb Conquers Hebron and Debir
(Judg 1.11–15)

13 As the LORD **commanded** Joshua,
part of the territory of Judah was given
to Caleb son of Jephunneh, from the tribe
of Judah. He received Hebron, the city
belonging to Arba, father of Anak.
14 Caleb drove the descendants of Anak
out of the city—the clans of Sheshai,
Ahiman, and Talmai. 15 From there he
went to attack the people living in Debir.
(This city used to be called Kiriath
Sepher.) 16 Caleb said, "I will give my
daughter Achsah in marriage to the man
who **succeeds** in capturing Kiriath
Sepher." 17 Othniel, the son of Caleb's
brother Kenaz, captured the city, so
Caleb gave him his daughter Achsah in
marriage. 18 On the **wedding** day Othniel
urged her[i] to ask her father for a field.
She got down from her donkey, and
Caleb asked her what she wanted. 19 She
answered, "I want some pools of water.
The land you have given me is in the dry
country." So Caleb gave her the upper
and lower springs.

The Cities of Judah

20 This is the land that the families of
the tribe of Judah received as their
possession. 21 The cities farthest south
that belonged to them, those that were
near the border of Edom, were Kabzeel,
Eder, Jagur, 22 Kinah, Dimonah, Adadah,
23 Kedesh, Hazor, Ithnan, 24 Ziph, Telem,
Bealoth, 25 Hazor Hadattah, Kerioth
Hezron (or Hazor), 26 Amam, Shema,
Moladah, 27 Hazar Gaddah, Heshmon,
Bethpelet, 28 Hazar Shual, Beersheba,
Biziothiah, 29 Baalah, Iim, Ezem, 30 Elto-
lad, Chesil, Hormah, 31 Ziklag, Madmannah, Sansannah, 32 Lebaoth, Shilhim,
Ain, and Rimmon: twenty-nine cities in
all, along with the towns round them.
33 The cities in the foothills were
Eshtaol, Zorah, Ashnah, 34 Zanoah, En-
gannim, Tappuah, Enam, 35 Jarmuth,
Adullam, Socoh, Azekah, 36 Shaaraim,
Adithaim, Gederah, and Gederothaim:
fourteen cities, along with the towns
round them.
37 There were also Zenan, Hadashah,
Migdalgad, 38 Dilean, Mizpah, Joktheel,
39 Lachish, Bozkath, Eglon, 40 Cabbon,
Lahmam, Chitlish, 41 Gederoth, Bethdagon, Naamah, and Makkedah: sixteen
cities, along with the towns round them.
42 There were also Libnah, Ether,
Ashan, 43 Iphtah, Ashnah, Nezib, 44 Keilah,
Achzib, and Mareshah: nine cities, along
with the towns round them.
45 There was Ekron with its towns
and villages, 46 and all the cities and
towns near Ashdod, from Ekron to the
Mediterranean Sea.
47 There were Ashdod and Gaza, with
their towns and villages, reaching to the
stream on the border of Egypt and the
coast of the Mediterranean Sea.
48 In the hill-country there were
Shamir, Jattir, Socoh, 49 Dannah, Kiriath
Sepher (or Debir), 50 Anab, Eshtemoa,
Anim, 51 Goshen, Holon, and Giloh:
eleven cities, along with the towns round
them.
52 There were Arab, Dumah, Eshan,
53 Janim, Beth Tappuah, Aphekah,
54 Humtah, Hebron, and Zior: nine cities,
along with the towns round them.
55 There were Maon, Carmel, Ziph,
Juttah, 56 Jezreel, Jokdeam, Zanoah,
57 Kain, Gibeah, and Timnah: ten cities,
along with the towns round them.
58 There were Halhul, Bethzur, Gedor,
59 Maarath, Bethanoth, and Eltekon: six
cities, along with the towns round them.
60 There were Kiriath Baal (or
Kiriath Jearim) and Rabbah: two cities,
along with the towns round them.
61 In the desert there were Beth
Arabah, Middin, Secacah, 62 Nibshan, the
city of Salt, and Engedi: six cities, along
with the towns round them.
63 But the people of Judah were not
able to drive out the Jebusites, who lived
in Jerusalem. The Jebusites still live
there with the people of Judah.

The Territory Assigned to Ephraim and West Manasseh

16 The southern boundary of the **force** (1) 7.4; 17.13
land assigned to the descendants **possess** [2] 15.20; 17.4
of Joseph started from the Jordan near **slave** 9.23; 24.17
Jericho, at a point east of the springs of
Jericho, and went into the desert. It went
from Jericho up into the hill-country as
far as Bethel. 2 From Bethel it went to

[i] *Probable text (see Judg 1.14)* Othniel urged her; *Hebrew* she urged Othniel.

15.13–14: Judg 1.20 **15.63:** Judg 1.21; 2 Sam 5.6; 1 Chr 11.4

Luz, passing on to Ataroth Addar, where
the Archites lived. 3 It then went west to
the area of the Japhletites, as far as the
area of Lower Beth Horon. It went on
from there to Gezer and ended at the
Mediterranean Sea.
4 The descendants of Joseph, the
tribes of Ephraim and West Manasseh,
received this land as their **possession**.

Ephraim

5 This was the territory of the
Ephraimite families: their border ran
from Ataroth Addar eastwards to Upper
Beth Horon, 6 and from there to the
Mediterranean Sea. Michmethath was on
their north. East of there the border bent
towards Taanath Shiloh and went past it
on the east to Janoah. 7 Then it went
down from Janoah to Ataroth and
Naarah, reaching Jericho and ending at
the Jordan. 8 The border went west from
Tappuah to the stream of Kanah and
ended at the Mediterranean Sea. This
was the land given to the families of the
tribe of Ephraim as their **possession**,
9 along with some towns and villages that
were within the borders of Manasseh, but
given to the Ephraimites. 10 But they did
not drive out the Canaanites who lived in
Gezer, so the Canaanites have lived
among the Ephraimites to this day, but
they have been **forced** to work as **slaves**.

West Manasseh

bless 14.13; 22.6
clear [2] Gen 44.16; 1 Sam 14.41
command [2] 15.13; 19.50
enough 14.11; 22.17
force (1) 16.10; Judg 1.28
possess [4] 16.4; 18.4
power 11.10; 23.9
priest 14.1; 18.7
share [2] 13.14; 18.2
strong [2] 14.11; Judg 1.28

17 A part of the land west of the
Jordan was assigned to some of
the families descended from Joseph's
elder son Manasseh. Machir, the father
of Gilead, was Manasseh's eldest son and
a military hero, so Gilead and Bashan,
east of the Jordan, were assigned to him.
2 Land west of the Jordan was assigned to
the rest of the families of Manasseh:
Abiezer, Helek, Asriel, Shechem, Hepher,
and Shemida. These were male descendants of Manasseh son of Joseph, and they
were heads of families. 3 Zelophehad, son
of Hepher, son of Gilead, son of Machir,
son of Manasseh, did not have any sons,
but only daughters. Their names were
Mahlah, Noah, Hoglah, Milcah, and
Tirzah. 4 They went to Eleazar the **priest**
and to Joshua son of Nun and to the
leaders, and said, "The LORD **commanded** Moses to give us, as well as our
male relatives, a part of the land to
possess." So, as the LORD had **commanded**, they were given land along with
their male relatives. 5 That is why
Manasseh received ten **shares** in addition
to Gilead and Bashan on the east side of
the Jordan, 6 since his female descendants as well as his male descendants
were assigned land. The land of Gilead
was assigned to the rest of the descendants of Manasseh.
7 The territory of Manasseh reached
from Asher to Michmethath, east of
Shechem. The border then went south to
include the people of Entappuah. 8 The
land round Tappuah belonged to Manasseh, but the town of Tappuah, on the
border, belonged to the descendants of
Ephraim. 9 The border then went down to
the stream of Kanah. The cities south of
the stream belonged to Ephraim, even
though they were in the territory of
Manasseh. The border of Manasseh proceeded along the north side of the
stream and ended at the Mediterranean
Sea. 10 Ephraim was to the south, and
Manasseh was to the north, with the
Mediterranean Sea as their western border. Asher was to the north-west, and
Issachar to the north-east. 11 Within the
territories of Issachar and Asher,
Manasseh **possessed** Beth Shan and
Ibleam, along with their surrounding
towns, as well as Dor (the one on the
coast),[j] Endor, Taanach, Megiddo, and
their surrounding towns. 12 The people of
Manasseh, however, were not able to
drive out the people living in those cities,
so the Canaanites continued to live there.
13 Even when the Israelites became
stronger, they did not drive out all the
Canaanites, but they did **force** them to
work for them.

Ephraim and West Manasseh Request More Land

14 The descendants of Joseph said to
Joshua, "Why have you given us only one
part of the land to **possess** as our own?
There are very many of us because the
LORD has **blessed** us."
15 Joshua answered, "If there are so
many of you and the hill-country of
Ephraim is too small for you, then go into
the forests and **clear** ground for yourselves in the land of the Perizzites and
the Rephaim."
16 They replied, "The hill-country is
not big **enough** for us, but the Canaanites
in the plains have iron chariots, both
those who live in Beth Shan and its surrounding towns and those who live in the
Valley of Jezreel."
17 Joshua said to the tribes of
Ephraim and West Manasseh, "There
are indeed many of you, and you are

[j] *Probable text* Dor (the one on the coast); *Hebrew unclear.*

16.10: Judg 1.29 **17.4:** Num 27.1–7 **17.12–13:** Judg 1.27–28

very **powerful**. You shall have more than
one **share**. [18]The hill-country will be
yours. Even though it is a forest, you will
clear it and take **possession** of it from
one end to the other. As for the Canaanites, you will drive them out, even though
they do have iron chariots and are a
strong people."

The Division of the Rest of the Land

community 9.15; 22.12
conquer 12.1; 23.4
consult [3] 9.14; 19.51
Levites 14.3; 21.1
lot (1) [3] 14.2; 19.51
possess [3] 17.4; 19.8
priest 17.4; 19.51
servant 14.7; 22.2
serve 6.22; 22.5
share [3] 17.5; 22.6
Tent (2) (of the Lord's presence) Deut 31.14; 19.51
turn [2] 15.3; 19.13

18 After they had **conquered** the
land, the entire **community** of
Israel assembled at Shiloh and set up the
Tent of the LORD's presence. [2]There
were still seven tribes of the people of
Israel who had not yet been assigned
their **share** of the land. [3]So Joshua said to
the people of Israel, "How long are you
going to wait before you go in and take
the land that the LORD, the God of your
ancestors, has given you? [4]Let me have
three men from each tribe. I will send
them out over the whole country to map
out the territory that they would like to
have as their **possession**. Then they are
to come back to me. [5]The land will be
divided among them in seven parts;
Judah will stay in its territory in the
south, and Joseph in its territory in the
north. [6]Write down a description of these
seven divisions and bring it to me. Then I
will draw **lots**[k] to **consult** the LORD our
God for you. [7]The **Levites**, however, will
not receive a **share** of the land with the
rest of you, because their **share** is to
serve as the LORD's **priests**. And of
course, the tribes of Gad, Reuben, and
East Manasseh have already received
their land east of the Jordan, which
Moses, the LORD's **servant**, gave to
them."

8 The men went on their way to map
out the land after Joshua had given them
these instructions: "Go all over the land
and map it out, and come back to me.
And then here in Shiloh I will **consult** the
LORD for you by drawing **lots**." [9]So the
men went all over the land and set down
in writing how they divided it into seven
parts, making a list of the towns. Then
they went back to Joshua in the camp at
Shiloh. [10]Joshua drew **lots** to **consult** the
LORD for them, and assigned each of the
remaining tribes of Israel a certain part
of the land.

The Territory Assigned to Benjamin

11 The territory belonging to the
families of the tribe of Benjamin was the
first to be assigned. Their land lay between the tribes of Judah and Joseph.
[12]On the north their border began at the
Jordan and then went up the slope north
of Jericho and westwards through the
hill-country as far as the desert of Bethaven. [13]The border then went to the
slope on the south side of Luz (also called
Bethel), then down to Ataroth Addar, on
the mountain south of Lower Beth Horon.
[14]The border then went in another
direction, **turning** south from the western
side of this mountain and going to
Kiriath Baal (or Kiriath Jearim), which
belongs to the tribe of Judah. This was
the western border. [15]The southern border started on the edge of Kiriath Jearim
and went[l] to the Springs of Nephtoah.
[16]It then went down to the foot of the
mountain that overlooks the Valley of
Hinnom, at the north end of the Valley of
Rephaim. It then went south through the
Valley of Hinnom, south of the Jebusite
ridge, towards Enrogel. [17]It then **turned**
north to Enshemesh and then on to Geliloth, opposite Adummim Pass. The border then went down to the Stone of
Bohan (Bohan was a son of Reuben)
[18]and passed north of the ridge overlooking the Jordan Valley. It then went down
into the valley, [19]passing north of the
ridge of Beth Hoglah, and ended at the
northern inlet on the Dead Sea, where
the River Jordan empties into it. This
was the southern border. [20]The Jordan
was the eastern border. These were the
borders of the land which the families of
the tribe of Benjamin received as their
possession.

21 The cities belonging to the families
of the tribe of Benjamin were Jericho,
Beth Hoglah, Emek Keziz, [22]Beth
Arabah, Zemaraim, Bethel, [23]Avvim,
Parah, Ophrah, [24]Chepharammoni,
Ophni, and Geba: twelve cities, along
with the towns round them. [25]There were
also Gibeon, Ramah, Beeroth, [26]Mizpah,
Chephirah, Mozah, [27]Rekem, Irpeel,
Taralah, [28]Zela, Haeleph, Jebus (or Jerusalem), Gibeah, and Kiriath Jearim:
fourteen cities, along with the towns
round them. This is the land which the
families of the tribe of Benjamin
received as their **possession**.

The Territory Assigned to Simeon

19 The second assignment made
was for the families of the tribe
of Simeon. Its territory extended into the
land assigned to the tribe of Judah. [2]It included Beersheba, Sheba, Moladah,
[3]Hazar Shual, Balah, Ezem, [4]Eltolad,

change Deut 21.13; Judg 7.19
claim Num 8.16; 22.4
command 17.4; 20.2
consult 18.6; 1 Sam 2.28
lot (1) 18.6; 21.8
need 7.3; Judg 18.7

[k] DRAW LOTS: *See 14.2.* [l] *Probable text* and went; *Hebrew* and went westwards.

19.2–8: 1 Chr 4.28–33

possess [6] 18.4; 21.12
priest 18.7; 21.1
Tent (2) (of the Lord's presence) 18.1; 22.19
turn [6] 18.14; 24.20

Bethul, Hormah, 5 Ziklag, Beth Marcaboth, Hazar Susah, 6 Beth Lebaoth, and
Sharuhen: thirteen cities, along with the
towns round them.
7 There were also Ain, Rimmon,
Ether, and Ashan: four cities, along with
the towns round them. 8 This included all
the towns round these cities as far as
Baalath Beer (or Ramah), in the south.
This was the land which the families of
the tribe of Simeon received as their
possession. 9 Since Judah's assignment
was larger than was **needed**, part of its
territory was given to the tribe of
Simeon.

The Territory Assigned to Zebulun

10 The third assignment made was for
the families of the tribe of Zebulun. The
land which they received reached as far
as Sarid. 11 From there the border went
west to Mareal, touching Dabbesheth
and the stream east of Jokneam. 12 On
the other side of Sarid it went east to the
border of Chisloth Tabor, then to
Daberath and up to Japhia. 13 It continued
east from there to Gath Hepher and Eth-
kazin, **turning** in the direction of Neah on
the way to Rimmon. 14 On the north the
border **turned** towards Hannathon, ending at the Valley of Iphtahel. 15 It included Kattath, Nahalal, Shimron, Idalah,
and Bethlehem: twelve cities, along with
the towns round them. 16 These cities and
their towns were in the land which the
families of the tribe of Zebulun received
as their **possession**.

The Territory Assigned to Issachar

17 The fourth assignment made was
for the families of the tribe of Issachar.
18 Its area included Jezreel, Chesulloth,
Shunem, 19 Hapharaim, Shion, Anaharath,
20 Rabbith, Kishion, Ebez, 21 Remeth,
Engannim, Enhaddah, and Bethpazzez.
22 The border also touched Tabor, Shaha-
zumah, and Beth Shemesh, ending at the
Jordan. It included sixteen cities along
with the towns round them. 23 These
cities and their towns were in the land
which the families of the tribe of Issachar received as their **possession**.

The Territory Assigned to Asher

24 The fifth assignment made was for
the families of the tribe of Asher. 25 Its
area included Helkath, Hali, Beten,
Achshaph, 26 Allam Melech, Amad, and
Mishal. On the west it touched Carmel
and Shihor Libnath. 27 As it **turned** east,
the border went to Bethdagon, touching
Zebulun and the Valley of Iphtahel on the
way north to Bethemek and Neiel. It continued north to Cabul, 28 Ebron, Rehob,
Hammon, and Kanah, as far as Sidon.
29 The border then **turned** to Ramah,
reaching the fortified city of Tyre; then it
turned to Hosah and ended at the
Mediterranean Sea. It included Mahalab,
Achzib, 30 Ummah, Aphek, and Rehob:
twenty-two cities, along with the towns
round them. 31 These cities and their
towns were in the land which the
families of the tribe of Asher received as
their **possession**.

The Territory Assigned to Naphtali

32 The sixth assignment made was for
the families of the tribe of Naphtali. 33 Its
border went from Heleph to the oak in
Zaanannim, on to Adaminekeb and to
Jamnia, as far as Lakkum, and ended at
the Jordan. 34 There the border **turned**
west to Aznoth Tabor, from there to
Hukkok, touching Zebulun on the south,
Asher on the west, and the Jordan[m] on
the east. 35 The fortified cities were
Ziddim, Zer, Hammath, Rakkath,
Chinnereth, 36 Adamah, Ramah, Hazor,
37 Kedesh, Edrei, Enhazor, 38 Yiron, Mig-
dalel, Horem, Bethanath, and Beth
Shemesh: nineteen cities, along with the
towns round them. 39 These cities and
their towns were in the land which the
families of the tribe of Naphtali received
as their **possession**.

The Territory Assigned to Dan

40 The seventh assignment made was
for the families of the tribe of Dan. 41 Its
area included Zorah, Eshtaol, Irshemesh,
42 Shaalbim, Aijalon, Ithlah, 43 Elon,
Timnah, Ekron, 44 Eltekeh, Gibbethon,
Baalath, 45 Jehud, Beneberak, Gathrimmon, 46 Mejarkon, and Rakkon, as
well as the territory round Joppa.
47 When the people of Dan lost their land,
they went to Laish and attacked it. They
captured it, killed its people, and **claimed**
it for themselves. They settled there and
changed the name of the city from Laish
to Dan, naming it after their ancestor
Dan. 48 These cities and their towns were
in the land which the families of the tribe
of Dan received as their **possession**.

The Final Assignment of the Land

49 When the people of Israel finished
dividing up the land, they gave Joshua
son of Nun a part of the land as his own.
50 As the LORD had **commanded**, they
gave him the city he asked for: Timnath

[m] *One ancient translation* the Jordan; *Hebrew* Judah at the Jordan.

19.47: Judg 18.27-29

Serah, in the hill-country of Ephraim. He rebuilt the city and settled there.

51 Eleazar the **priest**, Joshua son of Nun, and the leaders of the families of the tribes of Israel assigned these parts of the land by drawing **lots**[n] to **consult** the LORD at Shiloh, at the entrance of the **Tent** of the LORD's presence. In this way they finished dividing the land.

The Cities of Refuge

anger Deut 32.16; 22.18
choose [3] 9.27; 24.22
command 19.50; 21.2
death (1) 2.19; 24.31
escape 10.16; Judg 3.26
High Priest Num 35.25; 2 Kgs 12.10
judge 8.33; 23.2
protect [2] 9.26; Judg 2.14
refuge [2] Num 35.6; 2 Sam 22.33
revenge [3] Deut 32.35; Judg 11.36
try (2) [2] Deut 21.19; 2 Chr 19.10

20 Then the LORD told Joshua 2 to say to the people of Israel, "**Choose** the **cities of refuge** that I **commanded** Moses to tell you about. 3 A person who kills someone accidentally can go there and **escape** the man who is looking for **revenge**. 4 He can run away to one of these cities, go to the place of **judgement** at the entrance to the city, and explain to the leaders what happened. Then they will let him into the city and give him a place to live in, so that he can stay there. 5 If the man looking for **revenge** follows him there, the people of the city must not hand him over to him. They must **protect** him because he killed the person accidentally and not out of **anger**. 6 He may stay in the city until he has received a public **trial** and until the **death** of the man who is then the **High Priest**. Then the man may go back home to his own town, from which he had run away."

7 So, on the west side of the Jordan they set aside Kedesh in Galilee, in the hill-country of Naphtali; Shechem, in the hill-country of Ephraim; and Hebron, in the hill-country of Judah. 8 East of the Jordan, on the desert plateau east of Jericho, they **chose** Bezer in the territory of Reuben; Ramoth in Gilead, in the territory of Gad; and Golan in Bashan, in the territory of Manasseh. 9 These were the **cities of refuge chosen** for all the people of Israel and for any foreigner living among them. Anyone who killed a person accidentally could find **protection** there from the man looking for **revenge**; he could not be killed unless he had first received a public **trial**.

The Cities of the Levites

command [3] 20.2; 22.2
enemy [2] 11.8; 22.6
Levites [8] 18.7; Judg 17.7
lot (1) 19.51; Judg 20.9
peace 14.15; 22.4
possess [3] 19.8; 23.4
priest [4] 19.51; 22.13
promise [3] 14.9; 22.4
refuge [5] Mic 1.11

21 The leaders of the **Levite** families went to Eleazar the **priest**, Joshua son of Nun, and to the heads of the families of all the tribes of Israel. 2 There at Shiloh in the land of Canaan they said to them, "The LORD **commanded** through Moses that we were to be given cities to live in, as well as pasture land round them for our livestock." 3 So in accordance with the LORD's **command** the people of Israel gave the **Levites** certain cities and pasture lands out of their own territories.

solemn 9.15; Judg 8.19
victory 11.1; 24.8

4 The families of the **Levite** clan of Kohath were the first to be assigned cities. The families who were descended from Aaron the **priest** were assigned thirteen cities from the territories of Judah, Simeon, and Benjamin. 5 The rest of the clan of Kohath was assigned ten cities from the territories of Ephraim, Dan, and West Manasseh.

6 The clan of Gershon was assigned thirteen cities from the territories of Issachar, Asher, Naphtali, and East Manasseh.

7 The families of the clan of Merari were assigned twelve cities from the territories of Reuben, Gad, and Zebulun.

8 By drawing **lots**,[n] the people of Israel assigned these cities and their pasture lands to the **Levites**, as the LORD had **commanded** through Moses.

9 These are the names of the cities from the territories of Judah and Simeon which were given 10 to the descendants of Aaron who were of the clan of Kohath, which was descended from Levi. Their assignment was the first to be made. 11 They were given the city of Arba (Arba was Anak's father), now called Hebron, in the hill-country of Judah, along with the pasture land surrounding it. 12 However, the fields of the city, as well as its towns, had already been given to Caleb son of Jephunneh as his **possession**.

13 In addition to Hebron (one of the **cities of refuge**), the following cities were assigned to the descendants of Aaron the **priest**: Libnah, 14 Jattir, Eshtemoa, 15 Holon, Debir, 16 Ain, Juttah, and Beth Shemesh, with their pasture lands: nine cities from the tribes of Judah and Simeon. 17 From the territory of Benjamin they were given four cities: Gibeon, Geba, 18 Anathoth, and Almon, with their pasture lands. 19 Thirteen cities in all, with their pasture lands, were given to the **priests**, the descendants of Aaron.

20 The other families of the **Levite** clan of Kohath were assigned some cities from the territory of Ephraim. 21 They were given four cities: Shechem and its pasture lands in the hill-country of Ephraim (one of the **cities of refuge**), Gezer, 22 Kibzaim, and Beth Horon, with their pasture lands. 23 From the territory of Dan they were given four cities: Eltekeh, Gibbethon, 24 Aijalon, and

[n] DRAWING LOTS: *See 14.2.*

20.1-9: Num 35.9-34; Deut 4.41-43, 19.1-13 **21.2:** Num 35.1-8

Gathrimmon, with their pasture lands. 25 From the territory of West Manasseh they were given two cities: Taanach and Gathrimmon, with their pasture lands. 26 These families of the clan of Kohath received ten cities in all, with their pasture lands.

27 Another group of **Levites**, the clan of Gershon, received from the territory of East Manasseh two cities: Golan in Bashan (one of the **cities of refuge**) and Beeshterah, with their pasture lands. 28 From the territory of Issachar they received four cities: Kishion, Daberath, 29 Jarmuth, and Engannim, with their pasture lands. 30 From the territory of Asher they received four cities: Mishal, Abdon, 31 Helkath, and Rehob, with their pasture lands. 32 From the territory of Naphtali they received three cities: Kedesh in Galilee, with its pasture lands (one of the **cities of refuge**), Hammoth Dor, and Kartan, with their pasture lands. 33 The various families of the clan of Gershon received a total of thirteen cities with their pasture lands.

34 The rest of the **Levites**, the clan of Merari, received from the territory of Zebulun four cities: Jokneam, Kartah, 35 Dimnah, and Nahalal, with their pasture lands. 36 From the territory of Reuben they received four cities: Bezer, Jahaz, 37 Kedemoth, and Mephaath, with their pasture lands. 38 From the tribe of Gad they received four cities: Ramoth in Gilead, with its pasture lands (one of the **cities of refuge**), Mahanaim, 39 Heshbon, and Jazer, with their pasture lands. 40 So the clan of Merari was assigned a total of twelve cities.

41–42 From the land that the people of Israel **possessed**, a total of forty-eight cities, with the pasture lands round them, was given to the **Levites**.

Israel Takes Possession of the Land

43 So the LORD gave to Israel all the land that he had **solemnly promised** their ancestors he would give them. When they had taken **possession** of it, they settled down there. 44 The LORD gave them **peace** throughout the land, just as he had **promised** their ancestors. Not one of all their **enemies** had been able to stand against them, because the LORD gave the Israelites the **victory** over all their **enemies**. 45 The LORD kept every one of the **promises** that he had made to the people of Israel.

Joshua Sends the Eastern Tribes Home

22 Then Joshua called together the people of the tribes of Reuben, Gad, and East Manasseh. 2 He said to them, "You have done everything that Moses the LORD's **servant** ordered you to do, and you have **obeyed** all my **commands**. 3 All this time you have never once deserted your fellow-Israelites. You have been careful to **obey** the **commands** of the LORD your God. 4 Now, as he **promised**, the LORD your God has given your fellow-Israelites **peace**. So go back home to the land which you **claimed** for your own, the land on the east side of the Jordan, that Moses, the LORD's **servant**, gave you. 5 Make **sure** you **obey** the **law** that Moses **commanded** you: **love** the LORD your God, do his **will**, **obey** his **commandments**, be **faithful** to him, and **serve** him **with all your heart** and **soul**." 6–8 Joshua sent them home with his **blessing** and with these **words**: "You are going back home very **rich**, with a lot of livestock, silver, gold, bronze, iron, and many clothes. **Share** with your fellow-tribesmen what you took from your **enemies**." Then they left for home.

Moses had given land east of the Jordan to one half of the tribe of Manasseh, but to the other half Joshua had given land west of the Jordan, along with the other tribes.

9 So the people of the tribes of Reuben, Gad, and East Manasseh went back home. They left the rest of the people of Israel at Shiloh in the land of Canaan and started out for their own land, the land of Gilead, which they had taken as the LORD had **commanded** them through Moses.

The Altar by the Jordan

10 When the tribes of Reuben, Gad, and East Manasseh arrived at Geliloth, still on the west side[p] of the Jordan, they built a large, impressive **altar** there by the river. 11 The rest of the people of Israel were told, "Listen! The people of the tribes of Reuben, Gad, and East Manasseh have built an **altar** at Geliloth, on our side of the Jordan!" 12 When the people of Israel heard this, the whole **community** came together at Shiloh to go to war against the eastern tribes.

13 Then the people of Israel sent Phinehas, the son of Eleazar the **priest**, to the people of the tribes of Reuben, Gad, and East Manasseh in the land of Gilead. 14 Ten **leading** men went with

afraid 14.8; Judg 4.18
altar [10] 13.14; Judg 2.2
anger 20.5; 23.16
bless 17.14; 24.10
claim [2] 19.47; Judg 18.1
command [5] 21.2; 23.16
commandment 8.35; 2 Chr 19.10
community [4] 18.1; Ezra 8.17
condemn 11.20; Ruth 1.21
destroy 11.20; 24.8
devastate Judg 6.5
disobey 7.1; 1 Sam 12.15
enemy 21.44; 23.1
enough 17.16; Judg 6.38
evil Deut 32.16; Judg 2.19
faith Num 20.12; 2 Sam 15.11
faithful 14.8; 23.8
fellowship-offering [2] 8.31; 2 Sam 6.17
fit (1) Num 26.2; 1 Sam 25.36
God's people 1.3; Judg 5.11
grain-offering [2] Num 29.3; 1 Kgs 8.64
heart Deut 30.2; 23.14
idea 1 Sam 9.9
keep from Deut 32.11; 24.27
law 8.31; 23.6
leading [2] Ex 24.11; Judg 8.14
love Deut 33.3; 23.11
might [2] Deut 32.4; Judg 6.12
obey [5] 14.8; 23.6
offer [4] 13.33; Judg 2.5
peace 21.44; Judg 3.11
praise Deut 33.20; Judg 5.2
priest [3] 21.1; Judg 17.5
promise 21.43; 23.5
punish [4] 9.20; 23.16
rebel [7] Deut 32.15; 24.27
refuse (1) [2] Deut 31.18; Judg 2.19
remember [2] 1.9; Judg 8.15
rich 5.4; Judg 5.30
sacred Deut 26.13; Judg 9.6
sacrifice [5] 13.14; Judg 2.5
satisfy [2] Num 11.22; Ruth 2.14
save 10.6; Judg 2.16
servant [2] 18.7; 24.29
serve 18.7; 23.16
share 18.2; Judg 2.6
sign (1) [2] 2.12; 1 Sam 14.10
soul Deut 6.5; 23.14
suffer Deut 29.22; Judg 2.18
sure 3.10; 23.13
Tent (2) (of the Lord's presence) [3] 19.51; Judg 18.31
will (1) Deut 33.8; 2 Sam 7.21
witness [2] Deut 31.26; 24.22
word (1) 11.1; 24.9

[p] still on the west side; *or* on the east side.

22.2: Num 32.20–32; Josh 1.12–15

worship (1) (of God) [3] 9.27; Judg 2.12

Phinehas, one from each of the western
tribes and each one the head of a family
among the clans. 15 They came to the
land of Gilead, to the people of Reuben,
Gad, and East Manasseh, 16 and speaking
for the whole **community** of the LORD,
they said to them, "Why have you done
this **evil** thing against the God of Israel?
You have **rebelled** against the LORD by
building this **altar** for yourselves! You
are no longer following him! 17 **Remember** our sin at Peor, when the LORD **punished** his **own people** with an epidemic?
We are still **suffering** because of that.
Wasn't that sin **enough**? 18 Are you going
to **refuse** to follow him now? If you **rebel**
against the LORD today, he will **be angry**
with everyone in Israel tomorrow. 19 Now
then, if your land is not **fit** to **worship** in,
come over into the LORD's land, where
his **Tent** is. **Claim** some land among us.
But don't **rebel** against the LORD or make
rebels out of us by building an **altar** in
addition to the altar of the LORD our God.
20 **Remember** how Achan son of Zerah **refused** to **obey** the **command** about the
things **condemned** to **destruction**; the
whole **community** of Israel was **punished**
for that. Achan was not the only one who
died because of his sin."

21 The people of the tribes of Reuben,
Gad, and East Manasseh answered the
heads of the families of the western
tribes: 22 "The **Mighty** One is God! He is
the LORD! The **Mighty** One is God! He is
the LORD! He knows why we did this, and
we want you to know too! If we **rebelled**
and did not keep **faith** with the LORD, do
not let us live any longer! 23 If we **disobeyed** the LORD and built our own **altar**
to burn **sacrifices** on or to use for **grain-
offerings** or **fellowship-offerings**, let the
LORD himself **punish** us. 24 No! We did it
because we were **afraid** that in the future
your descendants would say to ours,
'What do you have to do with the LORD,
the God of Israel? 25 He made the Jordan
a boundary between us and you people of
Reuben and Gad. You have nothing to do
with the LORD.' Then your descendants
might make our descendants stop
worshipping the LORD. 26 So we built an
altar, not to burn **sacrifices** or make
offerings, 27 but instead, as a **sign** for our
people and yours, and for the genera-
tions after us, that we do indeed **worship**
the LORD before his **sacred Tent** with our
offerings to be burnt and with **sacrifices**
and **fellowship-offerings**. This was to
keep your descendants from saying that
ours have nothing to do with the LORD.
28 It was our **idea** that, if this should ever
happen, our descendants could say,
'Look! Our ancestors made an **altar** just
like the LORD's altar. It was not for burning **offerings** or for **sacrifice**, but as a
sign for our people and yours.' 29 We
would certainly not **rebel** against the
LORD or stop following him now by building an **altar** to burn **offerings** on or for
grain-offerings or **sacrifices**. We would
not build any other **altar** than the altar of
the LORD our God that stands in front of
the **Tent** of his presence."

30 Phinehas the **priest** and the ten
leading men of the **community** who were
with him, the heads of families of the
western tribes, heard what the people of
the tribes of Reuben, Gad, and East
Manasseh had to say, and they were
satisfied. 31 Phinehas, the son of Eleazar
the **priest**, said to them, "Now we know
that the LORD is with us. You have not **rebelled** against him, and so you have
saved the people of Israel from the
LORD's **punishment**."

32 Then Phinehas and the leaders left
the people of Reuben and Gad in the land
of Gilead and went back to Canaan, to
the people of Israel, and reported to
them. 33 The Israelites were **satisfied** and
praised God. They no longer talked about
going to war to **devastate** the land where
the people of Reuben and Gad had
settled.

34 The people of Reuben and Gad
said, "This **altar** is a **witness** to all of us
that the LORD is God." And so they
named it "**Witness**."

Joshua's Farewell Address

23 Much later the LORD gave Israel
security from their **enemies**
around them. By that time Joshua was
very old, 2 so he called all Israel, the
elders, leaders, **judges**, and officers of the
people, and said, "I am very old now.
3 You have seen everything that the LORD
your God has done to all these nations
because of you. The LORD your God has
been fighting for you. 4 I have assigned as
the **possession** of your tribes the land of
the nations that are still left, as well as of
all the nations that I have already **conquered**, from the River Jordan in the
east to the Mediterranean Sea in the
west. 5 The LORD your God will make
them retreat from you, and he will drive
them away as you advance. You shall
have their land, as the LORD your God
has **promised** you. 6 So be careful to **obey**
and do everything that is written in the
book of the **Law of Moses**. Do not **neglect**

anger 22.18; Judg 2.12
bow (2) Deut 33.3; Judg 2.12
command 22.2; 24.24
conquer 18.1; Judg 3.8
covenant 7.15; 24.25
danger Deut 28.66; 1 Sam 20.21
elder (2) 24.1
enemy 22.6; Judg 2.3
fail Deut 32.29; 1 Sam 26.16
faithful 22.5; 24.14
god (2) (other gods) [3] Deut 33.26; 24.2
heart 22.5; Judg 5.9
judge 20.4; 24.1
last (1) Deut 20.19; 2 Sam 7.16
law 22.5; 24.25
love 22.5; Judg 14.16
neglect 1.7; Neh 10.39
obey 22.2; 24.24
pain Deut 28.35; Judg 11.35
possess 21.12; 24.4
power 17.17; Judg 8.3
promise [5] 22.4; Judg 2.1
punish 22.17; 24.20

22.16: Deut 12.13–14 **22.17:** Num 25.1–9 **22.20:** Josh 7.1–26

secure Deut 33.25; Ruth 4.15
serve 22.5; 24.14
soul 22.5; 1 Kgs 2.4
sure 22.5; Judg 13.13
threat Deut 7.22; Judg 8.28
trap Ex 34.12; Judg 2.3
vow Deut 32.40; 1 Sam 19.6
worship (2) (of other gods) [2] Deut 31.16; 24.2

any part of it, [7]and then you will not associate with these peoples left among you
or speak the names of their **gods** or use
those names in taking **vows** or **worship**
those gods or **bow down** to them. [8]In-
stead, be **faithful** to the LORD, as you
have been till now. [9]The LORD has driven
great and **powerful** nations out as you advanced and no one has ever been able to
stand against you. [10]Any one of you can
make a thousand men run away, because
the LORD your God is fighting for you,
just as he **promised**. [11]Be careful, then, to
love the LORD your God. [12]If you are disloyal and join with the nations that are
still left among you and intermarry with
them, [13]you may be **sure** that the LORD
your God will no longer drive these
nations out as you advance. Rather, they
will be as **dangerous** for you as a **trap** or
a pit and as **painful** as a whip on your
back or thorns in your eyes. And this will
last until none of you are left in this good
land which the LORD your God has given
you.

14 "Now my time has come to die.
Every one of you knows in his **heart** and
soul that the LORD your God has given
you all the good things that he **promised**.
Every **promise** he made has been kept;
not one has **failed**. [15]But just as he kept
every **promise** that he made to you, so he
will carry out every **threat**. [16]If you do
not keep the **covenant** which the LORD
your God **commanded** you to keep and if
you **serve** and **worship other gods**, then
in his **anger** he will **punish** you, and soon
none of you will be left in this good land
that he has given you."

alive 14.10; Judg 2.7
bless 22.6; Judg 13.24
body 10.26; Judg 14.8
choose 20.2; Judg 5.8
command [2] 23.16; Judg 1.20
covenant 23.16; Judg 2.1
curse 8.34; Judg 1.17
dark Deut 5.23; Judg 19.9
death (1) 20.6; Judg 1.1
destroy [2] 22.20; Judg 1.17
elder (2) 23.2; 2 Kgs 6.32
faithful 23.8; Judg 5.13
forgive Deut 32.43; 1 Sam 15.25
god (2) (other gods) [7] 23.7; Judg 2.3
help 10.4; Judg 1.18
holy 5.15; 1 Sam 2.2
honour 7.9; Judg 9.9
inherit Num 36.8; Judg 11.2

Joshua Speaks to the People at Shechem

24 Joshua gathered all the tribes of
Israel together at Shechem. He
called the **elders**, the leaders, the **judges**,
and the officers of Israel, and they came
into the **presence** of God. [2]Joshua said to
all the people, "This is what the LORD,
the God of Israel, has to say: 'Long ago
your ancestors lived on the other side of
the River Euphrates and **worshipped**
other gods. One of those ancestors was
Terah, the father of Abraham and Nahor.
[3]Then I took Abraham, your ancestor,
from the land beyond the Euphrates and
led him through the whole land of
Canaan. I gave him many descendants. I
gave him Isaac, [4]and to Isaac I gave
Jacob and Esau. I gave Esau the hill-
country of Edom as his **possession**, but
your ancestor Jacob and his children
went down to Egypt. [5]Later I sent Moses
and Aaron, and I brought great **trouble**
on Egypt. But I led you out; [6]I brought
your ancestors out of Egypt, and the
Egyptians pursued them with chariots
and cavalry. But when your ancestors
got to the Red Sea [7]they cried out to me
for **help**, and I put **darkness** between
them and the Egyptians. I made the sea
come rolling over the Egyptians and
drown them. You know what I did to
Egypt.

" 'You lived in the desert a long time.
[8]Then I brought you to the land of the
Amorites, who lived on the east side of
the Jordan. They fought you, but I gave
you **victory** over them. You took their
land, and I **destroyed** them as you advanced. [9]Then the king of Moab, Balak
son of Zippor, fought against you. He sent
word to Balaam son of Beor and asked
him to put a **curse** on you. [10]But I would
not listen to Balaam, so he **blessed** you,
and in this way I **rescued** you from Balak.
[11]You crossed the Jordan and came to
Jericho. The men of Jericho fought
against you, as did the Amorites, the
Perizzites, the Canaanites, the Hittites,
the Girgashites, the Hivites, and the
Jebusites. But I gave you **victory** over
them all. [12]As you advanced, I threw
them into panic in order to drive out the
two Amorite kings. Your swords and
bows had nothing to do with it. [13]I gave
you a land that you had never cultivated
and cities that you had not built. Now you
are living there and eating grapes from
vines that you did not plant, and olives
from trees that you did not plant.' "

14 "Now then," Joshua continued,
"**honour** the LORD and **serve** him **sin-**
cerely and **faithfully**. Get **rid** of the **gods**
which your ancestors used to **worship** in
Mesopotamia and in Egypt, and **serve**
only the LORD. [15]If you are not willing to
serve him, decide today whom you will
serve, the **gods** your ancestors **wor-**
shipped in Mesopotamia or the **gods** of
the Amorites, in whose land you are now
living. As for my family and me, we will
serve the LORD."

16 The people replied, "We would
never leave the LORD to **serve** other
gods! [17]The LORD our God brought our
fathers and us out of **slavery** in Egypt,
and we saw the **miracles** that he performed. He kept us **safe** wherever we
went among all the nations through
which we passed. [18]As we advanced into
this land, the LORD drove out all the

judge 23.2; Judg 4.4
keep from 22.27; Judg 7.24
law [2] 23.6; 2 Sam 15.3
loyal Deut 33.9; Judg 9.28
miracle 3.5; 2 Kgs 8.4
obey 23.6; Judg 2.17
possess 23.4; Judg 1.18
presence 10.12; Judg 11.11
punish 23.16; Judg 8.16
rebel 22.16; Judg 9.23
rescue Deut 32.36; Judg 3.31
rid [2] 7.13; Judg 9.29
rival Deut 6.15; 1 Sam 1.6
safe 10.20; Judg 6.2
sanctuary 9.23; 1 Sam 3.3
servant 22.2; Judg 2.8
serve [13] 23.16; Judg 2.7
sincere Judg 9.16
slave 16.10; Judg 6.8
tolerate Deut 6.15; 2 Chr 19.7
trouble 15.7; Judg 10.14
turn 19.13; Judg 3.19
victory [2] 21.44; Judg 1.4
vine Deut 32.32; Judg 9.12
witness [4] 22.34; Judg 11.10
word (1) [2] 22.6; Judg 13.12
worship (2) (of other gods) [3] 23.7; Judg 2.3

23.10: Deut 3.22, 32.30 **24.2:** Gen 11.27 **24.3:** Gen 12.1–9, 21.1–3
24.4: Gen 25.24–26, 36.8, 46.1–7; Deut 2.5 **24.5:** Ex 3.1–12.42 **24.6–7:** Ex 14.1–31 **24.8:** Num 21.21–35
24.9–10: Num 22.1–24.25 **24.11:** Josh 3.14–17, 6.1–21 **24.12:** Ex 23.28; Deut 7.20 **24.13:** Deut 6.10–11

Amorites who lived here. So we also will
serve the LORD; he is our God."
19 Joshua said to the people, "But you
may not be able to **serve** the LORD. He is
a **holy** God and will not **forgive** your sins.
He will **tolerate** no **rivals**, [20]and if you
leave him to **serve** foreign **gods**, he will
turn against you and **punish** you. He will
destroy you, even though he was good to
you before."
21 The people said to Joshua, "No! We
will **serve** the LORD."
22 Joshua said to them, "You are your
own **witnesses** to the fact that you have
chosen to **serve** the LORD."
"Yes," they said, "we are **witnesses**."
23 "Then get **rid** of those foreign **gods**
that you have," he demanded, "and
pledge your **loyalty** to the LORD, the God
of Israel."
24 The people then said to Joshua,
"We will **serve** the LORD our God. We
will **obey** his **commands**."
25 So Joshua made a **covenant** for[q]
the people that day, and there at
Shechem he gave them **laws** and rules to
follow. [26]Joshua wrote these **commands**
in the book of the **Law** of God. Then he
took a large stone and set it up under the
oak-tree in the LORD's **sanctuary**. [27]He
said to all the people, "This stone will be
our **witness**. It has heard all the **words**
that the LORD has spoken to us. So it will
be a **witness** against you, to **keep you**
from rebelling against your God." [28]Then
Joshua sent the people away, and everyone returned to his own part of the land.

Joshua and Eleazar Die

29 After that, the LORD's **servant**
Joshua son of Nun died at the age of a
hundred and ten. [30]They buried him on
his own land at Timnath Serah in the hill-
country of Ephraim north of Mount
Gaash.
31 As long as Joshua lived, the people
of Israel **served** the LORD, and after his
death they continued to do so as long as
those leaders were **alive** who had seen
for themselves everything that the LORD
had done for Israel.
32 The **body** of Joseph, which the
people of Israel had brought from Egypt,
was buried at Shechem, in the piece of
land that Jacob had bought from the sons
of Hamor, the father of Shechem, for a
hundred pieces of silver. This land was
inherited by Joseph's descendants.
33 Eleazar son of Aaron died and was
buried at Gibeah, the town in the hill-
country of Ephraim which had been
given to his son Phinehas.

[q] for; *or* with.

24.30: Josh 19.49–50 **24.32:** Gen 33.19, 50.24–25; Ex 13.19; Jn 4.5; Acts 7.16

THE BOOK OF JUDGES

INTRODUCTION

The book of *Judges* is composed of stories from the lawless period of Israel's history between the invasion of Canaan and the establishment of the monarchy. These stories are about the exploits of national heroes called "judges," most of whom were military leaders, rather than judges in the legal sense of the word. One of the better known of them was Samson, whose deeds are recorded in chapters 13–16.

The great lesson of the book is that Israel's survival depended on loyalty to God, while disloyalty always led to disaster. But there was more than this: even when the nation was disloyal to God, and disaster came, God was always ready to save his people when they repented and turned to him again.

Outline of Contents

barren Josh 8.15; 2 Sam 1.21
command Josh 24.24; 2.17
control Deut 15.6; 6.34
curse Josh 24.9; 5.23
death (1) Josh 24.31; 2.7
destroy Josh 24.8; 4.24
force (1) [5] Josh 17.13; 11.2
help [2] Josh 24.7; 2.18
hurt Num 35.23; 1 Sam 20.3
possess Josh 24.4; 2.6
strong Josh 17.13; 3.12
succeed (1) Josh 15.16; 18.5
urge Josh 15.18; 19.7
victory Josh 24.8; 2.23
wedding Josh 15.18; 14.12

The Tribes of Judah and Simeon Capture Adonibezek

1 After Joshua's **death** the people of
Israel asked the LORD, "Which of
our tribes should be the first to go and
attack the Canaanites?"
2 The LORD answered, "The tribe of
Judah will go first. I am giving them
control of the land."
3 The people of Judah said to the
people of Simeon, "Go with us into the
territory assigned to us, and we will fight
the Canaanites together. Then we will go
with you into the territory assigned to
you." So the tribes of Simeon 4 and Judah
went into battle together. The LORD gave
them **victory** over the Canaanites and
the Perizzites, and they defeated ten
thousand men at Bezek. 5 They found
Adonibezek there and fought against
him. 6 He ran away, but they chased him,
caught him, and cut off his thumbs and
big toes. 7 Adonibezek said, "Seventy
kings with their thumbs and big toes cut
off have picked up scraps under my
table. God has now done to me what I did
to them." He was taken to Jerusalem,
where he died.

The Tribe of Judah Conquers Jerusalem and Hebron

8 The men of Judah attacked Jerusalem and captured it. They killed its
people and set fire to the city. 9 After this
they went on to fight the Canaanites who
lived in the hill-country, in the foothills,
and in the dry country to the south.
10 They marched against the Canaanites
living in the city of Hebron, which used
to be called Kiriath Arba. There they
defeated the clans of Sheshai, Ahiman,
and Talmai.

Othniel Conquers the City of Debir
(Josh 15.13–19)

11 From there the men of Judah
marched against the city of Debir, at that
time called Kiriath Sepher. 12 One of
them, called Caleb, said, "I will give my
daughter Achsah in marriage to the man
who **succeeds** in capturing Kiriath
Sepher." 13 Othniel, the son of Caleb's
younger brother Kenaz, captured the
city, so Caleb gave him his daughter
Achsah in marriage. 14 On the **wedding**
day Othniel **urged** her[a] to ask her father
for a field. She got down from her
donkey, and Caleb asked her what she
wanted. 15 She answered, "I want some
pools of water. The land you have given
me is in the dry country." So Caleb gave
her the upper and lower springs.

The Victories of the Tribes of Judah and Benjamin

16 The descendants of Moses' father-
in-law, the Kenite, went on with the
people of Judah from Jericho, the city of
palm-trees, into the **barren** country south
of Arad in Judah. There they settled
among the Amalekites.[b] 17 The people of
Judah went with the people of Simeon,
and together they defeated the Canaanites who lived in the city of Zephath.

[a] *Some ancient translations* Othniel urged her; *Hebrew* she urged Othniel.
[b] *Some ancient translations* Amalekites; *Hebrew* people.

They put a **curse** on the city, **destroyed** it,
and named it Hormah.[c] 18-19 The LORD
helped the people of Judah, and they
took **possession** of the hill-country. But
they did not capture[d] Gaza, Ashkelon, or
Ekron, with their surrounding territories.
These people living along the coast had
iron chariots, and so the people of Judah
were not able to drive them out. 20 As
Moses had **commanded**, Hebron was
given to Caleb, who drove out of the city
the three clans descended from Anak.
21 But the people of the tribe of Benjamin
did not drive out the Jebusites living in
Jerusalem, and the Jebusites have continued to live there with the people of
Benjamin ever since.

The Tribes of Ephraim and Manasseh Conquer Bethel

22-23 The tribes of Ephraim and
Manasseh went to attack the city of
Bethel, at that time called Luz. The LORD
helped them. They sent spies to the city,
24 who saw a man leaving and said to
him, "Show us how to get into the city,
and we won't **hurt** you." 25 So he showed
them, and the people of Ephraim and
Manasseh killed everyone in the city,
except this man and his family. 26 He
later went to the land of the Hittites, built
a city there, and named it Luz, which is
still its name.

People Who Were not Driven Out by the Israelites

27 The tribe of Manasseh did not drive
out the people living in the cities of Beth
Shan, Taanach, Dor, Ibleam, Megiddo,
and the nearby towns; the Canaanites
continued to live there. 28 When the
Israelites became **stronger**, they **forced**
the Canaanites to work for them, but still
they did not drive them all out.

29 The tribe of Ephraim did not drive
out the Canaanites living in the city of
Gezer, and so the Canaanites continued
to live there with them.

30 The tribe of Zebulun did not drive
out the people living in the cities of
Kitron and Nahalal, and so the Canaanites continued to live there with them
and were **forced** to work for them.

31 The tribe of Asher did not drive out
the people living in the cities of Acco,
Sidon, Ahlab, Achzib, Helbah, Aphek, and
Rehob. 32 The people of Asher lived with
the local Canaanites, since they did not
drive them out.

33 The tribe of Naphtali did not drive
out the people living in the cities of Beth
Shemesh and Bethanath. The people of
Naphtali lived with the local Canaanites,
but **forced** them to work for them.

34 The Amorites **forced** the people of
the tribe of Dan into the hill-country and
did not let them come down to the plain.
35 The Amorites continued to live at Aijalon, Shaalbim, and Mount Heres, but the
tribes of Ephraim and Manasseh kept
them under their rule and **forced** them to
work for them.

36 North of Sela, the Edomite[e] border
ran through Akrabbim Pass.

The Angel of the LORD at Bochim

2 The **angel of the LORD** went from
Gilgal to Bochim and said to the
Israelites, "I took you out of Egypt and
brought you to the **land that I promised**
to your ancestors. I said, 'I will never
break my **covenant** with you. 2 You must
not make any **covenant** with the people
who live in this land. You must tear down
their **altars**.' But you have not done what
I told you. You have done just the opposite! 3 So I tell you now that I will not
drive these people out as you advance.
They will be your **enemies**,[f] and you will
be **trapped** by the **worship of their gods**."
4 When the **angel** had said this, all the
people of Israel began to cry, 5 and that is
why the place is called Bochim.[g] There
they **offered sacrifices** to the LORD.

The Death of Joshua

6 Joshua sent the people of Israel on
their way, and each man went to take
possession of his own **share** of the land.
7 As long as Joshua lived, the people of
Israel **served** the LORD, and after his
death they continued to do so as long as
the leaders were **alive** who had seen for
themselves all the great things that the
LORD had done for Israel. 8 The LORD's
servant Joshua son of Nun died at the
age of a hundred and ten. 9 He was buried
in his own part of the land at Timnath
Serah in the hill-country of Ephraim
north of Mount Gaash. 10 That whole
generation also died, and the next
generation **forgot** the LORD and what he
had done for Israel.

alive Josh 24.31; 1 Sam 2.33
altar Josh 22.10;
angel [2] Deut 3 5.23
anger Josh 23.16
bow (2) Josh 23.7 Ruth 2.10
command [2] 1.2 3.4
covenant [3] Josh 24.25; 2 Sam 23.5
death (1) [2] 1.1;
distress Num 14 10.9
enemy [3] Josh 2 3.28
evil Josh 22.16; 1
forget Deut 32.1
fury [2] Josh 7.1; 14.19
god (2) (other go [4] Josh 24.2; 3.6
groan Ex 6.5; Job 3.24
help 1.18; 4.3
mercy Josh 11.2 6.13
new Josh 9.13; 5.
obey [2] Josh 24. 3.4
offer Josh 22.26;
oppress Deut 30. 10.8
possess 1.18; 11.2
promise Josh 23. 11.30
protect Josh 20.5 Ruth 2.12
refuse (1) Josh 2 8.15
rob Deut 28.29; 9.
sacrifice Josh 22 11.31
save [2] Josh 22.3 8.22
servant Josh 24. 3.19
serve [4] Josh 24. 4.4
share Josh 22.6; 1 Sam 1.4
suffer Josh 22.17; 9.57
trap Josh 23.13; 8

[c] HORMAH: *This name in Hebrew means "destruction."*
[d] *One ancient translation* But they did not capture; *Hebrew* And they captured.
[e] *One ancient translation* Edomite; *Hebrew* Amorite.
[f] *Some ancient translations* enemies; *Hebrew* sides.
[g] BOCHIM: *This name in Hebrew means "those who cry."*

1.21: Josh 15.63; 2 Sam 5.6; 1 Chr 11.4 **1.27-28:** Josh 17.11-13 **1.29:** Josh 16.10
2.2: Ex 34.12-13; Deut 7.2-5 **2.9:** Josh 19.49-50

faithful Deut 32.5; 43
ctory 1.4; 3.10
ay (3) [3] Deut 32.4; Kgs 13.33
orse Num 13.28; Sam 14.19
orship (1) (of God) Josh 22.19; 7.15
orship (2) (of her gods) [4] sh 24.2; 3.6

Israel Stops Worshipping the LORD

11 Then the people of Israel sinned against the LORD and began to **serve** the Baals. 12 They stopped **worshipping** the LORD, the God of their ancestors, the God who had brought them out of Egypt, and they began to **worship other gods**, the **gods** of the peoples round them. They **bowed down** to them and made the LORD **angry**. 13 They stopped **worshipping** the LORD and **served** the Baals and the Astartes. 14 And so the LORD became **furious** with Israel and let raiders attack and **rob** them. He let **enemies** all around overpower them, and the Israelites could no longer **protect** themselves. 15 Every time they went into battle, the LORD was against them, just as he had said he would be. They were in great **distress**.

16 Then the LORD gave the Israelites leaders who **saved** them from the raiders. 17 But the Israelites paid no attention to their leaders. Israel was **unfaithful** to the LORD and **worshipped other gods**. Their fathers had **obeyed** the LORD's **commands**, but this **new** generation soon stopped doing so. 18 Whenever the LORD gave Israel a leader, the LORD would **help** him and would **save** the people from their **enemies** as long as that leader lived. The LORD would have **mercy** on them because they **groaned** under their **suffering** and **oppression**. 19 But when the leader died, the people used to return to the old **ways** and behave **worse** than the previous generation. They would **serve** and **worship other gods**, and **refused** to give up their own **evil ways**. 20 Then the LORD would become **furious** with Israel and say, "This nation has broken the **covenant** that I **commanded** their ancestors to keep. Because they have not **obeyed** me, 21 I will no longer drive out any of the nations that were still in the land when Joshua died. 22 I will use them to find out whether or not these Israelites will follow my **ways**, as their ancestors did." 23 So the LORD allowed those nations to remain in the land; he did not give Joshua **victory** over them, nor did he drive them out soon after Joshua's **death**.

The Nations Remaining in the Land

3 So then, the LORD left some nations in the land to **test** the Israelites who had not been through the wars in Canaan. 2 He did this only in order to **teach** each generation of Israelites about war, especially those who had never been in battle before. 3 Those left in the land were the five Philistine cities, all the Canaanites, the Sidonians, and the Hivites who lived in the Lebanon Mountains from Mount Baal Hermon as far as Hamath Pass. 4 They were to be a **test** for Israel, to find out whether or not the Israelites would **obey** the **commands** that the LORD had given their ancestors through Moses. 5 And so the people of Israel settled down among the Canaanites, the Hittites, the Amorites, the Perizzites, the Hivites, and the Jebusites. 6 They intermarried with them and **worshipped their gods**.

lone [2] Deut 32.12; 1.37
nger 2.12; 6.39
est Josh 10.7; 14.20
ommand 2.17; 4.6
onquer Josh 23.4; 2
ead Josh 1.2; 4.22
nemy 2.3; 5.31
scape [2] Josh 20.3; 2.5
orget 2.10; Sam 1.11
ree [2] Deut 24.18; 0.1

Othniel

7 The people of Israel **forgot** the LORD their God; they sinned against him and **worshipped the idols** of Baal and Asherah. 8 So the LORD became **angry** with Israel and let King Cushan Rishathaim of Mesopotamia **conquer** them, and he ruled over them for eight years. 9 Then the Israelites cried out to the LORD, and he sent a man who **freed** them. This was Othniel, the son of Caleb's younger brother Kenaz. 10 The **spirit of the** LORD came upon him, and he became Israel's leader. Othniel went to war, and the LORD gave him **victory** over the king of Mesopotamia. 11 There was **peace** in the land for forty years, and then Othniel died.

Ehud

12 The people of Israel sinned against the LORD again. Because of this the LORD made King Eglon of Moab **stronger** than Israel. 13 Eglon joined the Ammonites and the Amalekites; they defeated Israel and captured Jericho, the city of palm-trees. 14 The Israelites were **subject** to Eglon for eighteen years.

15 Then the Israelites cried out to the LORD, and he sent a man to **free** them. This was Ehud, a left-handed man, who was the son of Gera, from the tribe of Benjamin. The people of Israel sent Ehud to King Eglon of Moab with **gifts** for him. 16 Ehud had made himself a double-edged sword nearly fifty centimetres long. He had it fastened on his **right** side under his clothes. 17 Then he took the **gifts** to Eglon, who was a very fat man. 18 When Ehud had given him the **gifts**, he told the men who had carried them to go back home. 19 But Ehud himself **turned** back at the carved stones near Gilgal, went back to Eglon, and said, "Your **Majesty**, I have a **secret message** for you."

So the king ordered his **servants**, "Leave us **alone**!" And they all went out.

20 Then, as the king was sitting there **alone** in his cool room on the roof, Ehud went over to him and said, "I have a **message** from God for you." The king

get away Josh 8.22; 1 Sam 19.11
gift [3] Deut 16.16; 1 Sam 6.3
god (2) (other gods) 2.3; 5.8
idol Deut 32.16; 8.27
Majesty Ex 15.7; 1 Sam 15.29
master Lev 25.53; 19.10
message [2] Josh 10.3; 6.8
obey 2.17; 1 Sam 12.14
peace [2] Josh 22.4; 4.17
rescue Josh 24.10; 6.9
right (2) [2] Deut 33.2; 7.20
secret Josh 2.1; 6.11
servant [2] 2.8; 6.27
Spirit (1) (God's Spirit) Num 24.2; 6.34
strong 1.28; 6.2
subject (1) Ex 21.22; 2 Sam 3.28
teach Deut 33.10; 1 Sam 12.23
test [2] Deut 33.8; 6.39
turn Josh 24.20; 9.18
victory [2] 2.23; 4.7
worship (2) (of other gods) [2] 2.3; 6.10

stood up. 21 With his left hand Ehud took
the sword from his **right** side and
plunged it into the king's belly. 22 The
whole sword went in, handle and all, and
the fat covered it up. Ehud did not pull it
out of the king's belly, and it stuck out
behind, between his legs.[h] 23 Then Ehud
went outside, closed the doors behind
him, locked them, 24 and left. The **servants** came and saw that the doors were
locked, but they only thought that the
king was inside, relieving himself. 25 They
waited as long as they thought they
should, but when he still did not open the
door, they took the key and opened it.
And there was their **master**, lying **dead**
on the floor.
26 Ehud **got away** while they were
waiting. He went past the carved stones
and **escaped** to Seirah. 27 When he
arrived there in the hill-country of
Ephraim, he blew a trumpet to call the
men of Israel to battle; then he led them
down from the hills. 28 He said, "Follow
me! The LORD has given you **victory**
over your **enemies**, the Moabites." So
they followed Ehud down and captured
the place where the Moabites were to
cross the Jordan; they did not allow a
single man to cross. 29 That day they
killed about ten thousand of the **best**
Moabite soldiers; none of them **escaped**.
30 That day the Israelites defeated Moab,
and there was **peace** in the land for
eighty years.

Shamgar

31 The next leader was Shamgar son
of Anath. He too **rescued** Israel, and did
so by killing six hundred Philistines with
an ox-goad.

Deborah and Barak

4 After Ehud died, the people of Israel
sinned against the LORD again. 2 So
the LORD let them **be conquered** by
Jabin, a Canaanite king who ruled in the
city of Hazor. The commander of his
army was Sisera, who lived at Harosheth-
of-the-Gentiles. 3 Jabin had nine hundred
iron chariots, and he ruled the people of
Israel with **cruelty** and **violence** for
twenty years. Then the people of Israel
cried out to the LORD for **help**.
4 Now Deborah, the wife of Lappidoth,
was a **prophet**, and she was **serving** as a
judge for the Israelites at that time. 5 She
used to sit under a certain palm-tree
between Ramah and Bethel in the hill-
country of Ephraim, and the people of
Israel would go there for her decisions.
6 One day she sent for Barak son of
Abinoam from the city of Kedesh in
Naphtali and said to him, "The LORD, the
God of Israel, has given you this **command**: 'Take ten thousand men from the
tribes of Naphtali and Zebulun and lead
them to Mount Tabor. 7 I will bring
Sisera, the commander of Jabin's army,
to fight against you at the River Kishon.
He will have his chariots and soldiers,
but I will give you **victory** over him.' "
8 Then Barak replied, "I will go if you
go with me, but if you don't go with me, I
won't go either."
9 She answered, "All right, I will go
with you, but you won't get any credit for
the **victory**, because the LORD will hand
Sisera over to a woman." So Deborah set
off for Kedesh with Barak. 10 Barak
called the tribes of Zebulun and Naphtali
to Kedesh, and ten thousand men followed him. Deborah went with him.
11 In the meantime Heber the Kenite
had set up his tent close to Kedesh near
the oak-tree at Zanannim. He had moved
away from the other Kenites, the descendants of Hobab, the brother-in-law of
Moses.
12 When Sisera **learnt** that Barak had
gone up to Mount Tabor, 13 he called out
his nine hundred iron chariots and all his
men, and sent them from Harosheth-of-
the-Gentiles to the River Kishon.
14 Then Deborah said to Barak, "Go!
The LORD is leading you! Today he has
given you **victory** over Sisera." So Barak
went down from Mount Tabor with his
ten thousand men. 15 When Barak attacked with his army, the LORD threw
Sisera into confusion together with all his
chariots and men. Sisera got down from
his chariot and **fled** on foot. 16 Barak pursued the chariots and the army to
Harosheth-of-the-Gentiles, and Sisera's
whole army was killed. Not a man was
left.
17 Sisera ran away to the tent of Jael,
the wife of Heber the Kenite, because
King Jabin of Hazor was at **peace** with
Heber's family. 18 Jael went out to meet
Sisera and said to him, "Come in, sir;
come into my tent. Don't be **afraid**." So
he went in, and she hid him behind a curtain.[i] 19 He said to her, "Please give me a
drink of water; I'm thirsty." She opened
a leather bag of milk, gave him a drink,
and hid him again. 20 Then he told her,
"Stand at the door of the tent, and if anyone comes and asks you if someone is
here, say no."
21 Sisera was so tired that he fell

afraid Josh 22.24; 6.23
command 3.4; 7.9
conquer 3.8; 10.7
cruel Num 11.15; 2 Sam 12.6
dead 3.25; 5.27
destroy 1.17; 6.4
flee Num 35.32; 9.40
hard Deut 28.23; 9.33
help 2.18; 5.23
judge Josh 24.1; 11.27
learn Josh 9.16; 15.6
peace 3.11; 5.31
prophet Deut 34.10; 6.8
serve 2.7; 8.34
sound (2) Gen 44.17; 8.9
victory [4] 3.10; 5.11
violent Deut 21.5; 1 Sam 2.33

[h] *Probable text* it stuck...legs; *Hebrew unclear.*
[i] hid him behind a curtain; *or* covered him with a rug.

sound asleep. Then Jael took a hammer and a tent-peg, went up to him quietly, and killed him by driving the peg right through the side of his head and into the ground. 22 When Barak came looking for Sisera, Jael went out to meet him and said to him, "Come here! I'll show you the man you're looking for." So he went in with her, and there was Sisera on the ground, **dead**, with the tent-peg through his head.

23 That day God gave the Israelites **victory** over Jabin, the Canaanite king. 24 They pressed **harder** and harder against him until they **destroyed** him.

The Song of Deborah and Barak

5 On that day Deborah and Barak son of Abinoam sang this song:

2 **Praise** the LORD!
The Israelites were **determined** to fight;
the people **gladly** volunteered.
3 Listen, you kings!
Pay attention, you rulers!
I will sing, I will play music
to Israel's God, the LORD.
4 LORD, when you left the mountains of Seir,
when you came out of the region of Edom,
the earth shook, and rain fell from the sky.
Yes, water poured down from the **clouds**.

5 The mountains quaked before the LORD of Sinai,
before the LORD, the God of Israel.

6 In the days of Shamgar son of Anath,
in the days of Jael,
caravans no longer went through the land,
and travellers used the side roads.
7 The towns of Israel stood **abandoned**, Deborah;
they stood empty until you came,[j]
came like a mother for Israel.
8 Then there was war in the land
when the Israelites **chose new gods**.
Of the forty thousand men in Israel,
did anyone carry shield or spear?
9 My **heart** is with the commanders of Israel,
with the people who **gladly** volunteered.
Praise the LORD!

10 Tell of[k] it, you that ride on white donkeys,
sitting on saddles,
and you that must walk wherever you go.
11 Listen! The noisy crowds round the wells
are telling of the LORD's **victories**,
the victories of Israel's people!

Then the **LORD's people** marched down from their cities.[l]
12 Lead on, Deborah, lead on!
Lead on! Sing a song! Lead on!
Forward, Barak son of Abinoam,
lead your **captives** away!
13 Then the **faithful** ones came down to their leaders;
the **LORD's people** came to him[m] ready to fight.
14 They came[n] from Ephraim into the valley,[o]
behind the tribe of Benjamin and its people.
The commanders came down from Machir,
the officers down from Zebulun.
15 The leaders of Issachar came with Deborah;
yes, Issachar came and Barak too,
and they followed him into the valley.
But the tribe of Reuben was divided;
they could not decide whether to come.
16 Why did they stay behind with the **sheep**?
to listen to **shepherds** calling the **flocks**?
Yes, the tribe of Reuben was divided;
they could not decide whether to come.
17 The tribe of Gad stayed east of the Jordan,
and the tribe of Dan remained by the ships.
The tribe of Asher stayed by the sea-coast;
they remained along the shore.
18 But the people of Zebulun and Naphtali
risked their **lives** on the battlefield.

19 At Taanach, by the stream of Megiddo,
the kings came and fought;
the kings of Canaan fought,
but they took no silver away.
20 The stars fought from the sky;
as they moved across the sky,
they fought against Sisera.

[j] abandoned, Deborah...you came; *or* abandoned; they stood empty until I, Deborah, came.
[k] Tell of; *or* Think about. [l] from their cities; *or* to their gates.
[m] *One ancient translation* him; *Hebrew* me. [n] *Probable text* They came; *Hebrew* Their root.
[o] *One ancient translation* into the valley; *Hebrew* in Amalek.

5.5: Ex 19.18

andon Josh 10.6; 13
gel 2.1; 6.11
ptive Num 24.22; Sam 30.8
oose Josh 24.22; 8
oud Deut 33.26; .38
rse [2] 1.17; 9.57
ad 4.22; 9.55
termine Josh 14.2; uth 1.18
emy 3.28; 7.11
ithful Josh 24.14; Sam 2.9
ock Josh 14.3; Sam 8.17
ood Josh 4.18; Sam 5.20
rtune [2] Kgs 10.8
iend Josh 9.15; 7.13
lad [2] Deut 30.9; 25
od (2) (other gods) 6; 6.10
od's people [2] osh 22.17; 11.23
eart Josh 23.14; .35
elp 4.3; 6.7
nee [2] 7.5
fe (1) Josh 9.24; 17
ew 2.17; 15.13
eace 4.17; 6.23
raise [2] Josh 22.33; 5.24
ich Josh 22.6; uth 2.1
ise Josh 8.20; Sam 25.42
heep Josh 7.24; 6.4
hepherd um 27.17; Sam 17.40
trength Deut 33.17; .14
trike Deut 32.25; .33
ictory 4.7; 7.2
ise Deut 18.17; Sam 14.20

21 A **flood** in the Kishon swept them
away—
the onrushing River Kishon.
I shall march, march on, with
strength!
22 Then the horses came galloping on,
stamping the ground with their
hooves.

23 "Put a **curse** on Meroz," says the **angel
of the** LORD,
"a **curse**, a curse on those who live
there.
They did not come to **help** the LORD,
come as soldiers to fight for him."

24 The most **fortunate** of women is Jael,
the wife of Heber the Kenite—
the most **fortunate** of women who
live in tents.
25 Sisera asked for water, but she gave
him milk;
she brought him cream in a
beautiful bowl.
26 She took a tent peg in one hand,
a workman's hammer in the other;
she **struck** Sisera and crushed his
skull;
she pierced him through the head.
27 He sank to his **knees**,
fell down and lay still at her feet.
At her feet he sank to his **knees** and
fell;
he fell to the ground, **dead**.

28 Sisera's mother looked out of the
window;
she gazed[p] from behind the lattice.
"Why is his chariot so late in
coming?" she asked.
"Why are his horses so slow to
return?"
29 Her **wisest** ladies answered her,
and she told herself over and over,
30 "They are only finding things to
capture and divide,
a girl or two for every soldier,
rich cloth for Sisera,
embroidered pieces for the neck of
the queen."[q]

31 May all your **enemies** die like that, O
LORD,
but may your **friends** shine like the
rising sun!

And there was **peace** in the land for forty years.

Gideon

6 Once again the people of Israel
sinned against the LORD, so he let
the people of Midian rule them for seven
years. 2 The Midianites were **stronger**
than Israel, and the people of Israel hid
from them in caves and other **safe** places
in the hills. 3 Whenever the Israelites
sowed any **seed**, the Midianites would
come with the Amalekites and the desert
tribes and attack them. 4 They would
camp on the land and **destroy** the crops
as far south as the area round Gaza.
They would take all the **sheep**, cattle,
and donkeys, and leave nothing for the
Israelites to live on. 5 They would come
with their livestock and tents, as thick as
locusts. They and their camels were too
many to count. They came and **devastated** the land, 6 and Israel was **helpless**
against them.
7 Then the people of Israel cried out
to the LORD for **help** against the Midianites, 8 and he sent them a **prophet** who
brought them this **message** from the
LORD, the God of Israel: "I brought you
out of **slavery** in Egypt. 9 I **rescued** you
from the Egyptians and from the people
who fought against you here in this land.
I drove them out as you advanced, and I
gave you their land. 10 I told you that I am
the LORD your God and that you should
not **worship the gods** of the Amorites,
whose land you are now living in. But you
did not listen to me."
11 Then the **LORD's angel** came to the
village of Ophrah and sat under the oak-
tree that belonged to Joash, a man of the
clan of Abiezer. His son Gideon was
threshing some wheat **secretly** in a winepress, so that the Midianites would not
see him. 12 The **LORD's angel** appeared to
him there and said, "The LORD is with
you, brave and **mighty** man!"
13 Gideon said to him, "If I may ask,
sir, why has all this happened to us if the
LORD is with us? What about all the
wonderful things that our fathers told us
the LORD used to do—how he brought
them out of Egypt? The LORD has **abandoned** us and left us to the **mercy** of the
Midianites."
14 Then the LORD ordered him, "Go
with all your great **strength** and **rescue**
Israel from the Midianites. I myself am
sending you."
15 Gideon replied, "But LORD, how can
I **rescue** Israel? My clan is the **weakest**
in the tribe of Manasseh, and I am the
least important member of my family."
16 The LORD answered, "You can do it
because I will **help** you. You will crush
the Midianites as easily as if they were
only one man."
17 Gideon replied, "If you are **pleased**

[p] *Some ancient translations* gazed; *Hebrew* cried out. [q] *Probable text* queen, *Hebrew* plunder.

abandon 5.7; 8.27
afraid [2] 4.18; 7.3
altar [8] 2.2; 13.19

angel [8] 5.23;
anger 3.8; 8.3
bread [4] Josh
7.13
control 1.2;
1 Sam 10.6
defend [3] Josh
1 Sam 2.25
destroy 4.24; 2
devastate
Josh 22.33; 16.2
each other Ex
7.22
enough Josh 2
21.14
god (2) (other
[2] 5.8; 8.33
goddess Deut
1 Sam 7.3
help [2] 5.23; 8.
helpless Deut
16.5
important
Num 22.15;
1 Sam 9.21
least 1 Sam 9.2
mercy 2.18;
2 Sam 1.22
message 3.19;
might Josh 22.
16.30
offer [2] 2.5; 11
peace [2] 5.31;
please Deut 33
17.6
prophet 4.4;
1 Sam 2.27
prove Deut 33.
1 Sam 10.1
rescue [5] 3.31;
safe Josh 24.17
secret 3.19; 16.
seed Deut 28.3
Job 4.8
servant 3.19; 7.
sheep 5.16;
1 Sam 14.32
slave Josh 24.1
1 Sam 2.27
Sovereign Josh
16.28
sow Deut 28.38
2 Kgs 19.29
**Spirit (1) (God'
Spirit)** 3.10; 11.
strength 5.21;
strong 3.12; 9.5
symbol [4]
Deut 16.21;
1 Kgs 14.23
terror Deut 32.
1 Sam 17.24
test 3.1; 1 Kgs
weak Deut 32.3
16.7
wonder (1)
Deut 34.11; 13.1
**worship (2) (of
other gods)** 3.6
yeast Josh 5.11
1 Sam 28.24

with me, give me some **proof** that you
are really the LORD. 18 Please do not
leave until I bring you an **offering** of
food."
He said, "I will stay until you come
back."
19 So Gideon went into his house and
cooked a young goat and used ten kilogrammes of flour to make **bread** without
any **yeast**. He put the meat in a basket
and the broth in a pot, brought them to
the **LORD's angel** under the oak-tree, and
gave them to him. 20 The **angel** ordered
him, "Put the meat and the **bread** on this
rock, and pour the broth over them."
Gideon did so. 21 Then the **LORD's angel**
reached out and touched the meat and
the **bread** with the end of the stick he
was holding. Fire came out of the rock
and burnt up the meat and the **bread**.
Then the **angel** disappeared.
22 Gideon then realized that it was the
LORD's angel he had seen, and he said in
terror, "**Sovereign LORD**! I have seen
your **angel** face to face!"
23 But the LORD said to him, "**Peace**.
Don't be **afraid**. You will not die."
24 Gideon built an **altar** to the LORD there
and named it "The LORD is **Peace**." (It is
still standing at Ophrah, which belongs to
the clan of Abiezer.)
25 That night the LORD told Gideon,
"Take your father's bull and another bull
seven years old,[r] tear down your father's
altar to Baal, and cut down the **symbol** of
the **goddess** Asherah, which is beside it.
26 Build a well-constructed **altar** to the
LORD your God on top of this mound.
Then take the second bull[s] and burn it
whole as an **offering**, using for firewood
the **symbol** of Asherah you have cut
down." 27 So Gideon took ten of his **servants** and did what the LORD had told
him. He was too **afraid** of his family and
the people of the town to do it by day, so
he did it at night.
28 When the people of the town got up
early the next morning, they found that
the **altar** to Baal and the **symbol** of
Asherah had been cut down, and that the
second bull had been burnt on the **altar**
that had been built there. 29 They asked
each other, "Who did this?" They investigated and found out that Gideon son of
Joash had done it. 30 Then they said to
Joash, "Bring your son out here, so that
we can kill him! He tore down the **altar**
to Baal and cut down the **symbol** of
Asherah beside it."
31 But Joash said to all those who confronted him, "Are you standing up for
Baal? Are you **defending** him? Anyone
who stands up for him will be killed
before morning. If Baal is a **god**, let him
defend himself. It is his **altar** that was
torn down." 32 From then on Gideon was
known as Jerubbaal,[t] because Joash said,
"Let Baal **defend** himself; it is his **altar**
that was torn down."
33 Then all the Midianites, the Amalekites, and the desert tribes assembled,
crossed the River Jordan, and camped in
the Valley of Jezreel. 34 The **spirit of the
LORD** took **control** of Gideon, and he blew
a trumpet to call the men of the clan of
Abiezer to follow him. 35 He sent messengers throughout the territory of both
parts of Manasseh to call them to follow
him. He sent messengers to the tribes of
Asher, Zebulun, and Naphtali, and they
also came to join him.
36 Then Gideon said to God, "You say
that you have decided to use me to
rescue Israel. 37 Well, I am putting some
wool on the ground where we thresh the
wheat. If in the morning there is dew
only on the wool but not on the ground,
then I will know that you are going to use
me to **rescue** Israel." 38 That is exactly
what happened. When Gideon got up
early the next morning, he squeezed the
wool and wrung **enough** dew out of it to
fill a bowl with water. 39 Then Gideon
said to God, "Don't be **angry** with me; let
me speak just once more. Please let me
make one more **test** with the wool. This
time let the wool be dry, and the ground
be wet." 40 That night God did that very
thing. The next morning the wool was
dry, but the ground was wet with dew.

Gideon Defeats the Midianites

7 One day Gideon and all his men got
up early and camped beside the
Spring of Harod. The Midianite camp
was in the valley to the north of them by
Moreh Hill.
2 The LORD said to Gideon, "The men
you have are too many for me to give
them **victory** over the Midianites. They
might think that they had **won** by themselves, and so give me no credit.
3 **Announce** to the people, 'Anyone who is
afraid should go back home, and we will
stay here at Mount Gilead.' " So twenty-
two thousand went back, but ten thous-
and stayed.
4 Then the LORD said to Gideon, "You
still have too many men. Take them
down to the water, and I will **separate**

afraid [2] 6.23; 9.21
announce Ex 32.5; 2 Sam 1.20
bread 6.19; 8.5
change Josh 19.47; 14.12
command 4.6; 1 Sam 12.14
courage Josh 7.5; 1 Sam 30.6
dream [3] Deut 23.10; 1 Sam 28.6
each other 6.29; 9.23
enemy [3] 5.31; 8.4
friend [2] 5.31; 11.37
keep from Josh 24.27; 12.5
knee [3] 5.27; 1 Sam 14.13
rescue 6.9; 10.13
right (2) 3.16; 1 Sam 11.2
separate [2] Num 26.62; Ruth 1.17
servant [2] 6.27; 9.18
victory [5] 5.11; 11.9

[r] bull and another bull seven years old; *or* bull, the seven-year-old one.
[s] the second bull; *or* the bull. [t] JERUBBAAL: *This name in Hebrew means "Let Baal defend himself."*

7.3: Deut 20.8

watch Deut 11.12; 16.27
win Ex 17.11; 1 Sam 13.12
worship (1) (of God) 2.12; 10.6

them for you there. If I tell you a man should go with you, he will go. If I tell you a man should not go with you, he will not go." 5 Gideon took the men down to the water, and the LORD said to him, "**Separate** everyone who laps up the water with his tongue like a dog, from everyone who gets down on his **knees** to drink." 6 There were three hundred men who scooped up water in their hands and lapped it; all the others got down on their **knees** to drink. 7 The LORD said to Gideon, "I will **rescue** you and give you **victory** over the Midianites with the three hundred men who lapped the water. Tell everyone else to go home." 8 So Gideon sent all the Israelites home, except the three hundred, who kept all the supplies and trumpets. The Midianite camp was below them in the valley.

9 That night the LORD **commanded** Gideon, "Get up and attack the camp; I am giving you **victory** over it. 10 But if you are **afraid** to attack, go down to the camp with your **servant** Purah. 11 You will hear what they are saying, and then you will have the **courage** to attack." So Gideon and his **servant** Purah went down to the edge of the **enemy** camp. 12 The Midianites, the Amalekites, and the desert tribesmen were spread out in the valley like a swarm of locusts, and they had as many camels as there were grains of sand on the seashore.

13 When Gideon arrived, he heard a man telling a **friend** about a **dream**. He was saying, "I **dreamt** that a loaf of barley **bread** rolled into our camp and hit a tent. The tent collapsed and lay flat on the ground."

14 His **friend** replied, "It's the sword of the Israelite, Gideon son of Joash! It can't mean anything else! God has given him **victory** over Midian and our whole army!"

15 When Gideon heard about the man's **dream** and what it meant, he fell to his **knees** and **worshipped** the LORD. Then he went back to the Israelite camp and said, "Get up! The LORD is giving you **victory** over the Midianite army!" 16 He divided his three hundred men into three groups and gave each man a trumpet and a jar with a torch inside it. 17 He told them, "When I get to the edge of the camp, **watch** me, and do what I do. 18 When my group and I blow our trumpets, then you blow yours all round the camp and shout, 'For the LORD and for Gideon!' "

19 Gideon and his hundred men came to the edge of the camp a short while before midnight, just after the guard had been **changed**. Then they blew the trumpets and broke the jars they were holding, 20 and the other two groups did the same. They all held the torches in their left hands, the trumpets in their **right**, and shouted, "A sword for the LORD and for Gideon!" 21 Every man stood in his place round the camp, and the whole **enemy** army ran away yelling. 22 While Gideon's men were blowing their trumpets, the LORD made the **enemy** troops attack **each other** with their swords. They ran towards Zarethan as far as Beth Shittah, as far as the town of Abel Meholah near Tabbath.

23 Then men from the tribes of Naphtali, Asher, and both parts of Manasseh were called out, and they pursued the Midianites. 24 Gideon sent messengers through all the hill-country of Ephraim to say, "Come down and fight the Midianites. Hold the River Jordan and the streams as far as Bethbarah, to **keep the Midianites from** crossing them." The men of Ephraim were called together, and they held the River Jordan and the streams as far as Bethbarah. 25 They captured the two Midianite chiefs, Oreb and Zeeb; they killed Oreb at Oreb Rock, and Zeeb at the Winepress of Zeeb. They continued to pursue the Midianites and brought the heads of Oreb and Zeeb to Gideon, who was now east of the Jordan.

The Final Defeat of the Midianites

8 Then the men of Ephraim said to Gideon, "Why didn't you call us when you went to fight the Midianites? Why did you treat us like this?" They **complained bitterly** about it.

2 But he said, "What I was able to do is nothing **compared** with what you have done. Even the little that you men of Ephraim did is **worth** more than what my whole clan has done. 3 After all, through the **power of God** you killed the two Midianite chiefs, Oreb and Zeeb. What have I done to **compare** with that?" When he said this, they were no longer so **angry**.

4 By this time Gideon and his three hundred men had come to the River Jordan and had crossed it. They were exhausted, but were still pursuing the **enemy**. 5 When they arrived at Sukkoth, he said to the men of the town, "Please give my men some loaves of **bread**. They are exhausted, and I am pursuing Zebah and Zalmunna, the Midianite kings."

6 But the leaders of Sukkoth said,

abandon 6.13; 10.6
anger 6.39; 9.30
bitter Deut 32.32; 21.2
bread 7.13; 19.19
compare [2] 1 Kgs 20.27
complain Josh 9.18; 1 Sam 8.18
concubine Lev 19.20; 19.1
death (1) 2.7; 10.1
enemy [2] 7.11; 11.3
glad 5.2; 1 Sam 19.5
god (2) (other gods 6.10; 9.9
grateful Deut 27.7; 2 Chr 32.25
help 6.7; Ruth 3.15
idol [2] 3.7; 17.3
leading Josh 22.14; 9.46
peace 6.23; 11.13
power Josh 23.9; 13.25
punish Josh 24.20; 20.10
question Josh 1.18; 1 Sam 9.9
refuse (1) 2.19; 1 Sam 1.7
remember Josh 22.17; 9.2
request Deut 18.17; 1 Sam 8.6
ripe Deut 33.14; 1 Chr 29.28

8.3–5: Ps 83.11

safe 6.2; 9.46
save [2] 2.16; 9.17
serve 4.4; 9.28
solemn Josh 21.43; 11.35
sound (2) 4.21; 1 Sam 26.12
swear Josh 5.4; 15.7
threat Josh 23.15; 1 Sam 3.12
tomb Gen 50.5; 16.31
trap 2.3; 20.43
unfaithful 2.17; 1 Chr 5.25
worship (2) (of other gods) [2] 6.10; 10.6
worth Gen 32.10; 2 Sam 18.3

"Why should we give your army any food? You haven't captured Zebah and Zalmunna yet."

7 So Gideon said, "All right! When the LORD has handed Zebah and Zalmunna over to me, I will beat you with thorns and briars from the desert!" 8 Gideon went on to Penuel and made the same **request** of the people there, but the men of Penuel gave the same answer as the men of Sukkoth. 9 So he said to them, "I am going to come back **safe and sound**, and when I do, I will tear your tower down!"

10 Zebah and Zalmunna were at Karkor with their army. Of the whole army of desert tribesmen, only about 15,000 were left; 120,000 soldiers had been killed. 11 Gideon went along the road by the edge of the desert, east of Nobah and Jogbehah, and attacked the army by surprise. 12 The two Midianite kings, Zebah and Zalmunna, ran away, but he pursued them and captured them, and caused their whole army to panic.

13 When Gideon was returning from the battle by way of Heres Pass, 14 he captured a young man from Sukkoth and **questioned** him. The young man wrote down for Gideon the names of the seventy-seven **leading** men of Sukkoth. 15 Then Gideon went to the men of Sukkoth and said, "**Remember** when you **refused** to **help** me? You said that you couldn't give any food to my exhausted army because I hadn't captured Zebah and Zalmunna yet. Well, here they are!" 16 He then took thorns and briars from the desert and used them to **punish** the leaders of Sukkoth. 17 He also tore down the tower at Penuel and killed the men of that city.

18 Then Gideon asked Zebah and Zalmunna, "What about the men you killed at Tabor?"

They answered, "They looked like you—every one of them like the son of a king."

19 Gideon said, "They were my brothers, my own mother's sons. I **solemnly swear** that if you had not killed them, I would not kill you." 20 Then he said to Jether, his eldest son, "Go ahead, kill them!" But the boy did not draw his sword. He hesitated, because he was still only a boy.

21 Then Zebah and Zalmunna said to Gideon, "Come on, kill us yourself. It takes a man to do a man's job." So Gideon killed them and took the ornaments that were on the necks of their camels.

22 After that, the Israelites said to Gideon, "Be our ruler—you and your descendants after you. You have **saved** us from the Midianites."

23 Gideon answered, "I will not be your ruler, nor will my son. The LORD will be your ruler." 24 But he went on to say, "Let me ask one thing of you. Every one of you give me the earrings you took." (The Midianites, like other desert people, wore gold earrings.)

25 The people answered, "We'll be **glad** to give them to you." They spread out a cloth, and everyone put on it the earrings that he had taken. 26 The gold earrings that Gideon received weighed nearly twenty kilogrammes, and this did not include the ornaments, necklaces, and purple clothes that the kings of Midian wore, nor the collars that were round the necks of their camels. 27 Gideon made an **idol** from the gold and put it in his home town, Ophrah. All the Israelites **abandoned** God and went there to **worship the idol**. It was a **trap** for Gideon and his family.

28 So Midian was defeated by the Israelites and was no longer a **threat**. The land was at **peace** for forty years, until Gideon died.

The Death of Gideon

29 Gideon went back to his own home and lived there. 30 He had seventy sons, because he had many wives. 31 He also had a **concubine** in Shechem; she bore him a son, and he named him Abimelech. 32 Gideon son of Joash died at a **ripe** old age and was buried in the **tomb** of his father Joash, at Ophrah, the town of the clan of Abiezer.

33 After Gideon's **death** the people of Israel were again **unfaithful** to God and **worshipped the Baals**. They made Baal-of-the-Covenant their **god**, 34 and no longer **served** the LORD their God, who had **saved** them from all their **enemies** round them. 35 They were not **grateful** to the family of Gideon for all the good that he had done for Israel.

Abimelech

9 Gideon's son Abimelech went to the town of Shechem, where all his mother's relatives lived, and told them 2 to ask the men of Shechem, "Which would you prefer? To be governed by all seventy of Gideon's sons or by just one man? **Remember** that Abimelech is your own **flesh and blood**." 3 His mother's relatives talked to the men of Shechem about this for him, and the men of Shechem decided to follow Abimelech because he was their relative. 4 They gave him

action Lev 18.25; 1 Sam 12.7
afraid 7.3; 1 Sam 3.15
anger 8.3; 10.7
blood Deut 32.42; 1 Sam 14.32
choose 5.8; 10.14
confident Josh 10.25; 1 Kgs 2.2
crime [2] Deut 25.2; 20.3
curse 5.23; 17.2
dead 5.27; 14.8
deserve Deut 9.4; 1 Sam 26.16
each other 7.22; 1 Sam 14.20

encourage Deut 13.6; 20.22
festival Deut 31.10; 21.19
flee 4.15; 11.3
flesh Num 12.12; 2 Sam 5.1
fortune-teller Josh 13.22; 1 Sam 28.3
god (2) (other gods) [3] 8.33; 10.6
grapevine *see* **vine**
happy [2] Deut 33.29; 18.20
hard 4.24; 20.34
honest [2] Josh 14.7; 1 Sam 8.3
honour Josh 24.14; 13.17
leading 8.14; 1 Kgs 21.8
life (1) 5.18; 12.3
loyal Josh 24.23; Ruth 3.10
plan Num 33.56; 20.32
proper Num 29.3; 1 Kgs 14.13
rebel Josh 24.27; 1 Sam 15.23
remember [2] 8.15; 16.28
respect Deut 5.16; 1 Sam 2.17
rid Josh 24.14; 10.16
rob 2.14; 14.15
sacred Josh 22.27; 18.18
safe 8.9; 18.7
save 8.22; 10.12
scorn [2] 1 Sam 17.42
seek Num 35.12; 2 Sam 22.31
servant 7.10; 19.3
serve [3] 8.34; 18.4
shelter Deut 31.10; Ruth 2.7
sincere [2] Josh 24.14; 1 Kgs 8.48
strong 6.2; 14.6
suffer 2.18; 1 Sam 9.16
temple (2) (of other gods) [3] 1 Sam 5.2
turn 3.19; 11.8
vine [2] Josh 24.13; 13.14
vineyard Deut 28.30; 14.5
wicked Deut 31.29; 1 Sam 2.9
wish Deut 28.67; 1 Sam 11.10
worthless Deut 13.13; 11.3

seventy pieces of silver from the **temple**
of Baal-of-the-Covenant, and with this
money he hired a bunch of **worthless**
scoundrels to join him. 5 He went to his
father's house at Ophrah, and there on
the top of a single stone he killed his
seventy brothers, Gideon's sons. But
Jotham, Gideon's youngest son, hid and
was not killed. 6 Then all the men of
Shechem and Bethmillo got together and
went to the **sacred** oak-tree at Shechem,
where they made Abimelech king.

7 When Jotham heard about this, he
went and stood on top of Mount Gerizim
and shouted out to them, "Listen to me,
you men of Shechem, and God may listen
to you! 8 Once upon a time the trees got
together to **choose** a king for themselves.
They said to the olive-tree, 'Be our king.'
9 The olive-tree answered, 'In order to
govern you, I would have to stop producing my oil, which is used to **honour**
gods and men.' 10 Then the trees said to
the fig-tree, 'You come and be our king.'
11 But the fig-tree answered, 'In order to
govern you, I would have to stop producing my good sweet fruit.' 12 So the
trees then said to the **grapevine**, 'You
come and be our king.' 13 But the **vine**
answered, 'In order to govern you, I
would have to stop producing my wine,
that makes **gods** and men **happy**.' 14 So
then all the trees said to the thorn-bush,
'You come and be our king.' 15 The thorn-
bush answered, 'If you really want to
make me your king, then come and take
shelter in my shade. If you don't, fire will
blaze out of my thorny branches and
burn up the cedars of Lebanon.'

16 "Now then," Jotham continued,
"were you really **honest** and **sincere**
when you made Abimelech king? Did
you **respect** Gideon's memory and treat
his family **properly**, as his **actions**
deserved? 17 **Remember** that my father
fought for you. He risked his **life** to **save**
you from the Midianites. 18 But today you
turned against my father's family. You
killed his sons—seventy men on a single
stone—and just because Abimelech, his
son by his **servant-girl**, is your relative,
you have made him king of Shechem.
19 Now then, if what you did today to
Gideon and his family was **sincere** and
honest, then be **happy** with Abimelech
and let him be happy with you. 20 But if
not, may fire blaze out from Abimelech
and burn up the men of Shechem and
Bethmillo. May fire blaze out from the
men of Shechem and Bethmillo and burn
Abimelech up." 21 Then because he was
afraid of his brother Abimelech, Jotham
ran away and went to live at Beer.

22 Abimelech ruled Israel for three
years. 23 Then God made Abimelech and
the men of Shechem hostile to **each**
other, and they **rebelled** against him.
24 This happened so that Abimelech and
the men of Shechem, who **encouraged**
him to murder Gideon's seventy sons,
would pay for their **crime**. 25 The men of
Shechem put men in ambush against
Abimelech on the mountain-tops, and
they **robbed** everyone who passed their
way. Abimelech was told about this.

26 Then Gaal son of Ebed came to
Shechem with his brothers, and the men
of Shechem put their **confidence** in him.
27 They all went out into their **vineyards**
and picked the grapes, made wine from
them, and held a **festival**. They went into
the **temple** of their **god**, where they ate
and drank and spoke **scornfully** of
Abimelech. 28 Gaal said, "What kind of
men are we in Shechem? Why are we
serving Abimelech? Who is he, anyway?
The son of Gideon! And Zebul takes
orders from him, but why should we
serve him? Be **loyal** to your ancestor
Hamor, who founded your clan! 29 I **wish**
I were leading this people! I would get
rid of Abimelech! I would say[u] to him,
'Reinforce your army, come on out and
fight!'"

30 Zebul, the ruler of the city, became
angry when he heard what Gaal had
said. 31 He sent messengers to Abimelech
at Arumah[v] to say, "Gaal son of Ebed
and his brothers have come to Shechem,
and they are not going to let you into the
city. 32 Now then, you and your men
should move by night and hide in the
fields. 33 Get up tomorrow morning at
sunrise and make a sudden attack on the
city. Then when Gaal and his men come
out against you, hit them as **hard** as you
can!"

34 So Abimelech and all his men made
their move at night and hid outside Shechem in four groups. 35 When Abimelech
and his men saw Gaal come out and
stand at the city gate, they got up from
their hiding places. 36 Gaal saw them and
said to Zebul, "Look! There are men
coming down from the mountain-tops!"

"Those are not men," Zebul answered.
"They are just shadows on the mountains."

37 Gaal said again, "Look! There are
men coming down the crest of the mountain and one group is coming along the
road from the oak-tree of the **fortune-**
tellers!"

[u] *One ancient translation* I would say; *Hebrew* He said. [v] *Probable text* Arumah; *Hebrew unclear.*

38 Then Zebul said to him, "Where is
all your big talk now? You were the one
who asked why we should **serve** this man
Abimelech. These are the men you were
treating so **scornfully**. Go on out now and
fight them." 39 Gaal led the men of
Shechem out and fought Abimelech.
40 Gaal **fled**, and Abimelech pursued him.
Many were wounded, even at the city
gate. 41 Abimelech lived in Arumah, and
Zebul drove Gaal and his brothers out of
Shechem, so that they could no longer
live there.

42 The next day Abimelech found out
that the people of Shechem were **planning** to go out into the fields, 43 so he took
his men, divided them into three groups,
and hid in the fields, waiting. When he
saw the people coming out of the city, he
came out of hiding to kill them. 44 While
Abimelech and his group hurried forward to guard the city gate, the other
two companies attacked the people in
the fields and killed them all. 45 The fighting continued all day long. Abimelech
captured the city, killed its people, tore it
down, and covered the ground with salt.

46 When all the **leading** men in the
fort at Shechem heard about this, they
sought safety in the stronghold of the
temple of Baal-of-the-Covenant. 47 Abimelech was told that they had gathered
there, 48 so he went up to Mount Zalmon
with his men. There he took an axe, cut a
branch off a tree, and put it on his
shoulder. He told his men to be quick and
do the same thing. 49 So every man cut off
a branch of a tree; then they followed
Abimelech and piled the wood up against
the stronghold. They set it on fire, with
the people inside, and all the people of
the fort died—about a thousand men and
women.

50 Then Abimelech went to Thebez,
surrounded that city, and captured it.
51 There was a **strong** tower there, and
every man and woman in the city, including the leaders, ran to it. They
locked themselves in and went up to the
roof. 52 When Abimelech came to attack
the tower, he went up to the door to set
the tower on fire. 53 But a woman threw a
millstone down on his head and fractured
his skull. 54 Then he quickly called the
young man who was carrying his
weapons and ordered, "Draw your sword
and kill me. I don't want it said that a
woman killed me." So the young man ran
him through, and he died. 55 When the
Israelites saw that Abimelech was **dead**,
they all went home.

56 In this way God paid Abimelech
back for the **crime** that he committed
against his father in killing his seventy
brothers. 57 God also made the men of
Shechem **suffer** for their **wickedness**, just
as Jotham, Gideon's son, said they would
when he **cursed** them.

Tola

10 After Abimelech's **death** Tola,
the son of Puah and grandson of
Dodo, came to **free** Israel. He was from
the tribe of Issachar and lived at Shamir
in the hill-country of Ephraim. 2 He was
Israel's leader for twenty-three years.
Then he died and was buried at Shamir.

Jair

3 After Tola came Jair from Gilead.
He led Israel for twenty-two years. 4 He
had thirty sons who rode thirty donkeys.
They had thirty cities in the land of
Gilead, which are still called the villages
of Jair. 5 Jair died and was buried at
Kamon.

Jephthah

6 Once again the Israelites sinned
against the LORD by **worshipping the
Baals** and the Astartes, as well as the
gods of Syria, of Sidon, of Moab, of Ammon, and of Philistia. They **abandoned**
the LORD and stopped **worshipping** him.
7 So the LORD became **angry** with the
Israelites, and let the Philistines and the
Ammonites **conquer** them. 8 For eighteen
years they **oppressed** and **persecuted** all
the Israelites who lived in Amorite country east of the River Jordan in Gilead.
9 The Ammonites even crossed the
Jordan to fight the tribes of Judah, Benjamin, and Ephraim. Israel was in great
distress.

10 Then the Israelites cried out to the
LORD and said, "We have sinned against
you, for we left you, our God, and **worshipped the Baals**."

11 The LORD gave them this answer:
"The Egyptians, the Amorites, the
Ammonites, the Philistines, 12 the Sidonians, the Amalekites, and the Maonites
oppressed you in the past, and you cried
out to me. Did I not **save** you from them?
13 But you still left me and **worshipped
other gods**, so I am not going to **rescue**
you again. 14 Go and cry out to the **gods**
you have **chosen**. Let them **rescue** you
when you get into **trouble**."

15 But the people of Israel said to the
LORD, "We have sinned. Do whatever
you like, but please, **save** us today." 16 So
they got **rid** of their foreign **gods** and

abandon 8.27; 1 Sam 12.22
anger 9.30; 18.25
choose 9.8; 18.2
conquer 4.2; 1 Sam 12.9
death (1) 8.33; 16.30
distress [2] 2.15; 1 Sam 1.9
free 3.9; 16.20
god (2) (other gods) [4] 9.9; 11.24
oppress [2] 2.18; 1 Sam 10.18
persecute Esth 7.6
rescue [2] 7.7; 12.2
rid 9.29; 1 Sam 7.3
save [2] 9.17; 18.27
trouble [2] Josh 24.5; 11.7
worship (1) (of God) [2] 7.15; 18.31
worship (2) (of other gods) [3] 8.27; 18.30

9.53: 2 Sam 11.21

worshipped the LORD; and he became
troubled over Israel's **distress**.
17 Then the Ammonite army prepared for battle and made camp in
Gilead. The men of Israel came together
and camped at Mizpah in Gilead. 18 There
the people and the leaders of the Israelite tribes asked one another, "Who will
lead the fight against the Ammonites?
Whoever does will be the leader of
everyone in Gilead."

11 Jephthah, a brave soldier from
Gilead, was the son of a **prostitute**. His father Gilead 2 had other sons by
his wife, and when they grew up, they
forced Jephthah to leave home. They
said to him, "You will not **inherit** anything from our father; you are the son of
another woman." 3 Jephthah **fled** from
his brothers and lived in the land of Tob.
There he attracted a group of **worthless**
men, and they went round with him.
4 It was some time later that the
Ammonites went to war against Israel.
5 When this happened, the leaders of
Gilead went to bring Jephthah back from
the land of Tob. 6 They said, "Come and
lead us, so that we can fight the Ammonites."
7 But Jephthah answered, "You **hated**
me so much that you **forced** me to leave
my father's house. Why come to me now
that you're in **trouble**?"
8 They said to Jephthah, "We are **turning** to you now because we want you to
go with us and fight the Ammonites and
lead all the people of Gilead."
9 Jephthah said to them, "If you take
me back home to fight the Ammonites
and the LORD gives me **victory**, I will be
your ruler."
10 They replied, "We **agree**. The LORD
is our **witness**." 11 So Jephthah went with
the leaders of Gilead, and the people
made him their ruler and leader. Jephthah stated his terms at Mizpah in the
presence of the LORD.
12 Then Jephthah sent messengers to
the king of Ammon to say, "What is your
quarrel with us? Why have you invaded
our country?"
13 The king of Ammon answered
Jephthah's messengers, "When the
Israelites came out of Egypt, they took
away my land from the River Arnon to
the River Jabbok and the River Jordan.
Now you must give it back **peacefully**."
14 Jephthah sent messengers back to
the king of Ammon 15 with this answer:
"It is not **true** that Israel took away the
land of Moab or the land of Ammon.
16 This is what happened: when the
Israelites left Egypt, they went through
the desert to the Gulf of Aqaba and came
to Kadesh. 17 Then they sent messengers
to the king of Edom to ask **permission** to
go through his land. But the king of
Edom would not let them. They also
asked the king of Moab, but neither
would he let them go through his land. So
the Israelites stayed at Kadesh. 18 Then
they went on through the desert, going
round the land of Edom and the land of
Moab until they came to the east side of
Moab, on the other side of the River
Arnon. They made camp there, but they
did not cross the Arnon because it was
the boundary of Moab. 19 Then the Israelites sent messengers to Sihon, the
Amorite king of Heshbon, and asked him
for **permission** to go through his country
to their own land. 20 But Sihon would not
let Israel do it. He brought his whole
army together, made camp at Jahaz, and
attacked Israel. 21 But the LORD, the God
of Israel, gave the Israelites **victory** over
Sihon and his army. So the Israelites took
possession of all the territory of the
Amorites who lived in that country.
22 They occupied all the Amorite territory
from the Arnon in the south to the Jabbok in the north and from the desert on
the east to the Jordan on the west. 23 So it
was the LORD, the God of Israel, who
drove out the Amorites for **his people**,
the Israelites. 24 Are you going to try to
take it back? You can keep whatever
your **god Chemosh** has given you. But we
are going to keep everything that the
LORD, our God, has given us. 25 Do you
think you are any better than Balak son
of Zippor, king of Moab? He never
challenged Israel, did he? Did he ever go
to war against us? 26 For three hundred
years Israel has occupied Heshbon and
Aroer, and the towns round them, and all
the cities on the banks of the River
Arnon. Why haven't you taken them
back in all this time? 27 No, I have not
done you any **wrong**. You are doing
wrong by making war on me. The LORD
is the **judge**. He will decide today between the Israelites and the Ammonites." 28 But the king of Ammon paid no
attention to this **message** from Jephthah.
29 Then the **spirit of the LORD** came
upon Jephthah. He went through Gilead
and Manasseh and returned to Mizpah in
Gilead and went on to Ammon. 30 Jephthah **promised** the LORD: "If you give me
victory over the Ammonites, 31 I will burn
as an **offering** the first person that comes
out of my house to meet me, when I

11.17: Num 20.14–21 **11.18:** Num 21.4 **11.19–22:** Num 21.21–24 **11.25:** Num 22.1–6

agree Josh 7.11; 17.11
alone 3.19; Ruth 1.3
challenge 1 Sam 17.4
custom Lev 20.23; 14.10
enemy 8.4; 16.23
flee 9.40; 1 Sam 7.10
force (1) [2] 1.28; 21.21
friend [2] 7.13; 14.16
god (2) (other gods) 10.6; 16.23
God's people 5.11; 20.2
grief [3] Josh 7.6; 1 Sam 4.12
hate Deut 32.41; 14.16
heart 5.9; 1 Sam 2.1
inherit Josh 24.32; Ruth 4.6
judge 4.4; 1 Sam 2.3
message 6.8; 16.18
offer [2] 6.18; 13.15
pain Josh 23.13; 1 Chr 4.9
peace 8.28; 18.7
permit [2] Num 31.24; 12.5
possess 2.6; 1 Kgs 8.36
presence Josh 24.1; 20.1
promise [4] 2.1; 21.1
prostitute Josh 6.17; 16.1
quarrel Lev 24.10; 12.2
revenge Josh 20.3; 1 Sam 14.24
sacrifice 2.5; 16.23
slaughter Josh 10.10; 1 Sam 4.8
solemn 8.19; 17.3
sorrow Josh 7.6; 2 Sam 1.11
Spirit (1) (God's Spirit) 6.34; 1 Sam 10.6
strike 5.26; 1 Sam 14.44
trouble 10.14; Ruth 1.21
true Josh 9.24; 13.12
turn 9.18; 15.5
unmarried Num 30.6; 2 Sam 13.1
victory [5] 7.2; 12.3
virgin [2] Deut 22.14; 19.24
witness Josh 24.22; Ruth 4.9
worthless 9.4; 1 Sam 1.16
wrong [2] Deut 27.18; 1 Sam 11.5

come back from the **victory**. I will **offer** that person to you as a **sacrifice**."

32 So Jephthah crossed the river to fight the Ammonites, and the LORD gave him **victory**. [33] He **struck** at them from Aroer to the area round Minnith, twenty cities in all, and as far as Abel Keramim. There was a great **slaughter**, and the Ammonites were defeated by Israel.

Jephthah's Daughter

34 When Jephthah went back home to Mizpah, there was his daughter coming out to meet him, dancing and playing the tambourine. She was his only child. [35] When he saw her, he tore his clothes in **sorrow** and said, "Oh, my daughter! You are breaking my **heart**! Why must it be you that causes me **pain**? I have made a **solemn promise** to the LORD, and I cannot take it back!"

36 She said to him, "If you have made a **promise** to the LORD, do what you said you would do to me, since the LORD has given you **revenge** on your **enemies**, the Ammonites." [37] But she asked her father, "Do this one thing for me. Leave me **alone** for two months, so that I can go with my **friends** to wander in the mountains and **grieve** that I must die a **virgin**." [38] He told her to go and sent her away for two months. She and her **friends** went up into the mountains and **grieved** because she was going to die **unmarried** and childless. [39] After two months she came back to her father. He did what he had **promised** the LORD, and she died still a **virgin**.

This was the origin of the **custom** in Israel [40] that the young women would go away for four days every year to **grieve** for the daughter of Jephthah of Gilead.

Jephthah and the Ephraimites

12 The men of Ephraim prepared for battle; they crossed the River Jordan to Zaphon and said to Jephthah, "Why did you cross the border to fight the Ammonites without calling us to go with you? We'll burn the house down over your head!"

2 But Jephthah said to them, "My people and I had a **serious quarrel** with the Ammonites. I did call you, but you would not **rescue** me from them. [3] When I saw that you were not going to, I risked my **life** and crossed the border to fight them, and the LORD gave me **victory** over them. So why are you coming to fight me now?" [4] Then Jephthah brought all the men of Gilead together, fought the men of Ephraim and defeated them. (The Ephraimites had said, "You Gileadites in Ephraim and Manasseh, you are deserters from Ephraim!") [5] In order to **keep the Ephraimites from escaping**, the Gileadites captured the places where the Jordan could be crossed. When any Ephraimite who was trying to **escape** asked **permission** to cross, the men of Gilead would ask, "Are you an Ephraimite?" If he said, "No," [6] they would tell him to say "Shibboleth." But he would say "Sibboleth," because he could not pronounce it correctly. Then they would seize him and kill him there at one of the crossings of the Jordan. At that time forty-two thousand of the Ephraimites were killed.

7 Jephthah led Israel for six years. Then he died and was buried in his home town[w] in Gilead.

Ibzan, Elon, and Abdon

8 After Jephthah, Ibzan from Bethlehem led Israel. [9] He had thirty sons and thirty daughters. He gave his daughters in marriage outside the clan and brought thirty girls from outside the clan for his sons to marry. Ibzan led Israel for seven years, [10] then he died and was buried at Bethlehem.

11 After Ibzan, Elon from Zebulun led Israel for ten years. [12] Then he died and was buried at Aijalon in the territory of Zebulun.

13 After Elon, Abdon son of Hillel from Pirathon led Israel. [14] He had forty sons and thirty grandsons, who rode on seventy donkeys. Abdon led Israel for eight years, [15] then he died and was buried at Pirathon in the territory of Ephraim in the hill-country of the Amalekites.

The Birth of Samson

13 The Israelites sinned against the LORD again, and he let the Philistines rule them for forty years.

2 At that time there was a man named Manoah from the town of Zorah. He was a member of the tribe of Dan. His wife had never been able to have children. [3] The **LORD's angel** appeared to her and said, "You have never been able to have children, but you will soon be pregnant and have a son. [4] Take **care** not to drink any wine or beer, or eat any **forbidden** food; [5] and after your son is born, you must never cut his hair, because from the day of his **birth** he will be **dedicated** to God as a **Nazirite**.[x] He will begin the

escape [2] 3.26; 20.42
keep from 7.24; Ruth 1.13
life (1) 9.17; 13.12
permit 11.17; 1 Sam 20.6
quarrel 11.12; 2 Sam 14.6
rescue 10.13; 13.5
serious Deut 15.21; 1 Sam 2.17
victory 11.9; 15.18

accept Josh 9.14; 1 Sam 2.15
altar [2] 6.24; 21.4
angel [10] 6.11; 1 Sam 29.9
birth [2] Deut 28.54; 1 Sam 1.20
bless Josh 24.10; 17.2
care Deut 32.10; 18.6
dedicate [2] Deut 20.5; 16.17
forbid [3] Deut 31.29; 1 Sam 12.23
fright Gen 32.7; 2 Sam 17.2
grapevine *see* **vine**
heaven Josh 2.11; 1 Sam 2.10
honour 9.9; 1 Sam 2.8
life (1) 12.3; 16.30
man of God [2] Josh 14.6; 1 Kgs 17.18
Nazirite [2] Num 6.2; 16.17

[w] *One ancient translation* his home town; *Hebrew* the towns.
[x] NAZIRITE: *A person who showed his devotion to God by taking vows not to drink wine or beer or cut his hair or touch corpses (see Num 6.1–8).*

11.35: Num 30.2 **13.5:** Num 6.1–5

offer [3] 11.31; 16.23
power 8.3; 14.6
pray Deut 9.20; 16.28
rescue 12.2; 1 Sam 7.3
strength 6.14; 16.9
sure [2] Josh 23.13; Ruth 2.2
true [2] 11.15; Ruth 3.12
vine 9.12; 1 Kgs 4.25
wonder (1) [2] 6.13; 2 Sam 1.23
word (1) [2] Josh 24.9; 15.12

work of **rescuing** Israel from the Philistines."

6 Then the woman went and said to her husband, "A **man of God** has come to me, and he looked as **frightening** as the **angel**[y] of God. I didn't ask him where he came from, and he didn't tell me his name. 7 But he did tell me that I would become pregnant and have a son. He told me not to drink any wine or beer, or eat any **forbidden** food, because the boy is to be **dedicated** to God as a **Nazirite** as long as he lives."

8 Then Manoah **prayed** to the LORD, "Please, LORD, let the **man of God** that you sent come back to us and tell us what we must do with the boy when he is born."

9 **God** did what Manoah asked, and his **angel** came back to the woman while she was sitting in the fields. Her husband Manoah was not with her, 10 so she ran at once and said to him, "Look! The man who came to me the other day has appeared to me again."

11 Manoah got up and followed his wife. He went to the man and asked, "Are you the man who was talking to my wife?"

"Yes," he answered.

12 Then Manoah asked, "When your **words** come **true**, what must the boy do? What kind of a **life** must he lead?"

13 The **LORD's angel** answered, "Your wife must be **sure** to do everything that I have told her. 14 She must not eat anything that comes from the **grapevine**; she must not drink any wine or beer, or eat any **forbidden** food. She must do everything that I have told her."

15–16 Manoah did not know that it was the **LORD's angel**, so he said to him, "Please do not go yet. Let us cook a young goat for you."

But the **angel** said, "If I do stay, I will not eat your food. But if you want to prepare it, burn it as an **offering** to the LORD."

17 Manoah replied, "Tell us your name, so that we can **honour** you when your **words** come **true**."

18 The **angel** asked, "Why do you want to know my name? It is a name of **wonder**."[z]

19 So Manoah took a young goat and some grain, and **offered** them on the rock **altar** to the LORD who works **wonders**.[a] 20–21 While the flames were going up from the **altar**, Manoah and his wife saw the **LORD's angel** go up towards **heaven** in the flames. Manoah realized then that the man had been the **LORD's angel**, and he and his wife threw themselves face downwards on the ground. They never saw the **angel** again.

22 Manoah said to his wife, "We are **sure** to die, because we have seen God!"

23 But his wife answered, "If the LORD had wanted to kill us, he would not have **accepted** our **offerings**; he would not have shown us all this or told us such things now."

24 The woman gave **birth** to a son and named him Samson. The child grew and the LORD **blessed** him. 25 And the **LORD's power** began to **strengthen** him while he was between Zorah and Eshtaol in the Camp of Dan.

Samson and the Girl from Timnah

14 One day Samson went down to Timnah, where he **noticed** a certain Philistine girl. 2 He went back home and said to his father and mother, "There is a Philistine girl down at Timnah who has caught my attention. Get her for me; I want to marry her."

3 But his father and mother asked him, "Why do you have to go to those **heathen** Philistines to get a wife? Can't you find a girl in our own clan, among all our people?"

But Samson said to his father, "She is the one I want you to get for me. I like her."

4 His parents did not know that it was the LORD who was leading Samson to do this, for the LORD was looking for a chance to fight the Philistines. At this time the Philistines were ruling Israel.

5 So Samson went down to Timnah with his father and mother. As they were going through the **vineyards** there, he heard a young lion roaring. 6 Suddenly the **power of the** LORD made Samson **strong**, and he tore the lion **apart** with his bare hands, as if it were a young goat. But he did not tell his parents what he had done.

7 Then he went and talked to the girl, and he liked her. 8 A few days later Samson went back to marry her. On the way he left the road to look at the lion he had killed, and he was surprised to find a swarm of bees and some honey inside the **dead body**. 9 He scraped the honey out into his hands and ate it as he walked along. Then he went to his father and

apart Josh 6.19; 2 Sam 22.10
banquet Gen 40.20; 2 Sam 13.27
best 3.29; 20.44
body [2] Josh 24.32; 16.31
change 7.19; 18.29
custom 11.39; Ruth 4.7
dead [2] 9.55; Ruth 2.20
feast [2] Num 25.2; 1 Sam 20.29
friend 11.37; 15.2
fury 2.14; 1 Sam 11.6
hate 11.7; 15.2
heathen 15.18
love Josh 23.11; 16.4
notice (1) Ex 2.5; 19.17
power [2] 13.25; 15.14
rob 9.25; 2 Sam 17.8
strip (1) Gen 30.37; 1 Sam 31.9
strong [4] 9.51; 15.14
tear (2) 2 Kgs 8.11
trick Gen 29.25; 16.5
vineyard 9.27; 21.20
wedding [2] 1.14; 1 Sam 18.26

[y] the angel; *or* an angel. [z] name of wonder; *or* mysterious name.
[a] *Some ancient translations* who works wonders; *Hebrew* and working wonders while Manoah and his wife watched.

13.18: Gen 32.29

mother and gave them some. They ate it,
but Samson did not tell them that he had
taken the honey from the **dead body** of a
lion.
10 His father went to the girl's house,
and Samson gave a **banquet** there. This
was a **custom** among the young men.
11 When the Philistines saw him, they
sent thirty young men to stay with him.
12-13 Samson said to them, "Let me ask
you a riddle. I'll bet each one of you a
piece of fine linen and a **change** of fine
clothes that you can't tell me its meaning
before the seven days of the **wedding
feast** are over."
"Tell us your riddle," they said. "Let's
hear it."
14 He said,

"Out of the eater came something to
eat;
Out of the **strong** came something
sweet."

Three days later they had still not solved
the riddle.
15 On the fourth[b] day they said to
Samson's wife, "**Trick** your husband into
telling us what the riddle means. If you
don't, we'll set fire to your father's house
and burn you with it.[c] You two invited us
so that you could **rob** us, didn't you?"
16 So Samson's wife went to him in
tears and said, "You don't **love** me! You
just **hate** me! You asked my **friends** a
riddle and didn't tell me what it means!"
He said, "Look, I haven't even told my
father and mother. Why should I tell
you?" 17 She cried about it for the whole
seven days of the **feast**. But on the
seventh day he told her what the riddle
meant, for she nagged him about it so
much. Then she told the Philistines. 18 So
on the seventh day, before Samson went
into the bedroom,[d] the men of the city
said to him,

"What could be sweeter than honey?
What could be **stronger** than a lion?"

Samson replied,

"If you hadn't been ploughing with my
cow,
You wouldn't know the answer now."

19 Suddenly the **power of the LORD** made
him **strong**, and he went down to Ashkelon, where he killed thirty men,
stripped them, and gave their fine
clothes to the men who had solved the
riddle. After that, he went back home,
furious about what had happened, 20 and
his wife was given to the man that had
been his **best** man at the **wedding**.

15 Some time later Samson went to
visit his wife during the wheat
harvest and took her a young goat. He
said to her father, "I want to go to my
wife's room."
But he wouldn't let him go in. 2 He said
to Samson, "I really thought that you
hated her, so I gave her to your **friend**.
But her younger sister is prettier, anyway. You can have her, instead."
3 Samson said, "This time I'm not
going to be responsible for what I do to
the Philistines!" 4 So he went and caught
three hundred foxes. Two by two, he tied
their tails together and put torches in the
knots. 5 Then he set fire to the torches
and **turned** the foxes loose in the Philistine cornfields. In this way he burnt up
not only the corn that had been **harvested** but also the corn that was still in
the fields, and the olive orchards as well.
6 When the Philistines asked who had
done this, they **learnt** that Samson had
done it because his father-in-law, a man
from Timnah, had given Samson's wife to
a **friend** of Samson's. So the Philistines
went and burnt the woman **to death** and
burnt down her father's house.[e]
7 Samson told them, "So this is how
you **act**! I **swear** that I won't stop until I
pay you back!" 8 He attacked them
fiercely and killed many of them. Then
he went and stayed in the cave in the
cliff at Etam.

Samson Defeats the Philistines

9 The Philistines came and made
camp in Judah, and attacked the town of
Lehi. 10 The men of Judah asked them,
"Why are you attacking us?"
They answered, "We came to take
Samson **prisoner** and to treat him as he
treated us." 11 So three thousand men of
Judah went to the cave in the cliff at
Etam and said to Samson, "Don't you
know that the Philistines are our rulers?
What have you done to us?"
He answered, "I did to them just what
they did to me."
12 They said, "We have come here to
tie you up, so that we can hand you over
to them."
Samson said, "Give me your **word** that
you won't kill me yourselves."
13 "All right," they said, "we are only
going to tie you up and hand you over to
them. We won't kill you." So they tied
him up with two **new** ropes and brought
him back from the cliff.
14 When he got to Lehi, the Philistines

act Josh 8.14; 20.6
death (3) (to death) Josh 11.11; 21.5
friend [2] 14.16; 19.23
harvest [2] Josh 3.14; Ruth 1.6
hate 14.16; 1 Sam 13.4
heathen 14.3; 1 Sam 14.6
learn 4.12; 1 Sam 26.3
new 5.8; 16.7
power 14.6; 1 Sam 2.10
prison Deut 32.42; 16.21
strong 14.6; 16.5
swear 8.19; Ruth 3.13
turn 11.8; 18.21
victory 12.3; 16.23
word (1) 13.12; 18.19

[b] *Some ancient translations* fourth; *Hebrew* seventh.
[c] set fire...you with it; *or* burn you and your family. [d] *Probable text* bedroom; *Hebrew* sun.
[e] burnt the woman...house; *or* burnt the woman and her family to death.

came running towards him, shouting at him. Suddenly the **power of the** LORD made him **strong**, and he broke the ropes round his arms and hands as if they were burnt thread. 15 Then he found the jaw-bone of a donkey that had recently died. He bent down and picked it up, and killed a thousand men with it. 16 So Samson sang,

"With the jaw-bone of a donkey I killed
a thousand men;
With the jaw-bone of a donkey I piled
them up in piles."[f]

17 After that, he threw the jaw-bone away. The place where this happened was named Ramath Lehi.[g]

18 Then Samson became very thirsty, so he called to the LORD and said, "You gave me this great **victory**; am I now going to die of thirst and be captured by these **heathen** Philistines?" 19 Then God opened a hollow place in the ground there at Lehi, and water came out of it. Samson drank it and began to feel much better. So the spring was named Hakkore;[h] it is still there at Lehi.

20 Samson led Israel for twenty years while the Philistines ruled the land.

Samson at Gaza

16 One day Samson went to the Philistine city of Gaza, where he met a **prostitute** and went to bed with her. 2 The people of Gaza found out that Samson was there, so they surrounded the place and waited for him all night long at the city gate. They were quiet all night, thinking to themselves, "We'll wait until daybreak, and then we'll kill him." 3 But Samson stayed in bed only until midnight. Then he got up and took hold of the city gate and pulled it up—doors, posts, lock, and all. He put them on his shoulders and carried them all the way to the top of the hill overlooking Hebron.

Samson and Delilah

4 After this, Samson fell in **love** with a woman named Delilah, who lived in the Valley of Sorek. 5 The five Philistine kings went to her and said, "**Trick** Samson into telling you why he is so **strong** and how we can overpower him, tie him up, and make him **helpless**. Each one of us will give you eleven hundred pieces of silver."

6 So Delilah said to Samson, "Please tell me what makes you so **strong**. If someone wanted to tie you up and make you **helpless**, how could he do it?"

7 Samson answered, "If they tie me up with seven **new** bowstrings that are not dried out, I'll be as **weak** as anybody else."

8 So the Philistine kings brought Delilah seven **new** bowstrings that were not dried out, and she tied Samson up. 9 She had some men waiting in another room, so she shouted, "Samson! The Philistines are coming!" But he snapped the bowstrings just as thread breaks when fire touches it. So they still did not know the **secret** of his **strength**.

10 Delilah said to Samson, "Look, you've been making a **fool** of me and not telling me the **truth**. Please tell me how someone could tie you up."

11 He answered, "If they tie me with **new** ropes that have never been used, I'll be as **weak** as anybody else."

12 So Delilah got some **new** ropes and tied him up. Then she shouted, "Samson! The Philistines are coming!" The men were waiting in another room. But he snapped the ropes off his arms like thread.

13 Delilah said to Samson, "You're still making a **fool** of me and not telling me the **truth**. Tell me how someone could tie you up."

He answered, "If you weave my seven locks of hair into a loom, and make it tight with a peg, I'll be as **weak** as anybody else."

14 Delilah then lulled him to sleep, took his seven locks of hair, and wove them into the loom.[i] She made it tight with a peg and shouted, "Samson! The Philistines are coming!" But he woke up and pulled his hair loose from the loom.

15 So she said to him, "How can you say you **love** me, when you don't mean it? You've made a **fool** of me three times, and you still haven't told me what makes you so **strong**." 16 She kept on asking him, day after day. He got so sick and tired of her nagging him about it 17 that he finally told her the **truth**. "My hair has never been cut," he said. "I have been **dedicated** to God as a **Nazirite**[j] from the time I was born. If my hair were cut, I would lose my **strength** and be as **weak** as anybody else."

18 When Delilah realized that he had told her the **truth**, she sent a **message** to the Philistine kings and said, "Come back just once more. He has told me the

secret 6.11; 1 Sam 19.2
Sovereign 6.22; 2 Sam 7.18
strength [4] 13.25; 1 Sam 2.9
strong [3] 15.14; 18.
tomb 8.32; 1 Sam 10.2
torment 1 Sam 1.6
trick 14.15; 1 Sam 19.17
truth [5] Josh 7.19; 2 Sam 14.18
victory [2] 15.18; 20.27
watch 7.17; 21.21
weak [4] 6.15; 1 Sam 2.4

body 14.8; 19.28
celebrate Deut 26.11; 1 Sam 11.15
death (1) 10.1; Ruth 1.17
dedicate 13.5; 17.3
devastate 6.5; 2 Chr 34.6
enemy [2] 11.36; 20.35
enjoy Deut 20.6; 19.6
fool [3] Deut 32.6; 1 Sam 6.6
free 10.1; 1 Sam 17.26
god (2) (other gods) [4] 11.24; 18.24
helpless [2] 6.6; 2 Chr 20.12
life (1) 13.12; Ruth 1.20
love [2] 14.16; Ruth 4.15
message 11.28; 1 Sam 2.27
might 6.12; 1 Sam 12.7
Nazirite 13.5; Amos 2.11
new [4] 15.13; Ruth 4.15
offer 13.15; 19.15
praise 5.2; Ruth 4.14
pray 13.8; 1 Sam 1.9
prison [2] 15.10; 2 Sam 8.2
prostitute 11.1; 1 Kgs 3.16
remember 9.2; Ruth 3.2
sacrifice 11.31; 20.26

[f] PILES: *This word sounds like the Hebrew for "donkey."*
[g] RAMATH LEHI: *This name in Hebrew means "Jaw-bone Hill."*
[h] HAKKORE: *This name in Hebrew means "caller."*
[i] *One ancient translation* and make it tight *(in verse 13)*...into the loom *(in verse 14); Hebrew does not have these words.* [j] NAZIRITE: *See 13.5.*

truth." Then they came and brought the
money with them. 19 Delilah lulled Samson to sleep in her lap and then called a
man, who cut off[k] Samson's seven locks
of hair. Then she began to **torment** him,
for he had lost his **strength**. 20 Then she
shouted, "Samson! The Philistines are
coming!" He woke up and thought, "I'll
get loose and go **free**, as always." He did
not know that the LORD had left him.
21 The Philistines captured him and put
his eyes out. They took him to Gaza,
chained him with bronze chains, and put
him to work grinding at the mill in the
prison. 22 But his hair started growing
again.

The Death of Samson

23 The Philistine kings met together
to **celebrate** and **offer a great sacrifice** to
their **god Dagon**. They sang, "Our **god** has
given us **victory** over our **enemy**
Samson!" 24-25 They were **enjoying** themselves, so they said, "Call Samson, and
let's make him entertain us!"[l] When
they brought Samson out of the **prison**,
they made him entertain them[m] and
made him stand between the pillars.
When the people saw him, they sang
praise to their **god**: "Our **god** has given
us **victory** over our **enemy**, who **devastated** our land and killed so many of us!"
26 Samson said to the boy who was leading him by the hand, "Let me touch the
pillars that hold up the building. I want to
lean on them." 27 The building was
crowded with men and women. All five
Philistine kings were there, and there
were about three thousand men and
women on the roof, **watching** Samson
entertain them.[n]
28 Then Samson **prayed**, "**Sovereign**
LORD, please **remember** me; please, God,
give me my **strength** just once more, so
that with this one blow I can get even
with the Philistines for putting out my
two eyes." 29 So Samson took hold of the
two middle pillars holding up the building. Putting one hand on each pillar, he
pushed against them 30 and shouted, "Let
me die with the Philistines!" He pushed
with all his **might**, and the building fell
down on the five kings and everyone
else. Samson killed more people at his
death than he had killed during his **life**.
31 His brothers and the rest of his
family came down to get his **body**. They
took him back and buried him between
Zorah and Eshtaol in the **tomb** of his
father Manoah. He had been Israel's
leader for twenty years.

Micah's Idols

17 There was once a man named
Micah, who lived in the hill-
country of Ephraim. 2 He said to his
mother, "When someone **stole** those
eleven hundred pieces of silver from you,
you put a **curse** on the **thief**. I heard you
do it. Look, I have the money. I am the
one who took it."
His mother said, "May the LORD **bless**
you, my son!" 3 He gave the money back
to his mother, and she said, "To stop the
curse from falling on my son, I myself
am **solemnly dedicating** the silver to the
LORD. It will be used to make a wooden
idol covered with silver. So now I will
give the pieces of silver back to you."
4 Then he gave them back to his mother.
She took two hundred of the pieces of silver and gave them to a metal-worker,
who made an **idol**, carving it from wood
and covering it with the silver. It was
placed in Micah's house.
5 This man Micah had his own **place
of worship**. He made some **idols** and an
ephod,[o] and appointed one of his sons as
his **priest**. 6 There was no king in Israel at
that time; everyone did just as he
pleased.
7 At that same time there was a young
Levite who had been living in the town of
Bethlehem in Judah. 8 He left Bethlehem
to find somewhere else to live. While he
was travelling, he came to Micah's house
in the hill-country of Ephraim. 9 Micah
asked him, "Where do you come from?"
He answered, "I am a **Levite** from
Bethlehem in Judah. I am looking for
somewhere to live."
10 Micah said, "Stay with me. Be my
adviser and **priest**, and I will give you ten
pieces of silver a year, some clothes, and
your food."[p] 11 The young **Levite agreed**
to stay with Micah and became like a son
to him. 12 Micah appointed him as his
priest, and he lived in Micah's home.
13 Micah said, "Now that I have a **Levite**
as my **priest**, I know that the LORD will
make things go well for me."

agree 11.10; 1 Sam 20.35
bless 13.24; Ruth 1.6
curse [2] 9.57; 21.18
dedicate 16.17; 1 Sam 1.11
ephod (1) Lev 8.7; 18.14
idol [3] 8.27; 18.14
Levites [4] Josh 21.1; 18.3
place of worship Deut 31.11; 20.18
please 6.17; 21.25
priest [4] Josh 22.13; 18.4
solemn 11.35; 21.1
steal Josh 7.11; 1 Sam 23.1
thief Ex 22.2; Job 12.6

Micah and the Tribe of Dan

18 There was no king in Israel at
that time. In those days the tribe
of Dan was looking for territory to **claim**
and occupy because they had not yet received any land of their own among the

anger 10.7; 19.2
care 13.4; 19.20
change 14.12; 1 Sam 14.21
choose 10.14; 20.9
claim Josh 22.4; 1 Sam 18.8

[k] *Probable text* who cut off; *Hebrew* and she cut off. [l] make him entertain us; *or* make fun of him.
[m] made him entertain them; *or* jeered at him. [n] entertain them; *or* and jeering at him.
[o] EPHOD: *See Word List.* [p] *Probable text* your food; *Hebrew* your food. So the Levite went.

17.6: Judg 21.25

dispute Deut 25.1;
1 Sam 7.6
ephod (1) [2] 17.5;
1 Sam 2.28
exile Lev 26.34;
2 Sam 14.13
god (2) (other gods)
16.23; Ruth 1.15
happy 9.13;
1 Sam 2.1
idol [6] 17.3;
1 Sam 7.4
Levites [2] 17.7; 19.1
matter [2]
2 Sam 13.4
need Josh 19.9; 19.19
neighbour
Deut 27.17;
1 Kgs 4.24
peace [2] 11.13;
1 Sam 1.17
priest [11] 17.5;
1 Sam 1.3
sacred [2] 9.6;
1 Sam 2.18
safe 9.46;
1 Sam 12.11
save 10.12; 1 Sam 4.3
serve [3] 9.28;
1 Sam 2.11
strong 16.5;
1 Sam 2.4
succeed (1) 1.12;
1 Sam 18.5
Tent (2) (of the Lord's presence)
Josh 22.19;
1 Sam 2.22
turn [3] 15.5; 19.15
word (1) 15.12; 21.13
worry Gen 45.20;
Ruth 3.11
worship (1) (of God)
10.6; 1 Sam 1.3
worship (2) (of other gods) 10.6;
1 Sam 5.5

tribes of Israel.
2 So the people of Dan
chose five qualified[q] men out of all the
families in the tribe and sent them from
the towns of Zorah and Eshtaol with instructions to explore the land. When they
arrived in the hill-country of Ephraim,
they stayed at Micah's house.
3 While
they were there, they recognized the
accent of the young **Levite**, so they went
up to him and asked, "What are you
doing here? Who brought you here?"
4 He answered, "I have an arrangement with Micah, who pays me to **serve**
as his **priest**."
5 They said to him, "Please ask God if
we are going to be **successful** on our
journey."
6 The **priest** answered, "You have
nothing to **worry** about. The LORD is
taking **care** of you on this journey."
7 So the five men left and went to the
town of Laish. They saw how **safely** the
people there were living, like the Sidonians. They were a **peaceful**, quiet people,
with no **disputes** with anyone; they had
all they **needed**.[r] They lived far away
from the Sidonians and had no dealings
with any other people.
8 When the five
men returned to Zorah and Eshtaol, their
countrymen asked them what they had
found out.
9 "Come on," they replied.
"Let's attack Laish. We saw the land, and
it's very good. Don't stay here doing
nothing; hurry! Go on in and take it
over!
10 When you get there, you will find
that the people don't suspect a thing. It is
a big country; it has everything a person
could want, and God has given it to you."
11 So six hundred men from the tribe
of Dan left Zorah and Eshtaol, ready for
battle.
12 They went up and made camp
west of Kiriath Jearim in Judah. That is
why the place is still called Camp of Dan.
13 They went on from there and came to
Micah's house in the hill-country of
Ephraim.
14 Then the five men who had gone to
explore the country round Laish said to
their companions, "Did you know that
here in one of these houses there is a
wooden **idol** covered with silver? There
are also other **idols** and an **ephod**. What
do you think we should do?"
15 So they
went into Micah's house, where the
young **Levite** lived, and asked the Levite
how he was getting on.
16 Meanwhile the
six hundred soldiers from Dan, ready for
battle, were standing at the gate.
17 The
five spies went straight on into the house
and took the wooden **idol** covered with
silver, the other **idols**, and the **ephod**,
while the **priest** stayed at the gate with
the six hundred armed men.
18 When the men went into Micah's
house and took the **sacred** objects, the
priest asked them, "What are you
doing?"
19 They said, "Keep quiet. Don't say a
word. Come with us and be our **priest** and
adviser. Wouldn't you rather be a **priest**
for a whole Israelite tribe than for the
family of one man?"
20 This made the
priest very **happy**, so he took the **sacred**
objects and went along with them.
21 They **turned** round and started off,
with their children, their livestock, and
their belongings going ahead.
22 They had
travelled a good distance from the house
when Micah called his **neighbours** out for
battle. They caught up with the men
from Dan
23 and shouted at them. The
men from Dan **turned** round and asked
Micah, "What's the **matter**? Why all this
mob?"
24 Micah answered, "What do you
mean, 'What's the **matter**?' You take my
priest and the **gods** that I made, and walk
off! What have I got left?"
25 The men from Dan said, "You had
better not say anything else unless you
want these men to get **angry** and attack
you. Then you and your whole family
would die."
26 Then they went on. Micah
saw that they were too **strong** for him, so
he **turned** and went back home.
27-28 After the men from Dan had
taken the **priest** and the things that
Micah had made, they went and attacked
Laish, that town of **peaceful**, quiet people
which was in the same valley as Bethrehob. They killed the inhabitants and
burnt the town. There was no one to **save**
them, because Laish was a long way
from Sidon, and they had no dealings
with any other people. The men from
Dan rebuilt the town and settled down
there.
29 They **changed** its name from
Laish to Dan, after their ancestor Dan,
the son of Jacob.
30 The men from Dan
set up the **idol** to be **worshipped**, and
Jonathan, the son of Gershom and grandson of Moses, **served** as a **priest** for the
tribe of Dan, and his descendants **served**
as their **priests** until the people were
taken away into **exile**.
31 Micah's **idol** re-
mained there all the time that the **Tent**
where God was **worshipped** remained at
Shiloh.

The Levite and His Concubine

19
In those days, before Israel had a
king, there was a **Levite** living
far back in the hill-country of Ephraim.

anger 18.25;
1 Sam 15.11
body [2] 16.31; 20.1
bread 8.5; Ruth 2.14

[q] qualified; *or* brave. [r] *Probable text* They were...needed; *Hebrew unclear.*

are 18.6; Ruth 2.20
oncubine [8] 8.31;
:0.4
lark Josh 24.7;
Sam 2.9
njoy [2] 16.24;
: Sam 7.29
vil 2.19; 20.6
riend 15.2; Ruth 4.1
mmoral Lev 19.29;
:0.6
.evites [6] 18.3; 20.4
naster [2] 3.25;
Sam 20.38
need 18.7; 1 Sam 2.8
notice (1) 14.1;
Ruth 3.4
ffer 16.23; 20.26
ersuade Deut 13.8;
: Kgs 18.30
ervert Lev 18.23;
:0.13
ape Deut 22.25; 20.5
ervant [5] 9.18;
Ruth 2.13
sex [2] Deut 27.21;
Sam 21.4
urn 18.21; 20.39
rge 1.14;
Sam 28.23
virgin 11.37; 21.11
welcome [2]
Sam 13.10

He took a girl from Bethlehem in Judah
to be his **concubine**, 2but she became
angry with him, went back to her
father's house in Bethlehem, and stayed
there four months. 3Then the man
decided to go after her and try to **persuade** her to return to him. He took his
servant and two donkeys with him. The
girl showed the **Levite** into the house,
and when her father saw him, he gave
him a warm **welcome**. 4The father
insisted that he stay, and so he stayed for
three days. The couple had their meals
and spent the nights there. 5On the morning of the fourth day they woke up early
and got ready to go. But the girl's father
said to the **Levite**, "Have something to
eat first. It will do you good. You can go
later."
6 So the two men sat down and ate
and drank together. Then the girl's
father said to him, "Please spend the
night here and **enjoy** yourself."
7 The **Levite** got up to go, but the
father **urged** him to stay, so he spent
another night there. 8Early in the morning of the fifth day he started to leave,
but the girl's father said, "Eat something,
please. Wait until later in the day." So the
two men ate together.
9 When the man, his **concubine**, and
the **servant** once more started to leave,
the father said, "Look, it's almost evening now; you might as well stay all night.
It will be **dark** soon; stay here and have a
good time. Tomorrow you can get up
early for your journey and go home."
10–11 But the man did not want to
spend another night there, so he and his
concubine started on their way, with
their **servant** and two donkeys with pack
saddles. It was late in the day when they
came near Jebus (that is, Jerusalem), so
the **servant** said to his **master**, "Why
don't we stop and spend the night here in
this Jebusite city?"
12–13 But his **master** said, "We're not
going to stop in a city where the people
are not Israelites. We'll pass on and go a
little farther and spend the night at
Gibeah or Ramah." 14So they went past
Jebus and continued on their way. It was
sunset when they came to Gibeah in the
territory of the tribe of Benjamin. 15They
turned off the road to go and spend the
night there. They went into the city and
sat down in the square, but no one
offered to take them home for the night.
16 While they were there, an old man
came by at the end of a day's work in the
fields. He was originally from the hill-
country of Ephraim, but he was now
living in Gibeah. (The other people there
were from the tribe of Benjamin.) 17The
old man **noticed** the traveller in the city
square and asked him, "Where do you
come from? Where are you going?"
18 The **Levite** answered, "We have
been to Bethlehem in Judah, and now we
are on our way home[s] deep in the hill-
country of Ephraim. No one will put us
up for the night, 19even though we have
fodder and straw for our donkeys, as well
as **bread** and wine for my **concubine** and
me and for my **servant**. We have everything we **need**."
20 The old man said, "You are
welcome in my home! I'll take **care** of
you; you don't have to spend the night in
the square." 21So he took them home
with him and fed their donkeys. His
guests washed their feet and had a meal.
22 They were **enjoying** themselves
when all of a sudden some **sexual perverts** from the town surrounded the
house and started beating on the door.
They said to the old man, "Bring out that
man that came home with you! We want
to have **sex** with him!"
23 But the old man went outside and
said to them, "No, my **friends**! Please!
Don't do such an **evil**, **immoral** thing!
This man is my guest. 24Look! Here is his
concubine and my own daughter, who is
a **virgin**. I'll bring them out now, and you
can have them. Do with them whatever
you want. But don't do such an awful
thing to this man!" 25But the men would
not listen to him. So the **Levite** took his
concubine and put her outside with them.
They **raped** her and abused her all night
long and didn't stop until morning.
26 At dawn the woman came and fell
down at the door of the old man's house,
where her husband was. She was still
there when daylight came. 27Her
husband got up that morning, and when
he opened the door to go on his way, he
found his **concubine** lying in front of the
house with her hands reaching for the
door. 28He said, "Get up. Let's go." But
there was no answer. So he put her **body**
across the donkey and started on his way
home. 29When he arrived, he went into
the house and got a knife. He took his
concubine's body, cut it into twelve
pieces, and sent one piece to each of the
twelve tribes of Israel. 30Everyone who
saw it said, "We have never heard of
such a thing! Nothing like this has ever
happened since the Israelites left Egypt!

[s] *One ancient translation* home; *Hebrew* to the house of the LORD.
19.22–24: Gen 19.5–8 **19.29:** 1 Sam 11.7

act [2] 15.7; 1 Sam 21.13
amaze Gen 45.7; 1 Kgs 9.8
best 14.20; Ruth 2.21
body [3] 19.28; 1 Sam 5.4
choose [3] 18.2; 21.23
cloud [2] 5.4; 2 Sam 22.10
concubine [3] 19.1; 2 Sam 3.7
Covenant Box Josh 8.33; 1 Sam 3.3
crime [2] 9.24; 1 Sam 20.1
destroy [3] 6.4; 1 Sam 2.10
encourage 9.24; 1 Sam 22.8
enemy [2] 16.23; 1 Sam 2.1
escape [2] 12.5; 1 Sam 4.16
evil [2] 19.23; 1 Sam 2.23
fellowship-sacrifice 21.4
God's people 11.23; Ruth 1.6
hard 9.33; 1 Sam 4.10
immoral [2] 19.23; Prov 2.16
intend Deut 9.5; 1 Sam 20.13
Levites 19.1; 1 Sam 6.15
lot (1) Josh 21.8; 1 Chr 6.61
mourn [2] Deut 34.8; 21.2
offer 19.15; 21.4
pervert 19.22; Prov 6.14
place of worship [2] 17.5; 1 Sam 9.14
plan 9.42; 1 Sam 18.25
presence [4] 11.11; 21.2
provide Deut 29.6; 21.7
punish 8.16; Ruth 1.17
purpose Deut 5.11; 2 Sam 7.21
rape 19.25; 2 Sam 13.14
rely 2 Kgs 18.21
sacrifice [2] 16.23; 21.4
special [2] Deut 12.11; 1 Sam 1.21
trap 8.27; 1 Sam 18.21
turn [4] 19.15; Ruth 1.13
victory [2] 16.23; 1 Sam 2.10

We have to do something about this!
What will it be?"

Israel Prepares for War

20 All the people of Israel from Dan
in the north to Beersheba in the
south, as well as from the land of Gilead
in the east, answered the call. They
gathered in one **body** in the LORD's
presence at Mizpah. 2 The leaders of all
the tribes of Israel were present at this
gathering of **God's people**, and there
were 400,000 foot-soldiers. 3 Meanwhile
the people of Benjamin heard that all the
other Israelites had gathered at Mizpah.
The Israelites asked, "Tell us, how was
this **crime** committed?" 4 The **Levite**
whose **concubine** had been murdered
answered, "My **concubine** and I went to
Gibeah in the territory of Benjamin to
spend the night. 5 The men of Gibeah
came to attack me and surrounded the
house at night. They **intended** to kill me;
instead they **raped** my **concubine**, and
she died. 6 I took her **body**, cut it in
pieces, and sent one piece to each of the
twelve tribes of Israel. These people
have committed an **evil** and **immoral act**
among us. 7 All of you here are Israelites.
What are we going to do about this?"
8 All the people stood up together and
said, "None of us, whether he lives in a
tent or in a house, will go home. 9 This is
what we will do: we will draw **lots** and
choose some men to attack Gibeah.[t]
10 One tenth of the men in Israel will **provide** food for the army, and the others
will go and **punish** Gibeah[u] for this
immoral act that they have committed in
Israel." 11 So all the men in Israel assembled with one **purpose**—to attack the
town.
12 The Israelite tribes sent messengers all through the territory of the tribe
of Benjamin to say, "What is this **crime**
that you have committed? 13 Now hand
over those **perverts** in Gibeah, so that we
can kill them and remove this **evil** from
Israel." But the people of Benjamin paid
no attention to the other Israelites.
14 From all the cities of Benjamin they
came to Gibeah to fight against the other
people of Israel. 15-16 They called out
twenty-six thousand soldiers from their
cities that day. Besides these, the citizens
of Gibeah gathered seven hundred
specially chosen men[v] who were left-
handed. Every one of them could sling a
stone at a strand of hair and never miss.
17 The rest of the Israelite tribes gathered
400,000 trained soldiers.

The War against the Benjaminites

18 The Israelites went to the **place of
worship** at Bethel, and there they asked
God, "Which tribe should attack the
Benjaminites first?"
The LORD answered, "The tribe of
Judah."
19 So the Israelites started out the
next morning and made camp near the
city of Gibeah. 20 They went to attack the
army of Benjamin, and placed the soldiers in position facing the city. 21 The
army of Benjamin came out of the city,
and before the day was over they had
killed twenty-two thousand Israelite
soldiers. 22-23 Then the Israelites went to
the **place of worship** and **mourned** in the
presence of the LORD until evening. They
asked him, "Should we go again into
battle against our brothers the Benjaminites?"
The LORD answered, "Yes."
So the Israelite army was **encouraged**,
and they placed their soldiers in the
same position as they had been the day
before. 24 They marched against the
army of Benjamin a second time. 25 And
for the second time the Benjaminites
came out of Gibeah, and this time they
killed eighteen thousand trained Israelite
soldiers. 26 Then all the people of Israel
went up to Bethel and **mourned**. They sat
there in the LORD's **presence** and did not
eat until evening. They **offered fellowship sacrifices** and burnt some **sacrifices**
whole—all in the **presence** of the LORD.
27-28 God's **Covenant Box** was there at
Bethel in those days, and Phinehas, the
son of Eleazar and grandson of Aaron,
was in charge of it. The people asked the
LORD, "Should we go out to fight our
brothers the Benjaminites again, or
should we give up?"
The LORD answered, "Fight. Tomorrow I will give you **victory** over
them."
29 So the Israelites put some soldiers
in hiding round Gibeah. 30 Then for the
third successive day they marched
against the army of Benjamin and placed
their soldiers in battle position facing
Gibeah, as they had done before. 31 The
Benjaminites came out to fight and were
led away from the city. As before, they
began killing some Israelites in the open
country on the road to Bethel and on the
road to Gibeah. They killed about thirty

[t] *One ancient translation* to attack Gibeah; *Hebrew* to Gibeah.
[u] *One ancient translation* Gibeah; *Hebrew* Geba.
[v] *Some ancient translations* men; *Hebrew* men. In all this number there were seven hundred specially chosen men.

Israelites. 32 The Benjaminites said, "We've beaten them just as we did before."

But the Israelites had **planned** to retreat and lead them away from the city on to the roads. 33 So when the main army of the Israelites pulled back and regrouped at Baaltamar, the men surrounding Gibeah suddenly rushed out of their hiding places in the rocky country round the city.[w] 34 Ten thousand men, **specially chosen** out of all Israel, attacked Gibeah, and the fighting was **hard**. The Benjaminites had not realized that they were about to be **destroyed**. 35 The LORD gave Israel **victory** over the army of Benjamin. The Israelites killed 25,100 of the **enemy** that day, 36 and the Benjaminites realized they were defeated.

How the Israelites Won

The main **body** of the Israelite army had retreated from the Benjaminites because they were **relying** on the men that they had put in hiding round Gibeah. 37 These men ran quickly towards Gibeah; they spread out in the city and killed everyone there. 38 The main Israelite army and the men in hiding had arranged a signal. When they saw a big **cloud** of smoke going up from the town, 39 the Israelites out on the battlefield were to **turn** round. By this time the Benjaminites had already killed the thirty Israelites. They told themselves, "Yes, we've beaten them just as we did before." 40 Then the signal appeared; a **cloud** of smoke began to go up from the town. The Benjaminites looked behind them and were **amazed** to see the whole city going up in flames. 41 Then the Israelites **turned** round, and the Benjaminites were thrown into a panic because they realized that they were about to be **destroyed**. 42 They retreated from the Israelites and ran towards the open country, but they could not **escape**. They were caught between the main army and the men who were now coming out of the city,[x] and they were **destroyed**. 43 The Israelites had the **enemy trapped**, and without stopping they pursued them as far as a point east of Gibeah, killing them as they went.[y] 44 Eighteen thousand of the **best** Benjaminite soldiers were killed. 45 The others **turned** and ran towards the open country to the Rock of Rimmon. Five thousand of them were killed along the road. The Israelites continued to pursue the rest to Gidom, killing two thousand. 46 In all, twenty-five thousand Benjaminites were killed that day—all of them brave soldiers.

47 But six hundred men were able to **escape** to the open country to the Rock of Rimmon, and they stayed there four months. 48 The Israelites **turned** back against the rest of the Benjaminites and killed them all—men, women, and children, and animals as well. They burnt every town in the area.

Wives for the Tribe of Benjamin

21 When the Israelites had gathered at Mizpah, they had made a **solemn promise** to the LORD: "None of us will allow a Benjaminite to marry a daughter of ours." 2 So now the people of Israel went to Bethel and sat there in the **presence** of God until evening. Loudly and **bitterly** they **mourned**: 3 "LORD God of Israel, why has this happened? Why is the tribe of Benjamin about to disappear from Israel?"

4 Early the next morning the people built an **altar** there, **offered fellowship sacrifices** and burnt some **sacrifices** whole. 5 They asked, "Is there any group out of all the tribes of Israel that did not go to the gathering in the LORD's **presence** at Mizpah?" (They had taken a **solemn oath** that anyone who had not gone to Mizpah would be put **to death**.) 6 The people of Israel felt **sorry** for their brothers the Benjaminites and said, "Today Israel has lost one of its tribes. 7 What shall we do to **provide** wives for the men of Benjamin who are left? We have made a **solemn promise** to the LORD that we will not give them any of our daughters."

8 When they asked if there was some group out of the tribes of Israel that had not gone to the gathering at Mizpah, they found out that no one from Jabesh in Gilead had been there; 9 at the roll call of the army no one from Jabesh had responded. 10 So the assembly sent twelve thousand of their bravest men with the orders, "Go and kill everyone in Jabesh, including the women and children. 11 Kill all the males, and also every woman who is not a **virgin**." 12 Among the people in Jabesh they found four hundred young **virgins**, so they brought them to the camp at Shiloh, which is in the land of Canaan.

13 Then the whole assembly sent **word** to the Benjaminites who were at the Rock of Rimmon and **offered** to end the

altar 13.19; 1 Sam 2.28
bitter 8.1; Ruth 1.20
choose 20.9; 1 Sam 2.10
curse 17.2; 1 Sam 14.24
death (3) (to death) 15.6; 1 Sam 11.13
enough 6.38; Ruth 3.14
fellowship-sacrifice 20.26; 1 Sam 10.8
festival [2] 9.27; 1 Sam 20.5
force (1) 11.2; 1 Sam 2.16
guilty Deut 25.1; 1 Sam 14.39
mourn 20.22; 1 Sam 6.19
oath Num 30.2; 1 Sam 14.24
offer [2] 20.26; 1 Sam 1.3
please 17.6; 1 Sam 18.5
presence [2] 20.1; Ruth 4.4
promise [3] 11.30; Ruth 2.20
provide [2] 20.10; 2 Sam 5.11
sacrifice [2] 20.26; 1 Sam 1.3
solemn [3] 17.3; 1 Sam 1.11
sorry [2] Ex 2.6; Ruth 1.13
unite Deut 33.7; 1 Chr 12.38
vineyard [2] 14.5; 1 Sam 8.14
virgin [2] 19.24; 2 Sam 13.2
watch 16.27; Ruth 2.9
word (1) 18.19; 1 Sam 2.3

[w] *One ancient translation* the city *(that is,* Gibeah*); Hebrew* Geba.
[x] *Probable text* city; *Hebrew* cities. [y] *Verse 43 in Hebrew is unclear.*

war. 14 The Benjaminites came back, and
the other Israelites gave them the girls
from Jabesh whom they had not killed.
But there were not **enough** of them.
15 The people felt **sorry** for the Benjaminites because the LORD had broken
the **unity** of the tribes of Israel. 16 So the
leaders of the gathering said, "There are
no more women in the tribe of Benjamin.
What shall we do to **provide** wives for the
men who are left? 17 Israel must not lose
one of its twelve tribes. We must find a
way for the tribe of Benjamin to survive,
18 but we cannot allow them to marry our
daughters, because we have put a **curse**
on anyone of us who allows a Benjaminite to marry one of our daughters."
19 Then they thought, "The yearly
festival of the LORD at Shiloh is coming
soon." (Shiloh is north of Bethel, south of
Lebonah, and east of the road between
Bethel and Shechem.) 20 They said to the
Benjaminites, "Go and hide in the **vineyards** 21 and **watch**. When the girls of
Shiloh come out to dance during the
festival, you come out of the **vineyards**.
Each of you take a wife by **force** from
among the girls and take her back to the
territory of Benjamin with you. 22 If their
fathers or brothers come to you[z] and
protest, you[a] can say, 'Please let us keep
them, because we did not take them
from you in battle to be our wives. And
since you did not give them to us, you are
not **guilty** of breaking your **promise**.' "
23 The Benjaminites did this; each of
them **chose** a wife from the girls who
were dancing at Shiloh and carried her
away. Then they went back to their own
territory, rebuilt their towns, and lived
there. 24 At the same time the rest of the
Israelites left, and every man went back
to his own tribe and family and to his
own property.
25 There was no king in Israel at that
time. Everyone did just as he **pleased**.

[z] *One ancient translation* you; *Hebrew* us. [a] *Probable text* you; *Hebrew* we.

21.25: Judg 17.6

THE BOOK OF
RUTH

INTRODUCTION

he peaceful story of *Ruth* is set in the violent times of the book of *Judges*. Ruth, a Moabite woman, is arried to an Israelite. When he dies, Ruth shows uncommon loyalty to her Israelite mother-in-law and eep devotion to the God of Israel. In the end, she finds a new husband among her former husband's relaves, and through this marriage becomes the great-grandmother of David, Israel's greatest king.

The stories of *Judges* show the disaster that came when God's people turned away from him. *Ruth* shows e blessing that came to a foreigner who turned to Israel's God, and so became part of his faithful people.

Outline of Contents

---

lmighty [2]
um 24.4; 1 Sam 1.3
one [2] Judg 11.37;
am 7.22
ter Judg 21.2;
am 1.9
ss Judg 17.2; 2.4
ndemn Josh 22.20;
am 1.16
ath (1) Judg 16.30;
am 2.33
termine Judg 5.2;
am 13.19
mine Gen 47.4;
am 21.1
d (2) (other gods)
dg 18.24; 1 Sam 4.7
d's people
dg 20.2; 1 Sam 2.29
rvest [2]
dg 15.1; 2.2
pe Deut 28.65;
am 2.33
possible
n 20.17; 2 Sam 13.2
ep from Judg 12.5;
am 1.5
ss [2] Ex 18.7;
am 10.1
e (1) Judg 16.30;
5
enty Deut 32.14;
Kgs 10.27
nish Judg 20.10;
am 3.13
parate Judg 7.4;
am 23.26
rry Judg 21.6;
am 15.11
uble Judg 11.7;
am 1.11
rn Judg 20.39; 3.8
rst Ex 9.24;
am 19.7

Elimelech and His Family Move to Moab

1 1-2 Long ago, in the days before
Israel had a king, there was a
famine in the land. So a man named
Elimelech, who belonged to the clan of
Ephrath and who lived in Bethlehem in
Judah, went with his wife Naomi and
their two sons Mahlon and Chilion to live
for a while in the country of Moab. While
they were living there, 3 Elimelech died,
and Naomi was left **alone** with her two
sons, 4 who married Moabite girls, Orpah
and Ruth. About ten years later 5 Mahlon
and Chilion also died, and Naomi was left
all **alone**, without husband or sons.

Naomi and Ruth Return to Bethlehem

6 Some time later Naomi heard that
the LORD had **blessed his people** by
giving them a good **harvest**; so she got
ready to leave Moab with her daughters-
in-law. 7 They started out together to go
back to Judah, but on the way 8 she said
to them, "Go back home and stay with
your mothers. May the LORD be as good
to you as you have been to me and to
those who have died. 9 And may the LORD
make it possible for each of you to marry
again and have a home."

So Naomi **kissed** them good-bye. But
they started crying 10 and said to her,
"No! We will go with you to your
people."

11 "You must go back, my daughters,"
Naomi answered. "Why do you want to
come with me? Do you think I could
have sons again for you to marry? 12 Go
back home, for I am too old to get
married again. Even if I thought there
was still **hope**, and so got married tonight
and had sons, 13 would you wait until they
had grown up? Would this **keep you from**
marrying someone else? No, my
daughters, you know that's **impossible**.
The LORD has **turned** against me, and I
feel very **sorry** for you."[a]

14 Again they started crying. Then
Orpah **kissed** her mother-in-law good-bye
and went back home,[b] but Ruth held on
to her. 15 So Naomi said to her, "Ruth,
your sister-in-law has gone back to her
people and to her **god**.[c] Go back home
with her."

16 But Ruth answered, "Don't ask me
to leave you! Let me go with you.
Wherever you go, I will go; wherever
you live, I will live. Your people will be
my people, and your God will be my God.
17 Wherever you die, I will die, and that is
where I will be buried. May the LORD's
worst punishment come upon me if I let
anything but **death**[d] **separate** me from
you!"

18 When Naomi saw that Ruth was
determined to go with her, she said
nothing more.

19 They went on until they came to
Bethlehem. When they arrived, the
whole town got excited, and the women
there exclaimed, "Is this really Naomi?"

20 "Don't call me Naomi," she answered; "call me Marah,[e] because
Almighty God has made my **life bitter**.

[a] sorry for you; *or* bitter about what has happened to you.
[b] *One ancient translation* and went back home; *Hebrew does not have these words.* [c] god; *or* gods.
[d] anything but death; *or* even death.
[e] NAOMI...MARAH: *In Hebrew Naomi means "pleasant" and Marah means "bitter."*

21 When I left here, I had **plenty**, but the
LORD has brought me back without a
thing. Why call me Naomi when the
LORD **Almighty** has **condemned** me and
sent me **trouble**?"
22 This, then, was how Naomi came
back from Moab with Ruth, her Moabite
daughter-in-law. The barley **harvest** was
just beginning when they arrived in
Bethlehem.

Ruth Works in the Field of Boaz

advice Deut 18.14; 2 Sam 15.31
best Judg 20.44; 3.3
bless [3] 1.6; 3.10
bow (2) Judg 2.12; 1 Sam 20.41
bread Judg 19.19; 1 Sam 10.3
care Judg 19.20; 3.9
concern Num 11.29; 1 Sam 22.8
dead Judg 14.8; 4.5
gentle Deut 32.2; Job 21.33
harvest [3] 1.6; 1 Sam 6.13
interest (1) Num 11.29; 1 Sam 8.3
kind [2] Josh 2.12; 1 Sam 1.18
promise Judg 21.1; 1 Sam 1.11
protect Judg 2.14; 1 Sam 2.2
reap Deut 28.38; Ps 107.37
rest (1) Josh 11.23; 3.18
reward [2] Num 24.11; 1 Sam 17.25
rich Judg 5.30; 3.10
satisfy Josh 22.30; 1 Sam 22.2
servant Judg 19.3; 1 Sam 1.11
shelter Judg 9.15; 2 Sam 21.10
sure Judg 13.13; 3.4
watch Judg 21.21; 1 Sam 1.12

2 Naomi had a relative named Boaz, a
rich and influential man who belonged to the family of her husband
Elimelech. 2 One day Ruth said to Naomi,
"Let me go to the fields to gather the
corn that the **harvest** workers leave. I
am **sure** to find someone who will let me
work with him."
Naomi answered, "Go ahead, my
daughter."
3 So Ruth went out to the fields and
walked behind the workers, picking up
the corn which they left. It so happened
that she was in a field that belonged to
Boaz.
4 Some time later Boaz himself
arrived from Bethlehem and greeted the
workers. "The LORD be with you!" he
said.
"The LORD **bless** you!" they answered.
5 Boaz asked the man in charge, "Who
is that young woman?"
6 The man answered, "She is the
foreign girl who came back from Moab
with Naomi. 7 She asked me to let her
follow the workers and pick up the corn.
She has been working since early morning and has just now stopped to **rest** for a
while under the **shelter**."
8 Then Boaz said to Ruth, "Let me
give you some **advice**. Don't pick up corn
anywhere except in this field. Work with
the women here; 9 **watch** them to see
where they are **reaping** and stay with
them. I have ordered my men not to
molest you. And whenever you are
thirsty, go and drink from the water jars
that they have filled."
10 Ruth **bowed down** with her face
touching the ground, and said to Boaz,
"Why should you be so **concerned** about
me? Why should you be so **kind** to a
foreigner?"
11 Boaz answered, "I have heard
about everything that you have done for
your mother-in-law since your husband
died. I know how you left your father and
mother and your own country and how
you came to live among a people you had
never known before. 12 May the LORD
reward you for what you have done. May
you have a full **reward** from the LORD
God of Israel, to whom you have come
for **protection**!"
13 Ruth answered, "You are very
kind[f] to me, sir. You have made me feel
better by speaking **gently** to me, even
though I am not the equal of one of your
servants."
14 At meal-time Boaz said to Ruth,
"Come and have a piece of **bread**, and
dip it in the sauce." So she sat with the
workers, and Boaz passed some roasted
grain to her. She ate until she was **satisfied**, and she still had some food left over.
15–16 After she had left to go on picking up
corn, Boaz ordered the workers, "Let her
pick it up even where the bundles are
lying, and don't say anything to stop her.
Besides that, pull out some corn from the
bundles and leave it for her to pick up."
17 So Ruth went on gathering corn in
the field until evening, and when she had
beaten it out, she found she had nearly
ten kilogrammes. 18 She took the corn
back into town and showed her mother-
in-law how much she had gathered. She
also gave her the food left over from the
meal. 19 Naomi asked her, "Where did
you gather all this? Whose field have
you been working in? May God **bless** the
man who took an **interest** in you!"
So Ruth told Naomi that she had been
working in a field belonging to a man
named Boaz.
20 "May the LORD **bless** Boaz!" Naomi
exclaimed. "The LORD always keeps his
promises to the living and the **dead**." And
she went on, "That man is a close relative of ours, one of those responsible for
taking **care** of us."
21 Then Ruth said, "**Best** of all, he told
me to keep picking up corn with his
workers until they finish the **harvest**."
22 Naomi said to Ruth, "Yes, my
daughter, it will be better for you to work
with the women in Boaz' field. You might
be molested if you went to someone
else's field." 23 So Ruth worked with them
and gathered corn until all the barley
and wheat had been **harvested**. And she
continued to live with her mother-in-law.

Ruth Finds a Husband

3 Some time later Naomi said to Ruth,
"I must find a husband for you, so
that you will have a home of your own.
2 **Remember** that this man Boaz, whose
women you have been working with, is
our relative. Now listen. This evening he

best 2.21; 1 Sam 1.23
bless 2.4; 4.13
care 2.20; 4.14
enough Judg 21.14; 1 Sam 21.15
help Judg 8.15; 1 Sam 2.1
light (1) Num 20.6; 1 Sam 29.10

[f] You are very kind; *or* Please be kind.

2.2: Lev 19.9–10; Deut 24.19 **2.20:** Lev 25.25

loyal Judg 9.28; 1 Sam 18.17
notice (1) Judg 19.17; 1 Sam 18.15
patient Num 21.4; Neh 9.30
poor Deut 28.18; 1 Sam 2.7
remember Judg 16.28; 1 Sam 1.11
rest (1) 2.7; 2 Sam 4.5
rich 2.1; 4.11
settle (2) Deut 25.1; 4.7
sure 2.2; 1 Sam 16.6
swear Judg 15.7; 1 Sam 18.3
true Judg 13.12; 1 Sam 1.23
turn [2] 1.13; 1 Sam 6.12
worry Judg 18.6; 1 Sam 9.5

will be threshing the barley. 3 So wash
yourself, put on some perfume, and get
dressed in your **best** clothes. Then go
where he is threshing, but don't let him
know you are there until he has finished
eating and drinking. 4 Be **sure** to **notice**
where he lies down, and after he falls
asleep, go and lift the covers and lie
down at his feet. He will tell you what to
do."
5 Ruth answered, "I will do everything
you say."
6 So Ruth went to the threshing-place
and did just what her mother-in-law had
told her. 7 When Boaz had finished eating
and drinking, he was in a good mood. He
went to the pile of barley and lay down to
sleep. Ruth slipped over quietly, lifted
the covers and lay down at his feet.
8 During the night he woke up suddenly,
turned over, and was surprised to find a
woman lying at his feet. 9 "Who are
you?" he asked.
"It's Ruth, sir," she answered.
"Because you are a close relative, you
are responsible for taking **care** of me. So
please marry me."
10 "The LORD **bless** you," he said.
"You are showing even greater family
loyalty in what you are doing now than in
what you did for your mother-in-law. You
might have gone looking for a young
man, either **rich** or **poor**, but you didn't.
11 Now don't **worry**, Ruth. I will do everything you ask; as everyone in town
knows, you are a fine woman. 12 It is **true**
that I am a close relative and am responsible for you, but there is a man who is a
closer relative than I am. 13 Stay here the
rest of the night, and in the morning we
will find out whether or not he will take
responsibility for you. If so, well and
good; if not, then I **swear** by the living
LORD that I will take the responsibility.
Now lie down and stay here till
morning."
14 So she lay there at his feet, but she
got up before it was **light enough** for her
to be seen, because Boaz did not want
anyone to know that she had been there.
15 Boaz said to her, "Take off your cloak
and spread it out here." She did, and he
poured out nearly twenty kilogrammes
of barley and **helped** her to lift it on her
shoulder. Then she returned to the town
with it. 16 When she arrived home, her
mother-in-law asked her, "How did you
get on, my daughter?"
Ruth told her everything that Boaz had
done for her. 17 She added, "He told me I
must not come back to you empty-
handed, so he gave me all this barley."
18 Naomi said to her, "Now be **patient**,
Ruth, until you see how this all **turns** out.
Boaz will not **rest** today until he **settles**
the matter."

Boaz Marries Ruth

4 Boaz went to the meeting place at
the town gate and sat down there.
Then Elimelech's nearest relative, the
man whom Boaz had mentioned, came
by, and Boaz called to him, "Come over
here, my **friend**, and sit down." So he
went over and sat down. 2 Then Boaz got
ten of the leaders of the town and asked
them to sit down there too. When they
were seated, 3 he said to his relative,
"Now that Naomi has come back from
Moab, she wants to sell the field that
belonged to our relative Elimelech, 4 and
I think you ought to know about it. Now
then, if you want it, buy it in the **presence**
of these men sitting here. But if you don't
want it, say so, because the **right** to buy it
belongs first to you and then to me."
The man said, "I will buy it."
5 Boaz said, "Very well, but if you buy
the field from Naomi, then you are also
buying Ruth,[g] the Moabite **widow**, so that
the field will stay in the **dead** man's
family."
6 The man answered, "In that case I
will give up my **right** to buy the field,
because it would mean that my own children would not **inherit** it. You buy it; I
would rather not."
7 Now in those days, to **settle** a sale or
an exchange of property, it was the **custom** for the seller to take off his sandal
and give it to the buyer. In this way the
Israelites showed that the matter was
settled.
8 So when the man said to Boaz, "You
buy it," he took off his sandal and gave it
to Boaz.[h] 9 Then Boaz said to the leaders
and all the others there, "You are all **witnesses** today that I have bought from
Naomi everything that belonged to
Elimelech and to his sons Chilion and
Mahlon. 10 In addition, Ruth the Moabite,
Mahlon's **widow**, becomes my wife. This
will keep the property in the **dead** man's
family, and his family line will continue
among his people and in his town. You
are **witnesses** to this today."
11 The leaders and the others said,
"Yes, we are **witnesses**. May the LORD
make your wife become like Rachel and
Leah, who bore many children to Jacob.

bless 3.10; 1 Sam 2.20
care [2] 3.9; 1 Sam 16.11
custom Judg 14.10; 1 Kgs 10.13
dead [2] 2.20; 1 Sam 4.19
friend Judg 19.23; 1 Sam 18.3
inherit Judg 11.2; 1 Kgs 21.3
life (1) 1.20; 1 Sam 1.11
love Judg 16.4; 1 Sam 1.5
new Judg 16.7; 1 Sam 6.7
praise Judg 16.24; 1 Sam 19.4
presence Judg 21.2; 1 Sam 2.35
rich 3.10; 1 Sam 2.7
right (3) [2] Deut 27.19; 1 Sam 2.28
secure Josh 23.1; 1 Kgs 2.45
settle (2) [2] 3.18; 1 Sam 7.6
widow [2] Deut 27.19; 1 Sam 27.3
witness [3] Judg 11.10; 1 Sam 6.18

[g] *Some ancient translations* Naomi...Ruth; *Hebrew* Naomi and from Ruth.
[h] *One ancient translation* and gave it to Boaz; *Hebrew does not have these words.*

3.12: Ruth 2.20 **4.7-8:** Deut 25.9 **4.10:** Deut 25.5-6 **4.11:** Gen 29.31

May you become rich in the clan of
Ephrath and famous in Bethlehem.
12 May the children that the LORD will
give you by this young woman make
your family like the family of Perez, the
son of Judah and Tamar."

Boaz and His Descendants

13 So Boaz took Ruth home as his wife.
The LORD blessed her, and she became
pregnant and had a son. 14 The women
said to Naomi, "Praise the LORD! He has
given you a grandson today to take care
of you. May the boy become famous in
Israel! 15 Your daughter-in-law loves you,
and has done more for you than seven
sons. And now she has given you a grandson, who will bring new life to you and
give you security in your old age."
16 Naomi took the child, held him close,[i]
and took care of him.

17 The women of the neighbourhood
named the boy Obed. They told everyone, "A son has been born to Naomi!"

Obed became the father of Jesse, who
was the father of David.

18–22 This is the family line from
Perez to David: Perez, Hezron, Ram,
Amminadab, Nahshon, Salmon, Boaz,
Obed, Jesse, David.

[i] held him close; *or* adopted him.

4.12: Gen 38.27–30

THE FIRST BOOK OF
SAMUEL

INTRODUCTION

The book of *First Samuel* records the transition in Israel from the period of the judges to the monarchy. This change in Israel's national life revolved mainly around three men: Samuel, the last of the great judges; Saul, Israel's first king; and David, whose early adventures before coming to power are interwoven with the accounts of Samuel and Saul.

The theme of this book, like that of other historical writings in the Old Testament, is that faithfulness to God brings success, while disobedience brings disaster. This is stated clearly in the Lord's message to the priest Eli in 2.30: "I will honour those who honour me, and I will treat with contempt those who despise me."

The book records mixed feelings about the establishment of the monarchy. The Lord himself was regarded as the real king of Israel, but in response to the people's request, the Lord chose a king for them. The important fact was that both the king and the people of Israel lived under the sovereignty and judgement of God (2.7-10). Under God's laws the rights of all people, rich and poor alike, were to be maintained.

Outline of Contents

Samuel as judge of Israel 1.1—7.17
Saul becomes king 8.1—10.27
The first years of Saul's reign 11.1—15.35
David and Saul 16.1—30.31
The death of Saul and his sons 31.1-13

Almighty [2] Ruth 1.20; 4.4
best Ruth 3.3; 2.29
birth Judg 13.5; 4.19
bitter Ruth 1.20; 8.18
dedicate [2] Judg 17.3; 2.20
despair Deut 28.53; 11.4
distress Judg 10.9; 20.34
excuse Deut 24.5; 2 Kgs 10.19
forget Judg 3.7; 6.6
humiliate Deut 25.3; 2 Sam 19.5
keep from Ruth 1.13; 3.17
kind Ruth 2.10; 15.6
life (1) [2] Ruth 4.15; 2.9
love Ruth 4.15; 18.1
misery Deut 26.7; 2.8
offer [3] Judg 21.4; 2.13
peace Judg 18.7; 7.14
pray [6] Judg 16.28; 2.1
prayer Ex 9.29; 7.9
priest [2] Judg 18.4; 2.11
promise [4] Ruth 2.20; 2.30
refuse (1) Judg 8.15; 22.17
remember [2] Ruth 3.2; 12.24
rival Josh 24.19; Is 19.2
sacrifice [4] Judg 21.4; 2.13

Elkanah and His Family at Shiloh

1 There was a man named Elkanah,
from the tribe of Ephraim, who
lived in the town of Ramah in the hill-
country of Ephraim. He was the son of
Jeroham and grandson of Elihu, and belonged to the family of Tohu, a part of
the clan of Zuph. 2 Elkanah had two
wives, Hannah and Peninnah. Peninnah
had children, but Hannah had none.
3 Every year Elkanah went from Ramah
to **worship** and **offer sacrifices** to the
LORD **Almighty** at Shiloh, where Hophni
and Phinehas, the two sons of Eli, were
priests of the LORD. 4 Each time Elkanah
offered his sacrifice, he would give one
share of the meat to Peninnah and one
share to each of her children. 5 And even
though he **loved** Hannah very much he
would give her only one **share**, because[a]
the LORD had **kept her from** having children. 6 Peninnah, her **rival**, would
torment and **humiliate** her, because the
LORD had kept her childless. 7 This went
on year after year; whenever they went
to the house of the LORD, Peninnah
would **upset** Hannah so much that she
would cry and **refuse** to eat anything.
8 Her husband Elkanah would ask her,
"Hannah, why are you crying? Why
won't you eat? Why are you always so
sad? Don't I mean more to you than ten
sons?"

Hannah and Eli

9-10 One day, after they had finished
their meal in the house of the LORD at
Shiloh, Hannah got up. She was deeply
distressed, and she cried **bitterly** as she
prayed to the LORD. Meanwhile, Eli the
priest was sitting in his place by the door.
11 Hannah made a **solemn promise**:
"**Almighty** LORD, look at me, your
servant! See my **trouble** and **remember**
me! Don't **forget** me! If you give me a
son, I **promise** that I will **dedicate** him to
you for his whole **life** and that he will
never have his hair cut."[b]
12 Hannah continued to **pray** to the
LORD for a long time, and Eli **watched**
her lips. 13 She was **praying** silently; her
lips were moving, but she made no
sound. So Eli thought that she was drunk,
14 and said to her, "Stop making a
drunken show of yourself! Stop your
drinking and sober up!"
15 "No, I'm not drunk, sir," she

sad [2] 2 Sam 13.4
servant Ruth 2.13; 2.13
share [3] Judg 2.6; 2.28
solemn Judg 21.1; 3.14
special Judg 20.15; 21.5
torment Judg 16.19; 16.14
trouble [2] Ruth 1.21; 2.32
true Ruth 3.12; 2.34
upset Gen 48.17; 2 Sam 11.25
watch Ruth 2.9; 6.9
worship (1) (of God) [3] Judg 18.31; 7.3
worthless Judg 11.3; 10.27

[a] And...because; *or* To Hannah, however, he would give a special share, because he loved her very much, even though. [b] NEVER HAVE HIS HAIR CUT: *A sign of dedication to the LORD (see Num 6.5).*

1.11: Num 6.5

answered. "I haven't been drinking! I am **desperate**, and I have been **praying**, pouring out my **troubles** to the LORD. 16 Don't think I am a **worthless** woman. I have been **praying** like this because I'm so **miserable**."

17 "Go in **peace**," Eli said, "and may the God of Israel give you what you have asked him for."

18 "May you always think **kindly** of me," she replied. Then she went away, ate some food, and was no longer **sad**.

Samuel's Birth and Dedication

19 The next morning Elkanah and his family got up early, and after **worshipping** the LORD, they went back home to Ramah. Elkanah had intercourse with his wife Hannah, and the LORD answered her **prayer**. 20 So it was that she became pregnant and gave **birth** to a son. She named him Samuel,[c] and explained, "I asked the LORD for him."

21 The time came again for Elkanah and his family to go to Shiloh and **offer** to the LORD the yearly **sacrifice** and the **special sacrifice** he had **promised**. 22 But this time Hannah did not go. She told her husband, "As soon as the child is weaned, I will take him to the house of the LORD, where he will stay all his **life**."

23 Elkanah answered, "All right, do whatever you think **best**; stay at home until you have weaned him. And may the LORD make your[d] **promise** come **true**." So Hannah stayed at home and nursed her child.

24 After she had weaned him, she took him to Shiloh, taking along a three-year-old bull,[e] ten kilogrammes of flour, and a leather bag full of wine. She took Samuel, young as he was, to the house of the LORD at Shiloh. 25 After they had killed the bull, they took the child to Eli. 26 Hannah said to him, "**Excuse** me, sir. Do you **remember** me? I am the woman you saw standing here, **praying** to the LORD. 27 I asked him for this child, and he gave me what I asked for. 28 So I am **dedicating** him to the LORD. As long as he lives, he will belong to the LORD."

Then they[f] **worshipped** the LORD there.

Hannah's Prayer

2 Hannah **prayed**:
"The LORD has filled my **heart** with
  joy;
  how **happy** I am because of what he
    has done!
I laugh at my **enemies**;
  how **joyful** I am because God has
    helped me!

2 "No one is **holy** like the LORD;
  there is none like him,
  no **protector** like our God.
3 Stop your loud **boasting**;
  silence your **proud words**.
For the LORD is a God who knows,
  and he **judges** all that people do.
4 The bows of **strong** soldiers are
    broken,
  but the **weak** grow strong.
5 The people who once were well fed
  now hire themselves out to get food,
  but the **hungry** are hungry no more.
The childless wife has borne seven
    children,
  but the mother of many is left with
    none.
6 The LORD kills and **restores to life**;
  he sends people to the **world of the**
    dead
  and brings them back again.
7 He makes some men **poor** and others
    rich;
  he **humbles** some and makes others
    great.
8 He lifts the **poor** from the dust
  and **raises** the **needy** from their
    misery.
He makes them companions of princes
  and puts them in places of **honour**.
The foundations of the earth belong to
    the LORD;
  on them he has built the **world**.

9 "He **protects** the **lives** of his **faithful**
    people,
  but the **wicked** disappear in
    darkness;
  a man does not **triumph** by his own
    strength.
10 The LORD's **enemies** will be **destroyed**;
  he will thunder against them from
    heaven.
The LORD will **judge** the whole **world**;
  he will give **power** to his king,
  he will make his **chosen king**
    victorious."

11 Then Elkanah went back home to Ramah, but the boy Samuel stayed in Shiloh and **served** the LORD under the **priest** Eli.

[c] SAMUEL: *This name, which in Hebrew means "name of God," is here related to the Hebrew verb for "ask."* [d] *Some ancient translations* your; *Hebrew* his.
[e] *Some ancient translations* a three-year-old bull; *Hebrew* three bulls.
[f] *Some ancient translations* they; *Hebrew* he.

2.1-10: Lk 1.46–55

accept Judg 13.23; 8.3
alive Judg 2.7; 15.8

altar [2] Judg 21.4; 7.17
beg Deut 33.29; 15.25
best 1.23; 3.18
bless [3] Ruth 4.13; 9.12
blind Deut 28.28; 3.2
boast Deut 32.27; 1 Kgs 20.11
choose [4] Judg 21.23; 8.18
consult Josh 19.51; 14.19
contempt Num 15.30; 2 Sam 12.14
dark Judg 19.9; 28.8
death (1) Ruth 1.17; 4.21
dedicate 1.11; 7.3
defend [2] Judg 6.31; 13.23
demand Deut 29.19; 2 Sam 14.7
despise Deut 23.7; 10.27
destroy Judg 20.34; 12.25
enemy [2] Judg 20.35; 4.3
envy Job 5.5
ephod (1) Judg 18.14; 14.3
evil Judg 20.6; 3.13
faithful [2] Judg 5.13; 12.24
favour Deut 33.23; 13.12
force (1) Judg 21.21; 28.3
God's people [2] Ruth 1.6; 9.16
greed Job 20.20
happy Judg 18.20; 2 Sam 19.6
heart Judg 11.35; 7.3
heaven Judg 13.20; 7.10
help [2] Ruth 3.15; 4.20
holy Josh 24.19; 6.20
honour [3] Judg 13.17; 6.5
hope Ruth 1.12; 2 Sam 14.7
humble Num 12.3; 2 Sam 22.28
hunger Deut 32.24; 14.24
incense Num 16.6; 1 Kgs 7.50
joy [2] Deut 28.47; 4.5
judge [2] Judg 11.27; 7.17
life (1) 1.11; 9.2
life (2) (to life) 2 Sam 12.23
message Judg 16.18; 3.1
misery 1.16; 2 Sam 16.12
need Judg 19.19; 17.47
offer [7] 1.3; 3.14
poor [2] Ruth 3.10; 18.23
power Judg 15.14; 4.8
pray 1.9; 7.5
presence Ruth 4.4; 12.3
priest [13] 1.3; 5.5
promise 1.11; 12.22
prophet Judg 6.8; 3.20
protect [2] Ruth 2.12; 10.1

proud Deut 8.14; 2 Sam 22.28
raise Deut 32.40; 1 Kgs 8.22
regulation Num 36.13; 2 Chr 35.13
require Deut 21.9; 17.25
respect Judg 9.16; 9.6
restore Num 36.4; 2 Sam 8.3
reveal Deut 33.8; 3.21
rich Ruth 4.11; 25.2
right (1) Josh 9.25; 12.23
right (3) Ruth 4.4; 10.25
sacred Judg 18.18; 3.3
sacrifice [7] 1.3; 3.14
serious Judg 12.2; 2 Kgs 1.2
servant [3] 1.11; 3.9
serve [6] Judg 18.4; 3.1
service Josh 9.8; 16.21
share 1.4; 30.24
sight Josh 10.10; 6.13
slave Judg 6.8; 4.9
strength Judg 16.9; 30.12
strong Judg 18.26; 13.6
Tent (2) (of the Lord's presence) Judg 18.31; 2 Sam 6.17
triumph Ex 15.7; 2 Chr 20.27
trouble 1.11; 10.19
true 1.23; 3.19
victory Judg 20.27; 14.6
violent Judg 4.3; 2 Sam 3.39
weak Judg 16.7; 14.24
wicked Judg 9.57; 15.18
word (1) Judg 21.13; 20.12
world [2] Deut 29.24; 17.46
world of the dead Deut 32.22; Job 11.8

The Sons of Eli

12 The sons of Eli were scoundrels. They paid no attention to the LORD 13 or to the **regulations** concerning what the **priests** could **demand** from the people. Instead, when a man was **offering his sacrifice**, the **priest's servant** would come with a three-pronged fork. While the meat was still cooking, 14 he would stick the fork into the cooking-pot, and whatever the fork brought out belonged to the **priest**. All the Israelites who came to Shiloh to **offer sacrifices** were treated like this. 15 In addition, even before the fat was taken off and burnt, the **priest's servant** would come and say to the man **offering the sacrifice**, "Give me some meat for the **priest** to roast; he won't **accept** boiled meat from you, only raw meat."

16 If the man answered, "Let us do what is **right** and burn the fat first; then take what you want," the **priest's servant** would say, "No! Give it to me now! If you don't, I will have to take it by **force**!"

17 This sin of the sons of Eli was extremely **serious** in the LORD's **sight**, because they treated the **offerings** to the LORD with such **disrespect**.

Samuel at Shiloh

18 In the meantime the boy Samuel continued to **serve** the LORD, wearing a **sacred** linen apron. 19 Each year his mother would make a little robe and take it to him when she accompanied her husband to **offer the yearly sacrifice**. 20 Then Eli would **bless** Elkanah and his wife, and say to Elkanah, "May the LORD give you other children by this woman to take the place of the one you **dedicated** to him."

After that they would go back home.

21 The LORD did **bless** Hannah, and she had three more sons and two daughters. The boy Samuel grew up in the **service** of the LORD.

Eli and His Sons

22 Eli was now very old. He kept hearing about everything his sons were doing to the Israelites and that they were even sleeping with the women who worked at the entrance to the **Tent** of the LORD's presence. 23 So he said to them, "Why are you doing these things? Everybody tells me about the **evil** you are doing. 24 Stop it, my sons! This is an awful thing the people of the LORD are talking about! 25 If a man sins against another man, God can **defend** him; but who can **defend** a man who sins against the LORD?"

But they would not listen to their father, for the LORD had decided to kill them.

26 The boy Samuel continued to grow and to gain **favour** both with the LORD and with men.

The Prophecy against Eli's Family

27 A **prophet** came to Eli with this **message** from the LORD: "When your ancestor Aaron and his family were **slaves** of the king of Egypt, I **revealed** myself to Aaron. 28 From all the tribes of Israel I **chose** his family to be my **priests**, to **serve** at the **altar**, to burn the **incense**, and to wear the **ephod**[g] to **consult** me. And I gave them the **right** to keep a **share** of the **sacrifices** burnt on the **altar**. 29 Why, then, do you look with **greed**[h] at the **sacrifices** and **offerings** which I **require** from **my people**? Why, Eli, do you **honour** your sons more than me by letting them fatten themselves on the **best** parts of all the **sacrifices my people offer** to me? 30 I, the LORD God of Israel, **promised** in the past that your family and your clan would **serve** me as **priests** for all time. But now I say that I won't have it any longer! Instead, I will **honour** those who honour me, and I will treat with **contempt** those who **despise** me. 31 Listen, the time is coming when I will kill all the young men in your family and your clan, so that no man in your family will live to be old. 32 You will be **troubled** and look with **envy**[i] on all the **blessings** I will give to the other people of Israel, but no one in your family will ever again live to old age. 33 Yet I will keep one of your descendants **alive**, and he will **serve** me as **priest**. But he[j] will become **blind** and lose all **hope**, and all your other descendants will die a **violent death**. 34 When your two sons Hophni and Phinehas both die on the same day, this will show you that everything I have said will come **true**. 35 I will **choose** a **priest** who will be **faithful** to me and do everything I want him to. I will give him descendants, who will always **serve** in the **presence** of my **chosen** king. 36 Any of your descendants who survive will have to go to that **priest** and ask him for money and food, and **beg** to be allowed to **help** the **priests**, in order to have something to eat."

[g] EPHOD: *See Word List.* [h] *One ancient translation* look with greed; *Hebrew unclear.*
[i] *Probable text* look with envy; *Hebrew unclear.* [j] *One ancient translation* he; *Hebrew* you.

2.26: Lk 2.52 **2.28:** Ex 28.1–4; Lev 7.35–36 **2.34:** 1 Sam 4.11

afraid Judg 9.21; 4.7
best 2.29; 8.14
blind 2.33; 4.15
Covenant Box Judg 20.27; 4.3
direct Num 27.21; 1 Chr 25.2
evil 2.23; 12.20
keep from 1.5; 13.19
message 2.27; 11.9
offer 2.13; 6.14
prophet 2.27; 9.9
punish [2] Ruth 1.17; 5.6
reveal 2.27; 2 Sam 7.17
sacred 2.18; 10.3
sacrifice 2.13; 6.15
sanctuary Josh 24.26; 1 Kgs 6.3
servant [2] 2.13; 8.16
serve 2.11; 7.17
solemn 1.11; 12.22
terrible [2] Josh 7.15; 4.17
threat Judg 8.28; 14.27
true 2.34; 9.6
vision [2] Num 24.4; 2 Chr 9.29

The LORD Appears to Samuel

3 In those days, when the boy Samuel was **serving** the LORD under the **direction** of Eli, there were very few **messages** from the LORD, and **visions** from him were quite rare. 2 One night Eli, who was now almost **blind**, was sleeping in his own room; 3 Samuel was sleeping in the **sanctuary**, where the **sacred Covenant Box** was. Before dawn, while the lamp was still burning, 4 the LORD called Samuel. He answered, "Yes, sir!" 5 and ran to Eli and said, "You called me, and here I am."

But Eli answered, "I didn't call you; go back to bed." So Samuel went back to bed.

6–7 The LORD called Samuel again. The boy did not know that it was the LORD, because the LORD had never spoken to him before. So he got up, went to Eli, and said, "You called me, and here I am."

But Eli answered, "My son, I didn't call you; go back to bed."

8 The LORD called Samuel a third time; he got up, went to Eli, and said, "You called me, and here I am."

Then Eli realized that it was the LORD who was calling the boy, 9 so he said to him, "Go back to bed; and if he calls you again, say, 'Speak, LORD, your **servant** is listening.' " So Samuel went back to bed.

10 The LORD came and stood there, and called as he had before, "Samuel! Samuel!"

Samuel answered, "Speak; your **servant** is listening."

11 The LORD said to him, "Some day I am going to do something to the people of Israel that is so **terrible** that everyone who hears about it will be stunned. 12 On that day I will carry out all my **threats** against Eli's family, from beginning to end. 13 I have already told him[k] that I am going to **punish** his family for ever because his sons have spoken **evil** things against me. Eli knew they were doing this, but he did not stop them. 14 So I **solemnly** declare to the family of Eli that no **sacrifice** or **offering** will ever be able to remove the consequences of this **terrible** sin."

15 Samuel stayed in bed until morning; then he got up and opened the doors of the house of the LORD. He was **afraid** to tell Eli about the **vision**. 16 Eli called him, "Samuel, my boy!"

"Yes, sir," answered Samuel.

17 "What did the LORD tell you?" Eli asked. "Don't **keep anything from** me. God will **punish** you severely if you don't tell me everything he said." 18 So Samuel told him everything; he did not keep anything back. Eli said, "He is the LORD; he will do whatever seems **best** to him."

19 As Samuel grew up, the LORD was with him and made everything that Samuel said come **true**. 20 So all the people of Israel, from one end of the country to the other, knew that Samuel was indeed a **prophet** of the LORD. 21 The LORD continued to **reveal** himself at Shiloh, where he had appeared to Samuel and had spoken to him. And when Samuel spoke, all Israel listened.

The Capture of the Covenant Box

4 At that time the Philistines gathered to go to war against Israel, so[l] the Israelites set out to fight them. The Israelites set up their camp at Ebenezer and the Philistines at Aphek. 2 The Philistines attacked, and after fierce fighting they defeated the Israelites and killed about four thousand men on the battlefield. 3 When the survivors came back to camp, the leaders of Israel said, "Why did the LORD let the Philistines defeat us today? Let's go and bring the LORD's **Covenant Box** from Shiloh, so that he[m] will go with us and **save** us from our **enemies**." 4 So they sent messengers to Shiloh and fetched the **Covenant Box** of the LORD **Almighty**; who is **enthroned** above the winged **creatures**.[x] And Eli's two sons, Hophni and Phinehas, came along with the **Covenant Box**.

5 When the **Covenant Box** arrived, the Israelites gave such a loud shout of **joy** that the earth shook. 6 The Philistines heard the shouting and said, "Listen to all that shouting in the **Hebrew** camp! What does it mean?" When they found out that the LORD's **Covenant Box** had arrived in the **Hebrew** camp, 7 they were **afraid**, and said, "A **god** has come into their camp! We're lost! Nothing like this has ever happened to us before! 8 Who can **save** us from those **powerful gods**? They are the **gods** who **slaughtered** the Egyptians in the desert! 9 Be brave, Philistines! Fight like men, or we will become slaves to the **Hebrews**, just as they were our **slaves**. So fight like men!"

10 The Philistines fought **hard** and defeated the Israelites, who went running to their homes. There was a

afraid 3.15; 7.7
Almighty 1.3; 15.1
anxious Deut 28.65; Ps 38.18
birth 1.20; 2 Sam 3.2
blind 3.2; 2 Sam 5.6
Covenant Box [12] 3.3; 5.1
creature Num 7.89; 2 Sam 6.2
dead Ruth 4.5; 14.44
death (1) 2.33; 20.3
enemy 2.1; 10.1
escape Judg 20.42; 19.10
fear Josh 9.24; 13.7
glory [2] Deut 5.24; 1 Chr 16.24
god (2) (other gods) [3] Ruth 1.15; 5.2
grief Judg 11.37; 15.35
hard Judg 20.34; 2 Sam 10.12
Hebrew [3] Ex 21.2; 13.3
help 2.1; 5.12
joy 2.1; 6.13
power 2.10; 7.3
save [2] Judg 18.27; 7.8
slaughter [2] Judg 11.33; 6.19
slave 2.27; 8.17
terrible 3.11; 6.9
throne Ex 12.29; 2 Sam 6.2

[k] *One ancient translation* I have already told him; *Hebrew* I will tell him.
[l] *One ancient translation* the Philistines...so; *Hebrew does not have these words.* [m] he; *or* it.
[x] WINGED CREATURES: *See Word List.*

4.4: Ex 25.22

great **slaughter**: thirty thousand Israelite soldiers were killed. [11]God's **Covenant Box** was captured, and Eli's sons, Hophni and Phinehas, were both killed.

The Death of Eli

12 A man from the tribe of Benjamin ran all the way from the battlefield to Shiloh and arrived there the same day. To show his **grief**, he had torn his clothes and put earth on his head. [13]Eli, who was very **anxious** about the **Covenant Box**, was sitting on a seat beside the road, staring. The man spread the news throughout the town, and everyone cried out in **fear**. [14]Eli heard the noise and asked, "What is all this noise about?" The man hurried to Eli to tell him the news. [15](Eli was now ninety-eight years old and almost completely **blind**.) [16]The man said, "I have **escaped** from the battle and have run all the way here today."

Eli asked him, "What happened, my son?"

17 The messenger answered, "Israel ran away from the Philistines; it was a **terrible** defeat for us! Besides that, your sons Hophni and Phinehas were killed, and God's **Covenant Box** was captured!"

18 When the man mentioned the **Covenant Box**, Eli fell backwards from his seat beside the gate. He was so old and fat that the fall broke his neck, and he died. He had been a leader in Israel for forty years.

The Death of the Widow of Phinehas

19 Eli's daughter-in-law, the wife of Phinehas, was pregnant, and it was almost time for her baby to be born. When she heard that God's **Covenant Box** had been captured and that her father-in-law and her husband were **dead**, she suddenly went into labour and gave **birth**. [20]As she was dying, the women **helping** her said to her, "Be brave! You have a son!" But she paid no attention and did not answer. [21]She named the boy Ichabod,[n] explaining, "God's **glory** has left Israel"—referring to the capture of the **Covenant Box** and the **death** of her father-in-law and her husband. [22]"God's **glory** has left Israel," she said, "because God's **Covenant Box** has been captured."

The Covenant Box among the Philistines

5 After the Philistines captured the **Covenant Box**, they carried it from Ebenezer to their city of Ashdod, [2]took it into the **temple** of their **god Dagon**, and set it up beside his statue. [3]Early next morning the people of Ashdod saw that the statue of Dagon had fallen face downwards on the ground in front of the LORD's **Covenant Box**. So they lifted it up and put it back in its place. [4]Early the following morning they saw that the statue had again fallen down in front of the **Covenant Box**. This time its head and both its arms were broken off and were lying in the doorway; only the **body** was left. [5](That is why even today the **priests** of Dagon and all his **worshippers** in Ashdod step over that place and do not walk on it.)

6 The LORD **punished** the people of Ashdod severely and **terrified** them. He **punished** them and the people in the surrounding territory by causing them to have tumours.[o] [7]When they saw what was happening, they said, "The God of Israel is **punishing** us and our **god Dagon**. We can't let the **Covenant Box** stay here any longer." [8]So they sent messengers and called together all five of the Philistine kings and asked them, "What shall we do with the **Covenant Box** of the God of Israel?"

"Take it over to Gath," they answered; so they took it to Gath, another Philistine city. [9]But after it arrived there, the LORD **punished** that city too and caused a great panic. He **punished** them with tumours which developed in all the people of the city, young and old alike. [10]So they sent the **Covenant Box** to Ekron, another Philistine city; but when it arrived there, the people cried out, "They have brought the **Covenant Box** of the God of Israel here, in order to kill us all!" [11]So again they sent for all the Philistine kings and said, "Send the **Covenant Box** of Israel back to its own place, so that it won't kill us and our families." There was panic throughout the city because God was **punishing** them so severely. [12]Even those who did not die developed tumours and the people cried out to their **gods** for **help**.

The Return of the Covenant Box

6 After the LORD's **Covenant Box** had been in Philistia for seven months, [2]the people called the **priests** and the **magicians** and asked, "What shall we do with the **Covenant Box** of the LORD? If we send it back where it belongs, what shall we send with it?"

3 They answered, "If you return the

body Judg 20.1; 17.44
Covenant Box [8] 4.3; 6.1

god (2) (other gods) [3] 4.7; 6.5
help 4.20; 7.2
priest 2.11; 6.2
punish [6] 3.13; 6.3
temple (2) (of other gods) Judg 9.4; 31.10
terrify Josh 9.24; 14.15
worship (2) (of other gods) Judg 18.30; 8.8

burnt-offering [2] Josh 8.31; 10.8
Covenant Box [11] 5.1; 7.1
disaster Deut 32.23; 25.17
fool Judg 16.10; 13.13
forget 1.11; 12.9
gift [5] Judg 3.15; 10.27
god (2) (other gods) 5.2; 7.3

[n] ICHABOD: *This name in Hebrew means "no glory."*
[o] TUMOURS: *The association of tumours with an abundance of mice suggests that this was a case of bubonic plague (see 6.5).*

harvest Ruth 2.2; 8.12
heal Josh 5.8; 1 Kgs 13.6
holy 2.2; 9.6
honour 2.8; 12.14
joy 4.5; 11.9
Levites Judg 20.4; 2 Sam 15.24
magic Num 23.23; 2 Kgs 21.6
mourn Judg 21.2; 25.1
new Ruth 4.15; 10.9
offer [2] 3.14; 7.6
plague [2] Deut 29.3; Ps 78.50
priest 5.5; 14.3
punish [2] 5.6; 15.2
sacrifice 3.14; 7.9
sight 2.17; 9.17
slaughter 4.8; 11.11
stubborn Deut 32.20; 2 Kgs 17.14
terrible 4.17; 14.29
turn Ruth 3.8; 7.3
watch [2] 1.12; 14.16
witness Ruth 4.9; 12.5

Covenant Box of the God of Israel, you
must, of course, send with it a **gift** to him
to pay for your sin. The **Covenant Box**
must not go back without a **gift**. In this
way you will be **healed**, and you will find
out why he has kept on **punishing** you."
4 "What **gift** shall we send him?" the
people asked.
They answered, "Five gold models of
tumours and five gold mice, one of each
for each Philistine king. The same
plague was sent on all of you and on the
five kings. 5 You must make these models
of the tumours and of the mice that are
ravaging your country, and you must
give **honour** to the God of Israel. Perhaps
he will stop **punishing** you, your **gods**, and
your land. 6 Why should you be **stubborn**,
as the king of Egypt and the Egyptians
were? Don't **forget** how God made **fools**
of them until they let the Israelites leave
Egypt. 7 So prepare a **new** wagon and two
cows that have never been yoked; hitch
them to the wagon and drive their calves
back to the barn. 8 Take the LORD's **Covenant Box**, put it on the wagon, and place
in a box beside it the gold models that
you are sending to him as a **gift** to pay
for your sins. Start the wagon on its way
and let it go by itself. 9 Then **watch** it go;
if it goes towards the town of Beth Shemesh, this means that it is the God of the
Israelites who has sent this **terrible
disaster** on us. But if it doesn't, then we
will know that he did not send the
plague; it was only a matter of chance."
10 They did what they were told: they
took two cows and hitched them to the
wagon, and shut the calves in the barn.
11 They put the **Covenant Box** in the
wagon, together with the box containing
the gold models of the mice and of the
tumours. 12 The cows started off on the
road to Beth Shemesh and headed
straight towards it, without **turning** off
the road. They were mooing as they
went. The five Philistine kings followed
them as far as the border of Beth
Shemesh.
13 The people of Beth Shemesh were
harvesting wheat in the valley, when suddenly they looked up and saw the **Covenant Box**. They were **overjoyed** at the
sight. 14 The wagon came to a field
belonging to a man named Joshua, who
lived in Beth Shemesh, and it stopped
there near a large rock. The people
chopped up the wooden wagon and killed
the cows and **offered them as a burnt-
sacrifice** to the LORD. 15 The **Levites** lifted
off the **Covenant Box** of the LORD and the
box with the gold models in it, and placed
them on the large rock. Then the people
of Beth Shemesh **offered burnt-sacrifices**
and other **sacrifices** to the LORD. 16 The
five Philistine kings **watched** them do
this and then went back to Ekron that
same day.
17 The Philistines sent the five gold
tumours to the LORD as a **gift** to pay for
their sins, one each for the cities of Ashdod, Gaza, Ashkelon, Gath, and Ekron.
18 They also sent gold mice, one for each
of the cities ruled by the five Philistine
kings, both the fortified towns and the
villages without walls. The large rock in
the field of Joshua of Beth Shemesh, on
which they placed the LORD's **Covenant
Box**, is still there as a **witness** to what
happened.
19 The LORD killed seventy of the men
of Beth Shemesh because they looked
inside the **Covenant Box**. And the people
mourned because the LORD had caused
such a great **slaughter** among them.

The Covenant Box at Kiriath Jearim

20 So the men of Beth Shemesh said,
"Who can stand before the LORD, this
holy God? Where can we send him to get
him away from us?" 21 They sent
messengers to the people of Kiriath
Jearim to say, "The Philistines have
returned the LORD's **Covenant Box**. Come
down and fetch it."
7 So the people of Kiriath Jearim
fetched the LORD's **Covenant Box**
and took it to the house of a man named
Abinadab, who lived on a hill. They
consecrated his son Eleazar to be in
charge of it.

Samuel Rules Israel

2 The **Covenant Box** of the LORD
stayed in Kiriath Jearim a long time,
some twenty years. During this time all
the Israelites cried to the LORD for **help**.
3 Samuel said to the people of Israel,
"If you are going to **turn to** the LORD **with
all your hearts**, you must get **rid** of all the
foreign **gods** and the **images** of the **goddess** Astarte. **Dedicate** yourselves completely to the LORD and **worship** only
him, and he will **rescue** you from the
power of the Philistines." 4 So the Israelites got **rid** of their **idols** of Baal and
Astarte, and **worshipped** only the LORD.
5 Then Samuel sent for all the Israelites to meet at Mizpah, saying, "I will
pray to the LORD for you there." 6 So they
all gathered at Mizpah. They drew some
water and poured it out as an **offering** to
the LORD and **fasted** that whole day.
They said, "We have sinned against the

7.1: 2 Sam 6.2–4; 1 Chr 13.5–7

afraid 4.7; 11.7
altar 2.28; 9.12
consecrate Num 8.17; 1 Kgs 8.6
Covenant Box [2] 6.1; 2 Sam 6.2
dedicate 2.20; 2 Sam 8.11
dispute [2] Judg 18.7; 2 Sam 15.2
fast (2) Lev 16.29; 31.13
flee Judg 11.3; 19.8
god (2) (other gods) 6.5; 8.8
goddess Judg 6.25; 31.10
heart 2.1; 10.26
heaven 2.10; 1 Kgs 8.23
help [4] 5.12; 9.16
idol Judg 18.14; 12.1
image Deut 5.8; 1 Kgs 14.9
judge 2.3; 8.1
lamb Deut 14.26; 15.
offer [2] 6.14; 9.12
peace 1.17; 16.4
power 4.8; 10.26
pray [3] 2.1; 8.6
prayer 1.19; 2 Sam 7.27
prevent Num 30.12; 2 Chr 32.3
rescue Judg 13.5; 9.16
rid [2] Judg 10.16; 1 Kgs 14.10
sacrifice [2] 6.15; 9.12
save 4.3; 9.24
serve 3.1; 8.11

settle (2) [2] Ruth 4.7; 2 Sam 15.2
turn 6.12; 8.8
worship (1) (of God) [2] 1.3; 12.10

LORD." (It was at Mizpah that Samuel
settled disputes among the Israelites.)
7 When the Philistines heard that the
Israelites had gathered at Mizpah, the
five Philistine kings started out with their
men to attack them. The Israelites heard
about it and were **afraid**, [8]and said to
Samuel, "Keep **praying** to the LORD our
God to **save** us from the Philistines."
[9]Samuel killed a young **lamb** and burnt it
whole as a **sacrifice** to the LORD. Then he
prayed to the LORD to **help** Israel, and
the LORD answered his **prayer**. [10]While
Samuel was **offering the sacrifice**, the
Philistines moved forward to attack; but
just then the LORD thundered from
heaven against them. They became completely confused and **fled** in panic. [11]The
Israelites marched out from Mizpah and
pursued the Philistines almost as far as
Bethcar, killing them along the way.
12 Then Samuel took a stone, set it up
between Mizpah and Shen, and said,
"The LORD has **helped** us all the way"—
and he named it "Stone of **Help**." [13]So the
Philistines were defeated, and the LORD
prevented them from invading Israel's
territory as long as Samuel lived. [14]All
the cities which the Philistines had captured between Ekron and Gath were returned to Israel, and so Israel got back
all its territory. And there was **peace**
also between the Israelites and the
Canaanites.
15 Samuel ruled Israel as long as he
lived. [16]Every year he would go round to
Bethel, Gilgal, and Mizpah, and in these
places he would **settle disputes**. [17]Then
he would go back to his home in Ramah,
where also he would **serve** as **judge**. In
Ramah he built an **altar** to the LORD.

The People Ask for a King

8 When Samuel grew old, he made his
sons **judges** in Israel. [2]The elder son
was named Joel and the younger one
Abijah; they were **judges** in Beersheba.
[3]But they did not follow their father's
example; they were **interested** only in
making money, so they **accepted bribes**
and did not decide **cases honestly**.
4 Then all the leaders of Israel met together, went to Samuel in Ramah, [5]and
said to him, "Look, you are getting old
and your sons don't follow your **example**.
So then, appoint a king to rule over us, so
that we will have a king, as other countries have." [6]Samuel was **displeased** with
their **request** for a king; so he **prayed** to
the LORD, [7]and the LORD said, "Listen to
everything the people say to you. You
are not the one they have **rejected**; I am
the one they have **rejected** as their king.
[8]Ever since I brought them out of Egypt,
they have **turned away** from me and **worshipped other gods**; and now they are
doing to you what they have always done
to me. [9]So then, listen to them, but give
them strict **warnings** and explain how
their kings will treat them."
10 Samuel told the people who were
asking him for a king everything that the
LORD had said to him. [11]"This is how
your king will treat you," Samuel explained. "He will make soldiers of your
sons; some of them will **serve** in his war
chariots, others in his cavalry, and others
will run before his chariots. [12]He will
make some of them officers in charge of
a thousand men, and others in charge of
fifty men. Your sons will have to plough
his fields, **harvest** his crops, and make his
weapons and the equipment for his
chariots. [13]Your daughters will have to
make perfumes for him and work as his
cooks and his bakers. [14]He will take your
best fields, **vineyards**, and olive-groves,
and give them to his officials. [15]He will
take a tenth of your corn and of your
grapes for his **court** officers and other
officials. [16]He will take your **servants** and
your **best** cattle[p] and donkeys, and make
them work for him. [17]He will take a tenth
of your **flocks**. And you yourselves will
become his **slaves**. [18]When that time
comes, you will **complain bitterly**
because of your king, whom you yourselves **chose**, but the LORD will not listen
to your **complaints**."
19 The people paid no attention to
Samuel, but said, "No! We want a king,
[20]so that we will be like other nations,
with our own king to rule us and to lead
us out to war and to fight our battles."
[21]Samuel listened to everything they said
and then went and told the LORD. [22]The
LORD answered, "Do what they want and
give them a king." Then Samuel told all
the men of Israel to go back home.

Saul Meets Samuel

9 There was a wealthy and influential
man named Kish, from the tribe of
Benjamin; he was the son of Abiel and
grandson of Zeror, and belonged to the
family of Becorath, a part of the clan of
Aphiah. [2]He had a son named Saul, a
handsome man in the prime of **life**. Saul
was a head taller than anyone else in
Israel and more handsome as well.
3 Some donkeys belonging to Kish had
wandered off, so he said to Saul, "Take

accept 2.15; 10.4
best [2] 3.18; 14.36
bitter 1.9; 15.32
bribe Deut 16.19; 12.3
case (2) Deut 22.26; 2 Sam 15.3
choose 2.10; 10.1
complain [2] Judg 8.1; 2 Kgs 6.1
court (1) Deut 25.1; 22.14
displease Num 32.13; 15.19
example [2] Deut 29.21; 1 Kgs 22.52
flock Judg 5.16; 25.16
god (2) (other gods) 7.3; 12.21
harvest 6.13; 23.1
honest Judg 9.16; 1 Kgs 3.6
interest (1) Ruth 2.19; Ezra 4.22
judge [2] 7.17; 16.7

pray 7.5; 12.17
reject [2] Deut 32.15; 10.19
request Judg 8.8; 2 Sam 14.22
servant 3.9; 9.3
serve 7.17; 12.14
slave 4.9; 17.8
turn 7.3; 10.9
vineyard Judg 21.20; 22.7
warn Josh 6.26; 11.7
worship (2) (of other gods) 5.5; 12.10

altar 7.17; 10.5
anoint Num 7.1; 10.1
bless 2.20; 15.13
God's people [3] 2.29; 10.1
help 7.2; 11.3
holy [2] 6.20; 10.25
idea Josh 22.28; 17.55
important Judg 6.15; 15.17
least Judg 6.15; Jer 31.34
life (1) 2.9; 15.9
offer 7.6; 10.3

[p] *One ancient translation* cattle; *Hebrew* young men.

8.5: Deut 17.14

place of worship [3] Judg 20.18; 2 Sam 15.32
prophet 3.20; 10.5
question [2] Judg 8.14; 17.29
rescue 7.3; 10.18
respect 2.17; 15.30
sacrifice [2] 7.9; 10.3
save 7.8; 12.7
servant [8] 8.16; 10.10
sight 6.13; 2 Sam 6.20
suffer Judg 9.57; 25.37
true 3.19; 20.2
worry [2] Ruth 3.11; 10.2

one of the **servants** with you and go and look for the donkeys." 4 They went through the hill-country of Ephraim and the region of Shalishah, but did not find them; so they went on through the region of Shaalim, but the donkeys were not there. Then they went through the territory of Benjamin, but still did not find them. 5 When they came into the region of Zuph, Saul said to his **servant**, "Let's go back home, or my father might stop thinking about the donkeys and start **worrying** about us."

6 The **servant** answered, "Wait! In this town there is a **holy** man who is highly **respected** because everything he says comes **true**. Let's go to him, and maybe he can tell us where we can find the donkeys."

7 "If we go to him, what can we give him?" Saul asked. "There is no food left in our packs, and we haven't anything to give him, have we?"

8 The **servant** answered, "I have a small silver coin. I can give him that, and then he will tell us where we can find them."

9–11 Saul replied, "A **good idea**! Let's go." So they went to the town where the **holy** man lived. As they were going up the hill to the town, they met some girls who were coming out to draw water. They asked the girls, "Is the seer in town?"

(At that time a **prophet** was called a seer, and so whenever someone wanted to ask God a **question**, he would say, "Let's go to the seer.")

12–13 "Yes, he is," the girls answered. "In fact, he is just ahead of you. If you hurry, you will catch up with him. As soon as you go into the town, you will find him. He arrived in town today because the people are going to **offer a sacrifice** on the **altar** on the hill. The people who are invited won't start eating until he gets there, because he has to **bless** the **sacrifice** first. If you go now, you will find him before he goes up the hill to eat." 14 So Saul and his **servant** went on to the town, and as they were going in, they saw Samuel coming out towards them on his way to the **place of worship**.

15 Now on the previous day the LORD had said to Samuel, 16 "Tomorrow about this time I will send you a man from the tribe of Benjamin; **anoint** him as ruler of **my people** Israel, and he will **rescue** them from the Philistines. I have seen the **suffering** of **my people** and have heard their cries for **help**."

17 When Samuel caught **sight** of Saul, the LORD said to him, "This is the man I told you about. He will rule **my people**." 18 Then Saul went over to Samuel, who was near the gate, and asked, "Tell me, where does the seer live?"

19 Samuel answered, "I am the seer. Go on ahead of me to the **place of worship**. Both of you are to eat with me today. Tomorrow morning I will answer all your **questions** and send you on your way. 20 As for the donkeys that were lost three days ago, don't **worry** about them; they have already been found. But who is it that the people of Israel want so much?[q] It is you—you and your father's family."

21 Saul answered, "I belong to the tribe of Benjamin, the smallest tribe in Israel, and my family is the **least important** one in the tribe. Why, then, do you talk like this to me?"

22 Then Samuel led Saul and his **servant** into the large room and gave them a place at the head of the table where the guests, about thirty in all, were seated. 23 Samuel said to the cook, "Bring the piece of meat I gave you, which I told you to set aside." 24 So the cook brought the choice piece of the leg and placed it before Saul. Samuel[r] said, "Look, here is the piece that was kept for you. Eat it. I **saved** it for you to eat at this time with the people I invited."[s]

So Saul ate with Samuel that day. 25 When they went down from the **place of worship** to the town, they made up a bed for Saul[t] on the roof,[u] 26 and he slept there.[v]

Samuel Anoints Saul as Ruler

At dawn Samuel called to Saul on the roof, "Get up, and I will send you on your way." Saul got up, and he and Samuel went out to the street together. 27 When they arrived at the edge of the town, Samuel said to Saul, "Tell the **servant** to go on ahead of us." The **servant** left, and Samuel continued, "Stay here a minute, and I will tell you what God has said."

10 Then Samuel took a jar of olive-oil and poured it on Saul's head, **kissed** him, and said, "The LORD **anoints** you as ruler of **his people** Israel. You will rule **his people** and **protect** them from all

accept 8.3; 11.1
altar [2] 9.12; 14.35
anoint 9.16; 15.1
bread Ruth 2.14; 16.20
burnt-offering 6.14; 13.9

[q] who is it...much?; *or* who is to have the most desirable thing in Israel?
[r] *Some ancient translations* Samuel; *Hebrew* He *(that is,* the cook).
[s] *Probable text* I saved it...invited; *Hebrew unclear.*
[t] *One ancient translation* they made up a bed for Saul; *Hebrew* he spoke with Saul.
[u] ON THE ROOF: *At that time houses had flat roofs, and it was common for people to sleep on them.*
[v] *Some ancient translations* and he slept there; *Hebrew* and they got up early.

ıoose [2] 8.18; 12.3
ontrol [2] Judg 6.34;
.6
espise 2.30;
Kgs 19.21
fficult Deut 30.11;
Kgs 10.1
ıty (1) Deut 25.5;
.16
nemy 4.3; 11.11
ellowship-sacrifice
udg 21.4; 11.15
ift 6.3; 1 Kgs 10.10
od's people [3] 9.16;
.22
eart 7.3; 12.20
oly 9.6; 11.15
iss Ruth 1.9; 20.41
ature Prov 10.6
ew 6.7; 23.1
ffer [3] 9.12; 11.15
ppress Judg 10.8;
.3
ower 7.3; 17.46
rophet [5] 9.9; 19.20
rotect 2.2; 17.6
rove Judg 6.17;
Kgs 18.36
eject 8.7; 12.12
eligion [2]
eut 12.30; 21.7
escue [2] 9.16; 11.9
ight (3) 2.28;
Sam 16.10
acred 3.3; 14.41
acrifice 9.12; 13.12
aying 19.24
ervant [2] 9.3; 16.15
pirit (1) (God's
pirit) [2] Judg 11.29;
.6
omb Judg 16.31;
Sam 2.32
rouble 2.32; 24.5
urn 8.8; 12.10
vorry 9.5; 25.35
vorthless 1.16; 15.9

their enemies. And this is the proof to
you that the LORD has chosen you[w] to be
the ruler of his people: 2 When you leave
me today, you will meet two men near
Rachel's tomb at Zelzah in the territory
of Benjamin. They will tell you that the
donkeys you were looking for have been
found, so that your father isn't worried
any more about them but about you, and
he keeps asking, 'What shall I do about
my son?' 3 You will go on from there
until you come to the sacred tree at
Tabor, where you will meet three men
on their way to offer a sacrifice to God at
Bethel. One of them will be leading three
young goats, another one will be carrying three loaves of bread, and the third
one will have a leather bag full of wine.
4 They will greet you and offer you two of
the loaves, which you are to accept.
5 Then you will go to the Hill of God in
Gibeah, where there is a Philistine camp.
At the entrance to the town you will
meet a group of prophets coming down
from the altar on the hill, playing harps,
drums, flutes, and lyres. They will be
dancing and shouting. 6 Suddenly the
spirit of the LORD will take control of
you, and you will join in their religious
dancing and shouting and will become a
different person. 7 When these things
happen, do whatever God leads you to
do. 8 You will go ahead of me to Gilgal,
where I will meet you and offer burnt-sacrifices and fellowship-sacrifices. Wait
there seven days until I come and tell
you what to do."

9 When Saul turned to leave Samuel,
God gave Saul a new nature. And everything Samuel had told him happened that
day. 10 When Saul and his servant arrived
at Gibeah, a group of prophets met him.
Suddenly the spirit of God took control of
him, and he joined in their ecstatic dancing and shouting. 11 People who had
known him before saw him doing this
and asked one another, "What has happened to the son of Kish? Has Saul
become a prophet?" 12 A man who lived
there asked, "How about these other prophets—who do you think their fathers
are?" This is how the saying originated,
"Has even Saul become a prophet?"
13 When Saul finished his ecstatic dancing
and shouting, he went to the altar on the
hill.

14 Saul's uncle saw him and the servant, and he asked them, "Where have
you been?"

"Looking for the donkeys," Saul
answered. "When we couldn't find them,
we went to see Samuel."

15 "And what did he tell you?" Saul's
uncle asked.

16 "He told us that the animals had
been found," Saul answered—but he did
not tell his uncle what Samuel had said
about his becoming king.

Saul Is Acclaimed as King

17 Samuel called the people together
for a religious gathering at Mizpah 18 and
said to them, "The LORD, the God of
Israel, says, 'I brought you out of Egypt
and rescued you from the Egyptians and
all the other peoples who were oppressing you. 19 I am your God, the one who
rescues you from all your troubles and
difficulties, but today you have rejected
me and have asked me to give you a
king. Very well, then, gather yourselves
before the LORD by tribes and by clans.'"

20 Then Samuel made each tribe
come forward, and the LORD picked the
tribe of Benjamin. 21 Then Samuel made
the families of the tribe of Benjamin
come forward, and the family of Matri
was picked out. Then the men of the
family of Matri came forward,[x] and Saul
son of Kish was picked out. They looked
for him, but when they could not find
him, 22 they asked the LORD, "Is there still
someone else?"

The LORD answered, "Saul is over
there, hiding behind the supplies."

23 So they ran and brought Saul out to
the people, and they could see that he
was a head taller than anyone else.
24 Samuel said to the people, "Here is the
man the LORD has chosen! There is no
one else among us like him."

All the people shouted, "Long live the
king!"

25 Samuel explained to the people the
rights and duties of a king, and then
wrote them in a book, which he
deposited in a holy place. Then he sent
everyone home. 26 Saul also went back
home to Gibeah. Some powerful men,[y]
whose hearts God had touched, went
with him. 27 But some worthless people
said, "How can this fellow do us any
good?" They despised Saul and did not
bring him any gifts.

Saul Defeats the Ammonites

11 About a month later King
Nahash of Ammon led his army

accept 10.4; 12.3
afraid 7.7; 12.18

[w] *Some ancient translations* as ruler of his people...the LORD has chosen you; *Hebrew does not have these words.*
[x] *One ancient translation* Then the men of the family of Matri came forward; *Hebrew does not have these words.* [y] *One ancient translation* Some powerful men; *Hebrew* The army.

10.12: 1 Sam 19.23–24

celebrate Judg 16.23; 18.7
control 10.6; 16.13
death (3) (to death) Judg 21.5; 14.39
despair 1.15; 13.6
disgrace Josh 5.9; 17.26
enemy 10.1; 12.10
fellowship-sacrifice 10.8; 13.9
fury Judg 14.19; 20.30
help 9.16; 12.8
holy 10.25; 1 Kgs 19.8
joy 6.13; 18.6
message 3.1; 16.22
offer 10.3; 13.9
proclaim [2] Deut 11.29; 2 Sam 22.47
rescue [2] 10.18; 12.10
right (2) Judg 7.20; 2 Sam 20.9
scatter Deut 30.1; 30.16
slaughter 6.19; 14.14
Spirit (1) (God's Spirit) 10.6; 16.13
warn 8.9; 15.6
wish Judg 9.29; 25.6
wrong Judg 11.27; 12.3

against the town of Jabesh in the territory of Gilead and besieged it. The men
of Jabesh said to Nahash, "Make a treaty
with us, and we will **accept** you as our
ruler."

2 Nahash answered, "I will make a
treaty with you on one condition: I will
put out everyone's **right** eye and so bring
disgrace on all Israel."

3 The leaders of Jabesh said, "Give us
seven days to send messengers throughout the land of Israel. If no one will **help**
us, then we will surrender to you."

4 The messengers arrived at Gibeah,
where Saul lived, and when they told the
news, the people started crying in
despair. 5 Saul was just coming in from
the field with his oxen, and he asked,
"What's **wrong**? Why is everyone crying?" They told him what the messengers from Jabesh had reported. 6 When
Saul heard this, the **spirit of God** took
control of him, and he became **furious**.
7 He took two oxen, cut them in pieces,
and sent messengers to carry the pieces
throughout the land of Israel with this
warning: "Whoever does not follow Saul
and Samuel into battle will have this
done to his oxen!"

The people of Israel were **afraid** of
what the LORD might do, and all of them,
without exception, came out together.
8 Saul gathered them at Bezek: there
were 300,000 from Israel and 30,000 from
Judah. 9 They said to the messengers
from Jabesh, "Tell your people that
before noon tomorrow they will be
rescued." When the people of Jabesh
received the **message**, they were **overjoyed** 10 and said to Nahash, "Tomorrow
we will surrender to you, and you can do
with us whatever you **wish**."

11 That night Saul divided his men
into three groups, and at dawn they
rushed into the **enemy** camp and
attacked the Ammonites. By noon they
had **slaughtered** them. The survivors
scattered, each man running off by
himself.

12 Then the people of Israel said to
Samuel, "Where are the people who said
that Saul should not be our king? Hand
them over to us, and we will kill them!"

13 But Saul said, "No one will be put to
death today, for this is the day the LORD
rescued Israel." 14 And Samuel said to
them, "Let us all go to Gilgal and once
more **proclaim** Saul as our king." 15 So
they all went to Gilgal, and there at the
holy place they **proclaimed** Saul king.
They **offered fellowship-sacrifices**, and
Saul and all the people of Israel **celebrated** the event.

Samuel Addresses the People

12 Then Samuel said to the people
of Israel, "I have done what you
asked me to do. I have given you a king
to rule you, 2 and now you have him to
lead you. As for me, I am old and grey,
and my sons are with you. I have been
your leader from my youth until now.
3 Here I am. If I have done anything
wrong, **accuse** me now in the **presence** of
the LORD and the king he has **chosen**.
Have I taken anybody's cow or anybody's
donkey? Have I **cheated** or **oppressed**
anyone? Have I **accepted** a **bribe** from
anyone? If I have done any of these
things, I will pay back what I have
taken."

4 The people answered, "No, you have
not **cheated** us or **oppressed** us; you have
not taken anything from anyone."

5 Samuel replied, "The LORD and the
king he has **chosen** are **witnesses** today
that you have found me to be completely
innocent."

"Yes, the LORD is our **witness**," they
answered.

6 Samuel continued, "The LORD is the
one who **chose** Moses and Aaron and
who brought your ancestors out of Egypt.
7 Now stand where you are, and I will
accuse you before the LORD by **reminding** you[z] of all the **mighty actions** the
LORD did to **save** you and your ancestors.
8 When Jacob and his family went to
Egypt and the Egyptians **oppressed**
them,[a] your ancestors cried to the LORD
for **help**, and he sent Moses and Aaron,
who brought them out of Egypt and
settled them in this land. 9 But the people
forgot the LORD their God, and so he let
the Philistines and the king of Moab and
Sisera, commander of the army of the
city of Hazor, fight against your ancestors and **conquer** them. 10 Then they
cried to the LORD for **help** and said, 'We
have sinned, because we **turned away**
from you, LORD, and **worshipped the
idols** of Baal and Astarte. **Rescue** us from
our **enemies**, and we will **worship** you!'
11 And the LORD sent Gideon, Barak,[b]
Jephthah, and finally me. Each of us
rescued you from your **enemies**, and you
lived in **safety**. 12 But when you saw that
King Nahash of Ammon was about to

abandon Judg 10 18.12
accept 11.1; 25.27
accuse [2] Deut 22.14; 22.15
action Judg 9.16; 21.15
afraid [2] 11.7; 14
bribe 8.3; 2 Chr 1
cheat [2] Deut 25. Job 31.21
choose [4] 10.1; 16
command [2] Judg 7.9; 13.13
conquer Judg 10. 2 Sam 5.6
destroy 2.10; 15.3
disobey Josh 22.2 13.14
enemy [2] 11.11; 14.24
evil 3.13; 16.14
faithful 2.9; 22.14
false Deut 22.14; 1 Kgs 14.23
forbid Judg 13.4;
forget 6.6; 24.21
god (2) (other go 8.8; 17.43
God's people 10.1 13.14
heart [2] 10.26; 16.
help [3] 11.3; 14.6
honour 6.5; 18.23
idol 7.4; 15.23
innocent Deut 27. 19.5
might Judg 16.30; 2 Sam 1.22
obey [2] Judg 3.4; 13.13
oppress [3] 10.18; 22.2
pray [4] 8.6; 2 Sam 7.18
presence 2.35; 16.
promise 2.30; 14.3
real Deut 32.17; 1 Kgs 3.26
reject 10.19; 15.23
remember 1.11; 2 Sam 3.18
remind Josh 4.6; 1 Kgs 17.18
rescue [2] 11.9; 17.
right (1) 2.16; 24.1
safe Judg 18.7; 20.
save [2] 9.24; 14.23
serve [3] 8.11; 18.1
solemn 3.14; 14.24
teach Judg 3.2; 2 Sam 1.18
turn [2] 10.9; 15.11
witness [2] 6.18; 20.12
worship (1) (of Go 7.3; 15.25
worship (2) (of other gods) 8.8; 26
wrong 11.5; 19.4

[z] *One ancient translation* by reminding you; *Hebrew does not have these words.*
[a] *One ancient translation* and the Egyptians oppressed them; *Hebrew does not have these words.*
[b] *Some ancient translations* Barak; *Hebrew* Bedan.

12.6: Ex 6.26 **12.8:** Ex 2.23 **12.9:** Judg 3.12, 4.2, 13.1 **12.10:** Judg 10.10–15
12.11: 1 Sam 3.20; Judg 4.6, 7.1, 11.29 **12.12:** 1 Sam 8.19

attack you, you **rejected** the LORD as
your king and said to me, 'We want a
king to rule us.'
13 "Now here is the king you **chose**;
you asked for him, and now the LORD has
given him to you. 14 All will go well with
you if you **honour** the LORD your God,
serve him, listen to him, and **obey** his
commands, and if you and your king
follow him. 15 But if you do not listen to
the LORD but **disobey** his **commands**, he
will be against you and your king.[c] 16 So
then, stand where you are, and you will
see the great thing which the LORD is
going to do. 17 It's the dry season, isn't it?
But I will **pray**, and the LORD will send
thunder and rain. When this happens,
you will realize that you committed a
great sin against the LORD when you
asked him for a king."
18 So Samuel **prayed**, and on that
same day the LORD sent thunder and
rain. Then all the people became **afraid**
of the LORD and of Samuel, 19 and they
said to Samuel, "Please, sir, **pray** to the
LORD your God for us, so that we won't
die. We now realize that, besides all our
other sins, we have sinned by asking for
a king."
20 "Don't be **afraid**," Samuel
answered. "Even though you have done
such an **evil** thing, do not **turn away** from
the LORD, but **serve** him **with all your
heart**. 21 Don't go after[d] **false gods**; they
cannot **help** you or **save** you, for they are
not **real**. 22 The LORD has made a **solemn
promise**, and he will not **abandon** you, for
he has decided to make you his **own
people**. 23 As for me, the LORD **forbid** that
I should sin against him by no longer
praying for you. Instead, I will **teach** you
what is good and **right** for you to do.
24 **Obey** the LORD and **serve** him **faithfully
with all your heart**. **Remember** the great
things he has done for you. 25 But if you
continue to sin, you and your king will be
destroyed."

War against the Philistines

13 [e]2 Saul picked three thousand
men, keeping two thousand of
them with him in Michmash and in the
hill-country of Bethel and sending one
thousand with his son Jonathan to
Gibeah, in the territory of the tribe of
Benjamin. The rest of the men Saul sent
home.
3 Jonathan killed the Philistine commander[f] in Geba, and all the Philistines
heard about it. Then Saul sent messengers to call the **Hebrews** to war by blowing a trumpet throughout the whole
country. 4 All the Israelites were told that
Saul had killed the Philistine commander
and that the Philistines **hated** them. So
the people answered the call to join Saul
at Gilgal.
5 The Philistines assembled to fight
the Israelites; they had thirty thousand
war chariots, six thousand horsemen,
and as many soldiers as there are grains
of sand on the seashore. They went to
Michmash, east of Bethaven, and
camped there. 6 Then they launched a
strong attack against the Israelites,
putting them in a **desperate** situation.
Some of the Israelites hid in caves and
holes or among the rocks or in pits and
wells; 7 others crossed the River Jordan
into the territories of Gad and Gilead.
Saul was still at Gilgal, and the people
with him were **trembling** with **fear**. 8 He
waited seven days for Samuel, as Samuel
had instructed him to do, but Samuel still
had not come to Gilgal. The people
began to desert Saul, 9 so he said to them,
"Bring me the **burnt-sacrifices** and the
fellowship-sacrifices." He **offered a
burnt-sacrifice**, 10 and just as he was
finishing, Samuel arrived. Saul went out
to meet him and **welcome** him, 11 but
Samuel said, "What have you done?"
Saul answered, "The people were
deserting me, and you had not come
when you said you would; besides that,
the Philistines are gathering at Michmash. 12 So I thought, 'The Philistines are
going to attack me here in Gilgal, and I
have not tried to **win** the LORD's **favour**.'
So I felt I had to **offer a sacrifice**."
13 "That was a **foolish** thing to do,"
Samuel answered. "You have not **obeyed**
the **command** the LORD your God gave
you. If you had **obeyed**, he would have let
you and your descendants rule over
Israel for ever. 14 But now your rule will
not continue. Because you have **disobeyed** him, the LORD will find the kind
of man he wants and make him ruler of
his people."
15 Samuel left Gilgal and went on his
way. The rest of the people followed Saul
as he went to join his soldiers. They went
from Gilgal[g] to Gibeah in the territory of

burnt-offering [2] 10.8; 2 Sam 24.25
command 12.14; 15.11
defend 2.25; 24.15
despair 11.4; 2 Sam 24.14
determine Ruth 1.18; 20.7
disobey 12.15; 15.11
favour 2.26; 20.8
fear 4.13; 14.15

fellowship-sacrifice 11.15
fool 6.6; 25.25
God's people 12.22; 15.1
hate Judg 15.2; 27.12
Hebrew [2] 4.6; 14.11
keep from 3.17; 14.6
obey [2] 12.14; 15.13
offer [2] 11.15; 15.15
sacrifice 10.3; 15.15
strong 2.4; 14.52
tremble Deut 2.25; 14.15
welcome Judg 19.3; 2 Sam 9.7
win Judg 7.2; 14.45

[c] *One ancient translation* your king; *Hebrew* your ancestors.
[d] *Some ancient translations* after; *Hebrew* because after.
[e] *One ancient translation does not have verse 1; Hebrew has as verse 1* Saul was...years old when he became king, and he was king of Israel for two years. *The Hebrew text is defective at two points in this verse.* [f] killed the Philistine commander; *or* defeated the Philistines camping.
[g] *Some ancient translations* on his way...went from Gilgal; *Hebrew does not have these words.*

13.8: 1 Sam 10.8 **13.14:** Acts 13.22

Benjamin. Saul inspected his troops, about six hundred men. 16 Saul, his son Jonathan, and their men camped in Geba in the territory of Benjamin; the Philistine camp was at Michmash. 17 The Philistine soldiers went out on raids from their camp in three groups: one group went towards Ophrah in the territory of Shual, 18 another went towards Beth Horon, and the other one went to the border overlooking the Valley of Zeboim and the wilderness.

19 There were no blacksmiths in Israel because the Philistines were **determined** to **keep the Hebrews from** making swords and spears. 20 (The Israelites had to go to the Philistines to get their ploughs, hoes, axes, and sickles[h] sharpened; 21 the charge was one small coin for sharpening axes and for repairing ox-goads,[i] and two coins for sharpening ploughs or hoes.) 22 And so on the day of battle none of the Israelite soldiers except Saul and his son Jonathan had swords or spears.

23 The Philistines sent a group of soldiers to **defend** the pass of Michmash.

Jonathan's Daring Deed

14 One day Jonathan said to the young man who carried his weapons, "Let's go across to the Philistine camp." But Jonathan did not tell his father Saul, 2 who was camping under a pomegranate-tree in Migron, not far from Gibeah; he had about six hundred men with him. 3 (The **priest** carrying the **ephod** was Ahijah, the son of Ichabod's brother Ahitub, who was the son of Phinehas and grandson of Eli, the **priest** of the LORD in Shiloh.) The men did not know that Jonathan had left.

4 In the pass of Michmash, which Jonathan had to go through to get over to the Philistine camp, there were two large jagged rocks, one on each side of the pass: one was called Bozez and the other Seneh. 5 One was on the north side of the pass, facing Michmash, and the other was on the south side, facing Geba.

6 Jonathan said to the young man, "Let's cross over to the camp of those **heathen** Philistines. Maybe the LORD will **help** us; if he does, nothing can **keep him from** giving us the **victory**, no matter how few of us there are."

7 The young man answered, "Whatever you want to do,[j] I'm with you."

8 "All right," Jonathan said. "We will go across and let the Philistines see us. 9 If they tell us to wait for them to come to us, then we will stay where we are. 10 But if they tell us to go to them, then we will, because that will be the **sign** that the LORD has given us **victory** over them."

11 So they let the Philistines see them, and the Philistines said, "Look! Some **Hebrews** are coming out of the holes they have been hiding in!" 12 Then they called out to Jonathan and the young man, "Come on up here! We have something to tell[k] you!"

Jonathan said to the young man, "Follow me. The LORD has given Israel **victory** over them." 13 Jonathan climbed up out of the pass on his hands and **knees**, and the young man followed him. Jonathan attacked the Philistines and knocked them down, and the young man killed them. 14 In that first **slaughter** Jonathan and the young man killed about twenty men in an area of about a quarter of a hectare.[l] 15 All the Philistines in the countryside were **terrified**; the raiders and the soldiers in the camp **trembled** with **fear**; the earth shook, and there was great panic.

The Defeat of the Philistines

16 Saul's men on **watch** at Gibeah in the territory of Benjamin saw the Philistines running in confusion. 17 So Saul said to his men, "Count the soldiers and find out who is missing." They did so and found that Jonathan and the young man who carried his weapons were missing. 18 "Bring the **ephod**[m] here," Saul said to Ahijah the **priest**. (On that day Ahijah was carrying it in front of the people of Israel.)[n] 19 As Saul was speaking to the **priest**, the confusion in the Philistine camp got **worse and worse**, so Saul said to him, "There's no time to **consult** the LORD!" 20 Then he and his men marched into battle against the Philistines, who were fighting **each other** in complete confusion. 21 Some **Hebrews**, who had been on the Philistine side and had gone with them to the camp, **changed** sides again[o] and joined Saul and Jonathan. 22 Others, who had been hiding in the hills of Ephraim, heard that the Philistines were running away, so they also joined in and attacked the Philistines, 23 fighting all the way beyond Bethaven. The LORD **saved** Israel that day.

[h] *One ancient translation* sickles; *Hebrew* ploughs.
[i] *Probable text* the charge...repairing ox-goads; *Hebrew unclear.*
[j] *One ancient translation* you want to do; *Hebrew* you want to do. Turn. [k] tell; *or* show.
[l] *Probable text* in an area of about a quarter of a hectare; *Hebrew unclear.*
[m] *One ancient translation* ephod *(see 2.28); Hebrew* Covenant Box.
[n] *One ancient translation* On that day...Israel; *Hebrew* Because on that day God's Covenant Box and the people of Israel. [o] *Some ancient translations* changed sides again; *Hebrew* around also.

afraid 12.18; 15.24
altar 10.5; 15.33
best [2] 8.14; 15.9
blood [3] Judg 9.2; 2 Sam 5.1
change Judg 18.29; 15.29
clear Josh 17.15; Job 26.13
consult [2] 2.28; 22.13
curse [4] Judg 21.18; 17.43
dead 4.19; 17.51
death (3) (to death) [4] 11.13; 17.35
each other Judg 9.23; 17.21
enemy [4] 12.10; 18.25
ephod (1) [2] 2.28; 21.9
fear 13.7; 15.32
guilty [2] Judg 21.22; 20.8
heathen Judg 15.18; 17.26
Hebrew [2] 13.3; 29.3
help [2] 12.8; 19.4
hunger [3] 2.5; 2 Sam 17.28
keep from 13.19; 24.6
knee Judg 7.5; 20.41
oath Judg 21.5; 1 Kgs 8.31
priest [5] 6.2; 21.1
promise [2] 12.22; 17.25
revenge Judg 11.36; 18.25
sacred 10.3; 20.8
save [3] 12.7; 17.37
sheep [2] Judg 6.4; 15.3

sign (1) Josh 22.27
2 Sam 15.30
slaughter [4] 11.11
22.21
solemn 12.22; 2 Sam 3.35
strike Judg 11.33; 20.13
strong 13.6; 28.22
terrible 6.9; 26.21
terrify 5.6; 17.11
threat [2] 3.12; 30.6
traitor 1 Kgs 1.21
tremble 13.7; 15.32
victory [7] 2.10; 17
watch 6.9; 17.28
weak [3] 2.4; 28.20
win 13.12; 17.9
worse Judg 2.19; 2

Events after the Battle

24 The Israelites were **weak** with
hunger that day, because Saul, with a
solemn oath, had given the order: "A
curse be on anyone who eats any food
today before I take **revenge** on my
enemies." So nobody had eaten anything
all day. 25 They all[p] came into a wooded
area and found honey everywhere. 26 The
woods were full of honey, but no one ate
any of it because they were all **afraid** of
Saul's **curse**. 27 But Jonathan had not
heard his father **threaten** the people with
a **curse**; so he reached out with the stick
he was carrying, dipped it in a honeycomb, and ate some honey. At once he
felt much better. 28 But one of the men
said, "We are all **weak** with **hunger**, but
your father **threatened** us and said, 'A
curse be on anyone who eats any food
today.' "

29 Jonathan answered, "What a
terrible thing my father has done to our
people! See how much better I feel because I ate some honey! 30 How much
better it would have been today if our
people had eaten the food they took
when they defeated the **enemy**. Just
think how many more Philistines they
would have killed!"

31 That day the Israelites defeated the
Philistines, fighting all the way from
Michmash to Aijalon. By this time the
Israelites were very **weak** with **hunger**,
32 and so they rushed over to what they
had captured from the **enemy**, took
sheep and cattle, **slaughtered** them on
the spot, and ate the meat with the **blood**
still in it. 33 Saul was told, "Look, the
people are sinning against the LORD by
eating meat with the **blood** in it."

"You are **traitors**!" Saul cried out.
"Roll a big stone over here[q] to me."
34 Then he gave another order: "Go
among the people and tell them all to
bring their cattle and **sheep** here. They
are to **slaughter** them and eat them
here; they must not sin against the LORD
by eating meat with **blood** in it." So that
night they all brought their cattle and
slaughtered them there. 35 Saul built an
altar to the LORD, the first one that he
built.

36 Saul said to his men, "Let's go down
and attack the Philistines in the night,
plunder them until dawn, and kill them
all."

"Do whatever you think **best**," they
answered.

But the **priest** said, "Let's **consult** God
first."

37 So Saul asked God, "Shall I attack
the Philistines? Will you give us **victory**?" But God did not answer that day.
38 Then Saul said to the leaders of the
people, "Come here and find out what sin
was committed today. 39 I **promise** by the
living LORD, who gives Israel **victory**,
that the **guilty** one will be put **to death**,
even if he is my son Jonathan." But no
one said anything. 40 Then Saul said to
them, "All of you stand over there, and
Jonathan and I will stand over here."

"Do whatever you think **best**," they
answered.

41 Saul said to the LORD, the God of
Israel, "LORD, why have you not
answered me today? LORD, God of
Israel, answer me by the **sacred** stones.
If the **guilt** is Jonathan's or mine, answer
by the Urim; but if it belongs to your
people Israel,[r] answer by the Thummim."[s] The answer indicated Jonathan
and Saul; and the people were **cleared**.
42 Then Saul said, "Decide between my
son Jonathan and me." And Jonathan
was indicated. 43 Then Saul asked Jonathan, "What have you done?"

Jonathan answered, "I ate a little
honey with the stick I was holding. Here I
am—I am ready to die."

44 Saul said to him, "May God **strike**
me **dead** if you are not put **to death**!"

45 But the people said to Saul, "Will
Jonathan, who **won** this great **victory** for
Israel, be put **to death**? No! We **promise**
by the living LORD that he will not lose
even a hair from his head. What he did
today was done with God's **help**." So the
people **saved** Jonathan from being put **to
death**.

46 After that, Saul stopped pursuing
the Philistines, and they went back to
their own territory.

Saul's Reign and Family

47 After Saul became king of Israel, he
fought against all his **enemies** everywhere: the people of Moab, of Ammon,
and of Edom, the kings of Zobah, and the
Philistines. Wherever he fought he was
victorious.[t] 48 He fought heroically and
defeated even the people of Amalek. He
saved the Israelites from all attacks.

49 Saul's sons were Jonathan, Ishvi,

[p] *Probable text* They all; *Hebrew* All the land. [q] *One ancient translation* here; *Hebrew* today.
[r] *Some ancient translations* answer me by the sacred stones....your people Israel; *Hebrew does not have these words.*
[s] URIM...THUMMIM: *Two stones used by the priest to determine God's will; it is not known precisely how they were used.* [t] *One ancient translation* was victorious; *Hebrew* acted wickedly.

14.33: Gen 9.4; Lev 7.26–27, 17.10–14, 19.26; Deut 12.16, 23, 15.23 **14.41:** Num 27.21; 1 Sam 28.6

and Malchishua. His elder daughter was named Merab, and the younger one Michal. 50 His wife was Ahinoam, the daughter of Ahimaaz; his army commander was his cousin Abner, the son of his uncle Ner. 51 Saul's father Kish and Abner's father Ner were sons of Abiel.

52 As long as he lived, Saul had to fight fiercely against the Philistines. So whenever he found a man who was **strong** or brave, he would enlist him in his army.

War against the Amalekites

15 Samuel said to Saul, "I am the one whom the LORD sent to **anoint** you king of **his people** Israel. Now listen to what the LORD **Almighty** says. 2 He is going to **punish** the people of Amalek because their ancestors opposed the Israelites when they were coming from Egypt. 3 Go and attack the Amalekites and completely **destroy** everything they have. Don't leave a thing; kill all the men, women, children, and babies; the cattle, **sheep**, camels, and donkeys."

4 Saul called his forces together and inspected them at Telem: there were 200,000 soldiers from Israel and 10,000 from Judah. 5 Then he and his men went to the city of Amalek and waited in ambush in a dry river-bed. 6 He sent a **warning** to the Kenites, a people whose ancestors had been **kind** to the Israelites when they came from Egypt: "Go away and leave the Amalekites, so that I won't kill you along with them." So the Kenites left.

7 Saul defeated the Amalekites, fighting all the way from Havilah to Shur, east of Egypt; 8 he captured King Agag of Amalek **alive** and killed all the people. 9 But Saul and his men **spared** Agag's **life** and did not kill the **best sheep** and cattle, the **best** calves and **lambs**,[u] or anything else that was good; they **destroyed** only what was **useless** or **worthless**.[v]

Saul Is Rejected as King

10 The LORD said to Samuel, 11 "I am **sorry** that I made Saul king; he has **turned away** from me and **disobeyed** my **commands**." Samuel was **angry**, and all night long he **pleaded** with the LORD. 12 Early the following morning he went off to find Saul. He heard that Saul had gone to the town of Carmel, where he had built a monument to himself, and then had gone on to Gilgal. 13 Samuel went up to Saul, who greeted him, saying, "The LORD **bless** you, Samuel! I have **obeyed** the LORD's **command**."

14 Samuel asked, "Why, then, do I hear cattle mooing and **sheep** bleating?"

15 Saul answered, "My men took them from the Amalekites. They kept the **best sheep** and cattle to **offer as a sacrifice** to the LORD your God, and the rest we have **destroyed** completely."[w]

16 "Stop," Samuel ordered, "and I will tell you what the LORD said to me last night."

"Tell me," Saul said.

17 Samuel answered, "Even though you consider yourself of no **importance**, you are the leader of the tribes of Israel. The LORD **anointed** you king of Israel, 18 and he sent you out with orders to **destroy** those **wicked** people of Amalek. He told you to fight until you had killed them all. 19 Why, then, did you not **obey** him? Why did you rush to seize the loot, and so do what **displeases** the LORD?"

20 "I did **obey** the LORD," Saul replied. "I went out as he told me to, brought back King Agag, and killed all the Amalekites. 21 But my men did not kill the **best sheep** and cattle that they captured; instead, they brought them here to Gilgal to **offer as a sacrifice** to the LORD your God."

22 Samuel said, "Which does the LORD prefer: **obedience** or **offerings** and **sacrifices**? It is better to **obey** him than to **sacrifice** the **best sheep** to him. 23 **Rebellion** against him is as **bad** as witchcraft, and **arrogance** is as sinful as **idolatry**. Because you **rejected** the LORD's **command**, he has rejected you as king."

24 "Yes, I have sinned," Saul replied. "I **disobeyed** the LORD's **command** and your instructions. I was **afraid** of my men and did what they wanted. 25 But now I **beg** you, **forgive** my sin and go back with me, so that I can **worship** the LORD."

26 "I will not go back with you," Samuel answered. "You **rejected** the LORD's **command**, and he has **rejected** you as king of Israel."

27 Then Samuel **turned** to leave, but Saul caught hold of his cloak, and it tore. 28 Samuel said to him, "The LORD has torn the kingdom of Israel away from you today and given it to someone who is a better man than you. 29 Israel's **majestic** God does not **lie** or **change his mind**. He is not a man—he does not **change his mind**."

afraid 14.26; 17.32
alive 2.33; 20.14
Almighty 4.4; 17.45
altar 14.35; 2 Sam 24.18
anger Judg 19.2; 17.28
anoint [2] 10.1; 16.3
arrogant Ex 9.17; 2 Chr 26.16
bad Num 13.19; 31.3
beg 2.36; 20.6
best [5] 14.36; 24.2
bitter 8.18; 30.6
bless 9.12; 23.21
change [2] 14.21; 26.19
command [5] 13.13; 18.13
destroy [4] 12.25; 20.15
disobey [2] 13.14; 28.18
displease 8.6; 29.7
fear 14.15; 2 Sam 17.10
forgive Josh 24.19; 25.28
God's people 13.14; 17.47
grief 4.12; 16.1
idol 12.10; 19.13
important 9.21; 20.2
kind 1.18; 23.21
lamb 7.9; 17.34
lie (2) Josh 7.11; 2 Sam 19.27
life (1) 9.2; 17.33
Majesty Judg 3.19; 17.32
mind (1) [2] Deut 28.28; 26.19
never again Deut 13.16; 2 Sam 21.17
obey [5] 13.13; 2 Sam 22.22
offer [3] 13.9; 16.2
plead Ex 32.11; 1 Kgs 20.32
punish 6.3; 20.16
rebel Judg 9.23; 20.30
reject [3] 12.12; 16.1
respect 9.6; 22.14
sacrifice [4] 13.12; 16.2
sheep [6] 14.32; 16.11
sorry [2] Ruth 1.13; 24.10
spare Josh 10.30; 24.21
tremble 14.15; 16.4
turn [2] 12.10; 17.30
useless 2 Sam 1.27
warn 11.7; 19.11
wicked 2.9; 2 Sam 22.27

worship (1) (of Go
[3] 12.10; 2 Sam 8.1
worthless 10.27; 30.22

[u] *One ancient translation* the best calves and lambs; *Hebrew unclear.*
[v] *Some ancient translations* useless or worthless; *Hebrew unclear.*
[w] DESTROYED COMPLETELY: *These animals had been unconditionally dedicated to the LORD and had to be destroyed (see Lev 27.28).*

15.1: 1 Sam 10.1 **15.2:** Ex 17.8–14; Deut 25.17–19 **15.27–28:** 1 Sam 28.17; 1 Kgs 11.30–31

30 "I have sinned," Saul replied. "But at least show me **respect** in front of the leaders of my people and all Israel. Go back with me so that I can **worship** the LORD your God." 31 So Samuel went back with him, and Saul **worshipped** the LORD.

32 "Bring King Agag here to me," Samuel ordered. Agag came to him, **trembling** with **fear**, thinking to himself, "What a **bitter** thing it is to die!"[x] 33 Samuel said, "As your sword has made many mothers childless, so now will your mother become childless." And he cut Agag to pieces in front of the **altar** in Gilgal.

34 Then Samuel went to Ramah, and King Saul went home to Gibeah. 35 As long as Samuel lived, he **never again** saw the king; but he **grieved** over him. The LORD was **sorry** that he had made Saul king of Israel.

David Is Anointed King

16 The LORD said to Samuel, "How long will you go on **grieving** over Saul? I have **rejected** him as king of Israel. But now get some olive-oil and go to Bethlehem, to a man named Jesse, because I have **chosen** one of his sons to be king."

2 "How can I do that?" Samuel asked. "If Saul hears about it, he will kill me!"

The LORD answered, "Take a calf with you and say that you are there to **offer a sacrifice** to the LORD. 3 Invite Jesse to the **sacrifice**, and I will tell you what to do. You will **anoint** as king the man I tell you to."

4 Samuel did what the LORD told him to do and went to Bethlehem, where the city leaders came **trembling** to meet him and asked, "Is this a **peaceful** visit, seer?"

5 "Yes," he answered. "I have come to **offer a sacrifice** to the LORD. **Purify** yourselves and come with me." He also told Jesse and his sons to **purify** themselves, and he invited them to the **sacrifice**.

6 When they arrived, Samuel saw Jesse's son Eliab and said to himself, "This man standing here in the LORD's **presence** is **surely** the one he has **chosen**." 7 But the LORD said to him, "Pay no attention to how tall and handsome he is. I have **rejected** him, because I do not **judge** as man judges. Man looks at the outward **appearance**, but I look at the **heart**."

8 Then Jesse called his son Abinadab and brought him to Samuel. But Samuel said, "No, the LORD hasn't **chosen** him either." 9 Jesse then brought Shammah. "No, the LORD hasn't **chosen** him either," Samuel said. 10 In this way Jesse brought seven of his sons to Samuel. And Samuel said to him, "No, the LORD hasn't **chosen** any of these." 11 Then he asked him, "Have you any more sons?"

Jesse answered, "There is still the youngest, but he is out taking **care** of the **sheep**."

"Tell him to come here," Samuel said. "We won't **offer the sacrifice** until he comes." 12 So Jesse sent for him. He was a handsome, healthy young man, and his eyes sparkled. The LORD said to Samuel, "This is the one—**anoint** him!" 13 Samuel took the olive-oil and **anointed** David in front of his brothers. Immediately the **spirit of the LORD** took **control** of David and was with him from that day on. Then Samuel returned to Ramah.

David in Saul's Court

14 The **LORD's spirit** left Saul, and an **evil spirit** sent by the LORD **tormented** him. 15 His **servants** said to him, "We know that an **evil spirit** sent by God is **tormenting** you. 16 So give us the order, sir, and we will look for a man who knows how to play the harp. Then when the **evil spirit** comes on you, the man can play his harp, and you will be all right again."

17 Saul ordered them, "Find me a man who plays well and bring him to me."

18 One of his attendants said, "Jesse, of the town of Bethlehem, has a son who is a good musician. He is also a brave and handsome man, a good soldier, and an able speaker. The LORD is with him."

19 So Saul sent messengers to Jesse to say, "Send me your son David, the one who takes **care** of the **sheep**." 20 Jesse sent David to Saul with a young goat, a donkey loaded with **bread**, and a leather bag full of wine. 21 David came to Saul and entered his **service**. Saul liked him very much and **chose** him as the man to carry his weapons. 22 Then Saul sent a **message** to Jesse: "I like David. Let him stay here in my **service**." 23 From then on, whenever the **evil spirit** sent by God came on Saul, David would get his harp and play it. The **evil spirit** would leave, and Saul would feel better and be all right again.

Goliath Challenges the Israelites

17 The Philistines gathered for battle in Socoh, a town in Judah; they camped at a place called Ephes

[x] trembling with fear...die; *or* confidently, thinking to himself, "Surely the bitter danger of death is past!"

anoint [3] 15.1; 2 Sam 2.4
appearance Prov 1.9
bread 10.3; 17.17
care [2] Ruth 4.14; 17.15
choose [6] 12.3; 17.8
control 11.6; 18.10
evil [5] 12.20; 18.10
grief 15.35; 20.41
heart 12.20; 1 Kgs 2.4
judge 8.1; 24.12
message 11.9; 25.9
offer [3] 15.15; 21.6
peace 7.14; 29.7
presence 12.3; 19.24
pure [2] Josh 7.13; 20.26
reject [2] 15.23; 1 Kgs 11.33
sacrifice [5] 15.15; 20.6
servant 10.10; 17.58
service [2] 2.21; 22.12
sheep [2] 15.3; 17.15
Spirit (1) (God's Spirit) [2] 11.6; 19.20
spirit (2) [5] Deut 18.11; 18.10
sure Ruth 3.4; 20.23
torment [2] 1.6; Job 15.20
tremble 15.32; 21.1

afraid 15.24; 18.12
Almighty 15.1; 2 Sam 5.10
anger 15.11; 18.8

Dammim, between Socoh and Azekah.
2 Saul and the Israelites assembled and
camped in the Valley of Elah, where
they got ready to fight the Philistines.
3 The Philistines lined up on one hill and
the Israelites on another, with a valley
between them.

4 A man named Goliath, from the city
of Gath, came out from the Philistine
camp to **challenge** the Israelites. He was
nearly three metres[y] tall 5 and wore
bronze armour that weighed about fifty-
seven kilogrammes and a bronze helmet.
6 His legs were also **protected** by bronze
armour, and he carried a bronze javelin
slung over his shoulder. 7 His spear was
as thick as the bar on a weaver's loom,
and its iron head weighed about seven
kilogrammes. A soldier walked in front
of him carrying his shield. 8 Goliath stood
and shouted at the Israelites, "What are
you doing there, lined up for battle? I am
a Philistine, you **slaves** of Saul! **Choose**
one of your men to fight me. 9 If he **wins**
and kills me, we will be your **slaves**; but
if I **win** and kill him, you will be our
slaves. 10 Here and now I **challenge** the
Israelite army. I **dare** you to pick someone to fight me!" 11 When Saul and his
men heard this, they were **terrified**.

David in Saul's Camp

12 David was the son of Jesse, who
was an Ephrathite from Bethlehem in
Judah. Jesse had eight sons, and at the
time Saul was king, he was already a
very old man.[z] 13 His three eldest sons
had gone with Saul to war. The eldest
was Eliab, the next was Abinadab, and
the third was Shammah. 14 David was the
youngest son, and while the three eldest
brothers stayed with Saul, 15 David would
go back to Bethlehem from time to time,
to take **care** of his father's **sheep**.

16 Goliath **challenged** the Israelites
every morning and evening for forty
days.

17 One day Jesse said to David, "Take
ten kilogrammes of this roasted grain
and these ten loaves of **bread**, and hurry
with them to your brothers in the camp.
18 And take these ten cheeses to the
commanding officer. Find out how your
brothers are getting on and bring back
something to show that you saw them
and that they are well. 19 King Saul, your
brothers, and all the other Israelites are
in the Valley of Elah fighting the Philistines."

20 David got up early the next
morning, left someone else in charge of
the **sheep**, took the food, and went as
Jesse had told him to. He arrived at the
camp just as the Israelites were going
out to their battle line, shouting the war-
cry. 21 The Philistine and the Israelite
armies took up positions for battle,
facing **each other**. 22 David left the food
with the officer in charge of the supplies,
ran to the battle line, went to his
brothers, and asked how they were
getting on. 23 As he was talking to them,
Goliath came forward and **challenged**
the Israelites as he had done before. And
David heard him. 24 When the Israelites
saw Goliath, they ran away in **terror**.
25 "Look at him!" they said to **each other**.
"Listen to his **challenge**! King Saul has
promised to give a big **reward** to the man
who kills him; the king will also give him
his daughter to marry and will not
require his father's family to pay **taxes**."[a]

26 David asked the men who were
near him, "What will the man get who
kills this Philistine and **frees** Israel from
this **disgrace**? After all, who is this
heathen Philistine to **defy** the army of
the living God?" 27 They told him what
would be done for the man who killed
Goliath.

28 Eliab, David's eldest brother, heard
David talking to the men. He was **angry**
with David and said, "What are you
doing here? Who is taking **care** of those
sheep of yours out there in the wilderness? You cheeky brat, you! You just
came to **watch** the fighting!"

29 "Now what have I done?" David
asked. "Can't I even ask a **question**?"
30 He **turned** to another man and asked
him the same **question**, and every time
he asked, he got the same answer.

31 Some men heard what David had
said, and they told Saul, who sent for him.
32 David said to Saul, "Your **Majesty**, no
one should be **afraid** of this Philistine! I
will go and fight him."

33 "No," answered Saul. "How could
you fight him? You're just a boy, and he
has been a soldier all his **life**!"

34 "Your **Majesty**," David said, "I take
care of my father's **sheep**. Whenever a
lion or a bear carries off a **lamb**, 35 I go
after it, attack it, and **rescue** the **lamb**.
And if the lion or bear **turns** on me, I
grab it by the throat and beat it **to death**.
36 I have killed lions and bears, and I will
do the same to this **heathen** Philistine,
who has **defied** the army of the living
God. 37 The LORD has **saved** me from

[y] *Hebrew* nearly three metres; *one ancient Hebrew manuscript and one ancient translation* about two metres. [z] *Some ancient translations* a very old man; *Hebrew unclear.*
[a] to pay taxes; *or* either to pay taxes or serve him.

body [2] 5.4; 31.8
bread 16.20; 21.3
care [3] 16.11; 2 Sam 12.3
challenge [6] Judg 11.25; 2 Sam 23.9
choose 16.1; 24.6
curse 14.24; 26.19
dare Josh 10.21; 2 Sam 1.14
dead 14.44; 18.25
death (3) (to death) 14.39; 22.19
defy [3] Num 26.9; 2 Sam 21.21
disgrace 11.2; 20.30
each other [2] 14.20; 20.16
forehead Deut 11.18; 2 Chr 26.19
free Judg 16.20; 26.24
god (2) (other gods) 12.21; 26.19
God's people 15.1; 2 Sam 3.18
heathen [2] 14.6; Ps 9.5
idea 9.9; Esth 1.21
lamb [2] 15.9; 2 Sam 12.3
life (1) 15.9; 19.5
Majesty [3] 15.29; 22.15
name (2) (name of God, of Jesus) Josh 9.18; 19.6
need 2.8; 27.5
power [2] 10.26; 23.7
promise 14.39; 20.8
protect 10.1; 23.16
question [2] 9.9; 20.12
require 2.29; 1 Kgs 15.22
rescue 12.10; 30.8
reward Ruth 2.12; 26.23
save [3] 14.23; 23.2
scorn Judg 9.27; Job 16.20
servant 16.15; 19.4
sheep [4] 16.11; 22.19
shepherd Judg 5.16; 25.7
slave [3] 8.17; 25.10
tax Num 31.28; 2 Sam 8.2
terrify 14.15; 28.5
terror Judg 6.22; Esth 7.6
turn [2] 15.11; 22.13
victory 14.6; 19.5
watch 14.16; 19.11
win [2] 14.45; 19.5
world 2.8; 2 Sam 7.9

lions and bears; he will **save** me from
this Philistine."
"All right," Saul answered. "Go, and
the LORD be with you." 38 He gave his
own armour to David for him to wear: a
bronze helmet, which he put on David's
head, and a coat of armour. 39 David
strapped Saul's sword over the armour
and tried to walk, but he couldn't,
because he wasn't used to wearing them.
"I can't fight with all this," he said to
Saul. "I'm not used to it." So he took it all
off. 40 He took his **shepherd's** stick and
then picked up five smooth stones from
the stream and put them in his bag. With
his sling ready, he went out to meet
Goliath.

David Defeats Goliath

41 The Philistine started walking
towards David, with his shield-bearer
walking in front of him. He kept coming
closer, 42 and when he got a good look at
David, he was filled with **scorn** for him
because he was just a nice, good-looking
boy. 43 He said to David, "What's that
stick for? Do you think I'm a dog?" And
he called down **curses** from his **god** on
David. 44 "Come on," he **challenged**
David, "and I will give your **body** to the
birds and animals to eat."
45 David answered, "You are coming
against me with sword, spear, and
javelin, but I come against you in the
name of the LORD Almighty, the God of
the Israelite armies, which you have
defied. 46 This very day the LORD will put
you in my **power**; I will defeat you and
cut off your head. And I will give the
bodies of the Philistine soldiers to the
birds and animals to eat. Then the whole
world will know that Israel has a God,
47 and everyone here will see that the
LORD does not **need** swords or spears to
save his people. He is **victorious** in battle,
and he will put all of you in our **power**."
48 Goliath started walking towards
David again, and David ran quickly towards the Philistine battle line to fight
him. 49 He put his hand into his bag and
took out a stone, which he slung at
Goliath. It hit him on the **forehead** and
broke his skull, and Goliath fell face
downwards on the ground. 50 And so,
without a sword, David defeated and
killed Goliath with a sling and a stone!
51 He ran to him, stood over him, took
Goliath's sword out of its sheath, and cut
off his head and killed him.
When the Philistines saw that their
hero was **dead**, they ran away. 52 The
men of Israel and Judah shouted and ran
after them, pursuing them all the way to
Gath[b] and to the gates of Ekron. The
Philistines fell wounded all along the
road that leads to Shaaraim, as far as
Gath and Ekron. 53 When the Israelites
came back from pursuing the Philistines,
they looted their camp. 54 David picked
up Goliath's head and took it to Jerusalem, but he kept Goliath's weapons in his
own tent.

David Is Presented to Saul

55 When Saul saw David going out to
fight Goliath, he asked Abner, the commander of his army, "Abner, whose son
is he?"
"I have no **idea**, Your **Majesty**," Abner
answered.
56 "Then go and find out," Saul
ordered.
57 So when David returned to camp
after killing Goliath, Abner took him to
Saul. David was still carrying Goliath's
head. 58 Saul asked him, "Young man,
whose son are you?"
"I am the son of your **servant** Jesse
from Bethlehem," David answered.

18 Saul and David finished their
conversation. After that, Saul's
son Jonathan was deeply attracted to
David and came to love him as much as
he **loved** himself. 2 Saul kept David with
him from that day on and did not let him
go back home. 3 Jonathan **swore eternal
friendship** with David because of his
deep **affection** for him. 4 He took off the
robe he was wearing and gave it to
David, together with his armour and also
his sword, bow, and belt. 5 David was
successful in all the missions on which
Saul sent him, and so Saul made him an
officer in his army. This **pleased** all of
Saul's officers and men.

Saul Becomes Jealous of David

6 As David was returning after killing
Goliath and as the soldiers were coming
back home, women from every town in
Israel came out to meet King Saul. They
were singing **joyful** songs, dancing, and
playing tambourines and lyres. 7 In their
celebration the women sang, "Saul has
killed thousands, but David tens of thousands." 8 Saul did not like this, and he
became very **angry**. He said, "For David
they **claim** tens of thousands, but only
thousands for me. They will be making
him king next!" 9 And so he was **jealous**
and suspicious of David from that day on.
10 The next day an **evil spirit** from

abandon 12.22; 28.15
affection Gen 34.3; Esth 2.17
afraid [3] 17.32; 21.12
anger 17.28; 20.7
bride Deut 22.29; 2 Sam 17.3
celebrate 11.15; 20.29
claim Judg 18.1; 2 Sam 15.4
command 15.11; 28.18
control 16.13; 19.9
dead 17.51; 19.11
delight Deut 28.63; 2 Chr 15.15
enemy [2] 14.24; 19.17
eternal Deut 33.27; 2 Sam 23.5
evil 16.14; 19.9
friend Ruth 4.1; 20.29
honour 12.14; 2 Sam 6.5
jealous Deut 32.16; Ps 37.1
joy 11.9; 2 Sam 6.15
love [4] 1.5; 20.17
loyal Ruth 3.10; 20.14
mad 21.13
notice (1) Ruth 3.4; 20.6
plan Judg 20.32; 19.1
please [3] Judg 21.25; 29.6
poor 2.7; 2 Sam 5.8
revenge 14.24; 25.26
serve 12.14; 19.7
spirit (2) 16.14; 19.9
succeed (1) [5] Judg 18.5; 26.25
swear Ruth 3.13; 20.3
trap Judg 20.43; 23.7
wedding Judg 14.12; 1 Kgs 9.16

[b] *One ancient translation* Gath; *Hebrew* a valley.
17.50: 2 Sam 21.19 **17.51:** 1 Sam 21.29 **18.7:** 1 Sam 21.11, 29.5

God suddenly took **control** of Saul, and he raved in his house like a **madman**. David was playing the harp, as he did every day, and Saul was holding a spear. 11 "I'll pin him to the wall," Saul said to himself, and he threw the spear at him twice; but David dodged each time.

12 Saul was **afraid** of David because the LORD was with David but had **abandoned** him. 13 So Saul sent him away and put him in **command** of a thousand men. David led his men in battle 14 and was **successful** in all he did, because the LORD was with him. 15 Saul **noticed** David's **success** and became even more **afraid** of him. 16 But everyone in Israel and Judah **loved** David because he was such a **successful** leader.

David Marries Saul's Daughter

17 Then Saul said to David, "Here is my elder daughter Merab. I will give her to you as your wife on condition that you **serve** me as a brave and **loyal** soldier, and fight the LORD's battles." (Saul was thinking that in this way the Philistines would kill David, and he would not have to do it himself.)

18 David answered, "Who am I and what is my family that I should become the king's son-in-law?" 19 But when the time came for Merab to be given to David, she was given instead to a man named Adriel from Meholah.

20 Saul's daughter Michal, however, fell in **love** with David, and when Saul heard of this, he was **pleased**. 21 He said to himself, "I'll give Michal to David; I will use her to **trap** him, and he will be killed by the Philistines." So for the second time Saul said to David, "You will be my son-in-law." 22 He ordered his officials to speak privately to David and tell him, "The king is **pleased** with you and all his officials like you; now is a good time for you to marry his daughter."

23 So they told David this, and he answered, "It's a great **honour** to become the king's son-in-law, too great for someone **poor** and insignificant like me."

24 The officials told Saul what David had said, 25 and Saul ordered them to tell David: "All the king wants from you as payment for the **bride** is the foreskins of a hundred **dead** Philistines, as **revenge** on his **enemies**." (This was how Saul **planned** to have David killed by the Philistines.) 26 Saul's officials reported to David what Saul had said, and David was **delighted** with the thought of becoming the king's son-in-law. Before the day set for the **wedding**, 27 David and his men went and killed two hundred Philistines. He took their foreskins to the king and counted them all out to him, so that he might become his son-in-law. So Saul had to give his daughter Michal in marriage to David.

28 Saul realized clearly that the LORD was with David and also that his daughter Michal **loved** him. 29 So he became even more **afraid** of David and was his **enemy** as long as he lived.

30 The Philistine armies would come and fight, but in every battle David was more **successful** than any of Saul's other officers. As a result David became very famous.

David Is Persecuted by Saul

19 Saul told his son Jonathan and all his officials that he **planned** to kill[c] David. But Jonathan was very fond of David, 2 and so he said to him, "My father is trying to kill you. Please be careful tomorrow morning; hide in some **secret** place and stay there. 3 I will go and stand by my father in the field where you are hiding, and I will speak to him about you. If I find out anything, I will let you know."

4 Jonathan **praised** David to Saul and said, "Sir, don't do **wrong** to your **servant** David. He has never done you any **wrong**; on the contrary, everything he has done has been a great **help** to you. 5 He risked his **life** when he killed Goliath, and the LORD **won** a great **victory** for Israel. When you saw it, you were **glad**. Why, then, do you now want to do **wrong** to an **innocent** man and kill David for no **reason** at all?"

6 Saul was **convinced** by what Jonathan said and made a **vow** in the **LORD's name** that he would not kill David. 7 So Jonathan called David and told him everything; then he took him to Saul, and David **served** the king as he had before.

8 War with the Philistines broke out again. David attacked them and defeated them so thoroughly that they **fled**.

9 One day an **evil spirit** from the LORD took **control** of Saul. He was sitting in his house with his spear in his hand, and David was there, playing his harp. 10 Saul tried to pin David to the wall with his spear, but David dodged, and the spear stuck in the wall. David ran away and **escaped**.

11 That same night Saul sent some

[c] that he planned to kill; *or* to kill.

19.11: Ps 59 (Title)

arrest Gen 39.20; 1 Kgs 22.26
control [3] 18.10; 2 Sam 2.1
convince Deut 29.19 24.7
dead 18.25; 20.13
enemy 18.25; 20.15
escape [5] 4.16; 22.20
evil 18.10; 24.13
flee 7.10; 20.1
get away Judg 3.26; 23.26
glad Judg 8.25; 2 Sam 1.20
help [2] 14.6; 25.21
idol [2] 15.23; 31.9
innocent 12.5; 2 Sam 3.28
life (1) 17.33; 26.21
naked Deut 28.48; Is 3.26
name (2) (name of God, of Jesus) 17.45; 24.21
plan 18.25; 20.3
praise Ruth 4.14; 25.32
presence 16.6; 2 Sam 24.4
prophet [2] 10.5; 22.5
reason Deut 29.24; 27.6
saying 10.12; 24.13
secret Judg 16.9; 2 Sam 12.12
servant 17.58; 20.21
serve 18.17; 27.12
Spirit (1) (God's Spirit) [2] 16.13; 2 Sam 23.2
spirit (2) 18.10; 28.8
trick Judg 16.5; 28.12
victory 17.47; 23.4
vow Josh 23.7; 28.10
warn 15.6; 1 Kgs 2.42
watch 17.28; 2 Sam 18.24
win 17.9; 29.4
wrong [3] 12.3; 20.1

men to **watch** David's house and kill him
the next morning. Michal, David's wife,
warned him, "If you don't **get away**
tonight, tomorrow you will be **dead**."
12 She let him down from a window, and
he ran away and **escaped**. 13 Then she
took the household **idol**, laid it on the bed,
put a pillow made of goats'-hair at its
head, and put a cover over it. 14 When
Saul's men came to get David, Michal
told them that he was ill. 15 But Saul sent
them back to see David for themselves.
He ordered them, "Carry him here in his
bed, and I will kill him." 16 They went
inside and found the household **idol** in the
bed and the goats'-hair pillow at its head.
17 Saul asked Michal, "Why have you
tricked me like this and let my **enemy**
escape?"

She answered, "He said he would kill
me if I didn't **help** him to **escape**."

18 David **escaped** and went to Samuel
in Ramah and told him everything that
Saul had done to him. Then he and
Samuel went to Naioth and stayed there.
19 Saul was told that David was in Naioth
in Ramah, 20 so he sent some men to
arrest him. They saw[d] the **group of**
prophets dancing and shouting, with
Samuel as their leader. Then the **spirit of**
God took **control** of Saul's men, and they
also began to dance and shout. 21 When
Saul heard of this, he sent more messengers, and they also began to dance and
shout. He sent messengers the third time,
and the same thing happened to them.
22 Then he himself started out for Ramah.
When he came to the large well in Secu,
he asked where Samuel and David were
and was told that they were at Naioth.
23 As he was going there, the **spirit of God**
took **control** of him also, and he danced
and shouted all the way to Naioth. 24 He
took off his clothes and danced and
shouted in Samuel's **presence**, and lay
naked all that day and all that night.
(This is how the **saying** originated, "Has
even Saul become a **prophet**?")

Jonathan Helps David

20 Then David **fled** from Naioth in
Ramah and went to Jonathan.
"What have I done?" he asked. "What
crime have I committed? What **wrong**
have I done to your father to make him
want to kill me?"

2 Jonathan answered, "God **forbid** that
you should die! My father tells me everything he does, **important** or not, and he
would not hide this from me. It isn't
true!"

3 But David answered,[e] "Your father
knows very well how much you like me,
and he has decided not to let you know
what he **plans** to do, because you would
be deeply **hurt**. I **swear** to you by the
living LORD that I am only a step away
from **death**!"

4 Jonathan said, "I'll do anything you
want."

5 "Tomorrow is the **New Moon**
Festival," David replied, "and I am supposed to eat with the king. But if it's all
right with you, I will go and hide in the
fields until the evening of the day after
tomorrow. 6 If your father **notices** that I
am not at table, tell him that I **begged**
your **permission** to hurry home to Bethlehem, since it's the time for the annual
sacrifice there for my whole family. 7 If
he says, 'All right,' I will be **safe**; but if he
becomes **angry**, you will know that he is
determined to **harm** me. 8 Please do me
this **favour**, and keep the **sacred promise**
you made to me. But if I'm **guilty**, kill me
yourself! Why take me to your father to
be killed?"

9 "Don't even think such a thing!"
Jonathan answered. "If I knew for
certain that my father was **determined** to
harm you, wouldn't I tell you?"

10 David then asked, "Who will let me
know if your father answers you
angrily?"

11 "Let's go out to the fields,"
Jonathan answered. So they went, 12 and
Jonathan said to David, "May the LORD
God of Israel be our **witness**![f] At this
time tomorrow and on the following day
I will **question** my father. If his attitude
towards you is good, I will send you **word**.
13 If he **intends** to **harm** you, may the
LORD **strike** me **dead** if I don't let you
know about it and get you **safely** away.
May the LORD be with you as he was with
my father! 14 And if I remain **alive**,
please keep your **sacred promise** and be
loyal to me; but if I die,[g] 15 show the same
kind of **loyalty** to my family for ever. And
when the LORD has completely **destroyed**
all your **enemies**, 16 may our **promise** to
each other still be unbroken. If it is
broken, the LORD will **punish** you."[h]

17 Once again Jonathan made David
promise to **love** him, for Jonathan **loved**
David as much as he loved himself.

[d] *Some ancient translations* They saw; *Hebrew* He saw.
[e] *One ancient translation* answered; *Hebrew* made a vow again.
[f] *One ancient translation* be our witness; *Hebrew does not have these words.*
[g] *Some ancient translations* if I die; *Hebrew* that I may not die.
[h] *Verses 15–16 in Hebrew are unclear.*

19.24: 1 Sam 10.11–12 **20.5:** Num 28.11 **20.15:** 2 Sam 9.1

agree Judg 17.11; 29.9
alive [2] 15.8; 2 Sam 12.21
anger [2] 18.8; 29.4
beg [2] 15.25; 23.11
bow (2) Ruth 2.10; 24.8
celebrate 18.7; 30.16
certain (1) Deut 8.11; 23.22

crime Judg 20.3; 25.33
danger Josh 23.13; 2 Sam 4.9
dead 19.11; 24.14
death (1) 4.21; 22.22
destroy 15.3; 23.10
determine [3] 13.19; 1 Kgs 2.2
disgrace 17.26; 2 Sam 1.21
distress 1.9; 2 Kgs 4.27
each other [4] 17.21; 23.18
enemy 19.17; 24.4
faithless Ezra 10.10
favour 13.12; 29.4
feast Judg 14.12; 25.8
festival [5] Judg 21.19; 1 Kgs 8.2
flee 19.8; 21.10
forbid 12.23; 26.11
friend 18.3; 23.18
fury 11.6; 2 Sam 2.17
grief 16.1; 2 Sam 1.2
guilty 14.39; 2 Sam 14.32
harm [3] Josh 9.19; 23.17
hurt Judg 1.24; 1 Kgs 20.37
important 15.17; 2 Kgs 24.16
insult Gen 39.14; 25.14
intend Judg 20.5; 1 Kgs 12.21
kiss 10.1; 2 Sam 14.33
knee 14.13; 1 Kgs 18.42
love [2] 18.1; 2 Sam 1.26
loyal [2] 18.17; 29.6
master Judg 19.10; 24.6
New Moon Festival [5] Num 10.10; 2 Kgs 4.23
notice (1) [3] 18.15; 2 Sam 12.19
permit Judg 12.5; 1 Kgs 20.31
plan 19.1; 23.9
promise [6] 17.25; 23.18
punish 15.2; 24.12
pure 16.5; 21.5
question 17.29; 2 Sam 14.18
rage Deut 9.3; 1 Kgs 22.35
rebel 15.23; 24.11
sacred [3] 14.41; 21.4
sacrifice [2] 16.2; 2 Sam 6.13
safe [3] 12.11; 22.23
servant 19.4; 23.10
strike 14.44; 25.22
sure [2] 16.6; 22.22
swear [2] 18.3; 25.26
true 9.6; 2 Sam 3.9
witness 12.5; 1 Chr 24.6
word (1) 2.3; 21.12
wrong 19.4; 24.11

18 Then Jonathan said to him, "Since tomorrow is the **New Moon Festival**, your absence will be **noticed** if you aren't at the meal. 19 The day after tomorrow your absence will be **noticed**[i] even more; so go to the place where you hid the other time, and hide behind the pile of stones there.[j] 20 I will then shoot three arrows at it, as though it were a target. 21 Then I will tell my **servant** to go and find them. And if I tell him, 'Look, the arrows are on this side of you; get them,' that means that you are **safe** and can come out. I **swear** by the living LORD that you will be in no **danger**. 22 But if I tell him, 'The arrows are on the other side of you,' then leave, because the LORD is sending you away. 23 As for the **promise** we have made to **each other**, the LORD will make **sure** that we will keep it for ever."

24 So David hid in the fields. At the **New Moon Festival**, King Saul came to the meal 25 and sat in his usual place by the wall. Abner sat next to him, and Jonathan sat opposite him.[k] David's place was empty, 26 but Saul said nothing that day, because he thought, "Something has happened to him, and he is not ritually **pure**." 27 On the following day, the day after the **New Moon Festival**, David's place was still empty, and Saul asked Jonathan, "Why didn't David come to the meal either yesterday or today?"

28 Jonathan answered, "He **begged** me to let him go to Bethlehem. 29 'Please let me go,' he said, 'because our family is **celebrating** the **sacrificial feast** in town, and my brother ordered me to be there. So then, if you are my **friend**, let me go and see my relatives.' That is why he isn't in his place at your table."

30 Saul was **furious** with Jonathan and said to him, "How **rebellious** and **faithless** your mother was! Now I know you are taking sides with David and are **disgracing** yourself and that mother of yours! 31 Don't you realize that as long as David is **alive**, you will never be king of this country? Now go and bring him here—he must die!"

32 "Why should he die?" Jonathan replied. "What has he done?"

33 At that, Saul threw his spear at Jonathan to kill him, and Jonathan realized that his father was really **determined** to kill David. 34 Jonathan got up from the table in a **rage** and ate nothing that day—the second day of the New Moon Festival. He was deeply **distressed** about David, because Saul had **insulted** him. 35 The following morning Jonathan went to the fields to meet David, as they had **agreed**. He took a young boy with him 36 and said to him, "Run and find the arrows I'm going to shoot." The boy ran, and Jonathan shot an arrow beyond him. 37 When the boy reached the place where the arrow had fallen, Jonathan shouted to him, "The arrow is further on! 38 Don't just stand there! Hurry up!" The boy picked up the arrow and returned to his **master**, 39 not knowing what it all meant; only Jonathan and David knew. 40 Jonathan gave his weapons to the boy and told him to take them back to the town.

41 After the boy had left, David got up from behind the pile of stones,[l] fell on his **knees** and **bowed** with his face to the ground three times. Both he and Jonathan were crying as they **kissed each other**; David's **grief** was even greater than Jonathan's.[m] 42 Then Jonathan said to David, "God be with you. The LORD will make **sure** that you and I, and your descendants and mine, will for ever keep the **sacred promise** we have made to **each other**." Then David left, and Jonathan went back to the town.

David Flees from Saul

21 David went to the **priest** Ahimelech in Nob. Ahimelech came out **trembling** to meet him and asked, "Why did you come here all by yourself?"

2 "I am here on the king's business," David answered. "He told me not to let anyone know what he sent me to do. As for my men, I have told them to meet me at a certain place. 3 Now, then, what supplies have you got? Give me five loaves of **bread** or anything else you have."

4 The **priest** said, "I haven't any ordinary **bread**, only **sacred** bread; you can have it if your men haven't had **sexual relations** recently."

5 "Of course they haven't," answered David. "My men always keep themselves ritually **pure** even when we go out on an ordinary mission; how much more this time when we are on a **special** mission!"

6 So the **priest** gave David the **sacred bread**, because the only **bread** he had was the loaves **offered** to God, which had

act Judg 20.6; 2 Sam 14.2
action 12.7; 24.12
afraid 18.12; 22.23
bread [5] 17.17; 25.1
enough Ruth 3.14; 23.3
ephod (1) 14.3; 22.18
flee 20.1; 22.1
fulfil Deut 23.18; 2 Sam 7.25
mad [3] 18.10; 2 Kgs 9.20
obligation Deut 29.12; Ezra 4.1
offer 16.2; 26.19
priest [3] 14.3; 22.11
pure 20.26; 2 Sam 11.4
relations Deut 27.2 1 Kgs 3.6
religion 10.6; 1 Kgs 12.32
sacred [3] 20.8; 23.18
sex Judg 19.22; Prov 31.3
special 1.21; 2 Chr 30.1
tremble 16.4; 2 Sam 22.8
word (1) 20.12; 2 Sam 3.11

[i] *Some ancient translations* your absence will be noticed; *Hebrew* go down.
[j] *Probable text* the pile of stones there; *Hebrew* the Ezel Stone.
[k] *One ancient translation* sat opposite him; *Hebrew* stood up.
[l] *Probable text* the pile of stones; *Hebrew* the south.
[m] *Probable text* David's grief was even greater than Jonathan's; *Hebrew unclear.*

21.1–6: Mt 12.3–4; Mk 2.25–26; Lk 6.3 **21.6:** Lev 24.5–9

been removed from the **sacred** table and replaced by fresh **bread**.

7 (Saul's chief herdsman, Doeg, who was from Edom, happened to be there that day, because he had to **fulfil** a **religious obligation**.)

8 David said to Ahimelech, "Have you got a spear or a sword you can give me? The king's orders made me leave in such a hurry that I didn't have time to get my sword or any other weapon."

9 Ahimelech answered, "I have the sword of Goliath the Philistine, whom you killed in the Valley of Elah; it is behind the **ephod**, wrapped in a cloth. If you want it, take it—it's the only weapon here."

"Give it to me," David said. "There is not a better sword anywhere!"

10 So David left, **fleeing** from Saul, and went to King Achish of Gath. 11 The king's officials said to Achish, "Isn't this David, the king of his country? This is the man about whom the women sang, as they danced, 'Saul has killed thousands, but David has killed tens of thousands.' "

12 Their **words** made a deep impression on David, and he became very much **afraid** of King Achish. 13 So whenever they were around, David pretended to be insane and **acted** like a **madman** when they tried to restrain him; he would scribble on the city[n] gates and dribble down his beard. 14 So Achish said to his officials, "Look! The man is **mad**! Why did you bring him to me? 15 Haven't I got **enough madmen** already? Why bring another one to annoy me with his daft **actions** right here in my own house?"

The Slaughter of the Priests

22 David **fled** from the city of Gath and went to a cave near the town of Adullam. When his brothers and the rest of the family heard that he was there, they joined him. 2 People who were **oppressed** or in **debt or dissatisfied** went to him, about four hundred men in all, and he became their leader.

3 David went on from there to Mizpah in Moab and said to the king of Moab, "Please let my father and mother come and stay with you until I find out what God is going to do for me." 4 So David left his parents with the king of Moab, and they stayed there as long as David was hiding in the cave.

5 Then the **prophet** Gad came to David and said, "Don't stay here; go at once to the land of Judah." So David left and went to the forest of Hereth.

6 One day Saul was in Gibeah, sitting under a tamarisk-tree on a hill, with his spear in his hand, and all his officers were standing round him. He was told that David and his men had been found, 7 and he said to his officers, "Listen, men of Benjamin! Do you think that David will give fields and **vineyards** to all of you, and make you officers in his army? 8 Is that why you are **plotting** against me? Not one of you told me that my own son had made an alliance with David. No one is **concerned** about me or tells me that David, one of my own men, is at this moment looking for a chance to kill me, and that my son has **encouraged** him!"

9 Doeg was standing there with Saul's officers, and he said, "I saw David when he went to Ahimelech son of Ahitub in Nob. 10 Ahimelech asked the LORD what David should do, and then he gave David some food and the sword of Goliath the Philistine."

11 So King Saul sent for the **priest** Ahimelech and all his relatives, who were also **priests** in Nob, and they came to him. 12 Saul said to Ahimelech, "Listen, Ahimelech!"

"At your **service**, sir," he answered.

13 Saul asked him, "Why are you and David **plotting** against me? Why did you give him some food and a sword, and **consult** God for him? Now he has **turned** against me and is waiting for a chance to kill me!"

14 Ahimelech answered, "David is the most **faithful** officer you have! He is your own son-in-law, captain of[o] your bodyguard, and highly **respected** by everyone in the royal **court**. 15 Yes, I **consulted** God for him, and it wasn't the first time.[p] As for **plotting** against you, Your **Majesty** must not **accuse** me or anyone else in my family. I don't know anything about this matter!"

16 The king said, "Ahimelech, you and all your relatives must die." 17 Then he said to the guards standing near him, "Kill the LORD's **priests**! They conspired with David and did not tell me that he had run away, even though they knew it all along." But the guards **refused** to lift a hand to kill the LORD's **priests**. 18 So Saul said to Doeg, "You kill them!"—and Doeg killed them all. On that day he killed eighty-five **priests** who were qualified to carry the **ephod**. 19 Saul also

[n] city; *or* palace. [o] *Some ancient translations* captain of; *Hebrew* he turned to.
[p] Yes, I consulted...time; *or* Now, have I done something wrong today by consulting God for him? Not at all!

21.9: 1 Sam 17.51 **21.11:** 1 Sam 18.7, 29.5 **21.12:** Ps 56 (Title) **21.13:** Ps 34 (Title)
22.1: Ps 57 (Title); Ps 142 (Title) **22.9–10:** 1 Sam 21.7–9; Ps 52 (Title)

accuse 12.3; 2 Sam 3.7
afraid 21.12; 23.3
concern Ruth 2.10; Job 39.16
consult [2] 14.19; 23.4
court (1) 8.15; 2 Sam 8.17
death (1) 20.3; 26.10
death (3) (to death) 17.35; 2 Sam 4.10
debt Deut 31.10; 2 Kgs 4.1
encourage Judg 20.22; 23.16
ephod (1) 21.9; 23.6
escape 19.10; 23.6
faithful 12.24; 26.23
flee 21.10; 27.4
Majesty 17.32; 23.20
oppress 12.3; 2 Sam 7.10
plot (1) [3] Ex 10.10; 2 Sam 15.11
priest [7] 21.1; 23.9
prophet 19.20; 28.6
refuse (1) 1.7; 28.23

respect 15.30; 24.8
safe 20.7; 25.29
satisfy Ruth 2.14; 2 Kgs 14.10
service 16.21; 2 Sam 9.2
sheep 17.15; 24.3
slaughter 14.14; 25.11
sure 20.23; 23.20
turn 17.30; 24.8
vineyard 8.14; 1 Kgs 21.1

ordered all the other inhabitants of Nob,
the city of **priests**, to be put **to death**:
men and women, children and babies,
cattle, donkeys, and **sheep**—they were all
killed.
20 But Abiathar, one of Ahimelech's
sons, **escaped**, and went and joined
David. 21 He told him how Saul had
slaughtered the **priests** of the LORD.
22 David said to him, "When I saw Doeg
there that day, I knew that he would be
sure to tell Saul. So I am responsible[r] for
the **death** of all your relatives. 23 Stay
with me and don't be **afraid**. Saul wants
to kill both you and me, but you will be
safe with me."

David Saves the Town of Keilah

23 David heard that the Philistines
were attacking the town of
Keilah and were **stealing** the **newly-**
harvested corn. 2 So he asked the LORD,
"Shall I go and attack the Philistines?"
"Yes," the LORD answered. "Attack
them and **save** Keilah."
3 But David's men said to him, "We
have **enough** to be **afraid** of here in
Judah; it will be much **worse** if we go to
Keilah and attack the Philistine forces!"
4 So David **consulted** the LORD again, and
the LORD said to him, "Go and attack
Keilah, because I will give you **victory**
over the Philistines." 5 So David and his
men went to Keilah and attacked the
Philistines; they killed many of them and
took their livestock. And that was how
David **saved** the town.
6 When Abiathar son of Ahimelech
escaped and joined David in Keilah, he
took the **ephod** with him.
7 Saul was told that David had gone to
Keilah, and he said, "God has put him in
my **power**. David has **trapped** himself by
going into a walled town with fortified
gates." 8 So Saul called his troops to war,
to march against Keilah and besiege
David and his men.
9 When David heard that Saul was
planning to attack him, he said to the
priest Abiathar, "Bring the **ephod** here."
10 Then David said, "LORD, God of Israel,
I have heard that Saul is **planning** to
come to Keilah and **destroy** it on account
of me, your **servant**. 11 Will the citizens of
Keilah hand me over to Saul? Will Saul
really come, as I have heard? LORD, God
of Israel, I **beg** you to answer me!"
The LORD answered, "Saul will come."
12 "And will the citizens of Keilah
hand my men and me over to Saul?"
David asked again.
"They will," the LORD answered.
13 So David and his men—about six
hundred in all—left Keilah at once and
kept on the move. When Saul heard that
David had **escaped** from Keilah, he gave
up his **plan**.

David in the Hill-Country

14 David stayed in hiding in the hill-
country, in the wilderness near Ziph. Saul
was always trying to find him, but God
did not hand David over to him. 15 David
saw that Saul was out to kill him.
David was at Horesh, in the wilderness
near Ziph. 16 Jonathan went to him there
and **encouraged** him with **assurances** of
God's **protection**, 17 saying to him, "Don't
be **afraid**. My father Saul won't be able to
harm you. He knows very well that you
are the one who will be the king of Israel
and that I will be next in rank to you."
18 The two of them made a **sacred**
promise of **friendship** to **each other**.
David stayed at Horesh, and Jonathan
went home.
19 Some people from Ziph went to
Saul at Gibeah and said, "David is hiding
in our territory at Horesh on Mount
Hachilah, in the southern part of the
Judaean wilderness. 20 We know, Your
Majesty, how much you want to capture
him; so come to our territory, and we
will make **sure** that you catch him."
21 Saul answered, "May the LORD
bless you for being so **kind** to me! 22 Go
and make **sure** once more; find out for
certain where he is and who has seen
him there. I hear that he is very cunning.
23 Find out exactly the places where he
hides, and be **sure** to bring back a report
to me straight away. Then I will go with
you, and if he is still in the region, I will
hunt him down, even if I have to search
the whole land of Judah."
24 So they left and returned to Ziph
ahead of Saul. David and his men were in
the wilderness of Maon, in a **desolate**
valley in the southern part of the
Judaean wilderness. 25 Saul and his men
set out to look for David, but he heard
about it and went to a rocky hill in the
wilderness of Maon and stayed there.
When Saul heard about this, he went
after David. 26 Saul and his men were on
one side of the hill, **separated** from David
and his men, who were on the other side.
They were hurrying to **get away** from
Saul and his men, who were closing in on
them and were about to capture them.
27 Just then a messenger arrived and said

afraid [2] 22.23; 28.13
assure Ps 44.3
beg 20.6; 2 Chr 33.12
bless 15.13; 24.19
certain (1) 20.9; Neh 6.7
consult 22.13; 28.7
desolate Deut 32.10; 2 Kgs 19.17
destroy 20.15; 28.18
each other 20.16; 2 Sam 12.19
encourage 22.8; 2 Sam 11.25
enough 21.15; 28.22
ephod (1) [2] 22.18; 30.7
escape [2] 22.20; 27.1
friend 20.29; 25.6
get away 19.11; 24.19
harm 20.7; 24.6
harvest 8.12; 2 Sam 9.10
kind 15.6; 25.8
Majesty 22.15; 24.8
new 10.9; 2 Sam 6.3
plan [3] 20.3; 2 Sam 17.21
power 17.46; 24.4
priest 22.11; 30.7
promise 20.8; 24.21
protect 17.6; 25.16
sacred 21.4; 28.10
save [2] 17.37; 24.15
separate Ruth 1.17; 2 Sam 14.6
servant 20.21; 25.8
steal Judg 17.2; 25.7
sure [3] 22.22; 24.20
trap 18.21; 28.9
victory 19.5; 30.23
worse 14.19; 2 Sam 4.11

[r] *Some ancient translations* I am responsible; *Hebrew* I have turned.

23.18: 1 Sam 18.3 **23.19:** Ps 54 (Title)

to Saul, "Come back at once! The Philistines are invading the country!" 28 So
Saul stopped pursuing David and went to
fight the Philistines. That is why that
place is called Separation Hill. 29 David
left and went to the region of Engedi,
where he stayed in hiding.

David Spares Saul's Life

24 When Saul came back from fighting the Philistines, he was told
that David was in the wilderness near
Engedi. 2 Saul took three thousand of the
best soldiers in Israel and went looking
for David and his men east of Wild Goat
Rocks. 3 He came to a cave close to some
sheep pens by the road and went in to
relieve himself. It happened to be the
very cave in which David and his men
were hiding far back in the cave. 4 They
said to him, "This is your chance! The
LORD has told you that he would put your
enemy in your **power** and you could do to
him whatever you wanted to." David
crept over and cut off a piece of Saul's
robe without Saul's knowing it. 5 But then
David's **conscience** began to **trouble** him,
6 and he said to his men, "May the LORD
keep me from doing any **harm** to my
master, whom the LORD **chose** as king! I
must not **harm** him in the least, because
he is the king **chosen** by the LORD!" 7 So
David **convinced** his men that they
should not attack Saul.

Saul got up, left the cave, and started
on his way. 8 Then David went out after
him and called to him, "Your **Majesty**!"
Saul **turned** round, and David **bowed
down** to the ground in **respect** 9 and said,
"Why do you listen to people who say
that I am trying to **harm** you? 10 You can
see for yourself that just now in the cave
the LORD put you in my **power**. Some of
my men told me to kill you, but I felt
sorry for you and said that I would not
harm you in the least, because you are
the one whom the LORD **chose** to be king.
11 Look, my father, look at the piece of
your robe I am holding! I could have
killed you, but instead I only cut this off.
This should **convince** you that I have no
thought of **rebelling** against you or of
harming you. You are hunting me down
to kill me, even though I have not done
you any **wrong**. 12 May the LORD **judge**
which one of us is **wrong**! May he **punish**
you for your **action** against me, for I will
not **harm** you in the least. 13 You know
the old **saying**, '**Evil** is done only by evil
men.' And so I will not **harm** you. 14 Look
at what the king of Israel is trying to kill!
Look at what he is chasing! A **dead** dog,
a flea! 15 The LORD will **judge**, and he will
decide which one of us is **wrong**. May he
look into the matter, **defend** me, and
save me from you."

16 When David had finished speaking,
Saul said, "Is that really you, David my
son?" And he started crying. 17 Then he
said to David, "You are **right**, and I am
wrong. You have been so good to me,
while I have done such **wrong** to you!
18 Today you have shown how good you
are to me, because you did not kill me,
even though the LORD put me in your
power. 19 How often does a man catch his
enemy and then let him **get away unharmed**? The LORD **bless** you for what
you have done to me today! 20 Now I am
sure that you will be king of Israel and
that the kingdom will continue under
your rule. 21 But **promise** me in the
LORD's name that you will **spare** my descendants, so that my name and my
family's name will not be completely **forgotten**." 22 David **promised** that he would.

Then Saul went back home, and David
and his men went back to their hiding
place.

action 21.15; 2 Kgs 21.21
best 15.9; 25.6
bless 23.21; 25.31
bow (2) 20.41; 25.41
choose [3] 17.8; 26.9
conscience Gen 20.5; 2 Sam 24.10
convince [2] 19.6; 2 Sam 16.3
dead 20.13; 25.22
defend 13.23; 2 Sam 18.13
enemy [2] 20.15; 25.26
evil 19.9; 25.28
forget 12.9; 25.31
get away 23.26; 30.17
harm [8] 23.17; 25.7
judge [2] 16.7; 2 Sam 15.4
keep from 14.6; 25.26
Majesty 23.20; 26.17
master 20.38; 25.14
name (2) (name of God, of Jesus) 19.6; 30.15
power [3] 23.7; 26.8
promise [2] 23.18; 25.30
punish 20.16; 25.26
rebel 20.30; 2 Sam 15.31
respect 22.14; 28.14
right (1) 12.23; 2 Sam 19.27
save 23.2; 2 Sam 3.8
saying 19.24; 1 Kgs 10.8
sheep 22.19; 25.2
sorry 15.11; 2 Chr 21.20
spare 15.9; 26.21
sure 23.20; 2 Sam 7.13
trouble 10.19; 26.24
turn 22.13; 26.19
wrong [5] 20.1; 25.28

The Death of Samuel

25 Samuel died, and all the Israelites came together and **mourned**
for him. Then they buried him at his
home in Ramah.

David and Abigail

After this, David went to the wilderness of Paran. 2-3 There was a man of the
clan of Caleb named Nabal, who was
from the town of Maon, and who owned
land near the town of Carmel. He was a
very **rich** man, the owner of three thous-
and **sheep** and one thousand goats. His
wife Abigail was beautiful and **intelligent**,
but he was a mean, bad-tempered man.

Nabal was shearing his **sheep** in Carmel, 4 and David, who was in the wilderness, heard about it, 5 so he sent ten
young men with orders to go to Carmel,
find Nabal, and give him his greetings.
6 He instructed them to say to Nabal:
"David sends you greetings, my **friend**,
with his **best wishes** for you, your family,
and all that is yours. 7 He heard that you
were shearing your **sheep**, and he wants
you to know that your **shepherds** have
been with us and we did not **harm** them.
Nothing that belonged to them was
stolen all the time they were at Carmel.
8 Just ask them, and they will tell you. We
have come on a **feast** day, and David
asks you to receive us **kindly**. Please give

accept [2] 12.3; 2 Sam 3.21
best 24.2; 26.2
blame Gen 45.5; 2 Sam 14.9
bless 24.19; 26.25
bow (2) 24.8; 28.14
bread [2] 21.3; 28.24
crime 20.1; 26.18
dead [2] 24.14; 31.5
dear 2 Sam 1.23
disaster 6.9; 2 Sam 17.14
enemy [3] 24.4; 26.8
evil [2] 24.13; 2 Sam 4.11
feast [2] 20.29; 2 Sam 3.20
fit (1) Josh 22.19; 2 Sam 3.29
flock 8.17; 30.20
fool 13.13; 26.21
forget 24.21; 2 Sam 19.19
forgive 15.25; 2 Sam 12.13
friend [2] 23.18; 27.5
harm [3] 24.6; 26.9
help 19.4; 2 Sam 3.12
insult [2] 20.34; 2 Kgs 19.4
intelligent 1 Kgs 7.14
keep from [4] 24.6; 2 Sam 13.2
kind 23.21; 2 Sam 2.6
last (2) Josh 13.12; 2 Sam 14.7
master [2] 24.6; 26.15
message 16.22; 30.26
mourn 6.19; 28.3
paralyse 1 Kgs 13.4
praise [2] 19.4; 2 Sam 18.28
promise 24.21; 28.10
protect [2] 23.16; 26.15
punish [2] 24.12; 26.9

24.3: Ps 57 (Title); Ps 142 (Title) **24.6:** 1 Sam 26.11 **24.14:** 1 Sam 26.20

revenge [4] 18.25; 2 Sam 3.30
rich 2.7; 2 Sam 1.24
rise Judg 5.31; 2 Sam 22.39
safe 22.23; 26.13
sense Deut 32.6; Esth 8.16
servant [9] 23.10; 26.18
sheep [4] 24.3; 27.9
shepherd 17.40; 1 Kgs 22.17
slaughter 22.21; 1 Kgs 3.3
slave 17.8; 30.13
steal [3] 23.1; 2 Sam 21.12
strike [2] 20.13; 26.8
suffer 9.16; 2 Sam 19.7
swear [2] 20.3; 26.16
thank Deut 8.10; 1 Chr 16.8
wish 11.10; 2 Sam 15.4
worry 10.2; 1 Kgs 17.13
wrong [2] 24.11; 26.21

what you can to us your **servants** and to your **dear friend** David."

9 David's men delivered this **message** to Nabal in David's name. Then they waited there, 10 and Nabal finally answered, "David? Who is he? I've never heard of him! The country is full of runaway **slaves** nowadays! 11 I'm not going to take my **bread** and water, and the animals I have **slaughtered** for my shearers, and give them to men who come from I don't know where!"

12 David's men went back to him and told him what Nabal had said. 13 "Buckle on your swords!" he ordered, and they all did. David also buckled on his sword and left with about four hundred of his men, leaving two hundred behind with the supplies.

14 One of Nabal's **servants** said to Nabal's wife Abigail, "Have you heard? David sent some messengers from the wilderness with greetings for our **master**, but he **insulted** them. 15 Yet they were very good to us; they never bothered us, and all the time we were with them in the fields, nothing that belonged to us was **stolen**. 16 They **protected** us day and night the whole time we were with them looking after our **flocks**. 17 Please think this over and decide what to do. This could be **disastrous** for our **master** and all his family. He is so pigheaded that he won't listen to anybody!"

18 Abigail quickly collected two hundred loaves of **bread**, two leather bags full of wine, five roasted **sheep**, seventeen kilogrammes of roasted grain, a hundred bunches of raisins, and two hundred cakes of dried figs, and loaded them on donkeys. 19 Then she said to the **servants**, "You go on ahead and I will follow you." But she said nothing to her husband.

20 She was riding her donkey round a bend on a hillside when suddenly she met David and his men coming towards her. 21 David had been thinking, "Why did I ever **protect** that fellow's property out here in the wilderness? Not a thing that belonged to him was **stolen**, and this is how he pays me back for the **help** I gave him! 22 May God **strike** me[s] **dead** if I don't kill every **last** one of those men before morning!"

23 When Abigail saw David, she quickly dismounted and threw herself on the ground 24 at David's feet, and said to him, "Please, sir, listen to me! Let me take the **blame**. 25 Please, don't pay any attention to Nabal, that good-for-nothing! He is exactly what his name means—a **fool**![t] I wasn't there when your **servants** arrived, sir. 26 It is the LORD who has **kept you from** taking **revenge** and killing your **enemies**. And now I **swear** to you by the living LORD that your **enemies** and all who want to **harm** you will be **punished** like Nabal. 27 Please, sir, **accept** this present I have brought you, and give it to your men. 28 Please **forgive** me, sir, for any **wrong** I have done. The LORD will make you king, and your descendants also, because you are fighting his battles; and you will not do anything **evil**[u] as long as you live. 29 If anyone should attack you and try to kill you, the LORD your God will keep you **safe**, as a man guards a precious treasure. As for your **enemies**, however, he will throw them away, as a man hurls stones with his sling. 30 And when the LORD has done all the good things he has **promised** you and has made you king of Israel, 31 then you will not have to feel regret or remorse, sir, for having killed without cause or for having taken your own **revenge**. And when the LORD has **blessed** you, sir, please do not **forget** me."

32 David said to her, "**Praise** the LORD, the God of Israel, who sent you today to meet me! 33 **Thank** God for your good **sense** and for what you have done today in **keeping me from** the **crime** of murder and from taking my own **revenge**. 34 The LORD has **kept me from harming** you. But I **swear** by the living God of Israel that if you had not hurried to meet me, all of Nabal's men would have been **dead** by morning!" 35 Then David **accepted** what she had brought him and said to her, "Go back home and don't **worry**. I will do what you want."

36 Abigail went back to Nabal, who was at home having a **feast fit** for a king. He was drunk and in a good mood, so she did not tell him anything until the next morning. 37 Then, after he had sobered up, she told him everything. He **suffered** a stroke and was completely **paralysed**. 38 Some ten days later the LORD **struck** Nabal and he died.

39 When David heard that Nabal had died, he said, "**Praise** the LORD! He has taken **revenge** on Nabal for **insulting** me and has **kept me his servant from** doing **wrong**. The LORD has **punished** Nabal for his **evil**."

Then David sent a proposal of marriage to Abigail. 40 His **servants** went

[s] *One ancient translation* me; *Hebrew* my enemies.
[t] A FOOL: *This is the meaning of the Hebrew name Nabal.*
[u] you will not do anything evil; *or* no evil will happen to you.

to her at Carmel and said to her, "David
sent us to take you to him to be his wife."
41 Abigail **bowed down** to the ground
and said, "I am his **servant**, ready to
wash the feet of his **servants**." 42 She **rose**
quickly and mounted her donkey.
Accompanied by her five maids, she
went with David's **servants** and became
his wife.
43 David had married Ahinoam from
Jezreel, and now Abigail also became his
wife. 44 Meanwhile, Saul had given his
daughter Michal, who had been David's
wife, to Palti son of Laish, who was from
the town of Gallim.

David Spares Saul's Life Again

26 Some men from Ziph came to
Saul at Gibeah and told him that
David was hiding on Mount Hachilah at
the edge of the Judaean wilderness. 2 Saul
went at once with three thousand of the
best soldiers in Israel to the wilderness of
Ziph to look for David, 3 and camped by
the road on Mount Hachilah. David was
still in the wilderness, and when he
learnt that Saul had come to look for
him, 4 he sent spies and found out that
Saul was indeed there. 5 He went at once
and located the exact place where Saul
and Abner son of Ner, commander of
Saul's army, slept. Saul slept inside the
camp, and his men camped round him.
6 Then David asked Ahimelech the
Hittite, and Abishai the brother of Joab
(their mother was Zeruiah), "Which of
you two will go to Saul's camp with me?"
"I will," Abishai answered.
7 So that night David and Abishai
entered Saul's camp and found Saul
sleeping in the centre of the camp with
his spear stuck in the ground near his
head. Abner and the troops were sleeping round him. 8 Abishai said to David,
"God has put your **enemy** in your **power**
tonight. Now let me plunge his own spear
through him and pin him to the ground
with just one blow—I won't have to **strike**
twice!"
9 But David said, "You must not **harm**
him! The LORD will certainly **punish**
whoever **harms** his **chosen** king. 10 By the
living LORD," David continued, "I know
that the LORD himself will kill Saul,
either when his time comes to die a
natural death or when he dies in battle.
11 The LORD **forbid** that I should try to
harm the one whom the LORD has made
king! Let's take his spear and his water
jar, and go." 12 So David took the spear
and the water jar from just beside Saul's
head, and he and Abishai left. No one
saw it or knew what had happened or
even woke up—they were all **sound
asleep**, because the LORD had sent a
heavy sleep on them all.
13 Then David crossed over to the
other side of the valley to the top of the
hill, a **safe** distance away, 14 and shouted
to Saul's troops and to Abner, "Abner!
Can you hear me?"
"Who is that shouting and waking up
the king?" Abner asked.
15 David answered, "Abner, aren't you
the greatest man in Israel? So why
aren't you **protecting** your **master**, the
king? Just now someone entered the
camp to kill your **master**. 16 You **failed** in
your **duty**, Abner! I **swear** by the living
LORD that all of you **deserve** to die,
because you have not **protected** your
master, whom the LORD made king.
Look! Where is the king's spear? Where
is the water jar that was beside his
head?"
17 Saul recognized David's voice and
asked, "David, is that you, my son?"
"Yes, Your **Majesty**," David answered.
18 And he added, "Why, sir, are you still
pursuing me, your **servant**? What have I
done? What **crime** have I committed?
19 Your **Majesty**, listen to what I have to
say. If it is the LORD who has **turned** you
against me, an **offering** to him will make
him **change his mind**; but if men have
done it, may the LORD's **curse** fall on
them. For they have driven me out from
the LORD's land to a country where I can
only **worship foreign gods**. 20 Don't let me
be killed on foreign soil, away from the
LORD. Why should the king of Israel
come to kill a flea like me? Why should
he hunt me down like a wild bird?"
21 Saul answered, "I have done **wrong**.
Come back, David, my son! I will never
harm you again, because you have
spared my **life** tonight. I have been a
fool! I have done a **terrible** thing!"
22 David replied, "Here is your spear,
Your **Majesty**. Let one of your men come
over and get it. 23 The LORD **rewards**
those who are **faithful** and **righteous**.
Today he put you in my **power**, but I did
not **harm** you, whom the LORD made
king. 24 Just as I have **spared** your **life**
today, may the LORD do the same to me
and **free** me from all **troubles**!"
25 Saul said to David, "God **bless** you,
my son! You will **succeed** in everything
you do!"
So David went on his way, and Saul
returned home.

25.44: 2 Sam 3.14–16 **26.1:** Ps 54 (Title) **26.11:** 1 Sam 24.6

best 25.6; 27.1
bless 25.31; 2 Sam 2.5
change 15.29; 2 Sam 12.20
choose 24.6; 2 Sam 1.14
crime 25.33; 2 Sam 3.34
curse 17.43; 2 Sam 16.5
death (1) 22.22; 29.4
deserve Judg 9.16; 2 Sam 3.39
duty (1) 10.25; 2 Sam 13.34
enemy 25.26; 28.16
fail Josh 23.14; 1 Kgs 11.22
faithful 22.14; 2 Sam 2.6
fool 25.25; 2 Sam 3.33
forbid 20.2; 1 Kgs 21.3
free 17.26; 2 Sam 7.23
god (2) (other gods) 17.43; 2 Sam 7.23
harm [5] 25.7; 2 Sam 12.18
learn Judg 15.6; 2 Sam 11.3
life (1) [2] 19.5; 27.12
Majesty [3] 24.8; 2 Sam 3.21
master [3] 25.14; 29.4
mind (1) 15.29; 2 Sam 7.3
natural Deut 14.21; 1 Kgs 2.6
offer 21.6; 2 Sam 6.13
power [2] 24.4; 2 Sam 3.6
protect [2] 25.16; 2 Sam 21.2
punish 25.26; 28.10
reward 17.25; 2 Sam 4.10
righteous Num 23.10; Job 4.7
safe 25.29; 27.1
servant 25.8; 28.2
sound (2) Judg 8.9; 2 Sam 4.7
spare [2] 24.21; 2 Sam 21.7
strike 25.22; 2 Sam 1.15
succeed (1) 18.5; 1 Kgs 2.33
swear 25.26; 29.6
terrible 14.29; 2 Sam 18.7
trouble 24.5; 28.15
turn 24.8; 29.4

worship (2) (of other gods) 12.10; 1 Kgs 9.6
wrong 25.28; 29.8

best 26.2; 2 Sam 6.1
escape 23.6; 30.17
flee 22.1; 31.1
friend 25.6; 30.26
hate 13.4; 2 Sam 5.8
life (1) 26.21; 28.21
need 17.47; 2 Sam 20.3
reason 19.5; 2 Sam 14.15
safe 26.13; 30.23
serve 19.7; 29.8
sheep 25.2; 2 Sam 7.8
trust Josh 2.12; 2 Sam 15.32
widow Ruth 4.5; 2 Sam 2.2

David among the Philistines

27 David said to himself, "One of these days Saul will kill me. The **best** thing for me to do is to **escape** to Philistia. Then Saul will give up looking for me in Israel, and I will be **safe**." 2 So David and his six hundred men went over at once to Achish son of Maoch, king of Gath. 3 David and his men settled there in Gath with their families. David had his two wives with him, Ahinoam from Jezreel, and Abigail, Nabal's **widow**, from Carmel. 4 When Saul heard that David had **fled** to Gath, he gave up trying to find him.

5 David said to Achish, "If you are my **friend**, let me have a small town to live in. There is no **need**, sir, for me to live with you in the capital city." 6 So Achish gave him the town of Ziklag, and for this **reason** Ziklag has belonged to the kings of Judah ever since. 7 David lived in Philistia for sixteen months.

8 During that time David and his men would attack the people of Geshur, Girzi, and Amalek, who had been living in the region a very long time. He would raid their land as far as Shur, all the way down to Egypt, 9 killing all the men and women and taking the **sheep**, cattle, donkeys, camels, and even the clothes. Then he would come back to Achish, 10 who would ask him, "Where did you go on a raid this time?" and David would tell him that he had gone to the southern part of Judah or to the territory of the clan of Jerahmeel or to the territory where the Kenites lived. 11 David would kill everyone, men and women, so that no one could go back to Gath and report what he and his men had really done. This is what David did the whole time he lived in Philistia. 12 But Achish **trusted** David and said to himself, "He is **hated** so much by his own people the Israelites that he will have to **serve** me all his **life**."

abandon [2] 18.12; 31.7
afraid 23.3; 2 Sam 3.11
bow (2) 25.41; 2 Sam 1.2
bread 25.11; 2 Sam 6.19
command 18.13; 2 Sam 5.25
consult [2] 23.4; 2 Sam 5.23
dark 2.9; 2 Sam 22.10
destroy 23.10; 2 Sam 14.7
disobey 15.11; 2 Sam 12.9
dream [2] Judg 7.13; 1 Kgs 3.5
enemy 26.8; 29.8

28 Some time later, the Philistines gathered their troops to fight Israel, and Achish said to David, "Of course you **understand** that you and your men are to fight on my side."

2 "Of course," David answered. "I am your **servant**, and you will see for yourself what I can do."

Achish said, "Good! I will make you my permanent bodyguard."

Saul Consults a Medium

3 Now Samuel had died, and all the Israelites had **mourned** for him and had buried him in his own city of Ramah. Saul had **forced** all the **fortune-tellers** and **mediums** to leave Israel.

4 The Philistine troops assembled and camped near the town of Shunem; Saul gathered the Israelites and camped at Mount Gilboa. 5 When Saul saw the Philistine army, he was **terrified**, 6 and so he asked the LORD what to do. But the LORD did not answer him at all, either by **dreams** or by the use of Urim and Thummim or by **prophets**. 7 Then Saul ordered his officials, "Find me a woman who is a **medium**, and I will go and **consult** her."

"There is one in Endor," they answered.

8 So Saul disguised himself; he put on different clothes, and after **dark** he went with two of his men to see the woman. "**Consult** the **spirits** for me and tell me what is going to happen," he said to her. "Call up the **spirit** of the man I name."

9 The woman answered, "Surely you know what King Saul has done, how he **forced** the **fortune-tellers** and **mediums** to leave Israel.[v] Why, then, are you trying to **trap** me and get me killed?"

10 Then Saul made a **sacred vow**. "By the living LORD I **promise** that you will not be **punished** for doing this," he told her.

11 "Whom shall I call up for you?" the woman asked.

"Samuel," he answered.

12 When the woman saw Samuel, she screamed and said to Saul, "Why have you **tricked** me? You are King Saul!"

13 "Don't be **afraid**!" the king said to her. "What do you see?"

"I see a **spirit** coming up from the earth," she answered.

14 "What does it look like?" he asked.

"It's an old man coming up," she answered. "He is wearing a cloak."

Then Saul knew that it was Samuel, and he **bowed** to the ground in **respect**.

15 Samuel said to Saul, "Why have you disturbed me? Why did you make me come back?"

Saul answered, "I am in great **trouble**! The Philistines are at war with me, and God has **abandoned** me. He doesn't answer me any more, either by **prophets** or by **dreams**. And so I have called you, for you to tell me what I must do."

16 Samuel said, "Why do you call me when the LORD has **abandoned** you and become your **enemy**? 17 The LORD has done to you what he told you through me: he has taken the kingdom away from you and given it to David instead.

enough 23.3; 2 Sam 3.29
force (1) [2] 2.16; 2 Sam 2.22
fortune-teller [2] Judg 9.37; 2 Kgs 17.17
life (1) 27.12; 2 Sam 1.23
medium [3] 2 Kgs 17.17
mourn 25.1; 2 Sam 1.12
promise 25.30; 30.1
prophet [2] 22.5; 2 Sam 7.2
punish 26.9; 2 Sam 3.29
refuse (1) 22.17; 2 Sam 12.16
respect 24.8; 2 Sam 1.2
sacred 23.18; 2 Sam 5.3
servant 26.18; 2 Sam 3.18
spirit (2) [3] 19.9; 1 Kgs 22.21
strong 14.52; 2 Sam 1.23
terrify [3] 17.11; 31
trap 23.7; 2 Sam 22
trick 19.17; 2 Kgs 10.19
trouble 26.24; 30.6
understand Deut 32.29; 2 Sam 3.37
unleavened Josh 5.11; 2 Kgs 23.
urge Judg 19.7; 1 Kgs 21.25
vow 19.6; 2 Sam 4.9
weak 14.24; 30.21
yeast Judg 6.19; 1 Chr 23.29

[v] he forced...Israel; *or* he put to death the fortune-tellers and mediums in Israel.

28.3: Lev 20.27; Deut 18.10–11; 1 Sam 25.1 **28.6:** Num 27.21 **28.17:** 1 Sam 15.28

18 You **disobeyed** the LORD's **command**
and did not completely **destroy** the
Amalekites and all they had. That is why
the LORD is doing this to you now. 19 He
will hand you and Israel over to the
Philistines. Tomorrow you and your sons
will join me, and the LORD will also hand
the army of Israel over to the Philistines."
20 At once Saul fell down and lay
stretched out on the ground, **terrified** by
what Samuel had said. He was **weak**,
because he had not eaten anything all
day and all night. 21 The woman went
over to him and saw that he was **terri-**
fied, so she said to him, "Please, sir, I
risked my **life** by doing what you asked.
22 Now please do what I ask. Let me
prepare some food for you. You must eat
so that you will be **strong enough** to
travel."
23 Saul **refused** and said he would not
eat anything. But his officers also **urged**
him to eat. He finally gave in, got up
from the ground, and sat on the bed.
24 The woman quickly killed a calf which
she had been fattening. Then she took
some flour, prepared it, and baked some
bread without yeast. 25 She set the food
before Saul and his officers, and they ate
it. And they left that same night.

David Is Rejected by the Philistines

29 The Philistines brought all their
troops together at Aphek, while
the Israelites camped at the spring in the
Valley of Jezreel. 2 The five Philistine
kings marched out with their units of a
hundred and of a thousand men; David
and his men marched in the rear with
King Achish. 3 The Philistine commanders saw them and asked, "What are
these **Hebrews** doing here?"
Achish answered, "This is David, an
official of King Saul of Israel. He has
been with me for quite a long time now.
He has done nothing I can find **fault** with
since the day he came over to me."
4 But the Philistine commanders were
angry with Achish and said to him, "Send
that fellow back to the town you gave
him. Don't let him go into battle with us;
he might **turn** against us during the fighting. What better way is there for him to
win back his **master's favour** than by the
death of our men? 5 After all, this is
David, the one about whom the women
sang, as they danced, 'Saul has killed
thousands, but David has killed tens of
thousands.'"
6 Achish called David and said to him,
"I **swear** by the living GOD of Israel that
you have been **loyal** to me; and I would
be **pleased** to let you go with me and
fight in this battle. I have not found any
fault in you from the day you came over
to me. But the other kings don't **approve**
of you. 7 So go back home in **peace**, and
don't do anything that would **displease**
them."
8 David answered, "What have I done
wrong, sir? If, as you say, you haven't
found any **fault** in me since the day I
started **serving** you, why shouldn't I go
with you, my **master** and king, and fight
your **enemies**?"
9 "I **agree**," Achish replied. "I
consider you as **loyal** as an **angel of God**.
But the other kings have said that you
can't go with us into battle. 10 So then,
David, tomorrow morning all of you who
left Saul and came over to me will have
to get up early and leave as soon as it's
light."
11 So David and his men started out
early the following morning to go back to
Philistia, and the Philistines went on to
Jezreel.

The War against the Amalekites

30 Two days later David and his
men arrived back at Ziklag. The
Amalekites had raided southern Judah
and attacked Ziklag. They had burnt
down the town 2 and captured all the
women; they had not killed anyone, but
had taken everyone with them when
they left. 3 When David and his men
arrived, they found that the town had
been burnt down and that their wives,
sons, and daughters had been carried
away. 4 David and his men started crying
and did not stop until they were completely exhausted. 5 Even David's two
wives, Ahinoam and Abigail, had been
taken away.
6 David was now in great **trouble**,
because his men were all very **bitter**
about losing their children, and they
were **threatening** to stone him; but the
LORD his God gave him **courage**. 7 David
said to the **priest** Abiathar son of Ahimelech, "Bring me the **ephod**," and Abiathar brought it to him. 8 David asked the
LORD, "Shall I go after those raiders?
And will I catch them?"
He answered, "Go after them; you will
catch them and **rescue** the **captives**."
9 So David and his six hundred men
started out, and when they arrived at the
brook of Besor, some of them stayed
there. 10 David continued on his way with
four hundred men; the other two hundred men were too tired to cross the

agree 20.35; 30.24
angel Judg 13.3; 2 Sam 14.17
anger 20.7; 2 Sam 6.7
approve Lev 10.19; 1 Kgs 1.27
death (1) 26.10; 2 Sam 1.1
displease 15.19; 1 Kgs 16.19
enemy 28.16; 30.26
fault [3] Josh 2.19; 2 Sam 3.8
favour 20.8; 2 Sam 7.29
Hebrew 14.11; 2 Kgs 18.26
light (1) Ruth 3.14; 2 Sam 22.29
loyal [2] 20.14; 2 Sam 2.5
master [2] 26.15; 30.13
peace 16.4; 2 Sam 10.19
please 18.5; 2 Sam 3.36
serve 27.12; 2 Sam 3.8
swear 26.16; 2 Sam 2.27
turn 26.19; 2 Sam 1.7
win 19.5; 2 Sam 3.12
wrong 26.21; 2 Sam 7.14

agree 29.9; 2 Sam 3.12
bitter 15.32; 2 Sam 2.26
captive Judg 5.12; Neh 7.5
celebrate 20.29; 2 Sam 6.12
courage Judg 7.11; 2 Sam 7.27
enemy 29.8; 31.3
ephod (1) 23.6; 1 Chr 15.27
escape 27.1; 2 Sam 1.3
flock 25.16; 1 Kgs 20.27
friend 27.5; 2 Sam 3.8
get away 24.19; 2 Sam 15.14
master [3] 29.4; 2 Sam 9.9
message 25.9; 2 Sam 2.5
name (2) (name of God, of Jesus) 24.21; 2 Sam 6.2
priest 23.9; 2 Sam 8.17
promise 28.10; 2 Sam 3.9
rescue [2] 17.35; 2 Sam 3.18
safe 27.1; 2 Sam 3.21
scatter 11.11; 2 Sam 17.19
share [2] 2.28; 2 Sam 19.29
slave 25.10; 2 Sam 7.23
strength 2.9; 2 Sam 15.12
threat 14.27; 2 Sam 14.10
trouble 28.15; 2 Sam 12.11
victory 23.4; 2 Sam 1.1
weak 28.20; 2 Sam 3.1

28.18: 1 Sam 15.3–9 **29.5:** 1 Sam 18.7, 21.11 **30.5:** 1 Sam 25.42–43 **30.7:** 1 Sam 22.20–23

worthless 15.9;
2 Sam 20.1

brook and so stayed behind. 11 The men
with David found an Egyptian boy out in
the country and brought him to David.
They gave him some food and water,
12 some dried figs, and two bunches of
raisins. After he had eaten, his **strength**
returned; he had not had anything to eat
or drink for three full days. 13 David
asked him, "Who is your **master**, and
where are you from?"

"I am an Egyptian, the **slave** of an
Amalekite," he answered. "My **master**
left me behind three days ago because I
was ill. 14 We had raided the territory of
the Cherethites in the southern part of
Judah and the territory of the clan of
Caleb, and we burnt down Ziklag."

15 "Will you lead me to those
raiders?" David asked him.

He answered, "I will if you **promise** me
in God's **name** that you will not kill me or
hand me over to my **master**." 16 And he
led David to them.

The raiders were **scattered** all over
the place, eating, drinking, and **celebrating** because of the enormous amount
of loot they had captured from Philistia
and Judah. 17 At dawn the next day David
attacked them and fought until evening.
Except for four hundred young men who
mounted camels and **got away**, none of
them **escaped**. 18 David **rescued** everyone
and everything the Amalekites had
taken, including his two wives; 19 nothing
at all was missing. David got back all his
men's sons and daughters, and all the
loot the Amalekites had taken. 20 He also
recovered all the **flocks** and herds; his
men drove all the livestock in front of
them[w] and said, "This belongs to
David!"

21 Then David went back to the two
hundred men who had been too **weak** to
go with him and had stayed behind at the
brook of Besor. They came forward to
meet David and his men, and David went
up to them and greeted them warmly.
22 But some mean and **worthless** men
who had gone with David said, "They
didn't go with us, and so we won't give
them any of the loot. They can take their
wives and children and go away."

23 But David answered, "My brothers,
you can't do this with what the LORD has
given us! He kept us **safe** and gave us
victory over the raiders. 24 No one can
agree with what you say! All must **share**
alike: whoever stays behind with the
supplies gets the same **share** as the one
who goes into battle." 25 David made this
a rule, and it has been followed in Israel
ever since.

26 When David returned to Ziklag, he
sent part of the loot to his **friends**, the
leaders of Judah, with the **message**,
"Here is a present for you from the loot
we took from the LORD's **enemies**." 27 He
sent it to the people in Bethel, to the
people in Ramah in the southern part of
Judah, and to the people in the towns of
Jattir, 28 Aroer, Siphmoth, Eshtemoa,
29 and Racal; to the clan of Jerahmeel, to
the Kenites, 30 and to the people in the
towns of Hormah, Borashan, Athach,
31 and Hebron. He sent it to all the places
where he and his men had roamed.

The Death of Saul and His Sons

(1 Chr 10.1–12)

31 The Philistines fought a battle
against the Israelites on Mount
Gilboa. Many Israelites were killed
there, and the rest of them, including
King Saul and his sons, **fled**. 2 But the
Philistines caught up with them and
killed three of Saul's sons, Jonathan,
Abinadab, and Malchishua. 3 The fighting
was heavy round Saul, and he himself
was hit by **enemy** arrows and **badly**
wounded. 4 He said to the young man
carrying his weapons, "Draw your sword
and kill me, so that these **godless** Philistines won't gloat over me and kill me."
But the young man was too **terrified** to do
it. So Saul took his own sword and threw
himself on it. 5 The young man saw that
Saul was **dead**, so he too threw himself on
his own sword and died with Saul. 6 And
that is how Saul, his three sons, and the
young man died; all of Saul's men died
that day. 7 When the Israelites on the
other side of the Valley of Jezreel and
east of the River Jordan heard that the
Israelite army had **fled** and that Saul and
his sons had been killed, they **abandoned**
their towns and **fled**. Then the Philistines
came and occupied them.

8 The day after the battle the Philistines went to plunder the corpses, and
they found the **bodies** of Saul and his
three sons lying on Mount Gilboa. 9 They
cut off Saul's head, **stripped** off his
armour, and sent messengers with them
throughout Philistia to tell the **good news**
to their **idols** and to their people. 10 Then
they put his weapons in the **temple** of the
goddess Astarte, and they nailed his **body**
to the wall of the city of Beth Shan.

11 When the people of Jabesh in

abandon 28.15;
2 Sam 1.27
bad 15.23; 2 Sam 1.9
body [3] 17.44;
2 Sam 2.32
dead 25.22; 2 Sam 1.
enemy 30.26;
2 Sam 1.6
fast (2) 7.6;
2 Sam 1.12
flee [3] 27.4;
2 Sam 2.8
goddess 7.3;
1 Kgs 11.5
godless 2 Sam 23.6
Good News
2 Sam 4.10
idol 19.13; 2 Sam 5.2
strip (1) Judg 14.19;
2 Sam 23.10
**temple (2) (of other
gods)** 5.2; 1 Kgs 16.3
terrify 28.5;
2 Kgs 3.27

[w] *Probable text* his men...front of them; *Hebrew unclear.*

Gilead heard what the Philistines had
done to Saul, [12]the bravest men started
out and marched all night to Beth Shan.
They took down the **bodies** of Saul and
his sons from the wall, brought them
back to Jabesh, and burnt them there.
[13]Then they took the bones and buried
them under the tamarisk-tree in the
town, and **fasted** for seven days.

THE SECOND BOOK OF
SAMUEL

INTRODUCTION

Second Samuel, the sequel to *First Samuel,* is the history of David's reign as king, first over Judah in the south (chapters 1–4), and then over the whole nation, including Israel in the north (chapters 5–24). It is a vivid account of how David, in order to extend his kingdom and consolidate his position, had to struggle with enemies within the nation as well as with foreign powers. David is shown to be a man of deep faith and devotion to God, and one who was able to win the loyalty of his people. Yet he is also shown as being sometimes ruthless, and willing to commit terrible sins to serve his own desires and ambitions. But when he is confronted with his sins, by the Lord's prophet Nathan, he confesses them and accepts the punishment that God sends.

The life and achievements of David impressed the people of Israel so much that in later times of national distress, when they longed for another king, it was for one who would be "a son of David," that is, a descendant of David who would be like him.

Outline of Contents

David Learns of Saul's Death

1 After Saul's **death** David came back
from his **victory** over the Amalekites and stayed in Ziklag for two days.
2 The next day a young man arrived from
Saul's camp. To show his **grief**, he had
torn his clothes and put earth on his
head. He went to David and **bowed** to the
ground in **respect**. 3 David asked him,
"Where have you come from?"
"I have **escaped** from the Israelite
camp," he answered.
4 "Tell me what happened," David
said.
"Our army ran away from the battle,"
he replied, "and many of our men were
killed. Saul and his son Jonathan were
also killed."
5 "How do you know that Saul and
Jonathan are **dead**?" David asked him.
6 He answered, "I happened to be on
Mount Gilboa, and I saw that Saul was
leaning on his spear and that the chariots
and horsemen of the **enemy** were closing
in on him. 7 Then he **turned** round, saw
me, and called to me. I answered, 'Yes,
sir!' 8 He asked who I was, and I told him
that I was an Amalekite. 9 Then he said,
'Come here and kill me! I have been
badly wounded, and I'm about to die.'
10 So I went up to him and killed him, because I knew that he would die anyway
as soon as he fell. Then I took the **crown**
from his head and the bracelet from his
arm, and I have brought them to you,
sir."
11 David tore his clothes in **sorrow**,
and all his men did the same. 12 They
grieved and **mourned** and **fasted** until
evening for Saul and Jonathan and for
Israel, the people of the LORD, because so
many had been killed in battle.
13 David asked the young man who
had brought him the news, "Where are
you from?"
He answered, "I'm an Amalekite, but I
live in your country."
14 David asked him, "How is it that
you **dared** to kill the LORD's **chosen**
king?" 15 Then David called one of his
men and said, "Kill him!" The man
struck the Amalekite and **mortally**
wounded him, 16 and David said to the
Amalekite, "You brought this on yourself.
You **condemned** yourself when you
admitted that you killed the one whom
the LORD **chose** to be king."

1.6-10: 1 Sam 31.1-6; 1 Chr 10.1-6

David's Lament for Saul and Jonathan

17 David sang this lament for Saul and

abandon 1 Sam 31.7; 1 Kgs 6.13
admit (1) Num 14.40; 2 Chr 12.6
announce Judg 7.3; 1 Kgs 1.24
bad 1 Sam 31.3; 1 Kgs 14.6
barren Judg 1.16; Job 3.7
bow (2) 1 Sam 28.14; 9.6
choose [2] 1 Sam 26.9; 3.39
condemn Ruth 1.21; 14.13
crown 12.30
dare 1 Sam 17.10; 17.17
dead [3] 1 Sam 31.5; 2.7
deadly Job 18.13
dear [2] 1 Sam 25.8; Ps 78.68
death (1) [2] 1 Sam 29.4; 4.4
disgrace 1 Sam 20.30; 6.22
enemy [2] 1 Sam 31.3; 3.18
escape 1 Sam 30.17; 15.14
fast (2) 1 Sam 31.13; 12.22
glad 1 Sam 19.5; 1 Chr 16.10
grief [3] 1 Sam 20.41; 15.30
life (1) 1 Sam 28.21; 19.5
love [2] 1 Sam 20.17; 11.4

mercy Judg 6.13; 12.22
might 1 Sam 12.7; 6.
mortal Gen 6.3; Job 21.4
mourn [2] 1 Sam 28.3; 3.31
pagan Deut 31.16; 1 Kgs 13.2
rejoice Gen 31.27; 1 Chr 16.10
respect 1 Sam 28.14 9.6
rich 1 Sam 25.2; 12.1
sorrow Judg 11.35; 13.31
strike [2] 1 Sam 26.8 2.23
strong 1 Sam 28.22; 2.7
teach 1 Sam 12.23; 7.21
turn 1 Sam 29.4; 6.10
useless 1 Sam 15.9; Job 13.12
victory 1 Sam 30.23; 5.19
wonder (1) [2] Judg 13.18; 7.23

his son Jonathan, [18] and ordered it[a] to be
taught to the people of Judah. (It is recorded in *The Book of Jashar*.)

[19] "On the hills of Israel our leaders are
dead!
The bravest of our soldiers have
fallen!
[20] Do not **announce** it in Gath
or in the streets of Ashkelon.
Do not make the women of Philistia
glad;
do not let the daughters of **pagans**
rejoice.

[21] "May no rain or dew fall on Gilboa's
hills;
may its fields be always **barren**!
For the shields of the brave lie there in
disgrace;
the shield of Saul is no longer
polished with oil.
[22] Jonathan's bow was **deadly**,
the sword of Saul was **merciless**,
striking down the **mighty**, killing the
enemy.

[23] "Saul and Jonathan, so **wonderful** and
dear;
together in **life**, together in **death**;
swifter than eagles, **stronger** than
lions.

[24] "Women of Israel, **mourn** for Saul!
He clothed you in **rich** scarlet
dresses
and adorned you with jewels and
gold.

[25] "The brave soldiers have fallen,
they were killed in battle.
Jonathan lies **dead** in the hills.

[26] "I **grieve** for you, my brother
Jonathan;
how **dear** you were to me!
How **wonderful** was your **love** for me,
better even than the **love** of women.

[27] "The brave soldiers have fallen,
their weapons **abandoned** and
useless."

David Is Made King of Judah

2 After this, David asked the LORD,
"Shall I go and take **control** of one of
the towns of Judah?"
"Yes," the LORD answered.
"Which one?" David asked.
"Hebron," the LORD said. [2] So David
went to Hebron, taking with him his two
wives: Ahinoam, who was from Jezreel,
and Abigail, Nabal's **widow**, who was
from Carmel. [3] He also took his men and
their families, and they settled in the
towns round Hebron. [4] Then the men of
Judah came to Hebron and **anointed**
David as king of Judah.
When David heard that the people of
Jabesh in Gilead had buried Saul, [5] he
sent some men there with the **message**:
"May the LORD **bless** you for showing
your **loyalty** to your king by burying him.
[6] And now may the LORD be **kind** and
faithful to you. I too will treat you well
because of what you have done. [7] Be
strong and brave! Saul your king is **dead**,
and the people of Judah have **anointed**
me as their king."

Ishbosheth Is Made King of Israel

8 The commander of Saul's army,
Abner son of Ner, had **fled** with Saul's son
Ishbosheth across the Jordan to
Mahanaim. [9] There Abner made Ish-
bosheth king of the territories of Gilead,
Asher,[b] Jezreel, Ephraim, and Benjamin,
and indeed over all Israel. [10] He was forty
years old when he was made king of
Israel, and he ruled for two years.
But the tribe of Judah was **loyal** to
David, [11] and he ruled in Hebron over
Judah for seven and a half years.

War between Israel and Judah

12 Abner and the officials of Ishbosheth went from Mahanaim to the city
of Gibeon. [13] Joab, whose mother was
Zeruiah, and David's other officials met
them at the pool, where they all sat
down, one group on one side of the pool
and the other group on the opposite side.
[14] Abner said to Joab, "Let's get some of
the young men from each side to fight an
armed contest."
"All right," Joab answered.
15 So twelve men, **representing** Ishbosheth and the tribe of Benjamin,
fought twelve of David's men. [16] Each
man caught his opponent by the head
and plunged his sword into his opponent's side, so that all twenty-four of
them fell down **dead** together. And so
that place in Gibeon is called "Field of
Swords."
17 Then a **furious** battle broke out, and
Abner and the Israelites were defeated
by David's men. [18] The three sons of
Zeruiah were there: Joab, Abishai, and
Asahel. Asahel, who could run as fast as a
wild deer, [19] started chasing Abner,

anoint [2] 1 Sam 16.3; 5.3
bitter 1 Sam 30.6; 13.36
bless 1 Sam 26.25; 6.11
body 1 Sam 31.8; 18.17
control 1 Sam 19.9; 8.1

dead [3] 1.5; 3.9
faithful 1 Sam 26.23; 15.20
flee 1 Sam 31.1; 4.3
force (1) 1 Sam 28.3; 12.31
fury 1 Sam 20.30; 3.8
kind 1 Sam 25.8; 9.1
loyal [2] 1 Sam 29.6; 3.6
message 1 Sam 30.26; 11.5
represent Num 17.3; 15.3
strike 1.15; 3.9
strong 1.23; 3.1
swear 1 Sam 29.6; 11.11
tomb 1 Sam 10.2; 4.12
widow 1 Sam 27.3; 3.3

[a] *One ancient translation* it; *Hebrew* the bow. [b] *One ancient translation* Asher; *Hebrew* Assyria.

1.18: Josh 10.13 **2.2:** 1 Sam 25.42–43 **2.4:** 1 Sam 31.11–13

running straight for him. 20 Abner looked
back and said, "Is that you, Asahel?"
"Yes," he answered.
21 "Stop chasing me!" Abner said.
"Run after one of the soldiers and take
what he has." But Asahel kept on chasing
him. 22 Once more Abner said to him,
"Stop chasing me! Why **force** me to kill
you? How could I face your brother
Joab?" 23 But Asahel would not give up;
so Abner, with a backward thrust[c] of his
spear, **struck** him through the belly so
that the spear came out at his back.
Asahel dropped to the ground **dead**, and
everyone who came to the place where
he was lying stopped and stood there.
24 But Joab and Abishai started out
after Abner, and at sunset they came to
the hill of Ammah, which is to the east of
Giah on the road to the wilderness of
Gibeon. 25 The men from the tribe of
Benjamin gathered round Abner again
and took their stand on the top of a hill.
26 Abner called out to Joab, "Do we have
to go on fighting for ever? Can't you see
that in the end there will be nothing but
bitterness? We are your fellow-countrymen. How long will it be before you order
your men to stop chasing us?"
27 "I **swear** by the living God," Joab
answered, "that if you had not spoken,
my men would have kept on chasing you
until tomorrow morning." 28 Then Joab
blew the trumpet as a signal for his men
to stop pursuing the Israelites; and so the
fighting stopped.
29 Abner and his men marched
through the Jordan Valley all that night;
they crossed the River Jordan, and after
marching all the next morning, they
arrived back at Mahanaim.
30 When Joab gave up the chase, he
gathered all his men and found that nineteen of them were missing, in addition to
Asahel. 31 David's men had killed 360 of
Abner's men from the tribe of Benjamin.
32 Joab and his men took Asahel's **body**
and buried it in the family **tomb** at
Bethlehem. Then they marched all night
and at dawn arrived back at Hebron.

3 The fighting between the forces
supporting Saul's family and those
supporting David went on for a long
time. As David became **stronger and
stronger**, his opponents became **weaker
and weaker**.

David's Sons

2 The following six sons, in the order
of their **birth**, were born to David at
Hebron: Amnon, whose mother was
Ahinoam, from Jezreel; 3 Chileab, whose
mother was Abigail, Nabal's **widow**, from
Carmel; Absalom, whose mother was
Maacah, the daughter of King Talmai of
Geshur; 4 Adonijah, whose mother was
Haggith; Shephatiah, whose mother was
Abital; 5 Ithream, whose mother was
Eglah. All of these sons were born in
Hebron.

Abner Joins David

6 As the fighting continued between
David's forces and the forces **loyal** to
Saul's family, Abner became more and
more **powerful** among Saul's **followers**.
7 One day Ishbosheth son of Saul
accused Abner of sleeping with Saul's
concubine Rizpah, the daughter of Aiah.
8 This made Abner **furious**. "Do you think
that I would **betray** Saul? Do you really
think I'm **serving** Judah?" he exclaimed.
"From the very first I have been **loyal** to
the **cause** of your father Saul, his
brothers, and his **friends**, and I have
saved you from being defeated by David;
yet today you find **fault** with me about a
woman! 9-10 The LORD **promised** David
that he would take the kingdom away
from Saul and his descendants and would
make David king of both Israel and
Judah, from one end of the country to the
other. Now may God **strike** me **dead** if I
don't make this come **true**!" 11 Ishbosheth
was so **afraid** of Abner that he could not
say a **word**.
12 Abner sent messengers to David,
who at that time was at Hebron,[d] to say,
"Who is going to rule this land? Make an
agreement with me, and I will **help** you
win all Israel over to your side."
13 "Good!" David answered. "I will
make an **agreement** with you on one condition: you must bring Saul's daughter
Michal to me when you come to see me."
14 And David also sent messengers to Ishbosheth to say, "Give me back my wife
Michal. I paid a hundred Philistine foreskins in order to marry her." 15 So Ishbosheth took her away from her husband
Paltiel son of Laish. 16 Paltiel followed
her all the way to the town of Bahurim,
crying as he went. But when Abner said,
"Go back home," he did.
17 Abner went to the leaders of Israel
and said to them, "For a long time you
have wanted David to be your king.
18 Now here is your chance. **Remember**
that the LORD has said, 'I will use my **servant** David to **rescue my people** Israel

accept 1 Sam 25.27; 16.23
accuse 1 Sam 22.15; 1 Kgs 8.31
afraid 1 Sam 28.13; 4.1
agree [3] 1 Sam 30.24; 23.5
betray 19.26
bind Num 15.15; 2 Chr 2.16
birth 1 Sam 4.19; 1 Kgs 3.17
cause (2) Ex 23.8; 1 Kgs 1.7
choose 1.14; 6.21
concubine Judg 2 5.13
crime [2] 1 Sam 26.18; 13.16
dead [2] 2.7; 9.8
deceive Josh 9.4; 1 Kgs 22.20
deserve 1 Sam 26. 19.28
disease Deut 32.2 1 Kgs 8.37
enemy 1.6; 4.8
enough 1 Sam 28. 5.8
fault 1 Sam 29.3; 22.24
feast 1 Sam 25.8; 1 Kgs 1.9
fit (1) 1 Sam 25.36 13.27
follower Deut 28. 15.12
fool 1 Sam 26.21; 6
friend 1 Sam 30.2 10.2
fury 2.17; 6.8
God's people 1 Sam 17.47; 5.2
grave Num 33.15; 17.23
guarantee [3] Esth 3.9
help 1 Sam 25.21;
innocent 1 Sam 1 4.11
loyal [2] 2.5; 9.3
Majesty 1 Sam 26. 4.8
mourn 1.12; 11.26
please [2] 1 Sam 29.6; 11.27
power 1 Sam 26.8; 22.18
promise [2] 1 Sam 30.15; 5.2
punish [2] 1 Sam 28.10; 6.8
remember 1 Sam 12.24; 11.21
rescue 1 Sam 30.8; 7.6
revenge 1 Sam 25 4.8
sackcloth Gen 37. 21.10
safe [3] 1 Sam 30.2 7.1
save 1 Sam 24.15;
servant 1 Sam 28. 6.20
serve 1 Sam 29.8; 12.20
solemn 1 Sam 14.2 1 Kgs 1.13
strike [2] 2.23; 19.1
strong 2.7; 5.10
subject (1) Judg 3. 8.2
true 1 Sam 20.2; 1 Kgs 2.27
understand 1 Sam 28.1; 12.21
violent 1 Sam 2.33; 7.10
weak [2] 1 Sam 30. 2 Kgs 19.3
weep [2] Gen 45.15 12.21
widow 2.2; 14.5
win [2] 1 Sam 29.4; 15.6
word (1) 1 Sam 21.12; 10.5

[c] *Probable text* with a backward thrust; *Hebrew unclear.*
[d] *One ancient translation* at Hebron; *Hebrew* where he (Abner) was.

3.9-10: 1 Sam 15.28 **3.14:** 1 Sam 18.27

from the Philistines and from all their
other **enemies**.’ ” 19 Abner spoke also to
the people of the tribe of Benjamin and
then went to Hebron to tell David what
the people of Benjamin and of Israel had
agreed to do.

20 When Abner came to David at
Hebron with twenty men, David gave a
feast for them. 21 Abner told David, “I will
go now and **win** all Israel over to Your
Majesty. They will **accept** you as king,
and then you will get what you have
wanted and will rule over the whole
land.” David gave Abner a **guarantee** of
safety and sent him on his way.

Abner Is Murdered

22 Later on Joab and David’s other
officials returned from a raid, bringing a
large amount of loot with them. Abner,
however, was no longer there at Hebron
with David, because David had sent him
away with a **guarantee of safety**. 23 When
Joab and his men arrived, he was told
that Abner had come to King David and
had been sent away with a **guarantee** of
safety. 24 So Joab went to the king and
said to him, “What have you done?
Abner came to you—why did you let him
go like that? 25 He came here to **deceive**
you and to find out everything you do and
everywhere you go. Surely you know
that!”

26 After leaving David, Joab sent
messengers to get Abner, and they
brought him back from the well of Sirah;
but David knew nothing about it. 27 When
Abner arrived in Hebron, Joab took him
aside at the gate, as though he wanted to
speak privately with him, and there he
stabbed him in the belly. And so Abner
was murdered because he had killed
Joab’s brother Asahel. 28 When David
heard the news, he said, “The LORD
knows that my **subjects** and I are completely **innocent** of the murder of Abner.
29 May the **punishment** for it fall on Joab
and all his family! In every generation
may there be some man in his family
who has gonorrhoea or a dreaded **skin
disease** or is **fit** only to do a woman’s
work or is killed in battle or hasn’t
enough to eat!” 30 So Joab and his brother
Abishai took **revenge** on Abner for killing
their brother Asahel in the battle at
Gibeon.

Abner Is Buried

31 Then David ordered Joab and his
men to tear their clothes, wear **sackcloth**, and **mourn** for Abner. And at the
funeral King David himself walked
behind the coffin. 32 Abner was buried at
Hebron, and the king **wept** aloud at the
grave, and so did all the people. 33 David
sang this lament for Abner:

“Why did Abner have to die like a
    fool?
34 His hands were not tied,
  And his feet were not **bound**;
  He died like someone killed by
    criminals!”

And the people **wept** for him again.

35 All day long the people tried to get
David to eat something, but he made a
solemn promise, “May God **strike** me
dead if I eat anything before the day is
over!” 36 They took note of this and were
pleased. Indeed, everything the king did
pleased the people. 37 All David’s people
and all the people in Israel **understood**
that the king had no part in the murder
of Abner. 38 The king said to his officials,
“Don’t you realize that this day a great
leader in Israel has died? 39 Even though
I am the king **chosen** by God, I feel **weak**
today. These sons of Zeruiah are too
violent for me. May the LORD **punish**
these **criminals** as they **deserve**!”

Ishbosheth Is Murdered

4 When Saul’s son Ishbosheth heard
that Abner had been killed in
Hebron, he was **afraid**, and all the people
of Israel were alarmed. 2 Ishbosheth had
two officers who were leaders of raiding
parties, Baanah and Rechab, sons of
Rimmon, from Beeroth in the tribe of
Benjamin. (Beeroth is counted as part of
Benjamin. 3 Its original inhabitants had
fled to Gittaim, where they have lived
ever since.)

4 Another descendant of Saul was
Jonathan’s son Mephibosheth, who was
five years old when Saul and Jonathan
were killed. When the news about their
death came from the city of Jezreel, his
nurse picked him up and **fled**; but she
was in such a hurry that she dropped
him, and he became **crippled**.

5 Rechab and Baanah set out for Ishbosheth’s house and arrived there about
noon, while he was taking his midday
rest. 6 The woman at the door had
become drowsy while she was sifting
wheat and had fallen asleep, so Rechab
and Baanah slipped in.[e] 7 Once inside,
they went to Ishbosheth’s bedroom,
where he was **sound asleep**, and killed
him. Then they cut off his head, took it

afraid 3.11; 6.9
cripple Josh 11.6; 5.6
danger 1 Sam 20.21; 22.6
death (1) [2] 1.1; 12.10
death (3) (to death) 1 Sam 22.19; 8.2
enemy 3.18; 5.20
evil 1 Sam 25.28; 12.9
flee [2] 2.8; 5.21
Good News [2] 1 Sam 31.9; 18.19
innocent 3.28; 14.9
Majesty 3.21; 9.11
present (1) Josh 8.31; 1 Kgs 3.16
rest (1) Ruth 3.18; 11.8
revenge [2] 3.30; 1 Kgs 2.5
reward 1 Sam 26.23; 18.22
save 3.8; 14.16
sound (2) 1 Sam 26.12; Neh 9.13
tomb 2.32; 1 Kgs 14.31
vow 1 Sam 28.10; Job 22.27
worse 1 Sam 23.3; 1 Kgs 17.17

[e] *Verse 6 follows one ancient translation; Hebrew* They went on into the house carrying wheat, and struck him in the belly. Then Rechab and his brother Baanah escaped.

4.4: 2 Sam 9.3

with them, and walked all night through the Jordan Valley. 8 They **presented** the head to King David at Hebron and said to him, "Here is the head of Ishbosheth, the son of your **enemy** Saul, who tried to kill you. Today the LORD has allowed Your **Majesty** to take **revenge** on Saul and his descendants."

9 David answered them, "I make a **vow** by the living LORD, who has **saved** me from all **dangers**! 10 The messenger who came to me at Ziklag and told me of Saul's **death** thought he was bringing **good news**. I seized him and had him put **to death**. That was the **reward** I gave him for his **good news**! 11 How much **worse** it will be for **evil** men who murder an **innocent** man asleep in his own house! I will now take **revenge** on you for murdering him and will wipe you off the face of the earth!" 12 David gave the order, and his soldiers killed Rechab and Baanah and cut off their hands and feet, which they hung up near the pool in Hebron. They took Ishbosheth's head and buried it in Abner's **tomb** there at Hebron.

David Becomes King of Israel and Judah

(1 Chr 11.1–9; 14.1–7)

5 Then all the tribes of Israel came to David at Hebron and said to him, "We are your own **flesh and blood**. 2 In the past, even when Saul was still our king, you led the people of Israel in battle, and the LORD **promised** you that you would lead **his people** and be their ruler." 3 So all the leaders of Israel came to King David at Hebron. He made a **sacred** alliance with them, they **anointed** him, and he became king of Israel. 4 David was thirty years old when he became king, and he ruled for forty years. 5 He ruled in Hebron over Judah for seven and a half years, and in Jerusalem over all Israel and Judah for thirty-three years.

6 The time came when King David and his men set out to attack Jerusalem. The Jebusites, who lived there, thought that David would not be able to **conquer** the city, and so they said to him, "You will never get in here; even the **blind** and the **crippled** could keep you out." 7 (But David did capture their fortress of Zion, and it became known as "David's City.")

8 That day David said to his men, "Does anybody here **hate** the Jebusites as much as I do? **Enough** to kill them? Then go up through the water tunnel and attack those **poor blind cripples**." (That is why it is said, "The **blind** and the **crippled** cannot enter the LORD's house.")[f]

9 After capturing the fortress, David lived in it and named it "David's City." He built the city round it, starting at the place where land was filled in on the east side of the hill. 10 He grew **stronger** all the time, because the LORD God **Almighty** was with him.

11 King Hiram of Tyre sent a trade mission to David; he **provided** him with cedar logs and with carpenters and stone-masons to build a palace. 12 And so David realized that the LORD had **established** him as king of Israel and was making his kingdom **prosperous** for the **sake of his people**.

13 After moving from Hebron to Jerusalem, David took more **concubines** and wives, and had more sons and daughters. 14 The following children were born to him in Jerusalem: Shammua, Shobab, Nathan, Solomon, 15 Ibhar, Elishua, Nepheg, Japhia, 16 Elishama, Eliada, and Eliphelet.

Victory over the Philistines

(1 Chr 14.8–17)

17 The Philistines were told that David had been made king of Israel, so their army set out to capture him. When David heard of it, he went down to a fortified place. 18 The Philistines arrived at the Valley of Rephaim and occupied it. 19 David asked the LORD, "Shall I attack the Philistines? Will you give me the **victory**?"

"Yes, attack!" the LORD answered. "I will give you the **victory**!"

20 So David went to Baal Perazim and there he defeated the Philistines. He said, "The LORD has broken through my **enemies** like a **flood**." And so that place is called Baal Perazim.[g] 21 When the Philistines **fled**, they left their **idols** behind, and David and his men carried them away.

22 Then the Philistines went back to the Valley of Rephaim and occupied it again. 23 Once more David **consulted** the LORD, who answered, "Don't attack them from here, but go round and get ready to attack them from the other side, near the balsam-trees. 24 When you hear the sound of marching in the tree-tops, then attack because I will be marching ahead of you to defeat the Philistine army." 25 David did what the LORD had **commanded**, and

Almighty 1 Sam 17.45; 6.2
anoint 2.4; 19.10
blind [3] 1 Sam 4.15; 1 Kgs 14.4
blood 1 Sam 14.32; 19.12
command 1 Sam 28.18; 9.11
concubine 3.7; 15.16
conquer 1 Sam 12.9; 8.11
consult 1 Sam 28.7; 21.1
cripple [3] 4.4; 8.4
enemy 4.8; 7.1
enough 3.29; 8.4
establish Deut 19.14; 1 Kgs 2.12
flee 4.3; 10.13
flesh Judg 9.2; 19.12
flood Judg 5.21; 1 Chr 14.11
God's people [2] 3.18; 6.21
hate 1 Sam 27.12; 13.15
idol 1 Sam 31.9; 12.30
poor 1 Sam 18.23; 12.1
promise 3.9; 7.10
prosper Josh 1.8; 1 Kgs 1.37
provide Judg 21.7; 9.10
sacred 1 Sam 28.10; 6.16
sake Gen 18.26; 9.1
strong 3.1; 7.12
victory [2] 1.1; 8.6

[f] *Verse 8 in Hebrew is unclear.*
[g] BAAL PERAZIM: *This name in Hebrew means "Lord of the Break-through."*

4.10: 2 Sam 1.1–16 **5.4–5:** 1 Kgs 2.11; 1 Chr 3.4, 29.27 **5.6:** Josh 15.63; Judg 1.21

was able to drive the Philistines back from Geba all the way to Gezer.

The Covenant Box Is Brought to Jerusalem
(1 Chr 13.1–14; 15.25—16.6, 43)

6 Once more David called together the **best** soldiers in Israel, a total of thirty thousand men, 2 and led them to Baalah[h] in Judah, in order to bring from there God's **Covenant Box**, bearing the **name of the** LORD **Almighty**, who is **enthroned** above the winged **creatures**.[x] 3 They took it from Abinadab's home on the hill and placed it on a **new** cart. Uzzah and Ahio, sons of Abinadab, were **guiding** the cart, 4 with Ahio walking in front. 5 David and all the Israelites were dancing and singing with all their **might**[i] to **honour** the LORD. They were playing harps, lyres, drums, rattles, and cymbals.

6 As they came to the threshing-place of Nacon, the oxen **stumbled**, and Uzzah reached out and took hold of the **Covenant Box**. 7 At once the LORD God became **angry** with Uzzah and killed him because of his irreverence.[j] Uzzah died there beside the **Covenant Box**, 8 and so that place has been called Perez Uzzah[k] ever since. David was **furious** because the LORD had **punished** Uzzah in **anger**.

9 Then David was **afraid** of the LORD and said, "How can I take the **Covenant Box** with me now?" 10 So he decided not to take it with him to Jerusalem; instead, he **turned** off the road and took it to the house of Obed Edom, a native of the city of Gath. 11 It stayed there three months, and the LORD **blessed** Obed Edom and his family.

12 King David heard that because of the **Covenant Box** the LORD had **blessed** Obed Edom's family and all that he had; so he fetched the **Covenant Box** from Obed's house to take it to Jerusalem with a great **celebration**. 13 After the men carrying the **Covenant Box** had gone six steps, David made them stop while he **offered the** LORD **a sacrifice** of a bull and a fattened calf. 14 David, wearing only a linen cloth round his waist, danced with all his **might** to **honour** the LORD. 15 And so he and all the Israelites took the **Covenant Box** up to Jerusalem with shouts of **joy** and the sound of trumpets.

16 As the **Box** was being brought into the city, Michal, Saul's daughter, looked out of the window and saw King David dancing and jumping around in the **sacred** dance, and she was **disgusted** with him. 17 They brought the **Box** and put it in its place in the **Tent** that David had set up for it. Then he **offered sacrifices** and **fellowship-offerings** to the LORD. 18 When he had finished **offering the sacrifices**, he **blessed** the people in the **name of the** LORD **Almighty** 19 and distributed food to them all. He gave each man and woman in Israel a loaf of **bread**, a piece of roasted meat,[l] and some raisins. Then everyone went home.

20 Afterwards, when David went home to greet his family, Michal came out to meet him. "The king of Israel made a big name for himself today!" she said. "He exposed himself like a **fool** in the **sight** of the **servant-girls** of his officials!"

21 David answered, "I was dancing to **honour** the LORD, who **chose** me instead of your father and his family to make me the leader of **his people** Israel. And I will go on dancing to **honour** the LORD, 22 and will **disgrace** myself even more. You[m] may think I am nothing, but those girls will think highly of me!"

23 Michal, Saul's daughter, never had any children.

Nathan's Message to David
(1 Chr 17.1–15)

7 King David was settled in his palace, and the LORD kept him **safe** from all his **enemies**. 2 Then the king said to the **prophet** Nathan, "Here I am living in a house built of cedar, but God's **Covenant Box** is kept in a **tent**!"

3 Nathan answered, "Do whatever you have in **mind**, because the LORD is with you." 4 But that night the LORD said to Nathan, 5 "Go and tell my **servant** David that I say to him, 'You are not the one to build a **temple** for me to live in. 6 From the time I **rescued** the people of Israel from Egypt until now, I have never lived in a **temple**; I have travelled round living in a **tent**. 7 In all my travelling with the people of Israel I never asked any of the leaders[n] that I appointed why they had not built me a **temple** made of cedar.'

8 "So tell my **servant** David that I, the LORD **Almighty**, say to him, 'I took you from looking after **sheep** in the fields and made you the ruler of **my people** Israel.

afraid 4.1; 9.7
Almighty [2] 5.10; 7.8
anger [2] 1 Sam 29.4; 11.20
best 1 Sam 27.1; 10.9
bless [3] 2.5; 7.29
box *see* **Covenant Box**
bread 1 Sam 28.24; 16.1
celebrate 1 Sam 30.16; 1 Kgs 8.65
choose 3.39; 7.10
Covenant Box [10] 1 Sam 7.1; 7.2
creature 1 Sam 4.4; 22.11
disgrace 1.21; 13.13
disgust Deut 29.17; 1 Kgs 11.5
fellowship-offering Josh 22.23; 24.25
fool 3.33; 24.10
fury 3.8; 13.21
God's people 5.2; 7.8
guide Num 10.31; 1 Chr 10.13
honour [4] 1 Sam 18.23; 10.3
joy 1 Sam 18.6; 19.2
might [2] 1.22; 2 Kgs 2.12
name (2) (name of God, of Jesus) [2] 1 Sam 30.15; 15.21
new 1 Sam 23.1; 15.19
offer [3] 1 Sam 26.19; 13.11
punish 3.29; 7.14
sacred 5.3; 11.11
sacrifice [3] 1 Sam 20.6; 15.12
servant 3.18; 7.5
sight 1 Sam 9.17; 13.17
stumble Lev 26.37; 1 Chr 13.9
Tent (2) (of the Lord's presence) 1 Sam 2.22; 7.2
throne 1 Sam 4.4; 1 Kgs 1.35
turn 1.7; 10.14

Almighty [3] 6.2; 22.14
alone Ruth 1.3; 16.11
bless [2] 6.11; 14.22
choose 6.21; 10.9
courage 1 Sam 30.6; 10.12
Covenant Box 6.2; 11.11
enemy [3] 5.20; 10.6
enjoy Judg 19.6; 1 Chr 17.27
Father (2) (God) Deut 32.6; Ps 2.7
favour 1 Sam 29.4; 19.28
free 1 Sam 26.24; 1 Kgs 20.34
fulfil 1 Sam 21.7; 1 Kgs 8.24
god (2) (other gods) 1 Sam 26.19; 12.30
God's people [4] 6.21; 14.13
last (1) Josh 23.13; 21.1
mind (1) 1 Sam 26.19; 13.32
oppress 1 Sam 22.2; 2 Kgs 13.4
pray [2] 1 Sam 12.17; 12.16
prayer 1 Sam 7.9; 21.14

[h] *Probable text (see 1 Chr 13.6)* to Baalah; *Hebrew* from Baaley, *or* from the leaders.
[x] WINGED CREATURES: *See Word List.*
[i] *One ancient translation (and see 1 Chr 13.8)* and singing with all their might; *Hebrew* with all the fir-trees. [j] *Probable text* his irreverence; *Hebrew unclear.*
[k] PEREZ UZZAH: *This name in Hebrew means "Punishment of Uzzah."*
[l] a piece of roasted meat; *or* a cake of dates. [m] *One ancient translation* You; *Hebrew* I.
[n] *Probable text (see 1 Chr 17.6)* leaders; *Hebrew* tribes.

6.2: Ex 25.22 **6.3:** 1 Sam 7.1–2 **6.11:** 1 Chr 26.4–5 **6.19–20:** 1 Chr 16.43

preserve Gen 50.20; 1 Chr 17.24
promise [6] 5.2; 9.3
prophet 1 Sam 28.6; 12.1
punish [2] 6.8; 16.8
purpose Judg 20.11; 2 Kgs 14.27
rescue [2] 3.18; 12.7
reveal [2] 1 Sam 3.21; 2 Kgs 8.10
safe [2] 3.21; 14.17
servant [4] 6.20; 9.2
sheep 1 Sam 27.9; 12.2
slave 1 Sam 30.13; 18.21
Sovereign [6] Judg 16.28; 1 Kgs 8.52
strong 5.10; 10.12
sure 1 Sam 24.20; 8.15
teach 1.18; 1 Kgs 8.36
Temple (1) (of God) [4] Ex 15.17; 22.7
Tent (2) (of the Lord's presence) [3] 6.17; 1 Kgs 1.39
violent 3.39; 12.10
will (1) Josh 22.5; 10.12
wonder (1) [2] 1.23; 1 Chr 16.9
world [2] 1 Sam 17.46; 1 Kgs 4.34
worthy Deut 32.5; 1 Chr 17.16
wrong 1 Sam 29.8; 14.13

9 I have been with you wherever you
have gone, and I have defeated all your
enemies as you advanced. I will make
you as famous as the greatest leaders in
the **world**. 10–11 I have **chosen** a place for
my people Israel and have settled them
there, where they will live without being
oppressed any more. Ever since they
entered this land, they have been
attacked by **violent** people, but this will
not happen again. I **promise** to keep you
safe from all your **enemies** and to give
you descendants. 12 When you die and are
buried with your ancestors, I will make
one of your sons king and will keep his
kingdom **strong**. 13 He will be the one to
build a **temple** for me, and I will make
sure that his dynasty continues for ever.
14 I will be his **father**, and he will be my
son. When he does **wrong**, I will **punish**
him as a father **punishes** his son. 15 But I
will not withdraw my support from him
as I did from Saul, whom I removed so
that you could be king. 16 You will always
have descendants, and I will make your
kingdom **last** for ever. Your dynasty will
never end.' "

17 Nathan told David everything that
God had **revealed** to him.

David's Prayer of Thanksgiving
(1 Chr 17.16–27)

18 Then King David went into the
Tent of the LORD's presence, sat down
and **prayed**, "I am not **worthy** of what
you have already done for me, **Sovereign**
LORD, nor is my family. 19 Yet now you
are doing even more, **Sovereign LORD**;
you have made **promises** about my descendants in the years to come. And you
let a man see this,[o] **Sovereign LORD**!
20 What more can I say to you! You know
me, your **servant**. 21 It was your **will** and
purpose to do this; you have done all
these great things in order to **teach** me.
22 How great you are, **Sovereign LORD**!
There is none like you; we have always
known that you **alone** are God. 23 There is
no other nation on earth like Israel,
whom you **rescued** from **slavery** to make
them your **own people**. The great and
wonderful things you did for them[p] have
spread your fame throughout the **world**.
You drove out[q] other nations and their
gods as your people advanced, the people
whom you **set free** from Egypt to be your
own. 24 You have made Israel your **own**
people for ever, and you, LORD, have
become their God.

25 "And now, LORD God, **fulfil** for all
time the **promise** you made about me
and my descendants, and do what you
said you would. 26 Your fame will be
great, and people will for ever say, 'The
LORD **Almighty** is God over Israel.' And
you will **preserve** my dynasty for all
time. 27 **Almighty** LORD, God of Israel! I
have the **courage** to **pray** this **prayer** to
you, because you have **revealed** all this
to me, your **servant**, and have told me
that you will make my descendants
kings.

28 "And now, **Sovereign LORD**, you are
God; you always keep your **promises**,
and you have made this **wonderful**
promise to me. 29 I ask you to **bless** my
descendants so that they will continue to
enjoy your **favour**. You, **Sovereign LORD**,
have **promised** this, and your **blessing**
will rest on my descendants for ever."

David's Military Victories
(1 Chr 18.1–17)

8 Some time later King David
attacked the Philistines again,
defeated them, and ended their **control**
over the land.[r]

2 Then he defeated the Moabites. He
made the **prisoners** lie down on the
ground and put two out of every three of
them **to death**. So the Moabites became
his **subjects** and paid **taxes** to him.

3 Then he defeated the king of the
Syrian state of Zobah, Hadadezer son of
Rehob, as Hadadezer was on his way to
restore his **control** over the territory by
the upper Euphrates. 4 David captured
seventeen hundred of his horsemen and
twenty thousand of his foot soldiers. He
kept **enough** horses for a hundred
chariots and **crippled** all the rest.

5 When the Syrians of Damascus sent
an army to **help** King Hadadezer, David
attacked it and killed twenty-two
thousand men. 6 Then he set up military
camps[s] in their territory, and they
became his **subjects** and paid **taxes** to
him. The LORD made David **victorious**
everywhere. 7 David captured the gold
shields carried by Hadadezer's officials
and took them to Jerusalem. 8 He also
took a great quantity of bronze from
Betah and Berothai, cities ruled by
Hadadezer.

conquer 5.6; 10.3
control [2] 2.1; 1 Kgs 2.46
court (1) 1 Sam 22.14; 12.17
cripple 5.6; 9.3
death (3) (to deatl 4.10; 14.32
dedicate 1 Sam 7.3 1 Kgs 7.51
enough 5.8; 12.8
help 3.12; 10.11
justice Deut 32.4; 15.4
priest [2] 1 Sam 30 15.24
prison Judg 16.21; 1 Kgs 8.46
restore 1 Sam 2.6; 16.3
subject (1) [3] 3.28; 10.19
sure 7.13; 13.13
tax [2] 1 Sam 17.25; 1 Kgs 4.21
victory [3] 5.19; 18.
worship (1) (of Go 1 Sam 15.25; 12.20

[o] *Probable text* you let a man see this; *Hebrew* this is a law for men.
[p] *Probable text* them; *Hebrew* you *(plural)*.
[q] *One ancient translation (and see 1 Chr 17.21);* You drove out; *Hebrew* for your land.
[r] *Probable text* over the land; *Hebrew unclear.*
[s] set up military camps in; *or* placed military commanders over.

7.12: Ps 89.3–4, 132.11; Jn 7.42; Acts 2.30 **7.14:** Ps 89.26–27; 2 Cor 6.18; Heb 1.5 **7.16:** Ps 89.36–37
7.23: Deut 4.34

9 King Toi of Hamath heard that David had defeated all of Hadadezer's army. 10 So he sent his son Joram to greet King David and congratulate him on his **victory** over Hadadezer, against whom Toi had fought many times. Joram took David presents made of gold, silver, and bronze. 11 King David **dedicated** them for use in **worship**, along with the silver and gold he took from the nations he had **conquered**—12 Edom, Moab, Ammon, Philistia, and Amalek—as well as part of the loot he had taken from Hadadezer.

13 David became even more famous when he returned from killing eighteen thousand Edomites in the Valley of Salt. 14 He set up military camps[t] throughout Edom, and the people there became his **subjects**. The LORD made David **victorious** everywhere.

15 David ruled over all Israel and made **sure** that his people were always treated fairly and **justly**. 16 Joab, whose mother was Zeruiah, was the commander of the army; Jehoshaphat son of Ahilud was in charge of the records; 17 Zadok son of Ahitub and Ahimelech son of Abiathar were **priests**; Seraiah was the **court** secretary; 18 Benaiah son of Jehoiada was in charge of[u] David's bodyguard and David's sons were **priests**.

David and Mephibosheth

afraid 6.9; 10.19
bow (2) [2] 1.2; 14.4
command 5.25; 10.10
cripple [2] 8.4; 19.26
dead 3.9; 12.18
harvest 1 Sam 23.1; 21.9
kind [3] 2.6; 15.20
loyal 3.6; 10.2
Majesty 4.8; 11.24
master [2] 1 Sam 30.13; 16.3
promise 7.10; 14.11
provide 5.11; 15.1
respect 1.2; 14.4
sake [2] 5.12; 18.5
servant [5] 7.5; 13.17
service [2] 1 Sam 22.12; 24.9
welcome 1 Sam 13.10; 14.33

9 One day David asked, "Is there anyone left of Saul's family? If there is, I would like to show him **kindness** for Jonathan's **sake**."

2 There was a **servant** of Saul's family named Ziba, and he was told to go to David. "Are you Ziba?" the king asked.

"At your **service**, sir," he answered.

3 The king asked him, "Is there anyone left of Saul's family to whom I can show **loyalty** and **kindness**, as I **promised** God I would?"

Ziba answered, "There is still one of Jonathan's sons. He is **crippled**."

4 "Where is he?" the king asked.

"At the home of Machir son of Ammiel in Lodebar," Ziba answered. 5 So King David sent for him.

6 When Mephibosheth, the son of Jonathan and grandson of Saul, arrived, he **bowed down** before David in **respect**. David said, "Mephibosheth," and he answered, "At your **service**, sir."

7 "Don't be **afraid**," David replied. "I will be **kind** to you for the **sake** of your father Jonathan. I will give you back all the land that belonged to your grandfather Saul, and you will always be **welcome** at my table."

8 Mephibosheth **bowed** again and said, "I am no better than a **dead** dog, sir! Why should you be so good to me?"

9 Then the king called Ziba, Saul's **servant**, and said, "I am giving Mephibosheth, your **master's** grandson, everything that belonged to Saul and his family. 10 You, your sons, and your **servants** will farm the land for your **master** Saul's family and bring in the **harvest**, to **provide** food for them. But Mephibosheth himself will always be a guest at my table." (Ziba had fifteen sons and twenty **servants**.)

11 Ziba answered, "I will do everything Your **Majesty commands**."

So Mephibosheth ate at the king's[v] table, just like one of the king's sons. 12 Mephibosheth had a young son named Mica. All the members of Ziba's family became **servants** of Mephibosheth. 13 So Mephibosheth, who was **crippled** in both feet, lived in Jerusalem, eating all his meals at the king's table.

David Defeats the Ammonites and the Syrians
(1 Chr 19.1–19)

afraid 9.7; 12.18
ashamed 19.3
best 6.1; 18.4
choose 7.10; 16.18
command [2] 9.11; 11.22
conquer 8.11; 12.29
courage 7.27; 22.46
enemy [3] 7.1; 11.16
flee [2] 5.21; 13.29
friend 3.8; 13.3
hard 1 Sam 4.10; 17.8
help [3] 8.5; 14.4
honour 6.5; 1 Kgs 3.13
loyal 9.3; 15.6
peace 1 Sam 29.7; 15.9
shave Deut 21.12; 1 Chr 19.4
strong 7.12; 11.16
subject (1) [2] 8.2; 22.44
sympathy [2] 1 Chr 19.2
turn 6.10; 14.7
will (1) 7.21; 1 Kgs 2.15
word (1) 3.11; 13.7

10 Some time later King Nahash of Ammon died, and his son Hanun became king. 2 King David said, "I must show **loyal friendship** to Hanun, as his father Nahash did to me." So David sent messengers to express his **sympathy**.

When they arrived in Ammon, 3 the Ammonite leaders said to the king, "Do you think that it is in your father's **honour** that David has sent these men to express **sympathy** to you? Of course not! He has sent them here as spies to explore the city, so that he can **conquer** us!"

4 Hanun seized David's messengers, **shaved** off one side of their beards, cut off their clothes at the hips, and sent them away. 5 They were too **ashamed** to return home. When David heard about what had happened, he sent **word** that they should stay in Jericho and not return until their beards had grown again.

6 The Ammonites realized that they had made David their **enemy**, so they hired twenty thousand Syrian soldiers from Bethrehob and Zobah, twelve thousand men from Tob, and the king of

[t] set up military camps; *or* placed military commanders.
[u] *Some ancient translations* was in charge of; *Hebrew does not have these words.*
[v] *One ancient translation* the king's; *Hebrew* my.

8.13: Ps 60 (Title) **9.1:** 1 Sam 20.15–17 **9.3:** 2 Sam 4.4

Maacah with a thousand men. [7] David heard of it and sent Joab against them with the whole army. [8] The Ammonites marched out and took up their position at the entrance to Rabbah, their capital city, while the others, both the Syrians and the men from Tob and Maacah, took up their position in the open countryside.

9 Joab saw that the **enemy** troops would attack him in front and from the rear, so he **chose** the **best** of Israel's soldiers and put them in position facing the Syrians. [10] He placed the rest of his troops under the **command** of his brother Abishai, who put them in position facing the Ammonites. [11] Joab said to him, "If you see that the Syrians are defeating me, come and **help** me, and if the Ammonites are defeating you, I will go and **help** you. [12] Be **strong** and **courageous**! Let's fight **hard** for our people and for the cities of our God. And may the **Lord's will** be done!"

13 Joab and his men advanced to attack, and the Syrians **fled**. [14] When the Ammonites saw the Syrians running away, they **fled** from Abishai and retreated into the city. Then Joab **turned** back from fighting the Ammonites and went back to Jerusalem.

15 The Syrians realized that they had been defeated by the Israelites, so they called all their troops together. [16] King Hadadezer sent for the Syrians who were on the east side of the River Euphrates, and they came to Helam under the **command** of Shobach, commander of the army of King Hadadezer of Zobah. [17] When David heard of it, he gathered the Israelite troops, crossed the River Jordan, and marched to Helam, where the Syrians took up their position facing him. The fighting began, [18] and the Israelites drove the Syrian army back. David and his men killed seven hundred Syrian chariot drivers and forty thousand horsemen, and they wounded Shobach, the **enemy** commander, who died on the battlefield. [19] When the kings who were **subject** to Hadadezer realized that they had been defeated by the Israelites, they made **peace** with them and became their **subjects**. And the Syrians were **afraid** to **help** the Ammonites any more.

David and Bathsheba

11 The following spring, at the time of the year when kings usually go to war, David sent out Joab with his officers and the Israelite army; they defeated the Ammonites and besieged the city of Rabbah. But David himself stayed in Jerusalem.

2 One day, late in the afternoon, David got up from his nap and went to the palace roof. As he walked about up there, he saw a woman having a bath. She was very beautiful. [3] So he sent a messenger to find out who she was, and **learnt** that she was Bathsheba, the daughter of Eliam and the wife of Uriah the Hittite. [4] David sent messengers to fetch her; they brought her to him and he made **love** to her. (She had just finished her monthly **ritual** of **purification**.) Then she went back home. [5] Afterwards she discovered that she was pregnant and sent a **message** to David to tell him.

6 David then sent a **message** to Joab: "Send me Uriah the Hittite." So Joab sent him to David. [7] When Uriah arrived, David asked him if Joab and the troops were well, and how the fighting was going. [8] Then he said to Uriah, "Go home and **rest** a while." Uriah left, and David sent a present to his home. [9] But Uriah did not go home; instead he slept at the palace gate with the king's guards. [10] When David heard that Uriah had not gone home, he asked him, "You have just returned after a long absence; why didn't you go home?"

11 Uriah answered, "The men of Israel and Judah are away at the war, and the **Covenant Box** is with them; my commander Joab and his officers are camping out in the open. How could I go home, eat and drink, and sleep with my wife? By all that's **sacred**, I **swear** that I could never do such a thing!"

12 So David said, "Then stay here the rest of the day, and tomorrow I'll send you back." So Uriah stayed in Jerusalem that day and the next. [13] David invited him to supper and made him drunk. But again that night Uriah did not go home; instead he slept on his blanket[w] in the palace guardroom.

14 The next morning David wrote a **letter** to Joab and sent it by Uriah. [15] He wrote: "Put Uriah in the front line, where the fighting is heaviest, then retreat and let him be killed." [16] So while Joab was besieging the city, he sent Uriah to a place where he knew the **enemy** was **strong**. [17] The **enemy** troops came out of the city and fought Joab's forces; some of David's officers were killed, and so was Uriah.

18 Then Joab sent a report to David telling him about the battle, [19] and he instructed the messenger, "After you have

[w] blanket; *or* bunk.

11.1: 1 Chr 20.1

learn 1 Sam 26.3; 2 Kgs 11.1
letter (2) 1 Kgs 21.8
love 1.26; 12.24
Majesty 9.11; 13.24
message [2] 2.5; 17.16
mourn [2] 3.31; 13.37
please 3.36; 14.22
pure 1 Sam 21.5; 22.27
remember 3.18; 1 Kgs 2.5
rest (1) 4.5; 16.14
ritual Num 35.33; 1 Kgs 18.28
sacred 6.16; 14.19
strong [3] 10.12; 13.1
swear 2.27; 12.5
upset 1 Sam 1.7; 13.20

anger 6.7; 12.5
command 10.10; 12.9
Covenant Box 7.2; 15.24
encourage 1 Sam 23.16; 16.21
enemy [3] 10.6; 16.21

told the king all about the battle, 20 he
may get **angry** and ask you, 'Why did you
go so near the city to fight them? Didn't
you realize that they would shoot arrows
from the walls? 21 Don't you **remember**
how Abimelech son of Gideon was
killed? It was at Thebez, where a woman
threw a millstone down from the wall
and killed him. Why, then, did you go so
near the wall?' If the king asks you this,
tell him, 'Your officer Uriah was also
killed.' "
22 So the messenger went to David
and told him what Joab had **commanded**
him to say. 23 He said, "Our **enemies** were
stronger than we were and came out of
the city to fight us in the open, but we
drove them back to the city gate. 24 Then
they shot arrows at us from the wall, and
some of Your **Majesty's** officers were
killed; your officer Uriah was also
killed."
25 David said to the messenger,
"**Encourage** Joab and tell him not to be
upset, since you never can tell who will
die in battle. Tell him to launch a
stronger attack on the city and capture
it."
26 When Bathsheba heard that her
husband had been killed, she **mourned**
for him. 27 When the time of **mourning**
was over, David sent for her to come to
the palace; she became his wife and bore
him a son. But the LORD was not **pleased**
with what David had done.

Nathan's Message and David's Repentance

12 The LORD sent the **prophet**
Nathan to David. Nathan went to
him and said, "There were two men who
lived in the same town; one was **rich** and
the other **poor**. 2 The **rich** man had many
cattle and **sheep**, 3 while the **poor** man
had only one **lamb**, which he had bought.
He took **care** of it, and it grew up in his
home with his children. He would feed it
with some of his own food, let it drink
from his **cup**, and hold it in his lap. The
lamb was like a daughter to him. 4 One
day a visitor arrived at the **rich** man's
home. The **rich** man didn't want to kill
one of his own animals to prepare a meal
for him; instead, he took the **poor** man's
lamb and cooked a meal for his guest."
5 David was very **angry** with the **rich**
man and said, "I **swear** by the living
LORD that the man who did this ought to
die! 6 For having done such a **cruel** thing,
he must pay back four times as much as
he took."
7 "You are that man," Nathan said to
David. "And this is what the LORD God of
Israel says: 'I made you king of Israel
and **rescued** you from Saul. 8 I gave you
his kingdom and his wives; I made you
king over Israel and Judah. If this had
not been **enough**, I would have given you
twice as much. 9 Why, then, have you **disobeyed** my **commands**? Why did you do
this **evil** thing? You had Uriah killed in
battle; you let the Ammonites kill him,
and then you took his wife! 10 Now, in
every generation some of your descendants will die a **violent death**
because you have **disobeyed** me and
have taken Uriah's wife. 11 I **swear** to you
that I will cause someone from your own
family to bring **trouble** on you. You will
see it when I take your wives from you
and give them to another man; and he
will have intercourse with them in broad
daylight. 12 You sinned in **secret**, but I will
make this happen in broad daylight for
all Israel to see.' "
13 "I have sinned against the LORD,"
David said.
Nathan replied, "The LORD **forgives**
you; you will not die. 14 But because you
have shown such **contempt** for the LORD
in doing this, your child will die." 15 Then
Nathan went home.

David's Son Dies

The LORD caused the child that Uriah's
wife had borne to David to become very
ill. 16 David **prayed** to God that the child
would get well. He **refused** to eat anything, and every night he went into his
room and spent the night lying on the
floor. 17 His **court** officials went to him
and tried to make him get up, but he
refused and would not eat anything with
them. 18 A week later the child died, and
David's officials were **afraid** to tell him
the news. They said, "While the child was
living, David wouldn't answer us when
we spoke to him. How can we tell him
that his child is **dead**? He might do himself some **harm**!"
19 When David **noticed** them whispering to **each other**, he realized that the
child had died. So he asked them, "Is the
child **dead**?"
"Yes, he is," they answered.
20 David got up from the floor, had a
bath, combed his hair, and **changed** his
clothes. Then he went and **worshipped** in
the house of the LORD. When he returned
to the palace, he asked for food and ate it
as soon as it was **served**. 21 "We don't
understand this," his officials said to him.
"While the child was **alive**, you **wept** for

afraid 10.19; 13.28
alive [2] 1 Sam 20.14; 14.7
anger 11.20; 19.42
care 1 Sam 17.15; 14.8
change 1 Sam 26.19; 23.5
comfort Deut 31.20; 1 Chr 7.22
command [2] 11.22; 17.25
conquer 10.3; 1 Kgs 11.15
contempt 1 Sam 2.30; 1 Kgs 9.7
court (1) 8.17; 20.25
crown [2] 1.10; 2 Kgs 11.12
cruel Judg 4.3; 2 Kgs 17.20
cup Ex 37.16; 1 Kgs 7.26
dead [3] 9.8; 13.32
death (1) 4.4; 13.39
disobey [2] 1 Sam 28.18; 18.13
each other 1 Sam 23.18; 21.7
enough 8.4; 19.30
evil 4.11; 14.17
fast (2) [2] 1.12; 1 Kgs 21.9
force (1) 2.22; 13.12
forgive 1 Sam 25.28; 24.10
god (2) (other gods) 7.23; 1 Kgs 8.23
harm 1 Sam 26.9; 14.11
idol 5.21; 1 Kgs 14.9
lamb [3] 1 Sam 17.34; 2 Kgs 3.4
life (2) (to life) 1 Sam 2.6; 14.14
love [2] 11.4; 13.1
mercy 1.22; 24.14
notice (1) 1 Sam 20.6; 13.28
poor [3] 5.8; 14.5
pray 7.18; 14.11
prophet [2] 7.2; 24.11
refuse (1) [2] 1 Sam 28.23; 14.29
rescue 7.6; 19.9
rich [5] 1.24; 19.32
secret 1 Sam 19.2; 2 Chr 22.11
serve 3.8; 13.5
sheep 7.8; 13.23
swear [2] 11.11; 14.19
trouble 1 Sam 30.6; 13.25
understand 3.37; 1 Kgs 3.12
violent 7.10; 19.43
weep [2] 3.32; 13.36
worship (1) (of God) 8.11; 15.8

11.21: Judg 9.53 **12.1:** Ps 51 (Title) **12.11-12:** 2 Sam 16.22

him and would not eat; but as soon as he
died, you got up and ate!"
22 "Yes," David answered, "I did **fast**
and **weep** while he was still **alive**. I
thought that the LORD might be **merciful**
to me and not let the child die. 23 But now
that he is **dead**, why should I **fast**? Could
I bring the child back **to life**? I will some
day go to where he is, but he can never
come back to me."

Solomon Is Born

24 Then David **comforted** his wife
Bathsheba. He had intercourse with her,
and she bore a son, whom David named
Solomon. The LORD **loved** the boy 25 and
commanded the **prophet** Nathan to name
the boy Jedidiah,[x] because the LORD
loved him.

David Captures Rabbah
(1 Chr 20.1–3)

26 Meanwhile Joab continued his campaign against Rabbah, the capital city of
Ammon, and was about to capture it.
27 He sent messengers to David to report:
"I have attacked Rabbah and have captured its water supply. 28 Now gather the
rest of your forces, attack the city and
take it yourself. I don't want to get the
credit for capturing it." 29 So David
gathered his forces, went to Rabbah,
attacked it, and **conquered** it. 30 From the
head of the **idol** of the Ammonite **god**
Molech[y] David took a gold **crown** which
weighed about thirty-five kilogrammes
and had a jewel in it. David took the
jewel and put it in his own **crown**.[m] He
also took a large amount of loot from the
city 31 and put its people to work with
saws, iron hoes, and iron axes, and
forced them to work at[z] making bricks.
He did the same to the people of all the
other towns of Ammon. Then he and his
men returned to Jerusalem.

Amnon and Tamar

13 David's son Absalom had a
beautiful **unmarried** sister
named Tamar. Amnon, another of
David's sons, fell in **love** with her. 2 He
was so much in **love** with her that he
became ill, because it seemed **impossible**
for him to have her; as a **virgin**, she was
kept from meeting men. 3 But he had a
friend, a very shrewd man named Jonadab, the son of David's brother Shammah. 4 Jonadab said to Amnon, "You are
the king's son, yet day after day I see you
looking **sad**. What's the **matter**?"
"I'm in **love** with Tamar, the sister of
my half-brother Absalom," he answered.
5 Jonadab said to him, "Pretend that
you are ill and go to bed. When your
father comes to see you, say to him,
'Please ask my sister Tamar to come and
feed me. I want her to prepare the food
here where I can see her, and then **serve**
it to me herself.' " 6 So Amnon pretended
that he was ill and went to bed.
King David went to see him, and
Amnon said to him, "Please let Tamar
come and make a few cakes here where
I can see her, and then **serve** them to me
herself."
7 So David sent **word** to Tamar in the
palace: "Go to Amnon's house and prepare some food for him." 8 She went
there and found him in bed. She took
some dough, prepared it, and made some
cakes there where he could see her.
Then she baked the cakes 9 and emptied
them out of the pan for him to eat, but he
wouldn't. He said, "Send everyone
away"—and they all left. 10 Then he said
to her, "Bring the cakes here to my bed
and **serve** them to me yourself." She took
the cakes and went over to him. 11 As she
offered them to him, he grabbed her and
said, "Come to bed with me!"
12 "No," she said. "Don't **force** me to
do such a degrading thing! That's awful!
13 How could I ever hold up my head in
public again? And you—you would be
completely **disgraced** in Israel. Please,
speak to the king, and I'm **sure** that he
will give me to you." 14 But he would not
listen to her; and since he was **stronger**
than she was, he overpowered her and
raped her.
15 Then Amnon was filled with a deep
hatred for her; he **hated** her now even
more than he had **loved** her before. He
said to her, "Get out!"
16 "No," she answered. "To send me
away like this is a greater **crime**[a] than
what you just did!"
But Amnon would not listen to her;
17 he called in his personal **servant** and
said, "Get this woman out of my **sight**!
Throw her out and lock the door!" 18 The
servant put her out and locked the door.
Tamar was wearing a long robe with
full sleeves,[b] the usual clothing for an **unmarried** princess in those days.[c] 19 She
sprinkled ashes on her head, tore her

[x] JEDIDIAH: *This name in Hebrew means "Beloved of the* LORD."
[y] idol of the Ammonite god Molech; *or* Ammonite king.
[m] jewel...crown; *or* crown and put it on his own head.
[z] *Probable text (see 1 Chr 20.3)* work at; *Hebrew* pass through.
[a] *Probable text* To send me...crime; *Hebrew unclear.*
[b] long robe with full sleeves; *or* decorated robe *(see Gen 37.3).*
[c] *Probable text* in those days; *Hebrew* garments.

afraid 12.18; 17.10
ash Num 19.9;
1 Kgs 13.3
banquet Judg 14.10;
Esth 1.3
believe Ex 19.9;
1 Kgs 10.7
bitter 2.26; 1 Kgs 2.8
crime 3.34; 14.11
dead [2] 12.18; 14.5
death (1) 12.10; 14.11
disgrace 6.22;
2 Kgs 19.3
duty (1) 1 Sam 26.16;
1 Kgs 8.11

fit (1) 3.29;
2 Kgs 24.16
flee [3] 10.13; 18.17
force (1) 12.31; 20.24
friend 10.2; 15.32
fury 6.8; 1 Kgs 19.11
hate [3] 5.8; 19.6
impossible
Ruth 1.13; Jer 33.22
keep from
1 Sam 25.26; 22.24
lonely Job 28.4
long (2) Job 7.2
love [4] 12.24; 19.6
Majesty [2] 11.24;
14.4
matter Judg 18.23;
Job 9.21
mind (1) 7.3; 24.16
mourn 11.26; 14.2
notice (1) 12.19;
16.12
offer 6.13; 15.12
rape [3] Judg 20.5;
Esth 7.8
sad [2] 1 Sam 1.8;
19.2
servant [5] 9.2; 14.30
serve [3] 12.20; 15.34
sheep [2] 12.2; 17.28
sight 6.20; 16.22
sorrow 1.11;
1 Kgs 8.38
sprinkle Num 19.4;
2 Chr 29.22
strong 11.16; 22.2
sure 8.15; 23.5
trouble 12.11; 14.10
unmarried [2]
Judg 11.38; Is 4.1
upset 11.25; 2 Kgs 5.8
virgin Judg 21.11;
Esth 2.2
weep 12.21; 15.30
word (1) 10.5; 16.23

robe, and with her face buried in her
hands went away crying. 20 When her
brother Absalom saw her, he asked, "Has
Amnon molested you? Please, sister,
don't let it **upset** you so much. He is your
half-brother, so don't tell anyone about
it." So Tamar lived in Absalom's house,
sad and **lonely**.
21 When King David heard what had
happened, he was **furious**. 22 And Absalom **hated** Amnon so much for having
raped his sister Tamar that he would no
longer even speak to him.

Absalom's Revenge

23 Two years later Absalom was
having his **sheep** sheared at Baal Hazor,
near the town of Ephraim, and he invited
all the king's sons to be there. 24 He went
to King David and said, "Your **Majesty**, I
am having my **sheep** sheared. Will you
and your officials come and take part in
the festivities?"
25 "No, my son," the king answered.
"It would be too much **trouble** for you if
we all went." Absalom insisted, but the
king would not give in, and he asked
Absalom to leave.
26 But Absalom said, "Well, then, will
you at least let my brother Amnon
come?"
"Why should he?" the king asked.
27 But Absalom kept on insisting until
David finally let Amnon and all his other
sons go with Absalom.
Absalom prepared a **banquet fit** for a
king[d] 28 and instructed his **servants**:
"**Notice** when Amnon has had too much
to drink, and then when I give the order,
kill him. Don't be **afraid**. I will take the
responsibility myself. Be brave and don't
hesitate!" 29 So the **servants** followed
Absalom's instructions and killed Amnon.
All the rest of David's sons mounted their
mules and **fled**.
30 While they were on their way
home, David was told: "Absalom has
killed all your sons—not one of them is
left!" 31 The king stood up, tore his
clothes in **sorrow**, and threw himself to
the ground. The **servants** who were there
with him tore their clothes also. 32 But
Jonadab, the son of David's brother
Shammah, said, "Your **Majesty**, they
haven't killed all your sons. Only Amnon
is **dead**. You could tell by looking at
Absalom that he had made up his **mind**
to do this from the time that Amnon
raped his sister Tamar. 33 So don't **believe**
the news that all your sons are **dead**;
only Amnon was killed."
34 In the meantime Absalom had **fled**.
Just then the soldier on sentry **duty**
saw a large crowd coming down the hill
on the road from Horonaim.[e] He went to
the king and reported what he had seen.[f]
35 Jonadab said to David, "Those are your
sons coming, just as I said they would."
36 As soon as he finished saying this,
David's sons came in; they started crying, and David and his officials also **wept**
bitterly.
37-38 Absalom **fled** and went to the
king of Geshur, Talmai son of Ammihud,
and stayed there three years. David
mourned a long time for his son Amnon;
39 but when he got over Amnon's **death**,
he was filled with **longing** for his son
Absalom.

Joab Arranges for Absalom's Return

14 Joab knew that King David
missed Absalom very much, 2 so
he sent for a clever woman who lived in
Tekoa. When she arrived, he said to her,
"Pretend that you are in **mourning**; put
on your **mourning** clothes, and don't
comb your hair. **Act** like a woman who
has been in **mourning** for a long time.
3 Then go to the king and say to him what
I tell you to say." Then Joab told her
what to say.
4 The woman went to the king, **bowed**
down to the ground in **respect**, and said,
"**Help** me, Your **Majesty**!"
5 "What do you want?" he asked her.
"I am a **poor widow**, sir," she
answered. "My husband is **dead**. 6 Sir, I
had two sons, and one day they got into a
quarrel out in the fields, where there was
no one to **separate** them, and one of
them killed the other. 7 And now, sir, all
my relatives have **turned** against me and
are **demanding** that I hand my son over
to them, so that they can kill him for
murdering his brother. If they do this, I
will be left without a son. They will **des-**
troy my **last hope** and leave my husband
without a son to keep his name **alive**."
8 "Go back home," the king answered,
"and I will take **care** of the matter."
9 "Your **Majesty**," she said, "whatever
you do, my family and I will take the
blame; you and the royal family are
innocent."
10 The king replied, "If anyone
threatens you, bring him to me, and he
will never **trouble** you again."

act 1 Sam 21.13; 24.10
alive 12.21; 18.14
angel [2] 1 Sam 29.9; 19.27
blame 1 Sam 25.24; 1 Kgs 2.37
bless 7.29; 16.12
bow (2) [2] 9.6; 15.5
care 12.3; 15.16
condemn 1.16; 2 Chr 21.12
crime 13.16; 16.7
dead [2] 13.32; 18.20
death (1) 13.39; 15.21
death (3) (to death) 8.2; 19.21
demand 1 Sam 2.13; 1 Kgs 20.2
destroy 1 Sam 28.18; 20.19
distinguish Deut 17.8; Ezra 3.13
evil 12.9; 1 Kgs 3.9
exile [2] Judg 18.30; 2 Kgs 17.23
God's people [2] 7.8; 21.3
grant 1 Kgs 8.28
guilty 1 Sam 20.8; 21.1
harm 12.18; 18.5
help 10.11; 15.33
hope [2] 1 Sam 2.33; 21.17
innocent 4.11; 22.21
kiss 1 Sam 20.41; 15.5
last (2) 1 Sam 25.22; 15.17
life (2) (to life) 12.23; 1 Kgs 17.21
Majesty [9] 13.24; 15.15
mourn [3] 13.37; 19.1
please 11.27; 15.25
poor 12.1; 24.17
pray 12.16; 15.31
promise [2] 9.3; 15.7
quarrel Judg 12.2; 19.9
question [2] 1 Sam 20.12; 1 Kgs 10.1
reason 1 Sam 27.6; 1 Kgs 9.13

[d] *Some ancient translations* Absalom prepared a banquet fit for a king; *Hebrew does not have these words.* [e] *Probable text* from Horonaim; *Hebrew* behind him.
[f] *One ancient translation* He went...had seen; *Hebrew does not have these words.*

13.37: 2 Sam 3.3

refuse (1) 12.16; 23.17
request 1 Sam 8.6; 1 Kgs 2.16
respect [2] 9.6; 1 Kgs 1.47
sacred 11.11; 15.24
safe 7.1; 17.3
save 4.9; 18.19
separate 1 Sam 23.26; 2 Kgs 17.21
servant [2] 13.17; 16.1
swear 12.5; 15.21
threat [2] 1 Sam 30.6; 2 Kgs 22.19
trouble 13.25; 19.22
truth Judg 16.10; 1 Kgs 22.16
turn 10.14; 15.31
welcome 9.7; 2 Kgs 20.13
widow 3.3; 20.3
wise Judg 5.29; 20.16
wrong 7.14; 19.19

11 She said, "Your **Majesty**, please **pray** to the LORD your God, so that my relative who is responsible for avenging the **death** of my son will not commit a greater **crime** by killing my other son."

"I **promise** by the living LORD," David replied, "that your son will not be **harmed** in the least."

12 "Please, Your **Majesty**, let me say just one more thing," the woman said.

"All right," he answered.

13 She said to him, "Why have you done such a **wrong** to **God's people**? You have not allowed your own son to return from **exile**, and so you have **condemned** yourself by what you have just said. 14 We will all die; we are like water spilt on the ground, which can't be gathered again. Even God does not bring the **dead** back **to life**, but the king can at least find a way to bring a man back from **exile**.[g] 15 Now, Your **Majesty**, the **reason** I have come to speak to you is that the people **threatened** me, and so I said to myself that I would speak to you in the **hope** that you would do what I ask. 16 I thought you would listen to me and **save** me from the one who is trying to kill my son and me and so remove us from the land God gave **his people**. 17 I said to myself that your **promise**, sir, would make me **safe**, because the king is like **God's angel** and can **distinguish** good from **evil**.[h] May the LORD your God be with you!"

18 The king answered, "I'm going to ask you a **question**, and you must tell me the whole **truth**."

"Ask me anything, Your **Majesty**," she answered.

19 "Did Joab put you up to this?" he asked her.

She answered, "I **swear** by all that is **sacred**, Your **Majesty**, that there is no way to avoid answering your **question**.[i] It was indeed your officer Joab who told me what to do and what to say. 20 But he did it in order to straighten out this whole matter. Your **Majesty** is as **wise** as the **angel of God** and knows everything that happens."

21 Later on the king said to Joab, "I have decided to do what you want. Go and get the young man Absalom and bring him back here."

22 Joab threw himself to the ground in front of David in **respect**, and said, "God **bless** you, Your **Majesty**! Now I know that you are **pleased** with me, because you have **granted** my **request**." 23 Then he got up and went to Geshur and brought Absalom back to Jerusalem. 24 The king, however, gave orders that Absalom should not live in the palace. "I don't want to see him," the king said. So Absalom lived in his own house and did not appear before the king.

Absalom Is Reconciled to David

25 There was no one in Israel as famous for his good looks as Absalom; he had no defect from head to foot. 26 His hair was very thick, and he had to cut it once a year, when it grew too long and heavy. It would weigh more than two kilogrammes according to the royal standard of weights. 27 Absalom had three sons and one daughter named Tamar, a very beautiful woman.

28 Absalom lived two years in Jerusalem without seeing the king. 29 Then he sent for Joab, to ask him to go to the king for him; but Joab would not come. Again Absalom sent for him, and again Joab **refused** to come. 30 So Absalom said to his **servants**, "Look, Joab's field is next to mine, and it has barley growing in it. Go and set fire to it." So they went and set the field on fire.

31 Joab went to Absalom's house and demanded, "Why did your **servants** set fire to my field?"

32 Absalom answered, "Because you wouldn't come when I sent for you. I wanted you to go to the king and ask him from me: 'Why did I leave Geshur and come here? It would have been better for me to have stayed there.' " And Absalom went on, "I want you to arrange for me to see the king, and if I'm **guilty**, then let him put me **to death**."

33 So Joab went to King David and told him what Absalom had said. The king sent for Absalom, who went to him and **bowed down** to the ground in front of him. The king **welcomed** him with a **kiss**.

Absalom Plans Rebellion

15 After this, Absalom **provided** a chariot and horses for himself, and an escort of fifty men. 2 He would get up early and go and stand by the road at the city gate. Whenever someone came there with a **dispute** that he wanted the king to **settle**, Absalom would call him over and ask him where he was from. And after the man had told him what tribe he was from, 3 Absalom would say, "Look, the **law** is on your side, but there

advice [2] Ruth 2.8; 16.20
bow (2) 14.4; 18.21
care 14.8; 16.21
case (2) 1 Sam 8.3; 1 Kgs 7.7
claim 1 Sam 18.8; 19.43
concubine 5.13; 16.21
Covenant Box [3] 11.11; 1 Kgs 2.26
death (1) 14.11; 22.5
depend Deut 25.2; 22.31
dispute [2] 1 Sam 7.6; 1 Kgs 3.28

[g] *Probable text* Even God...from exile; *Hebrew unclear.*
[h] can distinguish good from evil; *or* knows everything.
[i] there is...question; *or* you are absolutely right.

14.17: 2 Sam 19.27

is no **representative** of the king to hear
your **case**." 4 And he would add, "How I
wish I were a **judge**! Then anyone who
had a **dispute** or a **claim** could come to
me, and I would give him **justice**." 5 When
the man approached Absalom to **bow
down** before him, Absalom would reach
out, take hold of him, and **kiss** him.
6 Absalom did this with every Israelite
who came to the king for **justice**, and so
he **won** their **loyalty**.

7 After four[j] years Absalom said to
King David, "Sir, let me go to Hebron
and keep a **promise** I made to the LORD.
8 While I was living in Geshur in Syria, I
promised the LORD that if he would take
me back to Jerusalem, I would **worship**
him in Hebron."[k]

9 "Go in **peace**," the king said. So
Absalom went to Hebron. 10 But he sent
messengers to all the tribes of Israel to
say, "When you hear the sound of trumpets, shout, 'Absalom has become king at
Hebron!'" 11 There were two hundred
men who at Absalom's invitation had
gone from Jerusalem with him; they
knew nothing of the **plot** and went in all
good **faith**. 12 And while he was **offering
sacrifices**, Absalom also sent to the town
of Gilo for Ahithophel, who was one of
King David's advisers. The **plot** against
the king gained **strength**, and Absalom's
followers grew in number.

David Flees from Jerusalem

13 A messenger reported to David,
"The Israelites are pledging their **loyalty**
to Absalom."

14 So David said to all his officials who
were with him in Jerusalem, "We must
get away at once if we want to **escape**
from Absalom! Hurry! Or else he will
soon be here and defeat us and kill
everyone in the city!"

15 "Yes, Your **Majesty**," they answered. "We are ready to do whatever
you say." 16 So the king left, accompanied
by all his family and officials, except for
ten **concubines**, whom he left behind to
take **care** of the palace.

17 As the king and all his men were
leaving the city, they stopped at the **last**
house. 18 All his officials stood[l] next to
him as the royal bodyguard passed by in
front of him. The six hundred soldiers
who had followed him from Gath also
passed by, 19 and the king said to Ittai,
their leader, "Why are you going with
us? Go back and stay with the **new** king.
You are a foreigner, a **refugee** away
from your own country. 20 You have lived
here only a short time, so why should I
make you wander round with me? I
don't even know where I'm going. Go
back and take your fellow-countrymen
with you—and may the LORD be **kind** and
faithful to you."[m]

21 But Ittai answered, "Your **Majesty**,
I **swear** to you in the **LORD's name** that I
will always go with you wherever you go,
even if it means **death**."

22 "Fine!" David answered. "March
on!" So Ittai went on with all his men
and their **dependants**. 23 The people cried
loudly as David's **followers** left. The king
crossed the brook of Kidron, followed by
his men, and together they went out towards the wilderness.

24 Zadok the **priest** was there, and
with him were the **Levites**, carrying the
sacred Covenant Box. They set it down[n]
and didn't pick it up again until all the
people had left the city. The **priest** Abiathar was there too.[o] 25 Then the king said
to Zadok, "Take the **Covenant Box** back
to the city. If the LORD is **pleased** with
me, some day he will let me come back
to see it and the place where it stays.
26 But if he isn't **pleased** with me—well,
then, let him do to me what he **wishes**."
27 And he went on to say to Zadok,
"Look,[p] take your son Ahimaaz and Abiathar's son Jonathan and go back to the
city in **peace**. 28 Meanwhile, I will wait at
the river crossings in the wilderness until
I receive news from you." 29 So Zadok and
Abiathar took the **Covenant Box** back
into Jerusalem and stayed there.

30 David went on up the Mount of
Olives **weeping**; he was barefoot and had
his head covered as a **sign** of **grief**. All
who followed him covered their heads
and **wept** also. 31 When David was told[q]
that Ahithophel had joined Absalom's **rebellion**, he **prayed**, "Please, LORD, **turn**
Ahithophel's **advice** into nonsense!"

32 When David reached the top of the
hill, where there was a **place of worship**,
his **trusted friend** Hushai the Archite met
him with his clothes torn and with earth
on his head. 33 David said to him, "You
will be of no **help** to me if you come with
me, 34 but you can **help** me by returning
to the city and telling Absalom that you

[j] *Some ancient translations* four; *Hebrew* forty.
[k] *One ancient translation* in Hebron; *Hebrew does not have these words.*
[l] *Probable text* stood; *Hebrew* passed.
[m] *One ancient translation* and may the LORD be kind and faithful to you; *Hebrew* kindness and faithfulness. [n] *Probable text* set it down; *Hebrew* poured it out.
[o] *Probable text* was there too; *Hebrew* went up.
[p] *Some ancient translations* Look; *Hebrew* Are you the seer?
[q] *One ancient translation* was told; *Hebrew* told.

will now serve him as **faithfully** as you **served** his father. And do all you can to oppose any **advice** that Ahithophel gives. 35 The **priests** Zadok and Abiathar will be there; tell them everything you hear in the king's palace. 36 They have their sons Ahimaaz and Jonathan with them, and you can send them to me with all the information you gather."

37 So Hushai, David's **friend**, returned to the city just as Absalom was arriving.

David and Ziba

16 When David had gone a little beyond the top of the hill, he was suddenly met by Ziba, the **servant** of Mephibosheth, who had with him a couple of donkeys loaded with two hundred loaves of **bread**, a hundred bunches of raisins, a hundred bunches of fresh fruit, and a leather bag full of wine. 2 King David asked him, "What are you going to do with all that?"

Ziba answered, "The donkeys are for Your **Majesty's** family to ride, the **bread** and the fruit are for the men to eat, and the wine is for them to drink when they get tired in the wilderness."

3 "Where is Mephibosheth, the grandson of your **master** Saul?" the king asked him.

"He is staying in Jerusalem," Ziba answered, "because he is **convinced** that the Israelites will now **restore** to him the kingdom of his grandfather Saul."

4 The king said to Ziba, "Everything that belonged to Mephibosheth is yours."

"I am your **servant**," Ziba replied. "May I always **please** Your **Majesty**!"

David and Shimei

5 When King David arrived at Bahurim, one of Saul's relatives, Shimei son of Gera, came out to meet him, **cursing** him as he came. 6 Shimei started throwing stones at David and his officials, even though David was surrounded by his men and his bodyguard. 7 Shimei **cursed** him and said, "Get out! Get out! Murderer! **Criminal**! 8 You took Saul's kingdom, and now the LORD is **punishing** you for murdering so many of Saul's family. The LORD has given the kingdom to your son Absalom, and you are **ruined**, you murderer!"

9 Abishai, whose mother was Zeruiah, said to the king, "Your **Majesty**, why do you let this dog **curse** you? Let me go over there and cut off his head!"

10 "This is none of your business," the king said to Abishai and his brother Joab. "If he **curses** me because the LORD told him to, who has the **right** to ask why he does it?" 11 And David said to Abishai and to all his officials, "My own son is trying to kill me; so why should you be surprised at this Benjaminite? The LORD told him to **curse**; so leave him **alone** and let him do it. 12 Perhaps the LORD will **notice** my **misery**[r] and give me some **blessings** to take the place of his **curse**." 13 So David and his men continued along the road. Shimei kept up with them, walking on the hillside; he was **cursing** and throwing stones and earth at them as he went. 14 The king and all his men were worn out when they reached the Jordan,[s] and there they **rested**.

Absalom in Jerusalem

15 Absalom and all the Israelites with him entered Jerusalem, and Ahithophel was with them. 16 When Hushai, David's **trusted friend**, met Absalom, he shouted, "Long live the king! Long live the king!"

17 "What has happened to your **loyalty** to your **friend** David?" Absalom asked him. "Why didn't you go with him?"

18 Hushai answered, "How could I? I am on the side of the one **chosen** by the LORD, by these people, and by all the Israelites. I will stay with you. 19 After all, whom should I **serve**, if not my **master's** son? As I **served** your father, so now I will serve you."

20 Then Absalom **turned** to Ahithophel and said, "Now that we are here, what do you **advise** us to do?"

21 Ahithophel answered, "Go and have intercourse with your father's **concubines** whom he left behind to take **care** of the palace. Then everyone in Israel will know that your father regards you as his **enemy**, and your **followers** will be greatly **encouraged**." 22 So they set up a tent for Absalom on the palace roof, and in the **sight** of everyone Absalom went in and had intercourse with his father's **concubines**.

23 Any **advice** that Ahithophel gave in those days was **accepted** as though it were the very **word of God**; both David and Absalom followed it.

Hushai Misleads Absalom

17 Not long after that, Ahithophel said to Absalom, "Let me **choose** twelve thousand men, and tonight I will set out after David. 2 I will attack him while he is tired and **discouraged**. He will

accept 3.21; 24.23
advice [2] 15.31; 17.4
alone 7.22; 18.24
bless 14.22; 19.39
bread [2] 6.19; 1 Kgs 7.48
care 15.16; 18.22
choose 10.9; 17.1
concubine [2] 15.16; 19.5
convince 1 Sam 24.7; 2 Chr 33.13
crime 14.11; 2 Kgs 14.6
curse [7] 1 Sam 26.19; 19.21
encourage 11.25; 2 Chr 15.8
enemy 11.16; 18.3
follower 15.12; 1 Chr 12.23
friend [2] 15.32; 20.9
loyal 15.6; 19.14
Majesty [3] 15.15; 18.28
master [2] 9.9; 1 Kgs 11.23
misery 1 Sam 2.8; Neh 4.2
notice (1) 13.28; 17.19
please 15.25; 22.20
punish 7.14; 24.14
rest (1) 11.8; 1 Kgs 7.2
restore 8.3; 1 Kgs 12.21
right (3) 1 Sam 10.25; 19.28
ruin Josh 8.28; 20.19
servant [2] 14.30; 17.17
serve [2] 15.34; 19.37
sight 13.17; 1 Kgs 21.20
trust 15.32; 2 Kgs 17.14
turn 15.31; 18.3
word (1) 13.7; 19.14

advice [9] 16.20; 1 Kgs 1.12
afraid 13.28; 1 Kgs 1.43
bride 1 Sam 18.25; Ps 45.10
choose 16.18; 19.21

[r] *Some ancient translations* misery; *Hebrew* wickedness.
[s] *One ancient translation* the Jordan; *Hebrew does not have these words.*

16.1: 2 Sam 9.9–10 **16.3:** 2 Sam 19.26–27 **16.22:** 2 Sam 12.11–12

command 12.9; 18.1
dare 1.14; Esth 7.5
disaster 1 Sam 25.17; 19.7
discourage Josh 10.25; 2 Chr 15.7
experience Deut 29.4; 1 Kgs 7.14
fear 1 Sam 15.32; 1 Kgs 1.50
fright Judg 13.6; 2 Kgs 19.6
grave 3.32; 19.37
hang (2) Josh 10.26; 21.6
hard [2] 10.12; 1 Kgs 11.28
hunger 1 Sam 14.24; 2 Chr 32.11
message 11.5; 23.2
notice (1) 16.12; 1 Kgs 11.28
plan 1 Sam 23.9; 20.21
priest 15.24; 19.11
rob Judg 14.15; Ezra 9.7
safe 14.17; 18.29
scatter 1 Sam 30.16; 22.15
servant 16.1; 19.17
sheep 13.23; 1 Kgs 1.9

be **frightened**, and all his men will run away. I will kill only the king 3 and then bring back all his men to you, like a **bride** returning to her husband. You want to kill only one man;[t] the rest of the people will be **safe**." 4 This seemed like good **advice** to Absalom and all the Israelite leaders.

5 Absalom said, "Now call Hushai, and let us hear what he has to say." 6 When Hushai arrived, Absalom said to him, "This is the **advice** that Ahithophel has given us; shall we follow it? If not, you tell us what to do."

7 Hushai answered, "The **advice** Ahithophel gave you this time is no good. 8 You know that your father David and his men are **hard** fighters and that they are as fierce as a mother bear **robbed** of her cubs. Your father is an **experienced** soldier and does not stay with his men at night. 9 Just now he is probably hiding in a cave or some other place. As soon as David attacks your men, whoever hears about it will say that your men have been defeated. 10 Then even the bravest men, as **fearless** as lions, will be **afraid** because everyone in Israel knows that your father is a great soldier and that his men are **hard** fighters. 11 My **advice** is that you bring all the Israelites together from one end of the country to the other, as many as the grains of sand on the seashore, and that you lead them personally in battle. 12 We will find David wherever he is, and attack him before he knows what's happening. Neither he nor any of his men will survive. 13 If he retreats into a city, our people will all bring ropes and just pull the city[u] into the valley below. Not a single stone will be left there on top of the hill."

14 Absalom and all the Israelites said, "Hushai's **advice** is better than Ahithophel's." The LORD had decided that Ahithophel's good **advice** would not be followed, so that **disaster** would come on Absalom.

David Is Warned and Escapes

15 Then Hushai told the **priests** Zadok and Abiathar what **advice** he had given to Absalom and the Israelite leaders and what **advice** Ahithophel had given. 16 Hushai added, "Quick, now! Send a **message** to David not to spend the night at the river crossings in the wilderness, but to cross the Jordan at once, so that he and his men won't all be caught and killed."

17 Abiathar's son Jonathan and Zadok's son Ahimaaz were waiting at the spring of Enrogel, on the outskirts of Jerusalem, because they did not **dare** to be seen entering the city. A **servant-girl** would regularly go and tell them what was happening, and then they would go and tell King David. 18 But one day a boy happened to see them, and he told Absalom; so they hurried off to hide in the house of a certain man in Bahurim. He had a well near his house, and they got down into it. 19 The man's wife took a covering, spread it over the opening of the well and **scattered** grain over it, so that no one would **notice** anything. 20 Absalom's officials came to the house and asked the woman, "Where are Ahimaaz and Jonathan?"

"They crossed the river," she answered.

The men looked for them but could not find them, and so they returned to Jerusalem. 21 After they left, Ahimaaz and Jonathan came up out of the well and went and reported to King David. They told him what Ahithophel had **planned** against him and said, "Hurry up and cross the river." 22 So David and his men started crossing the Jordan, and by daybreak they had all gone across.

23 When Ahithophel saw that his **advice** had not been followed, he saddled his donkey and went back to his own city. After putting his affairs in order, he **hanged** himself. He was buried in the family **grave**.

24 David had reached the town of Mahanaim by the time Absalom and the Israelites had crossed the Jordan. 25 (Absalom had put Amasa in **command** of the army in the place of Joab. Amasa was the son of Jether the Ishmaelite;[v] his mother was Abigail, the daughter of Nahash and the sister of Joab's mother Zeruiah.) 26 Absalom and his men camped in the land of Gilead.

27 When David arrived at Mahanaim, he was met by Shobi son of Nahash, from the city of Rabbah in Ammon, and by Machir son of Ammiel, from Lodebar, and by Barzillai, from Rogelim in Gilead. 28-29 They brought bowls, clay pots, and bedding, and also food for David and his men: wheat, barley, meal, roasted grain, beans, peas,[w] honey, cheese, cream, and some **sheep**. They knew that David and his men would be **hungry**, thirsty, and tired in the wilderness.

[t] *One ancient translation* like a bride...only one man; *Hebrew* like the return of the whole, so is the man you seek. [u] *Some ancient translations* the city; *Hebrew* him.
[v] *One ancient translation (and see 1 Chr 2.17)* Ishmaelite; *Hebrew* Israelite.
[w] *Some ancient translations* peas; *Hebrew* peas and roasted grain.

alive [2] 14.7; 19.6
alone [3] 16.11; 22.32
best 10.9; 19.37
body 2.32; 20.11
bow (2) 15.5; 22.45
care 16.21; 19.33
command [4] 17.25; 20.23
dead 14.5; 19.6
defend 1 Sam 24.15; 22.3
disobey 12.9; 22.23
enemy [3] 16.21; 19.9
flee 13.29; 19.8
Good News [6] 4.10; 1 Kgs 1.42
grief 15.30; 2 Kgs 2.12
harm [2] 14.11; 1 Chr 16.22
help 15.33; 19.11
Majesty [2] 16.2; 19.19
praise 1 Sam 25.32; 22.4
rebel [3] 15.31; 20.21
reward 4.10; 19.36
safe [2] 17.3; 19.30
sake [2] 9.1; 1 Kgs 11.12
save 14.16; 19.5
slave [5] 7.23; 1 Kgs 2.39
terrible 1 Sam 26.21; 24.10
turn 16.20; 19.2
victory [2] 8.6; 19.2
watch [3] 1 Sam 19.11; 1 Kgs 8.29
weep 15.30; 19.1
wish 15.4; 23.15
worth Judg 8.2; Job 25.6

Absalom Is Defeated and Killed

18 King David brought all his men
together, divided them into units
of a thousand and of a hundred, and
placed officers in **command** of them.
2 Then he sent them out in three groups,
with Joab and Joab's brother Abishai and
Ittai from Gath, each in **command** of a
group. And the king said to his men, "I
will go with you myself."
3 "You mustn't go with us," they
answered. "It won't make any difference
to the **enemy** if the rest of us **turn** and
run, or even if half of us are killed; but
you are **worth** ten thousand of us. It will
be better if you stay here in the city and
send us **help**."
4 "I will do whatever you think **best**,"
the king answered. Then he stood by the
side of the gate as his men marched out
in units of a thousand and of a hundred.
5 He gave orders to Joab, Abishai, and
Ittai: "For my **sake** don't **harm** the young
man Absalom." And all the troops heard
David give this **command** to his officers.
6 David's army went out into the
countryside and fought the Israelites in
the forest of Ephraim. 7 The Israelites
were defeated by David's men; it was a
terrible defeat, with twenty thousand
men killed that day. 8 The fighting spread
over the countryside, and more men died
in the forest than were killed in battle.
9 Suddenly Absalom met some of
David's men. Absalom was riding a mule,
and as it went under a large oak-tree,
Absalom's head got caught in the
branches. The mule ran on and Absalom
was left hanging in mid air. 10 One of
David's men saw him and reported to
Joab, "Sir, I saw Absalom hanging in an
oak-tree!"
11 Joab answered, "If you saw him,
why didn't you kill him on the spot? I
myself would have given you ten pieces
of silver and a belt."
12 But the man answered, "Even if
you gave me a thousand pieces of silver,
I wouldn't lift a finger against the king's
son. We all heard the king **command** you
and Abishai and Ittai, 'For my **sake** don't
harm the young man Absalom.' 13 But if I
had **disobeyed** the king and killed Absalom, the king would have heard about
it—he hears about everything—and you
would not have **defended** me."
14 "I'm not going to waste any more
time with you," Joab said. He took three
spears and plunged them into Absalom's
chest while he was still **alive**, hanging in
the oak-tree. 15 Then ten of Joab's soldiers
closed in on Absalom and finished killing
him.
16 Joab ordered the trumpet to be
blown to stop the fighting, and his troops
came back from pursuing the Israelites.
17 They took Absalom's **body**, threw it into
a deep pit in the forest, and covered it
with a huge pile of stones. All the Israelites **fled**, each man to his own home.
18 During his lifetime Absalom had
built a monument for himself in King's
Valley, because he had no son to keep his
name **alive**. So he named it after himself,
and to this day it is known as Absalom's
Monument.

David Is Told of Absalom's Death

19 Then Ahimaaz son of Zadok said to
Joab, "Let me run to the king with the
good news that the LORD has **saved** him
from his **enemies**."
20 "No," Joab said, "today you will not
take any **good news**. Some other day you
may do so, but not today, for the king's
son is **dead**." 21 Then he said to his
Sudanese **slave**, "Go and tell the king
what you have seen." The **slave bowed**
and ran off.
22 Ahimaaz insisted, "I don't **care**
what happens; please let me take the
news also."
"Why do you want to do it, my son?"
Joab asked. "You will get no **reward** for
it."
23 "Whatever happens," Ahimaaz said
again, "I want to go."
"Then go," Joab said. So Ahimaaz ran
off down the road through the Jordan
Valley, and soon he passed the **slave**.
24 David was sitting in the space
between the inner and outer gates of the
city. The **watchman** went up to the top of
the wall and stood on the roof of the gateway; he looked out and saw a man running **alone**. 25 He called down and told the
king, and the king said, "If he is **alone**, he
is bringing **good news**." The runner came
nearer and nearer.
26 Then the **watchman** saw another
man running **alone**, and he called down
to the gatekeeper, "Look! There's
another man running!"
The king answered, "This one also is
bringing **good news**."
27 The **watchman** said, "I can see that
the first man runs like Ahimaaz."
"He's a good man," the king said, "and
he is bringing **good news**."
28 Ahimaaz called out a greeting to
the king, threw himself down to the
ground before him, and said, "**Praise** the
LORD your God, who has given you **victory** over the men who **rebelled** against
Your **Majesty**!"

29 "Is the young man Absalom **safe**?"
the king asked.
Ahimaaz answered, "Sir, when your
officer Joab sent me, I saw a great
commotion, but I couldn't tell what it
was."
30 "Stand over there," the king said;
and he went over and stood there.
31 Then the Sudanese **slave** arrived
and said to the king, "I have **good news**
for Your **Majesty**! Today the LORD has
given you **victory** over all who **rebelled**
against you!"
32 "Is the young man Absalom **safe**?"
the king asked.
The **slave** answered, "I **wish** that what
has happened to him would happen to all
your **enemies**, sir, and to all who **rebel**
against you."
33 The king was overcome with **grief**.
He went up to the room over the gateway and **wept**. As he went, he cried, "O
my son! My son Absalom! Absalom, my
son! If only I had died in your place, my
son! Absalom, my son!"

Joab Reprimands David

19 Joab was told that King David
was **weeping** and **mourning** for
Absalom. 2 And so the **joy of victory** was
turned into **sadness** for all David's troops
that day, because they heard that the
king was **mourning** for his son. 3 They
went back into the city quietly, like
soldiers who are **ashamed** because they
are running away from battle. 4 The king
covered his face and cried loudly, "O my
son! My son Absalom! Absalom, my
son!"
5 Joab went to the king's house and
said to him, "Today you have **humiliated**
your men—the men who **saved** your **life**
and the **lives** of your sons and daughters
and of your wives and **concubines**. 6 You
oppose those who **love** you and support
those who **hate** you! You have made it
clear that your officers and men mean
nothing to you. I can see that you would
be quite **happy** if Absalom were **alive**
today and all of us were **dead**. 7 Now go
and reassure your men. I **swear** by the
LORD's name that if you don't, not one of
them will be with you by tomorrow
morning. That would be the **worst dis**-
aster you have **suffered** in all your **life**."
8 Then the king got up, and went and sat
near the city gate. His men heard that he
was there, and they all gathered round
him.

David Starts Back to Jerusalem

Meanwhile all the Israelites had **fled**,
each man to his own home. 9 All over the
country they started **quarrelling** among
themselves. "King David **saved** us from
our **enemies**," they said to one another.
"He **rescued** us from the Philistines, but
now he has **fled** from Absalom and left
the country. 10 We **anointed** Absalom as
our king, but he has been killed in battle.
So why doesn't somebody try to bring
King David back?"
11 The news of what the Israelites
were saying reached King David.[x] So he
sent the **priests** Zadok and Abiathar to
ask the leaders of Judah, "Why should
you be the **last** to **help** bring the king
back to his palace? 12 You are my relatives, my own **flesh and blood**; why
should you be the **last** to bring me
back?" 13 David also told them to say to
Amasa, "You are my relative. From now
on I am putting you in charge of the
army in place of Joab. May God **strike**
me **dead** if I don't!" 14 David's **words won**
the complete **loyalty** of all the men of
Judah, and they sent him **word** to return
with all his officials.
15 On his way back the king was met
at the River Jordan by the men of Judah,
who had come to Gilgal to escort him
across the river. 16 At the same time the
Benjaminite Shimei son of Gera from
Bahurim hurried to the Jordan to meet
King David. 17 He had with him a thous-
and men from the tribe of Benjamin. And
Ziba, the **servant** of Saul's family, also
came with his fifteen sons and twenty
servants, and they arrived at the Jordan
before the king. 18 They crossed[y] the
river to escort the royal party across and
to do whatever the king wanted.

David Shows Kindness to Shimei

As the king was getting ready to cross,
Shimei threw himself down in front of
him 19 and said, "Your **Majesty**, please
forget the **wrong** I did that day you left
Jerusalem. Don't hold it against me or
think about it any more. 20 I know, sir,
that I have sinned, and this is why I am
the first one from the northern tribes to
come and meet Your **Majesty** today."
21 Abishai son of Zeruiah spoke up:
"Shimei should be put to **death** because
he **cursed** the one whom the LORD **chose**
as king."
22 But David said to Abishai and his
brother Joab, "Who asked your opinion?
Are you going to give me **trouble**? I am

alive 18.14; 21.5
angel 14.17; 24.16
anger 12.5; 22.8
anoint 5.3; 1 Kgs 1.34
ashamed 10.5; 1 Chr 19.5
best 18.4; 1 Kgs 12.21
betray 3.8; 1 Chr 12.17
bless 16.12; 21.3
blood 5.1; 20.12
burden Ex 18.22; 1 Kgs 12.4
care 18.22; 20.3
choose 17.1; 21.6
claim [2] 15.4; 1 Kgs 3.23
concubine 16.21; 20.3
cripple 9.3; 1 Kgs 15.23
curse 16.5; 1 Kgs 2.8
dead [2] 18.20; 23.10
death (3) (to death) [4] 14.32; 21.1
deserve [2] 3.39; 1 Kgs 2.26
disaster 17.14; 1 Kgs 9.9
enemy 18.3; 22.1
enough 12.8; 24.16
favour 7.29; 1 Kgs 2.20
flee [2] 18.17; 23.11
flesh 5.1; 2 Kgs 5.14
forget [2] 1 Sam 25.31; 2 Kgs 13.23
grave 17.23; 21.14
happy 1 Sam 2.1; 1 Kgs 4.20
hate 13.15; 22.18
help 18.3; 21.17
humiliate 1 Sam 1.6; Neh 6.13
joy 6.15; 1 Kgs 1.40
kiss 15.5; 20.9
last (2) [2] 15.17; 23.1
lie (2) 1 Sam 15.29; 1 Kgs 13.18

life (1) [3] 1.23; 20.3
look down on Neh 1.3
love 13.1; 21.20
loyal 16.17; 20.2
Majesty [11] 18.28; 24.3
mourn [2] 14.2; 1 Kgs 13.29
name (2) (name of God, of Jesus) 15.21; 1 Kgs 1.17
pleasure 1 Chr 28.4
priest 17.15; 20.25
quarrel 14.6; 21.4
rescue 12.7; 22.18
reward 18.22; 22.21
rich 12.1; 1 Kgs 10.23
right (1) 1 Sam 24.17; 22.21
right (3) [3] 16.10; 1 Chr 5.1
sad 13.4; Neh 2.1
safe 18.29; 22.3
save [2] 18.19; 22.1
servant [3] 17.17; 1 Kgs 1.1
serve 16.19; 1 Kgs 2.27
share 1 Sam 30.24; 1 Kgs 2.26
strike 3.9; 20.10
suffer 1 Sam 25.37; 1 Kgs 2.5
swear 15.21; 1 Kgs 1.51
trouble 14.10; 20.6
turn 18.3; 22.22
victory [2] 18.28; 22.40
violent 12.10; 22.3
weep 18.33; 2 Kgs 13.14
win 15.6; 23.10
word (1) [3] 16.23; 22.31
worst Ruth 1.17; 1 Kgs 14.24
wrong 14.13; 21.3

[x] *Some ancient translations* The news...David; *Hebrew* The news...David, to his palace, *and places this sentence at the end of the verse.* [y] *Probable text* They crossed; *Hebrew* The crossing crossed.

19.16: 2 Sam 16.5–13

the one who is king of Israel now, and no
Israelite will be put to death today."
23 And he said to Shimei, "I give you my
word that you will not be put to death."

David Shows Kindness to Mephibosheth

24 Then Mephibosheth, Saul's grandson, came down to meet the king. He had
not washed his feet, trimmed his beard,
or washed his clothes from the time the
king left Jerusalem until he returned victorious. 25 When Mephibosheth arrived
from[z] Jerusalem to meet the king, the
king said to him, "Mephibosheth, you
didn't go with me. Why not?"

26 He answered, "As you know, Your
Majesty, I am crippled. I told my servant
to saddle my donkey so that I could ride
along with you, but he betrayed me. 27 He
lied about me to Your Majesty, but you
are like God's angel, so do what seems
right to you. 28 All my father's family
deserved to be put to death by Your
Majesty, but you gave me the right to eat
at your table. I have no right to ask for
any more favours from Your Majesty."

29 The king answered, "You don't
have to say anything more. I have
decided that you and Ziba will share
Saul's property."

30 "Let Ziba have it all," Mephibosheth answered. "It's enough for me that
Your Majesty has come home safely."

David Shows Kindness to Barzillai

31 Barzillai, from Gilead, had also
come down from Rogelim to escort the
king across the Jordan. 32 Barzillai was a
very old man, eighty years old. He was
very rich and had supplied the king with
food while he was staying at Mahanaim.
33 The king said to him, "Come with me to
Jerusalem, and I will take care of you."

34 But Barzillai answered, "I haven't
long to live; why should I go with Your
Majesty to Jerusalem? 35 I am already
eighty years old, and nothing gives me
pleasure any more. I can't taste what I
eat and drink, and I can't hear the voices
of singers. I would only be a burden to
Your Majesty. 36 I don't deserve such a
great reward. So I will go just a little way
with you beyond the Jordan. 37 Then let
me go back home and die near my
parents' grave. Here is my son Chimham,
who will serve you; take him with you,
Your Majesty, and do for him as you
think best."

38 The king answered, "I will take him
with me and do for him whatever you
want. And I will do for you anything you
ask." 39 Then David and all his men
crossed the Jordan. He kissed Barzillai
and gave him his blessing, and Barzillai
went back home.

Judah and Israel Argue over the King

40 When the king had crossed,
escorted by all the men of Judah and half
the men of Israel, he went on to Gilgal,
and Chimham went with him. 41 Then all
the Israelites went to the king and said to
him, "Your Majesty, why did our
brothers, the men of Judah, think they
had the right to take you away and
escort you, your family, and your men
across the Jordan?"

42 The men of Judah answered, "We
did it because the king is one of us. So
why should this make you angry? He
hasn't paid for our food nor has he given
us anything."

43 The Israelites replied, "We have
ten times as many claims on King David
as you have, even if he is one of you. Why
do you look down on us? Don't forget
that we were the first to talk about bringing the king back!"

But the men of Judah were more
violent in making their claims than the
men of Israel.

Sheba's Rebellion

20 There happened to be in Gilgal a
worthless character named
Sheba son of Bikri, of the tribe of Benjamin. He blew the trumpet and called out,
"Down with David! We won't follow
him! Men of Israel, let's go home!" 2 So
the Israelites deserted David and went
with Sheba, but the men of Judah
remained loyal and followed David from
the Jordan to Jerusalem.

3 When David arrived at his palace in
Jerusalem, he took the ten concubines he
had left to take care of the palace, and
put them under guard. He provided for
their needs, but did not have intercourse
with them. They were kept confined for
the rest of their lives, living like widows.

4 The king said to Amasa, "Call the
men of Judah together and be back here
with them by the day after tomorrow."
5 Amasa went to call them, but he did not
get back by the time the king had set. 6 So
the king said to Abishai, "Sheba will give
us more trouble than Absalom. Take my
men and go after him, or else he may
occupy some fortified towns and escape
from us." 7 So Joab's men, the royal bodyguard, and all the other soldiers left
Jerusalem with Abishai to go after Sheba.

blood 19.12; 23.17
body [4] 18.17; 21.12
care 19.33; 1 Kgs 1.2
command 18.1; 21.14
concubine 19.5; 21.10
court (1) 12.17; 1 Kgs 1.33
destroy [2] 14.7; 21.2
escape 15.14; 1 Kgs 11.17
force (1) 13.12; 23.16
friend 16.16; 1 Kgs 2.13
kiss 19.39; 1 Kgs 19.18
life (1) 19.5; 23.17
loyal [2] 19.14; 1 Kgs 1.52
need 1 Sam 27.5; 1 Kgs 3.9
peace 15.9; 1 Kgs 2.5
plan [2] 17.21; 1 Kgs 6.38
priest [2] 19.11; 1 Kgs 1.7
provide 15.1; 1 Kgs 1.5
rebel 18.28; 22.44
right (2) 1 Sam 11.2; 1 Kgs 2.19
ruin [2] 16.8; 1 Kgs 9.8
strike 19.13; 22.39
trouble 19.22; 22.7
widow 14.5; 1 Kgs 11.26
wise 14.20; 1 Kgs 4.30
worthless 1 Sam 30.22; 2 Kgs 17.15

[z] *One ancient translation* from; *Hebrew* at.

19.24: 2 Sam 9.1-13, 16.1-4 **19.31:** 2 Sam 17.27-29 **20.1:** 1 Kgs 12.16; 2 Chr 10.16 **20.3:** 2 Sam 16.22

8 When they reached the large rock at Gibeon, Amasa met them. Joab was dressed for battle, with a sword in its sheath fastened to his belt. As he came forward, the sword fell out. 9 Joab said to Amasa, "How are you, my **friend**?" and took hold of his beard with his **right hand** in order to **kiss** him. 10 Amasa was not on guard against the sword that Joab was holding in his other hand, and Joab stabbed him in the belly, and his entrails spilt out on the ground. He died immediately, and Joab did not have to **strike** again.

Then Joab and his brother Abishai went on after Sheba. 11 One of Joab's men stood by Amasa's **body** and called out, "Everyone who is for Joab and David follow Joab!" 12 Amasa's **body**, covered with **blood**, was lying in the middle of the road. Joab's man saw that every**body** was stopping, so he dragged the **body** from the road into the field and threw a blanket over it. 13 After the body had been removed from the road, everyone followed Joab in pursuit of Sheba.

14 Sheba passed through the territory of all the tribes of Israel and came to the city of Abel Beth Maacah, and all the members of the clan of Bikri[a] assembled and followed him into the city. 15 Joab's men heard that Sheba was there, and so they went and besieged the city. They built ramps of earth against the outer wall and also began to dig under the wall to make it fall down. 16 There was a **wise** woman in the city who shouted from the wall, "Listen! Listen! Tell Joab to come here; I want to speak with him." 17 Joab went, and she asked, "Are you Joab?"

"Yes, I am," he answered.

"Listen to me, sir," she said.

"I'm listening," he answered.

18 She said, "Long ago they used to say, 'Go and get your answer in the city of Abel'—and that's just what they did. 19 Ours is a great city, one of the most **peaceful** and **loyal** in Israel. Why are you trying to **destroy** it? Do you want to **ruin** what belongs to the LORD?"

20 "Never!" Joab answered. "I will never **ruin** or **destroy** your city! 21 That is not our **plan**. A man named Sheba son of Bikri, who is from the hill-country of Ephraim, started a **rebellion** against King David. Hand over this one man, and I will withdraw from the city."

"We will throw his head over the wall to you," she said. 22 Then she went to the people of the city with her **plan**, and they cut off Sheba's head and threw it over the wall to Joab. He blew the trumpet as a signal for his men to leave the city, and they went back home. And Joab returned to Jerusalem to the king.

David's Officials

23 Joab was in **command** of the army of Israel; Benaiah son of Jehoiada was in charge of David's bodyguard; 24 Adoniram was in charge of the **forced labour**; Jehoshaphat son of Ahilud was in charge of the records; 25 Sheva was the **court** secretary; Zadok and Abiathar were the **priests**, 26 and Ira from the town of Jair was also one of David's **priests**.

Saul's Descendants Are Put to Death

21 During David's **reign** there was a severe **famine** which **lasted** for three full years. So David **consulted** the LORD about it, and the LORD said, "Saul and his family are **guilty** of murder; he put the people of Gibeon **to death**." 2 (The people of Gibeon were not Israelites; they were a small group of Amorites whom the Israelites had **promised to protect**, but Saul had tried to **destroy** them because of his zeal for the people of Israel and Judah.) 3 So David summoned the people of Gibeon and said to them, "What can I do for you? I want to make up for the **wrong** that was done to you, so that you will **bless** the **LORD's people**."

4 They answered, "Our **quarrel** with Saul and his family can't be **settled** with silver or gold, nor do we want to kill any Israelite."

"What, then, do you think I should do for you?" David asked.

5 They answered, "Saul wanted to **destroy** us and leave none of us **alive** anywhere in Israel. 6 So hand over seven of his male descendants, and we will **hang** them before the LORD at Gibeah, the town of Saul, the LORD's **chosen** king."

"I will hand them over," the king answered.

7 But because of the **sacred promise** that he and Jonathan had made to **each other**, David **spared** Jonathan's son Mephibosheth, the grandson of Saul. 8 However, he took Armoni and Mephibosheth, the two sons that Rizpah the daughter of Aiah had borne to Saul; he also took the five sons of Saul's daughter Merab, whom she had borne to Adriel son of Barzillai, who was from Meholah. 9 David handed them over to the people of Gibeon, who **hanged** them on the mountain before the LORD—and all seven of them died together. It was late

alive 19.6; 1 Kgs 17.23
bless 19.39; 22.21
body 20.11; 1 Kgs 13.22
choose 19.21; 22.51
command 20.23; 22.23
concubine 20.3; 1 Kgs 11.3
consult 5.23; 1 Kgs 12.6
death (3) (to death) [2] 19.21; 1 Kgs 1.51
defy 1 Sam 17.26; 1 Chr 20.7
destroy [2] 20.19; 22.5
each other 12.19; 1 Kgs 5.12
famine Ruth 1.1; 24.13
God's people 14.13; 1 Kgs 6.13
grave 19.37; 22.6
guilty 14.32; 24.17
hang (2) [4] 17.23; Esth 2.23
harvest [2] 9.10; 23.13
help 19.11; 22.7
hope 14.7; 2 Kgs 4.28
last (1) 7.16; 24.15
love 19.6; 22.51
never again 1 Sam 15.35; 1 Chr 19.19
new 15.19; 1 Kgs 11.30
prayer 7.27; 24.25
promise [3] 15.7; 23.5
protect [2] 1 Sam 26.15; 22.2
quarrel 19.9; 2 Kgs 5.7
reign Deut 17.20; 1 Kgs 1.37
sackcloth 3.31; 1 Kgs 20.31
sacred 15.24; 2 Kgs 10.22
settle (2) 15.2; 1 Kgs 3.28
shelter Ruth 2.7; 1 Kgs 8.2
spare 1 Sam 26.21; 1 Kgs 20.31
steal 1 Sam 25.7; 1 Chr 7.21
wrong 19.19; 22.24

[a] *Probable text* Bikri; *Hebrew* Beri.

21.2: Josh 9.3–15 **21.7:** 1 Sam 20.15–17; 2 Sam 9.1–7 **21.8:** 1 Sam 18.19

in the spring, at the beginning of the barley **harvest**, when they were put to **death**.
10 Then Saul's **concubine** Rizpah, the
daughter of Aiah, used **sackcloth** to make
a **shelter** for herself on the rock where
the corpses were, and she stayed there
from the beginning of **harvest** until the
autumn rains came. During the day she
would keep the birds away from the
corpses, and at night she would **protect**
them from wild animals.
11 When David heard what Rizpah
had done, 12 he went and got the bones of
Saul and of his son Jonathan from the
people of Jabesh in Gilead. (They had
stolen them from the public square in
Beth Shan, where the Philistines had
hanged the **bodies** on the day they killed
Saul on Mount Gilboa.) 13 David took the
bones of Saul and Jonathan and also
gathered up the bones of the seven men
who had been **hanged**. 14 Then they
buried the bones of Saul and Jonathan in
the **grave** of Saul's father Kish, in Zela in
the territory of Benjamin, doing all that
the king had **commanded**. And after that,
God answered their **prayers** for the
country.

Battles against Philistine Giants
(1 Chr 20.4–8)

15 There was another war between
the Philistines and Israel, and David and
his men went and fought the Philistines.
During one of the battles David grew
tired. 16 A giant named Ishbibenob, who
was carrying a bronze spear that
weighed about three and a half kilogrammes and who was wearing a **new**
sword, thought he could kill David. 17 But
Abishai son of Zeruiah came to David's
help, attacked the giant, and killed him.
Then David's men made David **promise**
that he would **never again** go out with
them to battle. "You are the **hope** of
Israel, and we don't want to lose you,"
they said.
18 After this there was a battle with
the Philistines at Gob, during which
Sibbecai from Hushah killed a giant
named Saph.
19 There was another battle with the
Philistines at Gob, and Elhanan son of
Jair[b] from Bethlehem killed Goliath
from Gath, whose spear had a shaft as
thick as the bar on a weaver's loom.
20 Then there was another battle at
Gath, where there was a giant who **loved**
to fight. He had six fingers on each hand
and six toes on each foot. 21 He **defied** the
Israelites, and Jonathan, the son of
David's brother Shammah, killed him.
22 These four were descendants of the
giants of Gath, and they were killed by
David and his men.

David's Song of Victory
(Psalm 18)

22 When the LORD **saved** David from Saul and his other **enemies**, David sang this song to the LORD:

2 The LORD is my **protector**;
he is my **strong** fortress.
3 My God is my **protection**,
and with him I am **safe**.
He **protects** me like a shield;
he **defends** me and keeps me **safe**.
He is my **saviour**;
he **protects** me and **saves** me from **violence**.
4 I call to the LORD,
and he **saves** me from my **enemies**.
Praise the LORD!

5 The waves of **death** were all round me;
the waves of **destruction** rolled over me.
6 The **danger** of **death** was round me,
and the **grave** set its **trap** for me.
7 In my **trouble** I called to the LORD;
I called to my God for **help**.
In his **temple** he heard my voice;
he listened to my cry for **help**.

8 Then the earth **trembled** and shook;
the foundations of the sky rocked and quivered
because God was **angry**!
9 Smoke poured out of his nostrils,
a consuming flame and burning coals from his mouth.
10 He tore the sky **apart** and came down,
with a **dark cloud** under his feet.
11 He flew swiftly on his winged **creature**;[x]
he travelled on the wings of the wind.
12 He covered himself with **darkness**;
thick **clouds**, full of[d] water,
surrounded him;
13 burning coals flamed up from the lightning before him.

14 Then the LORD thundered from the sky,
and the voice of **Almighty** God was heard.
15 He shot his arrows and **scattered** his **enemies**;

above Josh 2.11; 1 Kgs 8.23
Almighty 7.8; 1 Kgs 19.10
alone [2] 18.24; 1 Kgs 8.39
anger [2] 19.42; 24.1
apart Judg 14.6; 1 Kgs 13.3
bless 21.3; 23.5
bow (2) 18.21; 1 Kgs 1.16
choose 21.6; 23.1
cloud [2] Judg 20.38; 23.4
command 21.14; 24.19
constant Deut 28.33; 1 Kgs 3.6
courage 10.12; 1 Chr 17.25
creature 6.2; 1 Kgs 6.23
danger [2] 4.9; 1 Kgs 5.4
dark [3] 1 Sam 28.8; 1 Kgs 8.12
death (1) [2] 15.21; 1 Kgs 2.5
defend [4] 18.13; 23.12
depend 15.22; 2 Chr 20.15
destroy [3] 21.2; 24.1
disobey 18.13; 1 Kgs 2.43
enemy [11] 19.9; 24.13
faithful 15.20; 1 Kgs 2.4
fault 3.8; Job 4.18
grave 21.14; 1 Kgs 13.22
hate [2] 19.6; 1 Kgs 22.8
help [5] 21.17; 1 Kgs 8.39
humble [2] 1 Sam 2.7; 1 Kgs 8.33
innocent [2] 14.9; 1 Kgs 2.5
keep from [2] 13.2; 1 Chr 4.10
law [2] 15.3; 1 Kgs 2.3
light (1) 1 Sam 29.10; 1 Kgs 8.11
love 21.20; 1 Kgs 3.3
obey [2] 1 Sam 15.13; 23.3
observe Josh 5.10; 2 Chr 20.3
perfect [2] Deut 32.4; 2 Chr 5.11
please 16.4; 1 Kgs 3.10
power [2] 3.6; 1 Kgs 2.12
praise [4] 18.28; 1 Kgs 1.48
proclaim 1 Sam 11.14; 1 Kgs 16.16
protect [8] 21.2; 23.3
proud 1 Sam 2.3; 2 Kgs 14.10
pure 11.4; 1 Kgs 5.11
rebel 20.21; 1 Kgs 8.50

[b] *Probable text (see 1 Chr 20.5)* Jair; *Hebrew* Jaareoregim. [x] WINGED CREATURE: *See Word List.*
[d] *Some ancient translations (and see Ps 18.11)* full of; *Hebrew unclear.*

21.12: 1 Sam 31.8–13 **21.17:** 1 Kgs 11.36; Ps 132.17

rebuke Job 5.17
refuge Josh 20.2; 1 Kgs 20.30
rescue 19.9; 1 Kgs 1.29
reward [2] 19.36; 1 Kgs 13.7
right (1) [2] 19.27; 1 Kgs 8.18
rise 1 Sam 25.42; 2 Chr 6.41
safe [4] 19.30; 1 Kgs 4.25
save [10] 19.5; 1 Kgs 1.12
Saviour Deut 32.15; 1 Chr 16.35
scatter 17.19; 1 Kgs 13.3
seek Judg 9.46; Ps 18.30
strength [2] 15.12; 1 Kgs 19.8
strike 20.10; 1 Kgs 2.23
strong [5] 13.14; 1 Kgs 20.3
subject (1) 10.19; 1 Kgs 4.21
Temple (1) (of God) 7.5; 1 Kgs 3.1
trap 1 Sam 28.9; Job 5.12
tremble [2] 1 Sam 21.1; 1 Chr 16.30
trouble [2] 20.6; 24.1
turn 19.2; 1 Kgs 8.14
victory [4] 19.2; 23.5
violent [2] 19.43; 1 Chr 17.9
wicked 1 Sam 15.18; 1 Kgs 8.47
word (1) 19.14; 23.1
wrong 21.3; 24.17

with flashes of lightning he sent
them running.
16 The floor of the ocean was laid bare,
and the foundations of the earth
were uncovered
when the LORD **rebuked** his **enemies**
and roared at them in **anger**.

17 The LORD reached down from **above**
and took hold of me;
he pulled me out of the deep waters.
18 He **rescued** me from my **powerful**
enemies
and from all those who **hate** me—
they were too **strong** for me.
19 When I was in **trouble**, they attacked
me,
but the LORD **protected** me.
20 He **helped** me out of **danger**;
he **saved** me because he was **pleased**
with me.

21 The LORD **rewards** me because I do
what is **right**;
he **blesses** me because I am
innocent.
22 I have **obeyed** the **law** of the LORD;
I have not **turned away** from my
God.
23 I have **observed** all his **laws**;
I have not **disobeyed** his **commands**.
24 He knows that I am **faultless**,
that I have **kept myself from** doing
wrong.
25 And so he **rewards** me because I do
what is **right**,
because he knows that I am
innocent.

26 O LORD, you are **faithful** to those who
are faithful to you,
and completely good to those[f] who
are **perfect**.
27 You are **pure** to those who are pure,
but hostile to those who are **wicked**.
28 You **save** those who are **humble**,
but you **humble** those who are
proud.

29 You, LORD, are my **light**;
you dispel my **darkness**.
30 You give me **strength** to attack my
enemies
and **power** to overcome their
defences.

31 This God—how **perfect** are his deeds,
how **dependable** his **words**!
He is like a shield
for all who **seek** his **protection**.
32 The LORD **alone** is God;
God **alone** is our **defence**.
33 This God is my **strong refuge**;
he makes[g] my pathway **safe**.
34 He makes me sure-footed as a deer;
he keeps me **safe** on the mountains.
35 He trains me for battle,
so that I can use the **strongest** bow.

36 O LORD, you **protect** me and **save** me;
your **help** has made me great.
37 You have **kept me from** being
captured,
and I have never fallen.
38 I pursue my **enemies** and defeat them;
I do not stop until I **destroy** them.
39 I **strike** them down, and they cannot
rise;
they lie defeated before me.
40 You give me **strength** for the battle
and **victory** over my **enemies**.
41 You make my **enemies** run from me;
I **destroy** those who **hate** me.
42 They look for **help**, but no one **saves**
them;
they call to the LORD, but he does
not answer.
43 I crush them, and they become like
dust;
I trample on them like mud in the
streets.

44 You **saved** me from my **rebellious**
people
and maintained my rule over the
nations;
people I did not know have now
become my **subjects**.
45 Foreigners **bow** before me;
when they hear me, they **obey**.
46 They lose their **courage**
and come **trembling**[h] from their
fortresses.

47 The LORD lives! **Praise** my **defender**!
Proclaim the greatness of the **strong**
God who **saves** me!
48 He gives me **victory** over my **enemies**;
he subdues the nations under me
49 and **saves** me from my foes.

O LORD, you give me **victory** over my
enemies
and **protect** me from **violent** men.
50 And so I **praise** you among the nations;
I sing **praises** to you.
51 God gives great **victories** to his king;

[f] *Probable text (see Ps 18.25)* those; *Hebrew* the strong.
[g] *Probable text (see Ps 18.32)* he makes; *Hebrew unclear.*
[h] *Probable text (see Ps 18.45)* come trembling; *Hebrew* come ready to fight.

22.34: Hab 3.19 **22.50:** Rom 15.9

he shows **constant love** to the one he
has **chosen**,
to David and his descendants for
ever.

David's Last Words

23 David son of Jesse was the man
whom God made great, whom
the God of Jacob **chose** to be king, and
who was the composer of beautiful songs
for Israel. These are David's **last words**:

2 The **spirit of the** LORD speaks through
me;
his **message** is on my lips.
3 The God of Israel has spoken;
the **protector** of Israel said to me:
"The king who rules with **justice**,
who rules in **obedience** to God,
4 is like the sun shining on a **cloudless**
dawn,
the sun that makes the grass sparkle
after rain."

5 And that is how God will **bless** my
descendants,
because he has made an **eternal
covenant** with me,
an **agreement** that will not be
broken,
a **promise** that will not be **changed**.
That is all I **desire**;
that will be my **victory**,
and God will **surely** bring it about.
6 But **godless** men are like thorns that
are thrown away;
no one can touch them with bare
hands.
7 You must use an iron tool or a spear;
they will be burnt completely.[i]

David's Famous Soldiers
(1 Chr 11.10–41)

8 These are the names of David's
famous soldiers: the first was Josheb
Basshebeth from Tachemon, who was
the leader of "The Three";[j] he fought
with his spear[k] against eight hundred
men and killed them all in one battle.
9 The second of the famous three was
Eleazar son of Dodo, of the clan of Ahoh.
One day he and David **challenged** the
Philistines who had gathered for battle.
The Israelites fell back, 10 but he stood his
ground and fought the Philistines until
his hand was so stiff that he could not let
go of his sword. The LORD **won** a great
victory that day. After it was over, the
Israelites returned to where Eleazar was
and **stripped** the armour from the **dead**.
11 The third of the famous three was
Shammah son of Agee, from Harar. The
Philistines had gathered at Lehi, where
there was a field of peas. The Israelites
fled from the Philistines, 12 but Shammah
stood his ground in the field, **defended** it,
and killed the Philistines. The LORD **won**
a great **victory** that day.
13 Near the beginning of **harvest** time[l]
three of "The Thirty" went down to the
cave of Adullam, where David was, while
a band of Philistines was camping in the
Valley of Rephaim. 14 At that time David
was on a fortified hill, and a group of
Philistines had occupied Bethlehem.
15 David felt homesick and said, "How I
wish someone would bring me a drink of
water from the well by the gate at
Bethlehem!" 16 The three famous
soldiers **forced** their way through the
Philistine camp, drew some water from
the well, and brought it back to David.
But he would not drink it; instead he
poured it out as an **offering** to the LORD
17 and said, "LORD, I could never drink
this! It would be like drinking the **blood**
of these men who risked their **lives**!" So
he **refused** to drink it.
Those were the brave deeds of the
three famous soldiers.
18 Joab's brother Abishai (their
mother was Zeruiah) was the leader of
"The Famous Thirty." He fought with his
spear against three hundred men and
killed them, and became famous among
"The Thirty."[m] 19 He was the most
famous of "The Thirty"[n] and became
their leader, but he was not as famous as
"The Three."
20 Benaiah son of Jehoiada, from Kabzeel, was another famous soldier; he did
many brave deeds, including killing two
great Moabite warriors. He once went
down into a pit on a snowy day and killed
a lion. 21 He also killed an Egyptian, a
huge man who was armed with a spear.
Benaiah attacked him with his club,
snatched the spear from the Egyptian's
hand, and killed him with it. 22 Those
were the brave deeds of Benaiah, who
was one of "The Thirty."[n] 23 He was outstanding among them, but was not as
famous as "The Three." David put him in
charge of his bodyguard.
24–39 Other members of "The Thirty"
included:
Asahel, Joab's brother

agree 3.12; 1 Kgs 1.7
bless 22.21; 1 Kgs 2.45
blood 20.12; 1 Kgs 18.28
challenge 1 Sam 17.4; 2 Kgs 14.8
change 12.20; 24.16
choose 22.51; 24.11
cloud 22.10; 1 Kgs 8.10
covenant Judg 2.1; 1 Kgs 8.9
dead 19.6; 1 Kgs 1.5
defend 22.3; 2 Kgs 2.12
desire Deut 7.25; 1 Chr 28.9
eternal 1 Sam 18.3; 1 Kgs 10.9
flee 19.8; 1 Kgs 2.7
force (1) 20.24; 1 Kgs 4.6
godless 1 Sam 31.4; 1 Chr 10.4
harvest 21.9; 2 Kgs 4.18
justice 15.4; 1 Kgs 3.9
last (2) 19.11; 1 Kgs 2.1
life (1) 20.3; 1 Kgs 1.12
message 17.16; 1 Kgs 5.2
obey 22.22; 24.4
offer 15.12; 24.22
promise 21.2; 1 Kgs 1.13
protect 22.2; 1 Kgs 9.3
refuse (1) 14.29; 1 Kgs 2.16
Spirit (1) (God's Spirit) 1 Sam 19.20; 1 Kgs 18.12
strip (1) 1 Sam 31.9; 2 Kgs 18.16
sure 13.13; 1 Kgs 11.38
victory [3] 22.40; 1 Kgs 5.3
win [2] 19.14; 1 Kgs 11.19
wish 18.32; 24.22
word (1) 22.31; 1 Kgs 8.24

[i] *Verses 6–7 in Hebrew are unclear.* [j] *One ancient translation* "The Three"; *Hebrew* the third.
[k] *Probable text (see 1 Chr 11.11)* he fought with his spear; *Hebrew unclear.*
[l] *Probable text* Near the beginning of harvest time; *Hebrew unclear.*
[m] *One ancient translation* "The Thirty"; *Hebrew* "The Three."
[n] *Probable text* "The Thirty"; *Hebrew* "The Three."

Elhanan son of Dodo from
Bethlehem
Shammah and Elika from Harod
Helez from Pelet
Ira son of Ikkesh from Tekoa
Abiezer from Anathoth
Mebunnai from Hushah
Zalmon from Ahoh
Maharai from Netophah
Heleb son of Baanah from Netophah
Ittai son of Ribai from Gibeah in
Benjamin
Benaiah from Pirathon
Hiddai from the valleys near Gaash
Abialbon from Arabah
Azmaveth from Bahurim
Eliahba from Shaalbon
The sons of Jashen
Jonathan
Shammah from Harar
Ahiam son of Sharar from Harar
Eliphelet son of Ahasbai from
Maacah
Eliam son of Ahithophel from Gilo
Hezro from Carmel
Paarai from Arab
Igal son of Nathan from Zobah
Bani from Gad
Zelek from Ammon
Naharai from Beeroth, Joab's
armour bearer
Ira and Gareb from Jattir
Uriah the Hittite.

There were thirty-seven famous soldiers in all.

David Takes a Census
(1 Chr 21.1-27)

24 The LORD was **angry** with Israel
once more, and he made David
bring **trouble** on them. The LORD said to
him, "Go and count the people of Israel
and Judah." 2 So David gave orders to
Joab, the commander of his army: "Go
with your officers through all the tribes
of Israel from one end of the country to
the other, and count the people. I want to
know how many there are."
3 But Joab answered the king, "Your
Majesty, may the LORD your God make
the people of Israel a hundred times
more numerous than they are now, and
may you live to see him do it. But why
does Your **Majesty** want to do this?"
4 But the king made Joab and his officers
obey his order; they left his **presence** and
went out to count the people of Israel.
5 They crossed the Jordan and
camped south of Aroer, the city in the
middle of the valley, in the territory of
Gad.[p] From there they went north to
Jazer, 6 and on to Gilead and to Kadesh,
in Hittite territory.[q] Then they went to
Dan, and from Dan they went[r] west to
Sidon. 7 Then they went south to the fortified city of Tyre, on to all the cities of the
Hivites and the Canaanites, and finally to
Beersheba, in the southern part of Judah.
8 So after nine months and twenty days
they returned to Jerusalem, having
travelled through the whole country.
9 They reported to the king the total
number of men capable of **military service**: 800,000 in Israel and 500,000 in
Judah.
10 But after David had taken the
census, his **conscience** began to **trouble**
him, and he said to the LORD, "I have
committed a **terrible** sin in doing this!
Please **forgive** me. I have **acted
foolishly**."
11-12 The LORD said to Gad, David's
prophet, "Go and tell David that I am
giving him three **choices**. I will do whichever he **chooses**." The next morning,
after David got up, 13 Gad went to him,
told him what the LORD had said, and
asked, "Which is it to be? Three[s] years
of **famine** in your land or three months of
running away from your **enemies** or
three days of an epidemic in your land?
Now think it over, and tell me what
answer to take back to the LORD."
14 David answered, "I am in a
desperate situation! But I don't want to
be **punished** by men. Let the LORD himself be the one to **punish** us, for he is
merciful." 15 So the LORD sent an
epidemic on Israel, which **lasted** from
that morning until the time that he had
chosen. From one end of the country to
the other seventy thousand Israelites
died. 16 When the **LORD's angel** was about
to **destroy** Jerusalem, the LORD **changed
his mind** about **punishing** the people and
said to the **angel** who was killing them,
"Stop! That's **enough**!" The **angel** was by
the threshing-place of Araunah, a
Jebusite.
17 David saw the **angel** who was
killing the people, and said to the LORD,
"I am the **guilty** one. I am the one who
did **wrong**. What have these **poor** people
done? You should **punish** me and my
family."
18 That same day Gad went to David
and said to him, "Go up to Araunah's
threshing-place and build an **altar** to the
LORD." 19 David **obeyed** the LORD's **command** and went as Gad had told him.

[p] *Probable text* Aroer...Gad; *Hebrew unclear.*
[q] *One ancient translation* Kadesh, in Hittite territory; *Hebrew* to the land of Tahtim, Hodshi.
[r] *Probable text* and from Dan they went; *Hebrew unclear.*
[s] *Some ancient translations (and see 1 Chr 21.12)* Three; *Hebrew* Seven.

accept 16.23; 1 Kgs 7.14
act 14.2; 1 Chr 21.8
altar [4] 1 Sam 15.33; 1 Kgs 1.50
angel [4] 19.27; 1 Kgs 13.18
anger 22.8; 1 Kgs 8.46
burnt-offering 1 Sam 13.9; 1 Kgs 3.4
change 23.5; 2 Kgs 5.5
choose [3] 23.1; 1 Kgs 1.35
command 22.23; 1 Kgs 2.3
conscience 1 Sam 24.5; Job 27.6
despair 1 Sam 13.6; 1 Chr 21.13
destroy 22.5; 1 Kgs 8.37
enemy 22.1; 1 Kgs 3.11
enough 19.30; 1 Kgs 1.40
famine 21.1; 1 Kgs 8.37
fellowship-offering 6.17; 1 Kgs 3.15
fool 6.20; 2 Kgs 18.32

forgive 12.13; 1 Kgs 8.30
guilty 21.1; 1 Kgs 8.32
last (1) 21.1; 2 Kgs 8.1
Majesty [4] 19.19; 1 Kgs 1.2
mercy 12.22; 1 Kgs 8.49
mind (1) 13.32; 1 Kgs 18.21
obey [2] 23.3; 1 Kgs 2.3
offer [5] 23.16; 1 Kgs 1.9
poor 14.5; 2 Kgs 23.2
prayer 21.14; 1 Kgs 8.28
presence 1 Sam 19.24; 1 Kgs 8.11
prophet 12.1; 1 Kgs 1.8
punish [4] 16.8; 1 Kgs 2.9
sacrifice 15.12; 1 Kgs 1.9
service 9.2; 2 Kgs 25.14
terrible 18.7; 1 Kgs 17.20
trouble [2] 22.7; 1 Kgs 1.29
wish 23.15; 1 Kgs 19.4
wrong 22.24; 1 Kgs 2.44

20 Araunah looked down and saw the king
and his officials coming up to him. He
threw himself on the ground in front of
David 21 and asked, "Your **Majesty**, why
are you here?"
David answered, "To buy your
threshing-place and build an **altar** for the
LORD, in order to stop the epidemic."
22 "Take it, Your **Majesty**," Araunah
said, "and **offer** to the LORD whatever
you **wish**. Here are these oxen to burn as
an **offering** on the **altar**; here are their
yokes and the threshing-boards to use as
fuel." 23 Araunah gave it all to the king[t]
and said to him, "May the LORD your God
accept your **offering**."
24 But the king answered, "No, I will
pay you for it. I will not **offer** to the LORD
my God **sacrifices** that have cost me
nothing." And he bought the threshing-
place and the oxen for fifty pieces of
silver. 25 Then he built an **altar** to the
LORD and **offered burnt-offerings** and
fellowship-offerings. The LORD answered
his **prayer**, and the epidemic in Israel
was stopped.

[t] *Probable text* to the king; *Hebrew* to the king the king.

THE FIRST BOOK OF KINGS

INTRODUCTION

The *First book of Kings* continues the history of the Israelite monarchy begun in the books of *Samuel.* It may be divided into three parts: (1) The succession of Solomon as king of Israel and Judah, and the death of his father David. (2) The reign and achievements of Solomon. Especially noteworthy is the building of the Temple in Jerusalem. (3) The division of the nation into the northern and southern kingdoms, and the stories of the kings who ruled them down to the middle of the ninth century B.C.

In the two books of *Kings* each ruler is judged according to his loyalty to God, and national success is seen as depending on this loyalty. Idolatry and disobedience, on the other hand, lead to disaster. The kings of the northern kingdom all fail the test, while the record of Judah's kings is mixed.

Prominent in *First Kings* are the prophets of the Lord, those courageous spokesmen for God who warned the people not to worship idols and not to disobey God. Especially notable is Elijah and the story of his contest with the priests of Baal (chapter 18).

Outline of Contents

---

advice 2 Sam 17.4; 12.6
afraid [3] 2 Sam 17.10; 2.29
agree 2 Sam 23.5; 2.42
altar [3] 2 Sam 24.18; 2.28
announce 2 Sam 1.20; 2 Kgs 7.11
anoint [3] 2 Sam 19.10; 19.15
approve 1 Sam 29.6; 11.38
bow (2) [5] 2 Sam 22.45; 2.19
care [3] 2 Sam 20.3; 2.7
cause (2) 2 Sam 3.8; Ps 35.23
choose 2 Sam 24.11; 3.8
court (1) [2] 2 Sam 20.25; 4.3
dead [2] 2 Sam 23.10; 2.23
death (3) (to death) 2 Sam 21.1; 2.9
enough 2 Sam 24.16; 8.27
fear 2 Sam 17.10; Neh 1.5

King David in His Old Age

1 King David was now a very old
man, and although his **servants**
covered him with blankets, he could not
keep warm. 2 So his officials said to him,
"Your **Majesty**, let us find a young
woman to stay with you and take **care** of
you. She will lie close to you and keep
you warm." 3 A search was made all over
Israel for a beautiful girl, and in Shunem
they found such a girl named Abishag,
and brought her to the king. 4 She was
very beautiful, and waited on the king
and took **care** of him, but he did not have
intercourse with her.

Adonijah Claims the Throne

5–6 Now that Absalom was **dead**,
Adonijah, the son of David and Haggith,
was the eldest surviving son. He was a
very handsome man. David had never
reprimanded him about anything, and he
was ambitious to be king. He **provided**
for himself chariots, horses, and an
escort of fifty men. 7 He talked with Joab
(whose mother was Zeruiah) and with
Abiathar the **priest**, and they **agreed** to
support his **cause**. 8 But Zadok the **priest**,
Benaiah son of Jehoiada, Nathan the
prophet, Shimei, Rei, and David's bodyguard were not on Adonijah's side.
9 One day Adonijah **offered a sacrifice**
of **sheep**, bulls, and fattened calves at
Snake Rock, near the spring of Enrogel.
He invited the other sons of King David
and the king's officials who were from
Judah to come to this **sacrificial feast**,
10 but he did not invite his half brother
Solomon or Nathan the **prophet**, or
Benaiah, or the king's bodyguard.

Solomon Is Made King

11 Then Nathan went to Bathsheba,
Solomon's mother, and asked her,
"Haven't you heard that Haggith's son
Adonijah has made himself king? And
King David doesn't know anything about

feast [4] 2 Sam 3.20; 3.15
Good News 2 Sam 18.19; 2 Kgs 7.9
joy [2] 2 Sam 19.2; 2 Kgs 11.14
life (1) 2 Sam 23.17; 2.23
loyal 2 Sam 20.2; 3.6
Majesty [9] 2 Sam 24.3; 2.38
name (2) (name of God, of Jesus) [2] 2 Sam 19.7; 2.8
offer [3] 2 Sam 24.22; 3.2
praise 2 Sam 22.4; 5.7
pray 2 Sam 15.31; 8.12
priest [6] 2 Sam 20.25; 2.22
promise [4] 2 Sam 23.5; 2.4
prophet [3] 2 Sam 24.11; 11.29
prosper [2] 2 Sam 5.12; 2.3
provide 2 Sam 20.3; 4.7
reign [2] 2 Sam 21.1; 6.1

1.5: 2 Sam 3.4 **1.11:** 2 Sam 12.24

reprimand Num 20.12; Neh 13.11
rescue 2 Sam 22.18; 2 Kgs 11.2
respect 2 Sam 14.4; 3.28
sacrifice [4] 2 Sam 24.24; 3.2
save 2 Sam 22.1; 2 Kgs 12.4
servant 2 Sam 19.17; 3.6
sheep [3] 2 Sam 17.28; 4.23
solemn [2] 2 Sam 3.35; 2.8
swear 2 Sam 19.7; 2.24
Tent (2) (of the Lord's presence) [2] 2 Sam 7.2; 2.28
throne 2 Sam 6.2; 2.19
traitor 1 Sam 14.33; Ps 59.5
trouble 2 Sam 24.1; 2.26
worship (1) (of God) 2 Sam 15.8; 5.3

it! 12 If you want to **save** your **life** and the life of your son Solomon, I would **advise** you 13 to go at once to King David and ask him, 'Your **Majesty**, didn't you **solemnly promise** me that my son Solomon would succeed you as king? How is it, then, that Adonijah has become king?' " 14 And Nathan added, "Then, while you are still talking with King David, I will come in and confirm your story."

15 So Bathsheba went to see the king in his bedroom. He was very old, and Abishag, the girl from Shunem, was taking **care** of him. 16 Bathsheba **bowed** low before the king, and he asked, "What do you want?"

17 She answered, "Your **Majesty**, you made me a **solemn promise** in the **name of the** LORD your God that my son Solomon would be king after you. 18 But Adonijah has already become king, and you don't know anything about it. 19 He has **offered a sacrifice** of many bulls, **sheep**, and fattened calves, and he invited your sons, and Abiathar the **priest**, and Joab the commander of your army to the **feast**, but he did not invite your son Solomon. 20 Your **Majesty**, all the people of Israel are looking to you to tell them who is to succeed you as king. 21 If you don't, as soon as you are **dead** my son Solomon and I will be treated as **traitors**."

22 She was still speaking, when Nathan arrived at the palace. 23 The king was told that the **prophet** was there, and Nathan went in and **bowed** low before the king. 24 Then he said, "Your **Majesty**, have you **announced** that Adonijah would succeed you as king? 25 This very day he has gone and **offered a sacrifice** of many bulls, **sheep**, and fattened calves. He invited all your sons, Joab the commander of your army,[a] and Abiathar the **priest**, and just now they are **feasting** with him and shouting, 'Long live King Adonijah!' 26 But he did not invite me, sir, or Zadok the **priest**, or Benaiah, or Solomon. 27 Did Your **Majesty approve** all this and not even tell your officials who is to succeed you as king?"

28 King David said, "Ask Bathsheba to come back in"—and she came and stood before him. 29 Then he said to her, "I **promise** you by the living LORD, who has **rescued** me from all my **troubles**, 30 that today I will keep the **promise** I made to you in the **name of the** LORD, the God of Israel, that your son Solomon would succeed me as king."

31 Bathsheba **bowed** low and said, "May my lord the king live for ever!"

32 Then King David sent for Zadok, Nathan, and Benaiah. When they came in, 33 he said to them, "Take my **court** officials with you; let my son Solomon ride my own mule, and escort him down to the spring of Gihon, 34 where Zadok and Nathan are to **anoint** him as king of Israel. Then blow the trumpet and shout, 'Long live King Solomon!' 35 Follow him back here when he comes to sit on my **throne**. He will succeed me as king, because he is the one I have **chosen** to be the ruler of Israel and Judah."

36 "It shall be done," answered Benaiah, "and may the LORD your God confirm it. 37 As the LORD has been with Your **Majesty**, may he also be with Solomon, and make his **reign** even more **prosperous** than yours."

38 So Zadok, Nathan, Benaiah, and the royal bodyguard put Solomon on King David's mule, and escorted him to the spring of Gihon. 39 Zadok took the container of olive-oil which he had brought from the **Tent** of the LORD's presence, and **anointed** Solomon. They blew the trumpet, and all the people shouted, "Long live King Solomon!" 40 Then they all followed him back, shouting for **joy** and playing flutes, making **enough** noise to shake the ground.

41 As Adonijah and all his guests were finishing the **feast**, they heard the noise. And when Joab heard the trumpet, he asked, "What's the meaning of all that noise in the city?" 42 Before he finished speaking, Jonathan, the son of the **priest** Abiathar, arrived. "Come in," Adonijah said. "You're a good man—you must be bringing **good news**."

43 "I'm **afraid** not," Jonathan answered. "His **Majesty** King David has made Solomon king. 44 He sent Zadok, Nathan, Benaiah, and the royal bodyguard to escort him. They made him ride on the king's mule, 45 and Zadok and Nathan **anointed** him as king at the spring of Gihon. Then they went into the city, shouting for **joy**, and the people are now in an uproar. That's the noise you just heard. 46 Solomon is now the king. 47 What is more, the **court** officials went in to pay their **respects** to His **Majesty** King David, and said, 'May your God make Solomon even more famous than you, and may Solomon's **reign** be even more **prosperous** than yours.' Then King David **bowed** in **worship** on his bed 48 and **prayed**, 'Let us **praise** the LORD, the God of Israel, who has today made one of my descendants succeed me as king, and has let me live to see it!' "

[a] *One ancient translation* Joab the commander of your army; *Hebrew* your army commanders.

49 Then Adonijah's guests were afraid,
and they all got up and left, each going
his own way. 50 Adonijah, in great fear of
Solomon, went to the Tent of the LORD's
presence and took hold of the corners of
the altar.[b] 51 King Solomon was told that
Adonijah was afraid of him and that he
was holding on to the corners of the altar
and had said, "First, I want King Solomon to swear to me that he will not have
me put to death."
52 Solomon replied, "If he is loyal, not
even a hair on his head will be touched;
but if he is not, he will die." 53 King Solomon then sent for Adonijah and had him
brought down from the altar. Adonijah
went to the king and bowed low before
him, and the king said to him, "You may
go home."

David's Last Instructions to Solomon

2 When David was about to die, he
called his son Solomon and gave
him his last instructions: 2 "My time to
die has come. Be confident and determined, 3 and do what the LORD your God
orders you to do. Obey all his laws and
commands, as written in the Law of
Moses, so that wherever you go you may
prosper in everything you do. 4 If you
obey him, the LORD will keep the
promise he made when he told me that
my descendants would rule Israel as long
as they were careful to obey his commands faithfully with all their heart and
soul.
5 "There is something else. You
remember what Joab did to me by killing
the two commanders of Israel's armies,
Abner son of Ner and Amasa son of
Jether. You remember how he murdered
them in time of peace in revenge for
deaths they had caused in time of war.
He killed innocent men[c] and now I bear
the responsibility for what he did, and I
suffer[d] the consequences. 6 You know
what to do; you must not let him die a
natural death.
7 "But show kindness to the sons of
Barzillai from Gilead and take care of
them, because they were kind to me
when I was fleeing from your brother
Absalom.
8 "There is also Shimei son of Gera,
from the town of Bahurim in Benjamin.
He cursed me bitterly the day I went to
Mahanaim, but when he met me at the
River Jordan, I gave him my solemn
promise in the name of the LORD that I
would not have him killed. 9 But you must
not let him go unpunished. You know
what to do, and you must see to it that he
is put to death."

The Death of David

10 David died and was buried in
David's City. 11 He had been king of Israel
for forty years, ruling seven years in
Hebron and thirty-three years in Jerusalem. 12 Solomon succeeded his father
David as king, and his royal power was
firmly established.

The Death of Adonijah

13 Then Adonijah, whose mother was
Haggith, went to Bathsheba, who was
Solomon's mother. "Is this a friendly
visit?" she asked.
"It is," he answered, 14 and then he
added, "I have something to ask of you."
"What is it?" she asked.
15 He answered, "You know that I
should have become king and that everyone in Israel expected it. But it happened
differently, and my brother became king,
because it was the LORD's will. 16 And
now I have one request to make; please
do not refuse me."
"What is it?" Bathsheba asked.
17 He answered, "Please ask King
Solomon—I know he won't refuse you—to
let me have Abishag, the girl from
Shunem, as my wife."
18 "Very well," she answered. "I will
speak to the king for you."
19 So Bathsheba went to the king to
speak to him on behalf of Adonijah. The
king stood up to greet his mother and
bowed to her. Then he sat on his throne
and had another one brought in on which
she sat at his right. 20 She said, "I have a
small favour to ask of you; please do not
refuse me."
"What is it, mother?" he asked. "I will
not refuse you."
21 She answered, "Let your brother
Adonijah have Abishag as his wife."
22 "Why do you ask me to give
Abishag to him?" the king asked. "You
might as well ask me to give him the
throne too. After all, he is my elder
brother, and Abiathar the priest and
Joab are on his side!"[e] 23 Then Solomon
made a solemn promise in the LORD's

[b] CORNERS OF THE ALTAR: *Small projections at the four corners of the altar that looked like horns. Anyone holding on to them was safe from being killed.*
[c] *Some ancient translations* innocent men; *Hebrew* men in battle.
[d] *Some ancient translations* I bear...and I suffer; *Hebrew* he bears...and he suffers.
[e] *Some ancient translations* and Abiathar the priest...on his side; *Hebrew unclear.*

2.5: 2 Sam 3.27, 20.10 **2.7:** 2 Sam 17.27–29 **2.8:** 2 Sam 16.5–13, 19.16–23 **2.11:** 2 Sam 5.4–5; 1 Chr 3.4
2.12: 1 Chr 29.23 **2.17:** 1 Kgs 1.3–4

name, "May God **strike** me **dead** if I don't
make Adonijah pay with his **life** for
asking this! 24 The LORD has firmly **established** me on the **throne** of my father
David; he has kept his **promise** and given
the kingdom to me and my descendants.
I **swear** by the living LORD that Adonijah
will die this very day!"
25 So King Solomon gave orders to
Benaiah, who went out and killed
Adonijah.

Abiathar's Banishment and Joab's Death

26 Then King Solomon said to
Abiathar the **priest**, "Go to your country
home in Anathoth. You **deserve** to die,
but I will not have you put **to death** now,
for you were in charge of the LORD's
Covenant Box while you were with my
father David, and you **shared** in all his
troubles." 27 Then Solomon dismissed
Abiathar from **serving** as a **priest** of the
LORD, and so he made what the LORD
had said in Shiloh about the **priest** Eli and
his descendants come **true**.
28 Joab heard what had happened.
(He had supported Adonijah, but not
Absalom.) So he **fled** to the **Tent** of the
LORD's presence and took hold of the
corners of the **altar**.[f] 29 When the news
reached King Solomon that Joab had **fled**
to the **Tent** and was by the **altar**, Solomon sent a messenger to Joab to ask him
why he had **fled** to the **altar**. Joab
answered that he had **fled** to the LORD
because he was **afraid** of Solomon. So
King Solomon sent Benaiah[g] to kill Joab.
30 He went to the **Tent** of the LORD's
presence and said to Joab, "The king
orders you to come out."
"No," Joab answered. "I will die here."
Benaiah went back to the king and told
him what Joab had said.
31 "Do what Joab says," Solomon
answered. "Kill him and bury him. Then
neither I nor any other of David's descendants will any longer be held responsible for what Joab did when he killed
innocent men. 32 The LORD will **punish**
Joab for those murders, which he committed[h] without my father David's
knowledge. Joab killed two **innocent** men
who were better men than he: Abner,
commander of the army of Israel, and
Amasa, commander of the army of
Judah. 33 The **punishment** for their
murders will fall on Joab and on his descendants for ever. But the LORD will
always give **success** to David's descendants who sit on his **throne**."
34 So Benaiah went to the **Tent** of the
LORD's presence and killed Joab, and he
was buried at his home in the open
country. 35 The king made Benaiah commander of the army in Joab's place and
put Zadok the **priest** in Abiathar's place.

The Death of Shimei

36 Then the king sent for Shimei and
said to him, "Build a house for yourself
here in Jerusalem. Live in it and don't
leave the city. 37 If you ever leave and go
beyond the brook of Kidron, you will certainly die—and you yourself will be to
blame."
38 "Very well, Your **Majesty**," Shimei
answered. "I will do what you say." So he
lived in Jerusalem a long time.
39 Three years later, however, two of
Shimei's **slaves** ran away to the king of
Gath, Achish son of Maacah. When
Shimei heard that they were in Gath,
40 he saddled his donkey and went to King
Achish in Gath, to find his **slaves**. He
found them and brought them back
home. 41 When Solomon heard what
Shimei had done, 42 he sent for him and
said, "I made you **promise** in the **LORD's
name** not to leave Jerusalem. And I
warned you that if you ever did, you
would certainly die. Did you not **agree** to
it and say that you would **obey** me?
43 Why, then, have you broken your
promise and **disobeyed** my **command**?
44 You know very well all the **wrong** that
you did to my father David. The LORD
will **punish** you for it. 45 But he will **bless**
me and he will make David's kingdom
secure for ever."
46 Then the king gave orders to
Benaiah, who went out and killed Shimei.
Solomon was now in complete **control**.

Solomon Prays for Wisdom
(2 Chr 1.3–12)

3 Solomon made an alliance with the
king of Egypt by marrying his
daughter. He brought her to live in
David's City until he had finished building his palace, the **Temple**, and the wall
round Jerusalem. 2 A **temple** had not yet
been built for the LORD, and so the
people were still **offering sacrifices** at
many different **altars**. 3 Solomon **loved**
the LORD and followed the instructions of
his father David, but he also **slaughtered**

altar [3] 2.28; 6.20
argue Gen 44.16; Job 9.3
birth [2] 2 Sam 3.2; 2 Kgs 4.17
burnt-offering [2] 2 Sam 24.25; 9.25
choose 1.35; 5.9
claim 2 Sam 19.43; 2 Kgs 19.6
command 2.3; 5.17
constant 2 Sam 22.51; 5.3
Covenant Box 2.26; 6.19
dead [5] 2.23; 11.15
death (1) 2.5; 11.40

[f] CORNERS OF THE ALTAR: *See 1.50.*
[g] *One ancient translation* Solomon sent a messenger...sent Benaiah; *Hebrew* Solomon sent Benaiah. [h] will punish...committed; *or* will kill Joab, because he committed those murders.

2.26: 1 Sam 22.20–23; 2 Sam 15.24 **2.27:** 1 Sam 2.27–36

dispute 2 Sam 15.2; 1 Chr 23.4
dream [2] 1 Sam 28.6; 18.27
enemy 2 Sam 24.13; 5.3
evil 2 Sam 14.17; 11.21
feast 1.9; 10.5
fellowship-offering 2 Sam 24.25; 8.63
heart 2.4; 8.23
honest 1 Sam 8.3; 9.4
honour 2 Sam 10.3; 21.9
justice [2] 2 Sam 23.3; 10.9
law 2.3; 6.12
life (1) [3] 2.23; 4.21
love [4] 2 Sam 22.51; 8.23
loyal 1.52; 11.2
Majesty [2] 2.38; 8.13
need 2 Sam 20.3; 4.22
obey 2.3; 6.12
offer [5] 1.9; 7.48
please 2 Sam 22.20; 5.7
present (1) 2 Sam 4.8; 10.10
prostitute Judg 16.1; 14.24
real [2] 1 Sam 12.21; 20.11
relations 1 Sam 21.4; Mt 1.25
respect 1.47; 2 Kgs 3.14
riches 1 Chr 29.12
sacrifice [3] 1.9; 8.5
servant 1.1; 4.6
settle (2) 2 Sam 21.4; 1 Chr 26.29
slaughter 1 Sam 25.11; 11.24
Temple (1) (of God) [2] 2 Sam 22.7; 5.3
understand 2 Sam 12.21; 2 Kgs 18.26
wisdom [4] Deut 34.9; 4.29

animals and **offered them as sacrifices** on various **altars**.

4 On one occasion he went to Gibeon to **offer sacrifices** because that was where the most famous **altar** was. He had **offered** hundreds of **burnt-offerings** there in the past. 5 That night the LORD appeared to him in a **dream** and asked him, "What would you like me to give you?"

6 Solomon answered, "You always showed great **love** for my father David, your **servant**, and he was good, **loyal**, and **honest** in his **relations** with you. And you have continued to show him your great and **constant love** by giving him a son who today rules in his place. 7 O LORD God, you have let me succeed my father as king, even though I am very young and don't know how to rule. 8 Here I am among the people you have **chosen** to be your own, a people who are so many that they cannot be counted. 9 So give me the **wisdom** I **need** to rule your people with **justice** and to know the difference between good and **evil**. Otherwise, how would I ever be able to rule this great people of yours?"

10 The LORD was **pleased** that Solomon had asked for this, 11 and so he said to him, "Because you have asked for the **wisdom** to rule **justly**, instead of long **life** for yourself or **riches** or the **death** of your **enemies**, 12 I will do what you have asked. I will give you more **wisdom** and **understanding** than anyone has ever had before or will ever have again. 13 I will also give you what you have not asked for: all your **life** you will have wealth and **honour**, more than that of any other king. 14 And if you **obey** me and keep my **laws** and **commands**, as your father David did, I will give you a long **life**."

15 Solomon woke up and realized that God had spoken to him in the **dream**. Then he went to Jerusalem and stood in front of the LORD's **Covenant Box** and **offered burnt-offerings** and **fellowship-offerings** to the LORD. After that he gave a **feast** for all his officials.

Solomon Judges a Difficult Case

16 One day two **prostitutes** came and **presented** themselves before King Solomon. 17 One of them said, "Your **Majesty**, this woman and I live in the same house, and I gave **birth** to a baby boy at home while she was there. 18 Two days after my child was born she also gave **birth** to a baby boy. Only the two of us were there in the house—no one else was present. 19 Then one night she accidentally rolled over on her baby and smothered it. 20 She got up during the night, took my son from my side while I was asleep, and carried him to her bed; then she put the **dead** child in my bed. 21 The next morning, when I woke up and was going to feed my baby, I saw that it was **dead**. I looked at it more closely and saw that it was not my child."

22 But the other woman said, "No! The living child is mine, and the **dead** one is yours!"

The first woman answered, "No! The **dead** child is yours, and the living one is mine!"

And so they **argued** before the king.

23 Then King Solomon said, "Each of you **claims** that the living child is hers and that the **dead** child belongs to the other one." 24 He sent for a sword, and when it was brought, 25 he said, "Cut the living child in two and give each woman half of it."

26 The **real** mother, her **heart** full of **love** for her son, said to the king, "Please, Your **Majesty**, don't kill the child! Give it to her!"

But the other woman said, "Don't give it to either of us; go ahead and cut it in two."

27 Then Solomon said, "Don't kill the child! Give it to the first woman—she is its **real** mother."

28 When the people of Israel heard of Solomon's decision, they were all filled with deep **respect** for him, because they knew then that God had given him the **wisdom** to **settle disputes** fairly.

Solomon's Officials

4 Solomon was king of all Israel, 2 and these were his high officials:

The **priest**: Azariah son of Zadok
3 The **court** secretaries: Elihoreph and Ahijah, sons of Shisha
In charge of the records: Jehoshaphat son of Ahilud
4 Commander of the army: Benaiah son of Jehoiada
Priests: Zadok and Abiathar
5 Chief of the district governors: Azariah son of Nathan
Royal adviser: the **priest** Zabud son of Nathan
6 In charge of the palace **servants**: Ahishar
In charge of the **forced labour**: Adoniram son of Abda

7 Solomon appointed twelve men as district governors in Israel. They were to **provide** food from their districts for the king and his household, each man being responsible for one month out of the year. 8 The following are the names of

court (1) 1.33; 22.9
force (1) 2 Sam 23.16; 5.13
grapevine *see* **vine**
happy 2 Sam 19.6; 8.66
hyssop Num 19.6; Jn 19.29
insight Gen 41.33; 1 Chr 22.12
knowledge 2.32; 2 Chr 1.10
life (1) 3.11; 12.4
need [4] 3.9; 8.59
neighbour [2] Judg 18.22; 2 Kgs 4.3
peace 2.5; 5.4
priest [3] 2.22; 8.3
proverb Job 13.12
provide 1.5; 5.8
safe 2 Sam 22.3; 22.27
servant 3.6; 8.26
share 2.26; 2 Kgs 2.9
sheep 1.9; 8.5
subject (1) [2] 2 Sam 22.44; 12.4
tax 2 Sam 8.2; 10.15
vine Judg 13.14; 2 Kgs 4.39
wisdom [2] 3.9; 5.12
wise [4] 2 Sam 20.16; 5.7
world 2 Sam 7.9; 8.43

these twelve officers and the districts
they were in charge of:

Benhur: the hill-country of Ephraim
9 Bendeker: the cities of Makaz,
Shaalbim, Beth Shemesh, Elon,
and Beth Hanan
10 Benhesed: the cities of Arubboth and
Socoh and all the territory of
Hepher
11 Benabinadab, who was married to
Solomon's daughter Taphath: the
whole region of Dor
12 Baana son of Ahilud: the cities of
Taanach, Megiddo, and all the
region near Beth Shan, near the
town of Zarethan, south of the
town of Jezreel, as far as the city
of Abel Meholah and the city of
Jokmeam
13 Bengeber: the city of Ramoth in
Gilead, and the villages in Gilead
belonging to the clan of Jair, a
descendant of Manasseh, and the
region of Argob in Bashan, sixty
large towns in all, fortified with
walls and with bronze bars on the
gates
14 Ahinadab son of Iddo: the district of
Mahanaim
15 Ahimaaz, who was married to
Basemath, another of Solomon's
daughters: the territory of
Naphtali
16 Baana son of Hushai: the region of
Asher and the town of Bealoth
17 Jehoshaphat son of Paruah: the
territory of Issachar
18 Shimei son of Ela: the territory of
Benjamin
19 Geber son of Uri: the region of Gilead,
which had been ruled by King
Sihon of the Amorites and King Og
of Bashan

Besides these twelve, there was one
governor over the whole land.

Solomon's Prosperous Reign

20 The people of Judah and Israel
were as numerous as the grains of sand
on the seashore; they ate and drank, and
were **happy**. 21 Solomon's kingdom
included all the nations from the River
Euphrates to Philistia and the Egyptian
border. They paid him **taxes** and were
subject to him all his **life**.

22 The supplies Solomon **needed** each
day were five thousand litres of fine flour
and ten thousand litres of meal; 23 ten
stall-fed cattle, twenty pasture-fed cattle,
and a hundred **sheep**, besides deer,
gazelles, roebucks, and poultry.

24 Solomon ruled over all the land
west of the River Euphrates, from
Tiphsah on the Euphrates as far west as
the city of Gaza. All the kings west of the
Euphrates were **subject** to him, and he
was at **peace** with all the **neighbouring**
countries. 25 As long as he lived, the
people throughout Judah and Israel lived
in **safety**, each family with its own **grape-**
vines and fig-trees.

26 Solomon had forty thousand stalls
for his chariot-horses and twelve thousand cavalry horses. 27 His twelve
governors, each one in the month
assigned to him, supplied the food King
Solomon **needed** for himself and for all
who ate in the palace; they always
supplied everything **needed**. 28 Each
governor also supplied his **share** of
barley and straw, where it was **needed**,[i]
for the chariot-horses and the draught
animals.

29 God gave Solomon unusual **wisdom**
and **insight**, and **knowledge** too great to
be measured. 30 Solomon was wiser than
the **wise** men of the East or the **wise** men
of Egypt. 31 He was the **wisest** of all men:
wiser than Ethan the Ezrahite, and
Heman, Calcol, and Darda, the sons of
Mahol, and his fame spread throughout
all the **neighbouring** countries. 32 He composed three thousand **proverbs** and more
than a thousand songs. 33 He spoke of
trees and plants, from the Lebanon
cedars to the **hyssop** that grows on walls;
he talked about animals, birds, reptiles,
and fish. 34 Kings all over the **world** heard
of his **wisdom** and sent people to listen to
him.

Solomon Prepares to Build the Temple
(2 Chr 2.1–18)

5 King Hiram of Tyre had always
been a **friend** of David's, and when
he heard that Solomon had succeeded his
father David as king he sent ambassadors to him. 2 Solomon sent back this
message to Hiram: 3 "You know that
because of the **constant** wars my father
David had to fight against the **enemy**
countries all round him, he could not
build a **temple** for the **worship** of the
LORD his God until the LORD had given
him **victory** over all his **enemies**. 4 But
now the LORD my God has given me
peace on all my borders. I have no
enemies, and there is no **danger** of
attack. 5 The LORD **promised** my father

choose 3.8; 8.12
command 3.14; 6.12
constant 3.6;
Job 9.13
danger 2 Sam 22.6;
18.9
each other
2 Sam 21.7; 6.27
enemy [3] 3.11; 8.33
force (1) 4.6; 9.15
friend 2.13; 11.19
message [4]
2 Sam 23.2; 12.23
peace [2] 4.24; 8.56
please 3.10; 10.9
praise 1.48; 8.15
promise [2] 2.4; 6.12
provide [2] 4.7; 8.21
pure 2 Sam 22.27;
6.20
Temple (1) (of God)
[5] 3.1; 8.16
victory 2 Sam 23.5;
8.45

[i] where it was needed; *or* wherever King Solomon was.

4.21: Gen 15.18; 2 Chr 9.26 **4.26:** 1 Kgs 10.26; 2 Chr 1.14, 9.25 **4.31:** Ps 89 (Title)
4.32: Prov 1.1, 10.1, 25.1; Song 1.1 **5.5:** 2 Sam 7.12–13; 1 Chr 17.11–12

wisdom 4.29; 10.4
wise 4.30; 10.8
worship (1) (of God) [2] 1.47; 8.16

David, 'Your son, whom I will make king after you, will build a **temple** for me.' And I have now decided to build that **temple** for the **worship** of the LORD my God. 6 So send your men to Lebanon to cut down cedars for me. My men will work with them, and I will pay your men whatever you decide. As you well know, my men don't know how to cut down trees as well as yours do."

7 Hiram was extremely **pleased** when he received Solomon's **message**, and he said, "**Praise** the LORD today for giving David such a **wise** son to succeed him as king of that great nation!" 8 Then Hiram sent Solomon the following **message**: "I have received your **message** and I am ready to do what you ask. I will **provide** the cedars and the pine-trees. 9 My men will bring the logs down from Lebanon to the sea, and will tie them together in rafts to float them down the coast to the place you **choose**. There my men will untie them, and your men will take charge of them. On your part, I would like you to supply the food for my men."

10 So Hiram supplied Solomon with all the cedar and pine logs that he wanted, 11 and Solomon **provided** Hiram with two thousand metric tons of wheat and four hundred thousand litres[j] of **pure** olive-oil every year to feed his men.

12 The LORD kept his **promise** and gave Solomon **wisdom**. There was **peace** between Hiram and Solomon, and they made a treaty with **each other**.

13 King Solomon drafted 30,000 men as **forced labour** from all over Israel, 14 and put Adoniram in charge of them. He divided them into three groups of 10,000 men, and each group spent one month in Lebanon and two months back home. 15 Solomon also had 80,000 men in the hill-country quarrying stone, with 70,000 men to carry it, 16 and he placed 3,300 foremen in charge of them to supervise their work. 17 At King Solomon's **command** they quarried fine large stones for the foundation of the **Temple**. 18 Solomon's and Hiram's workmen and men from the city of Byblos prepared the stones and the timber to build the **Temple**.

Solomon Builds the Temple

abandon 2 Sam 1.27; 8.57
altar [2] 3.2; 7.48
command 5.17; 8.44
Covenant Box 3.15; 8.1

6 Four hundred and eighty years after the people of Israel left Egypt, during the fourth year of Solomon's **reign** over Israel, in the second month, the month of Ziv, Solomon began work on the Temple. 2 Inside it was 27 metres long, 9 metres wide, and 13.5 metres high. 3 The entrance room was 4.5 metres deep and 9 metres wide, as wide as the **sanctuary** itself. 4 The walls of the Temple had openings in them, narrower on the outside than on the inside. 5 Against the outside walls, on the sides and the back of the Temple, a three-storied annexe was built, each storey 2.2 metres high. 6 Each room in the lowest storey was 2.2 metres wide, in the middle storey 2.7 metres wide, and in the top storey 3.1 metres wide. The temple wall on each floor was thinner than on the floor below so that the rooms could rest on the wall without having their beams built into it.

7 The stones with which the Temple was built had been prepared at the quarry, so that there was no noise made by hammers, axes, or any other iron tools as the Temple was being built.

8 The entrance to the lowest[k] storey of the annexe was on the south side of the Temple, with stairs leading up to the second and third storeys. 9 So King Solomon finished building the Temple. He put in a ceiling made of beams and boards of cedar. 10 The three-storied annexe, each storey[l] 2.2 metres high, was built against the outside walls of the Temple, and was joined to them by cedar beams.

11 The LORD said to Solomon, 12 "If you **obey** all my **laws** and **commands**, I will do for you what I **promised** your father David. 13 I will live among **my people** Israel in this Temple that you are building, and I will never **abandon** them."

14 So Solomon finished building the Temple.

The Interior Furnishings of the Temple
(2 Chr 3.8–14)

15 The inside walls were covered with cedar panels from the floor to the ceiling, and the floor was made of pine. 16 An inner room, called the **Most Holy Place**, was built in the rear of the Temple. It was nine metres long and was partitioned off by cedar boards reaching from the floor to the ceiling.[m] 17 The room in front of the **Most Holy Place** was eighteen metres long. 18 The cedar panels were decorated with carvings of gourds and flowers; the whole interior was covered with cedar, so that the stones of the walls could not be seen.

creature [6] 2 Sam 22.11; 7.29
each other 5.12; 14.30
God's people 2 Sam 21.3; 8.16
Holy Place [6] Num 18.3; 7.49
law 3.14; 8.58
obey 3.14; 8.23
plan 2 Sam 20.21; 8.17
promise 5.5; 8.15
pure 5.11; 10.21
reign [3] 1.37; 10.27
sanctuary 1 Sam 3.3; 2 Kgs 10.25

[j] *Some ancient translations (and see 2 Chr 2.10)* four hundred thousand litres; *Hebrew* four thousand litres. [k] *Some ancient translations* lowest; *Hebrew* middle.
[l] *Probable text* three-storied annexe, each storey; *Hebrew* three-storied annexe.
[m] *One ancient translation* ceiling; *Hebrew* walls.

5.14: 1 Kgs 12.18 **6.16:** Ex 26.33–34

19 In the rear of the Temple an inner room was built, where the LORD's **Covenant Box** was to be placed. 20 This inner room was nine metres long, nine metres wide, and nine metres high, all covered with **pure** gold. The **altar** was covered with cedar panels.[n] 21 The inside of the Temple was covered with gold, and gold chains were placed across the entrance of the inner room, which was also covered with gold. 22 The whole interior of the Temple was covered with gold, as well as the **altar** in the **Most Holy Place**.

23 Two winged **creatures** were made of olive wood and placed in the **Most Holy Place**, each one 4.4 metres tall. 24–26 Both were of the same size and shape. Each had two wings, each wing 2.2 metres long, so that the distance from one wing-tip to the other was 4.4 metres. 27 They were placed side by side in the **Most Holy Place**, so that two of their outstretched wings touched **each other** in the middle of the room, and the other two wings touched the walls. 28 The two winged **creatures** were covered with gold.

29 The walls of the main room and of the inner room were all decorated with carved figures of winged **creatures**, palm-trees, and flowers. 30 Even the floor was covered with gold.

31 A double door made of olive wood was set in place at the entrance of the **Most Holy Place**; the top of the doorway was a pointed arch. 32 The doors were decorated with carved figures of winged **creatures**, palm-trees, and flowers. The doors, the winged **creatures**, and the palm-trees were covered with gold. 33 For the entrance to the main room a rectangular door-frame of olive wood was made. 34 There were two folding doors made of pine 35 and decorated with carved figures of winged **creatures**, palm-trees, and flowers, which were evenly covered with gold.

36 An inner court was built in front of the Temple, enclosed with walls which had one layer of cedar beams for every three layers of stone.

37 The foundation of the Temple was laid in the second month, the month of Ziv, in the fourth year of Solomon's **reign**. 38 In the eighth month, the month of Bul, in the eleventh year of Solomon's **reign**, the Temple was completely finished exactly as it had been **planned**. It had taken Solomon seven years to build it.

Solomon's Palace

7 Solomon also built a palace for himself, and it took him thirteen years. 2–3 The Hall of the Forest of Lebanon[o] was 44 metres long, 22 metres wide, and 13.5 metres high. It had three[p] rows of cedar pillars, fifteen in each row, with cedar beams **resting** on them. The ceiling was of cedar, extending over store-rooms, which were supported by the pillars. 4 In each of the two side walls there were three rows of windows. 5 The doorways and the windows[q] had rectangular frames, and the three rows of windows in each wall faced the opposite rows.

6 The Hall of Columns was 22 metres long and 13.5 metres wide. It had a covered porch, supported by columns.

7 The **Throne** Room, also called the **Hall of Judgement**, where Solomon decided **cases**, had cedar panels from the floor to the rafters.[r]

8 Solomon's own quarters, in another court behind the **Hall of Judgement**, were made like the other buildings. He also built the same kind of house for his wife, the daughter of the king of Egypt.

9 All these buildings and the great court were made of fine stones from the foundations to the eaves. The stones were prepared at the quarry and cut to measure, with their inner and outer sides trimmed with saws. 10 The foundations were made of large stones prepared at the quarry, some of them three and a half metres long and others four metres long. 11 On top of them were other stones, cut to measure, and cedar beams. 12 The palace court, the inner court of the Temple, and the entrance room of the Temple had walls with one layer of cedar beams for every three layers of cut stones.

Huram's Task

13 King Solomon sent for a man named Huram, a craftsman living in the city of Tyre, who was skilled in bronze work. 14 His father, who was no longer living, was from Tyre, and had also been a skilled bronze craftsman; his mother was from the tribe of Naphtali. Huram was an **intelligent** and **experienced** craftsman. He **accepted** King Solomon's

accept 2 Sam 24.23; 13.16
altar 6.20; 8.22
bread 2 Sam 16.1; 14.3
case (2) 2 Sam 15.3; 2 Chr 19.8
complete [2] Josh 5.8; 1 Chr 27.24
creature [2] 6.23; 8.6
cup [2] 2 Sam 12.3; 10.21
dedicate 2 Sam 8.11; 8.63
determine 2.2; 2 Kgs 19.31
experience 2 Sam 17.8; 9.27
Holy Place [2] 6.16; 8.6
incense 1 Sam 2.28; 9.25
intelligent 1 Sam 25.2; Prov 1.3
judge [2] 2 Sam 15.4; 8.32
offer 3.2; 8.62
rest (1) [2] 2 Sam 16.14; 2 Kgs 4.11
throne 2.19; 10.18

[n] *Verse 20 in Hebrew is unclear.*
[o] HALL OF THE FOREST OF LEBANON: *A large ceremonial hall in the palace, probably so called because it was panelled in cedar.* [p] *One ancient translation* three; *Hebrew* four.
[q] *One ancient translation* windows; *Hebrew* doorposts.
[r] *Some ancient translations* rafters; *Hebrew* floor.

6.22: Ex 30.1–3 **6.23–28:** Ex 25.18–20 **7.8:** 1 Kgs 3.1

invitation to be in charge of all the bronze work.

The Two Bronze Columns
(2 Chr 3.15–17)

15 Huram cast two bronze columns, each one 8 metres tall and 5.3 metres in circumference,[s] and placed them at the entrance of the Temple. 16 He also made two bronze capitals, each one 2.2 metres tall, to be placed on top of the columns. 17 The top of each column was decorated with a design of interwoven chains,[t] 18 and two rows of bronze pomegranates.

19 The capitals were shaped like lilies, 1.8 metres tall, 20 and were placed on a rounded section which was above the chain design. There were two hundred pomegranates in two rows round each[u] capital.

21 Huram placed these two bronze columns in front of the entrance of the Temple: the one on the south side was named Jachin,[v] and the one on the north was named Boaz.[w] 22 The lily-shaped bronze capitals were on top of the columns.

And so the work on the columns was **completed**.

The Bronze Tank
(2 Chr 4.2–5)

23 Huram made a round tank of bronze, 2.2 metres deep, 4.4 metres in diameter, and 13.2 metres in circumference. 24 All round the outer edge of the rim of the tank[x] were two rows of bronze gourds, which had been cast all in one piece with the rest of the tank. 25 The tank **rested** on the backs of twelve bronze bulls that faced outwards, three facing in each direction. 26 The sides of the tank were 75 millimetres thick. Its rim was like the rim of a **cup**, curving outwards like the petals of a lily. The tank held about forty thousand litres.

The Bronze Carts

27 Huram also made ten bronze carts; each was 1.8 metres long, 1.8 metres wide, and 1.3 metres high. 28 They were made of square panels which were set in frames, 29 with the figures of lions, bulls, and winged **creatures** on the panels; and on the frames, above and underneath the lions and bulls, there were spiral figures in relief. 30 Each cart had four bronze wheels with bronze axles. At the four corners were bronze supports for a basin; the supports were decorated with spiral figures in relief. 31 There was a circular frame on top for the basin. It projected upwards 45 centimetres from the top of the cart and 18 centimetres down into it. It had carvings round it. 32 The wheels were 66 centimetres high; they were under the panels, and the axles were of one piece with the carts. 33 The wheels were like chariot wheels; their axles, rims, spokes, and hubs were all of bronze. 34 There were four supports at the bottom corners of each cart, which were of one piece with the cart. 35 There was a 22 centimetre band round the top of each cart; its supports and the panels were of one piece with the cart. 36 The supports and panels were decorated with figures of winged **creatures**, lions, and palm-trees, wherever there was space for them, with spiral figures all round. 37 This, then, is how the carts were made; they were all alike, having the same size and shape.

38 Huram also made ten basins, one for each cart. Each basin was 1.8 metres in diameter, and held about 800 litres. 39 He placed five of the carts on the south side of the Temple, and the other five on the north side; the tank he placed at the south-east corner.

Summary List of Temple Furnishings
(2 Chr 4.11–5.1)

40–45 Huram also made pots, shovels, and bowls. He **completed** all his work for King Solomon for the LORD's Temple. This is what he made:

The two columns
The two bowl-shaped capitals on top of the columns
The design of interwoven chains on each capital
The four hundred bronze pomegranates, in two rows of a hundred each round the design on each capital
The ten carts
The ten basins
The tank
The twelve bulls supporting the tank
The pots, shovels, and bowls

All this equipment for the Temple, which Huram made for King Solomon, was of polished bronze. 46 The king had it all made in the foundry between Sukkoth

[s] *Some ancient translations* each one...circumference; *Hebrew* the first column was 8 metres tall and the second column was 5.3 metres in circumference. [t] *Verse 17 in Hebrew is unclear.*
[u] *One ancient translation* each; *Hebrew* the second.
[v] JACHIN: *This name sounds like the Hebrew for "he (God) establishes."*
[w] BOAZ: *This name sounds like the Hebrew for "by his (God's) strength."*
[x] *Probable text* All round...tank; *Hebrew unclear.*

7.38: Ex 30.17–21

and Zarethan, in the Jordan Valley. 47 Solomon did not have these bronze objects weighed, because there were too many of them, and so their weight was never **determined**.

48 Solomon also had gold furnishings made for the Temple: the **altar**, the table for the **bread offered** to God, 49 the ten lamp-stands that stood in front of the **Most Holy Place**, five on the south side and five on the north; the flowers, lamps, and tongs; 50 the **cups**, lamp snuffers, bowls, dishes for **incense**, and the pans used for carrying live coals; and the hinges for the doors of the **Most Holy Place** and of the outer doors of the Temple. All these furnishings were made of gold.

51 When King Solomon finished all the work on the Temple, he placed in the temple storerooms all the things that his father David had **dedicated** to the LORD—the silver, gold, and other articles.

The Covenant Box Is Brought to the Temple

(2 Chr 5.2–6.2)

8 Then King Solomon summoned all the leaders of the tribes and clans of Israel to come to him in Jerusalem in order to take the LORD's **Covenant Box** from Zion, David's City, to the Temple. 2 They all assembled during the **Festival of Shelters** in the seventh month, in the month of Ethanim. 3 When all the leaders had gathered, the **priests** lifted the **Covenant Box** 4 and carried it to the Temple. The **Levites** and the **priests** also moved the **Tent** of the LORD's presence and all its equipment to the Temple. 5 King Solomon and all the people of Israel assembled in front of the **Covenant Box** and **sacrificed** a large number of **sheep** and cattle—too many to count. 6 Then the **priests** carried the **Covenant Box** into the Temple and put it in the **Most Holy Place**, beneath the winged **creatures**. 7 Their outstretched wings covered the **box** and the poles it was carried by. 8 The ends of the poles could be seen by anyone standing directly in front of the **Most Holy Place**, but from nowhere else. (The poles are still there today.) 9 There was nothing inside the **Covenant Box** except the two stone **tablets** which Moses had placed there at Mount Sinai, when the LORD made a **covenant** with the people of Israel as they were coming from Egypt.

10 As the **priests** were leaving the Temple, it was suddenly filled with a **cloud** 11 shining with the **dazzling light** of the LORD's **presence**, and they could not go back in to perform their **duties**. 12 Then Solomon **prayed**:

"You, LORD, have placed the sun in the
sky,[y]
yet you have **chosen** to live in **clouds**
and **darkness**.
13 Now I have built a **majestic** temple for
you,
a place for you to live in for ever."

Solomon's Address to the People

(2 Chr 6.3–11)

14 As the people stood there, King Solomon **turned** to face them, and he asked God's **blessing** on them. 15 He said, "**Praise** the LORD God of Israel! He has kept the **promise** he made to my father David, when he said, 16 'From the time I brought **my people** out of Egypt, I have not **chosen** any city in all the land of Israel in which a **temple** should be built where I would be **worshipped**. But I **chose** you, David, to rule **my people**.' "

17 And Solomon continued, "My father David **planned** to build a **temple** for the **worship** of the LORD God of Israel, 18 but the LORD said to him, 'You were **right** in wanting to build a **temple** for me, 19 but you will never build it. It is your son, your own son, who will build my **temple**.'

20 "And now the LORD has kept his **promise**. I have succeeded my father as king of Israel, and I have built the **Temple** for the **worship** of the LORD God of Israel. 21 I have also **provided** a place in the **Temple** for the **Covenant Box** containing the stone **tablets** of the **covenant** which the LORD made with our ancestors when he brought them out of Egypt."

Solomon's Prayer

(2 Chr 6.12–42)

22 Then in the **presence** of the people Solomon went and stood in front of the **altar**, where he **raised** his arms 23 and **prayed**, "LORD God of Israel, there is no **god** like you in **heaven above** or on earth below! You keep your **covenant** with your people and show them your **love** when they live in **whole-hearted obedience** to you. 24 You have kept the **promise** you made to my father David; today every **word** has been **fulfilled**.

[y] *One ancient translation* You...sky; *Hebrew does not have these words.*

7.48: Ex 25.23-30, 30.1–3 **7.49:** Ex 25.31–40 **7.51:** 2 Sam 8.11; 1 Chr 18.11
8.1: 2 Sam 6.12–16; 1 Chr 15.25–29 **8.2:** Lev 23.24 **8.9:** Deut 10.5 **8.10–11:** Ex 40.34–35
8.12: Ps 18.11, 97.2 **8.16:** 2 Sam 7.4–11; 1 Chr 17.3–10 **8.17–18:** 2 Sam 7.1–3; 1 Chr 17.1–2
8.19: 2 Sam 7.12–13; 1 Chr 17.11–12

helter [2] ! Sam 21.10; ! Chr 5.3
incere Judg 9.16; Chr 29.17
orrow 2 Sam 13.31; ! Chr 6.29
overeign ! Sam 7.18; Ps 69.6
ablet [2] Deut 10.1; Chr 5.10
each 2 Sam 7.21; Kgs 4.38
Temple (1) (of God) 20] 5.3; 9.1
Tent (2) (of the ord's presence) .28; 1 Chr 6.32
rue [2] 2.27; 10.6
urn [2] 2 Sam 22.22; 1.3
ictory 5.3; 20.13
vatch 2 Sam 18.24; .3
vicked 2 Sam 22.27; 2.52
vord (1) 2 Sam 23.1; 3.20
vorld [2] 4.34; 10.24
vorship (1) (of God) 6] 5.3; 9.3
vrong 2.44; 11.33

25 And now, LORD God of Israel, I **pray** that you will also keep the other **promise** you made to my father when you told him that there would always be one of his descendants ruling as king of Israel, **provided** they **obeyed** you as carefully as he did. 26 So now, O God of Israel, let everything come **true** that you **promised** to my father David, your **servant**.

27 "But can you, O God, really live on earth? Not even all **heaven** is large **enough** to hold you, so how can this **Temple** that I have built be large **enough**? 28 LORD my God, I am your **servant**. Listen to my **prayer**, and **grant** the **requests** I make to you today. 29 **Watch** over this **Temple** day and night, this place where you have **chosen** to be **worshipped**. Hear me when I face this **Temple** and **pray**. 30 Hear my **prayers** and the prayers of your people when they face this place and **pray**. In your home in **heaven** hear us and **forgive** us.

31 "When a person is **accused** of **wronging** another and is brought to your **altar** in this **Temple** to take an **oath** that he is **innocent**, 32 O LORD, listen in **heaven** and **judge** your **servants**. **Punish** the **guilty** one as he **deserves**, and acquit the one who is **innocent**.

33 "When your people Israel are defeated by their **enemies** because they have sinned against you, and then when they **turn to** you and come to this **Temple**, **humbly praying** to you for **forgiveness**, 34 listen to them in **heaven**. **Forgive** the sins of your people, and bring them back to the land which you gave to their ancestors.

35 "When you hold back the rain because your people have sinned against you, and then when they **repent** and face this **Temple**, **humbly praying** to you, 36 listen to them in **heaven**. **Forgive** the sins of the king and of the people of Israel. **Teach** them to do what is **right**. Then, O LORD, send rain on this land of yours, which you gave to your people as a permanent **possession**.

37 "When there is **famine** in the land or an epidemic, or the crops are **destroyed** by scorching winds or swarms of locusts, or when your people are attacked by their **enemies**, or when there is **disease** or sickness among them, 38 listen to their **prayers**. If any of your people Israel, out of **heartfelt sorrow**, stretch out their hands in **prayer** towards this **Temple**, 39 hear their **prayer**. Listen to them in your home in **heaven**, **forgive** them, and **help** them. You **alone** know the thoughts of the **human heart**. Deal with each person as he **deserves**, 40 so that your people may **obey** you all the time they live in the land which you gave to our ancestors.

41–42 "When a foreigner who lives in a distant land hears of your fame and of the great things you have done for your people, and comes to **worship** you and to **pray** at this **Temple**, 43 listen to his **prayer**. In **heaven**, where you live, hear him and do what he asks you to do, so that all the peoples of the **world** may know you and **obey** you, as your people Israel do. Then they will know that this **Temple** I have built is the place where you are to be **worshipped**.

44 "When you **command** your people to go into battle against their **enemies** and they **pray** to you, wherever they are, facing this city which you have **chosen** and this **Temple** which I have built for you, 45 listen to their **prayers**. Hear them in **heaven**, and give them **victory**.

46 "When your people sin against you—and there is no one who does not sin—and in your **anger** you let their **enemies** defeat them and take them as **prisoners** to some other land, even if that land is far away, 47 listen to your people's **prayers**. If there in that land they **repent** and **pray** to you, **confessing** how sinful and **wicked** they have been, hear their **prayers** O LORD. 48 If in that land they **truly** and **sincerely repent**, and **pray** to you as they face towards this land which you gave to our ancestors, this city which you have **chosen**, and this **Temple** which I have built for you, 49 then listen to their **prayers**. In your home in **heaven** hear them and be **merciful** to them. 50 **Forgive** all their sins and their **rebellion** against you, and make their **enemies** treat them with **kindness**. 51 They are your **own people**, whom you brought out of Egypt, that blazing furnace.

52 "**Sovereign** LORD, may you always look with **favour** on your people Israel and their king, and hear their **prayer** whenever they call to you for **help**. 53 You **chose** them from all the peoples to be your **own people**, as you told them through your **servant** Moses when you brought our ancestors out of Egypt."

The Final Prayer

54 After Solomon had finished **praying** to the LORD, he stood up in front of the **altar**, where he had been **kneeling** with uplifted hands. 55 In a loud voice he asked God's **blessings** on all the people assembled there. He said, 56 "**Praise** the LORD who has given **his people peace**, as

8.25: 1 Kgs 2.4 **8.27:** 2 Chr 2.6 **8.29:** Deut 12.11 **8.56:** Deut 12.10; Josh 21.44–45

he **promised** he would. He has kept all
the **generous promises** he made through
his **servant** Moses. 57 May the LORD our
God be with us, as he was with our ancestors; may he never leave us, or **abandon**
us; 58 may he make us **obedient** to him, so
that we will always live as he wants us to
live, and keep all the **laws** and **com-**
mands he gave our ancestors. 59 May the
LORD our God **remember** at all times this
prayer and these petitions I have made
to him. May he always be **merciful** to the
people of Israel and to their king, according to their daily **needs**. 60 And so all the
nations of the **world** will know that the
LORD **alone** is God—there is no other.
61 May you, **his people**, always be **faithful**
to the LORD our God, **obeying** all his **laws**
and **commands**, as you do today."

The Dedication of the Temple
(2 Chr 7.4–10)

62 Then King Solomon and all the
people there **offered sacrifices** to the
LORD. 63 He **sacrificed** 22,000 head of
cattle and 120,000 **sheep** as **fellowship-**
offerings. And so the king and all the
people **dedicated** the **Temple**. 64 That
same day he also **consecrated** the
central part of the courtyard, the area in
front of the **Temple**, and then he **offered**
there the sacrifices burnt whole, the
grain-offerings, and the fat of the animals
for the **fellowship-offerings**. He did this
because the bronze **altar** was too small
for all these **offerings**.

65 There at the **Temple**, Solomon and
all the people of Israel **celebrated** the
Festival of Shelters for seven[z] days.
There was a huge crowd of people from
as far away as Hamath Pass in the north
and the Egyptian border in the south.
66 On the eighth day Solomon sent the
people home. They all **praised** him and
went home **happy** because of all the
blessings that the LORD had given his servant David and **his people** Israel.

God Appears to Solomon Again
(2 Chr 7.11–22)

9 After King Solomon had finished
building the **Temple** and the palace
and everything else he wanted to build,
2 the LORD appeared to him again, as he
had in Gibeon. 3 The LORD said to him, "I
have heard your **prayer**. I **consecrate**
this **Temple** which you have built as the
place where I shall be **worshipped** for
ever. I will **watch** over it and **protect** it
for all time. 4 If you will **serve** me in
honesty and integrity, as your father
David did, and if you **obey** my **laws** and
do everything I have **commanded** you, 5 I
will keep the **promise** I made to your
father David when I told him that Israel
would always be ruled by his descendants. 6 But if you or your descendants stop
following me, if you **disobey** the **laws** and
commands I have given you, and **worship**
other gods, 7 then I will remove **my**
people Israel from the land that I have
given them. I will also **abandon** this
Temple which I have **consecrated** as the
place where I am to be **worshipped**.
People everywhere will **ridicule** Israel
and treat her with **contempt**. 8 This
Temple will become a pile of **ruins**,[a] and
everyone who passes by will be shocked
and **amazed**. 'Why did the LORD do this to
this land and this **Temple**?' they will ask.
9 People will answer, 'It is because they
abandoned the LORD their God, who
brought their ancestors out of Egypt.
They gave their allegiance to other **gods**
and **worshipped** them. That is why the
LORD has brought this **disaster** on
them.'"

Solomon's Agreement with Hiram
(2 Chr 8.1–2)

10 It took Solomon twenty years to
build the **Temple** and his palace. 11 King
Hiram of Tyre had **provided** him with all
the cedar and pine and with all the gold
he wanted for this work. After it was
finished, King Solomon gave Hiram
twenty towns in the region of Galilee.
12 Hiram went to see them, and he did not
like them. 13 So he said to Solomon, "So
these, my brother, are the towns you
have given me!" For this **reason** the
area is still called Cabul.[b] 14 Hiram had
sent Solomon more than four thousand
kilogrammes of gold.

Further Achievements of Solomon
(2 Chr 8.3–18)

15 King Solomon used **forced labour** to
build the **Temple** and the palace, to fill in
land on the east side of the city, and to
build the city wall. He also used it to
rebuild the cities of Hazor, Megiddo, and
Gezer. 16 (The king of Egypt had attacked
Gezer and captured it, killing its inhabitants and setting fire to the city. Then he
gave it as a **wedding** present to his
daughter when she married Solomon,
17 and Solomon rebuilt it.) Using his

abandon [2] 8.57; 14.16
altar 8.22; 12.32
amaze Judg 20.40; 10.5
burnt-offering 3.4; 2 Kgs 5.17
command [2] 8.44; 11.2
consecrate [2] 8.64; 2 Chr 5.11

contempt 2 Sam 12.14; 2 Chr 7.20
disaster 2 Sam 1[…] 14.10
disobey 2.43; 11.1[…]
experience 7.14; 1 Chr 12.1
fellowship-offeri[…] 8.63; 2 Kgs 16.13
force (1) [4] 5.13; 11.28
god (2) (other go[…] [2] 8.23; 11.2
God's people 8.16[…] 14.7
honest 3.6; 2 Kgs 12.15
incense 7.50; 11.8
law [2] 8.58; 10.9
obey 8.23; 11.9
offer 8.62; 10.5
possess 8.36; 21.1
prayer 8.28; 17.22
promise 8.15; 11.[…]
protect 2 Sam 23.[…] 2 Kgs 11.7
provide 8.21; 11.1[…]
reason 2 Sam 14.[…] Neh 5.9
ridicule Deut 28.[…] 2 Kgs 19.22
ruin 2 Sam 20.19; 13.34
serve [3] 2.27; 10.[…]
slave [2] 2.39; 2 Kgs 4.1
Temple (1) (of G[…] [8] 8.16; 10.5
watch 8.29; 20.33
wedding 1 Sam 18.26; Song 3.11
worship (1) (of G[…] [2] 8.16; 11.36
worship (2) (of other gods) [2] 1 Sam 26.19; 11.4

[z] *One ancient translation* seven; *Hebrew* fourteen.
[a] *Some ancient translations* a pile of ruins; *Hebrew* high.
[b] CABUL: *This name sounds like "ke-bal," the Hebrew for "worthless."*

9.2: 1 Kgs 3.5; 2 Chr 1.7 **9.5:** 1 Kgs 2.4 **9.8:** 2 Kgs 25.9; 2 Chr 36.19

forced labour, Solomon also rebuilt Lower Beth Horon, 18 Baalath, Tamar in the wilderness of Judah, 19 the cities where his supplies were kept, the cities for his horses and chariots, and everything else he wanted to build in Jerusalem, in Lebanon, and elsewhere in his kingdom. 20-21 For his **forced labour** Solomon used the descendants of the people of Canaan whom the Israelites had not killed when they took **possession** of their land. These included Amorites, Hittites, Perizzites, Hivites, and Jebusites, whose descendants continue to be **slaves** down to the present time. 22 Solomon did not make **slaves** of Israelites; they **served** as his soldiers, officers, commanders, chariot captains, and horsemen.

23 There were 550 officials in charge of the **forced labour** working on Solomon's various building projects.

24 Solomon filled in the land on the east side of the city, after his wife, the daughter of the king of Egypt, had moved from David's City to the palace Solomon built for her.

25 Three times a year Solomon **offered burnt-offerings** and **fellowship-offerings** on the **altar** he had built to the LORD. He also burnt **incense**[c] to the LORD. And so he finished building the **Temple**.

26 King Solomon also built a fleet of ships at Eziongeber, which is near Elath, on the shore of the Gulf of Aqaba, in the land of Edom. 27 King Hiram sent some **experienced** seamen from his fleet to **serve** with Solomon's men. 28 They sailed to the land of Ophir, and brought back to Solomon more than fourteen thousand kilogrammes of gold.

The Visit of the Queen of Sheba
(2 Chr 9.1–12)

10 The queen of Sheba heard of Solomon's fame,[d] and she travelled to Jerusalem to **test** him with **difficult questions**. 2 She brought with her a large group of attendants, as well as camels loaded with spices, jewels, and a large amount of gold. When she and Solomon met, she asked him all the **questions** that she could think of. 3 He answered them all; there was nothing too **difficult** for him to explain. 4 The queen of Sheba heard Solomon's **wisdom** and saw the palace he had built. 5 She saw the food that was **served** at his table, the living quarters for his officials, the organization of his palace staff and the uniforms they wore, the **servants** who waited on him at **feasts**, and the **sacrifices** he **offered** in the **Temple**. It left her breathless and **amazed**. 6 She said to King Solomon, "What I heard in my own country about you[e] and your **wisdom** is **true**! 7 But I couldn't **believe** it until I had come and seen it all for myself. But I didn't hear even half of it; your **wisdom** and wealth are much greater than what I was told. 8 How **fortunate** are your wives![f] And how **fortunate** your **servants**, who are always in your **presence** and are **privileged** to hear your **wise sayings**! 9 **Praise** the LORD your God! He has shown how **pleased** he is with you by making you king of Israel. Because his **love** for Israel is **eternal**, he has made you their king so that you can maintain **law** and **justice**."

10 She **presented** to King Solomon the **gifts** she had brought: more than four thousand kilogrammes of gold and a very large amount of spices and jewels. The amount of spices she gave him was by far the greatest that he ever received at any time.

11 (Hiram's fleet, which had brought gold from Ophir, also brought from there a large amount of juniper wood and jewels. 12 Solomon used the wood to build railings in the **Temple** and the palace, and also to make harps and lyres for the musicians. It was the finest juniper wood ever imported into Israel; none like it has ever been seen again.)

13 King Solomon gave the queen of Sheba everything she asked for, besides all the other **customary gifts** that he had **generously** given her. Then she and her attendants returned to the land of Sheba.

King Solomon's Wealth
(2 Chr 9.13–28)

14 Every year King Solomon received almost twenty-three thousand kilogrammes of gold 15 in addition to the **taxes**[g] paid by merchants, the profits from trade, and **tribute** paid by the Arabian kings and the governors of the Israelite districts.

16 Solomon made two hundred large shields, and had each one overlaid with almost seven kilogrammes of gold. 17 He also made three hundred smaller shields, overlaying each one of them with almost two kilogrammes of gold. He had all these shields placed in the Hall of the Forest of Lebanon.[h]

justice 3.9; 1 Chr 18.14
law 9.4; 11.33
love 8.23; 11.1
offer 9.25; 11.8
please 5.7; 14.13
plenty Ruth 1.21; 2 Kgs 3.17
praise 8.15; 1 Chr 16.4
presence 8.11; 2 Kgs 19.14
present (1) 3.16; 18.1
privilege Deut 18.2; 2 Chr 9.7
pure 6.20; 2 Kgs 2.21
question [2] 2 Sam 14.18; 2 Kgs 8.6
reign 6.1; 11.12
rich 2 Sam 19.32; 2 Kgs 4.8
sacrifice 8.5; 11.8
saying 1 Sam 24.13; 2 Chr 9.7
servant [2] 8.26; 11.13
serve 9.4; 12.6
tax 4.21; 2 Kgs 23.35
Temple (1) (of God) [2] 9.1; 12.26
test Judg 6.39; 1 Chr 29.17
throne [4] 7.7; 22.10
tribute Gen 49.10; 2 Kgs 3.4
true 8.26; 11.6
value Lev 27.18; 20.6
wisdom [4] 5.12; 11.41
wise [2] 5.7; 2 Chr 2.12
world 8.43; 18.10

amaze 9.8; 2 Chr 7.21
believe 2 Sam 13.33; 2 Chr 9.6
control 2.46; 12.21
cup 7.26; 2 Kgs 12.13
custom Ruth 4.7; 2 Kgs 11.14
difficult [2] 1 Sam 10.19; 2 Kgs 2.10
eternal 2 Sam 23.5; 1 Chr 16.34
exist Gen 8.22; 2 Chr 9.19
feast 3.15; 2 Kgs 6.23
fortune [2] Judg 5.24; 2 Chr 9.7
generous 8.56; 1 Chr 29.5
gift [3] 1 Sam 10.27; 2 Kgs 5.15

[c] *Hebrew has two additional words, the meaning of which is unclear.*
[d] *Probable text (see 2 Chr 9.1)* Solomon's fame; *Hebrew* Solomon's fame concerning the name of the LORD. [e] you; *or* your deeds. [f] *Some ancient translations* wives; *Hebrew* men.
[g] *Some ancient translations* taxes; *Hebrew* men. [h] HALL OF THE FOREST OF LEBANON: *See 7.2–3.*

9.25: Ex 23.17, 34.23; Deut 16.16 **10.1-10:** Mt 12.42; Lk 11.31

18 He also had a large **throne** made. Part of it was covered with ivory and the rest of it was covered with the finest gold. 19-20 The **throne** had six steps leading up to it, with the figure of a lion at each end of every step, a total of twelve lions. At the back of the **throne** was the figure of a bull's head, and beside each of the two arms was the figure of a lion. No **throne** like this had ever **existed** in any other kingdom.

21 All of Solomon's drinking **cups** were made of gold, and all the utensils in the Hall of the Forest of Lebanon were of **pure** gold. No silver was used, since it was not considered **valuable** in Solomon's day. 22 He had a fleet of ocean-going ships sailing with Hiram's fleet. Every three years his fleet would return, bringing gold, silver, ivory, apes, and monkeys.

23 King Solomon was **richer** and **wiser** than any other king, 24 and the whole **world** wanted to come and listen to the **wisdom** that God had given him. 25 Everyone who came brought him a **gift**—articles of silver and gold, robes, weapons, spices, horses, and mules. This continued year after year.

26 Solomon built up a force of fourteen hundred chariots and twelve thousand cavalry **horses**. Some of them he kept in Jerusalem and the rest he stationed in various other cities. 27 During his **reign** silver was as common in Jerusalem as stone, and cedar was as **plentiful** as ordinary sycomore in the foothills of Judah. 28 The king's agents **controlled** the export of horses from Musri[i] and Cilicia,[j] 29 and the export of chariots from Egypt. They supplied the Hittite and Syrian kings with horses and chariots, selling chariots for 600 pieces of silver each and horses for 150 each.

Solomon Turns Away from God

11 Solomon **loved** many foreign women. Besides the daughter of the king of Egypt he married Hittite women and women from Moab, Ammon, Edom, and Sidon. 2 He married them even though the LORD had **commanded** the Israelites not to intermarry with these people, because they would cause the Israelites to give their **loyalty** to other **gods**. 3 Solomon married seven hundred princesses and also had three hundred **concubines**. They made him **turn** away from God, 4 and by the time he was old they had led him into the **worship of foreign** gods. He was not **faithful** to the LORD his God, as his father David had been. 5 He **worshipped Astarte** the **goddess** of Sidon, and Molech the **disgusting god of Ammon**. 6 He sinned against the LORD and was not **true** to him as his father David had been. 7 On the mountain east of Jerusalem he built a place to **worship** Chemosh, the **disgusting god of** Moab, and a place to **worship Molech**, the **disgusting god of Ammon**. 8 He also built **places of worship** where all his foreign wives could burn **incense** and **offer sacrifices** to their own **gods**.

9-10 Even though the LORD, the God of Israel, had appeared to Solomon twice and had **commanded** him not to **worship foreign gods**, Solomon did not **obey** the LORD, but **turned away** from him. So the LORD was **angry** with Solomon 11 and said to him, "Because you have deliberately broken your **covenant** with me and **disobeyed** my **commands**, I **promise** that I will take the kingdom away from you and give it to one of your officials. 12 However, for the **sake** of your father David I will not do this in your lifetime, but during the **reign** of your son. 13 And I will not take the whole kingdom away from him; instead, I will leave him one tribe for the **sake** of my **servant** David and for the **sake** of Jerusalem, the city I have made my own."

Solomon's Enemies

14 So the LORD caused Hadad, of the royal family of Edom, to **turn** against Solomon. 15-16 Long before this, when David had **conquered** Edom, Joab the commander of his army had gone there to bury the **dead**. He and his men remained in Edom six months, and during that time they killed every male in Edom 17 except Hadad and some of his father's Edomite **servants**, who **escaped** to Egypt. (At that time Hadad was just a child.) 18 They left Midian and went to Paran, where some other men joined them. Then they travelled to Egypt and went to the king, who gave Hadad some land and a house and **provided** him with food. 19 Hadad **won** the **friendship** of the king, and the king gave his sister-in-law, the sister of Queen Tahpenes, to Hadad in marriage. 20 She bore him a son, Genubath, who was brought up by the queen in the palace, where he lived with the king's sons.

21 When the news reached Hadad in

[i] *Probable text* Musri; *Hebrew* Egypt.
[j] MUSRI AND CILICIA: *Two ancient countries in what is now south-east Turkey, which were centres of horse breeding in Solomon's time.*

10.26: 1 Kgs 4.26 **10.28:** Deut 17.16 **11.1:** Deut 17.17 **11.2:** Ex 34.16; Deut 7.3–4

alone 8.39; 18.39
anger 8.46; 14.9
approve 1.27; 14.8
bitter 2.8; 2 Kgs 20.3
choose [3] 8.12; 12.31
command [6] 9.4; 12.24
concubine 2 Sam 21.10; 1 Chr 1.32
conquer 2 Sam 12.29; 2 Kgs 3.19
covenant 8.9; 19.10
dead [2] 3.20; 19.2
death (1) 3.11; 17.12
disgust [3] 2 Sam 6.16; 2 Kgs 16.3
disobey [2] 9.6; 13.21
enemy [2] 8.33; 20.39

escape [2] 2 Sam 20.6; 12.2
evil 3.9; 13.33
fail 1 Sam 26.16; 2 Kgs 3.26
faithful 8.61; 15.14
flee 2.7; 19.3
force (1) 9.15; 12.1
friend 5.1; 16.11
god (2) (other god [10] 9.6; 12.28
goddess [2] 1 Sam 31.10; 14.15
hard 2 Sam 17.8; 20.37
incense 9.25; 22.43
law [3] 10.9; 2 Kgs 10.31
love 10.9; 1 Chr 16.
loyal 3.6; 12.4
master 2 Sam 16.3 18.8
new 2 Sam 21.16; 2 Kgs 2.20
notice (1) 2 Sam 17.19; 21.29
obey [3] 9.4; 12.24
offer 10.5; 12.26
place of worship 2 Sam 15.32; 12.31
power 2.12; 15.16
promise 9.5; 17.16
prophet 1.8; 12.15
provide 9.11; 18.4
punish 8.32; 14.15
reign 10.27; 14.25
reject 1 Sam 16.1; 14.9
sacrifice 10.5; 12.2
sake [6] 2 Sam 18.5 15.4
servant [6] 10.5; 14
slaughter 3.3; 13.2
sure 2 Sam 23.5; 13.32
true 10.6; 13.32
turn [5] 8.14; 13.33
widow 2 Sam 20.3; 17.9
win [2] 2 Sam 23.10 16.22
wisdom 10.4; 1 Chr 22.12
worship (1) (of Go 9.3; 12.28
worship (2) (of other gods) [6] 9.6; 12.30
wrong 8.31; 21.20

Egypt that David had died and that Joab the commander of the army was **dead**, Hadad said to the king, "Let me go back to my own country."

22 "Why?" the king asked. "Have I **failed** to give you something? Is that why you want to go back home?"

"Just let me go," Hadad answered the king. And he went back to his country.[k]

As king of Edom, Hadad was an **evil, bitter enemy** of Israel.[l]

23 God also caused Rezon son of Eliada to **turn** against Solomon. Rezon had **fled** from his **master**, King Hadadezer of Zobah, 24 and had become the leader of a gang of outlaws. (This happened after David had defeated Hadadezer and had **slaughtered** his Syrian allies.) Rezon and his men went and lived in Damascus, where his men made him king of Syria. 25 He was an **enemy** of Israel during the lifetime of Solomon.

God's Promise to Jeroboam

26 Another man who **turned** against King Solomon was one of his officials, Jeroboam son of Nebat, from Zeredah in Ephraim. His mother was a **widow** named Zeruah. 27 This is the story of the revolt.

Solomon was filling in the land on the east side of Jerusalem and repairing the city walls. 28 Jeroboam was an able young man, and when Solomon **noticed** how **hard** he worked, he put him in charge of all the **forced labour** in the territory of the tribes of Manasseh and Ephraim. 29 One day, as Jeroboam was travelling from Jerusalem, the **prophet** Ahijah, from Shiloh, met him **alone** on the road in the open country. 30 Ahijah took off the **new** robe he was wearing, tore it into twelve pieces, 31 and said to Jeroboam, "Take ten pieces for yourself, because the LORD, the God of Israel, says to you, 'I am going to take the kingdom away from Solomon, and I will give you ten tribes. 32 Solomon will keep one tribe, for the **sake** of my **servant** David and for the **sake** of Jerusalem, the city I have **chosen** to be my own from the whole land of Israel. 33 I am going to do this because Solomon has **rejected** me and has[m] **worshipped foreign gods**: Astarte, the **goddess** of Sidon; Chemosh, the **god of Moab**; and Molech, the **god of Ammon**. Solomon has[n] **disobeyed** me; he has done **wrong**, and has not kept my **laws** and **commands** as his father David did. 34 But I will not take the whole kingdom away from Solomon, and I will keep him in **power** as long as he lives. This I will do for the **sake** of my **servant** David, whom I **chose** and who **obeyed** my **laws** and **commands**. 35 I will take the kingdom away from Solomon's son and will give you ten tribes, 36 but I will let Solomon's son keep one tribe, so that I will always have a descendant of my **servant** David ruling in Jerusalem, the city I have **chosen** as the place where I am **worshipped**. 37 Jeroboam, I will make you king of Israel, and you will rule over all the territory that you want. 38 If you **obey** me completely, live by my **laws**, and **win** my **approval** by doing what I **command**, as my **servant** David did, I will always be with you. I will make you king of Israel and will make **sure** that your descendants rule after you, just as I have done for David. 39 Because of Solomon's sin I will **punish** the descendants of David, but not for all time.'"

40 And so Solomon tried to kill Jeroboam, but he **escaped** to King Shishak of Egypt and stayed there until Solomon's **death**.

The Death of Solomon
(2 Chr 9.29–31)

41 Everything else that Solomon did, his career and his **wisdom**, are all recorded in *The History of Solomon*. 42 He was king in Jerusalem over all Israel for forty years. 43 He died and was buried in David's City, and his son Rehoboam succeeded him as king.

The Northern Tribes Revolt
(2 Chr 10.1–19)

12 Rehoboam went to Shechem, where all the people of northern Israel had gathered to make him king. 2 When Jeroboam son of Nebat, who had gone to Egypt to **escape** from King Solomon, heard this news, he returned from[o] Egypt. 3 The people of the northern tribes sent for him, and then they all went together to Rehoboam and said to him, 4 "Your father Solomon treated us harshly and placed heavy **burdens** on us. If you make these **burdens** lighter and make **life** easier for us, we will be your **loyal subjects**."

5 "Come back in three days and I will

advice [5] 1.12; 20.25
altar [2] 9.25; 13.1
best 2 Sam 19.37; 2 Kgs 7.1
bull-calf [3] Deut 9.16; 2 Kgs 10.29
burden [5] 2 Sam 19.35; 2 Chr 10.4
celebrate 8.65; 2 Kgs 23.21
choose 11.32; 13.33
command 11.2; 13.1
consult 2 Sam 21.1; 22.5
control 10.28; 2 Kgs 16.6
death (3) (to death) 2.9; 16.11
enough 8.27; 16.31

[k] *One ancient translation* And he went back to his country; *Hebrew does not have these words.*
[l] *One ancient translation* As king...Israel; *in Hebrew this sentence, with some differences, comes at the end of verse 25.*
[m] *Some ancient translations* Solomon has...and has; *Hebrew* they have...and have.
[n] *Some ancient translations* Solomon has; *Hebrew* They have.
[o] *Some ancient translations (and see 2 Chr 10.2)* returned from; *Hebrew* remained in.

escape [2] 11.17; 19.17
festival [3] 8.2; 2 Kgs 4.23
force (1) 11.28; 2 Kgs 3.26
god (2) (other gods) 11.2; 14.23
ignore [2] Deut 22.1; 1 Chr 13.3
intend 1 Sam 20.13; 1 Chr 12.17
life (1) 4.21; 15.14
loyal [3] 11.2; 14.8
message 5.2; 15.18
obey 11.9; 14.8
offer [3] 11.8; 13.1
place of worship [2] 11.8; 13.32
priest [2] 8.3; 13.2
prophet [2] 11.29; 13.1
rebel [2] 8.50; 2 Kgs 1.1
religion 1 Sam 21.7; 1 Chr 26.30
request 8.28; 2 Kgs 2.10
restore 2 Sam 16.3; 17.21
sacrifice [3] 11.8; 13.1
serve [4] 10.5; 13.2
subject (1) 4.21; 1 Chr 18.2
Temple (1) (of God) 10.5; 14.26
will (1) [2] 2.15; 1 Chr 5.22
worship (1) (of God) 11.36; 14.21
worship (2) (of other gods) 11.4; 14.9

give you my answer," he replied. So they
left.

6 King Rehoboam **consulted** the older
men who had **served** as his father
Solomon's advisers. "What answer do you
advise me to give these people?" he
asked.

7 They replied, "If you want to **serve**
this people well, give a favourable
answer to their **request**, and they will
always **serve** you **loyally**."

8 But he **ignored** the **advice** of the
older men and went instead to the young
men who had grown up with him and
who were now his advisers. 9 "What do
you **advise** me to do?" he asked. "What
shall I say to the people who are asking
me to make their **burdens** lighter?"

10 They replied, "This is what you
should tell them: 'My little finger is
thicker than my father's waist!' 11 Tell
them, 'My father placed heavy **burdens**
on you; I will make them even heavier.
He beat you with a whip; I'll flog you
with a horsewhip!' "

12 Three days later Jeroboam and all
the people returned to King Rehoboam,
as he had instructed them. 13 The king
ignored the **advice** of the older men and
spoke harshly to the people, 14 as the
younger men had **advised**. He said, "My
father placed heavy **burdens** on you; I
will make them even heavier. He beat
you with a whip; I'll flog you with a
horsewhip!" 15 It was the **will of the** LORD
to bring about what he had spoken to
Jeroboam son of Nebat through the
prophet Ahijah from Shiloh. This is why
the king did not pay any attention to the
people.

16 When the people saw that the king
would not listen to them, they shouted,
"Down with David and his family! What
have they ever done for us? Men of
Israel, let's go home! Let Rehoboam look
out for himself!"

So the people of Israel **rebelled**,
17 leaving Rehoboam as king only of the
people who lived in the territory of
Judah.

18 Then King Rehoboam sent Adoniram, who was in charge of the **forced
labour**, to go to the Israelites, but they
stoned him **to death**. At this, Rehoboam
hurriedly got into his chariot and
escaped to Jerusalem. 19 Ever since that
time the people of the northern kingdom
of Israel have been in **rebellion** against
the dynasty of David.

20 When the people of Israel heard
that Jeroboam had returned from Egypt,
they invited him to a meeting of the
people and made him king of Israel. Only
the tribe of Judah remained **loyal** to
David's descendants.

Shemaiah's Prophecy
(2 Chr 11.1–4)

21 When Rehoboam arrived in
Jerusalem, he called together 180,000 of
the **best** soldiers from the tribes of Judah
and Benjamin. He **intended** to go to war
and **restore** his **control** over the northern
tribes of Israel. 22 But God told the
prophet Shemaiah 23 to give this **message**
to Rehoboam and to all the people of the
tribes of Judah and Benjamin: 24 "Do not
attack your own brothers, the people of
Israel. Go home, all of you. What has
happened is my **will**." They all **obeyed**
the LORD's **command** and went back
home.

Jeroboam Turns Away from the LORD

25 King Jeroboam of Israel fortified
the town of Shechem in the hill-country
of Ephraim and lived there for a while.
Then he left and fortified the town of
Penuel. 26–27 He said to himself, "As things
are now, if my people go to Jerusalem
and **offer sacrifices** to the LORD in the
Temple there, they will transfer their
allegiance to King Rehoboam of Judah
and will kill me."

28 After thinking it over, he made two
bull-calves of gold and said to his people,
"You have been going long **enough** to
Jerusalem to **worship**. People of Israel,
here are your **gods** who brought you out
of Egypt!" 29 He placed one of the gold
bull-calves in Bethel and the other in
Dan. 30 And so the people sinned, going to
worship in Bethel and in Dan.[p] 31 Jeroboam also built **places of worship** on hill-
tops, and he **chose priests** from families
who were not of the tribe of Levi.

Worship at Bethel Is Condemned

32 Jeroboam also instituted a **religious
festival** on the fifteenth day of the eighth
month, like the **festival** in Judah. On the
altar in Bethel he **offered sacrifices** to
the gold **bull-calves** he had made, and he
placed there in Bethel the **priests serving**
at the **places of worship** he had built.
33 And on the fifteenth day of the eighth
month, the day that he himself had set,
he went to Bethel and **offered a sacrifice**
on the **altar** in **celebration** of the **festival**
he had instituted for the people of Israel.

13 At the LORD's **command** a
prophet from Judah went to

accept 7.14; 2 Kgs 5.15
altar [8] 12.32; 16.32

[p] *One ancient translation* in Bethel and in Dan; *Hebrew* in Dan.

12.16: 2 Sam 20.1 **12.28:** Ex 32.4 **12.32–33:** Lev 23.33–34

angel 2 Sam 24.16; 19.5
apart [2] 2 Sam 22.10; 2 Kgs 16.17
ash [2] 2 Sam 13.19; 2 Kgs 23.4
body [7] 2 Sam 21.12; 21.23
choose 12.31; 14.7
command [8] 12.24; 14.8
denounce Neh 5.7
destroy 8.37; 15.14
disobey [2] 11.11; 15.5
evil 11.21; 16.7
grave [3] 2 Sam 22.6; 2 Chr 34.4
heal [2] 1 Sam 6.3; 2 Kgs 20.5
human 8.39; 2 Kgs 19.18
lie (2) 2 Sam 19.27; 22.22
mourn [2] 2 Sam 19.1; 14.13
name (2) (name of God, of Jesus) 2.8; 17.1
offer [3] 12.26; 18.33
ordain Num 3.3; 2 Kgs 23.5
pagan 2 Sam 1.20; 14.24
paralyse 1 Sam 25.37; Ezek 3.26
place of worship 12.31; 14.23
pray [2] 8.12; 17.20
predict 2 Kgs 7.17
priest [3] 12.31; 2 Kgs 10.11
prophet [26] 12.15; 14.2
reward 2 Sam 22.21; 2 Chr 15.7
ruin 9.8; 20.7
sacrifice [2] 12.26; 18.36
scatter 2 Sam 22.15; 14.15
serve [2] 12.6; 14.24
slaughter 11.24; 2 Kgs 3.24
sure 11.38; 2 Kgs 4.9
true 11.6; 2 Kgs 3.12
turn 11.3; 22.32
way (3) Judg 2.19; 2 Kgs 8.18
word (1) [2] 8.24; 18.21

Bethel and arrived there as Jeroboam
stood at the **altar** to **offer the sacrifice**.
2 Following the LORD's **command**, the
prophet denounced the **altar**: "O **altar**,
altar, this is what the LORD says: A child,
whose name will be Josiah, will be born
to the family of David. He will **slaughter**
on you the **priests serving** at the **pagan**
altars who **offer sacrifices** on you, and he
will burn **human** bones on you." 3 And the
prophet went on to say, "This **altar** will
fall **apart**, and the **ashes** on it will be
scattered. Then you will know that the
LORD has spoken through me."
4 When King Jeroboam heard this, he
pointed at him and ordered, "Seize that
man!" At once the king's arm became
paralysed so that he couldn't pull it back.
5 The **altar** suddenly fell **apart** and the
ashes spilt to the ground, as the **prophet**
had **predicted** in the **name of the LORD**.
6 King Jeroboam said to the **prophet**,
"Please **pray** for me to the LORD your
God, and ask him to **heal** my arm!"
The **prophet prayed** to the LORD, and
the king's arm was **healed**. 7 Then the
king said to the **prophet**, "Come home
with me and have something to eat. I will
reward you for what you have done."
8 The **prophet** answered, "Even if you
gave me half your wealth, I would not go
with you or eat or drink anything with
you. 9 The LORD has **commanded** me not
to eat or drink a thing, and not to return
home the same way I came." 10 So he did
not go back the same way he had come,
but by another road.

The Old Prophet of Bethel

11 At that time there was an old
prophet living in Bethel. His sons[q] came
and told him what the **prophet** from
Judah had done in Bethel that day and
what he had said to King Jeroboam.
12 "Which way did he go when he left?"
the old **prophet** asked them. They
showed him[r] the road 13 and he told them
to saddle his donkey for him. They did so,
and he rode off 14 down the road after the
prophet from Judah and found him
sitting under an oak. "Are you the
prophet from Judah?" he asked.
"I am," the man answered.
15 "Come home and have a meal with
me," he said.
16 But the **prophet** from Judah
answered, "I can't go home with you or
accept your hospitality. And I won't eat
or drink anything with you here,
17 because the LORD has **commanded** me
not to eat or drink a thing, and not to
return home the same way I came."
18 Then the old **prophet** from Bethel
said to him, "I, too, am a **prophet** just like
you, and at the LORD's **command** an
angel told me to take you home with me
and **offer** you my hospitality." But the old
prophet was **lying**.
19 So the **prophet** from Judah went
home with the old prophet and had a
meal with him. 20 As they were sitting at
the table, the **word of the LORD** came to
the old **prophet**, 21 and he cried out to the
prophet from Judah, "The LORD says that
you **disobeyed** him and did not do what
he **commanded**. 22 Instead, you returned
and ate a meal in a place he had ordered
you not to eat in. Because of this you will
be killed, and your **body** will not be
buried in your family **grave**."
23 After they had finished eating, the
old **prophet** saddled the donkey for the
prophet from Judah, 24 who rode off. On
the way, a lion met him and killed him.
His **body** lay on the road, and the donkey
and the lion stood beside it. 25 Some men
passed by and saw the **body** on the road,
with the lion standing near by. They
went on into Bethel and reported what
they had seen.
26 When the old **prophet** heard about
it, he said, "That is the **prophet** who **disobeyed** the LORD's **command**! And so the
LORD sent the lion to attack and kill him,
just as the LORD said he would." 27 Then
he said to his sons, "Saddle my donkey
for me." They did so, 28 and he rode off
and found the **prophet's body** lying on the
road, with the donkey and the lion still
standing by it. The lion had not eaten the
body or attacked the donkey. 29 The old
prophet picked up the **body**, put it on the
donkey, and brought it back to Bethel to
mourn over it and bury it. 30 He buried it
in his own family **grave**, and he and his
sons **mourned** over it, saying, "Oh my
brother, my brother!" 31 After the burial,
the **prophet** said to his sons, "When I die,
bury me in this **grave** and lay my **body**
next to his. 32 The **words** that he spoke at
the LORD's **command** against the **altar** in
Bethel and against all the **places of worship** in the towns of Samaria will **surely**
come **true**."

Jeroboam's Fatal Sin

33 King Jeroboam of Israel still did
not **turn from** his **evil ways**, but continued to **choose priests** from ordinary
families to **serve** at the **altars** he had

[q] *Some ancient translations* sons; *Hebrew* son.
[r] *Some ancient translations* showed him; *Hebrew* saw.

13.2: 2 Kgs 23.15–16

built. He **ordained** as **priest** anyone who wanted to be one. 34 This sin on his part brought about the **ruin** and total **destruction** of his dynasty.

The Death of Jeroboam's Son

14 At that time King Jeroboam's son Abijah fell ill. 2 Jeroboam said to his wife, "Disguise yourself so that no one will recognize you, and go to Shiloh, where the **prophet** Ahijah lives, the one who said I would be king of Israel. 3 Take him ten loaves of **bread**, some cakes, and a jar of honey. Ask him what is going to happen to our son, and he will tell you."

4 So she went to Ahijah's home in Shiloh. Old age had made Ahijah **blind**. 5 The LORD had told him that Jeroboam's wife was coming to ask him about her son, who was ill. And the LORD told Ahijah what to say.

When Jeroboam's wife arrived, she pretended to be someone else. 6 But when Ahijah heard her coming in the door, he said, "Come in. I know you are Jeroboam's wife. Why are you pretending to be someone else? I have **bad** news for you. 7 Go and tell Jeroboam that this is what the LORD, the God of Israel, says to him: 'I **chose** you from among the people and made you the ruler of **my people** Israel. 8 I took the kingdom away from David's descendants and gave it to you. But you have not been like my **servant** David, who was completely **loyal** to me, **obeyed** my **commands**, and did only what I **approve** of. 9 You have committed far greater sins than those who ruled before you. You have **rejected** me and have aroused my **anger** by making **idols** and metal **images** to **worship**. 10 Because of this I will bring **disaster** on your dynasty and will kill all your male descendants, young and old alike. I will get **rid** of your family; they will be swept away like dung. 11 Any members of your family who die in the city will be eaten by dogs, and any who die in the open country will be eaten by vultures. I, the LORD, have spoken.' "

12 And Ahijah went on to say to Jeroboam's wife, "Now go back home. As soon as you enter the town your son will die. 13 All the people of Israel will **mourn** for him and bury him. He will be the only member of Jeroboam's family who will be **properly** buried, because he is the only one with whom the LORD, the God of Israel, is **pleased**. 14 The LORD is going to place a king over Israel who will put an end to Jeroboam's dynasty.[s] 15 The LORD will **punish** Israel, and she will shake like a reed shaking in a stream. He will uproot the people of Israel from this good land which he gave to their ancestors, and he will **scatter** them beyond the River Euphrates, because they have aroused his **anger** by making **idols** of the **goddess** Asherah. 16 The LORD will **abandon** Israel because Jeroboam sinned and led the people of Israel into sin."

17 Jeroboam's wife went back to Tirzah. Just as she entered her home, the child died. 18 The people of Israel **mourned** for him and buried him, as the LORD had said through his **servant**, the **prophet** Ahijah.

The Death of Jeroboam

19 Everything else that King Jeroboam did, the wars he fought and how he ruled, are all recorded in *The History of the Kings of Israel.* 20 Jeroboam ruled as king for twenty-two years. He died and was buried, and his son Nadab succeeded him as king.

King Rehoboam of Judah
(2 Chr 11.5—12.15)

21 Solomon's son Rehoboam was forty-one years old when he became king of Judah, and he ruled for seventeen years in Jerusalem, the city which the LORD had **chosen** from all the territory of Israel as the place where he was to be **worshipped**. Rehoboam's mother was Naamah from Ammon.

22 The people of Judah sinned against the LORD and did more to arouse his **anger** against them than all their ancestors had done. 23 They built **places of worship** for **false gods**, and put up stone pillars and **symbols** of Asherah to **worship** on the hills and under shady trees. 24 **Worst** of all, there were men and women who **served** as **prostitutes** at those **pagan places of worship**. The people of Judah **practised** all the **shameful** things done by the people whom the LORD had driven out of the land as the Israelites advanced into the country.

25 In the fifth year of Rehoboam's **reign** King Shishak of Egypt attacked Jerusalem. 26 He took away all the treasures in the **Temple** and in the palace, including the gold shields Solomon had made. 27 To replace them, King Rehoboam made bronze shields and **entrusted** them to the officers responsible for guarding the palace gates. 28 Every time the king went to the **Temple**, the

abandon 9.7; 2 Kgs 7.7
anger [3] 11.9; 15.30
approve 11.38; 18.24
bad 2 Sam 1.9; 22.8
blind 2 Sam 5.6; 2 Kgs 6.18
bread 7.48; 17.6
choose [2] 13.33; 2 Kgs 6.8
command 13.1; 15.5
disaster 9.9; 21.21
each other 6.27; 15.16
entrust 2 Chr 12.10
false 1 Sam 12.21; Job 36.4
god (2) (other gods) 12.28; 18.24
God's people 9.7; 16.2
goddess 11.5; 15.13
idol [2] 2 Sam 12.30; 15.12
image 1 Sam 7.3; 16.33
loyal 12.4; 15.3
mourn [2] 13.29; 1 Chr 7.22
obey 12.24; 17.5
pagan 13.2; 15.12
place of worship [2] 13.32; 15.12
please 10.9; 15.5
practice Deut 18.9; 2 Kgs 16.3
proper Judg 9.16; 2 Chr 30.1
prophet [2] 13.1; 15.29
prostitute 3.16; 15.12
punish 11.39; 2 Kgs 7.9
reign 11.12; 15.1
reject 11.33; 2 Kgs 17.20
rid 1 Sam 7.3; 21.21
scatter 13.3; 22.17
servant [2] 11.13; 15.29
serve 13.2; 15.12
shame Josh 7.15; 21.26
symbol Judg 6.25; 2 Kgs 21.7
Temple (1) (of God) [2] 12.26; 15.15
tomb 2 Sam 4.12; 15.24
worship (1) (of God) 12.28; 18.3
worship (2) (of other gods) [3] 12.30; 16.31
worst 2 Sam 19.7; 18.2

[s] *Hebrew has five additional words, the meaning of which is unclear.*

14.10: 1 Kgs 15.29 **14.23:** 2 Kgs 17.9–10 **14.24:** Deut 23.17 **14.26:** 1 Kgs 10.16–17; 2 Chr 9.15–16

guards carried the shields, and then returned them to the guard-room.

29 Everything else that King Rehoboam did is recorded in *The History of the Kings of Judah.* 30 During all this time Rehoboam and Jeroboam were constantly at war with **each other**. 31 Rehoboam died and was buried in the royal **tombs** in David's City, and his son Abijah succeeded him as king.

King Abijah of Judah
(2 Chr 13.1—14.1)

15 In the eighteenth year of the **reign** of King Jeroboam of Israel, Abijah became king of Judah, 2 and he ruled for three years in Jerusalem. His mother was Maacah, the daughter of Absalom. 3 He committed the same sins as his father and was not completely **loyal** to the LORD his God, as his great-grandfather David had been. 4 But for David's **sake**, the LORD his God gave Abijah a son to rule after him in Jerusalem and to keep Jerusalem **secure**. 5 The LORD did this because David had done what **pleased** him and had never **disobeyed** any of his **commands**, except in the case of Uriah the Hittite. 6 The war which had begun between Rehoboam and Jeroboam continued throughout Abijah's lifetime. 7 And everything else that Abijah did is recorded in *The History of the Kings of Judah.*

8 Abijah died and was buried in David's City, and his son Asa succeeded him as king.

King Asa of Judah
(2 Chr 15.16—16.6)

9 In the twentieth year of the **reign** of King Jeroboam of Israel, Asa became king of Judah, 10 and he ruled for forty-one years in Jerusalem. His grandmother was Maacah, the daughter of Absalom. 11 Asa did what **pleased** the LORD, as his ancestor David had done. 12 He expelled from the country all the male and female **prostitutes serving** at the **pagan places of worship**, and he removed all the **idols** his predecessors had made. 13 He removed his grandmother Maacah from her position as queen mother, because she had made an obscene **idol** of the fertility **goddess** Asherah. Asa cut down the **idol** and burnt it in the valley of the Kidron. 14 Even though Asa did not **destroy** all the **pagan places of worship**, he remained **faithful** to the LORD all his **life**. 15 He placed in the **Temple** all the objects his father had **dedicated** to God, as well as the gold and silver objects that he himself **dedicated**.

16 King Asa of Judah and King Baasha of Israel were constantly at war with **each other** as long as they were in **power**. 17 Baasha invaded Judah and started to fortify Ramah in order to cut off all traffic in and out of Judah. 18 So King Asa took all the silver and gold that was left in the **Temple** and the palace, and sent it by some of his officials to Damascus, to King Benhadad of Syria, the son of Tabrimmon and grandson of Hezion, with this **message**: 19 "Let us be allies, as our fathers were. This silver and gold is a present for you. Now break your alliance with King Baasha of Israel, so that he will have to pull his troops out of my territory."

20 King Benhadad **agreed** to Asa's proposal and sent his commanding officers and their armies to attack the cities of Israel. They captured Ijon, Dan, Abel Beth Maacah, the area near Lake Galilee, and the whole territory of Naphtali. 21 When King Baasha heard what had happened, he stopped fortifying Ramah and went to Tirzah.

22 Then King Asa sent out an order throughout all Judah **requiring** everyone, without exception, to **help** carry away from Ramah the stones and timber that Baasha had been using to fortify it. With this material Asa fortified Mizpah and Geba, a city in the territory of Benjamin.

23 Everything else that King Asa did, his brave deeds and the towns he fortified, are all recorded in *The History of the Kings of Judah.* But in his old age he was **crippled** by a foot **disease**. 24 Asa died and was buried in the royal **tombs** in David's City, and his son Jehoshaphat succeeded him as king.

King Nadab of Israel

25 In the second year of the **reign** of King Asa of Judah, King Jeroboam's son Nadab became king of Israel, and he ruled for two years. 26 Like his father before him, he sinned against the LORD and led Israel into sin.

27 Baasha son of Ahijah, of the tribe of Issachar, **plotted** against Nadab and killed him as Nadab and his army were besieging the city of Gibbethon in Philistia. 28 This happened during the third year of the **reign** of King Asa of Judah. And so Baasha succeeded Nadab as king of Israel. 29 At once he began killing all the members of Jeroboam's family. In accordance with what the LORD had said through his **servant**, the

agree 2.42; 18.6
anger 14.9; 16.2
command 14.8; 17.4
cripple 2 Sam 19.26; 1 Chr 18.4
dedicate [2] 8.63; 2 Kgs 12.18
destroy 13.34; 20.10
disease 8.37; 2 Kgs 5.1
disobey 13.21; 18.18
each other [2] 14.30; 20.29
faithful 11.4; 2 Kgs 18.6
goddess 14.15; 16.33
help 8.39; 19.21
idol [3] 14.9; 16.13
life (1) 12.4; 19.3
loyal 14.8; 19.18
message 12.23; 16.1
pagan [2] 14.24; 22.43
place of worship [2] 14.23; 22.43
please [2] 14.13; 2 Kgs 12.2
plot (1) 2 Sam 15.11; 16.9
power [2] 11.34; 18.46
prophet 14.2; 16.1
prostitute 14.24; 22.38
reign [5] 14.25; 16.8
require 1 Sam 17.25; 18.10
sake 11.12; 2 Kgs 19.34
secure 2.45; 2 Kgs 20.19
servant 14.8; 18.36
serve 14.24; 17.1
Temple (1) (of God) [2] 14.26; 2 Kgs 11.2
tomb 14.31; 22.50

15.4: 1 Kgs 11.36 **15.5:** 2 Sam 11.1–27 **15.29:** 1 Kgs 14.10

prophet Ahijah from Shiloh, all Jeroboam's family were killed; not one survived. 30 This happened because Jeroboam aroused the **anger of the LORD**, the
God of Israel, by the sins that he committed and that he caused Israel to
commit.

31 Everything else that Nadab did is
recorded in *The History of the Kings of
Israel.* 32 King Asa of Judah and King
Baasha of Israel were constantly at war
with **each other** as long as they were in
power.

King Baasha of Israel

33 In the third year of the **reign** of
King Asa of Judah, Baasha son of Ahijah
became king of all Israel, and he ruled in
Tirzah for twenty-four years. 34 Like King
Jeroboam before him, he sinned against
the LORD and led Israel into sin.

16 The LORD spoke to the **prophet**
Jehu son of Hanani and gave him
this **message** for Baasha: 2 "You were a
nobody, but I made you the leader of **my
people** Israel. And now you have sinned
like Jeroboam and have led **my people**
into sin. Their sins have aroused my
anger, 3 and so I will do away with you
and your family, just as I did with Jeroboam. 4 Any members of your family who
die in the city will be eaten by dogs, and
any who die in the open country will be
eaten by vultures."

5 Everything else that Baasha did and
all his brave deeds are recorded in *The
History of the Kings of Israel.* 6 Baasha
died and was buried in Tirzah, and his
son Elah succeeded him as king.

7 That **message** from the LORD
against Baasha and his family was given
by the **prophet** Jehu because of the sins
that Baasha committed against the
LORD. He aroused the **LORD's anger** not
only because of the **evil** he did, just as
King Jeroboam had done before him, but
also because he killed all Jeroboam's
family.

King Elah of Israel

8 In the twenty-sixth year of the **reign**
of King Asa of Judah, Elah son of Baasha
became king of Israel, and he ruled in
Tirzah for two years. 9 Zimri, one of his
officers who was in charge of half the
king's chariots, **plotted** against him. One
day in Tirzah, Elah was getting drunk in
the home of Arza, who was in charge of
the palace. 10 Zimri entered the house,
assassinated Elah, and succeeded him as
king. This happened in the twenty-
seventh year of the **reign** of King Asa of
Judah.

11 As soon as Zimri became king he
killed off all the members of Baasha's
family. Every male relative and **friend**
was put **to death**. 12 And so, in accordance
with what the LORD had said against
Baasha through the **prophet** Jehu, Zimri
killed all the family of Baasha. 13 Because
of their **idolatry** and because they led
Israel into sin, Baasha and his son Elah
had aroused the **anger of the LORD**, the
God of Israel. 14 Everything else that
Elah did is recorded in *The History of the
Kings of Israel.*

King Zimri of Israel

15 In the twenty-seventh year of the
reign of King Asa of Judah, Zimri ruled
in Tirzah over Israel for seven days. The
Israelite troops were besieging the city
of Gibbethon in Philistia, 16 and when
they heard that Zimri had **plotted** against
the king and assassinated him, then and
there they all **proclaimed** their commander Omri king of Israel. 17 Omri and
his troops left Gibbethon and went and
besieged Tirzah. 18 When Zimri saw that
the city had fallen, he went into the
palace's inner fortress, set the palace on
fire, and died in the flames. 19 This happened because of his sins against the
LORD. Like his predecessor Jeroboam he
displeased the LORD by his own sins and
by leading Israel into sin. 20 Everything
else that Zimri did, including the account
of his conspiracy, is recorded in *The History of the Kings of Israel.*

King Omri of Israel

21 The people of Israel were divided:
some of them wanted to make Tibni son
of Ginath king, and the others were in
favour of Omri. 22 In the end, those in
favour of Omri **won**; Tibni died and Omri
became king. 23 So in the thirty-first year
of the **reign** of King Asa of Judah, Omri
became king of Israel, and he ruled for
twelve years. The first six years he ruled
in Tirzah, 24 and then he bought the hill of
Samaria for six thousand pieces of silver
from a man named Shemer. Omri fortified the hill, built a town there, and
named it Samaria, after Shemer, the
former owner of the hill.

25 Omri sinned against the LORD more
than any of his predecessors. 26 Like Jeroboam before him, he aroused the **anger
of the LORD**, the God of Israel, by his sins
and by leading the people into sin and
idolatry. 27 Everything else that Omri did
and all his accomplishments are
recorded in *The History of the Kings of
Israel.* 28 Omri died and was buried in

altar 13.1; 18.26
anger [5] 15.30; 21.4
death (3) (to death) 12.18; 17.12
displease 1 Sam 29.7; 1 Chr 21.7
enough 12.28; 17.15
evil 13.33; 2 Kgs 8.18
favour [2] 8.52; 1 Chr 17.27
friend 11.19; 2 Kgs 9.17
God's people [2] 14.7; 2 Kgs 9.6
goddess 15.13; 18.19
idol [2] 15.12; 18.18
image 14.9; 2 Kgs 3.2
message [2] 15.18; 19.2
plot (1) [2] 15.27; 2 Kgs 9.14
proclaim 2 Sam 22.47; 21.9
prophet [3] 15.29; 17.1
reign [6] 15.1; 22.41
temple (2) (of other gods) [2] 1 Sam 31.10; 2 Kgs 5.18
win 11.19; 22.12
worship (2) (of other gods) 14.9; 18.18

Samaria, and his son Ahab succeeded
him as king.

King Ahab of Israel

29 In the thirty-eighth year of the
reign of King Asa of Judah, Ahab son of
Omri became king of Israel, and he ruled
in Samaria for twenty-two years. 30 He
sinned against the LORD more than any
of his predecessors. 31 It was not **enough**
for him to sin like King Jeroboam; he
went further and married Jezebel, the
daughter of King Ethbaal of Sidon, and
worshipped Baal. 32 He built a **temple** to
Baal in Samaria, made an **altar** for him,
and put it in the **temple**. 33 He also put up
an **image** of the **goddess** Asherah. He did
more to arouse the **anger of the LORD**,
the God of Israel, than all the kings of
Israel before him. 34 During his **reign** Hiel
from Bethel rebuilt Jericho. As the LORD
had foretold through Joshua son of Nun,
Hiel lost his eldest son Abiram when he
laid the foundation of Jericho, and his
youngest son Segub when he built the
gates.

Elijah and the Drought

alive 2 Sam 21.5; 18.5
bread [3] 14.3; 19.6
care 2.7; 2 Kgs 10.6
command [3] 15.5; 18.18
death (1) [2] 11.40; 22.40
death (3) (to death) 16.11; 18.12
enough [2] 16.31; 18.5
kind 8.50; 2 Kgs 13.23
last (2) 2.1; 19.19
life (2) (to life) 2 Sam 14.14; 2 Kgs 8.1
man of God [2] Judg 13.6; 2 Kgs 1.9
name (2) (name of God, of Jesus) 13.5; 22.16
obey 14.8; 2 Kgs 10.31
pray [2] 13.6; 18.24
prayer 9.3; 2 Kgs 6.17
promise 11.11; 18.15
prophet 16.1; 18.4
remind 1 Sam 12.7; Job 33.23
restore 12.21; 20.34
serve 15.12; 18.15
swear 2.24; 18.10
terrible 2 Sam 24.10; 2 Kgs 14.26
widow [5] 11.26; 2 Kgs 4.1
worry 1 Sam 25.35; 20.43
worse 2 Sam 4.11; 2 Kgs 21.11

17 A **prophet** named Elijah, from
Tishbe in Gilead, said to King
Ahab, "In the **name of the LORD**, the
living God of Israel, whom I **serve**, I tell
you that there will be no dew or rain for
the next two or three years until I say
so."
2 Then the LORD said to Elijah,
3 "Leave this place and go east and hide
yourself near the brook of Cherith, east
of the Jordan. 4 The brook will supply you
with water to drink, and I have **commanded** ravens to bring you food there."
5 Elijah **obeyed** the LORD's **command**,
and went and stayed by the brook of
Cherith. 6 He drank water from the
brook, and ravens brought him **bread**
and meat every morning and every
evening. 7 After a while the brook dried
up because of the lack of rain.

Elijah and the Widow in Zarephath

8 Then the LORD said to Elijah, 9 "Now
go to the town of Zarephath, near Sidon,
and stay there. I have **commanded** a
widow who lives there to feed you." 10 So
Elijah went to Zarephath, and as he
came to the gate of the town, he saw a
widow gathering firewood. "Please bring
me a drink of water," he said to her.
11 And as she was going to get it, he called
out, "And please bring me some **bread**,
too."
12 She answered, "By the living LORD
your God I **swear** that I haven't got any
bread. All I have is a handful of flour in a
bowl and a drop of olive-oil in a jar. I
came here to gather some firewood to
take back home and prepare what little I
have for my son and me. That will be our
last meal, and then we will starve **to
death**."
13 "Don't **worry**," Elijah said to her.
"Go ahead and prepare your meal. But
first make a small loaf from what you
have and bring it to me, and then
prepare the rest for you and your son.
14 For this is what the LORD, the God of
Israel, says: 'The bowl will not run out of
flour or the jar run out of oil before the
day that I, the LORD, send rain.' "
15 The **widow** went and did as Elijah
had told her, and all of them had **enough**
food for many days. 16 As the LORD had
promised through Elijah, the bowl did
not run out of flour nor did the jar run out
of oil.
17 Some time later the **widow's** son
fell ill; he got **worse and worse**, and
finally he died. 18 She said to Elijah, "**Man
of God**, why did you do this to me? Did
you come here to **remind** God of my sins
and so cause my son's **death**?"
19 "Give the boy to me," Elijah said.
He took the boy from her arms, carried
him upstairs to the room where he was
staying, and laid him on the bed. 20 Then
he **prayed** aloud, "O LORD my God, why
have you done such a **terrible** thing to
this **widow**? She has been **kind enough** to
take **care** of me, and now you kill her
son!" 21 Then Elijah stretched himself out
on the boy three times and **prayed**, "O
LORD my God, **restore** this child **to life**!"
22 The LORD answered Elijah's **prayer**;
the child started breathing again and
revived.
23 Elijah took the boy back downstairs
to his mother and said to her, "Look,
your son is **alive**!"
24 She answered, "Now I know that
you are a **man of God** and that the LORD
really speaks through you!"

Elijah and the Prophets of Baal

18 After some time, in the third
year of the drought, the LORD
said to Elijah, "Go and **present** yourself
to King Ahab, and I will send rain." 2 So
Elijah started out.
The **famine** in Samaria was at its
worst, 3 so Ahab called in Obadiah, who
was in charge of the palace. (Obadiah
was a devout **worshipper** of the LORD,
4 and when Jezebel was killing the LORD's
prophets, Obadiah took a hundred of

agree 15.20; 20.4
alive 17.23; 19.18
alone 11.29; 19.10
altar [6] 16.32; 19.10
approve 14.8; 2 Kgs 17.9
blood 2 Sam 23.17; 21.19
bow (2) [2] 2.19; 19.18
cloud [2] 8.10; 2 Chr 5.11
command [2] 17.4; 20.14
danger 5.4; Ps 3.3
dark 8.12; 2 Kgs 7.5

16.34: Josh 6.26 **17.1:** Jas 5.17 **17.9:** Lk 4.25–26 **17.21:** 2 Kgs 4.34–35

death (3) (to death) 17.12; 19.1
disobey 15.5; 20.36
dream 3.5; Job 7.14
enough [2] 17.15; 19.8
famine 8.37; 2 Kgs 4.38
get away 2 Sam 15.14; 2 Kgs 5.20
god (2) (other gods) [3] 14.23; 19.2
goddess 16.33; 2 Kgs 13.6
idol 16.13; 19.18
knee 1 Sam 20.41; 2 Kgs 1.13
master 11.23; 2 Kgs 2.3
mind (1) 2 Sam 24.16; 2 Kgs 23.25
offer 13.1; 21.6
power 15.16; 2 Kgs 2.9
pray [7] 17.20; 19.4
present (1) [2] 10.10; 2 Kgs 10.25
promise 17.16; 22.14
prophet [13] 17.1; 19.1
prove 1 Sam 10.1; 2 Kgs 10.10
provide 11.18; 2 Kgs 4.13
remember 8.59; 2 Kgs 9.25
require 15.22; 2 Kgs 12.15
ritual 2 Sam 11.4; 2 Chr 29.18
sacrifice [2] 13.1; 22.43
servant [4] 15.29; 19.3
serve 17.1; 19.10
Spirit (1) (God's Spirit) 2 Sam 23.2; 22.24
swear [2] 17.12; 2 Kgs 2.2
trouble [2] 2.26; 2 Kgs 4.13
word (1) 13.20; 20.5
world 10.24; 2 Kgs 19.15
worship (1) (of God) [4] 14.21; 2 Kgs 10.23
worship (2) (of other gods) [2] 16.31; 21.26
worst [2] 14.24; 2 Kgs 7.4

them, hid them in caves in two groups of
fifty, and **provided** them with food and
water.) 5 Ahab said to Obadiah, "Let us go
and look[t] at every spring and every
river-bed in the land to see if we can find
enough grass to keep the horses and
mules **alive**. Maybe we won't have to kill
any of our animals." 6 They **agreed** on
which part of the land each one would
explore, and set off in different
directions.

7 As Obadiah was on his way, he
suddenly met Elijah. He recognized him,
bowed low before him, and asked, "Is it
really you, sir?"

8 "Yes, I'm Elijah," he answered. "Go
and tell your **master** the king that I am
here."

9 Obadiah answered, "What have I
done that you want to put me in **danger**
of being killed by King Ahab? 10 By the
living LORD, your God, I **swear** that the
king has made a search for you in every
country in the **world**. Whenever the ruler
of a country reported that you were not
in his country, Ahab would **require** that
ruler to **swear** that you could not be
found. 11 And now you want me to go and
tell him that you are here? 12 What if the
spirit of the LORD carries you off to some
unknown place as soon as I leave? Then,
when I tell Ahab that you are here, and
he can't find you, he will put me **to death**.
Remember that I have been a devout
worshipper of the LORD ever since I was
a boy. 13 Haven't you heard that when
Jezebel was killing the **prophets** of the
LORD I hid a hundred of them in caves, in
two groups of fifty, and supplied them
with food and water? 14 So how can you
order me to go and tell the king that you
are here? He will kill me!"

15 Elijah answered, "By the living
LORD, whom I **serve**, I **promise** that I will
present myself to the king today."

16 So Obadiah went to King Ahab and
told him, and Ahab set off to meet Elijah.
17 When Ahab saw him, he said, "So there
you are—the **worst troublemaker** in
Israel!"

18 "I'm not the **troublemaker**," Elijah
answered. "You are—you and your
father. You are **disobeying** the LORD's
commands and **worshipping the idols** of
Baal. 19 Now order all the people of Israel
to meet me at Mount Carmel. Bring
along the 450 **prophets** of Baal and the
400 **prophets** of the **goddess** Asherah who
are supported by Queen Jezebel."

20 So Ahab summoned all the
Israelites and the **prophets** of Baal to
meet at Mount Carmel. 21 Elijah went up
to the people and said, "How much
longer will it take you to make up your
minds? If the LORD is God, **worship** him;
but if Baal is God, **worship** him!" But the
people didn't say a **word**. 22 Then Elijah
said, "I am the only **prophet** of the LORD
still left, but there are 450 **prophets** of
Baal. 23 Bring two bulls; let the **prophets**
of Baal take one, kill it, cut it in pieces,
and put it on the wood—but don't light
the fire. I will do the same with the other
bull. 24 Then let the **prophets** of Baal **pray**
to their **god**, and I will **pray** to the LORD,
and the one who answers by sending
fire—he is God."

The people shouted their **approval**.

25 Then Elijah said to the **prophets** of
Baal, "Since there are so many of you,
you take a bull and prepare it first. **Pray**
to your **god**, but don't set fire to the
wood."

26 They took the bull that was brought
to them, prepared it, and **prayed** to Baal
until noon. They shouted, "Answer us,
Baal!" and kept dancing round the **altar**
they had built. But no answer came.

27 At noon Elijah started making fun
of them: "**Pray** louder! He is a **god**!
Maybe he is **day-dreaming** or relieving
himself, or perhaps he's gone on a
journey! Or maybe he's sleeping, and
you've got to wake him up!" 28 So the
prophets prayed louder and cut themselves with knives and daggers, according to their **ritual**, until **blood** flowed.
29 They kept on ranting and raving until
the middle of the afternoon; but no
answer came, not a sound was heard.

30 Then Elijah said to the **people**,
"Come closer to me," and they all
gathered round him. He set about repairing the **altar** of the LORD which had been
torn down. 31 He took twelve stones, one
for each of the twelve tribes named after
the sons of Jacob, the man to whom the
LORD had given the name Israel. 32 With
these stones he rebuilt the **altar** for the
worship of the LORD. He dug a trench
round it, large **enough** to hold almost
fourteen litres of water. 33 Then he placed
the wood on the **altar**, cut the **bull** in
pieces, and laid it on the wood. He said,
"Fill four jars with water and pour it on
the **offering** and the wood." They did so,
34 and he said, "Do it again"—and they
did. "Do it once more," he said—and they
did. 35 The water ran down round the
altar and filled the trench.

36 At the hour of the afternoon
sacrifice the **prophet** Elijah approached

[t] *One ancient translation* Let us go and look; *Hebrew* You go and look.
18.31: Gen 32.28, 35.10

the **altar** and **prayed**, "O LORD, the God
of Abraham, Isaac, and Jacob, **prove** now
that you are the God of Israel and that I
am your **servant** and have done all this at
your **command**. 37 Answer me, LORD,
answer me, so that this people will know
that you, the LORD, are God, and that you
are bringing them back to yourself."[u]
38 The LORD sent fire down, and it
burnt up the **sacrifice**, the wood, and the
stones, scorched the earth and dried up
the water in the trench. 39 When the
people saw this, they threw themselves
on the ground and exclaimed, "The LORD
is God; the LORD **alone** is God!"
40 Elijah ordered, "Seize the **prophets**
of Baal; don't let any of them **get away**!"
The people seized them all, and Elijah
led them down to the River Kishon and
killed them.

The End of the Drought

41 Then Elijah said to King Ahab,
"Now, go and eat. I hear the roar of rain
approaching." 42 While Ahab went to eat,
Elijah climbed to the top of Mount
Carmel, where he **bowed down** to the
ground, with his head between his **knees**.
43 He said to his **servant**, "Go and look
towards the sea."
The **servant** went and returned,
saying, "I didn't see anything." Seven
times in all Elijah told him to go and
look. 44 The seventh time he returned and
said, "I saw a little **cloud** no bigger than a
man's hand, coming up from the sea."
Elijah ordered his **servant**, "Go to King
Ahab and tell him to get into his chariot
and go back home before the rain stops
him."
45 In a little while the sky was
covered with **dark clouds**, the wind
began to blow, and heavy rain began to
fall. Ahab got into his chariot and started
back to Jezreel. 46 The **power of the LORD**
came on Elijah; he fastened his clothes
tight round his waist and ran ahead of
Ahab all the way to Jezreel.

Elijah on Mount Sinai

19 King Ahab told his wife Jezebel
everything that Elijah had done
and how he had put all the **prophets** of
Baal **to death**. 2 She sent a **message** to
Elijah: "May the **gods strike** me **dead** if
by this time tomorrow I don't do the
same thing to you that you did to the
prophets." 3 Elijah was **afraid**, and **fled**
for his **life**; he took his **servant** and went
to Beersheba in Judah.
Leaving the **servant** there, 4 Elijah
walked a whole day into the wilderness.
He stopped and sat down in the shade of
a tree and **wished** he would die. "It's too
much, LORD," he **prayed**. "Take away my
life; I might as well be **dead**!"
5 He lay down under the tree and fell
asleep. Suddenly an **angel** touched him
and said, "Wake up and eat." 6 He looked
round, and saw a loaf of **bread** and a jar
of water near his head. He ate and drank,
and lay down again. 7 The **LORD's angel**
returned and woke him up a second time,
saying, "Get up and eat, or the journey
will be too much for you." 8 Elijah got up,
ate and drank, and the food gave him
enough strength to walk forty days to
Sinai, the **holy** mountain. 9 There he went
into a cave to spend the night.
Suddenly the LORD spoke to him,
"Elijah, what are you doing here?"
10 He answered, "LORD God **Almighty**,
I have always **served** you—you **alone**.
But the people of Israel have broken
their **covenant** with you, torn down your
altars, and killed all your **prophets**. I am
the only one left—and they are trying to
kill me!"
11 "Go out and stand before me on top
of the mountain," the LORD said to him.
Then the LORD passed by and sent a
furious wind that split the hills and
shattered the rocks—but the LORD was
not in the wind. The wind stopped blowing, and then there was an earthquake—
but the LORD was not in the earthquake.
12 After the earthquake, there was a
fire—but the LORD was not in the fire.
And after the fire, there was the soft
whisper of a voice.
13 When Elijah heard it, he covered
his face with his cloak and went out and
stood at the entrance of the cave. A voice
said to him, "Elijah, what are you doing
here?"
14 He answered, "LORD God **Almighty**,
I have always **served** you—you **alone**.
But the people of Israel have broken
their **covenant** with you, torn down your
altars, and killed all your **prophets**. I am
the only one left—and they are trying to
kill me."
15 The LORD said, "Return to the
wilderness near Damascus, then enter
the city and **anoint** Hazael as king of
Syria; 16 **anoint** Jehu son of Nimshi as
king of Israel, and **anoint** Elisha son of
Shaphat from Abel Meholah to succeed
you as **prophet**. 17 Anyone who **escapes**
being put **to death** by Hazael will be
killed by Jehu, and anyone who **escapes**
Jehu will be killed by Elisha. 18 Yet I will

dead [2] 11.15; 20.10
death (3) (to death) [2] 18.12; 21.10
enough 18.5; 20.10
escape [2] 12.2; 20.20
flee 11.23; 20.20
fury 2 Sam 13.21; 1 Chr 13.11
god (2) (other gods) 18.24; 20.10
help 15.22; 2 Kgs 3.13
holy 1 Sam 11.15; 2 Kgs 4.9
idol 18.18; 21.26
kiss [2] 2 Sam 20.9; Job 31.27
last (2) 17.12; 2 Kgs 4.6
life (1) [2] 15.14; 20.31
loyal 15.3; 2 Kgs 2.2
message 16.1; 20.7
pray 18.24; 2 Kgs 4.33
prophet [5] 18.4; 20.13
servant [2] 18.36; 20.32
serve [2] 18.15; 22.46
strength 2 Sam 22.30; 2 Kgs 9.24
strike 2.23; 20.10
wish 2 Sam 24.22; 2 Kgs 5.3

afraid 2.29; 20.13
alive 18.5; 20.18
Almighty [2] 2 Sam 22.14; 2 Kgs 20.16
alone [2] 18.39; 2 Kgs 4.27
altar [2] 18.26; 22.46
angel [2] 13.18; 22.19
anoint [3] 1.34; 2 Kgs 9.3
bow (2) 18.7; 2 Kgs 2.15
bread 17.6; 22.27
covenant [2] 11.11; 2 Kgs 11.17

[u] you are bringing them back to yourself; *or* you yourself made them turn away from you.

18.42-45: Jas 5.18 **19.4:** Jon 4.3 **19.10:** Rom 11.3 **19.15:** 2 Kgs 8.7-13 **19.16:** 2 Kgs 9.1-6 **19.18:** Rom 11.4

leave seven thousand people **alive** in Israel—all those who are **loyal** to me and have not **bowed** to Baal or **kissed** his **idol**."

The Call of Elisha

19 Elijah left and found Elisha ploughing with a team of oxen; there were eleven teams ahead of him, and he was ploughing with the **last** one. Elijah took off his cloak and put it on Elisha. 20 Elisha then left his oxen, ran after Elijah, and said, "Let me **kiss** my father and mother good-bye, and then I will go with you."

Elijah answered, "All right, go back. I'm not stopping you!"[v]

21 Then Elisha went to his team of oxen, killed them, and cooked the meat, using the yoke as fuel for the fire. He gave the meat to the people, and they ate it. Then he went and followed Elijah as his **helper**.

War with Syria

20 King Benhadad of Syria gathered all his troops, and supported by thirty-two other rulers with their horses and chariots, he marched up, laid siege to Samaria, and launched attacks against it. 2 He sent messengers into the city to King Ahab of Israel to say, "King Benhadad **demands** that 3 you surrender to him your silver and gold, your women and the **strongest** of your children."

4 "Tell my lord, King Benhadad, that I **agree**; he can have me and everything I own," Ahab answered.

5 Later the messengers came back to Ahab with another **demand** from Benhadad: "I sent you **word** that you were to hand over to me your silver and gold, your women and your children. 6 Now, however, I will send my officers to search your palace and the homes of your officials, and to take everything they[w] consider **valuable**. They will be there about this time tomorrow."

7 King Ahab called in all the leaders of the country and said, "You see that this man wants to **ruin** us. He sent me a **message demanding** my wives and children, my silver and gold, and I **agreed**."

8 The leaders and the people answered, "Don't pay any attention to him; don't give in."

9 So Ahab replied to Benhadad's messengers, "Tell my lord the king that I **agreed** to his first **demand**, but I cannot **agree** to the second."

The messengers left and then returned with another **message** 10 from Benhadad: "I will bring **enough** men to **destroy** this city of yours and carry off the rubble in their hands. May the **gods strike** me **dead** if I don't!"

11 King Ahab answered, "Tell King Benhadad that a **real** soldier does his **boasting** *after* a battle, not before it."

12 Benhadad received Ahab's answer as he and his allies, the other rulers, were drinking in their tents. He ordered his men to get ready to attack the city, so they moved into position.

13 Meanwhile, a **prophet** went to King Ahab and said, "The LORD says, 'Don't be **afraid** of that huge army! I will give you **victory** over it today, and you will know that I am the LORD.' "

14 "Who will lead the attack?" Ahab asked.

The **prophet** answered, "The LORD says that the young soldiers under the **command** of the district governors are to do it."

"Who will **command** the main force?" the king asked.

"You," the **prophet** answered.

15 So the king called out the young soldiers who were under the district commanders, 232 in all. Then he called out the Israelite army, a total of seven thousand men.

16 The attack began at noon, as Benhadad and his thirty-two allies were getting drunk in their tents. 17 The young soldiers advanced first. Scouts sent out by Benhadad reported to him that a group of soldiers was coming out of Samaria. 18 He ordered, "Take them **alive**, no matter whether they are coming to fight or to ask for **peace**."

19 The young soldiers led the attack, followed by the Israelite army, 20 and each one killed the man he fought. The Syrians **fled**, with the Israelites in hot pursuit, but Benhadad **escaped** on horseback, accompanied by some of the cavalry. 21 King Ahab took to the field, captured[x] the horses and chariots, and inflicted a severe defeat on the Syrians.

22 Then the **prophet** went to King Ahab and said, "Go back and build up your forces, and make careful **plans**, because the king of Syria will attack again next spring."

The Second Syrian Attack

23 King Benhadad's officials said to him, "The **gods** of Israel are mountain gods, and that is why the Israelites

[v] All right...you; *or* Go on, but come back, because what I have just done to you is important.
[w] *Some ancient translations* they; *Hebrew* you.
[x] *One ancient translation* captured; *Hebrew* destroyed.

advice 12.6; 1 Chr 26.14
afraid 19.3; 2 Kgs 1.15
agree [5] 18.6; 2 Kgs 6.3
alive [2] 19.18; 2 Kgs 7.12
boast 1 Sam 2.3; 2 Kgs 19.23
command [5] 18.18; 21.11
compare Judg 8.2; Job 8.7
dead 19.2; 21.15
demand [4] 2 Sam 14.7; 2 Kgs 18.14
destroy [2] 15.14; 22.43
disobey 18.18; 2 Kgs 17.12
each other 15.16; 2 Kgs 3.23
enemy 11.21; 21.20
enough 19.8; 2 Kgs 4.7
escape [6] 19.17; 2 Kgs 3.26
flee [2] 19.3; 2 Kgs 7.7
flock 1 Sam 30.20; 2 Chr 31.3
free 2 Sam 7.23; 2 Kgs 13.5
god (2) (other gods) [3] 19.2; 2 Kgs 1.2
hard 11.28; 1 Chr 19.13
hurt 1 Sam 20.3; 2 Kgs 4.19
life (1) [4] 19.3; 2 Kgs 1.13
Majesty 8.13; 2 Kgs 6.12
mercy 8.49; 2 Kgs 1.13
message [2] 19.2; 21.14
peace 8.56; 22.1
permit 1 Sam 20.6; 2 Kgs 6.2
plan 8.17; 2 Kgs 7.12

plead 1 Sam 15.11; 2 Kgs 1.13
prophet [13] 19.1; 21.17
real 3.26; Ps 127.3
refuge 2 Sam 22.33; 1 Chr 6.57
refuse (1) 2.16; 21.15
restore 17.21; 2 Kgs 6.20
ruin 13.34; 2 Kgs 3.19
sackcloth [2] 2 Sam 21.10; 21.27
sentence Deut 25.2; 2 Kgs 25.6
servant 19.3; 2 Kgs 4.12
sign (1) 2 Sam 15.30; 2 Kgs 4.31
spare 2 Sam 21.7; 2 Kgs 1.13
strike 19.2; 22.34
strong 2 Sam 22.2; 2 Kgs 2.16
value 10.21; 2 Kgs 8.6
victory [2] 8.45; 22.6
watch 9.3; 2 Kgs 9.17
word (1) [2] 18.21; 2 Kgs 3.7
worry 17.13; Neh 4.14

defeated us. But we will certainly defeat them if we fight them in the plains. 24 Now, remove the thirty-two rulers from their **commands** and replace them with field commanders. 25 Then call up an army as large as the one that deserted you, with the same number of horses and chariots. We will fight the Israelites in the plains, and this time we will defeat them."

King Benhadad **agreed** and followed their **advice**. 26 The following spring he called up his men and marched with them to the city of Aphek to attack the Israelites. 27 The Israelites were called up and equipped; they marched out and camped in two groups facing the Syrians. The Israelites looked like two small **flocks** of goats **compared** with the Syrians, who spread out over the countryside.

28 A **prophet** went to King Ahab and said, "This is what the LORD says: 'Because the Syrians say that I am a **god** of the hills and not of the plains, I will give you **victory** over their huge army, and you and your people will know that I am the LORD.' "

29 For seven days the Syrians and the Israelites stayed in their camps, facing **each other**. On the seventh day they started fighting, and the Israelites killed a hundred thousand Syrians. 30 The survivors **fled** into the city of Aphek, where the city walls fell on twenty-seven thousand of them.

Benhadad also **escaped** into the city and took **refuge** in the back room of a house. 31 His officials went to him and said, "We have heard that the Israelite kings are **merciful**. Give us **permission** to go to the king of Israel with **sackcloth** round our waists and ropes round our necks, and maybe he will **spare** your **life**." 32 So they wrapped **sackcloth** round their waists and ropes round their necks, went to Ahab and said, "Your **servant** Benhadad **pleads** with you for his **life**."

Ahab answered, "Is he still **alive**? Good! He's like a brother to me!"

33 Benhadad's officials were **watching** for a good **sign**, and when Ahab said "brother," they took it up at once, and said, "As you say, Benhadad is your brother!"

"Bring him to me," Ahab ordered. When Benhadad arrived, Ahab invited him to get in the chariot with him. 34 Benhadad said to him, "I will **restore** to you the towns my father took from your father, and you may set up a commercial centre for yourself in Damascus, just as my father did in Samaria."

Ahab replied, "On these terms, then, I will **set you free**." He made a treaty with him and let him go.

A Prophet Condemns Ahab

35 At the LORD's **command** a member of a **group of prophets** ordered a **fellow-prophet** to hit him. But he **refused**, 36 so he said to him, "Because you have **disobeyed** the LORD's **command**, a lion will kill you as soon as you leave me." And as soon as he left, a lion came along and killed him.

37 Then this same **prophet** went to another man and said, "Hit me!" This man did so; he hit him a **hard** blow and **hurt** him. 38 The **prophet** bandaged his face with a cloth, to disguise himself, and went and stood by the road, waiting for the king of Israel to pass. 39 As the king was passing by, the **prophet** called out to him and said, "Your **Majesty**, I was fighting in the battle when a soldier brought a captured **enemy** to me and said, 'Guard this man; if he **escapes**, you will pay for it with your **life** or else pay a fine of three thousand pieces of silver.' 40 But I got busy with other things, and the man **escaped**."

The king answered, "You have pronounced your own **sentence**, and you will have to pay the penalty."

41 The **prophet** tore the cloth from his face, and at once the king recognized him as one of the **prophets**. 42 The **prophet** then said to the king, "This is the **word of the LORD**: 'Because you allowed the man to **escape** whom I had ordered to be killed, you will pay for it with your **life**, and your army will be **destroyed** for letting his army **escape**.' "

43 The king went back home to Samaria, **worried** and depressed.

Naboth's Vineyard

21 Near King Ahab's palace in Jezreel there was a **vineyard** owned by a man named Naboth. 2 One day Ahab said to Naboth, "Let me have your **vineyard**; it is close to my palace, and I want to use the land for a vegetable garden. I will give you a better **vineyard** for it, or, if you prefer, I will pay you a fair price."

3 "I **inherited** this **vineyard** from my ancestors," Naboth replied. "The LORD **forbid** that I should let you have it!"

4 Ahab went home, depressed and **angry** over what Naboth had said to him. He lay down on his bed, facing the wall,

accuse [2] 8.31; 2 Chr 6.22
anger [2] 16.2; 22.53
blood 18.28; 22.35
body 13.22; 22.37
cheer (1) Job 29.24
command 20.14; 2 Kgs 1.3
curse [2] 2.8; 2 Kgs 2.24
dead 20.10; 2 Kgs 4.32
death (3) (to death) [3] 19.1; 2 Kgs 6.22
devote [2] 2 Kgs 10.16
disaster [3] 14.10; 22.23
enemy 20.39; 2 Kgs 3.23

20.36: 1 Kgs 13.24

fast (2) [2] 2 Sam 12.22; 1 Chr 10.12
forbid 1 Sam 26.11; 1 Chr 28.3
gloom Job 3.5
honour [2] 3.13; 2 Kgs 10.20
humble 8.33; 2 Kgs 22.19
idol 19.18; 2 Kgs 9.22
inherit Ruth 4.6; Job 42.15
leading [2] Judg 9.46; 2 Kgs 10.1
letter (2) [2] 2 Sam 11.14; 2 Kgs 5.5
message [2] 20.7; 2 Kgs 9.5
notice (1) 11.28; Job 1.8
offer 18.33; 22.43
possess [3] 9.20; 2 Kgs 17.24
proclaim [2] 16.16; 2 Kgs 9.3
prophet [2] 20.13; 22.6
refuse (1) [2] 20.35; 22.49
rid 14.10; 22.46
sackcloth [2] 20.31; 2 Kgs 6.30
seal Ex 24.8; Neh 6.5
shame 14.24; Job 10.15
sight [2] 2 Sam 16.22; 22.43
urge 1 Sam 28.23; 2 Kgs 6.3
vineyard [9] 1 Sam 22.7; 2 Kgs 5.26
worship (2) (of other gods) 18.18; 22.53
wrong [2] 11.33; 2 Kgs 4.41

and would not eat. 5 His wife Jezebel went
to him and asked, "Why are you so
depressed? Why won't you eat?"
6 He answered, "Because of what
Naboth said to me. I **offered** to buy his
vineyard, or, if he preferred, to give him
another one for it, but he told me that I
couldn't have it!"
7 "Well, are you the king or aren't
you?" Jezebel replied. "Get out of bed,
cheer up and eat. I will get you Naboth's
vineyard!"
8 Then she wrote some **letters**, signed
them with Ahab's name, **sealed** them
with his seal, and sent them to the
officials and **leading** citizens of Jezreel.
9 The **letters** said: "**Proclaim** a day of
fasting, call the people together, and give
Naboth the place of **honour**. 10 Get a
couple of scoundrels to **accuse** him to his
face of **cursing** God and the king. Then
take him out of the city and stone him to
death."
11 The officials and **leading** citizens of
Jezreel did what Jezebel had commanded. 12 They **proclaimed** a day of
fasting, called the people together, and
gave Naboth the place of **honour**. 13 The
two scoundrels publicly **accused** him of
cursing God and the king, and so he was
taken outside the city and stoned to
death. 14 The **message** was sent to
Jezebel: "Naboth has been put to **death**."
15 As soon as Jezebel received the
message, she said to Ahab, "Naboth is
dead. Now go and take **possession** of the
vineyard which he **refused** to sell to you."
16 At once Ahab went to the **vineyard** to
take **possession** of it.
17 Then the LORD said to Elijah, the
prophet from Tishbe, 18 "Go to King Ahab
of Samaria. You will find him in Naboth's
vineyard, about to take **possession** of it.
19 Tell him that I, the LORD, say to him,
'After murdering the man, are you taking
over his property as well?' Tell him that
this is what I say: 'In the very place that
the dogs licked up Naboth's **blood** they
will lick up your blood!'"
20 When Ahab saw Elijah, he said,
"Have you caught up with me, my
enemy?"
"Yes, I have," Elijah answered. "You
have **devoted** yourself completely to
doing what is **wrong** in the LORD's **sight**.
21 So the LORD says to you, 'I will bring
disaster on you. I will do away with you
and get **rid** of every male in your family,
young and old alike. 22 Your family will
become like the family of King Jeroboam son of Nebat and like the family of
King Baasha son of Ahijah, because you
have stirred up my **anger** by leading
Israel into sin.' 23 And concerning
Jezebel, the LORD says that dogs will eat
her **body** in the city of Jezreel. 24 Any of
your relatives who die in the city will be
eaten by dogs, and any who die in the
open country will be eaten by vultures."
25 (There was no one else who had
devoted himself so completely to doing
wrong in the LORD's **sight** as Ahab—all at
the **urging** of his wife Jezebel. 26 He committed the most **shameful** sins by **worshipping idols**, as the Amorites had done,
whom the LORD had driven out of the
land as the people of Israel advanced.)
27 When Elijah finished speaking,
Ahab tore his clothes, took them off, and
put on **sackcloth**. He **refused** food, slept
in the **sackcloth**, and went about **gloomy**
and depressed.
28 The LORD said to the **prophet**
Elijah, 29 "Have you **noticed** how Ahab
has **humbled** himself before me? Since
he has done this, I will not bring **disaster**
on him during his lifetime; it will be
during his son's lifetime that I will bring
disaster on Ahab's family."

The Prophet Micaiah Warns Ahab

(2 Chr 18.2–27)

22 There was **peace** between Israel
and Syria for the next two years,
2 but in the third year King Jehoshaphat
of Judah went to see King Ahab of Israel.
3 Ahab asked his officials, "Why is it
that we have not done anything to get
back Ramoth in Gilead from the king of
Syria? It belongs to us!" 4 And Ahab
asked Jehoshaphat, "Will you go with me
to attack Ramoth?"
"I am ready when you are," Jehoshaphat answered, "and so are my soldiers
and my cavalry. 5 But first let's **consult**
the LORD."
6 So Ahab called in the **prophets**,
about four hundred of them, and asked
them, "Should I go and attack Ramoth, or
not?"
"Attack it," they answered. "The Lord
will give you **victory**."
7 But Jehoshaphat asked, "Isn't there
another **prophet** through whom we can
consult the LORD?"
8 Ahab answered, "There is one more,
Micaiah son of Imlah. But I **hate** him,
because he never **prophesies** anything
good for me; it's always something **bad**."
"You shouldn't say that!" Jehoshaphat
replied.
9 Then Ahab called in a **court** official
and told him to go and fetch Micaiah at
once.

altar 19.10; 2 Kgs 11.18
angel [2] 19.5; 2 Kgs 1.3
anger 21.4; 2 Kgs 13.3
arrest 1 Sam 19.20; 2 Kgs 17.4
bad [2] 14.6; 2 Kgs 2.19
blood [2] 21.19; 2 Kgs 3.22
body 21.23; 2 Kgs 4.34
bread 19.6; 2 Kgs 4.42
clean Deut 23.14; 2 Kgs 21.13
consult [2] 12.6; 2 Kgs 1.2
court (1) 4.3; 2 Kgs 18.18
death (1) 17.12; 2 Kgs 1.1
deceive [3] 2 Sam 3.25; 2 Kgs 18.29
destroy 20.10; 2 Kgs 3.25
disaster 21.21; 2 Kgs 14.10
example 1 Sam 8.3; 2 Kgs 10.31
hate 2 Sam 22.18; 2 Chr 18.7
heaven 8.23; 2 Kgs 1.10
incense 11.8; 2 Kgs 12.3
lie (2) [2] 13.18; 2 Kgs 4.16
name (2) (name of God, of Jesus) 17.1; 2 Kgs 2.24
offer [3] 21.6; 2 Kgs 3.27
pagan [2] 15.12; 2 Kgs 12.3

21.19: 1 Kgs 22.38 **21.23:** 2 Kgs 9.36

eace [3] 20.18;
Kgs 5.19
lace of worship
5.12; 2 Kgs 12.3
rison 8.46;
Kgs 14.13
romise 18.15;
Kgs 8.19
rophecy [4]
Num 24.3; 2 Chr 9.29
rophet [8] 21.17;
Kgs 1.3
rostitute [2] 15.12;
Kgs 23.7
age 1 Sam 20.34;
Kgs 5.11
efuse (1) 21.15;
Kgs 14.11
eign [2] 16.8;
Kgs 1.17
id 21.21; 2 Kgs 9.8
ight (1) 8.18;
Chr 1.11
sacrifice 18.36;
Kgs 3.20
safe [2] 4.25;
Chr 15.5
scatter 14.15;
Kgs 8.21
serve [2] 19.10;
Kgs 3.14
sheep 8.5; 2 Kgs 3.4
shepherd
Sam 25.7;
Chr 14.15
sight 21.20;
2 Kgs 6.20
Spirit (1) (God's Spirit) 18.12;
2 Kgs 2.16
spirit (2) [2]
Sam 28.8;
2 Kgs 5.26
strike 20.10;
2 Kgs 2.8
succeed (1) [2] 2.33;
2 Kgs 18.7
throne [2] 10.18;
2 Kgs 11.19
tomb 15.24;
2 Kgs 8.24
truth 2 Sam 14.18;
2 Chr 18.15
turn [2] 13.33;
2 Kgs 2.24
victory [3] 20.13;
2 Kgs 3.18
wicked 8.47;
2 Kgs 14.24
win [2] 16.22;
2 Kgs 13.17
worship (2) (of other gods) 21.26;
2 Kgs 3.2

10 The two kings, dressed in their royal robes, were sitting on their **thrones** at the threshing-place just outside the gate of Samaria, and all the **prophets** were **prophesying** in front of them. 11 One of them, Zedekiah son of Chenaanah, made iron horns and said to Ahab, "This is what the LORD says: 'With these you will fight the Syrians and totally defeat them.' " 12 All the other **prophets** said the same thing. "March against Ramoth and you will **win**," they said. "The LORD will give you **victory**."

13 Meanwhile, the official who had gone to get Micaiah said to him, "All the other **prophets** have **prophesied success** for the king, and you had better do the same."

14 But Micaiah answered, "By the living LORD I **promise** that I will say what he tells me to!"

15 When he appeared before King Ahab, the king asked him, "Micaiah, should King Jehoshaphat and I go and attack Ramoth, or not?"

"Attack!" Micaiah answered. "Of course you'll **win**. The LORD will give you **victory**."

16 But Ahab replied, "When you speak to me in the **name of the LORD**, tell the **truth**! How many times do I have to tell you that?"

17 Micaiah answered, "I can see the army of Israel **scattered** over the hills like **sheep** without a **shepherd**. And the LORD said, 'These men have no leader; let them go home in **peace**.' "

18 Ahab said to Jehoshaphat, "Didn't I tell you that he never **prophesies** anything good for me? It's always something **bad**!"

19 Micaiah went on: "Now listen to what the LORD says! I saw the LORD sitting on his **throne in heaven**, with all his **angels** standing beside him. 20 The LORD asked, 'Who will **deceive** Ahab so that he will go and be killed at Ramoth?' Some of the **angels** said one thing, and others said something else, 21 until a **spirit** stepped forward, approached the LORD, and said, 'I will **deceive** him.' 22 'How?' the LORD asked. The **spirit** replied, 'I will go and make all Ahab's **prophets** tell **lies**.' The LORD said, 'Go and **deceive** him. You will **succeed**.' "

23 And Micaiah concluded: "This is what has happened. The LORD has made these **prophets** of yours **lie** to you. But he himself has decreed that you will meet with **disaster**!"

24 Then the **prophet** Zedekiah went up to Micaiah, slapped his face, and asked, "Since when did the LORD's **spirit** leave me and speak to you?"

25 "You will find out when you go into some back room to hide," Micaiah replied.

26 Then King Ahab ordered one of his officers, "**Arrest** Micaiah and take him to Amon, the governor of the city, and to Prince Joash. 27 Tell them to throw him in **prison** and to put him on **bread** and water until I return **safely**."

28 "If you return **safely**," Micaiah exclaimed, "then the LORD has not spoken through me!" And he added, "Listen, everyone, to what I have said!"

The Death of Ahab

(2 Chr 18.28–34)

29 Then King Ahab of Israel and King Jehoshaphat of Judah went to attack the city of Ramoth in Gilead. 30 Ahab said to Jehoshaphat, "As we go into battle, I will disguise myself, but you wear your royal garments." So the king of Israel went into battle in disguise.

31 The king of Syria had ordered his thirty-two chariot commanders to attack no one else except the king of Israel. 32 So when they saw King Jehoshaphat, they all thought that he was the king of Israel, and they **turned** to attack him. But when he cried out, 33 they realized that he was not the king of Israel, and they stopped their attack. 34 By chance, however, a Syrian soldier shot an arrow which **struck** King Ahab between the joints of his armour. "I'm wounded!" he cried out to his chariot driver. "**Turn** round and pull out of the battle!"

35 While the battle **raged** on, King Ahab remained propped up in his chariot, facing the Syrians. The **blood** from his wound ran down and covered the bottom of the chariot, and at evening he died. 36 Near sunset the order went out through the Israelite ranks: "Every man go back to his own country and city!"

37 So died King Ahab. His **body** was taken to Samaria and buried. 38 His chariot was **cleaned** up at the pool of Samaria, where dogs licked up his **blood** and **prostitutes** washed themselves, as the LORD had said would happen.

39 Everything else that King Ahab did, including an account of his palace decorated with ivory and all the cities he built, is recorded in *The History of the Kings of Israel*. 40 At his **death** his son Ahaziah succeeded him as king.

22.17: Num 27.17; Mt 9.36; Mk 6.34 **22.19:** Is 6.1; Job 1.6

King Jehoshaphat of Judah
(2 Chr 20.31—21.1)

41 In the fourth year of the **reign** of
King Ahab of Israel, Jehoshaphat son of
Asa became king of Judah 42 at the age of
thirty-five, and he ruled in Jerusalem for
twenty-five years. His mother was
Azubah, the daughter of Shilhi. 43 Like his
father Asa before him, he did what was
right in the **sight** of the LORD; but the
pagan places of worship were not **destroyed**, and the people continued to **offer
sacrifices** and burn **incense** there.
44 Jehoshaphat made **peace** with the king
of Israel.

45 Everything else that Jehoshaphat
did, all his bravery and his battles, are
recorded in *The History of the Kings of
Judah.* 46 He got **rid** of all the male and
female **prostitutes serving** at the **pagan
altars** who were still left from the days of
his father Asa.

47 The land of Edom had no king; it
was ruled by a deputy appointed by the
king of Judah.

48 King Jehoshaphat built ocean-going
ships to sail to the land of Ophir for gold;
but they were wrecked at Eziongeber
and never sailed. 49 Then King Ahaziah of
Israel **offered** to let his men sail with
Jehoshaphat's men, but Jehoshaphat
refused the **offer**.

50 Jehoshaphat died and was buried in
the royal **tombs** in David's City, and his
son Jehoram succeeded him as king.

King Ahaziah of Israel

51 In the seventeenth year of the **reign**
of King Jehoshaphat of Judah, Ahaziah
son of Ahab became king of Israel, and
he ruled in Samaria for two years. 52 He
sinned against the LORD, following the
wicked example of his father Ahab, his
mother Jezebel, and King Jeroboam,
who had led Israel into sin. 53 He **worshipped** and **served** Baal, and like his
father before him, he aroused the **anger**
of the LORD, the God of Israel.

THE SECOND BOOK OF
KINGS

INTRODUCTION

The *Second book of Kings* continues the history of the two Israelite kingdoms where *First Kings* leaves off. The book may be divided into two parts: (1) The story of the two kingdoms from the middle of the ninth century B.C. down to the fall of Samaria and the end of the northern kingdom in 722 B.C. (2) The story of the kingdom of Judah from the fall of the kingdom of Israel down to the capture and destruction of Jerusalem by King Nebuchadnezzar of Babylonia in 586 B.C. The book ends with an account of Gedaliah as governor of Judah under the Babylonians, and a report of the release of King Jehoiachin of Judah from prison in Babylon.

These national disasters took place because of the unfaithfulness of the kings and people of Israel and Judah. The destruction of Jerusalem and the exile of many of the people of Judah was one of the great turning points of Israelite history.

The prophet who stands out in *Second Kings* is Elijah's successor Elisha.

Outline of Contents

---

afraid 1 Kgs 20.13; 6.16
angel [2] 1 Kgs 22.19; 19.35
command [2] 1 Kgs 21.11; 7.17
consult [5] 1 Kgs 22.5; 3.11
death (1) 1 Kgs 22.40; 2.21
god (2) (other gods) [7] 1 Kgs 20.10; 3.27
heaven [3] 1 Kgs 22.19; 2.1
knee 1 Kgs 18.42; Job 3.12
life (1) 1 Kgs 20.31; 4.31
man of God [5] 1 Kgs 17.18; 4.16
mercy [2] 1 Kgs 20.31; 3.10
plead 1 Kgs 20.32; 16.9
prophet 1 Kgs 22.6; 2.3
rebel 1 Kgs 12.16; 3.5
reign 1 Kgs 22.41; 3.1
serious 1 Sam 2.17; Esth 7.4
spare 1 Kgs 20.31; 7.4

Elijah and King Ahaziah

1 After the **death** of King Ahab of
Israel, the country of Moab **rebelled**
against Israel.
2 King Ahaziah of Israel fell off the
balcony on the roof of his palace in
Samaria and was **seriously** injured. So he
sent some messengers to **consult** Baalzebub, the **god** of the Philistine city of
Ekron, in order to find out whether or
not he would recover. 3 But an **angel of
the LORD commanded** Elijah, the
prophet from Tishbe, to go and meet the
messengers of King Ahaziah and ask
them, "Why are you going to **consult**
Baalzebub, the **god of Ekron**? Is it
because you think there is no **god** in
Israel? 4 Tell the king that the LORD says,
'You will not recover from your injuries;
you will die!' "
Elijah did as the LORD **commanded**,
5 and the messengers returned to the
king. "Why have you come back?" he
asked.
6 They answered, "We were met by a
man who told us to come back and tell
you that the LORD says to you, 'Why are
you sending messengers to **consult** Baalzebub, the **god of Ekron**? Is it because
you think there is no **god** in Israel? You
will not recover from your injuries; you
will die!' "
7 "What did the man look like?" the
king asked.
8 "He was wearing a cloak made of
animal skins, tied with[a] a leather belt,"
they answered.
"It's Elijah!" the king exclaimed.
9 Then he sent an officer with fifty
men to get Elijah. The officer found him
sitting on a hill and said to him, "**Man of
God**, the king orders you to come down."
10 "If I am a **man of God**," Elijah
answered, "may fire come down from
heaven and kill you and your men!" At
once fire came down and killed the
officer and his men.
11 The king sent another officer with
fifty men, who went up[b] and said to

[a] was wearing...with; *or* was a hairy man and wore.
[b] *One ancient translation* went up; *Hebrew* answered.

1.8: Mt 3.4; Mk 1.6 **1.10-12:** Lk 9.54

Elijah, "**Man of God**, the king orders you to come down at once!"

12 "If I am a **man of God**," Elijah answered, "may fire come down from **heaven** and kill you and your men!" At once the fire of God came down and killed the officer and his men.

13 Once more the king sent an officer with fifty men. He went up the hill, fell on his **knees** in front of Elijah, and **pleaded**, "**Man of God**, be **merciful** to me and my men. **Spare** our **lives**! 14 The two other officers and their men were killed by fire from **heaven**; but please be **merciful** to me!"

15 The **angel of the** LORD said to Elijah, "Go down with him, and don't be **afraid**." So Elijah went with the officer to the king 16 and said to him, "This is what the LORD says: 'Because you sent messengers to **consult** Baalzebub, the **god of Ekron**—as if there were no **god** in Israel to **consult**—you will not get well; you will die!' "

17 Ahaziah died, as the LORD had said through Elijah. Ahaziah had no sons, so his brother[c] Joram succeeded him as king in the second year of the **reign** of Jehoram son of Jehoshaphat, king of Judah.

18 Everything else that King Ahaziah did is recorded in *The History of the Kings of Israel.*

Elijah Is Taken Up to Heaven

2 The time came for the LORD to take Elijah up to **heaven** in a whirlwind. Elijah and Elisha set out from Gilgal, 2 and on the way Elijah said to Elisha, "Now stay here; the LORD has ordered me to go to Bethel."

But Elisha answered, "I **swear** by my **loyalty** to the living LORD and to you that I will not leave you." So they went on to Bethel.

3 A **group of prophets** who lived there went to Elisha and asked him, "Do you know that the LORD is going to take your **master** away from you today?"

"Yes, I know," Elisha answered. "But let's not talk about it."

4 Then Elijah said to Elisha, "Now stay here; the LORD has ordered me to go to Jericho."

But Elisha answered, "I **swear** by my **loyalty** to the living LORD and to you that I will not leave you." So they went on to Jericho.

5 A **group of prophets** who lived there went to Elisha and asked him, "Do you know that the LORD is going to take your **master** away from you today?"

"Yes, I know," Elisha answered. "But let's not talk about it."

6 Then Elijah said to Elisha, "Now stay here; the LORD has ordered me to go to the River Jordan."

But Elisha answered, "I **swear** by my **loyalty** to the living LORD and to you that I will not leave you." So they went on, 7 and fifty of the **prophets** followed them to the Jordan. Elijah and Elisha stopped by the river, and the fifty **prophets** stood a short distance away. 8 Then Elijah took off his cloak, rolled it up, and **struck** the water with it; the water divided, and he and Elisha crossed to the other side on dry ground. 9 There, Elijah said to Elisha, "Tell me what you want me to do for you before I am taken away."

"Let me receive the **share** of your **power** that will make me your successor,"[d] Elisha answered.

10 "That is a **difficult request** to **grant**," Elijah replied. "But you will receive it if you see me as I am being taken away from you; if you don't see me, you won't receive it."

11 They kept talking as they walked on; then suddenly a chariot of fire pulled by horses of fire came between them, and Elijah was taken up to **heaven** by a whirlwind. 12 Elisha saw it and cried out to Elijah, "My father, my father! **Mighty defender** of Israel! You are gone!" And he never saw Elijah again.

In **grief**, Elisha tore his cloak in two. 13 Then he picked up Elijah's cloak that had fallen from him, and went back and stood on the bank of the Jordan. 14 He **struck** the water with Elijah's cloak, and said, "Where is the LORD, the God of Elijah?" Then he **struck** the water again, and it divided, and he walked over to the other side. 15 The fifty **prophets** from Jericho saw him and said, "The **power** of Elijah is on Elisha!" They went to meet him, **bowed down** before him, 16 and said, "There are fifty of us here, all **strong** men. Let us go and look for your **master**. Maybe the **spirit of the** LORD has carried him away and left him on some mountain or in some valley."

"No, you must not go," Elisha answered.

17 But they insisted until he gave in and let them go. The fifty of them went and looked high and low for Elijah for

[c] *Some ancient translations* his brother; *Hebrew does not have these words.*
[d] THE SHARE...SUCCESSOR: *Elisha asked for the share that the first-born son inherited by law from his father (see Deut 21.17).*

2.9: Deut 21.17 **2.12:** 2 Kgs 13.14

share 1 Kgs 4.28; 1 Chr 6.54
Spirit (1) (God's Spirit) 1 Kgs 22.24; 1 Chr 12.18
strike [3] 1 Kgs 22.34; 6.18
strong 1 Kgs 20.3; 1 Chr 5.2
swear [3] 1 Kgs 18.10; 3.14
turn 1 Kgs 22.32; 4.2

bad 1 Kgs 22.8; 3.2
bow (2) 1 Kgs 19.18; 4.27
curse 1 Kgs 21.10; 22.19
death (1) 1.1; 5.7
defend 2 Sam 23.12; 10.3
difficult 1 Kgs 10.1; 5.13
grant 1 Kgs 8.28; 2 Chr 6.19
grief 2 Sam 18.33; 18.37
heaven [2] 1.10; 1 Chr 16.26
loyal [3] 1 Kgs 19.18; 4.30
master [3] 1 Kgs 18.8; 5.3
might 2 Sam 6.5; 13.14
name (2) (name of God, of Jesus) 1 Kgs 22.16; 1 Chr 13.6
new 1 Kgs 11.30; 11.14
power [2] 1 Kgs 18.46; 3.15
prophet [5] 1.3; 3.11
pure [2] 1 Kgs 10.21; 1 Chr 15.12
request 1 Kgs 12.7; 2 Chr 6.19

three days, but didn't find him. 18 Then they returned to Elisha, who had waited at Jericho, and he said to them, "Didn't I tell you not to go?"

Miracles of Elisha

19 Some men from Jericho went to Elisha and said, "As you know, sir, this is a fine city, but the water is **bad** and causes miscarriages."

20 "Put some salt in a **new** bowl, and bring it to me," he ordered. They brought it to him, 21 and he went to the spring, threw the salt in the water, and said, "This is what the LORD says: 'I make this water **pure**, and it will not cause any more **deaths** or miscarriages.'" 22 And that water has been **pure** ever since, just as Elisha said it would be.

23 Elisha left Jericho to go to Bethel, and on the way some boys came out of a town and made fun of him. "Get out of here, baldy!" they shouted.

24 Elisha **turned** round, glared at them, and **cursed** them in the **name of the LORD**. Then two she-bears came out of the woods and tore forty-two of the boys to pieces.

25 Elisha went on to Mount Carmel, and later returned to Samaria.

War between Israel and Moab

3 In the eighteenth year of the **reign** of King Jehoshaphat of Judah, Joram son of Ahab became king of Israel, and he ruled in Samaria for twelve years. 2 He sinned against the LORD, but he was not as **bad** as his father or his mother Jezebel; he pulled down the **image** his father had made for the **worship of Baal**. 3 Yet, like King Jeroboam son of Nebat before him, he led Israel into sin, and would not stop.

4 King Mesha of Moab bred **sheep**, and every year he gave as **tribute** to the king of Israel 100,000 **lambs**, and the wool from 100,000 **sheep**. 5 But when King Ahab of Israel died, Mesha **rebelled** against Israel. 6 At once King Joram left Samaria and gathered all his troops. 7 He sent **word** to King Jehoshaphat of Judah: "The king of Moab has **rebelled** against me; will you join me in war against him?"

"I will," King Jehoshaphat replied. "I am at your disposal, and so are my men and my horses. 8 What route shall we take for the attack?"

"We will go the long way, through the wilderness of Edom," Joram answered.

9 So King Joram and the kings of Judah and Edom set out. After marching for seven days, they ran out of water, and there was none left for the men or the pack-animals. 10 "We're done for!" King Joram exclaimed. "The LORD has put the three of us at the **mercy** of the king of Moab!"

11 King Jehoshaphat asked, "Is there a **prophet** here through whom we can **consult** the LORD?"

An officer of King Joram's forces answered, "Elisha son of Shaphat is here. He was Elijah's assistant."

12 "He is a **true prophet**," King Jehoshaphat said. So the three kings went to Elisha.

13 "Why should I **help** you?" Elisha said to the king of Israel. "Go and **consult** those **prophets** that your father and mother **consulted**."

"No!" Joram replied. "It is the LORD who has put us three kings at the **mercy** of the king of Moab."

14 Elisha answered, "By the living LORD, whom I **serve**, I **swear** that I would have nothing to do with you if I didn't **respect** your ally King Jehoshaphat of Judah. 15 Now get me a musician."

As the musician played his harp, the **power of the LORD** came on Elisha, 16 and he said, "This is what the LORD says: 'Dig ditches all over this dry stream bed. 17 Even though you will not see any rain or wind, this stream bed will be filled with water, and you, your livestock, and your pack-animals will have **plenty** to drink.'" 18 And Elisha continued, "But this is an easy thing for the LORD to do; he will also give you **victory** over the Moabites. 19 You will **conquer** all their beautiful fortified cities; you will cut down all their fruit-trees, stop all their springs, and **ruin** all their fertile fields by covering them with stones."

20 The next morning, at the time of the regular morning **sacrifice**, water came flowing from the direction of Edom, and covered the ground.

21 When the Moabites heard that the three kings had come to attack them, all the men who could bear arms, from the oldest to the youngest, were called out and stationed at the border. 22 When they got up the following morning, the sun was shining on the water, making it look as red as **blood**. 23 "It's **blood**!" they exclaimed. "The three **enemy** armies must have fought and killed **each other**! Let's go and loot their camp!"

24 But when they reached the camp, the Israelites attacked them and drove them back. The Israelites kept up the pursuit,[e] **slaughtering** the Moabites 25 and

[e] *One ancient translation* kept up the pursuit; *Hebrew unclear.*

swear 2.2; 4.30
terrify 1 Sam 31.4; 10.4
tribute 1 Kgs 10.15; 17.3
true 1 Kgs 13.32; 10.10
victory 1 Kgs 22.6; 5.1
word (1) 1 Kgs 20.5; 4.13
worship (2) (of other gods) 1 Kgs 22.53; 5.18

bad 2.19; 25.3
blood [2] 1 Kgs 22.35; 9.33
conquer 1 Kgs 11.15; 10.32
consult [3] 1.2; 6.8
destroy 1 Kgs 22.43; 8.19
each other 1 Kgs 20.29; 7.9
enemy [2] 1 Kgs 21.20; 9.17
escape 1 Kgs 20.20; 8.21
fail 1 Kgs 11.22; 10.21
force (1) 1 Kgs 12.18; 15.20
god (2) (other gods) 1.2; 5.15
help 1 Kgs 19.21; 6.26
image 1 Kgs 16.33; 13.6
lamb 2 Sam 12.3; 1 Chr 29.21
mercy [2] 1.13; 13.23
offer 1 Kgs 22.43; 5.17
plenty 1 Kgs 10.27; 1 Chr 4.40
power 2.9; 5.7
prophet [3] 2.3; 4.1
rebel [2] 1.1; 18.7
reign 1.17; 8.16
respect 1 Kgs 3.28; 5.1
ruin 1 Kgs 20.7; Ezra 9.9
sacrifice [2] 1 Kgs 22.43; 5.17
serve 1 Kgs 22.46; 5.16
sheep [2] 1 Kgs 22.17; 5.26
slaughter 1 Kgs 13.2; 8.12

destroying their cities. As they passed a
fertile field, every Israelite would throw
a stone on it until finally all the fields
were covered; they also stopped up the
springs and cut down the fruit-trees. At
last only the capital city of Kir Heres[f]
was left, and the slingers surrounded it
and attacked it.
26 When the king of Moab realized
that he was losing the battle, he took
seven hundred swordsmen with him and
tried to **force** his way through the **enemy**
lines and **escape** to the king of Syria,[g] but
he **failed**. 27 So he took his eldest son, who
was to succeed him as king, and **offered**
him on the city wall as a **sacrifice** to the
god of Moab. The Israelites were **terrified**[h] and so they drew back from the
city and returned to their own country.

Elisha Helps a Poor Widow

4 The **widow** of a member of a **group
of prophets** went to Elisha and said,
"Sir, my husband has died! As you know,
he was a **God-fearing** man, but now a
man he **owed** money to has come to take
away my two sons as **slaves** in payment
for my husband's **debt**."
2 "What shall I do for you?" he asked.
"Tell me, what have you got at home?"
"Nothing at all, except a small jar of
olive-oil," she answered.
3 "Go to your **neighbours** and borrow
as many empty jars as you can," Elisha
told her. 4 "Then you and your sons go
into the house, close the door, and start
pouring oil into the jars. Set each one
aside as soon as it is full."
5 So the woman went into her house
with her sons, closed the door, took the
small jar of olive-oil, and poured oil into
the jars as her sons brought them to her.
6 When they had filled all the jars, she
asked if there were any more. "That was
the **last** one," one of her sons answered.
And the olive-oil stopped flowing. 7 She
went back to Elisha, the **prophet**, who
said to her, "Sell the olive-oil and pay all
your **debts**, and there will be **enough**
money left over for you and your sons to
live on."

Elisha and the Rich Woman from Shunem

8 One day Elisha went to Shunem,
where a **rich** woman lived. She invited
him to a meal, and from then on every
time he went to Shunem he would have
his meals at her house. 9 She said to her
husband, "I am **sure** that this man who
comes here so often is a **holy** man.
10 Let's build a small room on the roof,
put a bed, a table, a chair, and a lamp in
it, and he can stay there whenever he
visits us."
11 One day Elisha returned to Shunem
and went up to his room to **rest**. 12 He told
his **servant** Gehazi to go and call the
woman. When she came, 13 he said to
Gehazi, "Ask her what I can do for her in
return for all the **trouble** she has had in
providing for our **needs**. Maybe she
would like me to go to the king or the
army commander and put in a good
word for her."
"I have all I **need** here among my own
people," she answered.
14 Elisha asked Gehazi, "What can I
do for her then?"
He answered, "Well, she has no son,
and her husband is an old man."
15 "Tell her to come here," Elisha
ordered. She came and stood in the doorway, 16 and Elisha said to her, "By this
time next year you will be holding a son
in your arms."
"Oh!" she exclaimed. "Please, sir,
don't **lie** to me. You are a **man of God**!"
17 But, as Elisha had said, at about
that time the following year she gave
birth to a son.
18 Some years later, at **harvest** time,
the boy went out one morning to join his
father, who was in the field with the **harvest** workers. 19 Suddenly he cried out to
his father, "My head **hurts**! My head
hurts!"
"Carry the boy to his mother," the
father said to a **servant**. 20 The **servant**
carried the boy back to his mother, who
held him in her lap until noon, at which
time he died. 21 She carried him up to
Elisha's room, put him on the bed and
left, closing the door behind her. 22 Then
she called her husband and said to him,
"Send a **servant** here with a donkey. I
need to go to the **prophet** Elisha. I'll be
back as soon as I can."
23 "Why do you have to go today?"
her husband asked. "It's neither a **Sabbath** nor a **New Moon Festival**."[i]
"Never mind," she answered. 24 Then
she had the donkey saddled, and ordered
the **servant**, "Make the donkey go as fast

alone [2] 1 Kgs 19.10; 19.15
birth 1 Kgs 3.17; 19.3
body 1 Kgs 22.37; 9.10
bow (2) 2.15; 17.35
bread 1 Kgs 22.27; 18.32
dead 1 Kgs 21.15; 6.31
debt [2] 1 Sam 22.2; Neh 5.11
distress 1 Sam 20.34; 11.14
enough [2] 1 Kgs 20.10; 1 Chr 18.4
famine 1 Kgs 18.2; 7.12
festival 1 Kgs 12.32; 23.16
God-fearing Ex 18.21; Neh 7.2
harvest [3] 2 Sam 23.13; 19.29
holy 1 Kgs 19.8; 19.22
hope 2 Sam 21.17; 5.18
hurt [2] 1 Kgs 20.37; 1 Chr 12.17
last (2) 1 Kgs 19.19; 1 Chr 26.6
lie (2) 1 Kgs 22.22; 2 Chr 18.21
life (1) 1.13; 5.7
loyal 2.2; 20.3
man of God 1.9; 1 Chr 23.14
need [3] 1 Kgs 8.59; 12.5
neighbour 1 Kgs 4.24; 2 Chr 32.22
New Moon Festival 1 Sam 20.5; 1 Chr 23.31
owe Deut 15.1; Neh 5.11
pray 1 Kgs 19.4; 5.11
prophet [5] 3.11; 5.3
provide 1 Kgs 18.4; 6.23
raise 1 Kgs 8.22; 23.35

rest (1) 1 Kgs 7.2; 2 Chr 4.4
rich 1 Kgs 10.23; 15.20
Sabbath Deut 5.12; 11.5
servant [9] 1 Kgs 20.32; 5.2
sign (1) 1 Kgs 20.3 19.29
slave 1 Kgs 9.20; 1 Chr 17.21
sure 1 Kgs 13.32; 7
swear 3.14; 5.16
teach 1 Kgs 8.36; 17.27
trouble 1 Kgs 18.1 6.28
turn 2.24; 9.23
vine 1 Kgs 4.25; 18
widow 1 Kgs 17.9; 1 Chr 2.24
word (1) 3.7; 5.8
wrong 1 Kgs 21.20; 5.21

[f] *Probable text* only the capital city of Kir Heres; *Hebrew unclear.*
[g] *One ancient translation* Syria; *Hebrew* Edom.
[h] TERRIFIED, *either because of what Chemosh, the god of the Moabites, might do, or because of what the* LORD, *the God of the Israelites, might do.*
[i] SABBATH...NEW MOON FESTIVAL: *Such holy days were thought to be the best time to consult a prophet.*

4.16: Gen 18.14

as it can, and don't slow down, unless I
tell you to." 25 So she set out, and went to
Mount Carmel, where Elisha was.

Elisha saw her coming while she was
still some distance away, and said to his
servant Gehazi, "Look—there comes the
woman from Shunem! 26 Hurry to her
and find out if everything is all right with
her, her husband, and her son."

She told Gehazi that everything was all
right, 27 but when she came to Elisha she
bowed down before him and took hold of
his feet. Gehazi was about to push her
away, but Elisha said, "Leave her **alone**.
Can't you see she's deeply **distressed**?
And the LORD has not told me a thing
about it."

28 The woman said to him, "Sir, did I
ask you for a son? Didn't I tell you not to
raise my **hopes**?"

29 Elisha **turned** to Gehazi and said,
"Hurry! Take my stick and go. Don't stop
to greet anyone you meet, and if anyone
greets you, don't take time to answer. Go
straight to the house and hold my stick
over the boy."

30 The woman said to Elisha, "I **swear**
by my **loyalty** to the living LORD and to
you that I will not leave you!" So the two
of them started back together. 31 Gehazi
went on ahead and held Elisha's stick
over the child, but there was no sound or
any other **sign of life**. So he went back to
meet Elisha and said, "The boy didn't
wake up."

32 When Elisha arrived, he went **alone**
into the room and saw the boy lying **dead**
on the bed. 33 He closed the door and
prayed to the LORD. 34 Then he lay down
on the boy, placing his mouth, eyes, and
hands on the boy's mouth, eyes, and
hands. As he lay stretched out over the
boy, the boy's **body** started to get warm.
35 Elisha got up, walked about the room,
and then went back and again stretched
himself over the boy. The boy sneezed
seven times, and then opened his eyes.
36 Elisha called Gehazi and told him to
call the boy's mother. When she came in,
he said to her, "Here's your son." 37 She
fell at Elisha's feet, with her face touching the ground; then she took her son
and left.

Two More Miracles

38 Once, when there was a **famine**
throughout the land, Elisha returned to
Gilgal. While he was **teaching** a **group of**
prophets, he told his **servant** to put a big
pot on the fire and make some stew for
them. 39 One of them went out in the
fields to get some herbs. He found a wild
vine, and picked as many gourds as he
could carry. He brought them back and
sliced them up into the stew, not knowing
what they were. 40 The stew was poured
out for the men to eat, but as soon as
they tasted it they exclaimed to Elisha,
"It's poisoned!"—and wouldn't eat it.
41 Elisha asked for some meal, threw it
into the pot, and said, "Pour out some
more stew for them." And then there was
nothing **wrong** with it.

42 Another time, a man came from
Baal Shalishah, bringing Elisha twenty
loaves of **bread** made from the first
barley **harvested** that year, and some
freshly-cut ears of corn. Elisha told his
servant to feed the **group of prophets**
with this, 43 but he answered, "Do you
think this is **enough** for a hundred men?"

Elisha replied, "Give it to them to eat,
because the LORD says that they will eat
and still have some left over." 44 So the
servant set the food before them, and, as
the LORD had said, they all ate and there
was still some left over.

Naaman Is Cured

5 Naaman, the commander of the
Syrian army, was highly **respected**
and esteemed by the king of Syria,
because through Naaman the LORD had
given **victory** to the Syrian forces. He
was a great soldier, but he **suffered** from
a dreaded **skin-disease**. 2 In one of their
raids against Israel, the Syrians had
carried off a little Israelite girl, who
became a **servant** of Naaman's wife.
3 One day she said to her mistress, "I **wish**
that my **master** could go to the **prophet**
who lives in Samaria! He would **cure** him
of his **disease**." 4 When Naaman heard of
this, he went to the king and told him
what the girl had said. 5 The king said,
"Go to the king of Israel and take this
letter to him."

So Naaman set out, taking thirty thousand pieces of silver, six thousand pieces
of gold, and ten **changes** of fine clothes.
6 The **letter** that he took read: "This
letter will introduce my officer Naaman.
I want you to **cure** him of his **disease**."

7 When the king of Israel read the
letter, he tore his clothes in dismay and
exclaimed, "How can the king of Syria
expect me to **cure** this man? Does he
think that I am God,[j] with the **power** of
life and **death**? It's **plain** that he is trying
to start a **quarrel** with me!"

8 When the **prophet** Elisha heard what
had happened, he sent **word** to the king:

accept [6] 1 Kgs 13.16; 1 Chr 28.9
burnt-offering 1 Kgs 9.25; 10.24
change [3] 2 Sam 24.16; 23.34
cure [8] Deut 28.27; Jer 30.15
death (1) 2.21; 7.4
difficult 2.10; 2 Chr 9.1
disease [7] 1 Kgs 15.23; 7.3
flesh 2 Sam 19.12; 1 Chr 11.1
forgive [2] 1 Kgs 8.30; 24.4
get away 1 Kgs 18.40; Ps 139.7
gift [3] 1 Kgs 10.10; 8.8
god (2) (other gods) [3] 3.27; 10.18
hope 4.28; 2 Chr 14.11
letter (2) [4] 1 Kgs 21.8; 10.1
life (1) 4.31; 7.4
master [3] 2.3; 9.7
offer [2] 3.27; 10.19
peace 1 Kgs 22.1; 9.22
plain (1) Num 14.14; Ps 5.8
power 3.15; 8.13
pray 4.33; 6.17
prophet [5] 4.1; 6.1
quarrel 2 Sam 21.4; Job 9.32
rage 1 Kgs 22.35; 19.27
respect 3.14; 10.13
sacrifice 3.20; 10.19
servant [7] 4.12; 6.15
serve 3.14; 10.18
sheep 3.4; 1 Chr 4.39

[j] God; *or* a god.

4.34-35: 1 Kgs 17.21 **5.1-14:** Lk 4.27

spirit (2) 1 Kgs 22.21; 1 Chr 10.13
suffer 1 Kgs 2.5; 7.3
swear 4.30; 2 Chr 36.13
temple (2) (of other gods) 1 Kgs 16.32; 10.21
upset 2 Sam 13.20; 6.11
victory 3.18; 13.17
vineyard 1 Kgs 21.1; 18.32
wish 1 Kgs 19.4; 1 Chr 11.17
word (1) 4.13; 6.9
worship (2) (of other gods) 3.2; 10.19
wrong 4.41; 6.19

"Why are you so **upset**? Send the man to me, and I'll show him that there is a **prophet** in Israel!"

9 So Naaman went with his horses and chariot, and stopped at the entrance to Elisha's house. 10 Elisha sent a **servant** out to tell him to go and wash himself seven times in the River Jordan, and he would be completely **cured** of his **disease**. 11 But Naaman left in a **rage**, saying, "I thought that he would at least come out to me, **pray** to the LORD his God, wave his hand over the **diseased** spot,[k] and **cure** me! 12 Besides, aren't the rivers Abana and Pharpar, back in Damascus, better than any river in Israel? I could have washed in them and been **cured**!"

13 His **servants** went up to him and said, "Sir, if the **prophet** had told you to do something **difficult**, you would have done it. Now why can't you just wash yourself, as he said, and **be cured**?" 14 So Naaman went down to the Jordan, dipped himself in it seven times, as Elisha had instructed, and he was completely **cured**. His **flesh** became firm and healthy, like that of a child. 15 He returned to Elisha with all his men and said, "Now I know that there is no **god** but the God of Israel; so please, sir, **accept** a **gift** from me."

16 Elisha answered, "By the living LORD, whom I **serve**, I **swear** that I will not **accept a gift**."

Naaman insisted that he **accept** it, but he would not. 17 So Naaman said, "If you won't **accept** my **gift**, then let me have two mule-loads of earth to take home with me,[l] because from now on I will not **offer sacrifices** or **burnt-offerings** to any **god** except the LORD. 18 So I **hope** that the LORD will **forgive** me when I accompany my king to the **temple** of Rimmon, the **god of Syria**, and **worship** him. Surely the LORD will **forgive** me!"

19 "Go in **peace**," Elisha said. And Naaman left.

He had gone only a short distance, 20 when Elisha's **servant** Gehazi said to himself, "My **master** has let Naaman **get away** without paying a thing! He should have **accepted** what that Syrian **offered** him. By the living LORD, I will run after him and get something from him." 21 So he set off after Naaman. When Naaman saw a man running after him, he got down from his chariot to meet him, and asked, "Is something **wrong**?"

22 "No," Gehazi answered. "But my **master** sent me to tell you that just now two members of the **group of prophets** in the hill-country of Ephraim arrived, and he would like you to give them three thousand pieces of silver and two **changes** of fine clothes."

23 "Please take six thousand pieces of silver," Naaman replied. He insisted on it, tied up the silver in two bags, gave them and two **changes** of fine clothes to two of his **servants**, and sent them on ahead of Gehazi. 24 When they reached the hill where Elisha lived, Gehazi took the two bags and carried them into the house. Then he sent Naaman's **servants** back. 25 He went back into the house, and Elisha asked him, "Where have you been?"

"Oh, nowhere, sir," he answered.

26 But Elisha said, "Wasn't I there in **spirit** when the man got out of his chariot to meet you? This is no time to **accept** money and clothes, olive-groves and **vineyards**, **sheep** and cattle, or **servants**! 27 And now Naaman's **disease** will come upon you, and you and your descendants will have it for ever!"

When Gehazi left, he had the **disease**—his skin was as white as snow.

The Recovery of the Axe-head

6 One day the **group of prophets** that Elisha was in charge of **complained** to him, "The place where we live is too small! 2 Give us **permission** to go to the Jordan and cut down some trees, so that we can build a place to live."

"All right," Elisha answered.

3 One of them **urged** him to go with them; he **agreed**, 4 and they set out together. When they arrived at the Jordan, they began to work. 5 As one of them was cutting down a tree, suddenly his iron axe-head fell in the water. "What shall I do, sir?" he exclaimed to Elisha. "It was a borrowed axe!"

6 "Where did it fall?" Elisha asked.

The man showed him the place, and Elisha cut off a stick, threw it in the water, and made the axe-head float. 7 "Take it out," he ordered, and the man bent down and picked it up.

The Syrian Army Is Defeated

8 The king of Syria was at war with Israel. He **consulted** his officers and **chose** a place to set up his camp. 9 But Elisha sent **word** to the king of Israel, **warning** him not to go near that place, because the Syrians were waiting in ambush there. 10 So the king of Israel

afraid 1.15; 25.24
agree 1 Kgs 20.4; 11.4
blind [2] 1 Kgs 14.4; Job 9.24
choose 1 Kgs 14.7; 7.14
complain 1 Sam 8.18; Neh 5.1
consult 3.11; 8.8
dead 4.32; 8.5
death (3) (to death) 1 Kgs 21.10; 7.4
doom Deut 32.35; 7.13
dove Num 6.10; Ps 55.6
elder (2) [2] Josh 24.1; Job 29.7
feast 1 Kgs 10.5; 1 Chr 12.39
help [2] 3.13; 10.15
Majesty [2] 1 Kgs 20.39; 8.5
permit 1 Kgs 20.31; 25.29
pray [3] 5.11; 13.4
prayer [3] 1 Kgs 17.22; 13.4
prophet [2] 5.3; 8.8
provide [2] 4.13; 23.9
restore 1 Kgs 20.34; 8.3
sackcloth 1 Kgs 21.27; 19.1
servant [2] 5.2; 8.4
sight 1 Kgs 22.43; 17.17
strike [3] 2.8; 9.24
trouble [2] 4.13; 14.10
upset 5.8; Job 5.12
urge 1 Kgs 21.25; Esth 3.4
warn [2] 1 Kgs 2.42; 9.14

[k] the diseased spot; *or* this place.
[l] EARTH TO TAKE HOME WITH ME: *It was then believed that a god could be worshipped only on his own land.*

word (1) 5.8; 9.25
wrong 5.21; 17.17

warned the men who lived in that place, and they were on guard. This happened several times.

11 The Syrian king became greatly **upset** over this; he called in his officers and asked them, "Which one of you is on the side of the king of Israel?"

12 One of them answered, "No one is, Your **Majesty**. The **prophet** Elisha tells the king of Israel what you say even in the privacy of your own room."

13 "Find out where he is," the king ordered, "and I will capture him."

When he was told that Elisha was in Dothan, 14 he sent a large force there with horses and chariots. They reached the town at night and surrounded it. 15 Early the next morning Elisha's **servant** got up, went out of the house, and saw the Syrian troops with their horses and chariots surrounding the town. He went back to Elisha and exclaimed, "We are **doomed**, sir! What shall we do?"

16 "Don't be **afraid**," Elisha answered. "We have more on our side than they have on theirs." 17 Then he **prayed**, "O LORD, open his eyes and let him see!" The LORD answered his **prayer**, and Elisha's **servant** looked up and saw the hillside covered with horses and chariots of fire all round Elisha.

18 When the Syrians attacked, Elisha **prayed**, "O LORD, **strike** these men **blind**!" The LORD answered his **prayer** and **struck** them **blind**. 19 Then Elisha went to them and said, "You are on the **wrong** road; this is not the town you are looking for. Follow me, and I will lead you to the man you are after." And he led them to Samaria.

20 As soon as they had entered the city, Elisha **prayed**, "Open their eyes, LORD, and let them see." The LORD answered his **prayer**; he **restored** their **sight**, and they saw that they were inside Samaria.

21 When the king of Israel saw the Syrians, he asked Elisha, "Shall I kill them, sir? Shall I kill them?"

22 "No," he answered. "Not even soldiers you had captured in combat would you put **to death**. Give them something to eat and drink, and let them return to their king." 23 So the king of Israel **provided** a great **feast** for them; and after they had eaten and drunk, he sent them back to the king of Syria. From then on the Syrians stopped raiding the land of Israel.

The Siege of Samaria

24 Some time later King Benhadad of Syria led his entire army against Israel and laid siege to the city of Samaria. 25 As a result of the siege the food shortage in the city was so severe that a donkey's head cost eighty pieces of silver, and two hundred grammes of **dove's dung**[m] cost five pieces of silver.

26 The king of Israel was walking by on the city wall when a woman cried out, "**Help** me, Your **Majesty**!"

27 He replied, "If the LORD won't **help** you, what help can I **provide**? Have I got any wheat or wine? 28 What's your **trouble**?"

She answered, "The other day this woman here suggested that we eat my child, and then eat her child the next day. 29 So we cooked my son and ate him. The next day I told her that we would eat her son, but she had hidden him!"

30 Hearing this, the king tore his clothes in dismay, and the people who were close to the wall could see that he was wearing **sackcloth** under his clothes. 31 He exclaimed, "May God **strike** me **dead** if Elisha is not beheaded before the day is over!" 32 And he sent a messenger to get Elisha.

Meanwhile, Elisha was at home with some **elders** who were visiting him. Before the king's messenger arrived, Elisha said to the **elders**, "That murderer is sending someone to kill me! Now, when he gets here, shut the door and don't let him come in. The king himself will be just behind him." 33 He had hardly finished saying this, when the king[n] arrived and said, "It's the LORD who has brought this **trouble** on us! Why should I wait any longer for him to do something?"

7 Elisha answered, "Listen to what the LORD says! By this time tomorrow you will be able to buy in Samaria three kilogrammes of the **best** wheat or six kilogrammes of barley for one piece of silver."

2 The personal attendant of the king said to Elisha, "That can't happen—not even if the LORD himself were to send grain[x] at once!"

"You will see it happen, but you will never eat any of the food," Elisha replied.

The Syrian Army Leaves

3 Four men who were **suffering** from a dreaded **skin-disease** were outside the

abandon [2] 1 Kgs 14.16; 17.13
alive 1 Kgs 20.18; 10.11
announce 1 Kgs 1.24; 1 Chr 13.2
best [3] 1 Kgs 12.21; 10.3
choose 6.8; 10.3
command 1.3; 14.6
dark 1 Kgs 18.45; 2 Chr 6.1
death (1) 5.7; 13.24
death (3) (to death) [3] 6.22; 8.12
disease 5.1; 13.14
doom 6.15; Ps 1.6
each other 3.23; 2 Chr 3.11
famine 4.38; 8.1
flee [2] 1 Kgs 20.20; 9.10
Good News 1 Kgs 1.42; 1 Chr 10.9
life (1) [2] 5.7; 10.24

[m] DOVE'S DUNG: *This may be a popular term for a vegetable such as wild onions.*
[n] *Probable text* king; *Hebrew* messenger. [x] grain; *or* rain.

6.29: Deut 18.57; Lam 4.10

plan 1 Kgs 20.22; 11.4
predict 1 Kgs 13.5; 23.16
punish 1 Kgs 14.15; 9.7
spare 1.13; 10.17
suffer 5.1; 14.26
sure 4.9; 9.14
worst 1 Kgs 18.2; 2 Chr 28.22

gates of Samaria, and they said to one
another, "Why should we wait here until
we die? 4 It's no use going into the city,
because we would starve **to death** in
there; but if we stay here, we'll die also.
So let's go to the Syrian camp; the **worst**
they can do is kill us, but maybe they will
spare our **lives**." 5 So, as it began to get
dark, they went to the Syrian camp, but
when they reached it, no one was there.
6 The Lord had made the Syrians hear
what sounded like the advance of a large
army, with horses and chariots, and the
Syrians thought that the king of Israel
had hired Hittite and Egyptian kings and
their armies to attack them. 7 So that
evening the Syrians had **fled** for their
lives, **abandoning** their tents, horses, and
donkeys, and leaving the camp just as it
was.
8 When the four men reached the
edge of the camp, they went into a tent,
ate and drank what was there, grabbed
the silver, gold, and clothing they found,
and went off and hid them; then they
returned, entered another tent, and did
the same thing. 9 But then they said to
each other, "We shouldn't be doing this!
We have **good news** and we shouldn't
keep it to ourselves. If we wait until
morning to tell it, we are **sure** to be
punished. Let's go at once and tell the
king's officers!" 10 So they left the Syrian
camp, went back to Samaria and called
out to the guards at the gates: "We went
to the Syrian camp and didn't see or hear
anybody; the horses and donkeys have
not been untied, and the tents are just as
the Syrians left them."
11 The guards **announced** the news,
and it was reported in the palace. 12 It
was still night, but the king got out of bed
and said to his officials, "I'll tell you what
the Syrians are **planning**! They know
about the **famine** here, so they have left
their camp to go and hide in the countryside. They think that we will leave the
city to find food, and then they will take
us **alive** and capture the city."
13 One of his officials said, "The
people here in the city are **doomed** anyway, like those that have already died. So
let's send some men with five of the
horses that are left, so that we can find
out what has happened."[o] 14 They **chose**
some men, and the king sent them in two
chariots with instructions to go and find
out what had happened to the Syrian
army. 15 The men went as far as the
Jordan, and all along the road they saw
the clothes and equipment that the
Syrians had **abandoned** as they **fled**.
Then they returned and reported to the
king. 16 The people of Samaria rushed out
and looted the Syrian camp. And, as the
LORD had said, three kilogrammes of the
best wheat or six kilogrammes of barley
were sold for one piece of silver.
17 It so happened that the king of
Israel had put the city gate under the
command of the officer who was his
personal attendant. The officer was
trampled **to death** there by the people
and died, as Elisha had **predicted** when
the king went to see him. 18 Elisha had
told the king that by that time the following day three kilogrammes of the **best**
wheat or six kilogrammes of barley
would be sold in Samaria for one piece of
silver, 19 to which the officer had
answered, "That can't happen—not even
if the LORD himself were to send grain[x]
at once!" And Elisha had replied, "You
will see it happen, but you will never eat
any of the food." 20 And that is just what
happened to him—he died, trampled **to
death** by the people at the city gate.

The Woman from Shunem Returns

8 Now Elisha had told the woman
who lived in Shunem, whose son he
had brought back **to life**, that the LORD
was sending a **famine** on the land, which
would **last** for seven years, and that she
should leave with her family and go and
live somewhere else. 2 She had followed
his instructions, and had gone with her
family to live in Philistia for the seven
years.
3 At the end of the seven years, she
returned to Israel and went to the king to
ask for her house and her land to be
restored to her. 4 She found the king
talking with Gehazi, Elisha's **servant**; the
king wanted to know about Elisha's
miracles. 5 While Gehazi was telling the
king how Elisha had brought a **dead**
person back **to life**, the woman made her
appeal to the king. Gehazi said to him,
"Your **Majesty**, here is the woman and
here is her son whom Elisha brought
back **to life**!" 6 In answer to the king's
question, she confirmed Gehazi's story,
and so the king called an official and told
him to give back to her everything that
was hers, including the **value** of all the
crops that her fields had produced during
the seven years she had been away.

Elisha and King Benhadad of Syria

7 Elisha went to Damascus at a time
when King Benhadad of Syria was ill.

consult 6.8; 17.17
dead 6.31; 9.24
death (3) (to death 7.4; 10.11
destroy 3.25; 10.27
escape 3.26; 10.24
evil 1 Kgs 16.7; 13.
famine 7.12; 25.3
gift 5.15; 12.4
horror [2] Deut 28.59; 2 Chr 26.20
last (1) 2 Sam 24.1 1 Chr 16.15
life (2) (to life) [3] 1 Kgs 17.21; 13.21
Majesty 6.12; 1 Chr 16.27
miracle Josh 24.17 1 Chr 16.12
power 5.7; 14.5
promise 1 Kgs 22. 9.26
prophet 6.1; 9.1
question 1 Kgs 10. 9.19
reign [3] 3.1; 12.1
restore 6.20; 14.28
reveal 2 Sam 7.17; 1 Chr 17.15
scatter 1 Kgs 22.17 9.37
servant [3] 6.15; 9.7
slaughter 3.24; 2 Chr 18.2
tear (2) Judg 14.16 20.5
tomb 1 Kgs 22.50; 9.28
value 1 Kgs 20.6; 2 Chr 9.20
way (3) 1 Kgs 13.3 13.2

[o] *Verse 13 in Hebrew is unclear.* [x] grain; *or* rain.
8.1: 2 Kgs 4.8–37

When the king was told that Elisha was
there, 8 he said to Hazael, one of his
officials, "Take a **gift** to the **prophet**, and
ask him to **consult** the LORD to find out
whether or not I am going to get well."
9 So Hazael loaded forty camels with all
kinds of the finest products of Damascus
and went to Elisha. When Hazael met
him, he said, "Your **servant** King Benhadad has sent me to ask you whether or
not he will recover from his illness."
10 Elisha answered, "The LORD has
revealed to me that he will die; but go to
him and tell him that he will recover."
11 Then Elisha stared at him with a **horrified** look on his face until Hazael became
ill at ease. Suddenly Elisha burst into
tears. 12 "Why are you crying, sir?"
Hazael asked.
"Because I know the **horrible** things
you will do against the people of Israel,"
Elisha answered. "You will set their fortresses on fire, **slaughter** their finest
young men, batter their children **to
death**, and rip open their pregnant
women."
13 "How could I ever be that **powerful**?" Hazael asked. "I'm a nobody!"
"The LORD has shown me that you will
be king of Syria," Elisha replied.
14 Hazael went back to Benhadad,
who asked him, "What did Elisha say?"
"He told me that you would certainly
get well," Hazael answered. 15 But on the
following day Hazael took a blanket,
soaked it in water, and smothered the
king.
And Hazael succeeded Benhadad as
king of Syria.

King Jehoram of Judah
(2 Chr 21.1–20)

16 In the fifth year of the **reign** of
Joram son of Ahab as king of Israel,[p]
Jehoram son of Jehoshaphat became
king of Judah 17 at the age of thirty-two,
and he ruled in Jerusalem for eight
years. 18 His wife was Ahab's daughter,
and like the family of Ahab he followed
the **evil ways** of the kings of Israel. He
sinned against the LORD, 19 but the LORD
was not willing to **destroy** Judah, because
he had **promised** his **servant** David that
his descendants would always continue
to rule.
20 During Jehoram's **reign** Edom
revolted against Judah and became an
independent kingdom. 21 So Jehoram set
out with all his chariots for Zair, where
the Edomite army surrounded them.
During the night he and his chariot commanders managed to break out and
escape, and his soldiers **scattered** to their
homes. 22 Edom has been independent of[q]
Judah ever since. During this same
period the city of Libnah also revolted.
23 Everything else that Jehoram did is
recorded in *The History of the Kings of
Judah*. 24 Jehoram died and was buried in
the royal **tombs** in David's City, and his
son Ahaziah succeeded him as king.

King Ahaziah of Judah
(2 Chr 22.1–6)

25 In the twelfth year of the **reign** of
Joram son of Ahab as king of Israel,
Ahaziah son of Jehoram became king of
Judah 26 at the age of twenty-two, and he
ruled in Jerusalem for one year. His
mother was Athaliah, the daughter of
King Ahab and granddaughter of King
Omri of Israel. 27 Since Ahaziah was
related to King Ahab by marriage, he
sinned against the LORD, just as Ahab's
family did.
28 King Ahaziah joined King Joram of
Israel in a war against King Hazael of
Syria. The armies clashed at Ramoth in
Gilead, and Joram was wounded in
battle. 29 He returned to the city of Jezreel to recover from his wounds, and
Ahaziah went there to visit him.

Jehu Is Anointed King of Israel

9 Meanwhile the **prophet** Elisha
called one of the young prophets
and said to him, "Get ready and go to
Ramoth in Gilead. Take this jar of olive-
oil with you, 2 and when you get there
look for Jehu, the son of Jehoshaphat and
grandson of Nimshi. Take him to a
private room away from his companions,
3 pour this olive-oil on his **head**, and say,
'The LORD **proclaims** that he **anoints** you
king of Israel.' Then leave there as fast
as you can."
4 So the young **prophet** went to
Ramoth, 5 where he found the army
officers in a conference. He said, "Sir, I
have a **message** for you."
Jehu asked, "Which one of us are you
speaking to?"
"To you, sir," he replied. 6 Then the two
of them went indoors, and the young
prophet poured the olive-oil on Jehu's
head and said to him, "The LORD, the
God of Israel, **proclaims**: 'I **anoint** you
king of **my people** Israel. 7 You are to kill
your **master** the king, that son of Ahab,

anoint [3] 1 Kgs 19.15; 11.12
blood 3.22; 16.13
body [6] 4.34; 10.25
dead 8.5; 19.35
duty (1) 1 Kgs 8.11; 11.5
enemy 3.23; 14.19
flee [3] 7.7; 14.12
friend [2] 1 Kgs 16.11; 10.11
fulfil 1 Kgs 8.24; 15.12
God's people 1 Kgs 16.2; 11.17
heart 1 Kgs 8.23; 10.31
idol 1 Kgs 21.26; 11.18
mad 1 Sam 21.13; Job 16.14
master 5.3; 1 Chr 12.19
message 1 Kgs 21.14; 10.5
peace [2] 5.19; 13.5
plot (1) 1 Kgs 16.9; 10.9
proclaim [3] 1 Kgs 21.9; 10.20
promise [2] 8.19; 10.10
prophet [5] 8.8; 10.10
punish [2] 7.9; 17.20
question 8.6; 2 Chr 9.1
remember 1 Kgs 18.12; 20.3

[p] *Some ancient translations* Israel; *Hebrew* Israel, Jehoshaphat being king of Judah.
[q] independent of; *or* in revolt against.

8.13: 1 Kgs 19.15 **8.19:** 1 Kgs 11.36 **8.20:** Gen 27.40 **9.6:** 1 Kgs 19.16

rid 1 Kgs 22.46; Ezra 10.11
scatter 8.21; 23.6
servant [2] 8.4; 10.5
strength 1 Kgs 19.8; 15.19
strike 6.18; 13.18
sure 7.9; 10.23
tomb 8.24; 12.20
turn 4.29; 10.27
warn 6.9; 17.13
watch [2] 1 Kgs 20.33; 2 Chr 6.20
word (1) 6.9; 10.21

so that I may **punish** Jezebel for murdering my **prophets** and my other **servants**.
8 All Ahab's family and descendants are
to die; I will get **rid** of every male in his
family, young and old alike. 9 I will treat
his family as I did the families of King
Jeroboam of Israel and of King Baasha
of Israel. 10 Jezebel will not be buried; her
body will be eaten by dogs in the territory of Jezreel.' " After saying this, the
young **prophet** left the room and **fled**.
11 Jehu went back to his fellow-
officers, who asked him, "Is everything
all right? What did that crazy fellow
want with you?"
"You know what he wanted," Jehu
answered.
12 "No we don't!" they replied. "Tell
us what he said!"
"He told me that the LORD **proclaims**:
'I **anoint** you king of Israel.' "
13 At once Jehu's fellow-officers
spread their cloaks at the top of the steps
for Jehu to stand on, blew trumpets, and
shouted, "Jehu is king!"

King Joram of Israel Is Killed

14–15 Then Jehu **plotted** against King
Joram, who was in Jezreel, where he had
gone to recover from the wounds which
he had received in the battle at Ramoth
against King Hazael of Syria. So Jehu
said to his fellow-officers, "If you are
with me, make **sure** that no one slips out
of Ramoth to go and **warn** the people in
Jezreel." 16 Then he got into his chariot
and set off for Jezreel. Joram had still
not recovered, and King Ahaziah of
Judah was there, visiting him.
17 A guard on **duty** in the **watch-tower**
at Jezreel saw Jehu and his men
approaching. "I see some men riding
up!" he called out.
Joram replied, "Send a horseman to
find out if they are **friends or enemies**."
18 The messenger rode out to Jehu
and said to him, "The king wants to know
if you come as a **friend**."
"That's none of your business!" Jehu
answered. "Fall in behind me."
The guard on the **watch-tower**
reported that the messenger had
reached the group but was not returning.
19 Another messenger was sent out, who
asked Jehu the same **question**. Again
Jehu answered, "That's none of your
business! Fall in behind me."
20 Once more the guard reported that
the messenger had reached the group
but was not returning. And he added,
"The leader of the group is driving his
chariot like a **madman**, just like Jehu!"
21 "Get my chariot ready," King
Joram ordered. It was done, and he and
King Ahaziah rode out, each in his own
chariot, to meet Jehu. They met him at
the field which had belonged to Naboth.
22 "Are you coming in **peace**?" Joram
asked him.
"How can there be **peace**," Jehu
answered, "when we still have all the
witchcraft and **idolatry** that your mother
Jezebel started?"
23 "It's treason, Ahaziah!" Joram
cried out, as he **turned** his chariot round
and **fled**. 24 Jehu drew his bow, and with
all his **strength** shot an arrow that **struck**
Joram in the back and pierced his **heart**.
Joram fell **dead** in his chariot, 25 and Jehu
said to his aide Bidkar, "Get his **body** and
throw it in the field that belonged to
Naboth. **Remember** that when you and I
were riding together behind King
Joram's father Ahab, the LORD spoke
these **words** against Ahab: 26 'I saw the
murder of Naboth and his sons yester-
day. And I **promise** that I will **punish** you
here in this same field.' So take Joram's
body," Jehu ordered his aide, "and throw
it in the field that belonged to Naboth, so
as to **fulfil** the LORD's **promise**."

King Ahaziah of Judah Is Killed

27 King Ahaziah saw what happened,
so he **fled** in his chariot towards the town
of Beth Haggan, pursued by Jehu. "Kill
him too!" Jehu ordered his men, and
they wounded him[s] as he drove his
chariot on the road up to Gur, near the
town of Ibleam. But he managed to keep
going until he reached the city of
Megiddo, where he died. 28 His officials
took his **body** back to Jerusalem in a
chariot and buried him in the royal
tombs in David's City.
29 Ahaziah had become king of Judah
in the eleventh year that Joram son of
Ahab was king of Israel.

Queen Jezebel Is Killed

30 Jehu arrived in Jezreel. Jezebel,
having heard what had happened, put on
eyeshadow, arranged her hair, and stood
looking down at the street from a
window in the palace. 31 As Jehu came
through the gate, she called out, "You
Zimri![t] You assassin! Why are you
here?"
32 Jehu looked up and shouted, "Who
is on my side?" Two or three palace

[s] *Some ancient translations* and they wounded him; *Hebrew does not have these words.*
[t] ZIMRI: *An Israelite army officer who assassinated the king of Israel (see 1 Kgs 16.8–12).*

9.10: 1 Kgs 21.23 **9.26:** 1 Kgs 21.19

officials looked down at him from a
window, 33 and Jehu said to them, "Throw
her down!" They threw her down, and
her **blood** spattered the wall and the
horses. Jehu drove his horses and chariot
over her **body**, 34 entered the palace, and
had a meal. Only then did he say, "Take
that damned woman and bury her; after
all, she is a king's daughter." 35 But the
men who went out to bury her found
nothing except her skull, and the bones
of her hands and feet. 36 When they
reported this to Jehu, he said, "This is
what the LORD said would happen, when
he spoke through his **servant** Elijah:
'Dogs will eat Jezebel's **body** in the territory of Jezreel. 37 Her remains will be
scattered there like dung, so that no one
will be able to identify them.' "

The Descendants of Ahab Are Killed

10 There were seventy descendants
of King Ahab living in the city of
Samaria. Jehu wrote a **letter** and sent
copies to the rulers of the city,[u] to the
leading citizens, and to the guardians of
Ahab's descendants. The **letter** read:
2 "You are in charge of the king's descendants and you have at your disposal
chariots, horses, weapons, and fortified
cities. So then, as soon as you receive this
letter, 3 you are to **choose** the **best** qualified of the king's descendants, make him
king, and fight to **defend** him."

4 The rulers of Samaria were **terrified**.
"How can we oppose Jehu," they said,
"when neither King Joram nor King
Ahaziah could?" 5 So the officer in
charge of the palace and the official in
charge of the city, together with the **leading** citizens and the guardians, sent this
message to Jehu: "We are your **servants**
and we are ready to do anything you say.
But we will not make anyone king; do
whatever you think **best**."

6 Jehu wrote them another **letter**: "If
you are with me, and are ready to follow
my orders, bring the heads of King
Ahab's descendants to me at Jezreel by
this time tomorrow."

The seventy descendants of King Ahab
were under the **care** of the **leading**
citizens of Samaria, who were bringing
them up. 7 When Jehu's **letter** was
received, the leaders of Samaria killed
all seventy of Ahab's descendants, put
their heads in baskets, and sent them to
Jehu at Jezreel.

8 When Jehu was told that the heads
of Ahab's descendants had been brought,
he ordered them to be piled up in two
heaps at the city gate and to be left there
until the following morning. 9 In the
morning, he went out to the gate and said
to the people who were there, "I was the
one who **plotted** against King Joram and
killed him; you are not responsible for
that. But who killed all these? 10 This
proves that everything that the LORD
said about the descendants of Ahab will
come **true**. The LORD has done what he
promised through his **prophet** Elijah."
11 Then Jehu put to **death** all the other
relatives of Ahab living in Jezreel, and all
his officers, close **friends**, and **priests**; not
one of them was left **alive**.

The Relatives of King Ahaziah Are Killed

12 Jehu left Jezreel to go to Samaria.
On the way, at a place called "Shepherds'
Camp," 13 he met some relatives of the
late King Ahaziah of Judah and asked
them, "Who are you?"

"Ahaziah's relatives," they answered.
"We are going to Jezreel to pay our
respects to the children of Queen Jezebel
and to the rest of the royal family."
14 Jehu ordered his men, "Take them
alive!" They seized them, and he put
them **to death** near a pit there. There
were forty-two people in all, and not one
of them was left **alive**.

All Remaining Relatives of Ahab Are Killed

15 Jehu started out again, and on his
way he was met by Jonadab son of
Rechab. Jehu greeted him and said, "You
and I think alike. Will you support me?"

"I will," Jonadab answered.

"Give me your hand, then," Jehu
replied. They clasped hands, and Jehu
helped him up into the chariot, 16 saying,
"Come with me and see for yourself how
devoted I am to the LORD." And they
rode on together to Samaria. 17 When
they arrived there, Jehu killed all of
Ahab's relatives, not **sparing** even one.
This is what the LORD had told Elijah
would happen.

The Worshippers of Baal Are Killed

18 Jehu called the people of Samaria
together and said, "King Ahab **served** the
god Baal a little, but I will **serve** him
much more. 19 Call together all the **prophets** of Baal, all his **worshippers**, and all
his **priests**. No one is **excused**; I am going
to **offer** a **great sacrifice** to Baal, and
whoever is not **present** will be put **to
death**." (This was a **trick** on the part of

[u] *Some ancient translations* the city; *Hebrew* Jezreel.

9.36: 1 Kgs 21.23 **10.11:** Hos 1.4

alive [3] 7.12; 2 Chr 24.2
best [2] 7.1; 1 Chr 12.23
body 9.10; 13.21
bull-calf 1 Kgs 12.28; 17.16
burnt-offering 5.17; 16.3
care 1 Kgs 17.20; 11.3
choose 7.14; 17.32
conquer 3.19; 12.17
death (3) (to death) [3] 8.12; 14.6
defend 2.12; 13.14
destroy 8.19; 12.3
devote 1 Kgs 21.20; 16.7
escape [2] 8.21; 11.2
example 1 Kgs 22.52; 13.11
excuse 1 Sam 1.26; Job 19.28
fail 3.26; 2 Chr 29.7
friend 9.17; 1 Chr 12.17
god (2) (other gods) 5.15; 17.7
heart 9.24; 23.3
help 6.26; 13.23
honour 1 Kgs 21.9; 18.4
law 1 Kgs 11.33; 11.12
leading [3] 1 Kgs 21.8; 24.14
letter (2) [5] 5.5; 19.9
life (1) 7.4; 12.2
message 9.5; 14.9
obey 1 Kgs 17.5; 11.9
offer [3] 5.17; 12.3
plot (1) 9.14; 12.20
present (1) 1 Kgs 18.1; 1 Chr 6.49
priest [3] 1 Kgs 13.2; 11.4
proclaim [2] 9.3; 11.12
promise [2] 9.26; 14.25
prophet [2] 9.1; 13.14
prove 1 Kgs 18.36; 20.8
respect 5.1; 19.22
sacred [3] 2 Sam 21.7; 1 Chr 9.29
sacrifice [2] 5.17; 12.3
sanctuary 1 Kgs 6.3; Ps 60.6
servant 9.7; 14.25
serve [2] 5.16; 12.5
spare 7.4; 1 Chr 21.17
sure 9.14; 1 Chr 15.26
temple (2) (of other gods) [6] 5.18; 11.18
terrify 3.27; 22.19
trick 1 Sam 28.12; Neh 6.2
true 3.12; 2 Chr 6.17
turn 9.23; 19.25
word (1) 9.25; 18.20
worship (1) (of God) 1 Kgs 18.3; 12.9
worship (2) (of other gods) [8] 5.18; 17.7

Jehu by which he meant to kill all the
worshippers of Baal.) [20]Then Jehu
ordered, "**Proclaim** a day of **worship** in
honour of Baal!" The **proclamation** was
made, [21]and Jehu sent **word** throughout
all the land of Israel. All who **worshipped**
Baal came; not one of them **failed** to
come. They all went into the **temple** of
Baal, filling it from one end to the other.
[22]Then Jehu ordered the **priest** in charge
of the **sacred** robes to bring the robes out
and give them to the **worshippers.**
[23]After that, Jehu himself went into the
temple with Jonadab son of Rechab and
said to the people there, "Make **sure** that
only **worshippers of Baal** are present and
that no **worshipper** of the LORD has come
in." [24]Then he and Jonadab went in to
offer sacrifices and **burnt-offerings** to
Baal. He had stationed eighty men outside the **temple** and had instructed them:
"You are to kill all these people; anyone
who lets one of them **escape** will pay for
it with his **life**!"

25 As soon as Jehu had **presented** the
offerings, he said to the guards and
officers, "Go in and kill them all; don't
let anyone **escape**!" They went in with
drawn swords, killed them all, and
dragged the **bodies** outside. Then they
went on into the inner **sanctuary** of the
temple, [26]brought out the **sacred** pillar
that was there, and burnt it. [27]So they
destroyed the **sacred** pillar and the
temple, and **turned** the **temple** into a
latrine—which it still is today.

28 That was how Jehu wiped out the
worship of Baal in Israel. [29]But he
imitated the sin of King Jeroboam, who
led Israel into the sin of **worshipping** the
gold **bull-calves** he set up in Bethel and in
Dan. [30]The LORD said to Jehu, "You have
done to Ahab's descendants everything I
wanted you to do. So I **promise** you that
your descendants, down to the fourth
generation, will be kings of Israel." [31]But
Jehu did not **obey with all his heart** the
law of the LORD, the God of Israel;
instead, he followed the **example** of Jeroboam, who led Israel into sin.

The Death of Jehu

32 At that time the LORD began to
reduce the size of Israel's territory. King
Hazael of Syria **conquered** all the
Israelite territory [33]east of the Jordan, as
far south as the town of Aroer on the
River Arnon—this included the territories of Gilead and Bashan, where the
tribes of Gad, Reuben, and East
Manasseh lived.

34 Everything else that Jehu did,
including his brave deeds, is recorded in
The History of the Kings of Israel. [35]He
died and was buried in Samaria, and his
son Jehoahaz succeeded him as king.
[36]Jehu had ruled in Samaria as king of
Israel for twenty-eight years.

Queen Athaliah of Judah
(2 Chr 22.10—23.15)

11 As soon as King Ahaziah's
mother Athaliah **learnt** of her
son's murder, she gave orders for all the
members of the royal family to be killed.
[2]Only Ahaziah's son Joash **escaped.** He
was about to be killed with the others,
but was **rescued** by his aunt Jehosheba,
who was King Jehoram's daughter and
Ahaziah's half-sister. She took him and
his nurse into a bedroom in the **Temple**
and hid him from Athaliah, so that he
was not killed. [3]For six years Jehosheba
took **care** of the boy and kept him hidden
in the **Temple**, while Athaliah ruled as
queen.

4 But in the seventh year Jehoiada the
priest sent for the officers in charge of
the royal bodyguard and of the palace
guards, and told them to come to the
Temple, where he made them **agree**
under **oath** to what he **planned** to do. He
showed them King Ahaziah's son Joash
[5]and gave them the following orders:
"When you come on **duty** on the **Sabbath**,
one third of you are to guard the palace;
[6]another third are to stand guard at the
Sur Gate, and the other third are to stand
guard at the gate behind the other
guards.[v] [7]The two groups that go **off duty**
on the **Sabbath** are to stand guard at the
Temple to **protect** the king. [8]You are to
guard King Joash with drawn swords and
stay with him wherever he goes. Anyone
who comes near you is to be killed."

9 The officers **obeyed** Jehoiada's
instructions and brought their men to
him—those going off duty on the **Sabbath**
and those going on **duty.** [10]He gave the
officers the spears[w] and shields that had
belonged to King David and had been
kept in the **Temple**, [11]and he stationed
the men with drawn swords all round the
front of the **Temple**, to **protect** the king.
[12]Then Jehoiada led Joash out, placed
the **crown** on his head, and gave him a
copy of the **laws** governing kingship.

agree 6.3; 12.8
altar [2] 1 Kgs 22.46
12.9
anoint 9.3; 23.30
care 10.6; 1 Chr 23.2
covenant [2]
1 Kgs 19.10; 13.23
crown 2 Sam 12.30;
14.21
custom 1 Kgs 10.13;
17.8
distress 4.27;
2 Chr 15.6
duty (1) [4] 9.17; 12.9
escape 10.24; 19.11
God's people 9.6;
13.23
happy 1 Kgs 8.66;
1 Chr 29.9
idol 9.22; 16.3
joy 1 Kgs 1.40;
1 Chr 12.40
law 10.31; 14.6
learn 2 Sam 11.3;
17.4
new 2.20; 16.14
oath 1 Kgs 8.31;
2 Chr 6.22
obey 10.31; 17.13
plan 7.12; 19.25
priest [3] 10.11; 12.2
proclaim 10.20;
1 Chr 16.8
protect [2] 1 Kgs 9.3
19.34
rescue [2] 1 Kgs 1.29
14.27
Sabbath [3] 4.23;
1 Chr 9.32
Temple (1) (of God)
[11] 1 Kgs 15.15; 12.4
**temple (2) (of other
gods)** 10.21; 19.37
throne 1 Kgs 22.10;
16.18

[v] *Hebrew has an additional word, the meaning of which is unclear.*
[w] *Some ancient translations (and see 2 Chr 23.9)* spears; *Hebrew* spear.

10.29: 1 Kgs 12.28–30

Then Joash was **anointed** and **proclaimed** king. The people clapped their
hands and shouted, "Long live the king!"
13 Queen Athaliah heard the noise
being made by the guards and the
people, so she hurried to the **Temple**,
where the crowd had gathered. 14 There
she saw the **new** king standing by the
column at the entrance of the **Temple**, as
was the **custom**. He was surrounded by
the officers and the trumpeters, and the
people were all shouting **joyfully** and
blowing trumpets. Athaliah tore her
clothes in **distress** and shouted,
"Treason! Treason!"
15 Jehoiada did not want Athaliah
killed in the **temple** area, so he ordered
the army officers: "Take her out
between the rows of guards, and kill anyone who tries to **rescue** her." 16 They
seized her, took her to the palace, and
there at the Horse Gate they killed her.

Jehoiada's Reforms
(2 Chr 23.16–21)

17 The **priest** Jehoiada made King
Joash and the people enter into a **covenant** with the LORD that they would be the
LORD's people; he also made a **covenant**
between the king and the people. 18 Then
the people went to the **temple** of Baal
and tore it down; they smashed the
altars and the **idols**, and killed Mattan,
the **priest** of Baal, in front of the **altars**.
Jehoiada put guards on **duty** at the
Temple, 19 and then he, the officers, the
royal bodyguard, and the palace guards
escorted the king from the **Temple** to the
palace, followed by all the people. Joash
entered by the Guard Gate and took his
place on the **throne**. 20 All the people
were filled with **happiness**, and the city
was quiet, now that Athaliah had been
killed in the palace.
21 Joash became king of Judah at the
age of seven.

King Joash of Judah
(2 Chr 24.1–16)

12 In the seventh year of the **reign**
of King Jehu of Israel, Joash
became king of Judah, and he ruled in
Jerusalem for forty years. His mother
was Zibiah from the city of Beersheba.
2 Throughout his **life** he did what **pleased**
the LORD, because Jehoiada the **priest** instructed him. 3 However, the **pagan
places of worship** were not **destroyed**,
and the people continued to **offer sacrifices** and burn **incense** there.
4 Joash called the **priests** and ordered
them to **save** up the money paid in connection with the **sacrifices** in the **Temple**,
both the dues paid for the regular **sacrifices** and the money given as **free-will
gifts**. 5 Each **priest** was to be responsible
for the money brought by those he
served, and the money was to be used to
repair the **Temple**, as **needed**.
6 But by the twenty-third year of
Joash's **reign** the **priests** still had not
made any repairs to the **Temple**. 7 So he
called in Jehoiada and the other **priests**
and asked them, "Why aren't you repairing the **Temple**? From now on you are
not to keep the money you receive; you
must hand it over, so that the repairs can
be made." 8 The **priests agreed** to this
and also **agreed** not to make the repairs
in the **Temple**.
9 Then Jehoiada took a box, made a
hole in the lid, and placed the box by the
altar, on the **right** side as one enters the
Temple. The **priests** on **duty** at the
entrance put in the box all the money
given by the **worshippers**. 10 Whenever
there was a large amount of money in
the box, the royal secretary and the **High
Priest** would come, melt down the silver,
and weigh it.[x] 11 After recording the
exact amount, they would hand the silver
over to the men in charge of the work in
the **Temple**, and these would pay the carpenters, the builders, 12 the masons, and
the stone-cutters, buy the timber and the
stones used in the repairs, and pay all
other necessary expenses. 13 None of the
money, however, was used to pay for
making silver **cups**, bowls, trumpets, or
tools for tending the lamps, or any other
article of silver or of gold. 14 It was all
used to pay the workmen and to buy the
materials used in the repairs. 15 The men
in charge of the work were thoroughly
honest, so there was no **need** to **require**
them to account for the funds. 16 The
money given for the **repayment offerings**
and for the **offerings** for sin was not
deposited in the box; it belonged to the
priests.
17 At that time King Hazael of Syria
attacked the city of Gath and **conquered**
it; then he decided to attack Jerusalem.
18 King Joash of Judah took all the **offerings** that his predecessors Jehoshaphat,
Jehoram, and Ahaziah had **dedicated** to
the LORD, added to them his own
offerings and all the gold in the
treasuries of the **Temple** and the palace,
and sent them all as a **gift** to King
Hazael, who then led his army away
from Jerusalem.

[x] melt down the silver, and weigh it; *or* count the money, and tie it up in bags.

11.14: 2 Kgs 23.3 **12.4:** Ex 30.11–16 **12.15:** 2 Kgs 22.7 **12.16:** Lev 7.7

agree [2] 11.4; 1 Chr 13.4
altar 11.18; 16.10
conquer 10.32; 14.22
cup 1 Kgs 10.21; 2 Chr 4.5
dedicate 1 Kgs 15.15; 16.14
destroy 10.27; 13.7
duty (1) 11.5; 15.5
freewill Deut 16.10; Ezra 2.68
gift [2] 8.8; 1 Chr 26.20
High Priest Josh 20.6; 22.4
honest 1 Kgs 9.4; 22.7

incense 1 Kgs 22.43; 14.4
life (1) 10.24; 15.5
need [2] 4.13; 22.7
offer [5] 10.19; 14.4
pagan 1 Kgs 22.43; 14.4
place of worship 1 Kgs 22.43; 14.4
please 1 Kgs 15.5; 14.3
plot (1) 10.9; 14.19
priest [8] 11.4; 16.10
reign [2] 8.16; 13.1
repayment-offering Num 18.9; Ezek 40.39
require 1 Kgs 18.10; 22.7
right (2) 1 Kgs 2.19; 1 Chr 12.2
sacrifice [3] 10.19; 14.4
save 1 Kgs 1.12; 18.29
serve 10.18; 17.16
Temple (1) (of God) [8] 11.2; 14.14
tomb 9.28; 13.13
worship (1) (of God) 10.23; 17.25

19 Everything else that King Joash did
is recorded in *The History of the Kings of
Judah.*
20–21 King Joash's officials **plotted**
against him, and two of them, Jozacar
son of Shimeath and Jehozabad son of
Shomer, killed him at the house built on
the land that was filled in on the east side
of Jerusalem, on the road that goes down
to Silla. Joash was buried in the royal
tombs in David's City, and his son
Amaziah succeeded him as king.

King Jehoahaz of Israel

13 In the twenty-third year of the
reign of Joash son of Ahaziah as
king of Judah, Jehoahaz son of Jehu
became king of Israel, and he ruled in
Samaria for seventeen years. 2 Like King
Jeroboam before him he sinned against
the LORD and led Israel into sin; he never
gave up his **evil ways.** 3 So the LORD was
angry with Israel, and he allowed King
Hazael of Syria and his son Benhadad to
defeat Israel time after time. 4 Then
Jehoahaz **prayed** to the LORD, and the
LORD, seeing how harshly the king of
Syria was **oppressing** the Israelites,
answered his **prayer.** 5 The LORD sent
Israel a leader, who **freed** them from the
Syrians, and so the Israelites lived in
peace, as before. 6 But they still did not
give up the sins into which King Jeroboam had led Israel, but kept on[y] committing them; and the **image** of the **goddess** Asherah remained in Samaria.
7 Jehoahaz had no armed forces left
except fifty horsemen, ten chariots, and
ten thousand men on foot, because the
king of Syria had **destroyed** the rest,
trampling them down like dust.
8 Everything else that Jehoahaz did
and all his brave deeds are recorded in
The History of the Kings of Israel. 9 He
died and was buried in Samaria, and his
son Jehoash succeeded him as king.

King Jehoash of Israel

10 In the thirty-seventh year of the
reign of King Joash of Judah, Jehoash
son of Jehoahaz became king of Israel,
and he ruled in Samaria for sixteen
years. 11 He too sinned against the LORD
and followed the **evil example** of King
Jeroboam, who had led Israel into sin.
12 Everything else that Jehoash did,
including his bravery in the war against
King Amaziah of Judah, is recorded in
The History of the Kings of Israel.
13 Jehoash died and was buried in the
royal **tombs** in Samaria, and his son
Jeroboam II succeeded him as king.

The Death of Elisha

14 The **prophet** Elisha fell ill with a
fatal **disease**, and as he lay dying King
Jehoash of Israel went to visit him. "My
father, my father!" he exclaimed as he
wept. "You have been the **mighty
defender** of Israel!"
15 "Get a bow and some arrows,"
Elisha ordered him. Jehoash got them,
16 and Elisha told him to get ready to
shoot. The king did so, and Elisha placed
his hands on the king's hands. 17 Then,
following the **prophet's** instructions, the
king opened the window that faced
towards Syria. "Shoot the arrow!" Elisha
ordered. As soon as the king shot the
arrow, the **prophet** exclaimed, "You are
the LORD's arrow, with which he will **win
victory** over Syria. You will fight the
Syrians in Aphek until you defeat them."
18 Then Elisha told the king to take
the other arrows and **strike** the ground
with them. The king **struck** the ground
three times, and then stopped. 19 This
made Elisha **angry**, and he said to the
king, "You should have **struck** five or six
times, and then you would have **won**
complete **victory** over the Syrians; but
now you will defeat them only three
times."
20 Elisha died and was buried.
Every year bands of Moabites used to
invade the land of Israel. 21 Once, during
a funeral, one of those bands was seen,
and the people threw the corpse into
Elisha's **tomb** and ran off.[z] As soon as the
body came into contact with Elisha's
bones, the man came back **to life** and
stood up.

War between Israel and Syria

22 King Hazael of Syria **oppressed** the
Israelites during all of Jehoahaz' **reign**,
23 but the LORD was **kind** and **merciful** to
them. He would not let them **be destroyed**, but **helped** them, because of his
covenant with Abraham, Isaac, and
Jacob. He has never **forgotten his people**.
24 At the **death** of King Hazael of Syria
his son Benhadad became king. 25 Then
King Jehoash of Israel defeated Benhadad three times and recaptured the
cities that had been taken by Benhadad
during the **reign** of Jehoahaz, the father
of Jehoash.

anger [2] 1 Kgs 22.53; 17.11
body 10.25; 14.20
covenant 11.17; 17.15
death (1) 7.4; 14.17
defend 10.3; 19.34
destroy [2] 12.3; 14.27
disease 7.3; 15.5
evil [2] 8.18; 17.13
example 10.31; 14.24
forget 2 Sam 19.19; 17.38
free 1 Kgs 20.34; 1 Chr 9.33
God's people 11.17; 17.8
goddess 1 Kgs 18.19; 17.10
help 10.15; 14.26
image 3.2; 17.10
kind 1 Kgs 17.20; 25.27
life (2) (to life) 8.1; Neh 9.29
mercy 3.10; 1 Chr 21.13
might 2.12; 18.20
oppress [2] 2 Sam 7.10; 1 Chr 16.21
peace 9.22; 20.19
pray 6.17; 19.4
prayer 6.17; 19.20
prophet [3] 10.10; 14.25
reign [4] 12.1; 14.1
strike [3] 9.24; 15.5
tomb [2] 12.20; 14.16
victory [2] 5.1; 1 Chr 5.20
way (3) 8.18; 17.13
weep 2 Sam 19.1; 22.19
win [2] 1 Kgs 22.12; 2 Chr 13.12

[y] *Some ancient translations* kept on; *Hebrew* he kept on.
[z] *One ancient translation* and ran off; *Hebrew* and he ran off.

13.14: 2 Kgs 2.12

body 13.21; 23.30
challenge 2 Sam 23.9; 2 Chr 25.17
command 7.17; 16.16
conquer [2] 12.17; 18.13
crime [3] 2 Sam 16.7; 2 Chr 25.4
crown 11.12; 1 Chr 20.2
death (1) [2] 13.24; 15.18
death (3) (to death) [3] 10.11; 25.7
destroy 13.7; 15.4
disaster 1 Kgs 22.23; 21.12
enemy 9.17; 17.20
example 13.11; 15.3
execute Num 25.4; 2 Chr 25.3
flee [2] 9.10; 25.4
help 13.23; 17.4
incense 12.3; 15.4
law 11.12; 17.13
message 10.5; 16.7
offer 12.3; 15.4
pagan 12.3; 15.4
place of worship 12.3; 15.4
please 12.2; 15.3
plot (1) 12.20; 15.25
power 8.13; 15.19
prison 1 Kgs 22.27; 15.29
promise 10.10; 15.12
prophet 13.14; 17.13
proud 2 Sam 22.28; 19.28
purpose 2 Sam 7.21; 1 Chr 12.38
refuse (1) 1 Kgs 22.49; 17.15
reign [2] 13.1; 15.1
rescue 11.2; 16.7
restore 8.3; 1 Chr 11.8
sacrifice 12.3; 15.4
satisfy 1 Sam 22.2; Job 18.4
servant 10.5; 16.7
suffer 7.3; 19.3
Temple (1) (of God) 12.4; 15.35
terrible 1 Kgs 17.20; 17.21
tomb [3] 13.13; 15.38
trouble 6.28; 1 Chr 7.23
wicked 1 Kgs 22.52; 15.9

King Amaziah of Judah
(2 Chr 25.1–24)

14 In the second year of the **reign** of
Jehoash son of Jehoahaz as king
of Israel, Amaziah son of Joash became
king of Judah 2 at the age of twenty-five,
and he ruled in Jerusalem for twenty-
nine years. His mother was Jehoaddin,
from Jerusalem. 3 He did what was
pleasing to the LORD, but he was not like
his ancestor King David; instead, he did
what his father Joash had done. 4 He did
not tear down the **pagan places of worship**, and the people continued to **offer
sacrifices** and burn **incense** there.

5 As soon as Amaziah was firmly in
power, he **executed** the officials who had
killed his father, the king. 6 However, he
did not kill their children but followed
what the LORD had **commanded** in the
Law of Moses: "Parents are not to be put
to death for **crimes** committed by their
children, and children are not to be put
to death for **crimes** committed by their
parents; a person is to be put **to death**
only for a **crime** he himself has committed."

7 Amaziah killed ten thousand
Edomite soldiers in Salt Valley; he captured the city of Sela in battle and called
it Joktheel, the name it still has.

8 Then Amaziah sent messengers to
King Jehoash of Israel, **challenging** him
to fight.[a] 9 But King Jehoash sent back
the following reply: "Once a thorn bush
on the Lebanon Mountains sent a
message to a cedar: 'Give your daughter
in marriage to my son.' A wild animal
passed by and trampled the bush down.
10 Now Amaziah, you have defeated the
Edomites, and you are filled with **pride**.
Be **satisfied** with your fame and stay at
home. Why stir up **trouble** that will only
bring **disaster** on you and your people?"

11 But Amaziah **refused** to listen, so
King Jehoash marched out with his men
and fought against him at Beth Shemesh
in Judah. 12 Amaziah's army was
defeated, and all his soldiers **fled** to their
homes. 13 Jehoash took Amaziah **prisoner**,
advanced on Jerusalem, and tore down
the city wall from Ephraim Gate to the
Corner Gate, a distance of nearly two
hundred metres. 14 He took all the silver
and gold he could find, all the **temple**
equipment and all the palace treasures,
and carried them back to Samaria. He
also took hostages with him.

15 Everything else that Jehoash did,
including his bravery in the war against
King Amaziah of Judah, is recorded in
The History of the Kings of Israel.
16 Jehoash died and was buried in the
royal **tombs** in Samaria, and his son Jeroboam II succeeded him as king.

The Death of King Amaziah of Judah
(2 Chr 25.25–28)

17 King Amaziah of Judah lived fifteen
years after the **death** of King Jehoash of
Israel. 18 Everything else that Amaziah
did is recorded in *The History of the
Kings of Judah.*

19 There was a **plot** in Jerusalem to
assassinate Amaziah, so he **fled** to the
city of Lachish, but his **enemies** followed
him there and killed him. 20 His **body** was
carried back to Jerusalem on a horse
and was buried in the royal **tombs** in
David's City. 21 The people of Judah then
crowned his sixteen-year-old son Uzziah
as king. 22 Uzziah **reconquered** and
rebuilt Elath after his father's **death**.

King Jeroboam II of Israel

23 In the fifteenth year of the **reign** of
Amaziah son of Joash as king of Judah,
Jeroboam son of Jehoash became king of
Israel, and he ruled in Samaria for forty-
one years. 24 He sinned against the LORD,
following the **wicked example** of his predecessor King Jeroboam son of Nebat,
who led Israel into sin. 25 He **reconquered**
all the territory that had belonged to
Israel, from Hamath Pass in the north to
the Dead Sea in the south. This was what
the LORD, the God of Israel, had
promised through his **servant** the
prophet Jonah son of Amittai, from Gath
Hepher.

26 The LORD saw the **terrible**[b] **suffering** of the Israelites; there was no one at
all to **help** them. 27 But it was not the
LORD's **purpose** to **destroy** Israel completely and for ever, so he **rescued** them
through King Jeroboam II.

28 Everything else that Jeroboam II
did, his brave battles, and how he
restored Damascus and Hamath to
Israel,[c] are all recorded in *The History
of the Kings of Israel.* 29 Jeroboam died
and was buried in the royal **tombs**, and
his son Zechariah succeeded him as king.

King Uzziah of Judah
(2 Chr 26.1–23)

15 In the twenty-seventh year of the
reign of King Jeroboam II of
Israel, Uzziah son of Amaziah became

contribute Num 31.29; 2 Chr 24.8

[a] challenging him to fight; *or* inviting him to a conference.
[b] *Some ancient translations* terrible; *Hebrew* rebellious.
[c] *One ancient translation* to Israel; *Hebrew* for Judah in Israel.

14.6: Deut 24.16 **14.25:** Jon 1.1

death (1) [2] 14.17; 22.20
destroy [3] 14.27; 18.4
disease 13.14; 2 Chr 6.28
duty (1) 12.9; 22.4
example [6] 14.24; 16.2
force (1) 3.26; 24.1
fulfil 9.26; 1 Chr 17.23
incense [2] 14.4; 16.4
life (1) 12.2; 25.29
offer [2] 14.4; 16.4
pagan [2] 14.4; 16.4
place of worship [2] 14.4; 16.4
please [2] 14.3; 16.2
plot (1) [2] 14.19; 21.23
power 14.5; 17.36
prison 14.13; 16.9
promise 14.25; 19.34
reign [8] 14.1; 16.1
relieve (1) Gen 5.29; 2 Chr 26.21
rich 4.8; 23.2
sacrifice [2] 14.4; 16.3
strength 9.24; 17.36
strike 13.18; 2 Chr 13.20
Temple (1) (of God) 14.14; 16.8
tomb 14.16; 16.20
wicked [4] 14.24; 17.11

king of Judah 2 at the age of sixteen, and
he ruled in Jerusalem for fifty-two years.
His mother was Jecoliah from Jerusalem. 3 Following the **example** of his
father, he did what was **pleasing** to the
LORD. 4 But the **pagan places of worship**
were not **destroyed**, and the people continued to **offer sacrifices** and burn
incense there. 5 The LORD **struck** Uzziah
with a dreaded **skin-disease** that stayed
with him the rest of his **life**. He lived in a
house on his own, **relieved** of all **duties**,
while his son Jotham governed the
country.

6 Everything else that Uzziah did is
recorded in *The History of the Kings of
Judah.* 7 Uzziah died and was buried in
the royal burial ground in David's City,
and his son Jotham succeeded him as
king.

King Zechariah of Israel

8 In the thirty-eighth year of the **reign**
of King Uzziah of Judah, Zechariah son
of Jeroboam II became king of Israel,
and he ruled in Samaria for six months.
9 He, like his predecessors, sinned against
the LORD. He followed the **wicked
example** of King Jeroboam son of Nebat,
who led Israel into sin. 10 Shallum son of
Jabesh conspired against King Zechariah, assassinated him at Ibleam,[d]
and succeeded him as king.

11 Everything else that Zechariah did
is recorded in *The History of the Kings of
Israel.*

12 So the **promise** was **fulfilled** which
the LORD had made to King Jehu: "Your
descendants, down to the fourth generation,[e] will be kings of Israel."

King Shallum of Israel

13 In the thirty-ninth year of the **reign**
of King Uzziah of Judah, Shallum son of
Jabesh became king of Israel, and he
ruled in Samaria for one month.

14 Menahem son of Gadi went from
Tirzah to Samaria, assassinated Shallum,
and succeeded him as king. 15 Everything
else that Shallum did, including an
account of his conspiracy, is recorded in
The History of the Kings of Israel. 16 As
Menahem was on his way from Tirzah,
he completely **destroyed** the city of
Tappuah,[f] its inhabitants, and the surrounding territory, because the city did
not surrender to him. He even ripped
open the bellies of all the pregnant
women.

King Menahem of Israel

17 In the thirty-ninth year of the **reign**
of King Uzziah of Judah, Menahem son of
Gadi became king of Israel, and he ruled
in Samaria for ten years. 18 He sinned
against the LORD, for until the day of his
death he followed the **wicked example** of
King Jeroboam son of Nebat, who led
Israel into sin till the day of his **death**.
19 Tiglath Pileser, the emperor of Assyria,
invaded Israel, and Menahem gave him
thirty-four thousand kilogrammes of
silver to gain his support in **strengthening** Menahem's **power** over the country.
20 Menahem got the money from the **rich**
men of Israel by **forcing** each one to **contribute** fifty pieces of silver. So Tiglath
Pileser went back to his own country.

21 Everything else that Menahem did
is recorded in *The History of the Kings of
Israel.* 22 He died and was buried, and his
son Pekahiah succeeded him as king.

King Pekahiah of Israel

23 In the fiftieth year of the **reign** of
King Uzziah of Judah, Pekahiah son of
Menahem became king of Israel, and he
ruled in Samaria for two years. 24 He
sinned against the LORD, following the
wicked example of King Jeroboam son of
Nebat, who led Israel into sin. 25 An
officer of Pekahiah's forces, Pekah son of
Remaliah, **plotted** with fifty men from
Gilead, assassinated Pekahiah in the
palace's inner fortress[g] in Samaria, and
succeeded him as king.

26 Everything else that Pekahiah did
is recorded in *The History of the Kings of
Israel.*

King Pekah of Israel

27 In the fifty-second year of the **reign**
of King Uzziah of Judah, Pekah son of
Remaliah became king of Israel, and he
ruled in Samaria for twenty years. 28 He
sinned against the LORD, following the
wicked example of King Jeroboam son of
Nebat, who led Israel into sin.

29 It was while Pekah was king that
Tiglath Pileser, the emperor of Assyria,
captured the cities of Ijon, Abel Beth
Maacah, Janoah, Kedesh, and Hazor, and
the territories of Gilead, Galilee, and
Naphtali, and took the people to Assyria
as **prisoners**.

30 In the twentieth year of the **reign** of
Jotham son of Uzziah as king of Judah,
Hoshea son of Elah **plotted** against King
Pekah, assassinated him, and succeeded

[d] *One ancient translation* at Ibleam; *Hebrew* before people.
[e] FOURTH GENERATION: *Zechariah was Jehu's great-great-grandson.*
[f] *One ancient translation* Tappuah; *Hebrew* Tiphsah.
[g] *Hebrew has two additional words, the meaning of which is unclear.*

15.7: Is 6.1 **15.12:** 2 Kgs 10.30

him as king. [31]Everything else that
Pekah did is recorded in *The History of
the Kings of Israel.*

King Jotham of Judah
(2 Chr 27.1–9)

32 In the second year of the **reign** of
Pekah son of Remaliah as king of Israel,
Jotham son of Uzziah became king of
Judah [33]at the age of twenty-five, and he
ruled in Jerusalem for sixteen years. His
mother was Jerusha, the daughter of
Zadok. [34]Following the **example** of his
father Uzziah, Jotham did what was
pleasing to the LORD. [35]But the **pagan
places of worship** were not **destroyed**,
and the people continued to **offer sacrifices** and burn **incense** there. It was
Jotham who built the North Gate of the
Temple.

36 Everything else that Jotham did is
recorded in *The History of the Kings of
Judah.* [37]It was while he was king that
the LORD first sent King Rezin of Syria
and King Pekah of Israel to attack
Judah. [38]Jotham died and was buried in
the royal **tombs** in David's City, and his
son Ahaz succeeded him as king.

King Ahaz of Judah
(2 Chr 28.1–27)

16 In the seventeenth year of the
reign of Pekah son of Remaliah
as king of Israel, Ahaz son of Jotham
became king of Judah [2]at the age of
twenty, and he ruled in Jerusalem for sixteen years. He did not follow the good
example of his ancestor King David;
instead, he did what was not **pleasing** to
the LORD his God [3]and followed the
example of the kings of Israel. He even
sacrificed his own son as a **burnt-offering**
to **idols**, imitating the **disgusting practice**
of the people whom the LORD had driven
out of the land as the Israelites
advanced. [4]At the **pagan places of
worship**, on the hills, and under every
shady tree, Ahaz **offered sacrifices** and
burnt **incense**.

5 King Rezin of Syria and King Pekah
of Israel attacked Jerusalem and
besieged it, but could not defeat Ahaz.
[6](At the same time, the king of Edom[h]
regained **control** of the city of Elath, and
drove out the Judaeans who lived there.
The Edomites settled in Elath, and still
live there.) [7]Ahaz sent men to Tiglath
Pileser, the emperor of Assyria, with this
message: "I am your **devoted servant**.
Come and **rescue** me from the kings of
Syria and of Israel, who are attacking
me." [8]Ahaz took the silver and gold from
the **Temple** and the palace treasury and
sent it as a present to the emperor. [9]Tig-
lath Pileser, in answer to Ahaz' **plea**,
marched out with his army against
Damascus, captured it, killed King Rezin,
and took the people to Kir as **prisoners**.

10 When King Ahaz went to Damascus
to meet Emperor Tiglath Pileser, he saw
the **altar** there and sent back to Uriah
the **priest** an exact model of it, down to
the smallest details. [11]So Uriah built an
altar just like it, and finished it before
Ahaz returned. [12]On his return from
Damascus, Ahaz saw that the **altar** was
finished, [13]so he burnt animal **sacrifices**
and **grain-offerings** on it, and poured a
wine-offering and the **blood** of a **fellowship-offering** on it. [14]The bronze **altar**
dedicated to the LORD was between the
new altar and the **Temple**, so Ahaz
moved it to the north side of his **new
altar**. [15]Then he ordered Uriah: "Use this
large **altar** of mine for the morning
burnt-offerings and the evening **grain-
offerings**, for the **burnt-offerings** and
grain-offerings of the king and the
people, and for the people's **wine-
offerings**. Pour on it the **blood** of all the
animals that are **sacrificed**. But keep the
bronze **altar** for me to use for
divination." [16]Uriah did as the king
commanded.

17 King Ahaz took **apart** the bronze
carts used in the **Temple** and removed
the basins that were on them; he also
took the bronze tank from the backs of
the twelve bronze bulls, and placed it on
a stone foundation. [18]And in order to
please the Assyrian emperor, Ahaz also
removed from the **Temple** the platform
for the royal **throne** and closed up the
king's private entrance to the **Temple**.[i]

19 Everything else that King Ahaz did
is recorded in *The History of the Kings of
Judah.* [20]Ahaz died and was buried in the
royal **tombs** in David's City, and his son
Hezekiah succeeded him as king.

King Hoshea of Israel

17 In the twelfth year of the **reign** of
King Ahaz of Judah, Hoshea son
of Elah became king of Israel, and he
ruled in Samaria for nine years. [2]He
sinned against the LORD, but not as much
as the kings who had ruled Israel before
him. [3]Emperor Shalmaneser of Assyria
made war against him; Hoshea surrendered to Shalmaneser and paid him

[h] *Probable text* the king of Edom; *Hebrew* King Rezin of Syria. [i] *Verse 18 in Hebrew is unclear.*

16.3: Deut 12.31 **16.5:** Is 7.1 **16.14:** Ex 27.1–2; 2 Chr 4.1 **16.17:** 1 Kgs 7.23–39; 2 Chr 4.2–6
16.20: Is 14.28

wine-offering [2] Num 29.6; Ps 116.13

altar [8] 12.9; 17.11
apart 1 Kgs 13.3; 1 Chr 23.13
blood [2] 9.33; 21.16
burnt-offering [3] 10.24; 17.17
command 14.6; 17.12
control 1 Kgs 12.21; 24.7
dedicate 12.18; 23.8
devote 10.16; 17.17
disgust 1 Kgs 11.5; 21.2
divination Deut 18.10; 21.6
example [2] 15.3; 18.3
fellowship-offering 1 Kgs 9.25; 1 Chr 16.1
grain-offering [3] 1 Kgs 8.64; 2 Chr 7.7
idol 11.18; 17.12
incense 15.4; 17.11
message 14.9; 18.14
new [2] 11.14; 22.14
offer 15.4; 17.32
pagan 15.4; 17.9
place of worship 15.4; 17.9
plead 1.13; Esth 4.8
please [2] 15.3; 18.3
practice 1 Kgs 14.24; 17.11
priest 12.2; 17.27
prison 15.29; 17.4
reign 15.1; 17.1
rescue 14.27; 17.7
sacrifice [4] 15.4; 17.17
servant 14.25; 17.13
Temple (1) (of God) [5] 15.35; 18.15
throne 11.19; 19.15
tomb 15.38; 21.26

abandon [2] 7.7; 21.14
altar 16.10; 18.22
anger [3] 13.3; 21.6
approve 1 Kgs 18.24; 1 Chr 13.2
arrest 1 Kgs 22.26; 2 Chr 18.25
bow (2) [2] 4.27; 1 Chr 16.29
bull-calf 10.29; 2 Chr 11.15
burnt-offering [2] 16.3; 21.6

choose 10.3; 21.7
command [6] 16.16; 18.6
consult 8.8; 19.8
covenant [3] 13.23; 18.12
cruel 2 Sam 12.6; 2 Chr 16.10
custom [7] 11.14; 2 Chr 35.25
devote 16.7; 1 Chr 2.7
disobey [2] 1 Kgs 20.36; 18.6
enemy [2] 14.19; 21.14
evil 13.2; 1 Chr 2.3
exile [2] 2 Sam 14.13; 25.21
forget 13.23; 1 Chr 16.15
fortune-teller 1 Sam 28.3; 21.6
god (2) (other gods) [11] 10.18; 18.33
God's people 13.23; 20.5
goddess [2] 13.6; 18.4
help 14.26; 18.20
idol [9] 16.3; 21.11
image [2] 13.6; 18.4
incense 16.4; 18.4
law [7] 14.6; 18.12
learn 11.1; 19.8
medium 1 Sam 28.3; 21.6
obey [9] 11.9; 18.12
offer [3] 16.4; 22.17
pagan [4] 16.4; 18.4
place of worship [2] 16.4; 18.4
possess 1 Kgs 21.15; 1 Chr 16.18
power 15.19; 19.25
practice [2] 16.3; 21.2
priest [3] 16.10; 19.2
prison [3] 16.9; 18.11
prophet [3] 14.25; 19.2
punish 9.7; 19.3
refuse (1) 14.11; 18.7
reign [2] 16.1; 18.1
reject 1 Kgs 14.9; 21.22
rescue [2] 16.7; 18.32
sacrifice [5] 16.3; 21.6
separate 2 Sam 14.6; Ezra 9.1
servant [2] 16.7; 18.12
serve [3] 12.5; 20.3
shrine 18.22
sight [4] 6.20; 22.19
strength 15.19; 23.25
stubborn 1 Sam 6.6; 2 Chr 30.8
teach [2] 4.38; 22.13
terrible 14.26; 1 Chr 21.8
tribute [2] 3.4; 23.33
trust 2 Sam 16.16; 18.5
warn [3] 9.14; 18.29
way (3) 13.2; Ezra 6.21
wicked 15.9; 2 Chr 6.37
worship (1) (of God) [6] 12.9; 18.22
worship (2) (of other gods) [8] 10.19; 19.37
worthless 2 Sam 20.1; 2 Chr 13.7
wrong 6.19; 18.14

tribute every year. 4 But one year Hoshea
sent messengers to So, king of Egypt,[j]
asking for his help, and stopped paying
the annual tribute to Assyria. When Shalmaneser learnt of this, he had Hoshea
arrested and put in prison.

The Fall of Samaria

5 Then Shalmaneser invaded Israel
and besieged Samaria. In the third year
of the siege, 6 which was the ninth year of
the reign of Hoshea, the Assyrian
emperor[k] captured Samaria, took the
Israelites to Assyria as prisoners, and
settled some of them in the city of Halah,
some near the River Habor in the district
of Gozan, and some in the cities of
Media.

7 Samaria fell because the Israelites
sinned against the LORD their God, who
had rescued them from the king of Egypt
and had led them out of Egypt. They worshipped other gods, 8 followed the
customs of the people whom the LORD
had driven out as his people advanced,
and adopted customs introduced by the
kings of Israel.[l] 9 The Israelites did[m]
things that the LORD their God dis-
approved of. They built pagan places of
worship in all their towns, from the
smallest village to the largest city. 10 On
all the hills and under every shady tree
they put up stone pillars and images of
the goddess Asherah, 11 and they burnt
incense on all the pagan altars, following
the practice of the people whom the
LORD had driven out of the land. They
aroused the LORD's anger with all their
wicked deeds 12 and disobeyed the LORD's
command not to worship idols.

13 The LORD had sent his messengers
and prophets to warn Israel and Judah:
"Abandon your evil ways and obey my
commands, which are contained in the
Law I gave to your ancestors and which I
handed on to you through my servants
the prophets." 14 But they would not obey;
they were stubborn like their ancestors,
who had not trusted in the LORD their
God. 15 They refused to obey his instructions, they did not keep the covenant he
had made with their ancestors, and they
disregarded his warnings. They worshipped worthless idols and became
worthless themselves, and they followed
the customs of the surrounding nations
disobeying the LORD's command not to
imitate them. 16 They broke all the laws
of the LORD their God and made two
metal bull-calves to worship; they also
made an image of the goddess Asherah,
worshipped the stars, and served the god
Baal. 17 They sacrificed their sons and
daughters as burnt-offerings to pagan
gods; they consulted mediums and
fortune-tellers, and they devoted themselves completely to doing what is wrong
in the LORD's sight, and so aroused his
anger. 18 The LORD was angry with the
Israelites and banished them from his
sight, leaving only the kingdom of Judah.

19 But even the people of Judah did
not obey the laws of the LORD their God;
they imitated the customs adopted by the
people of Israel. 20 The LORD rejected all
the Israelites, punishing them and
handing them over to cruel enemies until
at last he had banished them from his
sight.

21 After the LORD had separated
Israel from Judah, the Israelites made
Jeroboam son of Nebat their king. Jeroboam made them abandon the LORD and
led them into terrible sins. 22 They
followed Jeroboam and continued to
practise all the sins he had committed,
23 until at last the LORD banished them
from his sight, as he had warned through
his servants the prophets that he would
do. So the people of Israel were taken
into exile to Assyria, where they still live.

The Assyrians Settle in Israel

24 The emperor of Assyria took
people from the cities of Babylon, Cuth,
Ivvah, Hamath, and Sepharvaim, and
settled them in the cities of Samaria,[n] in
place of the exiled Israelites. They took
possession of these cities and lived there.
25 When they first settled there, they did
not worship the LORD, and so he sent
lions, which killed some of them. 26 The
emperor of Assyria was told that the
people he had settled in the cities of
Samaria did not know the law of the god
of that land, and so the god had sent
lions, which were killing them. 27 So the
emperor commanded: "Send back one of
the priests we brought as prisoners;
make him[o] go back and live there, in
order to teach the people the law of the
god of that land." 28 So an Israelite priest
who had been deported from Samaria
went and lived in Bethel, where he
taught the people how to worship the
LORD.

[j] So, king of Egypt; *or* the king of Egypt at Sais.
[k] ASSYRIAN EMPEROR: *Probably Sargon II, the successor of Shalmaneser.*
[l] *Probable text* and adopted...Israel; *Hebrew unclear.* [m] did; *or* said.
[n] SAMARIA: *The name of its capital city was applied to the territory of the former kingdom of Israel.*
[o] *Some ancient translations* him; *Hebrew* them.

17.10: 1 Kgs 14.23 **17.16:** 1 Kgs 12.28 **17.17:** Deut 18.10

29 But the people who settled in
Samaria continued to make their own
idols, and they placed them in the
shrines that the Israelites had built. Each
different group made **idols** in the cities
they were living in: 30 The people of
Babylon made **idols** of the **god** Succoth
Benoth; the people of Cuth, **idols** of
Nergal; the people of Hamath, **idols** of
Ashima; 31 the people of Ivvah, **idols** of
Nibhaz and Tartak; and the people of
Sepharvaim **sacrificed** their children as
burnt-offerings to their **gods** Adrammelech and Anammelech. 32 These
people also **worshipped** the LORD and
chose from among their own number all
sorts of people to **serve** as **priests** at the
pagan places of worship and to **offer**
sacrifices for them there. 33 So they **wor-**
shipped the LORD, but they also **wor-**
shipped their own gods according to the
customs of the countries from which they
had come.
34 They still carry on their old
customs to this day. They do not **worship**
the LORD nor do they **obey** the **laws** and
commands which he gave to the descendants of Jacob, whom he named
Israel. 35 The LORD had made a **covenant**
with them and had ordered them: "Do
not **worship other gods**; do not **bow down**
to them or **serve** them or **offer sacrifices**
to them. 36 You shall **obey** me, the LORD,
who brought you out of Egypt with great
power and **strength**; you are to **bow**
down to me and **offer sacrifices** to me.
37 You shall always **obey** the **laws** and
commands that I wrote for you. You shall
not **obey** other **gods**, 38 and you shall not
forget the **covenant** I made with you.
39 You shall **obey** me, the LORD your God,
and I will **rescue** you from your
enemies." 40 But those people would not
listen, and they continued to follow their
old **customs**.
41 So those people **worshipped** the
LORD, but they also **worshipped their**
idols; and to this day their descendants
continue to do the same.

King Hezekiah of Judah
(2 Chr 29.1–2; 31.1)

18 In the third year of the **reign** of
Hoshea son of Elah as king of
Israel, Hezekiah son of Ahaz became
king of Judah 2 at the age of twenty-five,
and he ruled in Jerusalem for twenty-
nine years. His mother was Abijah, the
daughter of Zechariah. 3 Following the
example of his ancestor King David, he
did what was **pleasing** to the LORD. 4 He
destroyed the **pagan places of worship**,
broke the stone pillars, and cut down the
images of the **goddess** Asherah. He also
broke in pieces the bronze snake that
Moses had made, which was called
Nehushtan. Up to that time the people of
Israel had burnt **incense** in its **honour**.
5 Hezekiah **trusted** in the LORD, the God
of Israel; Judah never had another king
like him, either before or after his time.
6 He was **faithful** to the LORD and never
disobeyed him, but carefully kept all the
commands that the LORD had given
Moses. 7 So the LORD was with him, and
he was **successful** in everything he did.
He **rebelled** against the emperor of
Assyria and **refused** to **submit** to him.
8 He defeated the Philistines, and raided
their settlements, from the smallest
village to the largest city, including Gaza
and its surrounding territory.
9 In the fourth year of Hezekiah's
reign—which was the seventh year of
King Hoshea's **reign** over Israel—
Emperor Shalmaneser of Assyria
invaded Israel and besieged Samaria.
10 In the third year of the siege, Samaria
fell; this was the sixth year of Hezekiah's
reign, and the ninth year of Hoshea's
reign. 11 The Assyrian emperor[p] took the
Israelites to Assyria as **prisoners** and
settled some of them in the city of Halah,
some near the River Habor in the district
of Gozan, and some in the cities of
Media.
12 Samaria fell because the Israelites
did not **obey** the LORD their God, but
broke the **covenant** he had made with
them and **disobeyed** all the **laws** given by
Moses, the **servant** of the LORD. They
would not listen and they would not **obey**.

The Assyrians Threaten Jerusalem
(2 Chr 32.1–19; Is 36.1–22)

13 In the fourteenth year of the **reign**
of King Hezekiah, Sennacherib, the
emperor of Assyria, attacked the fortified cities of Judah and **conquered** them.
14 Hezekiah sent a **message** to Sennacherib, who was in Lachish: "I have done
wrong; please stop your attack, and I will
pay whatever you **demand**." The
emperor's answer was that Hezekiah
should send him ten thousand kilogrammes of silver and a thousand kilogrammes of gold. 15 Hezekiah sent him all
the silver in the **Temple** and in the
palace treasury; 16 he also **stripped** the
gold from the **temple** doors and the gold
with which he himself had covered the

[p] ASSYRIAN EMPEROR: *See 17.6.*

17.34: Gen 32.28, 35.10 **17.35:** Ex 20.5; Deut 5.9 **17.36:** Deut 6.13 **18.4:** Num 21.9

altar [2] 17.11; 21.3
bread 4.42; 23.9
command [4] 17.12; 21.8
confident 1 Kgs 2.2; 1 Chr 22.13
conquer 14.22; 19.23
court (1) 1 Kgs 22.9; 19.2
covenant 17.15; 23.2
deceive 1 Kgs 22.20; 19.10
demand 1 Kgs 20.2; 23.3
destroy [4] 15.4; 19.11
disobey [2] 17.12; 21.22
example 16.2; 22.2
faithful 1 Kgs 15.14; 20.3
fool 2 Sam 24.10; 1 Chr 21.8
god (2) (other gods) [4] 17.7; 19.12
goddess 17.10; 21.3
grief 2.12; 19.1
Hebrew [2] 1 Sam 29.3; 2 Chr 32.18
help [3] 17.4; 23.29
honour 10.20; 19.34
image 17.10; 19.18
incense 17.11; 25.14
law 17.13; 21.8
message 16.7; 19.3
might 13.14; 1 Chr 13.8
obey [2] 17.13; 21.8
pagan 17.9; 21.3
persuade Judg 19.3; 2 Chr 18.2
place of worship 17.9; 21.3
please 16.2; 22.2
prison 17.4; 23.33
rebel [2] 3.5; 24.1
refuse (1) 17.15; 1 Chr 11.19
reign [6] 17.1; 22.3
rely [3] Judg 20.36; 1 Chr 12.1
rescue 17.7; 19.19
save [6] 12.4; 19.6
servant 17.13; 19.34
shrine 17.29; 2 Chr 32.12
strip (1) 2 Sam 23.10; 1 Chr 10.9
submit Ex 10.3; 24.1
succeed (1) 1 Kgs 22.13; 1 Chr 12.18
Temple (1) (of God) [2] 16.8; 19.1
trust 17.14; 19.10
understand 1 Kgs 3.12; 20.19
vine 4.39; 19.29
vineyard 5.26; 25.12
warn 17.13; 1 Chr 16.21
word (1) [2] 10.21; 19.9
worship (1) (of God) 17.25; 21.4
wrong 17.17; 1 Chr 21.17

doorposts, and he sent it all to Sennacherib. [17] The Assyrian emperor sent a
large army from Lachish to attack
Hezekiah at Jerusalem; it was **commanded** by his three highest officials.
When they arrived at Jerusalem, they
occupied the road where the clothmakers work, by the ditch that brings
water from the upper pond. [18] Then they
sent for King Hezekiah, and three of his
officials went out to meet them: Eliakim
son of Hilkiah, who was in charge of the
palace; Shebna, the **court** secretary; and
Joah son of Asaph, who was in charge of
the records. [19] One of the Assyrian
officials told them that the emperor
wanted to know what made King
Hezekiah so **confident**. [20] He demanded,
"Do you think that **words** can take the
place of military skill and **might**? Who
do you think will **help** you **rebel** against
Assyria? [21] You are expecting Egypt to
help you, but that would be like using a
reed as a walking-stick—it would break
and jab your hand. That is what the king
of Egypt is like when anyone **relies** on
him."

22 The Assyrian official went on, "Or
will you tell me that you are **relying** on
the LORD your God? It was the LORD's
shrines and **altars** that Hezekiah **destroyed**, when he told the people of Judah
and Jerusalem to **worship** only at the
altar in Jerusalem. [23] I will make a
bargain with you in the name of the
emperor. I will give you two thousand
horses if you can find that many men to
ride them! [24] You are no match for even
the lowest ranking Assyrian official, and
yet you expect the Egyptians to send you
chariots and horsemen! [25] Do you think I
have attacked your country and **destroyed** it without the LORD's **help**? The
LORD himself told me to attack it and
destroy it."

26 Then Eliakim, Shebna, and Joah
told the official, "Speak Aramaic to us,
sir. We **understand** it. Don't speak
Hebrew; all the people on the wall are
listening."

27 He replied, "Do you think you and
the king are the only ones the emperor
sent me to say all these things to? No, I
am also talking to the people who are
sitting on the wall, who will have to eat
their excrement and drink their urine,
just as you will."

28 Then the official stood up and
shouted in **Hebrew**, "Listen to what the
emperor of Assyria is telling you! [29] He
warns you not to let Hezekiah **deceive**
you. Hezekiah can't **save** you. [30] And don't
let him **persuade** you to **rely** on the LORD.
Don't think that the LORD will **save** you,
and that he will stop our Assyrian army
from capturing your city. [31] Don't listen to
Hezekiah. The emperor of Assyria **commands** you to come out of the city and
surrender. You will all be allowed to eat
grapes from your own **vines**, and figs
from your own trees, and to drink water
from your own wells—[32] until the
emperor resettles you in a country much
like your own, where there are **vineyards**
to give wine and there is corn for making
bread; it is a land of olives, olive-oil, and
honey. If you do what he **commands**, you
will not die, but live. Don't let Hezekiah
fool you into thinking that the LORD will
rescue you. [33] Did the **gods** of any other
nations **save** their countries from the
emperor of Assyria? [34] Where are they
now, the **gods** of Hamath and Arpad?
Where are the **gods** of Sepharvaim,
Hena, and Ivvah? Did anyone **save**
Samaria? [35] When did any of the **gods** of
all these countries ever **save** their
country from our emperor? Then what
makes you think the LORD can **save**
Jerusalem?"

36 The people kept quiet, just as King
Hezekiah had told them to; they did not
say a **word**. [37] Then Eliakim, Shebna, and
Joah tore their clothes in **grief**, and went
and reported to the king what the
Assyrian official had said.

The King Asks Isaiah's Advice
(Is 37.1–7)

19 As soon as King Hezekiah heard
their report, he tore his clothes
in **grief**, put on **sackcloth**, and went to the
Temple of the LORD. [2] He sent Eliakim,
the official in charge of the palace,
Shebna, the **court** secretary, and the
senior **priests** to the **prophet** Isaiah son of
Amoz. They also were wearing **sack-
cloth**. [3] This is the **message** which he told
them to give Isaiah: "Today is a day of
suffering; we are being **punished** and are
in **disgrace**. We are like a woman who is
ready to give **birth**, but is too **weak** to do
it. [4] The Assyrian emperor has sent his
chief official to **insult** the living God. May
the LORD your God hear these **insults** and
punish those who spoke them. So **pray** to
God for those of our people who survive."

5 When Isaiah received King Hezekiah's **message**, [6] he sent back this
answer: "The LORD tells you not to let
the Assyrians **frighten** you with their
claims that he cannot **save** you. [7] The
LORD will cause the emperor to hear a
rumour that will make him go back to his
own country, and the LORD will have him
killed there."

honour 18.4; 20.6
human 1 Kgs 13.2; 23.14
image 18.4; 21.3
insult [4] 1 Sam 25.14; Neh 4.5
learn 17.4; 2 Chr 12.8
letter (2) [3] 10.1; 20.12
message [3] 18.14; 20.19
plan 11.4; 1 Chr 28.11
power [2] 17.36; 1 Chr 16.27
pray [2] 13.4; 20.2
prayer 13.4; 20.5
presence 1 Kgs 10.8; 1 Chr 13.10
priest 17.27; 22.4
promise 15.12; 20.6
prophet 17.13; 20.1
protect 11.7; 1 Chr 16.21
proud 14.10; 2 Chr 17.6
punish [2] 17.20; 21.13
rage [2] 5.11; 2 Chr 18.34
rescue 18.32; 20.6
respect 10.13; 1 Chr 4.9
ridicule 1 Kgs 9.7; 2 Chr 7.20
sackcloth [2] 6.30; 1 Chr 21.16
sake 1 Kgs 15.4; 20.6
save [2] 18.29; 1 Chr 16.23
servant 18.12; 20.6
sign (1) 4.31; 20.8
sow Judg 6.3; Job 4.8
suffer 14.26; 2 Chr 21.15
Temple (1) (of God) [2] 18.15; 20.5
temple (2) (of other gods) 11.18; 1 Chr 10.10
throne 16.18; 1 Chr 13.6
trust 18.5; 1 Chr 5.20
turn 10.27; 20.2
vine 18.31; Job 15.33
weak 2 Sam 3.1; 2 Chr 14.11
weed Deut 29.23; Job 8.16
word (1) 18.20; 25.24
world [2] 1 Kgs 18.10; 1 Chr 1.10
worship (2) (of other gods) 17.7; 21.3

The Assyrians Send Another Threat
(Is 37.8–20)

8 The Assyrian official **learnt** that the
emperor had left Lachish and was fighting against the nearby city of Libnah; so
he went there to **consult** him. 9 **Word**
reached the Assyrians that the Egyptian
army, led by King Tirhakah of Sudan,
was coming to attack them. When the
emperor heard this, he sent a **letter** to
King Hezekiah of Judah 10 to say to him,
"The god you are **trusting** in has told you
that you will not fall into my hands, but
don't let that **deceive** you. 11 You have
heard what an Assyrian emperor does to
any country he decides to **destroy**. Do
you think that you can **escape**? 12 My
ancestors **destroyed** the cities of Gozan,
Haran, and Rezeph, and killed the people
of Betheden who lived in Telassar, and
none of their **gods** could **save** them.
13 Where are the kings of the cities of
Hamath, Arpad, Sepharvaim, Hena, and
Ivvah?"
14 King Hezekiah took the **letter** from
the messengers and read it. Then he
went to the **Temple**, placed the **letter**
there in the **presence** of the LORD, 15 and
prayed, "O LORD, the God of Israel,
enthroned above the winged **creatures**,
you **alone** are God, ruling all the kingdoms of the **world**. You **created** the earth
and the sky. 16 Now, LORD, look at what is
happening to us. Listen to all the things
that Sennacherib is saying to **insult** you,
the living God. 17 We all know, LORD, that
the emperors of Assyria have **destroyed**
many nations, made their lands **desolate**,
18 and burnt up their **gods**—which were
no gods at all, only **images** of wood and
stone made by **human** hands. 19 Now,
LORD our God, **rescue** us from the
Assyrians, so that all the nations of the
world will know that only you, O LORD,
are God."

Isaiah's Message to the King
(Is 37.21–38)

20 Then Isaiah sent a **message** telling
King Hezekiah that in answer to the
king's **prayer** 21 the LORD had said, "The
city of Jerusalem laughs at you, Sennacherib, and **despises** you. 22 Whom do you
think you have been **insulting** and
ridiculing? You have been **disrespectful**
to me, the **holy** God of Israel. 23 You sent
your messengers to **boast** to me that with
all your chariots you had **conquered** the
highest mountains of Lebanon. You
boasted that there you cut down the
tallest cedars and the finest cypress-trees
and that you reached the deepest parts
of the forests. 24 You **boasted** that you dug
wells and drank water in foreign lands
and that the feet of your soldiers
tramped the River Nile dry.
25 "Have you never heard that I
planned all this long ago? And now I
have carried it out. I gave you the **power**
to **turn** fortified cities into piles of rubble.
26 The people who lived there were
powerless; they were **frightened** and
stunned. They were like grass in a field
or **weeds** growing on a roof when the hot
east wind blasts them.[p]
27 "But I know everything about you,
what you do and where you go. I know
how you **rage** against me. 28 I have
received the report of that **rage** and that
pride of yours, and now I will put a hook
through your nose and a bit in your
mouth, and take you back by the same
road you came."
29 Then Isaiah said to King Hezekiah,
"This is a **sign** of what will happen. This
year and next you will have only wild
grain to eat, but the following year you
will be able to **sow** your corn and **harvest**
it, and plant **vines** and eat grapes.
30 Those in Judah who survive will
flourish like plants that send roots deep
into the ground and produce fruit.
31 There will be people in Jerusalem and
on Mount Zion who will survive, because
the LORD is **determined** to make this
happen.
32 "This is what the LORD has said
about the Assyrian emperor: 'He will not
enter this city or shoot a single arrow
against it. No soldiers with shields will
come near the city, and no siege-mounds
will be built round it. 33 He will go back by
the same road he came, without entering
this city. I, the LORD, have spoken. 34 I
will **defend** this city and **protect** it, for the
sake of my own **honour** and because of
the **promise** I made to my **servant**
David.' "
35 That night an **angel of the LORD**
went to the Assyrian camp and killed
185,000 soldiers. At dawn the next day,
there they lay, all **dead**! 36 Then the
Assyrian emperor Sennacherib withdrew
and returned to Nineveh. 37 One day,
when he was **worshipping** in the **temple**
of his **god Nisroch**, two of his sons,
Adrammelech and Sharezer, killed him
with their swords, and then **escaped** to
the land of Ararat. Another of his sons,
Esarhaddon, succeeded him as emperor.

[p] *Probable text* when the hot east wind blasts them; *Hebrew* blasted before they are grown.

19.15: Ex 25.22

Almighty 1 Kgs 19.10; 1 Chr 11.9
bitter 1 Kgs 11.21; 2 Chr 25.10
defend 19.34; 2 Chr 32.5
faithful 18.6; 1 Chr 29.18
God's people 17.8; 21.2
heal [2] 1 Kgs 13.6; Job 5.18
honour 19.34; 23.21
letter (2) 19.9; 2 Chr 2.11
loyal 4.30; 1 Chr 12.23
message 19.3; 22.16
peace 13.5; 22.20
pray [2] 19.4; 1 Chr 4.10
prayer 19.20; 22.19
promise [2] 19.34; 23.3
prophet [2] 19.2; 21.10
prove [2] 10.10; Ezra 2.59
remember 9.25; 1 Chr 16.12
rescue 19.19; 1 Chr 16.35
sake 19.34; 1 Chr 14.2
secure 1 Kgs 15.4; 1 Chr 22.9
servant 19.34; 21.8
serve [2] 17.16; 23.9
sign (1) [2] 19.29; 2 Chr 32.24
tear (2) 8.11; Job 16.20
Temple (1) (of God) [2] 19.1; 21.4
turn 19.25; 21.13
understand 18.26; 2 Chr 2.12
welcome 2 Sam 14.33; 1 Chr 12.17

King Hezekiah's Illness and Recovery
(Is 38.1–8, 21–22; 2 Chr 32.24–26)

20 About this time King Hezekiah
fell ill and almost died. The
prophet Isaiah son of Amoz went to see
him and said to him, "The LORD tells you
that you are to put everything in order,
because you will not recover. Get ready
to die."
2 Hezekiah **turned** his face to the wall
and **prayed**: 3 "**Remember**, LORD, that I
have **served** you **faithfully** and **loyally**,
and that I have always tried to do what
you wanted me to." And he began to cry
bitterly.
4 Isaiah left the king, but before he
had passed through the central courtyard of the palace the LORD told him 5 to
go back to Hezekiah, ruler of the LORD's
people, and say to him, "I, the LORD, the
God of your ancestor David, have heard
your **prayer** and seen your **tears**. I will
heal you, and in three days you will go to
the **Temple**. 6 I will let you live fifteen
years longer. I will **rescue** you and this
city of Jerusalem from the emperor of
Assyria. I will **defend** this city, for the
sake of my own **honour** and because of
the **promise** I made to my **servant**
David."
7 Then Isaiah told the king's attendants to put on his boil a paste made of
figs, and he would get well.[q] 8 King
Hezekiah asked, "What is the **sign** to
prove that the LORD will **heal** me and
that three days later I will be able to go
to the **Temple**?"
9 Isaiah replied, "The LORD will give
you a **sign** to **prove** that he will keep his
promise. Now, would you prefer the
shadow on the stairway to go forward ten
steps or go back ten steps?"[r]
10 Hezekiah answered, "It's easy to
make the shadow go forward ten steps![s]
Make it go back ten steps."[s]
11 Isaiah **prayed** to the LORD, and the
LORD made the shadow go back ten
steps[s] on the stairway[t] set up by King
Ahaz.

Messengers from Babylonia
(Is 39.1–8)

12 About that same time the king of
Babylonia, Merodach Baladan, the son of
Baladan, heard that King Hezekiah had
been ill, so he sent him a **letter** and a
present. 13 Hezekiah **welcomed** the
messengers and showed them his
wealth—his silver and gold, his spices
and perfumes, and all his military equipment. There was nothing in his
storerooms or anywhere in his kingdom
that he did not show them. 14 Then the
prophet Isaiah went to King Hezekiah
and asked, "Where did these men come
from and what did they say to you?"
Hezekiah answered, "They came from
a very distant country, from Babylonia."
15 "What did they see in the palace?"
"They saw everything. There is
nothing in the storerooms that I didn't
show them."
16 Isaiah then said to the king, "The
LORD **Almighty** says that 17 a time is
coming when everything in your palace,
everything that your ancestors have
stored up to this day, will be carried off
to Babylonia. Nothing will be left. 18 Some
of your own direct descendants will be
taken away and made eunuchs to **serve**
in the palace of the king of Babylonia."
19 King Hezekiah **understood** this to
mean that there would be **peace** and
security during his lifetime, so he replied,
"The **message** you have given me from
the LORD is good."

The End of Hezekiah's Reign
(2 Chr 32.32–33)

20 Everything else that King Hezekiah
did, his brave deeds, and an account of
how he built a reservoir and dug a tunnel
to bring water into the city, are all
recorded in *The History of the Kings of
Judah*. 21 Hezekiah died, and his son
Manasseh succeeded him as king.

King Manasseh of Judah
(2 Chr 33.1–20)

21 Manasseh was twelve years old
when he became king of Judah,
and he ruled in Jerusalem for **fifty-five**
years. His mother was Hephzibah.
2 Following the **disgusting practices** of
the nations whom the LORD had driven
out of the land as **his people** advanced,
Manasseh sinned against the LORD. 3 He
rebuilt the **pagan places of worship** that
his father Hezekiah had **destroyed**; he
built **altars** for the **worship of Baal** and
made an **image** of the **goddess** Asherah,
as King Ahab of Israel had done.
Manasseh also **worshipped the stars**. 4 He
built **pagan altars** in the **Temple**, the
place that the LORD had said was where
he should be **worshipped**. 5 In the two
courtyards of the **Temple** he built **altars**

abandon 17.13; 1 Chr 10.7
action 1 Sam 24.12; 2 Chr 23.1
altar [3] 18.22; 23.5
anger [2] 17.11; 22.13
blood 16.13; 25.14
burnt-offering 17.17; 23.10
choose 17.32; 23.27
clean [2] 1 Kgs 22.38; 25.14
command [2] 18.6; 23.3
conquer 19.23; 1 Chr 1.10
consult 19.8; 22.13
destroy 19.11; 23.7
disaster 14.10; 1 Chr 2.7
disgust [2] 16.3; 23.13
disobey 18.6; 1 Chr 10.13
divination 16.15; 2 Chr 33.6
enemy 17.20; 1 Chr 5.21

[q] *One ancient translation (and see Is 38.21)* figs, and he would get well; *Hebrew* figs. They did so, and he got well. [r] stairway...steps...steps; *or* sundial...divisions...divisions. [s] steps; *or* divisions.
[t] stairway; *or* sundial. *Archaeological evidence suggests that the stairway referred to in this passage was one specially constructed to tell the time.*

20.17: 2 Kgs 24.13; 2 Chr 36.10 **20.18:** 2 Kgs 24.14–15; Dan 1.1–7 **21.2:** Jer 15.4 **21.4:** 2 Sam 7.13

ortune-teller 17.17;
3.24
God's people [3] 20.5;
Chr 11.2
goddess [2] 18.4; 23.4
dol [3] 17.12; 23.13
mage 19.18; 23.15
nnocent 1 Kgs 8.31;
24.4
aw 18.12; 22.2
magic 1 Sam 6.2;
2 Chr 33.6
medium 17.17; 23.24
obey [2] 18.12; 22.2
pagan [2] 18.4; 23.5
place of worship
18.4; 23.10
plot (1) 15.25;
2 Chr 24.25
practice [2] 17.11;
23.3
prophet 20.1; 22.14
punish 19.3; 22.16
reject 17.20; 22.17
sacrifice 17.17; 22.17
servant [2] 20.6; 22.9
symbol 1 Kgs 14.23;
23.6
Temple (1) (of God)
[4] 20.5; 22.3
tomb 16.20; 23.16
turn 20.2; 1 Chr 6.32
worse 1 Kgs 17.17;
2 Chr 21.15
worship (1) (of God)
[2] 18.22; 23.27
worship (2) (of other gods) [4] 19.37;
23.4

for the **worship of the stars.** 6 He sacrificed his son as a **burnt-offering.** He
practised divination and **magic** and **con-**
sulted[u] **fortune-tellers** and **mediums.** He
sinned greatly against the LORD and
stirred up his **anger.** 7 He placed the
symbol of the **goddess** Asherah in the
Temple, the place about which the LORD
had said to David and his son Solomon:
"Here in Jerusalem, in this **Temple**, is
the place that I have **chosen** out of all the
territory of the twelve tribes of Israel as
the place where I am to be **worshipped.**
8 And if the people of Israel will **obey** all
my **commands** and keep the whole **Law**
that my **servant** Moses gave them, then I
will not allow them to be driven out of
the land that I gave to their ancestors."
9 But the people of Judah did not **obey** the
LORD, and Manasseh led them to commit
even greater sins than those committed
by the nations whom the LORD had
driven out of the land as **his people**
advanced.

10 Through his **servants** the **prophets**
the LORD said, 11 "King Manasseh has
done these **disgusting** things, things far
worse than what the Canaanites did; and
with his **idols** he has led the people of
Judah into sin. 12 So I, the LORD God of
Israel, will bring such a **disaster** on
Jerusalem and Judah that everyone who
hears about it will be stunned. 13 I will
punish Jerusalem as I did Samaria, as I
did King Ahab of Israel and his descendants. I will wipe Jerusalem **clean** of
its people, as **clean** as a plate that has
been wiped and **turned** upside down. 14 I
will **abandon** the people who survive, and
will hand them over to their **enemies,**
who will **conquer** them and plunder their
land. 15 I will do this to **my people**
because they have sinned against me
and have stirred up my **anger** from the
time their ancestors came out of Egypt
to this day."

16 Manasseh killed so many **innocent**
people that the streets of Jerusalem were
flowing with **blood**; he did this in addition
to leading the people of Judah into
idolatry, causing them to sin against the
LORD.

17 Everything else that Manasseh did,
including the sins he committed, is
recorded in *The History of the Kings of*
Judah. 18 Manasseh died and was buried
in the palace garden, the garden of Uzza,
and his son Amon succeeded him as king.

King Amon of Judah
(2 Chr 33.21–25)

19 Amon was twenty-two years old
when he became king of Judah, and he
ruled in Jerusalem for two years. His
mother was Meshullemeth, the daughter
of Haruz, from the town of Jotbah. 20 Like
his father Manasseh, he sinned against
the LORD; 21 he imitated his father's
actions, and he **worshipped the idols** that
his father had worshipped. 22 He **rejected**
the LORD, the God of his ancestors, and
disobeyed the LORD's **commands.**

23 Amon's officials **plotted** against him
and assassinated him in the palace.
24 The people of Judah killed Amon's
assassins and made his son Josiah king.

25 Everything else that Amon did is
recorded in *The History of the Kings of*
Judah. 26 Amon was buried in the **tomb** in
the garden of Uzza, and his son Josiah
succeeded him as king.

King Josiah of Judah
(2 Chr 34.1–2)

22 Josiah was eight years old when
he became king of Judah, and he
ruled in Jerusalem for thirty-one years.
His mother was Jedidah, the daughter of
Adaiah, from the town of Bozkath.
2 Josiah did what was **pleasing** to the
LORD; he followed the **example** of his
ancestor King David, strictly **obeying** all
the **laws** of God.

The Book of the Law Is Discovered
(2 Chr 34.8–28)

3 In the eighteenth year of his **reign,**
King Josiah sent the **court** secretary
Shaphan, the son of Azaliah and grandson of Meshullam, to the **Temple** with the
order: 4 "Go to the **High Priest** Hilkiah
and get a report on the amount of money
that the **priests** on **duty** at the entrance to
the **Temple** have collected from the
people. 5 Tell him to give the money to
the men who are in charge of the repairs
in the **Temple.** They are to pay 6 the carpenters, the builders, and the masons,
and buy the timber and the stones used
in the repairs. 7 The men in charge of the
work are thoroughly **honest,** so there is
no **need** to **require** them to account for
the funds."

8 Shaphan delivered the king's order
to Hilkiah, and Hilkiah told him that he
had found the book of the **Law** in the
Temple. Hilkiah gave him the book, and
Shaphan read it. 9 Then he went back to
the king and reported: "Your **servants**
have taken the money that was in the

anger [3] 21.6; 23.19
consult [2] 21.6;
1 Chr 10.13
court (1) [2] 19.2;
1 Chr 18.16
curse 2.24;
2 Chr 34.24
death (1) 15.18;
1 Chr 2.19
duty (1) 15.5; 23.4
example 18.3; 23.32
god (2) (other gods)
19.12; 23.10
High Priest 12.10;
23.4
honest 12.15;
1 Chr 29.17
humble 1 Kgs 21.29;
2 Chr 6.24
law [2] 21.8; 23.3
message [2] 20.19;
1 Chr 25.1
need 12.5; 23.35
new 16.14;
1 Chr 12.22
obey 21.8; 23.3
offer 17.32; 23.5
peace 20.19;
1 Chr 4.40
please 18.3;
1 Chr 13.4
prayer 20.5;
1 Chr 5.20
priest [2] 19.2; 23.2
prophet 21.10; 23.2
punish [3] 21.13;
1 Chr 9.1
reign 18.1; 23.23
reject 21.22; 23.27
repent 1 Kgs 8.35;
2 Chr 6.26
require 12.15;
2 Chr 8.13
sacrifice 21.6; 23.5
servant 21.8; 24.2
sight 17.17; 23.27
teach 17.27;
2 Chr 6.27
Temple (1) (of God)
[6] 21.4; 23.2
terrify 10.4;
1 Chr 10.4

[u] consulted; *or* brought back.

21.7–8: 1 Kgs 9.3–5; 2 Chr 7.12–18 **22.1:** Jer 3.6 **22.7:** 2 Kgs 12.15

threat 2 Sam 14.10;
2 Chr 34.27
weep 13.14;
2 Chr 34.27

Temple and have handed it over to the
men in charge of the repairs." 10 And
then he said, "I have here a book that
Hilkiah gave me." And he read it aloud to
the king.
11 When the king heard the book
being read, he tore his clothes in dismay,
12 and gave the following order to Hilkiah
the **priest**, to Ahikam son of Shaphan, to
Achbor son of Micaiah, to Shaphan, the
court secretary, and to Asaiah, the king's
attendant: 13 "Go and **consult** the LORD
for me and for all the people of Judah
about the **teachings** of this book. The
LORD is **angry** with us because our ancestors have not done what this book says
must be done."
14 Hilkiah, Ahikam, Achbor, Shaphan,
and Asaiah went to **consult** a woman
named Huldah, a **prophet** who lived in
the **newer** part of Jerusalem. (Her husband Shallum, the son of Tikvah and
grandson of Harhas, was in charge of the
temple robes.) They described to her
what had happened, 15 and she told them
to go back to the king and give him 16 the
following **message** from the LORD: "I am
going to **punish** Jerusalem and all its
people, as written in the book that the
king has read. 17 They have **rejected** me
and have **offered sacrifices** to other **gods**,
and so have stirred up my **anger** by all
they have done. My **anger** is aroused
against Jerusalem, and it will not die
down. 18 As for the king himself, this is
what I, the LORD God of Israel, say: You
listened to what is written in the book,
19 and you **repented** and **humbled** yourself
before me, tearing your clothes and
weeping, when you heard how I
threatened to **punish** Jerusalem and its
people. I will make it a **terrifying sight**, a
place whose name people will use as a
curse. But I have heard your **prayer**,
20 and the **punishment** which I am going
to bring on Jerusalem will not come until
after your **death**. I will let you die in
peace."
The men returned to King Josiah with
this **message**.

Josiah Does Away with Pagan Worship
(2 Chr 34.3–7, 29–33)

altar [15] 21.3; 25.14
anger [2] 22.13; 24.20
anoint 11.12;
1 Chr 11.3
ash [2] 1 Kgs 13.3;
25.14
body 14.20;
1 Chr 10.8
bread 18.32;
1 Chr 9.32

23 King Josiah summoned all the
leaders of Judah and Jerusalem,
2 and together they went to the **Temple**,
accompanied by the **priests** and the
prophets and all the rest of the people,
rich and **poor** alike. Before them all, the
king read aloud the whole book of the
covenant which had been found in the
Temple. 3 He stood by the royal column
and made a **covenant** with the LORD to
obey him, to keep his **laws** and **commands with all his heart** and **soul**, and to
put into **practice** the **demands** attached
to the **covenant**, as written in the book.
And all the people **promised** to keep the
covenant.
4 Then Josiah ordered the **High Priest**
Hilkiah, his assistant **priests**, and the
guards on **duty** at the entrance to the
Temple to bring out of the **Temple** all the
objects used in the **worship of Baal**, of the
goddess Asherah, and of the stars. The
king burnt all these objects outside the
city near the valley of the Kidron, and
then had the **ashes** taken to Bethel. 5 He
removed from office the **priests** that the
kings of Judah had **ordained** to **offer**
sacrifices[v] on the **pagan altars** in the
cities of Judah and in places near Jerusalem—all the **priests** who **offered sacrifices** to Baal, to the sun, the moon, the
planets, and the stars. 6 He removed from
the **Temple** the **symbol** of the **goddess**
Asherah, took it out of the city to the
valley of the Kidron, burnt it, pounded its
ashes to dust, and **scattered** it over the
public burial-ground. 7 He **destroyed** the
living-quarters in the **Temple** occupied
by the temple **prostitutes**.[w] (It was there
that women wove robes used in the
worship of Asherah.) 8 He brought to
Jerusalem the **priests** who were in the
cities of Judah, and throughout the whole
country he desecrated the **altars** where
they had **offered sacrifices**. He also tore
down the **altars dedicated** to the **goat-
demons** near the gate built by Joshua,
the city governor, which was to the left
of the main gate as one enters the city.
9 Those **priests** were not allowed to **serve**
in the **Temple**, but they could eat the **unleavened bread provided** for their **fellow-
priests**.
10 King Josiah also desecrated
Topheth, the **pagan place of worship** in
the Valley of Hinnom, so that no one
could **sacrifice** his son or daughter as a
burnt-offering to the **god Molech**. 11 He
also removed the horses that the kings of
Judah had **dedicated** to the **worship of**
the sun, and he burnt the chariots used in
this **worship**. (These were kept in the
temple courtyard, near the gate and not
far from the living-quarters of Nathan
Melech, a high official.) 12 The **altars**
which the kings of Judah had built on the
palace roof above King Ahaz' quarters,

burnt-offering 21
1 Chr 21.26
celebrate [3]
1 Kgs 12.33;
1 Chr 15.25
change 5.5; 24.17
choose [2] 21.7;
1 Chr 9.22
command 21.8; 24
covenant [5] 18.12
1 Chr 16.15
dedicate [2] 16.14;
1 Chr 18.11
demand [2] 18.14;
2 Chr 34.31
demon Lev 17.7;
2 Chr 11.15
destroy 21.3; 24.2
disgust 21.2;
1 Chr 15.29
duty (1) 22.4; 24.16
example [2] 22.2; 2
festival 4.23;
1 Chr 23.31
fortune-teller 21.6
2 Chr 33.6
god (2) (other god
[4] 22.17; 1 Chr 5.25
goddess [4] 21.3;
2 Chr 14.3
heart [2] 10.31;
1 Chr 22.19
help 18.20; 1 Chr 5
High Priest [2] 22.
25.18
honour 20.6; 25.28
human [2] 19.18;
2 Chr 6.30
idol [2] 21.11;
1 Chr 10.9
image 21.3;
2 Chr 24.18
judge 1 Kgs 8.32;
1 Chr 16.12
law [3] 22.2;
1 Chr 16.40
medium 21.6;
2 Chr 33.6
mind (1) 1 Kgs 18.
1 Chr 17.2
need 22.7; 25.24
obey [2] 22.2;
1 Chr 21.4
offer [3] 22.17;
1 Chr 6.49
ordain 1 Kgs 13.33
pagan [5] 21.3;
2 Chr 11.15
Passover [3]
Josh 5.10; 2 Chr 30.
place of worship [
21.3; 1 Chr 6.31
poor 2 Sam 24.17;
24.14
practice 21.2;
2 Chr 28.3
predict [3] 7.17;
Ps 105.19
priest [8] 22.4; 25.18
prison 18.11; 24.12
promise 20.6;
1 Chr 11.2
prophet [5] 22.14;
24.2
prostitute
1 Kgs 22.38;
Prov 6.26
provide 6.23;
1 Chr 5.2
raise 4.28; 2 Chr 6.
reign [2] 22.3; 24.10
reject 22.17;
2 Chr 6.42
rich 15.20; 25.26
sacrifice [4] 22.17;
25.14
scatter 9.37;
1 Chr 12.15
serve [3] 20.3; 25.24
sight 22.19; 24.3

[v] *Some ancient translations* to offer sacrifices; *Hebrew* and he offered sacrifices.
[w] TEMPLE PROSTITUTES: *Men and women who practised prostitution in the worship of fertility gods.*

23.4-6: 2 Kgs 21.3; 2 Chr 33.3 **23.10:** Lev 18.21; Jer 7.31, 19.1-6, 32.35 **23.12:** 2 Kgs 21.5; 2 Chr 33.5

ꞏoul 1 Kgs 2.4;
Chr 22.19
ꞏtrength 17.36;
Chr 29.12
ꞏymbol [2] 21.7;
Chr 6.41
ax 1 Kgs 10.15;
Chr 18.2
Temple (1) (of God)
11] 22.3; 24.13
omb [5] 21.26;
Chr 12.16
ribute [2] 17.3;
Chr 26.8
ınleavened
Sam 28.24;
Chr 23.29
worship (1) (of God)
21.4; 1 Chr 6.49
worship (2) (of
other gods) [6] 21.3;
Chr 5.25

King Josiah tore down, along with the
altars put up by King Manasseh in the
two courtyards of the **Temple**; he
smashed the **altars** to bits[x] and threw
them into the valley of the Kidron.
13 Josiah desecrated the **altars** that King
Solomon had built east of Jerusalem,
south of the Mount of Olives,[y] for the
worship of disgusting idols—Astarte the
goddess of Sidon, Chemosh the **god of**
Moab, and Molech the **god of Ammon**.
14 King Josiah broke the stone pillars to
pieces, cut down the **symbols** of the **god-**
dess Asherah, and the ground where they
had stood he covered with **human** bones.
15 Josiah also tore down the **place of**
worship in Bethel which had been built
by King Jeroboam son of Nebat, who led
Israel into sin. Josiah pulled down the
altar, broke its stones into pieces,[z] and
pounded them to dust; he also burnt the
image of Asherah. 16 Then Josiah looked
round and saw some **tombs** there on the
hill; he had the bones taken out of them
and burnt on the **altar**. In this way he
desecrated the **altar**, doing what the
prophet had predicted long before during
the **festival** as King Jeroboam was
standing by the **altar**. King Josiah looked
round and saw the **tomb** of the **prophet**[a]
who had made this **prediction**. 17 "Whose
tomb is that?" he asked.
The people of Bethel answered, "It is
the **tomb** of the **prophet** who came from
Judah and **predicted** these things that
you have done to this **altar**."
18 "Leave it as it is," Josiah ordered.
"His bones are not to be moved."
So his bones were not moved, neither
were those of the **prophet** who had come
from Samaria.
19 In every city of Israel King Josiah
tore down all the **pagan places of**
worship which had been built by the
kings of Israel, who thereby aroused the
LORD's anger. He did to all those **altars**
what he had done in Bethel. 20 He killed
all the **pagan priests** on the **altars** where
they **served**, and he burnt **human** bones
on every **altar**. Then he returned to
Jerusalem.

Josiah Celebrates the Passover
(2 Chr 35.1–19)

21 King Josiah ordered the people to
celebrate the **Passover** in **honour** of the
LORD their God, as written in the book of
the **covenant**. 22 No **Passover** like this one
had ever been **celebrated** by any of the
kings of Israel or of Judah, since the time
when **judges** ruled the nation. 23 Now at
last, in the eighteenth year of the **reign** of
Josiah, the **Passover** was **celebrated** in
Jerusalem.

Other Changes Made by Josiah

24 In order to enforce the **laws** written
in the book that the **High Priest** Hilkiah
had found in the **Temple**, King Josiah
removed from Jerusalem and the rest of
Judah all the **mediums** and **fortune-**
tellers, and all the household **gods**, **idols**,
and all other **pagan** objects of **worship**.
25 There had never been a king like him
before, who **served** the LORD **with all his**
heart, mind, and **strength, obeying** all the
Law of Moses; nor has there been a king
like him since.
26 But the **LORD's fierce anger** had
been aroused against Judah by what
King Manasseh had done, and even now
it did not die down. 27 The LORD said, "I
will do to Judah what I have done to
Israel: I will banish the people of Judah
from my **sight**, and I will **reject** Jerusalem, the city I **chose**, and the **Temple**, the
place I said was where I should be **wor-**
shipped."

The End of Josiah's Reign
(2 Chr 35.20—36.1)

28 Everything else that King Josiah
did is recorded in *The History of the*
Kings of Judah. 29 While Josiah was king,
King Neco of Egypt led an army to the
River Euphrates to **help** the emperor of
Assyria. King Josiah tried to stop the
Egyptian army at Megiddo and was
killed in battle. 30 His officials placed his
body in a chariot and took it back to
Jerusalem, where he was buried in the
royal **tombs**.
The people of Judah **chose** Josiah's son
Joahaz and **anointed** him king.

King Joahaz of Judah
(2 Chr 36.2–4)

31 Joahaz was twenty-three years old
when he became king of Judah, and he
ruled in Jerusalem for three months. His
mother was Hamutal, the daughter of
Jeremiah from the city of Libnah.
32 Following the **example** of his ancestors,
he sinned against the LORD. 33 His **reign**
ended when King Neco of Egypt took
him **prisoner** in Riblah, in the land of

[x] *Probable text* smashed...to bits; *Hebrew unclear.*
[y] MOUNT OF OLIVES: *Hebrew here refers to it as "Mount of Destruction" or "Mount of Sin."*
[z] *One ancient translation* broke its stones into pieces; *Hebrew* burnt the altar.
[a] *One ancient translation* during the festival...the prophet; *Hebrew does not have these words.*

23.13: 1 Kgs 11.7 **23.15:** 1 Kgs 12.33 **23.16:** 1 Kgs 13.2 **23.17:** 1 Kgs 13.30–32

Hamath, and made Judah pay 3,400 kilogrammes of silver and thirty-four kilogrammes of gold as **tribute**. [34]King Neco
made Josiah's son Eliakim king of Judah
as successor to Josiah, and **changed** his
name to Jehoiakim. Joahaz was taken to
Egypt by King Neco, and there he died.

King Jehoiakim of Judah
(2 Chr 36.5–8)

35 King Jehoiakim collected a **tax**
from the people in proportion to their
wealth, in order to **raise** the amount
needed to pay the **tribute demanded** by
the king of Egypt.
36 Jehoiakim was twenty-five years
old when he became king of Judah, and
he ruled in Jerusalem for eleven years.
His mother was Zebidah, the daughter of
Pedaiah from the town of Rumah.
[37]Following the **example** of his ancestors,
Jehoiakim sinned against the LORD.

24 While Jehoiakim was king, King
Nebuchadnezzar of Babylonia invaded Judah, and for three years Jehoiakim was **forced** to **submit** to his rule;
then he **rebelled**. [2]The LORD sent armed
bands of Babylonians, Syrians, Moabites,
and Ammonites against Jehoiakim to
destroy Judah, as the LORD had said
through his **servants** the **prophets** that he
would do. [3]This happened at the LORD's
command, in order to banish the people
of Judah from his **sight** because of all the
sins that King Manasseh had committed,
[4]and especially because of all the **innocent** people he had killed. The LORD
could not **forgive** Manasseh for that.
5 Everything else that Jehoiakim did
is recorded in *The History of the Kings of
Judah*. [6]Jehoiakim died, and his son
Jehoiachin succeeded him as king.
7 The king of Egypt and his army
never marched out of Egypt again,
because the king of Babylonia now **controlled** all the territory that had belonged
to Egypt, from the River Euphrates to
the northern border of Egypt.

anger 23.19; 1 Chr 13.10
change 23.34; 25.29
command [2] 23.3; 25.19
control 16.6; 1 Chr 7.29
destroy 23.7; 1 Chr 4.41
duty (1) 23.4; 1 Chr 6.32
example 23.32; 2 Chr 17.3
fit (1) 2 Sam 13.27; Hos 5.3
force (1) 15.20; 1 Chr 8.6
forgive 5.18; 1 Chr 6.49
important 1 Sam 20.2; 25.9
innocent 21.16; 2 Chr 6.22
leading [2] 10.1; 1 Chr 5.12
poor 23.2; 25.12
prison [3] 23.33; 25.18
prophet 23.2; 1 Chr 9.22
rebel 18.7; 25.1
reign [2] 23.23; 25.1
servant 22.9; 1 Chr 2.34
sight [2] 23.27; 2 Chr 20.32
submit 18.7; 2 Chr 12.12
Temple (1) (of God) [2] 23.2; 25.9

King Jehoiachin of Judah
(2 Chr 36.9–10)

8 Jehoiachin was eighteen years old
when he became king of Judah, and he
ruled in Jerusalem for three months. His
mother was Nehushta, the daughter of
Elnathan from Jerusalem. [9]Following
the **example** of his father, Jehoiachin
sinned against the LORD.
10 It was during his **reign** that the
Babylonian army, **commanded** by King
Nebuchadnezzar's officers, marched
against Jerusalem and besieged it.
[11]During the siege Nebuchadnezzar himself came to Jerusalem, [12]and King
Jehoiachin, along with his mother, his
sons, his officers, and the palace officials,
surrendered to the Babylonians. In the
eighth year of Nebuchadnezzar's **reign**
he took Jehoiachin **prisoner** [13]and
carried off to Babylon all the treasures in
the **Temple** and the palace. As the LORD
had foretold, Nebuchadnezzar broke up
all the gold utensils which King Solomon
had made for use in the **Temple**. [14]Nebu-
chadnezzar carried away as **prisoners**
the people of Jerusalem, all the royal
princes, and all the **leading** men, ten
thousand in all. He also deported all the
skilled workmen, including the blacksmiths, leaving only the **poorest** of the
people behind in Judah.
15 Nebuchadnezzar took Jehoiachin to
Babylon as a **prisoner**, together with
Jehoiachin's mother, his wives, his
officials, and the **leading** men of Judah.
[16]Nebuchadnezzar deported all the
important men to Babylonia, seven thousand in all, and one thousand skilled
workers, including the blacksmiths, all of
them able-bodied men **fit** for military
duty.
17 Nebuchadnezzar made Jehoiachin's
uncle Mattaniah king of Judah and
changed his name to Zedekiah.

King Zedekiah of Judah
(2 Chr 36.11–12; Jer 52.1–3a)

18 Zedekiah was twenty-one years old
when he became king of Judah, and he
ruled in Jerusalem for eleven years. His
mother was Hamutal, the daughter of
Jeremiah from the city of Libnah. [19]King
Zedekiah sinned against the LORD, just as
King Jehoiakim had done. [20]The LORD
became so **angry** with the people of
Jerusalem and Judah that he banished
them from his **sight**.

The Fall of Jerusalem
(2 Chr 36.13–21; Jer 52.3b–11)

25 Zedekiah **rebelled** against King
Nebuchadnezzar of Babylonia, so
Nebuchadnezzar came with all his army
and attacked Jerusalem on the tenth day
of the tenth month of the ninth year of
Zedekiah's **reign**. They set up camp outside the city, built siege walls round it,
[2]and kept it under siege until Zedekiah's
eleventh year. [3]On the ninth day of the
fourth month[b] of that same year, when

afraid [2] 6.16; 1 Chr 12.19
altar 23.5; 1 Chr 6.4
ash 23.4; Esth 4.1
bad 3.2; 1 Chr 10.3
blood 21.16; 1 Chr 11.1
change 24.17; 1 Chr 21.15
clean 21.13; 2 Chr 13.11
command 24.3; 1 Chr 10.13
death (3) (to death) [2] 14.6; 2 Chr 10.18

[b] *Probable text (see Jer 52.6)* the fourth month; *Hebrew* the month.

23.34: Jer 22.11–12 **23.36:** Jer 22.18–19, 26.1–6, 35.1–19 **24.1:** Jer 25.1–38; Dan 1.1–2
24.12: Jer 22.24–30, 24.1–10, 29.1–2 **24.15:** Ezek 17.12 **24.17:** Jer 37.1; Ezek 17.13
24.18: Jer 27.1–22, 28.1–17 **24.20:** Ezek 17.15 **25.1:** Jer 21.1–10, 34.1–5; Ezek 24.2

the **famine** was so **bad** that the people had nothing left to eat, 4 the city walls were broken through. Although the Babylonians were surrounding the city, all the soldiers **escaped** during the night. They left by way of the royal garden, went through the gateway connecting the two walls, and **fled** in the direction of the Jordan Valley. 5 But the Babylonian army pursued King Zedekiah, captured him in the plains near Jericho, and all his soldiers deserted him. 6 Zedekiah was taken to King Nebuchadnezzar, who was in the city of Riblah, and there Nebuchadnezzar passed **sentence** on him. 7 While Zedekiah was looking on, his sons were put **to death**; then Nebuchadnezzar had Zedekiah's eyes put out, placed him in chains, and took him to Babylon.

The Destruction of the Temple
(Jer 52.12–23)

8 On the seventh day of the fifth month of the nineteenth year of King Nebuchadnezzar of Babylonia, Nebuzaradan, adviser to the king and commander of his army, entered Jerusalem. 9 He burnt down the **Temple**, the palace, and the houses of all the **important** people in Jerusalem, 10 and his soldiers tore down the city walls. 11 Then Nebuzaradan took away to Babylonia the people who were left in the city, the remaining skilled workmen,[c] and those who had deserted to the Babylonians. 12 But he left in Judah some of the **poorest** people, who owned no property, and put them to work in the **vineyards** and fields.

13 The Babylonians broke in pieces the bronze columns and the carts that were in the **Temple**, together with the large bronze tank, and they took all the bronze to Babylon. 14 They also took away the shovels and the **ash** containers used in **cleaning** the **altar**, the tools used in tending the lamps, the bowls used for catching the **blood** from the **sacrifices**, the bowls used for burning **incense**, and all the other bronze articles used in the **temple service**. 15 They took away everything that was made of gold or silver, including the small bowls and the pans used for carrying live coals. 16 The bronze objects that King Solomon had made for the **Temple**—the two columns, the carts, and the large tank—were too heavy to weigh. 17 The two columns were identical: each one was eight metres high, with a bronze capital on top, 1.3 metres high. All round each capital was a bronze grating decorated with pomegranates made of bronze.

The People of Judah Are Taken to Babylonia
(Jer 52.24–27)

18 In addition, Nebuzaradan, the commanding officer, took away as **prisoners** Seraiah the **High Priest**, Zephaniah the **priest** next in rank, and the three other **important temple** officials. 19 From the city he took the officer who had been in **command** of the troops, five of the king's personal advisers who were still in the city, the commander's assistant, who was in charge of military records, and sixty other **important** men. 20 Nebuzaradan took them to the king of Babylonia, who was in the city of Riblah 21 in the territory of Hamath. There the king had them beaten and put **to death**.

So the people of Judah were carried away from their land into **exile**.

Gedaliah, Governor of Judah
(Jer 40.7–9; 41.1–3)

22 King Nebuchadnezzar of Babylonia made Gedaliah, the son of Ahikam and grandson of Shaphan, governor of Judah, and placed him in charge of all those who had not been taken away to Babylonia. 23 When the Judaean officers and soldiers who had not surrendered heard about this, they joined Gedaliah at Mizpah. These officers were Ishmael son of Nethaniah, Johanan son of Kareah, Seraiah son of Tanhumeth, from the town of Netophah, and Jezaniah from Maacah. 24 Gedaliah said to them, "I give you my **word** that there is no **need** for you to be **afraid** of the Babylonian officials. Settle in this land, **serve** the king of Babylonia, and all will go well with you."

25 But in the seventh month of that year, Ishmael, the son of Nethaniah and grandson of Elishama, a member of the royal family, went to Mizpah with ten men, attacked Gedaliah and killed him. He also killed the Israelites and Babylonians who were there with him. 26 Then all the Israelites, **rich** and **poor** alike, together with the army officers, left and went to Egypt, because they were **afraid** of the Babylonians.

Jehoiachin Is Released from Prison
(Jer 52.31–34)

27 In the year that Evilmerodach became king of Babylonia, he showed

[c] *Probable text (see Jer 52.15)* skilled workmen; *Hebrew* crowd.

25.4: Ezek 33.21 **25.7:** Ezek 12.13 **25.13:** 1 Kgs 7.15–26; 2 Chr 3.15–17 **25.14:** 1 Kgs 7.45; 2 Chr 4.16 **25.26:** Jer 43.5–7

kindness to King Jehoiachin of Judah by
releasing him from **prison**. This
happened on the twenty-seventh day of
the twelfth month of the thirty-seventh
year after Jehoiachin had been taken
away as **prisoner**. 28 Evilmerodach
treated him **kindly**, and gave him a
position of greater **honour** than he gave
the other kings who were **exiles** with him
in Babylonia. 29 So Jehoiachin was **per-**
mitted to **change** from his **prison** clothes
and to dine at the king's table for the rest
of his **life**. 30 Each day, for as long as he
lived, he was given a regular allowance
for his **needs**.

THE FIRST BOOK OF CHRONICLES

INTRODUCTION

The books of *Chronicles* are largely a retelling of events recorded in the books of *Samuel* and *Kings*, but from a different point of view. Two main purposes govern the account of the history of the Israelite monarchy in the books of *Chronicles:*

1. To show that in spite of the disasters that had fallen upon the kingdoms of Israel and Judah, God was still keeping his promises to the nation and was working out his plan for his people through those who were living in Judah. As a basis for this assurance, the writer looked to the great achievements of David and Solomon, to the reforms of Jehoshaphat, Hezekiah, and Josiah, and to the people who remained faithful to God.

2. To describe the origin of the worship of God in the Temple at Jerusalem, and especially the organization of the priests and Levites, by which the worship was carried out. David is presented as the real founder of the Temple and its ritual, even though it is Solomon who builds the Temple.

Outline of Contents

---

concubine 1 Kgs 11.3; 2.46
conquer 2 Kgs 21.14; 2.23
world [2] 2 Kgs 19.15; 16.14

From Adam to Abraham
(Gen 5.1-32; 10.1-32; 11.10-26)

1 Adam was the father of Seth, Seth
was the father of Enosh, Enosh the
father of Kenan, 2 Kenan the father of
Mahalalel, Mahalalel the father of Jared.
3 Jared was the father of Enoch, who was
the father of Methuselah; Methuselah
was the father of Lamech, 4 who was the
father of Noah. Noah had three sons:
Shem, Ham, and Japheth.
5 The sons of Japheth—Gomer,
Magog, Madai, Javan, Tubal, Meshech,
and Tiras—were the ancestors of the
peoples who bear their names. 6 The descendants of Gomer were the people of
Ashkenaz, Riphath, and Togarmah. 7 The
descendants of Javan were the people of
Elishah, Spain, Cyprus, and Rhodes.
8 The sons of Ham—Cush, Egypt,
Libya, and Canaan—were the ancestors
of the peoples who bear their names.
9 The descendants of Cush were the
people of Seba, Havilah, Sabtah,
Raamah, and Sabteca. The descendants
of Raamah were the people of Sheba and
Dedan. 10 (Cush had a son named Nimrod,
who became the **world's** first great **conqueror.**) 11 The descendants of Egypt
were the people of Lydia, Anam, Lehab,
Naphtuh, 12 Pathrus, Casluh, and of Crete
(from whom the Philistines were descended). 13 Canaan's sons—Sidon, the
eldest, and Heth—were the ancestors of
the peoples who bear their names.
14 Canaan was also the ancestor of the
Jebusites, the Amorites, Girgashites,
15 Hivites, Arkites, Sinites, 16 Arvadites,
Zemarites, and Hamathites.
17 Shem's sons—Elam, Asshur,
Arpachshad, Lud, Aram, Uz, Hul, Gether,
and Meshek—were the ancestors of the
peoples who bear their names. 18 Arpachshad was the father of Shelah, who was
the father of Eber. 19 Eber had two sons;
one was named Peleg,[a] because during
his time the people of the **world** were
divided, and the other was named Joktan. 20 The descendants of Joktan were
the people of Almodad, Sheleph, Hazarmaveth, Jerah, 21 Hadoram, Uzal, Diklah,
22 Ebal, Abimael, Sheba, 23 Ophir, Havilah,
and Jobab.
24 The family line from Shem to
Abram is as follows: Shem, Arpachshad,
Shelah, 25 Eber, Peleg, Reu, 26 Serug,
Nahor, Terah, 27 and Abram (also known
as Abraham).

The Descendants of Ishmael
(Gen 25.12-16)

28 Abraham had two sons, Isaac and

[a] PELEG: *This name sounds like the Hebrew for "divide."*

Ishmael. [29] The sons of Ishmael became the heads of twelve tribes: Nebaioth (from the name of Ishmael's eldest son), Kedar, Adbeel, Mibsam, [30] Mishma, Dumah, Massa, Hadad, Tema, [31] Jetur, Naphish, and Kedemah.

32 Abraham had a **concubine** named Keturah, who bore him six sons: Zimran, Jokshan, Medan, Midian, Ishbak, and Shuah. Jokshan had two sons: Sheba and Dedan. [33] Midian had five sons: Ephah, Epher, Hanoch, Abida, and Eldaah.

The Descendants of Esau
(Gen 36.1–19)

34 Abraham's son Isaac had two sons, Esau and Jacob. [35] Esau's sons were Eliphaz, Reuel, Jeush, Jalam, and Korah. [36] Eliphaz became the ancestor of the following tribes: Teman, Omar, Zephi, Gatam, Kenaz, Timna, and Amalek. [37] And Reuel became the ancestor of the tribes of Nahath, Zerah, Shammah, and Mizzah.

The Original Inhabitants of Edom
(Gen 36.20–30)

38–42 The original inhabitants of Edom were descended from the following sons of Seir:

Lotan, who was the ancestor of the clans of Hori and Homam. (Lotan had a sister named Timna.)

Shobal, who was the ancestor of the clans of Alvan, Manahath, Ebal, Shephi, and Onam.

Zibeon, who had two sons, Aiah and Anah. Anah was the father of Dishon, and Dishon was the ancestor of the clans of Hamran, Eshban, Ithran, and Cheran.

Ezer, who was the ancestor of the clans of Bilhan, Zaavan, and Jaakan.

Dishan, who was the ancestor of the clans of Uz and Aran.

The Kings of Edom
(Gen 36.31–43)

43–50 The following kings ruled the land of Edom one after the other, in the time before there were any kings in Israel:

Bela son of Beor from Dinhabah
Johab son of Zerah from Bozrah
Husham from the region of Teman
Hadad son of Bedad from Avith (he defeated the Midianites in a battle in the country of Moab)
Samlah from Masrekah
Shaul from Rehoboth-on-the-River
Baal Hanan son of Achbor
Hadad from Pau (his wife was Mehetabel, the daughter of Matred and granddaughter of Mezahab)

51 The people of Edom were divided into the following tribes: Timna, Alvah, Jetheth, [52] Oholibamah, Elah, Pinon, [53] Kenaz, Teman, Mibzar, [54] Magdiel, and Iram.

The Descendants of Judah

2 Jacob had twelve sons: Reuben, Simeon, Levi, Judah, Issachar, Zebulun, [2] Dan, Joseph, Benjamin, Naphtali, Gad, and Asher.

3 Judah had five sons in all. By his wife Bathshua, a Canaanite, he had three sons: Er, Onan, and Shelah. His eldest son, Er, was so **evil** that the LORD killed him. [4] By his daughter-in-law Tamar, Judah had two more sons, Perez and Zerah.

5 Perez had two sons, Hezron and Hamul. [6] His brother Zerah had five sons: Zimri, Ethan, Heman, Calcol, and Darda. [7] Achan[b] son of Carmi, one of Zerah's descendants, brought **disaster** on the people of Israel by keeping loot that had been **devoted** to God.

8 Ethan had one son, Azariah.

The Family Tree of King David

9 Hezron had three sons: Jerahmeel, Ram, and Caleb.

10 The family line from Ram to Jesse is as follows: Ram, Amminadab, Nahshon (a prominent man of the tribe of Judah), [11] Salmon, Boaz, [12] Obed, and Jesse.

13 Jesse had seven sons. In order of age they were: Eliab, Abinadab, Shammah, [14] Nethanel, Raddai, [15] Ozem, and David. [16] He also had two daughters, Zeruiah and Abigail.

Jesse's daughter Zeruiah had three sons: Abishai, Joab, and Asahel. [17] His other daughter Abigail married Jether, a descendant of Ishmael, and they had a son named Amasa.

The Descendants of Hezron

18 Hezron's son Caleb married Azubah and had a daughter named Jerioth. She had[c] three sons: Jesher, Shobab, and Ardon. [19] After the **death** of Azubah, Caleb married Ephrath, and they had a son named Hur. [20] Hur's son was Uri, and his grandson was Bezalel.

21 When Hezron was sixty years old, he married Machir's daughter, the sister

concubine [2] 1.32; 3.9
conquer 1.10; 18.11
death (1) 2 Kgs 22.20; 21.12
devote 2 Kgs 17.17; 29.18
disaster 2 Kgs 21.12; 2 Chr 7.22
evil 2 Kgs 17.13; 4.10
servant 2 Kgs 24.2; 6.49
widow 2 Kgs 4.1; Job 22.9

[b] ACHAN: *This is his name in Josh 7.1. The Hebrew text here calls him "Achar," which means "disaster."* [c] *Some ancient translations* had a daughter... She had; *Hebrew unclear.*

2.7: Josh 7.1

of Gilead. They had a son named Segub,
22 and Segub had a son named Jair. Jair
ruled[d] twenty-three cities in the territory
of Gilead. 23 But the kingdoms of Geshur
and Aram **conquered** sixty towns there,
including the villages of Jair and Kenath,
and the towns near by. All the people
who lived there were descendants of
Machir, the father of Gilead. 24 After
Hezron died, his son Caleb married
Ephrath, his father's **widow**.[e] They had a
son named Ashhur, who founded the
town of Tekoa.

The Descendants of Jerahmeel

25 Jerahmeel, the eldest son of
Hezron, had five sons: Ram, the eldest,
Bunah, Oren, Ozem, and Ahijah. 26-27 Ram
had three sons: Maaz, Jamin, and Eker.
Jerahmeel had another wife, a woman
named Atarah, and they had a son,
Onam. 28 Onam had two sons, Shammai
and Jada, and Shammai also had two
sons, Nadab and Abishur.

29 Abishur married a woman named
Abihail, and they had two sons, Ahban
and Molid. 30 Abishur's brother Nadab
had two sons, Seled and Appaim, but
Seled died without having any sons.
31 Appaim was the father of Ishi, Ishi was
the father of Sheshan, and Sheshan the
father of Ahlai.

32 Jada, the brother of Shammai, had
two sons, Jether and Jonathan, but
Jether died without having any sons.
33 Jonathan had two sons, Peleth and
Zaza. All these were descendants of
Jerahmeel.

34 Sheshan had no sons, only
daughters. He had an Egyptian **servant**
named Jarha, 35 to whom he gave one of
his daughters in marriage. They had a
son named Attai. 36 The family line from
Attai to Elishama is as follows: Attai,
Nathan, Zabad, 37 Ephlal, Obed, 38 Jehu,
Azariah, 39 Helez, Eleasah, 40 Sismai,
Shallum, 41 Jekamiah, and Elishama.

Other Descendants of Caleb

42 The eldest son of Caleb, Jerahmeel's brother, was named Mesha.
Mesha was the father of Ziph, who was
the father of Mareshah, who was the
father of Hebron.[f] 43 Hebron had four
sons: Korah, Tappuah, Rekem, and
Shema. 44 Shema was the father of
Raham and the grandfather of Jorkeam.
Rekem, Shema's brother, was the father
of Shammai, 45 who was the father of
Maon, who was the father of Bethzur.

46 Caleb had a **concubine** named
Ephah, and by her he had three more
sons: Haran, Moza, and Gazez. Haran
also had a son named Gazez.

47 (A man named Jahdai had six sons:
Regem, Jotham, Geshan, Pelet, Ephah,
and Shaaph.)

48 Caleb had another **concubine**,
Maacah, who bore him two sons, Sheber
and Tirhanah. 49 Later she had two more
sons: Shaaph, who founded the town of
Madmannah; and Shevah, who founded
the towns of Machbenah and Gibea.

In addition, Caleb had a daughter
named Achsah.

50 The following are also descendants
of Caleb.

Hur was the eldest son of Caleb and his
wife Ephrath. Hur's son Shobal founded
Kiriath Jearim, 51 his second son Salma
founded Bethlehem, and his third son
Hareph founded Bethgader.

52 Shobal, the founder of Kiriath
Jearim, was the ancestor of the people of
Haroeh, of half the inhabitants of Menu-
hoth, 53 and of the following clans that
lived in Kiriath Jearim: the Ithrites,
Puthites, Shumathites, and Mishraites.
(The people of the cities of Zorah and
Eshtaol were members of these clans.)

54 Salma, the founder of Bethlehem,
was the ancestor of the people of Neto-
phath, of Atroth Beth Joab, and of the
Zorites, who were one of the two clans in
Manahath.

55 (The following clans of experts in
writing and copying documents lived in
the town of Jabez: the Tirathites,
Shimeathites, and Sucathites. They were
Kenites who had intermarried with the
Rechabites.)

King David's Children

3 1-3 The following, in order of age, are **concubine** 2.46; 5.1
David's sons who were born while **prison** 2 Kgs 25.18; 5.21
he was in Hebron:

Amnon, whose mother was Ahinoam
from Jezreel
Daniel, whose mother was Abigail
from Carmel
Absalom, whose mother was Maacah,
daughter of King Talmai of
Geshur
Adonijah, whose mother was Haggith
Shephatiah, whose mother was Abital
Ithream, whose mother was Eglah

4 All six were born in Hebron during the
seven and a half years that David ruled
there.

In Jerusalem he ruled as king for

[d] ruled; *or* owned. [e] *Some ancient translations* his son...widow; *Hebrew unclear.*
[f] *Probable text* father of Mareshah...Hebron; *Hebrew unclear.*

3.4: 2 Sam 5.4-5; 1 Kgs 2.11; 1 Chr 29.27

thirty-three years, 5 and many sons were
born to him there.
His wife Bathsheba, daughter of
Ammiel, bore him four sons: Shimea,
Shobab, Nathan, and Solomon.
6 He had nine other sons: Ibhar,
Elishua, Elpelet, 7 Nogah, Nepheg,
Japhia, 8 Elishama, Eliada, and Eliphelet.
9 In addition to all these sons, David had
sons by his **concubines**. He also had a
daughter, Tamar.

The Descendants of King Solomon

10 This is the line of King Solomon's
descendants from father to son: Solomon, Rehoboam, Abijah, Asa, Jehoshaphat, 11 Jehoram, Ahaziah, Joash,
12 Amaziah, Uzziah, Jotham, 13 Ahaz,
Hezekiah, Manasseh, 14 Amon, and
Josiah. 15 Josiah had four sons: Johanan,
Jehoiakim, Zedekiah, and Joahaz.
16 Jehoiakim had two sons: Jehoiachin
and Zedekiah.

The Descendants of King Jehoiachin

17 These are the descendants of King
Jehoiachin, who was taken **prisoner** by
the Babylonians. Jehoiachin had seven
sons: Shealtiel, 18 Malchiram, Pedaiah,
Shenazzar, Jekamiah, Hoshama, and
Nedabiah. 19 Pedaiah had two sons,
Zerubbabel and Shimei. Zerubbabel was
the father of two sons, Meshullam and
Hananiah, and one daughter, Shelomith.
20 He had five other sons: Hashubah,
Ohel, Berechiah, Hasadiah, and Jushab
Hesed.
21 Hananiah had two sons, Pelatiah
and Jeshaiah. Jeshaiah was the father of
Rephaiah, who was the father of Arnan,
the father of Obadiah, the father of She-
caniah.[g] 22 Shecaniah had one son,
Shemaiah, and five grandsons: Hattush,
Igal, Bariah, Neariah, and Shaphat.
23 Neariah had three sons: Elioenai,
Hizkiah, and Azrikam. 24 Elioenai had
seven sons: Hodaviah, Eliashib, Pelaiah,
Akkub, Johanan, Delaiah, and Anani.

The Descendants of Judah

4 These are some of the descendants
of Judah: Perez, Hezron, Carmi,
Hur, and Shobal. 2 Shobal was the father
of Reaiah, who was the father of Jahath,
the father of Ahumai and Lahad, the
ancestors of the people who lived in
Zorah.
3–4 Hur was the eldest son of his
father Caleb's wife Ephrath, and his de-
scendants founded the city of Bethlehem.
Hur had three sons: Etam, Penuel, and
Ezer. Etam had three sons:[h] Jezreel,
Ishma, and Idbash, and one daughter,
Hazzelelponi. Penuel founded the city of
Gedor, and Ezer founded Hushah.
5 Ashhur, who founded the town of
Tekoa, had two wives, Helah and
Naarah. 6 He and Naarah had four sons:
Ahuzzam, Hepher, Temeni, and Haahash-
tari. 7 Ashhur and Helah had three sons:
Zereth, Izhar, and Ethnan.
8 Koz was the father of Anub and
Zobebah, and the ancestor of the clans
descended from Aharhel son of Harum.
9 There was a man named Jabez, who
was the most **respected** member of his
family. His mother had given him the
name Jabez,[i] because his **birth** had been
very **painful**. 10 But Jabez **prayed** to the
God of Israel, "**Bless** me, God, and give
me much land. Be with me and **keep me**
from anything **evil** that might cause me
pain." And God gave him what he **prayed**
for.

Other Family Lists

11 Caleb, the brother of Shuhah, had a
son, Mehir. Mehir was the father of
Eshton, 12 who had three sons:
Bethrapha, Paseah, and Tehinnah.
Tehinnah was the founder of the city of
Nahash. The descendants of these men
lived in Recah.
13 Kenaz had two sons, Othniel and
Seraiah. Othniel also had two sons,
Hathath and Meonothai.[j] 14 Meonothai
was the father of Ophrah.
Seraiah was the father of Joab, the
founder of the Valley of Craftsmen,
where all the people were skilled workmen.
15 Caleb son of Jephunneh had three
sons: Iru, Elah, and Naam. And Elah was
the father of Kenaz.
16 Jehallelel had four sons: Ziph,
Ziphah, Tiria, and Asarel.
17–18 Ezrah had four sons: Jether,
Mered, Epher, and Jalon. Mered married
Bithiah, a daughter of the king of Egypt,
and they had a daughter, Miriam, and
two sons, Shammai and Ishbah. Ishbah
founded the town of Eshtemoa. Mered
also married a woman from the tribe of
Judah, and they had three sons: Jered,
who founded the town of Gedor; Heber,
founder of the town of Soco; and Jeku-
thiel, founder of the town of Zanoah.
19 Hodiah married the sister of
Naham. Their descendants founded the

[g] *Verse 21 in Hebrew is unclear.* [h] *Some ancient translations* sons; *Hebrew* fathers.
[i] JABEZ: *This name sounds like the Hebrew for "pain."*
[j] *Some ancient translations* Meonothai; *Hebrew does not have this name.*

3.5: 2 Sam 11.3

pray [2] 2 Kgs 20.2; 5.20
respect 2 Kgs 19.22; 29.28
service 2 Kgs 25.14; 7.4
sheep [2] 2 Kgs 5.26; 5.21

birth 2 Kgs 19.3; 7.16
bless 1 Kgs 8.14; 13.14
destroy 2 Kgs 24.2; 20.1
evil 2.3; 2 Chr 7.14
keep from 2 Sam 22.24; 10.4
pain [2] Judg 11.35; 2 Chr 21.15
peace 2 Kgs 22.20; 19.19
plenty [2] 2 Kgs 3.17; 2 Chr 1.15

clan of Garm, which lived in the town of Keilah, and the clan of Maacath, which lived in the town of Eshtemoa.[k]

20 Shimon had four sons: Amnon, Rinnah, Benhanan, and Tilon.

Ishi had two sons: Zoheth and Benzoheth.

The Descendants of Shelah

21 Shelah was one of Judah's sons. His descendants included Er, who founded the town of Lecah; Laadah, founder of the town of Mareshah; the clan of linen-weavers, who lived in the town of Beth Ashbea; 22 Jokim and the people who lived in the town of Cozeba; and Joash and Saraph, who married Moabite women and then settled in Bethlehem.[l] (These traditions are very old.) 23 They were potters in the **service** of the king and lived in the towns of Netaim and Gederah.

The Descendants of Simeon

24 Simeon had five sons: Nemuel, Jamin, Jarib, Zerah, and Shaul. 25 Shaul's son was Shallum, his grandson was Mibsam, and his great-grandson was Mishma. 26 Then from Mishma the line descended through Hammuel, Zaccur, and Shimei. 27 Shimei had sixteen sons and six daughters, but his relatives had fewer children, and the tribe of Simeon did not grow as much as the tribe of Judah did.

28 Down to the time of King David the descendants of Simeon lived in the following towns: Beersheba, Moladah, Hazarshual, 29 Bilhah, Ezem, Tolad, 30 Bethuel, Hormah, Ziklag, 31 Beth Marcaboth, Hazarsusim, Bethbiri, and Shaaraim. 32 They also lived in five other places: Etam, Ain, Rimmon, Tochen, and Ashan, 33 and the surrounding villages, as far south-west as the town of Baalath. These are the records which they kept of their families and of the places where they lived.

34–38 The following men were the heads of their clans:

Meshobab, Jamlech, Joshah son of Amaziah, Joel,
Jehu (the son of Joshibiah, the son of Seraiah, the son of Asiel),
Elioenai, Jaakobah, Jeshohaiah, Asaiah, Adiel, Jesimiel, Benaiah,
Ziza (the son of Shiphi, the son of Allon, a descendant of Jedaiah, Shimri, and Shemaiah).

Because their families continued to grow, 39 they spread out westwards almost to Gerar[m] and pastured their **sheep** on the eastern side of the valley in which that city is located. 40 They found **plenty** of fertile pasture lands there in a stretch of open country that was quiet and **peaceful**. The people who had lived there before were Hamites.

41 In the time of King Hezekiah of Judah, the men named above went to Gerar and **destroyed** the tents and huts of the people who lived there.[n] They drove the people out and settled there permanently because there was **plenty** of pasture for their **sheep**. 42 Five hundred other members of the tribe of Simeon went east to Edom. They were led by the sons of Ishi: Pelatiah, Neariah, Rephaiah, and Uzziel. 43 There they killed the surviving Amalekites, and they have lived there ever since.

The Descendants of Reuben

5 These are the descendants of Reuben, the eldest of Jacob's sons. (Because he had intercourse with one of his father's **concubines**, he lost the **rights** belonging to the **first-born** son, and those **rights** were given to Joseph. 2 It was the tribe of Judah, however, that became the **strongest** and **provided** a ruler for all the tribes.) 3 Reuben, the eldest of Jacob's sons, had four sons: Hanoch, Pallu, Hezron, and Carmi.

4–6 These are the descendants of Joel from generation to generation: Shemaiah, Gog, Shimei, Micah, Reaiah, Baal, and Beerah. The Assyrian emperor, Tiglath Pileser, captured Beerah, a leader of the tribe, and deported him.

7 The family records list the following clan leaders in the tribe of Reuben: Jeiel, Zechariah, 8 and Bela, the son of Azaz and grandson of Shema, of the clan of Joel. This clan lived in Aroer and in the territory from there north to Nebo and Baal Meon. 9 They had large herds in the land of Gilead, and so they occupied the land as far east as the desert that stretches all the way to the River Euphrates.

10 In the time of King Saul the tribe of Reuben attacked the Hagrites, killed them in battle, and occupied their land in the eastern part of Gilead.

concubine 3.9; 7.14
enemy [2] 2 Kgs 21.14; 10.3
exile 2 Kgs 25.21; 6.15
first-born Deut 21.16; Ps 78.51
god (2) (other gods) 2 Kgs 23.10; 10.10
help 2 Kgs 23.29; 11.10
important 2 Kgs 25.9; 26.6
leading 2 Kgs 24.14; 11.15
pray 4.10; 17.16
prayer 2 Kgs 22.19; 17.25
prison 3.17; 2 Chr 6.36
provide 2 Kgs 23.9; 7.4
right (3) [2] 2 Sam 19.28; 2 Chr 26.18
sheep 4.39; 12.40
strong 2 Kgs 2.16; 11.9
trust 2 Kgs 19.10; 2 Chr 20.20
unfaithful Judg 8.33; 10.13
victory 2 Kgs 13.17; 11.14
will (1) 1 Kgs 12.15; 13.2
worship (2) (of other gods) 2 Kgs 23.4; 2 Chr 7.19

[k] *Verse 19 in Hebrew is unclear.* [l] *Probable text* settled in Bethlehem; *Hebrew unclear.*
[m] *Some ancient translations* Gerar; *Hebrew* Gedor.
[n] the tents and huts...there; *or* the tents of the people who lived there, and the Meunites also.

4.28–33: Josh 19.2–8 **5.1:** Gen 35.22, 49.3–4 **5.2:** Gen 49.8–10 **5.6:** 2 Kgs 15.29

The Descendants of Gad

11 The tribe of Gad lived to the north of Reuben in the land of Bashan as far east as Salecah. [12]Joel was the founder of the **leading** clan, and Shapham of the second most **important** clan. Janai and Shaphat were founders of other clans in Bashan. [13]The other members of the tribe belonged to the following seven clans: Michael, Meshullam, Sheba, Jorai, Jacan, Zia, and Eber. [14]They were descendants of Abihail son of Huri, whose ancestors were traced back as follows: Abihail, Huri, Jaroah, Gilead, Michael, Jeshishai, Jahdo, Buz. [15]Ahi, the son of Abdiel and grandson of Guni, was head of these clans. [16]They lived in the territory of Bashan and Gilead, in the towns there and all over the pasture lands of Sharon. [17](These records were compiled in the days of King Jotham of Judah and King Jeroboam II of Israel.)

The Armies of the Eastern Tribes

18 In the tribes of Reuben, Gad, and East Manasseh there were 44,760 soldiers, well-trained in the use of shields, swords, and bows. [19]They went to war against the Hagrite tribes of Jetur, Naphish, and Nodab. [20]They put their **trust** in God and **prayed** to him for **help**, and God answered their **prayers** and made them **victorious** over the Hagrites and their allies. [21]They captured from the **enemy** 50,000 camels, 250,000 **sheep**, and 2,000 donkeys, and took 100,000 **prisoners** of war. [22]They killed many of the **enemy**, because the war was **God's will**. And they went on living in that territory until the **exile**.[o]

The People of East Manasseh

23 The people of East Manasseh settled in the territory of Bashan as far north as Baal Hermon, Senir, and Mount Hermon, and their population increased greatly. [24]The following were the heads of their clans: Epher, Ishi, Eliel, Azriel, Jeremiah, Hodaviah, and Jahdiel. They were all outstanding soldiers, well-known leaders of their clans.

The Eastern Tribes Are Deported

25 But the people were **unfaithful** to the God of their ancestors and deserted him to **worship the gods** of the nations whom God had driven out of the land. [26]So God made Emperor Pul of Assyria (also known as Tiglath Pileser) invade their country. He deported the tribes of Reuben, Gad, and East Manasseh and settled them permanently in Halah, Habor, and Hara, and by the River Gozan.

The Family Line of the High Priests

6 Levi had three sons: Gershon, Kohath, and Merari.

2 Kohath had four sons: Amram, Izhar, Hebron, and Uzziel.

3 Amram had two sons, Aaron and Moses, and one daughter, Miriam.

Aaron had four sons: Nadab, Abihu, Eleazar, and Ithamar.

4 The descendants of Eleazar from generation to generation are as follows: Phinehas, Abishua, [5]Bukki, Uzzi, [6]Zerahiah, Meraioth, [7]Amariah, Ahitub, [8]Zadok, Ahimaaz, [9]Azariah, Johanan, [10]Azariah (the one who **served** in the **Temple** which King Solomon built in Jerusalem), [11]Amariah, Ahitub, [12]Zadok, Shallum, [13]Hilkiah, Azariah, [14]Seraiah, Jehozadak. [15]King Nebuchadnezzar deported Jehozadak along with the other people of Judah and Jerusalem whom the LORD sent into **exile**.

Other Descendants of Levi

16 Levi had three sons: Gershon, Kohath, and Merari. [17]Each of them also had sons. Gershon was the father of Libni and Shimei; [18]Kohath was the father of Amram, Izhar, Hebron, and Uzziel; [19]and Merari was the father of Mahli and Mushi.

20 These are the descendants of Gershon from generation to generation: Libni, Jahath, Zimmah, [21]Joah, Iddo, Zerah, Jeatherai.

22 These are the descendants of Kohath from generation to generation: Amminadab, Korah, Assir, [23]Elkanah, Ebiasaph, Assir, [24]Tahath, Uriel, Uzziah, Shaul.

25 Elkanah had two sons, Amasai and Ahimoth. [26]These are Ahimoth's descendants from generation to generation: Elkanah, Zophai, Nahath, [27]Eliab, Jeroham, Elkanah.

28 Samuel had two sons: Joel,[p] the elder, and Abijah, the younger.

29 These are the descendants of Merari from generation to generation: Mahli, Libni, Shimei, Uzzah, [30]Shimea, Haggiah, Asaiah.

The Temple Musicians

31 These are the men whom King

altar 2 Kgs 25.14; 16.40
Covenant Box 1 Kgs 8.1; 13.3
duty (1) [2] 2 Kgs 24.16; 9.25
exile 5.22; 29.15
forgive 2 Kgs 24.4; 21.8
Holy Place 1 Kgs 8.6; 28.11
incense 2 Kgs 25.14; 9.29
Levites [3] 1 Kgs 8.4; 9.2
lot (1) [2] Judg 20.9; 24.5
offer 2 Kgs 23.5; 9.31
place of worship [2] 2 Kgs 23.10; 16.39
present (1) 2 Kgs 10.25; 2 Chr 2.4
refuge [2] 1 Kgs 20.30; Ps 9.9
sacrifice [2] 2 Kgs 25.14; 15.26
servant 2.34; 16.12
serve 2 Kgs 25.24; 12.21
share 2 Kgs 2.9; 23.24
Temple (1) (of God) [2] 2 Kgs 25.9; 9.2
Tent (2) (of the Lord's presence) 1 Kgs 8.4; 9.19
turn 2 Kgs 21.13; 9.25
worship (1) (of God) 2 Kgs 23.27; 9.28

[o] THE EXILE: *About 733 B.C. the Assyrians conquered northern Israel and the Israelite territory east of the River Jordan and deported the people (see 2 Kgs 15.29).*
[p] *Some ancient translations (see also 1 Sam 8.2)* Joel; *Hebrew does not have this name.*

5.26: 2 Kgs 15.19, 29, 17.6 **6.16–19:** Ex 6.16–19

David put in charge of the music at the
place of worship in Jerusalem after the
Covenant Box was moved there. [32]They
took regular **turns of duty** at the **Tent** of
the LORD's presence during the time
before King Solomon built the **Temple**.
[33]The family lines of those who held this
office are as follows:

The clan of Kohath: Heman, the
leader of the first choir, was the son of
Joel. His family line went back to Jacob
as follows: Heman, Joel, Samuel,
[34]Elkanah, Jeroham, Eliel, Toah, [35]Zuph,
Elkanah, Mahath, Amasai, [36]Elkanah,
Joel, Azariah, Zephaniah, [37]Tahath,
Assir, Ebiasaph, Korah, [38]Izhar, Kohath,
Levi, Jacob.

39 Asaph was leader of the second
choir. His family line went back to Levi
as follows: Asaph, Berechiah, Shimea,
[40]Michael, Baaseiah, Malchijah, [41]Ethni,
Zerah, Adaiah, [42]Ethan, Zimmah, Shimei,
[43]Jahath, Gershon, Levi.

44 Ethan of the clan of Merari was the
leader of the third choir. His family line
went back to Levi as follows: Ethan,
Kishi, Abdi, Malluch, [45]Hashabiah,
Amaziah, Hilkiah, [46]Amzi, Bani, Shemer,
[47]Mahli, Mushi, Merari, Levi.

48 Their **fellow-Levites** were assigned
all the other **duties** at the **place of
worship**.

The Descendants of Aaron

49 Aaron and his descendants **presented** the offerings of **incense** and
offered the sacrifices that were burnt on
the **altar**. They were responsible for all
the **worship** in the **Most Holy Place** and
for the **sacrifices** by which God **forgives**
Israel's sins. They did all this in accordance with the instructions given by
Moses, God's **servant**. [50]This is the line of
Aaron's descendants: Eleazar, Phinehas,
Abishua, [51]Bukki, Uzzi, Zerahiah,
[52]Meraioth, Amariah, Ahitub, [53]Zadok,
Ahimaaz.

Where the Levites Lived

54 This is the territory assigned to the
descendants of Aaron of the clan of
Kohath. They received the first **share** of
the land assigned to the **Levites**. [55]This
included Hebron in the territory of Judah
and the pasture lands round it. [56]The
fields and villages, however, that
belonged to the city were assigned to
Caleb son of Jephunneh. [57-59]The following towns were assigned to Aaron's descendants: Hebron, a **city of refuge**,[q]
Jattir, and the towns of Libnah,
Eshtemoa, Hilen, Debir, Ashan, and Beth
Shemesh, with their pasture lands. [60]In
the territory of Benjamin they were
assigned the following towns with their
pasture lands: Geba, Alemeth, and
Anathoth. This made a total of thirteen
towns for all their families to live in.
[61]Ten towns in the territory of West
Manasseh were assigned by **lot** to the
rest of the clan of Kohath, family by
family.

62 To the clan of Gershon, family by
family, were assigned thirteen towns in
the territories of Issachar, Asher,
Naphtali, and East Manasseh in Bashan.
[63]In the same way, twelve towns in the
territories of Reuben, Gad, and Zebulun
were assigned to the clan of Merari,
family by family. [64]In this way the people
of Israel assigned towns for the **Levites**
to live in, together with the pasture lands
round the towns. [65](The towns in the
territories of Judah, Simeon, and Benjamin, mentioned above, were also
assigned by drawing **lots**.)

66 Some of the families of the clan of
Kohath were assigned towns and pasture
lands in the territory of Ephraim:
[67]Shechem, the **city of refuge** in the hills
of Ephraim, Gezer, [68]Jokmeam, Beth
Horon, [69]Aijalon, and Gath Rimmon. [70]In
the territory of West Manasseh they
were assigned the towns of Aner and
Bileam with the surrounding pasture
lands.

71 The families of the clan of Gershon
were assigned the following towns, with
the surrounding pasture lands:

In the territory of East Manasseh:
Golan in Bashan, and Ashtaroth.

72 In the territory of Issachar:
Kedesh, Daberath, [73]Ramoth, and Anem.

74 In the territory of Asher: Mashal,
Abdon, [75]Hukok, and Rehob.

76 In the territory of Naphtali: Kedesh
in Galilee, Hammon, and Kiriathaim.

77 The remaining families of the clan
of Merari were assigned the following
towns with the surrounding pasture
lands:

In the territory of Zebulun: Rimmono
and Tabor.

78 In the territory of Reuben, east of
the River Jordan beyond Jericho: Bezer
on the plateau, Jahzah, [79]Kedemoth, and
Mephaath.

80 In the territory of Gad: Ramoth in
Gilead, Mahanaim, [81]Heshbon, and Jazer.

[q] CITY OF REFUGE: *If anyone accidentally killed someone, he could escape to one of these cities and be safe from revenge (see Josh 20.1–9).*

birth 4.9; Job 21.10
comfort 2 Sam 12.24; Job 2.11
concubine 5.1; 2 Chr 11.21
control 2 Kgs 24.7; 10.14
mourn 1 Kgs 14.13; 2 Chr 16.14
provide 5.2; 14.1
service [6] 4.23; 18.17
steal 2 Sam 21.12; Job 1.15
trouble 2 Kgs 14.10; 21.1

The Descendants of Issachar

7 Issachar had four sons: Tola, Puah,
Jashub, and Shimron.
2 Tola had six sons: Uzzi, Rephaiah,
Jeriel, Jahmai, Ibsam, and Shemuel.
They were heads of families of the clan
of Tola and were famous soldiers. At the
time of King David their descendants
numbered 22,600.
3 Uzzi had one son, Izrahiah. Izrahiah
and his four sons, Michael, Obadiah, Joel,
and Isshiah, were all heads of families.
4 They had so many wives and children
that their descendants were able to
provide 36,000 men for **military service**.
5 The official records of all the
families of the tribe of Issachar listed
87,000 men eligible for **military service**.

The Descendants of Benjamin and Dan

6 Benjamin had three sons: Bela,
Becher, and Jediael.
7 Bela had five sons: Ezbon, Uzzi,
Uzziel, Jerimoth, and Iri. They were
heads of families in the clan and were all
famous soldiers. Their descendants
included 22,034 men eligible for **military
service**.
8 Becher had nine sons: Zemirah,
Joash, Eliezer, Eleoenai, Omri, Jeremoth, Abijah, Anathoth, and Alemeth.
9 The official record of their descendants
by families listed 20,200 men eligible for
military service.
10 Jediael had one son, Bilhan, and
Bilhan had seven sons: Jeush, Benjamin,
Ehud, Chenaanah, Zethan, Tarshish, and
Ahishahar. 11 They were heads of families
in the clan and were all famous soldiers.
Their descendants included 17,200 men
eligible for **military service**. 12 Shuppim
and Huppim also belonged to this tribe.
Dan had one son, Hushim.[r]

The Descendants of Naphtali

13 Naphtali had four sons: Jahziel,
Guni, Jezer, and Shallum. (They were descendants of Bilhah.)[s]

The Descendants of Manasseh

14 By his Aramean **concubine**,
Manasseh had two sons, Asriel and
Machir. Machir was the father of Gilead.
15 Machir found a wife for Huppim and
one for Shuppim. His sister's name was
Maacah. Machir's second son was
Zelophehad, and he had only daughters.
16 Maacah, Machir's wife, gave **birth**
to two sons, whom they named Peresh
and Sheresh. Peresh had two sons, Ulam
and Rakem, 17 and Ulam had a son
named Bedan. These are all descendants
of Gilead, the son of Machir and grandson of Manasseh.
18 Gilead's sister Hammolecheth had
three sons: Ishod, Abiezer, and Mahlah.
19 (Shemida had four sons: Ahian,
Shechem, Likhi, and Aniam.)

The Descendants of Ephraim

20 These are the descendants of
Ephraim from generation to generation:
Shuthelah, Bered, Tahath, Eleadah,
Tahath, 21 Zabad, Shuthelah. Ephraim
had two other sons besides Shuthelah:
Ezer and Elead, who were killed when
they tried to **steal** the livestock belonging
to the native inhabitants of Gath. 22 Their
father Ephraim **mourned** for them for
many days, and his relatives came to
comfort him. 23 Then he had intercourse
with his wife again, and she became
pregnant and had a son. They named
him Beriah,[t] because of the **trouble** that
had come to their family.
24 Ephraim had a daughter named
Sheerah. She built the towns of Upper
and Lower Beth Horon, and Uzzen
Sheerah.
25 Ephraim also had a son named
Rephah, whose descendants were as
follows: Resheph, Telah, Tahan, 26 Ladan,
Ammihud, Elishama, 27 Nun, Joshua.
28 The territory which they took and
settled in included Bethel and the towns
round it, as far east as Naaran and as far
west as Gezer and the towns round it. It
also included the cities of Shechem and
Ayyah, and the towns round them.
29 The descendants of Manasseh **controlled** the cities of Beth Shan, Taanach,
Megiddo, and Dor, and the towns round
them.
All these are the places where the descendants of Joseph son of Jacob lived.

The Descendants of Asher

30 These are the descendants of
Asher. He had four sons: Imnah, Ishvah,
Ishvi, and Beriah; and one daughter,
Serah.
31 Beriah had two sons, Heber and
Malchiel. (Malchiel founded the city of
Birzaith.)
32 Heber had three sons: Japhlet,
Shomer, and Hotham; and one daughter,
Shua.
33 Japhlet also had three sons:
Pasach, Bimhal, and Ashvath.

[r] *Probable text* Shuppim...Hushim *(see Gen 46.23; Num 26.39,42); Hebrew* And Shuppim and Huppim, sons of Ir; Hushim sons of Aher.
[s] BILHAH: *A concubine of Jacob and the mother of his two sons Dan and Naphtali.*
[t] BERIAH: *This name sounds like the Hebrew for "in trouble."*

34 His brother Shomer had three sons:
Rohgah, Jehubbah, and Aram.
35 His brother Hotham[u] had four sons:
Zophah, Imna, Shelesh, and Amal.
36 The descendants of Zophah were
Suah, Harnepher, Shual, Beri, Imrah,
37 Bezer, Hod, Shamma, Shilshah, Ithran,
and Beera.
38 The descendants of Jether were
Jephunneh, Pispa, and Ara, 39 and the descendants of Ulla were Arah, Hanniel,
and Rizia.
40 All these were descendants of
Asher. They were heads of families,
famous fighting men, outstanding
leaders. Asher's descendants included
26,000 men eligible for **military service**.

The Descendants of Benjamin

divorce Deut 24.1; Ezra 10.19
force (1) 2 Kgs 24.1; 11.18

8 Benjamin had five sons. In order of
age they were Bela, Ashbel, Aharah,
2 Nohah, and Rapha.
3 The descendants of Bela were
Addar, Gera, Abihud, 4 Abishua, Naaman,
Ahoah, 5 Gera, Shephuphan, and Huram.
6–7 The descendants of Ehud were
Naaman, Ahijah, and Gera. They were
heads of families that lived in Geba, but
which were **forced** out and went to live in
Manahath. Gera, the father of Uzza and
Ahihud, led them in this move.
8–9 Shaharaim **divorced** two wives,
Hushim and Baara. Later, when he lived
in the country of Moab, he married
Hodesh and had seven sons: Jobab, Zibia,
Mesha, Malcam, 10 Jeuz, Sachia, and
Mirmah. His sons all became heads of
families.
11 He also had two sons by Hushim:
Abitub and Elpaal.
12 Elpaal had three sons: Eber,
Misham, and Shemed. It was Shemed
who built the cities of Ono and Lod and
the surrounding villages.

The Benjaminites in Gath and Aijalon

13 Beriah and Shema were heads of
families that settled in the city of Aijalon
and drove out the people who lived in the
city of Gath. 14 Beriah's descendants
included Ahio, Shashak, Jeremoth,
15 Zebadiah, Arad, Eder, 16 Michael,
Ishpah, and Joha.

The Benjaminites in Jerusalem

17 Elpaal's descendants included
Zebadiah, Meshullam, Hizki, Heber,
18 Ishmerai, Izliah, and Jobab.
19 Shimei's descendants included
Jakim, Zichri, Zabdi, 20 Elienai, Zillethai,
Eliel, 21 Adaiah, Beraiah, and Shimrath.
22 Shashak's descendants included
Ishpan, Eber, Eliel, 23 Abdon, Zichri,
Hanan, 24 Hananiah, Elam, Anthothijah,
25 Iphdeiah, and Penuel.
26 Jeroham's descendants included
Shamsherai, Shehariah, Athaliah,
27 Jaareshiah, Elijah, and Zichri.
28 These were the ancestral heads of
families and their principal descendants
who lived in Jerusalem.

The Benjaminites in Gibeon and Jerusalem

29 Jeiel[v] founded the city of Gibeon
and settled there. His wife was named
Maacah, 30 and his eldest son, Abdon. His
other sons were Zur, Kish, Baal, Ner,[w]
Nadab, 31 Gedor, Ahio, Zechariah, 32 and
Mikloth, the father of Shimeah. Their descendants lived in Jerusalem near other
families of their clan.

The Family of King Saul

33 Ner was the father of Kish, and
Kish was the father of King Saul. Saul
had four sons: Jonathan, Malchishua,
Abinadab, and Eshbaal.[a] 34 Jonathan was
the father of Meribbaal,[b] who was the
father of Micah.
35 Micah had four sons: Pithon,
Melech, Tarea, and Ahaz. 36 Ahaz was the
father of Jehoaddah, who was the father
of three sons: Alemeth, Azmaveth, and
Zimri. Zimri was the father of Moza,
37 Moza the father of Binea, Binea of
Raphah, Raphah of Eleasah, and Eleasah
of Azel.
38 Azel had six sons: Azrikam,
Bocheru, Ishmael, Sheariah, Obadiah,
and Hanan. 39 Azel's brother Eshek had
three sons: Ulam, Jeush, and Eliphelet.
40 Ulam's sons were outstanding
soldiers and archers. He had a hundred
and fifty sons and grandsons in all. All
those named above were members of the
tribe of Benjamin.

The People Who Returned from Captivity

9 All the people of Israel were listed
according to their families, and this
information was recorded in *The Book of
the Kings of Israel.*
The people of Judah had been
deported to Babylon as **punishment** for
their sins. 2 The first to return to their
property in the cities included Israelite

bread 2 Kgs 23.9; 16.3
choose 2 Kgs 23.27; 12.23
duty (1) [3] 6.32; 16.37
final Lev 27.12; 23.27
free 2 Kgs 13.5; Ezra 9.8
incense 6.49; 23.13
Levites [8] 6.48; 13.2
offer 6.49; 11.18

[u] *Probable text (see verse 32)* Hotham; *Hebrew* Helem.
[v] *Probable text (and see 9.35)* Jeiel; *Hebrew does not have this name.*
[w] *One ancient translation (and see 9.36)* Ner; *Hebrew does not have this name.*
[a] ESHBAAL: *Called Ishbosheth in 2 Sam 2.8 and elsewhere in 2 Sam.*
[b] MERIBBAAL: *Called Mephibosheth in 2 Sam 4.4 and elsewhere in 2 Sam.*

9.2–3: Ezra 2.27; Neh 7.73

priest [4] 2 Kgs 25.18; 13.2
prophet 2 Kgs 24.2; 16.22
punish 2 Kgs 22.16; 12.17
Sabbath 2 Kgs 11.5; 23.31
sacred [2] 2 Kgs 10.22; 11.3
Temple (1) (of God) [9] 6.10; 16.27
Tent (2) (of the Lord's presence) [2] 6.32; 15.1
turn 6.32; 24.6
worship (1) (of God) 6.49; 15.13

laymen, **priests**, **Levites**, and **temple** workmen. 3 People from the tribes of Judah, Benjamin, Ephraim, and Manasseh went to live in Jerusalem.

4–6 There were 690 families of the tribe of Judah who lived in Jerusalem.

The descendants of Judah's son Perez had as their leader Uthai, the son of Ammihud and grandson of Omri. His other ancestors included Imri and Bani.

The descendants of Judah's son Shelah had as their leader Asaiah, who was the head of his family.

The descendants of Judah's son Zerah had Jeuel as their leader.

7–8 The following members of the tribe of Benjamin lived in Jerusalem:

Sallu son of Meshullam, who was the son of Hodaviah, the son of Hassenuah
Ibneiah son of Jeroham
Elah, the son of Uzzi and grandson of Michri
Meshullam son of Shephatiah, who was the son of Reuel, the son of Ibnijah

9 There were 956 families of this tribe living there. All the men named above were heads of families.

The Priests Who Lived in Jerusalem

10–12 The following **priests** lived in Jerusalem:

Jedaiah, Jehoiarib, and Jachin
Azariah son of Hilkiah (the chief official in the **Temple**), whose ancestors included Meshullam, Zadok, Meraioth, and Ahitub
Adaiah son of Jeroham, whose ancestors included Pashhur and Malchijah
Maasai son of Adiel, whose ancestors included Jahzerah, Meshullam, Meshillemith, and Immer

13 The **priests** who were heads of families totalled 1,760. They were experts in all the work carried on in the **Temple**.

The Levites Who Lived in Jerusalem

14–16 The following **Levites** lived in Jerusalem:

Shemaiah son of Hasshub, whose ancestors included Azrikam and Hashabiah, of the clan of Merari
Bakbakkar, Heresh, and Galal
Mattaniah son of Mica, whose ancestors included Zichri and Asaph
Obadiah son of Shemaiah, whose ancestors included Galal and Jeduthun
Berechiah, the son of Asa and grandson of Elkanah, who lived in the territory that belonged to the town of Netophah

The Temple Guards Who Lived in Jerusalem

17 The following temple guards lived in Jerusalem: Shallum, Akkub, Talmon, and Ahiman. Shallum was their leader. 18 Down to that time members of their clans had been stationed at the eastern entrance to the King's Gate.[x] Formerly they had stood guard at the gates to the camps of the Levites.

19 Shallum, the son of Kore and grandson of Ebiasaph, together with his fellow-members of the clan of Korah, was responsible for guarding the entrance to the **Tent** of the LORD's presence, just as their ancestors had been when they were in charge of the LORD's camp. 20 Phineas son of Eleazar—may the LORD be with him!—had supervised them at one time.

21 Zechariah son of Meshelemiah was also a guard at the entrance to the **Tent** of the LORD's presence.

22 In all, 212 men were **chosen** as guards for the entrances and gates. They were registered according to the villages where they lived. It was King David and the **prophet** Samuel who had put their ancestors in these responsible positions. 23 They and their descendants continued to guard the gates to the **Temple**. 24 There was a gate facing in each direction, north, south, east, and west, and each had a chief guard. 25 These guards were assisted by their relatives, who lived in the villages and who had to take **turns** at guard **duty** for seven days at a time. 26 The four chief guards were **Levites** and had the **final** responsibility. They were also responsible for the rooms in the **Temple** and for the supplies kept there. 27 They lived near the **Temple**, because it was their **duty** to guard it and to open the gates every morning.

The Other Levites

28 Other **Levites** were responsible for the utensils used in **worship**. They checked them out and checked them back in every time they were used. 29 Others were in charge of the other **sacred** equipment, and of the flour, wine, olive-oil, **incense**, and spices. 30 But the responsibility for mixing the spices belonged to the **priests**.

31 A **Levite** named Mattithiah, eldest son of Shallum, of the clan of Korah, was responsible for preparing the baked **offerings**.[y] 32 Members of the clan of Kohath were responsible for preparing

[x] KING'S GATE: *The east gate of the Temple, through which the king usually entered.*
[y] BAKED OFFERINGS: *Thin cakes of flour and olive-oil which were baked and then presented as offerings to God (see Lev 2.4–6).*

the **sacred bread**[z] for the **Temple** every
Sabbath.
33 Some **Levite** families were responsible for the **temple** music. The
heads of these families lived in some of
the **temple** buildings and were **free** from
other **duties**, because they were on call
day and night.
34 The men named above were heads
of **Levite** families, according to their
ancestral lines. They were the leaders
who lived in Jerusalem.

The Ancestors and Descendants of King Saul
(8.29–38)

35 Jeiel founded the city of Gibeon
and settled there. His wife was named
Maacah. 36 His eldest son was Abdon, and
his other sons were Zur, Kish, Baal, Ner,
Nadab, 37 Gedor, Ahio, Zechariah, and
Mikloth, 38 the father of Shimeah. Their
descendants lived in Jerusalem near
other families of their clan.
39 Ner was the father of Kish, and
Kish was the father of Saul. Saul had four
sons: Jonathan, Malchishua, Abinadab,
and Eshbaal.[m] 40 Jonathan was the father
of Meribbaal,[n] who was the father of
Micah. 41 Micah had four sons: Pithon,
Melech, Tarea, and Ahaz.[a] 42 Ahaz was
the father of Jarah, who was the father of
three sons: Alemeth, Azmaveth, and
Zimri. Zimri was the father of Moza,
43 Moza the father of Binea, Binea of
Rephaiah, Rephaiah of Eleasah, and
Eleasah of Azel.
44 Azel had six sons: Azrikam,
Bocheru, Ishmael, Sheariah, Obadiah,
and Hanan.

The Death of King Saul
(1 Sam 31.1–13)

10 The Philistines fought a battle
against the Israelites on Mount
Gilboa. Many Israelites were killed
there, and the rest of them, including
King Saul and his sons, **fled**. 2 But the
Philistines caught up with them and
killed three of Saul's sons, Jonathan,
Abinadab, and Malchishua. 3 The fighting
was heavy round Saul, and he was hit by
enemy arrows and **badly** wounded. 4 He
said to the young man carrying his
weapons, "Draw your sword and kill me,
to **keep these godless Philistines from**
gloating over me." But the young man
was too **terrified** to do it. So Saul took his
own sword and threw himself on it. 5 The
young man saw that Saul was **dead**, so he
too threw himself on his sword and died.
6 So Saul and his three sons all died together and none of his descendants ever
ruled. 7 When the Israelites who lived in
the Valley of Jezreel heard that the army
had **fled** and that Saul and his sons had
died, they **abandoned** their towns and
ran off. Then the Philistines came and
occupied them.
8 The day after the battle, the Philistines went to plunder the corpses, and
they found the **bodies** of Saul and his sons
lying on Mount Gilboa. 9 They cut off
Saul's head, **stripped** off his armour, and
sent messengers with them throughout
Philistia to tell the **good news** to their
idols and to their people. 10 They put his
weapons in one of their **temples** and
hung his head in the **temple** of their **god**
Dagon. 11 When the people of Jabesh in
Gilead heard what the Philistines had
done to Saul, 12 the bravest men went and
fetched the **bodies** of Saul and his sons
and took them to Jabesh. They buried
them there under an oak and **fasted** for
seven days.
13 Saul died because he was **unfaithful**
to the LORD. He **disobeyed** the LORD's
commands; he tried to find **guidance** by
consulting the **spirits** of the **dead**
14 instead of **consulting** the LORD. So the
LORD killed him and gave **control** of the
kingdom to David son of Jesse.

David Becomes King of Israel and Judah
(2 Sam 5.1–10)

11 All the people of Israel went to
David at Hebron and said to him,
"We are your own **flesh and blood**. 2 In
the past, even when Saul was still our
king, you led the people of Israel in
battle, and the LORD your God **promised**
you that you would lead **his people** and
be their ruler." 3 So all the leaders of
Israel came to King David at Hebron. He
made a **sacred** alliance with them, they
anointed him, and he became king of
Israel, just as the LORD had **promised**
through Samuel.
4 King David and all the Israelites
went and attacked the city of Jerusalem.
It was then known as Jebus, and the
Jebusites, the original inhabitants of the
land, were still living there. 5 The
Jebusites told David he would never get

[z] SACRED BREAD: *Twelve loaves of bread which were placed on a table in the Temple each Sabbath as an offering to God (see Lev 24.5–9).*
[m] ESHBAAL: *Called Ishbosheth in 2 Sam 2.8 and elsewhere in 2 Sam.*
[n] MERIBBAAL: *Called Mephibosheth in 2 Sam 4.4 and elsewhere in 2 Sam.*
[a] *Some ancient translations* Ahaz *(see 1 Chr 8.35); Hebrew does not have this name.*

10.13: Lev 19.31, 20.6; 1 Sam 13.8–14, 15.1–24, 28.7–8 **11.4:** Josh 15.63; Judg 1.21

abandon 2 Kgs 21.14; 28.9
bad 2 Kgs 25.3; 2 Chr 18.7
body [2] 2 Kgs 23.30; 2 Chr 16.14
command 2 Kgs 25.19; 12.3
consult [2] 2 Kgs 22.13; 13.1
control 7.29; 12.18
dead [2] 2 Kgs 19.35; 2 Chr 20.24
disobey 2 Kgs 21.22; 2 Chr 7.19
enemy 5.21; 12.17
fast (2) 1 Kgs 21.9; 2 Chr 20.3
flee [2] 2 Kgs 25.4; 14.12
god (2) (other gods) 5.25; 16.25
godless 2 Sam 23.6; Job 8.13
Good News 2 Kgs 7.9; 16.23
guide 2 Sam 6.3; 13.7
idol 2 Kgs 23.13; 14.12
keep from 4.10; Ezra 4.4
spirit (2) 2 Kgs 5.26; 2 Chr 18.20
strip (1) 2 Kgs 18.16; Ps 29.9
temple (2) (of other gods) [2] 2 Kgs 19.37; 2 Chr 23.17
terrify 2 Kgs 22.19; 2 Chr 14.14
unfaithful 5.25; 2 Chr 21.13
Almighty 2 Kgs 20.16; 17.7
anoint 2 Kgs 23.30; 29.22
blood [2] 2 Kgs 25.14; 22.8
flesh 2 Kgs 5.14; Ps 50.13
force (1) 8.6; 2 Chr 8.7
God's people 2 Kgs 21.2; 14.2
help 5.20; 12.17
leading [2] 5.12; 12.23
life (1) 2 Kgs 25.29; 29.15
offer 9.31; 16.1
promise [3] 2 Kgs 23.3; 12.23
refuse (1) 2 Kgs 18.7; 2 Chr 24.19
restore 2 Kgs 14.28; 2 Chr 11.1
sacred 9.29; 22.19
strong [2] 5.2; 17.11
victory 5.20; 14.10
wish 2 Kgs 5.3; 21.23

inside the city, but David captured their
fortress of Zion, and it became known as
"David's City." 6 David said, "The first
man to kill a Jebusite will be commander
of the army!" Joab, whose mother was
Zeruiah, led the attack and became commander. 7 Because David went to live in
the fortress, it came to be called "David's
City." 8 He rebuilt the city, starting at the
place where land was filled in on the east
side of the hill, and Joab **restored** the rest
of the city. 9 David grew **stronger and
stronger**, because the LORD **Almighty**
was with him.

David's Famous Soldiers
(2 Sam 23.8–39)

10 This is the list of David's famous
soldiers. Together with the rest of the
people of Israel, they **helped** him to
become king, as the LORD had **promised**,
and they kept his kingdom **strong**.

11 First was Jashobeam of the clan of
Hachmon, the leader of "The Three."[b]
He fought with his spear against three
hundred men and killed them all in one
battle. 12 Next among the famous "Three"
was Eleazar son of Dodo, of the clan of
Ahoh. 13 He fought on David's side against
the Philistines at the battle of Pas
Dammim. He was in a barley-field when
the Israelites started to run away, 14 so he
and his men made a stand in the middle
of the field and fought the Philistines.
The LORD gave him a great **victory**.

15 One day three of the thirty **leading**
soldiers went to a rock where David was
staying near the cave of Adullam, while a
band of Philistines was camping in the
Valley of Rephaim. 16 At that time David
was on a fortified hill, and a group of
Philistines had occupied Bethlehem.
17 David got homesick and said, "How I
wish someone would bring me a drink of
water from the well by the gate in
Bethlehem!" 18 The three famous
soldiers **forced** their way through the
Philistine camp, drew some water from
the well, and brought it back to David.
But he would not drink it; instead he
poured it out as an **offering** to the LORD
19 and said, "I could never drink this! It
would be like drinking the **blood** of these
men who risked their **lives**!" So he
refused to drink it. These were the brave
deeds of the three famous soldiers.

20 Joab's brother Abishai was the
leader of "The Famous Thirty."[c] He
fought with his spear against three hundred men and killed them, and became
famous among "The Thirty."[d] 21 He was
the most famous of "The Thirty"[e] and
became their leader, but he was not as
famous as "The Three."

22 Benaiah son of Jehoiada from
Kabzeel was a famous soldier; he did
many brave deeds, including killing two
great Moabite warriors. He once went
down into a pit on a snowy day and killed
a lion. 23 He also killed an Egyptian, a
huge man over two metres tall, who was
armed with a gigantic spear. Benaiah
attacked him with a club, snatched the
spear from the Egyptian's hand, and
killed him with it. 24 Those were the
brave deeds of Benaiah, who was one of
"The Thirty."[f] 25 He was outstanding
among "The Thirty," but not as famous
as "The Three." David put him in charge
of his bodyguard.

26–47 These are the other outstanding
soldiers:

Asahel, Joab's brother
Elhanan son of Dodo from Bethlehem
Shammoth from Harod
Helez from Pelet
Ira son of Ikkesh from Tekoa
Abiezer from Anathoth
Sibbecai from Hushah
Ilai from Ahoh
Maharai from Netophah
Heled son of Baanah from Netophah
Ithai son of Ribai from Gibeah in Benjamin
Benaiah from Pirathon
Hurai from the valleys near Gaash
Abiel from Arbah
Azmaveth from Bahurum
Eliahba from Shaalbon
Hashem[g] from Gizon
Jonathan son of Shagee from Harar
Ahiam son of Sachar from Harar
Eliphal son of Ur
Hepher from Mecherah
Ahijah from Pelon
Hezro from Carmel
Naarai son of Ezbai
Joel brother of Nathan
Mibhar son of Hagri
Zelek from Ammon
Naharai, Joab's armour-bearer, from Beeroth
Ira and Gareb from Jattir
Uriah the Hittite
Zabad son of Ahlai

[b] *One ancient translation (see also 2 Sam 23.8)* "The Three"; *Hebrew* "The Thirty".
[c] *One ancient translation* Thirty; *Hebrew* Three.
[d] *One ancient translation (see also 2 Sam 23.18)* "The Thirty"; *Hebrew* "The Three".
[e] *Probable text (see 2 Sam 23.19)* most famous of "The Thirty"; *Hebrew unclear.*
[f] *Probable text* "The Thirty"; *Hebrew* "The Three".
[g] *Probable text* Hashem; *Hebrew* the sons of Hashem.

Adina son of Shiza (a **leading** member
of the tribe of Reuben, with his
own group of thirty soldiers)
Hanan son of Maacah
Joshaphat from Mithan
Uzzia from Ashterah
Shamma and Jeiel, sons of Hotham,
from Aroer
Jediael and Joha, sons of Shimri, from
Tiz
Eliel from Mahavah
Jeribai and Joshaviah, sons of Elnaam
Ithmah from Moab
Eliel, Obed, and Jaasiel from Zobah[h]

David's Early Followers from the Tribe of Benjamin

12 David was living in Ziklag,
where he had gone to **escape**
from King Saul. There he was joined by
many **experienced**, **reliable** soldiers,
2 members of the tribe of Benjamin, to
which Saul belonged. They could shoot
arrows and sling stones either **right-**
handed or left-handed. 3-7 They were
under the **command** of Ahiezer and
Joash, sons of Shemaah, from Gibeah.

These were the soldiers:
Jeziel and Pelet, sons of Azmaveth
Beracah and Jehu from Anathoth
Ishmaiah from Gibeon, a famous
soldier and one of the leaders of
"The Thirty"
Jeremiah, Jahaziel, Johannan, and
Jozabad, from Gederah
Eluzai, Jerimoth, Bealiah, Shemariah,
and Shephatiah, from Hariph
Elkanah, Isshiah, Azarel, Joezer, and
Jashobeam, of the clan of Korah
Joelah and Zebadiah, sons of Jeroham,
from Gedor

David's Followers from the Tribe of Gad

8 These are the names of the famous,
experienced soldiers from the tribe of
Gad who joined David's troops when he
was at the desert fort. They were experts
with shields and spears, as fierce-looking
as lions and as quick as mountain deer.
9-13 They were ranked in the following
order: Ezer, Obadiah, Eliab, Mish-
mannah, Jeremiah, Attai, Eliel, Johanan,
Elzabad, Jeremiah, and Machbannai.

14 Some of these men from the tribe
of Gad were senior officers in **command**
of a thousand men, and others were
junior officers in **command** of a hundred.
15 In the first month of one year, the time
when the River Jordan overflowed its
banks, they crossed the river, **scattering**
the people who lived in the valleys both
east and west of the river.

Followers from Benjamin and Judah

16 Once a group of men from the
tribes of Benjamin and Judah went out to
the fort where David was. 17 David went
to meet them and said, "If you are
coming as **friends** to **help** me, you are
welcome here. Join us! But if you **intend**
to **betray** me to my **enemies**, even though
I have not tried to **hurt** you, the God of
our ancestors will know it and **punish**
you."

18 **God's spirit** took **control** of one of
them, Amasai, who later became the
commander of "The Thirty," and he
called out,

"David son of Jesse, we are yours!
Success to you and those who **help**
you!
God is on your side."

David **welcomed** them and made them
officers in his army.

Followers from Manasseh

19 Some soldiers from the tribe of
Manasseh went over to David's side
when he was marching out with the
Philistines to fight King Saul. Actually he
did not **help** the Philistines, for their
kings were **afraid** that he would **betray**
them to his former **master** Saul, so they
sent him back to Ziklag. 20 These are the
soldiers from Manasseh who went over
to David's side when he was returning:
Adnah, Jozabad, Jediael, Michael, Jozabad, Elihu, and Zillethai. In Manasseh
they had all **commanded** units of a
thousand men. 21 They **served** David as
officers over his troops,[i] because they
were all outstanding soldiers. Later they
were officers in the Israelite army.
22 Almost every day **new** men joined
David's forces, so that his army was soon
enormous.

List of David's Forces

23-37 When David was at Hebron,
many trained soldiers joined his army to
help make him king in place of Saul, as
the LORD had **promised**. Their numbers
were as follows:

Judah: 6,800 well-equipped men,
armed with shields and spears;
Simeon: 7,100 well-trained men;
Levi: 4,600 men;
Followers of Jehoiada, descendant of
Aaron: 3,700 men;
Relatives of Zadok, an able young
fighter: 22 **leading** men;

[h] *Probable text* from Zobah; *Hebrew unclear.*
[i] They served David...troops; *or* They helped David fight against the bands of raiders.

afraid 2 Kgs 25.24; 13.12
best 2 Kgs 10.3; 19.10
betray [2] 2 Sam 19.26; Job 17.5
choose 9.22; 15.2
command [5] 10.13; 13.1
control 10.14; 18.1
determine 2 Kgs 19.31; 22.13
enemy 10.3; 14.11
escape 2 Kgs 25.4; 29.15
experience [2] 1 Kgs 9.27; 29.1
feast 2 Kgs 6.23; 2 Chr 9.4
follower 2 Sam 16.21; 2 Chr 24.7
friend 2 Kgs 10.11; 19.2
help [4] 11.10; 15.26
hurt 2 Kgs 4.19; 2 Chr 35.23
intend 1 Kgs 12.21; 2 Chr 2.5
joy 2 Kgs 11.14; 15.16
leading 11.15; 28.1
loyal [2] 2 Kgs 20.3; 19.2
master 2 Kgs 9.7; 2 Chr 2.13
new 2 Kgs 22.14; 13.7
promise 11.2; 16.16
punish 9.1; 13.11
purpose 2 Kgs 14.27; 17.19
rely [2] 2 Kgs 18.21; 2 Chr 13.18
right (2) 2 Kgs 12.9; Neh 8.4
scatter 2 Kgs 23.6; 2 Chr 18.16
serve 6.10; 15.2
sheep 5.21; 15.26
Spirit (1) (God's Spirit) 2 Kgs 2.16; 2 Chr 15.1
succeed (1) 2 Kgs 18.7; 22.11
unite Judg 21.15; 2 Chr 30.12
welcome [2] 2 Kgs 20.13; Job 2.10

Benjamin (Saul's own tribe): 3,000 men (most of the people of Benjamin had remained **loyal** to Saul);

Ephraim: 20,800 men famous in their own clans;

West Manasseh: 18,000 men **chosen** to go and make David king;

Issachar: 200 leaders, together with the men under their **command** (these leaders knew what Israel should do and the **best** time to do it);

Zebulun: 50,000 **loyal** and **reliable** men ready to fight, trained to use all kinds of weapons;

Naphtali: 1,000 leaders, together with 37,000 men armed with shields and spears;

Dan: 28,600 trained men;

Asher: 40,000 men ready for battle;

Tribes east of the Jordan—Reuben, Gad, and East Manasseh: 120,000 men trained to use all kinds of weapons.

38 All these soldiers, ready for battle,
went to Hebron, **determined** to make
David king over all Israel. All the rest of
the people of Israel were **united** in the
same **purpose**. 39 They spent three days
there with David, **feasting** on the food
and drink which their fellow-countrymen
had prepared for them. 40 From as far
away as the northern tribes of Issachar,
Zebulun, and Naphtali, people came
bringing donkeys, camels, mules, and
oxen loaded with food—flour, figs,
raisins, wine, and olive-oil. They also
brought cattle and **sheep** to kill and eat.
All this was an expression of the **joy** that
was felt throughout the whole country.

The Covenant Box Is Moved from Kiriath Jearim
(2 Sam 6.1–11)

13 King David **consulted** with all the
officers in **command** of units of a
thousand men and units of a hundred
men. 2 Then he **announced** to all the
people of Israel, "If you give your
approval and if it is the **will of the LORD**
our God, let us send messengers to the
rest of our countrymen and to the **priests
and Levites** in their towns, and tell them
to assemble here with us. 3 Then we will
go and fetch God's **Covenant Box**, which
was **ignored** while Saul was king." 4 The
people were **pleased** with the suggestion
and **agreed** to it.
5 So David assembled the people of
Israel from all over the country, from the
Egyptian border in the south to Hamath
Pass in the north, in order to bring the
Covenant Box from Kiriath Jearim to
Jerusalem. 6 David and the people went
to the city of Baalah, that is, to Kiriath
Jearim, in the territory of Judah, to fetch
the **Covenant Box** of God, which bears
the **name of the LORD enthroned** above
the winged **creatures**. 7 At Abinadab's
house they brought out the **Covenant Box**
and put it on a **new** cart. Uzzah and Ahio
guided the cart, 8 while David and all the
people danced with all their **might** to
honour God. They sang and played
musical instruments—harps, drums,
cymbals, and trumpets.
9 As they came to the threshing-place
of Chidon, the oxen **stumbled**, and Uzzah
stretched out his hand and took hold of
the **Covenant Box**. 10 At once the LORD
became **angry** with Uzzah and killed him
for touching the **box**. He died there in
God's **presence**, 11 and so that place has
been called Perez Uzzah[j] ever since.
David was **furious** because the LORD had
punished Uzzah in **anger**.
12 Then David was **afraid** of God and
said, "How can I take the **Covenant Box**
with me now?" 13 So David did not take it
with him to Jerusalem. Instead, he left it
at the house of a man named Obed
Edom, a native of the city of Gath. 14 It
stayed there three months, and the LORD
blessed Obed Edom's family and everything that belonged to him.

David's Activities in Jerusalem
(2 Sam 5.11–16)

14 King Hiram of Tyre sent a trade
mission to David; he **provided**
him with cedar logs and with stone-
masons and carpenters to build a palace.
2 And so David realized that the LORD
had **established** him as king of Israel and
was making his kingdom **prosperous** for
the **sake of his people**.
3 There in Jerusalem, David married
more wives and had more sons and
daughters. 4 The following children were
born to him in Jerusalem: Shammua,
Shobab, Nathan, Solomon, 5 Ibhar,
Elishua, Elpelet, 6 Nogah, Nepheg,
Japhia, 7 Elishama, Beeliada,[x] and
Eliphelet.

Victory over the Philistines
(2 Sam 5.17–25)

8 When the Philistines heard that
David had now been made king over the
whole country of Israel, their army went
out to capture him. So David marched
out to meet them. 9 The Philistines

[j] PEREZ UZZAH: *This name in Hebrew means "Punishment of Uzzah."*
[x] BEELIADA: *Called Eliada in 3.8.*

13.5: 1 Sam 7.1–2 **13.6:** Ex 25.22 **13.14:** 1 Chr 26.4–5

ignore 1 Kgs 12.8; 2 Chr 10.8
Levites 9.2; 15.2
might 2 Kgs 18.20; 16.24
name (2) (name o[f] God, of Jesus) 2 Kgs 2.24; 16.2
new 12.22; 2 Chr 2[…]
please 2 Kgs 22.2; 29.17
presence 2 Kgs 19.14; 28.8
priest 9.2; 15.11
punish 12.17; 15.13
stumble 2 Sam 6.6; Job 4.4
throne 2 Kgs 19.15; 29.23
will (1) 5.22; 17.19

afraid 12.19; 14.17
agree 2 Kgs 12.8; 2 Chr 15.12
anger [2] 2 Kgs 24.20; 2 Chr 6.36
announce 2 Kgs 7.11; 29.1
approve 2 Kgs 17.9; 21.6
bless 4.10; 16.2
box *see* **Covenant Box**
command 12.3; 14.16
consult 10.13; 14.14
Covenant Box [7] 6.31; 15.1
creature 2 Kgs 19.15; 16.32
fury 1 Kgs 19.11; Neh 4.1
guide 10.13; 2 Chr 20.3
honour 2 Kgs 25.28; 16.25

afraid 13.12; 21.30
command 13.1; 15
consult 13.1; 2 Chr 9.23
enemy 12.17; 17.8
establish 1 Kgs 2.[…] 24.19
flee 10.1; 19.14
flood 2 Sam 5.20; Job 11.16
God's people 11.2; 16.19
idol 10.9; 16.26
prosper 1 Kgs 2.3; 2 Chr 7.14
provide 7.4; 23.5
sake 2 Kgs 20.6; Ps 69.7
victory [2] 11.14; 1[…]

arrived at the Valley of Rephaim and
began plundering. 10 David asked God,
"Shall I attack the Philistines? Will you
give me the **victory**?"
The LORD answered, "Yes, attack! I
will give you the **victory**!"
11 So David attacked them at Baal
Perazim and defeated them. He said,
"God has used me to break through the
enemy army like a **flood**." So that place
is called Baal Perazim.[k] 12 When the
Philistines **fled**, they left their **idols**
behind, and David gave orders for them
to be burnt.
13 Soon the Philistines returned to the
valley and started plundering it again.
14 Once more David **consulted** God, who
answered, "Don't attack them from here,
but go round and get ready to attack
them from the other side, near the
balsam-trees. 15 When you hear the sound
of marching in the tree-tops, then attack,
because I will be marching ahead of you
to defeat the Philistine army." 16 David
did what God had **commanded**, and so he
drove the Philistines back from Gibeon
all the way to Gezer. 17 David's fame
spread everywhere, and the LORD made
every nation **afraid** of him.

Getting Ready to Move the Covenant Box

15 For his own use, David built
houses in David's City.[l] He also
prepared a place for God's **Covenant Box**
and put up a **tent** for it. 2 Then he said,
"Only **Levites** should carry the **Covenant
Box**, because they are the ones the LORD
chose to carry it and to **serve** him for
ever." 3 So David summoned all the
people of Israel to Jerusalem in order to
bring the **Covenant Box** to the place he
had prepared for it. 4 Next he sent for the
descendants of Aaron and for the
Levites. 5 From the **Levite** clan of Kohath
came Uriel, in charge of 120 members of
his clan; 6 from the clan of Merari came
Asaiah, in charge of 220; 7 from the clan
of Gershon, Joel, in charge of 130; 8 from
the clan of Elizaphan, Shemaiah, in
charge of 200; 9 from the clan of Hebron,
Eliel, in charge of 80; 10 and from the
clan of Uzziel, Amminadab, in charge of
112.
11 David called in the **priests** Zadok
and Abiathar and the six **Levites**, Uriel,
Asaiah, Joel, Shemaiah, Eliel, and
Amminadab. 12 He said to the **Levites**,
"You are the leaders of the **Levite** clans.
Purify yourselves and your **fellow-
Levites**, so that you can bring the **Covenant Box** of the LORD God of Israel to the
place I have prepared for it. 13 Because
you were not there to carry it the first
time, the LORD our God **punished** us for
not **worshipping** him as we should have
done."
14 Then the **priests and the Levites**
purified themselves in order to move the
Covenant Box of the LORD God of Israel.
15 The **Levites** carried it on poles on their
shoulders, as the LORD had **commanded**
through Moses.
16 David **commanded** the leaders of
the **Levites** to assign various Levites to
sing and to play **joyful** music on harps
and cymbals. 17-21 From the clans of
singers they **chose** the following men to
play the brass cymbals: Heman son of
Joel, his relative Asaph son of Berechiah,
and Ethan son of Kushaiah, of the clan of
Merari. To assist them they **chose** the
following **Levites** to play the high-pitched
harps: Zechariah, Jaaziel, Shemiramoth,
Jehiel, Unni, Eliab, Maaseiah, and
Benaiah.
To play the low-pitched harps they
chose the following **Levites**: Mattithiah,
Eliphelehu, Mikneiah, Azaziah, and the
temple guards, Obed Edom and Jeiel.
22 Because of his skill in music
Chenaniah was **chosen** to be in charge of
the **levitical** musicians. 23-24 Berechiah
and Elkanah, along with Obed Edom and
Jehiah, were **chosen** as guards for the
Covenant Box. The **priests** Shebaniah,
Joshaphat, Nethanel, Amasai, Zechariah,
Benaiah, and Eliezer were **chosen** to
blow trumpets in front of the **Covenant
Box**.

Moving the Covenant Box to Jerusalem
(2 Sam 6.12-22)

25 So King David, the leaders of Israel,
and the military commanders went to
the house of Obed Edom to fetch the
Covenant Box, and they had a great **celebration**. 26 They **sacrificed** seven bulls
and seven **sheep**, to make **sure** that God
would **help** the **Levites** who were carrying the **Covenant Box**. 27 David was
wearing a robe made of the finest linen,
and so were the musicians, Chenaniah
their leader, and the **Levites** who carried
the **Box**. David also wore a linen **ephod**.
28 So all the Israelites accompanied the
Covenant Box up to Jerusalem with
shouts of **joy**, the sound of trumpets,

box *see* **Covenant Box**
celebrate 2 Kgs 23.21; 2 Chr 7.8
choose [7] 12.23; 16.12
command [2] 14.16; 16.14
Covenant Box [12] 13.3; 16.1
disgust 2 Kgs 23.13; 2 Chr 28.3
ephod (1) 1 Sam 30.7
help 12.17; 16.11
joy [3] 12.40; 16.27
Levites [15] 13.2; 16.4
priest [3] 13.2; 16.6
punish 13.11; 21.7
pure [2] 2 Kgs 2.21; 28.17
sacrifice 6.49; 16.1
serve 12.21; 22.19
sheep 12.40; 17.7
sure 2 Kgs 10.23; 17.12
Tent (2) (of the Lord's presence) 9.19; 16.1
worship (1) (of God) 9.28; 16.4

[k] BAAL PERAZIM: *This name in Hebrew means "Lord of the Break-through."*
[l] DAVID'S CITY: That part of Jerusalem which David had captured from the original inhabitants, the Jebusites *(see 2 Sam 5.6-10)*.

15.2: Deut 10.8 **15.15:** Ex 25.14

horns, and cymbals, and the music of
harps.
29 As the Box was being brought into
the city, Michal, Saul's daughter, looked
out of the window and saw King David
dancing and leaping for **joy**, and she was
disgusted with him.

16 They took the **Covenant Box** to
the **tent** which David had prepared for it and put it inside. Then they
offered sacrifices and **fellowship-offerings** to God.
2 After David had
finished **offering the sacrifices**, he
blessed the people in the **name of the**
LORD 3 and distributed food to them all.
He gave each man and woman in Israel
a loaf of **bread**, a piece of roasted meat,[m]
and some raisins.
4 David appointed some of the **Levites**
to lead the **worship** of the LORD, the God
of Israel, in front of the **Covenant Box**, by
singing and **praising** him. 5 Asaph was
appointed leader, with Zechariah as his
assistant. Jeiel, Shemiramoth, Jehiel,
Mattithiah, Eliab, Benaiah, Obed Edom,
and Jeiel were to play harps. Asaph was
to sound the cymbals, 6 and two **priests**,
Benaiah and Jahaziel, were to blow trumpets regularly in front of the **Covenant**
Box. 7 It was then that David first gave
Asaph and his **fellow-Levites** the
responsibility for singing **praises** to the
LORD.

A Song of Praise
(Ps 105.1–15; 96.1–13; 106.1,47–48)

8 Give **thanks** to the LORD, **proclaim** his
greatness;
tell the nations what he has done.
9 Sing **praise** to the LORD;
tell the **wonderful** things he has
done.
10 Be **glad** that we belong to him;
let all who **worship** him **rejoice**!
11 Go to the LORD for **help**,
and **worship** him continually.
12–13 You descendants of Jacob, God's
servant,
descendants of Israel, whom God
chose,
remember the **miracles** that God
performed
and the **judgements** that he gave.
14 The LORD is our God;
his **commands** are for all the **world**.
15 Never **forget** God's **covenant**,
which he made to **last for ever**,
16 the **covenant** he made with Abraham,
the **promise** he made to Isaac.
17 The LORD made a **covenant** with
Jacob,
one that will **last** for ever.
18 "I will give you the land of Canaan," he
said.
"It will be your own **possession**."
19 **God's people** were few in number,
strangers in the land of Canaan.
20 They wandered from country to
country,
from one kingdom to another.
21 But God let no one **oppress** them;
to **protect** them, he **warned** the
kings:
22 "Don't **harm** my **chosen servants**;
do not touch my **prophets**."
23 Sing to the LORD, all the **world**!
Proclaim every day the **good news**
that he has **saved** us.
24 **Proclaim** his **glory** to the nations,
his **mighty** deeds to all peoples.
25 The LORD is great and is to be highly
praised;
he is to be **honoured** more than all
the **gods**.
26 The **gods** of all other nations are only
idols,
but the LORD **created** the **heavens**.
27 Glory and **majesty** surround him,
power and **joy** fill his **Temple**.

28 **Praise** the LORD, all people on earth,
praise his **glory** and **might**.
29 **Praise** the LORD's **glorious name**;
bring an **offering** and come into his
Temple.
Bow down before the **Holy One** when
he appears;[n]
30 **tremble** before him, all the earth!
The earth is set firmly in place and
cannot be moved.
31 Be **glad**, earth and sky!
Tell the nations that the LORD is
king.
32 Roar, sea, and every **creature** in you;
be **glad**, fields, and everything in
you!
33 The trees in the woods will shout for
joy
when the LORD comes to rule the
earth.

34 Give **thanks** to the LORD, because he is
good;
his **love** is **eternal**.
35 Say to him, "**Save** us, O God our
Saviour;

[m] a piece of roasted meat; *or* a cake of dates. [n] when he appears; *or* in garments of worship.

16.16: Gen 12.7, 26.3 **16.17–18:** Gen 28.13 **16.21–22:** Gen 20.3–7
16.34: 2 Chr 5.13, 7.3; Ezra 3.11; Ps 100.5, 106.1, 107.1, 118.1, 136.1; Jer 33.11

altar 6.49; 21.18
bless 13.14; 17.27
bow (2) 2 Kgs 17.35; 21.16
bread 9.32; 23.29
choose [3] 15.2; 17.9
command 15.15; 19.11
covenant [3] 2 Kgs 23.2; 2 Chr 5.10
Covenant Box [4] 15.1; 17.1
create 2 Kgs 19.15; Neh 4.8
creature 13.6; 28.18
duty (1) 9.25; 23.5
eternal [2] 1 Kgs 10.9; 2 Chr 5.11
fellowship-offering 2 Kgs 16.13; 21.26
forget 2 Kgs 17.38; 2 Chr 24.22
glad [3] 2 Sam 1.20; Job 22.19
glory [4] 1 Sam 4.21; 23.30
god (2) (other gods) [2] 10.10; 2 Chr 2.5
God's people 14.2; 17.7
Good News 10.9; Ps 40.9
harm 2 Sam 18.5; 2 Chr 30.20
heaven 2 Kgs 2.1; 21.26
help 15.26; 18.5
holy [2] 2 Kgs 19.22; 28.10
honour 13.8; 17.18
idol 14.12; 20.2
joy [2] 15.16; 2 Chr 23.13
judge 2 Kgs 23.22; 2 Chr 6.23
last (1) [2] 2 Kgs 8.1; 28.7
law 2 Kgs 23.3; 22.12
Levites [3] 15.2; 23.2
love [2] 1 Kgs 11.1; 29.3
Majesty 2 Kgs 8.5; 21.3
might [2] 13.8; 2 Chr 20.6
miracle 2 Kgs 8.4; Neh 9.10
name (2) (name of God, of Jesus) [3] 13.6; 23.13
offer [3] 11.18; 21.23
oppress 2 Kgs 13.4; 17.9
place of worship 6.31; 21.29
possess 2 Kgs 17.24; 28.8
power 2 Kgs 19.25; 25.5
praise [12] 1 Kgs 10.9; 23.5
priest [2] 15.11; 18.16
proclaim [3] 2 Kgs 11.12; 25.1
promise 12.23; 17.9
prophet 9.22; 17.1
protect 2 Kgs 19.34; 2 Chr 7.16

rejoice 2 Sam 1.20; Ps 5.11
remember 2 Kgs 20.3; 2 Chr 6.4
rescue 2 Kgs 20.6; 17.5
sacrifice [3] 15.26; 21.26
save [2] 2 Kgs 19.6; 2 Chr 22.11
Saviour 2 Sam 22.3; Ps 27.9
servant [2] 6.49; 17.
stranger Gen 15.13 29.15
Temple (1) (of God [2] 9.2; 17.4
Tent (2) (of the Lord's presence) 15.1; 17.1
thank [3] 1 Sam 25.33; 25.3
tremble 2 Sam 22.8 Ezra 10.9
warn 2 Kgs 18.29; 2 Chr 20.37
wonder (1) 2 Sam 7.23; 17.21
world [2] 1.10; 17.8
worship (1) (of God [5] 15.13; 18.11

gather us together; **rescue** us from
the nations,
so that we may be **thankful**
and **praise** your **holy name**."
36 **Praise** the LORD, the God of Israel!
Praise him now and for ever!

Then all the people said, "Amen," and
praised the LORD.

Worship at Jerusalem and Gibeon

37 King David put Asaph and his
fellow-Levites in permanent charge of
the **worship** that was held at the place
where the **Covenant Box** was kept. They
were to perform their **duties** there day
by day. 38 Obed Edom son of Jeduthun
and sixty-eight men of his clan were to
assist them. Hosah and Obed Edom were
in charge of guarding the gates.
39 Zadok the **priest** and his fellow-
priests, however, were in charge of the
worship of the LORD at the **place of worship** in Gibeon. 40 Every morning and
evening they were to burn **sacrifices**
whole on the **altar** in accordance with
what was written in the **Law** which the
LORD gave to Israel. 41 There with them
were Heman and Jeduthun and the
others who were specifically **chosen** to
sing **praises** to the LORD for his **eternal
love**. 42 Heman and Jeduthun also had
charge of the trumpets and cymbals and
the other instruments which were played
when the songs of **praise** were sung. The
members of Jeduthun's clan were in
charge of guarding the gates.
43 Then everyone went home, and
David went home to spend some time
with his family.

Nathan's Message to David
(2 Sam 7.1–17)

17 King David was now living in his
palace. One day he sent for the
prophet Nathan and said to him, "Here I
am living in a house built of cedar, but
the LORD's **Covenant Box** is kept in a
tent!"
2 Nathan answered, "Do whatever you
have in **mind**, because God is with you."
3 But that night God said to Nathan,
4 "Go and tell my **servant** David that I say
to him, 'You are not the one to build a
temple for me to live in. 5 From the time
I **rescued** the people of Israel from Egypt
until now, I have never lived in a **temple**;
I have always lived in tents and moved
from place to place. 6 In all my travelling
with the people of Israel I never asked
any of the leaders that I appointed why
they had not built me a **temple** made of
cedar.'
7 "So tell my **servant** David that I, the
LORD **Almighty**, say to him, 'I took you
from looking after **sheep** in the fields and
made you the ruler of **my people** Israel.
8 I have been with you wherever you
have gone, and I have defeated all your
enemies as you advanced. I will make
you as famous as the greatest leaders in
the **world**. 9-10 I have **chosen** a place for
my people Israel and have settled them
there, where they will live without being
oppressed any more. Ever since they
entered this land they have been
attacked by **violent** people, but this will
not happen again. I **promise** to defeat all
your **enemies** and to give you descendants. 11 When you die and are buried with
your ancestors, I will make one of your
sons king and will keep his kingdom
strong. 12 He will be the one to build a
temple for me, and I will make **sure** that
his dynasty continues for ever. 13 I will be
his father and he will be my son. I will
not withdraw my support from him as I
did from Saul, whom I removed so that
you could be king. 14 I will put him in
charge of **my people** and my kingdom for
ever. His dynasty will never end.' "
15 Nathan told David everything that
God had **revealed** to him.

David's Prayer of Thanksgiving
(2 Sam 7.18–29)

16 Then King David went into the
Tent of the LORD's presence, sat down,
and **prayed**, "I am not **worthy** of what
you have already done for me, LORD
God, nor is my family. 17 Yet now you are
doing even more; you have made
promises about my descendants in the
years to come, and you, LORD God, are
already treating me like a great man.[o]
18 What more can I say to you! You know
me well, and yet you **honour** me, your
servant. 19 It was your **will** and **purpose** to
do this for me and to show me my future
greatness. 20 LORD, there is none like you;
we have always known that you **alone**
are God. 21 There is no other nation on
earth like Israel, whom you **rescued** from
slavery to make them your **own people**.
The great and **wonderful** things you did
for them spread your fame throughout
the **world**. You **rescued** your people from
Egypt and drove out other nations as
your people advanced. 22 You have made
Israel your **own people** for ever, and you,
LORD, have become their God.
23 "And now, O LORD, **fulfil** for all time

Almighty [2] 11.9; Job 6.4
alone 2 Kgs 19.15; 2 Chr 6.30
bless [2] 16.2; 23.13
choose 16.12; 19.10
courage 2 Sam 22.46; 19.13
Covenant Box 16.1; 22.19
enemy [2] 14.11; 19.6
enjoy 2 Sam 7.29; 2 Chr 14.1
favour 1 Kgs 16.21; 2 Chr 11.22
fulfil 2 Kgs 15.12; 2 Chr 1.9
God's people [5] 16.19; 23.25
honour 16.25; 19.3
mind (1) 2 Kgs 23.25; 21.15
oppress 16.21; 2 Chr 15.6
pray [2] 5.20; 21.17
prayer 5.20; 21.28

preserve 2 Sam 7.26; 2 Chr 9.8
promise [4] 16.16; 22.9
prophet 16.22; 21.9
purpose 12.38; 23.5
rescue [3] 16.35; 2 Chr 18.31
reveal [2] 2 Kgs 8.10; Job 20.27
servant [4] 16.12; 21.3
sheep 15.26; 27.25
slave 2 Kgs 4.1; 2 Chr 8.7
strong 11.9; 19.13
sure 15.26; 18.14
Temple (1) (of God) [4] 16.27; 18.8
Tent (2) (of the Lord's presence) [2] 16.1; 21.29
violent 2 Sam 22.3; Job 5.22
will (1) 13.2; 19.13
wonder (1) [2] 16.9; Esth 10.2
world [2] 16.14; 2 Chr 6.33
worthy 2 Sam 7.18; Esth 2.18

[o] *Probable text* and you, LORD God...man; *Hebrew unclear.*

16.43: 2 Sam 6.19–20 **17.13:** 2 Cor 6.18; Heb 1.5

the **promise** you made about me and my
descendants, and do what you said you
would. 24 Your fame will be great, and
people will for ever say, 'The LORD
Almighty is God over Israel.' And you
will **preserve** my dynasty for all time. 25 I
have the **courage** to **pray** this **prayer** to
you, my God, because you have **revealed**
all this to me, your **servant**, and have told
me that you will make my descendants
kings. 26 You, LORD, are God, and you
have made this **wonderful promise** to
me. 27 I ask you to **bless** my descendants
so that they will continue to **enjoy** your
favour. You, LORD, have blessed them,
and your **blessing** will rest on them for
ever."

David's Military Victories
(2 Sam 8.1–18)

18 Some time later King David
attacked the Philistines again
and defeated them. He took out of their
control the city of Gath and its surrounding villages. 2 He also defeated the Moabites, who became his **subjects** and paid
taxes to him.
3 Next, David attacked King
Hadadezer of the Syrian state of Zobah,
near the territory of Hamath, because
Hadadezer was trying to gain **control** of
the territory by the upper Euphrates.
4 David captured a thousand of his
chariots, seven thousand horsemen, and
twenty thousand foot soldiers. He kept
enough horses for a hundred chariots
and **crippled** all the rest.
5 When the Syrians of Damascus sent
an army to **help** King Hadadezer, David
attacked it and killed twenty-two thousand men. 6 Then he set up military
camps in their territory, and they
became his **subjects** and paid **taxes** to
him. The LORD made David **victorious**
everywhere. 7 David captured the gold
shields carried by Hadadezer's officials
and took them to Jerusalem. 8 He also
took a great quantity of bronze from Tib-
hath and Kun, cities ruled by Hadadezer.
(Solomon later used this bronze to make
the tank, the columns, and the bronze
utensils for the **Temple**.)
9 King Toi of Hamath heard that
David had defeated Hadadezer's entire
army. 10 So he sent his son Joram to greet
King David and congratulate him for his
victory over Hadadezer, against whom
Toi had fought many times. Joram
brought David presents made of gold,
silver, and bronze. 11 King David **dedicated** them for use in **worship**, along with
the silver and gold he took from the
nations he **conquered**—Edom, Moab,
Ammon, Philistia, and Amalek.
12 Abishai, whose mother was
Zeruiah, defeated the Edomites in the
Valley of Salt and killed eighteen thousand of them. 13 He set up military camps
throughout Edom, and the people there
became King David's **subjects**. The LORD
made David **victorious** everywhere.
14 David ruled over all Israel and
made **sure** that his people were always
treated fairly and **justly**. 15 Abishai's
brother Joab was commander of the
army; Jehoshaphat son of Ahilud was in
charge of the records; 16 Zadok son of
Ahitub and Ahimelech son of Abiathar
were **priests**; Seraiah[p] was **court** secretary; 17 Benaiah son of Jehoiada was in
charge of David's bodyguard; and King
David's sons held high positions in his
service.

David Defeats the Ammonites and the Syrians
(2 Sam 10.1–19)

19 Some time later King Nahash of
Ammon died, and his son Hanun
became king. 2 King David said, "I must
show **loyal friendship** to Hanun, as his
father Nahash did to me." So David sent
messengers to express his **sympathy**.
When they arrived in Ammon and
called on King Hanun, 3 the Ammonite
leaders said to the king, "Do you think
that it is in your father's **honour** that
David has sent these men to express
sympathy to you? Of course not! He has
sent them here as spies to explore the
land, so that he can **conquer** it!"
4 Hanun seized David's messengers,
shaved off their beards, cut off their
clothes at the hips, and sent them away.
5 They were too **ashamed** to return home.
When David heard what had happened,
he sent **word** for them to stay in Jericho
and not return until their beards had
grown again.
6 King Hanun and the Ammonites
realized that they had made David their
enemy, so they paid thirty-four thousand
kilogrammes of silver to hire chariots
and charioteers from Upper Mesopotamia and from the Syrian states of
Maacah and Zobah. 7 The thirty-two thousand chariots they hired and the army of
the king of Maacah came and camped
near Medeba. The Ammonites too came
out from all their cities and got ready to
fight.
8 When David heard what was

conquer 2.23; 19.3
control [2] 12.18; 2 Chr 1.1
court (1) 2 Kgs 22.3; 2 Chr 18.8
cripple 1 Kgs 15.23; 2 Chr 16.12
dedicate 2 Kgs 23.8; 26.20
enough 2 Kgs 4.7; 21.15
help 16.11; 19.9
justice 1 Kgs 10.9; 2 Chr 9.8
priest 16.6; 23.2
service 7.4; 21.5
subject (1) [3] 1 Kgs 12.4; 19.19
sure 17.12; 2 Chr 2.18
tax [2] 2 Kgs 23.35; 2 Chr 9.14
Temple (1) (of God) 17.4; 22.1
victory [3] 14.10; 2 Chr 6.35
worship (1) (of God) 16.4; 21.30

ashamed 2 Sam 19. 2 Chr 30.15
best 12.23; 2 Chr 11
choose 17.9; 21.10
command [2] 16.14; 21.6
conquer 18.11; 22.1
courage 17.25; 2 Chr 19.11
enemy [2] 17.8; 21.1
flee [2] 14.12; 2 Chr 13.16
friend 12.17; 27.33
hard 1 Kgs 20.37; 2 Chr 24.13
help [4] 18.5; 22.17
honour 17.18; 22.7
loyal 12.23; 29.24
never again 2 Sam 21.17; Neh 13.25
peace 4.40; 22.9
shave 2 Sam 10.4; Job 1.20
strong 17.11; 29.12
subject (1) [2] 18.2; 22.18
sympathy [2] 2 Sam 10.2; Job 42.1
will (1) 17.19; 2 Chr 10.15
word (1) 2 Kgs 25.2 2 Chr 6.15

[p] *Probable text (see 2 Sam 8.17)* Seraiah; *Hebrew* Shavsha

18.8: 1 Kgs 7.40–47; 2 Chr 4.11–18 **18.12:** Ps 60 (Title)

happening, he sent out Joab and the
whole army. 9 The Ammonites marched
out and took up their position at the
entrance to Rabbah, their capital city,
and the kings who had come to **help** took
up their position in the open countryside.
10 Joab saw that the **enemy** troops
would attack him in front and from the
rear, so he **chose** the **best** of Israel's
soldiers and put them in position facing
the Syrians. 11 He placed the rest of his
troops under the **command** of his brother
Abishai, who put them in position facing
the Ammonites. 12 Joab said to him, "If
you see that the Syrians are defeating
me, come and **help** me, and if the
Ammonites are defeating you, I will go
and **help** you. 13 Be **strong** and
courageous! Let's fight **hard** for our
people and for the cities of our God. And
may the **LORD's will** be done."
14 Joab and his men advanced to
attack, and the Syrians **fled**. 15 When the
Ammonites saw the Syrians running
away, they **fled** from Abishai and retreated into the city. Then Joab went
back to Jerusalem.
16 The Syrians realized that they had
been defeated by the Israelites, so they
brought troops from the Syrian states on
the east side of the River Euphrates and
placed them under the **command** of Shobach, commander of the army of King
Hadadezer of Zobah. 17 When David
heard of it, he gathered the Israelite
troops, crossed the Jordan, and put them
in position facing the Syrians. The fighting began, 18 and the Israelites drove the
Syrian army back. David and his men
killed seven thousand Syrian chariot
drivers and forty thousand foot-soldiers.
They also killed the Syrian commander,
Shobach. 19 When the kings who were
subject to Hadadezer realized that they
had been defeated by Israel, they made
peace with David and became his
subjects. The Syrians were **never again**
willing to **help** the Ammonites.

David Captures Rabbah
(2 Sam 12.26–31)

20 The following spring, at the time
of the year when kings usually go
to war, Joab led out the army and
invaded the land of Ammon; King David,
however, stayed in Jerusalem. They
besieged the city of Rabbah, attacked it,
and **destroyed** it. 2 The Ammonite **idol**
Molech[q] had a gold **crown** which
weighed about thirty-four kilogrammes.
In it there was a jewel, which David took
and put in his own **crown**. He also took a
large amount of loot from the city. 3 He
took the people of the city and put them
to work with saws, iron hoes, and axes.
He did the same to the people of all the
other towns of Ammon. Then he and his
men returned to Jerusalem.

Battles against Philistine Giants
(2 Sam 21.15–22)

4 Later on, war broke out again with
the Philistines at Gezer. This was when
Sibbecai from Hushah killed a giant
named Sippai, and the Philistines were
defeated.
5 There was another battle with the
Philistines, and Elhanan son of Jair killed
Lahmi, the brother of Goliath from Gath,
whose spear had a shaft as thick as the
bar on a weaver's loom.
6 Another battle took place at Gath,
where there was a giant with six fingers
on each hand and six toes on each foot.
He was a descendant of the **ancient**
giants. 7 He **defied** the Israelites, and
Jonathan, the son of David's brother
Shammah, killed him.
8 These three, who were killed by
David and his men, were descendants of
the giants at Gath.

David Takes a Census
(2 Sam 24.1–25)

21 **Satan** wanted to bring **trouble** on
the people of Israel, so he made
David decide to take a census. 2 David
gave orders to Joab and the other
officers, "Go through Israel, from one
end of the country to the other, and count
the people. I want to know how many
there are."
3 Joab answered, "May the LORD
make the people of Israel a hundred
times more numerous than they are
now! Your **Majesty**, they are all your **servants**. Why do you want to do this and
make the whole nation **guilty**?" 4 But the
king made Joab **obey** the order. Joab
went out, travelled through the whole
country of Israel, and then returned to
Jerusalem. 5 He reported to King David
the total number of men capable of **military service**: 1,100,000 in Israel, and
470,000 in Judah. 6 Because Joab **dis-
approved** of the king's **command**, he did
not take any census of the tribes of Levi
and Benjamin.
7 God was **displeased** with what had
been done, so he **punished** Israel. 8 David
said to God, "I have committed a **terrible**

[q] Ammonite idol Molech; *or* Ammonite king.

20.1: 2 Sam 11.1 **20.5:** 1 Sam 17.4–7

ancient Deut 33.15; Ezra 4.15
crown [2] 2 Kgs 14.21; 2 Chr 23.11
defy 2 Sam 21.21; 2 Chr 26.16
destroy 4.41; 21.15
idol 16.26; 2 Chr 11.15

act 2 Sam 24.10; 2 Chr 6.32
afraid 14.17; 22.13
altar [7] 16.40; 22.1
angel [10] 2 Kgs 19.35; 2 Chr 18.18
approve 13.2; Neh 2.6
bow (2) [2] 16.29; 29.20
burnt-offering 2 Kgs 23.10; 22.1
change 2 Kgs 25.29; 2 Chr 36.4
choose [2] 19.10; 25.1
command [3] 19.11; 22.6
death (1) 2.19; 29.15
despair 2 Sam 24.14; Ezra 9.3
destroy [2] 20.1; 2 Chr 6.28
displease 1 Kgs 16.19; 2 Chr 29.6
enemy 19.6; 22.9
enough 18.4; 2 Chr 6.18
famine 2 Kgs 25.3; 2 Chr 6.28
fellowship-offering 16.1; 2 Chr 7.5
fool 2 Kgs 18.32; 2 Chr 16.9
forgive 6.49; 28.11
guilty 1 Kgs 8.32; 2 Chr 6.23
heaven 16.26; 29.11
Majesty [2] 16.27; 29.11

mercy 2 Kgs 13.23; 2 Chr 6.39
mind (1) 17.2; 28.9
obey [3] 2 Kgs 23.3; 22.13
offer [5] 16.1; 22.1
place of worship 16.39; 2 Chr 1.3
poor 2 Kgs 25.12; 2 Chr 34.30
pray [2] 17.16; 2 Chr 6.1
prayer 17.25; 2 Chr 6.12
prophet 17.1; 25.5
punish [4] 15.13; 27.24
sackcloth 2 Kgs 19.1; Neh 9.1
sacrifice [3] 16.1; 29.21
Satan Job 1.6
servant 17.4; 2 Chr 1.3
service 18.17; 23.27
spare 2 Kgs 10.17; 2 Chr 36.15
Tent (2) (of the Lord's presence) 17.1; 23.26
terrible 2 Kgs 17.21; Ps 14.1
trouble 7.23; 2 Chr 15.4
wish 11.17; Esth 6.6
worship (1) (of God) 18.11; 22.19
wrong 2 Kgs 18.14; 2 Chr 6.22

sin in doing this! Please **forgive** me. I
have **acted foolishly**."
9 Then the LORD said to Gad, David's
prophet, 10 "Go and tell David that I am
giving him three **choices**. I will do whichever he **chooses**."
11 Gad went to David, told him what
the LORD had said, and asked, "Which is
it to be? 12 Three years of **famine**? Or
three months of running away from the
armies of your **enemies**? Or three days
during which the LORD attacks you with
his sword and sends an epidemic on your
land, using his **angel** to bring **death**
throughout Israel? What answer shall I
give the LORD?"
13 David replied to Gad, "I am in a
desperate situation! But I don't want to
be **punished** by men. Let the LORD himself be the one to **punish** me, because he
is **merciful**."
14 So the LORD sent an epidemic on
the people of Israel, and seventy thousand of them died. 15 Then he sent an
angel to **destroy** Jerusalem, but he
changed his mind and said to the **angel**,
"Stop! That's **enough**!" The **angel** was
standing by the threshing-place of
Araunah, a Jebusite.
16 David saw the **angel** standing in
mid air, holding his sword in his hand,
ready to **destroy** Jerusalem. Then David
and the leaders of the people—all of
whom were wearing **sackcloth**—**bowed**
low, with their faces touching the ground.
17 David **prayed**, "O God, I am the one
who did **wrong**. I am the one who
ordered the census. What have these
poor people done? LORD, my God, **punish**
me and my family, and **spare** your
people."
18 **The angel of the LORD** told Gad to
command David to go and build an **altar**
to the LORD at Araunah's threshing-
place. 19 David **obeyed** the LORD's **command** and went, as Gad had told him to.
20 There at the threshing-place Araunah
and his four sons were threshing wheat,
and when they saw the **angel**, the sons
ran and hid. 21 As soon as Araunah saw
King David approaching, he left the
threshing-place and **bowed** low, with his
face touching the ground. 22 David said to
him, "Sell me your threshing-place, so
that I can build an **altar** to the LORD, to
stop the epidemic. I'll give you the full
price."
23 "Take it, Your **Majesty**," Araunah
said, "and do whatever you **wish**. Here
are these oxen to burn as an **offering** on
the **altar**, and here are the threshing-
boards to use as fuel, and wheat to give
as an **offering**. I give it all to you."
24 But the king answered, "No, I will
pay you the full price. I will not give as
an **offering** to the LORD something that
belongs to you, something that costs me
nothing." 25 And he paid Araunah six hundred gold coins for the threshing-place.
26 He built an **altar** to the LORD there and
offered burnt-offerings and **fellowship-
offerings**. He **prayed**, and the LORD
answered him by sending fire from
heaven to burn the **sacrifices** on the
altar.
27 The LORD told the **angel** to put his
sword away, and the **angel obeyed**.
28 David saw by this that the LORD had
answered his **prayer**, so he **offered sacrifices** on the **altar** at Araunah's threshing-
place. 29 The **Tent** of the LORD's presence
which Moses had made in the wilderness,
and the **altar** on which **sacrifices** were
burnt were still at the **place of worship** at
Gibeon at this time; 30 but David was not
able to go there to **worship** God, because
he was **afraid** of the sword of the LORD's
angel.

22 So David said, "This is where the
Temple of the LORD God will be.
Here is the **altar** where the people of
Israel are to **offer burnt-offerings**."

Preparations for Building the Temple

2 King David gave orders for all the
foreigners living in the land of Israel to
assemble, and he put them to work. Some
of them prepared stone blocks for building the **Temple**. 3 He supplied a large
amount of iron for making nails and
clamps for the wooden gates, and so
much bronze that no one could weigh it.
4 He arranged for the people of Tyre and
Sidon to bring him a large number of
cedar logs. 5 David thought, "The **Temple**
that my son Solomon is to build must be
splendid and world-famous. But he is
young and inexperienced, so I must
make preparations for it." So David got
large amounts of the materials ready
before he died.
6 He sent for his son Solomon and
commanded him to build a **temple** for
the LORD, the God of Israel. 7 David said
to him, "My son, I wanted to build a
temple to **honour** the LORD my God. 8 But
the LORD told me that I had killed too
many people and fought too many wars.
And so, because of all the **bloodshed** I
have caused, he would not let me build a
temple for him. 9 He did, however, make
me a **promise**. He said, 'You will have a
son who will rule in **peace**, because I will

22.7–10: 2 Sam 7.1–16; 1 Chr 17.1–14

afraid 21.30; 2 Chr 17.10
altar 21.18; 28.18
blood 11.1; 28.3
burnt-offering 21.26 2 Chr 2.4
command [2] 21.6; 24.19
confident 2 Kgs 18.19; 28.20
conquer 19.3; 2 Chr 12.8
Covenant Box 17.1; 28.2
determine 12.38; 25.8
enemy 21.12; 2 Chr 1.11
heart 2 Kgs 23.3; 28.
help 19.9; 23.28
honour 19.3; 28.2
insight 1 Kgs 4.29; Job 12.12
law [2] 16.40; 28.7
obey 21.4; 24.19
offer 21.23; 23.29
peace [4] 19.19; 23.25
promise [2] 17.9; 25.5
reign 2 Kgs 25.1; 2 Chr 1.15
sacred 11.3; 23.13
secure 2 Kgs 20.19; 2 Chr 11.23
serve 15.2; 23.13
soul 2 Kgs 23.3; 2 Chr 15.12
splendour Deut 33.26; 29.11
subject (1) 19.19; 2 Chr 10.4
succeed (1) [2] 12.18, 29.23
Temple (1) (of God) [10] 18.8; 23.4
wisdom 1 Kgs 11.41; 2 Chr 1.10
worship (1) (of God) 21.30; 23.13

give him **peace** from all his **enemies**. His
name will be Solomon,[r] because during
his **reign** I will give Israel **peace** and
security. 10 He will build a **temple** for me.
He will be my son, and I will be his
father. His dynasty will rule Israel for
ever.' "
11 David continued, "Now, my son,
may the LORD your God be with you, and
may he keep his **promise** to make you
successful in building a **temple** for him.
12 And may the LORD your God give you
insight and **wisdom** so that you may
govern Israel according to his **Law**. 13 If
you **obey** all the **laws** which the LORD
gave to Moses for Israel, you will be
successful. Be **determined** and **confident**,
and don't let anything make you **afraid**.
14 As for the **Temple**, by my efforts I have
accumulated more than 3,400 metric tons
of gold and over 34,000 metric tons of
silver to be used in building it. Besides
that, there is an unlimited supply of
bronze and iron. I also have wood and
stone ready, but you must get more.
15 You have many workmen. There are
men to work in the stone quarries, and
there are masons and carpenters, as well
as a large number of craftsmen of every
sort who can work 16 with gold, silver,
bronze, and iron. Now begin the work,
and may the LORD be with you."
17 David **commanded** all the leaders
of Israel to **help** Solomon. 18 He said, "The
LORD your God has been with you and
given you **peace** on all sides. He let me
conquer all the people who used to live in
this land, and they are now **subject** to you
and to the LORD. 19 Now **serve** the LORD
your God **with all your heart** and **soul**.
Start building the **Temple**, so that you
can place in it the **Covenant Box** of the
LORD and all the other **sacred** objects
used in **worshipping** him."

23 When David was very old, he
made his son Solomon king of
Israel.

The Work of the Levites

2 King David brought together all the
Israelite leaders and all the **priests and**
Levites. 3 He took a census of all the male
Levites aged thirty or older. The total
was thirty-eight thousand. 4 The king
assigned twenty-four thousand to
administer the work of the **Temple**, six
thousand to keep records and decide
disputes, 5 four thousand to do guard **duty**,
and four thousand to **praise** the LORD,
using the musical instruments **provided**
by the king for this **purpose**.
6 David divided the **Levites** into three
groups, according to their clans:
Gershon, Kohath, and Merari.
7 Gershon had two sons: Ladan and
Shimei. 8 Ladan had three sons: Jehiel,
Zetham, and Joel, 9 who were the heads
of the clans descended from Ladan.
(Shimei had three sons: Shelomoth,
Haziel, and Haran.)[s] 10-11 Shimei had four
sons: Jahath, Zina, Jeush, and Beriah, in
order of age. Jeush and Beriah did not
have many descendants, so they were
counted as one clan.
12 Kohath had four sons: Amram,
Izhar, Hebron, and Uzziel. 13 His eldest
son, Amram, was the father of Aaron and
Moses. (Aaron and his descendants were
set **apart** to be in charge of the **sacred**
objects for ever, to burn **incense** in the
worship of the LORD, to **serve** him, and to
bless the people **in his name**. 14 But the
sons of Moses, the **man of God**, were
included among the **Levites**.) 15 Moses
had two sons, Gershom and Eliezer.
16 The leader among Gershom's sons was
Shebuel. 17 Eliezer had only one son,
Rehabiah, but Rehabiah had many
descendants.
18 Kohath's second son, Izhar, had a
son, Shelomith, the head of the clan.
19 Kohath's third son, Hebron, had four
sons: Jeriah, Amariah, Jehaziel, and
Jekameam. 20 Kohath's fourth son, Uzziel,
had two sons, Micah and Isshiah.
21 Merari had two sons, Mahli and
Mushi. Mahli also had two sons, Eleazar
and Kish, 22 but Eleazar died without
having any sons, only daughters. His
daughters married their cousins, the sons
of Kish. 23 Merari's second son, Mushi,
had three sons: Mahli, Eder, and
Jeremoth.
24 These were the descendants of
Levi, by clans and families, every one of
them registered by name. Each of his descendants, twenty years of age or older,
had a **share** in the work of the LORD's
Temple.
25 David said, "The LORD God of
Israel has given **peace** to **his people**, and
he himself will live in Jerusalem for
ever. 26 So there is no longer any **need** for
the **Levites** to carry the **Tent** of the
LORD's presence and all the equipment
used in **worship**." 27 On the basis of
David's **final** instructions all **Levites** were
registered for **service** when they reached

[r] SOLOMON: *This name is formed from the Hebrew word "shalom," which means "peace and security."*
[s] SHIMEI...HARAN: *The relation of this list to the list of Shimei's sons in verse 10 is not clear.*

22.13: Josh 1.6–9 **23.1:** 1 Kgs 1.1–40 **23.13:** Ex 28.1 **23.26:** Deut 10.8

apart 2 Kgs 16.17; Job 30.27
bless 17.27; 26.4
bread 16.3; 28.16
care [2] 2 Kgs 11.3; 28.13
defile Deut 24.4; 2 Chr 29.5
dispute 1 Kgs 3.28; 26.29
duty (1) [3] 16.37; 24.3
festival 2 Kgs 23.16; 2 Chr 2.4
final 9.26; 27.24
glory 16.24; 29.11
God's people 17.7; 28.8
help 22.17; 28.21
incense 9.29; 28.18
Levites [8] 16.4; 24.6
man of God 2 Kgs 4.16; 2 Chr 8.14
name (2) (name of God, of Jesus) 16.2; 29.13
need 2 Kgs 25.24; 2 Chr 1.10
New Moon Festival 2 Kgs 4.23; 2 Chr 2.4
offer [5] 22.1; 28.16
peace 22.9; 2 Chr 14.1
praise [2] 16.4; 25.3
priest [3] 18.16; 24.2
provide 14.1; 28.4
purpose 17.19; Ps 33.10
Sabbath 9.32; 2 Chr 2.4
sacred [2] 22.19; 2 Chr 2.4
serve 22.19; 26.1
service 21.5; 25.1
share 6.54; 2 Chr 31.16
Temple (1) (of God) [6] 22.1; 24.5
Tent (2) (of the Lord's presence) [2] 21.29; 2 Chr 1.3
unleavened 2 Kgs 23.9; 2 Chr 8.13
worship (1) (of God) [5] 22.19; 25.1
yeast 1 Sam 28.24; Ezek 45.21

the age of twenty, [28]and were assigned the following **duties**: to **help** the **priests** descended from Aaron with the **temple worship**, to take **care** of its courtyards and its rooms, and to keep **undefiled** everything that is **sacred**; [29]to be responsible for the **bread offered** to God, the flour used in **offerings**, the wafers made **without yeast**, the baked **offerings**, and the flour mixed with olive-oil; to weigh and measure the **temple offerings**; [30]and to **praise** and **glorify** the LORD every morning and every evening [31]and whenever **offerings** to the LORD are **burnt** on the **Sabbath**, the **New Moon Festival**, and other **festivals**. Rules were made specifying the number of **Levites** assigned to do this work each time. The **Levites** were assigned the **duty** of **worshipping** the LORD for all time. [32]They were given the responsibility of taking **care** of the **Tent** of the LORD's presence and the **Temple**, and of assisting their relatives, the **priests** descended from Aaron, in the **temple worship**.

The Work Assigned to the Priests

command 22.6; 25.2
duty (1) [2] 23.5; 25.8
establish 14.2; 29.23
Levites [4] 23.2; 25.1
lot (1) [3] 6.61; 25.8
obey 22.13; 28.7
priest [5] 23.2; 27.2
spiritual Mt 5.3
Temple (1) (of God) [2] 23.4; 25.6
turn 9.25; 28.9
witness [2] 1 Sam 20.12; Job 10.17

24 These are the groups to which the descendants of Aaron belong. Aaron had four sons: Nadab, Abihu, Eleazar, and Ithamar. [2]Nadab and Abihu died before their father did, and left no descendants, so their brothers Eleazar and Ithamar became **priests**. [3]King David organized the descendants of Aaron into groups according to their **duties**. He was assisted in this by Zadok, a descendant of Eleazar, and by Ahimelech, a descendant of Ithamar. [4]The descendants of Eleazar were organized into sixteen groups, while the descendants of Ithamar were organized into eight; this was done because there were more male heads of families among the descendants of Eleazar. [5]Since there were **temple** officials and **spiritual** leaders among the descendants of both Eleazar and Ithamar, assignments were made by drawing **lots**. [6]The descendants of Eleazar and of Ithamar took **turns** in drawing **lots**. Then they were registered by Shemaiah son of Nethanel, a **Levite** secretary. The king, his officials, the **priest** Zadok, Ahimelech son of Abiathar, and the heads of the **priestly** families and of the **Levite** families, were all **witnesses**.

7–18 This is the order in which the twenty-four family groups were given their assignments:

1. Jehoiarib
2. Jedaiah
3. Harim
4. Seorim
5. Malchijah
6. Mijamin
7. Hakkoz
8. Abijah
9. Jeshua
10. Shecaniah
11. Eliashib
12. Jakim
13. Huppah
14. Jeshebeab
15. Bilgah
16. Immer
17. Hezir
18. Happizzez
19. Pethahiah
20. Jehezkel
21. Jachin
22. Gamul
23. Delaiah
24. Maaziah

19 These men were registered according to their assignments for going to the **Temple** and performing the **duties established** by their ancestor Aaron in **obedience** to the **commands** of the LORD God of Israel.

The List of the Levites

20 These are other heads of families descended from Levi:
Jehdeiah, a descendant of Amram through Shebuel;
21 Isshiah, a descendant of Rehabiah;
22 Jahath, a descendant of Izhar through Shelomith;
23 Jeriah, Amariah, Jehaziel, and Jekameam, sons of Hebron, in order of age;
24 Shamir, a descendant of Uzziel through Micah;
25 Zechariah, a descendant of Uzziel through Isshiah, Micah's brother;
26 Mahli, Mushi, and Jaaziah, descendants of Merari. [27]Jaaziah had three sons: Shoham, Zaccur, and Ibri. [28-29]Mahli had two sons, Eleazar and Kish. Eleazar had no sons, but Kish had one son, Jerahmeel. [30]Mushi had three sons: Mahli, Eder, and Jeremoth.

These are the families of the **Levites**.

31 The head of each family and one of his younger brothers drew **lots** for their assignments, just as their relatives, the **priests** descended from Aaron, had done. King David, Zadok, Ahimelech, and the heads of families of the **priests** and of the **Levites** were **witnesses**.

The Temple Musicians

25 King David and the leaders of the **Levites chose** the following

choose [2] 21.10; 26.32
command 24.19; 27.2

23.28–32: Num 3.5–9 **24.2:** Lev 10.1–2

determine 22.13; 28.10
direct [3] 1 Sam 3.1; 2 Chr 34.4
duty (1) [2] 24.3; 26.12
Levites [3] 24.6; 26.1
lot (1) 24.5; 26.13
message [3] 2 Kgs 22.16; 2 Chr 2.3
power 16.27; 29.11
praise 23.5; 29.10
proclaim [3] 16.8; 29.22
promise 22.9; 27.23
prophet 21.9; 26.28
service [2] 23.27; 2 Chr 5.11
Temple (1) (of God) 24.5; 26.12
thank 16.8; 29.13
worship (1) (of God) [3] 23.13; 2 Chr 1.5

Levite clans to lead the **services** of **worship**: Asaph, Heman, and Jeduthun. They were to **proclaim** God's **messages**, accompanied by the music of harps and cymbals. This is the list of persons **chosen** to lead the **worship**, with the type of **service** that each group performed:

2 The four sons of Asaph: Zaccur, Joseph, Nethaniah, and Asharelah. They were under the **direction** of Asaph, who **proclaimed** God's **messages** whenever the king **commanded**.

3 The six sons of Jeduthun: Gedaliah, Zeri, Jeshaiah, Shimei, Hashabiah, and Mattithiah. Under the **direction** of their father they **proclaimed** God's **message**, accompanied by the music of harps, and sang **praise** and **thanks** to the LORD.

4 The fourteen sons of Heman: Bukkiah, Mattaniah, Uzziel, Shebuel, Jerimoth, Hananiah, Hanani, Eliathah, Giddalti, Romamti Ezer, Joshbekashah, Mallothi, Hothir, and Mahazioth. 5 God gave to Heman, the king's **prophet**, these fourteen sons and also three daughters, as he had **promised**, in order to give **power** to Heman. 6 All his sons played cymbals and harps under their father's **direction**, to accompany the **temple worship**. And Asaph, Jeduthun, and Heman were under orders from the king.

7 All these twenty-four men were experts; and their **fellow-Levites** were trained musicians. There were 288 men in all.

8 To **determine** the assignment of **duties** they all drew **lots**, whether they were young or old, experts or beginners.

9–31 These 288 men were divided according to families into twenty-four groups of twelve, with a leader in charge of each group. This is the order in which they were on **duty**:

1. Joseph of the family of Asaph
2. Gedaliah
3. Zaccur
4. Zeri
5. Nethaniah
6. Bukkiah
7. Asharelah
8. Jeshaiah
9. Mattaniah
10. Shimei
11. Uzziel
12. Hashabiah
13. Shebuel
14. Mattithiah
15. Jerimoth
16. Hananiah
17. Joshbekashah
18. Hanani
19. Mallothi
20. Eliathah
21. Hothir
22. Giddalti
23. Mahazioth
24. Romamti Ezer

The Temple Guards

26 These are the assignments of work for the **Levites** who **served** as temple guards. From the clan of Korah there was Meshelemiah son of Kore, of the family of Asaph. 2 He had seven sons, listed in order of age: Zechariah, Jediael, Zebadiah, Jathniel, 3 Elam, Jehohanan, and Eliehoenai.

4 There was also Obed Edom, whom God **blessed** by giving him eight sons, listed in order of age: Shemaiah, Jehozabad, Joah, Sachar, Nethanel, 5 Ammiel, Issachar, and Peullethai.

6–7 Obed Edom's eldest son, Shemaiah, had six sons: Othni, Rephael, Obed, Elzabad, Elihu, and Semachiah. They were **important** men in their clan because of their great ability; the **last** two were especially talented.

8 Obed Edom's family furnished a total of sixty-two highly qualified men for this work.

9 Meshelemiah's family furnished eighteen qualified men.

10 From the clan of Merari there was Hosah, who had four sons: Shimri (his father made him the leader, even though he was not the eldest son), 11 Hilkiah, Tebaliah, and Zechariah. In all there were thirteen members of Hosah's family who were temple guards.

12 The temple guards were divided into groups, according to families, and they were assigned **duties** in the **Temple**, just as the other **Levites** were. 13 Each family, regardless of size, drew **lots** to see which gate it would be responsible for. 14 Shelemiah drew the east gate, and his son Zechariah, a man who always gave good **advice**, drew the north gate. 15 Obed Edom was allotted the south gate, and his sons were allotted to guard the storerooms. 16 Shuppim and Hosah were allotted the west gate and the Shallecheth Gate on the upper road. Guard **duty** was divided into assigned periods, one after another. 17 On the east, six guards were on **duty** each day, on the north, four, and on the south, four. Four guards were stationed at the storerooms daily, two at each storeroom. 18 Near the western pavilion there were four guards by the road and two at the pavilion itself. 19 This is the assignment of guard **duty** to the clan of Korah and the clan of Merari.

advice 1 Kgs 20.25; 2 Chr 10.6
bless 23.13; 2 Chr 1.1
choose 25.1; 28.4
dedicate [4] 18.11; 28.12
dispute 23.4; 2 Chr 19.8
duty (1) [6] 25.8; 27.1
gift [3] 2 Kgs 12.4; 28.12
important 5.12; 28.1
last (2) 2 Kgs 4.6; 2 Chr 7.9
Levites [3] 25.1; 28.13
lot (1) 25.8; Neh 10.34
prophet 25.5; 29.29
religion [2] 1 Kgs 12.32; 2 Chr 19.11
serve 23.13; 28.9
settle (2) 1 Kgs 3.28; Job 14.5
Temple (1) (of God) [6] 25.6; 29.16

26.4-5: 2 Sam 6.11; 1 Chr 13.14

Other Temple Duties

20 Others of their **fellow-Levites**[t] were
in charge of the **temple** treasury and the
storerooms for **gifts dedicated** to God.
21 Ladan, one of the sons of Gershon, was
the ancestor of several family groups,
including the family of his son Jehiel.
22 Ladan's two other sons, Zetham and
Joel, had charge of the **temple** treasury
and storerooms.

23 **Duties** were also assigned to the descendants of Amram, Izhar, Hebron, and
Uzziel.

24 Shebuel, of the clan of Moses' son
Gershom, was the chief official responsible for the **temple** treasury. 25 Through
Gershom's brother Eliezer he was
related to Shelomith. Eliezer was the
father of Rehabiah, who was the father
of Jeshiah, the father of Joram, the
father of Zichri, the father of Shelomith.
26 Shelomith and the members of his
family were in charge of all the **gifts
dedicated** to God by King David, the
heads of families, leaders of clan groups,
and army officers. 27 They took some of
the loot they captured in battle and **dedicated** it for use in the **Temple**. 28 Shelomith and his family were in charge of
everything that had been **dedicated** for
use in the **Temple**, including the **gifts**
brought by the **prophet** Samuel, by King
Saul, by Abner son of Ner, and by Joab
son of Zeruiah.

Duties of Other Levites

29 Among the descendants of Izhar,
Chenaniah and his sons were assigned
administrative **duties**: keeping records
and **settling disputes** for the people of
Israel.

30 Among the descendants of Hebron,
Hashabiah and seventeen hundred of his
relatives, all outstanding men, were put
in charge of the administration of all
religious and civil matters in Israel west
of the River Jordan. 31 Jeriah was the
leader of the descendants of Hebron. In
the fortieth year that David was king, an
investigation was made of the family line
of Hebron's descendants, and outstanding
soldiers belonging to this family were
found living at Jazer in the territory of
Gilead. 32 King David **chose** two thousand
seven hundred outstanding heads of
families from Jeriah's relatives and put
them in charge of administering all
religious and civil matters in Israel east
of the River Jordan—the territories of
Reuben, Gad, and East Manasseh.

Military and Civil Organization

27 This is the list of the Israelite heads of families and clan leaders and their officials who administered the work of the kingdom. Each month of the year a different group of twenty-four thousand men was on **duty** under the commander for that month.

2–15 The following were the commanders for each month:

First month: Jashobeam son of Zabdiel (he was a member of the clan of Perez, a part of the tribe of Judah)
Second month: Dodai, a descendant of Ahohi (Mikloth was his second in **command**)[u]
Third month: Benaiah son of Jehoiada the **priest**; he was the leader of "The Thirty" (his son Amizzabad succeeded him as commander of this group)
Fourth month: Asahel, brother of Joab (his son Zebadiah succeeded him)
Fifth month: Shamhuth, a descendant of Izhar
Sixth month: Ira son of Ikkesh from Tekoa
Seventh month: Helez, an Ephraimite from Pelon
Eighth month: Sibbecai from Hushah (he was a member of the clan of Zerah, a part of the tribe of Judah)
Ninth month: Abiezer from Anathoth in the territory of the tribe of Benjamin
Tenth month: Maharai from Netophah (he was a member of the clan of Zerah)
Eleventh month: Benaiah from Pirathon in the territory of the tribe of Ephraim
Twelfth month: Heldai from Netophah (he was a descendant of Othniel)

Administration of the Tribes of Israel

16–22 This is the list of the administrators of the tribes of Israel:

Tribe	*Administrator*
Reuben	Eliezer son of Zichri
Simeon	Shephatiah son of Maacah
Levi	Hashabiah son of Kemuel
Aaron	Zadok
Judah	Elihu, one of King David's brothers
Issachar	Omri son of Michael
Zebulun	Ishmaiah son of Obadiah
Naphtali	Jeremoth son of Azriel

[t] *One ancient translation* fellow-Levites; *Hebrew* Levites, Ahijah.
[u] *Probable text* Mikloth...command; *Hebrew unclear.*

command 25.2; 28.
complete 1 Kgs 7.
2 Chr 4.11
duty (1) 26.12; 28.1
final 23.27;
2 Chr 19.11
friend 19.2;
2 Chr 20.7
priest 24.2; 28.13
promise 25.5; 29.24
punish 21.7;
2 Chr 6.23
scholar Ezra 7.6
sheep 17.7; 2 Chr 5
vineyard
2 Kgs 25.12;
2 Chr 26.10

Ephraim	Hoshea son of Azaziah
West Manasseh	Joel son of Pedaiah
East Manasseh	Iddo son of Zechariah
Benjamin	Jaasiel son of Abner
Dan	Azarel son of Jeroham

23 King David did not take a census of
the people who were under the age of
twenty, because of the LORD's **promise** to
make the people of Israel as numerous
as the stars in the sky. 24 Joab, whose
mother was Zeruiah, began to take a
census, but he did not **complete** it. God
punished Israel because of this census, so
the **final** figures were never recorded in
King David's official records.

Administrators of the Royal Property

25–31 This is the list of those who administered the royal property:

Royal storerooms: Azmaveth son of Adiel
Local storerooms: Jonathan son of Uzziah
Farm labour: Ezri son of Chelub
Vineyards: Shimei from Ramah
Wine cellars: Zabdi from Shepham
Olives and sycomore-trees (in the western foothills): Baal Hanan from Geder
Olive-oil storage: Joash
Cattle in the Plain of Sharon: Shirtai from Sharon
Cattle in the valleys: Shaphat son of Adlai
Camels: Obil, an Ishmaelite
Donkeys: Jehdeiah from Meronoth
Sheep and goats: Jaziz, a Hagrite

David's Personal Advisers

32 Jonathan, King David's uncle, was
a skilful adviser and a **scholar**. He and
Jehiel son of Hachmoni were in charge
of the education of the king's sons.
33 Ahithophel was adviser to the king, and
Hushai the Archite was the king's **friend**
and counsellor. 34 After Ahithophel died,
Abiathar and Jehoiada son of Benaiah
became advisers. Joab was commander
of the royal army.

David's Instructions for the Temple

28 King David **commanded** all the
officials of Israel to assemble in
Jerusalem. So all the officials of the
tribes, the officials who administered the
work of the kingdom, the leaders of the
clans, the supervisors of the property and
livestock that belonged to the king and
his sons—indeed all the palace officials,
leading soldiers, and **important** men—
gathered in Jerusalem.

2 David stood before them and
addressed them: "My countrymen, listen
to me. I wanted to build a permanent
home for the **Covenant Box**, the **footstool**
of the LORD our God. I have made
preparations for building a temple to
honour him, 3 but he has **forbidden** me to
do it, because I am a soldier and have
shed too much **blood**. 4 The LORD, the God
of Israel, **chose** me and my descendants
to rule Israel for ever. He **chose** the tribe
of Judah to **provide** leadership, and out of
Judah he **chose** my father's family. From
all that family it was his **pleasure** to take
me and make me king over all Israel.
5 He gave me many sons, and out of them
all he **chose** Solomon to rule over Israel,
the **LORD's kingdom**.

6 "The LORD said to me, 'Your son
Solomon is the one who will build my
Temple. I have **chosen** him to be my son,
and I will be his father. 7 I will make his
kingdom **last** for ever if he continues to
obey carefully all my **laws** and **commands** as he does now.'

8 "So now, my people, in the **presence**
of our God and of this assembly of all
Israel, the **LORD's people**, I charge you to
obey carefully everything that the LORD
our God has **commanded** us, so that you
may continue to **possess** this good land
and so that you may hand it on to
succeeding generations for ever."

9 And to Solomon he said, "My son, I
charge you to **acknowledge** your father's
God and to **serve** him with an undivided
heart and a willing **mind**. He knows all
our thoughts and **desires**. If you go to
him, he will **accept** you; but if you **turn**
away from him, he will **abandon** you for
ever. 10 You must realize that the LORD
has **chosen** you to build his **holy** Temple.
Now do it—and do it with **determination**."

11 David gave Solomon the **plans** for
all the temple buildings, for the storerooms and all the other rooms, and for
the **Most Holy Place**, where sins are **forgiven**. 12 He also gave him the **plans** for
all he had in **mind** for the courtyards and
the rooms around them, and for the
storerooms for the temple equipment
and the **gifts dedicated** to the LORD.
13 David also gave him the **plans** for
organizing the **priests and Levites** to
perform their **duties**, to do the work of
the Temple, and to take **care** of all the
temple utensils. 14 He gave instructions as
to how much silver and gold was to be
used for making the utensils, 15 for each
lamp and lampstand, 16 for the silver
tables, and for each gold table on which

confident 22.13; 2 Chr 32.7
Covenant Box [2] 22.19; 2 Chr 1.4
creature 16.32; 2 Chr 3.7
dedicate 26.20; 29.21
desire 2 Sam 23.5; 29.19
determine [2] 25.8; 2 Chr 4.18
duty (1) [2] 27.1; 2 Chr 8.14
eager Neh 4.6
footstool 2 Chr 9.18
forbid 1 Kgs 21.3; Ezra 7.24
forgive 21.8; 2 Chr 6.21
gift 26.20; 29.14
God's people 23.25; 2 Chr 1.11
heart 22.19; 29.17
help 23.28; 2 Chr 13.14
holy 16.29; 29.16
Holy Place 6.49; 2 Chr 3.8
honour 22.7; 29.16
important 26.6; Ezra 10.9
incense 23.13; 2 Chr 2.4
Kingdom (1) (of God) Job 25.1
last (1) 16.15; Esth 1.5
law 22.12; 2 Chr 6.16
leading 12.23; 2 Chr 19.8
Levites [2] 26.1; 29.8
mind (1) [2] 21.15; Job 14.22
obey [2] 24.19; 29.19
offer 23.29; 29.5
plan [4] 2 Kgs 19.25; 2 Chr 2.12
pleasure 2 Sam 19.35; Ps 16.3
possess 16.18; 2 Chr 6.27
presence 13.10; 29.22
priest [2] 27.2; 29.22
provide 23.5; 29.3
pure [2] 15.12; 29.4
serve [2] 26.1; 2 Chr 7.17
turn 24.6; 2 Chr 6.3

abandon [2] 10.7; 2 Chr 7.20
accept 2 Kgs 5.15; 2 Chr 7.12
acknowledge Deut 26.3; Ps 83.16
altar 22.1; 29.21
blood 22.8; 2 Chr 29.22
bread 23.29; 2 Chr 2.4
care 23.28; 2 Chr 30.1
choose [6] 26.32; 29.1
command [4] 27.2; 29.19

27.23: Gen 15.5, 22.17, 26.4 **27.24:** 2 Sam 24.1–15; 1 Chr 21.1–14 **28.2–7:** 2 Sam 7.1–16; 1 Chr 17.1–14

were placed the loaves of **bread offered**
to God. 17 He also gave instructions as to
how much **pure** gold was to be used in
making forks, bowls, and jars, how much
silver and gold in making dishes, 18 and
how much **pure** gold in making the **altar**
on which **incense** was burnt and in
making the chariot for the winged
creatures that spread their wings over
the LORD's **Covenant Box**. 19 King David
said, "All this is contained in the **plan**
written according to the instructions
which the LORD himself gave me to
carry out."
20 King David said to his son Solomon,
"Be **confident** and **determined**. Start the
work and don't let anything stop you. The
LORD God, whom I **serve**, will be with
you. He will not **abandon** you, but he will
stay with you until you finish the work to
be done on his Temple. 21 The **priests and**
the Levites have been assigned **duties** to
perform in the Temple. Workmen with
every kind of skill are **eager** to **help** you,
and all the people and their leaders are
at your **command**."

Gifts for Building the Temple

29 King David **announced** to the
whole assembly: "My son
Solomon is the one whom God has
chosen, but he is still young and lacks
experience. The work to be done is tremendous, because this is not a palace for
men but a temple for the LORD God. 2 I
have made every effort to prepare
materials for the Temple—gold, silver,
bronze, iron, timber, precious stones and
gems, stones for mosaics, and quantities
of marble. 3 Over and above all this that I
have **provided**, I have given silver and
gold from my personal property because
of my **love** for God's Temple. 4 I have
given more than a hundred metric tons
of the finest gold and almost two hundred
and forty metric tons of **pure** silver for
decorating the walls of the Temple 5 and
for all the objects which the craftsmen
are to make. Now who else is willing to
give a **generous offering** to the LORD?"
6 Then the heads of the clans, the
officials of the tribes, the commanders of
the army, and the administrators of the
royal property volunteered to give 7 the
following for the work on the Temple:
more than 170 metric tons of gold, over
340 metric tons of silver, almost 620
metric tons of bronze, and more than
3,400 metric tons of iron. 8 Those who had
precious stones gave them to the temple
treasury, which was administered by
Jehiel of the **Levite** clan of Gershon.
9 The people had given willingly to the
LORD, and they were **happy** that so much
had been given. King David also was
extremely **happy**.

David Praises God

10 There in front of the whole
assembly King David **praised** the LORD.
He said, "LORD God of our ancestor
Jacob, may you be **praised** for ever and
ever! 11 You are great and **powerful**,
glorious, **splendid**, and **majestic**. Everything in **heaven and earth** is yours, and
you are king, **supreme** ruler over all.
12 All **riches** and wealth come from you;
you rule everything by your **strength** and
power; and you are able to make anyone
great and **strong**. 13 Now, our God, we
give you **thanks**, and we **praise** your
glorious name.
14 "Yet my people and I cannot really
give you anything, because everything is
a **gift** from you, and we have only given
back what is yours already. 15 You know,
O LORD, that we pass through **life** like
exiles and **strangers**, as our ancestors
did. Our days are like a passing shadow,
and we cannot **escape death**. 16 O LORD,
our God, we have brought together all
this wealth to build a **temple** to **honour**
your **holy name**, but it all came from you
and all belongs to you. 17 I know that you
test everyone's **heart** and are **pleased**
with people of integrity. In **honesty** and
sincerity I have willingly given all this to
you, and I have seen how your people
who are gathered here have been **happy**
to bring **offerings** to you. 18 LORD God of
our ancestors Abraham, Isaac, and
Jacob, keep such **devotion** for ever
strong in your people's **hearts** and keep
them always **faithful** to you. 19 Give my
son Solomon a **wholehearted desire** to
obey everything that you **command** and
to build the **Temple** for which I have
made these preparations."
20 Then David **commanded** the
people, "**Praise** the LORD your God!"
And the whole assembly **praised** the
LORD, the God of their ancestors, and
they **bowed** low and gave **honour** to the
LORD and also to the king.
21 The following day they killed
animals as **sacrifices**, **dedicating** them to
the LORD, and then gave them to the
people to eat. In addition, they **sacrificed**
a thousand bulls, a thousand rams, and a
thousand **lambs**, which they burnt whole
on the **altar**. They also brought the
offerings of wine. 22 So that day they were
very **happy** as they ate and drank in the
presence of the LORD.

29.1-2: 1 Chr 22.5 **29.11:** Mt 6.13

altar 28.18; 2 Chr 1.5
announce 13.2; 2 Chr 20.2
anoint 11.3; 2 Chr 23.11
awe Deut 28.58; Job 22.4
bow (2) 21.16; 2 Chr 20.18
choose 28.4; 2 Chr 1.11
command [2] 28.1; 2 Chr 1.3
death (1) 21.12; 2 Chr 1.11
dedicate 28.12; 2 Chr 5.1
desire 28.9; Ezra 7.13
devote 2.7; 2 Chr 31.21
escape 12.1; 2 Chr 10.2
establish 24.19; 2 Chr 12.1
exile 6.15; Ezra 1.4
experience 12.1; 2 Chr 8.18
faithful 2 Kgs 20.3; 2 Chr 7.17
generous 1 Kgs 10.13; 2 Chr 11.23
gift 28.12; 2 Chr 9.9
glory [3] 23.30; Neh 9.5
happy [4] 2 Kgs 11.20; 2 Chr 6.41
heart [3] 28.9; 2 Chr 6.14
heaven 21.26; 2 Chr 2.6
holy 28.10; 2 Chr 2.4
honest 2 Kgs 22.7; 2 Chr 34.12
honour [2] 28.2; 2 Chr 2.4
lamb 2 Kgs 3.4; 2 Chr 29.21

Levites 28.13; 2 Chr 5.4
life (1) 11.19; 2 Chr 1.11
love 16.34; 2 Chr 1.8
loyal 19.2; 2 Chr 10.4
Majesty 21.3; 2 Chr 6.2
name (2) (name of God, of Jesus) [3] 23.13; 2 Chr 9.8
obey [2] 28.7; 2 Chr 6.14
offer [3] 28.16; 2 Chr 1.6
please 13.4; 2 Chr 9.
power [3] 25.5; 2 Chr 1.1
praise [5] 25.3; 2 Chr 2.12
presence 28.8; 2 Chr 5.11
priest 28.13; 2 Chr 4.6
proclaim 25.1; Neh 6.7
promise 27.23; 2 Chr 1.9
prophet 26.28; 2 Chr 9.29
provide 28.4; 2 Chr 2.10
pure 28.17; 2 Chr 3.4
respect 4.9; 2 Chr 22.9
riches 1 Kgs 3.11; Esth 1.4
ripe Judg 8.32; Neh 10.35
sacrifice [2] 21.26; 2 Chr 1.6
sincere 1 Kgs 8.48; 2 Chr 6.38
splendour 22.5; Esth 1.4
stranger 16.19; Job 19.13
strength 2 Kgs 23.25; 2 Chr 11.17
strong [2] 19.13; 2 Chr 11.11
succeed (1) 22.11; 2 Chr 7.11
supreme Deut 10.17; 2 Chr 9.26
Temple (1) (of God) [2] 26.12; 2 Chr 2.1
test 1 Kgs 10.1; 2 Chr 9.1
thank 25.3; 2 Chr 29.31
throne 13.6; 2 Chr 9.17

For a second time they **proclaimed**
Solomon king. In the **name of the LORD**
they **anointed** him as their ruler and
Zadok as **priest**. 23 So Solomon succeeded
his father David on the **throne** which the
LORD had **established**. He was a **successful** king, and the whole nation of Israel
obeyed him. 24 All the officials and
soldiers, and even all of David's other
sons **promised** to be **loyal** to Solomon as
king. 25 The LORD made the whole nation
stand in **awe** of Solomon, and he made
him more **glorious** than any other king
that had ruled Israel.

29.23: 1 Kgs 2.12 **29.27:** 2 Sam 5.4–5; 1 Chr 3.4

Summary of David's Reign

26 David son of Jesse ruled over all
Israel 27 for forty years. He ruled in
Hebron for seven years and in Jerusalem
for thirty-three. 28 He died at a **ripe** old
age, wealthy and **respected**, and his son
Solomon succeeded him as king. 29 The
history of King David from beginning to
end is recorded in the records of the
three **prophets**, Samuel, Nathan, and
Gad. 30 The records tell how he ruled,
how **powerful** he was, and all the things
that happened to him, to Israel, and to
the surrounding kingdoms.

THE SECOND BOOK OF
CHRONICLES

INTRODUCTION

Second Chronicles begins where *First Chronicles* ends, starting with the account of the rule of King Solomon until his death. After recording the revolt of the northern tribes led by Jeroboam against Rehoboam, King Solomon's son and successor, the account confines itself to the history of the southern kingdom of Judah until the fall of Jerusalem in 586 B.C.

Outline of Contents

---

altar [2] 1 Chr 29.21; 4.1
bless 1 Chr 26.4; 6.3
box *see* **Covenant Box**
choose 1 Chr 29.1; 6.1
command 1 Chr 29.19; 2.4
control [2] 1 Chr 18.1; 11.1
Covenant Box [2] 1 Chr 28.2; 5.2
death (1) 1 Chr 29.15; 16.14
enemy 1 Chr 22.9; 6.24
fulfil 1 Chr 17.23; 6.15
God's people 1 Chr 28.8; 2.11
knowledge [3] 1 Kgs 4.29; Ezra 7.6
life (1) 1 Chr 29.15; 10.4
love 1 Chr 29.3; 2.11
need 1 Chr 23.26; 2.16
offer 1 Chr 29.5; 2.4
place of worship [2] 1 Chr 21.29; 11.15
plenty 1 Chr 4.40; 9.27
power 1 Chr 29.11; 6.32
promise 1 Chr 29.24; 2.15
reign 1 Chr 22.9; 9.27
right (1) 1 Kgs 22.43; 6.8
sacrifice 1 Chr 29.21; 4.6
servant 1 Chr 21.3; 6.17
Tent (2) (of the Lord's presence) [5] 1 Chr 23.26; 5.5
wisdom [3] 1 Chr 22.12; 9.3

King Solomon Prays for Wisdom
(1 Kgs 3.1-15)

1 Solomon, the son of King David,
took firm **control** of the kingdom of
Israel, and the LORD his God **blessed** him
and made him very **powerful**.
2 King Solomon gave an order to all
the officers in charge of units of a thousand men and of a hundred men, all the
government officials, all the heads of
families, and all the rest of the people,
3 **commanding** them to go with him to the
place of worship at Gibeon. They went
there because that was where the **Tent** of
the LORD's presence was located, which
Moses, the LORD's **servant**, had made in
the wilderness. 4 (The **Covenant Box**,
however, was in Jerusalem, kept in a
tent which King David had set up when
he brought the **Box** from Kiriath
Jearim.) 5 The bronze **altar** which had
been made by Bezalel, the son of Uri and
grandson of Hur, was also in Gibeon in
front of the **Tent** of the LORD's presence.
King Solomon and all the people **worshipped** the LORD there. 6 In front of the
Tent the king **worshipped** the LORD by
offering sacrifices on the bronze **altar**;
he had a thousand animals killed and
burnt whole on it.
7 That night God appeared to Solomon
and asked, "What would you like me to
give you?"
8 Solomon answered, "You always
showed great **love** for my father David,
and now you have let me succeed him as
king. 9 O LORD God, **fulfil** the **promise** you
made to my father. You have made me
king over a people who are so many that
they cannot be counted, 10 so give me the
wisdom and **knowledge** I **need** to rule
over them. Otherwise, how would I ever
be able to rule this great people of
yours?"
11 God replied to Solomon, "You have
made the **right choice**. Instead of asking
for wealth or treasure or fame or the
death of your **enemies** or even for long
life for yourself, you have asked for
wisdom and **knowledge** so that you can
rule **my people**, over whom I have made
you king. 12 I will give you **wisdom** and
knowledge. And in addition, I will give
you more wealth, treasure, and fame
than any king has ever had before or will
ever have again."

King Solomon's Power and Wealth
(1 Kgs 10.26-29)

13 So Solomon left[a] the **place of
worship** at Gibeon, where the **Tent** of the
LORD's presence was, and returned to
Jerusalem. There he ruled over Israel.
14 He built up a force of fourteen hundred
chariots and twelve thousand cavalry
horses. Some of them he kept in Jerusalem, and the rest he stationed in various
other cities. 15 During his **reign** silver and
gold became as common in Jerusalem as
stone, and cedar was as **plentiful** as

worship (1) (of God [2] 1 Chr 25.1; 2.1

[a] *Some ancient translations* left; *Hebrew* came to.

1.4: 2 Sam 6.1-17; 1 Chr 13.5-14, 15.25—16.1 **1.5:** Ex 38.1-7 **1.9:** Gen 13.16, 28.14 **1.14:** 1 Kgs 4.26

ordinary sycomore. [16] The king's agents **controlled** the export of horses from Musri[b] and Cilicia,[c] [17] and the export of chariots from Egypt. They supplied the Hittite and Syrian kings with horses and chariots, selling chariots for six hundred pieces of silver each and horses for a hundred and fifty each.[d]

Preparations for Building the Temple
(1 Kgs 5.1–18)

2 King Solomon decided to build a **temple** where the LORD would be **worshipped**, and also to build a palace for himself. [2] He put seventy thousand men to work transporting materials, and eighty thousand men to work quarrying stone. There were three thousand six hundred men responsible for supervising the work.

3 Solomon sent a **message** to King Hiram of Tyre: "Do business with me as you did with my father, King David, when you sold him cedar logs for building his palace. [4] I am building a **temple** to **honour** the LORD my God. It will be a **holy** place where my people and I will **worship** him by burning **incense** of fragrant spices, where we will **present offerings** of **sacred bread** to him continuously, and where we will **offer burnt-offerings** every morning and evening, as well as on **Sabbaths**, **New Moon Festivals**, and other **holy** days **honouring** the LORD our God. He has **commanded** Israel to do this for ever. [5] I **intend** to build a great **temple**, because our God is greater than any other **god**. [6] Yet no one can really build a **temple** for God, because even all the vastness of **heaven** cannot contain him. How then can I build a **temple** that would be anything more than a place to burn **incense** to God? [7] Now send me a man with skill in engraving, in working gold, silver, bronze, and iron, and in making blue, purple and red cloth. He will work with the craftsmen of Judah and Jerusalem whom my father David selected. [8] I know how skilful your woodmen are, so send me cedar, cypress, and juniper logs from Lebanon. I am ready to send my men to assist yours [9] in preparing large quantities of timber, because this **temple** I **intend** to build will be large and magnificent. [10] As **provisions** for your workmen, I will send you two thousand metric tons of wheat, two thousand metric tons of barley, four hundred thousand litres of wine, and four hundred thousand litres of olive-oil."

11 King Hiram sent Solomon a **letter** in reply. He wrote, "Because the LORD **loves his people**, he has made you their king. [12] **Praise** the LORD God of Israel, **Creator** of **heaven and earth**! He has given King David a **wise** son, full of **understanding** and skill, who now **plans** to build a **temple** for the LORD and a palace for himself. [13] I am sending you a **wise** and skilful **master** craftsman named Huram. [14] His mother was a member of the tribe of Dan and his father was a native of Tyre. He knows how to make things out of gold, silver, bronze, iron, stone, and wood. He can work with blue, purple, and red cloth, and with linen. He can do all sorts of engraving and can follow any design suggested to him. Let him work with your craftsmen and with those who worked for your father, King David. [15] So now send us the wheat, barley, wine, and olive-oil that you **promised**. [16] In the mountains of Lebanon we will cut down all the cedars you **need**, **bind** them together in rafts, and float them by sea as far as Joppa. From there you can take them to Jerusalem."

Construction of the Temple Begins
(1 Kgs 6.1–38)

17 King Solomon took a census of all the foreigners living in the land of Israel, similar to the census his father David had taken. There were 153,600 resident foreigners. [18] He assigned 70,000 of them to transport materials and 80,000 to cut stones in the mountains, and appointed 3,600 supervisors to make **sure** the work was done.

3 King David, Solomon's father, had already prepared a place for the Temple. It was in Jerusalem, on Mount Moriah, where the LORD appeared to David, the place which Araunah the Jebusite had used as a threshing-place. King Solomon began the construction [2] in the second month of the fourth year that he was king. [3] The Temple which King Solomon built was twenty-seven metres long and nine metres wide. [4] The entrance room was the full width of the Temple, nine metres, and was fifty-four metres high. The inside of the room was overlaid with **pure** gold. [5] The main room was panelled with cedar and overlaid with fine gold, in which were worked designs of palm-trees and chain patterns.

bind 2 Sam 3.34; Job 13.27
bread 1 Chr 28.16; 4.19
burnt-offering 1 Chr 22.1; 8.13
command 1.3; 4.11
Creator Deut 32.6; Job 4.17
festival 1 Chr 23.31; 5.3
god (2) (other gods) 1 Chr 16.25; 6.14
God's people 1.11; 6.5
heaven [2] 1 Chr 29.11; 6.13
holy [2] 1 Chr 29.16; 8.11
honour [2] 1 Chr 29.16; 6.31
incense [2] 1 Chr 28.18; 4.22
intend [2] 1 Chr 12.17; 11.1
letter (2) 2 Kgs 20.12; 21.12
love 1.8; 5.11
master 1 Chr 12.19; 4.11
message 1 Chr 25.1; 11.3
need 1.10; 35.15
New Moon Festival 1 Chr 23.31; 8.13
offer [2] 1.6; 4.19
plan 1 Chr 28.11; 4.20
praise 1 Chr 29.10; 5.11
present (1) 1 Chr 6.49; 9.9
promise 1.9; 4.11
provide 1 Chr 29.3; 6.16
Sabbath 1 Chr 23.31; 8.13
sacred 1 Chr 23.13; 14.3
sure 1 Chr 18.14; Ezra 7.23
Temple (1) (of God) [7] 1 Chr 29.16; 5.11
understand 2 Kgs 20.19; Neh 8.2
wise [2] 1 Kgs 10.8; 9.6
worship (1) (of God) [2] 1.5; 5.11

creature [3] 1 Chr 28.18; 5.7
each other 2 Kgs 7.9; 12.15
Holy Place [4] 1 Chr 28.11; 4.20
pure 1 Chr 29.4; 4.22

[b] *Probable text* Musri; *Hebrew* Egypt.
[c] MUSRI AND CILICIA: *Two ancient countries in what is now south-east Turkey which were centres of horse-breeding in Solomon's time.* [d] *Verses 16–17 in Hebrew are unclear.*

1.16: Deut 17.16 **2.6:** 1 Kgs 8.27; 2 Chr 6.18 **3.1:** Gen 22.2

6 The king decorated the Temple with beautiful precious stones and with gold imported from the land of Parvaim. 7 He used the gold to overlay the temple walls, the rafters, the thresholds, and the doors. On the walls the workmen carved designs of winged **creatures**.[e] 8 The inner room, called the **Most Holy Place**, was nine metres long and nine metres wide, which was the full width of the Temple. Over twenty metric tons of gold were used to cover the walls of the **Most Holy Place**; 9 570 grammes of gold were used for making nails, and the walls of the upper rooms were also covered with gold.

10 The king also ordered his workmen to make two winged **creatures** out of metal, cover them with gold, and place them in the **Most Holy Place**, 11-13 where they stood side by side facing the entrance. Each had two wings, each wing 2.2 metres long, which were spread out so that they touched **each other** in the centre of the room and reached the wall on either side of the room, stretching across the full width of about nine metres. 14 A curtain for the **Most Holy Place** was made of linen and of other material, which was dyed blue, purple, and red, with designs of the winged **creatures** worked into it.

The Two Bronze Columns
(1 Kgs 7.15–22)

15 The king made two columns, each one fifteen and a half metres tall, and placed them in front of the Temple. Each one had a capital 2.2 metres tall. 16 The tops of the columns were decorated with a design of interwoven chains and one hundred bronze pomegranates.[f] 17 The columns were set at the sides of the temple entrance: the one on the south side was named Jachin,[g] and the one on the north side was named Boaz.[h]

Equipment for the Temple
(1 Kgs 7.23–51)

4 King Solomon had a bronze **altar** made, which was nine metres square and four and a half metres high. 2 He also made a round tank of bronze, 2.2 metres deep, 4.4 metres in diameter, and 13.2 metres in circumference. 3 All round the outer edge of the rim of the tank[i] were two rows of decorations, one above the other. The decorations were in the shape of bulls, which had been cast all in one piece with the rest of the tank. 4 The tank **rested** on the backs of twelve bronze bulls that faced outwards, three facing in each direction. 5 The sides of the tank were 75 millimetres thick. Its rim was like the rim of a **cup**, curving outwards like the petals of a flower. The tank held about sixty thousand litres. 6 They also made ten basins, five to be placed on the south side of the Temple and five on the north side. They were to be used to rinse the parts of the animals that were burnt as **sacrifices**. The water in the large tank was for the **priests** to use for washing.

7-8 They made ten gold lampstands according to the usual pattern, and ten tables, and placed them in the main room of the Temple, five lampstands and five tables on each side. They also made a hundred gold bowls.

9 They made an inner courtyard for the **priests**, and also an outer courtyard. The doors in the gates between the courtyards were covered with bronze. 10 The tank was placed near the south-east corner of the Temple.

11-16 Huram also made pots, shovels, and bowls. He **completed** all the objects that he had **promised** King Solomon he would make for the Temple:

The two columns
The two bowl-shaped capitals on top of the columns
The design of interwoven chains on each capital
The four hundred bronze pomegranates arranged in two rows round the design of each capital
The ten[j] carts
The ten basins
The tank
The twelve bulls supporting the tank
The pots, shovels, and forks

Huram the **master** craftsman made all these objects[k] out of polished bronze, as King Solomon had **commanded**, for use in the Temple of the LORD.

17 The king had them all made in the foundry between Sukkoth and Zeredah[l] in the Jordan Valley. 18 So many objects

incense 2.4; 13.11
master 2.13; Esth 1.22
offer 2.4; 6.40
plan 2.12; 6.7
priest [2] 1 Chr 29 5.5
promise 2.15; 6.4
pure 3.4; 9.17
rest (1) 2 Kgs 4.11 36.21
sacrifice 1.6; 5.6

altar [2] 1.5; 5.11
bread 2.4; 8.13
command 2.4; 6.34
complete 1 Chr 27.24; 8.16
cup 2 Kgs 12.13; 9.20
determine 1 Chr 28.10; 30.12
Holy Place [2] 3.8; 5.7

[e] WINGED CREATURES: *See Word List.* [f] *Verse 16 in Hebrew is unclear.*
[g] JACHIN: *This name sounds like the Hebrew for "he (God) establishes."*
[h] BOAZ: *This name sounds like the Hebrew for "by his (God's) strength."*
[i] *Probable text* All round...tank; *Hebrew unclear.*
[j] *Probable text (see 1 Kgs 7.40–45)* ten; *Hebrew* he made.
[k] *One ancient translation* all these objects; *Hebrew* all their objects.
[l] Zeredah; *or* Zarethan *(see 1 Kgs 7.46).*

3.8: Ex 26.33–34 **3.10–13:** Ex 25.18–20 **3.14:** Ex 26.31 **4.1:** Ex 27.1–2 **4.6:** Ex 30.17–21
4.7: Ex 25.31–40 **4.8:** Ex 25.23–30

were made that no one determined the
total weight of the bronze used.
19 King Solomon also had gold furnishings made for the Temple: the altar and
the tables for the bread offered to God;
20 the lampstands and the lamps of fine
gold that were to burn in front of the
Most Holy Place, according to plan; 21 the
flower decorations, the lamps, and the
tongs; 22 the lamp snuffers, the bowls, the
dishes for incense, and the pans used for
carrying live coals. All these objects
were made of pure gold. The outer doors
of the Temple and the doors to the Most
Holy Place were overlaid with gold.

5 When King Solomon finished all the
work on the Temple, he placed in
the temple storerooms all the things that
his father David had dedicated to the
LORD—the silver, gold, and other
articles.

The Covenant Box Is Brought to the Temple
(1 Kgs 8.1–9)

2 Then King Solomon summoned all
the leaders of the tribes and clans of
Israel to assemble in Jerusalem, in order
to take the LORD's Covenant Box from
Zion, David's City,[m] to the Temple.
3 They all assembled at the time of the
Festival of Shelters. 4 When all the
leaders had gathered, then the Levites
lifted the Covenant Box 5 and carried it to
the Temple. The priests and the Levites
also moved the Tent of the LORD's
presence and all its equipment to the
Temple. 6 King Solomon and all the
people of Israel assembled in front of the
Covenant Box and sacrificed a large
number of sheep and cattle—too many to
count. 7 Then the priests carried the
Covenant Box of the LORD into the
Temple and put it in the Most Holy
Place, beneath the winged creatures.
8 Their outstretched wings covered the
Box and the carrying-poles. 9 The ends of
the poles could be seen by anyone standing directly in front of the Most Holy
Place, but from nowhere else. (The poles
are still there today.) 10 There was
nothing inside the Covenant Box except
the two stone tablets which Moses had
placed there at Mount Sinai, when the
LORD made a covenant with the people
of Israel as they were coming from
Egypt.

The Glory of the Lord

11–14 All the priests present, regardless of the group to which they belonged,
had consecrated themselves. And all the
Levite musicians—Asaph, Heman, and
Jeduthun, and the members of their
clans—were wearing linen clothing. The
Levites stood near the east side of the
altar with cymbals and harps, and with
them were a hundred and twenty priests
playing trumpets. The singers were
accompanied in perfect harmony by
trumpets, cymbals, and other instruments, as they praised the LORD, singing:
"Praise the LORD, because he is good,
And his love is eternal."
As the priests were leaving the
Temple, it was suddenly filled with a
cloud shining with the dazzling light of
the LORD's presence, and they could not
continue the service of worship.

Solomon's Address to the People
(1 Kgs 8.12–21)

6 Then King Solomon prayed,
"LORD, you have chosen to live in
clouds and darkness.
2 Now I have built a majestic temple for
you,
a place for you to live in for ever."
3 All the people of Israel were
standing there. The king turned to face
them and asked God's blessing on them.
4 He said, "Praise the LORD God of Israel!
He has kept the promise he made to my
father David when he said to him,
5 'From the time I brought my people out
of Egypt until now, I did not choose any
city in the land of Israel as the place to
build a temple where I would be worshipped, and I did not choose anyone to
lead my people Israel. 6 But now I have
chosen Jerusalem as the place where I
will be worshipped, and you, David, to
rule my people.' "
7 And Solomon continued, "My father
David planned to build a temple for the
worship of the LORD God of Israel, 8 but
the LORD said to him, 'You were right in
wanting to build a temple for me, 9 but
you will never build it. It is your son, your
own son, who will build my temple.'
10 "Now the LORD has kept his
promise: I have succeeded my father as
king of Israel, and I have built a temple
for the worship of the LORD God of Israel.
11 I have placed in the Temple the Covenant Box, which contains the stone tablets

[m] DAVID'S CITY: *See Word List.*

5.1: 2 Sam 8.11; 1 Chr 18.11 **5.2:** 2 Sam 6.12–15; 1 Chr 15.25–28 **5.10:** Deut 10.5
5.13: 1 Chr 16.34; 2 Chr 7.3; Ezra 3.11; Ps 100.5, 106.1, 107.1, 116.1, 136.1; Jer 33.11 **5.13–14:** Ex 40.34–35
6.4–9: 2 Sam 7.1–13; 1 Chr 17.1–12

innocent [2] 2 Kgs 24.4; Job 9.15
judge 1 Chr 16.12; 19.5
kneel 1 Kgs 8.54; 29.29
law 1 Chr 28.7; 7.17
love [2] 5.11; 7.3
Majesty 1 Chr 29.11; 20.15
mercy 1 Chr 21.13; 30.9
oath 2 Kgs 11.4; 15.14
obey [4] 1 Chr 29.19; 7.17
offer 4.19; 7.1
plan 4.20; 7.11
possess 1 Chr 28.8; 8.7
power [2] 1.1; 12.13
praise 5.11; 7.3
pray [10] 1 Chr 21.17; 7.14
prayer [12] 1 Chr 21.28; 7.1
presence 5.11; 7.1
priest 5.5; 7.2
prison 1 Chr 5.21; 18.26
promise [6] 4.11; 7.18
provide 2.10; 7.6
punish 1 Chr 27.24; 12.2
raise [2] 2 Kgs 23.35; 13.3
reject 2 Kgs 23.27; 34.25
remember 1 Chr 16.12; Neh 1.8
repent [3] 2 Kgs 22.19; 7.14
request 2 Kgs 2.10; Neh 2.5
right (1) [2] 1.11; 14.2
rise 2 Sam 22.39; 36.20
servant [5] 1.3; 9.4
sincere 1 Chr 29.17; 11.16
sorrow 1 Kgs 8.38; Neh 9.1
symbol 2 Kgs 23.6; 14.3
tablet 5.10; Hab 2.2
teach 2 Kgs 22.13; 14.4
Temple (1) (of God) [19] 5.11; 7.1
true [2] 2 Kgs 10.10; 9.5
turn [2] 1 Chr 28.9; 7.14
victory 1 Chr 18.6; 13.18
watch 2 Kgs 9.17; 7.15
wicked 2 Kgs 17.11; 19.2
word (1) 1 Chr 19.5; 20.20
world 1 Chr 17.8; 9.22
worship (1) (of God) [6] 5.11; 7.3
wrong 1 Chr 21.17; Ezra 9.13

of the covenant which the LORD made with the people of Israel."

Solomon's Prayer
(1 Kgs 8.22–53)

12 Then in the presence of the people
Solomon went and stood in front of the
altar and raised his arms in prayer.
13 (Solomon had made a bronze platform
and put it in the middle of the courtyard.
It was 2.2 metres square and 1.3 metres
high. He mounted this platform, knelt
down where everyone could see him, and
raised his hands towards heaven.) 14 He
prayed, "LORD God of Israel, in all
heaven and earth there is no god like
you. You keep your covenant with your
people and show them your love when
they live in wholehearted obedience to
you. 15 You have kept the promise you
made to my father David; today every
word has been fulfilled. 16 Now, LORD God
of Israel, keep the other promise you
made to my father when you told him
that there would always be one of his descendants
ruling as king of Israel,
provided that they carefully obeyed your
Law just as he did. 17 So now, LORD God of
Israel, let everything come true that you
promised to your servant David.

18 "But can you, O God, really live on
earth among men and women? Not even
all heaven is large enough to hold you, so
how can this Temple that I have built be
large enough? 19 LORD my God, I am
your servant. Listen to my prayer and
grant the requests I make to you.
20 Watch over this Temple day and night.
You have promised that this is where
you will be worshipped, so hear me when
I face this Temple and pray. 21 Hear my
prayers and the prayers of your people
Israel when they face this place and
pray. In your home in heaven hear us
and forgive us.

22 "When a person is accused of
wronging another and is brought to your
altar in this Temple to take an oath that
he is innocent, 23 O LORD, listen in heaven
and judge your servants. Punish the
guilty one as he deserves and acquit the
one who is innocent.

24 "When your people Israel are
defeated by their enemies because they
have sinned against you and then when
they turn to you and come to this
Temple, humbly praying to you for
forgiveness, 25 listen to them in heaven.
Forgive the sins of your people and bring
them back to the land which you gave to
them and to their ancestors.

26 "When you hold back the rain
because your people have sinned against
you and then when they repent and face
this Temple, humbly praying to you, 27 O
LORD, listen to them in heaven and
forgive the sins of your servants, the
people of Israel, and teach them to do
what is right. Then, O LORD, send rain on
this land of yours, which you gave to your
people as a permanent possession.

28 "When there is famine in the land
or an epidemic or the crops are destroyed
by scorching winds or swarms of
locusts, or when your people are
attacked by their enemies, or when there
is disease or sickness among them,
29 listen to their prayers. If any of your
people Israel, out of heartfelt sorrow,
stretch out their hands in prayer towards
this Temple, 30 hear their prayer. Listen
to them in your home in heaven and
forgive them. You alone know the
thoughts of the human heart. Deal with
each person as he deserves, 31 so that
your people may honour you and obey
you all the time they live in the land
which you gave to our ancestors.

32 "When a foreigner who lives in a
distant land hears how great and powerful
you are and how you are always
ready to act, and then he comes to pray
at this Temple, 33 listen to his prayer. In
heaven, where you live, hear him and do
what he asks you to do, so that all the
peoples of the world may know you and
obey you, as your people Israel do. Then
they will know that this Temple I have
built is where you are to be worshipped.

34 "When you command your people
to go into battle against their enemies
and they pray to you, wherever they are,
facing this city which you have chosen
and this Temple which I have built for
you, 35 listen to their prayers. Hear them
in heaven and give them victory.

36 "When your people sin against
you—and there is no one who does not
sin—and in your anger you let their
enemies defeat them and take them as
prisoners to some other land, even if that
land is far away, 37 listen to your people's
prayers. If there in that land they repent
and pray to you, confessing how sinful
and wicked they have been, hear their
prayers, O LORD. 38 If in that land they
truly and sincerely repent and pray to
you as they face towards this land which
you gave to our ancestors, this city which
you have chosen, and this Temple which
I have built for you, 39 then listen to their
prayers. In your home in heaven hear
them and be merciful to them and
forgive all the sins of your people.

6.16: 1 Kgs 2.4 **6.18:** 2 Chr 2.6 **6.20:** Deut 12.11

40 "Now, O my God, look on us and
listen to the **prayers offered** in this place.
41 **Rise** up now, LORD God, and with the
Covenant Box, the **symbol** of your **power**,
enter the **Temple** and stay here for ever.
Bless your **priests** in all they do, and may
all your people be **happy** because of your
goodness to them. 42 LORD God, do not
reject the king you have **chosen**. Remember the **love** you had for your **servant**
David."[n]

The Dedication of the Temple
(1 Kgs 8.62–66)

7 When King Solomon finished his
prayer, fire came down from
heaven and burnt up the **sacrifices** that
had been **offered**, and the **dazzling light**
of the LORD's **presence** filled the **Temple**.
2 Because the **Temple** was full of the
dazzling light, the **priests** could not enter
it. 3 When the people of Israel saw the
fire fall from **heaven** and the **light** fill the
Temple, they fell face downwards on the
pavement, **worshipping** God and **praising**
him for his goodness and his **eternal love**.
4 Then Solomon and all the people
offered sacrifices to the LORD. 5 He **sacrificed** 22,000 head of cattle and 120,000
sheep as **fellowship-offerings**. And so he
and all the people **dedicated** the **Temple**.
6 The **priests** stood in the places that
were assigned to them, and facing them
stood the **Levites**, **praising** the LORD with
the musical instruments that King David
had **provided** and singing the **hymn**, "His
Love Is Eternal!" as they had been commissioned by David. The **priests** blew
trumpets while all the people stood.
7 Solomon **consecrated** the central
part of the courtyard, the area in front of
the **Temple**, and then **offered** there the
sacrifices burnt whole, the **grain-
offerings**, and the fat from the **fellowship-
offerings**. He did this because the bronze
altar which he had made was too small
for all these **offerings**.
8 Solomon and all the people of Israel
celebrated the **Festival of Shelters** for
seven days. There was a huge crowd of
people from as far away as Hamath Pass
in the north and the Egyptian border in
the south. 9 They had spent seven days
for the **dedication** of the **altar** and then
seven more days for the **festival**. On the
last day they had a closing **celebration**,
10 and on the following day, the twenty-
third day of the seventh month, Solomon
sent the people home. They were **happy**
about all the **blessings** that the LORD had
given to **his people** Israel, to David, and
to Solomon.

God Appears to Solomon Again
(1 Kgs 9.1–9)

11 After King Solomon had finished
the **Temple** and the palace, **successfully**
completing all his **plans** for them, 12 the
LORD appeared to him at night. He said
to him, "I have heard your **prayer**, and I
accept this **Temple** as the place where
sacrifices are to be **offered** to me.
13 Whenever I hold back the rain or send
locusts to eat up the crops or send an
epidemic on **my people**, 14 if they **pray** to
me and **repent** and **turn away** from the
evil they have been doing, then I will
hear them in **heaven**, **forgive** their sins,
and make their land **prosperous** again.
15 I will **watch** over this **Temple** and be
ready to hear all the **prayers** that are
offered here, 16 because I have **chosen** it
and **consecrated** it as the place where I
will be **worshipped** for ever. I will **watch**
over it and **protect** it for all time. 17 If you
serve me **faithfully** as your father David
did, **obeying** my **laws** and doing everything I have **commanded** you, 18 I will
keep the **promise** I made to your father
David when I told him that Israel would
always be ruled by his descendants. 19 But
if you and your people ever **disobey** the
laws and **commands** I have given you,
and **worship other gods**, 20 then I will
remove you from the land that I gave
you, and I will **abandon** this **Temple** that
I have **consecrated** as the place where I
am to be **worshipped**. People everywhere will **ridicule** it and treat it with
contempt.
21 "The **Temple** is now greatly
honoured, but then everyone who passes
by it will be **amazed** and will ask, 'Why
did the LORD do this to this land and this
Temple?' 22 People will answer, 'It is
because they **abandoned** the LORD their
God, who brought their ancestors out of
Egypt. They gave their allegiance to
other **gods** and **worshipped** them. That is
why the LORD has brought this **disaster**
on them.'"

Solomon's Achievements
(1 Kgs 9.10–28)

8 It took Solomon twenty years to
build the **Temple** and his palace.
2 He also rebuilt the cities that King
Hiram had given him, and sent Israelites
to settle in them. 3 He captured the territory of Hamath and Zobah 4 and fortified

abandon [2] 1 Chr 28.9; 11.14
accept 1 Chr 28.9; 15.15
altar [2] 6.12; 8.12
amaze 1 Kgs 10.5; 9.4
bless 6.3; 17.3
celebrate [2] 1 Chr 15.25; 23.13
choose 6.1; 11.22
command [2] 6.34; 8.14
consecrate [3] 5.11; 13.9
contempt 1 Kgs 9.7; Ps 31.11
dazzling [2] 5.11; Job 37.21
dedicate [2] 5.1; 15.18
disaster 1 Chr 2.7; 18.22
disobey 1 Chr 10.13; 24.20
eternal [2] 5.11; 20.21
evil 1 Chr 4.10; 12.14
faithful 1 Chr 29.18; 15.17
fellowship-offering [2] 1 Chr 21.26; 31.2
festival [2] 5.3; 8.13
forgive 6.21; 30.19
god (2) (other gods) [2] 6.14; 13.8
God's people [2] 6.5; 9.8
grain-offering 2 Kgs 16.13; Neh 10.33
happy 6.41; 15.15
heaven [3] 6.13; 18.18
honour 6.31; 17.5
hymn 8.14
last (2) 1 Chr 26.6; Neh 3.32
law [2] 6.16; 8.13
Levites 5.4; 8.14
light (1) [3] 5.11; Neh 9.12
love [2] 6.14; 9.8
obey 6.14; 11.4
offer [6] 6.40; 8.12
plan 6.7; 8.6
praise [2] 6.4; 9.8
pray 6.1; 14.11
prayer [3] 6.12; 30.18
presence 6.12; 9.7
priest [3] 6.41; 8.14
promise 6.4; 21.7
prosper 1 Chr 14.2; 14.7
protect 1 Chr 16.21; 14.7
provide 6.16; 11.23
repent 6.26; 33.19
ridicule 2 Kgs 19.22; 30.10
sacrifice [5] 5.6; 8.12
serve 1 Chr 28.9; 8.9
sheep 5.6; 13.9

shelter 5.3; 8.13
succeed (1) 1 Chr 29.23; 8.16
Temple (1) (of God) [11] 6.2; 8.1
turn 6.3; 15.2
watch [2] 6.20; 16.9
worship (1) (of God) [3] 6.5; 11.16
worship (2) (of other gods) [2] 1 Chr 5.25; 11.15

altar 7.7; 14.3
bread 4.19; 13.11
burnt-offering 2.4; 28.3
command [2] 7.17; 11.4
complete [2] 4.11; 29.18

[n] the love you...David; *or* your servant David's loyal service.

6.41–42: Ps 132.8–10 **7.1:** Lev 9.23–24
7.3: 1 Chr 16.34; 2 Chr 5.13; Ezra 3.11; Ps 100.5, 106.1, 107.1, 118.1, 136.1; Jer 33.11 **7.18:** 1 Kgs 2.4

Covenant Box 6.11; 35.3
duty (1) 1 Chr 28.13; 13.10
experience 1 Chr 29.1; Ps 72.3
festival [3] 7.8; 30.1
force (1) [3] 1 Chr 11.18; 10.18
harvest 2 Kgs 19.29; Neh 10.35
holy [2] 2.4; 26.18
hymn 7.6; Neh 12.8
law 7.17; 9.8
Levites [2] 7.6; 11.13
man of God 1 Chr 23.14; 30.16
New Moon Festival 2.4; 31.3
offer [2] 7.1; 9.4
plan 7.11; 30.4
possess 6.27; 21.3
priest [3] 7.2; 11.13
require 2 Kgs 22.7; 24.6
Sabbath 2.4; 23.4
sacrifice 7.1; 9.4
serve 7.17; 9.4
shelter 7.8; Ezra 3.4
slave 1 Chr 17.21; 28.10
succeed (1) 7.11; 18.12
Temple (1) (of God) [3] 7.1; 9.4
unleavened 1 Chr 23.29; 30.13

the city of Palmyra in the desert. He
rebuilt all the cities in Hamath that were
centres for storing supplies. 5 Solomon
also rebuilt the following cities: Upper
Beth Horon and Lower Beth Horon (fortified cities with gates that could be
barred), 6 the city of Baalath, all the
cities where he stored supplies, and the
cities where his horses and chariots were
stationed. He carried out all his **plans** for
building in Jerusalem, in Lebanon, and
throughout the territory that he ruled
over. 7-8 Solomon employed in **forced**
labour all the descendants of the people
of Canaan whom the Israelites had not
killed when they took **possession** of the
land. These included Hittites, Amorites,
Perizzites, Hivites, and Jebusites, whose
descendants continue to be **slaves** down
to the present time. 9 Israelites were not
used in **forced labour**, but **served** as
soldiers, officers, chariot commanders,
and horsemen. 10 There were 250 officials
in charge of the **forced labour** working
on the various building projects.
11 Solomon moved his wife, the
daughter of the king of Egypt, from
David's City to a house he built for her.
He said, "She must not live in the palace
of King David of Israel, because any
place where the **Covenant Box** has been
is **holy**."
12 Solomon **offered sacrifices** to the
LORD on the **altar** which he had built in
front of the **Temple**. 13 He **offered burnt-**
offerings according to the **requirements**
of the **Law of Moses** for each **holy** day:
Sabbaths, **New Moon Festivals**, and the
three annual **festivals**—the Festival of
Unleavened Bread, the **Harvest Festival**,
and the **Festival of Shelters**. 14 Following
the rules laid down by his father David,
he organized the daily work of the **priests**
and of the **Levites** who assisted the
priests in singing **hymns** and in doing
their work. He also organized the temple
guards in sections for performing their
daily **duties** at each gate, in accordance
with the **commands** of David, the **man of**
God. 15 The instructions which David had
given the **priests and the Levites** concerning the storehouses and other
matters were carried out in detail.
16 By this time all Solomon's projects
had been **completed**. From the laying of
the foundation of the LORD's **Temple** to
its **completion**, all the work had been
successful.
17 Then Solomon went to Eziongeber
and Elath, ports on the shore of the Gulf
of Aqaba, in the land of Edom. 18 King
Hiram sent him ships under the **com-**
mand of his own officers and manned by
experienced sailors. They sailed with
Solomon's officers to the land of Ophir
and brought back to Solomon more than
fifteen thousand kilogrammes of gold.

The Visit of the Queen of Sheba
(1 Kgs 10.1–13)

9 The queen of Sheba heard of King
Solomon's fame, and she travelled
to Jerusalem to **test** him with **difficult**
questions. She brought with her a large
group of attendants, as well as camels
loaded with spices, jewels, and a large
amount of gold. When she and Solomon
met, she asked him all the **questions** that
she could think of. 2 He answered them
all; there was nothing too **difficult** for
him to explain. 3 The queen of Sheba
heard Solomon's **wisdom** and saw the
palace he had built. 4 She saw the food
that was **served** at his table, the living-
quarters for his officials, the organization
of his palace staff and the uniforms they
wore, the clothing of the **servants** who
waited on him at **feasts**, and the
sacrifices he **offered**[o] in the **Temple**. It
left her breathless and **amazed**.
5 She said to the king, "What I heard
in my own country about you[p] and your
wisdom is **true**! 6 I did not **believe** what
they told me until I came and saw for
myself. I had not heard of even half your
wisdom. You are even **wiser** than people
say. 7 How **fortunate** are the men who
serve you, who are always in your
presence and are **privileged** to hear your
wise sayings! 8 **Praise** the LORD your
God! He has shown how **pleased** he is
with you by making you king, to rule **in**
his name. Because he **loves his people**
Israel and wants to **preserve** them for
ever, he has made you their king so that
you can maintain **law** and **justice**."
9 She **presented** to King Solomon the
gifts she had brought: more than four
thousand kilogrammes of gold and a very
large amount of spices and jewels. There
have never been any other spices as fine
as those that the queen of Sheba gave to
King Solomon.
10 (The men of King Hiram and of
King Solomon who brought gold from
Ophir also brought juniper wood and
jewels. 11 Solomon used the wood to make
stairs for the **Temple** and for his palace,
and to make harps and lyres for the

amaze 7.21; Neh 9.10
believe 1 Kgs 10.7; 20.20
consult 1 Chr 14.14; 10.6
cup 4.5; Ezra 1.7
difficult [2] 2 Kgs 5.13; Neh 1.3
exist 1 Kgs 10.19; Job 10.19
feast 1 Chr 12.39; 18.2
footstool 1 Chr 28.2; Is 66.1
fortune 1 Kgs 10.8; Prov 11.10
gift [3] 1 Chr 29.14; 17.5
God's people 7.10; 23.16
justice 1 Chr 18.14; 12.6
law 8.13; 12.1
love 7.3; 11.21
name (2) (name of God, of Jesus) 1 Chr 29.13; 14.11
offer 8.12; 11.16
please 1 Chr 29.17; 10.7
plenty 1.15; Job 29.6
praise 7.3; 20.19
presence 7.1; Ezra 9.6
present (1) 2.4; 13.11
preserve 1 Chr 17.24; Ps 12.7
privilege 1 Kgs 10.8; Ezek 16.49
prophecy 1 Kgs 22.8; 15.8
prophet [2] 1 Chr 29.29; 10.15
pure [2] 4.22; 29.5
question [2] 2 Kgs 9.19; Esth 1.13
reign [2] 1.15; 12.2
rich 2 Kgs 25.26; 18.1
sacrifice 8.12; 11.16
saying 1 Kgs 10.8; Ps 78.2
servant 6.17; 24.6
serve [2] 8.9; 10.6
supreme 1 Chr 29.11; Ps 46.10
tax 1 Chr 18.2; 24.6
Temple (1) (of God) [2] 8.1; 12.9
test 1 Chr 29.17; 32.31
throne [4] 1 Chr 29.23; 18.9
true 6.17; 15.3
value 2 Kgs 8.6; 20.25
vision 1 Sam 3.1; 32.32
wisdom [4] 1.10; Ezra 7.25
wise [3] 2.12; 11.23
world 6.33; 16.9

[o] *Probable text (see 1 Kgs 10.5)* sacrifices he offered; *Hebrew* his upper rooms.
[p] you; *or* your deeds.

8.13: Ex 23.14–17, 34.22–23; Num 28.9, 29.39; Deut 16.16 **9.1–9:** Mt 12.42; Lk 11.31

musicians. Nothing like that had ever been seen before in the land of Judah.)

12 King Solomon gave the queen of Sheba everything she asked for. This was in addition to what he gave her in exchange for the **gifts**[q] she brought to him. Then she and her attendants returned to the land of Sheba.

King Solomon's Wealth
(1 Kgs 10.14–25)

13 Every year King Solomon received almost twenty-three thousand kilogrammes of gold, 14 in addition to the **taxes** paid by the traders and merchants. The kings of Arabia and the governors of the Israelite districts also brought him silver and gold. 15 Solomon made two hundred large shields, each of which was covered with about seven kilogrammes of beaten gold, 16 and three hundred smaller shields, each covered with about three kilogrammes of beaten gold. He had them all placed in the Hall of the Forest of Lebanon.[r]

17 The king also had a large **throne** made. Part of it was covered with ivory and the rest of it was covered with **pure** gold. 18 Six steps led up to the **throne**, and there was a **footstool** attached to it, covered with gold. There were arms on each side of the **throne**, and the figure of a lion stood at each side. 19 Twelve figures of lions were on the steps, one at either end of each step. No **throne** like this had ever **existed** in any other kingdom.

20 All King Solomon's **cups** were made of gold, and all the utensils in the Hall of the Forest of Lebanon were of **pure** gold. Silver was not considered **valuable** in Solomon's day. 21 He had a fleet of ocean-going ships sailing with King Hiram's fleet. Every three years his fleet would return, bringing gold, silver, ivory, apes, and monkeys.

22 King Solomon was **richer** and **wiser** than any other king in the **world**. 23 They all **consulted** him, to hear the **wisdom** that God had given him. 24 Each of them brought Solomon **gifts**—articles of silver and gold, robes, weapons, spices, horses, and mules. This continued year after year.

25 King Solomon also had four thousand stalls for his chariots and horses, and had twelve thousand cavalry horses. Some of them he kept in Jerusalem and the rest he stationed in various other cities. 26 He was **supreme** ruler of all the kings in the territory from the River Euphrates to Philistia and the Egyptian border. 27 During his **reign** silver was as common in Jerusalem as stone, and cedar was as **plentiful** as ordinary sycomore in the foothills of Judah. 28 Solomon imported horses from Musri[s] and from every other country.

Summary of Solomon's Reign
(1 Kgs 11.41–43)

29 The rest of the history of Solomon from beginning to end is recorded in *The History of Nathan the **Prophet**,* in *The **Prophecy** of Ahijah of Shiloh,* and in *The **Visions** of Iddo the **Prophet**,* which also deal with the **reign** of King Jeroboam of Israel. 30 Solomon ruled in Jerusalem over all Israel for forty years. 31 He died and was buried in David's City, and his son Rehoboam succeeded him as king.

The Northern Tribes Revolt
(1 Kgs 12.1–20)

10 Rehoboam went to Shechem, where all the people of northern Israel had gathered to make him king. 2 When Jeroboam son of Nebat, who had gone to Egypt to **escape** from King Solomon, heard this news, he returned home. 3 The people of the northern tribes sent for him, and they all went together to Rehoboam and said to him, 4 "Your father placed heavy **burdens** on us. If you make these **burdens** lighter and make **life** easier for us, we will be your **loyal subjects**."

5 Rehoboam replied, "Give me three days to consider the matter. Then come back." So the people left.

6 King Rehoboam **consulted** the older men who had **served** as his father Solomon's advisers. "What answer do you **advise** me to give these people?" he asked.

7 They replied, "If you are **kind** to these people and try to **please** them by giving a considerate answer, they will always **serve** you **loyally**."

8 But he **ignored** the **advice** of the older men and went instead to the young men who had grown up with him and who were now his advisers. 9 "What do you **advise** me to do?" he asked. "What shall I say to the people who are asking me to make their **burdens** lighter?"

10 They replied, "This is what you should tell them: 'My little finger is

advice [5] 1 Chr 26.14; 22.2
burden [5] 1 Kgs 12.4; Neh 4.10
consult 9.23; 18.4
death (3) (to death) 2 Kgs 25.7; 15.13
escape [2] 1 Chr 29.15; 12.5
force (1) 8.7; 12.7
ignore [2] 1 Chr 13.3; 25.16
kind 2 Kgs 25.27; 30.9
life (1) 1.11; 15.17
loyal [2] 1 Chr 29.24; 16.9
please 9.8; 14.2
prophet 9.29; 11.2
rebel [2] 2 Kgs 25.1; 13.6
serve [2] 9.4; 11.14
subject (1) 1 Chr 22.18; 21.19
will (1) 1 Chr 19.13; 11.4

[q] *Probable text* he gave her in exchange for the gifts; *Hebrew unclear.*
[r] HALL OF THE FOREST OF LEBANON: *A large ceremonial hall in the palace, probably so called because it was panelled in cedar.* [s] *Probable text (see 1.16)* Musri; *Hebrew* Egypt.

9.25: 1 Kgs 4.26 **9.26:** Gen 15.18; 1 Kgs 4.21 **9.28:** Deut 17.16

thicker than my father's waist.' 11 Tell
them, 'My father placed heavy **burdens**
on you; I will make them even heavier.
He beat you with a whip; I'll flog you
with a horsewhip!' "

12 Three days later Jeroboam and all
the people returned to King Rehoboam,
as he had instructed them. 13 The king
ignored the **advice** of the older men and
spoke harshly to the people, 14 as the
younger men had **advised**. He said, "My
father placed heavy **burdens** on you; I
will make them even heavier. He beat
you with a whip; I'll flog you with a
horsewhip!" 15 It was the **will of the LORD**
God to bring about what he had spoken
to Jeroboam son of Nebat through the
prophet Ahijah from Shiloh. This is why
the king did not pay any attention to the
people.

16 When the people saw that the king
would not listen to them, they shouted,
"Down with David and his family! What
have they ever done for us? Men of
Israel, let's go home! Let Rehoboam look
out for himself!"

So the people of Israel **rebelled**,
17 leaving Rehoboam as king only of the
people who lived in the territory of
Judah.

18 Then King Rehoboam sent
Adoniram, who was in charge of the
forced labour, to go to the Israelites, but
they stoned him **to death**. At this, Rehoboam hurriedly got into his chariot and
escaped to Jerusalem. 19 Ever since that
time the people of the northern kingdom
of Israel have been in **rebellion** against
the dynasty of David.

Shemaiah's Prophecy
(1 Kgs 12.21–24)

11 When King Rehoboam arrived in
Jerusalem, he called together a
hundred and eighty thousand of the **best**
soldiers from the tribes of Benjamin and
Judah. He **intended** to go to war and
restore his **control** over the northern
tribes of Israel. 2 But the LORD told the
prophet Shemaiah 3 to give this **message**
to King Rehoboam and to all the people
of the tribes of Judah and Benjamin:
4 "Do not attack your fellow-Israelites. Go
home, all of you. What has happened is
my **will**." They **obeyed** the LORD's **command** and did not go to fight Jeroboam.

Rehoboam Fortifies the Cities

5 Rehoboam remained in Jerusalem
and had fortifications built for the following cities of Judah and Benjamin:
6 Bethlehem, Etam, Tekoa, 7 Bethzur,
Soco, Adullam, 8 Gath, Mareshah, Ziph,
9 Adoraim, Lachish, Azekah, 10 Zorah,
Aijalon, and Hebron. 11 He had them
strongly fortified and appointed a commander for each of them, and in each
one he placed supplies of food, olive-oil,
and wine, 12 and also shields and spears.
In this way he kept Judah and Benjamin
under his **control**.

Priests and Levites Come to Judah

13 From all the territory of Israel
priests and Levites came south to Judah.
14 The **Levites abandoned** their pastures
and other land and moved to Judah and
Jerusalem, because King Jeroboam of
Israel and his successors would not let
them **serve** as **priests** of the LORD. 15 Jeroboam appointed **priests** of his own to
serve at the **pagan places of worship** and
to **worship demons** and the **idols** he made
in the form of **bull-calves**. 16 From all the
tribes of Israel people who **sincerely**
wanted to **worship** the LORD, the God of
Israel, followed the **Levites** to Jerusalem,
so that they could **offer sacrifices** to the
LORD, the God of their ancestors. 17 This
strengthened the kingdom of Judah, and
for three years they supported Rehoboam son of Solomon and lived as they
had under the rule of King David and
King Solomon.

Rehoboam's Family

18 Rehoboam married Mahalath,
whose father was Jerimoth son of David,
and whose mother was Abihail, the
daughter of Eliab and granddaughter of
Jesse. 19 They had three sons, Jeush,
Shemariah, and Zaham. 20 Later he
married Maacah, the daughter of Absalom, and they had four sons: Abijah,
Attai, Ziza, and Shelomith. 21 In all, Rehoboam had eighteen wives and sixty
concubines, and he fathered twenty-eight
sons and sixty daughters. Of all his wives
and **concubines** he **loved** Maacah **best**,
22 and he **favoured** her son Abijah over all
his other children, **choosing** him as the
one to succeed him as king. 23 Rehoboam
wisely assigned responsibilities to his
sons, and stationed them throughout
Judah and Benjamin in the fortified
cities. He **provided generously** for them
and also **secured** many wives for them.

An Egyptian Invasion of Judah
(1 Kgs 14.25–28)

12 As soon as Rehoboam had
established his **authority** as king,
he and all his people **abandoned** the **Law**

10.16: 2 Sam 20.1 **11.15:** 1 Kgs 12.31

abandon 7.20; 12.1
best [2] 1 Chr 19.10; 13.17
bull-calf 2 Kgs 17.16; 13.8
choose 7.16; 12.13
command 8.14; 13.11
concubine [2] 1 Chr 7.14; Esth 2.14
control [2] 1.1; 14.7
demon 2 Kgs 23.8; Is 34.14
favour 1 Chr 17.27; Ezra 7.28
generous 1 Chr 29.5; Esth 1.7
idol 1 Chr 20.2; 15.8
intend 2.5; 28.10
Levites [3] 8.14; 13.9
love 9.8; 20.21
message 2.3; 12.5
obey 7.17; 14.4
offer 9.4; 13.11
pagan 2 Kgs 23.5; 14.3
place of worship 1.3; 14.3
priest [3] 8.14; 13.9
prophet 10.15; 12.5

provide 7.6; 28.15
restore 1 Chr 11.8; 24.13
sacrifice 9.4; 13.11
secure 1 Chr 22.9; 14.7
serve [2] 10.6; 12.8
sincere 6.38; Job 16.17
strength 1 Chr 29.12; 16.9
strong 1 Chr 29.12; 15.7
will (1) 10.15; 12.14
wise 9.6; Esth 6.13
worship (1) (of God) 7.3; 12.13
worship (2) (of other gods) 7.19; 17.3

abandon [2] 11.14; 13.10
act 6.32; 16.9

admit (1) [2] 2 Sam 1.16; Job 28.22
anger [2] 6.36; 16.10
authority Josh 1.18; 13.8
choose 11.22; 22.7
conquer 1 Chr 22.18; 30.6
destroy [2] 6.28; 14.14
each other 3.11; 20.23
entrust 1 Kgs 14.27; Ezra 7.14
escape 10.2; 16.7
establish 1 Chr 29.23; 31.2
evil 7.14; 22.2
force (1) 10.18; 13.7
justice 9.8; Ezra 9.15
law 9.8; 15.3
learn 2 Kgs 19.8; 22.10
message 11.3; 16.2
power 6.32; 13.20
prophet [3] 11.2; 13.22
punish 6.23; 20.9
reign 9.27; 13.1
serve 11.14; 13.10
submit 2 Kgs 24.1; Ps 32.9
Temple (1) (of God) [2] 9.4; 15.8
tomb 2 Kgs 23.16; 14.1
will (1) 11.4; 13.7
worship (1) (of God) 11.16; 15.12

of the LORD. 2 In the fifth year of Rehoboam's **reign** their disloyalty to the LORD was **punished**. King Shishak of Egypt attacked Jerusalem 3 with an army of twelve hundred chariots, sixty thousand horsemen, and more soldiers than could be counted, including Libyan, Sukkite, and Sudanese troops. 4 He captured the fortified cities of Judah and advanced as far as Jerusalem.

5 Shemaiah the **prophet** went to King Rehoboam and the Judaean leaders who had gathered in Jerusalem to **escape** Shishak. He said to them, "This is the LORD's **message** to you: 'You have **abandoned** me, so now I have abandoned you to Shishak.' "

6 The king and the leaders **admitted** that they had sinned, and they said, "What the LORD is doing is **just**."

7 When the LORD saw this, he spoke again to Shemaiah and said to him, "Because they **admit** their sin, I will not **destroy** them. But when Shishak attacks, they will barely survive. Jerusalem will not feel the full **force** of my **anger**, 8 but Shishak will **conquer** them, and they will **learn** the difference between **serving** me and serving earthly rulers."

9 King Shishak came to Jerusalem and took the treasures from the **Temple** and from the palace. He took everything, including the gold shields that King Solomon had made. 10 To replace them, Rehoboam made bronze shields and **entrusted** them to the officers responsible for guarding the palace gates. 11 Every time the king went to the **Temple**, the guards carried the shields and then returned them to the guardroom. 12 Because he **submitted** to the LORD, the **LORD's anger** did not completely **destroy** him, and things went well for Judah.

Summary of Rehoboam's Reign

13 Rehoboam ruled in Jerusalem and increased his **power** as king. He was forty-one years old when he became king, and he ruled for seventeen years in Jerusalem, the city which the LORD had **chosen** from all the territory of Israel as the place where he was to be **worshipped**. Rehoboam's mother was Naamah, from the land of Ammon. 14 He did what was **evil**, because he did not try to find the **LORD's will**.

15 Rehoboam's **acts** from beginning to end and his family records are found in *The History of Shemaiah the Prophet* and *The History of Iddo the Prophet*. Rehoboam and Jeroboam were constantly at war with **each other**. 16 Rehoboam died and was buried in the royal **tombs** in David's City and his son Abijah succeeded him as king.

Abijah's War with Jeroboam

(1 Kgs 15.1–8)

13 In the eighteenth year of the **reign** of King Jeroboam of Israel, Abijah became king of Judah, 2 and he ruled for three years in Jerusalem. His mother was Micaiah daughter of Uriel, from the city of Gibeah.

War broke out between Abijah and Jeroboam. 3 Abijah **raised** an army of 400,000 soldiers, and Jeroboam opposed him with an army of 800,000.

4 The armies met in the hill-country of Ephraim. King Abijah went up Mount Zemaraim and called out to Jeroboam and the Israelites: "Listen to me!" he said. 5 "Don't you know that the LORD, the God of Israel, made an unbreakable **covenant** with David, giving him and his descendants kingship over Israel for ever? 6 Jeroboam son of Nebat **rebelled** against Solomon, his king. 7 Later he gathered together a group of **worthless** scoundrels, and they **forced** their **will** on Rehoboam son of Solomon, who was too young and inexperienced to **resist** them. 8 Now you propose to fight against the royal **authority** that the LORD gave to David's descendants. You have a huge army and have with you the gold **bull-calves** that Jeroboam made to be your **gods**. 9 You drove out the LORD's **priests**, the descendants of Aaron, and you drove out the **Levites**. In their place you appointed **priests** in the same way that other nations do. Anybody who comes along with a bull or seven **sheep** can get himself **consecrated** as a **priest** of those so-called **gods** of yours.

10 "But we still **serve** the LORD our God and have not **abandoned** him. **Priests** descended from Aaron perform their **duties**, and **Levites** assist them. 11 Every morning and every evening they **offer** him **incense** and animal **sacrifices** burnt whole. They **present** the **offerings** of **bread** on a table that is ritually **clean**, and every evening they light the lamps on the gold lampstand. We do what the LORD has **commanded**, but you have **abandoned** him. 12 God himself is our leader and his **priests** are here with trumpets, ready to blow them and call us to battle against you. People of Israel, don't fight against the LORD, the God of your ancestors! You can't **win**!"

13 Meanwhile Jeroboam had sent some of his troops to ambush the

abandon [2] 12.1; 15.2
authority 12.1; 19.6
best 11.1; Neh 5.18
bread 8.13; 18.26
bull-calf 11.15; Neh 9.18
clean 2 Kgs 25.14; 29.15
command 11.4; 14.4
consecrate 7.7; 23.6
covenant 6.11; 15.12
duty (1) 8.14; 19.9
flee 1 Chr 19.14; 14.12
force (1) 12.7; 19.10
god (2) (other gods) [2] 7.19; 25.15
help 1 Chr 28.21; 14.11
incense 4.22; 14.5
Levites [2] 11.13; 17.8
offer [2] 11.16; 15.11
power [2] 12.13; 14.11
present (1) 9.9; 29.27
priest [6] 11.13; 15.3
prophet 12.5; 16.7
raise 6.12; Ezra 9.6
rebel 10.16; 25.27
reign [2] 12.2; 15.19
rely 1 Chr 12.1; 14.11
resist Lev 26.21; 26.18
sacrifice 11.16; 15.11
serve 12.8; 17.4
sheep 7.5; 14.15
strike 2 Kgs 15.5; 18.33
victory 6.35; 16.8
will (1) 12.14; 14.4
win 2 Kgs 13.17; 18.11
worthless 2 Kgs 17.15; Job 11.11

12.9: 1 Kgs 10.16–17; 2 Chr 9.15–16

Judaean army from the rear, while the
rest faced them from the front. 14 The
Judaeans looked round and saw that they
were surrounded. They cried to the LORD
for **help**, and the **priests** blew the trumpets. 15 The Judaeans gave a loud shout,
and led by Abijah, they attacked; God
defeated Jeroboam and the Israelite
army. 16 The Israelites **fled** from the
Judaeans, and God let the Judaeans overpower them. 17 Abijah and his army dealt
the Israelites a crushing defeat—half a
million of Israel's **best** soldiers were
killed. 18 And so the people of Judah were
victorious over Israel, because they
relied on the LORD, the God of their
ancestors.
19 Abijah pursued Jeroboam's army
and occupied some of his cities: Bethel,
Jeshanah, and Ephron, and the villages
near each of these cities. 20 Jeroboam
never regained his **power** during Abijah's
reign. Finally the LORD **struck** him down,
and he died.
21 Abijah, however, grew more
powerful. He had fourteen wives and
fathered twenty-two sons and sixteen
daughters. 22 The rest of the history of
Abijah, what he said and what he did, is
written in *The History of Iddo the
Prophet*.

King Asa Defeats the Sudanese

14 King Abijah died and was buried
in the royal **tombs** in David's
City. His son Asa succeeded him as king,
and under Asa the land **enjoyed peace**
for ten years. 2 Asa **pleased** the LORD, his
God, by doing what was **right** and good.
3 He removed the foreign **altars** and the
pagan places of worship, broke down the
sacred stone columns, and cut down the
symbols of the **goddess** Asherah. 4 He
commanded the people of Judah to do
the **will of the LORD**, the God of their
ancestors, and to **obey** his **teachings** and
commands. 5 Because he abolished the
pagan places of worship and the **incense-
altars** from all the cities of Judah, the
kingdom was at **peace** under his rule.
6 He built fortifications for the cities of
Judah during this time, and for several
years there was no war, because the
LORD gave him **peace**. 7 He said to the
people of Judah, "Let us fortify the cities
by building walls and towers, and gates
that can be shut and barred. We have
control of the land because we have done
the **will of the LORD** our God. He has **protected** us and given us **security** on every
side." And so they built and **prospered**.
8 King Asa had an army of 300,000 men
from Judah, armed with shields and
spears, and 280,000 men from Benjamin,
armed with shields and bows. All of them
were brave, well-trained men.
9 A Sudanese named Zerah invaded
Judah with an army of a million men and
three hundred chariots and advanced as
far as Mareshah. 10 Asa went out to fight
him, and both sides took up their
positions in the Valley of Zephathah near
Mareshah. 11 Asa **prayed** to the LORD his
God, "O LORD, you can **help** a **weak** army
as easily as a **powerful** one. **Help** us now,
O LORD our God, because we are **relying**
on you, and in your **name** we have come
out to fight against this huge army. LORD,
you are our God; no one can **hope** to
defeat you."
12 The LORD defeated the Sudanese
army when Asa and the Judaean army
attacked them. They **fled**, 13 and Asa and
his troops pursued them as far as Gerar.
So many of the Sudanese were killed that
the army was unable to rally and fight.[f]
They were overpowered by the LORD
and his army, and the army took large
amounts of loot. 14 Then they were able to
destroy the cities in the area around
Gerar, because the people there were
terrified of the LORD. The army
plundered all those cities and captured
large amounts of loot. 15 They also
attacked the camps of some **shepherds**,
capturing large numbers of **sheep** and
camels. Then they returned to
Jerusalem.

Asa's Reforms

15 The **spirit of God** came upon
Azariah son of Oded, 2 and he
went to meet King Asa. He called out,
"Listen to me, King Asa, and all you
people of Judah and Benjamin! The
LORD is with you as long as you are with
him. If you look for him, he will let you
find him, but if you **turn away**, he will
abandon you. 3 For a long time Israel
lived without the **true** God, without
priests to **teach** them, and without a **law**.
4 But when **trouble** came, they **turned to**
the LORD, the God of Israel. They
searched for him and found him. 5 In
those days no one could come and go in
safety, because there was **trouble** and
disorder in every land. 6 One nation
oppressed another nation, and one city
oppressed another city, because God was
bringing **trouble** and **distress** on them.

[f] So many of the Sudanese...fight; *or* The Sudanese were completely defeated; not one of them was left alive.

weak 2 Kgs 19.3; 28.15
will (1) [2] 13.7; 19.3

altar [2] 8.12; 15.8
command [2] 13.11; 17.4
control 11.1; 17.5
destroy 12.7; 15.17
enjoy 1 Chr 17.27; Ezra 9.12
flee 13.16; 25.22
goddess 2 Kgs 23.4; 15.16
help [2] 13.14; 16.12
hope 2 Kgs 5.18; Ezra 10.2
incense 13.11; 25.14
name (2) (name of God, of Jesus) 9.8; 15.14
obey 11.4; 17.4
pagan [2] 11.15; 15.17
peace [3] 1 Chr 23.25; 15.15
place of worship [2] 11.15; 15.17
please 10.7; 24.2
power 13.20; 17.12
pray 7.14; 20.3
prosper 7.14; Ezra 9.12
protect 7.16; 23.10
rely 13.18; 16.7
right (1) 6.8; 19.2
sacred 2.4; 20.21
secure 11.23; 20.30
sheep 13.9; 15.11
shepherd 1 Kgs 22.17; 18.16
symbol 6.41; 17.6
teach 6.27; 15.3
terrify 1 Chr 10.4; 20.29
tomb 12.16; 16.14

abandon 13.10; 16.5
accept 7.12; 30.9
agree 1 Chr 13.4; 16.4
altar 14.3; 23.17
covenant [3] 13.5; 21.7
death (3) (to death) 10.18; 22.9
dedicate [2] 7.5; 29.19
delight 1 Sam 18.26; Ps 35.19
destroy 14.14; 17.6
discourage 2 Sam 17.2; 20.15
distress 2 Kgs 11.14; 23.13
encourage 2 Sam 16.21; 26.10
faithful 7.17; 19.9
goddess 14.3; 17.6
happy 7.10; 23.21
heart [2] 6.14; 16.9
idol [4] 11.15; 23.17
law 12.1; 17.9
life (1) 10.4; 17.3
name (2) (name of God, of Jesus) 14.11; 18.15
oath 6.22; Ezra 10.5
offer 13.11; 23.18

oppress 1 Chr 17.9; Neh 5.7
pagan 14.3; 17.6
peace 14.1; 18.16
place of worship 14.3; 17.6
priest 13.9; 17.8
prophecy 9.29; 18.7
reign 13.1; 16.1
reward 1 Kgs 13.7; Esth 6.3
sacrifice 13.11; 23.18
safe 1 Kgs 22.27; 18.26
sheep 14.15; 17.11
soul 1 Chr 22.19; 34.31
Spirit (1) (God's Spirit) 1 Chr 12.18; 18.23
strong 11.11; 25.8
teach 14.4; 17.7
Temple (1) (of God) [2] 12.9; 16.2
trouble [3] 1 Chr 21.1; 20.9
true 9.5; 36.22
turn [2] 7.14; 16.12
worship (1) (of God) [3] 12.13; 20.9

7 But you must be **strong** and not be **dis-**
couraged. The work that you do will be
rewarded."
8 When Asa heard the **prophecy** that
Azariah son of[u] Oded had spoken, he was
encouraged. He did away with all the
idols in the land of Judah and Benjamin
and all the **idols** in the cities he had captured in the hill-country of Ephraim. He
also repaired the **altar** of the LORD that
stood in the **temple** courtyard.
9 Many people had come over to Asa's
side from Ephraim, Manasseh, and
Simeon, and were living in his kingdom,
because they had seen that the LORD was
with him. Asa summoned all of them and
the people of Judah and Benjamin.
10 They assembled in Jerusalem in the
third month of the fifteenth year that Asa
was king. 11 On that day they **offered**
sacrifices to the LORD from the loot they
had brought back: seven hundred head
of cattle and seven thousand **sheep**.
12 They made a **covenant** in which they
agreed to **worship** the LORD, the God of
their ancestors, **with all their heart** and
soul. 13 Anyone, young or old, male or
female, who did not **worship** him was to
be put **to death**. 14 In a loud voice they
took an **oath** in the **LORD's name** that
they would keep the **covenant**, and then
they shouted and blew trumpets. 15 All the
people of Judah were **happy** because
they had made this **covenant with all**
their heart. They took **delight** in **wor-**
shipping the LORD, and he **accepted**
them and gave them **peace** on every
side.
16 King Asa removed his grandmother
Maacah from her position as queen
mother, because she had made
an obscene **idol** of the fertility **goddess**
Asherah. Asa cut down the **idol**, chopped
it up, and burnt the pieces in the valley of
the Kidron. 17 Even though Asa did not
destroy all the **pagan places of worship**
in the land, he remained **faithful** to the
LORD all his **life**. 18 He placed in the
Temple all the objects his father Abijah
had **dedicated** to God, as well as the gold
and silver objects that he himself **dedi-**
cated. 19 There was no more war until the
thirty-fifth year of his **reign**.

Troubles with Israel
(1 Kgs 15.17–22)

16 In the thirty-sixth year of the
reign of King Asa of Judah, King
Baasha of Israel invaded Judah and
started to fortify Ramah in order to cut
off all traffic in and out of Judah. 2 So Asa
took silver and gold from the treasuries
of the **Temple** and the palace and sent it
to Damascus, to King Benhadad of Syria,
with this **message**: 3 "Let us be allies, as
our fathers were. This silver and gold is a
present for you. Now break your alliance
with King Baasha of Israel so that he will
have to pull his troops out of my
territory."
4 Benhadad **agreed** to Asa's proposal
and sent his commanding officers and
their armies to attack the cities of Israel.
They captured Ijon, Dan, Abel Beth
Maacah, and all the cities of Naphtali
where supplies were stored. 5 When King
Baasha heard what was happening,
he stopped fortifying Ramah and
abandoned the work. 6 Then King Asa
gathered men from throughout Judah
and ordered them to carry off the stones
and timber that Baasha had been using
at Ramah, and they used them to fortify
the cities of Geba and Mizpah.

abandon 15.2; 21.10
act 12.15; 17.4
agree 15.12; 30.1
anger 12.7; 19.2
body 1 Chr 10.8; 22.9
cripple 1 Chr 18.4; Ps 35.16

The Prophet Hanani

7 At that time the **prophet** Hanani
went to King Asa and said, "Because you
relied on the king of Syria instead of
relying on the LORD your God, the army
of the king of Israel[v] has **escaped** from
you. 8 Didn't the Sudanese and the
Libyans have large armies with many
chariots and horsemen? But because
you **relied** on the LORD, he gave you
victory over them. 9 The LORD keeps
close **watch** over the whole **world**, to give
strength to those whose **hearts** are **loyal**
to him. You have **acted foolishly**, and so
from now on you will always be at war."
10 This made Asa so **angry** with the
prophet that he had him put in chains. It
was at this same time that Asa began
treating some of the people **cruelly**.

The End of Asa's Reign
(1 Kgs 15.23–24)

11 All the events of Asa's **reign** from
beginning to end are recorded in *The*
History of the Kings of Judah and Israel.
12 In the thirty-ninth year that Asa was
king, he was **crippled** by a severe foot
disease; but even then he did not **turn** to
the LORD for **help**, but to doctors. 13 Two
years later he died 14 and was buried in
the rock **tomb** which he had carved out
for himself in David's City. They used
spices and perfumed oils to prepare his
body for burial, and they built a huge
bonfire to **mourn** his **death**.

cruel 2 Kgs 17.20; Job 10.3
death (1) 1.11; 22.4
disease 6.28; 21.15
escape 12.5; 20.24
fool 1 Chr 21.8; Job 5.2
heart 15.12; 20.33
help 14.11; 19.2
loyal 10.4; 24.22
message 12.5; 25.17
mourn 1 Chr 7.22; 21.19
prophet [2] 13.22; 18.5
reign [2] 15.19; 17.7
rely [3] 14.11; Neh 7.2
strength 11.17; 17.1
Temple (1) (of God) 15.8; 20.5
tomb 14.1; 21.1
turn 15.2; 18.31
victory 13.18; 18.5
watch 7.15; Ezra 3.12
world 9.22; 20.6

[u] *Some ancient translations* Azariah son of; *Hebrew does not have these words.*
[v] *One ancient translation* Israel; *Hebrew* Syria.

act 16.9; 19.6
afraid 1 Chr 22.13; 20.15
bless 7.10; 26.5
command [3] 14.4; 24.20
control 14.7; 21.4
destroy 15.17; 20.10
example 2 Kgs 24.9; 21.6
gift [2] 9.9; 31.5
goddess 15.16; 19.3
honour 7.21; 18.2
law 15.3; 19.8
Levites [2] 13.9; 19.8
life (1) 15.17; 26.21
obey 14.4; 19.9
pagan 15.17; 20.33
place of worship 15.17; 20.33
power 14.11; 20.6
priest [2] 15.3; 19.8
proud 2 Kgs 19.28; 32.25
reign 16.1; 20.34
serve [4] 13.10; 22.9
sheep 15.11; 18.2
strength 16.9; 26.9
symbol 14.3; 19.3
teach [2] 15.3; 34.21
worship (2) (of other gods) 11.15; 19.3

Jehoshaphat Becomes King

17 Jehoshaphat succeeded his
father Asa as king and
strengthened his position against Israel.
2 He stationed troops in the fortified cities
of Judah, in the Judaean countryside, and
in the cities which Asa had captured in
the territory of Ephraim. 3 The LORD
blessed Jehoshaphat because he followed
the **example** of his father's early **life** and
did not **worship Baal**. 4 He **served** his
father's God, **obeyed** God's **commands**,
and did not **act** in the way the kings of
Israel did. 5 The LORD gave Jehoshaphat
firm **control** over the kingdom of Judah,
and all the people brought him **gifts**, so
that he became wealthy and highly
honoured. 6 He took **pride** in **serving** the
LORD and **destroyed** all the **pagan places
of worship** and the **symbols** of the
goddess Asherah in Judah.
7 In the third year of his **reign** he sent
out the following officials to **teach** in the
cities of Judah: Benhail, Obadiah,
Zechariah, Nethanel, and Micaiah. 8 They
were accompanied by nine **Levites** and
two **priests**. The **Levites** were Shemaiah,
Nethaniah, Zebadiah, Asahel, Shemiramoth, Jehonathan, Adonijah, Tobijah,
and Tobadonijah; and the **priests** were
Elishama and Jehoram. 9 They took the
book of the **Law** of the LORD and went
through all the towns of Judah, **teaching**
it to the people.

Jehoshaphat's Greatness

10 The LORD made all the surrounding
kingdoms **afraid** to go to war against
King Jehoshaphat. 11 Some of the Philistines brought Jehoshaphat a large
amount of silver and other **gifts**, and
some Arabs brought him 7,700 **sheep** and
7,700 goats. 12 So Jehoshaphat continued
to grow more and more **powerful**.
Throughout Judah he built fortifications
and cities, 13 where supplies were stored
in huge amounts.
In Jerusalem he stationed outstanding
officers, 14 according to their clans.
Adnah was the commander of the troops
from the clans of Judah, and he had
300,000 soldiers under him. 15 Second in
rank was Jehohanan, with 280,000
soldiers, 16 and third was Amasiah son of
Zichri, with 200,000. (Amasiah had volunteered to **serve** the LORD.) 17 The commander of the troops from the clans of
Benjamin was Eliada, an outstanding
soldier, in **command** of 200,000 men
armed with shields and bows. 18 His
second in **command** was Jehozabad with
180,000 men, well-equipped for battle.
19 These men **served** the king in Jerusalem, and in addition he stationed other
soldiers in the other fortified cities of
Judah.

The Prophet Micaiah Warns Ahab
(1 Kgs 22.1–28)

18 When King Jehoshaphat of
Judah became **rich** and famous,
he arranged a marriage between a
member of his family and the family of
King Ahab of Israel. 2 A number of years
later Jehoshaphat went to the city of
Samaria to visit Ahab. To **honour**
Jehoshaphat and those with him, Ahab
had a large number of **sheep** and cattle
slaughtered for a **feast**. He tried to **persuade** Jehoshaphat to join him in attacking the city of Ramoth in Gilead. 3 He
asked, "Will you go with me to attack
Ramoth?"
Jehoshaphat replied, "I am ready
when you are, and so is my army. We
will join you." 4 Then he added, "But first
let's **consult** the LORD."
5 So Ahab called in the **prophets**,
about four hundred of them, and asked
them, "Should I go and attack Ramoth, or
not?"
"Attack it," they answered. "God will
give you **victory**."
6 But Jehoshaphat asked, "Isn't there
another **prophet** through whom we can
consult the LORD?"
7 Ahab answered, "There is one more,
Micaiah son of Imlah. But I **hate** him
because he never **prophesies** anything
good for me; it's always something **bad**."
"You shouldn't say that!" Jehoshaphat
replied.
8 So King Ahab called in a **court**
official and told him to go and fetch
Micaiah at once.
9 The two kings, dressed in their royal
robes, were sitting on their **thrones** at the
threshing-place just outside the gate of
Samaria, and all the **prophets** were
prophesying in front of them. 10 One of
them, Zedekiah son of Chenaanah, made
iron horns and said to Ahab, "This is
what the LORD says, 'With these you will
fight the Syrians and totally defeat
them.'" 11 All the other **prophets** said the
same thing. "March against Ramoth and
you will **win**," they said. "The LORD will
give you **victory**."
12 Meanwhile, the official who had
gone to fetch Micaiah said to him, "All
the other **prophets** have **prophesied**
success for the king, and you had better
do the same."
13 But Micaiah answered, "By the
living LORD, I will say what my God tells
me to!"

angel [2] 1 Chr 21.1 32.21
arrest 2 Kgs 17.4; Job 11.10
bad [2] 1 Chr 10.3; 35.23
bread 13.11; 29.18
consult [2] 10.6; 20.2
court (1) 1 Chr 18.1 19.11
deceive [3] 2 Kgs 19.10; 32.11
disaster 7.22; 20.9
feast 9.4; Neh 8.10
hate 1 Kgs 22.8; 19.2
heaven 7.1; 20.6
honour 17.5; 19.7
lie (2) [2] 2 Kgs 4.16 Job 6.28
name (2) (name of God, of Jesus) 15.1 33.18
peace 15.15; 20.30
persuade 2 Kgs 18.30; 24.17
prison 6.36; 21.17
prophecy [4] 15.8; 24.27
prophet [8] 16.7; 19.
rage 2 Kgs 19.27; Neh 9.11
rescue 1 Chr 17.5; 20.9
rich 9.22; 34.30
safe [2] 15.5; 19.1
scatter 1 Chr 12.15; 34.4
sheep [2] 17.11; 29.2
shepherd 14.15; Job 1.16
slaughter 2 Kgs 8.1 28.9
Spirit (1) (God's Spirit) 15.1; 20.14
spirit (2) [2] 1 Chr 10.13; 31.21
strike 13.20; 20.9
succeed (1) [2] 8.16; 20.20
throne [2] 9.17; 23.20
truth 1 Kgs 22.16; Job 8.8
turn [3] 16.12; 20.23
victory [3] 16.8; 20.1
win [2] 13.12; Ezra 7.28

14 When he appeared before King Ahab, the king asked him, "Micaiah, should King Jehoshaphat and I go and attack Ramoth, or not?"

"Attack!" Micaiah answered. "Of course you'll **win**. The LORD will give you **victory**."

15 But Ahab replied, "When you speak to me in the **name of the LORD**, tell the **truth**! How many times do I have to tell you that?"

16 Micaiah answered, "I can see the army of Israel **scattered** over the hills like **sheep** without a **shepherd**. And the LORD said, 'These men have no leader; let them go home in **peace**.'"

17 Ahab said to Jehoshaphat, "I told you that he never **prophesies** anything good for me; it's always something **bad**!"

18 Micaiah went on: "Now listen to what the LORD says! I saw the LORD sitting on his **throne** in **heaven**, with all his **angels** standing beside him. 19 The LORD asked, 'Who will **deceive** Ahab so that he will go and get killed at Ramoth?' Some of the **angels** said one thing, and others said something else, 20 until a **spirit** stepped forward, approached the LORD, and said, 'I will **deceive** him.' 'How?' the LORD asked. 21 The **spirit** replied, 'I will go and make all Ahab's **prophets** tell **lies**.' The LORD said, 'Go and **deceive** him. You will **succeed**.'"

22 And Micaiah concluded: "This is what has happened. The LORD has made these **prophets** of yours **lie** to you. But he himself has decreed that you will meet with **disaster**!"

23 Then the **prophet** Zedekiah went up to Micaiah, slapped his face, and asked, "Since when did the **LORD's spirit** leave me and speak to you?"

24 "You will find out when you go into some back room to hide," Micaiah replied.

25 Then King Ahab ordered one of his officers, "**Arrest** Micaiah and take him to Amon, the governor of the city, and to Prince Joash. 26 Tell them to throw him in **prison** and to put him on **bread** and water until I return **safely**."

27 "If you return **safely**," Micaiah exclaimed, "then the LORD has not spoken through me!" And he added, "Listen, everyone, to what I have said!"

The Death of Ahab
(1 Kgs 22.29–35)

28 Then King Ahab of Israel and King Jehoshaphat of Judah went to attack the city of Ramoth in Gilead. 29 Ahab said to Jehoshaphat, "As we go into battle, I will disguise myself, but you wear your royal garments." So the king of Israel went into battle in disguise.

30 The king of Syria had ordered his chariot commanders to attack no one else except the king of Israel. 31 So when they saw King Jehoshaphat, they all thought that he was the king of Israel, and they **turned** to attack him. But Jehoshaphat gave a shout, and the LORD God **rescued** him and **turned** the attack away from him. 32 The chariot commanders saw that he was not the king of Israel, so they stopped pursuing him. 33 By chance, however, a Syrian soldier shot an arrow which **struck** King Ahab between the joints of his armour. "I'm wounded!" he cried out to his chariot driver. "**Turn** round and pull out of the battle!" 34 While the battle **raged** on, King Ahab remained propped up in his chariot, facing the Syrians. At sunset he died.

A Prophet Reprimands Jehoshaphat

19 King Jehoshaphat of Judah returned **safely** to his palace in Jerusalem. 2 A **prophet**, Jehu son of Hanani, went to meet the king and said to him, "Do you think it is **right** to **help** those who are **wicked** and to take the side of those who **hate** the LORD? What you have done has brought the **LORD's anger** on you. 3 But even so, there is some good in you. You have removed all the **symbols** of the **goddess** Asherah which people **worshipped**, and you have tried to follow **God's will**."

Jehoshaphat's Reforms

4 Even though King Jehoshaphat lived in Jerusalem, he travelled regularly among the people, from Beersheba in the south to the edge of the hill-country of Ephraim in the north, in order to call the people back to the LORD, the God of their ancestors. 5 He appointed **judges** in each of the fortified cities of Judah 6 and instructed them: "Be careful in pronouncing **judgement**; you are not **acting** on **human authority**, but on the **authority** of the LORD, and he is with you when you pass **sentence**. 7 **Honour** the LORD and **act** carefully, because the LORD our God does not **tolerate** fraud or **partiality** or the taking of **bribes**."

8 In Jerusalem Jehoshaphat appointed **Levites**, **priests**, and some of the **leading** citizens as **judges** in **cases** involving a violation of the **Law** of the LORD or legal **disputes** between inhabitants of the

18.16: Num 27.17; Ezek 34.5; Mt 9.36; Mk 6.34

act [2] 17.4; 24.5
anger [2] 16.10; 24.18
authority [4] 13.8; 31.13
bribe 1 Sam 12.3; Ezra 4.5
case (2) [4] 1 Kgs 7.7; Ezra 10.17
commandment Josh 22.5; Ezra 9.14
courage 1 Chr 19.13; 25.11
court (1) 18.8; 34.20
dispute 1 Chr 26.29; Job 13.3
duty (1) [2] 13.10; 23.4
faithful 15.17; 26.5
final [2] 1 Chr 27.24; Esth 1.22
force (1) 13.7; 26.20
goddess 17.6; 24.18
guilty [2] 6.23; 24.18
hate 18.7; Esth 9.16
help 16.12; 20.12
High Priest 2 Kgs 25.18; 24.11
honour 18.2; 20.8
human 6.30; 32.8
judge [3] 6.23; Ezra 4.9
law [2] 17.9; 23.11
leading 1 Chr 28.1; 23.20
Levites [2] 17.8; 20.14
obey 17.4; 23.6
partiality Deut 21.16; Ps 82.2
priest 17.8; 22.11
prophet 18.5; 20.20
religion 1 Chr 26.30; 26.5
reverence Lev 19.32; Job 28.28
right (1) [2] 14.2; 20.32
safe 18.26; 31.12
sentence 2 Kgs 25.6; 22.8
symbol 17.6; 31.1
tolerate Josh 24.19; Esth 3.4

try (2) Josh 20.6; Job 11.10
wicked 6.37; 20.35
will (1) 14.4; 25.20
worship (2) (of other gods) 17.3; 21.11

city.[w] [9]He gave them the following instructions: "You must perform your **duties** in **reverence** for the LORD, **faithfully obeying** him in everything you do. [10]Whenever your fellow-citizens from any of the cities bring before you a **case** of homicide or any other violation of a **law** or **commandment**, you must instruct them carefully how to conduct themselves during the **trial**, so that they do not become **guilty** of sinning against the LORD. Unless you do, you and your fellow-citizens will feel the **force** of the **LORD's anger**. But if you do your **duty**, you will not be **guilty**. [11]Amariah the **High Priest** will have **final authority** in all **religious cases**, and Zebadiah son of Ishmael, governor of Judah, will have **final authority** in all civil **cases**. The **Levites** have the responsibility of seeing that the decisions of the **courts** are carried out. Be **courageous** and carry out these instructions, and may the LORD be on the side of the **right**!"

War against Edom

afraid [2] 17.10; 32.7
announce 1 Chr 29.1; Esth 6.9
believe 9.6; 32.15
bow (2) [2] 1 Chr 29.20; Ezra 10.1
consult 18.4; 33.6
dead 1 Chr 10.5; 24.17
depend 2 Sam 22.31; 31.18
destroy [4] 17.6; 21.7
disaster 18.22; 24.20
discourage 15.7; 32.18
each other 12.15; Ps 12.2
enemy [3] 6.24; 24.25
escape 16.7; 21.9
eternal 7.3; Ezra 3.11
famine 6.28; Job 5.20
fast (2) 1 Chr 10.12; Ezra 8.21
friend 1 Chr 27.33; Esth 5.10
fright 2 Kgs 19.6; 29.8
guide [2] 1 Chr 13.7; Job 38.32
heart 16.9; 30.19
heaven 18.18; 30.27
help 19.2; 26.7
helpless Judg 16.5; Neh 5.5
honour 19.7; 30.1
Levites [2] 19.8; 23.2
love 11.21; 26.10
Majesty 6.2; Ezra 4.12
might 1 Chr 16.24; Ezra 3.11
new 1 Chr 13.7; 23.13
observe 2 Sam 22.23; 30.18
pagan 17.6; 21.11
peace 18.16; 32.22
place of worship 17.6; 21.11

20 Some time later the armies of Moab and Ammon, together with their allies, the Meunites,[x] invaded Judah. [2]Some messengers came and **announced** to King Jehoshaphat: "A large army from Edom has come from the other side of the Dead Sea to attack you. They have already captured Hazazon Tamar." (This is another name for Engedi.) [3]Jehoshaphat was **frightened** and **prayed** to the LORD for **guidance**. Then he gave orders for a **fast** to be **observed** throughout the country. [4]From every city of Judah people hurried to Jerusalem to ask the LORD for **guidance**, [5]and they and the people of Jerusalem gathered in the **new** courtyard of the **Temple**. King Jehoshaphat went and stood before them [6]and **prayed** aloud, "O LORD God of our ancestors, you rule in **heaven** over all the nations of the **world**. You are **powerful** and **mighty**, and no one can oppose you. [7]You are our God. When your people Israel moved into this land, you drove out the people who were living here and gave the land to the descendants of Abraham, your **friend**, to be theirs for ever. [8]They have lived here and have built a **temple** to **honour** you, knowing [9]that if any **disaster struck** them to **punish** them—a war,[y] an epidemic, or a **famine**—then they could come and stand in front of this **Temple** where you are **worshipped**. They could **pray** to you in their **trouble**, and you would hear them and **rescue** them.

10 "Now the people of Ammon, Moab, and Edom have attacked us. When our ancestors came out of Egypt, you did not allow them to enter those lands, so our ancestors went round them and did not **destroy** them. [11]This is how they **repay** us—they come to drive us out of the land that you gave us. [12]You are our God! **Punish** them, for we are **helpless** in the face of this large army that is attacking us. We do not know what to do, but we look to you for **help**."

13 All the men of Judah, with their wives and children, were standing there at the **Temple**. [14]The **spirit of the LORD** came upon a **Levite** who was present in the crowd. His name was Jahaziel son of Zechariah; he was a member of the clan of Asaph and was descended from Asaph through Mattaniah, Jeiel, and Benaiah. [15]Jahaziel said, "Your **Majesty** and all you people of Judah and Jerusalem, the LORD says that you must not be **discouraged** or be **afraid** to face this large army. The battle **depends** on God, not on you. [16]Attack them tomorrow as they come up the pass at Ziz. You will meet them at the end of the valley that leads to the wild country near Jeruel. [17]You will not have to fight this battle. Just take up your positions and wait; you will see the LORD give you **victory**. People of Judah and Jerusalem, do not hesitate or be **afraid**. Go out to battle, and the LORD will be with you!"

18 Then King Jehoshaphat **bowed** low, with his face touching the ground, and all the people **bowed** with him and **worshipped** the LORD. [19]The members of the **Levite** clans of Kohath and Korah stood up and with a loud shout **praised** the LORD, the God of Israel.

20 Early the next morning the people went out to the wild country near Tekoa. As they were starting out, Jehoshaphat addressed them with these **words**: "Men of Judah and Jerusalem! Put your **trust** in the LORD your God, and you will stand firm. **Believe** what his **prophets** tell you, and you will **succeed**." [21]After **consulting** with the people, the king ordered some musicians to put on the robes they wore on **sacred** occasions and to march ahead of the army, singing: "**Praise** the LORD! His **love** is **eternal**!"

22 When they began to sing, the LORD

power 17.12; 25.3
praise [3] 9.8; 29.2
pray [3] 14.11; 32.2
prophet 19.2; 21.1
punish [2] 12.2; 21.
reign 17.7; 21.8
repay Num 5.7; Neh 5.10
rescue 18.31; 22.1
right (1) 19.2; 31.2
sacred 14.3; 24.7
secure 14.7; Esth 9.30
sight 2 Kgs 24.3; Job 4.17
Spirit (1) (God's Spirit) 18.23; 24.20
strike 18.33; 35.23
succeed (1) 18.12; 31.21
Temple (1) (of Go [5] 16.2; 22.11
terrify 14.14; Neh 4.14
triumph 1 Sam 2.9 Esth 9.1
trouble 15.4; 25.19
trust 1 Chr 5.20; Ezra 8.22
turn [2] 18.31; 26.9
value 9.20; 21.3
victory 18.5; 25.8
warn 1 Chr 16.21; 24.19
wicked 19.2; 21.6
word (1) 6.15; 24.9
world 16.9; 36.23
worship (1) (of Go [3] 15.12; 24.18

[w] *Some ancient translations* between...city; *Hebrew unclear.*
[x] *One ancient translation* Meunites; *Hebrew* Ammonites.
[y] struck...war; *or* struck them—a devastating war.

20.7: Is 41.8; Jas 2.23 **20.10:** Deut 2.4-19 **20.15-17:** Deut 20.1-4 **20.17:** Ex 14.13-14

threw the invading armies into a panic.
23 The Ammonites and the Moabites
attacked the Edomite army and completely **destroyed** it, and then they **turned**
on **each other** in savage fighting. 24 When
the Judaean army reached a tower that
was in the desert, they looked towards
the **enemy** and saw that they were all
lying on the ground, **dead**. Not one had
escaped.

25 Jehoshaphat and his troops moved
in to take the loot, and they found many
cattle,[z] supplies, clothing, and other
valuable objects. They spent three days
gathering the loot, but there was so much
that they could not take everything. 26 On
the fourth day they assembled in the
Valley of Beracah and **praised** the LORD
for all he had done. That is why
the valley is called "Beracah."[a]
27 Jehoshaphat led his troops back to
Jerusalem in **triumph**, because the LORD
had defeated their **enemies**. 28 When they
reached the city, they marched to the
Temple, to the music of harps and
trumpets. 29 Every nation that heard how
the LORD had defeated Israel's **enemies**
was **terrified**, 30 so Jehoshaphat ruled in
peace, and God gave him **security** on
every side.

The End of Jehoshaphat's Reign
(1 Kgs 22.41–50)

31 Jehoshaphat had become king of
Judah at the age of thirty-five and had
ruled in Jerusalem for twenty-five years.
His mother was Azubah, the daughter of
Shilhi. 32 Like his father Asa before him,
he did what was **right** in the **sight** of the
LORD; 33 but the **pagan places of worship**
were not **destroyed**. The people still did
not **turn wholeheartedly** to the **worship**
of the God of their ancestors.

34 Everything else that Jehoshaphat
did, from the beginning of his **reign** to its
end, is recorded in *The History of Jehu
Son of Hanani,* which is a part of *The History of the Kings of Israel.*

35 At one time King Jehoshaphat of
Judah made an alliance with King
Ahaziah of Israel, who did many **wicked**
things. 36 At the port of Eziongeber they
built ocean-going ships. 37 But Eliezer son
of Dodavahu, from the town of Mareshah, **warned** Jehoshaphat, "Because you
have made an alliance with Ahaziah, the
LORD will **destroy** what you have built."
And the ships were wrecked and never
sailed.

21 Jehoshaphat died and was buried
in the royal **tombs** in David's City
and his son Jehoram succeeded him as
king.

King Jehoram of Judah
(2 Kgs 8.17–24)

2 Jehoram son of King Jehoshaphat of
Judah had six brothers: Azariah, Jehiel,
Zechariah, Azariahu, Michael, and
Shephatiah. 3 Their father gave them
large amounts of gold, silver, and other
valuable possessions, and placed each
one in charge of one of the fortified cities
of Judah. But because Jehoram was the
eldest, Jehoshaphat made him his
successor. 4 When Jehoram was in firm
control of the kingdom, he had all his
brothers killed, and also some Israelite
officials.

5 Jehoram became king at the age of
thirty-two, and he ruled in Jerusalem for
eight years. 6 He followed the **wicked
example** of King Ahab and the other
kings of Israel, because he had married
one of Ahab's daughters. He sinned
against the LORD, 7 but the LORD was not
willing to **destroy** the dynasty of David,
because he had made a **covenant** with
David and **promised** that his descendants
would always continue to rule.

8 During Jehoram's **reign** Edom
revolted against Judah and became an
independent kingdom. 9 So Jehoram and
his officers set out with chariots and
invaded Edom. There the Edomite army
surrounded them, but during the night
they managed to break out and **escape**.
10 Edom has been independent of[b] Judah
ever since. During this same period, the
city of Libnah also revolted, because
Jehoram had **abandoned** the LORD, the
God of his ancestors. 11 He even built
pagan places of worship in the Judaean
highlands and led the people of Judah
and Jerusalem to sin against the LORD.

12 The **prophet** Elijah sent Jehoram a
letter, which read as follows: "The LORD,
the God of your ancestor David, **condemns** you, because you did not follow
the **example** of your father, King
Jehoshaphat, or that of your grandfather,
King Asa. 13 Instead, you have followed
the **example** of the kings of Israel and
have led the people of Judah and Jerusalem into being **unfaithful** to God, just as
Ahab and his successors led Israel into
unfaithfulness. You even murdered your
brothers, who were better men than you
are. 14 As a result, the LORD will severely

[z] *One ancient translation* cattle; *Hebrew* among them.
[a] BERACAH: *This name in Hebrew means "praise."* [b] independent of; *or* in revolt against.

21.7: 1 Kgs 11.36 **21.8:** Gen 27.40

abandon 16.5; 24.20
condemn 2 Sam 14.13; Job 6.29
control 17.5; 24.20
covenant 15.12; 23.3
destroy [2] 20.10; 22.7
disease [2] 16.12; 26.19
escape 20.24; 36.16
example [3] 17.3; 22.2
letter (2) 2.11; 30.1
mourn 16.14; 35.24
pagan 20.33; 28.4
pain [2] 1 Chr 4.9; Neh 9.21
place of worship 20.33; 28.4
possess [2] 8.7; Ezra 8.21
prison 18.26; 25.12
promise 7.18; 23.3
prophet 20.20; 24.19
punish 20.9; 24.22
reign 20.34; 25.26
sorry 1 Sam 24.10; Job 30.25
subject (1) 10.4; Ps 18.43
suffer 2 Kgs 19.3; 32.25
tomb [2] 16.14; 24.16
unfaithful [2] 1 Chr 10.13; 29.6
value 20.25; 32.27
wicked 20.35; Ezra 9.14
worse [2] 2 Kgs 21.11; 32.16
worship (2) (of other gods) 19.3; 24.7

punish your people, your children, and
your wives, and will **destroy** your **pos-**
sessions. 15 You yourself will **suffer** a
painful disease of the intestines that will
grow **worse** day by day."

16 Some Philistines and Arabs lived
near where some Sudanese had settled
along the coast. The LORD incited them
to go to war against Jehoram. 17 They
invaded Judah, looted the royal palace,
and carried off as **prisoners** all the king's
wives and sons except Ahaziah, his
youngest son.

18 Then after all this, the LORD
brought on the king a **painful disease** of
the intestines. 19 For almost two years it
grew steadily **worse** until finally the king
died in agony. His **subjects** did not light a
bonfire in **mourning** for him as had been
done for his ancestors.

20 Jehoram had become king at the
age of thirty-two and had ruled in Jerusalem for eight years. Nobody was **sorry**
when he died. They buried him in
David's City, but not in the royal **tombs**.

King Ahaziah of Judah
(2 Kgs 8.25–29; 9.21–28)

22 Some Arabs had led a raid and
killed all King Jehoram's sons
except Ahaziah, the youngest. So now the
people of Jerusalem made Ahaziah king
as his father's successor. 2-3 Ahaziah
became king at the age of twenty-two,[c]
and he ruled in Jerusalem for one year.
Ahaziah also followed the **example** of
King Ahab's family, since his mother
Athaliah—the daughter of King Ahab
and granddaughter of King Omri of
Israel—gave him **advice** that led him
into **evil**. 4 He sinned against the LORD,
because after his father's **death** other
members of King Ahab's family became
his advisers, and they led to his **downfall**.
5 Following their **advice**, he joined King
Joram of Israel in a war against King
Hazael of Syria. The armies clashed at
Ramoth in Gilead, and Joram was
wounded in battle. 6 He returned to the
city of Jezreel to recover from his
wounds, and Ahaziah went there to visit
him.

7 God used this visit to Joram to bring
about Ahaziah's **downfall**. While Ahaziah
was there, he and Joram were confronted by a man named Jehu son of
Nimshi, whom the LORD had **chosen** to
destroy the dynasty of Ahab. 8 As Jehu
was carrying out God's **sentence** on the
dynasty, he came across a group made
up of Judaean leaders and of Ahaziah's
nephews that had accompanied Ahaziah
on his visit. Jehu killed them all. 9 A
search was made for Ahaziah, and he
was found hiding in Samaria. They took
him to Jehu and put him **to death**. But
they did bury his **body** out of **respect** for
his grandfather King Jehoshaphat, who
had done all he could to **serve** the LORD.

No member of Ahaziah's family was
left who could rule the kingdom.

advice [2] 10.6; 25.16
body 16.14; 25.28
choose 12.13; 24.3
death (1) 16.14; 26.2
death (2) (from death) Job 5.15
death (3) (to death) 15.13; 25.4
destroy 21.7; 25.16
downfall [2] 26.16
evil 12.14; 33.19
example 21.6; 26.4
learn 12.8; Neh 13.10
priest 19.8; 23.1
rescue 20.9; 23.14
respect 1 Chr 29.28; Esth 1.18
save 1 Chr 16.23; 25.15
secret 2 Sam 12.12; Esth 2.10
sentence 19.6; Ps 94.21
serve 17.4; 26.5
Temple (1) (of God) 20.5; 23.3

Queen Athaliah of Judah
(2 Kgs 11.1–3)

10 As soon as King Ahaziah's mother
Athaliah **learnt** of her son's murder, she
gave orders for all the members of the
royal family of Judah to be killed.
11 Ahaziah had a half-sister, Jehosheba,
who was married to a **priest** named
Jehoiada. She **secretly rescued** one of
Ahaziah's sons, Joash, took him away
from the other princes who were about
to be murdered and hid him and a nurse
in a bedroom at the **Temple**. By keeping
him hidden, she **saved** him **from death** at
the hands of Athaliah. 12 For six years he
remained there in hiding, while Athaliah
ruled as queen.

The Revolt against Athaliah
(2 Kgs 11.4–16)

23 After waiting six years Jehoiada
the **priest** decided that it was
time to take **action**. He made a pact with
five army officers: Azariah son of
Jeroham, Ishmael son of Jehohanan,
Azariah son of Obed, Maaseiah son of
Adaiah, and Elishaphat son of Zichri.
2 They travelled to all the cities of Judah
and brought back with them to Jerusalem the **Levites** and all the heads of the
clans.

3 They all gathered in the **Temple**,
and there they made a **covenant** with
Joash, the king's son. Jehoiada said to
them, "Here is the son of the late king!
He is now to be king, as the LORD
promised that King David's descendants
would be. 4 This is what we will do. When
the **priests and Levites** come on **duty** on
the **Sabbath**, one third of them will guard
the **temple** gates, 5 another third will
guard the royal palace, and the rest will
be stationed at the Foundation Gate. All
the people will assemble in the **temple**
courtyard. 6 No one is to enter the **temple**
buildings except the **priests and the**
Levites who are on **duty**. They may
enter, because they are **consecrated**, but
the rest of the people must **obey** the
LORD's instructions and stay outside.

action 2 Kgs 21.21; 28.12
altar [2] 15.8; 26.16
anoint 1 Chr 29.22; 36.1
celebrate [2] 7.8; 3
consecrate 13.9; 26.18
covenant [2] 21.7; 29.10
crown 1 Chr 20.2; Esth 1.11
distress 15.6; Neh 9.37
duty (1) [6] 19.9; 26.21
God's people 9.8; 31.8
happy 15.15; 29.36
idol 15.8; 24.18
joy 1 Chr 16.27; 29.
law [2] 19.8; 25.4
leading 19.8; 28.12
Levites [6] 20.14; 24
new 20.5; 34.22
obey 19.9; 27.6
offer 15.11; 24.14
priest [7] 22.11; 24.
promise 21.7; 34.32
protect 14.7; Ezra 8.21
rescue 22.11; 32.22
Sabbath [2] 8.13; 31
sacrifice 15.11; 24.1
Temple (1) (of God) [14] 22.11; 24.4
temple (2) (of other gods) 1 Chr 10.10; 32.21
throne 18.9; Esth 1.
unclean Deut 26.14; 26.21

[c] *Some ancient translations (and see 2 Kgs 8.26)* twenty-two; *Hebrew* forty-two.

23.3: 2 Sam 7.12

7 The **Levites** are to stand guard round the king, with their swords drawn, and are to stay with the king wherever he goes. Anyone who tries to enter the **Temple** is to be killed."

8 The **Levites** and the people of Judah carried out Jehoiada's instructions. The men were not dismissed when they went off **duty** on the **Sabbath**, so the commanders had available both those coming on **duty** and those going off. 9 Jehoiada gave the officers the spears and shields that had belonged to King David and had been kept in the **Temple**. 10 He stationed the men with drawn swords all round the front of the **Temple**, to **protect** the king. 11 Then Jehoiada led Joash out, placed the **crown** on his head, and gave him a copy of the **laws** governing kingship. And so he was made king. Jehoiada the **priest** and his sons **anointed** Joash, and everyone shouted, "Long live the king!"

12 Athaliah heard the people cheering for the king, so she hurried to the **Temple**, where the crowd had gathered. 13 There she saw the **new** king at the **temple** entrance, standing by the column reserved for kings and surrounded by the army officers and the trumpeters. All the people were shouting **joyfully** and blowing trumpets, and the **temple** musicians with their instruments were leading the **celebration**. She tore her clothes in **distress** and shouted, "Treason! Treason!"

14 Jehoiada did not want Athaliah killed in the **temple** area, so he called out the army officers and said, "Take her out between the rows of guards, and kill anyone who tries to **rescue** her."

15 They seized her, took her to the palace, and there at the Horse Gate they killed her.

Jehoiada's Reforms
(2 Kgs 11.17–20)

16 The **priest** Jehoiada got King Joash and the people to join him in making a **covenant** that they would be the LORD's **people**. 17 Then they all went to the **temple** of Baal and tore it down. They smashed the **altars** and **idols** there and killed Mattan, the **priest** of Baal, in front of the **altars**. 18 Jehoiada put the **priests and Levites** in charge of the work of the **Temple**. They were to carry out the **duties** assigned to them by King David and to burn the **sacrifices offered** to the LORD in accordance with the **Law of Moses**. They were also in charge of the music and the **celebrations**. 19 Jehoiada also put guards on **duty** at the **temple** gates to keep out anyone who was ritually **unclean**.

20 The army officers, the **leading** citizens, the officials, and all the rest of the people joined Jehoiada in a procession that brought the king from the **Temple** to the palace. They entered by the main gate, and the king took his place on the **throne**. 21 All the people were filled with **happiness**, and the city was quiet, now that Athaliah had been killed.

King Joash of Judah
(2 Kgs 12.1–16)

24 Joash became king of Judah at the age of seven, and he ruled in Jerusalem for forty years. His mother was Zibiah from the city of Beersheba. 2 He did what was **pleasing** to the LORD as long as Jehoiada the **priest** was **alive**. 3 Jehoiada **chose** two wives for King Joash, and they bore him sons and daughters.

4 After he had been king for a while, Joash decided to have the **Temple** repaired. 5 He ordered the **priests and the Levites** to go to the cities of Judah and collect from all the people **enough** money to make the annual repairs on the **Temple**. He told them to **act** promptly, but the **Levites** delayed, 6 so he called in Jehoiada, their leader, and demanded, "Why haven't you seen to it that the **Levites** collect from Judah and Jerusalem the **tax** which Moses, the **servant** of the LORD, **required** the people[d] to pay for support of the **Tent** of the LORD's presence?"

7 (The **followers** of Athaliah, that **corrupt** woman,[e] had damaged the **Temple** and had used many of the **sacred** objects in the **worship of Baal**.)

8 The king ordered the **Levites** to make a box for **contributions** and to place it at the **temple** gate. 9 They sent **word** throughout Jerusalem and Judah for everyone to bring to the LORD the **tax** which Moses, God's **servant**, had first collected in the wilderness. 10 This **pleased** the people and their leaders, and they brought their **tax** money and filled the box with it. 11 Every day the **Levites** would take the box to the royal official who was in charge of it. Whenever it was full, the royal secretary and the **High Priest's representative** would take the

abandon [2] 21.10; 28.5
act 19.6; Ezra 10.4
alive [2] 2 Kgs 10.11; Neh 5.2
anger 19.2; 25.10
choose 22.7; 26.1
command 17.4; 25.4
contribute 2 Kgs 15.20; 30.24
control 21.4; Ezra 4.16
corrupt Deut 32.32; Job 15.16
dead 20.24; Job 3.22
disaster 20.9; 25.19
disobey 7.19; Ezra 6.11
enemy 20.24; 25.8
enough 6.18; 28.13
follower 1 Chr 12.23; Ps 106.18
forget 1 Chr 16.15; Neh 4.5
goddess 19.3; 31.1
guilty 19.10; 28.13
hard 1 Chr 19.13; Ezra 4.15
High Priest 19.11; 31.10
idol 23.17; 25.14
image 2 Kgs 23.15; 28.2
Levites [5] 23.2; 29.4
loyal 16.9; 31.21
offer 23.18; 28.4
persuade 18.2; Ezra 7.28
please [2] 14.2; 25.2
plot (1) [2] 2 Kgs 21.23; 25.17
priest [4] 23.1; 26.17
prophecy 18.7; Jer 28.6
prophet 21.12; 25.7
punish [2] 21.14; 26.20
refuse (1) 1 Chr 11.19; 25.20
represent 2 Sam 15.3; Neh 11.24
require 8.13; 31.3
restore 11.1; Ezra 5.14
sacred 20.21; 29.18
sacrifice 23.18; 28.3
servant [2] 9.4; 32.16
service [2] 5.11; Ezra 6.18
Spirit (1) (God's Spirit) 20.14; Job 32.8
tax [3] 9.14; Ezra 4.13

[d] *Probable text* required the people; *Hebrew unclear.*
[e] that corrupt woman; *or* whom she corrupted.

24.6: Ex 30.11–16

Temple (1) (of God) [12] 23.3; 25.24
Tent (2) (of the Lord's presence) 5.5; Ps 78.60
tomb [2] 21.1; 25.28
warn 20.37; 33.10
word (1) 20.20; 30.1
worship (1) (of God) 20.9; 29.11
worship (2) (of other gods) [2] 21.11; 25.14

money out and return the box to its place. And so they collected a large sum of money.

12 The king and Jehoiada would give the money to those who were in charge of repairing the Temple, and they hired stonemasons, carpenters, and metalworkers to make the repairs. [13] All the workmen worked hard, and they restored the Temple to its original condition, as solid as ever. [14] When the repairs were finished, the remaining gold and silver was given to the king and Jehoiada, who used it to have bowls and other utensils made for the Temple.

Jehoiada's Policies Are Reversed

As long as Jehoiada was alive, sacrifices were offered regularly at the Temple. [15] After reaching the very old age of a hundred and thirty, he died. [16] They buried him in the royal tombs in David's City in recognition of the service he had done for the people of Israel, for God, and for the Temple.

17 But once Jehoiada was dead, the leaders of Judah persuaded King Joash to listen to them instead. [18] So the people stopped worshipping in the Temple of the LORD, the God of their ancestors, and began to worship idols and the images of the goddess Asherah. Their guilt for these sins brought the LORD's anger on Judah and Jerusalem. [19] The LORD sent prophets to warn them to return to him, but the people refused to listen. [20] Then the spirit of God took control of Zechariah son of Jehoiada the priest. He stood where the people could see him and called out, "The LORD God asks why you have disobeyed his commands and are bringing disaster on yourselves! You abandoned him, so he has abandoned you!" [21] King Joash joined in a conspiracy against Zechariah, and on the king's orders the people stoned Zechariah in the temple courtyard. [22] The king forgot about the loyal service that Zechariah's father Jehoiada had given him, and he had Zechariah killed. As Zechariah was dying, he called out, "May the LORD see what you are doing and punish you!"

The End of Joash's Reign

23 When autumn came that year, the Syrian army attacked Judah and Jerusalem, killed all the leaders, and took large amounts of loot back to Damascus. [24] The Syrian army was small, but the LORD let them defeat a much larger Judaean army because the people had abandoned him, the LORD God of their ancestors. In this way King Joash was punished. [25] He was severely wounded, and when the enemy withdrew, two of his officials plotted against him and killed him in his bed to avenge the murder of the son[f] of Jehoiada the priest. He was buried in David's City, but not in the royal tombs. [26] (Those who plotted against him were Zabad, the son of an Ammonite woman named Shimeath, and Jehozabad, the son of a Moabite woman named Shimrith). [27] The *Commentary on the Book of Kings* contains the stories of the sons of Joash, the prophecies spoken against him, and the record of how he rebuilt the Temple. His son Amaziah succeeded him as king.

King Amaziah of Judah
(2 Kgs 14.2–6)

25 Amaziah became king at the age of twenty-five, and he ruled in Jerusalem for twenty-nine years. His mother was Jehoaddin from Jerusalem. [2] He did what was pleasing to the LORD, but did it reluctantly. [3] As soon as he was firmly in power, he executed the officials who had murdered his father. [4] He did not, however, execute their children, but followed what the LORD had commanded in the Law of Moses: "Parents are not to be put to death for crimes committed by their children, and children are not to be put to death for crimes committed by their parents; a person is to be put to death only for a crime he himself has committed."

War against Edom
(2 Kgs 14.7)

5 King Amaziah organized all the men of the tribes of Judah and Benjamin into army units, according to the clans they belonged to, and placed officers in command of units of a thousand men and units of a hundred men. This included all men twenty years of age or older, 300,000 in all. They were picked troops, ready for battle, skilled in using spears and shields. [6] In addition, he hired 100,000 soldiers from Israel at a cost of about 3,400 kilogrammes of silver. [7] But a prophet went to the king and said to him, "Don't take these Israelite soldiers with you. The LORD is not with these men from the Northern Kingdom. [8] You may think that they will make you stronger[g] in battle, but it is God who has the power to give

advice [2] 22.2; Ezra 10.3
anger [2] 24.18; 26.1
bitter 2 Kgs 20.3; Ezra 10.1
boast 2 Kgs 19.23; Esth 5.11
body 22.9; Ezra 6.1
challenge 2 Kgs 14.8; Job 40.1
command [2] 24.20 26.12
courage 19.11; 26.1
crime [3] 2 Kgs 14. Job 13.23
death (3) (to death [3] 22.9; Esth 3.9
destroy 22.7; 31.1
disaster 24.20; 28.2
enemy [2] 24.25; 26.13
execute [2] 2 Kgs 14.5; Prov 24.11
flee [2] 14.12; Job 15.28
god (2) (other gods 13.8; 28.25
idol [2] 24.18; 28.3
ignore 10.8; 36.16
incense 14.5; 26.16
law 23.11; 29.15
message [2] 16.2; 32.9
please 24.2; 26.4
plot (1) [2] 24.25; 33.24
power [3] 20.6; 26.8
prison 21.17; 28.5
prophet [6] 24.19; 26.22
rebel 13.6; 36.13
refuse (1) 24.19; 33.10
reign 21.8; 26.22
save 22.11; 32.11
strong 15.7; 26.16
Temple (1) (of God [2] 24.4; 26.16
tomb 24.16; 26.23
trouble 20.9; 28.19
victory 20.17; Esth 8.16
will (1) 19.3; 30.12
worship (2) (of other gods) [3] 24.7 28.4

[f] *Some ancient translations* son; *Hebrew* sons.
[g] *Some ancient translations* You may...stronger; *Hebrew unclear.*

24.20–21: Mt 23.35; Lk 11.51 **25.4:** Deut 24.16

victory or defeat, and he will let your **enemies** defeat you."

9 Amaziah asked the **prophet**, "But what about all that silver I have already paid for them?"

The **prophet** replied, "The LORD can give you back more than that!" 10 So Amaziah sent the hired troops away and told them to go home. At this they went home, **bitterly angry** with the people of Judah.

11 Amaziah summoned up his **courage** and led his army to the Valley of Salt. There they fought and killed ten thousand Edomite soldiers 12 and captured another ten thousand. They took the **prisoners** to the top of the cliff at the city of Sela and threw them off, so that they were killed on the rocks below.

13 Meanwhile the Israelite soldiers that Amaziah had not allowed to go into battle with him attacked the Judaean cities between Samaria and Beth Horon, killed three thousand men, and captured quantities of loot.

14 When Amaziah returned from defeating the Edomites, he brought their **idols** back with him, set them up, **worshipped** them, and burnt **incense** to them. 15 This made the LORD **angry**, so he sent a **prophet** to Amaziah. The **prophet** demanded, "Why have you **worshipped foreign gods** that could not even **save** their own people from your **power**?"

16 "Since when," Amaziah interrupted, "have we made you adviser to the king? Stop talking, or I'll have you killed!"

The **prophet** stopped, but not before saying, "Now I know that God has decided to **destroy** you because you have done all this and have **ignored** my **advice**."

War against Israel
(2 Kgs 14.8–20)

17 King Amaziah of Judah and his advisers **plotted** against Israel. He then sent a **message** to King Jehoash of Israel, who was the son of Jehoahaz and grandson of Jehu, **challenging** him to fight.[h] 18 Jehoash sent this answer to Amaziah: "Once, a thorn bush in the Lebanon Mountains sent a **message** to a cedar: 'Give your daughter in marriage to my son.' A wild animal passed by and trampled the bush down. 19 Now Amaziah, you **boast** that you have defeated the Edomites, but I **advise** you to stay at home. Why stir up **trouble** that will only bring **disaster** on you and your people?"

20 But Amaziah **refused** to listen. It was **God's will** for Amaziah to be defeated, because he had **worshipped the Edomite idols**. 21 So King Jehoash of Israel went into battle against King Amaziah of Judah. They met at Beth Shemesh in Judah, 22 the Judaean army was defeated, and the soldiers **fled** to their homes. 23 Jehoash captured Amaziah and took him to Jerusalem. There he tore down the city wall from Ephraim Gate to the Corner Gate, a distance of nearly two hundred metres. 24 He took back to Samaria as loot all the gold and silver in the **Temple**, the **temple** equipment guarded by the descendants of Obed Edom, and the palace treasures. He also took hostages with him.

25 King Amaziah of Judah outlived King Jehoash of Israel by fifteen years. 26 All the other things that Amaziah did from the beginning to the end of his **reign** are recorded in *The History of the Kings of Judah and Israel.* 27 Ever since the time when he **rebelled** against the LORD, there had been a **plot** against him in Jerusalem. Finally he **fled** to the city of Lachish, but his **enemies** followed him there and killed him. 28 His **body** was carried to Jerusalem on a horse, and he was buried in the royal **tombs** in David's City.

King Uzziah of Judah
(2 Kgs 14.21–22; 15.1–7)

26 All the people of Judah **chose** Amaziah's sixteen-year-old son Uzziah to succeed his father as king. 2 (It was after the **death** of Amaziah that Uzziah recaptured Elath and rebuilt the city.)

3 Uzziah became king at the age of sixteen, and he ruled in Jerusalem for fifty-two years. His mother was Jecoliah from Jerusalem. 4 Following the **example** of his father, he did what was **pleasing** to the LORD. 5 As long as Zechariah, his **religious** adviser, was living, he **served** the LORD **faithfully**, and God **blessed** him.

6 Uzziah went to war against the Philistines. He tore down the walls of the cities of Gath, Jamnia, and Ashdod, and built fortified cities near Ashdod and in the rest of Philistia. 7 God **helped** him to defeat the Philistines, the Arabs living at Gurbaal, and the Meunites. 8 The Ammonites paid **tribute** to Uzziah, and he became so **powerful** that his fame spread even to Egypt.

9 Uzziah **strengthened** the fortifications of Jerusalem by building towers at the Corner Gate, at the Valley Gate, and

altar [2] 23.17; 28.24
anger 25.10; 28.9
arrogant
1 Sam 15.23; Ps 31.18
bless [2] 17.3; 30.27
choose 24.3; 29.11
command 25.4; 28.7
consecrate 23.6; 29.5
courage 25.11;
Ezra 7.28
death (1) 22.4; 32.26
defy 1 Chr 20.7; 28.19
disease [3] 21.15;
Job 18.13
downfall 22.4;
Ps 13.4
duty (1) 23.4; 31.2
encourage 15.8; 32.8
enemy 25.8; 32.22
example 22.2; 28.1
faithful 19.9; 27.6
force (1) 19.10; 27.5
forehead [2]
1 Sam 17.49; Ezek 9.4
help [2] 20.12; 28.16
holy 8.11; 30.8
horror 2 Kgs 8.11;
Ps 55.5
incense [4] 25.14;
27.2
life (1) 17.3;
Ezra 7.10
love 20.21; Ezra 3.11
please 25.2; 27.2
power [2] 25.3; 27.6
priest [5] 24.2; 29.4
prophet 25.7; 28.9
punish 24.22; 28.11
reign 25.26; 27.7

[h] challenging him to fight; *or* inviting him to a conference.

relieve (1) 2 Kgs 15.5; Esth 8.16
religion 19.11; Ecc 9.2
resist 13.7; Prov 2.16
right (3) 1 Chr 5.1; 28.19
serve 22.9; 32.1
strength 17.1; 30.21
strong [2] 25.8; Neh 6.9
Temple (1) (of God) [4] 25.24; 27.2
tomb 25.28; 28.27
tribute 2 Kgs 23.33; 27.5
turn 20.23; 29.6
unclean 23.19; 29.16
vineyard 1 Chr 27.25; Neh 5.3

where the wall **turned**. 10 He also built
fortified towers in the open country and
dug many cisterns, because he had large
herds of livestock in the western foothills
and plains. Because he **loved** farming, he
encouraged the people to plant **vineyards**
in the hill-country and to farm the fertile
land.

11 He had a large army ready for
battle. Its records were kept by his secretaries Jeiel and Maaseiah under the
supervision of Hananiah, a member of
the king's staff. 12 The army was **commanded** by 2,600 officers. 13 Under them
were 307,500 soldiers able to fight
effectively for the king against his
enemies. 14 Uzziah supplied the army
with shields, spears, helmets, coats of
armour, bows and arrows, and stones for
slinging. 15 In Jerusalem his inventors
made equipment for shooting arrows and
for throwing large stones from the
towers and corners of the city wall. His
fame spread everywhere, and he
became very **powerful** because of the
help he received from God.

Uzziah Is Punished for His Pride

16 But when King Uzziah became
strong, he grew **arrogant**, and that led to
his **downfall**. He **defied** the LORD his God
by going into the **Temple** to burn **incense**
on the **altar of incense**. 17 Azariah the
priest, accompanied by eighty **strong** and
courageous priests, followed the king 18 to
resist him. They said, "Uzziah! You have
no **right** to burn **incense** to the LORD.
Only the **priests** who are descended from
Aaron have been **consecrated** to do this.
Leave this **holy** place. You have offended
the LORD God, and you no longer have
his **blessing**."

19 Uzziah was standing there in the
Temple beside the **incense altar** and was
holding an **incense burner**. He became
angry with the **priests**, and immediately
a dreaded **skin-disease** broke out on his
forehead. 20 Azariah and the other **priests**
stared at the king's **forehead** in **horror**,
and then **forced** him to leave the **Temple**.
He hurried to get out, because the LORD
had **punished** him.

21 For the rest of his **life** King Uzziah
was ritually **unclean** because of his
disease. Unable to enter the **Temple**
again, he lived in his own house, **relieved**
of all **duties**, while his son Jotham
governed the country.

22 The **prophet** Isaiah son of Amoz
recorded all the other things that King
Uzziah did during his **reign**. 23 Uzziah died
and was buried in the royal burial-
ground, but because of his **disease** he was
not buried in the royal **tombs**. His son
Jotham succeeded him as king.

King Jotham of Judah
(2 Kgs 15.32–38)

27 Jotham became king at the age
of twenty-five, and he ruled in
Jerusalem for sixteen years. His mother
was Jerushah, the daughter of Zadok.
2 He did what was **pleasing** to the LORD,
just as his father had done; but unlike his
father he did not sin by burning **incense**[i]
in the **Temple**. The people, however,
went on sinning.

3 It was Jotham who built the North
Gate of the **Temple** and did extensive
work on the city wall in the area of
Jerusalem called Ophel. 4 In the
mountains of Judah he built cities, and in
the forests he built forts and towers. 5 He
fought against the king of Ammon and
his army and defeated them. Then he
forced the Ammonites to pay him the
following **tribute** each year for three
years: 3,400 kilogrammes of silver, 1,000
metric tons of wheat, and 1,000 metric
tons of barley. 6 Jotham grew **powerful**
because he **faithfully obeyed** the LORD
his God. 7 The other events of Jotham's
reign, his wars, and his policies, are all
recorded in *The History of the Kings of
Israel and Judah*. 8 Jotham was twenty-
five years old when he became king, and
he ruled in Jerusalem for sixteen years.
9 He died and was buried in David's City
and his son Ahaz succeeded him as king.

faithful 26.5; 29.34
force (1) 26.20; 36.13
incense 26.16; 28.3
obey 23.6; 29.31
please 26.4; 28.1
power 26.8; 32.7
reign 26.22; 28.26
Temple (1) (of God) [2] 26.16; 28.21
tribute 26.8; 36.3

King Ahaz of Judah
(2 Kgs 16.1–4)

28 Ahaz became king at the age of
twenty, and he ruled in Jerusalem for sixteen years. He did not follow
the good **example** of his ancestor King
David; instead, he did what was not
pleasing to the LORD 2 and followed the
example of the kings of Israel. He had
metal **images** of Baal made, 3 burnt
incense in the Valley of Hinnom, and
even **sacrificed** his own sons as **burnt-
offerings** to **idols**, imitating the **disgusting
practice** of the people whom the LORD
had driven out of the land as the
Israelites advanced. 4 At the **pagan
places of worship**, on the hills, and under
every shady tree Ahaz **offered sacrifices**
and burnt **incense**.

abandon 24.20; 29.6
action 23.1; Ezra 5.5
altar 26.16; 29.18
anger [4] 26.19; 29.8
burnt-offering 8.13; 29.7
command 26.12; 29.15
defy 26.16; 32.17
disaster 25.19; Esth 8.6
disgust 1 Chr 15.29; 33.2
enough [2] 24.5; 29.34
example [2] 26.4; 29.2
god (2) (other gods) 25.15; 32.13
guilty 24.18; Ezra 9.15
help [5] 26.7; 29.34
idol 25.14; 32.19
image 24.18; 33.3
incense [3] 27.2; 29.7
intend 11.1; 32.2
leading 23.20; 29.20
offer [2] 24.14; 29.7

[i] he did not sin by burning incense; *or* he did not take part in the worship.

26.18: Ex 30.7–8; Num 3.10 **26.23:** Is 6.1

pagan [2] 21.11; 31.1
permit 2 Kgs 25.29; Ezra 3.7
place of worship [2] 21.11; 31.1
please 27.2; 29.2
practice 2 Kgs 23.3; 33.2
prison [9] 25.12; 29.9
prophet 26.22; 29.25
provide 11.23; 31.3
punish [2] 26.20; 30.7
reign 27.7; 34.8
right (3) 26.18; Ezra 9.15
sacrifice [4] 24.14; 29.21
slaughter 18.2; Ezra 9.7
slave 8.7; 36.20
Temple (1) (of God) [3] 27.2; 30.1
tomb 26.23; 32.33
trouble [3] 25.19; Ezra 4.15
weak 14.11; Neh 4.10
worship (2) (of other gods) [2] 25.14; 33.3
worst 2 Kgs 7.4; Job 19.11

War with Syria and Israel
(2 Kgs 16.5)

5–6 Because King Ahaz sinned, the LORD his God let the king of Syria defeat him and take a large number of Judaeans back to Damascus as **prisoners**. The LORD also let the king of Israel, Pekah son of Remaliah, defeat Ahaz and kill 120,000 of the bravest Judaean soldiers in one day. The LORD, the God of their ancestors, **permitted** this to happen, because the people of Judah had **abandoned** him. 7 An Israelite soldier named Zichri killed King Ahaz' son Maaseiah, the palace administrator Azrikam, and Elkanah, who was second in **command** to the king. 8 Even though the Judaeans were their fellow-countrymen, the Israelite army captured 200,000 women and children as **prisoners** and took them back to Samaria, along with large amounts of loot.

The Prophet Oded

9 A man named Oded, a **prophet** of the LORD, lived in the city of Samaria. He met the returning Israelite army with its Judaean **prisoners** as it was about to enter the city, and he said, "The LORD God of your ancestors was **angry** with Judah and let you defeat them, but now he has heard of the vicious way you **slaughtered** them. 10 And now you **intend** to make the men and women of Jerusalem and Judah your **slaves**. Don't you know that you also have committed sins against the LORD your God? 11 Listen to me! These **prisoners** are your brothers and sisters. Let them go, or the LORD will **punish** you in his **anger**."

12 Four of the **leading** men of the Northern Kingdom, Azariah son of Jehohanan, Berechiah son of Meshillemoth, Jehizkiah son of Shallum, and Amasa son of Hadlai also opposed the **actions** of the army. 13 They said, "Don't bring those **prisoners** here! We have already sinned against the LORD and made him **angry enough** to **punish** us. Now you want to do something that will increase our **guilt**." 14 So then the army handed the **prisoners** and the loot over to the people and their leaders, 15 and the four men were appointed to **provide** the **prisoners** with clothing from the captured loot. They gave them clothes and sandals to wear, gave them **enough** to eat and drink, and put olive-oil on their wounds. Those who were too **weak** to walk were put on donkeys, and all the **prisoners** were taken back to Judaean territory at Jericho, the city of palm-trees. Then the Israelites returned home to Samaria.

Ahaz Asks Assyria for Help
(2 Kgs 16.7–9)

16–17 The Edomites began to raid Judah again and captured many **prisoners**, so King Ahaz asked Tiglath Pileser, the emperor of Assyria, to send **help**. 18 At this same time the Philistines were raiding the towns in the western foothills and in southern Judah. They captured the cities of Beth Shemesh, Aijalon, and Gederoth, and the cities of Soco, Timnah, and Gimzo with their villages, and settled there permanently. 19 Because King Ahaz of Judah had violated the **rights** of his people and had **defied** the LORD, the LORD brought **troubles** on Judah. 20 The Assyrian emperor, instead of **helping** Ahaz, opposed him and caused him **trouble**. 21 So Ahaz took the gold from the **Temple**, the palace, and the homes of the leaders of the people, and gave it to the emperor, but even this did not **help**.

The Sins of Ahaz

22 When his **troubles** were at their **worst**, that man Ahaz sinned against the LORD more than ever. 23 He **offered sacrifices** to the gods of the Syrians, who had defeated him. He said, "The Syrian gods **helped** the kings of Syria, so if I **sacrifice** to them, they may **help** me too." This brought **disaster** on him and on his nation. 24 In addition, he took all the **temple** equipment and broke it in pieces. He closed the **Temple** and set up **altars** in every part of Jerusalem. 25 In every city and town in Judah, he built **pagan places of worship**, where **incense** was to be burnt to foreign **gods**. In this way he brought on himself the **anger of the** LORD, the God of his ancestors.

26 All the other events of his **reign**, from beginning to end, are recorded in *The History of the Kings of Judah and Israel*. 27 King Ahaz died and was buried in Jerusalem, but not in the royal **tombs**. His son Hezekiah succeeded him as king.

King Hezekiah of Judah
(2 Kgs 18.1–3)

29 Hezekiah became king of Judah at the age of twenty-five, and he ruled in Jerusalem for twenty-nine years. His mother was Abijah, the daughter of Zechariah. 2 Following the **example** of his ancestor King David, he did what was **pleasing** to the LORD.

abandon 28.5; Neh 9.19
altar [5] 28.24; 30.14
anger [2] 28.9; 30.8
blood [2] 1 Chr 28.3; 30.16
bread 18.26; 30.13
burnt-offering [7] 28.3; 30.15
choose 26.1; 33.7

28.5–6: Is 7.1 **28.27:** Is 14.28

clean [5] 13.11; 30.1
command [2] 28.7; 30.6
complete 8.16; Ezra 4.13
consecrate 26.18; Ezek 43.20
covenant 23.3; 34.30
dedicate 15.18; 30.15
defile 1 Chr 23.28; 36.14
displease 1 Chr 21.7; Ezra 8.22
enough 28.13; 30.1
example 28.1; 34.2
fail 2 Kgs 10.21; Ezra 6.9
faithful 27.6; 31.15
fright 20.3; 32.18
happy 23.21; 30.25
help [2] 28.16; 32.8
incense [2] 28.3; 30.14
joy 23.13; 30.21
kneel [2] 6.13; Ezra 9.5
lamb [3] 1 Chr 29.21; 30.15
law 25.4; 30.5
leading 28.12; Ezra 8.24
Levites [10] 24.5; 30.15
obey 27.6; 30.8
offer [7] 28.4; 30.14
please 28.1; 30.4
praise [2] 20.19; 30.21
present (1) [2] 13.11; Ezra 1.4
priest [10] 26.17; 30.1
prison 28.5; 30.9
prophet [3] 28.9; 32.20
pure [4] 9.17; 30.18
ritual 1 Kgs 18.28; 30.18
sacred 24.7; 31.18
sacrifice [9] 28.3; 30.14
sheep [4] 18.2; 30.24
sin-offering Num 29.5; Ezek 44.29
sprinkle 2 Sam 13.19; 30.16
take away (sin) [2] Lev 23.26; Neh 10.33
thank 1 Chr 29.13; 31.2
turn 26.9; 33.12
unclean 26.21; Job 14.4
unfaithful [2] 21.13; 30.7
worship (1) (of God) [7] 24.18; 30.8

The Purification of the Temple

3 In the first month of the year after
Hezekiah became king, he re-opened the
gates of the Temple and had them
repaired. 4 He assembled a group of
priests and Levites in the east courtyard
of the Temple 5 and spoke to them there.
He said, "You **Levites** are to **consecrate**
yourselves and **purify** the Temple of the
LORD, the God of your ancestors.
Remove from the Temple everything
that **defiles** it. 6 Our ancestors were
unfaithful to the LORD our God and did
what was **displeasing** to him. They
abandoned him and **turned** their backs
on the place where he dwells. 7 They
closed the doors of the Temple, let the
lamps go out, and **failed** to burn **incense**
or **offer burnt-offerings** in the Temple of
the God of Israel. 8 Because of this the
LORD has been **angry** with Judah and
Jerusalem, and what he has done to
them has shocked and **frightened** everyone. You know this very well. 9 Our
fathers were killed in battle, and our
wives and children have been taken
away as **prisoners**.

10 "I have now decided to make a
covenant with the LORD, the God of
Israel, so that he will no longer **be angry**
with us. 11 My sons, do not lose any time.
You are the ones that the LORD has
chosen to burn **incense** to him and to
lead the people in **worshipping** him."

12–14 The following **Levites** were
there:

From the clan of Kohath, Mahath son of Amasai and Joel son of Azariah
From the clan of Merari, Kish son of Abdi and Azariah son of Jehallelel
From the clan of Gershon, Joah son of Zimnah and Eden son of Joah
From the clan of Elizaphan, Shimri and Jeuel
From the clan of Asaph, Zechariah and Mattaniah
From the clan of Heman, Jehuel and Shimei
From the clan of Jeduthun, Shemaiah and Uzziel

15 These men assembled their **fellow-**
Levites, and they all made themselves
ritually **clean**. Then, as the king had **com-**
manded them to do, they began to make
the Temple ritually **clean**, according to
the **Law of the** LORD.[j] 16 The **priests** went
inside the Temple to **purify** it, and they
carried out into the temple courtyard
everything that was ritually **unclean**.
From there the **Levites** took it all outside
the city to the valley of the Kidron.

17 The work was begun on the first
day of the first month, and by the eighth
day they had finished it all, including the
entrance room to the Temple. Then they
worked for the next eight days, until the
sixteenth of the month, preparing the
Temple for **worship**.

The Temple Is Rededicated

18 The **Levites** made the following
report to King Hezekiah: "We have **com-**
pleted the **ritual purification** of the whole
Temple, including the **altar** for **burnt-**
offerings, the table for the **sacred bread**,
and all their equipment. 19 We have also
brought back all the equipment which
King Ahaz took away during those years
he was **unfaithful** to God, and we have
rededicated it. It is all in front of the
LORD's **altar**."

20 Without delay King Hezekiah
assembled the **leading** men of the city,
and together they went to the Temple.
21 As an **offering** to **take away** the sins of
the royal family and of the people of
Judah and to **purify** the Temple, they
took seven bulls, seven **sheep**, seven
lambs, and seven goats. The king told the
priests, who were descendants of Aaron,
to **offer the animals as sacrifices** on the
altar. 22 The **priests** killed the bulls first,
then the **sheep**, and then the **lambs**, and
sprinkled the **blood** of each **sacrifice** on
the **altar**. 23 Finally they took the goats to
the king and to the other **worshippers**,
who laid their hands on them. 24 Then the
priests killed the goats and poured their
blood on the **altar** as a **sacrifice** to **take**
away the sin of all the people, for the
king had **commanded burnt-offerings** and
sin-offerings to be made for all Israel.

25 The king followed the instructions
that the LORD had given to King David
through Gad, the king's **prophet**, and
through the **prophet** Nathan; he
stationed **Levites** in the Temple, with
harps and cymbals, 26 instruments like
those that King David had used. The
priests also stood there with trumpets.
27 Hezekiah gave the order for the **burnt-**
offering to be **presented**; and as the
offering began, the people sang **praise** to
the LORD, and the musicians began to
play the trumpets and all the other
instruments. 28 Everyone who was there
joined in **worship**, and the singing and
the rest of the music continued until all
the **sacrifices** had been burnt. 29 Then
King Hezekiah and all the people **knelt**
down and **worshipped** God. 30 The king
and the leaders of the nation told the

[j] Then, as the king...LORD; *or* Then they began to make the Temple ritually clean, as the king, who was acting at the LORD's command, had ordered them to do.

Levites to sing to the LORD the songs of **praise** that were written by David and by Asaph the **prophet**. So everyone sang with great **joy** as they **knelt** and **worshipped** God.

31 Hezekiah said to the people, "Now that you are ritually **clean**, bring **sacrifices** as **offerings** of **thanksgiving** to the LORD." They **obeyed**, and some of them also voluntarily brought animals to be **sacrificed** as **burnt-offerings**. 32 They brought seventy bulls, a hundred **sheep**, and two hundred **lambs** as **burnt-offerings** for the LORD; 33 they also brought six hundred bulls and three thousand **sheep** as **sacrifices** for the people to eat. 34 Since there were not **enough priests** to kill all these animals, the **Levites helped** them until the work was finished. By then more **priests** had made themselves ritually **clean**. (The **Levites** were more **faithful** in keeping ritually **clean** than the **priests** were.) 35 In addition to **offering the sacrifices** that were burnt whole, the **priests** were responsible for burning the fat that was **offered from the sacrifices** which the people ate, and for pouring out the wine that was **presented** with the **burnt-offerings**.

And so **worship** in the Temple was begun again. 36 King Hezekiah and the people were **happy**, because God had **helped** them to do all this so quickly.

Preparations for Passover

30 1-3 The people had not been able to **celebrate** the **Passover Festival** at the **proper** time, in the first month, because not **enough priests** were ritually **clean** and not many people had assembled in Jerusalem. So King Hezekiah, his officials, and the people of Jerusalem **agreed** to **celebrate** it in the second month, and the king sent **word** to all the people of Israel and Judah. He took **special care** to send **letters** to the tribes of Ephraim and Manasseh, inviting them to come to the **Temple** in Jerusalem to **celebrate** the **Passover** in **honour** of the LORD, the God of Israel. 4 The king and the people were **pleased** with their **plan**, 5 so they invited all the Israelites, from Dan in the north to Beersheba in the south, to come together in Jerusalem and **celebrate** the **Passover** according to the **Law**, in larger numbers than ever before. 6 Messengers went out at the **command** of the king and his officials through all Judah and Israel with the following invitation:

"People of Israel, you have survived the Assyrian **conquest** of the land. Now return to the LORD, the God of Abraham, Isaac, and Jacob, and he will return to you. 7 Do not be like your ancestors and your fellow-Israelites who were **unfaithful** to the LORD their God. As you can see, he **punished** them severely. 8 Do not be **stubborn** as they were, but **obey** the LORD. Come to the **Temple** in Jerusalem, which the LORD your God has made **holy** for ever, and **worship** him so that he will no longer be **angry** with you. 9 If you return to the LORD, then those who have taken your relatives away as **prisoners** will take **pity** on them and let them come back home. The LORD your God is **kind** and **merciful**, and if you return to him, he will **accept** you."

10 The messengers went to every city in the territory of the tribes of Ephraim and Manasseh, and as far north as the tribe of Zebulun, but people laughed at them and **ridiculed** them. 11 Still, there were some from the tribes of Asher, Manasseh, and Zebulun who were willing to come to Jerusalem. 12 God was also at work in Judah and **united** the people in their **determination** to **obey** his **will** by following the **commands** of the king and his officials.

Passover Is Celebrated

13 A great number of people gathered in Jerusalem in the second month to **celebrate** the **Festival** of **Unleavened** Bread. 14 They took all the **altars** that had been used in Jerusalem for **offering** sacrifices and burning **incense** and threw them into the valley of the Kidron. 15 And on the fourteenth day of the month they killed the **lambs** for the **Passover sacrifice**. The **priests and Levites** who were not ritually **clean** were so **ashamed** that they **dedicated** themselves to the LORD, and now they could **sacrifice burnt-offerings** in the **Temple**. 16 They took their places in the **Temple** according to the instructions in the **Law of** Moses, the **man of God**. The **Levites** gave the **blood** of the **sacrifices** to the **priests**, who **sprinkled** it on the **altar**. 17 Because many of the people were not ritually **clean**, they could not kill the **Passover lambs**, so the **Levites** did it for them, and **dedicated** the **lambs** to the LORD. 18 In addition, many of those who had come from the tribes of Ephraim, Manasseh, Issachar, and Zebulun had not performed the **ritual** of **purification**, and so they were **observing Passover** improperly. King Hezekiah **offered** this **prayer** for them: 19 "O LORD, the God of our

accept [2] 15.15; 33.13
agree 16.4; Neh 9.38
altar [2] 29.18; 31.1
anger 29.8; 33.6
ashamed 1 Chr 19.5; Ezra 8.22
bless 26.5; 31.10
blood 29.22; 35.11
bread [2] 29.18; 35.17
burnt-offering 29.7; 31.2
care 1 Chr 28.13; Ezra 5.8
celebrate [8] 23.13; 35.1
clean [4] 29.15; 34.5
command [2] 29.15; 32.6
conquer 12.8; Ezra 5.12
contribute 24.8; 35.7
dedicate [2] 29.19; 31.6
determine 4.18; 32.7
enough 29.34; 31.10
festival [3] 8.13; 31.1
forgive [2] 7.14; Neh 4.5
happy 29.36; Neh 2.2
harm 1 Chr 16.22; Ezra 4.22
heart 20.33; 34.31
heaven 20.6; 36.23
holy 26.18; 36.14
honour 20.8; 32.23
incense 29.7; 32.12

joy [3] 29.30; Ezra 3.12
kind 10.7; Esth 5.8
lamb [3] 29.21; 35.6
law [2] 29.15; 31.3
letter (2) 21.12; 32.17
Levites [7] 29.4; 31.2
man of God 8.14; Ezra 3.2
mercy 6.39; 36.17
obey [2] 29.31; 33.8
observe 20.3; 31.21
offer [3] 29.7; 31.2
Passover [6] 2 Kgs 23.21; 35.1
pity Deut 13.8; Job 16.13
plan 8.6; Ezra 10.15
please 29.2; 31.20
praise [3] 29.27; 31.2
prayer [3] 7.1; 33.13
priest [7] 29.4; 31.2
prison 29.9; 36.3
proper 1 Kgs 14.13; Ezra 6.5
punish 28.11; 32.26
pure [2] 29.5; 34.8
ridicule 7.20; 36.16
ritual [2] 29.18; Neh 12.30
sacrifice [5] 29.21; 33.6
sheep [2] 29.21; 31.6
special 1 Sam 21.5; Esth 2.9
sprinkle 29.22; 35.11
strength 26.9; 32.5
stubborn 2 Kgs 17.14; 36.13
Temple (1) (of God) [4] 28.21; 31.2
unfaithful 29.6; Ezra 10.6
unite 1 Chr 12.38; Ezek 37.22
unleavened [2] 8.13; 35.17
will (1) 25.20; Ezra 5.17
word (1) 24.9; 32.8
worship (1) (of God) [3] 29.11; 31.2

30.2-3: Num 9.9-11

ancestors, in your goodness forgive those who are worshipping you with all their heart, even though they are not ritually clean.” 20 The LORD answered Hezekiah's prayer; he forgave the people and did not harm them. 21 For seven days the people who had gathered in Jerusalem celebrated the Festival of Unleavened Bread with great joy, and day after day the Levites and the priests praised the LORD with all their strength.[k] 22 Hezekiah praised the Levites for their skill in conducting the worship of the LORD.

A Second Celebration

After the seven days during which they offered sacrifices in praise of the LORD, the God of their ancestors, 23 they all decided to celebrate for another seven days. So they celebrated with joy. 24 King Hezekiah contributed a thousand bulls and seven thousand sheep for the people to kill and eat, and the officials gave them another thousand bulls and ten thousand sheep. A large number of priests went through the ritual of purification. 25 So everyone was happy—the people of Judah, the priests, the Levites, the people who had come from the north, and the foreigners who had settled permanently in Israel and Judah. 26 The city of Jerusalem was filled with joy, because nothing like this had happened since the days of King Solomon, the son of David. 27 The priests and the Levites asked the LORD's blessing on the people. In his home in heaven God heard their prayers and accepted them.

Hezekiah Reforms Religious Life

31 After the festival ended, all the people of Israel went to every city in Judah and broke the stone pillars, cut down the symbols of the goddess Asherah, and destroyed the altars and the pagan places of worship. They did the same thing throughout the rest of Judah, and the territories of Benjamin, Ephraim, and Manasseh; then they all returned home.

2 King Hezekiah re-established the organization of the priests and Levites, under which they each had specific duties. These included offering the burnt-offerings and the fellowship-offerings, taking part in the temple worship, and giving praise and thanks in the various parts of the Temple. 3 From his own flocks and herds he provided animals for the burnt-offerings each morning and evening, and for those offered on the Sabbath, at the New Moon Festival, and at the other festivals which are required by the Law of the LORD.

4 In addition, the king told the people of Jerusalem to bring the offerings to which the priests and the Levites were entitled, so that they could give all their time to the requirements of the Law of the LORD. 5 As soon as the order was given, the people of Israel brought gifts of their finest corn, wine, olive-oil, honey, and other farm produce, and they also brought the tithes[l] of everything they had. 6 All the people who lived in the cities of Judah brought tithes of their cattle and sheep, and they also brought large quantities of gifts, which they dedicated to the LORD their God. 7 The gifts started arriving in the third month and continued to pile up for the next four months. 8 When King Hezekiah and his officials saw how much had been given, they praised the LORD and praised his people Israel. 9 The king spoke to the priests and the Levites about these gifts, 10 and Azariah the High Priest, a descendant of Zadok, said to him, “Since the people started bringing their gifts to the Temple, there has been enough to eat and a large surplus besides. We have all this because the LORD has blessed his people.”

11 On the king's orders they prepared storerooms in the Temple area 12 and put all the gifts and tithes in them for safekeeping. They placed a Levite named Conaniah in charge and made his brother Shimei his assistant. 13 Ten Levites were assigned to work under them: Jehiel, Azaziah, Nahath, Asahel, Jerimoth, Jozabad, Eliel, Ismachiah, Mahath, and Benaiah. All this was done under the authority of King Hezekiah and Azariah the High Priest. 14 Kore son of Imnah, a Levite who was chief guard at the East Gate of the Temple, was in charge of receiving the gifts offered to the LORD and of distributing them. 15 In the other cities where priests lived, he was faithfully assisted in this by other Levites: Eden, Miniamin, Jeshua, Shemaiah, Amariah, and Shecaniah. They distributed the food equally to their fellow-Levites according to what their duties were, 16 and not by clans. They gave a share to all males thirty[m] years of

[k] *Probable text* with all their strength; *Hebrew* with mighty instruments.
[l] GIFTS...TITHES: *The gifts were for the priests, and the tithes for the Levites (see Num 18).*
[m] *Probable text* thirty; *Hebrew* three.

31.3: Num 28.1–29.39 **31.4–5:** Num 18.12–13, 21

altar 30.14; 32.12
authority 19.6; Ezra 4.19
bless 30.27; Ezra 6.10
burnt-offering [2] 30.15; 33.6
dedicate 30.15; 35.3
depend 20.15; Ps 18.30
destroy 25.16; 32.12
devote 1 Chr 29.18; 32.32
duty (1) [4] 26.21; 35.2
enough 30.1; Neh 5.3
establish 12.1; Ps 44.2
faithful 29.34; 32.1
fellowship-offering 7.5; 33.16
festival [3] 30.1; 35.1
flock 1 Kgs 20.27; 35.7
gift [7] 17.5; 32.23
God's people [2] 23.16; 32.17
goddess 24.18; 33.3

High Priest [2] 24.1[illegible] 34.9
law [3] 30.5; 33.8
Levites [10] 30.15; 34.9
loyal 24.22; 36.13
New Moon Festiva[illegible] 8.13; Ezra 3.5
observe 30.18; 36.21
offer [4] 30.14; 32.23
pagan 28.4; 33.3
place of worship 28.4; 33.3
please 30.4; 34.2
praise [2] 30.21; Ezra 3.10
priest [7] 30.1; 34.5
provide 28.15; 35.14
require [3] 24.6; 34.32
right (1) 20.32; Neh 5.9
Sabbath 23.4; 36.21
sacred 29.18; 35.3
safe 19.1; Ezra 9.8
share 1 Chr 23.24; Neh 2.20
sheep 30.24; 32.28
spirit (2) 18.20; Job 26.5
succeed (1) 20.20; 32.30
symbol 19.3; 33.19
Temple (1) (of God) [7] 30.1; 33.4
thank 29.31; Neh 11.17
tithe [3] Deut 26.12; Neh 10.37
worship (1) (of God 30.8; 32.12

age or older who had daily responsibilities in the **Temple** in accordance with
their positions. 17 The **priests** were
assigned their **duties** by clans, and the
Levites twenty years of age or older
were assigned theirs by work groups.
18 They were all registered together with
their wives, children, and other
dependants, because they were **required**
to be ready to perform their **sacred**
duties at any time. 19 Among the **priests**
who lived in the cities assigned to
Aaron's descendants, or in the pasture
lands belonging to these cities, there
were responsible men who distributed
the food to all the males in the **priestly**
families and to everyone who was on the
rolls of the **Levite** clans.
20 Throughout all Judah, King Hezekiah did what was **right** and what was
pleasing to the LORD his God. 21 He was
successful, because everything he did for
the **Temple** or in **observance** of the **Law**,
he did in a **spirit** of complete **loyalty** and
devotion to his God.

The Assyrians Threaten Jerusalem
(2 Kgs 18.13–37; 19.14–19, 35–37;
Is 36.1–22; 37.8–38)

32 After these events, in which King
Hezekiah **served** the LORD **faithfully**, Sennacherib, the emperor of
Assyria, invaded Judah. He besieged the
fortified cities and gave orders for his
army to break their way through the
walls. 2 When Hezekiah saw that Sennacherib **intended** to attack Jerusalem also,
3–4 he and his officials decided to cut off
the supply of water outside the city in
order to **prevent** the Assyrians from
having any water when they got near
Jerusalem. The officials led a large
number of people out and stopped up all
the springs, so that no more water flowed
out of them. 5 The king **strengthened** the
city's **defences** by repairing the wall,
building towers on it,[n] and building an
outer wall. In addition, he repaired the
defences built on the land that was filled
in on the east side of the old part of
Jerusalem. He also had a large number
of spears and shields made. 6 He placed
all the men in the city under the **command** of army officers and ordered them
to assemble in the open square at the
city gate. He said to them, 7 "Be **determined** and **confident**, and don't be **afraid**
of the Assyrian emperor or of the army
he is leading. We have more **power** on
our side than he has on his. 8 He has
human power, but we have the LORD our
God to **help** us and to fight our battles."
The people were **encouraged** by these
words of their king.
9 Some time later, while Sennacherib
and his army were still at Lachish, he
sent the following **message** to Hezekiah
and the people of Judah who were with
him in Jerusalem: 10 "I, Sennacherib,
Emperor of Assyria, ask what gives you
people the **confidence** to remain in
Jerusalem under siege. 11 Hezekiah tells
you that the LORD your God will **save** you
from our **power**, but Hezekiah is
deceiving you and will let you die of
hunger and thirst. 12 He is the one who
destroyed the LORD's **shrines** and **altars**
and then told the people of Judah and
Jerusalem to **worship** and burn **incense**
at one **altar** only. 13 Don't you know what
my ancestors and I have done to the
people of other nations? Did the **gods** of
any other nation **save** their people from
the emperor of Assyria? 14 When did any
of the **gods** of all those countries ever
save their country from us? Then what
makes you think that your god can **save**
you? 15 Now don't let Hezekiah **deceive**
you or **mislead** you like that. Don't
believe him! No **god** of any nation has
ever been able to **save** his people from
any Assyrian emperor. So certainly this
god of yours can't **save** you!"
16 The Assyrian officials said even
worse things about the LORD God and
Hezekiah, the LORD's **servant**. 17 The
letter that the emperor wrote **defied** the
LORD, the God of Israel. It said, "The
gods of the nations have not **saved** their
people from my **power**, and neither will
Hezekiah's god **save his people** from
me." 18 The officials shouted this in
Hebrew in order to **frighten** and **discourage** the people of Jerusalem who
were on the city wall, so that it would be
easier to capture the city. 19 They talked
about the God of Jerusalem in the same
way that they talked about the **gods** of
the other peoples, **idols** made by **human**
hands.
20 Then King Hezekiah and the
prophet Isaiah son of Amoz **prayed** to
God and cried out to him for **help**. 21 The
LORD sent an **angel** that killed the
soldiers and officers of the Assyrian
army. So the emperor went back to
Assyria **disgraced**. One day when he was
in the **temple** of his **god**, some of his sons
killed him with their swords.
22 In this way the LORD **rescued** King
Hezekiah and the people of Jerusalem
from the **power** of Sennacherib, the
emperor of Assyria, and also from their
other **enemies**. He let the people live in

[n] *Some ancient translations* building towers on it; *Hebrew* building on the towers.

afraid 20.15; Ezra 3.3
altar [2] 31.1; 33.3
angel 18.18; Job 4.18
believe 20.20; Job 9.16
command 30.6; 33.8
confident [2] 1 Chr 28.20; Job 4.6
death (1) [2] 26.2; 34.28
deceive [2] 18.19; Job 6.15
defend [2] 2 Kgs 20.6; Esth 8.11
defy 28.19; Ezra 6.12
destroy 31.1; 33.3
determine 30.12; 35.22
devote 31.21; 35.26
discourage 20.15; Ezra 4.4
disgrace 2 Kgs 19.3; Ezra 9.7
encourage 26.10; 35.2
enemy 26.13; 35.21
faithful 31.15; Neh 1.5
fright 29.8; Ezra 4.4
gift 31.5; Neh 12.47
god (2) (other gods) [6] 28.25; 33.15
God's people 31.8; 33.2
grateful Judg 8.35; Ecc 4.16
Hebrew 2 Kgs 18.26; Esth 2.7
help [2] 29.34; 33.12
honour [3] 30.1; 35.1
human [2] 19.6; Neh 9.5
humble 6.24; 33.12
hunger 2 Sam 17.28; Neh 9.15
idol 28.3; 33.19
incense 30.14; 34.4
intend 28.10; Neh 4.2

letter (2) 30.1; Ezra 4.7
message 25.17; 33.18
mislead Deut 13.13; Prov 4.24
neighbour 2 Kgs 4.3; Ezra 1.4
offer 31.2; 33.17
peace 20.30; 34.28
power [5] 27.6; Ezra 4.10
pray [2] 20.3; Ezra 6.10
prevent 1 Sam 7.13; Esth 8.5
prophet [2] 29.25; 33.18
proud 17.6; Neh 9.16
punish 30.7; 34.24
rescue 23.14; Neh 1.10
save [8] 25.15; Neh 6.11
servant 24.6; 33.8
serve 26.5; 34.13
sheep [2] 31.6; 35.7
shrine 2 Kgs 18.22; Is 15.2
sign (1) 2 Kgs 20.8; Neh 9.1
strength 30.21; Neh 1.10
succeed (1) 31.21; Ezra 9.12
suffer 21.15; 33.12
temple (2) (of other gods) 23.17; Ezra 1.7
test 9.1; Job 7.18
tomb 28.27; 35.24
value 21.3; Ezra 8.26
vision 9.29; Job 7.14
word (1) 30.1; 34.21
worse 21.15; Ps 39.2
worship (1) (of God) 31.2; 33.4

peace[o] with all the **neighbouring**
countries. 23 Many people came to Jerusalem, bringing **offerings** to the LORD and
gifts to Hezekiah, so that from then on all
the nations held Hezekiah in **honour**.

Hezekiah's Illness and Pride
(2 Kgs 20.1–3, 12–19; Is 38.1–3; 39.1–8)

24 About this time King Hezekiah fell
ill and almost died. He **prayed**, and the
LORD gave him a **sign** that he would
recover. 25 But Hezekiah was too **proud** to
show **gratitude** for what the LORD had
done for him, and Judah and Jerusalem
suffered for it. 26 Finally, however,
Hezekiah and the people of Jerusalem
humbled themselves, and so the LORD
did not **punish** the people until after
Hezekiah's **death**.

Hezekiah's Wealth and Splendour

27 King Hezekiah became very
wealthy, and everyone held him in
honour. He had storerooms built for his
gold, silver, precious stones, spices,
shields, and other **valuable** objects. 28 In
addition, he had storehouses built for his
corn, wine, and olive-oil; barns for his
cattle; and enclosures for his **sheep**.
29 Besides all this, God gave him **sheep**
and cattle and so much other wealth that
he built many cities. 30 It was King
Hezekiah who blocked the outlet for the
Spring of Gihon and channelled the
water to flow through a tunnel to a point
inside the walls of Jerusalem. Hezekiah
succeeded in everything he did, 31 and
even when the Babylonian ambassadors
came to inquire about the unusual event
that had happened in the land, God let
Hezekiah go his own way only in order to
test his character.

The End of Hezekiah's Reign
(2 Kgs 20.20–21)

32 Everything else that King Hezekiah
did and his **devotion** to the LORD are
recorded in *The Vision of the Prophet
Isaiah Son of Amoz* and in *The History of
the Kings of Judah and Israel.* 33 Hezekiah
died and was buried in the upper section
of the royal **tombs**. All the people of
Judah and Jerusalem paid him great
honour at his **death**. His son Manasseh
succeeded him as king.

King Manasseh of Judah
(2 Kgs 21.1–9)

33 Manasseh was twelve years old
when he became king of Judah,
and he ruled in Jerusalem for fifty-five
years. 2 Following the **disgusting**
practices of the nations whom the LORD
had driven out of the land as **his people**
advanced, Manasseh sinned against the
LORD. 3 He rebuilt the **pagan places of**
worship that his father Hezekiah had **des-**
troyed. He built **altars** for the **worship of**
Baal, made **images** of the **goddess**
Asherah, and **worshipped the stars**. 4 He
built **pagan altars** in the **Temple**, the
place that the LORD had said was where
he should be **worshipped** for ever. 5 In the
two courtyards of the **Temple** he built
altars for the **worship of the stars**. 6 He
sacrificed his sons in the Valley of
Hinnom as **burnt-offerings**. He **practised**
divination and **magic** and **consulted**
fortune-tellers and **mediums**. He sinned
greatly against the LORD and stirred up
his **anger**. 7 He placed an **image** in the
Temple, the place about which God had
said to David and his son Solomon: "Here
in Jerusalem, in this **Temple**, is the place
that I have **chosen** out of all the territory
of the twelve tribes of Israel as the place
where I am to be **worshipped**. 8 And if the
people of Israel will **obey** all my **com-**
mands and keep the whole **Law** that my
servant Moses gave them, then I will not
allow them to be driven out of the land
that I gave to their ancestors."
9 Manasseh led the people of Judah to
commit even greater sins than those
committed by the nations whom the
LORD had driven out of the land as **his**
people advanced.

Manasseh Repents

10 Although the LORD **warned**
Manasseh and his people, they **refused** to
listen. 11 So the LORD let the commanders
of the Assyrian army invade Judah. They
captured Manasseh, stuck hooks in him,
put him in chains, and took him to
Babylon. 12 In his **suffering** he became
humble, **turned to** the LORD his God, and
begged him for **help**. 13 God **accepted**
Manasseh's **prayer** and answered it by
letting him go back to Jerusalem and
rule again. This **convinced** Manasseh
that the LORD was God.

14 After this, Manasseh increased the
height of the outer wall on the east side
of David's City, from a point in the valley
near the spring of Gihon north to the
Fish Gate and the area of the city called
Ophel. He also stationed an army officer
in **command** of a unit of troops in each of
the fortified cities of Judah. 15 He
removed from the Temple the foreign
gods and the **image** that he had placed

[o] *Some ancient translations* He let the people live in peace; *Hebrew* He led the people.

33.2: Jer 15.4 **33.4:** 2 Chr 6.6 **33.7–8:** 1 Kgs 9.3–5; 2 Chr 7.12–18

accept 30.9; Ezra 2.61
altar [5] 32.12; 34.4
anger 30.8; 34.21

beg 1 Sam 23.11; Esth 4.8
burnt-offering 31.2; 35.12
choose 29.11; 36.1
command [3] 32.6; 34.16
consult 20.21; 34.21
convince 2 Sam 16.3; Ezra 4.16
destroy 32.12; 34.3
disgust 28.3; 34.33
divination 2 Kgs 21.6; Hos 3.4
evil 22.2; 36.8
fellowship-offering 31.2; Ezek 43.27
fortune-teller 2 Kgs 23.24; Is 3.2
god (2) (other gods) 32.13; 34.25
God's people [2] 32.17; 35.3
goddess [2] 31.1; 34.3
help 32.8; 35.5
humble [2] 32.26; 34.27
idol [2] 32.19; 34.3
image [3] 28.2; 34.4
law 31.3; 34.2
magic 2 Kgs 21.6; Ps 58.5
medium 2 Kgs 23.24; Is 8.19
message 32.9; 34.24
name (2) (name of God, of Jesus) 18.15; 36.13
obey 30.8; 34.2
offer [2] 32.23; 34.25
pagan [4] 31.1; 34.3
place of worship [3] 31.1; 34.3
plot (1) 25.17; Neh 4.8
practice [2] 28.3; 34.31
prayer [3] 30.18; 34.27
prophet [2] 32.20; 34.22
refuse (1) 25.20; 35.22
repent 7.14; 34.27
sacrifice [3] 30.14; 34.4
servant 32.16; 35.23
suffer 32.25; Neh 9.9
symbol 31.1; 34.3
Temple (1) (of God) [6] 31.2; 34.8
turn [2] 29.6; Ezra 8.22
warn 24.19; 36.15
worship (1) (of God) [4] 32.12; 34.3
worship (2) (of other gods) [5] 28.4; 34.4

there, and the **pagan altars** that were on
the hill where the **Temple** stood and in
other places in Jerusalem; he took all
these things outside the city and threw
them away. 16 He also repaired the **altar**
where the LORD was **worshipped**, and he
sacrificed fellowship-offerings and
thanksgiving-offerings on it. He **commanded** all the people of Judah to
worship the LORD, the God of Israel.
17 Although the people continued to **offer**
sacrifices at other **places of worship**,
they **offered** them only to the LORD.

The End of Manasseh's Reign
(2 Kgs 21.17–18)

18 Everything else that Manasseh did,
the **prayer** he made to his God, and the
messages of the **prophets** who spoke to
him in the **name of the LORD**, the God of
Israel, are all recorded in *The History of
the Kings of Israel.* 19 The king's **prayer**
and God's answer to it, and an account of
the sins he committed before he
repented—the **evil** he did, the **pagan**
places of worship and the **symbols** of the
goddess Asherah that he made and the
idols that he **worshipped**—are all
recorded in *The History of the Prophets.*
20 Manasseh died and was buried at the
palace, and his son Amon succeeded him
as king.

King Amon of Judah
(2 Kgs 21.19–26)

21 Amon was twenty-two years old
when he became king of Judah, and he
ruled in Jerusalem for two years. 22 Like
his father Manasseh, he sinned against
the LORD, and he **worshipped the idols**
that his father had worshipped. 23 But
unlike his father, he did not become
humble and **turn to** the LORD; he was
even more sinful than his father had
been.

24 Amon's officials **plotted** against him
and assassinated him in the palace.
25 The people of Judah killed Amon's
assassins and made his son Josiah king.

King Josiah of Judah
(2 Kgs 22.1–2)

34 Josiah was eight years old when
he became king of Judah, and he
ruled in Jerusalem for thirty-one years.
2 He did what was **pleasing** to the LORD;
he followed the **example** of his ancestor
King David, strictly **obeying** all the **laws**
of God.

Josiah Attacks Pagan Worship

3 In the eighth year that Josiah was
king, while he was still very young, he
began to **worship** the God of his ancestor
King David. Four years later he began to
destroy the **pagan places of worship**, the
symbols of the **goddess** Asherah, and all
the other **idols**. 4 Under his **direction** his
men smashed the **altars** where Baal was
worshipped and tore down the **incense-
altars** near them. They ground to dust
the **images** of Asherah and all the other
idols and then **scattered** the dust on the
graves of the people who had **sacrificed**
to them. 5 He burnt the bones of the
pagan priests on the **altars** where they
had **worshipped**. By doing all this, he
made Judah and Jerusalem ritually **clean**
again. 6 He did the same thing in the
cities and the **devastated** areas of
Manasseh, Ephraim, and Simeon, and as
far north as Naphtali. 7 Throughout the
territory of the Northern Kingdom he
smashed the **altars** and the **symbols** of
Asherah, ground the **idols** to dust, and
broke in pieces all the **incense-altars**.
Then he returned to Jerusalem.

The Book of the Law Is Discovered
(2 Kgs 22.3–20)

8 In the eighteenth year of his **reign**,
after he had **purified** the land and the
Temple by ending **pagan worship**, King
Josiah sent three men to repair the
Temple of the LORD God: Shaphan son of
Azaliah, Maaseiah, the governor of
Jerusalem, and Joah son of Joahaz, a
high official. 9 The money that the **Levite**
guards had collected in the **Temple** was
handed over to Hilkiah the **High Priest**.
(It had been collected from the people of
Ephraim and Manasseh and the rest of
the Northern Kingdom, and from the
people of Judah, Benjamin, and
Jerusalem.) 10 This money was then
handed over to the three men in charge
of the **temple** repairs, and they gave it to
11 the carpenters and the builders to buy
the stones and the timber used to repair
the buildings that the kings of Judah had
allowed to decay. 12 The men who did the
work were thoroughly **honest**. They were
supervised by four **Levites**: Jahath and
Obadiah of the clan of Merari, and
Zechariah and Meshullam of the clan of
Kohath. (The **Levites** were all skilful
musicians.) 13 Other **Levites** were in
charge of transporting materials and
supervising the workmen on various jobs,
and others kept records or **served** as
guards.

14 While the money was being taken
out of the storeroom, Hilkiah found the
book of the **Law** of the LORD, the **Law**

34.1: Jer 3.6 **34.4:** 2 Kgs 21.3; 2 Chr 33.3 **34.5:** 1 Kgs 13.2

altar [5] 33.3; 35.11
anger [3] 33.6; 36.16
clean 30.1; 35.6
command [3] 33.8; 35.10
consult [2] 33.6; Is 8.19
court (1) 19.11; Neh 11.24
covenant [5] 29.10; Neh 1.5
curse 2 Kgs 22.19; Neh 10.29
death (1) 32.26; 35.24

demand 2 Kgs 23.3; Ezra 10.3
destroy [2] 33.3; 35.21
devastate Judg 16.24; Is 1.7
direct 1 Chr 25.2; Neh 12.24
disgust 33.2; 36.8
example 29.2; 36.14
god (2) (other gods) 33.15; Ezra 1.7
goddess 33.3; Is 17.8
grave 1 Kgs 13.22; Job 3.17
heart 30.19; Ezra 1.5
High Priest 31.10; 35.8
honest 1 Chr 29.17; Neh 13.13
humble 33.12; 36.12
idol [4] 33.19; 36.14
image 33.3; Ps 106.20
incense [2] 32.12; Neh 13.5
law [4] 33.8; 35.12
Levites [5] 31.2; 35.3
message [2] 33.18; 35.21
new 23.13; Ezra 9.8
obey [4] 33.8; 35.26
offer 33.17; 35.9
pagan [3] 33.3; Ezra 6.21
peace 32.22; Ezra 5.7
place of worship 33.3; Ps 78.58
please 31.20; Ezra 5.17
poor 1 Chr 21.17; Esth 1.5
practice 33.2; 36.8
prayer 33.13; Ezra 8.23
priest [2] 31.2; 35.2
promise 23.3; Ezra 10.3
prophet 33.18; 35.15
punish [3] 32.26; Ezra 7.26
pure 30.18; Ezra 6.20
reign 28.26; 35.19
reject 6.42; Neh 9.29
repent 33.19; 36.13
require [2] 31.3; Ezra 3.4
rich 18.1; Esth 1.5
sacrifice [2] 33.6; 35.6
scatter 18.16; Neh 1.8
serve [2] 32.1; 35.3
soul 15.12; Ps 42.6
symbol [2] 33.19; Ps 74.9
teach 17.7; Ezra 7.10
Temple (1) (of God) [9] 33.4; 35.2
threat 2 Kgs 22.19; Job 26.11
weep 2 Kgs 22.19; Ezra 10.1
word (1) 32.8; 36.12
worship (1) (of God) 33.4; 35.16
worship (2) (of other gods) [3] 33.3; 36.14

that God had given to Moses. 15 He said to Shaphan, "I have found the book of the Law here in the **Temple**." He gave Shaphan the book, 16 and Shaphan took it to the king. He reported, "We have done everything that you **commanded**. 17 We have taken the money that was kept in the **Temple** and handed it over to the workmen and their supervisors." 18 Then he added, "I have here a book that Hilkiah gave me." And he read it aloud to the king.

19 When the king heard the book being read, he tore his clothes in dismay 20 and gave the following order to Hilkiah, to Ahikam son of Shaphan, to Abdon[p] son of Micaiah, to Shaphan, the **court** secretary, and to Asaiah, the king's attendant: 21 "Go and **consult** the LORD for me and for the people who still remain in Israel and Judah. Find out about the **teachings** of this book. The LORD is **angry** with us because our ancestors have not **obeyed** the **word of the LORD** and have not done what this book says must be done."

22 At the king's **command**, Hilkiah and the others went to **consult** a woman named Huldah, a **prophet** who lived in the **newer** part of Jerusalem. (Her husband Shallum, the son of Tikvah and grandson of Harhas, was in charge of the **temple** robes.) They described to her what had happened, 23 and she told them to go back to the king and give him 24 the following **message** from the LORD: "I am going to **punish** Jerusalem and all its people with the **curses** written in the book that was read to the king. 25 They have **rejected** me and have **offered sacrifices** to other **gods**, and so have stirred up my **anger** by all they have done. My **anger** is aroused against Jerusalem, and it will not die down. 26 As for the king himself, this is what I, the LORD God of Israel, say: You listened to what is written in the book, 27 and you **repented** and **humbled** yourself before me, tearing your clothes and **weeping**, when you heard how I **threatened** to **punish** Jerusalem and its people. I have heard your **prayer**, 28 and the **punishment** which I am going to bring on Jerusalem will not come until after your **death**. I will let you die in **peace**."

The men returned to King Josiah with this **message**.

Josiah Makes a Covenant to Obey The LORD
(2 Kgs 23.1-20)

29 King Josiah summoned all the leaders of Judah and Jerusalem, 30 and together they went to the **Temple**, accompanied by the **priests and the Levites** and all the rest of the people, **rich** and **poor** alike. Before them all, the king read aloud the whole book of the **covenant**, which had been found in the **Temple**. 31 He stood by the royal column[q] and made a **covenant** with the LORD to **obey** him, to keep his **laws** and **commands with all his heart** and **soul**, and to put into **practice** the **demands** attached to the **covenant**, as written in the book. 32 He made the people of Benjamin and everyone else present in Jerusalem **promise** to keep the **covenant**. And so the people of Jerusalem **obeyed** the **requirements** of the **covenant** they had made with the God of their ancestors. 33 King Josiah **destroyed** all the **disgusting idols** that were in the territory belonging to the people of Israel, and as long as he lived, he **required** the people to **serve** the LORD, the God of their ancestors.

Josiah Celebrates the Passover
(2 Kgs 23.21-23)

35 King Josiah **celebrated** the Passover at Jerusalem in **honour** of the LORD; on the fourteenth day of the first month they killed the animals for the **festival**. 2 He assigned to the **priests** the **duties** they were to perform in the **Temple** and **encouraged** them to do them well. 3 He also gave these instructions to the **Levites**, the **teachers** of Israel, who were **dedicated** to the LORD: "Put the **sacred Covenant Box** in the **Temple** that King Solomon, the son of David, built. You are no longer to carry it from place to place, but you are to **serve** the LORD your God and **his people** Israel. 4 Take your places in the **Temple** by clans, according to the responsibilities assigned to you by King David and his son King Solomon, 5 and arrange yourselves so that some of you will be available to **help** each family of the people of Israel. 6 You are to kill the **Passover lambs** and goats. Now make yourselves ritually **clean** and prepare the **sacrifices** in order that your fellow-Israelites may follow the instructions which the LORD gave through Moses."

7 For the use of the people at the **Passover**, King Josiah **contributed** from his

altar [2] 34.4; Ezra 3.2
bad 18.7; Ps 14.3
blood 30.16; Job 20.2
bread 30.13; Ezra 6.22
burnt-offering [2] 33.6; Ps 50.8
celebrate [5] 30.1; Ezra 3.4
clean 34.5; Ezra 6.20
command [2] 34.16; 36.22
contribute [3] 30.24; Neh 7.70
Covenant Box 8.11; Ps 78.61
custom 2 Kgs 17.8; Esth 1.13
death (1) 34.28; Ezra 7.26
dedicate 31.6; Ezra 6.16
destroy 34.3; Ezra 4.15
determine 32.7; Neh 10.34
devote 32.32; Ezra 7.10
duty (1) 31.2; Neh 7.3
encourage 32.8; Ezra 6.14
enemy 32.22; Ezra 4.1
festival [4] 31.1; Ezra 3.4
flock 31.3; Job 24.2
God's people 33.2; 36.15
help 33.12; Ezra 1.4
High Priest 34.9; Ezra 7.1

[p] ABDON: Achbor in 2 Kgs 22.12.
[q] *Probable text (see 2 Kgs 23.3)* by the royal column; *Hebrew* in his place.
35.4: 2 Chr 8.14

honour 32.23; Ezra 7.27
hurt 1 Chr 12.17; Job 1.12
lamb [5] 30.15; Ezra 6.9
law [2] 34.2; Ezra 3.2
Levites [11] 34.9; Ezra 1.5
message 34.24; Ezra 5.2
mourn [2] 21.19; Neh 1.4
need 2.16; Ezra 1.4
obey 34.2; Ezra 6.12
offer [4] 34.25; Ezra 1.4
Passover [10] 30.1; Ezra 6.19
priest [8] 34.5; 36.14
prophet [3] 34.22; 36.12
provide 31.3; Ezra 1.4
refuse (1) 33.10; 36.13
regulation 1 Sam 2.13; Ezra 3.4
reign 34.8; Ezra 4.5
sacred [2] 31.18; Ezra 8.28
sacrifice [5] 34.4; Ezra 3.2
servant 33.8; Ezra 2.55
serve 34.13; 36.20
sheep 32.28; Ezra 6.9
sprinkle 30.16; Job 18.15
strike 20.9; Job 1.16
teacher Ezra 8.16
Temple (1) (of God) [6] 34.8; 36.7
tomb 32.33; Neh 3.16
unleavened 30.13; Ezra 6.22
worship (1) (of God) 34.3; Ezra 1.3

own herds and **flocks** thirty thousand
sheep, lambs, and young goats, and three
thousand bulls. 8 His officials also made
contributions for the people, the **priests,**
and the Levites to use. And the officials
in charge of the **Temple**—Hilkiah, the
High Priest, Zechariah, and Jehiel—gave
the **priests** two thousand six hundred
lambs and young goats and three
hundred bulls for **sacrifices** during the
festival. 9 The leaders of the **Levites**—
Conaniah, Shemaiah and his brother
Nethanel, Hashabiah, Jeiel, and
Jozabad—**contributed** five thousand
lambs and young goats and five hundred
bulls for the **Levites** to **offer as sacrifices.**
10 When everything was arranged for
the **Passover**, the **priests and the Levites**
took their places, as **commanded** by the
king. 11 After the **lambs** and goats had
been killed, the **Levites** skinned them,
and the **priests sprinkled** the **blood** on the
altar. 12 Then they divided among the
people, by family groups, the animals for
burnt-offerings, so that they could **offer**
them according to the instructions in the
Law of Moses. 13 The **Levites** roasted the
Passover sacrifices over the fire, according to the **regulations**, and boiled the
sacred offerings in pots, cauldrons, and
pans, and quickly distributed the meat to
the people. 14 After this was done, the
Levites provided meat for themselves
and for the **priests** descended from
Aaron, for the **priests** were kept busy
until night, burning the animals that
were burnt whole and the fat of the
sacrifices. 15 The following musicians of
the **Levite** clan of Asaph were in the
places assigned to them by King David's
instructions: Asaph, Heman, and
Jeduthun, the king's **prophet**. The guards
at the **temple** gates did not **need** to leave
their posts, because the other **Levites**
prepared the **Passover** for them. 16 So, as
King Josiah had **commanded**, everything
was done that day for the **worship** of the
LORD, the keeping of the **Passover**
Festival, and the **offering** of **burnt-**
offerings on the **altar.** 17 For seven days
all the people of Israel who were present
celebrated the **Passover** and the **Festival**
of Unleavened Bread. 18 Since the days of
the **prophet** Samuel, the **Passover** had
never been **celebrated** like this. None of
the former kings had ever **celebrated** a
Passover like this one **celebrated** by
King Josiah, the **priests**, the **Levites**, and
the people of Judah, Israel, and Jerusalem 19 in the eighteenth year of Josiah's
reign.

The End of Josiah's Reign
(2 Kgs 23.28–30)

20 After King Josiah had done all this
for the **Temple**, King Neco of Egypt led
an army to fight at Carchemish on the
River Euphrates. Josiah tried to stop
him, 21 but Neco sent Josiah this
message: "This war I am fighting does
not concern you, King of Judah. I have
not come to fight you, but to fight my
enemies, and God has told me to hurry.
God is on my side, so don't oppose me, or
he will **destroy** you." 22 But Josiah was
determined to fight. He **refused** to listen
to what God was saying through King
Neco, so he disguised himself and went
into battle on the plain of Megiddo.
23 During the battle King Josiah was
struck by Egyptian arrows. He ordered
his **servants**, "Take me away; I'm **badly**
hurt!" 24 They lifted him out of his
chariot, placed him in a second chariot
which he had there, and took him to
Jerusalem. There he died and was buried
in the royal **tombs**. All the people of
Judah and Jerusalem **mourned** his **death**.
25 The **prophet** Jeremiah composed a
lament for King Josiah. It has become a
custom in Israel for the singers, both
men and women, to use this song when
they **mourn** for him. The song is found in
the collection of laments.
26 Everything that Josiah did—his
devotion to the LORD, his **obedience** to
the **Law**, 27 and his history from
beginning to end—is all recorded in *The*
History of the Kings of Israel and Judah.

King Joahaz of Judah
(2 Kgs 23.30–35)

36 The people of Judah **chose**
Josiah's son Joahaz and **anointed**
him king in Jerusalem. 2 Joahaz was
twenty-three years old when he became
king of Judah, and he ruled in Jerusalem
for three months. 3 King Neco of Egypt
took him **prisoner** and made Judah pay
3,400 kilogrammes of silver and 34 kilogrammes of gold as **tribute.** 4 Neco made
Joahaz' brother Eliakim king of Judah
and **changed** his name to Jehoiakim.
Joahaz was taken to Egypt by Neco.

King Jehoiakim of Judah
(2 Kgs 23.36—24.7)

5 Jehoiakim was twenty-five years old
when he became king of Judah, and he
ruled in Jerusalem for eleven years. He
sinned against the LORD his God. 6 King
Nebuchadnezzar of Babylonia invaded
Judah, captured Jehoiakim, and took him

anger 34.21; Ezra 5.12
anoint 23.11; Ps 89.20
change 1 Chr 21.15; Neh 9.7
choose 33.7; Ezra 6.12
command [2] 35.10; Ezra 1.1
defile 29.5; Neh 13.29
desolate 2 Kgs 19.17; Job 30.3
disgust 34.33; Ezra 9.1
escape 21.9; Ezra 9.8
evil 33.19; Ezra 4.12
example 34.2; Neh 13.27
force (1) 27.5; Ezra 4.23
fulfil 6.15; Job 23.14
God's people [3] 35.3; Ezra 1.3
heaven 30.27; Ezra 1.2
holy 30.8; Ezra 9.2
humble 34.27; Ezra 8.21
idol 34.3; Neh 9.18
ignore 25.16; Ezra 9.14

35.13: Ex 12.8–9 **35.15:** 1 Chr 25.1 **35.17:** Ex 12.1–20 **36.4:** Jer 22.11–12
36.5: Jer 22.18–19, 26.1–6, 35.1–19 **36.6:** Jer 25.1–38, 36.1–32, 45.1–5; Dan 1.1–2

loyal 31.21; Job 6.14
mercy 30.9; Neh 1.11
name (2) (name of God, of Jesus) 33.18; Ezra 5.1
observe 31.21; Esth 3.8
practice 34.31; Ezra 7.10
priest 35.2; Ezra 1.5
prison [2] 30.9; Ezra 2.1
prophet [5] 35.15; Ezra 1.1
rebel 25.27; Ezra 4.12
refuse (1) 35.22; Neh 3.5
repent 34.27; Neh 9.28
rest (1) 4.4; Ezra 8.32
ridicule 30.10; Neh 4.1
rise 6.41; Neh 8.7
Sabbath 31.3; Neh 9.14
serve 35.3; Ezra 8.17
slave 28.10; Ezra 9.8
spare 1 Chr 21.17; Neh 13.22
stubborn 30.8; Neh 9.16
swear 2 Kgs 5.16; Neh 5.12
Temple (1) (of God) [9] 35.2; Ezra 1.2
tribute 27.5; Hos 10.6
true 15.3; Ezra 1.1
warn 33.10; Neh 4.12
word (1) [2] 34.21; Job 2.13
world 20.6; Ezra 1.2
worship (2) (of other gods) 34.4; Job 31.26

to Babylonia in chains. 7 Nebuchadnezzar
carried off some of the treasures of the
Temple and put them in his palace in
Babylon. 8 Everything that Jehoiakim
did, including his **disgusting practices**
and the **evil** he committed, is recorded in
*The History of the Kings of Israel and
Judah*. His son Jehoiachin succeeded him
as king.

King Jehoiachin of Judah
(2 Kgs 24.8–17)

9 Jehoiachin was eighteen[x] years old
when he became king of Judah, and he
ruled in Jerusalem for three months and
ten days. He too sinned against the LORD.
10 When spring came, King Nebuchadnezzar took Jehoiachin to Babylonia as a
prisoner, and carried off the treasures of
the **Temple**. Then Nebuchadnezzar made
Jehoiachin's uncle[r] Zedekiah king of
Judah and Jerusalem.

King Zedekiah of Judah
(2 Kgs 24.18–20; Jer 52.1–3a)

11 Zedekiah was twenty-one years old
when he became king of Judah, and he
ruled in Jerusalem for eleven years. 12 He
sinned against the LORD and did not
listen **humbly** to the **prophet** Jeremiah,
who spoke the **word of the LORD**.

The Fall of Jerusalem
(2 Kgs 25.1–21; Jer 52.3b–11)

13 Zedekiah **rebelled** against King
Nebuchadnezzar, who had **forced** him to
swear in God's **name** that he would be
loyal. He **stubbornly refused** to **repent**
and return to the LORD, the God of Israel.
14 In addition, the leaders of Judah, the
priests, and the people followed the sinful
example of the nations round them in
worshipping idols, and so they **defiled** the
Temple, which the LORD himself had
made **holy**. 15 The LORD, the God of their
ancestors, had continued to send
prophets to **warn his people**, because he
wanted to **spare** them and the **Temple**.
16 But they **ridiculed** God's messengers,
ignoring his **words** and laughing at his
prophets, until at last the **LORD's anger**
against **his people** was so great that
there was no **escape**.

17 So the LORD brought the king of
Babylonia to attack them. The king killed
the young men of Judah, even in the
Temple. He had no **mercy** on anyone,
young or old, man or woman, sick or
healthy. God handed them all over to
him. 18 The king of Babylonia looted the
Temple, the **temple** treasury, and the
wealth of the king and his officials, and
took everything back to Babylon. 19 He
burnt down the **Temple** and the city, with
all its palaces and its wealth, and broke
down the city wall. 20 He took all the survivors to Babylonia, where they **served**
him and his descendants as **slaves** until
the **rise** of the Persian Empire. 21 And so
what the LORD had foretold through the
prophet Jeremiah was **fulfilled**: "The
land will lie **desolate** for seventy years, to
make up for the **Sabbath rest**[s] that has
not been **observed**."

Cyrus Commands the Jews to Return
(Ezra 1.1–4)

22 In the first year that Cyrus of
Persia was emperor,[t] the LORD made
what he had said through the **prophet**
Jeremiah come **true**. He prompted Cyrus
to issue the following **command** and send
it out in writing to be read aloud everywhere in his empire:
23 "This is the **command** of Cyrus,
Emperor of Persia. The LORD, the God of
Heaven, has made me ruler over the
whole **world** and has given me the
responsibility of building a **temple** for
him in Jerusalem in Judah. Now, all of
you who are **God's people**, go there, and
may the LORD your God be with you."

[x] *Some ancient translations (and see 2 Kgs 24.8)* eighteen; *Hebrew* eight.
[r] *Some ancient translations (and see 2 Kgs 24.17)* uncle; *Hebrew* brother.
[s] SABBATH REST: *A reference to the requirement of the Law that every seventh year the land was not to be farmed (see Lev 25.1–7).*
[t] EMPEROR: *King Cyrus of Persia occupied the city of Babylon in 539 B.C. and began to reign as the emperor of Babylonia.*

36.10: Jer 22.24–30, 24.1–10, 29.1–2, 37.1; Ezek 17.12, 13 **36.11:** Jer 27.1–22, 28.1–17 **36.13:** Ezek 17.15 **36.17:** Jer 21.1–10, 34.1–5 **36.21:** Jer 25.11, 29.10 **36.23:** Is 44.28

THE BOOK OF
EZRA

INTRODUCTION

The book of *Ezra* is a sequel to *Chronicles,* describing the return of some of the Jewish exiles from Babylon and the restoration of life and worship in Jerusalem. These events are presented in the following stages: (1) The first group of Jewish exiles returns from Babylonia at the order of Cyrus, the Persian emperor. (2) The Temple is rebuilt and dedicated, and the worship of God restored in Jerusalem. (3) Years later another group of Jews returns to Jerusalem under the leadership of Ezra, an expert in the Law of God, who helps the people reorganize their religious and social life in order to safeguard the spiritual heritage of Israel.

Outline of Contents

---

command [2] 2 Chr 36.22; 4.3
cup 2 Chr 9.20; Esth 1.7
exile [2] 1 Chr 29.15; 2.1
god (2) (other gods) 2 Chr 34.25; Neh 9.18
God's people [2] 2 Chr 36.15; 9.2
heart 2 Chr 34.31; Job 9.35
heaven 2 Chr 36.23; 5.11
help [3] 2 Chr 35.5; 2.68
Levites 2 Chr 35.3; 2.40
need 2 Chr 35.15; 4.3
neighbour [2] 2 Chr 32.22; 9.1
offer [4] 2 Chr 35.9; 2.63
present (1) 2 Chr 29.27; 7.19
priest 2 Chr 36.14; 2.36
prophet 2 Chr 36.12; 5.1
provide 2 Chr 35.14; 7.21
Temple (1) (of God) [6] 2 Chr 36.7; 2.40
temple (2) (of other gods) 2 Chr 32.21; 5.14
true 2 Chr 36.22; Neh 6.8
world 2 Chr 36.23; Job 9.24
worship (1) (of God) 2 Chr 35.16; 3.5

Cyrus Commands the Jews to Return

1 In the first year that Cyrus of Persia
was emperor,[a] the LORD made what
he had said through the **prophet**
Jeremiah come **true**. He prompted Cyrus
to issue the following **command** and send
it out in writing to be read aloud everywhere in his empire:
2 "This is the **command** of Cyrus,
Emperor of Persia. The LORD, the
God of **Heaven**, has made me ruler
over the whole **world** and has given
me the responsibility of building a
temple for him in Jerusalem in
Judah. 3 May God be with all of you
who are **his people**. You are to go to
Jerusalem and rebuild the **Temple**
of the LORD, the God of Israel, the
God who is **worshipped** in
Jerusalem. 4 If any of **his people** in
exile need help to return, their
neighbours are to give them this
help. They are to **provide** them with
silver and gold, supplies and pack
animals, as well as **offerings** to **present** in the **Temple** of God in
Jerusalem."
5 Then the heads of the clans of the
tribes of Judah and Benjamin, the **priests**
and Levites, and everyone else whose
heart God had moved got ready to go
and rebuild the LORD's **Temple** in
Jerusalem. 6 All their **neighbours helped**
them by giving them many things: silver
utensils, gold, supplies, pack animals,
other valuables, and **offerings** for the
Temple.
7 Cyrus gave them back the bowls and
cups that King Nebuchadnezzar had
taken from the **Temple** in Jerusalem and
had put in the **temple** of his **gods**. 8 He
handed them over to Mithredath, chief of
the royal treasury, who made an inven-
tory of them for Sheshbazzar, the governor of Judah, 9-10 as follows:

gold bowls for **offerings**	30
silver bowls for **offerings**	1,000
other bowls	29
small gold bowls	30
small silver bowls	410
other utensils	1,000

11 In all there were 5,400 gold and silver bowls and other articles which Sheshbazzar took with him when he and the
other **exiles** went from Babylon to Jerusalem.

The List of Those Who Returned from Exile
(Neh 7.4–73)

2 Many of the **exiles** left the province
of Babylon and returned to
Jerusalem and Judah, each to his own
city. Their families had been living in
exile in Babylonia ever since King
Nebuchadnezzar had taken them there
as **prisoners**. 2 Their leaders were Zerubbabel, Joshua, Nehemiah, Seraiah,
Reelaiah, Mordecai, Bilshan, Mispar,
Bigvai, Rehum, and Baanah.
This is the list of the clans of Israel,

accept 2 Chr 33.13; 6.10
exile [10] 1.4; 3.3
freewill 2 Kgs 12.4; 8.28
help 1.4; 3.9
Jew 4.4
Levites [2] 1.5; 3.8
offer [2] 1.4; 3.4
priest [7] 1.5; 3.2
prison 2 Chr 36.3; 7.26
prove [3] 2 Kgs 20.8; Neh 7.61
servant [3] 2 Chr 35.23; 4.11

[a] EMPEROR: *King Cyrus of Persia occupied the city of Babylon in 539 B.C. and began to reign as the emperor of Babylonia.*

1.1: Jer 25.11, 29.10 **1.2:** Is 44.28

Temple (1) (of God) [6] 1.2; 3.6

with the number of those from each clan who returned from **exile**:

3-20 Parosh – 2,172
Shephatiah – 372
Arah – 775
Pahath Moab (descendants of Jeshua and Joab) – 2,812
Elam – 1,254
Zattu – 945
Zaccai – 760
Bani – 642
Bebai – 623
Azgad – 1,222
Adonikam – 666
Bigvai – 2,056
Adin – 454
Ater (also called Hezekiah) – 98
Bezai – 323
Jorah – 112
Hashum – 223
Gibbar – 95

21-35 People whose ancestors had lived in the following towns also returned:

Bethlehem – 123
Netophah – 56
Anathoth – 128
Azmaveth – 42
Kiriath Jearim, Chephirah, and Beeroth – 743
Ramah and Geba – 621
Michmash – 122
Bethel and Ai – 223
Nebo – 52
Magbish – 156
The other Elam – 1,254
Harim – 320
Lod, Hadid, and Ono – 725
Jericho – 345
Senaah – 3,630

36-39 This is the list of the **priestly** clans that returned from **exile**:

Jedaiah (descendants of Jeshua) – 973
Immer – 1,052
Pashhur – 1,247
Harim – 1,017

40-42 Clans of **Levites** who returned from **exile**:

Jeshua and Kadmiel (descendants of Hodaviah) – 74
Temple musicians (descendants of Asaph) – 128
Temple guards (descendants of Shallum, Ater, Talmon, Akkub, Hatita, and Shobai) – 139

43-54 Clans of **temple** workmen who returned from **exile**:

Ziha, Hasupha, Tabbaoth,
Keros, Siaha, Padon,
Lebanah, Hagabah, Akkub,
Hagab, Shamlai, Hanan,
Giddel, Gahar, Reaiah,
Rezin, Nekoda, Gazzam,
Uzza, Paseah, Besai,
Asnah, Meunim, Nephisim,
Bakbuk, Hakupha, Harhur,
Bazluth, Mehida, Harsha,
Barkos, Sisera, Temah,
Neziah, and Hatipha

55-57 Clans of Solomon's **servants** who returned from **exile**:

Sotai, Hassophereth, Peruda,
Jaalah, Darkon, Giddel,
Shephatiah, Hattil, Pochereth Hazzebaim, and Ami

58 The total number of descendants of the **temple** workmen and of Solomon's **servants** who returned from **exile** was 392.

59–60 There were 652 belonging to the clans of Delaiah, Tobiah, and Nekoda who returned from the towns of Tel Melah, Tel Harsha, Cherub, Addan, and Immer; but they could not **prove** that they were descendants of Israelites.

61–62 The following **priestly** clans could find no record to **prove** their ancestry: Habaiah, Hakkoz, and Barzillai. (The ancestor of the **priestly** clan of Barzillai had married a woman from the clan of Barzillai of Gilead and had taken the name of his father-in-law's clan.) Since they were unable to **prove** who their ancestors were, they were not **accepted** as **priests**. 63 The **Jewish** governor told them that they could not eat the food **offered** to God until there was a **priest** who could use the Urim and Thummim.[b]

64–67 Total number of **exiles** who returned – 42,360
Their male and female **servants** – 7,337
Male and female musicians – 200
Horses – 736
Mules – 245
Camels – 435
Donkeys – 6,720

68 When the **exiles** arrived at the LORD's **Temple** in Jerusalem, some of the leaders of the clans gave **freewill offerings** to **help** rebuild the **Temple** on its old site. 69 They gave as much as they could for this work, and the total came to 500 kilogrammes of gold, 2,800 kilogrammes of silver, and 100 robes for **priests**.

70 The **priests**, the **Levites**, and some of the people settled in or near Jerusalem;[c] the musicians, the temple guards, and the **temple** workmen settled in nearby towns; and the rest of the

[b] URIM AND THUMMIM: *Two objects used by the priest to determine God's will; it is not known precisely how they were used.*
[c] *One ancient translation* in or near Jerusalem; *Hebrew does not have these words.*

2.63: Num 27.21 **2.70:** 1 Chr 9.2; Neh 11.3

Israelites settled in the towns where their ancestors had lived.

Worship Begins Again

3 By the seventh month the people of Israel were all settled in their towns. Then they all assembled in Jerusalem, 2 and Joshua son of Jehozadak, his **fellow-priests**, and Zerubbabel son of Shealtiel, together with his relatives, rebuilt the **altar** of the God of Israel, so that they could burn **sacrifices** on it according to the instructions written in the **Law of Moses**, the **man of God**. 3 Even though[d] the returning **exiles** were **afraid** of the people who were living in the land, they rebuilt the **altar** where it had stood before. Then they began once again to burn on it the regular morning and evening **sacrifices**. 4 They **celebrated** the **Festival of Shelters** according to the **regulations**; each day they **offered the sacrifices required** for that day; 5 and in addition they **offered the regular sacrifices** to be burnt whole and those to be **offered** at the **New Moon Festival** and at all the other regular assemblies at which the LORD is **worshipped**, as well as all the **offerings** that were given to the LORD voluntarily. 6 Although the people had not yet started to rebuild the **Temple**, they began on the first day of the seventh month to burn **sacrifices** to the LORD.

The Rebuilding of the Temple Begins

7 The people gave money to pay the stonemasons and the carpenters and gave food, drink, and olive-oil to be sent to the cities of Tyre and Sidon in exchange for cedar-trees from Lebanon, which were to be brought by sea to Joppa. All this was done with the **permission** of Cyrus, emperor of Persia. 8 So in the second month of the year after they came back to the site of the **Temple** in Jerusalem, they began work. Zerubbabel, Joshua, and the rest of their fellow-countrymen, the **priests, and the** Levites, in fact all the **exiles** who had come back to Jerusalem, joined in the work. All the **Levites** twenty years of age or older were put in charge of the work of rebuilding the **Temple**. 9 The Levite Jeshua and his sons and relatives, and Kadmiel and his sons (the clan of Hodaviah)[e] joined together in taking charge of the rebuilding of the **Temple**. (They were **helped** by the **Levites** of the clan of Henadad.)

10 When the men started to lay the foundation of the **Temple**, the **priests** in their robes took their places with trumpets in their hands, and the **Levites** of the clan of Asaph stood there with cymbals. They **praised** the LORD according to the instructions handed down from the time of King David. 11 They sang the LORD's **praises**, repeating the refrain:

"The LORD is good, and his **love** for
Israel is **eternal**."

Everyone shouted with all his **might**, **praising** the LORD, because the work on the foundation of the **Temple** had been started. 12 Many of the older **priests**, **Levites**, and heads of clans had seen the first **Temple**, and as they **watched** the foundation of this **Temple** being laid, they cried and **wailed**. But the others who were there shouted for **joy**. 13 No one could **distinguish** between the **joyful** shouts and the crying, because the noise they made was so loud that it could be heard far and wide.

Opposition to the Rebuilding of the Temple

4 The **enemies** of the people of Judah and Benjamin heard that those who had returned from **exile** were rebuilding the **Temple** of the LORD, the God of Israel. 2 So they went to see Zerubbabel and the heads of the clans and said, "Let us join you in building the **Temple**. We **worship** the same God you worship, and we have been **offering sacrifices** to him ever since Esarhaddon, emperor of Assyria, sent us here to live."

3 Zerubbabel, Joshua, and the heads of the clans said to them, "We don't **need** your **help** to build a **temple** for the LORD our God. We will build it ourselves, just as Cyrus, emperor of Persia, **commanded** us."

4 Then the people who had been living in the land tried to **discourage** and **frighten** the **Jews** and **keep them from** building. 5 They also **bribed** Persian government officials to work against them. They kept on doing this throughout the **reign** of Cyrus and into the **reign** of Darius.[f]

Opposition to the Rebuilding of Jerusalem

6 At the beginning of the **reign** of Xerxes the emperor, the **enemies** of the

afraid 2 Chr 32.7; Neh 4.14
altar [2] 2 Chr 35.11; 7.17
celebrate 2 Chr 35.1; 6.19
distinguish 2 Sam 14.17; Ezek 22.26
eternal 2 Chr 20.21; Ps 33.11
exile [2] 2.1; 4.1
festival [2] 2 Chr 35.1; 6.22
help 2.68; 4.3
joy [2] 2 Chr 30.21; 6.16
law 2 Chr 35.12; 7.6
Levites [6] 2.40; 6.16
love 2 Chr 26.10; Neh 1.5
man of God 2 Chr 30.16; Neh 12.24
might 2 Chr 20.6; Job 24.22
New Moon Festival 2 Chr 31.3; Neh 10.33
offer [4] 2.63; 4.2
permit 2 Chr 28.5; 7.13
praise [3] 2 Chr 31.2; 7.27
priest [4] 2.36; 6.9
regulation 2 Chr 35.13; 7.10
require 2 Chr 34.32; 7.23
sacrifice [5] 2 Chr 35.6; 4.2
shelter 2 Chr 8.13; Neh 8.14
Temple (1) (of God) [8] 2.40; 4.1
wail Esth 4.1
watch 2 Chr 16.9; 5.5
worship (1) (of God) 1.3; 4.2

ancient [2] 1 Chr 20.6; Job 3.14
authority 2 Chr 31.13; 5.9
bribe 2 Chr 19.7; Neh 6.12
charge (3) Deut 22.14; Job 10.2
command [2] 1.1; 6.3
complete [2] 2 Chr 29.18; 6.14
control 2 Chr 24.20; Neh 9.15
convince 2 Chr 33.13; Job 6.25
destroy 2 Chr 35.21; 5.12
discourage 2 Chr 32.18; Ps 34.18
enemy [2] 2 Chr 35.21; 8.22
evil 2 Chr 36.8; Neh 4.5
exile 3.3; 5.12
force (1) 2 Chr 36.13; Neh 5.8
fright 2 Chr 32.18; 9.4
hard 2 Chr 24.13; 10.9
harm 2 Chr 30.20; Neh 6.2
help 3.9; 5.2
interest (1) 1 Sam 8.3; Esth 3.8
Jew [3] 2.63; 5.1
judge 2 Chr 19.5; 7.25
keep from 1 Chr 10.4; Neh 5.3
letter (2) [6] 2 Chr 32.17; Neh 2.7
Majesty [4] 2 Chr 20.15; 5.8
need 1.4; 6.9

[d] Even though; *or* Because. [e] *Probable text (see 2.40)* Hodaviah; *Hebrew* Judah.
[f] DARIUS: *The account of these events is continued at verse 24. The material in verses 6–23 describes events which took place almost a century later.*

3.2: Ex 27.1 **3.3:** Num 28.1–8 **3.4:** Num 29.12–38 **3.5:** Num 28.11—29.39 **3.10:** 1 Chr 25.1
3.11: 1 Chr 16.34; 2 Chr 5.13, 7.3; Ps 100.5, 106.1, 107.1, 118.1, 136.1; Jer 33.11 **4.2:** 2 Kgs 17.24–41
4.6: Esth 1.1

obligation 1 Sam 21.7; Rom 1.14
offer 3.4; 6.3
power [2] 2 Chr 32.7; 5.11
rebel [3] 2 Chr 36.13; Neh 2.19
reign [6] 2 Chr 35.19; 5.13
sacrifice 3.2; 6.3
servant 2.55; 5.11
tax [2] 2 Chr 24.6; 6.8
Temple (1) (of God) [4] 3.6; 5.2
trouble [2] 2 Chr 28.19; Neh 2.17
worship (1) (of God) 3.5; 6.12

people living in Judah and Jerusalem
brought written **charges** against them.

7 Again, in the **reign** of Artaxerxes,
emperor of Persia, Bishlam, Mithredath,
Tabeel, and their associates wrote a
letter to the emperor. The **letter** was
written in Aramaic[h] and was to be translated when read.[i]

8 Also Rehum, the governor, and
Shimshai, the secretary of the province,
wrote the following **letter** to Artaxerxes
about Jerusalem:

9 “From Rehum, the governor,
from Shimshai, secretary of the province, from their associates, the
judges, and from all the other officials, who are men originally from
Erech, Babylon, and Susa in the land
of Elam, 10 together with the other
peoples whom the great and **powerful** Ashurbanipal moved from their
homes and settled in the city of
Samaria and elsewhere in the province of West Euphrates.”[j]

11 This is the text of the **letter**:

“To Emperor Artaxerxes from his
servants, the men of West
Euphrates.

12 “We want Your **Majesty** to know
that the **Jews** who came here from
your other territories have settled in
Jerusalem and are rebuilding that
evil and **rebellious** city. They have
begun to rebuild the walls and will
soon finish them. 13 Your **Majesty**, if
this city is rebuilt and its walls are
completed, the people will stop paying **taxes**, and your royal revenues
will decrease. 14 Now, because we
are under **obligation** to Your
Majesty, we do not want to see this
happen, and so we suggest 15 that
you order a search to be made in the
records your ancestors kept. If you
do, you will discover that this city
has always been **rebellious** and that
from **ancient** times it has given
trouble to kings and to rulers of
provinces. Its people have always
been **hard** to govern. This is why the
city was **destroyed**. 16 We therefore
are **convinced** that if this city is rebuilt and its walls are **completed**,
Your **Majesty** will no longer be able
to **control** the province of West
Euphrates.”

17 The emperor sent this answer:

“To Rehum, the governor, to
Shimshai, secretary of the province,
and to their associates who live in
Samaria and in the rest of West
Euphrates, greetings.

18 “The **letter** which you sent has
been translated and read to me. 19 I
gave orders for an investigation to
be made, and it has indeed been
found that from **ancient** times
Jerusalem has revolted against
royal **authority** and that it has been
full of **rebels** and **troublemakers**.
20 **Powerful** kings have **reigned** there
and have ruled over the entire province of West Euphrates, collecting
taxes and revenue. 21 Therefore you
are to issue orders that those men
are to stop rebuilding the city until I
give further **commands**. 22 Do this at
once, so that no more **harm** may be
done to my **interests**.”

23 As soon as this **letter** from
Artaxerxes was read to Rehum,
Shimshai, and their associates, they
hurried to Jerusalem and **forced** the
Jews to stop rebuilding the city.

Work on the Temple Begins Again

24 Work on the **Temple** had been
stopped and had remained at a standstill
until the second year of the **reign** of
5 Darius, emperor of Persia. 1 At that
time two **prophets**, Haggai and
Zechariah son of Iddo, began to speak in
the **name** of the God of Israel to the **Jews**
who lived in Judah and Jerusalem.
2 When Zerubbabel son of Shealtiel and
Joshua son of Jehozadak heard their
messages, they began to rebuild the
Temple in Jerusalem, and the two
prophets helped them.

3 Almost at once Tattenai, governor of
West Euphrates, Shethar Bozenai, and
their fellow-officials came to Jerusalem
and demanded: “Who gave you orders to
build this **Temple** and equip it?” 4 They[k]
also asked for the names of all the men
who were **helping** to build the **Temple**.
5 But God was **watching** over the **Jewish**
leaders, and the Persian officials decided
to take no **action** until they could write to
Darius and receive a reply. 6 This is the
report that they sent to the emperor:

7 “To Emperor Darius, may you
rule in **peace**.

8 “Your **Majesty** should know that
we went to the province of Judah
and found that the **Temple** of the
great God is being rebuilt with large
stone blocks and with wooden

action 2 Chr 28.12; 9.11
anger 2 Chr 36.16; 7.23
authority 4.19; Esth 1.22
care 2 Chr 30.1; Esth 2.3
conquer 2 Chr 30.6 Neh 9.22
destroy 4.15; 6.12
exile 4.1; 6.16
heaven [2] 1.2; 6.9
help [2] 4.3; 6.8
Jew [2] 4.4; 6.7
Majesty [2] 4.12; Neh 2.3
message 2 Chr 35.2 10.7
name (2) (name of God, of Jesus) 2 Chr 36.13; Neh 9.5
peace 2 Chr 34.28; Neh 9.28
please 2 Chr 34.2; 10.11
power 4.10; 7.28
prophet [2] 1.1; 6.14
reign 4.5; 6.3
restore 2 Chr 24.13 Neh 1.3
servant 4.11; 9.11
Temple (1) (of God [14] 4.1; 6.3
temple (2) (of othe gods) 1.7; Is 16.12
watch 3.12; Job 10.1
will (1) 2 Chr 30.12 7.18

[h] ARAMAIC: *From 4.8 to 6.18 this book is not in Hebrew, but Aramaic, the official language of the Persian Empire.* [i] The letter...read; *or* It was in Aramaic and was written in the Aramaic script.
[j] PROVINCE OF WEST EUPHRATES: *Under Persian rule the land of Judah was part of this large Persian province west of the River Euphrates.* [k] *Some ancient translations* They; *Aramaic* We.

4.24—5.1: Hag 1.1; Zech 1.1 **5.2:** Hag 1.12; Zech 4.6–9

beams set in the wall. The work is
being done with great care and is
moving ahead steadily.
9 “We then asked the leaders of
the people to tell us who had given
them authority to rebuild the
Temple and to equip it. 10 We also
asked them their names so that we
could inform you who the leaders of
this work are.
11 “They answered, ‘We are servants of the God of heaven and
earth, and we are rebuilding the
Temple which was originally built
and equipped many years ago by a
powerful king of Israel. 12 But because our ancestors made the God
of Heaven angry, he let them be conquered by King Nebuchadnezzar of
Babylonia, a king of the Chaldean
dynasty. The Temple was destroyed,
and the people were taken into exile
in Babylonia. 13 Then in the first year
of the reign of King Cyrus as emperor of Babylonia, Cyrus issued orders for the Temple to be rebuilt.
14 He restored the gold and silver
temple utensils which Nebuchadnezzar had taken from the
Temple in Jerusalem and had
placed in the temple in Babylon.
Cyrus handed these utensils over to
a man named Sheshbazzar, whom
he appointed governor of Judah.
15 The emperor told him to take
them and return them to the Temple
in Jerusalem, and to rebuild the
Temple where it had stood before.
16 So Sheshbazzar came and laid its
foundation; construction has continued from then until the present,
but the Temple is still not finished.’
17 “Now, if it please Your Majesty,
let a search be made in the royal
records in Babylon to find whether
or not Cyrus gave orders for this
Temple in Jerusalem to be rebuilt,
and then inform us what your will is
in this matter.”

Cyrus’ Order Is Rediscovered

6 So Darius the emperor issued orders
for a search to be made in the royal
records that were kept in Babylon. 2 But
it was in the city of Ecbatana in the province of Media that a scroll was found,
containing the following record:
3 “In the first year of his reign
Cyrus the emperor commanded that
the Temple in Jerusalem be rebuilt
as a place where sacrifices are
made and offerings are burnt. The
Temple is to be twenty-seven metres
high and twenty-seven metres wide.
4 The walls are to be built with one
layer of wood on top of every three
layers of stone. All expenses are to
be paid by the royal treasury. 5 Also
the gold and silver utensils which
King Nebuchadnezzar brought to
Babylon from the Temple in
Jerusalem are to be returned to
their proper place in the Jerusalem
Temple.”

Darius Orders the Work to Continue

6 Then Darius sent the following
reply:
“To Tattenai, governor of West
Euphrates, Shethar Bozenai, and
your fellow-officials in West
Euphrates.
“Stay away from the Temple 7 and
do not interfere with its construction. Let the governor of Judah and
the Jewish leaders rebuild the
Temple of God where it stood before. 8 I hereby command you to help
them rebuild it. Their expenses are
to be paid promptly out of the royal
funds received from taxes in West
Euphrates, so that the work is not interrupted. 9 Day by day, without fail,
you are to give the priests in
Jerusalem whatever they tell you
they need: young bulls, sheep, or
lambs to be burnt as offerings to the
God of Heaven, or wheat, salt, wine,
or olive-oil. 10 This is to be done so
that they can offer sacrifices that
are acceptable to the God of Heaven
and pray for his blessing on me and
my sons. 11 I further command that if
anyone disobeys this order, a
wooden beam is to be torn out of his
house, sharpened at one end, and
then driven through his body. And
his house is to be made a rubbish
heap. 12 May the God who chose
Jerusalem as the place where he is
to be worshipped overthrow any
king or nation that defies this command and tries to destroy the
Temple there. I, Darius, have given
this order. It is to be fully obeyed.”

The Temple Is Dedicated

13 Then Tattenai the governor,
Shethar Bozenai, and their fellow-
officials did exactly as the emperor had
commanded. 14 The Jewish leaders made
good progress with the building of the
Temple, encouraged by the prophets
Haggai and Zechariah. They completed

accept 2.61; 10.16
bless 2 Chr 31.10; 7.6
body 2 Chr 25.28; Esth 9.13
bread 2 Chr 35.17; Neh 9.15
celebrate [2] 3.4; Neh 8.18
choose 2 Chr 36.1; 8.24
clean 2 Chr 35.6; Job 14.4
command [6] 4.3; 7.11
complete 4.13; Ps 138.8
dedicate [2] 2 Chr 35.3; Neh 3.1
defy 2 Chr 32.17; Job 15.25
destroy 5.12; 9.14
disobey 2 Chr 24.20; 7.26
encourage 2 Chr 35.2; Job 4.4
exile [3] 5.12; 7.26
fail 2 Chr 29.7; 10.8
festival 3.4; Neh 8.18
heaven [2] 5.11; 7.12
help 5.2; 7.8
Jew [2] 5.1; 9.2
joy [3] 3.12; Neh 8.10
lamb [2] 2 Chr 35.6; 7.17
Levites [4] 3.8; 7.6
need 4.3; 7.20
obey 2 Chr 35.26; 7.14
offer [5] 4.2; 7.15
overthrow Ex 15.7; Job 34.25
pagan 2 Chr 34.3; Ps 106.35
Passover [2] 2 Chr 35.1; Ezek 45.21
pray 2 Chr 32.20; 8.23
priest [5] 3.2; 7.6
proper 2 Chr 30.1; Neh 13.31
prophet 5.1; 9.11
pure 2 Chr 34.8; 8.35
reign [2] 5.13; 7.6
sacrifice [5] 4.2; 8.35
scroll Esth 9.32
service 2 Chr 24.16; 7.19
sheep [2] 2 Chr 35.7; Neh 5.18
tax 4.13; 7.24
Temple (1) (of God) [13] 5.2; 7.6
unleavened 2 Chr 35.17; Ezek 45.21
way (3) 2 Kgs 17.13; Ps 7.12
worship (1) (of God) [2] 4.2; 8.36

5.12: 2 Kgs 25.8–12; 2 Chr 36.17–20; Jer 52.12–15 **5.13:** Ezra 1.2–11 **6.14:** Hag 1.1; Zech 1.1

the **Temple** as they had been **commanded** by the God of Israel and by
Cyrus, Darius, and Artaxerxes, emperors
of Persia. 15 They finished the **Temple** on
the third day of the month Adar in the
sixth year of the **reign** of Darius the emperor. 16 Then the people of Israel—the
priests, the **Levites**, and all the others
who had returned from **exile—joyfully
dedicated** the **Temple.** 17 For the **dedication** they **offered** a hundred bulls, two
hundred **sheep**, and four hundred **lambs**
as **sacrifices**, and twelve goats as **offerings** for sin, one for each tribe of Israel.
18 They also organized the **priests and the
Levites** for the **temple services** in
Jerusalem, according to the instructions
contained in the book of Moses.

The Passover

19 The people who had returned from
exile celebrated Passover on the fourteenth day of the first month of the
following year. 20 All the **priests and the
Levites** had **purified** themselves and
were ritually **clean**. The **Levites** killed
the animals for the **Passover sacrifices**
for all the people who had returned, for
the **priests**, and for themselves. 21 The
sacrifices were eaten by all the Israelites
who had returned from **exile** and by all
those who had given up the **pagan ways**
of the other people who were living in
the land and who had come to **worship**
the LORD God of Israel. 22 For seven days
they **joyfully celebrated** the **Festival** of
Unleavened Bread . They were full of **joy**
because the LORD had made the emperor
of Assyria [l] favourable to them, so that he
supported them in their work of rebuilding the **Temple** of the God of Israel.

Ezra Arrives in Jerusalem

7 Many years later, when Artaxerxes
was emperor of Persia, there was a
man named Ezra. He traced his ancestors back to Aaron, the **High Priest**, as
follows: Ezra was the son of Seraiah, son
of Azariah, son of Hilkiah, 2 son of
Shallum, son of Zadok, son of Ahitub,
3 son of Amariah, son of Azariah, son of
Meraioth, 4 son of Zerahiah, son of Uzzi,
son of Bukki, 5 son of Abishua, son of
Phinehas, son of Eleazar, son of Aaron.
6–7 Ezra was a **scholar** with a
thorough **knowledge** of the **Law** which
the LORD, the God of Israel, had given to
Moses. Because Ezra had the **blessing** of
the LORD his God, the emperor gave him
everything he asked for. In the seventh
year of the **reign** of Artaxerxes, Ezra set
out from Babylonia for Jerusalem with a
group of Israelites which included
priests, **Levites**, **temple** musicians,
temple guards, and workmen. 8–9 They
left Babylonia on the first day of the first
month, and with God's **help** they arrived
in Jerusalem on the first day of the fifth
month. 10 Ezra had **devoted** his **life** to
studying the **Law** of the LORD, to
practising it, and to **teaching** all its **laws**
and **regulations** to the people of Israel.

The Document Which Artaxerxes Gave to Ezra

11 Artaxerxes gave the following
document to Ezra, the **priest and scholar**,
who had a thorough **knowledge** of the
laws and commands which the LORD had
given to Israel:
12 "From Artaxerxes [m] the em-
peror to Ezra the **priest**, **scholar** in
the **Law** of the God of **Heaven**. [n]
13 "I **command** that throughout my
empire all the Israelite people,
priests, and Levites that so **desire** be
permitted to go with you to
Jerusalem. 14 I, together with my
seven counsellors, send you to investigate the conditions in Jerusalem
and Judah in order to see how well
the **Law** of your God, which has
been **entrusted** to you, is being
obeyed. 15 You are to take with you
the gold and silver **offerings** which I
and my counsellors **desire** to give to
the God of Israel, whose **Temple** is
in Jerusalem. 16 You are also to take
all the silver and gold which you collect throughout the province of
Babylon and the **offerings** which the
Israelite people and their **priests**
give for the **Temple** of their God in
Jerusalem.
17 "You are to spend this money
carefully and buy bulls, rams, **lambs**,
corn, and wine and **offer** them on
the **altar** of the **Temple** in
Jerusalem. 18 You may use the silver
and gold that is left over for whatever you and your fellow-
countrymen **desire**, in accordance
with the **will of your God**. 19 You are
to **present** to God in Jerusalem all
the utensils that have been given to
you for use in the **temple services**.
20 And anything else which you **need**

[l] EMPEROR OF ASSYRIA: *Apparently a reference to the Persian emperor who then also ruled the territory once occupied by Assyria, Israel's ancient enemy.*
[m] *Verses 12–26 are in Aramaic (see also 4.7).*
[n] *Aramaic has an additional word, the meaning of which is unclear.*

6.19: Ex 12.1–20

for the **Temple**, you may get from
the royal treasury.
21 “I **command** all the treasury
officials in the province of West
Euphrates to **provide** promptly for
Ezra, the **priest** and **scholar** in the
Law of the God of **Heaven**, everything he asks you for, 22 up to a limit
of 3,400 kilogrammes of silver, 10,000
kilogrammes of wheat, 2,000 litres of
wine, 2,000 litres of olive-oil, and as
much salt as necessary. 23 You must
be careful to **provide** everything
which the God of **Heaven requires**
for his **Temple**, and so make **sure**
that he is never **angry** with me or
with those who **reign** after me.
24 You are **forbidden** to collect any
taxes from the **priests**, **Levites**, musicians, guards, workmen, or anyone
else connected with this **Temple**.
25 “You, Ezra, using the **wisdom**
which your God has given you, are
to appoint administrators and **judges**
to govern all the people in West
Euphrates who live by the **Law** of
your God. You must **teach** that **Law**
to anyone who does not know it. 26 If
anyone **disobeys** the **laws** of your
God or the laws of the empire, he is
to be **punished** promptly: by **death**
or by **exile** or by confiscation of his
property or by **imprisonment**.”

Ezra Praises God

27 Ezra said, “**Praise** the LORD, the
God of our ancestors! He has made the
emperor willing to **honour** in this way the
Temple of the LORD in Jerusalem. 28 By
God’s **grace** I have **won** the **favour** of the
emperor, of his counsellors, and of all his
powerful officials; the LORD my God has
given me **courage**, and I have been able
to **persuade** many of the heads of the
clans of Israel to return with me.”

The People Who Returned from Exile

8 This is the list of the heads of the
clans who had been in **exile** in
Babylonia and who returned with Ezra to
Jerusalem when Artaxerxes was em-
peror:
2-14 Gershom, of the clan of Phinehas
Daniel, of the clan of Ithamar
Hattush son of Shecaniah, of the clan of David
Zechariah, of the clan of Parosh, with 150 men of his clan (there were records of their ancestry)
Eliehoenai son of Zerahiah, of the clan of Pahath Moab, with 200 men
Shecaniah son of Jahaziel, of the clan of Zattu,[o] with 300 men
Ebed son of Jonathan, of the clan of Adin, with 50 men
Jeshaiah son of Athaliah, of the clan of Elam, with 70 men
Zebadiah son of Michael, of the clan of Shephatiah, with 80 men
Obadiah son of Jehiel, of the clan of Joab, with 218 men
Shelomith son of Josiphiah, of the clan of Bani,[p] with 160 men
Zechariah son of Bebai, of the clan of Bebai, with 28 men
Johanan son of Hakkatan, of the clan of Azgad, with 110 men
Eliphelet, Jeuel, and Shemaiah, of the clan of Adonikam, with 60 men (they returned at a later date)
Uthai and Zaccur, of the clan of Bigvai, with 70 men

Ezra Finds Levites for the Temple

15 I assembled the entire group by the
canal that runs to the town of Ahava, and
we camped there three days. I found that
there were **priests** in the group, but no
Levites. 16 I sent for nine of the leaders:
Eliezer, Ariel, Shemaiah, Elnathan, Jarib,
Elnathan, Nathan, Zechariah, and Meshullam, and for two **teachers**, Joiarib
and Elnathan. 17 I sent them to Iddo, head
of the **community** at Casiphia, to ask him
and his associates, the **temple** workmen,
to send us people to **serve** God in the
Temple. 18 Through God’s **grace** they sent
us Sherebiah, an able man, a **Levite** from
the clan of Mahli, and eighteen of his
sons and brothers came with him. 19 They
also sent Hashabiah and Jeshaiah of the
clan of Merari, with twenty of their relatives. 20 In addition there were 220 **temple**
workmen whose ancestors had been
designated by King David and his officials to assist the **Levites**. They were all
listed by name.

Ezra Leads the People in Fasting and Prayer

21 There by the Ahava Canal I gave
orders for us all to **fast** and **humble** ourselves before our God and to ask him to
lead us on our journey and **protect** us and
our children and all our **possessions**. 22 I
would have been **ashamed** to ask the emperor for a troop of cavalry to guard us
from any **enemies** during our journey, because I had told him that our God **blesses**
everyone who **trusts** him, but that he is
displeased with and **punishes** anyone
who **turns away** from him. 23 So we **fasted**

[o] *One ancient translation (see also 2.8)* Zattu; *Hebrew does not have this name.*
[p] *One ancient translation (see also 2.10)* Bani; *Hebrew does not have this name.*

ashamed 2 Chr 30.15; 9.6
bless 7.6; Neh 9.35
choose 6.12; Neh 1.9
community Josh 22.12; 10.8
displease 2 Chr 29.6; Ps 85.4
enemy [2] 4.1; Neh 4.11
exile [2] 7.26; 9.4
fast (2) [2] 2 Chr 20.3; Neh 9.1
freewill 2.68
grace 7.28; 9.8
humble 2 Chr 36.12; Esth 7.3
lamb 7.17; Neh 10.36
leading 2 Chr 29.20; Neh 3.5
Levites [6] 7.6; 9.1
offer [4] 7.15; 9.4
possess 2 Chr 21.3; Esth 8.11
pray 6.10; Neh 1.4
prayer 2 Chr 34.27; 9.5
priest [7] 7.6; 9.1
protect [3] 2 Chr 23.10; Job 1.10
punish 7.26; 9.13
pure 6.20; Neh 12.30
rest (1) 2 Chr 36.21; Job 3.13
sacred 2 Chr 35.3; Neh 7.1
sacrifice [2] 6.3; 9.4
serve 2 Chr 36.20; Neh 5.18
teacher 2 Chr 35.3; Job 36.22
Temple (1) (of God) [8] 7.6; 9.9
trust 2 Chr 20.20; Neh 13.13
turn 2 Chr 33.12; 10.14
value 2 Chr 32.27; Job 28.13
worship (1) (of God) 6.12; Neh 1.9

and prayed for God to protect us, and he
answered our prayers.

The Gifts for the Temple

24 From among the leading priests I
chose Sherebiah, Hashabiah, and ten
others. 25 Then I weighed out the silver,
the gold, and the utensils which the emperor, his advisers and officials, and the
people of Israel had given to be used in
the Temple, and I gave it to the priests.
26-27 This is what I gave them:
silver – 22 metric tons
100 silver utensils – 70 kilogrammes
gold – 3,400 kilogrammes
20 gold bowls – 8.4 kilogrammes
2 fine bronze bowls, equal in value to
gold bowls
28 I said to them, "You are sacred to
the LORD, the God of your ancestors, and
so are all the silver and gold utensils
brought to him as freewill offerings.
29 Guard them carefully until you reach
the Temple. There in the priests' room
weigh them and hand them over to the
leaders of the priests and of the Levites,
and to the leaders of the people of Israel
in Jerusalem." 30 So the priests and the
Levites took charge of the silver, the
gold, and the utensils, to take them to the
Temple in Jerusalem.

The Return to Jerusalem

31 It was on the twelfth day of the first
month that we left the Ahava Canal to go
to Jerusalem. Our God was with us and
protected us from enemy attacks and
from ambush as we travelled. 32 When we
reached Jerusalem, we rested for three
days. 33 Then on the fourth day we went
to the Temple, weighed the silver, the
gold, and the utensils, and handed them
over to Meremoth the priest, son of
Uriah. With him were Eleazar son of
Phinehas and two Levites, Jozabad son of
Jeshua and Noadiah son of Binnui.
34 Everything was counted and weighed,
and a complete record was made at the
same time.
35 All those who had returned from
exile then brought offerings to be burnt
as sacrifices to the God of Israel. They
offered 12 bulls for all Israel, 96 rams,
and 77 lambs; they also offered 12 goats
to purify themselves from sin. All these
animals were burnt as sacrifices to the
LORD. 36 They also took the document the
emperor had given them and gave it to
the governors and officials of the province of West Euphrates, who then gave
their support to the people and the
temple worship.

Ezra Learns of Intermarriages with Non-Jews

9 After all this had been done, some of
the leaders of the people of Israel
came and told me that the people, the
priests, and the Levites had not kept
themselves separate from the people in
the neighbouring countries of Ammon,
Moab, and Egypt or from the Canaanites,
Hittites, Perizzites, Jebusites, and
Amorites. They were doing the same
disgusting things that those people did.
2 Jewish men were marrying foreign
women, and so God's holy people had become contaminated. The leaders and
officials were the chief offenders. 3 When
I heard this, I tore my clothes in despair,
tore my hair and my beard, and sat down
crushed with grief. 4 I sat there grieving
until the time for the evening sacrifice to
be offered, and people began to gather
round me—all those who were
frightened because of what the God of
Israel had said about the sins of those
who had returned from exile.
5 When the time came for the evening
sacrifice, I got up from where I had been
grieving, and still wearing my torn
clothes, I knelt in prayer and stretched
out my hands to the LORD my God. 6 I
said, "O God, I am too ashamed to raise
my head in your presence. Our sins pile
up, high above our heads; they reach as
high as the heavens. 7 From the days of
our ancestors until now, we, your people,
have sinned greatly. Because of our sins
we, our kings, and our priests have fallen
into the hands of foreign kings, and we
have been slaughtered, robbed, and
carried away as prisoners. We have been
totally disgraced, as we still are today.
8 Now for a short time, O LORD our God,
you have been gracious to us and have
let some of us escape from slavery and
live in safety in this holy place. You have
freed us from slavery and given us new
life. 9 We were slaves, but you did not
leave us in slavery. You made the emperors of Persia favour us and permit us
to go on living and to rebuild your
Temple, which was in ruins, and to find
safety here in Judah and Jerusalem.
10 "But now, O God, what can we say
after all that has happened? We have
again disobeyed the commands 11 that
you gave us through your servants, the
prophets. They told us that the land we
were going to occupy was an impure
land because the people who lived in it
filled it from one end to the other with
disgusting, filthy actions. 12 They told us

9.12: Ex 34.11–16; Deut 7.1–5

action 5.5; Ps 92.5
anger 7.23; 10.14
ashamed 8.22; Job 9.31
command 7.11; 10.3
commandment 2 Chr 19.10; Ps 50.16
confess 2 Chr 6.37; 10.1
deserve 2 Chr 6.23; Job 8.4
despair 1 Chr 21.13; Esth 9.22
destroy 6.12; Neh 2
disgrace 2 Chr 32.2; Neh 2.17
disgust [2] 2 Chr 36.8; Job 19.19
disobey 7.26; Neh 9.26
enjoy 2 Chr 14.1; Neh 9.25
escape 2 Chr 36.16; Job 1.15
exile 8.1; 10.6
favour 7.28; Neh 2.7
filthy Job 9.31
free 1 Chr 9.33; Job 3.18
fright 4.4; Neh 6.9
God's people 1.3; Neh 1.10
grace 8.18; Neh 9.1
grief [3] 2 Kgs 19.1; 10.6
guilty 2 Chr 28.13; 10.10
heaven 7.12; Neh 1.
help 7.8; Neh 2.18
holy [2] 2 Chr 36.14; Neh 8.9
ignore 2 Chr 36.16; Job 24.12
impure Lev 15.24; Ps 106.39
Jew 6.7; Neh 1.2
justice 2 Chr 12.6; Job 8.3
kneel 2 Chr 29.29; Neh 8.6
Levites 8.15; 10.5
life (1) 7.10; Neh 6.
neighbour 1.4; Neh 6.6
new 2 Chr 34.22; Esth 2.8
offer 8.28; 10.19
permit 7.13; Neh 13.1
prayer 8.23; 10.1
presence [2] 2 Chr 9.7; Esth 8.1
priest [2] 8.15; 10.5
prison 7.26; Neh 4.4
prophet 6.14; Neh 6.7
prosper 2 Chr 14.7; Job 20.21
punish [2] 8.22; Neh 6.14
raise 2 Chr 13.3; Neh 8.6
right (3) 2 Chr 28.19; 10.8
rob 2 Sam 17.8; Neh 4.4
ruin 2 Kgs 3.19; Neh 2.3
sacrifice [2] 8.35; 10.19
safe [2] 2 Chr 31.12; Esth 4.13
separate 2 Kgs 17.21; 10.11
servant 5.11; Neh 1.
slaughter 2 Chr 28.9; Esth 3.13
slave [4] 2 Chr 36.20; Neh 5.5

succeed (1) 2 Chr 32.30; Neh 1.11
Temple (1) (of God) 8.17; 10.1
wicked 2 Chr 21.6; Neh 1.7
wrong 2 Chr 6.22; Neh 5.9

that we were never to intermarry with those people and never to **help** them **prosper** or **succeed** if we wanted to **enjoy** the land and pass it on to our descendants for ever. 13 Even after everything that has happened to us in **punishment** for our sins and **wrongs**, we know that you, our God, have **punished** us less than we **deserve** and have allowed us to survive. 14 Then how can we **ignore** your **commandments** again and intermarry with these **wicked** people? If we do, you will be so **angry** that you will **destroy** us completely and let no one survive. 15 LORD God of Israel, you are **just**, but you have let us survive. We **confess** our **guilt** to you; we have no **right** to come into your **presence**."

The Plan for Ending Mixed Marriages

accept 6.10; Neh 7.63
act 2 Chr 24.5; Neh 1.7
advice 2 Chr 25.16; Esth 1.14
anger 9.14; Neh 4.7
bitter 2 Chr 25.10; Esth 4.1
bow (2) 2 Chr 20.18; Neh 9.6
case (2) 2 Chr 19.8; Job 5.8
command 9.10; Neh 1.5
community 8.17; Neh 13.3
confess [2] 9.15; Neh 1.6
demand 2 Chr 34.31; Neh 5.15
divorce [2] 1 Chr 8.8; Is 50.1
exile [3] 9.4; Neh 1.2
fail 6.9; Neh 9.35
faith 2 Sam 15.11; Ps 27.14
faithless 1 Sam 20.30; Prov 2.17
grief 9.3; Neh 9.1
guilty 9.15; Job 9.20
hard [2] 4.15; Job 7.1
honour 7.27; Neh 1.11
hope 2 Chr 14.11; Esth 9.1
important 1 Chr 28.1; Neh 6.3
judge 7.25; Job 9.15
law 7.6; Neh 1.7
Levites [3] 9.1; Neh 3.17
message 5.2; Neh 6.2
oath 2 Chr 15.14; Neh 10.29
offer 9.4; Neh 4.2
plan [2] 2 Chr 30.4; Neh 2.19
please 5.17; Neh 2.5
prayer 9.5; Neh 1.6
priest [4] 9.1; Neh 2.16
promise [2] 2 Chr 34.32; Neh 5.12
rid 2 Kgs 9.8; Esth 9.16
right (3) 9.15; Neh 2.20
sacrifice 9.4; Neh 4.2

10 While Ezra was **bowing** in **prayer** in front of the **Temple**, **weeping** and **confessing** these sins, a large group of Israelites—men, women, and children—gathered round him, **weeping bitterly**. 2 Then Shecaniah son of Jehiel, of the clan of Elam, said to Ezra, "We have broken **faith** with God by marrying foreign women, but even so there is still **hope** for Israel. 3 Now we must make a **solemn promise** to our God that we will send these women and their children away. We will do what you and the others who **honour** God's **commands advise** us to do. We will do what God's **Law demands**. 4 It is your responsibility to **act**. We are behind you, so go ahead and get it done."

5 So Ezra began by making the leaders of the **priests**, of the **Levites**, and of the rest of the people take an **oath** that they would do what Shecaniah had proposed. 6 Then he went from in front of the **Temple** into the living-quarters of Jehohanan son of Eliashib, and spent the night[r] there **grieving** over the **unfaithfulness** of the **exiles**. He did not eat or drink anything.

7 A **message** was sent throughout Jerusalem and Judah that all those who had returned from **exile** were to meet in Jerusalem 8 by order of the leaders of the people. If anyone **failed** to come within three days, all his property would be confiscated, and he would lose his **right** to be a member of the **community**. 9 Within the three days, on the twentieth day of the ninth month, all the men living in the territory of Judah and Benjamin came to Jerusalem and assembled in the **temple** square. It was raining **hard**, and because of the weather and the **importance** of the meeting everyone was **trembling**.

10 Ezra the **priest** stood up and spoke to them. He said, "You have been **faithless** and have brought **guilt** on Israel by marrying foreign women. 11 Now then, **confess** your sins to the LORD, the God of your ancestors, and do what **pleases** him. **Separate** yourselves from the foreigners living in our land and get **rid** of your foreign wives."

12 The people shouted in answer, "We will do whatever you say." 13 But they added, "The crowd is too big, and it's raining **hard**. We can't stand here in the open like this. This isn't something that can be done in one or two days, because so many of us are involved in this sin. 14 Let our officials stay in Jerusalem and take charge of the matter. Then let anyone who has a foreign wife come at a set time, together with the leaders and the **judges** of his city. In this way **God's anger** over this situation will be **turned** away." 15 No one was opposed to the **plan** except Jonathan son of Asahel and Jahzeiah son of Tikvah, who had the support of Meshullam and of Shabbethai, a **Levite**.

16 The returned **exiles accepted** the **plan**, so Ezra the **priest** appointed[s] men from among the heads of the clans and recorded their names. On the first day of the tenth month they began their investigation, 17 and within the next three months they investigated all the **cases** of men with foreign wives.

The Men Who Had Foreign Wives

18 This is the list of the men who had foreign wives:

Priests, listed by clans:

Clan of Joshua and his brothers, sons of Jehozadak: Maaseiah, Eliezer, Jarib, and Gedaliah. 19 They **promised** to **divorce** their wives, and they **offered** a ram as a **sacrifice** for their sins.

20 Clan of Immer: Hanani and Zebadiah

21 Clan of Harim: Maaseiah, Elijah, Shemaiah, Jehiel, and Uzziah

22 Clan of Pashhur: Elioenai, Maaseiah, Ishmael, Nethanel, Jozabad, and Elasah

23 *Levites:*

Jozabad, Shimei, Kelaiah (also called Kelita), Pethahiah, Judah, and Eliezer

24 *Musicians:*

Eliashib

Temple guards:

Shallum, Telem, and Uri

separate 9.1; Neh 4.19
solemn 1 Kgs 2.8; Neh 9.38
Temple (1) (of God) [3] 9.9; Neh 2.8
tremble 1 Chr 16.30; Job 4.14
turn 8.22; Neh 1.9
unfaithful 2 Chr 30.7; Neh 1.8
weep [2] 2 Chr 34.27; Neh 1.4

[r] *One ancient translation* spent the night; *Hebrew* went.
[s] *Some ancient translations* appointed; *Hebrew unclear.*

[25] *Others:*

Clan of Parosh: Ramiah, Izziah, Malchijah, Mijamin, Eleazar, Malchijah, and Benaiah

26 Clan of Elam: Mattaniah, Zechariah, Jehiel, Abdi, Jeremoth, and Elijah

27 Clan of Zattu: Elioenai, Eliashib, Mattaniah, Jeremoth, Zabad, and Aziza

28 Clan of Bebai: Jehohanan, Hananiah, Zabbai, and Athlai

29 Clan of Bani: Meshullam, Malluch, Adaiah, Jashub, Sheal, and Jeremoth

30 Clan of Pahath Moab: Adna, Chelal, Benaiah, Maaseiah, Mattaniah, Bezalel, Binnui, and Manasseh

31–32 Clan of Harim: Eliezer, Isshijah, Malchijah, Shemaiah, Shimeon, Benjamin, Malluch, and Shemariah

33 Clan of Hashum: Mattenai, Mattattah, Zabad, Eliphelet, Jeremai, Manasseh, and Shimei

34–37 Clan of Bani: Maadai, Amram, Uel, Benaiah, Bedeiah, Cheluhi, Vaniah, Meremoth, Eliashib, Mattaniah, Mattenai, and Jaasu

38–42 Clan of Binnui: Shimei, Shelemiah, Nathan, Adaiah, Machnadebai, Shashai, Sharai, Azarel, Shelemiah, Shemariah, Shallum, Amariah, and Joseph

43 Clan of Nebo: Jeiel, Mattithiah, Zabad, Zebina, Jaddai, Joel, and Benaiah

44 All these men had foreign wives. They **divorced** them and sent them and their children away.[t]

[t] *Verse 44 in Hebrew is unclear.*

THE BOOK OF NEHEMIAH

INTRODUCTION

The book of *Nehemiah* may be divided into four parts: (1) The return of Nehemiah to Jerusalem, where he has been sent by the Persian emperor to govern Judah. (2) The rebuilding of the walls of Jerusalem. (3) The solemn reading of the Law of God by Ezra, and the people's confession of sin. (4) Further activities of Nehemiah as governor of Judah.

A notable feature of the book is the record of Nehemiah's deep dependence on God and his frequent prayers to him.

Outline of Contents

---

act Ezra 10.4; 5.7
choose Ezra 8.24; 9.7
command [3] Ezra 10.3; 9.16
confess Ezra 10.1; 9.1
covenant 2 Chr 34.30; 9.8
difficult 2 Chr 9.1; Ps 73.16
exile Ezra 10.6; 7.6
faithful 2 Chr 32.1; 9.8
fear 1 Kgs 1.50; Job 3.25
God's people Ezra 9.2; 13.1
heaven Ezra 9.6; 2.4
honour Ezra 10.3; 5.15
Jew Ezra 9.2; 2.16
law Ezra 10.3; 8.1
look down on 2 Sam 19.43; Esth 1.17
love Ezra 3.11; 9.17
mercy 2 Chr 36.17; 9.17
mourn 2 Chr 35.24; 8.9
power Ezra 7.28; 9.6
pray [2] Ezra 8.23; 2.4
prayer [3] Ezra 10.1; 9.6
remember 2 Chr 6.42; 4.14
rescue 2 Chr 32.22; 9.27
restore Ezra 5.14; 7.70
scatter [2] 2 Chr 34.4; Esth 3.8
servant [4] Ezra 9.11; 2.20
strength 2 Chr 32.5; Job 4.3
succeed (1) Ezra 9.12; 2.20
turn Ezra 10.14; 3.19
unfaithful Ezra 10.6; Ps 73.27
weep Ezra 10.1; Esth 4.3

1 This is the account of what
Nehemiah son of Hacaliah accomplished.

Nehemiah's Concern for Jerusalem

In the month of Kislev in the twentieth
year that Artaxerxes was emperor of
Persia, I, Nehemiah, was in Susa, the
capital city. 2 Hanani, one of my brothers,
arrived from Judah with a group of other
men, and I asked them about Jerusalem
and about our **fellow-Jews** who had returned from **exile** in[a] Babylonia. 3 They
told me that those who had survived and
were back in the homeland[b] were in
great **difficulty** and that the foreigners
who lived near by **looked down on** them.
They also told me that the walls of Jerusalem were still broken down and that
the gates had not been **restored** since the
time they were burnt. 4 When I heard all
this, I sat down and **wept**.
For several days I **mourned** and did
not eat. I **prayed** to God, 5 "LORD God of
Heaven! You are great, and we stand in
fear of you. You **faithfully** keep your **covenant** with those who **love** you and do
what you **command**. 6 Look at me, LORD,
and hear my **prayer**, as I **pray** day and
night for your **servants**, the people of
Israel. I **confess** that we, the people of
Israel, have sinned. My ancestors and I
have sinned. 7 We have **acted wickedly**
against you and have not done what you
commanded. We have not kept the **laws**
which you gave us through Moses, your
servant. 8 **Remember** now what you told
Moses: 'If you people of Israel are **unfaithful** to me, I will **scatter** you among
the other nations. 9 But then if you **turn
back** to me and do what I have
commanded you, I will bring you back to
the place where I have **chosen** to be **worshipped**, even though you are **scattered**
to the ends of the earth.'
10 "Lord, these are your **servants**,
your **own people**. You **rescued** them by
your great **power** and **strength**. 11 Listen
now to my **prayer** and to the **prayers** of
all your other **servants** who want to
honour you. Give me **success** today and
make the emperor **merciful** to me."
In those days I was the emperor's wine
steward.

wicked Ezra 9.14; Job 3.17
worship (1) (of God) Ezra 8.36; 8.6

Nehemiah Goes to Jerusalem

2 One day four months later, when
Emperor Artaxerxes was dining, I
took the wine to him. He had never seen
me look **sad** before, 2 so he asked, "Why
are you looking so **sad**? You aren't ill, so
it must be that you're **unhappy**."
I was startled 3 and answered, "May
Your **Majesty** live for ever! How can I
help looking **sad** when the city where my
ancestors are buried is in **ruins** and its
gates have been **destroyed** by fire?"
4 The emperor asked, "What is it that
you want?"
I **prayed** to the God of **Heaven**, 5 and
then I said to the emperor, "If Your
Majesty is **pleased** with me and is willing

approve 1 Chr 21.6; Job 28.27
destroy [3] Ezra 9.14; 9.31
disgrace Ezra 9.7; Job 8.22
favour Ezra 9.9; Esth 2.9
grant [2] 2 Chr 6.19; Esth 5.6
happy 2 Chr 30.25; 8.17
heaven [2] 1.5; 9.6
help Ezra 9.12; 3.12
inspire 7.5
Jew 1.2; 4.1
letter (2) [3] Ezra 4.7; 6.5
Majesty [2] Ezra 5.8; 6.7
plan Ezra 10.15; 4.12
please Ezra 10.11; 9.24

[a] had returned from exile in; *or* had not been exiled to.
[b] had survived and...homeland; *or* had remained in the homeland and had not gone into exile.

1.8: Lev 26.33 **1.9:** Deut 30.1–5 **2.3:** 2 Kgs 25.8–10; 2 Chr 36.19; Jer 52.12–14

pray 1.4; 4.4
priest Ezra 10.5; 3.1
rebel Ezra 4.12; 9.26
request [2]
2 Chr 6.19; Esth 5.6
right (3) Ezra 10.8;
Job 24.4
ruin [2] Ezra 9.9; 6.13
sad [3] 2 Sam 19.2;
8.10
servant 1.6; 4.23
share 2 Chr 31.16;
8.10
succeed (1) 1.11;
Job 5.12
Temple (1) (of God)
Ezra 10.1; 3.25
trouble Ezra 4.15;
9.27

to **grant** my **request**, let me go to the land
of Judah, to the city where my ancestors
are buried, so that I can rebuild the city."
6 The emperor, with the empress
sitting at his side, **approved** my **request**.
He asked me how long I would be gone
and when I would return, and I told him.
7 Then I asked him to **grant** me the
favour of giving me **letters** to the governors of West Euphrates Province,[c]
instructing them to let me travel to
Judah. 8 I asked also for a **letter** to Asaph,
keeper of the royal forests, instructing
him to supply me with timber for the
gates of the fort that guards the **Temple**,
for the city walls, and for the house I was
to live in. The emperor gave me all I
asked for, because God was with me.
9 The emperor sent some army officers and a troop of horsemen with me,
and I made the journey to West Euphrates. There I gave the emperor's **letters**
to the governors. 10 But Sanballat, from
the town of Beth Horon, and Tobiah, an
official in the province of Ammon, heard
that someone had come to work for the
good of the people of Israel, and they
were highly indignant.
11 I went on to Jerusalem, and for
three days 12 I did not tell anyone what
God had **inspired** me to do for Jerusalem.
Then in the middle of the night I got up
and went out, taking a few of my companions with me. The only animal we
took was the donkey that I rode on. 13 It
was still night as I left the city through
the Valley Gate on the west and went
south past Dragon's Fountain to the
Rubbish Gate. As I went, I inspected the
broken walls of the city and the gates
that had been **destroyed** by fire. 14 Then
on the east side of the city I went north to
the Fountain Gate and the King's Pool.
The donkey I was riding could not find
any path through the rubble, 15 so I went
down into the valley of the Kidron and
rode along, looking at the wall. Then I returned the way I had come and went
back into the city through the Valley
Gate.
16 None of the local officials knew
where I had been or what I had been doing. So far I had not said anything to any
of my **fellow-Jews**—the **priests**, the leaders, the officials, or anyone else who
would be taking part in the work. 17 But
now I said to them, "See what **trouble** we
are in because Jerusalem is in **ruins** and
its gates are **destroyed**! Let's rebuild the
city walls and put an end to our **disgrace**." 18 And I told them how God had
been with me and **helped** me, and what
the emperor had said to me.
They responded, "Let's start rebuilding!" And they got ready to start the
work.
19 When Sanballat, Tobiah, and an
Arab named Geshem heard what we
were **planning** to do, they laughed at us
and said, "What do you think you're doing? Are you going to **rebel** against the
emperor?"
20 I answered, "The God of **Heaven**
will give us **success**. We are his **servants**,
and we are going to start building. But
you have no **right** to any property in
Jerusalem, and you have no **share** in its
traditions."

Rebuilding the Wall of Jerusalem

3 This is how the city wall was rebuilt.[d] The **High Priest** Eliashib and
his **fellow-priests** rebuilt the Sheep Gate,
dedicated it, and put the gates in place.
They **dedicated** the wall as far as the
Tower of the Hundred and the Tower of
Hananel.
2 The men of Jericho built the next
section.
Zaccur son of Imri built the next section.
3 The clan of Hassenaah built the Fish
Gate. They put the beams and the gates
in place, and put in the bolts and bars for
locking the gate.
4 Meremoth, the son of Uriah and
grandson of Hakkoz, built the next section.
Meshullam, the son of Berechiah and
grandson of Meshezabel, built the next
section.
Zadok son of Baana built the next section.
5 The men of Tekoa built the next section, but the **leading** men of the town **refused** to do the manual labour assigned to
them by the supervisors.
6 Joiada son of Paseah and Meshullam
son of Besodeiah rebuilt Jeshanah Gate.[e]
They put the beams and the gates in
place, and put in the bolts and bars for
locking the gate.
7 Melatiah from Gibeon, Jadon from
Meronoth, and the men of Gibeon and
Mizpah built the next section, as far as
the residence of the governor of West
Euphrates.

dedicate [2]
Ezra 6.16; 10.36
help 2.18; 4.22
High Priest [2]
Ezra 7.1; 11.11
last (2) 2 Chr 7.9;
8.18
leading Ezra 8.24;
11.3
Levites Ezra 10.5;
7.1
priest [4] 2.16; 5.12
refuse (1)
2 Chr 36.13; 9.16
Temple (1) (of God)
[4] 2.8; 6.10
tomb 2 Chr 35.24;
Job 21.32
turn 1.9; 9.26

[c] WEST EUPHRATES PROVINCE: *Under Persian rule the land of Israel was part of this large Persian province west of the River Euphrates.*
[d] CITY WALL WAS REBUILT: *According to the following report, the rebuilding of the wall started at the middle of the north side and proceeded anti-clockwise round the city. Many of the places mentioned cannot be identified.* [e] Jeshanah Gate; *or* the Old Gate.

8 Uzziel son of Harhaiah, a goldsmith, built the next section.

Hananiah, a maker of perfumes, built the next section, as far as Broad Wall.

9 Rephaiah son of Hur, ruler of half the Jerusalem District, built the next section.

10 Jedaiah son of Harumaph built the next section, which was near his own house.

Hattush son of Hashabneiah built the next section.

11 Malchijah son of Harim and Hasshub son of Pahath Moab built both the next section and the Tower of the Ovens.

12 Shallum son of Hallohesh, ruler of the other half of the Jerusalem District, built the next section. (His daughters **helped** with the work.)

13 Hanun and the inhabitants of the city of Zanoah rebuilt the Valley Gate. They put the gates in place, put in the bolts and the bars for locking the gate, and repaired the wall for 440 metres, as far as the Rubbish Gate.

14 Malchijah son of Rechab, ruler of the Beth Haccherem District, rebuilt the Rubbish Gate. He put the gates in place, and put in the bolts and the bars for locking the gate.

15 Shallum son of Colhozeh, ruler of the Mizpah District, rebuilt the Fountain Gate. He covered the gateway, put the gates in place, and put in the bolts and the bars. At the Pool of Shelah he built the wall next to the royal garden, as far as the steps leading down from David's City.

16 Nehemiah son of Azbuk, ruler of half the Bethzur District, built the next section, as far as David's **tomb**, the pool, and the barracks.

Levites Who Worked on the Wall

17 The following **Levites** rebuilt the next several sections of the wall:

Rehum son of Bani built the next section;

Hashabiah, ruler of half the Keilah District, built the next section on behalf of his district;

18 Bavvai son of Henadad, ruler of the other half of the Keilah District, built the next section;

19 Ezer son of Jeshua, ruler of Mizpah, built the next section in front of the armoury, as far as the place where the wall **turns**;

20 Baruch son of Zabbai built the next section, as far as the entrance to the house of the **High Priest** Eliashib;

21 Meremoth, the son of Uriah and grandson of Hakkoz, built the next section, up to the far end of Eliashib's house.

Priests Who Worked on the Wall

22 The following **priests** rebuilt the next several sections of the wall:

Priests from the area around Jerusalem built the next section;

23 Benjamin and Hasshub built the next section, which was in front of their houses;

Azariah, the son of Maaseiah and grandson of Ananiah, built the next section, which was in front of his house;

24 Binnui son of Henadad built the next section, from Azariah's house to the corner of the wall;

25–26 Palal son of Uzai built the next section, beginning at the corner of the wall and the tower of the upper palace near the court of the guard;

Pedaiah son of Parosh built the next section, to a point on the east near the Water Gate and the tower guarding the **Temple**. (This was near that part of the city called Ophel, where the **temple** workmen lived.)

Other Builders

27 The men of Tekoa built the next section, their second one, from a point opposite the large tower guarding the **Temple** as far as the wall near Ophel.

28 A group of **priests** built the next section, going north from the Horse Gate, each one building in front of his own house.

29 Zadok son of Immer built the next section, which was in front of his house.

Shemaiah son of Shecaniah, keeper of the East Gate, built the next section.

30 Hananiah son of Shelemiah and Hanun, the sixth son of Zalaph, built the next section, their second one.

Meshullam son of Berechiah built the next section, which was in front of his house.

31 Malchijah, a goldsmith, built the next section, as far as the building used by the **temple** workmen and the merchants, which was by the Miphkad[f] Gate, near the room on top of the north-east corner of the wall.

32 The goldsmiths and the merchants built the last section, from the room at the corner as far as the Sheep Gate.

Nehemiah Overcomes Opposition to His Work

4 When Sanballat heard that we **Jews**
had begun rebuilding the wall, he

afraid Ezra 3.3; Esth 8.17

[f]Miphkad; *or* Mustering, *or* Watch.

anger Ezra 10.14; 5.6
burden 2 Chr 10.4; 5.15
create 1 Chr 16.26; Job 31.15
eager 1 Chr 28.21; Job 39.21
enemy [5] Ezra 8.22; 5.9
evil Ezra 4.12; 13.17
forget 2 Chr 24.22; 9.17
forgive 2 Chr 30.19; 9.17
fury 1 Chr 13.11; 13.8
help 3.12; 6.16
insult 2 Kgs 19.4; 9.18
intend 2 Chr 32.2; 6.6
Jew [3] 2.16; 5.1
misery 2 Sam 16.12; Job 3.20
mock Job 11.3
offer Ezra 10.19; 7.65
plan [2] 2.19; 6.6
plot (1) [2] 2 Chr 33.24; Esth 2.21
pray [2] 2.4; 5.19
prison Ezra 9.7; 7.6
remember 1.8; 5.19
ridicule [2] 2 Chr 36.16; 5.9
rob Ezra 9.7; Job 15.21
sacrifice Ezra 10.19; 10.33
separate Ezra 10.11; 9.1
servant 2.20; 5.15
terrify 2 Chr 20.29; 9.32
warn 2 Chr 36.15; 6.12
weak 2 Chr 28.15; Job 4.4
worry 1 Kgs 20.43; Job 5.2

was **furious** and began to **ridicule** us. 2 In
front of his companions and the
Samaritan troops he said, "What do these
miserable Jews think they're doing? Do
they **intend** to rebuild the city? Do they
think that by **offering sacrifices** they can
finish the work in one day? Can they
make building-stones out of heaps of
burnt rubble?"
3 Tobiah was standing there beside
him, and he added, "What kind of wall
could they ever build? Even a fox could
knock it down!"
4 I **prayed**, "Listen to them **mocking**
us, O God! Let their **ridicule** fall on their
own heads. Let them be **robbed** of everything they have, and let them be taken as
prisoners to a foreign land. 5 Don't **forgive** the **evil** they do and don't **forget**
their sins, for they have **insulted** us who
are building."
6 So we went on rebuilding the wall,
and soon it was half its full height, because the people were **eager** to work.
7 Sanballat, Tobiah, and the people of
Arabia, Ammon, and Ashdod heard that
we were making progress in rebuilding
the wall of Jerusalem and that the gaps
in the wall were being closed, and they
were very **angry**. 8 So they all **plotted** together to come and attack Jerusalem
and **create** confusion, 9 but we **prayed** to
our God and kept men on guard against
them day and night.
10 The people of Judah had a song
they sang:
"We grow **weak** carrying **burdens**;
There's so much rubble to take away.
How can we build the wall today?"
11 Our **enemies** thought we would not
see them or know what was happening
until they were already upon us, killing
us and putting an end to our work. 12 But
time after time **Jews** who were living
among our **enemies** came to **warn** us of
the **plans** our **enemies** were making
against us.[g] 13 So I armed the people with
swords, spears, and bows, and stationed
them by clans behind the wall, wherever
it was still unfinished.
14 I saw that the people were **worried**,
so I said to them and to their leaders and
officials, "Don't be **afraid** of our **enemies**.
Remember how great and **terrifying** the
Lord is, and fight for your fellow-countrymen, your children, your wives, and your
homes." 15 Our **enemies** heard that we
had found out what they were **plotting**,
and they realized that God had defeated
their **plans**. Then all of us went back to
rebuilding the wall.
16 From then on half my men worked
and half stood guard, wearing coats of
armour and armed with spears, shields,
and bows. And our leaders gave their full
support to the people 17 who were rebuilding the wall. Even those who carried
building materials worked with one hand
and kept a weapon in the other, 18 and
everyone who was building kept a sword
strapped to his waist. The man who was
to sound the alarm on the bugle stayed
with me. 19 I told the people and their officials and leaders, "The work is spread
out over such a distance that we are
widely **separated** from one another on
the wall. 20 If you hear the bugle, gather
round me. Our God will fight for us." 21 So
every day, from dawn until the stars
came out at night, half of us worked on
the wall, while the other half stood guard
with spears.
22 During this time I told the men in
charge that they and all their **helpers**
had to stay in Jerusalem at night, so that
we could guard the city at night as well
as work in the daytime. 23 I didn't take off
my clothes even at night, neither did any
of my companions nor my **servants** nor
my bodyguard. And we all kept our
weapons to hand.[h]

Oppression of the Poor

5 Some time later many of the people,
both men and women, began to
complain against their **fellow-Jews**.
2 Some said, "We have large families, we
need corn to keep us **alive**."
3 Others said, "We have had to mort-
gage our fields and **vineyards** and houses
to get **enough** corn to **keep us from**
starving."
4 Still others said, "We had to **borrow**
money to pay the royal **tax** on our fields
and **vineyards**. 5 We are of the same **race**
as our **fellow-Jews**. Aren't our children
just as good as theirs? But we have to
make **slaves** of our children. Some of our
daughters have already been sold as
slaves. We are **helpless** because our
fields and **vineyards** have been taken
away from us."
6 When I heard their **complaints**, I
was **angry** 7 and decided to **act**. I **denounced** the leaders and officials of the
people and told them, "You are **oppressing** your brothers!"
I called a public assembly to deal with
the problem 8 and said, "As far as we

act [2] 1.7; Job 12.1
alive 2 Chr 24.2; Job 2.4
anger 4.7; 9.17
best 2 Chr 13.17; Esth 2.4
burden [2] 4.10; Job 7.20
claim [2] 2 Kgs 19.6 Job 11.4
complain [2] 2 Kgs 6.1; Job 2.10
debt [2] 2 Kgs 4.1; 10.31
demand Ezra 10.3; Job 27.8
denounce 1 Kgs 13 Job 15.13
enemy 4.11; 6.1
enough 2 Chr 31.10; 8.2
force (1) Ezra 4.23; 13.21
Gentile Lam 1.10
helpless 2 Chr 20.1 Job 14.1
honour 1.11; Esth 2.18
Jew [5] 4.1; 6.6
keep from Ezra 4.4 Job 3.9
need Ezra 7.20; 9.21
obey Ezra 7.14; 9.16
oppress [2] 2 Chr 15.6; 9.10
owe 2 Kgs 4.1; Job 22.6
praise Ezra 7.27; 8.

[g] *Probable text* the plans our enemies were making against us; *Hebrew unclear.*
[h] *Probable text* weapons to hand; *Hebrew unclear.*

5.7: Ex 22.25; Lev 25.35–37; Deut 23.19–20

pray 4.4; 6.9
priest 3.1; 7.39
promise [3]
Ezra 10.3; 9.8
provide Ezra 7.21; 9.21
race (1) Josh 14.12; Esth 3.8
reason 1 Kgs 9.13; Job 2.3
remember 4.14; 6.14
repay 2 Chr 20.11; Job 22.6
ridicule 4.1; Is 37.23
right (1) 2 Chr 31.20; 9.33
servant 4.23; 6.5
serve Ezra 8.17; 9.35
sheep Ezra 6.9; 10.36
slave [2] Ezra 9.8; 9.17
swear 2 Chr 36.13; Job 27.1
tax Ezra 7.24; Dan 11.20
vineyard [4]
2 Chr 26.10; 9.25
wrong Ezra 9.13; Job 6.30

have been able, we have been buying back our **Jewish** brothers who had to sell themselves to foreigners. Now you are **forcing** your own brothers to sell themselves to you, their **fellow-Jews**!" The leaders were silent and could find nothing to say.

9 Then I said, "What you are doing is **wrong**! You ought to **obey** God and do what's **right**. Then you would not give our **enemies**, the **Gentiles**, any **reason** to **ridicule** us. 10 I have let the people borrow money and corn from me, and so have my companions and the men who work for me. Now let's give up all our **claims** to **repayment**. 11 Cancel all the **debts**[i] they **owe** you—money or corn or wine or olive-oil. And give them back their fields, **vineyards**, olive-groves, and houses at once!"

12 The leaders replied, "We'll do as you say. We'll give the property back and not try to collect the **debts**."

I called in the **priests** and made the leaders **swear** in front of them to keep the **promise** they had just made. 13 Then I took off the sash[j] I was wearing round my waist and shook it out. "This is how God will shake any of you who don't keep your **promise**," I said. "God will take away your houses and everything you own, and will leave you with nothing."

Everyone who was present said, "Amen!" and **praised** the LORD. And the leaders kept their **promise**.

Nehemiah's Unselfishness

14 During all the twelve years that I was governor of the land of Judah, from the twentieth year that Artaxerxes was emperor until his thirty-second year, neither my relatives nor I ate the food I was entitled to have as governor. 15 Every governor who had been in office before me had been a **burden** to the people and had **demanded** forty silver coins a day[k] for food and wine. Even their **servants** had **oppressed** the people. But I **acted** differently, because I **honoured** God. 16 I put all my energy into rebuilding the wall and did not acquire any property. Everyone who worked for me joined in the rebuilding. 17 I regularly fed at my table a hundred and fifty of the **Jewish** people and their leaders, besides all the people who came to me from the surrounding nations. 18 Every day I **served** one ox, six of the **best sheep**, and many chickens, and every ten days I **provided** a fresh supply of wine. But I knew what heavy **burdens** the people had to bear, so I did not **claim** the allowance that the governor is entitled to.

19 I **pray** you, O God, **remember** to my credit everything that I have done for this people.

Plots against Nehemiah

6 Sanballat, Tobiah, Geshem, and the rest of our **enemies** heard that we had finished building the wall and that there were no gaps left in it, although we still had not set up the gates in the gateways. 2 So Sanballat and Geshem sent me a **message**, suggesting that I meet with them in one of the villages in the Plain of Ono. This was a **trick** of theirs to try to **harm** me. 3 I sent messengers to say to them, "I am doing **important** work and can't go down there. I am not going to let the work stop just to go and see you."

4 They sent me the same **message** four times, and each time I sent them the same reply.

5 Then Sanballat sent one of his **servants** to me with a fifth **message**, this one in the form of an **unsealed letter**.[l] 6 It read:

> "Geshem tells me that a rumour is going round among the **neighbouring** peoples that you and the **Jewish** people **intend** to revolt and that this is why you are rebuilding the wall. He also says you **plan** to make yourself king 7 and that you have arranged for some **prophets** to **proclaim** in Jerusalem that you are the king of Judah. His **Majesty** is **certain** to hear about this, so I suggest that you and I meet to talk the situation over."

8 I sent a reply to him: "Nothing of what you are saying is **true**. You have made it all up yourself."

9 They were trying to **frighten** us into stopping work. I **prayed**, "But now, God, make me **strong**!"

10 About this time I went to visit Shemaiah, the son of Delaiah and grandson of Mehetabel, who was unable to leave his house. He said to me, "You and I must go and hide together in the **Holy Place** of the **Temple** and lock the doors, because they are coming to kill you. Any night now they will come to kill you."

11 I answered, "I'm not the kind of

bribe Ezra 4.5; Job 6.22
certain (1)
1 Sam 23.22; Ps 112.8
enemy [2] 5.9; 9.27
fright [4] Ezra 9.4; Job 4.15
harm Ezra 4.22; Esth 9.2
help 4.22; 7.70
Holy Place
2 Chr 5.7; Ezek 41.1
humiliate
2 Sam 19.5; Ps 107.39
important Ezra 10.9; Esth 5.11
intend 4.2; 13.5
Jew [3] 5.1; 7.65
letter (2) [2] 2.7; Esth 8.9
life (1) Ezra 9.8; 9.6
Majesty 2.3; Esth 1.4
message [3]
Ezra 10.7; Esth 1.22
neighbour Ezra 9.1; Job 31.9
plan 4.12; Esth 3.6
pray [2] 5.19; 9.4
proclaim
1 Chr 29.22; Esth 1.19
prophet [2]
Ezra 9.11; 9.26
punish Ezra 9.13; 9.33
remember [2] 5.19; 9.32
reputation Job 19.9
ruin 2.3; Job 30.24
save 2 Chr 32.11; 9.28
seal 1 Kgs 21.8; 9.38
servant 5.15; 7.57
strong 2 Chr 26.16; 8.10
Temple (1) (of God)
[2] 3.25; 7.43
trick 2 Kgs 10.19; Prov 23.3
true Ezra 1.1; Esth 2.23
warn 4.12; 9.26

[i] *One ancient translation* debts; *Hebrew unclear.*
[j] SASH: *Clothing in those days had no pockets, so small items were tucked into the sash that was worn like a belt round the waist. Shaking it out was a symbol of losing everything.*
[k] *One ancient translation* a day; *Hebrew unclear.*
[l] UNSEALED LETTER: *Leaving a letter unsealed was a deliberate way of making certain that its contents would become widely known.*

man that runs and hides. Do you think I
would try to **save** my **life** by hiding in the
Temple? I won't do it."
12 When I thought it over, I realized
that God had not spoken to Shemaiah,
but that Tobiah and Sanballat had **bribed**
him to give me this **warning**. 13 They
hired him to **frighten** me into sinning, so
that they could **ruin** my **reputation** and
humiliate me.
14 I **prayed**, "God, **remember** what
Tobiah and Sanballat have done and
punish them. **Remember** that woman
Nodiah and all the other **prophets** who
tried to **frighten** me."

The Conclusion of the Work

15 After fifty-two days of work the entire wall was finished on the twenty-fifth
day of the month of Elul. 16 When our
enemies in the surrounding nations
heard this, they realized that they had
lost face, since everyone knew that the
work had been done with God's **help**.
17 During all this time the **Jewish**
leaders had been in correspondence with
Tobiah. 18 Many people in Judah were on
his side because of his **Jewish** father-in-
law, Shecaniah son of Arah. In addition,
his son Jehohanan had married the
daughter of Meshullam son of Berechiah.
19 People would talk in front of me about
all the good deeds Tobiah had done and
would tell him everything I said. And he
kept sending me **letters** to try to **frighten**
me.

7 And now the wall had been rebuilt,
the gates had all been put in place,
and the temple guards, the members of
the **sacred** choir, and the other **Levites**
had been assigned their work. 2 I put two
men in charge of governing the city of
Jerusalem: my brother Hanani and
Hananiah, commanding officer of the
fortress. Hananiah was a **reliable** and
God-fearing man without an equal. 3 I
told them not to have the gates of Jerusalem opened in the morning until well
after sunrise and to have them closed
and barred before the guards went off
duty at sunset. I also told them to appoint
guards from among the people who lived
in Jerusalem and to assign some of them
to specific posts and others to patrol the
area round their own houses.

The List of Those Who Returned from Exile
(Ezra 2.1-70)

4 Jerusalem was a large city, but not
many people were living in it, and not
many houses had been built yet. 5 God **inspired** me to assemble the people and
their leaders and officials and to check
their family records. I located the records of those who had first returned
from **captivity**, and this is the information I found:
6 Many of the **exiles** left the province
of Babylon and returned to Jerusalem
and Judah, each to his own city. Their
families had been living in **exile** in Babylonia ever since King Nebuchadnezzar
had taken them there as **prisoners**.
7 Their leaders were Zerubbabel, Joshua,
Nehemiah, Azariah, Raamiah, Naha-
mani, Mordecai, Bilshan, Mispereth,
Bigvai, Nehum, and Baanah.
8–25 This is the list of the clans of
Israel, with the number of those from
each clan who returned from **exile**:
Parosh – 2,172
Shephatiah – 372
Arah – 652
Pahath Moab (descendants of Jeshua
and Joab) – 2,818
Elam – 1,254
Zattu – 845
Zaccai – 760
Binnui – 648
Bebai – 628
Azgad – 2,322
Adonikam – 667
Bigvai – 2,067
Adin – 655
Ater (also called Hezekiah) – 98
Hashum – 328
Bezai – 324
Hariph – 112
Gibeon – 95
26–38 People whose ancestors had lived in
the following towns also returned:
Bethlehem and Netophah – 188
Anathoth – 128
Beth Azmaveth – 42
Kiriath Jearim, Chephirah,
and Beeroth – 743
Ramah and Geba – 621
Michmash – 122
Bethel and Ai – 123
The other Nebo – 52
The other Elam – 1,254
Harim – 320
Jericho – 345
Lod, Hadid, and Ono – 721
Senaah – 3,930
39–42 This is the list of the **priestly** clans
that returned from **exile**:
Jedaiah (descendants of Jeshua) – 973
Immer – 1,052
Pashhur – 1,247
Harim – 1,017
43–45 Clans of **Levites** who returned from
exile:
Jeshua and Kadmiel (descendants of
Hodaviah) – 74

accept Ezra 10.16; Esth 4.4
captive 1 Sam 30.8; 8.17
ceremony Lev 21.1; 8.18
contribute 2 Chr 35.7; 10.32
duty (1) 2 Chr 35.2; 10.39
exile [9] 1.2; 12.1
God-fearing 2 Kgs 4.1; Lk 2.25
help 6.16; 9.9
inspire 2.12; 9.30
Jew 6.6; 13.17
Levites [3] 3.17; 8.7
offer 4.2; 10.33
priest [8] 5.12; 8.1
prison 4.4; Job 3.18
prove [3] Ezra 2.59; Job 16.8
rely 2 Chr 16.7; Job 39.11
restore 1.3; Job 8.6
sacred Ezra 8.28; 10.33
servant [3] 6.5; 9.14
Temple (1) (of God) [5] 6.10; 8.16

Temple musicians (descendants of
Asaph) - 148
Temple guards (descendants of
Shallum, Ater, Talmon, Akkub,
Hatita, and Shobai) - 138

46-56 Clans of **temple** workmen who re-
turned from **exile**:
Ziha, Hasupha, Tabbaoth,
Keros, Sia, Padon,
Lebana, Hagaba, Shalmai,
Hanan, Giddel, Gahar,
Reaiah, Rezin, Nekoda,
Gazzam, Uzza, Paseah,
Besai, Meunim, Nephushesim,
Bakbuk, Hakupha, Harhur,
Bazlith, Mehida, Harsha,
Barkos, Sisera, Temah,
Neziah, and Hatipha.

57-59 Clans of Solomon's **servants** who re-
turned from **exile**:
Sotai, Sophereth, Perida,
Jaalah, Darkon, Giddel,
Shephatiah, Hattil, Pochereth
Hazzebaim, and Amon.

60 The total number of descendants of
the **temple** workmen and of Solomon's
servants who returned from **exile** was
392.

61–62 There were 642 belonging to the
clans of Delaiah, Tobiah, and Nekoda
who returned from the towns of Tel
Melah, Tel Harsha, Cherub, Addon, and
Immer; but they could not **prove** that
they were descendants of Israelites.

63–64 The following **priestly** clans
could find no record to **prove** their ancestry: Hobaiah, Hakkoz, and Barzillai.
(The ancestor of the **priestly** clan of
Barzillai had married a woman from the
clan of Barzillai of Gilead and taken the
name of his father-in-law's clan.) Since
they were unable to **prove** who their
ancestors were, they were not **accepted**
as **priests**. 65 The **Jewish** governor told
them that they could not eat the food
offered to God until there was a **priest**
who could use the Urim and Thummim.[m]

66–69 Total number of **exiles** who
returned - 42,360
Their male and female **servants** - 7,337
Male and female musicians - 245
Horses - 736
Mules - 245
Camels - 435
Donkeys - 6,720

70–72 Many of the people **contributed**
to **help** pay the cost of **restoring** the
Temple:

The governor 8 kilogrammes of gold
50 **ceremonial** bowls
530 robes for **priests**
Heads of clans 168 kilogrammes of gold
1,250 kilogrammes of
silver
The rest of the people
168 kilogrammes of gold
140 kilogrammes of
silver
67 robes for **priests**

73 The **priests**, the **Levites**, the temple
guards, the musicians, many of the
ordinary people, the **temple** workmen—
all the people of Israel—settled in the
towns and cities of Judah.

Ezra Reads the Law to the People

8 By the seventh month the people of
Israel were all settled in their
towns. On the first day of that month
they all assembled in Jerusalem, in the
square just inside the Water Gate. They
asked Ezra, the **priest** and **scholar** of the
Law which the LORD had given Israel
through Moses, to get the book of the
Law. 2 So Ezra brought it to the place
where the people had gathered—men,
women, and the children who were old
enough to **understand**. 3 There in the
square by the gate he read the **Law** to
them from dawn until noon, and they all
listened attentively.

4 Ezra was standing on a wooden plat-
form that had been built for the occasion.
The following men stood at his **right**:
Mattithiah, Shema, Anaiah, Uriah,
Hilkiah, and Maaseiah; and the following
stood at his left: Pedaiah, Mishael,
Malchijah, Hashum, Hashbaddanah,
Zechariah, and Meshullam.

5 As Ezra stood there on the platform
high above the people, they all kept their
eyes fixed on him. As soon as he opened
the book, they all stood up. 6 Ezra said,
"**Praise** the LORD, the great God!"

All the people **raised** their arms in the
air and answered, "Amen! Amen!" They
knelt in **worship**, with their faces to the
ground.

7 Then they **rose** and stood in their
places, and the following **Levites** explained the **Law** to them: Jeshua, Bani,
Sherebiah, Jamin, Akkub, Shabbethai,
Hodiah, Maaseiah, Kelita, Azariah,
Jozabad, Hanan, and Pelaiah. 8 They
gave an oral translation[n] of God's **Law**
and explained[o] it so that the people could
understand it.

9 When the people heard what the

calm Job 15.11
captive 7.5; Esth 2.6
celebrate Ezra 6.19; 12.27
ceremony 7.70; 12.45
enough [2] 5.3; 9.5
feast 2 Chr 18.2; Esth 8.17
festival Ezra 6.22; 10.33
happy 2.2; 12.43
holy [3] Ezra 9.2; 9.14
joy [2] Ezra 6.16; 12.43
kneel Ezra 9.5; Esth 3.2
last (2) 3.32; Esth 8.11
law [13] 1.7; 9.3
Levites [4] 7.1; 9.4
mourn 1.4; Esth 4.3
praise 5.13; 9.5
priest [3] 7.39; 9.32
raise Ezra 9.6; Job 5.11
require [2] Ezra 7.23; 10.29
right (2) 1 Chr 12.2; 12.31
rise 2 Chr 36.20; Esth 5.9
sad [2] 2.1; Job 30.29
scholar [2] Ezra 7.6; 12.26
share [2] 2.20; Job 26.3
shelter [4] Ezra 3.4; Job 24.8
strong 6.9; Job 12.16
study Ezra 7.10; Job 5.27
teach Ezra 7.10; 9.13
Temple (1) (of God) 7.43; 10.28
understand [3] 2 Chr 2.12; 10.28
worship (1) (of God) 1.9; 9.3

[m] URIM AND THUMMIM: *Two objects used by the priest to determine God's will; it is not known precisely how they were used.*
[n] TRANSLATION: *The Law was written in Hebrew, but in Babylonia the Jews had adopted Aramaic as the language for daily life. Because of this a translation was necessary.*
[o] They gave...explained; *or* They read God's Law and then translated it, explaining.

7.65: Ex 28.30; Deut 33.8 **7.73:** 1 Chr 9.2; Neh 11.3

Law required, they were so moved that
they began to cry. So Nehemiah, who
was the governor, Ezra, the priest and
scholar of the Law, and the Levites who
were explaining the Law told all the
people, "This day is holy to the LORD
your God, so you are not to mourn or cry.
10 Now go home and have a feast. Share
your food and wine with those who
haven't enough. Today is holy to our
Lord, so don't be sad. The joy that the
LORD gives you will make you strong."
11 The Levites went about calming
the people and telling them not to be sad
on such a holy day. 12 So all the people
went home and ate and drank joyfully
and shared what they had with others,
because they understood what had been
read to them.

The Festival of Shelters

13 The next day the heads of the
clans, together with the priests and the
Levites, went to Ezra to study the teachings of the Law. 14 They discovered that
the Law, which the LORD gave through
Moses, ordered the people of Israel to
live in temporary shelters during the
Festival of Shelters. 15 So they gave the
following instructions and sent them[p] all
through Jerusalem and the other cities
and towns: "Go out to the hills and get
branches from pines, olives, myrtles,
palms, and other trees to make shelters
according to the instructions written in
the Law."
16 So the people got branches and
built shelters on the flat roofs of their
houses, in their yards, in the temple
courtyard, and in the public squares by
the Water Gate and by the Ephraim
Gate. 17 All the people who had come
back from captivity built shelters and
lived in them. This was the first time it
had been done since the days of Joshua
son of Nun, and everybody was excited
and happy. 18 From the first day of the
festival to the last they read a part of
God's Law every day. They celebrated
for seven days, and on the eighth day
there was a closing ceremony, as required in the Law.

The People Confess Their Sins

9 1-2 On the twenty-fourth day of the
same month the people of Israel
assembled to fast in order to show sorrow for their sins. They had already
separated themselves from all
foreigners. They wore sackcloth and put
dust on their heads as signs of grief. Then
they stood and began to confess the sins
that they and their ancestors had committed. 3 For about three hours the Law
of the LORD their God was read to them,
and for the next three hours they confessed their sins and worshipped the
LORD their God.
4 There was a platform for the
Levites, and on it stood Jeshua, Bani,
Kadmiel, Shebaniah, Bunni, Sherebiah,
Bani, and Chenani. They prayed aloud to
the LORD their God.
5 The following Levites gave a call to
worship: Jeshua, Kadmiel, Bani,
Hashabneiah, Sherebiah, Hodiah,
Shebaniah, and Pethahiah. They said:

"Stand up and praise the LORD your
God;
praise him for ever and ever!
Let everyone praise his glorious name,
although no human praise is great
enough."

The Prayer of Confession

6 And then the people of Israel prayed
this prayer:

"You, LORD, you alone are LORD;
you made the heavens and the stars
of the sky.
You made land and sea and
everything in them;
you gave life to all.
The heavenly powers bow down and
worship you.
7 You, LORD God, chose Abram
and led him out of Ur in Babylonia;
you changed his name to Abraham.
8 You found that he was faithful to you,
and you made a covenant with him.
You promised to give him the land of
the Canaanites,
the land of the Hittites and the
Amorites,
the land of the Perizzites, the
Jebusites, and the Girgashites,
to be a land where his descendants
would live.
You kept your promise, because you
are faithful.

9 "You saw how our ancestors suffered
in Egypt;
you heard their call for help at the
Red Sea.
10 You worked amazing miracles against
the king,
against his officials and the people
of his land,

[p] *Probable text* So they...sent them; *Hebrew* It also ordered that the following instructions be sent.

8.14-15: Lev 23.33-36, 39-43; Deut 16.13-15 **9.7:** Gen 11.31, 12.1, 17.5 **9.8:** Gen 15.18-21
9.9: Ex 3.7, 14.10-12 **9.10:** Ex 7.8—12.32

abandon 2 Chr 29.6; Job 8.20
agree 2 Chr 30.1; Job 13.20
alone 2 Chr 6.30; Esth 3.6
amaze 2 Chr 9.4; Job 37.5

anger 5.6; 13.18
bless Ezra 8.22; 13.2
bow (2) Ezra 10.1; Esth 3.2
bread Ezra 6.22; 10.33
bull-calf 2 Chr 13.8; Ps 106.19
change 2 Chr 36.4; Esth 1.19
choose [2] 1.9; 11.1
cloud [2] 2 Chr 6.1; Job 3.5
command [2] 1.5; 10.29
confess [2] 1.6; Job 34.31
conquer [7] Ezra 5.12; Job 26.12
control Ezra 4.16; Esth 5.10
covenant [2] 1.5; 13.29
destroy 2.3; 13.18
disobey Ezra 9.10; 13.27
distress 2 Chr 23.13; Job 36.15
enemy [2] 6.1; Esth 3.10
enjoy Ezra 9.12; Job 3.18
enough 8.2; 10.28
fail Ezra 10.8; Job 8.3
faithful [4] 1.5; Job 1.1
fast (2) Ezra 8.21; Esth 4.3
forget [2] 4.5; Job 7.9
forgive 4.5; Job 7.21
forsake [2] Job 6.14
glory 1 Chr 29.11; Job 37.22
god (2) (other gods) Ezra 1.7; Job 12.6
grace [2] Ezra 9.8; Prov 5.19
grief Ezra 10.6; Esth 9.22
heaven [6] 2.4; Esth 4.14
help [2] 7.70; 10.32
holy 8.9; 10.31
human 2 Chr 32.8; Job 7.1
hunger 2 Chr 32.11; Job 5.5
idol 2 Chr 36.14; Ps 24.4
inspire 7.5; Job 26.4
insult [2] 4.5; Esth 1.16
law [7] 8.1; 10.28
Levites [3] 8.7; 10.9
life (1) [2] 6.11; Esth 4.11
life (2) (to life) 2 Kgs 13.21; Job 14.7
light (1) 2 Chr 7.1; Job 3.4
love 1.5; 13.22
manna Josh 5.12; Ps 78.24
mercy [6] 1.11; Esth 3.13
miracle [2] 1 Chr 16.12; Job 5.9
name (2) (name of God, of Jesus) Ezra 5.1; 13.25
need 5.2; 10.33
obey [4] 5.9; 10.28
oppress [2] 5.7; Job 5.15
pain 2 Chr 21.15; Job 6.10
patient Ruth 3.18; Job 32.11

because you knew how they
oppressed your people.
You **won** then the fame you still have
today.
11 Through the sea you made a path for
your people
and led them through on dry ground.
Those who pursued them drowned in
deep water,
as a stone sinks in the **raging** sea.
12 With a **cloud** you led them in day-time,
and at night you **lighted** their way
with fire.
13 At Mount Sinai you came down from
heaven;
you spoke to your people
and gave them good **laws** and **sound**
teachings.
14 You **taught** them to keep your
Sabbaths holy,
and through your **servant** Moses you
gave them your **laws**.

15 "When they were **hungry**, you gave
them **bread** from **heaven**,
and water from a rock when they
were thirsty.
You told them to take **control** of the
land
which you had **promised** to give
them.
16 But our ancestors grew **proud** and
stubborn
and **refused** to **obey** your **commands**.
17 They **refused** to **obey**; they **forgot** all
you did;
they **forgot** the **miracles** you had
performed.
In their **pride** they **chose** a leader
to take them back to **slavery** in
Egypt.
But you are a God who **forgives**;
you are **gracious** and **loving**, slow to
be **angry**.
Your **mercy** is great; you did not
forsake them.
18 They made an **idol** in the shape of a
bull-calf
and said it was the **god** who led them
from Egypt!
How much they **insulted** you, LORD!
19 But you did not **abandon** them there in
the desert,
for your **mercy** is great.
You did not take away the **cloud** or the
fire
that showed them the path by day
and night.
20 In your goodness you told them what
they should do;
you fed them with **manna** and gave
them water to drink.
21 Through forty years in the desert
you **provided** all that they **needed**;
their clothing never wore out,
and their feet were not swollen with
pain.

22 "You let them **conquer** nations and
kingdoms,
lands that bordered their own.
They **conquered** the land of Heshbon,
where Sihon ruled,
and the land of Bashan, where Og
was king.
23 You gave them as many children as
there are stars in the sky,
and let them **conquer** and live in the
land
that you had **promised** their
ancestors to give them.
24 They **conquered** the land of Canaan;
you overcame the people living
there.
You gave your people the **power** to do
as they **pleased**
with the people and kings of Canaan.
25 Your people captured fortified cities,
fertile land, houses full of wealth,
cisterns already dug,
olive-trees, fruit-trees, and
vineyards.
They ate all they wanted and grew fat;
they **enjoyed** all the good things you
gave them.

26 "But your people **rebelled** and
disobeyed you;
they **turned** their backs on your
Law.
They killed the **prophets** who **warned**
them,
who told them to **turn back** to you.
They **insulted** you time after time,
27 so you let their **enemies conquer** and
rule them.
In their **trouble** they called to you for
help,
and you answered them from
heaven.
In your great **mercy** you sent them
leaders
who **rescued** them from their foes.
28 When **peace** returned, they sinned
again,
and again you let their **enemies**
conquer them.
Yet when they **repented** and asked you
to **save** them,

9.11: Ex 14.21–29, 15.4–5 **9.12:** Ex 13.21–22 **9.13–14:** Ex 19.18—23.33
9.15: Ex 16.4–15, 17.1–7; Deut 1.21 **9.16–17:** Num 14.1–4; Deut 1.26–33 **9.17:** Ex 34.6; Num 14.18
9.18: Ex 32.1–4 **9.19–21:** Deut 8.2–4 **9.22:** Num 21.21–35 **9.23:** Gen 15.5, 22.17; Josh 3.14–17
9.24: Josh 11.23 **9.25:** Deut 6.10–11 **9.26–28:** Judg 2.11–16

in **heaven** you heard, and time after time
you **rescued** them in your great **mercy**.
29 You **warned** them to **obey** your **teachings**,
but in **pride** they **rejected** your laws,
although keeping your **Law** is the way **to life**.
Obstinate and **stubborn**, they **refused** to **obey**.
30 Year after year you **patiently warned** them.
You **inspired** your **prophets** to speak,
but your people were deaf,
so you let them be **conquered** by other nations.
31 And yet, because your **mercy** is great,
you did not **forsake** or **destroy** them.
You are a **gracious** and **merciful** God!

32 "O God, our God, how great you are!
How **terrifying**, how **powerful**!
You **faithfully** keep your **covenant promises**.
From the time when Assyrian kings **oppressed** us,
even till now, how much we have **suffered**!
Our kings, our leaders, our **priests** and **prophets**,
our ancestors, and all our people have **suffered**.
Remember how much we have **suffered**!
33 You have done **right** to **punish** us;
you have been **faithful**, even though we have sinned.
34 Our ancestors, our kings, leaders, and **priests**
have not kept your **Law**.
They did not listen to your **commands** and **warnings**.
35 With your **blessing**, kings ruled your people
when they lived in the broad, fertile land you gave them;
but they **failed to turn from** sin and **serve** you.
36 And now we are **slaves** in the land that you gave us,
this fertile land which gives us food.
37 What the land produces goes to the kings
that you put over us because we sinned.
They do as they **please** with us and our livestock,
and we are in deep **distress**!"

The People Sign an Agreement

38 Because of all that has happened, we, the people of Israel, hereby make a **solemn** written **agreement**, and our leaders, our **Levites**, and our **priests** put their **seals** to it.

10

The first to sign was the governor, Nehemiah son of Hacaliah, and then Zedekiah signed. The following also signed:

2-8 *Priests:*
Seraiah, Azariah, Jeremiah,
Pashhur, Amariah, Malchijah,
Hattush, Shebaniah, Malluch,
Harim, Meremoth, Obadiah,
Daniel, Ginnethon, Baruch,
Meshullam, Abijah, Mijamin,
Maaziah, Bilgai, and Shemaiah.

9-13 *Levites:*
Jeshua son of Azaniah,
Binnui of the clan of Henadad,
Kadmiel, Shebaniah, Hodiah,
Kelita, Pelaiah, Hanan,
Mica, Rehob, Hashabiah,
Zaccur, Sherebiah, Shebaniah,
Hodiah, Bani, and Beninu.

14-27 *Leaders of the people:*
Parosh, Pahath Moab,
Elam, Zattu, Bani,
Bunni, Azgad, Bebai,
Adonijah, Bigvai, Adin,
Ater, Hezekiah, Azzur,
Hodiah, Hashum, Bezai,
Hariph, Anathoth, Nebai,
Magpiash, Meshullam, Hezir,
Meshezabel, Zadok, Jaddua,
Pelatiah, Hanan, Anaiah,
Hoshea, Hananiah, Hasshub,
Hallohesh, Pilha, Shobek,
Rehum, Hashabnah, Maaseiah,
Ahiah, Hanan, Anan,
Malluch, Harim, and Baanah.

The Agreement

28 We, the people of Israel, the **priests**, the **Levites**, the temple guards, the **temple** musicians, the temple workmen, and all others who in **obedience** to God's **Law** have **separated** themselves from the foreigners living in our land, we, together with our wives and all our children old **enough** to **understand**,
29 do hereby join with our leaders in an **oath**, under penalty of a **curse** if we break it, that we will live according to God's **Law**, which God gave through his **servant** Moses; that we will **obey** all that the LORD, our Lord, **commands** us; and that we will keep all his **laws** and **requirements**.

30 We will not intermarry with the foreigners living in our land.

31 If foreigners bring corn or anything else to sell to us on the **Sabbath** or on any

bread 9.15; Ps 78.20
command 9.16; 12.4[?]
contribute [2] 7.70; 12.44
curse 2 Chr 34.24; 13.2
debt 5.11; Job 24.3
dedicate [2] 3.1; 12.2
determine 2 Chr 35.22; Esth 7.7
duty (1) 7.3; 12.45
enough 9.5; 13.10
festival 8.18; Ps 76.10
grain-offering 2 Chr 7.7; 13.9
harvest [2] 2 Chr 8.13; Job 4.8
help 9.9; Esth 4.14
holy 9.14; 11.1
lamb Ezra 8.35; Job 21.11
law [5] 9.3; 12.26
Levites [7] 9.4; 11.3
lot (1) 1 Chr 26.13; 11.1
need 9.21; Job 5.15
neglect Josh 23.6; 13.11
New Moon Festival Ezra 3.5; Is 1.13
oath Ezra 10.5; 13.25
obey [2] 9.16; Esth 1.15
offer [6] 7.65; 12.43
priest Rev 20.6; 11.10
priest [6] 9.32; 11.3
provide [2] 9.21; Esth 6.10
require [3] 8.9; 12.44
ripe 1 Chr 29.28; 12.44
Sabbath [2] 9.14; 13.15
sacred [3] 7.1; 12.47
sacrifice [2] 4.2; 12.43
separate 9.1; Is 7.17
servant 9.14; 11.3
sheep 5.18; Job 1.3
take away (sin) 2 Chr 29.21; Ps 40.6
Temple (1) (of God) [11] 8.16; 11.3
tithe [4] 2 Chr 31.5; 12.44
understand 8.2; Job 5.9
worship (1) (of God) 9.3; 13.14

9.29: Lev 18.5 **9.30:** 2 Kgs 17.13–18; 2 Chr 36.15–16 **9.32:** 2 Kgs 15.19, 29, 17.3–6; Ezra 4.2, 10
10.30: Ex 34.16; Deut 7.3 **10.31:** Ex 23.10–11; Lev 25.1–7; Deut 15.1–2

other holy day, we will not buy from
them.
Every seventh year we will not farm
the land, and we will cancel all debts.
32 Every year we will each contribute
five grammes of silver to help pay the
expenses of the Temple.
33 We will provide for the temple worship the following: the sacred bread, the
daily grain-offering, the animals to be
burnt each day as sacrifices, the sacred
offerings for Sabbaths, New Moon Festivals, and other festivals, the other sacred
offerings, the offerings to take away the
sins of Israel, and anything else needed
for the Temple.
34 We, the people, priests, and Levites,
will draw lots each year to determine
which clans are to provide wood to burn
the sacrifices offered to the LORD our
God, according to the requirements of
the Law.
35 We will take to the Temple each
year an offering of the first corn we harvest and of the first fruit that ripens on
our trees.
36 The first son born to each of us we
will take to the priests in the Temple and
there, as required by the Law, dedicate
him to God. We will also dedicate the
first calf born to each of our cows, and
the first lamb or kid born to each of our
sheep or goats.
37 We will take to the priests in the
Temple the dough made from the first
corn harvested each year and our other
offerings of wine, olive-oil, and all kinds
of fruit.
We will take to the Levites, who collect
tithes in our farming villages, the tithes
from the crops that grow on our land.
38 Priests who are descended from Aaron
are to be with the Levites when tithes
are collected, and for use in the Temple
the Levites are to take to the temple
storerooms one tenth of all the tithes
they collect. 39 The people of Israel and
the Levites are to take the contributions
of corn, wine, and olive-oil to the storerooms where the utensils for the Temple
are kept and where the priests who are
on duty, the temple guards, and the
members of the temple choir have their
quarters.
We will not neglect the house of our
God.

The People Who Lived in Jerusalem

11 The leaders settled in Jerusalem,
and the rest of the people drew
lots to choose one family out of every ten
to go and live in the holy city of
Jerusalem, while the rest were to live in
the other cities and towns. 2 The people
praised anyone else who volunteered to
live in Jerusalem. 3 In the other towns
and cities the people of Israel, the
priests, the Levites, the temple workmen,
and the descendants of Solomon's servants lived on their own property in their
own towns.
The following is the list of the leading
citizens of the province of Judah who
lived in Jerusalem:
4 *Members of the tribe of Judah:*
Athaiah, the son of Uzziah and grandson of Zechariah. His other ancestors included Amariah, Shephatiah, and
Mahalalel, descendants of Judah's son
Perez.
5 Maaseiah, the son of Baruch and
grandson of Colhozeh. His other ancestors included Hazaiah, Adaiah, Joiarib,
and Zechariah, descendants of Judah's
son Shelah.
6 Of the descendants of Perez, 468
outstanding men lived in Jerusalem.
7 *Members of the tribe of Benjamin:*
Sallu, the son of Meshullam and grandson of Joed. His other ancestors included
Pedaiah, Kolaiah, Maaseiah, Ithiel, and
Jeshaiah.
8 Gabbai and Sallai, close relatives[q] of
Sallu.
In all, 928 Benjaminites lived in
Jerusalem. 9 Joel son of Zichri was their
leader, and Judah son of Hassenuah was
the second senior official in the city.
10 *Priests:*
Jedaiah son of Joiarib, and Jachin.
11 Seraiah, the son of Hilkiah and
grandson of Meshullam. His ancestors included Zadok, Meraioth, and Ahitub, who
was the High Priest. 12 In all, 822 members of this clan served in the Temple.
Adaiah, the son of Jeroham and grandson of Pelaliah. His ancestors included
Amzi, Zechariah, Pashhur, and Malchijah. 13 In all, 242 members of this clan
were heads of families.
Amashsai, the son of Azarel and grandson of Ahzai. His ancestors included
Meshillemoth and Immer. 14 There were
128 members of this clan who were
outstanding soldiers. Their leader was
Zabdiel, a member of a leading family.[r]

choose 9.7; Esth 2.9
court (1) 2 Chr 34.20; Esth 1.4
High Priest 3.1; 12.1
holy [2] 10.31; 13.22
leading [2] 3.5; Prov 31.23
Levites [7] 10.9; 12.1
lot (1) 10.34; Esth 3.7
praise 9.5; 12.24
prayer 9.6; Job 6.8
priest [2] 10.28; 12.1
priest 10.2; 12.2
regulation Ezra 7.10; 12.45
represent 2 Chr 24.11; Esth 9.3
servant 10.29; Esth 1.8
serve 9.35; Esth 1.7
service Ezra 7.19; Esth 3.2
Temple (1) (of God) [7] 10.28; 12.25
thank 2 Chr 31.2; 12.8
turn 9.26; 13.2

[q] *One ancient translation* close relatives; *Hebrew* after him.
[r] a member of a leading family; *or* son of Haggedolim.

10.32: Ex 30.11-16 **10.35:** Ex 23.19, 34.26; Deut 26.2 **10.36:** Ex 13.2 **10.37:** Num 18.21
10.38: Num 18.26 **11.3:** Neh 7.73

15 *Levites:*
Shemaiah, the son of Hasshub and
grandson of Azrikam. His ancestors included Hashabiah and Bunni.
16 Shabbethai and Jozabad, prominent
Levites in charge of the work outside the
Temple.
17 Mattaniah, the son of Mica and
grandson of Zabdi, a descendant of
Asaph. He led the **temple** choir in singing
the **prayer of thanksgiving**.
Bakbukiah, who was Mattaniah's
assistant.
Abda, the son of Shammua and grandson of Galal, a descendant of Jeduthun.
18 In all, 284 **Levites** lived in the **holy
city** of Jerusalem.
19 *Temple guards:*
Akkub, Talmon, and their relatives,
172 in all.
20 The rest of the people of Israel and
the remaining **priests and Levites** lived
on their own property in the other cities
and towns of Judah.
21 The **temple** work-
men lived in the part of Jerusalem called
Ophel and worked under the supervision
of Ziha and Gishpa.
22 The supervisor of the **Levites** who
lived in Jerusalem was Uzzi, the son of
Bani and grandson of Hashabiah. His
ancestors included Mattaniah and Mica,
and he belonged to the clan of Asaph, the
clan that was responsible for the music
in the **temple services**.
23 There were
royal **regulations** stating how the clans
should take **turns** in leading the **temple**
music each day.
24 Pethahiah son of Meshezabel, of
the clan of Zerah and the tribe of Judah,
represented the people of Israel at the
Persian **court**.

The People in Other Towns and Cities

25 Many of the people lived in towns
near their farms. Those who were of the
tribe of Judah lived in Kiriath Arba,
Dibon, and Jekabzeel, and in the villages
near these cities.
26 They also lived in the
cities of Jeshua, Moladah, Bethpelet,
27 and Hazarshual, and in Beersheba and
the villages around it.
28 They lived in the
city of Ziklag, in Meconah and its
villages,
29 in Enrimmon, in Zorah, in
Jarmuth,
30 in Zanoah, in Adullam, and in
the villages near these towns. They lived
in Lachish and on the farms near by, and
in Azekah and its villages. That is to say,
the people of Judah lived in the territory
between Beersheba in the south and the
Valley of Hinnom in the north.
31 The people of the tribe of Benjamin
lived in Geba, Michmash, Ai, Bethel and
the nearby villages,
32 Anathoth, Nob,
Ananiah,
33 Hazor, Ramah, Gittaim,
34 Hadid, Zeboim, Neballat,
35 Lod, and
Ono, and in the Valley of Craftsmen.
36 Some groups of **Levites** that had lived
in the territory of Judah were assigned to
live with the people of Benjamin.

List of Priests and Levites

12 The following is a list of the
priests and Levites who returned
from **exile** with Zerubbabel son of
Shealtiel and with the **High Priest**
Joshua:
2-7 *Priests:*
Seraiah, Jeremiah, Ezra,
Amariah, Malluch, Hattush,
Shecaniah, Rehum, Meremoth,
Iddo, Ginnethoi, Abijah,
Mijamin, Maadiah, Bilgah,
Shemaiah, Joiarib, Jedaiah,
Sallu, Amok, Hilkiah, and Jedaiah.
These men were leaders among all
their **fellow-priests** in the days of Joshua.
8 *Levites:*
The following were in charge of the
singing of **hymns** of **thanksgiving**:
Jeshua, Binnui, Kadmiel, Sherebiah,
Judah, and Mattaniah.
9 The following formed the choir that
sang the responses: Bakbukiah, Unno,
and their **fellow-Levites**.

Descendants of the High Priest Joshua

10 Joshua was the father of Joiakim;
Joiakim was the father of Eliashib;
Eliashib was the father of Joiada;
11 Joiada was the father of Jonathan; and
Jonathan was the father of Jaddua.

Heads of the Priestly Clans

12-21 When Joiakim was **High Priest**,
the following priests were the heads of
the **priestly** clans:

Priest	*Clan*
Meraiah	Seraiah
Hananiah	Jeremiah
Meshullam	Ezra
Jehohanan	Amariah
Jonathan	Malluchi
Joseph	Shebaniah
Adna	Harim
Helkai	Meraioth
Zechariah	Iddo
Meshullam	Ginnethon
Zichri	Abijah
...[s]	Miniamin
Piltai	Moadiah
Shammua	Bilgah
Jehonathan	Shemaiah
Mattenai	Joiarib
Uzzi	Jedaiah

[s] *In Hebrew a name is missing from the list.*

celebrate [2] 8.18; Esth 9.23
ceremony 8.18; Lk 2.22
command 10.29; Esth 1.12
contribute [2] 10.32
dedicate [2] 10.36; Is 19.19
direct 2 Chr 34.4; Esth 9.31
duty (1) 10.39; 13.30
exile 7.6; Esth 2.6
gift 2 Chr 32.23; Esth 2.18
happy 8.17; Esth 5.9
High Priest [3] 11.11; 13.28
hymn 2 Chr 8.14; Ps 26.7
joy 8.10; Esth 8.15
law [2] 10.28; 13.1
Levites [12] 11.3; 13.5
man of God [2] Ezra 3.2
offer [2] 10.33; 13.5
please 9.24; Esth 1.19
praise [2] 11.2; Job 1.21
priest [11] 11.3; 13.4
priest [2] 11.10
pure [2] Ezra 8.35; 13.9
regulation 11.23; 13.30
require [2] 10.29; Ps 51.6
right (2) 8.4; Ps 45.9
ripe 10.35; 13.31
ritual [2] 2 Chr 30.18; Ezek 44.8
sacred 10.33; Ps 2.6
sacrifice 10.33; Job 1.5
scholar [2] 8.1; 13.13
Temple (1) (of God) [6] 11.3; 13.4
thank [7] 11.17; Ps 7.17
tithe 10.37; 13.5

Kallai	Sallai
Eber	Amok
Hashabiah	Hilkiah
Nethanel	Jedaiah

Record of the Priestly and Levite Families

22 A record was kept of the heads of the **Levite** families and of the **priestly** families during the lifetimes of the following **High Priests**: Eliashib, Joiada, Jonathan, and Jaddua. This record was finished when Darius was emperor of Persia.

23 The heads of the **Levite** families, however, were recorded in the official records only until the time of Jonathan, the grandson of Eliashib.

Assignment of Duties in the Temple

24 Under the **direction** of Hashabiah, Sherebiah, Jeshua, Binnui,[t] and Kadmiel, the **Levites** were organized into groups. Two groups at a time **praised** God responsively and gave **thanks** to him, in accordance with the instructions given by King David, the **man of God**.

25 The following temple guards were in charge of guarding the storerooms by the gates to the **Temple**: Mattaniah, Bakbukiah, Obadiah, Meshullam, Talmon, and Akkub.

26 These people lived during the time of Joiakim, the son of Joshua and grandson of Jehozadak, and the time of Nehemiah the governor, and the time of Ezra, the **priest** who was a **scholar** of the **Law**.

Nehemiah Dedicates the City Wall

27 When the city wall of Jerusalem
was **dedicated**, the **Levites** were brought
in from wherever they were living, so
that they could join in **celebrating** the
dedication with songs of **thanksgiving**
and with the music of cymbals and harps.
28 The **Levite** families of singers gathered
from the area where they had settled
round Jerusalem and from the towns
round Netophah, 29 and from Bethgilgal,
Geba, and Azmaveth. 30 The **priests and
the Levites** performed **ritual purification**
for themselves, the people, the gates, and
the city wall.

31 I assembled the leaders of Judah on top of the wall and put them in charge of two large groups to march round the city, giving **thanks** to God.

The first group went to the **right** on top
of the wall towards the Rubbish Gate.[u]
32 Hoshaiah marched behind the singers,
followed by half the leaders of Judah.
33-35 The following **priests**, blowing trumpets,
marched next: Azariah, Ezra,
Meshullam, Judah, Benjamin, Shemaiah,
and Jeremiah. Next came Zechariah, the
son of Jonathan and grandson of
Shemaiah. (His ancestors also included
Mattaniah, Micaiah, and Zaccur, of the
clan of Asaph.) 36 He was followed by
other members of his clan—Shemaiah,
Azarel, Milalai, Gilalai, Maai, Nethanel,
Judah, and Hanani—all of whom carried
musical instruments of the kind played
by King David, the **man of God**. Ezra the
scholar led this group in the procession.
37 At the Fountain Gate they went up the
steps that led to David's City, past
David's palace, and back to the wall at
the Water Gate, on the east side of the
city.

38 The other group of those who gave
thanks went to the left along the top of
the wall, and I followed with half the
people. We marched past the Tower of
the Ovens to the Broad Wall, 39 and from
there we went past Ephraim Gate,
Jeshanah Gate,[v] the Fish Gate, the
Tower of Hananel, and the Tower of the
Hundred, to the Sheep Gate. We ended
our march near the gate to the **Temple**.

40 So both the groups that were giving **thanks** to God reached the **temple** area.

In addition to the leaders who were
with me, 41 my group included the following
priests, blowing trumpets: Eliakim,
Maaseiah, Miniamin, Micaiah, Elioenai,
Zechariah, and Hananiah; 42 and they
were followed by Maaseiah, Shemaiah,
Eleazar, Uzzi, Jehohanan, Malchijah,
Elam, and Ezer. The singers, led by
Jezrahiah, sang at the top of their voices.

43 That day many **sacrifices** were **offered**, and the people were full of **joy** because God had made them very **happy**. The women and the children joined in the **celebration**, and the noise they all made could be heard far and wide.

Providing for Worship in the Temple

44 At that time men were put in charge of the storerooms where **contributions** for the **Temple** were kept, including the **tithes** and the first corn and fruit that **ripened** each year. These men were responsible for collecting from the farms near the various cities the **contributions** for the **priests and the** Levites which the **Law required**. All the people of Judah were **pleased** with the

[t] *Probable text (see 10.9 and 12.8)* Binnui; *Hebrew* son of.
[u] RUBBISH GATE: *The two groups started somewhere on the south-western part of the city wall and went in opposite directions until they met in front of the Temple in the north-eastern part of the city.* [v] Ephraim Gate, Jeshanah Gate; *or* Ephraim Gate (also called the Old Gate).

priests and the **Levites**, 45 because they
performed the **ceremonies** of **purifica-**
tion and the other **rituals** that God had
commanded. The **temple** musicians and
the temple guards also performed their
duties in accordance with the **regulations**
made by King David and his son
Solomon. 46 From the time of King David
and the musician Asaph long ago, the
musicians have led songs of **praise** and
thanksgiving to God. 47 In the time of
Zerubbabel and also in the time of
Nehemiah, all the people of Israel gave
daily **gifts** for the support of the **temple**
musicians and the temple guards. The
people gave a **sacred offering** to the
Levites, and the Levites gave the **re-**
quired portion to the **priests**.

Separation from Foreigners

13 When the **Law of Moses** was being read aloud to the people, they
came to the passage that said that no
Ammonite or Moabite was ever to be
permitted to join **God's people**. 2 This was
because the people of Ammon and Moab
did not give food and water to the
Israelites on their way out of Egypt. Instead, they paid money to Balaam to
curse Israel, but our God **turned** the
curse into a **blessing**. 3 When the people
of Israel heard this **law** read, they excluded all foreigners from the **com-**
munity.

Nehemiah's Reforms

4 The **priest** Eliashib, who was in
charge of the **temple** storerooms, had for
a long time been on good terms with
Tobiah. 5 He allowed Tobiah to use a
large room that was **intended** only for
storing **offerings** of corn and **incense**, the
equipment used in the **Temple**, the **offer-**
ings for the **priests**, and the **tithes** of
corn, wine, and olive-oil given to the
Levites, to the **temple** musicians, and to
the temple guards. 6 While this was going
on, I was not in Jerusalem, because in
the thirty-second year that Artaxerxes[w]
was king of Babylon I had gone back to
report to him. After some time I received
his **permission** 7 and returned to
Jerusalem. There I was shocked to find
that Eliashib had allowed Tobiah to use a
room in the **Temple**. 8 I was **furious** and
threw out all Tobiah's belongings. 9 I gave
orders for the rooms to be ritually **puri-**
fied and for the **temple** equipment, **grain-**
offerings, and **incense** to be put back.

10 I also **learnt** that the **temple** musicians and other **Levites** had left
Jerusalem and gone back to their farms,
because the people had not been giving
them **enough** to live on. 11 I **reprimanded**
the officials for letting the **Temple** be
neglected. And I brought the **Levites** and
musicians back to the **Temple** and put
them to work again. 12 Then all the
people of Israel again started bringing to
the **temple** storerooms their **tithes** of
corn, wine, and olive-oil. 13 I put the
following men in charge of the storerooms: Shelemiah, a **priest**; Zadok, a
scholar of the **Law**; and Pedaiah, a
Levite. Hanan, the son of Zaccur and
grandson of Mattaniah, was to be their
assistant. I knew I could **trust** these men
to be **honest** in distributing the supplies
to their fellow-workers.

14 **Remember**, my God, all these
things that I have done for your **Temple**
and its **worship**.

15 At that time I saw people in Judah
pressing juice from grapes on the
Sabbath. Others were loading corn, wine,
grapes, figs, and other things on their
donkeys and taking them into
Jerusalem; I **warned** them not to sell
anything on the **Sabbath**. 16 Some men
from the city of Tyre were living in
Jerusalem, and they brought fish and all
kinds of goods into the city to sell to our
people on the **Sabbath**. 17 I **reprimanded**
the **Jewish** leaders and said, "Look at the
evil you're doing! You're making the
Sabbath unholy. 18 This is exactly why
God **punished** your ancestors when he
brought **destruction** on this city. And yet
you insist on bringing more of **God's an-**
ger down on Israel by **profaning** the
Sabbath."

19 So I gave orders for the city gates
to be shut at the beginning of every
Sabbath, as soon as evening[x] began to
fall, and not to be opened again until the
Sabbath was over. I stationed some of my
men at the gates to make **sure** that
nothing was brought into the city on the
Sabbath. 20 Once or twice merchants who
sold all kinds of goods spent Friday night
outside the city walls. 21 I **warned** them,
"It's no use waiting out there for morning
to come. If you try this again, I'll use
force against you." From then on they
did not come back on the **Sabbath**. 22 I ordered the **Levites** to **purify** themselves
and to go and guard the gates to make
sure that the **Sabbath** was kept **holy**.

[w] ARTAXERXES: *As emperor of Persia, Artaxerxes also had the title "King of Babylon."*
[x] EVENING: *The Jewish day begins at sunset.*

12.45: 1 Chr 25.1–8, 26.12 **13.1–2:** Deut 23.3–5 **13.2:** Num 22.1–6 **13.10:** Deut 12.19 **13.12:** Mal 3.10
13.15: Ex 20.8–10; Deut 5.12–14; Jer 17.21–22

anger 9.17; Esth 1.18
bless 9.35; Job 1.10
community Ezra 10.8; Ezek 14.7
covenant 9.8; Ps 25.10
curse [3] 10.29; Job 1.11
defile 2 Chr 36.14; Ps 106.38
destroy 9.31; Esth 4.8
disobey 9.26; Esth 3.3
duty (1) 12.45; Job 33.23
enough 10.28; Esth 2.14
evil 4.5; Esth 7.6
example 2 Chr 36.14; Ps 1.1
force (1) 5.8; Esth 10.1
fury 4.1; Esth 1.12
God's people 1.10; Ps 1.5
grain-offering 10.33; Is 57.6
High Priest 12.1; Jer 52.24
holy 11.1; Job 6.10
honest 2 Chr 34.12; Job 6.25
incense [2] 2 Chr 34.4; Ps 141.2
intend 6.6; Is 7.6
Jew [2] 7.65; Esth 2.5
law [3] 12.26; Esth 1.13
learn 2 Chr 22.10; Esth 2.22
Levites [7] 12.1; Ps 135.20
love [2] 9.17; Job 10.12
name (2) (name of God, of Jesus) 9.5; Job 1.21
neglect 10.39; Job 20.19
never again 1 Chr 19.19; Esth 1.19
oath 10.29; Ps 144.8
offer [4] 12.43; Job 1.5
permit [2] Ezra 9.9; Jer 7.21
priest [6] 12.1; Job 12.19

profane Num 18.3
Is 43.28
proper Ezra 6.5; Esth 1.20
punish 9.33; Esth 3
pure [3] 12.30; Job 1.5
regulation 12.45; Ezek 43.11
remember [4] 9.32; Esth 9.28
reprimand [3] 1 Kgs 1.5; Job 13.10
ripe 12.44; Job 5.26
Sabbath [10] 10.31; Is 1.13
scholar 12.26; Is 19.11
spare 2 Chr 36.15; Esth 4.11
sure [2] Ezra 7.23; Job 5.7
Temple (1) (of Go
[10] 12.25; Ps 5.7
tithe [2] 12.44; Amos 4.4
trust Ezra 8.22; Job 4.18
turn 11.23; Esth 1.
unholy Num 26.61; Ezek 21.25
warn [2] 9.26; Esth 4.13
worship (1) (of Go
10.33; Job 1.1

Remember me, O God, for this also,
and **spare** me because of your great **love**.

23 At that time I also discovered that
many of the **Jewish** men had married
women from Ashdod, Ammon, and Moab.
24 Half their children spoke the language
of Ashdod or some other language and
didn't know how to speak our language.
25 I **reprimanded** the men, called down
curses on them, beat them, and pulled
out their hair. Then I made them take an
oath in God's **name** that **never again**
would they or their children intermarry
with foreigners. 26 I said, "It was foreign
women that made King Solomon sin. He
was a man who was greater than any of
the kings of other nations. God **loved** him
and made him king over all Israel, and
yet he fell into this sin. 27 Are we then to
follow your **example** and **disobey** our
God by marrying foreign women?"

28 Joiada was the son of Eliashib the
High Priest, but one of Joiada's sons
married the daughter of Sanballat, from
the town of Beth Horon, so I made Joiada
leave Jerusalem.

29 **Remember**, O God, how those
people **defiled** both the office of **priest**
and the **covenant** you made with the
priests and the Levites.

30 I **purified** the people from everything foreign; I prepared **regulations** for
the **priests and the Levites** so that each
one would know his **duty**; 31 I arranged
for the wood used for burning the **offerings** to be brought at the **proper** times,
and for the people to bring their **offerings** of the first corn and the first fruits
that **ripened**.

Remember all this, O God, and give
me credit for it.

13.23–25: Ex 34.11-16; Deut 7.1-5 **13.26:** 2 Sam 12.24-25; 1 Kgs 11.1-8 **13.28:** Neh 4.1

THE BOOK OF
ESTHER

INTRODUCTION

The events of the book of *Esther*, which take place at the winter residence of the Persian emperor, centre round a Jewish heroine named Esther, who by her great courage and devotion to her people saved them from being exterminated by their enemies. The book explains the background and meaning of the Jewish festival of Purim.

Outline of Contents

---

advice Ezra 10.3; 2.4
anger Neh 13.18; 2.1
authority Ezra 5.9; 9.29
banquet [4] 2 Sam 13.27; 2.18
change Neh 9.7; Job 14.5
command [3] Neh 12.45; 3.3
court (1) Neh 11.24; Job 5.4
crown 2 Chr 23.11; 2.17
cup Ezra 1.7; Ps 23.5
custom 2 Chr 35.25; 3.8
final 2 Chr 19.11; Job 30.12
fury Neh 13.8; 3.5
generous 2 Chr 11.23; Ps 37.21
idea 1 Sam 17.55; 5.14
insult Neh 9.18; Job 1.5
last (1) 1 Chr 28.7; 2.12
law [3] Neh 13.1; 3.8
look down on Neh 1.3; Job 41.34
Majesty [2] Neh 6.7; 3.9
master 2 Chr 4.11; Ps 45.11
message Neh 6.2; 4.10
never again Neh 13.25; Job 3.4
obey Neh 10.28; 2.20
please Neh 12.44; 3.9
poor [2] 2 Chr 34.30; 9.22
proclaim [2] Neh 6.7; 2.1
proper Neh 13.31; 9.27
question 2 Chr 9.1; Job 9.3
refuse (1) [3] Neh 9.16; 3.2
reign Ezra 7.6; Ps 146.10
respect [2] 2 Chr 22.9; 3.2

Queen Vashti Defies King Xerxes

1 1-2 From his royal **throne** in Persia's capital city of Susa, King Xerxes ruled over 127 provinces, all the way from India to Sudan.

3 In the third year of his **reign** he gave a **banquet** for all his officials and administrators. The armies of Persia and Media were present, as well as the governors and noblemen of the provinces. 4 For six whole months he made a show of the **riches** of the imperial **court** with all its **splendour** and **majesty**.

5 After that, the king gave a **banquet** for all the men in the capital city of Susa, **rich** and **poor** alike. It **lasted** a whole week and was held in the gardens of the royal palace. 6 The courtyard there was decorated with blue and white cotton curtains, tied by cords of fine purple linen to silver rings on marble columns. Couches made of gold and silver had been placed in the courtyard, which was paved with white marble, red feldspar, shining mother-of-pearl, and blue turquoise. 7 Drinks were **served** in gold **cups**, no two of them alike, and the king was **generous** with the royal wine. 8 There were no limits on the drinks; the king had given orders to the palace **servants** that everyone could have as much as he wanted.[a]

9 Meanwhile, inside the royal palace Queen Vashti was giving a **banquet** for the women.

10 On the seventh day of his **banquet** the king was drinking and feeling merry, so he called in the seven eunuchs who were his personal **servants**, Mehuman, Biztha, Harbona, Bigtha, Abagtha, Zethar, and Carkas. 11 He ordered them to bring in Queen Vashti, wearing her royal **crown**. The queen was a beautiful woman, and the king wanted to show off her beauty to the officials and all his guests. 12 But when the **servants** told Queen Vashti of the king's **command**, she **refused** to come. This made the king **furious**.

13 Now it was the king's **custom** to ask for expert opinion on **questions** of **law** and order, so he called for his advisers, who would know what should be done. 14 Those he most often **turned** to for **advice** were Carshena, Shethar, Admatha, Tarshish, Meres, Marsena, and Memucan—seven officials of Persia and Media who held the highest offices in the kingdom. 15 He said to these men, "I, King Xerxes, sent my **servants** to Queen Vashti with a **command**, and she **refused** to **obey** it! What does the **law** say that we should do with her?"

16 Then Memucan declared to the king and his officials: "Queen Vashti has **insulted** not only the king but also his officials—in fact, every man in the empire! 17 Every woman in the empire will begin to **look down on** her husband as soon as she hears what the queen has done. They'll say, 'King Xerxes **commanded** Queen Vashti to come to him, and she **refused**.' 18 When the wives of the royal officials of Persia and Media hear about the

rich [2] 2 Chr 34.30; 5.11
riches 1 Chr 29.12; Job 31.24
servant [4] Neh 11.3 4.4
serve Neh 11.12; 2.9
splendour 1 Chr 29.11; Is 33.17
throne 2 Chr 23.20; 5.1
turn Neh 13.2; 2.12

[a] There were no limits...wanted; *or* But no one was forced to drink; the king had given orders to the palace servants that everyone could have as much or as little as he wanted.

1.1: Ezra 4.6

queen's behaviour they will be telling their husbands about it before the day is out. Wives everywhere will have no **respect** for their husbands, and husbands will be **angry** with their wives. 19 If it **please** Your **Majesty**, issue a royal **proclamation** that Vashti may **never again** appear before the king. Order it to be written into the **laws** of Persia and Media, so that it can never be **changed**. Then give her place as queen to some better woman. 20 When your **proclamation** is made known all over this huge empire, every woman will treat her husband with **proper respect**, whether he's **rich** or **poor**."

21 The king and his officials liked this **idea**, and the king did what Memucan suggested. 22 To each of the royal provinces he sent a **message** in the language and the system of writing of that province, saying[b] that every husband should be the **master** of his home and speak with **final authority**.

Esther Becomes Queen

2 Later, even after the king's **anger** had cooled down, he kept thinking about what Vashti had done and about his **proclamation** against her. 2 So some of the king's advisers who were close to him suggested, "Why don't you make a search to find some beautiful young **virgins**? 3 You can appoint officials in every province of the empire and order them to bring all these beautiful young girls to your harem here in Susa, the capital city. Put them in the **care** of Hegai, the eunuch who is in charge of your women, and let them be given a beauty treatment. 4 Then take the girl you like **best** and make her queen in Vashti's place."

The king thought this was good **advice**, so he followed it.

5 There in Susa lived a **Jew** named Mordecai son of Jair; he was from the tribe of Benjamin and was a descendant of Kish and Shimei. 6 When King Nebuchadnezzar of Babylon took King Jehoiachin of Judah into **exile** from Jerusalem, along with a group of **captives**, Mordecai was among them. 7 He had a cousin, Esther, whose **Hebrew** name was Hadassah; she was a beautiful girl, and had a good figure. At the **death** of her parents, Mordecai had adopted her and brought her up as his own daughter.

8 When the king had issued his **new proclamation** and many girls were being brought to Susa, Esther was among them. She too was put in the royal palace in the **care** of Hegai, who had charge of the harem. 9 Hegai liked Esther, and she **won** his **favour**. He lost no time in beginning her beauty treatment of massage and **special** diet. He gave her the **best** place in the harem and assigned seven girls **specially chosen** from the royal palace to **serve** her.

10 Now, on the **advice** of Mordecai, Esther had kept it **secret** that she was **Jewish**. 11 Every day Mordecai would walk to and fro in front of the courtyard of the harem, in order to find out how she was getting on and what was going to happen to her.

12 The regular beauty treatment for the women **lasted** a year—massages with oil of myrrh for six months and with oil of balsam for six more. After that, each girl would be taken in **turn** to King Xerxes. 13 When she went from the harem to the palace, she could wear whatever she wanted. 14 She would go there in the evening, and the next morning she would be taken to another harem and put in the **care** of Shaashgaz, the eunuch in charge of the king's **concubines**. She would not go to the king again unless he liked her **enough** to ask for her by name.

15 The time came for Esther to go to the king. Esther—the daughter of Abihail and the cousin of Mordecai, who had adopted her as his daughter; Esther—admired by everyone who saw her. When her **turn** came, she wore just what Hegai, the eunuch in charge of the harem, **advised** her to wear. 16 So in Xerxes' seventh year as king, in the tenth month, the month of Tebeth, Esther was brought to King Xerxes in the royal palace. 17 The king liked her more than any of the other girls, and more than any of the others she **won** his **favour** and **affection**. He placed the royal **crown** on her head and made her queen in place of Vashti. 18 Then the king gave a great **banquet** in Esther's **honour** and invited all his officials and administrators. He **proclaimed** a holiday[c] for the whole empire and distributed **gifts worthy** of a king.

Mordecai Saves the King's Life

19 Meanwhile Mordecai had been appointed by the king to an administrative position. 20 As for Esther, she had still not let it be known that she was **Jewish**. Mordecai had told her not to tell anyone, and she **obeyed** him in this, just

advice [3] 1.14; Job 16.5
affection 1 Sam 18.3; Hos 11.4
anger 1.18; 7.10
banquet 1.3; 5.4
best [2] Neh 5.18; 3.8
captive Neh 8.17; Ps 68.18
care [4] Ezra 5.8; 8.5
choose Neh 11.1; Job 23.11
concubine 2 Chr 11.21; Song 6.8
crown 1.11; 8.15
death (1) Ezra 7.26; Job 3.21
enough Neh 13.10; 5.8
exile Neh 12.1; Ps 42.6
favour [2] Neh 2.7; 5.2
gift Neh 12.47; 9.19
hang (2) 2 Sam 21.6; 5.14
Hebrew 2 Chr 32.18; Is 19.18
honour Neh 5.15; 6.3
Jew [3] Neh 13.17; 3.4
last (1) 1.5; Job 15.29
learn Neh 13.10; 3.6
new Ezra 9.8; Job 10.17
obey [2] 1.15; 3.8
plot (1) Neh 4.8; 3.7
proclaim [3] 1.19; 3.10
secret 2 Chr 22.11; Job 10.13
serve 1.7; Job 21.15
special [2] 2 Chr 30.1; Jer 45.5
true Neh 6.8; Job 3.25
turn [2] 1.14; 9.22
virgin 2 Sam 13.2; Is 47.1
win [2] Neh 9.10; 5.2
worthy 1 Chr 17.16; Prov 22.29

[b] saying; *or* in order. [c] holiday; *or* remission of taxes.

2.6: 2 Kgs 24.10–16; 2 Chr 36.10

as she had **obeyed** him when she was a little girl under his **care**.

21 During the time that Mordecai held office in the palace, Bigthana and Teresh, two of the palace eunuchs who guarded the entrance to the king's rooms, became hostile to King Xerxes and **plotted** to assassinate him. 22 Mordecai **learnt** about it and told Queen Esther, who then told the king what Mordecai had found out. 23 There was an investigation, and it was discovered that the report was **true**, so both men were **hanged** on the gallows. The king ordered an account of this to be written down in the official records of the empire.

Haman Plots to Destroy the Jews

3 Some time later King Xerxes promoted a man named Haman to the position of prime minister. Haman was the son of Hammedatha, a descendant of Agag.[d] 2 The king ordered all the officials in his **service** to show their **respect** for Haman by **kneeling** and **bowing** to him. They all did so, except for Mordecai, who **refused** to do it. 3 The other officials in the royal **service** asked him why he was **disobeying** the king's **command**; 4 day after day they **urged** him to give in, but he would not listen to them. "I am a **Jew**," he explained, "and I cannot **bow** to Haman." So they told Haman about this, wondering if he would **tolerate** Mordecai's conduct. 5 Haman was **furious** when he realized that Mordecai was not going to **kneel** and **bow** to him, 6 and when he **learnt** that Mordecai was a **Jew**, he decided to do more than **punish** Mordecai **alone**. He made **plans** to kill every **Jew** in the whole Persian Empire.

7 In the twelfth year of King Xerxes' rule, in the first month, the month of Nisan, Haman ordered the **lots** to be cast ("purim," they were called) to find out the **right** day and month to carry out his **plot**. The thirteenth day of the twelfth month, the month of Adar, was decided on.

8 So Haman told the king, "There is a certain **race** of people **scattered** all over your empire and found in every province. They **observe customs** that are not like those of any other people. Moreover, they do not **obey** the **laws** of the empire, so it is not in your **best interests** to **tolerate** them. 9 If it **please** Your **Majesty**, issue a decree that they are to be put to **death**. If you do, I **guarantee** that I will be able to put more than 340,000 kilogrammes of silver into the royal treasury for the administration of the empire."

10 The king took off his ring, which was used to stamp **proclamations** and make them official, and gave it to the **enemy** of the **Jewish** people, Haman son of Hammedatha, the descendant of Agag. 11 The king told him, "The people and their money are yours; do as you like with them."

12 So on the thirteenth day of the first month Haman called the king's secretaries and dictated a **proclamation** to be translated into every language and system of writing used in the empire and to be sent to all the rulers, governors, and officials. It was issued in the name of King Xerxes and stamped with his ring. 13 Runners took this **proclamation** to every province of the empire. It contained the instructions that on a single day, the thirteenth day of Adar, all **Jews**—young and old, women and children—were to be killed. They were to be **slaughtered** without **mercy** and their belongings were to be taken. 14 The contents of the **proclamation** were to be made public in every province, so that everyone would be prepared when that day came.

15 At the king's **command** the decree was made public in the capital city of Susa, and runners carried the news to the provinces. The king and Haman sat down and had a drink while the city of Susa was being thrown into confusion.

alone Neh 9.6; 9.12
best 2.4; Job 27.22
bow (2) [3] Neh 9.6; Ps 2.12
command [2] 1.12; 7.9
custom 1.13; 9.23
death (3) (to death) 2 Chr 25.4; Job 5.2
disobey Neh 13.27; Ps 18.22
enemy Neh 9.27; 7.6
fury 1.12; 5.9
guarantee 2 Sam 3.21; Prov 20.16
interest (1) Ezra 4.22; Prov 18.1
Jew [5] 2.5; 4.3
kneel [2] Neh 8.6; Ps 95.6
law 1.13; 4.11
learn 2.22; 4.1
lot (1) Neh 11.1; 9.24
Majesty 1.4; 5.4
mercy Neh 9.17; 4.8
obey 2.20; Job 36.11
observe 2 Chr 36.21; 9.19
plan Neh 6.6; 9.24
please 1.19; 5.4
plot (1) 2.21; 6.2
proclaim [4] 2.1; 4.3
punish Neh 13.18; 7.7
race (1) Neh 5.5; Ps 22.27
refuse (1) 1.12; Job 10.14
respect 1.18; 5.9
right (1) Neh 9.33; 8.5
scatter Neh 1.8; Job 4.11
service [2] Neh 11.22; Job 7.1
slaughter Ezra 9.7; 7.4
tolerate [2] 2 Chr 19.7; Ps 101.3
urge 2 Kgs 6.3; Jer 17.16

Mordecai Asks for Esther's Help

4 When Mordecai **learnt** of all that had been done, he tore his clothes in **anguish**. Then he dressed in **sackcloth**, covered his head with **ashes**, and walked through the city, **wailing** loudly and **bitterly**, 2 until he came to the entrance of the palace. He did not go in because no one wearing **sackcloth** was allowed inside. 3 Throughout all the provinces, wherever the king's **proclamation** was made known, there was loud **mourning** among the **Jews**. They **fasted**, **wept** and **wailed**, and most of them put on **sackcloth** and lay in **ashes**.

4 When Esther's **servant-girls** and eunuchs told her what Mordecai was doing, she was deeply disturbed. She sent Mordecai some clothes to put on instead of the **sackcloth**, but he would not **accept** them. 5 Then she called Hathach, one of the palace eunuchs appointed as **her servant** by the king, and told him to go to Mordecai and find out what was happening and why. 6 Hathach went to Mordecai in the city square at the entrance of the palace. 7 Mordecai told him everything

accept Neh 7.63; Job 5.27
anguish Ps 48.6
ash [2] 2 Kgs 25.14; Job 13.12
beg 2 Chr 33.12; 7.7
bitter Ezra 10.1; Job 7.11
destroy Neh 13.18; 7.4
fast (2) [2] Neh 9.1; 5.1
heaven Neh 9.6; Job 1.6
help Neh 10.32; 9.3
Jew [6] 3.4; 5.13
law [3] 3.8; 8.13
learn 3.6; Job 5.27
life (1) Neh 9.6; 7.7
mercy 3.13; 7.8
message [2] 1.22; Job 4.12
mourn Neh 8.9; 9.31
plead 2 Kgs 16.9; Job 8.5
pray Neh 9.4; Job 15.4
proclaim [2] 3.10; 8.5
promise Neh 9.8; Job 31.1
sackcloth [4] Neh 9.1; Job 16.15
safe Ezra 9.8; Job 5.4
save Neh 9.28; 7.9
servant [3] 1.8; 6.3
spare Neh 13.22; Job 21.30
wail [2] Ezra 3.12; Job 2.12

[d] AGAG: *An Amalekite king; his people were traditional enemies of the people of Israel.*

warn Neh 13.15; Job 9.5
weep Neh 1.4; Job 2.12

that had happened to him and just how much money Haman had **promised** to put into the royal treasury if all the **Jews** were killed. 8 He gave Hathach a copy of the **proclamation** that had been issued in Susa, ordering the **destruction** of the **Jews**. Mordecai asked him to take it to Esther, explain the situation to her, and ask her to go and **plead** with the king and **beg** him to have **mercy** on her people. 9 Hathach did this, 10 and Esther gave him this **message** to take back to Mordecai: 11 "If anyone, man or woman, goes to the inner courtyard and sees the king without being summoned, that person must die. That is the **law**; everyone, from the king's advisers to the people in the provinces, knows that. There is only one way to get round this **law**: if the king holds out his gold sceptre to someone, then that person's **life** is **spared**. But it has been a month since the king sent for me."

12 When Mordecai received Esther's **message**, 13 he sent her this **warning**: "Don't imagine that you are **safer** than any other **Jew** just because you are in the royal palace. 14 If you keep quiet at a time like this, **help** will come from **heaven** to the **Jews**, and they will be **saved**, but you will die and your father's family will come to an end. Yet who knows—maybe it was for a time like this that you were made queen!"

15 Esther sent Mordecai this reply: 16 "Go and gather all the **Jews** in Susa together; hold a **fast** and **pray** for me. Don't eat or drink anything for three days and nights. My **servant-girls** and I will be doing the same. After that, I will go to the king, even though it is against the **law**. If I must die for doing it, I will die."

17 Mordecai then left and did everything that Esther had told him to do.

Esther Invites the King and Haman to a Banquet

5 On the third day of her **fast** Esther put on her royal robes and went and stood in the inner courtyard of the palace, facing the **throne** room. The king was inside, seated on the royal **throne**, facing the entrance. 2 When the king saw Queen Esther standing outside, she **won** his **favour**, and he held out to her the gold sceptre. She then came up and touched the tip of it. 3 "What is it, Queen Esther?" the king asked. "Tell me what you want, and you shall have it—even if it is half my empire."

4 Esther replied, "If it **please** Your **Majesty**, I would like you and Haman to be my guests tonight at a **banquet** I am preparing for you."

5 The king then ordered Haman to come quickly, so that they could be Esther's guests. So the king and Haman went to Esther's **banquet**. 6 Over the wine the king asked her, "Tell me what you want, and you shall have it. I will **grant** your **request**, even if you ask for half my empire."

7 Esther replied, 8 "If Your **Majesty** is **kind enough** to **grant** my **request**, I would like you and Haman to be my guests tomorrow at another **banquet** that I will prepare for you. At that time I will tell you what I want."

Haman Plots to Kill Mordecai

9 When Haman left the **banquet** he was **happy** and in a good mood. But then he saw Mordecai at the entrance of the palace, and when Mordecai did not **rise** or show any **sign** of **respect** as he passed, Haman was **furious** with him. 10 But he **controlled** himself and went home. Then he invited his **friends** to his house and asked his wife Zeresh to join them. 11 He **boasted** to them how **rich** he was, how many sons he had, how the king had promoted him to high office, and how much more **important** he was than any of the king's other officials. 12 "What is more," Haman went on, "Queen Esther gave a **banquet** for no one but the king and me, and we are invited back tomorrow. 13 But none of this means a thing to me as long as I see that **Jew** Mordecai sitting at the entrance of the palace."

14 So his wife and all his **friends** suggested, "Why don't you have a gallows built, twenty-two metres tall? Tomorrow morning you can ask the king to have Mordecai **hanged** on it, and then you can go to the **banquet** **happy**."

Haman thought this was a good **idea**, so he had the gallows built.

The King Honours Mordecai

6 That same night the king could not get to sleep, so he ordered the official records of the empire to be brought and read to him. 2 The part they read included the account of how Mordecai had uncovered a **plot** to assassinate the king—the **plot** made by Bigthana and Teresh, the two palace eunuchs who had guarded the king's rooms. 3 The king asked, "How have we **honoured** and **rewarded** Mordecai for this?"

His **servants** answered, "Nothing has been done for him."

6.2: Esth 2.21-22

Majesty [2] 3.9; 7.3
please 3.9; 7.3
request [2] Neh 2.5; 7.3
respect 3.2; Job 17.9
rich 1.5; Job 1.3
rise Neh 8.7; Job 9.7
sign (1) Neh 9.1; Ps 60.8
throne [2] 1.1; Job 12.18
win 2.9; Job 9.1

banquet [6] 2.18; 6.14
boast 2 Chr 25.19; Ps 12.3
control Neh 9.15; Job 3.8
enough 2.14; Job 1.10
fast (2) 4.3; 9.31
favour 2.9; Job 23.4
friend [2] 2 Chr 20.7; 6.13
fury 3.5; 7.7
grant [2] Neh 2.5; 7.3
hang (2) 2.23; 6.4
happy [2] Neh 12.43; 8.16
idea 1.21; Job 38.18
important Neh 6.3; Job 7.17
Jew 4.3; 6.10
kind 2 Chr 30.9; Job 24.21

announce [2] 2 Chr 20.2; Job 36.33
banquet 5.4; Ps 23.5
friend [2] 5.10; Job 2.11
hang (2) 5.14; 7.9
honour [6] 2.18; 10.3
Jew [2] 5.13; 8.1
plot (1) [2] 3.7; 8.3
power Neh 9.6; 9.1
provide Neh 10.33; Job 36.31
reward [3] 2 Chr 15.7; Job 8.6
servant [2] 4.4; Job 1.3
wise 2 Chr 11.23; Job 5.12

wish [3] 1 Chr 21.23; 7.3

4 "Are any of my officials in the
palace?" the king asked.
Now Haman had just entered the
courtyard; he had come to ask the king
to have Mordecai **hanged** on the gallows
that was now ready. 5 So the **servants**
answered, "Haman is here, waiting to
see you."
"Show him in," said the king.
6 So Haman came in, and the king
said to him, "There is someone I **wish**
very much to **honour**. What should I do
for this man?"
Haman thought to himself, "Now who
could the king want to **honour** so much?
Me, of course."
7–8 So he answered the king, "Order
royal robes to be brought for this man—
robes that you yourself wear. Order a
royal ornament[e] to be put on your own
horse. 9 Then get one of your highest
noblemen to dress the man in these
robes and lead him, mounted on the
horse, through the city square. Let the
nobleman **announce** as they go: 'See how
the king **rewards** a man he **wishes** to
honour!'"
10 Then the king said to Haman,
"Hurry and get the robes and the horse,
and **provide** these **honours** for Mordecai
the **Jew**. Do everything for him that you
have suggested. You will find him sitting
at the entrance of the palace."
11 So Haman got the robes and the
horse, and he put the robes on Mordecai.
Mordecai got on the horse, and Haman
led him through the city square,
announcing to the people as they went:
"See how the king **rewards** a man he
wishes to **honour**!"
12 Mordecai then went back to the
palace entrance while Haman hurried
home, covering his face in embarrass-
ment. 13 He told his wife and all his
friends everything that had happened to
him. Then she and those **wise friends** of
his said to him, "You are beginning to
lose **power** to Mordecai. He is a **Jew**, and
you cannot overcome him. He will certainly defeat you."

Haman Is Put to Death

14 While they were still talking, the
palace eunuchs arrived in a hurry to take
7 Haman to Esther's **banquet**. 1 And so
the king and Haman went to eat
with Esther 2 for a second time. Over the
wine the king asked her again, "Now,
Queen Esther, what do you want? Tell
me and you shall have it. I'll even give
you half the empire."
3 Queen Esther answered, "If it **please**
Your **Majesty** to **grant** my **humble request**, my **wish** is that I may live and that
my people may live. 4 My people and I
have been sold for **slaughter**. If it were
nothing more **serious** than being sold into
slavery, I would have kept quiet and not
bothered you about it;[f] but we are about
to be **destroyed**—exterminated!"
5 Then King Xerxes asked Queen
Esther, "Who **dares** to do such a thing?
Where is this man?"
6 Esther answered, "Our **enemy**, our
persecutor, is this **evil** man Haman!"
Haman stared at the king and queen in
terror. 7 The king got up in a **fury**, left the
room, and went outside to the palace gardens. Haman could see that the king was
determined to **punish** him for this, so he
stayed behind to **beg** Queen Esther for
his **life**. 8 He had just thrown himself
down on Esther's couch to **beg** for
mercy, when the king came back into
the room from the gardens. Seeing this,
the king cried out, "Is this man going to
rape the queen right here in front of me,
in my own palace?"
The king had no sooner said this than
the eunuchs covered Haman's head.
9 Then one of them, who was named
Harbonah, said, "Haman even went so
far as to build a gallows at his house so
that he could **hang** Mordecai, who **saved**
Your **Majesty's life**. And it's twenty-two
metres tall!"
"**Hang** Haman on it!" the king **commanded**.
10 So Haman was **hanged** on the
gallows that he had built for Mordecai.
Then the king's **anger** cooled down.

The Jews Are Told to Fight Back

8 That same day King Xerxes gave
Queen Esther all the property of
Haman, the **enemy** of the **Jews**. Esther
told the king that Mordecai was related
to her, and from then on Mordecai was
allowed to enter the king's **presence**.
2 The king took off his ring with his **seal**
on it (which he had taken back from
Haman) and gave it to Mordecai. Esther
put Mordecai in charge of Haman's property.
3 Then Esther spoke to the king again,
throwing herself at his feet and crying.
She **begged** him to do something to stop
the **evil plot** that Haman, the descendant
of Agag,[g] had made against the **Jews**.
4 The king held out the gold sceptre to
her, so she stood up and said, 5 "If it
please Your **Majesty**, and if you **care**

anger 2.1; Job 4.9
beg [2] 4.8; 8.3
command 3.3; 8.14
dare 2 Sam 17.17; Job 9.12
destroy 4.8; 8.5
determine Neh 10.34; 9.24
enemy 3.10; 8.1
evil Neh 13.17; 8.3

fury 5.9; Job 20.23
grant 5.6; Mal 1.8
hang (2) [3] 6.4; 8.7
humble Ezra 8.21; Job 5.11
life (1) [2] 4.11; Job 4.6
Majesty [2] 5.4; 8.5
mercy 4.8; Job 9.15
persecute Judg 10.8 Job 19.22
please 5.4; 8.5
punish 3.6; Job 8.4
rape 2 Sam 13.14; Is 13.16
request 5.6; Ps 20.5
save 4.14; Job 5.15
serious 2 Kgs 1.2; Prov 4.10
slaughter 3.13; 8.11
slave Neh 9.17; Job 3.19
terror 1 Sam 17.24; Job 6.4
wish 6.6; 8.8

afraid Neh 4.14; 9.2
beg 7.7; Job 9.15
care 2.3; Job 9.21
command 7.9; 9.31
crown 2.17; Job 31.36
defend 2 Chr 32.5; 9.16
destroy [2] 7.4; 9.24
disaster 2 Chr 28.23; Job 4.7
endure Num 11.15; Job 14.12
enemy [2] 7.6; 9.1
evil 7.6; Job 1.1
feast Neh 8.10; 9.17
hang (2) 7.9; 9.13
happy [2] 5.9; 9.22
Jew [16] 6.10; 9.1
joy [3] Neh 12.43; 9.17
last (2) Neh 8.18; Job 16.3
law 4.11; Job 38.33
letter (2) [4] Neh 6.5; 9.20
Majesty 7.3; 9.13
please 7.3; 9.13
plot (1) [2] 6.2; Ps 2.1

[e] ORNAMENT: *Probably a type of crown.* [f] *Probable text* and not...it; *Hebrew unclear.*
[g] AGAG: *See 3.1.*

possess Ezra 8.21; Ps 25.13
presence Ezra 9.6; Job 2.7
prevent 2 Chr 32.3; Job 24.4
proclaim [4] 4.3; 9.1
relieve (1) 2 Chr 26.21; Job 7.13
revenge 1 Kgs 2.5; Prov 6.34
right (1) 3.7; Job 6.29
seal [4] Neh 9.38; Job 38.14
sense 1 Sam 25.33; Job 5.2
slaughter [2] 7.4; 9.5
victory 2 Chr 25.8; Job 12.16
wish 7.3; 9.30

about me and if it seems **right** to you, please issue a **proclamation** to **prevent** Haman's orders from being carried out—those orders that the son of Hammedatha the descendant of Agag gave for the **destruction** of all the **Jews** in the empire. 6 How can I **endure** it if this **disaster** comes on my people, and my own relatives are killed?"

7 King Xerxes then said to Queen Esther and Mordecai, the **Jew**, "Look, I have **hanged** Haman for his **plot** against the **Jews**, and I have given Esther his property. 8 But a **proclamation** issued in the king's name and stamped with the royal **seal** cannot be revoked. You may, however, write to the **Jews** whatever you **wish**; and you may write it in my name and stamp it with the royal **seal**."

9 This happened on the twenty-third day of the third month, the month of Sivan. Mordecai called the king's secretaries and dictated **letters** to the **Jews** and to the governors, administrators, and officials of all the 127 provinces from India to Sudan. The **letters** were written to each province in its own language and system of writing and to the **Jews** in their language and system of writing. 10 Mordecai had the **letters** written in the name of King Xerxes, and he stamped them with the royal **seal**. They were delivered by riders mounted on fast horses from the royal stables.

11 These **letters** explained that the king would allow the **Jews** in every city to organize themselves for **self-defence**. If armed men of any nationality in any province attacked the **Jewish** men, their children or their women, the **Jews** could fight back and **destroy** the attackers; they could **slaughter** them to the **last** man and take their **possessions**. 12 This decree was to take effect throughout the Persian Empire on the day set for the **slaughter** of the **Jews**, the thirteenth of Adar, the twelfth month. 13 It was to be **proclaimed** as **law** and made known to everyone in every province, so that the **Jews** would be ready to take **revenge** on their **enemies** when that day came. 14 At the king's **command** the riders mounted royal horses and rode off at top speed. The decree was also made public in Susa, the capital city.

15 Mordecai left the palace, wearing royal robes of blue and white, a cloak of fine purple linen, and a magnificent gold **crown**. Then the streets of Susa rang with cheers and **joyful** shouts. 16 For the **Jews** there was **joy** and **relief, happiness** and a **sense** of **victory**. 17 In every city and province, wherever the king's **proclamation** was read, the **Jews** held a **joyful** holiday with **feasting** and **happiness**. In fact, many other people became **Jews**, because they were **afraid** of them now.

The Jews Destroy Their Enemies

9 The thirteenth day of Adar came, the day on which the royal **proclamation** was to take effect, the day when the **enemies** of the **Jews** were **hoping** to get them in their **power**. But instead, the **Jews triumphed** over them. 2 In the **Jewish** quarter of every city[h] in the empire the **Jews** organized themselves to attack anyone who tried to **harm** them. People everywhere were **afraid** of them, and no one could stand against them. 3 In fact, all the provincial officials—governors, administrators, and royal **representatives—helped** the **Jews** because they were all **afraid** of Mordecai. 4 It was well known throughout the empire that Mordecai was now a **powerful** man in the palace and was growing more **powerful**. 5 So the **Jews** could do what they wanted with their **enemies**. They attacked them with swords and **slaughtered** them.

6 In Susa, the capital city itself, the **Jews** killed five hundred people. 7-10 Among them were the ten sons of Haman son of Hammedatha, the **enemy** of the **Jews**: Parshandatha, Dalphon, Aspatha, Poratha, Adalia, Aridatha, Parmashta, Arisai, Aridai, and Vaizatha. However, there was no looting.

11 That same day the number of people killed in Susa was reported to the king. 12 He then said to Queen Esther, "In Susa **alone** the **Jews** have killed five hundred men, including Haman's ten sons. What must they have done out in the provinces! What do you want now? You shall have it. Tell me what else you want, and you shall have it."

13 Esther answered, "If it **please** Your **Majesty**, let the **Jews** in Susa do again tomorrow what they were allowed to do today. And order the **bodies** of Haman's ten sons to be **hung** from the gallows." 14 The king ordered this to be done, and the **proclamation** was issued in Susa. The **bodies** of Haman's ten sons were publicly displayed. 15 On the fourteenth day of Adar the **Jews** of Susa got together again and killed three hundred more men in the city. But again, they did no looting.

16 The **Jews** in the provinces also organized and **defended** themselves. They **rid** themselves of their **enemies** by killing seventy-five thousand people who **hated** them. But they did no looting.

afraid [2] 8.17; Job 5.22
alone 3.6; Job 7.16
authority 1.22; Ps 105.22
body [2] Ezra 6.11; Job 2.5
celebrate Neh 12.27; Ps 20.5
command [2] 8.14; Job 3.18
custom 3.8; Is 2.6
defend 8.11; Job 5.4
despair Ezra 9.3; Job 6.26
destroy 8.5; Job 4.9
determine 7.7; Job 22.15
direct Neh 12.24; Job 12.10
enemy [7] 8.1; Job 6.23
fast (2) 5.1; Ps 69.10
fate Job 6.21
feast [3] 8.17; Job 1.4
gift [2] 2.18; Job 6.22
grief Neh 9.1; Job 1.20
hang (2) [2] 8.7; Lam 5.12
happy 8.16; Job 3.22
harm Neh 6.2; Job 5.19
hate 2 Chr 19.2; Job 8.22
help 4.14; Job 6.13
hope Ezra 10.2; Job 3.9
Jew [25] 8.1; 10.3
joy [3] 8.15; Job 3.7
letter (2) [5] 8.9; Is 37.9
lot (1) 3.7; Prov 16.33
Majesty 8.5; Job 37.4
mourn 4.3; Job 3.24
observe [7] 3.8; Ps 18.22
peace Neh 9.28; Job 3.18
plan [2] 3.6; Job 5.12
please 8.5; Job 14.15
poor 1.5; Job 5.15
power [3] 6.13; Job 1.12
proclaim [2] 8.5; Ps 18.46
proper [2] 1.20; Ps 51.19
remember Neh 13.14; Job 3.4
represent Neh 11.24; Is 6.13
rid [2] Ezra 10.11; Ps 35.25
scroll Ezra 6.2; Is 29.11
secure 2 Chr 20.30; 10.3
slaughter [2] 8.11; Ps 37.14
suffer Neh 9.9; Job 2.10
triumph 2 Chr 20.27; Job 17.4
turn 2.12; Job 1.4
wish 8.8; Job 3.11

[h] In the Jewish quarter of every city; *or* In every Jewish city.

17 This was on the thirteenth day of Adar. On the next day, the fourteenth, there was no more killing, and they made it a **joyful** day of **feasting**. 18 The **Jews** of Susa, however, made the fifteenth a holiday, since they had **slaughtered** their **enemies** on the thirteenth and fourteenth and then stopped on the fifteenth. 19 This is why **Jews** who live in small towns **observe** the fourteenth day of the month of Adar as a **joyous** holiday, a time for **feasting** and giving **gifts** of food to one another.

The Festival of Purim

20 Mordecai had these events written down and sent **letters** to all the **Jews**, near and far, throughout the Persian Empire, 21 telling them to **observe** the fourteenth and fifteenth days of Adar as holidays every year. 22 These were the days on which the **Jews** had **rid** themselves of their **enemies**; this was a month that had been **turned** from a time of **grief** and **despair** into a time of **joy** and **happiness**. They were told to **observe** these days with **feasts** and parties, giving **gifts** of food to one another and to the **poor**. 23 So the **Jews** followed Mordecai's instructions, and the **celebration** became an annual **custom**.

24 Haman son of Hammedatha—the descendant of Agag and the **enemy** of the **Jewish** people—had cast **lots** (or "purim," as they were called) to **determine** the day for **destroying** the **Jews**; he had **planned** to wipe them out. 25 But Esther went to the king, and the king issued written orders with the result that Haman **suffered** the **fate** he had **planned** for the **Jews**—he and his sons were **hanged** from the gallows. 26 That is why the holidays are called Purim. Because of Mordecai's **letter** and because of all that had happened to them, 27 the **Jews** made it a rule for themselves, their descendants, and anyone who might become a **Jew**, that at the **proper** time each year these two days would be regularly **observed** according to Mordecai's instructions. 28 It was resolved that every **Jewish** family of every future generation in every province and every city should **remember** and **observe** the days of Purim for all time to come.

29 Then Queen Esther, the daughter of Abihail, along with Mordecai, also wrote a **letter**, putting her full **authority** behind the **letter** about Purim, which Mordecai had written earlier. 30 The **letter** was addressed to all the **Jews**, and copies were sent to all the 127 provinces of the Persian Empire. It **wished** the **Jews** **peace** and **security** 31 and **directed** them and their descendants to **observe** the days of Purim at the **proper** time, just as they had adopted rules for the **observance** of **fasts** and times of **mourning**. This was **commanded** by both Mordecai and Queen Esther. 32 Esther's **command**, confirming the rules for Purim, was written down on a **scroll**.

9.24: Esth 3.7

The Greatness of Xerxes and Mordecai

10 King Xerxes imposed **forced** **labour** on the people of the coastal regions of his empire as well as on those of the interior. 2 All the great and **wonderful** things he did, as well as the whole story of how he promoted Mordecai to high office, are recorded in the official records of the kings of Persia and Media. 3 Mordecai the **Jew** was second in rank only to King Xerxes himself. He was **honoured** and well-liked by his **fellow-Jews**. He worked for the good of his people and for the **security** of all their descendants.

force (1) Neh 13.21; Job 7.1
honour 6.3; Job 14.21
Jew [2] 9.1; Jer 40.15
secure 9.30; Job 5.3
wonder (1)
1 Chr 17.21; Job 37.5

THE BOOK OF
JOB

INTRODUCTION

The book of *Job* is the story of a good man who suffers total disaster—he loses all his children and property and is afflicted with a repulsive disease. Then in three series of poetic dialogues the author shows how Job's friends and Job himself react to these calamities. In the end, God himself, whose dealings with mankind have been a prominent part of the discussion, appears to Job.

The friends of Job explain his suffering in traditional religious terms. Since God, so they assume, always rewards good and punishes evil, the sufferings of Job can only mean that he has sinned. But for Job this is too simple; he does not deserve such cruel punishment, because he has been an unusually good and righteous man. He cannot understand how God can let so much evil happen to one like himself, and he boldly challenges God. Job does not lose his faith, but he does long to be justified before God and to regain his honour as a good man.

God does not give an answer to Job's questions, but he does respond to Job's faith by overwhelming him with a poetic picture of his divine power and wisdom. Job then humbly acknowledges God as wise and great, and repents of the wild and angry words he had used.

The prose conclusion records how Job is restored to his former condition, with even greater prosperity than before. God reprimands Job's friends for failing to understand the meaning of Job's suffering. Only Job had really sensed that God is greater than traditional religion had depicted him.

Outline of Contents

---

being Josh 10.14; 2.1
blame 1 Kgs 2.37; 4.6
bless Neh 13.2; 22.21
curse Neh 13.2; 2.5
enough Esth 5.8; 6.29
escape [4] Ezra 9.8; 11.20
evil [2] Esth 8.3; 2.3
faithful [2] Neh 9.8; 2.3
feast [4] Esth 9.17; 42.11
grief Esth 9.22; 2.12
heaven Esth 4.14; 2.1
hurt 2 Chr 35.23; 2.5
insult Esth 1.16; 19.3
name (2) (name of God, of Jesus) Neh 13.25; Ps 29.2
notice (1) 1 Kgs 21.29; 2.3
offer Neh 13.5; 15.11
power Esth 9.1; 2.6

Satan Tests Job

1 There was a man named Job, living
in the land of Uz,[a] who **worshipped**
God and was **faithful** to him. He was a
good man, careful not to do anything
evil. 2 He had seven sons and three
daughters, 3 and owned seven thousand
sheep, three thousand camels, one thousand head of cattle, and five hundred
donkeys. He also had a large number of
servants and was the **richest** man in the
East.
4 Job's sons used to take it in **turns** to
give a **feast**, to which all the others would
come, and they always invited their
three sisters to join them. 5 The morning
after each **feast**, Job would get up early
and **offer sacrifices** for each of his children in order to **purify** them. He always
did this because he thought that one of
them might have sinned by **insulting** God
unintentionally.
6 When the day came for the **heavenly**
beings[b] to appear before the LORD,
Satan[c] was there among them. 7 The
LORD asked him, "What have you been
doing?"
Satan answered, "I have been walking
here and there, roaming round the
earth."
8 "Did you **notice** my **servant** Job?"
the LORD asked. "There is no one on
earth as **faithful** and good as he is. He

praise Neh 12.24; 29.13
protect Ezra 8.21; 5.20
pure Neh 13.9; 4.17
rich Esth 5.11; 6.27
sacrifice Neh 12.43; 42.8
Satan [5] 1 Chr 21.1; 2.1
servant [7] Esth 6.3; 2.3
shave 1 Chr 19.4; Is 3.17
sheep [2] Neh 10.36; 5.24
shepherd 2 Chr 18.16; Ps 23.1
steal 1 Chr 7.21; 20.10
strike 2 Chr 35.23; 19.21
turn Esth 9.22; 3.4
unintentional Num 15.22; Ezek 45.20

[a] UZ: *An area whose exact location is unknown.*
[b] HEAVENLY BEINGS: *Supernatural beings who serve God in heaven.*
[c] SATAN: *A supernatural being whose name indicates he was regarded as man's opponent.*

1.6: Gen 6.2

worship (1) (of God) [3] Neh 13.14; 2.3

worships me and is careful not to do anything **evil**."

9 **Satan** replied, "Would Job **worship** you if he got nothing out of it? 10 You have always **protected** him and his family and everything he owns. You **bless** everything he does, and you have given him **enough** cattle to fill the whole country. 11 But now suppose you take away everything he has—he will **curse** you to your face!"

12 "All right," the LORD said to **Satan**, "everything he has is in your **power**, but you must not **hurt** Job himself." So **Satan** left.

Job's Children and Wealth Are Destroyed

13 One day when Job's children were having a **feast** at the home of their eldest brother, 14 a messenger came running to Job. "We were ploughing the fields with the oxen," he said, "and the donkeys were in a nearby pasture. 15 Suddenly the Sabeans[d] attacked and **stole** them all. They killed every one of your **servants** except me. I am the only one who **escaped** to tell you."

16 Before he had finished speaking, another **servant** came and said, "Lightning **struck** the **sheep** and the **shepherds** and killed them all. I am the only one who **escaped** to tell you."

17 Before he had finished speaking, another **servant** came and said, "Three bands of Chaldean[e] raiders attacked us, took away the camels, and killed all your **servants** except me. I am the only one who **escaped** to tell you."

18 Before he had finished speaking, another **servant** came and said, "Your children were having a **feast** at the home of your eldest son, 19 when a storm swept in from the desert. It blew the house down and killed them all. I am the only one who **escaped** to tell you."

20 Then Job stood up and tore his clothes in **grief**. He **shaved** his head and threw himself face downwards on the ground. 21 He said, "I was born with nothing, and I will die with nothing. The LORD gave, and now he has taken away. May his **name be praised**!"

22 In spite of everything that had happened, Job did not sin by **blaming** God.

Satan Tests Job Again

2 When the day came for the **heavenly beings** to appear before the LORD again, **Satan** was there among them. 2 The LORD asked him, "Where have you been?"

Satan answered, "I have been walking here and there, roaming round the earth."

3 "Did you **notice** my **servant** Job?" the LORD asked. "There is no one on earth as **faithful** and good as he is. He **worships** me and is careful not to do anything **evil**. You **persuaded** me to let you attack him for no **reason** at all, but Job is still as **faithful** as ever."

4 **Satan** replied, "A man will give up everything in order to stay **alive**. 5 But now suppose you **hurt** his **body**—he will **curse** you to your face!"

6 So the LORD said to **Satan**, "All right, he is in your **power**, but you are not to kill him."

7 Then **Satan** left the LORD's **presence** and made sores break out all over Job's **body**. 8 Job went and sat by the rubbish heap and took a piece of broken pottery to scrape his sores. 9 His wife said to him, "You are still as **faithful** as ever, aren't you? Why don't you **curse** God and die?"

10 Job answered, "You are talking nonsense! When God sends us something good, we **welcome** it. How can we **complain** when he sends us **trouble**?" In spite of everything he **suffered**, Job said nothing against God.

Job's Friends Come

11 Three of Job's **friends** were Eliphaz, from the city of Teman, Bildad, from the land of Shuah, and Zophar, from the land of Naamah. When they heard how much Job had been **suffering**, they decided to go and **comfort** him. 12 While they were still a long way off they saw Job, but did not recognize him. When they did, they began to **weep** and **wail**, tearing their clothes in **grief** and throwing dust into the air and on their heads. 13 Then they sat there on the ground with him for seven days and nights without saying a **word**, because they saw how much he was **suffering**.

Job's Complaint to God

3 Finally Job broke the silence and **cursed** the day on which he had been born.

Job

2-3 O God, put a **curse** on the day I was
born;
put a **curse** on the night when I was
conceived!

comfort 1 Chr 7.22; 15.11
complain Neh 5.1; 10.1
curse [2] 1.11; 3.1
evil 1.1; 3.17
faithful [3] 1.1; 8.20
friend Esth 6.13; 6.1
grief 1.20; 3.10
heaven 1.6; 4.18
hurt 1.12; 5.18
notice (1) 1.8; Ps 10.14
persuade Ezra 7.28; Prov 16.21
power 1.12; 9.4
presence Esth 8.1; 31.37
reason Neh 5.9; 9.17
Satan [5] 1.6; Zech 3.1
servant 1.3; 4.18
suffer [3] Esth 9.25; 9.27
trouble Neh 9.27; 3.10
wail Esth 4.1; Is 15.2
weep Esth 4.3; 30.25
welcome 1 Chr 12.17; 29.23
word (1) 2 Chr 36.12 4.4
worship (1) (of God) 1.1; 4.6

alive Neh 5.2; 4.20
being 1.6; 38.7
body [2] Esth 9.13; 4.14

ancient Ezra 4.15; 8.8
barren 2 Sam 1.21; Is 13.2
cloud Neh 9.12; 7.9
command Esth 9.31; 6.10
control Esth 5.10; 32.2
curse [5] 2.5; 5.3
dark [2] 2 Chr 6.1; 5.14

[d] SABEANS: *A tribe of wandering raiders from the south.*
[e] CHALDEANS: *A tribe of wandering raiders from the north.*

1.9–11: Rev 12.10 **3.1–19:** Jer 20.14–18

dead 2 Chr 24.17; 26.5
death (1) Esth 2.7; 5.2
enjoy Neh 9.25; 10.20
evil 2.3; 4.8
fear Neh 1.5; 4.14
free [2] Ezra 9.8; 5.23
gloom 1 Kgs 21.27; 10.21
grave [2] 2 Chr 34.4; 7.21
grief [2] 2.12; 6.1
groan Judg 2.18; 23.1
happy Esth 9.22; 5.17
hope Esth 9.1; 4.6
joy Esth 9.17; 5.11
keep from Neh 5.3; 9.7
knee 2 Kgs 1.13; Ps 109.24
Leviathan 41.1
light (1) [2] Neh 9.12; 10.22
misery Neh 4.2; 7.15
mourn Esth 9.31; 5.11
never again [2] Esth 1.19; 7.8
peace [2] Esth 9.30; 5.24
prison Neh 7.6; 12.14
remember Esth 9.28; 7.7
rest (1) [3] Ezra 8.32; 7.13
slave Esth 7.4; 6.27
trouble [2] 2.10; 4.5
true Esth 2.23; 5.27
turn 1.4; 4.5
wicked Neh 1.7; 4.8
wish Esth 9.30; 11.5
womb Gen 25.22; 10.10

4 **Turn** that day into **darkness**, God.
Never again remember that day;
never again let **light** shine on it.
5 Make it a day of **gloom** and thick
darkness;
cover it with **clouds**, and blot out the
sun.
6 Blot that night out of the year,
and never let it be counted again;
7 make it a **barren, joyless** night.
8 Tell the sorcerers to **curse** that day,
those who know how to **control**
Leviathan.[f]
9 **Keep the morning star from** shining;
give that night no **hope** of dawn.
10 **Curse** that night for letting me be born,
for exposing me to **trouble** and **grief**.

11 I **wish** I had died in my mother's **womb**
or died the moment I was born.
12 Why did my mother hold me on her
knees?
Why did she feed me at her breast?
13 If I had died then, I would be at **rest**
now,
14 sleeping like the kings and rulers
who rebuilt **ancient** palaces.
15 Then I would be sleeping like princes
who filled their houses with gold and
silver,
16 or sleeping like a still-born child.
17 In the **grave wicked** men stop their
evil,
and tired workmen find **rest** at last.
18 Even **prisoners enjoy peace**,
free from shouts and harsh
commands.
19 Everyone is there, the famous and the
unknown,
and **slaves** at last are **free**.

20 Why let men go on living in **misery**?
Why give **light** to men in **grief**?
21 They wait for **death**, but it never
comes;
they prefer a **grave** to any treasure.
22 They are not **happy** till they are **dead**
and buried;
23 God keeps their future hidden
and hems them in on every side.
24 Instead of eating, I **mourn**,
and I can never stop **groaning**.
25 Everything I **fear** and dread comes
true.
26 I have no **peace**, no **rest**,
and my **troubles** never end.

The First Dialogue

(4.1—14.22)

4 *Eliphaz*
1-2 Job, will you be annoyed if I
speak?
I can't keep quiet any longer.
3 You have **taught** many people
and given **strength** to feeble hands.
4 When someone **stumbled, weak** and
tired,
your **words encouraged** him to
stand.
5 Now it's your **turn** to be in **trouble**,
and you are too stunned to face it.
6 You **worshipped** God, and your **life** was
blameless;
and so you should have **confidence**
and **hope**.
7 Think back now. Name a single case
where a **righteous** man met with
disaster.
8 I have seen people plough fields of **evil**
and **sow wickedness** like **seed**;
now they **harvest wickedness** and
evil.
9 Like a storm, God **destroys** them in his
anger.
10 The **wicked** roar and growl like lions,
but God silences them and breaks
their teeth.
11 Like lions with nothing to kill and eat,
they die, and all their children are
scattered.

12 Once a **message** came quietly,
so quietly I could hardly hear it.
13 Like a nightmare it disturbed my
sleep.
14 I **trembled** and shuddered;
my whole **body** shook with **fear**.
15 A light breeze touched my face,
and my hair bristled with **fright**.
16 I could see something standing there;
I stared, but couldn't tell what it was.
Then I heard a voice out of the silence:
17 "Can anyone be **righteous** in the **sight**
of[g] God
or be **pure** before[h] his **Creator**?
18 God does not **trust** his **heavenly**
servants;
he finds **fault** even with his **angels**.
19 Do you think he will **trust** a **creature** of
clay,
a thing of dust that can be crushed
like a moth?
20 A man may be **alive** in the morning,
but die unnoticed before evening
comes.
21 All that he has is taken away;

alive 2.4; 5.20
angel 2 Chr 32.21; 5.1
anger Esth 7.10; 7.11
blame 1.22; 12.4
body 2.5; 6.4
confident 2 Chr 32.7; 29.24
Creator 2 Chr 2.12; 35.10
creature 2 Chr 5.7; 12.8
destroy Esth 9.24; 5.21
disaster Esth 8.6; 15.24
encourage Ezra 6.14; 29.24
evil [2] 3.17; 5.6
fault 2 Sam 22.24; 6.24
fear 3.25; 6.21
fright Neh 6.9; 13.25
harvest Neh 10.35; 5.26
heaven 2.1; 9.8
hope 3.9; 5.16
life (1) Esth 7.7; 7.1
message Esth 4.10; Ps 19.4
pure 1.5; 8.6
righteous [2] 1 Sam 26.23; 12.4
scatter Esth 3.8; Ps 18.14
seed Judg 6.3; Ps 126.5
servant 2.3; 19.15
sight 2 Chr 20.32; 11.4
sow 2 Kgs 19.29; Ps 107.37
strength Neh 1.10; 6.11
stumble 1 Chr 13.9; 18.7
teach Neh 9.13; 6.24
tremble Ezra 10.9; 18.20
trouble 3.10; 5.6
trust [2] Neh 13.13; 8.14
turn 3.4; 5.1
weak Neh 4.10; 14.1
wicked [3] 3.17; 5.16
wisdom Ezra 7.25; 8.8
word (1) 2.13; 6.3
worship (1) (of God) 2.3; 33.26

[f] LEVIATHAN: *Some take this to be the crocodile, others a legendary monster. Magicians were thought to be able to make him cause eclipses of the sun.*
[g] righteous in the sight of; *or* more righteous than. [h] be pure before; *or* be more pure than.

3.21: Rev 9.6 **4.13:** Job 33.15

accept Esth 4.4; 17.3
afraid Esth 9.2; 9.35
alive 4.20; 10.12
angel 4.18; 15.15
case (2) Ezra 10.17; 9.1
correct Deut 8.5; 33.19
court (1) Esth 1.4; 9.19
curse 3.1; 24.18
dark 3.4; 10.21
death (1) 3.21; 11.20
death (2) (from death) [2] 2 Chr 22.11; 33.18
death (3) (to death) Esth 3.9; Ps 94.21
defend Esth 9.16; 13.8
destroy 4.9; 9.5
envy 1 Sam 2.32; Prov 23.17
evil 4.8; 8.16
famine 2 Chr 20.9; Ps 33.19
fool [3] 2 Chr 16.9; 12.17
free 3.18; 12.14
happy 3.22; 7.7
harm Esth 9.2; 7.20
harvest 4.8; 24.6
heal 2 Kgs 20.5; 13.4
hope 4.6; 6.11
humble Esth 7.3; 12.19
hunger [2] Neh 9.15; 18.12
hurt 2.5; 10.16
joy 3.7; 6.10
learn Esth 4.1; 8.8
miracle Neh 9.10; 9.10
mourn 3.24; 16.15
need Neh 10.33; 6.14
oppress Neh 9.10; 15.20
peace 3.18; 12.6
plan Esth 9.24; 10.13
poor [2] Esth 9.22; 20.10
present (1) Ezra 7.19; 23.4
protect 1.10; 11.18
raise Neh 8.6; Ps 63.4
rebuke 2 Sam 22.16; Ps 6.1
rescue Neh 9.27; 22.30
ripe [2] Neh 13.31; 15.33
safe [2] Esth 4.13; 15.21
save [4] Esth 7.9; 6.13
scheme 10.3
secure Esth 10.3; 11.18
sense Esth 8.16; 7.16
sheep 1.3; 24.2
slander Ps 15.3
study Neh 8.13; Ps 1.2
succeed (1) Neh 2.20; 10.16
sure Neh 13.19; 38.21
trap 2 Sam 22.6; 18.9
trouble [2] 4.5; 6.1
true 3.25; 11.4
turn [2] 4.5; 6.13
understand Neh 10.28; 9.10
upset 2 Kgs 6.11; 20.1
violent 1 Chr 17.9; 16.17
wicked 4.8; 8.22
wise Esth 6.13; 8.10

he dies, still lacking wisdom."

5 Call out, Job. See if anyone answers.
Is there any angel to whom you can
turn?
2 To worry yourself to death with
resentment
would be a foolish, senseless thing to
do.
3 I have seen fools who looked secure,
but I called down a sudden curse on
their homes.
4 Their sons can never find safety;
no one stands up to defend them in
court.
5 Hungry people will eat the fool's
crops—
even the grain growing among
thorns[i]—
and thirsty people will envy his
wealth.
6 Evil does not grow in the soil,
nor does trouble grow out of the
ground.
7 No indeed! Man brings trouble on
himself,
as surely as sparks fly up from a
fire.[j]

8 If I were you, I would turn to God
and present my case to him.
9 We cannot understand the great things
he does,
and to his miracles there is no end.
10 He sends rain on the land
and he waters the fields.
11 Yes, it is God who raises the humble
and gives joy to all who mourn.
12-13 He upsets the plans of cunning men,
and traps wise men in their own
schemes,
so that nothing they do succeeds;
14 even at noon they grope in darkness.
15 But God saves the poor[k] from death;
he saves the needy from oppression.
16 He gives hope to the poor and silences
the wicked.

17 Happy is the person whom God
corrects!
Do not resent it when he rebukes
you.
18 God bandages the wounds he makes;
his hand hurts you, and his hand
heals.
19 Time after time he will save you from
harm;
20 when famine comes, he will keep
you alive,
and in war protect you from death.
21 God will rescue you from slander;
he will save you when destruction
comes.
22 You will laugh at violence and hunger
and not be afraid of wild animals.
23 The fields you plough will be free of
rocks;
wild animals will never attack you.
24 Then you will live at peace in your
tent;
when you look at your sheep, you
will find them safe.
25 You will have as many children
as there are blades of grass in a
pasture.
26 Like wheat that ripens till harvest
time,
you will live to a ripe old age.
27 Job, we have learnt this by long study.
It is true, so now accept it.

worry Neh 4.14; 30.27

Almighty 1 Chr 17.7; 8.5
body [2] 4.14; 7.5
bribe Neh 6.12; 15.34
command 3.18; 23.12
condemn 2 Chr 21.12; 9.20
convince Ezra 4.16; 17.9
deceive 2 Chr 32.11; 12.16
despair Esth 9.22; 11.20
enemy Esth 9.1; 9.13
enough 1.10; 7.19
fate Esth 9.25; 15.25
fault 4.18; 10.6
fear 4.14; 15.4
forsake Neh 9.17; 19.13
friend [3] 2.11; 12.4
gift Esth 9.19; Ps 16.6
grief 3.10; 7.3
help Esth 9.3; 8.6
holy Neh 13.22; Ps 5.7
honest Neh 13.13; 8.6
hope [2] 5.16; 7.6
joy 5.11; 8.19
lie (2) [2] 2 Chr 18.21; 13.4
loyal 2 Chr 36.13; Ps 32.6
need 5.15; 15.6
orphan Deut 27.19; 22.9
pain Neh 9.21; 7.13
prayer Neh 11.17; 12.4
rich 1.3; 15.29
right (1) [2] Esth 8.5; 8.3
save [2] 5.15; 10.7
slave 3.19; 7.2
strength [2] 4.3; 10.10
teach 4.3; 8.10
terror Esth 7.6; 9.34
trouble [2] 5.6; 10.15
turn 5.1; 8.5
unjust Deut 16.19; 34.12
word (1) [3] 4.4; 9.14
wrong Neh 5.9; 7.21

6 *Job*
1-2 If my troubles and griefs were
weighed on scales,
3 they would weigh more than the
sands of the sea,
so my wild words should not surprise
you.
4 Almighty God has pierced me with
arrows,
and their poison spreads through my
body.
God has lined up his terrors against
me.

5 A donkey is content when eating grass,
and a cow is quiet when eating hay.
6 But who can eat tasteless, unsalted
food?
What flavour is there in the white of
an egg?
7 I have no appetite for food like that,
and everything I eat makes me
sick.[l]

8 Why won't God give me what I ask?
Why won't he answer my prayer?
9 If only he would go ahead and kill me!
10 If I knew he would, I would leap for
joy,
no matter how great my pain.
I know that God is holy;
I have never opposed what he
commands.
11 What strength have I got to keep on
living?
Why go on living when I have no
hope?
12 Am I made of stone? Is my body
bronze?

[i] *Probable text* even...thorns; *Hebrew unclear.* [j] sparks fly up from a fire; *or* birds fly up to the sky.
[k] *Probable text* poor; *Hebrew unclear.* [l] *Probable text* sick; *Hebrew unclear.*

5.13: 1 Cor 3.19 **5.17:** Prov 3.11; Heb 12.5–6 **5.18:** Hos 6.1

[13] I have no **strength** left to **save** myself;
there is nowhere I can **turn** for **help**.

[14] **In trouble**[m] like this I **need loyal friends**—
whether I've **forsaken** God or not.
[15] But you, my **friends**, you **deceive** me like streams
that go dry when no rain comes.
[16] The streams are choked with snow and ice,
[17] but in the heat they disappear,
and the stream beds lie bare and dry.
[18] Caravans get lost looking for water;
they wander and die in the desert.
[19] Caravans from Sheba and Tema search,
[20] but their **hope** dies beside dry streams.
[21] You are like[n] those streams to me,[o]
you see my **fate** and draw back in **fear**.
[22] Have I asked you to give me a **gift**
or to **bribe** someone on my behalf
[23] or to **save** me from some **enemy** or tyrant?

[24] All right, **teach me**; tell me my **faults**.
I will be quiet and listen to you.
[25] **Honest words** are **convincing**,
but you are talking nonsense.
[26] You think I am talking nothing but wind;
then why do you answer my **words** of **despair**?
[27] You would even throw dice for **orphan slaves**
and make yourselves **rich** off your closest **friends**!
[28] Look me in the face. I won't lie.
[29] You have gone far **enough**. Stop being **unjust**.
Don't **condemn** me. I'm in the **right**.
[30] But you think I am **lying**—
you think I can't tell **right** from **wrong**.

7

Human life is like **forced army** service,
like a life of **hard** manual labour,
[2] like a **slave longing** for cool shade;
like a worker waiting for his pay.
[3] Month after month I have nothing to live for;
night after night brings me **grief**.
[4] When I lie down to sleep, the hours drag;
I toss all night and **long** for dawn.
[5] My **body** is full of worms;
it is covered with scabs;
pus runs out of my sores.
[6] My days pass by without **hope**,
pass faster than a weaver's shuttle.[p]

[7] **Remember**, O God, my **life** is only a breath;
my **happiness** has already ended.
[8] You see me now, but **never again**.
If you look for me, I'll be gone.
[9–10] Like a **cloud** that fades and is gone,
a man dies and never returns;
he is **forgotten** by all who knew him.
[11] No! I can't be quiet!
I am **angry** and **bitter**.
I have to speak.

[12] Why do you keep me under guard?
Do you think I am a **sea-monster**?[q]
[13] I lie down and try to **rest**;
I look for **relief** from my **pain**.
[14] But you—you **terrify** me with **dreams**;
you send me **visions** and nightmares
[15] until I would rather be strangled
than live in this **miserable body**.
[16] I give up; I am tired of living.
Leave me **alone**. My **life** makes no **sense**.

[17] Why is man so **important** to you?
Why pay attention to what he does?
[18] You inspect him every morning
and **test** him every minute.
[19] Won't you look away long **enough**
for me to swallow my spittle?
[20] Are you **harmed** by my sin, you **jailer**?
Why use me for your target-practice?
Am I so great a **burden** to you?
[21] Can't you ever **forgive** my sin?
Can't you pardon the **wrong** I do?
Soon I will be in my **grave**,
and I'll be gone when you look for me.

8

Bildad

[1–2] Are you finally through with your windy **speech**?
[3] God never twists **justice**;
he never **fails** to do what is **right**.
[4] Your children must have sinned against God,

[m] *Probable text* trouble; *Hebrew unclear.* [n] *Probable text* like; *Hebrew* because.
[o] *Some ancient translations and one Hebrew manuscript* to me; *most Hebrew manuscripts have two different expressions:* nothing *in the text and* to him *in the margin.*
[p] WEAVER'S SHUTTLE: *A small device in the loom which carries threads to and fro rapidly in weaving cloth.*
[q] SEA-MONSTER: *A reference to ancient stories in which sea-monsters had to be guarded so that they would not escape and do damage.*

7.17: Ps 8.4, 144.3

force (1) Esth 10.1; 9.19
forget Neh 9.17; 8.13
forgive Neh 9.17; 10.14
grave 3.17; 10.19
grief 6.1; 14.22
happy 5.17; 20.5
hard Ezra 10.9; 14.6
harm 5.19; 10.13
hope 6.11; 8.13
human Neh 9.5; 9.32
important Esth 5.11; 29.10
jail Gen 39.21; Mt 5.25
life (1) [3] 4.6; 8.9
long (2) [2] 2 Sam 13.39; Ps 38.9
misery 3.20; 10.15
monster Gen 1.21; 9.8
never again 3.4; Ps 77.7
pain 6.10; 9.27
relieve (1) Esth 8.16; 30.16
remember 3.4; 10.9
rest (1) 3.13; 11.18
sense 5.2; 12.3
service Esth 3.2; 38.35
slave 6.27; 24.9
terrify Neh 9.32; 41.14
test 2 Chr 32.31; 23.10
vision 2 Chr 32.32; 20.8
wrong 6.30; 11.14

alone Esth 9.12; 10.20
anger 4.9; 9.5
bitter Esth 4.1; 9.18
body [2] 6.4; 10.11
burden Neh 5.15; Ps 38.4
cloud 3.5; 20.6
dream 1 Kgs 18.27; 20.8
enough 6.29; 15.31

abandon Neh 9.19; Ps 9.10
Almighty 6.4; 15.25
ancient [2] 3.14; 20.4
compare 1 Kgs 20.27; 28.19
deserve Ezra 9.13; 11.6
disgrace Neh 2.17; 12.21

evil [3] 5.6; 11.11
fail Neh 9.35; 17.11
faithful 2.3; 9.20
forget 7.9; 9.27
godless 1 Chr 10.4; 12.6
hate Esth 9.16; 16.9
help [3] 6.13; 9.8
honest 6.25; 17.3
hope 7.6; 11.18
joy 6.10; 22.26
justice Ezra 9.15; 16.18
learn 5.27; 15.10
life (1) 7.1; 9.18
plead Esth 4.8; 16.21
punish Esth 7.7; 9.34
pure 4.17; 11.4
restore Neh 7.70; Ps 3.3
reward Esth 6.3; 15.31
right (1) 6.29; 10.3
speech Num 22.28; 11.3
teach 6.24; 12.7
trust 4.18; 12.20
truth 2 Chr 18.15; 15.18
turn 6.13; 12.15
vanish Num 16.33; 15.29
weed [2] 2 Kgs 19.26; 24.24
wicked 5.16; 9.24
wisdom 4.21; 11.6
wise 5.12; 9.4

and so he **punished** them as they
deserved.
5 But **turn** now and **plead** with **Almighty**
God;
6 if you are so **honest** and **pure**,
then God will come and **help** you
and **restore** your household as your
reward.
7 All the wealth you lost will be nothing
compared with what God will give
you then.

8 Look for a moment at **ancient wisdom**;
consider the **truths** our fathers
learnt.
9 Our **life** is short, we know nothing at
all;
we pass like shadows across the
earth.
10 But let the **ancient wise** men **teach**
you;
listen to what they had to say:

11 "Reeds can't grow where there is no
water;
they are never found outside a
swamp.
12 If the water dries up, they are the first
to wither,
while still too small to be cut and
used.
13 **Godless** men are like those reeds;
their **hope** is gone, once God is
forgotten.
14 They **trust** a thread—a spider's web.
15 If they lean on a web, will it hold
them up?
If they grab for a thread, will it **help**
them stand?"

16 **Evil** men sprout like **weeds** in the sun,
like **weeds** that spread all through
the garden.
17 Their roots wrap round the stones
and hold fast to[r] every rock.
18 But then pull them up—
no one will ever know they were
there.
19 Yes, that's all the **joy evil** men have;
others now come and take their
places.

20 But God will never **abandon** the
faithful
or ever give **help** to **evil** men.
21 He will let you laugh and shout again,
22 but he will bring **disgrace** on those
who **hate** you,
and the homes of the **wicked** will
vanish.

9

Job

1-2 Yes, I've heard all that before.
But how can a man **win** his **case**
against God?
3 How can anyone **argue** with him?
He can ask a thousand **questions**
that no one could ever answer.[s]
4 God is so **wise** and **powerful**;
no man can stand up against him.
5 Without **warning** he moves mountains
and in **anger** he **destroys** them.
6 God sends earthquakes and shakes the
ground;
he rocks the pillars that support the
earth.
7 He can **keep the sun from rising**,
and the stars from shining at night.
8 No one **helped** God spread out the
heavens
or trample the **sea-monster's** back.[t]
9 God hung the stars in the sky—the
Great Bear,
Orion, the Pleiades, and the stars of
the south.
10 We cannot **understand** the great things
he does,
and to his **miracles** there is no end.

11 God passes by, but I cannot see him.
12 He takes what he wants, and no one
can stop him;
no one **dares** ask him, "What are you
doing?"
13 **God's anger** is **constant**. He crushed
his **enemies**
who **helped** Rahab,[u] the **sea-monster**, oppose him.
14 So how can I find **words** to answer
God?
15 Though I am **innocent**, all I can do
is **beg** for **mercy** from God my **judge**.
16 Yet even then, if he lets me speak,
I can't **believe** he would listen to me.
17 He sends storms to batter and bruise
me
without any **reason** at all.
18 He won't let me get my breath;
he has filled my **life** with **bitterness**.
19 Should I try **force**? Try **force** on God?
Should I take him to **court**? Could
anyone make him go?[v]

afraid 5.22; 11.19
anger [2] 7.11; 10.17
argue 1 Kgs 3.22; 13.3
ashamed Ezra 9.6; 42.6
beg Esth 8.3; 19.16
believe 2 Chr 32.15; 22.17
bitter 7.11; 10.1
blind 2 Kgs 6.18; 17.7
care Esth 8.5; 10.12
case (2) 5.8; 13.3
condemn 6.29; 10.2
constant 1 Kgs 5.3; 10.12
court (1) [2] 5.4; 13.8
dare Esth 7.5; 13.16
destroy [2] 5.21; 10.8
enemy 6.23; 11.19
faithful 8.20; 23.11
filthy Ezra 9.11; Prov 30.12
force (1) [2] 7.1; 24.4
forget 8.13; 19.15
guilty [4] Ezra 10.10; 10.7
heart Ezra 1.5; 11.13
heaven 4.18; 16.19
help [2] 8.6; 11.19
human 7.1; 11.6
innocent [5] 2 Chr 6.22; 22.19
judge [3] Ezra 10.14; 14.3
keep from 3.9; 22.14
life (1) [2] 8.9; 10.5
matter 2 Sam 13.4; Ps 10.4
mercy Esth 7.8; 33.24
miracle 5.9; 10.16
monster [2] 7.12; 26.12
pain 7.13; 14.22
power 2.6; 11.7
punish 8.4; 11.6
quarrel 2 Kgs 5.7; 21.4
question Esth 1.13; 38.2
race (2) 39.24
reason 2.3; 17.4
rise Esth 5.9; 14.12
suffer 2.10; 17.5
terror 6.4; 13.11
understand 5.9; 13.1
warn Esth 4.13; 33.16
wicked 8.22; 10.3
win Esth 5.2; 14.21
wise 8.10; 11.12
word (1) [2] 6.3; 11.3
world Ezra 1.2; 11.15

[r] *Probable text* hold fast to; *Hebrew* see.
[s] He can ask...answer; *or* A man could ask him a thousand questions, and he would not answer.
[t] TRAMPLE THE SEA-MONSTER'S BACK: *A reference to ancient stories in which a sea-monster was killed and then trampled on (see also 26.13).*
[u] RAHAB: *A legendary sea-monster which represented the forces of chaos and evil.*
[v] *Probable text* make him go; *Hebrew* make me go.

9.2: Job 4.17 **9.9:** Job 38.31; Amos 5.8

20 I am **innocent** and **faithful**, but my
words sound **guilty**,
and everything I say seems to
condemn me.
21-22 I am **innocent**, but I no longer **care**.
I am sick of living. Nothing **matters**;
innocent or **guilty**, God will **destroy**
us.
23 When an **innocent** man suddenly dies,
God laughs.
24 God gave the **world** to the **wicked**.
He made all the **judges blind**.
And if God didn't do it, who did?

25 My days **race** by, not one of them good.
26 My **life** passes like the swiftest boat,
as fast as an eagle swooping down
on a rabbit.
27-28 If I smile and try to **forget** my **pain**,
all my **suffering** comes back to
haunt me;
I know that God does hold me **guilty**.
29 Since I am held **guilty**, why should I
bother?
30 No soap can wash away my sins.
31 God throws me into a pit of **filth**,
and even my clothes are **ashamed** of
me.
32 If God were **human**, I could answer
him;
we could go to **court** to decide our
quarrel.
33 But there is no one to step between
us—
no one to **judge** both God and me.
34 Stop **punishing** me, God!
Keep your **terrors** away!
35 I am not **afraid**. I am going to talk
because I know my own **heart**.

10 I am tired of living.
Listen to my **bitter complaint**.
2 Don't **condemn** me, God.
Tell me! What is the **charge** against
me?
3 Is it **right** for you to be so **cruel**?
To **despise** what you yourself have
made?
And then to smile on the **schemes** of
wicked men?
4 Do you see things as we do?
5 Is your **life** as short as ours?
6 Then why do you track down all my
sins
and hunt down every **fault** I have?
7 You know that I am not **guilty**,
that no one can **save** me from you.

8 Your hands formed and shaped me,
and now[w] those same hands **destroy**
me.
9 **Remember** that you made me from
clay;[x]
are you going to crush me back to
dust?
10 You gave my father **strength** to beget
me;
you made me grow in my mother's
womb.
11 You formed my **body** with bones and
sinews
and covered the bones with muscles
and skin.
12 You have given me **life** and **constant**
love,
and your **care** has kept me **alive**.
13 But now I know that all that time
you were **secretly planning** to **harm**
me.
14 You were **watching** to see if I would
sin,
so that you could **refuse** to **forgive**
me.
15 As soon as I sin, I'm in **trouble** with
you,
but when I do **right**, I get no credit.
I am **miserable** and covered with
shame.[y]
16 If I have any **success** at all,
you hunt me down like a lion;
to **hurt** me you even work **miracles**.
17 You always have some **witness** against
me;
your **anger** towards me grows and
grows;
you always **plan** some **new** attack.

18 Why, God, did you let me be born?
I should have died before anyone
saw me.
19 To go from the **womb** straight to the
grave
would have been as good as never
existing.
20 Isn't my **life** almost over? Leave me
alone!
Let me **enjoy** the time I have left.
21 I am going soon and will never come
back—
going to a land that is **dark** and
gloomy,
22 a land of darkness, shadows, and
confusion,
where the **light** itself is **darkness**.

11 *Zophar*
1-2 Will no one answer all this
nonsense?

[w] *Some ancient translations* and now; *Hebrew* together.
[x] *One ancient translation* from clay; *Hebrew* like clay.
[y] *Probable text* covered with shame; *Hebrew* see my shame.

alive 5.20; 33.28
alone 7.16; 14.6
anger 9.5; 14.13
bitter 9.18; 13.26
body 7.5; 14.22
care 9.21; 18.21
charge (3) Ezra 4.6; 13.23
complain 2.10; 23.1
condemn 9.20; 15.6
constant 9.13; Ps 13.5
cruel 2 Chr 16.10; 29.17
dark [2] 5.14; 11.17
despise 2 Kgs 19.21; 19.18
destroy 9.5; 12.23
enjoy 3.18; 12.11
exist 2 Chr 9.19; Ps 93.2
fault 6.24; 34.32
forgive 7.21; 14.17
gloom 3.5; 30.28
grave 7.21; 17.1
guilty 9.20; 16.8
harm 7.20; 35.6
hurt 5.18; 18.4

life (1) [3] 9.18; 11.17
light (1) 3.4; 12.22
love Neh 13.22; 19.19
miracle 9.10; Ps 77.14
misery 7.15; 20.22
new Esth 2.8; 32.19
plan [2] 5.12; 15.8
refuse (1) Esth 3.2; 22.7
remember 7.7; 11.16
right (1) [2] 8.3; 11.1
save 6.13; 13.16
scheme 5.12; Ps 73.7
secret Esth 2.10; 15.18
shame 1 Kgs 21.26; 19.3
strength 6.11; 12.6
succeed (1) 5.12; 20.22
trouble 6.1; 11.16
watch Ezra 5.5; 13.27
wicked 9.24; 11.20
witness 1 Chr 24.6; Ps 50.4
womb [2] 3.11; 38.8

afraid 9.35; 19.29
arrest 2 Chr 18.25; Is 53.8

Does talking so much put a man in
the **right**?
3 Job, do you think we can't answer
you?
That your **mocking words** will leave
us **speechless**?
4 You **claim** that what you say is **true**;
you **claim** you are **pure** in the **sight**
of God.
5 How I **wish** God would answer you!
6 He would tell you there are many sides
to **wisdom**;
there are things too deep for **human**
knowledge.
God is **punishing** you less than you
deserve.

7 Can you discover the limits and bounds
of the greatness and **power of God**?
8 The sky is no limit for God,
but it lies beyond your reach.
God knows the **world of the dead**,
but you do not know it.
9 God's greatness is broader than the
earth,
wider than the sea.
10 If God **arrests** you and brings you to
trial,
who is there to stop him?
11 God knows which men are **worthless**;
he sees all their **evil** deeds.
12 **Stupid** men will start being **wise**
when wild donkeys are born tame.

13 Put your **heart right**, Job. Reach out to
God.
14 Put away **evil** and **wrong** from your
home.
15 Then face the **world** again, firm and
courageous.
16 Then all your **troubles** will fade from
your memory,
like **floods** that are past and
remembered no more.
17 Your **life** will be brighter than
sunshine at noon,
and **life's darkest** hours will shine
like the dawn.
18 You will live **secure** and full of **hope**;
God will **protect** you and give you
rest.
19 You won't be **afraid** of your **enemies**;
many people will ask you for **help**.
20 But the **wicked** will look round in
despair
and find that there is no way to
escape.
Their one **hope** is that **death** will come.

12

Job

1-2 Yes, you are the voice of the
people.
When you die, **wisdom** will die with
you.
3 But I have as much **sense** as you have;
I am in no way inferior to you;
everyone knows all that you have
said.
4 Even my **friends** laugh at me now;
they laugh, although I am **righteous**
and **blameless**;
but there was a time when God
answered my **prayers**.
5 You have no **troubles**, and yet you
make fun of me;
you hit a man who is about to fall.
6 But **thieves** and **godless** men live in
peace,
though their only **god** is their own
strength.

7 Even birds and animals have much
they could **teach** you;
8 ask the **creatures** of earth and sea
for their **wisdom**.
9 All of them know that the LORD's hand
made them.
10 It is God who **directs the lives** of his
creatures;
every man's **life** is in his **power**.
11 But just as your tongue **enjoys** tasting
food,
your ears **enjoy** hearing **words**.

12-13 Old men have **wisdom**,
but God has wisdom and **power**.
Old men have **insight**;
God has **insight** and **power** to **act**.
14 When God tears down, who can
rebuild,
and who can **free** the man God
imprisons?
15 Drought comes when God withholds
rain;
floods come when he **turns** water
loose.

16 God is **strong** and always **victorious**;
both **deceived** and deceiver are in
his **power**.
17 He takes away the **wisdom** of rulers
and makes leaders **act** like **fools**.
18 He **dethrones** kings and makes them
prisoners;
19 he **humbles priests** and men of
power.
20 He silences men who are **trusted**,
and takes the **wisdom** of old men
away.
21 He **disgraces** those in **power**
and puts an end to the **strength** of
rulers.
22 He sends **light** to places **dark** as **death**.
23 He makes nations **strong** and great,

but then he defeats and **destroys**
them.
24 He makes their leaders **foolish**
and lets them wander confused and
lost;
25 they grope in the **dark** and stagger
like drunkards.

accuse 2 Chr 6.22; 21.31
agree Neh 9.38; 34.32
argue [3] 9.3; 23.4
ash Esth 4.1; 42.6
benefit Deut 10.13; 22.3
bind 2 Chr 2.16; 33.11
bitter 10.1; 17.2
bold Gen 18.27; Prov 7.11
case (2) [5] 9.1; 23.4
charge (3) [2] 10.2; 31.35
court (1) 9.19; 31.21
crime 2 Chr 25.4; Ps 35.11
dare 9.12; 41.10
defend 5.4; 15.3
dispute 2 Chr 19.8; Is 2.4
enemy 11.19; 16.8
fool 12.17; 15.31
fright 4.15; 27.23
heal 5.18; Ps 30.2
hope 11.18; 14.7
ignorant Num 15.24; 34.35
lie (2) [3] 6.28; 21.34
life (1) 12.10; 14.1
power 12.10; 15.24
proverb 1 Kgs 4.32; 17.5
punish 11.6; 20.23
reprimand Neh 13.11; 22.4
right (1) 11.1; 17.9
save 10.7; 20.26
terror [2] 9.34; 15.21
understand 9.10; 22.18
useless 2 Sam 1.27; 35.13
watch 10.14; 14.16
wicked 11.20; 15.5
wise 11.12; 15.3
word (1) 12.11; 15.1
wrong 11.14; 14.17

13 1-2 Everything you say, I have
heard before.
I **understand** it all; I know as much
as you do.
I'm not your inferior.
3 But my **dispute** is with God, not you;
I want to **argue** my **case** with him.
4 You cover up your **ignorance** with **lies**;
you are like doctors who can't **heal**
anyone.
5 Say nothing, and someone may think
you are **wise**!

6 Listen while I state my **case**.
7 Why are you **lying**?
Do you think your **lies** will **benefit**
God?
8 Are you trying to **defend** him?
Are you going to **argue** his **case** in
court?
9 If God looks at you closely, will he find
anything good?
Do you think you can **fool** God as
you fool men?
10 Even though your prejudice is hidden,
he will **reprimand** you,
11 and his **power** will fill you with
terror.
12 Your **proverbs** are as **useless** as **ashes**;
your **arguments** crumble like clay.
13 Be quiet and give me a chance to
speak,
and let the results be what they will.

14 I am[z] ready to risk my **life**.
15 I've lost all **hope**, so what if God kills
me?
I am going to state my **case** to him.
16 It may even be that my **boldness** will
save me,
since no **wicked** man would **dare** to
face God.
17 Now listen to my **words** of explanation.
18 I am ready to state my **case**,
because I know I am in the **right**.

19 Are you coming to **accuse** me, God?
If you do, I am ready to be silent and
die.
20 Let me ask for two things; **agree** to
them,
and I will not try to hide from you:
21 stop **punishing** me, and don't crush
me with **terror**.

22 Speak first, O God, and I will answer.
Or let me speak, and you answer
me.
23 What are my sins? What **wrongs** have
I done?
What **crimes** am I **charged** with?

24 Why do you avoid me?
Why do you treat me like an
enemy?
25 Are you trying to **frighten** me? I'm
nothing but a leaf;
you are attacking a piece of dry
straw.

26 You bring **bitter charges** against me,
even for what I did when I was
young.
27 You **bind** chains on my feet;
you **watch** every step I take,
and even examine my footprints.
28 As a result, I crumble like rotten wood,
like a moth-eaten coat.

14 We are all born **weak** and
helpless.
All lead the same short, **troubled**
life.
2 We grow and wither as quickly as
flowers;
we disappear like shadows.
3 Will you even look at me, God,
or put me on **trial** and **judge** me?
4 Nothing **clean** can ever come
from anything as **unclean** as man.
5 The length of his **life** is decided
beforehand—
the number of months he will live.
You have **settled** it, and it can't be
changed.
6 Look away from him and leave him
alone;[a]
let him **enjoy** his **hard life**—if he
can.[b]

7 There is **hope** for a tree that has been
cut down;
it can come back **to life** and sprout.
8 Even though its roots grow old,
and its stump dies in the ground,
9 with water it will sprout like a young
plant.
10 But a man dies, and that is the end of
him;
he dies, and where is he then?

alone 10.20; 15.8
anger 10.17; 15.12
body 10.11; 18.13
change Esth 1.19; 23.13
clean Ezra 6.20; 37.21
creature 12.8; 28.21
death (1) 12.22; 18.14
destroy 12.23; 15.28
disgrace 12.21; 36.14
endure Esth 8.6; Ps 13.2
enjoy 12.11; 20.12
forgive 10.14; Ps 25.7
grief 7.3; 17.7
hard 7.1; 28.9
helpless Neh 5.5; 30.11
honour Esth 10.3; 31.27
hope [2] 13.15; 15.22
judge 9.15; 19.29
life (1) [4] 13.14; 17.1
life (2) (to life) [2] Neh 9.29; Ps 16.11
mind (1) 1 Chr 28.9; 17.4
pain 9.27; 16.6
please Esth 9.13; 31.29
remember 11.16; 18.17
rise 9.7; 41.18
settle (2) 1 Chr 26.29; Prov 18.18
trouble [2] 12.5; 15.35
try (2) 11.10; 22.4
unclean 2 Chr 29.16; Jer 19.13
watch 13.27; 17.2
weak 4.4; 26.1
win 9.1; 31.21
wish 11.5; 19.23
world of the dead 11.8; 17.13
wrong 13.23; 16.18

[z] *One ancient translation* I am; *Hebrew* Why am I...?
[a] *One Hebrew manuscript* and leave him alone; *most Hebrew manuscripts* so that he may rest.
[b] let him...can; *or* until he finishes his day of hard work.

13.27: Job 33.11

11 Like rivers that stop running,
and lakes that go dry,
12 people die, never to **rise**.
They will never wake up while the sky **endures**;
they will never stir from their sleep.

13 I **wish** you would hide me in the **world of the dead**;
let me be hidden until your **anger** is over,
and then set a time to **remember** me.
14 If a man dies, can he come back to **life**?
But I will wait for better times,
wait till this time of **trouble** is ended.
15 Then you will call, and I will answer,
and you will be **pleased** with me,
your **creature**.
16 Then you will **watch** every step I take,
but you will not keep track of my sins.
17 You will **forgive** them and put them away;
you will wipe out all the **wrongs** I have done.

18 There comes a time when mountains fall
and solid cliffs are moved away.
19 Water will wear down rocks,
and heavy rain will wash away the soil;
so you **destroy** man's **hope** for **life**.
20 You overpower a man and send him away for ever;
his face is twisted in **death**.
21 His sons **win honour**, but he never knows it,
nor is he told when they are **disgraced**.
22 He feels only the **pain** of his own **body**
and the **grief** of his own **mind**.

The Second Dialogue
(15.1—21.34)

15

Eliphaz

1-2 Empty **words**, Job! Empty **words**!
3 No **wise** man would talk as you do
or **defend** himself with such meaningless **words**.
4 If you had your way, no one would **fear** God;
no one would **pray** to him.
5 Your **wickedness** is **evident** by what you say;
you are trying to hide behind clever **words**.
6 There is no **need** for me to **condemn** you;
you are **condemned** by every **word** you speak.

7 Do you think you were the first man born?
Were you there when God made the mountains?
8 Did you overhear the **plans** God made?
Does **human wisdom** belong to you **alone**?
9 There is nothing you know that we don't know.
10 We **learnt** our **wisdom** from grey-haired men—
men born before your father.

11 God **offers** you **comfort**; why still **reject** it?
We have spoken for him with **calm**, even **words**.
12 But you are excited and glare at us in **anger**.
13 You are **angry** with God and **denounce** him.

14 Can any man be really **pure**?
Can anyone be **right with God**?
15 Why, God does not **trust** even his **angels**;
even they are not **pure** in his **sight**.
16 And man drinks **evil** as if it were water;
yes, man is **corrupt**; man is **worthless**.

17 Now listen, Job, to what I know.
18 **Wise** men have **taught** me **truths**
which they **learnt** from their fathers,
and they kept no **secrets** hidden.
19 Their land was **free** from foreigners;
there was no one to lead them away from God.

20 A **wicked** man who **oppresses** others
will be in **torment** as long as he lives.
21 Voices of **terror** will scream in his ears,
and **robbers** attack when he thinks he is **safe**.
22 He has no **hope** of **escaping** from **darkness**,
for somewhere a sword is waiting to kill him,
23 and vultures[c] are waiting[d] to eat his corpse.
He knows his future is **dark**;
24 **disaster**, like a **powerful** king,

[c] *One ancient translation* vultures; *Hebrew* where is he?
[d] *One ancient translation* are waiting; *Hebrew* he wanders.

15.14–16: Job 25.4–6

Almighty 8.5; 21.20
alone 14.6; 21.14
angel 5.1; 25.3
anger [2] 14.13; 16.9
bribe 6.22; 36.18
calm Neh 8.11; 16.6
comfort 2.11; 16.1
condemn [2] 10.2; 17.8
corrupt 2 Chr 24.7; Ps 14.1
dark [3] 12.22; 17.12
deceive 12.16; 31.5
defend 13.8; 19.25
defy Ezra 6.12; Ps 9.19
denounce Neh 5.7; Ezek 11.4
destroy [2] 14.19; 19.9
disaster 4.7; 18.12
enough 7.19; 19.22
escape [2] 11.20; 19.20
evidence Deut 31.19; Prov 24.28
evil [3] 11.11; 16.11
fate 6.21; 18.20
fear 6.21; 18.20
flee 2 Chr 25.22; Ps 104.7
fool 13.9; 26.3
free 12.14; 33.9
godless 12.6; 17.8
heart 11.13; 20.25
hope 14.7; 17.11
human 11.6; 20.26
last (1) Esth 2.12; 19.24
learn [2] 8.8; 28.12
need 6.14; 21.15
offer 1.5; 42.8
oppress 5.15; 20.19
plan [2] 10.13; 17.11
power 13.11; 22.8
pray Esth 4.16; 21.15
proud Neh 9.16; 22.29
pure [2] 11.4; 23.10
rebel Neh 9.26; 23.1
reject Neh 9.29; 22.17
reward 8.6; 34.11
rich 6.27; 18.12
right with God Lk 18.14
ripe 5.26; Song 2.13
rob Neh 4.4; 22.9
safe 5.4; 41.11
secret 10.13; Ps 44.21
sight 11.4; 25.4
stubborn Neh 9.16; Ps 81.12
teach 12.7; 21.22
terror 13.11; 18.11
torment 1 Sam 16.14; 16.1
trouble 14.1; 19.5
trust [2] 12.20; 22.26
truth 8.8; 33.3
vanish 8.22; 20.8
vine 2 Kgs 19.29; Ps 78.47
wicked [2] 13.16; 18.5
wisdom [2] 12.1; 28.12
wise [2] 13.5; 16.4
word (1) [6] 13.17; 16.1
worthless 11.11; 30.1

is waiting to attack him.

25 That is the **fate** of the man
who shakes his fist at God
and **defies** the **Almighty**.
26–27 That man is **proud** and **rebellious**;
he **stubbornly** holds up his shield
and rushes to fight against God.

28 That is the man who captured cities
and seized houses whose owners had **fled**,
but war will **destroy** those cities and houses.
29 He will not remain **rich** for long;
nothing he owns will **last**.
Even his shadow[e] will **vanish**,
30 and he will not **escape** from **darkness**.
He will be like a tree
whose **branches** are burnt by fire,
whose blossoms[f] are blown away by the wind.
31 If he is **foolish enough** to **trust** in **evil**,
then evil will be his **reward**.
32 Before his time is up he will wither,[g]
wither like a branch and never be green again.
33 He will be like a **vine** that loses its **unripe** grapes;
like an olive-tree that drops its blossoms.
34 There will be no descendants for **godless** men,
and fire will **destroy** the homes built by **bribery**.
35 These are the men who **plan trouble** and do **evil**;
their **hearts** are always full of **deceit**.

16

Job

1–2 I have heard **words** like that before;
the **comfort** you give is only **torment**.
3 Are you going to keep on talking for ever?
Do you always have to have the **last word**?
4 If you were in my place and I in yours,
I could say everything you are saying.
I could shake my head **wisely**
and drown you with a **flood** of **words**.
5 I could **strengthen** you with **advice**
and keep talking to **comfort** you.

6 But nothing I say **helps**,
and being silent does not **calm** my **pain**.
7 You have worn me out, God;
you have let my family be killed.
8 You have seized me; you are my **enemy**.
I am skin and bones,
and people take that as **proof** of my **guilt**.[h]

9 In **anger** God tears me limb from limb;
he glares at me with **hate**.
10 People **sneer** at me;
they crowd round me and slap my face.
11 God has handed me over to **evil** men.
12 I was living in **peace**,
but God took me by the throat
and battered me and crushed me.
God uses me for target-practice
13 and shoots arrows at me from every side—
arrows that pierce and wound me;
and even then he shows no **pity**.
14 He wounds me again and again;
he attacks like a soldier gone **mad** with **hate**.

15 I **mourn** and wear clothes made of **sackcloth**,
and I sit here in the dust defeated.
16 I have cried until my face is red,
and my eyes are swollen and circled with shadows,
17 but I am not **guilty** of any **violence**,
and my **prayer** to God is **sincere**.

18 O Earth, don't hide the **wrongs** done to me!
Don't let my call for **justice** be silenced!
19 There is someone in **heaven**
to stand up for me and take my side.
20 My **friends scorn** me;
my eyes pour out **tears** to God.
21 I want someone to **plead** with God for me,
as a man **pleads** for his **friend**.
22 My years are passing now,
and I walk the road of no return.

17

The end of my **life** is near. I can hardly breathe;
there is nothing left for me but the **grave**.
2 I **watch** how **bitterly** everyone **mocks** me.
3 I am being **honest**, God. **Accept** my **word**.

advice Esth 2.4; 18.7
anger 15.12; 18.4
calm 15.11; 40.23
comfort [2] 15.11; 21.1
enemy 13.24; 19.11
evil 15.16; 18.21
flood 12.15; 20.28
friend [2] 12.4; 17.5
guilty [2] 10.7; 19.5
hate [2] 8.22; 34.17
heaven 9.8; 19.25
help 11.19; 19.16
justice 8.3; 19.7
last (2) Esth 8.11; 27.19
mad 2 Kgs 9.20; Prov 26.18
mourn 5.11; 27.15
pain 14.22; 30.17
peace 12.6; 21.13
pity 2 Chr 30.9; 19.21
plead [2] 8.5; 30.28
prayer 12.4; 24.12
prove Neh 7.61; 19.5
sackcloth Esth 4.1; Is 15.3
scorn 1 Sam 17.42; 31.34
sincere 2 Chr 11.16; 33.3
sneer 21.3
strength 12.6; 21.16
tear (2) 2 Kgs 20.5; Ps 6.6
torment 15.20; 19.1
violent 5.22; 19.7
wise 15.3; 17.10
word (1) [3] 15.1; 17.3
wrong 14.17; 19.4

accept 5.27; 21.16
betray 1 Chr 12.17; Ps 7.3
bitter 13.26; 20.14
blind 9.24; 23.16
claim [2] 11.4; 21.16
condemn 15.6; 34.17
convince 6.25; 32.1
dark [2] 15.22; 18.6
fail 8.3; 19.27
friend [2] 16.20; 19.14
godless 15.34; 27.8

[e] *One ancient translation* shadow; *Hebrew unclear.*
[f] *One ancient translation* blossoms; *Hebrew* mouth.
[g] *Some ancient translations* wither; *Hebrew* be filled.
[h] *Verses 7–8 in Hebrew are unclear.*

16.19: Job 19.25

grave [2] 10.19; 21.32
grief 14.22; Ps 6.6
honest [2] 8.6; 23.7
hope [4] 15.22; 19.10
life (1) 14.1; 19.20
light (1) 12.22; 18.5
mind (1) 14.22; 33.2
mock 11.3; 34.37
plan 15.8; 23.14
proverb [2] 13.12; Ps 49.4
reason 9.17; 21.4
respect Esth 5.9; 29.8
right (1) 13.18; 22.3
suffer 9.27; 21.13
triumph Esth 9.1; Ps 13.2
watch 14.16; 21.8
wise 16.4; 22.1
word (1) 16.1; 19.1
world of the dead [2] 14.13; 26.6

There is no one else to support what
I say.
4 You have closed their **minds** to
reason;
don't let them **triumph** over me now.
5 In the old **proverb** a man **betrays** his
friends for money,
and his children **suffer** for it.[i]
6 And now people use this **proverb**
against me;
they come and spit in my face.
7 My **grief** has almost made me **blind**;
my arms and legs are as thin as
shadows.
8 Those who **claim** to be **honest** are
shocked,
and they all **condemn** me as **godless**.
9 Those who **claim** to be **respectable**
are more and more **convinced** they
are **right**.
10 But if all of them came and stood
before me,
I would not find even one of them
wise.

11 My days have passed; my **plans** have
failed;
my **hope** is gone.
12 But my **friends** say night is **daylight**;
they say that light is near,
but I know I remain in **darkness**.
13 My only **hope** is the **world of the dead**,
where I will lie down to sleep in the
dark.
14 I will call the **grave** my father,
and the worms that eat me
I will call my mother and my sisters.
15 Where is there any **hope** for me?
Who sees any?
16 **Hope** will not go with me[j]
when I go down to the **world of the**
dead.

18

Bildad

1-2 Job, can't people like you ever
be quiet?
If you stopped to listen, we could
talk to you.
3 What makes you think we are as **stupid**
as cattle?
4 You are only **hurting** yourself with
your **anger**.
Will the earth be deserted because
you are **angry**?
Will God move mountains to **satisfy**
you?

advice 16.5; 26.3
anger [2] 16.9; 19.11
body 14.22; 19.26
care 10.12; 21.21
dark [2] 17.12; 19.8
deadly 2 Sam 1.22; 20.16
death (1) 14.20; 27.15
disaster 15.24; 21.9
disease 2 Chr 26.19; 19.26
evil 16.11; 20.12
fate [3] 15.25; 20.29
fear 15.4; 22.10
hunger 5.5; 22.7
hurt 10.16; 19.4
light (1) [2] 17.12; 21.17
put out 21.17

5 The **wicked** man's **light** will still be **put**
out;
its flame will never burn again.
6 The lamp in his tent will be **darkened**.
7 His steps were firm, but now he
stumbles;
he falls—a **victim** of his own **advice**.
8 He walks into a net, and his feet are
caught;
9 a **trap** catches his heels and holds
him.
10 On the ground a snare is hidden;
a **trap** has been set in his path.

11 All round him **terror** is waiting;
it follows him at every step.
12 He used to be **rich**, but now he goes
hungry;
disaster stands and waits at his side.
13 A **deadly disease** spreads over his **body**
and causes his arms and legs to rot.
14 He is torn from the tent where he lived
secure,
and is dragged off to face King
Death.
15 Now anyone may live in his tent—[k]
after sulphur is **sprinkled** to disinfect
it![l]
16 His roots and branches are withered
and dry.
17 His fame is ended at home and
abroad;
no one **remembers** him any more.
18 He will be driven out of the land of the
living,
driven from **light** into **darkness**.
19 He has no descendants, no survivors.
20 From east to west, all who hear of his
fate
shudder and **tremble** with **fear**.
21 That is the **fate** of **evil** men,
the **fate** of those who **care** nothing
for God.

remember 14.13; 19.23
rich 15.29; 27.19
satisfy 2 Kgs 14.10; 20.20
secure 11.18; 24.23
sprinkle 2 Chr 35.11; Ezek 36.25
stumble 4.4; Ps 20.8
stupid 11.12; Ps 32.9
terror 15.21; 20.25
trap [2] 5.12; 19.6
tremble 4.14; 21.6
victim Gen 49.9; 29.17
wicked 15.5; 20.5

19

Job

1-2 Why do you keep **tormenting**
me with **words**?
3 Time after time you **insult** me
and show no **shame** for the way you
abuse me.
4 Even if I have done **wrong**,
how does that **hurt** you?
5 You think you are better than I am,
and regard my **troubles** as **proof** of
my **guilt**.
6 Can't you see it is God who has done
this?
He has set a **trap** to catch me.

afraid 11.19; 23.16
anger 18.4; 20.23
beg 9.15; 30.24
body 18.13; 20.11
courage 11.15; 23.16
dark 18.6; 22.11
defend 15.3; 30.14
despise 10.3; 36.5
destroy 15.28; 20.26
disease 18.13; 27.15
disgust Ezra 9.1; 30.10
enemy 16.8; 22.21
enough 15.31; 21.5
escape 15.22; 20.24
excuse 2 Kgs 10.19; 33.10
fail 17.11; 29.20
forget 9.27; 41.8
forsake 6.14; Ps 102.17

[i] a man...suffer for it; *or* a man entertains his friends while his children go hungry.
[j] *One ancient translation* with me; *Hebrew unclear.*
[k] Now anyone may live in his tent; *Hebrew unclear.*
[l] TO DISINFECT IT: *Sulphur was used in the ancient world as a disinfectant and to clean rooms that had contained corpses.*

18.5–6: Job 21.17

riend [3] 17.5; 29.4
uilty 16.8; 33.9
eaven 16.19; 20.27
elp 16.6; 22.3
ope 17.11; 27.8
urt 18.4; Ps 7.16
nsult 1.5; 20.3
udge 14.3; 21.22
ustice 16.18; 24.1
ast (1) 15.29; Ps 21.4
ife (1) 17.1; 21.13
ove 10.12; Ps 4.2
ersecute Esth 7.6;
0.21
ity 16.13; 27.22
rove 16.8; 24.25
age Neh 9.11; 30.22
emember 18.17;
4.20
eputation Neh 6.13;
Prov 3.35
ervant [2] 4.18;
1.13
hame 10.15; Ps 6.10
tranger [3]
Chr 29.15; 29.16
trike 1.16; 27.20
orment [3] 16.1;
Ps 78.45
rap 18.9; 40.24
rouble 15.35; 21.10
urn 12.15; 20.11
iolent 16.17; 27.13
wish 14.13; 23.3
word (1) [3] 17.3;
2.22
worst 2 Chr 28.22;
Ps 41.7
wrong 16.18; 31.3

7 I protest against his **violence**,
but no one is listening;
no one hears my cry for **justice**.
8 God has blocked the way, and I can't
get through;
he has hidden my path in **darkness**.
9 He has taken away all my wealth
and **destroyed** my **reputation**.
10 He batters me from every side.
He uproots my **hope**
and leaves me to wither and die.
11 God is **angry** and **rages** against me;
he treats me like his **worst enemy**.
12 He sends his army to attack me;
they dig trenches and lay siege to
my tent.

13 God has made my brothers **forsake**
me;
I am a **stranger** to those who knew
me;
14 my relatives and **friends** are gone.
15 Those who were guests in my house
have **forgotten** me;
my **servant-girls** treat me like a
stranger and a foreigner.
16 When I call a **servant**, he doesn't
answer—
even when I **beg** him to **help** me.
17 My wife can't stand the smell of my
breath,
and my own brothers won't come
near me.
18 Children **despise** me and laugh when
they see me.
19 My closest **friends** look at me with
disgust;
those I **loved** most have **turned**
against me.
20 My skin hangs loose on my bones;
I have barely **escaped** with my **life**.[m]

21 You are my **friends**! Take **pity** on me!
The hand of God has **struck** me
down.
22 Why must you **persecute** me as God
does?
Haven't you **tormented** me **enough**?

23 How I **wish** that someone would
remember my **words**
and record them in a book!
24 Or with a chisel carve my **words** in
stone
and write them so that they would
last for ever.[n]
25 But I know there is someone in **heaven**
who will come at last to my **defence**.
26 Even after my skin is eaten by **disease**,
while still in this **body**[o] I will see
God.[p]
27 I will see him with my own eyes,
and he will not be a **stranger**.

My **courage failed** because you said,
28 "How can we **torment** him?"
You looked for some **excuse** to
attack me.
29 But now, be **afraid** of the sword—
the sword that brings God's wrath
on sin,
so that you will know there is one
who **judges**.[q]

20

Zophar

1-2 Job, you **upset** me. Now I'm
impatient to answer.
3 What you have said is an **insult**,
but I know how to reply to you.

4 Surely you know that from **ancient**
times,
when man was first placed on earth,
5 no **wicked** man has been **happy** for
long.
6 He may grow great, towering to the
sky,
so great that his head reaches the
clouds,
7 but he will be blown away like dust.
Those who used to know him
will wonder where he has gone.
8 He will **vanish** like a **dream**, like a
vision at night,
and never be seen again.
9 He will disappear from the place
where he used to live;
10 and his sons will make good what he
stole from the **poor**.
11 His **body** used to be young and
vigorous,
but soon it will **turn** to dust.

12-13 **Evil** tastes so good to him
that he keeps some in his mouth to
enjoy its flavour.
14 But in his stomach the food **turns**
bitter,
as bitter as any poison could be.
15 The **wicked** man vomits up the wealth
he **stole**;
God takes it back, even out of his
stomach.
16 What the **evil** man swallows is like
poison;
it kills him like the bite of a **deadly**
snake.
17 He will not live to see rivers of olive-
oil[r]

ancient 8.8; Ps 24.7
anger [2] 19.11; 21.17
bitter 17.2; 21.25
blood 2 Chr 35.11;
39.30
body [2] 19.26; 21.23
cloud 7.9; 22.13
deadly 18.13; Ps 5.9
destroy [2] 19.9; 22.20
dream 7.14; 33.15
enjoy [2] 14.6; 36.16
escape 19.20; 26.13
evil [2] 18.21; 21.7
fate [2] 18.20; 30.23
flood 16.4; 22.11
fury Esth 7.7; 30.11
greed 1 Sam 2.29;
Ps 10.3
happy 7.7; 21.21
heart 15.35; 21.25
heaven 19.25; 22.12
human 15.8; 28.4
insult 19.3; Ps 4.2
misery 10.15; 29.13
neglect Neh 13.11;
Ps 9.18
oppress 15.20; 34.30
poor [2] 5.15; 24.4
prosper Ezra 9.12;
21.7
punish 13.21; 21.17
reveal 1 Chr 17.15;
Ps 9.16
satisfy 18.4; 38.39
save 13.16; 22.29
steal [2] 1.15; 24.2
succeed (1) 10.16;
21.16
terror 18.11; 21.9
testimony Lev 19.16;
Prov 21.28
turn [2] 19.19; 28.28
upset 5.12; Ps 49.16
vanish 15.29; 24.19
vision 7.14; 33.15
wicked [3] 18.5; 21.14

[m] *Verse 20 in Hebrew is unclear.* [n] last for ever; *or* be on record.
[o] while still in this body; *or* although not in this body. [p] *Verse 26 in Hebrew is unclear.*
[q] one who judges; *or* a judgement. [r] *Probable text* He will...olive-oil; *Hebrew unclear.*

or streams that flow with milk and
honey.
18 He will have to give up all he has
worked for;
he will have no chance to **enjoy** his
wealth,
19 because he **oppressed** and **neglected**
the **poor**
and seized houses someone else had
built.
20 His **greed** is never **satisfied**.
21 When he eats, there is nothing left
over,
but now his **prosperity** comes to an
end.
22 At the height of his **success**
all the weight of **misery** will crush
him.
23 Let him eat all he wants!
God will **punish** him in **fury** and
anger.
24 When he tries to **escape** from an iron
sword,
a bronze bow will shoot him down.
25 An arrow sticks through his **body**;
its shiny point drips with his **blood**,
and **terror** grips his **heart**.
26 Everything he has **saved** is **destroyed**;
a fire not lit by **human** hands
burns him and all his family.
27 **Heaven reveals** this man's sin,
and the earth gives **testimony**
against him.
28 All his wealth will be **destroyed**
in the **flood** of **God's anger**.

29 This is the **fate** of **wicked** men,
the **fate** that God assigns to them.

21

Job

1-2 Listen to what I am saying;
that is all the **comfort** I ask from
you.
3 Give me a chance to speak and then,
when I am through, **sneer** if you like.

4 My **quarrel** is not with **mortal** men;
I have good **reason** to be impatient.
5 Look at me. Isn't that **enough**
to make you stare in shocked
silence?
6 When I think of what has happened to
me,
I am stunned, and I **tremble** and
shake.

7 Why does God let **evil** men live,
let them grow old and **prosper**?
8 They have children and grandchildren,
and live to **watch** them all grow up.
9 God does not bring **disaster** on their
homes;
they never have to live in **terror**.
10 Yes, all their cattle breed
and give **birth** without **trouble**.
11 Their children run and play like **lambs**
12 and dance to the music of harps and
flutes.
13 They live out their **lives** in **peace**
and quietly die without **suffering**.

14 The **wicked** tell God to leave them
alone;
they don't want to know his **will** for
their **lives**.
15 They think there is no **need** to **serve**
God
nor any **advantage** in **praying** to
him.
16 They **claim** they **succeed** by their own
strength,
but their way of thinking I can't
accept.

17 Was a **wicked** man's **light** ever **put
out**?
Did one of them ever meet with
disaster?
Did God ever **punish** the **wicked** in
anger
18 and blow them away like straw in
the wind,
or like dust carried away in a
storm?

19 You **claim** God **punishes** a child for the
sins of his father.
No! Let God **punish** the sinners
themselves;
let him show that he does it because
of *their* sins.
20 Let sinners bear their own
punishment;
let them feel the wrath of **Almighty**
God.
21 When a man's **life** is over,
does he really **care** whether his
children are **happy**?
22 Can a man **teach** God,
who **judges** even those in high
places?

23-24 Some men stay healthy till the day
they die;
they die **happy** and at ease,
their **bodies** well-nourished.
25 Others have no **happiness** at all;
they live and die with **bitter hearts**.
26 But all alike die and are buried;
they all are covered with worms.

27 I know what spiteful thoughts you
have.
28 You ask, "Where is the house of the
great man now,
the man who **practised evil**?"

accept 17.3; 22.22
accuse 13.19; 33.13
advantage Lev 19.13; Prov 22.22
Almighty 15.25; 22.25
alone 15.8; 28.23
anger [2] 20.23; 32.2
birth 1 Chr 7.16; 39.1
bitter 20.14; 27.1
body [2] 20.11; 33.19
care 18.21; 31.18
claim [2] 17.8; 27.6
comfort [2] 16.1; 29.18
disaster [2] 18.12; 31.3
enough 19.22; 27.14
evil [2] 20.12; 22.5
gentle Ruth 2.13; Prov 15.1
grave 17.1; Ps 18.5
happy [3] 20.5; 30.26
heart 20.25; 22.22
judge 19.29; 22.13
lamb Neh 10.36; Ps 114.4
lie (2) 13.4; 27.4
life (1) [3] 19.20; 27.1
light (1) 18.5; 22.28
mortal 2 Sam 1.15; Ps 9.20
need 15.6; 24.4
peace 16.12; 22.21
practice Ezra 7.10; Ps 7.14

pray 15.4; 22.27
prosper 20.21; 22.1
punish [5] 20.23; 22.19
put out 18.5; Song
quarrel 9.32; Ps 140.2
reason 17.4; 23.7
serve Esth 2.9; 24.1
sneer 16.10; Ps 10.5
spare Esth 4.11; 33.27
strength 16.5; 23.6
succeed (1) 20.22; 22.28
suffer 17.5; 30.16
teach 15.18; 22.22
terror 20.25; 24.17
tomb Neh 3.16; Ps 88.6
tremble 18.20; 23.1
trouble 19.5; 27.9
watch 17.2; 29.2
wicked [5] 20.5; 22.1
will (1) Ezra 7.18; 23.12

29 Haven't you talked with people who
travel?
Don't you know the reports they
bring back?
30 On the day God is **angry** and **punishes**,
it is the **wicked** man who is always
spared.
31 There is no one to **accuse** a **wicked**
man
or pay him back for all he has done.
32 When he is carried to the **graveyard**,
to his well-guarded **tomb**,
33 thousands join the funeral
procession,
and even the earth lies **gently** on his
body.

34 And you! You try to **comfort** me with
nonsense!
Every answer you give is a lie!

The Third Dialogue
(22.1—27.23)

22

Eliphaz

1-2 Is there any man, even the
wisest,
who could ever be of use to God?
3 Does your doing **right benefit** God,
or does your being good **help** him at
all?
4 It is not because you stand in **awe** of
God
that he **reprimands** you and brings
you to **trial**.
5 No, it's because you have sinned so
much;
it's because of all the **evil** you do.
6 To make your brother **repay** you the
money he **owed**,
you took away his clothes and left
him nothing to wear.
7 You **refused** water to those who were
tired,
and **refused** to feed those who were
hungry.
8 You used your **power** and your position
to take over the whole land.
9 You not only **refused** to **help widows**,
but you also **robbed** and **ill-treated**
orphans.
10 So now there are pitfalls all round you,
and suddenly you are full of **fear**.
11 It has grown so **dark** that you cannot
see,
and a **flood** overwhelms you.

12 Doesn't God live in the highest
heavens
and look down on the stars, even
though they are high?
13 And yet you ask, "What does God
know?
He is hidden by **clouds**—how can he
judge us?"
14 You think the thick **clouds keep him
from** seeing,
as he walks on the **dome** of the sky.

15 Are you **determined** to walk in the
paths
that **evil** men have always
followed?
16 Even before their time had come,
they were washed away by a **flood**.
17 These are the men who **rejected** God
and **believed** that he could do
nothing to them.
18 And yet it was God who made them
prosperous—
I can't **understand** the thoughts of
the **wicked**.
19 Good men are **glad** and **innocent** men
laugh
when they see the **wicked punished**.
20 All that the **wicked** own is **destroyed**,
and fire burns up anything that is
left.

21 Now, Job, make **peace** with God
and stop treating him like an
enemy;
if you do, then he will **bless** you.
22 **Accept** the **teaching** he gives;
keep his **words** in your **heart**.
23 Yes, you must **humbly**[s] return to God
and put an end to all the **evil**
that is done in your house.
24 Throw away your gold;
dump your finest gold in the dry
stream bed.
25 Let **Almighty** God be your gold,
and let him be silver, piled high for
you.
26 Then you will always **trust** in God
and find that he is the **source** of your
joy.
27 When you **pray**, he will answer you,
and you will keep the **vows** you
made.
28 You will **succeed** in all you do,
and **light** will shine on your path.
29 God brings down the **proud**[t]
and **saves** the **humble**.
30 He will **rescue** you if you are
innocent,[u]
if what you do is **right**.[v]

accept 21.16; Ps 19.14
Almighty 21.20; 23.16
awe 1 Chr 29.25; 25.1
believe 9.16; Ps 73.10
benefit 13.7; Prov 10.21
bless 1.10; 42.12
cloud [2] 20.6; 26.8
dark 19.8; 23.16
destroy 20.26; 23.16
determine Esth 9.24; 28.25
dome Gen 1.6; Ezek 1.22
enemy 19.11; 31.29
evil [3] 21.7; 24.9
fear 18.20; 23.15
flood [2] 20.28; 24.18
glad 1 Chr 16.10; 31.29
heart 21.25; 31.20
heaven 20.27; 25.1
help [2] 19.16; 26.1
humble [2] 12.19; 40.11
hunger 18.12; 24.10
ill-treat Num 20.15; 24.21
innocent [2] 9.15; 23.7
joy 8.19; 27.10
judge 21.22; 24.1
keep from 9.7; 24.7
light (1) 21.17; 24.13
orphan 6.27; 24.3
owe Neh 5.11; Amos 2.8
peace 21.13; 25.1
power 15.24; 25.1
pray 21.15; 27.10
prosper 21.7; 24.24
proud 15.26; 31.25
punish 21.17; 27.7
refuse (1) [3] 10.14; 27.1
reject 15.11; 24.13
repay Neh 5.10; 31.2
reprimand 13.10; Ps 50.8
rescue 5.21; 29.17
right (1) [2] 17.9; 27.5
rob 15.21; Ps 14.4
save 20.26; 33.17
source Num 27.16; 28.11
succeed (1) 21.16; Ps 1.3
teach 21.22; 27.11
trust 15.15; 31.24
try (2) 14.3; Ps 37.33
understand 13.1; 24.13
vow 2 Sam 4.9; Ps 132.2
wicked [3] 21.14; 24.6
widow 1 Chr 2.24; 24.3
wise 17.10; 28.28
word (1) 19.1; 24.25

[s] *One ancient translation* humbly; *Hebrew* be built up. [t] *Probable text* proud; *Hebrew unclear.*
[u] *Some ancient translations* innocent; *Hebrew* not innocent. [v] *Verse 30 in Hebrew is unclear.*

22.2-3: Job 35.6-8

afraid 19.29; 32.6
Almighty 22.25; 27.1
argue 13.3; 33.5
blind 17.7; 29.15
case (2) 13.3; 34.4
change 14.5; Ps 7.12
choose Esth 2.9; Ps 2.2
command 6.10; 34.27
complain 10.1; 31.13
courage 19.27; 41.9
dark [2] 22.11; 24.17
desire Ezra 7.13; 27.10
destroy 22.20; 24.20
faithful 9.20; Ps 16.3
favour Esth 5.2; 34.19
fear 22.10; 24.17
fulfil 2 Chr 36.21; Is 45.13
groan 3.24; 35.9
honest 17.3; 27.17
innocent 22.19; 27.5
plan [2] 17.11; 27.11
present (1) 5.8; Is 1.23
pure 15.14; 25.4
reason 21.4; 33.7
rebel 15.26; 34.37
strength 21.16; 24.22
test 7.18; 28.27
tremble 21.6; 26.5
will (1) 21.14; 34.9
wish 19.23; 36.20

23

Job

1–2 I still **rebel** and **complain**
against God;
I can't hold back my **groaning**.
3 How I **wish** I knew where to find him,
and knew how to go where he is.
4 I would state my **case** before him
and **present** all the **arguments** in my
favour.
5 I want to know what he would say
and how he would answer me.
6 Would God use all his **strength** against
me?
No, he would listen as I spoke.
7 I am **honest**; I could **reason** with God;
he would declare me **innocent**[w]
once and for all.

8 I have searched in the east, but God is
not there;
I have not found him when I
searched in the west.
9 God has been at work in the north and
the south,
but still I have not seen him.
10 Yet God knows every step I take;
if he **tests** me, he will find me **pure**.
11 I follow **faithfully** the road he **chooses**,
and never wander to either side.
12 I always do what God **commands**;
I follow his **will**, not my own **desires**.

13 He never **changes**. No one can oppose
him
or stop him from doing what he
wants to do.
14 He will **fulfil** what he has **planned** for
me;
that **plan** is just one of the many he
has;
15 I **tremble** with **fear** before him.
16–17 **Almighty** God has **destroyed** my
courage.
It is God, not the **dark**, that makes me
afraid—
even though the **darkness** has made
me **blind**.

act 12.12; 29.14
adultery Deut 5.18; Ps 50.18
curse 5.3; Ps 10.3
dark 23.16; 26.10
debt [2] Neh 10.31; Prov 6.1
deny Ex 23.6; 31.28
destroy [2] 23.16; 26.12
evil 22.5; 27.4
fear 23.15; 26.11
flock 2 Chr 35.7; 31.20
flood 22.11; 27.20
force (1) 9.19; 34.28

24

Why doesn't God set a time for
judging,
a day of **justice** for those who **serve**
him?

2 Men move **boundary stones** to get
more land;
they **steal sheep** and put them with
their own **flocks**.
3 They take donkeys that belong to
orphans,
and keep a **widow's** ox till she pays
her **debts**.
4 They **prevent** the **poor** from getting
their **rights**
and **force** the **needy** to run and hide.

5 So the **poor**, like wild donkeys,
search for food in the dry
wilderness;
nowhere else can they find food for
their children.
6 They have to **harvest** fields they don't
own,[x]
and gather grapes in **wicked** men's
vineyards.
7 At night they sleep with nothing to
cover them,
nothing to **keep them from** the cold.
8 They are drenched by the rain that
falls on the mountains,
and they huddle beside the rocks for
shelter.

9 **Evil** men make **slaves** of **fatherless**
infants
and take the **poor** man's children in
payment for **debts**.
10 But the **poor** must go out with no
clothes to **protect** them;
they must go **hungry** while
harvesting wheat.
11 They press olives for oil, and grapes
for wine,
but they themselves are thirsty.
12 In the cities the wounded and dying
cry out,
but God **ignores** their **prayers**.

13 There are men who **reject** the **light**;
they don't **understand** it or go where
it leads.
14 At dawn the murderer gets up
and goes out to kill the **poor**,
and at night he **steals**.
15 The **adulterer** waits for twilight to
come;
he covers his face so that no one can
see him.
16 At night **thieves** break into houses,
but by day they hide and avoid the
light.
17 They **fear** the **light** of day,
but **darkness** holds no **terror** for
them.

[Zophar][y]

18 The **wicked** man is swept away by
floods,
and the land he owns is under God's
curse;

harvest [2] 5.26; 39.12
hunger 22.7; 30.3
ignore Ezra 9.14; 34.27
ill-treat 22.9; Prov 19.26
judge 22.13; 31.14
justice 19.7; 27.1
keep from 22.14; 26.8
kind Esth 5.8; Ps 4.1
light (1) [3] 22.28; 25.3
might Ezra 3.11; 34.20
need 21.15; 27.16
orphan 22.9; 29.12
poor [5] 20.10; 26.1
prayer 16.17; 42.8
prevent Esth 8.5; Ps 106.23
prosper 22.18; 29.4
protect 11.18; 29.4
prove 19.5; 32.12
reject 22.17; Ps 1.1
remember 19.23; 36.22
right (3) Neh 2.20; 31.38
secure 18.14; 29.13
serve 21.15; 25.3
sheep 5.24; 30.1
shelter Neh 8.14; 40.22
slave 7.2; 27.18
steal [2] 20.10; 31.38
strength 23.6; 26.12
terror 21.9; 27.20
thief 12.6; 30.5
true 11.4; 26.14
understand 22.18; 28.12
vanish [2] 20.8; Ps 10.16
vineyard [2] Neh 9.25; Prov 24.30
weed 8.16; 31.40
wicked [4] 22.18; 27.7
widow [2] 22.9; 27.15
word (1) 22.22; 26.4

[w] he would declare me innocent; *or* then my rights would be safe.
[x] FIELDS THEY DON'T OWN: *Having been cheated out of their own land, the poor are forced to work for others for very small pay.*
[y] Zophar *is not named in the text, but this speech is usually assigned to him.*

he no longer goes to work in his
vineyards.
19 As snow **vanishes** in heat and drought,
so a sinner **vanishes** from the land of
the living.
20 Not even his mother **remembers** him
now;
he is eaten by worms and **destroyed**
like a fallen tree.
21 That happens because he **ill-treated**
widows
and showed no **kindness** to childless
women.
22 God, in his **strength**, **destroys** the
mighty;
God **acts**—and the **wicked** man dies.
23 God may let him live **secure**,
but keeps an eye on him all the time.
24 For a while the **wicked** man **prospers**,
but then he withers like a **weed**,
like an ear of corn that has been cut
off.
25 Can anyone **deny** that this is so?
Can anyone **prove** that my **words** are
not **true**?

25

Bildad

1-2 God is **powerful**; all must
stand in **awe** of him;
he keeps his **heavenly kingdom** in
peace.
3 Can anyone count the **angels** who
serve him?
Is there any place where God's **light**
does not shine?
4 Can anyone be **righteous** or **pure** in
God's **sight**?
5 In his eyes even the moon is not bright,
nor the stars **pure**.
6 Then what about man, that worm, that
insect?
What is man **worth** in God's eyes?

angel 15.15; 33.23
awe 22.4; 37.22
heaven 22.12; 38.7
Kingdom (1) (of God) 1 Chr 28.5; Ps 45.6
light (1) 24.13; 26.10
peace 22.21; 36.11
power 22.8; 26.14
pure [2] 23.10; 28.19
righteous 12.4; 27.7
serve 24.1; 36.11
sight 15.15; 26.6
worth 2 Sam 18.3; 28.17

26

Job

1-2 What a fine **help** you are to
me—
poor, **weak** man that I am!
3 You give such good **advice**
and **share** your **knowledge** with a
fool like me!
4 Who do you think will hear all your
words?
Who **inspired** you to speak like this?

[Bildad][z]

5 The **spirits of the dead tremble**
in the waters under the earth.
6 The **world of the dead** lies open to
God;
no covering shields it from his **sight**.
7 God stretched out the northern sky
and hung the earth in empty space.
8 It is God who fills the **clouds** with
water
and **keeps them from** bursting with
the weight.
9 He hides the full moon behind a **cloud**.
10 He divided **light** from **darkness**
by a circle drawn on the face of the
sea.
11 When he **threatens** the pillars that hold
up the sky,
they shake and **tremble** with **fear**.
12 It is his **strength** that **conquered** the
sea;[a]
by his skill he **destroyed** the **monster**
Rahab.[b]
13 It is his breath that made the sky
clear,
and his hand that killed the **escaping**
monster.[c]
14 But these are only hints of his **power**,
only the whispers that we have
heard.
Who can know how **truly** great God
is?

advice 18.7; 29.21
clear 1 Sam 14.41; 38.14
cloud [2] 22.13; 28.26
conquer Neh 9.22; Ps 44.3
dark 24.17; 28.3
dead 3.22; 39.30
destroy 24.20; 27.23
escape 20.24; 27.22
fear 24.17; 31.23
fool 15.31; 39.17
help 22.3; 29.12
inspire Neh 9.30; Ezek 13.3
keep from 24.7; 33.28
knowledge 11.6; 36.3
light (1) 25.3; 28.11
monster [2] 9.8; 40.15
poor 24.4; 29.12
power 25.1; 27.11
share Neh 8.10; 32.7
sight 25.4; 33.6
spirit (2) 2 Chr 31.21; Ps 51.10

strength 24.22; 29.20
threat 2 Chr 34.27; Ps 10.7
tremble [2] 23.15; 39.24
true 24.25; 28.13
weak 14.1; 30.2
word (1) 24.25; 29.22
world of the dead 17.13; 33.22

27

Job

1-2 I swear by the living **Almighty**
God,
who **refuses** me **justice** and makes
my **life bitter**—
3 as long as God gives me breath,
4 my lips will never say anything **evil**,
my tongue will never tell a **lie**.
5 I will never say that you men are
right;
I will insist on my **innocence** to my
dying day.
6 I will never give up my **claim** to be
right;
my **conscience** is clear.

7 May all who oppose me and fight
against me
be **punished** like **wicked**,
unrighteous men.
8 What **hope** is there for **godless** men
in the hour when God **demands** their
life?
9 When **trouble** comes, will God hear
their cries?
10 They should have **desired** the **joy** he
gives;
they should have constantly **prayed**
to him.

11 Let me **teach** you how great is **God's**
power,

Almighty [3] 23.16; 29.5
best Esth 3.8; Ps 41.9
bitter 21.25; Ps 6.10
claim 21.16; 32.13
conscience 2 Sam 24.10; Ps 16.7
death (1) 18.14; 28.22
demand Neh 5.15; Ps 7.6
desire 23.12; Ps 7.9
destroy 26.12; 28.22
disease 19.26; Ps 38.3
enough 21.5; 34.22
escape 26.13; 30.13
evil 24.9; 28.28
flood 24.18; 38.36
fright 13.25; 33.16
godless 17.8; 34.30
honest 23.7; 31.6
hope 19.10; 30.26
innocent 23.7; 31.6
joy 22.26; 30.31
justice 24.1; 29.14
last (2) 16.3; 42.12
lie (2) 21.34; 34.6
life (1) [2] 21.13; 29.2
mourn 16.15; 30.31
need 24.4; 30.25
pity 19.21; 30.24
plan 23.14; Ps 2.1
power [2] 26.14; 28.25
pray 22.27; 30.20
punish [2] 22.19; 31.11
refuse (1) 22.7; 31.16
rich 18.12; 34.19
right (1) [2] 22.3; 31.7
righteous 25.4; 34.17
slave 24.9; Ps 74.2
strike 19.21; 34.20
swear Neh 5.12; 31.5
teach 22.22; 33.33
terror 24.17; 30.15
trouble 21.10; 29.16
violent 19.7; 38.15
wicked [4] 24.6; 31.5
widow 24.3; 29.13

[z] Bildad *is not named in the text, but this speech is usually assigned to him.*
[a] CONQUERED THE SEA: *A reference to an ancient story in which the sea fought against God.*
[b] RAHAB: *See 9.13.* [c] ESCAPING MONSTER: *See 9.8.*

and explain what **Almighty** God has
planned.
12 But no, after all, you have seen for
yourselves;
so why do you talk such nonsense?

[Zophar][d]
13 This is how **Almighty** God
punishes wicked, **violent** men.
14 They may have many sons,
but all will be killed in war;
their children never have **enough** to
eat.
15 Those who survive will die from
disease,
and even their **widows** will not
mourn their **death**.
16 The **wicked** may have too much silver
to count
and more clothes than anyone
needs;
17 but some good man will wear the
clothes,
and some **honest** man will get the
silver.
18 The **wicked** build houses like a spider's
web[e]
or like the hut of a **slave** guarding
the fields.
19 One **last** time[f] they will lie down **rich**,
and when they wake up, they will
find their wealth gone.
20 **Terror** will **strike** like a sudden **flood**;
a wind in the night will blow them
away;
21 the east wind will sweep them from
their homes;
22 it will blow down on them without
pity
while they try their **best** to **escape**.
23 The wind howls at them as they run,
frightening them with **destructive**
power.

In Praise of Wisdom[g]

28 There are mines where silver is
dug;
There are places where gold is
refined.
2 Men dig iron out of the ground
And melt copper out of the stones.
3 Men explore the deepest **darkness**.
They search the depths of the earth
And dig for rocks in the **darkness**.
4 Far from where anyone lives
Or **human** feet ever travel,
Men dig the shafts of mines.
There they work in **loneliness**,
Clinging to ropes in the pits.
5 Food grows out of the earth,
But underneath the same earth
All is torn up and crushed.
6 The stones of the earth contain
sapphires,
And its dust contains gold.
7 No hawk sees the roads to the mines,
And no vulture ever flies over them.
8 No lion or other fierce **beast**
Ever travels those **lonely** roads.

9 Men dig the **hardest** rocks,
Dig mountains away at their base.
10 As they tunnel through the rocks,
They discover precious stones.
11 They dig to the **sources** of[h] rivers
And bring to **light** what is hidden.
12 But where can **wisdom** be found?
Where can we **learn** to **understand**?

13 **Wisdom** is not to be found among men;
No one knows its **true value**.
14 The depths of the oceans and seas
Say that **wisdom** is not found there.
15 It cannot be bought with silver or gold.
16 The finest gold and jewels
Cannot equal its **value**.
17 It is **worth** more than gold,
Than a gold vase or finest glass.
18 The **value** of **wisdom** is more
Than coral or crystal or rubies.
19 The finest topaz and the **purest** gold
Cannot **compare** with the **value** of
wisdom.

20 Where, then, is the **source** of **wisdom**?
Where can we **learn** to **understand**?
21 No living **creature** can see it,
Not even a bird in flight.
22 Even **death** and **destruction**
Admit they have heard only rumours.

23 God **alone** knows the way,
Knows the place where **wisdom** is
found,
24 Because he sees the ends of the earth,
Sees everything under the sky.
25 When God gave the wind its **power**
And **determined** the size of the sea;
26 When God decided where the rain
would fall,
And the path that the **thunderclouds**
travel;
27 It was then he saw **wisdom** and **tested**
its **worth**—
He gave it his **approval**.

28 God said to men,

admit (1) 2 Chr 12.6; 33.32
alone 21.14; Ps 4.8
approve Neh 2.6; Ps 101.6
beast (1) 40.20
cloud 26.8; 30.15
compare 8.7; 41.33
creature 14.15; 40.19
dark [2] 26.10; 29.3
death (1) 27.15; 30.23
destroy 27.23; 29.17
determine 22.15; Prov 11.19
evil 27.4; 31.7
hard 14.6; 37.18
human 20.26; 31.2
learn [2] 15.10; 39.26
light (1) 26.10; 29.3
lonely [2] 2 Sam 13.20; 30.29

power 27.11; 29.17
pure 25.4; Ps 18.26
refine Deut 28.54; Ps 12.6
reverence 2 Chr 19.9; 31.27
source [2] 22.26; 38.19
test 23.10; Ps 26.2
thundercloud *see* **cloud**
true 26.14; 31.35
turn 20.11; 29.12
understand [3] 24.13; 34.10
value [4] Ezra 8.26; Ps 44.12
wisdom [8] 15.8; 32.7
wise 22.1; 32.9
worth [2] 25.6; Ps 37.16

[d] Zophar *is not named in the text, but this speech is usually assigned to him.*
[e] *Some ancient translations* spider's web; *Hebrew* moth *or* bird's nest.
[f] *Some ancient translations* One last time; *Hebrew* They will not be gathered.
[g] *The Hebrew text does not indicate who is speaking in this chapter.*
[h] *Some ancient translations* dig to the sources of; *Hebrew* bind from trickling.

28.28: Ps 111.10; Prov 1.7, 9.10

"To be **wise**, you must have **reverence**
for the Lord.
To **understand**, you must **turn from**
evil."

Job's Final Statement of His Case

act 24.22; 31.5
advice 26.3; Ps 1.1
Almighty 27.1; 31.2
blind 23.16; 40.24
cheer (1) 1 Kgs 21.7; Ps 104.15
comfort [2] 21.1; 42.11
confident 4.6; Ps 57.7
cruel 10.3; 30.21
dark 28.3; 30.26
despair 11.20; 31.16
destroy 28.22; 30.13
elder (2) 2 Kgs 6.32; Is 3.14
encourage 4.4; Ps 64.5
fail 19.27; 32.12
friend 19.14; 32.3
help [3] 26.1; 30.1
important 7.17; Ps 118.22
justice 27.1; 34.5
life (1) [2] 27.1; 31.18
light (1) 28.11; 30.26
misery 20.22; Ps 90.15
orphan 24.3; 31.17
plenty 2 Chr 9.27; Ps 65.11
poor [2] 26.1; 30.3
power 28.25; 30.21
praise [2] 1.21; 31.20
prosper 24.24; 30.15
protect 24.10; 36.7
rescue 22.30; Ps 6.4
respect 17.9; 34.7
secure 24.23; 36.16
stranger 19.13; 31.31
strength 26.12; 36.19
trouble 27.9; 30.25
turn 28.28; 30.11
victim 18.7; Ps 10.8
watch 21.8; 33.11
welcome [2] 2.10; 31.31
widow 27.15; 31.16
word (1) 26.4; 31.35

29 Job began speaking again.
Job
2 If only my **life** could once again
be as it was when God **watched** over
me.
3 God was always with me then
and gave me **light** as I walked
through the **darkness**.
4 Those were the days when I was
prosperous,
and the **friendship** of God **protected**
my home.
5 **Almighty** God was with me then,
and I was surrounded by all my
children.
6 My cows and goats gave **plenty** of
milk,
and my olive-trees grew in the
rockiest soil.
7 Whenever the city **elders** met
and I took my place among them,
8 young men stepped aside as soon as
they saw me,
and old men stood up to show me
respect.
9 The leaders of the people would stop
talking;
10 even the most **important** men kept
silent.

11 Everyone who saw me or heard of me
had good things to say about what I
had done.
12 When the **poor** cried out, I **helped**
them;
I gave **help** to **orphans** who had
nowhere to **turn**.
13 Men who were in deepest **misery**
praised me,
and I **helped widows** find **security**.
14 I have always **acted justly** and fairly.
15 I was eyes for the **blind**,
and feet for the lame.
16 I was like a father to the **poor**
and took the side of **strangers** in
trouble.
17 I **destroyed** the **power** of **cruel** men
and **rescued** their **victims**.

18 I always expected to live a long **life**
and to die at home in **comfort**.
19 I was like a tree whose roots always
have water
and whose branches are wet with
dew.
20 Everyone was always **praising** me,
and my **strength** never **failed** me.
21 When I gave **advice**, people were silent
and listened carefully to what I said;
22 they had nothing to add when I had
finished.
My **words** sank in like drops of rain;
23 everyone **welcomed** them
just as farmers **welcome** rain in
spring.
24 I smiled on them when they had lost
confidence;
my **cheerful** face **encouraged** them.
25 I took charge and made the decisions;
I led them as a king leads his troops,
and gave them **comfort** in their
despair.

apart 1 Chr 23.13; 41.17
beg 19.16; 41.3
cloud 28.26; 35.5
cruel 29.17; Ps 41.5
dark [2] 29.3; 34.22
death (1) 28.22; 31.11
defend 19.25; Ps 4.1
desolate 2 Chr 36.21; Ps 68.6
destroy 29.17; 31.8
disgust 19.19; Ps 95.10
escape 27.22; Ps 22.5
fate 20.29; Ps 26.9
final Esth 1.22; Ecc 12.5
fury 20.23; Ps 2.5
gloom 10.21; Ps 107.10
happy 21.21; Ps 1.1
help [2] 29.12; 31.16
helpless 14.1; 34.29
hope 27.8; 35.10
hunger 24.10; 31.17
joy 27.10; 33.26
light (1) 29.3; 37.21
lonely 28.4; Ps 25.16
mourn 27.15; Ps 35.13
need 27.16; 31.19
pain [2] 16.6; 33.19
persecute 19.22; Ps 10.2
pity 27.22; Ps 6.2
plead 16.21; 41.3
poor 29.12; 31.16
power 29.17; 34.13
pray 27.10; 31.30
prosper 29.4; 36.11
rage 19.11; Ps 46.3
relieve (1) 7.13; Ps 25.17
ruin Neh 6.13; 31.3
sad Neh 8.10; Ps 30.11
sheep 24.2; 31.20
sorry 2 Chr 21.20; Ps 106.46
suffer [2] 21.13; 31.29
terror 27.20; Ps 10.18
thief 24.16; Ps 50.18
trouble [2] 29.16; 36.16
turn [2] 29.12; 31.7
weak [2] 26.1; 41.23
weep [2] 2.12; Ps 6.6
worry 5.2; Ps 25.17
worthless [2] 15.16; 34.18

30 But men younger than I am
make fun of me now!
Their fathers have always been so
worthless
that I wouldn't let them **help** my
dogs guard **sheep**.
2 They were a bunch of worn-out men,
too **weak** to do any work for me.
3 They were so **poor** and **hungry**
that they would gnaw dry roots—
at night, in wild, **desolate** places.
4 They pulled up the plants of the desert
and ate them,
even the tasteless roots of the
broom-tree!
5 Everyone drove them away with
shouts,
as if they were shouting at **thieves**.
6 They had to live in caves,
in holes dug in the sides of cliffs.
7 Out in the wilds they howled like
animals
and huddled together under the
bushes.
8 A **worthless** bunch of nameless
nobodies!
They were driven out of the land.

9 Now they come and laugh at me;
I am nothing but a joke to them.
10 They treat me with **disgust**;
they think they are too good for me,
and even come and spit in my face.
11 Because God has made me **weak** and
helpless,
they **turn** against me with all their
fury.
12 This mob attacks me head-on;
they send me running; they prepare
their **final** assault.
13 They cut off my **escape** and try to
destroy me;
and there is no one to stop[i] them.

[i] *Probable text* stop; *Hebrew* help.

14 They pour through the holes in my
defences
and come crashing down on top of
me;
15 I am overcome with **terror**;
my dignity is gone like a puff of
wind,
and my **prosperity** like a **cloud**.

16 Now I am about to die;
there is no **relief** for my **suffering**.
17 At night my bones all ache;
the **pain** that gnaws me never stops.
18 God seizes me by my collar
and twists my clothes out of shape.
19 He throws me down in the mud;
I am no better than dirt.

20 I call to you, O God, but you never
answer;
and when I **pray**, you pay no
attention.
21 You are treating me **cruelly**;
you **persecute** me with all your
power.
22 You let the wind blow me away;
you toss me about in a **raging** storm.
23 I know you are taking me off to my
death,
to the **fate** in store for everyone.
24 Why do you attack a **ruined** man,
one who can do nothing but **beg** for
pity?[j]
25 Didn't I **weep** with people in **trouble**
and feel **sorry** for those in **need**?
26 I **hoped** for **happiness** and **light**,
but **trouble** and **darkness** came
instead.
27 I am torn **apart** by **worry** and **pain**;
I have had day after day of
suffering.
28 I go about in **gloom**, without any
sunshine;
I stand up in public and **plead** for
help.
29 My voice is as **sad** and **lonely**
as the cries of a jackal or an ostrich.
30 My skin has **turned dark**; I am burning
with fever.
31 Where once I heard **joyful** music,
now I hear only **mourning** and
weeping.

31

I have made a **solemn promise**
never to look with **lust** at a girl.

2 What does **Almighty** God do to us?
How does he **repay human** deeds?
3 He sends **disaster** and **ruin**
to those who do **wrong**.
4 God knows everything I do;
he sees every step I take.
5 I **swear** I have never **acted wickedly**
and never tried to **deceive** others.
6 Let God weigh me on **honest** scales,
and he will see how **innocent** I am.
7 If I have **turned from** the **right** path
or let myself be attracted to **evil**,
if my hands are stained with sin,
8 then let my crops be **destroyed**,
or let others eat the food I grow.

9 If I have been attracted to my
neighbour's wife,
and waited, hidden, outside her door,
10 then let my wife cook another man's
food
and sleep in another man's bed.
11 Such **wickedness** should be **punished**
by **death**.
12 It would be like a **destructive**, **hellish**
fire,
consuming everything I have.

13 When one of my **servants complained**
against me,
I would listen and treat him fairly.
14 If I did not, how could I then face **God**?
What could I say when God came to
judge me?
15 The same God who **created** me
created my **servants** also.

16 I have never **refused** to **help** the **poor**;
never have I let **widows** live in
despair
17 or let **orphans** go **hungry** while I ate.
18 All my **life** I have taken **care** of them.[k]

19 When I found someone in **need**,
too **poor** to buy clothes,
20 I would give him clothing made of
wool
that had come from my own **flock** of
sheep.
Then he would **praise** me **with all his**
heart.

21 If I have ever **cheated** an **orphan**,
knowing I could **win in court**,
22 then may my arms be **broken**;
may they be torn from my
shoulders.
23 Because I **fear** God's **punishment**,
I could never do such a thing.

24 I have never **trusted** in **riches**
25 or taken **pride** in my wealth.
26 I have never **worshipped the sun** in its
brightness
or the moon in all its beauty.
27 I have not been led astray to **honour**
them

[j] *Verse 24 in Hebrew is unclear.* [k] All my life...them; *Hebrew unclear.*

act 29.14; 39.16
Almighty [3] 29.5; 32.8
care 21.21; Ps 8.4
charge (3) 13.23; Is 50.8
cheat 1 Sam 12.3; Ecc 7.7
complain 23.1; 33.13
court (1) 13.8; Ps 45.9
create Neh 4.8; 34.19
crown Esth 8.15; Ps 8.5
death (1) [3] 30.23; Ps 9.17
deceive 15.35; 36.18
deny 24.25; Ecc 2.10
despair 29.25; Ps 22.1
destroy [2] 30.13; 33.18
disaster [2] 21.9; Ps 78.33
enemy 22.21; 33.10
evil 28.28; 34.8
fear [3] 26.11; 33.7
flock 24.2; Ps 50.9
glad 22.19; 33.32
heart 22.22; 37.1
hell Mt 5.22
help 30.1; 32.9
honest 27.17; Ps 9.4
honour 14.21; 36.7
human 28.4; Ps 49.8
hunger 30.3; 38.39
innocent 27.5; 32.1
judge 24.1; 34.23
kiss 1 Kgs 19.18; Prov 5.3
life (1) 29.2; 33.4
lust Is 57.8
need 30.25; 34.23
neighbour Neh 6.6; Ps 15.3
orphan [2] 29.12; Ps 10.18
please 14.15; Ps 5.4
poor [2] 30.3; 34.19
praise 29.13; 36.24
pray 30.20; 33.26
presence 2.7; Ps 5.4
promise Esth 4.7; 34.31
proud [2] 22.29; 33.17
punish [3] 27.7; 32.22
refuse (1) 27.1; 34.5
repay 22.6; Ps 103.10
reverence 28.28; Ps 5.7
riches Esth 1.4; 36.18
right (1) 27.5; 32.9
right (3) 24.4; Ps 24.3
ruin 30.24; Ps 5.10
scorn 16.20; Ps 22.6
servant [2] 19.15; 41.5
sheep 30.1; 42.12
solemn Neh 9.38; Ps 95.11
steal 24.2; Ps 69.4
stranger 29.16; Ps 35.15
suffer 30.16; 35.8
swear [2] 27.1; Song 2.7
true 28.13; 36.4
trust 22.26; Ps 4.5
turn 30.11; 34.15
weed 24.24; 41.20
welcome 29.23; Ps 23.5
wicked [2] 27.7; 34.18
widow 29.13; Ps 68.5
win 14.21; 40.14
word (1) [2] 29.22; 32.15
worship (2) (of other gods) 2 Chr 36.14; Ps 10.16
wrong 19.4; 32.3

by **kissing** my hand in **reverence** to
them.
28 Such a sin should be **punished** by
death;
it **denies Almighty** God.

29 I have never been **glad** when my
enemies suffered,
or **pleased** when they met with
disaster;
30 I never sinned by **praying** for their
death.
31 All the men who work for me know
that I have always **welcomed**
strangers.
32 I invited travellers into my home
and never let them sleep in the
streets.

33 Other men try to hide their sins,
but I have never concealed mine.
34 I have never **feared** what people would
say;
I have never kept quiet or stayed
indoors
because I **feared** their **scorn**.

35 Will no one listen to what I am
saying?
I **swear** that every **word** is **true**.
Let **Almighty** God answer me.

If the **charges** my opponent brings
against me
were written down so that I could
see them,
36 I would wear them **proudly** on my
shoulder
and place them on my head like a
crown.
37 I would tell God everything I have
done,
and hold my head high in his
presence.

38 If I have **stolen** the land I farm
and taken it from its **rightful**
owners—
39 if I have eaten the food that grew
there
but let the farmers that grew it
starve—
40 then instead of wheat and barley,
may **weeds** and thistles grow.

The **words** of Job are ended.

Elihu's Speech
(32.1—37.24)

32 Because Job was **convinced** of
his own **innocence**, the three
men gave up trying to answer him. 2 But
a bystander named Elihu could not **con-**
trol his **anger** any longer, because Job
was justifying himself and **blaming** God.
(Elihu was the son of Barakel, a descendant of Buz, and belonged to the clan of
Ram.) 3 He was also **angry** with Job's
three **friends**. They could find no way to
answer Job, and this made it appear that
God was in the **wrong**. 4 Because Elihu
was the youngest one there, he had
waited until everyone finished speaking.
5 When he saw that the three men could
not answer Job, he was **angry** 6 and began to speak.

Elihu
I am young, and you are old,
so I was **afraid** to tell you what I
think.
7 I told myself that you ought to speak,
that you older men should **share**
your **wisdom**.
8 But it is the **spirit of Almighty God**
that comes to men and gives them
wisdom.
9 It is not growing old that makes men
wise
or **helps** them to know what is **right**.
10 So now I want you to listen to me;
let me tell you what I think.

11 I listened **patiently** while you were
speaking
and waited while you searched for
wise phrases.
12 I paid close attention and heard you
fail;
you have not **disproved** what Job has
said.
13 How can you **claim** you have
discovered **wisdom**?
God must answer Job, for you have
failed.
14 Job was speaking to you, not to me,
but I would never answer as you did.

15 **Words** have **failed** them, Job;
they have no answer for you.
16 Shall I go on waiting when they are
silent?
They stand there with nothing more
to say.
17 No, I will give my own answer now
and tell you what I think.
18 I can hardly wait to speak.
I can't hold back the **words**.
19 If I don't get a chance to speak,
I will burst like a wineskin full of
new wine.
20 I can't stand it; I have to speak.
21 I will not take sides in this debate;
I am not going to flatter anyone.
22 I don't know how to flatter,

afraid 23.16; 40.23
Almighty 31.2; 34.10
anger [3] 21.17; 36.13
blame 12.4;
Prov 19.3
claim 27.6; 34.5
control 3.8; Ps 2.3
convince 17.9;
Prov 25.15
fail [3] 29.20; Ps 10.6
friend 29.4; 35.4
help 31.16; 34.28
innocent 31.6; 33.9
new 10.17; Ps 19.7
patient Neh 9.30;
35.14
prove 24.25; 40.8
punish 31.11; 34.26
right (1) 31.7; 33.26
share 26.3; 42.15
Spirit (1) (God's Spirit) 2 Chr 24.20;
33.4
wisdom [3] 28.12;
38.2
wise [2] 28.28; 33.33
word (1) [2] 31.35;
33.3
wrong 31.3; 33.9

accuse 21.31; 36.23
admit (1) 28.22; 40.14
alive 10.12; Ps 33.19
angel [3] 25.3; Ps 34.7
argue 23.4; Prov 3.30
bind 13.27; 36.8
body [3] 21.23; 39.30
complain 31.13; Ps 55.17
correct 5.17; Ps 50.17
death (2) (from death) 5.15; Ps 6.4
destroy 31.8; 37.20
dream 20.8; Ps 73.20
duty (1) Neh 13.30; Jer 29.26
enemy 31.29; Ps 3.1
excuse 19.28; Ezek 8.12
fear 31.23; 39.22
free [2] 15.19; 39.5
fright 27.23; 39.20
glad 31.29; Ps 13.5
guilty 19.5; Ps 106.30
innocent 32.1; 34.5
joy [2] 30.31; 38.7
keep from 26.8; 34.30
life (1) [2] 31.18; 34.14
mercy 9.15; 41.3
mind (1) 17.4; 37.19
pain 30.17; Ps 12.5
pray 31.30; 36.13
proud 31.25; 35.12
reason 23.7; Ps 35.7
remind 1 Kgs 17.18; Ps 143.8
right (1) [3] 32.9; 35.1
save [3] 22.29; 35.9
sight 26.6; 35.1
sincere 16.17; Ps 15.2
spare 21.30; Ps 26.9
Spirit (1) (God's Spirit) 32.8; Ps 51.11
strong 12.16; 36.5
teach 27.11; 36.15
truth 15.18; 42.7
vision 20.8; Ps 89.19
warn 9.5; 36.10
watch 29.2; 34.21
wise 32.9; 34.1
word (1) 32.15; 34.3
world of the dead [3] 26.6; 36.12
worship (1) (of God) 4.6; Ps 5.7
wrong [2] 32.3; 34.6

and God would quickly **punish** me if
I did.

33

And now, Job, listen carefully
to all that I have to say.
2 I am ready to say what's on my **mind**.
3 All my **words** are **sincere**,
and I am speaking the **truth**.
4 **God's spirit** made me and gave me **life**.

5 Answer me if you can. Prepare your
arguments.
6 You and I are the same in God's **sight**,
both of us were formed from clay.
7 So you have no **reason** to **fear** me;
I will not overpower you.

8 Now this is what I heard you say:
9 "I am not **guilty**; I have done nothing
wrong.
I am **innocent** and **free** from sin.
10 But God finds **excuses** for attacking
me
and treats me like an **enemy**.
11 He **binds** chains on my feet;
he **watches** every move I make."

12 But I tell you, Job, you are **wrong**.
God is greater than any man.
13 Why do you **accuse** God
of never answering a man's
complaints?
14 Although God speaks again and again,
no one pays attention to what he
says.
15 At night when men are asleep,
God speaks in **dreams** and **visions**.
16 He makes them listen to what he says,
and they are **frightened** at his
warnings.
17 God speaks to make them stop their
sinning
and to **save** them from becoming
proud.
18 He will not let them be **destroyed**;
he **saves** them **from death** itself.
19 God **corrects** a man by sending
sickness
and filling his **body** with **pain**.
20 The sick man loses his appetite,
and even the finest food looks
revolting.
21 His **body** wastes away to nothing;
you can see all his bones;
22 he is about to go to the **world of the**
dead.

23 Perhaps an **angel** may come to his
aid—
one of God's thousands of **angels**,
who **remind** men of their **duty**.
24 In **mercy** the **angel** will say, "Release
him!
He is not to go down to the **world of**
the dead.
Here is the ransom to **set him free**."
25 His **body** will grow young and **strong**
again;
26 when he **prays**, God will answer
him;
he will **worship** God with **joy**;
God will set things **right** for him
again.
27 He will say in public, "I have sinned.
I have not done **right**, but God
spared me.
28 He **kept me from** going to the **world of**
the dead,
and I am still **alive**."

29 God does all this again and again;
30 he **saves** a person's **life**,
and gives him the **joy** of living.

31 Now, Job, listen to what I am saying;
be quiet and let me speak.
32 But if you have something to say, let
me hear it;
I would **gladly admit** you are in the
right.
33 But if not, be quiet and listen to me,
and I will **teach** you how to be **wise**.

34

1-2 You men are so **wise**, so
clever;
listen now to what I am saying.
3 You know good food when you taste it,
but not **wise words** when you hear
them.
4 It is up to us to decide the **case**.
5 Job **claims** that he is **innocent**,
that God **refuses** to give him **justice**.
6 He asks, "How could I **lie** and say I am
wrong?
I am fatally wounded, but I am
sinless."

7 Have you ever seen anyone like this
man Job?
He never shows **respect** for God.
8 He likes the company of **evil** men
and goes about with sinners.
9 He says that it never does any good
to try to follow **God's will**.

10 Listen to me, you men who
understand!
Will **Almighty** God do what is
wrong?
11 He **rewards** people for what they do
and treats them as they **deserve**.
12 **Almighty** God does not do **evil**;
he is never **unjust** to anyone.

agree [2] 13.20; 41.4
Almighty [2] 32.8; 35.13
case (2) 23.4; 35.14
claim 32.13; 37.24
command 23.12; 36.32
condemn [2] 17.8; Ps 1.5
confess Neh 9.1; Ps 32.3
create 31.15; 40.15
criticize Num 12.1; Prov 10.10
dark [2] 30.26; 35.10
deserve 11.6; 36.17
enough 27.14; 38.37
evil [4] 31.7; 35.12
fault 10.6; Ps 18.23
favour 23.4; 37.13
force (1) 24.4; Is 14.3
godless 27.8; 36.13
hate 16.9; Ps 5.5
help 32.9; 35.7
helpless 30.11; 41.25
ignorant 13.4; 36.12
ignore 24.12; 37.24
innocent 33.9; 35.1
judge 31.14; Ps 7.8
justice [2] 29.14; 36.3
keep from 33.28; 36.21
lie (2) 27.4; Ps 5.6
life (1) 33.4; 36.11
might 24.22; Ps 24.8
mock 17.2; Ps 2.4
need [2] 31.19; 35.7
oppress 20.19; 35.9
overthrow Ezra 6.12; Is 13.19
perish Num 24.20; 36.20
poor [2] 31.16; 36.6
power 30.21; 36.22

33.11: Job 13.27 **33.15:** Job 4.13 **34.3:** Job 12.11 **34.11:** Ps 62.12

promise 31.1; 41.4
punish 32.22; 35.15
rebel 23.1; Ps 2.1
refuse (1) 31.16; Ps 50.17
respect 29.8; Ps 112.9
reward 15.31; Ps 7.9
rich 27.19; Ps 45.12
righteous 27.7; 35.7
sense [2] 12.3; Ps 94.11
strike 27.20; Ps 18.38
turn 31.7; 35.10
understand 28.12; 36.5
unjust 6.29; 40.8
watch 33.11; 36.25
wicked 31.5; 38.13
will (1) 23.12; 37.12
wise [4] 33.33; 35.11
word (1) 33.3; 38.2
world 11.15; 37.12
worthless 30.1; Ps 4.2
wrong [2] 33.9; 35.6

13 Did God get his **power** from someone
else?
Did someone put him in charge of
the **world**?
14 If God took back the breath of **life**,
15 then everyone living would die
and **turn** into dust again.

16 Now listen to me, if you are **wise**.
17 Are you **condemning** the **righteous**
God?
Do you think that *he* **hates justice**?
18 God **condemns** kings and rulers
when they are **worthless** or **wicked**.
19 He does not take the side of rulers
nor **favour** the **rich** against the **poor**,
for he **created** everyone.
20 A man may suddenly die at night.
God **strikes** men down and they
perish;
he kills the **mighty** with no effort at
all.
21 He **watches** every step men take.
22 There is no **darkness dark enough**
to hide a sinner from God.
23 God does not **need** to set a time[l]
for men to go and be **judged** by him.
24 He does not **need** an investigation
to remove leaders and replace them
with others.
25 Because he knows what they do
he **overthrows** them and crushes
them by night.
26 He **punishes** sinners where all can see
it,
27 because they have stopped following
him
and **ignored** all his **commands**.
28 They **forced** the **poor** to cry out to God,
and he heard their calls for **help**.

29 If God decided to do nothing at all,
no one could **criticize** him.
If he hid his face, men would be
helpless.
30 There would be nothing that nations
could do
to **keep godless oppressors from**
ruling them.

31 Job, have you **confessed** your sins to
God
and **promised** not to sin again?
32 Have you asked God to show you your
faults,
and have you **agreed** to stop doing
evil?
33 Since you object to what God does,
can you expect him to do what you
want?
The decision is yours, not mine;
tell us now what you think.

34 Any **sensible** person will surely **agree**;
any **wise** man who hears me will say
35 that Job is speaking from **ignorance**
and that nothing he says makes
sense.
36 Think through everything that Job
says;
you will see that he talks like an **evil**
man.
37 To his sins he adds **rebellion**;
in front of us all he **mocks** God.

35

1-2 It is not **right**, Job, for you to
say
that you are **innocent** in God's **sight**,
3 or to ask God, "How does my sin affect
you?
What have I gained by not sinning?"
4 I am going to answer you and your
friends too.

5 Look at the sky! See how high the
clouds are!
6 If you sin, that does no **harm** to God.
If you do **wrong** many times, does
that affect him?
7 Do you **help** God by being so
righteous?
There is nothing God **needs** from
you.
8 It is your fellow-man who **suffers** from
your sins,
and the good you do **helps** him.

9 When men are **oppressed**, they **groan**;
they cry for someone to **save** them.
10 But they don't **turn to** God, their
Creator,
who gives them **hope** in their
darkest hours.
11 They don't **turn to** God, who makes us
wise,
wiser than any animal or bird.
12 They cry for **help**, but God doesn't
answer,
for they are **proud** and **evil** men.
13 It is **useless** for them to cry out;
Almighty God does not see or hear
them.

14 Job, you say you can't see God;
but wait **patiently**—your **case** is
before him.
15 You think that God does not **punish**,
that he pays little attention to sin.
16 It is **useless** for you to go on talking;
it is clear you don't know what you
are saying.

Almighty 34.10; 40.1
case (2) 34.4; Prov 22.23
cloud 30.15; 36.28
Creator 4.17; 36.3
dark 34.22; 36.30
evil 34.8; 36.10
friend 32.3; 42.7
groan 23.1; Ps 12.5
harm 10.13; 41.26
help [3] 34.28; 36.13
hope 30.26; Ps 9.18
innocent 34.5; Ps 7.8
need 34.23; Ps 9.18
oppress 34.30; 37.17
patient 32.11; 36.1
proud 33.17; 36.9
punish 34.26; 36.13
right (1) 33.26; 40.8
righteous 34.17; 36.7
save 33.17; Ps 3.7
sight 33.6; Ps 5.5
suffer 31.29; 36.8
turn [2] 34.15; 36.10
useless [2] 13.12; Ps 2.1
wise 34.1; 36.4
wrong 34.6; 40.8

[l] *Probable text* a time; *Hebrew* yet.
35.6–8: Job 22.2–3

abundant Deut 30.9; Ps 36.8
accuse 33.13; Ps 32.2
anger 32.2; 40.11
announce Esth 6.9; Ps 2.7
bind 33.11; 40.13
bribe 15.34; Ps 15.5
cloud [2] 35.5; 37.11
command 34.27; 37.5
Creator 35.10; 40.19
dark 35.10; 38.9
deceive 31.5; Ps 5.6
deserve 34.11; 42.8
despise 19.18; Ps 5.6
disgrace 14.21; 42.8
distress Neh 9.37; Ps 25.18
enjoy 20.12; Ps 34.12
evil [3] 35.12; Ps 1.1
false 1 Kgs 14.23; Ps 4.2
godless 34.30; Ps 74.18
help [3] 35.7; 37.18
honour 31.27; 40.10
ignorant 34.35; 38.2
justice [2] 34.5; 37.23
keep from 34.30; Ps 18.23
knowledge 26.3; Ps 19.11
life (1) [2] 34.14; 38.12
mankind Gen 6.1; Ps 7.8
mark (1) Deut 27.17; 38.10
obey Esth 3.8; Ps 1.2
patient 35.14; Ps 37.7
peace 25.1; Ps 4.8
perish 34.20; Ps 68.2
poor 34.19; Ps 9.18
power 34.13; 37.23
praise [2] 31.20; 40.14
pray 33.26; 42.8
prosper 30.15; 42.10
protect 29.4; Ps 1.6
proud 35.12; 40.10
provide Esth 6.10; Ps 36.8
punish [2] 35.15; 37.13
remember 24.20; Ps 4.3
riches 31.24; Ps 49.6
righteous 35.7; 37.23
secure 29.13; Ps 8.2
serve 25.3; 41.4
strength 29.20; 39.11
strong 33.25; 39.4
suffer [3] 35.8; 37.17
teach 33.33; 37.19
teacher Ezra 8.16; Ps 94.10
trouble 30.25; 38.23
true 31.35; Ps 5.11
turn [3] 35.10; 37.10
understand 34.10; 37.5
warn 33.16; Ps 2.5
watch 34.21; 39.1
wise 35.11; 37.24
wish 23.3; Ps 12.4
world of the dead 33.22; 38.17

36

1-2 Be **patient** and listen a little longer
to what I am saying on God's behalf.
3 My **knowledge** is wide; I will use what I know
to show that God, my **Creator**, is **just**.
4 Nothing I say to you is **false**;
you see before you a **truly wise** man.

5 How **strong** God is! He **despises** no one;
there is nothing he doesn't **understand**.
6 He does not let sinners live on,
and he always treats the **poor** with **justice**.
7 He **protects** those who are **righteous**;
he allows them to rule like kings
and lets them be **honoured** for ever.
8 But if people are **bound** in chains,
suffering for what they have done,
9 God shows them their sins and their **pride**.
10 He makes them listen to his **warning**
to **turn away** from **evil**.
11 If they **obey** God and **serve** him,
they live out their **lives in peace** and **prosperity**.
12 But if not, they will die in **ignorance**
and cross the stream into the **world of the dead**.

13 Those who are **godless** keep on being **angry**,
and even when **punished**, they don't **pray** for **help**.
14 They die while they are still young,
worn out by a **life of disgrace**.
15 But God **teaches** men through **suffering**
and uses **distress** to open their eyes.

16 God brought you out of **trouble**,
and let you **enjoy security**;
your table was piled high with food.
17 But now you are being **punished** as you **deserve**.
18 Be careful not to let **bribes deceive** you,
or **riches** lead you astray.
19 It will do you no good to cry out for **help**;
all your **strength** can't **help** you now.
20 Don't **wish** for night to come,
the time when nations will **perish**.
21 Be careful not to **turn to evil**;
your **suffering** was sent to **keep you from** it.

22 **Remember** how great is **God's power**;
he is the greatest **teacher** of all.
23 No one can tell God what to do
or **accuse** him of doing **evil**.
24 He has always been **praised** for what he does;
you also must **praise** him.
25 Everyone has seen what he has done;
but we can only **watch** from a distance.[m]
26 We cannot fully know his greatness
or count the number of his years.

27 It is God who takes water from the earth
and **turns** it into drops of rain.
28 He lets the rain pour from the **clouds**
in showers for all **mankind**.
29 No one knows how the **clouds** move
or how the thunder roars
through the sky, where God dwells.
30 He sends lightning through all the sky,
but the depths of the sea remain **dark**.
31 This is how he feeds[n] the people
and **provides** an **abundance** of food.
32 He seizes the lightning with his hands
and **commands** it to hit the **mark**.
33 Thunder **announces** the approaching storm,
and the cattle know it is coming.

37

The storm makes my **heart** beat wildly.
2 Listen, all of you, to the voice of God,
to the thunder that comes from his mouth.
3 He sends the lightning across the sky,
from one end of the earth to the other.
4 Then the roar of his voice is heard,
the **majestic** sound of thunder,
and all the while the lightning flashes.
5 At God's **command amazing** things happen,
wonderful things that we can't **understand**.
6 He **commands** snow to fall on the earth,
and sends torrents of drenching rain.
7 He brings the work of men to a stop;
he shows them what he can do.[x]
8 The wild animals go to their dens.
9 The storm winds come from the south,
and the biting cold from the north.
10 The breath of God freezes the waters,
and **turns** them to solid ice.
11 Lightning flashes from the **clouds**,[o]
12 as they move at **God's will**.
They do all that God **commands**,

amaze [2] Neh 9.10; 40.19
awe [2] 25.1; Ps 65.8
claim 34.5; Ps 35.26
clean 14.4; Ps 51.2
cloud [3] 36.28; 38.9
command [4] 36.32; 38.12
dazzling 2 Chr 7.1; Song 6.10
destroy 33.18; Ps 5.6
favour 34.19; Ps 7.8
glory Neh 9.5; 40.10
hard 28.9; 38.38
heart 31.20; 41.24
help 36.13; Ps 3.2
ignore 34.27; Ps 22.24
justice 36.3; Ps 7.6
light (1) 30.26; 38.15
Majesty Esth 9.13; 40.10
mind (1) 33.2; Ps 19.8
oppress 35.9; Ps 9.9
power 36.22; 38.11
punish 36.13; Ps 3.7
righteous 36.7; Ps 1.6
suffer 36.8; Ps 9.12
teach 36.15; Ps 25.4
turn 36.10; 38.30
understand 36.5; 42.3
will (1) 34.9; Ps 5.8
wise 36.4; 38.37
wonder (1) [2] Esth 10.2; Ps 9.1
world 34.13; 38.4

[m] but we can only watch from a distance; *or* no one understands it all.
[n] *Probable text* feeds; *Hebrew* judges.
[x] *One ancient translation* them what he can do; *Hebrew* this to those whom he has made.
[o] *Verse 11 in Hebrew is unclear.*

everywhere throughout the **world**.
13 God sends rain to water the earth;
he may send it to **punish** men,
or to show them his **favour**.

14 Pause a moment, Job, and listen;
consider the **wonderful** things God does.
15 Do you know how God gives the **command**
and makes lightning flash from the **clouds**?
16 Do you know how **clouds** float in the sky,
the work of God's **amazing** skill?
17 No, you can only **suffer** in the heat
when the south wind **oppresses** the land.
18 Can you **help** God stretch out the sky
and make it as **hard** as polished metal?
19 **Teach** us what to say to God;
our **minds** are blank; we have nothing to say.
20 I won't ask to speak with God;
why should I give him a chance to **destroy** me?

21 And now the **light** in the sky is **dazzling**,
too bright for us to look at it;
and the sky has been swept **clean** by the wind.
22 A golden glow is seen in the north,
and the **glory** of God fills us with **awe**.
23 **God's power** is so great that we cannot come near him;
he is **righteous** and **just** in his dealings with men.
24 No wonder, then, that everyone stands in **awe** of him,
and that he **ignores** those who **claim** to be **wise**.

The LORD Answers Job

38 Then out of the storm the LORD spoke to Job.

The LORD

2 Who are you to **question** my **wisdom**
with your **ignorant**, empty **words**?
3 Stand up now like a man
and answer the **questions** I ask you.
4 Were you there when I made the **world**?
If you know so much, tell me about it.
5 Who decided how large it would be?
Who stretched the measuring-line over it?
Do you know all the answers?
6 What holds up the pillars that support the earth?
Who laid the corner-stone of the **world**?
7 In the dawn of that day the stars sang together,
and the **heavenly beings**[q] shouted for **joy**.
8 Who closed the gates to hold back the sea[r]
when it burst from the **womb** of the earth?
9 It was I who covered the sea with **clouds**
and wrapped it in **darkness**.
10 I **marked** a boundary for the sea
and kept it behind bolted gates.
11 I told it, "So far and no farther!
Here your **powerful** waves must stop."
12 Job, have you ever in all your **life**
commanded a day to dawn?
13 Have you ordered the dawn to seize the earth
and shake the **wicked** from their hiding places?
14 Daylight makes the hills and valleys stand out
like the folds of a garment,
clear as the imprint of a **seal** on clay.
15 The **light** of day is too bright for the **wicked**
and restrains them from deeds of **violence**.

16 Have you been to the springs in the depths of the sea?
Have you walked on the floor of the ocean?
17 Has anyone ever shown you the gates
that guard the **dark world of the dead**?
18 Have you any **idea** how big the **world** is?
Answer me if you know.

19 Do you know where the **light** comes from
or what the **source of darkness** is?
20 Can you show them how far to go,
or send them back again?
21 I am **sure** you can, because you're so old
and were there when the **world** was made!

22 Have you ever visited the storerooms,
where I keep the snow and the hail?
23 I keep them ready for times of **trouble**,

[q] HEAVENLY BEINGS: *See 1.6.* [r] TO HOLD BACK THE SEA: *See 26.12.*

38.8-11: Jer 5.22

being 2.1; Ps 6.3
clear [2] 26.13; Ps 49.3
cloud [3] 37.11; Ps 18.9
command [2] 37.5; 39.25
dark [3] 36.30; Ps 18.9
direct 12.10; Prov 16.9
enough 34.22; 42.16
flood 27.20; Ps 32.6
guide 2 Chr 20.3; Ps 1.6
hard 37.18; 41.15
heaven 25.1; Ps 2.4
hunger [2] 31.17; Ps 34.10
idea Esth 5.14; Prov 10.20
ignorant 36.12; 42.3

joy 33.26; Ps 1.2
law Esth 8.13; Ps 1.2
life (1) 36.11; 42.12
light (1) [2] 37.21; 41.18
mark (1) 36.32; Ps 104.19
power 37.23; 40.16
question [2] 9.3; 40.7
satisfy 20.20; Ps 49.13
seal Esth 8.2; Is 29.11
service 7.1; Jer 52.18
source 28.11; Ps 36.9
sure 5.7; Ps 50.23
trouble 36.16; 42.11
turn 37.10; 39.5
violent 27.13; Ps 5.6
wicked [2] 34.18; 40.12
wisdom 32.7; 39.17
wise 37.24; Ps 14.2
womb 10.10; Ps 139.13
word (1) 34.3; Ps 5.1
world [4] 37.12; 39.3
world of the dead 36.12; 40.13

for days of battle and war.
24 Have you been to the place where the
sun comes up,
or the place from which the east
wind blows?

25 Who dug a channel for the pouring
rain
and **cleared** the way for the
thunderstorm?
26 Who makes rain fall where no one
lives?
27 Who waters the dry and thirsty land,
so that grass springs up?
28 Does either the rain or the dew have a
father?
29 Who is the mother of the ice and the
frost,
30 which **turn** the waters to stone
and freeze the face of the sea?

31 Can you tie the Pleiades together
or loosen the bonds that hold Orion?
32 Can you **guide** the stars season by
season
and **direct** the Great and the Little
Bear?
33 Do you know the **laws** that govern the
skies,
and can you make them apply to the
earth?

34 Can you shout orders to the **clouds**
and make them drench you with
rain?
35 And if you **command** the lightning to
flash,
will it come to you and say, "At your
service"?
36 Who tells the ibis[s] when the Nile will
flood,
or who tells the cock that rain will
fall?[t]
37 Who is **wise enough** to count the **clouds**
and tilt them over to pour out the
rain,
38 rain that **hardens** the dust into
lumps?

39 Do you find **food** for lions to eat,
and **satisfy hungry** young lions
40 when they hide in their caves,
or lie in wait in their dens?
41 Who is it that feeds the ravens
when they wander about **hungry**,
when their young cry to me for
food?

39

Do you know when mountain-
goats are born?
Have you **watched** wild deer give
birth?
2 Do you know how long they carry their
young?
Do you know the time for their
birth?
3 Do you know when they will crouch
down
and bring their young into the
world?
4 In the wilds their young grow **strong**;
they go away and don't come back.

5 Who gave the wild donkeys their
freedom?
Who **turned** them loose and let them
roam?
6 I gave them the desert to be their
home,
and let them live on the salt plains.
7 They keep far away from the noisy
cities,
and no one can tame them and
make them work.
8 The mountains are the pastures where
they feed,
where they search for anything
green to eat.

9 Will a wild ox work for you?
Is he willing to spend the night in
your stable?
10 Can you hold one with a rope and
make him plough?
Or make him pull a harrow in your
fields?
11 Can you **rely** on his great **strength**
and expect him to do your heavy
work?
12 Do you expect him to bring in your
harvest
and gather the grain from your
threshing-place?

13 How fast the wings of an ostrich beat!
But no ostrich can fly like a stork.[u]
14 The ostrich leaves her eggs on the
ground
for the heat in the soil to warm
them.
15 She is unaware that a foot may crush
them
or a wild animal break them.
16 She **acts** as if the eggs were not hers,
and is **unconcerned** that her efforts
were wasted.
17 It was I who made her **foolish**
and did not give her **wisdom**.
18 But when she begins to run,[v]

[s] IBIS: *A bird in ancient Egypt that was believed to announce the flooding of the River Nile.*
[t] *Verse 36 in Hebrew is unclear.* [u] *Verse 13 in Hebrew is unclear.*
[v] *Probable text* run; *Hebrew unclear.*

38.31: Job 9.9; Amos 5.8

act 31.5; Ps 24.4
birth [2] 21.10; Ps 22.9

blood 20.25; Ps 50.1
body 33.19; 40.16
command [2] 38.12
Ps 17.4
concern 1 Sam 22.
Ps 41.1
dead 26.5; Ps 22.15
eager Neh 4.6; Ps 19.5
fear 33.7; 41.24
fool 26.3; 40.3
free 33.9; Ps 2.3
fright 33.16; 41.25
harvest 24.6; Ps 65.11
learn 28.12; Ps 2.10
race (2) 9.25; Ps 19
rely Neh 7.2; Ps 13
strength [2] 36.19; 40.16
strong [2] 36.5; 40.9
tremble 26.5; Ps 2.
turn [2] 38.30; 41.32
watch [2] 36.25; Ps 11.4
wisdom 38.2; 42.3
world 38.4; 41.11

she can laugh at any horse and
rider.

[19] Was it you, Job, who made horses so
strong
and gave them their flowing
manes?
[20] Did you make them leap like locusts
and **frighten** men with their
snorting?
[21] They **eagerly** paw the ground in the
valley;
they rush into battle with all their
strength.
[22] They do not know the meaning of **fear**,
and no sword can **turn** them back.
[23] The weapons which their riders carry
rattle and flash in the sun.
[24] **Trembling** with excitement, the horses
race ahead;
when the trumpet blows, they can't
stand still.
[25] At each blast of the trumpet they
snort;
they can smell a battle before they
get near,
and they hear the officers shouting
commands.

[26] Does a hawk **learn** from you how to fly
when it spreads its wings towards
the south?
[27] Does an eagle wait for your **command**
to build its nest high in the
mountains?
[28] It makes its home on the highest rocks
and makes the sharp peaks its
fortress.
[29] From there it **watches** near and far
for something to kill and eat.
[30] Around **dead bodies** the eagles gather,
and the young eagles drink the
blood.

40

[1-2] Job, you **challenged Almighty**
God;
will you give up now, or will you
answer?

Job

[3-4] I spoke **foolishly**, LORD. What can I
answer?
I will not try to say anything else.
[5] I have already said more than I should.

6 Then out of the storm the LORD
spoke to Job once again.

The LORD

[7] Stand up now like a man,
and answer my **questions**.
[8] Are you trying to **prove** that I am
unjust—
to put me in the **wrong** and yourself
in the **right**?
[9] Are you as **strong** as I am?
Can your voice thunder as loud as
mine?
[10] If so, stand up in your **honour** and
pride;
clothe yourself with **majesty** and
glory.
[11] Look at those who are **proud**;
pour out your **anger** and **humble**
them.
[12] Yes, look at them and bring them
down;
crush the **wicked** where they stand.
[13] Bury them all in the ground;
bind them in the **world of the dead**.
[14] Then I will be the first to **praise** you
and **admit** that you **won** the **victory**
yourself.

[15] Look at the **monster** Behemoth;[w]
I **created** him and I created you.
He eats grass like a cow,
[16] but what **strength** there is in his
body,
and what **power** there is in his
muscles!
[17] His tail stands up like a cedar,
and the muscles in his legs are
strong.
[18] His bones are as **strong** as bronze,
and his legs are like iron bars.

[19] The most **amazing** of all my **creatures**!
Only his **Creator** can defeat him.
[20] Grass to feed him grows
on the hills where wild **beasts** play.[x]
[21] He lies down under the thorn-bushes,
and hides among the reeds in the
swamp.
[22] The thorn-bushes and the willows by
the stream
give him **shelter** in their shade.
[23] He is not **afraid** of a rushing river;
he is **calm** when the Jordan dashes
in his face.
[24] Who can **blind** his eyes and capture
him?
Or who can catch his snout in a
trap?

41

Can you catch **Leviathan**[y] with a
fish-hook
or tie his tongue down with a rope?
[2] Can you put a rope through his snout

Majesty 37.4; Ps 21.5
monster 26.12;
Ps 74.13
power 38.11; 41.22
praise 36.24; Ps 6.5
proud [2] 36.9; 41.34
prove 32.12; Ps 86.17
question 38.2; 42.3
right (1) 35.1; Ps 1.3
shelter 24.8; Ps 27.5
strength 39.11;
Ps 6.2
strong [3] 39.4; 41.12
trap 19.6; Ps 7.15
unjust 34.12; Ps 82.2
victory 12.16; Ps 3.3
wicked 38.13; Ps 5.5
win 31.21; Ps 33.16
world of the dead
38.17; Ps 6.5
wrong 35.6; Ps 5.4

admit (1) 33.32;
Ps 141.6
afraid 32.6; Ps 3.6
Almighty 35.13;
Ps 9.2
amaze 37.5; Ps 46.8
anger 36.13; 42.7
beast (1) 28.8; 41.34
bind 36.8; Ps 149.8
blind 29.15; Ps 69.23
body 39.30; Ps 38.3
calm 16.6; Ps 65.7
challenge
2 Chr 25.17; Ecc 8.4
create 34.19; Ps 8.6
Creator 36.3;
Ps 146.6
creature 28.21; 41.33
fool 39.17; Ps 11.1
glory 37.22; Ps 8.5
honour 36.7; Ps 8.5
humble 22.23;
Ps 14.6

agree 34.32; Ps 83.5
apart 30.27; Ps 1.5
beast (1) 40.20;
Dan 7.3
beg 30.24; Ps 30.8

[w] BEHEMOTH: *Some identify this with the hippopotamus, others with a legendary creature.*
[x] *Verse 20 in Hebrew is unclear.* [y] LEVIATHAN: *See 3.8.*

39.30: Mt 24.28; Lk 17.37 **41.1:** Ps 74.14, 104.26; Is 27.1

compare 28.19; Prov 3.15
courage 23.16; Ps 3.3
creature 40.19; Ps 8.8
dare 13.16; 42.3
fear [3] 39.22; Ps 2.11
forget 19.15; Ps 9.6
fright 39.20; Is 7.4
hard [3] 38.38; Ps 107.12
harm 35.6; Ps 3.7
heart 37.1; Ps 9.1
helpless 34.29; Ps 10.8
Leviathan [3] 3.8; Ps 74.14
light (1) 38.15; Ps 18.28
look down on Esth 1.17; Prov 12.8
mercy 33.24; Ps 6.4
plead 30.28; Ps 17.1
power 40.16; 42.2
promise 34.31; Ps 12.6
proud 40.10; Ps 5.5
rise [2] 14.12; Ps 7.6
safe 15.21; Ps 4.8
servant 31.13; 42.7
serve 36.11; Ps 2.11
strong [2] 40.9; Ps 18.2
terrify [2] 7.14; Ps 2.5
turn 39.5; Ps 3.1
weak 30.2; Ps 25.16
weed 31.40; Ps 58.7
world 39.3; 42.15

or put a hook through his jaws?
3 Will he **beg** you to let him go?
Will he **plead** with you for **mercy**?
4 Will he make an **agreement** with you
and **promise** to **serve** you for ever?
5 Will you tie him up like a pet bird,
like something to amuse your
servant-girls?
6 Will fishermen bargain over him?
Will merchants cut him up to sell?
7 Can you fill his hide with fishing-spears
or pierce his head with a harpoon?
8 Touch him once and you'll never try it
again;
you'll never **forget** the fight!

9 Anyone who sees **Leviathan**
loses **courage** and falls to the
ground.
10 When he is aroused, he is fierce;
no one would **dare** to stand before
him.
11 Who can attack him and still be **safe**?
No one in all the **world** can do it.[z]

12 Let me tell you about **Leviathan's** legs
and describe how great and **strong**
he is.
13 No one can tear off his outer coat
or pierce the armour[a] he wears.
14 Who can make him open his jaws,
ringed with those **terrifying** teeth?
15 His back[b] is made of rows of shields,
fastened together and **hard** as stone.
16 Each one is joined so tight to the next,
not even a breath can come
between.
17 They all are fastened so firmly
together
that nothing can ever pull them
apart.
18 **Light** flashes when he sneezes,
and his eyes glow like the **rising** sun.
19 Flames blaze from his mouth,
and streams of sparks fly out.
20 Smoke comes pouring out of his nose,
like smoke from **weeds** burning
under a pot.
21 His breath starts fires burning;
flames leap out of his mouth.
22 His neck is so **powerful**
that all who meet him are **terrified**.
23 There is not a **weak** spot in his skin;
it is as **hard** and unyielding as iron.
24 His stony **heart** is without **fear**,
as unyielding and **hard** as a
millstone.
25 When he **rises** up, even the **strongest**[c]
are **frightened**;
they are **helpless** with **fear**.
26 There is no sword that can wound him;
no spear or arrow or lance that can
harm him.
27 For him iron is as flimsy as straw,
and bronze as soft as rotten wood.
28 There is no arrow that can make him
run;
rocks thrown at him are like bits of
straw.
29 To him a club is a piece of straw,
and he laughs when men throw
spears.
30 The scales on his belly are like jagged
pieces of pottery;
they tear up the muddy ground like
a threshing-sledge.[d]
31 He churns up the sea like boiling water
and makes it bubble like a pot of oil.
32 He leaves a shining path behind him
and **turns** the sea to white foam.
33 There is nothing on earth to **compare**
with him;
he is a **creature** that has no **fear**.
34 He **looks down on** even the **proudest**
animals;
he is king of all wild **beasts**.

42

Then Job answered the LORD.

Job

2 I know, LORD, that you are **all-**
powerful;
that you can do everything you
want.
3 You ask how I **dare question** your
wisdom
when I am so very **ignorant**.
I talked about things I did not
understand,
about marvels too great for me to
know.
4 You told me to listen while you spoke
and to try to answer your **questions**.
5 In the past I knew only what others
had told me,
but now I have seen you with my
own eyes.
6 So I am **ashamed** of all I have said
and **repent** in dust and **ashes**.

Conclusion

7 After the LORD had finished speaking to Job, he said to Eliphaz, "I am
angry with you and your two **friends**, because you did not speak the **truth** about
me, as my **servant** Job did. 8 Now take
seven bulls and seven rams to Job and
offer them as a sacrifice for yourselves.

anger 40.11; Ps 2.5
ash 13.12; Ps 102.9
ashamed 9.31; Ps 86.17
bless [2] 22.21; Ps 3.
comfort 29.18; Ps 69.20
dare 41.10; Is 19.11
deserve 36.17; Ps 28.4
disgrace 36.14; Ps 31.17
enough 38.37; Ps 17.14
feast 1.4; Ps 36.8
friend [3] 35.4; Ps 7.
ignorant 38.2; Ps 14.4
inherit 1 Kgs 21.3; Ps 69.36
last (2) 27.19; Ps 75.
life (1) 38.12; Ps 16.11
offer 15.11; Ps 4.5
power 41.22; Ps 3.7
pray [2] 36.13; Ps 4.1
prayer [2] 24.12; Ps 4.1
prosper 36.11; Ps 14.7
question [2] 40.7; Prov 18.17
repent Neh 9.28; Ps 51.17
sacrifice 1.5; Ps 4.5
servant 41.5; Ps 19.11
share 32.7; Ps 41.9
sheep 31.20; Ps 8.7
sympathy 1 Chr 19.2; Ps 69.20
trouble 38.23; Ps 4.1
truth [2] 33.3; Ps 25.5
understand 37.5; Ps 10.5

[z] *Verse 11 in Hebrew is unclear.* [a] *One ancient translation* armour; *Hebrew* bridle.
[b] *Some ancient translations* back; *Hebrew* pride. [c] strongest; *or* gods.
[d] THRESHING SLEDGES: *These had sharp pieces of iron or stone fastened beneath them.*

42.3: Job 38.2 **42.4:** Job 38.3

wisdom 39.17; Ps 19.7
world 41.11; Ps 2.10

Job will **pray** for you, and I will answer
his **prayer** and not **disgrace** you as you
deserve. You did not speak the **truth**
about me as he did."
9 Eliphaz, Bildad, and Zophar did what
the LORD had told them to do, and the
LORD answered Job's **prayer**.
10 Then, after Job had **prayed** for his
three **friends**, the LORD made him **prosperous** again and gave him twice as
much as he had had before. 11 All Job's
brothers and sisters and former **friends**
came to visit him and **feasted** with him in
his house. They expressed their **sympathy** and **comforted** him for all the **troubles** the LORD had brought on him. Each
of them gave him some money and a
gold ring.
12 The LORD **blessed** the **last** part of
Job's **life** even more than he had **blessed**
the first. Job owned fourteen thousand
sheep, six thousand camels, two thousand
head of cattle, and one thousand donkeys. 13 He was the father of seven sons
and three daughters. 14 He called the eldest daughter Jemimah, the second
Keziah, and the youngest Keren
Happuch.[e] 15 There were no other
women in the whole **world** as beautiful as
Job's daughters. Their father gave them
a **share** of the **inheritance** along with
their brothers.
16 Job lived a hundred and forty years
after this, long **enough** to see his grandchildren and great-grandchildren. 17 And
then he died at a very great age.

[e] *In Hebrew the names of Job's daughters suggest beauty both by their sound and by their meaning.* JEMIMAH *means "dove";* KEZIAH *means "cassia," a variety of cinnamon used as a perfume; and* KEREN HAPPUCH *means a small box used for eye make-up.*

42.10: Job 1.1-3

THE PSALMS

INTRODUCTION

The book of *Psalms* is the hymn book and prayer book of the Bible. Composed by different authors over a long period of time, these hymns and prayers were collected and used by the people of Israel in their worship, and eventually this collection was included in their Scriptures.

These religious poems are of many kinds: there are hymns of praise and worship of God; prayers for help, protection, and salvation; pleas for forgiveness; songs of thanksgiving for God's blessings; and petitions for the punishment of enemies. These prayers are both personal and national; some portray the most intimate feelings of one person, while others represent the needs and feelings of all the people of God.

The psalms were used by Jesus, quoted by the writers of the New Testament, and became the treasured book of worship of the Christian Church from its beginning.

Outline of Contents

The 150 psalms are grouped into five collections, or books, as follows:

BOOK ONE

(Psalms 1–41)

True Happiness

1 **Happy** are those
who **reject** the **advice** of **evil** men,
who do not follow the **example** of
sinners
or join those who have no use for
God.
2 Instead, they find **joy** in **obeying** the
Law of the LORD,
and they **study** it day and night.
3 They are like trees that grow beside a
stream,
that bear fruit at the **right** time,
and whose leaves do not dry up.
They **succeed** in everything they do.

4 But **evil** men are not like this at all;
they are like straw that the wind
blows away.
5 Sinners will be **condemned** by God
and kept **apart** from **God's own
people**.
6 The **righteous** are **guided** and
protected by the LORD,
but the **evil** are on the way to their
doom.

God's Chosen King

2 Why do the nations **plan rebellion**?
Why do people make their **useless
plots**?
2 Their kings revolt,
their rulers **plot** together against the
LORD
and against the king he **chose**.
3 "Let us **free** ourselves from their rule,"
they say;
"let us throw off their **control**."

4 From his **throne** in **heaven** the Lord
laughs
and **mocks** their feeble **plans**.
5 Then he **warns** them in **anger**
and **terrifies** them with his **fury**.
6 "On Zion,[a] my **sacred** hill," he says,
"I have installed my king."

7 "I will **announce**," says the king, "what
the LORD has declared.
He said to me: 'You are my son;
today I have become your **father**.
8 Ask, and I will give you all the nations;
the whole earth will be yours.
9 You will break them with an iron rod;
you will shatter them in pieces like a
clay pot.' "

advice Job 29.21; 32.8
apart Job 41.17; 11.3
condemn Job 34.17; 5.10
doom 2 Kgs 7.13; 49.14
evil [3] Job 36.10; 5.4
example Neh 13.27; 71.7
God's people Neh 13.1; 3.8
guide Job 38.32; 16.7
happy Job 30.26; 2.12
joy Job 38.7; 4.7
law Job 38.33; 18.21
obey Job 36.11; 5.12
protect Job 36.7; 2.12
reject Job 24.13; 9.17
right (1) Job 40.8; 4.5
righteous Job 37.23; 4.3
study Job 5.27; 119.15
succeed (1) Job 22.28; 10.5

anger [2] Job 42.7; 6.1
announce Job 36.33; 19.2
bow (2) Esth 3.2; 5.7
choose Job 23.11; 4.3
control Job 32.2; 32.9
Father (2) (God) 2 Sam 7.14; 89.26
fear Job 41.24; 4.4
free Job 39.5; 19.13
fury Job 30.11; 7.6
happy 1.1; 5.11
heaven Job 38.7; 8.1
learn Job 39.26; 25.12
lesson Prov 6.6
mock Job 34.37; 35.15
plan [2] Job 27.11; 7.14
plot (1) [2] Esth 8.3; 5.10
protect 1.6; 3.5
rebel Job 34.37; 5.10
sacred Neh 12.47; 3.4
serve Job 41.4; 16.10
terrify Job 41.14; 14.5
throne Job 12.18; 9.7
tremble Job 39.24; 4.4
useless Job 35.13; 33.17
warn [2] Job 36.10; 16.7
world Job 42.15; 8.1

[a] ZION: *See Zion in Word List.*

1.3: Jer 17.8 **2.1-2:** Acts 4.25-26 **2.7:** Acts 13.33; Heb 1.5, 5.5 **2.9:** Rev 2.26-27, 12.5, 19.15

10 Now listen to this **warning**, you kings;
learn this **lesson**, you rulers of the **world**:
11 **Serve** the LORD with **fear**;
12 **tremble** and **bow down** to him;[b]
or else his **anger** will be quickly aroused,
and you will suddenly die.
Happy are all who go to him for **protection**.

tremble 2.11; 18.7
trouble Job 42.11; 6.3
trust Job 31.24; 5.9
worthless Job 34.18; 26.4

Morning Prayer for Help[c]

afraid Job 40.23; 9.20
bless Job 42.12; 4.6
courage Job 41.9; 10.17
danger 1 Kgs 18.9; 18.4
enemy [3] Job 33.10; 5.8
God's people 1.5; 14.4
harm Job 41.26; 71.24
help [2] Job 37.18; 4.1
power Job 42.2; 10.15
protect 2.12; 5.11
punish Job 37.13; 5.10
restore Job 8.6; 13.3
sacred 2.6; 15.1
save Job 35.9; 6.4
turn Job 41.32; 9.3
victory [2] Job 40.14; 14.7

3 I have so many **enemies**, LORD,
so many who **turn** against me!
2 They talk about me and say,
"God will not **help** him."

3 But you, O LORD, are always my shield
from **danger**;
you give me **victory**
and **restore** my **courage**.
4 I call to the LORD for **help**,
and from his **sacred** hill[d] he answers me.

5 I lie down and sleep,
and all night long the LORD **protects** me.
6 I am not **afraid** of the thousands of **enemies**
who surround me on every side.

7 Come, LORD! **Save** me, my God!
You **punish** all my **enemies**
and leave them **powerless** to **harm** me.
8 **Victory** comes from the LORD—
may he **bless his people**.

Evening Prayer for Help[e]

alone Job 28.23; 18.31
bless 3.8; 5.12
choose 2.2; 18.50
defend Job 30.14; 18.1
false Job 36.4; 24.4
fear 2.11; 27.1
help 3.2; 5.2
insult Job 20.3; 31.20
joy 1.2; 5.11
kind [2] Job 24.21; 25.6
love Job 19.19; 5.7
offer Job 42.8; 5.3
peace Job 36.11; 29.11
perfect 2 Chr 5.11; 18.25
pray [2] Job 42.8; 5.2
prayer Job 42.8; 5.3
remember Job 36.22; 6.5
right (1) 1.3; 14.1
righteous 1.6; 7.9
sacrifice Job 42.8; 16.4
safe Job 41.11; 5.11

4 Answer me when I **pray**,
O God, my **defender**!
When I was in **trouble**, you **helped** me.
Be **kind** to me now and hear my **prayer**.

2 How long will you people **insult** me?
How long will you **love** what is **worthless**
and go after what is **false**?

3 **Remember** that the LORD has **chosen**
the **righteous** for his own,
and he hears me when I call to him.

4 **Tremble** with **fear** and stop sinning;
think deeply about this,
when you lie in silence on your beds.
5 **Offer the right sacrifices** to the LORD,
and put your **trust** in him.

6 There are many who **pray**:
"Give us more **blessings**, O LORD.
Look on us with **kindness**!"
7 But the **joy** that you have given me
is more than they will ever have
with all their corn and wine.

8 When I lie down, I go to sleep in **peace**;
you **alone**, O LORD, keep me
perfectly safe.

A Prayer for Protection[f]

bless 4.6; 18.20
bow (2) 2.12; 18.44
condemn 1.5; 7.11
deadly Job 20.16; 7.13
deceive [2] Job 36.18; 7.14
despise Job 36.5; 10.13
destroy [2] Job 37.20; 9.5
enemy [2] 3.1; 6.7
evil 1.1; 6.8
happy 2.12; 14.7
hate Job 34.17; 10.7
help 4.1; 6.3
holy Job 6.10; 11.4
joy 4.7; 9.2
lie (2) Job 34.6; 10.7
love [3] 4.2; 11.7
obey 1.2; 7.10
offer 4.5; 20.3
plain (1) 2 Kgs 5.7; 19.1
please Job 31.29; 18.19
plot (1) 2.1; 21.11
pray 4.1; 14.4
prayer 4.1; 6.9
presence [2] Job 31.37; 11.7
protect [2] 3.5; 7.1
proud Job 41.34; 10.2
punish 3.7; 6.1
rebel 2.1; 18.43
rejoice 1 Chr 16.10; 9.14
reverence Job 31.27; 19.9
ruin Job 31.3; 38.12
safe 4.8; 8.2
sight Job 35.1; 39.5
Temple (1) (of God) Neh 13.4; 11.4
true Job 36.4; 15.2
trust 4.5; 9.10
violent Job 38.15; 7.3
wicked Job 40.12; 7.9
will (1) Job 37.12; 25.9
word (1) [2] Job 38.2; 10.7
worship (1) (of God) Job 33.26; 14.2
wrong Job 40.8; 7.3

5 Listen to my **words**, O LORD,
and hear my sighs.
2 Listen to my cry for **help**,
my God and king!

I **pray** to you, O LORD;
3 you hear my voice in the morning;
at sunrise I **offer** my **prayer**[g]
and wait for your answer.

4 You are not a God who is **pleased** with **wrongdoing**;
you allow no **evil** in your **presence**.
5 You cannot stand the **sight of proud** men;
you **hate** all **wicked** people.
6 You **destroy** all **liars**
and **despise violent**, **deceitful** men.

7 But because of your great **love**
I can come into your house;
I can **worship** in your **holy Temple**
and **bow down** to you in **reverence**.
8 LORD, I have so many **enemies**!
Lead me to do your **will**;
make your way **plain** for me to follow.

9 What my **enemies** say can never be **trusted**;
they only want to **destroy**.
Their **words** are flattering and smooth,
but full of **deadly deceit**.
10 **Condemn** and **punish** them, O God;
may their own **plots** cause their **ruin**.
Drive them out of your **presence**
because of their many sins
and their **rebellion** against you.

11 But all who find **safety** in you will **rejoice**;
they can always sing for **joy**.
Protect those who **love** you;
because of you they are **truly happy**.

[b] *Probable text* tremble...him; *Some other possible texts* with trembling kiss his feet *and* with trembling kiss the Son *and* tremble and kiss the mighty one; *Hebrew unclear*.
[c] HEBREW TITLE: *A psalm by David, after he ran away from his son Absalom.* [d] SACRED HILL: *See 2.6.*
[e] HEBREW TITLE: *A psalm by David.* [f] HEBREW TITLE: *A psalm by David.* [g] prayer; *or* sacrifice.

3 Title: 2 Sam 15.13—17.22 **4.4:** Eph 4.26 **5.9:** Rom 3.13

12 You bless those who obey you, LORD;
your love protects them like a
shield.

A Prayer for Help in Time of Trouble[h]

anger [2] 2.5; 7.6
being Job 38.7; 9.20
bitter Job 27.1; 73.21
death (2) (from death) Job 33.18; 9.13
enemy [2] 5.8; 7.3
evil 5.4; 7.9
grief Job 17.7; Prov 10.1
help [2] 5.2; 7.6
mercy Job 41.3; 9.13
pity Job 30.24; 17.10
praise Job 40.14; 7.17
prayer 5.3; 10.17
punish 5.10; 7.16
rebuke Job 5.17; 18.15
remember 4.3; 9.5
rescue Job 29.17; 7.1
save 3.7; 7.1
shame Job 19.3; 25.2
strength Job 40.16; 10.10
tear (2) Job 16.20; 30.5
trouble 4.1; 7.14
weep [3] Job 30.25; 31.10
world of the dead Job 40.13; 16.10

6 LORD, don't be angry and rebuke
me!
Don't punish me in your anger!
2 I am worn out, O LORD; have pity on
me!
Give me strength; I am completely
exhausted
3 and my whole being is deeply
troubled.
How long, O LORD, will you wait to
help me?

4 Come and save me, LORD;
in your mercy rescue me from
death.
5 In the world of the dead you are not
remembered;
no one can praise you there.

6 I am worn out with grief;
every night my bed is damp from
my weeping;
my pillow is soaked with tears.
7 I can hardly see;
my eyes are so swollen
from the weeping caused by my
enemies.

8 Keep away from me, you evil men!
The LORD hears my weeping;
9 he listens to my cry for help
and will answer my prayer.
10 My enemies will know the bitter
shame of defeat;
in sudden confusion they will be
driven away.

A Prayer for Justice[i]

above 1 Kgs 8.23; 18.16
anger 6.1; 18.7
betray Job 17.5; Prov 14.25
change Job 23.13; 30.11
condemn 5.10; 9.5
deadly 5.9; 17.9
deceive 5.6; 12.2
demand Job 27.8; 78.18
desire Job 27.10; 10.3
enemy [3] 6.7; 8.2
evil [3] 6.8; 10.3
favour Job 37.13; 9.4
friend Job 42.7; 15.3
fury 2.5; 48.7
help 6.3; 10.14
hurt Job 19.4; 38.12
innocent Job 35.1; 10.8

7 O LORD, my God, I come to you for
protection;
rescue me and save me from all who
pursue me,
2 or else like a lion they will carry me
off
where no one can save me,
and there they will tear me to
pieces.

3–4 O LORD, my God, if I have wronged
anyone,
if I have betrayed a friend
or without cause done violence to
my enemy[j]—
if I have done any of these things—
5 then let my enemies pursue me and
catch me,
let them cut me down and kill me
and leave me lifeless on the ground!

6 Rise in your anger, O LORD!
Stand up against the fury of my
enemies;
rouse yourself and help me!
Justice is what you demand,
7 so bring together all the peoples
round you,
and rule over them from above.[k]
8 You are the judge of all mankind.
Judge in my favour, O LORD;
you know that I am innocent.
9 You are a righteous God
and judge our thoughts and desires.
Stop the wickedness of evil men
and reward those who are good.

10 God is my protector;
he saves those who obey him.
11 God is a righteous judge
and always condemns the wicked.
12 If they do not change their ways,
God will sharpen his sword.
He bends his bow and makes it ready;
13 he takes up his deadly weapons
and aims his burning arrows.

14 See how wicked people think up evil;
they plan trouble and practise
deception.
15 But in the traps they set for others,
they themselves get caught.
16 So they are punished by their own evil
and are hurt by their own violence.

17 I thank the LORD for his justice,
I sing praises to the LORD, the Most
High.

judge [4] Job 34.23; 9.4
justice [2] Job 37.23; 9.8
mankind Job 36.28; 14.2
Most High Deut 32.8; 18.13
obey 5.12; 14.5
plan 2.1; 14.6
practice Job 21.28; Is 2.6
praise 6.5; 8.1
protect [2] 5.11; 14.6
punish 6.1; 9.12
rescue 6.4; 9.13
reward Job 34.11; 18.20
righteous [2] 4.3; 9.8
rise Job 41.18; 18.38
save [3] 6.4; 9.14
thank Neh 12.8; 16.9
trap Job 40.24; 9.15
trouble 6.3; 9.9
violent [2] 5.6; 17.4
way (3) Ezra 6.21; 25.4
wicked [3] 5.5; 9.5
wrong 5.4; 9.12

God's Glory and Man's Dignity[l]

care Job 31.18; 10.4
create Job 40.15; 33.6
creature Job 41.33; 18.10
crown Job 31.36; 21.3
enemy 7.3; 9.3
glory Job 40.10; 19.1
heaven 2.4; 11.4
honour Job 40.10; 15.4
praise 7.17; 9.1
safe 5.11; 9.9
secure Job 36.16; 12.5
sheep Job 42.12; 44.11
world [2] 2.10; 9.8

8 O LORD, our Lord,
your greatness is seen in all the
world!
Your praise reaches up to the
heavens;
2 it is sung by children and babies.
You are safe and secure from all your
enemies;
you stop anyone who opposes you.

3 When I look at the sky, which you have
made,

[h] HEBREW TITLE: *A psalm by David.*
[i] HEBREW TITLE: *A song which David sang to the LORD because of Cush the Benjaminite.*
[j] without...enemy; *or* shown mercy to someone who wronged me unjustly.
[k] *Probable text* rule over them from above; *Hebrew* return above over them.
[l] HEBREW TITLE: *A psalm by David.*

6.1: Ps 38.1 **6.8:** Mt 7.23; Lk 13.27 **7.9:** Rev 2.23 **8.2:** Mt 21.16

at the moon and the stars, which you
set in their places—
4 what is man, that you think of him;
mere man, that you **care** for him?

5 Yet you made him inferior only to
yourself;[m]
you **crowned** him with **glory** and
honour.
6 You appointed him ruler over
everything you made;
you placed him over all **creation**:
7 **sheep** and cattle, and the wild
animals too;
8 the birds and the fish
and the **creatures** in the seas.

9 O LORD, our Lord,
your greatness is seen in all the
world!

Thanksgiving to God for His Justice[n]

9 I will **praise** you, LORD, **with all my
heart**;
I will tell of all the **wonderful** things
you have done.
2 I will sing with **joy** because of you.
I will sing **praise** to you, **Almighty**
God.

3 My **enemies turn** back when you
appear;
they fall down and die.
4 You are fair and **honest** in your
judgements,
and you have **judged** in my **favour**.

5 You have **condemned** the **heathen**
and **destroyed** the **wicked**;
they will be **remembered** no more.
6 Our **enemies** are finished for ever;
you have **destroyed** their cities,
and they are completely **forgotten**.

7 But the LORD is king for ever;
he has set up his **throne** for
judgement.
8 He rules the **world** with **righteousness**;
he **judges** the nations with **justice**.

9 The LORD is a **refuge** for the
oppressed,
a place of **safety** in times of **trouble**.
10 Those who know you, LORD, will **trust**
you;
you do not **abandon** anyone who
comes to you.

11 Sing **praise** to the LORD, who rules in
Zion!
Tell every nation what he has done!
12 God **remembers** those who **suffer**;
he does not **forget** their cry,
and he **punishes** those who **wrong**
them.

13 Be **merciful** to me, O LORD!
See the **sufferings** my **enemies** cause
me!
Rescue me **from death**, O LORD,
14 that I may stand before the people
of Jerusalem
and tell them all the things for
which I **praise** you.
I will **rejoice** because you **saved** me.

15 The **heathen** have dug a pit and fallen
in;
they have been caught in their own
trap.
16 The LORD has **revealed** himself by his
righteous judgements,
and the **wicked** are **trapped** by their
own deeds.

17 **Death** is the destiny of all the **wicked**,
of all those who **reject** God.
18 The **needy** will not always be
neglected;
the **hope** of the **poor** will not be
crushed for ever.

19 Come, LORD! Do not let men **defy** you!
Bring the **heathen** before you
and pronounce **judgement** on them.
20 Make them **afraid**, O LORD;
make them know that they are only
mortal beings.

A Prayer for Justice

10 Why are you so far away, O
LORD?
Why do you hide yourself when we
are in **trouble**?
2 The **wicked** are **proud** and **persecute**
the **poor**;
catch them in the **traps** they have
made.

3 The **wicked** man is **proud** of his **evil**
desires;
the **greedy** man **curses** and **rejects**
the LORD.
4 A **wicked** man does not **care** about the
LORD;
in his **pride** he thinks that God
doesn't **matter**.

5 A **wicked** man **succeeds** in everything.
He cannot **understand** God's
judgements;
he **sneers** at his **enemies**.

[m] yourself; *or* the gods, *or* the angels. [n] HEBREW TITLE: *A psalm by David.*

8.4: Job 7.17–18; Ps 144.3; Heb 2.6–8 **8.6:** 1 Cor 15.27; Eph 1.22; Heb 2.8

world 8.1; 19.4
wrong 7.3; 10.15

abandon Job 8.20; 16.10
afraid 3.6; 23.4
Almighty Job 40.1; 21.7
being 6.3; 29.1
condemn 7.11; 28.3
death (1) Job 31.11; 16.10
death (2) (from death) 6.4; 33.19
defy Job 15.25; Is 1.20
destroy [2] 5.6; 18.4
enemy [3] 8.2; 10.5
favour 7.8; 10.18
forget [2] Job 41.8; 13.1
heart Job 41.24; 11.5
heathen [3] 1 Sam 17.26; 44.2
honest Job 31.6; 12.1
hope Job 35.10; 31.24
joy 5.11; 16.11
judge [5] 7.8; 10.5
justice 7.6; 17.1
mercy 6.4; 25.16
mortal Job 21.4; 10.18
need Job 35.7; 10.14
neglect Job 20.19; 22.24
oppress Job 37.17; 10.18
poor Job 36.6; 10.2
praise [4] 8.1; 12.7
punish 7.16; 10.12
refuge 1 Chr 6.57; 19.14
reject 1.1; 10.3
rejoice 5.11; 21.1
remember [2] 6.5; 10.12
rescue 7.1; 13.5
reveal Job 20.27; 17.7
righteous [2] 7.9; 11.7
safe 8.2; 11.1
save 7.1; 17.7
suffer [2] Job 37.17; 10.12
throne 2.4; 11.4
trap [2] 7.15; 10.2
trouble 7.14; 10.1
trust 5.9; 11.1
turn 3.1; 17.6
wicked [3] 7.9; 10.2
wonder (1) Job 37.5; 16.6

care [2] 8.4; 18.35
courage 3.3; 18.45
curse [2] Job 24.18; 37.22
desire 7.9; 17.3
despise 5.6; 15.4
enemy 9.3; 13.2
evil [3] 7.9; 12.7
fail Job 32.12; 89.33
favour 9.4; 17.2
god (2) (other gods) Job 12.6; 16.4
greed Job 20.20; Prov 11.6
hate 5.5; 11.5
help [2] 7.6; 12.1
helpless [3] Job 41.25; 22.21
innocent 7.8; 15.5
judge [2] 9.4; 17.2
lie (2) 5.6; 12.2
matter Job 9.21; 1 Cor 3.7
mortal 9.20; 22.29
need 9.18; 12.5
notice (1) Job 2.3; 28.5
oppress 9.9; 12.5
orphan Job 31.17; 68.5
persecute Job 30.21; 12.5
poor [2] 9.18; 22.24

power 3.7; 16.10
prayer 6.9; 17.1
proud [3] 5.5; 17.10
punish [3] 9.12; 11.6
reject 9.17; 15.4
remember 9.5; 22.27
sneer Job 21.3; 44.16
speech Job 11.3; 19.3
strength 6.2; 13.3
succeed (1) 1.3; 20.4
suffer [2] 9.12; 17.14
terror Job 30.15; 31.13
threat Job 26.11; 27.12
trap [2] 9.15; 18.5
trouble [3] 9.9; 13.2
understand Job 42.3; 19.8
vanish Job 24.19; 37.20
victim [2] Job 29.17; Prov 9.18
wicked [8] 9.5; 11.2
word (1) 5.1; 12.4
worship (2) (of other gods) Job 31.26; 16.4
wrong 9.12; 14.3

6 He says to himself, "I will never fail;
I will never be in trouble."
7 His speech is filled with curses, lies,
and threats;
he is quick to speak hateful, evil
words.

8 He hides himself in the villages,
waiting to murder innocent people.
He spies on his helpless victims;
9 he waits in his hiding place like a
lion.
He lies in wait for the poor;
he catches them in his trap and
drags them away.

10 The helpless victims lie crushed;
brute strength has defeated them.
11 The wicked man says to himself, "God
doesn't care!
He has closed his eyes and will
never see me!"

12 O LORD, punish those wicked men!
Remember those who are suffering!
13 How can a wicked man despise God
and say to himself, "He will not
punish me"?

14 But you do see; you take notice of
trouble and suffering
and are always ready to help.
The helpless man commits himself to
you;
you have always helped the needy.

15 Break the power of wicked and evil
men;
punish them for the wrong they
have done
until they do it no more.

16 The LORD is king for ever and ever.
Those who worship other gods
will vanish from his land.

17 You will listen, O LORD, to the prayers
of the lowly;
you will give them courage.
18 You will hear the cries of the
oppressed and the orphans;
you will judge in their favour,
so that mortal men may cause
terror no more.

Confidence in the LORD[o]

apart 1.5; 18.9
fool Job 40.3; 14.1
hate 10.7; 18.17
heart 9.1; 13.2

11 I trust in the LORD for safety.
How foolish of you to say to
me,
"Fly away like a bird to the
mountains,[p]
2 because the wicked have drawn
their bows and aimed their
arrows
to shoot from the shadows at good
men.
3 There is nothing a good man can do
when everything falls apart."

4 The LORD is in his holy temple;
he has his throne in heaven.
He watches people everywhere
and knows what they are doing.
5 He examines the good and the wicked
alike;
the lawless he hates with all his
heart.

6 He sends down flaming coals[q] and
burning sulphur on the wicked;
he punishes them with scorching
winds.
7 The LORD is righteous and loves good
deeds;
those who do them will live in his
presence.

heaven 8.1; 14.2
holy 5.7; 20.6
love 5.7; 13.5
presence 5.4; 16.8
punish 10.12; 17.14
righteous 9.8; 25.8
safe 9.9; 12.7
Temple (1) (of God) 5.7; 15.1
throne 9.7; 22.3
trust 9.10; 12.6
watch Job 39.1; 17.11
wicked [3] 10.2; 12.7

A Prayer for Help[r]

12 Help us, LORD!
There is not a good man left;
honest men can no longer be found.
2 All of them lie to one another;
they deceive each other with
flattery.

3 Silence those flattering tongues, O
LORD!
Close those boastful mouths that say,
4 "With our words we get what we want.
We will say what we wish,
and no one can stop us."

5 "But now I will come," says the LORD,
"because the needy are oppressed
and the persecuted groan in pain.
I will give them the security they long
for."

6 The promises of the LORD can be
trusted;
they are as genuine as silver
refined seven times in the furnace.

7–8 Wicked men are everywhere,
and everyone praises what is evil.
Keep us always safe, O LORD,
and preserve us from such people.

boast Esth 5.11; 38.16
deceive 7.14; 32.2
each other 2 Chr 20.23; 41.7
evil 10.3; 14.4
groan Job 35.9; 38.8
help 10.14; 17.1
honest 9.4; 17.1
lie (2) 10.7; 27.12
need 10.14; 16.5
oppress 10.18; 34.2
pain Job 33.19; 38.3
persecute 10.2; 31.15
praise 9.1; 16.7
preserve 2 Chr 9.8; 25.21
promise Job 41.4; 15.4
refine Job 28.1; Is 1.25
safe 11.1; 16.1
secure 8.2; 15.5
trust 11.1; 16.1
wicked 11.2; 17.9
wish Job 36.20; 31.8
word (1) 10.7; 15.2

[o] HEBREW TITLE: *By David.*
[p] *Some ancient translations* like a bird to the mountains; *Hebrew* bird, to your *(plural)* mountains.
[q] *One ancient translation* coals; *Hebrew* traps. [r] HEBREW TITLE: *A psalm by David.*

10.7: Rom 3.14

A Prayer for Help[s]

constant Job 10.12; 18.50
downfall 2 Chr 26.16; 38.16
endure Job 14.12; 33.11
enemy [2] 10.5; 17.7
forget 9.6; 31.12
glad Job 33.32; 16.9
heart 11.5; 17.3
love 11.7; 17.7
rely Job 39.11; 22.8
rescue 9.13; 18.17
restore 3.3; 30.3
sorrow Neh 9.1; 30.11
strength 10.10; 18.29
triumph Job 17.4; 20.5
trouble 10.1; 16.4

13 How much longer will you **forget**
me, LORD? For ever?
How much longer will you hide
yourself from me?
2 How long must I **endure trouble**?
How long will **sorrow** fill my **heart**
day and night?
How long will my **enemies triumph**
over me?

3 Look at me, O LORD my God, and
answer me.
Restore my **strength**; don't let me
die.
4 Don't let my **enemies** say, "We have
defeated him."
Don't let them gloat over my
downfall.

5 I **rely** on your **constant love**;
I will be **glad**, because you will
rescue me.
6 I will sing to you, O LORD,
because you have been good to me.

The Wickedness of Men[t]
(Ps 53)

bad 2 Chr 35.23; 37.19
corrupt Job 15.16; 53.1
evil [2] 12.7; 17.3
fool 11.1; 38.5
God's people 3.8; 22.31
happy 5.11; 19.5
heaven 11.4; 20.6
humble Job 40.11; 18.27
ignorant Job 42.3; 53.4
mankind 7.8; 33.13
obey 7.10; 15.2
plan 7.14; 20.4
pray [2] 5.2; 17.6
prosper Job 42.10; 22.26
protect 7.1; 16.1
right (1) [2] 4.5; 15.2
rob Job 22.9; 53.4
terrible 1 Chr 21.8; 53.1
terrify 2.5; 46.6
victory 3.3; 18.39
wise Job 38.37; 36.3
worship (1) (of God) 5.7; 15.1
wrong 10.15; 15.3

14 **Fools** say to themselves,
"There is no God."
They are all **corrupt**,
and they have done **terrible** things;
there is no one who does what is
right.

2 The LORD looks down from **heaven** at
mankind
to see if there are any who are **wise**,
any who **worship** him.
3 But they have all gone **wrong**;
they are all equally **bad**.
Not one of them does what is **right**,
not a single one.

4 "Don't they know?" asks the LORD.
"Are all these **evildoers ignorant**?
They live by **robbing my people**,
and they never **pray** to me."

5 But then they will be **terrified**,
for God is with those who **obey** him.
6 **Evildoers** frustrate the **plans** of the
humble man,
but the LORD is his **protection**.

7 How I **pray** that **victory**
will come to Israel from Zion.
How **happy** the people of Israel will be
when the LORD makes them
prosperous again!

What God Requires[u]

15 LORD, who may enter your
Temple?
Who may **worship** on Zion, your
sacred hill?[v]

2 A person who **obeys** God in everything
and always does what is **right**,
whose **words** are **true** and **sincere**,
3 and who does not **slander** others.
He does no **wrong** to his **friends**
nor spreads rumours about his
neighbours.
4 He **despises** those whom God **rejects**,
but **honours** those who **obey** the
LORD.
He always does what he **promises**,
no matter how much it may cost.
5 He makes loans without charging
interest
and cannot be **bribed** to **testify**
against the **innocent**.

Whoever does these things will always
be **secure**.

bribe Job 36.18; 26.10
despise 10.13; 22.6
friend 7.3; 25.14
honour 8.5; 22.23
innocent 10.8; 18.20
neighbour Job 31.9; 31.11
obey [2] 14.5; 17.4
promise 12.6; 22.25
reject 10.3; 36.1
right (1) 14.1; 17.2
sacred 3.4; 43.3
secure 12.5; 16.9
sincere Job 33.3; 41.6
slander Job 5.21; 64.4
Temple (1) (of God) 11.4; 18.6
testify Deut 17.6; 35.11
true 5.11; 33.4
word (1) 12.4; 17.6
worship (1) (of God) 14.2; 22.23
wrong 14.3; 17.15

A Prayer of Confidence[w]

16 **Protect** me, O God; I **trust** in you
for **safety**.
2 I say to the LORD, "You are my Lord;
all the good things I have come from
you."

3 How excellent are the LORD's **faithful**
people!
My greatest **pleasure** is to be with
them.

4 Those who rush to other **gods**
bring many **troubles** on themselves.[x]
I will not take part in their **sacrifices**;
I will not **worship their gods**.

5 You, LORD, are all I have,
and you give me all I **need**;
my future is in your hands.
6 How **wonderful** are your **gifts** to me;
how good they are!

7 I **praise** the LORD, because he **guides**
me,
and in the night my **conscience**
warns me.
8 I am always aware of the LORD's
presence;

abandon 9.10; 22.1
conscience Job 27.6; Prov 20.9
death (1) 9.17; 18.4
faithful [2] Job 23.11; 18.25
gift Job 6.22; 37.21
glad 13.5; 21.1
god (2) (other gods) [2] 10.16; 31.6
guide 1.6; 23.3
joy 9.2; 17.15
life (1) Job 42.12; 17.14
life (2) (to life) Job 14.7; Prov 2.19
need 12.5; 23.1
pleasure [2] 1 Chr 28.4; 62.4
power 10.15; 18.17
praise 12.7; 18.3
presence [2] 11.7; 17.15
protect [2] 14.6; 17.8
sacrifice 4.5; 20.3
safe 12.7; 17.7
secure 15.5; 21.7
serve 2.11; 22.30
thank 7.17; 26.7
trouble 13.2; 18.6
trust 12.6; 19.7
warn 2.5; 40.3
wonder (1) 9.1; 17.7
world of the dead 6.5; 28.1
worship (2) (of other gods) 10.16; 24.4

[s] HEBREW TITLE: *A psalm by David.* [t] HEBREW TITLE: *By David.* [u] HEBREW TITLE: *A psalm by David.*
[v] SACRED HILL: *See 2.6.* [w] HEBREW TITLE: *A psalm by David.*
[x] *Probable text* Those...themselves; *Hebrew unclear.*

14.1-3: Rom 3.10-12 **16.8-11:** Acts 2.25-28

he is near, and nothing can shake
me.

9 And so I am **thankful** and **glad**,
and I feel completely **secure**,
10 because you **protect** me from the
power of **death**.
I have **served** you **faithfully**,
and you will not **abandon** me to the
world of the dead.

11 You will show me the path that leads
to life;
your **presence** fills me with **joy**
and brings me **pleasure** for ever.

The Prayer of an Innocent Man[y]

17 Listen, O LORD, to my **plea** for
justice;
pay attention to my cry for **help**!
Listen to my **honest prayer**.
2 You will **judge** in my **favour**,
because you know what is **right**.

3 You know my **heart**.
You have come to me at night;
you have examined me completely
and found no **evil desire** in me.
4 I speak no **evil** as others do;
I have **obeyed** your **command**
and have not followed paths of
violence.
5 I have always walked in your way
and have never strayed from it.

6 I **pray** to you, O God, because you
answer me;
so **turn** to me and listen to my
words.
7 **Reveal** your **wonderful love** and **save**
me;
at your side I am **safe** from my
enemies.

8 **Protect** me as you would your very
eyes;
hide me in the shadow of your wings
9 from the attacks of the **wicked**.

Deadly enemies surround me;
10 they have no **pity** and speak **proudly**.
11 They are round me now, wherever I
turn,
watching for a chance to pull me
down.
12 They are like lions, waiting for me,
wanting to tear me to pieces.
13 Come, LORD! Oppose my **enemies** and
defeat them!
Save me from the **wicked** by your
sword;
14 **save** me from those who in this **life**
have all they want.
Punish them with the **sufferings** you
have stored up for them;
may there be **enough** for their
children
and some left over for their
children's children!

15 But I will see you, because I have done
no **wrong**;
and when I awake, your **presence**
will fill me with **joy**.

command Job 39.25; 18.22
deadly 7.13; 40.2
desire 10.3; 19.10
enemy [3] 13.2; 18.3
enough Job 42.16; 37.19
evil [2] 14.4; 19.13
favour 10.18; 45.12
heart 13.2; 21.2
help 12.1; 18.6
honest 12.1; 25.21
joy 16.11; 20.5
judge 10.5; 19.9
justice 9.8; 19.8
life (1) 16.11; 21.4
love 13.5; 18.1
obey 15.2; 18.21
pity 6.2; 72.13
plead Job 41.3; 35.23
pray 14.4; 31.1
prayer 10.17; 25.1
presence 16.8; 21.6
protect 16.1; 18.2
proud 10.2; 18.27
punish 11.6; 28.4
reveal 9.16; 19.1
right (1) 15.2; 18.20
safe 16.1; 18.2
save [3] 9.14; 18.3
suffer 10.12; 22.24
turn [2] 9.3; 18.21
violent 7.3; 18.48
watch 11.4; 33.18
wicked [2] 12.7; 18.26
wonder (1) 16.6; 26.7
word (1) 15.2; 18.30
wrong 15.3; 18.23

David's Song of Victory[z]
(2 Sam 22.1–51)

18 How I **love** you, LORD!
You are my **defender**.

2 The LORD is my **protector**;
he is my **strong** fortress.
My God is my **protection**,
and with him I am **safe**.
He **protects** me like a shield;
he **defends** me and keeps me **safe**.
3 I call to the LORD,
and he **saves** me from my **enemies**.
Praise the LORD!

4 The **danger** of **death** was all round me;
the waves of **destruction** rolled over
me.
5 The **danger** of **death** was round me,
and the **grave** set its **trap** for me.
6 In my **trouble** I called to the LORD;
I called to my God for **help**.
In his **temple** he heard my voice;
he listened to my cry for **help**.

7 Then the earth **trembled** and shook;
the foundations of the mountains
rocked and quivered,
because God was **angry**.
8 Smoke poured out of his nostrils,
a consuming flame and burning
coals from his mouth.
9 He tore the sky **apart** and came down
with a **dark cloud** under his feet.
10 He flew swiftly on a winged **creature**;[x]
he travelled on the wings of the
wind.
11 He covered himself with **darkness**;
thick **clouds**, full of water,
surrounded him.
12 Hailstones and flashes of fire

above 7.7; 78.23
alone [2] 4.8; 39.13
anger [2] 7.6; 21.9
apart 11.3; 60.2
bless 5.12; 21.3
bow (2) 5.7; 22.29
care 10.4; 27.10
choose 4.3; 20.6
cloud [3] Job 38.9; 68.4
command 17.4; 19.7
constant 13.5; 21.7
courage 10.17; 31.24
creature 8.8; 69.34
danger [3] 3.3; 22.5
dark [4] Job 38.9; 23.4
death (1) [2] 16.10; 30.9
defend [5] 4.1; 28.1
depend 2 Chr 31.18; 33.4
destroy [3] 9.5; 21.9
disobey Esth 3.3; 44.18
enemy [10] 17.7; 21.8
faithful 16.3; 25.10
fault Job 34.32; 19.12
grave Job 21.32; 30.3
hate [2] 11.5; 21.8
help [4] 17.1; 20.2
humble [2] 14.6; 25.9
innocent [2] 15.5; 24.5
keep from [2] Job 36.21; 25.20
law [2] 1.2; 19.7
light (1) Job 41.18; 27.1
love [2] 17.7; 21.7
Most High 7.17; 46.4
obey [2] 17.4; 19.8
observe Esth 9.19; 37.37
perfect [2] 4.8; 19.7
please 5.4; 20.3
power [3] 16.10; 20.6
praise [4] 16.7; 20.5
proclaim Esth 9.1; 30.9
protect [7] 17.8; 20.1
proud 17.10; 22.29
pure Job 28.19; 19.10
rebel 5.10; 25.3
rebuke 6.1; 39.11
rescue 13.5; 22.19
reward [2] 7.9; 19.11
right (1) [2] 17.2; 19.8
rise 7.6; 20.8

[y] HEBREW TITLE: *A prayer by David.*
[z] HEBREW TITLE: *The words that David, the LORD's servant, sang to the LORD on the day the LORD saved him from Saul and all his other enemies.* [x] WINGED CREATURE: *See Word List.*

16.10: Acts 13.35

safe [5] 17.7; 19.13
save [8] 17.7; 22.4
scatter Job 4.11; 44.11
seek 2 Sam 22.31; 37.4
strength [2] 13.3; 19.7
strike Job 34.20; 35.6
strong [4] Job 41.12; 24.8
subject (1) 2 Chr 21.19; 106.42
Temple (1) (of God) 15.1; 20.2
trap 10.2; 31.4
tremble [2] 4.4; 55.5
trouble [2] 16.4; 20.1
turn 17.6; 21.12
victory [4] 14.7; 20.5
violent 17.4; 46.3
wicked 17.9; 26.5
word (1) 17.6; 19.3
wrong 17.15; 32.1

came from the lightning before him
and broke through the dark clouds.

13 Then the LORD thundered from the sky;
and the voice of the Most High was heard.[a]
14 He shot his arrows and scattered his enemies;
with flashes of lightning he sent them running.
15 The floor of the ocean was laid bare,
and the foundations of the earth were uncovered,
when you rebuked your enemies, LORD,
and roared at them in anger.

16 The LORD reached down from above
and took hold of me;
he pulled me out of the deep waters.
17 He rescued me from my powerful enemies
and from all those who hate me—
they were too strong for me.
18 When I was in trouble, they attacked me,
but the LORD protected me.
19 He helped me out of danger;
he saved me because he was pleased with me.

20 The LORD rewards me because I do what is right;
he blesses me because I am innocent.
21 I have obeyed the law of the LORD;
I have not turned away from my God.
22 I have observed all his laws;
I have not disobeyed his commands.
23 He knows that I am faultless,
that I have kept myself from doing wrong.
24 And so he rewards me because I do what is right,
because he knows that I am innocent.

25 O LORD, you are faithful to those who are faithful to you;
completely good to those who are perfect.
26 You are pure to those who are pure,
but hostile to those who are wicked.
27 You save those who are humble,
but you humble those who are proud.

28 O LORD, you give me light;
you dispel my darkness.
29 You give me strength to attack my enemies
and power to overcome their defences.

30 This God—how perfect are his deeds!
How dependable his words!
He is like a shield
for all who seek his protection.
31 The LORD alone is God;
God alone is our defence.
32 He is the God who makes me strong,
who makes my pathway safe.
33 He makes me sure-footed as a deer;
he keeps me safe on the mountains.
34 He trains me for battle,
so that I can use the strongest bow.

35 O LORD, you protect me and save me;
your care has made me great,
and your power has kept me safe.
36 You have kept me from being captured,
and I have never fallen.
37 I pursue my enemies and catch them;
I do not stop until I destroy them.
38 I strike them down, and they cannot rise;
they lie defeated before me.
39 You give me strength for the battle
and victory over my enemies.
40 You make my enemies run from me;
I destroy those who hate me.
41 They cry for help, but no one saves them;
they call to the LORD, but he does not answer.
42 I crush them, so that they become like dust
which the wind blows away.
I trample on them like mud in the streets.

43 You saved me from a rebellious people
and made me ruler over the nations;
people I did not know have now become my subjects.
44 Foreigners bow before me;
when they hear me, they obey.
45 They lose their courage
and come trembling from their fortresses.

46 The LORD lives! Praise my defender!
Proclaim the greatness of the God who saves me.
47 He gives me victory over my enemies;
he subdues the nations under me
48 and saves me from my foes.

[a] *One ancient translation (and see 2 Sam 22.14)* was heard; *Hebrew* was heard hailstones and flashes of fire.

18.33: Hab 3.19

O LORD, you give me **victory** over my
enemies
and **protect** me from **violent** men.
49 And so I **praise** you among the nations;
I sing **praises** to you.

50 God gives great **victories** to his king;
he shows **constant love** to the one he
has **chosen**,
to David and his descendants for
ever.

God's Glory in Creation[b]

accept Job 22.22; 20.3
announce 2.7; 98.2
bridegroom Is 62.5
command [2] 18.22; 25.10
desire 17.3; 20.4
eager Job 39.21; 73.10
error Ex 28.38; 25.7
evil 17.3; 22.16
fault 18.23; 50.20
free 2.3; 31.8
glory 8.5; 21.5
happy [2] 14.7; 32.1
judge 17.2; 26.2
justice [2] 17.1; 33.5
knowledge Job 36.3; 94.10
law [2] 18.21; 37.31
message Job 4.12; 147.19
mind (1) Job 37.19; 45.1
new Job 32.19; 23.3
obey [2] 18.21; 25.10
perfect [2] 18.25; 50.2
plain (1) 5.8; 50.21
pure 18.26; 24.4
race (2) Job 39.24; Ecc 9.11
redeem 49.7
refuge 9.9; 31.2
reveal 17.7; 80.2
reverence 5.7; 25.12
reward 18.20; 58.11
right (1) 18.20; 23.3
safe 18.2; 22.9
servant Job 42.7; 22.23
speech 10.7; 36.3
strength 18.29; 21.1
trust 16.1; 20.7
understand 10.5; 71.15
wisdom Job 42.3; 49.3
word (1) [2] 18.30; 28.3
world 9.8; 22.27

19 How clearly the sky **reveals**
God's **glory**!
How **plainly** it shows what he has
done!
2 Each day **announces** it to the following
day;
each night repeats it to the next.
3 No **speech** or **words** are used,
no sound is heard;
4 yet their **message**[c] goes out to all the
world
and is heard to the ends of the earth.
God made a home in the sky for the
sun;
5 it comes out in the morning like a
happy bridegroom,
like an athlete **eager** to run a **race**.
6 It starts at one end of the sky
and goes across to the other.
Nothing can hide from its heat.

The Law of the LORD

7 The **law** of the LORD is **perfect**;
it gives **new strength**.
The **commands** of the LORD are
trustworthy,
giving **wisdom** to those who lack it.
8 The **laws** of the LORD are **right**,
and those who **obey** them are **happy**.
The **commands** of the LORD are **just**
and give **understanding** to the **mind**.
9 **Reverence** for the LORD is good;
it will continue for ever.
The **judgements** of the LORD are **just**;
they are always fair.
10 They are more **desirable** than the
finest gold;
they are sweeter than the **purest**
honey.
11 They give **knowledge** to me, your
servant;
I am **rewarded** for **obeying** them.

12 No one can see his own **errors**;
deliver me, LORD, from hidden
faults!
13 Keep me **safe**, also, from wilful sins;
don't let them rule over me.
Then I shall be **perfect**
and **free** from the **evil** of sin.

14 May my **words** and my thoughts be
acceptable to you,
O LORD, my **refuge** and my
redeemer!

A Prayer for Victory[d]

20 May the LORD answer you when
you are in **trouble**!
May the God of Jacob **protect** you!
2 May he send you **help** from his **Temple**
and give you aid from Mount Zion.
3 May he **accept** all your **offerings**
and be **pleased** with all your
sacrifices.
4 May he give you what you **desire**
and make all your **plans succeed**.
5 Then we will shout for **joy** over your
victory
and **celebrate** your **triumph** by
praising our God.
May the LORD answer all your
requests.

accept 19.14; 119.108
celebrate Esth 9.23; 118.24
choose 18.50; 28.8
desire 19.10; 21.2
heaven 14.2; 29.1
help 18.6; 21.5
holy 11.4; 22.3
joy 17.15; 21.6
offer 5.3; 22.25
plan 14.6; 21.11
please 18.19; 35.27
power [2] 18.17; 21.13
praise 18.3; 21.13
protect 18.2; 23.4
request Esth 7.3; 21.2
rise 18.38; 35.23
sacrifice 16.4; 22.25
stumble Job 18.7; 27.2
succeed (1) 10.5; 21.11
Temple (1) (of God) 18.6; 24.3
triumph 13.2; 24.10
trouble 18.6; 22.11
trust [2] 19.7; 21.7
victory [4] 18.39; 21.1

6 Now I know that the LORD gives
victory to his **chosen** king;
he answers him from his **holy**
heaven
and by his **power** gives him great
victories.
7 Some **trust** in their war-chariots
and others in their horses,
but we **trust** in the **power of the**
LORD our God.
8 Such people will **stumble** and fall,
but we will **rise** and stand firm.

9 Give **victory** to the king, O LORD;
answer[e] us when we call.

Praise for Victory[f]

21 The king is **glad**, O LORD,
because you gave him
strength;
he **rejoices** because you made him
victorious.
2 You have given him his **heart's desire**;
you have answered his **request**.

3 You came to him with great **blessings**
and set a **crown** of gold on his head.
4 He asked for life, and you gave it,
a long and **lasting life**.

Almighty 9.2; 46.7
anger 18.7; 27.9
bless [2] 18.20; 24.5
constant 18.50; 25.6
crown 8.5; 89.39
desire 20.4; 26.2
destroy 18.4; 26.9
devour Deut 28.42; Is 9.12
enemy 18.3; 22.12
glad 16.9; 28.7
glory 19.1; 26.8
hate 18.17; 25.19
heart 17.3; 22.14
help 20.2; 22.1
joy 20.5; 27.6
last (1) Job 19.24; 30.5

[b] HEBREW TITLE: *A psalm by David.*
[d] HEBREW TITLE: *A psalm by David.*
[f] HEBREW TITLE: *A psalm by David.*
[c] *Some ancient translations* message; *Hebrew* line.
[e] *Some ancient translations* answer; *Hebrew* he will answer.

18.49: Rom 15.9 **19.4:** Rom 10.18

life (1) 17.14; 22.20
love 18.1; 23.6
Majesty Job 40.10; 29.4
plan 20.4; 31.13
plot (1) 5.10; 31.13
power 20.6; 29.1
praise [2] 20.5; 22.3
presence 17.15; 22.25
rejoice 9.14; 31.7
request 20.5; Jer 21.1
secure 16.9; 27.5
strength [2] 19.7; 22.14
succeed (1) 20.4; 35.27
trust 20.7; 22.4
turn 18.21; 22.24
victory 20.5; 24.8

5 His **glory** is great because of your
help;
you have given him fame and
majesty.
6 Your **blessings** are with him for ever
and your **presence** fills him with **joy**.

7 The king **trusts** in the LORD **Almighty**;
and because of the LORD's **constant**
love
he will always be **secure**.
8 The king will capture all his **enemies**;
he will capture everyone who **hates**
him.
9 He will **destroy** them like a blazing fire
when he appears.

The LORD will **devour** them in his
anger,
and fire will consume them.
10 None of their descendants will survive;
the king will kill them all.

11 They make their **plans**, and **plot**
against him,
but they will not **succeed**.
12 He will shoot his arrows at them
and make them **turn** and run.

13 We **praise** you, LORD, for your great
strength!
We will sing and **praise** your **power**.

A Cry of Anguish and a Song of Praise[g]

22 My God, my God, why have you
abandoned me?
I have cried **desperately** for **help**,
but still it does not come.
2 During the day I call to you, my God,
but you do not answer;
I call at night,
but get no **rest**.
3 But you are **enthroned** as the **Holy**
One,
the one whom Israel **praises**.
4 Our ancestors put their **trust** in you;
they **trusted** you, and you **saved**
them.
5 They called to you and **escaped** from
danger;
they **trusted** you and were not
disappointed.

6 But I am no longer a man; I am a
worm,
despised and **scorned** by everyone!
7 All who see me **jeer** at me;
they stick out their tongues and
shake their heads.
8 "You **relied** on the LORD," they say.
"Why doesn't he **save** you?
If the LORD likes you,
why doesn't he **help** you?"

9 It was you who brought me **safely**
through **birth**,
and when I was a baby, you kept me
safe.
10 I have **relied** on you since the day I
was born,
and you have always been my God.
11 Do not stay away from me!
Trouble is near,
and there is no one to **help**.

12 Many **enemies** surround me like bulls;
they are all round me,
like fierce bulls from the land of
Bashan.
13 They open their mouths like lions,
roaring and tearing at me.

14 My **strength** is gone,
gone like water spilt on the ground.
All my bones are out of joint;
my **heart** is like melted wax.
15 My throat[h] is as dry as dust,
and my tongue sticks to the roof of
my mouth.
You have left me for **dead** in the dust.

16 A gang of **evil** men is round me;
like a pack of dogs they close in on
me;
they tear at[i] my hands and feet.
17 All my bones can be seen.
My **enemies** look at me and stare.
18 They gamble for my clothes
and divide them among themselves.

19 O LORD, don't stay away from me!
Come quickly to my **rescue**!
20 **Save** me from the sword;
save my **life** from these dogs.
21 **Rescue** me from these lions;
I am **helpless**[j] before these wild
bulls.

22 I will tell my people what you have
done;
I will **praise** you in their assembly:
23 "**Praise** him, you **servants** of the LORD!
Honour him, you descendants of
Jacob!
Worship him, you people of Israel!
24 He does not **neglect** the **poor** or **ignore**
their **suffering**;
he does not **turn** away from them,

abandon 16.10; 27.9
birth Job 39.1; Ecc 3.2
bow (2) [2] 18.44; 29.2
danger 18.4; 25.15
dead Job 39.30; 30.9
despair Job 31.16; 27.14
despise 15.4; 74.18
disappoint 34.5
enemy [2] 21.8; 23.5
escape Job 30.13; 60.4
evil 19.13; 26.5
God's people 14.4; 26.12
heart 21.2; 28.3
help [4] 21.5; 25.15
helpless 10.8; 34.6
holy 20.6; 24.3
honour 15.4; 23.5
ignore Job 37.24; 50.22
jeer 40.15
life (1) 21.4; 23.6
mortal 10.18; 78.39
neglect 9.18; 72.12
offer 20.3; 25.1
poor [2] 10.2; 35.10
praise [5] 21.13; 26.12
presence 21.6; 24.6
promise 15.4; 23.3
prosper 14.7; 25.13
proud 18.27; 31.18
race (1) Esth 3.8; Prov 8.31
rely [2] 13.5; 71.6
remember 10.12; 25.6
rescue [2] 18.17; 25.15
rest (1) Job 11.18; 23.2
sacrifice 20.3; 27.6
safe [2] 19.13; 25.20
save [5] 18.3; 24.5
scorn Job 31.34; 44.14
servant 19.11; 27.9
serve 16.10; 72.11
strength 21.1; 23.3
suffer 17.14; 25.18
throne 11.4; 45.9
trouble 20.1; 25.17
trust [3] 21.7; 25.2
turn [2] 21.12; 25.16
world 19.4; 24.1
worship (1) (of God) [3] 15.1; 26.6

[g] HEBREW TITLE: *A psalm by David.* [h] *Probable text* throat; *Hebrew* strength.
[i] *Some ancient translations* they tear at; *others* they tie; *Hebrew* like a lion.
[j] *Some ancient translations* I am helpless; *Hebrew* you answered me.

22.1: Mt 27.46; Mk 15.34 **22.7:** Mt 27.39; Mk 15.29; Lk 23.35 **22.8:** Mt 27.43
22.18: Mt 27.35; Mk 15.24; Lk 23.34; Jn 19.24 **22.22:** Heb 2.12

but answers when they call for
help."

25 In the full assembly I will **praise** you
for what you have done;
in the **presence** of those who
worship you
I will **offer the sacrifices I promised.**
26 The **poor** will eat as much as they
want;
those who come to the LORD will
praise him.
May they **prosper** for ever!

27 All nations will **remember** the LORD.
From every part of the **world** they
will **turn to** him;
all **races** will **worship** him.
28 The LORD is king,
and he rules the nations.

29 All **proud** men will **bow down** to him;[k]
all **mortal** men will **bow down** before
him.
30 Future generations will **serve** him;
men will speak of the Lord to the
coming generation.
31 People not yet born will be told:
"The Lord **saved his people.**"

The LORD Our Shepherd[l]

afraid 9.20; 27.1
banquet Esth 6.14; 69.22
cup Esth 1.7; 75.8
dark 18.9; 35.6
enemy 22.12; 25.2
guide 16.7; 26.3
honour 22.23; 31.19
life (1) 22.20; 27.4
love 21.7; 25.6
need 16.5; 32.6
new 19.7; 33.3
promise 22.25; 24.4
protect 20.1; 25.20
rest (1) 22.2; 55.6
right (1) 19.8; 25.9
shepherd [2] Job 1.16; 28.9
strength 22.14; 29.11
welcome Job 31.31; Prov 19.12

23 The LORD is my **shepherd**;
I have everything I **need**.
2 He lets me **rest** in fields of green grass
and leads me to quiet pools of fresh
water.
3 He gives me **new strength**.
He **guides** me in the **right** paths,
as he has **promised**.
4 Even if I go through the deepest
darkness,
I will not be **afraid**, LORD,
for you are with me.
Your **shepherd's** rod and staff **protect**
me.

5 You prepare a **banquet** for me,
where all my **enemies** can see me;
you **welcome** me as an **honoured** guest
and fill my **cup** to the brim.
6 I know that your goodness and **love**
will be with me all my **life**;
and your house will be my home as
long as I live.

The Great King[m]

act Job 39.16; 37.7
ancient [2] Job 20.4; 68.33

24 The **world** and all that is in it
belong to the LORD;
the earth and all who live on it are
his.
2 He built it on the deep waters beneath
the earth
and laid its foundations in the ocean
depths.

3 Who has the **right** to go up the LORD's
hill?[n]
Who may enter his **holy Temple**?
4 Those who are **pure in act** and in
thought,
who do not **worship idols**
or make **false promises**.
5 The LORD will **bless** them and **save**
them;
God will declare them **innocent**.
6 Such are the people who come to God,
who come into the **presence** of the
God of Jacob.

7 Fling wide the gates,
open the **ancient** doors,
and the great king will come in.
8 Who is this great king?
He is the LORD, **strong** and **mighty**,
the LORD, **victorious** in battle.

9 Fling wide the gates,
open the **ancient** doors,
and the great king will come in.
10 Who is this great king?
The **triumphant** LORD—he is the great
king!

bless 21.3; 28.9
false 4.2; 31.6
holy 22.3; 28.2
idol Neh 9.18; 40.4
innocent 18.20; 26
might Job 34.20; 2
presence 22.25; 3
promise 23.3; 25.1
pure 19.10; 51.10
right (3) Job 31.38; 82.3
save 22.4; 25.2
strong 18.2; 31.24
Temple (1) (of G 20.2; 27.5
triumph 20.5; 27.6
victory 21.1; 33.17
world 22.27; 33.8
worship (2) (of other gods) 16.4;

A Prayer for Guidance and Protection[o]

25 To you, O LORD, I **offer** my
prayer;
2 in you, my God, I **trust**.
Save me from the **shame** of defeat;
don't let my **enemies** gloat over me!
3 Defeat does not come to those who
trust in you,
but to those who are quick to **rebel**
against you.

4 **Teach** me your **ways**, O LORD;
make them known to me.
5 **Teach** me to live according to your
truth,
for you are my God, who **saves** me.
I always **trust** in you.

6 **Remember**, O LORD, your **kindness**
and **constant love**
which you have shown from long
ago.
7 **Forgive** the sins and **errors** of my
youth.

command 19.7; 33
constant [2] 21.7; 26.3
covenant [2] Neh 13.29; 44.17
danger 22.5; 26.12
distress Job 36.15; 38.16
enemy [2] 23.5; 27.
error 19.12; Eph 4
faithful 18.25; 26.3
forgive [3] Job 14.; 32.1
friend 15.3; 28.3
hate 21.8; 26.5
help 22.1; 27.9
honest 17.1; 55.22
humble 18.27; 37.1
keep from 18.23;
kind 4.1; 31.16
learn 2.10; 78.6
lonely Job 30.29;
love [3] 23.6; 26.3
mercy 9.13; 26.11
obey [2] 19.8; 32.11
offer 22.25; 27.6
possess Esth 8.11; 37.9
prayer 17.1; 39.12
preserve 12.7; 34.
promise 24.4; 31.3
prosper 22.26; 37.7
protect 23.4; 27.1
rebel 18.43; 66.7

[k] *Probable text* will bow down to him; *Hebrew* will eat and bow down.
[l] HEBREW TITLE: *A psalm by David.* [m] HEBREW TITLE: *A psalm by David.*
[n] THE LORD'S HILL: *The hill in Jerusalem on which the Temple was built.* [o] HEBREW TITLE: *By David.*

23.2: Rev 7.17 **24.1:** 1 Cor 10.26 **24.4:** Mt 5.8

elieve (1) Job 30.16; 14.3
emember [2] 22.27;).4
escue 22.19; 34.7
everence 19.9; 36.1
ight (1) 23.3; 26.1
ighteous 11.7; 31.1
afe 22.9; 26.12
ave [5] 24.5; 26.11
hame 6.10; 35.26
uffer 22.24; 31.7
each [4] Job 37.19; 7.11
rouble [2] 22.11; 27.5
rust [4] 22.4; 26.1
ruth Job 42.7; 43.3
urn 22.24; 27.9
ay (3) 7.12; 68.21
eak Job 41.23; 31.10
ill (1) 5.8; 40.8
orry Job 30.27; 37.1

In your constant love and goodness,
remember me, LORD!

8 Because the LORD is righteous and
good,
he teaches sinners the path they
should follow.
9 He leads the humble in the right way
and teaches them his will.
10 With faithfulness and love he leads
all who keep his covenant and obey
his commands.

11 Keep your promise, LORD, and forgive
my sins,
for they are many.
12 Those who have reverence for the
LORD
will learn from him the path they
should follow.
13 They will always be prosperous,
and their children will possess the
land.
14 The LORD is the friend of those who
obey him
and he affirms his covenant with
them.

15 I look to the LORD for help at all times,
and he rescues me from danger.
16 Turn to me, LORD, and be merciful to
me,
because I am lonely and weak.
17 Relieve me of my worries
and save me from all my troubles.
18 Consider my distress and suffering
and forgive all my sins.

19 See how many enemies I have;
see how much they hate me.
20 Protect me and save me;
keep me from defeat.
I come to you for safety.
21 May my goodness and honesty
preserve me,
because I trust in you.

22 From all their troubles, O God,
save your people Israel!

The Prayer of a Good Man[p]

ltar Ezra 7.17; 40.6
ribe 15.5; Prov 15.27
onstant 25.6; 31.7
anger 25.15; 27.1
esire 21.2; 37.4
estroy 21.9; 28.5
vil [2] 22.16; 27.2
aithful 25.10; 30.4
ate Job 30.23; 49.13
lory 21.5; 29.1
God's people 22.31; 8.8
uide 23.3; 27.4

26 Declare me innocent, O LORD,
because I do what is right
and trust you completely.
2 Examine me and test me, LORD;
judge my desires and thoughts.
3 Your constant love is my guide;
your faithfulness always leads me.[q]

4 I do not keep company with worthless
people;
I have nothing to do with hypocrites.
5 I hate the company of evil men
and avoid the wicked.

6 LORD, I wash my hands to show that I
am innocent
and march in worship round your
altar.
7 I sing a hymn of thanksgiving
and tell of all your wonderful deeds.

8 I love the house where you live, O
LORD,
the place where your glory dwells.
9 Do not destroy me with the sinners;
spare me from the fate of
murderers—
10 men who do evil all the time
and are always ready to take bribes.

11 As for me, I do what is right;
be merciful to me and save me!

12 I am safe from all dangers;
in the assembly of his people I
praise the LORD.

A Prayer of Praise[r]

27 The LORD is my light and my
salvation;
I will fear no one.
The LORD protects me from all
danger;
I will never be afraid.

2 When evil men attack me and try to
kill me,
they stumble and fall.
3 Even if a whole army surrounds me,
I will not be afraid;
even if enemies attack me,
I will still trust God.[s]

4 I have asked the LORD for one thing;
one thing only do I want:
to live in the LORD's house all my life,
to marvel there at his goodness,
and to ask for his guidance.
5 In times of trouble he will shelter me;
he will keep me safe in his Temple
and make me secure on a high rock.
6 So I will triumph over my enemies
around me.
With shouts of joy I will offer
sacrifices in his Temple;
I will sing, I will praise the LORD.

7 Hear me, LORD, when I call to you!
Be merciful and answer me!
8 When you said, "Come and worship
me,"

hate 25.19; 28.3
hymn Neh 12.8; 71.22
hypocrite 101.7
innocent [2] 24.5; 35.24
judge 19.9; 48.11
love [2] 25.6; 31.7
mercy 25.16; 27.7
praise 22.3; 27.6
right (1) [2] 25.9; 37.14
safe 25.20; 27.5
save 25.2; 28.8
spare Job 33.27; 34.22
test Job 28.27; 66.10
thank 16.9; 30.4
trust 25.2; 27.3
wicked 18.26; 28.3
wonder (1) 17.7; 31.19
worship (1) (of God) 22.23; 27.8
worthless 4.2; 60.11

abandon [3] 22.1; 37.25
afraid [2] 23.4; 30.7
anger 21.9; 30.5
care 18.35; 28.9
danger 26.12; 31.4
despair 22.1; 35.12
enemy [4] 25.2; 30.1
evil 26.5; 28.3
faith Ezra 10.2; 73.2
fear 4.4; 34.4
guide 26.3; 31.3
help 25.15; 28.2
joy 21.6; 28.7
lie (2) 12.2; 31.18
life (1) [2] 23.6; 30.3
light (1) 18.28; 36.9
mercy 26.11; 30.10
offer 25.1; 40.6
praise 26.12; 28.6
protect 25.20; 28.7
sacrifice 22.25; 40.6
safe [2] 26.12; 31.4
salvation 32.7
Saviour 1 Chr 16.35; 38.22
secure 21.7; 30.6
servant 22.23; 31.16
shelter Job 40.22; 31.4
stumble 20.8; 107.27
teach 25.4; 32.8
Temple (1) (of God) [2] 24.3; 28.2
threat 10.7; 38.12
triumph 24.10; 33.16
trouble 25.17; 31.7
trust [3] 26.1; 28.7
turn 25.16; 34.14
worship (1) (of God) 26.6; 33.8

[p] HEBREW TITLE: *By David.* [q] your faithfulness always leads me; *or* I live in loyalty to you.
[r] HEBREW TITLE: *By David.* [s] still trust God; *or* not lose courage.

I answered, "I will come, LORD;
9 don't hide yourself from me!"

Don't be **angry** with me;
don't **turn** your **servant** away.
You have been my **help**;
don't leave me, don't **abandon** me,
O God, my **saviour**.
10 My father and mother may **abandon** me,
but the LORD will take **care** of me.

11 **Teach** me, LORD, what you want me to do,
and lead me along a **safe** path,
because I have many **enemies**.
12 Don't **abandon** me to my **enemies**,
who attack me with **lies** and **threats**.

13 I know that I will live to see
the LORD's goodness in this present **life**.
14 **Trust** in the LORD.
Have **faith**, do not **despair**.
Trust in the LORD.

A Prayer for Help[t]

bless 24.5; 29.11
care 27.10; 31.5
choose 20.6; 33.12
condemn 9.5; 36.2
defend [3] 18.1; 31.2
deserve Job 42.8; 31.23
destroy 26.9; 35.8
evil [2] 27.2; 34.13
friend 25.14; 34.11
glad 21.1; 31.7
God's people 26.12; 29.11
hate 26.5; 31.6
heart 22.14; 34.14
help [3] 27.9; 30.2
holy 24.3; 29.2
joy 27.6; 30.5
notice (1) 10.14; 37.37
praise [2] 27.6; 29.1
protect [2] 27.1; 30.7
punish [3] 17.14; 31.23
save [2] 26.11; 30.1
shepherd 23.1; 49.14
Temple (1) (of God) 27.5; 29.9
trust 27.3; 31.6
wicked 26.5; 31.17
word (1) 19.3; 33.4
world of the dead 16.10; 31.17

28 O LORD, my **defender**, I call to you.
Listen to my cry!
If you do not answer me,
I will be among those who go down
to the **world of the dead**.
2 Hear me when I cry to you for **help**,
when I lift my hands towards your **holy Temple**.
3 Do not **condemn** me with the **wicked**,
with those who do **evil**—
men whose **words** are **friendly**,
but who have **hatred** in their **hearts**.

4 **Punish** them for what they have done,
for the **evil** they have committed.
Punish them for all their deeds;
give them what they **deserve**!
5 They take no **notice** of what the LORD has done
or of what he has made;
so he will **punish** them
and **destroy** them for ever.

6 Give **praise** to the LORD;
he has heard my cry for **help**.
7 The LORD **protects** and **defends** me;
I **trust** in him.
He gives me **help** and makes me **glad**;
I **praise** him with **joyful** songs.

8 The LORD **protects his people**;
he **defends** and **saves** his **chosen** king.
9 **Save** your people, LORD,
and **bless** those who are yours.
Be their **shepherd**,
and take **care** of them for ever.

The Voice of the LORD in the Storm[u]

29 Praise the LORD, you **heavenly beings**;
praise his **glory** and **power**.
2 **Praise** the LORD's **glorious name**;
bow down before the **Holy One** when he appears.[v]

being 9.20; 56.4
bless 28.9; 37.22
bow (2) 22.29; 35.1
glory [4] 26.8; 45.3
God's people 28.8 34.9
heaven 20.6; 33.6
holy 28.2; 30.4
Majesty 21.5; 45.3
might 24.8; 45.3
name (2) (name o God, of Jesus) Job 1.21; 33.21
peace 4.8; 34.14
power 21.13; 33.16
praise [3] 28.6; 30.
strength 23.3; 32.4
strip (1) 1 Chr 10. 76.5
Temple (1) (of Go 28.2; 43.3

3 The voice of the LORD is heard on the seas;
the **glorious** God thunders,
and his voice echoes over the ocean.
4 The voice of the LORD is heard
in all its **might** and **majesty**.

5 The voice of the LORD breaks the cedars,
even the cedars of Lebanon.
6 He makes the mountains of Lebanon
jump like calves
and makes Mount Hermon leap like
a young bull.

7 The voice of the LORD makes the
lightning flash.
8 His voice makes the desert shake;
he shakes the desert of Kadesh.
9 The LORD's voice shakes the oaks[w]
and **strips** the leaves from the trees
while everyone in his **Temple**
shouts, "**Glory** to God!"

10 The LORD rules over the deep waters;
he rules as king for ever.
11 The LORD gives **strength** to **his people**
and **blesses** them with **peace**.

A Prayer of Thanksgiving[x]

30 I praise you, LORD, because you have **saved** me
and **kept my enemies from** gloating over me.
2 I cried to you for **help**, O LORD my God,
and you **healed** me;
3 you **kept me from** the **grave**.
I was on my way to the depths below,[y]
but you **restored** my **life**.

4 Sing **praise** to the LORD,
all his **faithful** people!

afraid 27.1; 31.11
anger 27.9; 37.8
beg Job 41.3; 37.25
change 7.12; 55.19
dead 22.15; 31.12
death (1) 18.4; 38.7
enemy 27.3; 31.8
faithful 26.3; 31.5
grave [2] 18.5; 49.9
heal Job 13.4; 41.4
help [3] 28.2; 31.22
holy 29.2; 33.21
joy [3] 28.7; 32.11
keep from [2] 25.20 33.10
last (1) 21.4; 33.11
life (1) 27.4; 31.10
mercy 27.7; 31.9

[t] HEBREW TITLE: *By David.* [u] HEBREW TITLE: *A psalm by David.*
[v] when he appears; *or* in garments of worship; *or* in his beautiful Temple.
[w] *Probable text* shakes the oaks; *Hebrew* makes the deer give birth.
[x] HEBREW TITLE: *A song for the dedication of the Temple; a psalm by David.*
[y] THE DEPTHS BELOW: *The world of the dead (see 6.5).*

28.4: Rev 22.12 **29.1–2:** Ps 96.7–9

raise [4] 29.1; 31.21
roclaim 18.46; 34.3
rotect 28.7; 31.1
emember 25.6; 42.4
estore 13.3; 41.3
ad Job 30.29; 42.5
ave 28.8; 31.1
ecure 27.5; 31.19
orrow 13.2; 31.10
ear (2) 6.6; 42.3
hank [2] 26.7; 33.2

Remember what the **Holy One** has
done,
and give him **thanks**!
5 His **anger lasts** only a moment,
his goodness for a lifetime.
Tears may flow in the night,
but **joy** comes in the morning.

6 I felt **secure** and said to myself,
"I will never be defeated."
7 You were good to me, LORD;
you **protected** me like a mountain
fortress.
But then you hid yourself from me,
and I was **afraid**.

8 I called to you, LORD;
I **begged** for your **help**:
9 "What will you gain from my **death**?
What profit from my going to the
grave?
Are **dead** people able to **praise** you?
Can they **proclaim** your unfailing
goodness?
10 Hear me, LORD, and be **merciful**!
Help me, LORD!"

11 You have **changed** my **sadness** into a
joyful dance;
you have taken away my **sorrow**
and surrounded me with **joy**.
12 So I will not be silent;
I will sing **praise** to you.
LORD, you are my God,
I will give you **thanks** for ever.

A Prayer of Trust in God[z]

afraid [2] 30.7; 46.2
arrogant
2 Chr 26.16; 73.9
care [2] 28.9; 36.6
constant [2] 26.3;
32.10
contempt [2]
2 Chr 7.20; 44.14
courage 18.45; 40.12
danger 27.1; 34.7
dead 30.9; 58.8
defend [2] 28.1; 35.23
deserve 28.4; 94.2
disgrace [2] Job 42.8;
35.4
enemy [5] 30.1; 35.19
faithful [3] 30.4; 36.5
false 24.4; 40.4
forget 13.1; 34.16
free 19.13; 32.2
glad 28.7; 32.11
god (2) (other gods)
16.4; 40.4
guide 27.4; 37.23
hate 28.3; 34.21
help 30.2; 33.20
honour 23.5; 33.8
hope 9.18; 33.20
insult 4.2; 42.10
kind 25.6; 51.18
lie (2) 27.12; 34.13
life (1) 30.3; 34.12
love [4] 26.3; 32.10
mercy 30.10; 40.11
neighbour 15.3; 38.11

31 I come to you, LORD, for
protection;
never let me be defeated.
You are a **righteous** God;
save me, I **pray**!
2 Hear me! **Save** me now!
Be my **refuge** to **protect** me;
my **defence** to **save** me.

3 You are my **refuge** and **defence**;
guide me and lead me as you have
promised.
4 Keep me **safe** from the **trap** that has
been set for me;
shelter me from **danger**.
5 I place myself in your **care**.
You will **save** me, LORD;
you are a **faithful** God.

6 You **hate** those who **worship false
gods**,
but I **trust** in you.
7 I will be **glad** and **rejoice**
because of your **constant love**.
You see my **suffering**;
you know my **trouble**.
8 You have not let my **enemies** capture
me;
you have given me **freedom** to go
where I **wish**.

9 Be **merciful** to me, LORD,
for I am in **trouble**;
my eyes are tired from so much
crying;
I am completely worn out.
10 I am exhausted by **sorrow**,
and **weeping** has shortened my **life**.
I am **weak** from all my **troubles**;[a]
even my bones are wasting away.

11 All my **enemies**, and especially my
neighbours,
treat me with **contempt**;
those who know me are **afraid** of me;
when they see me in the street, they
run away.
12 Everyone has **forgotten** me, as though
I were **dead**;
I am like something thrown away.
13 I hear many **enemies** whispering;
terror is all round me.
They are making **plans** against me,
plotting to kill me.

14 But my **trust** is in you, O LORD;
you are my God.
15 I am always in your **care**;
save me from my **enemies**,
from those who **persecute** me.
16 Look on your **servant** with **kindness**;
save me in your **constant love**.
17 I call to you, LORD;
don't let me be **disgraced**.
May the **wicked** be **disgraced**;
may they go silently down to the
world of the dead.
18 Silence those **liars**—
all the **proud** and **arrogant**
who speak with **contempt** about
righteous men.

19 How **wonderful** are the good things
you keep for those who **honour** you!
Everyone knows how good you are,
how **securely** you **protect** those who
trust you.
20 You hide them in the **safety** of your
presence
from the **plots** of men;
in a **safe shelter** you hide them
from the **insults** of their **enemies**.

21 **Praise** the LORD!

persecute 12.5; 56.1
plan 21.11; 33.10
plot (1) [2] 21.11; 35.4
praise 30.1; 33.1
pray 17.6; 32.6
presence [2] 24.6;
41.12
promise 25.11; 35.3
protect [4] 30.7; 32.7
proud [2] 22.29; 36.11
punish 28.4; 32.4
refuge [2] 19.14; 46.7
rejoice 21.1; 32.11
righteous [2] 25.8;
32.11
safe [3] 27.5; 34.8
save [6] 30.1; 32.7
secure 30.6; 40.2
servant 27.9; 35.27
shelter [2] 27.5; 46.1
sorrow 30.11; 35.19
strong 24.8; 35.10
suffer 25.18; 32.10
terror 10.18; 55.4
trap 18.5; 35.7
trouble [3] 27.5; 32.6
trust [3] 28.7; 32.10
weak 25.16; 35.10
weep 6.6; 39.12
wicked 28.3; 32.10
wish 12.4; 55.6
wonder (1) [2] 26.7;
40.5
world of the dead
28.1; 49.14
worship (2) (of
other gods) 24.4; 40.4

[z] HEBREW TITLE: *A psalm by David.* [a] *Some ancient translations* troubles; *Hebrew* iniquity.

31.5: Lk 23.46

How **wonderfully** he showed his **love**
for me
when I was surrounded and
attacked!
22 I was **afraid** and thought
that he had driven me out of his
presence.
But he heard my cry,
when I called to him for **help**.

23 **Love** the LORD, all his **faithful** people.
The LORD **protects** the **faithful**,
but **punishes** the **proud** as they
deserve.
24 Be **strong**, be **courageous**,
all you that **hope** in the LORD.

Confession and Forgiveness[b]

32 **Happy** are those whose sins are
forgiven,
whose **wrongs** are pardoned.
2 **Happy** is the man whom the LORD does
not **accuse** of doing **wrong**
and who is **free** from all **deceit**.

3 When I did not **confess** my sins,
I was worn out from crying all day
long.
4 Day and night you **punished** me, LORD;
my **strength** was completely
drained,
as moisture is dried up by the
summer heat.

5 Then I **confessed** my sins to you;
I did not conceal my **wrongdoings**.
I decided to **confess** them to you,
and you **forgave** all my sins.

6 So all your **loyal** people should **pray** to
you in times of **need**;[c]
when a great **flood** of **trouble** comes
rushing in,
it will not reach them.
7 You are my hiding place;
you will **save** me from **trouble**.
I sing aloud of your **salvation**,
because you **protect** me.

8 The LORD says, "I will **teach** you the
way you should go;
I will instruct you and **advise** you.
9 Don't be **stupid** like a horse or a mule,
which must be **controlled** with a bit
and bridle
to make it **submit**."

10 The **wicked** will have to **suffer**,
but those who **trust** in the LORD
are **protected** by his **constant love**.

11 You that are **righteous**, be **glad** and
rejoice
because of what the LORD has done.
You that **obey** him, shout for **joy**!

A Song of Praise

33 All you that are **righteous**,
shout for **joy** for what the
LORD has done;
praise him, all you that **obey** him.
2 Give **thanks** to the LORD with harps,
sing to him with stringed
instruments.
3 Sing a **new** song to him,
play the harp with skill, and shout
for **joy**!

4 The **words of the LORD** are **true**
and all his works are **dependable**.
5 The LORD **loves** what is **righteous** and
just;
his **constant love** fills the earth.

6 The LORD **created** the **heavens** by his
command,
the sun, moon, and stars by his
spoken **word**.
7 He gathered all the seas into one
place;
he shut up the ocean depths in
storerooms.

8 **Worship** the LORD, all the earth!
Honour him, all peoples of the
world!
9 When he spoke, the **world** was
created;
at his **command** everything
appeared.

10 The LORD frustrates the **purposes** of
the nations;
he **keeps them from** carrying out
their **plans**.
11 But his **plans endure** for ever;
his **purposes last eternally**.
12 **Happy** is the nation whose God is the
LORD;
happy are the people he has **chosen**
for his own!

13 The LORD looks down from **heaven**
and sees all **mankind**.
14 From where he rules, he looks down
on all who live on earth.
15 He forms all their thoughts
and knows everything they do.

16 A king does not **win** because of his
powerful army;

[b] HEBREW TITLE: *A poem by David.* [c] *Some ancient translations* need; *Hebrew* finding only.

32.1-2: Rom 4.7-8

accuse Job 36.23; 35.11
advice 1.1; 106.13
confess [3] Job 34.31; 38.18
constant 31.7; 33.5
control 2.3; Prov 16.32
deceive 12.2; 105.25
flood Job 38.36; 38.4
forgive [2] 25.7; 65.3
free 31.8; 34.4
glad 31.7; 33.21
happy [2] 19.5; 33.12
joy 30.5; 33.1
love 31.7; 33.5
loyal Job 6.14; 40.10
need 23.1; 34.9
obey 25.10; 33.1
pray 31.1; 34.4
protect [2] 31.1; 33.20
punish 31.23; 34.21
rejoice 31.7; 63.11
righteous 31.1; 33.1
salvation 27.1; 40.10
save 31.1; 33.17
strength 29.11; 33.16
stupid Job 18.3; 49.10
submit 2 Chr 12.12; Jer 27.8
suffer 31.7; 34.19
teach 27.11; 34.11
trouble [2] 31.7; 34.6
trust 31.6; 33.18
wicked 31.17; 34.21
wrong [3] 18.23; 37.1

alive Job 33.28; 4
choose 28.8; 45.7
command [2] 25.1 37.34
constant [3] 32.10 36.5
create [2] 8.6; 51.1
death (2) (from death) 9.13; 49.12
depend 18.30; 52.7
endure 13.2; 55.12
eternal Ezra 3.11 52.1
famine Job 5.20; 37.19
glad 32.11; 34.2
happy [2] 32.1; 34.
heaven [2] 29.1; 3
help 31.22; 37.5
holy 30.4; 51.11
honour 31.19; 34.7
hope [2] 31.24; 34.
joy [2] 32.11; 35.27
justice 19.8; 36.6
keep from 30.1; 3
last (1) 30.5; 45.6
love [4] 32.10; 36.5
mankind 14.2; 53.
name (2) (name of God, of Jesus) 29. 34.3
new 23.3; 40.3
obey [2] 32.11; 34.
plan [2] 31.13; 36.4
power 29.1; 37.33
praise 31.21; 34.1
protect 32.7; 34.22
purpose [2] 1 Chr 23.5; Is 26.3
righteous [2] 32.1 34.15
save [2] 32.7; 34.6
strength [2] 32.4; 37.17
thank 30.4; 34.1
triumph 27.6; 41.1
true 15.2; 78.20
trust [2] 32.10; 37.
useless 2.1; 76.5
victory 24.8; 44.4
watch 17.11; 34.15
win Job 40.14; 44.3
word (1) [2] 28.3; 37.30
world [2] 24.1; 46.9
worship (1) (of G 27.8; 42.2

a soldier does not **triumph** because
of his **strength**.
17 War-horses are **useless** for **victory**;
their great **strength** cannot **save**.

18 The LORD **watches** over those who
obey him,
those who **trust** in his **constant love**.
19 He **saves** them **from death**;
he keeps them **alive** in times of
famine.

20 We put our **hope** in the LORD;
he is our **protector** and our **help**.
21 We are **glad** because of him;
we **trust** in his **holy name**.

22 May your **constant love** be with us,
LORD,
as we put our **hope** in you.

In Praise of God's Goodness[d]

angel Job 33.23; 35.5
danger 31.4; 40.2
disappoint 22.5; 119.116
discourage Ezra 4.4; 77.3
enjoy Job 36.16; 37.11
evil [4] 28.3; 35.11
fear 27.1; 47.2
forget 31.12; 40.17
free 32.2; 37.26
friend 28.3; 35.14
glad [2] 33.21; 35.9
God's people [2] 29.11; 44.12
happy [2] 33.12; 35.9
hate 31.6; 35.16
heart 28.3; 35.10
helpless 22.21; 44.19
honour [3] 33.8; 37.34
hope 33.20; 37.34
hunger Job 38.39; 50.12
lie (2) 31.18; 35.19
life (1) [2] 31.10; 35.17
name (2) (name of God, of Jesus) 33.21; 63.11
need 32.6; 37.14
obey [2] 33.1; 37.18
oppress [2] 12.5; 35.10
peace 29.11; 35.20
praise [3] 33.1; 35.18
pray 32.6; 35.13
preserve 25.21; 41.2
proclaim 30.9; 35.28
protect 33.20; 35.10
punish 32.4; 38.1
rescue [2] 25.15; 35.2
righteous [3] 33.1; 35.24
safe 31.4; 37.3
save [4] 33.17; 35.3
spare 26.9; 51.14
suffer 32.10; 35.26
teach 32.8; 40.3
thank 33.2; 35.18
trouble [3] 32.6; 35.15
turn 27.9; 35.4
watch 33.18; 37.32
wicked 32.10; 36.1

34 I will always **thank** the LORD;
I will never stop **praising** him.
2 I will **praise** him for what he has done;
may all who are **oppressed** listen
and be **glad**!
3 **Proclaim** with me the LORD's
greatness;
let us **praise** his **name** together!

4 I **prayed** to the LORD, and he answered
me;
he **freed** me from all my **fears**.
5 The **oppressed** look to him and are
glad;
they will never be **disappointed**.
6 The **helpless** call to him, and he
answers;
he **saves** them from all their
troubles.
7 His **angel** guards those who **honour** the
LORD
and **rescues** them from **danger**.

8 Find out for yourself how good the
LORD is.
Happy are those who find **safety**
with him.
9 **Honour** the LORD, all **his people**;
those who **obey** him have all they
need.
10 Even lions go **hungry** for lack of food,
but those who **obey** the LORD lack
nothing good.

11 Come, my young **friends**, and listen to
me,
and I will **teach** you to **honour** the
LORD.
12 Would you like to **enjoy life**?
Do you want long **life** and
happiness?
13 Then hold back from speaking **evil**
and from telling **lies**.
14 **Turn away** from **evil** and do good;
strive for **peace with all your heart**.

15 The LORD **watches** over the **righteous**
and listens to their cries;
16 but he opposes those who do **evil**,
so that when they die, they are soon
forgotten.
17 The **righteous** call to the LORD, and he
listens;
he **rescues** them from all their
troubles.
18 The LORD is near to those who are
discouraged;
he **saves** those who have lost all
hope.

19 The good man **suffers** many **troubles**,
but the LORD **saves** him from them
all;
20 the LORD **preserves** him completely;
not one of his bones is broken.
21 **Evil** will kill the **wicked**;
those who **hate** the **righteous** will be
punished.

22 The LORD will **save his people**;
those who go to him for **protection**
will be **spared**.

A Prayer for Help[e]

accuse [2] 32.2; 50.20
angel [2] 34.7; 78.25
bow (2) 29.2; 38.6
cause (2) 1 Kgs 1.7; 43.1
claim Job 37.24; Prov 1.19
crime Job 13.23; 55.10
cripple 2 Chr 16.12; Prov 25.19
dark 23.4; 44.19
defend 31.2; 42.9
delight 2 Chr 15.15; 111.2
despair 27.14; 61.2
destroy [2] 28.5; 37.13
disgrace [2] 31.17; 40.14
enemy [2] 31.8; 37.20
evil [2] 34.13; 36.4
friend [2] 34.11; 38.11
glad [2] 34.2; 40.16
happy 34.8; 37.4
hate [2] 34.21; 37.12
heart 34.14; 36.1
innocent 26.1; 43.1
joy 33.1; 40.16
lie (2) [2] 34.13; 36.3
life (1) 34.12; 36.9
mock [2] 2.4; 44.13
mourn [3] Job 30.31; 38.6
oppress 34.2; 55.3
peace 34.14; 37.11

35 Oppose those who oppose me,
LORD,
and fight those who fight against
me!
2 Take your shield and armour
and come to my **rescue**.
3 Lift up your spear and your axe
against those who pursue me.
Promise that you will **save** me.

4 May those who try to kill me
be defeated and **disgraced**!
May those who **plot** against me
be **turned** back and confused!
5 May they be like straw blown by the
wind
as the **angel of the LORD** pursues
them!
6 May their path be **dark** and slippery
while the **angel of the LORD strikes**
them down!

7 Without any **reason** they laid a **trap** for
me

[d] HEBREW TITLE: *By David, who left the presence of Abimelech after pretending to be mad and being sent away by him.* [e] HEBREW TITLE: *By David.*

34 Title: 1 Sam 21.13–15 **34.8:** 1 Pet 2.3 **34.12–16:** 1 Pet 3.10–12 **34.20:** Jn 19.36

plead 17.1; 55.1
please 20.3; 37.23
plot (1) 31.13; 37.12
poor 22.24; 37.14
praise [2] 34.1; 40.3
pray [2] 34.4; 44.20
proclaim 34.3; 50.6
promise 31.3; 50.14
protect 34.22; 36.7
reason [2] Job 33.7; 38.19
rescue [2] 34.7; 37.40
rid Esth 9.16; 101.5
righteous [2] 34.15; 36.6
rise 20.8; 36.12
save [3] 34.6; 37.39
servant 31.16; 69.17
shame 25.2; 44.15
sorrow 31.10; 42.6
stranger Job 31.31; 69.8
strike [2] 18.38; 38.2
strong 31.24; 38.19
succeed (1) 21.11; 37.7
suffer 34.19; 37.19
testify 15.5; 50.7
thank 34.1; 40.16
trap [2] 31.4; 38.12
trouble 34.6; 37.8
turn 34.14; 37.27
weak 31.10; 40.17

and dug a deep hole to catch me.
8 But **destruction** will catch them before
they know it;
they will be caught in their own **trap**
and fall to their **destruction**!

9 Then I will be **glad** because of the
LORD;
I will be **happy** because he **saved**
me.
10 **With all my heart** I will say to the
LORD,
"There is no one like you.
You **protect** the **weak** from the
strong,
the **poor** from the **oppressor**."

11 **Evil** men **testify** against me
and **accuse** me of **crimes** I know
nothing about.
12 They pay me back **evil** for good,
and I sink in **despair**.
13 But when they were sick, I dressed in
mourning;
I deprived myself of food;
I **prayed** with my head **bowed** low,
14 as I would **pray** for a **friend** or a
brother.
I went about bent over in **mourning**,
as one who **mourns** for his mother.

15 But when I was in **trouble**, they were
all **glad**
and gathered round to **mock** me;
strangers beat me
and kept **striking** me.
16 Like men who would **mock** a **cripple**,[f]
they glared at me with **hate**.

17 How much longer, Lord, will you just
look on?
Rescue me from their attacks;
save my **life** from these lions!
18 Then I will **thank** you in the assembly
of your people;
I will **praise** you before them all.

19 Don't let my **enemies**, those **liars**,
gloat over my defeat.
Don't let those who **hate** me for no
reason
smirk with **delight** over my **sorrow**.

20 They do not speak in a **friendly** way;
instead they invent all kinds of **lies**
about **peace-loving** people.
21 They **accuse** me, shouting,
"We saw what you did!"
22 But you, O LORD, have seen this.
So don't be silent, Lord;
don't keep yourself far away!
23 Rouse yourself, O Lord, and **defend**
me;
rise up, my God, and **plead** my
cause.
24 You are **righteous**, O LORD, so declare
me **innocent**;
don't let my **enemies** gloat over me.
25 Don't let them say to themselves,
"We are **rid** of him!
That's just what we wanted!"

26 May those who gloat over my **suffering**
be completely defeated and
confused;
may those who **claim** to be better than
I am
be covered with **shame** and
disgrace.

27 May those who want to see me
acquitted
shout for **joy** and say again and
again,
"How great is the LORD!
He is **pleased** with the **success** of his
servant."
28 Then I will **proclaim** your
righteousness,
and I will **praise** you all day long.

The Wickedness of Man[g]

36 Sin speaks to the **wicked** man
deep in his **heart**;
he **rejects** God and has no **reverence**
for him.
2 Because he thinks so highly of himself,
he thinks that God will not discover
his sin and **condemn** it.
3 His **speech** is **wicked** and full of **lies**;
he no longer does what is **wise** and
good.
4 He makes **evil plans** as he lies in bed;
nothing he does is good,
and he never **rejects** anything **evil**.

The Goodness of God

5 LORD, your **constant love** reaches the
heavens;
your **faithfulness** extends to the
skies.
6 Your **righteousness** is towering like the
mountains;
your **justice** is like the depths of the
sea.
Men and animals are in your **care**.

7 How precious, O God, is your **constant**
love!

abundant Job 36.31; 65.10
care 31.5; 37.18
condemn 28.3; 37.33
constant [2] 33.5; 38.17
evil [3] 35.11; 37.7
faithful 31.5; 37.28
feast Job 42.11; 63.5
heart 35.10; 37.4
heaven 33.6; 50.4
justice 33.5; 45.4
lie (2) 35.19; 43.1
life (1) 35.17; 39.4
light (1) 27.1; 43.3
love [3] 33.5; 37.28
plan 33.10; 37.7
protect 35.10; 37.17
proud 31.18; 47.4
provide Job 36.31; 65.9
reject [2] 15.4; 44.9
reverence 25.12; 60.4
righteous [2] 35.24; 37.6
rise 35.23; 59.5
source Job 38.19; 43.4
speech 19.3; 55.9
wicked [3] 34.21; 37.1
wise 14.2; 37.30

[f] *Probable text* Like men...cripple; *Hebrew unclear.*
[g] HEBREW TITLE: *By David, the LORD's servant.*

35.19: Ps 69.4; Jn 15.25 **36.1:** Rom 3.18

We find[x] **protection** under the
shadow of your wings.
8 We **feast** on the **abundant** food you
provide;
you let us drink from the river of
your goodness.
9 You are the **source** of all **life**,
and because of your **light** we see the
light.

10 Continue to **love** those who know you
and to do good to those who are
righteous.
11 Do not let **proud** men attack me
or **wicked** men make me run away.

12 See where **evil** men have fallen.
There they lie, unable to **rise**.

The Destiny of the Wicked and of the Good[h]

37 Don't be **worried** on account of
the **wicked**;
don't be **jealous** of those who do
wrong.
2 They will soon disappear like grass
that dries up;
they will die like plants that wither.

3 **Trust** in the LORD and do good;
live in the land and be **safe**.
4 **Seek** your **happiness** in the LORD,
and he will give you your **heart's**
desire.

5 Give yourself to the LORD;
trust in him, and he will **help** you;
6 he will make your **righteousness** shine
like the noonday sun.

7 Be **patient** and wait for the LORD to
act;
don't be **worried** about those who
prosper
or those who **succeed** in their **evil**
plans.

8 Don't give in to **worry** or **anger**;
it only leads to **trouble**.
9 Those who **trust** in the LORD will
possess the land,
but the **wicked** will be driven out.

10 Soon the **wicked** will disappear;
you may look for them, but you
won't find them;
11 the **humble** will **possess** the land
and **enjoy prosperity** and **peace**.

12 The **wicked** man **plots** against the good
man
and glares at him with **hate**.
13 But the Lord laughs at **wicked** men,
because he knows they will soon be
destroyed.

14 The **wicked** draw their swords and
bend their bows
to kill the **poor** and **needy**,
to **slaughter** those who do what is
right;
15 but they will be killed by their own
swords,
and their bows will be smashed.

16 The little that a good man owns
is **worth** more than the wealth of all
the **wicked**,
17 because the LORD will take away the
strength of the **wicked**,
but **protect** those who are good.

18 The LORD takes **care** of those who
obey him,
and the land will be theirs for ever.
19 They will not **suffer** when times are
bad;
they will have **enough** in time of
famine.
20 But the **wicked** will die;
the **enemies** of the LORD will **vanish**
like wild flowers;
they will disappear like smoke.

21 The **wicked** man borrows and never
pays back,
but the good man is **generous** with
his **gifts**.
22 Those who are **blessed** by the LORD
will **possess** the land,
but those who are **cursed** by him will
be driven out.

23 The LORD **guides** a man in the way he
should go
and **protects** those who **please** him.
24 If they fall, they will not stay down,
because the LORD will **help** them up.

25 I am an old man now; I have lived a
long time,
but I have never seen a good man
abandoned by the LORD
or his children **begging** for food.
26 At all times he gives **freely** and lends
to others,
and his children are a **blessing**.

27 **Turn away** from **evil** and do good,

[x] precious, O God, is...find; *or* precious is your constant love! Gods and men find.
[h] HEBREW TITLE: *By David*.

37.11: Mt 5.5

abandon [3] 27.9; 38.21
act 24.4; 66.5
anger 30.5; 38.1
bad 14.3; 41.6
beg 30.8; 116.4
bless [2] 29.11; 45.2
care 36.6; 54.3
command 33.6; 44.18
condemn 36.2; 51.4
curse 10.3; 59.12
desire 26.2; 45.11
destroy [2] 35.8; 39.11
enemy [2] 35.19; 38.16
enjoy 34.12; 72.3
enough 17.14; 49.8
evil [2] 36.4; 38.20
faithful 36.5; 40.10
famine 33.19; 105.16
free 34.4; 54.1
generous Esth 1.7; 112.5
gift 16.6; 45.12
guide 31.3; 67.4
happy 35.9; 39.13
hate 35.16; 38.19
heart [2] 36.1; 38.8
help [3] 33.20; 38.22
honour 34.7; 50.23
hope 34.18; 39.7
humble 25.9; 51.17
jealous 1 Sam 18.9; 73.3
law 19.7; 40.7
love 36.5; 39.11
need 34.9; 50.9
notice (1) 28.5; 48.13
obey [2] 34.9; 45.11
observe 18.22; Is 21.7
patient Job 36.1; 40.1
peace [2] 35.20; 85.8
plan 36.4; 40.5
please 35.27; 41.11
plot (1) 35.4; 38.12
poor 35.10; 40.17
possess [4] 25.13; 47.4
power 33.16; 41.2
prosper [2] 25.13; 44.2
protect [5] 36.7; 41.2
rescue 35.2; 49.15
right (1) [2] 26.1; 38.20
righteous [4] 36.6; 49.14
safe 34.8; 40.2
save [2] 35.3; 39.8
seek 18.30; 141.8
slaughter Esth 9.5; 44.11
strength 33.16; 38.10
succeed (1) 35.27; 49.18
suffer 35.26; 39.2
trouble [2] 35.15; 38.8
trust [3] 33.18; 38.15
try (2) Job 22.4; 95.9
turn 35.4; 40.4
vanish 10.16; 102.26
watch 34.15; 56.6
wicked [15] 36.1; 50.16
wise 36.3; 49.10
word (1) 33.4; 39.2
worry [3] 25.17; 55.2
worth Job 28.17; Prov 3.14
wrong 32.1; 58.3

and your descendants will always
live in the land;
28 for the LORD **loves** what is **right**
and does not **abandon** his **faithful**
people.
He **protects** them for ever,
but the descendants of the **wicked**
will be driven out.
29 The **righteous** will **possess** the land
and live in it for ever.

30 A good man's **words** are **wise**,
and he is always fair.
31 He keeps the **law** of his God in his
heart
and never departs from it.

32 A **wicked** man **watches** a good man
and tries to kill him;
33 but the LORD will not **abandon** him to
his **enemy's power**
or let him be **condemned** when he is
on **trial**.

34 Put your **hope** in the LORD and **obey**
his **commands**;
he will **honour** you by giving you the
land,
and you will see the **wicked** driven
out.

35 I once knew a **wicked** man who was a
tyrant;
he towered over everyone like a
cedar of Lebanon;[i]
36 but later I[j] passed by, and he wasn't
there;
I looked for him, but couldn't find
him.

37 **Notice** the good man, **observe** the
righteous man;
a **peaceful** man has descendants,
38 but sinners are completely **destroyed**,
and their descendants are wiped out.

39 The LORD **saves righteous** men
and **protects** them in times of
trouble.
40 He **helps** them and **rescues** them;
he **saves** them from the **wicked**,
because they go to him for
protection.

The Prayer of a Suffering Man[k]

38 O LORD, don't **punish** me in your
anger!
2 You have wounded me with your
arrows;
you have **struck** me down.
3 Because of your **anger**, I am in great
pain;
my whole **body** is **diseased** because
of my sins.
4 I am drowning in the **flood** of my sins;
they are a **burden** too heavy to bear.

5 Because I have been **foolish**,
my sores stink and rot.
6 I am **bowed down**, I am crushed;
I **mourn** all day long.
7 I am burning with fever
and I am near to **death**.
8 I am worn out and utterly crushed;
my **heart** is **troubled**, and I **groan**
with **pain**.

9 O Lord, you know what I **long** for;
you hear all my **groans**.
10 My **heart** is pounding, my **strength** is
gone,
and my eyes have lost their
brightness.
11 My **friends** and **neighbours** will not
come near me,
because of my sores;
even my family keeps away from
me.
12 Those who want to kill me lay **traps** for
me,
and those who want to **hurt** me
threaten to **ruin** me;
they never stop **plotting** against me.

13 I am like a deaf man and cannot hear,
like a dumb man and cannot speak.
14 I am like a man who does not answer,
because he cannot hear.

15 But I **trust** in you, O LORD;
and you, O Lord my God, will
answer me.
16 Don't let my **enemies** gloat over my
distress;
don't let them **boast** about my
downfall!
17 I am about to fall
and am in **constant pain**.

18 I **confess** my sins;
they fill me with **anxiety**.
19 My **enemies** are healthy and **strong**;
there are many who **hate** me for no
reason.
20 Those who pay back **evil** for good
are against me because I try to do
right.

21 Do not **abandon** me, O LORD;
do not stay away, my God!
22 **Help** me now, O Lord my **saviour**!

[i] *One ancient translation* like a cedar of Lebanon; *Hebrew unclear.*
[j] *Some ancient translations* I; *Hebrew* he. [k] HEBREW TITLE: *A psalm by David; a lament.*

abandon 37.25; 41.2
anger [2] 37.8; 55.3
anxious 1 Sam 4.13; 39.3
boast 12.3; 49.6
body Job 40.16; 49.14
bow (2) 35.13; 66.3

burden Job 7.20; 66.11
confess 32.3; 119.2
constant 36.5; 40.1
death (1) 30.9; 49.1
disease Job 27.15; 91.3
distress 25.18; 57.6
downfall 13.4; 69.2
enemy [2] 37.20; 41
evil 37.7; 39.1
flood 32.6; 42.6
fool 14.1; 39.8
friend 35.14; 41.9
groan [2] 12.5; 55.1
hate 37.12; 41.7
heart [2] 37.4; 40.8
help 37.5; 40.1
hurt 7.16; 52.4
long (2) Job 7.2; 42
mourn 35.13; 69.11
neighbour 31.11; 44.13
pain [3] 12.5; 69.29
plot (1) 37.12; 64.2
punish 34.21; 39.10
reason 35.7; 69.4
right (1) 37.14; 41.1
ruin 5.10; 52.2
Saviour 27.9; 40.17
strength 37.17; 44.
strike 35.6; 69.23
strong 35.10; 61.3
threat 27.12; 55.3
trap 35.7; 64.5
trouble 37.8; 39.3
trust 37.3; 40.3

alone 18.31; 62.1
anxious 38.18; 94.19
destroy 37.13; 46.5
evil 38.20; 43.1
fool 38.5; 49.10
happy 37.4; 40.4
hope [2] 37.34; 42.5
keep from 33.10; 49.9
life (1) [2] 36.9; 41.2
love 37.28; 40.8
prayer 25.1; 42.8
punish [2] 38.1; 44.2
rebuke 18.15; 68.30
save 37.39; 40.9
sight 5.5; 107.18
suffer [2] 37.19; 42.9
trouble 38.8; 40.12
weep 31.10; 126.5
word (1) [2] 37.30; 45.1
worse 2 Chr 32.16; Is 7.17

The Confession of a Suffering Man[l]

39 I said, "I will be careful what I do
and will not let my tongue
make me sin;
I will not say anything
while **evil** men are near."
2 I kept quiet, not saying a **word**,
not even about anything good!
But my **suffering** only grew **worse**,
3 and I was overcome with **anxiety**.
The more I thought, the more **troubled**
I became;
I could not **keep from** asking:
4 "LORD, how long will I live?
When will I die?
Tell me how soon my **life** will end."

5 How short you have made my **life**!
In your **sight** my lifetime seems
nothing.
Indeed every living man is no more
than a puff of wind,
6 no more than a shadow.
All he does is for nothing;
he gathers wealth, but doesn't know
who will get it.

7 What, then, can I **hope** for, Lord?
I put my **hope** in you.
8 **Save** me from all my sins,
and don't let **fools** laugh at me.
9 I will keep quiet, I will not say a **word**,
for you are the one who made me
suffer like this.
10 Don't **punish** me any more!
I am about to die from your blows.
11 You **punish** a man's sins by your
rebukes,
and like a moth you **destroy** what he
loves.
Indeed a man is no more than a puff of
wind!

12 Hear my **prayer**, LORD,
and listen to my cry;
come to my aid when I **weep**.
Like all my ancestors
I am only your guest for a little
while.
13 Leave me **alone** so that I may have
some **happiness**
before I go away and am no more.

A Song of Praise[m]

altar 26.6; 43.4
constant 38.17; 42.8
courage 31.24; 107.26
danger 34.7; 49.5
deadly 17.9; 91.3
disgrace 35.4; 44.15
faithful 37.28; 50.5
false 31.6; 52.3

40 I waited **patiently** for the LORD's
help;
then he listened to me and heard my
cry.
2 He pulled me out of a **dangerous** pit,
out of the **deadly** quicksand.
He set me **safely** on a rock
and made me **secure**.
3 He **taught** me to sing a **new** song,
a song of **praise** to our God.
Many who see this will take **warning**
and will put their **trust** in the LORD.

4 **Happy** are those who **trust** the LORD,
who do not **turn to idols**
or join those who **worship false gods**.
5 You have done many things for us, O
LORD our God;
there is no one like you!
You have made many **wonderful**
plans for us.
I could never speak of them all—
their number is so great!

6 You do not want **sacrifices** and
offerings;
you do not ask for animals burnt
whole on the **altar**
or for **sacrifices** to **take away** sins.
Instead, you have given me ears to
hear you,
7 and so I answered, "Here I am;
your instructions for me are in the
book of the **Law**.[n]
8 How I **love** to do your **will**, my God!
I keep your **teaching** in my **heart**."

9 In the assembly of all your people,
LORD,
I told the **good news** that you **save**
us.
You know that I will never stop
telling it.
10 I have not kept the news of **salvation** to
myself;
I have always spoken of your
faithfulness and **help**.
In the assembly of all your people I
have not been silent
about your **loyalty** and **constant love**.

11 LORD, I know you will never stop being
merciful to me.
Your **love** and **loyalty** will always
keep me **safe**.

A Prayer for Help
(Ps 70)

12 I am surrounded by many **troubles**—
too many to count!
My sins have caught up with me,
and I can no longer see;
they are more than the hairs of my
head,
and I have lost my **courage**.
13 **Save** me, LORD! **Help** me now!

forget 34.16; 41.5
glad 35.9; 45.15
god (2) (other gods) 31.6; 44.20
Good News 1 Chr 16.23; 96.2
happy [2] 39.13; 41.1
heart 38.8; 42.4
help [3] 38.22; 41.1
idol 24.4; 78.58
jeer 22.7; 70.3
joy 35.27; 45.15
law 37.31; 78.5
love [3] 39.11; 42.8
loyal [2] 32.6; 51.10
mercy 31.9; 41.4
new 33.3; 51.10
offer 27.6; 50.5
patient 37.7; 62.1
plan 37.7; 52.2
poor 37.14; 41.1
praise 35.18; 41.13
sacrifice [2] 27.6; 50.5
safe [2] 37.3; 48.3
salvation [2] 32.7; 51.12
save [2] 39.8; 44.6
Saviour 38.22; 42.5
secure 31.19; 52.7
take away (sin) Neh 10.33; Ezek 45.17
teach [2] 34.11; 51.13
thank 35.18; 44.8
trouble [2] 39.3; 41.1
trust [2] 38.15; 41.9
turn [2] 37.27; 41.9
warn 16.7; 60.4
weak 35.10; 69.23
will (1) 25.9; 67.2
wonder (1) 31.19; 65.5
worship (2) (of other gods) 31.6; 81.9

[l] HEBREW TITLE: *A psalm by David.* [m] HEBREW TITLE: *A psalm by David.*
[n] your instructions...Law; *or* my devotion to you is recorded in your book.

40.6–8: Heb 10.5–7

14 May those who try to kill me
be completely defeated and
confused.
May those who are **happy** because of
my **troubles**
be **turned** back and **disgraced**.
15 May those who **jeer** at me
be dismayed by their defeat.

16 May all who come to you
be **glad** and **joyful**.
May all who are **thankful** for your
salvation
always say, "How great is the
LORD!"

17 I am **weak** and **poor**, O Lord,
but you have not **forgotten** me.
You are my **saviour** and my God—
hurry to my aid!

The Prayer of a Sick Man[o]

41 **Happy** are those who are
concerned for the **poor**;
the LORD will **help** them when they
are in **trouble**.
2 The LORD will **protect** them and
preserve their **lives**;
he will make them **happy** in the
land;
he will not **abandon** them to the
power of their **enemies**.
3 The LORD will **help** them when they
are sick
and will **restore** them to health.

4 I said, "I have sinned against you,
LORD;
be **merciful** to me and **heal** me."
5 My **enemies** say **cruel** things about me.
They want me to die and be
forgotten.
6 Those who come to see me are not
sincere;
they gather **bad** news about me
and then go out and tell it
everywhere.
7 All who **hate** me whisper to **each other**
about me,
they imagine the **worst** about[p] me.
8 They say, "He is fatally ill;
he will never leave his bed again."
9 Even my **best friend**, the one I **trusted**
most,
the one who **shared** my food,
has **turned** against me.

10 Be **merciful** to me, LORD, and **restore**
my health,
and I will pay my **enemies** back.
11 They will not **triumph** over me,
and I will know that you are **pleased**
with me.
12 You will **help** me, because I do what is
right;
you will keep me in your **presence**
for ever.

13 **Praise** the LORD, the God of Israel!
Praise him now and for ever!

Amen! Amen!

BOOK TWO
(Psalms 42–72)

The Prayer of a Man in Exile[q]

42 As a deer **longs** for a stream of
cool water,
so I **long** for you, O God.
2 I thirst for you, the living God;
when can I go and **worship** in your
presence?
3 Day and night I cry,
and **tears** are my only food;
all the time my **enemies** ask me,
"Where is your God?"

4 My **heart** breaks when I **remember** the
past,
when I went with the crowds to the
house of God
and led them as they walked along,
a **happy** crowd, singing and shouting
praise to God.
5 Why am I so **sad**?
Why am I so **troubled**?
I will put my **hope** in God,
and once again I will **praise** him,
my **saviour** and my God.

6–7 Here in **exile** my **heart** is breaking,
and so I **turn** my thoughts to him.
He has sent waves of **sorrow** over my
soul;
chaos roars at me like a **flood**,
like waterfalls thundering down to
the Jordan
from Mount Hermon and Mount
Mizar.
8 May the LORD show his **constant love**
during the day,
so that I may have a song at night,
a **prayer** to the God of my **life**.

9 To God, my **defender**, I say,
"Why have you **forgotten** me?
Why must I go on **suffering**

abandon 38.21; 43.2
bad 37.19; 53.3
best Job 27.22; 78.31
concern Job 39.16; 131.1
cruel Job 30.21; 42.9
each other 12.2; 55.14
enemy [3] 38.16; 42.3
forget 40.17; 42.9
friend 38.11; 50.18
happy [2] 40.4; 42.4
hate 38.19; 44.7
heal 30.2; 60.2
help [3] 40.1; 46.1
life (1) 39.4; 42.8
mercy [2] 40.11; 51.1
please 37.23; 51.16
poor 40.17; 49.2
power 37.33; 44.3
praise [2] 40.3; 42.4
presence 31.20; 42.2
preserve 34.20; 80.17
protect 37.17; 43.2
restore [2] 30.3; 68.9
right (1) 38.20; 45.7
share Job 42.15; 72.1
sincere 15.2; 51.6
triumph 33.16; 49.14
trouble 40.12; 42.5
trust 40.3; 44.6
turn 40.4; 42.6
worst Job 19.11; Prov 29.24

constant 40.10; 44.26
cruel 41.5; 43.2
defend 35.23; 43.1
enemy [2] 41.2; 43.2
exile Esth 2.6; 147.2
flood 38.4; 66.12
forget 41.5; 44.17
happy 41.1; 43.4
heart [2] 40.8; 45.5
hope [2] 39.7; 43.5
insult 31.20; 44.16
life (1) 41.2; 49.8
long (2) [2] 38.9; 63.1
love 40.8; 44.3
praise [3] 41.13; 43.4
prayer 39.12; 54.2
presence 41.12; 44.3
remember 30.4; 63.6
sad [2] 30.11; 43.5
Saviour [2] 40.17; 43.5
sorrow 35.19; 80.5
soul 2 Chr 34.31; 57.8
suffer 39.2; 43.2
tear (2) 30.5; 56.8
trouble [2] 41.1; 43.5
turn 41.9; 49.4
worship (1) (of God) 33.8; 44.20

[o] HEBREW TITLE: *A psalm by David.* [p] imagine the worst about; *or* make evil plans to harm.
[q] HEBREW TITLE: *A poem by the clan of Korah.*

41.9: Mt 26.23; Mk 14.18; Lk 22.21; Jn 13.18 **41.13:** Ps 106.48

from the **cruelty** of my **enemies**?"
10 I am crushed by their **insults**,
as they keep on asking me,
"Where is your God?"

11 Why am I so **sad**?
Why am I so **troubled**?
I will put my **hope** in God,
and once again I will **praise** him,
my **saviour** and my God.

abandon 41.2; 44.19
altar 40.6; 51.19
cause (2) 35.23; 74.22
cruel 42.9; 54.3
defend 42.9; 45.4
enemy 42.3; 44.5
evil 39.1; 45.7
happy 42.4; 45.7
hope 42.5; 56.6
innocent 35.24; 94.21
lie (2) 36.3; 50.19
light (1) 36.9; 56.13
praise [2] 42.4; 44.8
protect 41.2; 57.1
sacred 15.1; 46.4
sad 42.5; 78.40
Saviour 42.5; 70.5
source 36.9; 87.7
suffer 42.9; 44.24
Temple (1) (of God) 29.9; 48.9
trouble 42.5; 44.24
truth 25.5; 45.4
ungodly Jer 23.15

The Prayer of a Man in Exile
(Continuation of Psalm 42)

43 O God, declare me **innocent**,
and **defend** my **cause** against
the **ungodly**;
deliver me from **lying** and **evil** men!
2 You are my **protector**;
why have you **abandoned** me?
Why must I go on **suffering**
from the **cruelty** of my **enemies**?

3 Send your **light** and your **truth**;
may they lead me
and bring me back to Zion, your
sacred hill,[r]
and to your **Temple**, where you live.
4 Then I will go to your **altar**, O God;
you are the **source** of my **happiness**.
I will play my harp and sing **praise** to
you,
O God, my God.

5 Why am I so **sad**?
Why am I so **troubled**?
I will put my **hope** in God,
and once again I will **praise** him,
my **saviour** and my God.

abandon 43.2; 71.9
assure 1 Sam 23.16; Ezek 13.16
command 37.34; 50.17
conquer Job 26.12; 78.54
constant 42.8; 48.9
contempt 31.11; 107.40
covenant 25.10; 50.5
dark 35.6; 49.19
disgrace 40.14; 69.6
disobey 18.22; 78.8
enemy [4] 43.2; 45.5
establish 2 Chr 31.2; 99.4
forget [2] 42.9; 45.10
god (2) (other gods) 40.4; 77.13
God's people 34.9; 47.4
hate [2] 41.7; 45.7
heathen 9.5; 59.5
helpless 34.6; 74.19
insult 42.10; 59.7
love [2] 42.8; 45.7
mock 35.15; 55.12
neighbour 38.11; 89.41

A Prayer for Protection[s]

44 With our own ears we have
heard it, O God—
our ancestors have told us about it,
about the great things you did in their
time,
in the days of long ago:
2 how you yourself drove out the
heathen
and **established** your people in their
land;
how you **punished** the other nations
and caused your own to **prosper**.
3 Your people did not **conquer** the land
with their swords;
they did not **win** it by their own
power;
it was by your **power** and your
strength,
by the **assurance** of your **presence**,
which showed that you **loved** them.

4 You are my king and my God;
you give[t] **victory** to your people,
5 and by your **power** we defeat our
enemies.
6 I do not **trust** in my bow
or in my sword to **save** me;
7 but you have **saved** us from our
enemies
and defeated those who **hate** us.
8 We will always **praise** you
and give **thanks** to you for ever.

9 But now you have **rejected** us and let
us be defeated;
you no longer march out with our
armies.
10 You made us run from our **enemies**,
and they took for themselves what
was ours.
11 You allowed us to be **slaughtered** like
sheep;
you **scattered** us in foreign
countries.
12 You sold your **own people** for a small
price
as though they had little **value**.[m]

13 Our **neighbours** see what you did to us,
and they **mock** us and laugh at us.
14 You have made us an object of
contempt among the nations;
they shake their heads at us in
scorn.
15 I am always in **disgrace**;
I am covered with **shame**
16 from hearing the **sneers** and **insults**
of my **enemies** and those who **hate**
me.

17 All this has happened to us,
even though we have not **forgotten**
you
or broken the **covenant** you made
with us.
18 We have not been disloyal to you;
we have not **disobeyed** your
commands.
19 Yet you left us **helpless** among wild
animals;
you **abandoned** us in deepest
darkness.

20 If we had stopped **worshipping** our God
and **prayed** to a foreign **god**,
21 you would surely have discovered it,
because you know our **secret**
thoughts.
22 But it is on your account that we are
being killed all the time,

power [3] 41.2; 47.9
praise 43.4; 45.17
pray 35.13; 53.4
presence 42.2; 51.11
prosper 37.7; 53.6
punish 39.10; 54.5
reject [2] 36.1; 50.17
save [3] 40.9; 49.12
scatter 18.14; 53.5
scorn 22.6; 68.16
secret Job 15.18; 83.3
shame 35.26; 64.4
sheep [2] 8.7; 49.14
slaughter [2] 37.14; Prov 7.22
sneer 10.5; Lam 2.16
strength 38.10; 45.4
suffer 43.2; 60.3
thank 40.16; 50.14
trouble 43.5; 46.1
trust 41.9; 49.6
value Job 28.13; Prov 3.15
victory 33.17; 45.4
win 33.16; 45.4
worship (1) (of God) 42.2; 53.2

[r] SACRED HILL: *See 2.6.* [s] HEBREW TITLE: *A poem by the clan of Korah.*
[t] *Some ancient translations* and my God; you give; *Hebrew* O God; give.
[m] as...value; *or* and made no profit from the sale.

44.22: Rom 8.36

that we are treated like **sheep** to be
slaughtered.

[23] Wake up, Lord! Why are you asleep?
Rouse yourself! Don't **reject** us for
ever!
[24] Why are you hiding from us?
Don't **forget** our **suffering** and
trouble!

[25] We fall crushed to the ground;
we lie defeated in the dust.
[26] Come to our aid!
Because of your **constant love save**
us!

A Royal Wedding Song[u]

alive 33.19; 55.15
bless 37.22; 62.4
bride 2 Sam 17.3; Song 4.8
choose 33.12; 47.4
court (1) Job 31.21; 94.15
defend 43.1; 54.4
desire 37.4; 63.1
enemy 44.5; 49.5
evil 43.1; 49.6
favour 17.2; 103.6
forget 44.17; 59.11
gift 37.21; 68.18
glad 40.16; 48.11
glory 29.1; 57.5
happy 43.4; 51.8
hate 44.7; 55.3
heart 42.4; 51.10
joy 40.16; 46.4
justice [2] 36.6; 48.10
Kingdom (1) (of God) Job 25.1; 89.14
last (1) 33.11; 49.19
love 44.3; 47.4
Majesty [2] 29.4; 68.34
master Esth 1.22; 123.2
might 29.4; 54.1
mind (1) 19.8; 51.6
obey 37.18; 50.23
praise 44.8; 47.1
rich Job 34.19; 49.2
right (1) 41.12; 48.11
right (2) Neh 12.31; 110.1
strength 44.3; 46.1
throne 22.3; 47.5
truth 43.3; 51.6
victory [2] 44.4; 47.3
win [2] 44.3; 60.12
word (1) 39.2; 49.3

45 Beautiful **words** fill my **mind**,
as I compose this song for the
king.
Like the pen of a good writer
my tongue is ready with a poem.

[2] You are the most handsome of men;
you are an eloquent speaker.
God has always **blessed** you.
[3] Buckle on your sword, **mighty** king;
you are **glorious** and **majestic**.

[4] Ride on in **majesty** to **victory**
for the **defence** of **truth** and **justice**![v]
Your **strength** will **win** you great
victories!
[5] Your arrows are sharp,
they pierce the **hearts** of your
enemies;
nations fall down at your feet.

[6] The **kingdom** that God has given you[w]
will **last** for ever and ever.
You rule over your people with **justice**;
[7] you **love** what is **right** and **hate** what
is **evil**.
That is why God, your God, has **chosen**
you
and has poured out more **happiness**
on you
than on any other king.
[8] The perfume of myrrh and aloes is on
your clothes;
musicians entertain you in palaces
decorated with ivory.
[9] Among the ladies of your **court** are
daughters of kings,
and on the **right** of your **throne**
stands the queen,
wearing ornaments of finest gold.

[10] **Bride** of the king, listen to what I say—
forget your people and your
relatives.
[11] Your beauty will make the king **desire**
you;
he is your **master**, so you must **obey**
him.
[12] The people of Tyre will bring you **gifts**;
rich people will try to **win** your
favour.

[13] The princess is in the palace—how
beautiful she is!
Her gown is made of gold thread.
[14] In her colourful gown she is led to the
king,
followed by her bridesmaids,
and they also are brought to him.
[15] With **joy** and **gladness** they come
and enter the king's palace.

[16] You, my king, will have many sons
to succeed your ancestors as kings,
and you will make them rulers over
the whole earth.
[17] My song will keep your fame **alive** for
ever,
and everyone will **praise** you for all
time to come.

God Is with Us[x]

afraid 31.11; 48.5
Almighty [2] 21.7; 48.8
amaze Job 40.19; 48.5
destroy [2] 39.11; 50.22
help 41.1; 51.15
joy 45.15; 47.1
Most High 18.13; 47.2
rage Job 30.22; 50.3
refuge [2] 31.2; 59.9
sacred 43.3; 47.8
shelter 31.4; 55.8
strength 45.4; 59.9
supreme 2 Chr 9.26; 47.9
terrify 14.5; 53.5
trouble 44.24; 50.15
violent 18.48; 55.9
world [2] 33.8; 47.2

46 God is our **shelter** and **strength**,
always ready to **help** in times
of **trouble**.
[2] So we will not be **afraid**, even if the
earth is shaken
and mountains fall into the ocean
depths;
[3] even if the seas roar and **rage**,
and the hills are shaken by the
violence.

[4] There is a river that brings **joy** to the
city of God,
to the **sacred** house of the **Most**
High.
[5] God is in that city, and it will never be
destroyed;
at early dawn he will come to its aid.
[6] Nations are **terrified**, kingdoms are
shaken;
God thunders, and the earth
dissolves.

[7] The LORD **Almighty** is with us;
the God of Jacob is our **refuge**.

[8] Come and see what the LORD has done.
See what **amazing** things he has
done on earth.

[u] HEBREW TITLE: *A poem by the clan of Korah; a love song.*
[v] *Probable text* and justice; *Hebrew* and meekness of justice.
[w] The kingdom that God has given you; *or* Your kingdom, O God; *or* Your divine kingdom.
[x] HEBREW TITLE: *A song by the clan of Korah.*

45.6–7: Heb 1.8–9

9 He stops wars all over the **world**;
he breaks bows, **destroys** spears,
and sets shields on fire.
10 "Stop fighting," he says, "and know
that I am God,
supreme among the nations,
supreme over the **world**."

11 The LORD **Almighty** is with us;
the God of Jacob is our **refuge**.

The Supreme Ruler[y]

47 Clap your hands for **joy**, all
peoples!
Praise God with loud songs!
2 The LORD, the **Most High**, is to be
feared;
he is a great king, ruling over all the
world.
3 He gave us **victory** over the peoples;
he made us rule over the nations.
4 He **chose** for us the land where we live,
the **proud possession of his people**,
whom he **loves**.

5 God goes up to his **throne**.
There are shouts of **joy** and the blast
of trumpets,
as the LORD goes up.
6 Sing **praise** to God;
sing **praise** to our king!
7 God is king over all the **world**;
praise him with songs!

8 God sits on his **sacred throne**;
he rules over the nations.
9 The rulers of the nations assemble
with the people[z] of the God of
Abraham.
More **powerful** than all armies is he;
he rules **supreme**.

choose 45.7; 65.4
fear 34.4; 48.6
God's people 44.12; 48.12
joy [2] 46.4; 48.2
love 45.7; 48.9
Most High 46.4; 57.2
possess 37.9; 69.35
power 44.3; 49.15
praise [4] 45.17; 48.1
proud 36.11; 54.3
sacred 46.4; 48.1
supreme 46.10; 83.18
throne [2] 45.9; 80.1
victory 45.4; 53.6
world [2] 46.9; 48.2

Zion, the City of God[a]

48 The LORD is great and is to be
highly **praised**
in the city of our God, on his **sacred**
hill.[b]
2 Zion, the mountain of God, is high and
beautiful;
the city of the great king brings **joy**
to all the **world**.
3 God has shown that there is **safety**
with him
inside the fortresses of the city.

4 The kings gathered together
and came to attack Mount Zion.
5 But when they saw it, they were
amazed;
they were **afraid** and ran away.
6 There they were seized with **fear** and
anguish,
like a woman about to bear a child,
7 like ships tossing in a **furious** storm.

8 We have heard what God has done,
and now we have seen it
in the city of our God, the LORD
Almighty;
he will keep the city **safe** for ever.

9 Inside your **Temple**, O God,
we think of your **constant love**.
10 You are **praised** by people
everywhere,
and your fame extends over all the
earth.
You rule with **justice**;
11 let the people of Zion be **glad**!
You give **right judgements**;
let there be **joy** in the cities of
Judah!

12 **People of God**, walk round Zion and
count the towers;
13 take **notice** of the walls and examine
the fortresses,
so that you may tell the next
generation:
14 "This God is our God for ever and
ever;
he will lead us for all time to come."

afraid 46.2; 49.5
Almighty 46.7; 50.1
amaze 46.8; 106.22
anguish Esth 4.1; Is 26.16
constant 44.26; 51.1
fear 47.2; 55.5
fury 7.6; 50.3
glad 45.15; 51.8
God's people 47.4; 50.4
joy [2] 47.1; 51.8
judge 26.2; 50.4
justice 45.4; 58.1
love 47.4; 51.1
notice (1) 37.37; 94.7
praise [2] 47.1; 49.18
right (1) 45.7; 51.4
sacred 47.8; 65.4
safe [2] 40.2; 52.7
Temple (1) (of God) 43.3; 55.14
world 47.2; 50.12

The Foolishness of Trusting in Riches[c]

49 Hear this, everyone!
Listen, all people everywhere,
2 great and small alike,
rich and **poor** together.
3 My thoughts will be **clear**;
I will speak **words of wisdom**.
4 I will **turn** my attention to **proverbs**
and explain their meaning as I play
the harp.

5 I am not **afraid** in times of **danger**
when I am surrounded by **enemies**,
6 by **evil** men who **trust** in their **riches**
and **boast** of their great wealth.
7 A person can never **redeem** himself;
he cannot pay God the price for his
life,
8 because the payment for a **human**
life is too great.
What he could pay would never be
enough
9 to **keep him from** the **grave**,
to let him live for ever.

afraid 48.5; 52.6
boast 38.16; 52.1
body 38.3; 63.10
clear Job 38.14; 80.9
danger 40.2; 91.3
dark 44.19; 74.20
death (1) [3] 38.7; 55.4
death (2) (from death) [2] 33.19; 56.13
doom 1.6; Prov 19.9
enemy 45.5; 53.5
enough 37.19; 59.15
evil 45.7; 50.19
fate 26.9; Ecc 1.13
fool 39.8; 53.1
grave [3] 30.3; 55.23
human Job 31.2; 56.4
keep from 39.3; 56.13
last (1) 45.6; 72.7
life (1) [2] 42.8; 51.14
poor 41.1; 68.10
power 47.9; 54.1
praise 48.1; 50.15
proverb Job 17.5; Prov 1.1
redeem 19.14; Mt 20.28
rescue 37.40; 54.7
rich [2] 45.12; 65.9
riches [2] Job 36.18; 62.10
righteous 37.6; 50.6
satisfy [2] Job 38.39; 63.5

[y] HEBREW TITLE: *A psalm by the clan of Korah.*
[z] *Probable text* with the people; *Hebrew* the people.
[a] HEBREW TITLE: *A psalm by the clan of Korah; a song.* [b] SACRED HILL: *See 2.6.*
[c] HEBREW TITLE: *A psalm by the clan of Korah.*

48.2: Mt 5.35

10 Anyone can see that even **wise** men
die,
as well as **foolish** and **stupid** men.
They all leave their **riches** to their
descendants.
11 Their **graves**[d] are their homes for
ever;
there they stay for all time,
though they once had lands of their
own.
12 A man's greatness cannot **save** him
from death;
he will still die like the animals.

13 See what happens to those who **trust** in
themselves,
the **fate** of those[e] who are **satisfied**
with their wealth—
14 they are **doomed** to die like **sheep**,
and **Death** will be their **shepherd**.
The **righteous** will **triumph** over them,
as their **bodies** quickly decay
in the **world of the dead** far from
their homes.[x]
15 But God will **rescue** me;
he will **save** me from the **power** of
death.

16 Don't be **upset** when a man becomes
rich,
when his wealth grows even
greater;
17 he cannot take it with him when he
dies;
his wealth will not go with him to
the **grave**.
18 Even if a man is **satisfied** with this **life**
and is **praised** because he is
successful,
19 he will join all his ancestors in **death**,
where the **darkness lasts** for ever.
20 A man's greatness cannot **save** him
from death;
he will still die like the animals.

True Worship[f]

50 The **Almighty** God, the LORD,
speaks;
he calls to the whole earth from east
to west.
2 God shines from Zion,
the city **perfect** in its beauty.

3 Our God is coming, but not in silence;
a **raging** fire is in front of him,
a **furious** storm is round him.
4 He calls **heaven and earth** as **witnesses**
to see him **judge his people**.
5 He says, "Gather my **faithful** people to
me,
those who made a **covenant** with me
by **offering a sacrifice**."
6 The **heavens proclaim** that God is
righteous,
that he himself is **judge**.

7 "Listen, **my people**, and I will speak;
I will **testify** against you, Israel.
I am God, your God.
8 I do not **reprimand** you because of
your **sacrifices**
and the **burnt-offerings** you always
bring me.
9 And yet I do not **need** bulls from your
farms
or goats from your **flocks**;
10 all the animals in the forest are mine
and the cattle on thousands of hills.
11 All the wild birds are mine
and all living things in the fields.

12 "If I were **hungry**, I would not ask you
for food,
for the **world** and everything in it is
mine.
13 Do I eat the **flesh** of bulls
or drink the **blood** of goats?
14 Let the giving of **thanks** be your
sacrifice to God,[g]
and give the **Almighty** all that you
promised.
15 Call to me when **trouble** comes;
I will **save** you,
and you will **praise** me."

16 But God says to the **wicked**,
"Why should you recite my
commandments?
Why should you talk about my
covenant?
17 You **refuse** to let me **correct** you;
you **reject** my **commands**.
18 You become the **friend** of every **thief**
you see
and you associate with **adulterers**.

19 "You are always ready to speak **evil**;
you never hesitate to tell **lies**.
20 You are ready to **accuse** your own
brothers
and to find **fault** with them.
21 You have done all this, and I have said
nothing,
so you thought that I was like you.
But now I **reprimand** you
and make the matter **plain** to you.

22 "Listen to this, you that **ignore** me,
or I will **destroy** you,
and there will be no one to **save** you.

[d] *Some ancient translations* graves; *Hebrew* inner thoughts.
[e] *One ancient translation* the fate of those; *Hebrew* after them. [x] in...homes; *Hebrew unclear.*
[f] HEBREW TITLE: *A psalm by Asaph.*
[g] Let the giving...to God; *or* Offer your thanksgiving sacrifice to God.

[23] Giving **thanks** is the **sacrifice** that
honours me,
and I will **surely save** all who **obey**
me."

A Prayer for Forgiveness[h]

altar 43.4; 66.15
burnt-offering [2] 50.8; 66.13
clean [2] Job 37.21; Is 1.6
command 50.17; 68.11
condemn 37.33; 75.7
constant 48.9; 52.8
create 33.6; 74.16
evil [4] 50.19; 52.1
fault 50.20; 59.4
glad [2] 48.11; 54.6
happy 45.7; 53.6
heart [2] 45.5; 55.15
help [2] 46.1; 54.4
holy 33.21; 68.17
humble [2] 37.11; 69.10
joy [2] 48.2; 63.7
judge 50.4; 58.1
kind 31.16; 67.1
life (1) 49.8; 55.23
love 48.9; 52.3
loyal 40.10; 78.37
mercy [2] 41.4; 56.1
mind (1) 45.1; 64.6
new 40.3; 81.3
obey 50.23; 78.7
offer 50.5; 54.6
please [2] 41.11; 69.31
praise 50.15; 56.4
presence 44.3; 52.9
proclaim 50.6; 52.9
proper Esth 9.27; Prov 5.2
pure 24.4; 66.10
reject 50.17; 53.5
repent Job 42.6; 78.34
require Neh 12.44; Is 45.19
right (1) 48.11; 53.1
righteous 50.6; 52.6
sacrifice [4] 50.5; 54.6
salvation 40.10; 62.7
save 50.15; 54.1
sincere 41.6; 78.36
spare 34.22; 78.50
Spirit (1) (God's Spirit) Job 33.4; Is 11.2
spirit (2) [2] Job 26.5; Prov 15.4
teach 40.3; 71.17
truth 45.4; 52.3
turn 49.4; 53.3
wisdom 49.3; 119.66

51 Be **merciful** to me, O God,
because of your **constant love**.
Because of your great **mercy**
wipe away my sins!
[2] Wash away all my **evil**
and make me **clean** from my sin!

[3] I recognize my **faults**;
I am always conscious of my sins.
[4] I have sinned against you—only
against you—
and done what you consider **evil**.
So you are **right** in **judging** me;
you are justified in **condemning** me.
[5] I have been **evil** from the day I was
born;
from the time I was conceived, I
have been sinful.

[6] **Sincerity** and **truth** are what you
require;
fill my **mind** with your **wisdom**.
[7] Remove my sin, and I will be **clean**;
wash me, and I will be whiter than
snow.
[8] Let me hear the sounds of **joy** and
gladness;
and though you have crushed me
and broken me,
I will be **happy** once again.
[9] Close your eyes to my sins
and wipe out all my **evil**.

[10] **Create** a **pure heart** in me, O God,
and put a **new** and **loyal spirit** in me.
[11] Do not banish me from your **presence**;
do not take your **holy spirit** away
from me.
[12] Give me again the **joy** that comes from
your **salvation**,
and make me willing to **obey** you.
[13] Then I will **teach** sinners your
commands,
and they will **turn back** to you.

[14] **Spare** my **life**, O God, and **save** me,[i]
and I will **gladly proclaim** your
righteousness.
[15] **Help** me to speak, Lord,
and I will **praise** you.

[16] You do not want **sacrifices**,
or I would **offer** them;
you are not **pleased** with **burnt-offerings**.
[17] My **sacrifice** is a **humble spirit**, O God;
you will not **reject** a **humble** and
repentant heart.

[18] O God, be **kind** to Zion and **help** her;
rebuild the walls of Jerusalem.
[19] Then you will be **pleased** with **proper**
sacrifices
and with our **burnt-offerings**;
and bulls will be **sacrificed** on your
altar.

God's Judgement and Grace[j]

afraid 49.5; 56.3
boast 49.6; 55.12
constant 51.1; 57.3
depend 33.4; 62.1
eternal 33.11; 55.19
evil [2] 51.2; 53.4
faithful 50.5; 54.5
false 40.4; 119.78
hurt 38.12; 56.5
lie (2) [2] 50.19; 55.23
love [3] 51.1; 57.3
plan 40.5; 56.5
presence 51.11; 56.13
proclaim 51.14; 68.34
righteous 51.14; 58.10
ruin [2] 38.12; 69.22
safe 48.3; 55.18
secure 40.2; 71.3
thank 50.14; 54.6
trust [2] 49.6; 55.23
truth 51.6; 111.8
wicked 50.16; 55.3
word (1) 49.3; 54.2
world 50.12; 58.11

52 Why do you **boast**, great man, of
your **evil**?
God's **faithfulness** is **eternal**.
[2] You make **plans** to **ruin** others;
your tongue is like a sharp razor.
You are always inventing **lies**.
[3] You **love evil** more than good
and **falsehood** more than **truth**.
[4] You **love** to **hurt** people with your
words, you **liar**!

[5] So God will **ruin** you for ever;
he will take hold of you and snatch
you from your home;
he will remove you from the **world**
of the living.
[6] **Righteous** people will see this and be
afraid;
then they will laugh at you and say,
[7] "Look, here is a man who did not
depend on God for **safety**,
but **trusted** instead in his great
wealth
and looked for **security** in being
wicked."

[8] But I am like an olive-tree growing in
the house of God;
I **trust** in his **constant love** for ever
and ever.
[9] I will always **thank** you, God, for what
you have done;
in the **presence** of your people
I will **proclaim** that you are good.

The Wickedness of Men[k]

(Ps 14)

bad 41.6; 112.7
corrupt 14.1; 82.5
enemy 49.5; 54.5
evil 52.1; 54.5
fool 49.10; 69.5
God's people [2] 50.4; 60.6
happy 51.8; 65.4
heaven 50.4; 57.3

53 **Fools** say to themselves,
"There is no God."
They are all **corrupt**,
and they have done **terrible** things;
there is no one who does what is
right.

[h] HEBREW TITLE: *A psalm by David, after the prophet Nathan had spoken to him about his adultery with Bathsheba.* [i] Spare my life...me; *or* O God my saviour, keep me from the crime of murder.
[j] HEBREW TITLE: *A poem by David, after Doeg the Edomite went to Saul and told him that David had gone to the house of Ahimelech.* [k] HEBREW TITLE: *A poem by David.*

51 Title: 2 Sam 12.1–15 **51.4:** Rom 3.4 **52 Title:** 1 Sam 22.9–10 **53.1–3:** Rom 3.10–12

ignorant 14.4; 82.5
mankind 33.13; Prov 8.4
pray [2] 44.20; 69.13
prosper 44.2; 72.3
reject 51.17; 60.1
right (1) [2] 51.4; 65.1
rob 14.4; 62.10
scatter 44.11; 59.11
terrible 14.1; 88.16
terrify 46.6; 55.3
turn 51.13; 55.1
victory 47.3; 63.11
wise 49.10; 78.2
worship (1) (of God) 44.20; 55.14

2 God looks down from **heaven** at
mankind
to see if there are any who are **wise**,
any who **worship** him.
3 But they have all **turned away**;
they are all equally **bad**.
Not one of them does what is **right**,
not a single one.

4 "Don't they know?" God asks.
"Are these **evildoers ignorant**?
They live by **robbing my people**,
and they never **pray** to me."

5 But then they will be **terrified**,
as they have never been before,
for God will **scatter** the bones of the
enemies of his people.
God has **rejected** them,
and so Israel will totally defeat
them.

6 How I **pray** that **victory**
will come to Israel from Zion.
How **happy** the people of Israel will be
when God makes them **prosperous**
again!

A Prayer for Protection from Enemies[l]

care 37.18; 65.9
cruel 43.2; 59.3
defend 45.4; 55.22
destroy 50.22; 55.11
enemy [2] 53.5; 55.3
evil 53.4; 55.15
faithful 52.1; 57.3
free 37.26; 68.6
glad 51.8; 58.10
help 51.15; 55.16
might 45.3; 60.5
offer 51.16; 56.12
power 49.15; 62.11
prayer 42.8; 55.1
proud 47.4; 59.12
punish 44.2; 56.7
rescue 49.15; 56.13
sacrifice 51.16; 66.15
save 51.14; 55.16
thank 52.9; 56.12
trouble 50.15; 55.3
word (1) 52.4; 55.21

54 Save me by your **power**, O God;
set me free by your **might**!
2 Hear my **prayer**, O God;
listen to my **words**!
3 **Proud** men are coming to attack me;
cruel men are trying to kill me—
men who do not **care** about God.

4 But God is my **helper**.
The Lord is my **defender**.
5 May God use their own **evil** to **punish**
my **enemies**.
He will **destroy** them because he is
faithful.

6 I will **gladly offer** you a **sacrifice**, O
LORD;
I will give you **thanks**
because you are good.
7 You have **rescued** me from all my
troubles,
and I have seen my **enemies**
defeated.

The Prayer of a Man Betrayed by a Friend[m]

alive 45.17; 66.9
anger 38.1; 56.7
boast 52.1; 75.5
change 30.11; 66.6
complain Job 33.13; 142.2

55 Hear my **prayer**, O God;
don't **turn** away from my **plea**!
2 Listen to me and answer me;
I am worn out by my **worries**.
3 I am **terrified** by the **threats** of my
enemies,
crushed by the **oppression** of the
wicked.
They bring **trouble** on me;
they are **angry** with me and **hate**
me.

4 I am **terrified**,
and the **terrors of death** crush me.
5 I am gripped by **fear** and **trembling**;
I am overcome with **horror**.
6 I **wish** I had wings, like a **dove**.
I would fly away and find **rest**.
7 I would fly far away
and live in the wilderness.
8 I would quickly find myself a **shelter**
from the **raging** wind and the storm.
9 Confuse the **speech** of my **enemies**, O
Lord!

I see **violence** and riots in the city,
10 surrounding it day and night,
filling it with **crime** and **trouble**.
11 There is **destruction** everywhere;
the streets are full of **oppression** and
fraud.

12 If it were an **enemy** that **mocked** me,
I could **endure** it;
if it were an opponent **boasting** over
me,
I could hide myself from him.
13 But it is you, my companion,
my colleague and close **friend**.
14 We had intimate talks with **each other**
and **worshipped** together in the
Temple.
15 May my **enemies** die before their
time;
may they go down **alive** into the
world of the dead!
Evil is in their homes and in their
hearts.

16 But I call to the LORD God for **help**,
and he will **save** me.
17 Morning, noon, and night
my **complaints** and **groans** go up to
him,
and he will hear my voice.
18 He will bring me **safely** back
from the battles that I fight
against so many **enemies**.
19 God, who has ruled from **eternity**,
will hear me and defeat them;
for they **refuse** to **change**,
and they do not **fear** him.

crime 35.11; 58.2
death (1) 49.14; 76.
defend 54.4; 59.17
destroy 54.5; 59.13
dove 2 Kgs 6.25; 68.13
each other 41.7; 64
endure 33.11; 89.50
enemy [5] 54.5; 56.1
eternal 52.1; 90.2
evil 54.5; 56.7
fear [2] 48.6; 66.3
friend [2] 50.18; 88.
grave 49.9; 69.15
groan 38.8; 79.11
hate [2] 45.7; 68.1
heart [2] 51.10; 62.4
help 54.4; 60.11
honest 25.21; 101.6
horror 2 Chr 26.20; 73.19
lie (2) 52.2; 58.3
life (1) 51.14; 58.3
mock 44.13; 59.8
oppress [2] 35.10; 57.3
plead 35.23; 142.1
prayer 54.2; 60.5
promise 50.14; 56.4
rage 50.3; 57.1
refuse (1) 50.17; 74.11
rest (1) 23.2; 94.13
safe 52.7; 57.1
save 54.1; 57.3
shelter 46.1; 59.16
speech 36.3; Prov 22.11
Temple (1) (of God 48.9; 65.4
terrify [2] 53.5; 76.1
terror 31.13; Prov 1.26
threat 38.12; 59.7
tremble 18.7; 60.2
trouble [3] 54.7; 56.
trust 52.7; 56.3
turn 53.3; 56.9
violent 46.3; 58.2
wicked 52.7; 58.10
wish 31.8; 81.8
word (1) [2] 54.2; 59.12
world of the dead 49.14; 63.9
worry 37.1; 77.4
worship (1) (of Go 53.2; 66.4

[l] HEBREW TITLE: *A poem by David, after the men from Ziph went to Saul and told him that David was hiding in their territory.* [m] HEBREW TITLE: *A poem by David.*

54 Title: 1 Sam 23.19, 26.1

[20] My former companion attacked his
friends;
he broke his **promises**.
[21] His **words** were smoother than cream,
but there was **hatred** in his **heart**;
his **words** were as soothing as oil,
but they cut like sharp swords.

[22] Leave your **troubles** with the LORD,
and he will **defend** you;
he never lets **honest** men be
defeated.

[23] But you, O God, will bring those
murderers and **liars** to their
graves
before half their **life** is over.
As for me, I will **trust** in you.

A Prayer of Trust in God[n]

afraid [3] 52.6; 64.1
Almighty 50.1; 59.5
anger 55.3; 58.9
being [2] 29.1; 63.1
death (2) (from death) 49.12; 68.20
enemy [3] 55.3; 57.4
evil 55.15; 58.2
hope 43.5; 62.5
human [2] 49.8; 60.11
hurt 52.4; 71.13
keep from 49.9; 71.20
light (1) 43.3; 58.8
mercy 51.1; 57.1
offer [2] 54.6; 61.8
persecute 31.15; 69.26
plan 52.2; 64.5
praise [2] 51.15; 57.7
presence 52.9; 61.7
promise [3] 55.20; 61.5
punish 54.5; 58.10
rescue 54.7; 59.2
tear (2) 42.3; 80.5
thank 54.6; 57.9
trouble [2] 55.3; 59.16
trust [3] 55.23; 62.8
turn 55.1; 60.1
watch 37.32; 78.12

56 Be **merciful** to me, O God,
because I am under attack;
my **enemies persecute** me all the
time.
[2] All day long my opponents attack me.
There are so many who fight against
me.
[3] When I am **afraid**, O LORD **Almighty**,
I put my **trust** in you.
[4] I **trust** in God and am not **afraid**;
I **praise** him for what he has
promised.
What can a mere **human being** do to
me?

[5] My **enemies** make **trouble** for me all
day long;
they are always **planning** how to
hurt me!
[6] They gather in hiding-places
and **watch** everything I do,
hoping to kill me.
[7] **Punish**[o] them, O God, for their **evil**;
defeat those people in your **anger**!

[8] You know how **troubled** I am;
you have kept a record of my **tears**.
Aren't they listed in your book?
[9] The day I call to you,
my **enemies** will be **turned** back.
I know this: God[p] is on my side—
[10] the LORD, whose **promises** I **praise**.
[11] In him I **trust**, and I will not be **afraid**.
What can a mere **human being** do to
me?

[12] O God, I will **offer** you what I have
promised;
I will give you my **offering** of
thanksgiving,
[13] because you have **rescued** me **from**
death
and **kept** me **from** defeat.
And so I walk in the **presence** of God,
in the **light** that shines on the living.

A Prayer for Help[q]

confident Job 29.24; 59.9
constant [2] 52.8; 59.16
distress 38.16; 78.49
enemy [2] 56.1; 59.1
faithful [2] 54.5; 61.7
glory [2] 45.3; 63.2
heaven [2] 53.2; 69.34
love [2] 52.3; 59.10
mercy 56.1; 59.5
Most High 47.2; 73.11
need 50.9; 69.33
oppress 55.3; 69.32
praise [2] 56.4; 59.17
protect 43.2; 59.1
rage 55.8; 78.49
safe 55.18; 61.2
save 55.16; 59.1
soul 42.6; 63.1
thank 56.12; 63.4

57 Be **merciful** to me, O God, be
merciful,
because I come to you for **safety**.
In the shadow of your wings I find
protection
until the **raging** storms are over.

[2] I call to God, the **Most High**,
to God, who supplies my every **need**.
[3] He will answer from **heaven** and **save**
me;
he will defeat my **oppressors**.
God will show me his **constant love**
and **faithfulness**.

[4] I am surrounded by **enemies**,
who are like man-eating lions.
Their teeth are like spears and
arrows;
their tongues are like sharp swords.

[5] Show your greatness in the sky, O God,
and your **glory** over all the earth.

[6] My **enemies** have spread a net to catch
me;
I am overcome with **distress**.
They dug a pit in my path,
but fell into it themselves.

[7] I have complete **confidence**, O God;
I will sing and **praise** you!
[8] Wake up, my **soul**!
Wake up, my harp and lyre!
I will wake up the sun.
[9] I will **thank** you, O Lord, among the
nations.
I will **praise** you among the peoples.
[10] Your **constant love** reaches the
heavens;
your **faithfulness** touches the skies.
[11] Show your greatness in the sky, O God,
and your **glory** over all the earth.

A Prayer for God to Punish the Wicked[r]

anger 56.7; 59.13
blood 50.13; 68.23
crime 55.10; 64.6
dead 31.12; 76.6

58 Do you rulers[s] ever give a **just**
decision?
Do you **judge** all men fairly?

[n] HEBREW TITLE: *A psalm by David, after the Philistines captured him in Gath.*
[o] *Probable text* Punish; *Hebrew* Save. [p] I know this: God; *or* Because I know that God.
[q] HEBREW TITLE: *A psalm by David, after he fled from Saul in the cave.*
[r] HEBREW TITLE: *A psalm by David.* [s] rulers; *or* gods.

56 Title: 1 Sam 21.13–15 **57 Title:** 1 Sam 22.1, 24.3

2 No! You think only of the evil you can
do,
and commit crimes of violence in
the land.

3 Evil men go wrong all their lives;
they tell lies from the day they are
born.
4 They are full of poison like snakes;
they stop up their ears like a deaf
cobra,
5 which does not hear the voice of the
snake-charmer,
or the chant of the clever magician.

6 Break the teeth of these fierce lions, O
God.
7 May they disappear like water
draining away;
may they be crushed like weeds on a
path.[t]
8 May they be like snails that dissolve
into slime;
may they be like a baby born dead
that never sees the light.
9 Before they know it, they are cut down
like weeds;
in his fierce anger God will blow
them away
while they are still living.[u]

10 The righteous will be glad when they
see sinners punished;
they will wade through the blood of
the wicked.
11 People will say, "The righteous are
indeed rewarded;
there is indeed a God who judges the
world."

A Prayer for Safety[v]

59 Save me from my enemies, my
God;
protect me from those who attack
me!
2 Save me from those evil men;
rescue me from those murderers!

3 Look! They are waiting to kill me;
cruel men are gathering against me.
It is not because of any sin or wrong I
have done,
4 nor because of any fault of mine, O
LORD,
that they hurry to their places.

5 Rise, LORD God Almighty, and come to
my aid;
see for yourself, God of Israel!
Wake up and punish the heathen;
show no mercy to evil traitors!

6 They come back in the evening,
snarling like dogs as they go about
the city.
7 Listen to their insults and threats.
Their tongues are like swords in their
mouths,
yet they think that no one hears
them.

8 But you laugh at them, LORD;
you mock all the heathen.
9 I have confidence in your strength;
you are my refuge, O God.
10 My God loves me and will come to me;
he will let me see my enemies
defeated.

11 Do not kill them, O God, or my people
may forget.
Scatter them by your strength and
defeat them,
O Lord, our protector.
12 Sin is on their lips; all their words are
sinful;
may they be caught in their pride!
Because they curse and lie,
13 destroy them in your anger;
destroy them completely.
Then everyone will know that God
rules in Israel,
that his rule extends over all the
earth.

14 My enemies come back in the evening,
snarling like dogs as they go about
the city,
15 like dogs roaming about for food
and growling if they do not find
enough.

16 But I will sing about your strength;
every morning I will sing aloud of
your constant love.
You have been a refuge for me,
a shelter in my time of trouble.
17 I will praise you, my defender.
My refuge is God,
the God who loves me.

A Prayer for Deliverance[w]

60 You have rejected us, God, and
defeated us;
you have been angry with us—but
now turn back to us.[x]
2 You have made the land tremble, and
you have cut it open;

[t] *Probable text* may...path; *Hebrew unclear.* [u] *Verse 9 in Hebrew is unclear.*
[v] HEBREW TITLE: *A psalm by David, after Saul sent men to watch his house in order to kill him.*
[w] HEBREW TITLE: *A psalm by David, for teaching, when he fought against the Arameans from Naharaim and from Zobah, and Joab turned back and killed 12,000 Edomites in the Valley of Salt.*
[x] angry with us...us; *or* angry with us and turned your back on us.

59 Title: 1 Sam 19.11 **60 Title:** 2 Sam 8.13; 1 Chr 18.12

help [2] 55.16; 63.7
human 56.4; 108.12
love 59.10; 61.7
might 54.1; 63.2
prayer 55.1; 61.1
reject [2] 53.5; 66.20
rescue 59.2; 68.20
reverence 36.1; Prov 1.7
sanctuary 2 Kgs 10.25; 61.4
save 59.1; 62.1
sign (1) Esth 5.9; 74.4
suffer 44.24; 69.26
tremble 55.5; 75.3
triumph [2] 49.14; 68.24
turn 56.9; 69.16
warn 40.3; 81.8
win 45.4; 98.1
worthless 26.4; 62.9

now **heal** its wounds, because it is
falling **apart**.
3 You have made your people **suffer**
greatly;
we stagger around as though we
were drunk.
4 You have **warned** those who show you
reverence,
so that they might **escape**
destruction.
5 **Save** us by your **might**; answer our
prayer,
so that the people you **love** may be
rescued.

6 From his **sanctuary**[y] God has said,
"In **triumph** I will divide Shechem
and distribute the Valley of Sukkoth
to **my people**.
7 Gilead is mine, and Manasseh too;
Ephraim is my helmet
and Judah my royal sceptre.
8 But I will use Moab as my wash-basin
and I will throw my sandals on
Edom,
as a **sign** that I own it.
Did the Philistines think they would
shout in **triumph** over me?"

9 Who, O God, will take me into the
fortified city?
Who will lead me to Edom?
10 Have you really **rejected** us?
Aren't you going to march out with
our armies?
11 **Help** us against the **enemy**;
human help is **worthless**.
12 With God on our side we will **win**;
he will defeat our **enemies**.

A Prayer for Protection[z]

constant 59.16; 62.12
defend 59.17; 62.2
despair 35.12; 69.20
enemy 60.11; 64.1
faithful 57.3; 71.22
honour 50.23; 62.4
life (1) [2] 58.3; 63.3
love 60.5; 62.12
offer 56.12; 66.2
praise 59.17; 63.3
prayer 60.5; 63.4
presence 56.13; 68.2
promise [2] 56.4; 63.11
protect [2] 59.1; 62.2
refuge 59.9; 62.8
safe [2] 57.1; 63.8
sanctuary 60.6; 63.2
strong 38.19; 62.3

61 Hear my cry, O God;
listen to my **prayer**!
2 In **despair** and far from home
I call to you!

Take me to a **safe refuge**,
3 for you are my **protector**,
my **strong defence** against my
enemies.

4 Let me live in your **sanctuary** all my
life;
let me find **safety** under your wings.
5 You have heard my **promises**, O God,
and you have given me what
belongs to those who **honour** you.

6 Add many years to the king's **life**;
let him live on and on!
7 May he rule for ever in your **presence**,
O God;
protect him with your **constant love**
and **faithfulness**.

8 So I will always sing **praises** to you,
as I **offer** you daily what I have
promised.

Confidence in God's Protection[a]

alone [4] 39.13; 71.16
bless 45.2; 65.4
constant 61.7; 63.3
curse 59.12; 89.50
defend [2] 61.3; 71.3
depend [4] 52.7; 104.27
heart 55.15; 64.6
honour [2] 61.5; 66.16
hope [2] 56.6; 69.20
lie (2) 59.12; 63.11
iove 61.7; 63.3
patient 40.1; 86.15
pleasure 16.3; 112.1
power 54.1; 65.6
protect [3] 61.3; 64.2
refuge 61.2; 71.3
reward 58.11; 91.16
riches 49.6; Prov 1.13
rob 53.4; Prov 1.19
salvation 51.12; 67.2
save [3] 60.5; 64.1
shelter 59.16; 71.3
strong [2] 61.3; 69.4
trouble 59.16; 64.1
trust [2] 56.3; 65.5
violent 58.2; 72.14
word (1) 59.12; 64.3
worthless 60.11; 108.12

62 I wait **patiently** for God to **save**
me;
I **depend** on him **alone**.
2 He **alone protects** and **saves** me;
he is my **defender**,
and I shall never be defeated.

3 How much longer will all of you attack
a man
who is no **stronger** than a broken-
down fence?
4 You only want to bring him down from
his place of **honour**;
you take **pleasure** in **lies**.
You speak **words** of **blessing**,
but in your **heart** you **curse** him.

5 I **depend** on God **alone**;
I put my **hope** in him.
6 He **alone protects** and **saves** me;
he is my **defender**,
and I shall never be defeated.
7 My **salvation** and **honour depend** on
God;
he is my **strong protector**;
he is my **shelter**.

8 **Trust** in God at all times, my people.
Tell him all your **troubles**,
for he is our **refuge**.

9 Men are all like a puff of breath;
great and small alike are **worthless**.
Put them on the scales, and they weigh
nothing;
they are lighter than a mere breath.
10 Don't put your **trust** in **violence**;
don't **hope** to gain anything by
robbery;
even if your **riches** increase,
don't **depend** on them.

11 More than once I have heard God say
that **power** belongs to him
12 and that his **love** is **constant**.
You yourself, O Lord, **reward** everyone
according to his deeds.

[y] From his sanctuary; *or* In his holiness. [z] HEBREW TITLE: *By David.*
[a] HEBREW TITLE: *A psalm by David.*

62.12: Job 34.11; Jer 17.10; Mt 16.27; Rom 2.6; Rev 2.23

being 56.4; 71.23
body 49.14; 73.26
constant 62.12; 66.20
desire 45.11; 102.4
feast 36.8; 69.22
glad 58.10; 67.4
glory 57.5; 66.2
help 60.11; 66.17
joy 51.8; 65.8
lie (2) 62.4; 64.4
life (1) 61.4; 64.1
long (2) 42.1; 84.2
love 62.12; 66.20
might 60.5; 65.6
name (2) (name of God, of Jesus) 34.3; 66.2
praise [3] 61.8; 64.10
prayer 61.1; 64.1
promise 61.5; 65.1
raise Job 5.11; 68.31
rejoice 32.11; 64.10
remember 42.4; 74.2
safe 61.2; 64.10
sanctuary 61.4; 65.4
satisfy 49.13; 65.4
soul [2] 57.8; 103.1
thank 57.9; 69.30
victory 53.6; 65.5
world of the dead 55.15; 139.8

Longing for God[b]

63 O God, you are my God,
and I long for you.
My whole being desires you;
like a dry, worn-out, and waterless
land,
my soul is thirsty for you.
2 Let me see you in the sanctuary;
let me see how mighty and glorious
you are.
3 Your constant love is better than life
itself,
and so I will praise you.
4 I will give you thanks as long as I live;
I will raise my hands to you in
prayer.
5 My soul will feast and be satisfied,
and I will sing glad songs of praise to
you.

6 As I lie in bed, I remember you;
all night long I think of you,
7 because you have always been my
help.
In the shadow of your wings I sing for
joy.
8 I cling to you,
and your hand keeps me safe.

9 Those who are trying to kill me
will go down into the world of the
dead.
10 They will be killed in battle,
and their bodies eaten by wolves.
11 Because God gives him victory,
the king will rejoice.
Those who make promises in God's
name will praise him,
but the mouths of liars will be shut.

afraid [2] 56.3; 76.8
crime 58.2; 94.4
cruel 59.3; 71.4
destroy [2] 60.4; 71.13
each other 55.14; Prov 7.18
encourage Job 29.24; 69.32
enemy 61.3; 66.3
evil [3] 59.2; 71.4
heart 62.4; 69.20
lie (2) 63.11; 69.4
life (1) 63.3; 71.6
mind (1) 51.6; 73.7
mystery 78.2
perfect 50.2; 119.45
plan [3] 56.5; 73.8
plot (1) [2] 38.12; 71.10
praise 63.3; 65.1
prayer 63.4; 65.2
protect 62.2; 68.5
rejoice 63.11; 66.6
righteous 58.10; 68.3

A Prayer for Protection[c]

64 I am in trouble, God—listen to
my prayer!
I am afraid of my enemies—save
my life!
2 Protect me from the plots of the
wicked,
from mobs of evil men.
3 They sharpen their tongues like
swords
and aim cruel words like arrows.
4 They are quick to spread their
shameless lies;
they destroy good men with
cowardly slander.
5 They encourage each other in their
evil plots;
they plan where to place their traps.
"No one can see them," they say.
6 They make evil plans and say,
"We have planned a perfect crime."
The heart and mind of man are a
mystery.

7 But God shoots his arrows at them,
and suddenly they are wounded.
8 He will destroy them because of those
words;[d]
all who see them will shake their
heads.
9 They will all be afraid;
they will think about what God has
done
and tell about his deeds.
10 All righteous people will rejoice
because of what the LORD has done.
They will find safety in him;
all good people will praise him.

safe 63.8; 66.12
save 62.1; 65.5
shame 44.15; 69.6
slander 15.3; Is 29.2
trap 38.12; 66.11
trouble 62.8; 66.14
wicked 58.10; 68.2
word (1) [2] 62.4; 78.36

Praise and Thanksgiving[e]

65 O God, it is right for us to praise
you in Zion
and keep our promises to you,
2 because you answer prayers.
People everywhere will come to you
3 on account of their sins.
Our faults defeat us,[f]
but you forgive them.
4 Happy are those whom you choose,
whom you bring to live in your
sanctuary.
We shall be satisfied with the good
things of your house,
the blessings of your sacred Temple.

5 You answer us by giving us victory
and you do wonderful things to save
us.
People all over the world
and across the distant seas trust in
you.
6 You set the mountains in place by your
strength,
showing your mighty power.
7 You calm the roar of the seas
and the noise of the waves;
you calm the uproar of the peoples.
8 The whole world stands in awe
of the great things that you have
done.
Your deeds bring shouts of joy
from one end of the earth to the
other.

9 You show your care for the land by
sending rain;

abundant 36.8; 68.9
awe Job 37.22; 68.35
bless 62.4; 67.1
calm [2] Job 40.23; 89.9
care 54.3; 68.5
choose 47.4; 68.16
fault 59.4; 101.2
flock 50.9; 78.48
forgive 32.1; 78.38
happy 53.6; 68.3
harvest Job 39.12; 67.6
joy [3] 63.7; 66.1
might 63.2; 66.7
plenty Job 29.6; 72.1
power 62.11; 66.3
praise 64.10; 66.1
prayer 64.1; 66.19
promise 63.11; 66.13
provide [2] 36.8; 68.10
rich [2] 49.2; 85.12
right (1) 53.1; 84.11
sacred 48.1; 68.5
sanctuary 63.2; 68.2
satisfy 63.5; 78.29
save 64.1; 68.19
sheep 49.14; 66.15
strength 59.9; 68.35
Temple (1) (of God) 55.14; 68.5
trust 62.8; 69.6
victory 63.11; 74.4
wonder (1) 40.5; 66.3
world [2] 58.11; 67.2

[b] HEBREW TITLE: *A psalm by David, when he was in the desert of Judah.*
[c] HEBREW TITLE: *A psalm by David.*
[d] *Probable text* He will destroy them because of those words; *Hebrew* They will destroy him, those words are against them. [e] HEBREW TITLE: *A psalm by David; a song.*
[f] *One ancient translation* us; *Hebrew* me.

63 Title: 1 Sam 23.14

you make it **rich** and fertile.
You fill the streams with water;
you **provide** the earth with crops.
This is how you do it:
10 you send **abundant** rain on the
ploughed fields
and soak them with water;
you soften the soil with showers
and cause the young plants to grow.
11 What a **rich harvest** your goodness
provides!
Wherever you go there is **plenty**.
12 The pastures are filled with **flocks**;
the hillsides are full of **joy**.
13 The fields are covered with **sheep**;
the valleys are full of wheat.
Everything shouts and sings for **joy**.

A Song of Praise and Thanksgiving[g]

66 **Praise** God with shouts of joy, all
people!
2 Sing to the **glory** of his **name**;
offer him **glorious praise**!
3 Say to God, "How **wonderful** are the
things you do!
Your **power** is so great
that your **enemies bow down** in **fear**
before you.
4 Everyone on earth **worships** you;
they sing **praises** to you,
they sing praises to your **name**."

5 Come and see what God has done,
his **wonderful acts** among men.
6 He **changed** the sea into dry land;
our ancestors crossed the river on
foot.
There we **rejoiced** because of what he
did.
7 He rules for ever by his **might**
and keeps his eyes on the nations.
Let no **rebels rise** against him.
8 **Praise** our God, all nations;
let your **praise** be heard.
9 He has kept us **alive**
and has not allowed us to fall.

10 You have put us **to the test**, God;
as silver is **purified** by fire
so you have **tested** us.
11 You let us fall into a **trap**
and placed heavy **burdens** on our
backs.
12 You let our **enemies** trample over us;
we went through fire and **flood**,
but now you have brought us to a
place of **safety**.[h]

13 I will bring **burnt-offerings** to your
house;

act 37.7; 71.17
alive 55.15; 69.25
altar 51.19; 84.3
bow (2) 38.6; 68.30
burden 38.4; 68.19
burnt-offering 51.16; Is 43.23
change 55.19; 90.3
constant 63.3; 69.16
enemy [2] 64.1; 68.1
fear 55.5; 76.7
flood 42.6; 69.15
glory [2] 63.2; 71.8
help 63.7; 69.3
honour 62.4; 67.7
ignore 50.22; Prov 1.25
joy 65.8; 67.4
love 63.3; 68.30
might 65.6; 68.15
name (2) (name of God, of Jesus) [2] 63.11; 68.4
offer [3] 61.8; 68.30
power 65.6; 68.28
praise [7] 65.1; 67.3
prayer [2] 65.2; 68.31
promise 65.1; 69.13
pure 51.10; 73.1
rebel 25.3; 68.6
reject 60.1; 71.9
rejoice 64.10; 68.3
rise 59.5; 68.1
sacrifice 54.6; 69.31
safe 64.10; 69.14
sheep 65.13; 68.13
test [2] 26.2; 78.18
trap 64.5; 94.13
trouble 64.1; 69.17
wonder (1) [2] 65.5; 71.17
worship (1) (of God) 55.14; 69.6

I will **offer** you what I **promised**.
14 I will give you what I said I would
when I was in **trouble**.
15 I will **offer sheep** to be burnt on the
altar;
I will **sacrifice** bulls and goats,
and the smoke will go up to the sky.

16 Come and listen, all who **honour** God,
and I will tell you what he has done
for me.
17 I cried to him for **help**;
I **praised** him with songs.
18 If I had **ignored** my sins,
the Lord would not have listened to
me.
19 But God has indeed heard me;
he has listened to my **prayer**.

20 I **praise** God,
because he did not **reject** my **prayer**
or keep back his **constant love** from
me.

A Song of Thanksgiving[i]

67 God, be **merciful** to us and **bless**
us;
look on us with **kindness**,
2 so that the whole **world** may know
your **will**;
so that all nations may know your
salvation.

3 May the peoples **praise** you, O God;
may all the peoples **praise** you!

4 May the nations be **glad** and sing for
joy,
because you **judge** the peoples with
justice
and **guide** every nation on earth.

5 May the peoples **praise** you, O God;
may all the peoples **praise** you!

6 The land has produced its **harvest**;
God, our God, has **blessed** us.
7 God has **blessed** us;
may all people everywhere **honour**
him.

bless [3] 65.4; 72.15
glad 63.5; 68.3
guide 37.23; 73.24
harvest 65.11; 85.12
honour 66.16; 73.24
joy 66.1; 68.3
judge 58.1; 72.1
justice 58.1; 72.1
kind 51.18; 84.11
mercy 59.5; 77.9
praise [4] 66.1; 68.4
salvation 62.7; 69.27
will (1) 40.8; 103.21
world 65.5; 68.32

A National Song of Triumph[j]

68 God **rises** up and **scatters** his
enemies.
Those who **hate** him run away in
defeat.
2 As smoke is blown away, so he drives
them off;
as wax melts in front of the fire,

abundant 65.10; 107.37
Almighty 59.5; 69.6
ancient 24.7; Is 19.11
awe 65.8; 89.7
blood 58.10; 78.44
bow (2) 66.3; 72.9
burden 66.11; 81.6
captive Esth 2.6; Song 6.5

[g] HEBREW TITLE: *A song.* [h] *Some ancient translations* safety; *Hebrew* overflowing.
[i] HEBREW TITLE: *A psalm; a song.* [j] HEBREW TITLE: *A psalm by David; a song.*

66.6: Ex 14.21; Josh 3.14–17

care 65.9; 78.72
choose 65.4; 69.13
cloud 18.9; 77.17
command 51.13; 78.23
death (2) (from death) 56.13; 86.2
desolate Job 30.3; Is 6.11
dove 55.6; Song 2.12
enemy [3] 66.3; 69.4
free 54.1; 79.11
gift [2] 45.12; 72.10
glad [2] 67.4; 69.32
God's people [2] 60.6; 69.33
happy [2] 65.4; 70.2
hate 55.3; 69.4
holy 51.11; 71.22
joy 67.4; 70.4
lonely 25.16; 102.7
love 66.20; 69.13
Majesty 45.3; 76.4
might [5] 66.7; 71.18
name (2) (name of God, of Jesus) [2] 66.2; 72.19
offer 66.2; 69.21
orphan 10.18; 82.3
perish Job 36.20; 73.27
poor 49.2; 70.5
power [3] 66.3; 71.4
praise [6] 67.3; 69.30
prayer 66.19; 72.15
presence [3] 61.7; 76.7
prison Job 12.14; 69.33
proclaim 52.9; 69.30
protect 64.2; 71.1
provide 65.9; 78.20
raise 63.4; 93.3
rebel [2] 66.7; 78.8
rebuke [2] 39.11; 103.9
rejoice 66.6; 89.16
rescue 60.5; 69.18
restore 41.3; 71.20
righteous 64.10; 71.2
rise 66.7; 76.9
sacred 65.4; 69.22
sanctuary [2] 65.4; 108.7
save [2] 65.5; 69.1
scatter [3] 59.11; 83.13
scorn 44.14; 109.25
sheep 66.15; 79.13
strength 65.6; 71.20
sure 50.23; 85.9
Temple (1) (of God) [2] 65.4; 69.9
triumph 60.6; 74.4
way (3) 25.4; 81.12
wicked 64.2; 71.4
widow Job 31.16; 78.64
world 67.2; 72.19

so do the **wicked perish** in God's
presence.
3 But the **righteous** are **glad** and **rejoice**
in his **presence**;
they are **happy** and shout for **joy**.

4 Sing to God, sing **praises** to his **name**;
prepare a way for him who rides on
the **clouds**.[k]
His **name** is the LORD—be **glad** in his
presence!

5 God, who lives in his **sacred Temple**,
cares for **orphans** and **protects**
widows.
6 He gives the **lonely** a home to live in
and leads **prisoners** out into **happy**
freedom,
but **rebels** will have to live in a
desolate land.

7 O God, when you led your people,
when you marched across the
desert,
8 the earth shook, and the sky poured
down rain,
because of the coming of the God of
Sinai,[l]
the coming of the God of Israel.
9 You caused **abundant** rain to fall
and **restored** your worn-out land;
10 your people made their home there;
in your goodness you **provided** for
the **poor**.

11 The Lord gave the **command**,
and many women carried the news:
12 "Kings and their armies are running
away!"
The women at home divided what
was captured:
13 figures of **doves** covered with silver,
whose wings glittered with fine gold.
(Why did some of you stay among the
sheep pens on the day of battle?)
14 When **Almighty** God **scattered** the
kings on Mount Zalmon,
he caused snow to fall there.

15 What a **mighty** mountain is Bashan,
a mountain of many peaks!
16 Why from your **mighty** peaks do you
look with **scorn**
on the mountain[m] on which God
chose to live?
The LORD will live there for ever!

17 With his many thousands of **mighty**
chariots
the Lord comes from Sinai[n] into the
holy place.
18 He goes up to the heights,
taking many **captives** with him;
he receives **gifts** from **rebellious**
men.
The LORD God will live there.

19 **Praise** the Lord,
who carries our **burdens** day after
day;
he is the God who **saves** us.
20 Our God is a God who **saves**;
he is the LORD, our Lord,
who **rescues** us **from death**.

21 God will **surely** break the heads of his
enemies,
of those who persist in their sinful
ways.
22 The Lord has said, "I will bring your
enemies back from Bashan;
I will bring them back from the
depths of the ocean,
23 so that you may wade in their **blood**,
and your dogs may lap up as much
as they want."

24 O God, your march of **triumph** is seen
by all,
the procession of God, my king, into
his **sanctuary**.
25 The singers are in front, the musicians
are behind,
in between are the girls beating the
tambourines.
26 "**Praise** God in the meeting of **his**
people;
praise the LORD, all you descendants
of Jacob!"
27 First comes Benjamin, the smallest
tribe,
then the leaders of Judah with their
group,
followed by the leaders of Zebulun
and Naphtali.

28 Show your **power**, O God,
the power you have used on our
behalf
29 from your **Temple** in Jerusalem,
where kings bring **gifts** to you.
30 **Rebuke** Egypt, that wild animal in the
reeds;
rebuke the nations, that herd of bulls
with their calves,
until they all **bow down** and **offer**
you their silver.

[k] on the clouds; *or* across the desert.
[l] GOD OF SINAI: *As the people of Israel went from Egypt to Canaan, God revealed himself to them at Mount Sinai (see Ex 19.16–25).* [m] MOUNTAIN: *See 2.6.*
[n] *Probable text* comes from Sinai; *Hebrew* in them, Sinai.

68.8: Ex 19.18 **68.18:** Eph 4.8

Scatter those people who **love** to make
war![o]
31 Ambassadors[p] will come from Egypt;
the Sudanese will **raise** their hands
in **prayer** to God.

32 Sing to God, kingdoms of the **world**,
sing **praise** to the Lord,
33 to him who rides in the sky,
the **ancient** sky.
Listen to him shout with a **mighty** roar.
34 **Proclaim God's power**;
his **majesty** is over Israel,
his **might** is in the skies.
35 How **awesome** is God as he comes
from his **sanctuary**—
the God of Israel!
He gives **strength** and **power** to **his
people**.

Praise God!

A Cry for Help[q]

69 Save me, O God!
The water is up to my neck;
2 I am sinking in deep mud,
and there is no solid ground;
I am out in deep water,
and the waves are about to drown
me.
3 I am worn out from calling for **help**,
and my throat is aching.
I have strained my eyes,
looking for your **help**.

4 Those who **hate** me for no **reason**
are more numerous than the hairs of
my head.
My **enemies** tell **lies** against me;
they are **strong** and want to kill me.
They made me give back things I did
not **steal**.
5 My sins, O God, are not hidden from
you;
you know how **foolish** I have been.
6 Don't let me bring **shame** on those who
trust in you,
Sovereign LORD **Almighty**!
Don't let me bring **disgrace** to those
who **worship** you,
O God of Israel!
7 It is for your **sake** that I have been
insulted
and that I am covered with **shame**.
8 I am like a **stranger** to my brothers,
like a foreigner to my family.

9 My **devotion** to your **Temple** burns in
me like a fire;
the **insults** which are hurled at you
fall on me.
10 I **humble** myself[r] by **fasting**,
and people **insult** me;
11 I dress myself in clothes of **mourning**,
and they laugh at me.
12 They talk about me in the streets,
and drunkards make up songs about
me.

13 But as for me, I will **pray** to you, LORD;
answer me, God, at a time you
choose.
Answer me because of your great **love**,
because you keep your **promise** to
save.
14 **Save** me from sinking in the mud;
keep me **safe** from my **enemies**,
safe from the deep water.
15 Don't let the **flood** come over me;
don't let me drown in the depths
or sink into the **grave**.

16 Answer me, LORD, in the goodness of
your **constant love**;
in your great **compassion turn** to
me!
17 Don't hide yourself from your **servant**;
I am in great **trouble**—answer me
now!
18 Come to me and **save** me;
rescue me from my **enemies**.

19 You know how I am **insulted**,
how I am **disgraced** and
dishonoured;
you see all my **enemies**.
20 **Insults** have broken my **heart**,
and I am in **despair**.
I had **hoped** for **sympathy**, but there
was none;
for **comfort**, but I found none.
21 When I was **hungry**, they gave me
poison;
when I was thirsty, they **offered** me
vinegar.
22 May their **banquets** cause their **ruin**;
may their **sacred feasts** cause their
downfall.
23 **Strike** them with **blindness**!
Make their backs always **weak**!
24 Pour out your **anger** on them;
let your indignation overtake them.
25 May their camps be left deserted;
may no one be left **alive** in their
tents.
26 They **persecute** those whom you have
punished;

[o] *Verse 30 in Hebrew is unclear.* [p] *Some ancient translations* Ambassadors; *Hebrew unclear.*
[q] HEBREW TITLE: *By David.* [r] *Some ancient translations* humble myself; *Hebrew* cry.

69.4: Ps 35.19; Jn 15.25 **69.9:** Jn 2.17; Rom 15.3 **69.21:** Mt 27.48; Mk 15.36; Lk 23.36; Jn 19.28–29
69.22–23: Rom 11.9–10 **69.25:** Acts 1.20

they talk about the **sufferings** of
those you have wounded.
27 Keep a record of all their sins;
don't let them have any part in your
salvation.
28 May their names be erased from the
book of the living;
may they not be included in the list
of your people.

29 But I am in **pain** and **despair**;
lift me up, O God, and **save** me!

30 I will **praise** God with a song;
I will **proclaim** his greatness by
giving him **thanks**.
31 This will **please** the LORD more than
offering him cattle,
more than **sacrificing** a full-grown
bull.
32 When the **oppressed** see this, they will
be **glad**;
those who **worship** God will be
encouraged.
33 The LORD listens to those in **need**
and does not **forget his people** in
prison.

34 **Praise** God, O **heaven and earth**,
seas and all **creatures** in them.
35 He will **save** Jerusalem
and rebuild the towns of Judah.
His people will live there and **possess**
the land;
36 the descendants of his **servants** will
inherit it,
and those who **love** him will live
there.

A Prayer for Help[s]
(Ps 40.13–17)

70 Save me, O God!
LORD, **help** me now!
2 May those who try to kill me
be defeated and confused.
May those who are **happy** because of
my **troubles**
be **turned** back and **disgraced**.
3 May those who **jeer** at me
be dismayed by their defeat.

4 May all who come to you
be **glad** and **joyful**.
May all who are **thankful** for your
salvation
always say, "How great is God!"

5 I am **weak** and **poor**;
come to me quickly, O God.

disgrace 69.6; 71.13
glad 69.32; 86.4
happy 68.3; 84.4
help 69.3; 71.2
jeer 40.15; Is 57.4
joy 68.3; 71.23
poor 68.10; 72.4
salvation 69.27; 71.15
save 69.1; 71.2
Saviour 43.5; 85.4
thank 69.30; 75.1
trouble 69.17; 71.20
turn 69.16; 73.10
weak 69.23; 72.13

You are my **saviour**, O LORD—
hurry to my aid!

An Old Man's Prayer

71 LORD, I have come to you for
protection;
never let me be defeated!
2 Because you are **righteous**, **help** me
and **rescue** me.
Listen to me and **save** me!
3 Be my **secure shelter**
and a **strong** fortress[t] to **protect** me;
you are my **refuge** and **defence**.

4 My God, **rescue** me from **wicked** men,
from the **power** of **cruel** and **evil**
men.
5 **Sovereign** LORD, I put my **hope** in you;
I have **trusted** in you since I was
young.
6 I have **relied** on you all my **life**;
you have **protected**[u] me since the
day I was born.
I will always **praise** you.

7 My **life** has been an **example** to many,
because you have been my **strong**
defender.
8 All day long I **praise** you
and **proclaim** your **glory**.
9 Do not **reject** me now that I am old;
do not **abandon** me now that I am
feeble.
10 My **enemies** want to kill me;
they talk and **plot** against me.
11 They say, "God has **abandoned** him;
let's go after him and catch him;
there is no one to **rescue** him."

12 Don't stay so far away, O God;
my God, hurry to my aid!
13 May those who attack me
be defeated and **destroyed**.
May those who try to **hurt** me
be **shamed** and **disgraced**.
14 I will always put my **hope** in you;
I will **praise** you more and more.
15 I will tell of your goodness;
all day long I will speak of your
salvation,
though it is more than I can
understand.
16 I will **praise** your **power**, **Sovereign**
LORD;
I will **proclaim** your goodness, yours
alone.

17 You have **taught** me ever since I was
young,

abandon [3] 44.19; 73.27
act 66.5; 73.15
alone 62.1; 72.18
being 63.1; 78.39
comfort 69.20; 77.2
cruel 64.3; 74.19
defend [2] 62.2; 74.22
destroy 64.4; 73.18
disgrace [2] 70.2; 83.17
enemy 69.4; 72.9
evil 64.2; 73.7
example 1.1; Prov 2.20
faithful 61.7; 78.8
glory 66.2; 72.19
grave 69.15; 86.13
harm 3.7; 91.7
help 70.1; 72.4
holy 68.17; 74.8
hope [2] 69.20; 79.8
hurt 56.5; 73.21
hymn 26.7; 147.7
joy 70.4; 81.1
keep from 56.13; 78.
life (1) [2] 64.1; 72.13
might 68.15; 74.13
plot (1) 64.2; 83.3
power [3] 68.28; 75.1
praise [6] 69.30; 72.1
proclaim [3] 69.30; 73.28
protect [3] 68.5; 73.2
refuge 62.8; Mic 1.11
reject 66.20; 77.7
rely 22.8; 78.57
rescue [3] 69.18; 72.12
restore 68.9; 122.3
righteous [3] 68.3; 72.1
salvation 70.4; Is 61.10
save [2] 70.1; 72.13
secure 52.7; 78.69
shame 69.6; 74.21
shelter 62.7; 144.2
Sovereign [2] 69.6; 73.28
strength 68.35; 73.26
strong [2] 69.4; 73.4
suffer 69.26; 73.4
teach 51.13; 72.1
trouble 70.2; 73.5
trust 69.6; 78.7
understand 19.8; 73.17
wicked 68.2; 73.3
wonder (1) 66.3; 72.18

[s] HEBREW TITLE: *A psalm by David; a lament.*
[t] *One ancient translation* a strong fortress; *Hebrew* to go always you commanded.
[u] *Some ancient translations* protected; *Hebrew unclear.*

69.28: Ex 32.32; Rev 3.5, 13.8, 17.8

share 41.9; 106.5
teach 71.17; 78.1
violent 62.10; 73.6
weak 70.5; 73.26
wonder (1) 71.17; 73.28
world 68.32; 76.8
worship (1) (of God) 69.6; 74.7

and I still tell of your **wonderful acts**.
18 Now that I am old and my hair is grey,
do not **abandon** me, O God!
Be with me while I **proclaim** your
power and **might**
to all generations to come.

19 Your **righteousness**, God, reaches the
skies.
You have done great things;
there is no one like you.
20 You have sent **troubles** and **suffering**
on me,
but you will **restore** my **strength**;
you will **keep me from** the **grave**.
21 You will make me greater than ever;
you will **comfort** me again.

22 I will indeed **praise** you with the harp;
I will **praise** your **faithfulness**, my
God.
On my harp I will play **hymns** to you,
the **Holy One** of Israel.
23 I will shout for **joy** as I play for you;
with my whole **being** I will sing
because you have **saved** me.
24 I will speak of your **righteousness** all
day long,
because those who tried to **harm** me
have been defeated and **disgraced**.

A Prayer for the King[v]

age (1) 119.90
alone 71.16; 83.18
bless [2] 67.1; 84.9
bow (2) [2] 68.30; 81.15
enemy 71.10; 74.3
enjoy 37.11; Prov 1.22
experience 2 Chr 8.18; Prov 20.30
forget 69.33; 74.19
gift 68.18; 76.11
glory [2] 71.8; 76.4
help 71.2; 74.11
judge [2] 67.4; 75.2
justice [2] 67.4; 82.5
last (1) [2] 49.19; 74.9
life (1) [2] 71.6; 78.33
light (1) [2] 58.8; 77.18
name (2) (name of God, of Jesus) 68.4; 74.10
need [3] 69.33; 73.26
neglect 22.24; 119.87
offer [2] 69.21; 96.8
oppress [3] 69.32; 73.8
pity 17.10; 90.13
plenty 65.11; 73.12
poor [3] 70.5; 74.21
praise [2] 71.6; 74.21
prayer [2] 68.31; 77.2
prosper [2] 53.6; 85.1
rescue [2] 71.2; 79.9
righteous [4] 71.2; 75.10
save 71.2; 74.12
serve 22.30; 86.11

72 **Teach** the king to **judge** with
your **righteousness**, O God;
share with him your own **justice**,
2 so that he will rule over your people
with **justice**
and govern the **oppressed** with
righteousness.
3 May the land **enjoy prosperity**;
may it **experience righteousness**.
4 May the king **judge** the **poor** fairly;
may he **help** the **needy**
and defeat their **oppressors**.
5 May your people **worship** you as long
as the sun shines,
as long as the moon gives **light**, for
ages to come.

6 May the king be like rain on the fields,
like showers falling on the land.
7 May **righteousness** flourish in his
lifetime,
and may **prosperity last** as long as
the moon gives **light**.

8 His kingdom will reach from sea to
sea,
from the Euphrates to the ends of
the earth.
9 The peoples of the desert will **bow
down** before him;
his **enemies** will throw themselves
to the ground.
10 The kings of Spain and of the islands
will **offer** him **gifts**;
the kings of Sheba and Seba[a] will
bring him **offerings**.
11 All kings will **bow down** before him;
all nations will **serve** him.

12 He **rescues** the **poor** who call to him,
and those who are **needy** and
neglected.
13 He has **pity** on the **weak** and **poor**;
he **saves** the **lives** of those in **need**.
14 He **rescues** them from **oppression** and
violence;
their **lives** are precious to him.

15 Long live the king!
May he be given gold from Sheba;
may **prayers** be said for him at all
times;
may God's **blessings** be on him
always!
16 May there be **plenty** of corn in the
land;
may the hills be covered with crops,
as fruitful as those of Lebanon.
May the cities be filled with people,
like fields full of grass.
17 May the king's name never be
forgotten;
may his fame **last** as long as the sun.
May all nations ask God to bless
them
as he has **blessed** the king.[b]

18 **Praise** the LORD, the God of Israel!
He **alone** does these **wonderful** things.
19 **Praise** his **glorious name** for ever!
May his **glory** fill the whole **world**.

Amen! Amen!

20 This is the end of the **prayers** of David
son of Jesse.

BOOK THREE
(Psalms 73–89)

The Justice of God[w]

abandon 71.9; 74.1
act 71.17; 77.12
arrogant 31.18; 75.4

73 God is indeed good to Israel,
to those who have **pure hearts**.
2 But I had nearly lost **confidence**;

[v] HEBREW TITLE: *By Solomon.*
[a] SHEBA AND SEBA: *Sheba was towards the south in Arabia and Seba was on the opposite side of the Red Sea.* [b] as he...king; *or* and may they wish happiness for the king. [w] HEBREW TITLE: *By Asaph.*

72.8: Zech 9.10

believe Job 22.17; 78.22
bitter 6.10; 106.33
body 63.10; 74.14
confident 59.9; 108.1
destroy [3] 71.13; 74.3
difficult Neh 1.3; 131.1
dream Job 33.15; 90.5
eager 19.5; 84.5
evil [3] 71.4; 82.4
faith 27.14; 78.22
God's people 69.33; 74.1
guide 67.4; 78.52
heart [2] 69.20; 86.12
heaven [2] 69.34; 76.8
honour 67.7; 76.1
horror 55.5; 116.3
hurt 71.13; 77.10
jealous 37.1; 106.16
mind (1) [2] 64.6; 139.23
Most High 57.2; 78.17
need 72.4; 74.21
oppress 72.2; 74.21
pain 69.29; 78.41
perish 68.2; 1 Cor 8.11
plan 64.5; 83.3
plenty 72.16; 104.16
proclaim 71.8; 75.1
protect 71.1; 78.35
proud [3] 59.12; 76.12
punish 69.26; 79.8
pure [2] 66.10; 101.2
scheme Job 10.3; 119.118
Sovereign 71.5; 109.21
strength 71.20; 74.13
strong 71.3; 75.8
stupid 49.10; 82.5
suffer [3] 71.20; 88.9
Temple (1) (of God) 69.9; 74.3
trouble 71.20; 77.2
turn 70.2; 78.6
understand [2] 71.15; 92.6
unfaithful Neh 1.8; 106.39
violent 72.14; 74.20
weak 72.13; 86.1
wicked [4] 71.4; 75.4
wonder (1) 72.18; 75.1

my faith was almost gone
3 because I was jealous of the proud
when I saw that things go well for
the wicked.

4 They do not suffer pain;
they are strong and healthy.
5 They do not suffer as other people do;
they do not have the troubles that
others have.
6 And so they wear pride like a necklace
and violence like a robe;
7 their hearts pour out evil,[x]
and their minds are busy with
wicked schemes.
8 They laugh at other people and speak
of evil things;
they are proud and make plans to
oppress others.
9 They speak evil of God in heaven
and give arrogant orders to men on
earth,
10 so that even God's people turn to them
and eagerly believe whatever they
say.[y]
11 They say, "God will not know;
the Most High will not find out."
12 That is what the wicked are like.
They have plenty and are always
getting more.

13 Is it for nothing, then, that I have kept
myself pure
and have not committed sin?
14 O God, you have made me suffer all
day long;
every morning you have punished
me.

15 If I had said such things,
I would not be acting as one of your
people.
16 I tried to think this problem through,
but it was too difficult for me
17 until I went into your Temple.
Then I understood what will happen to
the wicked.

18 You will put them in slippery places
and make them fall to destruction!
19 They are instantly destroyed;
they go down to a horrible end.
20 They are like a dream that goes away
in the morning;
when you rouse yourself, O Lord,
they disappear.

21 When my thoughts were bitter
and my feelings were hurt,
22 I was as stupid as an animal;
I did not understand you.
23 Yet I always stay close to you,
and you hold me by the hand.
24 You guide me with your instruction
and at the end you will receive me
with honour.
25 What else have I in heaven but you?
Since I have you, what else could I
want on earth?
26 My mind and my body may grow
weak,
but God is my strength;
he is all I ever need.

27 Those who abandon you will certainly
perish;
you will destroy those who are
unfaithful to you.
28 But as for me, how wonderful to be
near God,
to find protection with the Sovereign
LORD
and to proclaim all that he has
done!

A Prayer for National Deliverance[z]

74 Why have you abandoned us like
this, O God?
Will you be angry with your own
people for ever?
2 Remember your people, whom you
chose for yourself long ago,
whom you brought out of slavery to
be your own tribe.
Remember Mount Zion, where once
you lived.
3 Walk over these total ruins;
our enemies have destroyed
everything in the Temple.

4 Your enemies have shouted in triumph
in your Temple;
they have placed their flags there as
signs of victory.
5 They looked like woodmen
cutting down trees with their axes.[a]
6 They smashed all the wooden panels
with their axes and sledge-hammers.
7 They wrecked your Temple and set it
on fire;
they desecrated the place where you
are worshipped.
8 They wanted to crush us completely;
they burnt down every holy place in
the land.

9 All our sacred symbols are gone;
there are no prophets left,
and no one knows how long this will
last.

abandon [2] 73.27; 78.60
anger [2] 69.24; 75.8
body 73.26; 79.2
cause (2) 43.1; 119.154
choose 69.13; 78.68
covenant 50.5; 78.10
create 51.10; 86.9
cruel 71.4; 86.14
dark 49.19; 88.6
defend 71.3; 81.1
despise 22.6; 119.141
destroy 73.18; 78.38
enemy [6] 72.9; 76.3
forget [2] 72.17; 77.9
God's people 73.10; 78.20
godless [2] Job 36.13; Prov 11.9
help 72.4; 79.9
helpless 44.19; 82.3
holy 71.22; 77.13
insult 69.7; 79.4
last (1) 72.7; 78.66
Leviathan Job 41.1; 104.26
might 71.18; 77.12
monster [2] Job 40.15; 89.10
name (2) (name of God, of Jesus) 72.19; 76.1
need 73.26; 82.3
oppress 73.8; 76.9
persecute 69.26; 109.16
poor 72.4; 82.3
praise 72.18; 75.9
prophet Neh 9.26; 105.15
refuse (1) 55.19; 78.10
remember [5] 63.6; 77.5
ruin 69.22; 78.45
sacred 69.22; 87.1
save 72.13; 76.9
shame 71.13; 78.66
sign (1) 60.8; 108.9

[x] *Some ancient translations* their hearts pour out evil; *Hebrew unclear.*
[y] *Verse 10 in Hebrew is unclear.* [z] HEBREW TITLE: *A poem by Asaph.*
[a] *Verse 5 in Hebrew is unclear.*

10 How long, O God, will our **enemies**
laugh at you?
Will they **insult** your **name** for ever?
11 Why have you **refused** to **help** us?
Why do you keep your hands behind
you? [b]

12 But you have been our king from the
beginning, O God;
you have **saved** us many times.
13 With your **mighty strength** you divided
the sea
and smashed the heads of the **sea-monsters**;
14 you crushed the heads of the **monster**
Leviathan [c]
and fed his **body** to desert animals. [d]
15 You made springs and fountains flow;
you dried up large rivers.
16 You **created** the day and the night;
you set the sun and the moon in
their places;
17 you set the limits of the earth;
you made summer and winter.

18 But **remember**, O LORD, that your
enemies laugh at you,
that they are **godless** and **despise**
you.
19 Don't **abandon** your **helpless** people to
their **cruel enemies**;
don't **forget** your **persecuted** people!

20 **Remember** the **covenant** you made
with us.
There is **violence** in every **dark**
corner of the land.
21 Don't let the **oppressed** be put to
shame;
let those **poor** and **needy** people
praise you.

22 Rouse yourself, God, and **defend** your
cause!
Remember that **godless** people
laugh at you all day long.
23 Don't **forget** the **angry** shouts of your
enemies,
the continuous noise made by your
foes.

God the Judge [e]

75 We give **thanks** to you, O God, we
give thanks to you!
We **proclaim** how great you are
and tell of [f] the **wonderful** things you
have done.

2 "I have set a time for **judgement**," says
God,
"and I will **judge** with fairness.
3 Though every living **creature tremble**
and the earth itself be shaken,
I will keep its foundations firm.
4 I tell the **wicked** not to be **arrogant**;
5 I tell them to stop their **boasting**."

6 **Judgement** does not come from the
east or from the west,
from the north or from the south; [g]
7 it is God who is the **judge**,
condemning some and acquitting
others.
8 The LORD holds a **cup** in his hand,
filled with the **strong** wine of his
anger.
He pours it out, and all the **wicked**
drink it;
they drink it down to the **last** drop.

9 But I will never stop speaking of the
God of Jacob
or singing **praises** to him.
10 He will break the **power** of the **wicked**,
but the **power** of the **righteous** will
be increased.

God the Victor [h]

76 God is known in Judah;
his **name** is **honoured** in Israel.
2 He has his home in Jerusalem;
he lives on Mount Zion.
3 There he broke the arrows of the
enemy,
their shields and swords, yes, all
their weapons.

4 How **glorious** you are, O God!
How **majestic**, as you return from
the mountains
where you defeated your foes.
5 Their brave soldiers have been
stripped of all they had
and now are sleeping the sleep of
death;
all their **strength** and skill was
useless.
6 When you **threatened** them, O God of
Jacob,
the horses and their riders fell **dead**.

7 But you, LORD, are **feared** by all.
No one can stand in your **presence**
when you are **angry**.

[b] *Probable text* Why do you keep your hands behind you; *Hebrew unclear.*
[c] LEVIATHAN: *A legendary monster which was a symbol of the forces of chaos and evil.*
[d] animals; *or* people. [e] HEBREW TITLE: *A psalm by Asaph; a song.*
[f] *Some ancient translations* We proclaim how great you are and tell of; *Hebrew* Your name is near and they tell of.
[g] *Probable text* from the north or from the south; *Hebrew* from the wilderness of the mountains.
[h] HEBREW TITLE: *A psalm by Asaph; a song.*

74.13: Ex 14.21 **74.14:** Job 41.1; Ps 104.26; Is 27.1

[8] You made your **judgement** known
from **heaven**;
the **world** was **afraid** and kept silent,
[9] when you **rose** up to pronounce
judgement,
to **save** all the **oppressed** on earth.

[10] Men's **anger** only results in more
praise for you;
those who survive the wars will keep
your **festivals**.[i]

[11] Give the LORD your God what you
promised him;
bring **gifts** to him, all you nearby
nations.
God makes men **fear** him;
[12] he **humbles proud** princes
and **terrifies** great kings.

No **god** is as great as you.
[14] You are the God who works **miracles**;
you showed your **might** among the
nations.
[15] By your **power** you **saved** your people,
the descendants of Jacob and of
Joseph.

[16] When the waters saw you, O God, they
were **afraid**,
and the depths of the sea **trembled**.
[17] The **clouds** poured down rain;
thunder crashed from the sky,
and lightning flashed in all
directions.
[18] The crash of your thunder rolled out,
and flashes of lightning **lit** up the
world;
the earth **trembled** and shook.
[19] You walked through the waves;
you crossed the deep sea,
but your footprints could not be
seen.
[20] You led your people like a **shepherd**,
with Moses and Aaron in charge.

Comfort in Time of Distress[j]

77 I cry aloud to God;
I cry aloud, and he hears me.
[2] In times of **trouble** I **pray** to the Lord;
all night long I lift my hands in
prayer,
but I cannot find **comfort**.
[3] When I think of God, I sigh;
when I meditate, I feel **discouraged**.

[4] He keeps me awake all night;
I am so **worried** that I cannot speak.
[5] I think of days gone by
and **remember** years of long ago.
[6] I spend the night in deep thought;[k]
I meditate, and this is what I ask
myself:
[7] "Will the Lord always **reject** us?
Will he **never again** be **pleased** with
us?
[8] Has he stopped **loving** us?
Does his **promise** no longer stand?
[9] Has God **forgotten** to be **merciful**?
Has **anger** taken the place of his
compassion?"
[10] Then I said, "What **hurts** me most is
this—
that God is no longer **powerful**."[l]

[11] I will **remember** your great deeds,
LORD;
I will recall the **wonders** you did in
the past.
[12] I will think about all that you have
done;
I will meditate on all your **mighty**
acts.

[13] Everything you do, O God, is **holy**.

God and His People[m]

78 Listen, my people, to my
teaching,
and pay attention to what I say.
[2] I am going to use **wise sayings**
and explain **mysteries** from the past,
[3] things we have heard and known,
things that our fathers told us.
[4] We will not **keep them from** our
children;
we will tell the next generation
about the LORD's **power** and his
great deeds
and the **wonderful** things he has
done.

[5] He gave **laws** to the people of Israel
and **commandments** to the
descendants of Jacob.
He instructed our ancestors
to **teach** his **laws** to their children,
[6] so that the next generation might
learn them
and in **turn** should tell their children.
[7] In this way they also would put their
trust in God
and not **forget** what he has done,
but always **obey** his **commandments**.
[8] They would not be like their ancestors,
a **rebellious** and **disobedient** people,
whose **trust** in God was never firm
and who did not remain **faithful** to
him.

[i] *One ancient translation* will keep your festivals; *verse 10 in Hebrew is unclear.*
[j] HEBREW TITLE: *A psalm by Asaph.* [k] *Some ancient translations* deep thought; *Hebrew* song.
[l] *Verse 10 in Hebrew is unclear.* [m] HEBREW TITLE: *A poem by Asaph.*

78.2: Mt 13.35

fury [2] 50.3; 85.3
glory 76.4; 84.11
God's people [10] 74.1; 81.8
grapevine *see* **vine**
guide 73.24; 119.105
heathen 59.5; 79.1
heaven [2] 76.8; 80.14
holy [2] 77.13; 79.1
idol 40.4; 96.5
keep from 71.20; 89.48
last (1) 74.9; 81.15
law [3] 40.7; 81.4
learn 25.12; 94.8
lie (2) 69.4; 89.35
life (1) [2] 72.13; 82.7
light (1) 77.18; 89.15
love 77.8; 84.1
loyal 51.10; 85.11
manna Neh 9.20; Jn 6.31
mercy 77.9; 79.8
might 77.12; 86.10
miracle [4] 77.14; 88.10
mortal 22.29; 89.47
Most High 73.11; 82.6
mourn 69.11; Ecc 3.4
mystery 64.6; Prov 30.18
obey [3] 51.12; 81.11
pain 73.4; 116.15
place of worship 2 Chr 34.3; Jer 48.35
plague 1 Sam 6.4; 91.6
power [4] 77.10; 79.11
pray 77.2; 79.6
priest Job 12.19; 99.6
protect 73.28; 80.17
provide 68.10; 95.7
rage 57.1; 85.3
rebel [5] 68.6; 83.2
refuse (1) 74.11; 84.11
reject [2] 77.7; 88.14
rely 71.6; Prov 2.15
remember [2] 77.5; 89.47
repent 51.17; Is 1.27
ruin 74.3; 79.1
sad 43.5; 90.15
safe 69.14; 91.1
satisfy [2] 65.4; 81.16
save [2] 77.15; 79.9
saying 2 Chr 9.7; Prov 1.2
secure 71.3; 102.28
selfish Deut 15.7; Prov 28.22
servant 69.17; 79.2
shame 74.21; 83.16
shepherd [2] 77.20; 80.1
sincere 51.6; 145.18
spare 51.14; 119.80
strike 69.23; 91.6
strong [2] 75.8; 80.15
symbol 74.9; 132.8
teach [2] 72.1; 86.11
Temple (1) (of God) 74.3; 79.1
Tent (2) (of the Lord's presence) 2 Chr 24.6; Acts 7.44
test [3] 66.10; 81.7
torment Job 19.1; Rev 14.10
true 33.4; 103.18
trust [3] 71.5; 84.12
turn [3] 73.10; 79.6
vine Job 15.33; 80.8
violent 74.20; 91.10
watch 56.6; 89.36
widow 68.5; 94.6
wise 53.2; 90.12
wonder (1) 77.11; 86.10
word (1) 64.3; 105.19

9 The Ephraimites, armed with bows
and arrows,
ran away on the day of battle.
10 They did not keep their **covenant** with
God;
they **refused** to **obey** his **law**.
11 They **forgot** what he had done,
the **miracles** they had seen him
perform.
12 While their ancestors **watched**, God
performed **miracles**
in the plain of Zoan in the land of
Egypt.
13 He divided the sea and took them
through it;
he made the waters stand like walls.
14 By day he led them with a **cloud**
and all night long with the **light** of a
fire.
15 He split rocks open in the desert
and gave them water from the
depths.
16 He caused a stream to come out of the
rock
and made water flow like a river.

17 But they continued to sin against God,
and in the desert they **rebelled**
against the **Most High**.
18 They deliberately put God **to the test**
by **demanding** the food they wanted.
19 They spoke against God and said,
"Can God supply food in the desert?
20 It is **true** that he **struck** the rock,
and water flowed out in a torrent;
but can he also **provide** us with **bread**
and give **his people** meat?"

21 And so the LORD was **angry** when he
heard them;
he attacked **his people** with fire,
and his **anger** against them grew,
22 because they had no **faith** in him
and did not **believe** that he would
save them.
23 But he spoke to the sky **above**
and **commanded** its doors to open;
24 he gave them grain from **heaven**,
by sending down **manna** for them to
eat.
25 So they ate the food of **angels**,
and God gave them all they wanted.
26 He also caused the east wind to blow,
and by his **power** he stirred up the
south wind;
27 and to **his people** he sent down birds,
as many as the grains of sand on the
shore;
28 they fell in the middle of the camp
all round the tents.
29 So the people ate and were **satisfied**;
God gave them what they wanted.
30 But they had not yet **satisfied** their
craving
and were still eating,
31 when God became **angry** with them
and killed their **strongest** men,
the **best** young men of Israel.

32 In spite of all this the people kept
sinning;
in spite of his **miracles** they did not
trust him.
33 So he ended their days like a breath
and their **lives** with sudden **disaster**.
34 Whenever he killed some of them,
the rest would **turn to him**;
they would **repent** and **pray**
earnestly to him.
35 They **remembered** that God was their
protector,
that the **Almighty** came to their aid.
36 But their **words** were all **lies**;
nothing they said was **sincere**.
37 They were not **loyal** to him;
they were not **faithful** to their
covenant with him.

38 But God was **merciful** to **his people**.
He **forgave** their sin
and did not **destroy** them.
Many times he held back his **anger**
and restrained his **fury**.
39 He **remembered** that they were only
mortal beings,
like a wind that blows by and is
gone.

40 How often they **rebelled** against him in
the desert;
how many times they made him
sad!
41 Again and again they put God **to the**
test
and brought **pain** to the **Holy** God of
Israel.
42 They **forgot** his great **power**
and the day when he **saved** them
from their **enemies**
43 and performed his **mighty acts** and
miracles
in the plain of Zoan in the land of
Egypt.
44 He **turned** the rivers into **blood**,
and the Egyptians had no water to
drink.
45 He sent flies among them, that
tormented them,
and frogs that **ruined** their land.
46 He sent locusts to eat their crops
and to **destroy** their fields.
47 He killed their **grapevines** with hail

78.12: Ex 7.8—12.32 **78.13:** Ex 14.21–22 **78.14:** Ex 13.21–22 **78.15–16:** Ex 17.1–7; Num 20.2–13 **78.18–31:** Ex 16.2–15; Num 11.4–23, 31–35 **78.24:** Jn 6.31 **78.44:** Ex 7.17–21 **78.45:** Ex 8.1–6, 20–24 **78.46:** Ex 10.12–15 **78.47–48:** Ex 9.22–25

and their fig-trees with frost.
48 He killed their cattle with hail
and their **flocks** with lightning.[n]
49 He caused them great **distress**
by pouring out his **anger** and fierce **rage**,
which came as messengers of **death**.
50 He did not restrain his **anger**
or **spare** their **lives**,
but killed them with a **plague**.
51 He killed the **first-born** sons
of all the families of Egypt.

52 Then he led **his people** out like a **shepherd**
and **guided** them through the desert.
53 He led them **safely**, and they were not **afraid**;
but the sea came rolling over their **enemies**.
54 He brought them to his **holy** land,
to the mountains which he himself **conquered**.
55 He drove out the inhabitants as **his people** advanced;
he divided their land among the tribes of Israel
and gave their homes to **his people**.

56 But they **rebelled** against **Almighty** God
and put him **to the test**.
They did not **obey** his **commandments**,
57 but were **rebellious** and disloyal like their fathers,
unreliable as a crooked arrow.
58 They **angered** him with their **heathen places of worship**,
and with their **idols** they made him **furious**.
59 God was **angry** when he saw it,
so he **rejected his people** completely.
60 He **abandoned** his tent in Shiloh,[o]
the home where he had lived among us.
61 He allowed our **enemies** to capture the **Covenant Box**,
the **symbol** of his **power** and **glory**.
62 He was **angry** with his **own people**
and let them be killed by their **enemies**.
63 Young men were killed in war,
and young women had no one to marry.
64 **Priests** died by **violence**,
and their **widows** were not allowed to **mourn**.

65 At last the Lord woke up as though from sleep;
he was like a **strong** man excited by wine.
66 He drove his **enemies** back
in **lasting** and **shameful** defeat.
67 But he **rejected** the descendants of Joseph;
he did not select the tribe of Ephraim.
68 Instead he **chose** the tribe of Judah
and Mount Zion, which he **dearly loves**.
69 There he built his **Temple**
like his home in **heaven**;
he made it firm like the earth itself,
secure for all time.

70 He **chose** his **servant** David;
he took him from the pastures,
71 where he looked after his **flocks**,
and he made him king of Israel,
the **shepherd** of the **people of God**.
72 David took **care** of them with **unselfish devotion**
and led them with skill.

A Prayer for the Nation's Deliverance[p]

79

O God, the **heathen** have invaded your land.
They have desecrated your **holy Temple**
and left Jerusalem in **ruins**.
2 They left the **bodies** of your people for the vultures,
the **bodies** of your **servants** for wild animals to eat.
3 They shed your people's **blood** like water;
blood flowed like water all through Jerusalem,
and no one was left to bury the **dead**.
4 The surrounding nations **insult** us;
they laugh at us and **mock** us.

5 LORD, will you be **angry** with us for ever?
Will your **anger** continue to burn like fire?
6 **Turn** your **anger** on the nations that do not **worship** you,
on the people who do not **pray** to you.
7 For they have killed your people;
they have **ruined** your country.

8 Do not **punish** us for the sins of our ancestors.

[n] hail...lightning; *or* terrible disease...deadly plague.
[o] SHILOH: *The central place of worship for the people of Israel before the time of King David.*
[p] HEBREW TITLE: *A psalm by Asaph.*

78.51: Ex 12.29 **78.52:** Ex 13.17–22 **78.53:** Ex 14.26–28 **78.54:** Ex 15.17; Josh 3.14–17
78.55: Josh 11.16–23 **78.56:** Judg 2.11–15 **78.60:** Josh 18.1; Jer 7.12–14, 26.6 **78.61:** 1 Sam 4.4–22
78.70–71: 1 Sam 16.11–12; 2 Sam 7.8; 1 Chr 17.7 **79.1:** 2 Kgs 25.8–10; 2 Chr 36.17–19; Jer 52.12–14

Have **mercy** on us now;
we have lost all **hope**.
9 **Help** us, O God, and **save** us;
rescue us and **forgive** our sins
for the **sake** of your own **honour**.
10 Why should the nations ask us,
"Where is your God?"
Let us see you **punish** the nations
for shedding the **blood** of your
servants.

11 Listen to the **groans** of the **prisoners**,
and by your great **power free** those
who are **condemned** to die.
12 Lord, pay the other nations back seven
times
for all the **insults** they have hurled at
you.
13 Then we, your people, the **sheep** of
your **flock**,
will **thank** you for ever
and **praise** you for all time to come.

A Prayer for the Nation's Restoration[q]

80 Listen to us, O **Shepherd** of
Israel;
hear us, leader of your **flock**.
Seated on your **throne** above the
winged **creatures**,
2 **reveal** yourself to the tribes of
Ephraim, Benjamin, and
Manasseh.
Show us your **strength**;
come and **save** us!

3 Bring us back, O God!
Show us your **mercy**, and we will be
saved!

4 How much longer, LORD God
Almighty,
will you be **angry** with your people's
prayers?
5 You have given us **sorrow** to eat,
a large **cup of tears** to drink.
6 You let the surrounding nations fight
over our land;
our **enemies insult** us.

7 Bring us back, **Almighty** God!
Show us your **mercy**, and we will be
saved!

8 You brought a **grapevine** out of Egypt;
you drove out other nations and
planted it in their land.
9 You **cleared** a place for it to grow;
its roots went deep, and it spread out
over the whole land.
10 It covered the hills with its shade;
its branches overshadowed the giant
cedars.
11 It extended its branches to the
Mediterranean Sea
and as far as the River Euphrates.
12 Why did you break down the fences
round it?
Now anyone passing by can **steal** its
grapes;
13 wild pigs trample it down,
and wild animals feed on it.

14 **Turn** to us, **Almighty** God!
Look down from **heaven** at us;
come and **save** your people!
15 Come and **save** this **grapevine** that you
planted,
this young **vine** you made grow so
strong!

16 Our **enemies** have set it on fire and cut
it down;
look at them in **anger** and **destroy**
them!
17 **Preserve** and **protect** the people you
have **chosen**,
the nation you made so **strong**.
18 We will never **turn away** from you
again;
keep us **alive**, and we will **praise**
you.

19 Bring us back, LORD God **Almighty**.
Show us your **mercy**, and we will be
saved.

alive 69.25; 119.93
Almighty [4] 78.35; 84.1
anger [2] 79.5; 85.3
choose 78.68; 84.9
clear 49.3; Is 5.2
creature 75.3; 96.11
cup 75.8; Prov 23.31
destroy 78.38; 83.4
enemy [2] 78.42; 81.14
flock 79.13; 95.7
grapevine *see* **vine**
heaven 78.24; 82.1
insult 79.4; 89.50
mercy [3] 79.8; 85.1
praise 79.13; 81.1
prayer 77.2; 84.8
preserve 41.2; 89.4
protect 78.35; 83.3
reveal 19.1; 94.1
save [6] 79.9; 81.7
shepherd 78.52; Ecc 12.11
sorrow 42.6; 90.10
steal 69.4; 89.41
strength 76.5; 84.5
strong [2] 78.31; 83.8
tear (2) 56.8; 102.9
throne 47.5; 89.19
turn [2] 79.6; 86.16
vine [3] 78.47; 105.33

A Song for a Festival[r]

81 Shout for **joy** to God our
defender;
sing **praise** to the God of Jacob!
2 Start the music and beat the
tambourines;
play pleasant music on the harps
and the lyres.
3 Blow the trumpet for the **festival**,
when the moon is **new** and when the
moon is full.
4 This is the **law** in Israel,
an order from the God of Jacob.
5 He gave it to the people of Israel
when he attacked the land of Egypt.

I hear an unknown voice saying,
6 "I took the **burdens** off your backs;
I let you put down your loads of
bricks.
7 When you were in **trouble**, you called
to me, and I **saved** you.
From my hiding-place in the storm,
I answered you.

bow (2) 72.9; 86.9
burden 68.19; 88.15
conquer 78.54; Is 10.9
defend 74.22; 82.3
enemy 80.6; 83.2
fear 76.7; 89.7
festival 76.10; 118.27
god (2) (other gods) 77.13; 82.1
God's people [3] 78.20; 85.8
hate 69.4; 83.2
joy 71.23; 84.2
last (1) 78.66; 89.2
law 78.5; 89.30
new 51.10; 96.1
obey [2] 78.7; 86.11
praise 80.18; 84.4
punish 79.8; 88.15
satisfy 78.29; 104.28
save 80.2; 85.7
stubborn Job 15.26; 95.8
test 78.18; 95.9
trouble 77.2; 86.7
warn 60.4; 105.14
way (3) 68.21; 85.8
wish [3] 55.6; 115.3
worship (2) (of other gods) 40.4; 97.7

[q] HEBREW TITLE: *A psalm by Asaph; a testimony.* [r] HEBREW TITLE: *By Asaph.*

80.1: Ex 25.22 **81.3:** Num 10.10 **81.7:** Ex 17.7; Num 20.13

I put you to the test at the springs of
Meribah.
8 Listen, my people, to my warning;
Israel, how I wish you would listen to
me!
9 You must never worship another god.
10 I am the LORD your God,
who brought you out of Egypt.
Open your mouth, and I will feed you.

11 "But my people would not listen to me;
Israel would not obey me.
12 So I let them go their stubborn ways
and do whatever they wanted.
13 How I wish my people would listen to
me;
how I wish they would obey me!
14 I would quickly defeat their enemies
and conquer all their foes.
15 Those who hate me would bow in fear
before me;
their punishment would last for
ever.
16 But I would feed you with the finest
wheat
and satisfy you with wild honey."

God the Supreme Ruler[s]

corrupt 53.1; 94.20
Council 89.7
defend 81.1; 91.2
evil 73.7; 91.6
god (2) (other gods) [2] 81.9; 84.7
heaven 80.14; 85.11
helpless 74.19; 86.1
ignorant 53.4; 119.130
judge 76.8; 94.2
justice 72.1; 89.14
life (1) 78.33; 89.47
Most High 78.17; 91.9
need 74.21; 91.5
orphan 68.5; 94.6
partiality 2 Chr 19.7
poor 74.21; 109.16
power 79.11; 83.16
rescue 79.9; 91.15
right (3) 24.3; 103.6
stupid 73.22; 92.6
unjust Job 40.8; 119.161
wicked 75.4; 84.10
world [2] 77.18; 89.11

82 God presides in the heavenly
council;
in the assembly of the gods he gives
his decision:
2 "You must stop judging unjustly;
you must no longer be partial to the
wicked!
3 Defend the rights of the poor and the
orphans;
be fair to the needy and the helpless.
4 Rescue them from the power of evil
men.

5 "How ignorant you are! How stupid!
You are completely corrupt,
and justice has disappeared from
the world.
6 'You are gods,' I said;
'all of you are sons of the Most High.'
7 But you will die like men;
your life will end like that of any
prince."

8 Come, O God, and rule the world;
all the nations are yours.

A Prayer for the Defeat of Israel's Enemies[t]

acknowledge 1 Chr 28.9; 91.14
agree Job 41.4; 105.9
alone 72.18; 86.10

83 O God, do not keep silent;
do not be still, do not be quiet!
2 Look! Your enemies are in revolt,
and those who hate you are
rebelling.
3 They are making secret plans against
your people;
they are plotting against those you
protect.
4 "Come," they say, "let us destroy their
nation,
so that Israel will be forgotten for
ever."

5 They agree on their plan
and form an alliance against you:
6 the people of Edom and the
Ishmaelites;
the people of Moab and the
Hagrites;
7 the people of Gebal, Ammon, and
Amalek,
and of Philistia and Tyre.
8 Assyria has also joined them
as a strong ally of the Ammonites
and Moabites, the descendants of
Lot.

9 Do to them what you did to the
Midianites,
and to Sisera and Jabin at the River
Kishon.
10 You defeated them at Endor,
and their bodies rotted on the
ground.
11 Do to their leaders what you did to
Oreb and Zeeb;
defeat all their rulers as you did
Zebah and Zalmunna,
12 who said, "We will take for our own
the land that belongs to God."

13 Scatter them like dust, O God,
like straw blown away by the wind.
14 As fire burns the forest,
as flames set the hills on fire,
15 chase them away with your storm
and terrify them with your fierce
winds.
16 Cover their faces with shame, O LORD,
and make them acknowledge your
power.
17 May they be defeated and terrified for
ever;
may they die in complete disgrace.
18 May they know that you alone are the
LORD,
supreme ruler over all the earth.

body 79.2; 102.3
destroy 80.16; 88.1
disgrace 71.13; 89.
enemy 81.14; 89.10
forget 78.7; 88.5
hate 81.15; 86.17
plan [2] 73.8; 103.7
plot (1) 71.10; 94.21
power 82.4; 89.9
protect 80.17; 84.1
rebel 78.8; 106.7
scatter 68.1; 106.27
secret 44.21; 90.8
shame 78.66; 97.7
strong 80.15; 84.7
supreme 47.9; 92.8
terrify [2] 76.12; 90

Longing for God's House[u]

84 How I love your Temple, LORD
Almighty!
2 How I want to be there!

Almighty [4] 80.4; 87.5
altar 66.15; 118.27
being 78.39; 89.6

[s] HEBREW TITLE: *A psalm by Asaph.* [t] HEBREW TITLE: *A psalm by Asaph; a song.*
[u] HEBREW TITLE: *A psalm by the clan of Korah.*

81.9–10: Ex 20.2–3; Deut 5.6–7 **82.6:** Jn 10.34 **83.9:** Judg 4.6–22, 7.1–23 **83.11:** Judg 7.25, 8.12

less [2] 72.15; 87.7
hoose 80.17; 89.3
ager 73.10; 119.32
lory 78.61; 90.16
od (2) (other gods)
2.1; 86.8
appy [3] 70.2; 89.15
onour 79.9; 85.9
y 81.1; 89.12
ind 67.1; 86.15
ng (2) 63.1; 119.20
ve 78.68; 85.7
raise 81.1; 85.6
rayer 80.4; 86.4
rotect 83.3; 89.18
efuse (1) 78.10;
5.10
ight (1) 65.1; 99.4
trength 80.2; 86.16
trong 83.8; 85.6
emple (1) (of God)
] 79.1; 92.13
rust 78.7; 86.2
icked 82.2; 89.22

I long to be in the LORD's Temple.
With my whole being I sing for joy
to the living God.
3 Even the sparrows have built a nest,
and the swallows have their own
home;
they keep their young near your altars,
LORD Almighty, my king and my
God.
4 How happy are those who live in your
Temple,
always singing praise to you.

5 How happy are those whose strength
comes from you,
who are eager to make the
pilgrimage to Mount Zion.
6 As they pass through the dry valley of
Baca,
it becomes a place of springs;
the autumn rain fills it with pools.
7 They grow stronger as they go;
they will see the God of gods on
Zion.

8 Hear my prayer, LORD God Almighty.
Listen, O God of Jacob!
9 Bless our king, O God,
the king you have chosen.

10 One day spent in your Temple
is better than a thousand anywhere
else;
I would rather stand at the gate of the
house of my God
than live in the homes of the wicked.
11 The LORD is our protector and glorious
king,
blessing us with kindness and
honour.
He does not refuse any good thing
to those who do what is right.
12 LORD Almighty, how happy are those
who trust in you!

A Prayer for the Nation's Welfare[v]

nger [3] 80.4; 88.7
onstant 69.16; 86.5
isplease Ezra 8.22;
s 59.15
aithful 78.8; 86.11
ool 69.5; 92.6
orgive 79.9; 86.5
ury 78.38; 88.16
od's people 81.8;
4.14
arvest 67.6; 107.37
eaven 82.1; 89.5
elp 79.9; 86.6
onour 84.11; 91.15
ove [2] 84.1; 86.5
oyal 78.37; 86.2
ercy 80.3; 86.3
eace [2] 37.11; 120.6
raise 84.4; 86.9
resence 76.7; 101.7
romise 77.8; 89.3
rosper [2] 72.3; 92.7

85 LORD, you have been merciful to
your land;
you have made Israel prosperous
again.
2 You have forgiven your people's sins
and pardoned all their wrongs.
3 You stopped being angry with them
and held back your furious rage.

4 Bring us back, O God our saviour,
and stop being displeased with us!
5 Will you be angry with us for ever?
Will your anger never cease?
6 Make us strong again,
and we, your people, will praise you.
7 Show us your constant love, O LORD,
and give us your saving help.

8 I am listening to what the LORD God is
saying;
he promises peace to us, his own
people,
if we do not go back to our foolish
ways.
9 Surely he is ready to save those who
honour him,
and his saving presence will remain
in our land.

10 Love and faithfulness will meet;
righteousness and peace will
embrace.
11 Man's loyalty will reach up from the
earth,
and God's righteousness will look
down from heaven.
12 The LORD will make us prosperous,
and our land will produce rich
harvests.
13 Righteousness will go before the LORD
and prepare the path for him.

A Prayer for Help[w]

86 Listen to me, LORD, and answer
me,
for I am helpless and weak.
2 Save me from death, because I am
loyal to you;
save me, for I am your servant and I
trust in you.

3 You are my God, so be merciful to me;
I pray to you all day long.
4 Make your servant glad, O Lord,
because my prayers go up to you.
5 You are good to us and forgiving,
full of constant love for all who pray
to you.

6 Listen, LORD, to my prayer;
hear my cries for help.
7 I call to you in times of trouble,
because you answer my prayers.

8 There is no god like you, O Lord,
not one has done what you have
done.
9 All the nations that you have created
will come and bow down to you;
they will praise your greatness.
10 You are mighty and do wonderful
things;
you alone are God.

11 Teach me, LORD, what you want me to
do,

rage 78.49; 107.29
rich 65.9; 107.34
righteous [3] 75.10;
89.14
save [3] 81.7; 86.2
Saviour 70.5; 88.1
strong 84.7; 87.5
sure 68.21;
Prov 11.21
way (3) 81.12; 106.35
wrong 59.3; 89.32

alone 83.18; 115.1
ashamed Job 42.6;
119.46
bow (2) 81.15; 95.6
comfort 77.2; 94.19
constant [2] 85.7;
88.11
create 74.16; 89.12
cruel 74.19; 107.39
death (2) (from
death) 68.20; 116.8
devote 78.72;
Prov 2.8
faithful [2] 85.10;
88.11
forgive 85.2; 99.8
glad 70.4; 90.14
god (2) (other gods)
84.7; 95.3
grave 71.20; 88.5
hate 83.2; 89.23
heart 73.1; 109.22
help [2] 85.7; 88.2
helpless 82.3; 109.16
kind 84.11; 89.15
love [3] 85.7; 87.2
loyal 85.11; 89.24
mercy [3] 85.1; 102.13
might 78.43; 89.8
obey 81.11; 87.4
patient 62.1;
Prov 15.18
praise [2] 85.6; 88.10
pray [2] 79.6; 88.13
prayer [3] 84.8; 88.2
proclaim 75.1; 89.1
proud 76.12; 94.2
prove Job 40.8; 89.49
save [4] 85.7; 91.14
servant [2] 79.2; 89.3
serve [2] 72.11; 101.6
strength 84.5; 88.4
teach [2] 78.1; 90.12
trouble 81.7; 88.3
trust 84.12; 91.2
turn 80.14; 88.14
weak 73.26; 88.9
wonder (1) 78.4; 87.3

[v] HEBREW TITLE: *A psalm by the clan of Korah.* [w] HEBREW TITLE: *A prayer by David.*

86.9: Rev 15.4

and I will **obey** you **faithfully**;
teach me to **serve** you with
complete **devotion**.
12 I will **praise** you **with all my heart**, O
Lord my God;
I will **proclaim** your greatness for
ever.
13 How great is your **constant** love for
me!
You have **saved** me from the **grave**
itself.
14 **Proud** men are coming against me, O
God;
a gang of **cruel** men is trying to kill
me—
people who pay no attention to you.
15 But you, O Lord, are a **merciful** and
loving God,
always **patient**, always **kind** and
faithful.
16 **Turn** to me and have **mercy** on me;
strengthen me and **save** me,
because I **serve** you, just as my
mother did.
17 Show me **proof** of your goodness,
LORD;
those who **hate** me will be **ashamed**
when they see that you have given
me **comfort** and **help**.

In Praise of Jerusalem[x]

Almighty 84.1; 89.8
bless 84.9; 90.17
love 86.5; 88.11
obey 86.11; 95.10
sacred 74.9; 99.9
source 43.4; 119.92
strong 85.6; 89.21
wonder (1) 86.10; 89.5

87 The LORD built his city on the
sacred hill;[y]
2 more than any other place in Israel
he **loves** the city of Jerusalem.
3 Listen, city of God,
to the **wonderful** things he says
about you:

4 "I will include Egypt and Babylonia
when I list the nations that **obey** me;
I will number among the inhabitants of
Jerusalem
the people of Philistia, Tyre, and
Sudan."

5 Of Zion it will be said
that all nations belong there
and that the **Almighty** will make her
strong.
6 The LORD will write a list of the
peoples
and include them all as citizens of
Jerusalem.
7 They dance and sing,
"In Zion is the **source** of all our
blessings."

A Cry for Help[z]

abandon [3] 78.60; 94.14
anger [2] 85.3; 89.9
burden 81.6; Ecc 3.10
constant 86.5; 89.1
dark [3] 74.20; 91.6
dead [2] 79.3; 91.7
death (1) [2] 78.49; 107.18
destroy [2] 83.4; 90
escape 60.4; 124.7
faithful 86.11; 89.1
flood 69.15; 90.5
forget [2] 83.4; 89.5
friend [2] 55.13; 119.63
fury 85.3; 90.7
grave [2] 86.13; 89.
help [3] 86.6; 89.19
love 87.2; 89.1
miracle [2] 78.11; 105.5
praise 86.9; 89.16
pray 86.3; 99.6
prayer [2] 86.4; 10
punish 81.15; 89.32
reject 78.59; 89.38
rise 76.9; 94.2
Saviour 85.4; 89.26
strength 86.16; 89.
suffer [2] 73.4; 89.3
terrible 53.1; 106.
tomb Job 21.32; Is 14.18
trouble 86.7; 90.10
turn 86.16; 101.3
weak 86.1; 102.23

88 LORD God, my **saviour**, I cry out
all day,
and at night I come before you.
2 Hear my **prayer**;
listen to my cry for **help**!

3 So many **troubles** have fallen on me
that I am close to **death**.
4 I am like all others who are about to
die;
all my **strength** is gone.[a]
5 I am **abandoned** among the **dead**;
I am like the slain lying in their
graves,
those you have **forgotten** completely,
who are beyond your **help**.
6 You have thrown me into the depths of
the **tomb**,
into the **darkest** and deepest pit.
7 Your **anger** lies heavy on me,
and I am crushed **beneath** its waves.

8 You have caused my **friends** to
abandon me;
you have made me repulsive to
them.
I am closed in and cannot **escape**;
9 my eyes are **weak** from **suffering**.
LORD, every day I call to you
and lift my hands to you in **prayer**.

10 Do you perform **miracles** for the
dead?
Do they **rise** up and **praise** you?
11 Is your **constant love** spoken of in the
grave
or your **faithfulness** in the place of
destruction?
12 Are your **miracles** seen in that place of
darkness
or your goodness in the land of the
forgotten?

13 LORD, I call to you for **help**;
every morning I **pray** to you.
14 Why do you **reject** me, LORD?
Why do you **turn** away from me?
15 Ever since I was young, I have
suffered and been near **death**;
I am worn out[b] from the **burden** of
your **punishments**.
16 Your **furious anger** crushes me;
your **terrible** attacks **destroy** me.
17 All day long they surround me like a
flood;
they close in on me from every side.
18 You have made even my closest
friends abandon me,

[x] HEBREW TITLE: *A psalm by the clan of Korah; a song.* [y] SACRED HILL: *See 2.6.*
[z] HEBREW TITLE: *A psalm by the clan of Korah; a song. A poem by Heman the Ezrahite.*
[a] all my strength is gone; *or* there is no help for me.
[b] *Probable text* I am worn out; *Hebrew unclear.*

and darkness is my only companion.

A Hymn in Time of National Trouble[c]

89 O LORD, I will always sing of your
constant love;
I will proclaim your faithfulness for
ever.
2 I know that your love will last for all
time,
that your faithfulness is as
permanent as the sky.
3 You said, "I have made a covenant
with the man I chose;
I have promised my servant David,
4 'A descendant of yours will always be
king;
I will preserve your dynasty for
ever.' "

5 The heavens sing of the wonderful
things you do;
the holy ones sing of your
faithfulness, LORD.
6 No one in heaven is like you, LORD;
none of the heavenly beings is your
equal.
7 You are feared in the council of the
holy ones;
and all of them stand in awe of you.

8 LORD God Almighty, none is as mighty
as you;
in all things you are faithful, O LORD.
9 You rule over the powerful sea;
you calm its angry waves.
10 You crushed the monster Rahab[d] and
killed it;
with your mighty strength you
defeated your enemies.
11 Heaven is yours, the earth also;
you made the world and everything
in it.
12 You created the north and the south;
Mount Tabor and Mount Hermon
sing to you for joy.
13 How powerful you are!
How great is your strength!
14 Your kingdom is founded on
righteousness and justice;
love and faithfulness are shown in
all you do.

15 How happy are the people who
worship you with songs,
who live in the light of your
kindness!
16 Because of you they rejoice all day
long,
and they praise you for your
goodness.
17 You give us great victories;
in your love you make us
triumphant.
18 You, O LORD, chose our protector;
you, the Holy God of Israel, gave us
our king.

God's Promise to David

19 In a vision long ago you said to your
faithful servants,
"I have given help to a famous
soldier;
I have given the throne to one I
chose from the people.
20 I have made my servant David king
by anointing him with holy oil.
21 My strength will always be with him,
my power will make him strong.
22 His enemies will never succeed
against him;
the wicked will not defeat him.
23 I will crush his foes
and kill everyone who hates him.
24 I will love him and be loyal to him;
I will make him always victorious.
25 I will extend his kingdom
from the Mediterranean to the
River Euphrates.
26 He will say to me,
'You are my father and my God;
you are my protector and saviour.'
27 I will make him my first-born son,
the greatest of all kings.
28 I will always keep my promise to him,
and my covenant with him will last
for ever.
29 His dynasty will be as permanent as
the sky;
a descendant of his will always be
king.

30 "But if his descendants disobey my law
and do not live according to my
commands,
31 if they disregard my instructions
and do not keep my
commandments,
32 then I will punish them for their sins;
I will make them suffer for their
wrongs.
33 But I will not stop loving David
or fail to keep my promise to him.
34 I will not break my covenant with him
or take back even one promise I
made him.

[c] HEBREW TITLE: *A poem by Ethan the Ezrahite.*
[d] RAHAB: *A legendary sea-monster which represented the forces of chaos and evil.*

89.Title: 1 Kgs 4.31 **89.4:** 2 Sam 7.12–16; 1 Chr 17.11–14; Ps 132.11; Acts 2.30
89.20: 1 Sam 13.14; Acts 13.22; 1 Sam 16.12 **89.27:** Rev 1.5

35 “Once and for all I have **promised** by
my **holy name**:
I will never lie to David.
36 He will always have descendants,
and I will **watch** over his kingdom as
long as the sun shines.
37 It will be as permanent as the moon,
that **faithful witness** in the sky.”

Lament over the Defeat of the King

38 But you are **angry** with your **chosen**
king;
you have deserted and **rejected** him.
39 You have broken your **covenant** with
your **servant**
and thrown his **crown** in the mud.
40 You have torn down the walls of his
city
and left his forts in **ruins**.
41 All who pass by **steal** his belongings;
all his **neighbours** laugh at him.
42 You have given the **victory** to his
enemies;
you have made them all **happy**.
43 You have made his weapons **useless**
and let him be defeated in battle.
44 You have taken away his royal
sceptre[e]
and hurled his **throne** to the ground.
45 You have made him old before his
time
and covered him with **disgrace**.

A Prayer for Deliverance

46 LORD, will you hide yourself for ever?
How long will your **anger** burn like
fire?
47 **Remember** how short my **life** is;
remember that you **created** all of us
mortal!
48 Who can live and never die?
How can man **keep himself from** the
grave?

49 Lord, where are the former **proofs** of
your **love**?
Where are the **promises** you made
to David?
50 Don't **forget** how I, your **servant**, am
insulted,
how I **endure** all the **curses**[f] of the
heathen.
51 Your **enemies insult** your **chosen** king,
O LORD!
They **insult** him wherever he goes.

52 **Praise** the LORD for ever!

Amen! Amen!

BOOK FOUR
(Psalms 90–106)

Of God and Man[g]

90 O Lord, you have always been
our home.
2 Before you **created** the hills
or brought the **world** into **being**,
you were **eternally** God,
and will be God for ever.

3 You tell man to return to what he was;
you **change** him back to dust.
4 A thousand years to you are like one
day;
they are like yesterday, already
gone,
like a short hour in the night.
5 You carry us away like a **flood**;
we **last** no longer than a **dream**.
We are like **weeds** that sprout in the
morning,
6 that grow and burst into bloom,
then dry up and die in the evening.

7 We are **destroyed** by your **anger**;
we are **terrified** by your **fury**.
8 You place our sins before you,
our **secret** sins where you can see
them.

9 Our **life** is cut short by your **anger**;
it fades away like a whisper.
10 Seventy years is all we have—
eighty years, if we are **strong**;
yet all they bring us is **trouble** and
sorrow;
life is soon over, and we are gone.

11 Who has felt the full **power** of your
anger?
Who knows what **fear** your **fury** can
bring?
12 **Teach** us how short our **life** is,
so that we may become **wise**.

13 How much longer will your **anger**
last?
Have **pity**, O LORD, on your
servants!
14 Fill us each morning with your
constant love,
so that we may sing and be **glad** all
our **life**.
15 Give us now as much **happiness** as the
sadness you gave us
during all our years of **misery**.
16 Let us, your **servants**, see your **mighty**
deeds;

anger [4] 89.9; 94.1
being 89.6; 103.1
bless 87.7; 92.10
change 66.6; 107.3
constant 89.1; 92.2
create 89.12; 96.5
destroy 88.11; 92.7
dream 73.20; 126.1
eternal 55.19; 93.5
fear 89.7; 91.5
flood 88.17; 124.4
fury [2] 88.16; 102.9
glad 86.4; 92.4
glory 84.11; 96.3
happy 89.15; 92.10
last (1) [2] 89.2; 100
life (1) [4] 89.47; 91.16
love 89.1; 91.14
might [2] 89.8; 92.4
misery Job 29.13; 107.41
pity 72.13; 102.13
power 89.9; 93.4
sad 78.40; Prov 14.1
secret 83.3; 139.15
servant [2] 89.3; 102.14
sorrow 80.5; 119.28
strong 89.21; 92.10
succeed (1) 89.22; 118.25
teach 86.11; 94.12
terrify 83.15; Is 7.2
trouble 88.3; 91.15
weed 58.7; 92.7
wise 78.2; 104.24
world 89.11; 96.1

[e] *Probable text* royal sceptre; *Hebrew* purity. [f] *Probable text* curses; *Hebrew* crowds.
[g] HEBREW TITLE: *A prayer by Moses, the man of God.*

90.4: 2 Peter 3.8

let our descendants see your
glorious might.
17 LORD our God, may your blessings be
with us.
Give us success in all we do!

God Our Protector

91 Whoever goes to the LORD for
safety,
whoever remains under the
protection of the Almighty,
2 can say to him,
"You are my defender and
protector.
You are my God; in you I trust."
3 He will keep you safe from all hidden
dangers
and from all deadly diseases.
4 He will cover you with his wings;
you will be safe in his care;
his faithfulness will protect and
defend you.
5 You need not fear any dangers at night
or sudden attacks during the day
6 or the plagues that strike in the dark
or the evils that kill in daylight.

7 A thousand may fall dead beside you,
ten thousand all round you,
but you will not be harmed.
8 You will look and see
how the wicked are punished.

9 You have made the LORD your[x]
defender,
the Most High your protector,
10 and so no disaster will strike you,
no violence will come near your
home.
11 God will put his angels in charge of
you
to protect you wherever you go.
12 They will hold you up with their hands
to keep you from hurting your feet
on the stones.
13 You will trample down lions and
snakes,
fierce lions and poisonous snakes.

14 God says, "I will save those who love
me
and will protect those who
acknowledge me as LORD.
15 When they call to me, I will answer
them;
when they are in trouble, I will be
with them.
I will rescue them and honour them.
16 I will reward them with long life;
I will save them."

acknowledge 83.16; 100.3
Almighty 89.8; 97.9
angel 78.25; 103.20
care 78.72; 95.7
danger [2] 49.5; 107.26
dark 88.6; 97.2
dead 88.5; 115.17
deadly 40.2; 140.3
defend [3] 82.3; 94.22
disaster 78.33; Prov 3.25
disease 38.3; 103.3
evil 82.4; 94.16
faithful 89.1; 92.2
fear 90.11; 102.15
harm 71.24; 105.15
honour 85.9; 92.1
hurt 77.10; 109.22
keep from 89.48; 103.4
life (1) 90.9; 97.10
love 90.14; 92.2
Most High 82.6; 92.1
need 82.3; 104.27
plague 78.50; 106.30
protect [6] 89.18; 92.15
punish 89.32; 94.1
rescue 82.4; 97.10
reward 62.12; Prov 10.16
safe [3] 78.53; 102.28
save [2] 86.2; 96.2
strike [2] 78.20; Prov 1.26
trouble 90.10; 94.13
trust 86.2; 112.7
violent 78.64; 139.19
wicked 89.22; 92.7

A Song of Praise[h]

92 How good it is to give thanks to
you, O LORD,
to sing in your honour, O Most High
God,
2 to proclaim your constant love every
morning
and your faithfulness every night,
3 with the music of stringed instruments
and with melody on the harp.
4 Your mighty deeds, O LORD, make me
glad;
because of what you have done, I
sing for joy.

5 How great are your actions, LORD!
How deep are your thoughts!
6 This is something a fool cannot know;
a stupid man cannot understand:
7 the wicked may grow like weeds,
those who do wrong may prosper;
yet they will be totally destroyed,
8 because you, LORD, are supreme for
ever.

9 We know that your enemies will die,
and all the wicked will be defeated.
10 You have made me as strong as a wild
ox;
you have blessed me with happiness.
11 I have seen the defeat of my enemies
and heard the cries of the wicked.

12 The righteous will flourish like palm-
trees;
they will grow like the cedars of
Lebanon.
13 They are like trees planted in the
house of the LORD,
that flourish in the Temple of our
God,
14 that still bear fruit in old age
and are always green and strong.
15 This shows that the LORD is just,
that there is no wrong in my
protector.

action Ezra 9.11; 101.3
bless 90.17; 103.4
constant 90.14; 94.18
destroy 90.7; 94.23
enemy [2] 89.10; 97.3
faithful 91.4; 100.5
fool 85.8; 94.8
glad 90.14; 94.3
happy 90.15; 94.12
honour 91.15; 96.4
joy 89.12; 95.1
justice 89.14; 94.15
love 91.14; 94.18
might 90.16; 95.3
Most High 91.9; Mk 5.7
proclaim 89.1; 96.2
prosper 85.1; 106.5
protect 91.1; 94.22
righteous 89.14; 94.15
strong [2] 90.10; 103.5
stupid 82.5; 94.8
supreme 83.18; 93.4
Temple (1) (of God) 84.1; 93.5
thank 79.13; 95.2
understand 73.17; 106.7
weed 90.5; Prov 24.31
wicked [3] 91.8; 94.3
wrong [2] 89.32; 103.10

God the King

93 The LORD is king.
He is clothed with majesty and
strength.
The earth is set firmly in place
and cannot be moved.
2 Your throne, O LORD, has been firm
from the beginning,
and you existed before time began.

3 The ocean depths raise their voice, O
LORD;
they raise their voice and roar.

eternal 90.2; 100.5
exist Job 10.19; Prov 23.22
heaven 89.5; 96.5
holy 89.5; 96.9
law 89.30; 94.12
Majesty 76.4; 96.6
power 90.11; 96.6
raise [2] 68.31; 113.7
strength 89.10; 98.1
supreme 92.8; 99.2
Temple (1) (of God) 92.13; 96.6
throne 89.19; 99.1

[x] *Probable text* your; *Hebrew* my. [h] HEBREW TITLE: *A psalm; a song for the Sabbath.*

91.11: Mt 4.6; Lk 4.10 **91.12:** Mt 4.6; Lk 4.11 **91.13:** Lk 10.19

4 The LORD rules **supreme** in **heaven**,
greater than the roar of the ocean,
more **powerful** than the waves of the sea.

5 Your **laws** are **eternal**, LORD,
and your **Temple** is **holy** indeed,
for ever and ever.

God the Judge of All

94 LORD, you are a God who **punishes**;
reveal your **anger**!
2 You are the **judge** of all men;
rise and give the **proud** what they **deserve**!
3 How much longer will the **wicked** be **glad**?
How much longer, LORD?
4 How much longer will **criminals** be **proud**
and **boast** about their **crimes**?

5 They crush your people, LORD;
they **oppress** those who belong to you.
6 They kill **widows** and **orphans**,
and murder the **strangers** who live in our land.
7 They say, "The LORD does not see us;
the God of Israel does not **notice**."

8 My people, how can you be such **stupid fools**?
When will you ever **learn**?
9 God made our ears—can't he hear?
He made our eyes—can't he see?
10 He scolds the nations—won't he **punish** them?[x]
He is the **teacher** of all men—hasn't he any **knowledge**?
11 The LORD knows what they think;
he knows how **senseless** their **reasoning** is.

12 LORD, how **happy** is the person you instruct,
the one to whom you **teach** your **law**!
13 You give him **rest** from days of **trouble**
until a pit is dug to **trap** the **wicked**.
14 The LORD will not **abandon his people**;
he will not desert those who belong to him.
15 **Justice** will again be found in the **courts**,
and all **righteous** people will support it.

16 Who stood up for me against the **wicked**?
Who took my side against the **evildoers**?
17 If the LORD had not **helped** me,
I would have gone quickly to the land of silence.[i]
18 I said, "I am falling";
but your **constant love**, O LORD, held me up.
19 Whenever I am **anxious** and **worried**,
you **comfort** me and make me **glad**.

20 You have nothing to do with **corrupt judges**,
who make **injustice** legal,
21 who **plot** against good men
and **sentence** the **innocent to death**.
22 But the LORD **defends** me;
my God **protects** me.
23 He will **punish** them for their **wickedness**
and **destroy** them for their sins;
the LORD our God will **destroy** them.

A Song of Praise

95 Come, let us **praise** the LORD!
Let us sing for **joy** to God, who **protects** us!
2 Let us come before him with **thanksgiving**
and sing **joyful** songs of **praise**.
3 For the LORD is a **mighty** God,
a mighty king over all the **gods**.
4 He rules over the whole earth,
from the deepest caves to the highest hills.
5 He rules over the sea, which he made;
the land also, which he himself formed.

6 Come, let us **bow down** and **worship** him;
let us **kneel** before the LORD, our Maker!
7 He is our God;
we are the people he **cares** for,
the **flock** for which he **provides**.

Listen today to what he says:
8 "Don't be **stubborn**, as your ancestors were at Meribah,
as they were that day in the desert at Massah.
9 There they put me **to the test** and **tried** me,
although they had seen what I did for them.
10 For forty years I was **disgusted** with those people.
I said, 'How disloyal they are!
They **refuse** to **obey** my **commands**.'

[x] them; *or* our wicked leaders. [i] LAND OF SILENCE: *The world of the dead (see 6.5).*

94.11: 1 Cor 3.20 **95.7-8:** Heb 3.15, 4.7 **95.7-11:** Heb 3.7-11 **95.8-9:** Ex 17.1-7; Num 20.2-13

11 I was **angry** and made a **solemn promise**:
'You will never enter the land
where I would have given you
rest.' "

God the Supreme King
(1 Chr 16.23–33)

bow (2) 95.6; 97.7
create 90.2; 102.25
creature 80.1; 98.7
glad [2] 94.3; 97.1
glory [4] 90.16; 97.6
god (2) (other gods) [2] 95.3; 97.7
Good News 40.9; Prov 15.30
heaven 93.4; 97.6
holy 93.5; 97.12
honour 92.1; 103.11
idol 78.58; 97.7
joy 95.1; 98.4
judge 94.2; 97.8
justice [2] 94.15; 97.2
Majesty 93.1; 99.3
might [2] 95.3; 99.2
name (2) (name of God, of Jesus) 89.35; 99.3
new 81.3; 98.1
offer 72.10; 106.28
power 93.4; 97.10
praise [5] 95.1; 98.4
proclaim [2] 92.2; 97.6
save 91.14; 98.2
Temple (1) (of God) [2] 93.5; 100.4
tremble 77.16; 97.4
world [2] 90.2; 97.4

96 Sing a **new** song to the LORD!
Sing to the LORD, all the **world**!
2 Sing to the LORD, and **praise** him!
Proclaim every day the **good news**
that he has **saved** us.
3 **Proclaim** his **glory** to the nations,
his **mighty** deeds to all peoples.

4 The LORD is great and is to be highly **praised**;
he is to be **honoured** more than all
the **gods**.
5 The **gods** of all other nations are only **idols**,
but the LORD **created** the **heavens**.
6 **Glory** and **majesty** surround him;
power and beauty fill his **Temple**.

7 **Praise** the LORD, all people on earth;
praise his **glory** and **might**.
8 **Praise** the LORD's **glorious name**;
bring an **offering** and come into his
Temple.
9 **Bow down** before the **Holy One** when
he appears;[j]
tremble before him, all the earth!

10 Say to all the nations, "The LORD is
king!
The earth is set firmly in place and
cannot be moved;
he will **judge** the peoples with
justice."
11 Be **glad**, earth and sky!
Roar, sea, and every **creature** in
you;
12 be **glad**, fields, and everything in
you!
The trees in the woods will shout for
joy
13 when the LORD comes to rule the
earth.
He will rule the peoples of the **world**
with **justice** and fairness.

God the Supreme Ruler

Almighty 91.1; 106.7
bow (2) 96.9; 138.2
cloud 78.14; 99.7
dark 91.6; 104.20
enemy 92.9; 102.8
evil 94.16; 101.3
glad [4] 96.11; 104.34
glory 96.3; 104.1
god (2) (other gods) [2] 96.4; 106.28
God's people 94.14; 100.3
hate 89.23; 101.3
heaven 96.5; 102.19
holy 96.9; 98.1
idol 96.5; 106.19
judge 96.10; 103.6
justice 96.10; 98.9
life (1) 91.16; 101.2
light (1) [2] 89.15; 104.2
love 94.18; 98.3
power 96.6; 98.1
proclaim 96.2; 102.21
protect 95.1; 102.28
rejoice [2] 89.16; 105.3
remember 89.47; 102.12
rescue 91.15; 106.10
righteous [4] 94.15; 99.4
shame 83.16; 109.29
thank 95.2; 100.4
tremble 96.9; 99.1
wicked 94.3; 101.8
world 96.1; 98.9
worship (2) (of other gods) 81.9; 106.19

97 The LORD is king! Earth, be
glad!
Rejoice, you islands of the seas!
2 **Clouds** and **darkness** surround him;
he rules with **righteousness** and
justice.
3 Fire goes in front of him
and burns up his **enemies** round him.
4 His lightning **lights** up the **world**;
the earth sees it and **trembles**.
5 The hills melt like wax before the
LORD,
before the Lord of all the earth.
6 The **heavens proclaim** his
righteousness,
and all the nations see his **glory**.

7 Everyone who **worships idols** is put to
shame;
all the **gods bow down**[k] before the
LORD.
8 The people of Zion are **glad**,
and the cities of Judah **rejoice**
because of your **judgements**, O
LORD.
9 LORD **Almighty**, you are ruler of all the
earth;
you are much greater than all the
gods.

10 The LORD **loves** those who **hate evil**;[l]
he **protects** the **lives** of **his people**;
he **rescues** them from the **power** of
the **wicked**.
11 **Light** shines on the **righteous**,
and **gladness** on the good.
12 All you that are **righteous** be **glad**
because of what the LORD has done!
Remember what the **holy** God has
done,
and give **thanks** to him.

God the Ruler of the World[x]

announce 19.2; 119.46
constant 94.18; 103.8
creature 96.11; 99.1
holy 97.12; 99.3
joy [4] 96.12; 100.2
justice 97.2; 99.4
love 97.10; 99.4
loyal 89.24; 101.1
new 96.1; 104.30
power [2] 97.10; 102.15
praise [2] 96.2; 99.3
promise 95.11; 105.8
save 96.2; 106.4
strength 93.1; 104.15
victory [3] 89.17; 110.7
win 60.12; 108.13
wonder (1) 89.5; 105.2
world 97.4; 100.1

98 Sing a **new** song to the LORD;
he has done **wonderful** things!
By his own **power** and **holy strength**
he has **won** the **victory**.
2 The LORD **announced** his **victory**;
he made his **saving power** known to
the nations.
3 He kept his **promise** to the people of
Israel
with **loyalty** and **constant love** for
them.
All people everywhere have seen the
victory of our God.

4 Sing for **joy** to the LORD, all the earth;
praise him with songs and shouts of
joy!
5 Sing **praises** to the LORD!
Play music on the harps!
6 Blow trumpets and horns,

[j] when he appears; *or* in garments of worship. [k] all the gods bow down; *or* bow down, all gods.
[l] *Probable text* The LORD loves those who hate evil; *Hebrew* Hate evil, you who love the LORD.
[x] HEBREW TITLE: *A psalm.*

95.11: Num 14.20–23; Deut 1.34–36, 12.9–10; Heb 4.3–5 **96.7–9:** Ps 29.1–2

and shout for joy to the LORD, our
king.

7 Roar, sea, and every creature in you;
sing, earth, and all who live on you!
8 Clap your hands, you rivers;
you hills, sing together with joy
before the LORD,
9 because he comes to rule the earth.
He will rule the peoples of the world
with justice and fairness.

God the Supreme King

cloud 97.2; 104.3
command 95.10; 103.18
creature 98.7; 103.22
establish 44.2; Prov 22.28
forgive 86.5; 103.3
holy [3] 98.1; 102.19
justice 98.9; 101.1
law 94.12; 105.45
love 98.3; 100.5
Majesty 96.6; 104.1
might [2] 96.3; 103.7
name (2) (name of God, of Jesus) 96.8; 102.21
obey 95.10; 103.18
praise [3] 98.4; 100.4
pray 88.13; 109.4
priest 78.64; 110.4
punish 94.1; 103.10
right (1) 84.11; 102.13
righteous 97.2; 107.42
sacred 87.1; 105.42
supreme 93.4; 138.2
throne [2] 93.2; 103.19
tremble 97.4; 104.32
worship (1) (of God) [2] 95.6; 100.2

99 The LORD is king;
and the people tremble.
He is enthroned above the winged
creatures
and the earth shakes.
2 The LORD is mighty in Zion;
he is supreme over all the nations.
3 Everyone will praise his great and
majestic name.
Holy is he!

4 Mighty king,[m] you love what is right;
you have established justice in
Israel;
you have brought righteousness and
fairness.
5 Praise the LORD our God;
worship before his throne!
Holy is he!

6 Moses and Aaron were his priests,
and Samuel was one who prayed to
him;
they called to the LORD, and he
answered them.
7 He spoke to them from the pillar of
cloud;
they obeyed the laws and commands
that he gave them.

8 O LORD, our God, you answered your
people;
you showed them that you are a God
who forgives,
even though you punished them for
their sins.
9 Praise the LORD our God,
and worship at his sacred hill![n]
The LORD our God is holy.

A Hymn of Praise[o]

acknowledge 91.14; Is 19.21
eternal 93.5; 106.1
faithful 92.2; 101.6
flock 95.7; 107.41

100 Sing to the LORD, all the
world!
2 Worship the LORD with joy;
come before him with happy songs!

3 Acknowledge that the LORD is God.
He made us, and we belong to him;
we are his people, we are his flock.

4 Enter the temple gates with
thanksgiving,
go into its courts with praise.
Give thanks to him and praise him.

5 The LORD is good;
his love is eternal
and his faithfulness lasts for ever.

God's people 97.1 105.12
happy 94.12; 104.1
joy 98.4; 105.43
last (1) 90.5; 103.1
love 99.4; 102.14
praise [2] 99.3; 102
Temple (1) (of Go 96.6; 116.18
thank [2] 97.12; 10
world 98.9; 105.7
worship (1) (of G 99.5; 102.22

A King's Promise[p]

action 92.5; 106.29
approve Job 28.27 Jer 44.19
arrogant 75.4; 119.122
destroy 94.23; 102
dishonest Lev 6.4; Prov 10.2
evil [4] 97.10; 106.6
faithful 100.5; 103.
fault 65.3; 119.1
hate 97.10; 105.25
honest 55.22; 112.5
hypocrite 26.4; Prov 26.24
justice 99.4; 111.7
lie (2) 89.35; 109.2
life (1) 97.10; 102.3
loyal 98.3; 119.113
presence 85.9; 114
proud 94.2; 106.5
pure 73.1; 119.7
rid 35.25; Prov 20.9
serve 86.11; 116.16
tolerate [2] Esth 3. Prov 6.16
turn 88.14; 102.2
wicked 97.10; 104.3

101 My song is about loyalty and
justice,
and I sing it to you, O LORD.
2 My conduct will be faultless.
When will you come to me?

I will live a pure life in my house,
3 and will never tolerate evil.
I hate the actions of those who turn
away from God;
I will have nothing to do with them.
4 I will not be dishonest,[q]
and will have no dealings with evil.[r]
5 I will get rid of anyone
who whispers evil things about
someone else;
I will not tolerate a man
who is proud and arrogant.

6 I will approve of those who are faithful
to God
and will let them live in my palace.
Those who are completely honest
will be allowed to serve me.

7 No liar will live in my palace;
no hypocrite will remain in my
presence.
8 Day after day I will destroy
the wicked in our land;
I will expel all evil men
from the city of the LORD.

The Prayer of a Troubled Young Man[s]

abandon 94.14; 106.41
anger 95.11; 103.8
ash Job 42.6; Is 33.1
body 83.10; 109.18
condemn 79.11; 109.31
create 96.5; 104.19
curse 89.50; 109.17
desire 63.1; 119.36
destroy 101.8; 104.3
enemy 97.3; 105.24
fear [2] 91.5; 116.3
forsake Job 19.13; Is 1.28

102 Listen to my prayer, O LORD,
and hear my cry for help!
2 When I am in trouble,
don't turn away from me!
Listen to me,
and answer me quickly when I call!

3 My life is disappearing like smoke;
my body is burning like fire.
4 I am beaten down like dry grass;

[m] *Probable text* Mighty king; *Hebrew* The might of the king. [n] SACRED HILL: *See 2.6.*
[o] HEBREW TITLE: *A psalm of thanksgiving.* [p] HEBREW TITLE: *A psalm by David.*
[q] not be dishonest; *or* stay away from dishonest people. [r] evil; *or* evil men.
[s] HEBREW TITLE: *A prayer by a weary sufferer who pours out his complaints to the LORD.*

99.1: Ex 25.22 **99.7:** Ex 33.9
100.5: 1 Chr 16.34; 2 Chr 5.13, 7.3; Ezra 3.11; Ps 106.1, 107.1, 118.1, 136.1; Jer 33.11

free 79.11; 105.20
fury 90.7; 124.3
groan [2] 79.11; Prov 5.11
heaven [2] 97.6; 103.19
help 94.17; 105.4
holy 99.3; 103.1
insult 89.50; 119.22
life (1) [4] 101.2; 103.5
lonely 68.6; Is 30.17
love 100.5; 103.4
mercy 86.3; 103.4
mock 79.4; 123.4
name (2) (name of God, of Jesus) 99.3; 103.1
pity [2] 90.13; 135.14
power 98.1; 103.21
praise [2] 100.4; 103.1
prayer [2] 88.2; 108.6
prison 79.11; 107.10
proclaim 97.6; 105.1
protect 97.10; 105.14
remember 97.12; 103.14
reveal 94.1; 103.7
right (1) 99.4; 105.19
rise 94.2; 104.22
ruin [2] 89.40; 109.10
safe 91.1; 107.30
secure 78.69; 119.165
servant 90.13; 103.21
tear (2) 80.5; 116.8
trouble 94.13; 106.32
turn 101.3; 104.29
vanish 37.20; 109.23
weak 88.9; 109.24
worship (1) (of God) 100.2; 105.3

I have lost my desire for food.
5 I groan aloud;
I am nothing but skin and bones.
6 I am like a wild bird in the desert,
like an owl in abandoned ruins.
7 I lie awake;
I am like a lonely bird on a house-
top.
8 All day long my enemies insult me;
those who mock me use my name in
cursing.
9-10 Because of your anger and fury,
ashes are my food,
and my tears are mixed with my
drink.
You picked me up and threw me away.
11 My life is like the evening shadows;
I am like dry grass.

12 But you, O LORD, are king for ever;
all generations will remember you.
13 You will rise and take pity on Zion;
the time has come to have mercy on
her;
this is the right time.
14 Your servants love her,
even though she is destroyed;
they have pity on her,
even though she is in ruins.

15 The nations will fear the LORD;
all the kings of the earth will fear his
power.
16 When the LORD rebuilds Zion,
he will reveal his greatness.
17 He will hear his forsaken people
and listen to their prayer.

18 Write down for the coming generation
what the LORD has done,
so that people not yet born will
praise him.
19 The LORD looked down from his holy
place on high,
he looked down from heaven to
earth.
20 He heard the groans of prisoners
and set free those who were
condemned to die.
21 And so his name will be proclaimed in
Zion,
and he will be praised in Jerusalem
22 when nations and kingdoms come
together
and worship the LORD.

23 The LORD has made me weak while I
am still young;
he has shortened my life.
24 O God, do not take me away now
before I grow old.

O LORD, you live for ever;
25 long ago you created the earth,
and with your own hands you made
the heavens.
26 They will disappear, but you will
remain;
they will all wear out like clothes.
You will discard them like clothes,
and they will vanish.
27 But you are always the same,
and your life never ends.
28 Our children will live in safety,
and under your protection
their descendants will be secure.

The Love of God[t]

103

Praise the LORD, my soul!
All my being, praise his
holy name!
2 Praise the LORD, my soul,
and do not forget how kind he is.
3 He forgives all my sins
and heals all my diseases.
4 He keeps me from the grave
and blesses me with love and mercy.
5 He fills my life[u] with good things,
so that I stay young and strong like
an eagle.

6 The LORD judges in favour of the
oppressed
and gives them their rights.
7 He revealed his plans to Moses
and let the people of Israel see his
mighty deeds.
8 The LORD is merciful and loving,
slow to become angry and full of
constant love.
9 He does not keep on rebuking;
he is not angry for ever.
10 He does not punish us as we deserve
or repay us according to our sins
and wrongs.
11 As high as the sky is above the earth,
so great is his love for those who
honour him.
12 As far as the east is from the west,
so far does he remove our sins from
us.
13 As a father is kind to his children,
so the LORD is kind to those who
honour him.
14 He knows what we are made of;
he remembers that we are dust.

15 As for us, our life is like grass.
We grow and flourish like a wild
flower;

angel 91.11; 148.2
anger [2] 102.9; 106.23
being 90.2; 146.3
bless 92.10; 104.13
command [2] 99.7; 104.7
constant 98.3; 107.8
covenant 89.3; 105.8
creature 99.1; 104.24
deserve 94.2; Prov 1.31
disease 91.3; 106.15
endure 89.50; 119.90
faithful 101.6; 108.4
favour 45.12; 106.31
forget 89.50; 106.7
forgive 99.8; 109.14
grave 89.48; 107.20
heal 60.2; 107.20
heaven [2] 102.19; 104.2
holy 102.19; 106.16
honour [3] 96.4; 111.3
judge 97.8; 105.5
keep from 91.12; 104.9
kind [3] 89.15; 109.12
last (1) 100.5; 104.31
life (1) [2] 102.3; 104.30
love [5] 102.14; 106.1
mercy [2] 102.13; 111.4
might [2] 99.2; 105.27
name (2) (name of God, of Jesus) 102.21; 106.47
obey [2] 99.7; 105.28
oppress 94.5; 105.14
plan 83.3; 146.4
power 102.15; 105.22
praise [7] 102.18; 104.1
punish 99.8; 106.30
rebuke 68.30; 104.7
remember 102.12; 105.5
repay Job 31.2; Prov 17.13
reveal 102.16; Prov 25.9
right (3) 82.3; 140.12
servant 102.14; 104.4
soul [3] 63.1; 104.1
strong [2] 92.10; 105.24
throne 99.1; 132.7
true 78.20; 105.19
will (1) 67.2; 143.10
wrong 92.7; 119.3

[t] HEBREW TITLE: *By David.* [u] *Probable text* my life; *Hebrew unclear.*

102.25–27: Heb 1.10–12 **103.8:** Jas 5.11

16 then the wind blows on it, and it is
gone—
no one sees it again.
17 But for those who **honour** the LORD, his
love lasts for ever,
and his goodness **endures** for all
generations
18 of those who are **true** to his **covenant**
and who **faithfully obey** his
commands.

19 The LORD placed his **throne** in **heaven**;
he is king over all.
20 **Praise** the LORD, you **strong** and
mighty angels,
who **obey** his **commands,**
who listen to what he says.
21 **Praise** the LORD, all you **heavenly**
powers,
you **servants** of his, who do his **will**!
22 **Praise** the LORD, all his **creatures**
in all the places he rules.
Praise the LORD, my **soul**!

In Praise of the Creator

104 Praise the LORD, my **soul**!
O LORD, my God, how great
you are!
You are clothed with **majesty** and
glory;
2 you cover yourself with **light**.
You have spread out the **heavens** like
a tent
3 and built your home on the waters
above.[v]
You use the **clouds** as your chariot
and ride on the wings of the wind.
4 You use the winds as your messengers
and flashes of lightning as your
servants.

5 You have set the earth firmly on its
foundations,
and it will never be moved.
6 You placed the ocean over it like a
robe,
and the water covered the
mountains.
7 When you **rebuked** the waters, they
fled;
they rushed away when they heard
your shout of **command.**
8 They flowed over the mountains and
into the valleys,
to the place you had made for them.
9 You set a boundary they can never
pass,
to **keep them from** covering the
earth again.

10 You make springs flow in the valleys,
and rivers run between the hills.
11 They **provide** water for the wild
animals;
there the wild donkeys quench their
thirst.
12 In the trees near by,
the birds make their nests and sing.

13 From the sky you send rain on the
hills,
and the earth is filled with your
blessings.
14 You make grass grow for the cattle
and plants for man to use,
so that he can grow his crops
15 and produce wine to make him
happy,
olive-oil to make him **cheerful,**
and **bread** to give him **strength.**

16 The cedars of Lebanon get **plenty** of
rain—
the LORD's own trees, which he
planted.
17 There the birds build their nests;
the storks nest in the fir-trees.
18 The wild goats live in the high
mountains,
and the rock-badgers hide in the
cliffs.

19 You **created** the moon to **mark** the
months;
the sun knows the time to set.
20 You made the night, and in the
darkness
all the wild animals come out.
21 The young lions roar while they hunt,
looking for the food that God
provides.
22 When the sun **rises**, they go back
and lie down in their dens.
23 Then people go out to do their work
and keep working until evening.

24 LORD, you have made so many things!
How **wisely** you made them all!
The earth is filled with your
creatures.
25 There is the ocean, large and wide,
where countless **creatures** live,
large and small alike.
26 The ships sail on it, and in it plays
Leviathan,
that **sea-monster** which you made.[w]

27 All of them **depend** on you
to give them food when they **need** it.
28 You give it to them, and they eat it;

above 78.23; 113.5
afraid 78.53; 105.38
bless 103.4; 107.38
bread 78.20; Prov 6.26
cheer (1) Job 29.24; Prov 12.25
cloud 99.7; 105.39
command 103.18; 105.7
create [2] 102.25; 119.73
creature [2] 103.22; 136.25
dark 97.2; 105.28
depend 62.1; 111.7
destroy 102.14; 105.33
flee Job 15.28; Is 15.5
glad 97.1; 105.3
glory [2] 97.6; 106.20
happy [2] 100.2; 106.3
heaven 103.19; 105.40
keep from 103.4; 116.8
last (1) 103.17; 105.10
Leviathan 74.14; Is 27.1
life (1) [2] 103.5; 109.8
light (1) 97.4; 105.39
Majesty 99.3; 111.3
mark (1) Job 38.10; Is 44.5
monster 89.10; 148.7
need 91.5; 107.41
new 98.1; 119.40
please 77.7; Prov 3.4
plenty 73.12; 144.14
praise [4] 103.1; 105.2
provide [3] 95.7; 111.5
rebuke 103.9; 141.5
rise 102.13; Prov 8.29
satisfy 81.16; 105.40
servant 103.21; 105.5
soul [2] 103.1; 108.1
strength 98.1; 110.7
tremble 99.1; 114.7
turn 102.2; 105.29
wicked 101.8; 106.6
wise 90.12; 107.43

[v] THE WATERS ABOVE: *A reference to the waters above the celestial dome (Gen 1.6–7).*
[w] in it plays...made; *or* Leviathan is there, that sea-monster you made to amuse you.

104.4: Heb 1.7 **104.26:** Job 41.1; Ps 74.14; Is 27.1

you **provide** food, and they are
satisfied.
29 When you **turn** away, they are **afraid**;
when you take away your breath,
they die
and go back to the dust from which
they came.
30 But when you give them breath,[x] they
are **created**;
you give **new life** to the earth.

31 May the **glory** of the LORD **last** for
ever!
May the LORD be **happy** with what
he has made!
32 He looks at the earth, and it **trembles**;
he touches the mountains, and they
pour out smoke.

33 I will sing to the LORD all my **life**;
as long as I live I will sing **praises** to
my God.
34 May he be **pleased** with my song,
for my **gladness** comes from him.
35 May sinners be **destroyed** from the
earth;
may the **wicked** be no more.

Praise the LORD, my **soul**!
Praise the LORD!

God and His People
(1 Chr 16.8–22)

105 Give **thanks** to the LORD,
proclaim his greatness;
tell the nations what he has done.
2 Sing **praise** to the LORD;
tell of the **wonderful** things he has
done.
3 Be **glad** that we belong to him;
let all who **worship** him **rejoice**.
4 Go to the LORD for **help**;
and **worship** him continually.
5–6 You descendants of Abraham, his
servant;
you descendants of Jacob, the man
he **chose**:
remember the **miracles** that God
performed
and the **judgements** that he gave.

7 The LORD is our God;
his **commands** are for all the **world**.
8 He will keep his **covenant** for ever,
his **promises** for a thousand
generations.
9 He will keep the **agreement** he made
with Abraham
and his **promise** to Isaac.
10 The LORD made a **covenant** with
Jacob,
one that will **last** for ever.
11 "I will give you the land of Canaan," he
said.
"It will be your own **possession**."

12 **God's people** were few in number,
strangers in the land of Canaan.
13 They wandered from country to
country,
from one kingdom to another.
14 But God let no one **oppress** them;
to **protect** them, he **warned** the
kings:
15 "Don't **harm** my **chosen servants**;
do not touch my **prophets**."

16 The LORD sent **famine** to their country
and took away all their food.
17 But he sent a man ahead of them,
Joseph, who had been sold as a
slave.
18 His feet were kept in chains,
and an iron collar was round his
neck,
19 until what he had **predicted** came
true.
The **word of the LORD proved** him
right.
20 Then the king of Egypt had him
released;
the ruler of nations **set him free**.
21 He put him in charge of his
government
and made him ruler over all the
land,
22 with **power** over the king's officials
and **authority** to instruct his
advisers.

23 Then Jacob went to Egypt
and settled in that country.
24 The LORD gave many children to **his
people**
and made them **stronger** than their
enemies.
25 He made the Egyptians **hate his people**
and treat his **servants** with **deceit**.

26 Then he sent his **servant** Moses,
and Aaron, whom he had **chosen**.
27 They did God's **mighty acts**
and performed **miracles** in Egypt.
28 God sent **darkness** on the country,
but the Egyptians did not **obey**[y] his
command.
29 He **turned** their rivers into **blood**
and killed all their fish.

act 78.43; 106.7
afraid 104.29; 112.7
agree 83.5; Prov 18.1
authority Esth 9.29; Prov 16.10
blood 79.3; Prov 23.29
choose [4] 89.3; 106.23
cloud 104.3; 135.7
command [5] 104.7; 106.3
covenant [2] 103.18; 106.45
dark 104.20; 107.10
deceive 32.2; 119.118
destroy 104.35; 106.23
enemy 102.8; 106.10
famine 37.19; Is 14.30
first-born 89.27; 135.8
free 102.20; 111.9
glad [2] 104.34; 106.5
God's people [6] 100.3; 106.9
grapevine *see* **vine**
harm 91.7; 141.10
hate 101.3; 106.10
heaven 104.2; 108.4
help 102.1; 106.4
joy 100.2; 107.22
judge 103.6; 109.6
last (1) 104.31; 111.8
law 99.7; 119.1
light (1) 104.2; 112.4
might 103.7; 106.21

miracle [2] 88.10; 135.9
obey [2] 103.18; 106.3
oppress 103.6; 106.42
possess 69.35; 114.2
power 103.21; 106.8
praise [2] 104.1; 106.1
predict 2 Kgs 23.16; Is 41.22
proclaim 102.21; 107.32
promise [3] 98.3; 106.8
prophet 74.9; Is 3.2
protect 102.28; 115.9
prove 89.49; Prov 22.12
rejoice 97.1; 149.2
remember [2] 103.14; 106.4
right (1) 102.13; 106.3
sacred 99.9; 110.3
satisfy 104.28; 107.9
servant [5] 104.4; 106.16
slave 74.2; 129.4
stranger 94.6; 109.11
strong [2] 103.5; 112.7
thank 100.4; 106.1
true 103.18; 119.142
turn 104.29; 118.22
vine 80.8; 107.37
warn 81.8; 106.26
wonder (1) 98.1; 106.7
word (1) 78.36; 107.2
world 100.1; 116.9
worship (1) (of God) [2] 102.22; 115.11

[x] give them breath; *or* send out your spirit.
[y] *Some ancient translations* did not obey; *Hebrew* obeyed.

105.9: Gen 12.7, 17.8, 26.3 **105.10–11:** Gen 28.13 **105.14–15:** Gen 20.3–7 **105.16:** Gen 41.53–57 **105.17:** Gen 37.28, 45.5 **105.18–19:** Gen 39.20—40.23 **105.20:** Gen 41.14 **105.21:** Gen 41.39–41 **105.23:** Gen 46.6, 47.11 **105.24–25:** Ex 1.7–14 **105.26:** Ex 3.1—4.17 **105.28:** Ex 10.21–23 **105.29:** Ex 7.17–21

30 Their country was overrun with frogs,
even the palace was filled with
them.
31 God **commanded**, and flies and gnats
swarmed throughout the whole
country.
32 He sent hail and lightning on their land
instead of rain;
33 he **destroyed** their **grapevines** and fig-
trees
and broke down all the trees.
34 He **commanded**, and the locusts came,
countless millions of them;
35 they ate all the plants in the land;
they ate all the crops.
36 He killed the **first-born** sons
of all the families of Egypt.

37 Then he led the Israelites out;
they carried silver and gold,
and all of them were healthy and
strong.
38 The Egyptians were **afraid** of them
and were **glad** when they left.
39 God put a **cloud** over **his people**
and a fire at night to give them **light**.
40 They[z] asked, and he sent quails;
he gave them food from **heaven** to
satisfy them.
41 He opened a rock, and water gushed
out,
flowing through the desert like a
river.
42 He **remembered** his **sacred promise**
to Abraham his **servant**.

43 So he led his **chosen people** out,
and they sang and shouted for **joy**.
44 He gave them the lands of other
peoples
and let them take over their fields,
45 so that **his people** would **obey** his laws
and keep all his **commands**.

Praise the LORD!

The LORD's Goodness to His People

106

Praise the LORD!

Give **thanks** to the LORD, because he is
good;
his **love** is **eternal**.
2 Who can tell all the great things he has
done?
Who can **praise** him **enough**?
3 **Happy** are those who **obey** his
commands,
who always do what is **right**.

4 **Remember** me, LORD, when you **help**
your people;
include me when you **save** them.
5 Let me see the **prosperity** of your
people
and **share** in the **happiness** of your
nation,
in the **glad pride** of those who belong
to you.

6 We have sinned as our ancestors did;
we have been **wicked** and **evil**.
7 Our ancestors in Egypt did not
understand God's **wonderful acts**;
they **forgot** the many times he
showed them his **love**,
and they **rebelled** against the
Almighty[a] at the Red Sea.
8 But he **saved** them, as he had
promised,
in order to show his great **power**.
9 He gave a **command** to the Red Sea,
and it dried up;
he led **his people** across on dry land.
10 He **saved** them from those who **hated**
them;
he **rescued** them from their
enemies.
11 But the water drowned their **enemies**;
not one of them was left.
12 Then **his people believed** his **promises**
and sang **praises** to him.

13 But they quickly **forgot** what he had
done
and **acted** without waiting for his
advice.
14 They were filled with craving in the
desert
and put God **to the test**;
15 so he gave them what they asked for,
but also sent a **terrible disease**
among them.

16 There in the desert they were **jealous**
of Moses
and of Aaron, the LORD's **holy**
servant.
17 Then the earth opened up and
swallowed Dathan
and buried Abiram and his family;
18 fire came down on their **followers**
and burnt up those **wicked** people.

19 They made a gold **bull-calf** at Sinai

[z] *Some ancient translations* They; *Hebrew* He. [a] *Probable text* the Almighty; *Hebrew* the sea.

105.30: Ex 8.1–6 **105.31:** Ex 8.16–17, 20–24 **105.32–33:** Ex 9.22–25 **105.34–35:** Ex 10.12–15
105.36: Ex 12.29 **105.37–38:** Ex 12.33–36 **105.39:** Ex 13.21–22 **105.40:** Ex 16.2–15
105.41: Ex 17.1–7; Num 20.2–13 **105.44:** Josh 11.16–23
106.1: 1 Chr 16.34; 2 Chr 5.13, 7.3; Ezra 3.11; Ps 100.5, 107.1, 118.1, 136.1; Jer 33.11 **106.7:** Ex 14.10–12
106.9–12: Ex 14.21–31 **106.12:** Ex 15.1–21 **106.14–15:** Num 11.4–34 **106.16–18:** Num 16.1–35
106.19–23: Ex 32.1–14

abandon 102.6; 119.8
act [3] 105.27; 107.24
action [2] 101.3; 111.4
advice 32.8; Prov 1.2
Almighty 97.9; 107.11
amaze 48.5; Is 25.1
anger [4] 103.8; 110.5
believe [2] 78.22; 116.10
bitter 73.21; Prov 5.4
bull-calf Neh 9.18
choose [2] 105.5; 109.6

command [3] 105 107.11
covenant 105.8; 1
defile Neh 13.29; Is 24.5
destroy [3] 105.33 118.10
disease [2] 103.3; Is 10.16
disgust 95.10; 119.158
distress 78.49; 10
enemy [4] 105.24; 107.2
enough 59.15; 145
eternal 100.5; 107
evil 101.3; 107.17
favour 103.6; 146.
follower 2 Chr 24 Dan 11.24
forget [3] 103.2; 109.13
glad 105.3; 107.30
glory 104.1; 108.5
god (2) (other go 97.7; 115.4
God's people [7] 105.12; 107.38
guilty Job 33.9; 1
happy [2] 104.15; 112.1
hate 105.25; 109.5
heathen [3] 89.50; Is 52.1
help 105.4; 107.12
holy [2] 103.1; 111
idol [3] 97.7; 115.8
image 2 Chr 34.4; Is 10.11
impure Ezra 9.11 Prov 25.4
innocent 94.21; 14
jealous 73.3; Prov 3.31
love [3] 103.4; 107.
might 105.27; 107.
name (2) (name God, of Jesus) 10 113.1
notice (1) 94.7; 14
obey 105.28; 111.1
offer [2] 96.8; 116.
oppress [2] 105.14 107.39
pagan Ezra 6.21; Is 27.9
plague 91.6; Hos 13.14
power [2] 105.22; 110.2
praise [7] 105.2; 1
prevent Job 24.4; Prov 2.12
promise [3] 105.8; 109.21
prosper 92.7; 112.
proud 101.5; 119.2
punish 103.10; 109
rebel [2] 83.2; 107.
reject 89.38; 107.1
remember [3] 105 109.14
rescue [2] 97.10; 107.2
right (1) 105.19; 119.121
sacrifice [2] 69.31 107.22
sake 79.9; 122.8
save [5] 98.2; 107.2
scatter 83.13; 141.
servant [2] 105.5; 109.28
share 72.1; Prov

solemn 95.11; 110.4
sorry Job 30.25; Prov 23.29
subject (1) 18.43; Jer 34.1
terrible [2] 88.16; 119.107
test 95.9; 139.23
thank [2] 105.1; 107.1
trouble 102.2; 107.6
understand 92.6; 111.2
unfaithful 73.27; Prov 23.28
warn 105.14; Prov 3.11
way (3) 85.8; 119.3
wicked [2] 104.35; 107.34
wonder (1) [2] 105.2; 107.8
worship (2) (of other gods) [3] 97.7; Is 1.29

and worshipped that idol;
20 they exchanged the glory of God
for the image of an animal that eats grass.
21 They forgot the God who had saved them
by his mighty acts in Egypt.
22 What wonderful things he did there!
What amazing things at the Red Sea!
23 When God said that he would destroy his people,
his chosen servant, Moses, stood up against God
and prevented his anger from destroying them.

24 Then they rejected the pleasant land,
because they did not believe God's promise.
25 They stayed in their tents and grumbled
and would not listen to the LORD.
26 So he gave them a solemn warning
that he would make them die in the desert
27 and scatter their descendants among the heathen,
letting them die in foreign countries.

28 Then at Peor, God's people joined in the worship of Baal,
and ate sacrifices offered to lifeless gods.
29 They stirred up the LORD's anger by their actions,
and a terrible disease broke out among them.
30 But Phinehas stood up and punished the guilty,
and the plague was stopped.
31 This has been remembered in his favour ever since
and will be for all time to come.

32 At the springs of Meribah the people made the LORD angry,
and Moses was in trouble on their account.
33 They made him so bitter
that he spoke without stopping to think.

34 They did not kill the heathen,
as the LORD had commanded them to do,
35 but they intermarried with them
and adopted their pagan ways.
36 God's people worshipped idols,
and this caused their destruction.
37 They offered their own sons and daughters
as sacrifices to the idols of Canaan.
38 They killed those innocent children,
and the land was defiled by those murders.
39 They made themselves impure by their actions
and were unfaithful to God.

40 So the LORD was angry with his people;
he was disgusted with them.
41 He abandoned them to the power of the heathen,
and their enemies ruled over them.
42 They were oppressed by their enemies
and were in complete subjection to them.
43 Many times the LORD rescued his people,
but they chose to rebel against him
and sank deeper into sin.
44 Yet the LORD heard them when they cried out,
and he took notice of their distress.
45 For their sake he remembered his covenant,
and because of his great love he relented.
46 He made all their oppressors
feel sorry for them.

47 Save us, O LORD our God,
and bring us back from among the nations,
so that we may be thankful
and praise your holy name.

48 Praise the LORD, the God of Israel;
praise him now and for ever!
Let everyone say, "Amen!"

Praise the LORD!

BOOK FIVE
(Psalms 107–150)

In Praise of God's Goodness

107 "Give thanks to the LORD,
because he is good;
his love is eternal!"
2 Repeat these words in praise to the LORD,
all you whom he has saved.
He has rescued you from your enemies
3 and has brought you back from foreign countries,

abundant 68.9; Jer 33.6
act 106.7; 119.126
Almighty 106.7; Is 1.9
bless 104.13; 109.17
calm [2] 89.9; Prov 14.17
change 90.3; 114.8
command [3] 106.3; 111.7
constant [5] 103.8; 108.4

106.24–26: Num 14.1–35 **106.27:** Lev 26.33 **106.28–31:** Num 25.1–13 **106.32–33:** Num 20.2–13 **106.34–36:** Judg 2.1–3, 3.5–6 **106.37:** 2 Kgs 17.17 **106.38:** Num 35.33 **106.40–46:** Judg 2.14–18 **106.47–48:** 1 Chr 16.35–36
107.1: 1 Chr 16.34; 2 Chr 5.13, 7.3; Ezra 3.11; Ps 100.5, 106.1, 118.1, 136.1; Jer 33.11

contempt 44.14; 123.3
Council 89.7; Ecc 9.17
courage 40.12; Is 13.7
cruel 86.14; 119.150
danger 91.3; 116.3
dark [2] 105.28; 112.4
death (1) 88.3; 116.3
distress [4] 106.44; 118.5
enemy 106.10; 108.12
eternal 106.1; 111.3
evil 106.6; 109.3
flock 100.3; Song 1.7
fool 94.8; Prov 1.22
glad [2] 106.5; 109.28
gloom [2] Job 30.28; Prov 17.22
God's people [2] 106.9; 108.7
grapevine *see* **vine**
grave 103.4; 116.3
hard Job 41.15; 127.2
harvest 85.12; 126.5
heal 103.3; 147.3
help 106.4; 108.12
hope 79.8; 112.10
humiliate Neh 6.13; Is 2.9
hunger [3] 69.21; 146.7
joy 105.43; 119.92
love [6] 106.1; 108.4
might 106.21; 108.6
misery 90.15; 113.7
need 104.27; 109.16
oppress [2] 106.42; 119.122
praise [2] 106.1; 108.1
prison 102.20; 143.3
proclaim 105.1; 118.17
rage 85.3; 124.5
reap Ruth 2.9; Jer 9.22
rebel 106.7; 139.21
reject 106.24; 108.11
rescue [2] 106.10; 108.6
rich 85.12; 112.3
righteous 99.4; 111.3
sacrifice 106.28; 116.17
safe 102.28; 119.73
satisfy 105.40; 132.15
save [6] 106.4; 108.6
sight 39.5; 118.23
sow Job 4.8; 126.5
stumble 27.2; Prov 3.23
suffer [3] 89.32; 119.50
thank [6] 106.1; 108.3
trouble [4] 106.32; 119.143
useless 89.43; 119.83
vine 105.33; 128.3
wicked [2] 106.6; 109.2
wise 104.24; 111.10
wonder (1) [5] 106.7; 111.2
word (1) 105.19; 119.42

from east and west, from north and
south. [b]

4 Some wandered in the trackless desert
and could not find their way to a city
to live in.
5 They were **hungry** and thirsty
and had given up all **hope**.
6 Then in their **trouble** they called to the
LORD,
and he **saved** them from their
distress.
7 He led them by a straight road
to a city where they could live.
8 They must **thank** the LORD for his
constant love,
for the **wonderful** things he did for
them.
9 He **satisfies** those who are thirsty
and fills the **hungry** with good
things.

10 Some were living in **gloom** and
darkness,
prisoners suffering in chains,
11 because they had **rebelled** against the
commands of Almighty God
and had **rejected** his instructions.
12 They were worn out from **hard work**;
they would fall down, and no one
would **help**.
13 Then in their **trouble** they called to the
LORD,
and he **saved** them from their
distress.
14 He brought them out of their **gloom**
and **darkness**
and broke their chains in pieces.
15 They must **thank** the LORD for his
constant love,
for the **wonderful** things he did for
them.
16 He breaks down doors of bronze
and smashes iron bars.

17 Some were **fools**, **suffering** because of
their sins
and because of their **evil**;
18 they couldn't stand the **sight** of food
and were close to **death**.
19 Then in their **trouble** they called to the
LORD,
and he **saved** them from their
distress.
20 He **healed** them with his **command**
and **saved** them from the **grave**.
21 They must **thank** the LORD for his
constant love,
for the **wonderful** things he did for
them.
22 They must **thank** him with **sacrifices**,
and with songs of **joy** must tell all
that he has done.

23 Some sailed over the ocean in ships,
earning their living on the seas.
24 They saw what the LORD can do,
his **wonderful acts** on the seas.
25 He **commanded**, and a **mighty** wind
began to blow
and stirred up the waves.
26 The ships were lifted high in the air
and plunged down into the depths.
In such **danger** the men lost their
courage;
27 they **stumbled** and staggered like
drunken men—
all their skill was **useless**.
28 Then in their **trouble** they called to the
LORD,
and he **saved** them from their
distress.
29 He **calmed** the **raging** storm,
and the waves became quiet.
30 They were **glad** because of the **calm**,
and he brought them **safe** to the port
they wanted.
31 They must **thank** the LORD for his
constant love,
for the **wonderful** things he did for
them.
32 They must **proclaim** his greatness in
the assembly of the people
and **praise** him before the **council** of
the leaders.

33 The LORD made rivers dry up
completely
and stopped springs from flowing.
34 He made **rich** soil become a salty
wilderness
because of the **wickedness** of those
who lived there.
35 He **changed** deserts into pools of water
and dry land into flowing springs.
36 He let **hungry** people settle there,
and they built a city to live in.
37 They **sowed** the fields and planted
grapevines
and **reaped** an **abundant harvest**.
38 He **blessed his people**, and they had
many children;
he kept their herds of cattle from
decreasing.

39 When **God's people** were defeated and
humiliated
by **cruel oppression** and **suffering**,
40 he showed **contempt** for their
oppressors
and made them wander in trackless
deserts.

[b] *Probable text* south; *Hebrew* the Mediterranean Sea *(meaning "west")*.

41 But he **rescued** the **needy** from their
misery
and made their families increase
like **flocks**.
42 The **righteous** see this and are **glad**,
but all the **wicked** are put to silence.

43 May those who are **wise** think about
these things;
may they consider the LORD's
constant love.

A Prayer for Help against Enemies [d]
(Ps 57.7–11; 60.5–12)

108 I have complete **confidence**,
O God!
I will sing and **praise** you!
Wake up, my **soul**!
2 Wake up, my harp and lyre!
I will wake up the sun.
3 I will **thank** you, O LORD, among the
nations.
I will **praise** you among the peoples.
4 Your **constant love** reaches above the
heavens;
your **faithfulness** touches the skies.

5 Show your greatness in the sky, O God,
and your **glory** over all the earth.
6 **Save** us by your **might**; answer my
prayer,
so that the people you **love** may be
rescued.

7 From his **sanctuary** [e] God has said,
"In **triumph** I will divide Shechem
and distribute the Valley of Sukkoth
to **my people**.
8 Gilead is mine, and Manasseh too;
Ephraim is my helmet
and Judah my royal sceptre.
9 But I will use Moab as my wash-basin
and I will throw my sandals on
Edom,
as a **sign** that I own it.
I will shout in **triumph** over the
Philistines."

10 Who, O God, will take me into the
fortified city?
Who will lead me to Edom?
11 Have you really **rejected** us?
Aren't you going to march out with
our armies?
12 **Help** us against the **enemy**;
human help is **worthless**.
13 With God on our side we will **win**;
he will defeat our **enemies**.

confident 73.2; 116.7
constant 107.8; 109.26
enemy [2] 107.2; 109.6
faithful 103.18; 111.7
glory 106.20; 113.4
God's people 107.38; 111.1
heaven 105.40; 113.4
help [2] 107.12; 109.21
human 60.11; 115.4
love [2] 107.1; 109.4
might 107.25; 111.9
praise [2] 107.2; 109.1
prayer 102.1; 109.7
reject 107.11; 118.22
rescue 107.2; 109.21
sanctuary 68.24; 116.18
save 107.2; 109.26
sign (1) 74.4; Prov 24.26
soul 104.1; 143.6
thank 107.1; 109.30
triumph [2] 89.17; 149.5
win 98.1; Prov 7.25
worthless 62.9; 118.22

The Complaint of a Man in Trouble [f]

109 I **praise** you, God; don't
remain silent!
2 **Wicked** men and **liars** have attacked
me.
They tell **lies** about me
3 and they say **evil** things about me,
attacking me for no **reason**.
4 They oppose me, even though I **love**
them
and have **prayed** for them. [g]
5 They pay me back **evil** for good
and **hatred** for **love**.

6 **Choose** some **corrupt judge** to **try** my
enemy,
and let one of his own **enemies**
accuse him.
7 May he be **tried** and found **guilty**;
may even his **prayer** be considered
a **crime**!
8 May his **life** soon be ended;
may another man take his job!
9 May his children become **orphans**,
and his wife a **widow**!
10 May his children be homeless beggars;
may they be driven from [h] the **ruins**
they live in!
11 May his creditors take away all his
property,
and may **strangers** get everything
he worked for.
12 May no one ever be **kind** to him
or **care** for the **orphans** he leaves
behind.
13 May all his descendants die,
and may his name be **forgotten** in
the next generation.
14 May the LORD **remember** the **evil** of
his ancestors
and never **forgive** his mother's sins.
15 May the LORD always **remember** their
sins,
but may they themselves be
completely **forgotten**!

16 That man never thought of being **kind**;
he **persecuted** and killed
the **poor**, the **needy**, and the
helpless.
17 He **loved** to **curse**—may he be cursed!
He **hated** to give blessings—may no
one **bless** him!
18 He **cursed** as **naturally** as he dressed
himself;
may his own **curses** soak into his
body like water
and into his bones like oil!
19 May they cover him like clothes

accuse 50.20; 119.78
bless [2] 107.38; 112.2
body 102.3; Prov 14.30
care 95.7; 138.6
choose 106.23; 119.30
condemn 102.20; 130.3
constant 108.4; 115.1
corrupt 94.20; Prov 17.23
crime 94.4; Prov 29.16
curse [4] 102.8; 119.21
death (3) (to death) 94.21; Ecc 4.5
defend 94.22; 119.114
disgrace 89.45; Prov 3.35
enemy [5] 108.12; 110.1
evil [4] 107.17; 119.101
forget [2] 106.7; 111.4
forgive 103.3; 130.4
glad 107.30; 118.15
guilty 106.30; Prov 18.5
hate [2] 106.10; 112.10
heart 86.12; 111.1
help [2] 108.12; 115.9
helpless 86.1; 116.6
hurt 91.12; 121.6
judge 105.5; 110.6
kind [2] 103.2; 111.4
knee Job 3.12; Is 35.3
lie (2) [2] 101.7; 119.69
life (1) 104.30; 119.1
love [5] 108.4; 115.1
natural 1 Kgs 2.6; Prov 22.15
need [2] 107.41; 112.9
orphan [2] 94.6; 146.9
persecute [2] 74.19; 119.84
poor [3] 82.3; 113.7
praise [2] 108.1; 111.1
pray 99.6; 122.6
prayer 108.6; 116.1
promise 106.8; 110.4
punish 106.30; 118.18
reason 94.11; Prov 1.33
remember [2] 106.4; 112.6
rescue 108.6; 143.9
ruin 102.6; 146.9
save [3] 108.6; 116.4
scorn 68.16; 119.22
servant 106.16; 113.1
shame 97.7; 119.6
Sovereign 73.28; 140.7
stranger 105.12; 146.9
thank 108.3; 111.1
try (2) [2] 95.9; 143.2
vanish 102.26; Is 29.7
weak 102.23; Prov 24.10
wicked 107.34; 112.10
widow 94.6; 146.9

[d] HEBREW TITLE: *A psalm by David; a song.* [e] From his sanctuary; *or* In his holiness.
[f] HEBREW TITLE: *A psalm by David.* [g] *Probable text* have prayed for them; *Hebrew unclear.*
[h] *One ancient translation* be driven from; *Hebrew* seek.

109.8: Acts 1.20

and always be round him like a belt!
20 LORD, punish my enemies in that
way—
those who say such evil things
against me!
21 But my Sovereign LORD, help me as
you have promised,
and rescue me because of the
goodness of your love.
22 I am poor and needy;
I am hurt to the depths of my heart.
23 Like an evening shadow I am about to
vanish;
I am blown away like an insect.
24 My knees are weak from lack of food;
I am nothing but skin and bones.
25 When people see me, they laugh at
me;
they shake their heads in scorn.

26 Help me, O LORD my God;
because of your constant love, save
me!
27 Make my enemies know
that you are the one who saves me.
28 They may curse me, but you will bless
me.
May my persecutors be defeated,[i]
and may I, your servant, be glad.
29 May my enemies be covered with
disgrace;
may they wear their shame like a
robe.

30 I will give loud thanks to the LORD;
I will praise him in the assembly of
the people,
31 because he defends the poor man
and saves him from those who
condemn him to death.

The LORD and His Chosen King[j]

110 The LORD said to my lord, the
king,
"Sit here at my right
until I put your enemies under your
feet."
2 From Zion the LORD will extend your
royal power.
"Rule over your enemies," he says.
3 On the day you fight your enemies,
your people will volunteer.
Like the dew of early morning
your young men will come to you on
the sacred hills.[k]
4 The LORD made a solemn promise and
will not take it back:
"You will be a priest for ever
in the priestly order of
Melchizedek."[l]
5 The Lord is at your right side;
when he becomes angry, he will
defeat kings.
6 He will pass judgement on the nations
and fill the battlefield with corpses;
he will defeat kings all over the
earth.
7 The king will drink from the stream by
the road,
and strengthened, he will stand
victorious.

anger 106.23; 112.10
enemy [3] 109.6; 112.8
judge 109.6; 111.10
power 106.8; 111.6
priest 99.6; 115.10
promise 109.21; 116.14
right (2) [2] 45.9; Song 2.6
sacred 105.42; Prov 2.17
solemn 106.26; 119.106
strength 104.15; 119.28
victory 98.1; 118.15

In Praise of the LORD

111 Praise the LORD!
With all my heart I will thank the
LORD
in the assembly of his people.
2 How wonderful are the things the
LORD does!
All who are delighted with them
want to understand them.
3 All he does is full of honour and
majesty;
his righteousness is eternal.

4 The LORD does not let us forget his
wonderful actions;
he is kind and merciful.
5 He provides food for those who honour
him;
he never forgets his covenant.
6 He has shown his power to his people
by giving them the lands of
foreigners.

7 In all he does he is faithful and just;
all his commands are dependable.
8 They last for all time;
they were given in truth and
righteousness.
9 He set his people free
and made an eternal covenant with
them.
Holy and mighty is he!
10 The way to become wise is to honour
the LORD;[m]
he gives sound judgement to all who
obey his commands.
He is to be praised for ever.

action 106.29; 139.3
command [2] 107.11; 112.1
covenant [2] 106.45; 132.12
delight 35.19; 119.14
depend 104.27; 118.8
eternal [2] 107.1; 117.2
faithful 108.4; 115.1
forget [2] 109.13; 119.16
free 105.20; 118.5
God's people [3] 108.7; 113.8
heart 109.22; 116.7
holy 106.16; 114.2
honour [3] 103.11; 112.1
judge 110.6; 119.7
justice 101.1; 112.4
kind 109.12; 112.4
last (1) 105.10; 119.89
Majesty 104.1; 145.5
mercy 103.4; 112.4
might 108.6; 118.15
obey 106.3; 112.1
power 110.2; 112.2
praise [2] 109.1; 112.1
provide 104.11; 127.2
righteous [2] 107.42; 118.20
sound (2) Neh 9.13; Prov 3.24
thank 109.30; 115.18
truth 52.3; 119.18
understand 106.7; 119.27
wise 107.43; 119.98
wonder (1) [2] 107.8; 118.23

[i] *One ancient translation* May my persecutors be defeated; *Hebrew* They persecuted me and were defeated. [j] HEBREW TITLE: *A psalm by David.* [k] *Verse 3 in Hebrew is unclear.*
[l] in...Melchizedek; *or* like Melchizedek; *or* in the line of succession to Melchizedek.
[m] The way...the LORD; *or* The most important part of wisdom is honouring the LORD.

109.25: Mt 27.39; Mk 15.29
110.1: Mt 22.44; Mk 12.36; Lk 20.42–43; Acts 2.34–35; 1 Cor 15.25; Eph 1.20–22; Col 3.1; Heb 1.13, 10.12–13 **110.4:** Heb 5.6, 6.20, 7.17, 21 **111.10:** Job 28.28; Prov 1.7, 9.10

afraid [2] 105.38; 116.11
anger 110.5; 119.53
bad 53.3; 119.104
bless 109.17; 115.12
certain (1) Neh 6.7; 119.140
command 111.7; 119.2
dark 107.10; 139.11
enemy 110.1; 118.7
fail [2] 89.33; 119.157
faith 78.22; Is 7.9
generous [2] 37.21; Prov 11.25
happy [2] 106.3; 113.9
hate 109.5; 119.104
honest 101.6; Prov 1.3
honour 111.3; 113.9
hope 107.5; 119.5
justice 111.7; 119.106
kind [2] 111.4; 119.68
light (1) 105.39; 119.105
mercy 111.4; 116.5
need 109.16; 113.7
obey 111.10; 119.2
pleasure 62.4; 119.16
power [2] 111.6; 118.10
praise 111.1; 113.1
prosper 106.5; 122.6
remember 109.14; 115.12
respect Job 34.7; 119.48
rich 107.34; 119.36
strong 105.24; 117.2
trust 91.2; 115.8
wicked 109.2; 119.53
worry 94.19; Prov 3.25

The Happiness of a Good Person

112 Praise the LORD!

Happy is the person who honours the
LORD,
who takes pleasure in obeying his
commands.
2 The good man's children will be
powerful in the land;
his descendants will be blessed.
3 His family will be wealthy and rich,
and he will be prosperous for ever.

4 Light shines in the darkness for good
men,
for those who are merciful, kind,
and just.
5 Happy is the person who is generous
with his loans,
who runs his business honestly.
6 A good person will never fail;
he will always be remembered.

7 He is not afraid of receiving bad news;
his faith is strong, and he trusts in
the LORD.
8 He is not worried or afraid;
he is certain to see his enemies
defeated.
9 He gives generously to the needy,
and his kindness never fails;
he will be powerful and respected.
10 The wicked see this and are angry;
they glare in hate and disappear;
their hopes are gone for ever.

above 104.3; 138.6
glory 108.5; 115.1
God's people 111.1; 114.2
happy 112.1; 118.24
heaven [2] 108.4; 115.3
honour 112.1; 115.13
misery 107.41; Prov 1.27
name (2) (name of God, of Jesus) [3] 106.47; 118.26
need 112.9; 128.2
poor 109.16; 132.15
praise [5] 112.1; 115.17
raise 93.3; 134.2
servant 109.28; 116.16

In Praise of the LORD's Goodness

113 Praise the LORD!

You servants of the LORD,
praise his name!
2 May his name be praised,
now and for ever.
3 From the east to the west
praise the name of the LORD!
4 The LORD rules over all nations;
his glory is above the heavens.

5 There is no one like the LORD our God.
He lives in the heights above,
6 but he bends down
to see the heavens and the earth.
7 He raises the poor from the dust;
he lifts the needy from their misery
8 and makes them companions of
princes,
the princes of his people.
9 He honours the childless wife in her
home;
he makes her happy by giving her
children.

Praise the LORD!

change 107.35; 119.159
God's people 113.8; 116.14
holy 111.9; 138.2
lamb [2] Job 21.11; Is 5.17
possess 105.11; 119.111
presence 101.7; 116.9
tremble 104.32; Ecc 12.3

A Passover Song

114 When the people of Israel left
Egypt,
when Jacob's descendants left that
foreign land,
2 Judah became the Lord's holy people,
Israel became his own possession.

3 The Red Sea looked and ran away;
the River Jordan stopped flowing.
4 The mountains skipped like goats;
the hills jumped about like lambs.

5 What happened, Sea, to make you run
away?
And you, O Jordan, why did you stop
flowing?
6 You mountains, why did you skip like
goats?
You hills, why did you jump about
like lambs?

7 Tremble, earth, at the Lord's coming,
at the presence of the God of Jacob,
8 who changes rocks into pools of water
and solid cliffs into flowing springs.

alone [2] 86.10; 136.4
bless [4] 112.2; 118.26
constant 109.26; 119.64
dead 91.7; Prov 1.12
faithful 111.7; 117.2
glory 113.4; 138.5
god (2) (other gods) 106.28; 135.5
heaven [3] 113.4; 119.89
help [3] 109.21; 118.7
honour 113.9; 119.74
human 108.12; 118.9
idol 106.19; 135.18
love 109.4; 116.1
praise [2] 113.1; 116.18
priest [2] 110.4; 118.3
protect [3] 105.14; 116.6
remember 112.6; 119.49
thank 111.1; 116.13
trust [4] 112.7; 116.11
wish 81.8; 135.6
worship (1) (of God) 105.3; 118.4

The One True God

115 To you alone, O LORD, to you
alone,
and not to us, must glory be given
because of your constant love and
faithfulness.

2 Why should the nations ask us,
"Where is your God?"
3 Our God is in heaven;
he does whatever he wishes.
4 Their gods are made of silver and gold,
formed by human hands.
5 They have mouths, but cannot speak,
and eyes, but cannot see.
6 They have ears, but cannot hear,
and noses, but cannot smell.
7 They have hands, but cannot feel,
and feet, but cannot walk;
they cannot make a sound.
8 May all who made them and who trust
in them
become[n] like the idols they have
made.

9 Trust in the LORD, you people of Israel.
He helps you and protects you.
10 Trust in the LORD, you priests of God.

[n] May all...become; *or* All who made them and who trust in them will become.

112.9: 2 Cor 9.9 **114.1:** Ex 12.51 **114.3:** Ex 14.21; Josh 3.16 **114.8:** Ex 17.1–7; Num 20.2–13
115.4–8: Ps 135.15–18; Rev 9.20

He **helps** you and **protects** you.
11 **Trust** in the LORD, all you that **worship** him.
He **helps** you and **protects** you.

12 The LORD **remembers** us and will **bless** us;
he will **bless** the people of Israel
and all the **priests** of God.
13 He will **bless** everyone who **honours** him,
the great and the small alike.

14 May the LORD give you children—
you and your descendants!
15 May you be **blessed** by the LORD,
who made **heaven and earth**!

16 **Heaven** belongs to the LORD **alone**,
but he gave the earth to man.
17 The LORD is not **praised** by the **dead**,
by any who go down to the land of silence.[o]
18 But we, the living, will give **thanks** to him
now and for ever.

Praise the LORD!

A Man Saved from Death Praises God

116 I **love** the LORD, because he hears me;
he listens to my **prayers**.
2 He listens to me
every time I call to him.
3 The **danger** of **death** was all round me;
the **horrors** of the **grave** closed in on me;
I was filled with **fear** and **anxiety**.
4 Then I called to the LORD,
"**I beg** you, LORD, **save me**!"

5 The LORD is **merciful** and good;
our God is **compassionate**.
6 The LORD **protects** the **helpless**;
when I was in **danger**, he **saved** me.
7 Be **confident**, my **heart**,
because the LORD has been good to me.

8 The LORD **saved** me **from death**;
he stopped my **tears**
and **kept me from** defeat.
9 And so I walk in the **presence** of the LORD
in the **world** of the living.
10 I kept on **believing**, even when I said,
"I am completely crushed,"
11 even when I was **afraid** and said,
"No one can be **trusted**."
12 What can I **offer** the LORD
for all his goodness to me?
13 I will bring a **wine-offering** to the LORD,
to **thank** him for **saving** me.
14 In the assembly of all **his people**
I will give him what I have **promised**.

15 How **painful** it is to the LORD
when one of **his people** dies!
16 I am your **servant**, LORD;
I **serve** you, just as my mother did.
You have **saved** me **from death**.
17 I will give you a **sacrifice** of **thanksgiving**
and **offer** my **prayer** to you.
18–19 In the assembly of all your people,
in the **sanctuary** of your **Temple** in Jerusalem,
I will give you what I have **promised**.

Praise the LORD!

In Praise of the LORD

117 **Praise** the LORD, all nations!
Praise him, all peoples!
2 His **love** for us is **strong**
and his **faithfulness** is **eternal**.

Praise the LORD!

A Prayer of Thanks for Victory

118 Give **thanks** to the LORD,
because he is good,
and his **love** is **eternal**.
2 Let the people of Israel say,
"His **love** is **eternal**."
3 Let the **priests** of God say,
"His **love** is **eternal**."
4 Let all who **worship** him say,
"His **love** is **eternal**."

5 In my **distress** I called to the LORD;
he answered me and **set me free**.
6 The LORD is with me, I will not be **afraid**;
what can anyone do to me?
7 It is the LORD who **helps** me,
and I will see my **enemies** defeated.
8 It is better to **trust** in the LORD
than to **depend** on man.
9 It is better to **trust** in the LORD
than to **depend** on **human** leaders.

10 Many **enemies** were round me;
but I **destroyed** them by the **power** of the LORD!
11 They were round me on every side;

[o] LAND OF SILENCE: *The world of the dead (see 6.5).*

115.13: Rev 11.18, 19.5 **116.10:** 2 Cor 4.13 **117.1:** Rom 15.11
118.1: 1 Chr 16.34; 2 Chr 5.13, 7.3; Ezra 3.11; Ps 100.5, 106.1, 107.1, 136.1; Jer 33.11 **118.6:** Heb 13.6

but I destroyed them by the power
of the LORD!
12 They swarmed round me like bees,
but they burnt out as quickly as a
fire among thorns;
by the power of the LORD I
destroyed them.
13 I was fiercely attacked and was being
defeated,
but the LORD helped me.
14 The LORD makes me powerful and
strong;
he has saved me.

15 Listen to the glad shouts of victory in
the tents of God's people:
"The LORD's mighty power has done
it!
16 His power has brought us victory—
his mighty power in battle!"

17 I will not die; instead, I will live
and proclaim what the LORD has
done.
18 He has punished me severely,
but he has not let me die.

19 Open to me the gates of the Temple;
I will go in and give thanks to the
LORD!

20 This is the gate of the LORD;
only the righteous can come in.

21 I praise you, LORD, because you heard
me,
because you have given me victory.

22 The stone which the builders rejected
as worthless
turned out to be the most important
of all.
23 This was done by the LORD;
what a wonderful sight it is!
24 This is the day of the LORD's victory;
let us be happy, let us celebrate!
25 Save us, LORD, save us!
Give us success, O LORD!

26 May God bless the one who comes in
the name of the LORD!
From the Temple of the LORD we
bless you.
27 The LORD is God; he has been good to
us.
With branches in your hands, start the
festival
and march round the altar.

28 You are my God, and I give you
thanks;
I will proclaim your greatness.

29 Give thanks to the LORD, because he is
good,
and his love is eternal.

The Law of the LORD

119 Happy are those whose lives
are faultless,
who live according to the law of the
LORD.
2 Happy are those who follow his
commands,
who obey him with all their heart.
3 They never do wrong;
they walk in the LORD's ways.
4 LORD, you have given us your laws
and told us to obey them faithfully.
5 How I hope that I shall be faithful
in keeping your instructions!
6 If I pay attention to all your
commands,
then I will not be put to shame.
7 As I learn your righteous judgements,
I will praise you with a pure heart.
8 I will obey your laws;
never abandon me!

Obedience to the Law of the LORD

9 How can a young man keep his life
pure?
By obeying your commands.
10 With all my heart I try to serve you;
keep me from disobeying your
commandments.
11 I keep your law in my heart,
so that I will not sin against you.
12 I praise you, O LORD;
teach me your ways.
13 I will repeat aloud
all the laws you have given.
14 I delight in following your commands
more than in having great wealth.
15 I study your instructions;
I examine your teachings.
16 I take pleasure in your laws;
your commands I will not forget.

Happiness in the Law of the LORD

17 Be good to me, your servant,
so that I may live and obey your
teachings.
18 Open my eyes, so that I may see
the wonderful truths in your law.
19 I am here on earth for just a little
while;
do not hide your commands from
me.
20 My heart aches with longing;
I want to know your judgements at
all times.

118.14: Ex 15.2; Is 12.2 **118.22:** Lk 20.17; Acts 4.11; 1 Pet 2.7 **118.22–23:** Mt 21.42; Mk 12.10–11
118.25: Mt 21.9; Mk 11.9; Jn 12.13 **118.26:** Mt 21.9, 23.39; Mk 11.9; Lk 13.35, 19.38; Jn 12.13

21 You reprimand the proud;
cursed are those who disobey your commands.
22 Free me from their insults and scorn,
because I have kept your laws.
23 The rulers meet and plot against me,
but I will study your teachings.
24 Your instructions give me pleasure;
they are my advisers.

Determination to Obey the Law of the LORD

25 I lie defeated in the dust;
revive me, as you have promised.
26 I confessed all I have done, and you answered me;
teach me your ways.
27 Help me to understand your laws,
and I will meditate on your wonderful teachings.[p]
28 I am overcome by sorrow;
strengthen me, as you have promised.
29 Keep me from going the wrong way,
and in your goodness teach me your law.
30 I have chosen to be obedient;
I have paid attention to your judgements.
31 I have followed your instructions, LORD;
don't let me be put to shame.
32 I will eagerly obey your commands,
because you will give me more understanding.

A Prayer for Understanding

33 Teach me, LORD, the meaning of your laws,
and I will obey them at all times.
34 Explain your law to me, and I will obey it;
I will keep it with all my heart.
35 Keep me obedient to your commandments,
because in them I find happiness.
36 Give me the desire to obey your laws
rather than to get rich.
37 Keep me from paying attention to what is worthless;
be good to me, as you have promised.
38 Keep your promise to me, your servant—
the promise you make to those who obey you.
39 Save me from the insults I fear;
how wonderful are your judgements!
40 I want to obey your commands;
give me new life, for you are righteous.

[p] teachings; *or* deeds.

Trusting the Law of the LORD

41 Show me how much you love me, LORD,
and save me according to your promise.
42 Then I can answer those who insult me
because I trust in your word.
43 Enable me to speak the truth at all times,
because my hope is in your judgements.
44 I will always obey your law,
for ever and ever.
45 I will live in perfect freedom,
because I try to obey your teachings.
46 I will announce your commands to kings
and I will not be ashamed.
47 I find pleasure in obeying your commands,
because I love them.
48 I respect and love your commandments;
I will meditate on your instructions.

Confidence in the Law of the LORD

49 Remember your promise to me, your servant;
it has given me hope.
50 Even in my suffering I was comforted
because your promise gave me life.
51 The proud are always scornful of me,
but I have not departed from your law.
52 I remember your judgements of long ago,
and they bring me comfort, O LORD.
53 When I see the wicked breaking your law,
I am filled with anger.
54 During my brief earthly life
I compose songs about your commands.
55 In the night I remember you, LORD,
and I think about your law.
56 I find my happiness
in obeying your commands.

Devotion to the Law of the LORD

57 You are all I want, O LORD;
I promise to obey your laws.
58 I ask you with all my heart
to have mercy on me, as you have promised!
59 I have considered my conduct,
and I promise to follow your instructions.
60 Without delay I hurry
to obey your commands.
61 The wicked have laid a trap for me,
but I do not forget your law.
62 In the middle of the night I wake up

to praise you for your righteous
judgements.
63 I am a friend of all who serve you,
of all who obey your laws.
64 LORD, the earth is full of your constant
love;
teach me your commandments.

The Value of the Law of the LORD

65 You have kept your promise, LORD,
and you are good to me, your
servant.
66 Give me wisdom and knowledge,
because I trust in your commands.
67 Before you punished me, I used to go
wrong,
but now I obey your word.
68 How good you are—how kind!
Teach me your commands.
69 Proud men have told lies about me,
but with all my heart I obey your
instructions.
70 These men have no understanding,
but I find pleasure in your law.
71 My punishment was good for me,
because it made me learn your
commands.
72 The law that you gave means more to
me
than all the money in the world.

The Justice of the Law of the LORD

73 You created me, and you keep me
safe;
give me understanding, so that I
may learn your laws.
74 Those who honour you will be glad
when they see me,
because I trust in your promise.
75 I know that your judgements are
righteous, LORD,
and that you punished me because
you are faithful.
76 Let your constant love comfort me,
as you have promised me, your
servant.
77 Have mercy on me, and I will live
because I take pleasure in your law.
78 May the proud be ashamed for falsely
accusing me;
as for me, I will meditate on your
instructions.
79 May those who honour you come to
me—
all those who know your commands.
80 May I perfectly obey your
commandments
and be spared the shame of defeat.

A Prayer for Deliverance

81 I am worn out, LORD, waiting for you
to save me;
I place my trust in your word.
82 My eyes are tired from watching for
what you promised,
while I ask, "When will you help
me?"
83 I am as useless as a discarded
wineskin;
yet I have not forgotten your
commands.
84 How much longer must I wait?
When will you punish those who
persecute me?
85 Proud men, who do not obey your law,
have dug pits to trap me.
86 Your commandments are all
trustworthy;
men persecute me with lies—help
me!
87 They have almost succeeded in killing
me,
but I have not neglected your
commands.
88 Because of your constant love be good
to me,
so that I may obey your laws.

Faith in the Law of the LORD

89 Your word, O LORD, will last for ever;
it is eternal in heaven.
90 Your faithfulness endures through all
the ages;
you have set the earth in place, and
it remains.
91 All things remain to this day because
of your command,
because they are all your servants.
92 If your law had not been the source of
my joy,
I would have died from my
sufferings.
93 I will never neglect your instructions,
because by them you have kept me
alive.
94 I am yours—save me!
I have tried to obey your commands.
95 Wicked men are waiting to kill me,
but I will meditate on your laws.
96 I have learnt that everything has
limits;
but your commandment is perfect.

Love for the Law of the LORD

97 How I love your law!
I think about it all day long.
98 Your commandment is with me all the
time
and makes me wiser than my
enemies.
99 I understand more than all my
teachers,
because I meditate on your
instructions.
100 I have greater wisdom than old men,
because I obey your commands.

[101] I have avoided all evil conduct,
because I want to obey your word.
[102] I have not neglected your instructions,
for you yourself are my teacher.
[103] How sweet is the taste of your instructions—
sweeter even than honey!
[104] I gain wisdom from your laws,
and so I hate all bad conduct.

Light from the Law of the LORD

[105] Your word is a lamp to guide me
and a light for my path.
[106] I will keep my solemn promise
to obey your just instructions.
[107] My sufferings, LORD, are terrible indeed;
keep me alive, as you have promised.
[108] Accept my prayer of thanks, O LORD,
and teach me your commands.
[109] I am always ready to risk my life;
I[q] have not forgotten your law.
[110] Wicked men lay a trap for me,
but I have not disobeyed your commands.
[111] Your commandments are my eternal possession;
they are the joy of my heart.
[112] I have decided to obey your laws
until the day I die.

Safety in the Law of the LORD

[113] I hate those who are not completely loyal to you,
but I love your law.
[114] You are my defender and protector;
I put my hope in your promise.
[115] Go away from me, you sinful people.
I will obey the commands of my God.
[116] Give me strength, as you promised,
and I shall live;
don't let me be disappointed in my hope!
[117] Hold me, and I will be safe,
and I will always pay attention to your commands.
[118] You reject everyone who disobeys your laws;
their deceitful schemes are useless.
[119] You treat all the wicked like rubbish,
and so I love your instructions.
[120] Because of you I am afraid;
I am filled with fear because of your judgements.

Obedience to the Law of the LORD

[121] I have done what is right and good;
don't abandon me to my enemies!
[122] Promise that you will help your servant;
don't let arrogant men oppress me!
[123] My eyes are tired from watching for your saving help,
for the deliverance you promised.
[124] Treat me according to your constant love,
and teach me your commands.
[125] I am your servant; give me understanding,
so that I may know your teachings.
[126] LORD, it is time for you to act,
because people are disobeying your law.
[127] I love your commands more than gold,
more than the finest gold.
[128] And so I follow all your instructions;[r]
I hate all wrong ways.

Desire to Obey the Law of the LORD

[129] Your teachings are wonderful;
I obey them with all my heart.
[130] The explanation of your teachings gives light
and brings wisdom to the ignorant.
[131] In my desire for your commands
I pant with open mouth.
[132] Turn to me and have mercy on me
as you do on all those who love you.
[133] As you have promised, keep me from falling;
don't let me be overcome by evil.
[134] Save me from those who oppress me,
so that I may obey your commands.
[135] Bless me with your presence
and teach me your laws.
[136] My tears pour down like a river,
because people do not obey your law.

The Justice of the Law of the LORD

[137] You are righteous, LORD,
and your laws are just.
[138] The rules that you have given
are completely fair and right.
[139] My anger burns in me like a fire,
because my enemies disregard your commands.
[140] How certain your promise is!
How I love it!
[141] I am unimportant and despised,
but I do not neglect your teachings.
[142] Your righteousness will last for ever,
and your law is always true.
[143] I am filled with trouble and anxiety,
but your commandments bring me joy.
[144] Your instructions are always just;
give me understanding, and I shall live.

[q] I am always ready to risk my life; I; *or* My life is in constant danger, but I.
[r] *Some ancient translations* all your instructions; *Hebrew unclear.*

A Prayer for Deliverance

[145] With all my heart I call to you;
answer me, LORD, and I will obey
your commands!
[146] I call to you;
save me, and I will keep your laws.
[147] Before sunrise I call to you for help;
I place my hope in your promise.
[148] All night long I lie awake,
to meditate on your instructions.
[149] Because your love is constant, hear
me, O LORD;
show your mercy, and preserve my
life!
[150] My cruel persecutors are coming
closer,
people who never keep your law.
[151] But you are near to me, LORD,
and all your commands are
permanent.
[152] Long ago I learnt about your
instructions;
you made them to last for ever.

A Plea for Help

[153] Look at my suffering, and save me,
because I have not neglected your
law.
[154] Defend my cause, and set me free;
save me, as you have promised.
[155] The wicked will not be saved,
for they do not obey your laws.
[156] But your compassion, LORD, is great;
show your mercy and save me!
[157] I have many enemies and oppressors,
but I do not fail to obey your laws.
[158] When I look at those traitors, I am
filled with disgust,
because they do not keep your
commands.
[159] See how I love your instructions, LORD.
Your love never changes, so save
me!
[160] The heart of your law is truth,
and all your righteous judgements
are eternal.

Dedication to the Law of the LORD

[161] Powerful men attack me unjustly,
but I respect your law.
[162] How happy I am because of your
promises—
as happy as someone who finds rich
treasure.
[163] I hate and detest all lies,
but I love your law.
[164] Seven times each day I thank you
for your righteous judgements.
[165] Those who love your law have perfect
security,
and there is nothing that can make
them fall.
[166] I wait for you to save me, LORD,
and I do what you command.
[167] I obey your teachings;
I love them with all my heart.
[168] I obey your commands and your
instructions;
you see everything I do.

A Prayer for Help

[169] Let my cry for help reach you, LORD!
Give me understanding, as you have
promised.
[170] Listen to my prayer,
and save me according to your
promise!
[171] I will always praise you,
because you teach me your laws.
[172] I will sing about your law,
because your commands are just.
[173] Always be ready to help me,
because I follow your commands.
[174] How I long for your saving help, O
LORD!
I find happiness in your law.
[175] Give me life, so that I may praise you;
may your instructions help me.
[176] I wander about like a lost sheep;
so come and look for me, your
servant,
because I have not neglected your
laws.

A Prayer for Help

120 When I was in trouble, I
called to the LORD,
and he answered me.
[2] Save me, LORD,
from liars and deceivers.

[3] You liars, what will God do to you?
How will he punish you?
[4] With a soldier's sharp arrows,
with red-hot charcoal!

[5] Living among you is as bad as living in
Meshech
or among the people of Kedar.[s]
[6] I have lived too long
with people who hate peace!
[7] When I speak of peace,
they are for war.

bad 119.104; Prov 1.16
deceive 119.118; Prov 6.13
hate 119.104; 129.5
lie (2) [2] 119.69; 144.8
peace [2] 85.8; 122.6
punish 119.67; 125.5
save 119.39; 130.7
trouble 119.143; 138.7

The LORD Our Protector

121 I look to the mountains;
where will my help come
from?
[2] My help will come from the LORD,
who made heaven and earth.

[3] He will not let you fall;
your protector is always awake.

danger 116.3; Prov 6.29
heaven 119.89; 123.1
help [2] 119.27; 124.8
hurt 109.22; Prov 3.29
protect [5] 119.114; 127.1
safe 119.73; 122.7

[s] MESHECH...KEDAR: *Two distant regions, whose people were regarded as savages.*

[4] The protector of Israel
never dozes or sleeps.
[5] The LORD will guard you;
he is by your side to protect you.
[6] The sun will not hurt you during the
day,
nor the moon during the night.

[7] The LORD will protect you from all
danger;
he will keep you safe.
[8] He will protect you as you come and
go
now and for ever.

In Praise of Jerusalem[t]

122 I was glad when they said to
me,
"Let us go to the LORD's house."
[2] And now we are here,
standing inside the gates of
Jerusalem!

[3] Jerusalem is a city restored
in beautiful order and harmony.
[4] This is where the tribes come,
the tribes of Israel,
to give thanks to the LORD
according to his command.
[5] Here the kings of Israel
sat to judge their people.

[6] Pray for the peace of Jerusalem:
"May those who love you prosper.
[7] May there be peace inside your
walls
and safety in your palaces."
[8] For the sake of my relatives and
friends
I say to Jerusalem, "Peace be with
you!"
[9] For the sake of the house of the LORD
our God
I pray for your prosperity.

command 119.2; 125.4
friend 119.63; Prov 6.16
glad 119.74; 149.2
judge 119.7; 127.5
love 119.41; 127.2
peace [3] 120.6; 125.5
pray [2] 109.4; 141.5
prosper [2] 112.3; 126.4
restore 71.20; 147.2
safe 121.7; 138.7
sake [2] 106.45; Is 37.35
thank 119.108; 124.6

A Prayer for Mercy

123 LORD, I look up to you,
up to heaven, where you
rule.
[2] As a servant depends on his master,
as a maid depends on her mistress,
so we will keep looking to you, O LORD
our God,
until you have mercy on us.

[3] Be merciful to us, LORD, be merciful;
we have been treated with so much
contempt.
[4] We have been mocked too long by the
rich
and scorned by proud oppressors.

contempt 107.40; Song 8.7
depend [2] 118.8; 146.5
heaven 121.2; 124.8
master 45.11; Prov 17.2
mercy [2] 119.58; 145.8
mock 102.8; Prov 1.26
oppress 119.122; 143.12
proud 119.21; 131.1
rich 119.36; 132.15
scorn 119.22; Prov 1.22
servant 119.17; 132.10

God the Protector of His People[u]

124 What if the LORD had not
been on our side?
Answer, O Israel!

[2] "If the LORD had not been on our side
when our enemies attacked us,
[3] then they would have swallowed us
alive
in their furious anger against us;
[4] then the flood would have carried us
away,
the water would have covered us,
[5] the raging torrent would have
drowned us."

[6] Let us thank the LORD,
who has not let our enemies destroy
us.
[7] We have escaped like a bird from a
hunter's trap;
the trap is broken, and we are free!
[8] Our help comes from the LORD,
who made heaven and earth.

alive 119.93; Prov 1.12
anger 119.53; 138.7
destroy 118.10; 135.10
enemy [2] 119.98; 127.5
escape 88.8; 130.3
flood 90.5; Song 8.7
free 119.22; 129.4
fury 102.9; Is 13.9
heaven 123.1; 134.3
help 121.1; 130.2
rage 107.29; Song 8.
thank 122.4; 136.1
trap [2] 119.61; 140.5

The Security of God's People

125 Those who trust in the LORD
are like Mount Zion,
which can never be shaken, never
be moved.
[2] As the mountains surround Jerusalem,
so the LORD surrounds his people
now and for ever.

[3] The wicked will not always rule over
the land of the righteous;
if they did, the righteous themselves
might do evil.
[4] LORD, do good to those who are good,
to those who obey your commands.
[5] But when you punish the wicked,
punish also those who abandon your
ways.

Peace be with Israel!

abandon 119.8; Prov 2.13
command 122.4; 128.1
evil 119.101; 139.20
God's people 118.15; 130.8
obey 119.2; 128.1
peace 122.6; 128.6
punish [2] 120.3; 135.9
righteous [2] 119.7; 129.4
trust 119.42; 130.5
way (3) 119.3; Prov 8.13
wicked [2] 119.53; 139.19

A Prayer for Deliverance

126 When the LORD brought us
back to Jerusalem,[v]
it was like a dream!
[2] How we laughed, how we sang for joy!
Then the other nations said about us,
"The LORD did great things for
them."
[3] Indeed he did great things for us;
how happy we were!

[4] LORD, make us prosperous again,[m]

dream 90.5; Ecc 5.3
happy 119.1; 127.5
harvest [2] 107.37; Prov 10.5
joy [3] 119.92; 132.9
prosper 122.6; 128.2
seed [2] Job 4.8; Prov 22.8
sow 107.37; Prov 22.8
weep [2] 39.12; 137.1

[t] HEBREW TITLE: *By David.* [u] HEBREW TITLE: *By David.*
[v] brought us back to Jerusalem; *or* made Jerusalem prosperous again.
[m] make...again; *or* take us back to our land.

just as the rain brings water back to
dry river-beds.
5 Let those who wept as they sowed
their seed,
gather the harvest with joy!

6 Those who wept as they went out
carrying the seed
will come back singing for joy,
as they bring in the harvest.

In Praise of God's Goodness[w]

bless 119.135; 128.4
enemy 124.2; 129.1
gift 76.11; Prov 6.35
happy 126.3; 128.1
hard 107.12; Prov 2.4
judge 122.5; 146.7
love 122.6; 130.7
protect 121.3; 139.5
provide 111.5; 128.2
real 1 Kgs 20.11; Prov 17.27
useless [3] 119.83; Prov 12.11

127 If the LORD does not build the
house,
the work of the builders is useless;
if the LORD does not protect the city,
it is useless for the sentries to stand
guard.
2 It is useless to work so hard for a
living,
getting up early and going to bed
late.
For the LORD provides for those he
loves,
while they are asleep.

3 Children are a gift from the LORD;
they are a real blessing.
4 The sons a man has when he is young
are like arrows in a soldier's hand.
5 Happy is the man who has many such
arrows.
He will never be defeated
when he meets his enemies in the
place of judgement.

The Reward of Obedience to the LORD

bless [2] 127.3; 129.8
command 125.4; 132.12
happy [2] 127.5; 137.8
life (1) 119.1; 133.3
need 113.7; 132.15
obey [2] 125.4; 148.8
peace 125.5; 131.2
prosper [2] 126.4; 132.18
provide 127.2; 132.5
vine 107.37; Song 2.13

128 Happy are those who obey
the LORD,
who live by his commands.

2 Your work will provide for your needs;
you will be happy and prosperous.
3 Your wife will be like a fruitful vine in
your home,
and your sons will be like young
olive-trees round your table.
4 A man who obeys the LORD
will surely be blessed like this.

5 May the LORD bless you from Zion!
May you see Jerusalem prosper
all the days of your life!
6 May you live to see your
grandchildren!

Peace be with Israel!

A Prayer against Israel's Enemies

bless [2] 128.4; 132.16
cruel 119.150; 144.11

129 Israel, tell us how your
enemies have persecuted you
ever since you were young.

2 "Ever since I was young,
my enemies have persecuted me
cruelly,
but they have not overcome me.
3 They cut deep wounds in my back
and made it like a ploughed field.
4 But the LORD, the righteous one,
has freed me from slavery."

5 May everyone who hates Zion
be defeated and driven back.
6 May they all be like grass growing on
the house-tops,
which dries up before it can grow;
7 no one gathers it up
or carries it away in bundles.
8 No one who passes by will say,
"May the LORD bless you!
We bless you in the name of the
LORD."

enemy [2] 127.5; 132.18
free 124.7; 136.24
hate 120.6; 139.21
name (2) (name of God, of Jesus) 118.26; 135.1
persecute [2] 119.84; Is 14.6
righteous 125.3; 140.13
slave 105.17; Prov 12.24

A Prayer for Help

130 From the depths of my
despair I call to you,
LORD.
2 Hear my cry, O Lord;
listen to my call for help!
3 If you kept a record of our sins,
who could escape being
condemned?
4 But you forgive us,
so that we should stand in awe of
you.

5 I wait eagerly for the LORD's help,
and in his word I trust.
6 I wait for the Lord
more eagerly than watchmen wait
for the dawn—
than watchmen wait for the dawn.

7 Israel, trust in the LORD,
because his love is constant
and he is always willing to save.
8 He will save his people Israel
from all their sins.

awe 89.7; Ecc 3.14
condemn 109.31; Prov 12.2
constant 119.64; 138.2
despair 69.20; 142.6
eager [2] 119.32; Prov 18.15
escape 124.7; 139.7
forgive 109.14; Prov 14.9
God's people 125.2; 133.1
help [2] 124.8; 139.10
love 127.2; 136.0
save [2] 120.2; 138.7
trust [2] 125.1; 131.3
watch 119.82; Prov 1.17
word (1) 119.42; 140.3

A Prayer of Humble Trust[x]

131 LORD, I have given up my
pride
and turned away from my
arrogance.
I am not concerned with great matters
or with subjects too difficult for me.
2 Instead, I am content and at peace.
As a child lies quietly in its mother's
arms,
so my heart is quiet within me.

arrogant 119.122; Prov 8.13
concern 41.1; Prov 1.32
difficult 73.16; 139.17
heart 119.2; 138.1
peace 128.6; Prov 10.10
proud 123.4; 138.6
trust 130.5; 135.18
turn 119.132; 139.11

[w] HEBREW TITLE: *By Solomon.* [x] HEBREW TITLE: *By David.*
130.8: Mt 1.21; Tit 2.14

3 Israel, **trust** in the LORD
now and for ever!

In Praise of the Temple

bless 129.8; 133.3
choose [3] 119.30; 135.4
command 128.1; 138.2
covenant 111.5; Is 24.5
Covenant Box [2] 78.61; Jer 3.16
endure 119.90; 147.17
enemy 129.1; 136.24
forget 119.16; 136.23
joy [2] 126.2; 137.6
might [2] 118.15; 136.3
need 128.2; 140.12
poor 113.7; 140.12
power 119.161; 135.10
preserve 119.149; Prov 18.21
priest [2] 118.3; 135.19
promise [3] 119.25; 133.3
prosper 128.2; Prov 3.2
provide [2] 128.2; 147.8
reject 119.118; Prov 1.32
remember 119.49; 135.13
rest (1) 95.11; 139.3
rich 123.4; Prov 10.4
right (1) 119.121; 147.1
satisfy 107.9; 145.16
servant 123.2; 134.1
shame 119.6; Prov 4.25
solemn 119.106; Prov 30.1
symbol 78.61; Is 11.10
Temple (1) (of God) 118.19; 134.1
throne 103.19; Ecc 4.13
true 119.142; 141.6
vow Job 22.27; Prov 2.17
worship (1) (of God) 118.4; 135.20

132 LORD, do not **forget** David
and all the hardships he
endured.
2 **Remember**, LORD, what he **promised**,
the **vow** he made to you, the **Mighty**
God of Jacob:
3 "I will not go home or go to bed;
4 I will not **rest** or sleep,
5 until I **provide** a place for the LORD,
a home for the **Mighty** God of
Jacob."

6 In Bethlehem we heard about the
Covenant Box,
and we found it in the fields of
Jearim.
7 We said, "Let us go to the LORD's
house;
let us **worship** before his **throne**."

8 Come to the **Temple**, LORD, with the
Covenant Box,
the **symbol** of your **power**,
and stay here for ever.
9 May your **priests** do always what is
right;
may your people shout for **joy**!

10 You made a **promise** to your **servant**
David;
do not **reject** your **chosen** king,
LORD.
11 You made a **solemn promise** to
David—
a promise you will not take back:
"I will make one of your sons king,
and he will rule after you.
12 If your sons are **true** to my **covenant**
and to the **commands** I give them,
their sons, also, will succeed you for
all time as kings."

13 The LORD has **chosen** Zion;
he wants to make it his home:
14 "This is where I will live for ever;
this is where I want to rule.
15 I will **richly provide** Zion with all she
needs;
I will **satisfy** her **poor** with food.
16 I will **bless** her **priests** in all they do,
and her people will sing and shout
for joy.
17 Here I will make one of David's
descendants a great king;
here I will **preserve** the rule of my
chosen king.
18 I will cover his **enemies** with **shame**,
but his kingdom will **prosper** and
flourish."

In Praise of Brotherly Love[y]

anoint 89.20; Zech 4.14
bless 132.16; 134.3
God's people 130.8; 135.12
life (1) 128.5; 142.5
promise 132.2; 138
wonder (1) 119.18; 135.9

133 How **wonderful** it is, how
pleasant,
for **God's people** to live together in
harmony!
2 It is like the precious **anointing** oil
running down from Aaron's head
and beard,
down to the collar of his robes.
3 It is like the dew on Mount Hermon,
falling on the hills of Zion.
That is where the LORD has **promised**
his **blessing**—
life that never ends.

A Call to Praise God

bless 133.3; 147.13
heaven 124.8; 135.6
praise [2] 119.7; 135
prayer 119.108; 141
raise 113.7; 147.6
servant 132.10; 135
serve 119.10; Prov 23.3
Temple (1) (of God
[2] 132.8; 135.2

134 Come, **praise** the LORD,
all his **servants**,
all who **serve** in his **Temple** at night.
2 **Raise** your hands in **prayer** in the
Temple,
and **praise** the LORD!

3 May the LORD, who made **heaven and**
earth,
bless you from Zion!

A Hymn of Praise

choose 132.10; Prov 8.10
cloud 105.39; 147.8
defend 119.114; 140.
destroy 124.6; 137.8
first-born 105.36; 136.10
god (2) (other gods) [2] 115.4; 136.2
God's people [2] 133.1; 136.14
heaven 134.3; 136.5
human 118.9; 146.3
idol 115.8; Is 2.8
kind 119.68; 141.5
Levites Neh 13.5; Is 66.21
miracle 105.5; 136.4
name (2) (name of God, of Jesus) [2] 129.8; 138.2
pity 102.13; Prov 20.26
power 132.8; 136.12
praise [10] 134.1; 138.1
priest 132.9; Ecc 5.6
proclaim 118.17; 145.1
punish 125.5; 141.5
remember 132.2; 137.1
servant [2] 134.1; 136.22
Temple (1) (of God) 134.1; 138.2
trust 131.3; 141.8
wish 115.3; 139.19
wonder (1) 133.1; 139.14
worship (1) (of God) 132.7; Prov 14.31

135 Praise the LORD!

Praise his **name**, you **servants** of the
LORD,
2 who stand in the LORD's house,
in the **Temple** of our God.
3 **Praise** the LORD, because he is good;
sing **praises** to his **name**, because he
is **kind**.[z]
4 He **chose** Jacob for himself,
the people of Israel for his own.

5 I know that our LORD is great,
greater than all the **gods**.
6 He does whatever he **wishes**
in **heaven and on earth**,
in the seas and in the depths below.
7 He brings storm **clouds** from the ends
of the earth;
he makes lightning for the storms,
and he brings out the wind from his
storeroom.

8 In Egypt he killed all the **first-born**
of men and animals alike.
9 There he performed **miracles** and
wonders
to **punish** the king and all his
officials.
10 He **destroyed** many nations

[y] HEBREW TITLE: *By David.* [z] he is kind; *or* it is pleasant to do so.

132.6–10: 2 Chr 6.41–42 **132.11:** 2 Sam 7.12–16; 1 Chr 17.11–14; Ps 89.3–4; Acts 2.30 **132.17:** 1 Kgs 11.36

and killed **powerful** kings:
11 Sihon, king of the Amorites,
Og, king of Bashan,
and all the kings in Canaan.
12 He gave their lands to **his people**;
he gave them to Israel.

13 LORD, you will always be **proclaimed** as God;
all generations will **remember** you.
14 The LORD will **defend his people**;
he will take **pity** on his **servants**.

15 The **gods** of the nations are made of silver and gold;
they are formed by **human** hands.
16 They have mouths, but cannot speak,
and eyes, but cannot see.
17 They have ears, but cannot hear;
they are not even able to breathe.
18 May all who made them and who **trust** in them
become[a] like the **idols** they have made!

19 **Praise** the LORD, people of Israel;
praise him, you **priests** of God!
20 **Praise** the LORD, you **Levites**;
praise him, all you that **worship** him!
21 **Praise** the LORD in Zion,
in Jerusalem, his home.

Praise the LORD!

A Hymn of Thanksgiving

136 Give **thanks** to the LORD,
because he is good;
his **love** is **eternal**.
2 Give **thanks** to the greatest of all **gods**;
his love is eternal.
3 Give **thanks** to the **mightiest** of all lords;
his love is eternal.

4 He **alone** performs great **miracles**;
his love is eternal.
5 By his **wisdom** he made the **heavens**;
his love is eternal;
6 he built the earth on the deep waters;
his love is eternal.
7 He made the sun and the moon;
his love is eternal;
8 the sun to rule over the day;
his love is eternal;
9 the moon and the stars to rule over the night;
his love is eternal.
10 He killed the **first-born** sons of the Egyptians;
his love is eternal.
11 He led the people of Israel out of Egypt;
his love is eternal;
12 with his **strong** hand, his **powerful** arm;
his love is eternal.
13 He divided the Red Sea;
his love is eternal;
14 he led **his people** through it;
his love is eternal;
15 but he drowned the king of Egypt and his army;
his love is eternal.

16 He led **his people** through the desert;
his love is eternal.
17 He killed **powerful** kings;
his love is eternal;
18 he killed famous kings;
his love is eternal;
19 Sihon, king of the Amorites;
his love is eternal;
20 and Og, king of Bashan;
his love is eternal.
21 He gave their lands to **his people**;
his love is eternal;
22 he gave them to Israel, his **servant**;
his love is eternal.

23 He did not **forget** us when we were defeated;
his love is eternal;
24 he **freed** us from our **enemies**;
his love is eternal.
25 He gives food to every living **creature**;
his love is eternal.

26 Give **thanks** to the God of **heaven**;
his love is eternal.

A Lament of Israelites in Exile

137 By the rivers of Babylon we sat down;
there we **wept** when we **remembered** Zion.
2 On the willows near by
we hung up our harps.
3 Those who captured us told us to sing;
they told us to entertain them:
"Sing us a song about Zion."

4 How can we sing a song to the LORD
in a foreign land?
5 May I never be able to play the harp again
if I **forget** you, Jerusalem!

alone 115.1; 139.19
creature 104.24; 145.10
enemy 132.18; 138.7
eternal [26] 119.89; 138.8
first-born 135.8; Ezek 20.26
forget 132.1; 137.5
free 129.4; 142.7
god (2) (other gods) 135.5; 138.1
God's people [3] 135.12; 147.19
heaven [2] 135.6; 139.8
love [26] 130.7; 138.2
might 132.2; 145.4
miracle 135.9; Jer 21.2
power [2] 135.10; 138.7
servant 135.1; 143.2
strong 118.14; 140.7
thank [4] 124.6; 138.1
wisdom 119.66; 147.5

destroy 135.10; 140.11
forget 136.23; Prov 2.1
happy 128.1; 144.15
joy 132.9; 149.5
remember [4] 135.13; 143.5
weep 126.5; Ecc 4.1

[a] May all...become; *or* All who made them and who trust in them will become.

135.15–18: Ps 115.4–8; Rev 9.20
136.1: 1 Chr 16.34; 2 Chr 5.13, 7.3; Ezra 3.11; Ps 100.5, 106.1, 107.1, 118.1; Jer 33.11 **136.5:** Gen 1.1
136.6: Gen 1.2 **136.7–9:** Gen 1.16 **136.10:** Ex 12.29 **136.11:** Ex 12.51 **136.13–15:** Ex 14.21–29
136.19: Num 21.21–30 **136.20:** Num 21.31–35

6 May I never be able to sing again
if I do not **remember** you,
if I do not think of you as my
greatest **joy**!

7 **Remember**, LORD, what the Edomites
did
the day Jerusalem was captured.
Remember how they kept saying,
"Tear it down to the ground!"

8 Babylon, you will be **destroyed**.
Happy is the man who pays you back
for what you have done to us—
9 who takes your babies
and smashes them against a rock.

A Prayer of Thanksgiving [b]

138 I thank you, LORD, **with all my heart**;
I sing **praise** to you before the **gods**.
2 I face your **holy Temple**,
bow down, and **praise** your **name**
because of your **constant love** and
faithfulness,
because you have shown that your
name and your **commands** are
supreme. [c]
3 You answered me when I called to
you;
with your **strength** you strengthened
me.

4 All the kings in the **world** will **praise**
you, LORD,
because they have heard your
promises.
5 They will sing about what you have
done
and about your great **glory**.
6 Even though you are so high **above**,
you **care** for the lowly,
and the **proud** cannot hide from you.

7 When I am surrounded by **troubles**,
you keep me **safe**.
You oppose my **angry enemies**
and **save** me by your **power**.
8 You will do everything you have
promised;
LORD, your **love** is **eternal**.
Complete the work that you have
begun.

God's Complete Knowledge and Care [d]

139 LORD, you have examined me
and you know me.
2 You know everything I do;
from far away you **understand** all
my thoughts.
3 You see me, whether I am working or
resting;
you know all my **actions**.
4 Even before I speak,
you already know what I will say.
5 You are all round me on every side;
you **protect** me with your **power**.
6 Your **knowledge** of me is too deep;
it is beyond my **understanding**.

7 Where could I go to **escape** from you?
Where could I **get away** from your
presence?
8 If I went up to **heaven**, you would be
there;
if I lay down in the **world of the
dead**, you would be there.
9 If I flew away beyond the east
or lived in the farthest place in the
west,
10 you would be there to lead me,
you would be there to **help** me.
11 I could ask the **darkness** to hide me
or the **light** round me to **turn** into
night,
12 but even **darkness** is not dark for you,
and the night is as bright as the day.
Darkness and **light** are the same to
you.

13 You **created** every part of me;
you put me together in my mother's
womb.
14 I **praise** you because you are to be
feared;
all you do is **strange** and **wonderful**.
I know it **with all my heart**.
15 When my bones were being formed,
carefully put together in my
mother's **womb**,
when I was growing there in **secret**,
you knew that I was there—
16 you saw me before I was born.
The days allotted to me
had all been recorded in your book,
before any of them ever began.
17 O God, how **difficult** I find your
thoughts; [e]
how many of them there are!
18 If I counted them, they would be more
than the grains of sand.
When I awake, I am still with you.

19 O God, how I **wish** you would kill the
wicked!
How I **wish violent** men would leave
me **alone**!

above 113.5; 144.7
anger 124.3; 145.8
bow (2) 97.7;
Prov 14.19
care 109.12; 142.4
command 132.12;
147.15
complete Ezra 6.14;
Is 28.21
constant 130.7; 143.8
enemy 136.24; 139.22
eternal 136.0; 145.13
faithful 119.4; 143.1
glory 115.1; 145.5
god (2) (other gods)
136.2; Is 14.13
heart 131.2; 139.14
holy 114.2; 145.21
love [2] 136.0; 143.8
**name (2) (name of
God, of Jesus)** [2]
135.1; 139.20
power 136.12; 139.5
praise [3] 135.1;
139.14
promise [2] 133.3;
143.11
proud 131.1; 140.5
safe 122.7; 140.1
save 130.7; 140.1
strength 119.28;
150.1
supreme 99.2; 150.2
Temple (1) (of God)
135.2; 150.1
thank 136.1; 145.1
trouble 120.1; 142.2
world 119.72;
Prov 8.23

action 111.4;
Prov 1.31
alone 136.4;
Prov 5.15

create 119.73; 148.5
dark [3] 112.4; 143.3
despise 119.141;
Prov 6.30
difficult 131.1;
Prov 15.19
enemy 138.7; 140.9
escape 130.3;
Prov 6.5
everlasting
Gen 49.26; Is 40.28
evil [2] 125.3; 140.1
fear 119.39; Prov 2.
get away 2 Kgs 5.2
Prov 3.21
guide 119.105; 143.1
hate [2] 129.5;
Prov 3.32
heart 138.1; 147.3
heaven 136.5; 146.6
help 130.2; 140.6
knowledge 119.66;
Prov 1.5
light (1) [2] 119.105;
Prov 6.23
mind (1) 73.7; 143.5
**name (2) (name of
God, of Jesus)** 138.
145.21
power 138.7; 140.4
praise 138.1; 140.13
presence 119.135;
140.13
protect 127.1; 140.4
rebel 107.11;
Prov 24.21
rest (1) 132.4;
Prov 6.4
secret 90.8;
Prov 11.13
strange Ex 18.3;
Is 28.11
test 106.14; Prov 17
turn 131.1; Prov 4.2
understand [2]
119.27; 145.3
violent 91.10; 140.1
wicked [2] 125.3;
140.4
wish [2] 135.6;
Prov 13.12
womb [2] Job 38.8;
Ecc 11.5
wonder (1) 135.9;
145.5
world of the dead
63.9; 143.7

[b] HEBREW TITLE: *By David.*
[c] *Probable text* your name and your commands are supreme; *Hebrew* your command is greater than all your name. [d] HEBREW TITLE: *A psalm by David.*
[e] how difficult I find your thoughts; *or* how precious are your thoughts to me.

137.8: Rev 18.6

20 They say **wicked** things about you;
they speak **evil** things against your **name**.[f]
21 O LORD, how I **hate** those who hate you!
How I **despise** those who **rebel** against you!
22 I **hate** them with a total hatred;
I regard them as my **enemies**.

23 Examine me, O God, and know my **mind**;
test me, and discover my thoughts.
24 Find out if there is any **evil** in me
and **guide** me in the **everlasting** way.[g]

A Prayer for Protection[h]

140 Save me, LORD, from evil men;
keep me **safe** from **violent** men.
2 They are always **plotting evil**,
always stirring up **quarrels**.
3 Their tongues are like **deadly** snakes;
their **words** are like a cobra's poison.

4 **Protect** me, LORD, from the **power** of the **wicked**;
keep me **safe** from **violent** men
who **plot** my **downfall**.
5 **Proud** men have set a **trap** for me;
they have laid their snares
and along the path they have set
traps to catch me.

6 I say to the LORD, "You are my God."
Hear my cry for **help**, LORD!
7 My **Sovereign LORD**, my **strong defender**,
you have **protected** me in battle.
8 LORD, don't give the **wicked** what they **want**;
don't let their **plots succeed**.

9 Don't let my **enemies** be **victorious**;[i]
make their **threats** against me fall back on them.
10 May red-hot coals fall on them;
may they be thrown into a pit and never get out.
11 May those who **accuse** others **falsely**
not **succeed**;
may **evil** overtake **violent** men and **destroy** them.

12 LORD, I know that you **defend** the **cause** of the **poor**
and the **rights** of the **needy**.

accuse 119.78; Prov 25.18
cause (2) 119.154; Is 49.4
deadly 91.3; Prov 23.27
defend [2] 135.14; 144.2
destroy 137.8; 143.12
downfall 69.22; Prov 11.5
enemy 139.22; 142.3
evil [3] 139.20; 141.4
false 119.78; Prov 8.8
help 139.10; 141.1
need 132.15; 145.15
plot (1) [3] 119.23; Is 7.5
poor 132.15; Prov 6.11
power 139.5; 144.7
praise 139.14; 142.7
presence 139.7; Prov 8.30
protect [2] 139.5; 141.8
proud 138.6; Prov 3.12
quarrel Job 21.4; Prov 18.19
right (3) 103.6; Prov 29.7
righteous 129.4; 143.1
safe [2] 138.7; 143.10
save 138.7; 142.6
Sovereign 109.21; 141.8
strong 136.12; 142.6
succeed (1) [2] 119.87; Prov 2.5
threat 76.6; Prov 12.6
trap [2] 124.7; 141.9
victory 118.15; 144.10
violent [3] 139.19; Prov 1.19
wicked [2] 139.19; 141.4
word (1) 130.5; 141.6

13 The **righteous** will **praise** you indeed;
they will live in your **presence**.

An Evening Prayer[j]

141 I call to you, LORD; **help** me now!
Listen to me when I call to you.
2 Receive my **prayer** as **incense**,
my uplifted hands as an evening **sacrifice**.

3 LORD, place a guard at my mouth,
a sentry at the door of my lips.
4 **Keep me from** wanting to do **wrong**
and from joining evil men in their **wickedness**.
May I never take part in their **feasts**.

5 A good man may **punish** me and **rebuke** me in **kindness**,
but I will never **accept honour** from **evil** men,
because I am always **praying** against their evil deeds.
6 When their rulers are thrown down from rocky cliffs,
the people will **admit** that my **words** were **true**.
7 Like wood that is split and chopped into bits,
so their bones are **scattered** at the edge of the **grave**.[k]

8 But I keep **trusting** in you, my **Sovereign LORD**.
I **seek** your **protection**;
don't let me die!
9 **Protect** me from the **traps** they have set for me,
from the snares of those **evildoers**.
10 May the **wicked** fall into their own **traps**
while I go by **unharmed**.

accept 119.108; Prov 6.35
admit (1) Job 40.14; Prov 10.17
evil [4] 140.1; Prov 2.14
feast 69.22; Prov 9.2
grave 116.3; Prov 5.23
harm 105.15; Prov 3.30
help 140.6; 142.1
honour 119.74; 145.19
incense Neh 13.5; Song 3.6
keep from 119.10; Prov 10.3
kind 135.3; 145.7
pray 122.6; Prov 15.8
prayer 134.2; 143.1
protect [2] 140.4; 142.4
punish 135.9; 149.7
rebuke 104.7; Prov 17.10
sacrifice 116.17; Prov 7.14
scatter 106.27; 144.6
seek 37.4; Prov 30.5
Sovereign 140.7; Is 3.15
trap [2] 140.5; 142.3
true 132.12; 144.15
trust 135.18; 143.8
wicked [2] 140.4; 145.20
word (1) 140.3; Prov 4.20
wrong 119.3; Prov 2.12

A Prayer for Help[l]

142 I call to the LORD for **help**;
I **plead** with him.
2 I bring him all my **complaints**;
I tell him all my **troubles**.
3 When I am ready to give up,
he knows what I should do.
In the path where I walk,
my **enemies** have hidden a **trap** for me.
4 When I look beside me,
I see that there is no one to **help** me,
no one to **protect** me.
No one **cares** for me.

care 138.6; Prov 12.10
complain 55.17; Prov 20.14
despair 130.1; 143.4
distress 118.5; 144.14
enemy [2] 140.9; 143.3
free 136.24; 146.7
help [4] 141.1; 145.14
life (1) 133.3; 146.2
plead 55.1; 143.1
praise 140.13; 144.1
protect [2] 141.8; 143.9
save 140.1; 143.11
strong 140.7; 144.12
trap 141.9; Prov 1.18
trouble 138.7; 143.11

[f] *Probable text* they speak...name; *Hebrew unclear.*
[g] the everlasting way; *or* the ways of my ancestors. [h] HEBREW TITLE: *A psalm by David.*
[i] *Probable text* Don't let my enemies be victorious; *Hebrew unclear.*
[j] HEBREW TITLE: *A psalm by David.* [k] *Verses 5–7 in Hebrew are unclear.*
[l] HEBREW TITLE: *A poem by David, when he was in the cave; a prayer.*

140.3: Rom 3.13 **141.2:** Rev 5.8 **142 Title:** 1 Sam 22.1, 24.3

[5] LORD, I cry to you for **help**;
you, LORD, are my **protector**;
you are all I want in this **life**.
[6] Listen to my cry for **help**,
for I am sunk in **despair**.
Save me from my **enemies**;
they are too **strong** for me.
[7] **Set me free** from my **distress**;[m]
then in the assembly of your people
I will **praise** you
because of your goodness to me.

A Prayer for Help[n]

143 LORD, hear my **prayer**!
In your **righteousness** listen to
my **plea**;
answer me in your **faithfulness**!
[2] Don't put me, your **servant**, on trial;
no one is **innocent** in your **sight**.

[3] My **enemy** has hunted me down
and completely defeated me.
He has put me in a **dark prison**,
and I am like those who died long
ago.
[4] So I am ready to give up;
I am in deep **despair**.

[5] I **remember** the days gone by;
I think about all that you have done,
I bring to **mind** all your deeds.
[6] I lift up my hands to you in **prayer**;
like dry ground my **soul** is thirsty for
you.

[7] Answer me now, LORD!
I have lost all **hope**.
Don't hide yourself from me,
or I will be among those who go
down to the **world of the dead**.
[8] **Remind** me each morning of your
constant love,
for I put my **trust** in you.
My **prayers** go up to you;
show me the way I should go.

[9] I go to you for **protection**, LORD;
rescue me from my **enemies**.
[10] You are my God;
teach me to do your **will**.
Be good to me, and **guide** me on a **safe**
path.

[11] **Rescue** me, LORD, as you have
promised;
in your goodness **save** me from my
troubles!
[12] Because of your **love** for me, kill my
enemies
and **destroy** all my **oppressors**,
for I am your **servant**.

constant 138.2; 145.8
dark 139.11; Prov 2.13
despair 142.6; Prov 21.15
destroy 140.11; 145.20
enemy [3] 142.3; 144.6
faithful 138.2; 145.13
guide 139.24; Prov 1.5
hope 119.5; 145.15
innocent 106.38; Prov 1.11
love [2] 138.2; 145.8
mind (1) 139.23; Prov 6.14
oppress 123.4; 146.7
plead 142.1; Prov 2.3
prayer [3] 141.2; Prov 28.9
prison 107.10; 146.7
promise 138.4; 145.13
protect 142.4; 144.1
remember 137.1; Prov 3.1
remind Job 33.23; Prov 25.26
rescue [2] 109.21; 144.7
righteous 140.13; 145.17
safe 140.1; 144.2
save 142.6; 144.7
servant [2] 136.22; 144.10
sight 118.23; 146.8
soul 108.1; 146.1
teach 119.12; Prov 1.3
trouble 142.2; 145.14
trust 141.8; 144.2
try (2) 109.6; Prov 23.29
will (1) 103.21; Prov 16.33
world of the dead 139.8; Prov 2.18

A King Thanks God for Victory[o]

144 Praise the LORD, my
protector!
He trains me for battle
and prepares me for war.
[2] He is my **protector** and **defender**,
my **shelter** and **saviour**,
in whom I **trust** for **safety**.
He subdues the nations under me.

[3] LORD, what is man, that you **notice**
him;
mere man, that you pay attention to
him?
[4] He is like a puff of wind;
his days are like a passing shadow.

[5] O LORD, tear the sky **apart** and come
down;
touch the mountains, and they will
pour out smoke.
[6] Send flashes of lightning and **scatter**
your **enemies**;
shoot your arrows and send them
running.
[7] Reach down from **above**,
pull me out of the deep water, and
rescue me;
save me from the **power** of
foreigners,
[8] who never tell the **truth**
and **lie** even under **oath**.

[9] I will sing you a **new** song, O God;
I will play the harp and sing to you.
[10] You give **victory** to kings
and **rescue** your **servant** David.
[11] **Save** me from my **cruel enemies**;
rescue me from the **power** of
foreigners,
who never tell the **truth**
and **lie** even under **oath**.

[12] May our sons in their youth
be like plants that grow up **strong**.
May our daughters be like stately
pillars
which adorn the corners of a palace.
[13] May our barns be filled
with crops of every kind.
May the **sheep** in our fields
bear young by the tens of thousands.
[14] May our cattle reproduce **plentifully**
without miscarriage or **loss**.
May there be no cries of **distress** in our
streets.

[15] **Happy** is the nation of whom this is
true;

above 138.6; 148.1
apart 60.2; Is 64.1
cruel 129.2; Prov 11.17
defend 140.7; Prov 21.22
distress 142.7; Is 5.3
enemy [2] 143.3; Prov 16.7
happy [2] 137.8; 146.
lie (2) [2] 120.2; Prov 4.24
loss Lev 12.4; Is 47.8
new 119.40; 149.1
notice (1) 106.44; Prov 7.7
oath [2] Neh 13.25; Ecc 9.2
plenty 104.16; Prov 7.20
power [2] 140.4; 145.11
praise 142.7; 145.2
protect [2] 143.9; 145.20
rescue [3] 143.9; Prov 11.6
safe 143.10; 147.14
save [2] 143.11; 145.19
Saviour 89.26; Is 12.2
scatter 141.7; 147.16
servant 143.2; Prov 9.3
sheep 119.176; Prov 27.23
shelter 71.3; Is 4.6
strong 142.6; 147.10
true 141.6; Prov 4.24
trust 143.8; 146.3
truth [2] 119.18; Prov 8.7
victory 140.9; 149.4

[m] distress; *or* prison. [n] HEBREW TITLE: *A psalm by David.* [o] HEBREW TITLE: *By David.*

143.2: Rom 3.20; Gal 2.16 **144.3:** Job 7.17–18; Ps 8.4

act [3] 119.126; Prov 3.31
anger 138.7; Prov 6.34
compassion 119.156; Is 30.19
constant 143.8; 147.11
creature [2] 136.25; 150.6
destroy 143.12; Prov 1.32
enough 106.2; Prov 13.25
eternal 138.8; Is 9.6
faithful 143.1; 149.1
glory [3] 138.5; 148.13
help 142.1; 146.5
holy 138.2; Prov 9.10
honour 141.5; 147.11
hope 143.7; Prov 10.28
kind 141.5; Prov 10.32
Kingdom (1) (of God) 89.14; Is 9.7
love [3] 143.8; 146.8
Majesty [2] 111.3; Song 5.15
mercy [3] 123.2; Prov 5.9
might [4] 136.3; 147.5
name (2) (name of God, of Jesus) 139.20; 148.5
need [3] 140.12; Prov 3.27
power 144.7; Prov 6.3
praise [6] 144.1; 146.1
proclaim [3] 135.13; Is 14.28
promise 143.11; 146.6
protect 144.1; 146.9
righteous 143.1; 146.8
satisfy 132.15; 147.14
save 144.7; 146.3
sincere 78.36; Jer 3.10
thank [3] 138.1; Is 12.4
trouble 143.11; Prov 1.26
understand 139.2; Prov 1.2
wicked 141.4; 146.9
wonder (1) 139.14; Song 5.9

happy are the people whose God is
the LORD!

A Hymn of Praise[p]

145 I will **proclaim** your
greatness, my God and
king;
I will **thank** you for ever and ever.
2 Every day I will **thank** you;
I will **praise** you for ever and ever.
3 The LORD is great and is to be highly
praised;
his greatness is beyond
understanding.

4 What you have done will be **praised**
from one generation to the next;
they will **proclaim** your **mighty acts**.
5 They will speak of your **glory** and
majesty,
and I will meditate on your
wonderful deeds.
6 People will speak of your **mighty**
deeds,
and I will **proclaim** your greatness.
7 They will tell about all your goodness
and sing about your **kindness**.
8 The LORD is **loving** and **merciful**,
slow to become **angry** and full of
constant love.
9 He is good to everyone
and has **compassion** on all he made.

10 All your **creatures**, LORD, will **praise**
you,
and all your people will give you
thanks.
11 They will speak of the **glory** of your
royal **power**
and tell of your **might**,
12 so that everyone will know your
mighty deeds
and the **glorious majesty** of your
kingdom.
13 Your rule is **eternal**,
and you are king for ever.

The LORD is **faithful** to his **promises**,
and he is **merciful** in all his **acts**.
14 He **helps** those who are in **trouble**;
he lifts those who have fallen.

15 All living things look **hopefully** to you,
and you give them food when they
need it.
16 You give them **enough**
and **satisfy** the **needs** of all.

17 The LORD is **righteous** in all he does,
merciful in all his **acts**.
18 He is near to those who call to him,
who call to him with **sincerity**.
19 He supplies the **needs** of those who
honour him;
he hears their cries and **saves** them.
20 He **protects** everyone who **loves** him,
but he will **destroy** the **wicked**.

21 I will always **praise** the LORD;
let all his **creatures praise** his **holy**
name for ever.

In Praise of God the Saviour

146 Praise the LORD!
Praise the LORD, my **soul**!
2 I will **praise** him as long as I live;
I will sing to my God all my **life**.

3 Don't put your **trust** in **human** leaders;
no **human being** can **save** you.
4 When they die, they return to the dust;
on that day all their **plans** come to
an end.

5 **Happy** is the man who has the God of
Jacob to **help** him
and who **depends** on the LORD his
God,
6 the **Creator** of **heaven**, earth, and
sea,
and all that is in them.
He always keeps his **promises**;
7 he **judges** in **favour** of the **oppressed**
and gives food to the **hungry**.

The LORD sets **prisoners free**
8 and gives **sight** to the **blind**.
He lifts those who have fallen;
he **loves** his **righteous** people.
9 He **protects** the **strangers** who live in
our land;
he **helps widows** and **orphans**,
but takes the **wicked** to their **ruin**.

10 The LORD is king for ever.
Your God, O Zion, will **reign** for all
time.

Praise the LORD!

In Praise of God the Almighty

147 Praise the LORD!

It is good to sing **praise** to our God;
it is pleasant and **right** to **praise** him.
2 The LORD is **restoring** Jerusalem;
he is bringing back the **exiles**.
3 He **heals** the **broken-hearted**
and bandages their wounds.

4 He has decided the number of the stars
and calls each one by name.

being 103.1; Ecc 3.19
blind 69.23; Is 6.10
Creator Job 40.19; 149.2
depend 123.2; Prov 11.28
favour 106.31; Prov 3.34
free 142.7; Prov 11.24
happy 144.15; Prov 3.13
heaven 139.8; 148.1
help [2] 145.14; Prov 1.2
human [2] 135.15; Prov 8.31
hunger 107.5; Prov 6.30
judge 127.5; Prov 8.12
life (1) 142.5; Prov 1.19
love 145.8; 147.11
oppress 143.12; Prov 14.31
orphan 109.9; Prov 23.10
plan 103.7; Prov 3.29
praise [4] 145.2; 147.1
prison 143.3; Ecc 4.13
promise 145.13; Prov 6.1
protect 145.20; Prov 2.7
reign Esth 1.3; Jer 1.3
righteous 145.17; Prov 2.7
ruin 109.10; Prov 7.26
save 145.19; Prov 10.2
sight 143.2; Prov 23.33
soul 143.6; Prov 24.14
stranger 109.11; Prov 5.10
trust 144.2; 147.11
wicked 145.20; 147.6
widow 109.9; Prov 15.25

bless 134.3; Prov 3.33
cloud 135.7; 148.8
command [2] 138.2; 148.5
constant 145.8; Prov 15.15
delight 119.14; Song 1.16
endure 132.1; Prov 28.2
exile 42.6; Is 27.8
God's people 136.14; 148.14
heal 107.20; Prov 3.8

[p] HEBREW TITLE: *A song of praise by David.*
146.6: Acts 4.24, 14.15

heart 139.14; Prov 3.3
honour 145.19; 149.4
humble 76.12; 149.4
hymn 71.22; Mt 26.30
law [2] 119.1; Prov 8.15
love 146.8; Prov 3.12
message 19.4; Prov 26.6
might 145.4; 150.2
pleasure [2] 119.16; 149.4
praise [7] 146.1; 148.1
provide 132.5; Prov 2.7
raise 134.2; Prov 1.6
restore 122.3; Song 2.5
right (1) 132.9; Prov 2.9
safe 144.2; Prov 1.33
satisfy 145.16; Prov 6.35
scatter 144.6; Is 11.12
strong [2] 144.12; 148.8
trust 146.3; Prov 2.15
wicked 146.9; Prov 2.22
wisdom 136.5; Prov 1.2

5 Great and **mighty** is our Lord;
his **wisdom** cannot be measured.
6 He **raises** the **humble**,
but crushes the **wicked** to the
ground.

7 Sing **hymns** of **praise** to the LORD;
play music on the harp to our God.
8 He spreads **clouds** over the sky;
he **provides** rain for the earth
and makes grass grow on the hills.
9 He gives animals their food
and feeds the young ravens when
they call.

10 His **pleasure** is not in **strong** horses,
nor his **delight** in brave soldiers;
11 but he takes **pleasure** in those who
honour him,
in those who **trust** in his **constant**
love.

12 **Praise** the LORD, O Jerusalem!
Praise your God, O Zion!
13 He keeps your gates **strong**;
he **blesses** your people.
14 He keeps your borders **safe**
and **satisfies** you with the finest
wheat.

15 He gives a **command** to the earth,
and what he says is quickly done.
16 He spreads snow like a blanket
and **scatters** frost like dust.
17 He sends hail like gravel;
no one can **endure** the cold he
sends!
18 Then he gives a **command**, and the ice
melts;
he sends the wind, and the water
flows.

19 He gives his **message** to **his people**,
his instructions and **laws** to Israel.
20 He has not done this for other nations;
they do not know his **laws**.

Praise the LORD!

A Call for the Universe to Praise God

above 144.7; Is 24.21
angel 103.20; Is 37.36
cloud 147.8; Prov 3.20
command [3] 147.15; 149.9
create 139.13; Prov 3.19
dear 78.68; Prov 31.2
disobey 119.10; Is 65.12
glory 145.5; Prov 4.9
God's people 147.19; 149.4

148

Praise the LORD!

Praise the LORD from **heaven**,
you that live in the heights **above**.
2 **Praise** him, all his **angels**,
all his **heavenly** armies.

3 **Praise** him, sun and moon;
praise him, shining stars.
4 **Praise** him, highest **heavens**,
and the waters above the sky.[q]

5 Let them all **praise** the **name of the**
LORD!
He **commanded**, and they were
created;
6 by his **command** they were fixed in
their places for ever,
and they cannot **disobey**.[r]

7 **Praise** the LORD from the earth,
sea-monsters and all ocean depths;
8 lightning and hail, snow and **clouds**,
strong winds that **obey** his
command.

9 **Praise** him, hills and mountains,
fruit-trees and forests;
10 all animals, tame and wild,
reptiles and birds.

11 **Praise** him, kings and all peoples,
princes and all other rulers;
12 girls and young men,
old people and children too.

13 Let them all **praise** the **name of the**
LORD!
His **name** is greater than all others;
his **glory** is above **earth and heaven**.
14 He made his nation **strong**,
so that all **his people praise** him—
the people of Israel, so **dear** to him.

Praise the LORD!

heaven [4] 146.6; 150.1
monster 104.26; Is 27.1
name (2) (name of God, of Jesus) [3] 145.21; 149.3
obey 128.1; Prov 1.2
praise [13] 147.1; 149.1
strong [2] 147.10; Prov 8.14

A Hymn of Praise

149

Praise the LORD!

Sing a **new** song to the LORD;
praise him in the assembly of his
faithful people!
2 Be **glad**, Israel, because of your
Creator;
rejoice, people of Zion, because of
your king!
3 **Praise** his **name** with dancing;
play drums and harps in **praise** of
him.

4 The LORD takes **pleasure** in **his people**;
he **honours** the **humble** with **victory**.
5 Let **God's people rejoice** in their
triumph
and sing **joyfully** all night long.
6 Let them shout aloud as they **praise**
God,
with their sharp swords in their
hands
7 to defeat the nations

bind Job 40.13; Is 52.2
command 148.5; Ecc 8.5
Creator 146.6; Ecc 12.1
faithful 145.13; Prov 3.3
glad 122.1; Prov 22.18
God's people [3] 148.14; Is 1.3
honour 147.11; Prov 3.9
humble 147.6; Prov 3.34
joy 137.6; Prov 5.18
name (2) (name of God, of Jesus) 148.5; Is 19.18
new 144.9; Prov 19.4
pleasure 147.10; Prov 2.10
praise [6] 148.1; 150.1
punish [2] 141.5; Prov 10.13
rejoice [2] 105.3; Prov 24.17
triumph 108.7; Is 41.2
victory [2] 144.10; Prov 21.31

[q] WATERS ABOVE THE SKY: *See Gen 1.6–7.*
[r] by his command...disobey; *or* he has fixed them in their places for all time, by a command that lasts for ever.

and to **punish** the peoples;
8 to **bind** their kings in chains,
their leaders in chains of iron;
9 to **punish** the nations as God has
commanded.
This is the **victory** of God's **people**.

Praise the LORD!

Praise the LORD!

creature 145.10; Ecc 3.19
heaven 148.1; Prov 30.4
might 147.5; Is 9.6

150

Praise the LORD!

Praise God in his **Temple**!
Praise his **strength** in **heaven**!
2 Praise him for the **mighty** things he
has done.
Praise his **supreme** greatness.

3 **Praise** him with trumpets.
Praise him with harps and lyres.
4 Praise him with drums and dancing.
Praise him with harps and flutes.
5 Praise him with cymbals.
Praise him with loud cymbals.
6 **Praise** the LORD, all living **creatures**!

Praise the LORD!

praise [13] 149.1; Prov 11.26
strength 138.3; Prov 20.29
supreme 138.2; Dan 3.26
Temple (1) (of God) 138.2; Ecc 5.1

THE BOOK OF PROVERBS

INTRODUCTION

The book of *Proverbs* is a collection of moral and religious teachings in the form of sayings and proverbs. Much of it has to do with practical, everyday concerns. It begins with the reminder that "To have knowledge, you must first have reverence for the LORD," and then goes on to deal with matters not only of religious morality, but also of common sense and good manners. Its many short sayings reveal the insights of ancient Israelite teachers about what a wise person will do in certain situations. Some of these concern family relations, others business dealings. Some deal with matters of etiquette in social relationships, and others with the need for self-control. Much is said about such qualities as humility, patience, respect for the poor, and loyalty to friends.

Outline of Contents

In praise of wisdom 1.1—9.18
The proverbs of Solomon 10.1—29.27
The words of Agur 30.1-33
Various sayings 31.1-31

---

action Ps 139.3; 16.9
advice [4] Ps 106.13; 6.22
afraid Ps 119.120; 3.24
alive Ps 124.3; 26.21
appearance 1 Sam 16.7; Is 11.3
bad Ps 120.5; 6.24
claim Ps 35.26; 19.6
concern Ps 131.1; 23.17
correct [2] Ps 50.17; 3.11
dead Ps 115.17; 27.22
deserve Ps 103.10; 12.14
destroy Ps 145.20; 6.32
enjoy Ps 72.3; 2.14
fool [2] Ps 107.17; 7.7
guide Ps 143.10; 11.3
help Ps 146.5; 2.7
honest Ps 112.5; 2.7
ignore Ps 66.18; 4.5
innocent Ps 143.2; 6.16
intelligent 1 Kgs 7.14; 10.13
justice Ps 119.106; 2.9
knowledge [5] Ps 139.6; 2.3
learn [2] Ps 119.7; 2.1
life (1) Ps 146.2; 2.13
misery Ps 113.7; 23.29
mock Ps 123.4; Is 14.4
obey Ps 148.8; 3.7
pain Ps 116.15; 3.8
proverb [4] Ps 49.4; 10.1
raise Ps 147.6; Song 2.4
reason Ps 109.3; 3.30
refuse (1) [2] Ps 95.10; 3.7
reject Ps 132.10; 9.12

The Value of Proverbs

1 The **proverbs** of Solomon, son of
David and king of Israel.
2 Here are **proverbs** that will **help** you
to recognize **wisdom** and good **advice**,
and **understand sayings** with deep meaning. 3 They can **teach** you how to live
intelligently and how to be **honest**, **just**,
and fair. 4 They can make an inexperi-
enced person clever and **teach** young
men how to be resourceful. 5 These **pro-**
verbs can even add to the **knowledge** of
wise men and give **guidance** to the educated, 6 so that they can **understand** the
hidden meanings of **proverbs** and the
problems that **wise** men **raise**.

Advice to Young Men

7 To have **knowledge**, you must first
have **reverence** for the LORD.[a] **Stupid**
people have no **respect** for **wisdom** and
refuse to **learn**.
8 Pay attention to what your father
and mother tell you, my son. 9 Their
teaching will improve your character as
a handsome turban or a necklace im-
proves your **appearance**.
10 When sinners **tempt** you, my son,
don't give in. 11 Suppose they say, "Come
on; let's find someone to kill! Let's
attack some **innocent** people for the fun
of it! 12 They may be **alive** and well when
we find them, but they'll be **dead** when
we're through with them! 13 We'll find all
kinds of **riches** and fill our houses with
loot! 14 Come and join us, and we'll all
share what we **steal**."
15 Don't go with people like that, my
son. Stay away from them. 16 They can't
wait to do something **bad**. They're always ready to kill. 17 It does no good to
spread a net when the bird you want to
catch is **watching**, 18 but men like that are
setting a **trap** for themselves, a **trap** in
which they will die. 19 **Robbery** always
claims the **life** of the robber—this is what
happens to[b] anyone who lives by **vio-**
lence.

Wisdom Calls

20 Listen! **Wisdom** is calling out in the
streets and market-places, 21 calling
loudly at the city gates and wherever
people come together:
22 "**Foolish** people! How long do you
want to be **foolish**? How long will you
enjoy pouring **scorn** on **knowledge**? Will
you never **learn**? 23 Listen when I **repri-**
mand you; I will give you good **advice**
and **share** my **knowledge** with you. 24 I
have been calling you, inviting you to
come, but you would not listen. You paid
no attention to me. 25 You have **ignored**
all my **advice** and have not been willing
to let me **correct** you. 26 So when you get
into **trouble**, I will laugh at you. I will
mock you when **terror strikes**—27 when it
comes on you like a storm, bringing

reprimand Ps 119.21; 9.7
respect Ps 119.48; 5.9
reverence Ps 60.4; 9.10
riches Ps 62.10; 8.18
rob Ps 62.10; 6.11
safe Ps 147.14; 3.17
saying Ps 78.2; 22.20
scorn Ps 123.4; 11.12
secure Ps 119.165; 10.9
share [2] Ps 106.5; 14.10
steal Ps 89.41; 6.30
strike Ps 91.6; 6.15
stupid [2] Ps 94.8; 3.35
teach [3] Ps 143.10; 2.1
tempt Deut 4.19; 6.25
terror Ps 55.4; Is 17.14
trap [2] Ps 142.3; 3.26
trouble [2] Ps 145.14; 2.12
understand [2] Ps 145.3; 2.2
violent Ps 140.1; 3.31
watch Ps 130.6; 5.21
wisdom [5] Ps 147.5; 2.6
wise [2] Ps 119.98; 2.2

[a] To...LORD; *or* The most important part of knowledge is having reverence for the LORD.
[b] *One ancient translation* what happens to; *Hebrew* the path of.

1.1: 1 Kgs 4.32 **1.7:** Job 28.28; Ps 111.10; Prov 9.10 **1.20-21:** Prov 8.1-3

fierce winds of trouble, and you are in
pain and misery. 28 Then you will call for
wisdom, but I will not answer. You may
look for me everywhere, but you will not
find me. 29 You have never had any use
for knowledge and have always refused
to obey the LORD. 30 You have never
wanted my advice or paid any attention
when I corrected you. 31 So then, you will
get what you deserve, and your own
actions will make you sick. 32 Inexperienced people die because they reject wisdom. Stupid people are destroyed by
their own lack of concern. 33 But whoever
listens to me will have security. He will
be safe, with no reason to be afraid."

The Rewards of Wisdom

2 Learn what I teach you, my son, and
never forget what I tell you to do.
2 Listen to what is wise and try to understand it. 3 Yes, beg for knowledge; plead
for insight. 4 Look for it as hard as you
would for silver or some hidden treasure.
5 If you do, you will know what it means
to fear the LORD and you will succeed in
learning about God. 6 It is the LORD who
gives wisdom; from him come knowledge and understanding. 7 He provides
help and protection for righteous, honest
men. 8 He protects those who treat others
fairly, and guards those who are devoted
to him.
9 If you listen to me, you will know
what is right, just, and fair. You will
know what you should do. 10 You will become wise, and your knowledge will give
you pleasure. 11 Your insight and understanding will protect you 12 and prevent
you from doing the wrong thing. They
will keep you away from people who stir
up trouble by what they say—13 men who
have abandoned a righteous life to live in
the darkness of sin, 14 men who find pleasure in doing wrong and who enjoy
senseless evil, 15 unreliable men who cannot be trusted.
16 You will be able to resist any
immoral woman who tries to seduce you
with her smooth talk, 17 who is faithless to
her own husband and forgets her sacred
vows. 18 If you go to her house, you are
travelling the road to death. To go there
is to approach the world of the dead.
19 No one who visits her ever comes back.
He never returns to the road to life. 20 So
you must follow the example of good
men and live a righteous life. 21 Righteous
men—men of integrity—will live in this
land of ours. 22 But God will snatch
wicked men from the land and pull sinners out of it like plants from the ground.

abandon Ps 125.5; 4.6
beg Ps 116.4; 6.3
dark Ps 143.3; 4.19
death (1) Ps 116.3; 5.5
devote Ps 86.11; Ecc 7.25
enjoy 1.22; 10.23
evil Ps 141.4; 3.32
example Ps 71.7; 4.14
faithless Ezra 10.10; Jer 31.22
fear Ps 139.14; 10.24
forget [2] Ps 137.5; 3.1
hard Ps 127.2; 10.4
help 1.2; 3.28
honest 1.3; 4.25
immoral Judg 20.6; 23.27
insight [2] Job 12.12; 3.21
justice 1.3; 8.20
knowledge [3] 1.5; 3.19
learn [2] 1.7; 4.13
life (1) [3] 1.19; 3.2
life (2) (to life) Ps 16.11; 5.6
plead Ps 143.1; Jer 3.21
pleasure [2] Ps 149.4; 10.23
prevent Ps 106.23; 18.5
protect [3] Ps 146.9; 4.6
provide Ps 147.8; 3.22
rely Ps 78.57; 3.5
resist 2 Chr 26.18; 25.15
right (1) Ps 147.1; 3.6
righteous [4] Ps 146.8; 3.32
sacred Ps 110.3; Is 1.29
sense Ps 94.11; 6.32
succeed (1) Ps 140.8; 8.18
teach 1.3; 3.1
trouble 1.26; 6.14
trust Ps 147.11; 3.5
understand [3] 1.2; 3.13
vow Ps 132.2; Is 45.23
wicked Ps 147.6; 3.25
wisdom 1.2; 3.15
wise [2] 1.5; 3.7
world of the dead Ps 143.7; 5.5
wrong [2] Ps 141.4; 3.7

Advice to Young Men

3 Don't forget what I teach you, my
son. Always remember what I tell
you to do. 2 My teaching will give you a
long and prosperous life. 3 Never let go of
loyalty and faithfulness. Tie them round
your neck; write them on your heart. 4 If
you do this, both God and man will be
pleased with you.
5 Trust in the LORD with all your
heart. Never rely on what you think you
know. 6 Remember the LORD in everything you do, and he will show you the
right way. 7 Never let yourself think that
you are wiser than you are; simply obey
the LORD and refuse to do wrong. 8 If you
do, it will be like good medicine, healing
your wounds and easing your pains.
9 Honour the LORD by making him an
offering from the best of all that your
land produces. 10 If you do, your barns
will be filled with grain, and you will
have too much wine to be able to store it
all.
11 When the LORD corrects you, my
son, pay close attention and take it as a
warning. 12 The LORD corrects those he
loves, as a father corrects a son of whom
he is proud. 13 Happy is the man who becomes wise—who gains understanding.
14 There is more profit in it than there is
in silver; it is worth more to you than
gold. 15 Wisdom is more valuable than
jewels; nothing you could want can compare with it. 16 Wisdom offers you long
life, as well as wealth and honour. 17 Wisdom can make your life pleasant and
lead you safely through it. 18 Those who
become wise are happy; wisdom will
give them life.
19 The LORD created the earth by his
wisdom;
by his knowledge he set the sky in
place.
20 His wisdom caused the rivers to flow
and the clouds to give rain to the
earth.
21 Hold on to your wisdom and insight,
my son. Never let them get away from
you. 22 They will provide you with life—a
pleasant and happy life. 23 You can go
safely on your way and never even
stumble. 24 You will not be afraid when
you go to bed, and you will sleep soundly
through the night. 25 You will not have to
worry about sudden disasters, such as
come on the wicked like a storm. 26 The
LORD will keep you safe. He will not let
you fall into a trap.
27 Whenever you possibly can, do
good to those who need it. 28 Never tell

act Ps 145.4; 13.16
afraid 1.33; 26.13
argue Job 33.5; 15.18
best Ps 78.31; 21.29
bless Ps 147.13; 10.6
cloud Ps 148.8; 8.28
compare Job 41.33; 8.11
conceited 9.7
confident Ps 116.7; 4.25
correct [2] 1.25; 5.12
create Ps 148.5; 8.22
curse Ps 119.21; 11.26
disaster Ps 91.10; 6.15
disgrace Ps 109.29; 5.14
evil 2.14; 4.14
faithful Ps 149.1; 5.15
favour Ps 146.7; 11.17
forget 2.1; 4.4
get away Ps 139.7; 4.21
happy [3] Ps 146.5; 5.18
harm Ps 141.10; 16.27
hate Ps 139.21; 6.16
heal Ps 147.3; 12.18
heart [2] Ps 147.3; 4.21
help 2.7; 5.17
honour [3] Ps 149.4; 4.8
humble Ps 149.4; 14.19
hurt Ps 121.6; 4.16
insight 2.3; 4.5
jealous Ps 106.16; 6.34
knowledge 2.3; 5.2
life (1) [5] 2.13; 4.10
love Ps 147.11; 4.6
loyal Ps 119.113; 16.6
need Ps 145.15; 10.13
neighbour [2] Ps 89.41; 14.20
obey 1.29; 10.27
offer [2] Ps 116.12; 7.14
pain 1.27; 5.4
plan Ps 146.4; 4.26
please Ps 104.34; 8.31
prosper Ps 132.18; 8.18
proud Ps 140.5; 6.16
provide 2.7; 27.27
reason 1.33; 8.1
refuse (1) 1.7; 4.15
rely 2.15; 13.17
remember [2] Ps 143.5; 4.2
reputation Job 19.9; 22.1
right (1) 2.9; 4.11
righteous [2] 2.7; 4.18
safe [3] 1.33; 4.6
sound (2) Ps 111.10; 8.12
stumble Ps 107.27; 4.12
stupid 1.7; 5.23
teach [2] 2.1; 4.1
trap 1.18; 5.22
trust [2] 2.15; 11.3
understand 2.2; 4.1
value Ps 44.12; 20.15
violent 1.19; 4.17
warn Ps 106.26; 6.15
wicked [2] 2.22; 4.14
wisdom [7] 2.6; 4.5
wise [4] 2.2; 4.12
worry Ps 112.8; 12.25
worth Ps 37.16; 23.23
wrong 2.12; 4.16

3.4: Lk 2.52 **3.7:** Rom 12.16 **3.11:** Job 5.17 **3.11–12:** Heb 12.5–6 **3.12:** Rev 3.19

your neighbour to wait until tomorrow if
you can help him now. 29Don't plan anything that will hurt your neighbour; he
lives beside you, trusting you. 30Don't
argue with someone for no reason when
he has never done you any harm. 31Don't
be jealous of violent people or decide to
act as they do, 32because the LORD hates
people who do evil, but he takes righteous men into his confidence. 33The
LORD puts a curse on the homes of
wicked men, but blesses the homes of the
righteous. 34He has no use for conceited
people, but shows favour to those who
are humble. 35Wise men will gain an honourable reputation, but stupid men will
only add to their own disgrace.

The Benefits of Wisdom

4 Listen to what your father teaches
you, my sons. Pay attention, and you
will have understanding. 2What I am
teaching you is good, so remember it all.
3When I was only a little boy, my
parents' only son, 4my father would
teach me. He would say, "Remember
what I say and never forget it. Do as I tell
you, and you will live. 5Get wisdom and
insight! Do not forget or ignore what I
say. 6Do not abandon wisdom, and she
will protect you; love her, and she will
keep you safe. 7Getting wisdom is the
most important thing you can do. Whatever else you get, get insight. 8Love wisdom, and she will make you great. Embrace her,[c] and she will bring you honour. 9She will be your crowning glory."
10 Listen to me, my son. Take
seriously what I am telling you, and you
will live a long life. 11I have taught you
wisdom and the right way to live. 12Noth-
ing will stand in your way if you walk
wisely, and you will not stumble when
you run. 13Always remember what you
have learnt. Your education is your life—
guard it well. 14Do not go where evil men
go. Do not follow the example of the
wicked. 15Don't do it! Keep away from
evil! Refuse it and go on your way.
16Wicked people cannot sleep unless they
have done something wrong. They lie
awake unless they have hurt someone.
17Wickedness and violence are like food
and drink to them.
18 The road the righteous travel is like
the sunrise, getting brighter and brighter
until daylight has come. 19The road of
the wicked, however, is dark as night.
They fall, but cannot see what they have
stumbled over.
20 Pay attention to what I say, my son.
Listen to my words. 21Never let them get
away from you. Remember them and
keep them in your heart. 22They will give
life and health to anyone who understands them. 23Be careful how you think;
your life is shaped by your thoughts.
24Never say anything that isn't true.
Have nothing to do with lies and misleading words. 25Look straight ahead with
honest confidence; don't hang your head
in shame. 26Plan carefully what you do,
and whatever you do will turn out right.
27Avoid evil and walk straight ahead.
Don't go one step off the right way.

Warning against Adultery

5 Pay attention, my son, and listen to
my wisdom and insight. 2Then you
will know how to behave properly, and
your words will show that you have
knowledge. 3The lips of another man's
wife may be as sweet as honey and her
kisses as smooth as olive-oil, 4but when it
is all over, she leaves you nothing but
bitterness and pain. 5She will take you
down to the world of the dead; the road
she walks is the road to death. 6She does
not stay on the road to life; but wanders
off, and does not realize what is happening.
7 Now listen to me, my sons, and
never forget what I am saying. 8Keep
away from such a woman! Don't even go
near her door! 9If you do, others will
gain the respect that you once had, and
you will die young at the hands of merciless men. 10Yes, strangers will take all
your wealth, and what you have worked
for will belong to someone else. 11You
will lie groaning on your deathbed, your
flesh and muscles being eaten away,
12and you will say, "Why would I never
learn? Why would I never let anyone
correct me? 13I wouldn't listen to my
teachers. I paid no attention to them.
14And suddenly I found myself[d] publicly
disgraced."
15 Be faithful to your own wife and
give your love to her alone. 16Children
that you have by other women will do
you no good. 17Your children should
grow up to help you, not strangers. 18So
be happy with your wife and find your
joy with the girl you married—19pretty
and graceful as a deer. Let her charms
keep you happy; let her surround you
with her love. 20Why should you give
your love to another woman, my son?
Why should you prefer the charms of
another man's wife? 21The LORD sees
everything you do. Wherever you go, he

abandon 2.13; Is 2.20
confident 3.32; 11.7
crown Ps 89.39; 16.31
dark 2.13; 7.9
evil [3] 3.32; 6.14
example 2.20; 23.26
forget [2] 3.1; 5.7
get away 3.21; Ecc 7.26
glory Ps 148.13; 16.31
heart 3.3; 6.21
honest 2.7; 10.2
honour 3.9; 8.13
hurt 3.29; 8.36
ignore 1.25; 12.16
important Ps 119.141; 18.16
insight [2] 3.21; 5.1
learn 2.1; 5.12
lie (2) Ps 144.8; 6.12
life (1) [4] 3.2; 5.6
love [2] 3.12; 5.15
mislead 2 Chr 32.15; 8.8
plan 3.29; 6.14
protect 2.7; 6.22
refuse (1) 3.7; 13.13
remember [4] 3.1; 7.1
right (1) [3] 3.6; 8.6
righteous 3.32; 8.20
safe 3.17; 10.9
serious Esth 7.4; 23.19
shame Ps 132.18; 7.11
stumble [2] 3.23; 24.17
teach [4] 3.1; 6.20
true Ps 144.15; 8.8
turn Ps 139.11; 13.19
understand [2] 3.13; 8.14
violent 3.31; 10.6
wicked [4] 3.25; 5.22
wisdom [5] 3.15; 5.1
wise 3.7; 8.33
word (1) [2] Ps 141.6; 5.2
wrong 3.7; 10.17

alone Ps 139.19; Ecc 4.8
bitter Ps 106.33; 14.10
correct 3.11; 6.23
death (1) [2] 2.18; 7.26
disgrace 3.35; 6.33
faithful 3.3; 16.6
flesh Ps 50.13; Lam 3.4
forget 4.4; 6.20
grace Neh 9.17; 11.16
grave Ps 141.7; 28.17
groan Ps 102.5; Is 16.11
happy [2] 3.13; 7.18
help 3.28; 8.15
insight 4.5; 7.4
joy Ps 149.5; 8.30
kiss Job 31.27; 7.13
knowledge 3.19; 8.10
learn 4.13; 6.6
life (1) 4.10; 7.23
life (2) (to life) 2.19; 12.28
love [3] 4.6; 7.18
mercy Ps 145.8; 21.10
pain 3.8; 20.30
proper Ps 51.19; Ecc 10.17
respect 1.7; 9.8
self-control Acts 24.25
stranger [2] Ps 146.9; 11.15
stupid 3.35; 9.13
teacher Ps 119.99; 23.12
trap 3.26; 6.2
watch 1.17; 14.15
wicked 4.14; 6.12
wisdom 4.5; 7.4
word (1) 4.20; 6.2
world of the dead 2.18; 7.27

[c] Embrace her; *or* Prize her highly. [d] And suddenly...myself; *or* I was about to be.

3.34: Jas 4.6; 1 Pet 5.5 **4.26:** Heb 12.13

is **watching**. 22 The sins of a **wicked** man are a **trap**. He gets caught in the net of his own sin. 23 He dies because he has no **self-control**. His utter **stupidity** will send him to his **grave**.

More Warnings

6 Have you **promised** to be responsible for someone else's **debts**, my son? 2 Have you been caught by your own **words**, **trapped** by your own **promises**? 3 Well then, my son, you are in that man's **power**, but this is how to get out of it: hurry to him, and **beg** him to release you. 4 Don't let yourself go to sleep or even stop to **rest**. 5 Get out of the **trap** like a bird or a deer **escaping** from a hunter.

6 Lazy people should **learn** a **lesson** from the way ants live. 7 They have no leader, chief, or ruler, 8 but they store up their food during the summer, getting ready for winter. 9 How long is the lazy man going to lie in bed? When is he ever going to get up? 10 "I'll just take a short nap," he says; "I'll fold my hands and **rest** a while." 11 But while he sleeps, **poverty** will attack him like an armed **robber**.

12 **Worthless**, **wicked** people go around telling **lies**. 13 They wink and make gestures to **deceive** you, 14 all the while **planning** **evil** in their **perverted** **minds**, stirring up **trouble** everywhere. 15 Because of this, **disaster** will **strike** them without **warning**, and they will be fatally wounded.

16–19 There are seven things that the LORD **hates** and cannot **tolerate**:

A **proud** look,
a **lying** tongue,
hands that kill **innocent** people,
a **mind** that thinks up **wicked** **plans**,
feet that hurry off to do evil,
a **witness** who tells one **lie** after another,
and a man who stirs up **trouble** among **friends**.

Warning against Adultery

20 Do what your father tells you, my son, and never **forget** what your mother **taught** you. 21 Keep their **words** with you always, locked in your **heart**. 22 Their **teaching** will lead you when you travel, **protect** you at night, and **advise** you during the day. 23 Their instructions are a shining **light**; their **correction** can **teach** you how to live. 24 It can keep you away from **bad** women, from the seductive **words** of other men's wives. 25 Don't be **tempted** by their beauty; don't be **trapped** by their flirting eyes. 26 A man can hire a **prostitute** for the price of a loaf of **bread**, but **adultery** will cost him all he has.

27 Can you carry fire against your chest without burning your clothes? 28 Can you walk on hot coals without burning your feet? 29 It is just as **dangerous** to sleep with another man's wife. Whoever does it will **suffer**. 30 People don't **despise** a **thief** if he **steals** food when he is **hungry**;[e] 31 yet if he is caught, he must pay back seven times more—he must give up everything he has. 32 But a man who **commits** **adultery** hasn't any **sense**. He is just **destroying** himself. 33 He will be **dishonoured** and beaten up; he will be permanently **disgraced**. 34 A husband is never **angrier** than when he is **jealous**; his **revenge** knows no limits. 35 He will not **accept** any payment; no amount of **gifts** will **satisfy** his **anger**.

7 **Remember** what I say, my son, and never **forget** what I tell you to do. 2 Do what I say, and you will live. Be as careful to follow my **teaching** as you are to **protect** your eyes. 3 Keep my **teaching** with you all the time; write it on your **heart**. 4 Treat **wisdom** as your sister, and **insight** as your closest **friend**. 5 They will keep you away from other men's wives, from women with seductive **words**.

The Immoral Woman

6 Once I was looking out of the window of my house, 7 and I saw many inexperienced young men, but **noticed** one **foolish** fellow in particular. 8 He was walking along the street near the corner where a certain woman lived. He was passing near her house 9 in the evening after it was **dark**. 10 And then she met him; she was dressed like a **prostitute** and was making **plans**. 11 She was a **bold** and **shameless** woman who always walked the streets 12 or stood waiting at a corner, sometimes in the streets, sometimes in the market-place. 13 She threw her arms round the young man, **kissed** him, looked him straight in the eye, and said, 14 "I made my **offerings** today and have the meat from the **sacrifices**. 15 So I came out looking for you. I wanted to find you, and here you are! 16 I've covered my bed with sheets of coloured linen from Egypt. 17 I've perfumed it with myrrh, aloes, and cinnamon. 18 Come on!

[e] People don't despise...hungry; *or* Don't people despise...hungry?

6.10–11: Prov 24.33–34

accept Ps 141.5; 10.8
adultery [2] Ps 50.18; 22.14
advice 1.2; 10.8
anger [2] Ps 145.8; 11.23
bad 1.16; 12.21
beg 2.3; 14.19
bread Ps 104.15; 9.17
commit Deut 27.24; 30.20
correct 5.12; 9.7
danger Ps 121.7; 7.23
debt Job 24.3; 11.15
deceive Ps 120.2; 12.5
despise Ps 139.21; 14.21
destroy 1.32; 10.15
disaster 3.25; 16.29
disgrace 5.14; 10.5
dishonour Ps 69.19; Is 48.11
escape Ps 139.7; 11.21
evil [2] 4.14; 8.13
forget 5.7; 7.1
friend Ps 122.8; 7.4
gift Ps 127.3; 18.16
hate 3.32; 8.7
heart 4.21; 7.3
hunger Ps 146.7; 10.3
innocent 1.11; 13.6
jealous 3.31; 14.30
learn 5.12; 8.5
lesson Ps 2.10; 19.25
lie (2) [3] 4.24; 8.7
light (1) Ps 139.11; 13.9
mind (1) [2] Ps 143.5; 14.30
pervert Judg 20.13; 17.26
plan [2] 4.26; 7.10
poor Ps 140.12; 10.4
poverty *see* **poor**
power Ps 145.11; 12.24
promise [2] Ps 146.6; 11.15
prostitute 2 Kgs 23.7; 7.10
protect 4.6; 7.2
proud 3.12; 8.13
rest (1) [2] Ps 139.3; 24.33
revenge Esth 8.13; Is 1.24
rob 1.19; 12.25
satisfy Ps 147.14; 15.14
sense 2.14; 8.5
steal 1.14; 9.17
strike 1.26; 28.22
suffer Ps 119.50; 9.12
teach [3] 4.1; 7.2
tempt 1.10; 7.21
thief Ps 50.18; 28.24
tolerate Ps 101.3; 16.12
trap [3] 5.22; 7.22
trouble [2] 2.12; 10.10
warn 3.11; 25.12
wicked [2] 5.22; 10.3
witness Ps 89.37; 14.5
word (1) [3] 5.2; 7.5
worthless Ps 119.37; 10.20

bold Job 13.16; Dan 11.25
danger 6.29; 10.17
dark 4.19; 20.20
death (1) [2] 5.5; 8.36
each other Ps 64.5; 18.18
fool 1.22; 8.5
forget 6.20; 10.7
friend 6.16; 12.26
happy 5.18; 8.31
heart [3] 6.21; 13.12
insight 5.1; 8.9
kiss 5.3; Ecc 3.5
life (1) 5.6; 8.35
love 5.15; 8.17
notice (1) Ps 144.3; Ecc 3.16
offer 3.9; 20.25
plan 6.14; 8.14
plenty Ps 144.14; 12.11
prostitute 6.26; 23.27
protect 6.22; 10.15
remember 4.2; 10.7
ruin Ps 146.9; 10.8
sacrifice Ps 141.2; 15.8
shame 4.25; 9.13
slaughter Ps 44.11; Is 14.21
teach [2] 6.20; 8.33
tempt 6.25; 23.31
trap 6.2; 11.6
win Ps 108.13; 13.15
wisdom 5.1; 8.1
word (1) 6.2; 8.6
world of the dead 5.5; 9.18

Let's make **love** all night long. We'll be
happy in **each other's** arms. 19 My husband isn't at home. He's gone away on a
long journey. 20 He took **plenty** of money
with him and won't be back for two
weeks." 21 So she **tempted** him with her
charms, and he gave in to her smooth
talk. 22 Suddenly he was going with her
like an ox on the way to be **slaughtered**,
like a deer prancing into a **trap**[f] 23 where
an arrow would pierce its **heart**. He was
like a bird going into a net—he did not
know that his **life** was in **danger**.

24 Now then, my sons, listen to me.
Pay attention to what I say. 25 Do not let
such a woman **win** your **heart**; don't go
wandering after her. 26 She has been the
ruin of many men and caused the **death**
of too many to count. 27 If you go to her
house, you are on the way to the **world of
the dead**. It is a short cut to **death**.

In Praise of Wisdom

8 Listen! **Wisdom** is calling out.
Reason is making herself heard.
2 On the hilltops near the road
and at the cross-roads she stands.
3 At the entrance to the city,
beside the gates, she calls:
4 "I appeal to you, **mankind**;
I call to everyone on earth.
5 Are you immature? **Learn** to be
mature.
Are you **foolish**? **Learn** to have
sense.
6 Listen to my excellent **words**;
all I tell you is **right**.
7 What I say is the **truth**;
lies are **hateful** to me.
8 Everything I say is **true**;
nothing is **false** or **misleading**.
9 To the man with **insight**, it is all clear;
to the well-informed, it is all **plain**.
10 **Choose** my instruction instead of
silver;
choose knowledge rather than the
finest gold.

11 "I am **Wisdom**, I am better than
jewels;
nothing you want can **compare** with
me.
12 I am **Wisdom**, and I have **insight**;
I have **knowledge** and **sound
judgement**.
13 To **honour** the LORD is to **hate evil**;
I **hate pride** and **arrogance**,
evil ways and **false words**.
14 I make **plans** and carry them out.
I have **understanding**, and I am
strong.
15 I **help** kings to govern
and rulers to make good **laws**.
16 Every ruler on earth governs with my
help,
statesmen and noblemen alike.
17 I **love** those who love me;
whoever looks for me can find me.
18 I have **riches** and **honour** to give,
prosperity and **success**.
19 What you get from me is better than
the finest gold,
better than the **purest** silver.
20 I walk the way of **righteousness**;
I follow the paths of **justice**,
21 giving wealth to those who **love** me,
filling their houses with treasures.

22 "The LORD **created** me first of all,
the first of his works, long ago.
23 I was made in the very beginning,
at the first, before the **world** began.
24 I was born before the oceans,
when there were no springs of
water.
25 I was born before the mountains,
before the hills were set in place,
26 before God made the earth and its
fields
or even the first handful of soil.
27 I was there when he set the sky in
place,
when he stretched the horizon
across the ocean,
28 when he placed the **clouds** in the sky,
when he opened the springs of the
ocean
29 and ordered the waters of the sea
to **rise** no further than he said.
I was there when he laid the earth's
foundations.
30 I was beside him like an architect,[g]
I was his daily **source of joy**,
always happy in his **presence**—
31 **happy** with the **world**
and **pleased** with the **human race**.

32 "Now, young men, listen to me.
Do as I say, and you will be **happy**.
33 Listen to what you are **taught**.
Be **wise**; do not **neglect** it.
34 The man who listens to me will be
happy—
the man who stays at my door every
day,
waiting at the entrance to my home.
35 The man who finds me finds **life**,
and the LORD will be **pleased** with
him.
36 The man who does not find me **hurts**
himself;
anyone who **hates** me **loves death**."

arrogant Ps 131.1; 13.1
choose [2] Ps 135.4; 22.1
cloud 3.20; 16.15
compare 3.15; 27.3
create 3.19; Ecc 12.13
death (1) 7.26; 11.4
evil [2] 6.14; 9.7
false [2] Ps 140.11; 25.18
fool 7.7; 9.4
happy [3] 7.18; 11.1
hate [4] 6.16; 9.8
help [2] 5.17; 11.25
honour [2] 4.8; 15.33
human Ps 146.3; 21.30
hurt 4.16; 9.7
insight [2] 7.4; 17.27
joy 5.18; 10.28
judge Ps 146.7; 11.22
justice 2.9; 12.17
knowledge [2] 5.2; 9.6
law Ps 147.19; 19.16
learn [2] 6.6; 13.18
lie (2) 6.12; 10.18
life (1) 7.23; 9.11
love [3] 7.18; 10.12
mankind Ps 53.2; Is 40.5
mature 16.21
mislead 4.24; 24.28
neglect Ps 119.87; 19.27
plain (1) Ps 50.21; Ecc 7.29
plan 7.10; 12.2
please [2] 3.4; 12.2
presence Ps 140.13; Ecc 8.3
prosper 3.2; 11.25
proud 6.16; 10.1
pure Ps 119.7; 10.20
race (1) Ps 22.27; Jer 34.1
reason 3.30; 23.24
riches 1.13; 11.4
right (1) 4.11; 11.18
righteous 4.18; 9.9
rise Ps 104.22; Ecc 1.5
sense 6.32; 10.5
sound (2) 3.24; Jon 1.5

source Ps 119.92; 18.4
strong Ps 148.8; 16.12
succeed (1) 2.5; 15.2
teach 7.2; 13.14
true 4.24; 13.12
truth Ps 144.8; 10.1
understand 4.1; 9.1
way (3) Ps 125.5; 15
wisdom [3] 7.4; 9.1
wise 4.12; 9.8
word (1) [2] 7.5; 10.6
world [2] Ps 138.4; 30.24

[f] *Probable text* like a deer prancing into a trap; *Hebrew unclear.* [g] an architect; *or* a little child.

8.1-3: Prov 1.20-21 **8.22:** Rev 3.14

Wisdom and Stupidity

9 **Wisdom** has built her house and made seven pillars for it. 2 She has had an animal killed for a **feast**, mixed spices in the wine, and laid the table. 3 She has sent her **servant-girls** to call out from the highest place in the town: 4 "Come in, **ignorant** people!" And to the **foolish** man she says, 5 "Come, eat my food and drink the wine that I have mixed. 6 Leave the company of **ignorant** people, and live. Follow the way of **knowledge**."

7 If you **correct** a **conceited** man, you will only be **insulted**. If you **reprimand** an **evil** man, you will only get **hurt**. 8 Never **correct** a **conceited** man; he will **hate** you for it. But if you **correct** a **wise** man, he will **respect** you. 9 Anything you say to a **wise** man will make him wiser. Whatever you tell a **righteous** man will add to his **knowledge**.

10 To be **wise** you must first have **reverence** for the LORD. If you know the **Holy One**, you have **understanding**. 11 **Wisdom** will add years to your **life**. 12 You are the one who will profit if you have **wisdom**, and if you **reject** it, you are the one who will **suffer**.

13 **Stupidity** is like a loud, **ignorant**, **shameless** woman.[h] 14 She sits at the door of her house or on a seat in the highest part of the town, 15 and calls out to people passing by, who are minding their own business: 16 "Come in, **ignorant** people!" To the **foolish** man she says, 17 "**Stolen** water is sweeter. **Stolen bread** tastes better." 18 Her **victims** do not know that the people die who go to her house, that those who have already entered are now deep in the **world of the dead**.

bread 6.26; 17.1
conceited [2] 3.34; 14.6
correct [3] 6.23; 10.17
evil 8.13; 10.31
feast Ps 141.4; Ecc 10.16
fool [2] 8.5; 10.1
hate 8.7; 10.12
holy Ps 145.21; Is 1.4
hurt 8.36; 10.32
ignorant [4] Ps 119.130; 12.23
insult Ps 119.22; 12.16
knowledge [2] 8.10; 10.14
life (1) 8.35; 10.2
reject 1.32; Is 1.4
reprimand 1.23; 30.6
respect 5.9; 11.16
reverence 1.7; 14.2
righteous 8.20; 10.24
servant Ps 144.10; 11.29
shame 7.11; 12.4
steal [2] 6.30; 28.24
stupid 5.23; 10.13
suffer 6.29; 21.18
understand 8.14; 16.21
victim Ps 10.8; Is 5.7
wisdom [3] 8.1; 10.23
wise [3] 8.33; 10.1
world of the dead 7.27; 15.11

Solomon's Proverbs

10 These are Solomon's **proverbs**: A **wise** son makes his father **proud** of him; a **foolish** one brings his mother **grief**.

2 Wealth that you get by **dishonesty** will do you no good, but **honesty** can **save** your **life**.

3 The LORD will not let good people go **hungry**, but he will **keep the wicked from** getting what they want.

4 Being lazy will make you **poor**, but **hard work** will make you **rich**.

5 A **sensible** man gathers the crops when they are ready; it is a **disgrace** to sleep through the time of **harvest**.

6 A good man will receive **blessings**. A **wicked** man's **words** hide a **violent nature**.

7 Good people will be **remembered** as a **blessing**, but the **wicked** will soon be **forgotten**.

8 **Sensible** people **accept** good **advice**. People who talk **foolishly** will come to **ruin**.

9 **Honest** people are **safe** and **secure**, but the **dishonest** will be caught.

10 Someone who holds back the **truth** causes **trouble**, but one who openly **criticizes** works for **peace**.[i]

11 A good man's **words** are a fountain of **life**, but a **wicked** man's **words** hide a **violent nature**.

12 **Hate** stirs up **trouble**, but **love** overlooks all offences.

13 **Intelligent** people talk **sense**, but **stupid** people **need** to be **punished**.

14 The **wise** get all the **knowledge** they can, but when **fools** speak, **trouble** is not far off.

15 Wealth **protects** the **rich**; poverty **destroys** the **poor**.

16 The **reward** for doing good is **life**, but sin leads only to more sin.

17 People who listen when they are **corrected** will live, but those who will not **admit** that they are **wrong** are in **danger**.

18 A man who hides his **hatred** is a **liar**. Anyone who spreads gossip is a **fool**.

19 The more you talk, the more likely you are to sin. If you are **wise**, you will keep quiet.

20 A good man's **words** are like **pure** silver; a **wicked** man's **ideas** are **worthless**.

21 A good man's **words** will **benefit** many people, but you can kill yourself with **stupidity**.

22 It is the LORD's **blessing** that makes you wealthy. **Hard work** can make you no **richer**.[j]

23 It is **foolish** to **enjoy** doing **wrong**. **Intelligent** people take **pleasure** in **wisdom**.

24 The **righteous** get what they want, but the **wicked** will get what they **fear** most.

25 Storms come, and the **wicked** are blown away, but **honest** people are always **safe**.

26 Never get a lazy man to do something for you; he will be as irritating as vinegar on your teeth or smoke in your eyes.

27 **Obey** the LORD, and you will live longer. The **wicked** die before their time.

accept 6.35; 15.5
admit (1) Ps 141.6; 13.1
advice 6.22; 12.15
benefit Job 22.3; Ezek 13.18
bless [3] 3.33; 11.11
correct 9.7; 12.1
criticize Job 34.29; 27.11
danger 7.23; 13.14
destroy [2] 6.32; 11.3
disgrace 6.33; 11.2
dishonest [2] Ps 101.4; 11.1
enjoy 2.14; 15.15
evil 9.7; 11.20
fear 2.5; 15.16
fool [5] 9.4; 11.12
forget 7.1; 27.10
grief Ps 6.6; 17.25
hard [2] 2.4; 12.11
harvest Ps 126.5; 20.4

hate [2] 9.8; 11.1
honest [4] 4.25; 11.1
hope Ps 145.15; 11.7
hunger 6.30; 12.9
hurt 9.7; 11.17
idea Job 38.18; 17.4
intelligent [2] 1.3; 12.8
joy 8.30; 11.10
keep from Ps 141.4; 13.23
kind Ps 145.7; 11.17
knowledge 9.6; 12.1
lie (2) 8.7; 12.17
life (1) [3] 9.11; 11.4
love 8.17; 11.20
nature [2] 1 Sam 10.9; Acts 17.29
need 3.27; 23.35
obey 3.7; 16.6
peace Ps 131.2; 13.17
pleasure 2.10; 17.5
poor [2] 6.11; 11.24
protect [2] 7.2; 11.8
proud 8.13; 11.2
proverb 1.1; 25.1
punish Ps 149.7; 11.21
pure 8.19; 22.11
remember 7.1; 17.9
reward Ps 91.16; 11.18
rich [3] Ps 132.15; 11.16
righteous [4] 9.9; 11.6
ruin 7.26; 11.9
safe [2] 4.6; 13.13
save Ps 146.3; 11.4
secure [2] 1.33; 11.14
sense [3] 8.5; 11.12
stupid [2] 9.13; 12.1
trouble [3] 6.14; 11.8
truth 8.7; 12.17
violent [2] 4.17; 11.30
wicked [11] 6.12; 11.5
wisdom [2] 9.1; 11.9
wise [3] 9.8; 11.2
word (1) [5] 8.6; 11.11
worthless 6.12; 17.2
wrong [3] 4.16; 11.19

[h] *Verse 13 in Hebrew is unclear.*
[i] *One ancient translation* but one...peace; *Hebrew repeats verse 8b.*
[j] Hard work...richer; *or* And the LORD does not add sorrow to your wealth.

9.10: Job 28.28; Ps 111.10; Prov 1.7 **10.12:** Jas 5.20; 1 Pet 4.8

28 The **hopes** of good men lead to **joy**, but **wicked** people can look forward to nothing.

29 The LORD **protects honest** people, but **destroys** those who do **wrong**.

30 **Righteous** people will always have **security**, but the **wicked** will not survive in the land.

31 **Righteous** people speak **wisdom**, but the tongue that speaks **evil** will be stopped.

32 **Righteous** people know the **kind** thing to say, but the **wicked** are always saying things that **hurt**.

secret Ps 139.15; 17.23
secure 10.9; 12.3
sense 10.5; 12.16
servant 9.3; 17.2
stranger 5.10; 20.1
sure [2] Ps 85.9; 17
trap 7.22; 12.13
trouble [3] 10.10; 12.13
trust [4] 3.5; 13.15
violent 10.6; 13.2
wicked [8] 10.3; 12
wisdom 10.23; 14.1
wise [2] 10.1; 12.15
word (1) 10.6; 12.6
wrong 10.17; 12.1

anger 6.34; 15.1
bless 10.6; 16.3
certain (1) Ps 119.140; Is 28.15
confident [2] 4.25; 14.26
cruel Ps 144.11; 12.10
curse 3.33; 20.20
death (1) 8.36; 12.28
debt 6.1; 17.18
depend Ps 146.5; 12.14
destroy 10.15; 13.3
determine Job 28.25; 16.33
disgrace [2] 10.5; 13.5
dishonest [2] 10.2; 14.2
downfall Ps 140.4; 12.7
escape 6.5; 13.14
evil [2] 10.31; 12.2
favour 3.34; 14.19
fool [2] 10.1; 12.16
fortune 2 Chr 9.7; 12.27
free Ps 146.7; 29.6
generous Ps 112.5; 21.26
godless Ps 74.18; Is 9.17
grace 5.19; 22.11
greed Ps 10.3; 19.22
guide [2] 1.5; 12.26
happy [2] 8.31; 12.20
hate [2] 10.12; 12.1
help 8.15; 13.14
honest [6] 10.2; 12.5
hope 10.28; 13.12
hurt 10.32; 15.32
joy 10.28; 12.4
judge 8.12; 16.2
kind 10.32; 12.25
life (1) [3] 10.2; 12.19
love 10.12; 12.1
poor 10.4; 13.7
praise Ps 150.1; 12.8
promise 6.1; 17.18
prosper [2] 8.18; 19.8
protect 10.15; 13.3
proud 10.1; 12.4
punish [2] 10.13; 13.24
rescue Ps 144.7; 12.6
respect [2] 9.8; 13.15
reward [2] 10.16; 12.14
rich [2] 10.4; 13.7
riches [2] 8.18; 21.6
right (1) [3] 8.6; 12.15
righteous [7] 10.24; 12.3
ruin [2] 10.8; 13.15
save [2] 10.2; 13.8
scorn 1.22; 18.3

11 The LORD **hates** people who use **dishonest** scales. He is **happy** with **honest** weights.

2 People who are **proud** will soon be **disgraced**. It is **wiser** to be modest.

3 If you are good, you are **guided** by **honesty**. People who can't be **trusted** are **destroyed** by their own **dishonesty**.

4 **Riches** will do you no good on the day you face **death**, but **honesty** can save your **life**.

5 **Honesty** makes a good man's **life** easier, but a **wicked** man will cause his own **downfall**.

6 **Righteousness rescues** the **honest** man, but someone who can't be **trusted** is **trapped** by his own **greed**.

7 When a **wicked** man dies, his **hope** dies with him. **Confidence** placed in **riches** comes to nothing.

8 The **righteous** are **protected** from **trouble**; it comes to the **wicked** instead.

9 You can be **ruined** by the talk of **godless** people, but the **wisdom** of the **righteous** can **save** you.

10 A city is **happy** when **honest** people have good **fortune**, and there are **joyful** shouts when **wicked** men die.

11 A city becomes great when **righteous** men give it their **blessing**; but a city is brought to **ruin** by the **words** of the **wicked**.

12 It is **foolish** to speak **scornfully** of others. If you are **sensible**, you will keep quiet.

13 No one who gossips can be **trusted** with a **secret**, but you can put **confidence** in someone who is **trustworthy**.

14 A nation will fall if it has no **guidance**. Many advisers mean **security**.

15 If you **promise** to pay a **stranger's debt**, you will regret it. You are better off if you don't get involved.

16 A **gracious** lady is **respected**, but a woman without virtue is a **disgrace**. A lazy man will never have money,[k] but an aggressive man will get **rich**.

17 You do yourself a **favour** when you are **kind**. If you are **cruel**, you only **hurt** yourself.

18 **Wicked** people do not really gain anything, but if you do what is **right**, you are **certain** to be **rewarded**.

19 Anyone who is **determined** to do **right** will live, but anyone who insists on doing **wrong** will die.

20 The LORD **hates evil-minded** people, but **loves** those who do **right**.

21 You can be **sure** that **evil** men will be **punished**, but **righteous** men will **escape**.

22 Beauty in a woman without good **judgement** is like a gold ring in a pig's snout.

23 What good people want always results in good; when the **wicked** get what they want, everyone is **angry**.[l]

24 Some people spend their money **freely** and still grow **richer**. Others are cautious, and yet grow **poorer**.

25 Be **generous**, and you will be **prosperous**. **Help** others, and you will be helped.

26 People **curse** a man who hoards grain, waiting for a higher price, but they **praise** the one who puts it up for sale.

27 If your goals are good, you will be **respected**, but if you are looking for **trouble**, that is what you will get.

28 Those who **depend** on their wealth will fall like the leaves of autumn, but the **righteous** will **prosper** like the leaves of summer.

29 The man who brings **trouble** on his family will have nothing at the end.

Foolish men will always be **servants** to the **wise**.

30 **Righteousness**[m] gives **life**, but **violence**[n] takes it away.

31 Those who are good are **rewarded** here on earth, so you can be **sure** that **wicked** and sinful people will be **punished**.

advice 10.8; 13.10
bad 6.24; 14.14
care Ps 142.4; 14.9
cheer (1) Ps 104.15; 17.22
condemn Ps 130.3; 17.15
correct 10.17; 13.1
cruel 11.17; 15.4
death (1) 11.4; 14.1
deceive 6.13; 13.2
depend 11.28; 14.28
deserve 1.31; 14.14
downfall 11.5; 13.6
evil [3] 11.20; 13.19

12 Anyone who **loves knowledge** wants to be told when he is **wrong**. It is **stupid** to **hate** being **corrected**.

2 The LORD is **pleased** with good people, but **condemns** those who **plan evil**.

3 **Wickedness** does not give **security**, but **righteous** people stand firm.

4 A good wife is her husband's **pride**

[k] *One ancient translation* but a woman...money; *Hebrew does not have these words.*
[l] everyone is angry; *or* God punishes them.
[m] *One ancient translation* Righteousness; *Hebrew* A righteous man.
[n] *Probable text* violence; *Hebrew* a wise man.

11.31: 1 Pet 4.18

and joy; but a wife who brings **shame** on her husband is like a cancer in his bones.

5 **Honest** people will treat you fairly; the **wicked** only want to **deceive** you.

6 The **words** of **wicked** men are murderous, but the **words** of the **righteous rescue** those who are **threatened**.

7 **Wicked** men meet their **downfall** and leave no descendants, but the families of **righteous** men live on.

8 If you are **intelligent**, you will be **praised**; if you are **stupid**, people will **look down on** you.

9 It is better to be an ordinary man working for a living than to play the part of a great man but go **hungry**.

10 A good man takes **care** of his animals, but **wicked** men are **cruel** to theirs.

11 A **hard-working** farmer has **plenty** to eat, but it is **stupid** to waste time on **useless** projects.

12 All that **wicked** people want is to find **evil** things to do, but the **righteous** stand firm.[o]

13 A **wicked** man is **trapped** by his own **words**, but an **honest** man gets himself out of **trouble**.

14 Your **reward depends** on what you say and what you do; you will get what you **deserve**.

15 **Stupid** people always think they are **right**. **Wise** people listen to **advice**.

16 When a **fool** is annoyed, he quickly lets it be known. **Sensible** people will **ignore an insult**.

17 When you tell the **truth**, **justice** is done, but **lies** lead to **injustice**.

18 Thoughtless **words** can wound as deeply as any sword, but **wisely** spoken **words** can **heal**.

19 A **lie** has a short **life**, but **truth** lives on for ever.

20 Those who **plan evil** are in for a rude surprise, but those who work for good will find **happiness**.

21 Nothing **bad** happens to **righteous** people, but the **wicked** have nothing but **trouble**.

22 The LORD **hates liars**, but is **pleased** with those who keep their **word**.

23 **Sensible** people keep quiet about what they know, but **stupid** people advertise their **ignorance**.

24 **Hard work** will give you **power**; being lazy will make you a **slave**.

25 **Worry** can **rob** you of **happiness**, but **kind words** will **cheer** you up.

26 The **righteous** man is a **guide** to his **friend**, but the path of the **wicked** leads them astray.

27 If you are lazy, you will never get what you are after, but if you work **hard**, you will get a **fortune**.[p]

28 **Righteousness** is the road **to life**; **wickedness**[q] is the road to **death**.

13

A **wise** son pays attention when his father **corrects** him, but an **arrogant** person never **admits** he is **wrong**.

2 Good people will be **rewarded** for what they say, but those who are **deceitful** are **hungry** for **violence**.

3 Be careful what you say and **protect** your **life**. A careless talker **destroys** himself.

4 No matter how much a lazy person may want something, he will never get it. A **hard worker** will get everything he wants.

5 **Honest** people **hate lies**, but the **words** of **wicked** people are **shameful** and **disgraceful**.

6 **Righteousness protects** the **innocent**; **wickedness** is the **downfall** of sinners.

7 Some people pretend to be **rich**, but have nothing. Others pretend to be **poor**, but own a **fortune**.

8 A **rich** man has to use his money to **save** his **life**, but no one **threatens** a **poor** man.

9 The **righteous** are like a **light** shining brightly; the **wicked** are like a lamp flickering out.

10 **Arrogance** causes nothing but **trouble**. It is **wiser** to ask for **advice**.

11 The more easily you get your wealth, the sooner you will lose it. The **harder** it is to earn, the more you will have.

12 When **hope** is crushed, the **heart** is crushed, but a **wish** come **true** fills you with **joy**.

13 If you **refuse** good **advice**, you are asking for **trouble**; follow it and you are **safe**.

14 The **teachings** of the **wise** are a fountain of **life**; they will **help** you **escape** when your **life** is in **danger**.

15 **Intelligence wins respect**, but those who can't be **trusted** are on the road to **ruin**.[r]

16 **Sensible** people always think before they **act**, but **stupid** people advertise their **ignorance**.

17 **Unreliable** messengers cause **trouble**, but those who can be **trusted** bring **peace**.

[o] *Verse 12 in Hebrew is unclear.* [p] *Verse 27 in Hebrew is unclear.*
[q] *One ancient translation* wickedness; *Hebrew* path.
[r] *One ancient translation* road to ruin; *Hebrew* permanent road.

18 Someone who will not **learn** will be **poor** and **disgraced**. Anyone who listens to **correction** is **respected**.

19 How good it is to get what you want! **Stupid** people **refuse** to **turn away** from **evil**.

20 Keep company with the **wise** and you will become wise. If you make **friends** with **stupid** people, you will be **ruined**.

21 **Trouble** follows sinners everywhere, but **righteous** people will be **rewarded** with good things.

22 A good man will have wealth to leave to his grandchildren, but the wealth of sinners will go to **righteous** men.

23 Unused fields could yield **plenty** of food for the **poor**, but **unjust** men **keep them from** being farmed.[s]

24 If you don't **punish** your son, you don't **love** him. If you do **love** him, you will **correct** him.

25 The **righteous** have **enough** to eat, but the **wicked** are always **hungry**.

14

Homes are made by the **wisdom** of women, but are **destroyed** by **foolishness**.

2 Be **honest** and you show that you have **reverence** for the LORD; be **dishonest** and you show that you do not.

3 A **fool's pride** makes him talk too much; a **wise** man's **words protect** him.

4 Without any oxen to pull the plough your barn will be empty, but with them it will be full of corn.[t]

5 A **reliable witness** always tells the **truth**, but an **unreliable** one tells nothing but **lies**.

6 **Conceited** people can never become **wise**, but **intelligent** people **learn** easily.

7 Stay away from **foolish** people; they have nothing to **teach** you.

8 Why is a clever person **wise**? Because he knows what to do. Why is a **stupid** person **foolish**? Because he only thinks he knows.

9 **Foolish** people don't **care** if they sin, but good people want to be **forgiven**.[u]

10 Your **joy** is your own; your **bitterness** is your own. No one can **share** them with you.

11 A good man's house will still be standing after an **evil** man's house has been **destroyed**.

12 What you think is the **right** road may lead to **death**.

13 Laughter may hide **sadness**. When **happiness** is gone, **sorrow** is always there.

14 **Bad** people will get what they **deserve**. Good people will be **rewarded** for their deeds.[v]

15 A **fool** will **believe** anything; **sensible** people **watch** their step.

16 **Wise** people are careful to stay out of **trouble**, but **stupid** people are careless and **act** too quickly.

17 People with a hot temper do **foolish** things; **wiser** people remain **calm**.[w]

18 **Ignorant** people get what their **foolishness deserves**, but the clever are **rewarded** with **knowledge**.

19 **Evil** people will have to **bow down** to the **righteous** and **humbly beg** their **favour**.

20 No one, not even his **neighbour**, likes a **poor** man, but the **rich** have many **friends**.

21 If you want to be **happy**, be **kind** to the **poor**; it is a sin to **despise** anyone.

22 You will earn the **trust** and **respect** of others if you work for good; if you work for **evil**, you are making a **mistake**.

23 Work and you will earn a living; if you sit around talking you will be **poor**.

24 **Wise** people are **rewarded** with wealth, but fools are known by[x] their **foolishness**.

25 A **witness saves lives** when he tells the **truth**; when he tells **lies**, he **betrays** people.

26 **Reverence** for the LORD gives **confidence** and **security** to a man and his family.

27 Do you want to avoid **death**? **Reverence** for the LORD is a fountain of **life**.

28 A king's greatness **depends** on how many people he rules; without them he is nothing.

29 If you stay **calm**, you are **wise**, but if you have a hot temper, you only show how **stupid** you are.

30 **Peace** of **mind** makes the **body** healthy, but **jealousy** is like a cancer.

31 If you **oppress poor** people, you **insult** the God who made them; but **kindness** shown to the **poor** is an **act** of **worship**.

32 **Wicked** people bring about their own **downfall** by their **evil** deeds, but good people are **protected** by their integrity.[y]

[s] *Verse 23 in Hebrew is unclear.*
[t] your barn will be...corn; *or* you may grow a little corn, but with them you can grow much more.
[u] *Verse 9 in Hebrew is unclear.* [v] *Probable text* for their deeds; *Hebrew* from upon them.
[w] *One ancient translation* remain calm; *Hebrew* are hated.
[x] *Probable text* are known by; *Hebrew unclear.*
[y] *Some ancient translations* integrity; *Hebrew* death.

14.12: Prov 16.25

act [2] 13.16; 21.5
bad 12.21; 18.9
beg 6.3; 18.23
believe Ps 116.10; 17.8
betray Ps 7.3; Is 21.2
bitter 5.4; 17.25
body Ps 109.18; Ecc 12.7
bow (2) Ps 138.2; Is 44.17
calm [2] Ps 107.29; 17.27
care 12.10; 18.2
conceited 9.7; 15.12
confident 11.7; 31.11
death (1) [2] 12.28; 15.24
depend 12.14; 25.19
deserve [2] 12.14; 26.2
despise 6.30; 15.20
destroy [2] 13.3; 15.25
disgrace 13.5; 19.22
dishonest 11.1; 15.27
downfall 13.6; 16.18
evil [4] 13.19; 15.3
fail Ps 119.157; 15.22
favour 11.17; 16.13
fool [10] 12.16; 15.5
forgive Ps 130.4; 16.6
friend 13.20; 15.26
happy [2] 12.20; 15.13
honest 13.5; 15.19
humble 3.34; 15.33
ignorant 13.16; 15.14
insult 12.16; 17.5
intelligent [2] 13.15; 15.14
jealous 6.34; 27.4
joy 13.12; 15.23
kind [2] 12.25; 15.4
knowledge 12.1; 15.2
learn 13.18; 15.14
lie (2) [2] 13.5; 17.4
life (1) [2] 13.3; 15.4
mind (1) 6.14; 17.1

mistake Num 32
Ecc 7.20
neighbour 3.28; 2
oppress Ps 146.7
22.8
peace 13.17; 15.1
please 12.2; 15.8
poor [5] 13.7; 15.1
protect [2] 13.3; 1
proud 12.4; 16.18
punish 13.24; 15.
rely [2] 13.17; 21.
respect 13.15; 17.
reverence [3] 9.1
15.33
reward [3] 13.2; 1
rich 13.7; 15.16
right (1) 12.15; 15
righteous [2] 13.6
15.6
sad Ps 90.15; 15.1
save 13.8; 16.17
secure 12.3; Ecc
sense 13.16; 17.16
share 1.14; 16.19
sorrow Ps 119.28;
17.21
stupid [3] 13.16; 1
teach 13.14; 15.5
trouble 13.10; 15.
trust 13.15; 16.20
truth [2] 12.17; 16.
watch 5.21; 15.3
wicked 13.5; 15.6
wisdom [3] 11.9;
16.16
wise [7] 13.1; 15.2
witness [2] 6.16;
19.28
word (1) 13.5; 15.
worship (1) (of G
Ps 135.20; 28.5

33 **Wisdom** is in every thought of an **intelligent** man; **fools** know nothing[m] about **wisdom**.

34 **Righteousness** makes a nation great; sin is a **disgrace** to any nation.

35 Kings are **pleased** with competent officials, but they **punish** those who **fail** them.

15 A **gentle** answer quietens **anger**, but a harsh one stirs it up.

2 When **wise** people speak, they make **knowledge** attractive, but **stupid** people spout nonsense.

3 The LORD sees what happens everywhere; he is **watching** us, whether we do good or **evil**.

4 **Kind words** bring **life**, but **cruel** words crush your **spirit**.

5 It is **foolish** to **ignore** what your father **taught** you; it is **wise** to **accept** his **correction**.

6 **Righteous** men keep their wealth, but **wicked** men lose theirs when **hard** times come.

7 **Knowledge** is spread by people who are **wise**, not by **fools**.

8 The LORD is **pleased** when good men **pray**, but **hates** the **sacrifices** that **wicked** men bring him.

9 The LORD **hates** the **ways** of **evil** people, but **loves** those who do what is **right**.

10 If you do what is **wrong**, you will be severely **punished**; you will die if you do not let yourself be **corrected**.

11 Not even the **world of the dead** can **keep the** LORD **from** knowing what is there; how then can a man hide his thoughts from God?

12 **Conceited** people do not like to be **corrected**; they never ask for **advice** from those who are **wiser**.

13 When people are **happy**, they smile, but when they are **sad**, they look depressed.

14 **Intelligent** people want to **learn**, but **stupid** people are **satisfied** with **ignorance**.

15 The **life** of the **poor** is a **constant struggle**, but **happy** people always **enjoy life**.

16 Better to be **poor** and **fear** the LORD than to be **rich** and in **trouble**.

17 Better to eat vegetables with people you **love** than to eat the finest meat where there is **hate**.

18 Hot tempers cause **arguments**, but **patience brings peace**.

19 If you are lazy, you will meet **difficulty** everywhere, but if you are **honest**, you will have **no trouble**.

20 A **wise** son makes his father **happy**. Only a **fool despises** his mother.

21 **Stupid** people are **happy** with their **foolishness**, but the **wise** will do what is **right**.

22 Get all the **advice** you can, and you will **succeed**; without it you will **fail**.

23 What a **joy** it is to find just the **right word** for the right occasion!

24 **Wise** people walk the road that leads upwards **to life**, not the road that leads downwards to **death**.

25 The LORD will **destroy** the homes of **arrogant** men, but he will **protect** a **widow's** property.

26 The LORD **hates evil** thoughts, but he is **pleased** with **friendly words**.

27 If you try to make a profit **dishonestly**, you will get your family into **trouble**. Don't take **bribes** and you will live longer.

28 Good people think before they answer. **Evil** people have a quick reply, but it causes **trouble**.

29 When good people **pray**, the LORD listens, but he **ignores** those who are **evil**.

30 Smiling faces make you **happy**, and **good news** makes you feel better.

31 If you pay attention when you are **corrected**, you are **wise**.

32 If you **refuse** to **learn**, you are **hurting** yourself. If you **accept correction**, you will become **wiser**.

33 **Reverence** for the LORD is an education in itself. You must **be humble** before you can ever receive **honours**.

16 We may make our **plans**, but God has the **last word**.[z]

2 You may think everything you do is **right**, but the LORD **judges** your **motives**.

3 Ask the LORD to **bless** your **plans**, and you will be **successful** in carrying them out.

4 Everything the LORD has made has its destiny; and the destiny of the **wicked** is **destruction**.

5 The LORD **hates** everyone who is **arrogant**; he will never let them **escape punishment**.

6 Be **loyal** and **faithful**, and God will **forgive** your sin. **Obey** the LORD and nothing **evil** will happen to you.

7 When you **please** the LORD, you can make[a] your **enemies** into **friends**.

8 It is better to have a little, **honestly** earned, than to have a large income gained **dishonestly**.

9 You may make your **plans**, but God **directs** your **actions**.

10 The king speaks with **divine authority**; his decisions are always **right**.

[m] *One ancient translation* nothing; *Hebrew does not have this word.*
[z] God...word; *or* God inspires our words. [a] you can make; *or* he will make.

cept [2] 10.8; 17.23
vice [2] 13.10;
.20
ger 11.23; 16.14
gue 3.30; 17.14
rogant 13.1; 16.5
ibe Ps 26.10; 17.8
nceited 14.6; 19.29
nstant Ps 147.11;
51.13
rrect [5] 13.1; 19.25
uel 12.10; 17.11
ath (1) 14.12; 16.25
spise 14.21; 30.17
stroy 14.1; 16.4
fficult Ps 139.17;
r 32.17
shonest 14.2; 16.8
joy 10.23; 20.17
il [5] 14.11; 16.6
il 14.35; Ecc 2.9
ar 10.24; 20.2
ol [4] 14.1; 17.7
iend 14.20; 16.7
ntle Job 21.33;
.26
ood News Ps 96.2;
.25
ppy [5] 14.13; 16.14
rd 13.4; 16.26
te [4] 13.5; 16.5
nest 14.2; 16.8
nour 8.13; 18.3
mble 14.19; 16.19
rt 11.17; 19.28
norant 14.18;
44.9
nore [2] 12.16; 19.11
telligent 14.6;
.23
y 14.10; Ecc 3.4
ep from 13.23; 30.8
nd 14.21; 16.24
owledge [2] 14.18;
.16
arn [2] 14.6; 16.33
e (1) [4] 14.25;
.15
e (2) (to life) 12.28;
26.19
ve [2] 13.24; 17.17
tient Ps 86.15;
.32
ace 14.30; 17.1
ease [2] 14.35; 16.7
or [2] 14.20; 16.19
ay [2] Ps 141.5;
1.15
otect 14.3; 18.11
nish 14.35; 16.5
fuse (1) 13.13; 21.7
verence 14.2; 23.17
ch 14.20; 18.11
ght (1) [3] 14.12;
.2
ghteous 14.19;
.31
crifice 7.14; 21.3
d 14.13; 17.21
tisfy 6.35; 16.26
irit (2) Ps 51.10;
cc 3.21
ruggle Gen 32.25;
19.2
upid [3] 14.8; 16.22
cceed (1) 8.18; 16.3
ach 14.7; 16.20
ouble [4] 14.16;
.28

watch 14.15; 16.17
way (3) 8.13; 20.30
wicked [2] 14.32; 16.4
widow Ps 146.9;
Is 1.17
wise [9] 14.3; 16.14
word (1) [3] 14.3; 16.1
world of the dead
9.18; 27.20
wrong 13.1; 17.9

action 1.31; 17.24
anger 15.1; 19.12
arrogant [3] 15.25;
18.12
authority Ps 105.22;
17.2
bless 11.11; 22.9
cloud 8.28; 25.14
control Ps 32.9; 19.11
crown 4.9; Song 3.11
death (1) 15.24; 17.11
deceive 13.2; 31.30
destroy [2] 15.25;
18.9
determine 11.19;
19.28
direct Job 38.32; 21.1
disaster 6.15; 17.20
dishonest 15.27;
20.10
divine Ezek 28.2
downfall 14.32; 29.16
enemy Ps 144.6;
24.17
escape 13.14; 19.5
evil [6] 15.3; 17.4
faithful 5.15; 20.6
favour [2] 14.19; 18.5
forgive 14.9; 17.9
friend [3] 15.26; 17.9
glory 4.9; Is 2.10
happy [2] 15.13; 21.15
hard 15.6; 19.7
harm 3.30; 19.23
hate 15.8; 17.15
honest [2] 15.19; 19.1
humble 15.33; 18.12

11 The LORD wants weights and measures to be **honest** and every sale to be **fair**.

12 Kings cannot **tolerate evil**,[b] because **justice** is what makes a government **strong**.

13 A king wants to hear the **truth** and will **favour** those who speak it.

14 A **wise** man will try to keep the king **happy**; if the king becomes **angry**, someone may die.

15 The king's **favour** is like the **clouds** that bring rain in the springtime—**life** is there.

16 It is better—much better—to have **wisdom** and **knowledge** than gold and silver.

17 Those who are good travel a road that avoids **evil**; so **watch** where you are going—it may **save** your **life**.

18 **Pride** leads to **destruction**, and **arrogance** to **downfall**.

19 It is better to be **humble** and stay **poor** than to be one of the **arrogant** and get a **share** of their loot.

20 Pay attention to what you are **taught**, and you will be **successful**; **trust** in the LORD and you will be **happy**.

21 A **wise**, **mature** person is known for his **understanding**. The more pleasant his **words**, the more **persuasive** he is.

22 **Wisdom** is a fountain of **life** to the **wise**, but trying to educate **stupid** people is a waste of time.

23 **Intelligent** people think before they speak; what they say is then more **persuasive**.

24 **Kind words** are like honey—sweet to the taste and good for your health.

25 What you think is the **right** road may lead to **death**.

26 A labourer's appetite makes him work **harder**, because he wants to **satisfy** his **hunger**.

27 **Evil** people look for ways to **harm** others; even their **words** burn with **evil**.

28 Gossip is spread by **wicked** people; they stir up **trouble** and break up **friendships**.

29 **Violent** people **deceive** their **friends** and lead them to **disaster**.

30 **Watch** out for people who grin and wink at you; they have thought of something **evil**.

31 Long **life** is the **reward** of the **righteous**; grey hair is a **glorious crown**.

32 It is better to be **patient** than **powerful**. It is better to **win control** over yourself than over whole cities.

33 Men cast **lots** to **learn God's will**, but God himself **determines** the answer.

17

Better to eat a dry crust of **bread** with **peace** of **mind** than to have a **banquet** in a house full of **trouble**.

2 A shrewd **servant** will gain **authority** over a **master's worthless** son and receive a part of the **inheritance**.

3 Gold and silver are **tested** by fire, and a person's **heart** is **tested** by the LORD.

4 **Evil** people listen to evil **ideas**, and liars listen to **lies**.

5 If you laugh at **poor** people, you **insult** the God who made them. You will be **punished** if you take **pleasure** in someone's misfortune.

6 Old men are **proud** of their grandchildren, just as boys are **proud** of their fathers.

7 **Respected** people do not tell **lies**, and **fools** have nothing worthwhile to say.

8 Some people think a **bribe** works like **magic**; they **believe** it can do anything.

9 If you want people to like you, **forgive** them when they **wrong** you. **Remembering wrongs** can break up a **friendship**.

10 An **intelligent** person **learns** more from one **rebuke** than a **fool learns** from being beaten a hundred times.

11 **Death** will come like a **cruel** messenger to **wicked** people who are always stirring up **trouble**.

12 It is better to meet a mother bear **robbed** of her cubs than to meet some **fool** busy with a **stupid** project.

13 If you **repay** good with **evil**, you will never get **evil** out of your house.

14 The start of an **argument** is like the first break in a dam; stop it before it goes any further.

15 **Condemning** the **innocent** or letting the **wicked** go—both are **hateful** to the LORD.

16 It does a **fool** no good to spend money on an education, because he has no common **sense**.

17 **Friends** always show their **love**. What are brothers for if not to **share trouble**?

18 Only a man with no **sense** would **promise** to be responsible for someone else's **debts**.

19 To like sin is to like making **trouble**. If you brag all the time,[c] you are asking for **trouble**.

20 Anyone who thinks and speaks **evil** can expect to find nothing good—only **disaster**.

21 There is nothing but **sadness** and

[b] Kings...evil; *or* It is intolerable for kings to do evil.
16.25: Prov 14.12

[c] brag...time; *or* make a show of your wealth.

sorrow for a father whose son does **foolish** things.
22 Being **cheerful** keeps you healthy.
It is slow **death** to be **gloomy** all the time.
23 **Corrupt judges accept secret
bribes**, and then **justice** is not done.
24 An **intelligent** person aims at **wise
action**, but a **fool** starts off in many directions.
25 A **foolish** son brings **grief** to his
father and **bitter** regrets to his mother.
26 It is not **right** to make an **innocent**
person pay a fine; **justice** is **perverted**
when good people are **punished**.
27 Someone who is **sure** of himself
does not talk all the time. People who
stay **calm** have **real insight**. 28 After all,
even a **fool** may be thought **wise** and
intelligent if he stays quiet and keeps his
mouth shut.

18 People who do not get along with
others are **interested** only in
themselves; they will **disagree** with what
everyone else knows is **right**.
2 A **fool** does not **care** whether he
understands a thing or not; all he wants
to do is to show how clever he is.
3 Sin and **shame** go together. Lose
your **honour**, and you will get **scorn** in its
place.
4 A person's **words** can be a **source** of
wisdom, deep as the ocean, fresh as a
flowing stream.
5 It is not **right** to **favour** the **guilty** and
prevent the **innocent** from receiving
justice.
6 When some **fool** starts an **argument**,
he is asking for a beating.
7 When a **fool** speaks, he is **ruining**
himself; he gets caught in the **trap** of his
own **words**.
8 Gossip is so tasty—how we **love** to
swallow it!
9 A lazy person is as **bad** as someone
who is **destructive**.
10 The LORD is like a **strong** tower,
where the **righteous** can go and be **safe**.
11 **Rich** people, however, imagine that
their wealth **protects** them like high,
strong walls round a city.
12 No one is **respected** unless he is
humble; **arrogant** people are on the way
to **ruin**.
13 Listen **before** you answer. If you
don't you are being **stupid** and **insulting**.
14 Your **will** to live can sustain you
when you are sick, but if you lose it, your
last hope is gone.
15 **Intelligent** people are always **eager**
and ready to **learn**.
16 Do you want to meet an **important**
person? Take him a **gift** and it will be
easy.
17 The first man to speak in **court**
always seems **right** until his opponent
begins to **question** him.
18 If two **powerful** men are opposing
each other in **court**, casting **lots** can
settle the issue.
19 **Help** your brother and he will **protect** you like a **strong** city wall,[d] but if
you **quarrel** with him, he will close his
doors to you.
20 You will have to live with the consequences of everything you say. 21 What
you say can **preserve life or destroy** it; so
you must **accept** the consequences of
your **words**.
22 Find a wife and you find a good
thing; it shows that the LORD is good to
you.
23 When the **poor** man speaks, he has
to **beg** politely, but when the **rich** man
answers, he is rude.
24 Some **friendships** do[e] not **last**, but
some **friends** are more **loyal** than
brothers.

19 It is better to be **poor** but **honest**
than to be a **lying fool**.
2 Enthusiasm without **knowledge** is
not good; impatience will get you into
trouble.
3 Some people **ruin** themselves by
their own **stupid actions** and then **blame**
the LORD.
4 **Rich** people are always finding **new
friends**, but the **poor** cannot keep the few
they have.
5 If you tell **lies** in **court**, you will be
punished—there will be no **escape**.
6 Everyone tries to gain the **favour** of
important people; everyone **claims** the
friendship of those who give out **favours**.
7 Even the brothers of a **poor** man
have no use for him; no wonder he has
no **friends**. No matter how **hard** he tries,
he cannot **win** any.[f]
8 Do yourself a **favour** and **learn** all
you can; then **remember** what you **learn**
and you will **prosper**.
9 No one who tells **lies** in **court** can
escape punishment; he is **doomed**.
10 **Fools** should not live in **luxury**, and
slaves should not rule over noblemen.
11 If you are **sensible**, you will **control**
your temper. When someone **wrongs** you,
it is a great virtue to **ignore** it.
12 The king's **anger** is like the roar of
a lion, but his **favour** is like **welcome**
rain.

[d] *Some ancient translations* Help...wall; *Hebrew unclear.*
[e] *Some ancient translations* Some friendships do; *Hebrew* A man of friends does.
[f] *Probable text* No matter...any; *Hebrew unclear.*

safe 13.13; 19.23
scorn 11.12; 24.9
settle (2) Job 14.5; 25.9
shame 13.5; 19.26
source 8.30; Is 22.23
strong [3] 16.12; 21.22
stupid 17.12; 19.3
trap 12.13; 22.5
understand 16.21; 20.24
will (1) 16.33; 19.21
wisdom 16.16; 21.30
word (1) [3] 16.1; 21.28

action 17.24; Ecc 3.17
advice 15.12; 20.18
anger 16.14; 20.2
arrogant 18.12; 21.4
blame Job 32.2; Ezek 18.13
claim 1.19; 26.18
conceited 15.12; 21.4
control 16.32; 21.1
correct 15.5; 27.5
court (1) [2] 18.17; 22.22
destroy 18.9; 21.22
determine 16.33; 20.24
discipline Deut 8.5; 23.13
disgrace [2] 14.34; 28.7
doom Ps 49.14; 21.7
enough 13.25; 20.16
escape [2] 16.5; Ecc 8.8
evil 17.4; 20.8
favour [4] 18.5; Is 49.8
fool [3] 18.2; 20.1
friend [3] 18.24; 22.11
greed 11.6; 23.3
hard 16.26; 28.19
harm 16.27; 31.12
help 18.19; 21.13
honest 16.8; 20.7
hunger 16.26; 21.10
hurt 15.32; 24.2
ignore [2] 15.5; 31.5
ill-treat Job 24.21; Jer 22.3
important 18.16; 23.1
inherit 17.2; Ecc 7.11
justice 18.5; 20.28
knowledge 16.16; 22.20
law 8.15; 28.4
learn [7] 18.15; 21.11
lesson 6.6; 21.11
lie (2) [4] 17.4; 21.28
life (1) 18.21; 20.20

ccept 17.23; 21.28
gree Ps 105.9;
s 28.15
rgue 17.14; 20.3
rrogant 16.5; 19.25
ad 14.14; 25.27
eg 14.19; Jer 36.25
are 14.9; 27.5
ourt (1) [2] Ps 94.15;
9.5
estroy [2] 16.4;
9.18
ach other 7.18;
s 6.3
ager Ps 130.5;
ong 6.12
avour 16.13; 19.6
ool [3] 17.7; 19.1
riend [2] 17.9; 19.4
ift 6.35; 21.14
uilty Ps 109.7; 21.8
elp 13.14; 19.18
onour 15.33; 20.3
ope 13.12; 29.20
umble 16.19; 22.4
mportant 4.7; 19.6
nnocent 17.15; 21.8
nsult 17.5; Ecc 7.21
ntelligent 17.10;
6.16
nterest (1) Esth 3.8;
s 58.3
ustice 17.23; 19.28
ast (1) Ps 119.89;
7.24
ast (2) 16.1; Is 24.13
earn 17.10; 19.8
ife (1) 16.15; 19.23
ot (1) 16.33;
zek 47.22
ove 17.17; 19.28
oyal 16.6; 20.6
oor 17.5; 19.1
ower 16.32; 20.28
reserve Ps 132.17;
s 8.16
revent 2.12; Is 5.23
rotect [2] 15.25;
9.10
uarrel Ps 140.2;
2.10
uestion Job 42.3;
6.4
espect 17.7; 20.29
ich [2] 15.16; 19.4
ight (1) [3] 17.26;
0.4
ighteous 16.31;
1.12
uin [2] 13.15; 19.3

love 18.8; 22.5
luxury 21.17
neglect 8.33; Mt 6.16
new Ps 149.1; 23.29
obey 16.6; 22.4
plan 16.1; 20.18
poor [5] 18.23; 20.13
prosper 11.25; 24.25
punish [3] 17.5; 20.26
remember 17.9; 21.2
rich 18.11; 21.17
ruin [2] 18.7; 21.12
safe 18.10; 22.12
sense [2] 17.16; 21.16
shame 18.3; 25.10
slave 12.24; 22.7
stupid [2] 18.13; 20.1
sure 17.27; 21.29
trouble [2] 17.1; 21.23
turn 13.19; 26.14
welcome Ps 23.5; Song 8.12
wicked 17.11; 21.4
will (1) 18.14; 29.26
win 16.32; 24.6
wise [2] 17.24; 20.26
witness 14.5; 25.8
wrong 17.9; 20.22

13 A **stupid** son can bring his father to **ruin**. A nagging wife is like water going drip-drip-drip.

14 A man can **inherit** a house and money from his parents, but only the LORD can give him a **sensible** wife.

15 Be lazy if you want to; sleep on, but you will go **hungry**.

16 Keep God's **laws** and you will live longer; if you **ignore** them, you will die.

17 When you give to the **poor**, it is like lending to the LORD, and the LORD will pay you back.

18 **Discipline** your children while they are young **enough** to **learn**. If you don't, you are **helping** them to **destroy** themselves.[g]

19 If someone has a hot temper, let him take the consequences. If you get him out of **trouble** once, you will have to do it again.[h]

20 If you listen to **advice** and are willing to **learn**, one day you will **be wise**.

21 People may **plan** all kinds of things, but the **LORD's will** is going to be done.

22 It is a **disgrace** to be **greedy**;[i] **poor** people are better off than **liars**.

23 **Obey** the LORD and you will live a long **life**, content and **safe** from **harm**.

24 Some people are too lazy to put food in their own mouths.

25 **Arrogance** should be **punished**, so that people who don't know any better can **learn** a **lesson**. If you are **wise**, you will **learn** when you are **corrected**.

26 Only a **shameful**, **disgraceful** person would **ill-treat** his father or **turn** his mother away from his home.

27 Son, when you stop **learning**, you will soon **neglect** what you already know.

28 There is no **justice** where a **witness** is **determined** to **hurt** someone. **Wicked** people **love** the taste of **evil**.

29 A **conceited fool** is **sure** to get a beating.

advice 19.20; 22.20
anger [2] 19.12; 21.14
argue 18.6; 22.10
change Ps 119.159; 22.25
complain Ps 142.2; 21.19
conscience [2] Ps 16.7; Acts 23.1
curse 11.26; 24.24
dark 7.9; Ecc 2.13
debt 17.18; 22.26
determine 19.28; Ecc 1.13
dishonest [3] 16.8; 21.6
enjoy 15.15; 24.25
enough 19.18; 21.5
evil 19.28; 21.10
experience Ps 72.3; 25.12
faithful 16.6; Is 1.21

20 Drinking too much makes you loud and **foolish**. It's **stupid** to get drunk.

2 **Fear** an **angry** king as you would a growling lion; making him **angry** is suicide.

3 Any **fool** can start **arguments**; the **honourable** thing is to stay out of them.

4 A farmer who is too lazy to plough his fields at the **right** time will have nothing to **harvest**.

5 A person's thoughts are like water in a deep well, but someone with **insight** can draw them out.

6 Everyone talks about how **loyal** and **faithful** he is, but just try to find someone who really is!

7 Children are **fortunate** if they have a father who is **honest** and does what is **right**.

8 The king sits in **judgement** and knows **evil** when he sees it.

9 Can anyone really say that his **conscience** is clear, that he has got **rid** of his sin?

10 The LORD **hates** people who use **dishonest** weights and measures.

11 Even a child shows what he is by what he does; you can tell if he is **honest** and good.

12 The LORD has given us eyes to see with and ears to listen with.

13 If you spend your time sleeping, you will be **poor**. Keep busy and you will have **plenty** to eat.

14 The customer always **complains** that the price is too high, but then he goes off and brags about the bargain he got.

15 If you know what you are talking about, you have something more **valuable** than gold or jewels.

16 Anyone **stupid enough** to **promise** to be responsible for a **stranger's debts** ought to have his own property held to **guarantee** payment.

17 What you get by **dishonesty** you may **enjoy** like the finest food, but sooner or later it will be like a mouthful of sand.

18 Get good **advice** and you will **succeed**; don't go charging into battle without a **plan**.

19 A gossip can never keep a **secret**. Stay away from people who talk too much.

20 If you **curse** your parents, your **life** will end like a lamp that goes out in the **dark**.

21 The more easily you get your wealth, the less good it will do you.

22 Don't take it on yourself to **repay** a **wrong**. **Trust** the LORD and he will make it **right**.

23 The LORD **hates** people who use **dishonest** scales and weights.

24 The LORD has **determined** our path; how then can anyone **understand** the direction his own **life** is taking?

25 Think carefully before you **promise** an **offering** to God. You might regret it later.

26 A **wise** king will find out who is doing **wrong**, and will **punish** him without **pity**.

fear 15.16; Is 5.22
fool [2] 19.1; 23.9
fortune 13.7; Ecc 10.17
guarantee Esth 3.9; 27.13
harvest 10.5; 25.13
hate [2] 17.15; 21.27
honest [3] 19.1; 21.2
honour 18.3; 22.4
insight 17.27; 21.30
judge 17.23; 21.2
justice 19.28; 21.15
life (1) [2] 19.23; 21.
loyal 18.24; Is 38.3
mind (1) 17.1; 21.1
offer 7.14; 21.27
pain 5.4; Ecc 11.10
pity Ps 135.14; Is 9.
plan 19.21; 21.5
plenty 13.23; 21.5
poor 19.1; 21.13
power 18.18; 23.11
promise [2] 17.18; 22.26
punish 19.5; 21.11
repay 17.13; Is 65.6
respect 18.12; 21.21
rid Ps 101.5; 22.10
right (1) [3] 18.1; 21
secret 17.23; 21.14
stranger 11.15; 27.2
strength Ps 150.1; 24.5
stupid [2] 19.3; 21.20
succeed (1) 16.3; 28.13
trust 16.20; 22.19
understand 18.2; 24.3
value 3.15; 23.23
way (3) 15.9; Is 55.8
wise 19.20; 21.11
wrong [2] 19.11; 24.2

[g] If you...themselves; *or* But don't beat them so hard that you kill them.
[h] get him out...again; *or* try to get him out of trouble, you only make things worse.
[i] It...greedy; *or* Loyalty is what is desired in a person.

accept 18.21; Is 1.23
act 14.16; 30.20
anger 20.2; 22.14
arrogant [2] 19.25; 29.23
believe 17.8; 26.25
best 3.9; 31.29
calm 17.27; 29.8
complain 20.14; 23.29
conceited [3] 19.29; 22.10
control [2] 19.11; 25.28
death (1) [2] 17.11; Ecc 3.2
defend Ps 144.2; 23.11
despair Ps 143.4; Is 16.7
destroy 19.18; 24.16
direct 16.9; Is 48.17
dishonest 20.10; 28.6
doom 19.9; Is 1.4
enough 20.16; 23.4
evil [3] 20.8; 24.1
generous 11.25; 22.9
gift 18.16; 22.16
guilty 18.5; 24.24
happy 16.14; 23.15
hate 20.10; 24.9
help [2] 19.18; 27.10
honest 20.7; 24.15
human 8.31; 27.20
hunger 19.15; 25.21
innocent 18.5; 24.24
insight 20.5; 28.11
judge 20.8; 24.12
justice 20.28; 25.5
kind 16.24; 28.8
learn [2] 19.8; 22.25
lesson 19.25; 24.32
lie (2) 19.1; 22.12
life (1) 20.20; 22.4
luxury [2] 19.10; Lam 4.5
mercy 5.9; 28.13
mind (1) 20.27; 23.1
motive [2] 16.2; 24.12
offer 20.25; Ecc 5.1
plan 20.18; 24.6
please 16.7; Ecc 2.26
plenty 20.13; 28.19
poor 20.13; 22.2
proud 17.6; 23.16
punish 20.26; 24.18
refuse (1) [3] 15.32; 27.7
rely 14.5; 25.13
remember 19.8; 22.6
respect 20.29; 29.23
rich 19.4; 22.2
riches 11.4; 22.4
right (1) [4] 20.4; 22.21
righteous [3] 18.10; 23.24
ruin 19.3; 24.22
sacrifice [2] 15.8; Ecc 5.1
secret 20.19; 25.9
sense 19.11; 22.3
share 17.17; 22.9
strong 18.10; 24.5
stupid 20.1; 24.7
suffer 9.12; 30.10
sure 19.29; 24.14
teach 16.20; 22.6
testimony Job 20.27; Zech 8.17
trouble 19.2; 22.3
victory Ps 149.4; Is 26.18

27 The LORD gave us **mind** and **con**-
science; we cannot hide from ourselves.
28 A king will remain in **power** as long
as his rule is **honest**, **just**, and fair.
29 We admire the **strength** of youth
and **respect** the grey hair of age.
30 Sometimes it takes a **painful experi**-
ence to make us **change** our **ways**.

21

The LORD **controls** the **mind** of a
king as easily as he **directs** the
course of a stream.
2 You may think that everything you
do is **right**, but **remember** that the LORD
judges your **motives**.
3 Do what is **right** and fair; that
pleases the LORD more than bringing
him **sacrifices**.
4 **Wicked** people are **controlled** by
their **conceit** and **arrogance**, and this is
sinful.
5 **Plan** carefully and you will have
plenty; if you **act** too quickly, you will
never have **enough**.
6 The **riches** you get by **dishonesty**
soon disappear, but not before they lead
you into the jaws of **death**.
7 The **wicked** are **doomed** by their
own **violence**; they **refuse** to do what is
right.
8 **Guilty** people walk a crooked path;
the **innocent** do what is **right**.
9 Better to live on the roof than **share**
the house with a nagging wife.
10 **Wicked** people are always **hungry**
for **evil**; they have no **mercy** on anyone.
11 When someone who is **conceited**
gets his **punishment**, even an unthinking
person **learns** a **lesson**. One who is **wise**
will **learn** from what he is **taught**.
12 God, the **righteous** one, knows what
goes on in the homes of the **wicked**, and
he will bring the **wicked** down to **ruin**.
13 If you **refuse** to listen to the cry of
the **poor**, your own cry for **help** will not
be heard.
14 If someone is **angry** with you, a **gift**
given **secretly** will **calm** him down.
15 When **justice** is done, good people
are **happy**, but **evil** people are brought to
despair.
16 **Death** is waiting for anyone who
wanders away from good **sense**.
17 Indulging in **luxuries**, wine, and
rich food will never make you wealthy.
18 The **wicked** bring on themselves
the **suffering** they try to cause good
people.
19 Better to live out in the desert than
with a nagging, **complaining** wife.
20 **Wise** people live in wealth and
luxury, but **stupid** people spend their
money as fast as they get it.
21 Be **kind** and **honest** and you will
live a long **life**; others will **respect** you
and treat you fairly.
22 A shrewd general can take a city
defended by **strong** men, and **destroy** the
walls they **relied** on.
23 If you want to stay out of **trouble**, be
careful what you say.
24 Show me a **conceited** person and I
will show you someone who is **arrogant**,
proud, and inconsiderate.
25 A lazy man who **refuses** to work is
only killing himself; 26 all he does is think
about what he would like to have. A
righteous man, however, can give, and
give **generously**.
27 The LORD **hates** it when **wicked**
men **offer him sacrifices**, especially if
they do it from **evil motives**.
28 The **testimony** of a **liar** is not **be**-
lieved, but the **word** of someone who
thinks matters through is **accepted**.
29 **Righteous** people are **sure** of themselves; the **wicked** have to pretend as
best they can.
30 **Human wisdom**, brilliance, **in**-
sight—they are of no **help** if the LORD is
against you.
31 You can get horses ready for battle,
but it is the LORD who gives **victory**.

22

If you have to **choose** between a
good **reputation** and great
wealth, **choose** a good **reputation**.
2 The **rich** and the **poor** have this in
common: the LORD made them both.
3 **Sensible** people will see **trouble**
coming and avoid it, but an unthinking
person will walk right into it and regret it
later.
4 **Obey** the LORD, be **humble**, and you
will get **riches**, **honour**, and a long **life**.
5 If you **love** your **life**, stay away from
the **traps** that catch the **wicked** along the
way.
6 **Teach** a child how he should live,
and he will **remember** it all his **life**.
7 **Poor** people are the **rich** man's
slaves. Borrow money and you are the
lender's **slave**.
8 If you **sow** the **seeds** of **injustice**,
disaster will spring up, and your **op**-
pression of others will end.
9 Be **generous** and **share** your food
with the **poor**. You will be **blessed** for it.
10 Get **rid** of a **conceited** person, and
then there will be no more **arguments**,
quarrelling, or calling of names.
11 If you **love purity** of **heart** and
graciousness of **speech**, the king will be
your **friend**.
12 The LORD sees to it that **truth** is
kept **safe** by **disproving** the **words** of
liars.
13 The lazy man stays at home; he

violent 16.29; 22.24
wicked [8] 19.28; 22.5
wisdom 18.4; 23.16
wise [2] 20.26; 22.17
word (1) 18.4; 22.12

adultery 6.26; 30.20
advantage [2] Job 21.15; 28.8
advice 20.18; 24.6
anger 21.14; 25.23
argue [2] 20.3; 23.11
bless 16.3; Is 19.24
case (2) Job 35.14; 23.11
change 20.30; Is 43.13
choose [2] 8.10; Ecc 3.1
conceited 21.4; Is 2.12
court (1) 19.5; 25.1
debt 20.16; 27.13
disaster 17.20; 24.16
establish Ps 99.4; 24.27
friend [2] 19.4; 24.1
generous 21.26; 31.20
gift 21.14; Ecc 3.13
glad Ps 149.2; 24.17
grace 11.16; Song 7.7
heart 17.3; 26.25
helpless Ps 116.6; 25.28
honour 20.3; 24.21
humble 18.12; 29.23
injustice 12.17; Ecc 4.1
knowledge 19.2; 24.4
learn 21.11; 23.12
lie (2) 21.28; 26.28
life (1) [4] 21.21; 23.14
love [2] 19.28; 26.22
natural Ps 109.18; Ecc 10.2
obey 19.23; 28.4
oppress [2] 14.31; 28.3
poor [5] 21.13; 23.21
promise 20.16; 25.14
prove Ps 105.19; 25.8
pure 10.20; 30.12
quarrel 18.19; 26.20
remember [2] 21.2; 23.35

says a lion might get him if he goes outside.

14 **Adultery** is a **trap**—it catches those with whom the LORD is **angry**.

15 Children just **naturally** do silly, careless things, but a good spanking will **teach** them how to behave.

16 If you make **gifts** to **rich** people or **oppress** the poor to get **rich**, you will become **poor** yourself.

The Thirty Wise Sayings

17 Listen, and I will **teach** you what **wise** men have said. **Study** their **teachings**, 18 and you will be **glad** if you **remember** them and can quote them. 19 I want you to put your **trust** in the LORD; that is why I am going to tell them to you now. 20 I have written down thirty **sayings** for you. They contain **knowledge** and good **advice**, 21 and will **teach** you what the **truth** really is. Then when you are sent to find it out, you will bring back the **right** answer.

-1-

22 Don't take **advantage** of the **poor** just because you can; don't take **advantage** of those who stand **helpless in court**. 23 The LORD will **argue** their **case** for them and **threaten** the **life** of anyone who **threatens** theirs.

-2-

24 Don't make **friends** with people who have hot, **violent** tempers. 25 You might **learn** their habits and not be able to **change**.

-3-

26 Don't **promise** to be responsible for someone else's **debts**. 27 If you should be unable to pay, they will take away even your bed.

-4-

28 Never move an old boundary-mark that your ancestors **established**.

-5-

29 Show me a man who does a good job, and I will show you a man who is better than most and **worthy** of the company of kings.

-6-

23 When you sit down to eat with an **important** man, keep in **mind** who he is.[j] 2 If you have a big appetite, restrain yourself. 3 Don't be **greedy** for the fine food he **serves**; he may be trying to **trick** you.

-7-

4 Be **wise enough** not to wear yourself out trying to get **rich**. 5 Your money can be gone in a flash, as if it had grown wings and flown away like an eagle.

-8-

6 Don't eat at the table of a stingy man or be **greedy** for the fine food he **serves**. 7 "Come on and have some more," he says, but he doesn't mean it. What he thinks is what he really is. 8 You will vomit up what you have eaten, and all your flattery will be wasted.

-9-

9 Don't try to talk **sense** to a **fool**; he can't appreciate it.

-10-

10 Never move an old boundary-mark or take over land owned by **orphans**. 11 The LORD is their **powerful defender**, and he will **argue** their **case** against you.

-11-

12 Pay attention to your **teacher** and **learn** all you can.

-12-

13 Don't hesitate to **discipline** a child. A good spanking won't kill him. 14 As a matter of fact, it may **save** his **life**.

-13-

15 Son, if you become **wise**, I will be very **happy**. 16 I will be **proud** when I hear you speaking **words** of **wisdom**.

-14-

17 Don't be **envious** of sinful people; let **reverence** for the LORD be the **concern** of your **life**. 18 If it is, you have a bright future.

-15-

19 Listen, my son, be **wise** and give **serious** thought to the way you live. 20 Don't associate with people who drink too much wine or stuff themselves with food. 21 Drunkards and gluttons will be reduced to **poverty**. If all you do is eat and sleep, you will soon be wearing rags.

-16-

22 Listen to your father; without him

[j] keep...is; *or* notice carefully what is before you.

you would not **exist**. When your mother is old, show her your appreciation.

23 **Truth**, **wisdom**, **learning**, and good **sense**—these are **worth** paying for, but too **valuable** for you to sell.

24 A **righteous** man's father has good **reason** to be **happy**. You can take **pride** in a **wise** son.

25 Make your father and mother **proud** of you; give your mother that **happiness**.

–17–

26 Pay close attention, son, and let my **life** be your **example**. 27 **Prostitutes** and **immoral** women are a **deadly trap**. 28 They wait for you like **robbers** and cause many men to be **unfaithful**.

–18–

29–30 Show me someone who drinks too much, who has to **try** out some **new** drink, and I will show you someone **miserable** and **sorry** for himself, always causing **trouble** and always **complaining**. His eyes are **bloodshot**, and he has bruises that could have been avoided. 31 Don't let wine **tempt** you, even though it is **rich** red, though it sparkles in the **cup**, and it goes down smoothly. 32 The next morning you will feel as if you had been bitten by a poisonous snake. 33 Weird **sights** will appear before your eyes, and you will not be able to think or speak clearly. 34 You will feel as if you were out on the ocean, sea-sick, swinging high up in the rigging of a tossing ship. 35 "I must have been hit," you will say; "I must have **been beaten** up, but I don't **remember** it. Why can't I wake up? I **need** another drink."

–19–

24 Don't be **envious** of **evil** people, and don't try to make **friends** with them. 2 Causing **trouble** is all they ever think about; every time they open their mouth someone is going to be **hurt**.

–20–

3 Homes are built on the foundation of **wisdom** and **understanding**.[k] 4 Where there is **knowledge**, the rooms are furnished with **valuable**, beautiful things.

–21–

5 Being **wise** is better than being **strong**;[l] yes, **knowledge** is more **important** than **strength**. 6 After all, you must make careful **plans** before you fight a battle, and the more good **advice** you get, the more likely you are to **win**.

–22–

7 **Wise sayings** are too deep for a **stupid** person to **understand**. He has nothing to say when **important** matters are being **discussed**.

–23–

8 If you are always **planning evil**, you will earn a **reputation** as a **troublemaker**. 9 Any **scheme** a **fool** thinks up is sinful. People **hate** a person who has nothing but **scorn** for others.

–24–

10 If you are **weak** in a crisis, you are weak indeed.

–25–

11 Don't hesitate to **rescue** someone who is about to be **executed unjustly**. 12 You may say that it is none of your business, but God knows and **judges** your **motives**. He keeps **watch** on you; he knows. And he will **reward** you according to what you do.

–26–

13 Son, eat honey; it is good. And just as honey from the comb is sweet on your tongue, 14 you may be **sure** that **wisdom** is good for the **soul**. Get **wisdom** and you have a bright future.

–27–

15 Don't be like the **wicked** who **scheme** to **rob** an **honest** man or to take away his home. 16 No matter how often an **honest** man falls, he always gets up again; but **disaster destroys** the **wicked**.

–28–

17 Don't be **glad** when your **enemy** meets **disaster**, and don't **rejoice** when he **stumbles**. 18 The LORD will know if you are gloating, and he will not like it; and then he might not **punish** him.

–29–

19 Don't let **evil** people **worry** you; don't be **envious** of them. 20 A **wicked** person has no future—nothing to look forward to.

[k] Homes...understanding; *or* It takes care to lay the foundations of a house, and craftsmanship to build it.
[l] *Some ancient translations* Being wise is better than being strong; *Hebrew* A man is wise in strength.

advice 22.20; Ecc 4.13
curse 20.20; 26.2
destroy 21.22; 27.4
disaster [3] 22.8; Is 10.3
discuss Mt 16.7
enemy 16.7; 25.21
enjoy 20.17; Ecc 2.1
envy [2] 23.17; Ecc 4.2
establish 22.28; Is 14.32
evidence Job 15.5; Ecc 10.3
evil [3] 21.10; 25.5
execute 2 Chr 25.3; Jer 39.6
fool 23.9; 26.1
friend [2] 22.11; 27.6
glad 22.18; Ecc 7.14
guilty [2] 21.8; 28.17
hate [2] 21.27; 25.17

honest [3] 21.21; 28.1
honour 22.4; 25.2
hurt 19.28; 26.2
important [2] 23.1; 25.6
innocent 21.8; 28.10
judge [3] 21.2; 28.21
knowledge [2] 22.20; 30.4
learn 23.12; 25.10
lesson 21.11; Is 28.10
mislead 8.8; 26.18
motive 21.2; Dan 11.27
plan [2] 21.5; 30.32
poor 23.21; 28.3
poverty *see* **poor**
prosper 19.8; Is 26.12
punish [2] 21.11; 28.20
reason 23.24; 26.16
rebel Ps 139.21; Is 1.2
rejoice Ps 149.2; Is 9.3
reputation [2] 22.1; 27.21
rescue 12.6; Is 17.10
rest (1) 6.4; Ecc 2.23
reverence 23.17; Ecc 7.18
reward 16.31; 25.22
rob [2] 23.28; Is 33.1
ruin 21.12; 26.28
saying 22.20; 26.9
scheme [2] Ps 119.118; Is 8.12
scorn 18.3; Jer 20.8
sign (1) Ps 108.9; Is 7.11
soul Ps 146.1; Lam 1.20
strength 20.29; Ecc 9.16
strong 21.22; 25.15
stumble 4.12; Is 5.27
stupid [2] 21.20; 26.8
sure [2] 21.29; 25.23
trouble [2] 23.29; 26.6
true 13.12; Is 10.20
understand [2] 20.24; 28.5
unjust 13.23; Is 10.1
value 23.23; 25.12
vineyard Job 24.6; 31.16
watch 16.17; 27.6
weak Ps 109.24; 30.25
weed Ps 92.7; Is 5.6
wicked [3] 22.5; 28.1
win 19.7; 25.27
wisdom [3] 23.16; 29.3
wise [3] 23.4; 26.9
worry 12.25; 31.21
wrong 20.22; 25.8

-30-

21 Have **reverence** for the LORD, my son, and **honour** the king. Have nothing to do with people who **rebel** against them; 22 such men could be **ruined** in a moment. Do you realize the **disaster** that God or the king can cause?

More Wise Sayings

23 **Wise** men have also said these things:

It is **wrong** for a **judge** to be prejudiced. 24 If he pronounces a **guilty** person **innocent**, he will be **cursed** and **hated** by everyone. 25 **Judges** who **punish** the **guilty**, however, will be **prosperous** and **enjoy** a good **reputation**.

26 An **honest** answer is a **sign** of **true friendship**.

27 Don't build your house and **establish** a home until your fields are ready, and you are **sure** that you can earn a living.

28 Don't give **evidence** against someone else without good **reason**, or say **misleading** things about him. 29 Don't say, "I'll do to him just what he did to me! I'll get even with him!"

30 I walked through the fields and **vineyards** of a lazy, **stupid** man. 31 They were full of thorn bushes and overgrown with **weeds**. The stone wall round them had fallen down. 32 I looked at this, thought about it, and **learned** a **lesson** from it: 33 Have a nap and sleep if you want to. Fold your hands and **rest** awhile, 34 but while you are asleep, **poverty** will attack you like an armed **robber**.

More of Solomon's Proverbs

25 Here are more of Solomon's **proverbs**, copied by men at the **court** of King Hezekiah of Judah.

2 We **honour** God for what he conceals; we **honour** kings for what they explain.

3 You never know what a king is thinking; his thoughts are beyond us, like the heights of the sky or the depths of the ocean.

4 Take the **impurities** out of silver and the artist can produce a thing of beauty. 5 Keep **evil** advisers away from the king and his government will be known for its **justice**.

6 When you stand before the king, don't try to impress him and pretend to be **important**. 7 It is better to be asked to take a higher position than to be told to give your place to someone more **important**.

8 Don't be too quick to go to **court** about something you have seen. If another **witness** later **proves** you **wrong**, what will you do then?

9 If you and your **neighbour** have a difference of opinion, **settle** it between yourselves and do not **reveal** any **secrets**. 10 Otherwise everyone will **learn** that you can't keep a **secret**, and you will never live down the **shame**.

11 An **idea** well-expressed is like a design of gold, set in silver.

12 A **warning** given by an **experienced** person to someone willing to listen is more **valuable** than gold rings or jewellery made of the finest gold.

13 A **reliable** messenger is refreshing to the one who sends him, like cold water in the heat of **harvest** time.

14 People who **promise** things that they never give are like **clouds** and wind that bring no rain.

15 **Patient persuasion** can break down the **strongest resistance** and can even **convince** rulers.

16 Never eat more honey than you **need**; too much may make you vomit. 17 Don't visit your **neighbour** too often; he may get tired of you and come to **hate** you.

18 A **false accusation** is as **deadly** as a sword, a club, or a sharp arrow.

19 **Depending** on an **unreliable** person in a crisis is like trying to chew with a loose tooth or walk with a **crippled** foot.

20 Singing to a person who is depressed is like taking off his clothes on a cold day or like rubbing salt in a wound.

21 If your **enemy** is **hungry**, feed him; if he is thirsty, give him a drink. 22 You will make him burn with **shame**, and the LORD will **reward** you.

23 Gossip brings **anger** just as **surely** as the north wind brings rain.

24 Better to live on the roof than **share** the house with a nagging wife.

25 Finally, hearing **good news** from a distant land is like a drink of cold water when you are dry and thirsty.

26 A good person who gives in to someone who is **evil reminds** you of a polluted spring or a poisoned well.

27 Too much honey is **bad** for you, and so is trying to **win** too much **praise**. [m]

28 If you cannot **control** your **anger**, you are as **helpless** as a city without walls, open to attack.

26 **Praise** for a **fool** is out of place, like snow in summer or rain at **harvest** time.

2 **Curses** cannot **hurt** you unless you

[m] *Probable text* and so...praise; *Hebrew unclear.*

24.33–34: Prov 6.10–11 **25.6–7:** Lk 14.8–10 **25.21–22:** Rom 12.20

accuse Ps 140.11; Is 3.14
anger [2] 22.14; 27.4
bad 18.9; 28.12
cloud 16.15; Ecc 11.3
control 21.1; 30.16
convince Job 32.1; Ecc 8.15
court (1) [2] 22.22; 29.24
cripple Ps 35.16; 26.7
deadly 23.27; 26.18
depend 14.28; Ecc 5.9
enemy 24.17; 27.6
evil [2] 24.1; 26.26
experience 20.30; Mic 2.4
false 8.8; 29.12
Good News 15.30; Is 21.10
harvest 20.4; 26.1
hate 24.9; 26.24
helpless 22.22; 28.15
honour [2] 24.21; 27.18
hunger 21.10; 27.7
idea 17.4; Is 44.20
important [2] 24.5; Is 10.15

impure Ps 106.39; Is 1.25
justice 21.15; 28.5
learn 24.32; 27.17
need 23.35; 28.27
neighbour [2] 14.20; 27.10
patient 16.32; 29.11
persuade 16.21; Is 36.15
praise 12.8; 26.1
promise 22.26; 27.13
prove 22.12; Is 38.7
proverb 10.1; 26.7
rely [2] 21.22; Is 8.2
remind Ps 143.8; 26.9
resist 2.16; Ecc 4.12
reveal Ps 103.7; Is 1.1
reward 24.12; 28.10
secret [2] 21.14; Ecc 12.14
settle (2) 18.18; Is 1.18
shame [2] 19.26; Is 3.24
share 22.9; Ecc 6.3
strong 24.5; 28.2
sure 24.14; Ecc 3.21
value 24.4; 31.18
warn 6.15; Is 8.11
win 24.6; Ecc 9.11
witness 19.28; Is 8.2
wrong 24.23; 28.21

afraid 3.24; 30.30
alive 1.12; Ecc 3.12
argue [2] 23.11; Ecc 6.10
believe 21.28; Is 43.10

claim 19.6; 30.6
cripple 25.19; Mic 4.7
curse 24.24; 27.14
deadly 25.18; Is 27.1
deserve 14.14; 27.13
evil 25.5; 28.5
fool [8] 24.9; 27.22
harvest 25.13; Ecc 5.9
hate [4] 25.17; 28.9
heart 22.11; 27.19
hurt [3] 24.2; 27.6
hypocrite Ps 101.7; Mt 6.2
intelligent 18.15; 28.2
lie (2) 22.12; 29.12
love 22.5; 30.19
mad Job 16.14; Ecc 1.17
message Ps 147.19; Ecc 10.20
mislead 24.28; Is 3.12
praise [2] 25.27; 27.2
proverb 25.1; Ecc 12.9
quarrel 22.10; 29.22
question [2] 18.17; Ecc 7.10
reason 24.28; 29.17
remind 25.26; Ecc 7.2
ruin 24.22; 28.14
saying 24.7; Ecc 12.11
sense 23.9; 27.12
stupid [3] 24.7; 27.3
trap 23.27; 28.10
trouble [2] 24.2; 27.3
turn 19.26; Ecc 12.5
wise [2] 24.5; 27.11
word (1) 23.16; 30.1

deserve them. They are like birds that fly
by and never settle.

3 You have to whip a horse, you have
to bridle a donkey, and you have to beat
a **fool**.

4 If you answer a silly **question**, you
are just as silly as the person who asked
it.

5 Give a silly answer to a silly **question**, and the one who asked it will realize
that he's not as clever as he thinks.

6 If you let a **fool** deliver a **message**,
you might as well cut off your own feet;
you are asking for **trouble**.

7 A **fool** can use a **proverb** about as
well as a **crippled** man can use his legs.

8 **Praising** someone who is **stupid**
makes as much **sense** as tying a stone in
a sling.

9 A **fool** quoting a **wise saying reminds**
you of a drunk man trying to pick a thorn
out of his hand.

10 An employer who hires any **fool**
that comes along is only **hurting** everybody concerned.[n]

11 A **fool** doing some **stupid** thing a
second time is like a dog going back to
its vomit.

12 The most **stupid fool** is better off
than someone who thinks he is **wise**
when he is not.

13 Why doesn't the lazy man ever get
out of the house? What is he **afraid** of?
Lions?

14 The lazy man **turns** over in bed. He
gets no farther than a door swinging on
its hinges.

15 Some people are too lazy to put
food in their own mouths.

16 A lazy man will think he is more
intelligent than seven men who can give
good **reasons** for their opinions.

17 Getting involved in an **argument**
that is none of your business is like going
down the street and grabbing a dog by
the ears.

18–19 A man who **misleads** someone
and then **claims** that he was only joking
is like a **madman** playing with a **deadly**
weapon.

20 Without wood, a fire goes out; without gossip, **quarrelling** stops.

21 Charcoal keeps the embers glowing, wood keeps the fire burning, and
troublemakers keep **arguments alive**.

22 Gossip is so tasty! How we **love** to
swallow it!

23 Insincere[o] talk that hides what you
are really thinking is like a fine glaze[p] on
a cheap clay pot.

24 A **hypocrite** hides his **hate** behind
flattering **words**. 25 They may sound fine,
but don't **believe** him, because his **heart**
is filled to the brim with **hate**. 26 He may
disguise his **hatred**, but everyone will see
the **evil** things he does.

27 People who set **traps** for others get
caught themselves. People who start
landslides get crushed.

28 You have to **hate** someone to want
to **hurt** him with **lies**. Insincere talk
brings nothing but **ruin**.

27

Never **boast** about tomorrow.
You don't know what will happen
between now and then.

2 Let other people **praise** you—even
strangers; never do it yourself.

3 The weight of stone and sand is
nothing **compared** to the **trouble** that **stupidity** can cause.

4 **Anger** is **cruel** and **destructive**, but it
is nothing **compared** to **jealousy**.

5 Better to **correct** someone openly
than to let him think you don't **care** for
him at all.

6 A **friend** means well, even when he
hurts you. But when an **enemy** puts his
arm round your shoulder—**watch** out!

7 When you are full, you will **refuse**
honey, but when you are **hungry**, even
bitter food tastes sweet.

8 A man away from home is like a
bird away from its nest.

9 Perfume and fragrant oils make you
feel **happier**, but **trouble** shatters your
peace of mind.[q]

10 Do not **forget** your **friends** or your
father's friends. If you are in **trouble**,
don't ask your brother for **help**; a **neighbour** near by can **help** you more than a
brother who is far away.

11 Be **wise**, my son, and I will be
happy; I will have an answer for anyone
who **criticizes** me.

12 **Sensible** people will see **trouble**
coming and avoid it, but an unthinking
person will walk right into it and regret it
later.

13 Anyone **stupid enough** to **promise** to
be responsible for a **stranger's debts**[r] **deserves** to have his own property held to
guarantee payment.

14 You might as well **curse** your **friend**
as wake him up early in the morning
with a loud greeting.

15 A nagging wife is like water going
drip-drip-drip on a rainy day. 16 How can

anger 25.23; 29.11
bitter 17.25; Ecc 7.26
boast Ps 94.4; Is 10.8
care [3] 18.2; Song 1.6
compare [2] 8.11; Song 2.3
correct 19.25; 28.23
criticize 10.10; 30.10
cruel 17.11; 28.16
curse 26.2; 28.27
dead 1.12; Ecc 4.2
debt 22.26; Amos 2.6
deserve 26.2; 31.31
desire Ps 119.36; Ecc 2.3
destroy 24.16; 28.3
enemy 25.21; 29.24
enough 23.4; 30.32
fool [2] 26.1; 28.26
forget 10.7; 31.5
friend [3] 24.1; 28.7
guarantee 20.16; Ezek 34.25
happy [2] 23.15; 28.14
heart 26.25; Ecc 2.23
help [2] 21.13; Ecc 4.1
honour 25.2; 31.30
human 21.30; Ecc 3.19
hunger 25.21; Is 5.14
hurt 26.2; Ecc 1.18
jealous 14.30; Is 11.13
last (1) 18.24; Ecc 3.14
learn 25.10; 30.3
master 17.2; 30.4
mind (1) 23.1; Ecc 2.23
neighbour 25.9; Ecc 4.4
peace 17.1; Ecc 3.8
praise 26.1; 31.28
promise 25.14; 30.5
provide 3.22; Is 55.10
refuse (1) 21.7; Is 7.12
reputation 24.8; Ecc 7.1
self Mt 16.24
sense 26.8; 28.2
servant [2] 17.2; 29.19
sheep [2] Ps 144.13; Ecc 12.11
stranger [2] 20.16; Ecc 6.2
stupid [2] 26.8; 29.11
test [2] 17.3; Ecc 3.18
trouble [4] 26.6; 28.25
watch 24.12; 30.29
wise 26.9; 28.11
world of the dead 15.11; 30.16

[n] *Verse 10 in Hebrew is unclear.* [o] *One ancient translation* Insincere; *Hebrew* Burning.
[p] *Probable text* fine glaze; *Hebrew* unrefined silver.
[q] *One ancient translation* but trouble...mind; *Hebrew unclear.*
[r] *One ancient translation* stranger's debts; *Hebrew* stranger's debts or those of an immoral woman.

27.1: Jas 4.13–16

you keep her quiet? Have you ever tried to stop the wind or ever tried to hold a handful of oil?[s]

17 People **learn** from one another, just as iron sharpens iron.

18 Take **care** of a fig-tree and you will have figs to eat. A **servant** who takes **care** of his **master** will be **honoured**.

19 It is your own face that you see reflected in the water and it is your own **self** that you see in your **heart**.

20 **Human desires** are like the **world of the dead**—there is always room for more.

21 Fire **tests** gold and silver; a person's **reputation** can also be **tested**.

22 Even if you beat a **fool** until he's half **dead**, you still can't beat his **foolishness** out of him.

23 Look after your **sheep** and cattle as carefully as you can, 24 because wealth is not permanent. Not even nations **last** for ever. 25 You cut the hay and then cut the grass on the hillsides while the next crop of hay is growing. 26 You can make clothes from the wool of your **sheep** and buy land with the money you get from selling some of your goats. 27 The rest of the goats will **provide** milk for you and your family, and for your **servant-girls** as well.

28

The **wicked** run when no one is chasing them, but an **honest** person is as brave as a lion.

2 When a nation sins, it will have one ruler after another. But a nation will be **strong** and **endure** when it has **intelligent**, **sensible** leaders.

3 A man in **authority** who **oppresses** **poor** people is like a driving rain that **destroys** the crops.

4 If you have no regard for the **law**, you are on the side of the **wicked**; but if you **obey** it, you are against them.

5 **Evil** people do not know what **justice** is, but those who **worship** the LORD **understand** it well.

6 Better to be **poor** and **honest** than **rich** and **dishonest**.

7 A young man who **obeys** the **law** is **intelligent**. One who makes **friends** with good-for-nothings is a **disgrace** to his father.

8 If you get **rich** by charging interest and taking **advantage** of people, your wealth will go to someone who is **kind** to the **poor**.

9 If you do not **obey** the **law**, God will find your **prayers** too **hateful** to hear.

10 If you **trick** an **honest** person into doing **evil**, you will fall into your own **trap**.

The **innocent** will be well **rewarded**.

11 **Rich** people always think they are **wise**, but a **poor** person who has **insight** into character knows better.

12 When good men come to **power**, everybody **celebrates**, but when **bad** men rule, people stay in hiding.

13 You will never **succeed in life** if you try to hide your sins. **Confess** them and give them up; then God will show **mercy** to you.

14 Always **obey** the LORD and you will be **happy**. If you are **stubborn**, you will be **ruined**.

15 **Poor** people are **helpless** against a **wicked** ruler; he is as **dangerous** as a growling lion or a prowling bear.

16 A ruler without good **sense** will be a **cruel** tyrant. One who **hates dishonesty** will rule a long time.

17 A man **guilty** of murder is digging his own **grave** as fast as he can. Don't try to stop him.

18 Be **honest** and you will be **safe**. If you are **dishonest**, you will suddenly fall.

19 A **hard-working** farmer has **plenty** to eat. People who waste time will always be **poor**.

20 **Honest** people will lead a full, **happy life**. But if you are in a hurry to get **rich**, you are going to be **punished**.

21 Prejudice is **wrong**. But some **judges** will do **wrong** to get even the smallest **bribe**.

22 **Selfish** people are in such a hurry to get **rich** that they do not know when **poverty** is about to **strike**.

23 **Correct** someone, and afterwards he will appreciate it more than flattery.

24 Anyone who thinks it isn't **wrong** to **steal** from his parents is no better than a common **thief**.

25 **Selfishness** only causes **trouble**. You are much better off to **trust** the LORD.

26 It is **foolish** to follow your own opinions. Be **safe**, and follow the **teachings of wiser** people.

27 Give to the **poor** and you will never be in **need**. If you close your eyes to the **poor**, many people will **curse** you.

28 People stay in hiding when **bad** men come to **power**. But when they fall from **power**, **righteous** men will rule again.

29

If you get more **stubborn** every time you are **corrected**, one day you will be crushed and never recover.

2 Show me a **righteous** ruler and I will show you a **happy** people. Show me a **wicked** ruler and I will show you a **miserable** people.

[s] *Probable text* or ever...oil; *Hebrew unclear.*

crime Ps 109.7; Ecc 8.11
curse 28.27; 30.10
danger 28.15; Ecc 8.3
defend 23.11; Is 1.8
discipline [2] 23.13; Zeph 3.2
downfall [2] 16.18; Jer 20.10
enemy 27.6; Is 1.24
evil [2] 28.5; 30.32
false 25.18; Is 59.13
fool [3] 28.26; 30.22
free 11.24; Is 5.18
friend 28.7; Is 1.23
guide 12.26; Ecc 12.11
happy [3] 28.14; 31.7
hate [2] 28.9; 30.23
honest [2] 28.1; Ecc 12.9
hope 18.14; Ecc 9.4
humble 22.4; Is 2.12
intelligent 28.2; Ecc 4.13
justice [2] 28.5; Ecc 3.16
law 28.4; 31.5
lie (2) 26.28; 30.6
life (1) 28.13; Ecc 1.2
misery 23.29; 31.6
oppress 28.3; Ecc 4.1
patient 25.15; Ecc 7.8
poor [3] 28.3; 30.8
power 28.12; Ecc 4.1
prostitute 23.27; Is 23.15
protect 18.11; 30.5
proud [2] 23.16; Ecc 2.10
punish 28.20; Ecc 8.11
quarrel 26.20; Is 58.4
reason 26.16; Is 14.29
respect 21.21; 31.25
right (3) [2] Ps 140.12; 31.5
righteous [4] 28.28; 31.9
ruin 28.14; Ecc 7.7
safe 28.18; Ecc 7.12
sense 28.2; 30.2
servant [2] 27.18; 30.10
strong 28.2; 30.26
stubborn 28.14; Is 46.12
stupid [2] 27.3; Ecc 7.5
thief 28.24; Is 1.23
trap [2] 28.10; Ecc 7.26
trouble 28.25; 30.33
trust 28.25; Is 8.17
truth 23.23; Ecc 12.9
understand [2] 28.5; 30.18
wicked [4] 28.1; Ecc 3.16
will (1) 19.21; Is 11.2
wisdom 24.3; 30.3
wise 28.11; Ecc 1.16
worst Ps 41.7; Jer 2.33

3 If you appreciate **wisdom**, your father will be **proud** of you.

It is a **foolish** waste to spend money on **prostitutes**.

4 When the king is **concerned** with **justice**, the nation will be **strong**, but when he is only **concerned** with money, he will **ruin** his country.

5 If you flatter your **friends**, you set a **trap** for yourself.[t]

6 **Evil** people are **trapped** in their own sins, while **honest** people are **happy** and **free**.

7 A good person knows the **rights** of the **poor**, but **wicked** people cannot **understand** such things.

8 People with no regard for others can throw whole cities into turmoil. Those who are **wise** keep things **calm**.

9 When an **intelligent** man brings a lawsuit against a **fool**, the fool only laughs and becomes loud and abusive.

10 Bloodthirsty people **hate** anyone who's **honest**, but **righteous** people will **protect**[u] the **life** of such a person.

11 **Stupid** people express their **anger** openly, but **sensible** people are **patient** and hold it back.

12 If a ruler pays attention to **false** information, all his officials will be **liars**.

13 A **poor** man and his **oppressor** have this in common—the LORD gave eyes to both of them.

14 If a king **defends** the **rights** of the **poor**, he will rule for a long time.

15 **Correction** and **discipline** are good for children. If a child has his own way, he will make his mother **ashamed** of him.

16 When **evil** men are in **power**, **crime** increases. But the **righteous** will live to see the **downfall** of such men.

17 **Discipline** your son and you can always be **proud** of him. He will never give you **reason** to be **ashamed**.

18 A nation without God's **guidance** is a nation without order. **Happy** is the man who keeps God's **law**!

19 You cannot **correct** a **servant** just by talking to him. He may **understand** you, but he will pay no attention.

20 There is more **hope** for a **stupid fool** than for someone who speaks without thinking.

21 If you give your **servant** everything he wants from childhood on, some day he will take over everything you own.[v]

22 People with quick tempers cause a lot of **quarrelling** and **trouble**.

23 **Arrogance** will bring your **downfall**, but if you are **humble**, you will be **respected**.

24 A **thief's** partner is his own **worst enemy**. He will be **punished** if he tells the **truth** in **court**, and God will **curse** him if he doesn't.

25 It is **dangerous** to be **concerned** with what others think of you, but if you **trust** the LORD, you are **safe**.

26 Everybody wants the **good will** of the ruler, but only from the LORD can you get **justice**.

27 The **righteous hate** the **wicked**, and the **wicked** hate the righteous.

The Words of Agur

30 These are the **solemn words** of Agur son of Jakeh:
"God is not with me, God is not with me,
and I am **helpless**.[w]
2 I am more like an animal than a man;
I do not have the **sense** a man should have.
3 I have never **learned** any **wisdom**,
and I know nothing at all about God.
4 Who has ever **mastered heavenly knowledge**?
Who has ever caught the wind in his hand?
Or wrapped up water in a piece of cloth?
Or fixed the boundaries of the earth?
Who is he, if you know? Who is his son?

5 "God keeps every **promise** he
makes. He is like a shield for all who
seek his **protection**. 6 If you **claim** that he
said something that he never said, he will
reprimand you and show that you are a
liar."

More Proverbs

7 I ask you, God, to let me have two
things before I die: 8 **keep me from lying**,
and let me be neither **rich** nor **poor**. So
give me only as much food as I **need**. 9 If I
have more, I might say that I do not **need**
you. But if I am **poor**, I might **steal** and
bring **disgrace** on my God.

10 Never **criticize** a **servant** to his **master**. You will be **cursed** and **suffer** for it.

11 There are people who **curse** their fathers and do not show their appreciation for their mothers.

12 There are people who think they are **pure** when they are as **filthy** as they can be.

13 There are people who think they are so good—oh, how good they think they are!

act 21.5; Ecc 7.7
adultery 22.14; Is 57.3
advantage 28.8; Ecc 7.12
afraid 26.13; 31.25
anger 29.11; Ecc 5.6
arrogant 29.23; Is 2.11
claim 26.18; Ecc 8.17
commit 6.32; Is 5.7
control 25.28; Ecc 7.9
criticize 27.11; Ecc 10.20
cruel 28.16; Is 13.9
curse [2] 29.24; Is 8.21
despise 15.20; Is 37.22
disgrace 28.7; Is 2.9
enough 27.13; Ecc 1.8
evil 29.6; Ecc 3.17
filthy Job 9.31; Is 30.22
fool [2] 29.3; Ecc 1.17
hate 29.10; Ecc 3.8
heaven Ps 150.1; Ecc 5.2
helpless 28.15; 31.8
keep from 15.11; Ecc 8.8
knowledge 24.4; Ecc 1.16
learn 27.17; Ecc 1.17
lie (2) [2] 29.12; Is 9.15
love 26.22; Ecc 3.5
master [2] 27.18; Is 1.3
mystery Ps 78.2; Is 28.21
need [4] 28.27; 31.5
plan 24.6; Ecc 10.10
poor [3] 29.7; 31.7
promise 27.13; Ecc 5.2
protect 29.10; 31.8
pure 22.11; Ecc 10.13
reprimand 9.7; Ecc 7.5
rich 28.6; Ecc 5.10
satisfy 16.26; Ecc 1.8
seek Ps 141.8; Is 56.11
sense 29.11; Ecc 10.10
servant [2] 29.19; 31.15
slave 22.7; Ecc 2.7
solemn Ps 132.11; 31.1
steal 28.24; Song 4.9
strong [2] 29.4; 31.17
suffer 21.18; Ecc 2.15
tolerate 16.12; Ezek 44.6

[t] yourself; *or* them. [u] *Probable text* protect; *Hebrew* seek.
[v] he...own; *or* you will not be able to control him. [w] *Probable text* God...helpless; *Hebrew unclear.*

trouble 29.22; Ecc 2.17
understand 29.7; Ecc 3.11
unfaithful 23.28; Is 54.4
watch 27.6; Ecc 12.12
weak 24.10; Ecc 12.3
wisdom 29.3; 31.26
word (1) 26.24; 31.1
world 8.23; Ecc 1.4
world of the dead 27.20; Ecc 9.10
wrong 28.21; Ecc 5.1

14 There are people who take **cruel**
advantage of the **poor** and **needy**; that is
the way they make their living.
15 A leech has two daughters, and
both are named "Give me!"
There are four things that are never
satisfied:
16 the **world of the dead**,
a woman without children,
dry ground that **needs** rain,
and a fire burning out of **control**.
17 Anyone who makes fun of his
father or **despises** his mother in her old
age[x] ought to be eaten by vultures or
have his eyes picked out by wild ravens.
18 There are four things that are too
mysterious for me to **understand**:
19 an eagle flying in the sky,
a snake moving on a rock,
a ship finding its way over the sea,
and a man and a woman falling in
love.
20 This is how an **unfaithful** wife **acts**:
she **commits adultery**, has a bath, and
says, "But I haven't done anything
wrong!"
21 There are four things that the earth
itself cannot **tolerate**:
22 a **slave** who becomes a king,
a **fool** who has all he wants to eat,
23 a **hateful** woman who gets married,
and a **servant-girl** who takes the
place of her mistress.
24 There are four animals in the **world**
that are small, but very, very clever:
25 Ants: they are **weak**, but they store
up their food in the summer.
26 Rock-badgers: they are not **strong**
either, but they make their
homes among the rocks.
27 Locusts: they have no king, but
they move in formation.
28 Lizards: you can hold one in your
hand, but you can find them
in palaces.
29 There are four things that are impressive to **watch** as they walk:
30 lions, **strongest** of all animals and
afraid of none;
31 goats,
strutting cocks,
and kings in front of their people.[y]
32 If you have been **foolish enough** to be
arrogant and **plan evil**, stop and think!
33 If you churn milk, you get butter. If you
hit someone's nose, it bleeds. If you stir
up **anger**, you get into **trouble**.

Advice to a King

31 These are the **solemn words**
which King Lemuel's mother
said to him:
2 "You are my own **dear** son, the
answer to my **prayers**. What shall I tell
you? 3 Don't spend all your energy on **sex**
and all your money on women; they
have **destroyed** kings. 4 Listen, Lemuel.
Kings should not drink wine or have a
craving for alcohol. 5 When they drink,
they **forget** the **laws** and **ignore** the **rights**
of people in **need**. 6 Alcohol is for people
who are dying, for those who are in
misery. 7 Let them drink and **forget** their
poverty and **unhappiness**.
8 "Speak up for people who cannot
speak for themselves. **Protect** the **rights**
of all who are **helpless**. 9 Speak for them
and be a **righteous judge**. **Protect** the
rights of the **poor** and **needy**."

The Capable Wife

10 How **hard** it is to find a capable
wife! She is **worth** far more than jewels!
11 Her husband puts his **confidence** in
her, and he will never be **poor**.
12 As long as she lives, she does him
good and never **harm**.
13 She keeps herself busy making
wool and linen cloth.
14 She brings home food from out-of-
the-way places, as merchant ships do.
15 She gets up before daylight to prepare food for her family and to tell her
servant-girls what to do.
16 She looks at land and buys it, and
with money she has earned she plants a
vineyard.
17 She is a **hard worker**, **strong** and
industrious.
18 She knows the **value** of everything
she makes, and works late into the night.
19 She spins her own thread and
weaves her own cloth.
20 She is **generous** to the **poor** and
needy.
21 She doesn't **worry** when it snows,
because her family has warm clothing.
22 She makes bedspreads and wears
clothes of fine purple linen.
23 Her husband is well known, one of
the **leading** citizens.
24 She makes clothes and belts, and
sells them to merchants.
25 She is **strong** and **respected** and not
afraid of the future.
26 She speaks with a **gentle wisdom**.
27 She is always busy and looks after
her family's **needs**.

afraid 30.30; Ecc 12.5
best 21.29; Ecc 2.3
confident 14.26; Is 2.22
dear Ps 148.14; Song 1.16
deceive 16.29; Is 28.15
deserve 27.13; Is 10.22
destroy 28.3; Ecc 5.6
forget [2] 27.10; Ecc 2.16
generous 22.9; Mt 20.15
gentle 15.1; Is 40.11
happy 29.2; Ecc 2.1
hard [2] 28.19; Ecc 2.11
harm 19.23; Is 11.8
helpless 30.1; Is 11.4
honour 27.18; Ecc 6.2
ignore 19.11; Ecc 10.6
judge 28.21; Ecc 3.17
law 29.18; Is 10.1
leading Neh 11.3; Jer 27.19
misery 29.2; Ecc 1.13
need [4] 30.8; Ecc 5.13
poor [4] 30.8; Ecc 4.13
poverty *see* **poor**
praise [2] 27.2; Ecc 7.5
prayer 28.9; Is 1.15
protect [2] 30.5; Ecc 5.8
respect [2] 29.23; Ecc 7.28
right (3) [3] 29.7; Ecc 5.8
righteous 29.2; Ecc 3.17
servant 30.10; Ecc 7.21
sex 1 Sam 21.4; Is 57.5
solemn 30.1; Is 19.21
strong [2] 30.26; Ecc 6.10
value 25.12; Is 58.13
vineyard 24.30; Ecc 2.4
wisdom 30.3; Ecc 1.16
word (1) 30.1; Ecc 1.1
worry 24.19; Ecc 1.18
worth 23.23; Is 2.22

[x] *One ancient translation* mother in her old age; *Hebrew* mother's obedience.
[y] *Verse 31 in Hebrew is unclear.*

28 Her children show their appreciation, and her husband **praises** her.

29 He says, "Many women are good wives, but you are the **best** of them all."

30 Charm is **deceptive** and beauty disappears, but a woman who **honours** the LORD should be **praised**.

31 Give her credit for all she does. She **deserves** the **respect** of everyone.

ECCLESIASTES

INTRODUCTION

The book of *Ecclesiastes* contains the thoughts of "the Philosopher," a man who reflected deeply on how short and contradictory human life is, with its mysterious injustices and frustrations, and concluded that "life is useless." He could not understand the ways of God, who controls human destiny. Yet, in spite of this, he advised people to work hard, and to enjoy the gifts of God as much and as long as they could.

Many of the Philosopher's thoughts appear negative and even depressing. But the fact that this book is in the Bible shows that biblical faith is broad enough to take into account such pessimism and doubt. Many have taken comfort in seeing themselves in the mirror of *Ecclesiastes*, and have discovered that the same Bible which reflects these thoughts also offers the hope in God that gives life its greater meaning.

Outline of Contents

---

determine [2] Prov 20.24; 6.10
enough [2] Prov 30.32; 5.12
fate Ps 49.13; 2.14
fool Prov 30.22; 2.2
hurt Prov 27.6; 10.9
knowledge [2] Prov 30.4; 2.21
learn Prov 30.3; 4.4
life (1) [2] Prov 29.10; 2.3
mad Prov 26.18; 9.3
misery Prov 31.6; 4.8
new [2] Prov 23.29; 11.5
remember [2] Prov 23.35; 2.16
rise Prov 8.29; 4.13
satisfy Prov 30.15; 3.11
study Prov 22.17; 7.25
useless [3] Prov 12.11; 2.1
wisdom [2] Prov 31.26; 2.3
wise [2] Prov 29.8; 2.12
word (1) [2] Prov 31.1; 5.6
world [4] Prov 30.24; 2.19
worry Prov 31.21; 2.22

Life Is Useless

1 These are the **words** of the Philosopher, David's son, who was king in
Jerusalem.
2 It is **useless, useless,** said the Philosopher. **Life** is **useless**, all useless. 3 You
spend your **life** working, labouring, and
what do you have to show for it? 4 Generations come and generations go, but the
world stays just the same. 5 The sun still
rises, and it still goes down, going
wearily back to where it must start all
over again. 6 The wind blows south, the
wind blows north—round and round and
back again. 7 Every river flows into the
sea, but the sea is not yet full. The water
returns to where the rivers began, and
starts all over again. 8 Everything leads
to weariness—a weariness too great for
words. Our eyes can never see **enough** to
be **satisfied**; our ears can never hear
enough. 9 What has happened before will
happen again. What has been done before will be done again. There is nothing
new in the whole **world**. 10 "Look," they
say, "here is something **new**!" But no, it
has all happened before, long before we
were born. 11 No one **remembers** what
has happened in the past, and no one in
days to come will **remember** what happens between now and then.

The Philosopher's Experience

12 I, the Philosopher, have been king
over Israel in Jerusalem. 13 I **determined**
that I would examine and **study** all the
things that are done in this **world**.
God has laid a **miserable fate** upon us.
14 I have seen everything done in this
world, and I tell you, it is all **useless**. It is
like chasing the wind. 15 You can't
straighten out what is crooked; you can't
count things that aren't there.
16 I told myself, "I have become a
great man, far **wiser** than anyone who
ruled Jerusalem before me. I know what
wisdom and **knowledge** really are." 17 I
was **determined** to **learn** the difference
between **knowledge** and **foolishness, wisdom** and **madness**. But I found out that I
might as well be chasing the wind. 18 The
wiser you are, the more **worries** you
have; the more you know, the more it
hurts.

2 I decided to **enjoy** myself and find
out what **happiness** is. But I found
that this is **useless**, too. 2 I discovered that
laughter is **foolish**, that **pleasure** does you
no good. 3 Driven on by my **desire** for **wisdom**, I decided to **cheer** myself up with
wine and have a good time. I thought
that this might be the **best** way people
can spend their short **lives** on earth.
4 I accomplished great things. I built
myself houses and planted **vineyards**. 5 I
planted gardens and orchards, with all
kinds of fruit-trees in them; 6 I dug ponds
to irrigate them. 7 I bought many **slaves**,
and there were slaves born in my house-

best [2] Prov 31.29; 3.12
cheer (1) Prov 17.2[illegible]; 9.7
dark Prov 20.20; 5.[illegible]
deny Job 31.28; 4.8
desire Prov 27.20; 3.11
enjoy [3] Prov 24.2[illegible]; 3.13
fail Prov 15.22; Is 5[illegible]
fate [2] 1.13; 3.19
fool [8] 1.17; 4.5
forget Prov 31.5; 6.[illegible]
happy [2] Prov 31.7; 3.12
hard [2] Prov 31.10; 4.4
heart Prov 27.19; 11.9
knowledge [2] 1.16; 5.11

1.16: 1 Kgs 4.29-31 **2.4-8:** 1 Kgs 10.23-27; 2 Chr 9.22-27 **2.7:** 1 Kgs 4.23

fe (1) [3] 1.2; 3.19
ght (1) Prov 13.9;
5
ind (1) Prov 27.9;
6
ease [2] Prov 21.3;
26
easure [2]
rov 17.5; 4.8
roud Prov 29.3; 7.8
emember 1.11; 7.14
st (1) Prov 24.33;
5
eward Prov 28.10;
14
ght (1) Prov 22.21;
11
ave Prov 23.14; 3.6
ave Prov 30.22;
.7
uffer Prov 30.10;
9
ouble Prov 30.33;
14
seless [6] 1.2; 4.4
ineyard Prov 31.16;
ng 1.6
isdom [6] 1.16; 7.12
ise [6] 1.16; 6.8
orld 1.4; 3.1
orry [2] 1.18; 5.3

hold. I owned more livestock than anyone else who had ever lived in Jerusalem. 8 I also piled up silver and gold
from the royal treasuries of the lands I
ruled. Men and women sang to entertain
me, and I had all the women a man could
want.
9 Yes, I was great, greater than anyone else who had ever lived in Jerusalem, and my **wisdom** never **failed** me.
10 Anything I wanted, I got. I did not **deny**
myself any **pleasure**. I was **proud** of
everything I had worked for, and all this
was my **reward**. 11 Then I thought about
all that I had done and how **hard** I had
worked doing it, and I realized that it
didn't mean a thing. It was like chasing
the wind—of no use at all. 12 After all, a
king can only do what previous kings
have done.
So I started thinking about what it
meant to be **wise** or reckless or **foolish**.
13 Oh, I know, "**Wisdom** is better than
foolishness, just as **light** is better than
darkness. 14 **Wise** men can see where
they are going, and **fools** cannot." But I
also know that the same **fate** is waiting
for us all. 15 I thought to myself, "I will
suffer the same **fate** as **fools**. So what
have I gained from being so **wise**?"
"Nothing," I answered, "not a thing."
16 No one **remembers wise** men, and no
one remembers **fools**. In days to come,
we will all be **forgotten**. We must all
die—**wise** and **foolish** alike. 17 So **life**
came to mean nothing to me, because
everything in it had brought me nothing
but **trouble**. It had all been **useless**; I had
been chasing the wind.
18 Nothing that I had worked for and
earned meant a thing to me, because I
knew that I would have to leave it to my
successor, 19 and he might be **wise**, or he
might be **foolish**—who knows? Yet he
will own everything I have worked for,
everything my **wisdom** has earned for
me in this **world**. It is all **useless**. 20 So I
came to regret that I had worked so
hard. 21 You work for something with all
your **wisdom**, **knowledge**, and skill, and
then you have to leave it all to someone
who hasn't had to work for it. It is **useless**, and it isn't **right**! 22 You work and
worry your way through **life**, and what do
you have to show for it? 23 As long as you
live, everything you do brings nothing
but **worry** and **heartache**. Even at night
your **mind** can't **rest**. It is all **useless**.
24 The **best** thing a man can do is to
eat and drink and **enjoy** what he has
earned. And yet, I realized that even this
comes from God. 25 How else could you
have anything to eat or **enjoy** yourself at
all? 26 God gives **wisdom**, **knowledge**, and
happiness to those who **please** him, but
he makes sinners work, earning and **saving**, so that what they get can be given to
those who **please** him. It is all **useless**. It
is like chasing the wind.

A Time for Everything

3 Everything that happens in this
world happens at the time God
chooses.

2 He sets the time for **birth** and the time
for **death**,
the time for planting and the time
for pulling up,
3 the time for killing and the time for
healing,
the time for tearing down and the
time for building.
4 He sets the time for **sorrow** and the
time for **joy**,
the time for **mourning** and the time
for dancing,
5 the time for making **love** and the
time for not making **love**,
the time for **kissing** and the time for
not kissing.
6 He sets the time for finding and the
time for losing,
the time for **saving** and the time for
throwing away,
7 the time for tearing and the time for
mending,
the time for silence and the time for
talk.
8 He sets the time for **love** and the time
for **hate**,
the time for war and the time for
peace.

9 What do we gain from all our work?
10 I know the heavy **burdens** that God has
laid on us. 11 He has set the **right** time for
everything. He has given us a **desire** to
know the future, but never gives us the
satisfaction of fully **understanding** what
he does. 12 So I realized that all we can do
is to be **happy** and do the **best** we can
while we are still **alive**. 13 All of us should
eat and drink and **enjoy** what we have
worked for. It is God's **gift**.
14 I know that everything God does
will **last** for ever. You can't add anything
to it or take anything away from it. And
one thing God does is to make us stand in
awe of him. 15 Whatever happens or can
happen has already happened before.
God makes the same thing happen again
and again.

action Prov 19.3; 9.1
alive Prov 26.21; 4.2
awe Ps 130.4; 5.7
being Ps 146.3; Is 44.11
best [2] 2.3; 5.18
birth Ps 22.9; Is 26.18
burden Ps 88.15; Is 1.14
choose Prov 22.1; Is 2.3
creature Ps 150.6; Is 6.2
death (1) Prov 21.6; 4.5
desire 2.3; 11.9
enjoy [2] 2.1; 5.18
evil Prov 30.32; 7.15
fate 2.14; 5.18
gift Prov 22.16; 5.19
happy 2.1; 5.20
hate Prov 30.23; 9.1
heal Prov 12.18; Is 6.10
human Prov 27.20; Is 2.11
joy Prov 15.23; Song 3.11
judge Prov 31.9; 11.9
justice Prov 29.4; 5.8
kiss Prov 7.13; Song 1.2
last (1) Prov 27.24; 12.11
life (1) 2.3; 4.7
love [3] Prov 30.19; 5.10
mourn Ps 78.64; 7.2
notice (1) Prov 7.7; 4.7
peace Prov 27.9; 4.6
right (1) [2] 2.21; 5.1
righteous Prov 31.9; 8.14
satisfy 1.8; 4.8
save 2.26; 5.13
sorrow Prov 17.21; 7.3
spirit (2) [2] Prov 15.4; Is 8.19
sure Prov 25.23; Is 47.10
test Prov 27.21; 7.23
understand Prov 30.18; 7.3
wicked Prov 29.2; 7.17
world [2] 2.19; 4.1

2.8: 1 Kgs 10.10, 14–22 **2.9:** 1 Chr 29.25 **2.23:** Job 5.7, 14.1
2.24: Ecc 3.13, 5.18, 9.7; Lk 12.19; 1 Cor 15.32 **2.26:** Job 32.8; Prov 2.6

Injustice in the World

16 In addition, I have also **noticed** that in this **world** you find **wickedness** where **justice** and **right** ought to be. [17]I told myself, "God is going to **judge** the **righteous** and the **evil** alike, because every thing, every **action**, will happen at its own set time."[a] [18]I concluded that God is **testing** us, to show us that we are no better than animals. [19]After all, the same **fate** awaits man and animal alike. One dies just like the other. They are both the same kind of **creature**. A **human being** is no better off than an animal, because **life** has no meaning for either. [20]They are both going to the same place—the dust. They both came from it; they will both go back to it. [21]How can anyone be **sure** that a man's **spirit** goes upwards while an animal's **spirit** goes down into the ground? [22]So I realized then that the **best** thing we can do is to **enjoy** what we have worked for. There is nothing else we can do.[b] There is no way for us to know what will happen after we die.

4 Then I looked again at all the **injustice** that goes on in this **world**. The **oppressed** were **weeping**, and no one would **help** them. No one would **help** them, because their **oppressors** had **power** on their side. [2]I **envy** those who are **dead** and gone; they are better off than those who are still **alive**. [3]But better off than either are those who have never been born, who have never seen the **injustice** that goes on in this **world**.

4 I have also **learnt** why people work so **hard** to **succeed**: it is because they **envy** their **neighbours**. But it is **useless**. It is like chasing the wind. [5]They say that a man would be a **fool** to fold his hands and let himself starve **to death**. [6]Perhaps so, but it is better to have only a little, with **peace of mind**, than to be busy all the time with both hands, trying to catch the wind.

7 I have **noticed** something else in **life** that is **useless**. [8]Here is a man who lives **alone**. He has no son, no brother, yet he is always working, never **satisfied** with the wealth he has. For whom is he working so **hard** and **denying** himself any **pleasure**? This is **useless**, too—and a **miserable** way to live.

9 Two are better off than one, because together they can work more effectively. [10]If one of them falls down, the other can **help** him up. But if someone is **alone** and falls, it's just too **bad**, because there is no one to **help** him. [11]If it is cold, two can sleep together and stay warm, but how can you keep warm by yourself? [12]Two men can **resist** an attack that would defeat one man **alone**. A rope made of three cords is **hard** to break.

13–14 A man may **rise** from **poverty** to become king of his country, or go from **prison** to the **throne**, but if in his old age he is too **foolish** to take **advice**, he is not as well off as a young man who is **poor** but **intelligent**. [15]I thought about all the people who live in this **world**, and I realized that somewhere among them there is a young man who will take the king's place. [16]There may be no limit to the number of people a king rules; when he is gone, no one will be **grateful** for what he has done. It is **useless**. It is like chasing the wind.

Don't Make Rash Promises

5 Be careful about going to the **Temple**. It is better to go there to **learn** than to **offer sacrifices** as **foolish** people do, people who don't know **right** from **wrong**. [2]Think before you speak, and don't make any rash **promises** to God. He is in **heaven** and you are on earth, so don't say any more than you have to. [3]The more you **worry**, the more likely you are to have **bad dreams**, and the more you talk, the more likely you are to say something **foolish**. [4]So when you make a **promise** to God, keep it as quickly as possible. He has no use for a **fool**. Do what you **promise** to do. [5]Better not to **promise** at all than to make a **promise** and not keep it. [6]Don't let your own **words** lead you into sin, so that you have to tell God's **priest** that you didn't mean it. Why make God **angry** with you? Why let him **destroy** what you have worked for? [7]No matter how much you **dream**, how much **useless** work you do, or how much you talk, you must still stand in **awe** of God.

Life Is Useless

8 Don't be surprised when you see that the government **oppresses** the **poor** and **denies** them **justice** and their **rights**. Every official is **protected** by the one over him, and both are **protected** by still higher officials.

9 Even a king **depends** on the **harvest**.[c]

10 If you **love** money, you will never be **satisfied**; if you **long** to be **rich**, you

[a] *Probable text* its own set time; *Hebrew* its own set time there.
[b] what we have...do; *or* our work, because we are going to have to do it anyway.
[c] *Verse 9 in Hebrew is unclear.*

5.4: Ps 66.13–14

advice Prov 24.6; Is 19.3
alive 3.12; 9.4
alone [3] Prov 5.15; Is 1.8
bad Prov 28.12; 5.3
dead Prov 27.22; 6.3
death (1) 3.2; 7.2
death (3) (to death) Ps 109.31; Is 5.13
deny 2.10; 5.8
envy [2] Prov 24.1; Ezek 31.9
fool [2] 2.2; 5.1
grateful 2 Chr 32.25; 5.19
hard [3] 2.11; 7.24
help [4] Prov 27.10; Song 6.1
injustice [2] Prov 22.8; 6.1
intelligent Prov 29.9; 7.10
learn 1.17; 5.1
life (1) 3.19; 5.17
mind (1) 2.23; 9.3
misery 1.13; Is 50.11
neighbour Prov 27.10; Is 19.2
notice (1) 3.16; 6.1
oppress [2] Prov 29.13; 5.8
peace 3.8; Song 8.10
pleasure 2.2; 8.15
poor [2] Prov 31.7; 5.8
poverty *see* **poor**
power Prov 29.16; 8.9
prison Ps 146.7; Is 5.13
resist Prov 25.15; Jer 1.18
rise 1.5; 9.11
satisfy 3.11; 5.10
succeed (1) Prov 28.13; 7.18
throne Ps 132.7; Song 3.7
useless [4] 2.1; 5.7

weep Ps 137.1; Is 15.2
world [3] 3.1; 5.13

anger [2] Prov 30 10.4
awe 3.14; Is 8.14
bad 4.10; 9.2
best 3.12; 6.12
dark 2.13; 6.4
deny 4.8; Jer 2.35
depend Prov 25.1 Is 3.1
destroy Prov 31.3 10.12
dream [2] Ps 126.1 Song 3.1
enjoy [3] 3.13; 6.2
enough 1.8; 6.7
fate 3.19; 9.2
fool [3] 4.5; 6.8
gift 3.13; Is 1.23
grateful 4.16; 11.8
grief Prov 17.25; Is 15.2
happy 3.12; 6.3
harvest Prov 26.1 11.4
heaven Prov 30.4 Is 7.11
justice 3.16; Is 1.1
knowledge 2.21; 7
learn 4.4; 7.25
life (1) [3] 4.7; 6.5
long (2) Ps 119.20; Is 21.4
love 3.5; 7.26
need Prov 31.5; Song 1.7
offer Prov 21.27; 7
oppress 4.1; Is 1.1
poor 4.13; 6.8
priest Ps 135.19; Is 8.2
promise [5] Prov 30.5; 8.2
protect [2] Prov 3 12.3
rich [4] Prov 30.8; 9.11
right (1) [2] 3.11; 7
right (3) Prov 31.5 Is 1.17
sacrifice Prov 21. 9.2
satisfy 4.8; 6.9
save 3.6; 9.15
Temple (1) (of Go Ps 150.1; Is 1.12

rrible Ps 119.107;
14.30
eless [2] 4.4; 6.2
ord (1) 1.1; 9.17
orld [2] 4.1; 6.1
orry [4] 2.22; 11.10
rong Prov 30.20;
2

will never get all you want. It is **useless.**
11 The **richer** you are, the more mouths
you must feed. All you gain is the **knowledge** that you are **rich.** 12 A working man
may or may not have **enough** to eat, but
at least he can get a good night's sleep. A
rich man, however, has so much that he
stays awake **worrying.**

13 Here is a **terrible** thing that I have
seen in this **world**: people **save** up their
money for a time when they may **need**
it,[d] 14 and then lose it all in some unlucky
deal and end up with nothing left to pass
on to their children. 15 We leave this
world just as we entered it—with nothing. In spite of all our work there is nothing we can take with us. 16 It isn't **right**!
We go just as we came. We labour, trying
to catch the wind, and what do we get?
17 We have to live our **lives** in **darkness**
and **grief**,[e] **worried**, **angry**, and sick.

18 This is what I have found out: the
best thing anyone can do is to eat and
drink and **enjoy** what he has worked for
during the short **life** that God has given
him; this is man's **fate.** 19 If God gives a
man wealth and property and lets him
enjoy them, he should be **grateful** and
enjoy what he has worked for. It is a **gift**
from God. 20 Since God has allowed him
to be **happy**, he will not **worry** too much
about how short **life** is.

rgue [2] Prov 26.17;
s 41.21
est 5.18; Song 4.16
ark 5.17; Song 1.5
ead 4.2; 9.4
etermine 1.13; 7.23
njoy [3] 5.18; 8.15
nough 5.12; 8.11
ool 5.1; 7.4
orget 2.16; 9.5
appy 5.20; 7.4
onour Prov 31.30;
0.12
njustice 4.1; 10.5
ife (1) [4] 5.17; 7.15
ight (1) 2.13; 11.7
otice (1) 4.7; Is 53.2
oor 5.8; 9.15
est (1) 2.23; 12.5
atisfy 5.10; Is 9.20
erious Prov 23.19;
0.4
hare Prov 25.24;
Song 8.12
stranger Prov 27.2;
0.3
strong Prov 31.17;
2.3
useless [4] 5.7; 7.15
wise 2.12; 7.4
world [2] 5.13; 8.9
wrong 5.1; 9.3

6 I have **noticed** that in this **world** a
serious injustice is done. 2 God will
give someone wealth, **honour**, and
property, yes, everything he wants, but
then will not let him **enjoy** it. Some
stranger will **enjoy** it instead. It is **useless**, and it's all **wrong.** 3 A man may have
a hundred children and live a long time,
but no matter how long he lives, if he
does not get his **share** of **happiness** and
does not receive a decent burial, then I
say that a baby born **dead** is better off.
4 It does that baby no good to be born; it
disappears into **darkness**, where it is **forgotten.** 5 It never sees the **light** of day or
knows what **life** is like, but at least it has
found **rest**— 6 more so than the man who
never **enjoys life**, though he may live two
thousand years. After all, both of them
are going to the same place.

7 A man does all his work just to get
something to eat, but he never has
enough. 8 How is a **wise** man better off
than a **fool**? What good does it do a **poor**
man to know how to face **life**? 9 It is **useless**; it is like chasing the wind. It is
better to be **satisfied** with what you have
than to be always wanting something
else.

10 Everything that happens was already **determined** long ago, and we all
know that a man[f] cannot **argue** with
someone who is **stronger** than he. 11 The
longer you **argue**, the more **useless** it is,
and you are no better off. 12 How can anyone know what is **best** for a man in this
short, **useless life** of his—a life that
passes like a shadow? How can anyone
know what will happen in the **world** after
he dies?

Thoughts about Life

7 A good **reputation** is better than expensive perfume; and the day you
die is better than the day you are born.

2 It is better to go to a home where
there is **mourning** than to one where
there is a party, because the living
should always **remind** themselves that
death is waiting for us all.

3 **Sorrow** is better than laughter; it
may **sadden** your face, but it sharpens
your **understanding.**

4 Someone who is always thinking
about **happiness** is a **fool.** A **wise** person
thinks about **death.**

5 It is better to have **wise** people **reprimand** you than to have **stupid** people sing
your **praises.**

6 When a **fool** laughs, it is like thorns
crackling in a fire. It doesn't mean a
thing.

7 When a **wise** man **cheats** someone,
he is **acting** like a **fool.** If you take a
bribe, you **ruin** your character.

8 The end of anything is better than its
beginning.

Patience is better than **pride.**

9 Keep your temper under **control**; it
is **foolish** to harbour a grudge.

10 Never ask, "Oh, why were things so
much better in the old days?" It's not an
intelligent question.

11 Everyone who lives ought to be
wise; it is as good as receiving an **inheritance** 12 and will give you as much
security as money can. **Wisdom** keeps
you **safe**—this is the **advantage** of **knowledge.**

13 Think about what God has done.
How can anyone straighten out what God
has made crooked? 14 When things are
going well for you, be **glad**, and when
trouble comes, just **remember**: God
sends both **happiness** and **trouble**; you

act Prov 30.20; 8.4
advantage
Prov 30.14; Is 3.5
bitter Prov 27.7;
Is 5.20
bribe Prov 28.21;
Is 1.23
cheat Job 31.21; 8.8
control Prov 30.16;
9.1
death (1) [3] 4.5; 8.8
determine [2] 6.10;
Is 9.7
devote Prov 2.8;
Is 53.11
evil 3.17; 8.10
fool [6] 6.8; 9.17
get away Prov 4.21;
Jer 9.2
glad Prov 24.17;
Song 3.11
happy [2] 6.3; 9.7
hard 4.4; 8.17
inherit Prov 19.14
insult [2] Prov 18.13;
Is 3.8
intelligent 4.13; 9.11
knowledge [2] 5.11;
9.10
learn [2] 5.1; 8.16
life (1) [2] 6.5; 8.13
love 5.10; 9.1
mistake Prov 14.22;
Jer 42.20
mourn 3.4; 12.5
offer 5.1; 9.2
patient Prov 29.11;
Is 7.13
plain (1) Prov 8.9;
Hos 6.5
please 2.26; Is 42.1
praise Prov 31.28;
8.10
proud 2.10; Is 2.11
question [2]
Prov 26.4; Is 41.28
remember 2.16; 11.8
remind Prov 26.9;
Is 19.17
reprimand
Prov 30.6; Is 17.13
reputation
Prov 27.21; Mk 6.14
respect Prov 31.25;
Is 3.5
reverence
Prov 24.21; 12.13
right (1) 5.1; 8.6
ruin Prov 29.4;
Song 2.15
sad Prov 17.21;
Is 16.11
safe Prov 29.25; 8.5
secure Prov 14.26;
Is 28.17

[d] for...it; *or* to their own hurt.
[e] *Some ancient translations* in darkness and grief; *Hebrew* eating in darkness.
[f] and we...man; *or* and a man's nature is already known; a man.

5.15: Job 1.21; Ps 49.17; 1 Tim 6.7 **7.1:** Prov 22.1 **7.9:** Jas 1.19

servant Prov 31.15; Is 20.3
sorrow 3.4; Is 25.7
study 1.13; 12.9
stupid [2] Prov 29.11; 10.1
succeed (1) 4.4; Is 8.10
test 3.18; 12.9
trap Prov 29.5; 9.12
trouble [2] 2.17; 9.9
understand [2] 3.11; 8.17
useless 6.2; 8.10
wicked [2] 3.16; 8.10
wisdom [4] 2.3; 8.1
wise [6] 6.8; 8.1

never know what is going to happen next.[g]

15 My life has been useless, but in it I have seen everything. A good man may die while another man lives on, even though he is evil. 16 So don't be too good or too wise—why kill yourself? 17 But don't be too wicked or too foolish, either—why die before you have to? 18 Avoid both extremes. If you have reverence for God, you will be successful anyway.

19 Wisdom does more for a person than ten rulers can do for a city.

20 There is no one on earth who does what is right all the time and never makes a mistake.

21 Don't pay attention to everything people say—you may hear your servant insulting you, 22 and you know yourself that you have insulted other people many times.

23 I used my wisdom to test all of this. I was determined to be wise, but it was beyond me. 24 How can anyone discover what life means? It is too deep for us, too hard to understand. 25 But I devoted myself to knowledge and study; I was determined to find wisdom and the answers to my questions, and to learn how wicked and foolish stupidity is.

26 I found something more bitter than death—woman. The love she offers you will catch you like a trap or like a net; and her arms round you will hold you like a chain. A man who pleases God can get away, but she will catch the sinner. 27 Yes, said the Philosopher, I found this out little by little while I was looking for answers. 28 I have looked for other answers but have found none. I found one man in a thousand that I could respect, but not one woman. 29 This is all that I have learnt: God made us plain and simple, but we have made ourselves very complicated.

act 7.7; Is 31.3
authority Prov 28.3; 10.6
challenge Job 40.1; Jer 49.19
cheat 7.7; Is 3.12
claim Prov 30.6; Is 10.15
command Ps 149.9; 12.13
convince Prov 25.15; Ezek 5.13
crime [3] Prov 29.16; Is 29.21
danger Prov 29.25; 12.5
death (1) 7.2; Song 8.6

8 Only a wise man knows what things really mean. Wisdom makes him smile and makes his frowns disappear.

Obey the King

2 Do what the king says,[h] and don't make any rash promises to God. 3 The king can do anything he likes, so depart from his presence; don't stay in such a dangerous place. 4 The king acts with authority, and no one can challenge what he does. 5 As long as you obey his commands, you are safe, and a wise man knows how and when to do it. 6 There is a right time and a right way to do everything, but we know so little! 7 None of us knows what is going to happen, and there is no one to tell us. 8 No one can keep himself from dying or put off the day of his death. That is a battle we cannot escape; we cannot cheat our way out.

The Wicked and the Righteous

9 I saw all this when I thought about the things that are done in this world, a world where some men have power and others have to suffer under them. 10 Yes, I have seen wicked men buried and in their graves, but on the way back from the cemetery people praise them in the very city where they did their evil. It is useless.[i]

11 Why do people commit crimes so readily? Because crime is not punished quickly enough. 12 A sinner may commit a hundred crimes and still live. Oh yes, I know what they say: "If you obey God, everything will be all right, 13 but it will not go well for the wicked. Their life is like a shadow and they will die young, because they do not obey God." 14 But this is nonsense. Look at what happens in the world: sometimes righteous men get the punishment of the wicked, and wicked men get the reward of the righteous. I say it is useless.

15 So I am convinced that a man should enjoy himself, because the only pleasure he has in this life is eating and drinking and enjoying himself. He can at least do this as he labours during the life that God has given him in this world.

16 Whenever I tried to become wise and learn what goes on in the world, I realized that you could stay awake night and day 17 and never be able to understand what God is doing. However hard you try, you will never find out. Wise men may claim to know, but they don't.

9 I thought long and hard about all this and saw that God controls the actions of wise and righteous men, even their love and their hate. No one knows anything about what lies ahead of him. 2 It makes no difference.[j] The same fate comes to the righteous and the wicked, to the good and the bad,[k] to those who are religious and those who are not, to those who offer sacrifices and those who do not. A good man is no better off than a

enjoy [2] 6.2; 9.9
enough 6.7; Is 1.1
escape Prov 19.5; Is 2.10
evil 7.15; 9.3
grave Prov 28.17; Is 26.19
hard 7.24; 9.1
keep from Prov 30.8; Is 29.21
learn 7.25; Is 1.17
life (1) [3] 7.15; 9.
obey [3] Prov 28.4; 12.13
pleasure 4.8; Is 1
power 4.1; 9.14
praise 7.5; Song 6
presence Prov 8.; Is 19.20
promise 5.2; Song
punish [2] Prov 29.24; Is 1.5
reward 2.10; 9.5
right (1) 7.20; 10.2
righteous [2] 3.17
safe 7.12; Is 4.6
suffer 2.15; Is 14.
understand 7.3; 1
useless [2] 7.15; 9
wicked [4] 7.17; 9.
wisdom 7.12; 9.10
wise [4] 7.4; 9.1
world [4] 6.1; 9.3

action [2] 3.17; Is
alive 4.2; Is 14.30
bad [2] 5.3; 11.2
cheer (1) [2] 2.3; 10.19
control 7.9; 10.17
Council Ps 107.32; Mt 5.22
dead [2] 6.3; 10.1
enjoy [2] 8.15; 11.7
evil [2] 8.10; Is 1.4
example Prov 23.; Ezek 14.8
fate [2] 5.18; Is 17.
fool 7.4; 10.2
forget 6.4; Is 17.10

[g] you...next; *or* you cannot find fault with him.
[h] *Some ancient translations* Do what the king says; *Hebrew unclear.*
[i] *Verse 10 in Hebrew is unclear.*
[j] men, even their...difference; *or* men, but no one knows whether it is out of love or hate. 2 It makes no difference what lies ahead of us.
[k] *Some ancient translations* and the bad; *Hebrew does not have these words.*

appy [2] 7.4; 10.19
ard [2] 8.17; 10.10
ate [2] 3.8; Is 1.14
ope Prov 29.20;
s 6.5
ntelligent 7.10;
nan 1.4
nowledge 7.12;
s 11.2
fe (1) [2] 8.13; 11.5
ove [3] 7.26; Song 1.2
nad 1.17; 10.13
nind (1) 4.6; Is 1.5
ever again Ps 77.7;
s 2.4
ath Ps 144.8;
s 14.24
ffer 7.26; Is 1.11
assion Song 2.5
oor [2] 6.8; Is 3.14
ower 8.9; Song 8.6
ace (2) Ps 19.5;
ong 2.8
eligion 2 Chr 26.5;
s 1.13
eward 8.14; Is 49.4
ich 5.10; 10.6
ighteous [2] 8.14;
s 1.21
ise 4.13; Is 8.8
acrifice 5.1; Is 1.11
ave 5.13; Is 1.27
trength Prov 24.5;
ong 2.5
rap [2] 7.26; Is 8.14
rouble 7.14; 10.16
seless [2] 8.10; 12.8
icked 8.10; Is 9.17
in [2] Prov 25.27;
s 26.18
isdom [4] 8.1; 10.1
ise [4] 8.1; 10.2
ord (1) 5.6; 10.12
orld [6] 8.9; 10.5
orld of the dead
rov 30.16; Is 5.14
rong 6.2; 10.2

sinner; a man who takes an **oath** is no
better off than one who does not. 3 One
fate comes to all alike, and this is as
wrong as anything that happens in this
world. As long as people live, their **minds**
are full of **evil** and **madness**, and suddenly they die. 4 But anyone who is **alive**
in the **world** of the living has some **hope**;
a live dog is better off than a **dead** lion.
5 Yes, the living know they are going to
die, but the **dead** know nothing. They
have no further **reward**; they are completely **forgotten**. 6 Their **loves**, their
hates, their **passions**, all died with them.
They will **never again** take part in anything that happens in this **world**.
7 Go ahead—eat your food and be
happy; drink your wine and be **cheerful**.
It's all right with God. 8 Always look
happy and **cheerful**. 9 **Enjoy life** with the
woman you **love**, as long as you live the
useless life that God has given you in this
world. **Enjoy** every **useless** day of it, because that is all you will get for all your
trouble. 10 Work **hard** at whatever you do,
because there will be no **action**, no
thought, no **knowledge**, no **wisdom** in the
world of the dead—and that is where you
are going.
11 I realized another thing, that in this
world fast runners do not always **win** the
race, and the brave do not always **win**
the battle. **Wise** men do not always earn
a living, **intelligent** men do not always
get **rich**, and capable men do not always
rise to high positions. **Bad** luck happens
to everyone. 12 You never know when
your time is coming. Like birds suddenly
caught in a **trap**, like fish caught in a net,
we are **trapped** at some **evil** moment
when we least expect it.

Thoughts on Wisdom and Foolishness

13 There is something else I saw, a
good **example** of how **wisdom** is
regarded in this **world**. 14 There was a
little town without many people in it. A
powerful king attacked it. He surrounded
it and prepared to break through the
walls. 15 A man lived there who was **poor**,
but so clever that he could have **saved**
the town. But no one thought about him.[l]
16 I have always said that **wisdom** is
better than **strength**, but no one thinks of
a **poor** man as **wise** or pays any attention
to what he says. 17 It is better to listen to
the quiet **words** of a **wise** man than to the
shouts of a ruler at a **council** of **fools**.
18 **Wisdom** does more good than weapons,
but one sinner can undo a lot of good.

10 Dead **flies** can make a whole
bottle of perfume stink, and a
little **stupidity** can cancel out the
greatest **wisdom**.
2 It is **natural** for a **wise** man to do the
right thing and for a **fool** to do the **wrong**
thing. 3 His **stupidity** will be **evident** even
to **strangers** he meets along the way; he
lets everyone know that he is a **fool**.
4 If your ruler becomes **angry** with
you, do not hand in your resignation;
serious wrongs may be pardoned if you
keep **calm**.[m]
5 Here is an **injustice** I have seen in
the **world**—an **injustice** caused by rulers.
6 **Stupid** people are given positions of
authority while **rich** men are **ignored**. 7 I
have seen **slaves** on horseback while
noblemen go on foot like slaves.
8 If you dig a pit, you fall in it; if you
break through a wall, a snake bites you.
9 If you work in a stone quarry, you get
hurt by stones. If you split wood, you get
hurt doing it. 10 If your axe is blunt and
you don't sharpen it, you have to work
harder to use it. It is more **sensible** to
plan ahead. 11 Knowing how to charm a
snake is of no use if you let the snake bite
first. 12 What a **wise** man says brings him
honour, but a **fool** is **destroyed** by his own
words. 13 He starts out with silly talk and
ends up with **pure madness**. 14 A **fool** talks
on and on.
No one knows what is going to happen
next, and no one can tell us what will
happen after we die.
15 Only someone too **stupid** to find his
way home would wear himself out with
work.
16 A country is in **trouble** when its
king is a youth and its leaders **feast** all
night long. 17 But a country is **fortunate** to
have a king who makes his own decisions
and leaders who eat at the **proper** time,
who **control** themselves and don't get
drunk.
18 When a man is too lazy to repair
his roof, it will leak, and the house will
fall in.
19 **Feasting** makes you **happy** and
wine **cheers** you up, but you can't have
either without money.
20 Don't **criticize** the king, even
silently, and don't **criticize** the **rich**, even
in the privacy of your bedroom. A bird
might carry the **message** and tell them
what you said.

anger 5.6; Song 1.6
authority 8.4;
Is 22.21
calm Prov 29.8;
Is 7.4
cheer (1) 9.7;
Mk 10.49
control 9.1; Is 3.3
criticize [2]
Prov 30.10; Mk 14.5
dead 9.4; 11.8
destroy 5.6; Is 1.9
evidence Prov 24.28;
Mt 26.59
feast [2] Prov 9.2;
Is 5.12
fool [4] 9.17; Is 19.11
fortune Prov 20.7;
Hos 12.8
happy 9.7; 11.9
hard 9.1; Is 5.28
honour 6.2; Is 9.1
hurt [2] 1.18; Is 43.2
ignore Prov 31.5;
Is 30.12
injustice [2] 6.1;
Is 40.27
mad 9.3; Jer 29.26
message Prov 26.6;
Is 1.1
natural Prov 22.15;
Jer 31.36
plan Prov 30.32;
Is 5.19
proper Prov 5.2;
Is 28.27
pure Prov 30.12;
Is 1.25
rich [2] 9.11; Is 10.18
right (1) 8.6; 11.4
sense Prov 30.2;
Is 28.6
serious 6.1; Mal 2.2
slave 2.7; Is 14.2
stranger 6.2;
Jer 5.19
stupid [4] 7.5; Is 19.11
trouble 9.9; Is 1.24
wisdom 9.10; Is 11.2
wise [2] 9.1; 12.9
word (1) 9.17; 12.10
world 9.3; 11.2
wrong [2] 9.3;
Is 19.14

[l] he could have...him; *or* he saved the town. But later on no one remembered him.
[m] keep calm; *or* submit to him.

10.8: Ps 7.15; Prov 26.27

bad 9.2; 12.14
cloud Prov 25.14; 12.2
dead 10.1; Is 8.19
desire 3.11; 12.5
enjoy [2] 9.9; 12.1
grateful 5.19; Lk 6.35
happy 10.19; Song 1.4
harvest 5.9; Is 9.3
heart 2.23; Song 4.9
judge 3.17; 12.14
life (1) 9.9; 12.1
light (1) 6.5; 12.2
new 1.9; Song 6.11
pain Prov 20.30; Is 13.6
remember [2] 7.14; 12.1
right (1) 10.2; Is 1.17
sow [3] Prov 22.8; Is 19.7
understand [2] 8.17; Is 1.3
womb Ps 139.13; Jer 20.17
world 10.5; Is 6.3
worry 5.3; Is 32.9

What a Wise Man Does

11 Invest your money in foreign
trade, and one of these days you
will make a profit. 2 Put your investments
in several places—many places, in fact—
because you never know what kind of
bad luck you are going to have in this
world.
3 No matter in which direction a tree
falls, it will lie where it fell. When the
clouds are full, it rains. 4 If you wait until
the wind and the weather are just **right**,
you will never **sow** anything and never
harvest anything. 5 God made everything,
and you can no more **understand** what he
does than you **understand** how **new life**
begins in the **womb** of a pregnant
woman. 6 Do your **sowing** in the morning
and in the evening, too. You never know
whether it will all grow well or whether
one **sowing** will do better than the other.
7 It is good to be able to **enjoy** the
pleasant **light** of day. 8 Be **grateful** for
every year you live. No matter how long
you live, **remember** that you will be **dead**
much longer. There is nothing at all to
look forward to.

Advice to Young People

9 Young people, **enjoy** your youth. Be
happy while you are still young. Do what
you want to do, and follow your **heart's**
desire. But **remember** that God is going
to **judge** you for whatever you do.
10 Don't let anything **worry** you or
cause you **pain**. You aren't going to be
young very long.

12 So **remember** your **Creator**[n]
while you are still young, before
those dismal days and years come when
you will say, "I don't **enjoy life**." 2 That is
when the **light** of the sun, the moon, and
the stars will grow dim for you, and the
rain **clouds** will never pass away. 3 Then
your arms, that have **protected** you, will
tremble, and your legs, now **strong**, will
grow **weak**. Your teeth will be too few to
chew your food, and your eyes too dim to
see clearly. 4 Your ears will be deaf to the
noise of the street. You will barely be
able to hear the mill as it grinds or music
as it plays, but even the song of a bird
will wake you from sleep. 5 You will be
afraid of high places, and walking will be
dangerous. Your hair will **turn** white; you
will hardly be able to drag yourself
along, and all **desire** will have gone.
We are going to our **final resting place**,
and then there will be **mourning** in the
streets. 6 The silver chain will snap, and
the golden lamp will fall and break; the
rope at the well will break, and the water
jar will be shattered. 7 Our **bodies** will return to the dust of the earth, and the
breath of **life** will go back to God, who
gave it to us.
8 **Useless**, **useless**, said the Philosopher. It is all **useless**.

The Summing Up

9 But because the Philosopher was
wise, he kept on **teaching** the people
what he knew. He **studied proverbs** and
honestly **tested** their **truth**. 10 The
Philosopher tried to find **comforting**
words, but the **words** he wrote were
honest. 11 The **sayings** of **wise** men are
like the sharp sticks that **shepherds** use
to **guide sheep**, and collected **proverbs**
are as **lasting** as firmly driven nails.
They have been given by God, the one
Shepherd of us all.
12 My son, there is something else to
watch out for. There is no end to the
writing of books, and too much **study** will
wear you out.
13 After all this, there is only one
thing to say: Have **reverence** for God,
and **obey** his **commands**, because this is
all that man was **created** for. 14 God is
going to **judge** everything we do, whether
good or **bad**, even things done in **secret**.

[n] *The Hebrew expression for* your Creator *sounds like the Hebrew for* your grave.

afraid Prov 31.25; Is 8.9
bad 11.2; Is 7.13
body Prov 14.30; Song 5.14
cloud 11.3; Is 4.5
comfort Ps 119.50; Is 12.1
command 8.5; Is 11.4
create Prov 8.22; Is 19.25
Creator Ps 149.2; Is 17.7

danger 8.3; Is 7.4
desire 11.9; Song 7.10
enjoy 11.7; Is 3.10
final Job 30.12; Is 51.6
guide Prov 29.18; Is 58.11
honest [2] Prov 29.
Is 28.17
judge 11.9; Is 3.2
last (1) 3.14; Is 24.5
life (1) [2] 11.5; Is 10.31
light (1) 11.7; Is 2.5
mourn 7.2; Is 3.26
obey 8.5; Is 1.19
protect 5.8; Song 8.
proverb [2] Prov 26.7; Is 28.20
remember 11.8; Is 8.13
rest (1) 6.5; Song 1.
reverence 7.18; Is 11.2
saying Prov 26.9; Is 29.17
secret Prov 25.9; Song 4.12
sheep Prov 27.23; Song 4.2
shepherd [2] Ps 80.
Song 1.7
strong 6.10; Song 5.10
study [2] 7.25; Is 47.13
teach Prov 28.26; Song 8.2
test 7.23; Is 7.12
tremble Ps 114.7; Song 6.12
truth Prov 29.24; Is 43.9
turn Prov 26.14; Song 6.5
useless [2] 9.9; Is 1.13
watch Prov 30.29; Song 3.3
weak Prov 30.25; Song 2.5
wise [2] 10.2; Is 5.21
word (1) [2] 10.12; Is 6.5

THE SONG OF SONGS

INTRODUCTION

The *Song of Songs* is a series of love poems, for the most part in the form of songs addressed by a man to a woman, and by the woman to the man. In some translations, the book is called *The Song of Solomon,* because it is attributed to Solomon in the Hebrew.

These songs have often been interpreted by Jews as a picture of the relationship between God and his people, and by Christians as a picture of the relationship between Christ and the Church.

Outline of Contents

---

anger Ecc 10.4; Is 2.10
care Prov 27.5; Is 11.6
dark [2] Ecc 6.4; 2.17
dear Prov 31.2; 2.3
delight Ps 147.10; 4.10
flock [3] Ps 107 41; 2.16
happy Ecc 11.9; Is 3.10
kiss Ecc 3.5; 5.16
look down on Prov 12.8; Dan 9.16
love [8] Ecc 9.1; 2.3
need Ecc 5.13; Is 7.22
rest (1) Ecc 12.5; Is 14.7
shepherd [2] Ecc 12.11; Is 13.14
vineyard [2] Ecc 2.4; 2.15

1 The most beautiful of songs, by Solomon.[a]

The First Song

The Woman

2 Your lips cover me with **kisses**;
your **love** is better than wine.
3 There is a fragrance about you;
the sound of your name recalls it.
No woman could help **loving** you.
4 Take me with you, and we'll run away;
be my king and take me to your room.
We will be **happy** together,
drink deep, and lose ourselves in **love**.
No wonder all women **love** you!
5 Women of Jerusalem, I am **dark** but[b] beautiful,
dark as the desert tents of Kedar,
but beautiful as the curtains in Solomon's palace.
6 Don't **look down on** me because of my colour,
because the sun has tanned me.
My brothers were **angry** with me
and made me work in the **vineyard**.
I had no time to **care** for myself.
7 Tell me, my **love**,
Where will you lead your **flock** to graze?
Where will they **rest** from the noonday sun?
Why should I **need** to look for you
among the **flocks** of the other **shepherds**?[c]

The Man

8 Don't you know the place, loveliest of women?
Go and follow the **flock**;
find pasture for your goats
near the tents of the **shepherds**.

9 You, my **love**, excite men
as a mare excites the stallions of Pharaoh's chariots.
10 Your hair is beautiful upon your cheeks
and falls along your neck like jewels.
11 But we will make for you a chain of gold
with ornaments of silver.

The Woman

12 My king was lying on his couch,
and my perfume filled the air with fragrance.
13 My lover has the scent of myrrh
as he lies upon my breasts.
14 My lover is like the wild flowers
that bloom in the **vineyards** at Engedi.

The Man

15 How beautiful you are, my **love**;
how your eyes shine with **love**!

[a] by Solomon; *or* dedicated to Solomon, *or* about Solomon. [b] but; *or* and.
[c] *Probable text* Why should I...shepherds; *Hebrew unclear.*

1.1: 1 Kgs 4.32

The Woman

16 How handsome you are, my **dearest**;
how you **delight** me!
The green grass will be our bed;
17 the cedars will be the beams of our house,
and the cypress-trees the ceiling.

2 I am only a wild flower in Sharon,
a lily in a mountain valley.

The Man

2 Like a lily among thorns
is my darling among women.

The Woman

3 Like an apple-tree among the trees of the forest,
so is my **dearest compared** with other men.
I **love** to sit in its shadow,
and its fruit is sweet to my taste.
4 He brought me to his **banqueting** hall
and **raised** the banner of **love** over me.
5 **Restore** my **strength** with raisins
and refresh me with apples!
I am **weak** from **passion**.
6 His left hand is under my head,
and his **right hand** caresses me.
7 **Promise** me, women of Jerusalem;
swear by the swift deer and the gazelles
that you will not interrupt our **love**.

banquet Prov 17.1; Is 21.5
compare Prov 27.3; Is 40.18
dark 1.5; 4.6
dear 1.16; Jer 31.20
dove [2] Ps 68.13; 5.2
flock 1.7; 4.1
love [5] 1.2; 3.1
passion Ecc 9.6; 5.8
promise Ecc 8.2; 3.5
race (2) Ecc 9.11; Jer 12.5
raise Prov 1.6; Is 11.12
restore Ps 147.2; Is 49.6
right (2) Ps 110.1; 8.3
ripe Job 15.33; Is 5.2
ruin Ecc 7.7; Is 1.7
strength Ecc 9.16; Is 12.2
swear Job 31.5; 3.5
vine Ps 128.3; 6.11
vineyard 1.6; 8.11
weak Ecc 12.3; 5.8

The Second Song

The Woman

8 I hear my lover's voice.
He comes running over the mountains,
racing across the hills to me.
9 My lover is like a gazelle,
like a young stag.
There he stands beside the wall.
He looks in through the window
and glances through the lattice.
10 My lover speaks to me.

The Man

Come then, my **love**;
my darling, come with me.
11 The winter is over; the rains have stopped;
12 in the countryside the flowers are in bloom.
This is the time for singing;
the song of **doves** is heard in the fields.
13 Figs are beginning to **ripen**;
the air is fragrant with blossoming **vines**.
Come then, my **love**;
my darling, come with me.

14 You are like a **dove** that hides
in the crevice of a rock.
Let me see your lovely face
and hear your enchanting voice.

15 Catch the foxes, the little foxes,
before they **ruin** our **vineyard** in bloom.

The Woman

16 My lover is mine, and I am his.
He feeds his **flock** among the lilies
17 until the morning breezes blow
and the **darkness** disappears.
Return, my darling, like a gazelle,
like a stag on the mountains of Bether.[d]

3 Asleep on my bed, night after night
I **dreamt** of the one I **love**;
I was looking for him, but couldn't find him.
2 I went wandering through the city,
through its streets and alleys.
I looked for the one I **love**.
I looked, but couldn't find him.
3 The **watchmen** patrolling the city saw me.
I asked them, "Have you found my lover?"
4 As soon as I left them, I found him.
I held him and wouldn't let him go
until I took him to my mother's house,
to the room where I was born.

5 **Promise** me, women of Jerusalem;
swear by the swift deer and the gazelles
that you will not interrupt our **love**.

The Third Song

The Woman

6 What is this coming from the desert
like a column of smoke,
fragrant with **incense** and myrrh,
the **incense** sold by the traders?
7 Solomon is coming, carried on his **throne**;
sixty soldiers form the bodyguard,
the finest soldiers in Israel.
8 All of them are skilful with the sword;
they are battle-hardened veterans.
Each of them is armed with a sword,
on guard against a night attack.
9 King Solomon is carried on a **throne**
made of the finest wood.
10 Its posts are covered with silver;
over it is cloth embroidered with gold.
Its cushions are covered with purple cloth,

crown Prov 16.31; Is 28.1
dream Ecc 5.3; 5.2
glad Ecc 7.14; Is 14.29
incense [2] Ps 141.2; 4.6
joy Ecc 3.4; Is 9.3
love [4] 2.3; 4.1
promise 2.7; 5.8
swear 2.7; Is 14.24
throne [2] Ecc 4.13; Is 6.1
watch Ecc 12.12; 5.7
wedding 1 Kgs 9.16; Is 61.10

[d] mountains of Bether; *or* rugged mountains.

lovingly woven by the women of
Jerusalem.
11 Women of Zion, come and see King
Solomon.
He is wearing the **crown** that his
mother placed on his head
on his **wedding** day,
on the day of his **gladness** and **joy**.

The Man

best Ecc 6.12; Is 30.24
bride [4] Ps 45.10; 5.1
dark 2.17; Is 5.20
delight 1.16; 7.6
flock 2.16; 6.2
heart Ecc 11.9; 5.2
incense [2] 3.6; Is 1.13
love [5] 3.1; 5.1
perfect [2] Ps 119.45; 6.6
secret Ecc 12.14; Is 26.21
sheep Ecc 12.11; 6.6
steal Prov 30.9; Is 10.6

4 How beautiful you are, my **love**!
How your eyes shine with **love**
behind your veil.
Your hair dances, like a **flock** of goats
bounding down the hills of Gilead.
2 Your teeth are as white as **sheep**
that have just been shorn and
washed.
Not one of them is missing;
they are all **perfectly** matched.
3 Your lips are like a scarlet ribbon;
how lovely they are when you speak.
Your cheeks glow behind your veil.
4 Your neck is like the tower of David,
round and smooth,[e]
with a necklace like a thousand
shields hung round it.
5 Your breasts are like gazelles,
twin deer feeding among lilies.
6 I will stay on the hill of myrrh,
the hill of **incense**,
until the morning breezes blow
and the **darkness** disappears.
7 How beautiful you are, my **love**;
how **perfect** you are!

8 Come with me from the Lebanon
Mountains, my **bride**;
come with me from Lebanon.
Come down from the top of Mount
Amana,
from Mount Senir and Mount
Hermon,
where the lions and leopards live.
9 The look in your eyes, my sweetheart
and **bride**,
and the necklace you are wearing
have **stolen** my **heart**.
10 Your **love delights** me,
my sweetheart and **bride**.
Your **love** is better than wine;
your perfume more fragrant than
any spice.
11 The taste of honey is on your lips, my
darling;
your tongue is milk and honey for
me.
Your clothing has all the fragrance of
Lebanon.

12 My sweetheart, my **bride**, is a **secret**
garden,
a walled garden, a private spring;
13 there the plants flourish.
They grow like an orchard of
pomegranate-trees
and bear the finest fruits.
There is no lack of henna and nard,
14 of saffron, calamus, and cinnamon,
or **incense** of every kind.
Myrrh and aloes grow there
with all the most fragrant perfumes.
15 Fountains water the garden,
streams of flowing water,
brooks gushing down from the
Lebanon Mountains.

The Woman

16 Wake up, North Wind.
South Wind, blow on my garden;
fill the air with fragrance.
Let my lover come to his garden
and eat the **best** of its fruits.

The Man

5 I have entered my garden,
my sweetheart, my **bride**.
I am gathering my spices and myrrh;
I am eating my honey and
honeycomb;
I am drinking my wine and milk.

The Women

Eat, lovers, and drink
until you are drunk with **love**!

body Ecc 12.7; Is 1.6
bride 4.8; Is 49.18
dove [3] 2.12; 6.9
dream 3.1; Is 29.7
heart 4.9; 8.6
kiss 1.2; 8.1
love 4.1; 6.4
Majesty Ps 145.5; Is 30.30
passion 2.5; 8.6
promise [2] 3.5; 8.4
strike Prov 28.22; Is 28.19
strong Ecc 12.3; 8.6
watch 3.3; 6.13
weak 2.5; Is 14.10
wonder (1) Ps 145.5; 7.1

The Fourth Song

The Woman

2 While I slept, my **heart** was awake.
I **dreamt** my lover knocked at the
door.

The Man

Let me come in, my darling,
my sweetheart, my **dove**.
My head is wet with dew,
and my hair is damp from the mist.

The Woman

3 I have already undressed;
why should I get dressed again?
I have washed my feet;
why should I get them dirty again?

4 My lover put his hand to the door,
and I was thrilled that he was near.
5 I was ready to let him come in.
My hands were covered with myrrh,
my fingers with liquid myrrh,
as I grasped the handle of the door.
6 I opened the door for my lover,
but he had already gone.
How I wanted to hear his voice!

[e] round and smooth; *Hebrew unclear.*

I looked for him, but couldn't find him;
I called to him, but heard no answer.

7 The **watchmen** patrolling the city
found me;
they **struck** me and bruised me;
the guards at the city wall tore off
my cape.
8 **Promise** me, women of Jerusalem,
that if you find my lover,
you will tell him I am **weak** from
passion.

The Women
9 Most beautiful of women,
is your lover different from
everyone else?
What is there so **wonderful** about him
that we should give you our
promise?

The Woman
10 My lover is handsome and **strong**;
he is one in ten thousand.
11 His face is bronzed and smooth;
his hair is wavy,
black as a raven.
12 His eyes are as beautiful as **doves** by a
flowing brook,
doves washed in milk and standing
by the stream.[f]
13 His cheeks are as lovely as a garden
that is full of herbs and spices.
His lips are like lilies,
wet with liquid myrrh.
14 His hands are well-formed,
and he wears rings set with gems.
His **body** is like smooth ivory,[g]
with sapphires set in it.
15 His thighs are columns of alabaster
set in sockets of gold.
He is **majestic**, like the Lebanon
Mountains
with their towering cedars.
16 His mouth is sweet to **kiss**;
everything about him enchants me.
This is what my lover is like,
women of Jerusalem.

The Women
6 Most beautiful of women,
where has your lover gone?
Tell us which way your lover went,
so that we can **help** you find him.

The Woman
2 My lover has gone to his garden,
where the balsam-trees grow.
He is feeding his **flock** in the garden
and gathering lilies.
3 My lover is mine, and I am his;
he feeds his **flock** among the lilies.

The Fifth Song

The Man
4 My **love**, you are as beautiful as
Jerusalem,
as lovely as the city of Tirzah,
as breathtaking as these great
cities.[h]
5 **Turn** your eyes away from me;
they are holding me **captive**.
Your hair dances, like a **flock** of goats
bounding down the hills of Gilead.
6 Your teeth are as white as a **flock** of
sheep
that have just been washed.
Not one of them is missing;
they are all **perfectly** matched.
7 Your cheeks glow behind your veil.
8 Let the king have sixty queens, eighty
concubines,
young women without number!
9 But I **love** only one,
and she is as lovely as a **dove**.
She is her mother's only daughter,
her mother's favourite child.
All women look at her and **praise** her;
queens and **concubines** sing her
praises.

10 Who is this whose glance is like the
dawn?
She is beautiful and bright,
as **dazzling** as the sun or the moon.[i]
11 I have come down among the almond-
trees
to see the young plants in the valley,
to see the **new** leaves on the **vines**
and the blossoms on the
pomegranate-trees.
12 I am **trembling**; you have made me as
eager for love
as a chariot driver is for battle.[j]

The Women
13 Dance, dance,[k] girl of Shulam.
Let us **watch** you as you dance.

The Woman
Why do you want to **watch** me
as I dance between the rows of
onlookers?

The Man
7 What a **wonderful** girl you are!
How beautiful are your feet in
sandals.
The curve of your thighs

[f] and standing by the stream; *Hebrew unclear.* [g] like smooth ivory; *Hebrew unclear.*
[h] as breathtaking as...cities; *Hebrew unclear.* [i] as dazzling as...moon; *Hebrew unclear.*
[j] *Verse 12 in Hebrew is unclear.* [k] Dance, dance; *or* Come back, come back.

sheep 4.2; Is 1.11
tremble Ecc 12.3; Is 7.2
turn Ecc 12.5; Is 1.4
vine 2.13; 7.12
watch [2] 5.7; Is 1.8

captive Ps 68.18; 7.5
concubine [2] Esth 2.14; Dan 5.2
dazzling Job 37.21; Ezek 1.22
dove 5.2; Is 38.14
eager Prov 18.15; Is 42.4
flock [4] 4.1; Is 13.20
help Ecc 4.1; Is 1.17
love [3] 5.1; 7.6
new Ecc 11.5; 7.13
perfect 4.2; Is 26.3
praise [2] Ecc 8.10; Is 12.1

captive 6.5; Is 45.13
delight [2] 4.10; Is 4.2
desire Ecc 12.5; Is 26.8
grace Prov 22.11; Lk 1.30

love [2] 6.4; 8.2
new 6.11; Is 6.13
vine 6.11; Is 5.2
wonder (1) 5.9; Is 9.6

is like the work of an artist.
2 A bowl is there,
that never runs out of spiced wine.
A sheaf of wheat is there,
surrounded by lilies.
3 Your breasts are like twin deer,
like two gazelles.
4 Your neck is like a tower of ivory.
Your eyes are like the pools in the city of Heshbon,
near the gate of that great city.
Your nose is as lovely as the tower of Lebanon
that stands guard at Damascus.
5 Your head is held high like Mount Carmel.
Your braided hair shines like the finest satin;
its beauty[l] could hold a king **captive**.

6 How pretty you are, how beautiful;
how complete the **delights** of your **love**.
7 You are as **graceful** as a palm-tree,
and your breasts are clusters of dates.
8 I will climb the palm-tree
and pick its fruit.
To me your breasts are like bunches of grapes,
your breath like the fragrance of apples,
9 and your mouth like the finest wine.

The Woman

Then let the wine flow straight to my lover,
flowing over his lips and teeth.[m]
10 I belong to my lover, and he **desires** me.
11 Come, darling, let's go out to the countryside
and spend the night in the villages.[n]
12 We will get up early and look at the **vines**
to see whether they've started to grow,
whether the blossoms are opening
and the pomegranate-trees are in bloom.
There I will give you my **love**.
13 You can smell the scent of mandrakes,
and all the pleasant fruits are near our door.
Darling, I have kept for you
the old **delights** and the **new**.

contempt Ps 123.3; Is 29.20
death (1) [2] Ecc 8.8; Is 5.13

8 I **wish** that you were my brother,
that my mother had nursed you at her breast.
Then, if I met you in the street,
I could **kiss** you and no one would mind.
2 I would take you to my mother's house,
where you could **teach** me **love**.
I would give you spiced wine,
my pomegranate wine to drink.

3 Your left hand is under my head,
and your **right hand** caresses me.

4 **Promise** me, women of Jerusalem,
that you will not interrupt our **love**.

The Sixth Song

The Women

5 Who is this coming from the desert,
arm in arm with her lover?

The Woman

Under the apple-tree I woke you,
in the place where you were born.
6 Close your **heart** to every **love** but mine;
hold no one in your arms but me.
Love is as **powerful** as **death**;
passion is as **strong** as **death** itself.
It bursts into flame
and burns like a **raging** fire.
7 Water cannot **put it out**;
no **flood** can drown it.
But if anyone tried to buy **love** with his wealth,
contempt is all he would get.

The Woman's Brothers

8 We have a young sister,
and her breasts are still small.
What will we do for her
when a young man comes courting?
9 If she is a wall,
we will build her a silver tower.
But if she is a gate,
we will **protect** her with panels of cedar.

The Woman

10 I am a wall,
and my breasts are its towers.
My lover knows that with him
I find contentment and **peace**.

The Man

11 Solomon has a **vineyard**
in a place called Baal Hamon.
There are farmers who rent it from him;
each one pays a thousand silver coins.

flood Ps 124.4; Is 8.7
heart 5.2; Is 1.5
kiss 5.16; Hos 13.2
love [6] 7.6; Is 16.5
passion 5.8; Rom 1.26
peace Ecc 4.6; Is 9.6
power Ecc 9.14; Is 1.24
promise 5.8; Is 19.21
protect Ecc 12.3; Is 4.5
put out Job 21.17; Is 42.3
rage Ps 124.5; Is 29.6
right (2) 2.6; Is 30.21
share Ecc 6.3; Is 33.22
strong 5.10; Is 3.25
teach Ecc 12.9; Is 1.10
vineyard [2] 2.15; Is 1.8
welcome Prov 19.12; Is 14.9
wish Prov 13.12; Jer 9.1

[l] beauty; *Hebrew unclear.*
[m] *Some ancient translations* lips and teeth; *Hebrew* lips of those who sleep.
[n] villages; *or* fields.

12 Solomon is welcome to his thousand
coins,
and the farmers to two hundred as
their share;
I have a vineyard of my own!

13 Let me hear your voice from the
garden, my love;
my companions are waiting to hear
you speak.

The Woman

14 Come to me, my lover, like a gazelle,
like a young stag on the mountains
where spices grow.

THE BOOK OF
ISAIAH

INTRODUCTION

The book of *Isaiah* is named after a great prophet who lived in Jerusalem in the latter half of the eighth century B.C. This book may be divided into three principal parts:

1. *Chapters 1-39* come from a time when Judah, the southern kingdom, was threatened by a powerful neighbour, Assyria. Isaiah saw that the real threat to the life of Judah was not simply the might of Assyria, but the nation's own sin and disobedience to God, and their lack of trust in him. In vivid words and actions the prophet called the people and their leaders to a life of righteousness and justice, and warned that failure to listen to God would bring doom and destruction. Isaiah also foretold a time of world-wide peace and the coming of a descendant of David who would be the ideal king.

2. *Chapters 40-55* come from a time when many of the people of Judah were in exile in Babylon, crushed and without hope. The prophet proclaimed that God would set his people free and take them home to Jerusalem, to begin a new life. A notable theme of these chapters is that God is the Lord of history, and his plan for his people includes their mission to all nations, who will be blessed through Israel. The passages about "the Servant of the Lord" are among the best known in the Old Testament.

3. *Chapters 56-66* for the most part speak to a time when people were back in Jerusalem and needed reassurance that God was going to fulfil his promises to the nation. Concern is expressed for righteousness and justice, and also for Sabbath observance, sacrifice, and prayer. A notable passage is 61.1-2, words used by Jesus at the beginning of his ministry to express his calling.

Outline of Contents

---

accept Prov 21.28; 33.15
action Ecc 9.1; 28.21
Almighty [2] Ps 107.11; 2.12
alone Ecc 4.8; 2.11
blood [2] Prov 23.29; 4.4
body Song 5.14; 5.25
bribe Ecc 7.7; 5.23
burden Ecc 3.10; 9.4
case (2) Prov 23.11; 3.13
clean [3] Ps 51.2; 28.8
corrupt [2] Prov 17.23; Jer 6.28
court (1) Prov 29.24; 36.3
defend [3] Prov 29.14; 11.4
defy Ps 9.19; Ezek 2.6
destroy [3] Ecc 10.12; 2.11
devastate 2 Chr 34.6; 13.5
disgust Ps 119.158; 41.24
doom [2] Prov 21.7; 3.8
enemy Prov 29.24; 9.11
enough Ecc 8.11; 7.13

1 This book contains the **messages**
about Judah and Jerusalem which
God **revealed** to Isaiah son of Amoz during the time when Uzziah, Jotham, Ahaz,
and Hezekiah were kings of Judah.

God Reprimands His People

2 The LORD said, "Earth and sky,
listen to what I am saying! The children
I brought up have **rebelled** against me.
3 Cattle know who owns them, and donkeys know where their **master** feeds
them. But that is more than **my people**
Israel know. They don't **understand** at
all."

4 You are **doomed**, you sinful nation,
you **corrupt** and **evil** people! Your sins
drag you down! You have **rejected** the
LORD, the **holy** God of Israel, and have
turned your backs on him. 5 Why do you
keep on **rebelling**? Do you want to be
punished even more? Israel, your head
is already covered with wounds, and
your **heart** and **mind** are sick. 6 From
head to foot there is not a healthy spot on
your **body**. You are covered with bruises
and sores and open wounds. Your
wounds have not been **cleaned** or bandaged. No ointment has been put on them.

7 Your country has been **devastated**,
and your cities have been burnt to the
ground. While you look on, foreigners
take over your land and bring everything
to **ruin**. 8 Jerusalem **alone** is left, a city
under siege—as **defenceless** as a **watchman's** hut in a **vineyard** or a shed in a
cucumber field. 9 If the LORD **Almighty**
had not let some of the people survive,
Jerusalem would have been totally **destroyed**, just as Sodom and Gomorrah
were.

10 Jerusalem, your rulers and your
people are like those of Sodom and
Gomorrah. Listen to what the LORD is
saying to you. Pay attention to what our
God is **teaching** you. 11 He says, "Do you

evil [4] Ecc 9.3; 3.11
faithful [2] Prov 20.6; 16.5
festival [2] Ps 118.27; 29.1
forsake Ps 102.17; 2.6
friend Prov 29.5; 5.1
gift Ecc 5.19; 30.6
God's people Ps 149.4; 2.3
hate Ecc 9.1; 45.24
heart Song 8.6; 10.34
help Song 6.1; 3.7
holy [2] Prov 9.10; 4.3
impure Prov 25.4; Rom 6.19
incense Song 4.6; 17.8
justice Ecc 5.8; 5.7
learn Ecc 8.16; 23.1
master Prov 30.4; 22.18
message Ecc 10.20; 2.1
mind (1) Ecc 9.3; 5.19
New Moon Festival [2] Neh 10.33; 66.23
obey Ecc 12.13; 11.3
offer [2] Ecc 9.2; 18.7
oppress Ecc 5.8; 3.12

1.1: 2 Kgs 15.1-7, 15.32-16.20, 18.1-20.21; 2 Chr 26.1-32.33 **1.9:** Gen 19.24; Rom 9.29
1.11-14: Amos 5.21-22

think I want all these **sacrifices** you keep
offering to me? I have had more than
enough of the **sheep** you burn as **sacrifices** and of the fat of your fine animals. I
am tired of the **blood** of bulls and **sheep**
and goats. 12 Who asked you to bring me
all this when you come to **worship** me?
Who asked you to do all this tramping
about in my **Temple**? 13 It's **useless** to
bring your **offerings**. I am **disgusted** with
the smell of the **incense** you burn. I cannot stand your **New Moon Festivals**, your
Sabbaths, and your **religious** gatherings;
they are all **corrupted** by your sins. 14 I
hate your **New Moon Festivals** and **holy**
days; they are a **burden** that I am tired of
bearing.

15 "When you lift your hands in
prayer, I will not look at you. No matter
how much you **pray**, I will not listen, for
your hands are covered with **blood**.
16 Wash yourselves **clean**. Stop all this **evil**
that I see you doing. Yes, stop doing **evil**
17 and **learn** to do **right**. See that **justice** is
done—**help** those who are **oppressed**,
give **orphans** their **rights**, and **defend**
widows."

18 The LORD says, "Now, let's **settle**
the matter. You are stained red with sin,
but I will wash you as **clean** as snow.[a]
Although your stains are deep red, you
will be as white as wool.[b] 19 If you will
only **obey** me, you will eat the good
things the land produces. 20 But if you
defy me, you are **doomed** to die. I, the
LORD, have spoken."

The Sinful City

21 The city that once was **faithful** is
behaving like a whore! At one time it
was filled with **righteous** men, but now
only murderers remain. 22 Jerusalem, you
were once like silver, but now you are
worthless; you were like good wine, but
now you are only water. 23 Your leaders
are **rebels** and **friends** of **thieves**; they
are always **accepting gifts** and **bribes**.
They never **defend orphans** in **court** or
listen when **widows present** their **case**.

24 So now, listen to what the LORD
Almighty, Israel's **powerful** God, is saying: "I will take **revenge** on you, my
enemies, and you will cause me no more
trouble. 25 I will take **action** against you. I
will **purify** you just as metal is **refined**,
and will remove all your **impurity**. 26 I
will give you rulers and advisers like
those you had long ago. Then Jerusalem
will be called the **righteous**, **faithful** city."

27 Because the LORD is **righteous**, he
will **save** Jerusalem and everyone there
who **repents**. 28 But he will crush everyone who sins and **rebels** against him; he
will kill everyone who **forsakes** him.

29 You will be **sorry** that you ever
worshipped trees and planted **sacred**
gardens.[c] 30 You will wither like a dying
oak, like a garden that no one waters.
31 Just as straw is set on fire by a spark,
so **powerful** men will be **destroyed** by
their own **evil** deeds, and no one will be
able to stop the **destruction**.

Everlasting Peace
(Mic 4.1-3)

2 This is the **message** which God gave
to Isaiah son of Amoz about Judah
and Jerusalem:

2 In days to come
the mountain where the **Temple**
stands
will be the highest one of all,
towering above all the hills.
Many nations will come streaming to
it,
3 and their people will say,
"Let us go up the hill of the LORD,[d]
to the **Temple** of Israel's God.
He will **teach** us what he wants us to
do;
we will walk in the paths he has
chosen.
For the LORD's **teaching** comes from
Jerusalem;
from Zion he speaks to **his people**."

4 He will **settle disputes** among great
nations.
They will hammer their swords into
ploughs
and their spears into pruning-knives.
Nations will **never again** go to war,
never prepare for battle again.

5 Now, descendants of Jacob, let us
walk in the **light** which the LORD gives
us!

Arrogance Will Be Destroyed

6 O God, you have **forsaken** your
people, the descendants of Jacob! The
land is full of **magic practices** from the
east and from Philistia.[e] The people
follow foreign **customs**. 7 Their land is full
of silver and gold, and there is no end to

[a] sin, but...snow; *or* sin; do you think I will wash you as clean as snow?
[b] Although your...wool; *or* Your stains are deep red; do you think you will be as white as wool?
[c] SACRED GARDENS: *People believed that dedicating a garden to a fertility god would cause him to bless their crops.*
[d] HILL OF THE LORD: *Mount Zion, the hill in Jerusalem on which the Temple was built.*
[e] *Probable text* The land...Philistia; *Hebrew unclear.*

2.4: Joel 3.10

worth Prov 31.10; 7.23

their treasures. Their land is full of
horses, and there is no end to their
chariots. 8 Their land is full of **idols**, and
they **worship objects** that they have
made with their own hands.
9 Everyone will be **humiliated** and **dis-**
graced. Do not **forgive** them, LORD!
10 They will hide in caves in the rocky
hills or dig holes in the ground to try to
escape from the **LORD's anger** and to
hide from his **power** and **glory**! 11 A day
is coming when human **pride** will be
ended and **human arrogance destroyed**.
Then the LORD **alone** will be exalted.
12 On that day the LORD **Almighty** will
humble everyone who is **powerful**, everyone who is **proud** and **conceited**. 13 He will
destroy the tall cedars of Lebanon and
all the oaks in the land of Bashan. 14 He
will level the high mountains and hills,
15 every high tower, and the walls of
every fortress. 16 He will sink even the
largest and most beautiful ships.
17–18 **Human pride** will be ended, and
human **arrogance** will be **destroyed**. **Idols**
will completely disappear, and the LORD
alone will be exalted on that day.
19 People will hide in caves in the
rocky hills or dig holes in the ground to
try to **escape** from the **LORD's anger** and
to hide from his **power** and **glory**, when
he comes to shake the earth. 20 When that
day comes, they will throw away the gold
and silver **idols** they have made, and
abandon them to the moles and the bats.
21 When the LORD comes to shake the
earth, people will hide in holes and caves
in the rocky hills to try to **escape** from
his **anger** and to hide from his **power** and
glory.
22 Put no more **confidence** in **mortal**
men. What are they **worth**?

Chaos in Jerusalem

3 Now the Lord, the **Almighty** LORD, is
about to take away from Jerusalem
and Judah everything and everyone that
the people **depend** on. He is going to take
away their food and their water, 2 their
heroes and their soldiers, their **judges**
and their **prophets**, their **fortune-tellers**
and their statesmen, 3 their military and
civilian leaders, their politicians and
everyone who uses **magic** to **control**
events. 4 The LORD will let the people be
governed by immature boys. 5 Everyone
will take **advantage** of everyone else.
Young people will not **respect** their
elders, and **worthless** people will not
respect their superiors.
6 A time will come when the members
of a clan will **choose** one of their number
and say to him, "You at least have something to wear, so be our leader in this
time of **trouble**."
7 But he will answer, "Not me! I can't
help you. I haven't any food or clothes
either. Don't make me your leader!"
8 Yes, Jerusalem is **doomed**! Judah is
collapsing! Everything they say and do
is against the LORD; they openly **insult**
God himself. 9 Their prejudices will be
held against them. They sin as openly as
the people of Sodom did. They are
doomed, and they have brought it on
themselves.
10 **Righteous** men will be **happy**,[f] and
things will go well for them. They will be
able to **enjoy** what they have worked for.
11 But **evil** men are **doomed**; what they
have done to others will now be done to
them.
12 Money-lenders **oppress my people**,
and their creditors **cheat** them.
My people, your leaders are **mis-**
leading you, so that you do not know
which way to **turn**.

The LORD Judges His People

13 The LORD is ready to state his **case**;
he is ready to **judge his people**.[g] 14 The
LORD is bringing the **elders** and leaders
of **his people** to **judgement**. He makes
this **accusation**: "You have plundered
vineyards, and your houses are full of
what you have taken from the **poor**.
15 You have no **right** to crush **my people**
and take **advantage** of the **poor**. I, the
Sovereign LORD **Almighty**, have spoken."

A Warning to the Women of Jerusalem

16 The LORD said, "Look how **proud**
the women of Jerusalem are! They walk
along with their noses in the air. They
are always flirting. They take dainty
little steps, and the bracelets on their
ankles jingle. 17 But I will **punish** them—I
will **shave** their heads and leave them
bald."
18 A day is coming when the Lord will
take away from the women of Jerusalem
everything they are so **proud** of—the
ornaments they wear on their ankles, on
their heads, on their necks, 19 and on
their wrists. He will take away their veils
20 and their hats; the **magic** charms they
wear on their arms and at their waists;
21 the rings they wear on their fingers
and in their noses; 22 all their fine robes,

accuse Prov 25.18; 43.26
advantage [2] Ecc 7.12; 56.11
Almighty [2] 2.12; 5.7
case (2) 1.23; 28.7
cheat Ecc 8.8; 33.15
choose 2.3; 4.3
control Ecc 10.17; 45.12
depend Ecc 5.9; 22.24
doom [3] 1.4; 5.8
elder (2) Job 29.7; Jer 19.1
enjoy Ecc 12.1; 14.7
evil 1.4; 5.20
fortune-teller 2 Chr 33.6; 8.19
God's people [5] 2.3; 5.16
happy Song 1.4; 9.3
help 1.17; 10.3

insult Ecc 7.21; 32.6
judge [3] Ecc 12.14; 4.4
magic [2] 2.6; 47.9
mislead Prov 26.18; 9.16
mourn Ecc 12.5; 15.3
naked 1 Sam 19.24; 20.2
oppress 1.17; 9.4
poor [2] Ecc 9.15; 10.2
prophet Ps 105.15; 9.15
proud [2] 2.11; 4.2
punish 1.5; 5.25
respect [2] Ecc 7.28; 33.8
right (3) 1.17; 10.2
righteous 1.21; 24.16
shame Prov 25.10; 4.1
shave Job 1.20; 7.20
Sovereign Ps 141.8; 10.23
strip (1) Ps 76.5; 32.11
strong Song 8.6; 7.8
trouble 1.24; 7.17
turn [2] 1.4; 5.20
vineyard 1.8; 5.1
worthless 1.22; 33.11

[f] *Probable text* Righteous men will be happy; *Hebrew* Say to the righteous.
[g] *Some ancient translations* his people; *Hebrew* the peoples.

2.10: Rev 6.15; 2 Thes 1.9

gowns, cloaks, and purses; 23 their revealing garments, their linen handkerchiefs,
and the scarves and long veils they wear
on their heads.
24 Instead of using perfumes, they will
stink; instead of fine belts, they will wear
coarse ropes; instead of having beautiful
hair, they will be bald; instead of fine
clothes, they will be dressed in rags;
their beauty will be **turned** to **shame**!
25 The men of the city, yes, even the
strongest men, will be killed in war.
26 The city gates will **mourn** and cry, and
the city itself will be like a woman sitting
on the ground, **stripped naked**.

4 When that time comes, seven
women will grab hold of one man
and say, "We can feed and clothe ourselves, but please let us say you are our
husband, so that we won't have to **endure**
the **shame** of being **unmarried**."

Jerusalem Will Be Restored

2 The time is coming when the LORD
will make every plant and tree in the
land grow large and beautiful. All the
people of Israel who survive will take **de-**
light and **pride** in the crops that the land
produces. 3 Everyone who is left in Jerusalem, whom God has **chosen** for survival, will be called **holy**. 4 By his **power**
the Lord will **judge** and **purify** the nation
and wash away the **guilt** of Jerusalem
and the **blood** that has been shed there.
5 Then over Mount Zion and over all who
are gathered there, the LORD will send a
cloud in the daytime and smoke and a
bright flame at night. God's **glory** will
cover and **protect** the whole city. 6 His
glory will shade the city from the heat of
the day and make it a place of **safety**,
sheltered from the rain and storm.

The Song of the Vineyard

5 Listen while I sing you this song,
a song of my **friend** and his
vineyard:
My **friend** had a **vineyard**
on a very fertile hill.
2 He dug the soil and **cleared** it of
stones;
he planted the finest **vines**.
He built a tower to guard them,
dug a pit for treading the grapes.
He waited for the grapes to **ripen**,
but every grape was sour.

3 So now my **friend** says, "You people
who live in Jerusalem and Judah, **judge**
between my **vineyard** and me. 4 Is there
anything I **failed** to do for it? Then why
did it produce sour grapes and not the
good grapes I expected?
5 "This is what I am going to do to my
vineyard; I will take away the hedge
round it, break down the wall that **pro-**
tects it, and let wild animals eat it and
trample it down. 6 I will let it be overgrown with **weeds**. I will not prune the
vines or hoe the ground; instead I will let
briars and thorns cover it. I will even **for-**
bid the **clouds** to let rain fall on it."

7 Israel is the **vineyard** of the LORD
Almighty;
the people of Judah are the **vines** he
planted.
He expected them to do what was
good,
but instead they **committed murder**.
He expected them to do what was
right,
but their **victims** cried out for
justice.

The Evil That Men Do

8 You are **doomed**! You buy more
houses and fields to add to those you
already have. Soon there will be nowhere
for anyone else to live, and you **alone** will
live in the land. 9 I have heard the LORD
Almighty say, "All these big, fine houses
will be empty **ruins**. 10 The **grapevines**
growing on ten hectares of land will yield
only eight litres of wine. A hundred and
eighty litres of **seed** will produce only
eighteen litres of corn."
11 You are **doomed**! You get up early
in the morning to start drinking, and you
spend long evenings getting drunk. 12 At
your **feasts** you have harps and tambourines and flutes—and wine. But you
don't **understand** what the LORD is doing,
13 and so you will be carried away as
prisoners. Your leaders will starve **to**
death, and the common people will die of
thirst. 14 The **world of the dead** is **hungry**
for them, and it opens its mouth wide. It
gulps down the nobles of Jerusalem
along with the noisy crowd of common
people.
15 Everyone will be **disgraced**, and all
who are **proud** will be **humbled**. 16 But the
LORD **Almighty** shows his greatness by
doing what is **right**, and he **reveals** his
holiness by **judging his people**. 17 In the
ruins of the cities **lambs** will eat grass
and young goats will find pasture.[h]
18 You are **doomed**! You are unable
to break **free** from your sins. 19 You say,
"Let the LORD hurry up and do what he
says he will, so that we can see it. Let

[h] *Verse 17 in Hebrew is unclear.*

4.5: Ex 13.21, 24.16 **5.1-2:** Mt 21.33; Mk 12.1; Lk 20.9

blood 1.11; 9.5
choose 3.6; 14.1
cloud Ecc 12.2; 5.6
delight Song 7.6; 62.5
endure Prov 28.2; 7.9
glory [2] 2.10; 6.3
guilty Prov 28.17; 5.23
holy 1.4; 5.16
judge 3.2; 5.3
power 2.10; 8.11
protect Song 8.9; 5.5
proud 3.16; 5.15
pure 1.25; 66.17
safe Ecc 8.5; 14.30
shame 3.24; 13.8
shelter Ps 144.2; 25.4
unmarried 2 Sam 13.1; Ezek 44.25

Almighty [4] 3.1; 6.3
alone 2.11; 22.4
anger [2] 2.10; 7.4
bitter Ecc 7.26; 22.4
body 1.6; 6.2
bribe 1.23; 33.15
clear Ps 80.9; 40.3
cloud 4.5; 14.14
commit Prov 30.20; 33.15
dark [3] Song 4.6; 8.22
death (1) Song 8.6; 25.8
death (3) (to death) Ecc 4.5; 13.15
disgrace 2.9; 9.1
distress Ps 144.14; 54.6
doom [6] 3.8; 6.5
evil 3.11; 9.17
fail Ecc 2.9; 13.7
fear Prov 20.2; 8.9
feast Ecc 10.16; 29.1

forbid Ezra 7.24; 52.11
free [2] Prov 29.6; 10.27
friend [3] 1.23; 41.
God's people [2] 3 6.13
grapevine *see* vi
guilty 4.4; 6.7
hard Ecc 10.10; 14
holy [3] 4.3; 6.3
humble 2.12; 13.11
hunger Prov 27.7; 8.21
innocent Prov 28. 50.8
judge [2] 4.4; 9.8
justice [2] 1.17; 9.7
lamb Ps 114.4; 16.
light (1) [2] 2.5; 9.2
mind (1) 1.5; 6.10
plan Ecc 10.10; 8.
prevent Prov 18.5 10.2
prison Ecc 4.13; 1
protect 4.5; 8.8
proud 4.2; 9.9
punish [2] 3.17; 9.1
reject 1.4; 8.6
reveal 1.1; 19.21
right (1) [2] 1.17; 9
ripe Song 2.13; 18.
ruin [2] 1.7; 6.11
seed Prov 22.8; 28.
stumble Prov 24.1 8.14
teach 2.3; 8.20
turn [2] 3.12; 6.10
understand 1.3; 6.
victim Prov 9.18; 33.1
vine [4] Song 7.12; 7.23
vineyard [5] 3.14; 7.23
weed Prov 24.31; 37.27
wise Ecc 12.9; 10.1
world of the dead Ecc 9.10; 7.11

Israel's holy God carry out his plans; let's
see what he has in mind."
20 You are doomed! You call evil
good and call good evil. You turn darkness into light and light into darkness.
You make what is bitter sweet, and what
is sweet you make bitter.
21 You are doomed! You think you
are wise, so very clever.
22 You are doomed! Heroes of the
wine bottle! Brave and fearless when it
comes to mixing drinks! 23 But for just a
bribe you let guilty men go free, and you
prevent the innocent from getting justice. 24 So now, just as straw and dry grass
shrivel and burn in the fire, your roots
will rot and your blossoms will dry up
and blow away, because you have rejected what the LORD Almighty, Israel's
holy God, has taught us. 25 The LORD is
angry with his people and has stretched
out his hand to punish them. The mountains will shake, and the bodies of those
who die will be left in the streets like rubbish. Yet even then the LORD's anger will
not be ended, but his hand will still be
stretched out to punish.
26 The LORD gives a signal to call for
a distant nation.[o] He whistles for them to
come from the ends of the earth. And
here they come, swiftly, quickly! 27 None
of them grows tired; none of them stumbles. They never doze or sleep. Not a belt
is loose; not a sandal strap is broken.
28 Their arrows are sharp, and their bows
are ready to shoot. Their horses' hooves
are as hard as flint, and their chariot-
wheels turn like a whirlwind. 29 The
soldiers roar like lions that have killed an
animal and are carrying it off where no
one can take it away from them.
30 When that day comes, they will
roar over Israel as loudly as the sea.
Look at this country! Darkness and distress! The light is swallowed by darkness.

God Calls Isaiah to Be a Prophet

6 In the year that King Uzziah died, I
saw the Lord. He was sitting on his
throne, high and exalted, and his robe
filled the whole Temple. 2 Round him
flaming creatures were standing, each of
which had six wings. Each creature
covered its face with two wings, and its
body with two, and used the other two for
flying. 3 They were calling out to each
other:
"Holy, holy, holy!
The LORD Almighty is holy!
His glory fills the world."
4 The sound of their voices made the
foundation of the Temple shake, and the
Temple itself was filled with smoke.
5 I said, "There is no hope for me! I
am doomed because every word that
passes my lips is sinful, and I live among
a people whose every word is sinful. And
yet, with my own eyes, I have seen the
King, the LORD Almighty!"
6 Then one of the creatures flew down
to me, carrying a burning coal that he
had taken from the altar with a pair of
tongs. 7 He touched my lips with the burning coal and said, "This has touched your
lips, and now your guilt is gone, and your
sins are forgiven."
8 Then I heard the Lord say, "Whom
shall I send? Who will be our messenger?"
I answered, "I will go! Send me!"
9 So he told me to go and give the
people this message: "No matter how
much you listen, you will not understand.
No matter how much you look, you will
not know what is happening." 10 Then he
said to me, "Make the minds of these
people dull, their ears deaf, and their
eyes blind, so that they cannot see or
hear or understand. If they did, they
might turn to me and be healed."
11 I asked, "How long will it be like
this, Lord?"
He answered, "Until the cities are
ruined and empty—until the houses are
uninhabited—until the land itself is a
desolate waste. 12 I will send the people
far away and make the whole land desolate. 13 Even if one person out of ten remains in the land, he too will be destroyed; he will be like the stump of an
oak-tree that has been cut down."
(The stump represents a new beginning for God's people.)

A Message for King Ahaz

7 When King Ahaz, the son of Jotham
and grandson of Uzziah, ruled
Judah, war broke out. Rezin, king of
Syria, and Pekah son of Remaliah, king
of Israel, attacked Jerusalem, but were
unable to capture it.
2 When word reached the king of
Judah that the armies of Syria were
already in the territory of Israel, he and
all his people were so terrified that they
trembled like trees shaking in the wind.
3 The LORD said to Isaiah, "Take your
son Shear Jashub,[i] and go to meet King
Ahaz. You will find him on the road

heal Ecc 3.3; 19.22
holy [2] 5.16; 8.13
hope Ecc 9.4; 8.17
message 2.1; 7.10
mind (1) 5.19; 10.7
new Song 7.13; 11.1
represent Esth 9.3; Jer 40.10
ruin 5.9; 13.21
Temple (1) (of God) [3] 2.2; 30.29
throne Song 3.7; 7.6
turn 5.20; 14.17
understand [2] 5.12; 27.11
word (1) [2] Ecc 12.10; 7.2
world Ecc 11.2; 10.14

Almighty [2] 5.7; 8.13
altar Ps 118.27; 17.8
blind Ps 146.8; 29.9
body 5.25; 7.20
creature [3] Ecc 3.19; 34.16
desolate [2] Ps 68.6; 17.5
destroy 2.11; 9.5
doom 5.8; 10.1
each other Prov 18.18; 9.21
forgive 2.9; 22.14
glory 4.5; 24.23
God's people 5.16; 8.17
guilty 5.23; 30.13

alert Dan 4.13
anger 5.25; 8.21
bad Ecc 12.14; 30.14
body 6.2; 10.16
calm Ecc 10.4; Ezek 16.42
danger Ecc 12.5; 21.15
endure 4.1; 40.7
enough [2] 1.11; 8.4
faith Ps 112.7; 28.16
fright Job 41.25; 31.9
heaven Ecc 5.2; 13.13
intend Neh 13.5; 28.21
message 6.9; 8.16
need Song 1.7; 22.9
patient Ecc 7.8; 28.16

[o] *Probable text* a distant nation; *Hebrew* distant nations.
[i] SHEAR JASHUB: *This name in Hebrew means "A few will come back" (see also 10.20–22).*

6.1: 2 Kgs 15.7; 2 Chr 26.23 **6.3:** Rev 4.8 **6.4:** Rev 15.8
6.9–10: Mt 13.14–15; Mk 4.12; Lk 8.10; Jn 12.40; Acts 28.26–27 **7.1:** 2 Kgs 16.5; 2 Chr 28.5–6

plot (1) Ps 140.2; 32.7
refuse (1) Prov 27.7; 26.10
save 1.27; 12.3
separate Neh 10.28; 27.12
shave 3.17; 15.2
sheep 1.11; 11.6
sign (1) [3] Prov 24.26; 20.3
strong [4] 3.25; 10.13
terrify [3] Ps 90.7; 8.22
test Ecc 12.9; 48.10
throne 6.1; 8.18
tremble Song 6.12; 8.6
trouble 3.6; 8.22
vine 5.2; 16.8
vineyard 5.1; 16.8
word (1) 6.5; 28.16
world of the dead 5.14; 14.9
worse Ps 39.2; 14.29
worth 2.22; Zech 11.13

where the cloth makers work, at the end of the ditch that brings water from the upper pool. 4 Tell him to keep **alert**, to stay **calm**, and not to be **frightened** or disturbed. The **anger** of King Rezin and his Syrians and of King Pekah is no more **dangerous** than the smoke from two smouldering sticks. 5 Syria, together with Israel and its king, has made a **plot**. 6 They **intend** to invade Judah, **terrify** the people into joining their side, and then put Tabeel's son on the **throne**.

7 "But I, the LORD, declare that this will never happen. 8 Why? Because Syria is no **stronger** than Damascus, its capital city, and Damascus is no **stronger** than King Rezin. As for Israel, within sixty-five years it will be too shattered to survive as a nation. 9 Israel is no **stronger** than Samaria, its capital city, and Samaria is no **stronger** than King Pekah.

"If your **faith** is not **enduring**, you will not endure."

The Sign of Immanuel

10 The LORD sent another **message** to Ahaz: 11 "Ask the LORD your God to give you a **sign**. It can be from deep in the **world of the dead** or from high up in **heaven**."

12 Ahaz answered, "I will not ask for a **sign**. I **refuse** to put the LORD **to the test**."

13 To that Isaiah replied, "Listen, now, descendants of King David. It's **bad enough** for you to wear out the **patience** of men—must you wear out God's patience too? 14 Well then, the Lord himself will give you a **sign**: a young woman[x] who is pregnant will have a son and will name him 'Immanuel.'[j] 15 By the time he is old **enough** to make his own decisions, people will be drinking milk and eating honey.[k] 16 Even before that time comes, the lands of those two kings who **terrify** you will be deserted.

17 "The LORD is going to bring on you, on your people, and on the whole royal family, days of **trouble worse** than any that have come since the kingdom of Israel **separated** from Judah—he is going to bring the king of Assyria.

18 "When that time comes, the LORD will whistle as a signal for the Egyptians to come like flies from the farthest branches of the Nile, and for the Assyrians to come from their land like bees. 19 They will swarm in the rugged valleys and in the caves in the rocks, and they will cover every thorn-bush and every pasture.

20 "When that time comes, the Lord will hire a barber from across the Euphrates—the emperor of Assyria!—and he will **shave** off your beards, and the hair on your heads and your **bodies**.

21 "When that time comes, even if a farmer has been able to **save** only one young cow and two goats, 22 they will give so much milk that he will have all he **needs**. Yes, the few survivors left in the land will have milk and honey to eat.

23 "When that time comes, the fine **vineyards**, each with a thousand **vines** and each **worth** a thousand pieces of silver, will be overgrown with thorn-bushes and briars. 24 People will go hunting there with bows and arrows. Yes, the whole country will be full of briars and thorn-bushes. 25 All the hills where crops used to grow will be so overgrown with thorns that no one will go there. It will be a place where cattle and **sheep** graze."

Isaiah's Son as a Sign to the People

8 The LORD said to me, "Take a large piece of writing material and write on it in large letters:[l] 'Quick Loot, Fast Plunder.' 2 Get two **reliable** men, the **priest** Uriah and Zechariah son of Jeberechiah, to **serve as witnesses**."

3 Some time later my wife became pregnant. When our son was born, the LORD said to me, "Name him 'Quick-Loot-Fast-Plunder.' 4 Before the boy is old **enough** to say 'Mummy' and 'Daddy,' all the wealth of Damascus and all the loot of Samaria will be carried off by the king of Assyria."

The King of Assyria Is Coming

5 The LORD spoke to me again. 6 He said, "Because these people have **rejected** the quiet waters from the brook of Shiloah,[m] and **tremble**[n] before King Rezin and King Pekah, 7 I, the Lord, will bring the emperor of Assyria and all his forces to attack Judah. They will advance like the **flood** waters of the River Euphrates, overflowing all its banks. 8 They will sweep through Judah in a **flood**, **rising** shoulder high and covering everything."

afraid [3] Ecc 12.5; 10.24
Almighty [2] 6.3; 9.
anger 7.4; 9.12
awe Ecc 5.7; 29.23
consult 2 Chr 34.21 19.3
curse Prov 30.10; 24.6
dark [2] 5.20; 9.2
dead Ecc 11.8; 14.1
disciple Jer 35.4
discourage Ps 77.3 35.4
enough 7.13; 30.14
fear [3] 5.22; 13.8
flood [2] Song 8.7; 28.2
fortune-teller 3.2; 44.25
God's people 6.13; 10.1
holy [2] 6.3; 10.17
hope 6.5; 20.5
hunger [2] 5.14; 9.20
medium [2] 2 Chr 33.6; 19.3
message [4] 7.10; 13.1
plan 5.19; 10.7
power 4.4; 9.7
preserve Prov 18.2 Jer 32.14
priest Ecc 5.6; 24.2
protect 5.5; 16.3
reject 5.24; 41.9
rely Prov 25.13; 10.20
remember Ecc 12.1 16.7
rise Ecc 9.11; 13.10

[x] YOUNG WOMAN: *The Hebrew word here translated "young woman" is not the specific term for "virgin", but refers to any young woman of marriageable age. The use of "virgin" in Mat 1.23 reflects a Greek translation of the Old Testament, made some 500 years after Isaiah.*
[j] IMMANUEL: *This name in Hebrew means "God is with us."*
[k] MILK AND HONEY: *These foods were associated with the earlier days of Israel's history.*
[l] large letters; *or* letters that everyone can read.
[m] BROOK OF SHILOAH *A stream which flowed from the large spring on the eastern side of Jerusalem.*
[n] *Probable text* tremble; *Hebrew* rejoice.

7.14: Mt 1.23

scheme Prov 24.9; 29.15
serve Prov 23.3; 14.2
spirit (2) Ecc 3.21; 19.3
stumble [2] 5.27; 28.7
succeed (1) Ecc 7.18; 28.29
teach 5.24; 9.15
terrify 7.2; 10.29
throne 7.6; 14.9
trap [2] Ecc 9.12; 24.17
tremble 7.2; 13.13
trouble 7.17; 9.1
trust Prov 29.25; 10.20
useless 1.13; 19.8
warn Prov 25.12; 28.22
witness Prov 25.8; 43.9

God is with us! His outspread wings
protect the land.[o]
9 Gather together in **fear**, you
nations! Listen, you distant parts of the
earth. Get ready to fight, but be **afraid**!
Yes, get ready, but be **afraid**! 10 Make
your **plans**! But they will never **succeed**.
Talk as much as you like! But it is all
useless, because God is with us.

The LORD Warns the Prophet

11 With his great **power** the LORD
warned me not to follow the path which
the people were following. He said, 12 "Do
not join in the **schemes** of the people and
do not be **afraid** of the things that they
fear. 13 **Remember** that I, the LORD
Almighty, am **holy**; I am the one you
must **fear**. 14 Because of my **awesome**
holiness I am like a stone that people
stumble over; I am like a **trap** that will
catch the people of the kingdoms of
Judah and Israel and the people of Jerusalem. 15 Many will **stumble**; they will fall
and be crushed. They will be caught in a
trap."

Warning against Consulting the Dead

16 You, my **disciples** are to guard and
preserve the **messages** that God has
given me. 17 The LORD has hidden himself
from **his people**, but I **trust** him and place
my **hope** in him.
18 Here I am with the children the
LORD has given me. The LORD **Almighty**,
whose **throne** is on Mount Zion, has sent
us as living **messages** to the people of
Israel.
19 But people will tell you to ask for
messages from **fortune-tellers** and
mediums, who chirp and mutter. They
will say, "After all, people should ask for
messages from the **spirits** and **consult** the
dead on behalf of the living."
20 You are to answer them, "Listen to
what the LORD is **teaching** you! Don't
listen to **mediums**—what they tell you
will do you no good."[p]

A Time of Trouble

21 The people will wander through the
land, **discouraged** and **hungry**. In their
hunger and their **anger** they will **curse**
their king and their God. They may look
up to the sky 22 or stare at the ground, but
they will see nothing but **trouble** and
darkness, terrifying darkness into which
they are being driven.

9 1 There will
be no way for them to **escape** from
this time of **trouble**.

The Future King

The land of the tribes of Zebulun and
Naphtali was once **disgraced**, but the
future will bring **honour** to this region,
from the Mediterranean eastwards to the
land on the other side of the Jordan, and
even to Galilee itself, where the
foreigners live.
2 The people who walked in **darkness**
have seen a great **light**.
They lived in a land of shadows,
but now **light** is shining on them.
3 You have given them great **joy**,[q]
LORD;
you have made them **happy**.
They **rejoice** in what you have done,
as people **rejoice** when they **harvest**
their corn
or when they divide captured
wealth.
4 For you have broken the yoke that
burdened them
and the rod that beat their
shoulders.
You have defeated the nation
that **oppressed** and exploited your
people,
just as you defeated the army of
Midian long ago.
5 The boots of the invading army
and all their **bloodstained** clothing
will be **destroyed** by fire.
6 A child is born to us!
A son is given to us!
And he will be our ruler.
He will be called, "**Wonderful**[r]
Counsellor,"
"**Mighty** God," "**Eternal** Father,"
"Prince of **Peace**."
7 His royal **power** will continue to grow;
his **kingdom** will always be at **peace**.
He will rule as King David's successor,
basing his **power** on **right** and
justice,
from now until the end of time.
The LORD **Almighty** is **determined** to
do all this.

The LORD Will Punish Israel

8 The Lord has pronounced **judgement** on the kingdom of Israel, on the
descendants of Jacob. 9 All the people of
Israel, everyone who lives in the city of
Samaria, will know that he has done this.

Almighty [3] 8.13; 10.16
anger [4] 8.21; 10.4
arrogant 2.11; 13.11
blood 4.4; 15.9
burden 1.14; 10.27
dark 8.22; 13.10
destroy [3] 6.13; 10.7
determine Ecc 7.23; 10.7
devour Ps 21.9; 56.9
disgrace 5.15; 17.3
each other 6.3; 13.8
enemy 1.24; 10.28
escape [2] 2.10; 13.14
eternal Ps 145.13; 60.19
evil 5.20; 11.4
godless Prov 11.9; 10.6
happy 3.10; 16.10
harvest Ecc 11.4; 16.9
honour [2] Ecc 10.12; 11.10
hunger 8.21; 29.8
joy Song 3.11; 12.3
judge 5.3; 11.3
justice 5.7; 10.2
Kingdom (1) (of God) Ps 145.12; Dan 2.44
lie (2) Prov 30.6; 28.15
light (1) [2] 5.20; 10.17
might Ps 150.2; 10.21
mislead 3.12; 19.13
oppress 3.12; 10.1
orphan 1.17; 10.2
peace [2] Song 8.10; 11.6
pity Prov 20.26; 13.18
power [2] 8.11; 10.27
prophet 3.2; 28.7
proud 5.15; 10.12
punish [6] 5.25; 10.3
rejoice [2] Prov 24.17; 12.3
repent 1.27; 57.15
right (1) 5.7; 16.5
satisfy Ecc 6.9; 32.10
teach 8.20; 28.9
trouble 8.22; 16.7
wicked [2] Ecc 9.2; 13.11
widow 1.17; 10.2
wonder (1) Song 7.1; 52.7

[o] everything." God.....land; *or* everything. They will spread out over the land. God be with us!"
[p] *Verse 20 in Hebrew is unclear.*
[q] *Probable text* You have given them great joy; *Hebrew* You have increased the nation.
[r] Wonderful; *or* Wise.

8.12–13: 1 Pet 3.14–15 **8.14–15:** 1 Pet 2.8 **8.17:** Heb 2.13 **8.18:** Heb 2.13 **9.1:** Mt 4.15
9.2: Mt 4.16; Lk 1.79 **9.7:** Lk 1.32–33

Now they are **proud** and **arrogant**. They say, 10 “The brick buildings have fallen down, but we will replace them with stone buildings. The beams of sycomore wood have been cut down, but we will replace them with the finest cedar.”

11 The LORD has stirred up their **enemies**[s] to attack them. 12 Syria on the east and Philistia on the west have opened their mouths to **devour** Israel. Yet even so the **LORD's anger** is not ended; his hand is still stretched out to **punish**.

13 The people of Israel have not **repented**; even though the LORD **Almighty** has **punished** them, they have not returned to him. 14 In a single day the LORD will **punish** Israel's leaders and its people; he will cut them off, head and tail. 15 The old and **honourable** men are the head—and the tail is the **prophets** whose **teachings** are **lies**! 16 Those who lead these people have **misled** them and totally confused them. 17 And so the Lord will not let any of the young men **escape**, and he will not show **pity** to any of the **widows** and **orphans**, because all the people are **godless** and **wicked** and everything they say is **evil**. Yet even so the **LORD's anger** will not be ended, but his hand will still be stretched out to **punish**.

18 The **wickedness** of the people burns like a fire that **destroys** thorn-bushes and thistles. It burns like a forest fire that sends up columns of smoke. 19 Because the LORD **Almighty** is **angry**, his **punishment** burns like a fire throughout the land and **destroys** the people, and it is every man for himself. 20 Everywhere in the country people snatch and eat any bit of food they can find, but their **hunger** is never **satisfied**. They even eat their own children! 21 The people of Manasseh and the people of Ephraim attack **each other**, and together they attack Judah. Yet even so the **LORD's anger** is not ended; his hand is still stretched out to **punish**.

10 You are **doomed**! You make **unjust laws** that **oppress my people**. 2 That is how you **prevent** the **poor** from having their **rights** and from getting **justice**. That is how you take the property that belongs to **widows** and **orphans**. 3 What will you do when God **punishes** you? What will you do when he brings **disaster** on you from a distant country? Where will you run to find **help**? Where will you hide your wealth? 4 You will be killed in battle or dragged off as **prisoners**. Yet even so the **LORD's anger** will not be ended; his hand will still be stretched out to **punish**.

The Emperor of Assyria as the Instrument of God

5 The LORD said, “Assyria! I use Assyria like a club to **punish** those with whom I am **angry**. 6 I sent Assyria to attack a **godless** nation, people who have made me **angry**. I sent them to loot and **steal** and trample on the people like dirt in the streets.”

7 But the Assyrian emperor has his own **violent plans** in **mind**. He is **determined** to **destroy** many nations. 8 He **boasts**, “Every one of my commanders is a king! 9 I **conquered** the cities of Calno and Carchemish, the cities of Hamath and Arpad. I **conquered** Samaria and Damascus. 10 I stretched out my hand to **punish** those kingdoms that **worship idols**, **idols** more numerous than those of Jerusalem and Samaria. 11 I have **destroyed** Samaria and all its **idols**, and I will do the same to Jerusalem and the **images** that are **worshipped** there.”

12 But the Lord says, “When I finish what I am doing on Mount Zion and in Jerusalem, I will **punish** the emperor of Assyria for all his **boasting** and all his **pride**.”

13 The emperor of Assyria **boasts**, “I have done it all myself. I am **strong** and **wise** and clever. I wiped out the boundaries between nations and took the supplies they had stored. Like a bull I have trampled on the people who live there. 14 The nations of the **world** were like a bird's nest, and I gathered their wealth as easily as gathering eggs. Not a wing fluttered to scare me off; no beak opened to scream at me!”

15 But the LORD says, “Can an axe **claim** to be greater than the man who uses it? Is a saw more **important** than the man who saws with it? A club doesn't lift up a man; a man lifts up a club.”

16 The LORD **Almighty** is going to send **disease** to **punish** those who are now well-fed. In their **bodies** there will be a fire that burns and burns. 17 God, the **light** of Israel, will become a fire. Israel's **holy** God will become a flame, which in a single day will burn up everything, even the thorns and thistles. 18 The **rich** forests and farmlands will be totally **destroyed**, in the same way that a fatal sickness **destroys** a man. 19 There will be so few trees left that even a child will be able to count them.

[s] *Probable text* their enemies; *Hebrew* the enemies of Rezin.

10.5–34: Is 14.24–27; Nah 1.1–3.19; Zeph 2.13–15

afraid 8.9; 12.2
Almighty [5] 9.7; 13.6
anger [3] 9.12; 12.1
boast [3] Prov 27.1; 16.6
body 7.20; 14.19
burden 9.4; 14.25
claim Ecc 8.17; 29.13
conquer [2] Ps 81.14; 11.14
deserve Prov 31.31; 53.6
destroy [8] 9.5; 13.6
determine 9.7; 14.13
disaster Prov 24.16; 13.11
disease Ps 106.15; Jer 14.12
doom 6.5; 28.1

enemy [2] 9.11; 11.1
free 5.18; 14.17
God's people [2] 8.
11.11
godless 9.17; Jer 23.11
heart 1.5; 15.5
help 3.7; 12.4
holy [2] 8.13; 12.6
humiliate 2.9; 23.9
idol [3] 2.8; 19.1
image Ps 106.20; 37.19
important Prov 25
19.15
justice 9.7; 11.5
law Prov 31.5; 24.5
life (1) Ecc 12.1; 32
light (1) 9.2; 13.10
might 9.6; 17.10
mind (1) 6.10; 44.18
oppress [2] 9.4; 14.2
orphan 9.17; Jer 5.2
plan 8.10; 14.24
poor 3.14; 11.4
power 9.7; 11.11
prevent 5.23; 29.21
prison 5.13; 14.17
proud [2] 9.9; 13.2
punish [8] 9.12; 11.4
rely 8.2; 17.8
rich Ecc 10.6; 19.15
right (3) 3.15; 11.4
Sovereign [2] 3.15; 22.5
steal Song 4.9; Jer 7.9
strong 7.8; 18.2
terrify 8.22; 13.8
true Prov 24.26; 42.
trust 8.17; 12.2
unjust Prov 24.11; 59.8
violent Prov 22.24; 29.6
widow 9.17; 47.8
wise 5.21; 19.11
world 6.3; 12.5
worship (2) (of other gods) [2] 2.8; 17.10

A Few Will Come Back

20 A time is coming when the people
of Israel who have survived will no longer **rely** on the nation that almost **destroyed** them. They will **truly** put their
trust in the LORD, Israel's **holy** God. 21 A
few of the people of Israel will come
back to their **mighty** God. 22 Even though
now there are as many people of Israel
as there are grains of sand by the sea,
only a few will come back. **Destruction** is
in store for the people, and it is fully **deserved**. 23 Yes, throughout the whole
country the **Sovereign** LORD **Almighty**
will bring **destruction**, as he said he
would.

The LORD Will Punish Assyria

24 The **Sovereign** LORD **Almighty** says
to **his people** who live in Zion, "Do not be
afraid of the Assyrians, even though they
oppress you as the Egyptians used to do.
25 In only a little while I will finish **punishing** you, and then I will **destroy** them. 26 I,
the LORD **Almighty**, will beat them with
my whip as I beat the people of Midian at
the Rock of Oreb. I will **punish** Assyria as
I punished Egypt. 27 When that time
comes, I will **free** you from the **power** of
Assyria, and their yoke will no longer be
a **burden** on your shoulders."[s]

The Invader Attacks

28 The **enemy** army has captured the
city of Ai![t] They have passed through
Migron! They left their supplies at
Michmash! 29 They have crossed the pass
and are spending the night at Geba! The
people in the town of Ramah are **terrified**, and the people in King Saul's town
of Gibeah have run away. 30 Shout, people
of Gallim! Listen, people of Laishah!
Answer, people of Anathoth! 31 The
people of Madmenah and Gebim are running for their **lives**. 32 Today the **enemy**
are in the town of Nob, and there they
are shaking their fists at Mount Zion, at
the city of Jerusalem.

33 The LORD **Almighty** will bring them
crashing down like branches cut off a
tree. The **proudest** and highest of them
will be cut down and **humiliated**. 34 The
LORD will cut them down as trees in the
heart of the forest are cut down with an
axe, as even the finest trees of Lebanon
fall!

The Peaceful Kingdom

11 The royal line of David is like a
tree that has been cut down; but
just as **new** branches sprout from a
stump, so a **new** king will arise from
among David's descendants.

2 The **spirit of the LORD** will give him
wisdom,
and the **knowledge** and skill to rule
his people.
He will know the **LORD's will** and have
reverence for him,
3 and find **pleasure** in **obeying** him.
He will not **judge** by **appearance** or
hearsay;
4 he will **judge** the **poor** fairly
and **defend** the **rights** of the **helpless**.
At his **command** the people will be
punished,
and **evil** persons will die.
5 He will rule his people with **justice** and
integrity.

6 Wolves and **sheep** will live together in
peace,
and leopards will lie down with
young goats.
Calves and lion cubs will feed[u]
together,
and little children will take **care** of
them.
7 Cows and bears will eat together,
and their calves and cubs will lie
down in **peace**.
Lions will eat straw as cattle do.
8 Even a baby will not be **harmed**
if it plays near a poisonous snake.
9 On Zion, God's **sacred** hill,
there will be nothing **harmful** or
evil.
The land will be as full of **knowledge** of
the LORD
as the seas are full of water.

The Exiled People Will Return

10 A day is coming when the **new** king
from the royal line of David will be a
symbol to the nations. They will gather in
his royal city and give him **honour**.
11 When that day comes, the Lord will
once again use his **power** and bring back
home those of **his people** who are left in
Assyria and Egypt, in the lands of
Pathros, Sudan, Elam, Babylonia, and
Hamath, and in the coastlands and on the
islands of the sea. 12 The LORD will **raise** a
signal flag to show the nations that he is
gathering together again the **scattered**

appearance Prov 1.9; Mt 6.16
care Song 1.6; 13.17
command Ecc 12.13; 21.5
conquer 10.9; 14.6
defend 1.8; 17.3
enemy 10.28; 18.5
evil [2] 9.17; 14.5
God's people [2] 10.1; 12.3
harm [2] Prov 31.12; 27.3
helpless Prov 31.8; 13.16
honour 9.1; 14.11
jealous Prov 27.4; Ezek 16.42
judge [2] 9.8; 26.9
justice 10.2; 16.5
knowledge [2] Ecc 9.10; 33.6
new [3] 6.13; 28.19
obey [2] 1.19; 20.2
peace [2] 9.6; 14.7
pleasure Ecc 8.15; 47.8
poor 10.2; 14.30
power 10.27; 12.2
punish 10.3; 13.3
raise Song 2.4; 13.2
reverence Ecc 12.13; 33.6
right (3) 10.2; 22.16
sacred 1.29; 17.10
scatter Ps 147.16; 13.14
sheep 7.25; 13.14
Spirit (1) (God's Spirit) Ps 51.11; 32.15
symbol Ps 132.8; 17.8
will (1) Prov 29.26; 26.8
wisdom Ecc 10.1; 28.29

[s] *Hebrew has three additional words, the meaning of which is unclear.*
[t] AI: *This and the other places mentioned in verses 28–32 were located near Jerusalem, along the way by which an invader would come to attack from the north.*
[u] *Some ancient translations* will feed; *Hebrew* and well-fed cattle.

10.22–23: Rom 9.27 **11.1:** Rev 5.5, 22.16 **11.4:** 2 Thes 2.8 **11.5:** Eph 6.14 **11.6–9:** Is 65.25
11.9: Hab 2.14 **11.10:** Rom 15.12

people of Israel and Judah and bringing
them back from the four corners of the
earth. 13 The kingdom of Israel will not be
jealous of Judah any more, and Judah
will not be the **enemy** of Israel. 14 Together they will attack the Philistines on
the west and plunder the people who live
to the east. They will **conquer** the people
of Edom and Moab, and the people of
Ammon will **obey** them. 15 The LORD will
dry up the Gulf of Suez, and he will bring
a hot wind to dry up the Euphrates,
leaving only seven tiny streams, so that
anyone will be able to walk across.
16 There will be a highway out of Assyria
for those of **his people** Israel who have
survived there, just as there was for their
ancestors when they left Egypt.

Hymn of Thanksgiving

afraid 10.24; 35.4
anger [2] 10.4; 13.3
comfort Ecc 12.10; 22.4
God's people [2] 11.11; 14.1
help 10.3; 14.2
holy 10.17; 13.3
joy 9.3; 14.7
power 11.11; 14.5
praise Song 6.9; 24.15
rejoice 9.3; 14.8
save 7.21; 25.9
Saviour [2] Ps 144.2; 44.24
strength Song 2.5; 31.1
thank Ps 145.1; 51.3
trust 10.20; 17.8
world 10.14; 14.7

12 A day is coming when people
will sing,

"I **praise** you, LORD! You were **angry**
with me,
but now you **comfort** me and are
angry no longer.
2 God is my **saviour**;
I will **trust** him and not be **afraid**.
The LORD gives me **power** and
strength;
he is my **saviour**.
3 As fresh water brings **joy** to the thirsty,
so **God's people rejoice** when he
saves them."

4 A day is coming when people will
sing,

"Give **thanks** to the LORD! Call for him
to **help** you!
Tell all the nations what he has
done!
Tell them how great he is!
5 Sing to the LORD because of the great
things he has done.
Let the whole **world** hear the news.
6 Let everyone who lives in Zion shout
and sing!
Israel's **holy** God is great,
and he lives among **his people**."

God Will Punish Babylon

Almighty [2] 10.16; 14.14
anger [4] 12.1; 14.6
arrogant 9.9; 16.6
barren Job 3.7; 21.13
care 11.6; 34.15
confident 2.22; 36.4
courage Ps 107.26; 15.4
cruel [2] Prov 30.14; 14.4

13 This is a **message** about Babylon,
which Isaiah son of Amoz re-
ceived from God.

2 On the top of a **barren** hill **raise** the
battle flag! Shout to the soldiers and
raise your arm as the signal for them to
attack the gates of the **proud** city. 3 The
LORD has called out his **proud** and **confi-**
dent soldiers to fight a **holy** war and **pun-**
ish those he is **angry** with.

4 Listen to the noise on the mountains—the sound of a great crowd of
people, the sound of nations and kingdoms gathering. The LORD of Armies is
preparing his troops for battle. 5 They are
coming from far-off countries at the ends
of the earth. In his **anger** the LORD is
coming to **devastate** the whole country.

6 Howl in **pain**! The **day of the LORD** is
near, the day when the **Almighty** brings
destruction. 7 Everyone's hands will hang
limp, and everyone's **courage** will **fail**.
8 They will all be **terrified** and overcome
with **pain**, like the pain of a woman in
labour. They will look at **each other** in
fear, and their faces will burn with
shame. 9 The **day of the LORD** is coming—
that **cruel** day of his fierce **anger** and
fury. The earth will be made a wilderness, and every sinner will be **destroyed**.
10 Every star and every constellation will
stop shining, the sun will be **dark** when it
rises, and the moon will give no **light**.

11 The LORD says, "I will bring **dis-**
aster on the earth and **punish** all **wicked**
people for their sins. I will **humble** everyone who is **proud** and **punish** everyone
who is **arrogant** and **cruel**. 12 Those who
survive will be scarcer than gold. 13 I will
make the **heavens tremble**, and the earth
will be shaken out of its place on that day
when I, the LORD **Almighty**, show my **an-**
ger.

14 "The foreigners living in Babylon
will run away to their own countries,
scattering like deer **escaping** from hunters, like **sheep** without a **shepherd**.
15 Anyone who is caught will be stabbed
to death. 16 While they look on **helplessly**,
their babies will be battered **to death**,
their houses will be looted, and their
wives will be **raped**."

17 The LORD says, "I am stirring up
the Medes[v] to attack Babylon. They **care**
nothing for silver and are not **tempted** by
gold. 18 With their bows and arrows they
will kill the young men. They will show
no **mercy** to babies and take no **pity** on
children. 19 Babylonia is the most beautiful kingdom of all; it is the **pride** of its
people. But I, the LORD, will **overthrow**
Babylon as I did Sodom and Gomorrah!
20 No one will ever live there again. No
wandering Arab will ever pitch his tent
there, and no **shepherd** will ever pasture
his **flock** there. 21 It will be a place where
desert animals live and where owls build

dark 9.2; 24.23
Day of the Lord [2] Ezek 13.5
death (3) (to death) [2] 5.13; 53.8
destroy [2] 10.7; 14.17
devastate 1.7; 16.4
disaster 10.3; 21.1
each other 9.21; 19.2
escape 9.1; 15.5
fail 5.4; 30.5
fear 8.9; 18.2
flock Song 6.2; 40.11
fury Ps 124.3; 51.13
heaven 7.11; 14.12
helpless 11.4; 25.4
holy 12.6; 17.7
humble 5.15; 26.5
light (1) 10.17; 30.26
mercy Prov 28.13; 14.1
message 8.16; 14.28
overthrow Job 34.25; 23.11
pain [2] Ecc 11.10; 14.3
pity 9.17; 27.11
proud [4] 10.12; 16.6
punish [3] 11.4; 14.26
raise [2] 11.12; 18.3
rape Esth 7.8; Jer 13.22
rise 8.8; 14.9
ruin 6.11; 14.20
scatter 11.12; 24.1
shame 4.1; 20.4
sheep 11.6; 17.2
shepherd [2] Song 1.7; 14.30
tempt Prov 23.31; Mt 4.1
terrify 10.29; 14.31
tremble 8.6; 14.16
wicked 9.17; 26.10

[v] MEDES: *People of a nation north-east of Babylonia, which became part of the Persian empire.*

11.15: Rev 16.12 **12.2:** Ex 15.2; Ps 118.14 **13.1–14.23:** Is 47.1–15; Jer 50.1–51.64 **13.6:** Joel 1.15
13.10: Ezek 32.7; Mt 24.29; Mk 13.24–25; Lk 21.25; Rev 6.12–13 **13.19:** Gen 19.24
13.21: Is 34.14; Zeph 2.14; Rev 18.2

their nests. Ostriches will live there, and
wild goats will prance through the ruins.
22 The towers and palaces will echo with
the cries of hyenas and jackals.
Babylon's time has come! Her days are
almost over."

The Return from Exile

14 The LORD will once again be
merciful to his people Israel and
choose them as his own. He will let them
live in their own land again, and
foreigners will come and live there with
them. 2 Many nations will help the people
of Israel to return to the land which the
LORD gave them, and there the nations
will serve Israel as slaves. Those who
once captured Israel will now be captured by Israel, and the people of Israel
will rule over those who once oppressed
them.

The King of Babylonia in the World of the Dead

3 The LORD will give the people of
Israel relief from their pain and suffering, and from the hard work they were
forced to do. 4 When he does this, they
are to mock the king of Babylonia and
say:
"The cruel king has fallen! He will
never oppress anyone again! 5 The LORD
has ended the power of the evil rulers
6 who angrily oppressed the peoples and
never stopped persecuting the nations
they had conquered. 7 Now at last the
whole world enjoys rest and peace, and
everyone sings for joy. 8 The cypress-
trees and the cedars of Lebanon rejoice
over the fallen king, because there is no
one to cut them down, now that he is
gone!
9 "The world of the dead is getting
ready to welcome the king of Babylonia.
The ghosts of those who were powerful
on earth are stirring about. The ghosts of
kings are rising from their thrones.
10 They all call out to him, 'Now you are
as weak as we are! You are one of us!
11 You used to be honoured with the
music of harps, but now here you are in
the world of the dead. You lie on a bed of
maggots and are covered with a blanket
of worms.'
12 "King of Babylonia, bright morning
star, you have fallen from heaven! In the
past you conquered nations, but now you
have been thrown to the ground. 13 You
were determined to climb up to heaven
and to place your throne above the highest stars. You thought you would sit like a
king on that mountain in the north where
the gods assemble. 14 You said you would
climb to the tops of the clouds and be like
the Almighty. 15 But instead, you have
been brought down to the deepest part of
the world of the dead.
16 "The dead will stare and gape at
you. They will ask, 'Is this the man who
shook the earth and made kingdoms
tremble? 17 Is this the man who destroyed cities and turned the world into a
desert? Is this the man who never freed
his prisoners or let them go home?' 18 All
the kings of the earth lie in their magnificent tombs, 19 but you have no tomb, and
your corpse is thrown out to rot. It is
covered by the bodies of soldiers killed in
battle, thrown with them into a rocky pit,
and trampled down. 20 Because you
ruined your country and killed your own
people, you will not be buried like other
kings. None of your evil family will survive. 21 Let the slaughter begin! The sons
of this king will die because of their
ancestors' sins. None of them will ever
rule the earth or cover it with cities."

God Will Destroy Babylon

22 The LORD Almighty says, "I will
attack Babylon and bring it to ruin. I will
leave nothing—no children, no survivors
at all. I, the LORD, have spoken. 23 I will
turn Babylon into a marsh, and owls will
live there. I will sweep Babylon with a
broom that will sweep everything away.
I, the LORD Almighty, have spoken."

God Will Destroy the Assyrians

24 The LORD Almighty has sworn an
oath: "What I have planned will happen.
What I have determined to do will be
done. 25 I will destroy the Assyrians in my
land of Israel and trample upon them on
my mountains. I will free my people
from the Assyrian yoke and from the burdens they have had to bear. 26 This is my
plan for the world, and my arm is
stretched out to punish the nations."
27 The LORD Almighty is determined to do
this; he has stretched out his arm to punish, and no one can stop him.

God Will Destroy the Philistines

28 This is a message that was proclaimed in the year that King Ahaz died.
29 People of Philistia, the rod that
beat you is broken, but you have no
reason to be glad. When one snake dies,
a worse one comes in its place. A snake's
egg hatches a flying dragon. 30 The LORD

alive Ecc 9.4; 24.6
Almighty [5] 13.6; 17.3
anger 13.3; 26.20
body 10.16; 26.19
burden 10.27; 22.24
choose 4.3; 19.25
cloud [2] 5.6; 19.1
conquer [2] 11.14; 37.24
cruel 13.9; 19.4
dead 8.19; 19.3
destroy [2] 13.6; 15.1
determine [3] 10.7; 37.32
dragon 27.1
enjoy 3.10; 24.9
establish Prov 24.27; 23.7
evil [2] 11.4; 22.14
famine Ps 105.16; Jer 5.12
force (1) Job 34.28; 30.30
free [2] 10.27; 32.9
ghost [2] 26.14
glad Song 3.11; 16.9
god (2) (other gods) Ps 138.1; 17.10
God's people [3] 12.3; 19.25
hard 5.28; 28.22
heaven [2] 13.13; 18.4
help [2] 12.4; 17.7
honour 11.10; 22.23
joy 12.3; 16.10
mercy 13.18; 27.11
message 13.1; 15.1
mock Prov 1.26; 66.5
oath Ecc 9.2; 19.18
oppress [3] 10.1; 16.4
pain 13.6; 17.11
peace 11.6; 26.3
persecute Ps 129.1; Jer 15.15
plan [2] 10.7; 19.3
poor 11.4; 17.4
power [2] 12.2; 17.12
prison 10.4; 20.4
proclaim Ps 145.1; 40.6
punish [2] 13.3; 19.16
reason Prov 29.17; Ezek 14.23
rejoice 12.3; 35.1
relieve (1) Ps 25.17; Mic 1.12
rest (1) Song 1.7; 16.3
rise 13.10; 24.20
ruin [2] 13.21; 17.1
safe [2] 4.6; 23.12
serve 8.2; 28.6
shepherd 13.14; 31.4
slaughter Prov 7.22; 15.9
slave Ecc 10.7; 24.2
suffer [2] Ecc 8.9; 16.7
swear Song 3.5; 48.1
terrible Ecc 5.13; Jer 5.30
terrify 13.8; 19.17
throne [2] 8.18; 37.16
tomb Ps 88.6; 22.16
tremble 13.13; 15.4
turn [2] 6.10; 17.7
weak Song 5.8; 16.14

welcome Song 8.12; 39.2
world [3] 12.5; 18.2
world of the dead [3] 7.11; 28.15
worse 7.17; 15.9

14.12: Rev 8.10, 9.1 **14.13–15:** Mt 11.23; Lk 10.15 **14.24–27:** Is 10.5–34; Nah 1.1–3.19; Zeph 2.13–15
14.28: 2 Kgs 16.20; 2 Chr 28.27
14.29–31: Jer 47.1–7; Ezek 25.15–17; Joel 3.4–8; Amos 1.6–8; Zeph 2.4–7; Zech 9.5–7

will be a **shepherd** to the **poor** of **his** **people** and will let them live in **safety**. But he will send a **terrible famine** on you Philistines, and it will not leave any of you **alive**.

31 Howl and cry for **help**, all you Philistine cities! Be **terrified**, all of you! A **cloud** of dust is coming from the north—it is an army with no cowards in its ranks.

32 How shall we answer the messengers that come to us from Philistia? We will tell them that the LORD has **established** Zion and that his **suffering** people will find **safety** there.

God Will Destroy Moab

15 This is a **message** about Moab.
The cities of Ar and Kir are **destroyed** in a single night, and silence covers the land of Moab. 2 The people of Dibon[w] climb the hill to **weep** at the **shrine**. The people of Moab **wail** in **grief** over the cities of Nebo and Medeba; they have **shaved** their heads and their beards in **grief**. 3 The people in the streets are dressed in **sackcloth**; in the city squares and on the house-tops people **mourn** and cry. 4 The people of Heshbon and Elealeh cry out, and their cry can be heard as far away as Jahaz. Even the soldiers **tremble**; their **courage** is gone. 5 My **heart** cries out for Moab! The people have **fled** to the town of Zoar, and to Eglath Shelishiyah. Some climb the road to Luhith, **weeping** as they go; some **escape** to Horonaim, **grieving** loudly. 6 The brook of Nimrim is dry, the grass beside it has withered, and nothing green is left. 7 The people go across the Valley of Willows, trying to **escape** with all their **possessions**. 8 Everywhere at Moab's borders the sound of crying is heard. It is heard at the towns of Eglaim and Beerelim. 9 At the town of Dibon the river is red with **blood**, and God has something even **worse** in store for the people there. Yes, there will be a **bloody slaughter** of everyone left in Moab.

blood [2] 9.5; 29.2
courage 13.7; 19.1
destroy 14.17; 16.4
escape [2] 13.14; 21.15
flee Ps 104.7; 17.9
grief [3] Ecc 5.17; 16.11
heart 10.34; 26.9
message 14.28; 16.13
mourn 3.26; 22.12
possess Ps 119.111; 60.21
sackcloth Job 16.15; 20.2
shave 7.20; 22.12
shrine 2 Chr 32.12; 16.12
slaughter 14.21; 34.6
tremble 14.16; 19.1
wail Job 2.12; 23.2
weep [2] Ecc 4.1; 16.7
worse 14.29; 24.16

Moab's Hopeless Situation

16 From the city of Sela in the desert the people of Moab send a **lamb** as a present to the one who rules in Jerusalem. 2 They wait on the banks of the River Arnon and move aimlessly to and fro, like birds driven from their nest.

3 They say to the people of Judah, "Tell us what to do. **Protect** us like a tree that casts a cool shadow in the heat of noon, and let us **rest** in your shade. We are **refugees**; hide us where no one can find us. 4 Let us stay in your land. **Protect** us from those who want to **destroy** us."

(**Oppression** and **destruction** will end, and those who are **devastating** the country will be gone. 5 Then one of David's descendants will be king, and he will rule the people with **faithfulness** and **love**. He will be quick to do what is **right**, and he will see that **justice** is done.)

6 The people of Judah say, "We have heard how **proud** the people of Moab are. We know that they are **arrogant** and **conceited**, but their **boasts** are empty."

7 The people of Moab will **weep** because of the **troubles** they **suffer**. They will all **weep** when they **remember** the fine food they used to eat in the city of Kir Heres. They will be driven to **despair**. 8 The farms near Heshbon and the **vineyards** of Sibmah are **destroyed**—those vineyards whose wine used to make the rulers of the nations drunk. At one time the **vines** spread as far as the city of Jazer, and eastwards into the desert, and westwards to the other side of the Dead Sea. 9 Now I **weep** for Sibmah's **vines** as I weep for Jazer. My **tears** fall for Heshbon and Elealeh, because there is no **harvest** to make the people **glad**. 10 No one is **happy** now in the fertile fields. No one shouts or sings in the **vineyards**. No one tramples grapes to make wine; the shouts of **joy** are ended.[y] 11 I **groan** with **sadness** for Moab, with **grief** for Kir Heres. 12 The people of Moab wear themselves out going to their mountain **shrines** and to their **temples** to **pray**, but it will do them no good.

13 That is the **message** the LORD gave earlier about Moab. 14 And now the LORD says, "In exactly three years Moab's great wealth will disappear. Of its many people, only a few will survive, and they will be **weak**."

arrogant 13.11; 28.14
boast 10.8; 20.5
conceited 2.12; Jer 48.29
despair Prov 21.15; 19.9
destroy [3] 15.1; 18.5
devastate 13.5; 24.1
faithful 1.21; 25.1
glad 14.29; 29.24
grief 15.2; 23.1

groan Prov 5.11; 19
happy 9.3; 23.12
harvest 9.3; 17.5
joy 14.7; 23.7
justice 11.5; 26.9
lamb 5.17; 34.6
love Song 8.2; 26.11
message 15.1; 18.2
oppress 14.2; 19.20
pray 1.15; 26.16
protect [2] 8.8; 17.1
proud 13.2; 22.18
refugee 2 Sam 15.1 21.14
remember 8.13; 26.14
rest (1) 14.7; 27.10
right (1) 9.7; 26.2
sad Ecc 7.3; 24.7
shrine 15.2; 36.7
suffer 14.3; 21.2
tear (2) Ps 119.136; 25.8
temple (2) (of othe gods) Ezra 5.14; 37.38
trouble 9.1; 17.11
vine [2] 7.23; 18.5
vineyard [2] 7.23; 27.2
weak 14.10; 24.4
weep [3] 15.2; 22.4

God Will Punish Syria and Israel

17 The LORD said, "Damascus will not be a city any longer; it will be only a pile of **ruins**. 2 The cities of Syria will be deserted for ever.[z] They will be a pasture for **sheep** and cattle, and no one will drive them away. 3 Israel will be **defenceless**, and Damascus will lose its independence. Those Syrians who survive will be in **disgrace** like the people

abandon 2.20; 31.9
Almighty 14.14; 18.
altar [2] 6.6; 19.19
Creator Ecc 12.1; 27.11
defend [2] 11.4; 22.8
desolate 6.11; 24.1
disgrace 9.1; 22.18
fate Ecc 9.2; 19.17
flee 15.5; 21.15
forget Ecc 9.5; 23.1
god (2) (other gods 14.13; 31.3

[w] *Probable text* people of Dibon; *Hebrew* people and Dibon.
[y] *One ancient translation* the shouts of joy are ended; *Hebrew* I have ended the shouts of joy.
[z] *One ancient translation* The cities...for ever; *Hebrew* The cities of Aroer are deserted.

15.1–16.14: Is 25.10–12; Jer 48.1–47; Ezek 25.8–11; Amos 2.1–3; Zeph 2.8–11
17.1–3: Jer 49.23–27; Amos 1.3–5; Zech 9.1

goddess 2 Chr 34.3; 27.9
harvest [2] 16.9; 18.4
help 14.2; 19.3
holy 13.3; 29.19
incense 1.13; 27.9
might 10.21; 36.5
pain 14.3; 21.3
poor 14.30; 19.15
poverty *see* **poor**
power 14.5; 18.2
protect 16.3; 20.6
rely 10.20; 20.6
reprimand Ecc 7.5; 54.9
rescue Prov 24.11; 19.20
ruin [2] 14.20; 23.1
sacred 11.9; 27.13
sheep 13.14; 22.13
symbol 11.10; 19.20
terror Prov 1.26; 19.16
trouble 16.7; 25.4
trust 12.2; 20.5
turn 14.17; 19.2
worship (2) (of other gods) 10.10; 21.9

of Israel. I, the LORD **Almighty**, have
spoken."
4 The LORD said, "A day is coming
when Israel's greatness will come to an
end, and its wealth will be replaced by
poverty. 5 Israel will be like a field where
the corn has been cut and **harvested**, as
desolate as a field in the valley of
Rephaim when it has been picked bare.
6 Only a few people will survive, and
Israel will be like an olive-tree from
which all the olives have been picked except two or three at the very top, or a
few that are left on the lower branches. I,
the LORD God of Israel, have spoken."
7 When that day comes, people will
turn for **help** to their **Creator**, the **holy**
God of Israel. 8 They will no longer **rely**
on the **altars** they made with their own
hands, or **trust** in their own handiwork—
symbols of the **goddess** Asherah and **altars** for burning **incense**.
9 When that day comes, **well-defended**
cities will be deserted and left in **ruins**
like the cities that the Hivites and the
Amorites[a] **abandoned** as they **fled** from
the people of Israel.
10 Israel, you have **forgotten** the God
who **rescues** you and who **protects** you
like a **mighty** rock. Instead, you plant
sacred gardens[b] in order to **worship** a
foreign god. 11 But even if they sprouted
and blossomed the very morning you
planted them, there would still be no **harvest**. There would be only **trouble** and incurable **pain**.

Enemy Nations Are Defeated

12 **Powerful** nations are in commotion
with a sound like the roar of the sea, like
the crashing of huge waves. 13 The
nations advance like rushing waves, but
God **reprimands** them and they retreat,
driven away like dust on a hillside, like
straw in a whirlwind. 14 In the evening
they cause **terror**, but by morning they
are gone. That is the **fate** of everyone
who plunders our land.

God Will Punish Sudan

Almighty [2] 17.3; 19.4
destroy 16.4; 19.3
enemy 11.13; 25.2
fear [2] 13.8; 21.4
harvest 17.5; 24.13
heaven 14.12; 26.21
message 16.13; 19.1
offer 1.11; 19.15
power [2] 17.12; 19.2
raise 13.2; 42.2
ripe 5.2; 28.4
strong [2] 10.13; 26.1
vine 16.8; 24.7

18 Beyond the rivers of Sudan there
is a land where the sound of
wings is heard. 2 From that land ambassadors come down the Nile in boats
made of reeds. Go back home, swift
messengers! Take a **message** back to
your land divided by rivers, to your
strong and **powerful** nation, to your tall
and smooth-skinned people, who are
feared all over the **world**.
3 Listen, everyone who lives on earth!
Look for a signal flag to be **raised** on the
tops of the mountains! Listen for the
blowing of the bugle! 4 The LORD said to
me, "I will look down from **heaven** as
quietly as the dew forms in the warm
nights of **harvest** time, as serenely as the
sun shines in the heat of the day. 5 Before
the grapes are gathered, when the
blossoms have all fallen and the grapes
are **ripening**, the **enemy** will **destroy** the
Sudanese as easily as a knife cuts
branches from a **vine**. 6 The corpses of
their soldiers will be left exposed to the
birds and the wild animals. In summer
the birds will feed on them, and in winter, the animals."
7 A time is coming when the LORD **Almighty** will receive **offerings** from this
land divided by rivers, this **strong** and
powerful nation, this tall and smooth-
skinned people, who are **feared** all over
the **world**. They will come to Mount Zion,
where the LORD **Almighty** is **worshipped**.

world [2] 14.7; 19.24
worship (1) (of God) 1.12; 19.21

God Will Punish Egypt

19 This is a **message** about Egypt.
The LORD is coming to Egypt,
riding swiftly on a **cloud**. The Egyptian
idols tremble before him, and the people
of Egypt lose their **courage**. 2 The LORD
says, "I will stir up civil war in Egypt and
turn brother against brother and **neighbour** against neighbour. **Rival** cities will
fight **each other**, and **rival** kings will
struggle for **power**. 3 I am going to frustrate the **plans** of the Egyptians and **destroy** their morale. They will ask their
idols to **help** them, and they will go and
consult mediums and ask the **spirits** of
the **dead** for **advice**. 4 I will hand the
Egyptians over to a tyrant, to a **cruel**
king who will rule them. I, the LORD **Almighty**, have spoken."
5 The water will be low in the Nile,
and the river will gradually dry up. 6 The
channels of the river will stink as they
slowly go dry. Reeds and rushes will
wither, 7 and all the crops **sown** along the
banks of the Nile will dry up and be
blown away. 8 Everyone who earns his
living by fishing in the Nile will **groan**
and cry; their hooks and their nets will
be **useless**. 9 Those who make linen cloth
will be in **despair**; 10 weavers and skilled
workmen will be broken and depressed.
11 The leaders of the city of Zoan are
fools! Egypt's **wisest** men give **stupid advice**! How **dare** they tell the king that
they are successors to the **ancient**

acknowledge Ps 100.3; 29.23
advice [3] Ecc 4.13; 30.2
Almighty [7] 18.7; 21.10
altar 17.8; 27.9
ancient Ps 68.33; 44.8
bless [3] Prov 22.9; 44.3
choose 14.1; 40.20
cloud 14.14; 25.5
consult 8.19; 37.8
courage 15.4; 28.6
create Ecc 12.13; 34.11
cruel 14.4; 21.2
dare Job 42.3; 45.9
dead 14.16; 22.13
dedicate Neh 12.27; 23.18
despair 16.7; 32.10
destroy 18.5; 21.2
each other 13.8; 34.14
fate 17.14; 24.2
fool [2] Ecc 10.2; 29.14
God's people [2] 14.1; 21.10
groan 16.11; Jer 45.3
heal [2] 6.10; 30.26
Hebrew Esth 2.7; 36.11
help [3] 17.7; 22.5
idol [2] 10.10; 21.9
important 10.15; 22.17
medium 8.19
message 18.2; 21.1
mislead 9.16; 35.8
name (2) (name of God, of Jesus) Ps 149.3; 25.1
neighbour Ecc 4.4; Jer 5.8
oath 14.24; 65.16
offer [2] 18.7; 28.12
oppress 16.4; 23.12
plan [2] 14.24; 22.11

[a] *One ancient translation* the Hivites and the Amorites; *Hebrew* woodland and hill-country.
[b] SACRED GARDENS: *See 1.29.*

18.1–7: Zeph 2.12 **19.1–25:** Jer 46.2–26; Ezek 29.1–32.32

poor 17.4; 23.16
power 18.2; 24.21
prayer 1.15; 37.21
presence Ecc 8.3; 37.14
promise [2] Song 8.4; 37.35
punish [2] 14.26; 24.21
remind Ecc 7.2; 55.13
rescue 17.10; 25.9
reveal 5.16; 26.21
rich 10.18; 24.2
rival [2] 1 Sam 1.6; Ezek 26.2
sacrifice 1.11; 31.9
scholar Neh 13.13; 1 Cor 1.19
solemn Prov 31.1; 45.23
sow Ecc 11.4; 28.24
spirit (2) 8.19; 65.4
struggle Prov 15.15; 29.4
stupid Ecc 10.1; 29.9
symbol 17.8; 27.9
terrify 14.31; 21.1
terror 17.14; 21.3
tremble [2] 15.4; 21.4
turn [2] 17.7; 25.2
useless 8.10; 29.14
wise 10.13; 28.29
world 18.2; 23.17
worship (1) (of God) [2] 18.7; 23.18
wrong Ecc 10.2; 26.10

scholars and kings? [12]King of Egypt, where are those clever advisers of yours? Perhaps they can tell you what **plans** the LORD **Almighty** has for Egypt. [13]The leaders of Zoan and Memphis are **fools**. They were supposed to lead the nation, but they have **misled** it. [14]The LORD has made them give confusing **advice**. As a result, Egypt does everything **wrong** and staggers like a drunken man slipping on his own vomit. [15]No one in Egypt, **rich** or **poor**, **important** or unknown, can **offer help**.

Egypt Will Worship the LORD

16 A time is coming when the people of Egypt will be as timid as women. They will **tremble in terror** when they see that the LORD **Almighty** has stretched out his hand to **punish** them. [17]The people of Egypt will be **terrified** of Judah every time they are **reminded** of the **fate** that the LORD **Almighty** has prepared for them.

18 When that time comes, the **Hebrew** language will be spoken in five Egyptian cities. The people there will take their **oaths** in the **name of the LORD Almighty**. One of the cities will be called, "City of the Sun."

19 When that time comes, there will be an **altar** to the LORD in the land of Egypt and a stone pillar **dedicated** to him at the Egyptian border. [20]They will be **symbols** of the LORD **Almighty's presence** in Egypt. When the people there are **oppressed** and call out to the LORD **for help**, he will send someone to **rescue** them. [21]The LORD will **reveal** himself to the Egyptian people, and then they will **acknowledge** and **worship** him, and bring him **sacrifices** and **offerings**. They will make **solemn promises** to him and do what they **promise**. [22]The LORD will **punish** the Egyptians, but then he will **heal** them. They will **turn to** him, and he will hear their **prayers** and **heal** them.

23 When that time comes, there will be a highway between Egypt and Assyria. The people of those two countries will travel to and fro between them, and the two nations will **worship** together. [24]When that time comes, Israel will rank with Egypt and Assyria, and these three nations will be a **blessing** to all the **world**. [25]The LORD **Almighty** will **bless** them and say, "I will **bless** you, Egypt, **my people**; you, Assyria, whom I **created**; and you, Israel, my **chosen people**."

The Sign of the Naked Prophet

20 Under the orders of Sargon, emperor of Assyria, the commander-in-chief of the Assyrian army attacked the Philistine city of Ashdod. [2]Three years earlier the LORD had told Isaiah son of Amoz to take off his sandals and the **sackcloth** he was wearing. He **obeyed** and went about **naked** and barefoot. [3]When Ashdod was captured, the LORD said, "My **servant** Isaiah has been going about **naked** and barefoot for three years. This is a **sign** of what will happen to Egypt and Sudan. [4]The emperor of Assyria will lead away **naked** the **prisoners** he captures from those two countries. Young and old, they will walk barefoot and **naked**, with their buttocks exposed, bringing **shame** on Egypt. [5]Those who have put their **trust** in Sudan and have **boasted** about Egypt will be disillusioned, their **hopes** shattered. [6]When that time comes, the people who live along the coast of Philistia will say, 'Look at what has happened to the people we **relied** on to **protect** us from the emperor of Assyria! How will we ever survive?' "

boast 16.6; 28.15
hope 8.17; 24.16
naked [4] 3.26; 47.3
obey 11.3; 42.24
prison 14.17; 24.22
protect 17.10; 23.10
rely 17.8; 23.14
sackcloth 15.3; 22.12
servant Ecc 7.21; 22.20
shame 13.8; 26.11
sign (1) 7.11; 37.30
trust 17.8; 25.9

A Vision of the Fall of Babylon

21 This is a **message** about Babylonia.

Like a whirlwind sweeping across the desert, **disaster** will come from a **terrifying** land. [2]I have seen a **vision** of **cruel** events, a vision of **betrayal** and **destruction**.

Army of Elam, attack! Army of Media, lay siege to the cities! God will put an end to the **suffering** which Babylon has caused.

3 What I saw and heard in the **vision** has filled me with **terror** and **pain**, pain like that of a woman in labour. [4]My head is spinning, and I am **trembling** with **fear**. I had been **longing** for evening to come, but it has brought me nothing but **terror**.

5 In the **vision** a **banquet** is ready; rugs are spread for the guests to sit on. They are eating and drinking. Suddenly the **command** rings out: "Officers! Prepare your shields!"

6 Then the Lord said to me, "Go and post a sentry, and tell him to report what he sees. [7]If he sees men coming on horseback, two by two, and men riding on donkeys and camels, he is to **observe** them carefully."

8 The sentry calls out, "Sir, I have been standing guard at my post day and night."

Almighty 19.4; 22.5
announce Ps 119.46; 40.9
banquet Song 2.4; 25.6
barren 13.2; 32.2
betray Prov 14.25; 24.16
command 11.4; 34.16
cruel 19.4; 25.3
danger 7.4; 30.6
destroy 19.3; 23.1
disaster 13.11; 28.15
escape 15.5; 23.6
fear 18.2; 25.3
flee 17.9; 25.4
God's people 19.25; 22.4
Good News Prov 25.25; 40.9
idol 19.1; 30.22
long (2) Ecc 5.10; 26.9
message [3] 19.1; 22.1
observe Ps 37.37; 56.2
pain 17.11; 26.17
refugee 16.3; Jer 44.14
suffer 16.7; 25.8
terrify 19.17; 29.5
terror [2] 19.16; 24.17
tremble 19.1; 32.11
vision [3] Ps 89.19; 22.1
worship (2) (of other gods) 17.10; 37.38

9 Suddenly, here they come! Men on
horseback, two by two. The sentry gives
the news, "Babylon has fallen! All the
idols they **worshipped** lie shattered on
the ground."
10 **My people** Israel, you have been
threshed like wheat, but now I have **announced** to you the **good news** that I have
heard from the LORD **Almighty**, the God
of Israel.

A Message about Edom

11 This is a **message** about Edom.
Someone calls to me from Edom,
"Sentry, how soon will the night be over?
Tell me how soon it will end."
12 I answer, "Morning is coming, but
night will come again. If you want to ask
again, come back and ask."

A Message about Arabia

13 This is a **message** about Arabia.
You people of Dedan, whose caravans
camp in the **barren** country of Arabia,
14 give water to the thirsty people who
come to you. You people of the land of
Tema, give food to the **refugees**. 15 People
are **fleeing** to **escape** from swords that
are ready to kill them, from bows that
are ready to shoot, from all the **dangers**
of war.
16 Then the Lord said to me, "In exactly one year the greatness of the tribes
of Kedar will be at an end. 17 The bowmen are the bravest men of Kedar, but
few of them will be left. I, the LORD God
of Israel, have spoken."

A Message about Jerusalem

22 This is a **message** about the
Valley of **Vision**.
What is happening? Why are all the
people of the city **celebrating** on the
roofs of the houses? 2 The whole city is in
an uproar, filled with noise and excitement.
Your men who died in this war did not
die fighting. 3 All your leaders ran away
and were captured before they shot a
single arrow. 4 Now leave me **alone** to
weep bitterly over all those of **my people**
who have died. Don't try to **comfort** me.
5 This is a time of panic, defeat, and confusion in the Valley of **Vision**, and the
Sovereign LORD **Almighty** has sent it on
us. The walls of our city have been battered down, and cries for **help** have
echoed among the hills.
6 The soldiers from the land of Elam
came riding on horseback, armed with
bows and arrows. Soldiers from the land
of Kir had their shields ready. 7 The fertile valleys of Judah were filled with
chariots; soldiers on horseback stood in
front of Jerusalem's gates. 8 All Judah's
defences crumbled.
When that happened, you brought
weapons out of the arsenal. 9-10 You found
the places where the walls of Jerusalem
needed repair. You inspected all the
houses in Jerusalem and tore some of
them down to get stones to repair the
city walls. In order to store water, 11 you
built a reservoir inside the city to hold
the water flowing down from the old
pool. But you paid no attention to God,
who **planned** all this long ago and who
caused it to happen.
12 The **Sovereign** LORD **Almighty** was
calling you then to **weep** and **mourn**, to
shave your heads and wear **sackcloth**.
13 Instead, you laughed and **celebrated**.
You killed **sheep** and cattle to eat, and
you drank wine. You said, "We might as
well eat and drink! Tomorrow we'll be
dead."
14 The **Sovereign** LORD **Almighty** himself spoke to me and said, "This **evil** will
never be **forgiven** them as long as they
live. I, the **Sovereign** LORD **Almighty**,
have spoken."

A Warning to Shebna

15 The **Sovereign** LORD **Almighty** told
me to go to Shebna, the manager of the
royal household, and say to him, 16 "Who
do you think you are? What **right** have
you to carve a **tomb** for yourself out of
the rocky hillside? 17 You may be **important**, but the LORD will pick you up and
throw you away. 18 He will pick you up
like a ball and throw you into a much larger country. You will die there beside the
chariots you were so **proud** of. You are a
disgrace to your **master's** household.
19 The LORD will remove you from office
and bring you down from your high position."
20 The LORD said to Shebna, "When
that happens, I will send for my **servant**
Eliakim son of Hilkiah. 21 I will put your
official robe and belt on him and give
him all the **authority** you have had. He
will be like a father to the people of Jerusalem and Judah. 22 I will give him complete **authority** under the king, the
descendant of David. He will have the
keys of office; what he opens, no one will
shut, and what he shuts, no one will open.
23 I will fasten him firmly in place like a
peg, and he will be a **source** of **honour** to
his whole family.
24 "But all his relatives and **dependants** will become a **burden** to him. They

source Prov 18.4; 49.5
Sovereign [5] 10.23; 25.8
tomb 14.18; 65.4
vision [2] 21.2; 28.7
weep [2] 16.7; 29.2

Almighty [5] 21.10; 23.9
alone 5.8; 26.13
authority [2] Ecc 10.6; Jer 1.10
bitter 5.20; 33.7
burden 14.25; 43.23
celebrate [2] Prov 28.12; 33.20
comfort 12.1; 28.12
dead 19.3; 26.14
defend 17.3; 26.1
depend 3.1; 28.15
disgrace 17.3; 23.4
evil 14.5; 30.8
forgive 6.7; 27.9
God's people 21.10; 25.8
help 19.3; 30.2
honour 14.11; 23.8
important 19.15; 29.16
master 1.3; 24.2
message 21.1; 23.1
mourn 15.3; 50.3
need 7.22; 23.18
plan 19.3; 23.8
proud 16.6; 23.9
right (3) 11.4; 32.7
sackcloth 20.2; 37.1
servant 20.3; 37.24
shave 15.2; Jer 16.6
sheep 17.2; 32.14

21.9: Rev 14.8, 18.2 **22.13:** 1 Cor 15.32 **22.22:** Rev 3.7

will hang on him like pots and bowls
hanging from a peg! 25 When that happens, the peg that was firmly fastened
will work loose and fall. And that will be
the end of everything that was hanging
on it." The LORD has spoken.

A Message about Phoenicia

Almighty 22.5; 24.23
dedicate 19.19; Jer 4.4
destroy [4] 21.2; 25.2
disgrace 22.18; 25.8
escape [2] 21.15; 24.18
establish 14.32; 42.4
forget [2] 17.10; 44.21
grief [3] 16.11; 32.12
happy 16.10; 24.7
honour [2] 22.23; 25.1
humiliate 10.33; 25.11
joy 16.10; 24.8
learn [2] 1.17; 26.9
message 22.1; 28.9
need 22.9; 28.9
oppress 19.20; 26.6
overthrow 13.19; Jer 1.10
plan [3] 22.11; 25.1
poor 19.15; 24.2
prostitute Prov 29.3; 57.3
protect 20.6; 25.10
proud 22.18; 26.5
rely 20.6; 30.5
ruin [2] 17.1; 24.3
safe 14.30; 24.10
wail 15.2; 29.2
world 19.24; 24.4
worship (1) (of God) 19.21; 27.13

23 This is a **message** about Tyre.
Howl with **grief**, you sailors out
on the ocean! Your home port of Tyre
has been **destroyed**; its houses and its
harbour are in **ruins**. As your ships return
from Cyprus, you **learn** the news. 2 **Wail**,
you merchants of Sidon! You sent men
3 across the sea to buy and sell the corn
that grew in Egypt and to do business
with all the nations.
4 City of Sidon, you are **disgraced**!
The sea and the great ocean depths dis-
own you and say, "I never had any children. I never brought up sons or
daughters."
5 Even the Egyptians will be shocked
and dismayed when they **learn** that Tyre
has been **destroyed**.
6 Howl with **grief**, you people of
Phoenicia! Try to **escape** to Spain! 7 Can
this be the **joyful** city of Tyre, founded so
long ago? Is this the city that sent
settlers across the sea to **establish**
colonies? 8 Who was it that **planned** to
bring all this on Tyre, that imperial city,
whose merchant princes were the most
honoured men on earth? 9 The LORD
Almighty planned it. He **planned** it in order to put an end to their **pride** in what
they had done and to **humiliate** their
honoured men.
10 Go and farm the land, you people in
the colonies in Spain! There is no one to
protect you any more.[c] 11 The LORD has
stretched out his hand over the sea and
overthrown kingdoms. He has ordered
the Phoenician centres of commerce to
be **destroyed**. 12 City of Sidon, your **happiness** has ended, and your people are **oppressed**. Even if they **escape** to Cyprus,
they will still not be **safe**.
13 (It was the Babylonians, not the
Assyrians, who let the wild animals overrun Tyre. It was the Babylonians who put
up siege-towers, tore down the fortifications of Tyre, and left the city in **ruins**.[d])
14 Howl with **grief**, you sailors out on
the ocean! The city you **relied** on has
been **destroyed**.
15 A time is coming when Tyre will be
forgotten for seventy years, the lifetime
of a king. When those years are over,
Tyre will be like the **prostitute** in the
song:

16 Take your harp, go round the town,
you **poor forgotten** whore!
Play and sing your songs again
to bring men back once more.

17 When the seventy years are over,
the LORD will let Tyre go back to her old
trade, and she will hire herself out to all
the kingdoms of the **world**. 18 The money
she earns by commerce will be **dedicated** to the LORD. She will not store it
away, but those who **worship** the LORD
will use her money to buy the food and
the clothing they **need**.

The LORD Will Punish the Earth

24 The LORD is going to **devastate**
the earth and leave it **desolate**.
He will twist the earth's surface and **scatter** its people. 2 Everyone will meet the
same **fate**—the **priests** and the people,
slaves and **masters**, buyers and sellers,
lenders and borrowers, **rich** and **poor**.
3 The earth will lie shattered and **ruined**.
The LORD has spoken and it will be done.
4 The earth dries up and withers; the
whole **world** grows **weak**; both earth and
sky decay. 5 The people have **defiled** the
earth by breaking God's **laws** and by
violating the **covenant** he made to **last**
for ever. 6 So God has pronounced a **curse**
on the earth. Its people are paying for
what they have done. Fewer and fewer
remain **alive**. 7 The **grapevines** wither,
and wine is becoming scarce. Everyone
who was once **happy** is now **sad**, 8 and the
joyful music of their harps and drums
has ceased. 9 There is no more **happy**
singing over wine; no one **enjoys** its taste
any more. 10 In the city everything is in
chaos, and people lock themselves in
their houses for **safety**. 11 People shout in
the streets because there is no more
wine. **Happiness** is gone for ever; it has
been banished from the land. 12 The city
is in **ruins**, and its gates have been
broken down. 13 This is what will happen
in every nation all over the **world**. It will
be like the end of **harvest**, when the
olives have been beaten off every tree
and the **last** grapes picked from the
vines.
14 Those who survive will sing for **joy**.
Those in the west will tell how great the
LORD is, 15 and those in the east will
praise him. The people who live along
the sea will **praise** the LORD, the God of
Israel. 16 From the most distant parts of
the **world** we will hear songs in **praise** of
Israel, the **righteous** nation.

above Ps 148.1; Lam 1.13
alive 14.30; Jer 15.9
Almighty 23.9; 25.6
betray 21.2; 33.1
covenant Ps 132.12; 42.6
curse 8.21; 65.15
dark 13.10; 29.18
defile Ps 106.38; Jer 2.7
desolate 17.5; 37.18
devastate 16.4; 51.19
enjoy 14.7; 55.2
escape [2] 23.6; 28.22
fate 19.17; 50.11
glory 6.3; 28.1
grapevine *see* **vine**
happy [3] 23.12; 25.9
harvest 18.4; 30.23
hope 20.5; 26.8
joy [2] 23.7; 25.9
last (1) Ecc 12.11; 40.6
last (2) Prov 18.14; 44.6
law 10.1; 42.21
master 22.18; Jer 10.23
poor 23.16; 25.4
power 19.2; 25.3
praise [3] 12.1; 25.1
priest 8.2; 28.7
prison [2] 20.4; 28.13
punish [2] 19.16; 26.11
rich 19.15; 25.6
righteous 3.10; 26.10
rise 14.9; 26.14
ruin [2] 23.1; 25.2
sad 16.11; 63.10
safe 23.12; 25.4
scatter 13.14; 41.2
slave 14.2; 31.8
terror [2] 21.3; 28.19
traitor Ps 119.158; Jer 9.2
trap [2] 8.14; 28.13
vine [2] 18.5; 34.4
weak 16.14; 31.3
world [4] 23.17; 25.6
worse 15.9; Jer 7.24

[c] *Verse 10 in Hebrew is unclear.* [d] *Verse 13 in Hebrew is unclear.*

23.1–18: Ezek 26.1–28.19; Joel 3.4–8; Amos 1.9–10; Zech 9.1–4; Mt 11.21–22; Lk 10.13–14

But there is no hope for me! I am
wasting away! Traitors continue to betray, and their treachery grows worse
and worse. [17]Listen to me, everyone!
There are terrors, pits, and traps waiting
for you. [18]Anyone who tries to escape
from the terror will fall into a pit, and
anyone who escapes from the pit will be
caught in a trap. Torrents of rain will
pour from the sky, and earth's foundations will shake. [19]The earth will crack
and shatter and split open. [20]The earth itself will stagger like a drunken man and
sway like a hut in a storm. The world is
weighed down by its sins; it will collapse
and never rise again.
21 A time is coming when the LORD
will punish the powers above and the
rulers of the earth. [22]God will crowd
kings together like prisoners in a pit. He
will shut them in prison until the time of
their punishment comes. [23]The moon will
grow dark, and the sun will no longer
shine, for the LORD Almighty will be
king. He will rule in Jerusalem on Mount
Zion, and the leaders of the people will
see his glory.

A Hymn of Praise

25 LORD, you are my God;
I will honour you and praise
your name.
You have done amazing things;
you have faithfully carried out
the plans you made long ago.
[2]You have turned cities into ruins
and destroyed their fortifications.
The palaces which our enemies built
are gone for ever.
[3]The people of powerful nations will
praise you;
you will be feared in the cities of
cruel nations.
[4]The poor and the helpless have fled to
you
and have been safe in times of
trouble.
You give them shelter from storms
and shade from the burning heat.
Cruel men attack like a winter storm,[e]
5 like drought in a dry land.
But you, LORD, have silenced our
enemies;
you silence the shouts of cruel men,
as a cloud cools a hot day.

God Prepares a Banquet

6 Here on Mount Zion the LORD Almighty will prepare a banquet for all the
nations of the world—a banquet of the
richest food and the finest wine. [7]Here
he will suddenly remove the cloud of sorrow that has been hanging over all the
nations. [8]The Sovereign LORD will destroy death for ever! He will wipe away
the tears from everyone's eyes and take
away the disgrace his people have suffered throughout the world. The LORD
himself has spoken!
9 When it happens, everyone will say,
"He is our God! We have put our trust in
him, and he has rescued us. He is the
LORD! We have put our trust in him, and
now we are happy and joyful because he
has saved us."

God Will Punish Moab

10 The LORD will protect Mount Zion,
but the people of Moab will be trampled
down, just as straw is trampled in
manure. [11]They will stretch out their
hands as if they were trying to swim, but
God will humiliate them, and their hands
will sink helplessly. [12]He will destroy the
fortresses of Moab with their high walls
and bring them tumbling down into the
dust.

God Will Give His People Victory

26 A day is coming when the people will sing this song in the land of Judah:
Our city is strong!
God himself defends its walls!
[2]Open the city gates
and let the faithful nation enter,
the nation whose people do what is
right.
[3]You, LORD, give perfect peace
to those who keep their purpose
firm
and put their trust in you.
[4]Trust in the LORD for ever;
he will always protect us.
[5]He has humbled those who were
proud;
he destroyed the strong city they
lived in,
and sent its walls crashing into the
dust.
[6]Those who were oppressed walk over
it now
and trample it under their feet.

[7]LORD, you make the path smooth for
good men;
the road they travel is level.
[8]We follow your will and put our hope
in you;
you are all that we desire.

Almighty 24.23; 28.5
amaze Ps 106.22; 52.15
banquet [2] 21.5; Dan 5.1
cloud [2] 19.1; 30.30
cruel [3] 21.2; 27.8
death (1) 5.13; 28.15
destroy [3] 23.1; 26.5
disgrace 23.4; 29.22
enemy [2] 18.5; 26.11
faithful 16.5; 26.2
fear 21.4; 32.11
flee 21.15; Jer 9.10
God's people 22.4; 26.20
happy 24.7; 29.19
helpless [2] 13.16; 54.11
honour 23.8; 26.15
humiliate 23.9; 42.17
joy 24.8; 26.19
name (2) (name of God, of Jesus) 19.18; 44.5
plan 23.8; 28.29
poor 24.2; 29.19
power 24.21; 27.1
praise [2] 24.15; 38.9
protect 23.10; 26.4
rescue 19.20; 29.6
rich 24.2; 30.23
ruin 24.3; 27.10
safe 24.10; 28.15
save 12.3; 33.2
shelter 4.6; 32.2
sorrow Ecc 7.3; 35.10
Sovereign 22.5; 28.16
suffer 21.2; 26.11
tear (2) 16.9; 38.5
trouble 17.11; 29.22
trust [2] 20.5; 26.3
turn 19.2; 29.14
world [2] 24.4; 37.16

alone 22.4; 37.16
anger 14.6; 27.4
anguish Ps 48.6; Jer 6.24
birth Ecc 3.2; 37.3
body 14.19; 66.24
dead [2] 22.13; 37.36
defend 22.8; 28.6
desire Song 7.10; 59.17
destroy [2] 25.2; 28.17
enemy 25.2; 27.5
faithful 25.1; 38.3
ghost 14.9; 29.4
God's people 25.8; 27.5
grave Ecc 8.10; 53.9
heart 15.5; 29.13
heaven 18.4; 34.5
honour 25.1; 29.23
hope 24.16; 33.2
humble 13.11; 29.19
joy 25.9; 35.2
judge 11.3; 28.6
justice 16.5; 28.6
kind Prov 28.8; Jer 24.5
learn [2] 23.1; 29.24
life (2) (to life) Prov 15.24; Jer 21.8
long (2) 21.4; 59.11
love 16.5; 43.4
oppress 23.12; 29.20
pain [2] 21.3; 38.13
peace 14.7; 27.5
perfect Song 6.6; Jer 17.14
pray 16.12; 37.4
prosper Prov 24.25; 54.13
protect 25.10; 27.5
proud 23.9; 28.1
punish [5] 24.21; 27.1
purpose Ps 33.10; 45.13
refuse (1) 7.12; 28.12

[e] *Probable text* winter storm; *Hebrew* storm against a wall.

25.8: 1 Cor 15.54; Rev 7.17, 21.4
25.10-12: Is 15.1-16.14; Jer 48.1-47; Ezek 25.8-11; Amos 2.1-3; Zeph 2.8-11

remember 16.7; 38.3
reveal 19.21; 40.5
right (1) [2] 16.5; 30.10
righteous 24.16; 32.16
rise 24.20; 34.10
secret Song 4.12; 29.15
shame 20.4; 29.22
strong [2] 18.2; 28.2
suffer [2] 25.8; 37.3
trust [2] 25.9; 30.2
victory Prov 21.31; 41.2
wicked 13.11; 55.7
will (1) 11.2; 30.1
win Ecc 9.11; 59.4
wrong 19.14; 43.24

9 At night I long for you with all my
heart;
when you judge the earth and its
people,
they will all learn what justice is.
10 Even though you are kind to wicked
men,
they never learn to do what is right.
Even here in a land of righteous
people they still do wrong;
they refuse to recognize your
greatness.
11 Your enemies do not know that you
will punish them.
LORD, put them to shame and let them
suffer;
let them suffer the punishment you
have prepared.
Show them how much you love your
people.

12 You will give us prosperity, LORD;
everything that we achieve
is the result of what you do.[f]
13 LORD our God, we have been ruled by
others,
but you alone are our LORD.
14 Now they are dead and will not live
again;
their ghosts will not rise,
for you have punished them and
destroyed them.
No one remembers them any more.
15 LORD, you have made our nation grow,
enlarging its territory on every side,
and this has brought you honour.
16 You punished your people, LORD,
and in anguish they prayed to you.[g]
17 You, LORD, have made us cry out,
as a woman in labour cries out in
pain.
18 We were in pain and agony,
but we gave birth to nothing.
We have won no victory for our land;
we have accomplished nothing.[h]

19 Those of our people who have died will
live again!
Their bodies will come back to life.
All those sleeping in their graves
will wake up and sing for joy.
As the sparkling dew refreshes the
earth,
so the LORD will revive those who
have long been dead.

Judgement and Restoration

20 Go into your houses, my people,
and shut the door behind you. Hide yourselves for a little while until God's anger
is over. 21 The LORD is coming from his
heavenly dwelling-place to punish the
people of the earth for their sins. The
murders that were secretly committed
on the earth will be revealed, and the
ground will no longer hide those who
have been killed.

27 On that day the LORD will use his
powerful and deadly sword to
punish Leviathan, that wriggling, twist-
ing dragon, and to kill the monster[i] that
lives in the sea.
2 On that day the LORD will say of his
pleasant vineyard, 3 "I watch over it and
water it continually. I guard it night and
day so that no one will harm it. 4 I am no
longer angry with the vineyard. If only
there were thorns and briars to fight
against, then I would burn them up completely. 5 But if the enemies of my people
want my protection, let them make
peace with me. Yes, let them make
peace with me."
6 In days to come the people of Israel,
the descendants of Jacob, will take root
like a tree, and they will blossom and
bud. The earth will be covered with the
fruit they produce.
7 Israel has not been punished by the
LORD as severely as its enemies, nor has
she lost as many men. 8 The LORD punished his people by sending them into exile. He took them away with a cruel wind
from the east.[k] 9 But Israel's sins will be
forgiven only when the stones of pagan
altars are ground up like chalk, and no
more incense-altars or symbols of the
goddess Asherah are left.
10 The fortified city lies in ruins. It is
deserted like an empty wilderness. It has
become a pasture for cattle, where they
can rest and graze. 11 The branches of the
trees are withered and broken, and
women gather them for firewood. Because the people have understood
nothing, God their Creator will not pity
them or show them any mercy.
12 On that day, from the Euphrates to
the Egyptian border, the LORD will
gather his people one by one, like someone separating the wheat from the chaff.
13 When that day comes, a trumpet
will be blown to call back from Assyria
and Egypt all the Israelites who are in
exile there. They will come and worship
the LORD in Jerusalem, on his sacred
hill.[l]

altar [2] 19.19; 29.1
anger 26.20; 30.27
Creator 17.7; 44.24
cruel 25.3; Jer 6.23
deadly Prov 26.18; 59.5
dragon 14.29; 30.6
enemy [2] 26.11; 30.16
exile [2] Ps 147.2; 49.20
forgive 22.14; 33.24
God's people [3] 26.20; 28.5
goddess 17.8; Jer 7.18
harm 11.8; 65.25
incense 17.8; 43.23
Leviathan Ps 104.26
mercy 14.1; 30.18
monster Ps 148.7; 34.14
pagan Ps 106.35; 65.3
peace [2] 26.3; 32.17
pity 13.18; 30.18
power 25.3; 28.2
protect 26.4; 30.2
punish [3] 26.11; 29.21
rest (1) 16.3; 28.12
ruin 25.2; 28.28
sacred 17.10; 30.29
separate 7.17; 59.2
symbol 19.20; Jer 9.25
understand 6.9; 28.7
vineyard [2] 16.8; 32.12
watch 1.8; 43.19
worship (1) (of God) 23.18; 29.13

[f] everything that...do; *or* you treat us according to what we do. [g] *Verse 16 in Hebrew is unclear.*
[h] We have won...nothing; *Hebrew unclear.*
[i] LEVIATHAN...MONSTER: *Legendary monsters which were symbols of the nations oppressing Israel.*
[k] *Verse 8 in Hebrew is unclear.* [l] SACRED HILL: *See 2.3.*

26.11: Heb 10.27 **26.19:** Dan 12.2 **27.1:** Job 41.1; Ps 74.14, 104.26

action 1.25; 45.13
agree [2] Prov 18.1; 33.8
Almighty [3] 25.6; 29.6
arrogant 16.6; 33.19
boast 20.5; 37.24
case (2) 3.13; 41.1
certain (1) Prov 11.18; Ezek 39.8
clean 1.6; 66.20
comfort 22.4; 40.1
complain Prov 23.29; 33.24
complete Ps 138.8; Hag 2.18
courage 19.1; 42.4
crown [2] Song 3.11; 62.3
death (1) [2] 25.8; 53.10
deceive Prov 31.30; 30.12
defend 26.1; 30.29
depend [2] 22.24; 48.2
destroy [2] 26.5; 29.20
disaster [2] 21.1; 29.2
doom 10.1; 29.1
escape 24.18; 30.16
faith 7.9; Mt 6.30
flood [2] 8.7; 30.28
glory [3] 24.23; 30.27
God's people 27.5; 29.22
hard 14.3; 30.20
honest Ecc 12.9; 29.21
intend 7.6; 46.10
judge 26.9; 33.14
justice [2] 26.9; 29.21
lesson [3] Prov 24.32; Zeph 3.7
lie (2) [2] 9.15; 29.21
message [2] 23.1; 30.6
mystery Prov 30.18; Dan 2.18
need 23.18; 32.3
new 11.1; 41.15
offer 19.15; 34.6
patient 7.13; Jer 15.15
plan 25.1; 29.15
power 27.1; 30.3
priest [2] 24.2; 37.2
prison 24.22; 42.7
proper Ecc 10.17; Jer 33.20
prophet [2] 9.15; 29.10
proud [3] 26.5; 37.29
proverb Ecc 12.9; Ezek 12.22
refuse (1) 26.10; 30.9
rest (1) 27.10; 34.14
ripe 18.5; Jer 24.2
ruin 27.10; 32.7
safe 25.4; 32.18
secure Ecc 7.12; 30.15
seed [2] 5.10; 30.23
sense Ecc 10.10; 44.19
serve 14.2; 38.3
Sovereign 25.8; 30.15
sow [4] 19.7; 30.23
spare Ps 119.80; 66.19
strange [2] Ps 139.14; Hos 8.12
strike Song 5.7; 30.32
strong [2] 26.1; 30.15
stumble [2] 8.14; 59.10
succeed (1) 8.10; 48.15
teach [5] 9.15; 29.24

A Warning to the Northern Kingdom

28 The kingdom of Israel is
doomed! Its **glory** is fading like
the **crowns** of flowers on the heads of its
drunken leaders. Their **proud** heads are
well perfumed, but there they lie, dead
drunk. 2 The Lord has someone **strong**
and **powerful** ready to attack them,
someone who will come like a hailstorm,
like a torrent of rain, like a rushing, over-
powering **flood**, and will overwhelm the
land. 3 The **pride** of those drunken
leaders will be trampled underfoot. 4 The
fading **glory** of those **proud** leaders will
disappear like the first figs of the season,
picked and eaten as soon as they are
ripe.
5 A day is coming when the LORD **Almighty** will be like a **glorious crown** of
flowers for **his people** who survive. 6 He
will give a **sense of justice** to those who
serve as **judges**, and **courage** to those
who **defend** the city gates from attack.

Isaiah and the Drunken Prophets of Judah

7 Even the **prophets** and the **priests**
are so drunk that they stagger. They
have drunk so much wine and liquor that
they **stumble** in confusion. The **prophets**
are too drunk to **understand** the **visions**
that God sends, and the **priests** are too
drunk to decide the **cases** that are
brought to them. 8 The tables where they
sit are all covered with vomit, and not a
clean spot is left.
9 They **complain** about me. They say,
"Who does that man think he's **teaching**? Who **needs** his **message**? It's only
good for babies that have just been
weaned! 10 He is trying to **teach** us letter
by letter, line by line, **lesson by lesson**."
11 If you won't listen to me, then God
will use foreigners speaking some
strange-sounding language to **teach** you a
lesson. 12 He **offered rest** and **comfort** to
all of you, but you **refused** to listen to
him. 13 That is why the LORD is going to
teach you letter by letter, line by line,
lesson by lesson. Then you will **stumble**
with every step you take. You will be
wounded, **trapped**, and taken **prisoner**.

A Cornerstone for Zion

14 Now you **arrogant** men who rule
here in Jerusalem over this people, listen
to what the LORD is saying. 15 You **boast**
that you have made a treaty with **death**
and reached an **agreement** with the
world of the dead. You are **certain** that
disaster will **spare** you when it comes, because you **depend** on **lies** and **deceit** to
keep you **safe**. 16 This, now, is what the
Sovereign LORD says: "I am placing in
Zion a foundation that is firm and **strong**.
In it I am putting a solid cornerstone on
which are written the **words**, '**Faith** that
is firm is also **patient**.' 17 **Justice** will be
the measuring-line for the foundation,
and **honesty** will be its plumb-line."
Hailstorms will sweep away all the **lies**
you **depend** on, and **floods** will **destroy**
your **security**. 18 The treaty you have
made with **death** will be abolished, and
your **agreement** with the **world of the
dead** will be cancelled. When **disaster**
sweeps down, you will be overcome. 19 It
will **strike** you again and again, morning
after morning. You will have to bear it
day and night. Each **new message** from
God will bring new **terror**! 20 You will be
like the man in the **proverb**, who tries to
sleep in a bed too short to stretch out on,
with a blanket too narrow to wrap himself in. 21 The LORD will fight as he did at
Mount Perazim and in the valley of
Gibeon, in order to do what he **intends** to
do—**strange** as his **actions** may seem. He
will **complete** his work, his **mysterious**
work.
22 Don't laugh at the **warning** I am
giving you! If you do, it will be even
harder for you to **escape**. I have heard
the LORD **Almighty's** decision to **destroy**
the whole country.

God's Wisdom

23 Listen to what I am saying; pay
attention to what I am telling you. 24 No
farmer goes on constantly ploughing his
fields and getting them ready for **sowing**.
25 Once he has prepared the soil, he **sows**
the **seeds** of herbs such as dill and cumin.
He **sows** rows of wheat and barley,[m] and
at the edges of his fields he **sows** other
grain. 26 He knows how to do his work, because God has **taught** him. 27 He never
uses a heavy club to beat out dill **seeds** or
cumin seeds; instead he uses light sticks
of the **proper** size. 28 He does not **ruin** the
wheat by threshing it endlessly, and he
knows how to thresh it by driving a cart
over it without bruising the grains. 29 All
this **wisdom** comes from the LORD **Almighty**. The **plans** God makes are **wise**,
and they always **succeed**!

The Fate of Jerusalem

29 God's **altar**, Jerusalem itself, is
doomed! The city where David

terror 24.17; 31.9
trap 24.17; Jer 5.26
understand 27.11; 29.24
vision 22.1; 29.11
warn 8.11; 36.14
wisdom 11.2; 33.6
wise 19.11; 29.14
word (1) 7.2; 29.13
world of the dead [2] 14.9; 38.10

acknowledge 19.21; 33.13
Almighty 28.5; 31.4

[m] *Hebrew has an additional word, the meaning of which is unclear.*

28.11-12: 1 Cor 14.21 **28.16:** Ps 118.22-23; Rom 9.33, 10.11; 1 Pet 2.6
28.21: Josh 10.10-12; 2 Sam 5.20; 1 Chr 14.11

camped is **doomed**! Let another year or
two come and go, with its **feasts** and **festi-**
vals, 2 and then God will bring **disaster** on
the city that is called "**God's altar**."
There will be **weeping** and **wailing**, and
the whole city will be like an **altar**
covered with **blood**. 3 God will attack the
city, surround it, and besiege it. 4 Jerusalem will be like a **ghost struggling** to
speak from under the ground, a muffled
voice coming from the dust.
5 Jerusalem, all the foreigners who
attack you will be blown away like dust,
and their **terrifying** armies will fly away
like straw. Suddenly and unexpectedly
6 the LORD **Almighty** will **rescue** you with
violent thunderstorms and earthquakes.
He will send tempests and **raging** fire;
7 then all the armies of the nations
attacking the city of **God's altar**, all their
weapons and equipment—everything—
will **vanish** like a **dream**, like something
imagined in the night. 8 All the nations
that assemble to attack Jerusalem will
be like a starving man who **dreams** he is
eating and wakes up **hungry**, or like a
man dying of thirst who **dreams** he is
drinking and wakes with a dry throat.

Disregarded Warnings

9 Go ahead and be **stupid**! Go ahead
and be **blind**! Get drunk without any
wine! Stagger without drinking a drop!
10 The LORD has made you drowsy, ready
to fall into a deep sleep. The **prophets**
should be the eyes of the people, but God
has blindfolded them. 11 The meaning of
every **prophetic vision** will be hidden
from you; it will be like a **sealed scroll**. If
you take it to someone who knows how to
read and ask him to read it to you, he will
say he can't because it is **sealed**. 12 If you
give it to someone who can't read and
ask him to read it to you, he will answer
that he doesn't know how.
13 The Lord said, "These people **claim**
to **worship** me, but their **words** are
meaningless, and their **hearts** are somewhere else. Their **religion** is nothing but
human rules and traditions, which they
have simply memorized. 14 So I will
startle them with one unexpected blow
after another. Those who are **wise** will
turn out to be **fools**, and all their cleverness will be **useless**."

Hope for the Future

15 Those who try to hide their **plans**
from the LORD are **doomed**! They carry
out their **schemes** in **secret** and think no
one will see them or know what they are
doing. 16 They **turn** everything upside
down. Which is more **important**, the potter or the clay? Can something a man
has made say to him, "You didn't make
me"? Or can it say to him, "You don't
know what you are doing"?
17 As the **saying** goes, before long the
dense forest will become farmland, and
the farmland will go back to forest.
18 When that day comes, the deaf will
be able to hear a book being read aloud,
and the **blind**, who have been living in
darkness, will open their eyes and see.
19 **Poor** and **humble** people will once
again find the **happiness** which the LORD,
the **holy** God of Israel, gives. 20 It will be
the end of those who **oppress** others and
show **contempt** for God. Every sinner
will be **destroyed**. 21 God will **destroy**
those who **slander** others, those who **pre-**
vent the **punishment** of **criminals**, and
those who tell **lies** to **keep honest men**
from getting **justice**.
22 So now the LORD, the God of Israel,
who **rescued** Abraham from **trouble**,
says, "**My people**, you will not be **dis-**
graced any longer, and your faces will no
longer be pale with **shame**. 23 When you
see the children that I will give you, then
you will **acknowledge** that I am the **holy**
God of Israel. You will **honour** me and
stand in **awe** of me. 24 **Foolish** people will
learn to **understand**, and those who are
always grumbling will be **glad** to be
taught."

A Useless Treaty with Egypt

30 The LORD has spoken: "Those
who rule Judah are **doomed** because they **rebel** against me. They follow
plans that I did not make, and sign
treaties against my **will**, piling one sin on
another. 2 They go to Egypt for **help** without asking for my **advice**. They want
Egypt to **protect** them, so they put their
trust in Egypt's king. 3 But the king will
be **powerless** to **help** them, and Egypt's
protection will end in **disaster**. 4 Although
their ambassadors have already arrived
at the Egyptian cities of Zoan and Hanes,
5 the people of Judah will regret that they
ever **trusted** that **unreliable** nation, a
nation that **fails** them when they expect
help."
6 This is God's **message** about the
animals of the southern desert: "The ambassadors travel through **dangerous**
country, where lions live and where
there are poisonous snakes and flying
dragons. They load their donkeys and
camels with expensive **gifts** for a nation
that cannot give them any **help**. 7 The
help that Egypt gives is **useless**. So I have

29.10: Rom 11.8 **29.13:** Mt 15.8–9; Mk 7.6–7 **29.14:** 1 Cor 1.19 **29.16:** Is 45.9

idol [2] 21.9; 31.7
ignore Ecc 10.6; 53.3
lie (2) 29.21; 32.7
light (1) 13.10; 42.6
lonely Ps 102.7; 54.4
Majesty Song 5.15; Jer 37.20
mercy 27.11; 33.2
message 28.9; 37.3
pity 27.11; 49.13
plan [3] 29.15; 33.11
plenty Prov 28.19; 32.20
power [2] 28.2; 31.8
prophet 29.10; 37.2
protect [2] 27.5; 31.2
punish 29.21; 31.2
rebel [2] 1.2; 36.5
refuse (1) [2] 28.12; 58.7
rely [2] 23.14; 31.1
rich 25.6; 32.15
right (1) [3] 26.2; 32.8
right (2) Song 8.3; Jer 22.24
sacred 27.13; 56.7
secure 28.17; 32.17
seed 28.25; 55.10
sight Prov 23.33; 66.24
Sovereign 28.16; 40.10
sow 28.24; 37.30
strike 28.19; 34.5
strong 28.2; 31.3
teach [2] 29.24; 40.13
Temple (1) (of God) 6.1; 37.1
terrify 29.5; 41.10
trust [4] 26.3; 37.10
useless 29.14; 33.11
violent 29.6; 42.25
weep 29.2; 32.13
will (1) 26.8; 52.4
word (1) 29.13; 36.5

nicknamed Egypt, 'The Harmless **Dragon**.' "

The Disobedient People

8 God told me to write down in a book what the people are like, so that there would be a permanent record of how **evil** they are. 9 They are always **rebelling** against God, always **lying**, always **refusing** to listen to the LORD's **teachings**. 10 They tell the **prophets** to keep quiet. They say, "Don't talk to us about what's **right**. Tell us what we want to hear. Let us keep our illusions. 11 Get out of our way and stop blocking our path. We don't want to hear about your **holy** God of Israel."

12 But this is what the **holy** God of Israel says: "You **ignore** what I tell you and **rely** on **violence** and **deceit**. 13 You are **guilty**. You are like a high wall with a crack running down it; suddenly you will collapse. 14 You will be shattered like a clay pot, so **badly** broken that there is no piece big **enough** to pick up hot coals with, or to scoop water from a cistern."

15 The **Sovereign** LORD, the **holy** God of Israel, says to the people, "Come back and quietly **trust** in me. Then you will be **strong** and **secure**." But you **refuse** to do it! 16 Instead, you **plan** to **escape** from your **enemies** by riding fast horses. And you are **right**—**escape** is what you will have to do! You think your horses are fast **enough**, but those who pursue you will be faster! 17 A thousand of you will run away when you see one **enemy** soldier, and five soldiers will be **enough** to make you all run away. Nothing will be left of your army except a **lonely** flagstaff on the top of a hill! 18 And yet the LORD is waiting to be **merciful** to you. He is ready to take **pity** on you because he always does what is **right**. **Happy** are those who put their **trust** in the LORD.

God Will Bless His People

19 You people who live in Jerusalem will not **weep** any more. The LORD is **compassionate**, and when you cry to him for **help**, he will answer you. 20 The Lord will make you go through **hard** times, but he himself will be there to **teach** you, and you will not have to search for him any more. 21 If you wander off the road to the **right** or the left, you will hear his voice behind you saying, "Here is the road. Follow it." 22 You will take your **idols** plated with silver and your **idols** covered with gold, and will throw them away like **filth**, shouting, "Out of my **sight**!" 23 Whenever you **sow** your **seeds**, the LORD will send rain to make them grow and will give you a **rich harvest**, and your livestock will have **plenty** of pasture. 24 The oxen and donkeys that plough your fields will eat the finest and **best** fodder. 25 On the day when the forts of your **enemies** are captured and their people are killed, streams of water will flow from every mountain and every hill. 26 The moon will be as bright as the sun, and the sun will be seven times brighter than usual, like the **light** of seven days in one. This will all happen when the LORD bandages and **heals** the wounds he has given **his people**.

God Will Punish Assyria

27 The LORD's **power** and **glory** can be seen in the distance. Fire and smoke show his **anger**. He speaks, and his **words** burn like fire. 28 He sends the wind in front of him like a **flood** that carries everything away. It sweeps nations to **destruction** and puts an end to their **evil plans**. 29 But you, **God's people**, will be **happy** and sing as you do on the night of a **sacred festival**. You will be as **happy** as those who walk to the music of flutes on their way to the **Temple** of the LORD, the **defender** of Israel.

30 The LORD will let everyone hear his **majestic** voice and feel the **force** of his **anger**. There will be flames, **cloudbursts**, hailstones, and torrents of rain. 31 The Assyrians will be **terrified** when they hear the LORD's voice and feel the **force** of his **punishment**. 32 As the LORD **strikes** them again and again, **his people** will keep time with the music of drums and harps. God himself will fight against the Assyrians. 33 Long ago a place was prepared where a huge fire will burn the emperor of Assyria. It is deep and wide, and piled high with wood. The LORD will breathe out a stream of flame to set it on fire.

God Will Protect Jerusalem

31 Those who go to Egypt for **help** are **doomed**! They are **relying** on Egypt's vast military **strength**—horses, chariots, and soldiers. But they do not **rely** on the LORD, the **holy** God of Israel, or ask him for **help**. 2 He knows what he is doing! He sends **disaster**. He carries out his **threats** to **punish evil** men and those who **protect** them. 3 The Egyptians are not **gods**—they are only **human**. Their horses are not supernatural. When the LORD **acts**, the **strong** nation will crumble, and the **weak** nation it **helped** will fall. Both of them will be **destroyed**.

4 The LORD said to me, "No matter how **shepherds** yell and shout, they can't

abandon 17.9; 32.14
act Ecc 8.4; 32.4
Almighty [2] 29.6; 37.16
defend 30.29; 37.35
destroy [2] 30.28; 32.12
disaster 30.3; 41.23
doom 30.1; 33.1
evil 30.8; 32.6
fright 7.4; 33.14
god (2) (other gods) 17.10; 36.18
help [3] 30.2; 33.7
holy 30.11; 35.8
human [2] 29.13; 37.19
idol 30.22; 40.19
power 30.3; 33.10
protect [4] 30.2; 33.2
punish 30.31; 35.4
rely [2] 30.5; 36.6
sacrifice 19.21; 34.6
shepherd 14.30; 40.11

slave 24.2; 45.14
strength 12.2; 35.3
strong 30.15; 33.16
terror 28.19; 54.14
threat Prov 22.23; Jer 11.17
weak 24.4; 35.3
worship (1) (of God) 29.13; 36.7

scare away a lion from an animal that it has killed; in the same way, there is nothing that can keep me, the LORD Almighty, from protecting Mount Zion. 5 Just as a bird hovers over its nest to protect its young, so I, the LORD Almighty, will protect Jerusalem and defend it."

6 The LORD said, "People of Israel, you have sinned against me and opposed me. But now, come back to me! 7 A time is coming when all of you will throw away the sinful idols you made out of silver and gold. 8 Assyria will be destroyed in war, but not by human power. The Assyrians will run from battle, and their young men will be made slaves. 9 Their emperor will run away in terror, and the officers will be so frightened that they will abandon their battle flags." The LORD has spoken—the LORD who is worshipped in Jerusalem and whose fire burns there for sacrifices.

A King with Integrity

abandon 31.9; 41.17
act [2] 31.3; 33.10
barren 21.13; 34.11
despair 19.9; 54.4
destroy 31.3; 33.11
evil [2] 31.2; 33.15
fear 25.3; 33.18
fool [2] 29.14; 35.8
free [3] 14.17; 35.10
God's people [2] 30.26; 33.6
grief 23.1; 35.10
happy [2] 30.18; 35.10
honest [2] 29.21; 59.14
honour [2] 29.23; 37.35
hunger 29.8; 44.12
insult 3.8; 37.4
justice [2] 29.21; 33.5
lie (2) 30.9; 53.9
life (1) [3] 10.31; 38.10
need 28.9; 41.17
peace [2] 27.5; 33.7
plenty 30.23; 58.11
plot (1) 7.5; 50.11
poor 29.19; 33.15
prevent 29.21; 48.5
rich 30.23; 53.9
right (1) [2] 30.10; 33.15
right (3) 22.16; 45.11
righteous 26.10; Jer 23.5
ruin [2] 28.28; 44.26
safe [2] 28.15; 33.16
satisfy 9.20; 43.24
secure 30.15; 33.16
sheep 22.13; 43.23
shelter 25.4; Ezek 17.23
Spirit (1) (God's Spirit) 11.2; 33.11
strip (1) 3.26; 45.1
stupid 29.9; 44.18
tremble 21.4; 33.14
understand 29.24; 33.19
vineyard 27.2; 36.17
weep 30.19; 65.19
worry [3] Ecc 11.10; Jer 17.8

32 Some day there will be a king who rules with integrity, and national leaders who govern with justice. 2 Each of them will be like a shelter from the wind and a place to hide from storms. They will be like streams flowing in a desert, like the shadow of a giant rock in a barren land. 3 Their eyes and ears will be open to the needs of the people. 4 They will not be impatient any longer, but they will act with understanding and will say what they mean. 5 No one will think that a fool is honourable or say that a scoundrel is honest. 6 A fool speaks foolishly and thinks up evil things to do. What he does and what he says are an insult to the LORD, and he never feeds the hungry or gives thirsty people anything to drink. 7 A stupid person is evil and does evil things; he plots to ruin the poor with lies and to prevent them getting their rights. 8 But an honourable person acts honestly and stands firm for what is right.

Judgement and Restoration

9 You women who live an easy life, free from worries, listen to what I am saying. 10 You may be satisfied now, but this time next year you will be in despair because there will be no grapes for you to gather. 11 You have been living an easy life, free from worries; but now, tremble with fear! Strip off your clothes and tie rags round your waist. 12 Beat your breasts in grief because the fertile fields and the vineyards have been destroyed, 13 and thorn-bushes and briars are growing on my people's land. Weep for all the houses where people were happy and for the city that was full of life. 14 Even the palace will be abandoned and the capital city totally deserted. Homes and the forts that guarded them will be in ruins for ever. Wild donkeys will roam there, and sheep will find pasture there.

15 But once more God will send us his spirit. The waste land will become fertile, and fields will produce rich crops. 16 Everywhere in the land righteousness and justice will be done. 17 Because everyone will do what is right, there will be peace and security for ever. 18 God's people will be free from worries, and their homes peaceful and safe. (19 But hail will fall on the forests, and the city will be torn down.) 20 How happy everyone will be with plenty of water for the crops and safe pasture everywhere for the donkeys and cattle.

A Prayer for Help

33 Our enemies are doomed! They have robbed and betrayed, although no one has robbed them or betrayed them. But their time to rob and betray will end, and they themselves will become victims of robbery and treachery.

2 LORD, have mercy on us. We have put our hope in you. Protect us day by day and save us in times of trouble. 3 When you fight for us, nations run away from the noise of battle. 4 Their belongings are pounced upon and taken as loot.

5 How great the LORD is! He rules over everything. He will fill Jerusalem with justice and integrity 6 and give stability to the nation. He always protects his people and gives them wisdom and knowledge. Their greatest treasure is their reverence for the LORD.

7 Brave men are calling for help. The ambassadors who tried to bring about peace are crying bitterly. 8 The highways are so dangerous that no one travels on them. Treaties are broken and agreements are violated. No one is respected any more. 9 The land lies idle and deserted. The forests of Lebanon have withered, the fertile valley of Sharon is like a desert, and in Bashan and on Mount Carmel the leaves are falling from the trees.

The LORD Warns His Enemies

10 The LORD says to the nations, "Now I will act. I will show how powerful I am. 11 You make worthless plans and everything you do is useless. My spirit is like a

accept 1.23; 56.7
acknowledge 29.23; 46.9
act 32.4; 42.14
agree 28.15; Jer 34.8
arrogant 28.14; Jer 43.2
ash Ps 102.9; 44.20
betray [2] 24.16; Jer 5.11
bitter 22.4; 38.3
bribe 5.23; 45.13
celebrate 22.1; Ezek 7.7
cheat 3.12; Jer 6.13
commit 5.7; Jer 3.9
complain 28.9; 40.27
danger 30.6; 38.17
destroy 32.12; 34.2
doom 31.1; Jer 4.13
enemy [2] 30.16; 34.8
evil 32.6; 47.10
fear 32.11; 41.5
festival 30.29; 66.23
forgive 27.9; 38.17
fright 31.9; 37.6
glory 30.27; 40.5
God's people 32.13; 40.1
help 31.1; 36.5
hope 26.8; 42.4
judge 28.6; 57.3
justice 32.1; 42.1
knowledge 11.2; 47.10
mercy 30.18; 47.6
peace 32.17; 38.17
plan [2] 30.1; 37.26
poor 32.7; 58.7
power [3] 31.8; 35.2
protect [3] 31.2; 37.35
religion 29.13; Jer 10.3
respect 3.5; 37.23
reverence 11.2; Zeph 3.7
right (1) 32.8; 41.1
rob [4] Prov 24.15; 42.22
safe [2] 32.18; 41.3
save 25.9; 36.14
secure 32.17; 39.8
share Song 8.12; 34.17
Spirit (1) (God's Spirit) 32.15; 42.1
splendour Esth 1.4; 35.2

strong 31.3; 35.4
tax collector Mt 5.46
tremble 32.11; 35.3
trouble 29.22; 38.14
understand 32.4; 36.11
useless [2] 30.7; 41.29
victim 5.7; 59.15
wisdom 28.29; 44.25
worthless 3.5; 44.9

fire that will **destroy** you.[x] 12 You will crumble like rocks burnt to make lime, like thorns burnt to **ashes**. 13 Let everyone near and far hear what I have done and **acknowledge** my **power**."

14 The sinful people of Zion are **trembling** with **fright**. They say, "God's **judgement** is like a fire that burns for ever. Can any of us survive a fire like that?" 15 You can survive if you say and do what is **right**. Don't use your **power** to **cheat** the **poor** and don't **accept bribes**. Don't join with those who **plan** to **commit murder** or to do other **evil** things. 16 Then you will be **safe**; you will be as **secure** as if you were in a **strong** fortress. You will have food to eat and water to drink.

The Glorious Future

17 Once again you will see a king ruling in **splendour** over a land that stretches in all directions. 18 Your old **fears** of foreign **tax-collectors** and spies will be only a memory. 19 You will no longer see any **arrogant** foreigners who speak a language that you can't **understand**. 20 Look at Zion, the city where we **celebrate** our **religious festivals**. Look at Jerusalem! What a **safe** place it will be to live in! It will be like a tent that is never moved, whose pegs are never pulled up and whose ropes never break. 21 The LORD will show us his **glory**. We will live beside broad rivers and streams, but hostile ships will not sail on them.[n] 22-23 All the rigging on those ships is **useless**; the sails cannot be spread! We will seize all the wealth of **enemy** armies, and there will be so much that even lame men can have a **share**. The LORD himself will be our king; he will rule over us and **protect** us. 24 No one who lives in our land will ever again **complain** of being ill, and all sins will be **forgiven**.

God Will Punish His Enemies

age (1) [2] Ps 119.90; Ezek 25.15
anger 30.27; 41.11
barren 32.2; 41.18
blood [4] 29.2; 63.3
care 13.17; 40.11
command 21.5; 36.16
condemn [2] Prov 17.15; Jer 2.19
create 19.25; 37.16
creature [2] 6.2; 37.16
demon 2 Chr 11.15; Jer 50.39
destroy [2] 33.11; 36.7

34 Come, people of all nations! Gather round and listen. Let the whole earth and everyone living on it come here and listen. 2 The LORD is **angry** with all the nations and all their armies. He has **condemned** them to **destruction**. 3 Their corpses will not be buried, but will lie there rotting and stinking; and the mountains will be red with **blood**. 4 The sun, moon, and stars will crumble to dust. The sky will disappear like a **scroll** being rolled up, and the stars will fall like leaves dropping from a **vine** or a fig-tree.

5 The LORD has prepared his sword in **heaven**, and now it will **strike** Edom, those people whom he has **condemned** to **destruction**. 6 His sword will be covered with their **blood** and fat, like the **blood** and fat of **lambs** and goats that are **sacrificed**. The LORD will **offer this sacrifice** in the city of Bozrah; he will make this a great **slaughter** in the land of Edom. 7 The people will fall like wild oxen and young bulls, and the earth will be red with **blood** and covered with fat. 8 This is the time when the LORD will **rescue** Zion and take vengeance on her **enemies**.

9 The rivers of Edom will **turn** into tar, and the soil will **turn** into sulphur. The whole country will burn like tar. 10 It will burn day and night, and smoke will **rise** from it for ever. The land will lie waste **age after age**, and no one will ever travel through it again. 11 Owls and ravens will take over the land. The LORD will make it a **barren** waste again, as it was before the **creation**. 12 There will be no king to rule the country, and the leaders will all be gone.[o] 13 Thorns and thistles will grow up in all the palaces and walled towns, and jackals and owls will live in them. 14 Wild animals will roam there, and **demons** will call to **each other**. The night **monster**[p] will come there looking for a place to **rest**. 15 Owls will build their nests, lay eggs, hatch their young, and **care** for them there. Vultures will gather there, one after another.

16 Search in the LORD's book of living **creatures** and read what it says. Not one of these **creatures** will be missing, and not one will be without its mate. The LORD has **commanded** it to be so; he himself will bring them together. 17 It is the LORD who will divide the land among them and give each of them a **share**. They will live in the land **age after age**, and it will belong to them for ever.

each other 19.2; 49.26
enemy 33.1; 35.4
heaven 26.21; 38.14
lamb 16.1; 40.11
monster 27.1; 51.9
offer 28.12; 43.23
rescue 29.6; 35.4
rest (1) 28.12; 57.2
rise 26.14; 40.31
sacrifice [2] 31.9; 40.16
scroll 29.11; Jer 36.2
share 33.22; 42.8
slaughter 15.9; 53.7
strike 30.32; 41.2
turn [2] 29.14; 37.26
vine 24.7; 36.16

The Road of Holiness

35 The desert will **rejoice**,
and flowers will bloom in the wilderness.
2 The desert will sing and shout for **joy**;
it will be as beautiful as the Lebanon Mountains

afraid 12.2; 40.9
blind 29.9; 42.7
discourage 8.21; Jer 14.3
enemy 34.8; 42.13
fool 32.5; 36.18
free 32.9; 42.7
glad 29.24; 48.20
grief 32.12; 36.22

[x] *One ancient translation* My spirit...you; *Hebrew* You are destroying yourselves.
[n] *Verse 21 in Hebrew is unclear.*
[o] *Verse 12 in Hebrew begins with a word, the meaning of which is unclear.*
[p] NIGHT MONSTER: *A female demon, believed to live in desolate places.*

34.4: Mt 24.29; Mk 13.25; Lk 21.26; Rev 6.13–14
34.5–17: Is 63.1–6; Jer 49.7–22; Ezek 25.12–14, 35.1–15; Amos 1.11–12; Obad 1–14; Mal 1.2–5
34.10: Rev 14.11, 19.3

happy 32.13; 41.16
holy 31.1; 37.23
joy [3] 26.19; 42.11
knee Ps 109.24; Ezek 7.17
mislead 19.13; 44.20
power 33.10; 37.26
punish 31.2; 37.3
rejoice 14.8; 61.10
rescue [2] 34.8; 36.18
sorrow 25.7; 51.11
splendour 33.17; 52.1
strength 31.1; 40.29
strong 33.16; 41.10
tremble 33.14; 41.5
weak 31.3; 37.3

and as fertile as the fields of Carmel
and Sharon.
Everyone will see the LORD's
splendour,
see his greatness and **power**.

3 Give **strength** to hands that are tired
and to **knees** that **tremble** with
weakness.
4 Tell everyone who is **discouraged**,
"Be **strong** and don't be **afraid**!
God is coming to your **rescue**,
coming to **punish** your **enemies**."

5 The **blind** will be able to see,
and the deaf will hear.
6 The lame will leap and dance,
and those who cannot speak will
shout for **joy**.
Streams of water will flow through the
desert;
7 the burning sand will become a lake,
and dry land will be filled with
springs.
Where jackals used to live,
marsh grass and reeds will grow.

8 There will be a highway there,
called "The Road of **Holiness**."
No sinner will ever travel that road;
no **fools** will **mislead** those who
follow it.[q]
9 No lions will be there;
no fierce animals will pass that way.
Those whom the LORD has **rescued**
will travel home by that road.
10 They will reach Jerusalem with
gladness,
singing and shouting for **joy**.
They will be **happy** for ever,
for ever **free** from **sorrow** and **grief**.

The Assyrians Threaten Jerusalem
(2 Kgs 18.13–27; 2 Chr 32.1–19)

altar [2] 29.1; 56.7
bread Prov 17.1; 44.15
command 34.16; 38.4
confident 13.3; 57.15
court (1) 1.23; 37.2
deceive 30.12; 37.10
demand Ps 78.18; 43.23
destroy [3] 34.2; 37.11
fool 35.8; 44.20
god (2) (other gods) [4] 31.3; 37.12
grief 35.10; 37.1
Hebrew [2] 19.18; Jer 34.9
help [3] 33.7; 40.31
might 17.10; 43.17
persuade Prov 25.15; Mt 27.20
rebel 30.1; 48.8
rely [3] 31.1; 50.10
rescue 35.4; 37.20
save [6] 33.2; 37.6

36 In the fourteenth year that
Hezekiah was king of Judah,
Sennacherib, the emperor of Assyria,
attacked the fortified cities of Judah and
captured them. 2 Then he ordered his
chief official to go from Lachish to Jerusalem with a large military force to **demand** that King Hezekiah should surrender. The official occupied the road where
the clothmakers work, by the ditch that
brings water from the upper pond.
3 Three Judaeans came out to meet him:
the official in charge of the palace,
Eliakim son of Hilkiah; the **court** secretary, Shebna; and the official in charge
of the records, Joah son of Asaph. 4 The
Assyrian official told them that the emperor wanted to know what made King
Hezekiah so **confident**. 5 He demanded,
"Do you think that **words** can take the
place of military skill and **might**? Who
do you think will **help** you **rebel** against
Assyria? 6 You are expecting Egypt to
help you, but that would be like using a
reed as a walking-stick—it would break
and jab your hand. That is what the king
of Egypt is like when anyone **relies** on
him."
7 The Assyrian official went on, "Or
will you tell me that you are **relying** on
the LORD your God? It was the LORD's
shrines and **altars** that Hezekiah **destroyed** when he told the people of Judah
and Jerusalem to **worship** at one **altar**
only. 8 I will make a bargain with you in
the name of the emperor. I will give you
two thousand horses if you can find that
many men to ride them. 9 You are no
match for even the lowest ranking
Assyrian official, and yet you expect the
Egyptians to send you chariots and
cavalry. 10 Do you think I have attacked
your country and **destroyed** it without the
LORD's **help**? The LORD himself told me
to attack it and **destroy** it."
11 Then Eliakim, Shebna, and Joah
said to the official, "Speak Aramaic to us.
We **understand** it. Don't speak **Hebrew**;
all the people on the wall are listening."
12 He replied, "Do you think you and
the king are the only ones the emperor
sent me to say all these things to? No, I
am also talking to the people who are sitting on the wall, who will have to eat
their excrement and drink their urine,
just as you will."
13 Then the official stood up and
shouted in **Hebrew**, "Listen to what the
emperor of Assyria is telling you. 14 He
warns you not to let Hezekiah **deceive**
you. Hezekiah can't **save** you. 15 And don't
let him **persuade** you to **rely** on the LORD.
Don't think that the LORD will **save** you
and that he will stop our Assyrian army
from capturing your city. 16 Don't listen to
Hezekiah! The emperor of Assyria **commands** you to come out of the city and
surrender. You will all be allowed to eat
grapes from your own **vines** and figs
from your own trees, and to drink water
from your own wells—17 until the emperor resettles you in a country much
like your own, where there are **vineyards**
to give wine and there is corn for making
bread. 18 Don't let Hezekiah **fool** you into
thinking that the LORD will **rescue** you.
Did the **gods** of any other nations **save**
their countries from the emperor of

shrine 16.12; 65.7
understand 33.19; 39.8
vine 34.4; 37.30
vineyard 32.12; 61.
warn 28.22; 56.10
word (1) [2] 30.27; 37.9
worship (1) (of Go
31.9; 43.22

[q] *Probable text* no fools...follow it; *Hebrew unclear.*

35.3: Heb 12.12 **35.5–6:** Mt 11.5; Lk 7.22 **36.6:** Ezek 29.6–7

Assyria? 19 Where are they now, the **gods**
of Hamath and Arpad? Where are the
gods of Sepharvaim? Did anyone **save**
Samaria? 20 When did any of the **gods** of
all these countries ever **save** their
country from our emperor? Then what
makes you think the LORD can **save** Jerusalem?"

21 The people kept quiet, just as King
Hezekiah had told them to; they did not
say a **word**. 22 Then Eliakim, Shebna, and
Joah tore their clothes in **grief** and went
and reported to the king what the
Assyrian official had said.

The King Asks Isaiah's Advice
(2 Kgs 19.1–7)

37 As soon as King Hezekiah heard
their report, he tore his clothes
in **grief**, put on **sackcloth**, and went to the
Temple of the LORD. 2 He sent Eliakim,
the official in charge of the palace,
Shebna, the **court** secretary, and the
senior **priests** to the **prophet** Isaiah son of
Amoz. They also were wearing **sack-
cloth**. 3 This is the **message** which he told
them to give to Isaiah: "Today is a day of
suffering; we are being **punished** and are
in **disgrace**. We are like a woman who is
ready to give **birth**, but is too **weak** to do
it. 4 The Assyrian emperor has sent his
chief official to **insult** the living God. May
the LORD your God hear these **insults** and
punish those who spoke them. So **pray** to
God for those of our people who survive."

5 When Isaiah received King Hezekiah's **message**, 6 he sent back this answer: "The LORD tells you not to let the
Assyrians **frighten** you by their **claims**
that he cannot **save** you. 7 The LORD will
cause the emperor to hear a rumour that
will make him go back to his own
country, and the LORD will have him
killed there."

The Assyrians Send Another Threat
(2 Kgs 19.8–19)

8 The Assyrian official **learnt** that the
emperor had left Lachish and was fighting against the nearby city of Libnah; so
he went there to **consult** him. 9 **Word**
reached the Assyrians that the Egyptian
army, led by King Tirhakah of Sudan,
was coming to attack them. When the
emperor heard this, he sent a **letter** to
King Hezekiah 10 of Judah to say to him,
"The god you are **trusting** in has told you
that you will not fall into my hands, but
don't let that **deceive** you. 11 You have
heard what an Assyrian emperor does to
any country he decides to **destroy**. Do
you think that you can **escape**? 12 My
ancestors **destroyed** the cities of Gozan,
Haran, and Rezeph, and killed the people
of Betheden who lived in Telassar, and
none of their **gods** could **save** them.
13 Where are the kings of the cities of
Hamath, Arpad, Sepharvaim, Hena, and
Ivvah?"

14 King Hezekiah took the **letter** from
the messengers and read it. Then he
went to the **Temple**, placed the **letter**
there in the **presence** of the LORD, 15 and
prayed, 16 "**Almighty** LORD, God of Israel,
enthroned above the winged **creatures**,
you **alone** are God, ruling all the kingdoms of the **world**. You **created** the earth
and the sky. 17 Now, LORD, hear us and
look at what is happening to us. Listen to
all the things that Sennacherib is saying
to **insult** you, the living God. 18 We all
know, LORD, that the emperors of
Assyria have **destroyed** many nations,
made their lands **desolate**, 19 and burnt up
their **gods**—which were no gods at all,
only **images** of wood and stone made by
human hands. 20 Now, LORD our God, **rescue** us from the Assyrians, so that all the
nations of the **world** will know that you
alone are God."

Isaiah's Message to the King
(2 Kgs 19.20–37)

21 Then Isaiah sent a **message** telling
King Hezekiah that in answer to the
king's **prayer** 22 the LORD had said, "The
city of Jerusalem laughs at you,
Sennacherib, and **despises** you. 23 Whom
do you think you have been **insulting** and
ridiculing? You have been **disrespectful**
to me, the **holy** God of Israel. 24 You sent
your **servants** to **boast** to me that with all
your chariots you had **conquered** the
highest mountains of Lebanon. You
boasted that there you cut down the tallest cedars and the finest cypress-trees,
and that you reached the deepest parts
of the forests. 25 You **boasted** that you dug
wells and drank water in foreign lands,
and that the feet of your soldiers
tramped the River Nile dry.

26 "Have you never heard that I
planned all this long ago? And now I
have carried it out. I gave you the **power**
to **turn** fortified cities into piles of rubble.
27 The people who lived there were
powerless; they were **frightened** and
stunned. They were like grass in a field
or **weeds** growing on a roof when the hot
east wind blasts them.[q]

28 "But I know everything about you,
what you do and where you go. I know

[q] *Probable text* when...them; *Hebrew* blasted before they are grown.

37.16: Ex 25.22

how you **rage** against me. 29 I have received the report of that **rage** and that
pride of yours, and now I will put a hook
through your nose and a bit in your
mouth and will take you back by the road
on which you came."
30 Then Isaiah said to King Hezekiah,
"This is a **sign** of what will happen. This
year and next you will have only wild
grain to eat, but the following year you
will be able to **sow** your corn and **harvest**
it, and plant **vines** and eat grapes.
31 Those in Judah who survive will
flourish like plants that send roots deep
into the ground and produce fruit.
32 There will be people in Jerusalem and
on Mount Zion who will survive, because
the LORD **Almighty** is **determined** to
make this happen.
33 "This is what the LORD has said
about the Assyrian emperor: 'He will not
enter this city or shoot a single arrow
against it. No soldiers with shields will
come near the city, and no siege-mounds
will be built round it. 34 He will go back by
the road on which he came, without
entering this city. I, the LORD, have
spoken. 35 I will **defend** this city and **protect** it, for the **sake** of my own **honour**
and because of the **promise** I made to my
servant David.' "
36 An **angel of the** LORD went to the
Assyrian camp and killed 185,000 soldiers. At dawn the next day there they
lay, all **dead**! 37 Then the Assyrian emperor Sennacherib withdrew and returned to Nineveh. 38 One day when he
was **worshipping** in the **temple** of his **god**
Nisroch, two of his sons, Adrammelech
and Sharezer, killed him with their
swords and then **escaped** to the land of
Ararat. Another of his sons, Esarhaddon,
succeeded him as emperor.

King Hezekiah's Illness and Recovery
(2 Kgs 20.1-11; 2 Chr 32.24-26)

38 About this time King Hezekiah
fell ill and almost died. The **prophet** Isaiah son of Amoz went to see him
and said to him, "The LORD tells you that
you are to put everything in order because you will not recover. Get ready to
die."
2 Hezekiah **turned** his face to the wall
and **prayed**: 3 "**Remember**, LORD, that I
have **served** you **faithfully** and **loyally**,
and that I have always tried to do what
you wanted me to." And he began to cry
bitterly.
4 Then the LORD **commanded** Isaiah
5 to go back to Hezekiah and say to him,
"I, the LORD, the God of your ancestor
David, have heard your **prayer** and seen
your **tears**; I will let you live fifteen years
longer. 6 I will **rescue** you and this city of
Jerusalem from the emperor of Assyria,
and I will continue to **protect** the city."
21 [r] Isaiah told the king to put a paste
made of figs on his boil, and he would get
well. 22 Then King Hezekiah asked, "What
is the **sign** to **prove** that I will be able to
go to the **Temple**?"
7 Isaiah replied, "The LORD will give
you a **sign** to **prove** that he will keep his
promise 8 On the stairway built by King
Ahaz, the LORD will make the shadow go
back ten steps." And the shadow moved
back ten steps.[s]
9 After Hezekiah recovered from his
illness, he wrote this song of **praise**:

10 I thought that in the prime of **life**
I was going to the **world of the dead**,
Never to live out my **life**.
11 I thought that in this **world** of
the living
I would never again see the LORD
Or any living person.
12 My **life** was cut off and ended,
Like a tent that is taken down,
Like cloth that is cut from a loom.
I thought that God was ending my **life**.[t]
13 All night I cried out with pain,
As if a lion were breaking my **bones**.
I thought that God was ending my **life**.[u]
14 My voice was thin and **weak**,
And I moaned like a **dove**.
My eyes grew tired from looking to
heaven.
LORD, **rescue** me from all this **trouble**.
15 What can I say? The LORD has done
this.
My **heart** is bitter, and I cannot sleep.

16 LORD, I will live for you, for you **alone**;
Heal me and let me live.[v]
17 My **bitterness** will turn into **peace**.
You **save**[w] my life from all **danger**;
You **forgive** all my sins.
18 No one in the **world of the dead** can
praise you;
The **dead** cannot trust in your
faithfulness
19 It is the living who **praise** you,
As I praise you now.
Fathers tell their children how **faithful**
you are.
20 LORD, you have **healed** me.
We will play harps and sing your **praise**,

[r] *Verses 21–22 are moved here from the end of the chapter (see 2 Kgs 20.6–9).*
[s] stairway....ten steps...steps; *or* sundial...ten degrees...degrees *(see 2 Kgs 20.9–11).*
[t] I thought...my life; *Hebrew unclear.* [u] *Verse 13 in Hebrew is unclear.*
[v] *Verses 15–16 in Hebrew are unclear.* [w] *Some ancient translations* save; *Hebrew* love.

alone 37.16; 42.8
bitter [3] 33.7;
Jer 2.19
command 36.16;
44.27
danger 33.8; 65.25
dead 37.36; 50.3
dove Song 6.9; 60.8
faithful [3] 26.2; 56.4
forgive 33.24; 40.2
heal [2] 30.26; 53.5
heart 29.13; 47.7
heaven 34.5; 42.5
life (1) [6] 32.9; 42.5
loyal Prov 20.6; 45.23
never again 2.4; 54.9
pain 26.17; 53.3
peace 33.7; 39.8
praise [4] 25.1; 41.16

pray 37.4; 44.17
prayer 37.21; 41.17
promise 37.35; 40.5
prophet 37.2; 39.3
protect 37.35; 41.10
prove [2] Prov 25.8;
43.9
remember 26.14;
44.21
rescue [2] 37.20;
40.10
save 37.6; 41.10
serve 28.6; 39.7
sign (1) [2] 37.30;
55.13
tear (2) 25.8; Jer 6.2
Temple (1) (of God)
[2] 37.1; 44.28
trouble 33.2; 40.27
trust 37.10; 40.31
turn [2] 37.26; 41.18
weak 37.3; 40.29
world 37.16; 40.21
world of the dead [2
28.15; 57.9

Almighty 37.16; 44.6
letter (2) 37.9; Jer 29.1
message 37.3; 40.6
peace 38.17; 52.7
prophet 38.1; Jer 1.5
secure 33.16; 47.8
serve 38.3; 56.6
understand 36.11; 40.14
welcome 14.9; 64.5

Sing praise in your **Temple** as long as
we live.[y]

Messengers from Babylonia
(2 Kgs 20.12–19)

39 About this time, the king of
Babylonia, Merodach Baladan,
son of Baladan, heard that King
Hezekiah had been ill, so he sent him a
letter and a present. 2 Hezekiah **wel-**
comed the messengers and showed them
his wealth—his silver and gold, his spices
and perfumes, and all his military equipment. There was nothing in his
storerooms or anywhere in his kingdom
that he did not show them. 3 Then the
prophet Isaiah went to King Hezekiah
and asked, "Where did these men come
from and what did they say to you?"
Hezekiah answered, "They came from
a very distant country, from Babylonia."
4 "What did they see in the palace?"
"They saw everything. There is
nothing in the storerooms that I didn't
show them."
5 Isaiah then told the king, "The LORD
Almighty says that 6 a time is coming
when everything in your palace, everything that your ancestors have stored up
to this day, will be carried off to
Babylonia. Nothing will be left. 7 Some of
your own direct descendants will be
taken away and made eunuchs to **serve**
in the palace of the king of Babylonia."
8 King Hezekiah **understood** this to
mean that there would be **peace** and
security during his lifetime, so he replied,
"The **message** you have given me from
the LORD is good."

advice 30.2; 47.13
afraid 35.4; 41.10
announce 21.10; 48.5
care [2] 34.15; 42.23
choose 19.25; 41.8
clear 5.2; 62.10
comfort [2] 28.12; 49.13
compare [2] Song 2.3; 46.5
complain 33.24; 45.9
consult 37.8; 45.21
create [2] 37.16; 42.5
cup Prov 23.31; 51.17
encourage Ps 69.32; 41.6
endure [2] 7.9; 50.7
enough [2] 30.14; 56.11
everlasting Ps 139.24; 63.12
flock 13.20; 61.5

Words of Hope

40 "**Comfort my people**," says our
God. "**Comfort** them!
2 **Encourage** the people of Jerusalem.
Tell them they have **suffered** long
enough
and their sins are now **forgiven**.[z]
I have **punished** them in full for all
their sins."

3 A voice cries out,
"Prepare in the wilderness a road for
the LORD!
Clear the way in the desert for our
God!
4 Fill every valley;
level every mountain.
The hills will become a plain,
and the rough country will be made
smooth.
5 Then the **glory** of the LORD will be
revealed,
and all **mankind** will see it.
The LORD himself has **promised** this."

6 A voice cries out, "**Proclaim** a
message!"
"What **message** shall I **proclaim**?" I
ask.
"**Proclaim** that all **mankind** are like
grass;
they **last** no longer than wild
flowers.
7 Grass withers and flowers fade,
when the LORD sends the wind
blowing over them.
People are no more **enduring** than
grass.
8 Yes, grass withers and flowers fade,
but the **word of our God endures** for
ever."

9 Jerusalem, go up on a high mountain
and **proclaim** the **good news**!
Call out with a loud voice, Zion;
announce the **good news**![a]
Speak out and do not be **afraid**.
Tell the towns of Judah
that their God is coming!

10 The **Sovereign** LORD is coming to rule
with **power**,
bringing with him the people he has
rescued.[b]
11 He will take **care** of his **flock** like a
shepherd;
he will gather the **lambs** together
and carry them in his arms;
he will **gently** lead their mothers.

Israel's Incomparable God

12 Can anyone measure the ocean by
handfuls
or measure the sky with his hands?
Can anyone hold the soil of the earth in
a **cup**
or weigh the mountains and hills on
scales?
13 Can anyone tell the LORD what to do?
Who can **teach** him or give him
advice?
14 With whom does God **consult**
in order to know and **understand**

forgive 38.17; 43.25
gentle Prov 31.26; Jer 4.11
glory 33.21; 42.8
God's people 33.6; 41.17
Good News [2] 21.10; 52.7
help 36.5; 41.6
holy 37.23; 41.14
idol 31.7; 41.7
image 37.19; 42.17
injustice Ecc 10.5; 58.6
lamb 34.6; 53.7
last (1) 24.5; 42.3
learn 37.8; 42.25
mankind [2] Prov 8.4; 45.12
message [2] 39.8; Jer 2.2
power [3] 37.26; 41.29
proclaim [4] 14.28; 61.2
promise 38.7; 42.16
punish 37.3; 51.17
rescue 38.6; 42.22
reveal 26.21; 44.26
rise 34.10; 43.17
sacrifice 34.6; 43.23
shepherd 31.4; Jer 25.34
Sovereign 30.15; 48.16
strength [2] 35.3; 41.13
suffer [2] 37.3; 42.25
teach 30.9; 42.4
throne 37.16; 47.1
trouble 38.14; 43.2
trust 38.18; 42.17
understand [2] 39.8; 41.20
weak [3] 38.14; 41.14
word (1) 37.9; 41.26
world [2] 38.11; 42.10

[y] *Verses 21–22 are placed after verse 6.*
[z] and their sins are now forgiven; *or* they have paid for what they did.
[a] Jerusalem, go up...news!; *or* Go up on a high mountain and proclaim the good news to Jerusalem! Call out with a loud voice and announce the good news to Zion!
[b] the people he has rescued; *or* the rewards he has for his people.

39.7: Dan 1.1–7; 2 Kgs 24.10–16; 2 Chr 36.10 **40.3:** Mt 3.3; Mk 1.3; Jn 1.23 **40.3–5:** Lk 3.4–6
40.6–8: Jas 1.10–11; 1 Pet 1.24–25 **40.10:** Is 62.11; Rev 22.12 **40.11:** Ezek 34.15; Jn 10.11
40.13: Rom 11.34; 1 Cor 2.16

and to **learn** how things should be
done?

15 To the LORD the nations are nothing,
no more than a drop of water;
the distant islands are as light as
dust.
16 All the animals in the forests of
Lebanon
are not **enough** for a **sacrifice** to our
God,
and its trees are too few to kindle
the fire.
17 The nations are nothing at all to him.

18 To whom can God be **compared**?
How can you describe what he is
like?
19 He is not like an **idol** that workmen
make,
that metalworkers cover with gold
and set in a base of silver.
20 The man who cannot afford silver or
gold[d]
chooses wood that will not rot.
He finds a skilful craftsman
to make an **image** that won't fall
down.

21 Do you not know?
Were you not told long ago?
Have you not heard how the **world**
began?
22 It was made by the one who sits on his
throne
above the earth and beyond the sky;
the people below look as tiny as
ants.
He stretched out the sky like a curtain,
like a tent in which to live.
23 He brings down **powerful** rulers
and reduces them to nothing.
24 They are like young plants,
just set out and barely rooted.
When the LORD sends a wind,
they dry up and blow away like
straw.

25 To whom can the **holy** God be
compared?
Is there anyone else like him?
26 Look up at the sky!
Who **created** the stars you see?
The one who leads them out like an
army,
he knows how many there are
and calls each one by name!
His **power** is so great—
not one of them is ever missing!

27 Israel, why then do you **complain**
that the LORD doesn't know your
troubles
or **care** if you **suffer injustice**?
28 Don't you know? Haven't you heard?
The LORD is the **everlasting** God;
he **created** all the **world**.
He never grows tired or weary.
No one **understands** his thoughts.
29 He **strengthens** those who are **weak**
and tired.
30 Even those who are young grow **weak**;
young men can fall exhausted.
31 But those who **trust** in the LORD for
help
will find their **strength** renewed.
They will **rise** on wings like eagles;
they will run and not get weary;
they will walk and not grow **weak**.

God's Assurance to Israel

41 God says,
"Be silent and listen to me, you
distant lands!
Get ready to **present** your **case** in
court;
you will have your chance to speak.
Let us come together to decide who is
right.

2 "Who was it that brought the
conqueror from the east,[e]
and makes him **triumphant**
wherever he goes?
Who gives him **victory** over kings and
nations?
His sword **strikes** them down as if
they were dust.
His arrows **scatter** them like straw
before the wind.
3 He follows in pursuit and marches
safely on,
so fast that he hardly touches the
ground!
4 Who was it that made this **happen**?
Who has **determined** the course of
history?
I, the LORD, was there at the
beginning,
and I, the LORD, will be there at the
end.

5 "The people of distant lands have seen
what I have done;
they are **frightened** and **tremble**
with **fear**.
So they all assemble and come.
6 The craftsmen **help** and **encourage**
one another.

[d] *Verses 19-20a in Hebrew are unclear.*
[e] THE CONQUEROR FROM THE EAST: *Cyrus, the emperor of Persia (see 45.1).*

40.18-19: Acts 17.29

triumph Ps 149.5; 46.13
turn 38.2; 42.15
understand 40.14; 43.10
useless 33.11; 44.9
victory 26.18; 45.8
weak [2] 40.29; 50.2
word (1) 40.8; 43.9
worship (2) (of other gods) 37.38; 44.9

7 The carpenter says to the goldsmith,
'Well done!'
The man who beats the **idol** smooth
encourages the one who nails it
together.
They say, 'The soldering is good'—
and they fasten the idol in place with
nails.

8 "But you, Israel my **servant**,
you are the people that I have
chosen,
the descendants of Abraham, my
friend.
9 I brought you from the ends of the
earth;
I called you from its farthest corners
and said to you, 'You are my
servant.'
I did not **reject** you, but **chose** you.
10 Do not be **afraid**—I am with you!
I am your God—let nothing **terrify**
you!
I will make you **strong** and **help** you;
I will **protect** you and **save** you.

11 "Those who are **angry** with you
will know the **shame** of defeat.
Those who fight against you will die
12 and will disappear from the earth.
13 I am the LORD your God;
I **strengthen** you and say,
'Do not be **afraid**; I will **help** you.' "

14 The LORD says,
"Small and **weak** as you are, Israel,
don't be **afraid**; I will **help** you.
I, the **holy** God of Israel, am the one
who **saves** you.
15 I will make you like a threshing-board,
with spikes that are **new** and sharp.
You will thresh mountains and **destroy**
them;
hills will crumble into dust.
16 You will toss them in the air;
the wind will carry them off,
and they will be **scattered** by the
storm.
Then you will be **happy** because I am
your God;
you will **praise** me, the **holy** God of
Israel.

17 "When **my people** in their **need** look
for water,
when their throats are dry with
thirst,
then I, the LORD, will answer their
prayer;
I, the God of Israel, will never
abandon them.

18 I will make rivers flow among **barren**
hills
and springs of water run in the
valleys.
I will **turn** the desert into pools of
water
and the dry land into flowing
springs.
19 I will make cedars grow in the desert,
and acacias and myrtles and olive-
trees.
Forests will grow in **barren** land,
forests of pine and juniper and
cypress.
20 People will see this and know
that I, the LORD, have done it.
They will come to **understand**
that Israel's **holy** God has made it
happen."

The LORD's Challenge to False Gods

21 The LORD, the king of Israel, has
this to say:
"You **gods** of the nations, **present** your
case.
Bring the **best arguments** you have!
22 Come here and **predict** what will
happen,
so that we will know it when it takes
place.
Explain to the **court** the events of the
past,
and tell us what they mean.
23 Tell us what the future holds—
then we will know that you are
gods!
Do something good or bring some
disaster;
fill us with **fear** and **awe**!
24 You and all you do are nothing;
those who **worship** you are
disgusting!

25 "I have **chosen** a man who lives in the
east;[f]
I will bring him to attack from the
north.
He tramples on rulers as if they were
mud,
like a potter trampling clay.
26 Which of you **predicted** that this would
happen,
so that we could say that you were
right?
None of you said a **word** about it;
no one heard you say a thing!
27 I, the LORD, was the first to tell Zion
the news;
I sent a messenger to Jerusalem to
say,

[f] A MAN WHO LIVES IN THE EAST: *See 41.2.*
41.8: 2 Chr 20.7; Jas 2.23

'Your people are coming! They are
coming home!'[g]
28 When I looked among the **gods**,
none of them had a thing to say;
not one could answer the **questions** I
asked.
29 All these **gods** are **useless**;
they can do nothing at all—
these **idols** are **weak** and **powerless**."

The LORD's Servant

42 The LORD says,
"Here is my **servant**, whom I
strengthen—
the one I have **chosen**, with whom I
am **pleased**.
I have filled him with my **spirit**,
and he will bring **justice** to every
nation.
2 He will not shout or **raise** his voice
or make loud **speeches** in the
streets.
3 He will not break off a bent reed
or **put out** a flickering lamp.
He will bring **lasting justice** to all.
4 He will not lose **hope** or **courage**;
he will **establish justice** on the earth.
Distant lands **eagerly** wait for his
teaching."

5 God **created** the **heavens** and
stretched them out;
he fashioned the earth and all that
lives there;
he gave **life** and breath to all its
people.
And now the LORD God says to his
servant,
6 "I, the LORD, have called you and
given you **power**
to see that **justice** is done on earth.
Through you I will make a **covenant**
with all peoples;
through you I will bring **light** to the
nations.
7 You will open the eyes of the **blind**
and **set free** those who sit in **dark**
prisons.

8 "I **alone** am the LORD your God.
No other **god** may **share** my **glory**;
I will not let **idols share** my **praise**.
9 The things I **predicted** have now come
true.
Now I will tell you of **new** things
even before they begin to happen."

A Song of Praise

10 Sing a **new** song to the LORD;
sing his **praise**, all the **world**!
Praise him, you that sail the sea;
praise him, all **creatures** of the sea!
Sing, distant lands and all who live
there!
11 Let the desert and its towns **praise**
God;
let the people of Kedar **praise** him!
Let those who live in the city of Sela
shout for **joy** from the tops of the
mountains!
12 Let those who live in distant lands
give **praise** and **glory** to the LORD!
13 The LORD goes out to fight like a
warrior;
he is ready and **eager** for battle.
He gives a war-cry, a battle-shout;
he shows his **power** against his
enemies.

God Promises to Help His People

14 God says,
"For a long time I kept silent;
I did not answer **my people**.
But now the time to **act** has come;
I cry out like a woman in labour.
15 I will **destroy** the hills and mountains
and dry up the grass and trees.
I will **turn** the river valleys into
deserts[h]
and dry up the pools of water.

16 "I will lead my **blind** people
by roads they have never travelled.
I will **turn** their **darkness** into **light**
and make rough country smooth
before them.
These are my **promises**,
and I will keep them without **fail**.
17 All who **trust** in **idols**,
who call **images** their **gods**,
will be **humiliated** and **disgraced**."

Israel's Failure to Learn

18 The LORD says,
"Listen, you deaf people!
Look closely, you that are **blind**!
19 Is anyone more **blind** than my **servant**,
more deaf than the messenger I
send?
20 Israel, you have seen so much,
but what has it meant to you?
You have ears to hear with,
but what have you really heard?"

21 The LORD is a God who is **eager** to
save,
so he exalted his **laws** and **teachings**,
and he wanted **his people** to **honour**
them.

act 33.10; 57.18
alone 38.16; 43.11
anger [2] 41.11; 47.6
blind [4] 35.5; 43.8
care 40.11; 46.3
choose 41.8; 43.10
courage 28.6; Jer 4.9
covenant 24.5; 49.8
create 40.26; 43.1
creature 37.16; Jer 51.62
dark [2] 29.18; 45.3
destroy 41.15; 43.17
disgrace 37.3; 44.9
eager [3] Song 6.12; 50.4
enemy 35.4; 47.12
establish 23.7; Jer 30.20
fail 30.5; 46.10
force (1) 30.30; 51.20
free 35.10; 43.3
glory [2] 40.5; 43.7
god (2) (other gods) [2] 41.21; 43.9
God's people [3] 41.17; 43.6
heaven 38.14; 44.23
honour 37.35; 43.4
hope 33.2; 49.4
humiliate 25.11; 44.11
idol [2] 41.7; 44.9
image 40.20; 44.10
joy 35.2; 44.23
justice [4] 33.5; 45.8
last (1) 40.6; 45.17
law 24.5; 51.4
learn 40.14; Jer 2.19
life (1) 38.10; 43.4
light (1) [2] 30.26; 45.7
new [2] 41.15; 43.19
obey 20.2; 50.10
please Ecc 7.26; 53.11
power [2] 41.29; 43.13
praise [7] 41.16; 43.20
predict 41.22; 43.9
prison [2] 28.13; 49.9
promise 40.5; 45.23
put out Song 8.7; 66.24
raise 18.3; Jer 50.15
rescue 40.10; 45.25
rob 33.1; Jer 7.11
save 41.10; 43.1
servant [3] 41.8; 43.10
share [2] 34.17; 48.11
speech Prov 22.11; 52.15
Spirit (1) (God's Spirit) 33.11; 44.3
strength 41.13; 45.5
suffer 40.2; 44.11
teach [3] 40.13; 48.17
true 10.20; 44.26
trust 40.31; 48.8
turn [2] 41.18; 43.14
violent 30.12; 58.4
world 40.21; 43.6

[g] *Verse 27 in Hebrew is unclear.* [h] *Probable text* deserts; *Hebrew* coastlands.

42.1: Mt 3.17, 17.5; Mk 1.11; Lk 3.22, 9.35 **42.1-4:** Mt 12.18-21 **42.5:** Acts 17.24-25
42.6: Is 49.6; Lk 2.32; Acts 13.47, 26.23

22 But now his people have been
plundered;
they are locked up in dungeons
and hidden away in prisons.
They were robbed and plundered,
with no one to come to their rescue.

23 Will any of you listen to this?
From now on will you listen with
care?
24 Who gave Israel up to the looters?
It was the LORD himself, against
whom we sinned!
We would not live as he wanted us to
live
or obey the teachings he gave us.
25 So he made us feel the force of his
anger
and suffer the violence of war.
Like fire his anger burned throughout
Israel,
but we never knew what was
happening;
we learnt from it nothing at all.

God Promises to Rescue His People

43 Israel, the LORD who created you
says,
"Do not be afraid—I will save you.
I have called you by name—you are
mine.
2 When you pass through deep waters, I
will be with you;
your troubles will not overwhelm
you.
When you pass through fire, you will
not be burnt;
the hard trials that come will not
hurt you.
3 For I am the LORD your God,
the holy God of Israel, who saves
you.
I will give up Egypt to set you free;
I will give up Sudan and Seba.
4 I will give up whole nations to save
your life,
because you are precious to me
and because I love you and give you
honour.
5 Do not be afraid—I am with you!

"From the distant east and the farthest
west,
I will bring your people home.
6 I will tell the north to let them go
and the south not to hold them back.
Let my people return from distant
lands,
from every part of the world.
7 They are my own people,
and I created them to bring me
glory."

Israel Is the LORD's Witness

8 God says,
"Summon my people to court.
They have eyes, but they are blind;
they have ears, but they are deaf!
9 Summon the nations to come to the
trial.
Which of their gods can predict the
future?
Which of them foretold what is
happening now?
Let these gods bring in their witnesses
to prove that they are right,
to testify to the truth of their words.

10 "People of Israel, you are my
witnesses;
I chose you to be my servant,
so that you would know me and
believe in me
and understand that I am the only
God.
Besides me there is no other god;
there never was and never will be.

11 "I alone am the LORD,
the only one who can save you.
12 I predicted what would happen,
and then I came to your aid.
No foreign god has ever done this;
you are my witnesses.
13 I am God and always will be.
No one can escape from my power;
no one can change what I do."

Escape from Babylon

14 Israel's holy God, the LORD who
saves you, says,
"To save you, I will send an army
against Babylon;
I will break down the city gates,
and the shouts of her people will
turn into crying.
15 I am the LORD, your holy God.
I created you, Israel, and I am your
king."

16 Long ago the LORD made a road
through the sea,
a path through the swirling waters.
17 He led a mighty army to destruction,
an army of chariots and horses.
Down they fell, never to rise,
snuffed out like the flame of a lamp!

18 But the LORD says,
"Do not cling to events of the past
or dwell on what happened long ago.
19 Watch for the new thing I am going to
do.
It is happening already—you can
see it now!

accuse 3.14; 50.8
afraid [2] 41.10; 44.2
alone 42.8; 44.24
believe Prov 26.25; 53.1
blind 42.7; 44.9
burden [2] 22.24; 46.1
burnt-offering Ps 66.13; Jer 7.22
case (2) 41.1; 45.21
change Prov 22.25; 45.23
choose [2] 42.1; 44.1
court (1) [2] 41.1; 45.21
create [3] 42.5; 44.2
demand 36.2; Ezek 24.8
destroy [2] 42.15; 48.9
escape 37.11; 52.12
forgive 40.2; 53.10
free 42.7; 45.8
glory 42.8; 48.11
god (2) (other gods) [4] 42.8; 44.6
God's people [5] 42.14; 44.1
hard 30.20; Jer 5.12
holy [3] 41.14; 45.11
honour [3] 42.21; 45.4
hurt Ecc 10.9; 49.10
incense [2] 27.9; 60.6
insult 37.4; 50.6
life (1) 42.5; 47.15
love 26.11; 44.2
might 36.5; 60.16
new 42.9; 48.6
offer 34.6; 56.7
power 42.6; 44.8
praise [2] 42.8; 45.25
predict [2] 42.9; 44.7
present (1) 41.1; 45.20
profane Neh 13.18; Ezek 7.22
prove [2] 38.7; 48.4
right (1) [2] 41.1; 45.13
rise 40.31; 44.26
sacrifice 40.16; 53.10
sanctuary Ps 116.18; 63.18
satisfy 32.10; 44.16
save [6] 42.21; 44.17
servant 42.1; 44.1
sheep 32.14; 49.9
testify Ps 50.7; Mic 1.2
trouble 40.27; 65.10
truth Ecc 12.9; 44.18
try (2) [2] Prov 23.29; 44.11
turn 42.15; 45.22
understand 41.20; 50.5
watch 27.3; 56.10
witness [3] 8.2; 44.8
word (1) 41.26; 44.25
world 42.10; 45.6
worship (1) (of God) 36.7; 48.1
wrong 26.10; 59.11

I will make a road through the
wilderness
and give you streams of water there.
20 Even the wild animals will honour me;
jackals and ostriches will praise me
when I make rivers flow in the desert
to give water to my chosen people.
21 They are the people I made for myself,
and they will sing my praises!"

Israel's Sin

22 The LORD says,
"But you were tired of me, Israel;
you did not worship me.
23 You did not bring me your burnt-offerings of sheep;
you did not honour me with your sacrifices.
I did not burden you by demanding offerings
or wear you out by asking for incense.
24 You didn't buy incense for me
or satisfy me with the fat of your animals.
Instead you burdened me with your sins;
you wore me out with the wrongs you committed.
25 And yet, I am the God who forgives your sins,
and I do this because of who I am.
I will not hold your sins against you.

26 "Let us go to court; bring your accusation!
Present your case to prove you are in the right!
27 Your earliest ancestor[i] sinned;
your leaders sinned against me,
28 and your rulers profaned[j] my sanctuary.
So I brought destruction on Israel;
I let my own people be insulted."

The LORD Is the Only God

44 The LORD says,
"Listen now, Israel, my servant,
my chosen people, the descendants of Jacob.
2 I am the LORD who created you;
from the time you were born, I have helped you.
Do not be afraid; you are my servant,
my chosen people whom I love.

3 "I will give water to the thirsty land
and make streams flow on the dry ground.
I will pour out my spirit on your children
and my blessing on your descendants.
4 They will thrive like well-watered grass,
like willows by streams of running water.

5 "One by one, people will say, 'I am the LORD's.'
They will come to join the people of Israel.
Each one will mark the name of the LORD on his arm
and call himself one of God's people."

6 The LORD, who rules and protects Israel,
the LORD Almighty, has this to say:
"I am the first, the last, the only God;
there is no other god but me.
7 Could anyone else have done what I did?
Who could have predicted all that would happen
from the very beginning to the end of time?[k]
8 Do not be afraid, my people!
You know that from ancient times until now
I have predicted all that would happen,
and you are my witnesses.
Is there any other god?
Is there some powerful god I never heard of?"

Idolatry Is Ridiculed

9 All those who make idols are worthless, and the gods they prize so highly are useless. Those who worship these gods are blind and ignorant—and they will be disgraced. 10 It's no good making a metal image to worship as a god! 11 Everyone who worships it will be humiliated. The people who make idols are human beings and nothing more. Let them come and stand trial—they will be terrified and will suffer disgrace.

12 The metalworker takes a piece of metal and works with it over a fire. His strong arm swings a hammer to pound the metal into shape. As he works, he gets hungry, thirsty, and tired.

13 The carpenter measures the wood. He outlines a figure with chalk, carves it out with his tools, and makes it in the

[i] YOUR EARLIEST ANCESTOR: *A reference either to Jacob or to Abraham, or possibly to Adam.*
[j] *One ancient translation* your rulers profaned; *Hebrew* I profaned the rulers of.
[k] *Verse 7 in Hebrew is unclear.*

44.6: Is 48.12; Rev 1.17, 22.13

form of a man, a handsome **human**
figure, to be placed in his house. 14 He
might cut down cedars to use, or **choose**
oak or cypress wood from the forest. Or
he might plant a laurel-tree and wait for
the rain to make it grow. 15 A man uses
part of a tree for fuel and part of it for
making an **idol**. With one part he builds a
fire to warm himself and bake **bread**;
with the other part he makes a **god** and
worships it. 16 With some of the wood he
makes a fire; he roasts meat, eats it, and
is **satisfied**. He warms himself and says,
"How nice and warm! What a beautiful
fire!" 17 The rest of the wood he makes
into an **idol**, and then he **bows down** and
worships it. He **prays** to it and says, "You
are my **god**—**save** me!"

18 Such people are too **stupid** to know
what they are doing. They close their
eyes and their **minds** to the **truth**. 19 The
maker of **idols** hasn't the wit or the **sense**
to say, "Some of the wood I burnt up. I
baked some **bread** on the embers and I
roasted meat and ate it. And the rest of
the wood I made into an **idol**. Here I am
bowing down to a block of wood!"

20 It makes as much **sense**[l] as eating
ashes. His **foolish ideas** have so **misled**
him that he is beyond **help**. He won't **admit** to himself that the **idol** he holds in his
hand is not a **god** at all.

The Lord, the Creator and Saviour

21 The Lord says,
"Israel, **remember** this;
remember that you are my **servant**.
I **created** you to be my **servant**,
and I will never **forget** you.
22 I have swept your sins away like a
cloud.
Come back to me; I am the one who
saves you."

23 Shout for **joy**, you **heavens**!
Shout, deep places of the earth!
Shout for **joy**, mountains, and every
tree of the forest!
The Lord has shown his greatness
by **saving his people** Israel.

24 "I am the Lord, your **saviour**;
I am the one who **created** you.
I am the Lord, the **Creator** of all
things.
I **alone** stretched out the **heavens**;
when I made the earth, no one
helped me.
25 I make **fools of fortune-tellers**
and frustrate the **predictions** of
astrologers.
The **words** of the **wise** I refute
and show that their **wisdom** is
foolishness.
26 But when my **servant** makes a
prediction,
when I send a messenger to **reveal**
my **plans**,
I make those **plans** and **predictions**
come **true**.
I tell Jerusalem that people will live
there again,
and the cities of Judah that they will
be rebuilt.
Those cities will **rise** from the **ruins**.
27 With a **word** of **command** I dry up the
ocean.
28 I say to Cyrus, 'You are the one who
will rule for me;
you will do what I want you to do:
you will order Jerusalem to be
rebuilt
and the **Temple** foundations to be
laid.' "

The Lord Appoints Cyrus

45 The Lord has **chosen** Cyrus to be
king!
He has appointed him to **conquer**
nations;
he sends him to **strip** kings of their
power;
the Lord will open the gates of cities
for him.
To Cyrus the Lord says,
2 "I myself will prepare your way,
levelling mountains and hills.
I will break down bronze gates
and smash their iron bars.
3 I will give you treasures from **dark**,
secret places;
then you will know that I am the
Lord,
and that the God of Israel has called
you by name.
4 I appoint you to **help** my **servant**
Israel,
the people that I have **chosen**.
I have given you great **honour**,
although you do not know me.

5 "I am the Lord; there is no other **god**.
I will give you the **strength** you **need**,
although you do not know me.
6 I do this so that everyone
from one end of the **world** to the
other
may know that I am the Lord
and that there is no other **god**.
7 I create both **light** and **darkness**;
I bring both **blessing** and **disaster**.
I, the Lord, do all these things.

[l] It makes as much sense; *or* It will do as much good.

44.25: 1 Cor 1.20 **44.28:** 2 Chr 36.23; Ezra 1.2

power [2] 44.8; 47.6
praise 43.20; 48.9
pray 44.17; 46.7
predict 44.7; 46.10
present (1) [2] 43.26; 48.13
promise [2] 42.16; 49.7
purpose [2] 26.3; 53.10
question 41.28; Jer 12.1
require Ps 51.6; Jer 5.4
rescue 42.22; 46.4
right (1) [2] 43.9; 48.6
right (3) 32.7; Jer 5.28
save [5] 44.17; 46.2
secret [2] 29.15; Jer 13.17
servant 44.1; 48.20
slave 31.8; 47.1
solemn 19.21; 62.8
strength [2] 42.1; 49.4
strip (1) 32.11; 47.2
suffer 44.11; 47.8
true 44.26; 48.16
truth 44.18; 58.3
try (2) 44.11; Jer 22.16
turn 43.14; 47.2
victory [3] 41.2; 46.12
vow Prov 2.17; Jer 44.24
world [2] 43.6; 49.6

8 I will send **victory** from the sky like
rain;
the earth will open to receive it
and will blossom with **freedom** and
justice.
I, the LORD, will make this happen."

The LORD of Creation and History

9 Does a clay pot **dare** to **argue** with its
maker,
a pot that is like all the others?
Does the clay ask the potter what he is
doing?
Does the pot **complain** that its
maker has no skill?
10 Does anyone **dare** to say to his parents,
"Why did you make me like this?"
11 The LORD, the **holy** God of Israel,
the one who shapes the future, says:
"You have no **right** to **question** me
about my children
or to tell me what I ought to do!
12 I am the one who made the earth
and **created mankind** to live there.
By my **power** I stretched out the
heavens;
I **control** the sun, the moon, and the
stars.
13 I myself have stirred Cyrus to **action**
to **fulfil** my **purpose** and put things
right.
I will straighten every road that he
travels.
He will rebuild my city, Jerusalem,
and set my **captive** people **free**.
No one has hired him or **bribed** him to
do this."
The LORD **Almighty** has spoken.

14 The LORD says to Israel,
"The wealth of Egypt and Sudan will
be yours,
and the tall men of Seba will be your
slaves;
they will follow you in chains.
They will **bow down** to you and
confess,
'God is with you—he **alone** is God.
15 The God of Israel, who **saves his
people**,
is a God who conceals himself.
16 Those who make **idols** will all be
ashamed;
all of them will be **disgraced**.
17 But Israel is **saved** by the LORD,
and her **victory lasts** for ever;
her people will never be
disgraced.' "

18 The LORD **created** the **heavens**—
he is the one who is God!
He formed and made the earth—
he made it firm and **lasting**.
He did not make it a **desolate** waste,
but a place for people to live in.
It is he who says, "I am the LORD,
and there is no other **god**.
19 I have not spoken in **secret**
or kept my **purpose** hidden.
I did not **require** the people of Israel
to look for me in a **desolate** waste.
I am the LORD, and I speak the **truth**;
I make known what is **right**."

The LORD of the World and the Idols of Babylon

20 The LORD says,
"Come together, people of the nations,
all who survive the fall of the
empire;
present yourselves for the **trial**!
The people who parade with their **idols**
of wood
and **pray** to **gods** that cannot **save**
them—
those people know nothing at all!
21 Come and **present** your **case** in **court**;
let the defendants **consult** one
another.
Who **predicted** long ago what would
happen?
Was it not I, the LORD, the God who
saves his people?
There is no other **god**.

22 "**Turn** to me now and be **saved**,
people all over the **world**!
I am the only God there is.
23 My **promise** is **true**,
and it will not be **changed**.
I **solemnly promise** by all that I am:
Everyone will come and **kneel**
before me
and **vow** to be **loyal** to me.

24 "They will say that only through me
are **victory** and **strength** to be found;
but all who **hate** me will **suffer**
disgrace.
25 I, the LORD, will **rescue** all the
descendants of Jacob,
and they will give me **praise**.

46 "This is the end for Babylon's
gods!
Bel and Nebo once were
worshipped,
but now they are loaded on donkeys,
a **burden** for the backs of tired
animals.
2 The **idols** cannot **save** themselves;
they are captured and carried away.
This is the end for Babylon's **gods**!

acknowledge 33.13; 52.6
alone 45.14; 48.11
bow (2) 45.14; 49.7
burden 43.23; Jer 23.33
care [3] 42.23; 53.8
compare 40.18; Jer 23.28
disaster 45.7; 47.11
fail 42.16; 50.2
god (2) (other gods) [3] 45.5; 48.14
God's people 45.15; 47.6

45.9: Rom 9.20 **45.23:** Rom 14.11; Phil 2.10–11

help 45.4; 47.12
honour 45.4; 49.5
idol 45.16; 48.5
intend 28.21; Jer 13.11
plan [2] 44.26; 55.11
pray 45.20; 53.12
predict 45.21; 48.3
remember [2] 44.21; 56.5
rescue 45.25; 49.24
save [3] 45.15; 47.13
stubborn Prov 29.1; 48.4
triumph 41.2; Jer 19.7
victory [2] 45.8; 48.18
worship (2) (of other gods) [2] 44.9; 57.5

3 "Listen to me, descendants of Jacob,
all who are left of **my people**.
I have **cared** for you from the time you
were born.
4 I am your God and will take **care** of
you
until you are old and your hair is
grey.
I made you and will **care** for you;
I will give you **help** and **rescue** you.

5 "With whom will you **compare** me?"
says the LORD.
"Is there anyone else like me?
6 People open their purses and pour out
gold;
they weigh out silver on the scales.
They hire a goldsmith to make a **god**;
then they **bow down** and **worship** it!
7 They lift it to their shoulders and carry
it;
they put it in place, and there it
stands,
unable to move from where it is.
If anyone **prays** to it, it cannot answer
or **save** him from **disaster**.

8 "**Remember** this, you sinners;
consider what I have done.
9 **Remember** what happened long ago;
acknowledge that I **alone** am God
and that there is no one else like me.
10 From the beginning I **predicted** the
outcome;
long ago I foretold what would
happen.
I said that my **plans** would never **fail**,
that I would do everything I
intended to do.
11 I am calling a man to come from the
east;[m]
he will swoop down like a hawk
and accomplish what I have
planned.
I have spoken, and it will be done.

12 "Listen to me, you **stubborn** people
who think that **victory** is far away.
13 I am bringing the day of **victory**
near—
it is not far away at all.
My **triumph** will not be delayed.
I will **save** Jerusalem
and bring **honour** to Israel there."

Judgement on Babylon

advice 40.13; Jer 38.15
Almighty 45.13; 48.2
anger 42.25; 48.9
claim 37.6; 48.1

47 The LORD says,
"Babylon, come down from your
throne,
and sit in the dust on the ground.
You were once like a **virgin**, a city
unconquered,
but you are soft and delicate no
longer!
You are now a **slave**!
2 **Turn** the millstone! Grind the flour!
Off with your veil! **Strip** off your fine
clothes!
Lift up your skirts to cross the
streams![n]
3 People will see you **naked**;
they will see you **humbled** and
shamed.
I will take vengeance, and no one will
stop me."

4 The **holy** God of Israel **sets us free**—
his **name** is the LORD **Almighty**.

5 The LORD says to Babylon,
"Sit in silence and **darkness**;
no more will they call you the queen
of nations!
6 I was **angry** with **my people**;
I treated them as no longer mine:
I put them in your **power**,
and you showed them no **mercy**;
even the aged you treated harshly.
7 You thought you would always be a
queen,
and did not take these things to
heart
or think how it all would end.

8 "Listen to this, you lover of **pleasure**,
you that think you are **safe** and
secure.
You **claim** you are as great as God—
that there is no one else like you.
You thought that you would never be a
widow
or **suffer** the **loss** of your children.
9 But in a moment, in a single day,
both of these things will happen.
In spite of all the **magic** you use,
you will lose your husband and
children.

10 "You felt **sure** of yourself in your **evil**;
you thought that no one could see
you.
Your **wisdom** and **knowledge** led you
astray,
and you said to yourself, 'I am God—
there is no one else like me.'
11 **Disaster** will come upon you,
and none of your **magic** can stop it.
Ruin will come on you suddenly—
ruin you never **dreamt** of!

conquer 45.1; Jer 13.21
consult 45.21; 65.4
dark 45.3; 49.9
disaster 46.7; 51.19
dream 29.7; 56.10
enemy 42.13; 59.18
evil 33.15; 53.5
free 45.8; 48.20
fright 41.5; 59.11
God's people 46.3; 48.21
heart 38.15; 51.7
heaven 45.12; 48.13
help 46.4; 49.8
holy 45.11; 48.2
humble 29.19; 49.23
knowledge 33.6; Dan 1.17
life (1) 43.4; 51.14
loss Ps 144.14; Hos 10.5
magic [3] 3.3; Jer 27.9
mercy 33.2; 55.7
naked 20.2; Lam 1.8
name (2) (name of God, of Jesus) 44.5; 48.1
pleasure 11.3; 58.2
power [2] 45.1; 48.16
ruin 44.26; 49.19
safe 41.3; 48.22
save [3] 46.2; 48.17
secure 39.8; Jer 22.23
shame 41.11; 61.7
slave 45.14; 50.1
strip (1) 45.1; Jer 5.10
study Ecc 12.9; Ezek 43.10
suffer 45.24; 48.10
sure Ecc 3.21; 48.19
throne 40.22; 52.2
turn 45.22; 50.2
virgin Esth 2.2; 62.5
widow 10.2; 54.4
wisdom 44.25; Jer 3.15

[m] A MAN TO COME FROM THE EAST: *See 41.2.*
[n] CROSS THE STREAMS: *This probably refers to going into exile.*

47.1-15: Is 13.1–14.23; Jer 50.1, 51.64 **47.8-9:** Rev 18.7–8

12 Keep all your **magic** spells and
charms;
you have used them since you were
young.
Perhaps they will be of some **help** to
you;
perhaps you can **frighten** your
enemies.
13 You are **powerless** in spite of the
advice you get.
Let your astrologers come forward
and **save** you—
those people who **study** the stars,
who map out the zones of the
heavens
and tell you from month to month
what[x] is going to happen to you.

14 "They will be like bits of straw,
and a fire will burn them up!
They will not even be able to **save**
themselves—
the flames will be too hot for them,
not a cosy fire to warm themselves
by.
15 That is all the good they will do you—
those astrologers you've **consulted**
all your **life**.
They all will leave you and go their
own way,
and none will be left to **save** you."

God Is LORD of the Future

48 Listen to this, people of Israel,
you that are descended from
Judah:
You **swear** by the **name of the LORD**
and **claim** to **worship** the God of
Israel—
but you don't mean a **word** you say.
2 And yet you are **proud** to say
that you are citizens of the **holy city**
and that you **depend** on Israel's God,
whose **name** is the LORD **Almighty**.

3 The LORD says to Israel,
"Long ago I **predicted** what would take
place;
then suddenly I made it happen.
4 I knew that you would **prove** to be
stubborn,
as rigid as iron and unyielding as
bronze.
5 And so I **predicted** your future long
ago,
announcing events before they took
place,
to **prevent** you from **claiming**
that your **idols** and **images** made
them happen.
6 "All I foretold has now taken place;
you have to **admit** my **predictions**
were **right**.
Now I will tell you of **new** things to
come,
events that I did not **reveal** before.
7 Only now am I making them happen;
nothing like this took place in the
past.
If it had, you would **claim** that you
knew all about it.
8 I knew that you couldn't be **trusted**,
that you have always been known as
a **rebel**.
That is why you never heard of this at
all,
why no **word** of it ever came to your
ears.

9 "In order that people will **praise** my
name,
I am holding my **anger** in check;
I am keeping it back and will not
destroy you.
10 I have **tested** you in the fire of
suffering,
as silver is **refined** in a furnace.
But I have found that you are
worthless.
11 What I do is done for my own **sake**—
I will not let my **name** be
dishonoured
or let anyone else **share** the **glory**
that should be mine and mine
alone."

Cyrus, the LORD's Chosen Leader

12 The LORD says,
"Listen to me, Israel, the people I have
called!
I am God, the first, the **last**, the only
God!
13 My hands made the earth's
foundations
and spread the **heavens** out.
When I summon earth and sky,
they come at once and **present**
themselves.

14 "Assemble and listen, all of you!
None of the **gods** could **predict**
that the man I have **chosen** would
attack Babylon;
he will do what I want him to do.
15 I am the one who spoke and called
him;
I led him out and gave him **success**.

16 "Now come close to me and hear what
I say.

[x] *Some ancient translations* what; *Hebrew* from what.

48.12: Is 44.6; Rev 1.17, 22.13

admit (1) 44.20; Jer 3.13
Almighty 47.4; 51.15
alone 46.9; 49.21
anger 47.6; 51.17
announce 40.9; 52.7
bless 45.7; 51.2
choose 45.1; 49.1
claim [3] 47.8; 58.2
command 44.27; 50.2
depend 28.15; 59.4
destroy [2] 43.17; 49.17
direct Prov 21.1; Hab 1.14
dishonour Prov 6.33; Jer 34.16
free 47.4; 49.9
glad 35.10; 51.3
glory 43.7; 55.5
god (2) (other gods) 46.1; 57.5
God's people 47.6; 49.5
heaven 47.13; 49.13
holy [2] 47.4; 49.7
idol 46.2; 57.8
image 44.10; Jer 50.2
last (2) 44.6; Jer 25.19
name (2) (name of God, of Jesus) [4] 47.4; 51.15
new 43.19; 60.3
power 47.6; 49.26
praise 45.25; 49.3
predict [4] 46.10; Jer 14.14
present (1) 45.20; 66.3

prevent 32.7; Jer 11.15
proud 37.29; 49.18
prove 43.9; 50.8
rebel 36.5; 50.5
refine 1.25; Jer 6.29
reveal 44.26; 60.21
right (1) 45.13; 51.7
safe 47.8; 54.14
sake 37.35; 53.11
save [2] 47.13; 49.6
servant 45.4; 49.1
share 42.8; 53.12
Sovereign 40.10; 49.22
stubborn 46.12; 57.1
succeed (1) 28.29; 52.13
suffer [2] 47.8; 49.13
sure 47.10; 49.18
swear 14.24; 65.16
teach 42.4; 50.4
test 7.12; Jer 6.27
true 45.23; Jer 1.12
trust 42.17; 49.4
victory 46.12; 51.5
word (1) [3] 44.25; 49.2
worship (1) (of God 43.22; 56.3
worthless 44.9; Jer 2.5

From the beginning I have spoken
openly,
and have always made my **words**
come **true**."
(Now the **Sovereign** LORD has given me
his **power** and sent me.)

The LORD's Plan for His People

17 The **holy** God of Israel,
the LORD who **saves** you, says:
"I am the LORD your God,
the one who wants to **teach** you for
your own good
and **direct** you in the way you should
go.

18 "If only you had listened to my
commands!
Then **blessings** would have flowed for
you
like a stream that never goes dry!
Victory would have come to you
like the waves that roll on the shore.
19 Your descendants would be as
numerous as grains of sand,
and I would have made **sure** they
were never **destroyed**."

20 Go out from Babylon, go **free**!
Shout the news **gladly**; make it known
everywhere:
"The LORD has **saved** his **servant**
Israel!"
21 When the LORD led **his people** through
a hot, dry desert,
they did not **suffer** from thirst.
He made water come from a rock for
them;
he split the rock open, and water
flowed out.

22 "There is no **safety** for sinners," says
the LORD.

Israel, A Light to the Nations

49 Listen to me, distant nations,
you people who live far away!
Before I was born, the LORD **chose** me
and appointed me to be his **servant**.
2 He made my **words** as sharp as a
sword.
With his own hand he **protected**
me.[o]
He made me like an arrow,
sharp and ready for use.
3 He said to me, "*Israel*, you are my
servant;
because of you, people will **praise**
me."
4 I said, "I have worked, but how
hopeless it is!
I have used up my **strength**, but have
accomplished nothing."
Yet I can **trust** the LORD to **defend** my
cause;
he will **reward** me for what I do.

5 Before I was born, the LORD appointed
me;
he made me his **servant** to bring
back **his people**,
to bring back the **scattered** people of
Israel.
The LORD gives me **honour**;
he is the **source** of my **strength**.

6 The LORD said to me,
"I have a greater **task** for you, my
servant.
Not only will you **restore** to
greatness
the people of Israel who have
survived,
but I will also make you a **light** to the
nations—
so that all the **world** may be **saved**."

7 Israel's **holy** God and **saviour** says
to the one who is deeply **despised**,
who is **hated** by the nations
and is the **servant** of rulers:
"Kings will see you released
and will **rise** to show their **respect**;
princes also will see it,
and they will **bow** low to **honour**
you."

This will happen because the LORD has
chosen his **servant**;
the **holy** God of Israel keeps his
promises.

The Restoration of Jerusalem

8 The LORD says to **his people**,
"When the time comes to **save** you, I
will show you **favour**
and answer your cries for **help**.
I will guard and **protect** you
and through you make a **covenant**
with all peoples.
I will let you settle once again
in your land that is now laid waste.
9 I will say to the **prisoners**, 'Go **free**!'
and to those who are in **darkness**,
'Come out to the **light**!'
They will be like **sheep** that graze on
the hills;
10 they will never be **hungry** or thirsty.
Sun and desert heat will not **hurt** them,

[o] With his own hand...me; *or* He kept me hidden in his hand.

48.20: Rev 18.4 **48.22:** Is 57.21 **49.1:** Jer 1.5 **49.2:** Heb 4.12; Rev 1.16
49.6: Is 42.6; Lk 2.32; Acts 13.47, 26.23 **49.8:** 2 Cor 6.2 **49.10:** Rev 7.16–17

abandon 41.17; 57.17
alone 48.11; Jer 2.3
bow (2) [2] 46.6; 58.5
bride Song 5.1; 61.10
cause (2) Ps 140.12; Jer 11.20
choose [2] 48.14; 61.1
comfort 40.1; 52.9
covenant 42.6; 55.3
dark 47.5; 50.3
defend 37.35; 50.9
desolate 45.18; 60.15
despise 37.22; 53.3
destroy 48.9; 50.11
disappoint Ps 119.116; Jer 2.36
each other 34.14; Jer 23.30
exile [2] 27.8; 56.8
favour Prov 19.6; 58.8
forget [4] 44.21; 51.13
free [2] 48.20; 51.11
God's people [6] 48.21; 50.1
hate 45.24; 60.15
heaven 48.13; 51.6
help [2] 47.12; 50.7
holy [2] 48.2; 52.1
honour [3] 46.13; 50.10
hope 42.4; 51.5
humble 47.3; 53.7
hunger 44.12; 55.2
hurt 43.2; 50.7
joy 44.23; 51.3
light (1) [2] 45.7; 51.4
love [2] 44.2; 54.7
mankind 45.12; 66.24
need 45.5; 51.14
oppress 29.20; 51.13
pity 30.18; Jer 13.14
power 48.16; 51.9
praise 48.9; 51.3
prison [3] 42.7; 51.14
promise 45.23; 54.9
protect [2] 44.6; 51.16
proud 48.2; 61.6
rage 37.28; Jer 2.30
rescue [2] 46.4; 51.11
respect [2] 37.23; 60.14
restore Song 2.5; 57.15
reward Ecc 9.5; 61.8
rise 44.26; 52.2
ruin [2] 47.11; 51.3
save [3] 48.17; 50.2
Saviour 44.24; Hos 13.4
scatter 41.2; Jer 8.3
servant [6] 48.20; 50.10
sheep 43.23; 53.6
source 22.23; Jer 33.9
Sovereign 48.16; 50.4
strength [2] 45.5; 50.4
suffer 48.10; 50.11
sure 48.19; 52.11
task Num 4.19; 52.13
trust 48.8; 50.10
word (1) 48.1; 50.10
world 45.6; 52.10

for they will be led by one who **loves** them.
He will lead them to springs of water.

11 "I will make a highway across the mountains
and prepare a road for **my people** to travel.
12 **My people** will come from far away,
from the north and the west,
and from Aswan[p] in the south."

13 Sing, **heavens**! Shout for **joy**, earth!
Let the mountains burst into song!
The LORD will **comfort his people**;
he will have **pity** on his **suffering** people.

14 But the people of Jerusalem said,
"The LORD has **abandoned** us!
He has **forgotten** us."
15 So the LORD answers,
"Can a woman **forget** her own baby
and not **love** the child she bore?
Even if a mother should **forget** her child,
I will never **forget** you.
16 Jerusalem, I can never forget you!
I have written your name on the palms of my hands.

17 "Those who will rebuild you are coming soon,
and those who **destroyed** you will leave.
18 Look around and see what is happening!
Your people are assembling—they are coming home!
As **surely** as I am the living God,
you will be **proud** of your people,
as proud as a **bride** is of her jewels.

19 "Your country was **ruined** and **desolate**—
but now it will be too small
for those who are coming to live there.
And those who left you in **ruins**
will be far removed from you.
20 Your people who were born in **exile**
will one day say to you,
'This land is too small—
we **need** more room to live in!'
21 Then you will say to yourself,
'Who bore all these children for me?
I lost my children and could have no more.
I was **exiled** and driven away—
who brought these children up?
I was left all **alone**—
where did these children come from?'"

22 The **Sovereign** LORD says to **his people**:
"I will signal to the nations,
and they will bring your children home.
23 Kings will be like fathers to you;
queens will be like mothers.
They will **bow** low before you and **honour** you;
they will **humbly** show their **respect** for you.
Then you will know that I am the LORD;
no one who waits for my **help** will be **disappointed**."

24 Can you take away a soldier's loot?
Can you **rescue** the **prisoners** of a tyrant?

25 The LORD replies,
"That is just what is going to happen.
The soldier's **prisoners** will be taken away,
and the tyrant's loot will be seized.
I will fight against whoever fights you,
and I will **rescue** your children.
26 I will make your **oppressors** kill **each other**;
they will be drunk with murder and **rage**.
Then all **mankind** will know that I am the LORD,
the one who **saves** you and **sets you free**.
They will know that I am Israel's **powerful** God."

50

The LORD says,
"Do you think I sent **my people** away
like a man who **divorces** his wife?
Where, then, are the papers of **divorce**?
Do you think I sold you into **captivity**
like a man who sells his children as **slaves**?
No, you went away **captive** because of your sins;
you were sent away because of your **crimes**.

2 "Why did **my people fail** to respond
when I went to them to **save** them?
Why did they not answer when I called?
Am I too **weak** to **save** them?
I can dry up the sea with a **command**
and **turn** rivers into a desert,

accuse [2] 43.26; 54.17
captive [2] 45.13; 52.2
charge (3) Job 31.35; Jer 2.9
command 48.18; Jer 1.7
court (1) 45.21; 59.4
crime 29.21; 53.9
dare 45.9; Jer 6.25
dark [2] 49.9; 58.10
dead 38.18; 65.4
defend 49.4; 51.22
destroy 49.17; 51.13
disgrace 45.16; 54.4
divorce [2] Ezra 10.19; Jer 3.1
eager 42.4; 58.2
endure 40.7; 51.8
fail 46.10; 55.11
fate 24.2; 53.8
God's people [2] 49.5; 51.4
guilty 30.13; 59.3
help 49.8; 51.1
honour 49.5; 52.13
hurt 49.10; 54.17
innocent 5.23; 59.7
insult [2] 43.28; 51.7
misery Ecc 4.8; Jer 49.24

[p] ASWAN: *A city in southern Egypt, where a large Jewish community had settled.*

mourn 22.12; 57.18
obey 42.24; 58.2
plot (1) [2] 32.7; 59.5
prove [2] 48.4; Jer 3.11
rebel 48.8; 59.13
rely 36.6; Ezek 29.6
save [2] 49.6; 51.1
servant 49.1; 52.13
slave 47.1; 52.3
Sovereign [3] 49.22; 52.3
strength 49.4; 51.12
suffer 49.13; 51.21
teach [2] 48.17; 51.4
trust 49.4; 57.13
turn [3] 47.2; 54.8
understand 43.10; 52.15
vanish 29.7; 51.8
weak 41.14; 51.20
word (1) 49.2; 53.7

so that the fish in them die for lack
of water.
3 I can make the sky turn dark,
as if it were in mourning for the
dead."

The Obedience of the LORD's Servant

4 The Sovereign LORD has taught me
what to say,
so that I can strengthen the weary.
Every morning he makes me eager
to hear what he is going to teach
me.
5 The LORD has given me
understanding,
and I have not rebelled
or turned away from him.
6 I bared my back to those who beat me.
I did not stop them when they
insulted me,
when they pulled out the hairs of my
beard
and spat in my face.

7 But their insults cannot hurt me
because the Sovereign LORD gives
me help.
I brace myself to endure them.
I know that I will not be disgraced,
8 for God is near,
and he will prove me innocent.
Does anyone dare to bring charges
against me?
Let us go to court together!
Let him bring his accusation!
9 The Sovereign LORD himself defends
me—
who, then, can prove me guilty?
All my accusers will disappear;
they will vanish like moth-eaten
cloth.

10 All of you that honour the LORD
and obey the words of his servant,
the path you walk may be dark indeed,
but trust in the LORD, rely on your
God.
11 All of you that plot to destroy others
will be destroyed by your own plots.
The LORD himself will make this
happen;
you will suffer a miserable fate.

Words of Comfort to Jerusalem

afraid 44.2; 54.4
Almighty 48.2; 54.5
ancient 44.8; 64.5
anger [3] 48.9; 54.8
bless 48.18; 55.3
compassion 30.19; 63.9
constant Prov 15.15; 63.7

51 The LORD says,
"Listen to me, you that want to
be saved,
you that come to me for help.
Think of the rock from which you
came,
the quarry from which you were
dug.
2 Think of your ancestor, Abraham,
and of Sarah, from whom you are
descended.
When I called Abraham, he was
childless,
but I blessed him and gave him
children;
I made his descendants numerous.

3 "I will show compassion to Jerusalem,
to all who live in her ruins.
Though her land is a desert, I will
make it a garden,
like the garden I planted in Eden.
Joy and gladness will be there,
and songs of praise and thanks to
me.

4 "Listen to me, my people,
listen to what I say:
I give my teaching to the nations;
my laws will bring them light.
5 I will come quickly and save them;
the time of my victory is near.
I myself will rule over the nations.
Distant lands wait for me to come;
they wait with hope for me to save
them.
6 Look up at the heavens; look at the
earth!
The heavens will disappear like
smoke;
the earth will wear out like old
clothing,
and all its people will die like flies.
But the deliverance I bring will last for
ever;
my victory will be final.

7 "Listen to me, you that know what is
right,
who have my teaching fixed in your
hearts.
Do not be afraid when people taunt
and insult you;
8 they will vanish like moth-eaten
clothing!
But the deliverance I bring will last for
ever;
my victory will endure for all time."

9 Wake up, LORD, and help us!
Use your power and save us;
use it as you did in ancient times.
It was you that cut the sea-monster
Rahab[q] to pieces.
10 It was you also who dried up the sea
and made a path through the water,

cup [2] 40.12; Jer 25.15
defend 50.9; 54.17
destroy 50.11; 59.7
devastate 24.1; Jer 9.12
disaster 47.11; 65.23
endure [2] 50.7; 53.3
fear [2] 41.5; 59.19
final Ecc 12.5; Ezek 21.25
force (1) 42.25; 52.4
forget 49.14; 54.4
free [2] 49.9; 52.2
fury [2] 13.9; Jer 21.5
glad [2] 48.20; 61.3
God's people [2] 50.1; 52.3
grief 37.1; 60.20
happy 41.16; 65.13
heart 47.7; 61.1
heaven [4] 49.13; 55.9
help [2] 50.7; 57.12
hope 49.4; 57.15
insult 50.6; Jer 15.15
joy [2] 49.13; 52.8
last (1) [2] 45.17; 55.3
law 42.21; 58.2
life (1) 47.15; 53.10
light (1) 49.6; 59.9
monster 34.14; Jer 51.34
mortal 2.22; Jer 17.5
name (2) (name of God, of Jesus) 48.1; 54.5
need 49.20; 58.10
oppress [2] 49.26; 54.14
power 49.26; 52.10
praise 49.3; 60.18
prison 49.9; 61.1
protect 49.2; 52.12
punish 40.2; 53.4
rescue 49.24; 52.9
right (1) 48.6; 54.14
ruin 49.19; 52.9
save [5] 50.2; 52.10
sorrow 35.10; 61.3
strength 50.4; 54.2
suffer 50.11; 53.3
sympathy Ps 69.20; Jer 16.7
teach [3] 50.4; 54.13
thank 12.4; Jer 33.11
vanish 50.9; Ezek 27.34
victory [3] 48.18; 52.7
weak 50.2; 57.10

[q] RAHAB: *A legendary sea-monster, which represented the forces of chaos and evil, and was sometimes a symbol of Egypt.*

50.6: Mt 26.67; Mk 14.65 **50.8–9:** Rom 8.33–34

so that those you were **saving** could
cross.
11 Those whom you have **rescued**
will reach Jerusalem with **gladness**,
singing and shouting for **joy**.
They will be **happy** for ever,
for ever **free** from **sorrow** and **grief**.

12 The LORD says,
"I am the one who **strengthens** you.
Why should you **fear mortal** man,
who is no more **enduring** than
grass?
13 Have you **forgotten** the LORD who
made you,
who stretched out the **heavens**
and laid the earth's foundations?
Why should you live in **constant fear**
of the **fury** of those who **oppress** you,
of those who are ready to **destroy**
you?
Their **fury** can no longer touch you.
14 Those who are **prisoners** will soon be
set free;
they will live a long **life**
and have all the food they **need**.

15 "I am the LORD your God;
I stir up the sea
and make its waves roar.
My **name** is the LORD **Almighty**!
16 I stretched out[r] the **heavens**
and laid the earth's foundations;
I say to Jerusalem, 'You are **my
people**!
I have given you my **teaching**,
and I **protect** you with my hand.' "

The End of Jerusalem's Suffering

17 Jerusalem, wake up!
Rouse yourself and get up!
You have drunk the **cup** of **punishment**
that the LORD in his **anger** gave you
to drink;
you drank it down, and it made you
stagger.
18 There is no one to lead you,
no one among your people
to take you by the hand.

19 A double **disaster** has fallen on you:
your land has been **devastated** by
war,
and your people have starved.
There is no one to show you
sympathy.
20 At the corner of every street
your people collapse from
weakness;
they are like deer caught in a
hunter's net.
They have felt the **force** of **God's**
anger.

21 You **suffering** people of Jerusalem,
you that stagger as though you were
drunk,
22 the LORD your God **defends** you and
says,
"I am taking away the **cup**
that I gave you in my **anger**.
You will no longer have to drink
the wine that makes you stagger.
23 I will give it to those who **oppressed**
you,
to those who made you lie down in
the streets
and trampled on you as if you were
dirt."

God Will Rescue Jerusalem

52 Jerusalem, be **strong** and great
again!
Holy city of God, clothe yourself
with **splendour**!
The **heathen** will never enter your
gates again.
2 Shake yourself **free**, Jerusalem!
Rise from the dust and sit on your
throne!
Undo the chains that **bind** you,
captive people of Zion!

3 The **Sovereign** LORD says to **his**
people, "When you became **slaves**, no
money was paid for you; in the same
way nothing will be paid to **set you free**.
4 When you went to live in Egypt as
foreigners, you did so of your own **free**
will; Assyria, however, took you away by
force and paid nothing for you. 5 And now
in Babylonia the same thing has happened: you are **captives**, and nothing was
paid for you. Those who rule over you
boast and brag and constantly show **contempt** for me. 6 In time to come you will
acknowledge that I am God and that I
have spoken to you."

7 How **wonderful** it is to see
a messenger coming across the
mountains,
bringing **good news**, the news of
peace!
He **announces victory** and says to Zion,
"Your God is king!"
8 Those who guard the city are shouting,
shouting together for **joy**!
They can see with their own eyes
the return of the LORD to Zion!

9 Break into shouts of **joy**,

acknowledge 46.9; 63.16
amaze 25.1; 63.5
announce 48.5; 61.1
bind Ps 149.8; Lam 3.7
boast 37.24; Jer 9.23
captive [2] 50.1; 61.1
comfort 49.13; 54.11
contempt 29.20; 58.9
escape 43.13; Jer 6.1
forbid 5.6; Lam 1.10
force (1) 51.20; Jer 21.2
free [3] 51.11; 58.6
God's people [3] 51.4 55.3
Good News 40.9; 60.
heathen Ps 106.27; Ezek 34.28
holy [3] 49.7; 54.5
honour 50.10; 53.12
human 44.11; 66.3
joy [2] 51.3; 53.11
peace 39.8; 54.10
power 51.9; 53.12
protect 51.16; 58.8
rescue 51.11; 59.16
rise 49.7; Jer 21.13
ruin 51.3; 58.12
save 51.1; 54.5
servant 50.10; 53.2
slave 50.1; Jer 2.14
Sovereign 50.4; 56.8
speech 42.2; Ezek 3.27
splendour 35.2; 63.1
strong 44.12; 54.14
succeed (1) 48.15; 53.10
sure 49.18; 61.11
task 49.6; Rom 15.28
Temple (1) (of God) 44.28; 56.5
throne 47.1; 66.1
understand 50.5; 56.11
victory 51.5; 54.17
will (1) 30.1; 53.2
wonder (1) 9.6; Jer 28.6
world 49.6; 54.5

[r] *One ancient translation* stretched out; *Hebrew* planted.

51.17: Rev 14.10, 16.19 **52.1:** Rev 21.2, 27 **52.5:** Rom 2.24 **52.7:** Nah 1.15; Rom 10.15; Eph 6.15

you **ruins** of Jerusalem!
The LORD will **rescue** his city
and **comfort his people**.
10 The LORD will use his **holy power**;
he will **save his people**,
and all the **world** will see it.
11 Make **sure** you leave Babylonia,
all you that carry the **temple**
equipment!
Touch no **forbidden** thing;[s]
keep yourselves **holy** and leave.
12 This time you will not have to leave in
a hurry;
you will not be trying to **escape**.
The LORD your God will lead you
and **protect** you on every side.

The Suffering Servant

13 The LORD says,
"My **servant** will **succeed** in his **task**;
he will be highly **honoured**.[t]
14 Many people were shocked when they
saw him;
he was so disfigured that he hardly
looked **human**.
15 But now many nations will marvel at
him,
and kings will be **speechless** with
amazement.
They will see and **understand**
something they had never known."

53

The people reply,
"Who would have **believed** what
we now report?
Who could have seen the LORD's
hand in this?
2 It was the **will of the LORD** that his
servant
should grow like a plant taking root
in dry ground.
He had no dignity or beauty
to make us take **notice** of him.
There was nothing attractive about
him,
nothing that would draw us to him.
3 We **despised** him and **rejected** him;
he **endured suffering** and **pain**.
No one would even look at him—
we **ignored** him as if he were
nothing.

4 "But he **endured** the **suffering** that
should have been ours,
the **pain** that we should have borne.
All the while we thought that his
suffering
was **punishment** sent by God.
5 But because of our sins he was
wounded,
beaten because of the **evil** we did.
We are **healed** by the **punishment** he
suffered,
made whole by the blows he
received.
6 All of us were like **sheep** that were lost,
each of us going his own way.
But the LORD made the **punishment**
fall on him,
the **punishment** all of us **deserved**.

7 "He was treated harshly, but **endured**
it **humbly**;
he never said a **word**.
Like a **lamb** about to be **slaughtered**,
like a **sheep** about to be sheared,
he never said a **word**.
8 He was **arrested** and **sentenced** and
led off to die,
and no one **cared** about his **fate**.
He was put **to death** for the sins of our
people.
9 He was placed in a **grave** with **evil**
men,
he was buried with the **rich**,
even though he had never committed
a **crime**
or ever told a **lie**."

10 The LORD says,
"It was my **will** that he should **suffer**;
his **death** was a **sacrifice** to bring
forgiveness.
And so he will see his descendants;
he will live a long **life**,
and through him my **purpose** will
succeed.
11 After a **life** of **suffering**, he will again
have **joy**;
he will know that he did not **suffer** in
vain.
My **devoted servant**, with whom I am
pleased,
will bear the **punishment** of many
and for his **sake** I will **forgive** them.
12 And so I will give him a place of
honour,
a place among great and **powerful**
men.
He willingly gave his **life**
and **shared** the **fate** of **evil** men.
He took the place of many sinners
and **prayed** that they might be
forgiven."[u]

arrest Job 11.10; Jer 36.26
believe 43.10; Jer 7.4
care 46.3; 57.1
crime 50.1; 59.12
death (1) 28.15; 57.2
death (3) (to death) 13.15; 65.15
deserve 10.22; 65.7
despise 49.7; 60.14
devote Ecc 7.25; Hos 10.12
endure [3] 51.8; 64.12
evil [3] 47.10; 56.2
fate [2] 50.11; 65.11
forgive [3] 43.25; 55.7
grave 26.19; Jer 8.1
heal 38.16; 57.18
honour 52.13; 55.5
humble 49.23; 57.15
ignore 30.12; 63.15
joy 52.8; 54.1
lamb 40.11; 65.25
lie (2) 32.7; 57.4
life (1) [3] 51.14; 55.3
notice (1) Ecc 6.1; 58.3
pain [2] 38.13; Jer 4.19
please 42.1; 56.4
power 52.10; 55.4
pray 46.7; 55.6
punish [5] 51.17; 54.9
purpose 45.13; Jer 32.39
reject 41.9; 59.13
rich 32.15; 63.7
sacrifice 43.23; 56.7
sake 48.11; 63.17

sentence Ps 94.21; 65.6
servant [2] 52.13; 54.17
share 48.11; 58.7
sheep [2] 49.9; 60.7
slaughter 34.6; Jer 5.17
succeed (1) 52.13; 65.23
suffer [7] 51.21; 54.11
will (1) [2] 52.4; Jer 29.23
word (1) [2] 50.10; 55.10

[s] FORBIDDEN THING: *Any object that was considered ritually unclean.*
[t] he will be highly honoured; *or* he will be restored to greatness and honour.
[u] prayed that they might be forgiven; *or* suffered the punishment they deserved.

52.11: 2 Cor 6.17 **52.15:** Rom 15.21 **53.1:** Jn 12.38; Rom 10.16 **53.4:** Mt 8.17 **53.5:** 1 Pet 2.24
53.6: 1 Pet 2.25 **53.7:** Rev 5.6 **53.7–8:** Acts 8.32–33 **53.9:** 1 Pet 2.22 **53.12:** Mk 15.28; Lk 22.37

The LORD's Love for Israel

54 Jerusalem, you have been like a
childless woman,
but now you can sing and shout for
joy.
Now you will have more children
than a woman whose husband never
left her!
2 Make the tent you live in larger;
lengthen its ropes and **strengthen**
the pegs!
3 You will extend your boundaries on all
sides;
your people will get back the land
that the other nations now occupy.
Cities now deserted will be filled
with people.

4 Do not be **afraid**—you will not be
disgraced again;
you will not be **humiliated**.
You will **forget** your **unfaithfulness** as
a young wife,
and your **desperate loneliness** as a
widow.
5 Your **Creator** will be like a husband to
you—
the LORD **Almighty** is his **name**.
The **holy** God of Israel will **save** you—
he is the ruler of all the **world**.

6 Israel, you are like a young wife,
deserted by her husband and deeply
distressed.
But the LORD calls you back to him
and says:
7 "For one brief moment I left you;
with deep **love** I will take you back.
8 I **turned** away **angry** for only a
moment,
but I will show you my **love** for
ever."
So says the LORD who **saves** you.

9 "In the time of Noah I **promised**
never again to **flood** the earth.
Now I **promise** not to be **angry** with
you again;
I will not **reprimand** or **punish** you.
10 The mountains and hills may crumble,
but my **love** for you will never end;
I will keep for ever my **promise** of
peace."
So says the LORD who **loves** you.

The Future Jerusalem

11 The LORD says,
"O Jerusalem, you **suffering, helpless**
city,
with no one to **comfort** you,
I will rebuild your foundations with
precious stones.
12 I will build your towers with rubies,
your gates with stones that glow like
fire,
and the wall around you with jewels.

13 "I myself will **teach** your people,
and give them **prosperity** and **peace**.
14 **Justice** and **right** will make you **strong**.
You will be **safe** from **oppression**
and **terror**.
15 If anyone attacks you,
he does it without my consent;
whoever fights against you will fall.

16 "I **create** the blacksmith,
who builds a fire and forges
weapons.
I also **create** the soldier,
who uses the weapons to kill.
17 But no weapon will be able to **hurt** you;
you will have an answer for all who
accuse you.
I will **defend** my **servants**
and give them **victory**."
The LORD has spoken.

God's Offer of Mercy

55 The LORD says,
"Come, everyone who is
thirsty—
here is water!
Come, you that have no money—
buy corn and eat!
Come! Buy wine and milk—
it will cost you nothing!
2 Why spend money on what does not
satisfy?
Why spend your **wages** and still be
hungry?
Listen to me and do what I say,
and you will **enjoy** the **best** food of
all.

3 "Listen now, **my people**, and come to
me;
come to me, and you will have **life**!
I will make a **lasting covenant** with
you
and give you the **blessings** I
promised to David.
4 I made him a leader and commander
of nations,
and through him I showed them my
power.
5 Now you will summon foreign nations;
at one time they did not know you,
but now they will come running to
join you!

54.1: Gal 4.27 **54.9:** Gen 9.8–17 **54.11–12:** Rev 21.18–21 **54.13:** Jn 6.45 **55.1:** Rev 21.6; 22.17
55.3: Acts 13.34

I, the LORD your God, the **holy** God of
Israel,
will make all this happen;
I will give you **honour** and **glory**."

6 **Turn to** the LORD and **pray** to him,
now that he is near.
7 Let the **wicked** leave their way of **life**
and **change** their way of thinking.
Let them **turn to** the LORD, our God;
he is **merciful** and quick to **forgive**.
8 "My thoughts," says the LORD, "are not
like yours,
and my **ways** are different from
yours.
9 As high as the **heavens** are above the
earth,
so high are my **ways** and thoughts
above yours.

10 "My **word** is like the snow and the rain
that come down from the sky to
water the earth.
They make the crops grow
and **provide seed** for **sowing** and
food to eat.
11 So also will be the **word** that I speak—
it will not **fail** to do what I **plan** for it;
it will do everything I send it to do.

12 "You will leave Babylon with **joy**;
you will be led out of the city in
peace.
The mountains and hills will burst into
singing,
and the trees will shout for **joy**.
13 Cypress-trees will grow where now
there are briars;
myrtle-trees will come up in place of
thorns.
This will be a **sign** that will **last** for
ever,
a **reminder** of what I, the LORD,
have done."

God's People Will Include All Nations

56 The LORD says to **his people**, "Do
what is **just** and **right**, for soon I
will **save** you. 2 I will **bless** those who always **observe** the **Sabbath** and do not
misuse it. I will **bless** those who do
nothing **evil**."
3 A foreigner who has joined the
LORD's people should not say, "The LORD
will not let me **worship** with **his people**."
A man who has been castrated should
never think that because he cannot have
children, he can never be part of **God's**
people. 4 The LORD says to such a man,
"If you **honour** me by **observing** the
Sabbath and if you do what **pleases** me
and **faithfully** keep my **covenant**, 5 then
your name will be **remembered** in my
Temple and among **my people** longer
than if you had sons and daughters. You
will never be **forgotten**."
6 And the LORD says to those
foreigners who become part of **his**
people, who **love** him and **serve** him, who
observe the **Sabbath** and **faithfully** keep
his **covenant**: 7 "I will bring you to Zion,
my **sacred** hill,[v] give you **joy** in my house
of **prayer**, and **accept** the **sacrifices** you
offer on my **altar**. My **Temple** will be
called a house of **prayer** for the people of
all nations."
8 The **Sovereign** LORD, who has
brought **his people** Israel home from
exile, has **promised** that he will bring still
other people to join them.

Israel's Leaders Are Condemned

9 The LORD has told the foreign
nations to come like wild animals and **de-**
vour his people. 10 He says, "All the
leaders, who are supposed to **warn my**
people, are **blind**! They know nothing.
They are like **watchdogs** that don't
bark—they only lie about and **dream**.
How they **love** to sleep! 11 They are like
greedy dogs that never get **enough**.
These leaders have no **understanding**.
Every one of them does as he **pleases**
and **seeks** his own **advantage**. 12 'Let's get
some wine,' these drunkards say, 'and
drink all we can hold! Tomorrow will be
even better than today!' "

Israel's Idolatry Is Condemned

57 Good people die, and no one
understands or even **cares**. But
when they die, no calamity can **hurt**
them. 2 Those who live good **lives** find
peace and rest in **death**.
3 Come here to be **judged**, you sinners! You are no better than sorcerers,
adulterers, and **prostitutes**. 4 Who are you
making fun of? Who are you **liars jeering**
at? 5 You **worship the fertility gods** by
having **sex** under those **sacred** trees of
yours. You **offer your children as sacri-**
fices in the rocky caves near the bed of a
stream. 6 You take smooth stones from
there and **worship them as gods**. You
pour out wine as **offerings** to them and
bring them **grain-offerings**. Do you think
I am **pleased** with all this? 7 You go to
the high mountains to **offer sacrifices**
and have **sex**. 8 You set up your obscene
idols just inside your front doors. You **for-**
sake me; you take off your clothes and
climb into your large beds with your

[v] SACRED HILL: *See 2.3.*

55.10: 2 Cor 9.10 **56.7:** Mt 21.13; Mk 11.17; Lk 19.46

accept 33.15; Jer 3.19
advantage 3.5; Jer 7.6
altar 36.7; 60.7
bless [2] 55.3; 61.9
blind 44.9; 59.10
covenant [2] 55.3; 59.21
devour 9.12; Jer 5.17
dream 47.11; Jer 23.25
enough 40.2; Jer 9.12
evil 53.5; 57.20
exile 49.20; Jer 1.3
faithful [2] 38.3; 61.8
forget 54.4; 57.11
God's people [9] 55.3; 57.14
greed Prov 23.3; 57.17
honour 55.5; 57.11

joy 55.12; 58.14
justice 54.14; 58.2
love [2] 54.7; 61.8
observe [3] 21.7; Jer 17.22
offer 43.23; 57.5
please [2] 53.11; 57.6
prayer [2] 41.17; 58.4
promise 55.3; 62.6
remember 46.8; 63.11
right (1) 54.14; 57.12
Sabbath [3] 1.13; 58.13
sacred 30.29; 57.5
sacrifice 53.10; 57.5
save 54.5; 57.13
seek Prov 30.5; Jer 29.13
serve 39.7; 58.14
Sovereign 52.3; 61.1
Temple (1) (of God) [2] 52.11; 57.13
understand 52.15; 57.1
warn 36.14; Jer 4.16
watch 43.19; Jer 1.12
worship (1) (of God) 48.1; 57.13

abandon 49.14; 64.7
accuse 54.17; 59.12
act 42.14; Jer 3.2
adultery Prov 30.20; Jer 3.9
afraid 54.4; 66.4
anger [2] 54.8; 60.10
care 53.8; 60.16
comfort 54.11; 61.2
confident 36.4; Ezek 7.24
death (1) 53.10; 65.12
evil 56.2; 58.9
filthy 30.22; 64.6
forget 56.5; 62.6
forsake 2.6; 60.15
god (2) (other gods) [6] 48.14; 65.11
God's people [3] 56.1; 58.1
grain-offering Neh 13.9; 66.3
greed 56.11; Jer 51.39
heal [2] 53.5; 58.8
help [3] 51.1; 58.7
holy [2] 55.5; 58.13
honour 56.4; 58.13
hope 51.5; 59.9
humble 53.7; 60.22
hurt 54.17; 59.4
idol [4] 48.5; 66.3
jeer Ps 70.3; Jer 20.7
judge 33.14; Jer 4.12

lie (2) [2] 53.9; 59.3
life (1) [2] 55.3; 65.20
lust Job 31.1; Jer 5.8
mourn 50.3; 61.2
offer [4] 56.7; 60.7
peace [2] 55.12; 60.17
please 56.4; 58.5
prostitute 23.15; Jer 3.2
punish 54.9; 59.17
repent 9.13; 66.2
rest (1) [2] 34.14; 62.7
restore 49.6; 58.12
right (1) 56.1; 59.14
sacred 56.7; 58.13
sacrifice [2] 56.7; 60.7
safe 54.14; 59.8
satisfy 55.2; 58.10
save 56.1; 58.8
sex [2] Prov 31.3; Ezek 16.43
strength 54.2; 63.1
stubborn 48.4; 63.17
Temple (1) (of God) 56.5; 60.7
trust 50.10; Jer 2.37
understand 56.11; Jer 3.15
weak 51.20; 59.1
world of the dead 38.10; 59.10
worship (1) (of God) 56.3; 58.2
worship (2) (of other gods) [4] 46.1; 65.11

lovers, whom you pay to sleep with you. And there you **satisfy** your **lust**. 9 You put on your perfumes and ointments and go to **worship the god Molech**. To find **gods** to **worship**, you send messengers far and wide, even to the **world of the dead**. 10 You wear yourselves out looking for other **gods**, but you never give up. You think your obscene **idols** give you **strength**, and so you never grow **weak**.

11 The LORD says, "Who are these **gods** that make you **afraid**, so that you tell me **lies** and **forget** me completely? Have you stopped **honouring** me because I have kept silent for so long? 12 You think that what you do is **right**, but I will expose your conduct, and your **idols** will not be able to **help** you. 13 When you cry for **help**, let those **idols** of yours **save** you! A puff of wind will carry them off! But those who **trust** in me will live in the land and will **worship** me in my **Temple**."

God's Promise of Help and Healing

14 The LORD says, "Let **my people** return to me. Remove every obstacle from their path! Build the road, and make it ready!

15 "I am the high and **holy** God, who lives for ever. I live in a high and **holy** place, but I also live with people who are **humble** and **repentant**, so that I can **restore** their **confidence** and **hope**. 16 I gave **my people life**, and I will not continue to **accuse** them or be **angry** with them for ever.[w] 17 I was **angry** with them because of their sin and **greed**, and so I **punished** them and **abandoned** them. But they were **stubborn** and kept on going their own way.

18 "I have seen how they **acted**, but I will **heal** them. I will lead them and **help** them, and I will **comfort** those who **mourn**. 19 I **offer peace** to all, both near and far! I will **heal my people**. 20 But **evil** men are like the **restless** sea, whose waves never stop rolling in, bringing **filth** and muck. 21 There is no **safety** for sinners," says the LORD.

True Fasting

ash 44.20; Jer 6.26
bow (2) 49.7; 60.14
claim 48.1; Jer 5.2
contempt 52.5; Jer 33.24
dark 50.3; 59.9
eager 50.4; Acts 17.11
enjoy 55.2; 61.6
evil 57.20; 59.5
fast (2) [7] Ps 69.10; Jer 14.12
favour 49.8; 60.10

58 The LORD says, "Shout as loud as you can! Tell **my people** Israel about their sins! 2 They **worship** me every day, **claiming** that they are **eager** to know my **ways** and **obey** my **laws**. They say they want me to give them **just laws** and that they take **pleasure** in **worshipping** me."

3 The people ask, "Why should we **fast** if the LORD never **notices**? Why should we go without food if he pays no attention?"

The LORD says to them, "The **truth** is that at the same time as you **fast**, you pursue your own **interests** and **oppress** your workers. 4 Your **fasting** makes you **violent**, and you **quarrel** and fight. Do you think this kind of **fasting** will make me listen to your **prayers**? 5 When you **fast**, you make yourselves **suffer**; you **bow** your heads low like a blade of grass, and spread out **sackcloth** and **ashes** to lie on. Is that what you call **fasting**? Do you think I will be **pleased** with that?

6 "The kind of **fasting** I want is this: Remove the chains of **oppression** and the yoke of **injustice**, and let the **oppressed** go **free**. 7 **Share** your food with the **hungry** and open your homes to the homeless **poor**. Give clothes to those who have nothing to wear, and do not **refuse** to **help** your own relatives.

8 "Then my **favour** will shine on you like the morning sun, and your wounds will be quickly **healed**. I will always be with you to **save** you; my **presence** will **protect** you on every side. 9 When you **pray**, I will answer you. When you call to me, I will respond.

"If you put an end to **oppression**, to every gesture of **contempt**, and to every evil **word**; 10 if you give food to the **hungry** and **satisfy** those who are in **need**, then the **darkness** around you will **turn** to the brightness of noon. 11 And I will always **guide** you and **satisfy** you with good things. I will keep you **strong** and well. You will be like a garden that has **plenty** of water, like a spring of water that never runs dry. 12 Your people will rebuild what has long been in **ruins**, building again on the old foundations. You will be known as the people who rebuilt the walls, who **restored** the **ruined** houses."

The Reward for Keeping the Sabbath

13 The LORD says, "If you treat the **Sabbath** as **sacred** and do not pursue your own **interests** on that day; if you **value** my **holy** day and **honour** it by not travelling, working, or talking idly on that day, 14 then you will find the **joy** that comes from **serving** me. I will make you **honoured** all over the **world**, and you will **enjoy** the land I gave to your ancestor, Jacob. I, the LORD, have spoken."

free 52.2; 60.16
God's people 57.14; 59.20
guide Ecc 12.11; Jer 10.21
heal 57.18; 61.1
help 57.12; 59.1
holy 57.15; 60.9
honour [2] 57.11; 60.9
hunger [2] 55.2; 65.13
injustice 40.27; Jer 22.13
interest (1) [2] Prov 18.1; Jer 22.17
joy 56.7; 60.5
justice 56.1; 59.4
law [2] 51.4; Jer 8.7
need 51.14; Jer 3.16
notice (1) 53.2; Jer 33.24
obey 50.10; 59.21
oppress [4] 54.14; 59.9
please 57.6; 60.7
pleasure 47.8; 66.3
plenty 32.20; 65.13
poor 33.15; 61.1
pray 55.6; 65.1
prayer 56.7; 64.7
presence 37.14; 60.2
protect 52.12; 60.18
quarrel Prov 29.22; Jer 15.10
refuse (1) 30.9; 59.13
restore 57.15; 62.7
ruin [2] 52.9; 59.7
Sabbath 56.2; 66.23
sackcloth 37.1; Jer 4.8
sacred 57.5; 64.10
satisfy [2] 57.8; Jer 31.14
save 57.13; 59.1
serve 56.6; 60.10
share 53.12; Jer 37.12
strong 54.14; 59.17
suffer 54.11; 59.17
truth 45.19; 59.14
turn 55.6; 59.13
value Prov 31.18; Hos 13.15
violent 42.25; 59.3
way (3) 55.8; 63.17
word (1) 55.10; 59.13
world 54.5; 62.7
worship (1) (of God) [2] 57.13; 59.2

[w] I gave my people...for ever; *or* I will not continue to accuse them or be angry with them for ever, for then they would die — the very people to whom I gave life.

57.19: Eph 2.17 **57.21:** Is 48.22 **58.7:** Mt 25.35

accuse 57.16; Jer 2.5
blind 56.10; Jer 31.8
case (2) 45.21; Jer 2.9
court (1) 50.8; Jer 36.10
covenant 56.4; 61.8
crime [2] 53.9; 61.8
dark [2] 58.10; 60.2
deadly 27.1; Jer 9.8
defend 54.17; 60.18
depend 48.2; Jer 49.11
desire 26.8; Jer 5.8
destroy 51.13; 60.12
displease Ps 85.4; Jer 32.30
distress 54.6; Jer 15.11
enemy 47.12; 61.2
evil [3] 58.9; 65.7
false Prov 29.12; Jer 10.14
fear 51.12; 64.1
fright 47.12; Jer 48.41
God's people 58.1; 60.9
guilty 50.9; 66.16
help [2] 58.7; 63.3
honest [2] 32.5; Ezek 18.5
hope 57.15; 64.4
hurt 57.1; Jer 2.3
innocent 50.8; Jer 2.34
justice [4] 58.2; 60.17
lie (2) [3] 57.4; Jer 5.31
light (1) 51.4; 60.2
long (2) 26.9; Jer 22.27
obey [2] 58.2; 65.13
oppress [4] 58.3; 60.14
plan [2] 55.11; Jer 11.19
plot (1) [2] 50.11; Jer 11.9
power [4] 55.4; 60.22
punish [2] 57.17; 60.10
rebel 50.5; 63.10
refuse (1) 58.7; Jer 2.20
reject 53.3; Jer 2.20
rescue 52.9; 62.11
right (1) [2] 57.12; 60.21
ruin 58.12; 61.4
safe [2] 57.21; Jer 4.6
save [5] 58.8; 60.16
separate 27.12; Ezek 34.17
strong [2] 58.11; 63.5
stumble [2] 28.7; 63.12
suffer 58.5; 63.9
teach [2] 54.13; Jer 6.19
truth 58.3; Jer 8.6
turn [2] 58.10; 63.17
unjust 10.1; Dan 9.26
useless 44.9; Jer 2.8
victim 33.1; Jer 3.2
victory 54.17; 61.10
violent 58.4; 60.18
weak 57.10; Jer 31.25
win [2] 26.18; 63.5
word (1) 58.9; Jer 1.9
world of the dead 57.9; Ezek 26.20
worship (1) (of God) 58.2; 60.14
wrong [2] 43.24; 64.5

The Prophet Condemns the People's Sins

59 Don't think that the LORD is too
weak to **save** you or too deaf to
hear your call for **help**! 2 It is because of
your sins that he doesn't hear you. It is
your sins that **separate** you from God
when you try to **worship** him. 3 You are
guilty of **lying**, **violence**, and murder.
4 You go to **court**, but you haven't got
justice on your side. You **depend** on **lies**
to **win** your **case**. You carry out your
plans to **hurt** others. 5-6 The **evil plots** you
make are as **deadly** as the eggs of a
poisonous snake. Crush an egg, out
comes a snake! But your **plots** will do
you no good—they are as **useless** as
clothing made of cobwebs! 7 You are always **planning** something **evil**, and you
can hardly wait to do it. You never hesitate to murder **innocent** people. You
leave **ruin** and **destruction** wherever you
go, 8 and no one is **safe** when you are
about. Everything you do is **unjust**. You
follow a crooked path, and no one who
walks that path will ever be **safe**.

The People Confess Their Sin

9 The people say, "Now we know why
God does not **save** us from those who **oppress** us. We **hope** for **light** to walk by,
but there is only **darkness**, 10 and we
grope about like **blind** people. We
stumble at noon, as if it were night, as if
we were in the **dark world of the dead**.
11 We are **frightened** and **distressed**. We
long for God to **save** us from **oppression**
and **wrong**, but nothing happens.
12 "LORD, our **crimes** against you are
many. Our sins **accuse** us. We are well
aware of them all. 13 We have **rebelled**
against you, **rejected** you, and **refused** to
follow you. We have **oppressed** others
and **turned away** from you. Our thoughts
are **false**; our **words** are **lies**. 14 **Justice** is
driven away, and **right** cannot come
near. **Truth stumbles** in the public
square, and **honesty** finds no place there.
15 There is so little **honesty** that anyone
who stops doing **evil** finds himself the **victim** of **crime**."

The LORD Prepares to Rescue His People

The LORD has seen this, and he is **displeased** that there is no **justice**. 16 He is
astonished to see that there is no one to
help the **oppressed**. So he will use his own
power to **rescue** them and to **win** the **victory**. 17 He will wear **justice** like a coat of
armour and **saving power** like a helmet.
He will clothe himself with the **strong desire** to set things **right** and to **punish** and
avenge the **wrongs** that people **suffer**.
18 He will **punish** his **enemies** according to
what they have done, even those who
live in distant lands. 19 From east to west
everyone will **fear** him and his great
power. He will come like a rushing river,
like a **strong** wind.
20 The LORD says to **his people**, "I will
come to Jerusalem to **defend** you and to
save all of you that **turn from** your sins.
21 And I make a **covenant** with you: I
have given you my **power** and my **teachings** to be yours for ever, and from now
on you are to **obey** me and **teach** your
children and your descendants to **obey**
me for all time to come."

The Future Glory of Jerusalem

60 Arise, Jerusalem, and shine like
the sun;
The **glory** of the LORD is shining on
you!
2 Other nations will be covered by
darkness,
But on you the **light** of the LORD will
shine;
The brightness of his **presence** will be
with you.
3 Nations will be drawn to your **light**,
And kings to the dawning of your **new**
day.

4 Look around you and see what is
happening:
Your people are gathering to come
home!
Your sons will come from far away;
Your daughters will be carried like
children.
5 You will see this and be filled with **joy**;
You will **tremble** with excitement.
The wealth of the nations will be
brought to you;
From across the sea their **riches** will
come.

6 Great caravans of camels will come,
from Midian and Ephah.
They will come from Sheba, bringing
gold and **incense**.
People will tell the **good news** of what
the LORD has done!
7 All the **sheep** of Kedar and Nebaioth
Will be brought to you as **sacrifices**
And **offered** on the **altar** to **please** the
LORD.
The LORD will make his **Temple** more
glorious than ever.

8 What are these ships that skim along
like **clouds**,

altar 56.7; 65.3
anger 57.16; 63.3
bow (2) 58.5; Jer 8.19
care 57.1; 61.5
cloud 44.22; Jer 4.13
dark 59.9; Jer 2.31
defend 59.20; Jer 21.13
desolate 49.19; Jer 12.11
despise 53.3; Jer 10.15
destroy [2] 59.7; 64.11
dove 38.14; Jer 8.7
eternal [2] 9.6; 61.8
favour 58.8; Jer 26.19
forsake 57.8; 62.4
free 58.6; 61.1
glory [4] 55.5; 62.2
God's people [2] 59.20; 61.2
Good News 52.7; 61.1
grief 51.11; 61.3
hate 49.7; 61.8
holy [2] 58.13; 62.12
honour [2] 58.13; 63.14
humble 57.15; 66.2
incense 43.23; 65.3
joy [2] 58.14; 61.3
justice 59.4; 61.8
last (1) 55.3; 61.7
light (1) [7] 59.9; Jer 4.23
mercy 55.7; 63.7
might 43.17; Jer 5.16
name (2) (name of God, of Jesus) 54.5; 63.14
new 48.6; 62.2
offer 57.5; 65.3
oppress [2] 59.9; 61.8
peace 57.2; Jer 4.10
please 58.5; 62.4
possess 15.7; 65.9
power 59.16; 62.8
praise 51.3; 61.3
presence 58.8; 64.2
protect 58.8; Jer 1.8
punish 59.17; 63.4
respect 49.7; Jer 49.15
reveal 48.6; 64.2
riches Prov 22.4; Jer 17.11
right (1) [2] 59.14; 61.3
sacrifice 57.5; 65.3
save [2] 59.1; 61.2
serve [2] 58.14; 61.5
sheep 53.6; 65.10
Temple (1) (of God) [2] 57.13; 62.9

59.7-8: Rom 3.15-17 **59.16:** Is 63.5 **59.17:** Eph 6.14, 17; 1 Thes 5.8 **59.20:** Rom 11.26

tremble 41.5; 64.2
violent 59.3; 65.12
worship (1) (of God) 59.2; 65.10

Like doves returning home?
9 They are ships coming from distant
lands,
Bringing God's people home.
They bring with them silver and gold
To honour the name of the LORD,
The holy God of Israel,
Who has made all nations honour his
people.

10 The LORD says to Jerusalem,
"Foreigners will rebuild your walls,
And their kings will serve you.
In my anger I punished you,
But now I will show you my favour and
mercy.
11 Day and night your gates will be open,
So that the kings of the nations
May bring you their wealth.
12 But nations that do not serve you
Will be completely destroyed.

13 "The wood of the pine, the juniper, and
the cypress,
The finest wood from the forests of
Lebanon,
Will be brought to rebuild you,
Jerusalem,
To make my Temple beautiful,
To make my city glorious.
14 The sons of those who oppressed you
will come
And bow low to show their respect.
All who once despised you will worship
at your feet.
They will call you 'The City of the
LORD,'
'Zion, the City of Israel's Holy God.'

15 "You will no longer be forsaken and
hated,
A city deserted and desolate.
I will make you great and beautiful,
A place of joy for ever and ever.
16 Nations and kings will care for you
As a mother nurses her child.
You will know that I, the LORD, have
saved you,
That the mighty God of Israel sets you
free.

17 "I will bring you gold instead of
bronze,
Silver and bronze instead of iron and
wood,
And iron instead of stone.
Your rulers will no longer oppress you;
I will make them rule with justice and
peace.
18 The sounds of violence will be heard
no more;
Destruction will not shatter your
country again.
I will protect and defend you like a
wall;
You will praise me because I have
saved you.

19 "No longer will the sun be your light
by day
Or the moon be your light by night;
I, the LORD, will be your eternal light;
The light of my glory will shine on you.
20 Your days of grief will come to an end.
I, the LORD, will be your eternal light,
More lasting than the sun and moon.
21 Your people will all do what is right,
And will possess the land for ever.
I planted them, I made them,
To reveal my greatness to all.
22 Even your smallest and humblest
family
Will become as great as a powerful
nation.
When the right time comes,
I will make this happen quickly.
I am the LORD!"

The Good News of Deliverance

61 The Sovereign LORD has filled
me with his spirit.
He has chosen me and sent me
To bring good news to the poor,
To heal the broken-hearted,
To announce release to captives
And freedom to those in prison.
2 He has sent me to proclaim
That the time has come
When the LORD will save his people
And defeat their enemies.
He has sent me to comfort all who
mourn,
3 To give to those who mourn in Zion
Joy and gladness instead of grief,
A song of praise instead of sorrow.
They will be like trees
That the LORD himself has planted.
They will all do what is right,
And God will be praised for what he
has done.
4 They will rebuild cities that have long
been in ruins.

5 My people, foreigners will serve you.
They will take care of your flocks
And farm your land and tend your
vineyards.
6 And you will be known as the priests of
the LORD,
The servants of our God.
You will enjoy the wealth of the
nations

announce 52.7; 62.11
bless 56.2; 63.7
bride 49.18; 62.5
captive 52.2; Jer 13.17
care 60.16; 63.9
choose 49.1; 65.9
comfort 57.18; 66.13
covenant 59.21; Jer 4.4
crime 59.12; Jer 16.10
disgrace 54.4; 65.13
enemy 59.18; 62.8
enjoy 58.14; 65.21
eternal 60.19; Jer 10.10
faithful 56.4; 65.16
flock 40.11; Jer 3.24
free 60.16; Jer 31.11
glad 51.3; 65.18
God's people [4] 60.9; 62.12
Good News 60.6; Nah 1.15
grief 60.20; Jer 15.5
hate 60.15; 66.5
heal 58.8; Jer 3.22
heart 51.7; 65.14
joy [2] 60.5; 64.5
justice 60.17; Jer 5.28
last (1) 60.20; 66.12
love 56.6; 62.12
mourn [2] 57.18; 66.10
oppress 60.14; Jer 5.28
poor 58.7; Jer 2.34
praise [3] 60.18; 62.7
priest 37.2; 66.21
prison 51.14; Jer 15.2
proclaim 40.6; 66.19
proud 49.18; Jer 13.9
rejoice 35.1; 65.18
reward 49.4; Jer 31.16
right (1) 60.21; 64.5
ruin 59.7; 64.10

60.11: Rev 21.25–26 **60.14:** Rev 3.9 **60.19:** Rev 21.23, 22.5 **61.1:** Mt 11.5; Lk 7.22 **61.1–2:** Lk 4.18–19
61.2: Mt 5.4

salvation Ps 71.15; Jer 23.6
save [2] 60.16; 62.1
seed 55.10; Jer 2.21
servant 54.17; 63.11
serve 60.10; 63.17
shame 47.3; 65.3
sorrow 51.11; Jer 8.18
Sovereign [2] 56.8; 65.15
Spirit (1) (God's Spirit) 44.3; 63.10
sure 52.11; Jer 3.7
victory 59.16; 62.1
vineyard 36.17; 65.21
wedding Song 3.11; Jer 2.32

And be **proud** that it is yours.
7 Your **shame** and **disgrace** are ended.
You will live in your own land,
And your wealth will be doubled;
Your **joy** will **last** for ever.

8 The LORD says,
"I **love justice** and I **hate oppression** and **crime**.
I will **faithfully reward my people**
And make an **eternal covenant** with them.
9 They will be famous among the nations;
Everyone who sees them will know
That they are a people whom I have **blessed**."

10 Jerusalem **rejoices** because of what the LORD has done.
She is like a **bride** dressed for her **wedding**.
God has clothed her with **salvation** and **victory**.
11 As **surely** as **seeds** sprout and grow,
The **Sovereign** LORD **will save his people**,
And all the nations will **praise** him.

announce 61.1; 63.1
bread 44.15; Jer 37.21
bride [2] 61.10; Jer 2.32
bridegroom Ps 19.5; Mt 9.15
clear 40.3; Ezek 32.14
crown 28.1; Jer 13.18
delight [2] 4.2; Jer 3.19
encourage 41.6; Acts 4.36
enemy 61.2; 63.4
forget 57.11; 65.16
forsake [2] 60.15; 65.11
glory 60.1; 63.15
God's people 61.2; 63.4
groom *see* **bridegroom**
harvest 37.30; Jer 2.7
holy 60.9; 63.10
love 61.8; 63.7
new [2] 60.3; 65.15
please [2] 60.7; 66.2
power 60.22; 63.1
praise [2] 61.3; 63.7
promise [2] 56.8; Jer 11.5
remind 55.13; Ezek 20.4
rescue 59.16; 63.9
rest (1) 57.2; 63.14
restore 58.12; Jer 27.22
save [3] 61.2; 63.1
solemn 45.23; Jer 11.7
sow 55.10; Jer 2.2
Temple (1) (of God) 60.7; 64.11

62 I will speak out to **encourage** Jerusalem;
I will not be silent until she is **saved**,
And her **victory** shines like a torch in the night.
2 Jerusalem, the nations will see you **victorious**!
All their kings will see your **glory**.
You will be called by a **new** name,
A name given by the LORD himself.
3 You will be like a beautiful **crown** for the LORD.
4 No longer will you be called "**Forsaken**,"
Or your land be called "The Deserted Wife."
Your **new** name will be "God Is **Pleased** with Her."
Your land will be called "Happily Married,"
Because the LORD is **pleased** with you
And will be like a husband to your land.
5 Like a young man taking a **virgin** as his **bride**,
He who formed you will marry you.
As a **groom** is **delighted** with his **bride**,
So your God will **delight** in you.

6 On your walls, Jerusalem, I have placed sentries;
They must never be silent day or night.
They must **remind** the LORD of his **promises**
And never let him **forget** them.
7 They must give him no **rest** until he **restores** Jerusalem
And makes it a city the whole **world praises**.

8 The LORD has made a **solemn promise**,
And by his **power** he will carry it out:
"Your corn will no longer be food for your **enemies**,
And foreigners will no longer drink your wine.
9 But you that **sowed** and **harvested** the corn
Will eat the **bread** and **praise** the LORD.
You that tended and gathered the grapes
Will drink the wine in the courts of my **Temple**."

10 People of Jerusalem, go out of the city
And build a road for your returning people!
Prepare a highway; **clear** it of stones!
Put up a signal so that the nations can know
11 That the LORD is **announcing** to all the earth:
"Tell the people of Jerusalem
That the LORD is coming to **save** you,
Bringing with him the people he has **rescued**."
12 You will be called "**God's Holy People**,"
"The People the LORD Has **Saved**."
Jerusalem will be called "The City That God **Loves**,"
"The City That God Did Not **Forsake**."

victory [2] 61.10; 63.1
virgin 47.1; Ezek 23.3
world 58.14; 66.16

The LORD's Victory over the Nations

acknowledge 52.6; Jer 9.3
amaze 52.15; Jer 2.12
angel 37.36; Ezek 28.14
anger [3] 60.10; 64.5
announce 62.11; Jer 4.15
bless 61.9; 65.9
blood [2] 34.3; 66.3
care 61.5; Jer 2.6
compassion [2] 51.3; Jer 13.14
concern Prov 29.4; Jer 29.10
constant 51.13; Jer 9.24

63 "Who is this coming from the city of Bozrah in Edom? Who is
this so **splendidly** dressed in red, march-
ing along[x] in **power** and **strength**?"
"It is the LORD, **powerful** to **save**,
coming to **announce** his **victory**."
2 "Why is his clothing so red, like that
of a man who tramples grapes to make
wine?"
3 The LORD answers, "I have trampled
the nations like grapes, and no one came
to **help** me. I trampled them in my **anger**,

[x] *Some ancient translations* marching along; *Hebrew* bowed down.

61.10: Rev 21.2 **62.11:** Is 40.10; Rev 22.12
63.1-6: Is 34.5-17; Jer 49.7-22; Ezek 25.12-14, 35.1-15; Amos 1.11-12; Obad 1-14; Mal 1.2-5
63.3: Rev 14.20, 19.13, 15

deceive 37.10; Jer 4.10
enemy [3] 62.8; 64.2
everlasting 40.28; Jer 23.40
Father (2) (God) [2] Ps 89.26; 64.8
glory 62.2; Jer 14.21
God's people [7] 62.12; 65.1
heaven 55.9; 65.17
help [2] 59.1; 64.7
holy [3] 62.12; 65.5
honour 60.9; Jer 2.11
ignore 53.3; 65.11
love [4] 62.12; 64.11
mercy 60.10; 64.9
name (2) (name of God, of Jesus) 60.9; 65.16
power [4] 62.8; 64.2
praise 62.7; 64.11
punish 60.10; 65.6
rebel 59.13; 66.24
remember 56.5; 64.5
rescue [2] 62.11; Jer 2.6
rest (1) 62.7; Jer 22.23
rich 53.9; Jer 5.27
sad 24.7; Mt 6.16
sake [2] 53.11; Jer 15.15
sanctuary 43.28; Ezek 8.16
save [5] 62.1; 65.8
servant 61.6; Jer 7.25
serve 61.5; 65.8
Spirit (1) (God's Spirit) [2] 61.1; Ezek 2.2
splendour 52.1; Jer 46.20
strength 57.10; Jer 1.18
strong 59.17; 66.14
stubborn 57.17; 65.2
stumble 59.10; Jer 6.21
suffer 59.17; 64.12
turn 59.13; 64.7
victory [2] 62.1; Jer 43.12
way (3) 58.2; 66.3
win [2] 59.4; Jer 26.19

and their **blood** has stained all my
clothing. 4 I decided that the time to **save**
my people had come; it was time to **pun-**
ish their **enemies**. 5 I was **amazed** when I
looked and saw that there was no one to
help me. But my **anger** made me **strong**,
and I **won** the **victory** myself. 6 In my **an-**
ger I trampled whole nations and shattered them. I poured out their **life-blood**
on the ground."

The LORD's Goodness to Israel

7 I will tell of the LORD's unfailing **love**;
I **praise** him for all he has done for
us.
He has **richly blessed** the people of
Israel
because of his **mercy** and **constant**
love.
8 The LORD said, "They are **my**
people; they will not **deceive** me." And so
he **saved** them 9 from all their **suffering**.
It was not an **angel**, but the LORD himself
who **saved** them. In his **love** and **com-**
passion he **rescued** them. He had always
taken **care** of them in the past, 10 but they
rebelled against him and made his **holy**
spirit sad. So the LORD became their
enemy and fought against them.
11 But then they[y] **remembered** the
past, the days of Moses, the **servant** of
the LORD, and they asked, "Where now is
the LORD, who **saved** the leaders of **his**
people from the sea? Where is the LORD,
who gave his **spirit** to Moses? 12–13 Where
is the LORD, who by his **power** did great
things through Moses, dividing the
waters of the sea and leading **his people**
through the deep water, to **win ever-**
lasting fame for himself?"
Led by the LORD, they were as sure-
footed as wild horses, and never
stumbled. 14 As cattle are led into a fertile
valley, so the LORD gave **his people rest**.
He led **his people** and brought **honour** to
his **name**.

A Prayer for Mercy and Help

15 LORD, look upon us from **heaven**,
where you live in your **holiness** and
glory. Where is your great **concern** for
us? Where is your **power**? Where are
your **love** and **compassion**? Do not **ig-**
nore us. 16 You are our **father**. Our ancestors Abraham and Jacob do not **acknow-**
ledge us, but you, LORD, are our **father**,
the one who has always **rescued** us.
17 Why do you let us stray from your
ways? Why do you make us so **stubborn**
that we **turn away** from you? Come
back, for the **sake** of those who **serve**
you, for the **sake** of the people who have
always been yours.
18 We, your **holy people**, were driven
out by our **enemies** for a little while: they
trampled down your **sanctuary**.[z] 19 You
treat us as though you had never been
our ruler, as though we had never been
your people.

64 Why don't you tear the sky **apart**
and come down? The mountains
would see you and shake with **fear**.
2 They would **tremble** like water boiling
over a hot fire. Come and **reveal** your
power to your **enemies**, and make the
nations **tremble** at your **presence**!
3 There was a time when you came and
did **terrifying** things that we did not expect; the mountains saw you and shook
with **fear**. 4 No one has ever seen or
heard of a God like you, who does such
deeds for those who put their **hope** in
him. 5 You **welcome** those who find **joy** in
doing what is **right**, those who **remember**
how you want them to live. You were
angry with us, but we went on sinning; in
spite of your great **anger** we have continued to do **wrong** since **ancient** times.[a]
6 All of us have been sinful; even our **best**
actions are **filthy** through and through.
Because of our sins we are like leaves
that wither and are blown away by the
wind. 7 No one **turns to** you in **prayer**; no
one goes to you for **help**. You have hidden yourself from us and have **aban-**
doned[b] us because of our sins.
8 But you are our **father**, LORD. We
are like clay, and you are like the potter.
You **created** us, 9 so do not be too **angry**
with us or hold our sins against us for
ever. We are your people; be **merciful** to
us. 10 Your **sacred** cities are like a desert;
Jerusalem is a deserted **ruin**, 11 and our
Temple, the **sacred** and beautiful place
where our ancestors **praised** you, has
been **destroyed** by fire. All the places we
loved are in **ruins**. 12 LORD, are you un-
moved by all this? Are you going to do
nothing and make us **suffer** more than
we can **endure**?

abandon 57.17; Jer 1.16
action 45.13; Jer 32.19
ancient 51.9; Jer 3.2
anger [3] 63.3; 65.3
apart Ps 144.5; Jer 5.6
best 55.2; Jer 2.21
create 54.16; 65.18
destroy 60.12; 65.8
endure 53.3; 66.22
enemy 63.4; 66.6
Father (2) (God) 63.16; Jer 3.4
fear [2] 59.19; 66.2
filthy 57.20; Lam 1.8
help 63.3; 65.1
hope 59.9; Jer 8.15
joy 61.3; 65.14
love 63.7; 66.10
mercy 63.7; Jer 3.12
power 63.1; 66.18
praise 63.7; Jer 4.2
prayer 58.4; 65.1
presence 60.2; Jer 7.10
remember 63.11; Jer 2.2
reveal 60.21; Ezek 7.26
right (1) 61.3; Jer 1.12
ruin [2] 61.4; Jer 2.7
sacred [2] 58.13; 65.3
suffer 63.9; 66.8
Temple (1) (of God) 62.9; 66.6
terrify 44.11; Jer 10.2
tremble [2] 60.5; Jer 5.22
turn 63.17; Jer 2.5
welcome 39.2; 65.2
wrong 59.11; 65.2

God's Punishment of the Rebellious

65 The LORD said, "I was ready to
answer **my people's prayers**, but
they did not pray. I was ready for them
to find me, but they did not even try. The
nation did not **pray** to me, even though I
was always ready to answer, 'Here I am;

altar 60.7; Jer 7.21
anger [2] 64.5; 66.14
bless [3] 63.7; Jer 4.2
choose [3] 61.1; 66.4
consult 47.15; Jer 8.2
create 64.8; 66.2
curse 24.6; Jer 11.3
danger 38.17; Jer 2.6

[y] *Probable text* they; *Hebrew* he. [z] *Verse 18 in Hebrew is unclear.*
[a] *Probable text* in spite of...ancient times; *Hebrew unclear.*
[b] *Some ancient translations* abandoned; *Hebrew* melted.

63.5: Is 59.16 **63.12:** Ex 14.21 **64.4:** 1 Cor 2.9 **65.1:** Rom 10.20

dead 50.3; 66.24
death (1) 57.2; Jer 9.21
death (3) (to death) 53.8; 66.16
deserve 53.6; Jer 10.7
destroy [2] 64.11; Jer 1.10
disaster 51.19; 66.4
disgrace 61.7; 66.5
disobey Ps 148.6; 66.4
enjoy [2] 61.6; 66.11
evil [3] 59.5; 66.4
faithful [2] 61.8; 66.5
fate [2] 53.8; Jer 13.25
forget [2] 62.6; Jer 2.32
forsake 62.4
glad 61.3; 66.10
god (2) (other gods) 57.5; Jer 1.16
God's people [6] 63.4; 66.9
happy [2] 51.11; Jer 7.34
harm 27.3; Jer 10.5
heart 61.1; Jer 3.17
heaven 63.15; 66.1
help [2] 64.7; 66.14
holy 63.10; 66.7
hunger 58.7; Jer 31.25
ignore 63.15; Ezek 3.27
incense [2] 60.6; 66.3
joy [3] 64.5; Jer 7.34
lamb 53.7; 66.3
life (1) [2] 57.2; Jer 1.5
name (2) (name of God, of Jesus) 63.14; Jer 4.2
new [3] 62.2; 66.22
oath 19.18; Jer 7.9
obey [2] 59.21; 66.2
offer [2] 60.7; 66.3
pagan [4] 27.9; 66.17
plenty 58.11; Jer 44.17
possess 60.21; Jer 2.3
pray [3] 58.9; 66.3
prayer [2] 64.7; Lam 3.44
punish [3] 63.4; 66.6
rejoice 61.10; 66.5
repay Prov 20.22; Jer 51.24
sacred [3] 64.10; 66.17
sacrifice [2] 60.7; 66.3
save 63.1; 66.5
sentence 53.8; Jer 26.11
serve [2] 63.17; Jer 5.19
shame 61.7; Jer 2.37
sheep 60.7; Jer 12.3
shrine 36.7; Ezek 7.7
sign (1) 55.13; Jer 31.21
Sovereign 61.1; Jer 1.6
spirit (2) 19.3; Jer 27.9
stubborn 63.17; Jer 3.17
succeed (1) 53.10; Jer 12.1
swear 48.1; Jer 4.2
tomb 22.16; Jer 48.9
trouble [2] 43.2; Jer 2.24
vineyard 61.5; Jer 5.10
violent 60.18; Jer 6.7
weep 32.13; Jer 4.8

I will help you.' 2 I have always been ready to welcome my people, who stubbornly do what is wrong and go their own way. 3 They shamelessly keep on making me angry. They offer pagan sacrifices in sacred gardens[c] and burn incense on pagan altars. 4 At night they go to caves and tombs to consult the spirits of the dead. They eat pork and drink broth made from meat offered in pagan sacrifices. 5 And then they say to others, 'Keep away from us; we are too holy for you to touch!' I cannot stand people like that—my anger against them is like a fire that never goes out.

6 "I have already decided on their punishment, and their sentence is written down. I will not overlook what they have done, but will repay them 7 for their sins and the sins of their ancestors. They have burnt incense at pagan hill shrines and spoken evil of me. So I will punish them as their past deeds deserve."

8 The LORD says, "No one destroys good grapes; instead, they make wine with them. Neither will I destroy all my people—I will save those who serve me. 9 I will bless the Israelites who belong to the tribe of Judah, and their descendants will possess my land of mountains. My chosen people, who serve me, will live there. 10 They will worship me and will lead their sheep and cattle to pasture in the Plain of Sharon in the west and in the Valley of Trouble in the east.

11 "But it will be different for you that forsake me, who ignore Zion, my sacred hill,[e] and worship Gad and Meni, the gods of luck and fate. 12 It will be your fate to die a violent death, because you did not answer when I called you or listen when I spoke. You chose to disobey me and do evil. 13 And so I tell you that those who worship and obey me will have plenty to eat and drink, but you will be hungry and thirsty. They will be happy, but you will be disgraced. 14 They will sing for joy, but you will cry with a broken heart. 15 My chosen people will use your name as a curse. I, the Sovereign LORD, will put you to death. But I will give a new name to those who obey me. 16 Anyone in the land who asks for a blessing will ask to be blessed by the Faithful God. Whoever takes an oath will swear by the name of the Faithful God. The troubles of the past will be gone and forgotten."

The New Creation

17 The LORD says, "I am making a new earth and new heavens. The events of the past will be completely forgotten. 18 Be glad and rejoice for ever in what I create. The new Jerusalem I make will be full of joy, and her people will be happy. 19 I myself will be filled with joy because of Jerusalem and her people. There will be no weeping there, no calling for help. 20 Babies will no longer die in infancy, and all people will live out their life span. Those who live to be a hundred will be considered young. To die before that would be a sign that I had punished them. 21-22 People will build houses and live in them themselves—they will not be used by someone else. They will plant vineyards and enjoy the wine—it will not be drunk by others. Like trees, my people will live long lives. They will fully enjoy the things that they have worked for. 23 The work they do will be successful, and their children will not meet with disaster. I will bless them and their descendants for all time to come. 24 Even before they finish praying to me, I will answer their prayers. 25 Wolves and lambs will eat together; lions will eat straw, as cattle do, and snakes will no longer be dangerous. On Zion, my sacred hill,[e] there will be nothing harmful or evil."

The LORD Judges the Nations

66 The LORD says, "Heaven is my throne, and the earth is my footstool. What kind of house, then, could you build for me, what kind of place for me to live in? 2 I myself created the whole universe! I am pleased with those who are humble and repentant, who fear me and obey me.

3 "The people do as they please. It's all the same to them whether they kill a bull as a sacrifice or sacrifice a human being; whether they sacrifice a lamb or break a dog's neck; whether they present a grain-offering or offer pigs' blood; whether they offer incense or pray to an idol. They take pleasure in disgusting ways of worship. 4 So I will bring disaster upon them—the very things they are afraid of—because no one answered when I called or listened when I spoke. They chose to disobey me and do evil."

5 Listen to what the LORD says, you that fear him and obey him: "Because you are faithful to me, some of your own people hate you and will have nothing to

welcome 64.5; Lam 4.15
worship (1) (of God) [2] 60.14; 66.23
worship (2) (of other gods) 57.5; 66.3
wrong 64.5; Jer 2.19

afraid 57.11; Jer 1.8
anger [2] 65.3; Jer 2.35
being 44.11; Ezek 29.11
birth [2] 37.3; Jer 13.21
blood 63.3; Jer 2.34
body 26.19; Jer 9.22
choose 65.9; Jer 1.5
clean 28.8; Jer 6.9
comfort 61.2; Jer 16.7
create 65.18; Jer 10.12
dead 65.4; Jer 7.28
death (3) (to death) 65.15; Jer 14.18
disaster 65.23; Jer 2.3
disgrace 65.13; Jer 2.26
disgust [3] 41.24; Jer 6.15
disobey 65.12; Jer 18.10
endure [2] 64.12; Jer 10.10
enemy [2] 64.2; Jer 2.14
enjoy 65.21; Jer 2.7
evil 65.7; Jer 2.19
faithful 65.16; Jer 2.2
fear [2] 64.1; Jer 5.22
festival 33.20; Ezek 36.38

[c] SACRED GARDENS: *See 1.29.* [e] SACRED HILL: *See 2.3.*

65.2: Rom 10.21 **65.10:** Josh 7.24–26 **65.17:** Is 66.22; 2 Pet 3.13; Rev 21.1 **65.19:** Rev 21.4
65.25: Is 11.6–9 **66.1:** Mt 5.34, 35, 23.22 **66.1–2a:** Acts 7.49–50

footstool 2 Chr 9.18; Lk 20.43
gift 30.6; Jer 31.12
glad [2] 65.18; Jer 7.34
God's people 65.1; Jer 1.16
grain-offering [2] 57.6; Jer 14.12
guilty 59.3; Jer 2.22
hate 61.8; Jer 4.1
heaven [2] 65.17; Jer 7.18
help 65.1; Jer 3.23
holy 65.5; Jer 22.3
human 52.14; Jer 17.9
humble 60.22; Jer 13.15
idol 57.8; Jer 1.16
incense 65.3; Jer 6.20
lamb 65.25; Jer 11.19
last (1) 61.7; Jer 31.36
Levites Ps 135.20; Ezek 44.10
love [2] 64.11; Jer 2.2
mankind 49.26; Jer 27.5
mock 14.4; Jer 20.7
mourn 61.2; Jer 4.28
new 65.15; Jer 8.10
New Moon Festival 1.13; Ezek 45.17
obey [3] 65.13; Jer 2.20
offer [2] 65.3; Jer 1.16
pagan 65.3; Jer 3.23
please [2] 62.4; Jer 2.31
pleasure 58.2; Jer 32.41
power [3] 64.2; Jer 5.5
pray 65.1; Jer 7.16
present (1) 48.13; Dan 2.48
priest 61.6; Jer 1.1
proclaim 61.2; Jer 2.2
prosper [2] 54.13; Jer 12.1
punish [4] 65.6; Jer 1.16
pure 4.4; Jer 13.27
put out 42.3; Jer 4.4
rebel 63.10; Jer 2.8
rejoice [3] 65.18; Jer 31.13
repent 57.15; Lam 2.14

do with you. They **mock** you and say, 'Let the LORD show his greatness and **save** you, so that we may see you **rejoice**.' But they themselves will be **disgraced**!
6 Listen! That loud noise in the city, that sound in the **Temple**, is the sound of the LORD **punishing** his **enemies**!

7 "My **holy city** is like a woman who suddenly gives **birth** to a child, without ever going into labour.
8 Has anyone ever seen or heard of such a thing? Has a nation ever been born in a day? Zion will not have to **suffer** long, before the nation is born.
9 Do not think that I will bring **my people** to the point of **birth** and not let them be born." The LORD has spoken.

10 **Rejoice** with Jerusalem; be **glad** for
her,
all you that **love** this city!
Rejoice with her now,
all you that have **mourned** for her!
11 You will **enjoy** her **prosperity**,
like a child at its mother's breast.

12 The LORD says, "I will bring you **lasting prosperity**; the wealth of the nations will flow to you like a river that never goes dry. You will be like a child that is nursed by its mother, carried in her arms, and treated with **love**.
13 I will **comfort** you in Jerusalem, as a mother comforts her child.
14 When you see this happen, you will be **glad**; it will make you **strong** and healthy. Then you will know that I, the LORD, **help** those who **obey** me, and I show my **anger** against my **enemies**."

15 The LORD will come with fire. He will ride on the wings of a storm to **punish** those he is **angry** with.
16 By fire and sword he will **punish** all the people of the **world** whom he finds **guilty**—and many will be put **to death**.

17 The LORD says, "The end is near for those who **purify** themselves for **pagan worship**, who go in procession to **sacred** gardens,[g] and who eat pork and mice and other **disgusting** foods.
18 I know[h] their thoughts and their deeds. I am coming[i] to gather the people of all the nations. When they come together, they will see what my **power** can do
19 and will know that I am the one who **punishes** them.

"But I will **spare** some of them and send them to the nations and the distant lands that have not heard of my fame or seen my greatness and **power**: to Spain, Libya,[j] and Lydia, with its skilled bowmen, and to Tubal and Greece. Among these nations they will **proclaim** my greatness.
20 They will bring back all your fellow-countrymen from the nations as a **gift** to me. They will bring them to my **sacred** hill[k] in Jerusalem on horses, mules, and camels, and in chariots and wagons, just as Israelites bring **grain-offerings** to the **Temple** in ritually **clean** containers.
21 I will make some of them **priests and Levites**.

22 "Just as the **new** earth and the new **heavens** will **endure** by my **power**, so your descendants and your name will endure.
23 On every **New Moon Festival** and every **Sabbath**, people of every nation will come to **worship** me here in Jerusalem," says the LORD.
24 "As they leave, they will see the **dead bodies** of those who have **rebelled** against me. The worms that eat them will never die, and the fire that burns them will never be **put out**. The **sight** of them will be **disgusting** to all **mankind**."

Sabbath 58.13; Jer 17.21
sacred [2] 65.3; Jer 2.3
sacrifice [2] 65.3; Jer 1.16
save 65.8; Jer 2.27
sight 30.22; Jer 7.15
spare 28.15; Jer 6.11
strong 63.5; Jer 2.22
suffer 64.12; Jer 2.3
Temple (1) (of God) [2] 64.11; Jer 7.1
throne 52.2; Jer 1.15
universe Gen 2.1; Gal 4.3
way (3) 63.17; Jer 10.2
world 62.7; Jer 3.19
worship (1) (of God) 65.10; Jer 2.20
worship (2) (of other gods) [2] 65.11; Jer 1.16

[g] SACRED GARDENS: *See 1.29.* [h] *Some ancient translations* I know; *Hebrew* I.
[i] *Some ancient translations* I am coming; *Hebrew* He is coming.
[j] *One ancient translation* Libya; *Hebrew* Pul. [k] SACRED HILL: *See 2.3.*

66.7: Rev 12.5 **66.22:** Is 65.17; 2 Pet 3.13; Rev 21.1 **66.24:** Mk 9.48

THE BOOK OF JEREMIAH

INTRODUCTION

The prophet Jeremiah lived during the latter part of the seventh century and the first part of the sixth century B.C. During his long ministry he warned God's people of the catastrophe that was to fall upon the nation because of their idolatry and sin. He lived to see this prediction come true with the fall of Jerusalem to the Babylonian king, Nebuchadnezzar, the destruction of the city and the Temple, and the exile to Babylonia of Judah's king and many of the people. He also foretold the eventual return of the people from exile and the restoration of the nation.

The Book of Jeremiah may be divided into the following parts: (1) The call of Jeremiah. (2) Messages from God to the nation of Judah and its rulers during the reigns of Josiah, Jehoiakim, Jehoiachin, and Zedekiah. (3) Material from the memoirs of Baruch, Jeremiah's secretary, including various prophecies and important events from the life of Jeremiah. (4) Messages from the Lord about various foreign nations. (5) A historical appendix, giving an account of the fall of Jerusalem, and the exile to Babylon.

Jeremiah was a sensitive man who deeply loved his people, and who hated to have to pronounce judgement upon them. In many passages he spoke with deep emotion about the things he suffered because God had called him to be a prophet. The word of the Lord was like fire in his heart—he could not keep it back.

Some of the greatest words in the book point beyond Jeremiah's own troubled time to the day when there would be a new covenant, one that God's people would keep without a teacher to remind them, because it would be written on their hearts (31.31-34).

Outline of Contents

---

abandon Is 64.7; 2.15
afraid [3] Is 66.4; 3.8
authority Is 22.21; 2.20
choose Is 66.4; 7.12
command [2] Is 50.2; 2.12
destroy [2] Is 65.8; 4.6
exile Is 56.8; 3.18
god (2) (other gods) Is 65.11; 2.11
God's people Is 66.9; 2.9
idol Is 66.3; 2.5
life (1) Is 65.20; 3.21
offer Is 66.3; 6.20
overthrow Is 23.11; 31.28
priest [2] Is 66.21; 2.8
prophet Is 39.3; 2.8
protect [2] Is 60.18; 15.20
punish Is 66.6; 2.19
reign Ps 146.10; 52.4
resist Ecc 4.12; Dan 8.7
right (1) Is 64.5; 4.2
sacrifice Is 66.3; 6.20
Sovereign Is 65.15; 2.19
strength Is 63.1; 9.23
throne Is 66.1; 3.17

Jeremiah

1 This book is the account of what
was said by Jeremiah son of Hilkiah,
one of the **priests** of the town of Anathoth
in the territory of Benjamin. 2 The LORD
spoke to Jeremiah in the thirteenth year
that Josiah son of Amon was king of
Judah, 3 and he spoke to him again when
Josiah's son Jehoiakim was king. After
that, the LORD spoke to him many times,
until the eleventh year of the **reign** of
Zedekiah son of Josiah. In the fifth month
of that year the people of Jerusalem
were taken into **exile**.

The Call of Jeremiah

4 The LORD said to me, 5 "I **chose** you
before I gave you **life**, and before you
were born I selected you to be a **prophet**
to the nations."

6 I answered, "**Sovereign** LORD, I don't
know how to speak; I am too young."

7 But the LORD said to me, "Do not say
that you are too young, but go to the
people I send you to, and tell them everything I **command** you to say. 8 Do not be
afraid of them, for I will be with you to
protect you. I, the LORD, have spoken!"

9 Then the LORD stretched out his
hand, touched my lips, and said to me,
"Listen, I am giving you the **words** you
must speak. 10 Today I give you **authority**
over nations and kingdoms to uproot and
to pull down, to **destroy** and to **overthrow**, to build and to plant."

Two Visions

11 The LORD asked me, "Jeremiah,
what do you see?"

I answered, "A branch of an almond-
tree."

12 "You are **right**," the LORD said,
"and I am **watching**[a] to see that my
words come **true**."

13 Then the LORD spoke to me again.
"What else do you see?" he asked.

true Is 48.16; 10.10
watch Is 56.10; 6.17
word (1) [2] Is 59.13; 5.13
worship (2) (of other gods) Is 66.3; 2.5

[a] WATCHING: *This word in Hebrew sounds like the Hebrew for "almond."*

1.2: 2 Kgs 22.3-23.27; 2 Chr 34.8-35.19 **1.3:** 2 Kgs 23.36—24.7, 18—25.21; 2 Chr 36.5-8, 11.21

I answered, "I see a pot boiling in the
north, and it is about to tip over this
way."
14 He said to me, "Destruction will
boil over from the north on all who live
in this land, 15 because I am calling all the
nations in the north to come. Their kings
will set up their thrones at the gates of
Jerusalem and round its walls, and also
round the other cities of Judah. 16 I will
punish my people because they have
sinned; they have abandoned me, have
offered sacrifices to other gods, and have
made idols and worshipped them. 17 Get
ready, Jeremiah; go and tell them everything I command you to say. Do not be
afraid of them now, or I will make you
even more afraid when you are with
them. 18-19 Listen, Jeremiah! Everyone in
this land—the kings of Judah, the officials, the priests, and the people—will be
against you. But today I am giving you
the strength to resist them; you will be
like a fortified city, an iron pillar, and a
bronze wall. They will not defeat you, for
I will be with you to protect you. I, the
LORD, have spoken."

God's Care for Israel

2 The LORD told me 2 to proclaim this
message to everyone in Jerusalem.
"I remember how faithful you were
when you were young,
how you loved me when we were
first married;
you followed me through the desert,
through a land that had not been
sown.
3 Israel, you belonged to me alone;
you were my sacred possession.
I sent suffering and disaster
on everyone who hurt you.
I, the LORD, have spoken."

The Sin of Israel's Ancestors

4 Listen to the LORD's message, you
descendants of Jacob, you tribes of
Israel. 5 The LORD says:
"What accusation did your ancestors
bring against me?
What made them turn away from
me?
They worshipped worthless idols
and became worthless themselves.
6 They did not care about me,
even though I rescued them from
Egypt
and led them through the
wilderness:
a land of deserts and sand-dunes,
a dry and dangerous land
where no one lives
and no one will even travel.
7 I brought them into a fertile land,
to enjoy its harvests and its other
good things.
But instead they ruined my land;
they defiled the country I had given
them.
8 The priests did not ask, 'Where is the
LORD?'
My own priests did not know me.
The rulers rebelled against me;
the prophets spoke in the name of
Baal
and worshipped useless idols.

The LORD's Case against His People

9 "And so I, the LORD, will state my case
against my people again.
I will bring charges against their
descendants.
10 Go west to the island of Cyprus,
and send someone eastwards to the
land of Kedar.
You will see that nothing like this
has ever happened before.
11 No other nation has ever changed its
gods,
even though they were not real.
But my people have exchanged me,
the God who has brought them
honour,
for gods that can do nothing for
them.
12 And so I command the sky to shake
with horror,
to be amazed and astonished,
13 for my people have committed two
sins:
they have turned away from me,
the spring of fresh water,
and they have dug cisterns,
cracked cisterns that can hold no
water at all.

The Results of Israel's Unfaithfulness

14 "Israel is not a slave;
he was not born into slavery.
Why then do his enemies hunt him
down?
15 They have roared at him like lions;
they have made his land a desert,
and his towns lie in ruins,
completely abandoned.
16 Yes, the men of Memphis and
Tahpanhes
have cracked his skull.
17 Israel, you brought this on yourself!
You deserted me, the LORD your
God,
while I was leading you along the
way.
18 What do you think you will gain by
going to Egypt
to drink water from the Nile?

abandon [2] 1.16; 5.7
accuse Is 59.12; 14.7
Almighty Is 54.5; 5.13
alone Is 49.21; 29.11
amaze Is 63.5; 18.16
anger Is 66.14; 3.5
authority 1.10; 5.5
best Is 64.6; 6.16
bitter Is 38.3; 6.26
blood [2] Is 66.3; 19.4
bride Is 62.5; Jn 3.29
care Is 63.9; 6.20
case (2) Is 59.4; 12.1
change Is 55.7; 4.28
charge (3) Is 50.8; 18.18
command 1.7; 3.13
complain Is 45.9; 30.15
condemn Is 34.2; 8.14
control Is 45.12; 10.23
correct Prov 29.1; 10.24
danger [2] Is 65.25; 38.24
dark Is 60.2; 4.28
defile [2] Is 24.5; 3.1
deny Ecc 5.8; 5.12
disappoint Is 49.23; 15.18
disaster Is 66.4; 4.6
disgrace [3] Is 66.5; 3.25
enemy Is 66.6; 4.13
enjoy Is 66.11; 22.15
evil Is 66.4; 3.5
faithful Is 66.5; 3.20
forget [2] Is 65.16; 3.21
god (2) (other gods) [8] 1.16; 3.13
God's people [4] 1.16; 4.12
guilty Is 66.16; 3.13
harvest Is 62.9; 5.24
honour Is 63.14; 5.24
horror Ps 116.3; 15.4
hurt Is 59.4; 7.18

idol [2] 1.16; 4.1
innocent [2] Is 59.7; 7.6
learn [2] Is 42.25; 5.3
love [2] Is 66.10; 3.4
loyal Is 45.23; Ezek 14.5
message [2] Is 40.6; 5.13
obey Is 66.2; 3.13
please Is 66.2; 6.20
poor Is 61.1; 5.4
possess Is 65.9; 3.18
priest [3] 1.1; 4.9
proclaim Is 66.19; 11.6
prophet [3] 1.5; 4.9
punish [3] 1.16; 5.9
rage Is 49.26; 4.21
real Prov 17.27; 5.7
rebel [2] Is 66.24; 3.1
refuse (1) Is 59.13; 5.3
reject [2] Is 59.13; 4.30
remember Is 64.5; 3.16
rescue Is 63.9; 6.9
ruin [2] Is 64.10; 4.7
sacred Is 66.17; 17.2
save [2] Is 66.5; 4.14
seed Is 61.11; 4.3
shame Is 65.3; 3.3
slave [2] Is 52.3; 25.1
Sovereign [2] 1.6; 4.10
sow Is 62.9; 4.3
strong Is 66.14; 4.12
suffer Is 66.8; 4.18
thief Is 1.23; Joel 2.9
trouble [3] Is 65.10; 6.8
trust Is 57.13; 5.17
turn [8] Is 64.7; 3.6
useless Is 59.5; 6.29
vine [2] Is 37.30; 5.17
wedding Is 61.10; 7.34
worship (1) (of God Is 66.23; 3.17
worship (2) (of other gods) [4] 1.16; 3.9
worst Prov 29.24; Ezek 14.21
worthless [2] Is 48.10; 6.30
wrong Is 65.2; 8.6

What do you think you will gain by
going to Assyria
to drink water from the Euphrates?
19 Your own evil will punish you,
and your turning from me will
condemn you.
You will learn how bitter and wrong it
is
to abandon me, the LORD your God,
and no longer to remain loyal to me.
I, the Sovereign LORD Almighty, have
spoken."

Israel Refuses to Worship the LORD

20 The Sovereign LORD says,
"Israel, long ago you rejected my
authority;
you refused to obey me and worship
me.
On every high hill
and under every green tree
you worshipped fertility gods.
21 I planted you like a choice vine
from the very best seed.
But look what you have become!
You are like a rotten, worthless
vine.
22 Even if you washed with the strongest
soap,
I would still see the stain of your
guilt.
23 How can you say you have not defiled
yourself,
that you have never worshipped
Baal?
Look how you sinned in the valley;
see what you have done.
You are like a wild camel on heat,
running about loose,
24 rushing into the desert.[b]
When she is on heat, who can control
her?
No male that wants her has to trouble
himself;
she is always available at mating
time.
25 Israel, don't wear your feet out,
or let your throat become dry
from chasing after other gods.
But you say, 'No! I can't turn back.
I have loved foreign gods
and will go after them.' "

Israel Deserves to be Punished

26 The LORD says, "Just as a thief is
disgraced when caught, so all you people
of Israel will be disgraced—your kings
and officials, your priests and prophets.
27 You will all be disgraced—you that say
that a tree is your father and that a rock
is your mother. This will happen because
you turned away from me instead of
turning to me. But when you are in
trouble, you ask me to come and save
you.

28 "Where are the gods that you made
for yourselves? When you are in trouble,
let them save you—if they can! Judah,
you have as many gods as you have
cities. 29 What is your complaint? Why
have you rebelled against me? 30 I
punished you, but it did no good; you
would not let me correct you. Like a
raging lion, you have murdered your prophets. 31 People of Israel, listen to what I
am saying. Have I been like a desert to
you, like a dark and dangerous land?
Why, then, do you say that you will do as
you please, that you will never come
back to me? 32 Does a young woman forget her jewellery, or a bride her wed-
ding-dress? But my people have forgotten me for more days than can be
counted. 33 You certainly know how to
chase after lovers. Even the worst of
women can learn from you. 34 Your
clothes are stained with the blood of the
poor and innocent, not with the blood of
burglars.

"But in spite of all this, 35 you say, 'I am
innocent; surely the LORD is no longer
angry with me.' But I, the LORD, will
punish you because you deny that you
have sinned. 36 You have cheapened
yourself by turning to the gods of other
nations. You will be disappointed by
Egypt, just as you were by Assyria. 37 You
will turn away from Egypt, hanging your
head in shame. I, the LORD, have
rejected those you trust; you will not gain
anything from them."

Unfaithful Israel

3 The LORD says, "If a man divorces
his wife, and she leaves him and
becomes another man's wife, he cannot
take her back again. This would completely defile the land. But, Israel, you
have had many lovers, and now you want
to return to me! 2 Look up at the hill-tops.
Is there any place where you have not
acted like a prostitute? You waited for
lovers along the roadside, as an Arab
waits for victims in the desert. You have
defiled the land with your prostitution.
3 That is why the rains were held back,
and the spring showers did not come.
You even look like a prostitute; you have
no shame.

4 "And now you say to me, 'You are
my father, and you have loved me ever
since I was a child. 5 You won't always be
angry; you won't be cross with me for

accept Is 56.7; 6.20
act [2] Is 57.18; 6.14
admit (1) Is 48.6; Dan 4.25
adultery Is 57.3; 5.7
afraid 1.8; 10.5
ancient Is 64.5; 5.15
anger [3] 2.35; 4.4
ashamed Is 45.16; 6.15
command [2] 2.12; 4.12
commit Is 33.15; 5.7
confess Is 45.14; 14.20
Covenant Box Ps 132.6; Heb 9.4
defile [3] 2.7; 7.30
delight Is 62.5; 31.12
disgrace 2.26; 9.19
divorce [2] Is 50.1; Ezek 44.22
evil [2] 2.19; 4.4
exile 1.3; 13.19
faithful [2] 2.2; 4.1
Father (2) (God) [2] Is 64.8; 31.9
flock Is 61.5; 5.17
forget 2.32; 13.25

[b] *Probable text* rushing into the desert; *Hebrew* a wild donkey used to the desert.

god (2) (other gods) [2] 2.11; 5.7
guilty 2.22; 16.10
heal Is 61.1; 8.15
heart Is 65.14; 4.14
help [2] Is 66.14; 11.11
life (1) 1.5; 10.23
love [2] 2.2; 8.2
mercy Is 64.9; 5.16
need Is 58.10; 15.19
never again Is 54.9; 22.10
obey [3] 2.20; 5.5
pagan Is 66.17; 13.27
plead Prov 2.3; 7.16
possess 2.3; 7.7
prostitute [6] Is 57.3; 5.7
prove Is 50.8; 12.1
rebel 2.8; 4.17
remember 2.2; 11.19
shame [3] 2.37; 7.19
sincere Ps 145.18; Hos 7.14
stubborn Is 65.2; 5.3
sure Is 61.11; 5.3
throne 1.15; 13.18
turn [5] 2.5; 4.1
understand Is 57.1; 4.22
unfaithful [8] Is 54.4; 9.2
victim Is 59.15; 46.10
wisdom Is 47.10; 8.9
world Is 66.16; 10.10
worship (1) (of God) 2.20; 5.2
worship (2) (of other gods) [3] 2.5; 5.7

ever.' Israel, that is what you said, but
you did all the evil you could."

Israel and Judah Must Repent

6 When Josiah was king, the LORD
said to me, "Have you seen what Israel,
that unfaithful woman, has done? She
has turned away from me, and on every
high hill and under every green tree she
has acted like a prostitute. 7 I thought
that after she had done all this, she would
surely return to me. But she did not
return, and her unfaithful sister Judah
saw it all. 8 Judah also saw that I divorced
Israel and sent her away because she
had turned from me and had become a
prostitute. But Judah, Israel's unfaithful
sister, was not afraid. She too became a
prostitute 9 and was not at all ashamed.
She defiled the land, and she committed
adultery by worshipping stones and
trees. 10 And after all this, Judah, Israel's
unfaithful sister, only pretended to return
to me; she was not sincere. I, the LORD,
have spoken."

11 Then the LORD told me that, even
though Israel had turned away from him,
she had proved to be better than unfaithful Judah. 12 He told me to go and say to
Israel, "Unfaithful Israel, come back to
me. I am merciful and will not be angry;
I will not be angry with you for ever.
13 Only admit that you are guilty and that
you have rebelled against the LORD, your
God. Confess that under every green tree
you have given your love to foreign gods
and that you have not obeyed my commands. I, the LORD, have spoken.

14 "Unfaithful people, come back; you
belong to me. I will take one of you from
each town and two from each clan, and I
will bring you back to Mount Zion. 15 I will
give you rulers who obey me, and they
will rule you with wisdom and understanding. 16 Then when you have become
numerous in that land, people will no
longer talk about my Covenant Box.
They will no longer think about it or
remember it; they will not even need it,
nor will they make another one. 17 When
that time comes, Jerusalem will be
called 'The Throne of the LORD,' and all
nations will gather there to worship me.
They will no longer do what their stubborn and evil hearts tell them. 18 Israel
will join with Judah, and together they
will come from exile in the country in
the north and will return to the land that
I gave your ancestors as a permanent
possession."

The Idolatry of God's People

19 The LORD says,
"Israel, I wanted to accept you as my
son
and give you a delightful land,
the most beautiful land in all the
world.
I wanted you to call me father,
and never again turn away from me.
20 But like an unfaithful wife,
you have not been faithful to me.
I, the LORD, have spoken."

21 A noise is heard on the hill-tops:
it is the people of Israel crying and
pleading,
because they have lived sinful lives
and have forgotten the LORD their
God.
22 Return, all of you who have turned
away from the LORD;
he will heal you and make you
faithful.

You say, "Yes, we are coming to the
LORD, because he is our God. 23 We were
not helped at all by our pagan worship on
the hill-tops. Help for Israel comes only
from the LORD our God. 24 But the worship of Baal, the god of shame, has made
us lose flocks and herds, sons and daughters—everything that our ancestors have
worked for since ancient times. 25 We
should lie down in shame and let our disgrace cover us. We and our ancestors
have always sinned against the LORD our
God; we have never obeyed his commands."

A Call to Repentance

4 The LORD says, "People of Israel, if
you want to turn, then turn back to
me. If you are faithful to me and remove
the idols I hate, 2 it will be right for you to
swear by my name. Then[c] all the nations
will ask me to bless them, and they will
praise me."

3 The LORD says to the people of
Judah and Jerusalem, "Plough up your
unploughed fields; do not sow your seeds
among thorns. 4 Keep your covenant with
me, your LORD, and dedicate yourselves
to me, you people of Judah and Jerusalem. If you don't, my anger will burn
like fire because of the evil things you
have done. It will burn, and there will be
no one to put it out."

Judah Is Threatened with Invasion

5 Blow the trumpet throughout the land!

anger [3] 3.5; 6.11
announce Is 63.1; 7.1
bad Is 30.14; 10.19
barren Is 41.18; Hos 2.3
bless Is 65.9; 16.5
change 2.11; 7.1
cloud Is 60.8; 10.13
command 3.13; 5.31
courage Is 42.4; 38.4
covenant Is 61.8; 9.25
dark 2.31; 13.16
deceive Is 63.8; 7.4
dedicate Is 23.18; Ezek 43.18
destroy [5] 1.10; 5.10
disaster [2] 2.3; 6.1
doom [3] Is 33.1; 13.27
enemy [3] 2.14; 5.10
evil [3] 3.5; 5.26
fail Is 55.11; 10.21
faithful 3.20; 5.1
fool Is 44.20; 5.4
gentle Is 40.11; Mt 10.16
God's people [2] 2.9; 5.7

[c] it will be right...name. Then; *or* and if you swear by my name and are truthful, just, and righteous, then.

3.6: 2 Kgs 22.1—23.30; 2 Chr 34.1—35.27 **4.3:** Hos 10.12

hate Is 66.5; 7.10
heart [4] 3.17; 7.24
idol 2.5; 7.30
judge Is 57.3; 11.20
light (1) Is 60.2; 13.16
mind (1) Is 44.18; 7.31
mourn Is 66.10; 6.26
name (2) (name of God, of Jesus) Is 65.16; 10.6
pain [2] Is 53.3; 6.24
peace Is 60.17; 6.16
praise Is 64.11; 13.11
priest 2.8; 5.31
prophet 2.8; 5.13
put out Is 66.24; 7.20
rage 2.30; 23.19
rebel 3.13; 5.23
reject 2.20; 5.5
right (1) 1.12; 5.1
ruin [3] 2.7; 6.19
sackcloth Is 58.5; 6.26
safe Is 59.8; 6.1
save 2.27; 8.20
seed 2.21; 50.16
Sovereign 2.19; 7.20
sow 2.2; 12.13
strong 2.22; 5.15
stupid Is 44.18; 5.21
suffer 2.3; 15.8
swear Is 65.16; 12.16
turn [3] 3.6; 5.3
understand 3.15; 9.12
wail Is 29.2; Ezek 2.10
warn Is 56.10; 6.8
weep Is 65.19; 9.10

Shout loud and clear!
Tell the people of Judah and
Jerusalem
to run to the fortified cities.
6 Point the way to Zion!
Run for **safety**! Don't delay!
The LORD is bringing **disaster**
and great **destruction** from the
north.
7 Like a lion coming from its hiding
place,
a **destroyer** of nations has set out.
He is coming to **destroy** Judah.
The cities of Judah will be left in **ruins**,
and no one will live in them.
8 So put on **sackcloth**, and **weep** and **wail**
because the fierce **anger of the
LORD**
has not **turned** away from Judah.

9 The LORD said, "On that day kings
and officials will lose their **courage**;
priests will be shocked and **prophets** will
be astonished."
10 Then I said, "**Sovereign** LORD, you
have completely **deceived** the people of
Jerusalem! You have said there would
be **peace**, but a sword is at their throats."
11 The time is coming when the
people of Jerusalem will be told that a
scorching wind is blowing in from the
desert towards them. It will not be a
gentle wind that only blows away the
chaff—12 the wind that comes at the
LORD's **command** will be much **stronger**
than that! It is the LORD himself who is
pronouncing **judgement on his people**.

Judah Is Surrounded by Enemies

13 Look, the **enemy** is coming like
clouds. His war-chariots are like a whirlwind, and his horses are faster than
eagles. We are lost! We are **doomed**!
14 Jerusalem, wash the **evil** from your
heart, so that you may be **saved**. How
long will you go on thinking sinful
thoughts?
15 Messengers from the city of Dan
and from the hills of Ephraim **announce**
the **bad** news. 16 They have come to **warn**
the nations and to tell Jerusalem that
enemies are coming from a country far
away. These **enemies** will shout against
the cities of Judah 17 and will surround
Jerusalem like men guarding a field,
because her people have **rebelled** against
the LORD. The LORD has spoken.
18 Judah, you have brought this on
yourself by the way you have lived and
by the things you have done. Your sin
has caused this **suffering**; it has stabbed
you through the **heart**.

Jeremiah's Sorrow for His People

19 The **pain**! I can't bear the **pain**!
My **heart**! My **heart** is beating wildly!
I can't keep quiet;
I hear the trumpets
and the shouts of battle.
20 One **disaster** follows another;
the whole country is left in **ruins**.
Suddenly our tents are **destroyed**;
their curtains are torn to pieces.
21 How long must I see the battle **raging**
and hear the blasts of trumpets?
22 The LORD says, "**My people** are **stupid**;
they don't know me.
They are like **foolish** children;
they have no **understanding**.
They are experts at doing what is **evil**,
but **failures** at doing what is good."

Jeremiah's Vision of the Coming Destruction

23 I looked at the earth—it was a **barren**
waste;
at the sky—there was no **light**.
24 I looked at the mountains—they were
shaking,
and the hills were rocking to and
fro.
25 I saw that there were no people;
even the birds had flown away.
26 The fertile land had become a desert;
its cities were in **ruins**
because of the **LORD's fierce anger**.
27 (The LORD has said that the whole
earth will become a wilderness, but that
he will not completely **destroy** it.)
28 The earth will **mourn**;
the sky will grow **dark**.
The LORD has spoken
and will not **change his mind**.
He has made his decision
and will not **turn** back.
29 At the noise of the horsemen and
bowmen
everyone will run away.
Some will run to the forest,
others will climb up among the
rocks.
Every town will be left empty,
and no one will live in them again.
30 Jerusalem, you are **doomed**!
Why do you dress in scarlet?
Why do you put on jewellery and
paint your eyes?
You are making yourself beautiful for
nothing!
Your lovers have **rejected** you
and want to kill you.
31 I heard a cry, like a woman in labour,
a scream like a woman bearing her
first child.
It was the cry of Jerusalem gasping for
breath,

stretching out her hand and saying,
"I am **doomed**!
They are coming to kill me!"

The Sin of Jerusalem

5 People of Jerusalem, run through
your streets!
Look around! See for yourselves!
Search the market-places!
Can you find one person
who does what is **right**
and tries to be **faithful** to God?
If you can, the LORD will **forgive**
Jerusalem.
[2] Even though you **claim** to **worship** the
LORD,
you do not mean what you say.
[3] **Surely** the LORD looks for **faithfulness**.
He **struck** you, but you paid no
attention;
he crushed you, but you **refused** to
learn.
You were **stubborn** and would not **turn**
from your sins.
[4] Then I thought, "These are only the
poor and **ignorant**.
They behave **foolishly**;
they don't know what their God
requires,
what the LORD wants them to do.
[5] I will go to the people in **power**,
and talk with them.
Surely they know what their God
requires,
what the LORD wants them to do."
But all of them have **rejected** the
LORD's **authority**
and **refuse** to **obey** him.
[6] That is why lions from the forest will
kill them;
wolves from the desert will tear
them to pieces,
and leopards will prowl through
their towns.
If those people go out, they will be torn
apart
because their sins are numerous
and time after time they have
turned from God.
[7] The LORD asked, "Why should I **forgive**
the sins of **my people**?
They have **abandoned** me
and have **worshipped gods** that are
not **real**.
I fed **my people** until they were full,
but they **committed adultery**
and spent their time with
prostitutes.
[8] They were like well-fed stallions wild
with **desire**,
each **lusting** for his **neighbour's** wife.
[9] Shouldn't I **punish** them for these
things
and take **revenge** on a nation such
as this?
[10] I will send **enemies** to cut down **my
people's vineyards**,
but not to **destroy** them completely.
I will tell them to **strip** away the
branches,
because those branches are not
mine.
[11] The people of Israel and Judah
have **betrayed** me completely.
I, the LORD, have spoken."

The LORD Rejects Israel

12 The **LORD's people** have **denied** him
and have said, "He won't really do anything.[d] We won't have **hard** times; we
won't have war or **famine**." [13-14] They
have said that the **prophets** are nothing
but windbags and that they have no
message from the LORD. The LORD God
Almighty said to me, "Jeremiah, because
these people have said such things, I will
make my **words** like a fire in your mouth.
The people will be like wood, and the fire
will burn them up."
15 People of Israel, the LORD is bringing a nation from afar to attack you. It is
a **strong** and **ancient** nation, a nation
whose language you do not know. [16] Their
bowmen are **mighty** soldiers who kill
without **mercy**. [17] They will **devour** your
crops and your food; they will kill your
sons and your daughters. They will
slaughter your **flocks** and your herds and
destroy your **vines** and fig-trees. The
fortified cities in which you **trust** will be
destroyed by their army.
18 The LORD says, "Yet even in those
days I will not completely **destroy my
people**. [19] When they ask why I did all
these things, tell them, Jeremiah, that
just as they **turned away** from me and
served foreign **gods** in their own land, so
they will **serve strangers** in a land that is
not theirs."

God Warns His People

20 The LORD says, "Tell the descendants of Jacob, tell the people of Judah:
[21] Pay attention, you **foolish** and **stupid**
people, who have eyes, but cannot see,
and have ears, but cannot hear. [22] I am
the LORD; why don't you **fear** me? Why
don't you **tremble** before me? I placed
the sand as the boundary of the sea, a
permanent boundary that it cannot cross.
The sea may toss, but it cannot go beyond it; the waves may roar, but they

[d] He won't...anything; *or* We don't want anything to do with him.

5.21: Is 6.9–10; Ezek 12.2; Mk 8.18 **5.22:** Job 38.8–11

abandon 2.15; 6.8
adultery 3.9; 7.9
Almighty 2.19; 6.6
ancient 3.24; 6.16
apart Is 64.1; Ezek 22.27
authority 2.20; Dan 7.6
betray Is 33.1; 12.6
claim Is 58.2; 23.25
command 4.12; 7.22
commit 3.9; 7.9
deny 2.35; Lam 3.35
desire Is 59.17; 24.7
destroy [4] 4.6; 6.1
devour Is 56.9; 15.3
enemy 4.13; 6.25
evil [2] 4.4; 6.7
faithful [2] 4.1; 7.28
famine Is 14.30; 21.7
fear Is 66.2; 30.5
flock 3.24; 31.10
fool [2] 4.22; 10.8
forgive [2] Is 55.7; 18.23
god (2) (other gods) [2] 3.13; 7.6
God's people [7] 4.12; 6.14
hard Is 43.2; 6.28
harvest 2.7; 8.13
honour 2.11; 10.7
ignorant Is 44.9; Ezek 45.20
justice Is 61.8; 9.24
keep from Is 29.21; 10.4
learn 2.19; 6.18
lie (2) Is 59.3; 7.9
lust Is 57.8; 13.27
mercy 3.12; 6.23
message 2.2; 6.10
might Is 60.16; 6.22
neighbour Is 19.2; 6.21
obey 3.13; 6.19
oppress Is 61.8; 6.6
orphan Is 10.2; 7.6
poor 2.34; 16.6
power [2] Is 66.18; 10.6
priest 4.9; 6.13
prophet [3] 4.9; 6.13
prostitute 3.2; Ezek 16.16
punish [2] 2.19; 6.6
real 2.11; 23.36
rebel 4.17; 6.28
refuse (1) [2] 2.20; 6.10
reject 4.30; 6.19
require [2] Is 45.19; Mic 6.8
revenge [2] Is 1.24; 9.9
rich Is 63.7; 9.23
right (1) 4.2; 9.24
right (3) Is 45.11; 11.15
serve [2] Is 65.8; 8.2
slaughter Is 53.7; 7.32
stranger Ecc 10.3; 14.8
strike Is 41.2; 14.15
strip (1) Is 47.2; 6.9
strong 4.12; 9.23
stubborn [2] 3.17; 6.10
stupid 4.22; 10.8
sure 3.7; 22.24
terrible Is 14.30; 13.22

trap Is 28.13; 8.9
tremble Is 64.2; 8.1
trust 2.37; 7.8
turn [4] 4.1; 6.8
vine 2.21; 8.13
vineyard Is 65.21; 6
word (1) 1.9; 6.19
worship (1) (of Goc 3.17; 7.1
worship (2) (of other gods) 3.9; 7.6

cannot break through. 23 But you people!
You are stubborn and rebellious; you
have turned aside and left me. 24 You
never thought to honour me, even though
I send the autumn rains and the spring
rains and give you the harvest season
each year. 25 Instead, your sins have kept
these good things from you.
26 "Evil men live among my people;
they lie in wait like men who spread nets
to catch birds,[e] but they have set their
traps to catch men. 27 Just as a hunter
fills his cage with birds, they have filled
their houses with loot. That is why they
are powerful and rich, 28 why they are fat
and well fed. There is no limit to their
evil deeds. They do not give orphans
their rights or show justice to the
oppressed.
29 "But I, the LORD, will punish them
for these things; I will take revenge on
this nation. 30 A terrible and shocking
thing has happened in the land: 31 prophets speak nothing but lies; priests rule
as the prophets command, and my
people offer no objections. But what will
they do when it all comes to an end?"

Jerusalem Is Surrounded by Enemies

6 People of Benjamin, run for safety!
Escape from Jerusalem! Sound the
trumpet in Tekoa and build a signal fire
in Beth Haccherem. Disaster and
destruction are about to come from the
north. 2 The city of Zion is beautiful, but it
will be destroyed; 3 kings will camp there
with their armies. They will pitch their
tents round the city, and each one will
camp wherever he wants. 4 They will say,
"Prepare to attack Jerusalem! Get
ready! We'll attack at noon!" But then
they will say, "It's too late, the day is almost over, and the evening shadows are
growing long. 5 We'll attack by night;
we'll destroy the city's fortresses."
6 The LORD Almighty has ordered
these kings to cut down trees and build
mounds in order to besiege Jerusalem.
He has said, "I will punish this city because it is full of oppression. 7 As a well
keeps its water fresh, so Jerusalem keeps
its evil fresh. I hear violence and destruction in the city; sickness and wounds are
all I see. 8 People of Jerusalem, let these
troubles be a warning to you, or else I
will abandon you; I will turn your city
into a desert, a place where no one
lives."

Rebellious Israel

9 The LORD Almighty said to me,
"Israel will be stripped clean like a vineyard from which every grape has been
picked. So you must rescue everyone you
can while there is still time."
10 I answered, "Who would listen to
me if I spoke to them and warned them?
They are stubborn and refuse to listen to
your message; they laugh at what you
tell me to say. 11 Your anger against them
burns in me too, LORD, and I can't hold it
in any longer."
Then the LORD said to me, "Pour out
my anger on the children in the streets
and on the gatherings of the young men.
Husbands and wives will be taken away,
and even the very old will not be spared.
12 Their houses will be given to others,
and so will their fields and their wives. I
am going to punish the people of this
land. 13 Everyone, great and small, tries
to make money dishonestly; even prophets and priests cheat the people.
14 They act as if my people's wounds were
only scratches. 'All is well,' they say,
when all is not well. 15 Were they
ashamed because they did these disgusting things? No, they were not at all
ashamed; they don't even know how to
blush. And so they will fall as others have
fallen; when I punish them, that will be
the end of them. I, the LORD, have
spoken."

Israel Rejects God's Way

16 The LORD said to his people, "Stand
at the crossroads and look. Ask for the
ancient paths and where the best road is.
Walk on it, and you will live in peace."
But they said, "No, we will not!"
17 Then the LORD appointed watchmen to
listen for the trumpet's warning. But they
said, "We will not listen."
18 So the LORD said, "Listen, you
nations, and learn what is going to happen to my people. 19 Listen, earth! As
punishment for all their schemes I am
bringing ruin on these people, because
they have rejected my teaching and
have not obeyed my words. 20 What do I
care about the incense they bring me
from Sheba, or the spices from a distant
land? I will not accept their offerings or
be pleased with their sacrifices. 21 And so
I will make these people stumble and
fall. Fathers and sons will die, and so will
friends and neighbours."

Invasion from the North

22 The LORD says, "People are coming
from a country in the north; a mighty
nation far away is preparing for war.

[e] *Probable text* they...birds; *Hebrew unclear.*

6.12–15: Jer 8.10–12 **6.14:** Ezek 13.10

refine Is 48.10; 9.7
refuse (1) 5.3; 7.13
reject [2] 5.5; 7.29
rescue 2.6; 12.14
ruin 4.7; 9.11
sackcloth 4.8; 48.37
sacrifice 1.16; 7.9
safe 4.6; 7.4
scheme Is 29.15; Mic 7.3
spare Is 66.19; 17.18
strip (1) 5.10; 13.26
stubborn [2] 5.3; 7.24
stumble Is 63.12; 13.16
teach Is 59.21; 9.5
tear (2) Is 38.5; 9.1
terror Is 54.14; 8.15
test Is 48.10; 9.7
trouble 2.24; 11.14
turn 5.3; 8.4
useless 2.8; 8.19
vineyard 5.10; 12.10
violent Is 65.12; 9.5
warn [3] 4.16; 11.7
watch 1.12; 8.17
word (1) 5.13; 7.4
worthless 2.5; 10.3

abandon 5.7; 9.13
accept 3.19; 12.16
act 3.2; 8.11
Almighty [2] 5.13; 7.1
ancient 5.15; 30.20
anger [2] 4.4; 7.20
anguish Is 26.16; 15.8
ash Is 58.5; 51.25
ashamed [2] 3.9; 8.12
best 2.21; 20.9
bitter 2.19; 9.15
care 2.6; 12.2
cheat Is 33.15; 8.10
clean Is 66.20; 43.12
corrupt Is 1.4; Ezek 16.51
cruel Is 27.8; 50.42
dare Is 50.8; 30.21
destroy [5] 5.10; 7.6
disaster 4.6; 11.15
disgust Is 66.3; 8.12
dishonest Prov 28.6; 8.8
enemy 5.10; 8.16
escape Is 52.12; 11.11
evil [2] 5.26; 7.24
friend Is 41.8; 9.4
God's people [6] 5.7; 7.12
hard 5.12; 10.24
incense Is 66.3; 17.26
learn 5.3; 7.28
mercy 5.16; 12.15
message 5.13; 10.1
might 5.16; 10.6
mourn 4.28; 7.29
neighbour 5.8; 9.8
obey 5.5; 7.23
offer 1.16; 7.9
oppress 5.28; 20.13
pain 4.19; 13.21
peace 4.10; 8.15
please 2.31; 9.24
priest 5.31; 8.1
prophet 5.13; 7.25
punish [4] 5.9; 7.28
rebel 5.23; 7.26

23 They have taken up their bows and
swords; they are cruel and merciless.
They sound like the roaring sea, as they
ride their horses. They are ready for
battle against Jerusalem."
24 "We have heard the news," say the
people of Jerusalem, "and our hands
hang limp; we are seized by anguish and
pain like a woman in labour. 25 We dare
not go to the countryside or walk on the
roads, because our enemies are armed
and terror is all round us."
26 The LORD says to his people, "Put
on sackcloth and roll in ashes. Mourn
with bitter tears as you would for an only
son, because the one who comes to destroy you will suddenly attack.
27 Jeremiah, test my people, as you would
test metal, and find out what they are
like. 28 They are all stubborn rebels, hard
as bronze and iron. They are all corrupt,
going round and spreading gossip. 29 The
furnace burns fiercely, but the waste
metals do not melt and run off. It is useless to go on refining my people, because
those who are evil are not taken away.
30 They will be called worthless dross, because I, the LORD, have rejected them."

Jeremiah Preaches in the Temple

7 1-3 The LORD sent me to the gate of
the Temple where the people of
Judah went in to worship. He told me to
stand there and announce what the LORD
Almighty, the God of Israel, had to say to
them: "Change the way you are living
and the things you are doing, and I will
let you go on living here. 4 Stop believing
those deceitful words, 'We are safe! This
is the LORD's Temple, this is the LORD's
Temple, this is the LORD's Temple!'
5 "Change the way you are living and
stop doing the things you are doing. Be
fair in your treatment of one another.
6 Stop taking advantage of aliens, orphans, and widows. Stop killing innocent
people in this land. Stop worshipping
other gods, for that will destroy you. 7 If
you change, I will let you go on living
here in the land which I gave your ancestors as a permanent possession.
8 "Look, you put your trust in deceitful
words. 9 You steal, murder, commit adultery, tell lies under oath, offer sacrifices
to Baal, and worship gods that you had
not known before. 10 You do these things I
hate, and then you come and stand in my
presence, in my own Temple, and say,
'We are safe!' 11 Do you think that my
Temple is a hiding place for robbers? I
have seen what you are doing. 12 Go to
Shiloh,[f] the first place where I chose to
be worshipped, and see what I did to it
because of the sins of my people Israel.
13 You have committed all these sins, and
even though I spoke to you over and over
again, you refused to listen. You would
not answer when I called you. 14 And so,
what I did to Shiloh I will do to this
Temple of mine, in which you trust. Here
in this place that I gave to your ancestors
and to you, I will do the same thing that I
did to Shiloh. 15 I will drive you out of my
sight as I drove out your relatives, the
people of Israel. I, the LORD, have
spoken."

The People's Disobedience

16 The LORD said, "Jeremiah, do not
pray for these people. Do not cry or pray
on their behalf; do not plead with me, for
I will not listen to you. 17 Don't you see
what they are doing in the cities of Judah
and in the streets of Jerusalem? 18 The
children gather firewood, the men build
fires, and the women mix dough to bake
cakes for the goddess they call the Queen
of Heaven. They also pour out wine-
offerings to other gods, in order to hurt
me. 19 But am I really the one they are
hurting? No, they are hurting themselves and bringing shame on themselves. 20 And so I, the Sovereign LORD,
will pour out my fierce anger on this
Temple. I will pour it out on people and
animals alike, and even on the trees and
the crops. My anger will be like a fire
that no one can put out.
21 "My people, some sacrifices you
burn completely on the altar, and some
you are permitted to eat. But what I, the
LORD, say is that you might as well eat
them all. 22 I gave your ancestors no commands about burnt-offerings or any other
kinds of sacrifices, when I brought them
out of Egypt. 23 But I did command them
to obey me, so that I would be their God
and they would be my people. And I told
them to live as I had commanded them,
so that things would go well for them.
24 But they did not obey or pay any attention. Instead, they did whatever their
stubborn and evil hearts told them to do,
and they became worse instead of better.
25 From the day that your ancestors came
out of Egypt until this very day, I have
kept on sending my servants, the prophets, to you. 26 Yet no one listened or
paid any attention. Instead, you became

permit Neh 13.1; 52.33
plead 3.21; 11.14
possess 3.18; 20.5
pray [2] Is 66.3; 11.1
presence Is 64.2; 28.1
prophet 6.13; 8.1
punish 6.6; 8.12
put out 4.4; 17.27
rebel 6.28; 28.16
refuse (1) 6.10; 8.5
reject 6.19; 8.9
rob Is 42.22; 48.27
sacrifice [4] 6.20; 11.12
safe [2] 6.1; 15.20
servant Is 63.11; 14.
shame 3.3; 8.9
sight Is 66.24; 10.2
slaughter 5.17; 12.3
Sovereign 4.10; 14.1
steal Is 10.6; 51.44
stubborn [2] 6.10; 9.14
Temple (1) (of God) [8] Is 66.6; 11.15
trust [2] 5.17; 9.4
wedding 2.32; 16.9
widow Is 54.4; 15.8
wine-offering Ps 116.13; 32.29
word (1) [3] 6.19; 8.9
worse Is 24.16; 16.12
worship (1) (of God) [2] 5.2; 10.25
worship (2) (of other gods) [2] 5.7; 8.2

adultery 5.7; 23.14
advantage Is 56.11; Ezek 16.15
Almighty 6.6; 8.3
altar [2] Is 65.3; 11.13
anger [3] 6.11; 8.19
announce 4.15; 17.19
believe Is 53.1; 28.15
burnt-offering Is 43.23; 14.12
change [3] 4.28; 8.8
choose 1.5; 10.16
command [4] 5.31; 10.13
commit 5.7; 23.14
dead Is 66.24; 9.22
deceive [2] 4.10; 9.4
defile 3.1; 16.18
destroy 6.1; 8.16
evil [2] 6.7; 8.3
faithful 5.1; 23.28
feast Is 29.1; 12.9
glad Is 66.10; 16.9
god (2) (other gods) [3] 5.7; 8.19
God's people [5] 6.14; 8.4
goddess Is 27.9; 17.2
happy Is 65.13; 11.15
hate [2] 4.1; 12.8
heart 4.14; 8.18
heaven Is 66.1; 10.12
hurt [3] 2.3; 10.19
idol 4.1; 8.5
innocent 2.34; 19.4
joy Is 65.14; 15.16
learn 6.18; 10.8
lie (2) 5.31; 9.3
mind (1) 4.28; 17.10
mourn 6.26; 8.21
oath Is 65.16; Ezek 17.16
obey [3] 6.19; 9.13
offer 6.20; 11.12
orphan 5.28; 22.3

[f] SHILOH: *The city where the Covenant Box was kept in the time of Eli (see 1 Sam 1.3). The city was destroyed, probably by the Philistines.*

7.11: Mt 21.13; Mk 11.17; Lk 19.46 **7.12–14:** Josh 18.1; Ps 78.60; Jer 26.6 **7.18:** Jer 44.7–19

more **stubborn** and **rebellious** than your
ancestors.
27 "So, Jeremiah, you will speak all
these **words** to **my people**, but they will
not listen to you; you will call them, but
they will not answer. 28 You will tell them
that their nation does not **obey** me, the
LORD their God, or **learn** from their
punishment. **Faithfulness** is **dead**. No
longer is it even talked about.

Sinful Deeds in the Valley of Hinnom

29 "**Mourn**, people of Jerusalem;
cut off your hair and throw it away.
Sing a funeral song on the hill-tops,
because I, the LORD, am **angry**,
and have **rejected my people**.
30 "The people of Judah have done an
evil thing. They have placed their **idols**,
which I **hate**, in my **Temple** and have **defiled** it. 31 In the Valley of Hinnom they
have built an **altar** called Topheth, so
that they can **sacrifice** their sons and
daughters in the fire. I did not **command**
them to do this—it did not even enter my
mind. 32 And so, the time will come when
it will no longer be called Topheth or the
Valley of Hinnom, but the Valley of
Slaughter. They will bury people there
because there will be nowhere else to
bury them. 33 The corpses will be food for
the birds and wild animals, and there will
be no one to scare them off. 34 The land
will become a desert. In the cities of
Judah and in the streets of Jerusalem I
will put an end to the sounds of **joy** and
gladness and to the **happy** sounds of **wedding feasts**.

act 6.14; 9.5
Almighty 7.1; 9.7
anger 7.20; 10.10
ashamed [2] 6.15; 31.19
bow (2) Is 60.14; Lam 2.10
change 7.1; 13.23
cheat 6.13; 21.11
condemn 2.19; 17.5
consult Is 65.4; Ezek 14.1
destroy 7.6; 9.16
disgust 6.15; 11.13
dishonest [2] 6.13; 9.3
dove Is 60.8; 48.28
enemy [2] 6.25; 11.18
evil 7.24; 9.3
god (2) (other gods) 7.6; 10.11
God's people [10] 7.12; 9.1
grave Is 53.9; 20.17
harvest [2] 5.24; 50.16
heal [3] 3.22; 10.19
heart [2] 7.24; 12.16
hope Is 64.4; 13.16
idol [2] 7.30; 9.14
law [3] Is 58.2; 31.33
love 3.4; 9.24
mourn 7.29; 9.10

8

"At that time the bones of the kings
and of the officials of Judah, as well
as the bones of the **priests**, of the **prophets**, and of the other people who lived
in Jerusalem, will be taken out of their
graves. 2 Instead of being gathered and
buried, their bones will be like manure
lying on the ground. They will be spread
out before the sun, the moon, and the
stars, which these people have **loved** and
served, and which they have **consulted**
and **worshipped**. 3 And the people of this
evil nation who survive, who live in the
places where I have **scattered** them, will
prefer to die rather than to go on living.
I, the LORD **Almighty**, have spoken."

Sin and Punishment

4 The LORD told me to say to **his
people**, "When someone **falls** down,
doesn't he get back up? If someone
misses the road, doesn't he **turn** back?
5 Why then, **my people**, do you **turn away**
from me without ever **turning back**?
You cling to your **idols** and **refuse** to return to me. 6 I listened carefully, but you
did not speak the **truth**. Not one of you
has been **sorry** for his **wickedness**; not
one of you has asked, 'What have I done
wrong?' Everyone keeps on going his
own way, like a horse rushing into battle.
7 Even storks know when it is time to return; **doves**, swallows, and thrushes know
when it is time to migrate. But, **my
people**, you do not know the **laws** by
which I rule you. 8 How can you say that
you are **wise**, and that you know my
laws? Look, the **laws** have been **changed**
by **dishonest** scribes. 9 Your **wise** men are
put to **shame**; they are confused and
trapped. They have **rejected** my **words**;
what **wisdom** have they got now? 10 So I
will give their fields to **new** owners and
their wives to other men. Everyone,
great and small, tries to make money **dishonestly**. Even **prophets** and **priests**
cheat the people. 11 They **act** as if **my
people's** wounds were only scratches. 'All
is well,' they say, when all is not well.
12 **My people**, were you **ashamed** because
you did these **disgusting** things? No, you
were not **ashamed** at all; you don't even
know how to blush! And so you will fall
as others have fallen; when I **punish** you,
that will be the end of you. I, the LORD,
have spoken.
13 "I wanted to gather **my people**, as a
man gathers his **harvest**; but they are
like a **vine** with no grapes, like a fig-tree
with no figs; even the leaves have
withered. Therefore, I have allowed outsiders to take over the land."[g]
14 "Why are we sitting still?" **God's
people** ask. "Come on, we will run to the
fortified cities, and die there. The LORD
our God has **condemned** us to die; he has
given us poison to drink, because we
have sinned against him. 15 We **hoped** for
peace and a time of **healing**, but it was no
use; **terror** came instead. 16 Our **enemies**
are already in the city of Dan; we hear
the snorting of their horses. The whole
land **trembles** when their horses neigh.
Our **enemies** have come to **destroy** our
land and everything in it, our city and all
its people."
17 "**Watch** out!" the LORD says, "I am
sending snakes among you, poisonous
snakes that cannot be charmed, and they
will bite you."

new Is 66.22; 31.22
peace 6.16; 12.12
priest [2] 6.13; 13.13
prophet [2] 7.25; 13.13
punish 7.28; 9.9
refuse (1) 7.13; 11.8
reject 7.29; 9.5
save 4.14; 11.12
scatter Is 49.5; 9.16
serve 5.19; 13.10
shame 7.19; 13.26
sorrow Is 61.3; 14.2
sorry Is 1.29; Jon 1.6
terror 6.25; 14.19
trap 5.26; 9.8
tremble 5.22; 10.10
truth Is 59.14; 9.3
turn [3] 6.8; 10.22
useless 6.29; 16.19
vine 5.17; 48.32
watch 6.17; 11.20
wicked Is 55.7; 12.1
wisdom 3.15; 9.23
wise [2] Is 44.25; 9.12
word (1) 7.4; 9.8
worship (2) (of other gods) [2] 7.6; 9.14
wrong 2.19; 11.17

[g] Therefore...land; *Hebrew unclear.*

7.31: Lev 18.21; 2 Kgs 23.10; Jer 32.35 **7.34:** Jer 16.9, 25.10; Rev 18.23 **8.10-12:** Jer 6.12-15
8.11: Ezek 13.10

Jeremiah's Sorrow for His People

18 My sorrow cannot be healed;[h]
I am sick at heart.
19 Listen! Throughout the land
I hear my people crying out,
"Is the LORD no longer in Zion?
Is Zion's king no longer there?"
The LORD, their king, replies,
"Why have you made me angry by
worshipping your idols
and by bowing down to your useless
foreign gods?"
20 The people cry out,
"The summer is gone, the harvest is
over,
but we have not been saved."

21 My heart has been crushed
because my people are crushed;
I mourn; I am completely dismayed.
22 Is there no medicine in Gilead?[i]
Are there no doctors there?
Why, then, have my people not been
healed?

9 I wish my head were a well of
water,
and my eyes a fountain of tears,
so that I could cry day and night
for my people who have been killed.
2 I wish I had a place to stay in the
desert
where I could get away from my
people.
They are all unfaithful,
a mob of traitors.
3 They are always ready to tell lies;
dishonesty instead of truth rules the
land.

The LORD says,
"My people do one evil thing after
another,
and do not acknowledge me as their
God."

4 Everyone must be on guard against his
friend,
and no one can trust his brother;
for every brother is as deceitful as
Jacob,
and everyone slanders his friends.
5-6 They all mislead their friends,
and no one tells the truth;
they have taught their tongues to lie
and will not give up their sinning.
They do one violent thing after
another,
and one deceitful act follows
another.
The LORD says that his people reject
him.
7 Because of this the LORD Almighty
says,
"I will refine my people like metal
and put them to the test.
My people have done evil—
what else can I do with them?
8 Their tongues are like deadly arrows;
they always tell lies.
Everyone speaks friendly words to his
neighbour,
but is really setting a trap for him.
9 Will I not punish them for these
things?
Will I not take revenge on a nation
like this?
I, the LORD, have spoken."

10 I said, "I will mourn for the mountains
and weep for the pastures,
because they have dried up,
and no one travels through them.
The sound of livestock is no longer
heard;
birds and wild animals have fled and
gone."

11 The LORD says, "I will make Jerusalem
a pile of ruins,
a place where jackals live;
the cities of Judah will become a
desert,
a place where no one lives."

12 I asked, "LORD, why is the land devastated and dry as a desert, so that no
one travels through it? Who is wise
enough to understand this? To whom
have you explained it so that he can tell
others?"
13 The LORD answered, "This has happened because my people have abandoned the teaching that I gave them.
They have not obeyed me or done what I
told them. 14 Instead, they have been stubborn and have worshipped the idols of
Baal as their fathers taught them to do.
15 So then, listen to what I, the LORD Almighty, the God of Israel, will do: I will
give my people bitter plants to eat and
poison to drink. 16 I will scatter them
among nations that neither they nor
their ancestors have heard about, and I
will send armies against them until I
have completely destroyed them."

The People of Jerusalem Cry Out for Help

17 The LORD Almighty said,
"Think about what is happening!

[h] *Probable text* My sorrow...healed; *Hebrew unclear.*
[i] GILEAD: *A region east of the Jordan, famous for plants that were used for medicinal purposes.*

Call for the **mourners** to come,
for the women who sing funeral songs."

18 The people said,
"Tell them to hurry and sing a funeral song for us,
until our eyes fill with **tears**,
and our eyelids are wet from crying."

19 Listen to the sound of crying in Zion,
"We are **ruined**!
We are completely **disgraced**!
We must leave our land;
our homes have been torn down."

20 I said,
"Listen to the LORD, you women,
and pay attention to his **words**.
Teach your daughters how to **mourn**,
and your **friends** how to sing a funeral song.
21 **Death** has come in through our windows
and entered our palaces;
it has cut down the children in the streets
and the young men in the market-places.
22 **Dead bodies** are **scattered** everywhere,
like piles of manure on the fields,
like corn cut and left behind by the **reapers**,
corn that no one gathers.
This is what the LORD has told me to say."

23 The LORD says,
"**Wise** men should not **boast** of their **wisdom**,
nor **strong** men of their **strength**,
nor **rich** men of their wealth.
24 If anyone wants to **boast**,
he should **boast** that he knows and **understands** me,
because my **love is constant**,
and I do what is **just** and **right**.
These are the things that **please** me.
I, the LORD, have spoken."

25–26 The LORD says, "The time is
coming when I will **punish** the people of
Egypt, Judah, Edom, Ammon, Moab, and
the desert people, who have their hair
cut short.[j] All these people are **circumcised**, but have not kept the **covenant** it
symbolizes. None of these people and
none of the people of Israel have kept my
covenant."

Idolatry and True Worship

10 People of Israel, listen to the
message that the LORD has for
you. 2 He says,
"Do not follow the **ways** of other nations;
do not be disturbed by unusual **sights** in the sky,
even though other nations are **terrified**.
3 The **religion** of these people is **worthless**.
A tree is cut down in the forest;
it is carved by the tools of the woodcarver,
4 and decorated with silver and gold.
It is fastened down with nails
to **keep it from** falling over.
5 Such **idols** are like scarecrows in a field of melons;
they cannot speak;
they have to be carried
because they cannot walk.
Do not be **afraid** of them:
they can cause you no **harm**,
and they can do you no good."

6 LORD, there is no one like you;
you are **mighty**,
and your **name** is great and **powerful**.
7 Who would not **honour** you, the king of all nations?
You **deserve** to be **honoured**.
There is no one like you
among all the **wise** men of the nations
or among any of their kings.
8 All of them are **stupid** and **foolish**.
What can they **learn** from wooden **idols**?[k]
9 Their **idols** are covered with silver from Spain
and with gold from Uphaz,
all the work of artists;
they are dressed in violet and purple cloth
woven by skilled weavers.
10 But you, LORD, are the **true** God,
you are the living God
and the **eternal** king.
When you are **angry**, the **world trembles**;
the nations cannot **endure** your **anger**.

[j] HAIR CUT SHORT: *The desert people cut their hair short in honour of their god, a pagan practice forbidden to the Israelites (see Lev 19.27).*
[k] What can...idols?; *or* What their idols teach is worthless.

9.24: 1 Cor 1.31; 2 Cor 10.17 **10.7:** Rev 15.4

11 (You people must tell them that the
gods who did not make the earth and the
sky will be **destroyed**. They will no
longer **exist** anywhere on earth.)

A Hymn of Praise to God

12 The LORD made the earth by his
power;
by his **wisdom** he **created** the **world**
and stretched out the **heavens**.
13 At his **command** the waters above the
sky[l] roar;
he brings **clouds** from the ends of
the earth.
He makes lightning flash in the rain
and sends the wind from his
storeroom.
14 At the **sight** of this, men feel **stupid** and
senseless;
those who make **idols** are
disillusioned,
because the **gods** they make are
false and lifeless.
15 They are **worthless** and should be
despised;
they will be **destroyed** when the
LORD comes to deal with them.
16 The God of Jacob is not like them;
he is the one who made everything,
and he has **chosen** Israel to be his
very **own people**.
The LORD **Almighty** is his **name**.

The Coming Exile

17 People of Jerusalem, you are under
siege! Gather up your belongings. 18 The
LORD is going to throw you out of this
land; he is going to crush you until not
one of you is left. The LORD has spoken.
19 The people of Jerusalem cried out,
"How **badly** we are **hurt**!
Our wounds will not **heal**.
And we thought this was something we
could **endure**!
20 Our tents are **ruined**;
the ropes that held them have
broken.
Our children have all gone away;
there is no one left to put up our
tents again;
there is no one to hang their
curtains."

21 I answered, "Our leaders are **stupid**;
they do not ask the LORD for
guidance.
This is why they have **failed**,
and our people have been **scattered**.
22 Listen! News has come!
There is a great commotion in a
nation to the north;
its army will **turn** the cities of Judah
into a desert,
a place where jackals live."

23 LORD, I know that no one is the **master**
of his own destiny;
no person has **control** over his own
life.
24 **Correct** your people, LORD;
but do not be too **hard** on us
or **punish** us when you are **angry**;
that would be the end of us.
25 **Turn** your **anger** on the nations that do
not **worship** you
and on the people who **reject** you.
They have killed your people;
they have **destroyed** us completely
and left our country in **ruins**.

Jeremiah and the Covenant

11 The LORD said to me, 2 "Listen to
the terms of the **covenant**. Tell
the people of Judah and of Jerusalem
3 that I, the LORD God of Israel, have
placed a **curse** on everyone who does not
obey the terms of this **covenant**. 4 It is the
covenant I made with their ancestors
when I brought them out of Egypt, the
land that was like a blazing furnace to
them. I told them to **obey** me and to do
everything that I had **commanded**. I told
them that if they **obeyed**, they would be
my people and I would be their God.
5 Then I would keep the **promise** I made
to their ancestors that I would give them
the **rich** and fertile land which they now
have."
I said, "Yes, LORD."
6 Then the LORD said to me, "Go to
the cities of Judah and to the streets of
Jerusalem. **Proclaim** my **message** there
and tell the people to listen to the terms
of the **covenant** and to **obey** them. 7 When
I brought their ancestors out of Egypt, I
solemnly warned them to **obey** me, and I
have kept on **warning** the people until
this day. 8 But they did not listen or **obey**.
Instead, everyone continued to be as
stubborn and **evil** as ever. I had **commanded** them to keep the **covenant**, but
they **refused**. So I brought on them all the
punishments described in it."
9 Then the LORD said to me, "The
people of Judah and of Jerusalem are
plotting against me. 10 They have gone
back to the sins of their ancestors, who
refused to do what I said; they have **worshipped** other **gods**. Both Israel and
Judah have broken the **covenant** that I
made with their ancestors. 11 So now, I,
the LORD, **warn** them that I am going to
bring **destruction** on them, and they will

Almighty [3] 10.16; 15.16
altar 7.21; 17.1
anger 10.10; 12.13
cause (2) Is 49.4; 20.12
command [2] 10.13; 14.17
covenant [6] 9.25; 14.21
curse Is 65.15; 15.10
destroy [2] 10.11; 12.10
disaster [3] 6.1; 14.8
disgust 8.12; 32.34
enemy 8.16; 12.7
escape 6.1; 16.17
evil [3] 9.3; 12.3
god (2) (other gods) [5] 10.11; 13.10
God's people 10.16; 12.8
happy 7.34; 15.10
help [3] 3.23; 14.2
judge 4.12; 23.1
justice 9.24; 12.1
lamb Is 66.3; 51.40
love 9.24; 12.3
message [2] 10.1; 15.19
obey [6] 9.13; 12.17
offer [3] 7.9; 14.12
plan Is 59.4; 18.11
plead 7.16; 15.1
plot (1) [2] Is 59.5; 18.23
pray [2] 7.16; 18.19
prevent Is 48.5; Ezek 13.22
proclaim [2] 2.2; 15.19
promise [2] Is 62.6; 14.7
punish [2] 10.24; 14.10
refuse (1) [2] 8.5; 13.10
remember 3.16; 14.10
revenge 9.9; 15.15
rich 9.23; 14.3
right (3) 5.28; 18.6
sacrifice [4] 7.9; 17.26
save 8.20; 14.8
solemn Is 62.8; 44.24
stubborn 9.14; 13.10
Temple (1) (of God) 7.1; 17.12
test 9.7; 17.10
threat Is 31.2; 17.15
trouble 6.8; 15.11

[l] WATERS ABOVE THE SKY: *See Gen 1.6–8.*

trust 9.4; 12.6
warn [3] 6.8; 18.22
watch 8.17; 24.6
worship (2) (of other gods) 9.14; 13.10
wrong 8.6; 14.10

not escape. And when they cry out to me
for help, I will not listen to them. 12 Then
the people of Judah and of Jerusalem
will go to the gods to whom they offer
sacrifices and will cry out to them for
help. But those gods will not be able to
save them when this destruction comes.
13 The people of Judah have as many
gods as they have cities, and the inhabitants of Jerusalem have set up as many
altars for sacrifices to that disgusting god
Baal as there are streets in the city.
14 Jeremiah, don't pray to me or plead
with me on behalf of these people. When
they are in trouble and call to me for
help, I will not listen to them."

15 The LORD says, "The people I love
are doing evil things. What right have
they to be in my Temple? Do they think
they can prevent disaster by making
promises[m] and by offering animal sacrifices? Will that make them happy? 16 I
once called them a leafy olive-tree, full of
beautiful fruit; but now, with a roar like
thunder I will set its leaves on fire and
break its branches.

17 "I, the LORD Almighty, planted
Israel and Judah; but now I threaten
them with disaster. They have brought
this on themselves because they have
done wrong; they have made me angry
by offering sacrifices to Baal."

A Plot against Jeremiah's Life

18 The LORD informed me of the plots
that my enemies were making against
me. 19 I was like a trusting lamb taken out
to be killed, and I did not know that it
was against me that they were planning
evil things. They were saying, "Let's
chop down the tree while it is still
healthy;[x] let's kill him so that no one will
remember him any more."

20 Then I prayed, "Almighty LORD,
you are a just judge; you test people's
thoughts and feelings. I have placed my
cause in your hands; so let me watch you
take revenge on these people."

21 The men of Anathoth wanted me
killed, and they told me that they would
kill me if I kept on proclaiming the
LORD's message. 22 So the LORD Almighty
said, "I will punish them! Their young
men will be killed in war; their children
will die of starvation. 23 I have set a time
for bringing disaster on the people of
Anathoth, and when that time comes,
none of them will survive."

Jeremiah Questions the LORD

12 "LORD, if I argued my case with
you,
you would prove to be right.
Yet I must question you about matters
of justice.
Why are wicked men so prosperous?
Why do dishonest men succeed?
2 You plant them, and they take root;
they grow and bear fruit.
They always speak well of you,
yet they do not really care about
you.
3 But, LORD, you know me;
you see what I do,
and how I love you.
Drag these evil men away like sheep
to be butchered;
guard them until it is time for them
to be slaughtered.
4 How long will our land be dry,
and the grass in every field be
withered?
Animals and birds are dying
because of the wickedness of our
people,
people who say, 'God doesn't see
what we are doing.'"[n]

5 The LORD said,
"Jeremiah, if you get tired racing
against men,
how can you race against horses?
If you can't even stand up in open
country,
how will you manage in the jungle
by the Jordan?
6 Even your brothers, members of your
own family, have betrayed you;
they join in the attacks against you.
Do not trust them, even though they
speak friendly words."

The LORD's Sorrow because of His People

7 The LORD says,
"I have abandoned Israel;
I have rejected my chosen nation.
I have given the people I love
into the power of their enemies.
8 My chosen people have turned against
me;
like a lion in the forest
they have roared at me,
and so I hate them.
9 My chosen people are like a bird
attacked from all sides by hawks.
Call the wild animals
to come and join in the feast!

abandon 9.13; 14.5
accept 6.20; Lam 3.30
anger 11.17; 15.6
argue Is 45.9; 15.10
betray 5.11; Lam 1.2
care [2] 6.20; 13.20
case (2) 2.9; 25.31
choose [3] 10.16; 21.8
desolate Is 60.15; 22.6
destroy [3] 11.11; 13.9
dishonest 9.3; 17.11
enemy 11.18; 13.20
evil 11.8; 13.10
fail 10.21; 14.6
feast 7.34; 16.8
friend 9.4; 13.21
God's people [7] 11.4; 13.11
hard 10.24; Lam 5.5
hate 7.10; 13.27
heart 8.18; 14.4
justice 11.20; 20.12
love [2] 11.15; 14.10
mercy 6.23; 13.14
neighbour 9.8; 13.27
obey 11.3; 13.10
peace 8.15; 14.13
power 10.6; 14.9
prosper [2] Is 66.11; 22.15
prove 3.11; 44.29
question Is 45.11; 38.14
race (2) [2] Song 2.8; 1 Cor 9.24
reject 10.25; 14.19
religion 10.3; Ezek 44.24
rescue 6.9; 15.21
right (1) 9.24; 13.23
ruin 10.20; 13.7
sheep Is 65.10; 31.12
slaughter 7.32; 19.6
sow 4.3; 50.16
succeed (1) Is 65.23; 15.15
swear [2] 4.2; 16.14
teach 9.5; 16.11
trust 11.19; 13.25
turn [2] 10.22; 13.16
vineyard 6.9; 31.5
weed Is 37.27; Hos 9.6
wicked [3] 8.6; 13.10
word (1) 9.8; 14.14

[m] *One ancient translation* promises; *Hebrew* many.
[x] *Probable text* while it is still healthy; *Hebrew* with its bread.
[n] *Some ancient translations* what we are doing; *Hebrew* our latter end.

10 Many foreign rulers have destroyed
my vineyard;
they have trampled down my fields;
they have turned my lovely land into
a desert.
11 They have made it a wilderness;
it lies desolate before me.
The whole land has become a desert,
and no one cares.
12 Across all the desert highlands
men have come to plunder.
I have sent war to destroy the entire
land;
no one can live in peace.
13 My people sowed wheat, but gathered
weeds;
they have worked hard, but got
nothing for it.
Because of my fierce anger
their crops have failed."

The LORD's Promise to Israel's Neighbours

14 The LORD says, "I have something
to say about Israel's neighbours who
have ruined the land I gave to my people
Israel. I will take those wicked people
away from their countries like an uprooted plant, and I will rescue Judah
from them. 15 But after I have taken them
away, I will have mercy on them; I will
bring each nation back to its own land
and to its own country. 16 If with all their
hearts they will accept the religion of my
people and will swear, 'As the LORD
lives'—as they once taught my people to
swear by Baal—then they will also be a
part of my people and will prosper. 17 But
if any nation will not obey, then I will
completely uproot it and destroy it. I, the
LORD, have spoken."

The Linen Shorts

13 The LORD told me to go and buy
myself some linen shorts and to
put them on; but he told me not to put
them in water. 2 So I bought them and put
them on. 3 Then the LORD spoke to me
again, and said, 4 "Go to the River
Euphrates and hide the shorts in a hole
in the rocks." 5 So I went and hid them
near the Euphrates.

6 Some time later the LORD told me to
go back to the Euphrates and get the
shorts. 7 So I went back, and when I found
the place where I had hidden them, I saw
that they were ruined and were no longer any good.

8 Then the LORD spoke to me again.
He said, 9 "This is how I will destroy the
pride of Judah and the great pride of
Jerusalem. 10 These evil people have refused to obey me. They have been as
stubborn and wicked as ever, and have
worshipped and served other gods. So
then, they will become like these shorts
that are no longer any good. 11 Just as
shorts fit tightly round the waist, so I intended all the people of Israel and Judah
to hold tightly to me. I did this so that
they would be my people and would
bring praise and honour to my name; but
they would not obey me."

The Wine-Jar

12 The LORD God said to me,
"Jeremiah, tell the people of Israel that
every wine-jar should be filled with wine.
They will answer that they know every
wine-jar should be filled with wine.
13 Then tell them that I, the LORD, am going to fill the people in this land with
wine until they are drunk: the kings, who
are David's descendants, the priests, the
prophets, and all the people of
Jerusalem. 14 Then I will smash them like
jars against one another, old and young
alike. No pity, compassion, or mercy will
stop me from killing them."

Jeremiah Warns against Pride

15 People of Israel, the LORD has spoken!
Be humble and listen to him.
16 Honour the LORD, your God,
before he brings darkness,
and you stumble on the mountains;
before he turns into deep darkness
the light you hoped for.
17 If you will not listen,
I will cry in secret because of your
pride;
I will cry bitterly, and my tears will
flow
because the LORD's people have
been taken away as captives.

18 The LORD said to me, "Tell the king
and his mother to come down from their
thrones, because their beautiful crowns
have fallen from their heads.[o] 19 The
towns of southern Judah are under siege;
no one can get through to them. All the
people of Judah have been taken away
into exile."

20 Jerusalem, look! Your enemies are
coming down from the north! Where are
the people entrusted to your care, your
people you were so proud of? 21 What
will you say when people you thought
were your friends conquer you and rule
over you?[p] You will be in pain like a
woman giving birth. 22 If you ask why all
this has happened to you—why your
clothes have been torn off and you have

[o] *Some ancient translations* from their heads; *Hebrew unclear.*
[p] *Probable text* What...over you; *Hebrew unclear.*

raped—it is because your sin is so
terrible. 23 Can a black man **change** the
colour of his skin, or a leopard remove its
spots? If they could, then you that do
nothing but **evil** could **learn** to do what is
right. 24 The LORD will **scatter** you like
straw that is blown away by the desert
wind. 25 He has said that this will be your
fate. This is what he has decided to do
with you, because you have **forgotten**
him and have **trusted** in **false gods.** 26 The
LORD himself will **strip** off your clothes
and expose you to **shame.** 27 He has seen
you do the things he **hates.** He has seen
you go after **pagan gods** on the hills and
in the fields, like a man **lusting** after his
neighbour's wife or like a stallion after a
mare. People of Jerusalem, you are
doomed! When will you ever be **pure**?

The Terrible Drought

14 The LORD said to me concerning
the drought,

2 "Judah is in **mourning**;
its cities are dying,
its people lie on the ground in **sorrow**,
and Jerusalem cries out for **help**.
3 The **rich** people send their **servants** for
water;
they go to the cisterns,
but find no water;
they come back with their jars
empty.
Discouraged and confused,
they hide their faces.
4 Because there is no rain
and the ground is dried up,
the farmers are sick at **heart**;
they hide their faces.
5 In the field the mother deer
abandons her new-born fawn
because there is no grass.
6 The wild donkeys stand on the hill-tops
and pant for breath like jackals;
their **eyesight fails** them
because they have no food.

7 **My people** cry out to me,
'Even though our sins **accuse** us,
help us, LORD, as you have
promised.
We have **turned away** from you many
times;
we have sinned against you.
8 You are Israel's only **hope**;
you are the one who **saves** us from
disaster.
Why are you like a **stranger** in our
land,
like a traveller who stays for only
one night?
9 Why are you like a man taken by
surprise,
like a soldier **powerless** to **help**?
Surely, LORD, you are with us!
We are your people;
do not **abandon** us.' "

10 The LORD says about these people,
"They **love** to run away from me, and
they will not **control** themselves. So I am
not **pleased** with them. I will **remember**
the **wrongs** they have done and **punish**
them because of their sins."

11 The LORD said to me, "Do not ask
me to **help** these people. 12 Even if they
fast, I will not listen to their cry for **help**;
and even if they **offer** me **burnt-offerings**
and **grain-offerings**, I will not be **pleased**
with them. Instead, I will kill them in war
and by starvation and **disease**."

13 Then I said, "**Sovereign** LORD, you
know that the **prophets** are telling the
people that there will be no war or
starvation, because you have **promised**,
they say, that there will be only **peace** in
our land."

14 But the LORD replied, "The **prophets** are telling **lies in my name**; I did
not send them, nor did I give them any
orders or speak one **word** to them. The
visions they talk about have not come
from me; their **predictions** are **worthless**
things that they have imagined. 15 I, the
LORD, tell you what I am going to do to
those **prophets** whom I did not send but
who speak **in my name** and say war and
starvation will not **strike** this land—I will
kill them in war and by starvation. 16 The
people to whom they have said these
things will be killed in the same way.
Their **bodies** will be thrown out into the
streets of Jerusalem, and there will be no
one to bury them. This will happen to all
of them—including their wives, their
sons, and their daughters. I will make
them pay for their **wickedness**."

17 The LORD **commanded** me to tell
the people about my **sorrow** and to say:
"May my eyes flow with **tears** day and
night,
may I never stop **weeping**,
for **my people** are deeply wounded
and are **badly hurt**.
18 When I go out into the fields,
I see the **bodies** of men killed in
war;
when I go into the towns,
I see people starving **to death**.
Prophets and **priests** carry on their
work,
but they don't know what they are
doing."[q]

[q] Prophets...doing; *or* Prophets and priests have been dragged away to a land they know nothing about.

abandon [2] 12.7; 16.11
accuse 2.5; 32.3
bad [2] 10.19; 23.14
body [2] 9.22; 15.3
burnt-offering 7.22; 17.26
command 11.4; 17.22
confess 3.13; Dan 9.4
control 10.23; 15.6
covenant 11.2; 22.9
death (1) 9.21; 18.21
death (3) (to death) Is 66.16; 18.21
despise 10.15; 18.16
disaster 11.15; 17.16
discourage Is 35.4; Ezek 13.22
disease Is 10.16; 15.2
disgrace 9.19; 15.9
eyesight *see* **sight**
fail 12.13; 20.11
fast (2) Is 58.3; 36.6
glory Is 63.15; 17.12
God's people [2] 13.11; 15.7
grain-offering Is 66.3; 17.26
hate 13.27; 44.4
heal [2] 10.19; 15.18
heart 12.16; 15.9
help [5] 11.11; 15.15
hope [3] 13.16; 17.13
hurt [2] 10.19; 38.4
idol 10.5; 16.18
lie (2) 9.3; 20.6
love 12.3; 16.5
mourn 9.10; 16.4
name (2) (name of God, of Jesus) [2] 13.11; 20.9
offer 11.12; 19.4
peace [2] 12.12; 16.5
please [2] 9.24; 34.15
power 12.7; 15.21
predict Is 48.3; 27.9
priest 13.13; 18.18
promise [3] 11.5; 19.12
prophet [4] 13.13; 15.19
punish 11.8; 15.13
reject 12.7; 15.6
remember [2] 11.19; 15.15
rich 11.5; 16.6
save 11.12; 30.11
servant 7.25; 15.19
sight 10.2; 15.1
sorrow [2] 8.18; 20.18
Sovereign 7.20; 32.17

stranger 5.19; 35.7
strike 5.3; 15.8
tear (2) 13.17; 31.16
terror 8.15; 15.8
throne 13.18; 17.12
turn 13.16; 15.6
vision Is 29.11; 38.21
weep 9.10; 22.10
wicked 13.10; 15.21
word (1) 12.6; 15.16
worthless 10.3; 51.18
wrong 11.17; 23.14

The People Plead with the LORD

19 LORD, have you completely **rejected**
Judah?
Do you **hate** the people of Zion?
Why have you **hurt** us so **badly**
that we cannot be **healed**?
We looked for **peace**, but nothing good
happened;
we **hoped** for **healing**, but **terror**
came instead.
20 We have sinned against you, LORD;
we **confess** our own sins
and the sins of our ancestors.
21 **Remember** your **promises** and do not
despise us;
do not bring **disgrace** on Jerusalem,
the place of your **glorious throne**.
Do not break the **covenant** you made
with us.
22 None of the **idols** of the nations can
send rain;
the sky by itself cannot make
showers fall.
We have put our **hope** in you, O LORD
our God,
because you are the one who does
these things.

Doom for the People of Judah

15 Then the LORD said to me, "Even
if Moses and Samuel were stand-
ing here **pleading** with me, I would not
show these people any **mercy**. Make
them go away; make them get out of my
sight. 2 When they ask you where they
should go, tell them that I have said:
Some are **doomed** to die by **disease**—
that's where they will go!
Others are **doomed** to die in war—
that's where they will go!
Some are **doomed** to die of
starvation—
that's where they will go!
Others are **doomed** to be taken away
as **prisoners**—
that's where they will go!
3 I, the LORD, have decided that four
terrible things will happen to them: they
will be killed in war; their **bodies** will be
dragged off by dogs; birds will eat them,
and wild animals will **devour** what is left
over. 4 I will make all the people of the
world horrified at them because of what
Hezekiah's son Manasseh did in Jerusalem when he was king of Judah."
5 The LORD says,
"Who will **pity** you, people of
Jerusalem,
and who will **grieve** over you?
Who will stop long **enough**
to ask how you are?
6 You people have **rejected** me;
you have **turned** your backs on me.
So I stretched out my hand and
crushed you
because I was tired of **controlling**
my **anger**.[r]
7 In every town in the land
I threw you to the wind like straw.
I **destroyed** you, **my people**,
I killed your children
because you did not stop your **evil**
ways.
8 There are more **widows** in your land
than grains of sand by the sea.
I killed your young men in their prime
and made their mothers **suffer**.
I suddenly **struck** them
with **anguish** and **terror**.
9 The mother who lost her seven
children has fainted,
gasping for breath.
Her daylight has **turned** to **darkness**;
she is **disgraced** and sick at **heart**.
I will let your **enemies** kill
those of you who are still **alive**.
I, the LORD, have spoken."

Jeremiah Complains to the LORD

10 What an **unhappy** man I am! Why
did my mother bring me into the **world**?
I have to **quarrel** and **argue** with everyone in the land. I have not lent any
money or borrowed any; yet everyone
curses me. 11 LORD, may all their **curses**
come **true** if I have not **served**[s] you well,
if I have not **pleaded** with you on behalf
of my **enemies** when they were in **trouble**
and **distress**. 12 (No one can break iron,
especially the iron from the north that is
mixed with bronze.)
13 The LORD said to me, "I will send
enemies to carry away the wealth and
treasures of **my people**, in order to
punish them for the sins they have committed throughout the land. 14 I will make
them **serve** their **enemies** in a land they
know nothing about, because my **anger** is
like fire, and it will burn for ever."
15 Then I said, "LORD, you **understand**.
Remember me and **help** me. Let me
have **revenge** on those who **persecute**
me. Do not be so **patient** with them that
they **succeed** in killing me. **Remember**
that it is for your **sake** that I am **insulted**.
16 You spoke to me, and I listened to
every **word**. I belong to you, LORD God
Almighty, and so your **words** filled my
heart with **joy** and **happiness**. 17 I did not

[r] you because...anger; *or* you; I was tired of feeling sorry for you.
[s] *Probable text* LORD...served; *Hebrew unclear.*

15.1: Ex 32.11–14; Num 14.13–19; 1 Sam 7.5–9 **15.2:** Rev 13.10 **15.4:** 2 Kgs 21.1–16; 2 Chr 33.1–9

spend my time with other people, laughing and having a good time. In **obedience** to your orders I stayed by myself and was filled with **anger**. 18 Why do I keep on **suffering**? Why are my wounds incurable? Why won't they **heal**? Do you **intend** to **disappoint** me like a stream that goes dry in the summer?"

19 To this the LORD replied, "If you return, I will take you back, and you will be my **servant** again. If instead of talking nonsense you **proclaim** a worthwhile **message**, you will be my **prophet** again. The people will come back to you, and you will not **need** to go to them. 20 I will make you like a solid bronze wall as far as they are concerned. They will fight against you, but they will not defeat you. I will be with you to **protect** you and keep you **safe**. 21 I will **rescue** you from the **power** of **wicked** and **violent** men. I, the LORD, have spoken."

The LORD's Will for Jeremiah's Life

16 Again the LORD spoke to me and said, 2 "Do not marry or have children in a place like this. 3 I will tell you what is going to happen to the children who are born here and to their parents. 4 They will die of **terrible diseases**, and no one will **mourn** for them or bury them. Their **bodies** will lie like piles of manure on the ground. They will be killed in war or die of starvation, and their **bodies** will be food for the birds and the wild animals.

5 "You must not enter a house where there is **mourning**. Do not **grieve** for anyone. I will no longer **bless my people** with **peace** or show them **love** and **mercy**. 6 The **rich** and the **poor** will die in this land, but no one will bury them or **mourn** for them. No one will gash himself or **shave** his head to show his **grief**. 7 No one will eat or drink with anyone to **comfort** him when a **loved** one dies. No one will show **sympathy**, not even for someone who has lost his father or mother.

8 "Do not enter a house where people are **feasting**. Do not sit down with them to eat and drink. 9 Listen to what I, the LORD **Almighty**, the God of Israel, have to say. I will silence the sounds of **joy** and **gladness** and the **happy** sounds of **wedding feasts**. The people here will live to see this happen.

10 "When you tell them all this, they will ask you why I have decided to **punish** them so harshly. They will ask what **crime** they are **guilty** of and what sin they have committed against the LORD their God. 11 Then tell them that the LORD has said, 'Your ancestors **turned away** from me and **worshipped and served other gods**. They **abandoned** me and did not **obey** my **teachings**. 12 But you have done even **worse** than your ancestors. All of you are **stubborn** and **evil**, and you do not **obey** me. 13 So then, I will throw you out of this land into a land that neither you nor your ancestors have ever known. And there you will **serve** other **gods** day and night, and I will show you no **mercy**.' "

abandon 14.5; 17.13
Almighty 15.16; 19.3
bless 4.2; 17.7
body [2] 15.3; 25.33
comfort Is 66.13; 31.13
crime Is 61.8; 37.18
defile 7.30; 19.4
disease 15.2; 18.21
escape 11.11; 21.9
evil 15.7; 18.8
false [2] 13.25; 23.16
feast [2] 12.9; 25.10
glad 7.34; 20.15
god (2) (other gods) [6] 13.10; 19.4
God's people 15.7; 18.15
grief [2] 15.5; 31.18
guilty 3.13; 26.15
happy 15.10; 25.10
help 15.15; 18.17
idol [2] 14.22; 18.15
joy 15.16; 25.10
love [2] 14.10; 17.21
mercy [2] 15.1; 20.16
might 10.6; 20.11
mourn [3] 14.2; 22.10
obey [2] 15.17; 17.23
peace 14.13; 23.6
poor 5.4; 22.16
power 15.21; 17.25
protect 15.20; 21.11
punish 15.13; 18.11
rich 14.3; 31.14
scatter 13.24; 18.17
serve [2] 15.11; 17.4
shave Is 22.12; 41.5
sight 15.1; 25.9
strength 9.23; 17.5
stubborn 13.10; 17.23
swear [2] 12.16; 22.5
sympathy Is 51.19; Dan 1.9
teach 12.16; 26.4
terrible 15.3; 18.13
trouble 15.11; 17.16
turn 15.6; 17.5
useless 8.19; 46.11
wedding 7.34; 25.10
wicked 15.21; 23.10
worse 7.24; 23.14
worship (2) (of other gods) 13.10; 17.2

The Return from Exile

14 The LORD says, "The time is coming when people will no longer **swear** by me as the living God who brought the people of Israel out of the land of Egypt. 15 Instead, they will **swear** by me as the living God who brought the people of Israel out of a northern land and out of all the other countries where I had **scattered** them. I will bring them back to their own country, to the land that I gave their ancestors. I, the LORD, have spoken."

The Coming Punishment

16 The LORD says, "I am sending for many fishermen to come and catch these people. Then I will send for many hunters to hunt them down on every mountain and hill and in the caves among the rocks. 17 I see everything they do. Nothing is hidden from me; their sins do not **escape** my **sight**. 18 I will make them pay double for their sin and **wickedness**, because they have **defiled** my land with **idols** that are as lifeless as corpses, and have filled it with their **false gods**."

Jeremiah's Prayer of Confidence in the LORD

19 LORD, you are the one who **protects** me and gives me **strength**; you **help** me in times of **trouble**. Nations will come to you from the ends of the earth and say, "Our ancestors had nothing but **false gods**, nothing but **useless idols**. 20 Can a man make his own **gods**? No, if he did, they would not really be **gods**."

21 "So then," says the LORD, "once and for all I will make the nations know my **power** and my **might**; they will know that I am the LORD."

The Sin and Punishment of Judah

17 The LORD says, "People of Judah, your sin is written with an iron pen; it is engraved on your **hearts** with a diamond point and carved on the

abandon [2] 16.11; 19.4
afraid 10.5; 22.25
altar [2] 11.13; 19.5
anger 15.6; 18.20

16.9: Jer 7.34, 25.10; Rev 18.23

announce 7.1; 32.3
bless 16.5; 30.19
burnt-offering 14.12; 33.18
command [2] 14.17; 19.5
condemn 8.14; 22.30
deceive 9.4; 20.7
disaster [2] 14.8; 18.17
disgrace 15.9; 20.11
dishonest 12.1; 22.13
enemy [2] 15.9; 18.17
fool 10.8; 50.36
glory 14.21; 48.17
goddess 7.18; 44.17
grain-offering 14.12; 33.18
heal [2] 15.18; 30.12
heart [3] 15.9; 20.12
hope 14.8; 23.16
human Is 66.3; Ezek 1.5
incense 6.20; 18.15
learn 13.23; 32.33
life (1) [2] 10.23; 18.11
love 16.5; 31.3
message 15.19; 18.2
mind (1) 7.31; 19.5
mortal Is 51.12; Ezek 2.1
obey [3] 16.11; 22.5
observe [3] Is 56.2; Dan 6.11
perfect Is 26.3; Ezek 16.14
persecute 15.15; 20.11
power 16.21; 20.4
praise 13.11; 20.13
put out 7.20; 21.11
rescue 15.21; 20.13
riches Is 60.5; Obad 13
Sabbath [6] Is 66.23; Lam 2.6
sacred [3] 2.3; 31.23
sacrifice 11.12; 19.4
safe [2] 15.20; 23.6
serve 16.11; 22.9
shame 13.26; 22.22
spare 6.11; 21.7
strength 16.19; 27.5
stubborn 16.12; 18.12
symbol 9.25; 1 Pet 3.21
Temple (1) (of God) [2] 11.15; 19.14
terrify 10.2; 23.4
terror [2] 15.8; 18.22
test 11.20; 20.12
threat 11.17; 25.13
throne 14.21; 30.9
trouble [2] 16.19; 20.18
trust [2] 13.25; 39.18
turn 16.11; 18.4
understand 15.15; 23.18
urge Esth 3.4; Lk 3.18
wish 9.1; 38.5
worry Is 32.9; 49.23
worship (2) (of other gods) 16.11; 22.9

corners of your altars. 2 Your people worship at the altars and the symbols that
have been set up for the goddess Asherah
by every green tree, on the hill-tops 3 and
on the mountains in the open country. I
will make your enemies take away your
wealth and your treasures because of all
the sins you have committed[t] throughout
your land. 4 You will have to give up[u] the
land I gave you, and I will make you
serve your enemies in a land you know
nothing about, because my anger is like a
fire, and it will burn for ever."

Various Sayings

5 The LORD says,
"I will condemn the person
who turns away from me
and puts his trust in man,
in the strength of mortal man.
6 He is like a bush in the desert,
which grows in the dry wilderness,
on salty ground where nothing else
grows.
Nothing good ever happens to him.

7 "But I will bless the person
who puts his trust in me.
8 He is like a tree growing near a
stream
and sending out roots to the water.
It is not afraid when hot weather
comes,
because its leaves stay green;
it has no worries when there is no
rain;
it keeps on bearing fruit.

9 "Who can understand the human
heart?
There is nothing else so deceitful;
it is too sick to be healed.
10 I, the LORD, search the minds
and test the hearts of men.
I treat each one according to the way
he lives,
according to what he does."

11 The person who gets money
dishonestly
is like a bird that hatches eggs it
didn't lay.
In the prime of life he will lose his
riches,
and in the end he is nothing but a
fool.

12 Our Temple is like a glorious throne,
standing on a high mountain from
the beginning.

13 LORD, you are Israel's hope;
all who abandon you will be put to
shame.
They will disappear like names written
in the dust,[a]
because they have abandoned you,
the LORD,
the spring of fresh water.

Jeremiah Asks the LORD for Help

14 LORD, heal me and I will be completely well; rescue me and I will be perfectly safe. You are the one I praise!
15 The people say to me, "Where are
those threats the LORD made against us?
Let him carry them out now!"
16 But, LORD, I never urged you to
bring disaster on them;[b] I did not wish a
time of trouble for them. LORD, you know
this; you know what I have said. 17 Do not
be a terror to me; you are my place of
safety when trouble comes. 18 Bring disgrace on those who persecute me, but
spare me, LORD. Fill them with terror,
but do not terrify me. Bring disaster on
them and break them to pieces.

On Observing the Sabbath

19 The LORD said to me, "Jeremiah,
go and announce my message at the
People's Gate, through which the kings
of Judah enter and leave the city; then
go to all the other gates of Jerusalem.
20 Tell the kings and all the people of
Judah and everyone who lives in
Jerusalem and enters these gates, to listen to what I say. 21 Tell them that if they
love their lives, they must not carry any
load on the Sabbath; they must not carry
anything in through the gates of
Jerusalem 22 or carry anything out of
their houses on the Sabbath. They must
not work on the Sabbath; they must observe it as a sacred day, as I commanded
their ancestors. 23 Their ancestors did not
listen to me or pay any attention. Instead, they became stubborn; they would
not obey me or learn from me.
24 "Tell these people that they must
obey all my commands. They must not
carry any load in through the gates of
this city on the Sabbath. They must observe the Sabbath as a sacred day and
must not do any work at all. 25 Then their
kings and princes will enter the gates of
Jerusalem and have the same royal

[t] *Probable text* because of all the sins you have committed; *Hebrew* your high places for sins.
[u] *Probable text* You...give up; *Hebrew unclear.* [a] disappear...dust; *or* go to the world of the dead.
[b] *Probable text* bring disaster on them; *Hebrew* from being a shepherd after you.

17.8: Ps 1.3 **17.10:** Ps 62.12; Rev 2.23 **17.21:** Neh 13.15–22 **17.22:** Ex 20.8–10; Deut 5.12–14

power that David had. Together with the
people of Judah and of Jerusalem, they
will ride in chariots and on horses, and
the city of Jerusalem will always be filled
with people. 26 People will come from the
towns of Judah and from the villages
round Jerusalem; they will come from
the territory of Benjamin, from the foothills, from the mountains, and from
southern Judah. They will bring to my
Temple burnt-offerings and **sacrifices**,
grain-offerings and **incense**, as well as
thank-offerings. 27 But they must **obey** me
and **observe** the **Sabbath** as a **sacred** day.
They must not carry any load through
the gates of Jerusalem on that day, for if
they do, I will set the gates of Jerusalem
on fire. Fire will burn down the palaces
of Jerusalem, and no one will be able to
put it out."

Jeremiah at the Potter's House

18 The LORD said to me, 2 "Go down
to the potter's house, where I will
give you my **message**." 3 So I went there
and saw the potter working at his wheel.
4 Whenever a piece of pottery **turned** out
imperfect, he would take the clay and
make it into something else.

5 Then the LORD said to me, 6 "Haven't
I the **right** to do with you people of Israel
what the potter did with the clay? You
are in my hands just like clay in the potter's hands. 7 If at any time I say that I
am going to uproot, break down, or **destroy** any nation or kingdom, 8 but then
that nation **turns from** its **evil**, I will not
do what I said I would. 9 On the other
hand, if I say that I am going to plant or
build up any nation or kingdom, 10 but
then that nation **disobeys** me and does
evil, I will not do what I said I would.
11 Now then, tell the people of Judah and
of Jerusalem that I am making **plans**
against them and getting ready to **punish**
them. Tell them to stop living sinful
lives—to **change** their **ways** and the
things they are doing. 12 They will answer, 'No, why should we? We will all be
just as **stubborn** and **evil** as we want to
be.' "

amaze 2.12; 19.8
anger [2] 17.4; 21.5
change 13.23; 26.3
charge (3) 2.9;
Ezek 23.45
death (1) 14.18; 21.8
death (3) (to death)
14.18; 20.4
despise 14.21; 51.18
destroy 15.7; 19.8
disaster 17.16; 19.3
disease 16.4; 21.6
disobey Is 66.4; 23.38
enemy [2] 17.3; 19.7
evil [5] 16.12; 20.13
forget 13.25; 20.9
forgive 5.1; 31.34
God's people [2] 16.5;
23.1
help 16.19; 23.14
horror 15.4; 25.38
idol 16.18; 25.6
incense 17.26; 19.13
life (1) 17.11; 20.18
mark (1) Is 44.5;
31.21
message [2] 17.19;
19.2
plan 11.19; 19.7
plot (1) 11.9; 48.2
pray 11.14; 29.7
priest 14.18; 19.1
proclaim 15.19; 19.2
prophet 15.19; 23.11
punish 16.10; 19.15
remember 15.15;
31.34
right (3) 11.15; 32.7
scatter 16.15; 23.1
stubborn 17.23; 19.15
stumble 13.16; 23.12
terrible 16.4; 19.8
terror 17.17; 20.3
trap 9.8; 48.43
turn [3] 17.5; 23.27
warn 11.7; 26.15
way (3) [2] 15.7; 26.3
wise 10.7; 23.5

The People Reject the LORD

13 The LORD says,
"Ask every nation if such a thing
has ever happened before.
The people of Israel have done a
terrible thing!
14 Are Lebanon's rocky heights ever
without snow?
Do its cool mountain streams ever
run dry?
15 Yet **my people** have **forgotten me**;
they burn **incense** to **idols**.
They have **stumbled** in the way they
should go,
they no longer follow the old **ways**;
they walk on **unmarked** paths.
16 They have made this land a thing of
horror,
to be **despised** for ever.
All who pass by will be shocked at
what they see;
they will shake their heads in
amazement.
17 I will **scatter my people** before their
enemies,
like dust blown by the east wind.
I will **turn** my back on them;
I will not **help** them when the
disaster comes."

A Plot against Jeremiah

18 Then the people said, "Let's do
something about Jeremiah! There will
always be **priests** to instruct us, **wise** men
to give us counsel, and **prophets** to **proclaim** God's **message**. Let's bring **charges**
against him, and stop listening to what
he says."

19 So I **prayed**, "LORD, hear what I am
saying and listen to what my **enemies**
are saying about me. 20 Is **evil** the payment for good? Yet they have dug a pit
for me to fall in. **Remember** how I came
to you and spoke on their behalf, so that
you would not deal with them in **anger**.
21 But now, LORD, let their children starve
to death; let them be killed in war. Let
the women lose their husbands and children; let the men die of **disease** and the
young men be killed in battle. 22 Send a
mob to plunder their homes without
warning; make them cry out in **terror**.
They have dug a pit for me to fall in and
have set **traps** to catch me. 23 But, LORD,
you know all their **plots** to kill me. Do not
forgive their **evil** or pardon their sin.
Throw them down in defeat and deal
with them while you are **angry**."

The Broken Jar

19 The LORD told me to go and buy
a clay jar. He also told me to
take some of the **elders** of the people and
some of the older **priests**, 2 and to go
through Potsherd Gate out to the Valley
of Hinnom. There I was to **proclaim** the
message that he would give me. 3 The
LORD told me to say, "Kings of Judah and
people of Jerusalem, listen to what I, the
LORD **Almighty**, the God of Israel, have
to say. I am going to bring such a **disaster** on this place that everyone who

abandon 17.13; 22.9
Almighty [3] 16.9;
20.12
altar 17.1; 32.35
amaze 18.16; 50.13
blood 2.34; 46.10
command 17.22; 22.3
dead 9.22; 27.9
defile 16.18; 32.34
destroy 18.7; 20.8
disaster 18.17; 23.12
elder (2) Is 3.14;
26.17
enemy [2] 18.17; 20.4
god (2) (other gods)
[2] 16.11; 22.9
incense 18.15; 32.29

19.2: 2 Kgs 23.10; Jer 7.30–32, 32.34–35

innocent 7.6; 22.3
message [2] 18.2; 20.8
mind (1) 17.10; 20.12
offer [2] 14.12; 33.18
plan 18.11; 26.3
priest 18.18; 20.1
proclaim [2] 18.18; 20.1
promise 14.7; 29.10
punish 18.11; 21.14
sacrifice [2] 17.26; 32.35
slaughter 12.3; 25.34
stubborn 18.12; 23.17
Temple (1) (of God) 17.12; 20.1
terrible [2] 18.13; 21.6
triumph Is 46.13; Zech 9.9
unclean Job 14.4; 50.39

hears about it will be stunned. [4]I am going to do this because the people have
abandoned me and **defiled** this place by
offering sacrifices here to other **gods**—
gods that neither they nor their ancestors nor the kings of Judah have known
anything about. They have filled this
place with the **blood** of **innocent** people,
[5]and they have built **altars** for Baal in order to burn their children in the fire as
sacrifices. I never **commanded** them to
do this; it never even entered my **mind**.
[6]So then, the time will come when this
place will no longer be called Topheth or
the Valley of Hinnom. Instead, it will be
known as the Valley of **Slaughter**. [7]In this
place I will frustrate all the **plans** of the
people of Judah and Jerusalem. I will let
their **enemies triumph** over them and kill
them in battle. I will give their corpses to
the birds and the wild animals as food. [8]I
will bring such **terrible destruction** on
this city that everyone who passes by will
be shocked and **amazed**. [9]The **enemy**
will surround the city and try to kill its
people. The siege will be so **terrible** that
the people inside the city will eat one
another and even their own children."
10 Then the LORD told me to break the
jar in front of the men who had gone
with me [11]and to tell them that the LORD
Almighty had said, "I will break this
people and this city, and it will be like
this broken clay jar that cannot be put together again. People will bury their **dead**
even in Topheth because there will be
nowhere else to bury them. [12]I **promise**
that I will make this city and its inhabitants like Topheth. [13]The houses of
Jerusalem, the houses of the kings of
Judah, and indeed all the houses on
whose roofs **incense** has been burnt to
the stars and where wine has been
poured out as an **offering** to other **gods**—
they will all be as **unclean** as Topheth."
14 Then I left Topheth, where the
LORD had sent me to **proclaim** his
message. I went and stood in the court of
the **Temple** and told all the people [15]that
the LORD **Almighty**, the God of Israel,
had said, "I am going to bring on this city
and on every nearby town all the **punishment** that I said I would, because you are
stubborn and will not listen to what I
say."

Jeremiah's Conflict with Pashhur the Priest

Almighty 19.3; 23.15
authorities Mt 27.18
best 6.16; 31.20
birth 13.21; 30.6
cause (2) 11.20; 50.34

20 When the **priest** Pashhur son of
Immer, who was the chief officer
of the **Temple**, heard me **proclaim** these
things, [2]he ordered me to be beaten and
placed in chains near the upper
Benjamin Gate in the **Temple**. [3]The next
morning, after Pashhur had released me
from the chains, I said to him, "The LORD
did not name you Pashhur. The name he
has given you is '**Terror** Everywhere.'
[4]The LORD himself has said, 'I am going
to make you a **terror** to yourself and to
your **friends**, and you will see them all
killed by the swords of their **enemies**. I
am going to put all the people of Judah
under the **power** of the king of
Babylonia; he will take some away as
prisoners to his country and put others **to
death**. [5]I will also let their **enemies** plunder all the wealth of this city and seize all
its **possessions** and property, even the
treasures of the kings of Judah, and
carry everything off to Babylonia. [6]As
for you, Pashhur, you and all your family
will also be captured and taken off to
Babylonia. There you will die and be
buried, along with all your **friends** to
whom you have told so many **lies**.' "

Jeremiah Complains to the LORD

[7]LORD, you have **deceived** me,
and I was deceived.
You are **stronger** than I am,
and you have overpowered me.
Everyone **jeers** at me;
they **mock** me all day long.

[8]Whenever I speak, I have to cry out
and shout, "**Violence! Destruction!**"
LORD, I am **ridiculed** and **scorned** all
the time
because I **proclaim** your **message**.
[9]But when I say, "I will **forget** the LORD
and no longer speak **in his name**,"
then your **message** is like a fire
burning deep within me.
I try my **best** to hold it in,
but can no longer keep it back.
[10]I hear everybody whispering,
"**Terror** is everywhere!
So let's report him to the
authorities!"
Even my close **friends** wait for my
downfall.
"Perhaps he can be **tricked**," they say;
"then we can catch him and get
revenge."
[11]But you, LORD, are on my side, **strong**
and **mighty**,
and those who **persecute** me will
fail.
They will be **disgraced** for ever,
because they cannot **succeed**.
Their **disgrace** will never be **forgotten**.
[12]But, **Almighty** LORD, you **test** men
justly;

curse [2] 15.10; 23.10
death (3) (to death) 18.21; 21.7
deceive 17.9; 27.10
destroy [2] 19.8; 21.10
disgrace [3] 17.18; 22.22
downfall Prov 29.16; Lam 1.7
enemy [3] 19.7; 21.7
evil 18.8; 21.11
fail 14.6; 25.3
forget [3] 18.15; 23.2
friend [3] 13.21; 22.1
glad 16.9; 25.10
grave 8.1; Ezek 28.8
heart 17.1; 23.9
jeer Is 57.4; 48.27
justice 12.1; 21.11
lie (2) 14.14; 23.14
life (1) 18.11; 21.8
mercy 16.5; 21.7
message [2] 19.2; 21.11
might 16.21; 21.5
mind (1) 19.5; 21.10
mock Is 66.5; 24.9
name (2) (name of God, of Jesus) 14.14; 23.21
oppress 6.6; 22.3
pain 13.21; 22.23
persecute 17.18; Dan 12.7
possess 7.7; 25.5
power [2] 17.25; 23.1
praise 17.14; 30.19
priest 19.1; 21.1
prison 15.2; 22.22
proclaim [2] 19.2; 23.22
rescue 17.14; 30.10
revenge [2] 15.15; 46.10
ridicule Is 37.23; 24.
scorn Prov 24.9; 42.18
sorrow 14.2; 31.13
strong [2] 9.23; 50.9
succeed (1) 15.15; 22.30
Temple (1) (of God) [2] 19.14; 23.11
terror [3] 18.22; 26.21
test 17.10; 48.14
trick Prov 28.10; Dan 11.21
trouble 17.16; 44.17
violent 15.21; 22.17
womb Ecc 11.5; Hos 12.3

19.5: Lev 18.21

you know what is in their **hearts** and
minds.
So let me see you take **revenge** on my
enemies,
for I have placed my **cause** in your
hands.
13 Sing to the LORD!
Praise the LORD!
He **rescues** the **oppressed** from the
power of **evil** men.

14 **Curse** the day I was born!
Forget the day my mother gave me
birth!
15 **Curse** the man who made my father
glad
when he brought him the news,
"It's a boy! You have a son!"
16 May he be like those cities
that the LORD **destroyed** without
mercy.
May he hear cries of **pain** in the
morning
and the battle alarm at noon,
17 because he didn't kill me before I
was born.
Then my mother's **womb** would have
been my **grave**.
18 Why was I born?
Was it only to have **trouble** and
sorrow,
to end my **life** in **disgrace**?

Jerusalem's Defeat Is Predicted

21 King Zedekiah of Judah sent
Pashhur son of Malchiah and the
priest Zephaniah son of Maaseiah to me
with this **request**: 2 "Please speak to the
LORD for us, because King Nebuchadnezzar of Babylonia and his army are besieging the city. Maybe the LORD will
perform one of his **miracles** for us and
force Nebuchadnezzar to retreat."
3 Then the LORD spoke to me, and I
told the men who had been sent to me
4 to tell Zedekiah that the LORD, the God
of Israel, had said, "Zedekiah, I am going
to defeat your army that is fighting
against the king of Babylonia and his
army. I will pile up your soldiers'
weapons in the centre of the city. 5 I will
fight against you with all my **might**, my
anger, my wrath, and my **fury**. 6 I will kill
everyone living in this city; people and
animals alike will die of a **terrible**
disease. 7 But as for you, your officials,
and the people who survive the war, the
famine, and the **disease**—I will let
all of you be captured by King
Nebuchadnezzar and by your **enemies**,
who want to kill you. Nebuchadnezzar
will put you **to death**. He will not **spare**
any of you or show **mercy** or **pity** to any
of you. I, the LORD, have spoken."
8 Then the LORD told me to say to the
people, "Listen! I, the LORD, am giving
you a **choice** between the way that leads
to life and the way that leads to **death**.
9 Anyone who stays in the city will be
killed in war or by starvation or **disease**.
But whoever goes out and surrenders to
the Babylonians, who are now attacking
the city, will not be killed; he will at least
escape with his **life**. 10 I have made up my
mind not to **spare** this city, but to **destroy**
it. It will be given over to the king of
Babylonia and he will burn it to the
ground. I, the LORD, have spoken."

Judgement on the Royal House of Judah

11–12 The LORD told me to give this
message to the royal house of Judah, the
descendants of David: "Listen to what I,
the LORD, am saying. See that **justice** is
done every day. **Protect** the person who
is being **cheated** from the one who is
cheating him. If you don't, the **evil** you
are doing will make my **anger** burn like
a fire that cannot be **put out**. 13 You,
Jerusalem, are sitting[c] high above the
valleys, like a rock **rising** above the
plain. But I will fight against you. You
say that no one can attack you or break
through your **defences**. 14 But I will
punish you for what you have done. I will
set your palace on fire, and the fire will
burn down everything round it. I, the
LORD, have spoken."

Jeremiah's Message to the Royal House of Judah

22 1–2 The LORD told me to go to the
palace of the king of Judah, the
descendant of David, and there tell the
king, his officials, and the people of
Jerusalem to listen to what the LORD had
said: 3 "I, the LORD, **command** you to do
what is **just** and **right**. **Protect** the person
who is being **cheated** from the one who is
cheating him. Do not **ill-treat** or **oppress**
foreigners, **orphans**, or **widows**; and do
not kill **innocent** people in this **holy**
place. 4 If you really do as I have **commanded**, then David's descendants will
continue to be kings. And they, together
with their officials and their people, will
continue to pass through the gates of this
palace in chariots and on horses. 5 But if
you do not **obey** my **commands**, then I
swear to you that this palace will fall into
ruins. I, the LORD, have spoken.
6 "To me, Judah's royal palace is as

anger [2] 18.20; 23.19
cheat 8.10; 22.3
choose 12.7; 23.5
death (1) 18.21; 22.10
death (3) (to death) 20.4; 25.31
defend Is 60.18; 46.14
destroy 20.8; 22.7
disease [3] 18.21; 24.10
enemy 20.4; 30.14
escape 16.17; 25.35
evil 20.13; 22.22
famine 5.12; 52.6
force (1) Is 52.4; 22.26
fury Is 51.13; 23.19
justice 20.12; 22.3
life (1) [2] 20.18; 22.15
life (2) (to life) Is 26.19; Ezek 37.3
mercy 20.16; 30.18
message 20.8; 23.18
might 20.11; 31.11
mind (1) 20.12; 25.16
miracle Ps 136.4; 32.20
pity 15.5; 48.1
priest 20.1; 23.11
protect 16.19; 22.3
punish 19.15; 23.2
put out 17.27; Ezek 20.47
request Ps 21.2; 32.7
rise Is 52.2; 46.7
spare [2] 17.18; 38.17
terrible 19.8; 22.18

abandon 19.4; 25.38
afraid 17.8; 23.4
bitter 13.17; 23.15
cheat 21.11; Ezek 18.7
command [3] 19.5; 23.38
condemn 17.5; Lam 1.22
covenant 14.21; 31.31
death (1) [2] 21.8; 31.2
desolate 12.11; Ezek 26.19
destroy 21.10; 23.1
disgrace 20.11; 23.40
dishonest 17.11; Dan 6.4
doom [2] 15.2; 43.11
enjoy 2.7; Ezek 18.23
evil 21.11; 23.2
exile [2] 13.19; 28.4
force (1) 21.2; 34.11
friend 20.4; 23.35
god (2) (other gods) 19.4; 25.6
holy Is 66.7; 23.9
honour 13.11; 26.19
ill-treat Prov 19.26; Ezek 22.29

[c] You, Jerusalem, are sitting; *or* You are enthroned.

20.14–18: Job 3.1–19 **21.2:** 2 Kgs 25.1–11; 2 Chr 36.17–21 **22.5:** Mt 23.38; Lk 13.35

injustice Is 58.6; Hos 10.4
innocent [2] 19.4; 26.15
interest (1) Is 58.3; Dan 6.2
justice [2] 21.11; 23.5
life (1) [2] 21.8; 23.10
long (2) Is 59.11; 31.2
mourn [2] 16.4; 23.10
never again [2] 3.19; 31.40
obey [2] 17.23; 25.6
oppress [2] 20.13; 30.16
orphan 7.6; 49.11
pain [2] 20.16; 49.24
poor 16.6; 39.10
prison 20.4; 24.1
prosper [2] 12.1; 29.7
protect 21.11; 31.22
refuse (1) 13.10; 23.17
rest (1) Is 63.14; 31.2
right (1) 13.23; 23.5
right (2) Is 30.21; Ezek 1.10
ruin 13.7; 25.9
secure Is 47.8; 30.10
selfish Prov 28.22; Dan 11.34
serve 17.4; 25.6
shame 17.13; 23.40
strike 15.8; 33.5
succeed (1) 20.11; 32.5
sure 5.3; 26.15
swear 16.14; 23.7
terrible 21.6; 23.1
try (2) Is 45.20; 25.31
violent 20.8; 48.3
wage Is 55.2; Zech 11.12
weep [3] 14.17; 31.9
widow 15.8; 49.11
worship (2) (of other gods) 17.2; 25.6

beautiful as the land of Gilead and as the
Lebanon Mountains; but I will make it a
desolate place where no one lives. [7] I am
sending men to **destroy** it. They will all
bring their axes, cut down its beautiful
cedar pillars, and throw them into the
fire.

8 "Afterwards many foreigners will
pass by and ask one another why I, the
LORD, have done such a thing to this
great city. [9] Then they will answer that it
is because you have **abandoned** your
covenant with me, your God, and have
worshipped and served other gods."

Jeremiah's Message concerning Joahaz

[10] People of Judah, do not **weep** for King
Josiah;
do not **mourn** his **death**.
But **weep bitterly** for Joahaz, his son;
they are taking him away, never to
return,
never again to see the land where
he was born.

11 The LORD says concerning Josiah's
son Joahaz, who succeeded his father as
king of Judah, "He has gone away from
here, never to return. [12] He will die in the
country where they have taken him, and
he will **never again** see this land."

Jeremiah's Message concerning Jehoiakim

[13] **Doomed** is the man who builds his
house by **injustice**
and enlarges it by **dishonesty**;
who makes his countrymen work for
nothing
and does not pay their **wages**.
[14] **Doomed** is the man who says,
"I will build myself a mansion
with spacious rooms upstairs."
So he puts windows in his house,
panels it with cedar,
and paints it red.
[15] Does it make you a better king
if you build houses of cedar,
finer than those of others?
Your father **enjoyed** a full **life**.
He was always **just** and fair,
and he **prospered** in everything he
did.
[16] He gave the **poor** a fair **trial**,
and all went well with him.
That is what it means to know the
LORD.
[17] But you can only see your **selfish**
interests;
you kill the **innocent**
and **violently oppress** your people.
The LORD has spoken.

18 So then, the LORD says about
Josiah's son Jehoiakim, king of Judah,
"No one will **mourn** his **death** or say,
'How **terrible**, my **friend**, how
terrible!'
No one will **weep** for him or cry,
'My lord! My king!'
[19] With the funeral **honours** of a donkey,
he will be dragged away
and thrown outside Jerusalem's
gates."

Jeremiah's Message about the Fate of Jerusalem

[20] People of Jerusalem, go to Lebanon
and shout,
go to the land of Bashan and cry;
call out from the mountains of Moab,
because all your allies have been
defeated.
[21] The LORD spoke to you when you were
prosperous,
but you **refused** to listen.
That is what you've done all your **life**;
you never would **obey** the LORD.
[22] Your leaders will be blown away by
the wind,
your allies taken as **prisoners** of war,
your city **disgraced** and put to
shame
because of all the **evil** you have
done.
[23] You **rest secure** among the cedars
brought from Lebanon;
but how pitiful you'll be when **pains**
strike you,
pains like those of a woman in
labour.

God's Judgement on Jehoiachin

24 The LORD said to King Jehoiachin,
son of King Jehoiakim of Judah, "As
surely as I am the living God, even if you
were the signet-ring on my **right hand**, I
would pull you off [25] and give you to
people you are **afraid** of, people who
want to kill you. I will give you to King
Nebuchadnezzar of Babylonia and his
soldiers. [26] I am going to **force** you and
your mother into **exile**. You will go to a
country where neither of you was born,
and both of you will die there. [27] You will
long to see this country again, but you
will never return."

28 I said, "Has King Jehoiachin become like a broken jar that is thrown
away and that no one wants? Is that why
he and his children have been taken into
exile to a land they know nothing
about?"
[29] O land, land, land!

22.11: 2 Kgs 23.31–34; 2 Chr 36.1–4 **22.18:** 2 Kgs 23.36—24.6; 2 Chr 36.5–7
22.24: 2 Kgs 24.8–15; 2 Chr 36.9–10

Listen to what the LORD has said:
30 "This man is condemned to lose his
children,
to be a man who will never succeed.
He will have no descendants
who will rule in Judah
as David's successors.
I, the LORD, have spoken."

Hope for the Future

23 How terrible will be the LORD's
judgement on those rulers who
destroy and scatter his people! 2 This is
what the LORD, the God of Israel, says
about the rulers who were supposed to
take care of his people: "You have not
taken care of my people; you have scattered them and driven them away. Now I
am going to punish you for the evil you
have done. 3 I will gather the rest of my
people from the countries where I have
scattered them, and I will bring them
back to their homeland. They will have
many children and increase in number.
4 I will appoint rulers to take care of
them. My people will no longer be afraid
or terrified, and I will not punish them
again.[d] I, the LORD, have spoken."

5 The LORD says, "The time is coming
when I will choose as king a righteous descendant of David. That king will rule
wisely and do what is right and just
throughout the land. 6 When he is king,
the people of Judah will be safe, and the
people of Israel will live in peace. He will
be called 'The LORD Our Salvation.'

7 "The time is coming," says the
LORD, "when people will no longer swear
by me as the living God who brought the
people of Israel out of the land of Egypt.
8 Instead, they will swear by me as the
living God who brought the people of
Israel out of a northern land and out of
all the other countries where I had scattered them. Then they will live in their
own land."

Jeremiah's Message about the Prophets

9 My heart is crushed,
and I am trembling.
Because of the LORD,
because of his holy words,
I am like a man who is drunk,
a man who has had too much wine.
10 The land is full of people unfaithful to
the LORD;
they live wicked lives and misuse
their power.
Because of the LORD's curse the land
mourns
and the pastures are dry.
11 The LORD says,
"The prophets and the priests are
godless;
I have caught them doing evil in the
Temple itself.
12 The paths they follow will be slippery
and dark;
I will make them stumble and fall.
I am going to bring disaster on them;
the time of their punishment is
coming.
I, the LORD, have spoken.
13 I have seen the sin of Samaria's
prophets:
they have spoken in the name of
Baal
and have led my people astray.
14 But I have seen the prophets in
Jerusalem do even worse:
they commit adultery and tell lies;
they help people to do wrong,
so that no one stops doing what is
evil.
To me, they are all as bad
as the people of Sodom and
Gomorrah.

15 "So then, this is what I, the LORD Almighty, say about the prophets of
Jerusalem:
I will give them bitter plants to eat
and poison to drink,
because they have spread ungodliness
throughout the land."

16 The LORD Almighty said to the
people of Jerusalem, "Do not listen to
what the prophets say; they are filling
you with false hopes. They tell you what
they have imagined and not what I have
said. 17 To the people who refuse to listen
to what I have said, they keep saying that
all will go well with them. And they tell
everyone who is stubborn that disaster
will never touch him."

18 I said, "None of these prophets has
ever known the LORD's secret thoughts.
None of them has ever heard or understood his message, or ever listened or
paid attention to what he said. 19 His anger is a storm, a furious wind that will
rage over the heads of the wicked, 20 and
it will not end until he has done everything he intends to do. In days to come
his people will understand this clearly."

21 The LORD said, "I did not send
these prophets, but even so they went. I
did not give them any message, but still
they spoke in my name. 22 If they had
known my secret thoughts, then they
could have proclaimed my message to
my people and could have made them

[d] I will not punish them again; *or* not one of them will be missing.

23.5–6: Jer 33.14–16 **23.14:** Gen 18.20; Ezek 16.49

give up the **evil lives** they live and the **wicked** things they do.

23 "I am a God who is everywhere and not in one place only. 24 No one can hide where I cannot see him. Do you not know that I am everywhere in **heaven and on earth**? 25 I know what those **prophets** have said who speak **lies in my name** and **claim** that I have given them my **messages** in their **dreams**. 26 How much longer will those **prophets mislead my people** with the **lies** they have invented? 27 They think that the **dreams** they tell will make **my people** forget me, just as their fathers **forgot** me and **turned** to Baal. 28 The **prophet** who has had a **dream** should say it is only a **dream**, but the **prophet** who has heard my **message** should **proclaim** that message **faithfully**. What good is straw **compared** with wheat? 29 My **message** is like a fire, and like a hammer that breaks rocks in pieces. 30 I am against those **prophets** who take **each other's words** and **proclaim** them as my **message**. 31 I am also against those **prophets** who speak their own **words** and **claim** they came from me. 32 Listen to what I, the LORD, say! I am against the **prophets** who tell their **dreams** that are full of **lies**. They tell these **dreams** and lead **my people** astray with their **lies** and their **boasting**. I did not send them or order them to go, and they are of no **help** at all to the people. I, the LORD, have spoken."

The LORD's Burden

33 The LORD said to me, "Jeremiah, when one of **my people** or a **prophet** or a **priest** asks you, 'What is the LORD's **message**?' you are to tell him, 'You are a **burden**[e] to the LORD, and he is going to get **rid of** you.' 34 If one of **my people** or a **prophet** or a **priest** even uses the **words** 'the LORD's **burden**,' I will **punish** him and his family. 35 Instead, each one should ask his **friends** and his relatives, 'What answer has the LORD given? What has the LORD said?' 36 So they must no longer use the **words** 'the LORD's **burden**,' because if anyone does, I will make my **message** a **real burden** to him. The people have **perverted** the **words** of their God, the living God, the LORD **Almighty**. 37 Jeremiah, ask the **prophets**, 'What answer did the LORD give you? What did the LORD say?' 38 And if they **disobey** my **command** and use the **words** 'the LORD's **burden**,' then tell them that 39 I will certainly pick them up[f] and throw them far away from me, both them and the city that I gave to them and their ancestors. 40 I will bring on them **everlasting shame** and **disgrace** that will never be **forgotten**."

Two Baskets of Figs

24 The LORD showed me two baskets of figs placed in front of the **Temple**. (This was after King Nebuchadnezzar of Babylonia had taken away Jehoiakim's son, King Jehoiachin of Judah, as a **prisoner** from Jerusalem to Babylonia, together with the leaders of Judah, the craftsmen, and the skilled workers.) 2 The first basket contained good figs, those that **ripen** early; the other one contained **bad** figs, too **bad** to eat. 3 Then the LORD said to me, "Jeremiah, what do you see?"

I answered, "Figs. The good ones are very good, and the bad ones are very bad, too bad to eat."

4 So the LORD said to me, 5 "I, the LORD, the God of Israel, consider that the people who were taken away to Babylonia are like these good figs, and I will treat them with **kindness**. 6 I will **watch** over them and bring them back to this land. I will build them up and not tear them down; I will plant them and not pull them up. 7 I will give them the **desire** to know that I am the LORD. Then they will be **my people**, and I will be their God, because they will return to me **with all their heart**.

8 "As for King Zedekiah of Judah, the politicians round him, and the rest of the people of Jerusalem who have stayed in this land or moved to Egypt—I, the LORD, will treat them all like these figs that are too **bad** to be eaten. 9 I will bring such a **disaster** on them that all the nations of the **world** will be **terrified**. People will **mock** them, make jokes about them, **ridicule** them, and use their name as a **curse** everywhere I **scatter** them. 10 I will bring war, starvation, and **disease** on them until there is not one of them left in the land that I gave to them and their ancestors."

bad [3] 23.14; 49.23
curse 23.10; 25.18
desire 5.8; 34.16
disaster 23.12; 25.13
disease 21.6; 27.8
God's people 23.1; 25.30
heart 23.9; 29.13
kind Is 26.10; 52.31
mock 20.7; 29.18
prison 22.22; 28.6
ridicule 20.8
ripe Is 28.4; Hos 8.7
scatter 23.1; 25.33
Temple (1) (of God) 23.11; 26.2
terrify 23.4; 29.18
watch 11.20; 31.6
world 15.4; 26.6

The Enemy from the North

25 In the fourth year that Jehoiakim son of Josiah was king of Judah, I received a **message** from the LORD concerning all the people of Judah. (This was the first year that Nebuchadnezzar was king of Babylonia.) 2 I said to all the

abandon 22.9; 51.5
Almighty [5] 23.15; 26.18
anger [5] 23.19; 30.23
body 16.4; 26.23
case (2) 12.1; Ezek 44.24
command 23.38; 26.2

[e] *The Hebrew word for* message *and* burden *is the same.*
[f] *The Hebrew verb for* pick up *comes from the same root as the Hebrew word for* message *and* burden.

24.1: 2 Kgs 24.12–16; 2 Chr 36.10 **25.1:** 2 Kgs 24.1; 2 Chr 36.5–7; Dan 1.1–2

cup [4] Is 51.17; 35.5
curse 24.9; 26.6
death (3) (to death) 21.7; 26.11
destroy [4] 23.1; 26.3
disaster [3] 24.9; 26.19
distress 15.11; 30.7
escape 21.9; 26.21
evil 23.2; 26.3
fail 20.11; 49.4
feast 16.8; 33.11
glad 20.15; 31.13
god (2) (other gods) 22.9; 32.29
God's people [3] 24.7; 29.31
happy 16.9; 31.13
heaven 23.24; 44.17
horror 18.16; 29.18
idol [2] 18.15; 32.34
joy 16.9; 30.19
last (2) Is 48.12; Ezek 5.12
life (1) 23.10; 32.39
message 23.18; 27.3
mind (1) 21.10; 26.3
mourn [2] 23.10; 31.13
neighbour [3] 13.27; Ezek 11.12
obey 22.5; 26.4
peace 23.6; 28.9
possess 20.5; 30.3
proclaim 23.22; 26.2
prophet 23.11; 26.5
punish [6] 23.2; 27.8
refuse (1) [2] 23.17; 29.19
ruin [4] 22.5; 26.18
scatter 24.9; 29.14
servant [2] 15.19; 26.5
serve [2] 22.9; 27.6
shepherd Is 40.11; 31.10
sight [3] 16.17; 42.18
slaughter 19.6; 48.15
slave 2.14; 30.8
terrible [2] 23.1; 26.19
threat 17.15; 36.7
try (2) 22.16; Mt 5.21
turn [2] 23.27; 27.22
wedding 16.9; 33.11
wicked [2] 23.10; 26.3
worship (2) (of other gods) [2] 22.9; 35.15

people of Judah and of Jerusalem, 3 "For
twenty-three years, from the thirteenth
year that Josiah son of Amon was king of
Judah until this very day, the LORD has
spoken to me, and I have never **failed** to
tell you what he said. But you have paid
no attention. 4 You would not listen or
pay attention, even though the LORD has
continued to send you his **servants** the
prophets. 5 They told you to **turn from**
your **wicked** way of **life** and from the **evil**
things you are doing, so that you could go
on living in the land that the LORD gave
you and your ancestors as a permanent
possession. 6 They told you not to **worship**
and serve other gods and not to make the
LORD **angry by worshipping the idols** you
had made. If you had **obeyed** the LORD,
then he would not have **punished** you.
7 But the LORD himself says that you **re-**
fused to listen to him. Instead, you made
him **angry** with your **idols** and have
brought his **punishment** on yourselves.

8 "So then, because you would not listen to him, the LORD **Almighty** says, 9 'I
am going to send for all the peoples from
the north and for my **servant**, King
Nebuchadnezzar of Babylonia. I am going to bring them to fight against Judah
and its inhabitants and against all the
neighbouring nations. I am going to **des-**
troy this nation and its **neighbours** and
leave them in **ruins** for ever, a **terrible**
and shocking **sight**. I, the LORD, have
spoken. 10 I will silence their shouts of **joy**
and **gladness** and the **happy** sounds of
wedding feasts. They will have no oil for
their lamps, and there will be no more
corn. 11 This whole land will be left in
ruins and will be a shocking **sight**, and
the **neighbouring** nations will **serve** the
king of Babylonia for seventy years.
12 After that I will **punish** Babylonia and
its king for their sin. I will **destroy** that
country and leave it in **ruins** for ever. 13 I
will **punish** Babylonia with all the **dis-**
asters that I **threatened** to bring on the
nations when I spoke through
Jeremiah—all the **disasters** recorded in
this book. 14 I will pay the Babylonians
back for what they have done, and many
nations and great kings will make **slaves**
of them.' "

God's Judgement on the Nations

15 The LORD, the God of Israel, said to
me, "Here is a wine **cup** filled with my
anger. Take it to all the nations to whom
I send you, and make them drink from it.
16 When they drink from it, they will stagger and go out of their **minds** because of
the war I am sending against them."

17 So I took the **cup** from the LORD's
hand, gave it to all the nations to whom
the LORD had sent me, and made them
drink from it. 18 Jerusalem and all the
towns of Judah, together with its kings
and leaders, were made to drink from it,
so that they would become a desert, a
terrible and shocking **sight**, and so that
people would use their name as a **curse**—
as they still do.

19–26 Here is the list of all the others
who had to drink from the **cup**:

the king of Egypt, his officials and
leaders;
all the Egyptians and all the foreigners
in Egypt;
all the kings of the land of Uz;
all the kings of the Philistine cities of
Ashkelon, Gaza, Ekron, and what
remains of Ashdod;
all the people of Edom, Moab, and
Ammon;
all the kings of Tyre and Sidon;
all the kings of the Mediterranean
lands;
the cities of Dedan, Tema, and Buz;
all the people who cut their hair short;
all the kings of Arabia;
all the kings of the desert tribes;
all the kings of Zimri, Elam, and
Media;
all the kings of the north, far and near,
one after another.

Every nation on the face of the earth
had to drink from it. **Last** of all, the king
of Babylonia will drink from it.

27 Then the LORD said to me, "Tell the
people that I, the LORD **Almighty**, the
God of Israel, am **commanding** them to
drink until they are drunk and vomit, until they fall down and cannot get up, because of the war that I am sending
against them. 28 And if they **refuse** to take
the **cup** from your hand and drink from
it, then tell them that the LORD **Almighty**
has said that they will still have to drink
from it. 29 I will begin my work of **destruc-**
tion in my own city. Do they think they
will go **unpunished**? No, they will be **pun-**
ished, for I am going to send war on all
the people on earth. I, the LORD **Al-**
mighty, have spoken.

30 "You, Jeremiah, must **proclaim**
everything I have said. You must tell
these people,

'The LORD will roar from **heaven**
and thunder from the heights of
heaven.
He will roar against **his people**;
he will shout like a man treading
grapes.
Everyone on earth will hear him,

25.10: Jer 7.34, 16.9; Rev 18.22–23 **25.11:** 2 Chr 36.21; Jer 29.10; Dan 9.2

31 and the sound will echo to the ends
of the earth.
The LORD has a **case** against the
nations.
He will bring all people to **trial**
and put the **wicked to death**.
The LORD has spoken.' "

32 The LORD **Almighty** says that **dis-**
aster is coming on one nation after
another, and a great storm is gathering
at the far ends of the earth. 33 On that day
the **bodies** of those whom the LORD has
killed will lie **scattered** from one end of
the earth to the other. No one will **mourn**
for them, and they will not be taken
away and buried. They will lie on the
ground like piles of manure.
34 Cry, you leaders, you **shepherds** of
my people, cry out loud! **Mourn** and roll
in the dust. The time has come for you to
be **slaughtered**,[g] and you will be
butchered like rams.[h] 35 There will be no
way for you to **escape**. 36–37 You moan and
cry out in **distress** because the LORD in
his **anger** has **destroyed** your nation and
left your **peaceful** country in **ruins**. 38 The
LORD has **abandoned his people**[i] like a
lion that leaves its cave. The **horrors** of
war and the **LORD's fierce anger** have
turned the country into a desert.

Jeremiah Is Brought to Trial

26 Soon after Jehoiakim son of
Josiah became king of Judah,
2 the LORD said to me, "Stand in the court
of the **Temple** and **proclaim** all I have
commanded you to say to the people who
come from the towns of Judah to **worship**
there. Do not leave out anything. 3 Perhaps the people will listen and give up
their **evil ways**. If they do, then I will
change my mind about the **destruction** I
plan to bring on them for all their **wicked**
deeds."
4 The LORD told me to say to the
people, "I, the LORD, have said that you
must **obey** me by following the **teaching**
that I gave you, 5 and by paying attention
to the **words** of my **servants**, the **pro-**
phets, whom I have kept on sending to
you. You have never **obeyed** what they
said. 6 If you continue to **disobey**, then I
will do to this **Temple** what I did to
Shiloh,[j] and all the nations of the **world**
will use the name of this city as a **curse**."
7 The **priests**, the **prophets**, and all the
people heard me saying these things in
the **Temple**, 8 and as soon as I had finished all that the LORD had **commanded**
me to speak, they seized me and shouted,
"You ought to be killed for this! 9 Why
have you said in the **LORD's name** that
this **Temple** will become like Shiloh and
that this city will be **destroyed** and no
one will live in it?" Then the people
crowded round me.
10 When the leaders of Judah heard
what had happened, they hurried from
the royal palace to the **Temple** and took
their places at the New Gate. 11 Then the
priests and the **prophets** said to the
leaders and to the people, "This man **de-**
serves to be **sentenced to death** because
he has spoken against our city. You
heard him with your own ears."
12 Then I said, "The LORD sent me to
proclaim everything that you heard me
say against this **Temple** and against this
city. 13 You must **change** the way you are
living and the things you are doing, and
must **obey** the LORD your God. If you do,
he will **change his mind** about the
destruction that he said he would bring
on you. 14 As for me, I am in your **power**!
Do with me whatever you think is fair
and **right**. 15 But be **sure** of this: if you kill
me, you and the people of this city will be
guilty of killing an **innocent** man, because it is the LORD who sent me to give
you this **warning**."
16 Then the leaders and the people
said to the **priests** and the **prophets**,
"This man spoke to us in the **name of the**
LORD our God; he should not be put **to**
death."
17 After that, some of the **elders** stood
up and said to the people who had
assembled, 18 "When Hezekiah was king
of Judah, the **prophet** Micah of
Moresheth told all the people that the
LORD **Almighty** had said,

'Zion will be ploughed like a field,
Jerusalem will become a pile of
ruins,
and the **Temple** hill will become a
forest.'

19 King Hezekiah and the people of Judah
did not put Micah **to death**. Instead,
Hezekiah **honoured** the LORD and tried to
win his **favour**. And the LORD **changed**
his mind about the **disaster** that he said
he would bring on them. Now we are
about to bring a **terrible disaster** on ourselves."
20 (There was another man, Uriah son
of Shemaiah from Kiriath Jearim, who
spoke in the **name of the LORD** against

Almighty 25.8; 27.4
body 25.33; 41.7
change [4] 18.11; 34.11
command [2] 25.27; 27.4
curse 25.18; 29.18
death (3) (to death) [3] 25.31; 29.21
deserve 10.7; 49.12
destroy [3] 25.9; 27.8
disaster [2] 25.13; 29.11
disobey 23.38; 34.17
elder (2) 19.1; Ezek 7.26
escape 25.35; 31.2
evil 25.5; 32.32
favour Is 60.10; 36.9
flee 9.10; 49.24
guilty 16.10; 29.23
honour 22.19; 30.19
innocent 22.3; Lam 4.13
mind (1) [3] 25.16; 32.35
name (2) (name of God, of Jesus) [3] 23.21; 27.15
obey [3] 25.6; 29.19
plan 19.7; 29.11
power 23.10; 27.5
priest [3] 23.11; 27.16
proclaim [2] 25.30; 31.10
prophet [5] 25.4; 27.9
right (1) 23.5; 33.10
ruin 25.9; 27.17
sentence Is 65.6; 39.5
servant 25.4; 27.6
sure 22.24; 33.26
teach 16.11; 31.18
Temple (1) (of God) [7] 24.1; 27.16
terrible 25.9; 29.23
terror 20.3; 30.5
warn 18.22; 29.8
way (3) 18.11; 35.15
wicked 25.5; 30.14
win Is 63.5; Lam 1.9
word (1) 23.9; 31.10
world 24.9; 27.5
worship (1) (of God) 10.25; 32.34

[g] *Hebrew has an additional word, the meaning of which is unclear.*
[h] *One ancient translation* rams; *Hebrew* vessels.
[i] The LORD...people; *or* The LORD's people run away. [j] SHILOH: *See 7.12.*

26.1: 2 Kgs 23.36—24.6; 2 Chr 36.5–7 **26.6:** Josh 18.1; Ps 78.60; Jer 7.12–14 **26.18:** Mic 3.12

this city and nation just as Jeremiah did.
21 When King Jehoiakim and his soldiers
and officials heard what Uriah had said,
the king tried to have him killed. But
Uriah heard about it; so he **fled in terror**
and **escaped** to Egypt. 22 King Jehoiakim,
however, sent Elnathan son of Achbor
and some other men to Egypt to get
Uriah. 23 They brought him back to King
Jehoiakim, who had him killed and his
body thrown into the public burial-
ground.)

24 But because I had the support of
Ahikam son of Shaphan, I was not
handed over to the people and killed.

Jeremiah Wears an Ox Yoke

Almighty [3] 26.18; 28.2
choose 23.5; 33.15
claim 23.25; 29.8
command 26.2; 32.23
create 10.12; 31.22
dead 19.11; 31.40
deceive [2] 20.7; 29.8
destroy [2] 26.3; 30.11
disease [2] 24.10; 28.8
dream 23.25; 29.8
leading Prov 31.23; Nah 3.10
lie (2) [3] 23.14; 28.15
magic Is 47.9; Ezek 13.18
mankind Is 66.24; 32.27
message [2] 25.1; 29.19
name (2) (name of God, of Jesus) 26.9; 29.9
power [3] 26.14; 28.2
predict 14.14; 28.8
priest 26.7; 28.1
prophet [5] 26.5; 28.1
punish 25.6; 29.31
restore Is 62.7; 29.14
ruin 26.18; 44.2
servant 26.5; 29.19
serve [6] 25.6; 28.14
spirit (2) Is 65.4; 50.39
strength 17.5; 46.18
submit [6] Ps 32.9; Lam 3.29
Temple (1) (of God) [4] 26.2; 28.1
turn 25.5; 31.13
world 26.6; 29.18

27 Soon after Josiah's son Zedekiah
became king of Judah, the LORD
told me 2 to make myself a yoke out of
leather straps and wooden crossbars and
to put it on my neck. 3 Then the LORD told
me to send a **message**[k] to the kings of
Edom, Moab, Ammon, Tyre, and Sidon
through their ambassadors who had
come to Jerusalem to see King Zedekiah.
4 The LORD **Almighty**, the God of Israel,
told me to **command** them to tell their
kings that the LORD had said: 5 "By my
great **power** and **strength** I **created** the
world, **mankind**, and all the animals that
live on the earth; and I give it to anyone
I **choose**. 6 I am the one who has placed
all these nations under the **power** of
my **servant**, King Nebuchadnezzar of
Babylonia, and I have made even the
wild animals **serve** him. 7 All nations will
serve him, and they will **serve** his son
and his grandson until the time comes
for his own nation to fall. Then his nation
will **serve powerful** nations and great
kings.

8 "But if any nation or kingdom will
not **submit** to his rule, then I will **punish**
that nation by war, starvation, and
disease until I have let Nebuchadnezzar
destroy it completely. 9 Do not listen to
your **prophets** or to anyone who **claims**
he can **predict** the future, either by
dreams or by calling up the **spirits** of the
dead or by **magic**. They all tell you not to
submit to the king of Babylonia. 10 They
are **deceiving** you and will cause you to
be taken far away from your country. I
will drive you out, and you will be **destroyed**. 11 But if any nation **submits** to the
king of Babylonia and **serves** him, then I
will let it stay on in its own land, to farm
it and live there. I, the LORD, have
spoken."

12 I said the same thing to King
Zedekiah of Judah, "**Submit** to the king of
Babylonia. **Serve** him and his people, and
you will live. 13 Why should you and your
people die in war or of starvation or
disease? That is what the LORD has said
will happen to any nation that does not
submit to the king of Babylonia. 14 Do not
listen to the **prophets** who tell you not to
surrender to him. They are **deceiving**
you. 15 The LORD himself has said that he
did not send them and that they are **lying**
to you **in his name**. And so he will drive
you out, and you will be killed, you and
the **prophets** who are telling you these
lies."

16 Then I told the **priests** and the
people that the LORD had said: "Do not
listen to the **prophets** who say that the
temple treasures will soon be brought
back from Babylonia. They are **lying** to
you. 17 Don't listen to them! **Submit** to the
king of Babylonia and you will live! Why
should this city become a pile of **ruins**?
18 If they are really **prophets** and if they
have my **message**, let them ask me, the
LORD **Almighty**, not to allow the
treasures that remain in the **Temple** and
in the royal palace to be taken to
Babylonia."

19–20 (When King Nebuchadnezzar
took away to Babylonia the king of
Judah, Jehoiachin son of Jehoiakim, and
the **leading** men of Judah and Jerusalem,
he left the columns, the bronze tank, the
carts, and some of the other **temple**
treasures.)

21 "Listen to what I, the LORD **Almighty**, the God of Israel, say about the
treasures that are left in the **Temple** and
in the royal palace in Jerusalem: 22 They
will be taken to Babylonia and will remain there until I **turn** my attention to
them. Then I will bring them back and
restore them to this place. I, the LORD,
have spoken."

Jeremiah and the Prophet Hananiah

28 That same year,[l] in the fifth
month of the fourth year that
Zedekiah was king, Hananiah son of
Azzur, a **prophet** from the town of
Gibeon, spoke to me in the **Temple**. In
the **presence** of the **priests** and of the
people he told me 2 that the LORD **Almighty**, the God of Israel, had said: "I
have broken the **power** of the king of
Babylonia. 3 Within two years I will bring
back to this place all the **temple**
treasures that King Nebuchadnezzar

Almighty [2] 27.4; 29.4
believe 7.4; 29.31
disease 27.8; 29.17
exile 22.26; 29.2
hope [2] 23.16; 29.11
lie (2) 27.15; 29.9
peace 25.36; 30.5
power [3] 27.5; 29.21
predict [3] 27.9; 29.8
presence [3] 7.10; 32.12
priest [2] 27.16; 29.1
prison 24.1; 29.1
prophecy 2 Chr 24.27; Ezek 4.7
prophet [5] 27.9; 29.1

[k] *Probable text* a message; *Hebrew* them.
[l] *One ancient translation* That same year; *Hebrew* That same year at the beginning of his reign.

27.1: 2 Kgs 24.18–20; 2 Chr 36.11–13 **28.1:** 2 Kgs 24.18–20; 2 Chr 36.11–13

rebel 7.26; 29.31
rid 23.33; Ezek 11.18
serve [2] 27.6; 30.9
Temple (1) (of God) [4] 27.16; 29.26
true [3] 15.11; 32.24
wonder (1) Is 52.7; 32.20

took to Babylonia. 4 I will also bring back
the king of Judah, Jehoiachin son of
Jehoiakim, along with all the people of
Judah who went into **exile** in Babylonia.
Yes, I will break the **power** of the king of
Babylonia. I, the LORD, have spoken."
5 Then in the **presence** of the **priests**
and of all the people who were standing
in the **Temple**, I said to Hananiah:
6 "**Wonderful**! I **hope** the LORD will do
this! I certainly **hope** he will make your
prophecy come **true** and will bring back
from Babylonia all the **temple** treasures
and all the people who were taken away
as **prisoners**. 7 But listen to what I say to
you and to the people. 8 The **prophets**
who spoke long ago, before my time and
yours, **predicted** that war, starvation, and
disease would come to many nations and
powerful kingdoms. 9 But a **prophet** who
predicts peace can only be recognized as
a **prophet** whom the LORD has **truly** sent
when that **prophet's predictions** come
true."
10 Then Hananiah took the yoke off
my neck, broke it in pieces, 11 and said in
the **presence** of all the people: "The
LORD has said that this is how he
will break the yoke that King
Nebuchadnezzar has put on the neck of
all the nations; and he will do this within
two years." Then I left.
12 Some time after this the LORD told
me 13 to go and say to Hananiah: "The
LORD has said that you may be able to
break a wooden yoke, but he[m] will replace it with an iron yoke. 14 The LORD
Almighty, the God of Israel, has said that
he will put an iron yoke on all these
nations and that they will **serve** King
Nebuchadnezzar of Babylonia. The LORD
has said that he will make even the wild
animals **serve** Nebuchadnezzar."
15 Then I told Hananiah this, and
added, "Listen, Hananiah! The LORD did
not send you, and you are making these
people **believe** a **lie**. 16 And so the LORD
himself says that he is going to get **rid** of
you. Before this year is over you will die
because you have told the people to **rebel**
against the LORD."
17 And Hananiah died in the seventh
month of that same year.

Jeremiah's Letter to the Jews in Babylonia

adultery 23.14; Ezek 16.17
alive 15.9; Lam 1.11
Almighty [5] 28.2; 30.8

29 I wrote a **letter** to the **priests**, the
prophets, the leaders of the
people, and to all the others whom
Nebuchadnezzar had taken away as
prisoners from Jerusalem to Babylonia.
2 I wrote it after King Jehoiachin, his
mother, the palace officials, the leaders
of Judah and of Jerusalem, the craftsmen, and the skilled workmen had been
taken into **exile**. 3 I gave the **letter** to
Elasah son of Shaphan and to Gemariah
son of Hilkiah, whom King Zedekiah of
Judah was sending to King
Nebuchadnezzar of Babylonia. It said:
4 "The LORD **Almighty**, the God of
Israel, says to all those people whom
he allowed Nebuchadnezzar to take
away as **prisoners** from Jerusalem
to Babylonia: 5 'Build houses and
settle down. Plant gardens and eat
what you grow in them. 6 Marry and
have children. Then let your children get married, so that they also
may have children. You must increase in numbers and not decrease.
7 Work for the good of the cities
where I have made you go as
prisoners. **Pray** to me on their behalf, because if they are **prosperous**,
you will be prosperous too. 8 I, the
LORD, the God of Israel, **warn** you
not to let yourselves be **deceived** by
the **prophets** who live among you or
by any others who **claim** they can
predict the future. Do not pay any
attention to their[x] **dreams**. 9 They
are telling you **lies in my name**. I did
not send them. I, the LORD **Almighty**,
have spoken.'
10 "The LORD says, 'When
Babylonia's seventy years are over,
I will show my **concern** for you and
keep my **promise** to bring you back
home. 11 I **alone** know the **plans** I
have for you, **plans** to bring you
prosperity and not **disaster**, **plans** to
bring about the future you **hope for**.[n]
12 Then you will call to me. You will
come and **pray** to me, and I will answer you. 13 You will **seek** me, and
you will find me because you will
seek me **with all your heart**. 14 Yes, I
say, you will find me, and I will **restore** you to your land. I will gather
you from every country and from
every place to which I have **scattered** you, and I will bring you back
to the land from which I had sent
you away into **exile**. I, the LORD,
have spoken.'
15 "You say that the LORD has
given you **prophets** in Babylonia.
16 Listen to what the LORD says about
the king who rules the kingdom that

alone 2.3; Lam 3.28
believe 28.15; 40.14
claim 27.9; 48.14
commit 23.14; Ezek 9.9
concern Is 63.15; Lam 1.9
curse [2] 26.6; 42.18
death (3) (to death) 26.11; 38.4
deceive 27.10; 37.9
disaster 26.19; 32.42
disease [2] 28.8; 32.24
dream 27.9; Dan 1.17
duty (1) Job 33.23; 37.13
exile [3] 28.4; 48.7
fate 13.25; Lam 1.9
God's people 25.30; 30.3
guilty 26.15; Lam 4.13
heart 24.7; 31.20
hope 28.6; 30.13
horror 25.38; 34.17
letter (2) [5] Is 39.1; Acts 9.2
lie (2) [4] 28.15; 43.2
mad Ecc 10.13; Zech 12.4
message [3] 27.3; 33.1
mock 24.9; Lam 2.16
name (2) (name of God, of Jesus) [3] 27.15; 31.35
obey 26.4; 31.18
plan [3] 26.3; 32.19
power 28.2; 30.20
pray [2] 18.19; 31.9
predict 28.8; Ezek 12.22
priest [3] 28.1; 31.14
prison [7] 28.6; 30.10
promise 19.12; 31.36
prophet [7] 28.1; 32.32
prosper [2] 22.15; 33.7
punish 27.8; 30.11
rebel 28.16; 33.8
refuse (1) 25.7; 31.15
restore 27.22; 30.3
scatter [2] 25.33; 30.11
seek [2] Is 56.11; Hos 8.9
servant 27.6; 33.21
Temple (1) (of God) 28.1; 32.34
terrible 26.19; 30.7
terrify 24.9; 30.10
warn 26.15; 35.15
will (1) Is 53.2; Lam 3.37
witness Is 44.8; 32.10
world 27.5; 33.9

[m] *One ancient translation* he; *Hebrew* you. [x] *Probable text* their; *Hebrew* your.
[n] the future you hope for; *or* a future full of hope.

29.1-2: 2 Kgs 24.12-16; 2 Chr 36.10 **29.10:** 2 Chr 36.21; Jer 25.11; Dan 9.2 **29.13:** Deut 4.29

David ruled and about the people of
this city, that is, your relatives who
were not taken away as **prisoners**
with you. 17 The LORD **Almighty** says,
'I am bringing war, starvation, and
disease on them, and I will make
them like figs that are too rotten to
be eaten. 18 I will pursue them with
war, starvation, and **disease**, and all
the nations of the **world** will be
horrified at what they see. Everywhere I **scatter** them, people will be
shocked and **terrified** at what has
happened to them. People will **mock**
them and use their name as a **curse**.
19 This will happen to them because
they did not **obey** the **message** that I
kept on sending to them through my
servants the **prophets**. They **refused**
to listen. 20 All of you whom I sent
into **exile** in Babylonia, listen to
what I, the LORD, say.'

21 "The LORD **Almighty**, the God of
Israel, has spoken about Ahab son of
Kolaiah and Zedekiah son of
Maaseiah, who are telling you **lies in
his name**. He has said that he will
hand them over to the **power** of
King Nebuchadnezzar of Babylonia,
who will **put** them **to death** before
your eyes. 22 When the people who
were taken away as **prisoners** from
Jerusalem to Babylonia want to
bring a **curse** on someone, they will
say, 'May the LORD treat you like
Zedekiah and Ahab, whom the king
of Babylonia roasted **alive**!' 23 This
will be their **fate** because they are
guilty of **terrible** sins—they have
committed adultery and have told
lies in the **LORD's name**. This was
against the **LORD's will**; he knows
what they have done, and he is a **witness** against them.[o] The LORD has
spoken."

The Letter of Shemaiah

24-25 The LORD **Almighty**, the God of
Israel, gave me a **message** for Shemaiah
of Nehelam, who had sent a **letter** in his
own name to all the people of Jerusalem
and to the priest Zephaniah son of
Maaseiah and to all the other **priests**.
In this **letter**, Shemaiah wrote to
Zephaniah:

26 "The LORD made you a **priest** in
place of Jehoiada, and you are now
the chief officer[p] in the **Temple**. It is
your **duty** to see that every **madman**
who pretends to be a **prophet** is
placed in chains with an iron collar
round his neck. 27 Why haven't you
done this to Jeremiah of Anathoth,
who has been speaking as a **prophet**
to the people? 28 He must be stopped
because he told the people in
Babylonia that they would be
prisoners there a long time and
should build houses, settle down,
plant gardens, and eat what they
grow."

29 Zephaniah read the **letter** to me,
30 and then the LORD told me 31-32 to send
to all the **prisoners** in Babylon this
message about Shemaiah: "I, the LORD,
will **punish** Shemaiah and all his descendants. I did not send him, but he spoke to
you as if he were a **prophet**, and he made
you **believe lies**. He will have no descendants among you. He will not live to see
the good things that I am going to do for
my people, because he told them to **rebel**
against me. I, the LORD, have spoken."

The LORD's Promises to His People

30 The LORD, the God of Israel,
2 said to me: "Write down in a
book everything that I have told you, 3 because the time is coming when I will **restore my people**, Israel and Judah. I will
bring them back to the land that I gave
their ancestors, and they will take
possession of it again. I, the LORD, have
spoken."

4 The LORD says to the people of
Israel and Judah:

5 "I heard a cry of **terror**,
a cry of **fear** and not of **peace**.
6 Now stop and think!
Can a man give **birth** to a child?
Why then do I see every man with his
hands on his stomach
like a woman in labour?
Why is everyone so pale?
7 A **terrible** day is coming;
no other day can **compare** with it—
a time of **distress** for **my people**,
but they will survive."

8 The LORD **Almighty** says: "When
that day comes, I will break the yoke
that is round their necks and remove
their chains, and they will no longer be
the **slaves** of foreigners. 9 Instead, they
will **serve** me, the LORD their God, and a
descendant of David, whom I will
enthrone as king.

10 "**My people**, do not be **afraid**;
people of Israel, do not be **terrified**.

[o] done, and he...them; *or* done; he saw them do it.
[p] *Some ancient translations* officer; *Hebrew* officers.

30.10-11: Jer 46.27-28

terrible 29.23; 36.7
terrify 29.18; 32.21
terror 26.21; 46.5
throne 17.12; 43.10
understand 23.18; Ezek 3.6
wicked [3] 26.3; 36.3

I will **rescue** you from that distant
land,
from the land where you are
prisoners.
You will come back home and live in
peace;
you will be **secure**, and no one will
make you **afraid**.
11 I will come to you and **save** you.
I will **destroy** all the nations
where I have **scattered** you,
but I will not **destroy** you.
I will not let you go **unpunished**;
but when I **punish** you, I will be fair.
I, the LORD, have spoken."

12 The LORD says to **his people**,
"Your wounds are incurable,
your injuries cannot be **healed**.
13 There is no one to take **care** of you,
no remedy for your sores,
no **hope** of **healing** for you.
14 All your lovers have **forgotten** you;
they no longer **care** about you.
I have attacked you like an **enemy**;
your **punishment** has been harsh
because your sins are many
and your **wickedness** is great.
15 **Complain** no more about your injuries;
there is no **cure** for you.
I **punished** you like this
because your sins are many
and your **wickedness** is great.
16 But now, all who **devour** you will be
devoured,
and all your **enemies** will be taken
away as **prisoners**.
All who **oppress** you will be oppressed,
and all who plunder you will be
plundered.
17 I will make you well again;
I will **heal** your wounds,
though your **enemies** say,
'Zion is an **outcast**;
no one **cares** about her.'
I, the LORD, have spoken."

18 The LORD says,
"I will **restore my people** to their land
and have **mercy** on every family;
Jerusalem will be rebuilt,
and its palace **restored**.
19 The people who live there will sing
praise;
they will shout for **joy**.
By my **blessing** they will increase in
numbers;
my **blessing** will bring them **honour**.
20 I will **restore** the nation's **ancient**
power
and **establish** it firmly again;
I will **punish** all who **oppress** them.
21-22 Their ruler will come from their own
nation,
their prince from their own people.
He will approach me when I invite
him,
for who would **dare** come
uninvited?
They will be **my people**,
and I will be their God.
I, the LORD, have spoken."

23-24 The LORD's **anger** is a storm, a
furious wind that will **rage** over the
heads of the **wicked**. It will not end until
he has done all that he **intends** to do. In
days to come **his people** will **understand**
this clearly.

Israel's Return Home

31 The LORD says, "The time is
coming when I will be the God of
all the tribes of Israel, and they will be
my people. 2 In the desert I showed
mercy to those people who had **escaped**
death. When the people of Israel **longed**
for **rest**, 3 I appeared to them[q] from far
away. People of Israel, I have always
loved you, so I continue to show you my
constant love. 4 Once again I will rebuild
you. Once again you will take up your
tambourines and dance **joyfully**. 5 Once
again you will plant **vineyards** on the
hills of Samaria, and those who plant
them will eat what the **vineyards** produce. 6 Yes, the time is coming when
watchmen will call out on the hills of
Ephraim, 'Let's go up to Zion, to the
LORD our God.' "

7 The LORD says,
"Sing with **joy** for Israel,
the greatest of the nations.
Sing your song of **praise**,
'The LORD has **saved his**[x] people;
he has **rescued** all who are left.'
8 I will bring them from the north
and gather them from the ends of
the earth.
The **blind** and the lame will come with
them,
pregnant women and those about to
give **birth**.
They will come back a great nation.
9 **My people** will return **weeping**,
praying as I lead them back.
I will **guide** them to streams of water,
on a smooth road where they will
not **stumble**.
I am like a **father** to Israel,
and Ephraim is my eldest son."

10 The LORD says,

Almighty [2] 30.8; 32.14
ashamed 8.12; 51.51
best 20.9; 38.22
birth 30.6; Hos 1.3
bitter 23.15; 47.2
bless 30.19; Ezek 16.27
blind Is 59.10; Lam 4.14
care [2] 30.13; 39.12
comfort [2] 16.7; Lam 1.2
constant 9.24; 32.18
covenant [4] 22.9; 32.40
create 27.5; 51.15
dead 27.9; 34.5
dear Song 2.3; Hos 9.16
death (1) 22.10; 44.28
delight 3.19; Lam 2.4
destroy [2] 30.11; 32.23
disgrace 23.40; 48.20
enemy 30.14; 32.21
escape 26.21; 32.4
faithless Prov 2.17; Ezek 6.9
Father (2) (God) 3.4; Mal 1.6
flock [2] 5.17; 49.29
forgive 18.23; 33.8
free Is 61.1; 34.8
gift [2] Is 66.20; Ezek 16.41
glad 25.10; 33.11
God's people [6] 30.3; 32.38
grief [2] 16.5; Lam 2.11
guide 10.21; Zeph 1.6
happy 25.10; 33.11
heart [2] 29.13; 32.40
holy 23.9; 50.29
hope 30.13; Lam 2.13
hunger Is 65.13; 42.13
joy [4] 30.19; 33.9
last (1) Is 66.12; 48.30
law 8.7; 33.25
least 1 Sam 9.21; 50.12
light (1) 13.16; Ezek 1.27
long (2) 22.27; 44.14
love [4] 17.21; 32.18
mark (1) 18.15; 50.9
mercy [2] 30.18; 33.26
might 21.5; 32.17
mourn 25.33; 34.5

[q] *One ancient translation* them; *Hebrew* me.
[x] *Some ancient translations* The LORD...his; *Hebrew* LORD, save your.

name (2) (name of God, of Jesus) 29.9; 33.2
natural Ecc 10.2; Ezek 4.14
need [2] 15.19; 40.9
never again 22.10; 44.26
new [3] 8.10; 46.17
obey 29.19; 32.23
overthrow 1.10; Dan 7.24
praise 30.19; 51.41
pray 29.7; 32.16
priest 29.1; 32.32
proclaim 26.2; 46.14
promise 29.10; 32.22
protect 22.3; 39.17
provide Is 55.10; Ezek 13.3
punish 30.11; 32.18
refuse (1) 29.19; 35.12
reject 15.6; 33.24
rejoice Is 66.5; Ezek 21.10
remember 18.20; 42.22
rescue 30.10; 33.16
rest (1) 22.23; 45.3
restore 30.3; 32.44
reward Is 61.8; 32.19
rich 16.6; 32.22
sacred [2] 17.22; 43.13
satisfy [2] Is 58.10; 46.10
save [2] 30.11; 46.28
scatter 30.11; 32.37
sheep 12.3; 33.12
shepherd [2] 25.34; 33.12
sign (1) Is 65.20; 36.24
sorrow 20.18; 36.24
stumble 23.12; 46.6
teach [2] 26.4; 32.23
tear (2) 14.17; Lam 1.2
turn [2] 27.22; 32.33
vineyard [2] 12.10; 32.15
watch 24.6; Lam 4.18
weak Is 59.1; 49.15
weep [2] 22.10; 41.6
word (1) 26.5; 36.8
wrong 23.14; 38.9

"Nations, listen to me,
and proclaim my words on the far-off shores.
I scattered my people, but I will gather them
and guard them as a shepherd guards his flock.
11 I have set Israel's people free
and have saved them from a mighty nation.
12 They will come and sing for joy on Mount Zion
and be delighted with my gifts—
gifts of corn and wine and olive-oil,
gifts of sheep and cattle.
They will be like a well-watered garden;
they will have everything they need.
13 Then the girls will dance and be happy,
and men, young and old, will rejoice.
I will comfort them and turn their mourning into joy,
their sorrow into gladness.
14 I will fill the priests with the richest food
and satisfy all the needs of my people.
I, the LORD, have spoken."

The LORD's Mercy on Israel

15 The LORD says,
"A sound is heard in Ramah,
the sound of bitter weeping.
Rachel is crying for her children;
they are gone,
and she refuses to be comforted.
16 Stop your crying
and wipe away your tears.
All that you have done for your children
will not go unrewarded;
they will return from the enemy's land.
17 There is hope for your future;
your children will come back home.
I, the LORD, have spoken.

18 "I hear the people of Israel say in grief,
'LORD, we were like an untamed animal,
but you taught us to obey.
Bring us back;
we are ready to return to you,
the LORD our God.
19 We turned away from you,
but soon we wanted to return.
After you had punished us,
we hung our heads in grief.
We were ashamed and disgraced,
because we sinned when we were young.'

20 "Israel, you are my dearest son,
the child I love best.
Whenever I mention your name,
I think[r] of you with love.
My heart goes out to you;
I will be merciful.
21 Set up signs and mark the road;
find again the way by which you left.
Come back, people of Israel,
come home to the towns you left.
22 How long will you hesitate, faithless people?
I have created something new and different,
as different as a woman protecting a man."[s]

The Future Prosperity of God's People

23 The LORD Almighty, the God of Israel, says, "When I restore the people to their land, they will once again say in the land of Judah and in its towns,
'May the LORD bless the sacred hill[t] of Jerusalem,
the holy place where he lives.'
24 People will live in Judah and in all its
towns, and there will be farmers, and
shepherds with their flocks. 25 I will refresh those who are weary and will
satisfy with food everyone who is weak
from hunger. 26 So then, people will say, 'I
went to sleep and woke up refreshed.'
27 "I, the LORD, say that the time is
coming when I will fill the land of Israel
and Judah with people and animals.
28 And just as I took care to uproot, to pull
down, to overthrow, to destroy, and to de-
molish them, so I will take care to plant
them and to build them up. 29 When that
time comes, people will no longer say,
'The parents ate the sour grapes,
But the children got the sour taste.'
30 Instead, whoever eats sour grapes will
have his own teeth set on edge; and
everyone will die because of his own
sin."
31 The LORD says, "The time is
coming when I will make a new
covenant with the people of Israel and
with the people of Judah. 32 It will not be
like the old covenant that I made with
their ancestors when I took them by the
hand and led them out of Egypt. Although I was like a husband to them,

[r] I mention...I think; *or* I threaten to punish, I still think. [s] as different...man; *Hebrew unclear.*
[t] SACRED HILL: *Mount Zion, the hill in Jerusalem which formed part of the Temple and palace area.*

31.15: Gen 35.16–19; Mt 2.18 **31.29:** Ezek 18.2
31.31: Mt 26.28; Mk 14.24; Lk 22.20; 1 Cor 11.25; 2 Cor 3.6 **31.31–34:** Heb 8.8–12

they did not keep that **covenant**. [33] The **new covenant** that I will make with the people of Israel will be this: I will put my **law** within them and write it on their **hearts**. I will be their God, and they will be **my people**. [34] None of them will have to **teach** his fellow-countryman to know the LORD, because all will know me, from the **least** to the greatest. I will **forgive** their sins and I will no longer **remember** their **wrongs**. I, the LORD, have spoken."

[35] The LORD **provides** the sun for **light** by
    day,
  the moon and the stars to shine at
    night.
He stirs up the sea and makes it roar;
  his **name** is the LORD **Almighty**.
[36] He **promises** that as long as the **natural**
    order **lasts**,
  so long will Israel be a nation.
[37] If one day the sky could be measured
  and the foundations of the earth
    explored,
  only then would he **reject** the people
    of Israel
  because of all they have done.
The LORD has spoken.

38 "The time is coming," says the LORD, "when all Jerusalem will be rebuilt as my city, from Hananel Tower west to the Corner Gate. [39] And the boundary line will continue from there on the west to the hill of Gareb and then round to Goah. [40] The entire valley, where the **dead** are buried and refuse is thrown, and all the fields above the brook of Kidron as far as the Horse Gate to the east, will be **sacred** to me. The city will **never again** be torn down or **destroyed**."

Jeremiah Buys a Field

32 The LORD spoke to me in the tenth year that Zedekiah was king of Judah, which was also the eighteenth year of King Nebuchadnezzar of Babylonia. [2] At that time the army of the king of Babylonia was attacking Jerusalem, and I was locked up in the courtyard of the royal palace. [3] King Zedekiah had **imprisoned** me there and had **accused** me of **announcing** that the LORD had said, "I am going to let the king of Babylonia capture this city, [4] and King Zedekiah will not **escape**. He will be handed over to the king of Babylonia; he will see him face to face and will speak to him in person. [5] Zedekiah will be taken to Babylonia, and he will remain there until I deal with him. Even if he fights the Babylonians, he will not be **successful**. I, the LORD, have spoken."

6 The LORD told me [7] that Hanamel, my uncle Shallum's son, would come to me with the **request** to buy his field at Anathoth in the territory of Benjamin, because I was his nearest relative and had the **right** to buy it for myself. [8] Then, just as the LORD had said, Hanamel came to me there in the courtyard and asked me to buy the field. So I knew that the LORD had really spoken to me. [9] I bought the field from Hanamel and weighed out the money to him; the price came to seventeen pieces of silver. [10] I signed and **sealed** the deed, had it **witnessed**, and weighed out the money on scales. [11] Then I took both copies of the deed of purchase—the **sealed** copy containing the contract and its conditions, and the open copy—[12] and gave them to Baruch, the son of Neriah and grandson of Mahseiah. I gave them to him in the **presence** of Hanamel and of the **witnesses** who had signed the deed of purchase and of the men who were sitting in the courtyard. [13] Before them all I said to Baruch, [14] "The LORD **Almighty**, the God of Israel, has ordered you to take these deeds, both the **sealed** deed of purchase and the open copy, and to place them in a clay jar, so that they may be **preserved** for years to come. [15] The LORD **Almighty**, the God of Israel, has said that houses, fields, and **vineyards** will again be bought in this land."

Jeremiah's Prayer

16 After I had given the deed of purchase to Baruch, I **prayed**, [17] "**Sovereign** LORD, you made the earth and the sky by your great **power** and **might**; nothing is too **difficult** for you. [18] You have shown **constant love** to thousands, but you also **punish** people for the sins of their parents. You are a great and **powerful** God; you are the LORD **Almighty**. [19] You make **wise plans** and do **mighty** things; you see everything that people do, and you **reward** them according to their actions. [20] Long ago, you performed **miracles** and **wonders** in Egypt, and you have continued to perform them to this day, both in Israel and among all the other nations, so that you are now known everywhere. [21] **By means of miracles** and **wonders** that **terrified** our **enemies**, you used your **power** and **might** to bring your people Israel out of Egypt. [22] You gave them this **rich** and fertile land, as you had **promised** their ancestors. [23] But when they came into this land and took

accuse 14.7; Ezek 23.36
action Is 64.6; Ezek 12.16
Almighty [3] 31.23; 33.11
altar 19.5; 52.18
anger [4] 30.23; 33.5
announce 17.19; 48.20
command [2] 27.4; 35.7
constant 31.3; Lam 1.13
covenant 31.31; 33.20
defile 19.4; Lam 4.7
destroy [2] 31.28; 35.17
difficult [2] Prov 15.19; Ezek 3.5
disaster 29.11; 36.31
disease [2] 29.17; 34.17
disgust 11.13; 50.2
displease Is 59.15; 1 Thes 2.15
enemy 31.16; 34.20

escape 31.2; 34.3
establish 30.20; Ezek 23.38
eternal 10.10; 33.11
evil 26.3; 33.5
fear 30.5; 33.9
fury [2] 30.23; 33.5
god (2) (other gods) [2] 25.6; 35.15
God's people 31.1; 33.24
heart 31.20; 48.10
honour 30.19; 33.9
idol 25.6; 44.8
incense 19.13; 34.5
learn 17.23; Lam 3.27
life (1) 25.5; 38.2
love 31.3; 33.11
mankind 27.5; 45.5
means Deut 24.6; Mk 4.11
might [3] 31.11; 44.26
mind (1) 26.3; 34.11
miracle [2] 21.2; Dan 4.2
obey 31.18; 35.8
plan 29.11; 49.20
pleasure Is 66.3; Lam 3.33
possess 30.3; 37.12
power [3] 30.20; 42.11
pray 31.9; 36.7
presence [2] 28.1; 34.15
preserve Is 8.16; Eph 4.3
priest 31.14; 33.18
prison 30.10; 33.1
promise [2] 31.36; 33.14
prophet 29.1; 35.4
punish 31.19; 36.31
purpose Is 53.10; Mal 2.15
request 21.1; 42.9
restore 31.23; 33.6
reward 31.16; Ezek 18.20
rich 31.14; 51.13
right (3) 18.6; Lam 3.35
sacrifice 19.4; 33.18
safe 23.6; 33.16
scatter 31.10; 40.12
seal [4] Is 29.11; Dan 6.17
Sovereign [2] 14.13; 44.26
succeed (1) 22.30; Lam 1.5
teach [2] 31.18; Lam 2.9
Temple (1) (of God) 29.26; 33.11
terrify 30.10; 46.27
true 28.6; 40.16
turn [2] 31.13; 33.5
vineyard 31.5; 35.7
wine-offering 7.18; 44.17
wise 23.5; Ezek 28.3
witness [4] 29.23; 42.5
wonder (1) [2] 28.6; 33.3
worship (1) (of God) 26.2; 34.15

31.33: Heb 10.16 **31.34:** Heb 10.17 **32.1:** 2 Kgs 25.1-7

possession of it, they did not **obey** your
commands or live according to your
teaching; they did nothing that you had
ordered them to do. And so you brought
all this **destruction** on them.

24 "The Babylonians have built siege
mounds round the city to capture it, and
they are attacking. War, starvation, and
disease will make the city fall into their
hands. You can see that all you have said
has come **true**. 25 Yet, **Sovereign** LORD,
you are the one who ordered me to buy
the field in the **presence** of **witnesses**,
even though the city is about to be captured by the Babylonians."

26 Then the LORD said to me, 27 "I am
the LORD, the God of all **mankind**.
Nothing is too **difficult** for me. 28 I am going to give this city over to King
Nebuchadnezzar of Babylonia and his
army; they will capture it 29 and set it on
fire. They will burn it down, together
with the houses where people have made
me **angry** by burning **incense** to Baal on
the roof-tops and by pouring out **wine-**
offerings to other **gods**. 30 From the very
beginning of their history the people of
Israel and the people of Judah have **dis-**
pleased me and made me **angry** by what
they have done. 31 The people of this city
have made me **angry** and **furious** from
the day it was built. I have decided to
destroy it 32 because of all the **evil** that
has been done by the people of Judah
and Jerusalem, together with their kings
and leaders, their **priests** and **prophets**.
33 They **turned** their backs on me; and
though I kept on **teaching** them, they
would not listen and **learn**. 34 They even
placed their **disgusting idols** in the
Temple built for my **worship**, and they
have **defiled** it. 35 They have built **altars**
to Baal in the Valley of Hinnom, to **sacri-**
fice their sons and daughters to the **god**
Molech. I did not **command** them to do
this, and it did not even enter my **mind**
that they would do such a thing and
make the people of Judah sin."

A Promise of Hope

36 The LORD, the God of Israel, said to
me, "Jeremiah, the people are saying
that war, starvation, and **disease** will
make this city fall into the hands of the
king of Babylonia. Now listen to what
else I have to say. 37 I am going to gather
the people from all the countries where I
have **scattered** them in my **anger** and
fury, and I am going to bring them back
to this place and let them live here in
safety. 38 Then they will be **my people**,
and I will be their God. 39 I will give them
a single **purpose** in **life**: to **honour** me for
all time, for their own good and the good
of their descendants. 40 I will make an
eternal covenant with them. I will never
stop doing good things for them, and I
will make them **fear** me **with all their**
heart, so that they will never **turn away**
from me. 41 I will take **pleasure** in doing
good things for them, and I will **establish**
them permanently in this land.

42 "Just as I have brought this **disaster**
on these people, so I am going to give
them all the good things that I have
promised. 43 The people are saying that
this land will be like a desert where
neither people nor animals live, and that
it will be given over to the Babylonians.
But fields will once again be bought in
this land. 44 People will buy them, and the
deeds will be signed, **sealed**, and **wit-**
nessed. This will take place in the territory of Benjamin, in the villages round
Jerusalem, in the towns of Judah, and in
the towns in the hill-country, in the foothills, and in southern Judah. I will **restore**
the people to their land. I, the LORD, have
spoken."

Another Promise of Hope

33 While I was still in **prison** in the
courtyard, the LORD's **message**
came to me again. 2 The LORD, who made
the earth, who formed it and set it in
place, spoke to me. He whose **name** is
the LORD said, 3 "Call to me, and I will answer you; I will tell you **wonderful** and
marvellous things that you know nothing
about. 4 I, the LORD, the God of Israel, say
that the houses of Jerusalem and the
royal palace of Judah will be torn down
as a result of the siege and the attack.
5 Some will fight against the Babylonians,
who will fill the houses [w] with the corpses
of those whom I am going to **strike** down
in my **anger** and **fury**. I have **turned**
away from this city because of the **evil**
things that its people have done. 6 But I
will **heal** this city and its people and **res-**
tore them to health. I will show them
abundant peace and **security**. 7 I will
make Judah and Israel **prosperous**, and I
will rebuild them as they were before. 8 I
will **purify** them from the sins that they
have committed against me, and I will
forgive their sins and their **rebellion**.
9 Jerusalem will be a **source** of **joy**,
honour, and **pride** to me; and every
nation in the **world** will **fear** and **tremble**

abundant Ps 107.37; Ezek 27.12
Almighty [2] 32.14; 35.12
anger 32.29; 36.7
burnt-offering 17.26; 48.35
choose [3] 27.5; 40.4
contempt Is 58.9; Lam 1.8
control 15.6; 49.28
covenant [7] 32.40; 34.13
eternal 32.40; 50.5
evil 32.32; 35.15
fear 32.40; 42.16
feast 25.10; 51.39
forgive 31.34; 36.3
fulfil Is 45.13; Lk 9.31
fury 32.31; 36.7
glad 31.13; 41.13
God's people [2] 32.38; 46.27
grain-offering 17.26; Ezek 42.13
happy 31.13; 48.33
heal 30.12; 46.11
honour 32.39; 44.10
impossible 2 Sam 13.2; Zech 8.6
joy [2] 31.4; 48.33
justice 23.5; Lam 1.18
law 31.33; 44.10
love 32.18; Lam 2.13
mercy 31.2; 42.12
message 29.19; 34.6
name (2) (name of God, of Jesus) 31.35; 44.16
notice (1) Is 58.3; Ezek 12.3

[w] as a result...houses; *Hebrew unclear.*

32.28: 2 Kgs 25.1–11; 2 Chr 36.17–21 **32.34:** 2 Kgs 23.10; Jer 7.30–31, 19.1–6
32.35: Lev 18.21; 2 Kgs 23.10; Jer 7.31

offer 19.4; 35.2
peace 30.5; 34.5
priest [3] 32.32; 34.18
prison 32.3; 37.4
promise [2] 32.22; 35.17
proper Is 28.27; Ezek 44.20
prosper [4] 29.7; 39.16
proud 13.9; 48.29
pure 13.27; Lam 4.7
rebel 29.31; 48.26
reject 31.37; Lam 2.7
rescue 31.7; 34.13
restore 32.44; 50.19
right (1) [2] 26.14; 35.15
righteous 23.5; Ezek 18.5
sacrifice 32.35; 44.3
safe 32.37; 39.14
salvation 23.6; Jon 2.9
secure 30.10; 46.27
servant [3] 29.19; 35.15
serve [2] 30.9; 34.14
sheep [2] 31.12; 50.6
shepherd [2] 31.10; 43.12
source Is 49.5; 51.36
strike 22.23; 46.15
sure 26.15; 37.20
Temple (1) (of God) 32.34; 34.15
thank Is 51.3; Amos 4.5
tremble 23.9; 51.29
turn 32.33; 36.3
wedding 25.10; Mt 9.15
wonder (1) 32.20; Dan 4.2
world 29.18; 34.17

when they hear about the good things that I do for the people of Jerusalem and about the **prosperity** that I bring to the city."

10 The LORD said, "People are saying that this place is like a desert, that it has no people or animals living in it. And they are **right**; the towns of Judah and the streets of Jerusalem are empty; no people or animals live there. But in these places you will hear again 11 the shouts of **gladness** and **joy** and the **happy** sounds of **wedding feasts**. You will hear people sing as they bring thank-offerings to my **Temple**; they will say,

'Give **thanks** to the LORD **Almighty**,
because he is good
and his **love** is **eternal**.'

I will make this land as **prosperous** as it was before. I, the LORD, have spoken."

12 The LORD **Almighty** said, "In this land that is like a desert and where no people or animals live, there will once again be pastures where **shepherds** can take their **sheep**. 13 In the towns of the hill-country, in the foothills, and in southern Judah, in the territory of Benjamin, in the villages round Jerusalem, and in the towns of Judah, **shepherds** will once again count their **sheep**. I, the LORD, have spoken."

14 The LORD said, "The time is coming when I will **fulfil** the **promise** that I made to the people of Israel and Judah. 15 At that time I will **choose** as king a **righteous** descendant of David. That king will do what is **right** and **just** throughout the land. 16 The people of Judah and of Jerusalem will be **rescued** and will live in **safety**. The city will be called 'The LORD Our **Salvation**.' 17 I, the LORD, **promise** that there will always be a descendant of David to be king of Israel 18 and that there will always be **priests** from the tribe of Levi to **serve** me and to **offer** **burnt-offerings**, **grain-offerings**, and **sacrifices**."

19 The LORD said to me, 20 "I have made a **covenant** with the day and with the night, so that they always come at their **proper** times; and that **covenant** can never be broken. 21 In the same way I have made a **covenant** with my **servant** David that he would always have a descendant to be king, and I have made a **covenant** with the **priests** from the tribe of Levi that they would always **serve** me; and those **covenants** can never be broken. 22 I will increase the number of descendants of my **servant** David and the number of **priests** from the tribe of Levi, so that it will be as **impossible** to count them as it is to count the stars in the sky or the grains of sand on the sea-shore."

23 The LORD said to me, 24 "Have you **noticed** how people are saying that I have **rejected** Israel and Judah, the two families that I **chose**? And so they look with **contempt** on **my people** and no longer consider them a nation. 25 But I, the LORD, have a **covenant** with day and night, and I have made the **laws** that **control** earth and sky. 26 And just as **surely** as I have done this, so I will maintain my **covenant** with Jacob's descendants and with my **servant** David. I will **choose** one of David's descendants to rule over the descendants of Abraham, Isaac, and Jacob. I will be **merciful** to **my people** and make them **prosperous** again."

A Message for Zedekiah

34 The LORD spoke to me when King Nebuchadnezzar of Babylonia and his army, supported by troops from all the nations and **races** that were **subject** to him, were attacking Jerusalem and its nearby towns. 2 The LORD, the God of Israel, told me to go and say to King Zedekiah of Judah, "I, the LORD, will hand this city over to the king of Babylonia, and he will burn it down. 3 You will not **escape**; you will be captured and handed over to him. You will see him face to face and talk to him in person; then you will go to Babylonia. 4 Zedekiah, listen to what I say about you. You will not be killed in battle. 5 You will die in **peace**, and as people burnt **incense** when they buried your ancestors, who were kings before you, in the same way they will burn **incense** for you. They will **mourn** over you and say, 'Our king is **dead**!' I, the LORD, have spoken."

6 Then I gave this **message** to King Zedekiah in Jerusalem 7 while the army of the king of Babylonia was attacking the city. The army was also attacking Lachish and Azekah, the only other fortified cities left in Judah.

Deceitful Treatment of Slaves

8 King Zedekiah and the people of Jerusalem had made an **agreement** to **set free** 9 their **Hebrew slaves**, both male and female, so that no one would have a fellow-Israelite as a **slave**. 10 All the people and their leaders **agreed** to **free** their **slaves** and never to enslave them again. They did **set them free**, 11 but later they **changed their minds**, took them

agree [3] Is 33.8; Ezek 20.12
change [3] 26.3; 52.33
covenant [4] 33.20; 50.5
dead 31.40; Lam 2.21
desire 24.7; Ezek 7.19
disease 32.24; 38.2
dishonour Is 48.11; Ezek 13.19
disobey 26.6; 40.3
enemy 32.21; 44.30
escape 32.4; 38.2
force (1) [2] 22.26; Lam 1.3
free [10] 31.11; 37.4
Hebrew [2] Is 36.11; Jon 1.9
horror 29.18; 42.18
incense [2] 32.29; 41.5
message 33.1; 36.32
mind (1) [3] 32.35; 51.7
mourn 31.13; 47.5
peace 33.6; 46.27
please 14.10; 42.6
presence 32.12; Ezek 1.28
priest 33.18; 37.3
race (1) Prov 8.31; Dan 3.4
rescue 33.16; 42.11
serve 33.18; 35.15
slave [8] 30.8; Lam 1.1
subject (1) Ps 106.42; 1 Cor 9.20
Temple (1) (of God) 33.11; 35.2
world 33.9; 46.8
worship (1) (of God) 32.34; 44.3

33.11: 1 Chr 16.34; 2 Chr 5.13, 7.3; Ezra 3.11; Ps 100.5, 106.1, 107.1, 118.1, 136.1 **33.14–16:** Jer 23.5–6
33.17: 2 Sam 7.12–16; 1 Kgs 2.4; 1 Chr 17.11–14 **33.18:** Num 3.5–10 **34.1:** 2 Kgs 25.1–11; 2 Chr 36.17–21

back, and **forced** them to become **slaves**
again.
12 Then the LORD, [13] the God of Israel,
told me to say to the people: "I made a
covenant with your ancestors when I **rescued** them from Egypt and **set them free**
from **slavery** I told them that [14] every
seven years they were to **set free** any
Hebrew slave who had **served** them for
six years. But your ancestors would not
pay any attention to me or listen to what
I said. [15] Just a few days ago you **changed
your minds** and did what **pleased** me. All
of you **agreed** to set your fellow-Israelites
free, and you made a **covenant** in my
presence, in the **Temple** where I am **worshipped**. [16] But then you **changed your
minds** again and **dishonoured** me. All of
you took back the **slaves** whom you had
set free as they **desired**, and you **forced**
them into **slavery** again. [17] So now, I, the
LORD, say that you have **disobeyed** me:
you have not given your fellow-Israelites
their **freedom**. Very well, then, I will give
you **freedom**: the **freedom** to die by war,
disease, and starvation. I will make
every nation in the **world horrified** at
what I do to you. [18-19] The officials of
Judah and of Jerusalem, together with
the palace officials, the **priests**, and all
the leaders, made a **covenant** with me by
walking between the two halves of a bull
that they had cut in two. But they broke
the **covenant** and did not keep its terms.
So I will do to these people what they did
to the bull. [20] I will hand them over to
their **enemies**, who want to kill them, and
their corpses will be eaten by birds and
wild animals. [21] I will also hand over King
Zedekiah of Judah and his officials to
those who want to kill them. I will hand
them over to the Babylonian army,
which has stopped its attack against you.
[22] I will give the order, and they will return to this city. They will attack it, capture it, and burn it down. I will make the
towns of Judah like a desert where no
one lives. I, the LORD, have spoken."

Jeremiah and the Rechabites

35 When Jehoiakim son of Josiah
was king of Judah, the LORD said
to me, [2] "Go to the members of the
Rechabite clan and talk to them. Then
bring them into one of the rooms in the
Temple and **offer** them some wine." [3] So I
took the entire Rechabite clan—
Jaazaniah (the son of another Jeremiah,
who was Habazziniah's son) and all his
brothers and sons—[4] and brought them to
the **Temple**. I took them into the room of
the **disciples** of the **prophet** Hanan son of
Igdaliah. This room was above the room
of Maaseiah son of Shallum, an **important** official in the **Temple**, and near the
rooms of the other officials. [5] Then I
placed **cups** and bowls full of wine before
the Rechabites, and I said to them,
"Have some wine."
6 But they answered, "We do not drink
wine. Our ancestor Jonadab son of
Rechab told us that neither we nor our
descendants were ever to drink any
wine. [7] He also told us not to build houses
or farm the land, and not to plant **vineyards** or buy them. He **commanded** us always to live in tents, so that we might remain in this land where we live like
strangers. [8] We have **obeyed** all the
instructions that Jonadab gave us. We
ourselves never drink wine, and neither
do our wives, our sons, or our daughters.
[9-10] We do not build houses for homes—
we live in tents—and we own no **vineyards**, fields, or corn. We have fully
obeyed everything that our ancestor
Jonadab **commanded** us. [11] But when
King Nebuchadnezzar invaded the
country, we decided to come to
Jerusalem to **get away** from the
Babylonian and Syrian armies. That is
why we are living in Jerusalem."
12-13 Then the LORD **Almighty**, the
God of Israel, told me to go and say to
the people of Judah and Jerusalem, "I,
the LORD, ask you why you **refuse** to listen to me and to **obey** my instructions.
[14] Jonadab's descendants have **obeyed** his
command not to drink wine, and to this
very day none of them drink any. But I
have kept on speaking to you, and you
have not **obeyed** me. [15] I have continued
to send you all my **servants** the **prophets**,
and they have told you to give up your
evil ways and to do what is **right**. They
warned you not to **worship and serve
other gods**, so that you could go on living
in the land that I gave you and your
ancestors. But you would not listen to me
or pay attention to me. [16] Jonadab's
descendants have **obeyed** the **command**
that their ancestor gave them, but you
people have not **obeyed** me. [17] So now, I,
the LORD **Almighty**, the God of Israel,
will bring on you people of Judah and of
Jerusalem all the **destruction** that I **promised**. I will do this because you would
not listen when I spoke to you, and you
would not answer when I called you."
18 Then I told the Rechabite clan that
the LORD **Almighty**, the God of Israel,
had said, "You have **obeyed** the **command** that your ancestor Jonadab gave

34.14: Ex 21.2; Deut 15.12 **35.1:** 2 Kgs 23.36—24.6; 2 Chr 36.5-7

prophet [2] 32.32; 37.19
refuse (1) 31.15; 38.21
right (1) 33.10; 51.10
servant 33.21; 43.10
serve [2] 34.14; 40.9
stranger 14.8; Lam 5.2
Temple (1) (of God) [3] 34.15; 36.5
vineyard [2] 32.15; 39.10
warn 29.8; 36.31
way (3) 26.3; 36.3
worship (2) (of other gods) 25.6; 44.8

Almighty [4] 33.11; 38.17
command [6] 32.23; 39.11
cup 25.15; 49.12
destroy 32.23; 36.3
disciple Is 8.16; Mt 5.1
evil 33.5; 36.3
get away 9.2; 41.15
god (2) (other gods) 32.29; 43.12
important Is 29.16; 50.12
obey [8] 32.23; 37.2
offer 33.18; 41.5
promise [2] 33.14; 38.16

you; you have followed all his instructions, and you have done everything he **commanded** you. 19 So I, the LORD Almighty, the God of Israel, **promise** that Jonadab son of Rechab will always have a male descendant to **serve** me."

Baruch Reads the Scroll in the Temple

36 In the fourth year that Jehoiakim son of Josiah was king of Judah, the LORD said to me, 2 "Get a **scroll** and write on it everything that I have told you about Israel and Judah and all the nations. Write everything that I have told you from the time I first spoke to you, when Josiah was king, up to the present. 3 Perhaps when the people of Judah hear about all the **destruction** that I **intend** to bring on them, they will **turn from** their **evil ways**. Then I will **forgive** their **wickedness** and their sins."

4 So I called Baruch son of Neriah and dictated to him everything that the LORD had said to me. And Baruch wrote it all down on a **scroll**. 5 Then I gave Baruch the following instructions: "I am no longer allowed to go into the **Temple**. 6 But I want you to go there the next time the people are **fasting**. You are to read the **scroll** aloud, so that they will hear everything that the LORD has said to me and that I have dictated to you. Do this where everyone can hear you, including the people of Judah who have come in from their towns. 7 Perhaps they will **pray** to the LORD and **turn from** their **evil ways**, because the LORD has **threatened** this people with his **terrible anger** and **fury**." 8 So Baruch read the **LORD's words** in the **Temple** exactly as I had told him to do.

9 In the ninth month of the fifth year that Jehoiakim was king of Judah, the people **fasted** to gain the LORD's **favour**. The **fast** was kept by all who lived in Jerusalem and by all who came there from the towns of Judah. 10 Then, while all the people were listening, Baruch read from the **scroll** everything that I had said. He did this in the **Temple**, from the room of Gemariah son of Shaphan, the **court** secretary. His room was in the upper court near the entrance of the New Gate of the **Temple**.

The Scroll Is Read to the Officials

11 Micaiah, the son of Gemariah and grandson of Shaphan, heard Baruch read from the **scroll** what the LORD had said. 12 Then he went to the royal palace, to the room of the **court** secretary, where all the officials were in session. Elishama, the **court** secretary, Delaiah son of Shemaiah, Elnathan son of Achbor, Gemariah son of Shaphan, Zedekiah son of Hananiah, and all the other officials were there. 13 Micaiah told them everything that he had heard Baruch read to the people. 14 Then the officials sent Jehudi (the son of Nethaniah, grandson of Shelemiah, and great-grandson of Cushi) to tell Baruch to bring the **scroll** that he had read to the people. Baruch brought them the **scroll**. 15 "Sit down," they said, "and read the **scroll** to us." So Baruch did. 16 After he had read it, they **turned** to one another in alarm, and said to Baruch, "We must report this to the king." 17 Then they asked him, "Tell us, now, how did you come to write all this? Did Jeremiah dictate it to you?"

18 Baruch answered, "Jeremiah dictated every **word** of it to me, and I wrote it down in ink on this **scroll**."

19 Then they said to him, "You and Jeremiah must go and hide. Don't let anyone know where you are."

The King Burns the Scroll

20 The officials put the **scroll** in the room of Elishama, the **court** secretary, and went to the king's **court**, where they reported everything to the king. 21 Then the king sent Jehudi to get the **scroll**. He took it from the room of Elishama and read it to the king and all the officials who were standing round him. 22 It was winter and the king was sitting in his winter palace in front of the fire. 23 As soon as Jehudi finished reading three or four columns, the king cut them off with a small knife and threw them into the fire. He kept doing this until the entire **scroll** was burnt up. 24 But neither the king nor any of his officials who heard all this was **afraid** or showed any **sign** of **sorrow**. 25 Although Elnathan, Delaiah, and Gemariah **begged** the king not to burn the **scroll**, he paid no attention to them. 26 Then he ordered Prince Jerahmeel, together with Seraiah son of Azriel and Shelemiah son of Abdeel, to **arrest** me and my secretary Baruch. But the LORD had hidden us.

Jeremiah Writes Another Scroll

27 After King Jehoiakim had burnt the **scroll** that I had dictated to Baruch, the LORD told me 28 to take another **scroll** and write on it everything that had been on the first one. 29 The LORD told me to say to the king, "You have burnt the **scroll**, and you have asked Jeremiah why he wrote that the king of Babylonia would come and **destroy** this land and

afraid 30.10; 38.19
anger 33.5; 42.18
arrest Is 53.8; 37.14
beg Prov 18.23; 37.20
court (1) [5] Is 59.4; 37.15
destroy [2] 35.17; 39.16
disaster 32.42; 40.15
evil [2] 35.15; 44.3
fast (2) [3] 14.12; Dan 9.3
favour 26.19; Lam 3.59
forgive 33.8; 50.20
fury 33.5; 37.15
intend 30.23; 49.20
message 34.6; 37.2
pray 32.16; 37.3
punish 32.18; 44.13
scroll [18] Is 34.4; Ezek 2.9
sign (1) 31.21; Ezek 4.3
sorrow 31.13; 42.10
Temple (1) (of God) [4] 35.2; 38.14
terrible 30.7; 44.4
threat [2] 25.13; 40.2
turn [3] 33.5; 41.14
warn 35.15; 37.9
way (3) [2] 35.15; Lam 3.40
wicked 30.14; 44.9
word (1) [2] 31.10; 40.9

36.1: 2 Kgs 24.1; 2 Chr 36.5–7; Dan 1.1–2

kill its people and its animals. 30 So now, I, the LORD, say to you, King Jehoiakim, that no descendant of yours will ever rule over David's kingdom. Your corpse will be thrown out where it will be exposed to the sun during the day and to the frost at night. 31 I will **punish** you, your descendants, and your officials because of the sins all of you commit. Neither you nor the people of Jerusalem and of Judah have paid any attention to my **warnings**, and so I will bring on all of you the **disaster** that I have **threatened**."

32 Then I took another **scroll** and gave it to my secretary Baruch, and he wrote down everything that I dictated. He wrote everything that had been on the first **scroll** and similar **messages** that I dictated to him.

Zedekiah's Request to Jeremiah

37 King Nebuchadnezzar of Babylonia made Zedekiah son of Josiah king of Judah in the place of Jehoiachin son of Jehoiakim. 2 But neither Zedekiah nor his officials nor the people **obeyed** the **message** which the LORD had given me.

3 King Zedekiah sent Jehucal son of Shelemiah and the **priest** Zephaniah son of Maaseiah to ask me to **pray** to the LORD our God on behalf of our nation. 4 I had not yet been put in **prison** and was still moving about **freely** among the people. 5 The Babylonian army had been besieging Jerusalem, but when they heard that the Egyptian army had crossed the Egyptian border, they retreated.

6 Then the LORD, the God of Israel, told me 7 to say to Zedekiah, "The Egyptian army is on its way to **help** you, but it will return home. 8 Then the Babylonians will come back, attack the city, capture it, and burn it down. 9 I, the LORD, **warn** you not to **deceive** yourselves into thinking that the Babylonians will not come back, because they will. 10 Even if you defeat the whole Babylonian army, so that only wounded men are left, lying in their tents, those men would still get up and burn this city to the ground."

Jeremiah Is Arrested and Imprisoned

11 The Babylonian army retreated from Jerusalem because the Egyptian army was approaching. 12 So I started to leave Jerusalem and go to the territory of Benjamin to take **possession** of my **share** of the family property. 13 But when I reached the Benjamin Gate, the officer in charge of the soldiers on **duty** there, a man by the name of Irijah, the son of Shelemiah and grandson of Hananiah, stopped me and said, "You are deserting to the Babylonians!"

14 I answered, "That's not so! I'm not deserting." But Irijah would not listen to me. Instead, he **arrested** me and took me to the officials. 15 They were **furious** with me and ordered me to be beaten and locked up in the house of Jonathan, the **court** secretary, whose house had been made into a **prison**. 16 I was put in an underground cell and kept there a long time.

17 Later on King Zedekiah sent for me, and there in the palace he asked me privately, "Is there any **message** from the LORD?"

"There is," I answered, and added, "You will be handed over to the king of Babylonia." 18 Then I asked, "What **crime** have I committed against you or your officials or this people, to make you put me in **prison**? 19 What happened to your **prophets** who told you that the king of Babylonia would not attack you or the country? 20 And now, Your **Majesty**, I **beg** you to listen to me and do what I ask. Please do not send me back to the **prison** in Jonathan's house. If you do, I will **surely** die there."

21 So King Zedekiah ordered me to be locked up in the palace courtyard. I stayed there, and each day I was given a loaf of **bread** from the bakeries until all the **bread** in the city was gone.

37.1: 2 Kgs 24.17; 2 Chr 36.10

arrest 36.26; Dan 6.16
beg 36.25; 38.20
bread [2] Is 62.9; Ezek 4.9
court (1) 36.10; 38.7
crime 16.10; 41.11
deceive 29.8; 49.16
duty (1) 29.26; Ezek 44.11
free 34.8; 40.1
fury 36.7; 42.18
help 23.14; 38.4
Majesty Is 30.30; 38.9
message [2] 36.32; 38.20
obey 35.8; 38.20
possess 32.23; Ezek 11.15
pray 36.7; 42.2
priest 34.18; 48.7
prison [4] 33.1; 38.23
prophet 35.4; 44.4
share Is 58.7; Ezek 16.27
sure 33.26; 38.9
warn 36.31; 42.19

Jeremiah in a Dry Well

38 Shephatiah son of Mattan, Gedaliah son of Pashhur, Jehucal son of Shelemiah, and Pashhur son of Malchiah heard that I was telling the people that 2 the LORD had said, "Whoever stays on in the city will die in war or of starvation or **disease**. But whoever goes out and surrenders to the Babylonians will not be killed; he will at least **escape** with his **life**." 3 I was also telling them that the LORD had said, "I am going to give the city to the Babylonian army, and they will capture it."

4 Then the officials went to the king and said, "This man must be put **to death**. By talking like this he is making the soldiers in the city lose their **courage**, and he is doing the same thing to everyone else left in the city. He is not trying to **help** the people; he only wants to **hurt** them."

5 King Zedekiah answered, "Very

advice Is 47.13; Ezek 7.26
afraid 36.24; 39.17
Almighty 35.12; 39.16
beg [2] 37.20; Lam 2.19
best 31.20; Lam 3.26
courage 4.9; 51.30
court (1) 37.15; Lam 3.36
danger 2.6; Lam 3.47
death (3) (to death) [4] 29.21; 39.6
disease 34.17; 42.17
escape [3] 34.3; 39.4
friend [2] 23.35; Lam 1.2
help 37.7; 47.2
hurt [2] 14.17; Ezek 13.22
life (1) [5] 32.39; 39.18
Majesty 37.20; Dan 2.4
message 37.2; 49.14
mislead 23.26; Ezek 12.24
obey 37.2; 42.5
prison [2] 37.4; 39.9
promise [2] 35.17; 42.20
question [2] 12.1; Dan 1.20

refuse (1) 35.12; 42.13
secret 23.18; 50.2
spare [3] 21.7; 41.8
sure 37.20; 51.61
swear 23.7; 44.26
Temple (1) (of God) 36.5; 41.5
truth [2] 9.3; Dan 9.13
vision 14.14; Lam 2.9
wish 17.16; 40.4
wrong 31.34; 50.7

well, then, do what you **wish** with him; I can't stop you." 6 So they took me and let me down by ropes into Prince Malchiah's well, which was in the palace **courtyard**. There was no water in the well, only mud, and I sank down in it.

7 However, Ebedmelech the Sudanese, a eunuch who worked in the royal palace, heard that they had put me in the well. At that time the king was holding court at the Benjamin Gate. 8 So Ebedmelech went there and said to the king, 9 "Your **Majesty**, what these men have done is **wrong**. They have put Jeremiah in the well, where he is **sure** to die of starvation, since there is no more food in the city." 10 Then the king ordered Ebedmelech to take with him three men and to pull me out of the well before I died. 11 So Ebedmelech went with the men to the palace storeroom and got some worn-out clothing which he let down to me by ropes. 12 He told me to put the rags under my arms, so that the ropes wouldn't **hurt** me. I did this, 13 and they pulled me up out of the well. After that I was kept in the courtyard.

Zedekiah Asks Jeremiah's Advice

14 On another occasion King Zedekiah had me brought to him at the third entrance to the **Temple**, and he said, "I am going to ask you a **question**, and I want you to tell me the whole **truth**."

15 I answered, "If I tell you the **truth**, you will put me **to death**, and if I give you **advice**, you won't pay any attention."

16 So King Zedekiah **promised** me in **secret**, "I **swear** by the living God, the God who gave us **life**, that I will not put you **to death** or hand you over to the men who want to kill you."

17 Then I told Zedekiah that the LORD **Almighty**, the God of Israel, had said, "If you surrender to the king of Babylonia's officers, your **life** will be **spared**, and this city will not be burnt down. Both you and your family will be **spared**. 18 But if you do not surrender, then this city will be handed over to the Babylonians, who will burn it down, and you will not **escape** from them."

19 But the king answered, "I am **afraid** of our countrymen who have deserted to the Babylonians. I may be handed over to them and tortured."

20 I said, "You will not be handed over to them. I **beg** you to **obey** the LORD's **message**; then all will go well with you, and your **life** will be **spared**. 21 But the LORD has shown me in a **vision** what will happen if you **refuse** to surrender. 22 In it I saw all the women left in Judah's royal palace being led out to the king of Babylonia's officers. Listen to what they were saying as they went:

'The king's **best friends misled** him,
they overruled him.
And now that his feet have sunk in the mud,
his **friends** have left him.' "

23 Then I added, "All your women and children will be taken out to the Babylonians, and you yourself will not **escape** from them. You will be taken **prisoner** by the king of Babylonia, and this city will be burnt to the ground."

24 Zedekiah replied, "Don't let anyone know about this conversation, and your **life** will not be in **danger**. 25 If the officials hear that I have talked with you, they will come and ask you what we said. They will **promise** not to put you **to death** if you tell them everything. 26 Just tell them you were **begging** me not to send you back to **prison** to die there." 27 Then all the officials came and **questioned** me, and I told them exactly what the king had told me to say. There was nothing else they could do, because no one had overheard the conversation. 28 And I was kept in the palace courtyard until the day Jerusalem was captured.

The Fall of Jerusalem

39 In the tenth month of the ninth year that Zedekiah was king of Judah, King Nebuchadnezzar of Babylonia came with his whole army and attacked Jerusalem. 2 On the ninth day of the fourth month of Zedekiah's eleventh year as king, the city walls were broken through.

3 (When Jerusalem was captured,[z] all the high officials of the king of Babylonia came and took their places at the Middle Gate, including Nergal Sarezer, Samgar Nebo, Sarsechim, and another Nergal Sarezer.)[a]

4 When King Zedekiah and all his soldiers saw what was happening, they tried to **escape** from the city during the night. They left by way of the royal garden, went through the gateway connecting the two walls, and **escaped** in the direction of the Jordan Valley. 5 But the Babylonian army pursued them and captured Zedekiah in the plains near Jericho. Then they took him to King Nebuchadnezzar, who was in the city of

afraid 38.19; 40.9
Almighty 38.17; 42.13
care [2] 31.28; 40.4
command 35.7; 42.5
death (3) (to death) [2] 38.4; 52.10
destroy 36.3; 40.2
escape [3] 38.2; 41.15
execute Prov 24.11; 52.10
harm 10.5; Ezek 44.19
life (1) 38.2; 45.5
poor 22.16; 40.7
prison [2] 38.23; 40.1
prosper 33.7; 44.17
protect 31.22; 48.45
safe [2] 33.16; 49.31
sentence 26.11; 52.9
trust 17.5; 46.25
vineyard 35.7; 52.16

[z] When Jerusalem was captured; *these words are moved here from the end of chapter 38.*
[a] *The names and titles of these men are unclear.*

38.28: Ezek 33.21

Riblah in the territory of Hamath, and
there Nebuchadnezzar passed **sentence**
on him. [6]At Riblah he put Zedekiah's
sons **to death** while Zedekiah was looking
on, and he also **executed** the officials of
Judah. [7]After that, he had Zedekiah's
eyes put out and had him placed in
chains to be taken to Babylonia. [8]Mean-
while, the Babylonians burnt down the
royal palace and the houses of the people
and tore down the walls of Jerusalem.
[9]Finally Nebuzaradan, the commanding
officer, took away as **prisoners** to
Babylonia the people who were left in
the city, together with those who had deserted to him. [10]He left in the land of
Judah some of the **poorest** people, who
owned no property, and he gave them
vineyards and fields.

Jeremiah's Release

11 But King Nebuchadnezzar **commanded** Nebuzaradan, the commanding
officer, to give the following order: [12]"Go
and find Jeremiah and take good **care** of
him. Do not **harm** him, but do for him
whatever he wants." [13]So Nebuzaradan,
together with the high officials Nebu-
shazban and Nergal Sarezer and all the
other officers of the king of Babylonia,
[14]brought me from the palace courtyard.
They put me under the **care** of Gedaliah,
the son of Ahikam and grandson of
Shaphan, who was to see that I got home
safely. And so I stayed there among the
people.

Hope for Ebedmelech

15 While I was still **imprisoned** in the
palace courtyard, the LORD told me [16]to
tell Ebedmelech the Sudanese that the
LORD **Almighty**, the God of Israel, had
said, "Just as I said I would, I am going to
bring upon this city **destruction** and not
prosperity. And when this happens, you
will be there to see it. [17]But I, the LORD,
will **protect** you, and you will not be
handed over to the men you are **afraid**
of. [18]I will keep you **safe**, and you will not
be put **to death**. You will **escape** with
your **life** because you have put your **trust**
in me. I, the LORD, have spoken."

Jeremiah Stays with Gedaliah

40 The LORD spoke to me after
Nebuzaradan, the commanding
officer, had **set me free** at Ramah. I had
been taken there in chains, along with all
the other people from Jerusalem and
Judah who were being taken away as
prisoners to Babylonia.

2 The commanding officer took me
aside and said, "The LORD your God
threatened this land with **destruction**,
[3]and now he has done what he said he
would. All this happened because your
people sinned against the LORD and **disobeyed** him. [4]Now, I am taking the
chains off your wrists and **setting you
free**. If you want to go to Babylonia with
me, you may do so, and I will take **care**
of you. But if you don't want to go, you
don't have to. You have the whole
country to **choose** from, and you may go
wherever you **wish**."

5 When I did not answer,[c] Nebuzaradan said, "Go back to Gedaliah,
the son of Ahikam and grandson of
Shaphan, whom the king of Babylonia
has made governor of the towns of
Judah. You may stay with him and live
among the people, or you may go anywhere you think you should." Then he
gave me a present and some food to take
with me, and let me go on my way. [6]I
went to stay with Gedaliah in Mizpah and
lived among the people who were left in
the land.

Gedaliah, Governor of Judah
(2 Kgs 25.22–24)

7 Some of the Judaean officers and
soldiers had not surrendered. They heard
that the king of Babylonia had made
Gedaliah governor of the land and had
placed him in charge of all those who
had not been taken away to Babylonia—
the **poorest** people in the land. [8]So Ishmael son of Nethaniah, Johanan son of
Kareah, Seraiah son of Tanhumeth, the
sons of Ephai from Netophah, and Jezaniah from Maacah went with their men
to Gedaliah at Mizpah. [9]Gedaliah said to
them, "I give you my **word** that there is
no **need** for you to be **afraid** to surrender
to the Babylonians. Settle down in this
land, **serve** the king of Babylonia, and all
will go well with you. [10]I myself will stay
in Mizpah and be your **representative**
when the Babylonians come here. But
you can gather and store up wine, fruit,
and olive-oil, and live in the villages you
occupy." [11]Meanwhile, all the Israelites
who were in Moab, Ammon, Edom, and
other countries, heard that the king of
Babylonia had allowed some Israelites to
stay on in Judah and that he had made
Gedaliah their governor. [12]So they left
the places where they had been **scattered**, and returned to Judah. They came
to Gedaliah at Mizpah, and there they

[c] When I did not answer; *or* Then, before he left.

40.7–9: 2 Kgs 25.22–24

afraid 39.17; 41.17
believe 29.31; Lam 4.12
care 39.12; 41.10
choose 33.15; 49.19
destroy 39.16; 42.10
disaster 36.31; 42.17
disobey 34.17; 42.13
free [2] 37.4; Ezek 13.20

Jew Esth 10.3; Ezek 1.1
need 31.12; 52.34
poor 39.10; 52.16
prison 39.9; 41.10
represent Is 6.13; Ezek 4.1
scatter [2] 32.37; 43.5
serve 35.15; 44.3
threat 36.7; Lam 2.17
true 32.24; 42.5
wish 38.5; Ezek 1.12
word (1) 36.8; 44.28

gathered in large amounts of wine and
fruit.

Gedaliah Is Murdered
(2 Kgs 25.25–26)

13 After this, Johanan and the leaders
of the soldiers who had not surrendered
came to Gedaliah at Mizpah 14 and said to
him, "Don't you know that King Baalis of
Ammon has sent Ishmael to murder
you?" But Gedaliah did not **believe** it.
15 Then Johanan said privately to him,
"Let me go and kill Ishmael, and no one
will know who did it. Why should he be
allowed to murder you? That would
cause all the **Jews** who have gathered
round you to be **scattered**, and it would
bring **disaster** on all the people who are
left in Judah."
16 But Gedaliah answered, "Don't do
it! What you are saying about Ishmael is
not **true**!"

afraid 40.9; 42.11
body [3] 26.23; Lam 2.10
care 40.4; 43.6
crime 37.18; Ezek 9.9
escape 39.4; 42.17
get away [2] 35.11; 46.6
glad 33.11; 50.11
incense 34.5; 52.18
offer 35.2; 44.3
prison [4] 40.1; 43.11
shave 16.6; 48.37
spare 38.17; 50.20
Temple (1) (of God) 38.14; 50.28
turn 36.3; 44.11
weep 31.9; 48.20

41 In the seventh month of that
year, Ishmael, the son of
Nethaniah and grandson of Elishama, a
member of the royal family and one of
the king's chief officers, went to Mizpah
with ten men to see Gedaliah. While they
were all eating a meal together,
2 Ishmael and the ten men with him
pulled out their swords and killed
Gedaliah. 3 Ishmael also killed all the
Israelites who were with Gedaliah at
Mizpah and the Babylonian soldiers who
happened to be there.
4 The next day, before anyone knew
about Gedaliah's murder, 5 eighty men
arrived from Shechem, Shiloh, and Samaria. They had **shaved** off their beards,
torn their clothes, and gashed themselves. They were taking corn and **incense** to **offer** in the **Temple**. 6 So Ishmael
went out from Mizpah to meet them,
weeping as he went. When he came to
them, he said, "Please come in to see
Gedaliah." 7 As soon as they were inside
the city, Ishmael and his men killed them
and threw their **bodies** in a well.
8 But there were ten men in the group
who said to Ishmael, "Please don't kill
us! We have wheat, barley, olive-oil, and
honey hidden in the fields." So he **spared**
them. 9 The well into which Ishmael
threw the **bodies** of the men he had killed
was the large one[e] that King Asa had
dug when he was being attacked by King
Baasha of Israel. Ishmael filled the well
with the **bodies**. 10 Then he made
prisoners of the king's daughters and all
the rest of the people in Mizpah, whom
Nebuzaradan the commanding officer
had placed under the **care** of Gedaliah.
Ishmael took them **prisoner** and started
off in the direction of the territory of
Ammon.
11 Johanan and all the army leaders
with him heard of the **crime** that Ishmael
had committed. 12 So they went after him
with their men and overtook him near
the large pool at Gibeon. 13 When Ishmael's **prisoners** saw Johanan and the
leaders of the forces with him, they were
glad, 14 and **turned** and ran to them. 15 But
Ishmael and eight of his men **got away**
from Johanan and **escaped** to the land of
Ammon.
16 Then Johanan and the leaders of
the forces with him took charge of the
people whom Ishmael had taken away as
prisoners from Mizpah after murdering
Gedaliah—soldiers, women, children,
and eunuchs. 17–18 They were **afraid** of the
Babylonians because Ishmael had murdered Gedaliah, whom the king of
Babylonia had made governor of the
land. So they set out for Egypt, in order
to **get away** from the Babylonians. On the
way, they stopped at Chimham, near
Bethlehem.

The People Ask Jeremiah to Pray for Them

42 Then all the army leaders, including Johanan son of Kareah
and Azariah[f] son of Hoshaiah, came with
people of every class 2 and said to me,
"Please do what we ask you! **Pray** to the
LORD our God for us. **Pray** for all of us
who have survived. Once there were
many of us; but now only a few of us are
left, as you can see. 3 **Pray** that the LORD
our God will show us the way we should
go and what we should do."
4 I answered, "Very well, then. I will
pray to the LORD our God, just as you
have asked, and whatever he says, I will
tell you. I will not keep back anything
from you."
5 Then they said to me, "May the
LORD be a **true** and **faithful witness**
against us if we do not **obey** all the **commands** that the LORD our God gives you
for us. 6 Whether it **pleases** us or not, we
will **obey** the LORD our God, to whom we
are asking you to **pray**. All will go well
with us if we **obey** him."

The LORD's Answer to Jeremiah's Prayer

7 Ten days later the LORD spoke to

afraid 41.17; 46.27
Almighty 39.16; 43.10
anger 36.7; 44.3
command [2] 39.11; 43.4
curse 29.18; 44.8
destroy 40.2; 43.13
determine [2] Is 41.4; 44.12
disaster 40.15; 44.23
disease [2] 38.2; 43.11
disobey [2] 40.3; 43.7
escape 41.15; 44.14
faithful 23.28; 50.7
fear 33.9; 46.5
fury [2] 37.15; 44.6
horror 34.17; 44.6
hunger [2] 31.25; Lam 1.6
mercy [2] 33.26; 50.42
mistake Ecc 7.20; Heb 5.2
obey [3] 38.20; 43.4
please 34.15; Ezek 20.39
power 32.17; 43.3
pray [6] 37.3; 51.62
promise 38.16; 44.24
refuse (1) 38.21; 44.16
remember 31.34; 48.27
request 32.7; Dan 2.49
rescue 34.13; 46.27
scorn 20.8; 44.8
sight 25.9; 44.6
sorrow 36.24; 45.3
true 40.16; 44.28
warn 37.9; 49.30

[e] *One ancient translation* was the large one; *Hebrew* by means of Gedaliah.
[f] *One ancient translation (see also 43.2)* Azariah; *Hebrew* Jezaniah.

41.1–3: 2 Kgs 25.25

witness 32.10; Mt 18.16

me; 8 so I called together Johanan, all the army leaders who were with him, and all the other people. 9 I said to them, "The LORD, the God of Israel, to whom you sent me with your **request** has said, 10 'If you are willing to go on living in this land, then I will build you up and not tear you down; I will plant you and not pull you up. The **destruction** I brought on you has caused me great **sorrow**. 11 Stop being **afraid** of the king of Babylonia. I am with you, and I will **rescue** you from his **power**. 12 Because I am **merciful**, I will make him have **mercy** on you and let you go back home. I, the LORD, have spoken.'

13–15 "But you people who are left in Judah must not **disobey** the LORD your God and **refuse** to live in this land. You must not say, 'No, we will go and live in Egypt, where we won't face war any more or hear the call to battle or go **hungry**.' If you say this, then the LORD **Almighty**, the God of Israel, says, 'If you are **determined** to go and live in Egypt, 16 then the war that you **fear** will overtake you, and the **hunger** you dread will follow you, and you will die there in Egypt. 17 All the people who are **determined** to go and live in Egypt will die either in war or of starvation or **disease**. Not one of them will survive, not one will **escape** the **disaster** that I am going to bring on them.'

18 "The LORD, the God of Israel, says, 'Just as my **anger** and **fury** were poured out on the people of Jerusalem, so my **fury** will be poured out on you if you go to Egypt. You will be a **horrifying sight**; people will treat you with **scorn** and use your name as a **curse**. You will never see this place again.' "

19 Then I continued, "The LORD has told you people who are left in Judah not to go to Egypt. And so I **warn** you now 20 that you are making a fatal **mistake**. You asked me to **pray** to the LORD our God for you, and you **promised** that you would do everything that he **commands**. 21 And now I have told you, but you are **disobeying** everything that the LORD our God sent me to tell you. 22 So then, **remember** this: you will die in war or of starvation or **disease** in the land where you want to go and live."

Jeremiah Is Taken to Egypt

Almighty 42.13; 44.2
arrogant Is 33.19; 48.29
care 41.10; 49.11
clean [2] 6.9; 52.18

43 I finished telling the people everything that the LORD their God had sent me to tell them. 2 Then Azariah son of Hoshaiah and Johanan son of Kareah and all the other **arrogant** men said to me, "You are **lying**. The LORD our God did not send you to tell us not to go and live in Egypt. 3 Baruch son of Neriah has stirred you up against us, so that the Babylonians will gain **power** over us and can either kill us or take us away to Babylonia." 4 So neither Johanan nor any of the army officers nor any of the people would **obey** the LORD's **command** to remain in the land of Judah. 5 Then Johanan and all the army officers took everybody left in Judah away to Egypt, together with all the people who had returned from the nations where they had been **scattered**: 6 the men, the women, the children, and the king's daughters. They took everyone whom Nebuzaradan the commanding officer had left under the **care** of Gedaliah, including Baruch and me. 7 They **disobeyed** the LORD's **command** and went into Egypt as far as the city of Tahpanhes.

8 There the LORD said to me, 9 "Get some large stones and bury them in the mortar of the pavement[g] in front of the entrance to the government building here in the city, and let some of the Israelites see you do it. 10 Then tell them that I, the LORD **Almighty**, the God of Israel, am going to bring my **servant** King Nebuchadnezzar of Babylonia to this place, and he[h] will put his **throne** over these stones that you[i] buried, and will spread the royal tent over them. 11 Nebuchadnezzar will come and defeat Egypt. Those people who are **doomed** to die of **disease** will die of disease, those **doomed** to be taken away as **prisoners** will be taken away as prisoners, and those **doomed** to be killed in war will be killed in war. 12 I will set fire to the **temples** of Egypt's **gods**, and the king of Babylonia will either burn their **gods** or carry them off. As a **shepherd** picks his clothes **clean** of lice, so the king of Babylonia will pick the land of Egypt **clean** and then leave **victorious**. 13 He will **destroy** the **sacred** stone monuments at Heliopolis in Egypt and will burn down the **temples** of the Egyptian **gods**."

command [2] 42.5; 44.23
destroy 42.10; 44.2
disease 42.17; 44.13
disobey 42.13; Lam 1.18
doom [3] 22.13; 46.21
god (2) (other gods) [3] 35.15; 44.3
lie (2) 29.9; 50.36
obey 42.5; 44.23
power 42.11; 48.17
prison 41.10; 46.19
sacred 31.23; Ezek 34.26
scatter 40.12; 46.28
servant 35.15; 44.4
shepherd 33.12; 50.6
temple (2) (of other gods) [2] Is 37.38; Dan 1.2
throne 30.9; 49.38
victory Is 63.1; 51.14

The LORD's Message to the Israelites in Egypt

44 The LORD spoke to me concerning all the Israelites living in Egypt, in the cities of Migdol, Tahpanhes, and Memphis, and in the southern part of the country. 2 The LORD **Almighty**, the God of Israel, said, "You yourselves have

Almighty [4] 43.10; 46.10
anger [3] 42.18; 49.37
approve Ps 101.6; Hos 8.4
command 43.4; 46.9
curse [3] 42.18; 48.10
death (1) 31.2; 50.35

[g] *Probable text* bury them...pavement; *Hebrew unclear.*
[h] *Some ancient translations* he; *Hebrew* I. [i] *Some ancient translations* you; *Hebrew* I.

43.5–7: 2 Kgs 25.26

destroy [7] 43.13; 46.8
determine 42.13; Lam 2.8
disaster 42.17; 45.5
disease [2] 43.11; Ezek 6.11
endure 10.10; Ezek 16.52
enemy [2] 34.20; 46.10
escape [2] 42.17; 45.5
evil [4] 36.3; 50.39
forget [2] 30.14; 50.6
fury 42.18; Lam 2.3
god (2) (other gods) [5] 43.12; 46.15
goddess 17.2; Mic 5.14
hate 14.19; Lam 2.16
heaven [4] 25.30; 51.15
honour 33.9; 48.18
horror [3] 42.18; 49.13
humble 13.15; Dan 4.37
idol 32.34; 50.2
law 33.25; Lam 2.9
long (2) 31.2; Amos 5.18
might 32.17; 46.15
name (2) (name of God, of Jesus) [3] 33.2; 50.34
never again 31.40; 50.39
obey 43.4; Ezek 5.7
offer [7] 41.5; 48.35
plenty Is 65.13; Ezek 16.49
practice [2] Is 2.6; Ezek 16.24
promise [5] 42.20; 48.40
prophet 37.19; 50.36
prosper [2] 39.16; 48.47
prove 12.1; 46.11
punish [3] 36.31; 46.10
refugee Is 21.14; 48.45
refuse (1) 42.13; Lam 1.19
ruin [3] 27.17; 46.19
sacrifice [10] 33.18; 46.10
scorn [2] 42.18; Lam 2.15
servant 43.10; Ezek 28.25
serve 40.9; Ezek 20.24
sight [3] 42.18; 49.13
solemn 11.7; Ezek 32.2
Sovereign 32.17; 46.10
swear 38.16; 49.13
terrible 36.7; 49.17
trouble 20.18; 45.3
true [2] 42.5; Ezek 3.20
turn 41.14; 46.5
vow [3] Is 45.23; Ezek 20.23
wicked [2] 36.3; 50.20
wine-offering [4] 32.29; Ezek 45.17
word (1) 40.9; 51.64
worship (1) (of God) 34.15; Lam 1.4
worship (2) (of other gods) 35.15; 48.46

seen the destruction I brought on
Jerusalem and all the other cities of
Judah. Even now they are still in ruins,
and no one lives in them 3 because their
people had done evil and had made me
angry. They offered sacrifices to other
gods and served gods that neither they
nor you nor your ancestors ever worshipped. 4 I kept sending you my servants
the prophets, who told you not to do this
terrible thing that I hate. 5 But you would
not listen or pay any attention. You
would not give up your evil practice of
sacrificing to other gods. 6 So I poured out
my anger and fury on the towns of Judah
and on the streets of Jerusalem, and I set
them on fire. They were left in ruins and
became a horrifying sight, as they are today.

7 "And so I, the LORD Almighty, the
God of Israel, now ask why you are doing
such an evil thing to yourselves. Do you
want to bring destruction on men and
women, children and babies, so that none
of your people will be left? 8 Why do you
make me angry by worshipping idols and
by sacrificing to other gods here in
Egypt, where you have come to live?
Are you doing this just to destroy yourselves, so that every nation on earth will
treat you with scorn and use your name
as a curse? 9 Have you forgotten all the
wicked things that have been done in the
towns of Judah and in the streets of
Jerusalem by your ancestors, by the
kings of Judah and their wives, and by
you and your wives? 10 But to this day
you have not humbled yourselves. You
have not honoured me or lived according
to all the laws that I gave you and your
ancestors.

11 "So then, I, the LORD Almighty, the
God of Israel, will turn against you and
destroy all Judah. 12 As for the people of
Judah who are left and are determined
to go and live in Egypt, I will see to it
that all of them are destroyed. All of
them, great and small, will die in Egypt,
either in war or of starvation. They will
be a horrifying sight; people will treat
them with scorn and use their name as a
curse. 13 I will punish those who live in
Egypt, just as I punished Jerusalem—
with war, starvation, and disease. 14 None
of the people of Judah who are left and
have come to Egypt to live will escape or
survive. Not one of them will return to
Judah, where they long to live once
again. No one will return except a few
refugees."

15 Then all the men who knew that
their wives offered sacrifices to other
gods, and all the women who were standing there, including the Israelites who
lived in southern Egypt—a large crowd
in all—said to me, 16 "We refuse to listen
to what you have told us in the name of
the LORD. 17 We will do everything that
we said we would. We will offer sacrifices to our goddess, the Queen of
Heaven, and we will pour out wine-offerings to her, just as we and our ancestors,
our king and our leaders, used to do in
the towns of Judah and in the streets of
Jerusalem. Then we had plenty of food,
we were prosperous, and had no
troubles. 18 But ever since we stopped
sacrificing to the Queen of Heaven and
stopped pouring out wine-offerings to
her, we have had nothing, and our people
have died in war and of starvation."

19 And the women added, "When we
baked cakes shaped like the Queen of
Heaven, offered sacrifices to her, and
poured out wine-offerings to her, our husbands approved of what we were doing."

20 Then I said to all the men and the
women who had answered me in this
way, 21 "As for the sacrifices which you
and your ancestors, your kings and your
leaders, and the people of the land
offered in the towns of Judah and in the
streets of Jerusalem—do you think that
the LORD did not know about them or
that he forgot them? 22 This very day
your land lies in ruins and no one lives in
it. It has become a horrifying sight, and
people use its name as a curse because
the LORD could no longer endure your
wicked and evil practices. 23 This present
disaster has come on you because you
offered sacrifices to other gods and
sinned against the LORD by not obeying
all his commands."

24-25 I told all the people, especially
the women, what the LORD Almighty, the
God of Israel, was saying to the people of
Judah living in Egypt: "Both you and
your wives have made solemn promises
to the Queen of Heaven. You promised
that you would offer sacrifices to her and
pour out wine-offerings to her, and you
have kept your promises. Very well,
then! Keep your promises! Carry out
your vows! 26 But now listen to the vow
that I, the LORD, have made in my
mighty name to all you Israelites in
Egypt: Never again will I let any of you
use my name to make a vow by saying, 'I
swear by the living Sovereign LORD!' 27 I
will see to it that you will not prosper, but
will be destroyed. All of you will die,
either in war or of disease, until not one
of you is left. 28 But a few of you will escape death and return from Egypt to
Judah. Then the survivors will know

whose **words** have come **true**, mine or
theirs. 29 I, the LORD, will give you **proof**
that I will **punish** you in this place and
that my **promise** to bring **destruction** on
you will come **true**. 30 I will hand over
King Hophra of Egypt to his **enemies**
who want to kill him, just as I handed
over King Zedekiah of Judah to King
Nebuchadnezzar of Babylonia, who was
his **enemy** and wanted to kill him."

God's Promise to Baruch

45 In the fourth year that Jehoiakim
son of Josiah was king of Judah,
Baruch wrote down what I had dictated
to him. Then I told him 2 that the LORD,
the God of Israel, had said, "Baruch, 3 you
are saying, 'I give up! The LORD has
added **sorrow** to my **troubles**. I am worn
out from **groaning**, and I can't find any
rest!'
4 "But I, the LORD, am tearing down
what I have built and pulling up what I
have planted. I will do this to the entire
earth. 5 Are you looking for **special** treatment for yourself? Don't do it. I am
bringing **disaster** on all **mankind**, but you
will at least **escape** with your **life**, wherever you go. I, the LORD, have spoken."

Egypt's Defeat at Carchemish

46 The LORD spoke to me about the
nations, 2 beginning with Egypt.
This is what he said about the army of
King Neco of Egypt, which King
Nebuchadnezzar of Babylonia defeated
at Carchemish near the River Euphrates
in the fourth year that Jehoiakim was
king of Judah:

3 "The Egyptian officers shout,
'Get your shields ready
and march into battle!
4 Harness your horses and mount them!
Fall in line and put on your helmets!
Sharpen your spears!
Put on your armour!'

5 "But what do I see?" asks the LORD.
"They are **turning** back in **terror**.
Their soldiers are beaten back;
overcome with **fear**, they run as fast
as they can
and do not look back.
6 Those who run fast cannot **get away**;
the soldiers cannot **escape**.
In the north, by the Euphrates,
they **stumble** and fall.
7 Who is this that **rises** like the Nile,
like a river **flooding** its banks?
8 It is Egypt, **rising** like the Nile,
like a river **flooding** its banks.
Egypt said, 'I will **rise** and cover the
world;
I will **destroy** cities and the people
who live there.
9 **Command** the horses to go
and the chariots to roll!
Send out the soldiers:
men from Sudan and Libya, carrying
shields,
and skilled bowmen from Lydia.' "

10 This is the day of the **Sovereign** LORD
Almighty:
today he will take **revenge**;
today he will **punish** his **enemies**.
His sword will eat them until it is full,
and drink their **blood** until it is
satisfied.
Today the **Almighty sacrifices** his
victims
in the north, by the Euphrates.
11 People of Egypt, go to Gilead[j]
and look for medicine!
All your medicine has **proved useless**;
nothing can **heal** you.
12 Nations have heard of your **shame**;
everyone has heard you cry.
One soldier trips over another,
and both of them fall to the ground.

The Coming of Nebuchadnezzar

13 When King Nebuchadnezzar of
Babylonia came to attack Egypt, the
LORD spoke to me. He said,

14 "**Proclaim** it in the towns of Egypt,
in Migdol, Memphis, and
Tahpanhes:
'Get ready to **defend** yourselves;
all you have will be **destroyed** in
war!
15 Why has your **mighty god Apis** fallen?
The LORD has **struck** him down!'
16 Your soldiers have **stumbled** and
fallen;[k]
each one says to the other,
'Hurry! Let's go home to our people
and **escape** the **enemy's** sword!'

17 "Give the king of Egypt a **new** name—
'Noisy Braggart Who Missed His
Chance.'
18 I, the LORD **Almighty**, am king.
I am the living God.
As Mount Tabor towers above the
mountains
and Mount Carmel stands high
above the sea,
so will be the **strength** of the one who
attacks you.

splendour Is 63.1; 48.2
strength 27.5; 48.7
strike 33.5; Ezek 17.10
stumble [2] 31.9; 50.32
terrify 32.21; 49.17
terror 30.5; 48.43
trust 39.18; 48.7
turn [2] 44.11; 47.3
useless 16.19; Ezek 13.4
victim 3.2; Ezek 7.15
world 34.17; 50.23

disaster 44.23; 49.32
escape 44.14; 46.6
groan Is 19.8; 51.52
life (1) 39.18; 48.6
mankind 32.27; Zeph 1.3
rest (1) 31.2; 47.6
sorrow 42.10; 47.5
special Esth 2.9; Ezek 16.34
trouble 44.17; 49.23

afraid [2] 42.11; 49.37
Almighty [4] 44.2; 48.1
blood 19.4; 52.18
command 44.23; 47.7
conquer 13.21; 48.7
defend 21.13; 49.1
destroy [6] 44.2; 47.4
doom 43.11; 48.16
enemy [3] 44.30; 48.2
escape [2] 45.5; 48.8
fear 42.16; 49.16
flood [2] Is 54.9; 47.2
get away 41.15; Ezek 17.15
god (2) (other gods) [3] 44.3; 48.7
God's people 33.24; 50.6
heal 33.6; 51.8
helpless Is 54.11; 48.45
might 44.26; 48.1
new 31.22; Ezek 11.19
peace 34.5; 50.34
prison [2] 43.11; 48.46
proclaim 31.10; 50.2
prove 44.29; Mt 8.4
punish [4] 44.13; 49.8
rescue 42.11; 50.34
revenge 20.10; 50.15
rise [3] 21.13; 47.2
ruin 44.2; 48.8
sacrifice 44.3; 48.35
satisfy 31.14; Ezek 5.13
save 31.7; Lam 3.26
scatter 43.5; 49.32
secure 33.6; 48.11
shame [2] 23.40; 48.1
Sovereign 44.26; 50.25

[j] GILEAD: *See 8.22.* [k] *Probable text* Your soldiers...fallen; *Hebrew unclear.*

44.30: 2 Kgs 25.1–7 **45.1:** 2 Kgs 24.1; 2 Chr 36.5–7; Dan 1.1–2 **46.2–26:** Is 19.1–25; Ezek 29.1—32.32
46.13: Jer 43.10–13

19 Get ready to be taken **prisoner**,
you people of Egypt!
Memphis will be made a desert,
a **ruin** where no one lives.
20 Egypt is like a **splendid** cow,
attacked by a stinging fly from the
north.
21 Even her hired soldiers
are **helpless** as calves.
They did not stand and fight;
all of them **turned** and ran.
The day of their **doom** had arrived,
the time of their **destruction**.
22 Egypt runs away, hissing like a snake,
as the **enemy's** army approaches.
They attack her with axes,
like men cutting down trees
23 and **destroying** a thick forest.
Their men are too many to count;
their soldiers outnumber the locusts.
24 The people of Egypt are put to **shame**;
they are **conquered** by the people of
the north.
I, the LORD, have spoken."

25 The LORD **Almighty**, the God of
Israel, says, "I am going to **punish** Amon,
the **god of Thebes**, together with Egypt
and its **gods** and kings. I am going to take
the king of Egypt and all who put their
trust in him,
26 and hand them over to
those who want to kill them, to King
Nebuchadnezzar of Babylonia and his
army. But later on, people will live in
Egypt again, as they did in times past. I,
the LORD, have spoken."

The LORD Will Save His People

27 "**My people**, do not be **afraid**,
people of Israel, do not be **terrified**.
I will **rescue** you from that distant
land,
from the land where you are
prisoners.
You will come back home and live in
peace;
you will be **secure**, and no one will
make you **afraid**.
28 I will come to you and **save** you.
I will **destroy** all the nations
where I have **scattered** you,
but I will not **destroy** you.
I will not let you go **unpunished**;
but when I **punish** you, I will be fair.
I, the LORD, have spoken."

The LORD's Message about Philistia

47 Before the king of Egypt
attacked Gaza, the LORD spoke
to me about Philistia.
2 He said:

"Look! Waters are **rising** in the north
and will rush like a river in **flood**.
They will cover the land and
everything on it,
cities and the people who live there.
People will call out for **help**;
everyone on earth will cry **bitterly**.
3 They will hear the hoof beats of
horses,
the clatter of chariots,
the rumble of wheels.
Fathers will not **turn** back for their
children;
their hands will hang limp at their
sides.
4 The time has come to **destroy** Philistia,
to cut off from Tyre and Sidon
all the **help** that remains.
I, the LORD, will **destroy** the
Philistines,
all who came from the shores of
Crete.
5 Great **sorrow** has come to the people
of Gaza,
and Ashkelon's people are silent.
How long will the rest of Philistia
mourn?
6 You cry out, 'Sword of the LORD!
How long will you go on slashing?
Go back to your scabbard,
stay there and **rest**!'
7 But how can it **rest**,
when I have given it work to do?
I have **commanded** it to attack
Ashkelon
and the people who live on the
coast."

The Destruction of Moab

48 This is what the LORD **Almighty**
said about Moab:
"Pity the people of Nebo—
their town is **destroyed**!
Kiriathaim is captured,
its **mighty** fortress torn down,
and its people put to **shame**;
2 the **splendour** of Moab is gone.
The **enemy** have captured Heshbon
and **plot** to **destroy** the nation of
Moab.
The town of Madmen will be **silenced**;
armies will march against it.
3 The people of Horonaim cry out,
'**Violence**! **Destruction**!'

4 "Moab has been **destroyed**;
listen to the children crying.
5 Hear the sound of their sobs
along the road up to Luhith,
the cries of **distress**

bitter 31.15;
Lam 3.15
command 46.9; 50.21
destroy [2] 46.8; 48.1

flood 46.7;
Ezek 30.16
help [2] 38.4; 50.32
mourn 34.5; 48.17
rest (1) [2] 45.3; 49.23
rise 46.7; 51.64
sorrow 45.3;
Lam 1.20
turn 46.5; 49.8

Almighty [2] 46.10;
49.7
announce 32.3; 50.2
arrogant [2] 43.2;
Dan 8.4
boast 23.32; 49.4
burnt-offering 33.18;
Ezek 43.27
claim 29.8; Ezek 13.6
conceited Is 16.6;
1 Cor 13.4
conquer 46.24; 49.28
curse [2] 44.8; 49.13
destroy [14] 47.4;
49.3
disgrace [2] 31.19;
50.12
distress 30.7;
Ezek 4.16
doom 46.21; 50.27
dove 8.7; Ezek 7.16
enemy 46.10; 49.22
escape [2] 46.6; 50.28
exile [2] 29.2; 49.3
fright Is 59.11; 49.22
glory 17.12; Lam 5.21
god (2) (other gods)
[4] 46.15; 49.3
happy 33.11; 49.25
heart [2] 32.40;
Lam 1.20

46.27-28: Jer 30.10-11
47.1-7: Is 14.29-31; Ezek 25.15-17; Joel 3.4-8; Amos 1.6-8; Zeph 2.4-7; Zech 9.5-7
48.1-47: Is 15.1—16.14, 25.10-12; Ezek 25.8-11; Amos 2.1-3; Zeph 2.8-11

helpless 46.21; 51.51
honour 44.10; 52.32
jeer [2] 20.7; 49.13
joy [2] 33.9; 51.48
judge [2] 23.1; 49.7
last (1) 31.36; Ezek 4.4
life (1) 45.5; 49.5
might [3] 46.15; 50.41
mourn [3] 47.5; 49.3
offer 44.3; 52.19
pity [2] 21.7; Ezek 9.10
place of worship Ps 78.58; Ezek 16.16
plot (1) 18.23; 49.30
power [2] 43.3; 49.4
priest 37.3; 49.3
prison 46.19; 52.11
promise 44.24; Lam 1.21
prosper 44.17; 49.6
protect 39.17; 49.31
proud [2] 33.9; 49.16
rebel [2] 33.8; 52.3
refugee 44.14; 49.36
remember 42.22; 51.50
rob 7.11; 49.9
ruin [6] 46.19; 49.2
sackcloth 6.26; 49.3
sacrifice 46.10; 52.18
secure 46.27; 49.31
shame 46.12; 50.2
shave 41.5; Ezek 5.1
slaughter 25.34; 50.27
splendour 46.20; Lam 1.6
strength 46.18; 49.4
terror [2] 46.5; 49.5
test 20.12; Ezek 21.13
tomb Is 65.4; Ezek 32.23
trap [2] 18.22; 50.24
trust [2] 46.25; 49.4
vine 8.13; 49.9
violent 22.17; 51.35
weep [2] 41.6; 50.4
worship (2) (of other gods) 44.8; 49.1

on the way down to Horonaim.
6 'Quick, run for your **lives**!' they say.
'Run like a wild desert donkey!'

7 "Moab, you **trusted** in your **strength**
and your wealth,
but now even you will be **conquered**;
your **god Chemosh** will go into **exile**,
along with his princes and **priests**.
8 Not a town will **escape** the **destruction**;
both valley and plain will be **ruined**.
I, the LORD, have spoken.
9 Set up a **tombstone** for Moab;
it will soon be **destroyed**.
Its towns will be left in **ruins**,
and no one will live there again."
10 (**Curse** the man who does not do the
LORD's work **with all his heart**! **Curse** the
man who does not slash and kill!)

The Cities of Moab Are Destroyed

11 The LORD said, "Moab has always
lived **secure** and has never been taken
into **exile**. Moab is like wine left to settle
undisturbed and never poured from jar
to jar. Its flavour has never been **ruined**,
and it tastes as good as ever.
12 "So now, the time is coming when I
will send people to pour Moab out like
wine. They will empty its wine-jars and
break them in pieces.
13 Then the Moab-
ites will be disillusioned with their **god**
Chemosh, just as the Israelites were disillusioned with Bethel, a **god** in whom
they **trusted**.
14 "Men of Moab, why do you **claim** to be
heroes,
brave soldiers **tested** in war?
15 Moab and its cities are **destroyed**;
its finest young men have been
slaughtered.
I am the king, the LORD **Almighty**,
and I have spoken.
16 Moab's **doom** approaches;
its **ruin** is coming soon.

17 "**Mourn** for that nation, you that live
near by,
all of you that know its fame.
Say, 'Its **powerful** rule has been
broken;
its **glory** and **might** are no more.'
18 You that live in Dibon,
come down from your place of
honour
and sit on the ground in the dust;
Moab's **destroyer** is here
and has left its forts in **ruins**.
19 You that live in Aroer,
stand by the road and wait;
ask those who are running away,
find out from them what has
happened.
20 'Moab has fallen,' they will answer,
'**weep** for it; it is **disgraced**.
Announce along the River Arnon
that Moab is **destroyed**!'

21 "**Judgement** has come on the cities
of the plateau: on Holon, Jahzah, Meph-
ath,
22 Dibon, Nebo, Beth Diblathaim,
23 Kiriathaim, Bethgamul, Bethmeon,
24 Kerioth, and Bozrah. **Judgement** has
come on all the cities of Moab, far and
near.
25 Moab's **might** has been crushed;
its **power** has been **destroyed**. I, the
LORD, have spoken."

Moab Will Be Humbled

26 The LORD said, "Make Moab drunk,
because it has **rebelled** against me. Moab
will roll in its own vomit, and people will
laugh.
27 Moab, **remember** how you
jeered at the people of Israel? You
treated them as though they had been
caught with a gang of **robbers**.
28 "You people who live in Moab,
leave your towns! Go and live on the
cliffs! Be like the **dove** that makes its
nest in the sides of a ravine.
29 Moab is
very **proud**! I have heard how **proud**,
arrogant, and **conceited** the people are,
how much they think of themselves.
30 I,
the LORD, know of their **arrogance**. Their
boasts amount to nothing, and the things
they do will not **last**.
31 And so I will **weep**
for everyone in Moab and for the people
of Kir Heres.
32 I will cry for the people of
Sibmah, even more than for the people of
Jazer. City of Sibmah, you are like a **vine**
whose branches reach across the Dead
Sea and go as far as Jazer. But now your
summer fruits and your grapes have
been **destroyed**.
33 **Happiness** and **joy**
have been taken away from the fertile
land of Moab. I have made the wine stop
flowing from the winepresses; there is no
one to make the wine and shout for **joy**.
34 "The people of Heshbon and
Elealeh cry out,[l] and their cry can be
heard as far as Jahaz; it can be heard by
the people in Zoar, and it is heard as far
as Horonaim and Eglath Shelishiyah.
Even the brook of Nimrim has dried up.
35 I will stop the people of Moab from
making **burnt-offerings** at their **places of**
worship and from **offering sacrifices** to
their **gods**. I, the LORD, have spoken.
36 "So my **heart mourns** for Moab and
for the people of Kir Heres, like someone
playing a funeral song on a flute, because
everything they owned is gone.
37 All of
them have **shaved** their heads and cut off

[l] *Probable text* Heshbon...cry out; *Hebrew unclear.*

their beards. They have all made gashes
on their hands, and everyone is wearing
sackcloth. 38 On all the house-tops of
Moab and in all its public squares there is
nothing but **mourning**, because I have
broken Moab like a jar that no one
wants. 39 Moab has been shattered! Cry
out! Moab has been **disgraced**. It is in
ruins, and all the surrounding nations
jeer at it. I, the LORD, have spoken."

No Escape for Moab

40 The LORD has **promised** that a
nation will swoop down on Moab like an
eagle with its outspread wings, 41 and the
towns and fortresses will be captured. On
that day Moab's soldiers will be as
frightened as a woman in labour. 42 Moab
will be **destroyed** and will no longer be a
nation, because it **rebelled** against me.
43 **Terror**, pits, and **traps** are waiting for
the people of Moab. The LORD has
spoken. 44 Whoever tries to **escape** the
terror will fall into the pits, and whoever
climbs out of the pits will be caught in
the **traps**, because the LORD has set the
time for Moab's **destruction**. 45 **Helpless**
refugees try to find **protection** in
Heshbon, the city that King Sihon once
ruled, but it is in flames.[m] Fire has burnt
up the frontiers and the mountain
heights of the war-loving people of Moab.
46 **Pity** the people of Moab! The people
who **worshipped Chemosh** have been **des-**
troyed, and their sons and daughters
have been taken away as **prisoners**.
47 But in days to come the LORD will
make Moab **prosperous** again. All of this
is what the LORD has said will happen to
Moab.

The LORD's Judgement on Ammon

49 This is what the LORD said about
Ammon: "Where are the men of
Israel? Is there no one to **defend** their
land? Why have they let the people who
worship Molech take the territory of the
tribe of Gad and settle there? 2 But the
time is coming when I will make the
people of the capital city of Rabbah hear
the noise of battle, and it will be left in
ruins and its villages burnt to the ground.
Then Israel will take its land back from
those who took it from them. 3 People of
Heshbon, cry out! Ai is **destroyed**!
Women of Rabbah, go into **mourning**!
Put on **sackcloth** and **mourn**. Run about
in confusion. Your **god Molech** will be
taken into **exile**, together with his **priests**
and princes. 4 Why do you **unfaithful**
people **boast**? Your **strength** is **failing**.
Why do you **trust** in your **power** and say
that no one would **dare** attack you? 5 I
will bring **terror** on you from every side.
You will all run away. Each one will run
for his **life**, and there will be no one to
bring your troops together again.
6 "But later on I will make Ammon
prosperous again. I, the LORD, have
spoken."

The LORD's Judgement on Edom

7 This is what the LORD **Almighty** said
about Edom: "Have the people of Edom
lost their good **judgement**? Can their advisers no longer tell them what to do?
Has all their **wisdom** disappeared?
8 People of Dedan, **turn** and run! Hide! I
am going to **destroy** Esau's descendants,
because the time has come for me to
punish them. 9 When men pick grapes,
they leave a few on the **vines**, and when
robbers come at night, they take only
what they want. 10 But I[o] have **stripped**
Esau's descendants completely and uncovered their hiding places, so that they
can no longer hide. All the people of
Edom are **destroyed**. Not one of them is
left. 11 Leave your **orphans** with me, and I
will take **care** of them. Your **widows** can
depend on me.
12 "If even those who did not **deserve**
to be **punished** had to drink from the **cup**
of **punishment**, do you think that you will
go **unpunished**? No, you must drink from
the **cup**! 13 I myself have **sworn** that the
city of Bozrah will become a **horrifying**
sight and a desert; people will **jeer** at it
and use its name as a **curse**. All the nearby villages will be in **ruins** for ever. I, the
LORD, have spoken."
14 I said, "Edom, I have received a
message from the LORD. He has sent a
messenger to tell the nations to assemble
their armies and to get ready to attack
you. 15 The LORD is going to make you
weak, and no one will **respect** you.
16 Your **pride** has **deceived** you. No one
fears you as much as you think they do.
You live on the rocky cliffs, high on top
of the mountain; but even though you
live as high up as an eagle, the LORD will
bring you down. The LORD has spoken."
17 The LORD said, "The **destruction**
that will come on Edom will be so
terrible that everyone who passes by will

afraid 46.27; 50.16
Almighty [3] 48.1; 50.18
anger 44.3; 50.13
anxious Ps 119.143; Ezek 4.16
bad 24.2; 52.6
boast 48.30; Ezek 27.3
care 43.6; Ezek 16.49
challenge Ecc 8.4; 50.44
choose 40.4; 50.44
compare 30.7; 50.44
conquer 48.7; 50.9
control 33.25; 51.28
cup [2] 35.5; 51.7
curse 48.10; Lam 3.65
dare [2] 30.21; 50.44
deceive 37.9; Lam 2.14
defend 46.14; Lam 2.2
depend Is 59.4; Ezek 29.16
deserve 26.11; 51.6
destroy [9] 48.1; 50.21
disaster 45.5; Lam 1.21
enemy [2] 48.2; 50.7
exile 48.7; 52.27
fail 25.3; Ezek 21.7
fear 46.5; Lam 3.47
flee 26.21; 52.7
flock 31.10; 51.23
fright 48.41; Ezek 7.16
god (2) (other gods) 48.7; 50.2
happy 48.33; 50.11
horror [2] 44.6; 50.45
intend 36.3; 50.45
jeer 48.27; Lam 1.15
judge 48.21; Lam 3.59
life (1) 48.6; 50.20
message 38.20; 50.1
misery Is 50.11; Lam 1.11
mourn [2] 48.17; 51.8
orphan 22.3; Ezek 22.7
pain 22.23; 50.43
plan 32.19; 50.45
plot (1) 48.2; Lam 3.60
power [2] 48.17; 51.15
priest 48.7; 52.24
prosper [2] 48.47; Ezek 16.53
protect 48.45; Lam 4.20
proud 48.29; 50.29
punish [4] 46.10; 50.18
refugee 48.45; 50.28
respect Is 60.14; Lam 5.12
rest (1) 47.6; Lam 5.5
rob 48.27; Lam 1.10
ruin [2] 48.8; 50.13
sackcloth 48.37; Lam 2.10
safe 39.14; Ezek 28.26
scatter [2] 46.28; 50.17
secure 48.11; Ezek 18.7
sight 44.6; 51.17
strength 48.7; 51.12
strip (1) 13.26; Ezek 12.19
swear 44.26; 51.14
terrible 44.4; Lam 1.8
terrify 46.27; 50.36
terror [3] 48.43; Lam 2.22
throne 43.10; Ezek 1.26
trouble 45.3; 50.34
trust 48.7; 50.7
turn 47.3; Lam 2.1
unfaithful 23.10; Ezek 5.13
vine 48.32; Ezek 15.2
warn 42.19; Lam 2.17
weak [2] 31.25; 50.37
widow 22.3; Lam 1.1
wisdom 10.12; 50.35
worry 17.8; Dan 2.1
worship (2) (of other gods) 48.46; 51.44

[m] Heshbon, the city...flames; *or* the city of Heshbon, but it is in flames and the palace of King Sihon is burning.
[o] they leave a few...they take only what they want.[10] But I; *or* they leave nothing...they take everything.[10] And so I.

49.1-6: Ezek 21.28-32, 25.1-7; Amos 1.13-15; Zeph 2.8-11
49.7-22: Is 34.5-17, 63.1-6; Ezek 25.12-14, 35.1-15; Amos 1.11-12; Obad 1-14; Mal 1.2-5

be shocked and **terrified**. 18 The same
thing will happen to Edom as happened
to Sodom and Gomorrah, when they and
the near-by towns were **destroyed**. No
one will ever live there again. I, the
LORD, have spoken. 19 Like a lion coming
out of the thick woods along the Jordan
up to the green pasture land, I will come
and make the Edomites run away suddenly from their country. Then the
leader I **choose** will rule the nation. Who
can be **compared** to me? Who would
dare challenge me? What ruler could oppose me? 20 So listen to the **plan** that I
have made against the people of Edom,
and to what I **intend** to do to the people
of the city of Teman. Even their children
will be dragged off, and everyone will be
horrified. 21 When Edom falls, there will
be such a noise that the entire earth will
shake, and the cries of alarm will be
heard as far away as the Gulf of Aqaba.
22 The **enemy** will attack Bozrah like an
eagle swooping down with outspread
wings. On that day Edom's soldiers will
be as **frightened** as a woman in labour."

The LORD's Judgement on Damascus

23 This is what the LORD said about
Damascus: "The people in the cities of
Hamath and Arpad are **worried** and
troubled because they have heard **bad**
news. **Anxiety** rolls over them like a sea,
and they cannot **rest**. 24 The people of
Damascus are **weak** and have **fled** in terror. They are in **pain** and **misery** like a
woman in labour. 25 The famous city that
used to be **happy**[p] is completely deserted. 26 On that day her young men will
be killed in the city streets, and all her
soldiers **destroyed**. 27 I will set the walls
of Damascus on fire and will burn down
King Benhadad's palaces. I, the LORD Almighty, have spoken."

Judgement on the Tribe of Kedar and the City of Hazor

28 This is what the LORD said about
the tribe of Kedar and the districts **controlled** by Hazor, which were **conquered**
by King Nebuchadnezzar of Babylonia:
"Attack the people of Kedar and **destroy**
that tribe of eastern people! 29 Seize their
tents and their **flocks**, their tent curtains
and everything in their tents. Take their
camels and tell the people, '**Terror** is all
round you!'

30 "People of Hazor, I, the LORD, **warn**
you to run far away and hide. King
Nebuchadnezzar of Babylonia has **plotted**
against you, and this is what he says,
31 'Come on! We'll attack those people
that feel **safe** and **secure**! Their city has
no gates or locks and is completely **unprotected**.'

32 "Take their camels and all their
livestock! I will **scatter** in every direction those people who cut their hair
short, and I will bring **disaster** on them
from every side. 33 Hazor will be made a
desert for ever, a place where only
jackals live. No one will ever live there
again. I, the LORD, have spoken."

The LORD's Judgement on Elam

34 Soon after Zedekiah became king
of Judah, the LORD **Almighty** spoke to me
about the country of Elam. 35 He said, "I
will kill all the bowmen who have made
Elam so **powerful**. 36 I will make winds
blow against Elam from all directions,
and I will **scatter** her people everywhere,
until there is no country where her **refugees** have not gone. 37 I will make the
people of Elam **afraid** of their **enemies**,
who want to kill them. In my great **anger**
I will **destroy** the people of Elam and
send armies against them until I have
wiped them out. 38 I will **destroy** their
kings and leaders, and set up my **throne**
there. 39 But later on I will make the
people of Elam **prosperous** again. I, the
LORD, have spoken."

Babylon's Capture

50 This is the **message** that the
LORD gave me about the city of
Babylon and its people:

2 "Tell the news to the nations!
Proclaim it!
Give the signal and **announce** the
news!
Do not keep it a **secret**!
Babylon has fallen!
Her **god Marduk** has been
shattered!
Babylon's **idols** are put to **shame**,
her **disgusting images** are crushed!

3 "A nation from the north has come
to attack Babylonia and will make it a
desert. Men and animals will run away,
and no one will live there."

Israel's Return

4 The LORD says, "When that time
comes, the people of both Israel and
Judah will come **weeping**, looking for
me, their God. 5 They will ask the way to
Zion and then go in that direction. They
will make an **eternal covenant** with me
and never break it.

6 "**My people** are like **sheep** whose

act 9.5; Ezek 16.51
afraid 49.37; 51.46
Almighty [5] 49.7; 51.5
amaze 19.8; Dan 3.24
anger [2] 49.37; 51.45
anguish 15.8; Lam 1.20
announce 48.20; Ezek 3.18
cause (2) 20.12; 51.36
challenge 49.19; Dan 11.2
choose 49.19; 51.19
command 47.7; 51.11
compare 49.19; Ezek 15.2
conquer 49.28; Lam 1.7
covenant 34.13; Ezek 16.8
cruel 6.23; Lam 4.3
dare 49.4; Mic 1.11
death (1) [5] 44.28; 51.49
demon Is 34.14; Mt 4.24
destroy [8] 49.3; 51.1
disgrace 48.20; 51.51
disgust 32.34; Ezek 5.11
doom 48.16; Lam 5.16
enemy 49.22; 51.25
escape [2] 48.8; 51.50
eternal 33.11; Ezek 26.20
evil 44.3; 51.24
faithful 42.5; Ezek 11.20

[p] *Some ancient translations* happy; *Hebrew* my happiness.

49.18: Gen 19.24–25 **49.23–27:** Is 17.1–3; Amos 1.3–5; Zech 9.1 **50.1—51.64:** Is 13.1—14.23, 47.1–15

fool [2] 17.11; Ezek 13.3
forget 44.9; Lam 3.17
forgive 36.3; Lam 3.42
glad 41.13; Lam 1.21
god (2) (other gods) 49.3; 51.17
God's people 46.27; 51.10
happy 49.25; 51.39
harvest 8.13; Ezek 44.30
help 47.2; 51.9
holy 31.23; 51.5
horror 49.13; 51.37
humiliate Is 54.4; Ezek 36.6
idol [2] 44.8; 51.17
image Is 48.5; Ezek 8.12
important 35.4; 52.13
intend 49.20; 51.11
least 31.34; Dan 4.17
lie (2) 43.2; Lam 2.14
life (1) 49.5; 51.6
mark (1) 31.21; Ezek 9.4
mercy 42.12; Lam 1.9
message 49.14; Ezek 6.2
might 48.1; 51.9
name (2) (name of God, of Jesus) 44.16; 51.19
never again 44.26; Ezek 19.14
oppress 30.16; Ezek 18.16
pain 49.24; Lam 1.12
peace 46.27; Lam 3.17
plan 49.20; 51.29
proclaim 46.14; Dan 4.14
prophet 44.4; Lam 2.9
proud [3] 49.16; Lam 2.15
punish [4] 49.8; 51.6
raise Is 42.2; Lam 4.5
refugee 49.36; Ezek 12.3
rescue 46.27; Lam 3.58
restore 33.6; Lam 5.21
revenge [3] 46.10; 51.6
ruin 49.2; 51.26
scatter 49.32; Lam 4.1
secret 38.16; Ezek 8.12
seed 4.3; Ezek 17.23
shame 48.1; 51.47
sheep [3] 33.12; Ezek 24.5
shepherd 43.12; 51.23
slaughter 48.15; 51.23
Sovereign [2] 46.10; Ezek 2.4
sow 12.13; Ezek 36.9
spare 41.8; 51.3
spirit (2) 27.9; Lam 3.20
strong [2] 20.7; 51.53
stumble 46.6; Ezek 21.15
Temple (1) (of God) 41.5; 51.11
terrify [2] 49.17; 51.37
trap 48.43; Lam 1.13
trouble 49.23; Ezek 5.7
trust 49.4; Lam 3.25

shepherds have let them get lost in the mountains. They have wandered like **sheep** from one mountain to another, and they have **forgotten** where their home is.
7 They are attacked by all who find them. Their **enemies** say, 'They sinned against the LORD, and so what we have done is not **wrong**. Their ancestors **trusted** in the LORD, and they themselves should have remained **faithful** to him.'

8 "People of Israel, run away from Babylonia! Leave the country! Be the first to leave!
9 I am going to stir up a group of **strong** nations in the north and make them attack Babylonia. They will line up in battle against the country and **conquer** it. They are skilful hunters, shooting arrows that never miss the **mark**.
10 Babylonia will be looted, and those who loot it will take everything they want. I, the LORD, have spoken."

Babylon's Fall

11 The LORD says, "People of Babylonia, you plundered my nation. You are **happy** and **glad**, going about like a cow threshing corn or like a neighing horse,
12 but your own great city will be **humiliated** and **disgraced**. Babylonia will be the **least important** nation of all; it will become a dry and waterless desert.
13 Because of my **anger** no one will live in Babylon; it will be left in **ruins**, and all who pass by will be shocked and **amazed**.

14 "Bowmen, line up for battle against Babylon and surround it. Shoot all your arrows at Babylon, because it has sinned against me, the LORD.
15 **Raise** the war cry all round the city! Now Babylon has surrendered. Its walls have been broken through and torn down.[q] I am taking my **revenge** on the Babylonians. So take your **revenge** on them, and treat them as they have treated others.
16 Do not let **seeds** be **sown** in that country or let a **harvest** be gathered. Every foreigner living there will be **afraid** of the attacking army and will go back home."

Israel's Return

17 The LORD says, "The people of Israel are like **sheep**, chased and **scattered** by lions. First, they were attacked by the emperor of Assyria, and then King Nebuchadnezzar of Babylonia gnawed their bones.
18 Because of this, I, the LORD **Almighty**, the God of Israel, will **punish** King Nebuchadnezzar and his country, just as I **punished** the emperor of Assyria.
19 I will **restore** the people of Israel to their land. They will eat the food that grows on Mount Carmel and in the region of Bashan, and they will eat all they want of the crops that grow in the territories of Ephraim and Gilead.
20 When that time comes, no sin will be found in Israel and no **wickedness** in Judah, because I will **forgive** those people whose **lives** I have **spared**. I, the LORD, have spoken."

God's Judgement on Babylonia

21 The LORD says, "Attack the people of Merathaim and of Pekod. Kill and **destroy** them.[r] Do everything I **command** you. I, the LORD, have spoken.
22 The noise of battle is heard in the land, and there is great **destruction**.
23 Babylonia hammered the whole **world** to pieces, and now that hammer is shattered! All the nations are shocked at what has happened to that country.
24 Babylonia, you fought against me, and you have been caught in the **trap** I set for you, even though you did not know it.
25 I have opened the place where my weapons are stored, and in my **anger** I have taken them out, because I, the **Sovereign** LORD **Almighty**, have work to do in Babylonia.
26 Attack it from every side and break open the places where its grain is stored! Pile up the loot like piles of grain! **Destroy** the country! Leave nothing at all!
27 Kill all their soldiers! **Slaughter** them! The people of Babylonia are **doomed**! The time has come for them to be **punished**!"

28 (**Refugees escape** from Babylonia and come to Jerusalem, and they tell how the LORD our God took **revenge** for what the Babylonians had done to his **Temple**.)

29 "Tell the bowmen to attack Babylon. Send out everyone who knows how to use the bow and arrow. Surround the city and don't let anyone **escape**. Pay it back for all it has done, and treat it as it has treated others, because it **acted** with **pride** against me, the **Holy One** of Israel.
30 So its young men will be killed in the city streets, and all its soldiers will be **destroyed** on that day. I, the LORD, have spoken.

31 "Babylonia, you are filled with **pride**, so I, the **Sovereign** LORD **Almighty**, am against you! The time has come for me to **punish** you.
32 Your **proud** nation will **stumble** and fall, and no one will **help** you up. I will set your cities on fire, and everything around will be **destroyed**."

unclean 19.13; Lam 1.9
weak 49.15; Lam 1.6
weep 48.20; Lam 2.11
wicked 44.9; Lam 1.22
wisdom 49.7; 51.15
world 46.8; 51.7
wrong 38.9; Lam 3.59

[q] *Hebrew has an additional word, the meaning of which is unclear.*
[r] *One ancient translation* them; *Hebrew* after them.

50.8: Rev 18.4 **50.29:** Rev 18.6

33 The LORD **Almighty** says, "The
people of Israel and of Judah are **oppressed**. All who captured them are
guarding them closely and will not let
them go. 34 But the one who will **rescue**
them is **strong**—his **name** is the LORD **Almighty**. He himself will take up their
cause and will bring **peace** to the earth,
but **trouble** to the people of Babylonia."

35 The LORD says,
"**Death** to Babylonia!
Death to its people,
to its rulers, to its men of **wisdom**.
36 **Death** to its **lying prophets**—
what **fools** they are!
Death to its soldiers—
how **terrified** they are!
37 **Destroy** its horses and chariots!
Death to its hired soldiers—
how **weak** they are!
Destroy its treasures;
plunder and loot.
38 Bring a drought on its land
and dry up its rivers.
Babylonia is a land of **terrifying idols**,
that have made **fools** of the people.

39 "And so Babylon will be haunted by
demons and evil spirits,[t] and by **unclean**
birds. **Never again** will people live there,
not for all time to come. 40 The same
thing will happen to Babylon as happened to Sodom and Gomorrah, when I
destroyed them and the near-by towns.
No one will ever live there again. I, the
LORD, have spoken.

41 "People are coming from a country in
the north,
a **mighty** nation far away;
many kings are preparing for war.
42 They have taken their bows and
swords;
they are **cruel** and **merciless**.
They sound like the roaring sea,
as they ride their horses.
They are ready for battle against
Babylonia.
43 The king of Babylonia hears the news,
and his hands hang limp.
He is seized by **anguish**,
by **pain** like a woman in labour.

44 "Like a lion coming out of the thick
woods along the Jordan up to the green
pasture land, I, the LORD, will come and
make the Babylonians run away suddenly from their city. Then the leader I
choose will rule the nation. Who can be
compared to me? Who would **dare
challenge** me? What ruler could oppose
me? 45 So listen to the **plan** that I have
made against the city of Babylon and to
what I **intend** to do to its people. Even
their children will be dragged off, and
everyone will be **horrified**. 46 When
Babylon falls, there will be such a noise
that the entire earth will shake, and the
cries of alarm will be heard by the other
nations."

Further Judgement on Babylonia

51 The LORD says, "I am bringing a
destructive wind[u] against Babylonia and its people. 2 I will send
foreigners to **destroy** Babylonia like a
wind that blows straw away. When that
day of **destruction** comes, they will
attack from every side and leave the
land bare. 3 Don't give its soldiers time to
shoot their arrows or to put on their armour. Do not **spare** the young men! **Destroy** the whole army! 4 They will be
wounded and die in the streets of their
cities. 5 I, the LORD God **Almighty**, have
not **abandoned** Israel and Judah, even
though they have sinned against me, the
Holy One of Israel. 6 Run away from
Babylonia! Run for your **lives**! Do not be
killed because of Babylonia's sin. I am
now taking my **revenge** and **punishing** it
as it **deserves**. 7 Babylonia was like a gold
cup in my hand, making the whole **world**
drunk. The nations drank its wine and
went out of their **minds**. 8 Babylonia has
suddenly fallen and is **destroyed**! **Mourn**
over it! Get medicine for its wounds, and
perhaps it can be **healed**. 9 Foreigners
living there said, 'We tried to **help**
Babylonia, but it was too late. Let's leave
her now and go back home. God has **punished** Babylonia with all his **might** and
has **destroyed** it completely.' "

10 The LORD says, "**My people** shout,
'The LORD has shown that we are in the
right. Let's go and tell the people in
Jerusalem what the LORD our God has
done.' "

11 The LORD has stirred up the kings
of Media, because he **intends** to **destroy**
Babylonia. That is how he will take **revenge** for the **destruction** of his **Temple**.

The attacking officers **command**,
"Sharpen your arrows! Get your shields
ready! 12 Give the signal to attack
Babylon's walls. **Strengthen** the guard!
Post the sentries! Place men in am-
bush!"

The LORD has done what he said he
would do to the people of Babylonia.
13 That country has many rivers and **rich**
treasures, but its time is up, and its
thread of **life** is cut. 14 The LORD **Almighty**
has **sworn** by his own **life** that he will

abandon 25.38; Lam 1.13
afraid 50.16; Lam 3.57
Almighty [6] 50.18; Ezek 1.24
anger 50.13; 52.3
ash 6.26; 52.18
ashamed 31.19; Ezek 16.54
cause (2) 50.34; Acts 26.9
choose 50.44; Lam 4.20
cloud 10.13; Lam 3.44
command [2] 50.21; 52.25
control 49.28; Ezek 1.20
courage [2] 38.4; Lam 1.16
create 31.22; Ezek 21.30
creature Is 42.10; Ezek 1.5
cup 49.12; Ezek 4.11
death (1) [3] 50.35; Lam 1.20
deserve [2] 49.12; Ezek 13.19
despise 18.16; Ezek 2.6
destroy [18] 50.21; Lam 1.15
disgrace 50.12; Lam 2.2
enemy [4] 50.7; Lam 1.3
escape 50.28; 52.7
evil [2] 50.39; Lam 3.38
false 23.16; Ezek 12.24
feast 33.11; Ezek 39.17
flock 49.29; Ezek 34.17
god (2) (other gods) [2] 50.2; Ezek 8.14
God's people [3] 50.6; Lam 1.15
greed Is 57.17; Ezek 33.31
groan 45.3; Lam 1.4
happy 50.11; Lam 3.17
heal 46.11; Ezek 30.21
heaven 44.17; Lam 2.1
help 50.32; Lam 1.7
helpless 48.45; Lam 1.3
holy [2] 50.29; Lam 1.4
horror [3] 50.45; Lam 4.10
idol [3] 50.2; Ezek 6.3
intend 50.45; Ezek 13.14
joy 48.33; Lam 2.4
lamb 11.19; Ezek 27.21
life (1) [4] 50.20; 52.33
might [2] 50.41; Ezek 17.9

[t] demons and evil spirits; *or* wildcats and jackals.
[u] destructive wind; *or* destroying spirit.

50.39: Rev 18.2 **50.40:** Gen 19.24–25 **51.7:** Rev 17.2–4, 18.3 **51.9:** Rev 18.5 **51.13:** Rev 17.1

bring many men to attack Babylonia like a swarm of locusts, and they will shout with **victory**.

A Hymn of Praise to God

15 The LORD made the earth by his
power;
by his **wisdom** he **created** the **world**
and stretched out the **heavens**.
16 At his **command** the waters above the
sky[v] roar;
he brings **clouds** from the ends of
the earth.
He makes lightning flash in the rain
and sends the wind from his
storeroom.
17 At the **sight** of this, men feel **stupid** and
senseless;
those who make **idols** are
disillusioned
because the **gods** they make are
false and lifeless.
18 They are **worthless** and should be
despised;
they will be **destroyed** when the
LORD comes to deal with them.
19 The God of Jacob is not like them;
he is the one who made everything,
and he has **chosen** Israel to be his
very **own people**.
The LORD **Almighty** is his **name**.

The LORD's Hammer

20 The LORD says,
"Babylonia, you are my hammer, my
weapon of war.
I used you to crush nations and
kingdoms,
21 to shatter horses and riders,
to shatter chariots and their drivers,
22 to kill men and women,
to slay old and young,
to kill boys and girls,
23 to **slaughter shepherds** and their
flocks,
to **slaughter** ploughmen and their
horses,
to crush rulers and high officials."

Babylonia's Punishment

24 The LORD says, "You will see me
repay Babylonia and its people for all the
evil they did to Jerusalem. 25 Babylonia,
you are like a mountain that **destroys** the
whole **world**, but I, the LORD, am your
enemy. I will take hold of you, level you
to the ground, and leave you in **ashes**.
26 None of the stones from your **ruins** will
ever be used again for building. You will
be like a desert for ever. I, the LORD,
have spoken.
27 "Give the signal to attack! Blow
the trumpet so that the nations can hear!
Prepare the nations for war against
Babylonia! Tell the kingdoms of Ararat,
Minni, and Ashkenaz to attack. Appoint
an officer to lead the attack. Bring up the
horses like a swarm of locusts. 28 Prepare
the nations for war against Babylonia.
Send for the kings of Media, their leaders
and officials, and the armies of all the
countries they **control**. 29 The earth
trembles and shakes because the LORD is
carrying out his **plan** to make Babylonia
a desert, where no one lives. 30 The
Babylonian soldiers have stopped fighting and remain in their forts. They have
lost their **courage** and have become like
women. The city gates are broken down,
and the houses are on fire. 31 Messenger
after messenger runs to tell the king of
Babylonia that his city has been broken
into from every side. 32 The **enemy** have
captured the river-crossing and have set
the fortresses on fire. The Babylonian
soldiers have panicked. 33 Soon the
enemy will cut them down and trample
them like corn on a threshing-place. I,
the LORD **Almighty**, the God of Israel,
have spoken."
34 The king of Babylonia cut Jerusalem
up
and ate it.
He emptied the city like a jar;
like a **monster** he swallowed it.
He took what he wanted
and threw the rest away.
35 Let the people of Zion say,
"May Babylonia be held responsible
for the **violence** done to us!"
Let the people of Jerusalem say,
"May Babylonia be held responsible
for what we have **suffered**!"

The LORD Will Help Israel

36 And so the LORD said to the people
of Jerusalem, "I will take up your **cause**
and will make your **enemies** pay for
what they did to you. I will dry up the
source of Babylonia's water and make its
rivers go dry. 37 That country will become a pile of **ruins** where wild animals
live. It will be a **horrible sight**; no one
will live there, and all who see it will be
terrified. 38 The Babylonians all roar like
lions and growl like lion cubs. 39 Are they
greedy? I will prepare them a **feast** and
make them drunk and **happy**. They will
go to sleep and never wake up. 40 I will
take them to be **slaughtered**, like **lambs**,
goats, and rams. I, the LORD, have
spoken."

[v] WATERS ABOVE THE SKY: *See Gen 1.6–8.*

Babylon's Fate

41 The LORD says about Babylon:
"The city that the whole **world praised**
has been captured! What a **horrifying**
sight Babylon has become to the nations!
42 The sea has rolled over Babylon and
covered it with roaring waves. 43 The
towns have become a **horrifying sight**
and are like a waterless desert, where no
one lives or even travels. 44 I will **punish**
Bel, the **god of Babylonia**, and make him
give up his **stolen** goods; the nations will
not **worship** him any more.
"Babylon's walls have fallen. 45 People
of Israel, run away from there! Run for
your **life** from my fierce **anger**. 46 Do not
lose **courage** or be **afraid** because of the
rumours you hear. Every year a different
rumour spreads—rumours of **violence** in
the land and of one king fighting another.
47 And so the time is coming when I will
deal with Babylonia's **idols**. The whole
country will be put to **shame**, and all its
people will be killed. 48 Everything on
earth and in the sky will shout for **joy**
when Babylonia falls to the people who
come from the north to **destroy** it.
49 Babylonia caused the **death** of people
all over the **world**, and now Babylonia
will fall because it caused the **death** of so
many Israelites. I, the LORD, have
spoken."

God's Message to the Israelites in Babylonia

50 The LORD says to **his people** in
Babylonia: "You have **escaped death**!
Now go! Don't wait! Though you are far
from home, think about me, your LORD,
and **remember** Jerusalem. 51 You say,
'We've been **disgraced** and made
ashamed; we feel completely **helpless**
because foreigners have taken over the
holy places in the **Temple**.' 52 So then, I
say that the time is coming when I will
deal with Babylon's **idols**, and the
wounded will **groan** throughout the
country. 53 Even if Babylon could climb to
the sky and build a **strong** fortress there,
I would still send people to **destroy** it. I,
the LORD, have spoken."

Further Destruction of Babylon

54 The LORD says,
"Listen to the sound of crying in
Babylon,
of **mourning** for the **destruction** in
the land.
55 I am **destroying** Babylon
and putting it to silence.
The armies rush in like roaring waves
and attack with noisy shouts.
56 They have come to **destroy** Babylon;
its soldiers are captured,
and their bows are broken.
I am a God who **punishes evil**,
and I will treat Babylon as it
deserves.
57 I will make its rulers drunk—
men of **wisdom**, leaders, and
soldiers.
They will go to sleep and never wake
up.
I, the king, have spoken,
I am the LORD **Almighty**.
58 The walls of **mighty** Babylon will be
thrown to the ground,
and its towering gates burnt down.
The work of the nations is all for
nothing;
their efforts go up in flames.
I, the LORD **Almighty**, have spoken."

Jeremiah's Message Is Sent to Babylonia

59 King Zedekiah's personal attendant
was Seraiah, the son of Neriah and
grandson of Mahseiah. In the fourth year
that Zedekiah was king of Judah, Seraiah
was going to Babylonia with him, and I
gave him some instructions. 60 I wrote in
a book an account of all the **destruction**
that would come on Babylonia, as well as
all these other things about Babylonia.
61 I told Seraiah, "When you get to
Babylon, be **sure** to read aloud to the
people everything that is written here.
62 Then **pray**, 'LORD, you have said that
you would **destroy** this place, so that
there would be no living **creature** in it,
neither man nor animal, and it would be
like a desert for ever.' 63 Seraiah, when
you finish reading this book to the
people, then tie it to a stone and throw it
into the River Euphrates, 64 and say, 'This
is what will happen to Babylonia—it will
sink and never **rise** again, because of the
destruction that the LORD is going to
bring on it.' "[w]
The **words** of Jeremiah end here.

The Fall of Jerusalem
(2 Kgs 24.18—25.7)

52 Zedekiah was twenty-one years
old when he became king of
Judah, and he ruled in Jerusalem for
eleven years. His mother's name was
Hamutal, the daughter of the Jeremiah
who lived in the city of Libnah. 2 King
Zedekiah sinned against the LORD, just as
King Jehoiakim had done. 3 The LORD became so **angry** with the people of

altar 32.35; Lam 2.7
anger 51.45; Lam 1.12
ash [2] 51.25; Ezek 27.30
bad 49.23; Ezek 7.26
blood [2] 46.10; Lam 4.14
change 34.11; Ezek 3.18
clean 43.12; Ezek 22.26

[w] *One ancient translation* on it; *Hebrew* on it and they will become tired out.

51.48: Rev 18.20 **51.49:** Rev 18.24 **51.63–64:** Rev 18.21

command 51.11; Lam 3.38
death (3) (to death) [2] 39.6; Lam 2.19
escape 51.50; Lam 1.3
execute 39.6; Dan 2.12
exile [2] 49.3; Lam 2.9
famine 21.7; Ezek 6.11
flee 49.24; Lam 1.6
High Priest Neh 13.28; Dan 11.22
honour 48.18; Lam 1.1
important [3] 50.12; Ezek 17.13
incense [2] 41.5; Ezek 6.4
kind [2] 24.5; Joel 2.13
life (1) 51.6; Lam 3.58
need 40.9; Lam 2.14
offer 48.35; Ezek 16.18
permit 7.21; Ezek 40.46
poor 40.7; Ezek 16.49
priest 49.3; Lam 1.4
prison [6] 48.46; Lam 3.5
rebel 48.26; Lam 3.42
reign 1.3; Dan 6.28
sacrifice [2] 48.35; Ezek 6.13
sentence 39.5; Ezek 4.4
service Job 38.35; Ezek 29.20
sight 51.17; Ezek 32.31
Temple (1) (of God) [5] 51.11; Lam 1.4
vineyard 39.10; Ezek 28.26

Jerusalem and Judah that he banished them from his **sight**.

Zedekiah **rebelled** against King Nebuchadnezzar of Babylonia, 4 and so Nebuchadnezzar came with all his army and attacked Jerusalem on the tenth day of the tenth month of the ninth year of Zedekiah's **reign**. They set up camp outside the city, built siege walls round it, 5 and kept it under siege until Zedekiah's eleventh year. 6 On the ninth day of the fourth month of that same year, when the **famine** was so **bad** that the people had nothing left to eat, 7 the city walls were broken through. Although the Babylonians were surrounding the city, all the soldiers **escaped** during the night. They left by way of the royal garden, went through the gateway connecting the two walls, and **fled** in the direction of the Jordan Valley. 8 But the Babylonian army pursued King Zedekiah, captured him in the plains near Jericho, and all his soldiers deserted him. 9 Zedekiah was taken to King Nebuchadnezzar, who was in the city of Riblah in the territory of Hamath, and there Nebuchadnezzar passed **sentence** on him. 10 At Riblah he put Zedekiah's sons **to death** while Zedekiah was looking on and he also had the officials of Judah **executed**. 11 After that, he had Zedekiah's eyes put out and had him placed in chains and taken to Babylon. Zedekiah remained in **prison** in Babylon until the day he died.

The Destruction of the Temple
(2 Kgs 25.8–17)

12 On the tenth day of the fifth month of the nineteenth year of King Nebuchadnezzar of Babylonia, Nebuzaradan, adviser to the king and commander of his army, entered Jerusalem. 13 He burnt down the **Temple**, the palace, and the houses of all the **important** people in Jerusalem; 14 and his soldiers tore down the city walls. 15 Then Nebuzaradan took away to Babylonia[x] the people who were left in the city, the remaining skilled workmen, and those who had deserted to the Babylonians. 16 But he left in Judah some of the **poorest** people, who owned no property, and he put them to work in the **vineyards** and fields.

17 The Babylonians broke in pieces the bronze columns and the carts that were in the **Temple**, together with the large bronze tank, and they took all the bronze to Babylon. 18 They also took away the shovels and the **ash** containers used in **cleaning** the **altar**, the tools used in tending the lamps, the bowls used for catching the **blood** from the **sacrifices**, the bowls used for burning **incense**, and all the other bronze articles used in the **temple service**. 19 They took away everything that was made of gold or silver: the small bowls, the pans used for carrying live coals, the bowls for holding the **blood** from the **sacrifices**, the **ash** containers, the lampstands, the bowls used for **incense**, and the bowls used for pouring out **offerings** of wine. 20 The bronze objects that King Solomon had made for the **Temple**—the two columns, the carts, the large tank, and the twelve bulls that supported it—were too heavy to weigh. 21-22 The two columns were identical: each one was 8 metres high and 5.3 metres round. They were hollow, and the metal was 75 millimetres thick. On top of each column was a bronze capital 2.2 metres high, and all round it was a grating decorated with pomegranates, all of which was also made of bronze. 23 On the grating of each column there were a hundred pomegranates in all, and ninety-six of these were visible from the ground.

The People of Judah Are Taken to Babylonia
(2 Kgs 25.18–21, 27–30)

24 In addition, Nebuzaradan, the commanding officer, took away as **prisoners** Seraiah the **High Priest**, Zephaniah the **priest** next in rank, and the three other **important temple** officials. 25 From the city he took the officer who had been in **command** of the troops, seven of the king's personal advisers who were still in the city, the commander's assistant, who was in charge of military records, and sixty other **important** men. 26 Nebuzaradan took them to the king of Babylonia, who was in the city of Riblah 27 in the territory of Hamath. There the king had them beaten and put **to death**.

So the people of Judah were carried away from their land into **exile**. 28 This is the record of the people that Nebuchadnezzar took away as **prisoners**: in his seventh year as king he carried away 3,023; 29 in his eighteenth year, 832 from Jerusalem; 30 and in his twenty-third year, 745—taken away by Nebuzaradan. In all, 4,600 people were taken away.

31 In the year that Evilmerodach became king of Babylonia, he showed **kindness** to King Jehoiachin of Judah by releasing him from **prison**. This happened on the twenty-fifth day of the

[x] *Probable text* Babylonia; *Hebrew* Babylonia some of the poorest of the people.

52.4: Ezek 24.2 **52.7:** Ezek 33.21 **52.11:** Ezek 12.13 **52.13:** 1 Kgs 9.8 **52.17–23:** 1 Kgs 7.15–47

twelfth month of the thirty-seventh year
after Jehoiachin had been taken away as
a **prisoner**. 32 Evilmerodach treated him
kindly and gave him a position of greater
honour than he gave the other kings who
were **exiles** with him in Babylonia. 33 So
Jehoiachin was **permitted** to **change**
from his **prison** clothes and to dine at the
king's table for the rest of his **life**. 34 Each
day for as long as he lived, he was given
a regular allowance for his **needs**.

LAMENTATIONS

INTRODUCTION

The book of *Lamentations* is a collection of five poems lamenting the destruction of Jerusalem in 586 B.C., and its aftermath of ruin and exile. In spite of the mournful nature of most of the book, there is also the note of trust in God and hope for the future. These poems are used by the Jews in worship on the annual days of fasting and mourning which commemorate the national disaster of 586 B.C.

Outline of Contents

The sorrows of Jerusalem 1.1–22
The punishment of Jerusalem 2.1–22
Punishment and hope 3.1–66
Jerusalem in ruins 4.1–22
A prayer for mercy 5.1–22

The Sorrows of Jerusalem

1 How **lonely** lies Jerusalem, once so
full of people!
Once **honoured** by the **world**, she is
now like a **widow**;
The noblest of cities has fallen into
slavery.

2 All night long she cries; **tears** run
down her cheeks.
Of all her former **friends**, not one is
left to **comfort** her.
Her allies have **betrayed** her and all
are now against her.

3 Judah's people are **helpless slaves**,
forced away from home.[a]
They live in other lands, with no
place to call their own—
Surrounded by **enemies**, with no way
to **escape**.

4 No one comes to the **Temple** now to
worship on the **holy** days.
The girls who sang there **suffer**, and
the **priests** can only **groan**.
The city gates stand empty, and
Zion is in agony.

5 Her **enemies succeeded**; they hold her
in their **power**.
The LORD has made her **suffer** for
all her many sins;
Her children have been captured
and taken away.

6 The **splendour** of Jerusalem is a thing
of the past.
Her leaders are like deer that are
weak from **hunger**,
Whose **strength** is almost gone as
they **flee** from the hunters.

7 A **lonely ruin** now, Jerusalem recalls
her **ancient splendour**.
When she fell to the **enemy**, there
was no one to **help** her;
Her **conquerors** laughed at her
downfall.

8 Her **honour** is gone; she is **naked** and
held in **contempt**.
She **groans** and hides her face in
shame.
Jerusalem made herself **filthy** with
terrible sin.

9 Her **uncleanness** was easily seen, but
she showed no **concern** for her
fate.
Her **downfall** was **terrible**; no one
can **comfort** her.
Her **enemies** have **won**, and she
cries to the LORD for **mercy**.

10 Her **enemies robbed** her of all her
treasures.
She saw them enter the **Temple**
itself,
Where the LORD had **forbidden**
Gentiles to go.

11 Her people **groan** as they look for
something to eat;
They exchange their treasures for
food to keep themselves **alive**.

[a] are helpless...home; *or* fled from home, from the misery of slavery.

abandon Jer 51.5; 2.1
above Is 24.21; Ezek 1.22
alive [2] Jer 29.22; 3.53
ancient Jer 30.20; 5.21
anger Jer 52.3; 2.1
anguish Jer 50.43; 2.11
betray Jer 12.6; Ezek 37.23
captive Jer 13.17; Ezek 12.11
comfort [4] Jer 31.13; 2.13
concern Jer 29.10; 4.16
condemn Jer 22.30; Ezek 16.38
conquer [2] Jer 50.9; Ezek 25.4
constant Jer 32.18; Ezek 35.5
contempt Jer 33.24; Ezek 35.12
courage Jer 51.30; Ezek 21.7
death (1) Jer 51.49; 2.19
destroy Jer 51.1; 2.2
disaster Jer 49.32; 2.13
disobey Jer 43.7; Ezek 5.6
downfall [2] Jer 20.10; 2.17
enemy [9] Jer 51.25; 2.3
escape Jer 52.7; 2.22
fate Jer 29.23; Ezek 23.10
filthy [2] Is 64.6; Ezek 11.18
flee Jer 52.7; Ezek 29.12
forbid Is 52.11; Ezek 4.13
force (1) Jer 34.11; 2.6
friend Jer 38.22; Dan 1.11
Gentile Neh 5.9; Mt 4.15
glad Jer 50.11; 4.21

God's people [2] Jer 51.10; 2.11
groan [5] Jer 51.52; Ezek 2.10
heart [2] Jer 48.10; 2.19
help [3] Jer 51.9; 2.3
helpless [2] Jer 51.51; Ezek 38.11
holy Jer 51.5; 2.6
honour [2] Jer 52.32; Ezek 16.60
hunger Jer 42.13; 2.12
jeer Jer 49.13; 3.63
justice Jer 33.15; 3.36
lonely [2] Is 54.4; 5.1
mercy Jer 50.42; 2.2
misery [2] Jer 49.24; 3.5
naked Is 47.3; 4.21
pain [4] Jer 50.43; 3.19
power Jer 51.15; 5.8
priest [2] Jer 52.24; 2.6
promise Jer 48.40; Ezek 16.8
punish Jer 51.6; 3.1
refuse (1) Jer 44.16; 2.3
rob Jer 49.9; Ezek 7.21
ruin Jer 51.26; 2.1
shame Jer 51.47; 4.2
slave [2] Jer 34.9; 5.8
sorrow Jer 47.5; 2.5
soul Prov 24.14; 2.11
splendour [2] Jer 48.2; 2.1
strength Jer 51.12; 2.3
strong Jer 51.53; 3.3
succeed (1) Jer 32.5; Ezek 17.15
suffer [3] Jer 51.35; 2.13
tear (2) [2] Jer 31.16; 2.18
Temple (1) (of God) [2] Jer 52.13; 2.1
terrible [2] Jer 49.17; Ezek 9.9
trap Jer 50.24; 3.52
unclean Jer 50.39; Ezek 4.14

"Look at me, LORD," the city cries;
"see me in my **misery**."

12 "Look at me!" she cries to everyone
who passes by.[b]
"No one has ever had **pain** like
mine,
Pain that the LORD brought on me in
the time of his **anger**.

13 "He sent fire from **above**, a fire that
burnt inside me.
He set a **trap** for me and brought me
to the ground.
Then he **abandoned** me and left me
in **constant pain**.

14 "He took note of all my sins and tied
them all together;
He hung them round my neck, and I
grew **weak** beneath the weight.
The Lord gave me to my foes, and I
was **helpless** against them.

15 "The Lord **jeered** at all my **strongest**
soldiers;
He sent an army to **destroy** my
young men.
He crushed **my people** like grapes in
a winepress.

16 "That is why my eyes are overflowing
with **tears**.
No one can **comfort** me; no one can
give me **courage**.
The **enemy** has **conquered** me; **my**
people have nothing left.

17 "I stretch out my hands, but no one
will **help** me.
The LORD has called **enemies**
against me from every side;
They treat me like some **filthy** thing.

18 "But the LORD is **just**, for I have
disobeyed him.
Listen to me, people everywhere;
look at me in my **pain**.
My young men and women have
been taken away **captive**.

19 "I called to my allies, but they **refused**
to **help** me.
The **priests** and the leaders died in
the city streets,
Looking for food to keep themselves
alive.

20 "Look, O LORD, at my agony, at the
anguish of my **soul**!
My **heart** is broken in **sorrow** for my
sins.
There is murder in the streets; even
indoors there is **death**.

21 "Listen[c] to my **groans**; there is no one
to **comfort** me.
My **enemies** are **glad** that you
brought **disaster** on me.
Bring[d] the day you **promised**; make
my **enemies suffer** as I do.

22 "**Condemn** them for all their
wickedness;
Punish them as you punished me for
my sins.
I **groan** in **misery**, and I am sick at
heart."

The LORD's Punishment of Jerusalem

2 The Lord in his **anger** has covered
Zion with **darkness**.
Its **heavenly splendour** he has
turned into **ruins**.
On the day of his **anger** he
abandoned even his **Temple**.

2 The Lord **destroyed** without **mercy**
every village in Judah
And tore down the forts that
defended the land.
He brought **disgrace** on the kingdom
and its rulers.

3 In his **fury** he shattered the **strength** of
Israel;
He **refused** to **help** us when the
enemy came.
He **raged** against us like fire,
destroying everything.

4 He aimed his arrows at us like an
enemy;
He killed all those who were our **joy**
and **delight**.
Here in Jerusalem we felt his
burning anger.

5 Like an **enemy**, the Lord has **destroyed**
Israel;
He has left her forts and palaces in
ruins.
He has brought on the people of
Judah unending **sorrow**.

6 He smashed to pieces the **Temple**
where we **worshipped** him;
He has put an end to **holy** days and
Sabbaths.

[b] Look...by; *or* May this not happen to you that pass by; *or* Does this mean nothing to you that pass by? [c] *One ancient translation* Listen; *Hebrew* They listened.
[d] *One ancient translation* Bring; *Hebrew* You brought.

prophet [3] Jer 50.36; 4.13
proud Jer 50.29; 5.16
rage Jer 30.23; Ezek 5.13
refuse (1) 1.19; 3.8
reject Jer 33.24; 3.31
repent Is 66.2; Ezek 18.23
ruin [4] 1.7; 3.47
Sabbath Jer 17.21; Ezek 20.12
sackcloth Jer 49.3; Ezek 7.18
scorn Jer 44.8; Ezek 23.32
slaughter Jer 51.23; Ezek 6.8
sneer Ps 44.16; Ezek 5.14
sorrow 1.20; 3.32
soul 1.20; Mt 10.28
splendour 1.6; Ezek 7.11
strength 1.6; Ezek 17.9
suffer 1.4; 3.15
sure Jer 51.61; 3.23
teach Jer 32.23; Ezek 7.26
tear (2) 1.2; 3.48
Temple (1) (of God) [4] 1.4; 4.1
terror Jer 49.5; Ezek 30.2
threat Jer 40.2; Ezek 6.10
turn Jer 49.8; 3.9
victory [2] Jer 51.14; Ezek 39.13
vision Jer 38.21; Ezek 1.1
warn Jer 49.30; Ezek 3.17
weep [2] Jer 50.4; Ezek 8.14
world 1.1; 3.45
worship (1) (of God) [2] 1.4; Ezek 7.24

King and **priest** alike have felt the
force of his **anger**.

7 The Lord **rejected** his **altar** and
deserted his **holy Temple**;
He allowed the **enemy** to tear down
its walls.
They shouted in **victory** where once
we had **worshipped** in **joy**.

8 The LORD was **determined** that the
walls of Zion should fall;
He measured them off to make **sure**
of total **destruction**.
The towers and walls now lie in
ruins together.

9 The gates lie buried in rubble, their
bars smashed to pieces.
The king and the **noblemen** now are
in **exile**.
The **Law** is no longer **taught**, and the
prophets have no **visions** from the
LORD.

10 Jerusalem's old men sit on the ground
in silence,
With dust on their heads and
sackcloth on their **bodies**.
Young girls **bow** their heads to the
ground.

11 My eyes are worn out with **weeping**;
my **soul** is in **anguish**.
I am exhausted with **grief** at the
destruction of my people.
Children and babies are fainting in
the streets of the city.

12 **Hungry** and thirsty, they cry to their
mothers;
They fall in the streets as though
they were wounded,
And slowly die in their mothers'
arms.

13 O Jerusalem, **beloved** Jerusalem, what
can I say?
How can I **comfort** you? No one has
ever **suffered** like this.
Your **disaster** is boundless as the
ocean; there is no possible **hope**.

14 Your **prophets** had nothing to tell you
but **lies**;
Their **preaching deceived** you by
never exposing your sin.
They made you think you did not
need to repent.

15 People passing by the city look at you
in **scorn**.
They shake their heads and laugh at
the **ruins** of Jerusalem.
"Is this that lovely city? Is this the
pride of the world?"

16 All your **enemies mock** you and glare
at you with **hate**.
They curl their lips and **sneer**, "We
have **destroyed** it!
This is the day we have waited for!"

17 The LORD has finally done what he
threatened to do:
He has **destroyed** us without **mercy**,
as he **warned** us long ago.
He gave our **enemies victory**, gave
them **joy** at our **downfall**.

18 O Jerusalem, let your very walls cry
out to the Lord! [e]
Let your **tears** flow like rivers night
and day;
Wear yourself out with **weeping** and
grief!

19 All through the night get up again and
again to cry out to the Lord;
Pour out your **heart** and **beg** him for
mercy on your children—
Children starving **to death** on every
street corner!

20 Look, O LORD! Look at those you are
torturing!
Women are eating the **bodies** of the
children they **loved**!
Priests and **prophets** are being killed
in the **Temple** itself!

21 Young and old alike lie **dead** in the
streets,
Young men and women, killed by
enemy swords.
You **slaughtered** them without
mercy on the day of your **anger**.

22 You invited my **enemies** to hold a
carnival of **terror** all round me,
And no one could **escape** on that day
of your **anger**.
They murdered my children, whom
I had reared and **loved**.

Punishment, Repentance, and Hope

3 I am one who knows what it is to be
punished by God.
2 He drove me deeper and deeper into
darkness

accept Jer 12.16; Ezek 20.41
afraid Jer 51.46; Ezek 2.6
alive 1.11; 4.9

[e] *Probable text* O Jerusalem...Lord; *Hebrew* Their hearts cried out to the Lord, O wall of Jerusalem.

3 And beat me again and again with
merciless blows.

4 He has left my **flesh** open and raw, and
has broken my bones.
5 He has shut me in a **prison** of **misery**
and **anguish**.
6 He has **forced** me to live in the
stagnant **darkness** of **death**.

7 He has **bound** me in chains; I am a
prisoner with no **hope** of **escape**.
8 I cry aloud for **help**, but God **refuses**
to listen;
9 I stagger as I walk; stone walls
block me wherever I **turn**.

10 He waited for me like a bear; he
pounced on me like a lion.
11 He chased me off the road, tore me
to pieces, and left me.
12 He drew his bow and made me the
target for his arrows.

13 He shot his arrows deep into my **body**.
14 People laugh at me all day long; I
am a joke to them all.
15 **Bitter suffering** is all he has given
me for food and drink.

16 He rubbed my face in the ground and
broke my teeth on the gravel.
17 I have **forgotten** what health and
peace and **happiness** are.
18 I have not much longer to live; my
hope in the LORD is gone.

19 The thought of my **pain**, my
homelessness, is **bitter** poison;
20 I think of it constantly and my **spirit**
is depressed.
21 Yet **hope** returns when I **remember**
this one thing:

22 The LORD's unfailing **love** and **mercy**
still continue,
23 Fresh as the morning, as **sure** as the
sunrise.
24 The LORD is all I have, and so I put
my **hope** in him.

25 The LORD is good to everyone who
trusts in him,
26 So it is **best** for us to wait in
patience—to wait for him to **save**
us—
27 And it is **best** to **learn** this **patience**
in our youth.

28 When we **suffer**, we should sit **alone** in
silent **patience**;
29 We should **bow** in **submission**, for
there may still be **hope**.
30 Though beaten and **insulted**, we
should **accept** it all.

31 The Lord is **merciful** and will not
reject us for ever.
32 He may bring us **sorrow**, but his **love**
for us is **sure** and **strong**.
33 He takes no **pleasure** in causing us
grief or **pain**.

34 The Lord knows when our **spirits** are
crushed in **prison**;
35 He knows when we are **denied** the
rights he gave us;
36 When **justice** is **perverted** in **court**,
he knows.

37 The **will of the Lord alone** is always
carried out.[f]
38 Good and **evil** alike take place at his
command.
39 Why should we ever **complain** when
we are **punished** for our sin?[g]

40 Let us examine our **ways** and **turn**
back to the LORD.
41 Let us open our **hearts** to God in
heaven and **pray**,
42 "We have sinned and **rebelled**, and
you, O LORD, have not **forgiven** us.

43 "You pursued us and killed us; your
mercy was hidden by your **anger**,
44 By a **cloud** of **fury** too thick for our
prayers to get through.
45 You have made us the refuse heap
of the **world**.

46 "We are **insulted** and **mocked** by all
our **enemies**.
47 We have been through **disaster** and
ruin; we live in **danger** and **fear**.
48 My eyes flow with rivers of **tears** at
the **destruction** of **my people**.

49 "My **tears** will pour out in a ceaseless
stream
50 Until the LORD looks down from
heaven and sees us.
51 My **heart** is **grieved** when I see what
has happened to the women of the
city.

52 "I was **trapped** like a bird by **enemies**
who had no cause to **hate** me.

[f] The will...out; *or* No one can make anything happen unless the LORD is willing.
[g] Why should...sin; *or* Why should we complain about being punished for sin, as long as we are still alive?

alone [2] Jer 29.11; Ezek 9.8
anger 2.1; 5.22
anguish 2.11; Mt 26.37
beg 2.19; 4.4
best [2] Jer 38.22; Ezek 16.10
bind Is 52.2; Nah 1.13
bitter [2] Jer 47.2; Ezek 3.14
body 2.10; Ezek 1.9
bow (2) 2.10; Ezek 8.16
cloud Jer 51.16; Ezek 1.4
command Jer 52.25; Ezek 5.6
complain Jer 30.15; Ezek 20.49
court (1) Jer 38.7; Ezek 12.14
curse Jer 49.13; Dan 9.11
danger Jer 38.24; Ezek 3.20
dark [2] 2.1; Ezek 12.6
death (1) [2] 2.19; 4.8
deny Jer 5.12; Mt 26.70
despair Is 54.4; Ezek 4.17
destroy 2.2; Ezek 5.16
disaster 2.13; 4.10
enemy [3] 2.3; 4.18
escape 2.22; Ezek 6.8
evil Jer 51.24; Ezek 3.18
favour Jer 36.9; Ezek 16.19
fear Jer 49.16; Ezek 7.27
flesh Prov 5.11; Mic 3.2
force (1) 2.6; 4.11
forget Jer 50.6; Ezek 16.43
forgive Jer 50.20; Ezek 16.63
fury 2.3; 4.11
God's people 2.11; 4.3
grief [2] 2.11; 5.15
happy Jer 51.39; 5.15
hate [2] 2.16; Ezek 5.9
heart [2] 2.19; 5.17
heaven [2] 2.1; Ezek 3.12
help 2.3; 4.17
hope [5] 2.13; Ezek 7.27
insult [3] Jer 15.15; Ezek 8.17
jeer 1.15; Mt 27.41
judge Jer 49.7; Ezek 5.8
justice 1.18; Ezek 39.21
learn Jer 32.33; Ezek 19.6
life (1) Jer 52.33; 4.20
love [2] 2.13; 4.10
mercy [4] 2.2; Ezek 5.11
misery 1.11; Ezek 23.33
mock 2.16; Ezek 5.15
pain [2] 1.12; Ezek 5.16
patient [3] Jer 15.15; Hos 12.6
peace Jer 50.34; Ezek 7.25
pervert Jer 23.36; Hab 1.4
plan Jer 51.29; Ezek 11.2

pleasure Jer 32.41; Mic 7.18
plot (1) [2] Jer 49.30; Hos 7.3
pray Jer 51.62; Dan 2.18
prayer Is 65.1; Ezek 8.18
prison [3] Jer 52.11; Ezek 30.17
punish [3] 1.22; 4.6
rebel Jer 52.3; Ezek 2.3
refuse (1) 2.3; Ezek 5.6
reject 2.7; 5.22
remember Jer 51.50; 5.1
rescue Jer 50.34; Ezek 13.23
right (3) Jer 32.7; Dan 11.21
ruin 2.1; 5.18
save [2] Jer 46.28; 5.8
sorrow 2.5; Ezek 6.11
spirit (2) [2] Jer 50.39; Dan 4.8
strong 1.15; 4.7
submit Jer 27.8; 5.11
suffer [2] 2.13; 5.7
sure [2] 2.8; Ezek 14.16
tear (2) [2] 2.18; 5.17
trap 1.13; Ezek 12.13
trust Jer 50.7; 4.20
turn [2] 2.1; 4.11
way (3) Jer 36.3; Ezek 3.18
will (1) Jer 29.23; Ezek 14.1
world 2.15; Ezek 5.5
wrong Jer 50.7; Ezek 16.63

53 They threw me **alive** into a pit and
closed the opening with a stone.
54 Water began to close over me, and I
thought **death** was near.

55 "From the bottom of the pit, O LORD, I
cried out to you,
56 And when I **begged** you to listen to
my cry, you heard.
57 You answered me and told me not to
be **afraid**.

58 "You came to my **rescue**, Lord, and
saved my **life**.
59 **Judge** in my **favour**; you know the
wrongs done against me.
60 You know how my **enemies hate** me
and how they **plot** against me.

61 "You have heard them **insult** me, O
LORD; you know all their **plots**.
62 All day long they talk about me and
make their **plans**.
63 From morning till night they **jeer** at
me.

64 "**Punish** them for what they have done,
O LORD;
65 **Curse** them and fill them with
despair!
66 Hunt them down and wipe them off
the earth!"

Jerusalem after its Fall

4 Our glittering gold has grown dull;
the stones of the **Temple** lie
scattered in the streets.

2 Zion's young men were as precious to
us as gold,
but now they are treated like
common clay pots.

3 Even a mother wolf will nurse her
cubs,
but **my people** are like ostriches,
cruel to their young.

4 They let their babies die of **hunger** and
thirst;
children are **begging** for food that no
one will give them.

5 People who once ate the finest foods
die starving in the streets;
those **raised** in **luxury** are pawing
through refuse for food.

6 **My people** have been **punished** even
more than the inhabitants of
Sodom,
which met with a sudden **downfall** at
the hands of God.

7 Our princes[i] were **undefiled** and **pure**
as snow,
vigorous and **strong**, glowing with
health.

8 Now they lie unknown in the streets,
their faces blackened in **death**;
their skin, dry as wood, has
shrivelled on their bones.

9 Those who died in the war were better
off than those who died later,
who starved slowly **to death**, with no
food to keep them **alive**.

10 The **disaster** that came to **my people**
brought **horror**;
loving mothers boiled their own
children for food.

11 The LORD **turned** loose the full **force** of
his **fury**;
he lit a fire in Zion that burnt it to
the ground.

12 No one anywhere, not even rulers of
foreign nations,
believed that any invader could
enter Jerusalem's gates.

13 But it happened because her **prophets**
sinned and her **priests** were **guilty**
of causing the **death** of **innocent**
people.

14 Her leaders wandered through the
streets like **blind** men,
so stained with **blood** that no one
would touch them.

15 "Go away!" people shouted. "You're
defiled! Don't touch me!"
So they wandered from nation to
nation, **welcomed** by no one.

16 The LORD had no more **concern** for
them; he **scattered** them himself.
He showed no regard for our **priests**
and leaders.

17 We looked until we could look no
longer for **help** that never came.
We kept waiting for **help** from a
nation that had none to give.

18 The **enemy** was **watching** for us; we
could not even walk in the streets.

[i] princes *or* Nazirites.

4.6: Gen 19.24 **4.10:** Deut 28.57; Ezek 5.10

alive 3.53; 5.6
beg 3.56; 5.6
believe Jer 40.14; Ezek 13.19
blind Jer 31.8; Zeph 1.17
blood Jer 52.18; Ezek 16.6
choose Jer 51.19; Ezek 20.5
concern 1.9; Ezek 36.21
cruel Jer 50.42; Ezek 25.12
death (1) [3] 3.6; Ezek 3.18
death (3) (to death) 2.19; Ezek 6.12
defile [2] Jer 32.34; Ezek 4.14
disaster [2] 3.47; Ezek 7.5
downfall 2.17; Ezek 31.16
enemy 3.46; 5.3
exile 2.9; Ezek 1.1
force (1) 3.6; 5.11
fury 3.44; Ezek 5.15
glad 1.21; Ezek 25.4
God's people [3] 3.48; Ezek 11.20
guilty [2] Jer 29.23; Ezek 4.4
help [2] 3.8; Ezek 17.17
horror Jer 51.37; Dan 7.7
hunger 2.12; 5.10
innocent Jer 26.15; Ezek 16.51

life (1) 3.58; 5.9
love 3.22; Ezek 11.21
luxury Prov 21.17; Ezek 26.12
naked 1.8; Ezek 16.7
priest [2] 2.6; Ezek 1.1
prophet 2.9; Ezek 2.
protect Jer 49.31; Ezek 11.3
punish [2] 3.1; Ezek 4.4
pure Jer 33.8; Ezek 16.52
raise Jer 50.15; Ezek 1.11
scatter [2] Jer 50.17; Ezek 4.13
shame 1.8; Ezek 16.30
source Jer 51.36; Ezek 47.11
strong 3.32; Ezek 7.24
Temple (1) (of God) 2.1; Ezek 5.11
trust 3.25; Ezek 22.6
turn 3.9; Ezek 1.9
watch Jer 31.6; Ezek 3.17
welcome Is 65.2; Ezek 32.21

Our days were over; the end had
come.

19 Swifter than eagles swooping from the
sky, they chased us down.
They tracked us down in the hills;
they took us by surprise in the
desert.

20 They captured the **source** of our **life**,
the king the LORD had **chosen**,
the one we had **trusted** to **protect** us
from every invader.

21 Laugh on, people of Edom and Uz; be
glad while you can.
Your **disaster** is coming too; you too
will stagger **naked** in **shame**.

22 Zion has paid for her sin; the LORD will
not keep us in **exile** any longer.
But Edom, the LORD will **punish** you;
he will expose your **guilty** deeds.

A Prayer for Mercy

5 **Remember**, O LORD, what has
happened to us.
Look at us, and see our **disgrace**.

2 Our property is in the hands of
strangers;
foreigners are living in our homes.

3 Our fathers have been killed by the
enemy,
and now our mothers are **widows**.

4 We must pay for the water we drink;
we must buy the wood we **need** for
fuel.

5 Driven **hard** like donkeys or camels,
we are tired, but are allowed no **rest**.

6 To get food **enough** to stay **alive**,
we went **begging** to Egypt and
Assyria.

7 Our ancestors sinned, but now they are
gone,
and we are **suffering** for their sins.

8 We are ruled by men who are no
better than **slaves**,
and no one can **save** us from their
power.

9 Murderers roam through the
countryside;
we risk our **lives** when we look for
food.

10 **Hunger** has made us burn with fever,
until our skin is as hot as an oven.

11 Our wives have been **raped** on Mount
Zion itself;
in every Judaean village our
daughters have been **forced** to
submit.

12 Our leaders have been taken and
hanged;
our old men are shown no **respect**.

13 Our young men are **forced** to grind
corn like **slaves**;
boys go staggering under heavy
loads of wood.

14 The old people no longer sit at the city
gate,
and the young people no longer
make music.

15 **Happiness** has gone out of our **lives**;
grief has taken the place of our
dances.

16 Nothing is left of all we were **proud** of.
We sinned, and now we are **doomed**.

17 We are sick at our very **hearts**
and can hardly see through our
tears,

18 because Mount Zion lies **lonely** and
deserted,
and wild jackals prowl through its
ruins.

19 But you, O LORD, are king for ever,
and will rule to the end of time.

20 Why have you **abandoned** us so long?
Will you ever **remember** us again?

21 Bring us back to you, LORD! Bring us
back!
Restore our **ancient glory**.

22 Or have you **rejected** us for ever?
Is there no limit to your **anger**?

abandon 2.1; Ezek 8.12
alive 4.9; Ezek 3.21
ancient 1.7; Ezek 26.20
anger 3.43; Ezek 3.14
beg 4.4; Ezek 7.26
disgrace 2.2; Ezek 6.9
doom Jer 50.27; Ezek 13.3
enemy 4.18; Ezek 5.8
enough Jer 15.5; Ezek 7.13
force (1) [2] 4.11; Ezek 3.14
glory Jer 48.17; Ezek 3.12
grief 3.33; Ezek 2.10
hang (2) Esth 9.13; Mt 27.5
happy 3.17; Dan 12.12
hard Jer 12.13; Ezek 3.9
heart 3.41; Ezek 6.9
hunger 4.4; Ezek 5.12
life (1) [2] 4.20; Ezek 3.18
lonely 1.1; Mt 14.13
need 2.14; Ezek 27.33
power 1.5; Ezek 1.3
proud 2.15; Ezek 7.10
rape Jer 13.22; Zech 14.2
reject 3.31; Ezek 5.6
remember [2] 3.21; Ezek 2.7
respect Jer 49.15; Ezek 2.4
rest (1) Jer 49.23; Ezek 31.6
restore Jer 50.19; Ezek 16.55
ruin 3.47; Ezek 13.4
save 3.26; Ezek 3.18
slave [2] 1.1; Ezek 27.13
stranger Jer 35.7; Ezek 16.32
submit 3.29; Rom 10.3
suffer 3.15; Ezek 4.4
tear (2) 3.48; Ezek 24.16
widow 1.1; Ezek 22.7

THE BOOK OF
EZEKIEL

INTRODUCTION

The prophet Ezekiel lived in exile in Babylon during the period before and after the fall of Jerusalem in 586 B.C. His message was addressed both to the exiles in Babylonia and to the people of Jerusalem. *The Book of Ezekiel* has six principal parts: (1) God's call to Ezekiel to be a prophet. (2) Warnings to the people about God's judgement on them and about the coming fall and destruction of Jerusalem. (3) Messages from the Lord regarding his judgement upon the various nations that oppressed and misled his people. (4) Comfort for Israel after the fall of Jerusalem and the promise of a brighter future. (5) The prophecy against Gog. (6) Ezekiel's picture of a restored Temple and nation.

Ezekiel was a man of deep faith and great imagination. Many of his insights came in the form of visions, and many of his messages were expressed in vivid symbolic actions. Ezekiel emphasized the need for inner renewal of the heart and spirit, and the responsibility of each individual for his own sins. He also proclaimed his hope for the renewal of the life of the nation. As a priest, as well as prophet, he had special interest in the Temple and in the need for holiness.

Outline of Contents

---

above Lam 1.13; 3.12
Almighty Jer 51.5; 10.5
body [3] Lam 3.13; 8.2
cloud Lam 3.44; 10.3
control Jer 51.28; 10.17
creature [17] Jer 51.62; 3.13
dazzling [2] Song 6.10; 8.4
dome [4] Job 22.14; 10.1
exile [2] Lam 4.22; 3.11
human [3] Jer 17.9; 4.12
Jew Jer 40.15; Dan 2.25
light (1) [2] Jer 31.35; 8.4
power Lam 5.8; 3.14
presence Jer 34.15; 3.22
priest Lam 4.13; 7.26
raise Lam 4.5; 2.2
right (2) Jer 22.24; 4.6
rise [2] Jer 51.64; 8.11
throne [2] Jer 49.38; 10.1
turn [2] Lam 4.11; 2.3
vision Lam 2.9; 8.2
wish [2] Jer 40.4; 13.22

EZEKIEL'S FIRST VISION OF GOD
(1.1-7.27)

God's Throne

1 On the fifth day of the fourth month
of the thirtieth year,[a] I, Ezekiel the
priest, son of Buzi, was living with the
Jewish exiles by the River Chebar in
Babylonia. The sky opened, and I saw a
vision of God. 2 (It was the fifth year since
King Jehoiachin had been taken into
exile.) 3 There in Babylonia beside the
River Chebar, I heard the LORD speak to
me and I felt his **power**.

4 I looked up and saw a storm coming
from the north. Lightning was flashing
from a huge **cloud**, and the sky round it
was glowing. Where the lightning was
flashing, something shone like bronze.
5 At the centre of the storm, I saw what
looked like four living **creatures** in
human form, 6 but each of them had four
faces and four wings. 7 Their legs were
straight, and they had hoofs like those of
a bull. They shone like polished bronze.
8 In addition to their four faces and four
wings, they each had four **human** hands,
one under each wing. 9 Two wings of
each **creature** were spread out so that
the **creatures** formed a square with their
wing tips touching. When they moved,
they moved as a group without **turning**
their **bodies**.

10 Each living **creature** had four
different faces: a **human** face in front, a
lion's face at the **right**, a bull's face at the
left, and an eagle's face at the back.
11 Two wings[b] of each **creature** were
raised so that they touched the tips of the
wings of the **creatures** next to it, and
their other two wings were folded
against their **bodies**. 12 Each **creature**
faced all four directions, and so the
group could go wherever they **wished**,
without having to **turn**.

13 Among[c] the **creatures** there was
something that looked like a blazing
torch, constantly moving. The fire would
blaze up and shoot out flashes of lightning. 14 The **creatures** themselves darted
to and fro with the speed of lightning.

15 As I was looking at the four
creatures, I saw four wheels touching the
ground, one beside each of them.[d] 16 All

[a] THIRTIETH YEAR: *It is not known to what year this refers.*
[b] *Some ancient translations* Two wings; *Hebrew* Their faces, their wings.
[c] *Some ancient translations* Among; *Hebrew* And the likeness of.
[d] *Some ancient translations* them; *Hebrew* their faces.

1.1: Rev 19.11 **1.2:** 2 Kgs 24.10–16; 2 Chr 36.9–10 **1.5:** Rev 4.6 **1.10:** Ezek 10.14; Rev 4.7
1.15–21: Ezek 10.9–13

four wheels were alike; each one shone
like a precious stone, and each had
another wheel intersecting it at right
angles, [17]so that the wheels could move
in any of the four directions. [18]The rims
of the wheels were covered with eyes.[e]
[19]Whenever the **creatures** moved, the
wheels moved with them, and if the
creatures rose up from the earth, so did
the wheels. [20]The **creatures** went
wherever they **wished**, and the wheels
did exactly what the **creatures** did,
because the creatures **controlled** them.
[21]So every time the **creatures** moved or
stopped or **rose** in the air, the wheels did
exactly the same.

22 **Above** the heads of the **creatures**
there was something that looked like a
dome made of **dazzling** crystal. [23]There
under the **dome** stood the **creatures**,
each stretching out two wings towards
the ones next to it and covering its **body**
with the other two wings. [24]I heard the
noise their wings made in flight; it
sounded like the roar of the sea, like the
noise of a huge army, like the voice of
Almighty God. When they stopped flying,
they folded their wings, [25]but there was
still a sound coming from above the
dome over their heads.

26 Above the **dome** there was something
that looked like a **throne** made of
sapphire, and sitting on the **throne** was a
figure that looked like a man. [27]The
figure seemed to be shining like bronze
in the middle of a fire. It shone all over
with a bright **light** [28]that had in it all the
colours of the rainbow. This was the **dazzling
light** that shows the **presence** of the
LORD.

God Calls Ezekiel to Be a Prophet

When I saw this, I fell face downwards
2 on the ground. Then I heard a voice
[1]saying, "**Mortal man**, stand up. I
want to talk to you." [2]While the voice
was speaking, **God's spirit** entered me
and **raised** me to my feet, and I heard the
voice continue, [3]"**Mortal man**, I am sending
you to the people of Israel. They have
rebelled and **turned** against me and are
still **rebels**, just as their ancestors were.
[4]They are **stubborn** and do not **respect**
me, so I am sending you to tell them
what I, the **Sovereign** LORD, am saying to
them. [5]Whether those **rebels** listen to you
or not, they will know that a **prophet** has
been among them.

6 "But you, **mortal man**, must not be
afraid of them or of anything they say.
They will **defy** and **despise** you; it will be
like living among scorpions. Still, don't be
afraid of those **rebels** or of anything they
say. [7]You will tell them whatever I tell
you to say, whether they listen or not.
Remember what **rebels** they are.

8 "**Mortal man**, listen to what I tell
you. Don't be **rebellious** like them. Open
your mouth and eat what I am going to
give you." [9]I saw a hand stretched out towards
me, and it was holding a **scroll**.
[10]The hand unrolled the **scroll**, and I saw
that there was writing on both sides—
cries of **grief** were written there, and
wails and **groans**.

3 God said, "**Mortal man**, eat this
scroll; then go and speak to the
people of Israel."

2 So I opened my mouth, and he gave
me the **scroll** to eat. [3]He said, "**Mortal
man**, eat this **scroll** that I give you; fill
your stomach with it." I ate it, and it
tasted as sweet as honey.

4 Then God said, "**Mortal man**, go to
the people of Israel and say to them
whatever I tell you to say. [5]I am not
sending you to a nation that speaks a
difficult foreign language, but to the
Israelites. [6]If I sent you to great nations
that spoke **difficult** languages you didn't
understand, they would listen to you.
[7]But none of the people of Israel will be
willing to listen; they will not even listen
to me. All of them are **stubborn** and
defiant. [8]Now I will make you as **stubborn**
and as tough as they are. [9]I will
make you as firm as a rock, as **hard** as a
diamond; don't be **afraid** of those **rebels**."

10 God continued, "**Mortal man**, pay
close attention and **remember** everything
I tell you. [11]Then go to your
countrymen who are in **exile** and tell
them what I, the **Sovereign** LORD, am
saying to them, whether they pay attention
to you or not."

12 Then **God's spirit** lifted me up, and I
heard behind me the loud roar of a voice
that said, "**Praise** the **glory** of the LORD
in **heaven above**!" [13]I heard the wings of
the **creatures** beating together in the air,
and the noise of the wheels, as loud as an
earthquake. [14]The **power of the** LORD
came on me with great **force**, and as his
spirit carried me off, I felt **bitter** and
angry. [15]So I came to Tel Abib beside the
River Chebar, where the **exiles** were
living, and for seven days I stayed there,
overcome by what I had seen and heard.

afraid [2] Lam 3.57; 3.9
defy Is 1.20; 3.7
despise Jer 51.18; 25.6
grief Lam 5.15; 21.12
groan Lam 1.4; 21.6
mortal [4] Jer 17.5; 3.1
prophet Lam 4.13; 7.26
raise 1.11; 3.24
rebel [6] Lam 3.42; 3.9
remember Lam 5.1; 3.10
respect Lam 5.12; 22.8
scroll [2] Jer 36.2; 3.1
Sovereign Jer 50.25; 3.11
Spirit (1) (God's Spirit) Is 63.10; 3.12
stubborn Jer 23.17; 3.7

turn 1.9; 4.6
wail Jer 4.8; Hos 7.14

above 1.22; Lk 24.49
afraid 2.6; 11.8
alive Lam 5.6; 5.10
anger Lam 5.22; 5.13
announce Jer 50.2; 20.9
bitter Lam 3.15; 27.30
change Jer 52.33; 33.8
creature 1.5; 9.3
danger Lam 3.47; 14.15
death (1) [2] Lam 4.8; 4.14
defy 2.6; 20.8
difficult [2] Jer 32.17; Dan 2.11
evil [3] Lam 3.38; 5.11
exile [2] 1.1; 6.9
force (1) Lam 5.11; 5.13
glory [2] Lam 5.21; 7.11
hard Lam 5.5; Dan 10.1
heaven Lam 3.41; 32.8
ignore Is 65.11; 16.59
life (1) [3] Lam 5.9; 13.18
mortal [6] 2.1; 4.1
paralyse 1 Kgs 13.4; Mt 4.24
power [3] 1.3; 8.1
praise Jer 51.41; 28.22
presence 1.28; 8.4
raise 2.2; 16.27
rebel [3] 2.3; 5.6
remember [2] 2.7; 6.9
save Lam 5.8; 7.19
scroll [3] 2.9; Zech 5.1
Sovereign [2] 2.4; 4.14
spare [2] Jer 51.3; 6.14
speech Is 52.15; 24.27
Spirit (1) (God's Spirit) [3] 2.2; 8.3
stubborn [2] 2.4; 11.19
true Jer 44.28; 12.23
understand Jer 30.23; Dan 2.21
warn [6] Lam 2.17; 6.10
watch Lam 4.18; 10.2
way (3) Lam 3.40; 33.8

[e] *Verse 18 in Hebrew is unclear.*

1.18: Rev 4.8 **1.22:** Rev 4.6 **1.24:** Rev 1.15, 19.6 **1.26:** Ezek 10.1; Rev 4.2–3 **1.27:** Ezek 8.2
2.9–10: Rev 5.1 **3.1–3:** Rev 10.9–10

The LORD Appoints Ezekiel as a Watchman
(Ezek 33.1–9)

16 After the seven days had passed,
the LORD spoke to me. 17 "**Mortal man**,"
he said, "I am making you a **watchman**
for the nation of Israel. You will pass on
to them the **warnings** I give you. 18 If I **an-**
nounce that an **evil** man is going to die
but you do not **warn** him to **change** his
ways so that he can **save** his **life**, he will
die, still a sinner, and I will hold you
responsible for his **death**. 19 If you do
warn an **evil** man and he doesn't stop sinning, he will die, still a sinner, but your
life will be **spared**.
20 "If a **truly** good man starts doing
evil and I put him in a **dangerous** situation, he will die if you do not **warn** him.
He will die because of his sins—I will not
remember the good he did—and I will
hold you responsible for his **death**. 21 If
you do **warn** a good man not to sin and
he listens to you and doesn't sin, he will
stay **alive**, and your **life** will also be
spared."

Ezekiel Will Be Unable to Talk

22 I felt the **powerful presence** of the
LORD and heard him say to me, "Get up
and go out into the valley. I will talk to
you there."
23 So I went out into the valley, and
there I saw the **glory** of the LORD, just as
I had seen it beside the River Chebar. I
fell face downwards on the ground, 24 but
God's spirit entered me and **raised** me to
my feet. The LORD said to me, "Go home
and shut yourself up in the house. 25 You
will be tied with ropes, **mortal man**, and
you will not be able to go out in public. 26 I
will **paralyse** your tongue so that you
won't be able to **warn** these **rebellious**
people. 27 Then, when I speak to you
again and give you back the **power** of
speech, you will tell them what I, the
Sovereign LORD, am saying. Some of
them will listen, but some will **ignore**
you, for they are a nation of **rebels**."

Ezekiel Acts Out the Siege of Jerusalem

4 God said, "**Mortal man**, get a brick,
put it in front of you, and scratch
lines on it to **represent** the city of Jerusalem. 2 Then, to **represent** a siege, put
trenches, earthworks, camps, and
battering-rams all round it. 3 Take an iron
pan and set it up like a wall between you
and the city. Face the city. It is under
siege, and you are the one besieging it.
This will be a **sign** to the nation of Israel.
4–5 "Then lie down on your left side,
and I[g] will place on you the **guilt** of the
nation of Israel. For 390 days you will
stay there and **suffer** because of their
guilt. I have **sentenced** you to one day for
each year their **punishment** will **last**.
6 When you finish that, **turn** over on your
right side and **suffer** for the **guilt** of Judah
for forty days—one day for each year of
their **punishment**.
7 "Fix your eyes on the siege of Jerusalem. Shake your fist at the city and **pro-**
phesy against it. 8 I will tie you up so that
you cannot **turn** from one side to the
other until the siege is over.
9 "Now take some wheat, barley,
beans, peas, millet, and spelt. Mix them
all together and make **bread**. That is
what you are to eat during the 390 days
you are lying on your left side. 10 You will
be allowed 230 grammes of **bread** a day,
and it will have to **last** until the next day.
11 You will also have a limited amount of
water to drink, two **cups** a day. 12 You are
to build a fire out of dried **human** excrement, bake **bread** on the fire, and eat it
where everyone can see you."
13 The LORD said, "This **represents**
the way the Israelites will have to eat
food which the **Law forbids**,[h] when I
scatter them to foreign countries."
14 But I replied, "No, **Sovereign** LORD!
I have never **defiled** myself. From childhood on I have never eaten meat from
any animal that died a **natural death** or
was killed by wild animals. I have never
eaten any food considered **unclean**."
15 So God said, "Very well. I will let
you use cow dung instead, and you can
bake your **bread** on that."
16 And he added, "**Mortal man**, I am
going to cut off the supply of **bread** for
Jerusalem. The people there will be **dis-**
tressed and **anxious** as they measure out
the food they eat and the water they
drink. 17 They will run out of **bread** and
water; they will be in **despair**, and they
will waste away because of their sins."

Ezekiel Cuts His Hair

5 The LORD said, "**Mortal man**, take a
sharp sword and use it to **shave** off
your beard and all your hair. Then weigh
the hair on scales and divide it into three
parts. 2 Burn a third of it in the city when
the siege is over. Take another third and
chop it up with your sword as you move

guilty [3] Lam 4.13; 9.9
human 1.5; 8.2
last (1) [2] Jer 48.30 16.60
law Lam 2.9; 5.6
mortal [2] 3.1; 5.1
natural Jer 31.36; 44.31
prophecy Jer 28.6; 11.13
punish [2] Lam 4.6; 5.9
represent [3] Jer 40.10; 23.4
right (2) 1.10; 21.16
scatter Lam 4.1; 5.2
sentence Jer 52.9; 11.9
sign (1) Jer 36.24; 12.11
Sovereign 3.11; 5.5
suffer [2] Lam 5.7; 16.58
turn [2] 2.3; 8.16
unclean Lam 1.9; 8.10

anxious Jer 49.23; Dan 6.20
bread [6] Jer 37.21; 13.19
cup Jer 51.7; 23.31
death (1) 3.18; 6.12
defile Lam 4.7; 5.11
despair Lam 3.65; 7.25
distress Jer 48.5; 9.4
forbid Lam 1.10; 18.6

alive 3.21; 13.19
anger [2] 3.14; 6.12
command [3] Lam 3.38; 10.6
convince Ecc 8.15; 14.22
custom Is 2.6; 20.18
defile 4.14; 7.21
destroy Lam 3.48; 6.3

[g] *Probable text* I; *Hebrew* you.
[h] FOOD WHICH THE LAW FORBIDS: *The Law of Moses prohibited the eating of certain foods as being ritually unclean (see Lev. 11).*

disgust [2] Jer 50.2; 6.9
disobey Lam 1.18; 11.12
enemy Lam 5.3; 21.3
evil 3.18; 6.9
force (1) 3.14; 6.12
fury Lam 4.11; 7.19
hate Lam 3.52; 13.20
hunger [3] Lam 5.10; 7.15
judge Lam 3.59; 7.3
last (2) Jer 25.19; 40.15
law [2] 4.13; 11.12
mercy Lam 3.3; 7.4
mock Lam 3.46; 22.4
mortal 4.1; 6.2
obey Jer 44.23; 11.19
pain Lam 3.19; Hos 8.10
punish [3] 4.4; 6.9
rage Lam 2.3; 22.20
rebel 3.9; 12.2
refuse (1) Lam 3.8; 18.8
reject Lam 5.22; 20.13
satisfy Jer 46.10; 7.19
scatter [3] 4.13; 6.5
shave Jer 48.37; 7.18
sneer Lam 2.16; 22.4
Sovereign [4] 4.14; 6.3
Temple (1) (of God) Lam 4.1; 7.22
terrify Jer 51.37; 19.7
trouble Jer 50.34; 9.4
unfaithful Jer 49.4; 14.13
violent Jer 51.35; 7.10
wicked Lam 1.22; 7.11
word (1) Jer 51.64; 6.3
world Lam 3.45; 20.23

about outside the city. **Scatter** the remaining third to the winds, and I will pursue it with my sword. 3 Keep back a few
hairs and wrap them in the hem of your
clothes. 4 Then take a few of them out
again, throw them in the fire, and let
them burn up. From them fire will
spread to the whole nation of Israel."
5 The **Sovereign LORD** said, "Look at
Jerusalem. I put her at the centre of the
world, with other countries all round her.
6 But Jerusalem **rebelled** against my **commands** and showed that she was more
wicked than the other nations, more **disobedient** than the countries around her.
Jerusalem **rejected** my **commands** and
refused to keep my **laws**. 7 Now listen,
Jerusalem, to what I, the **Sovereign
LORD**, am saying. By not **obeying** my
laws or keeping my **commands**, you have
caused more **trouble** than the nations
around you. You have followed the **customs** of other nations. 8 And so I, the
Sovereign LORD, am telling you that I am
your **enemy**. I will pass **judgement** on you
where all the nations can see it.
9 Because of all the things you do that I
hate, I will **punish** Jerusalem as I have
never done before and will never do
again. 10 As a result, parents in Jerusalem
will eat their children, and children will
eat their parents. I will **punish** you and
scatter in every direction any who are
left **alive**.
11 "Therefore, as I am the living
God—this is the **word of the Sovereign
LORD**—because you **defiled** my **Temple**
with all the **evil**, **disgusting** things you
did, I will cut you down without **mercy**.
12 A third of your people will die from
sickness and **hunger** in the city; a third
will be cut down by swords outside the
city; and I will **scatter** the **last** third to
the winds and pursue them with a sword.
13 "You will feel all the **force** of my
anger and **rage** until I am **satisfied**. When
all this happens, you will be **convinced**
that I, the LORD, have spoken to you
because I am outraged at your **unfaithfulness**. 14 Everyone from the nations
around you who passes by will **sneer** at
you and keep his distance.
15 "When I am **angry** and **furious** with
you and **punish** you, all the nations
around you will be **terrified**. They will
look at you with **disgust** and will **mock**
you. 16 I will cut off your supply of food
and let you starve. You[i] will feel the
pains of hunger like sharp arrows sent to
destroy you. 17 I will send **hunger** and wild
animals to kill your children, and will
send sickness, **violence**, and war to kill
you. I, the LORD, have spoken."

The LORD Condemns Idolatry

6 The LORD spoke to me. 2 "**Mortal**
man," he said, "look towards the
mountains of Israel and give them my
message. 3 Tell the mountains of Israel to
hear the **word of the LORD**—to hear what
I, the **Sovereign LORD**, am telling the
mountains, the hills, the gorges, and the
valleys: I will send a sword to **destroy** the
places where people **worship idols**. 4 The
altars will be torn down and the **incense-
altars** broken. All the people there will
be killed in front of their **idols**. 5 I will
scatter the corpses of the people of
Israel; I will **scatter** their bones all round
the **altars**. 6 All the cities of Israel will be
destroyed, so that all their **altars** and
their **idols** will be smashed to pieces,
their **incense-altars** will be shattered, and
everything they made will disappear.
7 People will be killed everywhere, and
those who survive will **acknowledge** that
I am the LORD.
8 "I will let some **escape** the **slaughter**
and be **scattered** among the nations,
9 where they will live in **exile**. There they
will **remember** me and know that I have
punished them and **disgraced** them,[j]
because their **faithless hearts** deserted
me and they preferred **idols** to me. And
they will be **disgusted** with themselves
because of the **evil** and degrading things
they have done. 10 They will know that I
am the LORD and that my **warnings** were
not empty **threats**."
11 The **Sovereign LORD** said, "Wring
your hands! Stamp your feet! Cry in
sorrow because of all the **evil**, **disgusting**
things the Israelites have done. They are
going to die in war, by **famine**, and by
disease. 12 Those far away will fall ill and
die; those near by will be killed in war;
those who survive will starve **to death**.
They will feel all the **force** of my **anger**.
13 Corpses will be **scattered** among the
idols and round the **altars**, **scattered** on
every high hill, on the top of every mountain, under every green tree and every
large oak, in every place where they
burnt **sacrifices** to their **idols**. Then
everyone will know that I am the LORD.
14 Yes, I will stretch out my hand and **destroy** their country. I will make it a waste
from the southern desert to the city of
Riblah in the north, not **sparing** any

acknowledge Jer 9.3; 12.16
altar [5] Lam 2.7; 8.5
anger 5.13; 7.3
death (1) 4.14; 8.14
death (3) (to death) Lam 4.9; 11.9
destroy [3] 5.16; 12.20
disease Jer 44.13; 12.16
disgrace Lam 5.1; 7.18
disgust [2] 5.11; 7.3
escape Lam 3.7; 7.16
evil [2] 5.11; 7.13
exile 3.11; 8.1
faithless Jer 31.22
famine Jer 52.6; 12.16
force (1) 5.13; 7.8
heart Lam 5.17; 11.19
idol [6] Jer 51.17; 7.20
incense [2] Jer 52.18; 8.11
message Jer 50.1; 11.5
mortal 5.1; 7.2
punish 5.9; 7.4
remember 3.10; 16.22
sacrifice Jer 52.18; 16.19
scatter [5] 5.2; 10.2
slaughter Lam 2.21; 21.14
sorrow Lam 3.32; 19.1
Sovereign [2] 5.5; 7.2
spare 3.19; 7.4
threat Lam 2.17; 21.15
warn 3.17; 12.6
word (1) 5.11; 13.2
worship (2) (of other gods) Jer 51.44; 8.10

[i] *Probable text* You; *Hebrew* They.
[j] *Some ancient translations* disgraced them; *Hebrew* I am disgraced.

5.10: Lam 4.10 **5.17:** Rev 6.8

advice Jer 38.15; 11.2
anger [4] 6.12; 8.17
bad Jer 52.6; 11.2
beg Lam 5.6; Mt 8.5
celebrate Is 33.20; 45.21
confident Is 57.15; Mic 7.7
defile [2] 5.11; 9.7
desire Jer 34.16; Zech 13.2
despair 4.17; 21.6
disaster [3] Lam 4.10; 34.12
disgrace 6.9; 8.6
disgust [5] 6.9; 8.6
dove Jer 48.28; Hos 11.11
elder (2) Jer 26.17; Mt 16.21
enough Lam 5.6; 16.5
escape 6.8; 12.12
evil [2] 6.9; 8.9
fear Lam 3.47; 12.18
force (1) 6.12; 8.18
fright Jer 49.22; 32.10
fury 5.15; 16.38
glory 3.12; 27.10
hope Lam 3.7; 14.5
hunger [2] 5.12; 18.7
idol 6.3; 8.3
judge [3] 5.8; 18.30
knee Is 35.3; 21.7
mercy [2] 5.11; 8.18
mortal 6.2; 8.5
mourn Jer 51.8; 24.17
peace Lam 3.17; 16.49
priest 1.1; 22.26
profane [2] Is 43.28; 20.13
prophet 2.5; 13.2
proud [2] Lam 5.16; 16.49
punish [5] 6.9; 9.1
reveal Is 64.2; 20.5
rob [2] Lam 1.10; 18.7
sackcloth Lam 2.10; 27.31
satisfy 5.13; 8.17
save 3.18; 13.22
shave 5.1; 27.31
shrine Is 65.7; 18.6
Sovereign [2] 6.3; 8.1
spare [2] 6.14; 8.18
splendour Lam 2.1; Dan 2.48
strong Lam 4.7; 13.11
teach Lam 2.9; 19.3
Temple (1) (of God) 5.11; 8.3
tremble Jer 51.29; 12.18
victim Jer 46.10; Dan 7.7
violent [3] 5.17; 8.17
weak Lam 1.6; 29.6
wicked 5.6; 20.44
worship (1) (of God) Lam 2.6; 11.15

place where the Israelites live. Then
everyone will know that I am the LORD.”

The End Is Near for Israel

7 The LORD spoke to me. 2 “**Mortal**
man,” he said, “this is what I, the
Sovereign LORD, am saying to the land of
Israel: This is the end for the whole
land!
3 “Israel, the end has come. You will
feel my **anger**, because I am **judging** you
for what you have done. I will pay you
back for all your **disgusting** conduct. 4 I
will not **spare** you or show you any
mercy. I am going to **punish** you for the
disgusting things you have done, so that
you will know that I am the LORD.”
5 This is what the **Sovereign** LORD is
saying, “One **disaster** after another is
coming on you. 6 It's all over. This is the
end. You are finished. 7 The end is
coming for you people who live in the
land. The time is near when there will be
no more **celebrations** at the mountain
shrines, only confusion.[k]
8 “Very soon now you will feel all the
force of my **anger**. I am **judging** you for
what you have done, and I will pay you
back for all your **disgusting** conduct. 9 I
will not **spare** you or show you any
mercy. I am going to **punish** you for the
disgusting things you have done, so that
you will know that I am the LORD, and
that I am the one who **punishes** you.”
10 The day of **disaster** is coming for
Israel. **Violence** is flourishing. **Pride** is at
its height.[l] 11 **Violence** produces more
wickedness. Nothing of theirs will remain, nothing of their wealth, their **splendour**, or their **glory**.
12 The time is coming. The day is
near when buying and selling will have
no more meaning, because God's **punishment** will fall on everyone alike. 13 No
merchant will live long **enough** to get
back what he has lost, because **God's
anger** is on everyone. Those who are **evil**
cannot survive.[n] 14 The trumpet sounds,
and everyone gets ready. But no one
goes off to war, for **God's anger** will fall
on everyone alike.

Punishment for Israel's Sins

15 There is fighting in the streets, and
sickness and **hunger** in the houses. Anyone who is out in the country will die in
the fighting, and anyone in the city will
be a **victim** of sickness and **hunger**.
16 Some will **escape** to the mountains like
doves frightened from the valleys. All of
them will moan over their sins.[o] 17 Everyone's hands will be **weak**, and their **knees**
will shake. 18 They will put on **sackcloth**
and they will **tremble** all over. Their
heads will be **shaved**, and they will all be
disgraced. 19 They will throw their gold
and silver away in the streets like refuse,
because neither silver nor gold can **save**
them when the LORD pours out his **fury**.
They cannot use it to **satisfy** their **desires**
or fill their stomachs. Gold and silver led
them into sin. 20 Once they were **proud** of
their beautiful jewels, but they used them
to make **disgusting idols**. That is why the
LORD has made their wealth repulsive to
them.
21 “I will let foreigners **rob** them,”
says the LORD, “and law-breakers will
take all their wealth and **defile** it. 22 I will
not interfere when my treasured **Temple**
is **profaned**, when **robbers** break into it
and **defile** it.
23 “Everything is in confusion[q] —the
land is full of murders and the cities are
full of **violence**. 24 I will bring the most
evil nations here and let them have your
homes. Your **strongest** men will lose
their **confidence** when I let the nations
profane the places where you **worship**.
25 **Despair** is coming. You will look for
peace and never find it. 26 One **disaster**
will follow another, and a steady stream
of **bad** news will pour in. You will **beg** the
prophets to **reveal** what they foresee.
The **priests** will have nothing to **teach** the
people, and the **elders** will have no **advice** to give. 27 The king will **mourn**, the
prince will give up **hope**, and the people
will shake with **fear**. I will **punish** you for
all you have done, and will judge you in
the same way as you have **judged** others.
This will show you that I am the LORD.”

EZEKIEL'S SECOND VISION OF GOD
(8.1–10.22)

Idolatry in Jerusalem

8 On the fifth day of the sixth month
of the sixth year of our **exile**, the
leaders of the **exiles** from Judah were
sitting in my house with me. Suddenly the
power of the Sovereign LORD came on
me. 2 I looked up and saw a **vision** of a
fiery **human** form. From the waist down
his **body** looked like fire, and from the
waist up he was shining like polished
bronze. 3 He stretched out what seemed

abandon Lam 5.20; 9.9
altar [2] 6.4; 9.2
anger [2] 7.3; 9.8
body 1.9; 10.12
bow (2) Lam 3.29; 46.3
dazzling 1.22; 9.3
death (1) 6.12; 13.18
disgrace 7.18; 16.52
disgust [5] 7.3; 9.4
evil 7.13; 11.2
excuse Job 33.10; Mk 7.12

[k] *Probable text* celebrations...confusion; *Hebrew unclear.*
[l] *Probable text* Pride is at its height; *Hebrew unclear.* [n] *Verse 13 in Hebrew is unclear.*
[o] *Verse 16 in Hebrew is unclear.*
[q] *One ancient translation* Everything is in confusion; *Hebrew unclear.*

8.2: Ezek 1.27

exile [2] 6.9; 11.15
force (1) 7.8; 13.15
god (2) (other gods) Jer 51.17; 20.7
holy Lam 2.6; 20.12
human 4.12; 10.8
idol [2] 7.20; 11.18
image Jer 50.2; 16.17
incense [2] 6.4; 16.18
insult Lam 3.30; 20.27
light (1) 1.27; 9.3
mercy 7.4; 9.5
mortal [6] 7.2; 11.2
power 3.14; 13.18
prayer Lam 3.44; Dan 2.23
presence 3.22; 9.3
rise [2] 1.19; 9.3
sanctuary [2] Is 63.18; Heb 6.19
satisfy 7.19; 16.28
secret Jer 50.2; 28.3
Sovereign 7.2; 9.8
spare 7.4; 9.5
Spirit (1) (God's Spirit) 3.12; 11.1
Temple (1) (of God) [4] 7.22; 9.2
turn 4.6; 10.11
unclean 4.14; 20.7
violent 7.10; 28.16
vision [2] 1.1; 10.13
weep Lam 2.11; 27.31
worship (2) (of other gods) [3] 6.3; 11.21

to be a hand and seized me by the hair. Then in this **vision God's spirit** lifted me high in the air and took me to Jerusalem. He took me to the inner entrance of the north gate of the **Temple**, where there was an **idol** that was an outrage to God.

4 There I saw the **dazzling light** that shows the **presence** of Israel's God, just as I had seen it when I was by the River Chebar. 5 God said to me, "**Mortal man**, look towards the north." I looked, and there near the **altar** by the entrance of the gateway I saw the **idol** that was an outrage to God.

6 God said to me, "**Mortal man**, do you see what is happening? Look at the **disgusting** things the people of Israel are doing here, driving me farther and farther away from my **holy** place. You will see even more **disgraceful** things than this."

7 He took me to the entrance of the outer courtyard and showed me a hole in the wall. 8 He said, "**Mortal man**, break through the wall here." I broke through it and found a door. 9 He said to me, "Go in and look at the **evil, disgusting** things they are doing there." 10 So I went in and looked. The walls were covered with drawings of snakes and other **unclean** animals,[r] and of the other things which the Israelites were **worshipping**. 11 Seventy Israelite leaders were there, including Jaazaniah son of Shaphan. Each one was holding an **incense-burner**, and smoke was **rising** from the **incense**. 12 God asked me, "**Mortal man**, do you see what the Israelite leaders are doing in **secret**? They are all **worshipping** in a room full of **images**. Their **excuse** is: 'The LORD doesn't see us! He has **abandoned** the country.' "

13 Then the LORD said to me, "You are going to see them do even more **disgusting** things than that." 14 So he took me to the north gate of the **Temple** and showed me women **weeping** over the **death** of the **god Tammuz**.[s]

15 He asked, "**Mortal man**, do you see that? You will see even more **disgusting** things." 16 So he took me to the inner courtyard of the **Temple**. There near the entrance of the **sanctuary**, between the **altar** and the passage, were about twenty-five men. They had **turned** their backs to the **sanctuary** and were **bowing** low towards the east, **worshipping** the **rising** sun.

17 The LORD said to me, "**Mortal man**, do you see that? These people of Judah are not **satisfied** with merely doing all the **disgusting** things you have seen here and with spreading **violence** throughout the country. No, they must come and do them here in the **Temple** itself and make me even more **angry**. Look how they insult me in the most offensive way possible![m] 18 They will feel all the **force** of my **anger**. I will not **spare** them or show them any **mercy**. They will shout **prayers** to me as loud as they can, but I will not listen to them."

Jerusalem Is Punished

9 Then I heard God shout, "Come here, you men who are going to **punish** the city. Bring your weapons with you." 2 At once six men came from the outer north gate of the **Temple**, each one carrying a weapon. With them was a man dressed in linen clothes, carrying something to write with. They all came and stood by the bronze **altar**.

3 Then the **dazzling light** of the **presence** of the God of Israel **rose** up from the winged **creatures**,[t] where it had been, and moved to the entrance of the **Temple**. The LORD called to the man dressed in linen, 4 "Go through the whole city of Jerusalem and put a **mark** on the **forehead** of everyone who is **distressed** and **troubled** because of all the **disgusting** things being done in the city."

5 And I heard God say to the other men, "Follow him through the city, and kill. **Spare** no one; have **mercy** on no one. 6 Kill the old men, young men, young women, mothers, and children. But don't touch anyone who has the **mark** on his **forehead**. Start here at my **Temple**." So they began with the leaders who were standing there at the **Temple**.

7 God said to them, "**Defile** the **Temple**. Fill its courtyards with corpses. Get to work!" So they began to kill the people in the city.[u]

8 While the killing was going on, I was there **alone**. I threw myself face downwards on the ground and shouted, "**Sovereign** LORD, are you so **angry** with Jerusalem that you are going to kill everyone left in Israel?"

9 God answered, "The people of Israel

abandon 8.12; 39.9
alone Lam 3.28; 44.16
altar 8.5; 40.46
anger 8.17; 13.13
commit Jer 29.23; 16.17
creature 3.13; 10.1
crime Jer 41.11; Hos 4.2
dazzling 8.4; 10.4
defile 7.21; 14.11
disgust 8.6; 11.18
distress 4.16; 30.4
forehead [2] 2 Chr 26.19; Mt 23.5
guilty 4.4; 21.24
light (1) 8.4; 10.4
mark (1) [2] Jer 50.9; 21.19
mercy 8.18; 24.14
pity Jer 48.1; 16.5
presence 8.4; 10.4
punish 7.4; 11.11
rise 8.11; 10.4
Sovereign 8.1; 11.7
spare 8.18; 33.9
Temple (1) (of God) [5] 8.3; 10.3
terrible Lam 1.8; Dan 8.24
trouble 5.7; 29.18

[r] UNCLEAN ANIMALS: *The Law of Moses prohibited the eating of certain animals as being ritually unclean (see 4.13; Lev 11).*
[s] TAMMUZ: *A god who was thought to die when vegetation died and to come to life the next year. Women would mourn his ritual death.*
[m] IN THE MOST OFFENSIVE WAY POSSIBLE: *A reference to a pagan rite of putting a branch to the nose.*
[t] WINGED CREATURES: *See 1.5–12.*
[u] work!" So they...city.; *or* work! Go on and start killing the people in the city!"

8.4: Ezek 1.28 **9.4:** Rev 7.3, 9.4, 14.1

and Judah are **guilty** of **terrible** sins. They have **committed murder** all over the land and have filled Jerusalem with **crime**. They say that I, the LORD, have **abandoned** their country and that I don't see them. 10 But I will not have **pity** on them; I will do to them what they have done to others."

11 Then the man wearing linen clothes returned and reported to the LORD, "I have carried out your orders."

The Glory of the LORD Leaves the Temple

Almighty 1.24; Hos 12.5
body 8.2; 16.8
cloud [2] 1.4; 19.11
command 5.6; 11.12
control 1.20; 11.5
creature [19] 9.3; 11.22
dazzling [3] 9.3; 11.22
dome 1.22; Amos 9.6
human [3] 8.2; 29.11
light (1) [4] 9.3; 11.22
presence [2] 9.3; 11.22
rise [2] 9.3; 17.14
scatter 6.5; 11.16
Temple (1) (of God) [5] 9.2; 11.1
throne 1.26; 17.16
turn [2] 8.16; 14.5
vision 8.2; 11.24
watch [2] 3.17; 12.4

10 I looked at the **dome** over the heads of the living **creatures**[v] and above them was something that seemed to be a **throne** made of sapphire. 2 God said to the man wearing linen clothes, "Go between the wheels under the **creatures** and fill your hands with burning coals. Then **scatter** the coals over the city."

I **watched** him go. 3 The **creatures** were standing to the south of the **Temple** when he went in, and a **cloud** filled the inner courtyard. 4 The **dazzling light** of the LORD's **presence rose** up from the **creatures** and moved to the entrance of the **Temple**. Then the **cloud** filled the **Temple**, and the courtyard was blazing with the **light**. 5 The noise made by the **creatures'** wings was heard even in the outer courtyard. It sounded like the voice of **Almighty** God.

6 When the LORD **commanded** the man wearing linen clothes to take some fire from between the wheels that were under the **creatures**, the man went in and stood by one of the wheels. 7 One of the **creatures** put his hand into the fire that was there among them, picked up some coals, and put them in the hands of the man in linen. The man took the coals and left.

8 I saw that each **creature** had what looked like a **human** hand under each of its wings. 9-10 I also saw that there were four wheels, all alike, one beside each **creature**. The wheels shone like precious stones, and each one had another wheel which intersected it at right angles. 11 When the **creatures** moved, they could go in any direction without **turning**. They all moved together in the direction they wanted to go, without having to **turn** round. 12 Their **bodies**, backs, hands, wings, and wheels were covered with eyes. 13 These wheels were the same as those I had seen in my first **vision**.

14 Each **creature** had four faces. The first was the face of a bull, the second a **human** face, the third the face of a lion, and the fourth the face of an eagle. 15 (They were the same **creatures** that I had seen by the River Chebar.) When the **creatures rose** in the air 16 and moved, the wheels went with them. Whenever they spread their wings to fly, the wheels still went with them. 17 When the **creatures** stopped, the wheels stopped; and when the **creatures** flew, the wheels went with them, because the **creatures controlled** them.

18 Then the **dazzling light** of the LORD's **presence** left the entrance of the **Temple** and moved to a place above the **creatures**. 19 They spread their wings and flew up from the earth while I was **watching**, and the wheels went with them. They paused at the east gate of the **Temple**, and the **dazzling light** was over them. 20 I recognized them as the same **creatures** which I had seen beneath the God of Israel at the River Chebar.

21 Each of them had four faces, four wings, and what looked like a **human** hand under each wing. 22 Their faces looked exactly like the faces[w] I had seen by the River Chebar. Each **creature** moved straight ahead.

Jerusalem Is Condemned

advice 7.26; Dan 4.2
afraid 3.9; 27.36
bad 7.26; 16.20
command [2] 10.6; 18.9
control 10.17; 13.20
creature 10.1; 41.18
dazzling [2] 10.4; 16.13
dead Lam 2.21; 26.2
death (3) (to death) 6.12; 22.9
denounce Job 15.13; 13.2
disgust [2] 9.4; 12.16
disobey 5.6; 44.9
evil 8.9; 13.22
exile [5] 8.1; 12.4
faithful Jer 50.7; 37.24
filthy [2] Lam 1.8; Nah 3.6
God's people Lam 4.3; 13.9
heart [3] 6.9; 14.3
idol [2] 8.3; 14.3
law [3] 5.6; 18.9
light (1) [2] 10.4; 32.
love Lam 4.10; 16.5
message 6.2; 12.10
mind (1) Jer 51.7; 18.31
mortal [3] 8.5; 12.2
neighbour Jer 25.9; 16.26
new Jer 46.17; 18.31

11 **God's spirit** lifted me up and took me to the east gate of the **Temple**. There near the gate I saw twenty-five men, including Jaazaniah son of Azzur and Pelatiah son of Benaiah, two leaders of the nation.

2 God said to me, "**Mortal man**, these men make **evil plans** and give **bad advice** in this city. 3 They say, 'We will soon be building houses again.[x] The city is like a cooking-pot, and we are like the meat in it, but at least it **protects** us from the fire.' 4 Now then, **denounce** them, **mortal** man."

5 The **spirit of the LORD** took **control** of me, and the LORD told me to give the people this **message**: "People of Israel, I know what you are saying and what you are **planning**. 6 You have murdered so many people here in the city that the streets are full of corpses.

7 "So this is what I, the **Sovereign** LORD, am saying to you. This city is indeed a cooking-pot, but what is the

[v] LIVING CREATURES: *See 1.5–12.* [w] *Probable text* the faces; *Hebrew* the faces and them.
[x] We will...again; *or* We won't be building houses for a while.

10.1: Ezek 1.26; Rev 4.2 **10.2:** Rev 8.5 **10.9-13:** Ezek 1.15–21 **10.12:** Rev 4.8
10.14: Ezek 1.10; Rev 4.7

obey [2] 5.7; 18.9
plan [2] Lam 3.62; 38.10
possess Jer 37.12; 13.18
presence 10.4; 20.9
prophecy 4.7; 12.24
protect [3] Lam 4.20; 20.44
punish [3] 9.1; 13.9
rid Jer 28.16; 34.25
scatter [2] 10.2; 12.14
sentence 4.4; 20.4
Sovereign [4] 9.8; 12.10
Spirit (1) (God's Spirit) [3] 8.3; 36.27
stubborn 3.7; 16.50
Temple (1) (of God) 10.3; 23.38
vision [2] 10.13; 12.24
worship (1) (of God) 7.24; 20.40
worship (2) (of other gods) 8.10; 14.7

meat? The corpses of those you have
killed! You will not be here—I will throw
you out of the city! 8 Are you **afraid** of
swords? I will bring men with swords to
attack you. 9 I will take you out of the city
and hand you over to foreigners. I have
sentenced you **to death**, 10 and you will be
killed in battle in your own country. Then
everyone will know that I am the LORD.
11 This city will not **protect** you as a pot
protects the meat in it. I will **punish** you
wherever you may be in the land of
Israel. 12 You will know that I am the
LORD and that while you were keeping
the **laws** of the **neighbouring** nations, you
were breaking *my* **laws** and **disobeying**
my **commands**."
13 While I was **prophesying**, Pelatiah
dropped **dead**. I threw myself face downwards on the ground and shouted, "No,
Sovereign LORD! Are you going to kill
everyone left in Israel?"

God's Promise to the Exiles

14 The LORD spoke to me. 15 "**Mortal**
man," he said, "the people who live in
Jerusalem are talking about you and
your fellow-Israelites who are in **exile**.
They say, 'The **exiles** are too far away to
worship the LORD. He has given us **possession** of the land.'
16 "Now tell your **fellow-exiles** what I
am saying. I am the one who sent them
to live in far-off nations and **scattered**
them in other countries. Yet, for the time
being I will be present with them in the
lands where they have gone.
17 "So tell them what I, the **Sovereign**
LORD, am saying. I will gather them out
of the countries where I **scattered** them,
and will give the land of Israel back to
them. 18 When they return, they are to
get **rid** of all the **filthy**, **disgusting idols**
they find. 19 I will give them a **new heart**
and a new **mind**. I will take away their
stubborn heart of stone and will give
them an **obedient heart**. 20 Then they will
keep my **laws** and **faithfully obey** all my
commands. They will be **my people**, and
I will be their God. 21 But I will **punish** the
people who **love** to **worship filthy**, **disgusting idols**. I will **punish** them for what
they have done." The **Sovereign** LORD
has spoken.

God's Glory Leaves Jerusalem

22 The living **creatures** began to fly,
and the wheels went with them. The
dazzling light of the **presence** of the God
of Israel was over them. 23 Then the **dazzling light** left the city and moved to the
mountain east of it. 24 In the **vision** the
spirit of God lifted me up and brought me
back to the **exiles** in Babylonia. Then the
vision faded, 25 and I told the **exiles** everything that the LORD had shown me.

The Prophet as a Refugee

12 The LORD spoke to me. 2 "**Mortal**
man," he said, "you are living
among **rebellious** people. They have
eyes, but they see nothing; they have
ears, but they hear nothing, because they
are **rebellious**.
3 "Now, **mortal man**, pack a bundle
just as a **refugee** would, and start out
before nightfall. Let everyone see you
leaving and going to another place.
Maybe those **rebels** will **notice** you.[y]
4 While it is still daylight, pack your
bundle for **exile**, so that they can see you,
and then let them **watch** you leave in the
evening as if you were going into **exile**.
5 While they are **watching**, break a hole
through the wall of your house and take
your pack out through it. 6 Let them
watch you putting your pack on your
shoulder and going out into the **dark** with
your eyes covered, so that you can't see
where you are going. What you do will be
a **warning** to the Israelites."
7 I did what the LORD told me to do.
That day I packed a bundle as a **refugee**
would, and that evening as it was getting
dark I dug a hole in the wall with my
hands and went out. While everyone
watched, I put the pack on my shoulder
and left.
8 The next morning the LORD spoke to
me. 9 "**Mortal man**," he said, "now that
those Israelite **rebels** are asking you
what you're doing, 10 tell them what I, the
Sovereign LORD, am saying to them. This
message is for the prince ruling in Jerusalem and for all the people who live
there. 11 Tell them that what you have
done is a **sign** of what will happen to
them—they will be **refugees** and **captives**. 12 The prince who is ruling them
will shoulder his pack in the **dark** and **escape** through a hole that they dig for him
in the wall. He will cover his eyes and not
see where he is going. 13 But I will spread
out my net and **trap** him in it. Then I will
take him to the city of Babylon, where he
will die without having seen it. 14 I will
scatter in every direction all the members of his **court** and his advisers and
bodyguard, and people will search for
them to kill them.

acknowledge 6.7; Dan 4.26
action Jer 32.19; 16.27
captive Lam 1.18; 39.28
court (1) Lam 3.36; Dan 1.4
dark [3] Lam 3.2; 30.18
destroy 6.3; 13.13
disease 6.11; 14.21
disgust 11.18; 14.6
escape 7.16; 13.21
exile [2] 11.15; 20.1
false Jer 51.17; 13.6
famine 6.11; 14.13
fear [2] 7.27; 21.7
message [2] 11.5; 13.6
mislead Jer 38.22; 13.9
mortal [6] 11.2; 13.2
notice (1) Jer 33.24; Mt 8.18
predict [2] Jer 29.8; 13.6
prophecy [2] 11.13; 13.2
proverb [2] Is 28.20; 16.44
rebel [5] 5.6; 17.12
refugee [3] Jer 50.28; 29.12
scatter [2] 11.16; 17.21
sign (1) 4.3; 20.12
Sovereign [6] 11.7; 13.3
strip (1) Jer 49.10; 16.36
trap Lam 3.52; 19.4
tremble [2] 7.18; 21.7
true 3.20; 13.6
vision [2] 11.24; 13.3
warn [2] 6.10; 20.18
watch [4] 10.2; 21.6

[y] Maybe those...you; *or* Maybe they will then realize that they are rebels.

11.19-20: Ezek 36.26-28 **11.22-23:** Ezek 43.2-5 **12.2:** Is 6.9-10; Jer 5.21; Mk 8.18
12.13: 2 Kgs 25.7; Jer 52.11

15 "When I scatter them among the
other nations and in foreign countries,
they will know that I am the LORD. 16 I
will let a few of them survive the war,
the famine, and the diseases, so that
there among the nations they will realize
how disgusting their actions have been
and will acknowledge that I am the
LORD."

The Sign of the Trembling Prophet

17 The LORD spoke to me. 18 "Mortal
man," he said, "tremble when you eat,
and shake with fear when you drink.
19 Tell the whole nation that this is the
message of the Sovereign LORD to the
people of Jerusalem who are still living
in their land: They will tremble when
they eat and shake with fear when they
drink. Their land will be stripped bare,
because everyone who lives there is lawless. 20 Cities that are now full of people
will be destroyed, and the country will be
made a wilderness. Then they will know
that I am the LORD."

A Popular Proverb and an Unpopular Message

21 The LORD spoke to me. 22 "Mortal
man," he said, "why do the people of
Israel repeat this proverb: 'Time goes
by, and predictions come to nothing'?
23 Now tell them what I, the Sovereign
LORD, have to say about that. I will put
an end to that proverb. It won't be repeated in Israel any more. Tell them instead: The time has come, and the predictions are coming true!

24 "Among the people of Israel there
will be no more false visions or misleading prophecies. 25 I, the LORD, will speak
to them, and what I say will be done.
There will be no more delay. In your own
lifetime, you rebels, I will do what I have
warned you I would do. I have spoken,"
says the Sovereign LORD.

26 The LORD said to me, 27 "Mortal
man, the Israelites think that your
visions and prophecies are about the distant future. 28 So tell them that I, the
Sovereign LORD, am saying: There will
be no more delay. What I have said will
be done. I, the Sovereign LORD, have
spoken!"

Prophecy against False Male Prophets

13 The LORD spoke to me. 2 "Mortal
man," he said, "denounce the
prophets of Israel who make up their
own prophecies. Tell them to listen to the
word of the LORD."

3 This is what the Sovereign LORD
says: "These foolish prophets are
doomed! They provide their own inspira-
tion and invent their own visions.
4 People of Israel, your prophets are as
useless as foxes living among the ruins of
a city. 5 They don't guard the places
where the walls have crumbled, nor do
they rebuild the walls, and so Israel cannot be defended when war comes on the
day of the LORD. 6 Their visions are false,
and their predictions are lies. They claim
that they are speaking my message, but I
have not sent them. Yet they expect
their words to come true! 7 I tell them:
Those visions you see are false, and the
predictions you make are lies. You say
that they are my words, but I haven't
spoken to you!"

8 So the Sovereign LORD says to them,
"Your words are false, and your visions
are lies. I am against you. 9 I am about to
punish you prophets who have false
visions and make misleading predictions.
You will not be there when my people
gather to make decisions; your names
will not be included in the list of the citizens of Israel; you will never return to
your land. Then you will know that I am
the Sovereign LORD.

10 "The prophets mislead my people
by saying that all is well. All is certainly
not well! My people have put up a wall of
loose stones, and then the prophets have
come and covered it with whitewash.
11 Tell the prophets that their wall is
going to fall down. I will send a pouring
rain. Hailstones will fall on it, and a
strong wind will blow against it. 12 The
wall will collapse, and everyone will ask
you what good the whitewash did."

13 Now this is what the Sovereign
LORD says: "In my anger I will send a
strong wind, pouring rain, and hailstones
to destroy the wall. 14 I intend to break
down the wall they whitewashed, to
shatter it, and to leave the foundation
stones bare. It will collapse and kill you
all. Then everyone will know that I am
the LORD.

15 "The wall and those who covered it
with whitewash will feel the force of my
anger. Then I will tell you that the wall is
gone and so are those who whitewashed
it— 16 those prophets who assured Jerusalem that all was well, when all was not
well!" The Sovereign LORD has spoken.

Prophecy against False Female Prophets

17 The LORD said, "Now, mortal man,
look at the women among your people
who make up predictions. Denounce

13.10: Jer 6.14, 8.11

alive 5.10; 23.25
anger [2] 9.8; 14.19
assure Ps 44.3; Mt 6.2
believe Lam 4.12; 21.23
benefit Prov 10.21; 1 Cor 9.11

bread 4.9; 16.13
claim Jer 48.14; 22.28
control [2] 11.5; 20.37
Day of the Lord Is 13.6; Joel 1.15
death (1) [2] 8.14; 16.38
defend Lam 2.2; 22.30
denounce [2] 11.4; 21.2
deserve [2] Jer 51.6; 14.4
destroy 12.20; 14.13
discourage Jer 14.3; Hag 2.4
dishonour Jer 34.16; 20.9
doom [2] Lam 5.16; 16.23
escape 12.12; 15.7
evil 11.2; 14.22
false [5] 12.24; 14.9
fool Jer 50.36; 28.17
force (1) 8.18; 16.34
free Jer 40.1; 34.27
God's people [8] 11.20; 14.8
hate 5.9; 16.27
hurt Jer 38.4; 28.24
inspire Job 26.4; Hos 9.7
intend Jer 51.11; 38.13
lie (2) [5] Lam 2.14; 21.29
life (1) [4] 3.18; 14.14
magic Jer 27.9; Dan 1.20
message 12.10; 24.21
mislead [3] 12.24; Mic 3.6
mortal [2] 12.2; 14.3
possess 11.15; 35.10
power [4] 8.1; 16.39
predict [5] 12.22; 21.23
prevent Jer 11.15; Hos 5.4
prophecy 12.24; 20.46
prophet [8] 7.26; 14.4
provide Jer 31.35; 45.17
punish 11.11; 14.10
rescue Lam 3.58; 34.10
ruin Lam 5.18; 19.7
save 7.19; 14.14
Sovereign [7] 12.10; 14.4
strong [2] 7.24; 16.7
true 12.23; 18.5
useless Jer 46.11; 15.5
vision [6] 12.24; 21.29
wish 1.12; Dan 4.19
word (1) [4] 6.3; 22.14

them [18]and tell them what the **Sovereign** LORD is saying to them:

"You women are **doomed**! You sew **magic** wristbands for everyone and make magic scarves for everyone to wear on their heads, so that they can have **power** over other people's **lives**. You want to **possess** the **power of life** and **death** over **my people** and to use it for your own **benefit**. [19]You **dishonour** me in front of **my people** in order to get a few handfuls of barley and a few pieces of **bread**. You kill people who don't **deserve** to die, and you keep people **alive** who don't **deserve** to live. So you tell **lies** to **my people**, and they **believe** you."

20 Now this is what the **Sovereign** LORD says: "I **hate** the wristbands that you use in your attempt to **control life** and **death**. I will rip them off your arms and **set free** the people that you were **controlling**.[z] [21]I will rip off your scarves and let **my people escape** from your **power** once and for all. Then you will know that I am the LORD.

22 "By your **lies** you **discourage** good people, whom I do not **wish** to **hurt**. You **prevent evil** people from giving up evil and **saving** their **lives**. [23]So now your **false visions** and **misleading predictions** are over. I am **rescuing my people** from your **power**, so that you will know that I am the LORD."

God Condemns Idolatry

14 Some of the leaders of the Israelites came to **consult** me about the **LORD's will**. [2]Then the LORD spoke to me. [3]"**Mortal man**," he said, "these men have given their **hearts** to **idols** and are letting **idols** lead them into sin. Do they think I will give them an answer?

4 "Now speak to them and tell them what I, the **Sovereign LORD**, am saying to them: Every Israelite who has given his **heart to idols** and lets them lead him into sin and who then comes to **consult** a **prophet**, will get an answer from me—the answer that his many **idols deserve**! [5]All those **idols** have **turned** the Israelites away from me, but by my answer I **hope** to **win** back their **loyalty**.

6 "Now then, tell the Israelites what I, the **Sovereign LORD**, am saying: **Turn** back and leave your **disgusting idols**.

7 "Whenever one of the Israelites or one of the foreigners who live in the Israelite **community turns away** from me and **worships idols**, and then goes to **consult** a **prophet**, I, the LORD, will give him his answer! [8]I will oppose him. I will make an **example** of him. I will remove him from the **community** of **my people**, so that you will know that I am the LORD.

9 "If a **prophet** is **deceived** into giving a **false** answer, it is because I, the LORD, have **deceived** him. I will remove him from the people of Israel. [10]Both the **prophet** and the one who **consults** him will get the same **punishment**. [11]I will do this to **keep the Israelites from** deserting me and **defiling** themselves by their sins. They are to be **my people**, and I will be their God." The **Sovereign LORD** has spoken.

Noah, Danel, and Job

12 The LORD spoke to me. [13]"**Mortal man**," he said, "if a country sins and is **unfaithful** to me, I will stretch out my hand and **destroy** its supply of food. I will send a **famine** and kill people and animals alike. [14]Even if those three men, Noah, Danel,[a] and Job, were living there, their goodness would **save** only their own **lives**." The **Sovereign LORD** has spoken.

15 "Or I might send wild animals to kill the people, making the land so **dangerous** that no one could travel through it, [16]and even if those three men lived there—as **surely** as I, the **Sovereign** LORD, am the living God—they would not be able to **save** even their own children. They would **save** only their own **lives**, and the land would become a wilderness.

17 "Or I might bring war on that country and send **destructive** weapons to wipe out people and animals alike, [18]and even if those three men lived there—as **surely** as I, the **Sovereign LORD**, am the living God—they would not be able to **save** even their children, but only their own **lives**.

19 "If I send an epidemic on that country and in my **anger** take many **lives**, killing people and animals, [20]even if Noah, Danel, and Job lived there—as **surely** as I, the **Sovereign LORD**, am the living God—they would not be able to **save** even their own children. Their goodness would **save** only their own **lives**."

21 This is what the **Sovereign LORD** is saying: "I will send my four **worst punishments** on Jerusalem—war, **famine**, wild animals, and **disease**—to **destroy** people and animals alike. [22]If anyone does survive and **save** his children, look at them when they come to you. See how **evil**

save [7] 13.22; 18.27
Sovereign [9] 13.3; 15.6
sure [3] Lam 3.23; 16.48
turn [3] 10.11; 17.7
unfaithful 5.13; 15.8
will (1) Lam 3.37; 20.1
win Lam 1.9; 16.19
worship (2) (of other gods) 11.21; 16.24
worst Jer 2.33; Dan 12.1

anger 13.13; 16.26
community [2] Neh 13.3; 20.1
consult [4] Jer 8.2; 20.1
convince 5.13; Mt 21.26
danger 3.20; 34.25
deceive [2] Lam 2.14; Dan 8.23
defile 9.7; 20.18
deserve 13.19; 16.59
destroy [3] 13.13; 16.50
disease 12.16; 28.23
disgust 12.16; 16.2
evil 13.22; 16.23
example Ecc 9.13; 18.14
false 13.6; 20.7
famine [2] 12.16; 36.29
God's people [2] 13.9; 21.10
heart [2] 11.19; 18.31
hope 7.27; 17.7
idol [7] 11.18; 16.19
keep from Jer 10.4; 17.14
life (1) [5] 13.18; 16.22
loyal Jer 2.19; 17.13
mortal [2] 13.2; 15.2
prophet [4] 13.2; 22.28
punish [3] 13.9; 15.7
reason Is 14.29; Dan 11.34

[z] *In verse 20 in Hebrew a word occurs twice, the meaning of which is unclear.*
[a] DANEL: *or* Daniel, an ancient hero, known for his righteous life.

14.21: Rev 6.8

compare [2] Jer 50.44; 16.51
escape 13.21; 17.18
grapevine *see* vine
mortal 14.3; 16.2
punish [2] 14.10; 16.27
Sovereign [2] 14.4; 16.3
unfaithful 14.13; 16.20
useless [2] 13.4; 22.19
vine [3] Jer 49.9; 17.6

act [2] Jer 50.29; 20.44
action [2] 12.16; 20.44
adultery [3] Jer 29.23; 22.11
advantage Jer 7.6; 22.7
anger [5] 14.19; 19.12
ashamed [3] Jer 51.51; 43.10
bad 11.2; 23.13
best [3] Lam 3.26; 17.21
bless Jer 31.23; 34.26
blood [4] Lam 4.14; 21.32
body 10.12; 29.5
bread 13.19; 44.30
bribe Is 45.13; Amos 5.12
calm Is 7.4; 32.14
care Jer 49.11; 23.42
commit [2] 9.9; 22.6
compare 15.2; 27.32
condemn Lam 1.22; 20.35
corrupt Jer 6.28; 28.18
covenant [6] Jer 50.5; 20.20
crown Jer 13.18; 21.26
dazzling 11.22; 43.2
death (1) 13.18; 18.13
deserve 14.4; 20.44
destroy 14.13; 18.30
disgrace [2] 8.6; 20.43
disgust [8] 14.6; 18.12

they are, and be convinced that the punishment I am bringing on Jerusalem is
justified; 23 then you will know that there
was good reason for everything I did."
The Sovereign LORD has spoken.

A Parable about a Vine

15 The LORD spoke to me. 2 "Mortal
man," he said, "how does a vine
compare with a tree? What good is a
branch of a grapevine compared with
the trees of the forest? 3 Can you use it to
make anything? Can you even make a
peg out of it to hang things on? 4 It is only
good for building a fire. And when the
ends are burnt up and the middle is
charred, can you make anything out of
it? 5 It was useless even before it was
burnt. Now that the fire has burnt it and
charred it, it is even more useless."
6 Now this is what the Sovereign LORD
is saying, "Just as a vine is taken from
the forest and burnt, so I will take the
people who live in Jerusalem 7 and will
punish them. They have escaped one
fire, but now fire will burn them up.
When I punish them, you will know that I
am the LORD. 8 They have been unfaithful
to me, and so I will make the country a
wilderness." The Sovereign LORD has
spoken.

Jerusalem the Unfaithful

16 The LORD spoke to me again.
2 "Mortal man," he said, "point
out to Jerusalem what disgusting things
she has done. 3 Tell Jerusalem what the
Sovereign LORD is saying to her:
"You were born in the land of Canaan.
Your father was an Amorite, and your
mother was a Hittite.[b] 4 When you were
born, no one cut your umbilical cord or
washed you[c] or rubbed you with salt or
wrapped you in cloth. 5 No one took
enough pity on you to do any of these
things for you. When you were born, no
one loved you. You were thrown out in
an open field.
6 "Then I passed by and saw you
squirming in your own blood. You were
covered with blood, but I wouldn't let you
die. 7 I made you grow like a healthy
plant. You grew strong and tall and became a young woman.[d] Your breasts
were well-formed, and your hair had
grown, but you were naked.
8 "As I passed by again, I saw that the
time had come for you to fall in love. I
covered your naked body with my coat
and promised to love you. Yes, I made a
marriage covenant with you, and you
became mine." This is what the
Sovereign LORD says.
9 "Then I took water and washed the
blood off you. I rubbed olive-oil on your
skin. 10 I dressed you in embroidered
gowns and gave you shoes of the best
leather, a linen headband, and a silk
cloak. 11 I put jewels on you—bracelets
and necklaces. 12 I gave you a nose-ring
and earrings and a beautiful crown to
wear. 13 You had ornaments of gold and
silver, and you always wore clothes of
embroidered linen and silk. You ate
bread made from the best flour, and had
honey and olive-oil to eat. Your beauty
was dazzling, and you became a queen.
14 You became famous in every nation for
your perfect beauty, because I was the
one who made you so lovely." This is
what the Sovereign LORD says.
15 "But you took advantage of your
beauty and fame to sleep with everyone
who came along.[e] 16 You used some of
your clothes to decorate your places of
worship, and just like a prostitute,[f] you
gave yourself to everyone. 17 You took
the silver and gold jewellery that I had
given you, used it to make male images,
and committed adultery with them.
18 You took the embroidered clothes I
gave you and put them on the images,
and you offered to the images the olive-
oil and incense I had given you. 19 I gave
you food—the best flour, olive-oil, and
honey—but you offered it as a sacrifice
to win the favour of idols." This is what
the Sovereign LORD says.
20 "Then you took the sons and the
daughters you had borne me and offered
them as sacrifices to idols. Wasn't it bad
enough to be unfaithful to me, 21 without
taking my children and sacrificing them
to idols? 22 During your disgusting life as
a prostitute you never once remembered
your childhood—when you were naked,
squirming in your own blood."

Jerusalem's Life as a Prostitute

23 The Sovereign LORD said, "You are
doomed! Doomed! You did all that evil,
and then 24 by the side of every road you
built places to worship idols and practise
prostitution. 25 You dragged your beauty
through the mud. You offered yourself to
everyone who came by, and you were
more of a prostitute every day. 26 You let
your lustful neighbours, the Egyptians, go

doom [2] 13.3; 24.6
endure Jer 44.22; Mic 7.9
enough [2] 7.13; 19.1
evil [3] 14.22; 18.8
favour Lam 3.59; Dan 7.22
force (1) 13.15; 20.8
forget Lam 3.17; 22.12
forgive Lam 3.42; 18.22
fury 7.19; 25.14
gift Jer 31.12; 20.31
hate [5] 13.20; 23.28
honour Lam 1.1; 20.44
idol [8] 14.3; 18.6
ignore 3.27; 22.26
image [2] 8.12; 23.14
immoral [2] Prov 23.27; 23.13
incense 8.11; 23.41
innocent [2] Lam 4.13; Dan 6.22
jealous Is 11.13; 35.11
last (1) 4.4; 25.12
life (1) 14.14; 18.4
love [4] 11.21; 20.7
lust Jer 13.27; 22.9
mortal 15.2; 17.2
naked [5] Lam 4.21; 18.7
neighbour [2] 11.12; 28.26
offer [4] Jer 52.19; 18.6
peace 7.25; 38.11
perfect Jer 17.14; 27.3
pity 9.10; 20.17
place of worship Jer 48.35; 28.18
plenty Jer 44.17; 19.10
poor Jer 52.16; 18.12
power 13.18; 17.17
practice [2] Jer 44.5; 18.14
privilege 2 Chr 9.7; Rom 1.5
promise [2] Lam 1.21; 20.5
prosper [3] Jer 49.6; 36.11
prostitute [15] Jer 5.7; 23.3
proud [3] 7.10; 24.21
proverb 12.22; 18.2
punish [3] 15.7; 17.15
pure Lam 4.7; 24.11
raise 3.24; 21.26
remember [3] 6.9; 18.24
restore Lam 5.21; Dan 8.14
sacrifice [4] 6.13; 18.6
satisfy [3] 8.17; 22.9
sex Is 57.5; 23.17
shame [2] Lam 4.21; 36.32
share Jer 37.12; 27.36
Sovereign [11] 15.6; 17.3
special Jer 45.5; 48.8
stranger Lam 5.2; Obad 11
strip (1) [2] 12.19; 23.10
strong 13.11; 19.11
stubborn 11.19; 36.26
suffer 4.4; 18.19
sure 14.16; 17.14
unfaithful 15.8; 17.20
win 14.5; 27.10

[b] AMORITE...HITTITE: *The Israelites regarded these people as immoral and idolatrous.*
[c] *Hebrew has an additional word, the meaning of which is unclear.*
[d] *Probable text* young woman; *Hebrew unclear.*
[e] *Hebrew has two additional words, the meaning of which is unclear.*
[f] *Hebrew has four additional words, the meaning of which is unclear.*

worse [2] Jer 23.14; 29.12
worship (2) (of other gods) [3] 14.7; 18.6
wrong Lam 3.59; 29.16

to bed with you, and you used your prostitution to make me angry.

27 "Now I have raised my hand to punish you and to take away your share of my blessing. I have handed you over to the Philistines, who hate you and are disgusted with your immoral actions.

28 "Because you were not satisfied by the others, you went running after the Assyrians. You were their prostitute, but they didn't satisfy you either. 29 You were also a prostitute for the Babylonians, that nation of businessmen, but they didn't satisfy you either."

30 [g] This is what the Sovereign LORD is saying: "You have done all this like a shameless prostitute. 31 On every street you built places to worship idols and practise prostitution. But you are not out for money like a common prostitute. 32 You are like a woman who commits adultery with strangers instead of loving her husband. 33 A prostitute is paid, but you gave presents to all your lovers and bribed them to come from everywhere to sleep with you. 34 You are a special kind of prostitute. No one forced you to become one. You didn't get paid; you paid them! Yes, you are different."

God's Judgement on Jerusalem

35 Now then, Jerusalem, you whore! Hear what the LORD is saying.

36 This is what the Sovereign LORD says: "You stripped off your clothes and, like a prostitute, you gave yourself to your lovers and to all your disgusting idols, and you killed your children as sacrifices to idols. 37 Because of this I will bring all your former lovers together—the ones you liked and the ones you hated. I will bring them round you in a circle, and then I will strip off your clothes and let them see you naked. 38 I will condemn you for adultery and murder, and in my anger and fury I will punish you with death. 39 I will put you in their power, and they will tear down the places where you engage in prostitution and worship idols. They will take away your clothes and jewels and leave you completely naked.

40 "They will stir up a crowd to stone you, and they will cut you to pieces with their swords. 41 They will burn your houses down and let crowds of women see your punishment. I will make you stop being a prostitute and make you stop giving gifts to your lovers. 42 Then my anger will be over, and I will be calm. I will not be angry or jealous any more. 43 You have forgotten how I treated you when you were young, and you have made me angry by all the things you did. That is why I have made you pay for them all. Why did you add sexual immorality to all the other disgusting things you did?" The Sovereign LORD has spoken.

Like Mother, Like Daughter

44 The LORD said, "People will use this proverb about you, Jerusalem: 'Like mother, like daughter.' 45 You really are your mother's daughter. She detested her husband and her children. You are like your sisters, who hated their husbands and their children. You and your sister cities had a Hittite mother and an Amorite[h] father.

46 "Your elder sister is Samaria, in the north, with her villages. Your younger sister, with her villages, is Sodom, in the south. 47 Were you content to follow in their footsteps and copy their disgusting actions? No, in only a little while you were behaving worse than they were in everything you did.

48 "As sure as I am the living God," the Sovereign LORD says, "your sister Sodom and her villages never did the evil that you and your villages have done. 49 She and her daughters were proud because they had plenty to eat and lived in peace and quiet, but they did not take care of the poor and the underprivileged. 50 They were proud and stubborn and did the things that I hate, so I destroyed them, as you well know.

51 "Samaria did not sin half as much as you have. You have acted more disgustingly than she ever did. Your corruption makes your sisters look innocent by comparison. 52 And now you will have to endure your disgrace. Your sins are so much worse than those of your sisters that they look innocent beside you. Now blush and bear your shame, because you make your sisters look pure."

Sodom and Samaria Will Be Restored

53 The LORD said to Jerusalem, "I will make them prosperous again—Sodom and her villages and Samaria and her villages. Yes, I will make you prosperous too. 54 You will be ashamed of yourself, and your disgrace will show your sisters how well-off they are. 55 They will become prosperous again, and you and your villages will also be restored. 56 Didn't you joke about Sodom in those days when you were proud 57 and before

[g] *Verse 30 in Hebrew begins with three words, the meaning of which is unclear.*
[h] HITTITE...AMORITE: *See* 16.3.

the evil you did had been exposed? Now
you are just like her—a joke to the
Edomites, the Philistines, and your other
neighbours who hate you. 58 You must
suffer for the obscene, disgusting things
you have done." The LORD has spoken.

A Covenant That Lasts For Ever

59 The Sovereign LORD says, "I will
treat you as you deserve, because you ignored your promises and broke the
covenant. 60 But I will honour the covenant I made with you when you were
young, and I will make a covenant with
you that will last for ever. 61 You will
remember how you have acted, and be
ashamed of it when you get your elder
sister and your younger sister back. I will
let them be like daughters to you, even
though this was not part of my covenant
with you. 62 I will renew my covenant
with you, and you will know that I am the
LORD. 63 I will forgive all the wrongs you
have done, but you will remember them
and be too ashamed to open your
mouth." The Sovereign LORD has spoken.

The Parable of the Eagles and the Vine

17 The LORD spoke to me. 2 "Mortal
man," he said, "tell the Israelites
a parable 3 to let them know what I, the
Sovereign LORD, am saying to them:
There was a giant eagle with beautiful
feathers and huge wings, spread wide.
He flew to the Lebanon Mountains and
broke off the top of a cedar-tree, 4 which
he carried to a land of commerce, and
placed in a city of merchants. 5 Then he
took a young plant from the land of
Israel and planted it in a fertile field,[i]
where there was always water to make it
grow. 6 The plant sprouted and became a
low, wide-spreading grapevine. The
branches grew upward towards the
eagle, and the roots grew deep. The vine
was covered with branches and leaves.

7 "There was another giant eagle with
huge wings and thick plumage. And now
the vine sent its roots towards him and
turned its leaves towards him, in the
hope that he would give it more water
than there was in the garden where it
was growing.[j] 8 But the vine had already
been planted in a fertile, well-watered
field so that it could grow leaves and
bear grapes and be a magnificent vine.

9 "So I, the Sovereign LORD, ask: Will
this vine live and grow? Won't the first
eagle pull it up by its roots, pull off the
grapes, and break off the branches and
let them wither? It will not take much
strength or a mighty nation to pull it up.
10 Yes, it is planted, but will it live and
grow? Won't it wither when the east
wind strikes it? Won't it wither there
where it is growing?"

The Parable Is Explained

11 The LORD said to me, 12 "Ask these
rebels if they know what the parable
means. Tell them that the king of Babylonia came to Jerusalem and took the
king and his officials back with him to
Babylonia. 13 He took one of the king's
family, made a treaty with him, and
made him swear to be loyal. He took important men as hostages 14 to keep the
nation from rising again and to make
sure that the treaty would be kept. 15 But
the king of Judah rebelled and sent
agents to Egypt to get horses and a large
army. Will he succeed? Can he get away
with that? He cannot break the treaty
and go unpunished!

16 "As surely as I am the living God,"
says the Sovereign LORD, "this king will
die in Babylonia because he broke his
oath and the treaty he had made with the
king of Babylonia, who put him on the
throne. 17 Even the powerful army of the
king of Egypt will not be able to help him
fight when the Babylonians build earthworks and dig trenches in order to kill
many people. 18 He broke his oath and
the treaty he had made. He did all these
things, and now he will not escape."

19 The Sovereign LORD says, "As
surely as I am the living God, I will punish him for breaking the treaty which he
swore in my name to keep. 20 I will
spread out a hunter's net and catch him
in it. I will take him to Babylonia and
punish him there, because he was unfaithful to me. 21 His best soldiers will be
killed in battle, and the survivors will be
scattered in every direction. Then you
will know that I, the LORD, have spoken."

God's Promise of Hope

22 This is what the Sovereign LORD
says:

"I will take the top of a tall cedar
and break off a tender sprout;
I will plant it on a high mountain,
23 on Israel's highest mountain.
It will grow branches and bear seed
and become a magnificent cedar.
Birds of every kind will live there

[i] *Hebrew has an additional word, the meaning of which is unclear.*
[j] And now the vine...growing; *or* And now the vine turned away from the garden where it was growing and sent its roots towards him and turned its leaves towards him, in the hope that he would give it water.

17.12–15: 2 Kgs 24.15–20; 2 Chr 36.10–13

and find **shelter** in its shade.
24 All the trees in the land will know
that I am the LORD.
I cut down the tall trees
and make the small trees grow tall.
I wither up the green trees
and make the dry trees become
green.
I, the LORD, have spoken. I will do what I
have said I would do."

Individual Responsibility

18 The LORD spoke to me 2 and said,
"What is this **proverb** people
keep repeating in the land of Israel?
'The parents ate the sour grapes,
But the children got the sour taste.'
3 "As **surely** as I am the living God,"
says the **Sovereign** LORD, "you will not
repeat this **proverb** in Israel any more.
4 The **life** of every person belongs to me,
the **life** of the parent as well as that of
the child. The person who sins is the one
who will die.
5 "Suppose there is a **truly** good man,
righteous and **honest**. 6 He doesn't
worship the idols of the Israelites or eat
the **sacrifices offered** at **forbidden**
shrines. He doesn't seduce another man's
wife or have intercourse with a woman
during her period. 7 He doesn't **cheat** or
rob anyone. He returns what a borrower
gives him as **security**; he feeds the
hungry and gives clothing to the **naked**.
8 He doesn't lend money for profit. He
refuses to do **evil** and gives an **honest**
decision in any **dispute**. 9 Such a man
obeys my **commands** and carefully keeps
my **laws**. He is **righteous**, and he will
live," says the **Sovereign** LORD.
10 "Then suppose this man has a son
who **robs** and kills, who does any[k] of
these things 11 that the father never did.
He eats **sacrifices offered** at **forbidden**
shrines and seduces other men's wives.
12 He **cheats** the **poor**, he **robs**, he keeps
what a borrower gives him as **security**.
He goes to **pagan shrines**, **worships dis-**
gusting idols, 13 and lends money for
profit. Will he live? No, he will not. He
has done all these **disgusting** things, and
so he will die. He will be to **blame** for his
own **death**.
14 "Now suppose this second man has
a son. He sees all the sins his father
practised, but does not follow his
example. 15 He doesn't **worship the idols**
of the Israelites or eat the **sacrifices**
offered at **forbidden shrines**. He doesn't
seduce another man's wife 16 or **oppress**
anyone or **rob** anyone. He returns what a
borrower gives him as **security**. He feeds
the **hungry** and gives clothing to the
naked. 17 He **refuses** to do **evil**[l] and
doesn't lend money for profit. He keeps
my **laws** and **obeys** my **commands**. He
will not die because of his father's sins,
but he will certainly live. 18 His father, on
the other hand, **cheated** and **robbed**,[m]
and always did **evil** to everyone. And so
he died because of the sins he himself
had committed.
19 "But you ask: 'Why shouldn't the
son **suffer** because of his father's sins?'
The answer is that the son did what was
right and good. He kept my **laws** and
followed them carefully, and so he will
certainly live. 20 It is the one who sins
who will die. A son is not to **suffer**
because of his father's sins, nor a father
because of the sins of his son. A good
man will be **rewarded** for doing good,
and an evil man will **suffer** for the **evil** he
does.
21 "If an **evil** man stops sinning and
keeps my **laws**, if he does what is **right**
and good, he will not die; he will certainly live. 22 All his sins will be **forgiven**,
and he will live, because he did what is
right. 23 Do you think I **enjoy** seeing an
evil man die?" asks the **Sovereign** LORD.
"No, I would rather see him **repent** and
live.
24 "But if a **righteous** man stops doing
good and starts doing all the **evil**, **disgust-**
ing things that evil men do, will he go on
living? No! None of the good he did will
be **remembered**. He will die because of
his **unfaithfulness** and his sins.
25 "But you say, 'What the Lord does
isn't **right**.' Listen to me, you Israelites.
Do you think my way of doing things isn't
right? It is your way that isn't **right**.
26 When a **righteous** man stops doing
good and starts doing **evil** and then dies,
he dies because of the **evil** he has done.
27 When an **evil** man stops sinning and
does what is **right** and good, he **saves** his
life. 28 He realizes what he is doing and
stops sinning, so he will certainly not die,
but go on living. 29 And you Israelites say,
'What the Lord does isn't **right**.' You
think my way isn't **right**, do you? It is
your way that isn't **right**.
30 "Now I, the **Sovereign** LORD, am
telling you Israelites that I will **judge**
each of you by what he has done. **Turn**
away from all the **evil** you are doing, and

blame Prov 19.3; 33.4
cheat [3] Jer 22.3; 22.7
command [2] 11.12; 20.11
death (1) 16.38; 33.4
destroy 16.50; 20.13
disgust [3] 16.2; 20.4
dispute Is 2.4; 44.24
enjoy Jer 22.15; 33.11
evil [12] 16.23; 20.43
example 14.8; 26.21
forbid [3] 4.13; Hos 9.3
forgive 16.63; 33.16
heart 14.3; 21.6
honest [2] Is 59.14; 45.10
hunger [2] 7.15; 34.29
idol [3] 16.19; 20.7
judge 7.3; 21.30
law [4] 11.12; 20.11
life (1) [3] 16.22; 20.11
mind (1) 11.19; 20.32
naked [2] 16.7; 23.10
new 11.19; 36.26
obey [2] 11.19; 20.11
offer [3] 16.18; 20.26
oppress Jer 50.33; 45.8
pagan Jer 13.27; Hos 4.14
poor 16.49; 21.26
practice 16.24; 23.45
proverb [2] 16.44; Hos 4.14
refuse (1) [2] 5.6; 20.8
remember 16.22; 20.43
repent Lam 2.14; 21.13
reward Jer 32.19; Dan 2.6
right (1) [10] Jer 51.10; 33.14
righteous [4] Jer 33.15; 23.45
rob [5] 7.21; 22.13
sacrifice [3] 16.19; 20.26
save 14.14; 33.8
secure [3] Jer 49.31; 28.26
shrine [4] 7.7; Hos 10.8
Sovereign [5] 17.3; 20.3
suffer [3] 16.58; 23.35
sure 17.14; 20.3
true 13.6; 33.33
turn [2] 17.7; 21.16
unfaithful 17.20; 20.27
worship (2) (of other gods) [3] 16.24; 20.16

[k] *Some ancient translations* who does any; *Hebrew unclear.*
[l] *Some ancient translations (see also v. 8)* to do evil; *Hebrew* from the poor.
[m] *Some ancient translations* robbed; *Hebrew unclear.*

18.2: Jer 31.29 **18.9:** Lev 18.5 **18.20:** Deut 24.16

don't let your sin **destroy** you. 31 Give up
all the **evil** you have been doing, and get
yourselves **new minds** and **hearts**. Why
do you Israelites want to die? 32 I do not
want anyone to die," says the **Sovereign**
LORD. "**Turn away** from your sins and
live."

A Song of Sorrow

anger 16.26; 20.8
cloud 10.3; 26.10
enough 16.5; 22.14
grapevine *see* **vine**
hope 17.7; 37.11
learn Lam 3.27; Dan 1.4
never again Jer 50.39; 26.20
plenty 16.49; 36.29
ruin 13.4; 21.27
sorrow [2] 6.11; 21.6
strong [2] 16.7; 20.33
teach 7.26; 20.11
terrify 5.15; 21.14
trap [2] 12.13; Hos 5.1
vine [4] 17.6; Hos 2.12

19 The LORD told me to sing this
song of **sorrow** for two princes of
Israel:

2 What a lioness your mother was!
She reared her cubs among the fierce
male lions.
3 She reared a cub and **taught** him to
hunt;
he became a man-eater.
4 The nations heard about him
and **trapped** him in a pit.
With hooks they dragged him off to
Egypt.
5 She waited until she saw all **hope** was
gone.
Then she reared another of her cubs,
and he grew into a fierce lion.
6 When he was full-grown,
he prowled with the other lions.
He too **learnt** to hunt and became a
man-eater.
7 He wrecked forts,[o] he **ruined** towns.
The people of the land were **terrified**
every time he roared.
8 The nations gathered to fight him;
people came from everywhere.
They spread their hunting nets
and caught him in their **trap**.
9 They put him in a cage
and took him to the king of
Babylonia.
They kept him under guard,
so that his roar would never be
heard again
on the hills of Israel.

10 Your mother was like a **grapevine**[p]
planted near a stream.
Because there was **plenty** of water,
the **vine** was covered with leaves
and fruit.
11 Its branches were **strong**,
and grew to be royal sceptres.
The **vine** grew tall **enough** to reach the
clouds;
everyone saw how leafy and tall it
was.
12 But **angry** hands pulled it up by the
roots
and threw it to the ground.
The east wind dried up its fruit.
Its branches were broken off;
they dried up and were burnt.
13 Now it is planted in the desert,
in a dry and waterless land.
14 The stem of the **vine** caught fire;
fire burnt up its branches and fruit.
The branches will **never again** be
strong,
will never be royal sceptres.
This is a song of **sorrow**; it has been sung
again and again.

The LORD's Will and Man's Defiance

accept Lam 3.30; Dan 11.39
act 16.51; 23.19
action 16.27; 21.24
agree Jer 34.8; Dan 1.14
anger [6] 19.12; 21.17
announce 3.18; 21.28
best 17.21; 24.4
choose [2] Lam 4.20; 21.27
command [7] 18.9; 28.10
community 14.7; Mal 2.12
complain Lam 3.39; 24.16
condemn [3] 16.38; 21.24
consult 14.1; 21.21
control 13.20; Dan 2.21
covenant [2] 16.8; 34.25
custom 5.7; Zeph 1.8
defile [4] 14.11; 22.3
defy [3] 3.7; Dan 8.11
deserve 16.59; 31.11
destroy 18.30; 21.28
disgrace 16.52; 32.24
disgust [4] 18.12; 22.2
dishonour [4] 13.19; 22.16
evil [2] 18.8; 21.3
exile 12.4; 24.1
false 14.9; 21.29
first-born Ps 136.10; Mic 6.7
force (1) [3] 16.34; 22.10
gift [3] 16.41; Dan 2.6
god (2) (other gods) [2] 8.14; 28.2
holy [6] 8.6; 22.8
honour 16.60; 22.7
idol [9] 18.6; 21.21
insult 8.17; 21.28
law [8] 18.9; 22.26
life (1) [4] 18.4; 32.10
love 16.5; 24.16
mind (1) 18.31; 36.26
mortal [4] 17.2; 21.2
name (2) (name of God, of Jesus) [4] 17.19; 36.20
obey [6] 18.9; 33.32
offer [6] 18.6; 22.9
pity 16.5; 24.14
please [2] Jer 42.6; 31.16
power [2] 17.17; 21.26
presence 11.22; 33.22
profane [4] 7.22; 23.38
promise [7] 16.8; 33.13
prophecy 13.2; 21.9
protect 11.3; 23.24
punish 17.15; 21.10

20 It was the tenth day of the fifth
month of the seventh year of our
exile. Some of the leaders of the Israelite
community came to **consult** me about the
LORD's **will**, and they sat down in front of
me. 2 Then the LORD spoke to me.
3 "**Mortal man**," he said, "speak to these
men and tell them that the **Sovereign**
LORD is saying: You have come to ask
my **will**, have you? As **surely** as I am the
living God, I will not let you ask me anything. I, the **Sovereign** LORD, have
spoken.
4 "Are you ready to pass **sentence** on
them, **mortal man**? Then do so. **Remind**
them of the **disgusting** things their
fathers did. 5 Tell them what I am saying.
When I **chose** Israel, I made them a **pro**-
mise. I **revealed** myself to them in Egypt
and told them: I am the LORD your God.
6 It was then that I **promised** to take them
out of Egypt and lead them to a land I
had **chosen** for them, a **rich** and fertile
land, the finest land of all. 7 I told them to
throw away the **disgusting idols** they
loved and not to make themselves **un**-
clean with the **false gods** of Egypt, because I am the LORD their God. 8 But they
defied me and **refused** to listen. They did
not throw away their **disgusting idols** or
give up the Egyptian **gods**. I was ready to
let them feel the full **force** of my **anger**
there in Egypt. 9 But I did not, since that
would have brought **dishonour** to my
name, for in the **presence** of the people
among whom they were living I had **an**-
nounced to Israel that I was going to lead
them out of Egypt.
10 "And so I led them out of Egypt into
the desert. 11 I gave them my **commands**
and **taught** them my **laws**, which bring
life to anyone who **obeys** them. 12 I made
the keeping of the **Sabbath** a **sign** of the
agreement between us, to **remind** them
that I, the LORD, make them **holy**. 13 But
even in the desert they **defied** me. They
broke my **laws** and **rejected** my

[o] *One ancient translation* wrecked forts; *Hebrew unclear.*
[p] *Hebrew has an additional word, the meaning of which is unclear.*

20.5–6: Ex 6.2–8 **20.11, 13:** Lev 18.5 **20.12:** Ex 31.13–17

commands, which bring **life** to anyone who **obeys** them. They completely **profaned** the **Sabbath**. I was ready to let them feel the **force** of my **anger** there in the desert and **destroy** them. 14 But I did not, since that would have brought **dishonour** to my **name** among the nations which had seen me lead Israel out of Egypt. 15 So I made a **promise** in the desert that I would not take them to the land I had given them, a **rich** and fertile land, the finest land of all. 16 I made the **promise** because they had **rejected** my **commands**, broken my **laws**, and **profaned** the **Sabbath**—they preferred to **worship their idols**.

17 "But then I took **pity** on them. I decided not to kill them there in the desert. 18 Instead, I **warned** the young people among them: Do not keep the **laws** your ancestors made; do not follow their **customs** or **defile** yourselves with their **idols**. 19 I am the LORD your God. **Obey** my **laws** and my **commands**. 20 Make the **Sabbath** a **holy** day, so that it will be a **sign** of the **covenant** we made, and will **remind** you that I am the LORD your God.

21 "But that generation also **defied** me. They broke my **laws** and did not keep my **commands**, which bring **life** to anyone who **obeys** them. They **profaned** the **Sabbath**. I was ready to let them feel the **force** of my **anger** there in the desert and kill them all. 22 But I did not, since that would have brought **dishonour** to my **name** among the nations which had seen me bring Israel out of Egypt. 23 So I made another **promise** in the desert. I **vowed** that I would **scatter** them all over the **world**. 24 I did this because they had **rejected** my **commands**, broken my **laws**, **profaned** the **Sabbath**, and **worship ped** the same **idols** their ancestors had **served**.

25 "Then I gave them **laws** that are not good and **commands** that do not bring **life**. 26 I let them **defile** themselves with their own **offerings**, and I let them **sacrifice** their **first-born** sons. This was to **punish** them and show them that I am the LORD.

27 "Now then, **mortal man**, tell the Israelites what I, the **Sovereign** LORD, am saying to them. This is another way their fathers **insulted** me by their **unfaithfulness**. 28 I brought them to the **land I had promised** to give them. When they saw the high hills and green trees, they **offered sacrifices** at all of them. They made me **angry** by the **sacrifices** they burnt and by the wine they brought as **offerings**. 29 I asked them: What are these high places where you go? So they have been called 'High Places'[q] ever since. 30 Now tell the Israelites what I, the **Sovereign** LORD, am saying: Why must you commit the same sins your fathers did and go running after their **idols**? 31 Even today you **offer** the same **gifts** and **defile** yourselves with the same **idols** by **sacrificing** your children to them in the fire. And then you Israelites still come to ask what my **will** is! As **surely** as I, the **Sovereign** LORD, am the living God, I will not let you ask me anything. 32 You have made up your **minds** that you want to be like the other nations, like the people who live in other countries and **worship trees** and rocks. But that will never be.

God Punishes and Forgives

33 "As **surely** as I, the **Sovereign** LORD, am the living God, I **warn** you that in my **anger** I will rule over you with a **strong** hand, with all my **power**. 34 I will show you my **power** and my **anger** when I gather you together and bring you back from all the countries where you have been **scattered**. 35 I will bring you into the 'Desert of the Nations,' and there I will **condemn** you to your face. 36 I will now **condemn** you just as I **condemned** your fathers in the Sinai Desert," says the **Sovereign** LORD.

37 "I will take firm **control** of you and make you **obey** my **covenant**. 38 I will take away from among you those who are **rebellious** and sinful. I will take them out of the lands where they are living now, but I will not let them return to the land of Israel. Then you will know that I am the LORD."

39 The **Sovereign** LORD said, "And now, all you Israelites, **please** yourselves! Go on and **serve your idols**! But I **warn** you that after this you will have to **obey** me and stop **dishonouring** my **holy name** by **offering gifts to your idols**. 40 There in the land, on my **holy** mountain,[s] the high mountain of Israel, all you people of Israel will **worship** me. I will be **pleased** with you and will expect you to bring me your **sacrifices**, your **best offerings**, and your **holy gifts**. 41 After I bring you out of the countries where you have been **scattered** and gather you together, I will **accept** the **sacrifices** that you burn,

[q] HIGH PLACES: *Pagan places of worship which the Hebrews were forbidden to use. The Hebrew word translated "High Places" sounds like the Hebrew for "where you go."*
[s] HOLY MOUNTAIN: *Mount Zion, the hill in Jerusalem which formed part of the Temple and palace area.*

20.15: Num 14.26–35 **20.23:** Lev 26.33

and the nations will see that I am holy.
42 When I bring you back to Israel, the
land that I promised I would give to your
ancestors, then you will know that I am
the LORD. 43 Then you will remember all
the disgraceful things you did and how
you defiled yourselves. You will be disgusted with yourselves because of all the
evil things you did. 44 When I act to protect my honour, you Israelites will know
that I am the LORD, because I do not deal
with you as your wicked, evil actions deserve." The Sovereign LORD has spoken.

Fire in the South

45 The LORD spoke to me. 46 "Mortal
man," he said, "look towards the south.
Speak against the south and prophesy
against the forest of the south. 47 Tell the
southern forest to hear what the
Sovereign LORD is saying: Look! I am
starting a fire, and it will burn up every
tree in you, whether green or dry. Nothing will be able to put it out. It will spread
from south to north, and everyone will
feel the heat of the flames. 48 They will all
see that I, the LORD, set it on fire and
that no one can put it out."

49 But I protested, "Sovereign LORD,
don't make me do it! Everyone is
already complaining that I always speak
in riddles."

The LORD's Sword

21 The LORD spoke to me. 2 "Mortal
man," he said, "denounce Jerusalem. Denounce the places where people
worship. Warn the land of Israel 3 that I,
the LORD, am saying: I am your enemy. I
will draw my sword and kill all of you,
good and evil alike. 4 I will use my sword
against everyone from north to south.
5 Everyone will know that I, the LORD,
have drawn my sword and that I will not
put it away.

6 "Mortal man, groan as if your heart
is breaking with despair. Groan in
sorrow where everyone can watch you.
7 When they ask you why you are groaning, tell them it is because of the news
that is coming. When it comes, their
hearts will be filled with fear, their hands
will hang limp, their courage will fail,
and their knees will tremble. The time
has come; it is here." The Sovereign
LORD has spoken.

8 The LORD said to me, 9 "Mortal man,
prophesy. Tell the people what I, the
Lord, am saying:

A sword, a sword is sharpened and
polished.
10 It is sharpened to kill,
polished to flash like lightning.
There can be no rejoicing,
for my people have disregarded
every warning and punishment.[t]
11 The sword is being polished,
to make it ready for use.
It is sharpened and polished,
to be put in the hands of a killer.
12 Howl in grief, mortal man;
this sword is meant for my people
and for all the leaders of Israel.
They are going to be killed
with all the rest of my people.
Beat your breast in despair!
13 I am testing my people,
and if they refuse to repent,
all these things will happen to
them.[u]

14 "Now, mortal man, prophesy. Clap
your hands, and the sword will strike
again and again. It is a sword that kills, a
sword that terrifies[v] and slaughters. 15 It
makes my people lose courage and stumble. I am threatening their city with a
sword[w] that flashes like lightning and is
ready to kill. 16 Cut to the right and the
left, you sharp sword! Cut wherever you
turn.[x] 17 I also will clap my hands, and
my anger will be over. I, the LORD, have
spoken."

The Sword of the King of Babylonia

18 The LORD spoke to me. 19 "Mortal
man," he said, "mark out two roads by
which the king of Babylonia can come
with his sword. Both of them are to start
in the same country. Put up a signpost
where the roads fork.[y] 20 One will show
the king the way to the Ammonite city of
Rabbah, and the other the way to Judah,
to the fortified city, Jerusalem. 21 The
king of Babylonia stands by the signpost
at the fork of the road. To discover which
way to go, he shakes the arrows;[z] he consults his idols; he examines the liver of a
sacrificed animal. 22 Now! His right hand
holds the arrow marked 'Jerusalem'! It
tells him to go and set up battering-rams,
to shout the battle-cry, to place battering-
rams against the gates, to throw up
earthworks, and to dig trenches. 23 The
people of Jerusalem won't believe this,
because of the treaties they have made.

[t] *Probable text* There...punishment; *Hebrew unclear.* [u] *Verse 13 in Hebrew is unclear.*
[v] *Some ancient translations* terrifies; *Hebrew unclear.*
[w] *Probable text* threatening...sword; *Hebrew unclear.* [x] *Verse 16 in Hebrew is unclear.*
[y] *Probable text* Put...fork; *Hebrew unclear.*
[z] SHAKES THE ARROWS: *When faced with a decision, people in ancient times would sometimes take a handful of arrows, throw them down, and study the pattern in which they fell, in order to learn what to do.*

action 20.44; 22.15
anger [2] 20.8; 22.20
announce 20.9; 25.13
believe 13.19; Jon 3.5
blood 16.6; 23.45
choose 20.5; 33.2
condemn 20.35; 23.45
consult 20.1; Zech 10.2
courage [2] Lam 1.16; 22.14
create Jer 51.15; 28.13
crown 16.12; 23.42
denounce [2] 13.2; 25.2
despair [2] 7.25; Mic 1.10
destroy [3] 20.13; 22.30
enemy [2] 5.8; 25.15
evil [2] 20.43; 22.15
fail Jer 49.4; Mic 3.7
false 20.7; 22.28
fear 12.18; 23.33
final [2] Is 51.6; 35.5
God's people [5] 14.8; 25.14
grief 2.10; 28.12
groan [3] 2.10; 24.23
guilty 9.9; 22.4
heart [2] 18.31; 27.31
idol 20.7; 22.3
insult 20.27; 36.3
judge 18.30; 22.2

knee 7.17; 47.4
lie (2) 13.6; 22.9
mark (1) [2] 9.4; 39.15
mortal [7] 20.3; 22.2
poor 18.12; 22.29
power 20.33; 24.27
predict [2] 13.6; 22.28
prophecy [3] 20.46; 30.2
punish [4] 20.26; 22.24
raise 16.27; 26.10
refuse (1) 20.8; Dan 3.14
rejoice Jer 31.13; 35.14
remember 20.43; 33.13
remind 20.4; 29.16
repent 18.23; Joel 2.12
right (2) [2] 4.6; 39.3
ruin [2] 19.7; 23.33
sacrifice 20.26; 22.9
slaughter 6.8; 26.15
sorrow 19.1; Joel 2.13
Sovereign [4] 20.3; 22.3
strike 17.10; Dan 2.34
stumble Jer 50.32; Hos 5.5
terrify 19.7; 26.15
test Jer 48.14; Dan 1.12
threat 6.10; 39.26
tremble 12.18; 26.16
turn [2] 18.30; 22.31
unholy Neh 13.17; 22.24
vision 13.3; 22.28
warn [3] 20.18; 23.48
watch 12.4; 33.2
wicked [2] 20.44; 31.11
worship (2) (of other gods) 20.16; 22.3

But this prediction is to remind them of
their sins and to warn them that they will
be captured. 24 This then is what I, the
Sovereign LORD, am saying: Your sins
are exposed. Everyone knows how guilty
you are. You show your sins in your
every action. You stand condemned, and
I will hand you over to your enemies.
25 "You wicked, unholy ruler of Israel,
your day, the day of your final punishment,
is coming. 26 I, the Sovereign LORD,
have spoken. Take off your crown and
your turban. Nothing will be the same
again. Raise the poor to power! Bring
down those who are ruling! 27 Ruin, ruin!
Yes, I will make the city a ruin. But this
will not happen until the one whom I
have chosen to punish the city has come.
Then I will give it to him.

A Sword and the Ammonites

28 "Mortal man, prophesy. Announce
what I, the Sovereign LORD, am saying to
the Ammonites, who are insulting Israel.
Say to them:

'A sword is ready to destroy;
It is polished to kill, to flash like
lightning.

29 The visions that you see are false, and
the predictions you make are lies. You
are wicked and evil, and your day is
coming, the day of your final
punishment. The sword is going to fall on
your necks.
30 " 'Put up the sword! I will judge
you in the place where you were created,
in the land where you were born. 31 You
will feel my anger when I turn it loose on
you like a blazing fire. And I will hand
you over to brutal men, experts at destruction.
32 You will be destroyed by fire.
Your blood will be shed in your own
country, and no one will remember you
any more.' " The LORD has spoken.

The Crimes of Jerusalem

22 The LORD spoke to me. 2 "Mortal
man," he said, "are you ready to
judge the city that is full of murderers?
Make clear to her all the disgusting
things she has done. 3 Tell the city what I,
the Sovereign LORD, am saying: Because
you have murdered so many of your own
people and have defiled yourself by worshipping
idols, your time is coming. 4 You
are guilty of those murders and are defiled
by the idols you made, and so your
day is coming, your time is up! That is
why I have let the nations mock you and
all the countries sneer at you. 5 Countries
near by and countries far away sneer at
you because of your lawlessness. 6 All
Israel's leaders trust in their own
strength and commit murder. 7 No one in
the city honours his parents. You cheat
foreigners and take advantage of widows
and orphans. 8 You have no respect for
the holy places, and you don't keep the
Sabbath. 9 Some of your people tell lies
about others in order to have them put to
death. Some of them eat sacrifices
offered to idols. Some are always satisfying
their lusts. 10 Some of them sleep
with their father's wife. Some force
women to have intercourse with them
during their period. 11 Some commit adultery,
and others seduce their daughters-in-law
or their half-sisters. 12 Some of
your people murder for pay. Some
charge interest on the loans they make
to their fellow-Israelites and get rich by
taking advantage of them. They have forgotten
me." The Sovereign LORD has
spoken.
13 "I will bring my fist down on your
robberies and murders. 14 Do you think
you will have any courage left or have
strength enough to lift your hand when I
am finished with you? I, the LORD, have
spoken, and I keep my word. 15 I will
scatter your people to every country and
nation and will put an end to your evil
actions. 16 And so the other nations will
dishonour you, but you will know that I
am the LORD."

God's Refining Furnace

17 The LORD said to me, 18 "Mortal
man, the Israelites are of no use to me.
They are like the waste metal—copper,
tin, iron, and lead—left over after silver
has been refined in a furnace. 19 So now I,
the Sovereign LORD, am telling them that
they are just as useless as that. I will
bring them all together in Jerusalem 20 in
the same way that the ore of silver,
copper, iron, lead, and tin is put in a refining
furnace. My anger and rage will
melt them just as fire melts ore. 21 Yes, I
will gather them in Jerusalem, build a
fire under them, and melt them with my
anger. 22 They will be melted in Jerusalem
just as silver is melted in a furnace,
and then they will know that they
are feeling the anger of the LORD."

The Sins of Israel's Leaders

23 The LORD spoke to me again.
24 "Mortal man," he said, "tell the Israelites
that their land is unholy, and so I am
punishing it in my anger. 25 The leaders[a]
are like lions roaring over the animals

[a] *One ancient translation* The leaders; *Hebrew* A conspiracy of her prophets.

21.28–32: Jer 49.1–6; Ezek 25.1–7; Amos 1.13–15; Zeph 2.8–11 **22.7:** Ex 20.12, 22.21–22; Deut 5.16, 24.17 **22.8:** Lev 19.30, 26.2 **22.10–11:** Lev 18.7–20 **22.12:** Ex 22.25, 23.8; Lev 25.36–37; Deut 16.19, 23.19

action 21.24; 24.13
adultery 16.17; 23.37
advantage [3] 16.15; Zeph 3.4
anger [6] 21.17; 23.22
apart Jer 5.6; 44.29
cheat [2] 18.7; Hos 7.1
claim 13.6; 28.2
clean Jer 52.18; 24.6
commit [3] 16.17; 23.37
courage 21.7; Mic 3.8
death (3) (to death) 11.9; Dan 2.24
defend 13.5; 25.9
defile [2] 20.18; 23.7
destroy [2] 21.28; 24.26
disgust 20.4; 23.17
dishonour 20.9; Amos 2.1

distinguish Ezra 3.13; Col 3.11
enough 19.11; 30.21
evil 21.3; 28.15
false 21.29; 30.13
force (1) 20.8; 24.13
forget 16.43; 23.35
guilty 21.24; 23.21
holy [3] 20.12; 28.14
honour 20.44; 32.27
idol [3] 21.21; 23.7
ignore 16.59; 24.14
ill-treat Jer 22.3; 34.22
judge 21.30; 23.24
law 20.11; 23.24
lie (2) 21.29; Dan 2.9
lust 16.26; 23.5
mock 5.15; 23.32
mortal [3] 21.2; 23.2
offer 20.26; 36.38
orphan Jer 49.11; Zech 7.10
poor 21.26; Dan 4.27
predict 21.23; Mic 3.6
priest 7.26; 40.45
prophet 14.4; 33.33
punish 21.10; 23.31
rage 5.13; Dan 2.12
refine [2] Jer 9.7; Mal 3.2
respect [3] 2.4; Dan 3.29
rich [2] 20.6; 27.33
rob [2] 18.7; 23.46
Sabbath [2] 20.12; 23.38
sacrifice 21.21; 23.37
satisfy 16.28; 34.18
scatter 20.23; 28.25
sneer [2] 5.14; 34.29
Sovereign [5] 21.7; 23.22
strength [2] 17.9; 24.21
teach 20.11; 44.23
trust Lam 4.20; Dan 3.28
turn 21.16; 23.35
unclean 20.7; 36.17
unholy 21.25
useless 15.5; Hos 8.8
vision 21.29; 40.2
widow [2] Lam 5.3; 44.22
word (1) [2] 13.2; 30.2
worship (2) (of other gods) 21.2; 23.7

they have killed. They kill the people, take all the money and property they can get, and by their murders leave many **widows**. 26 The **priests** break my **law** and have no **respect** for what is **holy**. They make no **distinction** between what is **holy** and what is not. They do not **teach** the difference between **clean** and **unclean** things, and they **ignore** the **Sabbath**. As a result the people of Israel do not **respect** me. 27 The government officials are like wolves tearing **apart** the animals they have killed. They **commit murder** in order to get **rich**. 28 The **prophets** have hidden these sins like men covering a wall with whitewash. They see **false visions** and make false **predictions**. They **claim** to speak the **word of the Sovereign** LORD, but I, the LORD, have not spoken to them. 29 The wealthy **cheat** and **rob**. They **ill-treat** the **poor** and take **advantage** of foreigners. 30 I looked for someone who could build a wall, who could stand in the places where the walls have crumbled and **defend** the land when my **anger** is about to **destroy** it, but I could find no one. 31 So I will **turn** my **anger** loose on them, and like a fire I will **destroy** them for what they have done." The **Sovereign** LORD has spoken.

The Sinful Sisters

23 The LORD spoke to me. 2 "**Mortal** man," he said, "there were once two sisters. 3 When they were young, living in Egypt, they lost their **virginity** and became **prostitutes**. 4 The older one was named Oholah[x] (she **represents** Samaria), and the younger one was named Oholibah[y] (she **represents** Jerusalem). I married both of them, and they bore me children. 5 Although she was mine, Oholah continued to be a **prostitute** and was full of **lust** for her lovers from Assyria. 6 They were soldiers in uniforms of purple, noblemen and high-ranking officers; all of them were handsome young cavalry officers. 7 She was the whore for all the Assyrian officers, and her **lust** led her to **defile** herself by **worshipping Assyrian idols**. 8 She continued what she had begun as a **prostitute** in Egypt, where she lost her **virginity**. From the time she was a girl, men slept with her and treated her like a **prostitute**. 9 So I handed her over to her Assyrian lovers whom she wanted so much. 10 They **stripped** her **naked**, seized her sons and daughters, and then killed her with a sword. Women everywhere gossiped about her **fate**.

11 "Even though her sister Oholibah saw this, she was wilder and more of a **prostitute** than Oholah had ever been. 12 She too was full of **lust** for the Assyrian noblemen and officers—soldiers in bright uniforms—and for the cavalry officers, all those handsome young men. 13 I saw that she was completely **immoral**, that the second sister was as **bad** as the first.

14–15 "She sank deeper and deeper in her **immorality**. She was attracted by the **images** of high Babylonian officials carved into the wall and painted bright red, with sashes round their waists and fancy turbans on their heads. 16 As soon as she saw them, she was filled with **lust** and sent messengers to them in Babylonia. 17 The Babylonians came to have **sex** with her. They used her and **defiled** her so much that finally she became **disgusted** with them. 18 She exposed herself publicly and let everyone know she was a whore. I was as **disgusted** with her as I had been with her sister. 19 She became more of a **prostitute** than ever, **acting** just as she did as a girl, when she was a **prostitute** in Egypt. 20 She was filled with **lust** for **oversexed** men who had all the **lustfulness** of donkeys or stallions." 21 (Oholibah, you wanted to repeat the **immorality** you were **guilty** of as a girl in Egypt, where men played with your breasts and you lost your **virginity**.)

God's Judgement on the Younger Sister

22 "Now then, Oholibah, this is what I, the **Sovereign** LORD, am saying to you. You are tired of those lovers, but I will make them **angry** with you and bring them to surround you. 23 I will bring all the Babylonians and Chaldeans, men from Pekod, Shoa, and Koa, and all the Assyrians. I will gather all those handsome young noblemen and officers, all those **important** officials and high-ranking cavalry officers. 24 They will attack you from the north,[b] bringing a large army with chariots and supply wagons. **Protected** by shields and helmets, they will surround you. I will hand you over to them, and they will **judge** you by their own **laws**. 25 Because I am **angry** with you, I will let them deal with you in their **anger**. They will cut off your nose and your ears and kill your children. Yes, they will take your sons and daughters from you and burn them **alive**. 26 They

accuse Jer 32.3; Dan 6.5
act 20.44; 24.14
adultery [5] 22.11; 33.26
alive 13.19; Dan 5.19
anger [3] 22.20; 24.8
bad 16.20; 34.17
blood 21.32; 24.7
care 16.49; 34.2
charge (3) Jer 18.18; Acts 19.38
commit [2] 22.6; 33.25
condemn 21.24; 36.19
crown 21.26; Zech 6.11
cup [4] 4.11; Dan 5.2
defile [3] 22.3; 24.13
disgust [4] 22.2; 33.26
establish Jer 32.41; 37.26
fate Lam 1.9; 26.16
fear 21.7; 27.35
forget 22.12; 39.26
guilty 22.4; 25.12
hate [2] 16.27; 25.15
idol [7] 22.3; 30.13
image 16.17; Dan 11.8
immoral [6] 16.27; 24.13
important 17.13; 29.15
incense 16.18; Hos 2.13
judge [2] 22.2; 33.20
law 22.26; 33.15
lust [9] 22.9; 2 Cor 12.21
misery Lam 3.5; Jas 5.1
mock 22.4; 36.4
mortal [2] 22.2; 24.2
naked [2] 18.7; Hos 2.3
practice 18.14; Mic 6.16
profane [2] 20.13; 24.21
prostitute [13] 16.16
Hos 2.2
protect 20.44; 34.30
punish [2] 22.24; 24.14
represent [2] 4.1; 37.19
righteous 18.5; 33.1
rob 22.13; 25.7
ruin 21.27; 26.10
Sabbath 22.8; 44.24
sacrifice [2] 22.9; 36.38
scorn Lam 2.15; 28.24
sex [2] 16.43; Mt 1.2
Sovereign [7] 22.3; 24.3
strip (1) [2] 16.36; Dan 4.14
suffer 18.19; Dan 9.18
Temple (1) (of God [2] 11.1; 24.21
turn 22.31; 25.5
virgin [3] Is 62.5; 44.22
warn 21.2; 28.17
worship (2) (of other gods) [2] 22.3; 33.25

[x] *This name in Hebrew means "her sanctuary".*
[y] *This name in Hebrew means "my sanctuary is in her".*
[b] *One ancient translation* north; *Hebrew unclear.*

22.26: Lev 10.10

will tear off your clothes and take your
jewels. 27 I will put a stop to your lust and
to the obscenities you have committed
ever since you were in Egypt. You won't
look at any more idols or think about
Egypt any more."

28 This is what the Sovereign LORD
says: "I will hand you over to people you
hate and are disgusted with. 29 And because they hate you, they will take away
everything you have worked for and
leave you stripped naked, exposed like a
prostitute. Your lust and your prostitution 30 have brought this on you. You
were a prostitute for the nations and defiled yourself with their idols. 31 You
followed in your sister's footsteps, and so
I will give you the same cup of punishment to drink."

32 The Sovereign LORD says,
"You will drink from your sister's cup;
it is large and deep.
Everyone will scorn and mock you;
the cup is full.
33 It will make you miserable and drunk,
that cup of fear and ruin,
your sister Samaria's cup.
34 You will drink and drain it dry,
and with its broken pieces
tear your breast.
I, the Sovereign LORD, have spoken."

35 Now this is what the Sovereign
LORD is saying: "Because you forgot me
and turned your back on me, you will
suffer for your lust and your prostitution."

God's Judgement on Both Sisters

36 The LORD said to me, "Mortal man,
are you ready to judge Oholah and
Oholibah? Accuse them of the disgusting
things they have done. 37 They have committed adultery and murder—adultery
with idols and murder of the sons they
bore me. They sacrificed my sons to
their idols. 38 And that is not all they did.
They profaned my Temple and broke the
Sabbath, which I had established. 39 The
very day that they killed my children as
sacrifices to idols, they came to my
Temple and profaned it!

40 "Again and again they sent messengers to invite men to come from a
great distance, and the men came. The
two sisters would bathe and put on eyeshadow and jewellery. 41 They would sit
on a beautiful couch, and in front of them
they would have a table covered with
good things, including the incense and
the olive-oil that I had given them. 42 The
sound of a carefree crowd could be
heard, a group of men brought in from
the desert. They put bracelets on the
women's arms and beautiful crowns on
their heads. 43 And I said to myself that
they were using as a prostitute a woman
worn out by adultery.[c] 44 They went back
to these prostitutes again and again.
They went back to Oholah and Oholibah,
those immoral women. 45 Righteous men
will condemn them on the charge of
adultery and murder, because they practise adultery and their hands are stained
with blood."

46 This is what the Sovereign LORD
says: "Bring a mob to terrorize them and
rob them. 47 Let the mob stone them and
attack them with swords, kill their children, and burn down their houses.
48 Throughout the land I will put a stop to
immorality, as a warning to every
woman not to commit adultery as they
did. 49 And you two sisters—I will punish
you for your immorality and your sin of
worshipping idols. Then you will know
that I am the Sovereign LORD."

The Corroded Cooking-Pot

24 On the tenth day of the tenth
month of the ninth year of our
exile, the LORD spoke to me. 2 "Mortal
man," he said, "write down today's date,
because this is the day that the king of
Babylonia is beginning the siege of Jerusalem. 3 Tell my rebellious people this
parable that I, the Sovereign LORD, have
for them:
Set the pot on the fire
and fill it up with water.
4 Put in the best pieces of meat—
the shoulders and the legs—
fill it with choice bony pieces too.
5 Use the meat of the finest sheep;
pile the wood[d] under the pot.
Let the water boil;
boil the bones and the meat."

6 This is what the Sovereign LORD is
saying: "The city of murderers is
doomed! It is like a corroded pot that is
never cleaned. Piece after piece of meat
is taken out, and not one is left. 7 There
was murder in the city, but the blood was
not spilt on the ground where the dust
could hide it; it was spilt on a bare rock.
8 I have left the blood there, where it cannot be hidden, where it demands angry
revenge."

9 This is what the Sovereign LORD is
saying: "The city of murderers is
doomed! I myself will pile up the firewood. 10 Bring more wood! Fan the
flames! Cook the meat! Boil away the

act [2] 23.19; 28.17
action 22.15; 33.26
anger [2] 23.22; 25.14
best 20.40; 34.18
blood [2] 23.45; 28.23
clean 22.26; 36.25
complain 20.49; Hos 4.4
defile [2] 23.7; 36.17
demand Is 43.23; Dan 2.10
destroy 22.30; 25.7
doom [2] 16.23; 31.14
escape 17.18; 33.5
exile 20.1; 25.3
force (1) 22.10; 28.16
groan 21.6; 30.24
ignore 22.26; Dan 11.37
immoral 23.13; Mt 15.19
joy Lam 2.4; 25.6
love 20.7; 33.31
mercy 9.5; 39.25
message 13.6; 32.2
mortal [3] 23.2; 25.2
mourn [4] 7.27; 27.30
parable 17.2; Mt 13.3
pity 20.17; Hos 13.14
power 21.26; 26.2
profane 23.38; 25.3
proud [2] 16.49; 28.2
punish 23.31; 25.11
pure [3] 16.52; 37.23
rebel 20.38; 44.6
revenge Jer 51.6; 25.12
sheep Jer 50.6; 25.5
sign (1) [3] 20.12; 31.15
Sovereign [6] 23.22; 25.3
speech 3.27; 33.22
strength 22.6; 30.18
strong 20.33; 29.21
tear (2) Lam 5.17; Mal 2.13
Temple (1) (of God) [2] 23.38; 25.3

[c] *Verses 42–43 in Hebrew are unclear.* [d] *Probable text* wood; *Hebrew* bones.

24.2: 2 Kgs 25.1; Jer 52.4

broth![e] Burn up the bones! 11 Now set the empty bronze pot on the coals and let it get red-hot. Then the pot will be ritually **pure** again after the corrosion is burnt off, 12 although all that corrosion will not disappear in the flames.[f] 13 Jerusalem, your **immoral actions** have **defiled** you. Although I tried to **purify** you, you remained **defiled**. You will not be **pure** again until you have felt the full **force** of my **anger**. 14 I, the **Sovereign** LORD, have spoken. The time has come for me to **act**. I will not **ignore** your sins or show **pity** or be **merciful**. You will be **punished** for what you have done." The **Sovereign** LORD has spoken.

The Death of the Prophet's Wife

15 The LORD spoke to me. 16 "**Mortal** man," he said, "with one blow I am going to take away the person you **love** most. You are not to **complain** or cry or shed any **tears**. 17 Don't let your sobbing be heard. Do not go bareheaded or barefoot as a **sign** of **mourning**. Don't cover your face or eat the food that **mourners** eat."

18 Early in the day I was talking with the people. That evening my wife died, and the next day I did as I had been told. 19 The people asked me, "Why are you **acting** like this?"

20 So I said to them, "The LORD spoke to me and told me 21 to give you Israelites this **message**: You are **proud** of the **strength** of the **Temple**. You like to look at it and to visit it, but the LORD is going to **profane** it. And the younger members of your families who are left in Jerusalem will be killed in war. 22 Then you will do what I have done. You will not cover your faces or eat the food that **mourners** eat. 23 You will not go bareheaded or barefoot or **mourn** or cry. You will waste away because of your sins, and you will **groan** to one another. 24 Then I will be a **sign** to you; you will do everything I have done. The LORD says that when this happens, you will know that he is the **Sovereign** LORD."

25 The LORD said, "Now, **mortal man**, I will take away from them the **strong Temple** that was their **pride** and **joy**, which they liked to look at and to visit. And I will take away their sons and daughters. 26 On the day that I do this, someone who **escapes** the **destruction** will come and tell you about it. 27 That same day you will get back the **power** of **speech** which you had lost, and you will talk with him. In this way you will be a **sign** to the people, and they will know that I am the LORD."

Prophecy against Ammon

25 The LORD spoke to me. 2 "**Mortal** man," he said, "**denounce** the country of Ammon. 3 Tell them to listen to what I, the **Sovereign** LORD, am saying: You were **delighted** to see my **Temple profaned**, to see the land of Israel **devastated**, to see the people of Judah go into **exile**. 4 Because you were **glad**, I will let the tribes from the eastern desert **conquer** you. They will set up their camps in your country and settle there. They will eat the fruit and drink the milk that should have been yours. 5 I will **turn** the city of Rabbah into a place to keep camels, and the whole country of Ammon into a place to keep **sheep**, so that you will know that I am the LORD.

6 "This is what the **Sovereign** LORD is saying: You clapped your hands and jumped for **joy**. You **despised** the land of Israel. 7 Because you did, I will hand you over to other nations who will **rob** you and plunder you. I will **destroy** you so completely that you will not be a nation any more or have a country of your own. Then you will know that I am the LORD."

Prophecy against Moab

8 The **Sovereign** LORD said, "Because Moab[g] has said that Judah is like all the other nations, 9 I will let the cities that **defend** the border of Moab be attacked, including even the finest cities—Beth Jeshimoth, Baal Meon, and Kiriathaim. 10 I will let the tribes of the eastern desert **conquer** Moab, together with Ammon, so that Moab[h] will no longer be a nation. 11 I will **punish** Moab, and they will know that I am the LORD."

Prophecy against Edom

12 The **Sovereign** LORD said, "The people of Edom took **cruel revenge** on Judah, and that **revenge** has brought **lasting guilt** on Edom. 13 Now I **announce** that I will **punish** Edom and kill every man and animal there. I will make it a waste, from the city of Teman to the city of Dedan, and the people will be killed in battle. 14 **My people** Israel will take **revenge** on Edom for me, and they will

age (1) Is 34.10; Mt 13.39
anger [2] 24.8; 35.11
announce [2] 21.28; 30.2
conquer [2] Lam 1.7; 26.15
cruel [2] Lam 4.3; 32.12
defend 22.30; 30.6
delight Lam 2.4; Hos 4.18
denounce 21.2; 28.21
despise 2.6; Joel 2.17
destroy [3] 24.26; 26.4
devastate Jer 9.12; 30.11
enemy 21.3; 26.3
exile 24.1; 26.1
fury 16.38; 30.15
glad Lam 4.21; Joel 2.21
God's people 21.10; 30.5
guilty 23.21; 35.6
hate 23.28; 35.11
joy 24.25; Dan 6.23
last (1) 16.60; 39.9
mortal 24.2; 26.2
profane 24.21; 44.7
punish [3] 24.14; 28.22
revenge [6] 24.8; Mic 5.15
rob 23.46; 36.13
sheep 24.5; 27.21
Sovereign [6] 24.3; 26.3
Temple (1) (of God) 24.21; 37.26
turn 23.35; 38.4

[e] *Some ancient translations* Boil away the broth; *Hebrew unclear.*
[f] *Verse 12 in Hebrew begins with two words, the meaning of which is unclear.*
[g] *Some ancient translations* Moab; *Hebrew* Moab and Seir.
[h] *Probable text* Moab; *Hebrew* Ammon.

25.1-7: Jer 49.1-6; Ezek 21.28-32; Amos 1.13-15; Zeph 2.8-11
25.8-11: Is 15.1—16.14, 25.10-12; Jer 48.1-47; Amos 2.1-3; Zeph 2.8-11
25.12-14: Is 34.5-17, 63.1-6; Jer 49.7-22; Ezek 35.1-15; Amos 1.11-12; Obad 1-14; Mal 1.2-5

make Edom feel my **furious anger**. Edom
will know what it means to be the object
of my **revenge**." The **Sovereign** LORD has
spoken.

Prophecy against Philistia

15 The **Sovereign** LORD said, "The
Philistines have taken **cruel revenge** on
their **age-long enemies** and **destroyed**
them in their **hate**. 16 And so I am
announcing that I will attack the Philistines and wipe them out. I will **destroy**
everyone left living there on the Philistine Plain. 17 I will **punish** them severely
and take full **revenge** on them. They will
feel my **anger**. Then they will know that I
am the LORD."

Prophecy against Tyre

ancient Lam 5.21; 32.27
cloud 19.11; 30.3
conquer 25.4; Dan 1.21
dead 11.13; 32.24
desolate Jer 22.6; 29.12
destroy [3] 25.7; 28.7
enemy [3] 25.15; 28.7
eternal Jer 50.5; Dan 9.24
example 18.14; 28.12
exile 25.3; 29.1
fate 23.10; 27.35
luxury Lam 4.5; 27.24
might 17.9; Dan 2.37
mortal 25.2; 27.2
never again 19.14; 29.15
power 24.27; 30.12
raise 21.26; Dan 1.20
rival Is 19.2; Nah 1.2
ruin [3] 23.33; 29.12
slaughter 21.14; 32.13
Sovereign [7] 25.3; 27.3
terrify [4] 21.14; 27.35
throne 17.16; 28.2
tremble [3] 21.7; 32.10
world of the dead [2] Is 59.10; 31.14

26 On the first day of the ... month[i]
of the eleventh year of our **exile**,
the LORD spoke to me. 2 "**Mortal man**," he
said, "this is what the people in the city
of Tyre are cheering about. They shout,
'Jerusalem is shattered! Her commercial
power is gone! She won't be our **rival**
any more!'

3 "Now then, this is what I, the
Sovereign LORD, am saying: I am your
enemy, city of Tyre. I will bring many
nations to attack you, and they will come
like the waves of the sea. 4 They will **destroy** your city walls and tear down your
towers. Then I will sweep away all the
dust and leave only a bare rock. 5 Fishermen will dry their nets on it, there where
it stands in the sea. I, the **Sovereign**
LORD, have spoken. The nations will
plunder Tyre, 6 and with their swords
they will kill those who live in her towns
on the mainland. Then Tyre will know
that I am the LORD."

7 The **Sovereign** LORD says, "I am
going to bring the greatest king of all—
King Nebuchadnezzar of Babylonia—to
attack Tyre. He will come from the north
with a huge army, with horses and
chariots and with cavalry. 8 Those who
live in the towns on the mainland will be
killed in the fighting. The **enemy** will dig
trenches, build earthworks, and make a
solid wall of shields against you. 9 They
will pound in your walls with battering-
rams and tear down your towers with
iron bars. 10 The **clouds** of dust **raised** by
their horses will cover you. The noise of
their horses pulling wagons and chariots
will shake your walls as they pass
through the gates of the **ruined** city.
11 Their horsemen will storm through
your streets, killing your people with
their swords. Your **mighty** pillars will be
thrown to the ground. 12 Your **enemies**
will help themselves to your wealth and
merchandise. They will pull down your
walls and shatter your **luxurious** houses.
They will take the stones and wood and
all the rubble, and dump them into the
sea. 13 I will put an end to all your songs,
and I will silence the music of your
harps. 14 I will leave only a bare rock
where fishermen can dry their nets. The
city will never be rebuilt. I, the **Sovereign**
LORD, have spoken."

15 The **Sovereign** LORD has this to say
to the city of Tyre: "When you are being
conquered, the people who live along the
coast will be **terrified** at the screams of
those who are **slaughtered**. 16 All the
kings of the seafaring nations will come
down from their **thrones**. They will take
off their robes and their embroidered
clothes and sit **trembling** on the ground.
They will be so **terrified** at your **fate** that
they will not be able to stop **trembling**.
17 They will sing this funeral song for you:

> The famous city is **destroyed**!
> Her ships have been swept[j] from the
> seas.
> The people of this city ruled the seas
> And **terrified** all who lived on the
> coast.
> 18 Now, on the day it has fallen,
> The islands are **trembling**,
> And their people are shocked at such
> **destruction**."

19 The **Sovereign** LORD says: "I will
make you as **desolate** as **ruined** cities
where no one lives. I will cover you with
the water of the ocean depths. 20 I will
send you down to the **world of the dead**
to join the people who lived in **ancient**
times. I will make you stay in that **underground world** among **eternal ruins**, keeping company with the **dead**. As a result
you will **never again** be inhabited and
take your place[l] in the land of the living.
21 I will make you a **terrifying example**,
and that will be the end of you. People
may look for you, but you will never be
found." The **Sovereign** LORD has spoken.

A Funeral Song for Tyre

27 The LORD said to me, 2 "**Mortal**
man, sing a funeral song for
Tyre, 3 that city which stands at the edge

abundant Jer 33.6; Joel 2.14
afraid 11.8; 28.19
ash Jer 52.18; 28.18

[i] month; *the Hebrew text does not specify the month.*
[j] *Some ancient translations* swept; *Hebrew* inhabited.
[l] *One ancient translation* and take your place; *Hebrew unclear.*

25.15-17: Is 14.29-31; Jer 47.1-7; Joel 3.4-8; Amos 1.6-8; Zeph 2.4-7; Zech 9.5-7
26.1—28.19: Is 23.1-18; Joel 3.4-8; Amos 1.9-10; Zech 9.1-4; Mt 11.21-22; Lk 10.13-14 **26.13:** Rev 18.22
26.16-18: Rev 18.9-10 **26.21:** Rev 18.21

bitter [2] 3.14; Hos 12.14
boast Jer 49.4; 35.13
compare 16.51; 31.2
fate [2] 26.16; 28.12
fear 23.33; 32.10
glory 7.11; 39.21
heart 21.6; 36.26
lamb Jer 51.40; 39.18
luxury 26.12; Amos 3.12
mortal 26.2; 28.2
mourn 24.17; 31.15
need Lam 5.4; 34.26
perfect 16.14; 28.12
rich 22.12; 28.4
sackcloth 7.18; Dan 9.3
serve 20.24; 40.45
share 16.27; 28.19
shave 7.18; 44.20
sheep 25.5; 34.2
slave Lam 5.8; 34.27
Sovereign 26.3; 28.2
terrify [2] 26.15; 28.14
vanish Is 51.8; Hos 6.4
weep 8.14; Hos 10.5
win 16.19; Dan 11.32
world 20.23; 29.12

of the sea and does business with the
people living on every seacoast. Tell her
what the **Sovereign** LORD is saying:

Tyre, you **boasted** of your **perfect**
beauty.
4 Your home is the sea.
Your builders made you like a
beautiful ship;
5 They used fir-trees from Mount
Hermon for timber
And a cedar from Lebanon for your
mast.
6 They took oak-trees from Bashan to
make oars;
They made your deck out of pine from
Cyprus
And inlaid it with ivory.
7 Your sails were made of linen,
Embroidered linen from Egypt,
Easily recognized from afar.
Your awnings were made of finest
cloth,
Of purple from the island of Cyprus.
8 Your oarsmen were from the cities of
Sidon and Arvad.
Your own skilful men were the sailors.
9 The ship's carpenters
Were well-trained men from Byblos.
Sailors from every sea-going ship
Did business in your shops.

10 "Soldiers from Persia, Lydia, and
Libya **served** in your army. They hung
their shields and their helmets in your
barracks. They are the men who **won**
glory for you. 11 Soldiers from Arvad
guarded your walls, and men from
Gamad guarded your towers. They hung
their shields on your walls. They are the
men who made you beautiful.

12 "You did business in Spain and took
silver, iron, tin, and lead in payment for
your **abundant** goods. 13 You did business
in Greece, Tubal, and Meshech and
traded your goods for **slaves** and for
articles of bronze. 14 You sold your goods
for draught-horses, war-horses, and
mules from Beth Togarmah. 15 The
people of Rhodes[m] traded with you;
people of many coastal lands gave you
ivory and ebony in exchange for your
goods. 16 The people of Syria bought your
merchandise and your many products.
They gave emeralds, purple cloth, embroidery, fine linen, coral, and rubies in
payment for your wares. 17 Judah and
Israel paid for your goods with wheat,[n]
honey, olive-oil, and spices. 18-19 The
people of Damascus bought your merchandise and your products, paying for
them with wine from Helbon and wool
from Sahar.[o] They exchanged wrought
iron and spices for your goods. 20 The
people of Dedan exchanged saddle-cloths
for your goods. 21 The Arabians and the
rulers of the land of Kedar paid for your
merchandise with **lambs**, **sheep**, and
goats. 22 For your goods the merchants of
Sheba and Raamah exchanged jewels,
gold, and the finest spices. 23 The cities of
Haran, Canneh, and Eden, the merchants
of Sheba, the cities of Asshur and
Chilmad—they all traded with you.
24 They sold you **luxurious** clothing,
purple cloth, and embroidery, brightly
coloured carpets, and well-made cords
and ropes. 25 Your merchandise was
carried in fleets of the largest cargo
ships.

You were like a ship at sea
Loaded with heavy cargo.
26 When your oarsmen brought you out to
sea,
An east wind wrecked you far from
land.
27 All your wealth of merchandise,
All the sailors in your crew,
Your ship's carpenters and your
merchants,
Every soldier on board the ship—
All, all were lost at sea
When your ship was wrecked.
28 The shouts of the drowning sailors
Echoed on the shore.

29 "Every ship is now deserted,
And every sailor has gone ashore.
30 They all **mourn bitterly** for you,
Throwing dust on their heads and
rolling in **ashes**.
31 They **shave** their heads for you
And dress themselves in **sackcloth**.
Their **hearts** are **bitter** as they **weep**.
32 They chant a funeral song for you:
'Who can be **compared** to Tyre,
To Tyre now silent in the sea?
33 When your merchandise went
overseas,
You filled the **needs** of every nation.
Kings were made **rich**
By the wealth of your goods.
34 Now you are wrecked in the sea;
You have sunk to the ocean depths.
Your goods and all who worked for
you
Have **vanished** with you in the sea.'

35 "Everyone who lives along the
coast is shocked at your **fate**. Even their
kings are **terrified**, and **fear** is written on

[m] *One ancient translation* Rhodes; *Hebrew* Dedan.
[n] *Hebrew has two additional words, the meaning of which is unclear.*
[o] *Hebrew has three additional words, the meaning of which is unclear.*

27.25–36: Rev 18.11–19

their faces. [36] You are gone, gone for ever, and merchants all over the **world** are **terrified**, **afraid** that they will **share** your **fate**."

Prophecy against the King of Tyre

28 The LORD spoke to me. [2] "**Mortal man**," he said, "tell the ruler of Tyre what I, the **Sovereign** LORD, am saying to him: Puffed up with **pride**, you **claim** to be a **god**. You say that like a **god** you sit on a **throne**, surrounded by the seas. You may pretend to be a **god**, but, no, you are mortal, not **divine**. [3] You think you are **wiser** than Danel,[p] that no **secret** can be kept from you. [4] Your **wisdom** and skill made you **rich** with treasures of gold and silver. [5] You made clever business deals and kept on making profits. How **proud** you are of your wealth!

6 "Now then, this is what I, the **Sovereign** LORD, am saying: Because you think you are as **wise** as a **god**, [7] I will bring ruthless **enemies** to attack you. They will **destroy** all the beautiful things you have acquired by your skill and **wisdom**. [8] They will kill you and send you to a watery **grave**. [9] When they come to kill you, will you still **claim** that you are a **god**? When you face your murderers, you will be mortal and not at all **divine**. [10] You will die like a dog at the hand of **godless** foreigners. I, the **Sovereign** LORD, have given the **command**."

The Fall of the King of Tyre

11 The LORD spoke to me again. [12] "**Mortal man**," he said, "**grieve** for the **fate** that is waiting for the king of Tyre. Tell him what I, the **Sovereign** LORD, am saying: You were once an **example** of **perfection**. How **wise** and handsome you were! [13] You lived in Eden, the garden of God, and wore gems of every kind: rubies and diamonds; topaz, beryl, carnelian, and jasper; sapphires, emeralds, and garnets. You had ornaments of gold. They were made for you[q] on the day you were **created**. [14] I put a **terrifying angel** there to guard you.[r] You lived on my **holy** mountain and walked among sparkling gems. [15] Your conduct was **perfect** from the day you were **created** until you began to do **evil**. [16] You were busy buying and selling, and this led you to **violence** and sin. So I **forced** you to leave my **holy** mountain, and the **angel** who guarded you drove you away from the sparkling gems. [17] You were **proud** of being handsome, and your fame made you **act** like a **fool**. Because of this I hurled you to the ground and left you as a **warning** to other kings. [18] You did such **evil** in buying and selling that your **places of worship** were **corrupted**. So I set fire to the city and burnt it to the ground. All who look at you now see you reduced to **ashes**. [19] You are gone, gone for ever, and all the nations that had come to know you are **terrified**, **afraid** that they will **share** your **fate**."

Prophecy against Sidon

20 The LORD said to me, [21] "**Mortal man**, **denounce** the city of Sidon. [22] Tell the people there what I, the **Sovereign** LORD, say about them: I am your **enemy**, Sidon; people will **praise** me because of what I do to you. They will know that I am the LORD, when I show how **holy** I am by **punishing** those who live in you. [23] I will send **diseases** on you and make **blood** flow in your streets. You will be attacked from every side, and your people will be killed. Then you will know that I am the LORD."

Israel Will Be Blessed

24 The LORD said, "None of the surrounding nations that treated Israel with **scorn** will ever again be like thorns and briars to **hurt** Israel. And they will know that I am the **Sovereign** LORD."

25 The **Sovereign** LORD said, "I will bring back the people of Israel from the nations where I **scattered** them, and all the nations will know that I am **holy**. The people of Israel will live in their own land, the land that I gave to my **servant** Jacob. [26] They will live there in **safety**. They will build houses and plant **vineyards**. I will **punish** all their **neighbours** who treated them with **scorn**, and Israel will be **secure**. Then they will know that I am the LORD their God."

Prophecy against Egypt

29 On the twelfth day of the tenth month of the tenth year of our **exile**, the LORD spoke to me. [2] "**Mortal man**," he said, "**denounce** the king of Egypt. Tell him how he and all the land of Egypt will be **punished**. [3] Say that this is what the **Sovereign** LORD is telling the king of Egypt: I am your **enemy**, you **monster** crocodile, lying in the river. You say that the Nile is yours and that you made it.[s] [4] I am going to put a hook

act 24.14; 30.3
afraid 27.36; Dan 1.10
angel [2] Is 63.9; Dan 3.25
ash 27.30; Dan 9.3
blood 24.7; 32.6
claim [2] 22.28; Hos 8.2
command 20.11; 36.27
corrupt 16.51; 37.23
create [2] 21.30; Amos 4.13
denounce 25.2; 29.2
destroy 26.4; 30.6
disease 14.21; 33.27
divine [2] Prov 16.10; Acts 2.22
enemy [2] 26.3; 29.3
evil [2] 22.15; 30.12
example 26.21; Mic 2.4
fate [2] 27.35; 29.16
fool 13.3; Hos 7.5
force (1) 24.13; 36.18
god (2) (other gods) [5] 20.7; 30.13
godless Jer 23.11; Mt 12.39
grave Jer 20.17; 32.22
grief 21.12; Joel 1.11
holy [4] 22.8; 36.20
hurt 13.22; 34.4
mortal [3] 27.2; 29.2
neighbour 16.26; 36.3
perfect [2] 27.3; Mt 5.48
place of worship 16.16; Amos 2.8
praise 3.12; Dan 2.19
proud [3] 24.21; 30.6
punish [2] 25.11; 29.2
rich 27.33; Dan 10.3
safe Jer 49.31; 34.14
scatter 22.15; 29.13
scorn [2] 23.32; Hab 2.6
secret 8.12; Dan 2.22
secure 18.7; 33.15
servant Jer 44.4; 34.23
share 27.36; 32.25
Sovereign [7] 27.3; 29.3
terrify [2] 27.35; 30.9
throne 26.16; 43.7
vineyard Jer 52.16; Hos 2.12
violent 8.17; 45.9
warn 23.48; 32.2
wisdom [2] Jer 51.15; Dan 2.21
wise [3] Jer 32.19; Dan 2.20

being Is 66.3; 38.20
body 16.8; 32.27
denounce 28.21; 34.2
depend Jer 49.11; Mic 5.7
desolate 26.19; 30.7
enemy [2] 28.7; 30.22
exile [2] 26.1; 30.20
fate 28.12; 32.25
flee Lam 1.6; Hos 12.12
help 17.17; 36.37
human 10.8; 38.20
important 23.23; Dan 4.17

[p] Danel; *or* Daniel *(see 14.14).* [q] *Probable text* They were made for you; *Hebrew unclear.*
[r] *One ancient translation* I put...you; *Hebrew unclear.*
[s] *Some ancient translations* you made it; *Hebrew* you made yourself.

28.20-26: Joel 3.4-8; Zech 9.1-2; Mt 11.21-22; Lk 10.13-14 **29.1—32.32:** Is 19.1-25; Jer 46.2-26

monster Jer 51.34; Amos 9.3
mortal [2] 28.2; 30.2
never again [2] 26.20; 34.10
punish 28.22; 30.14
refugee 12.3; Heb 11.13
rely [2] Is 50.10; 33.26
remind 21.23; Rom 15.15
ruin 26.10; 30.4
scatter 28.25; 30.23
service Jer 52.18; 46.17
Sovereign [6] 28.2; 30.2
strong 24.25; 30.21
trouble 9.4; 30.3
weak [3] 7.17; 30.25
will (1) 20.1; Dan 4.35
world 27.36; 30.7
worse 16.47; Jon 1.11
wrong 16.63; 33.10

through your jaw and make the fish in
your river stick fast to you. Then I will
pull you up out of the Nile, with all the
fish sticking to you. 5 I will throw you and
all those fish into the desert. Your **body**
will fall on the ground and be left un-
buried. I will give it to the birds and
animals for food. 6 Then all the people of
Egypt will know that I am the LORD."

The LORD says, "The Israelites **relied**
on you Egyptians for support, but you
were no better than a **weak** stick. 7 When
they leaned on you, you broke, pierced
their armpits, and made them wrench
their backs.[t] 8 Now then, I, the **Sovereign**
LORD, am telling you that I will get men
to attack you with swords, and they will
kill your people and your animals.
9 Egypt will become an empty waste.
Then you will know that I am the LORD.

"Because you said that the Nile is
yours and you made it, 10 I am your
enemy and the enemy of your Nile. I will
make all of Egypt an empty waste, from
the city of Migdol in the north to the city
of Aswan in the south, all the way to the
Sudanese border. 11 No **human being** or
animal will walk through it. For forty
years nothing will live there. 12 I will
make Egypt the most **desolate** country in
the **world**. For forty years the cities of
Egypt will lie in **ruins**, ruins **worse** than
those of any other city. I will make the
Egyptians **refugees**. They will **flee** to
every country and live among other
peoples."

13 The **Sovereign** LORD says, "After
forty years I will bring the Egyptians
back from the nations where I have **scattered** them, 14 and I will let them live in
southern Egypt, their original home.
There they will be a **weak** kingdom, 15 the
weakest kingdom of all, and they will
never again rule over other nations. I
will make them so **unimportant** that they
will not be able to bend any other nation
to their will. 16 Israel will **never again** de-
pend on them for **help**. Egypt's **fate** will
remind Israel how **wrong** it was to **rely**
on them. Then Israel will know that I am
the **Sovereign** LORD."

King Nebuchadnezzar Will Conquer Egypt

17 On the first day of the first month of
the twenty-seventh year of our **exile**, the
LORD spoke to me. 18 "**Mortal man**," he
said, "King Nebuchadnezzar of Babylonia launched an attack on Tyre. He
made his soldiers carry such heavy loads
that their heads were rubbed bald and
their shoulders were worn raw, but
neither the king nor his army got anything for all their **trouble**. 19 So now this is
what I, the **Sovereign** LORD, am saying: I
am giving the land of Egypt to King
Nebuchadnezzar. He will loot and
plunder it and carry off all the wealth of
Egypt as his army's pay. 20 I am giving
him Egypt in payment for his **services**,
because his army was working for me. I,
the **Sovereign** LORD, have spoken.

21 "When that happens, I will make
the people of Israel **strong** and let you,
Ezekiel, speak out where everyone can
hear you, so that they will know that I
am the LORD."

The LORD Will Punish Egypt

30 The LORD spoke again. 2 "**Mortal**
man," he said, "**prophesy** and
announce what I, the **Sovereign** LORD,
am saying. You are to shout these **words**:

A day of **terror** is coming!
3 The day is near, the day when the
LORD will **act**,
A day of **clouds** and **trouble** for the
nations.
4 There will be war in Egypt
And great **distress** in Sudan.
Many in Egypt will be killed;
The country will be plundered
And left in **ruins**.

5 "That war will also kill the soldiers
hired from Sudan, Lydia, Libya, Arabia,
Kub, and even from among **my own**
people."

6 The LORD says, "From Migdol in the
north to Aswan in the south, all Egypt's
defenders will be killed in battle. Egypt's
proud army will be **destroyed**. I, the
Sovereign LORD, have spoken. 7 The land
will be the most **desolate** in the **world**,
and its cities will be left totally in **ruins**.
8 When I set fire to Egypt and all her **defenders** are killed, then they will know
that I am the LORD.

9 "When that day comes and Egypt is
destroyed, I will send messengers in
ships to arouse the unsuspecting people
of Sudan, and they will be **terrified**. That
day is coming!"

10 The **Sovereign** LORD says, "I will
use King Nebuchadnezzar of Babylonia
to put an end to Egypt's wealth. 11 He and
his ruthless army will come to **devastate**
the land. They will attack Egypt with
swords, and the land will be full of corpses. 12 I will dry up the Nile and put Egypt
under the **power** of **evil** men. Foreigners
will **devastate** the whole country. I, the
LORD, have spoken."

act 28.17; 32.2
announce 25.13; 33.8
cloud [2] 26.10; 31.3
dark 12.6; 31.15
defend [2] 25.9; 38.11
desolate [2] 29.12; 32.15
destroy [4] 28.7; 32.7
devastate [2] 25.3; 35.15
distress 9.4; Dan 5.9
enemy [2] 29.3; 33.3
enough 22.14; 32.27
evil 28.15; 33.8
exile 29.1; 31.1
false 22.28; Hos 7.13
flood Jer 47.2; Dan 9.26
fury 25.14; 38.18
god (2) (other gods) 28.2; 43.7
God's people 25.14; 33.31
groan 24.23; Amos 2.13
heal Jer 51.8; 34.4
idol 23.7; 33.25
mortal [2] 29.2; 31.2
power [2] 26.2; 31.2
prison [2] Lam 3.5; Dan 1.2
prophecy 21.9; 34.2
proud [2] 28.2; 31.10
punish [2] 29.2; 33.12
ruin [2] 29.12; 33.24
scatter [2] 29.13; 31.17
Sovereign [5] 29.3; 31.10
strength [2] 24.21; Dan 2.23
strong [2] 29.21; 34.16
terrify [2] 28.14; 32.23
terror Lam 2.22; 32.24
trouble 29.18; 32.9
weak 29.6; 34.4
word (1) 22.14; 33.30
world [3] 29.12; 31.6

[t] *One ancient translation* wrench their backs; *Hebrew* make their backs stand.

29.6: Is 36.6

13 The **Sovereign** LORD says, "I will
destroy the **idols** and the **false gods** in
Memphis. There will be no one to rule
over Egypt, and I will **terrify** all the
people. 14 I will make southern Egypt
desolate and set fire to the city of Zoan in
the north. I will **punish** the capital city of
Thebes. 15 I will let the city of Pelusium,
Egypt's great fortress, feel my **fury**. I will
destroy the wealth of Thebes. 16 I will set
fire to Egypt, and Pelusium will be in
agony. The walls of Thebes will be
broken down, and the city will be
flooded.[u] 17 The young men of the cities
of Heliopolis and Bubastis will die in the
war, and the other people will be taken
prisoner. 18 **Darkness** will fall on
Tahpanhes when I break the **power** of
Egypt and put an end to the **strength**
they were so **proud** of. A **cloud** will cover
Egypt, and the people of all her cities
will be taken **prisoner**. 19 When I **punish**
Egypt in this way, they will know that I
am the LORD."

The Broken Power of the King of Egypt

20 On the seventh day of the first
month of the eleventh year of our **exile**,
the LORD spoke to me. 21 "**Mortal man**,"
he said, "I have broken the arm of the
king of Egypt. No one has bandaged it or
put it in a sling so that it could **heal** and
be **strong enough** to hold a sword again.
22 Now then, this is what I, the **Sovereign**
LORD, say: I am the **enemy** of the king of
Egypt. I am going to break both his
arms—the good one and the one already
broken—and the sword will fall from his
hand. 23 I am going to **scatter** the Egyptians throughout the **world**. 24 Then I will
make the arms of the king of Babylonia
strong and put my sword in his hands.
But I will break the arms of the king of
Egypt, and he will **groan** and die in front
of his **enemy**. 25 Yes, I will **weaken** him
and **strengthen** the king of Babylonia.
When I give him my sword and he points
it towards Egypt, everyone will know
that I am the LORD. 26 I will **scatter** the
Egyptians throughout the **world**. Then
they will know that I am the LORD."

Egypt Is Compared to a Cedar Tree

31 On the first day of the third
month of the eleventh year of
our **exile**, the LORD spoke to me. 2 "**Mortal man**," he said, "say to the king of
Egypt and all his people:

How **powerful** you are!
What can I **compare** you to?
3 You are like[v] a cedar in Lebanon,
With beautiful, shady branches,
A tree so tall it reaches the **clouds**.[w]
4 There was water to make it grow,
And underground rivers to feed it.
They watered the place where the tree
was growing
And sent streams to all the trees of the
forest.
5 Because it was well-watered,
It grew taller than other trees.
Its branches grew thick and long.
6 Every kind of bird built nests in its
branches;
The wild animals bore their young in
its **shelter**;
The nations of the **world rested** in its
shade.
7 How beautiful the tree was—
So tall, with such long branches.
Its roots reached down to the deep-
flowing streams.
8 No cedar in God's garden could
compare with it.
No fir-tree ever had such branches,
And no plane-tree such boughs.
No tree in God's own garden was so
beautiful.
9 I made it beautiful, with spreading
branches.
It was the **envy** of every tree in Eden,
the garden of God.

10 "Now then, I, the **Sovereign** LORD,
will tell you what is going to happen to
that tree that grew until it reached the
clouds.[w] As it grew taller it grew **proud**;
11 so I have **rejected** it and will let a
foreign ruler have it. He will give that
tree what it **deserves** for its **wickedness**.
12 Ruthless foreigners will cut it down and
leave it. Its branches and broken boughs
will fall on every mountain and valley in
the country. All the nations that have
been living in its shade will go away.
13 The birds will come and perch on the
fallen tree, and the wild animals will
walk over its branches. 14 And so from
now on, no tree, no matter how well-
watered it is, will grow as tall as that
again or push its top through the **clouds**[w]
and reach such a height. All of them are
doomed to die like mortal men, **doomed**
to join those who go down to the **world of
the dead**."

15 This is what the **Sovereign** LORD
says: "On the day when the tree goes to

[u] *One ancient translation* flooded; *Hebrew unclear.*
[v] *Probable text* You are like; *Hebrew* Assyria is.
[w] *One ancient translation* clouds; *Hebrew* thick branches.

31.8: Gen 2.9

cloud [3] 30.3; 32.7
compare [2] 27.32; Dan 1.13
dark 30.18; 32.8
deserve 20.44; 39.24
doom [2] 24.6; 34.2
downfall [2] Lam 4.6; 35.14

envy Ecc 4.2; Acts 8.23
exile 30.20; 32.1
mortal 30.2; 32.2
mourn 27.30; 32.16
please 20.39; 43.27
power 30.12; 32.18
proud 30.6; 32.12
reject 20.13; Dan 9.5
rest (1) Lam 5.5; 32.30
scatter 30.23; 34.5
shelter 17.23; 45.25
sign (1) 24.17; Dan 3.25
Sovereign [3] 30.2; 32.8
ungodly Jer 23.15; 32.19
wicked 21.25; 39.24
world 30.7; 32.4
world of the dead [6] 26.20; 32.18

the **world of the dead**, I will make the underground waters cover it as a **sign** of **mourning**. I will hold back the rivers and not let the many streams flow out. Because the tree has died, I will bring **darkness** over the Lebanon Mountains and make all the trees of the forest wither. 16 When I send it down to the **world of the dead**, the noise of its **downfall** will shake the nations. All the trees of Eden and all the choice, well-watered trees of Lebanon who have gone to the **world below** will be **pleased** at its **downfall**. 17 They will go with it to the **world of the dead** to join those that have already fallen. And all who live under its shadow will be **scattered** among the nations.[y]

18 "The tree is the king of Egypt and all his people. Not even the trees in Eden were so tall and impressive. But now, like the trees of Eden, it will go down to the **world of the dead** and join the **ungodly** and those killed in battle. I have spoken," says the **Sovereign** LORD.

The King of Egypt Is Compared to a Crocodile

32 On the first day of the twelfth month of the twelfth year of our **exile**, the LORD spoke to me. 2 "**Mortal man**," he said, "give a **solemn warning** to the king of Egypt. Give him this **message** from me: You **act** like a lion among the nations, but you are more like a crocodile splashing through a river. You muddy the water with your feet and pollute the rivers. 3 When many nations gather, I will catch you in my net and let them drag the net ashore. 4 I will throw you out on the ground and bring all the birds and animals of the **world** to feed on you. 5 I will cover mountains and valleys with your rotting corpse. 6 I will pour out your **blood** until it spreads over the mountains and fills the streams. 7 When I **destroy** you, I will cover the sky and blot out the stars. The sun will hide behind the **clouds**, and the moon will give no **light**. 8 I will **put out** all the **lights** of **heaven** and plunge your **world** into **darkness**. I, the **Sovereign** LORD, have spoken.

9 "Many nations will be **troubled** when I spread the news of your **destruction** through countries you never heard of. 10 What I do to you will shock many nations. When I swing my sword, kings will shudder with **fright**. On the day you fall, all of them will **tremble** in **fear** for their own **lives**."

11 The **Sovereign** LORD says to the king of Egypt, "You will face the sword of the king of Babylonia. 12 I will let soldiers from **cruel** nations draw their swords and kill all your people. All your people and everything else that you are **proud** of will be **destroyed**. 13 I will **slaughter** your cattle at every water-hole. There will be no people or cattle to muddy the water any more. 14 I will let your waters settle and become **clear** and let your rivers run **calm**. I, the **Sovereign** LORD, have spoken. 15 When I make Egypt a **desolate** waste and **destroy** all who live there, they will know that I am the LORD. 16 This **solemn warning** will become a funeral song. The women of the nations will sing it to **mourn** for Egypt and all its people. I, the **Sovereign** LORD, have spoken."

The World of the Dead

17 On the fifteenth day of the first month[z] of the twelfth year of our **exile**, the LORD spoke to me. 18 "**Mortal man**," he said, "**mourn** for all the many people of Egypt. Send them down with the other **powerful** nations to the **world of the dead**. 19 Say to them:

"Do you think you are more beautiful
than anyone else?
You will go down to the **world of the dead**
and lie there among the **ungodly**.

20 "The people of Egypt will fall with those who are killed in battle. A sword is ready to kill them all.[a] 21 The greatest heroes and those who fought on the Egyptian side **welcome** the Egyptians to the **world of the dead**. They shout: 'The **ungodly** who were killed in battle have come down here, and here they lie!'

22 "Assyria is there, with the **graves** of her soldiers all around. They were all killed in battle, 23 and their **graves** are in the deepest parts of the **world of the dead**. All her soldiers fell in battle, and their **graves** surround her **tomb**. Yet once they **terrified** the land of the living.

24 "Elam is there, with the **graves** of her soldiers all around. They were all killed in battle, and they went down, **uncircumcised**, to the **world of the dead**. In **life** they spread **terror**, but now they lie **dead** and **disgraced**. 25 Elam lies down among those killed in battle, and the **graves** of her soldiers are all around her. They are all **uncircumcised**, all killed in battle. In **life** they spread **terror**, but now

[y] *Probable text* And all...nations; *Hebrew unclear.*
[z] *One ancient translation* of the first month; *Hebrew does not have these words.*
[a] *Probable text* A sword...all; *Hebrew unclear.*

32.7: Is 13.10; Mt 24.29; Mk 13.24–25; Lk 21.25; Rev 6.12–13, 8.12

act 30.3; 36.17
ancient 26.20; 36.2
blood 28.23; 33.25
body 29.5; 35.8
calm 16.42; Jon 1.12
circumcise [7] Jer 9.25; 44.7
clear Is 62.10; 34.18
cloud 31.3; 38.9
comfort Lam 2.13; Dan 4.4
cruel 25.12; 34.4
dark 31.15; 34.12
dead [2] 26.20; 37.9
desolate 30.7; 33.28
destroy [4] 30.6; 34.16
disgrace [4] 20.43; 36.20
enough 30.21; 33.13
exile [2] 31.1; 33.21
fate 29.16; 35.6
fear 27.35; 38.8
fright 7.16; Dan 4.5
grave [6] 28.8; 37.12
heaven 3.12; Dan 2.18
honour 22.7; 39.13
life (1) [3] 20.11; 33.8
light (1) [2] 11.22; 43.2
message 24.21; 36.1
mortal [2] 31.2; 33.2
mourn [2] 31.15; Dan 10.2
power [4] 31.2; 33.22
proud 31.10; 33.28
put out 20.47; Amos 5.6
rest (1) [2] 31.6; 34.15
share [2] 28.19; 44.28
sight Jer 52.3; Hab 1.13
slaughter 26.15; 35.5
solemn [2] Jer 44.24; 36.7
Sovereign [6] 31.10; 33.11

terrify [3] 30.9; 34.28
terror [3] 30.2; Joel 1.15
tomb Jer 48.9; Mt 23.27
tremble 26.16; 38.20
trouble 30.3; Dan 9.18
ungodly [2] 31.18; Tit 2.12
warn [2] 28.17; 33.3
welcome Lam 4.15; Dan 4.36
world [2] 31.6; 35.14
world of the dead [8 31.14; Hos 13.14

they lie **dead** and **disgraced**, **sharing** the **fate** of those killed in battle.

26 "Meshech and Tubal are there, with the **graves** of their soldiers all around. They are all **uncircumcised**, all killed in battle. Yet once they **terrified** the living. 27 They were not given **honourable** burial like the heroes of **ancient** times,[b] who went fully armed to the **world of the dead**, their swords placed under their heads and their shields[c] over their **bodies**. These heroes were once **powerful enough** to **terrify** the living.

28 "That is how the Egyptians will lie crushed among the **uncircumcised** who were killed in battle.

29 "Edom is there with her kings and rulers. They were **powerful** soldiers, but now they lie in the **world of the dead** with the **uncircumcised** who were killed in battle.

30 "All the princes of the north are there, and so are the Sidonians. Their **power** once spread **terror**, but now they go down in **disgrace** with those killed in battle and are laid to **rest**, **uncircumcised**. They **share** the **disgrace** of those who go down to the **world of the dead**.

31 "The **sight** of all these who were killed in battle will be a **comfort** to the king of Egypt and his army," says the **Sovereign LORD**.

32 "I made the king of Egypt terrorize the living, but he and all his army will be killed and laid to **rest** with all the **uncircumcised** who die in battle." The **Sovereign LORD** has spoken.

God Appoints Ezekiel as a Watchman
(Ezek 3.16–21)

33 The LORD spoke to me. 2 "**Mortal man**," he said, "tell your people what happens when I bring war to a land. The people of that country **choose** one of their number to be a **watchman**. 3 When he sees the **enemy** approaching, he sounds the alarm to **warn** everyone. 4 If someone hears it but pays no attention and the **enemy** comes and kills him, then he is to **blame** for his own **death**. 5 His **death** is his own **fault**, because he paid no attention to the **warning**. If he had paid attention, he could have **escaped**. 6 If, however, the **watchman** sees the **enemy** coming and does not sound the alarm, the **enemy** will come and kill those sinners, but I will hold the **watchman** responsible for their **death**.

7 "Now, **mortal man**, I am making you a **watchman** for the nation of Israel. You must pass on to them the **warnings** I give you. 8 If I **announce** that an **evil** man is going to die but you do not **warn** him to **change** his **ways** so that he can **save** his **life**, then he will die, still a sinner, and I will hold you responsible for his **death**. 9 If you do **warn** an **evil** man and he doesn't stop sinning, he will die, still a sinner, but your **life** will be **spared**."

Individual Responsibility

10 The LORD spoke to me. "**Mortal man**," he said, "repeat to the Israelites what they are saying: 'We are **burdened** with our sins and the **wrongs** we have done. We are wasting away. How can we live?' 11 Tell them that as **surely** as I, the **Sovereign LORD**, am the living God, I do not **enjoy** seeing a sinner die. I would rather see him stop sinning and live. Israel, stop the **evil** you are doing. Why do you want to die?

12 "Now, **mortal man**, tell the Israelites that when a good man sins, the good he has done will not **save** him. If an **evil** man stops doing evil, he won't be **punished**, and if a good man starts sinning, his **life** will not be **spared**. 13 I may **promise life** to a good man, but if he starts thinking that his past goodness is **enough** and begins to sin, I will not **remember** any of the good he did. He will die because of his sins. 14 I may **warn** an **evil** man that he is going to die, but if he stops sinning and does what is **right** and good—15 for example, if he returns the **security** he took for a loan or gives back what he **stole**—if he stops sinning and follows the **laws** that give **life**, he will not die, but live. 16 I will **forgive** the sins he has committed, and he will live because he has done what is **right** and good.

17 "And your people say that what I do isn't **right**! No, it's their way that isn't **right**. 18 When a **righteous** man stops doing good and starts doing **evil**, he will die for it. 19 When an **evil** man gives up sinning and does what is **right** and good, he has **saved** his **life**. 20 But Israel, you say that what I do isn't **right**. I am going to **judge** you by what you do."

The News of Jerusalem's Fall

21 On the fifth day of the tenth month of the twelfth year of our **exile**, a man who had **escaped** from Jerusalem came and told me that the city had fallen. 22 The evening before he came, I had felt the **powerful presence** of the LORD. When

[b] *Some ancient translations* of ancient times; *Hebrew* of the uncircumcised.
[c] *Probable text* shields; *Hebrew* iniquities.

33.21: 2 Kgs 25.3–10; Jer 39.2–8, 52.4–14

action 24.13; 43.10
adultery 23.37; Hos 2.2
announce 30.2; 36.3
blame 18.13; Jon 1.7
blood 32.6; 38.22
burden Jer 23.33; Mic 6.3
change 3.18; Dan 2.9
choose 21.27; 37.28
commit [2] 23.37; Hos 3.1
death (1) [4] 18.13; 35.6
desolate 32.15; 35.3
disease 28.23; 38.22
disgust 23.17; 36.31
enemy [4] 30.22; 34.10
enjoy 18.23; Dan 4.4
enough 32.27; 37.10
escape [2] 24.26; 35.6
evil [7] 30.12; 36.31
exile 32.1; 39.23
fault Ps 119.1; Jon 1.12
forgive 18.22; 45.13
God's people 30.5; 34.27

greed Jer 51.39; Hab 2.5
idol 30.13; 36.18
judge 23.24; 34.17
law 23.24; 36.27
life (1) [6] 32.10; 47.9
love [2] 24.16; Dan 9.4
mortal [6] 32.2; 34.2
obey 20.11; 36.26
power [3] 32.18; 37.1
presence 20.9; 37.1
promise 20.5; 36.7
prophet 22.28; 38.17
proud 32.12; Dan 4.37
punish [2] 30.14; 35.5
rely 29.6; Dan 6.4
remember 21.32; 36.31
right (1) [6] 18.19; 34.16
righteous 23.45; Hos 10.12
ruin [2] 30.4; 35.4
save [3] 18.27; 36.29
secure 28.26; 34.25
Sovereign [3] 32.8; 34.2
spare [2] 9.5; Dan 11.42
speech 24.27; Dan 10.15
steal Jer 51.44; Hos 4.2
sure [2] 20.3; 34.8
true 18.5; 36.13
warn [7] 32.2; Dan 8.25
watch [4] 21.6; 37.8
way (3) [2] 3.18; Dan 8.25
word (1) [4] 30.2; 37.4
worship (2) (of other gods) 23.7; 43.7
wrong 29.16; 36.31

the man arrived the next morning, the LORD gave me back the power of speech.

The Sins of the People

23 The LORD spoke to me. 24 "Mortal man," he said, "the people who are living in the ruined cities of the land of Israel are saying: 'Abraham was only one man, and he was given the whole land. There are many of us, so now the land is ours.'

25 "Tell them what I, the Sovereign LORD, am saying: You eat meat with the blood still in it. You worship idols. You commit murder. What makes you think that the land belongs to you? 26 You rely on your swords. Your actions are disgusting. Everyone commits adultery. What makes you think that the land is yours?

27 "Tell them that I, the Sovereign LORD, warn them that as surely as I am the living God, the people who live in the ruined cities will be killed. Those living in the country will be eaten by wild animals. Those hiding in the mountains and in caves will die of disease. 28 I will make the country a desolate waste, and the power they were so proud of will come to an end. The mountains of Israel will be so wild that no one will be able to travel through them. 29 When I punish the people for their sins and make the country a waste, then they will know that I am the LORD."

The Results of the Prophet's Message

30 The LORD said, "Mortal man, your people are talking about you when they meet by the city walls or in the doorways of their houses. They say to one another, 'Let's go and hear what word has come from the LORD now.' 31 So my people crowd in to hear what you have to say, but they don't do what you tell them to do. Loving words are on their lips, but they continue their greedy ways. 32 To them you are nothing more than an entertainer singing love songs or playing a harp. They listen to all your words and don't obey a single one of them. 33 But when all your words come true—and they will come true—then they will know that a prophet has been among them."

The Shepherds of Israel

34 The LORD spoke to me. 2 "Mortal man," he said, "denounce the rulers of Israel. Prophesy to them, and tell them what I, the Sovereign LORD, say to them: You are doomed, you shepherds of Israel! You take care of yourselves, but never tend the sheep. 3 You drink the milk, wear clothes made from the wool, and kill and eat the finest sheep. But you never tend the sheep. 4 You have not taken care of the weak ones, healed those that are sick, bandaged those that are hurt, brought back those that wandered off, or looked for those that were lost. Instead, you treated them cruelly. 5 Because the sheep had no shepherd, they were scattered, and wild animals killed and ate them. 6 So my sheep wandered over the high hills and the mountains. They were scattered over the face of the earth, and no one looked for them or tried to find them.

7 "Now, you shepherds, listen to what I, the LORD, am telling you. 8 As surely as I am the living God, you had better listen to me. My sheep have been attacked by wild animals that killed and ate them because there was no shepherd. My shepherds did not try to find the sheep. They were taking care of themselves and not the sheep. 9 So listen to me, you shepherds. 10 I, the Sovereign LORD, declare that I am your enemy. I will take my sheep away from you and never again let you be their shepherds; never again will I let you take care only of yourselves. I will rescue my sheep from you and not let you eat them.

The Good Shepherd

11 "I, the Sovereign LORD, tell you that I myself will look for my sheep and take care of them 12 in the same way as a shepherd takes care of his sheep that were scattered and are brought together again. I will bring them back from all the places where they were scattered on that dark, disastrous day. 13 I will take them out of foreign countries, gather them together, and bring them back to their own land. I will lead them back to the mountains and the streams of Israel and will feed them in pleasant pastures. 14 I will let them graze in safety in the mountain meadows and the valleys and in all the green pastures of the land of Israel. 15 I myself will be the shepherd of my sheep, and I will find them a place to rest. I, the Sovereign LORD, have spoken.

16 "I will look for those that are lost, bring back those that wander off, bandage those that are hurt, and heal those that are sick; but those that are fat and strong I will destroy, because I am a shepherd who does what is right.

17 "Now then, my flock, I, the Sovereign LORD, tell you that I will judge each of you and separate the good from the bad, the sheep from the goats.

34.5: Num 27.17; 1 Kgs 22.17; Mt 9.36; Mk 6.34

bad [2] 23.13; Obad 11
best 24.4; 44.30
bless [2] 16.27; 44.30
care [7] 23.42; Hos 11.3
clear 32.14; Mt 7.5
covenant 20.20; 37.26
cruel 32.12; Dan 5.20
danger 14.15; Jon 1.4
dark 32.8; Dan 2.22

denounce 29.2; 35.2
destroy 32.7; 43.3
disaster 7.5; 35.5
doom 31.14; Hos 4.6
enemy 33.3; 35.3
flock [3] Jer 51.23; 36.37
free 13.20; 37.23
God's people [3] 33.31; 35.11
guarantee Prov 27.13; 37.26
heal [2] 30.21; 47.12
heathen Is 52.1; Hos 7.14
hunger 18.7; Hos 4.10
hurt [2] 28.24; Dan 3.25
ill-treat 22.29; Amos 4.1
judge [3] 33.20; Dan 3.2
mortal 33.2; 35.2
need 27.33; 44.28
never again [2] 29.15; 36.12
prophecy 30.2; 36.3
protect 23.24; 39.25
rescue [2] 13.23; Dan 3.28
rest (1) 32.30; Dan 4.12
rid 11.18; Zech 11.8
right (1) 33.14; 45.9
sacred Jer 43.13; 43.12
safe [4] 28.26; 38.8
satisfy 22.9; Hos 9.4
scatter [4] 31.17; 36.19
secure 33.15; 37.26
separate [2] Is 59.2; 42.20
servant [2] 28.25; 37.24
sheep [20] 27.21; 36.37
shepherd [11] Jer 51.23; Amos 1.1
slave 27.13; Dan 10.17
sneer 22.4; 36.15
Sovereign [8] 33.11; 35.3
strong [2] 30.21; Dan 1.15
sure 33.11; 35.6
terrify 32.23; 38.21
weak [2] 30.25; Dan 2.42

[18]Some of you are not satisfied with eating the best grass; you even trample
down what you don't eat! You drink the
clear water and muddy what you don't
drink! [19]My other sheep have to eat the
grass you trample down and drink the
water you muddy.
20 "So now, I, the Sovereign LORD, tell
you that I will judge between you strong
sheep and the weak sheep. [21]You pushed
the sick ones aside and butted them
away from the flock. [22]But I will rescue
my sheep and not let them be ill-treated
any more. I will judge each of my sheep
and separate the good from the bad. [23]I
will give them a king like my servant
David to be their one shepherd, and he
will take care of them. [24]I, the LORD, will
be their God, and a king like my servant
David will be their ruler. I have spoken.
[25]I will make a covenant with them that
guarantees their security. I will get rid of
all the dangerous animals in the land, so
that my sheep can live safely in the fields
and sleep in the forests.
26 "I will bless them and let them live
round my sacred hill.[e] There I will bless
them with showers of rain when they
need it. [27]The trees will bear fruit, the
fields will produce crops, and everyone
will live in safety on his own land. When I
break my people's chains and set them
free from those who made them slaves,
then they will know that I am the LORD.
[28]The heathen nations will not plunder
them any more, and the wild animals
will not kill and eat them. They will live
in safety, and no one will terrify them. [29]I
will give them fertile fields and put an
end to hunger in the land. The other
nations will not sneer at them any more.
[30]Everyone will know that I protect
Israel and that they are my people. I, the
Sovereign LORD, have spoken.
31 "You, my sheep, the flock that I
feed, are my people, and I am your God,"
says the Sovereign LORD.

God's Punishment of Edom

35 The LORD spoke to me. [2]"Mortal
man," he said, "denounce the
country of Edom. [3]Tell the people what I,
the Sovereign LORD, am saying:

I am your enemy, mountains of Edom!
I will make you a desolate waste.
[4]I will leave your cities in ruins
And your land desolate;
Then you will know that I am the
LORD.

5 "You were Israel's constant enemy
and let her people be slaughtered in the
time of her disaster, the time of final
punishment for her sins. [6]So then—as
surely as I, the Sovereign LORD, am the
living God—death is your fate, and you
cannot escape it. You are guilty of[f]
murder, and murder will follow you. [7]I
will make the hill-country of Edom a
waste and kill everyone who travels
through it. [8]I will cover the mountains
with corpses, and the bodies of those who
are killed in battle will cover the hills
and valleys. [9]I will make you desolate for
ever, and no one will live in your cities
again. Then you will know that I am the
LORD.
10 "You said that the two nations,
Judah and Israel, together with their
lands, belonged to you and that you
would possess them, even though I, the
Lord, was their GOD. [11]So then, as surely
as I, the Sovereign LORD, am the living
God, I will pay you back for your anger,
your jealousy, and your hatred towards
my people. They will know that I am
punishing you for what you did to them.
[12]Then you will know that I, the LORD,
heard you say with contempt that the
mountains of Israel were desolate and
that they were yours to devour. [13]I have
heard the wild, boastful way you have
talked against me."
14 The Sovereign LORD says, "I will
make you so desolate that the whole
world will rejoice at your downfall, [15]just
as you rejoiced at the devastation of
Israel, my own possession. The mountains of Seir, yes, all the land of Edom,
will be desolate. Then everyone will
know that I am the LORD."

God's Blessing on Israel

36 The LORD said, "Mortal man,
speak to the mountains of Israel
and tell them to listen to the message
which I, [2]the Sovereign LORD, have for
them: Israel's enemies gloated and said,
'Now those ancient hills are ours!'
3 "Prophesy, then, and announce what
I, the Sovereign LORD, am saying. When
the neighbouring nations captured and
plundered the mountains of Israel, all of
them insulted Israel. [4]So now listen to
what I, the Sovereign LORD, say to you
mountains and hills, to you brooks and
valleys, to you places that were left in
ruins, and to you deserted cities which
were plundered and mocked by all the
surrounding nations.
5 "I, the Sovereign LORD, have spoken

[e] SACRED HILL: *See 20.40.* [f] *One ancient translation* are guilty of; *Hebrew* hate.

34.23: Rev 7.17 **34.24:** Ezek 37.24
35.1-15: Is 34.5-17, 63.1-6; Jer 49.7-22; Ezek 25.12-14; Amos 1.11-12; Obad 1-14; Mal 1.2-5

disaster 34.12; Hos 9.6
downfall 31.16; Zeph 1.3
enemy [2] 34.10; 36.2
escape 33.5; Dan 8.4
fate 32.25; Mt 24.51
final 21.25; Dan 11.40
God's people 34.27; 36.8
guilty 25.12; Hos 4.15
hate 25.15; Hos 7.4
jealous 16.42; 36.6
mortal 34.2; 36.1
possess [2] 13.18; 36.5
punish [2] 33.12; 38.22
rejoice [2] 21.10; Joel 2.23
ruin 33.24; 36.4
slaughter 32.13; Zeph 1.8
Sovereign [4] 34.2; 36.2
sure [2] 34.8; 36.9
world 32.4; 38.12

anger 25.14; 36.5
boast 27.3; Dan 7.8
body 32.27; 37.8
constant Lam 1.13; Dan 9.4
contempt Lam 1.8; 36.5
death (1) 33.4; 44.31
denounce 34.2; 38.2
desolate [6] 33.28; 38.8
devastate 30.11; Zech 11.6
devour Jer 30.16; Hos 13.8

act [2] 32.2; Dan 4.37
ancient 32.27; Mic 5.2
anger [3] 35.11; 38.19
announce 33.8; 38.17
clean [3] 24.6; 39.12
command [2] 28.10; 37.9
concern Lam 4.16; Joel 2.18
condemn 23.45; Zech 3.2
contempt 35.12; Mic 6.16
defile [4] 24.13; 37.23
disgrace [6] 32.24; 39.7
disgust 33.26; 37.23
enemy 35.3; 38.3
evil 33.8; 38.10
famine [2] 14.13; Amos 4.6
festival Is 66.23; 44.24
flock 34.17; Joel 1.18
force (1) 28.16; Dan 8.6

God's people [3] 35.11; 37.12
heart [3] 27.31; Dan 3.23
help 29.16; 39.13
holy [5] 28.14; 38.16
humiliate [2] Jer 50.12; Mic 3.7
idol [2] 33.25; 37.23
insult [2] 21.28; Zeph 2.8
jealous 35.11; Mt 20.15
law 33.15; 37.24
message [2] 32.2; Dan 4.1
mind (1) 20.32; Dan 1.8
mock [2] 23.32; Joel 2.17
mortal [2] 35.2; 37.3
name (2) (name of God, of Jesus) [4] 20.9; 39.7
neighbour [2] 28.26; Dan 9.16
never again 34.10; 39.29
new 18.31; 39.2
obey 33.32; 37.24
offer 22.9; 40.39
plenty 19.10; Joel 2.22
possess 35.10; 45.5
promise [2] 33.13; 37.14
prophecy [2] 34.2; 37.4
prosper 16.53; 39.25
remember 33.13; Dan 9.15
rob [3] 25.7; Dan 11.33
ruin [6] 35.4; 38.12
sacrifice 23.37; 39.17
sake [3] Jer 15.15; Amos 2.9
save 33.8; Dan 3.15
scatter 34.5; Dan 4.14
seed 17.23; Joel 1.17
shame 16.30; Dan 9.8
sheep [2] 34.2; 45.13
sneer 34.29; Lk 16.14
solemn 32.2; 44.12
Sovereign [14] 35.3; 37.3
sow Jer 50.16; Hos 8.7
Spirit (1) (God's Spirit) 11.1; 37.1
sprinkle Job 18.15; 43.18
stubborn 16.50; Dan 5.20
sure 35.6; 39.7
true 33.33; Dan 2.45
unclean 22.26; 39.24
wrong 33.10; 48.11

out in the heat of my **anger** against the surrounding nations, and especially against Edom. With glee and **contempt**, they captured my land and took **possession** of its pastures.

6 "So **prophesy** to the land of Israel; tell the mountains, hills, brooks, and valleys what I, the **Sovereign** LORD, am saying in **jealous anger** because of the way the nations have **insulted** and **humiliated** them. 7 I, the **Sovereign** LORD, **solemnly promise** that the surrounding nations will be **humiliated**. 8 But on the mountains of Israel the trees will again grow leaves and bear fruit for you, **my people** Israel. You are going to come home soon. 9 I am on your side, and I will make **sure** that your land is ploughed again and that **seeds** are **sown** there. 10 I will make your population grow. You will live in the cities and rebuild everything that was left in **ruins**. 11 I will make people and cattle increase in number. There will be more of you than ever before, and you will have many children. I will let you live there as you used to live, and I will make you more **prosperous** than ever. Then you will know that I am the LORD. 12 I will bring you, **my people** Israel, back to live again in the land. It will be your own land, and it will **never again** let your children starve.

13 "I, the **Sovereign** LORD, say: It is **true** that people call the land a man-eater, and they say that it **robs** the nation of its children. 14 But from now on it will no longer be a man-eater who **robs** you of your children. I, the **Sovereign** LORD, have spoken. 15 The land will no longer have to listen to the nations **mocking** it or see the peoples **sneer** at it. The land will no longer **rob** the nation of its children. I, the **Sovereign** LORD, have spoken."

Israel's New Life

16 The LORD spoke to me. 17 "**Mortal** man," he said, "when the Israelites were living in their land, they **defiled** it by the way they lived and **acted**. I regarded their behaviour as being as ritually **unclean** as a woman is during her monthly period.[g] 18 I let them feel the **force** of my **anger** because of the murders they had committed in the land and because of the **idols** by which they had **defiled** it. 19 I **condemned** them for the way they lived and **acted**, and I **scattered** them through foreign countries. 20 Wherever they went, they brought **disgrace** on my **holy name**, because people would say, 'These are the people of the LORD, but they had to leave his land.' 21 That made me **concerned** for my **holy name**, since the Israelites brought **disgrace** on it everywhere they went.

22 "Now then, give the Israelites the **message** that I, the **Sovereign** LORD, have for them: What I am going to do is not for the **sake** of you Israelites, but for the **sake** of my **holy name**, which you have **disgraced** in every country where you have gone. 23 When I demonstrate to the nations the **holiness** of my great **name**—the name you **disgraced** among them—then they will know that I am the LORD. I, the **Sovereign** LORD, have spoken. I will use you to show the nations that I am **holy**. 24 I will take you from every nation and country and bring you back to your own land. 25 I will **sprinkle clean** water on you and make you **clean** from all your **idols** and everything else that has **defiled** you. 26 I will give you a **new heart** and a new **mind**. I will take away your **stubborn heart** of stone and give you an **obedient heart**. 27 I will put my **spirit** in you and I will see to it that you follow my **laws** and keep all the **commands** I have given you. 28 Then you will live in the land I gave your ancestors. You will be **my people**, and I will be your God. 29 I will **save** you from everything that **defiles** you. I will **command** the corn to be **plentiful**, so that you will not have any more **famines**. 30 I will increase the yield of your fruit-trees and your fields, so that there will be no more **famines** to **disgrace** you among the nations. 31 You will **remember** your **evil** conduct and the **wrongs** that you committed, and you will be **disgusted** with yourselves because of your sins and your iniquities. 32 Israel, I want you to know that I am not doing all this for your **sake**. I want you to feel the **shame** and **disgrace** of what you are doing. I, the **Sovereign** LORD, have spoken."

33 The **Sovereign** LORD says, "When I make you **clean** from all your sins, I will let you live in your cities again and let you rebuild the **ruins**. 34 Everyone who used to walk by your fields saw how overgrown and wild they were, but I will let you farm them again. 35 Everyone will say how this land, which was once a wilderness, has become like the Garden of Eden, and how the cities which were torn down, looted, and left in **ruins**, are now inhabited and fortified. 36 Then the **neighbouring** nations that have survived

[g] RITUALLY UNCLEAN...PERIOD: *This is based on the view of ritual uncleanness described in the Law of Moses (see Lev 15.19).*

36.26-28: Ezek 11.19-20

will know that I, the LORD, rebuild **ruined**
cities and replant waste fields. I, the
LORD, have **promised** that I would do
this—and I will."
37 The **Sovereign** LORD says, "I will
once again let the Israelites ask me for
help, and I will let them increase in
numbers like a **flock** of **sheep**. 38 The
cities that are now in **ruins** will then be
as full of people as Jerusalem was once
full of the **sheep** which were **offered as
sacrifices** at a **festival**. Then they will
know that I am the LORD."

The Valley of Dry Bones

37 I felt the **powerful presence** of
the LORD, and his **spirit** took me
and set me down in a valley where the
ground was covered with bones. 2 He led
me all round the valley, and I could see
that there were very many bones and
that they were very dry. 3 He said to me,
"**Mortal man**, can these bones come back
to life?"
I replied, "**Sovereign** LORD, only you
can answer that!"
4 He said, "**Prophesy** to the bones. Tell
these dry bones to listen to the **word of
the** LORD. 5 Tell them that I, the
Sovereign LORD, am saying to them: I
am going to put breath into you and
bring you back **to life**. 6 I will give you
sinews and muscles, and cover you with
skin. I will put breath into you and bring
you back **to life**. Then you will know that
I am the LORD."
7 So I **prophesied** as I had been told.
While I was speaking, I heard a rattling
noise, and the bones began to join together. 8 While I **watched**, the bones were
covered with sinews and muscles, and
then with skin. But there was no breath
in the **bodies**.
9 God said to me, "**Mortal man**, **prophesy** to the wind.[h] Tell the wind that the
Sovereign LORD **commands** it to come
from every direction, to breathe into
these **dead bodies**, and to bring them
back **to life**."
10 So I **prophesied** as I had been told.
Breath entered the **bodies**, and they
came **to life** and stood up. There were
enough of them to form an army.
11 God said to me, "**Mortal man**, the
people of Israel are like these bones.
They say that they are dried up, without
any **hope** and with no future. 12 So **prophesy** to **my people** Israel and tell them
that I, the **Sovereign** LORD, am going to
open their **graves**. I am going to take
them out and bring them back to the
land of Israel. 13 When I open the **graves**
where **my people** are buried and bring
them out, they will know that I am the
LORD. 14 I will put my breath in them,
bring them back **to life**, and let them live
in their own land. Then they will know
that I am the LORD. I have **promised** that
I would do this— and I will. I, the LORD,
have spoken."

Judah and Israel in One Kingdom

15 The LORD spoke to me again.
16 "**Mortal man**," he said, "take a wooden
stick and write on it the **words**, 'The kingdom of Judah.' Then take another stick
and write on it the **words**, 'The kingdom
of Israel.' 17 Then hold the two sticks end
to end in your hand so that they look like
one stick. 18 When your people ask you to
tell them what this means, 19 tell them
that I, the **Sovereign** LORD, am going to
take the stick **representing** Israel and put
it with the one that **represents** Judah. Out
of the two I will make one stick and hold
it in my hand.
20 "Hold in your hand the two sticks
and let the people see them. 21 Then tell
them that I, the **Sovereign** LORD, am going to take all **my people** out of the
nations where they have gone, gather
them together, and bring them back to
their own land. 22 I will **unite** them into
one nation in the land, on the mountains
of Israel. They will have one king to rule
over them, and they will no longer be
divided into two nations or split into two
kingdoms. 23 They will not **defile** themselves with **disgusting idols** any more or
corrupt themselves with sin. I will **free**
them from all the ways in which they sin
and **betray** me. I will **purify** them; they
will be **my people**, and I will be their
God. 24 A king like my **servant** David will
be their king. They will all be **united**
under one ruler and will **obey** my **laws
faithfully**. 25 They will live on the land I
gave to my **servant** Jacob, the land
where their ancestors lived. They will
live there for ever, and so will their children and all their descendants. A king
like my **servant** David will rule over
them for ever. 26 I will make a **covenant**
with them that **guarantees** their **security**
for ever. I will **establish** them and increase their population, and put my
Temple in their land, where it will stay
for ever. 27 I will live there with them; I
will be their God, and they will be **my
people**. 28 When I place my **Temple** there
to be among them for ever, then the

betray Lam 1.2; 39.26
body [3] 35.8; 39.4
choose 33.2; 39.14
command 36.27; 38.7
corrupt 28.18; Zeph 3.1
covenant 34.25; 44.7
dead 32.24; 39.4
defile 36.17; Hos 6.10
disgust 36.31; 43.8
enough 33.13; 39.9
establish 23.38; Dan 2.44
faithful 11.20; 44.15
free 34.27; Dan 1.4
God's people [6] 36.8; 38.14
grave [2] 32.22; 39.15
guarantee 34.25; Rom 4.16
hope 19.5; Dan 2.9
idol 36.18; 44.10
law 36.27; 43.12
life (2) (to life) [6] Jer 21.8; Mt 10.8
mortal [4] 36.1; 38.2
obey 36.26; 44.7
power 33.22; 38.15
presence 33.22; 40.1
promise 36.7; 47.14
prophecy [5] 36.3; Dan 9.22
pure 24.11; 43.20
represent [2] 23.4; Dan 8.20
secure 34.25; 38.11
servant [3] 34.23; 38.17
Sovereign [6] 36.2; 38.3
Spirit (1) (God's Spirit) 36.27; 39.29
Temple (1) (of God) [2] 25.3; Dan 1.2
unite [2] 2 Chr 30.12; Dan 2.43
watch 33.2; 40.4
word (1) [3] 33.30; Dan 2.14

[h] wind; *or* spirit. *The same Hebrew word may mean* wind, *or* spirit, *or* breath.

37.10: Rev 11.11 **37.24:** Ezek 34.24 **37.27:** 2 Cor 6.16; Rev 21.3

nations will know that I, the LORD, have
chosen Israel to be my own people."

Gog as the Instrument of God

anger 36.5; 43.8
announce 36.3; Dan 3.4
being 29.11; 44.2
blood 33.25; 39.17
cloud 32.7; Dan 7.13
command 37.9; 43.19
defend 30.6; Dan 3.16
denounce [2] 35.2; 39.1
desolate 35.3; Mic 1.7
disease 33.27; Hab 3.5
enemy 36.2; 39.1
evil 36.31; Dan 9.5
fear [2] 32.10; Dan 6.26
fury 30.15; Dan 11.44
God's people [2] 37.12; 39.7
helpless Lam 1.3; Joel 1.16
holy [2] 36.20; 39.7
human 29.11; 39.15
intend 13.14; Gal 4.17
mortal 37.3; 39.1
peace 16.49; Dan 11.8
plan 11.2; 43.10
power 37.1; 39.21
prophet 33.33; Dan 9.2
punish 35.5; 44.10
ruin 36.4; Dan 2.5
safe 34.14; 39.26
secure [2] 37.26; Amos 2.8
servant 37.24; 46.24
Sovereign [6] 37.3; 39.1
terrify 34.28; Dan 2.31
tremble 32.10; Dan 5.19
turn [2] 25.5; 39.2
world 35.14; Dan 4.1

38 The LORD spoke to me. 2 "Mortal
man," he said, "denounce Gog,
chief ruler of the nations of Meshech and
Tubal in the land of Magog. Denounce
him, 3 and tell him that I, the Sovereign
LORD, am his enemy. 4 I will turn him
round, put hooks in his jaws, and drag
him and all his troops away. His army,
with its horses and uniformed riders, is
enormous, and every soldier carries a
shield and is armed with a sword. 5 Men
from Persia, Sudan, and Libya are with
him, and all have shields and helmets.
6 All the fighting men of the lands of
Gomer and Beth Togarmah in the north
are with him, and so are men from many
other nations. 7 Tell him to get ready and
have all his troops ready at his
command. 8 After many years I will
order him to invade a country where the
people were brought back together from
many nations and have lived without
fear of war. He will invade the mountains
of Israel, which were desolate and deserted so long, but where all the people
now live in safety. 9 He and his army and
the many nations with him will attack
like a storm and cover the land like a
cloud."

10 This is what the Sovereign LORD
says to Gog: "When that time comes, you
will start thinking up an evil plan. 11 You
will decide to invade a helpless country
where the people live in peace and
security in unwalled towns that have no
defences. 12 You will plunder and loot the
people who live in cities that were once
in ruins. They have been gathered from
the nations, and now they have livestock
and property and live at the crossroads
of the world. 13 The people of Sheba and
Dedan and the merchants from the
towns of Spain will ask you, 'Have you
assembled your army and attacked in
order to loot and plunder? Do you intend
to get silver and gold, livestock and property, and to march off with all those
spoils?'"

14 So the Sovereign LORD sent me to
tell Gog what he was saying to him:
"Now while my people Israel live in security, you will set out[j] 15 from your place in
the far north, leading a large, powerful
army of soldiers from many nations, all
of them on horseback. 16 You will attack
my people Israel like a storm moving
across the land. When the time comes, I
will send you to invade my land in order
to show the nations who I am, to show
my holiness by what I do through you.
17 You are the one I was talking about
long ago, when I announced through my
servants, the prophets of Israel, that in
days to come I would bring someone to
attack Israel." The Sovereign LORD has
spoken.

God's Punishment of Gog

18 The Sovereign LORD says, "On the
day when Gog invades Israel, I will be
furious. 19 I declare in the heat of my
anger that on that day there will be a
severe earthquake in the land of Israel.
20 Every fish and bird, every animal large
and small, and every human being on the
face of the earth will tremble for fear of
me. Mountains will fall, cliffs will crumble, and every wall will collapse. 21 I will
terrify Gog with all sorts of calamities.[k]
I, the Sovereign LORD, have spoken. His
men will turn their swords against one
another. 22 I will punish him with disease
and bloodshed. Torrents of rain and hail,
together with fire and sulphur, will pour
down on him and his army and on the
many nations that are on his side. 23 In
this way I will show all the nations that I
am great and that I am holy. They will
know then that I am the LORD."

The Defeat of Gog

39 The Sovereign LORD said, "Mortal man, denounce Gog, the chief
ruler of the nations of Meshech and
Tubal, and tell him that I am his enemy.
2 I will turn him in a new direction and
lead him out of the far north until he
comes to the mountains of Israel. 3 Then I
will knock his bow out of his left hand
and his arrows out of his right hand.
4 Gog and his army and his allies will fall
dead on the mountains of Israel, and I
will let their bodies be food for all the
birds and wild animals. 5 They will fall
dead in the open field. I, the Sovereign
LORD, have spoken. 6 I will start a fire in
the land of Magog and along all the
coasts where people live undisturbed,
and everyone will know that I am the
LORD. 7 I will make sure that my people
Israel know my holy name, and I will not
let my name be disgraced any more.
Then the nations will know that I, the
LORD, am the Holy God of Israel."

8 The Sovereign LORD said, "The day I
spoke about is certain to come. 9 The

abandon [2] 9.9; Dan 11.30
betray 37.23; Mt 10.4
blood [3] 38.22; 43.18
body [3] 37.8; Dan 4.33
captive 12.11; Joel 3.3
certain (1) Is 28.15; Mt 6.1
choose 37.28; Dan 1.6
clean [3] 36.25; 44.23
dead [2] 37.9; Joel 2.20
denounce 38.2; Dan 3.8
deserve 31.11; Hos 9.7
disgrace [2] 36.20; 43.7
enemy [3] 38.3; Dan 4.19
enough 37.10; Dan 4.12
exile 33.21; 40.1
feast Jer 51.39; 46.11
forget 23.35; Hos 2.13
glory 27.10; 43.5
God's people [3] 38.14; 44.7
grave 37.12; Nah 1.14
help 36.37; Dan 1.8
holy [4] 38.16; 42.13
honour 32.27; Dan 2.6

[j] *One ancient translation* set out; *Hebrew* know.
[k] *One ancient translation* terrify...calamities; *Hebrew unclear.*

38.2: Rev 20.8

human 38.20; 41.19
justice Lam 3.36; 45.9
lamb 27.21; 46.4
last (1) 25.12; Dan 2.44
mark (1) 21.19; Lk 11.44
mercy 24.14; Dan 2.18
mortal [2] 38.2; 40.4
name (2) (name of God, of Jesus) [3] 36.20; 43.7
never again 36.12; 45.9
new 36.26; 40.1
power 38.15; 40.1
prosper 36.11; Dan 4.4
protect 34.30; Dan 5.21
right (2) 21.16; Zech 11.17
sacrifice [2] 36.38; 40.38
safe 38.8; Hos 2.18
Sovereign [9] 38.3; 43.18
Spirit (1) (God's Spirit) 37.1; 43.5
sure 36.9; Dan 3.18
threat 21.15; Mic 3.5
turn [4] 38.4; 41.19
unclean 36.17; 44.25
victory Lam 2.7; Dan 11.12
wicked 31.11; Dan 8.23

people who live in the cities of Israel will
go out and collect the **abandoned**
weapons for firewood. They will build
fires with the shields, bows, arrows,
spears, and clubs, and will have **enough**
to **last** for seven years. 10 They will not
have to gather firewood in the fields or
cut down trees in the forest, because they
will have the **abandoned** weapons to
burn. They will loot and plunder those
who looted and plundered them." The
Sovereign LORD has spoken.

The Burial of Gog

11 The LORD said, "When all this happens, I will give Gog a burial-ground
there in Israel, in Travellers' Valley, east
of the Dead Sea.[l] Gog and all his army
will be buried there, and the valley will
be called 'The Valley of Gog's Army.' 12 It
will take the Israelites seven months to
bury all the corpses and make the land
clean again. 13 Everyone in the land will
help to bury them, and they will be
honoured for this on the day of my **victory**. I, the **Sovereign** LORD, have spoken.
14 After the seven months are over, men
will be **chosen** to travel through the land
in order to find and bury those **bodies**[m]
remaining on the ground, so that they
can make the land **clean**. 15 As they go up
and down the country, every time they
find a **human** bone, they will put a
marker beside it so that the **grave-
diggers** can come and bury it in the
Valley of Gog's Army. 16 (There will be a
town near by named after the army.)
And so the land will be made **clean**
again."

17 The **Sovereign** LORD said to me,
"**Mortal man**, call all the birds and
animals to come from all round to eat
the **sacrifice** I am preparing for them. It
will be a huge **feast** on the mountains of
Israel, where they can eat meat and
drink **blood**. 18 They are to eat the **bodies**
of soldiers and drink the **blood** of the
rulers of the earth, all of whom will be
killed like rams or **lambs** or goats or fat
bulls. 19 When I kill these people like
sacrifices, the birds and animals are to
eat all the fat they can hold and to drink
blood until they are drunk. 20 At my table
they will eat all they can hold of horses
and their riders and of soldiers and fighting men. I, the **Sovereign** LORD, have
spoken."

The Restoration of Israel

21 The LORD said, "I will let the
nations see my **glory** and show them how
I use my **power** to carry out my **just** decisions. 22 The Israelites will know from
then on that I am the LORD their God.
23 And the nations will know that the
Israelites went into **exile** because of the
sins which they committed against me. I
turned away from them and let their
enemies defeat them and kill them in
battle. 24 I gave them what they **deserved**
for their **uncleanness** and their **wickedness**, and I **turned** away from them."

25 The **Sovereign** LORD said, "But now
I will be **merciful** to Jacob's descendants,
the people of Israel, and make them **prosperous** again. I will **protect** my **holy
name**. 26 When they are once more living
in **safety** in their own land, with no one to
threaten them, they will be able to **forget**
how they were **disgraced** for having **betrayed** me. 27 In order to show the many
nations that I am **holy**, I will bring **my
people** back from all the countries where
their **enemies** live. 28 Then **my people** will
know that I am the LORD their God. They
will know this, because I sent them into
captivity and now gather them and bring
them back into their own land, not leaving even one of them behind. 29 I will pour
out my **spirit** on the people of Israel and
never again turn away from them. I, the
Sovereign LORD, have spoken."

A VISION OF THE FUTURE TEMPLE
(40.1–48.35)

Ezekiel Is Taken to Jerusalem

40 It was the tenth day of the **new**
year, which was the twenty-fifth
year after we had been taken into **exile**
and the fourteenth year after Jerusalem
was captured. On that day I felt the
powerful presence of the LORD, and he
carried me away. 2 In a **vision** God took
me to the land of Israel and put me on a
high mountain. I saw in front of me[n] a
group of buildings that looked like a city.
3 He took me closer, and I saw a man who
shone like bronze. He was holding a linen
tape-measure and a measuring-rod and
was standing by a gateway.

4 He said to me, "**Watch, mortal man**.
Listen carefully and pay close attention
to everything I show you, because this is
why you were brought here. You are to

altar [2] 9.2; 41.22
exile 39.23; Dan 1.3
last (2) 5.12; Zeph 1.4
mortal 39.1; 43.7
new 39.2; Dan 1.7
offer [3] 36.38; 42.13
permit Jer 52.33; Dan 2.16
power 39.21; Dan 2.10
presence [2] 37.1; 41.22
priest [3] 22.26; 41.8
repayment-offering 2 Kgs 12.16; 42.13
sacrifice [6] 39.17; 42.13
serve [3] 27.10; 42.14
vision 22.28; 43.3
watch 37.8; Dan 4.13

[l] *Hebrew has four additional words, the meaning of which is unclear.*
[m] *Some ancient translations* those bodies; *Hebrew* the travellers.
[n] *One ancient translation* in front of me; *Hebrew* in the south.

39.17-20: Rev 19.17-18 **40.2:** Rev 21.10 **40.3:** Rev 11.1, 21.15

tell the people of Israel everything you
see."

The East Gate

5 What I saw was the Temple, and
there was a wall round it. The man took
his measuring-rod, which was three
metres long, and measured the wall. It
was three metres high and three metres
thick. 6 Then he went to the gateway that
faced east. He went up the steps, and at
the top he measured the entrance; it was
three metres deep.[o] 7 Beyond it there
was a passage, which had three guardrooms on each side. Each of the rooms
was square, three metres on each side,
and the walls between them were two
and a half metres thick. Beyond the
guardrooms there was a passage three
metres long that led to an entrance room
which faced the Temple. 8-9 He measured
this room, and found it was four metres
deep. It formed that end of the gateway
which was nearest the Temple, and at its
far end the walls were one metre thick.
10 (These guardrooms on each side of the
passage were all the same size, and the
walls between them were all of the same
thickness.)

11 Next, the man measured the width
of the passage in the gateway. It was six
and a half metres altogether, and the
space between the open gates was five
metres. 12 In front of each of the guardrooms there was a low wall fifty centimetres high and fifty centimetres thick.
(The rooms were three metres square.)
13 Then he measured the distance from
the back wall[x] of one room to the back
wall[x] of the room across the passage
from it, and it was twelve and a half
metres. 14 The room at the far end led out
to a courtyard. He measured that room
and found it was ten metres wide.[p] 15 The
total length of the gateway from the outside wall of the gate to the far side of the
last room was twenty-five metres.
16 There were small openings in the outside walls of all the rooms and also in the
inner walls between the rooms. There
were palm-trees carved on the inner
walls that faced the passage.

The Outer Courtyard

17 The man took me through the gateway into the courtyard. There were
thirty rooms built against the outer wall,
and in front of them there was an area
paved with stones, 18 which extended
round the courtyard. This outer courtyard was at a lower level than the inner
courtyard.

19 There was a gateway at a higher
level that led to the inner courtyard. The
man measured the distance between the
two gateways, and it was fifty metres.[q]

The North Gate

20 Then the man measured the gateway on the north side that led into the
outer courtyard. 21 The three guardrooms
on each side of the passage, the walls between them, and the entrance room all
had the same measurements as those in
the east gateway. The total length of the
gateway was twenty-five metres and the
width twelve and a half metres. 22 The
entrance room, the windows, and the
carved palm-trees were like those in the
east gate. Here seven steps led up to the
gate, and the entrance room was at the
end facing the courtyard. 23 Across the
courtyard from this north gateway was
another gateway leading to the inner
courtyard, just as there was on the east
side. The man measured the distance between these two gateways, and it was
fifty metres.

The South Gate

24 Next, the man took me to the south
side, and there we saw another gateway.
He measured its inner walls and its
entrance room, and they were the same
as the others. 25 There were windows in
the rooms of this gateway just as in the
others. The total length of the gateway
was twenty-five metres, and the width
twelve and a half metres. 26 Seven steps
led up to it, and its entrance room was
also at the end facing the courtyard.
There were palm-trees carved on the
inner walls that faced the passage.
27 Here, too, there was a gateway leading
to the inner courtyard. The man
measured the distance to this second
gateway, and it was fifty metres.

The Inner Courtyard: The South Gate

28 The man took me through the south
gateway into the inner courtyard. He
measured the gateway, and it was the
same size as the gateways in the outer
wall. 29-30 Its guardrooms, its entrance
room, and its inner walls were the same
size as those in the other gateways.
There were also windows in the rooms of
this gateway. The total length was
twenty-five metres and the width twelve

[o] *One ancient translation* deep; *Hebrew* deep, one entrance three metres deep.
[x] *Probable text* back wall; *Hebrew* roof. [p] *Verse 14 in Hebrew is unclear.*
[q] *Hebrew has two additional words, the meaning of which is unclear.*

40.5—42.20: 1 Kgs 6.1–38; 2 Chr 3.1–9

and a half metres. 31 Its entrance room
faced the other courtyard, and palm-
trees were carved on the walls along the
passage. Eight steps led up to this gate.

The Inner Courtyard: The East Gate

32 The man took me through the east
gateway into the inner courtyard. He
measured the gateway, and it was the
same size as the others. 33 Its guardrooms, its entrance room, and its inner
walls measured the same as those in the
other gateways. There were windows all
round, and in the entrance room also.
The total length was twenty-five metres
and the width twelve and a half metres.
34 The entrance room faced the outer
courtyard. Palm-trees were carved on
the walls along the passage. Eight steps
led up to this gate.

The Inner Courtyard: The North Gate

35 Then the man took me to the north
gateway. He measured it, and it was the
same size as the others. 36 Like them, it
also had guardrooms, decorated inner
walls, an entrance room, and windows all
round. Its total length was twenty-five
metres and its width twelve and a half
metres. 37 The entrance room[r] faced the
outer courtyard. Palm-trees were carved
on the walls along the passage. Eight
steps led up to this gate.

Buildings Near the North Gate

38 In the outer courtyard there was an
annexe attached to the inner gateway on
the north side. It opened into the
entrance room that faced the courtyard,
and there they washed the carcasses of
the animals to be burnt whole as **sacrifices**. 39 In this entrance room there were
four tables, two on each side of the room.
It was on these tables that they killed the
animals to be **offered as sacrifices**, either
to be burnt whole or to be **sacrifices** for
sin or as **repayment-offerings**. 40 Outside
the room there were four similar tables,
two on either side of the entrance of the
north gate. 41 Altogether there were eight
tables on which the animals to be **sacrificed** were killed: four inside the room
and four out in the courtyard. 42 The four
tables in the annexe, used to prepare the
offerings to be burnt whole, were of cut
stone. They were fifty centimetres high,
and their tops were seventy-five centimetres square. All the equipment used in
killing the **sacrificial** animals was kept
on these tables. 43 Ledges seventy-five
millimetres wide ran round the edge of
the tables. All the meat to be **offered in
sacrifice** was placed on the tables.[s]

44 Then he brought me into the inner
courtyard. There were two rooms
opening on the inner courtyard, one
facing south beside the north gateway
and the other facing north beside the
south gateway.[t] 45 The man told me that
the room which faced south was for the
priests who **served** in the Temple, 46 and
the room which faced north was for the
priests who **served** at the **altar**. All the
priests are descended from Zadok; they
are the only members of the tribe of Levi
who are **permitted** to go into the LORD's
presence to **serve** him.

The Inner Courtyard and the Temple Building

47 The man measured the inner courtyard, and it was fifty metres square. The
Temple was on the west side, and in
front of it was an **altar**. 48 Then he took
me into the entrance room of the
Temple. He measured the entrance: it
was two and a half metres deep and
seven metres wide,[u] with walls one and a
half metres thick on either side. 49 Steps
led up to the entrance room, which was
ten metres wide and six metres deep.
There were two columns, one on each
side of the entrance.

41 Next, the man took me into the
central room, the **Holy Place**. He
measured the passage leading into it: it
was three metres deep[v] 2 and five metres
wide, with walls two and a half metres
thick on either side. He measured the
room itself: it was twenty metres long,
and ten metres wide.

altar 40.46; 43.13
creature [4] 11.22; Gal 6.15
Holy Place [9] Neh 6.10; 44.13
human 39.15; 44.2
presence 40.1; 42.13
priest 40.45; 42.13
turn [2] 39.2; 44.15

3 Then he went to the innermost
room. He measured the passage leading
into it: it was one metre deep and three
metres wide, with walls on either side
three and a half metres thick.[w] 4 He
measured the room itself, and it was ten
metres square. This room was beyond
the central room. Then he said to me,
"This is the **Most Holy Place**."

The Rooms Built against the Temple Walls

5 The man measured the thickness of
the inner wall of the temple building, and
it was three metres. Against this wall, all
round the Temple, was a series of small

[r] *Some ancient translations* entrance room; *Hebrew* inner wall. [s] *Verse 43 in Hebrew is unclear.*
[t] *One ancient translation* Then...south gateway; *verse 44 in Hebrew is unclear.*
[u] *One ancient translation* and seven metres wide; *Hebrew does not have these words.*
[v] *Hebrew has two additional words, the meaning of which is unclear.*
[w] *One ancient translation* with walls on either side three and a half metres thick; *Hebrew* and three and a half metres thick.

rooms two metres wide. 6 These rooms
were in three storeys, with thirty rooms
on each floor. The Temple's outer wall
on each floor was thinner than on the
floor below, so that the rooms could rest
on the wall without being anchored into
it. 7 And so the temple walls, when seen
from the outside, seemed to have the
same thickness all the way to the top.
Against the Temple's outer wall, on the
outside of the rooms, two wide stairways
were built, so that it was possible to go
from the lower storey to the middle and
the upper storeys.[x] 8–11 The outside wall
of these rooms was two and a half
metres thick; there was one door into the
rooms on the north side of the Temple,
and one into those on the south side. I
saw that there was a terrace two and a
half metres wide all round the Temple; it
was three metres above the ground and
it was level with the foundation of the
rooms by the temple walls. Between the
terrace and the buildings used by the
priests there was an open space ten
metres across, along the sides of the
Temple.

The Building on the West

12 At the far end of the open space on
the west side of the Temple there was a
building forty-five metres long and thirty-five metres wide; its walls were two and
a half metres thick all round.

The Total Measurements of the Temple Building

13 The man measured the outside of
the Temple, and it was fifty metres long.
And from the back of the Temple, across
the open space to the far side of the
building to the west, the distance was
also fifty metres. 14 The distance across
the front of the Temple, including the
open space on either side, was also fifty
metres. 15 He measured the length of the
building to the west, including its corridors on both sides, and it was also fifty
metres.

Details of the Temple Building

The entrance room of the Temple, the
Holy Place, and the **Most Holy Place**
16 were all panelled with wood from the
floor to the windows. These windows
could be covered.[z] 17 The inside walls of
the Temple, up as high as above the
doors, were completely covered with
carvings[a] 18 of palm-trees and winged
creatures. Palm-trees alternated with
creatures, one following the other, all the
way round the room. Each **creature** had
two faces: 19 a **human** face that was
turned towards the palm-tree on one
side, and a lion's face that was **turned** towards the tree on the other side. It was
like this all round the wall, 20 from the
floor to above the doors. 21 The door-posts
of the **Holy Place** were square.

The Wooden Altar

In front of the entrance of the **Most
Holy Place** there was something that
looked like 22 a wooden **altar**. It was one
and a half metres high and one metre
wide. Its corner-posts, its base,[c] and its
sides were all made of wood. The man
said to me, "This is the table which
stands in the **presence** of the LORD."

The Doors

23 There was a door at the end of the
passage leading to the **Holy Place** and
one also at the end of the passage leading to the **Most Holy Place**. 24 They were
double doors that swung open in the
middle. 25 There were palm-trees and
winged **creatures** carved on the doors of
the **Holy Place**, just as there were on the
walls. And there was a wooden covering
over the outside of the doorway of the entrance room. 26 At the sides of this room
there were windows, and the walls were
decorated with palm-trees.[e]

Two Buildings Near the Temple

42 Then the man took me into the
outer courtyard and led me to a
building on the north side of the Temple,
not far from the building at the west end
of the Temple. 2 This building was fifty
metres long and twenty-five metres wide.
3 On one side it faced the space ten
metres wide which was alongside the
Temple, and on the other side it faced
the pavement of the outer court. It was
built on three levels, each one set further
back than the one below it. 4 Along the
north side of this building was a passage
five metres wide and fifty metres long,[f]
with entrances on that side. 5 The rooms
at the upper level of the building were
narrower than those at the middle and
lower levels because they were set
further back. 6 The rooms at all three
levels were on terraces and were not
supported by columns like the other
buildings in the courtyard. 7–8 At the
lower level the outer wall of the building
was solid for twenty-five metres, half its

grain-offering Jer 33.18; 44.29
holy [6] 39.7; 43.7
offer [3] 40.39; 43.19
presence 41.22; 43.2
priest [3] 41.8; 43.19
repayment-offering 40.39; 44.29
sacrifice 40.38; 43.15
separate 34.17; Zech 12.12
serve [2] 40.45; 43.19

[x] *Verse 7 in Hebrew is unclear.* [z] *Verse 16 in Hebrew is unclear.* [a] *Verse 17 in Hebrew is unclear.*
[c] *Some ancient translations* base; *Hebrew* length.
[e] *Hebrew has three additional words, the meaning of which is unclear.*
[f] *Some ancient translations* fifty metres long; *Hebrew* a way of fifty centimetres.

length; and there were rooms in the remaining twenty-five metres. At the top level there were rooms in the entire length of the building. 9-10 Below these two rooms at the east end of the building, where the wall of the courtyard began,[g] there was an entrance into the outer courtyard.

At the south[h] side of the Temple there was an identical building not far from the building at the west end of the Temple. 11 In front of the rooms there was a passage just like the one on the north side. It had the same measurements, the same design, and the same kind of entrances. 12 There was a door under the rooms on the south side of the building, at the east end where the wall began.

13 The man said to me, "Both these buildings are **holy**. In them the **priests** who enter the LORD's **presence** eat the **holiest offerings**. Because the rooms are **holy**, the **priests** will place the **holiest offerings** there: the **grain-offerings** and the **sacrifices offered** for sin or as **repayment-offerings**. 14 When **priests** have been in the Temple and want to go to the outer courtyard, they must leave in these rooms the **holy** clothing they wore while **serving** the LORD. They must put on other clothes before going out to the area where the people gather."

The Measurements of the Temple Area

15 When the man had finished measuring inside the temple area, he took me out through the east gate and then measured the outside of the area. 16 He took the measuring-rod and measured the east side, and it was 250 metres. 17-19 Then he measured the north side, the south side, and the west side; each side had the same length, 250 metres,[i] 20 so that the wall enclosed a square 250 metres on each side. The wall **served** to **separate** what was **holy** from what was not.

The LORD Returns to the Temple

43 The man took me to the gate that faces east, 2 and there I saw coming from the east the **dazzling light** of the **presence** of the God of Israel. God's voice sounded like the roar of the sea, and the earth shone with the **dazzling light**. 3 This **vision** was like the one I had seen when God came to **destroy** Jerusalem, and the one I saw by the River Chebar. Then I threw myself face downwards on the ground. 4 The **dazzling light** passed through the east gate and went into the Temple.

5 The **LORD's spirit** lifted me up and took me into the inner courtyard, where I saw that the Temple was filled with the **glory** of the LORD. 6 The man stood beside me there, and I heard the LORD speak to me out of the Temple: 7 "**Mortal man**, here is my **throne**. I will live here among the people of Israel and rule over them for ever. Neither the people of Israel nor their kings will ever again **disgrace** my **holy name** by **worshipping other gods** or by burying the corpses of[j] their kings in this place. 8 The kings built the thresholds and door-posts of their palace right against the thresholds and door-posts of my Temple, so that there was only a wall between us. They **disgraced** my **holy name** by all the **disgusting** things they did, and so in my **anger** I **destroyed** them. 9 Now they must stop **worshipping other gods** and remove the corpses of[k] their kings. If they do, I will live among them for ever."

10 And the LORD continued, "**Mortal man**, tell the people of Israel about the Temple, and let them **study** its **plan**. Make them **ashamed** of their sinful **actions**. 11 Then if they are **ashamed** of what they have done, explain the **plan** of the Temple to them: its design, its entrances and exits, its shape, the arrangement of everything, and all its rules and **regulations**. Write all this down for them so that they can see how everything is arranged and can carry out all the rules. 12 This is the **law** of the Temple: All the area surrounding it on the top of the mountain is **sacred** and **holy**."

The Altar

13 These are the measurements of the **altar**, using the same unit of measurement as in measuring the Temple. All round the base of the **altar** there was a gutter fifty centimetres deep and fifty centimetres wide, with a rim at the outside edge twenty-five centimetres high. 14 The lowest section of the **altar**, from the top of the base, was one metre high. The next section was set back from the edge fifty centimetres all round, and was two metres high. The section after that was also set back from the edge fifty centimetres all round. 15 This top section, on which the **sacrifices** were burnt, was also two metres high. The projections on

[g] *One ancient translation* where...began; *Hebrew* in the breadth of the wall of the courtyard.
[h] *One ancient translation* south; *Hebrew* east. [i] *Verses 16–19 in Hebrew are unclear.*
[j] by burying the corpses of; *or* putting up monuments to.
[k] remove the corpses of; *or* remove the monuments to.

43.2: Ezek 10.3–4, 18–19, 11.22–23; Rev 1.15 **43.13–17:** Ex 27.1–2; 2 Chr 4.1

action 33.26; Jon 3.8
altar [12] 41.22; 44.16
anger 38.19; Dan 3.19
ashamed [2] 16.54; Hos 4.19
blood [3] 39.17; 44.7
burnt-offering Jer 48.35; 44.11
command 38.7; 45.13
consecrate [2] 2 Chr 29.5; Hag 2.12
dazzling [3] 16.13; 44.4
dedicate Jer 4.4; 45.1
destroy [2] 34.16; Dan 2.44
disgrace [2] 39.7; Dan 5.19
disgust 37.23; 44.6
fellowship-offering 2 Chr 33.16; 45.13
glory 39.21; Dan 4.30
god (2) (other gods) [2] 30.13; Dan 1.2
holy [3] 42.13; 44.3
law 37.24; 44.24
light (1) [3] 32.7; 44.4
mortal [3] 40.4; 44.5
name (2) (name of God, of Jesus) [2] 39.7; Dan 9.6
offer [6] 42.13; 44.7
plan [2] 38.10; Dan 11.17
please 31.16; Dan 8.4
presence [2] 42.13; 44.3
priest [4] 42.13; 44.13
pure [2] 37.23; 44.27
regulation Neh 13.30; 44.5
sacred 34.26; 44.8
sacrifice [7] 42.13; 44.7
serve 42.14; 44.11
Sovereign [3] 39.1; 44.6
Spirit (1) (God's Spirit) 39.29; Joel 2.28
sprinkle [2] 36.25; Mt 11.21
study Is 47.13; Dan 9.2
throne 28.2; Dan 5.20
vision 40.2; Dan 1.17
worship (2) (of other gods) [2] 33.25; 44.10

the four corners were higher than the
rest of the top. [16] The top of the **altar** was
a square, six metres on each side. [17] The
middle section was also a square, seven
metres on each side, with a rim at the
outside edge twenty-five centimetres
high. (The gutter was fifty centimetres
wide.) The steps going up the **altar** were
on the east side.

The Consecration of the Altar

18 The **Sovereign** LORD said to me,
"**Mortal man**, listen to what I tell you.
When the **altar** is built, you are to **dedi-**
cate it by burning **sacrifices** on it and by
sprinkling on it the **blood** of the animals
that were **sacrificed**. [19] Those **priests** belonging to the tribe of Levi who are descended from Zadok are the only ones
who are to come into my **presence** to
serve me. I, the **Sovereign** LORD,
command this. You will give them a
young bull to **offer as a sacrifice** for sin.
[20] You are to take some of its **blood** and
put it on the projections on the top
corners of the **altar**, and on the corners
of the middle section of the **altar**, and all
round its edges. In this way you will
purify the **altar** and **consecrate** it. [21] You
are to take the bull that is **offered as a**
sacrifice for sin and burn it at the speci-
fied place outside the temple area. [22] The
next day you are to take a male goat
without any defects and **offer it as a**
sacrifice for sin. **Purify** the **altar** with its
blood in the same way as you did with
the bull. [23] When you have finished doing
that, take a young bull and a young ram,
both of them without any defects, [24] and
bring them to me. The **priests** will
sprinkle salt on them and burn them as
an **offering** to me. [25] Each day for seven
days you are to **offer** a goat, a bull, and a
ram as **sacrifices** for sin. All of them
must be without any defects. [26] For seven
days the **priests** are to **consecrate** the
altar and make it ready for use. [27] When
the week is over, the **priests** are to begin
offering on the **altar** the **burnt-offerings**
and the **fellowship-offerings** of the
people. Then I will be **pleased** with all of
you. I, the **Sovereign** LORD, have spoken."

The Use of the East Gate

44 The man led me to the outer
gate at the east side of the
temple area. The gate was closed, [2] and
the LORD said to me, "This gate will stay
closed and will never be opened. No
human being is allowed to use it, because
I, the LORD God of Israel, have entered
through it. It is to remain closed. [3] The
ruling prince, however, may go there to
eat a **holy** meal in my **presence**. He is to
enter and leave the gateway through the
entrance room at the inner end."

Rules for Admission to the Temple

4 Then the man took me through the
north gate to the front of the Temple. As
I looked, I saw that the Temple of the
LORD was filled with the **dazzling light** of
his **presence**. I threw myself face downwards on the ground, [5] and the LORD said
to me, "**Mortal man**, pay attention to
everything you see and hear. I am going
to tell you the rules and **regulations** for
the Temple. Note carefully which persons are allowed to go in and out of the
Temple and which persons are not.

6 "Tell those **rebellious** people of
Israel that I, the **Sovereign** LORD, will no
longer **tolerate** the **disgusting** things that
they have been doing. [7] They have **pro-**
faned my Temple by letting **uncircum-**
cised foreigners, people who do not **obey**
me, enter the Temple when the fat and
the **blood** of the **sacrifices** are being
offered to me. So **my people** have broken
my **covenant** by all the **disgusting** things
they have done. [8] They have not taken
charge of the **sacred rituals** in my
Temple, but instead have put foreigners
in charge.

9 "I, the **Sovereign** LORD, declare that
no **uncircumcised** foreigner, no one who
disobeys me, will enter my Temple, not
even a foreigner who lives among the
people of Israel."

The Levites Are Excluded from the Priesthood

10 The LORD said to me, "I am **punish-**
ing those **Levites** who, together with the
rest of the people of Israel, deserted me
and **worshipped idols**. [11] They may **serve**
me in the Temple by taking charge of
the gates and by performing the work of
the Temple. They may kill the animals
which the people **offer** for **burnt-offerings**
and for **sacrifices**, and they are to be on
duty to **serve** the people. [12] But because
they conducted the **worship of idols** for
the people of Israel and in this way led
the people into sin, I, the **Sovereign**
LORD, **solemnly swear** that they must be
punished. [13] They are not to **serve** me as
priests or to go near anything that is **holy**
to me or to enter the **Most Holy Place**.
This is the **punishment** for the **disgusting**
things they have done. [14] I am assigning
to them the menial work that is to be
done in the Temple."

43.27: Ex 29.35–37

alone 9.8; Dan 10.8
altar 43.13; 45.19
apart 22.27; 48.8
being 38.20; Dan 2.11
best 34.18; 48.14
bless 34.26;
Hos 10.12
blood [2] 43.18; 45.19
bread 16.13; 45.21
burnt-offering 43.27;
Amos 5.22

case (2) Jer 25.31;
Mic 6.1
circumcise [2] 32.2
Lk 1.59
clean [2] 39.12;
Zech 3.5
covenant 37.26;
Dan 9.4
dazzling 43.2;
Mt 17.2
death (1) 35.6;
Hos 7.16
disgust [3] 43.8;
Hos 9.10
disobey 11.12;
Dan 3.12
dispute 18.8; Mic 4.
divorce Jer 3.1;
Mal 2.16
duty (1) [3] Jer 37.1
45.17
faithful 37.24; 48.11
festival 36.38; 45.17
God's people [2] 39.
45.9
grain-offering 42.1
45.13
harm Jer 39.12; 46.2
harvest Jer 50.16;
45.13
holy [5] 43.7; 45.1
Holy Place 41.1;
Mt 24.15
human 41.19;
Dan 2.11
idol [2] 37.23; Hos 3.
keep from 17.14;
Lk 4.42
law 43.12; Dan 6.8
Levites Is 66.21; 45.
light (1) 43.2;
Dan 2.22
mortal 43.7; 47.6
natural 4.14; Jn 1.13
need 34.26; Amos 4.
obey 37.24; Dan 6.13
offer [6] 43.19; 45.13
presence [3] 43.2;
Dan 2.25
priest [14] 43.19; 45.4
profane 25.3;
Amos 2.7
proper Jer 33.20;
Dan 8.12
punish [3] 38.22;
Dan 2.9
pure 43.20; 45.18
rebel 24.3; Dan 9.9
regulation [2] 43.11;
Heb 7.16
religion Jer 12.16;
Dan 6.5
repayment-offering
42.13; 46.20
ritual Neh 12.30;
Jn 2.6
Sabbath 23.38; 45.17
sacred [2] 43.12;
Dan 9.2
sacrifice [4] 43.15;
45.18
serve [7] 43.19; 45.4
share 32.25; 45.1
shave 27.31;
Amos 8.10
sin-offering
2 Chr 29.24; 45.17
solemn 36.7; 47.14
Sovereign [5] 43.18;
45.9
swear 17.13;
Amos 8.7
teach 22.26; Dan 1.4
tolerate Prov 30.21;
Nah 1.2
turn 41.19; Dan 3.19
unclean 39.24;
Dan 1.8
unmarried Is 4.1;
Acts 21.9
virgin 23.3; Amos 5.2
widow 22.7;
Zech 7.10

worship (1) (of God) 20.40; 46.2
worship (2) (of other gods) [2] 43.7; Dan 3.5

The Priests

15 The Sovereign LORD said, "Those
priests belonging to the tribe of Levi who
are descended from Zadok, however,
continued to serve me faithfully in the
Temple when the rest of the people of
Israel turned away from me. So now they
are the ones who are to serve me and
come into my presence to offer me the
fat and the blood of the sacrifices. 16 They
alone will enter my Temple, serve at my
altar, and conduct the temple worship.
17 When they enter the gateway to the
inner courtyard of the Temple, they are
to put on linen clothing. They must not
wear anything made of wool when they
are on duty in the inner courtyard or in
the Temple. 18 So that they won't per-
spire, they are to wear linen turbans and
linen trousers, but no belt. 19 Before they
go to the outer courtyard where the
people are, they must first take off the
clothes they wore on duty in the Temple
and leave them in the holy rooms. They
are to put on other clothing in order to
keep their sacred clothing from harming
the people.[l]

20 "Priests must neither shave their
heads nor let their hair grow long. They
are to keep it a proper length. 21 Priests
must not drink any wine before going
into the inner courtyard. 22 No priest may
marry a divorced woman; he is to marry
only an Israelite virgin or the widow of
another priest.

23 "The priests are to teach my people
the difference between what is holy and
what is not, and between what is ritually
clean and what is not. 24 When a legal dispute arises, the priests are to decide the
case according to my laws. They are to
keep the religious festivals according to
my rules and regulations, and they are to
keep the Sabbaths holy.

25 "A priest is not to become ritually
unclean by touching a corpse, unless it is
one of his parents, one of his children or
a brother or an unmarried sister. 26 After
he has become clean again, he must wait
seven days 27 and then go into the inner
courtyard of the Temple and offer a
sacrifice for his purification, so that he
can serve in the Temple again. I, the
Sovereign LORD, have spoken.

28 "The priests have the priesthood as
their share of what I have given Israel to
be handed down from one generation to
another. They are not to hold property in
Israel; I am all they need. 29 The grain-
offerings, the sin-offerings and the repayment-offerings will be the priests' food,
and they are to receive everything in
Israel that is set apart for me. 30 The
priests are to have the best of all the first
harvest and of everything else that is
offered to me. Each time the people bake
bread, they are to give the priests the
first loaf as an offering, and my blessing
will rest on their homes. 31 The priests
must not eat any bird or animal that dies
a natural death or is killed by another
animal."

The LORD's Portion of the Country

45 When the land is divided to give
each tribe a share, one part is to
be dedicated to the LORD. It is to be
twelve and a half kilometres long by ten
kilometres[m] wide. The entire area will
be holy. 2 In this area there is to be a
square plot of land for the Temple, 250
metres along each side, entirely surrounded by an open space twenty-five
metres wide. 3 Half of this area, a section
twelve and a half kilometres by five kilometres, is to be measured off; it will contain the Temple, the holiest place of all.
4 It will be a holy part of the country, set
aside for the priests who serve the LORD
in his Temple. It will contain their houses
and the section of land for the Temple.
5 The other half of the area is to be set
aside as the possession of the Levites,
who do the work in the Temple. There
will be towns there for them to live in.[n]

6 Next to the holy area, another section, twelve and a half kilometres long
and two and a half kilometres wide, is to
be set aside for a city where any of the
people of Israel may live.

Land for the Prince

7 Land is also to be set aside for the
ruling prince. From the western boundary of the holy area it will extend west
to the Mediterranean Sea; and from the
eastern boundary it will extend to the
eastern border of the country, so that its
length will be the same as the length of
one of the areas allotted to the tribes of
Israel. 8 This area will be the share the
ruling prince will have in the land of
Israel, so that he will no longer oppress
the people, but will let the rest of the
country belong to the tribes of Israel.

altar 44.16; 47.1
blood 44.7; Joel 2.30
bread 44.30; Hos 7.8
celebrate 7.7; Hos 2.11
command 43.19; 46.16
dedicate 43.18; 48.9
duty (1) 44.11; Zech 3.7
fellowship-offering [2] 43.27; 46.2
festival [5] 44.24; 46.1
forgive 33.16; Dan 9.9
God's people 44.7; 46.18
grain-offering [3] 44.29; 46.5
harvest [2] 44.30; Hos 2.9
holy [6] 44.3; 46.19
honest 18.5; Amos 2.6
ignorant Jer 5.4; Acts 3.17
justice 39.21; Dan 4.37
Levites 44.10; 48.12
never again 39.29; Hos 14.3
New Moon Festival Is 66.23; 46.1
offer [8] 44.7; 46.2
oppress [2] 18.16; 46.18
Passover Ezra 6.19; Mt 26.2
possess 36.5; 47.14
priest [2] 44.13; 46.2
provide [2] 13.3; 47.12
pure 44.27; Dan 7.9
right (1) 34.16; Dan 4.27
Sabbath 44.24; 46.1
sacrifice [6] 44.7; 46.2
serve 44.11; 48.11
share [2] 44.28; 47.22
sheep [2] 36.37; Hos 5.6
shelter 31.6; Hos 14.8
sin-offering [3] 44.29
Sovereign [4] 44.6; 46.1
take away (sin) Ps 40.6; Zech 3.4
unintentional Job 1.5

[l] HARMING THE PEOPLE: *It was believed that ordinary people would be harmed by touching something holy.* [m] *One ancient translation* ten kilometres; *Hebrew* five kilometres.
[n] *One ancient translation* towns there for them to live in; *Hebrew* twenty rooms.

44.17–18: Ex 28.39–43; Lev 16.4 **44.19:** Lev 16.23 **44.20:** Lev 21.5 **44.21:** Lev 10.9
44.22: Lev 21.7, 13–14 **44.23:** Lev 10.10 **44.25:** Lev 21.1–4 **44.28:** Num 18.20 **44.29–30:** Num 18.8–19
44.31: Lev 22.8

unleavened Ezra 6.22; Mt 26.17
violent 28.16; Dan 11.14
wine-offering Jer 44.17
yeast 1 Chr 23.29; Mt 13.33

Rules for the Prince

9 The Sovereign LORD said, "You have
sinned too long, you rulers of Israel! Stop
your violence and oppression. Do what is
right and just. You must never again
drive my people off their land. I, the
Sovereign LORD, am telling you this.
10 "Everyone must use honest weights
and measures:
11 "The *ephah* for dry measure is to
be equal to the *bath* for liquid measure.
The standard is the *homer.*[o] The resulting measures are as follows:

1 homer = 10 ephahs = 10 baths

12 "Your weights are to be as follows:

20 gerahs = 1 shekel[p]
60 shekels = 1 mina

13-15 "This is the basis on which you
are to make your offerings:

Wheat: $\frac{1}{60}$th of your harvest
Barley: $\frac{1}{60}$th of your harvest
Olive-oil: $\frac{1}{100}$th of the yield of your trees

(Measure it by the *bath: 10 baths = 1 homer = 1 kor.)*

Sheep: 1 sheep out of every 200 from the meadows of Israel

"You are to bring grain-offerings,
animals to be burnt whole, and animals
for fellowship-offerings, so that your sins
will be forgiven. I, the Sovereign LORD,
command it.
16 "All the people of the land must
take[q] these offerings to the ruling prince
of Israel. 17 It will be his duty to provide
the animals to be burnt whole, the grain-
offerings, and the wine-offerings for the
whole nation of Israel at the New Moon
Festivals, the Sabbaths, and the other festivals. He is to provide the sin-offerings,
the grain-offerings, the offerings to be
burnt whole, and the fellowship-offerings,
to take away the sins of the people of
Israel."

The Festivals
(Ex 12.1–20; Lev 23.33–43)

18 The Sovereign LORD said, "On the
first day of the first month you are to
sacrifice a bull without any defects and
purify the Temple. 19 The priest will take
some of the blood of this sin-offering and
put it on the door-posts of the Temple, on
the four corners of the altar, and on the
posts of the gateways to the inner courtyard. 20 On the seventh day of the month
you are to do the same thing on behalf of
anyone who sins unintentionally or
through ignorance. In this way, you will
keep the Temple holy.
21 "On the fourteenth day of the first
month you will begin the celebration of
the Passover Festival. For seven days
everyone will eat bread made without
yeast. 22 On the first day of the festival
the ruling prince must offer a bull as a
sacrifice for his sins and for those of all
the people. 23 On each of the seven days
of the festival he is to sacrifice to the
LORD seven bulls and seven rams without
any defects and burn them whole. He is
also to sacrifice a male goat each day as
a sin-offering. 24 For each bull and each
ram that is sacrificed, there is to be an
offering of seventeen and a half litres of
corn and three litres of olive-oil.
25 "For the Festival of Shelters, which
begins on the fifteenth day of the seventh
month, the prince will offer on each of
the seven days the same sacrifice for sin,
the same offerings to be burnt whole, and
the same offerings of corn and olive-oil."

The Prince and the Festivals

46 The Sovereign LORD says, "The
east gateway to the inner courtyard must be kept closed during the six
working days, but it is to be opened on
the Sabbath and at the New Moon
Festival. 2 The ruling prince will go from
the outer courtyard into the entrance
room of the gateway and stand beside
the posts of the gate while the priests
burn his sacrifices whole and offer his
fellowship-offerings. There at the gate he
must worship and then go out again. The
gate must not be shut until evening.
3 Each Sabbath and each New Moon Festival all the people are also to bow down
and worship the LORD in front of the
gate.
4 On the Sabbath the prince is to bring
to the LORD, as sacrifices to be burnt
whole, six lambs and one ram, all without
any defects. 5 With each ram he is to
bring an offering of seventeen and a half
litres of corn, and with each lamb he is to
bring whatever he wants to give. For
each such grain-offering he is to bring
three litres of olive-oil. 6 At the New
Moon Festival he will offer a young bull,
six lambs, and a ram, all without any defects. 7 With each bull and each ram the
offering is to be seventeen and a half
litres of corn, and with each lamb the
offering is to be whatever the prince
wants to give. Three litres of olive-oil are

bow (2) 8.16; Dan 2.46
command 45.13; Dan 2.24
feast 39.17; Amos 6.4
fellowship-offering [2] 45.13
festival [5] 45.17; Dan 7.25
God's people 45.9; Dan 7.21
grain-offering [4] 45.13; Amos 5.22
harm 44.19; Dan 3.27
holy [2] 45.1; 48.10
lamb [7] 39.18; Hos 4.16
New Moon Festival [3] 45.17; Col 2.16
offer [18] 45.13; Dan 2.46
oppress 45.8; Dan 7.25
priest [3] 45.4; 48.10
repayment-offering 44.29
Restoration Num 36.4
Sabbath [4] 45.17; Hos 2.11
sacrifice [4] 45.18; Dan 2.46
servant 38.17; Dan 3.26
service 29.20; Lk 1.8
Sovereign [2] 45.9; 47.13
worship (1) (of God) [5] 44.16; Dan 11.38

[o] HOMER: *A unit of dry or liquid measure, about 175 litres; so an* ephah *or a* bath *would be about 17.5 litres.* [p] SHEKEL: *In Ezekiel's time this unit of weight was about 11.4 grammes.*
[q] *Probable text* must take; *Hebrew unclear.*

45.10: Lev 19.36 **45.21:** Ex 12.1–20; Num 28.16–25 **45.25:** Lev 23.33–36; Num 29.12–38

to be **offered** with each such **grain-offering** of corn. 8 The prince must leave the
entrance room of the gateway and go out
by the same way as he went in.

9 "When the people come to **worship**
the LORD at any **festival**, those who enter
by the north gate are to leave by the
south gate after they have **worshipped**,
and those who enter by the south gate
are to leave by the north gate. No one
may go out by the same way as he entered, but must leave by the opposite
gate. 10 The prince is to come in when the
people come, and leave when they leave.
11 On the **feast** days and at the **festivals**
the **grain-offering** will be seventeen and
a half litres with each bull or ram, and
whatever the **worshipper** wants to give
with each **lamb**. Three litres of olive-oil
are to be **offered** with each such **grain-
offering**.

12 "When the ruling prince wants to
make a voluntary **offering** to the LORD,
either an **offering** to be burnt whole or a
fellowship-offering, the east gate to the
inner courtyard will be opened for him.
He is to make the **offering** in the same
way as he does on the **Sabbath**, and the
gate is to be closed after he goes out
again."

The Daily Offering

13 The LORD says, "Every morning a
one-year-old **lamb** without any defects is
to be burnt whole as an **offering** to the
LORD. This **offering** must be made every
day. 14 Also an **offering** of two kilogrammes of flour is to be made every
morning, together with one litre of olive-
oil for mixing with the flour. The rules
for this **offering** to the LORD are to be in
force for ever. 15 The **lamb**, the flour, and
the olive-oil are to be **offered** to the LORD
every morning for ever."

The Prince and the Land

16 The **Sovereign** LORD **commands**:
"If the ruling prince gives any of the land
he owns to one of his sons as a present, it
will belong to that son as a part of his
family property. 17 But if the ruling prince
gives any of his land to anyone who is in
his **service**, it will become the prince's
property again when the **Year of
Restoration**[s] comes round. It belongs to
him, and only he and his sons can own it
permanently. 18 The ruling prince must
not take any of the people's property
away from them. Any land he gives to his
sons must be from the land that is
assigned to him, so that he will not **oppress** any of **my people** by taking their
land."

The Temple Kitchens

19 Then the man took me to the entrance of the rooms facing north near
the gate on the south side of the inner
courtyard. These are **holy** rooms for the
priests. He pointed out a place on the
west side of the rooms 20 and said, "This
is the place where the **priests** are to boil
the meat **offered as sacrifices** for sin or
as **repayment-offerings**, and to bake the
offerings of flour, so that nothing **holy** is
carried to the outer courtyard, where it
might **harm** the people."[t]

21–22 Then he led me to the outer
courtyard and showed me that in each of
its four corners there was a smaller[u]
courtyard, twenty metres long and fifteen metres wide. 23 Each one had a
stone wall round it, with fireplaces built
against the wall. 24 The man told me,
"These are the kitchens where the
temple **servants** are to boil the **sacrifices**
the people **offer**."

The Stream Flowing from the Temple

47 The man led me back to the entrance of the Temple. Water was
coming out from under the entrance and
flowing east, the direction the Temple
faced. It was flowing down from under
the south part of the temple past the
south side of the **altar**. 2 The man then
took me out of the temple area by way of
the north gate and led me round to the
gate that faces east. A small stream of
water was flowing out at the south side of
the gate. 3 With his measuring-rod the
man measured five hundred metres
downstream to the east and told me to
wade through the stream there. The
water came only to my ankles. 4 Then he
measured another five hundred metres,
and the water came up to my **knees**.
Another five hundred metres further
down, the water was up to my waist. 5 He
measured five hundred metres more,
and there the stream was so deep I could
not wade through it. It was too deep to
cross except by swimming. 6 He said to
me, "**Mortal man**, note all this carefully."

Then the man took me back to the
bank of the river, 7 and when I got there I
saw that there were very many trees on
each bank. 8 He said to me, "This water

altar 45.19; Hos 8.11
heal 34.4; Hos 5.13
knee 21.7; Dan 5.6
life (1) 33.8; Dan 3.28
lot (1) Prov 18.18; Jon 1.7
mortal 44.5; Dan 8.17
possess [2] 45.5; 48.29
promise 37.14; Dan 8.9
provide [2] 45.17; Dan 1.16
share [3] 45.1; Dan 11.33
solemn 44.12; Dan 12.7
source Lam 4.20; Hos 14.8
Sovereign [2] 46.1; 48.29

[s] YEAR OF RESTORATION: *Every fifty years, all Israelites were required to give freedom to any of their fellow-countrymen who had become slaves because of debts; they were also to give back to the original owner, or his heirs, any ancestral land that had been sold for debt (see Lev 25.8–55).*
[t] HARM THE PEOPLE: *See 44.19.* [u] *One ancient translation* smaller; *Hebrew* enclosed.

46.17: Lev 25.10 **47.1:** Zech 14.8; Jn 7.38; Rev 22.1

flows through the land to the east and
down into the Jordan Valley and to the
Dead Sea. When it flows into the Dead
Sea, it replaces the salt water of that sea
with fresh water. 9 Wherever the stream
flows, there will be all kinds of animals
and fish. The stream will make the water
of the Dead Sea fresh, and wherever it
flows, it will bring **life**. 10 From the
Springs of Engedi all the way to the
Springs of Eneglaim, there will be fishermen on the shore of the sea, and they
will spread out their nets there to dry.
There will be as many different kinds of
fish there as there are in the Mediterranean Sea. 11 But the water in the
marshes and ponds along the shore will
not be made fresh. They will remain
there as a **source** of salt. 12 On each bank
of the stream all kinds of trees will grow
to **provide** food. Their leaves will never
wither, and they will never stop bearing
fruit. They will have fresh fruit every
month, because they are watered by the
stream that flows from the Temple. The
trees will **provide** food, and their leaves
will be used for **healing** people."

The Boundaries of the Land

13 The **Sovereign** LORD said, "These
are the boundaries of the land that is to
be divided among the twelve tribes, with
the tribe of Joseph receiving two sections.[v] 14 I **solemnly promised** your
ancestors that I would give them **possession** of this land; now divide it equally
among you.

15 "The northern boundary runs eastwards from the Mediterranean Sea to the
city of Hethlon, to Hamath Pass, to the
city of Zedad,[w] 16 to the cities of Berothah
and Sibraim (they are located between
the territory of the kingdom of
Damascus and that of the kingdom of
Hamath), and to the city of Ticon
(located by the border of the district of
Hauran). 17 So the northern boundary
runs from the Mediterranean eastwards
to the city of Enon, with the border regions of Damascus and Hamath to the
north of it.

18 "The eastern boundary runs south
from a point between the territory of
Damascus and that of Hauran, with the
River Jordan forming the boundary between the land of Israel on the west and
Gilead on the east, as far as Tamar[x] on
the Dead Sea.

19 "The southern boundary runs south-
west from Tamar to the oasis of Kadesh
Meribah, and then north-west along the
Egyptian border to the Mediterranean
Sea.

20 "The western boundary is formed
by the Mediterranean and runs north to a
point west of Hamath Pass.

21 "Divide this land among your
tribes; 22 it is to be your permanent
possession. The foreigners who are living
among you and who have had children
born here are also to receive their **share**
of the land when you divide it. They are
to be treated like full Israelite citizens
and are to draw **lots** for **shares** of the
land along with the tribes of Israel.
23 Each foreign resident will receive his
share with the people of the tribe among
whom he is living. I, the **Sovereign** LORD,
have spoken."

The Division of the Land among the Tribes

48 1-7 The northern boundary of the
land runs eastwards from the
Mediterranean Sea to the city of Hethlon,
to Hamath Pass, to the city of Enon, to
the boundary between the kingdoms of
Damascus and Hamath. Each tribe is to
receive one section of land extending
from the eastern boundary westwards to
the Mediterranean Sea,[y] in the following
order from north to south:

Dan
Asher
Naphtali
Manasseh
Ephraim
Reuben
Judah

The Special Section in the Centre of the Land

8 The next section of the land is to be
set **apart** for **special** use. It is to be twelve
and a half kilometres wide from north to
south, and the same length from east to
west as the sections given to the tribes.
The Temple will be in this section.

9 In the centre of this section, a
special area twelve and a half kilometres
by ten kilometres[z] is to be **dedicated** to
the LORD. 10 The **priests** are to have a
portion of this **holy** area. From east to
west their portion is to measure twelve
and a half kilometres, and from north to
south, five kilometres. The Temple of the

apart [2] 44.29; Mic 7.14
best 44.30; Dan 6.14
dedicate [2] 45.1; Dan 3.2
faithful 44.15; Dan 9.4
holy [6] 46.19; Dan 4.8
Levites [3] 45.5; Lk 10.32
possess 47.14; Dan 11.43
priest [4] 46.2; Hos 4.4
serve 45.4; Dan 1.4
Sovereign 47.13; Amos 3.7
special [6] 16.34; Zech 2.12
wrong 36.31; Dan 6.

[v] TWO SECTIONS: *The tribes of Manasseh and Ephraim, the sons of Joseph, were each given one section.* [w] *One ancient translation* Hamath...Zedad; *Hebrew* Zedad Pass to the city of Hamath.
[x] *Some ancient translations* Tamar; *Hebrew unclear.*
[y] *One ancient translation* extending...Sea; *Hebrew* having an eastern boundary and a western boundary. [z] *Probable text (see 45.1)* ten kilometres; *Hebrew* five kilometres.

47.12: Rev 22.2

LORD is to be in the middle of this area.
11 This **holy** area is to be for the **priests**
who are descendants of Zadok. They **served** me **faithfully** and did not join the rest
of the Israelites in doing **wrong**, as the
other members of the tribe of Levi did.
12 So they are to have a **special** area next
to the area belonging to the **Levites**, and
it will be the **holiest** of all. 13 The **Levites**
also are to have a **special** area, south of
that of the **priests**. It too is to be twelve
and a half kilometres from east to west,
by five kilometres from north to south.
14 The area **dedicated** to the LORD is the
best part of all the land, and none of it
may be sold or exchanged or transferred
to anyone else. It is **holy** and belongs to
the LORD.

15 The part of the **special** area that is
left, twelve and a half kilometres by two
and a half kilometres, is not **holy**, but is
for the general use of the people. They
may live there and use the land. The city
is to be in the centre of it, 16 and it will be
a square, measuring 2,250 metres on
each side. 17 All round the city on each
side there will be an open space 125
metres across. 18 The land that is left
after the city has been built in the area
immediately to the south of the **holy**
area—five kilometres by two and a half
kilometres on the east and five kilometres by two and a half kilometres on
the west—is to be used as farm land by
the people who live in the city. 19 Anyone
who lives in the city, no matter which
tribe he comes from, may farm that land.

20 And so the total area in the centre of the section which was set **apart** will be a square measuring twelve and a half kilometres on each side, and it will include the area occupied by the city.

21–22 To the east and to the west of this area which contains the Temple, the **priests'** land, the **Levites'** land, and the city, the remaining land belongs to the ruling prince. It extends eastwards to the eastern boundary and westwards to the Mediterranean Sea, and is bounded on the north by the section belonging to Judah and on the south by the section belonging to Benjamin.

48.30–34: Rev 21.12–13

Land for the Other Tribes

23–27 South of this **special** section, each of the remaining tribes is to receive one section of land running from the eastern boundary westwards to the Mediterranean Sea, in the following order from north to south:

Benjamin
Simeon
Issachar
Zebulun
Gad

28 On the south side of the portion given to the tribe of Gad, the boundary runs south-west from Tamar to the oasis of Kadesh, and then north-west along the Egyptian border to the Mediterranean Sea.

29 The **Sovereign** LORD said, "That is the way the land is to be divided into sections for the tribes of Israel to **possess**."

The Gates of Jerusalem

30–34 There are twelve entrances to
the city of Jerusalem. Each of the four
walls measures 2,250 metres and has
three gates in it, each named after one of
the tribes. The gates in the north wall
are named after Reuben, Judah, and
Levi; those in the east wall, after Joseph,
Benjamin, and Dan; those in the south
wall, after Simeon, Issachar, and
Zebulun; and those in the west wall are
named after Gad, Asher, and Naphtali.
35 The total length of the wall on all four
sides of the city is nine thousand metres.
The name of the city from now on will
be, "The-LORD-Is-Here!"

THE BOOK OF
DANIEL

INTRODUCTION

The book of *Daniel* was written during a time when the Jews were suffering greatly under the persecution and oppression of a pagan king. Using stories and accounts of visions, the writer encourages the people of his time with the hope that God will bring the tyrant down and restore sovereignty to God's people.

The book has two main parts: (1) Stories about Daniel and some of his fellow-exiles, who through their faith in God and obedience to him triumph over their enemies. These stories are set in the time of the Babylonian and Persian Empires. (2) A series of visions seen by Daniel, which in the form of symbols present the successive rise and fall of several empires, beginning with Babylonia, and predict the downfall of the pagan oppressor and the victory of God's people.

Outline of Contents

THE STORY OF DANIEL AND HIS FRIENDS
(1.1—6.28)

The Young Men at Nebuchadnezzar's Court

afraid Ezek 28.19; 5.19
agree Ezek 20.12; 2.9
choose Ezek 39.14; 2.14
compare Ezek 31.2; Mt 11.16
conquer Ezek 26.15; 2.44
court (1) [6] Ezek 12.14; 2.49
dream Jer 29.8; 2.1
exile Ezek 40.1; 2.25
fortune-teller Is 44.25; 2.2
free Ezek 37.23; 9.24
friend Lam 1.2; 2.13
god (2) (other gods) Ezek 43.7; 2.11
help Ezek 39.13; 9.22
intelligent Ecc 9.11; Mt 15.16
interpret Deut 13.1; 5.12
knowledge Is 47.10; 5.11
learn Ezek 19.6; 2.30
magic Ezek 13.18; 2.2
mind (1) Ezek 36.26; 2.5
new Ezek 40.1; 8.3
physical Lev 21.17; Jn 3.6
prison Ezek 30.17; 11.33
provide Ezek 47.12; Hab 1.16
question Jer 38.14; 4.35

1 In the third year that Jehoiakim was
king of Judah, King Nebuchadnezzar of Babylonia attacked Jerusalem
and surrounded the city. 2 The Lord let
him capture King Jehoiakim and seize
some of the **temple** treasures. He took
some **prisoners** back with him to the
temple of his **gods** in Babylon, and put
the captured treasures in the **temple**
storerooms.
3 The king ordered Ashpenaz, his
chief official, to select from among the
Israelite **exiles** some young men of the
royal family and of the noble families.
4 They had to be handsome, **intelligent**,
well-trained, quick to **learn**, and **free**
from **physical** defects, so that they would
be qualified to **serve** in the royal **court**.
Ashpenaz was to **teach** them to read and
write the Babylonian language. 5 The
king also gave orders that every day
they were to be given the same food and
wine as the members of the royal **court**.
After three years of this training they
were to appear before the king. 6 Among
those **chosen** were Daniel, Hananiah,
Mishael, and Azariah, all of whom were
from the tribe of Judah. 7 The chief
official gave them **new** names: Belteshazzar, Shadrach, Meshach, and
Abednego.
8 Daniel made up his **mind** not to let
himself become ritually **unclean** by
eating the food and drinking the wine of
the royal **court**, so he asked Ashpenaz to
help him, 9 and God made Ashpenaz
sympathetic to Daniel. 10 Ashpenaz, however, was **afraid** of the king, so he said to
Daniel, "The king has decided what you
are to eat and drink, and if you don't look
as fit as the other young men, he may kill
me."
11 So Daniel went to the guard whom
Ashpenaz had placed in charge of him
and his three **friends**. 12 "**Test** us for ten
days," he said. "Give us vegetables to eat
and water to drink. 13 Then **compare** us
with the young men who are eating the
food of the royal **court**, and base your
decision on how we look."
14 He **agreed** to let them try it for ten
days. 15 When the time was up, they
looked healthier and **stronger** than all
those who had been eating the royal
food. 16 So from then on the guard let
them continue to eat vegetables instead
of what the king **provided**.
17 God gave the four young men
knowledge and skill in literature and

raise Ezek 26.10; 8.18
serve Ezek 48.11; 3.17
strong Ezek 34.16; 2.40
sympathy Jer 16.7; Nah 3.7
teach Ezek 44.23; 12.3
Temple (1) (of God) Ezek 37.26; 5.2
temple (2) (of other gods) [2] Jer 43.12; Joel 3.5
test Ezek 21.13; Zech 13.9
unclean Ezek 44.25; Mt 15.11
vision Ezek 43.3; 2.19

1.1: 2 Kgs 24.1; 2 Chr 36.5-7 **1.2-4:** 2 Kgs 20.17-18, 24.10-16; 2 Chr 36.10; Is 39.7-8

philosophy. In addition, he gave Daniel skill in **interpreting visions** and **dreams**.

18 At the end of the three years set by the king, Ashpenaz took all the young men to Nebuchadnezzar. 19 The king talked with them all, and Daniel, Hananiah, Mishael, and Azariah impressed him more than any of the others. So they became members of the king's **court**. 20 No matter what **question** the king asked, or what problem he **raised**, these four knew ten times more than any **fortune-teller** or **magician** in his whole kingdom. 21 Daniel remained at the royal **court** until Cyrus the emperor of Persia **conquered** Babylonia.

Nebuchadnezzar's Dream

2 In the second year that Nebuchadnezzar was king, he had a **dream**. It **worried** him so much that he couldn't sleep, 2 so he sent for his **fortune-tellers**, **magicians**, sorcerers, and wizards to come and explain the **dream** to him. When they came and stood before the king, 3 he said to them, "I'm **worried** about a **dream** I have had. I want to know what it means."

4 They answered the king in Aramaic,[a] "May Your **Majesty** live for ever! Tell us your **dream**, and we will explain it to you."

5 The king said to them, "I have made up my **mind** that you must tell me the **dream** and then tell me what it means. If you can't, I'll have you torn limb from limb and make your houses a pile of **ruins**. 6 But if you can tell me both the **dream** and its meaning, I will **reward** you with **gifts** and great **honour**. Now then, tell me what the **dream** was and what it means."

7 They answered the king again, "If Your **Majesty** will only tell us what the **dream** was, we will explain it."

8 At that, the king exclaimed, "Just as I thought! You are trying to gain time, because you see that I have made up my **mind** 9 to give all of you the same **punishment** if you don't tell me the **dream**. You have **agreed** among yourselves to go on telling me **lies** because you **hope** that in time things will **change**. Tell me what the **dream** was, and then I will know that you can also tell me what it means."

10 The advisers replied, "There is no one on the face of the earth who can tell Your **Majesty** what you want to know. No king, not even the greatest and most **powerful**, has ever made such a **demand** of his **fortune-tellers**, **magicians**, and wizards. 11 What Your **Majesty** is asking for is so **difficult** that no one can do it for you except the **gods**, and they do not live among **human beings**."

12 At that, the king flew into a **rage** and ordered the **execution** of all the royal advisers in Babylon. 13 So the order was issued for all of them to be killed, including Daniel and his **friends**.

God Shows Daniel What the Dream Means

14 Then Daniel went to Arioch, commander of the king's bodyguard, who had been ordered to carry out the **execution**. **Choosing** his **words** carefully, 15 he asked Arioch why the king had issued such a harsh order. So Arioch told Daniel what had happened.

16 Daniel went at once and obtained royal **permission** for more time, so that he could tell the king what the **dream** meant. 17 Then Daniel went home and told his **friends** Hananiah, Mishael, and Azariah what had happened. 18 He told them to **pray** to the God of **heaven** for **mercy** and to ask him to explain the **mystery** to them so that they would not be killed along with the other advisers in Babylon. 19 Then that same night the **mystery** was **revealed** to Daniel in a **vision**, and he **praised** the God of **heaven**:

20 "God is **wise** and **powerful**!
 praise him for ever and ever.
21 He **controls** the times and the seasons;
 he makes and unmakes kings;
 it is he who gives **wisdom** and
  understanding.
22 He **reveals** things that are deep and
  secret;
 he knows what is hidden in
  darkness,
 and he himself is surrounded by
  light.
23 I **praise** you and **honour** you, God of
  my ancestors.
 You have given me **wisdom** and
  strength;
 you have answered my **prayer**
 and shown us what to tell the king."

Daniel Tells the King the Dream and Explains It

24 So Daniel went to Arioch, whom the king had **commanded** to **execute** the royal advisers. He said to him, "Don't put them **to death**. Take me to the king, and I will tell him what his **dream** means."

25 At once Arioch took Daniel into King Nebuchadnezzar's **presence** and told the king, "I have found one of the

[a] *From here to the end of chapter 7, the language used is Aramaic, not Hebrew.*

2.2: Gen 41.8

agree 1.14; 6.7
being Ezek 44.2; 4.12
bow (2) Ezek 46.3; 3.5
change Ezek 33.8; 6.8
choose 1.6; 4.17
command Ezek 46.16; 3.20
conquer 1.21; 7.21
control Ezek 20.37; 4.25
court (1) 1.4; 7.10
dark Ezek 34.12; Joel 2.2
death (3) (to death) Ezek 22.9; 11.33
demand Ezek 24.8; Amos 4.1
destroy Ezek 43.3; 4.23
difficult Ezek 3.5; Acts 27.7
dream [19] 1.17; 4.5
establish Ezek 37.26; 9.24
execute [3] Jer 52.10; Rev 20.4
exile 1.3; 5.13
fortune-teller [3] 1.20; 4.7
friend [2] 1.11; Amos 1.9
gift [2] Ezek 20.31; 5.17
god (2) (other gods) [2] 1.2; 3.12
heaven [5] Ezek 32.8; 4.13
honour [3] Ezek 39.13; 4.34
hope Ezek 37.11; Hos 2.15
human Ezek 44.2; 4.16
Jew Ezek 1.1; 3.8
Kingdom (1) (of God) Is 9.7; 4.34
last (1) Ezek 39.9; 4.34
learn 1.4; 6.10
lie (2) Ezek 22.9; 11.27
light (1) Ezek 44.4; 5.5
magic [3] 1.20; 4.7
Majesty [13] Jer 38.9; 3.9
mercy Ezek 39.25; 4.27
might Ezek 26.11; 4.30
mind (1) [2] 1.8; 4.16
mystery [7] Is 28.21; 4.9
offer Ezek 46.2; 8.11
permit Ezek 40.46; 6.7
power [3] Ezek 40.1; 3.17
praise [3] Ezek 28.22; 3.28
pray Lam 3.41; 6.10
prayer Ezek 8.18; 9.17
presence Ezek 44.3; 5.13
present (1) Is 66.3; 7.13
punish Ezek 44.10; 8.23
rage Ezek 22.20; 3.13
request Jer 42.9; 6.7
reveal [6] Ezek 20.5; 10.1
reward Ezek 18.20; 11.39
ruin Ezek 38.12; 3.29
sacrifice Ezek 46.2; 8.11
secret Ezek 28.3; 8.26
splendour Ezek 7.11; Hos 10.5
strength [2] Ezek 30.18; 8.7
strike [2] Ezek 21.14; Amos 3.6
strong [2] 1.15; 3.20
terrify Ezek 38.21; 4.5
true Ezek 36.13; 3.14
understand [2] Ezek 3.6; 4.9
unite Ezek 37.22; Hos 1.11
vision [3] 1.17; 4.5
weak Ezek 34.4; 10.16
wisdom [2] Ezek 28.4; 5.11
wise [2] Ezek 28.3; 5.12
word (1) Ezek 37.4; 4.31
worry [2] Jer 49.23; 10.19

Jewish exiles, who can tell Your **Majesty**
the meaning of your **dream**."
26 The king said to Daniel (who was
also called Belteshazzar), "Can you tell
me what I **dreamt** and what it means?"
27 Daniel replied, "Your **Majesty**,
there is no wizard, **magician**, **fortune-**
teller, or astrologer who can tell you
that. 28 But there is a God in **heaven**, who
reveals mysteries. He has informed Your
Majesty what will happen in the future.
Now I will tell you the **dream**, the **vision**
you had while you were asleep.
29 "While Your **Majesty** was sleeping,
you **dreamt** about the future; and God,
who **reveals mysteries**, showed you what
is going to happen. 30 Now, this **mystery**
was **revealed** to me, not because I am
wiser than anyone else, but so that Your
Majesty may **learn** the meaning of your
dream and **understand** the thoughts that
have come to you.
31 "Your **Majesty**, in your **vision** you
saw standing before you a giant statue,
bright and shining, and **terrifying** to look
at. 32 Its head was made of the finest
gold; its chest and arms were made of
silver; its waist and hips of bronze; 33 its
legs of iron, and its feet partly of iron and
partly of clay. 34 While you were looking
at it, a great stone broke loose from a
cliff without anyone touching it, **struck**
the iron and clay feet of the statue, and
shattered them. 35 At once the iron, clay,
bronze, silver, and gold crumbled and
became like the dust on a threshing-
place in summer. The wind carried it all
away, leaving not a trace. But the stone
grew to be a mountain that covered the
whole earth.
36 "This was the **dream**. Now I will tell
Your **Majesty** what it means. 37 Your
Majesty, you are the greatest of all kings.
The God of **heaven** has made you
emperor and given you **power**, **might**,
and **honour**. 38 He has made you ruler of
all the inhabited earth and ruler over all
the animals and birds. You are the head
of gold. 39 After you there will be another
empire, not as great as yours, and after
that a third, an empire of bronze, which
will rule the whole earth. 40 And then
there will be a fourth empire, as **strong**
as iron, which shatters and breaks everything. And just as iron shatters everything, it will shatter and crush all the
earlier empires. 41 You also saw that the
feet and the toes were partly clay and
partly iron. This means that it will be a
divided empire. It will have something of
the **strength** of iron, because there was
iron mixed with the clay. 42 The toes—
partly iron and partly clay—mean that
part of the empire will be **strong** and
part of it **weak**. 43 You also saw that the
iron was mixed with the clay. This
means that the rulers of that empire will
try to **unite** their families by intermarriage, but they will not be able to,
any more than iron can mix with clay.
44 At the time of those rulers the God of
heaven will **establish** a **kingdom** that will
never end. It will never be **conquered**,
but will completely **destroy** all those
empires, and then **last** for ever. 45 You
saw how a stone broke loose from a cliff
without anyone touching it and how it
struck the statue made of iron, bronze,
clay, silver, and gold. The great God is
telling Your **Majesty** what will happen in
the future. I have told you exactly what
you **dreamt**, and have given you its **true**
meaning."

The King Rewards Daniel

46 Then King Nebuchadnezzar **bowed**
to the ground and gave orders for **sacri-**
fices and **offerings** to be made to Daniel.
47 The king said, "Your God is the
greatest of all **gods**, the Lord over kings,
and the one who **reveals mysteries**. I
know this because you have been able to
explain this **mystery**." 48 Then he gave
Daniel a high position, **presented** him
with many **splendid gifts**, put him in
charge of the province of Babylon, and
made him the head of all the royal
advisers. 49 At Daniel's **request** the king
put Shadrach, Meshach, and Abednego in
charge of the affairs of the province of
Babylon; Daniel, however, remained at
the royal **court**.

Nebuchadnezzar Commands Everyone to Worship a Gold Statue

3 King Nebuchadnezzar had a gold
statue made, twenty-seven metres
high and nearly three metres wide, and
he had it set up in the plain of Dura in the
province of Babylon. 2 Then the king
gave orders for all his officials to come
together—the princes, governors, lieutenant-governors, commissioners, treas-
urers, **judges**, magistrates, and all the
other officials of the provinces. They
were to attend the **dedication** of the
statue which King Nebuchadnezzar had
set up. 3 When all these officials gathered
for the **dedication** and stood in front of
the statue, 4 a herald **announced** in a loud
voice, "People of all nations, **races**, and
languages! 5 You will hear the sound of
the trumpets, followed by the playing of
oboes, lyres, zithers, and harps; and then
all the other instruments will join in. As
soon as the music starts, you are to **bow**

amaze Jer 50.13; 10.8
angel [2] Ezek 28.14; 4.13
anger Ezek 43.8; 8.7
announce Ezek 38.17; Joel 3.9
bow (2) [10] 2.46; Mt 20.20
command [2] 2.24; 6.26
dedicate [2] Ezek 48.9; 9.24
defend Ezek 38.11; 9.16
denounce Ezek 39.1
disobey [2] Ezek 44.9; Mt 5.19
god (2) (other gods) [6] 2.11; 4.8
harm Ezek 46.20; Hos 2.18
heart Ezek 36.26; Hos 10.2
hurt Ezek 34.4; 6.22
Jew [2] 2.25; 5.13
judge Ezek 34.17; 7.22
life (1) Ezek 47.9; 12.2
Majesty [6] 2.4; 4.19
power 2.10; 4.3

praise 2.19; 4.34
race (1) [3] Jer 34.1; 4.1
rage 2.12; 11.30
refuse (1) Ezek 21.13; 9.11
rescue [2] Ezek 34.10; 6.14
respect Ezek 22.8; 6.13
ruin 2.5; 9.2
save [2] Ezek 36.29; 6.20
servant Ezek 46.24; 5.29
serve [2] 1.4; 6.16
sign (1) Ezek 31.15; Zech 3.8
strong 2.40; 4.22
supreme Ps 150.2; 4.2
sure Ezek 39.7; Hos 5.9
true 2.45; 4.33
trust Ezek 22.6; 6.23
turn Ezek 44.15; 5.6
worship (2) (of other gods) [10] Ezek 44.10; 11.39

down and **worship the gold statue** that
King Nebuchadnezzar has set up.
6 Anyone who does not **bow down** and
worship will immediately be thrown into
a blazing furnace." 7 And so, as soon as
they heard the sound of the instruments,
the people of all the nations, **races**, and
languages **bowed down** and **worshipped**
the gold statue which King Nebuchadnezzar had set up.

Daniel's Three Friends Are Accused of Disobedience

8 It was then that some Babylonians
took the opportunity to **denounce** the
Jews. 9 They said to King Nebuchadnezzar, "May Your **Majesty** live for ever!
10 Your **Majesty** has issued an order that
as soon as the music starts, everyone is
to **bow down** and **worship the gold statue**,
11 and that anyone who does not **bow**
down and **worship** it is to be thrown into
a blazing furnace. 12 There are some
Jews whom you put in charge of
the province of Babylon—Shadrach,
Meshach, and Abednego—who are **dis-**
obeying Your **Majesty's** orders. They do
not **worship your god** or **bow down** to the
statue you set up."

13 At that, the king flew into a **rage**
and ordered the three men to be brought
before him. 14 He said to them, "Shadrach, Meshach, and Abednego, is it **true**
that you **refuse to worship my god** and to
bow down to the gold statue I have set
up? 15 Now then, as soon as you hear the
sound of the trumpets, oboes, lyres,
zithers, harps, and all the other instruments, **bow down** and **worship the statue**.
If you do not, you will immediately be
thrown into a blazing furnace. Do you
think there is any **god** who can **save**
you?"

16 Shadrach, Meshach, and Abednego
answered, "Your **Majesty**, we will not try
to **defend** ourselves. 17 If the God whom
we **serve** is able to **save** us from the
blazing furnace and from your **power**,
then he will.[d] 18 But even if he doesn't,
Your **Majesty** may be **sure** that we will
not **worship your god**, and we will not
bow down to the gold statue that you
have set up."

Daniel's Three Friends Are Sentenced to Death

19 Then Nebuchadnezzar lost his
temper, and his face **turned** red with
anger at Shadrach, Meshach, and
Abednego. So he ordered his men to heat
the furnace seven times hotter than
usual. 20 And he **commanded** the
strongest men in his army to tie the
three men up and throw them into the
blazing furnace. 21 So they tied them up,
fully dressed—shirts, robes, caps, and
all—and threw them into the blazing
furnace. 22 Now because the king had
given strict orders for the furnace to be
made extremely hot, the flames burnt up
the guards who took the men to the furnace. 23 Then Shadrach, Meshach, and
Abednego, still tied up, fell into the **heart**
of the blazing fire.

24 Suddenly Nebuchadnezzar leapt to
his feet in **amazement**. He asked his
officials, "Didn't we tie up three men and
throw them into the blazing furnace?"

They answered, "Yes, we did, Your
Majesty."

25 "Then why do I see four men
walking about in the fire?" he asked.
"They are not tied up, and they show no
sign of being **hurt**—and the fourth one
looks like an **angel**."[x]

The Three Men Are Released and Promoted

26 So Nebuchadnezzar went up to the
door of the blazing furnace and called
out, "Shadrach! Meshach! Abednego!
Servants of the **Supreme** God! Come
out!" And they came out at once. 27 All
the princes, governors, lieutenant-
governors, and other officials of the king
gathered to look at the three men, who
had not been **harmed** by the fire. Their
hair was not singed, their clothes were
not burnt, and there was no smell of
smoke on them.

28 The king said, "**Praise** the God of
Shadrach, Meshach, and Abednego! He
sent his **angel** and **rescued** these men
who **serve** and **trust** him. They **disobeyed**
my orders and risked their **lives** rather
than **bow down** and **worship** any **god**
except their own.

29 "And now I **command** that if
anyone of any nation, **race**, or language
speaks **disrespectfully** of the God of
Shadrach, Meshach, and Abednego, he is
to be torn limb from limb, and his house
is to be made a pile of **ruins**. There is no
other **god** who can **rescue** like this."

30 And the king promoted Shadrach,
Meshach, and Abednego to higher positions in the province of Babylon.

[d] If the God...will; *or* If it is true that we refuse to worship your god or bow down to the gold statue you set up, the God whom we serve is able to save us from the blazing furnace and from your power—and he will. [x] an angel; *or* a son of the gods; *or* a son of God.

Nebuchadnezzar's Second Dream

4 King Nebuchadnezzar sent the following message to the people of all nations, races, and languages in the world:

"Greetings! 2 Listen to my account of the wonders and miracles which the Supreme God has shown me.

3 "How great are the wonders God
shows us!
How powerful are the miracles he
performs!
God is king for ever; he will rule for all
time.

4 "I was living comfortably in my palace, enjoying great prosperity. 5 But I had a frightening dream and saw terrifying visions while I was asleep. 6 I ordered all the royal advisers in Babylon to be brought to me so that they could tell me what the dream meant. 7 Then all the fortune-tellers, magicians, wizards, and astrologers were brought in, and I told them my dream, but they could not explain it to me. 8 Then Daniel came in. (He is also called Belteshazzar, after the name of my god.) The spirit of the holy gods[e] is in him, so I told him what I had dreamt. I said to him: 9 Belteshazzar, chief of the fortune-tellers, I know that the spirit of the holy gods[f] is in you, and that you understand all mysteries. This is[g] my dream. Tell me what it means.

10 "While I was asleep, I had a vision of a huge tree in the middle of the earth. 11 It grew bigger and bigger until it reached the sky and could be seen by everyone in the world. 12 Its leaves were beautiful, and it was loaded down with fruit—enough for the whole world to eat. Wild animals rested in its shade, birds built nests in its branches, and every kind of living being ate its fruit.

13 "While I was thinking about the vision, I saw coming down from heaven an angel, alert and watchful. 14 He proclaimed in a loud voice, 'Cut the tree down and chop off its branches; strip off its leaves and scatter its fruit. Drive the animals from under it and the birds out of its branches. 15 But leave the stump in the ground with a band of iron and bronze round it. Leave it there in the field with the grass.

" 'Now let the dew fall on this man, and let him live with the animals and the plants. 16 For seven years he will not have a human mind, but the mind of an animal. 17 This is the decision of the alert and watchful angels. So then, let all people everywhere know that the Supreme God has power over human kingdoms and that he can give them to anyone he chooses—even to the least important of men.'

18 "This is the dream I had," said King Nebuchadnezzar. "Now, Belteshazzar, tell me what it means. None of my royal advisers could tell me, but you can, because the spirit of the holy gods[h] is in you."

Daniel Explains the Dream

19 At this, Daniel, who is also called Belteshazzar, was so alarmed that he could not say anything. The king said to him, "Belteshazzar, don't let the dream and its message alarm you."

Belteshazzar replied, "Your Majesty, I wish that the dream and its explanation applied to your enemies and not to you. 20 The tree, so tall that it reached the sky, could be seen by everyone in the world. 21 Its leaves were beautiful, and it had enough fruit on it to feed the whole world. Wild animals rested under it, and birds made their nests in its branches.

22 "Your Majesty, you are the tree, tall and strong. You have grown so great that you reach the sky, and your power extends over the whole world. 23 While Your Majesty was watching, an angel came down from heaven and said, 'Cut the tree down and destroy it, but leave the stump in the ground. Wrap a band of iron and bronze round it, and leave it there in the field with the grass. Let the dew fall on this man, and let him live there with the animals for seven years.'

24 "This, then, is what it means, Your Majesty, and this is what the Supreme God has declared will happen to you. 25 You will be driven away from human society and will live with wild animals. For seven years you will eat grass like an ox, and sleep in the open air, where the dew will fall on you. Then you will admit that the Supreme God controls all human kingdoms, and that he can give them to anyone he chooses. 26 The angel ordered the stump to be left in the ground. This means that you will become king again when you acknowledge that God rules all the world. 27 So then, Your Majesty, follow my advice. Stop sinning, do what is right, and be merciful to the poor.[i] Then you will continue to be prosperous."

28 All this did happen to King Nebuchadnezzar. 29 Only twelve months later, while he was walking about on the

[e] gods; *or* God. [f] gods; *or* God. [g] *Probable text* This is; *Aramaic* Visions of. [h] gods; *or* God.
[i] Stop sinning...to the poor; *or* Make up for your sins by doing what is right and by being merciful to the poor.

roof of his royal palace in Babylon, 30 he
said, "Look how great Babylon is! I built
it as my capital city to display my power
and might, my glory and majesty."
31 Before the words were out of his
mouth, a voice spoke from heaven, "King
Nebuchadnezzar, listen to what I say!
Your royal power is now taken away
from you. 32 You will be driven away
from human society, live with wild
animals, and eat grass like an ox for
seven years. Then you will acknowledge
that the Supreme God has power over
human kingdoms and that he can give
them to anyone he chooses."
33 The words came true immediately.
Nebuchadnezzar was driven out of
human society and ate grass like an ox.
The dew fell on his body, and his hair
grew as long as eagles' feathers and his
nails as long as birds' claws.

Nebuchadnezzar Praises God

34 "When the seven years had
passed," said the king, "I looked up at the
sky, and my sanity returned. I praised
the Supreme God and gave honour and
glory to the one who lives for ever.

"He will rule for ever,
and his kingdom will last for all time.
35 He looks on the people of the earth as nothing;
angels in heaven and people on earth
are under his control.
No one can oppose his will
or question what he does.

36 "When my sanity returned, my
honour, my majesty, and the glory of my
kingdom were given back to me. My
officials and my noblemen welcomed
me, and I was given back my royal
power, with even greater honour than
before.
37 "And now, I, Nebuchadnezzar,
praise, honour, and glorify the King of
Heaven. Everything he does is right and
just, and he can humble anyone who acts
proudly."

Belshazzar's Banquet

5 One night King Belshazzar invited a
thousand noblemen to a great
banquet, and they drank wine together.
2 While they were drinking, Belshazzar
gave orders to bring in the gold and
silver cups and bowls which his father[x]
Nebuchadnezzar had carried off from
the Temple in Jerusalem. The king sent
for them so that he, his noblemen, his
wives, and his concubines could drink out
of them. 3 At once the gold cups and
bowls were brought in, and they all
drank wine out of them 4 and praised
gods made of gold, silver, bronze, iron,
wood, and stone.
5 Suddenly a human hand appeared
and began writing on the plaster wall of
the palace, where the light from the
lamps was shining most brightly. And the
king saw the hand as it was writing. 6 He
turned pale and was so frightened that
his knees began to shake. 7 He shouted
for someone to bring in the magicians,
wizards, and astrologers. When they
came in, the king said to them, "Anyone
who can read this writing and tell me
what it means will be dressed in robes of
royal purple, wear a gold chain of honour
round his neck, and be the third in power
in the kingdom." 8 The royal advisers
came forward, but none of them could
read the writing or tell the king what it
meant. 9 In his distress King Belshazzar
grew even paler, and his noblemen had
no idea what to do.
10 The queen mother heard the noise
made by the king and his noblemen and
entered the banqueting-hall. She said,
"May Your Majesty live for ever! Please
do not be so disturbed and look so pale.
11 There is a man in your kingdom who
has the spirit of the holy gods[k] in him.
When your father was king, this man
showed good sense, knowledge, and
wisdom like the wisdom of the gods. And
King Nebuchadnezzar, your father,[x]
made him chief of the fortune-tellers,
magicians, wizards, and astrologers. 12 He
has unusual ability and is wise and skilful
in interpreting dreams, solving riddles,
and explaining mysteries; so send for
this man Daniel, whom the king named
Belteshazzar, and he will tell you what all
this means."

Daniel Explains the Writing

13 Daniel was brought at once into the
king's presence, and the king said to him,
"Are you Daniel, that Jewish exile whom
my father the king brought here from
Judah? 14 I have heard that the spirit of
the holy gods[k] is in you and that you are
skilful and have knowledge and wisdom.
15 The advisers and magicians were
brought in to read this writing and tell
me what it means, but they could not discover the meaning. 16 Now I have heard
that you can find hidden meanings and

[x] *There were several kings of Babylonia between Nebuchadnezzar and Belshazzar.* Father *may mean predecessor, or the name* Nebuchadnezzar *may be used for Nabinodus.*
[k] gods; *or* God.

act 4.37; 9.8
admit (1) 4.25; Amos 6.3
afraid 1.10; 10.12
alive Ezek 23.25; Hos 9.12
banquet [2] Is 25.6; Amos 6.7
choose 4.17; 6.2
concubine [2] Song 6.8
control [2] 4.25; Mk 5.4
cruel Ezek 34.4; Amos 1.3
cup [3] Ezek 23.31; Obad 16
determine Lam 2.8; 11.28
disgrace Ezek 43.7; 9.7
distress Ezek 30.4; Joel 1.18
dream 4.5; 7.1
exile 2.25; 6.13
fortune-teller 4.7; Mic 5.12
fright 4.5; 7.28
gift 2.6; 11.38
god (2) (other gods) [6] 4.8; 6.7
heaven 4.13; 6.27
holy [2] 4.8; 9.20
honour [6] 4.34; 7.14
human [3] 4.16; 7.4
humble 4.37; 10.12
idea Is 44.20; Mt 15.19
interpret 1.17; Mic 3.11
Jew 3.8; Zech 8.23
knee Ezek 47.4; 10.10
knowledge [2] 1.17; Hab 2.14
light (1) 2.22; Amos 5.18
magic [3] 4.7; Mic 5.12
Majesty [3] 4.19; 6.6
mind (1) 4.16; 7.4
mystery [2] 4.9; 2 Thes 2.7
power [4] 4.3; 6.26
praise [2] 4.34; Hos 14.2
presence 2.25; Hos 6.2
protect Ezek 39.25; 11.38
proud 4.37; 7.8
race (1) 4.1; 6.25
sense Jer 51.17; Hos 4.11
servant 3.26; 6.20
spirit (2) [2] 4.8; Zech 12.10
stubborn Ezek 36.26; 8.23
supreme [2] 4.2; 7.18
Temple (1) (of God) [2] 1.2; 8.11
throne Ezek 43.7; 7.9
tremble Ezek 38.20; 10.10
turn 3.19; 7.28
wisdom [2] 2.21; 11.33
wise 2.20; 11.33
word (1) 4.31; 12.9

explain **mysteries**. If you can read this writing and tell me what it means, you will be dressed in robes of royal purple, wear a gold chain of **honour** round your neck, and be the third in **power** in the kingdom."

17 Daniel replied, "Keep your **gifts** for yourself or give them to someone else. I will read for Your **Majesty** what has been written and tell you what it means.

18 "The **Supreme** God made your father Nebuchadnezzar a great king and gave him dignity and **majesty**. 19 He was so great that people of all nations, **races**, and languages were **afraid** of him and **trembled**. If he wanted to kill someone, he did; if he wanted to keep someone **alive**, he did. He **honoured** or **disgraced** anyone he wanted to. 20 But because he became **proud**, **stubborn**, and **cruel**, he was removed from his royal **throne** and lost his place of **honour**. 21 He was driven away from **human** society, and his **mind** became like that of an animal. He lived with wild donkeys, ate grass like an ox, and slept in the open air with nothing to **protect** him from the dew. Finally he **admitted** that the **Supreme** God **controls** all **human** kingdoms and can give them to anyone he **chooses**.

22 "But you, his son, have not **humbled** yourself, even though you knew all this. 23 You **acted** against the Lord of **heaven** and brought in the **cups** and bowls taken from his **Temple**. You, your noblemen, your wives, and your **concubines** drank wine out of them and **praised gods** made of gold, silver, bronze, iron, wood, and stone—**gods** that cannot see or hear and that do not know anything. But you did not **honour** the God who **determines** whether you live or die and who **controls** everything you do. 24 That is why God has sent the hand to write these **words**.

25 "This is what was written: 'Number, number, weight, divisions.' 26 And this is what it means: *number,* God has numbered the days of your kingdom and brought it to an end; 27 *weight,* you have been weighed on the scales and found to be too light; 28 *divisions,* your kingdom is divided up and given to the Medes and Persians."[l]

29 Immediately Belshazzar ordered his **servants** to dress Daniel in a robe of royal purple and to hang a gold chain of **honour** round his neck. And he made him the third in **power** in the kingdom. 30 That same night Belshazzar, the king of Babylonia, was killed; 31 and Darius the Mede, who was then sixty-two years old, seized the royal **power**.

Daniel in the Pit of Lions

6 Darius decided to appoint a hundred and twenty governors to hold office throughout his empire. 2 In addition, he **chose** Daniel and two others to supervise the governors and to look after the king's **interests**. 3 Daniel soon showed that he could do better work than the other supervisors or the governors. Because he was so outstanding, the king considered putting him in charge of the whole empire. 4 Then the other supervisors and the governors tried to find something **wrong** with the way Daniel administered the empire, but they couldn't, because Daniel was **reliable** and did not do anything **wrong** or **dishonest**. 5 They said to one another, "We are not going to find anything of which to **accuse** Daniel unless it is something in connection with his **religion**."

6 So they went to see the king and said, "King Darius, may Your **Majesty** live for ever! 7 All of us who administer your empire—the supervisors, the governors, the lieutenant-governors, and the other officials—have **agreed** that Your **Majesty** should issue an order and enforce it strictly. Give orders that for thirty days no one be **permitted** to **request** anything from any **god** or from any man except from Your **Majesty**. Anyone who violates this order is to be thrown into a pit filled with lions. 8 So let Your **Majesty** issue this order and sign it, and it will be in force, a **law** of the Medes and Persians, which cannot be **changed**." 9 And so King Darius signed the order. 10 When Daniel **learnt** that the order had been signed, he went home. In an upstairs room of his house there were windows that faced towards Jerusalem. There, just as he had always done, he **knelt** down at the open windows and **prayed** to God three times a day.

11 When Daniel's **enemies observed** him **praying** to God, 12 all of them went together to the king to **accuse** Daniel. They said, "Your **Majesty**, you signed an order that for the next thirty days anyone who **requested** anything from any **god** or from any man except you, would be thrown into a pit filled with lions."

The king replied, "Yes, a strict order, a **law** of the Medes and Persians, which cannot be **changed**."

13 Then they said to the king, "Daniel,

accuse [3] Ezek 23.36; Hos 4.1
agree 2.9; 9.27
angel 4.13; 8.13
anxious Ezek 4.16; Mic 1.12
arrest [2] Jer 37.14; Mt 10.17
best Ezek 48.14; 11.15
change [3] 2.9; 7.25
choose 5.21; 9.25
command 3.20; 9.4
destroy 4.23; 7.11
dishonest Jer 22.13; Hos 12.7
enemy 4.19; 11.10
exile 5.13; Amos 1.9
fear Ezek 38.8; Hos 3.5
god (2) (other gods) [2] 5.4; 11.8
heaven 5.23; 7.26
hurt [2] 3.25; Hos 6.1
innocent Ezek 16.51; Joel 3.19
interest (1) Jer 22.17; 1 Cor 10.24
joy Ezek 25.6; Joel 1.12
Kingdom (1) (of God) 4.34; 7.14
kneel Is 45.23; Mt 2.11
law [3] Ezek 44.24; 7.25
learn 2.30; Mal 2.7
loyal [2] Ezek 17.13; Hos 12.6
Majesty [9] 5.10; Mic 5.4
miracle 4.2; Mic 7.15
obey Ezek 44.7; 7.27
observe Jer 17.22; 1 Cor 4.6
permit 2.16; 7.12
power 5.7; 7.7
pray [3] 2.18; 9.3
prosper 4.4; Hos 1.11
race (1) 5.19; 7.14
reign [2] Jer 52.4; 9.2
religion Ezek 44.24; 7.25
rely Ezek 33.26; Hos 7.8
request [2] 2.49; Jn 19.31
rescue [4] 3.28; Hos 12.13
respect [2] 3.29; Mal 1.6
save [3] 3.15; 8.7
seal [2] Jer 32.10; 12.4
servant 5.29; 9.6
serve [2] 3.17; 7.10
trust 3.28; Hos 10.13
upset Ps 49.16; Mt 2.3
wonder (1) 4.2; Joel 2.26
wrong [3] Ezek 48.11; 9.5

[l] PERSIANS: *In Aramaic the word for "Persians" sounds like the word for "division."*

5.29: Gen 41.42

one of the **exiles** from Judah, does not **respect** Your **Majesty** or **obey** the order you issued. He **prays** regularly three times a day."

14 When the king heard this, he was **upset** and did his **best** to find some way to **rescue** Daniel. He kept trying until sunset. 15 Then the men came back to the king and said to him, "Your **Majesty** knows that according to the **laws** of the Medes and Persians no order which the king issues can be **changed**."

16 So the king gave orders for Daniel to be **arrested** and he was thrown into the pit filled with lions. He said to Daniel, "May your God, whom you **serve** so **loyally**, **rescue** you." 17 A stone was put over the mouth of the pit, and the king placed his own royal **seal** and the **seal** of his noblemen on the stone, so that no one could **rescue** Daniel. 18 Then the king returned to the palace and spent a sleepless night, without food or any form of entertainment.

19 At dawn the king got up and hurried to the pit. 20 When he got there, he called out **anxiously**, "Daniel, **servant** of the living God! Was the God you **serve** so **loyally** able to **save** you from the lions?"

21 Daniel answered, "May Your **Majesty** live for ever! 22 God sent his **angel** to shut the mouths of the lions so that they would not **hurt** me. He did this because he knew that I was **innocent** and because I have not **wronged** you, Your **Majesty**."

23 The king was **overjoyed** and gave orders for Daniel to be pulled up out of the pit. So they pulled him up and saw that he had not been **hurt** at all, for he **trusted** God. 24 Then the king gave orders to **arrest** all the men who had **accused** Daniel, and they were thrown, together with their wives and their children, into the pit filled with lions. Before they even reached the bottom of the pit, the lions pounced on them and broke all their bones.

25 Then King Darius wrote to the people of all nations, **races**, and languages on earth:

"Greetings! 26 I **command** that throughout my empire everyone should **fear** and **respect** Daniel's God.

"He is a living God,
and he will rule for ever.
His **kingdom** will never be **destroyed**,
and his **power** will never come to an end.
27 He **saves** and **rescues**;
he performs **wonders** and **miracles**
in **heaven** and **on earth**.
He **saved** Daniel from being killed by the lions."

28 Daniel **prospered** during the **reign** of Darius and the **reign** of Cyrus the Persian.

DANIEL DESCRIBES HIS VISIONS
(7.1—12.13)

Daniel's Vision of the Four Beasts

7 In the first year that Belshazzar was king of Babylonia, I had a **dream** and saw a **vision** in the night. I wrote the **dream** down, and this is the record 2 of what I saw that night:

Winds were blowing from all directions and lashing the surface of the ocean. 3 Four huge **beasts** came up out of the ocean, each one different from the others. 4 The first one looked like a lion, but had wings like an eagle. While I was **watching**, the wings were torn off. The **beast** was lifted up and made to stand like a man. And then a **human mind** was given to it.

5 The second **beast** looked like a bear standing on its hind legs. It was holding three ribs between its teeth, and a voice said to it, "Go on, eat as much meat as you can!"

6 While I was **watching**, another **beast** appeared. It looked like a leopard, but on its back there were four wings, like the wings of a bird, and it had four heads. It had a look of **authority** about it.

7 As I was **watching**, a fourth **beast** appeared. It was **powerful**, **horrible**, **terrifying**. With its huge iron teeth it crushed its **victims**, and then it trampled on them. Unlike the other **beasts**, it had ten horns. 8 While I was staring at the horns, I saw a little horn coming up among the others. It tore out three of the horns that were already there. This horn had **human** eyes and a mouth that was **boasting proudly**.

The Vision of the One Who Has Been Living For Ever

9 While I was looking, **thrones** were put in place. One who had been living for ever sat down on one of the **thrones**. His clothes were white as snow, and his hair was like **pure** wool. His **throne**, mounted on fiery wheels, was blazing with fire, 10 and a stream of fire was pouring out from it. There were many thousands of people there to **serve** him, and millions of people stood before him. The **court**

authority [3] Jer 5.5; Mt 7.29
beast (1) [12] Job 41.34; 1 Cor 15.32
being 4.12; Zeph 1.3
boast [3] Ezek 35.13; 11.36
body 4.33; 10.6
change 6.8; 10.8
cloud Ezek 38.9; Joel 2.2
conquer 2.44; 11.18
court (1) [2] 2.49; Amos 5.10
destroy [2] 6.26; 8.24
dream [2] 5.12; Joel 2.28
favour Ezek 16.19; Zech 11.7
festival Ezek 46.1; Hos 2.11
fright 5.6; 10.19
God's people [4] Ezek 46.18; 8.24
heaven 6.27; 8.10
honour 5.7; 9.4
horror Lam 4.10; Hos 6.10
human [3] 5.5; 8.25
judge [2] 3.2; Hos 5.1
Kingdom (1) (of God) 6.26; Mt 3.2
last (1) 4.34; 11.6
law 6.8; 9.10
mind (1) 5.21; Hos 13.2
obey 6.13; Joel 2.11
oppress Ezek 46.18; 11.20
overthrow Jer 31.28; Hag 2.7
permit 6.7; Mt 16.19
power [9] 6.26; 8.4
present (1) 2.48; Mic 4.13
proud [2] 5.20; 8.25
pure Ezek 45.18; 11.35
race (1) 6.25; Zech 9.6
religion 6.5; 8.12
serve [3] 6.16; 11.37
supreme [4] 5.18; 11.36
terrify [3] 4.5; 8.17
throne [3] 5.20; Jon 3.6
turn 5.6; 9.5
victim [2] Ezek 7.15; Amos 3.4
vision [3] 4.5; 8.1
watch [4] 4.13; 8.4

7.3: Rev 13.1, 17.8 **7.4–6:** Rev 13.2 **7.7:** Rev 12.3, 13.1 **7.8:** Rev 13.5–6 **7.9:** Rev 20.4, 1.14
7.10: Rev 5.11, 20.12

began its session, and the books were
opened.

11 While I was looking, I could still
hear the little horn bragging and
boasting. As I **watched**, the fourth **beast**
was killed, and its **body** was thrown into
the flames and **destroyed**. 12 The other
beasts had their **power** taken away, but
they were **permitted** to go on living for a
limited time.

13 During this **vision** in the night, I
saw what looked like a **human being**. He
was approaching me, surrounded by
clouds, and he went to the one who had
been living for ever and was **presented** to
him. 14 He was given **authority**, **honour**,
and royal **power**, so that the people of all
nations, **races**, and languages would
serve him. His **authority** would **last** for
ever, and his **kingdom** would never end.

The Visions Are Explained

15 The **visions** I saw alarmed me, and
I was deeply disturbed.[m] 16 I went up to
one of those standing there and asked
him to explain it all. So he told me the
meaning. 17 He said, "These four huge
beasts are four empires which will arise
on earth. 18 And the people of the
Supreme God will receive royal **power**
and keep it for ever and ever."

19 Then I wanted to know more about
the fourth **beast**, which was not like any
of the others—the **terrifying beast** which
crushed its **victims** with its bronze claws
and iron teeth and then trampled on
them. 20 And I wanted to know about the
ten horns on its head and the horn that
had come up afterwards and had made
three of the horns fall. It had eyes and a
mouth and was **boasting proudly**. It was
more **terrifying** than any of the others.

21 While I was looking, that horn
made war on **God's people** and **conquered** them. 22 Then the one who had
been living for ever came and pronounced **judgement** in **favour** of[n] the
people of the **Supreme** God. The time
had arrived for **God's people** to receive
royal **power**.

23 This is the explanation I was given:
"The fourth **beast** is a fourth empire that
will be on the earth and will be different
from all other empires. It will crush the
whole earth and trample it down. 24 The
ten horns are ten kings who will rule that
empire. Then another king will appear;
he will be very different from the earlier
ones and will **overthrow** three kings.
25 He will speak against the **Supreme** God
and **oppress God's people**. He will try to
change their **religious laws** and **festivals**,
and **God's people** will be under his **power**
for three and a half years. 26 Then the
heavenly court will sit in **judgement**, take
away his **power**, and **destroy** him completely. 27 The **power** and greatness of all
the kingdoms on earth will be given to
the people of the **Supreme** God. Their
royal **power** will never end and all rulers
on earth will **serve** and **obey** them."

28 This is the end of the account. I was
so **frightened** that I **turned** pale, and I
kept everything to myself.

Daniel's Vision of a Ram and a Goat

8 In the third year that Belshazzar
was king, I saw a second **vision**.[o] 2 In
the **vision** I suddenly found myself in the
walled city of Susa in the province of
Elam. I was standing by the River Ulai,
3 and there beside the river I saw a ram
that had two long horns, one of which
was longer and **newer** than the other. 4 I
watched the ram butting with his horns
to the west, the north, and the south. No
animal could stop him or **escape** his
power. He did as he **pleased** and grew
arrogant.

5 While I was wondering what this
meant, a goat came rushing out of the
west, moving so fast that his feet didn't
touch the ground. He had one prominent
horn between his eyes. 6 He came
towards the ram, which I had seen standing beside the river, and rushed at him
with all his **force**. 7 I **watched** him attack
the ram. He was so **angry** that he
smashed into him and broke the two
horns. The ram had no **strength** to **resist**.
He was thrown to the ground and
trampled on, and there was no one who
could **save** him.

8 The goat grew more and more
arrogant, but at the height of his **power**
his horn was broken. In its place four
prominent horns came up, each pointing
in a different direction. 9 Out of one of
these four horns grew a little horn,
whose **power** extended towards the south
and the east and towards the **Promised**
Land. 10 It grew **strong enough** to attack
the army of **heaven**, the stars themselves, and it threw some of them to the
ground and trampled on them. 11 It even
defied the Prince of the **heavenly** army,

angel [2] 6.22; 10.11
anger [2] 3.19; 9.16
arrogant [2] Jer 48.29; 11.18
deceive [2] Ezek 14.9; 11.23
defy [2] Ezek 20.8
destroy [4] 7.11; 9.17
enough 4.12; 11.15
escape Ezek 35.6; 11.41
force (1) Ezek 36.18; 11.9
God's people 7.21; 9.4
heaven [3] 7.26; Amos 9.2
human 7.4; Hos 13.2
mortal Ezek 47.6; Acts 2.26
new 1.7; Hos 4.11
offer [3] 2.46; 9.21
please Ezek 43.27; 9.13
power [6] 7.7; 9.15
promise Ezek 47.14; 11.16
proper Ezek 44.20; 11.13
proud 7.8; 11.12
punish 2.9; 9.12
raise 1.20; 10.10
religion 7.25; 11.28
represent [3] Ezek 37.19; Zech 5.8
resist Jer 1.18; Acts 7.51
restore Ezek 16.55; 9.17
sacrifice [5] 2.46; 9.21
save 6.20; 12.1
secret 2.22; 12.9
strength 2.23; 10.8
strong [3] 4.22; 9.25
stubborn 5.20; Hos 4.16
succeed (1) [3] Ezek 17.15; 11.17
Temple (1) (of God) [3] 5.2; 9.17
terrible Ezek 9.9; Hos 9.12
terrify 7.7; 10.7
true [3] 4.33; 9.7
understand [3] 4.9; 9.22
vision [8] 7.1; 9.21
warn Ezek 33.3; 11.24

[m] *Aramaic has two additional words, the meaning of which is unclear.*
[n] pronounced judgement in favour of; *or* gave the right to judge to.
[o] *Beginning at 8.1, the rest of this book is in Hebrew (see 2.4).*

7.13: Mt 24.30, 26.64; Mk 13.26, 14.62; Lk 21.27; Rev 1.7, 13, 14.14 **7.14:** Rev 11.15 **7.18:** Rev 22.5
7.21: Rev 13.7 **7.22:** Rev 20.4 **7.24:** Rev 17.12 **7.25:** Rev 12.14, 13.5–6 **7.27:** Rev 20.4, 22.5
8.10: Rev 12.4

watch [2] 7.4; 10.8
way (3) Ezek 33.8; Hos 14.9
wicked Ezek 39.24; 12.10
world 4.1; 12.4

stopped the daily sacrifices offered to him, and desecrated the Temple. [12]People sinned there instead of offering the proper daily sacrifices,[p] and true religion was thrown to the ground. The horn was successful in everything it did.

13 Then I heard one angel ask another, "How long will these things that were seen in the vision continue? How long will an awful sin replace the daily sacrifices? How long will the army of heaven and the Temple be trampled on?"

14 I heard the other angel answer, "It will continue for 1,150 days, during which evening and morning[x] sacrifices will not be offered. Then the Temple will be restored."

The Angel Gabriel Explains the Vision

15 I was trying to understand what the vision meant, when suddenly someone was standing in front of me. [16]I heard a voice call out over the River Ulai, "Gabriel, explain to him the meaning of what he saw." [17]Gabriel came and stood beside me, and I was so terrified that I fell to the ground.

He said to me, "Mortal man, understand the meaning. The vision has to do with the end of the world." [18]While he was talking, I fell to the ground unconscious. But he took hold of me, raised me to my feet, [19]and said, "I am showing you what the result of God's anger will be. The vision refers to the time of the end.

20 "The ram you saw that had two horns represents the kingdoms of Media and Persia. [21]The goat represents the kingdom of Greece, and the prominent horn between his eyes is the first king. [22]The four horns that came up when the first horn was broken represent the four kingdoms into which that nation will be divided and which will not be as strong as the first kingdom.

23 "When the end of those kingdoms is near and they have become so wicked that they must be punished, there will be a stubborn, vicious, and deceitful king. [24]He will grow strong—but not by his own power. He will cause terrible destruction and be successful in everything he does. He will bring destruction on powerful men and on God's own people. [25]Because he is cunning, he will succeed in his deceitful ways. He will be proud of himself and destroy many people without warning. He will even defy the greatest King of all, but he will be destroyed without the use of any human power. [26]This vision about the evening and morning sacrifices which has been explained to you will come true. But keep it secret now, because it will be a long time before it does come true."

27 I was depressed and ill for several days. Then I got up and went back to the work that the king had assigned to me, but I was puzzled by the vision and could not understand it.

Daniel Prays for His People

9 Darius the Mede, who was the son of Xerxes, ruled over the kingdom of Babylonia. [2]In the first year of his reign, I was studying the sacred books and thinking about the seventy years that Jerusalem would be in ruins, according to what the LORD had told the prophet Jeremiah. [3]And I prayed earnestly to the Lord God, pleading with him, fasting, wearing sackcloth, and sitting in ashes. [4]I prayed to the LORD my God and confessed the sins of my people.

I said, "Lord God, you are great, and we honour you. You are faithful to your covenant and show constant love to those who love you and do what you command.

5 "We have sinned, we have been evil, we have done wrong. We have rejected what you commanded us to do and have turned away from what you showed us was right. [6]We have not listened to your servants the prophets, who spoke in your name to our kings, our rulers, our ancestors, and our whole nation. [7]You, Lord, always do what is right, but we have always brought disgrace on ourselves. This is true of all of us who live in Judaea and in Jerusalem and of all the Israelites whom you scattered in countries near and far because they were unfaithful to you. [8]Our kings, our rulers, and our ancestors have acted shamefully and sinned against you, Lord. [9]You are merciful and forgiving, although we have rebelled against you. [10]We did not listen to you, O LORD our God, when you told us to live according to the laws which you gave us through your servants the prophets. [11]All Israel broke your laws and refused to listen to what you said. We sinned against you, and so you brought on us the curses that are written in the Law of Moses, your servant. [12]You did what you said you would do to us and our rulers. You punished Jerusalem more severely than any other city on earth, [13]giving us all the punishment described in the Law of

act [2] 5.23; Hos 12.1
agree 6.7; Mt 3.15
anger 8.7; 11.11
ash Ezek 28.18; Amos 2.1
Awful Horror 11.31
choose [2] 6.2; Hos 1.11
command [3] 6.26; Joel 2.11
confess [2] Jer 14.20; Zech 13.9
constant Ezek 35.5; Hos 2.19
covenant Ezek 44.7; Hos 2.18
curse Lam 3.65; Mic 2.7
dedicate 3.2; 11.8
defend [2] 3.16; 11.1
destroy [3] 8.24; 11.17
disgrace 5.19; 12.2
earnest Ps 78.34; Jon 3.8
establish 2.44; Hos 2.23
eternal Ezek 26.20; 12.2
evil [3] Ezek 38.10; 11.21
faithful Ezek 48.11; 12.12
fast (2) Jer 36.6; Joel 1.14
flood Ezek 30.16; 11.10
forgive [3] Ezek 45.13; Hos 1.6
free 1.4; Mic 2.13
God's people [2] 8.24; 11.28
help 1.8; 10.13
holy [3] 5.11; Hos 6.9
honour 7.14; 11.38
justice 4.37; Hos 5.1
law [4] 7.25; Mic 3.11
look down on Song 1.6; 1 Cor 1.28
love [2] Ezek 33.31; 10.11
mercy [2] 4.27; Hos 2.4
name (2) (name of God, of Jesus) [2] Ezek 43.7; 12.7
neighbour Ezek 36.3; Mic 7.5
offer [2] 8.11; 11.17
plead [4] Jer 15.1; Hos 2.2
please 8.4; 11.16
power [3] 8.4; 11.2
pray [5] 6.10; Hos 7.7
prayer 2.23; 10.12
prophecy [2] Ezek 37.4; Amos 7.13
prophet [3] Ezek 38.17; Hos 4.5
punish [3] 8.23; 11.36
rebel Ezek 44.6; 11.14

[p] People...sacrifices; *Hebrew unclear.* [x] 1,150 days...morning; *or* 2,300 days, during which.

8.16: Lk 1.19, 26 **9.2:** Jer 25.11, 29.10

refuse (1) 3.14; Hos 4.6
reign 6.28
reject Ezek 31.11; Hos 4.6
remember Ezek 36.31; Hos 7.2
restore [3] 8.14; Joel 3.1
right (1) [4] 4.27; 12.3
ruin 3.29; 11.26
sackcloth Ezek 27.31; Joel 1.13
sacred [2] Ezek 44.8; Hos 3.4
sacrifice [2] 8.11; 11.31
scatter 4.14; Hos 9.6
servant [3] 6.20; 11.6
shame Ezek 36.32; Hos 2.4
strong 8.10; 10.18
study Ezek 43.10; Mt 2.1
suffer Ezek 23.35; 12.2
Temple (1) (of God) [5] 8.11; 11.31
trouble [2] Ezek 32.9; 12.1
true [2] 8.12; 10.1
truth Jer 38.14; 10.20
turn [2] 7.28; 11.18
understand [2] 8.15; 10.1
unfaithful Ezek 20.27; Hos 1.2
unjust Is 59.8; Rom 9.14
vision [3] 8.1; 10.1
wrong [2] 6.4; Amos 6.12

Moses. But even now, O LORD our God, we have not tried to please you by turning from our sins or by following your truth. 14 You, O LORD our God, were prepared to punish us, and you did, because you always do what is right, and we did not listen to you.

15 "O Lord our God, you showed your power by bringing your people out of Egypt, and your power is still remembered. We have sinned; we have done wrong. 16 You have defended us in the past, so do not be angry with Jerusalem any longer. It is your city, your sacred hill.[q] All the people in the neighbouring countries look down on Jerusalem and on your people because of our sins and the evil our ancestors did. 17 O God, hear my prayer and pleading. Restore your Temple, which has been destroyed; restore it so that everyone will know that you are God. 18 Listen to us, O God; look at us, and see the trouble we are in and the suffering of the city that bears your name. We are praying to you because you are merciful, not because we have done right. 19 Lord, hear us. Lord, forgive us. Lord, listen to us, and act! In order that everyone will know that you are God, do not delay! This city and these people are yours."

Gabriel Explains the Prophecy

20 I went on praying, confessing my sins and the sins of my people Israel, and pleading with the LORD my God to restore his holy Temple. 21 While I was praying, Gabriel, whom I had seen in the earlier vision, came flying down to where I was. It was the time for the evening sacrifice to be offered. 22 He explained, "Daniel, I have come here to help you understand the prophecy. 23 When you began to plead with God, he answered you. He loves you, and so I have come to tell you the answer. Now pay attention while I explain the vision.

24 "Seven times seventy years is the length of time God has set for freeing your people and your holy city from sin and evil. Sin will be forgiven and eternal justice established, so that the vision and the prophecy will come true, and the holy Temple[r] will be rededicated. 25 Note this and understand it: From the time the command is given to rebuild Jerusalem, until God's chosen leader comes, seven times seven years will pass. Jerusalem will be rebuilt with streets and strong defences, and will stand for seven times sixty-two years, but this will be a time of troubles. 26 And at the end of that time God's chosen leader will be killed unjustly.[s] The city and the Temple will be destroyed by the invading army of a powerful ruler. The end will come like a flood, bringing the war and destruction which God has prepared. 27 That ruler will have a firm agreement with many people for seven years, and when half this time is past, he will put an end to sacrifices and offerings. The Awful Horror[t] will be placed on the highest point of the Temple and will remain there until the one who put it there meets the end which God has prepared for him."

Daniel's Vision by the River Tigris

10 (In the third year that Cyrus was emperor of Persia, a message was revealed to Daniel, who is also called Belteshazzar. The message was true but extremely hard to understand.[u] It was explained to him in a vision.)

2 At that time, I was mourning for three weeks. 3 I did not eat any rich food or any meat, drink any wine, or comb my hair until the three weeks were past.

4 On the twenty-fourth day of the first month of the year, I was standing on the bank of the mighty River Tigris. 5 I looked up and saw someone who was wearing linen clothes and a belt of fine gold. 6 His body shone like a jewel. His face was as bright as a flash of lightning, and his eyes blazed like fire. His arms and legs shone like polished bronze, and his voice sounded like the roar of a great crowd.

7 I was the only one who saw the vision. The men who were with me did not see anything, but they were terrified and ran and hid. 8 I was left there alone, watching this amazing vision. I had no strength left, and my face was so changed that no one could have recognized me. 9 When I heard his voice, I fell to the ground unconscious and lay there face downwards. 10 Then a hand took hold of me and raised me to my hands and knees; I was still trembling.

11 The angel said to me, "Daniel, God loves you. Stand up and listen carefully to what I am going to say. I have been sent to you." When he had said this, I stood up, still trembling.

12 Then he said, "Daniel, don't be

afraid 5.19; Hos 10.5
alone [2] Ezek 44.16; Hos 13.4
amaze 3.24; 12.6
angel [7] 8.13; 11.2
body 7.11; Joel 2.20
change 7.25; Joel 2.7
fright 7.28; 11.30
hard Ezek 3.9; Hos 10.11
help [2] 9.22; 11.1
humble 5.22; Mic 6.8
knee 5.6; Nah 2.10
love [2] 9.4; 11.37
master Jer 10.23; Zeph 1.9
message [2] 4.1; Hos 1.1
might 4.30; Joel 2.11
mourn Ezek 32.16; Hos 10.5
prayer [2] 9.17; Hos 2.21
raise 8.18; 11.25
reveal [2] 2.19; Hos 4.12
rich Ezek 28.4; 11.2
slave Ezek 34.27; Hos 12.13
speech Ezek 33.22; Amos 7.10
strength [2] 8.7; 11.15
strong [2] 9.25; 11.5
terrify 8.17; Joel 2.6
tremble [3] 5.19; Joel 2.1
true 9.7; 11.2
truth 9.13; Amos 5.10
understand [3] 9.22; 12.4
vision [5] 9.21; 11.14
watch 8.4; Amos 9.8
weak 2.42; Joel 3.10
worry 2.1; Mt 6.25

[q] SACRED HILL: *Mount Zion (see Zion in Word List).* [r] Temple; *or* altar.
[s] *One ancient translation* unjustly; *Hebrew unclear.*
[t] THE AWFUL HORROR: *A pagan image set up in the Jerusalem Temple by foreign conquerors (see 1 Macc 1.54–61).* [u] but extremely hard to understand; *or* and it was about a great war.

9.21: Lk 1.19, 26 **9.27:** Dan 11.31, 12.11; Mt 24.15; Mk 13.14 **10.5–6:** Rev 1.13–15, 2.18, 19.12

afraid. God has heard your **prayers** ever
since the first day you decided to **humble**
yourself in order to gain **understanding**. I
have come in answer to your **prayer**.
13 The **angel** prince of the kingdom of
Persia opposed me for twenty-one days.
Then Michael, one of the chief **angels**,
came to **help** me, because I had been left
there **alone** in Persia. 14 I have come to
make you **understand** what will happen
to your people in the future. This is a
vision about the future."

15 When he said this, I stared at the
ground, **speechless**. 16 Then the **angel**,
who looked like a man, stretched out his
hand and touched my lips. I said to him,
"Sir, this **vision** makes me so **weak** that I
can't stop **trembling**. 17 I am like a **slave**
standing before his **master**. How can I
talk to you? I have no **strength** or breath
left in me."

18 Once more he took hold of me, and
I felt **stronger**. 19 He said, "God **loves** you,
so don't let anything **worry** you or
frighten you."

When he had said this, I felt even
stronger and said, "Sir, tell me what you
have to say. You have made me feel
better."

20–21 He said, "Do you know why I
came to you? It is to **reveal** to you what
is written in the **Book of Truth**. Now I
have to go back and fight the guardian
angel of Persia. After that, the guardian
angel of Greece will appear. There is no
one to **help** me except Michael, Israel's
11 guardian **angel**.[v] 1 He is[w] responsible for **helping** and **defending**
me. 2 And what I am now going to tell you
is **true**."

The Kingdoms of Egypt and Syria

The **angel** said, "Three more kings will
rule over Persia, followed by a fourth,
who will be **richer** than all the others. At
the height of his **power** and wealth he
will **challenge** the kingdom of Greece.

3 "Then a heroic king will appear. He
will rule over a huge empire and do
whatever he wants. 4 But at the height of
his **power** his empire will break up and
be divided into four parts. Kings not
descended from him will rule in his
place, but they will not have the **power**
that he had.

5 "The king of Egypt will be **strong**.
One of his generals, however, will be
even **stronger** and rule a greater
kingdom. 6 After a number of years the
king of Egypt will make an alliance with
the king of Syria and give him his
daughter in marriage. But the alliance
will not **last**, and she, her husband, her
child,[x] and the **servants** who went with
her will all be killed. 7 Soon afterwards,
one of her relatives will become king. He
will attack the army of the king of Syria,
enter their fortress, and defeat them.
8 He will carry back to Egypt the **images**
of their **gods** and the articles of gold and
silver **dedicated** to those **gods**. After
several years of **peace** 9 the king of Syria
will invade Egypt, but he will be **forced**
to retreat.

10 "The sons of the king of Syria will
prepare for war and gather a large
army. One of them will sweep on like a
flood and attack an **enemy** fortress. 11 In
his **anger** the king of Egypt will go to war
against the king of Syria and capture his
huge army. 12 He will be **proud** of his
victory and of the many soldiers he has
killed, but he will not continue to be
victorious.

13 "The king of Syria will go back and
gather a larger army than he had before.
When the **proper** time comes, he will
return with a large, well-equipped army.
14 Then many people will **rebel** against
the king of Egypt. And some **violent** men
from your nation, Daniel, will **rebel**
because of a **vision** they have seen, but
they will be defeated. 15 So the king of
Syria will lay siege to a fortified city and
capture it. The soldiers of Egypt will not
continue to fight; even the **best** of them
will not have **enough strength**. 16 The
Syrian invader will do with them as he
pleases, without opposition. He will stand
in the **Promised Land** and have it completely in his **power**.

17 "The king of Syria will **plan** an
expedition, using his whole army. Then,
in order to **destroy** his **enemy's** kingdom,
he will make an alliance with him and
offer him his daughter[y] in marriage; but
his **plan** will not **succeed**. 18 After that he
will attack the nations by the sea and
conquer many of them. But a foreign
leader will defeat him and put an end to
his **arrogance**; indeed he will **turn** the
arrogance of Syria's king back on him.[z]
19 The king will return to the fortresses of
his own land, but he will be defeated, and
that will be the end of him.

20 "He will be followed by another
king, who will send an officer to **oppress**
the people with **taxes** in order to

[v] *Probable text* guardian angel; *Hebrew* guardian angel. And I, in the first year of Darius the Mede.
[w] *One ancient translation* He is; *Hebrew* I am.
[x] *Some ancient translations* her child; *Hebrew* her father. [y] his daughter; *or* a young woman.
[z] *Probable text* his arrogance...on him: *Hebrew unclear.*

10.13, 21: Rev 12.7

abandon [2] Ezek 39.9; Hos 5.15
accept Ezek 20.41; Hos 14.2
advice 4.27; Hos 10.6
angel [2] 10.11; 12.1
anger 9.16; Hos 5.10
arrogant [2] 8.4; Hos 5.5
Awful Horror 9.27; 12.11
best 6.14; Hos 11.6
boast 7.8; Amos 4.5
bold Prov 7.11; Mk 15.42
challenge Jer 50.44; Amos 5.10
conquer [2] 7.21; Joel 3.17
death (3) (to death) 2.24; Hos 10.14
deceive [3] 8.23; Hos 7.3
dedicate 9.24; Zech 14.20
defend [2] 9.16; Joel 2.8
destroy [3] 9.17; Hos 1.5
determine 5.23; Amos 9.4
each other Jer 23.30; Joel 2.8

enemy [2] 6.11; Hos 8.1
enough 8.10; Hos 5.15
escape 8.4; Joel 2.3
evil [2] 9.5; Hos 4.9
final Ezek 35.5; Jn 11.4
flood [2] 9.26; Hos 5.10
follower Ps 106.18; Hab 3.13
force (1) 8.6; Mic 5.6
fright [2] 10.19; Mt 8.26
fury Ezek 38.18; Hos 8.5
gift 5.17; Hos 2.9
god (2) (other gods) [9] 6.7; Hos 3.1
God's people [3] 9.4; 12.7
help [3] 10.13; Hos 5.11
High Priest Jer 52.24; Hag 1.1
honour [2] 9.4; Hos 4.7
ignore [2] Ezek 24.14; Hos 14.9
image Ezek 23.14; Hos 3.4
last (1) 7.14; Mt 5.18
lie (2) 2.9; Hos 4.2
love 10.11; Hos 1.6
motive Prov 24.12; 1 Cor 15.32
offer [2] 9.21; Hos 3.1
oppress 7.25; Hos 5.11
peace Ezek 38.11; Hos 2.18
plan [4] Ezek 43.10; Amos 3.7
please [3] 9.13; Hos 8.13
possess Ezek 48.29; Obad 17
power [7] 9.15; Hos 1.5
prison 1.2; Amos 1.5
prize Is 44.9; Mt 22.4
promise [2] 8.9; 12.7
proper 8.12; Mt 15.2
protect 5.21; Hos 8.9
proud 8.25; Hos 13.6
punish 9.12; Hos 1.4
pure 7.9; 12.10
rage 3.13; Amos 1.14
raise 10.10; 12.7
reason Ezek 14.23; Mic 7.8
rebel [2] 9.9; Hos 7.13
religion [4] 8.12; Hos 2.11
reward 2.6; 12.13
rich [2] 10.3; Hos 4.8
right (3) Lam 3.35; Hos 5.11
rob Ezek 36.13; Hos 4.11
ruin 9.2; Hos 4.14
sacrifice 9.21; 12.11
selfish Jer 22.17; Mt 23.25
servant 9.6; Joel 2.29
serve 7.10; Hos 2.12
share Ezek 47.22; Hos 4.10
spare Ezek 33.9; Joel 3.20
strength 10.8; Hos 7.9
strong [3] 10.18; Hos 7.15
succeed (1) [2] 8.12; Zech 4.6

supreme 7.18; 1 Cor 11.3
tax Neh 5.4; Mt 17.24
Temple (1) (of God) [2] 9.17; Hos 9.4
trick Jer 20.10; Mt 2.16
true 10.1; Hos 2.19
turn [3] 9.5; Hos 2.12
victory [2] Ezek 39.13; Obad 21
violent Ezek 45.9; Hos 7.16
vision 10.1; Hos 12.10
warn 8.25; Hos 9.8
win Ezek 27.10; Hos 2.14
wisdom 5.11; Obad 8
wise [2] 5.12; 12.3
worship (1) (of God) Ezek 46.2; Hos 5.3
worship (2) (of other gods) 3.5; Hos 2.8

increase the wealth of his kingdom. In a
short time that king will be killed, but not
publicly and not in battle."

The Evil King of Syria

21 The angel went on to explain: "The
next king of Syria will be an evil man
who has no right to be king, but he will
come unexpectedly and seize power by
trickery. [22] Anyone who opposes him,
even God's High Priest, will be swept
away and wiped out. [23] By making
treaties, he will deceive other nations,
and he will grow stronger and stronger,
even though he rules only a small nation.
[24] He will invade a wealthy province without warning and will do things that none
of his ancestors ever did. Then he will
divide among his followers the goods and
property he has captured in war. He will
make plans to attack fortresses, but his
time will soon run out.

25 "He will boldly raise a large army
to attack the king of Egypt, who will
prepare to fight back with a huge and
powerful army. But the king of Egypt will
be deceived and will not be successful.
[26] His closest advisers will ruin him. Many
of his soldiers will be killed, and his army
will be wiped out. [27] Then the two kings
will sit down to eat at the same table, but
their motives will be evil, and they will
lie to each other. They will not get what
they want, because the time for it has not
yet come. [28] The king of Syria will return
home with all the loot he has captured,
determined to destroy the religion of
God's people. He will do as he pleases
and then return to his own land.

29 "Later on he will invade Egypt
again, but this time things will turn out
differently. [30] The Romans will come in
ships and oppose him, and he will be
frightened.

"Then he will turn back in a rage and
try to destroy the religion of God's
people. He will follow the advice of those
who have abandoned that religion.
[31] Some of his soldiers will desecrate the
Temple. They will stop the daily
sacrifices and set up The Awful Horror.[a]
[32] By deceit the king will win the support
of those who have already abandoned
their religion, but those who follow God
will fight back. [33] Wise leaders of the
people will share their wisdom with
many others. But for a while some of
them will be killed in battle or be burnt
to death, and some will be robbed and
made prisoners. [34] While the killing is
going on, God's people will receive a
little help, even though many who join
them will do so for selfish reasons.
[35] Some of those wise leaders will be
killed, but as a result of this the people
will be purified. This will continue until
the end comes, the time that God has set.

36 "The king of Syria will do as he
pleases. He will boast that he is greater
than any god, superior even to the
Supreme God. He will be able to do this
until the time when God punishes him.
God will do exactly what he has planned.
[37] The king will ignore the god his ancestors served, and also the god that women
love. In fact, he will ignore every god,
because he will think he is greater than
any of them. [38] Instead, he will honour the
god who protects fortresses. He will offer
gold, silver, jewels, and other rich gifts to
a god his ancestors never worshipped.
[39] To defend his fortresses, he will use
people who worship a foreign god. He
will give great honour to those who
accept him as ruler, put them into high
offices, and give them land as a reward.

40 "When the king of Syria's final hour
has almost come, the king of Egypt will
attack him, and the king of Syria will
fight back with all his power, using
chariots, horses, and many ships. He will
invade many countries, like the waters of
a flood. [41] He will even invade the
Promised Land and kill tens of
thousands, but the countries of Edom,
Moab, and what is left of Ammon will
escape. [42] When he invades all those
countries, even Egypt will not be spared.
[43] He will take away Egypt's hidden
treasures of gold and silver and its other
prized possessions. He will conquer Libya
and Sudan. [44] Then news that comes from
the east and the north will frighten him,
and he will fight furiously, killing many
people. [45] He will even set up his huge
royal tents between the sea and the
mountain on which the Temple stands.
But he will die, with no one there to help
him."

The Time of the End

12 The angel wearing linen clothes
said, "At that time the great
angel Michael, who guards your people,
will appear. Then there will be a time of
troubles, the worst since nations first
came into existence. When that time
comes, all the people of your nation
whose names are written in God's book
will be saved. [2] Many of those who have

amaze 10.8; Mt 7.28
angel [4] 11.2; Hos 12.4
Awful Horror 11.31; Mt 24.15
disgrace 9.7; Hos 4.7
enjoy 4.4; Zech 1.15
eternal [3] 9.24; Hab 1.12
exist Jer 10.11; Mt 11.23
faithful [2] 9.4; Hos 2.19

[a] THE AWFUL HORROR: *See 9.27.*

11.31: Dan 9.27, 12.11; Mt 24.15; Mk 13.14 **11.36:** 2 Thes 2.3–4; Rev 13.5–6
12.1: Mt 24.21; Mk 13.19; Rev 7.14, 12.7 **12.2:** Is 26.19; Mt 25.46; Jn 5.29

God's people 11.28; Hos 1.2
happy Lam 5.15; Jon 4.1
life (1) 3.28; Amos 2.14
name (2) (name of God, of Jesus) 9.6; Hos 4.15
persecute Jer 20.11; Amos 5.12
promise 11.16; Hos 2.20
pure 11.35; Zech 13.1
raise 11.25; Hos 5.8
reward 11.39; Mt 5.12
right (1) 9.5; Hos 14.9
rise Ezek 17.14; Amos 5.2
sacrifice 11.31; Hos 3.4
save 8.7; Hos 1.7
seal 6.17; Zech 9.11
secret 8.26; Hab 3.14
solemn Ezek 47.14; Amos 6.8
suffer 9.18; Hos 4.9
teach 1.4; Hos 4.6
trouble 9.18; Hos 2.15

already died will live again: some will
enjoy eternal life, and some will **suffer**
eternal disgrace. 3 The **wise** leaders will
shine with all the brightness of the sky.
And those who have **taught** many people
to do what is **right** will shine like the
stars for ever."
4 He said to me, "And now, Daniel,
close the book and put a **seal** on it until
the end of the **world**. Meanwhile, many
people will waste their efforts trying to
understand what is happening."
5 Then I saw two men standing by a
river, one on each bank. 6 One of them
asked the **angel** who was standing
further upstream, "How long will it be
until these **amazing** events come to an
end?"
7 The **angel raised** both hands towards
the sky and made a **solemn promise** in
the **name** of the **Eternal** God. I heard him
say, "It will be three and a half years.
When the **persecution** of **God's people**
ends, all these things will have
happened."
8 I heard what he said, but I did not
understand it. So I asked, "But, sir, how
will it all end?"
9 He answered, "You must go now,
Daniel, because these **words** are to be
kept **secret** and hidden until the end
comes. 10 Many people will be **purified**.
Those who are **wicked** will not **understand** but will go on being **wicked**; only
those who are **wise** will **understand**.
11 "From the time the daily **sacrifices**
are stopped, that is, from the time of The
Awful Horror,[b] 1,290 days will pass.
12 **Happy** are those who remain **faithful**
until 1,335 days are over!
13 "And you, Daniel, be **faithful** to the
end. Then you will die, but you will **rise** to
receive your **reward** at the end of time."

understand [4] 10.1; Hos 14.9
wicked [2] 8.23; Hos 7.1
wise [2] 11.33; Hos 14.9
word (1) 5.24; Hos 2.14
world 8.17; Amos 9.5
worst Ezek 14.21; Mt 10.36

[b] THE AWFUL HORROR: *See 9.27.*

12.4: Rev 22.10 **12.7:** Rev 10.5, 12.14 **12.10:** Rev 22.11 **12.11:** Dan 9.27, 11.31; Mt 24.15; Mk 13.14

THE BOOK OF HOSEA

INTRODUCTION

The prophet Hosea preached in the northern kingdom of Israel, after the prophet Amos, during the troubled times before the fall of Samaria in 721 B.C. He was especially concerned about the idolatry of the people and their faithlessness towards God. Hosea boldly pictured this faithlessness in terms of his own disastrous marriage to an unfaithful woman. Just as his wife Gomer turned out to be unfaithful to him, so God's people had deserted the Lord. For this, judgement would fall on Israel. Yet in the end God's constant love for his people would prevail, and he would win the nation back to himself and restore the relationship. This love is expressed in the moving words: "How can I give you up, Israel? How can I abandon you?...My heart will not let me do it! My love for you is too strong" (11.8).

Outline of Contents

---

birth Jer 31.8; Mic 4.10
choose Dan 9.25; 8.4
destroy Dan 11.17; 2.12
forgive Dan 9.9; 14.2
God's people [3] Dan 12.7; 2.1
love [2] Dan 11.37; 2.14
message Dan 10.1; 6.5
power Dan 11.2; 2.10
prosper Dan 6.28; 2.23
punish Dan 11.36; 2.13
save Dan 12.1; 2.10
unfaithful [2] Dan 9.7; 4.15
unite Dan 2.43; Mic 5.3

1 This is the **message** which the LORD
gave Hosea son of Beeri during the
time that Uzziah, Jotham, Ahaz, and
Hezekiah were kings of Judah, and Jeroboam son of Jehoash was king of Israel.

Hosea's Wife and Children

2 When the LORD first spoke to Israel
through Hosea, he said to Hosea, "Go and
get married; your wife will be **unfaithful**,
and your children will be just like her.[a]
In the same way, **my people** have left me
and become **unfaithful**."
3 So Hosea married a woman named
Gomer, the daughter of Diblaim. After
the **birth** of their first child, a son, 4 the
LORD said to Hosea, "Name him 'Jezreel,'
because it will not be long before I
punish the king of Israel for the murders
that his ancestor Jehu committed at
Jezreel.[b] I am going to put an end to
Jehu's dynasty.[x] 5 And in the Valley of
Jezreel I will at that time **destroy** Israel's
military **power**."
6 Gomer had a second child—this
time it was a girl. The LORD said to
Hosea, "Name her 'Unloved,' because I
will no longer show **love** to the people of
Israel or **forgive** them. 7 But to the people
of Judah I will show **love**. I, the LORD
their God, will **save** them, but I will not
do it by war—with swords or bows and
arrows or with horses and horsemen."
8 After Gomer had weaned her
daughter, she became pregnant again
and had another son. 9 The LORD said to
Hosea, "Name him 'Not-My-People,'
because the people of Israel are not **my
people**, and I am not their God."

Israel Is to Be Restored

10 The people of Israel will become
like the sand of the sea, more than can
be counted or measured. Now God says
to them, "You are not **my people**," but
the day is coming when he will say to
them, "You are the children of the living
God!" 11 The people of Judah and the
people of Israel will be **reunited**. They
will **choose** for themselves a single
leader, and once again they will grow
and **prosper** in their land. Yes, the day of
2 Jezreel[c] will be a great day! 1 So
call your fellow-Israelites "**God's
People**" and "Loved-by-the-Lord."

Unfaithful Gomer—Unfaithful Israel

2 My children, **plead** with your
mother—though she is no longer a wife
to me, and I am no longer her husband.
Plead with her to stop her **adultery** and
prostitution. 3 If she does not, I will **strip**
her as **naked** as she was on the day she

acknowledge [2] Dan 4.26; 4.1
adultery Ezek 33.26; 3.1
barren Jer 4.23; 9.14
celebrate Ezek 45.21; 7.5
constant Dan 9.4; 6.6
covenant Dan 9.4; 6.7
destroy [2] 1.5; 4.5
establish Dan 9.24; 1 Cor 1.6
faithful Dan 12.12; 4.1
festival Dan 7.25; 9.1

[a] get married; your wife...her; *or* marry a prostitute, and have children by her who will be just as bad as she is.
[b] JEZREEL: *At this city Jehu assassinated the king of Israel and all the rest of the royal family, and became the first king of a new dynasty (see 2 Kgs 9–10).*
[x] Jehu's dynasty; *or* the kingdom of Israel.
[c] JEZREEL: *This name in Hebrew means "God sows" and suggests growth and prosperity.*

1.1: 2 Kgs 14.23—15.7, 15.32—16.20, 18.1—20.21; 2 Chr 26.1—27.8, 28.1—32.33 **1.4:** 2 Kgs 10.11
1.10: Rom 9.26

forget Ezek 39.26; 8.14
gift Dan 11.38; 3.5
God's people [6] 1.2; 4.6
grapevine *see* **vine**
harm Dan 3.27; Amos 9.10
harvest Ezek 45.13; 10.13
hope Dan 2.9; 9.9
incense Ezek 23.41; 4.13
love [3] 1.6; 3.1
mercy [2] Dan 9.9; 14.3
naked [2] Ezek 23.10; Mic 1.8
peace Dan 11.8; Obad 7
plead [2] Dan 9.3; Lk 18.3
power 1.5; 5.4
prayer Dan 10.12; 14.2
promise Dan 12.7; 4.2
prosper 1.11; 7.1
prostitute [2] Ezek 23.3; 3.3
punish 1.4; 4.9
religion Dan 11.28; Amos 5.21
Sabbath Ezek 46.1; Amos 8.5
safe Ezek 39.26; 13.12
save 1.7; 5.14
serve Dan 11.37; 4.13
shame Dan 9.8; 10.6
strip (1) [2] Dan 4.14; 10.5
trouble Dan 12.1; Mic 2.3
true Dan 11.2; Amos 2.11
turn Dan 11.18; 3.1
vine Ezek 19.10; 10.1
vineyard [2] Ezek 28.26; 14.7
win Dan 11.32; 12.4
word (1) Dan 12.9; 10.4
worship (2) (of other gods) Dan 11.39; 4.10

was born. I will make her like a dry and **barren** land, and she will die of thirst. 4-5 I will not show **mercy** to her children; they are the children of a **shameless prostitute.**[d] She herself said, "I will go to my lovers—they give me food and water, wool and linen, olive-oil and wine."

6 So I am going to fence her in with thorn-bushes and build a wall to block her way. 7 She will run after her lovers but will not catch them. She will look for them but will not find them. Then she will say, "I am going back to my first husband—I was better off then than I am now."

8 She would never **acknowledge** that I am the one who gave her the corn, the wine, the olive-oil, and all the silver and gold that she used in the **worship of Baal.** 9 So at **harvest** time I will take back my **gifts** of corn and wine, and will take away the wool and the linen I gave her for clothing. 10 I will **strip** her **naked** in front of her lovers, and no one will be able to **save** her from my **power.** 11 I will put an end to all her festivities—her annual and monthly **festivals** and her **Sabbath celebrations**—all her **religious** meetings. 12 I will **destroy** her **grapevines** and her fig-trees, which she said her lovers gave her for **serving** them. I will **turn** her **vineyards** and orchards into a wilderness; wild animals will **destroy** them. 13 I will **punish** her for the times that she **forgot** me when she burnt **incense** to Baal and put on her jewellery to go chasing after her lovers. The LORD has spoken.

The LORD's Love for His People

14 So I am going to take her into the desert again; there I will **win** her back with **words of love.** 15 I will give back to her the **vineyards** she had and make **Trouble** Valley a door of **hope.** She will respond to me there as she did when she was young, when she came from Egypt. 16 Then once again she will call me her husband—she will no longer call me her Baal.[e] 17 I will never let her speak the name of Baal again.

18 At that time I will make a **covenant** with all the wild animals and birds, so that they will not **harm my people.** I will also remove all weapons of war from the land, all swords and bows, and will let **my people** live in **peace** and **safety.**

19 Israel, I will make you my wife;
I will be **true** and **faithful**;
I will show you **constant love** and **mercy**
and make you mine for ever.
20 I will keep my **promise** and make you mine,
and you will **acknowledge** me as LORD.
21-22 At that time I will answer the **prayers** of **my people** Israel.[f]
I will make rain fall on the earth,
and the earth will produce corn and grapes and olives.
23 I will **establish my people** in the land
and make them **prosper.**
I will show **love** to those who were called "Unloved,"
and to those who were called "Not-My-People"
I will say, "You are **my people,**"
and they will answer, "You are our God."

Hosea and the Unfaithful Woman

3 The LORD said to me, "Go again[x] and show your **love** for a woman who is **committing adultery** with a lover. You must **love** her just as I still love the people of Israel, even though they **turn to** other **gods** and like to take **offerings** of raisins to **idols.**"[g]

2 So I paid fifteen pieces of silver and 150 kilogrammes of barley to buy her. 3 I told her that for a long time she would have to wait for me without being a **prostitute** or **committing adultery**; and during this time I would wait for her. 4 In just this way the people of Israel will have to live for a long time without kings or leaders, without **sacrifices** or **sacred** stone pillars, without **idols** or **images** to use for **divination.** 5 But the time will come when the people of Israel will once again **turn to** the LORD their God, and to a descendant of David their king. Then they will **fear** the LORD and will receive his good **gifts.**

adultery [2] 2.2; 4.2
commit [2] Ezek 33.25; 4.2
divination 2 Chr 33.6
fear Dan 6.26; 10.3
gift 2.9; Zech 6.10
god (2) (other gods) Dan 11.8; 4.10
idol [2] Ezek 44.10; 4.17
image Dan 11.8; 13.2
love [2] 2.14; 4.1
offer Dan 11.17; 4.13
prostitute 2.2; 4.12
sacred Dan 9.2; 4.13
sacrifice Dan 12.11; 4.10
turn [2] 2.12; 4.7

The LORD's Accusation against Israel

4 The LORD has an **accusation** to bring against the people who live in this land. Listen, Israel, to what he says: "There is no **faithfulness** or **love** in the land, and the people do not **acknowledge** me as God. 2 They make **promises** and break them; they **lie,** murder, **steal,** and

accuse [2] Dan 6.5; 12.2
acknowledge [4] 2.8; 5.4
adultery [2] 3.1; Mal 3.5
ashamed Ezek 43.10; Mic 1.11
commit [2] 3.1; 6.9

[d] the children of a shameless prostitute; *or* as shameless as their mother, a prostitute.
[e] BAAL: *This title of the Canaanite god means "Lord"; another meaning of the word is "husband."*
[f] ISRAEL: *The Hebrew text here refers to Israel as Jezreel (see 1.4,11).*
[x] The LORD...again; *or* The LORD spoke to me again. He said, "Go".
[g] OFFERINGS OF RAISINS TO IDOLS: *Dried grapes were used in the worship of fertility gods, who were believed to give abundant harvests to their worshippers.*

2.15: Josh 7.24-26 **2.23:** Rom 9.25; 1 Pet 2.10

commit adultery. Crimes increase, and
there is one murder after another. 3 And
so the land will dry up, and everything
that lives on it will die. All the animals
and birds, and even the fish, will die."

The LORD Accuses the Priests

4 The LORD says, "Let no one accuse
the people or reprimand them—my
complaint is against you priests.[h] 5 Night
and day you blunder on, and the prophets
do no better than you. I am going to
destroy Israel, your mother. 6 My people
are doomed because they do not acknowledge me. You priests have refused to
acknowledge me and have rejected my
teaching, and so I reject you and will not
acknowledge your sons as my priests.

7 "The more of you priests there are,
the more you sin against me, and so I will
turn your honour into disgrace. 8 You
grow rich from the sins of my people,
and so you want them to sin more and
more. 9 You will suffer the same punishment as the people! I will punish you and
make you pay for the evil you do. 10 You
will eat your share of the sacrifices, but
still be hungry. You will worship the
fertility gods, but still have no children,
because you have turned away from me
to follow other gods."

The LORD Condemns Pagan Worship

11 The LORD says, "Wine, both old and
new, is robbing my people of their
senses! 12 They ask for revelations from
a piece of wood! A stick tells them what
they want to know! They have left me.
Like a woman who becomes a prostitute,
they have given themselves to other
gods. 13 At sacred places on the mountain-
tops they offer sacrifices, and on the hills
they burn incense under tall, spreading
trees, because the shade is so pleasant!

"As a result, your daughters serve as
prostitutes, and your daughters-in-law
commit adultery. 14 Yet I will not punish
them for this, because you yourselves go
off with temple prostitutes,[i] and together
with them you offer pagan sacrifices. As
the proverb says, 'A people without sense
will be ruined.'

15 "Even though you people of Israel
are unfaithful to me, may Judah not be
guilty of the same thing. Don't worship at
Gilgal or Bethaven,[j] or make promises
there in the name of the living LORD.
16 The people of Israel are as stubborn as
mules. How can I feed them like lambs in
a meadow? 17 The people of Israel are
under the spell of idols. Let them go their
own way. 18 After drinking much wine,
they delight in their prostitution,
preferring disgrace to honour. 19 They
will be carried away as by the wind, and
they will be ashamed of their pagan
sacrifices.[k]

5 "Listen to this, you priests! Pay
attention, people of Israel! Listen,
you that belong to the royal family! You
are supposed to judge with justice—so
judgement will fall on you! You have
become a trap at Mizpah, a net spread on
Mount Tabor, 2 a deep pit at Acacia City,[l]
and I will punish all of you. 3 I know what
Israel is like—she cannot hide from me.
She has been unfaithful, and her people
are unfit to worship me."

Hosea Warns against Idolatry

4 The evil that the people have done
prevents them from returning to their
God. Idolatry has a powerful hold on
them, and they do not acknowledge the
LORD. 5 The arrogance of the people of
Israel cries out against them. Their sins
make them stumble and fall, and the
people of Judah fall with them. 6 They
take their sheep and cattle to offer as
sacrifices to the LORD, but it does them
no good. They cannot find him, for he has
left them. 7 They have been unfaithful to
the LORD; their children do not belong to
him. So now they and their lands will
soon be destroyed.

War between Judah and Israel

8 Blow the war trumpets in Gibeah!
Sound the alarm in Ramah! Raise the
war-cry at Bethaven! Into battle, men of
Benjamin! 9 The day of punishment is
coming, and Israel will be ruined. People
of Israel, this will surely happen!

10 The LORD says, "I am angry
because the leaders of Judah have
invaded Israel and stolen land from her.
So I will pour out punishment on them
like a flood. 11 Israel is suffering
oppression; she has lost land that was
rightfully hers, because she insisted on
going for help to those who had none to
give.[m] 12 I will bring destruction on Israel
and ruin on the people of Judah.

13 "When Israel saw how sick she was

[h] *Probable text* my complaint is against you priests; *Hebrew* your people are like those with a complaint against the priests.
[i] TEMPLE PROSTITUTES: *These women were found in Canaanite temples, where fertility gods were worshipped. It was believed that intercourse with these prostitutes assured fertile fields and herds.*
[j] BETHAVEN: *This name means "house of evil" or "house of idolatry" and in this passage refers to the city of Bethel, a name which means "house of God." See also 5.8 and 10.8*
[k] sacrifices; *some ancient translations* altars. *Verses 17–19 in Hebrew are unclear.*
[l] *Probable text* a deep pit at Acacia City; *Hebrew unclear.*
[m] *Probable text* those who had none to give; *Hebrew* command.

and when Judah saw her own wounds,
then Israel went to Assyria to ask the
great emperor for **help**, but he could not
cure them or **heal** their wounds. 14 I will
attack the people of Israel and Judah like
a lion. I myself will tear them to pieces
and then leave them. When I drag them
off, no one will be able to **save** them.
15 "I will **abandon my people** until
they have **suffered enough** for their sins
and come looking for me. Perhaps in
their **suffering** they will try to find me."

The People's Insincere Repentance

6 The people say, "Let's return to the
LORD! He has **hurt** us, but he will be
sure to **heal** us; he has wounded us, but
he will bandage our wounds, won't he?
2 In two or three days he will revive us,
and we will live in his **presence**. 3 Let us
try to know the LORD. He will come to us
as **surely** as the day dawns, as **surely** as
the spring rains that water the earth."
4 But the LORD says, "Israel and
Judah, what am I going to do with you?
Your **love** for me disappears as quickly
as morning mist; it is like dew, that
vanishes early in the day. 5 That is why I
have sent my **prophets** to you with my
message of **judgement** and **destruction**.
What I want from you is **plain** and clear:
6 I want your **constant love**, not your
animal **sacrifices**. I would rather have
my people know me than burn **offerings**
to me.
7 "But as soon as they entered the
land at Adam,[n] they broke the **covenant**
I had made with them. 8 Gilead is a city
full of **evil** men and murderers. 9 The
priests are like a gang of **robbers** who
wait in ambush for a man. Even on the
road to the **holy** place at Shechem they
commit murder. And they do all this **evil**
deliberately! 10 I have seen a **horrible**
thing in Israel: **my people** have **defiled**
themselves by **worshipping idols**.
11 "And as for you, people of Judah, I
have set a time to **punish** you also for
what you are doing.

7 "Whenever I want to **heal my**
people Israel and make them **pros-**
perous again, all I can see is their
wickedness and the **evil** they do. They
cheat one another; they break into
houses and **steal**; they **rob** people in the
streets. 2 It never enters their heads that
I will **remember** all this **evil**; but their
sins surround them, and I cannot avoid
seeing them."

commit 4.2; Mic 7.2
constant 2.19; Mic 6.8
covenant 2.18; 8.1
defile Ezek 37.23; 9.4
destroy 5.7; 7.13
evil [2] 5.4; 7.1
God's people [2] 5.15; 7.1
heal 5.13; 7.1
holy Dan 9.20; 11.9
horror Dan 7.7; Nah 3.6
hurt Dan 6.22; Zech 11.16
idol 5.4; 8.4
judge 5.1; Joel 3.2
love [2] 4.1; 9.1
message 1.1; Joel 1.1
offer 5.6; 8.13
plain (1) Ecc 7.29; Mt 16.21
presence Dan 5.13; Jon 2.4
priest 5.1; 10.5
prophet 4.5; 9.7
punish 5.2; 7.12
rob 4.11; 7.1
sacrifice 5.6; 8.13
sure [3] 5.9; Zeph 2.9
vanish Ezek 27.34; 13.3
worship (2) (of other gods) 4.10; 8.5

anger [2] 5.10; 11.9
arrogant [2] 5.5; Zeph 2.10
bread Ezek 45.21; 8.7
celebrate 2.11; 9.1
cheat Ezek 22.7; 12.7
death (1) Ezek 44.31; 12.14
deceive Dan 11.23; 10.2
destroy 6.5; 8.4
doom 4.6; Amos 5.5
evil [4] 6.8; 9.9
false Ezek 30.13; 10.4

Conspiracy in the Palace

3 The LORD says, "People **deceive** the
king and his officers by their **evil plots**.
4 They are all treacherous and disloyal.
Their **hatred** smoulders like the fire in an
oven, which is not stirred by the baker
until the dough is ready to bake. 5 On the
day of the king's **celebration** they made
the king and his officials drunk and
foolish with wine. 6 Yes, they burned[o] like
an oven with their **plotting**. All night
their **anger** smouldered, and in the
morning it burst into flames.
7 "In the heat of their **anger** they murdered their rulers. Their kings have been
assassinated one after another, but no
one **prays** to me for **help**."

Israel and the Nations

8 The LORD says, "The people of Israel
are like a half-baked loaf of **bread**. They
rely on the nations around them 9 and do
not realize that this **reliance** on
foreigners has **robbed** them of their
strength. Their days are numbered, but
they don't even know it. 10 The **arrogance**
of the people of Israel cries out against
them. In spite of everything that has
happened, they have not returned to me,
the LORD their God. 11 Israel flits about
like a silly pigeon; first her people call on
Egypt for **help**, and then they run to
Assyria! 12 But I will spread out a net and
catch them like birds as they go by. I will
punish them for the **evil** they have done.[p]
13 "They are **doomed**! They have left
me and **rebelled** against me. They will be
destroyed. I wanted to **save** them, but
their **worship** of me was **false**. 14 They
have not **prayed** to me **sincerely**, but
instead they throw themselves down and
wail as the **heathen** do. When they **pray**
for corn and wine, they gash themselves
like **pagans**. What **rebels** they are!
15 Even though I was the one who brought
them up and made them **strong**, they
plotted against me. 16 They keep on
turning away from me to a **god** that is
powerless.[q] They are as **unreliable** as a
crooked bow. Because their leaders talk
arrogantly, they will die a **violent death**,
and the Egyptians will laugh."

The LORD Condemns Israel for Idol Worship

8 The LORD says, "Sound the alarm!
Enemies are swooping down on my
land like eagles! **My people** have broken
the **covenant** I made with them and have

fool Ezek 28.17; 9.7
god (2) (other gods) 4.10; 8.6
God's people 6.6; 8.1
hate Ezek 35.11; 8.5
heal 6.1; Mic 1.9
heathen Ezek 34.28; Amos 7.17
help [2] 5.11; 8.9
pagan 4.14; 9.1
plot (1) [3] Lam 3.60; Amos 7.10
power 5.4; 13.14
pray [3] Dan 9.3; Joel 2.17
prosper 2.23; 10.1
punish 6.11; 8.10
rebel [2] Dan 11.14; 8.1
rely [3] Dan 6.4; 2 Cor 1.9
remember Dan 9.15; 8.13
rob [2] 6.9; Amos 5.11
save 5.14; 13.10
sincere Jer 3.10; Joel 2.12
steal 5.10; Mic 2.8
strength Dan 11.15; Amos 2.14
strong Dan 11.5; 11.8
turn 4.7; 9.1
violent Dan 11.14; 12.1
wail Ezek 2.10; 10.5
wicked Dan 12.10; Joel 3.13
worship (1) (of God) 5.3; 12.5

altar Ezek 47.1; 10.1
approve Jer 44.19; Mt 16.1
bread 7.8; Amos 4.5
choose 1.11; Joel 2.32

[n] *Probable text* But...at Adam; *Hebrew* But like Adam.
[o] *One ancient translation* burned; *Hebrew* drew near.
[p] *Probable text* the evil they have done; *Hebrew* the report to their congregation.
[q] *Probable text* a god...powerless; *Hebrew unclear.*

6.6: Mt 9.13, 12.7

claim Ezek 28.2; Amos 5.14
covenant 6.7; Zech 9.11
destroy 7.13; 10.2
enemy [2] Dan 11.10; 9.8
forget 2.13; 13.6
fury Dan 11.44; 13.11
god (2) (other gods) 7.16; 9.1
God's people [3] 7.1; 9.8
hate 7.4; 9.7
help 7.7; 13.9
idol [3] 6.10; 10.5
offer 6.6; 9.4
oppress 5.11; Amos 4.1
pain Ezek 5.16; Zech 9.5
please Dan 11.16; Jon 4.6
protect Dan 11.38; 14.3
punish [2] 7.12; 9.7
reap Jer 9.22; 10.12
rebel 7.13; 9.15
reject [2] 4.6; 9.17
remember 7.2; 9.9
ripe Jer 24.2; 9.10
sacrifice 6.6; 9.4
seek Jer 29.13; Mt 7.7
sow Ezek 36.9; Mic 6.15
strange Is 28.11; Mk 16.17
stubborn 4.16; Zech 7.11
teach [2] 4.6; 11.3
useless Ezek 22.19; 10.4
worship (2) (of other gods) [2] 6.10; 9.10

rebelled against my **teaching**. [2]Even though they call me their God and **claim** that they are **my people** and that they know me, [3]they have **rejected** what is good. Because of this their **enemies** will pursue them.

4 "**My people chose** kings, but they did it on their own. They appointed leaders, but without my **approval**. They took their silver and gold and made **idols**—for their own **destruction**. [5]I **hate** the gold bull **worshipped** by the people of the city of Samaria. I am **furious** with them. How long will it be before they give up their **idolatry**? [6]An Israelite craftsman made the **idol**, and it is not a **god** at all! The gold bull **worshipped** in Samaria will be smashed to pieces! [7]When they **sow** the wind, they will **reap** a storm! A field of corn that doesn't **ripen** can never produce any **bread**. But even if it did, foreigners would eat it up. [8]Israel has become like any other nation and is as **useless** as a broken pot. [9]**Stubborn** as wild donkeys, the people of Israel go their own way. They have gone off to **seek help** from Assyria, and have paid other nations to **protect** them. [10]But now I am going to gather them together and **punish** them. Soon they will writhe in **pain**, when the emperor of Assyria **oppresses** them.

11 "The more **altars** the people of Israel build for removing sin, the more places they have for sinning! [12]I write down countless **teachings** for the people, but they **reject** them as **strange** and foreign. [13]They **offer sacrifices** to me and eat the meat of the **sacrifices**.[r] But I, the LORD, am not **pleased** with them, and now I will **remember** their sin and **punish** them for it; I will send them back to Egypt!

14 "The people of Israel have built palaces, but they have **forgotten** their own Maker. The people of Judah have built fortified cities. But I will send fire that will burn down their palaces and their cities."

Hosea Announces Punishment for Israel

abandon 5.15; 11.8
alive Dan 5.19; 14.6
barren 2.3; Joel 2.3
celebrate 7.5; Nah 1.15
dear Jer 31.20; Mt 3.17
defile 6.10; Zeph 3.4

9 People of Israel, stop **celebrating** your **festivals** like **pagans**. You have **turned away** from your God and have been **unfaithful** to him. All over the land you have sold yourselves like **prostitutes** to the **god Baal** and have **loved** the corn you thought he paid you with! [2]But soon you will not have **enough** corn and olive-oil, and there will be no wine. [3]The people of Israel will not remain in the LORD's land, but will have to go back to Egypt and will have to eat **forbidden** food[s] in Assyria. [4]In those foreign lands they will not be able to make **offerings** of wine to the LORD, or bring their **sacrifices** to him. Their food will **defile** everyone who eats it, like food eaten at funerals. It will be used only to **satisfy** their **hunger**; none of it will be taken as an **offering** to the LORD's **Temple**. [5]And when the time comes for the appointed **festivals** in **honour** of the LORD, what will they do then? [6]When the **disaster** comes and the people are **scattered**, the Egyptians will gather them up—gather them for burial there at Memphis! Their treasures of silver and the places where their homes once stood will be overgrown with **weeds** and thorn-bushes.

7 The time for **punishment** has come, the time when people will get what they **deserve**. When that happens, Israel will know it! "This **prophet**," you say, "is a **fool**. This **inspired** man is insane." You people **hate** me so much because your sin is so great. [8]God has sent me as a **prophet** to **warn his people** Israel. Yet wherever I go, you try to **trap** me like a bird. Even in God's **Temple** the people are the **prophet's enemies**. [9]They are **hopelessly evil** in what they do, just as they were at Gibeah.[t] God will **remember** their sin and **punish** them for it.

Israel's Sin and Its Consequences

10 The LORD says, "When I first found Israel, it was like finding grapes growing in the desert. When I first saw your ancestors, it was like seeing the first **ripe** figs of the season. But when they came to Mount Peor, they began to **worship Baal**, and soon became as **disgusting** as the **gods** they **loved**. [11]Israel's greatness will fly away like a bird, and there will be no more children born to them, no more women pregnant, no more children conceived. [12]But even if they did bring up children, I would take them away and not leave one **alive**. When I **abandon** these people, **terrible** things will happen to them."

13 LORD, I can see their children being hunted down[u] and killed. [14]What shall I

deserve Ezek 39.24; 12.14
disaster Ezek 35.5; Amos 3.6
disgust Ezek 44.6; 1 Pet 4.3
enemy 8.1; 11.10
enough 5.15; Joel 2.13
evil [3] 7.1; 10.13
festival [2] 2.11; Amos 5.21
fool 7.5; 13.13
forbid Ezek 18.6; Jon 3.7
god (2) (other gods) [2] 8.6; Amos 2.4
God's people [2] 8.1; 11.2
hate [2] 8.5; Amos 5.10
honour 4.7; Hab 2.16
hope 2.15; Amos 4.8
hunger 4.10; Amos 8.11
inspire Ezek 13.3; Hag 1.14
love [3] 6.4; 11.1
offer [2] 8.13; 13.2
pagan 7.14; Zeph 1.4
prophet [3] 6.5; 12.10
prostitute 4.12; Joel 3.3
punish [2] 8.10; 10.10
rebel 8.1; 11.12
reject 8.3; Zech 10.6
remember 8.13; Mic 6.5
ripe 8.7; Nah 3.12
sacrifice 8.13; 11.2
satisfy Ezek 34.18; 13.6
scatter Dan 9.7; Joel 3.2
serve 4.13; 10.5
Temple (1) (of God) [2] Dan 11.31; Joel 1.9
terrible Dan 8.24; 10.15
trap 5.1; Amos 3.5
turn 7.16; 10.12
unfaithful 5.3; Mt 5.32
warn Dan 11.24; 12.10
weed Jer 12.13; 10.4
worship (2) (of other gods) 8.5; 10.1

[r] They offer...the sacrifices; *Hebrew unclear.*
[s] FORBIDDEN FOOD: *The Law of Moses prohibited the eating of certain foods as being ritually unclean (see Lev 11).*
[t] GIBEAH: *At this city some Israelites of the tribe of Benjamin raped a Levite's concubine; this caused a civil war that almost wiped out the Benjaminites (see Judg 19–21).*
[u] *Probable text* being hunted down; *Hebrew unclear.*

9.7: Lk 21.22 **9.9:** Judg 19.1-30 **9.10:** Num 25.1-5

ask you to do to these people? Make
their women **barren**! Make them unable
to nurse their babies!

The LORD's Judgement on Israel

15 The LORD says, "All their **evil-doing**
began in Gilgal. It was there that I began
to **hate** them. And because of the **evil**
they have done, I will drive them out of
my land. I will not **love** them any more;
all their leaders have **rebelled** against
me. 16 The people of Israel are like a
plant whose roots have dried up and
which bears no fruit. They will have no
children, but even if they did, I would kill
the children so **dear** to them."

The Prophet Speaks about Israel

17 The God I **serve** will **reject his**
people, because they have not listened to
him. They will become wanderers
10 among the nations. 1 The people
of Israel were like a **grapevine**
that was full of grapes. The more **pros-**
perous they were, the more **altars** they
built. The more productive their land
was, the more beautiful they made the
sacred stone pillars they **worship**. 2 The
people whose **hearts** are **deceitful** must
now **suffer** for their sins. God will break
down their **altars** and **destroy** their
sacred pillars.

3 These people will soon be saying,
"We have no king because we did not
fear the LORD. But what could a king do
for us anyway?" 4 They utter empty
words and make **false promises** and
useless treaties. **Justice** has become
injustice, growing like poisonous **weeds**
in a ploughed field.

5 The people who live in the city of
Samaria will be **afraid** and will **mourn**
the **loss** of the gold bull[n] at Bethaven[o].
They and the **priests** who **serve** the **idol**
will **weep** over it. They will **wail** when it
is **stripped** of its golden **splendour**. 6 The
idol will be carried off to Assyria as
tribute to the great emperor. Israel will
be **disgraced** and put to **shame** because
of the **advice** she followed. 7 Her king will
be carried off, like a chip of wood on
water. 8 The hilltop **shrines** of Aven,
where the people of Israel **worship idols**,
will be **destroyed**. Thorns and **weeds** will
grow up over their **altars**. The people will
call out to the mountains, "Hide us!" and
to the hills, "Cover us!"

The LORD Pronounces Judgement on Israel

9 The LORD says, "The people of Israel
have not stopped sinning against me
since the time of their sin at Gibeah.[v] So
at Gibeah war will catch up with them.
10 I will attack[w] this sinful people and
punish them. Nations will join together
against them, and they will be **punished**
for their many sins.

11 "Israel was once like a well-trained
young cow, ready and willing to thresh
grain. But I decided to put a yoke[x] on her
beautiful neck and to harness her for
harder work. I made Judah pull the
plough and Israel pull the harrow. 12 I
said, 'Plough **new** ground for yourselves,
plant **righteousness**, and **reap** the
blessings that your **devotion** to me will
produce. It is time for you to **turn to** me,
your LORD, and I will come and pour out
blessings upon you.' 13 But instead you
planted **evil** and **reaped** its **harvest**. You
have eaten the fruit produced by your
lies.

"Because you **trusted** in your chariots[y]
and in the large number of your soldiers,
14 war will come to your people, and all
your fortresses will be **destroyed**. It will
be like the day when King Shalman
destroyed the city of Betharbel in battle,
and mothers and their children were
crushed **to death**. 15 That is what will
happen to you, people of Bethel, because
of the **terrible evil** that you have done. As
soon as the battle begins, the king of
Israel will die."

God's Love for His Rebellious People

11 The LORD says,
"When Israel was a child, I **loved**
him
and called him out of Egypt as my
son.[z]
2 But the more I[a] called to him,
the more he **turned away** from me.[b]
My people sacrificed to Baal;
they burnt **incense** to **idols**.
3 Yet I was the one who **taught** Israel to
walk.
I took **my people** up in my arms,[c]
but they did not **acknowledge** that I
took **care** of them.

[n] *Some ancient translations* bull; *Hebrew* cows.
[o] BETHAVEN: *This name means "house of evil" or "house of idolatry" and in this passage refers to the city of Bethel, a name which means "house of God." In verse 8, Bethaven is called Aven. See also 4.15 and 5.8.* [v] GIBEAH: *See 9.9.* [w] *One ancient translation* I will attack; *Hebrew* In my desire.
[x] *Probable text* put a yoke; *Hebrew* spare. [y] *One ancient translation* chariots; *Hebrew* way.
[z] him, and called him...son; *or* him; from the time he left Egypt I have called him my son.
[a] *One ancient translation* I; *Hebrew* they. [b] *One ancient translation* me; *Hebrew* them.
[c] *One ancient translation* I...my arms; *Hebrew* He...his arms.

10.8: Lk 23.30; Rev 6.16 **10.9:** Judg 19.1–30 **10.12:** Jer 4.3 **11.1:** Ex 4.22; Mt 2.15

advice Dan 11.30; Jn 18.14
afraid Dan 10.12; 13.1
altar [3] 8.11; 12.11
bless [2] Ezek 44.30; 12.4
death (3) (to death) Dan 11.33; Amos 9.4
deceive 7.3; 11.12
destroy [4] 8.4; 11.6
devote Is 53.11; Jn 2.17
disgrace 4.7; 12.14
evil [2] 9.9; Amos 5.13
false 7.13; 12.7
fear 3.5; Mic 6.9
grapevine *see* **vine**
hard Dan 10.1; Amos 9.1
harvest 2.9; Joel 3.13
heart Dan 3.23; 11.8
idol [3] 8.4; 11.2
injustice Jer 22.13; Amos 5.10
justice 5.1; 12.6
lie (2) 4.2; 11.12
loss Is 47.8; Acts 27.10
mourn Dan 10.2; Joel 1.8
new 4.11; 14.6
priest 6.9; Joel 1.9
promise 4.2; 14.2
prosper 7.1; Joel 3.1
punish [2] 9.7; 11.9
reap [2] 8.7; Mt 25.24
righteous Ezek 33.18; 14.9
sacred [2] 4.13; Joel 2.1
serve 9.17; Joel 1.13
shame 2.4; Nah 3.5
shrine Ezek 18.6
splendour Dan 2.48; Hab 3.3
strip (1) 2.3; Joel 1.7
suffer 5.11; Joel 1.18
terrible 9.12; Joel 2.11
tribute 2 Chr 36.3

trust Dan 6.23; 12.6
turn 9.1; 11.2
useless 8.8; 12.1
vine 2.12; Joel 1.7
wail 7.14; Amos 5.16
weed [2] 9.6; 13.15
weep Ezek 27.31; 12.4
word (1) 2.14; Amos 1.1
worship (2) (of other gods) [2] 9.10; 12.11

abandon 9.12; Amos 5.2
acknowledge 5.4; Mic 5.4
affection Esth 2.17; 2 Cor 9.14
anger [2] 7.6; 12.14
best Dan 11.15; Jon 4.2
care Ezek 34.2; 12.12
deceive 10.2; Obad 3
destroy [3] 10.2; 12.1
dove Ezek 7.16; Nah 2.7
enemy 9.8; Amos 3.11
faithful 4.1; Mic 7.20
God's people [4] 9.8; 12.10
heart 10.2; 14.4

4 I drew them to me with **affection** and
love.
I picked them up and held them to
my cheek;
I bent down to them and fed them.[d]

5 "They **refuse** to return to me, and so
they must return to Egypt, and Assyria
will rule them. 6 War will sweep through
their cities and break down the city
gates. It will **destroy my people** because
they do what they themselves think **best**.
7 They insist on **turning away** from me.
They will cry out because of the yoke
that is on them, but no one will lift it
from them.[e]

8 "How can I give you up, Israel?
How can I **abandon** you?
Could I ever **destroy** you as I did
Admah,
or treat you as I did Zeboiim?
My **heart** will not let me do it!
My **love** for you is too **strong**.
9 I will not **punish** you in my **anger**;
I will not **destroy** Israel again.
For I am God and not man.
I, the **Holy One**, am with you.
I will not come to you in **anger**.

10 "**My people** will follow me when I
roar like a lion at their **enemies**. They
will hurry to me from the west. 11 They
will come from Egypt, as swiftly as birds,
and from Assyria, like **doves**. I will bring
them to their homes again. I, the LORD,
have spoken."

Israel and Judah Are Condemned

12 The LORD says, "The people of
Israel have surrounded me with **lies** and
deceit, and the people of Judah are still
rebelling against me, the **faithful** and
12 **holy** God. 1 Everything that the
people of Israel do from morning
to night is **useless** and **destructive**.
Treachery and **acts** of **violence** increase
among them. They make treaties with
Assyria and do business with Egypt."

2 The LORD has an **accusation** to bring
against the people of Judah; he is also
going to **punish** Israel for the way her
people **act**. He will pay them back for
what they have done. 3 Their ancestor
Jacob **struggled** with his twin brother
Esau while the two of them were still in
their mother's **womb**; when Jacob grew
up, he fought against God—4 he fought
against an **angel** and **won**. He **wept** and
asked for a **blessing**. And at Bethel God
came to our ancestor Jacob and spoke
with him.[f] 5 This was the LORD God
Almighty—the LORD is the **name** by
which he is to be **worshipped**. 6 So now,
descendants of Jacob, **trust** in your God
and return to him. Be **loyal** and **just**, and
wait **patiently** for your God to **act**.

Further Words of Judgement

7 The LORD says, "The people of Israel
are as **dishonest** as the Canaanites; they
love to **cheat** their customers with **false**
scales. 8 'We are **rich**,' they say. 'We've
made a **fortune**. And no one can **accuse**
us of getting **rich dishonestly**.' 9 But I, the
LORD your God who led you out of Egypt,
I will make you live in tents again, as you
did when I came to you in the desert.

10 "I spoke to the **prophets** and gave
them many **visions**, and through the
prophets I gave **my people warnings**.
11 Yet **idols** are **worshipped** in Gilead, and
those who **worship** them will die. Bulls
are **sacrificed** in Gilgal, and the **altars**
there will become piles of stone in the
open fields."

12 Our ancestor Jacob had to **flee** to
Mesopotamia, where, in order to get a
wife, he worked for another man and
took **care** of his **sheep**. 13 The LORD sent a
prophet to **rescue** the people of Israel
from **slavery** in Egypt and to take **care** of
them. 14 The people of Israel have made
the LORD **bitterly angry**; they **deserve**
death for their **crimes**. The LORD will
punish them for the **disgrace** they have
brought on him.

Final Judgement on Israel

13 In the past, when the tribe of
Ephraim spoke, the other tribes
of Israel were **afraid**; they looked up to
Ephraim. But the people sinned by **worshipping** Baal, and for this they will die.
2 They still keep on sinning by making
metal **images** to **worship-idols** of silver,
designed by **human minds**, made by
human hands. And then they say, "**Offer**
sacrifices to them!" How can men **kiss**
those **idols**—idols in the shape of bulls![g]
3 And so these people will disappear like
morning mist, like the dew that **vanishes**
early in the day. They will be like chaff
which the wind blows from the threshing-
place, like smoke from a chimney.

4 The LORD says, "I am the LORD your
God, who led you out of Egypt. You have
no God but me. I **alone** am your **saviour**.

[d] *Verse 4 in Hebrew is unclear.* [e] *Verse 7 in Hebrew is unclear.*
[f] *Some ancient translations* him; *Hebrew* us.
[g] *Probable text* And then they...bulls; *Hebrew unclear.*

11.8: Deut 29.23 **12.3:** Gen 25.26 **12.3-4:** Gen 32.24-26 **12.4:** Gen 28.10-22 **12.9:** Lev 23.42-43
12.12: Gen 29.1-20 **12.13:** Ex 12.50-51

plague Ps 106.30; Amos 4.10
power 7.16; Joel 1.6
proud Dan 11.12; Amos 6.8
punish 12.2; Joel 2.13
rebel 11.12; Mic 1.5
refuse (1) 11.5; Amos 6.3
rescue 12.13; Mic 5.8
sacrifice 12.11; Amos 4.4
safe 2.18; Amos 6.1
satisfy 9.4; Joel 2.19
save [2] 7.13; 14.3
Saviour Is 49.7; Hab 3.18
value Is 58.13; Lk 16.15
vanish 6.4; Obad 16
weed 10.4; Mic 7.4
womb 12.3; Jn 3.4
world of the dead [2] Ezek 32.18; Amos 9.2
worship (2) (of other gods) [2] 12.11; Amos 2.8

5 I took **care** of you in a dry, desert land.
6 But when you entered the good land,
you became full and **satisfied**, and then
you grew **proud** and **forgot** me. 7 So I will
attack you like a lion. Like a leopard I
will lie in wait along your path. 8 I will
attack you like a bear that has lost her
cubs, and I will tear you open. Like a lion
I will **devour** you on the spot, and will
tear you to pieces like a wild animal.

9 "I will **destroy** you, people of Israel!
Then who can **help** you? [h] 10 You asked
for a king and for leaders, but how can
they **save** the nation? [i] 11 In my **anger** I
have given you kings, and in my **fury** I
have taken them away.

12 "Israel's sin and **guilt** are on record,
and the records are **safely** stored away.
13 Israel has a chance to live, but is too
foolish to take it—like a child about to be
born, who **refuses** to come out of the
womb. 14 I will not **save** this people from
the **world of the dead** or **rescue** them
from the **power** of **death**. Bring on[k] your
plagues, death! Bring on[k] your **destruction, world of the dead**! I will no longer
have **pity** for this people. 15 Even though
Israel flourishes like **weeds**,[l] I will send
a hot east wind from the desert, and it
will dry up their springs and wells. It
will take away everything of **value**.
16 Samaria must be **punished** for **rebelling**
against me. Her people will die in war;
babies will be dashed to the ground, and
pregnant women will be ripped open."

Hosea's Plea to Israel

accept Dan 11.39; Amos 5.22
alive 9.12; Amos 5.15
anger 13.11; Amos 1.11
bless 12.4; Joel 2.14
care 13.5; Joel 1.11
forgive 1.6; Joel 2.13

14 Return to the LORD your God,
people of Israel. Your sin has
made you **stumble** and fall. 2 Return to
the LORD, and let this **prayer** be your
offering to him: "**Forgive** all our sins and
accept our **prayer**, and we will **praise** you
as we have **promised**. 3 Assyria can never
save us, and war-horses cannot **protect**
us. We will **never again** say to our **idols**
that they are our God. O LORD, you show
mercy to those who have no one else to
turn to."

The LORD Promises New Life for Israel

4 The LORD says,
"I will bring **my people** back to me.
I will **love** them **with all my heart**;
no longer am I **angry** with them.
5 I will be to the people of Israel
like rain in a dry land.
They will blossom like flowers;
they will be firmly rooted
like the trees of Lebanon.
6 They will be **alive** with **new** growth,
and beautiful like olive-trees.
They will be fragrant
like the cedars of Lebanon.
7 Once again they will live under my
protection.
They will grow corn
and be fruitful like a **vineyard**.
They will be as famous as the wine
of Lebanon.
8 The people of Israel[n] will have nothing
more to do with **idols**;
I will answer their **prayers** and take
care of them;
Like an evergreen tree I will **shelter**
them;
I am the **source** of all their
blessings."

Conclusion

9 May those who are **wise understand**
what is written here, and may they take
it to **heart**. The LORD's **ways** are **right**,
and **righteous** people live by following
them, but sinners **stumble** and fall
because they **ignore** them.

God's people 12.10; Joel 2.18
heart [2] 11.8; Joel 2.13
idol [2] 13.2; Amos 8.14
ignore Dan 11.37; 2 Pet 3.5
love 12.7; Amos 4.5
mercy 2.4; Joel 2.13
never again Ezek 45.9; Mic 4.3
new 10.12; Joel 1.5
offer 13.2; Joel 1.9
praise Dan 5.4; Joel 2.26
prayer [3] 2.21; Mic 3.4
promise 10.4; Joel 2.13
protect [2] 8.9; Nah 1.7
right (1) Dan 12.3; Joel 2.23
righteous 10.12; Amos 5.24
save 13.10; Joel 2.32
shelter Ezek 45.25; Jon 4.5
source Ezek 47.11; Jn 1.4
stumble [2] 5.5; Nah 2.5
turn 11.2; Joel 1.3
understand Dan 12.4; Mt 13.13
vineyard 2.12; Joel 1.11
way (3) Dan 8.25; Lk 3.18
wise Dan 12.3; Mic 6.9

[h] *One ancient translation* who can help you?; *Hebrew* in me is your help.
[i] *Verse 10 in Hebrew is unclear.* [k] *Some ancient translations* Bring on; *Hebrew* I will be.
[l] *Probable text* like weeds; *Hebrew* among brothers.
[n] *One ancient translation* The people of Israel; *Hebrew* Israel, I.

13.5–6: Deut 8.11–17 **13.10:** 1 Sam 8.5–6 **13.11:** 1 Sam 10.17–24, 15.26 **13.14:** 1 Cor 15.55

THE BOOK OF JOEL

INTRODUCTION

Little is known about the prophet Joel, and it is not clear just when he lived. But it seems likely that the book comes from the fifth or fourth century B.C. during the time of the Persian Empire. Joel describes a terrible invasion of locusts and a devastating drought in Palestine. In these events he sees a sign of the coming Day of the Lord, a time when the Lord will punish those who oppose his righteous will. The prophet conveys the Lord's call to the people to repent, and his promise of restoration and blessing for his people. Noteworthy is the promise that God will send his spirit upon all the people, men and women, young and old alike.

Outline of Contents

---

1 This is the LORD's **message** to Joel son of Pethuel.

The People Mourn the Destruction of the Crops

2 Pay attention, you older people;
everyone in Judah, listen.
Has anything like this ever happened
in your time or the time of your fathers?
3 Tell your children about it;
they will tell their children,
who in **turn** will tell the next generation.

4 Swarm after swarm of locusts settled on the crops;
what one swarm left, the next swarm **devoured**.
5 Wake up and **weep**, you drunkards;
cry, you wine-drinkers;
the grapes for making **new** wine have been **destroyed**.

6 An army of locusts has attacked our land;
they are **powerful** and too many to count;
their teeth are as sharp as those of a lion.
7 They have **destroyed** our **grapevines**
and chewed up our fig-trees.
They have **stripped** off the bark,
till the branches are white.

8 Cry, you people, like a girl who **mourns** the **death**
of the man she was going to marry.
9 There is no corn or wine to **offer** in the **Temple**;
the **priests mourn** because they have no **offerings** for the LORD.
10 The fields are bare;
the ground **mourns**
because the corn is **destroyed**,
the grapes are dried up,
and the olive-trees are withered.

11 **Grieve**, you farmers;
cry, you that take **care** of the **vineyards**,
because the wheat, the barley,
yes all the crops are **destroyed**.
12 The **grapevines** and fig-trees have withered;
all the fruit-trees have wilted and died.
The **joy** of the people is gone.
13 Put on **sackcloth** and **weep**,
you **priests** who **serve** at the **altar**!
Go into the **Temple** and **mourn** all night!
There is no corn or wine to **offer** your God.
14 Give orders for a **fast**;
call an assembly!
Gather the leaders
and all the people of Judah
into the **Temple** of the LORD your God
and cry out to him.
15 The **day of the LORD** is near;
the day when the **Almighty** brings **destruction**.
What **terror** that day will bring!

1.6: Rev 9.8 **1.15:** Is 13.6

Almighty Hos 12.5; Amos 3.13
altar Hos 12.11; 2.17
care Hos 14.8; Amos 3.2
Day of the Lord Ezek 13.5; 2.1
death (1) Hos 13.14; Jon 1.14
destroy [6] Hos 13.9; 2.20
devour Hos 13.8; 1 Pet 5.8
distress Dan 5.9; Amos 8.8
fast (2) Dan 9.3; 2.12
flock Ezek 36.37; Zeph 2.7
grapevine *see* **vine**
grief Ezek 28.12; Amos 8.10
helpless Ezek 38.11; Amos 2.7
joy [2] Dan 6.23; 2.21
message Hos 6.5; 2.28
mourn [4] Hos 10.5; 2.12
new Hos 14.6; 2.16
offer [3] Hos 14.2; 2.14
power Hos 13.14; Mic 3.8
priest [2] Hos 10.5; 2.17
ruin Hos 5.9; 3.19
sackcloth Dan 9.3; Amos 8.10
seed Ezek 36.9; Mt 6.26
serve Hos 10.5; 2.17
sheep Hos 12.12; Amos 3.12
strip (1) Hos 10.5; Mic 3.3
suffer Hos 10.2; Obad 13
Temple (1) (of God) [4] Hos 9.4; 2.17
terror Ezek 32.24; Nah 2.6
turn Hos 14.3; 2.6
vine [2] Hos 10.1; Mic 1.6
vineyard Hos 14.7; 3.18

weep [2] Hos 12.4; 2.12

16 We look on **helpless** as our crops are
destroyed.
There is no **joy** in the **Temple** of our
God.
17 The **seeds** die in the dry earth.
There is no grain to be stored,
and so the empty granaries are in
ruins.
18 The cattle are bellowing in **distress**
because there is no pasture for
them;
the **flocks of sheep** also **suffer.**
19 I cry out to you, LORD,
because the pastures and trees are
dried up,
as though a fire had burnt them.
20 Even the wild animals cry out to you
because the streams have become
dry.

The Locusts as a Warning of the Day of the LORD

2 Blow the trumpet; sound the alarm
on Zion, God's **sacred** hill.[a]
Tremble, people of Judah!
The **day of the LORD** is coming soon.
2 It will be a **dark** and **gloomy** day,
a black and **cloudy** day.
The great army of locusts advances
like **darkness** spreading over the
mountains.
There has never been anything like it,
and there never will be again.

3 Like fire they eat up the plants.
In front of them the land is like the
Garden of Eden,
but behind them it is a **barren**
desert.
Nothing **escapes** them.
4 They look like horses;
they run like war-horses.
5 As they leap on the tops of the
mountains,
they rattle like chariots;
they crackle like dry grass on fire.
They are lined up like a great army
ready for battle.
6 As they approach, everyone is
terrified;
every face **turns** pale.
7 They attack like warriors;
they climb the walls like soldiers.
They all keep marching straight ahead
and do not **change** direction
8 or get in **each other's** way.
They swarm through **defences**,
and nothing can stop them.
9 They rush against the city;
they run over the walls;
they climb up the houses
and go in through the windows like
thieves.

10 The earth shakes as they advance;
the sky **trembles.**
The sun and the moon grow **dark**,
and the stars no longer shine.
11 The LORD thunders **commands** to his
army.
The troops that **obey** him
are many and **mighty.**
How **terrible** is the **day of the LORD**!
Who will survive it?

A Call to Repentance

12 "But even now," says the LORD,
"**repent sincerely** and return to me
with **fasting** and **weeping** and
mourning.
13 Let your broken **heart** show your
sorrow;
tearing your clothes is not **enough.**"

Come back to the LORD your God.
He is **kind** and full of **mercy**;
he is **patient** and keeps his **promise**;
he is always ready to **forgive** and not
punish.
14 Perhaps the LORD your God will
change his mind
and **bless** you with **abundant** crops.
Then you can **offer** him corn and wine.

15 Blow the trumpet on Mount Zion;
give orders for a **fast** and call an
assembly!
16 Gather the people together;
prepare them for a **sacred** meeting;
bring the old people;
gather the children
and the babies too.
Even **newly** married couples
must leave their room and come.
17 The **priests, serving** the LORD
between the **altar** and the entrance
of the **Temple**,
must **weep** and **pray**:
"Have **pity** on your people, LORD.
Do not let other nations **despise** us
and **mock** us
by saying, 'Where is your God?' "

God Restores Fertility to the Land

18 Then the LORD showed **concern** for his
land;
he had **mercy** on **his people.**
19 He answered them:
"Now I am going to give you
corn and wine and olive-oil,
and you will be **satisfied.**

[a] SACRED HILL: *Mount Zion (see Zion in Word List).*

2.4-5: Rev 9.7-9 **2.10:** Rev 8.12 **2.11:** Rev 6.17

abundant Ezek 27.12; Zech 14.14
afraid [2] Hos 13.1; Amos 3.6
altar 1.13; Amos 3.14
barren Hos 9.14
bless Hos 14.8; Mic 2.9
blood [2] Ezek 45.19; Zeph 1.17
body Dan 10.6; Amos 4.10
change [2] Dan 10.8; Amos 4.13
choose Hos 8.4; Amos 2.11
cloud [2] Dan 7.13; Nah 1.3
command Dan 9.4; Amos 2.4
concern Ezek 36.21; Mic 3.1
dark [4] Dan 2.22; 3.15
Day of the Lord [3] 1.15; 3.14
dead Ezek 39.4; Amos 4.10
defend Dan 11.1; 3.16
despise [4] Ezek 25.6; Amos 2.4
destroy 1.5; Amos 2.9
dream Dan 7.1; Zech 10.2
each other Dan 11.27; Mt 12.25
enough Hos 9.2; Amos 4.8
escape [2] Dan 11.41; Amos 2.14
fast (2) [2] 1.14; Jon 3.5
forgive Hos 14.2; Amos 7.2
glad [2] Ezek 25.4; Amos 8.10
gloom Prov 17.22; Amos 5.20
God's people [3] Hos 14.4; 3.2
heart Hos 14.4; Nah 2.10
help Hos 13.9; Amos 5.2
joy 1.12; Nah 3.19

kind Jer 52.31; Jon 4.2
mercy [2] Hos 14.3; Amos 1.11
message 1.1; Amos 2.12
might Dan 10.4; Amos 4.4
mind (1) Hos 13.2; Amos 7.3
mock Ezek 36.4; Mt 20.19
mourn 1.8; Amos 5.16
new 1.5; Mic 4.7
obey Dan 7.27; Jon 3.3
offer 1.9; Amos 4.5
patient Hos 12.6; Jon 4.2
pity Hos 13.14; Jon 4.11
plenty [2] Ezek 36.29; 3.18
praise Hos 14.2; Jon 2.9
pray Hos 7.7; Jon 1.6
priest 1.9; Amos 7.10
proclaim Dan 4.14; Amos 3.8
promise Hos 14.2; Amos 4.2
punish Hos 13.16; Amos 1.3
rejoice Ezek 35.14; Zeph 3.14
repent Ezek 21.13; Jon 3.5
right (1) Hos 14.9; Amos 5.14
sacred [2] Hos 10.1; 3.17
satisfy [2] Hos 13.6; Mic 6.14
save Hos 14.3; Amos 2.14
servant Dan 11.6; Amos 3.7
serve 1.13; Amos 2.4
sincere Hos 7.14; Lk 20.20
sorrow Ezek 21.6; Amos 5.16
Spirit (1) (God's Spirit) [2] Ezek 43.5; Mic 3.8
Temple (1) (of God) 1.9; 3.18
terrible [2] Hos 10.15; Amos 3.2
terrify Dan 10.7; Obad 9
thief Jer 2.26; Obad 5
tremble [2] Dan 10.10; 3.16
turn [2] 1.3; Amos 1.2
vision Hos 12.10; Amos 7.1
warn Hos 12.10; Amos 3.13
weep [2] 1.5; Mic 1.10
wonder (1) Dan 6.27; Mt 21.15

Other nations will no longer **despise**
you.
20 I will remove the locust army that
came from the north
and will drive some of them into the
desert.
Their front ranks will be driven into
the Dead Sea,
their rear ranks into the
Mediterranean.
Their **dead bodies** will stink.
I will **destroy** them because of all they
have done to you.

21 "Fields, don't be **afraid**,
but be **joyful** and **glad**
because of all the LORD has done for
you.
22 Animals, don't be **afraid**.
The pastures are green;
the trees bear their fruit,
and there are **plenty** of figs and
grapes.

23 "Be **glad**, people of Zion,
rejoice at what the LORD your God
has done for you.
He has given you the **right** amount
of autumn rain;[b]
he has poured down the winter rain
for you
and the spring rain as before.
24 The threshing-places will be full of
corn;
the pits beside the presses will
overflow with wine and olive-oil.
25 I will give you back what you lost
in the years when swarms of locusts
ate your crops.
It was I who sent this army against
you.
26 Now you will have **plenty** to eat, and
be **satisfied**.
You will **praise** the LORD your God,
who has done **wonderful** things for
you.
My people will never be **despised**
again.
27 Then, Israel, you will know that I am
among you,
and that I, the LORD, am your God
and there is no other.
My people will never be **despised**
again.

The Day of the LORD

28 "Afterwards I will pour out my **spirit**
on everyone:
your sons and daughters will
proclaim my **message**;
your old men will have **dreams**,
and your young men will see **visions**.
29 At that time I will pour out my **spirit**
even on **servants**, both men and
women.

30 "I will give **warnings** of that day
in the sky and on the earth;
there will be **bloodshed**, fire, and
clouds of smoke.
31 The sun will be **darkened**,
and the moon will **turn** red as **blood**
before the great and **terrible day of
the LORD** comes.
32 But all who ask the LORD for **help** will
be **saved**.
As the LORD has said,
'Some in Jerusalem will **escape**;
those whom I **choose** will survive.' "

God Will Judge the Nations

3 The LORD says,
"At that time I will **restore**
the **prosperity** of Judah and
Jerusalem.
2 I will gather all the nations
and bring them to the **Valley of
Judgement**.
There I will **judge** them
for all they have done to **my people**.
They have **scattered** the Israelites in
foreign countries
and divided up Israel, my land.
3 They threw dice to decide
who would get the **captives**.
They sold boys and girls into **slavery**
to pay for **prostitutes** and wine.
4 "What are you trying to do to me,
Tyre, Sidon, and all the regions of
Philistia? Are you trying to pay me back
for something? If you are, I will quickly
pay you back!
5 You have taken my
silver and gold and carried my **rich**
treasures into your **temples**.
6 You have
taken the people of Judah and Jerusalem
far from their own country and sold
them to the Greeks.
7 Now I am going to
bring them out of the places to which you
have sold them. I will do to you what you
have done to them.
8 I will let your sons
and daughters be sold to the people of
Judah; they will sell them to the far-off
Sabeans. I, the LORD, have spoken.

9 "Make this **announcement** among the
nations:
'Prepare for war;

announce Dan 3.4; Amos 3.9
captive Ezek 39.28; Amos 9.4
conquer Dan 11.18; Amos 9.12
dark 2.2; Amos 5.8
Day of the Lord 2.1; Amos 5.18
defend 2.8; Amos 3.11
God's people [2] 2.18; Amos 2.9
guilty Hos 13.12; Mic 1.5
harvest Hos 10.13; Amos 9.13
innocent Dan 6.22; Jon 4.11
judge [5] Hos 6.5; Amos 4.12
plenty 2.22; Zech 8.12
prosper Hos 10.1; Zeph 2.7
prostitute Hos 9.1; Amos 7.17
restore Dan 9.17; Amos 9.11
rich Hos 12.8; Mic 6.12
ruin 1.17; Amos 3.15
sacred [2] 2.1; Obad 16
scatter Hos 9.6; Nah 3.18
slave Hos 12.13; Amos 1.6
spare Dan 11.42; Jon 1.6
Temple (1) (of God) 2.17; Amos 9.1
temple (2) (of other gods) Dan 1.2; Amos 2.8
tremble 2.1; Mic 7.17
vineyard 1.11; Amos 4.9
weak Dan 10.16; Amos 2.7
wicked Hos 7.1; Jon 1.2

[b] right amount of autumn rain; *or* autumn rain because he is just.

2.28-32: Acts 2.17-21 **2.31:** Mt 24.29; Mk 13.24-25; Lk 21.25; Rev 6.12-13 **2.32:** Rom 10.13
3.4-8: Is 14.29-31, 23.1-18; Jer 47.1-7; Ezek 25.15—28.26; Amos 1.6-10; Zeph 2.4-7; Zech 9.1-7; Mt 11.21-22; Lk 10.13-14

call your warriors;
gather all your soldiers and march!
10 Hammer the points of your ploughs
into swords
and your pruning-knives into spears.
Even the **weak** must fight.
11 Hurry[c] and come,
all you surrounding nations,
and gather in the valley.' "

Send down, O LORD, your army to
attack them.

12 "The nations must get ready
and come to the **Valley of Judgement**.
There I, the LORD, will sit to **judge**
all the surrounding nations.
13 They are very **wicked**;
cut them down like corn
at **harvest** time;
crush them as grapes are crushed
in a full winepress
until the wine runs over."

14 Thousands and thousands
are in the **Valley of Judgement**.
It is there that the **day of the LORD**
will soon come.
15 The sun and the moon grow **dark**,
and the stars no longer shine.

God Will Bless His People

16 The LORD roars from Mount Zion;
his voice thunders from Jerusalem;
earth and sky **tremble**.
But he will **defend his people**.
17 "Then, Israel, you will know that I am
the LORD your God.
I live on Zion, my **sacred** hill.
Jerusalem will be a **sacred** city;
foreigners will never **conquer** it
again.

18 "At that time the mountains will be
covered with **vineyards**,
and cattle will be found on every
hill;
there will be **plenty** of water for all
the streams of Judah.
A stream will flow from the **Temple** of
the LORD,
and it will water the Valley of
Acacia.

19 "Egypt will become a desert,
and Edom a **ruined** waste,
because they attacked the land of
Judah
and killed its **innocent** people.
20-21 I will avenge[e] those who were killed;
I will not **spare** the **guilty**.
But Judah and Jerusalem will be
inhabited for ever,
and I the LORD, will live on Mount
Zion."

[c] *Probable text* Hurry; *Hebrew* Help.
[e] *Some ancient translations* avenge; *Hebrew* declare innocent.

3.10: Is 2.4; Mic 4.3 **3.13:** Rev 14.14–16, 19–20, 19.15 **3.16:** Amos 1.2

THE BOOK OF
AMOS

INTRODUCTION

Amos was the first prophet in the Bible whose message was recorded at length. Although he came from a town in Judah, he preached to the people of the northern kingdom of Israel, about the middle of the eighth century B.C. It was a time of great prosperity, notable religious piety, and apparent security. But Amos saw that prosperity was limited to the wealthy, and that it fed on injustice and on oppression of the poor. Religious observance was insincere, and security more apparent than real. With passion and courage he preached that God would punish the nation. He called for justice to "flow like a stream," and said, "Perhaps the Lord will be merciful to the people of this nation who are still left alive" (5.15).

Outline of Contents

---

anger Hos 14.4; Jon 3.9
cruel Dan 5.20; Nah 3.19
exile [2] Dan 6.13; 5.5
friend Dan 2.13; Obad 7
mercy Joel 2.13; 5.15
prison Dan 11.33; Mt 4.12
punish [6] Joel 2.13; 2.1
rage Dan 11.30; Lk 6.11
reveal Hos 4.12; 3.7
shepherd Ezek 34.2; 3.12
slave Joel 3.3; 2.6
turn Joel 2.6; 5.8
word (1) Hos 10.4; Zech 1.13

1 These are the **words** of Amos, a
shepherd from the town of Tekoa.
Two years before the earthquake, when
Uzziah was king of Judah and Jeroboam
son of Jehoash was king of Israel, God
revealed to Amos all these things about
Israel.
2 Amos said,

"The LORD roars from Mount Zion;
his voice thunders from Jerusalem.
The pastures dry up,
and the grass on Mount Carmel
turns brown."

God's Judgement on Israel's Neighbours

Syria

3 The LORD says, "The people of
Damascus have sinned again and again,
and for this I will certainly **punish** them.
They treated the people of Gilead with
savage **cruelty**. 4 So I will send fire upon
the palace built by King Hazael and I will
burn down the fortresses of King
Benhadad. 5 I will smash the city gates of
Damascus and remove the inhabitants of
the Valley of Aven and the ruler of
Betheden. The people of Syria will be
taken away as **prisoners** to the land of
Kir."

Philistia

6 The LORD says, "The people of Gaza
have sinned again and again, and for this
I will certainly **punish** them. They
carried off a whole nation and sold them
as **slaves** to the people of Edom. 7 So I will
send fire upon the city walls of Gaza and
burn down its fortresses. 8 I will remove
the rulers of the cities of Ashdod and
Ashkelon. I will **punish** the city of Ekron,
and all the Philistines who are left will
die."

Tyre

9 The LORD says, "The people of Tyre
have sinned again and again, and for this
I will certainly **punish** them. They
carried off a whole nation into **exile** in
the land of Edom, and did not keep the
treaty of **friendship** they had made. 10 So I
will send fire upon the city walls of Tyre
and burn down its fortresses."

Edom

11 The LORD says, "The people of
Edom have sinned again and again, and
for this I will certainly **punish** them. They
hunted down their brothers,[b] the Israelites, and showed them no **mercy**. Their
anger had no limits, and they never let it
die. 12 So I will send fire upon the city of
Teman and burn down the fortresses of
Bozrah."

Ammon

13 The LORD says, "The people of

[b] THEIR BROTHERS: *The Israelites were descended from Jacob, who was the brother of Esau, the ancestor of the Edomites.*

1.1: 2 Kgs 15.1-7; 2 Chr 26.1-23; 2 Kgs 14.23-29 **1.2:** Joel 3.16 **1.3-5:** Is 17.1-3; Jer 49.23-27; Zech 9.1
1.6-8: Is 14.29-31; Jer 47.1-7; Ezek 25.15-17; Joel 3.4-8; Zeph 2.4-7; Zech 9.5-7
1.9-10: Is 23.1-18; Ezek 26.1—28.19; Joel 3.4-8; Zech 9.1-4; Mt 11.21-22; Lk 10.13-14
1.11-12: Is 34.5-17, 63.1-6; Jer 49.7-22; Ezek 25.12-14, 35.1-15; Obad 1-14; Mal 1.2-5
1.13-15: Jer 49.1-6; Ezek 21.28-32, 25.1-7; Zeph 2.8-11

Ammon have sinned again and again, and for this I will certainly **punish** them. In their wars for more territory they even ripped open pregnant women in Gilead. 14 So I will send fire upon the city walls of Rabbah and burn down its fortresses. Then there will be shouts on the day of battle, and the fighting will **rage** like a storm. 15 Their king and his officers will go into **exile**."

Moab

2 The LORD says, "The people of Moab have sinned again and again, and for this I will certainly **punish** them. They **dishonoured** the bones of the king of Edom by burning them to **ashes**. 2 I will send fire upon the land of Moab and burn down the fortresses of Kerioth. The people of Moab will die in the noise of battle while soldiers are shouting and trumpets are sounding. 3 I will kill the ruler of Moab and all the leaders of the land."

Judah

4 The LORD says, "The people of Judah have sinned again and again, and for this I will certainly **punish** them. They have **despised** my **teachings** and have not kept my **commands**. They have been led astray by the same **false gods** that their ancestors **served**. 5 So I will send fire upon Judah and burn down the fortresses of Jerusalem."

God's Judgement on Israel

6 The LORD says, "The people of Israel have sinned again and again, and for this I will certainly **punish** them. They sell into **slavery honest** men who cannot pay their **debts**, **poor** men who cannot **repay** even the price of a pair of sandals. 7 They trample[c] down the **weak** and **helpless** and push the **poor** out of the way. A man and his father have intercourse with the same **slave-girl**, and so **profane** my **holy name**. 8 At every **place of worship** men sleep on clothing that they have taken from the **poor** as **security** for **debts**. In the **temple** of their God they drink wine which they have taken from those who **owe** them money.

9 "And yet, **my people**, it was for your **sake** that I totally **destroyed** the Amorites, men who were as tall as cedar-trees and as **strong** as oaks. 10 I brought you out of Egypt, led you through the desert for forty years, and gave you the land of the Amorites to be your own. 11 I **chose** some of your sons to be **prophets**, and some of your young men to be **Nazirites**.[e] Isn't this **true**, people of Israel? I, the LORD, have spoken. 12 But you made the **Nazirites** drink wine, and ordered the **prophets** not to speak my **message**. 13 And now I will crush you to the ground, and you will **groan** like a cart loaded with corn. 14 Not even fast runners will **escape**; **strong** men will lose their **strength**, and soldiers will not be able to **save** their own **lives**. 15 Bowmen will not stand their ground, fast runners will not **get away**, and men on horses will not **escape** with their **lives**. 16 On that day even the bravest soldiers will drop their weapons and run." The LORD has spoken.

3 People of Israel, listen to this **message** which the LORD has spoken about you, the entire nation that he brought out of Egypt: 2 "Of all the nations on earth, you are the only one I have known and **cared** for. That is what makes your sins so **terrible**, and that is why I must **punish** you for them."

The Prophet's Task

3 Do two men start travelling together without arranging to meet?

4 Does a lion roar in the forest unless he has found a **victim**?

Does a young lion growl in his den unless he has caught something?

5 Does a bird get caught in a **trap** if the **trap** has not been baited?

Does a trap spring unless something sets it off?

6 Does the war trumpet sound in a city without making the people **afraid**?

Does **disaster strike** a city unless the LORD sends it?

7 The **Sovereign** LORD never does anything without **revealing** his **plan** to his **servants**, the **prophets**.

8 When a lion roars, who can avoid being **afraid**?

When the **Sovereign** LORD speaks, who can avoid **proclaiming** his **message**?

The Doom of Samaria

9 **Announce** to those who live in the palaces of Egypt and Ashdod: "Gather together in the hills surrounding Samaria and see the great disorder and the **crimes** being committed there."

10 The LORD says, "These people fill their mansions with things taken by **crime** and **violence**. They don't even know how to be **honest**. 11 And so an

worship (2) (of other gods) Hos 13.1; 5.26

ash Dan 9.3; Jon 3.6
choose Joel 2.32; Mic 4.2
command Joel 2.11; 6.11
debt [2] Prov 27.13; 8.6
despise Joel 2.17; 6.8
destroy Joel 2.20; 3.11
dishonour Ezek 22.16; Obad 10
escape [2] Joel 2.3; 9.1
false Hos 12.7; 8.5
get away Ezek 17.15; 9.1
god (2) (other gods) Hos 9.1; 5.26
God's people Joel 3.2; 7.4
groan Ezek 30.24; Mic 4.10
helpless Joel 1.16; Zech 1.11
holy Hos 11.9; 4.2
honest Ezek 45.10; 3.10
life (1) [2] Dan 12.2; 6.1
message Joel 2.28; 3.1
name (2) (name of God, of Jesus) Hos 12.5; 4.13
Nazirite [2] Judg 16.17
owe Job 22.6; Mt 18.24
place of worship Ezek 28.18; 7.13
poor [3] Dan 4.27; 4.1
profane Ezek 44.7; Eph 5.4
prophet [2] Hos 12.10; 3.7
punish [3] 1.3; 3.2
repay Jer 51.24; Zech 9.12
sake Ezek 36.22; Mt 10.18
save Joel 2.32; 4.11
secure Ezek 38.11; Zeph 3.13
serve Joel 2.17; Jon 1.16
slave [2] 1.6; 8.6
strength Hos 7.9; Mic 5.4
strong [2] Hos 11.8; 6.13
teach Hos 11.3; Mic 4.2
temple (2) (of other gods) Joel 3.5; 7.13
true Hos 2.19; Hab 2.3
weak Joel 3.10; 4.1

afraid [2] Joel 2.21; Jon 1.16
Almighty Joel 1.15; 4.13
altar [2] Joel 2.17; 9.1
announce Joel 3.9; Nah 1.15
care Joel 1.11; 7.14
crime [2] Hos 12.14; 5.12
defend Joel 3.16; Mic 5.5
destroy [4] 2.9; 4.11
disaster Hos 9.6; 6.3
enemy Hos 11.10; 6.8
honest 2.6; Mic 7.2
luxury Ezek 27.24; 6.4
message [2] 2.12; 8.11
plan Dan 11.17; Mic 2.1
proclaim Joel 2.28; Jon 3.2
prophet 2.11; 7.12
punish [2] 2.1; 4.12
reveal 1.1; Mic 1.1
ruin Joel 3.19; 6.6
servant Joel 2.29; Nah 2.7
sheep Joel 1.18; Jon 3.7
shepherd 1.1; 7.15
Sovereign [3] Ezek 48.29; 4.2
strike Dan 2.34; 9.1
terrible Joel 2.11; 5.12
trap [2] Hos 9.8; Obad 7
victim Dan 7.7
violent Hos 12.1; Jon 1.4
warn Joel 2.30; 6.8

[c] trample; *Hebrew unclear.*
[e] NAZIRITES: *Israelites who showed their devotion to God by taking vows not to drink wine or beer or cut their hair or touch corpses (see Num 6.1–8).*

2.1–3: Is 15.1—16.14, 25.10–12; Jer 48.1–47; Ezek 25.8–11; Zeph 2.8–11 **2.9:** Deut 3.8–11 **2.11:** Num 6.1–8

enemy will surround their land, **destroy**
their **defences**, and plunder their
mansions."
12 The LORD says, "As a **shepherd**
recovers only two legs or an ear of a
sheep that a lion has eaten, so only a few
will survive of Samaria's people, who
now recline on **luxurious** couches.[f]
13 Listen now, and **warn** the descendants
of Jacob," says the **Sovereign** LORD
Almighty. 14 "On the day when I **punish**
the people of Israel for their sins, I will
destroy the **altars** of Bethel. The corners
of every **altar** will be broken off and will
fall to the ground. 15 I will **destroy** winter
houses and summer houses. The houses
decorated with ivory will fall in **ruins**;
every large house will be **destroyed**."

4 Listen to this, you women of
Samaria, who grow fat like the well-
fed cows of Bashan, who **ill-treat** the
weak, **oppress** the **poor**, and **demand** that
your husbands keep you supplied with
liquor! 2 As the **Sovereign** LORD is **holy**,
he has **promised**, "The days will come
when they will drag you away with
hooks; every one of you will be like a fish
on a hook. 3 You will be dragged to the
nearest break in the wall and thrown
out."[g]

Israel's Failure to Learn

4 The **Sovereign** LORD says, "People of
Israel, go to the **holy** place in Bethel and
sin, if you must! Go to Gilgal and sin with
all your **might**! Go ahead and bring
animals to be **sacrificed** morning after
morning, and bring your **tithes** every
third day. 5 Go ahead and **offer** your
bread in **thanksgiving** to God, and **boast**
about the extra **offerings** you bring! This
is the kind of thing you **love** to do.
6 "I was the one who brought **famine**
to all your cities, yet you did not come
back to me. 7 I held back the rain when
your crops **needed** it most. I sent rain on
one city, but not on another. Rain fell on
one field, but another field dried up.
8 **Weak** with thirst, the people of several
cities went to a city where they **hoped** to
find water, but there was not **enough** to
drink. Still you did not come back to me.
9 "I sent a scorching wind to dry up
your crops. The locusts ate up all your
gardens and **vineyards**, your fig-trees
and olive-trees. Still you did not come
back to me.
10 "I sent a **plague** on you like the one
I sent on Egypt. I killed your young men
in battle and took your horses away. I
filled your nostrils with the stink of **dead**
bodies in your camps. Still you did not
come back to me.
11 "I **destroyed** some of you as I destroyed Sodom and Gomorrah. Those of
you who survived were like a burning
stick **saved** from a fire. Still you did not
come back to me," says the LORD. 12 "So
then, people of Israel, I am going to
punish you. And because I am going to do
this, get ready to face my **judgement**!"

13 God is the one who made the
mountains
and **created** the winds.
He makes his thoughts known to man;
he **changes** day into night.
He walks on the heights of the earth.
This is his **name**: the LORD God
Almighty!

A Call to Repentance

5 Listen, people of Israel, to this
funeral song which I sing over you:

2 **Virgin** Israel has fallen,
Never to **rise** again!
She lies **abandoned** on the ground,
And no one **helps** her up.

3 The **Sovereign** LORD says, "A city in
Israel sends out a thousand soldiers, but
only a hundred return; another city
sends out a hundred, but only ten come
back."
4 The LORD says to the people of
Israel, "Come to me, and you will live.
5 Do not go to Beersheba to **worship**. Do
not try to find me at Bethel—Bethel will
come to nothing. Do not go to Gilgal—
her people are **doomed** to **exile**."
6 Go to the LORD, and you will live. If
you do not go, he will sweep down like
fire on the people of Israel. The fire will
burn up the people of Bethel, and no one
will be able to **put it out**. 7 You are
doomed, you that twist **justice** and **cheat**
people out of their **rights**!

8 The LORD made the stars,
the Pleiades and Orion.
He **turns darkness** into daylight,
and day into night.
He calls for the waters of the sea
and pours them out on the earth.
His **name** is the LORD.
9 He brings **destruction** on the **mighty**
and their strongholds.

10 You people **hate** anyone who

[f] luxurious couches; *Hebrew unclear.*
[g] *Hebrew has an additional word, the meaning of which is unclear.*

3.14: 2 Kgs 23.15 **4.11:** Gen 19.24 **5.8:** Job 9.9, 38.31

Almighty 3.13; 5.14
boast Dan 11.36; 6.13
body Joel 2.20; 6.10
bread Hos 8.7; 8.11
change Joel 2.7; 7.3
create Ezek 28.13; 7.1
dead Joel 2.20; 5.16
demand Dan 2.10; 5.25
destroy 3.11; 5.9
enough Joel 2.13; 6.13
famine Ezek 36.29; 8.11
holy [2] 2.7; 7.9
hope Hos 9.9; Mic 5.8
ill-treat Ezek 34.22; Mt 17.12
judge Joel 3.2; Obad 15
love Hos 14.4; 5.15
might Joel 2.11; 5.9
name (2) (name of God, of Jesus) 2.7; 5.8
need Ezek 44.28; 8.4
offer [2] Joel 2.14; 5.22
oppress Hos 8.10; 5.11
plague Hos 13.14; Lk 21.11
poor 2.6; 5.11
promise Joel 2.13; Jon 1.16
punish 3.2; 5.17
sacrifice Hos 13.2; 5.25
save 2.14; Mic 4.10
Sovereign [2] 3.7; 5.3
thank Jer 33.11; Mt 11.25
tithe Neh 13.5; Mal 3.8
vineyard Joel 3.18; 5.11
weak [2] 2.7; 7.2

abandon Hos 11.8; Jon 2.8
accept [2] Hos 14.2; Zeph 3.2
alive Hos 14.6; Jon 2.6
Almighty [3] 4.13; 6.8
bribe Ezek 16.33; Mic 3.11
burnt-offering Ezek 44.11
challenge Dan 11.2
cheat Hos 12.7; 8.5
claim Hos 8.2; Mic 3.11
court (1) [3] Dan 7.10; Zech 8.16
crime 3.9; Hab 2.12
dark [3] Joel 3.15; 8.9
Day of the Lord [2] Joel 3.14; Zeph 1.14
dead 4.10; 6.10
demand 4.1; Nah 2.13
destroy 4.11; 7.9
doom [2] Hos 7.13; Mic 2.10
evil [3] Hos 10.13; 8.7
exile [2] 1.9; 6.7
festival Hos 9.1; 8.10
gloom Joel 2.2; Zeph 1.15
god (2) (other gods) 2.4; 8.14
grain-offering Ezek 46.5
hate [3] Hos 9.7; 6.8
help Joel 2.32; 6.1
image [2] Hos 13.2; Mic 1.7
injustice Hos 10.4; Mic 3.10
justice [4] Hos 12.6; 6.12
light (1) [2] Dan 5.5; Mic 7.8
long (2) Jer 44.14; Zech 8.2
love 4.5; Jon 4.2
mercy 1.11; Jon 4.2
might 4.4; Jon 1.13
mourn Joel 2.12; 6.6
name (2) (name of God, of Jesus) [2] 4.13; 6.10
offer [2] 4.5; Jon 1.16
oppress 4.1; 6.14

persecute Dan 12.7; Mt 5.10
poor [2] 4.1; 8.4
prevent Hos 5.4; Mal 1.10
punish 4.12; 7.4
put out Ezek 32.8; Mt 12.20
religion Hos 2.11; Mt 6.1
right (1) [2] Joel 2.23; 6.12
right (3) Hos 5.11; Obad 17
righteous Hos 14.9; Hab 1.4
rise Dan 12.13; 8.8
rob Hos 7.1; Obad 10
sacrifice 4.4; Jon 1.16
sorrow Joel 2.13; Mic 1.8
Sovereign [2] 4.2; 6.8
terrible [2] 3.2; 6.1
truth Dan 10.20; Zech 8.16
turn 1.2; 6.12
vineyard [2] 4.9; 9.14
virgin Ezek 44.22; Mt 1.23
wail [2] Hos 10.5; Mic 1.8
worship (1) (of God) Hos 12.5; 7.9
worship (2) (of other gods) 2.8; Jon 2.8

challenges injustice and speaks the whole **truth** in **court**. [11]You have **oppressed** the **poor** and **robbed** them of their grain. And so you will not live in the fine stone houses you build or drink wine from the beautiful **vineyards** you plant. [12]I know how **terrible** your sins are and how many **crimes** you have committed. You **persecute** good men, take **bribes**, and **prevent** the **poor** from getting **justice** in the **courts**. [13]And so, keeping quiet in such **evil** times is the clever thing to do!

14 Make it your aim to do what is **right**, not what is **evil**, so that you may live. Then the LORD God **Almighty** really will be with you, as you **claim** he is. [15]**Hate** what is **evil**, **love** what is **right**, and see that **justice** prevails in the **courts**. Perhaps the LORD will be **merciful** to the people of this nation who are still left **alive**.

16 And so the **Sovereign** LORD **Almighty** says, "There will be **wailing** and cries of **sorrow** in the city streets. Even farmers will be called to mourn the **dead** along with those who are paid to **mourn**. [17]There will be **wailing** in all the **vineyards**. All this will take place because I am coming to **punish** you." The LORD has spoken.

18 How **terrible** it will be for you who **long** for the **day of the LORD**! What good will that day do you? For you it will be a day of **darkness** and not of **light**. [19]It will be like a man who runs from a lion and meets a bear! Or like a man who comes home and puts his hand on the wall—only to be bitten by a snake! [20]The **day of the LORD** will bring **darkness** and not **light**; it will be a day of **gloom**, without any brightness.

21 The LORD says, "I **hate** your **religious festivals**; I cannot stand them! [22]When you bring me **burnt-offerings** and **grain-offerings**, I will not **accept** them; I will not **accept** the animals you have fattened to bring me as **offerings**. [23]Stop your noisy songs; I do not want to listen to your harps. [24]Instead, let **justice** flow like a stream, and **righteousness** like a river that never goes dry.

25 "People of Israel, I did not **demand sacrifices** and **offerings** during those forty years that I led you through the desert. [26]But now, because you have **worshipped images** of Sakkuth, your king **god**, and of Kaiwan, your star god, you will have to carry those **images** [27]when I take you into **exile** in a land beyond Damascus," says the LORD, whose **name** is **Almighty** God.

The Destruction of Israel

6 How **terrible** it will be for you that have such an easy **life** in Zion and for you that feel **safe** in Samaria—you great men of this great nation Israel, you to whom the people go for **help**! [2]Go and look at the city of Calneh. Then go on to the great city of Hamath and on down to the Philistine city of Gath. Were they any better than the kingdoms of Judah and Israel? Was their territory larger than yours? [3]You **refuse** to **admit** that a day of **disaster** is coming, but what you do only brings that day closer. [4]How **terrible** it will be for you that stretch out on your **luxurious** couches, **feasting** on veal and **lamb**! [5]You like to compose songs, as David did, and play them on harps. [6]You drink wine by the bowlful and use the finest perfumes, but you do not **mourn** over the **ruin** of Israel. [7]So you will be the first to go into **exile**. Your **feasts** and **banquets** will come to an end.

8 The **Sovereign** LORD **Almighty** has given this **solemn warning**: "I **hate** the **pride** of the people of Israel; I **despise** their **luxurious** mansions. I will give their capital city and everything in it to the **enemy**."

9 If there are ten men left in a family, they will die. [10]The **dead** man's relative, the one in charge of the funeral, will take the **body** out of the house. The relative will call to whoever is still left in the house, "Is anyone else there with you?"

A voice will answer, "No!"

Then the relative will say, "Be quiet! We must be careful not even to mention the **LORD's name**."[h]

11 When the LORD gives the **command**, houses large and small will be smashed to pieces. [12]Do horses gallop on rocks? Do men plough the sea with oxen? Yet you have **turned justice** into poison, and **right** into **wrong**.

13 You **boast** about capturing the town of Lodebar.[i] You **boast**, "We were **strong enough** to take Karnaim."[j]

14 The LORD God **Almighty** himself says, "People of Israel, I am going to send a foreign army to occupy your country. It will **oppress** you from Hamath Pass in the north to the brook of the Arabah in the south."

admit (1) Dan 5.21; Mt 23.31
Almighty [2] 5.14; 9.5
banquet Dan 5.1
boast [2] 4.5; Zeph 2.8
body 4.10; 8.3
command 2.4; 9.1
dead 5.16; 8.3
despise 2.4; Obad 2
disaster 3.6; Obad 13
enemy 3.11; 9.4
enough 4.8; 7.12
exile 5.5; 7.11
feast [2] Ezek 46.11; Mt 8.11
hate 5.10; Mic 3.2
help 5.2; 7.7
justice 5.7; Mic 3.1
lamb Hos 4.16; Mk 14.12
life (1) 2.14; Jon 1.6
luxury [2] 3.12; Lk 7.25
mourn 5.16; 8.3
name (2) (name of God, of Jesus) 5.8; 9.6
oppress 5.11; Hab 3.14
proud Hos 13.6; Obad 3
refuse (1) Hos 13.13; Zech 7.11
right (1) 5.14; Mic 2.7
ruin 3.15; 7.9
safe Hos 13.12; Mic 2.2
solemn Dan 12.7; Nah 1.15
Sovereign 5.3; 7.1
strong 2.9; Jon 1.4
terrible [2] 5.12; Mic 2.1
turn 5.8; 8.10
warn 3.13; Mic 7.4
wrong Dan 9.5; Mic 3.9

[h] *Verse 10 in Hebrew is unclear.* [i] LODEBAR: *This name sounds like the Hebrew for "nothing."*
[j] KARNAIM: *The name of this small town means "horns," a symbol of strength.*

5.21–22: Is 1.11–14 **5.25–27:** Acts 7.42–43

care 3.2; Nah 1.7
change [3] 4.13; 8.2
create 4.13; Zech 12.1
destroy [2] 5.9; 8.4
enough 6.13; Jon 4.9
exile [2] 6.7; Obad 20
forgive Joel 2.13; Mic 6.11
God's people [3] 2.9; 8.2
heathen Hos 7.14; Mt 20.25
help 6.1; 9.4
holy 4.2; 8.5
mind (1) [3] Joel 2.14; 8.2
place of worship 2.8; Acts 17.23
plot (1) Hos 7.3; Nah 1.9
preach Lam 2.14; Mic 2.6
priest Joel 2.17; Mic 3.11
prophecy [4] Dan 9.22; Obad 1
prophet [2] 3.7; Mic 2.11
prostitute Joel 3.3; Mic 1.7
punish [2] 5.17; 8.2
ruin 6.6; 9.11
share Hos 4.10; Mic 2.5
shepherd 3.12; Mic 4.8
Sovereign [4] 6.8; 8.1
speech Dan 10.15; Mt 12.19
temple (2) (of other gods) 2.8; Nah 1.14
vision [4] Joel 2.28; 8.1
weak [2] 4.1; Obad 2
worship (1) (of God) 5.5; Jon 1.9

A Vision of Locusts

7 I had a **vision** from the **Sovereign**
LORD. In it I saw him **create** a
swarm of locusts just after the king's
share of the hay had been cut and the
grass was starting to grow again. 2 In my
vision I saw the locusts eat up every
green thing in the land, and then I said,
"**Sovereign** LORD, **forgive** your people!
How can they survive? They are so
small and **weak**!"
3 The LORD **changed his mind** and
said, "What you saw will not take place."

A Vision of Fire

4 I had another **vision** from the
Sovereign LORD. In it I saw him preparing to **punish his people** with fire. The
fire burnt up the great ocean under the
earth, and started to burn up the land.
5 Then I said, "Stop, **Sovereign** LORD!
How can your people survive? They are
so small and **weak**!"
6 The LORD **changed his mind** again
and said, "This will not take place
either."

A Vision of a Plumb-Line

7 I had another **vision** from the Lord.
In it I saw him standing beside a wall
that had been built with the **help** of a
plumb-line, and there was a plumb-line in
his hand. 8 He asked me, "Amos, what do
you see?"
"A plumb-line," I answered.
Then he said, "I am using it to show
that **my people** are like a wall that is out
of line. I will not **change my mind** again
about **punishing** them. 9 The places
where Isaac's descendants **worship** will
be **destroyed**. The **holy** places of Israel
will be left in **ruins**. I will bring the
dynasty of King Jeroboam to an end."

Amos and Amaziah

10 Amaziah, the **priest** of Bethel, then
sent a report to King Jeroboam of Israel:
"Amos is **plotting** against you among the
people. His **speeches** will **destroy** the
country. 11 This is what he says: 'Jeroboam will die in battle, and the people of
Israel will be taken away from their land
into **exile**.'"
12 Amaziah then said to Amos, "That's
enough, **prophet**! Go on back to Judah
and do your **preaching** there. Let *them*
pay you for it. 13 Don't **prophesy** here at
Bethel any more. This is the king's **place
of worship**, the national **temple**."
14 Amos answered, "I am not the kind
of **prophet** who **prophesies** for pay. I am
a herdsman, and I take **care** of fig-trees.
15 But the LORD took me from my work as
a **shepherd** and ordered me to come and
prophesy to his people Israel. 16 So now
listen to what the LORD says. You tell me
to stop **prophesying**, to stop raving
against the people of Israel. 17 And so,
Amaziah, the LORD says to you, 'Your
wife will become a **prostitute** on the
streets, and your children will be killed in
war. Your land will be divided up and
given to others, and you yourself will die
in a **heathen** country. And the people of
Israel will certainly be taken away from
their own land into **exile**.'"

A Vision of a Basket of Fruit

8 I had another **vision** from the
Sovereign LORD. In it I saw a basket
of fruit. 2 The LORD asked, "Amos, what
did you see?"
"A basket of fruit," I answered.
The LORD said to me, "The end[l] has
come for **my people** Israel. I will not
change my mind again about **punishing**
them. 3 On that day the songs in the
palace will become cries of **mourning**.
There will be **dead bodies** everywhere.
They will be thrown out in silence."[m]

Israel's Doom

4 Listen to this, you that trample on
the **needy** and try to **destroy** the **poor** of
the country. 5 You say to yourselves, "We
can hardly wait for the **holy** days to be
over so that we can sell our corn. When
will the **Sabbath** end, so that we can start
selling again? Then we can overcharge,
use **false** measures, and tamper with the
scales to **cheat** our customers. 6 We can
sell **worthless** wheat at a high price.
We'll find a **poor** man who can't pay his
debts, not even the price of a pair of
sandals, and we'll buy him as a **slave**."
7 The LORD, the God of Israel, has
sworn, "I will never **forget** their **evil**
deeds. 8 And so the earth will quake, and
everyone in the land will be in **distress**.
The whole country will be shaken; it will
rise and fall like the River Nile. 9 The
time is coming when I will make the sun
go down at noon and the earth grow **dark**
in daytime. I, the **Sovereign** LORD, have
spoken. 10 I will **turn** your **festivals** into
funerals and **change** your **glad** songs into
cries of **grief**. I will make you **shave** your
heads and wear **sackcloth**, and you will
be like parents **mourning** for their only
son. That day will be **bitter** to the end.
11 "The time is coming when I will
send **famine** on the land. People will be
hungry, but not for **bread**; they will be
thirsty, but not for water. They will

bitter Hos 12.14; Obad 16
body 6.10; Nah 3.3
bread 4.5; Hag 2.12
change [2] 7.3; Jon 3.9
cheat 5.7; Mal 1.14
dark 5.8; Mic 7.8
dead 6.10; Jon 4.3
debt 2.6; Hab 2.6
destroy 7.9; 9.4
distress Joel 1.18; Obad 12
evil 5.13; Jon 3.8
false 2.4; Mic 6.10
famine 4.6; Mt 24.7
festival 5.21; Nah 1.15
forget Hos 13.6; Zeph 3.7
glad Joel 2.21; Obad 12
god (2) (other gods) [2] 5.26; Jon 1.5
God's people 7.4; 9.10
grief Joel 1.11; Zech 11.3
holy 7.9; Jon 2.4
hunger [2] Hos 9.4; Mic 6.14
idol Hos 14.3; Jon 2.8
message [2] 3.1; Obad 15
mind (1) 7.3; Jon 3.9
mourn [2] 6.6; 9.5
need 4.7; Zeph 3.11
poor [2] 5.11; Mic 6.12
punish 7.4; Obad 8
rise [2] 5.2; 9.5
Sabbath Hos 2.11; Mt 12.1
sackcloth Joel 1.13; Jon 3.5
shave Ezek 44.20; Acts 18.18
slave 2.6; Mic 6.4
Sovereign [3] 7.1; 9.5
swear [2] Ezek 44.12 Zeph 1.5
turn 6.12; Mic 3.9
vision 7.1; Mic 3.6
worthless Jer 51.18; 9.9

[l] END: *The Hebrew words for "end" and "fruit" sound alike.* [m] out in silence; *or* out. Silence!

hunger and thirst for a message from the
LORD. I, the Sovereign LORD, have
spoken. 12 People will wander from the
Dead Sea to the Mediterranean and then
on from the north to the east. They will
look everywhere for a message from the
LORD, but they will not find it. 13 On that
day even healthy young men and women
will collapse from thirst. 14 Those who
swear by the idols of Samaria, who say,
'By the god of Dan,' or, 'By the god of
Beersheba'—those people will fall and
not rise again."

The Lord's Judgements

9 I saw the Lord standing by the altar.
He gave the command: "Strike the
tops of the temple columns so hard that
the whole porch will shake. Break them
off and let them fall on the heads of the
people. I will kill the rest of the people in
war. No one will get away; not one will
escape. 2 Even if they dig their way down
to the world of the dead, I will catch
them. Even if they climb up to heaven, I
will bring them down. 3 If they hide on
the top of Mount Carmel, I will search for
them and catch them. If they hide from
me at the bottom of the sea, I will command the sea-monster[o] to bite them. 4 If
they are taken away into captivity by
their enemies, I will order them to be put
to death. I am determined to destroy
them, not to help them."

5 The Sovereign LORD Almighty touches
the earth,
and it quakes;
all who live there mourn.
The whole world rises and falls like the
River Nile.
6 The LORD builds his home in the
heavens,
and over the earth he puts the dome
of the sky.
He calls for the waters of the sea
and pours them out on the earth.
His name is the LORD!

7 The LORD says, "People of Israel, I
think as much of the people of Sudan as I
do of you. I brought the Philistines from
Crete and the Syrians from Kir, just as I
brought you from Egypt. 8 I, the
Sovereign LORD, am watching this sinful
kingdom of Israel, and I will destroy it
from the face of the earth. But I will not
destroy all the descendants of Jacob.
9 "I will give the command and shake
the people of Israel like corn in a sieve. I
will shake them among the nations to
remove all who are worthless. 10 The
sinners among my people will be killed
in war—all those who say, 'God will not
let any harm come near us.' "

The Future Restoration of Israel

11 The LORD says, "A day is coming
when I will restore the kingdom of
David, which is like a house fallen into
ruins. I will repair its walls and restore it.
I will rebuild it and make it as it was long
ago. 12 And so the people of Israel will
conquer what is left of the land of Edom
and all the nations that were once mine,"
says the LORD, who will cause this to
happen.

13 "The days are coming," says the LORD,
"when corn will grow faster than it
can be harvested,
and grapes will grow faster than the
wine can be made.
The mountains will drip with sweet
wine,
and the hills will flow with it.
14 I will bring my people back to their
land.
They will rebuild their ruined cities
and live there;
they will plant vineyards and drink
the wine;
they will plant gardens and eat what
they grow.
15 I will plant my people on the land I
gave them,
and they will not be pulled up
again."
The LORD your God has spoken.

[o] SEA-MONSTER: *It was believed that the sea was inhabited by a great monster. This creature, like all others, was regarded as under God's control.*

9.11-12: Acts 15.16-18

Almighty 6.8; Mic 4.4
altar 3.14; Hag 2.14
captive Joel 3.3; Mic 2.4
command [3] 6.11; Jon 1.17
conquer Joel 3.17; Obad 7
death (3) (to death) Hos 10.14; Nah 3.10
destroy [3] 8.4; Obad 8
determine Dan 11.28; Zech 1.6
dome Ezek 10.1
enemy 6.8; Obad 5
escape 2.14; Obad 14
get away 2.15; Jon 1.3
God's people [3] 8.2; Obad 13
hard Hos 10.11; Zech 7.12
harm Hos 2.18; Mic 3.11
harvest Joel 3.13; Mic 6.15
heaven [2] Dan 8.10; Jon 1.9
help 7.7; Jon 1.5
monster Ezek 29.3
mourn 8.3; Mic 1.8
name (2) (name of God, of Jesus) 6.10; Hag 2.23
restore [2] Joel 3.1; Nah 2.2
rise 8.8; Jon 4.8
ruin [2] 7.9; Obad 12
Sovereign [2] 8.1; Obad 15
strike 3.6; Hab 3.13
Temple (1) (of God) Joel 3.18; Jon 2.4
vineyard 5.11; Mic 4.4
watch Dan 10.8; Mic 4.8

world Dan 12.4; Mic 4.13
world of the dead Hos 13.14; Jon 2.2
worthless 8.6; Jon 2.8

THE BOOK OF OBADIAH

INTRODUCTION

This short book comes from some undetermined time after the fall of Jerusalem in 586 B.C., when Edom, Judah's age-old enemy to the south-east, not only rejoiced over the fall of Jerusalem, but took advantage of Judah's plight to loot the city and help the invader. Obadiah prophesied that Edom would be punished and defeated, along with other nations that were the enemies of Israel.

Outline of Contents

The punishment of Edom 1–14
The day of the Lord 15–21

---

1 This is the **prophecy** of Obadiah—what the **Sovereign** LORD said about the nation of Edom.

The LORD Will Punish Edom

The LORD has sent his messenger to
the nations,
and we have heard his **message**:
"Get ready! Let us go to war against
Edom!"
2 The LORD says to Edom,
"I will make you **weak**;
everyone will **despise** you.
3 Your **pride** has **deceived** you.
Your capital is a fortress of solid rock;
your home is high in the mountains,
and so you say to yourself,
'Who can ever pull me down?'
4 Even though you make your home
as high as an eagle's nest,
so that it seems to be among the
stars,
yet I will pull you down.

5 "When **thieves** come at night,
they take only what they want.
When people gather grapes,
they always leave a few.
But your **enemies** have wiped you out
completely.
6 Descendants of Esau, your treasures
have been looted.
7 Your allies have **deceived** you;
they have driven you from your
country.
People who were at **peace** with you
have now **conquered** you.
Those **friends** who ate with you have
laid a **trap** for you;
they say of you, 'Where is all that
cleverness he had?'
8 "On the day I **punish** Edom,
I will **destroy** their clever men
and wipe out all their **wisdom**.
9 The fighting men of Teman will be
terrified,
and every soldier in Edom will be
killed.

Reasons for Edom's Punishment

10 "Because you **robbed** and killed
your brothers,[a] the descendants of
Jacob,
you will be **destroyed** and
dishonoured for ever.
11 You stood aside on that day
when **enemies** broke down their
gates.
You were as **bad** as those **strangers**
who carried off Jerusalem's wealth
and divided it among themselves.
12 You should not have gloated
over the misfortune of your brothers
in Judah.
You should not have been **glad**
on the day of their **ruin**.
You should not have laughed at them
in their **distress**.
13 You should not have entered the city
of **my people**
to gloat over their **suffering**
and to seize their **riches**
on the day of their **disaster**.
14 You should not have stood at the cross-
roads
to catch those trying to **escape**.
You should not have handed them
over to the **enemy**

[a] YOUR BROTHERS: *The Israelites were descended from Jacob, who was the brother of Esau, the ancestor of the Edomites.*

1–14: Is 34.5–17, 63.1–6; Jer 49.7–22; Ezek 25.12–14, 35.1–15; Amos 1.11–12; Mal 1.2–5

bad Ezek 34.17; Zeph 3.7
bitter [2] Amos 8.10; Zeph 1.14
conquer [2] Amos 9.12; Mic 5.6
cup [2] Dan 5.2; Hab 2.16
deceive [2] Hos 11.12; Mic 2.11
despise Amos 6.8; Mic 6.16
destroy [3] Amos 9.4; Jon 3.4
disaster Amos 6.3; Mic 1.12
dishonour Amos 2.1; Mal 1.12
distress [2] Amos 8.8; Jon 2.2
enemy [3] Amos 9.4; Mic 1.7
escape [2] Amos 9.1; Mic 2.3
exile [2] Amos 7.11; Mic 1.11
friend Amos 1.9; Mic 7.5
glad Amos 8.10; Hab 3.18
God's people [2] Amos 9.10; Mic 1.9
judge Amos 4.12; Mic 7.3
message Amos 8.11; Jon 3.2
peace Hos 2.18; Mic 3.5
possess [2] Dan 11.43; Zech 2.12
prophecy Amos 7.13; Mic 2.11
proud Amos 6.8; Mic 2.3
punish [3] Amos 8.2; Jon 1.14
riches Jer 17.11; Mt 6.19
right (3) Amos 5.7; Jon 4.4
rob Amos 5.11; Mic 2.9
ruin Amos 9.11; Mic 1.6
sacred [2] Joel 3.17; Mic 5.13
Sovereign Amos 9.5; Mic 1.2
stranger Ezek 16.32; Mt 25.35
suffer Joel 1.18; Mic 1.9
terrify Joel 2.6; Jon 1.5
thief Joel 2.9; Zech 5.3
trap Amos 3.5; Mt 16.1
vanish Hos 13.3; 1 Cor 14.9
victory Dan 11.12; Nah 1.15
weak Amos 7.2; Hab 1.4
wisdom Dan 11.33; Mt 11.19

on the day of their **distress**.

God Will Judge the Nations

15 "The day is near when I, the LORD,
will **judge** all nations.
Edom, what you have done
will be done to you.
You will get back what you have given.
16 **My people** have drunk a **bitter cup** of **punishment**
on my **sacred hill**.[b]
But all the surrounding nations will drink
a still more **bitter cup** of **punishment**;
they will drink it all and **vanish** away.

The Victory of Israel

17 "But on Mount Zion some will **escape**,
and it will be a **sacred** place.
The people of Jacob will **possess**
the land that is theirs by **right**.
18 The people of Jacob and of Joseph will be like fire;
they will **destroy** the people of Esau
as fire burns stubble.
No descendant of Esau will survive.
I, the LORD, have spoken.

19 "People from southern Judah will occupy Edom;
those from the western foothills will capture Philistia;
Israelites will **possess** the territory of Ephraim and Samaria;
the people of Benjamin will take Gilead.
20 The army of **exiles** from northern Israel
will return and **conquer** Phoenicia
as far north as Zarephath.
The **exiles** from Jerusalem who are in Sardis
will capture the towns of southern Judah.
21 The **victorious** men of Jerusalem
will attack Edom and rule over it.
And the LORD himself will be King."

[b] SACRED HILL: *Mount Zion (see Zion in Word List).*

THE BOOK OF JONAH

INTRODUCTION

The book of *Jonah* is unlike other prophetic books of the Bible in that it is a narrative, describing the adventures of a prophet who tried to disobey God's command. God told him to go to Nineveh, the capital of the great empire of Assyria, Israel's deadly enemy. But Jonah did not want to go there with God's message, because he was convinced that God would not carry out his threat to destroy the city. After a series of dramatic events, he reluctantly obeyed, and finally sulked when his message of doom did not come true.

The book portrays God's absolute sovereignty over his creation. But above all it portrays God as a God of love and mercy, who would rather forgive and save even the enemies of his people, than punish and destroy them.

Outline of Contents

---

afraid Amos 3.6; Mic 4.4
blame [2] Ezek 33.4; Mic 1.5
calm [2] Ezek 32.14; Zech 6.8
command Amos 9.1; 4.7
danger [3] Ezek 34.25; Hab 2.9
death (1) Joel 1.8; Nah 1.8
fault Ezek 33.5; Mal 1.9
get away Amos 9.1; Mal 3.15
god (2) (other gods) [2] Amos 8.14; Mic 4.5
heaven Amos 9.2; Mic 1.2
Hebrew Jer 34.9; Jn 5.2
help [2] Amos 9.4; 2.2
life (1) [2] Amos 6.1; 2.7
lot (1) Ezek 47.22; Lk 1.9
might Amos 5.9; 2.3
offer Amos 5.22; 2.9
pray [2] Joel 2.17; 2.1
promise Amos 4.2; 2.9
punish Obad 8; 3.10
sacrifice Amos 5.25; 2.9
serve Amos 2.4; Zeph 1.4
sorry Jer 8.6; 4.10
sound (2) Prov 8.12; Mt 6.22
spare Joel 3.20; Mk 12.44
strong Amos 6.13; Mic 4.13
terrify [2] Obad 9; Hab 1.9
violent [2] Amos 3.10; Mic 4.13

Jonah Disobeys the LORD

1 One day, the LORD spoke to Jonah
son of Amittai. 2 He said, "Go to
Nineveh, that great city, and speak out
against it; I am aware how **wicked** its
people are." 3 Jonah, however, set out in
the opposite direction in order to **get
away** from the LORD. He went to Joppa,
where he found a ship about to go to
Spain. He paid his fare and went aboard
with the crew to sail to Spain, where he
would be away from the LORD. 4 But the
LORD sent a **strong** wind on the sea, and
the storm was so **violent** that the ship
was in **danger** of breaking up. 5 The
sailors were **terrified** and cried out for
help, each one to his own **god**. Then, in
order to lessen the **danger**,[a] they threw
the cargo[b] overboard. Meanwhile, Jonah
had gone below and was lying in the
ship's hold, **sound asleep**.

6 The captain found him there and
said to him, "What are you doing asleep?
Get up and **pray** to your **god** for **help**.
Maybe he will feel **sorry** for us and **spare**
our **lives**."

7 The sailors said to one another,
"Let's draw **lots** and find out who is to
blame for getting us into this **danger**."
They did so, and Jonah's name was
drawn. 8 So they said to him: "Now then,
tell us! Who is to **blame** for this? What
are you doing here? What country do
you come from? What is your
nationality?"

9 "I am a **Hebrew**," Jonah answered.
"I **worship** the LORD, the God of **heaven**,
who made land and sea." 10 Jonah went
on to tell them that he was running away
from the LORD.

The sailors were **terrified**, and said to
him, "That was an awful thing to do!"[c]
11 The storm was getting **worse** all the
time, so the sailors asked him, "What
should we do to you to stop the storm?"

12 Jonah answered, "Throw me into
the sea, and it will **calm** down. I know it
is my **fault** that you are caught in this
violent storm."

13 Instead, the sailors tried to get the
ship to shore, rowing with all their **might**.
But the storm was getting **worse and
worse**, and they got nowhere. 14 So they
cried out to the LORD, "O LORD, we **pray**,
don't **punish** us with **death** for taking this
man's **life**! You, O LORD, are responsible
for all this; it is your doing." 15 Then they
picked Jonah up and threw him into the
sea, and it **calmed** down at once. 16 This
made the sailors so **afraid** of the LORD
that they **offered a sacrifice** and **promised** to **serve** him.

17 At the LORD's **command** a large
fish swallowed Jonah, and he was inside
the fish for three days and nights.

wicked Joel 3.13; 3.8
worse [2] Ezek 29.12; Zech 1.15
worship (1) (of God) Amos 7.9; Mic 4.5

[a] lessen the danger; *or* lighten the ship. [b] cargo; *or* equipment.
[c] and said...to do; *or* and asked him, "Why did you have to run away like that?"

1.1: 2 Kgs 14.25 **1.17:** Mt 12.40

Jonah's Prayer

2 From deep inside the fish Jonah
prayed to the LORD his God:
2 "In my **distress**, O LORD, I called to
you,
and you answered me.
From deep in the **world of the dead**
I cried for **help**, and you heard me.
3 You threw me down into the depths,
to the very bottom of the sea,
where the waters were all round
me,
and all your **mighty** waves rolled
over me.
4 I thought I had been banished from
your **presence**
and would never see your **holy**
Temple again.
5 The water came over me and choked
me;
the sea covered me completely,
and seaweed was wrapped round
my head.
6 I went down to the very roots of the
mountains,
into the land whose gates lock shut
for ever.[e]
But you, O LORD my God,
brought me back from the depths
alive.
7 When I felt my **life** slipping away,
then, O LORD, I **prayed** to you,
and in your **holy Temple** you heard
me.
8 Those who **worship worthless idols**
have **abandoned** their **loyalty** to you.
9 But I will sing **praises** to you;
I will **offer** you a **sacrifice**
and do what I have **promised**.
Salvation comes from the LORD!"
10 Then the LORD ordered the fish to
spew Jonah up on the beach, and it did.

abandon Amos 5.2; Mic 5.3
alive Amos 5.15; 4.3
distress Obad 12; Zeph 1.15
help 1.5; Mic 1.14
holy [2] Amos 8.5; Mic 1.3
idol Amos 8.14; Mic 1.5
life (1) 1.6; Hab 2.19
loyal Hos 12.6; Mic 7.2
might 1.13; Hab 3.15
offer 1.16; Mic 6.6
praise Joel 2.26; Hab 3.3
pray [2] 1.6; 3.8
presence Hos 6.2; Nah 1.5
promise 1.16; Mic 3.5
sacrifice 1.16; Hab 1.16
salvation Jer 33.16; Mk 16.10
Temple (1) (of God) [2] Amos 9.1; Mic 1.2
world of the dead Amos 9.2; Acts 2.27
worship (2) (of other gods) Amos 5.26; Mic 4.5
worthless Amos 9.9; Mic 7.4

Jonah Obeys the LORD

3 Once again the LORD spoke to
Jonah. 2 He said, "Go to Nineveh,
that great city, and **proclaim** to the
people the **message** I have given you."
3 So Jonah **obeyed** the LORD and went to
Nineveh, a city so large that it took three
days to walk through it. 4 Jonah started
through the city, and after walking a
whole day, he **proclaimed**, "In forty days
Nineveh will be **destroyed**!"
5 The people of Nineveh **believed**
God's **message**. So they decided that
everyone should **fast**, and all the people,
from the greatest to the **least**, put on
sackcloth to show that they had **repented**.
6 When the king of Nineveh heard
about it, he got up from his **throne**, took
off his robe, put on **sackcloth**, and sat
down in **ashes**. 7 He sent out a **proclamation** to the people of Nineveh: "This is an
order from the king and his officials: No
one is to eat anything; all persons, cattle,
and **sheep** are **forbidden** to eat or drink.
8 All persons and animals must wear
sackcloth. Everyone must **pray earnestly**
to God and must give up his **wicked** behaviour and his **evil actions**. 9 Perhaps
God will **change his mind**; perhaps he
will stop being **angry**, and we will not
die!"
10 God saw what they did; he saw that
they had given up their **wicked** behaviour. So he **changed his mind** and did
not **punish** them as he had said he would.

action Ezek 43.10; Mt 23.3
anger Amos 1.11; 4.1
ash Amos 2.1; Mt 11.21
believe Ezek 21.23; Mic 7.5
change [2] Amos 8.2; 4.2
destroy Obad 8; Mic 1.7
earnest Dan 9.3; Mk 5.23
evil Amos 8.7; Mic 2.1
fast (2) Joel 2.12; Zech 7.3
forbid Hos 9.3; Zech 9.7

least Dan 4.17; Mt 2.6
message [2] Obad 15; Mic 1.1
mind (1) [2] Amos 8.2; 4.2
obey Joel 2.11; Mic 4.5
pray 2.1; 4.2
proclaim [3] Amos 3.8; Zech 1.14
punish 1.14; 4.2
repent Joel 2.12; Hag 2.17
sackcloth [3] Amos 8.10; Mt 11.21
sheep Amos 3.12; Mic 2.12
throne Dan 7.9; Zech 6.13
wicked [2] 1.2; Mic 7.13

Jonah's Anger and God's Mercy

4 Jonah was very **unhappy** about this
and became **angry**. 2 So he **prayed**,
"LORD, didn't I say before I left home
that this is just what you would do?
That's why I did my **best** to run away to
Spain! I knew that you are a **loving** and
merciful God, always **patient**, always
kind, and always ready to **change your**
mind and not **punish**. 3 Now, LORD, let me
die. I am better off **dead** than **alive**."
4 The LORD answered, "What **right**
have you to be **angry**?"
5 Jonah went out east of the city and
sat down. He made a **shelter** for himself
and sat in its shade, waiting to see what
would happen to Nineveh. 6 Then the
LORD God made a plant grow up over
Jonah to give him some shade, so that he
would be more **comfortable**. Jonah was
extremely **pleased** with the plant. 7 But at
dawn the next day, at God's **command**, a
worm attacked the plant, and it died.
8 After the sun had **risen**, God sent a hot
east wind, and Jonah was about to faint
from the heat of the sun beating down on
his head. So he **wished** he were **dead**.[f] "I
am better off **dead** than **alive**," he said.
9 But God said to him, "What **right**
have you to be **angry** about the plant?"
Jonah replied, "I have every **right** to
be **angry**—**angry enough** to die!"
10 The LORD said to him, "This plant
grew up in one night and disappeared the
next; you didn't do anything for it, and

alive [2] 2.6; Mic 3.2
anger [4] 3.9; Mic 5.15
best Hos 11.6; Mic 6.6
change 3.9; Zeph 3.9
comfort Dan 4.4; Nah 3.7
command 1.17; Nah 1.4
dead [3] Amos 8.3; Mic 4.9
enough Amos 7.12; Hag 1.6
happy Dan 12.12; Zech 10.7
innocent Joel 3.19; Mt 12.37
kind Joel 2.13; Mic 2.7
love Amos 5.15; Mic 1.16
mercy Amos 5.15; Mic 7.19
mind (1) 3.9; Mic 4.12
patient Joel 2.13; Mic 2.7
pity Joel 2.17; Zech 11.5
please Hos 8.13; Mic 6.7
pray 3.8; Zeph 3.9
punish 3.10; Mic 4.6
right (3) [3] Obad 17; Mt 20.15
rise Amos 9.5; Mic 7.8
shelter Hos 14.8; Zech 14.16
sorry 1.6; Mal 3.14
wish Dan 4.19; Mal 1.10

[e] THE LAND WHOSE GATES LOCK SHUT FOR EVER: *A reference to the world of the dead (see 2.2).*
[f] wished he were dead; *or* prayed that he would die.

3.4–5: Mt 12.41; Lk 11.32 **4.2:** Ex 34.6 **4.3:** 1 Kgs 19.4

you didn't make it grow—yet you feel sorry for it! 11 How much more, then, should I have pity on Nineveh, that great city. After all, it has more than 120,000 innocent children in it, as well as many animals!"

THE BOOK OF MICAH

INTRODUCTION

The prophet Micah, a contemporary of Isaiah, was from a country town in Judah, the southern kingdom. He was convinced that Judah was about to face the same kind of national catastrophe that Amos had predicted for the northern kingdom, and for the same reason—God would punish the hateful injustice of the people. Micah's message, however, contains more clear and notable signs of hope for the future.

Passages especially worth noting are the picture of universal peace under God (4.1-4); the prediction of a great king who would come from the family line of David and bring peace to the nation (5.2-5a); and, in a single verse (6.8), the summary of much that the prophets of Israel had to say: "What he requires of us is this: to do what is just, to show constant love, and to live in humble fellowship with our God."

Outline of Contents

Judgement on Israel and Judah 1.1—3.12
Restoration and peace 4.1—5.15
Message of warning and hope 6.1—7.20

---

anxious Dan 6.20; Phil 2.26
ashamed Hos 4.19; Zeph 3.5
blame Jon 1.7; Acts 18.6
dare Jer 50.44; Mt 7.4
desolate Ezek 38.8; Nah 2.10
despair Ezek 21.6; 2.4
destroy [2] Jon 3.4; 2.10
disaster Obad 13; 2.3
enemy [3] Obad 5; 2.8
exile [2] Obad 20; 2.13
God's people Obad 13; 2.5
grapevine *see* **vine**
guilty Joel 3.20; Nah 1.3
heal Hos 7.1; Nah 3.19
heaven Jon 1.9; 6.6
help Jon 2.2; Hab 1.2
holy Jon 2.4; Hab 1.12
idol [2] Jon 2.8; 5.13
image Amos 5.26; 5.14
love Jon 4.2; 2.9
message Jon 3.2; Nah 1.1
mourn [3] Amos 9.5; Zech 7.3
naked [2] Hos 2.3; Nah 3.5
prostitute [2] Amos 7.17; Mt 21.31
rebel [2] Hos 13.16; Zeph 3.1
refuge Ps 71.3; Josh 21.13
relieve (1) Is 14.3; 2 Cor 8.13
reveal Amos 3.7; 3.11
rite Lev 9.1

1 During the time that Jotham, Ahaz,
and Hezekiah were kings of Judah,
the LORD gave this **message** to Micah,
who was from the town of Moresheth.
The LORD **revealed** to Micah all these
things about Samaria and Jerusalem.

A Lament for Samaria and Jerusalem

2 Hear this, all you nations;
listen to this, all who live on earth!
The **Sovereign** LORD will **testify** against
you.
Listen! He speaks from his **heavenly**
temple.
3 The LORD is coming from his **holy**
place;
he will come down and walk on the
tops of the mountains.
4 Then the mountains will melt under
him
like wax in a fire;
they will pour down into the valleys
like water pouring down a hill.

5 All this will happen because the
people of Israel have sinned and **rebelled**
against God. Who is to **blame** for Israel's
rebellion? Samaria, the capital city itself! Who is **guilty** of **idolatry** in Judah?
Jerusalem itself! 6 So the LORD says, "I
will make Samaria a pile of **ruins** in the
open country, a place for planting **grapevines**. I will pour the rubble of the city
down into the valley, and will lay bare
the city's foundations. 7 All its precious
idols will be smashed to pieces, everything given to its temple **prostitutes** will
be **destroyed** by fire, and all its **images**
will become a **desolate** heap. Samaria
acquired these things for its fertility
rites, and now her **enemies** will carry
them off for temple **prostitutes** elsewhere."

8 Then Micah said, "Because of this I
will **mourn** and lament. To show my
sorrow, I will walk about barefoot and
naked. I will howl like a jackal and **wail**
like an ostrich. 9 Samaria's wounds cannot be **healed**, and Judah is about to **suffer** in the same way; **destruction** has
reached the gates of Jerusalem itself,
where **my people** live."

The Enemy Approaches Jerusalem

10 Don't tell our **enemies** in Gath
about our defeat; don't let them see you
weeping. People of Beth Leaphrah,[a]
show your **despair** by rolling in the dust!
11 You people of Shaphir, go into **exile**,
naked and **ashamed**. Those who live in
Zaanan **dare** not come out of their city.
When you hear the people of Bethezel
mourn, you will know that there is no **refuge** there. 12 The people of Maroth wait
anxiously for **relief**, because the LORD
has brought **disaster** close to Jerusalem.
13 You that live in Lachish, hitch the
horses to the chariots. You imitated the
sins of Israel and so caused Jerusalem to
sin. 14 And now, people of Judah, say

ruin Obad 12; 2.4
sorrow Amos 5.16; Nah 2.7
Sovereign Obad 15; Hab 3.19
suffer Obad 13; 4.6
Temple (1) (of God) Jon 2.4; 3.12
testify Is 43.9; Mal 3.5
vine Joel 1.7; 7.1
wail Amos 5.16; Zeph 1.10
weep Joel 2.12; Zech 11.2

[a] BETH LEAPHRAH: *The prophet speaks of outlying towns (verses 10-14) which an enemy army approaching Jerusalem would attack.*

1.1: 2 Kgs 15.32—16.20, 18.1—20.21; 2 Chr 27.1-7, 28.1—32.33

good-bye to the town of Moresheth Gath.
The kings of Israel will get no **help** from
the town of Achzib.
15 People of Mareshah, the LORD will
hand you over to an **enemy**, who is going
to capture your town. The leaders of
Israel will go and hide in the cave at
Adullam. 16 People of Judah, cut off your
hair in **mourning** for the children you
love. Make yourselves as bald as vultures, because your children will be
taken away from you into **exile**.

The Fate of Those Who Oppress the Poor

2 How **terrible** it will be for those who
lie awake and **plan evil**! When
morning comes, as soon as they have the
chance, they do the **evil** they **planned**.
2 When they want fields, they seize them;
when they want houses, they take them.
No man's family or property is **safe**.
3 And so the LORD says, "I am **planning** to bring **disaster** on you, and you
will not be able to **escape** it. You are going to find yourselves in **trouble**, and then
you will not walk so **proudly** any more.
4 When that time comes, people will use
your story as an **example of disaster**, and
they will sing this song of **despair** about
your **experience**:

We are completely **ruined**!
The LORD has taken our land away
And given it to those who took us
captive."[b]

5 So then, when the time comes for
the land to be given back to the LORD's
people, there will be no **share** for any of
you.
6 The people **preach** at me and say,
"Don't **preach** at us. Don't preach about
all that. God is not going to **disgrace** us.
7 Do you think the people of Israel are under a **curse**?[c] Has the LORD lost his
patience? Would he really do such
things? Doesn't he[d] speak **kindly** to
those who do **right**?"
8 The LORD replies, "You attack **my
people**[e] like **enemies**. Men return from
battle, thinking they are **safe** at home,
but there you are, waiting to **steal** the
coats off their backs. 9 You drive the
women of **my people** out of the homes
they **love**, and you have **robbed** their children of my **blessings** for ever. 10 Get up
and go; there is no **safety** here any more.
Your sins have **doomed** this place to
destruction.
11 "These people want the kind of **prophet** who goes about full of **lies** and **deceit** and says, 'I **prophesy** that wine and
liquor will flow for you.'
12 "But I will gather you together, all
you people of Israel that are left. I will
bring you together like **sheep** returning
to the fold. Like a pasture full of **sheep**,
your land will once again be filled with
many people."
13 God will open the way for them and
lead them out of **exile**. They will break
out of the city gates and go **free**. Their
king, the LORD himself, will lead them
out.

Micah Denounces Israel's Leaders

3 Listen, you rulers of Israel! You are
supposed to be **concerned** about **justice**, 2 yet you **hate** what is good and you
love what is **evil**. You skin **my people
alive** and tear the **flesh** off their bones.
3 You eat **my people** up. You **strip** off
their skin, break their bones, and chop
them up like meat for the pot. 4 The time
is coming when you will cry out to the
LORD, but he will not answer you. He will
not listen to your **prayers**, for you have
done **evil**.
5 **My people** are **deceived** by **prophets**
who **promise peace** to those who pay
them, but **threaten** war for those who
don't. To these **prophets** the LORD says,
6 "**Prophets**, your day is almost over; the
sun is going down on you. Because you
mislead my people, you will have no
more **prophetic visions**, and you will not
be able to **predict** anything." 7 Those who
predict the future will be **disgraced** by
their **failure**. They will all be **humiliated**
because God does not answer them.
8 But as for me, the LORD fills me with
his **spirit** and **power**, and gives me a
sense of **justice** and the **courage** to tell
the people of Israel what their sins are.
9 Listen to me, you rulers of Israel, you
that **hate justice** and **turn right** into
wrong. 10 You are building God's city,
Jerusalem, on a foundation of murder
and **injustice**. 11 The city's rulers govern
for **bribes**, the **priests interpret** the **Law**
for pay, the **prophets** give their **revelations** for money—and they all **claim** that
the LORD is with them. "No **harm** will
come to us," they say. "The LORD is with
us."
12 And so, because of you, Zion will be

bless Joel 2.14; Hag 2.19
captive Amos 9.4; Nah 2.7
curse Dan 9.11; Zech 5.3
deceive Obad 3; 3.5
despair 1.10; Zeph 1.14
destroy 1.7; 4.11
disaster [2] 1.12; Zeph 1.17
disgrace Hos 12.14; 3.7
doom Amos 5.5; Nah 3.1
enemy 1.7; 4.10
escape Obad 14; Nah 3.11
evil [2] Jon 3.8; 3.2
example Ezek 28.12; Jn 13.15
exile 1.11; 4.6
experience Prov 25.12; Rom 4.1
free Dan 9.24; Zech 9.11
God's people [3] 1.9; 3.2
kind Jon 4.2; Zech 7.9
lie (2) Hos 11.12; 6.12
love 1.16; 3.2
patient Jon 4.2; Zech 11.8
plan [3] Amos 3.7; 6.5
preach [2] Amos 7.12; Mt 3.1
prophecy Obad 1; Zech 13.3
prophet Amos 7.12; 3.5
proud Obad 3; Hab 1.7
right (1) Amos 6.12; 3.9
rob Obad 10; Mt 6.19
ruin 1.6; 3.12
safe [3] Amos 6.1; 5.4
share Amos 7.1; Zech 8.23
sheep [2] Jon 3.7; 5.8
steal Hos 7.1; Zeph 1.9
terrible Amos 6.1; Nah 1.6
trouble Hos 2.15; Nah 1.7

alive Jon 4.3; Zech 1.5
bribe Amos 5.12; 7.3
claim Amos 5.14; Zech 1.17
concern Joel 2.18; Zech 1.14
courage Ezek 22.14; Zech 8.9
deceive 2.11; Hab 2.5
disgrace 2.6; 7.10
evil [2] 2.1; 6.10
fail Ezek 21.7; Hab 3.17
flesh Lam 3.4; Nah 2.12
God's people [4] 2.5; 4.2
harm Amos 9.10; Hab 2.9
hate [2] Amos 6.8; 6.10
humiliate Ezek 36.6; Hab 2.15
injustice Amos 5.10; Zech 8.17
interpret Dan 5.12; Zech 10.2
justice [3] Amos 6.12; 6.8
law Dan 9.10; Hab 1.4
love 2.9; 6.8
mislead Ezek 13.9; Zech 10.2
peace Obad 7; 4.4
power Joel 1.6; 4.3
prayer Hos 14.2; Hab 3.1
predict [2] Ezek 22.28; Mt 11.14
priest Amos 7.10; Zeph 1.4
promise Jon 2.9; 4.4
prophet [5] 2.11; 7.4
reveal 1.1; Hab 1.1
right (1) 2.7; 7.9
ruin 2.4; 4.11
sense Hos 4.11; Zeph 2.1
Spirit (1) (God's Spirit) Joel 2.28; Zech 4.6
strip (1) Joel 1.7; Nah 3.5
Temple (1) (of God) 1.2; 4.1
threat Ezek 39.26; Zeph 3.18
turn Amos 8.10; 7.17

[b] *Probable text* those who took us captive; *Hebrew* rebels.
[c] *Probable text* under a curse; *Hebrew unclear.*
[d] *One ancient translation* Doesn't he; *Hebrew* Don't I.
[e] *Probable text* You attack my people; *Hebrew* Recently my people have attacked.

3.12: Jer 26.18

vision Amos 8.1; Nah 1.1
wrong Amos 6.12; 7.9

ploughed like a field, Jerusalem will become a pile of **ruins**, and the **Temple** hill will become a forest.

The LORD's Universal Reign of Peace
(Is 2.1–4)

4 In days to come
the mountain where the **Temple** stands
will be the highest one of all,
towering above all the hills.
Many nations will come streaming to it,
2 and their people will say,
"Let us go up the hill of the LORD,[f]
to the **Temple** of Israel's God.
For he will **teach** us what he wants us to do;
we will walk in the paths he has **chosen**.
For the LORD's **teaching** comes from Jerusalem;
from Zion he speaks to **his people**."

3 He will **settle disputes** among the nations,
among the great **powers** near and far.
They will hammer their swords into ploughs
and their spears into pruning-knives.
Nations will **never again** go to war,
never prepare for battle again.
4 Everyone will live in **peace**
among his own **vineyards** and fig-trees,
and no one will make him **afraid**.
The LORD **Almighty** has **promised** this.

5 Each nation **worships** and **obeys** its
own **god**, but we will **worship** and **obey**
the LORD our God for ever and ever.

Israel Will Return from Exile

6 "The time is coming," says the
LORD, "when I will gather together the
people I **punished**, those who have **suf**-
fered in **exile**. 7 They are **crippled** and far
from home, but I will make a **new** beginning with those who are left, and they
will become a great nation. I will rule
over them on Mount Zion from that time
on and for ever."
8 And you, Jerusalem, where God, like
a **shepherd**, **watches** over **his people**, will
once again be the capital of the kingdom
that was yours. 9 Why do you cry out so
loudly? Why are you **suffering** like a
woman in labour? Is it because you have
no king, and your counsellors are **dead**?
10 Twist and **groan**,[g] people of Jerusalem,
like a woman giving **birth**, for now you
will have to leave the city and live in the
open country. You will have to go to
Babylon, but there the LORD will **save**
you from your **enemies**. 11 Many nations
have gathered to attack you. They say,
"Jerusalem must be **destroyed**! We will
see this city in **ruins**!" 12 But these
nations do not know what is in the LORD's
mind. They do not realize that they have
been gathered together to be **punished** in
the same way that corn is brought in to
be threshed.
13 The LORD says, "People of Jerusalem, go and **punish** your **enemies**!
I will make you as **strong** as a bull with
iron horns and bronze hoofs. You will
crush many nations, and the wealth they
got by **violence** you will **present** to me,
the Lord of the whole **world**."

5 People of Jerusalem, gather your
forces![h] We are besieged! They are
attacking the leader of Israel!

God Promises a Ruler from Bethlehem

2 The LORD says, "Bethlehem Ephra-
thah, you are one of the smallest towns in
Judah, but out of you I will bring a ruler
for Israel, whose family line goes back to
ancient times."
3 So the LORD will **abandon his people**
to their **enemies** until the woman who is
to give **birth** has her son. Then his fellow-
countrymen who are in **exile** will be **re-**
united with their own people. 4 When he
comes, he will rule **his people** with the
strength that comes from the LORD and
with the **majesty** of the LORD God himself. **His people** will live in **safety** because
people all over the earth will **acknow-**
ledge his greatness, 5 and he will bring
peace.

Deliverance and Punishment

When the Assyrians invade our
country and break through our **defences**,
we will send our **strongest** leaders to
fight them. 6 By **force** of arms they will
conquer Assyria, the land of Nimrod, and
they[i] will **save** us from the Assyrians
when they invade our territory.
7 The people of Israel who survive will
be like refreshing dew sent by the LORD
for many nations, like showers on growing plants. They will **depend** on God, not
man. 8 Those who are left among the
nations will be like a lion hunting for food
in a forest or a pasture: he gets in among
the **sheep**, pounces on them, and tears

[f] HILL OF THE LORD: *Mount Zion (see Zion in Word List).* [g] *Probable text* groan; *Hebrew* bring forth. [h] *Probable text* People...forces; *Hebrew unclear.* [i] *Probable text* they; *Hebrew* he.

4.3: Joel 3.10 **4.4:** Zech 3.10 **5.2:** Mt 2.6; Jn 7.42 **5.6:** Gen 10.8–11

afraid Jon 1.16; 7.17
Almighty Amos 9.5; Nah 2.13
birth Hos 1.3; 5.3
choose Amos 2.11; 7.14
cripple Prov 26.7; Mt 15.30
dead Jon 4.3; Nah 3.3
destroy 2.10; 5.9
dispute Ezek 44.24; Mt 5.25
enemy [2] 2.8; 5.3
exile 2.13; 5.3
god (2) (other gods) Jon 1.5; 7.18
God's people [2] 3.2; 5.3
groan Amos 2.13; Mk 7.34
mind (1) Jon 4.2; Zeph 3.8
never again Hos 14.3; Zeph 3.11
new Joel 2.16; Zeph 1.10
obey [2] Jon 3.3; 5.15
peace 3.5; 5.5
power 3.8; Nah 1.3
present (1) Dan 7.13; 6.1
promise 3.5; 7.20
punish [3] Jon 4.2; 7.4
ruin 3.12; 6.13
save Amos 4.11; 5.6
settle (2) Is 2.4; Mt 5.25
shepherd Amos 7.15; 7.14
strong Jon 1.4; 5.5
suffer [2] 1.9; Nah 1.12
teach [2] Amos 2.4; Zeph 3.7
Temple (1) (of God) [2] 3.12; Hab 2.20
vineyard Amos 9.14; Zeph 1.13
violent Jon 1.4; Hab 1.2
watch Amos 9.8; 7.4
world Amos 9.5; Nah 1.5
worship (1) (of God) Jon 1.9; 6.6
worship (2) (of other gods) Jon 2.8; 5.13

abandon Jon 2.8; Zech 11.17
acknowledge Hos 11.3; Zech 1.6
ancient Ezek 36.2; Hab 3.6
anger Jon 4.1; 7.9
birth 4.10; Mt 1.12
conquer [2] Obad 7; Hab 1.6
defend [2] Amos 3.11; 7.9
depend Ezek 29.16; Mt 22.40
destroy [6] 4.11; 6.13
enemy [2] 4.10; 7.6
exile 4.6; Nah 3.10
force (1) Dan 11.9; Hab 2.6
fortune-teller Dan 5.11; Zech 10.2
God's people [3] 4.2; 6.2
goddess Jer 44.17; Acts 19.24
hope Amos 4.8; 7.1
idol 1.5; Nah 1.14
image 1.7; Acts 7.43
magic Dan 5.7; Mal 3.5
Majesty Dan 6.6; Acts 26.7
obey 4.5; Zeph 2.3
peace 4.4; Hag 2.9
rescue Hos 13.14; 6.4
revenge Ezek 25.12; Mt 5.39
sacred Obad 16; Zeph 3.4
safe 2.2; Nah 2.11
save 4.10; 6.5
sheep 2.12; 6.7
strength Amos 2.14; 7.16
strong 4.13; Nah 1.12
unite Hos 1.11; Zech 11.7
worship (2) (of other gods) 4.5; Hab 1.16

them to pieces—and there is no hope of rescue. 9 Israel will conquer her enemies and destroy them all.

10 The LORD says, "At that time I will take away your horses and destroy your chariots. 11 I will destroy the cities in your land and tear down all your defences. 12 I will destroy the magic charms you use and leave you without any fortune-tellers. 13 I will destroy your idols and sacred stone pillars; no longer will you worship the things that you yourselves have made. 14 I will pull down the images of the goddess Asherah in your land and destroy your cities. 15 And in my great anger I will take revenge on all nations that have not obeyed me."

The LORD's Case Against Israel

6 Listen to the LORD's case against Israel.

Arise, O LORD, and present your case; let the mountains and the hills hear what you say.

2 You mountains, you everlasting foundations of the earth, listen to the LORD's case! The LORD has a case against his people. He is going to bring an accusation against Israel.

3 The LORD says, "My people, what have I done to you? How have I been a burden to you? Answer me. 4 I brought you out of Egypt; I rescued you from slavery; I sent Moses, Aaron, and Miriam to lead you. 5 My people, remember what King Balak of Moab planned to do to you and how Balaam son of Beor answered him. Remember the things that happened on the way from the camp at Acacia to Gilgal. Remember these things and you will realize what I did in order to save you."

What the LORD Requires

6 What shall I bring to the LORD, the God of heaven, when I come to worship him? Shall I bring the best calves to burn as offerings to him? 7 Will the LORD be pleased if I bring him thousands of sheep or endless streams of olive-oil? Shall I offer him my first-born child to pay for my sins? 8 No, the LORD has told us what is good. What he requires of us is this: to do what is just, to show constant love, and to live in humble fellowship with our God.

9 It is wise to fear the LORD. He calls to the city, "Listen, you people who assemble in the city![j] 10 In the houses of evil men are treasures which they got dishonestly. They use false measures, a thing that I hate.[k] 11 How can I forgive men who use false scales and weights? 12 Your rich men exploit the poor, and all of you are liars. 13 So I have already begun[l] your ruin and destruction because of your sins. 14 You will eat, but not be satisfied—in fact you will still be hungry. You will carry things off, but you will not be able to save them; anything you do save I will destroy in war. 15 You will sow corn, but not harvest the crop. You will press oil from olives, but never be able to use it. You will make wine, but never drink it. 16 This will happen because you have followed the evil practices of King Omri and of his son, King Ahab. You have continued their policies, and so I will bring you to ruin, and everyone will despise you. People[m] everywhere will treat you with contempt."[n]

Israel's Moral Corruption

7 It's hopeless! I am like a hungry man who finds no fruit left on the trees and no grapes on the vines. All the grapes and all the tasty figs have been picked. 2 There is not an honest person left in the land, no one loyal to God. Everyone is waiting for a chance to commit murder. Everyone hunts down his fellow-countryman. 3 They are all experts at doing evil. Officials and judges ask for bribes. The influential man tells them what he wants, and so they scheme together.[o] 4 Even the best and most honest of them are as worthless as weeds.

The day has come when God will punish the people, as he warned them through their watchmen, the prophets. Now they are in confusion. 5 Don't believe your neighbour or trust your friend. Be careful what you say even to your wife. 6 In these times sons treat their fathers like fools, daughters oppose their mothers, and young women quarrel with their mothers-in-law; a man's enemies are the members of his own family.

7 But I will watch for the LORD; I will wait confidently for God, who will save me. My God will hear me.

The LORD Brings Salvation

8 Our enemies have no reason to gloat

[j] *Probable text* who assemble in the city; *Hebrew* and who appointed it. Yet.
[k] *Verse 10 in Hebrew is unclear.* [l] *Some ancient translations* begun; *Hebrew* made ill.
[m] *One ancient translation* People; *Hebrew* My people.
[n] People...contempt; *or* As my people you will everywhere be treated with contempt.
[o] and so they scheme together; *Hebrew unclear.*

6.4: Ex 4.10–16, 12.50–51, 15.20 **6.5:** Num 22.2–24.25; Josh 3.1–4.19 **6.16:** 1 Kgs 16.23–34, 21.25–26
7.6: Mt 10.35–36; Lk 12.53

require Jer 5.4; Mt 3.15
rescue 5.8; Zeph 3.1
rich Joel 3.5; 7.14
ruin [2] 4.11; Nah 3.
satisfy Joel 2.19; Hab 2.5
save [3] 5.6; 7.7
sheep 5.8; Hab 3.17
slave Amos 8.6; Nah 3.4
sow Hos 8.7; Hag 1.
wise Hos 14.9; Mt 7.24
worship (1) (of God 4.5; Zeph 1.5

accuse Hos 12.2; Zeph 3.8
best Jon 4.2; 7.4
burden Ezek 33.10; Acts 15.28
case (2) [4] Ezek 44.24; Acts 24.22
constant Hos 6.6; 7.18
contempt Ezek 36.5; Nah 3.6
despise Obad 2; Mal 1.6
destroy [2] 5.9; Nah 1.8
dishonest Hos 12.7; Lk 16.8
everlasting Jer 23.40; Hab 3.6
evil [2] 3.2; 7.3
false [2] Amos 8.5; Zech 8.17
fear Hos 10.3; 7.17
fellowship Gen 6.9; Acts 2.42
first-born Ezek 20.26; Zech 12.10
forgive Amos 7.2; 7.18
God's people [3] 5.3; Nah 1.7
harvest Amos 9.13; Hag 1.6
hate 3.2; Zech 8.17
heaven 1.2; Hab 3.3
humble Dan 10.12; Zeph 2.3
hunger Amos 8.11; 7.1
justice 3.1; Hab 1.4
lie (2) 2.11; Nah 3.1
love 3.2; 7.18
offer [2] Jon 2.9; Hab 1.16
plan 2.1; Zech 7.10
please Jon 4.6; Hag 1.8
poor Amos 8.4; Hab 3.14
practice Ezek 23.45; Zeph 1.8
present (1) 4.13; Mt 2.11
remember [3] Hos 9.9; Zeph 1.4

afraid 4.4; Hab 3.7
anger [2] 5.15; Nah 1.2
apart Ezek 48.8; Zech 14.21
believe Jon 3.5; Hab 1.5
best 6.6; Hab 1.16
bribe 3.11; Lk 20.20
choose 4.2; Hab 1.12
commit Hos 6.9; Mt 5.21
confident Ezek 7.24; Zeph 1.12
constant [2] 6.8; Acts 10.2
dark Amos 8.9; Zeph 1.15
defend 5.5; Nah 2.1
disgrace 3.7; Hab 2.15
endure Ezek 16.52; Hab 1.3
enemy [4] 5.3; Nah 1.8
evil 6.10; Hab 1.4
faithful Hos 11.12; Hab 2.4
fear 6.9; Nah 2.10
fool Hos 13.13; Mt 5.22
forgive 6.11; Mt 6.12
friend Obad 7; Zech 13.6
god (2) (other gods) 4.5; Nah 1.14
honest [2] Amos 3.10; Mt 23.23
hope 5.8; Hag 1.9
hunger 6.14; Hab 1.8
judge Obad 15; Zeph 1.7
light (1) [2] Amos 5.18; Hab 3.4
love [2] 6.8; Zeph 3.17

loyal Jon 2.8; Zeph 1.5
mercy Jon 4.2; Hab 1.17
miracle Dan 6.27; Mt 7.22
neighbour Dan 9.16; Hab 2.15
pleasure Lam 3.33; Lk 8.14
promise 4.4; Nah 1.15
prophet 3.5; Hab 1.1
punish 4.6; Nah 1.2
quarrel Jer 15.10; Hab 1.3
reason Dan 11.34; Zeph 3.15
rich 6.12; Hab 2.6
right (1) 3.9; Zeph 2.3
rise Jon 4.8; Hab 3.10
save [2] 6.5; Hab 1.2
scheme Jer 6.19; Nah 1.11
shepherd 4.8; Zeph 2.6
strength 5.4; Nah 2.10
tremble Joel 3.16; Nah 1.5
trust Hos 12.6; Hab 2.18
turn 3.9; Nah 1.4
vine 1.6; Hab 3.17
warn Amos 6.8; Zech 1.6
watch [2] 4.8; Hab 1.5

over us. We have fallen, but we will **rise**
again. We are in **darkness** now, but the
LORD will give us **light**. 9 We have sinned
against the LORD, so now we must **en-**
dure his **anger** for a while. But in the end
he will **defend** us and **right** the **wrongs**
that have been done to us. He will bring
us out to the **light**; we will live to see him
save us. 10 Then our **enemies** will see this
and be **disgraced**—the same **enemies**
who taunted us by asking, "Where is the
LORD your God?" We will see them defeated, trampled[p] down like mud in the
streets.

11 People of Jerusalem, the time to rebuild the city walls is coming. At that
time your territory will be enlarged.
12 Your people will return to you from
everywhere—from Assyria in the east,
from Egypt in the south, from the region
of the Euphrates, from distant seas and
far-off mountains. 13 But the earth will become a desert because of the **wickedness**
of those who live on it.

The LORD's Compassion on Israel

14 Be a **shepherd** to your people,
LORD, the people you have **chosen**. Although they live **apart** in the wilderness,
there is fertile land around them. Let
them go and feed in the **rich** pastures of
Bashan and Gilead, as they did long ago.

15 Work **miracles** for us,[q] LORD, as
you did in the days when you brought us
out of Egypt. 16 The nations will see this
and be frustrated in spite of all their
strength. In dismay they will close their
mouths and cover their ears. 17 They will
crawl in the dust like snakes; they will
come from their fortresses, **trembling**
and **afraid**. They will **turn** in **fear** to the
LORD our God.

18 There is no other **god** like you, O
LORD; you **forgive** the sins of your people
who have survived. You do not stay
angry for ever, but you take **pleasure** in
showing us your **constant love**. 19 You will
be **merciful** to us once again. You will
trample our sins underfoot and send
them to the bottom of the sea! 20 You will
show your **faithfulness** and **constant love**
to your people, the descendants of
Abraham and of Jacob, as you **promised**
our ancestors long ago.

weed Hos 13.15; Zeph 2.9
wicked Jon 3.8; Nah 1.11
worthless Jon 2.8; Zech 11.15
wrong 3.9; Hab 1.3

[p] We will see...trampled; *or* We will gloat over them as they lie trampled.
[q] *Probable text* Work miracles for us; *Hebrew* I will work miracles for him.

THE BOOK OF NAHUM

INTRODUCTION

The book of *Nahum* is a poem celebrating the fall of Nineveh, the capital city of Israel's ancient and oppressive enemy, the Assyrians. The fall of Nineveh, near the end of the seventh century B.C., is seen as the judgement of God upon a cruel and arrogant nation.

Outline of Contents

anger [4] Mic 7.9; Hab 3.2
announce Amos 3.9; Mt 10.27
bind Lam 3.7; Mt 23.16
care Amos 7.14; Zech 10.3
celebrate Hos 9.1; Zech 14.16
cloud Joel 2.2; Hab 3.8
command Jon 4.7; Hab 3.5
death (1) Jon 1.14; Hab 2.5
deserve Hos 12.14; Zech 1.6
destroy [5] Mic 6.13; 2.10
enemy Mic 7.6; 2.2
festival Amos 8.10; Zeph 3.18
flood Hos 5.10; Mt 24.38
fury Hos 13.11; Hab 2.15
god (2) (other gods) Mic 7.18; Hab 1.11
God's people [3] Mic 6.2; Hab 1.5
Good News Is 61.1; Mt 4.23
grave Ezek 39.15; Mt 27.52
guilty Mic 1.5; Mt 5.28
idol Mic 5.13; Hab 2.18
message Mic 1.1; Hab 1.1
plot (1) [2] Amos 7.10; Mt 12.15
power [2] Mic 4.3; 2.1
presence Jon 2.4; Hab 2.20
promise Mic 7.20; Hag 1.13
protect Hos 14.3; 3.8
punish [2] Mic 7.4; 3.4
raise Hos 5.8; Zech 5.7
rival Ezek 26.2
scheme Mic 7.3; Hab 2.10
solemn Amos 6.8; Lk 1.73
strong Mic 5.5; Hab 1.12
suffer Mic 4.6; Zech 1.6

1 This is a **message** about Nineveh, the account of a **vision** seen by Nahum, who was from Elkosh.

The LORD's Anger against Nineveh

2 The LORD God **tolerates** no **rivals**;
he **punishes** those who oppose him.
In his **anger** he pays them back.
3 The LORD does not easily become
angry,
but he is **powerful**
and never lets the **guilty** go
unpunished.

Where the LORD walks, storms arise;
the **clouds** are the dust **raised** by his
feet!
4 He **commands** the sea, and it dries up!
He makes the rivers go dry.
The fields of Bashan wither,
Mount Carmel **turns** brown,
and the flowers of Lebanon fade.
5 Mountains quake in the **presence** of
the LORD;
hills melt before him.
The earth shakes when the LORD
appears;
the **world** and all its people **tremble**.
6 When he is **angry**, who can survive?
Who can survive his **terrible fury**?
He pours out his flaming **anger**;
rocks crumble to dust before him.

7 The LORD is good;
he **protects his people** in times of
trouble;
he takes **care** of those who **turn** to
him.
8 Like a great rushing **flood** he
completely **destroys** his **enemies**;[a]
he sends to their **death** those who
oppose him.
9 What are you **plotting** against the
LORD?
He will **destroy** you.
No one opposes him more than
once.
10 Like tangled thorns and dry straw,
you drunkards will be burnt up!

11 From you, Nineveh, there came a
man full of **wicked schemes**, who **plotted**
against the LORD. 12 This is what the
LORD says to **his people** Israel: "Even
though the Assyrians are **strong** and
numerous, they will be **destroyed** and disappear. **My people**, I made you **suffer**,
but I will not do it again. 13 I will now end
Assyria's **power** over you and break the
chains that **bind** you."
14 This is what the LORD has decreed
about the Assyrians: "They will have no
descendants to carry on their name. I
will **destroy** the **idols** that are in the
temples of their **gods**. I am preparing a
grave for the Assyrians—they don't
deserve to live!"
15 Look, a messenger is coming over
the mountains with **good news**! He is on
his way to **announce** the **victory**! People
of Judah, **celebrate** your **festivals** and
give God what you **solemnly promised**
him. The **wicked** will never invade your
land again. They have been totally
destroyed!

temple (2) (of other gods) Amos 7.13; Zech 5.11
terrible Mic 2.1; Zech 14.12
tolerate Ezek 44.6; Rom 2.4
tremble Mic 7.17; 2.10
trouble Mic 2.3; Hab 1.3
turn [2] Mic 7.17; 2.8
victory Obad 21; Hab 3.8
vision Mic 3.6; Zech 1.7
wicked [2] Mic 7.13; Hab 3.13
world Mic 4.13; Hab 1.6

The Fall of Nineveh

2 Nineveh, you are under attack!
The **power** that will shatter you
has come.
Man the **defences**!
Guard the road!
Prepare for battle!
2 (The LORD is about to **restore** the **glory**

Almighty Mic 4.4; 3.5
captive Mic 2.4; Hab 1.9
defend Mic 7.9; 3.8
demand Amos 5.25; Mk 6.25
desolate Mic 1.7; Zeph 2.15
destroy 1.8; 3.13

[a] *Some ancient translations* his enemies; *Hebrew* its place.

1.1–3.19: Is 10.5–34, 14.24–27; Zeph 2.13–15 **1.15:** Is 52.7

dove Hos 11.11; Mt 3.16
enemy [3] 1.8; 3.11
fear Mic 7.17; Hab 1.7
flesh Mic 3.2; Zech 14.12
glory Dan 4.30; Hab 2.14
heart Joel 2.13; Zeph 3.14
knee Dan 10.10; Mt 18.26
power 1.3; 3.9
restore Amos 9.11; Zech 1.16
safe Mic 5.4; Hab 2.9
servant Amos 3.7; Hag 2.23
sorrow Mic 1.8; Mt 26.38
strength Mic 7.16; 3.14
stumble Hos 14.1; 3.3
terror Joel 1.15; Hab 1.7
tremble 1.5; Hab 2.7
turn 1.4; Hab 2.16

of Israel, as it was before her **enemies** plundered her.)

3 The **enemy** soldiers carry red shields
and wear uniforms of red.
They are preparing to attack!
Their chariots flash like fire!
Their horses[c] prance!

4 Chariots dash wildly through the streets,
rushing to and fro through the city squares.
They flash like torches
and dart about like lightning.
5 The officers are summoned;
they **stumble** as they press forward.

The attackers rush to the wall
and set up the shield for the battering-ram.
6 The gates by the river burst open;
the palace is filled with **terror**.
7 The queen is taken **captive**;
her **servants** moan like **doves**
and beat their breasts in **sorrow**.
8 Like water from a broken dam
the people rush from Nineveh![e]
"Stop! Stop!" the cry rings out—
but no one **turns** back.

9 Plunder the silver!
Plunder the gold!
The city is full of treasure!

10 Nineveh is **destroyed**, deserted, **desolate**!
Hearts melt with **fear**;
knees tremble, **strength** is gone;
faces grow pale.

11 Where now is the city
that was like a den of lions,
the place where young lions were fed,
where the lion and the lioness would go
and their cubs would be **safe**?
12 The lion killed his prey
and tore it to pieces for his mate and her cubs;
he filled his den with torn **flesh**.

13 "I am your **enemy**!" says the LORD
Almighty. "I will burn up your chariots.
Your soldiers will be killed in war, and I
will take away everything that you took
from others. The **demands** of your
envoys will no longer be heard."

Almighty 2.13; Hab 2.13

3

Doomed is the **lying**, murderous city,
full of wealth to be looted and plundered!
2 Listen! The crack of the whip,
the rattle of wheels,
the gallop of horses,
the jolting of chariots!
3 Horsemen charge,
swords flash, spears gleam!
Corpses are piled high,
dead bodies without number—
men **stumble** over them!
4 Nineveh the whore is being **punished**.
Attractive and full of **deadly** charms,
she enchanted nations and **enslaved**[f] them.

5 The LORD **Almighty** says,
"I will **punish** you, Nineveh!
I will **strip** you **naked**
and let the nations see you,
see you in all your **shame**.
6 I will treat you with **contempt**
and cover you with **filth**.
People will stare at you in **horror**.
7 All who see you will shrink back.
They will say, 'Nineveh lies in **ruins**!
Who has any **sympathy** for her?
Who will want to **comfort** her?' "

8 Nineveh, are you any better than
Thebes, the capital of Egypt? She too
had a river to **protect** her like a wall—
the Nile was her **defence**. 9 She ruled
Sudan and Egypt, there was no limit to
her **power**; Libya was her ally. 10 Yet the
people of Thebes were carried off into
exile. At every street corner their children were beaten **to death**. Their **leading**
men were carried off in chains and
divided among their captors.
11 Nineveh, you too will fall into a
drunken stupor! You too will try to
escape from your **enemies**. 12 All your fortresses will be like fig-trees with **ripe**
figs: shake the trees, and the fruit falls
right into your mouth! 13 Your soldiers
are like women, and your country stands
defenceless before your **enemies**. Fire
will **destroy** the bars across your gates.
14 Draw water to prepare for a siege, and
strengthen your fortresses! Trample the
clay to make bricks, and get the brick
moulds ready! 15 No matter what you do,
you will still be burnt **to death** or killed in
battle. You will be wiped out like crops
eaten up by locusts.
You multiplied like locusts! 16 You produced more merchants than there are
stars in the sky! But now they are gone,
like locusts that spread their wings and
fly away. 17 Your officials are like a

body Amos 8.3; Hab 3.16
comfort Jon 4.6; Zech 1.13
contempt Mic 6.16; Hab 1.10
cruel Amos 1.3; Mal 2.16
dead [2] Mic 4.9; Zeph 1.11
deadly Jer 9.8; Rom 3.13
death (3) (to death) [2] Amos 9.4; Zeph 2.12
defend [2] 2.1; Zech 14.14
destroy [2] 2.10; Hab 1.3
doom Mic 2.10; Hab 2.6
enemy [2] 2.2; Hab 2.7
escape [2] Mic 2.3; Zeph 2.3
exile Mic 5.3; Zeph 3.19
filthy Ezek 11.18; Zech 3.3
heal Mic 1.9; Zech 11.16
horror Hos 6.10; Zeph 2.15
joy Joel 2.21; Hab 1.15
leading Jer 27.19; Mt 2.6
lie (2) Mic 6.12; Hab 2.18
naked Mic 1.8; Mt 25.36
power 2.1; Hab 1.6
protect 1.7; Hab 1.12
punish [2] 1.2; Hab 1.12
ripe Hos 9.10; Zech 12.6
ruin Mic 6.13; Hab 2.10
scatter Joel 3.2; Hab 3.14
shame Hos 10.6; Hab 2.10
slave Mic 6.4; Mt 6.24
strength 2.10; Hab 3.19
strip (1) Mic 3.3; Zeph 2.14
stumble 2.5; Hab 3.16
sympathy Dan 1.9; Heb 4.15

[c] *Some ancient translations* horses; *Hebrew* cypresses.
[e] *Probable text* Like water...Nineveh; *Hebrew unclear.*
[f] enslaved; *or* seduced.

swarm of locusts that stay in the walls on a cold day. But when the sun comes out, they fly away, and no one knows where they have gone!

18 Emperor of Assyria, your governors are **dead**, and your noblemen are asleep for ever! Your people are **scattered** on the mountains, and there is no one to bring them home again.
19 There is no remedy for your injuries, and your wounds cannot be **healed**. All those who hear the news of your **destruction** clap their hands for **joy**. Did anyone **escape** your endless **cruelty**?

THE BOOK OF HABAKKUK

INTRODUCTION

The words of the prophet Habakkuk come from near the end of the seventh century B.C., at a time when the Babylonians were in power. He was deeply disturbed by the violence of these cruel people, and asked the Lord, "So why are you silent while they destroy people who are more righteous than they are?" (1.13). The Lord's answer was that he would take action in his own good time, and meanwhile "those who are righteous will live because they are faithful to God" (2.4).

The rest of the book is a prophecy of doom on the unrighteous, with a concluding psalm celebrating the greatness of God and expressing the undying faith of the poet.

Outline of Contents

---

believe Mic 7.5; Mt 8.13
best Mic 7.4; Mt 23.6
captive Nah 2.7; Lk 4.18
choose Mic 7.14; 3.13
conquer [2] Mic 5.6; 2.5
contempt Nah 3.6; Mal 1.7
destroy [3] Nah 3.13; 2.10
direct Is 48.17; 1 Cor 12.28
endure Mic 7.9; Mal 3.2
eternal Dan 12.2; 3.6
evil [3] Mic 7.3; 2.4
fear Nah 2.10; 3.16
god (2) (other gods) Nah 1.14; 2.18
God's people Nah 1.7; Zeph 1.7
help Mic 1.14; Zeph 3.2
holy [2] Mic 1.3; 2.20
hunger Mic 7.1; Zeph 3.3
joy Nah 3.19; 3.18
justice [2] Mic 6.8; Zeph 3.5
law [2] Mic 3.11; Zeph 3.4
mercy Mic 7.19; 3.2
message Nah 1.1; 2.4
offer Mic 6.6; Zeph 3.10
pervert Lam 3.36; Rom 1.26
power [2] Nah 3.9; 3.4
prophet Mic 7.4; 3.1
protect Nah 3.8; Zech 2.5
proud Mic 2.3; 2.5
provide Dan 1.16; Mt 6.33
punish Nah 3.4; 2.16
quarrel Mic 7.6; Acts 6.1
rest (1) Dan 4.12; 2.5
reveal Mic 3.11; 2.2
righteous [2] Amos 5.24; 2.4

1 This is the message that the LORD
revealed to the prophet Habakkuk.

Habakkuk Complains of Injustice

2 O LORD, how long must I call for
help before you listen, before you save us
from violence? 3 Why do you make me
see such trouble? How can you endure to
look on such wrongdoing? Destruction
and violence are all round me, and there
is fighting and quarrelling everywhere.
4 The law is weak and useless, and justice
is never done. Evil men get the better of
the righteous, and so justice is perverted.

The LORD's Reply

5 Then the LORD said to his people,
"Keep watching the nations round you,
and you will be astonished at what you
see. I am going to do something that you
will not believe when you hear about it.
6 I am bringing the Babylonians to power,
those fierce, restless people. They are
marching out across the world to conquer other lands. 7 They spread fear and
terror, and in their pride they are a law
to themselves.

8 "Their horses are faster than leopards, fiercer than hungry wolves. Their
horsemen come riding from distant
lands; their horses paw the ground. They
come swooping down like eagles attacking their prey.

9 "Their armies advance in violent
conquest, and everyone is terrified as
they approach.[b] Their captives are as
numerous as grains of sand. 10 They treat
kings with contempt and laugh at high
officials. No fortress can stop them—they
pile up earth against it and capture it.
11 Then they sweep on like the wind and
are gone, these men whose power is
their god."

Habakkuk Complains to the LORD Again

12 LORD, from the very beginning you
are God. You are my God, holy and eternal. LORD, my God and protector, you
have chosen the Babylonians and made
them strong so that they can punish us.
13 But how can you stand these treacherous, evil men? Your eyes are too holy to
look at evil, and you cannot stand the
sight of people doing wrong. So why are
you silent while they destroy people who
are more righteous than they are?

14 How can you treat people like fish
or like a swarm of insects that have no
ruler to direct them? 15 The Babylonians
catch people with hooks, as though they
were fish. They drag them off in nets and
shout for joy over their catch! 16 They
even worship their nets and offer sacrifices to them, because their nets provide
them with the best of everything.

17 Are they going to use their swords
for ever and keep on destroying nations
without mercy?

The LORD's Answer to Habakkuk

2 I will climb my watch-tower and
wait to see what the LORD will tell
me to say and what answer he[x] will give
to my complaint.

sacrifice Jon 2.9; Zeph 1.7
save Mic 7.7; 3.13
sight Ezek 32.31; Mt 9.30
strong Nah 1.12; Zech 9.17
terrify Jon 1.5; 2.17
terror Nah 2.6
trouble Nah 1.7; Zeph 1.15
useless Hos 12.1; 2.13
violent [3] Mic 4.13; 2.8
watch Mic 7.4; 2.1
weak Obad 2; Zech 12.8
world Nah 1.5; 2.8
worship (2) (of other gods) Mic 5.13; Zeph 1.4
wrong [2] Mic 7.9; Zeph 3.5

Almighty Nah 3.5; Zeph 2.8
complain Hos 4.4; Lk 5.30
conquer [4] 1.6; Rom 12.21

[b] *Probable text* and everyone...approach; *Hebrew unclear.*
[x] *One ancient translation* he; *Hebrew* I.

1.5: Acts 13.41 **1.6:** 2 Kgs 24.2

crime Amos 5.12; Mt 27.23
cup Obad 16; Zech 12.2
danger Jon 1.4; Zech 9.16
death (1) Nah 1.8; 3.5
debt [2] Amos 8.6; Mt 18.25
deceive Mic 3.5; Zeph 3.13
destroy 1.3; 3.13
disgrace [2] Mic 7.10; Zeph 3.18
doom [5] Nah 3.1; Zeph 2.5
enemy Nah 3.11; Zeph 1.7
evil 1.4; Zech 1.4
faithful Mic 7.20; Zech 8.3
force (1) [2] Mic 5.6; Zeph 3.8
fury Nah 1.6; 3.8
glory Nah 2.2; Zech 2.5
god (2) (other gods) 1.11; Zeph 1.5
greed Ezek 33.31; Zeph 3.3
harm Mic 3.11; Zech 7.10
holy 1.12; 3.3
honour [2] Hos 9.5; Zeph 3.19
humiliate Mic 3.7; Acts 8.33
idol [2] Nah 1.14; Zech 10.2
knowledge Dan 5.11; Mal 2.7
lie (2) Nah 3.1; Zeph 3.13
life (1) Jon 2.7; Zeph 3.17
message 1.1; Zeph 1.1
neighbour Mic 7.5; Zech 3.10
presence Nah 1.5; Zeph 1.7
proud 1.7; Zeph 2.10
punish 1.12; 3.16
rest (1) 1.6; Zeph 2.15
reveal [2] 1.1; Zech 3.8
rich [2] Mic 7.14; Zech 11.5
righteous 1.4; Zeph 3.5
ruin Nah 3.7; Zeph 1.15
safe Nah 2.11; 3.19
satisfy Mic 6.14; Zeph 1.12
scheme Nah 1.11
scorn Ezek 28.24; Heb 11.26
shame [2] Nah 3.5; Zeph 2.1
tablet 2 Chr 6.11; Lk 1.63
Temple (1) (of God) Mic 4.1; Hag 1.2
terrify 1.9; Zeph 2.11
tremble Nah 2.10; 3.6
true [2] Amos 2.11; Mal 2.7
trust Mic 7.5; Zeph 3.2
turn [2] Nah 2.8; Zeph 1.6
useless 1.4; Zech 10.2
violent [3] 1.2; Zech 8.17

2 The LORD gave me this answer:
"Write down clearly on clay **tablets** what
I **reveal** to you, so that it can be read at a
glance. 3 Put it in writing, because it is
not yet time for it to come **true**. But the
time is coming quickly, and what I show
you will come **true**. It may seem slow in
coming, but wait for it; it will certainly
take place, and it will not be delayed.
4 And this is the **message**: 'Those who are
evil will not survive,[c] but those who are
righteous will live because they are **faithful** to God.' "

Doom on the Unrighteous

5 Wealth is **deceitful**. **Greedy** men are
proud and **restless**—like **death** itself they
are never **satisfied**. That is why they **conquer** nation after nation for themselves.
6 The conquered people will taunt their
conquerors and show their **scorn** for
them. They will say, "You take what isn't
yours, but you are **doomed**! How long
will you go on getting **rich** by **forcing**
your **debtors** to pay up?"
7 But before you know it, you that
have **conquered** others will be in **debt**
yourselves and be **forced** to pay interest.
Enemies will come and make you
tremble. They will plunder you! 8 You
have plundered the people of many
nations, but now those who have survived will plunder you because of the
murders you have committed and because of your **violence** against the people
of the **world** and its cities.[d]
9 You are **doomed**! You have made
your family **rich** with what you took by
violence, and have tried to make your
own home **safe** from **harm** and **danger**!
10 But your **schemes** have brought **shame**
on your family; by **destroying** many
nations you have only brought **ruin** on
yourself. 11 Even the stones of the walls
cry out against you, and the rafters echo
the cry.
12 You are **doomed**! You founded a
city on **crime** and built it up by murder.
13 The nations you **conquered** wore themselves out in **useless** labour, and all they
have built goes up in flames. The LORD
Almighty has done this. 14 But the earth
will be as full of the **knowledge** of the
LORD's **glory** as the seas are full of water.
15 You are **doomed**! In your **fury** you
humiliated and **disgraced** your **neighbours**; you made them stagger as though
they were drunk. 16 You in **turn** will be
covered with **shame** instead of **honour**.
You yourself will drink and stagger. The
LORD will make you drink your own **cup**
of **punishment**, and your **honour** will be
turned to **disgrace**. 17 You have cut down
the forests of Lebanon; now you will be
cut down. You killed its animals; now
animals will **terrify** you. This will happen
because of the murders you have committed and because of your **violence**
against the people of the **world** and its
cities.[d]
18 What's the use of an **idol**? It is only
something that a man has made, and it
tells you nothing but **lies**. What good does
it do for its maker to **trust** it—a **god** that
can't even talk! 19 You are **doomed**! You
say to a piece of wood, "Wake up!" or to
a block of stone, "Get up!" Can an **idol**
reveal anything to you? It may be
covered with silver and gold, but there is
no **life** in it.
20 The LORD is in his **holy Temple**; let
everyone on earth be silent in his **presence**.

A Prayer of Habakkuk

3 This is a **prayer** of the **prophet**
Habakkuk:[e]

2 O LORD, I have heard of what you have
done,
and I am filled with **awe**.
Now do again in our times
the great deeds you used to do.
Be **merciful**, even when you are **angry**.

3 God is coming again from Edom;
the **holy** God is coming from the
hills of Paran.
His **splendour** covers the **heavens**;
and the earth is full of his **praise**.
4 He comes with the brightness of
lightning;
light flashes from his hand,
there where his **power** is hidden.
5 He sends **disease** before him
and **commands death** to follow him.
6 When he stops, the earth shakes;
at his glance the nations **tremble**.
The **eternal** mountains are shattered;
the **everlasting** hills sink down,
the hills where he walked in **ancient**
times.

7 I saw the people of Cushan **afraid**
and the people of Midian **tremble**.
8 Was it the rivers that made you **angry**,
LORD?

watch 1.5; Zech 5.7
world [2] 1.6; Zeph 2.15

afraid Mic 7.17; Zeph 3.13
ancient Mic 5.2; Heb 11.2
anger [3] Nah 1.2; Zeph 1.18
awe Is 41.23; Acts 2.43
body Nah 3.3; Zeph 1.17
choose 1.12; Hag 2.23
cloud [2] Nah 1.3; Zeph 1.15
command Nah 1.4; Zeph 2.3
death (1) 2.5; Mt 4.16
destroy 2.10; Zeph 1.2
disease Ezek 38.22; Zech 14.12
eternal 1.12; Mt 18.8
everlasting Mic 6.2; Zeph 2.9
fail Mic 3.7; Zeph 3.5
fear 1.7; Mal 1.14
follower Dan 11.24; Mt 5.11
fury [2] 2.15; Zeph 1.15
glad Obad 12; Zech 4.10
heaven Mic 6.6; Hag 2.6
holy 2.20; Zech 1.14
joy 1.15; Zeph 3.14
light (1) Mic 7.8; Mt 4.16
mercy 1.17; Zech 1.12
might Jon 2.3; Zech 4.6
oppress Amos 6.14; Zeph 3.1
poor Mic 6.12; Mt 5.3
power 1.6; Zeph 2.13
praise Jon 2.9; Zeph 3.19

[c] *Probable text* will not survive; *Hebrew unclear.*
[d] the people...cities; *or* the land, the city, and those who live in it.
[e] *Hebrew has an additional phrase, the meaning of which is unclear.*

2.3: Heb 10.37 **2.4:** Rom 1.17; Gal 3.11; Heb 10.38 **2.14:** Is 11.9

prayer Mic 3.4; Zech 3.7
prophet 1.1; Zeph 3.4
punish 2.16; Zeph 1.4
rise Mic 7.8; Zeph 3.8
safe 2.9; Zeph 2.15
save [2] 1.2; Zeph 1.18
Saviour Hos 13.4; Lk 1.47
scatter Nah 3.18; Zeph 3.10
secret Dan 12.9; Mt 2.7
sheep Mic 6.7; Zeph 2.6
Sovereign Mic 1.2; Zech 9.14
splendour Hos 10.5; Hag 2.3
strength Nah 3.14; Zech 4.6
strike Amos 9.1; Zech 2.8
stumble Nah 3.3; Jn 11.9
tremble [4] 2.7; Mt 28.4
victory Nah 1.15; Zeph 3.17
vine Mic 7.1; Hag 2.19
wicked Nah 1.11; Zeph 1.3

Was it the sea that made you
furious?
You rode upon the clouds;
the storm cloud was your chariot,
as you brought victory to your
people.
9 You got ready to use your bow,
ready to shoot your arrows.[f]
Your lightning split open the earth.
10 When the mountains saw you, they
trembled;
water poured down from the skies.
The waters under the earth roared,
and their waves rose high.
11 At the flash of your speeding arrows
and the gleam of your shining spear,
the sun and the moon stood still.
12 You marched across the earth in
anger;
in fury you trampled the nations.
13 You went out to save your people,
to save your chosen king.
You struck down the leader of the
wicked
and completely destroyed his
followers.[h]
14 Your arrows pierced the commander
of his army
when it came like a storm to scatter
us,
gloating like those who secretly
oppress the poor.[i]
15 You trampled the sea with your
horses,
and the mighty waters foamed.

16 I hear all this, and I tremble;
my lips quiver with fear.
My body goes limp,
and my feet stumble[j] beneath me.

I will quietly wait for the time to come
when God will punish those who
attack us.

17 Even though the fig-trees have no fruit
and no grapes grow on the vines,
even though the olive-crop fails
and the fields produce no corn,
even though the sheep all die
and the cattle-stalls are empty,
18 I will still be joyful and glad,
because the LORD God is my
saviour.
19 The Sovereign LORD gives me
strength.
He makes me sure-footed as a deer,
and keeps me safe on the mountains.

[f] *Probable text* ready to shoot your arrows; *Hebrew unclear.*
[h] *Probable text* completely...followers; *Hebrew unclear.* [i] *Verse 14 in Hebrew is unclear.*
[j] *Probable text* my feet stumble; *Hebrew* I am excited, because.

3.19: 2 Sam 22.34; Ps 18.33

THE BOOK OF ZEPHANIAH

INTRODUCTION

The prophet Zephaniah preached in the latter part of the seventh century B.C., probably in the decade before King Josiah's religious reforms of 621 B.C. The book contains the familiar prophetic themes: A day of doom and destruction is threatened, when Judah will be punished for her worship of other gods. The Lord will punish other nations also. Although Jerusalem is doomed, in time the city will be restored, with a humble and righteous people living there.

Outline of Contents

---

1 This is the **message** that the LORD
gave to Zephaniah during the time
that Josiah son of Amon was king of
Judah. (Zephaniah was descended from
King Hezekiah through Amariah, Gedaliah, and Cushi.)

The Day of the LORD's Judgement

2 The LORD said, "I am going to destroy everything on earth, 3 all human beings and animals, birds and fish. I will
bring about the downfall of[a] the wicked.
I will destroy all mankind, and no survivors will be left. I, the LORD, have
spoken.
4 "I will punish the people of
Jerusalem and of all Judah. I will destroy
the last trace of the worship of Baal
there, and no one will even remember
the pagan priests who serve him. 5 I will
destroy anyone who goes up on the roof
and worships the sun, the moon, and the
stars. I will also destroy those who worship me and swear loyalty to me, but
then take oaths in the name of the god
Molech. 6 I will destroy those who have
turned back and no longer follow me,
those who do not come to me or ask me
to guide them."
7 The day is near when the LORD will
sit in judgement; so be silent in his presence. The LORD is preparing to sacrifice
his people and has invited enemies to
plunder Judah. 8 "On that day of
slaughter," says the LORD, "I will punish
the officials, the king's sons, and all who
practise foreign customs. 9 I will punish
all who worship like pagans and who
steal and kill in order to fill their master's house[b] with loot.
10 "On that day," says the LORD, "you
will hear the sound of crying at the Fish
Gate in Jerusalem. You will hear wailing
in the newer part of the city and a great
crashing sound in the hills. 11 Wail and
cry when you hear this, you that live in
the lower part of the city, because all the
merchants will be dead!
12 "At that time I will take a lamp and
search Jerusalem. I will punish the
people who are self-satisfied and confident, who say to themselves, 'The LORD
never does anything, one way or the
other.' 13 Their wealth will be looted and
their houses destroyed. They will never
live in the houses they are building or
drink wine from the vineyards they are
planting."
14 The great day of the LORD is near—
very near and coming fast! That will be
a bitter day, for even[c] the bravest soldiers will cry out in despair! 15 It will be a
day of fury, a day of trouble and distress,
a day of ruin and destruction, a day of
darkness and gloom, a black and cloudy
day, 16 a day filled with the sound of war-
trumpets and the battle-cry of soldiers
attacking fortified cities and high towers.
17 The LORD says, "I will bring such
disasters on mankind that everyone will
grope about like a blind man. They have
sinned against me, and now their blood
will be poured out like water, and their

[a] *Probable text* I will bring about the downfall of; *Hebrew* the stumbling blocks.
[b] their master's house; *or* the temple of their god.
[c] That...even; *or* Listen! That terrible day is coming when even.

1.1: 2 Kgs 22.1—23.30; 2 Chr 34.1—35.27

anger Hab 3.2; 2.2
being Dan 7.13; Mt 16.17
bitter Obad 16; Zech 12.10
blind Lam 4.14; Zech 11.17
blood Joel 2.30; Zech 9.7
body Hab 3.16; Hag 2.13
cloud Hab 3.8; Zech 10.1
confident Mic 7.7; Rom 1.16
custom Ezek 20.18; Lk 1.9
dark Mic 7.8; Zech 14.7
Day of the Lord Amos 5.18; Mal 4.5
dead [2] Nah 3.3; Hag 2.13
despair Mic 2.4; Lk 21.25
destroy [9] Hab 3.13; 2.5
disaster Mic 2.3; Zech 8.13
distress Jon 2.2; Mk 14.33
downfall Ezek 35.14
enemy Hab 2.7; 3.15
fury [2] Hab 3.8; 2.2
gloom Amos 5.20; Mk 10.22
god (2) (other gods) Hab 2.18; 2.11
God's people Hab 1.5; 2.8
guide Jer 31.9; Mt 2.6
human Hos 13.2; Mt 16.17
judge Mic 7.3; 3.3
last (2) Ezek 40.15; Zech 4.7
loyal Mic 7.2; Mt 6.24
mankind [2] Jer 45.5; Mt 5.13
master Dan 10.17; Mal 1.6
message Hab 2.4; Hag 1.1
new Mic 4.7; 3.17

oath Ezek 17.16; Zech 5.3
pagan [2] Hos 9.1; Mt 5.47
practice Mic 6.16; Mal 3.5
presence Hab 2.20; Zech 2.13
priest Mic 3.11; 3.4
punish [4] Hab 3.16; 2.3
remember Mic 6.5; Hag 2.3
ruin Hab 2.10; 2.9
sacrifice Hab 1.16; Hag 2.12
satisfy Hab 2.5; Zech 7.6
save Hab 3.13; Zech 8.13
serve Jon 1.16; Zech 4.14
slaughter Ezek 35.5; Acts 7.42
steal Mic 2.8; Mal 1.13
swear Amos 8.7; 2.9
trouble Hab 1.3; Zech 10.2
turn Hab 2.16; 2.3
vineyard Mic 4.4; Hag 1.11
wail [2] Mic 1.8; Zech 11.2
wicked Hab 3.13; Zech 5.8
worship (1) (of God) Mic 6.6; 2.11
worship (2) (of other gods) [3] Hab 1.16; Zech 13.2

dead bodies will lie rotting on the
ground."
18 On the day when the LORD shows
his **fury**, not even all their silver and gold
will **save** them. The whole earth will be
destroyed by the fire of his **anger**. He will
put an end—a sudden end—to everyone
who lives on earth.

A Plea for Repentance

2 **Shameless** nation, come to your
senses 2 before you are driven away
like chaff blown by the wind, before the
burning **anger of the** LORD comes upon
you, before the day when he shows his
fury. 3 **Turn to** the LORD, all you **humble**
people of the land, who **obey** his **commands**. Do what is **right**, and **humble**
yourselves before the LORD. Perhaps you
will **escape punishment** on the day when
the LORD shows his **anger**.

The Doom of the Nations round Israel

4 No one will be left in the city of
Gaza. Ashkelon will be deserted. The
people of Ashdod will be driven out in
half a day,[x] and the people of Ekron will
be driven from their city. 5 You
Philistines are **doomed**, you people who
live along the coast. The LORD has
passed **sentence** on you. He will **destroy**
you, and not one of you will be left. 6 Your
land by the sea will become open fields
with **shepherds'** huts and **sheep** pens.
7 The people of Judah who survive will
occupy your land. They will pasture their
flocks there and sleep in the houses of
Ashkelon. The LORD their God will be
with them and make them **prosper** again.
8 The LORD **Almighty** says, "I have
heard the people of Moab and Ammon
insulting and taunting **my people**, and
boasting that they would seize their land.
9 As **surely** as I am the living LORD, the
God of Israel, I **swear** that Moab and
Ammon are going to **be destroyed** like
Sodom and Gomorrah. They will become
a place of salt pits and **everlasting ruin**,
overgrown with **weeds**. Those of **my
people** who survive will plunder them
and take their land."
10 That is how the people of Moab and
Ammon will be **punished** for their **pride**
and **arrogance** and for **insulting** the
people of the LORD **Almighty**. 11 The LORD
will **terrify** them. He will reduce the **gods**
of the earth to nothing, and then every
nation will **worship** him, each in its own
land.
12 The LORD will also put the people
of Sudan **to death**.
13 The LORD will use his **power** to **destroy** Assyria. He will make the city of
Nineveh a deserted **ruin**, a waterless
desert. 14 It will be a place where **flocks**,
herds, and animals of every kind will lie
down. Owls will live among its **ruins** and
hoot from the windows. Crows[e] will caw
on the doorsteps. The cedar-wood of her
buildings will be **stripped** away. 15 That is
what will happen to the city that is so
proud of its own **power** and thinks it is
safe. Its people think that their city is the
greatest in the **world**. What a **desolate**
place it will become, a place where wild
animals will **rest**! Everyone who passes
by will shrink back in **horror**.

Jerusalem's Sin and Redemption

3 Jerusalem is **doomed**, that **corrupt**,
rebellious city that **oppresses** its
own people. 2 It has not listened to the
LORD or **accepted** his **discipline**. It has
not put its **trust** in the LORD or asked for
his **help**. 3 Its officials are like roaring
lions; its **judges** are like **hungry** wolves,
too **greedy** to leave a bone until morning.
4 The **prophets** are irresponsible and
treacherous; the **priests defile** what is
sacred, and twist the **law** of God to their
own **advantage**. 5 But the LORD is still in
the city; he does what is **right** and never
what is **wrong**. Every morning without
fail, he brings **justice** to **his people**. And
yet the **unrighteous** people there keep on
doing **wrong** and are not **ashamed**.
6 The LORD says, "I have wiped out
whole nations; I have **destroyed** their
cities and left their walls and towers in
ruins. The cities are deserted; the streets
are empty—no one is left. 7 I thought that
then **my people** would have **reverence**
for me and **accept** my **discipline**, that
they would never **forget**[f] the **lesson** I
taught them. But soon they were behaving as **badly** as ever.
8 "Just wait," the LORD says. "Wait for
the day when I **rise** to **accuse** the nations.
I have made up my **mind** to gather
nations and kingdoms, in order to let
them feel the **force** of my **anger**. The
whole earth will be **destroyed** by the fire
of my **fury**.
9 "Then I will **change** the people of
the nations, and they will **pray** to me

[x] in half a day; *or* by a surprise attack at noon.
[e] *Some ancient translations* Crows; *Hebrew* Desolation.
[f] *Some ancient translations* they would never forget; *Hebrew* their dwelling would not be cut off.

2.4-7: Is 14.29-31; Jer 47.1-7; Ezek 25.15-17; Joel 3.4-8; Amos 1.6-8; Zech 9.5-7
2.8-11: Is 15.1-16.14, 25.10-12; Jer 48.1-49.6; Ezek 21.28-32, 25.1-11; Amos 1.13-15 **2.9:** Gen 19.24
2.12: Is 18.1-7 **2.13-15:** Is 10.5-34, 14.24-27; Nah 1.1—3.19

help [2] Hab 1.2; Zech 1.17
honour Hab 2.16; Zech 6.13
humble 2.3; Zech 9.6
hunger Hab 1.8; Mt 4.2
joy [3] Hab 3.18; Zech 2.10
judge 1.7; Zech 14.1
justice Hab 1.4; Zech 7.9
law Hab 1.4; Zech 3.7
lesson Is 28.10; Mt 24.32
lie (2) Hab 2.18; Zech 5.3
life (1) Hab 2.19; Zech 1.4
love Mic 7.18; Zech 1.14
mind (1) Mic 4.12; Zech 7.11
need Amos 8.4; Zech 7.10
never again Mic 4.3; Mal 2.12
new 1.10; Hag 2.9
obey 2.3; Hag 1.12
offer Hab 1.16; Hag 2.14
oppress [2] Hab 3.14; Zech 7.10
power 2.13; Hag 2.22
praise Hab 3.3; Zech 11.5
pray Jon 4.2; Zech 7.2
priest 1.4; Hag 2.11
prophet Hab 3.1; Hag 1.1

alone and not to other **gods**. They will all
obey me. 10 Even from distant Sudan my
scattered people will bring **offerings** to
me. 11 At that time you, **my people**, will
no longer **need** to be **ashamed** that you
rebelled against me. I will remove everyone who is **proud** and **arrogant**, and you
will **never again rebel** against me on my
sacred hill.[g] 12 I will leave there a **humble**
and lowly people, who will come to me
for **help**. 13 The people of Israel who survive will do no **wrong** to anyone, tell no
lies, nor try to **deceive**. They will be **prosperous** and **secure**, **afraid** of no one."

A Song of Joy

14 Sing and shout for **joy**, people of
Israel!
Rejoice with all your heart,
Jerusalem!
15 The LORD has ended your **punishment**;
he has removed all your **enemies**.
The LORD, the king of Israel, is with
you;
there is no **reason** now to be **afraid**.
16 The time is coming when they will say
to Jerusalem,
"Do not be **afraid**, city of Zion!
Do not let your hands hang limp!
17 The LORD your God is with you;
his **power** gives you **victory**.
The LORD will take **delight** in you,
and in his love he will give you **new
life**.[h]
He will sing and be **joyful** over you,
18 as **joyful** as people at a **festival**."
The LORD says,
"I have ended the **threat of doom**
and taken away your **disgrace**.[i]
19 The time is coming!
I will **punish** your **oppressors**;
I will **rescue** all the lame
and bring the **exiles** home.
I will **turn** their **shame** to **honour**,
and all the **world** will **praise** them.
20 The time is coming!
I will bring your **scattered** people
home;
I will make you famous throughout
the **world**
and make you **prosperous** once
again."
The LORD has spoken.

prosper [2] 2.7; Hag 2.9
proud 2.10; Zech 9
punish [2] 2.3; Zech 1.6
reason Mic 7.8; Mt 13.13
rebel [3] Mic 1.5; Mk 15.7
rejoice Joel 2.23; Zech 9.9
rescue Mic 6.4; Zech 8.7
reverence Is 33.6; Acts 9.31
right (1) 2.3; Hag
righteous Hab 2.4; Mal 3.18
rise Hab 3.10; Mal 4.2
ruin 2.9; Hag 1.4
sacred [2] Mic 5.13
Zech 2.12
scatter [2] Hab 3.1
Zech 1.19
secure Amos 2.8; Zech 3.10
shame 2.1; Mk 12.4
teach Mic 4.2; Zech 7.12
threat Mic 3.5; Zech 11.16
trust Hab 2.18; Mt 27.43
turn 2.3; Hag 1.9
victory Hab 3.8; Zech 9.9
world [2] 2.15; Hag 2.8
wrong [3] Hab 1.3; Mal 1.8

[g] SACRED HILL: *Mount Zion (see Zion in Word List).*
[h] *Some ancient translations* give you new life; *Hebrew* be silent. [i] *Verse 18 in Hebrew is unclear.*

3.13: Rev 14.5

THE BOOK OF HAGGAI

INTRODUCTION

The book of *Haggai* is a collection of brief messages that came from the Lord through the prophet Haggai in 520 B.C. The people had returned from exile and had lived in Jerusalem for some years, but the Temple still lay in ruins. The messages urge the leaders of the people to rebuild the Temple, and the Lord promises prosperity and peace in the future for a renewed and purified people.

Outline of Contents

---

afraid Zeph 3.13; 2.5
Almighty [2] Zeph 2.8; 2.9
enough [4] Jon 4.9; Mt 3.11
exile [2] Zeph 3.19; Zech 2.6
God's people Zeph 3.5; 2.9
harvest [3] Mic 6.15; Mt 6.26
High Priest [2] Dan 11.22; 2.2
hope Mic 7.1; Zech 9.5
inspire Hos 9.7; Mt 22.43
message [3] Zeph 1.1; 2.20
obey Zeph 3.9; Zech 1.4
please Mic 6.7; Mal 1.8
promise Nah 1.15; 2.5
prophet [3] Zeph 3.4; 2.1
right (1) Zeph 3.5; Mal 2.6
ruin [2] Zeph 3.6; 2.17
sow Mic 6.15; Zech 8.12
Temple (1) (of God) [6] Hab 2.20; 2.3
turn Zeph 3.19; Zech 8.10
vineyard Zeph 1.13; Zech 3.10
worship (1) (of God) Zeph 2.11; Zech 5.11

The LORD's Command to Rebuild the Temple

1 During the second year that Darius
was emperor of Persia, on the first
day of the sixth month, the LORD spoke
through the **prophet** Haggai. The **message** was for the governor of Judah,
Zerubbabel son of Shealtiel, and for the
High Priest, Joshua son of Jehozadak.
2 The LORD **Almighty** said to Haggai,
"These people say that this is not the
right time to rebuild the **Temple**." 3 The
LORD then gave this **message** to the
people through the **prophet** Haggai:
4 "**My people**, why should you be living in
well-built houses while my **Temple** lies in
ruins? 5 Don't you see what is happening
to you? 6 You have **sown** much corn, but
have **harvested** very little. You have food
to eat, but not **enough** to make you full.
You have wine to drink, but not **enough**
to get drunk on! You have clothing, but
not **enough** to keep you warm. And the
working man cannot earn **enough** to live
on. 7 Can't you see why this has
happened? 8 Now go up into the hills, get
timber, and rebuild the **Temple**; then I
will be **pleased** and will be **worshipped** as
I should be.
9 "You **hoped** for large **harvests**, but
they **turned** out to be small. And when
you brought the **harvest** home, I blew it
away.[a] Why did I do that? Because my
Temple lies in **ruins** while every one of
you is busy working on his own house.
10 That is why there is no rain and
nothing can grow. 11 I have brought
drought on the land—on its hills, cornfields, **vineyards**, and olive orchards—on
every crop the ground produces, on men
and animals, on everything you try to
grow."

The People Obey the LORD's Command

12 Then Zerubbabel and Joshua and
all the people who had returned from the
exile[b] in Babylonia, did what the LORD
their God told them to do. They were
afraid and **obeyed** the **prophet** Haggai,
the LORD's messenger. 13 Then Haggai
gave the LORD's **message** to the people:
"I will be with you—that is my **promise**."
14 The LORD **inspired** everyone to work on
the **Temple**: Zerubbabel, the governor of
Judah; Joshua, the **High Priest**, and all
the people who had returned from the
exile.[b] They began working on the
Temple of the LORD **Almighty**, their God,
15 on the twenty-fourth day of the sixth
month of the second year that Darius
was emperor.

The Splendour of the New Temple

afraid 1.12; Zech 8.13
Almighty [3] 1.2; Zech 1.2
altar Amos 9.1; Zech 9.15
bless Mic 2.9; Zech 7.2
body Zeph 1.17; Mal 2.15
bread Amos 8.11; Mt 4.3
choose Hab 3.13; Zech 4.14
complete Is 28.21; Mt 20.25
consecrate [2] Ezek 43.20
dead Zeph 1.11; Mt 2.18
defile [3] Zeph 3.4; Mal 2.11
discourage Ezek 13.22; Lk 18.1

2 On the twenty-first day of the
seventh month of that same year,
the LORD spoke again through the **prophet** Haggai. 2 He told Haggai to speak to
Zerubbabel, the governor of Judah, to
Joshua, the **High Priest**, and to the
people, and to say to them, 3 "Is there
anyone among you who can still **remember** how **splendid** the **Temple** used to be?
How does it look to you now? It must
seem like nothing at all. 4 But now don't
be **discouraged**, any of you. Do the work,
for I am with you. 5 When you came out
of Egypt, I **promised** that I would always
be with you. I am still with you, so do not
be **afraid**.
6 "Before long I will shake **heaven and**

[a] I blew it away; *or* I spoilt it. [b] who had returned from the exile; *or* who had not gone into exile.
[b] *See 1.12.*

1.1: Ezra 4.24–5.2, 6.14 **2.3:** Ezra 3.12 **2.5:** Ex 29.45–46 **2.6:** Heb 12.26

God's people 1.4; Zech 1.15
heaven [2] Hab 3.3; Zech 3.4
High Priest 1.1; Zech 3.1
message 1.1; Zech 1.1
name (2) (name of God, of Jesus) Amos 9.6; Zech 14.9
new Zeph 3.17; Zech 3.4
offer Zeph 3.10; Zech 14.21
overthrow [2] Dan 7.24; Zech 1.21
peace Mic 5.5; Zech 1.15
power Zeph 3.17; Zech 1.19
priest [3] Zeph 3.4; Zech 3.8
promise 1.13; Zech 2.5
prophet [2] 1.1; Zech 1.1
prosper Zeph 3.13; Zech 1.17
question [2] Dan 4.35; Zech 7.3
remember Zeph 1.4; Zech 10.7
repent Jon 3.5; Zech 1.6
ruin 1.4; Zech 5.4
sacrifice Zeph 1.7; Zech 9.11
servant Nah 2.7; Zech 1.6
splendour [2] Hab 3.3; Rev 18.1
Temple (1) (of God) [5] 1.2; Zech 1.16
vine Hab 3.17; Zech 8.12
world Zeph 3.19; Zech 1.11

earth, land and sea. 7 I will overthrow all
the nations, and their treasures will be
brought here, and the Temple will be
filled with wealth. 8 All the silver and gold
of the world is mine. 9 The new Temple
will be more splendid than the old one,
and there I will give my people
prosperity and peace." The LORD
Almighty has spoken.

The Prophet Consults the Priests

10 On the twenty-fourth day of the
ninth month of the second year that
Darius was emperor, the LORD Almighty
spoke again to the prophet Haggai. 11 He
said, "Ask the priests for a ruling on this
question: 12 Suppose someone takes a
piece of consecrated meat from a sacrifice and carries it in a fold of his robe. If
he then lets his robe touch any bread,
cooked food, wine, olive-oil, or any kind
of food at all, will it make that food
consecrated also?"

When the question was asked, the
priests answered, "No."

13 Then Haggai asked, "Suppose a
man is defiled because he has touched a
dead body. If he then touches any of
these foods, will that make them defiled
too?"

The priests answered, "Yes."

14 Then Haggai said, "The LORD says
that the same thing applies to the people
of this nation and to everything they produce; and so everything they offer on the
altar is defiled."

2.13: Num 19.11-22

The LORD Promises His Blessing

15 The LORD says, "Can't you see what
has happened to you? Before you started
to rebuild the Temple, 16 you would go to
a heap of corn expecting to find two
hundred kilogrammes, but there would
be only a hundred. You would go to draw
a hundred litres of wine from a vat, but
find only forty. 17 I sent scorching winds
and hail to ruin everything you tried to
grow, but still you did not repent. 18 Today is the twenty-fourth day of the ninth
month, the day that the foundation of the
Temple has been completed. See what is
going to happen from now on. 19 Although
there is no corn left, and the grapevines,
fig-trees, pomegranates, and olive-trees
have not yet produced, yet from now on I
will bless you."

The LORD's Promise to Zerubbabel

20 On that same day, the twenty-
fourth of the month, the LORD gave Haggai a second message 21 for Zerubbabel,
the governor of Judah: "I am about to
shake heaven and earth 22 and overthrow
kingdoms and end their power. I will
overturn chariots and their drivers; the
horses will die, and their riders will kill
one another. 23 On that day I will take
you, Zerubbabel my servant, and I will
appoint you to rule in my name. You are
the one I have chosen." The LORD
Almighty has spoken.

THE BOOK OF
ZECHARIAH

INTRODUCTION

The book of *Zechariah* has two distinct parts: (1) *Chapters 1-8* Prophecies from the prophet Zechariah, dated at various times in the years from 520 to 518 B.C. These are largely in the form of visions, and deal with the restoration of Jerusalem, the rebuilding of the Temple, the purification of God's people, and the messianic age to come. (2) *Chapters 9-14* A collection of messages about the expected Messiah and the final judgement.

Outline of Contents

acknowledge Mic 5.4; 1 Jn 4.2
alive Mic 3.2; 14.12
Almighty [5] Hag 2.9; 2.8
angel [7] Hos 12.4; 2.3
anger [4] Zeph 3.8; 6.8
claim Mic 3.11; 13.2
comfort Nah 3.7; 10.2
command Zeph 2.3; 3.5
concern Mic 3.1; Mt 6.32
deserve Nah 1.14; Mt 8.8
determine Amos 9.4; Jn 5.18
enjoy Dan 12.2; 3.10
evil Hab 2.4; Mal 1.4
God's people [2] Hag 2.9; 2.6
help Zeph 3.2; 6.15
helpless Amos 2.7; Mt 9.36
holy Hab 3.3; 2.13
life (1) Zeph 3.17; 12.1
love Zeph 3.17; 2.12
mercy [2] Hab 3.2; 7.9
message [3] Hag 2.20; 2.8
obey Hag 1.12; 3.7
overthrow Hag 2.7; Jn 12.31
peace Hag 2.9; 3.10
power Hag 2.22; 5.9
proclaim [2] Jon 3.2; Mal 3.1
prophet [4] Hag 2.1; 7.3
prosper Hag 2.9; 7.7
punish Zeph 3.15; 9.1
repent Hag 2.17; Mt 3.11
restore Nah 2.2; Mt 9.30
scatter [2] Zeph 3.10; 2.6
servant Hag 2.23; 2.9
stand for 4.4
suffer [2] Nah 1.12; 9.5

The LORD Calls His People to Return to Him

1 In the eighth month of the second
year that Darius was emperor of
Persia, the LORD gave this **message** to
the **prophet** Zechariah, the son of
Berechiah and grandson of Iddo. [2]The
LORD **Almighty** told Zechariah to say to
the people, "I, the LORD, was very **angry**
with your ancestors, [3]but now I say to
you, 'Return to me, and I will return to
you. [4]Do not be like your ancestors. Long
ago the **prophets** gave them my **message**, telling them not to live **evil**, sinful
lives any longer. But they would not listen to me or **obey** me. [5]Your ancestors
and those **prophets** are no longer **alive**.
[6]Through my **servants** the **prophets** I
gave your ancestors **commands** and
warnings, but they disregarded them and
suffered the consequences. Then they **repented** and **acknowledged** that I, the
LORD **Almighty**, had **punished** them as
they **deserved** and as I had **determined**
to do."

The Prophet's Vision of the Horses

7 In the second year that Darius was
emperor, on the twenty-fourth day of the
eleventh month (the month of Shebat),
the LORD gave me a **message** in a **vision**
at night. [8]I saw an **angel of the LORD**
riding a red horse. He had stopped
among some myrtle-trees in a valley, and
behind him were other horses—red,
dappled, and white. [9]I asked him, "Sir,
what do these horses mean?"
He answered, "I will show you what
they mean. [10]The LORD sent them to go
and inspect the earth."
11 They reported to the **angel**: "We
have been all over the **world** and have
found that the whole **world** lies **helpless**
and subdued."
12 Then the **angel** said, "**Almighty**
LORD, you have been **angry** with Jerusalem and the cities of Judah for seventy
years now. How much longer will it be
before you show them **mercy**?"
13 The LORD answered the **angel** with
comforting words, [14]and the **angel** told
me to **proclaim** what the LORD **Almighty**
had said: "I have a deep **love** and **concern** for Jerusalem, my **holy city**, [15]and I
am very **angry** with the nations that
enjoy quiet and **peace**. For while I was
holding back my **anger** against **my
people**, those nations made the **sufferings**
of **my people worse**. [16]So I have come
back to Jerusalem to show **mercy** to the
city. My **Temple** will be **restored**, and the
city will be rebuilt."
17 The **angel** also told me to **proclaim**:
"The LORD **Almighty** says that his cities
will be **prosperous** again and that he will
once again **help** Jerusalem and **claim** the
city as his own."

The Vision of the Horns

18 In another **vision** I saw four ox
horns. [19]I asked the **angel** that had been
speaking to me, "What do these horns
mean?"
He answered, "They **stand for** the
world powers that have **scattered** the
people of Judah, Israel, and Jerusalem."
20 Then the LORD showed me four

1.1: Ezra 4.24–5.1, 6.14 **1.8:** Rev 6.2–8

Temple (1) (of God) Hag 2.3; 3.7
terrify Zeph 2.11; 12.4
vision [2] Nah 1.1; 2.1
warn Mic 7.4; Mt 2.12
word (1) Amos 1.1; 8.9
world [3] Hag 2.8; 12.3
worse Jon 1.11; Mt 10.25

workmen with hammers. 21 I asked, "What have these men come to do?"

He answered, "They have come to **terrify** and **overthrow** the nations that completely crushed the land of Judah and **scattered** its people."

The Vision of the Measuring-Line

Almighty [2] 1.2; 3.7
angel [2] 1.8; 3.1
escape Zeph 2.3; 14.5
exile Hag 1.12; 6.10
glory Hab 2.14; 11.2
God's people [3] 1.15; 4.9
holy 1.14; 8.3
joy Zeph 3.14; 8.19
love 1.14; 3.2
message 1.1; 4.6
possess Obad 17; Mt 5.28
presence Zeph 1.7; 3.7
promise Hag 2.5; Mal 1.14
protect Hab 1.12; 9.15
sacred Zeph 3.4; 8.3
scatter 1.19; 10.9
servant 1.6; 3.8
special Ezek 48.8; Rom 9.21
strike Hab 3.13; 10.11
vision 1.7; 3.1

2 In another **vision** I saw a man with a measuring-line in his hand. 2 "Where are you going?" I asked.

"To measure Jerusalem," he answered, "to see how long and how wide it is."

3 Then I saw the **angel** who had been speaking to me step forward, and another **angel** came to meet him. 4 The first one said to the other, "Run and tell that young man with the measuring-line that there are going to be so many people and so much livestock in Jerusalem that it will be too big to have walls. 5 The LORD has **promised** that he himself will be a wall of fire round the city to **protect** it and that he will live there in all his **glory**."

The Exiles Are Called to Come Home

6–7 The LORD said to **his people**, "I **scattered** you in all directions. But now, you **exiles**, **escape** from Babylonia and return to Jerusalem. 8 Anyone who **strikes** you strikes what is most precious to me."

So the LORD **Almighty**[a] sent me with this **message** for the nations that had plundered **his people**: 9 "The LORD himself will fight against you, and you will be plundered by the people who were once your **servants**."

When this happens, everyone will know that the LORD **Almighty** sent me.

10 The LORD said, "Sing for **joy**, people of Jerusalem! I am coming to live among you!"

11 At that time many nations will come to the LORD and become **his people**. He will live among you, and you will know that he has sent me to you. 12 Once again Judah will be the **special possession** of the LORD in his **sacred** land, and Jerusalem will be the city he **loves** most of all.

13 Be silent, everyone, in the **presence** of the LORD, for he is coming from his **holy** dwelling-place.

The Prophet's Vision of the High Priest

3 In another **vision** the LORD showed me the **High Priest** Joshua standing before the **angel of the** LORD. And there beside Joshua stood **Satan**,[b] ready to bring an **accusation** against him. 2 The **angel of the** LORD[c] said to **Satan**, "May the LORD **condemn** you, Satan! May the LORD, who **loves** Jerusalem, **condemn** you. This man is like a stick snatched from the fire."

3 Joshua was standing there, wearing **filthy** clothes. 4 The **angel** said to his **heavenly** attendants, "Take away the **filthy** clothes this man is wearing." Then he said to Joshua, "I have **taken away** your sin and will give you **new** clothes to wear."

5 He **commanded** the attendants to put[d] a **clean** turban on Joshua's head. They did so, and then they put the **new** clothes on him while the **angel of the** LORD stood there.

6 Then the **angel** told Joshua that 7 the LORD **Almighty** had said: "If you **obey** my **laws** and perform the **duties** I have assigned to you, then you will continue to be in charge of my **Temple** and its courts, and I will hear your **prayers**, just as I hear the **prayers** of the **angels** who are in my **presence**. 8 Listen then, Joshua, you who are the **High Priest**; and listen, you **fellow-priests** of his, you that are the **sign** of a good future: I will **reveal** my **servant**, who is called The Branch! 9 I am placing in front of Joshua a single stone with seven facets. I will engrave an inscription on it, and in a single day I will **take away** the sin of this land. 10 When that day comes, each of you will invite his **neighbour** to come and **enjoy peace** and **security**, surrounded by your **vineyards** and fig-trees."

accuse Zeph 3.8; Mt 12.10
Almighty 2.8; 5.4
angel [6] 2.3; 4.1
clean Ezek 44.23; Mt 8.2
command 1.6; 6.15
condemn [2] Ezek 36.19; Mt 12.7
duty (1) Ezek 45.17; Mal 2.7
enjoy 1.15; Lk 12.19
filthy [2] Nah 3.6; Rom 1.24
heaven Hag 2.6; Mal 3.10
High Priest [2] Hag 2.2; 6.11
law Zeph 3.4; Mal 3.
love 2.12; 8.2
neighbour Hab 2.15; Mt 19.19
new [2] Hag 2.9; Mt 9.16
obey 1.4; 6.15
peace 1.15; 6.13
prayer [2] Hab 3.1; 10.6
presence 2.13; 6.5
priest Hag 2.11; 6.13
reveal Hab 2.2; Mt 11.27
Satan [2] Job 2.1; Mt 4.10
secure Zeph 3.13; Mt 27.65
servant 2.9; Mal 1.6
sign (1) Dan 3.25; Mt 16.3
take away (sin) [2] Ezek 45.17; Jn 1.29
Temple (1) (of God) 1.16; 4.7
vineyard Hag 1.11; Mt 20.1
vision 2.1; 6.1

The Vision of the Lamp-Stand

4 The **angel** who had been speaking to me came again and roused me as if I had been sleeping. 2 "What do you see?" he asked.

"A lamp-stand made of gold," I answered. "At the top is a bowl for the oil. On the lamp-stand are seven lamps, each one with places for seven wicks. 3 There are two olive-trees beside the lamp-stand, one on each side of it." 4 Then I asked the **angel**, "What do these things **stand for**, sir?"

5 "Don't you know?" he asked me.

angel [4] 3.1; 5.2
anoint Ps 133.2; Mk 16.1
choose Hag 2.23; Mt 11.27
disappoint Jer 15.18; Rom 5.5
glad Hab 3.18; 8.19
God's people 2.6; 7.9
last (2) Zeph 1.4; Mt 5.26
message [2] 2.8; 6.9
might Hab 3.15; 10.11
serve Zeph 1.4; Mal 3.14
Spirit (1) (God's Spirit) Mic 3.8; Mt 1.18

[a] *Hebrew has two additional words, the meaning of which is unclear.*
[b] SATAN: *A supernatural being whose name indicates he was regarded as man's opponent.*
[c] *One ancient translation* The angel of the LORD; *Hebrew* The LORD.
[d] *Some ancient translations* He commanded the attendants to put; *Hebrew* I said, "Let them put.

3.1: Ezra 5.2; Rev 12.10 **3.2:** Jude 9 **3.8:** Jer 23.5, 33.15; Zech 6.12 **3.10:** Mic 4.4 **4.3:** Rev 11.4

stand for 1.19; 5.6
strength Hab 3.19; 12.5
succeed (1) Dan 11.17; Mt 23.15
Temple (1) (of God) [3] 3.7; 6.12

"No, I don't, sir," I replied.[e]

10b The **angel** said to me, "The seven lamps are the seven eyes of the LORD, which see all over the earth."

11 Then I asked him, "What do the two olive-trees on either side of the lamp-stand mean? 12 And what is the meaning of the two olive branches beside the two gold pipes from which the olive-oil pours?"

13 He asked me, "Don't you know?"

"No, I don't, sir," I answered.

14 Then he said, "These are the two men whom God has **chosen** and **anointed** to **serve** him, the Lord of the whole earth."

God's Promise to Zerubbabel

6 The **angel** told me to give Zerubbabel this **message** from the LORD: "You will **succeed**, not by military **might** or by your own **strength**, but by my **spirit**. 7 Obstacles as great as mountains will disappear before you. You will rebuild the **Temple**, and as you put the **last** stone in place, the people will shout, 'Beautiful, beautiful!' "

8 Another **message** came to me from the LORD 9 He said, "Zerubbabel has laid the foundation of the **Temple**, and he will finish the building. When this happens, **my people** will know that it is I who sent you to them. 10 They are **disappointed** because so little progress is being made. But they will see Zerubbabel continuing to build the **Temple**, and they will be **glad**."

The Vision of the Flying Scroll

Almighty 3.7; 6.12
angel [4] 4.1; 6.4
curse [2] Mic 2.7; 8.13
lie (2) [2] Zeph 3.13; 8.17
oath [2] Zeph 1.5; 8.17
power 1.19; 8.22
raise Nah 1.3; Mt 16.21
represent Dan 8.20; 2 Cor 8.23
ruin Hag 2.17; Mt 9.17
scroll [3] Ezek 3.1; Lk 4.17
stand for 4.4; Mt 13.20
temple (2) (of other gods) [2] Nah 1.14; Acts 14.13
thief [2] Obad 5; Mt 21.13
watch Hab 2.1; 11.11
wicked Zeph 1.3; Mal 3.18

5 I looked again, and this time I saw a **scroll** flying through the air. 2 The **angel** asked me what I saw. I answered, "A **scroll** flying through the air; it is nine metres long and four and a half metres wide."

3 Then he said to me, "On it is written the **curse** that is to go out over the whole land. On one side of the **scroll** it says that every **thief** will be removed from the land; and on the other side it says that everyone who tells **lies** under **oath** will also be taken away. 4 The LORD **Almighty** says that he will send this **curse** out, and it will enter the house of every **thief** and the house of everyone who tells **lies** under **oath**. It will remain in their houses and leave them in **ruins**."

The Vision of the Woman in the Basket

worship (1) (of God) Hag 1.8; 8.21

5 The **angel** appeared again and said, "Look! Something else is coming!"

6 "What is it?" I asked.

He replied, "It is a basket, and it **stands for** the sin[f] of the whole land."

7 The basket had a lid made of lead. As I **watched**, the lid was **raised**, and there in the basket sat a woman!

8 The **angel** said, "This woman **represents** **wickedness**." Then he pushed her down into the basket and put the lid back down. 9 I looked up and saw two women flying towards me with **powerful** wings like those of a stork. They picked up the basket and flew off with it.

10 I asked the **angel**, "Where are they taking it?"

11 He answered, "To Babylonia, where they will build a **temple** for it. When the **temple** is finished, the basket will be placed there to be **worshipped**."

The Vision of the Four Chariots

Almighty [2] 5.4; 7.2
angel [3] 5.2; 12.8
anger 1.2; 7.12
calm Jon 1.12; Mt 8.26
command 3.5; 7.9
crown [2] Ezek 23.42; 9.16
exile [2] 2.6; 9.11
gift Hos 3.5; Mt 2.11
help 1.17; 8.2
High Priest 3.1; Mt 26.3
honour [2] Zeph 3.19; 7.5
message 4.6; 7.1
obey 3.7; 10.12
peace 3.10; 8.12
presence 3.7; Mal 3.16
priest 3.8; 7.3
Temple (1) (of God) [3] 4.7; 7.2
throne Jon 3.6; Mt 5.34
vision 3.1; 13.4

6 I had another **vision**. This time I saw four chariots coming out from between two bronze mountains. 2 The first chariot was pulled by red horses, the second by black horses, 3 the third by white horses, and the fourth by dappled horses. 4 Then I asked the **angel**, "Sir, what do these chariots mean?"

5 He answered, "These are the four winds; they have just come from the **presence** of the Lord of all the earth."

6 The chariot pulled by the black horses was going north to Babylonia, the white horses were going to the west, and the dappled horses were going to the country in the south. 7 As the dappled horses came out, they were impatient to go and inspect the earth. The **angel** said, "Go and inspect the earth!"—and they did. 8 Then the **angel** cried out to me, "The horses that went north to Babylonia have **calmed** down the **LORD's anger**."

The Command to Crown Joshua

9 The LORD gave me this **message**. 10 He said, "Take the **gifts** given by the **exiles** Heldai, Tobijah, and Jedaiah, and go at once to the home of Josiah son of Zephaniah. All these men have returned from **exile** in Babylonia. 11 Make a **crown** out of the silver and gold they have given, and put it on the head of the **High Priest**, Joshua son of Jehozadak. 12 Tell him that the LORD **Almighty** says, 'The

[e] *Verses 10b–14 are moved here from the end of the chapter in order to retain the natural order of the narrative.* [f] *Some ancient translations* sin; *Hebrew* eye.

4.10b: Rev 5.6 **4.11:** Rev 11.4 **4.6:** Ezra 5.2 **6.2:** Rev 6.4, 5 **6.3:** Rev 6.2 **6.5:** Rev 7.1
6.12: Jer 23.5, 33.15; Zech 3.8

man who is called The Branch will flourish where he is and rebuild the LORD's Temple. 13 He is the one who will build it and receive the honour due to a king, and he will rule his people. A priest will stand by his throne, and they will work together in peace and harmony.' 14 The crown will be a memorial in the LORD's Temple in honour of Heldai,[g] Tobijah, Jedaiah, and Josiah."[h]

15 Men who live far away will come and help to rebuild the Temple of the LORD. And when it is rebuilt, you will know that the LORD Almighty sent me to you. This will all happen if you fully obey the commands of the LORD your God.

The LORD Condemns Insincere Fasting

7 In the fourth year that Darius was emperor, on the fourth day of the ninth month (the month of Kislev), the LORD gave me a message.

2 The people of Bethel had sent Sharezer and Regemmelech and their men to the Temple of the LORD Almighty to pray for the LORD's blessing 3 and to ask the priests and the prophets this question: "Should we continue to mourn because of the destruction of the Temple, by fasting in the fifth month as we have done for so many years now?"

4 This is the message of the LORD that came to me. 5 He said, "Tell the people of the land and the priests that when they fasted and mourned in the fifth and seventh months during these seventy years, it was not in honour of me. 6 And when they ate and drank, it was for their own satisfaction."

7 This is what the LORD said through the earlier prophets at the time when Jerusalem was prosperous and filled with people and when there were many people living not only in the towns round the city but also in the southern region and in the western foothills.

Disobedience, the Cause of Exile

8 The LORD gave this message to Zechariah: 9 "Long ago I gave these commands to my people: 'You must see that justice is done, and must show kindness and mercy to one another. 10 Do not oppress widows, orphans, foreigners who live among you, or anyone else in need. And do not plan ways of harming one another.'

11 "But my people stubbornly refused to listen. They closed their minds 12 and made their hearts as hard as rock. Because they would not listen to the teaching which I sent through the prophets who lived long ago, I became very angry. 13 Because they did not listen when I spoke, I did not answer when they prayed. 14 Like a storm I swept them away to live in foreign countries. This good land was left a desolate place, with no one living in it."

The LORD Promises to Restore Jerusalem

8 The LORD Almighty gave this message to Zechariah: 2 "I have longed to help Jerusalem because of my deep love for her people, a love which has made me angry with her enemies. 3 I will return to Jerusalem, my holy city, and live there. It will be known as the faithful city, and the hill of the LORD Almighty[i] will be called the sacred hill. 4 Once again old men and women, so old that they use a stick when they walk, will be sitting in the city squares. 5 And the streets will again be full of boys and girls playing.

6 "This may seem impossible to those of the nation who are now left, but it's not impossible for me. 7 I will rescue my people from the lands where they have been taken, 8 and will bring them back from east and west to live in Jerusalem. They will be my people, and I will be their God, ruling over them faithfully and justly.

9 "Have courage! You are now hearing the same words the prophets spoke at the time the foundation was being laid for rebuilding my Temple. 10 Before that time no one could afford to hire either men or animals, and no one was safe from his enemies. I turned people against one another. 11 But now I am treating the survivors of this nation differently. 12 They will sow their crops in peace. Their vines will bear grapes, the earth will produce crops, and there will be plenty of rain. I will give all these blessings to the people of my nation who survive. 13 People of Judah and Israel! In the past foreigners have cursed one another by saying, 'May the same disasters fall on you that fell on Judah and Israel!' But I will save you, and then those foreigners will say to one another, 'May you receive the same blessings that came to Judah and Israel!' So have courage and don't be afraid."

14 The LORD Almighty says, "When your ancestors made me angry, I planned disaster for them and did not change my mind, but carried out my plans. 15 But

Almighty 6.12; 8.1
anger 6.8; 8.2
bless Hag 2.19; 8.12
command 6.15; Mal 2.1
desolate Zeph 2.15
destroy Zeph 3.6; 9.10
fast (2) [2] Jon 3.5; 8.19
God's people [2] 4.9; 8.7
hard Amos 9.1; Mt 6.13
harm Hab 2.9; 8.17
heart Zeph 3.14; Mt 5.8
honour 6.13; 12.7
justice Zeph 3.5; 8.8
kind Mic 2.7; Mt 9.13
mercy 1.12; 12.10
message [3] 6.9; 8.1
mind (1) Zeph 3.8; 8.14
mourn [2] Mic 1.8; 12.10
need Zeph 3.11; Mt 4.4
oppress Zeph 3.1; 9.8
orphan Ezek 22.7; Mal 3.5
plan Mic 6.5; 8.14
pray [2] Zeph 3.9; 8.21
priest [2] 6.13; Mal 1.6
prophet [3] 1.1; 8.9
prosper 1.17; Mal 3.15
question Hag 2.11; Mt 21.24
refuse (1) Amos 6.3; 14.17
satisfy Zeph 1.12; Mt 5.6
stubborn Hos 8.9; Mk 3.5
teach Zeph 3.7; Mal 2.6
Temple (1) (of God) [2] 6.12; 8.9
widow Ezek 44.22; Mal 3.5

afraid [2] Hag 2.5; 9.5
Almighty [7] 7.2; 9.15
anger [2] 7.12; 10.3
bless [5] 7.2; 9.12
change Zeph 3.9; Mal 3.6
courage [2] Mic 3.8; Mt 9.2
court (1) Amos 5.10; Mt 5.25
curse 5.3; Mal 1.14
disaster [2] Zeph 1.17
enemy [2] Zeph 3.15; 9.15
faithful [2] Hab 2.4; Mal 2.14
false Mic 6.10; Mal 3.5
fast (2) 7.3; Mt 6.16
festival Zeph 3.18; 14.16
glad 4.10; 10.7
God's people [2] 7.9; 9.7
harm 7.10; Mk 3.4
hate Mic 6.10; 11.8
help 6.15; 11.16
holy 2.13; Mt 4.5
impossible [2] Jer 33.22; Mt 19.26
injustice Mic 3.10
Jew Dan 5.13; Mt 2.2
joy 2.10; 9.9
justice [2] 7.9; Mal 2.17
lie (2) 5.3; 10.2
long (2) Amos 5.18; Mal 3.1
love [3] 3.2; Mal 1.2
message [2] 7.1; 9.1
mind (1) 7.11; Mt 3.14
oath 5.3; Mt 26.63
peace [3] 6.13; 9.10
plan [4] 7.10; Mt 1.19
plenty Joel 3.18; Mal 3.10
power 5.9; 10.3
pray [2] 7.2; 13.9
prophet 7.3; 13.2
real Jer 23.36; Mk 6.52
rescue Zeph 3.19; 10.6
sacred 2.12; 14.20
safe Zeph 2.15; 9.12
save Zeph 1.18; 9.16
share Mic 2.5; Mt 10.41
sow Hag 1.6; Mt 6.26
Temple (1) (of God) 7.2; 11.13
testimony Prov 21.28; Mal 3.5
truth [2] Amos 5.10; Mt 16.17
turn Hag 1.9; Mal 1.13
vine Hag 2.19; Mal 3.11
violent Hab 2.8; Mt 11.12
word (1) 1.13; 13.3

[g] *One ancient translation* Heldai; *Hebrew* Helem. [h] *One ancient translation* Josiah; *Hebrew* Hen.
[i] HILL OF THE LORD ALMIGHTY: *Mount Zion (see Zion in Word List).*

worship (1) (of God) [2] 5.11; 10.12

now I am planning to bless the people of
Jerusalem and Judah. So don't be afraid.
16 These are the things you should do:
Speak the truth to one another. In the
courts, give real justice—the kind that
brings peace. 17 Do not plan ways of
harming one another. Do not give false
testimony under oath. I hate lying, injustice, and violence."
18 The LORD Almighty gave this
message to Zechariah: 19 "The fasts held
in the fourth, fifth, seventh, and tenth
months will become festivals of joy and
gladness for the people of Judah. You
must love truth and peace."
20 The LORD Almighty says, "The time
is coming when people from many[x]
cities will come to Jerusalem. 21 Those
from one city will say to those from
another, 'We are going to worship the
LORD Almighty and pray for his blessing.
Come with us!' 22 Many[x] peoples and
powerful nations will come to Jerusalem
to worship the LORD Almighty, and to
pray for his blessing. 23 In those days ten
foreigners will come to one Jew and say,
'We want to share in your destiny,
because we have heard that God is with
you.' "

Judgement on Neighbouring Nations

9 This is the LORD's message:
He has decreed punishment for the
land of Hadrach and for the city of
Damascus. Not only the tribes of Israel,
but also the capital of Syria belong to the
LORD. 2 Hamath, which borders on Hadrach, also belongs to him, and so do the
cities of Tyre and Sidon, with all their
skill. 3 Tyre has built fortifications for
herself and has piled up so much silver
and gold that it is as common as dirt!
4 But the Lord will take away everything
she has. He will throw her wealth into
the sea, and the city will be burnt to the
ground.
5 The city of Ashkelon will see this
and be afraid. The city of Gaza will see it
and suffer great pain. So will Ekron, and
her hopes will be shattered. Gaza will
lose her king, and Ashkelon will be left
deserted. 6 People of mixed race will live
in Ashdod. The LORD says, "I will humble
all these proud Philistines. 7 They will no
longer eat meat with blood in it, or other
forbidden food. All the survivors will
become part of my people and be like a
clan in the tribe of Judah. Ekron will
become part of my people, as the Jebusites[j] did. 8 I will guard my land and keep
armies from passing through it. I will not
allow tyrants to oppress my people any
more. I have seen how my people have
suffered."

The Future King

9 Rejoice, rejoice, people of Zion!
Shout for joy, you people of
Jerusalem!
Look, your king is coming to you!
He comes triumphant and victorious,
but humble and riding on a
donkey—
on a colt, the foal of a donkey.
10 The LORD says,
"I will remove the war-chariots from
Israel
and take the horses from Jerusalem;
the bows used in battle will be
destroyed.
Your king will make peace among the
nations;
he will rule from sea to sea,
from the River Euphrates to the
ends of the earth."

The Restoration of God's People

11 The LORD says,
"Because of my covenant with you
that was sealed by the blood of
sacrifices,
I will set your people free—
free from the waterless pit of exile.
12 Return, you exiles who now have
hope;
return to your place of safety.
I tell you now, I will repay you twice
over
with blessing for all you have
suffered.
13 I will use Judah like a soldier's bow
and Israel like the arrows.
I will use the men of Zion like a sword,
to fight the men of Greece."

14 The LORD will appear above his
people;
he will shoot his arrows like
lightning.
The Sovereign LORD will sound the
trumpet;
he will march in the storms from the
south.

afraid 8.13; 14.13
Almighty 8.1; 10.3
altar Hag 2.14; 14.20
bless 8.12; Mt 21.9
blood [4] Zeph 1.17; Mt 26.28
covenant Hos 8.1; 11.10
crown 6.11; Mt 27.29
danger Hab 2.9; Mt 5.22
destroy [2] 7.3; 11.2
enemy [2] 8.2; 10.5
exile [2] 6.10; 14.2
flock Zeph 2.7; 11.4
forbid Jon 3.7; Mt 16.22
free Mic 2.13; Mal 4.2
God's people [7] 8.7; 10.3
hope [2] Hag 1.9; Mt 12.21
humble [2] Zeph 3.12; 10.11
joy 8.19; Mt 2.9
message 8.1; 12.1
oppress 7.10; Lk 4.18
pain Hos 8.10; Mt 24.8
peace 8.12; Mt 5.9
protect 2.5; 12.8
proud Zeph 3.11; 10.11
punish 1.6; 10.3
race (1) Dan 7.14; Acts 7.8
rejoice Zeph 3.14; Lk 1.58

repay Amos 2.6; Lk 14.14
sacrifice [2] Hag 2.12; 14.21
safe 8.10; 12.6
save [2] 8.13; 11.6
seal Dan 12.4; Mt 26.28
shepherd Zeph 2.6; 11.4
Sovereign Hab 3.19
strong Hab 1.12; 10.6
suffer [3] 1.6; Mt 4.24
triumph Jer 19.7; Mt 12.20
victory Zeph 3.17; 10.5

[x] many; *or* great.
[j] JEBUSITES: *The original inhabitants of Jerusalem, who became David's subjects after he captured the city.*

8.16: Eph 4.25 **9.1:** Is 17.1–3; Jer 49.23–27; Amos 1.3–5
9.1–4: Is 23.1–18; Ezek 26.1–28.26; Joel 3.4–8; Amos 1.9–10; Mt 11.21–22; Lk 10.13–14
9.5–7: Is 14.29–31; Jer 47.1–7; Ezek 25.15–17; Joel 3.4–8; Amos 1.6–8; Zeph 2.4–7 **9.9:** Mt 21.5; Jn 12.15
9.10: Ps 72.8 **9.11:** Ex 24.8

15 The LORD **Almighty** will **protect his people**,
and they will **destroy** their **enemies**.
They will shout in battle like drunken men
and will shed the **blood** of their **enemies**;
it will flow like the **blood** of a **sacrifice**
poured on the **altar** from a bowl.[k]

16 When that day comes, the LORD will **save his people**,
as a **shepherd saves** his **flock** from **danger**.
They will shine in his land
like the jewels of a **crown**.
17 How good and beautiful the land will be!
The young people will grow **strong**
on its corn and wine.

The LORD Promises Deliverance

10 Ask the LORD for rain in the
spring of the year. It is the LORD
who sends rain **clouds** and showers,
making the fields green for everyone.
2 People **consult idols** and **fortune-tellers**,
but the answers they get are **lies** and
nonsense. Some **interpret dreams**, but
only **mislead** you; the **comfort** they give
is **useless**. So the people wander about
like lost **sheep**. They are in **trouble**
because they have no leader.
3 The LORD says, "I am **angry** with
those foreigners who rule **my people**, and
I am going to **punish** them. The people of
Judah are mine, and I, the LORD
Almighty, will take **care** of them. They
will be my **powerful** war-horses. 4 From
among them will come rulers, leaders,
and commanders to govern **my people**.[l]
5 The people of Judah will be **victorious**
like soldiers who trample their **enemies**
into the mud of the streets. They will
fight because the LORD is with them, and
they will defeat even the **enemy**
horsemen.

6 "I will make the people of Judah **strong**;
I will **rescue** the people of Israel.
I will have **compassion** on them
and bring them all back home.
They will be as though I had never **rejected** them.
I am the LORD their God; I will answer their **prayers**.

Almighty 9.15; 12.5
anger 8.2; Mal 1.4
care Nah 1.7; 11.7
cloud Zeph 1.15; Mt 17.5
comfort 1.13; Mt 2.18
compassion Jer 13.14; Phil 2.1
consult Ezek 21.21
dream Joel 2.28; Mt 1.20
enemy [2] 9.15; 12.4
fortune-teller Mic 5.12; Acts 16.16
glad 8.19; Mt 5.12
God's people [4] 9.7; 12.5
happy Jon 4.1; Mal 3.12
humble 9.6; Mt 5.5
idol Hab 2.18; 13.1
interpret Mic 3.11; Mt 16.3
lie (2) 8.17; 13.3
might 4.6; Mal 1.5
mislead Mic 3.6; Lk 23.2
obey 6.15; Mal 2.9
power [2] 8.22; 11.6
prayer 3.7; 12.10
proud 9.6; 13.4
punish 9.1; 11.5
reject Hos 9.17; Mt 10.33
remember [2] Hag 2.3; 13.2
rescue [2] 8.7; Lk 1.73
scatter 2.6; 13.7
sheep Zeph 2.6; 11.4
strike 2.8; 14.5
strong [3] 9.17; 12.8
trouble [2] Zeph 1.15; Mt 6.34
useless Hab 2.13; Mal 1.10
victory [2] 9.9; 12.7
worship (1) (of God) 8.21; 14.9

7 The people of Israel will be **strong** like soldiers,
happy like men who have been drinking wine.
Their descendants will **remember** this **victory**
and be **glad** because of what the LORD has done.

8 "I will call **my people**
and gather them together.
I will **rescue** them
and make them as numerous as they used to be.
9 Though I have **scattered** them among the nations,
yet in far-off places they will **remember** me.
They and their children will survive
and return home together.
10 From Egypt and Assyria I will bring them home
and settle them in their own country.
I will settle them in Gilead and Lebanon also;
the whole land will be filled with people.
11 When they pass through their sea of **trouble**,
I, the LORD, will **strike** the waves,
and the depths of the Nile will go dry.
Proud Assyria will be **humbled**,
and **mighty** Egypt will lose her **power**.
12 I will make **my people strong**;
they will **worship** and **obey** me."
The LORD has spoken.

The Fall of the Tyrants

11 Open your doors, Lebanon,
so that fire can burn down
your cedar-trees![m]
2 Weep and wail, cypress-trees—
the cedars have fallen;
those **glorious** trees have been **destroyed**!
Weep and wail, oaks of Bashan—
the dense forest has been cut down!
3 The rulers cry out in **grief**;
their **glory** is gone!
Listen to the roaring of the lions;
their forest home along the Jordan is **destroyed**!

The Two Shepherds

4 The LORD my God said to me, "**Act**
the part of the **shepherd**[n] of a **flock** of

abandon Mic 5.3; Mal 1.3
act [2] Hos 12.1; 13.4
blind Zeph 1.17; 12.4
care 10.3; Mt 6.26
covenant [2] 9.11; Mal 2.4
destroy [6] 9.10; 12.6
devastate Ezek 35.15; Mal 1.3
doom Zeph 3.1; Rom 9.22
favour [2] Dan 7.22; Mal 1.8
flock [5] 9.16; Mal 1.14
glory [2] 2.5; Mt 16.27
grief Amos 8.10; Mt 26.37
hate 8.17; Mal 1.3
heal Nah 3.19; Mal 4.2
help 8.2; Mal 2.6
hurt Hos 6.1; 12.3
patient Mic 2.7; Mal 3.15

[k] *Verse 15 in Hebrew is unclear.*
[l] *From among...people; or* All oppressors–rulers, leaders, and commanders–will depart together from Judah. [m] CEDAR-TREES: *Trees are used here as symbols of powerful nations or their kings.*
[n] SHEPHERD: *Shepherd is used here as a symbol of a king or leader, and sheep as symbols of his people or followers.*

pity [2] Jon 4.11; Mt 9.27
power [3] 10.3; Mal 4.2
praise Zeph 3.19; Mt 5.16
punish 10.3; 14.19
rich Hab 2.6; Mt 19.22
rid Ezek 34.25; 13.2
right (2) Ezek 39.3; Mt 5.29
save 9.16; Mal 4.2
sheep [6] 10.2; 13.7
shepherd [8] 9.16; 13.7
Temple (1) (of God) [2] 8.9; 14.20
threat Zeph 3.18; 14.11
unite [3] Mic 5.3; Mt 19.5
wage [2] Jer 22.13; Mal 3.5
wail [2] Zeph 1.10; Mal 2.13
watch 5.7; 12.4
weep [2] Mic 1.10; Mal 2.13
worth Is 7.23; Mt 6.25
worthless [2] Mic 7.4; Mal 1.7

sheep that are going to be butchered.
[5]Their owners kill them and go unpunished. They sell the meat and say, 'Praise
the LORD! We are rich!' Even their own
shepherds have no pity on them."
6 (The LORD said, "I will no longer
pity anyone on earth. I myself will put all
the people in the power of their rulers.
Those rulers will devastate the earth,
and I will not save it from their power.")
7 Those who bought and sold the
sheep hired me, and I became the shepherd of the sheep that were going to be
butchered. I took two sticks: one I called
"Favour," and the other "Unity." And I
took care of the flock. [8]I lost patience
with three other shepherds, who hated
me, and I got rid of them all in a single
month. [9]Then I said to the flock, "I will
not be your shepherd any longer. Let
those who are to die, die. Let those who
are to be destroyed, be destroyed. Those
who are left will destroy one another."
[10]Then I took the stick called "Favour"
and broke it, to cancel the covenant
which the LORD had made with all the
nations. [11]So the covenant was cancelled
on that day. Those who bought and sold
the sheep were watching me, and they
knew that the LORD was speaking
through what I did. [12]I said to them, "If
you are willing, give me my wages. But if
not, keep them." So they paid me thirty
pieces of silver as my wages.
13 The LORD said to me, "Put them in
the temple treasury."[o] So I took the
thirty pieces of silver—the magnificent
sum they thought I was worth—and put
them in the temple treasury. [14]Then I
broke the second stick, the one called
"Unity," and the unity of Judah and
Israel was shattered.
15 Then the LORD said to me, "Once
again act the part of a shepherd, this
time a worthless one. [16]I have put a shepherd in charge of my flock, but he does
not help the sheep that are threatened by
destruction; nor does he look for the lost,
or heal those that are hurt, or feed the
healthy. Instead, he eats the meat of the
fattest sheep and tears off their hoofs.
[17]That worthless shepherd is doomed!
He has abandoned his flock. War will
totally destroy his power. His arm will
wither, and his right eye will go blind."

The Future Deliverance of Jerusalem

Almighty 10.3; 13.1
angel 6.4; 14.5

12 This is a message about Israel
from the LORD, the LORD who
spread out the skies, created the earth,
and gave life to man. He says, [2]"I will
make Jerusalem like a cup of wine; the
nations round her will drink and stagger
like drunken men. And when they
besiege Jerusalem, the cities of the rest
of Judah will also be besieged. [3]But when
that time comes, I will make Jerusalem
like a heavy stone—any nation that tries
to lift it will be hurt. All the nations of the
world will join forces to attack her. [4]At
that time I will terrify all their horses
and make all their riders go mad. I will
watch over the people of Judah, but I will
make the horses of their enemies blind.
[5]Then the clans of Judah will say to
themselves, 'The LORD God Almighty
gives strength to his people who live in
Jerusalem.'
6 "At that time I will make the clans
of Judah like a fire in a forest or in a field
of ripe corn—they will destroy all the
surrounding nations. The people of Jerusalem will remain safe in the city.
7 "I, the LORD, will give victory to the
armies of Judah first, so that the honour
which the descendants of David and the
people of Jerusalem will receive will be
no greater than that of the rest of Judah.
[8]At that time the LORD will protect those
who live in Jerusalem, and even the
weakest among them will become as
strong as David was. The descendants of
David will lead them like the angel of the
LORD, like God himself. [9]At that time I
will destroy every nation that tries to
attack Jerusalem.
10 "I will fill the descendants of David
and the other people of Jerusalem with
the spirit of mercy and the spirit of
prayer. They will look at the one whom
they stabbed to death, and they will
mourn for him like those who mourn for
an only child. They will mourn bitterly,
like those who have lost their first-born
son. [11]At that time the mourning in Jerusalem will be as great as the mourning
for Hadad-rimmon[p] in the plain of
Megiddo. [12-14]Each family in the land will
mourn by itself: the family descended
from David, the family descended from
Nathan, the family descended from Levi,
the family descended from Shimei, and
all the other families. Each family will
mourn by itself, and the men of each
family will mourn separately from the
women.

13 "When that time comes," says
the LORD Almighty, "a fountain

bitter Zeph 1.14; Mt 2.18
blind 11.17; Mal 1.8
create Amos 7.1; Mal 2.10
cup Hab 2.16; Mt 20.22
death (3) (to death) Zeph 2.12; 13.3
destroy [2] 11.2; 14.11
enemy 10.5; 14.15
first-born Mic 6.7; Lk 2.23
God's people 10.3; 13.7
honour 7.5; Mal 1.6
hurt 11.16; Mt 4.6
life (1) 1.4; 13.5
mad Jer 29.26; Mk 3.21
mercy 7.9; Mal 3.17
message 9.1; Mal 1.1
mourn [7] 7.3; Mt 5.4
prayer 10.6; Mal 1.9
protect 9.15; Jn 17.12
ripe Nah 3.12; Mk 4.29
safe 9.12; 14.11
separate Ezek 42.20; Mt 19.6
spirit (2) Dan 5.11; Mal 2.15
strength 4.6; Mk 12.30
strong 10.6; Mal 3.2
terrify 1.21; Mt 14.26
victory 10.5; Rom 8.37
watch 11.11; Mt 10.17
weak Hab 1.4; Mt 26.41
world 1.11; Mal 1.11

act 11.4; Mal 3.17
Almighty [2] 12.5; 14.16

[o] *Some ancient translations* Put them in the temple treasury; *Hebrew* Give them to the potter.
[p] HADAD-RIMMON: *Probably a name for Baal, the god of vegetation in Canaan and Syria. When the vegetation died each year, the worshippers thought that the god had died too, and they mourned his death.*

11.12: Mt 26.15 **11.12–13:** Mt 27.9–10 **12.10:** Jn 19.37; Rev 1.7 **12.10–14:** Mt 24.30; Rev 1.7

claim [2] 1.17; Mt 22.23
confess Dan 9.4; Mt 3.6
death (3) (to death) [2] 12.10; Mt 10.21
deceive Zeph 3.13; Mt 24.4
desire Ezek 7.19; Mt 5.6
friend Mic 7.5; Mt 5.43
God's people [2] 12.5; Mal 1.2
idol [3] 10.2; Acts 7.41
lie (2) 10.2; Mt 5.11
life (1) 12.1; Mal 2.5
pray 8.21; Mt 5.44
prophecy [2] Mic 2.11; Mt 13.14
prophet [5] 8.9; Mal 4.5
proud 10.11; Mal 3.15
pure [3] Dan 12.10; Mal 3.3
remember 10.7; Mal 4.4
rid 11.8; 1 Cor 7.27
scatter 10.9; Mt 12.30
sheep 11.4; Mt 7.15
shepherd 11.4; Mt 9.36
test [2] Dan 1.12; Mal 3.10
vision 6.1; Mt 17.9
word (1) 8.9; 14.20
worship (2) (of other gods) Zeph 1.4; Mal 2.11

will be opened to purify the descendants
of David and the people of Jerusalem
from their sin and idolatry. 2 At that time
I will remove the names of the idols from
the land, and no one will remember them
any more. I will get rid of anyone who
claims to be a prophet and will take
away the desire to worship idols. 3 Then if
anyone still insists on prophesying, his
own father and mother will tell him that
he must be put to death, because he
claimed to speak the LORD's word, but
spoke lies instead. When he prophesies,
his own father and mother will stab him
to death. 4 When that time comes, no prophet will be proud of his visions, or act
like a prophet, or wear a prophet's
coarse garment in order to deceive
people. 5 Instead, he will say, 'I am not a
prophet. I am a farmer—I have farmed
the land all my life.' 6 Then if someone
asks him, 'What are those wounds on
your chest?' he will answer, 'I got them
at a friend's house.' "

The Command to Kill God's Shepherd

7 The LORD Almighty says, "Wake up,
sword, and attack the shepherd[q] who
works for me! Kill him, and the sheep
will be scattered. I will attack my people
8 and throughout the land two-thirds of
the people will die. 9 And I will test the
third that survives and will purify them
as silver is purified by fire. I will test
them as gold is tested. Then they will
pray to me, and I will answer them. I will
tell them that they are my people, and
they will confess that I am their God."

Jerusalem and the Nations

abundant Joel 2.14; Mal 3.10
afraid 9.5; Mt 1.20
alive 1.5; Mt 6.25
Almighty [4] 13.1; Mal 1.6
altar 9.15; Mal 1.7
angel 12.8; Mt 1.20
apart Mic 7.14; Mt 12.25
celebrate [3] Nah 1.15; Mt 26.18
dark Zeph 1.15; Mt 4.16
dedicate Dan 11.8; Lk 2.23
defend Nah 3.8; Lk 12.11
destroy 12.6; Mal 1.4
disease [3] Hab 3.5; Mt 4.23
enemy 12.4; Mt 5.43
escape 2.6; Mt 2.13
exile 9.11; Mt 1.6
festival [3] 8.19; Mt 26.2
flee Hos 12.12; Acts 7.29
flesh Nah 2.12; Mt 26.41

14 The day when the LORD will sit
in judgement is near. Then Jerusalem will be looted, and the loot will be
divided up before your eyes. 2 The LORD
will bring all the nations together to
make war on Jerusalem. The city will be
taken, the houses looted, and the women
raped. Half the people will go into exile,
but the rest of them will not be taken
away from the city. 3 Then the LORD will
go out and fight against those nations, as
he has fought in times past. 4 At that time
he will stand on the Mount of Olives, to
the east of Jerusalem. Then the Mount of
Olives will be split in two from east to
west by a large valley. Half the mountain
will move northwards and half of it
southwards. 5 You will escape through
this valley that divides the mountain in
two.[r] You will flee as your ancestors did
when the earthquake struck in the time
of King Uzziah of Judah. The LORD my
God will come, bringing all the angels
with him.
6 When that time comes, there will no
longer be cold or frost,[s] 7 nor any darkness. There will always be daylight, even
at night-time. When this will happen is
known only to the LORD.
8 When that day comes, fresh water
will flow from Jerusalem, half of it to the
Dead Sea and the other half to the
Mediterranean. It will flow all the year
round, in the dry season as well as the
wet. 9 Then the LORD will be king over all
the earth; everyone will worship him as
God and know him by the same name.
10 The whole region, from Geba in the
north to Rimmon in the south, will be
made level. Jerusalem will tower above
the land round it; the city will reach
from the Benjamin Gate to the Corner
Gate, where there had been an earlier
gate, and from the Tower of Hananel to
the royal winepresses. 11 The people will
live there in safety, no longer threatened
by destruction.
12 The LORD will bring a terrible
disease on all the nations that make war
on Jerusalem. Their flesh will rot away
while they are still alive; their eyes and
their tongues will rot away.
13 At that time the LORD will make
them so confused and afraid that everyone will seize the man next to him and
attack him. 14 The men of Judah will fight
to defend Jerusalem. They will take as
loot the wealth of all the nations—gold,
silver, and clothing in great abundance.
15 A terrible disease will also fall on
the horses, the mules, the camels, and
the donkeys—on all the animals in the
camps of the enemy.
16 Then all the survivors from the
nations that have attacked Jerusalem
will go there each year to worship the
LORD Almighty as king, and to celebrate
the Festival of Shelters. 17 If any nation
refuses to go and worship the LORD Almighty as king, then rain will not fall on
their land. 18 If the Egyptians refuse to
celebrate the Festival of Shelters, then
they will be struck by the same disease
that the LORD will send on every nation
that refuses to go. 19 This will be the punishment that will fall on Egypt and on all
the other nations if they do not celebrate
the Festival of Shelters.
20 At that time even the harness bells
of the horses will be inscribed with the

judge Zeph 3.3; Mal 3.3
name (2) (name of God, of Jesus) Hag 2.23; Mt 1.21
offer Hag 2.14; Mal 1.7
punish 11.5; Mal 2.3
rape Lam 5.11
refuse (1) [3] 7.11; Mt 2.18
sacred 8.3; Mk 16.10
sacrifice [2] 9.11; Mal 1.8
safe 12.6; Mt 6.13
shelter [3] Jon 4.5; Jn 7.2
strike [2] 10.11; Mt 26.51
Temple (1) (of God) [2] 11.13; Mal 1.10
terrible [2] Nah 1.6; Mal 3.13
threat 11.16; Acts 4.29
word (1) 13.3; Mt 4.4
worship (1) (of God) [4] 10.12; Mt 2.2

[q] SHEPHERD: *See 11.4.* [r] *Probable text* You will escape...in two; *Hebrew unclear.*
[s] *Probable text* cold or frost; *Hebrew unclear.*

13.7: Mt 26.31; Mk 14.27 **14.8:** Ezek 47.1; Jn 7.38; Rev 22.1 **14.11:** Rev 22.3 **14.16:** Lev 23.39–43

words "**Dedicated to the** LORD." The
cooking-pots in the **Temple** will be as
sacred as the bowls before the **altar**.
21 Every cooking-pot in Jerusalem and in
all Judah will be set **apart** for use in the
worship of the LORD **Almighty**. The
people who **offer sacrifices** will use them
for boiling the meat of the **sacrifices**.
When that time comes, there will no
longer be any merchant in the **Temple** of
the LORD **Almighty**.

THE BOOK OF MALACHI

INTRODUCTION

The book of *Malachi* comes from some time in the fifth century B.C. after the Temple in Jerusalem was rebuilt. The prophet's main concern is to call priests and people to renew their faithfulness to their covenant with God. It is clear that there is laxity and corruption in the life and worship of God's people. Priests and people are cheating God by not giving him the offerings that are rightly due to him, and by not living according to his teaching. But the Lord will come to judge and purify his people, sending ahead of him his messenger to prepare the way and to proclaim his covenant.

Outline of Contents

Israel's sins 1.1—2.16

God's judgement and his mercy 2.17—4.6

---

1 This is the message that the LORD
gave Malachi to tell the people of
Israel.

The LORD's Love for Israel

2 The LORD says to his people, "I have
always loved you."
But they reply, "How have you shown
your love for us?"
The LORD answers, "Esau and Jacob
were brothers, but I have loved Jacob
and his descendants, 3 and have hated
Esau and his descendants. I have devastated Esau's hill-country and abandoned
the land to jackals."
4 If Esau's descendants, the Edomites,
say, "Our towns have been destroyed, but
we will rebuild them," then the LORD will
reply, "Let them rebuild—I will tear
them down again. People will call them
'The evil country' and 'The nation with
whom the LORD is angry for ever.' "
5 The people of Israel are going to see
this with their own eyes, and they will
say, "The LORD is mighty even outside
the land of Israel!"

The LORD Reprimands the Priests

6 The LORD Almighty says to the
priests, "A son honours his father, and a
servant honours his master. I am your
father—why don't you honour me? I am
your master—why don't you respect
me? You despise me, and yet you ask,
'How have we despised you?' 7 This is
how—by offering worthless food on my
altar. Then you ask, 'How have we failed
to respect you?' I will tell you—by showing contempt for my altar. 8 When you
bring a blind or sick or lame animal to
sacrifice to me, do you think there's
nothing wrong with that? Try giving an
animal like that to the governor! Would
he be pleased with you or grant you any
favours?"
9 Now, you priests, try asking God to
be good to us. He will not answer your
prayer, and it will be your fault. 10 The
LORD Almighty says, "I wish one of you
would close the temple doors so as to
prevent you from lighting useless fires on
my altar. I am not pleased with you; I
will not accept the offerings you bring
me. 11 People from one end of the world
to the other honour me. Everywhere
they burn incense to me and offer
acceptable sacrifices. All of them honour
me! 12 But you dishonour me when you
say that my altar is worthless and when
you offer on it food that you despise.
13 You say, 'How tired we are of all this!'
and you turn up your nose at me. As your
offering to me you bring a stolen animal
or one that is lame or sick. Do you think I
will accept that from you? 14 A curse on
the cheat who sacrifices a worthless animal to me, when he has in his flock a
good animal that he promised to give
me! For I am a great king, and people of
all nations fear me."

2 The LORD Almighty says to the
priests, "This command is for you:
2 You must honour me by what you do. If
you will not listen to what I say, then I
will bring a curse on you. I will put a
curse on the things you receive for your
support. In fact, I have already put a
curse on them, because you do not take

abandon Zech 11.17; Mt 23.38
accept [3] Zeph 3.2; 2.13
Almighty [2] Zech 14.16; 2.1
altar [4] Zech 14.20; 2.13
anger Zech 10.3; Mt 5.22
blind Zech 12.4; Mt 9.27
cheat Amos 8.5; 3.5
contempt Hab 1.10; Lk 23.11
curse Zech 8.13; 2.2
despise [2] Mic 6.16; 2.9
destroy Zech 14.11; 3.11
devastate Zech 11.6
dishonour Obad 10; Jn 8.49
evil Zech 1.4; 2.6
fail Zeph 3.5; Lk 22.32
Father (2) (God) Jer 31.9; 2.10
fault Jon 1.12; Mt 18.15
favour Zech 11.7; Mt 20.20
fear Hab 3.16; 2.5
flock Zech 11.4; Mt 26.31
God's people Zech 13.7; 2.9
grant Esth 7.3; Mt 14.9
hate Zech 11.8; 2.16
honour [4] Zech 12.7; 2.2
incense Hos 11.2; Lk 1.9
love [3] Zech 8.2; 2.11
master [2] Zeph 1.9; Mt 6.24
message Zech 12.1; Mt 4.17
might Zech 10.11; Lk 1.17
offer [5] Zech 14.21; 2.12
please [2] Hag 1.8; 3.4
prayer Zech 12.10; Mt 6.7
prevent Amos 5.12; Rom 1.18

priest [2] Zech 7.3; 2.1
promise Zech 2.5; 2.5
respect [2] Dan 6.13; 2.5
sacrifice [3] Zech 14.21; 2.3
servant Zech 3.8; 4.4
steal Zeph 1.9; Mt 6.19
Temple (1) (of God) Zech 14.20; 2.11
turn Zech 8.10; 2.8
useless Zech 10.2; 3.14
wish Jon 4.8; Mt 14.9
world Zech 12.3; Mt 4.8
worthless [3] Zech 11.15; Mt 5.13
wrong Zeph 3.5; 2.6

accept [2] 1.10; Mt 19.12
Almighty [4] 1.6; 3.1
altar 1.7; Mt 5.23
body Hag 2.13; Mt 5.29
command [3] Zech 7.9; 4.4
community Ezek 20.1
covenant [4] Zech 11.10; 3.1

1.2-3: Rom 9.13 **1.2-5:** Is 34.5-17, 63.1-6; Jer 49.7-22; Ezek 25.12-14, 35.1-15; Amos 1.11-12; Obad 1-14
1.8: Deut 15.21

create Zech 12.1; Mt 13.35
cruel Nah 3.19; Acts 7.19
curse [3] 1.14; 3.9
defile Hag 2.13; Acts 10.14
despise [2] 1.6; Mt 6.24
divorce Ezek 44.22; Mt 5.31
duty (1) Zech 3.7; Mt 6.1
evil [2] 1.4; 3.15
faithful [2] Zech 8.3; Mt 5.20
Father (2) (God) 1.6; Mt 5.16
fear 1.14; 3.16
god (2) (other gods) Zeph 3.9; Mt 6.7
God's people [2] 1.2; 3.17
hate [2] 1.3; Mt 5.43
help Zech 11.16; Mt 4.11
honour 1.6; Mt 6.9
horror Zeph 2.15; Rev 8.13
justice Zech 8.8; Mt 12.20
knowledge Hab 2.14; Mt 13.11
learn Dan 6.10; Mt 2.16
life (1) Zech 13.5; Mt 6.25
love 1.2; Mt 5.43
never again Zeph 3.11
obey Zech 10.12; 4.2
offer [2] 1.7; 3.3
priest [4] 1.6; 3.3
promise [8] 1.14; Mt 5.5
punish Zech 14.19; Mt 3.7
purpose Jer 32.39; Lk 7.30
respect [2] 1.6; 3.5
right (1) [3] Hag 1.2; 3.3
sacrifice 1.8; Mt 8.4
serious Ecc 10.4; Acts 19.23
spirit (2) Zech 12.10; Mt 8.16
sure [2] Zeph 2.9; Mt 6.30
teach [4] Zech 7.12; 4.4
tear (2) Ezek 24.16; Lk 7.38
Temple (1) (of God) 1.10; 3.1
true [2] Hab 2.3; Mt 1.22
turn [2] 1.13; 3.7
wail Zech 11.2; Mk 5.38
weep Zech 11.2; Mt 2.18
will (1) [2] Dan 4.35; Mt 6.10
worship (2) (of other gods) Zech 13.2; Mt 4.9
wrong [2] 1.8; Mt 5.39

my **command seriously**. 3 I will **punish**
your children and rub your faces in the
dung of the animals you **sacrifice**—and
you will be taken out to the dunghill.
4 Then you will know that I have given
you this **command**, so that my **covenant**
with the **priests**, the descendants of Levi,
will not be broken.
5 "In my **covenant** I **promised** them
life and well-being, and this is what I
gave them, so that they might **respect**
me. In those days they did **respect** and
fear me. 6 They **taught** what was **right**,
not what was **wrong**. They lived in harmony with me; they not only did what
was **right** themselves, but they also
helped many others to stop doing **evil**. 7 It
is the **duty** of **priests** to **teach** the **true**
knowledge of God. People should go to
them to **learn** my **will**, because they are
the messengers of the LORD **Almighty**.
8 "But now you **priests** have **turned**
away from the **right** path. Your **teaching**
has led many to do **wrong**. You have
broken the **covenant** I made with you.
9 So I, in **turn**, will make the people of
Israel **despise** you because you do not
obey my **will**, and when you **teach my**
people, you do not treat everyone alike."

The People's Unfaithfulness to God

10 Don't we all have the same **father**?
Didn't the same God **create** us all? Then
why do we break our **promises** to one
another, and why do we **despise** the
covenant that God made with our ancestors? 11 The people of Judah have broken
their **promise** to God and done a **horrible**
thing in Jerusalem and all over the
country. They have **defiled** the **Temple**
which the LORD **loves**. Men have married
women who **worship foreign gods**. 12 May
the LORD remove from the **community** of
Israel those who did this, and **never**
again let them participate in the **offer-**
ings our nation brings to the LORD **Al-**
mighty.[a]
13 This is another thing you do. You
drown the LORD's **altar** with **tears**, **weep-**
ing and **wailing** because he no longer **ac-**
cepts the **offerings** you bring him. 14 You
ask why he no longer **accepts** them. It is
because he knows you have broken your
promise to the wife you married when
you were young. She was your partner,
and you have broken your **promise** to
her, although you **promised** before God
that you would be **faithful** to her. 15 Didn't
God make you one **body** and **spirit** with
her?[b] What was his **purpose** in this? It
was that you should have children who
are **truly God's people**. So make **sure** that
none of you breaks his **promise** to his
wife. 16 "I **hate divorce**," says the LORD
God of Israel. "I **hate** it when one of you
does such a **cruel** thing to his wife. Make
sure that you do not break your **promise**
to be **faithful** to your wife."

The Day of Judgement Is Near

17 You have tired the LORD out with
your talk. But you ask, "How have we
tired him?" By saying, "The LORD **Al-**
mighty thinks all **evildoers** are good; in
fact he likes them." Or by asking,
"Where is the God who is supposed to be
just?"

3

1 The LORD **Almighty** answers, "I will
send my messenger to prepare the
way for me. Then the Lord you are looking for will suddenly come to his **Temple**.
The messenger you **long** to see will come
and **proclaim** my **covenant**."
2 But who will be able to **endure** the
day when he comes? Who will be able to
survive when he appears? He will be
like **strong** soap, like a fire that **refines**
metal. 3 He will come to **judge** like one
who **refines** and **purifies** silver. As a
metal-worker **refines** silver and gold, so
the LORD's messenger will **purify** the
priests, so that they will bring to the
LORD the **right** kind of **offerings**. 4 Then
the **offerings** which the people of Judah
and Jerusalem bring to the LORD will be
pleasing to him, as they used to be in the
past.
5 The LORD **Almighty** says, "I will
appear among you to **judge**, and I will
testify at once against those who **practise**
magic, against **adulterers**, against those
who give **false testimony**, those who
cheat employees out of their **wages**, and
those who take **advantage** of **widows**,
orphans, and foreigners—against all who
do not **respect** me.

The Payment of Tithes

6 "I am the LORD, and I do not **change**.
And so you, the descendants of Jacob,
are not yet completely lost. 7 You, like
your ancestors before you, have **turned**
away from my **laws** and have not kept
them. **Turn back** to me, and I will turn to
you. But you ask, 'What must we do to
turn back to you?' 8 I ask you, is it **right**
for a person to **cheat** God? Of course not,
yet you are **cheating** me. 'How?' you ask.

abundant Zech 14.14; Rom 5.17
act Zech 13.4; 4.3
adultery Hos 4.2; Mt 5.27
advantage Zeph 3.4; Mk 12.40
Almighty [4] 2.1; 4.1
change Zech 8.14; Mt 3.14
cheat [4] 1.14; Mt 20.13
covenant 2.4; Mt 26.28
curse 2.2; Mt 15.4
destroy 1.4; 4.6
endure Hab 1.3; Jn 15.16
evil [2] 2.6; 4.1
false Zech 8.17; Mt 7.15
fear [2] 2.5; Mt 14.26
get away Jon 1.3; Mt 7.23
God's people [2] 2.9; Mt 1.21
happy [2] Zech 10.7; 4.2
heaven Zech 3.4; Mt 3.16
judge [2] Zech 14.1; Mt 5.25
law Zech 3.7; 4.4
long (2) Zech 8.2; Rom 8.19
magic Mic 5.12; Acts 8.9
mercy [2] Zech 12.10; Mt 5.7
offer [3] 2.12; Mt 5.23
orphan Zech 7.10; Jas 1.27
patient Zech 11.8; Mt 18.26
please 1.8; Mt 3.17
plenty Zech 8.12; Jn 2.10
practice Zeph 1.8; Mt 23.3
presence Zech 6.5; Mt 18.10
priest 2.1; Mt 8.4
proclaim Zech 1.14; Lk 1.2
prosper Zech 7.7; Acts 19.25
proud Zech 13.4; 4.1
pure [2] Zech 13.1; Mt 5.8
refine [3] Ezek 22.18; Rev 1.15

[a] *One ancient translation* May...Almighty; *Hebrew unclear.*
[b] *Probable text* Didn't God...her; *Hebrew unclear.*

2.4: Num 3.11–13 **2.5:** Num 25.12 **3.1:** Mt 11.10; Mk 1.2; Lk 1.76, 7.27 **3.2:** Joel 2.11; Rev 6.17

respect [2] 2.5; Mt 9.13
right (1) [2] 2.6; Mt 1.19
righteous Zeph 3.5; Mt 25.33
serve [3] Zech 4.14; Mt 4.10
sorry Jon 4.10; Mt 15.32
strong Zech 12.8; Mt 12.29
Temple (1) (of God) [2] 2.11; Mt 4.5
terrible Zech 14.12; 4.5
test [2] Zech 13.9; Mt 4.7
testify Mic 1.2; Jn 5.31
testimony Zech 8.17; Mt 18.16
tithe [2] Amos 4.4
turn [3] 2.8; Mt 3.2
useless 1.10; Mt 12.36
vine Zech 8.12; Jn 15.1
wage Zech 11.12; Mt 20.2
wicked Zech 5.8; 4.3
widow Zech 7.10; Mt 22.24

In the matter of **tithes** and **offerings.** 9 A
curse is on all of you because the whole
nation is **cheating** me. 10 Bring the full
amount of your **tithes** to the **Temple**, so
that there will be **plenty** of food there.
Put me **to the test** and you will see that I
will open the windows of **heaven** and
pour out on you in **abundance** all kinds of
good things. 11 I will not let insects **des-**
troy your crops, and your **grapevines** will
be loaded with grapes. 12 Then the people
of all nations will call you **happy**, because
your land will be a good place to live in.

God's Promise of Mercy

13 "You have said **terrible** things
about me," says the LORD. "But you ask,
'What have we said about you?' 14 You
have said, 'It's **useless** to **serve** God.
What's the use of doing what he says or
of trying to show the LORD **Almighty** that
we are **sorry** for what we have done?
15 As we see it, **proud** people are the ones
who are **happy**. **Evil** men not only **pros-**
per, but they **test** God's **patience** with
their **evil** deeds and **get away** with it.' "
16 Then the people who **feared** the
LORD **spoke** to one another, and the LORD
listened and heard what they said. In his
presence, there was written down in a
book a record of those who **feared** the
LORD and **respected** him. 17 "They will be
my people," says the LORD **Almighty**. "On
the day when I **act**, they will be my very
own. I will be **merciful** to them, as a
father is **merciful** to the son who **serves**
him. 18 Once again **my people** will see the
difference between what happens to the
righteous and to the **wicked**, to the person who **serves** me and the one who does
not."

The Day of the LORD Is Coming

4 The LORD **Almighty** says, "The day
is coming when all **proud** and **evil**
people will burn like straw. On that day
they will burn up, and there will be
nothing left of them. 2 But for you who
obey me, my **saving power** will **rise** on
you like the sun and bring **healing** like
the sun's rays. You will be as **free** and
happy as calves let out of a stall. 3 On the
day when I **act**, you will overcome the
wicked, and they will be like dust under
your feet.
4 "**Remember** the **teachings** of my
servant Moses, the **laws** and **commands**
which I gave him at Mount Sinai for all
the people of Israel to **obey**.
5 "But before the great and **terrible**
day of the LORD comes, I will send you
the **prophet** Elijah. 6 He will bring fathers
and children together again; otherwise I
would have to come and **destroy** your
country."

3.10: Lev 27.30; Num 18.21-24; Deut 12.6, 14.22-29; Neh 13.12
4.5: Mt 11.14, 17.10-13; Mk 9.11-13; Lk 1.17; Jn 1.21

act 3.17; Lk 10.36
Almighty 3.1; Mt 26.64
command 2.1; Mt 15.3
Day of the Lord Zeph 1.14; Lk 21.34
destroy 3.11; Mt 6.19
evil 3.15; Mt 5.11
free Zech 9.11; Mt 27.15
happy 3.12; Mt 2.9
heal Zech 11.16; Mt 4.23
law 3.7; Mt 5.17
obey [2] 2.9; Mt 5.19
power Zech 11.6; Mt 9.34
prophet Zech 13.2; Mt 1.22
proud 3.15; Mk 7.22
remember Zech 13.2; Mt 5.18
rise Zeph 3.8; Mt 13.33
save Zech 11.6; Mt 1.21
servant 1.6; Mt 8.6
teach 2.6; Mt 4.19
terrible 3.13; Mt 6.23
wicked 3.18; Mt 7.23

THE NEW TESTAMENT

THE GOSPEL ACCORDING TO
MATTHEW

INTRODUCTION

The Gospel according to Matthew tells the good news that Jesus is the promised Saviour, the one through whom God fulfilled the promises he made to his people in the Old Testament. This good news is not only for the Jewish people, among whom Jesus was born and lived, but for the whole world.

Matthew is carefully arranged. It begins with the birth of Jesus, describes his baptism and temptation, and then takes up his ministry of preaching, teaching, and healing in Galilee. After this the Gospel records Jesus' journey from Galilee to Jerusalem and the events of Jesus' last week, culminating in his crucifixion and resurrection.

This Gospel presents Jesus as the great Teacher, who has the authority to interpret the Law of God, and who teaches about God's kingdom. Much of his teaching is gathered by subject matter into five collections: (1) the Sermon on the Mount, which concerns the character, duties, privileges, and destiny of the citizens of the Kingdom of heaven (chapters 5–7); (2) instructions to the twelve disciples for their mission (chapter 10); (3) parables about the Kingdom of heaven (chapter 13); (4) teaching on the meaning of discipleship (chapter 18); and (5) teaching about the end of the present age and the coming of the Kingdom of heaven (chapters 24–25).

Outline of Contents

---

afraid Zech 14.13; 2.22
angel [2] Zech 14.5; 2.13
birth [4] Mic 5.3; Lk 1.15
disgrace Zeph 3.18; Lk 1.25
dream Zech 10.2; 2.12
exile [3] Zech 14.2; Acts 7.43
God's people Mal 3.17; 2.6
Messiah [2] 2.4
name (2) (name of God, of Jesus) Zech 14.9; 6.9
plan Zech 8.14; 12.14
prophet Mal 4.5; 2.5
relations 1 Kgs 3.6; Rom 1.27
right (1) Mal 3.3; 8.29
save Mal 4.2; 8.25
sex Ezek 23.17; Acts 15.20
Spirit (1) (God's Spirit) [2] Zech 4.6; 3.11
true Mal 2.7; 2.15
virgin Amos 5.2; Lk 1.34

The Ancestors of Jesus Christ
(Luke 3.23-38)

1 This is the list of the ancestors of
Jesus Christ, a descendant of David,
who was a descendant of Abraham.
2-6a From Abraham to King David,
the following ancestors are listed: Abraham, Isaac, Jacob, Judah and his
brothers; then Perez and Zerah (their
mother was Tamar), Hezron, Ram,
Amminadab, Nahshon, Salmon, Boaz (his
mother was Rahab), Obed (his mother
was Ruth), Jesse, and King David.
6b-11 From David to the time when
the people of Israel were taken into **exile**
in Babylon, the following ancestors are
listed: David, Solomon (his mother was
the woman who had been Uriah's wife),
Rehoboam, Abijah, Asa, Jehoshaphat,
Jehoram, Uzziah, Jotham, Ahaz, Hezekiah, Manasseh, Amon, Josiah, and
Jehoiachin and his brothers.
12-16 From the time after the **exile** in
Babylon to the **birth** of Jesus, the following ancestors are listed: Jehoiachin,
Shealtiel, Zerubbabel, Abiud, Eliakim,
Azor, Zadok, Achim, Eliud, Eleazar,
Matthan, Jacob, and Joseph, who
married Mary, the mother of Jesus, who
was called the **Messiah**.
17 So then, there were fourteen
generations from Abraham to David, and
fourteen from David to the **exile** in
Babylon, and fourteen from then to the
birth of the **Messiah**.

The Birth of Jesus Christ
(Luke 2.1-7)

18 This was how the **birth** of Jesus
Christ took place. His mother Mary was
engaged to Joseph, but before they were
married, she found out that she was going to have a baby by the **Holy Spirit**.
19 Joseph was a man who always did what
was **right**, but he did not want to **disgrace**
Mary publicly; so he made **plans** to
break the engagement privately. 20 While
he was thinking about this, an **angel of
the Lord** appeared to him in a **dream** and
said, "Joseph, descendant of David, do
not be **afraid** to take Mary to be your
wife. For it is by the **Holy Spirit** that she

1.11: 2 Kgs 24.14-15; 2 Chr 36.10; Jer 27.20 **1.18:** Lk 1.27

has conceived. 21 She will have a son, and
you will **name** him Jesus—because he
will **save his people** from their sins."
22 Now all this happened in order to
make what the Lord had said through the
prophet come **true**, 23 "A **virgin** will become pregnant and have a son, and he
will be called Immanuel" (which means,
"God is with us").
24 So when Joseph woke up, he
married Mary, as the **angel of the Lord**
had told him to do. 25 But he had no
sexual relations with her before she gave
birth to her son. And Joseph named him
Jesus.

Visitors from the East

2 Jesus was born in the town of
Bethlehem in Judaea, during the
time when Herod was king. Soon afterwards, some men who **studied** the stars
came from the east to Jerusalem 2 and
asked, "Where is the baby born to be the
king of the Jews? We saw his star when
it came up in the east, and we have come
to **worship** him."
3 When King Herod heard about this,
he was very **upset**, and so was everyone
else in Jerusalem. 4 He called together all
the **chief priests** and the **teachers of the
Law** and asked them, "Where will the
Messiah be born?"
5 "In the town of Bethlehem in
Judaea," they answered. "For this is
what the **prophet** wrote:
6 'Bethlehem in the land of Judah,
you are by no means the **least** of the
leading cities of Judah;
for from you will come a leader
who will **guide my people** Israel.' "
7 So Herod called the visitors from the
east to a **secret** meeting and found out
from them the exact time the star had
appeared. 8 Then he sent them to
Bethlehem with these instructions: "Go
and make a careful search for the child,
and when you find him, let me know, so
that I too may go and **worship** him."
9–10 And so they left, and on their way
they saw the same star they had seen in
the east. When they saw it, how **happy**
they were, what **joy** was theirs! It went
ahead of them until it stopped over the
place where the child was. 11 They went
into the house, and when they saw the
child with his mother Mary, they **knelt**
down and **worshipped** him. They brought
out their **gifts** of gold, frankincense, and
myrrh, and **presented** them to him.
12 Then they returned to their country
by another road, since God had **warned**
them in a **dream** not to go back to Herod.

The Escape to Egypt

13 After they had left, an **angel of the
Lord** appeared in a **dream** to Joseph and
said, "Herod will be looking for the child
in order to kill him. So get up, take the
child and his mother and **escape** to
Egypt, and stay there until I tell you to
leave."
14 Joseph got up, took the child and
his mother, and left during the night for
Egypt, 15 where he stayed until Herod
died. This was done to make what the
Lord had said through the **prophet** come
true, "I called my **Son** out of Egypt."

The Killing of the Children

16 When Herod realized that the visitors from the east had **tricked** him, he
was **furious**. He gave orders to kill all the
boys in Bethlehem and its neighbourhood
who were two years old and younger—
this was done in accordance with what
he had **learned** from the visitors about
the time when the star had appeared.
17 In this way what the **prophet**
Jeremiah had said came **true**:
18 "A sound is heard in Ramah,
the sound of **bitter weeping**.
Rachel is crying for her children;
she **refuses** to be **comforted**,
for they are **dead**."

The Return from Egypt

19 After Herod died, an **angel of the
Lord** appeared in a **dream** to Joseph in
Egypt 20 and said, "Get up, take the child
and his mother, and go back to the land
of Israel, because those who tried to kill
the child are **dead**." 21 So Joseph got up,
took the child and his mother, and went
back to Israel.
22 But when Joseph heard that Ar-
chelaus had succeeded his father Herod
as king of Judaea, he was **afraid** to go
there. He was given more instructions in
a **dream**, so he went to the province of
Galilee 23 and made his home in a town
named Nazareth. And so what the **prophets** had said came **true**: "He will be
called a Nazarene."

The Preaching of John the Baptist
(Mark 1.1–8; Luke 3.1–18; John 1.19–28)

3 At that time John the Baptist came
to the desert of Judaea and started
preaching. 2 "**Turn away from your sins**,"
he said, "because the **Kingdom of heaven**

afraid 1.20; 9.8
angel [2] 1.20; 4.6
bitter Zech 12.10; 26.75
chief priests 16.21
comfort Zech 10.2; 5.4
dead [2] Hag 2.13; 8.22
dream [4] 1.20; 27.19
escape Zech 14.5; 3.7
fury Zeph 3.8; Lk 14.21
gift Zech 6.10; 5.23
God's people 1.21; 13.17
guide Zeph 1.6; 23.16
happy Mal 4.2; 5.3
Jew Zech 8.23; 9.18
joy Zech 9.9; 28.8
kneel Dan 6.10; 4.9
leading Nah 3.10; Mk 6.21
learn Mal 2.7; 11.25
least Jon 3.5; 5.18
Messiah 1.12; 16.16
present (1) Mic 6.1; Lk 2.22
prophet [4] 1.22; 3.3
refuse (1) Zech 14.17; 18.30
secret Hab 3.14; 10.26
Son of God 3.17
study Dan 9.2; Lk 1.3
teacher of the Law 5.20
trick Dan 11.21; Mk 12.15
true [3] 1.22; 4.14
upset Dan 6.14; 18.31
warn Zech 1.6; 16.12
weep Mal 2.13; 24.30
worship (1) (of God) [3] Zech 14.9; 4.10

after me Mk 1.7
agree Dan 9.27; 18.19
baptize [7] 21.25
change Mal 3.6; 17.2
confess Zech 13.9; Mk 1.5

1.21: Lk 1.31 **1.23:** Is 7.14 (LXX) **1.25:** Lk 2.21 **2.6:** Mic 5.2 **2.15:** Hos 11.1 **2.18:** Jer 31.15
2.23: Mk 1.24; Lk 2.39; Jn 1.45 **3.2:** Mt 4.17; Mk 1.15

dear Hos 9.16; 17.5
dove Nah 2.7; 10.16
enough Hag 1.6; 6.34
escape [2] 2.13; 23.33
heaven [2] Mal 3.10; 5.12
Kingdom (1) (of God) Dan 7.14; 4.17
mind (1) Zech 8.14; 13.15
Pharisees 5.20
please Mal 3.4; 7.4
preach Mic 2.6; 4.17
prophet 2.5; 4.14
punish [2] Mal 2.3; 8.29
repent Zech 1.6; 27.3
require Mic 6.8; 5.6
Sadducees 16.1
Son of God 2.15; 4.3
Spirit (1) (God's Spirit) [2] 1.18; 4.1
turn [2] Mal 3.7; 4.3

is near!" 3 John was the man the **prophet**
Isaiah was talking about when he said,

"Someone is shouting in the desert,
'Prepare a road for the Lord;
make a straight path for him to
travel!' "

4 John's clothes were made of camel's
hair; he wore a leather belt round his
waist, and his food was locusts and wild
honey. 5 People came to him from
Jerusalem, from the whole province of
Judaea, and from all the country near
the River Jordan. 6 They **confessed** their
sins, and he **baptized** them in the Jordan.
7 When John saw many **Pharisees** and
Sadducees coming to him to be **baptized**,
he said to them, "You snakes—who told
you that you could **escape** from the
punishment God is about to send? 8 Do
those things that will show that you have
turned from your sins. 9 And don't think
you can **escape punishment** by saying
that Abraham is your ancestor. I tell you
that God can take these stones and make
descendants for Abraham! 10 The axe is
ready to cut down the trees at the roots;
every tree that does not bear good fruit
will be cut down and thrown in the fire.
11 I **baptize** you with water to show that
you have **repented**, but the one who will
come **after me** will **baptize** you with the
Holy Spirit and fire. He is much greater
than I am; and I am not good **enough**
even to carry his sandals. 12 He has his
winnowing shovel with him to thresh out
all the grain. He will gather his wheat
into his barn, but he will burn the chaff in
a fire that never goes out."

The Baptism of Jesus
(Mark 1.9–11; Luke 3.21–22)

13 At that time Jesus arrived from
Galilee and came to John at the Jordan
to be **baptized** by him. 14 But John tried to
make him **change** his **mind**. "I ought to
be **baptized** by you," John said, "and yet
you have come to me!"
15 But Jesus answered him, "Let it be
so for now. For in this way we shall do all
that God **requires**." So John **agreed**.
16 As soon as Jesus was **baptized**, he
came up out of the water. Then **heaven**
was opened to him, and he saw the **Spirit
of God** coming down like a **dove** and
alighting on him. 17 Then a voice said
from **heaven**, "This is my own **dear Son**,
with whom I am **pleased**."

The Temptation of Jesus
(Mark 1.12–13; Luke 4.1–13)

4 Then the **Spirit** led Jesus into the
desert to be **tempted** by the **Devil**.
2 After spending forty days and nights
without food, Jesus was **hungry**. 3 Then
the **Devil** came to him and said, "If you
are **God's Son**, order these stones to **turn**
into **bread**."
4 But Jesus answered, "The **scripture**
says, 'Man cannot live on **bread alone**,
but **needs** every **word** that God speaks.' "
5 Then the **Devil** took Jesus to
Jerusalem, the **Holy City**, set him on the
highest point of the **Temple**, 6 and said to
him, "If you are **God's Son**, throw yourself down, for the **scripture** says,
'God will give orders to his **angels**
about you;
they will hold you up with their
hands,
so that not even your feet will be
hurt on the stones.' "
7 Jesus answered, "But the **scripture**
also says, 'Do not put the Lord your God
to the test.' "
8 Then the **Devil** took Jesus to a very
high mountain and showed him all the
kingdoms of the **world** in all their greatness. 9 "All this I will give you," the **Devil**
said, "if you **kneel** down and **worship**
me."
10 Then Jesus answered, "Go away,
Satan! The **scripture** says, '**Worship** the
Lord your God and **serve** only him!' "
11 Then the **Devil** left Jesus; and
angels came and **helped** him.

Jesus Begins His Work in Galilee
(Mark 1.14–15; Luke 4.14–15)

12 When Jesus heard that John had
been put in **prison**, he went away to
Galilee. 13 He did not stay in Nazareth,
but went to live in Capernaum, a town by
Lake Galilee, in the territory of Zebulun
and Naphtali. 14 This was done to make
what the **prophet** Isaiah had said come
true,
15 "Land of Zebulun and land of Naphtali,
on the road to the sea, on the other
side of the Jordan,
Galilee, land of the **Gentiles**!
16 The people who live in **darkness**
will see a great **light**.
On those who live in the **dark** land of
death
the **light** will shine."
17 From that time Jesus began to
preach his **message**: "**Turn away from**

alone Zeph 3.9; 14.23
angel [2] 2.13; 13.39
bread [2] Hag 2.12; 7.9
dark [2] Zech 14.7; 6.23
death (1) Hab 3.5; 16.18
demon Jer 50.39; 7.22
Devil [6] 13.39
disease [2] Zech 14.12; 8.2
Gentile Lam 1.10; 10.5
Good News Nah 1.15; 9.35
heal [2] Mal 4.2; 8.3
help Mal 2.6; 6.3
holy Zech 8.3; 6.9
hunger Zeph 3.3; 12.1
hurt Zech 12.3; 15.12
Kingdom (1) (of God) [2] 3.2; 5.3
kneel 2.11; 8.2
light (1) [2] Hab 3.4; 5.14
message Mal 1.1; 7.22
need Zech 7.10; 6.2
paralyse Ezek 3.26; 9.2
preach [2] 3.1; 9.35
prison Amos 1.5; 11.2
prophet 3.3; 5.12
Satan Zech 3.1; 12.26
scripture [4] 9.13
serve Mal 3.14; 6.24
Son of God [2] 3.17; 8.29
Spirit (1) (God's Spirit) 3.11; 10.20
suffer Zech 9.5; 8.2
synagogue 9.35
teach [2] Mal 4.4; 5.2
Temple (1) (of God) Mal 3.1; 12.5
tempt Is 13.17; 26.41
test Mal 3.10; 6.13
true 2.15; 5.17
turn [2] 3.2; 7.6
word (1) Zech 14.20; 6.7
world Mal 1.11; 5.14
worship (1) (of God) 2.2; 6.2
worship (2) (of other gods) Mal 2.11; Lk 4.7

3.3: Is 40.3 (LXX) **3.4:** 2 Kgs 1.8 **3.7:** Mt 12.34, 23.33 **3.9:** Jn 8.33 **3.10:** Mt 7.19
3.17: Gen 22.2; Ps 2.7; Is 42.1; Mt 12.18, 17.5; Mk 1.11; Lk 9.35 **4.1:** Heb 2.18, 4.15 **4.4:** Deut 8.3
4.6: Ps 91.11-12 **4.7:** Deut 6.16 **4.10:** Deut 6.13 **4.12:** Mt 14.3; Mk 6.17; Lk 3.19-20 **4.13:** Jn 2.12
4.15-16: Is 9.1-2 **4.17:** Mt 3.2

your sins, because the **Kingdom** of
heaven is near!"

Jesus Calls Four Fishermen
(Mark 1.16–20; Luke 5.1–11)

18 As Jesus walked along the shore of
Lake Galilee, he saw two brothers who
were fishermen, Simon (called Peter)
and his brother Andrew, catching fish in
the lake with a net. 19 Jesus said to them,
"Come with me, and I will **teach** you to
catch men." 20 At once they left their nets
and went with him.
21 He went on and saw two other
brothers, James and John, the sons of
Zebedee. They were in their boat with
their father Zebedee, getting their nets
ready. Jesus called them, 22 and at once
they left the boat and their father, and
went with him.

Jesus Teaches, Preaches, and Heals
(Luke 6.17–19)

23 Jesus went all over Galilee,
teaching in the **synagogues**, **preaching**
the **Good News** about the **Kingdom**, and
healing people who had all kinds of **disease** and sickness. 24 The news about him
spread through the whole country of
Syria, so that people brought to him all
those who were sick, **suffering** from all
kinds of **diseases** and disorders: people
with **demons**, and epileptics, and **para-
lytics**—and Jesus **healed** them all.
25 Large crowds followed him from
Galilee and the Ten Towns, from
Jerusalem, Judaea, and the land on the
other side of the Jordan.

The Sermon on the Mount

5 Jesus saw the crowds and went up a
hill, where he sat down. His **disciples** gathered round him, 2 and he began to **teach** them:

True Happiness
(Luke 6.20–23)

3 "**Happy** are those who know they are
spiritually poor;
the **Kingdom of heaven** belongs to
them!
4 "**Happy** are those who **mourn**;
God will **comfort** them!
5 "**Happy** are those who are **humble**;
they will receive what God has
promised!
6 "**Happy** are those whose greatest
desire is to do what God **requires**;
God will **satisfy** them fully!
7 "**Happy** are those who are **merciful** to
others;
God will be **merciful** to them!
8 "**Happy** are the **pure in heart**;
they will see God!
9 "**Happy** are those who work for **peace**;
God will call them **his children**!
10 "**Happy** are those who are **persecuted**
because they do what God
requires;
the **Kingdom of heaven** belongs to
them!
11 "**Happy** are you when people **insult**
you and **persecute** you and tell all kinds
of **evil lies** against you because you are
my **followers**. 12 Be **happy** and **glad**, for a
great **reward** is kept for you in **heaven**.
This is how the **prophets** who lived before you were **persecuted**.

Salt and Light
(Mark 9.50; Luke 14.34–35)

13 "You are like salt for all **mankind**.
But if salt loses its saltiness, there is no
way to make it salty again. It has become **worthless**, so it is thrown out and
people trample on it.
14 "You are like **light** for the whole
world. A city built on a hill cannot be hidden. 15 No one lights a lamp and puts it
under a bowl; instead he puts it on the
lampstand, where it gives **light** for everyone in the house. 16 In the same way your
light must shine before people, so that
they will see the good things you do and
praise your **Father** in **heaven**.

Teaching about the Law

17 "Do not think that I have come to
do away with the **Law of Moses** and the
teachings of the **prophets**. I have not
come to do away with them, but to make
their **teachings** come **true**. 18 **Remember**
that as long as **heaven and earth last**, not
the **least** point nor the smallest detail of
the **Law** will be done away with—not until the end of all things.[a] 19 So then, whoever **disobeys** even the **least important** of
the **commandments** and **teaches** others
to do the same, will be **least** in the **Kingdom of heaven**. On the other hand, whoever **obeys** the **Law** and **teaches** others to
do the same, will be great in the **Kingdom of heaven**. 20 I tell you, then, that you
will be able to enter the **Kingdom of
heaven** only if you are more **faithful** than
the **teachers of the Law** and the
Pharisees in doing what God **requires**.

adultery [4] Mal 3.5; 15.19
altar [2] Mal 2.13; 23.18
anger Mal 1.4; 18.34
bad Zeph 3.7; 7.11
body [3] Mal 2.15; 6.22
child of God [2] Lk 6.35
comfort 2.18; Jn 11.19
commandment Ps 119.10; 19.17
commit [5] Mic 7.2; 15.19
Council Ecc 9.17; 26.59
court (1) [3] Zech 8.16; 10.17
danger Zech 9.16; 8.24
desire Zech 13.2; Mk 4.19
disciple Jer 35.4; 8.18
disobey Dan 3.12; 15.2

dispute Mic 4.3; Lk 12.58
divorce [2] Mal 2.16; 19.3
enemy [2] Zech 14.15; 10.36
evil [2] Mal 4.1; 9.4
Evil One 6.13
faithful Mal 2.14; 24.45
Father (2) (God) [3] Mal 2.10; 6.1
follower Hab 3.13; 9.14
fool Mic 7.6; 7.26
force (1) Zeph 3.8; 27.32
friend [2] Zech 13.6; 6.3
gift [3] 2.11; 23.18
glad Zech 10.7; 13.20
guilty [2] Nah 1.3; 12.5
happy [10] 2.9; 11.6
hate Mal 2.16; 6.24
heart [2] Zech 7.12; 6.21
heaven [6] 3.16; 6.1
hell [3] Job 31.12; 7.13
humble Zech 10.11; 11.29
important Dan 4.17; 21.42
insult Zeph 2.8; 27.39
jail Job 7.20; 18.30
judge Mal 3.3; 7.1
Kingdom (1) (of God) [5] 4.17; 6.10
last (1) Dan 11.6; 12.25
last (2) Zech 4.7; 19.30
law [3] Mal 4.4; 7.12
least [3] 2.6; 10.42
lie (2) Zech 13.3; 15.19
light (1) [3] 4.16; 6.22
love [3] Mal 2.11; 6.5
mankind Zeph 1.3; 24.9
mercy [2] Mal 3.17; 10.15
mourn Zech 12.10; Mk 16.10
obey Mal 4.2; 7.24
offer [2] Mal 3.3; 8.4
pagan Zeph 1.4; 6.7
peace [2] Zech 9.10; 10.12
perfect Ezek 28.12; 19.21
persecute [4] Amos 5.12; 10.23
Pharisees 3.7; 9.11
poor Hab 3.14; 7.17
possess Zech 2.12; 25.34
praise Zech 11.5; 6.2
pray Zech 13.9; 6.5
promise [3] Mal 2.5; 14.7
prophet [2] 4.14; 7.12
pure Mal 3.3; Mk 9.49
remember [2] Mal 4.4; 16.9
require [3] 3.15; 6.33
rest (1) Zeph 2.15; 8.20
revenge Mic 5.15; Acts 7.24
reward [2] Dan 12.13; 6.1
right (2) [3] Zech 11.17; 20.21
satisfy Zech 7.6; 10.25

[a] the end of all things; *or* all its teachings come true.

4.23: Mt 9.35; Mk 1.39 **5.4:** Is 61.2 **5.5:** Ps 37.11 **5.6:** Is 55.1-2 **5.8:** Ps 24.3-4 **5.10:** 1 Pet 3.14
5.11: 1 Pet 4.14 **5.12:** 2 Chr 36.16; Acts 7.52 **5.14:** Jn 8.12, 9.5 **5.15:** Mk 4.21; Lk 8.16, 11.33
5.16: 1 Pet 2.12 **5.18:** Lk 16.17

settle (2) Mic 4.3; 25.19
son *see* child of God
spiritual 1 Chr 24.5; Jn 3.6
swear [2] Zeph 2.9; 14.7
tax collector Is 33.18; 9.9
teach [5] 4.19; 7.12
teacher of the Law 2.4; 7.29
throne Zech 6.13; 19.28
true 4.14; 8.17
try (2) [2] Jer 25.31; 10.18
unfaithful Hos 9.1; 19.9
vow [2] Ezek 20.23; 23.16
world 4.8; 10.34
worthless [2] Mal 1.7; 13.48
wrong Mal 2.6; 6.12

Teaching about Anger

21 "You have heard that people were told in the past, 'Do not **commit murder**; anyone who does will be brought to **trial**.' 22 But now I tell you: whoever is **angry**[b] with his brother will be brought to **trial**, whoever calls his brother 'You good-for-nothing!' will be brought before the **Council**, and whoever calls his brother a **worthless fool** will be in **danger** of going to the fire of **hell**. 23 So if you are about to **offer** your **gift** to God at the **altar** and there you **remember** that your brother has something against you, 24 leave your **gift** there in front of the **altar**, go at once and make **peace** with your brother, and then come back and **offer** your **gift** to God.

25 "If someone brings a lawsuit against you and takes you to **court**, **settle** the **dispute** with him while there is time, before you get to **court**. Once you are there, he will hand you over to the **judge**, who will hand you over to the police, and you will be put in **jail**. 26 There you will stay, I tell you, until you pay the **last** penny of your fine.

Teaching about Adultery

27 "You have heard that it was said, 'Do not **commit adultery**.' 28 But now I tell you: anyone who looks at a woman and wants to **possess** her is **guilty** of **committing adultery** with her in his **heart**. 29 So if your **right** eye causes you to sin, take it out and throw it away! It is much better for you to lose a part of your **body** than to have your whole **body** thrown into **hell**. 30 If your **right hand** causes you to sin, cut it off and throw it away! It is much better for you to lose one of your limbs than for your whole **body** to go to **hell**.

Teaching about Divorce

(Matt. 19.9; Mark 10.11–12; Luke 16.18)

31 "It was also said, 'Anyone who divorces his wife must give her a written **notice of divorce**.' 32 But now I tell you: if a man **divorces** his wife, for any cause other than her **unfaithfulness**, then he is **guilty** of making her **commit adultery** if she marries again; and the man who marries her **commits adultery** also.

Teaching about Vows

33 "You have also heard that people were told in the past, 'Do not break your **promise**, but do what you have **vowed** to the Lord to do.' 34 But now I tell you: do not use any **vow** when you make a **promise**. Do not **swear** by **heaven**, for it is God's **throne**; 35 nor by earth, for it is the **resting place** for his feet; nor by Jerusalem, for it is the city of the great King. 36 Do not even **swear** by your head, because you cannot make a single hair white or black. 37 Just say 'Yes' or 'No'—anything else you say comes from the **Evil One**.

Teaching about Revenge

(Luke 6.29–30)

38 "You have heard that it was said, 'An eye for an eye, and a tooth for a tooth.' 39 But now I tell you: do not take **revenge** on someone who **wrongs** you. If anyone slaps you on the **right** cheek, let him slap your left cheek too. 40 And if someone takes you to **court** to sue you for your shirt, let him have your coat as well. 41 And if one of the occupation troops **forces** you to carry his pack one kilometre, carry it two kilometres. 42 When someone asks you for something, give it to him; when someone wants to borrow something, lend it to him.

Love for Enemies

(Luke 6.27–28, 32–36)

43 "You have heard that it was said, '**Love** your **friends**, **hate** your **enemies**.' 44 But now I tell you: **love** your **enemies** and **pray** for those who **persecute** you, 45 so that you may become the **sons** of your **Father** in **heaven**. For he makes his sun to shine on **bad** and good people alike, and gives rain to those who do good and to those who do **evil**. 46 Why should God **reward** you if you **love** only the people who love you? Even the **tax collectors** do that! 47 And if you speak only to your **friends**, have you done anything out of the ordinary? Even the **pagans** do that! 48 You must be **perfect**—just as your **Father** in **heaven** is perfect!

Teaching about Charity

6 "Make **certain** you do not perform your **religious duties** in public so that people will see what you do. If you do these things publicly, you will not have any **reward** from your **Father** in **heaven**.

2 "So when you give something to a **needy** person, do not make a big show of it, as the **hypocrites** do in the houses of **worship** and on the streets. They do it so that people will **praise** them. I **assure**

alive Zech 14.12; 27.63
appearance Is 11.3; 28.3
assure [3] Ezek 13.16; 8.11
body [5] 5.29; 10.28
care Zech 11.7; 8.33
certain (1) Ezek 39.8; Lk 11.35
concern [2] Zech 1.14; Lk 12.29
dark [2] 4.16; 8.12
despise Mal 2.9; 18.10

[b] whoever is angry; *some manuscripts have* whoever without cause is angry.

5.21: Ex 20.13; Deut 5.17 **5.27:** Ex 20.14; Deut 5.18 **5.29:** Mt 18.9; Mk 9.47 **5.30:** Mt 18.8; Mk 9.43
5.31: Deut 24.1-4; Mt 19.7; Mk 10.4 **5.32:** Mt 19.9; Mk 10.11-12; Lk 16.18; 1 Cor 7.10-11
5.33: Lev 19.12; Num 30.2; Deut 23.21 **5.34:** Jas 5.12; Is 66.1; Mt 23.22 **5.35:** Is 66.1; Ps 48.2
5.38: Ex 21.24; Lev 24.20; Deut 19.21 **5.43:** Lev 19.18 **5.48:** Lev 19.2; Deut 18.13 **6.1:** Mt 23.5

destroy [2] Mal 4.6; 10.28
duty (1) Mal 2.7; Lk 17.10
enough 3.11; 13.6
Evil One 5.37; 13.19
faith Is 28.16; 8.10
fast (2) [3] Zech 8.19; 9.14
Father (2) (God) [12] 5.16; 7.11
forgive [6] Mic 7.18; 9.2
friend 5.43; 11.19
god (2) (other gods) Mal 2.11; Jn 10.34
hard Zech 7.12; 7.14
harvest Hag 1.6; 9.37
hate 5.43; 10.22
heart 5.8; 9.36
heaven [7] 5.12; 7.11
help 4.11; 8.5
holy 4.5; 7.6
honour Mal 2.2; 15.6
hypocrite [3] Prov 26.24; 7.5
Kingdom (1) (of God) [2] 5.3; 7.21
life (1) Mal 2.5; 7.14
light (1) [2] 5.14; Lk 2.32
love [2] 5.43; 10.37
loyal Zeph 1.5; Lk 16.13
master Mal 1.6; 10.24
name (2) (name of God, of Jesus) 1.21; 7.22
need [7] 4.4; 9.12
neglect Prov 19.27; 23.23
pagan [2] 5.47; 18.17
praise 5.16; 9.8
pray [6] 5.44; 9.38
prayer Mal 1.9; 21.13
provide Hab 1.16; Lk 1.69
religion Amos 5.21; Jn 5.1
require 5.6; Lk 2.24
reward [4] 5.12; 10.41
riches [3] Obad 13; 13.22
rob [2] Mic 2.9; 15.19
sad Is 63.10; 9.15
safe Zech 14.11; Mk 6.20
seed Joel 1.17; 13.4
serve 4.10; 20.28
slave Nah 3.4; 8.9
sound (2) Jon 1.5; Lk 9.32
sow Zech 8.12; 13.3
steal [2] Mal 1.13; 19.18
sure Mal 2.15; 10.42
terrible Mal 4.5; 7.27
test 4.7; Lk 4.12
trouble Zech 10.2; 13.21
will (1) Mal 2.7; 22.16
word (1) 4.4; 7.24
worry [6] Dan 10.19; 9.36
worship (1) (of God) [2] 4.10; 14.33
worth [3] Zech 11.13; 10.31
wrong [4] 5.39; 12.10

you, they have already been paid in full.
3 But when you **help** a **needy** person, do it
in such a way that even your closest
friend will not know about it. 4 Then it
will be a private matter. And your
Father, who sees what you do in private,
will **reward** you.

Teaching about Prayer
(Luke 11.2–4)

5 “When you **pray**, do not be like the
hypocrites! They **love** to stand up and
pray in the houses of **worship** and on the
street corners, so that everyone will see
them. I **assure** you, they have already
been paid in full. 6 But when you **pray**, go
to your room, close the door, and **pray** to
your **Father**, who is unseen. And your
Father, who sees what you do in private,
will **reward** you.
7 “When you **pray**, do not use a lot of
meaningless **words**, as the **pagans** do,
who think that their **gods** will hear them
because their **prayers** are long. 8 Do not
be like them. Your **Father** already knows
what you **need** before you ask him. 9 This,
then, is how you should **pray**:
‘**Our Father** in **heaven**:
May your **holy name** be **honoured**;
10 may your **Kingdom** come;
may your **will** be done on earth as it
is in **heaven**.
11 Give us today the food we **need**.[c]
12 **Forgive** us the **wrongs** we have
done,
as we **forgive** the **wrongs** that
others have done to us.
13 Do not bring us to **hard testing**,
but keep us **safe** from the **Evil**
One.’[x]
14 “If you **forgive** others the **wrongs**
they have done to you, your **Father** in
heaven will also **forgive** you. 15 But if you
do not **forgive** others, then your **Father**
will not **forgive** the **wrongs** you have
done.

Teaching about Fasting

16 “And when you **fast**, do not put on a
sad face as the **hypocrites** do. They
neglect their **appearance** so that everyone will see that they are **fasting**. I
assure you, they have already been paid
in full. 17 When you go without food, wash
your face and comb your hair, 18 so that
others cannot know that you are **fasting**—only your **Father**, who is unseen,
will know. And your **Father**, who sees
what you do in private, will **reward** you.

Riches in Heaven
(Luke 12.33–34)

19 “Do not store up **riches** for yourselves here on earth, where moths and
rust **destroy**, and **robbers** break in and
steal. 20 Instead, store up **riches** for yourselves in **heaven**, where moths and rust
cannot **destroy**, and **robbers** cannot
break in and steal. 21 For your **heart** will
always be where your **riches** are.

The Light of the Body
(Luke 11.34–36)

22 “The eyes are like a lamp for the
body. If your eyes are **sound**, your whole
body will be full of **light**; 23 but if your
eyes are no good, your **body** will be in
darkness. So if the **light** in you is darkness, how **terribly dark** it will be!

God and Possessions
(Luke 16.13; 12.22–31)

24 “No one can be a **slave** of two
masters; he will **hate** one and **love** the
other; he will be **loyal** to one and **despise**
the other. You cannot **serve** both God
and money.
25 “This is why I tell you not to be
worried about the food and drink you
need in order to stay **alive**, or about
clothes for your **body**. After all, isn't **life**
worth more than food? And isn't the
body worth more than clothes? 26 Look
at the birds: they do not **sow seeds**,
gather a **harvest** and put it in barns; yet
your **Father** in **heaven** takes **care** of
them! Aren't you **worth** much more than
birds? 27 Can any of you live a bit longer[d]
by **worrying** about it?
28 “And why **worry** about clothes?
Look how the wild flowers grow: they do
not work or make clothes for themselves.
29 But I tell you that not even King
Solomon with all his wealth had clothes
as beautiful as one of these flowers. 30 It is
God who clothes the wild grass—grass
that is here today and gone tomorrow,
burnt up in the oven. Won't he be all the
more **sure** to clothe you? How little **faith**
you have!
31 “So do not start **worrying**: ‘Where
will my food come from? or my drink?
or my clothes?’ 32 (These are the things
the **pagans** are always **concerned** about.)
Your **Father** in **heaven** knows that you
need all these things. 33 Instead, be **concerned** above everything else with the
Kingdom of God and with what he **requires** of you, and he will **provide** you

[c] we need; *or* for today; *or* for tomorrow.
[x] *Some manuscripts add* For yours is the kingdom, and the power, and the glory for ever. Amen.
[d] live a bit longer; *or* grow a bit taller.

6.5: Lk 18.10-14 **6.14-15:** Mk 11.25-26 **6.19:** Jas 5.2-3 **6.29:** 1 Kgs 10.4-7; 2 Chr 9.3-6

with all these other things. 34 So do not **worry** about tomorrow; it will have **enough worries** of its own. There is no **need** to add to the **troubles** each day brings.

Judging Others
(Luke 6.37–38, 41–42)

amaze Dan 12.6; 8.27
authority Dan 7.6; 8.9
bad [3] 5.45; 12.33
bread 4.3; 12.4
clear Ezek 34.18; Mk 1.2
dare Mic 1.11; 8.28
Day of Judgement 10.15
demon 4.24; 8.16
false [2] Mal 3.5; 19.18
Father (2) (God) [2] 6.1; 10.20
fool 5.22; 23.17
get away Mal 3.15; 16.23
hard [3] 6.13; 19.8
heaven [2] 6.1; 10.32
hell 5.22; 10.28
holy 6.9; 23.17
hypocrite 6.2; 15.7
judge [3] 5.25; 12.18
Kingdom (1) (of God) 6.10; 8.11
law 5.17; 11.13
life (1) 6.25; 10.39
message 4.17; 11.12
miracle Mic 7.15; 11.20
name (2) (name of God, of Jesus) [2] 6.9; 18.5
obey [2] 5.19; 8.27
please 3.17; 12.18
poor [2] 5.3; 11.5
prophet [3] 5.12; 8.17
seek [2] Hos 8.9; Lk 11.9
sheep Zech 13.7; 9.36
teach [3] 5.2; 9.35
teacher of the Law 5.20; 8.19
terrible 6.23; 8.6
turn 4.3; 9.22
wicked Mal 4.3; Mk 8.38
wise Mic 6.9; 11.25
word (1) [2] 6.7; 8.16

7 "Do not **judge** others, so that God will not **judge** you, 2 for God will **judge** you in the same way as you judge others, and he will apply to you the same rules you apply to others. 3 Why, then, do you look at the speck in your brother's eye, and pay no attention to the log in your own eye? 4 How **dare** you say to your brother, '**Please**, let me take that speck out of your eye,' when you have a log in your own eye? 5 You **hypocrite**! First take the log out of your own eye, and then you will be able to see **clearly** to take the speck out of your brother's eye.

6 "Do not give what is **holy** to dogs—they will only **turn** and attack you. Do not throw your pearls in front of pigs—they will only trample them underfoot.

Ask, Seek, Knock
(Luke 11.9–13)

7 "Ask, and you will receive; **seek**, and you will find; knock, and the door will be opened to you. 8 For everyone who asks will receive, and anyone who **seeks** will find, and the door will be opened to him who knocks. 9 Would any of you who are fathers give your son a stone when he asks for **bread**? 10 Or would you give him a snake when he asks for a fish? 11 **Bad** as you are, you know how to give good things to your children. How much more, then, will your **Father** in **heaven** give good things to those who ask him!

12 "Do for others what you want them to do for you: this is the meaning of the **Law of Moses** and of the **teachings** of the **prophets**.

The Narrow Gate
(Luke 13.24)

13 "Go in through the narrow gate, because the gate to **hell** is wide and the road that leads to it is easy, and there are many who travel it. 14 But the gate to **life** is narrow and the way that leads to it is **hard**, and there are few people who find it.

A Tree and Its Fruit
(Luke 6.43–44)

15 "Be on your guard against **false prophets**; they come to you looking like **sheep** on the outside, but on the inside they are really like wild wolves. 16 You will know them by what they do. Thorn bushes do not bear grapes, and briars do not bear figs. 17 A healthy tree bears good fruit, but a **poor** tree bears **bad** fruit. 18 A healthy tree cannot bear **bad** fruit, and a **poor** tree cannot bear good fruit. 19 And any tree that does not bear good fruit is cut down and thrown in the fire. 20 So then, you will know the **false prophets** by what they do.

I Never Knew You
(Luke 13.25–27)

21 "Not everyone who calls me 'Lord, Lord' will enter the **Kingdom of heaven**, but only those who do what **my Father** in **heaven** wants them to do. 22 When **Judgement Day** comes, many will say to me, 'Lord, Lord! **In your name** we spoke God's **message**, by your **name** we drove out many **demons** and performed many **miracles**!' 23 Then I will say to them, 'I never knew you. **Get away** from me, you **wicked** people!'

The Two House Builders
(Luke 6.47–49)

24 "So then, anyone who hears these **words** of mine and **obeys** them is like a **wise** man who built his house on rock. 25 The rain poured down, the rivers overflowed, and the wind blew **hard** against that house. But it did not fall, because it was built on rock.

26 "But anyone who hears these **words** of mine and does not **obey** them is like a **foolish** man who built his house on sand. 27 The rain poured down, the rivers overflowed, the wind blew **hard** against that house, and it fell. And what a **terrible** fall that was!"

The Authority of Jesus

28 When Jesus finished saying these things, the crowd was **amazed** at the way he **taught**. 29 He wasn't like the **teachers of the Law**; instead, he **taught** with **authority**.

Jesus Heals a Man
(Mark 1.40–45; Luke 5.12–16)

8 When Jesus came down from the hill, large crowds followed him. 2 Then a man **suffering** from a dreaded **skin-disease** came to him, **knelt** down before him, and said, "Sir, if you want to, you can make me **clean**."[e]

3 Jesus stretched out his hand and

amaze 7.28; 9.33
assure 6.2; 10.15
authority 7.29; 9.6
beg [3] Ezek 7.26; 14.36
believe Hab 1.5; 9.28
calm Zech 6.8; Mk 4.39
care 6.26; 16.6

[e] MAKE ME CLEAN: *This disease was considered to make a person ritually unclean.*

7.2: Mk 4.24 **7.12:** Lk 6.31 **7.19:** Mt 3.10; Lk 3.9 **7.20:** Mt 12.33 **7.23:** Ps 6.8 **7.28-29:** Mk 1.22; Lk 4.32

clean [2] Zech 3.5; 11.5
cure Hos 5.13; Mk 1.44
danger 5.22; Lk 8.23
dare 7.4; 22.46
dark 6.23; 10.27
dead 2.18; 9.24
demon [4] 7.22; 9.32
deserve Zech 1.6; 22.8
disciple [4] 5.1; 9.10
disease [3] 4.23; 9.35
faith [2] 6.30; 9.2
feast Amos 6.4; 22.2
fright Dan 11.30; Mk 4.40
heal [3] 4.23; 9.28
help 6.3; 12.12
Kingdom (1) (of God) [2] 7.21; 9.35
kneel 4.9; 9.18
notice (1) Ezek 12.3; 14.30
obey 7.24; 19.20
offer 5.23; 12.4
priest Mal 3.3; 12.4
prophet 7.12; 11.9
prove Jer 46.11; 9.6
punish 3.7; 18.34
rest (1) 5.35; 11.28
right (1) 1.19; 14.4
sacrifice Mal 2.3; 9.13
save 1.21; 10.22
servant [3] Mal 4.4; 12.18
slave 6.24; 10.24
Son of God 4.3; 11.27
Son of Man 9.6
spirit (2) Mal 2.15; 10.1
suffer [2] 4.24; 9.20
teacher Prov 23.12; 9.11
teacher of the Law 7.29; 9.3
terrible 7.27; 11.21
true 5.17; 11.19
word (1) 7.24; 10.20

touched him. "I do want to," he answered. "Be **clean**!" At once the man
was **healed** of his **disease**.
4 Then Jesus
said to him, "Listen! Don't tell anyone,
but go straight to the **priest** and let him
examine you; then in order to **prove** to
everyone that you are **cured**, **offer the sacrifice** that Moses ordered."

Jesus Heals a Roman Officer's Servant
(Luke 7.1–10)

5 When Jesus entered Capernaum, a
Roman officer met him and **begged** for
help:
6 "Sir, my **servant** is sick in bed at
home, unable to move and **suffering terribly**."
7 "I will go and make him well," Jesus
said.
8 "Oh no, sir," answered the officer. "I
do not **deserve** to have you come into my
house. Just give the order, and my **servant** will get well.
9 I, too, am a man
under the **authority** of superior officers,
and I have soldiers under me. I order this
one, 'Go!' and he goes; and I order that
one, 'Come!' and he comes; and I order
my **slave**, 'Do this!' and he does it."
10 When Jesus heard this, he was surprised and said to the people following
him, "I tell you, I have never found anyone in Israel with **faith** like this.
11 I
assure you that many will come from the
east and the west and sit down with
Abraham, Isaac, and Jacob at the **feast** in
the **Kingdom of heaven**.
12 But those who
should be in the **Kingdom** will be thrown
out into the **darkness**, where they will cry
and grind their teeth."
13 Then Jesus said
to the officer, "Go home, and what you
believe will be done for you."
And the officer's **servant** was **healed**
that very moment.

Jesus Heals Many People
(Mark 1.29–34; Luke 4.38–41)

14 Jesus went to Peter's home, and
there he saw Peter's mother-in-law sick
in bed with a fever.
15 He touched her
hand; the fever left her, and she got up
and began to wait on him.
16 When evening came, people
brought to Jesus many who had **demons**
in them. Jesus drove out the **evil spirits**
with a **word** and **healed** all who were
sick.
17 He did this to make what the **prophet** Isaiah had said come **true**, "He himself took our sickness and carried away
our **diseases**."

The Would-be Followers of Jesus
(Luke 9.57–62)

18 When Jesus **noticed** the crowd
round him, he ordered his **disciples** to go
to the other side of the lake.
19 A **teacher of the Law** came to him. "**Teacher**," he
said, "I am ready to go with you
wherever you go."
20 Jesus answered him, "Foxes have
holes, and birds have nests, but the **Son of Man** has nowhere to lie down and **rest**."
21 Another man, who was a **disciple**,
said, "Sir, first let me go back and bury
my father."
22 "Follow me," Jesus answered, "and
let the **dead** bury their own dead."

Jesus Calms a Storm
(Mark 4.35–41; Luke 8.22–25)

23 Jesus got into a boat, and his **disciples** went with him.
24 Suddenly a fierce
storm hit the lake, and the boat was in
danger of sinking. But Jesus was asleep.
25 The **disciples** went to him and woke
him up. "**Save** us, Lord!" they said. "We
are about to die!"
26 "Why are you so **frightened**?"
Jesus answered. "How little **faith** you
have!" Then he got up and ordered the
winds and the waves to stop, and there
was a great **calm**.
27 Everyone was **amazed**. "What kind
of man is this?" they said. "Even the
winds and the waves **obey** him!"

Jesus Heals Two Men with Demons
(Mark 5.1–20; Luke 8.26–39)

28 When Jesus came to the territory of
Gadara on the other side of the lake, he
was met by two men who came out of the
burial caves there. These men had
demons in them and were so fierce that
no one **dared** travel on that road.
29 At
once they screamed, "What do you want
with us, you **Son of God**? Have you come
to **punish** us before the **right** time?"
30 Not far away there was a large
herd of pigs feeding.
31 So the **demons**
begged Jesus, "If you are going to drive
us out, send us into that herd of pigs."
32 "Go," Jesus told them; so they left
and went off into the pigs. The whole
herd rushed down the side of the cliff
into the lake and was drowned.
33 The men who had been taking **care**
of the pigs ran away and went into the
town, where they told the whole story
and what had happened to the men with
the **demons**.
34 So everyone from the town
went out to meet Jesus; and when they
saw him, they **begged** him to leave their
territory.

8.4: Lev 14.1-32 **8.11:** Lk 13.29 **8.12:** Mt 22.13, 25.30; Lk 13.28 **8.17:** Is 53.4

afraid 2.22; 10.26
amaze 8.27; 12.23
authority [2] 8.9; 10.1
believe [2] 8.13; 11.14
blasphemy 26.65
blind [2] Mal 1.8; 11.5
bridegroom [2] Is 62.5; 25.1
courage [2] Zech 8.9; 14.27
dead 8.22; 10.8
demon [4] 8.16; 10.8
disciple [5] 8.18; 10.1
disease 8.2; 10.1
evil 5.11; 12.31
faith [2] 8.10; 13.58
fast (2) [2] 6.16; 11.18
follower 5.11; 10.42
forgive [3] 6.12; 12.31
Good News 4.23; 10.18
harvest [3] 6.26; 13.30
heal [2] 8.3; 10.1
heart 6.21; 12.34
helpless Zech 1.11; Rom 5.6
Jew 2.2; 14.5
kind Zech 7.9; 12.7
Kingdom (1) (of God) 8.11; 10.7
kneel 8.2; 17.14
need 6.2; 10.10
new [4] Zech 3.4; 13.52
outcast [2] Jer 30.17; 11.19
paralyse [3] 4.24; 12.10
Pharisees [3] 5.20; 12.2
pity [2] Zech 11.5; 14.14
power Mal 4.2; 12.24
praise 6.2; 15.31
pray 6.5; 14.23
preach 4.17; 10.7
prove 8.4; 12.27
respect Mal 3.5; 13.57
restore Zech 1.16; Acts 15.16
ruin Zech 5.4; Mk 2.22
sacrifice 8.4; 12.7
sad 6.16; 14.9
scripture 4.4; 11.10
sheep 7.15; 10.6
shepherd Zech 13.7; 25.32
sight Hab 1.13; 20.33
Son of David 12.23
Son of Man 8.20; 10.23
suffer 8.2; 10.8
synagogue 4.23; 10.17
tax collector [2] 5.46; 10.3
teach 7.12; 11.1
teacher 8.19; 10.24
teacher of the Law 8.19; 12.38
turn 7.6; 10.21
wedding Jer 33.11; 11.17
worry 6.25; 10.19

Jesus Heals a Paralysed Man
(Mark 2.1–12; Luke 5.17–26)

9 Jesus got into the boat and went back across the lake to his own town,[f] 2 where some people brought to him a **paralysed** man, lying on a bed. When Jesus saw how much **faith** they had, he said to the **paralysed** man, "**Courage**, my son! Your sins are **forgiven**."

3 Then some **teachers of the Law** said to themselves, "This man is speaking **blasphemy**!"

4 Jesus perceived what they were thinking, so he said, "Why are you thinking such **evil** things? 5 Is it easier to say, 'Your sins are **forgiven**,' or to say, 'Get up and walk'? 6 I will **prove** to you, then, that the **Son of Man** has **authority** on earth to **forgive** sins." So he said to the **paralysed** man, "Get up, pick up your bed, and go home!"

7 The man got up and went home. 8 When the people saw it, they were **afraid**, and **praised** God for giving such **authority** to men.

Jesus Calls Matthew
(Mark 2.13–17; Luke 5.27–32)

9 Jesus left that place, and as he walked along, he saw a **tax collector**, named Matthew, sitting in his office. He said to him, "Follow me."

Matthew got up and followed him.

10 While Jesus was having a meal in Matthew's house,[g] many **tax collectors** and other **outcasts** came and joined Jesus and his **disciples** at the table. 11 Some **Pharisees** saw this and asked his **disciples**, "Why does your **teacher** eat with such people?"

12 Jesus heard them and answered, "People who are well do not **need** a doctor, but only those who are sick. 13 Go and find out what is meant by the **scripture** that says: 'It is **kindness** that I want, not animal **sacrifices**.' I have not come to call **respectable** people, but **outcasts**."

The Question about Fasting
(Mark 2.18–22; Luke 5.33–39)

14 Then the **followers** of John the Baptist came to Jesus, asking, "Why is it that we and the **Pharisees** fast often, but your **disciples** don't **fast** at all?"

15 Jesus answered, "Do you expect the guests at a **wedding party** to be **sad** as long as the **bridegroom** is with them? Of course not! But the day will come when the **bridegroom** will be taken away from them, and then they will **fast**.

16 "No one patches up an old coat with a piece of **new** cloth, for the **new** patch will shrink and make an even bigger hole in the coat. 17 Nor does anyone pour **new** wine into used wineskins, for the skins will burst, the wine will pour out, and the skins will be **ruined**. Instead, **new** wine is poured into fresh wineskins, and both will keep in good condition."

The Official's Daughter and the Woman Who Touched Jesus' Cloak
(Mark 5.21–43; Luke 8.40–56)

18 While Jesus was saying this, a **Jewish** official came to him, **knelt** down before him, and said, "My daughter has just died; but come and place your hands on her, and she will live."

19 So Jesus got up and followed him, and his **disciples** went along with him.

20 A woman who had **suffered** from severe bleeding for twelve years came up behind Jesus and touched the edge of his cloak. 21 She said to herself, "If I only touch his cloak, I will get well."

22 Jesus **turned round** and saw her, and said, "**Courage**, my daughter! Your **faith** has made you well." At that very moment the woman became well.

23 Then Jesus went into the official's house. When he saw the musicians for the funeral and the people all stirred up, 24 he said, "Get out, everybody! The little girl is not **dead**—she is only sleeping!" Then they all laughed at him. 25 But as soon as the people had been put out, Jesus went into the girl's room and took hold of her hand, and she got up. 26 The news about this spread all over that part of the country.

Jesus Heals Two Blind Men

27 Jesus left that place, and as he walked along, two **blind** men started following him. "Take **pity** on us, **Son of David**!" they shouted.

28 When Jesus had gone indoors, the two **blind** men came to him, and he asked them, "Do you **believe** that I can **heal** you?"

"Yes, sir!" they answered.

29 Then Jesus touched their eyes and said, "Let it happen, then, just as you **believe**!"—30 and their **sight** was **restored**. Jesus spoke sternly to them, "Don't tell this to anyone!"

31 But they left and spread the news about Jesus all over that part of the country.

[f] HIS OWN TOWN: *Capernaum (see 4.13).* [g] in Matthew's house; *or* in his *(that is,* Jesus') house.

9.10-11: Lk 15.1-2 **9.13:** Mt 12.7; Hos 6.6

Jesus Heals a Man Who Could Not Speak

32 As the men were leaving, some people brought to Jesus a man who could not talk because he had a **demon**. 33 But as soon as the **demon** was driven out, the man started talking, and everyone was **amazed**. "We have never seen anything like this in Israel!" they exclaimed.

34 But the **Pharisees** said, "It is the chief of the **demons** who gives him the **power** to drive out **demons**."

Jesus Has Pity for the People

35 Jesus went round visiting all the towns and villages. He **taught** in the **synagogues**, **preached** the **Good News** about the **Kingdom**, and **healed** people with every kind of **disease** and sickness. 36 As he saw the crowds, his **heart** was filled with **pity** for them, because they were **worried** and **helpless**, like **sheep** without a **shepherd**. 37 So he said to his **disciples**, "The **harvest** is large, but there are few workers to gather it in. 38 **Pray** to the owner of the **harvest** that he will send out workers to gather in his **harvest**."

The Twelve Apostles
(Mark 3.13–19; Luke 6.12–16)

10 Jesus called his twelve **disciples** together and gave them **authority** to drive out **evil spirits** and to **heal** every **disease** and every sickness. 2 These are the names of the twelve **apostles**: first, Simon (called Peter) and his brother Andrew; James and his brother John, the sons of Zebedee; 3 Philip and Bartholomew; Thomas and Matthew, the **tax collector**; James son of Alphaeus, and Thaddaeus; 4 Simon the Patriot, and Judas Iscariot, who **betrayed** Jesus.

The Mission of the Twelve
(Mark 6.7–13; Luke 9.1–6)

5 These twelve men were sent out by Jesus with the following instructions: "Do not go to any **Gentile** territory or any Samaritan towns. 6 Instead, you are to go to the lost **sheep** of the people of Israel. 7 Go and **preach**, 'The **Kingdom of heaven** is near!' 8 **Heal** the sick, bring the **dead** back **to life**, **heal** those who **suffer** from dreaded **skin-diseases**, and drive out **demons**. You have received without paying, so give without being paid. 9 Do not carry any gold, silver, or copper money in your pockets; 10 do not carry a beggar's bag for the journey or an extra shirt or shoes or a stick. A worker should be given what he **needs**.

11 "When you come to a town or village, go in and look for someone who is willing to **welcome** you, and stay with him until you leave that place. 12 When you go into a house, say, '**Peace** be with you.' 13 If the people in that house **welcome** you, let your greeting of **peace** remain; but if they do not **welcome** you, then take back your greeting. 14 And if some home or town will not **welcome** you or listen to you, then leave that place and shake the dust off your feet. 15 I **assure** you that on the **Judgement Day** God will show more **mercy** to the people of Sodom and Gomorrah than to the people of that town!

Coming Persecutions
(Mark 13.9–13; Luke 21.12–17)

16 "Listen! I am sending you out just like **sheep** to a pack of wolves. You must be as cautious as snakes and as **gentle** as **doves**. 17 **Watch** out, for there will be men who will **arrest** you and take you to **court**, and they will whip you in the **synagogues**. 18 For my **sake** you will be brought to **trial** before rulers and kings, to tell the **Good News** to them and to the **Gentiles**. 19 When they bring you to **trial**, do not **worry** about what you are going to say or how you will say it; when the time comes, you will be given what you will say. 20 For the **words** you will speak will not be yours; they will come from the **Spirit** of your **Father** speaking through you.

21 "Men will hand over their own brothers to be put **to death**, and fathers will do the same to their children; children will **turn** against their parents and have them put **to death**. 22 Everyone will **hate** you because of me. But whoever holds out to the end will be **saved**. 23 When they **persecute** you in one town, run away to another one. I **assure** you that you will not finish your work in all the towns of Israel before the **Son of Man** comes.

24 "No pupil is greater than his **teacher**; no **slave** is greater than his **master**. 25 So a pupil should be **satisfied** to become like his **teacher**, and a **slave** like his **master**. If the head of the family is

afraid [4] 9.8; 14.5
announce Nah 1.15; 12.18
apostle Mk 3.14
arrest Dan 6.16; 14.3
assure [2] 8.11; 11.11
authority 9.6; 20.25
betray Ezek 39.26; 24.10
body [2] 6.22; 14.12
court (1) 5.25; Mk 13.9
cross (1) 16.24
dark 8.12; 16.3
Day of Judgement 7.22; 11.22
dead 9.24; 11.5
death (3) (to death) [2] Zech 13.3; 15.4
declare 12.37
demon 9.32; 11.18
destroy 6.19; Mk 1.24
disciple [4] 9.10; 11.1
disease [2] 9.35; 11.5
dove 3.16; Mk 1.10
enemy 5.43; 13.25
Father (2) (God) [4] 7.11; 11.25
fit (1) [3] Hos 5.3; Mk 7.19
follower 9.14; 12.27
Gentile [2] 4.15; 20.19
gentle Jer 4.11; 11.29
Good News 9.35; 11.5
hate 6.24; 24.9
heal [3] 9.28; 12.10
heaven [2] 7.11; 11.23
hell 7.13; 11.23
Kingdom (1) (of God) 9.35; 11.11
least 5.18; 11.11
life (1) [2] 7.14; 13.22

life (2) (to life) Ezek 37.3; 11.5
love [2] 6.5; 12.18
master [2] 6.24; 15.2
mercy 5.7; 11.22
need 9.12; 15.6
peace [4] 5.9; 26.49
persecute 5.10; 13.2
preach 9.35; 11.1
reject [2] Zech 10.6; 13.57
reward [3] 6.1; 16.27
sake [2] Amos 2.9; 16.25
satisfy 5.6; Rom 8.4
save 8.25; 14.30
secret 2.7; 13.11
share [2] Zech 8.23; 21.34
sheep [2] 9.36; 12.11
slave [2] 8.9; 18.25
Son of Man 9.6; 11.1
soul [2] Lam 2.11; 22.37
Spirit (1) (God's Spirit) 4.1; 11.29
spirit (2) 8.16; 12.43
suffer 9.20; 11.5
sure 6.30; 11.24
synagogue 9.35; 12.
tax collector 9.9; 11.19
teacher [2] 9.11; 12.38
try (2) [2] 5.21; Lk 12.11
turn 9.22; 11.20
watch Zech 12.4; 21.33
welcome [8] Dan 4.36; 18.5
word (1) 8.16; 12.36
world 5.14; 13.35
worry 9.36; 13.22
worse Zech 1.15; 12.45
worst Dan 12.1; 1 Tim 1.15
worth 6.25; 12.12

9.34: Mt 10.25, 12.24; Mk 3.22; Lk 11.15 **9.35:** Mt 4.23; Mk 1.39; Lk 4.44
9.36: Num 27.17; 1 Kgs 22.17; 2 Chr 18.16; Ezek 34.5; Mk 6.34 **9.37-38:** Lk 10.2 **10.7-15:** Lk 10.4-12
10.10: 1 Cor 9.14; 1 Tim 5.18 **10.14:** Acts 13.51 **10.15:** Mt 11.24; Gen 19.24-28 **10.16:** Lk 10.3
10.17-20: Mk 13.9-11; Lk 12.11-12, 21.12-15 **10.21:** Mk 13.12; Lk 21.16
10.22: Mt 24.9, 13; Mk 13.13; Lk 21.17 **10.24:** Lk 6.40; Jn 13.16, 15.20
10.25: Mt 9.34, 12.24; Mk 3.22; Lk 11.15

called Beelzebul, the members of the
family will be called even **worse** names!

Whom to Fear
(Luke 12.2–7)

26 "So do not be **afraid** of people.
Whatever is now covered up will be uncovered, and every **secret** will be made
known. 27 What I am telling you in the
dark you must repeat in broad daylight,
and what you have heard in private you
must **announce** from the housetops. 28 Do
not be **afraid** of those who kill the **body**
but cannot kill the **soul**; rather be **afraid**
of God, who can **destroy** both **body** and
soul in **hell**. 29 For only a penny you can
buy two sparrows, yet not one sparrow
falls to the ground without your **Father's**
consent. 30 As for you, even the hairs of
your head have all been counted. 31 So do
not be **afraid**; you are **worth** much more
than many sparrows!

Confessing and Rejecting Christ
(Luke 12.8–9)

32 "If anyone **declares** publicly that he
belongs to me, I will do the same for him
before **my Father** in **heaven**. 33 But if anyone **rejects** me publicly, I will **reject** him
before **my Father** in **heaven**.

Not Peace, but a Sword
(Luke 12.51–53; 14.26–27)

34 "Do not think that I have come to
bring **peace** to the **world**. No, I did not
come to bring **peace**, but a sword. 35 I
came to set sons against their fathers,
daughters against their mothers,
daughters-in-law against their mothers-
in-law; 36 a man's **worst enemies** will be
the members of his own family.

37 "Whoever **loves** his father or
mother more than me is not **fit** to be my
disciple; whoever **loves** his son or
daughter more than me is not **fit** to be
my **disciple**. 38 Whoever does not take up
his **cross** and follow in my steps is not **fit**
to be my **disciple**. 39 Whoever tries to gain
his own **life** will lose it; but whoever loses
his **life** for my **sake** will gain it.

Rewards
(Mark 9.41)

40 "Whoever **welcomes** you **welcomes**
me; and whoever **welcomes** me **wel-**
comes the one who sent me. 41 Whoever
welcomes God's messenger because he is
God's messenger, will **share** in his **re-**
ward. And whoever **welcomes** a good
man because he is good, will **share** in his
reward. 42 You can be **sure** that whoever
gives even a drink of cold water to one of
the **least** of these my **followers** because
he is my follower, will certainly receive a
reward."

The Messengers from John the Baptist
(Luke 7.18–35)

11 When Jesus finished giving these
instructions to his twelve **dis-**
ciples, he left that place and went off to
teach and **preach** in the towns near
there.

2 When John the Baptist heard in
prison about the things that **Christ** was
doing, he sent some of his **disciples** to
him. 3 "Tell us," they asked Jesus, "are
you the one John said was going to come,
or should we expect someone else?"

4 Jesus answered, "Go back and tell
John what you are hearing and seeing:
5 the **blind** can see, the lame can walk,
those who **suffer** from dreaded **skin-**
diseases are made **clean**,[h] the deaf hear,
the **dead** are brought back **to life**, and the
Good News is **preached** to the **poor**.
6 How **happy** are those who have no
doubts about me!"

7 While John's **disciples** were leaving,
Jesus spoke about him to the crowds:
"When you went out to John in the
desert, what did you expect to see? A
blade of grass bending in the wind?
8 What did you go out to see? A man
dressed up in fancy clothes? People who
dress like that live in palaces! 9 Tell me,
what did you go out to see? A **prophet**?
Yes indeed, but you saw much more than
a **prophet**. 10 For John is the one of whom
the **scripture** says: 'God said, I will send
my messenger **ahead of you** to open the
way for you.' 11 I **assure** you that John the
Baptist is greater than any man who has
ever lived. But he who is **least** in the
Kingdom of heaven is greater than John.
12 From the time John **preached** his **mes-**
sage until this very day the **Kingdom of**
heaven has **suffered violent** attacks,[i] and
violent men try to seize it. 13 Until the
time of John all the **prophets** and the
Law of Moses spoke about the **Kingdom**;
14 and if you are willing to **believe** their
message, John is Elijah, whose coming
was **predicted**. 15 Listen, then, if you have
ears!

16 "Now, to what can I **compare** the
people of this day? They are like children sitting in the market-place. One
group shouts to the other, 17 'We played

ahead of you 21.2
ash Jon 3.6; Lk 10.13
assure [2] 10.15; 12.42
believe 9.28; 21.21
blind 9.27; 12.22
choose Zech 4.14; 12.18
Christ Lk 2.11
clean 8.2; 12.44
compare Dan 1.13; Lk 7.31
Day of Judgement [2] 10.15; 12.36
dead 10.8; 22.24
demon 10.8; 12.22
disciple [3] 10.1; 12.1
disease 10.1; 26.6
doubt 14.31
exist Dan 12.1; Jn 1.1
fast (2) 9.14; Mk 2.18
Father (2) (God) [5] 10.20; 12.50
friend 6.3; 20.13
gentle 10.16; 1 Cor 4.21
Good News 10.18; 24.14
happy 5.3; 13.44
heaven [2] 10.32; 12.50
hell 10.28; 18.9
humble 5.5; 18.4
Kingdom (1) (of God) [3] 10.7; 12.28
law 7.12; 12.2
learn [3] 2.16; 13.18
least 10.42; 25.40
life (2) (to life) 10.8; 16.21
mercy [2] 10.15; 15.22
message [2] 7.22; 13.19
miracle [3] 7.22; 12.38
outcast 9.10; Mk 2.15
poor 7.17; 12.33
preach [3] 10.7; 12.41
predict Mic 3.6; 16.3
prison 4.12; 14.3
prophet [3] 8.17; 12.17
rest (1) [2] 8.20; 12.43
result 23.35
reveal Zech 3.8; Lk 2.32
sackcloth Jon 3.5; Lk 10.13
scripture 9.13; 12.7
Son of God [3] 8.29; 14.33
Son of Man 10.23; 12.8
Spirit (1) (God's Spirit) 10.20; 12.18
sprinkle Ezek 43.18; Lk 10.13
suffer [2] 10.8; 16.21
sure 10.42; 12.36
tax collector 10.3; 18.17
teach 9.35; 12.42
terrible [2] 8.6; 15.22
thank Amos 4.5; 14.19
true 8.17; 12.17
turn [2] 10.21; 12.41

[h] MADE CLEAN: *See 8.2.* [i] has suffered violent attacks; *or* has been coming violently.

10.26: Mk 4.22; Lk 8.17 **10.33:** 2 Tim 2.12 **10.35-36:** Mic 7.6 **10.38:** Mt 16.24; Mk 8.34; Lk 9.23
10.39: Mt 16.25; Mk 8.35; Lk 9.24, 17.33; Jn 12.25 **10.40:** Mk 9.37; Lk 9.48, 10.16; Jn 13.20
11.5: Is 35.5-6, 61.1 **11.10:** Mal 3.1 **11.12-13:** Lk 16.16 **11.14:** Mal 4.5; Mt 17.10-13; Mk 9.11-13

violent [2] Zech 8.17; 23.25
wedding 9.15; 22.2
wisdom Obad 8; 13.54
wise 7.24; 12.42

wedding music for you, but you wouldn't
dance! We sang funeral songs, but you
wouldn't cry!' 18 When John came, he
fasted and drank no wine, and everyone
said, 'He has a **demon** in him!' 19 When
the **Son of Man** came, he ate and drank,
and everyone said, 'Look at this man! He
is a glutton and a drinker, a **friend** of **tax
collectors** and other **outcasts**!' God's **wisdom**, however, is shown to be **true** by its
results."

The Unbelieving Towns
(Luke 10.13–15)

20 The people in the towns where
Jesus had performed most of his **miracles** did not **turn from their sins**, so he
reproached those towns. 21 "How **terrible**
it will be for you, Chorazin! How **terrible**
for you too, Bethsaida! If the **miracles**
which were performed in you had been
performed in Tyre and Sidon, the people
there would long ago have put on **sackcloth** and **sprinkled ashes** on themselves,
to show that they had **turned from their
sins**! 22 I **assure** you that on the **Judgement Day** God will show more **mercy** to
the people of Tyre and Sidon than to you!
23 And as for you, Capernaum! Did you
want to lift yourself up to **heaven**? You
will be thrown down to **hell**! If the **miracles** which were performed in you had
been performed in Sodom, it would still
be in **existence** today! 24 You can be **sure**
that on the **Judgement Day** God will
show more **mercy** to Sodom than to
you!"

Come to Me and Rest
(Luke 10.21–22)

25 At that time Jesus said, "**Father**,
Lord of **heaven and earth**! I **thank** you
because you have shown to the **un-
learned** what you have hidden from the
wise and **learned**. 26 Yes, **Father**, this was
how you wanted it to happen.
27 "**My Father** has given me all things.
No one knows the **Son** except the **Father**,
and no one knows the **Father** except the
Son and those to whom the **Son chooses**
to **reveal** him.
28 "Come to me, all of you who are
tired from carrying heavy loads, and I
will give you **rest**. 29 Take my yoke and
put it on you, and **learn** from me, because
I am **gentle** and **humble** in **spirit**; and you
will find **rest**. 30 For the yoke I will give
you is easy, and the load I will put on you
is light."

The Question about the Sabbath
(Mark 2.23–28; Luke 6.1–5)

12 Not long afterwards Jesus was
walking through some cornfields
on the **Sabbath**. His **disciples** were
hungry, so they began to pick ears of
corn and eat the grain. 2 When the **Pharisees** saw this, they said to Jesus, "Look, it
is against our **Law** for your **disciples** to
do this on the **Sabbath**!"
3 Jesus answered, "Have you never
read what David did that time when he
and his men were **hungry**? 4 He went
into the house of God, and he and his
men ate the **bread offered** to God, even
though it was against the **Law** for them
to eat it—only the **priests** were allowed
to eat that **bread**. 5 Or have you not read
in the **Law of Moses** that every **Sabbath**
the **priests** in the **Temple** actually break
the **Sabbath law**, yet they are not **guilty**?
6 I tell you that there is something here
greater than the **Temple**. 7 The **scripture**
says, 'It is **kindness** that I want, not
animal **sacrifices**.' If you really knew
what this means, you would not **condemn**
people who are not **guilty**; 8 for the **Son of
Man** is Lord of the **Sabbath**."

The Man with a Paralysed Hand
(Mark 3.1–6; Luke 6.6–11)

9 Jesus left that place and went to a
synagogue, 10 where there was a man
who had a **paralysed** hand. Some people
were there who wanted to **accuse** Jesus
of doing **wrong**, so they asked him, "Is it
against our **Law** to **heal** on the
Sabbath?"
11 Jesus answered, "What if one of
you has a **sheep** and it falls into a deep
hole on the **Sabbath**? Will he not take
hold of it and lift it out? 12 And a man is
worth much more than a **sheep**! So then,
our **Law** does allow us to **help** someone
on the **Sabbath**." 13 Then he said to the
man with the **paralysed** hand, "Stretch
out your hand."
He stretched it out, and it became well
again, just like the other one. 14 Then the
Pharisees left and made **plans** to kill
Jesus.

God's Chosen Servant

15 When Jesus heard about the **plot**
against him, he went away from that
place; and large crowds followed him.
He **healed** all those who were ill 16 and
gave them orders not to tell others about
him. 17 He did this so as to make what

accuse [3] Zech 3.1; 18.16
amaze 9.33; 13.54
announce 10.27; Mk 1.7
apart [2] Zech 14.21; 27.51
argue Jer 15.10; 21.25
assure 11.11; 13.17
bad [3] 7.11; 22.10
blind 11.5; 15.14
bread [2] 7.9; 15.34
choose 11.27; 20.23
clean 11.5; 23.25
condemn Zech 3.2; 20.18
Day of Judgement [3] 11.22; Lk 10.12
declare 10.32; Mk 7.19
demon [4] 11.18; 15.22
disciple [3] 11.1; 13.10
each other [2] Joel 2.8; 24.7
evil [5] 9.4; 13.41
Father (2) (God) 11.25; 13.43
follower [2] 10.42; 19.28
forgive [4] 9.2; 18.21
godless Ezek 28.10; 16.4
guilty [3] 5.28; 26.66
heal [3] 10.1; 13.15
heart 9.36; 14.14
heaven 11.23; 14.19
help [2] 8.5; 15.5
hope Zech 9.5; Lk 3.15
hunger [2] 4.2; 21.18
innocent Jon 4.11; 23.35
judge [2] 7.1; 27.19
justice Mal 2.17; 23.23
kind 9.13; Mk 5.19
Kingdom (1) (of God) 11.11; 13.11
last (1) 5.18; 13.21
law [6] 11.13; 15.9
love 10.37; 13.22
miracle [4] 11.20; 13.54
offer 8.4; 21.16
paralyse [2] 9.2; Mk 2.3
Pharisees [4] 9.11; 15.1
plan 1.19; 22.15
please 7.4; 14.6
plot (1) Nah 1.9; Acts 4.25
poor 11.5; 19.21
power [4] 9.34; 14.2
preach 11.1; 23.3
priest [2] 8.4; Mk 1.44
prophet [2] 11.9; 13.17
prove [2] 9.6; Mk 1.44
put out Amos 5.6; Mk 9.48
rest (1) 11.28; 26.45
Sabbath [8] Amos 8.5; 24.20
sacrifice 9.13; Mk 1.44
Satan 4.10; 16.23
scatter Zech 13.7; 13.4
scripture 11.10; 18.16
servant 8.6; 13.27
sheep [2] 10.6; 15.24

11.21: Is 23.1-18; Ezek 26.1–28.26; Joel 3.4-8; Amos 1.9-10; Zech 9.2-4 **11.23:** Is 14.13-15; Gen 19.24-28 **11.24:** Mt 10.15; Lk 10.12 **11.27:** Jn 3.35, 1.18, 10.15 **11.29:** Jer 6.16 **12.1:** Deut 23.25 **12.3-4:** I Sam 21.1-6 **12.4:** Lev 24.9 **12.5:** Num 28.9-10 **12.7:** Mt 9.13; Hos 6.6 **12.11:** Lk 14.5

Son of David 9.27; 15.22
Son of Man [3] 11.19; 13.37
speech Amos 7.10; Mk 7.35
Spirit (1) (God's Spirit) [4] 11.29; 22.43
spirit (2) [2] 10.1; 26.41
strong [2] Mal 3.2; 14.30
sure 11.24; 19.28
synagogue 10.17; 13.54
teach 11.1; 13.1
teacher 10.24; 17.24
teacher of the Law 9.3; 13.52
Temple (1) (of God) [2] 4.5; 17.24
triumph Zech 9.9; Jas 2.13
true 11.19; 13.35
turn 11.20; 13.15
useless Mal 3.14; 25.30
wise 11.25; 23.34
word (1) [2] 10.20; 15.8
worse [2] 10.25; 27.64
worth 10.31; 17.27
wrong [2] 6.12; 17.17

God had said through the **prophet** Isaiah come **true**:

18 "Here is my **servant**, whom I have
chosen,
the one I **love**, and with whom I am
pleased.
I will send my **Spirit** upon him,
and he will **announce** my **judgement**
to the nations.
19 He will not **argue** or shout,
or make loud **speeches** in the
streets.
20 He will not break off a bent reed,
or **put out** a flickering lamp.
He will persist until he causes **justice**
to **triumph**,
21 and in him all peoples will put their
hope."

Jesus and Beelzebul
(Mark 3.20–30; Luke 11.14–23)

22 Then some people brought to Jesus a man who was **blind** and could not talk because he had a **demon**. Jesus **healed** the man, so that he was able to talk and see. 23 The crowds were all **amazed** at what Jesus had done. "Could he be the **Son of David**?" they asked.

24 When the **Pharisees** heard this, they replied, "He drives out **demons** only because their ruler Beelzebul gives him **power** to do so."

25 Jesus knew what they were thinking, so he said to them, "Any country that divides itself into groups which fight **each other** will not **last** very long. And any town or family that divides itself into groups which fight **each other** will fall **apart**. 26 So if one group is fighting another in **Satan's** kingdom, this means that it is already divided into groups and will soon fall **apart**! 27 You say that I drive out **demons** because Beelzebul gives me the **power** to do so. Well, then, who gives your **followers** the **power** to drive them out? What your own **followers** do **proves** that you are **wrong**! 28 No, it is not Beelzebul, but **God's Spirit**, who gives me the **power** to drive out **demons**, which **proves** that the **Kingdom of God** has already come upon you.

29 "No one can break into a **strong** man's house and take away his belongings unless he first ties up the **strong** man; then he can plunder his house.

30 "Anyone who is not for me is really against me; anyone who does not **help** me gather is really **scattering**. 31 And so I tell you that people can **be forgiven** any sin and any **evil** thing they say;*j* but whoever says **evil** things against the **Holy Spirit** will not be **forgiven**. 32 Anyone who says something against the **Son of Man** can be **forgiven**; but whoever says something against the **Holy Spirit** will not be **forgiven**—now or ever.

A Tree and Its Fruit
(Luke 6.43–45)

33 "To have good fruit you must have a healthy tree; if you have a **poor** tree, you will have **bad** fruit. A tree is known by the kind of fruit it bears. 34 You snakes—how can you say good things when you are **evil**? For the mouth speaks what the **heart** is full of. 35 A good person brings good things out of his treasure of good things; a **bad** person brings **bad** things out of his treasure of bad things.

36 "You can be sure that on **Judgement Day** everyone will have to give account of every **useless word** he has ever spoken. 37 Your **words** will be used to **judge** you—to **declare** you either **innocent** or guilty."

The Demand for a Miracle
(Mark 8.11–12; Luke 11.29–32)

38 Then some **teachers of the Law** and some **Pharisees** spoke up. "**Teacher**," they said, "we want to see you perform a **miracle**."

39 "How **evil** and **godless** are the people of this day!" Jesus exclaimed. "You ask me for a **miracle**? No! The only **miracle** you will be given is the **miracle** of the **prophet** Jonah. 40 In the same way that Jonah spent three days and nights in the big fish, so will the **Son of Man** spend three days and nights in the depths of the earth. 41 On **Judgement Day** the people of Nineveh will stand up and **accuse** you, because they **turned from their sins** when they heard Jonah **preach**; and I tell you that there is something here greater than Jonah! 42 On **Judgement Day** the Queen of Sheba will stand up and **accuse** you, because she travelled all the way from her country to listen to King Solomon's **wise teaching**; and I **assure** you that there is something here greater than Solomon!

The Return of the Evil Spirit
(Luke 11.24–26)

43 "When an **evil spirit** goes out of a person, it travels over dry country looking for a place to **rest**. If it can't find one,

j evil thing they say; *or* evil thing they say against God.

12.18-21: Is 42.1-4 (LXX) **12.24:** Mt 9.34, 10.25 **12.30:** Mk 9.40 **12.32:** Lk 12.10 **12.33:** Mt 7.20; Lk 6.44 **12.34:** Mt 3.7, 23.33, 15.18; Lk 3.7, 6.45 **12.38:** Mt 16.1; Mk 8.11; Lk 11.16 **12.39:** Mt 16.4; Mk 8.12 **12.40:** Jon 1.17 **12.41:** Jon 3.5 **12.42:** 1 Kgs 10.1-10; 2 Chr 9.1-12

44 it says to itself, 'I will go back to my house.' So it goes back and finds the house empty, clean, and all tidy. 45 Then it goes out and brings along seven other spirits even worse than itself, and they come and live there. So when it is all over, that person is in a worse state than he was at the beginning. This is what will happen to the evil people of this day."

Jesus' Mother and Brothers
(Mark 3.31–35; Luke 8.19–21)

46 Jesus was still talking to the people when his mother and brothers arrived. They stood outside, asking to speak with him. 47 So one of the people there said to him, "Look, your mother and brothers are standing outside, and they want to speak with you."[k]

48 Jesus answered, "Who is my mother? Who are my brothers?" 49 Then he pointed to his disciples and said, "Look! Here are my mother and my brothers! 50 Whoever does what my Father in heaven wants him to do is my brother, my sister, and my mother."

The Parable of the Sower
(Mark 4.1–9; Luke 8.4–8)

13 That same day Jesus left the house and went to the lake-side, where he sat down to teach. 2 The crowd that gathered round him was so large that he got into a boat and sat in it, while the crowd stood on the shore. 3 He used parables to tell them many things.

"Once there was a man who went out to sow corn. 4 As he scattered the seed in the field, some of it fell along the path, and the birds came and ate it up. 5 Some of it fell on rocky ground, where there was little soil. The seeds soon sprouted, because the soil wasn't deep. 6 But when the sun came up, it burnt the young plants; and because the roots had not grown deep enough, the plants soon dried up. 7 Some of the seed fell among thorn bushes, which grew up and choked the plants. 8 But some seeds fell in good soil, and the plants produced corn; some produced a hundred grains, others sixty, and others thirty."

9 And Jesus concluded, "Listen, then, if you have ears!"

The Purpose of the Parables
(Mark 4.10–12; Luke 8.9–10)

10 Then the disciples came to Jesus and asked him, "Why do you use parables when you talk to the people?"

11 Jesus answered, "The knowledge about the secrets of the Kingdom of heaven has been given to you, but not to them. 12 For the person who has something will be given more, so that he will have more than enough; but the person who has nothing will have taken away from him even the little he has. 13 The reason I use parables in talking to them is that they look, but do not see, and they listen, but do not hear or understand. 14 So the prophecy of Isaiah applies to them:

'This people will listen and listen, but
not understand;
they will look and look, but not see,
15 because their minds are dull,
and they have stopped up their ears
and have closed their eyes.
Otherwise, their eyes would see,
their ears would hear,
their minds would understand,
and they would turn to me, says God,
and I would heal them.'

16 "As for you, how fortunate you are! Your eyes see and your ears hear. 17 I assure you that many prophets and many of God's people wanted very much to see what you see, but they could not, and to hear what you hear, but they did not.

Jesus Explains the Parable of the Sower
(Mark 4.13–20; Luke 8.11–15)

18 "Listen, then, and learn what the parable of the sower means. 19 Those who hear the message about the Kingdom but do not understand it are like the seeds that fell along the path. The Evil One comes and snatches away what was sown in them. 20 The seeds that fell on rocky ground stand for those who receive the message gladly as soon as they hear it. 21 But it does not sink deep into them, and they don't last long. So when trouble or persecution comes because of the message, they give up at once. 22 The seeds that fell among thorn bushes stand for those who hear the message; but the worries about this life and the love for riches choke the message, and they don't bear fruit. 23 And the seeds sown in the good soil stand for those who hear the message and understand it: they bear fruit, some as much as a hundred, others sixty, and others thirty."

The Parable of the Weeds

24 Jesus told them another parable: "The Kingdom of heaven is like this. A man sowed good seed in his field. 25 One night, when everyone was asleep, an enemy came and sowed weeds among the wheat and went away. 26 When the

[k] *Some manuscripts do not have verse 47.*

13.2: Lk 5.1-3 **13.12:** Mt 25.29; Mk 4.25; Lk 8.18, 19.26 **13.14-15:** Is 6.9-10 (LXX) **13.16-17:** Lk 10.23-24

age (1) [3] Ezek 25.15; 19.28
amaze 12.23; 15.31
angel [3] 4.6; 16.27
assure 12.42; 16.28
create Mal 2.10; 19.8
Devil 4.1; 25.41
disciple [3] 12.1; 14.12
enemy [3] 10.36; 22.44
enough [2] 6.34; 14.20
evil [2] 12.31; 15.19
Evil One [2] 6.13; Jn 17.15
faith 9.2; 14.31
Father (2) (God) 12.50; 15.13
fortune Hos 12.8; Lk 10.23
give up 24.10
glad 5.12; Mk 4.16
God's people [2] 2.6; 24.22
happy 11.6; 18.13
harvest [4] 9.37; 21.34
heal 12.10; 14.14
Kingdom (1) (of God) [12] 12.28; 16.19
knowledge Mal 2.7; Lk 8.10
last (1) 12.25; 27.45
learn 11.25; 27.3
life (1) 10.39; 14.2
love 12.18; 19.19
message [6] 11.12; 22.4
mind (1) [2] 3.14; 21.29
miracle [2] 12.38; 14.2
new 9.16; 19.28
parable [12] Ezek 24.3; 21.33
persecute 10.23; Mk 4.17

prophecy Zech 13.3 15.7
prophet [3] 12.17; 14.5
reason Zeph 3.15; 19.3
reject 10.33; 21.42
respect 9.13; 15.4
riches 6.19; 19.21
rise Mal 4.2; 22.23
scatter 12.30; 25.24
secret 10.26; 26.4
seed [14] 6.26; 17.20
servant 12.18; 18.23
Son of Man [2] 12.8; 16.13
sow [10] 6.26; 25.24
stand for [3] Zech 5.6; Lk 8.12
synagogue 12.9; 23.6
teach [2] 12.42; 15.2
teacher of the Law 12.38; 15.1
trouble 6.34; 24.6
true 12.17; 14.33
turn 12.41; 16.23
understand [6] Hos 14.9; 15.10
weed [11] Zeph 2.9; Heb 6.8
wisdom 11.19; Mk 6.2
world [2] 10.34; 16.26
worry 10.19; 15.14
worthless 5.13; 18.32
yeast Ezek 45.21; 16.6

plants grew and the ears of corn began
to form, then the **weeds** showed up. 27 The
man's **servants** came to him and said,
'Sir, it was good **seed** you **sowed** in your
field; where did the **weeds** come from?'
28 'It was some **enemy** who did this,' he
answered. 'Do you want us to go and pull
up the **weeds**?' they asked him. 29 'No,' he
answered, 'because as you gather the
weeds you might pull up some of the
wheat along with them. 30 Let the wheat
and the **weeds** both grow together until
harvest. Then I will tell the **harvest**
workers to pull up the **weeds** first, tie
them in bundles and burn them, and then
to gather in the wheat and put it in my
barn.'"

The Parable of the Mustard Seed
(Mark 4.30–32; Luke 13.18–19)

31 Jesus told them another **parable**:
"The **Kingdom of heaven** is like this. A
man takes a mustard **seed** and **sows** it in
his field. 32 It is the smallest of all **seeds**,
but when it grows up, it is the biggest of
all plants. It becomes a tree, so that birds
come and make their nests in its
branches."

The Parable of the Yeast
(Luke 13.20–21)

33 Jesus told them still another
parable: "The **Kingdom of heaven** is like
this. A woman takes some **yeast** and
mixes it with forty litres of flour until the
whole batch of dough **rises**."

Jesus' Use of Parables
(Mark 4.33–34)

34 Jesus used **parables** to tell all these
things to the crowds; he would not say a
thing to them without using a **parable**.
35 He did this to make what the **prophet**
had said come **true**,

"I will use **parables** when I speak to
them;
I will tell them things unknown since
the **creation** of the **world**."

Jesus Explains the Parable of the Weeds

36 When Jesus had left the crowd and
gone indoors, his **disciples** came to him
and said, "Tell us what the **parable** about
the **weeds** in the field means."

37 Jesus answered, "The man who
sowed the good **seed** is the **Son of Man**;
38 the field is the **world**; the good **seed** is
the people who belong to the **Kingdom**;
the **weeds** are the people who belong to
the **Evil One**; 39 and the **enemy** who
sowed the **weeds** is the **Devil**. The
harvest is the end of the **age**, and the **harvest** workers are **angels**. 40 Just as the
weeds are gathered up and burnt in the
fire, so the same thing will happen at the
end of the **age**: 41 the **Son of Man** will
send out his **angels** to gather up out of his
Kingdom all those who cause people to
sin and all others who do **evil** things,
42 and they will throw them into the fiery
furnace, where they will cry and grind
their teeth. 43 Then **God's people** will
shine like the sun in their **Father's Kingdom**. Listen, then, if you have ears!

The Parable of the Hidden Treasure

44 "The **Kingdom of heaven** is like
this. A man happens to find a treasure
hidden in a field. He covers it up again,
and is so **happy** that he goes and sells
everything he has, and then goes back
and buys that field.

The Parable of the Pearl

45 "Also, the **Kingdom of heaven** is
like this. A man is looking for fine pearls,
46 and when he finds one that is unusually
fine, he goes and sells everything he has,
and buys that pearl.

The Parable of the Net

47 "Also, the **Kingdom of heaven** is
like this. Some fishermen throw their net
out in the lake and catch all kinds of fish.
48 When the net is full, they pull it to
shore and sit down to divide the fish: the
good ones go into their buckets, the
worthless ones are thrown away. 49 It will
be like this at the end of the **age**: the
angels will go out and gather up the **evil**
people from among the good 50 and will
throw them into the fiery furnace, where
they will cry and grind their teeth.

New Truths and Old

51 "Do you **understand** these things?"
Jesus asked them.

"Yes," they answered.

52 So he replied, "This means, then,
that every **teacher of the Law** who becomes a **disciple** in the **Kingdom of
heaven** is like the owner of a house who
takes **new** and old things out of his
storeroom."

Jesus is Rejected at Nazareth
(Mark 6.1–6; Luke 4.16–30)

53 When Jesus finished telling these
parables, he left that place 54 and went
back to his home town. He **taught** in the
synagogue, and those who heard him
were **amazed**. "Where did he get such
wisdom?" they asked. "And what about

13.35: Ps 78.2

his **miracles**? 55 Isn't he the carpenter's son? Isn't Mary his mother, and aren't James, Joseph, Simon, and Judas his brothers? 56 Aren't all his sisters living here? Where did he get all this?" 57 And so they **rejected** him.

Jesus said to them, "A **prophet** is **respected** everywhere except in his home town and by his own family." 58 Because they did not have **faith**, he did not perform many **miracles** there.

The Death of John the Baptist
(Mark 6.14–29; Luke 9.7–9)

14 At that time Herod, the ruler of Galilee, heard about Jesus. 2 "He is really John the Baptist, who has come back to **life**," he told his officials. "That is why he has this **power** to perform **miracles**."

3 For Herod had earlier ordered John's **arrest**, and he had him chained and put in **prison**. He had done this because of Herodias, his brother Philip's wife. 4 For some time John the Baptist had told Herod, "It isn't **right** for you to be married to Herodias!" 5 Herod wanted to kill him, but he was **afraid** of the **Jewish** people, because they **considered** John to be a **prophet**.

6 On Herod's birthday the daughter of Herodias danced in front of the whole group. Herod was so **pleased** 7 that he **promised** her, "I **swear** that I will give you anything you ask for!"

8 At her mother's suggestion she asked him, "Give me here and now the head of John the Baptist on a dish!"

9 The king was **sad**, but because of the **promise** he had made in front of all his guests he gave orders that her **wish** be **granted**. 10 So he had John beheaded in **prison**. 11 The head was brought in on a dish and given to the girl, who took it to her mother. 12 John's **disciples** came, carried away his **body**, and buried it; then they went and told Jesus.

Jesus Feeds Five Thousand Men
(Mark 6.30–44; Luke 9.10–17; John 6.1–14)

13 When Jesus heard the news about John, he left there in a boat and went to a **lonely** place by himself. The people heard about it, so they left their towns and followed him by land. 14 Jesus got out of the boat, and when he saw the large crowd, his **heart** was filled with **pity** for them, and he **healed** those who were ill.

15 That evening his **disciples** came to him and said, "It is already very late, and this is a **lonely** place. Send the people away and let them go to the villages to buy food for themselves."

16 "They don't have to leave," answered Jesus. "You yourselves give them something to eat!"

17 "All we have here are five loaves and two fish," they replied.

18 "Then bring them here to me," Jesus said. 19 He ordered the people to sit down on the grass; then he took the five loaves and the two fish, looked up to **heaven**, and gave **thanks** to God. He broke the loaves and gave them to the **disciples**, and the **disciples** gave them to the people. 20 Everyone ate and had **enough**. Then the **disciples** took up twelve baskets full of what was left over. 21 The number of men who ate was about five thousand, not counting the women and children.

Jesus Walks on the Water
(Mark 6.45–52; John 6.15–21)

22 Then Jesus made the **disciples** get into the boat and go on ahead to the other side of the lake, while he sent the people away. 23 After sending the people away, he went up a hill by himself to **pray**. When evening came, Jesus was there **alone**; 24 and by this time the boat was far out in the lake, tossed about by the waves, because the wind was blowing against it.

25 Between three and six o'clock in the morning Jesus came to the **disciples**, walking on the water. 26 When they saw him walking on the water, they were **terrified**. "It's a **ghost**!" they said, and screamed with **fear**.

27 Jesus spoke to them at once. "**Courage**!" he said. "It is I. Don't be **afraid**!"

28 Then Peter spoke up. "Lord, if it is really you, order me to come out on the water to you."

29 "Come!" answered Jesus. So Peter got out of the boat and started walking on the water to Jesus. 30 But when he **noticed** the **strong** wind, he was **afraid** and started to sink down in the water. "**Save** me, Lord!" he cried.

31 At once Jesus reached out and grabbed hold of him and said, "How little **faith** you have! Why did you **doubt**?"

32 They both got into the boat, and the wind died down. 33 Then the **disciples** in the boat **worshipped** Jesus. "**Truly** you are the **Son of God**!" they exclaimed.

Jesus Heals the Sick in Gennesaret
(Mark 6.53–56)

34 They crossed the lake and came to

afraid [3] 10.26; 17.7
alone 4.4; 17.1
arrest 10.17; 21.46
beg 8.5; 15.23
body 10.28; 15.17
consider 21.46
courage 9.2; Mk 6.50
disciple [8] 13.10; 15.2
doubt 11.6; 21.21
enough 13.6; 15.33
faith 13.58; 15.28
fear Mal 3.16; Mk 5.33
ghost Is 29.4; Mk 6.49
grant Mal 1.8; Acts 4.30
heal 13.15; 15.28
heart 12.34; 15.8
heaven 12.50; 15.13
Jew 9.18; 27.11
life (1) 13.22; 16.25
lonely [2] Lam 5.18; Mk 1.35
miracle 13.54; 16.1
notice (1) 8.18; 23.5
pity 9.27; 20.30
please 12.18; 17.5
power 12.24; 20.25
pray 9.38; 18.19
prison [2] 11.2; 25.36
promise [2] 5.5; 20.21
prophet 13.17; 16.14
right (1) 8.29; 15.7
sad 9.15; 17.23
save 10.22; 16.25
Son of God 11.27; 16.16
strong 12.29; Mk 3.27
swear 5.34; 23.16
terrify Zech 12.4; 17.6
thank 11.25; 15.36
true 13.35; 15.27
wish Mal 1.10; 17.4
worship (1) (of God) 6.2; 15.9

13.57: Jn 4.44 **14.3-4:** Lk 3.19-20 **14.4:** Lev 18.16, 20.21

land at Gennesaret, 35 where the people
recognized Jesus. So they sent for the
sick people in all the surrounding
country and brought them to Jesus.
36 They **begged** him to let those who were
ill at least touch the edge of his cloak;
and all who touched it were made well.

The Teaching of the Ancestors
(Mark 7.1-13)

15 Then some **Pharisees** and
teachers of the Law came from
Jerusalem to Jesus and asked him,
2 "Why is it that your **disciples disobey**
the **teaching** handed down by our ancestors? They don't wash their hands in the
proper way before they eat!"

3 Jesus answered, "And why do you
disobey God's **command** and follow your
own **teaching**? 4 For God said, '**Respect**
your father and your mother,' and 'Whoever **curses** his father or his mother is to
be put **to death**.' 5 But you **teach** that if a
person has something he could use to
help his father or mother, but says, 'This
belongs to God,' 6 he does not **need** to
honour his father.[l] In this way you disregard God's **command**, in order to follow your own **teaching**. 7 You **hypocrites**!
How **right** Isaiah was when he **prophesied** about you!

8 'These people, says God, **honour** me
with their **words**,
but their **heart** is really far away
from me.
9 It is no use for them to **worship** me,
because they **teach man-made** rules
as though they were my **laws**!' "

The Things That Make a Person Unclean
(Mark 7.14-23)

10 Then Jesus called the crowd to him
and said to them, "Listen and **understand**! 11 It is not what goes into a person's mouth that makes him ritually **unclean**; rather, what comes out of it
makes him **unclean**."

12 Then the **disciples** came to him and
said, "Do you know that the **Pharisees**
had their feelings **hurt** by what you
said?"

13 "Every plant which **my Father** in
heaven did not plant will be pulled up,"
answered Jesus. 14 "Don't **worry** about
them! They are **blind** leaders of the
blind; and when one blind man leads
another, both fall into a ditch."

15 Peter spoke up, "Explain this **saying** to us."

16 Jesus said to them, "You are still no
more **intelligent** than the others. 17 Don't
you **understand**? Anything that goes into
a person's mouth goes into his stomach
and then on out of his **body**. 18 But the
things that come out of the mouth come
from the **heart**, and these are the things
that make a person ritually **unclean**.
19 For from his **heart** come the **evil ideas**
which lead him to kill, **commit adultery**,
and do other **immoral** things; to **rob**, **lie**,
and **slander** others. 20 These are the
things that make a person **unclean**. But
to eat without washing your hands as
they say you should—this doesn't make a
person **unclean**."

A Woman's Faith
(Mark 7.24-30)

21 Jesus left that place and went off to
the territory near the cities of Tyre and
Sidon. 22 A Canaanite woman who lived in
that region came to him. "**Son of David**!"
she cried out. "Have **mercy** on me, sir!
My daughter has a **demon** and is in a
terrible condition."

23 But Jesus did not say a **word** to her.
His **disciples** came to him and **begged**
him, "Send her away! She is following us
and making all this noise!"

24 Then Jesus replied, "I have been
sent only to the lost **sheep** of the people
of Israel."

25 At this the woman came and fell at
his feet. "**Help** me, sir!" she said.

26 Jesus answered, "It isn't **right** to
take the children's food and throw it to
the dogs."

27 "That's **true**, sir," she answered;
"but even the dogs eat the leftovers that
fall from their **masters**' table."

28 So Jesus answered her, "You are a
woman of great **faith**! What you want
will be done for you." And at that very
moment her daughter was **healed**.

Jesus Heals Many People

29 Jesus left there and went along by
Lake Galilee. He climbed a hill and sat
down. 30 Large crowds came to him,
bringing with them the lame, the **blind**,
the **crippled**, the dumb, and many other
sick people, whom they placed at Jesus'
feet; and he **healed** them. 31 The people
were **amazed** as they saw the dumb
speaking, the **crippled** made whole, the
lame walking, and the **blind** seeing; and
they **praised** the God of Israel.

Jesus Feeds Four Thousand Men
(Mark 8.1-10)

32 Jesus called his **disciples** to him and

[l] his father; *some manuscripts have* his father or mother.

15.4: Ex 20.12, 21.17; Deut 5.16; Lev 20.9 **15.8-9:** Is 29.13 (LXX) **15.14:** Lk 6.39 **15.18:** Mt 12.34

adultery 5.27; 19.9
amaze 13.54; 19.25
beg 14.36; 18.26
blind [4] 12.22; 20.30
body 14.12; 24.28
bread 12.4; 16.5
command [2] Mal 4.4; 17.18
commit 5.21; 19.9
cripple [2] Mic 4.7; 21.14
curse Mal 3.9; 25.41
death (3) (to death) 10.21; 16.21
demon 12.22; 17.18
disciple [8] 14.12; 16.5
disobey [2] 5.19; Lk 1.17
enough [2] 14.20; 17.20
evil 13.41; 16.4
faith 14.31; 16.8
Father (2) (God) 13.43; 16.17
heal [2] 14.14; 17.16
heart [3] 14.14; 18.35
heaven 14.19; 16.17
help [2] 12.12; 23.4
honour [2] 6.9; Mk 7.6
hurt 4.6; Lk 4.11
hypocrite 7.5; 22.18
idea Dan 5.9; Mk 7.21
immoral Ezek 24.13; Mk 7.21
intelligent Dan 1.4; Mk 7.18
law 12.2; 19.3
lie (2) 5.11; 26.60
man-made Mk 7.7
master 10.24; 21.3
mercy 11.22; 17.15
need 10.10; 19.20
Pharisees [2] 12.2; 16.1
praise 9.8; 21.9
proper Dan 11.13; 21.43
prophecy 13.14; 26.68
respect 13.57; 19.19
right (1) [2] 14.4; 21.32
rob 6.19; Mk 7.21
saying Is 29.17; Mk 7.17
sheep 12.11; 18.12
slander Jer 9.4; Mk 7.22
Son of David 12.23; 20.30
sorry Mal 3.14; 18.27
teach [5] 13.1; 16.12
teacher of the Law 13.52; 16.21
terrible 11.21; 17.15
thank 14.19; 26.26
true 14.33; 21.4
unclean [5] Dan 1.8; Mk 7.2
understand [2] 13.13; 16.9
word (1) [2] 12.36; 24.35

worry 13.22; 22.16
worship (1) (of God) 14.33; 28.9

said, "I feel **sorry** for these people, because they have been with me for three days and now have nothing to eat. I don't want to send them away without feeding them, for they might faint on their way home."

33 The **disciples** asked him, "Where will we find **enough** food in this desert to feed this crowd?"

34 "How much **bread** have you?" Jesus asked.

"Seven loaves," they answered, "and a few small fish."

35 So Jesus ordered the crowd to sit down on the ground. 36 Then he took the seven loaves and the fish, gave **thanks** to God, broke them, and gave them to the **disciples**; and the **disciples** gave them to the people. 37 They all ate and had **enough**. Then the **disciples** took up seven baskets full of pieces left over. 38 The number of men who ate was four thousand, not counting the women and children.

39 Then Jesus sent the people away, got into a boat, and went to the territory of Magadan.

The Demand for a Miracle

(Mark 8.11–13; Luke 12.54–56)

16 Some **Pharisees** and **Sadducees** who came to Jesus wanted to **trap** him, so they asked him to perform a **miracle** for them, to show that God **approved** of him. 2 But Jesus answered, "When the sun is setting, you say, 'We are going to have fine weather, because the sky is red.' 3 And early in the morning you say, 'It is going to rain, because the sky is red and **dark**.' You can **predict** the weather by looking at the sky, but you cannot **interpret** the **signs** concerning these times! [m] 4 How **evil** and **godless** are the people of this day! You ask me for a **miracle**? No! The only **miracle** you will be given is the miracle of Jonah."

So he left them and went away.

The Yeast of the Pharisees and Sadducees

(Mark 8.14–21)

5 When the **disciples** crossed over to the other side of the lake, they **forgot** to take any **bread**. 6 Jesus said to them, "Take **care**; be on your guard against the **yeast** of the **Pharisees** and **Sadducees**."

7 They started **discussing** among themselves, "He says this because we didn't bring any **bread**."

8 Jesus knew what they were saying, so he asked them, "Why are you **discussing** among yourselves about not having any **bread**? How little **faith** you have! 9 Don't you **understand** yet? Don't you **remember** when I broke the five loaves for the five thousand men? How many baskets did you fill? 10 And what about the seven loaves for the four thousand men? How many baskets did you fill? 11 How is it that you don't **understand** that I was not talking to you about **bread**? Guard yourselves from the **yeast** of the **Pharisees** and **Sadducees**!"

12 Then the **disciples understood** that he was not **warning** them to guard themselves from the **yeast** used in **bread** but from the **teaching** of the **Pharisees** and **Sadducees**.

Peter's Declaration about Jesus

(Mark 8.27–30; Luke 9.18–21)

13 Jesus went to the territory near the town of Caesarea Philippi, where he asked his **disciples**, "Who do people say the **Son of Man** is?"

14 "Some say John the Baptist," they answered. "Others say Elijah, while others say Jeremiah or some other **prophet**."

15 "What about you?" he asked them. "**Who** do you say I am?"

16 Simon Peter answered, "You are the **Messiah**, the **Son of the living God**."

17 "Good for you, Simon son of John!" answered Jesus. "For this **truth** did not come to you from any **human being**, but it was given to you directly by **my Father** in **heaven**. 18 And so I tell you, Peter: you are a rock, and on this rock foundation I will build my **church**, and not even **death** will ever be able to overcome it. 19 I will give you the keys of the **Kingdom of heaven**; what you prohibit on earth will be prohibited in **heaven**, and what you permit on earth will be **permitted** in **heaven**."

20 Then Jesus ordered his **disciples** not to tell anyone that he was the **Messiah**.

Jesus Speaks about His Suffering and Death

(Mark 8.31—9.1; Luke 9.22–27)

21 From that time on Jesus began to say **plainly** to his **disciples**, "I must go to Jerusalem and **suffer** much from the **elders**, the **chief priests**, and the **teachers of the Law**. I will be put **to death**, but three days later I will be **raised to life**."

22 Peter took him aside and began to

[m] *Some manuscripts do not have the words of Jesus in verses 2 and 3.*

16.1: Mt 12.38; Lk 11.16 **16.4:** Mt 12.39; Lk 11.29 **16.6:** Lk 12.1 **16.9:** Mt 14.17-21 **16.10:** Mt 15.34-38 **16.14:** Mt 14.1-2; Mk 6.14-15; Lk 9.7-8 **16.16:** Jn 6.68-69 **16.19:** Mt 18.18; Jn 20.23

angel 13.39; 18.10
approve Hos 8.4; Mk 8.11
assure 13.17; 17.20
being Zeph 1.3; Jn 1.14
bread [5] 15.34; 26.23
care 8.33; 25.36
chief priests 2.4; 20.18
church 18.17
cross (1) 10.38; 27.32
dark 10.27; 22.13
death (1) 4.16; 27.4
death (3) (to death) 15.4; 24.9
deed (2) Jn 3.19
disciple [6] 15.2; 17.3
discuss [2] Prov 24.7; Mk 8.16
elder (2) Ezek 7.26; 21.23
evil 15.19; 21.41
faith 15.28; 17.20
Father (2) (God) [2] 15.13; 18.10
forbid Zech 9.7; 1 Cor 14.39
forget [2] Zeph 3.7; Mk 8.14
get away 7.23; Mk 8.33
glory Zech 11.2; 19.28
godless 12.39; Mk 8.38
heaven [3] 15.13; 18.10
human Zeph 1.3; Jn 1.13
interpret Zech 10.2; Lk 10.26
Kingdom (1) (of God) 13.11; 18.1
life (1) [4] 14.2; 18.8

life (2) (to life) 11.5 17.23
Messiah [2] 2.4; 22.4
miracle [3] 14.2; 24.24
permit Dan 7.12; 18.18
Pharisees [4] 15.1; 19.3
plain (1) Hos 6.5; Lk 1.66
predict 11.14; Lk 12.56
prophet 14.5; 21.4
raise Zech 5.7; 17.9
rebuke Prov 17.10; Mk 8.32
remember 5.18; 24.34
reward 10.41; Mk 9.41
Sadducees [4] 3.7; 22.23
sake 10.18; 19.12
Satan 12.26; Mk 1.1
save 14.30; 19.25
self Prov 27.19; Mk 8.34
sign (1) Zech 3.8; 24.30
Son of God 14.33; 17.5
Son of Man [3] 13.3 17.9
suffer 11.5; 20.22
teach 15.2; 19.8
teacher of the Law 15.1; 17.10
trap Obad 7; 19.3
truth Zech 8.16; 22.16
turn 13.15; 21.42
understand [3] 15.1 17.13
warn 2.12; Mk 6.11
who Mk 8.29
win Hos 12.4; 18.15
world 13.35; 17.25
yeast [3] 13.33; Mk 8.15

rebuke him. "God **forbid** it, Lord!" he
said. "That must never happen to you!"
23 Jesus **turned** around and said to
Peter, "**Get away** from me, **Satan**! You
are an obstacle in my way, because these
thoughts of yours don't come from God,
but from man."
24 Then Jesus said to his **disciples**, "If
anyone wants to come with me, he must
forget self, carry his **cross**, and follow
me. 25 For whoever wants to **save** his own
life will lose it; but whoever loses his **life**
for my **sake** will find it. 26 Will a person
gain anything if he **wins** the whole **world**
but loses his **life**? Of course not! There is
nothing he can give to regain his **life**.
27 For the **Son of Man** is about to come in
the **glory** of his **Father** with his **angels**,
and then he will **reward** each one according to his **deeds**. 28 I **assure** you that
there are some here who will not die until they have seen the **Son of Man** come
as King."

The Transfiguration
(Mark 9.2–13; Luke 9.28–36)

17 Six days later Jesus took with
him Peter and the brothers
James and John and led them up a high
mountain where they were **alone**. 2 As
they looked on, a **change** came over
Jesus: his face was shining like the sun,
and his clothes were **dazzling** white.
3 Then the three **disciples** saw Moses and
Elijah talking with Jesus. 4 So Peter spoke
up and said to Jesus, "Lord, how good it
is that we are here! If you **wish**, I will
make three tents here, one for you, one
for Moses, and one for Elijah."
5 While he was talking, a shining
cloud came over them, and a voice from
the **cloud** said, "This is my own **dear Son**,
with whom I am **pleased**—listen to him!"
6 When the **disciples** heard the voice,
they were so **terrified** that they threw
themselves face downwards on the
ground. 7 Jesus came to them and
touched them. "Get up," he said. "Don't
be **afraid**!" 8 So they looked up and saw
no one there but Jesus.
9 As they came down the mountain,
Jesus ordered them, "Don't tell anyone
about this **vision** you have seen until the
Son of Man has been **raised from death**."
10 Then the **disciples** asked Jesus,
"Why do the **teachers of the Law** say that
Elijah has to come first?"
11 "Elijah is indeed coming first," answered Jesus, "and he will get everything
ready. 12 But I tell you that Elijah has already come and people did not recognize
him, but treated him just as they **pleased**.
In the same way they will also **ill-treat**
the **Son of Man**."
13 Then the **disciples understood** that
he was talking to them about John the
Baptist.

Jesus Heals a Boy with a Demon
(Mark 9.14–29; Luke 9.37–43a)

14 When they returned to the crowd, a
man came to Jesus, **knelt** before him,
15 and said, "Sir, have **mercy** on my son!
He is an epileptic and has such **terrible**
fits that he often falls in the fire or into
water. 16 I brought him to your **disciples**,
but they could not **heal** him."
17 Jesus answered, "How **unbelieving**
and **wrong** you people are! How long
must I stay with you? How long do I
have to put up with you? Bring the boy
here to me!" 18 Jesus gave a **command** to
the **demon**, and it went out of the boy,
and at that very moment he was **healed**.
19 Then the **disciples** came to Jesus in
private and asked him, "Why couldn't we
drive the **demon** out?"
20 "It was because you haven't **enough**
faith," answered Jesus. "I **assure** you that
if you have **faith** as big as a mustard
seed, you can say to this hill, 'Go from
here to there!' and it will go. You could
do anything!"[n]

Jesus Speaks Again about His Death
(Mark 9.30–32; Luke 9.43b–45)

22 When the **disciples** all came together in Galilee, Jesus said to them,
"The **Son of Man** is about to be handed
over to men 23 who will kill him; but
three days later he will be **raised to life**."
The **disciples** became very **sad**.

Payment of the Temple-Tax

24 When Jesus and his **disciples** came
to Capernaum, the collectors of the
temple-tax came to Peter and asked,
"Does your **teacher** pay the **temple-**
tax?"
25 "Of course," Peter answered.
When Peter went into the house, Jesus
spoke up first, "Simon, what is your
opinion? Who pays duties or **taxes** to the
kings of **this world**? The citizens of the
country or the foreigners?"
26 "The foreigners," answered Peter.
"Well, then," replied Jesus, "that
means that the citizens don't have to pay.

world 16.26; 18.7
worth 12.12; Mk 12.42
wrong 12.10; 22.29

afraid 14.5; 21.26
alone 14.23; 24.36
assure 16.28; 18.3
change 3.14; 18.3
cloud [2] Zech 10.1; 24.30
command 15.3; 27.10
dazzling Ezek 44.4; Lk 9.29
dear 3.17; Mk 1.11
death (2) (from death) Ps 116.8; 22.23
demon [2] 15.22; Mk 1.32
disciple [9] 16.5; 18.1
enough [2] 15.33; 18.25
faith [2] 16.8; 18.6
heal [2] 15.28; 19.2
ill-treat Amos 4.1; Lk 6.28
kneel 9.18; 27.29
life (2) (to life) 16.21; 20.19
mercy 15.22; 18.33
please [2] 14.6; Mk 1.11
raise [2] 16.21; 20.19
sad 14.9; 19.22
seed 13.4; 25.24
Son of God 16.16; 24.36
Son of Man [3] 16.13; 19.28
tax [5] Dan 11.20; 22.17
teacher 12.38; 19.16
teacher of the Law 16.21; 20.18
Temple (1) (of God) [3] 12.5; 21.12
terrible 15.22; 18.7
terrify 14.26; 27.54
unbeliever Mk 9.19
understand 16.9; 24.15
vision Zech 13.4; Lk 1.22
wish 14.9; 19.3

[n] *Some manuscripts add verse 21:* But only prayer and fasting can drive this kind out; nothing else can *(see Mk 9.29)*.

16.24: Mt 10.38; Lk 14.27 **16.25:** Mt 10.39; Lk 17.33; Jn 12.25 **16.27:** Mt 25.31; Ps 62.12; Rom 2.6
17.1-5: 2 Pet 1.17-18 **17.5:** Gen 22.2; Deut 18.15; Ps 2.7; Is 42.1; Mt 3.17, 12.18; Mk 1.11; Lk 3.22
17.10: Mal 4.5 **17.12:** Mt 11.14 **17.20:** Mt 21.21; Mk 11.23; 1 Cor 13.2 **17.24:** Ex 30.13, 38.26

27 But we don't want to offend these people. So go to the lake and drop in a line. Pull up the first fish you hook, and in its mouth you will find a coin **worth enough** for my **temple-tax** and yours. Take it and pay them our **taxes**."

Who Is the Greatest?
(Mark 9.33–37; Luke 9.46–48)

18 At that time the **disciples** came to Jesus, asking, "Who is the greatest in the **Kingdom of heaven**?"

2 So Jesus called a child, made him stand in front of them, 3 and said, "I **assure** you that unless you **change** and become like children, you will never enter the **Kingdom of heaven**. 4 The greatest in the **Kingdom of heaven** is the one who **humbles** himself and becomes like this child. 5 And whoever **welcomes in my name** one such child as this, **welcomes** me.

Temptations to Sin
(Mark 9.42–48; Luke 17.1–2)

6 "If anyone should cause one of these little ones to lose his **faith** in me, it would be better for that person to have a large millstone tied round his neck and be drowned in the deep sea. 7 How **terrible** for the **world** that there are things that make people lose their **faith**! Such things will always happen—but how **terrible** for the one who causes them!

8 "If your hand or your foot makes you lose your **faith**, cut it off and throw it away! It is better for you to enter **life** without a hand or a foot than to keep both hands and both feet and be thrown into the **eternal** fire. 9 And if your eye makes you lose your **faith**, take it out and throw it away! It is better for you to enter **life** with only one eye than to keep both eyes and be thrown into the fire of **hell**.

The Parable of the Lost Sheep
(Luke 15.3–7)

10 "See that you don't **despise** any of these little ones. Their **angels in heaven**, I tell you, are always in the **presence** of **my Father in heaven**.[o]

12 "What do you think a man does who has a hundred **sheep** and one of them gets lost? He will leave the other ninety-nine grazing on the hillside and go and look for the lost **sheep**. 13 When he finds it, I tell you, he feels far **happier** over this one **sheep** than over the ninety-nine that did not get lost. 14 In just the same way your[p] **Father in heaven** does not want any of these little ones to be lost.

A Brother Who Sins

15 "If your brother sins against you,[q] go to him and show him his **fault**. But do it privately, just between yourselves. If he listens to you, you have **won** your brother back. 16 But if he will not listen to you, take one or two other persons with you, so that 'every **accusation** may be upheld by the **testimony** of two or more **witnesses**,' as the **scripture** says. 17 And if he will not listen to them, then tell the whole thing to the **church**. Finally, if he will not listen to the **church**, treat him as though he were a **pagan** or a **tax collector**.

Prohibiting and Permitting

18 "And so I tell all of you: what you prohibit on earth will be prohibited in **heaven**, and what you permit on earth will be **permitted** in **heaven**.

19 "And I tell you more: whenever two of you on earth **agree** about anything you **pray** for, it will be done for you by **my Father** in **heaven**. 20 For where two or three come together **in my name**, I am there with them."

The Parable of the Unforgiving Servant

21 Then Peter came to Jesus and asked, "Lord, if my brother keeps on sinning against me, how many times do I have to **forgive** him? Seven times?"

22 "No, not seven times," answered Jesus, "but seventy times seven,[r] 23 because the **Kingdom of heaven** is like this. Once there was a king who decided to check on his **servants'** accounts. 24 He had just begun to do so when one of them was brought in who **owed** him millions of pounds. 25 The **servant** did not have **enough** to pay his **debt**, so the king ordered him to be sold as a **slave**, with his wife and his children and all that he had, in order to pay the **debt**. 26 The **servant** fell on his **knees** before the king. 'Be **patient** with me,' he **begged**, 'and I will pay you everything!' 27 The king felt **sorry** for him, so he **forgave** him the **debt** and let him go.

28 "Then the man went out and met one of his **fellow-servants** who **owed** him a few pounds. He grabbed him and started choking him. 'Pay back what you **owe** me!' he said. 29 His **fellow-servant**

accuse 12.10; 19.18
agree 3.15; 20.2
angel 16.27; 22.30
anger 5.22; 20.24
assure 17.20; 19.23
beg [2] 15.23; Mk 1.40
change 17.2; 21.29
church [2] 16.18; Acts 5.11
debt [4] Hab 2.6; Lk 7.42
despise 6.24; Lk 16.13
disciple 17.3; 19.10
enough 17.20; 25.9
eternal Hab 3.6; 19.16
faith [4] 17.20; 24.10
Father (2) (God) [4] 16.17; 20.23
fault Mal 1.9; Rom 9.19
forgive [4] 12.31; 26.28
happy 13.44; 24.46
heart 15.8; 22.37
heaven [7] 16.17; 19.21
hell 11.23; 23.15
humble 11.29; 21.5
jail [2] 5.25; Lk 12.58
Kingdom (1) (of God) [4] 16.19; 19.12
knee Nah 2.10; Mk 5.6
life (1) [2] 16.25; 19.16
mercy [2] 17.15; 23.23
name (2) (name of God, of Jesus) [2] 7.22; 21.9
owe [4] Amos 2.8; Lk 7.41
pagan 6.7; Lk 12.30
patient [2] Mal 3.15; Acts 18.14
permit 16.19; 19.8
pray 14.23; 19.13
presence Mal 3.16; 27.58
punish 8.29; 23.35
refuse (1) 2.18; 25.45
scripture 12.7; 19.4
servant [9] 13.27; 20.26
sheep [3] 15.24; 25.32
slave [2] 10.24; 20.27
sorry 15.32; Mk 3.5
tax collector 11.19; 21.31
terrible [2] 17.15; 23.13
testimony Mal 3.5; Jn 1.32
upset 2.3; 26.22
welcome 10.11; 25.38
win 16.26; 23.15
witness Jer 42.5; 24.14
world 17.25; 24.14
worthless 13.48; 21.42

[o] *Some manuscripts add verse 11:* For the Son of Man came to save the lost *(see Lk 19.10).*
[p] your; *some manuscripts have* my. [q] *Some manuscripts do not have* against you.
[r] seventy times seven; *or* seventy-seven times.

18.1: Lk 22.24 **18.3:** Mk 10.15; Lk 18.17 **18.8:** Mt 5.30 **18.9:** Mt 5.29 **18.15:** Lk 17.3 **18.16:** Deut 19.15 **18.18:** Mt 16.19; Jn 20.23 **18.21-22:** Lk 17.3-4 **18.22:** Gen 4.24

fell down and **begged** him, 'Be **patient**
with me, and I will pay you back!' 30 But
he **refused**; instead, he had him thrown
into **jail** until he should pay the **debt**.
31 When the other **servants** saw what had
happened, they were very **upset** and
went to the king and told him everything.
32 So he called the **servant** in. 'You **worth-**
less slave!' he said. 'I **forgave** you the
whole amount you **owed** me, just because
you asked me to. 33 You should have had
mercy on your **fellow-servant**, just as I
had **mercy** on you.' 34 The king was very
angry, and he sent the **servant** to **jail** to
be **punished** until he should pay back the
whole amount."
35 And Jesus concluded, "That is how
my Father in heaven will treat every one
of you unless you **forgive** your brother
from your **heart**."

Jesus Teaches About Divorce
(Mark 10.1–12)

19 When Jesus finished saying these
things, he left Galilee and went
to the territory of Judaea on the other
side of the River Jordan. 2 Large crowds
followed him, and he **healed** them there.
3 Some **Pharisees** came to him and
tried to **trap** him by asking, "Does our
Law allow a man to **divorce** his wife for
whatever **reason** he **wishes**?"
4 Jesus answered, "Haven't you read
the **scripture** that says that in the beginning the **Creator** made people male and
female? 5 And God said, 'For this **reason**
a man will leave his father and mother
and **unite** with his wife, and the two will
become one.' 6 So they are no longer two,
but one. Man must not **separate**, then,
what God has joined together."
7 The **Pharisees** asked him, "Why,
then, did Moses give the **law** for a man to
hand his wife a **divorce notice** and send
her away?"
8 Jesus answered, "Moses gave you
permission to **divorce** your wives because you are so **hard** to **teach**. But it was
not like that at the time of **creation**. 9 I
tell you, then, that any man who **divorces**
his wife for any cause other than her **un-**
faithfulness, **commits adultery** if he
marries some other woman."
10 His **disciples** said to him, "If this is
how it is between a man and his wife, it is
better not to marry."
11 Jesus answered, "This **teaching**
does not apply to everyone, but only to
those to whom God has given it. 12 For
there are different **reasons** why men cannot marry: some, because they were
born that way; others, because men
made them that way; and others do not
marry for the **sake** of the **Kingdom of**
heaven. Let him who can **accept** this
teaching do so."

Jesus Blesses Little Children
(Mark 10.13–16; Luke 18.15–17)

13 Some people brought children to
Jesus for him to place his hands on them
and to **pray** for them, but the **disciples**
scolded the people. 14 Jesus said, "Let the
children come to me and do not stop
them, because the **Kingdom of heaven**
belongs to such as these."
15 He placed his hands on them and
then went away.

The Rich Young Man
(Mark 10.17–31; Luke 18.18–30)

16 Once a man came to Jesus.
"**Teacher**," he asked, "what good thing
must I do to receive **eternal life**?"
17 "Why do you ask me concerning
what is good?" answered Jesus. "There
is only One who is good. Keep the **com-**
mandments if you want to enter **life**."
18 "What **commandments**?" he asked.
Jesus answered, "Do not **commit mur-**
der; do not **commit adultery**; do not
steal; do not **accuse** anyone **falsely**;
19 **respect** your father and your mother;
and love your **neighbour** as you **love**
yourself."
20 "I have **obeyed** all these **command-**
ments," the young man replied. "What
else do I **need** to do?"
21 Jesus said to him, "If you want to be
perfect, go and sell all you have and give
the money to the **poor**, and you will have
riches in **heaven**; then come and follow
me."
22 When the young man heard this, he
went away **sad**, because he was very
rich.
23 Jesus then said to his **disciples**, "I
assure you: it will be very **hard** for **rich**
people to enter the **Kingdom of heaven**.
24 I repeat: it is much **harder** for a **rich**
person to enter the **Kingdom of God** than
for a camel to go through the eye of a
needle."
25 When the **disciples** heard this, they
were completely **amazed**. "Who, then,
can be **saved**?" they asked.
26 Jesus looked straight at them and
answered, "This is **impossible** for man,
but for God everything is possible."
27 Then Peter spoke up. "Look," he
said, "we have left everything and followed you. What will we have?"

accept Mal 2.13; Mk 4.20
accuse 18.16; 26.62
adultery [2] 15.19; Mk 7.22
age (1) 13.39; 24.3
amaze 15.31; 22.22
assure 18.3; 21.21
commandment [3] 5.19; 22.36
commit [3] 15.19; 27.23
create 13.35; 25.34
Creator Is 54.5; Acts 4.24
disciple [4] 18.1; 20.17
divorce [4] 5.31; Mk 10.2
eternal [2] 18.8; 25.41
false 7.15; 24.11
follower 12.27; Mk 2.18
glory 16.27; 24.30
hard [3] 7.14; 23.4
heal 17.16; 21.14
heaven 18.10; 22.30
impossible Zech 8.6; Mk 10.27
Kingdom (1) (of God) [4] 18.1; 20.1
last (2) [2] 5.26; 20.8
law [2] 15.9; 22.17
life (1) [3] 18.8; 20.28
love 13.22; 22.37
need 15.6; 21.3
neighbour Zech 3.10; 22.39
new 13.52; 26.29
obey 8.27; 23.3
perfect 5.48; 21.16
permit 18.18; Mk 10.4
Pharisees [2] 16.1; 21.45
poor 12.33; 26.9
pray 18.19; 24.20
reason [3] 13.13; Mk 10.7
respect 15.4; 21.37
rich [3] Zech 11.5; 27.57
riches 13.22; Mk 4.19
sad 17.23; Mk 6.26
sake [2] 16.25; 24.22
save 16.25; 24.13

scripture 18.16; 21.13
separate Zech 12.12; 25.32
Son of Man 17.9; 20.18
steal 6.19; 27.64
sure 12.36; 24.15
teach [3] 16.12; 21.23
teacher 17.24; 22.16
throne [2] 5.34; 23.22
trap 16.1; 22.15
unfaithful 5.32; Jas 4.4
unite Zech 11.7; Mk 10.7
wish 17.4; 20.15

19.4: Gen 1.27, 5.2 **19.5:** Gen 2.24 **19.7:** Deut 24.1-4; Mt 5.31 **19.9:** Mt 5.32; 1 Cor 7.10-11
19.18: Ex 20.13-16; Deut 5.17-20 **19.19:** Ex 20.12; Deut 5.16; Lev 19.18

28 Jesus said to them, "You can be **sure** that when the **Son of Man** sits on his **glorious throne** in the **New Age**, then you twelve **followers** of mine will also sit on **thrones**, to rule the twelve tribes of Israel. 29 And everyone who has left houses or brothers or sisters or father or mother or children or fields for my **sake**, will receive a hundred times more and will be given **eternal life**. 30 But many who now are first will be **last**, and many who now are **last** will be first.

The Workers in the Vineyard

20 "The **Kingdom of heaven** is like this. Once there was a man who went out early in the morning to hire some men to work in his **vineyard**. 2 He **agreed** to pay them the regular **wage**, a silver coin a day, and sent them to work in his **vineyard**. 3 He went out again to the market-place at nine o'clock and saw some men standing there doing nothing, 4 so he told them, 'You also go and work in the **vineyard**, and I will pay you a fair **wage**.' 5 So they went. Then at twelve o'clock and again at three o'clock he did the same thing. 6 It was nearly five o'clock when he went to the market-place and saw some other men still standing there. 'Why are you wasting the whole day here doing nothing?' he asked them. 7 'No one hired us,' they answered. 'Well, then, you also go and work in the **vineyard**,' he told them.

8 "When evening came, the owner told his foreman, 'Call the workers and pay them their **wages**, starting with those who were hired **last** and ending with those who were hired first.' 9 The men who had begun to work at five o'clock were paid a silver coin each. 10 So when the men who were the first to be hired came to be paid, they thought they would get more; but they too were given a silver coin each. 11 They took their money and started grumbling against the employer. 12 'These men who were hired **last** worked only one hour,' they said, 'while we put up with a whole day's work in the hot sun—yet you paid them the same as you paid us!'

13 " 'Listen, **friend**,' the owner answered one of them, 'I have not **cheated** you. After all, you **agreed** to do a day's work for one silver coin. 14 Now take your pay and go home. I want to give this man who was hired **last** as much as I have given you. 15 Don't I have the **right** to do as I **wish** with my own money? Or are you **jealous** because I am **generous**?' "

16 And Jesus concluded, "So those who are **last** will be first, and those who are first will be **last**."

Jesus Speaks a Third Time about His Death
(Mark 10.32–34; Luke 18.31–34)

17 As Jesus was going up to Jerusalem, he took the twelve **disciples** aside and spoke to them privately, as they walked along. 18 "Listen," he told them, "we are going up to Jerusalem, where the **Son of Man** will be handed over to the **chief priests** and the **teachers of the Law**. They will **condemn** him to death 19 and then hand him over to the **Gentiles**, who will **mock** him, whip him, and **crucify** him; but three days later he will be **raised to life**."

A Mother's Request
(Mark 10.35–45)

20 Then the wife of Zebedee came to Jesus with her two sons, **bowed** before him, and asked him a **favour**.

21 "What do you want?" Jesus asked her.

She answered, "**Promise** me that these two sons of mine will sit at your **right** and your left when you are King."

22 "You don't know what you are asking for," Jesus answered the sons. "Can you drink the **cup of suffering** that I am about to drink?"

"We can," they answered.

23 "You will indeed drink from my **cup**," Jesus told them, "but I do not have the **right** to **choose** who will sit at my **right** and my left. These places belong to those for whom **my Father** has prepared them."

24 When the other ten **disciples** heard about this, they became **angry** with the two brothers. 25 So Jesus called them all together and said, "You know that the rulers of the **heathen** have **power** over them, and the leaders have **complete authority**. 26 This, however, is not the way it shall be among you. If one of you wants to be great, he must be the **servant** of the rest; 27 and if one of you wants to be first, he must be your **slave**—28 like the **Son of Man**, who did not come to be **served**, but to serve and to give his **life** to **redeem** many people."

Jesus Heals Two Blind Men
(Mark 10.46–52; Luke 18.35–43)

29 As Jesus and his **disciples** were leaving Jericho, a large crowd was

agree [2] 18.19; 27.7
anger 18.34; 21.15
authority 10.1; 28.18
blind 15.14; 21.14
bow (2) Dan 3.5; Mk 15.19
cheat Mal 3.5; Mk 10.19
chief priests 16.21; 21.15
choose 12.18; 22.14
complete Hag 2.18; Mk 10.42
condemn 12.7; 23.33
crucify 23.34
cup [2] Zech 12.2; 23.25
disciple [3] 19.10; 21.1
Father (2) (God) 18.10; 23.9
favour Mal 1.8; Mk 15.8
friend 11.19; 22.12
generous Prov 31.20; Lk 6.38
Gentile 10.5; Mk 7.26
heathen Amos 7.17; Mk 10.42
jealous Ezek 36.6; 27.18
Kingdom (1) (of God) 19.12; 21.31
last (2) [5] 19.30; 21.37
life (1) 19.16; 23.29
life (2) (to life) 17.23; 22.28
mock Joel 2.17; 27.29
pity [3] 14.14; Mk 1.41
power 14.2; 22.29
promise 14.7; Mk 14.11
raise 17.9; 26.32
redeem Ps 49.7; Mk 10.45
right (2) [2] 5.29; 22.44
right (3) [2] Jon 4.4; 21.23
servant 18.23; 22.3
serve 6.24; Mk 10.45
sight 9.30; 21.42
slave 18.25; 21.34
Son of David [2] 15.22; 21.9
Son of Man [2] 19.28; 24.27
suffer 16.21; 26.6
teacher of the Law 17.10; 21.15
vineyard [4] Zech 3.10; 21.28
wage [3] Mal 3.5; Rom 4.4
wish 19.3; Lk 12.49

19.28: Mt 25.31; Lk 22.30 **19.30:** Mt 20.16; Lk 13.30 **20.8:** Lev 19.13; Deut 24.15
20.16: Mt 19.30; Mk 10.31; Lk 13.30 **20.25-26:** Lk 22.25-26 **20.26-27:** Mt 23.11; Mk 9.35; Lk 22.26

following. 30 Two **blind** men who were sitting by the road heard that Jesus was passing by, so they began to shout, "**Son of David**! Take **pity** on us, sir!"

31 The crowd scolded them and told them to be quiet. But they shouted even more loudly, "**Son of David**! Take **pity** on us, sir!"

32 Jesus stopped and called them. "What do you want me to do for you?" he asked them.

33 "Sir," they answered, "we want you to give us our **sight**!"

34 Jesus had **pity** on them and touched their eyes; at once they were able to see, and they followed him.

The Triumphant Entry into Jerusalem
(Mark 11.1–11; Luke 19.28–40; John 12.12–19)

21 As Jesus and his **disciples** approached Jerusalem, they came to Bethphage at the Mount of Olives. There Jesus sent two of the **disciples** on ahead 2 with these instructions: "Go to the village there **ahead of you**, and at once you will find a donkey tied up with her colt beside her. Untie them and bring them to me. 3 And if anyone says anything, tell him, 'The **Master**[s] **needs** them'; and then he will let them go at once."

4 This happened in order to make what the **prophet** had said come **true**:

5 "Tell the city of Zion,
Look, your king is coming to you!
He is **humble** and rides on a donkey
and on a colt, the foal of a donkey."

6 So the **disciples** went and did what Jesus had told them to do: 7 they brought the donkey and the colt, threw their cloaks over them, and Jesus got on. 8 A large crowd of people spread their cloaks on the road while others cut branches from the trees and spread them on the road. 9 The crowds walking in front of Jesus and those walking behind began to shout, "**Praise** to **David's Son**! God **bless** him who comes **in the name of** the Lord! **Praise** God!"

10 When Jesus entered Jerusalem, the whole city was thrown into an uproar. "Who is he?" the people asked.

11 "This is the **prophet** Jesus, from Nazareth in Galilee," the crowds answered.

Jesus Goes to the Temple
(Mark 11.15–19; Luke 19.45–48; John 2.13–22)

12 Jesus went into the **Temple** and drove out all those who were buying and selling there. He overturned the tables of the money-changers and the stools of those who sold pigeons, 13 and said to them, "It is written in the **Scriptures** that God said, 'My **Temple** will be called a house of **prayer**.' But you are making it a hideout for **thieves**!"

14 The **blind** and the **crippled** came to him in the **Temple**, and he **healed** them. 15 The **chief priests** and the **teachers of the Law** became **angry** when they saw the **wonderful** things he was doing and the children shouting in the **Temple**, "**Praise** to **David's Son**!" 16 So they asked Jesus, "Do you hear what they are saying?"

"Indeed I do," answered Jesus. "Haven't you ever read this **scripture**? 'You have trained children and babies to **offer perfect praise**.'"

17 Jesus left them and went out of the city to Bethany, where he spent the night.

Jesus Curses the Fig-Tree
(Mark 11.12–14, 20–24)

18 On his way back to the city early next morning, Jesus was **hungry**. 19 He saw a fig-tree by the side of the road and went to it, but found nothing on it except leaves. So he said to the tree, "You will never again bear fruit!" At once the fig-tree dried up.

20 The **disciples** saw this and were astounded. "How did the fig-tree dry up so quickly?" they asked.

21 Jesus answered, "I **assure** you that if you **believe** and do not **doubt**, you will be able to do what I have done to this fig-tree. And not only this, but you will even be able to say to this hill, 'Get up and throw yourself in the sea,' and it will. 22 If you **believe**, you will receive whatever you ask for in **prayer**."

The Question about Jesus' Authority
(Mark 11.27–33; Luke 20.1–8)

23 Jesus came back to the **Temple**; and as he **taught**, the **chief priests** and the **elders** came to him and asked, "What **right** have you to do these things? Who gave you this **right**?"

24 Jesus answered them, "I will ask you just one **question**, and if you give me an answer, I will tell you what **right** I

afraid [2] 17.7; 25.25
ahead of you [2] 11.10; 26.32
anger 20.24; 22.7
argue 12.19; Mk 8.11
arrest 14.3; 24.9
assure 19.23; 26.13
baptize 3.6; 28.19
believe [6] 11.14; 24.23
bless Zech 9.12; 23.39
blind 20.30; 23.16
change [2] 18.3; Mk 9.2
chief priests [3] 20.18; 26.3
consider 14.5; 22.24
convince Ezek 14.22; 28.14
cripple 15.30; Lk 14.13
disciple [4] 20.17; 22.16
doubt 14.31; 28.17
elder (2) 16.21; 26.3
evil 16.4; 22.18
harvest [2] 13.30; 25.24
heal 19.2; Mk 1.34
humble 18.4; 23.12
hunger 12.1; 25.35
important 5.19; 22.38
Kingdom (1) (of God) [2] 20.1; 22.2
last (2) 20.8; 22.27
master 15.27; 24.45
mind (1) [2] 13.15; 22.37
name (2) (name of God, of Jesus) 18.5; 23.39
need 19.20; 26.65
offer 12.4; 27.34
parable [2] 13.3; 22.1
perfect 19.21; Acts 23.1
Pharisees 19.3; 22.15
praise [4] 15.31; Mk 2.12
prayer [2] 6.7; 26.26
proper 15.2; 24.45
prophet [4] 16.14; 22.40
prostitute [2] Mic 1.7; Lk 15.30
question Zech 7.3; 22.15

reject 13.57; Mk 6.3
respect 19.19; 23.7
right (1) [2] 15.7; Mk 1.15
right (3) [5] 20.15; Mk 10.40
scripture [3] 19.4; 22.29
share [2] 10.41; 24.51
sight 20.33; Mk 8.25
slave [3] 20.27; 26.51
Son of David [2] 20.30; Mk 10.47
tax collector [2] 18.17; Mk 2.14
teach 19.8; 22.16
teacher of the Law 20.18; 22.35
Temple (1) (of God) [5] 17.24; 23.16
thief Zech 5.3; 24.43
true 15.27; 26.54
turn 16.23; Mk 1.4
vineyard [6] 20.1; Mk 12.1
watch 10.17; 26.38
wonder (1) [2] Joel 2.26; 24.24
worthless 18.32; Mk 12.10

[s] The Master; *or* Their owner.

21.5: Zech 9.9 **21.9:** Ps 118.25, 26 **21.13:** Is 56.7; Jer 7.11 **21.16:** Ps 8.2 (LXX)
21.21: Mt 17.20; 1 Cor 13.2

have to do these things. 25 Where did
John's **right** to **baptize** come from: was it
from God or from man?"
They started to **argue** among themselves, "What shall we say? If we answer, 'From God,' he will say to us, 'Why,
then, did you not **believe** John?' 26 But if
we say, 'From man,' we are **afraid** of
what the people might do, because they
are all **convinced** that John was a **prophet**." 27 So they answered Jesus, "We
don't know."
And he said to them, "Neither will I
tell you, then, by what **right** I do these
things.

The Parable of the Two Sons

28 "Now, what do you think? There
was once a man who had two sons. He
went to the elder one and said, 'Son, go
and work in the **vineyard** today.' 29 'I
don't want to,' he answered, but later he
changed his **mind** and went. 30 Then the
father went to the other son and said the
same thing. 'Yes, sir,' he answered, but
he did not go. 31 Which one of the two did
what his father wanted?"
"The elder one," they answered.
So Jesus said to them, "I tell you: the
tax collectors and the **prostitutes** are going into the **Kingdom of God ahead of
you**. 32 For John the Baptist came to you
showing you the **right** path to take, and
you would not **believe** him; but the **tax
collectors** and the **prostitutes believed**
him. Even when you saw this, you did not
later **change** your **minds** and **believe**
him.

The Parable of the Tenants in the Vineyard

(Mark 12.1–12; Luke 20.9–19)

33 "Listen to another **parable**," Jesus
said. "There was once a landowner who
planted a **vineyard**, put a fence around it,
dug a hole for the winepress, and built a
watch-tower. Then he let out the **vineyard** to tenants and went on a journey.
34 When the time came to gather the
grapes, he sent his **slaves** to the tenants
to receive his **share** of the **harvest**. 35 The
tenants seized his **slaves**, beat one, killed
another, and stoned another. 36 Again the
man sent other **slaves**, more than the
first time, and the tenants treated them
the same way. 37 **Last** of all he sent his
son to them. 'Surely they will **respect** my
son,' he said. 38 But when the tenants saw
the son, they said to themselves, 'This is
the owner's son. Come on, let's kill him,
and we will get his property!' 39 So they
seized him, threw him out of the **vineyard**, and killed him.
40 "Now, when the owner of the **vineyard** comes, what will he do to those
tenants?" Jesus asked.
41 "He will certainly kill those **evil**
men," they answered, "and let the **vineyard** out to other tenants, who will give
him his **share** of the **harvest** at the **right**
time."
42 Jesus said to them, "Haven't you
ever read what the **Scriptures** say?

'The stone which the builders **rejected**
as **worthless**
turned out to be the most **important**
of all.
This was done by the Lord;
what a **wonderful sight** it is!'

43 "And so I tell you," added Jesus,
"the **Kingdom of God** will be taken away
from you and given to a people who will
produce the **proper** fruits."[t]
45 The **chief priests** and the **Pharisees**
heard Jesus' **parables** and knew that he
was talking about them, 46 so they tried to
arrest him. But they were **afraid** of the
crowds, who **considered** Jesus to be a
prophet.

The Parable of the Wedding Feast

(Luke 14.15–24)

22 Jesus again used **parables** in talking to the people. 2 "The **King-
dom of heaven** is like this. Once there
was a king who prepared a **wedding feast**
for his son. 3 He sent his **servants** to tell
the invited guests to come to the **feast**,
but they did not want to come. 4 So he
sent other **servants** with this **message** for
the guests: 'My **feast** is ready now; my
bullocks and **prize** calves have been
butchered, and everything is ready.
Come to the **wedding feast**!' 5 But the invited guests paid no attention and went
about their business: one went to his
farm, another to his shop, 6 while others
grabbed the **servants**, beat them, and
killed them. 7 The king was very **angry**;
so he sent his soldiers, who killed those
murderers and burnt down their city.
8 Then he called his **servants** and said to
them, 'My **wedding feast** is ready, but the
people I invited did not **deserve** it. 9 Now
go to the main streets and invite to the
feast as many people as you find.' 10 So
the **servants** went out into the streets and
gathered all the people they could find,
good and **bad** alike; and the **wedding** hall
was filled with people.

amaze [2] 19.25; Mk 1.22
angel 18.10; 24.31
anger 21.15; 26.8
bad 12.33; 24.48
choose 20.23; 24.22
claim Zech 13.2; 23.30
commandment [4] 19.17; Mk 10.19
consider 21.46; Mk 10.42
dare 8.28; Mk 2.7
dark 16.3; 24.29
dead [5] 11.5; 24.28
death (2) (from death) 17.9; 27.53
depend Mic 5.7; Lk 11.22
deserve 8.8; 23.15
disciple 21.1; 23.1
enemy 13.25; Mk 12.36
evil 21.41; 24.12
feast [6] 8.11; 23.6
friend 20.13; 26.50
heart 18.35; 26.38
heaven 19.21; 23.9
hypocrite 15.7; 23.13
I am Ex 3.14; Mk 12.26
important [2] 21.42; 23.17
inspire Hag 1.14; Mk 12.36
Kingdom (1) (of God) 21.31; 23.13
last (2) 21.37; 27.19
law [3] 19.3; 23.2
life (2) (to life) [3] 20.19; 26.32
love [2] 19.19; 23.6

[t] *Some manuscripts add verse 44:* Whoever falls on this stone will be cut to pieces; and if the stone falls on someone, it will crush him to dust *(see Lk 20.18).*

21.32: Lk 3.12, 7.29-30 **21.33:** Is 5.1-2 **21.42:** Ps 118.22-23

message 13.19; 27.19
Messiah [2] 16.16; 23.10
mind (1) 21.29; Mk 5.15
neighbour 19.19; Mk 12.31
parable 21.33; Mk 3.23
Pharisees [3] 21.45; 23.2
plan [2] 12.14; 26.4
power 20.25; 24.29
prize Dan 11.43; Lk 15.23
prophet 21.4; 23.29
question [3] 21.24; 27.11
right (2) 20.21; 25.33
rise [4] 13.33; 27.53
Sadducees [2] 16.1; Mk 12.18
scripture 21.13; 23.5
servant [6] 20.26; 23.11
soul 10.28; Mk 12.30
Spirit (1) (God's Spirit) 12.18; 28.19
tax [2] 17.24; Mk 12.14
teach [3] 21.23; 23.16
teacher [3] 19.16; 23.7
teacher of the Law 21.15; 23.2
trap [3] 19.3; Mk 8.11
truth [2] 16.17; 26.74
wedding [6] 11.17; 25.10
widow [2] Mal 3.5; Mk 12.19
will (1) 6.10; 26.42
worry 15.14; 28.14
wrong 17.17; Mk 3.2

11 "The king went in to look at the
guests and saw a man who was not wearing wedding clothes. 12 'Friend, how did
you get in here without wedding
clothes?' the king asked him. But the
man said nothing. 13 Then the king told
the servants, 'Tie him up hand and foot,
and throw him outside in the dark. There
he will cry and grind his teeth.' "
14 And Jesus concluded, "Many are invited, but few are chosen."

The Question about Paying Taxes
(Mark 12.13–17; Luke 20.20–26)

15 The Pharisees went off and made a
plan to trap Jesus with questions. 16 Then
they sent to him some of their disciples
and some members of Herod's party.
"Teacher," they said, "we know that you
tell the truth. You teach the truth about
God's will for man, without worrying
about what people think, because you
pay no attention to a man's status. 17 Tell
us, then, what do you think? Is it against
our Law to pay taxes to the Roman Emperor, or not?"
18 Jesus, however, was aware of their
evil plan, and so he said, "You hypocrites! Why are you trying to trap me?
19 Show me the coin for paying the tax!"
They brought him the coin, 20 and he
asked them, "Whose face and name are
these?"
21 "The Emperor's," they answered.
So Jesus said to them, "Well, then, pay
the Emperor what belongs to the Emperor, and pay God what belongs to
God."
22 When they heard this, they were
amazed; and they left him and went
away.

The Question about Rising from Death
(Mark 12.18–27; Luke 20.27–40)

23 That same day some Sadducees
came to Jesus and claimed that people
will not rise from death. 24 "Teacher,"
they said, "Moses said that if a man who
has no children dies, his brother must
marry the widow so that they can have
children who will be considered the dead
man's children. 25 Now, there were seven
brothers who used to live here. The
eldest got married and died without
having children, so he left his widow to
his brother. 26 The same thing happened
to the second brother, to the third, and
finally to all seven. 27 Last of all, the
woman died. 28 Now, on the day when the
dead rise to life, whose wife will she be?
All of them had married her."
29 Jesus answered them, "How wrong
you are! It is because you don't know the
Scriptures or God's power. 30 For when
the dead rise to life, they will be like the
angels in heaven and will not marry.
31 Now, as for the dead rising to life:
haven't you ever read what God has told
you? He said, 32 'I am the God of
Abraham, the God of Isaac, and the God
of Jacob.' He is the God of the living, not
of the dead."
33 When the crowds heard this, they
were amazed at his teaching.

The Great Commandment
(Mark 12.28–34; Luke 10.25–28)

34 When the Pharisees heard that
Jesus had silenced the Sadducees, they
came together, 35 and one of them, a
teacher of the Law, tried to trap him
with a question. 36 "Teacher," he asked,
"which is the greatest commandment in
the Law?"
37 Jesus answered, " 'Love the Lord
your God with all your heart, with all
your soul, and with all your mind.' 38 This
is the greatest and the most important
commandment. 39 The second most
important commandment is like it: 'Love
your neighbour as you love yourself.'
40 The whole Law of Moses and the teachings of the prophets depend on these two
commandments."

The Question about the Messiah
(Mark 12.35–37; Luke 20.41–44)

41 When some Pharisees gathered together, Jesus asked them, 42 "What do
you think about the Messiah? Whose
descendant is he?"
"He is David's descendant," they answered.
43 "Why, then," Jesus asked, "did the
Spirit inspire David to call him 'Lord'?
David said,
44 'The Lord said to my Lord:
Sit here on my right
until I put your enemies under your
feet.'
45 If, then, David called him 'Lord,' how
can the Messiah be David's descendant?"
46 No one was able to give Jesus any
answer, and from that day on no one
dared to ask him any more questions.

Jesus Warns against the Teachers of the Law and the Pharisees
(Mark 12.38–39; Luke 11.43, 46; 20.45–46)

23 Then Jesus spoke to the crowds
and to his disciples. 2 "The

abandon Mal 1.3; 27.46

22.13: Mt 8.12, 25.30; Lk 13.28 22.23: Acts 23.8 22.24: Deut 25.5 22.32: Ex 3.6 22.35-40: Lk 10.25-28
22.37: Deut 6.5 22.39: Lev 19.18 22.44: Ps 110.1

action Jon 3.8; Lk 12.35
admit (1) Amos 6.3; Lk 11.48
altar [5] 5.23; Lk 1.9
best Hab 1.16; Mk 12.39
bind [4] Nah 1.13; Lk 13.16
bless 21.9; 25.34
blind [5] 21.14; Mk 8.22
claim 22.23; 24.5
clean [3] 12.44; Mk 1.40
condemn 20.18; 27.3
crucify 20.19; 26.2
cup [2] 20.22; 26.27
deserve 22.8; Lk 7.4
disciple 22.16; 24.1
escape 3.7; Lk 3.7
Father (2) (God) 20.23; 24.36
feast 22.2; 25.10
fool 7.26; 25.2
forehead Ezek 9.4; Rev 7.3
gift [3] 5.23; Lk 21.1
guide [2] 2.6; Lk 1.79
hard 19.8; 25.24
heaven [2] 22.30; 24.29
hell [2] 18.9; Mk 9.43
help 15.5; 25.44
holy [2] 7.6; 27.53
honest Mic 7.2; Jn 7.18
humble [2] 21.5; Lk 14.11
hypocrite [7] 22.18; 24.51
important [3] 22.38; 25.40
innocent [2] 12.37; 27.4
justice 12.20; Lk 11.42
Kingdom (1) (of God) 22.2; 24.14
law 22.17; 27.6
life (1) 20.28; 25.46
love [2] 22.37; 24.12
mercy 18.33; Lk 1.50
Messiah 22.42; 24.5
name (2) (name of God, of Jesus) 21.9; 26.63
neglect [2] 6.16; Lk 11.42
notice (1) [2] 14.30; Mk 7.2
obey [2] 19.20; 28.20
one another 24.7
Pharisees [8] 22.15; 27.62
practice [2] Mal 3.5; Lk 11.42
preach 12.41; 24.14
prophet [5] 22.40; 24.11
punish [2] 18.34; 24.9
respect 21.37; Mk 2.17
result 11.19; 27.14
scripture 22.29; 26.24
selfish Dan 11.34; Rom 2.8
servant 22.3; 24.45
succeed (1) Zech 4.6; Lk 23.23
swear [10] 14.7; 26.72
synagogue [2] 13.54; Mk 1.21
tassel Deut 22.12
teach [3] 22.16; 24.32
teacher [4] 22.16; 26.18
teacher of the Law [7] 22.35; 26.57
Temple (1) (of God) [6] 21.12; 24.1
terrible [7] 18.7; 24.19
throne 19.28; 25.31
tomb [2] Ezek 32.23; 27.60
violent 11.12; 28.2
vow [2] 5.33; Mk 6.23
win 18.15; Mk 8.36
wise 12.42; 24.45

teachers of the Law and the Pharisees
are the authorized interpreters of Moses'
Law. [3] So you must obey and follow
everything they tell you to do; do not,
however, imitate their actions, because
they don't practise what they preach.
[4] They tie on to people's backs loads that
are heavy and hard to carry, yet they
aren't willing even to lift a finger to help
them carry those loads. [5] They do everything so that people will see them. Look
at the straps with scripture verses on
them which they wear on their foreheads
and arms, and notice how large they
are! Notice also how long are the tassels
on their cloaks! [u] [6] They love the best
places at feasts and the reserved seats in
the synagogues; [7] they love to be greeted
with respect in the market-places and to
be called 'Teacher.' [8] You must not be
called 'Teacher', because you are all
brothers of one another and have only
one Teacher. [9] And you must not call anyone here on earth 'Father', because you
have only the one Father in heaven.
[10] Nor should you be called 'Leader', because your one and only leader is the
Messiah. [11] The greatest one among you
must be your servant. [12] Whoever makes
himself great will be humbled, and whoever humbles himself will be made great.

Jesus Condemns Their Hypocrisy

(Mark 12.40; Luke 11.39–42, 44, 52; 20.47)

13 "How terrible for you, teachers of
the Law and Pharisees! You hypocrites!
You lock the door to the Kingdom of
heaven in people's faces, and you yourselves don't go in, nor do you allow in
those who are trying to enter! [v]
15 "How terrible for you, teachers of
the Law and Pharisees! You hypocrites!
You sail the seas and cross whole
countries to win one convert; and when
you succeed, you make him twice as
deserving of going to hell as you yourselves are!
16 "How terrible for you, blind guides!
You teach, 'If someone swears by the
Temple, he isn't bound by his vow; but if
he swears by the gold in the Temple, he
is bound.' [17] Blind fools! Which is more
important, the gold or the Temple which
makes the gold holy? [18] You also teach,
'If someone swears by the altar, he isn't
bound by his vow; but if he swears by the
gift on the altar, he is bound.' [19] How blind
you are! Which is the more important,
the gift or the altar which makes the gift
holy? [20] So then, when a person swears
by the altar, he is swearing by it and by
all the gifts on it; [21] and when he swears
by the Temple, he is swearing by it and
by God, who lives there; [22] and when
someone swears by heaven, he is swearing by God's throne and by him who sits
on it.
23 "How terrible for you, teachers of
the Law and Pharisees! You hypocrites!
You give to God a tenth even of the
seasoning herbs, such as mint, dill, and
cumin, but you neglect to obey the really
important teachings of the Law, such as
justice and mercy and honesty. These
you should practise, without neglecting
the others. [24] Blind guides! You strain a
fly out of your drink, but swallow a
camel!
25 "How terrible for you, teachers of
the Law and Pharisees! You hypocrites!
You clean the outside of your cup and
plate, while the inside is full of what you
have obtained by violence and selfishness. [26] Blind Pharisee! Clean what is inside the cup first, and then the outside
will be clean too!
27 "How terrible for you, teachers of
the Law and Pharisees! You hypocrites!
You are like whitewashed tombs, which
look fine on the outside but are full of
bones and decaying corpses on the inside. [28] In the same way, on the outside
you appear good to everybody, but inside
you are full of hypocrisy and sins.

Jesus Predicts Their Punishment

(Luke 11.47–51)

29 "How terrible for you, teachers of
the Law and Pharisees! You hypocrites!
You make fine tombs for the prophets
and decorate the monuments of those
who lived good lives; [30] and you claim
that if you had lived during the time of
your ancestors, you would not have done
what they did and killed the prophets.
[31] So you actually admit that you are the
descendants of those who murdered the
prophets! [32] Go on, then, and finish what
your ancestors started! [33] You snakes
and sons of snakes! How do you expect
to escape from being condemned to
hell? [34] And so I tell you that I will send
you prophets and wise men and
teachers; you will kill some of them,
crucify others, and whip others in the
synagogues and chase them from town to

[u] TASSELS ON THEIR CLOAKS: *These tassels were worn as a sign of devotion to God (see Num 15.37-41).*
[v] *Some manuscripts add verse 14:* How terrible for you, teachers of the Law and Pharisees! You hypocrites! You take advantage of widows and rob them of their homes, and then make a show of saying long prayers! Because of this your punishment will be all the worse! *(see Mk 12.40).*

23.5: Mt 6.1; Num 15.38; Deut 6.8 **23.11:** Mt 20.26-27; Mk 9.35, 10.43-44; Lk 22.26 **23.12:** Lk 14.11, 18.14 **23.22:** Is 66.1; Mt 5.34 **23.23:** Lev 27.30 **23.27:** Acts 23.3 **23.33:** Mt 3.7, 12.34; Lk 3.7

town. 35 As a **result**, the **punishment** for
the murder of all **innocent** men will fall
on you, from the murder of **innocent** Abel
to the murder of Zachariah son of
Berachiah, whom you murdered between
the **Temple** and the **altar**. 36 I tell you indeed: the **punishment** for all these murders will fall on the people of this day!

Jesus' Love for Jerusalem
(Luke 13.34–35)

37 "Jerusalem, Jerusalem! You kill
the **prophets** and stone the messengers
God has sent you! How many times have
I wanted to put my arms round all your
people, just as a hen gathers her chicks
under her wings, but you would not let
me! 38 And so your **Temple** will be **abandoned** and empty. 39 From now on, I tell
you, you will never see me again until
you say, 'God **bless** him who comes **in the
name of the Lord**.' "

Jesus Speaks of the Destruction of the Temple
(Mark 13.1–2; Luke 21.5–6)

24 Jesus left and was going away
from the **Temple** when his **disciples** came to him to call his attention to
its buildings. 2 "Yes," he said, "you may
well look at all these. I tell you this: not a
single stone here will be left in its place;
every one of them will be thrown down."

Troubles and Persecutions
(Mark 13.3–13; Luke 21.7–19)

3 As Jesus sat on the Mount of Olives,
the **disciples** came to him in private.
"Tell us when all this will be," they
asked, "and what will happen to show
that it is the time for your coming and
the end of the **age**."
4 Jesus answered, "Be on your guard,
and do not let anyone **deceive** you.
5 Many men, **claiming** to speak for me,
will come and say, 'I am the **Messiah**!'
and they will **deceive** many people. 6 You
are going to hear the noise of battles
close by and the news of battles far
away; but do not be **troubled**. Such things
must happen, but they do not mean that
the end has come. 7 Countries will fight
each other, kingdoms will attack **one
another**. There will be **famines** and
earthquakes everywhere. 8 All these
things are like the first **pains** of childbirth.
9 "Then you will be **arrested** and
handed over to be **punished** and be put **to
death**. All **mankind** will **hate** you because
of me. 10 Many will **give up** their **faith** at
that time; they will **betray one another**
and **hate** one another. 11 Then many **false
prophets** will appear and **deceive** many
people. 12 Such will be the spread of **evil**
that many people's **love** will grow cold.
13 But whoever holds out to the end will
be **saved**. 14 And this **Good News** about
the **Kingdom** will be **preached** through
all the **world** for a **witness** to all **mankind**; and then the end will come.

The Awful Horror
(Mark 13.14–23; Luke 21.20–24)

15 "You will see 'The **Awful Horror**' of
which the **prophet** Daniel spoke. It will
be standing in the **holy place**." (Note to
the reader: be **sure** to **understand** what
this means!) 16 "Then those who are in
Judaea must run away to the hills. 17 A
man who is on the roof of his house must
not take the time to go down and get his
belongings from the house. 18 A man who
is in the field must not go back to get his
cloak. 19 How **terrible** it will be in those
days for women who are pregnant and
for mothers with little babies! 20 **Pray** to
God that you will not have to run away
during the winter or on a **Sabbath**! 21 For
the **trouble** at that time will be far more
terrible than any there has ever been,
from the beginning of the **world** to this
very day. Nor will there ever be anything
like it again. 22 But God has already reduced the number of days; had he not
done so, nobody would survive. For the
sake of his **chosen people**, however, God
will reduce the days.
23 "Then, if anyone says to you, 'Look,
here is the **Messiah**!' or 'There he is!'—
do not **believe** him. 24 For false **Messiahs**
and **false prophets** will appear; they will
perform great **miracles** and **wonders** in
order to **deceive** even God's **chosen
people**, if possible. 25 Listen! I have told
you this before the time comes.
26 "Or, if people should tell you, 'Look,
he is out in the desert!'—don't go there;
or if they say, 'Look, he is hiding here!'—
don't **believe** it. 27 For the **Son of Man** will
come like the lightning which flashes
across the whole sky from the east to the
west.
28 "Wherever there is a **dead body**,
the vultures will gather.

The Coming of the Son of Man
(Mark 13.24–27; Luke 21.25–28)

29 "Soon after the **trouble** of those
days, the sun will grow **dark**, the moon
will no longer shine, the stars will fall

age (1) 19.28; 28.20
alone 17.1; Mk 4.10
angel [2] 22.30; 25.31
arrest 21.46; 26.4
Awful Horror Dan 12.11; Mk 13.14
bad 22.10; 25.26
believe [2] 21.21; 27.42
betray 10.4; 26.15
body 15.17; 26.12
choose [3] 22.14; Mk 3.14
claim 23.30; 27.43
cloud 17.5; 26.64
dark 22.13; 25.30
dead 22.24; 28.4
death (3) (to death) 16.21; 26.4
deceive [4] Zech 13.4; Mk 7.22
disciple [2] 23.1; 26.1
each other 12.25; Mk 3.24
evil 22.18; Mk 3.28
faith 18.6; Mk 2.5
faithful 5.20; 25.21
false [2] 19.18; 26.59
famine Amos 8.11; Mk 13.8
fate Ezek 35.6; Lk 12.46
Father (2) (God) 23.9; 25.34
flood [2] Nah 1.8; Lk 6.49
give up 13.21; Mk 4.17
glory 19.28; Mk 8.38
God's people [3] 13.17; 27.52
Good News 11.5; Mk 1.1
happy 18.13; 25.21
hate [2] 10.22; Mk 13.13
heaven [4] 23.9; 26.64
Holy Place Ezek 44.13; Lk 11.51
hypocrite 23.13; Mk 7.6

Kingdom (1) (of God) 23.13; 25.1
lesson Zeph 3.7; Mk 13.28
love 23.6; Mk 4.19
mankind [2] 5.13; Mk 16.15
master [6] 21.3; 25.18
Messiah [3] 23.10; 26.63
miracle 16.1; Mk 6.2
one another [2] 23.8; Mk 1.27
pain Zech 9.5; Mk 13.8
power [2] 22.29; 26.45
pray 19.13; 26.36
preach 23.3; 26.13
proper 21.43; Mk 7.3
prophet [3] 23.29; 26.56
punish 23.35; 25.46
remember 16.9; 26.75
Sabbath 12.1; 27.62
sake 19.12; Mk 5.7
save 19.25; 27.40
servant [8] 23.11; 25.14
share 21.34; 25.21
sign (1) 16.3; Lk 1.22
Son of God 17.5; 26.63
Son of Man [6] 20.18; 25.31
sure [2] 19.28; Mk 12.6
teach 23.16; 26.1
Temple (1) (of God) 23.16; 26.55
terrible [2] 23.13; 26.24
thief [2] 21.13; Mk 11.17
trouble [3] 13.21; Mk 4.17
understand 17.13; Mk 4.12
weep 2.18; 26.75
wise 23.34; 25.2
witness 18.16; 26.65
wonder (1) 21.15; Mk 12.11
word (1) 15.8; 26.44
world [3] 18.7; 25.34

23.35: Gen 4.8; 2 Chr 24.20-21 **23.38:** Jer 22.5 **23.39:** Ps 118.26 **24.9:** Mt 10.22 **24.13:** Mt 10.22
24.15: Dan 9.27, 11.31, 12.11 **24.17-18:** Lk 17.31 **24.21:** Dan 12.1; Rev 7.14 **24.26-27:** Lk 17.23-24
24.28: Lk 17.37 **24.29:** Is 13.10, 34.4; Ezek 32.7; Joel 2.10, 31, 3.15; Rev 6.12-13

from **heaven**, and the **powers in space** will be driven from their courses. 30 Then the **sign** of the **Son of Man** will appear in the sky; and all the peoples of earth will **weep** as they see the **Son of Man** coming on the **clouds** of **heaven** with **power** and great **glory**. 31 The great trumpet will sound, and he will send out his **angels** to the four corners of the earth, and they will gather his **chosen people** from one end of the **world** to the other.

The Lesson of the Fig-Tree
(Mark 13.28–31; Luke 21.29–33)

32 "Let the fig-tree **teach** you a **lesson**. When its branches become green and tender and it starts putting out leaves, you know that summer is near. 33 In the same way, when you see all these things, you will know that the time is near, ready to begin.[w] 34 **Remember** that all these things will happen before the people now living have all died. 35 **Heaven and earth** will pass away, but my **words** will never pass away.

No One Knows the Day and Hour
(Mark 13.32–37; Luke 17.26–30, 34–36)

36 "No one knows, however, when that day and hour will come—neither the **angels** in **heaven** nor the **Son**;[x] the **Father alone** knows. 37 The coming of the **Son of Man** will be like what happened in the time of Noah. 38 In the days before the **flood** people ate and drank, men and women married, up to the very day Noah went into the boat; 39 yet they did not realize what was happening until the **flood** came and swept them all away. That is how it will be when the **Son of Man** comes. 40 At that time two men will be working in a field: one will be taken away, the other will be left behind. 41 Two women will be at a mill grinding meal: one will be taken away, the other will be left behind.

42 "Be on your guard, then, because you do not know what day your Lord will come. 43 If the owner of a house knew the time when the **thief** would come, you can be **sure** that he would stay awake and not let the **thief** break into his house. 44 So then, you also must always be ready, because the **Son of Man** will come at an hour when you are not expecting him.

The Faithful or the Unfaithful Servant
(Luke 12.41–48)

45 "Who, then, is a **faithful** and **wise** **servant**? He is the one that his **master** has placed in charge of the other **servants** to give them their food at the **proper** time. 46 How **happy** that **servant** is if his **master** finds him doing this when he comes home! 47 Indeed, I tell you, the **master** will put that **servant** in charge of all his property. 48 But if he is a **bad servant**, he will tell himself that his **master** will not come back for a long time, 49 and he will begin to beat his **fellow-servants** and to eat and drink with drunkards. 50 Then that **servant's master** will come back one day when the **servant** does not expect him and at a time he does not know. 51 The **master** will cut him in pieces[y] and make him **share** the **fate** of the **hypocrites**. There he will cry and grind his teeth.

The Parable of the Ten Girls

25 "At that time the **Kingdom of heaven** will be like this. Once there were ten girls who took their oil lamps and went out to meet the **bridegroom**. 2 Five of them were **foolish**, and the other five were **wise**. 3 The **foolish** ones took their lamps but did not take any extra oil with them, 4 while the **wise** ones took containers full of oil for their lamps. 5 The **bridegroom** was late in coming, so the girls began to nod and fall asleep.

6 "It was already midnight when the cry rang out, 'Here is the **bridegroom**! Come and meet him!' 7 The ten girls woke up and trimmed their lamps. 8 Then the **foolish** ones said to the **wise** ones, 'Let us have some of your oil, because our lamps are going out.' 9 'No, indeed,' the **wise** ones answered, 'there is not **enough** for you and for us. Go to the shop and buy some for yourselves.' 10 So the **foolish** girls went off to buy some oil; and while they were gone, the **bridegroom** arrived. The five girls who were ready went in with him to the **wedding feast**, and the door was closed.

11 "Later the other girls arrived. 'Sir, sir! Let us in!' they cried out. 12 'Certainly not! I don't know you,' the **bridegroom** answered."

13 And Jesus concluded, "Be on your guard, then, because you do not know the day or the hour.

The Parable of the Three Servants
(Luke 19.11–27)

14 "At that time the **Kingdom of heaven** will be like this. Once there was a

afraid 21.26; 28.4
angel [2] 24.31; 26.53
bad 24.48; Mk 9.26
bless 23.39; Mk 10.16
bridegroom [5] 9.15; Mk 2.19
care [2] 16.6; 27.4
create 19.8; Mk 10.6
curse 15.4; Mk 7.10
dark 24.29; 27.45
Devil 13.39; Lk 4.2
enough [2] 18.25; Mk 1.7
eternal [3] 19.16; Mk 3.29
faithful [4] 24.45; Lk 12.42
Father (2) (God) 24.36; 26.29
feast 23.6; Mk 6.21
fool [4] 23.17; Lk 11.40
happy [2] 24.46; Lk 1.14
hard 23.4; Mk 1.26
harvest [2] 21.34; Mk 4.29
help [3] 23.4; 26.53
hunger [4] 21.18; Mk 2.25
important [2] 23.17; Mk 12.10
Kingdom (1) (of God) [3] 24.14; 26.29
least [2] 11.11; Lk 7.28
life (1) 23.29; Mk 3.4
master [5] 24.45; Mk 11.3
naked [4] Nah 3.5; Mk 14.52
possess 5.28; Acts 2.45
prison [4] 14.3; 27:15
punish 24.9; 26.74
reap [2] Hos 10.12; Lk 19.21
refuse (1) [2] 18.30; 27.14
right (2) [2] 22.44; 26.64
righteous [3] Mal 3.18; Lk 1.17
scatter [2] 13.4; 26.31
seed [2] 17.20; Mk 4.4
separate 19.6; Mk 10.9
servant [12] 24.45; 26.69

[w] the time is near, ready to begin; *or* he is near, ready to come.
[x] *Some manuscripts do not have* nor the Son. [y] cut him in pieces; *or* throw him out.

24.30: Dan 7.13; Zech 12.10-14; Rev 1.7 **24.37:** Gen 6.5-8 **24.39:** Gen 7.6-24 **24.43-44:** Lk 12.39-40
25.1: Lk 12.35 **25.11-12:** Lk 13.25 **25.14-30:** Lk 19.11-27

settle (2) 5.25; Lk 12.58
share [2] 24.51; Mk 12.2
sheep 18.12; 26.31
shepherd 9.36; 26.31
Son of Man 24.27; 26.2
sow [2] 13.3; Mk 4.3
stranger [4] Obad 11; Rom 12.13
throne 23.22; Mk 10.37
useless 12.36; Acts 4.25
wedding 22.2; Mk 2.19
welcome [2] 18.5; Mk 6.10
wise [4] 24.45; Mk 12.34
world 24.14; 26.13

man who was about to go on a journey; he called his **servants** and put them in charge of his property. 15 He gave to each one according to his ability: to one he gave five thousand gold coins, to another he gave two thousand, and to another he gave one thousand. Then he left on his journey. 16 The **servant** who had received five thousand coins went at once and invested his money and earned another five thousand. 17 In the same way the **servant** who had received two thousand coins earned another two thousand. 18 But the **servant** who had received one thousand coins went off, dug a hole in the ground, and hid his **master's** money.

19 "After a long time the **master** of those **servants** came back and **settled** accounts with them. 20 The **servant** who had received five thousand coins came in and handed over the other five thousand. 'You gave me five thousand coins, sir,' he said. 'Look! Here are another five thousand that I have earned.' 21 'Well done, you good and **faithful servant**!' said his **master**. 'You have been **faithful** in managing small amounts, so I will put you in charge of large amounts. Come on in and **share** my **happiness**!'

22 "Then the **servant** who had been given two thousand coins came in and said, 'You gave me two thousand coins, sir. Look! Here are another two thousand that I have earned.' 23 'Well done, you good and **faithful servant**!' said his **master**. 'You have been **faithful** in managing small amounts, so I will put you in charge of large amounts. Come on in and **share** my **happiness**!'

24 "Then the **servant** who had received one thousand coins came in and said, 'Sir, I know you are a **hard** man; you **reap harvests** where you did not **sow**, and you gather crops where you did not **scatter seed**. 25 I was **afraid**, so I went off and hid your money in the ground. Look! Here is what belongs to you.'

26 " 'You **bad** and lazy **servant**!' his **master** said. 'You knew, did you, that I **reap harvests** where I did not **sow**, and gather crops where I did not **scatter seed**? 27 Well, then, you should have deposited my money in the bank, and I would have received it all back with interest when I returned. 28 Now, take the money away from him and give it to the one who has ten thousand coins. 29 For to every person who has something, even more will be given, and he will have more than **enough**; but the person who has nothing, even the little that he has will be taken away from him. 30 As for this **useless servant**—throw him outside in the **darkness**; there he will cry and grind his teeth.'

The Final Judgement

31 "When the **Son of Man** comes as King and all the **angels** with him, he will sit on his royal **throne**, 32 and the people of all the nations will be gathered before him. Then he will divide them into two groups, just as a **shepherd separates** the **sheep** from the goats. 33 He will put the **righteous** people on his **right** and the others on his left. 34 Then the King will say to the people on his **right**, 'Come, you that are **blessed** by **my Father**! Come and **possess** the **kingdom** which has been prepared for you ever since the **creation** of the **world**. 35 I was **hungry** and you fed me, thirsty and you gave me a drink; I was a **stranger** and you received me in your homes, 36 **naked** and you clothed me; I was sick and you took **care** of me, in **prison** and you visited me.'

37 "The **righteous** will then answer him, 'When, Lord, did we ever see you **hungry** and feed you, or thirsty and give you a drink? 38 When did we ever see you a **stranger** and **welcome** you in our homes, or **naked** and clothe you? 39 When did we ever see you sick or in **prison**, and visit you?' 40 The King will reply, 'I tell you, whenever you did this for one of the **least important** of these brothers of mine, you did it for me!'

41 "Then he will say to those on his left, 'Away from me, you that are under God's **curse**! Away to the **eternal** fire which has been prepared for the **Devil** and his **angels**! 42 I was **hungry** but you would not feed me, thirsty but you would not give me a drink; 43 I was a **stranger** but you would not **welcome** me in your homes, **naked** but you would not clothe me; I was sick and in **prison** but you would not take **care** of me.'

44 "Then they will answer him, 'When, Lord, did we ever see you **hungry** or thirsty or a **stranger** or **naked** or sick or in **prison**, and would not **help** you?' 45 The King will reply, 'I tell you, whenever you **refused** to **help** one of these **least important** ones, you **refused** to **help** me.' 46 These, then, will be sent off to **eternal punishment**, but the **righteous** will go to **eternal life**."

The Plot against Jesus
(Mark 14.1–2; Luke 22.1–2; John 11.45–53)

26 When Jesus had finished **teaching** all these things, he said to his **disciples**, 2 "In two days, as you know, it

accuse 19.18; 27.12
ahead of you 21.2; 28.7

25.29: Mt 13.12; Mk 4.25; Lk 8.18 **25.30:** Mt 8.12, 22.13; Lk 13.28 **25.31:** Mt 16.27, 19.28 **25.46:** Dan 12.2 **26.2:** Ex 12.1-27

Almighty Mal 4.1; Mk 14.62
angel 25.31; 28.2
anger 22.7; Mk 3.5
anguish Lam 3.5; Mk 14.33
arrest [5] 24.9; Mk 6.17
assure 21.21; Mk 3.28
betray [5] 24.10; 27.4
bitter 2.18; 27.34
blasphemy [2] 9.3; Mk 2.7
blood [2] Zech 9.7; 27.6
body [2] 24.28; 27.58
bread [2] 16.5; Mk 2.26
celebrate Zech 14.16; Lk 15.6
chief priests [4] 21.15; 27.1
cloud 24.30; Mk 9.7
Council 5.22; Mk 14.55
covenant Mal 3.1; Mk 14.24
crucify 23.34; 27.22
cup [3] 23.25; Mk 7.4
death (3) (to death) [2] 24.9; 27.1
deny [2] Lam 3.35; Mk 14.68
disciple [16] 24.1; 27.57
disease 11.5; Mk 1.34
elder (2) [3] 21.23; 27.1
evidence Ecc 10.3; Mk 14.55
false 24.11; Mk 10.19
Father (2) (God) [4] 25.34; 28.19
festival [3] Zech 14.16; 27.15
flesh Zech 14.12; Mk 14.38
flock Mal 1.14; Mk 10.1
forgive 18.21; Mk 1.4
friend 22.12; Mk 9.50
gospel Mk 8.35
grief Zech 11.3; Lk 22.45
guilty 12.5; Mk 14.64
heart 22.37; Mk 6.34
heaven 24.29; 28.2
help 25.44; 27.55
High Priest [8] Zech 6.11; Mk 2.26
hymn Ps 147.7; Mk 14.26
Kingdom (1) (of God) 25.1; Mk 1.15
kiss [2] Hos 13.2; Mk 14.44
lie (2) 15.19; 27.63
life (2) (to life) 22.28; 27.52
Messiah [2] 24.5; 27.17
name (2) (name of God, of Jesus) 23.39; 28.19
need 21.3; Mk 2.17
new 19.28; 27.59
oath Zech 8.17; Lk 1.73
Passover [4] Ezek 45.21; 27.15
peace 10.12; 28.9
plan 22.15; 27.1
poor [2] 19.21; Mk 10.21
power 24.29; Mk 3.22
pray [5] 24.20; Mk 1.35
prayer 21.13; Mk 9.29
preach 24.14; Mk 1.4
prophecy 15.7; Mk 7.6

will be the **Passover Festival**, and the **Son of Man** will be handed over to be **crucified**."

3 Then the **chief priests** and the **elders** met together in the palace of Caiaphas, the **High Priest**, 4 and made **plans** to **arrest** Jesus **secretly** and put him **to death**. 5 "We must not do it during the **festival**," they said, "or the people will riot."

Jesus Is Anointed at Bethany
(Mark 14.3-9; John 12.1-8)

6 Jesus was in Bethany at the house of Simon, a man who had **suffered** from a dreaded **skin-disease**. 7 While Jesus was eating, a woman came to him with an alabaster jar filled with an expensive perfume, which she poured on his head. 8 The **disciples** saw this and became **angry**. "Why all this waste?" they asked. 9 "This perfume could have been sold for a large amount and the money given to the **poor**!"

10 Jesus knew what they were saying, so he said to them, "Why are you bothering this woman? It is a fine and beautiful thing that she has done for me. 11 You will always have **poor** people with you, but you will not always have me. 12 What she did was to pour this perfume on my **body** to get me ready for burial. 13 Now, I **assure** you that wherever this **gospel** is **preached** all over the **world**, what she has done will be told in memory of her."

Judas Agrees to Betray Jesus
(Mark 14.10-11; Luke 22.3-6)

14 Then one of the twelve **disciples**—the one named Judas Iscariot—went to the **chief priests** 15 and asked, "What will you give me if I **betray** Jesus to you?" They counted out thirty silver coins and gave them to him. 16 From then on Judas was looking for a good chance to hand Jesus over to them.

Jesus Eats the Passover Meal with His Disciples
(Mark 14.12-21; Luke 22.7-13, 21-23; John 13.21-30)

17 On the first day of the **Festival** of **Unleavened Bread** the **disciples** came to Jesus and asked him, "Where do you want us to get the **Passover** meal ready for you?"

18 "Go to a certain man in the city," he said to them, "and tell him: 'The **Teacher** says, My hour has come; my **disciples** and I will **celebrate** the **Passover** at your house.' "

19 The **disciples** did as Jesus had told them and prepared the **Passover** meal.

20 When it was evening, Jesus and the twelve **disciples** sat down to eat. 21 During the meal Jesus said, "I tell you, one of you will **betray** me."

22 The **disciples** were very **upset** and began to ask him, one after the other, "Surely, Lord, you don't mean me?"

23 Jesus answered, "One who dips his **bread** in the dish with me will **betray** me. 24 The **Son of Man** will die as the **Scriptures** say he will, but how **terrible** for that man who **betrays** the **Son of Man**! It would have been better for that man if he had never been born!"

25 Judas, the **traitor**, spoke up. "Surely, **Teacher**, you don't mean me?" he asked.

Jesus answered, "So you say."

The Lord's Supper
(Mark 14.22-26; Luke 22.14-20; 1 Cor. 11.23-25)

26 While they were eating, Jesus took a piece of **bread**, gave a **prayer** of **thanks**, broke it, and gave it to his **disciples**. "Take and eat it," he said; "this is my **body**."

27 Then he took a **cup**, gave **thanks** to God, and gave it to them. "Drink it, all of you," he said; 28 "this is my **blood**, which **seals** God's **covenant**, my **blood** poured out for many for the **forgiveness** of sins. 29 I tell you, I will never again drink this wine until the day I drink the **new** wine with you in **my Father's Kingdom**."

30 Then they sang a **hymn** and went out to the Mount of Olives.

Jesus Predicts Peter's Denial
(Mark 14.27-31; Luke 22.31-34; John 13.36-38)

31 Then Jesus said to them, "This very night all of you will run away and leave me, for the **scripture** says, 'God will kill the **shepherd**, and the **sheep** of the **flock** will be **scattered**.' 32 But after I am **raised to life**, I will go to Galilee **ahead of you**."

33 Peter spoke up and said to Jesus, "I will never leave you, even though all the rest do!"

34 Jesus said to Peter, "I tell you that before the cock crows tonight, you will say three times that you do not know me."

35 Peter answered, "I will never say that, even if I have to die with you!"

And all the other **disciples** said the same thing.

prophet 24.11; 27.9
punish 25.46; Mk 5.7
raise 20.19; 27.52
remember 24.34; 27.63
rest (1) 12.43; Mk 6.31
right (2) 25.33; 27.29
scatter 25.24; Mk 4.4
scripture [4] 23.5; Mk 9.12
seal Zech 9.11; 27.66
secret 13.11; Mk 4.11
servant [2] 25.14; Mk 9.35
sheep 25.32; Mk 6.34
shepherd 25.32; Mk 6.34
slave 21.34; Mk 10.44
Son of God 24.36; 27.40
Son of Man [5] 25.31; Mk 2.10
sorrow Nah 2.7; Mk 14.34
spirit (2) 12.43; Mk 1.23
strike Zech 14.5; Mk 14.47
suffer [3] 20.22; 27.19
swear [2] 23.16; Mk 6.23
teach [2] 24.32; 28.20
teacher [3] 23.7; Mk 4.38
teacher of the Law 23.2; 27.41
Temple (1) (of God) [2] 24.1; 27.5
tempt 4.1; Mk 1.13
terrible 24.19; Mk 4.41
thank [2] 15.36; Mk 6.41
traitor [2] Jer 9.2; 27.3
true [2] 21.4; 27.9
truth 22.16; Mk 5.33
unleavened Ezek 45.21; Mk 14.1
upset 18.31; Mk 14.19
watch [3] 21.33; 27.36
weak Zech 12.8; Mk 14.38
weep 24.30; Lk 6.21
will (1) 22.16; Mk 12.14
witness 24.14; Mk 14.56
word (1) 24.35; 27.14
world 25.34; Mk 4.31

26.7: Lk 7.37-38 **26.11:** Deut 15.11 **26.15:** Zech 11.12 **26.23:** Ps 41.9 **26.28:** Ex 24.8; Jer 31.31-34 **26.31:** Zech 13.7 **26.32:** Mt 28.16

Jesus Prays in Gethsemane
(Mark 14.32–42; Luke 22.39–46)

36 Then Jesus went with his **disciples**
to a place called Gethsemane, and he
said to them, "Sit here while I go over
there and **pray**." 37 He took with him
Peter and the two sons of Zebedee. **Grief**
and **anguish** came over him, 38 and he
said to them, "The **sorrow** in my **heart** is
so great that it almost crushes me. Stay
here and keep **watch** with me."

39 He went a little farther on, threw
himself face downwards on the ground,
and **prayed**, "**My Father**, if it is possible,
take this **cup of suffering** from me! Yet
not what I want, but what you want."

40 Then he returned to the three **disciples** and found them asleep; and he
said to Peter, "How is it that you three
were not able to keep **watch** with me
even for one hour? 41 Keep **watch** and
pray that you will not fall into **temptation**. The **spirit** is willing, but the **flesh** is
weak."

42 Once more Jesus went away and
prayed, "**My Father**, if this **cup of suffering** cannot be taken away unless I drink
it, your **will** be done." 43 He returned once
more and found the **disciples** asleep;
they could not keep their eyes open.

44 Again Jesus left them, went away,
and **prayed** the third time, saying the
same **words**. 45 Then he returned to the
disciples and said, "Are you still sleeping
and **resting**? Look! The hour has come
for the **Son of Man** to be handed over to
the **power** of sinful men. 46 Get up, let us
go. Look, here is the man who is **betraying** me!"

The Arrest of Jesus
(Mark 14.43–50; Luke 22.47–53;
John 18.3–12)

47 Jesus was still speaking when
Judas, one of the twelve **disciples**,
arrived. With him was a large crowd
armed with swords and clubs and sent by
the **chief priests** and the **elders**. 48 The
traitor had given the crowd a signal:
"The man I **kiss** is the one you want.
Arrest him!"

49 Judas went straight to Jesus and
said, "**Peace** be with you, **Teacher**," and
kissed him.

50 Jesus answered, "Be quick about it,
friend!"[z]

Then they came up, **arrested** Jesus,
and held him tight. 51 One of those who
were with Jesus drew his sword and
struck at the **High Priest's slave**, cutting
off his ear. 52 "Put your sword back in its
place," Jesus said to him. "All who take
the sword will die by the sword. 53 Don't
you know that I could call on **my Father**
for **help**, and at once he would send me
more than twelve armies of **angels**?
54 But in that case, how could the **Scriptures** come **true** which say that this is
what must happen?"

55 Then Jesus spoke to the crowd,
"Did you have to come with swords and
clubs to capture me, as though I were an
outlaw? Every day I sat down and **taught**
in the **Temple**, and you did not **arrest** me.
56 But all this has happened in order to
make what the **prophets** wrote in the
Scriptures come **true**."

Then all the **disciples** left him and ran
away.

Jesus Before the Council
(Mark 14.53–65; Luke 22.54–55, 63–71;
John 18.13–14, 19–24)

57 Those who had **arrested** Jesus took
him to the house of Caiaphas, the **High
Priest**, where the **teachers of the Law**
and the **elders** had gathered together.
58 Peter followed from a distance, as far
as the courtyard of the **High Priest's**
house. He went into the courtyard and
sat down with the guards to see how it
would all come out. 59 The **chief priests**
and the whole **Council** tried to find some
false evidence against Jesus to put him **to
death**; 60 but they could not find any, even
though many people came forward and
told **lies** about him. Finally two men
stepped up 61 and said, "This man said, 'I
am able to tear down God's **Temple** and
three days later build it up again.'"

62 The **High Priest** stood up and said
to Jesus, "Have you no answer to give to
this **accusation** against you?" 63 But Jesus
kept quiet. Again the **High Priest** spoke
to him, "**In the name of** the living God I
now put you on **oath**: tell us if you are the
Messiah, the **Son of God**."

64 Jesus answered him, "So you say.
But I tell all of you: from this time on you
will see the **Son of Man** sitting on the
right of the **Almighty** and coming on the
clouds of heaven!"

65 At this the **High Priest** tore his
clothes and said, "**Blasphemy**! We don't
need any more **witnesses**! You have just
heard his **blasphemy**! 66 What do you
think?"

They answered, "He is **guilty** and must
die."

67 Then they spat in his face and beat
him; and those who slapped him 68 said,

[z] Be quick about it, friend! *or* Why are you here, friend?

26.55: Lk 19.47, 21.37 **26.61:** Jn 2.19 **26.64:** Dan 7.13 **26.65-66:** Lev 24.16 **26.67:** Is 50.6

"**Prophesy** for us, **Messiah**! Guess who hit you!"

Peter Denies Jesus
(Mark 14.66–72; Luke 22.56–62; John 18.15–18, 25–27)

69 Peter was sitting outside in the courtyard when one of the **High Priest's servant-girls** came to him and said, "You, too, were with Jesus of Galilee."

70 But he **denied** it in front of them all. "I don't know what you are talking about," he answered, 71 and went on out to the entrance of the courtyard. Another **servant-girl** saw him and said to the men there, "He was with Jesus of Nazareth."

72 Again Peter **denied** it and answered, "I **swear** that I don't know that man!"

73 After a little while the men standing there came to Peter. "Of course you are one of them," they said. "After all, the way you speak gives you away!"

74 Then Peter said, "I **swear** that I am telling the **truth**! May God **punish** me if I am not! I do not know that man!"

Just then a cock crowed, 75 and Peter **remembered** what Jesus had told him: "Before the cock crows, you will say three times that you do not know me." He went out and **wept bitterly**.

Jesus Is Taken to Pilate
(Mark 15.1; Luke 23.1–2; John 18.28–32)

27 Early in the morning all the **chief priests** and the **elders** made their **plans** against Jesus to put him **to death**. 2 They put him in chains, led him off, and handed him over to Pilate, the Roman governor.

The Death of Judas
(Acts 1.18–19)

3 When Judas, the **traitor**, **learnt** that Jesus had been **condemned**, **he repented** and took back the thirty silver coins to the **chief priests** and the **elders**. 4 "I have sinned by **betraying** an **innocent** man to **death**!" he said.

"What do we **care** about that?" they answered. "That is your business!"

5 Judas threw the coins down in the **Temple** and left; then he went off and **hanged** himself.

6 The **chief priests** picked up the coins and said, "This is **blood money**, and it is against our **Law** to put it in the **temple** treasury." 7 After reaching an **agreement** about it, they used the money to buy Potter's Field, as a cemetery for foreigners. 8 That is why that field is called "**Field of Blood**" to this very day.

9 Then what the **prophet** Jeremiah had said came **true**: "They took the thirty silver coins, the amount the people of Israel had **agreed** to pay for him, 10 and used the money to buy the potter's field, as the Lord had **commanded** me."

Pilate Questions Jesus
(Mark 15.2–5; Luke 23.3–5; John 18.33–38)

11 Jesus stood before the Roman governor, who **questioned** him. "Are you the **king of the Jews**?" he asked.

"So you say," answered Jesus. 12 But he said nothing in response to the **accusations** of the **chief priests** and **elders**.

13 So Pilate said to him, "Don't you hear all these things they **accuse** you of?"

14 But Jesus **refused** to answer a single **word**, with the **result** that the Governor was greatly surprised.

Jesus Is Sentenced to Death
(Mark 15.6–15; Luke 23.13–25; John 18.39—19.16)

15 At every **Passover Festival** the Roman governor was in the habit of **setting free** any one **prisoner** the crowd asked for. 16 At that time there was a well-known **prisoner** named Jesus Barabbas. 17 So when the crowd gathered, Pilate asked them, "Which one do you want me to **set free** for you? Jesus Barabbas or Jesus called the **Messiah**?" 18 He knew very well that the **Jewish authorities** had handed Jesus over to him because they were **jealous**.

19 While Pilate was sitting in the **judgement** hall, his wife sent him a **message**: "Have nothing to do with that **innocent** man, because in a **dream last** night I **suffered** much on account of him."

20 The **chief priests** and the **elders** **persuaded** the crowd to ask Pilate to **set** Barabbas **free** and have Jesus put to **death**. 21 But Pilate asked the crowd, "Which one of these two do you want me to **set free** for you?"

"Barabbas!" they answered.

22 "What, then, shall I do with Jesus called the **Messiah**?" Pilate asked them.

"**Crucify** him!" they all answered.

23 But Pilate asked, "What **crime** has he **committed**?"

Then they started shouting at the top of their voices: "**Crucify** him!"

24 When Pilate saw that it was no use to go on, but that a riot might break out, he took some water, washed his hands in front of the crowd, and said, "I am not responsible for the **death** of this man! This is your doing!"

27.3-8: Acts 1.18-19 **27.9-10:** Zech 11.12-13 **27.24:** Deut 21.6-9

abandon 23.38; Mk 15.34
accuse [3] 26.62; Mk 3.2
agree [2] 20.2; Mk 14.56
alive 6.25; Mk 16.11
apart 12.25; Mk 3.24
authorities Jer 20.10; Jn 1.19
believe 24.23; Mk 1.15
betray 26.15; Mk 3.19
bitter 26.75; Lk 11.53
blood [2] 26.28; Mk 14.24
body [3] 26.12; 28.13
care 25.36; Mk 4.38
chief priests [7] 26.3; 28.11
claim 24.5; Mk 13.6
command 17.18; 28.20
commit 19.9; Mk 3.29
condemn 23.33; Mk 10.33
crime Hab 2.12; Mk 15.14
cross (1) [3] 16.24; Mk 8.34
crown Zech 9.16; Mk 15.17
crucify [7] 26.2; 28.5
dark 25.30; Mk 13.24
death (1) [3] 16.18; Lk 1.79
death (2) (from death) [2] 22.23; 28.7
death (3) (to death) [2] 26.4; Mk 7.10
disciple [2] 26.1; 28.7

dream 2.12; Acts 2.17
elder (2) [5] 26.3; 28.12
festival 26.2; Mk 14.1
force (1) 5.41; Mk 15.21
free [5] Mal 4.2; Mk 15.6
God's people 24.22; Mk 13.20
grave [2] Nah 1.14; Lk 11.44
hang (2) Lam 5.12; Lk 23.39
help 26.53; Mk 1.13
holy 23.17; Mk 1.24
innocent [2] 23.35; 28.14
insult [2] 5.11; Mk 15.29
jealous 20.15; Mk 7.22
jeer Lam 3.63; Mk 15.31
Jew [4] 14.5; 28.15
judge 12.18; Mk 4.24
kneel 17.14; Mk 1.40
last (1) 13.21; Mk 3.26
last (2) [3] 22.27; Mk 9.35
law 23.2; Mk 2.24
learn 13.18; Lk 10.21
lie (2) [2] 26.60; Mk 14.56
life (2) (to life) [2] 26.32; Mk 8.31
message 22.4; Mk 2.2
Messiah [2] 26.63; Mk 8.29
mock [2] 20.19; Mk 10.34
new 26.29; Mk 1.27
offer 21.16; Mk 1.44
Passover 26.2; Mk 14.1
persuade Is 36.15; Acts 10.23
Pharisees 23.2; Mk 2.16
plan 26.4; 28.12
presence 18.10; Mk 15.42
prison [2] 25.36; Mk 1.14
prophet 26.56; Mk 1.2
question 22.15; Mk 10.3
raise [3] 26.32; 28.6
refuse (1) 25.45; Mk 6.26
remember 26.75; 28.7
repent 3.11; Lk 5.32
result 23.35; Lk 16.8
rich 19.22; Mk 10.22
right (2) [2] 26.64; Mk 10.37
rise 22.23; Mk 8.31
Sabbath 24.20; 28.1
save [4] 24.13; Mk 3.4
seal 26.28; Mk 14.24
secure [2] Zech 3.10; Acts 27.16
Son of God [3] 26.63; 28.19
steal 19.18; 28.13
strip (1) Zeph 2.14; Lk 10.30
suffer 26.6; Mk 1.40
teacher of the Law 26.57; Mk 1.22
Temple (1) (of God) [4] 26.55; Mk 11.11
terrify 17.6; Mk 6.50
tomb [6] 23.27; 28.1
traitor 26.25; Mk 14.44
true 26.54; Mk 12.32
trust Zeph 3.2; Lk 16.11

watch [3] 26.38; Mk 2.12
word (1) 26.44; Mk 7.6
worse 12.45; Mk 5.26

25 The whole crowd answered, "Let the responsibility for his **death** fall on us and our children!"

26 Then Pilate **set Barabbas free** for them; and after he had Jesus whipped, he handed him over to be **crucified**.

The Soldiers Mock Jesus
(Mark 15.16–20; John 19.2–3)

27 Then Pilate's soldiers took Jesus into the governor's palace, and the whole company gathered round him. 28 They **stripped** off his clothes and put a scarlet robe on him. 29 Then they made a **crown** out of thorny branches and placed it on his head, and put a stick in his **right hand**; then they **knelt** before him and **mocked** him. "Long live the **King of the Jews**!" they said. 30 They spat on him, and took the stick and hit him over the head. 31 When they had finished **mocking** him, they took the robe off and put his own clothes back on him. Then they led him out to **crucify** him.

Jesus Is Crucified
(Mark 15.21–32; Luke 23.26–43; John 19.17–27)

32 As they were going out, they met a man from Cyrene named Simon, and the soldiers **forced** him to carry Jesus' **cross**. 33 They came to a place called Golgotha, which means, "The Place of the Skull." 34 There they **offered** Jesus wine mixed with a **bitter** substance; but after tasting it, he would not drink it.

35 They **crucified** him and then divided his clothes among them by throwing dice. 36 After that they sat there and **watched** him. 37 Above his head they put the written notice of the **accusation** against him: "This is Jesus, the **King of the Jews**." 38 Then they **crucified** two bandits with Jesus, one on his **right** and the other on his left.

39 People passing by shook their heads and hurled **insults** at Jesus: 40 "You were going to tear down the **Temple** and build it up again in three days! **Save** yourself if you are **God's Son**! Come on down from the **cross**!"

41 In the same way the **chief priests** and the **teachers of the Law** and the **elders jeered** at him: 42 "He **saved** others, but he cannot save himself! Isn't he the king of Israel? If he comes down off the **cross** now, we will **believe** in him! 43 He **trusts** in God and **claims** to be **God's Son**. Well, then, let us see if God wants to **save** him now!"

44 Even the bandits who had been **crucified** with him **insulted** him in the same way.

The Death of Jesus
(Mark 15.33–41; Luke 23.44–49; John 19.28–30)

45 At noon the whole country was covered with **darkness**, which **lasted** for three hours. 46 At about three o'clock Jesus cried out with a loud shout, *"Eli, Eli, lema sabachthani?"* which means, "My God, my God, why did you **abandon** me?"

47 Some of the people standing there heard him and said, "He is calling for Elijah!" 48 One of them ran up at once, took a sponge, soaked it in cheap wine, put it on the end of a stick, and tried to make him drink it.

49 But the others said, "Wait, let us see if Elijah is coming to **save** him!"

50 Jesus again gave a loud cry and breathed his **last**.

51 Then the curtain hanging in the **Temple** was torn in two from top to bottom. The earth shook, the rocks split **apart**, 52 the **graves** broke open, and many of **God's people** who had died were **raised to life**. 53 They left the **graves**, and after Jesus **rose from death**, they went into the **Holy City**, where many people saw them.

54 When the army officer and the soldiers with him who were **watching** Jesus saw the earthquake and everything else that happened, they were **terrified** and said, "He really was the **Son of God**!"

55 There were many women there, looking on from a distance, who had followed Jesus from Galilee and **helped** him. 56 Among them were Mary Magdalene, Mary the mother of James and Joseph, and the wife of Zebedee.

The Burial of Jesus
(Mark 15.42–47; Luke 23.50–56; John 19.38–42)

57 When it was evening, a **rich** man from Arimathea arrived; his name was Joseph, and he also was a **disciple** of Jesus. 58 He went into the **presence** of Pilate and asked for the **body** of Jesus. Pilate gave orders for the **body** to be given to Joseph. 59 So Joseph took it, wrapped it in a **new** linen sheet, 60 and placed it in his own **tomb**, which he had just recently dug out of solid rock. Then he rolled a large stone across the entrance to the **tomb** and went away. 61 Mary Magdalene and the other Mary were sitting there, facing the **tomb**.

27.34: Ps 69.21 **27.35:** Ps 22.18 **27.39:** Ps 22.7, 109.25 **27.40:** Mt 26.61; Jn 2.19 **27.43:** Ps 22.8
27.46: Ps 22.1 **27.48:** Ps 69.21 **27.51:** Ex 26.31-33 **27.55-56:** Lk 8.2-3

The Guard at the Tomb

62 The next day, which was a **Sabbath**,
the **chief priests** and the **Pharisees** met
with Pilate 63 and said, "Sir, we **remember** that while that **liar** was still **alive** he
said, 'I will be **raised to life** three days
later.' 64 Give orders, then, for his **tomb** to
be carefully guarded until the third day,
so that his **disciples** will not be able to go
and **steal** the **body**, and then tell the
people that he was **raised from death**.
This **last lie** would be even **worse** than
the first one."

65 "Take a guard," Pilate told them;
"go and make the **tomb** as **secure** as you
can."

66 So they left and made the **tomb**
secure by putting a **seal** on the stone and
leaving the guard on **watch**.

The Resurrection
(Mark 16.1–10; Luke 24.1–12;
John 20.1–10)

28 After the **Sabbath**, as Sunday
morning was dawning, Mary
Magdalene and the other Mary went to
look at the **tomb**. 2 Suddenly there was a
violent earthquake; an **angel of the Lord**
came down from **heaven**, rolled the
stone away, and sat on it. 3 His **appearance** was like lightning, and his clothes
were white as snow. 4 The guards were so
afraid that they **trembled** and became
like **dead** men.

5 The **angel** spoke to the women. "You
must not be **afraid**," he said. "I know you
are looking for Jesus, who was **crucified**.
6 He is not here; he has been **raised**, just
as he said. Come here and see the place
where he was lying. 7 Go quickly now,
and tell his **disciples**, 'He has been **raised
from death**, and now he is going to
Galilee **ahead of you**; there you will see
him!' **Remember** what I have told you."

8 So they left the **tomb** in a hurry,
afraid and yet filled with **joy**, and ran to
tell his **disciples**.

9 Suddenly Jesus met them and said,
"**Peace** be with you." They came up to
him, took hold of his feet, and **worshipped** him. 10 "Do not be **afraid**," Jesus
said to them. "Go and tell my brothers to
go to Galilee, and there they will see
me."

The Report of the Guard

11 While the women went on their
way, some of the soldiers guarding the
tomb went back to the city and told the
chief priests everything that had happened. 12 The **chief priests** met with the
elders and made their **plan**; they gave a
large sum of money to the soldiers 13 and
said, "You are to say that his **disciples**
came during the night and **stole** his **body**
while you were asleep. 14 And if the
Governor should hear of this, we will
convince him that you are **innocent**, and
you will have nothing to **worry** about."

15 The guards took the money and did
what they were told to do. And so that is
the report spread round by the **Jews** to
this very day.

Jesus Appears to His Disciples
(Mark 16.14–18; Luke 24.36–49;
John 20.19–23; Acts 1.6–8)

16 The eleven **disciples** went to the hill
in Galilee where Jesus had told them to
go. 17 When they saw him, they **worshipped** him, even though some of them
doubted. 18 Jesus drew near and said to
them, "I have been given all **authority** in
heaven and on earth. 19 Go, then, to all
peoples everywhere and make them my
disciples: **baptize** them **in the name of**
the **Father**, the **Son**, and the **Holy Spirit**,
20 and **teach** them to **obey** everything I
have **commanded** you. And I will be with
you always, to the end of the **age**."

27.63: Mt 16.21, 17.23, 20.19; Mk 8.31, 9.31, 10.33-34; Lk 9.22, 18.31-33 **28.16:** Mt 26.32; Mk 14.28
28.19: Acts 1.8

afraid [4] 25.25; Mk 4.41
age (1) 24.3; Mk 10.30
ahead of you 26.32; Mk 1.2
angel [2] 26.53; Mk 1.13
appearance 6.16; Lk 9.29
authority 20.25; Mk 1.22
baptize 21.25; Mk 1.4
body 27.58; Mk 6.29
chief priests [2] 27.1; Mk 8.31
command 27.10; Mk 4.39
convince 21.26; Mk 11.32
crucify 27.22; Mk 15.13
dead 24.28; Mk 5.39
death (2) (from death) 27.53; Mk 9.9
disciple [5] 27.57; Mk 1.21
doubt 21.21; Mk 11.23
elder (2) 27.1; Mk 8.31
Father (2) (God) 26.29; Mk 8.38
heaven [2] 26.64; Mk 1.10
innocent 27.4; Rom 4.5
Jew 27.11; Mk 7.3
joy 2.9; Lk 2.10
name (2) (name of God, of Jesus) 26.63; Mk 9.37
obey 23.3; Mk 1.27
peace 26.49; Mk 5.34
plan 27.1; Mk 3.6
raise [2] 27.52; Mk 12.26
remember 27.63; Mk 8.18
Sabbath 27.62; Mk 1.21
Son of God 27.40; Mk 1.1
Spirit (1) (God's Spirit) 22.43; Mk 1.8
steal 27.64; Mk 10.19
teach 26.1; Mk 1.17
tomb [3] 27.60; Mk 5.3
tremble Hab 3.6; Mk 5.33
violent 23.25; Lk 11.39
worry 22.16; Mk 4.19
worship (1) (of God) [2] 15.9; Mk 7.7

THE GOSPEL ACCORDING TO MARK

INTRODUCTION

The Gospel according to Mark begins with the statement that it is "the Good News about Jesus Christ, the Son of God." Jesus is pictured as a man of action and authority. His authority is seen in his teaching, in his power over demons, and in forgiving people's sins. Jesus speaks of himself as the Son of Man, who came to give his life to set people free from sin.

Mark presents the story of Jesus in a straightforward, vigorous way, with emphasis on what Jesus did, rather than on his words and teachings. After a brief prologue about John the Baptist and the baptism and temptation of Jesus, the writer immediately takes up Jesus' ministry of healing and teaching. As time goes on, the followers of Jesus come to understand him better, but Jesus' opponents become more hostile. The closing chapters report the events of Jesus' last week of earthly life, especially his crucifixion and resurrection.

The two endings to the Gospel, which are enclosed in brackets, are generally regarded as written by someone other than the author of *Mark*.

Outline of Contents

---

after me Mt 3.11; Jn 1.15
ahead of you Mt 28.7; 11.2
amaze [2] Mt 22.22; 2.12
angel Mt 28.2; 8.38
announce Mt 12.18; Lk 4.19
authority [2] Mt 28.18; 2.10
baptize [6] Mt 28.19; 10.38
beg Mt 18.26; 5.7
believe Mt 27.42; 5.36
clean [3] Mt 23.25; Lk 5.12
clear Mt 7.5; 8.25
confess Mt 3.6; Rom 10.9
cure Mt 8.4; Lk 5.14
dear Mt 17.5; 9.7
demon [4] Mt 17.18; 3.15
destroy Mt 10.28; 3.4
disciple [2] Mt 28.7; 2.15
disease [3] Mt 26.6; 14.3
dove Mt 10.16; Lk 2.24
enough Mt 25.9; 4.6
forgive Mt 26.28; 2.5
Good News [3] Mt 24.14; 13.9

The Preaching of John the Baptist
(Matt. 3.1-12; Luke 3.1-18; John 1.19-28)

1 This is the **Good News** about Jesus Christ, the **Son of God**.[a] 2 It began as the **prophet** Isaiah had written:

"God said, 'I will send my messenger
ahead of you
to **clear** the way for you.'
3 Someone is shouting in the desert,
'Get the road ready for the Lord;
make a straight path for him to
travel!' "

4 So John appeared in the desert, **baptizing** and **preaching**.[b] "**Turn away from** your sins and be **baptized**," he told the people, "and God will **forgive** your sins." 5 Many people from the province of Judaea and the city of Jerusalem went out to hear John. They **confessed** their sins, and he **baptized** them in the River Jordan.

6 John wore clothes made of camel's hair, with a leather belt round his waist, and his food was locusts and wild honey. 7 He **announced** to the people, "The man who will come **after me** is much greater than I am. I am not good **enough** even to bend down and untie his sandals. 8 I **baptize** you with water, but he will **baptize** you with the **Holy Spirit**."

The Baptism and Temptation of Jesus
(Matt. 3.13—4.11; Luke 3.21-22; 4.1-13)

9 Not long afterwards Jesus came from Nazareth in the province of Galilee, and was **baptized** by John in the Jordan. 10 As soon as Jesus came up out of the water, he saw **heaven** opening and the **Spirit** coming down on him like a **dove**. 11 And a voice came from **heaven**, "You are my own **dear Son**. I am **pleased** with you."

12 At once the **Spirit** made him go into the desert, 13 where he stayed forty days, being **tempted** by **Satan**. Wild animals were there also, but **angels** came and **helped** him.

Jesus Calls Four Fishermen
(Matt. 4.12-22; Luke 4.14-15; 5.1-11)

14 After John had been put in **prison**, Jesus went to Galilee and **preached** the

hard Mt 25.24; 10.5
heal Mt 21.14; 3.2
heaven [2] Mt 28.2; 6.41
help [3] Mt 27.55; 3.4
holy Mt 27.53; 6.20
Kingdom (1) (of God) Mt 26.29; 4.11
kneel Mt 27.29; 5.33
lonely [2] Mt 14.13; 6.32
new Mt 27.59; 2.21
obey Mt 28.20; 4.41
offer Mt 27.34; 2.26
one another Mt 24.7; 4.41
pity Mt 20.30; 6.34
please Mt 17.5; 5.23
pray Mt 26.36; 6.46
preach [4] Mt 26.13; 2.2
priest Mt 12.4; 2.26
prison Mt 27.15; 6.17
prophet Mt 27.9; 6.4
prove Mt 12.27; 2.10
right (1) Mt 21.32; 5.15
Sabbath Mt 28.1; 2.23
sacrifice Mt 12.7; 9.49
Satan Mt 16.23; 3.23
Son of God [2] Mt 28.19; 3.11
Spirit (1) (God's Spirit) [3] Mt 28.19; 3.29
spirit (2) [4] Mt 26.41; 3.11
suffer Mt 27.19; 5.25

[a] *Some manuscripts do not have* the Son of God.
[b] John appeared in the desert, baptizing and preaching; *some manuscripts have* John the Baptist appeared in the desert, preaching.

1.2: Mal 3.1 **1.3:** Is 40.3 (LXX) **1.6:** 2 Kgs 1.8
1.11: Gen 22.2; Ps 2.7; Is 42.1; Mt 3.17, 12.18; Mk 9.7; Lk 3.22

synagogue [4] Mt 23.6; 3.1
teach [5] Mt 28.20; 2.13
teacher of the Law Mt 27.41; 2.6
tempt Mt 26.41; 14.38
turn [2] Mt 21.42; 4.12

Good News from God. 15 "The right time
has come," he said, "and the Kingdom of
God is near! Turn away from your sins
and believe the Good News!"
16 As Jesus walked along the shore of
Lake Galilee, he saw two fishermen,
Simon and his brother Andrew, catching
fish with a net. 17 Jesus said to them,
"Come with me, and I will teach you to
catch men." 18 At once they left their nets
and went with him.
19 He went a little farther on and saw
two other brothers, James and John, the
sons of Zebedee. They were in their boat
getting their nets ready. 20 As soon as
Jesus saw them, he called them; they left
their father Zebedee in the boat with the
hired men and went with Jesus.

A Man with an Evil Spirit
(Luke 4.31–37)

21 Jesus and his disciples came to the
town of Capernaum, and on the next
Sabbath Jesus went to the synagogue and
began to teach. 22 The people who heard
him were amazed at the way he taught,
for he wasn't like the teachers of the
Law; instead, he taught with authority.
23 Just then a man with an evil spirit
in him came into the synagogue and
screamed, 24 "What do you want with us,
Jesus of Nazareth? Are you here to destroy us? I know who you are—you are
God's holy messenger!"
25 Jesus ordered the spirit, "Be quiet,
and come out of the man!"
26 The evil spirit shook the man hard,
gave a loud scream, and came out of
him. 27 The people were all so amazed
that they started saying to one another,
"What is this? Is it some kind of new
teaching? This man has authority to give
orders to the evil spirits, and they obey
him!"
28 And so the news about Jesus spread
quickly everywhere in the province of
Galilee.

Jesus Heals Many People
(Matt. 8.14–17; Luke 4.38–41)

29 Jesus and his disciples, including
James and John, left the synagogue and
went straight to the home of Simon and
Andrew. 30 Simon's mother-in-law was
sick in bed with a fever, and as soon as
Jesus arrived, he was told about her.
31 He went to her, took her by the hand,
and helped her up. The fever left her,
and she began to wait on them.
32 After the sun had set and evening
had come, people brought to Jesus all the
sick and those who had demons. 33 All the
people of the town gathered in front of
the house. 34 Jesus healed many who
were sick with all kinds of diseases and
drove out many demons. He would not
let the demons say anything, because
they knew who he was.

Jesus Preaches in Galilee
(Luke 4.42–44)

35 Very early the next morning, long
before daylight, Jesus got up and left the
house. He went out of the town to a
lonely place, where he prayed. 36 But
Simon and his companions went out
searching for him, 37 and when they
found him, they said, "Everyone is looking for you."
38 But Jesus answered, "We must go
on to the other villages round here. I
have to preach in them also, because
that is why I came."
39 So he travelled all over Galilee,
preaching in the synagogues and driving
out demons.

Jesus Heals a Man
(Matt. 8.1–4; Luke 5.12–16)

40 A man suffering from a dreaded
skin-disease came to Jesus, knelt down,
and begged him for help. "If you want
to," he said, "you can make me clean."[c]
41 Jesus was filled with pity,[d] and
stretched out his hand and touched him.
"I do want to," he answered. "Be clean!"
42 At once the disease left the man, and
he was clean. 43 Then Jesus spoke sternly
to him and sent him away at once,
44 after saying to him, "Listen, don't tell
anyone about this. But go straight to the
priest and let him examine you; then in
order to prove to everyone that you are
cured, offer the sacrifice that Moses
ordered."
45 But the man went away and began
to spread the news everywhere. Indeed,
he talked so much that Jesus could not go
into a town publicly. Instead, he stayed
out in lonely places, and people came to
him from everywhere.

Jesus Heals a Paralysed Man
(Matt. 9.1–8; Luke 5.17–26)

2 A few days later Jesus went back to
Capernaum, and the news spread
that he was at home. 2 So many people
came together that there was no room
left, not even out in front of the door.
Jesus was preaching the message to

amaze 1.22; 5.20
authority 1.22; 3.15
blasphemy Mt 26.65; 14.64
bread [2] Mt 26.23; 6.8
bridegroom [2] Mt 25.1; Lk 5.34
dare Mt 22.46; 12.34

[c] MAKE ME CLEAN: *This disease was considered to make a person ritually unclean.*
[d] pity; *some manuscripts have* anger.

1.15: Mt 3.2 1.22: Mt 7.28–29 1.39: Mt 4.23, 9.35 1.44: Lev 14.1–32

disciple [6] 1.21; 3.7
faith Mt 24.10; 4.40
fast (2) [3] Mt 11.18; Lk 2.36
follower Mt 19.28; Lk 11.19
forgive [4] 1.4; 3.28
High Priest Mt 26.3; 14.47
hunger Mt 25.35; 11.12
law [2] Mt 27.6; 3.4
message Mt 27.19; 3.31
need [2] Mt 26.65; 10.21
new [4] 1.27; 14.25
offer 1.44; 12.33
outcast [3] Mt 11.19; Lk 5.30
paralyse [4] Mt 12.10; 3.1
Pharisees [4] Mt 27.62; 3.6
praise Mt 21.9; 11.9
preach 1.4; 3.14
priest 1.44; Lk 1.5
prove 1.44; 8.12
respect Mt 23.7; 6.4
ruin Mt 9.17; Lk 5.37
Sabbath [5] 1.21; 3.2
Son of Man [2] Mt 26.2; 8.31
tax collector [3] Mt 21.31; Lk 3.12
teach 1.17; 4.1
teacher of the Law [2] 1.22; 3.22
watch Mt 27.36; 3.2
wedding Mt 25.10; Lk 5.34

them 3 when four men arrived, carrying a **paralysed** man to Jesus. 4 Because of the crowd, however, they could not get the man to him. So they made a hole in the roof right above the place where Jesus was. When they had made an opening, they let the man down, lying on his mat. 5 Seeing how much **faith** they had, Jesus said to the **paralysed** man, "My son, your sins are **forgiven**."

6 Some **teachers of the Law** who were sitting there thought to themselves, 7 "How does he **dare** to talk like this? This is **blasphemy**! God is the only one who can **forgive** sins!"

8 At once Jesus knew what they were thinking, so he said to them, "Why do you think such things? 9 Is it easier to say to this **paralysed** man, 'Your sins are **forgiven**', or to say, 'Get up, pick up your mat, and walk'? 10 I will **prove** to you, then, that the **Son of Man** has **authority** on earth to **forgive** sins." So he said to the **paralysed** man, 11 "I tell you, get up, pick up your mat, and go home!"

12 While they all **watched**, the man got up, picked up his mat, and hurried away. They were all completely **amazed** and **praised** God, saying, "We have never seen anything like this!"

Jesus Calls Levi
(Matt. 9.9–13; Luke 5.27–32)

13 Jesus went back again to the shore of Lake Galilee. A crowd came to him, and he started **teaching** them. 14 As he walked along, he saw a **tax collector**, Levi son of Alphaeus, sitting in his office. Jesus said to him, "Follow me." Levi got up and followed him.

15 Later on Jesus was having a meal in Levi's house.[e] A large number of **tax collectors** and other **outcasts** were following Jesus, and many of them joined him and his **disciples** at the table. 16 Some **teachers of the Law**, who were **Pharisees**, saw that Jesus was eating with these **outcasts** and **tax collectors**, so they asked his **disciples**, "Why does he eat with such people?"

17 Jesus heard them and answered, "People who are well do not **need** a doctor, but only those who are sick. I have not come to call **respectable** people, but **outcasts**."

The Question about Fasting
(Matt. 9.14–17; Luke 5.33–39)

18 On one occasion the **followers** of John the Baptist and the **Pharisees** were **fasting**. Some people came to Jesus and asked him, "Why is it that the **disciples** of John the Baptist and the **disciples** of the **Pharisees fast**, but yours do not?"

19 Jesus answered, "Do you expect the guests at a **wedding party** to go without food? Of course not! As long as the **bridegroom** is with them, they will not do that. 20 But the day will come when the **bridegroom** will be taken away from them, and then they will **fast**.

21 "No one uses a piece of **new** cloth to patch up an old coat, because the **new** patch will shrink and tear off some of the old cloth, making an even bigger hole. 22 Nor does anyone pour **new** wine into used wineskins, because the wine will burst the skins, and both the wine and the skins will be **ruined**. Instead, **new** wine must be poured into fresh wineskins."

The Question about the Sabbath
(Matt. 12.1–8; Luke 6.1–5)

23 Jesus was walking through some cornfields on the **Sabbath**. As his **disciples** walked along with him, they began to pick the ears of corn. 24 So the **Pharisees** said to Jesus, "Look, it is against our **Law** for your **disciples** to do that on the **Sabbath**!"

25 Jesus answered, "Have you never read what David did that time when he **needed** something to eat? He and his men were **hungry**, 26 so he went into the house of God and ate the **bread offered** to God. This happened when Abiathar was the **High Priest**. According to our **Law** only the **priests** may eat this **bread**—but David ate it and even gave it to his men."

27 And Jesus concluded, "The **Sabbath** was made for the good of man; man was not made for the **Sabbath**. 28 So the **Son of Man** is Lord even of the **Sabbath**."

The Man with a Paralysed Hand
(Matt. 12.9–14; Luke 6.6–11)

3 Then Jesus went back to the **synagogue**, where there was a man who had a **paralysed** hand. 2 Some people were there who wanted to **accuse** Jesus of doing **wrong**; so they **watched** him closely to see whether he would **heal** the man on the **Sabbath**. 3 Jesus said to the man, "Come up here to the front." 4 Then he asked the people, "What does our **Law** allow us to do on the **Sabbath**? To **help** or to **harm**? To **save** a man's **life** or to **destroy** it?"

But they did not say a thing. 5 Jesus was **angry** as he looked round at them, but at the same time he felt **sorry** for

accuse Mt 27.12; 10.19
anger Mt 26.8; 10.14
apart [3] Mt 27.51; Lk 11.17
apostle Mt 10.2; 6.30
assure Mt 26.13; 9.41
authority 2.10; 6.7
betray Mt 27.4; 14.10
choose [3] Mt 24.22; 10.40
commit Mt 27.23; 7.22
demon [2] 1.32; 5.15
destroy 1.24; Lk 2.34
disciple [3] 2.15; 4.10
each other [2] Mt 24.7; 13.8
eternal Mt 25.41; 10.17
evil [2] Mt 24.12; 7.21
forgive [2] 2.5; 4.12

[e] in Levi's house; *or* in his (*that is*, Jesus') house.

2.23: Deut 23.25 **2.25–26:** 1 Sam 21.1–6 **2.26:** Lev 24.9

harm Zech 8.17; 16.18
heal [2] 1.34; 5.29
help 1.13; 7.11
last (1) Mt 27.45; 4.17
law 2.24; 7.7
life (1) Mt 25.46; 4.19
mad Zech 12.4; Jn 10.20
message 2.2; 4.14
parable Mt 22.1; 4.2
paralyse 2.3; Lk 5.18
Pharisees 2.16; 7.1
plan Mt 28.12; 15.1
power Mt 26.45; 5.30
preach 2.2; 4.33
Sabbath [2] 2.23; 6.2
Satan [2] 1.13; 4.15
save Mt 27.40; 8.35
Son of God 1.1; 5.7
sorry Mt 18 27; 8.2
Spirit (1) (God's Spirit) 1.8; 12.36
spirit (2) [3] 1.23; 5.2
strong [2] Mt 14.30; 4.37
stubborn Zech 7.11; 16.14
synagogue [2] 1.21; 5.22
teacher of the Law 2.6; 7.1
watch 2.12; 12.1
wrong [2] Mt 22.29; 11.25

them, because they were so **stubborn** and
wrong. Then he said to the man, "Stretch
out your hand." He stretched it out, and it
became well again. 6 So the **Pharisees** left
the **synagogue** and met at once with
some members of Herod's party, and
they made **plans** to kill Jesus.

A Crowd by the Lake

7 Jesus and his **disciples** went away to
Lake Galilee, and a large crowd followed
him. They had come from Galilee, from
Judaea, 8 from Jerusalem, from the territory of Idumea, from the territory on the
east side of the Jordan, and from the
region round the cities of Tyre and Sidon.
All these people came to Jesus because
they had heard of the things he was doing. 9 The crowd was so large that Jesus
told his **disciples** to get a boat ready for
him, so that the people would not crush
him. 10 He had **healed** many people, and
all those who were ill kept pushing their
way to him in order to touch him. 11 And
whenever the people who had **evil spirits**
in them saw him, they would fall down
before him and scream, "You are the **Son
of God**!"

12 Jesus sternly ordered the **evil
spirits** not to tell anyone who he was.

Jesus Chooses the Twelve Apostles
(Matt. 10.1–4; Luke 6.12–16)

13 Then Jesus went up a hill and
called to himself the men he wanted.
They came to him, 14 and he **chose**
twelve, whom he named **apostles**. "I
have **chosen** you to be with me," he told
them. "I will also send you out to **preach**,
15 and you will have **authority** to drive out
demons."

16 These are the twelve he **chose**:
Simon (Jesus gave him the name Peter);
17 James and his brother John, the sons of
Zebedee (Jesus gave them the name
Boanerges, which means "Men of Thun-
der"); 18 Andrew, Philip, Bartholomew,
Matthew, Thomas, James son of
Alphaeus, Thaddaeus, Simon the Patriot,
19 and Judas Iscariot, who **betrayed** Jesus.

Jesus and Beelzebul
(Matt. 12.22–32; Luke 11.14–23; 12.10)

20 Then Jesus went home. Again such
a large crowd gathered that Jesus and
his **disciples** had no time to eat. 21 When
his family heard about it, they set out to
take charge of him, because people were
saying, "He's gone **mad**!"

22 Some **teachers of the Law** who had
come from Jerusalem were saying, "He
has Beelzebul in him! It is the chief of
the **demons** who gives him the **power** to
drive them out."

23 So Jesus called them to him and
spoke to them in **parables**: "How can
Satan drive out Satan? 24 If a country
divides itself into groups which fight
each other, that country will fall **apart**.
25 If a family divides itself into groups
which fight **each other**, that family will
fall **apart**. 26 So if **Satan's** kingdom divides
into groups, it cannot **last**, but will fall
apart and come to an end.

27 "No one can break into a **strong**
man's house and take away his belongings unless he first ties up the **strong**
man; then he can plunder his house.

28 "I **assure** you that people can be
forgiven all their sins and all the **evil**
things they may say.[f] 29 But whoever says
evil things against the **Holy Spirit** will
never be **forgiven**, because he has **committed** an **eternal** sin." 30 (Jesus said this
because some people were saying, "He
has an **evil spirit** in him.")

Jesus' Mother and Brothers
(Matt. 12.46–50; Luke 8.19–21)

31 Then Jesus' mother and brothers
arrived. They stood outside the house
and sent in a **message**, asking for him.
32 A crowd was sitting round Jesus, and
they said to him, "Look, your mother and
your brothers and sisters are outside, and
they want you."

33 Jesus answered, "Who is my
mother? Who are my brothers?" 34 He
looked at the people sitting round him
and said, "Look! Here are my mother
and my brothers! 35 Whoever does what
God wants him to do is my brother, my
sister, my mother."

The Parable of the Sower
(Matt. 13.1–9; Luke 8.4–8)

4 Again Jesus began to **teach** beside
Lake Galilee. The crowd that
gathered round him was so large that he
got into a boat and sat in it. The boat was
out in the water, and the crowd stood on
the shore at the water's edge. 2 He used
parables to **teach** them many things, saying to them:

3 "Listen! Once there was a man who
went out to **sow** corn. 4 As he **scattered**
the **seed** in the field, some of it fell along
the path, and the birds came and ate it
up. 5 Some of it fell on rocky ground,
where there was little soil. The **seeds**
soon sprouted, because the soil wasn't
deep. 6 Then, when the sun came up, it

accept Mt 19.12; Lk 7.35
afraid Mt 28.4; 5.15
alone [2] Mt 24.36; 6.31
calm Mt 8.26; Lk 8.2
care Mt 27.4; 5.14
command Mt 28.20; 7.8
desire Mt 5.6; Jn 8.4
disciple [6] 3.7; 5.1
enough 1.7; 6.42
faith 2.5; 5.34
forgive 3.28; 11.25
fright Mt 8.26; 9.6
give up Mt 24.10; Lk 12.20
glad Mt 13.20; 12.3
harvest Mt 25.24; 12.2
judge [2] Mt 27.19; Lk 6.37
Kingdom (1) (of God) [3] 1.15; 9.1

[f] evil things they may say; *or* evil things they may say against God.

3.9–10: Mk 4.1; Lk 5.1–3 **3.22:** Mt 9.34, 10.25 **3.29:** Lk 12.10 **4.1:** Lk 5.1–3

last (1) 3.26; 15.33
life (1) 3.4; 6.14
love Mt 24.12; 10.21
means Jer 32.21; Lk 8.10
message [8] 3.31; 16.7
obey 1.27; 7.8
one another 1.27; 9.50
parable [8] 3.23; 12.1
persecute Mt 13.21; 10.30
preach 3.14; 6.12
riches Mt 19.21; 10.21
ripe Zech 12.6; Lk 8.14
Satan 3.23; 8.33
scatter [2] Mt 26.31; 14.27
secret Mt 26.4; 14.1
seed [11] Mt 25.24; Lk 8.5
sow [4] Mt 25.24; Lk 8.5
strong 3.27; 5.4
teach [2] 2.13; 6.2
teacher Mt 26.18; 5.35
terrible Mt 26.24; 5.25
trouble Mt 24.6; 5.29
turn 1.4; 5.30
understand [4] Mt 24.15; 6.52
world Mt 26.13; 8.36
worry Mt 28.14; 12.14

burnt the young plants; and because the roots had not grown deep **enough**, the plants soon dried up. 7 Some of the **seed** fell among thorn bushes, which grew up and choked the plants, and they didn't produce any corn. 8 But some **seeds** fell in good soil, and the plants sprouted, grew, and produced corn: some had thirty grains, others sixty, and others a hundred."

9 And Jesus concluded, "Listen, then, if you have ears!"

The Purpose of the Parables
(Matt. 13.10–17; Luke 8.9–10)

10 When Jesus was **alone**, some of those who had heard him came to him with the twelve **disciples** and asked him to explain the **parables**. 11 "You have been given the **secret** of the **Kingdom of God**," Jesus answered. "But the others, who are on the outside, hear all things **by means of parables**, 12 so that,

'They may look and look,
yet not see;
they may listen and listen,
yet not **understand**.
For if they did, they would **turn to God**,
and he would **forgive** them.' "

Jesus Explains the Parable of the Sower
(Matt. 13.18–23; Luke 8.11–15)

13 Then Jesus asked them, "Don't you **understand** this **parable**? How, then, will you ever **understand** any **parable**? 14 The **sower** sows God's **message**. 15 Some people are like the **seeds** that fall along the path; as soon as they hear the **message**, **Satan** comes and takes it away. 16 Other people are like the **seeds** that fall on rocky ground. As soon as they hear the **message**, they receive it **gladly**. 17 But it does not sink deep into them, and they don't **last** long. So when **trouble** or **persecution** comes because of the **message**, they **give up** at once. 18 Other people are like the **seeds sown** among the thorn bushes. These are the ones who hear the **message**, 19 but the **worries** about this **life**, the **love** for **riches**, and all other kinds of **desires** crowd in and choke the **message**, and they don't bear fruit. 20 But other people are like the **seeds sown** in good soil. They hear the **message**, **accept** it, and bear fruit: some thirty, some sixty, and some a hundred."

A Lamp under a Bowl
(Luke 8.16–18)

21 Jesus continued, "Does anyone ever bring in a lamp and put it under a bowl or under the bed? Doesn't he put it on the lampstand? 22 Whatever is hidden away will be brought out into the open, and whatever is covered up will be uncovered. 23 Listen, then, if you have ears!"

24 He also said to them, "Pay attention to what you hear! The same rules you use to **judge** others will be used by God to **judge** you—but with even greater severity. 25 The person who has something will be given more, and the person who has nothing will have taken away from him even the little he has."

The Parable of the Growing Seed

26 Jesus went on to say, "The **Kingdom of God** is like this. A man **scatters seed** in his field. 27 He sleeps at night, is up and about during the day, and all the while the **seeds** are sprouting and growing. Yet he does not know how it happens. 28 The soil itself makes the plants grow and bear fruit; first the tender stalk appears, then the ear, and finally the ear full of corn. 29 When the corn is **ripe**, the man starts cutting it with his sickle, because **harvest** time has come.

The Parable of the Mustard Seed
(Matt. 13.31–32, 34; Luke 13.18–19)

30 "What shall we say the **Kingdom of God** is like?" asked Jesus. "What **parable** shall we use to explain it? 31 It is like this. A man takes a mustard **seed**, the smallest seed in the **world**, and plants it in the ground. 32 After a while it grows up and becomes the biggest of all plants. It puts out such large branches that the birds come and make their nests in its shade."

33 Jesus **preached** his **message** to the people, using many other **parables** like these; he told them as much as they could **understand**. 34 He would not speak to them without using **parables**, but when he was **alone** with his **disciples**, he would explain everything to them.

Jesus Calms a Storm
(Matt. 8.23–27; Luke 8.22–25)

35 On the evening of that same day Jesus said to his **disciples**, "Let us go across to the other side of the lake." 36 So they left the crowd; the **disciples** got into the boat in which Jesus was already sitting, and they took him with them. Other boats were there too. 37 Suddenly a **strong** wind blew up, and the waves began to spill over into the boat, so that it was about to fill with water. 38 Jesus was in the back of the boat, sleeping with his

4.12: Is 6.9–10 (LXX) **4.21:** Mt 5.15; Lk 11.33 **4.22:** Mt 10.26; Lk 12.2 **4.24:** Mt 7.2; Lk 6.38 **4.25:** Mt 13.12, 25.29; Lk 19.26 **4.29:** Joel 3.13

head on a pillow. The **disciples** woke him
up and said, "**Teacher**, don't you **care**
that we are about to die?"
39 Jesus stood up and **commanded** the
wind, "Be quiet!" and he said to the
waves, "Be still!" The wind died down,
and there was a great **calm**. 40 Then Jesus
said to his **disciples**, "Why are you
frightened? Have you still no **faith**?"
41 But they were **terribly afraid** and
said to **one another**, "Who is this man?
Even the wind and the waves **obey** him!"

Jesus Heals a Man with Evil Spirits

(Matt. 8.28-34; Luke 8.26-39)

5 Jesus and his **disciples** arrived on
the other side of Lake Galilee, in the
territory of Gerasa. 2 As soon as Jesus got
out of the boat, he was met by a man who
came out of the burial caves there. This
man had an **evil spirit** in him 3 and lived
among the **tombs**. Nobody could keep
him chained up any more; 4 many times
his feet and hands had been chained, but
every time he broke the chains and
smashed the irons on his feet. He was too
strong for anyone to **control** him. 5 Day
and night he wandered among the **tombs**
and through the hills, screaming and cutting himself with stones.
6 He was some distance away when
he saw Jesus; so he ran, fell on his **knees**
before him, 7 and screamed in a loud
voice, "Jesus, **Son of the Most High God**!
What do you want with me? For God's
sake, I **beg** you, don't **punish** me!" 8 (He
said this because Jesus was saying, "**Evil
spirit**, come out of this man!")
9 So Jesus asked him, "What is your
name?"
The man answered, "My name is
'Mob'—there are so many of us!" 10 And
he kept **begging** Jesus not to send the **evil
spirits** out of that region.
11 There was a large herd of pigs near
by, feeding on a hillside. 12 So the **spirits
begged** Jesus, "Send us to the pigs, and
let us go into them." 13 He let them go,
and the **evil spirits** went out of the man
and entered the pigs. The whole herd—
about two thousand pigs in all—rushed
down the side of the cliff into the lake
and was drowned.
14 The men who had been taking **care**
of the pigs ran away and spread the news
in the town and among the farms. People
went out to see what had happened,
15 and when they came to Jesus, they saw
the man who used to have the mob of
demons in him. He was sitting there,
clothed and in his **right mind**; and they
were all **afraid**. 16 Those who had seen it
told the people what had happened to the
man with the **demons**, and about the
pigs.
17 So they asked Jesus to leave their
territory.
18 As Jesus was getting into the boat,
the man who had had the **demons
begged** him, "Let me go with you!"
19 But Jesus would not let him. Instead, he told him, "Go back home to
your family and tell them how much the
Lord has done for you and how **kind** he
has been to you."
20 So the man left and went all
through the Ten Towns, telling what
Jesus had done for him. And all who
heard it were **amazed**.

Jairus' Daughter and the Woman Who Touched Jesus' Cloak

(Matt. 9.18-26; Luke 8.40-56)

21 Jesus went back across to the other
side of the lake. There at the lakeside a
large crowd gathered round him.
22 Jairus, an official of the local **synagogue**, arrived, and when he saw Jesus,
he threw himself down at his feet 23 and
begged him **earnestly**, "My little
daughter is very ill. **Please** come and
place your hands on her, so that she will
get well and live!"
24 Then Jesus started off with him. So
many people were going along with
Jesus that they were crowding him from
every side.
25 There was a woman who had **suffered terribly** from severe bleeding for
twelve years, 26 even though she had
been treated by many doctors. She had
spent all her money, but instead of getting better she got **worse** all the time.
27 She had heard about Jesus, so she came
in the crowd behind him, 28 saying to herself, "If I just touch his clothes, I will get
well."
29 She touched his cloak, and her
bleeding stopped at once; and she had
the feeling inside herself that she was
healed of her **trouble**. 30 At once Jesus
knew that **power** had gone out of him, so
he **turned round** in the crowd and asked,
"Who touched my clothes?"
31 His **disciples** answered, "You see
how the people are crowding you; why
do you ask who touched you?"
32 But Jesus kept looking round to see
who had done it. 33 The woman realized
what had happened to her, so she came,
trembling with **fear**, **knelt** at his feet, and
told him the whole **truth**. 34 Jesus said to
her, "My daughter, your **faith** has made
you well. Go in **peace**, and be **healed** of
your **trouble**."
35 While Jesus was saying this, some

afraid [2] 4.41; 6.20
amaze [2] 2.12; 6.2
beg [5] 1.40; 6.56
believe 1.15; 11.23
care 4.38; 8.15
control Dan 5.21; Acts 5.3
dead Mt 28.4; 9.26
demon [3] 3.15; 6.13
disciple [3] 4.10; 6.1
earnest Jon 3.8; Lk 7.4
faith 4.40; 6.6
fear Mt 14.26; Lk 1.65
heal [2] 3.2; 6.5
kind Mt 12.7; Lk 10.37
knee Mt 18.26; 15.19
kneel 1.40; 10.17
mind (1) Mt 22.37; 6.52
Most High Ps 92.1; Lk 1.32
peace Mt 28.9; 9.50
please 1.11; 6.22
power 3.22; 6.14
punish Mt 26.74; 12.40
right (1) 1.15; 6.18
sake Mt 24.22; 13.9
Son of God 3.11; 9.7
spirit (2) [5] 3.11; 6.7
strong 4.37; 14.31
suffer 1.40; 8.31
synagogue 3.1; 6.2
teacher 4.38; 9.5
terrible 4.41; 13.17
tomb [2] Mt 28.1; 15.46
tremble Mt 28.4; Lk 8.47
trouble [2] 4.17; 7.35
truth Mt 26.74; 12.14
turn 4.12; 6.12
wail Mal 2.13; Lk 23.27
worse Mt 27.64; 12.40

messengers came from Jairus' house and told him, "Your daughter has died. Why bother the **Teacher** any longer?"

36 Jesus paid no attention to[g] what they said, but told him, "Don't be **afraid**, only **believe**." 37 Then he did not let anyone else go on with him except Peter and James and his brother John. 38 They arrived at Jairus' house, where Jesus saw the confusion and heard all the loud crying and **wailing**. 39 He went in and said to them, "Why all this confusion? Why are you crying? The child is not **dead**—she is only sleeping!"

40 They laughed at him, so he put them all out, took the child's father and mother and his three **disciples**, and went into the room where the child was lying. 41 He took her by the hand and said to her, "*Talitha, koum,*" which means, "Little girl, I tell you to get up!"

42 She got up at once and started walking around. (She was twelve years old.) When this happened, they were completely **amazed**. 43 But Jesus gave them strict orders not to tell anyone, and he said, "Give her something to eat."

Jesus Is Rejected at Nazareth
(Matt. 13.53–58; Luke 4.16–30)

6 Jesus left that place and went back to his home town, followed by his **disciples**. 2 On the **Sabbath** he began to **teach** in the **synagogue**. Many people were there; and when they heard him, they were all **amazed**. "Where did he get all this?" they asked. "What **wisdom** is this that has been given him? How does he perform **miracles**? 3 Isn't he the carpenter, the son of Mary, and the brother of James, Joseph, Judas, and Simon? Aren't his sisters living here?" And so they **rejected** him.

4 Jesus said to them, "A **prophet** is **respected** everywhere except in his own home town and by his relatives and his family."

5 He was not able to perform any **miracles** there, except that he placed his hands on a few sick people and **healed** them. 6 He was greatly surprised, because the people did not have **faith**.

Jesus Sends out the Twelve Disciples
(Matt. 10.5–15; Luke 9.1–6)

Then Jesus went to the villages round there, **teaching** the people. 7 He called the twelve **disciples** together and sent them out two by two. He gave them **authority** over the **evil spirits** 8 and ordered them, "Don't take anything with you on your journey except a stick—no **bread**, no beggar's bag, no money in your pockets. 9 Wear sandals, but don't carry an extra shirt." 10 He also said, "Wherever you are **welcomed**, stay in the same house until you leave that place. 11 If you come to a town where people do not **welcome** you or will not listen to you, leave it and shake the dust off your feet. That will be a **warning** to them!"

12 So they went out and **preached** that people should **turn away from their sins**. 13 They drove out many **demons**, and rubbed olive-oil on many sick people and **healed** them.

The Death of John the Baptist
(Matt. 14.1–12; Luke 9.7–9)

14 Now King Herod[h] heard about all this, because Jesus' **reputation** had spread everywhere. Some people were saying, "John the Baptist has come back to **life**! That is why he has this **power** to perform **miracles**."

15 Others, however, said, "He is Elijah."

Others said, "He is a prophet, like one of the **prophets** of long ago."

16 When Herod heard it, he said, "He is John the Baptist! I had his head cut off, but he has come back to **life**!" 17 Herod himself had ordered John's **arrest**, and he had him chained and put in **prison**. Herod did this because of Herodias, whom he had married, even though she was the wife of his brother Philip. 18 John the Baptist kept telling Herod, "It isn't **right** for you to be married to your brother's wife!"

19 So Herodias held a grudge against John and wanted to kill him, but she could not because of Herod. 20 Herod was **afraid** of John because he knew that John was a good and **holy** man, and so he kept him **safe**. He liked to listen to him, even though he became greatly disturbed every time he heard him.

21 Finally Herodias got her chance. It was on Herod's birthday, when he gave a **feast** for all the chief government officials, the military commanders, and the **leading** citizens of Galilee. 22 The daughter of Herodias[i] came in and danced, and **pleased** Herod and his guests. So the king said to the girl, "What would you like to have? I will give you

[g] paid no attention to; *or* overheard. [h] KING HEROD: *Herod Antipas, ruler of Galilee.*
[i] The daughter of Herodias; *some manuscripts have* His daughter Herodias.

6.4: Jn 4.44 **6.8–11:** Lk 10.4–11 **6.11:** Acts 13.51 **6.13:** Jas 5.14 **6.14–15:** Mt 16.14; Mk 8.28; Lk 9.19 **6.17–18:** Lk 3.19–20

anything you want." 23 With many **vows** he said to her, "I **swear** that I will give you anything you ask for, even as much as half my kingdom!"

24 So the girl went out and asked her mother, "What shall I ask for?"

"The head of John the Baptist," she answered.

25 The girl hurried back at once to the king and **demanded**, "I want you to give me here and now the head of John the Baptist on a dish!"

26 This made the king very **sad**, but he could not **refuse** her because of the **vows** he had made in front of all his guests. 27 So he sent off a guard at once with orders to bring John's head. The guard left, went to the **prison**, and cut John's head off; 28 then he brought it on a dish and gave it to the girl, who gave it to her mother. 29 When John's **disciples** heard about this, they came and took away his **body**, and buried it.

Jesus Feeds Five Thousand Men
(Matt. 14.13–21; Luke 9.10–17; John 6.1–14)

30 The **apostles** returned and met with Jesus, and told him all they had done and **taught**. 31 There were so many people coming and going that Jesus and his **disciples** didn't even have time to eat. So he said to them, "Let us go off by ourselves to some place where we will be **alone** and you can **rest** for a while." 32 So they started out in a boat by themselves for a **lonely** place.

33 Many people, however, saw them leave and knew at once who they were; so they went from all the towns and ran ahead by land and arrived at the place ahead of Jesus and his **disciples**. 34 When Jesus got out of the boat, he saw this large crowd, and his **heart** was filled with **pity** for them, because they were like **sheep** without a **shepherd**. So he began to **teach** them many things. 35 When it was getting late, his **disciples** came to him and said, "It is already very late, and this is a **lonely** place. 36 Send the people away, and let them go to the nearby farms and villages in order to buy themselves something to eat."

37 "You yourselves give them something to eat," Jesus answered.

They asked, "Do you want us to go and spend two hundred silver coins[j] on **bread** in order to feed them?"

38 So Jesus asked them, "How much **bread** have you got? Go and see."

When they found out, they told him, "Five loaves and also two fish."

39 Jesus then told his **disciples** to make all the people divide into groups and sit down on the green grass. 40 So the people sat down in rows, in groups of a hundred and groups of fifty. 41 Then Jesus took the five loaves and the two fish, looked up to **heaven**, and gave **thanks** to God. He broke the loaves and gave them to his **disciples** to distribute to the people. He also divided the two fish among them all. 42 Everyone ate and had **enough**. 43 Then the **disciples** took up twelve baskets full of what was left of the **bread** and the fish. 44 The number of **men** who were fed was five thousand.

Jesus Walks on the Water
(Matt. 14.22–33; John 6.15–21)

45 At once Jesus made his **disciples** get into the boat and go ahead of him to Bethsaida, on the other side of the lake, while he sent the crowd away. 46 After saying good-bye to the people he went away to a hill to **pray**. 47 When evening came, the boat was in the middle of the lake, while Jesus was **alone** on land. 48 He saw that his **disciples** were straining at the oars, because they were rowing against the wind; so some time between three and six o'clock in the morning he came to them, walking on the water. He was going to pass them by,[k] 49 but they saw him walking on the water. "It's a **ghost**!" they thought, and screamed. 50 They were all **terrified** when they saw him.

Jesus spoke to them at once, "**Courage**!" he said. "It is I. Don't be **afraid**!" 51 Then he got into the boat with them, and the wind died down. The **disciples** were completely **amazed**, 52 because they had not **understood** the **real** meaning of the feeding of the five thousand; their **minds** could not grasp it.

Jesus Heals the Sick in Gennesaret
(Matt. 14.34–36)

53 They crossed the lake and came to land at Gennesaret, where they tied up the boat. 54 As they left the boat, people recognized Jesus at once. 55 So they ran throughout the whole region; and wherever they heard he was, they brought to him sick people lying on their mats. 56 And everywhere Jesus went, to villages, towns, or farms, people would take those who were ill to the market-places and **beg** him to let them at least

[j] SILVER COINS: *A silver coin was the daily wage of a rural worker (see Mt 20.2).*
[k] pass them by; *or* join them.

6.34: Num 27.17; 1 Kgs 22.17; 2 Chr 18.16; Ezek 34.5; Mt 9.36

touch the edge of his cloak; and all who
touched it were made well.

The Teaching of the Ancestors
(Matt. 15.1–9)

7 Some **Pharisees** and **teachers of the**
Law who had come from Jerusalem
gathered round Jesus. 2 They **noticed** that
some of his **disciples** were eating their
food with hands that were ritually **un-**
clean—that is, they had not washed them
in the way the **Pharisees** said people
should.
3 (For the **Pharisees**, as well as the
rest of the **Jews**, follow the **teaching** they
received from their ancestors: they do
not eat unless they wash their hands in
the **proper** way; 4 nor do they eat anything that comes from the market unless
they wash it first.[l] And they follow many
other rules which they have received,
such as the **proper** way to wash **cups**,
pots, copper bowls, and beds.[m])
5 So the **Pharisees** and the **teachers of**
the Law asked Jesus, "Why is it that your
disciples do not follow the **teaching**
handed down by our ancestors, but instead eat with ritually **unclean** hands?"
6 Jesus answered them, "How **right**
Isaiah was when he **prophesied** about
you! You are **hypocrites**, just as he
wrote:
'These people, says God, **honour** me
with their **words**,
but their **heart** is really far away
from me.
7 It is no use for them to **worship** me,
because they **teach man-made** rules
as though they were God's **laws**!'
8 "You put aside God's **command** and
obey the **teachings** of men."
9 And Jesus continued, "You have a
clever way of **rejecting** God's **law** in
order to uphold your own **teaching**. 10 For
Moses **commanded**, '**Respect** your father
and your mother,' and, 'Whoever **curses**
his father or his mother is to be put to
death.' 11 But you **teach** that if a person
has something he could use to **help** his
father or mother, but says, 'This is
Corban' (which means, it belongs to
God), 12 he is **excused** from **helping** his
father or mother. 13 In this way the **teach-**
ing you pass on to others cancels out the
word of God. And there are many other
things like this that you do."

The Things that Make a Person Unclean
(Matt. 15.10–20)

14 Then Jesus called the crowd to him
once more and said to them, "Listen to
me, all of you, and **understand**. 15 There is
nothing that goes into a person from the
outside which can make him ritually **un-**
clean. Rather, it is what comes out of a
person that makes him **unclean**."[n]
17 When he left the crowd and went
into the house, his **disciples** asked him to
explain this **saying**. 18 "You are no more
intelligent than the others," Jesus said to
them. "Don't you **understand**? Nothing
that goes into a person from the outside
can really make him **unclean**, 19 because
it does not go into his **heart** but into his
stomach and then goes on out of the
body." (In saying this, Jesus **declared**
that all foods are **fit** to be eaten.)
20 And he went on to say, "It is what
comes out of a person that makes him
unclean. 21 For from the inside, from a
person's **heart**, come the **evil ideas** which
lead him to do **immoral** things, to **rob**,
kill, 22 **commit adultery**, be **greedy**, and
do all sorts of **evil** things; **deceit**, indecency, **jealousy**, **slander**, **pride**, and
folly—23 all these **evil** things come from
inside a person and make him **unclean**."

A Woman's Faith
(Matt. 15.21–28)

24 Then Jesus left and went away to
the territory near the city of Tyre. He
went into a house and did not want anyone to know he was there, but he could
not stay hidden. 25 A woman, whose
daughter had an **evil spirit** in her, heard
about Jesus and came to him at once and
fell at his feet. 26 The woman was a **Gen-**
tile, born in the region of Phoenicia in
Syria. She **begged** Jesus to drive the
demon out of her daughter. 27 But Jesus
answered, "Let us first feed the children.
It isn't **right** to take the children's food
and throw it to the dogs."
28 "Sir," she answered, "even the dogs
under the table eat the children's leftovers!"
29 So Jesus said to her, "Because of
that answer, go back home, where you
will find that the **demon** has gone out of
your daughter!"
30 She went home and found her child
lying on the bed; the **demon** had indeed
gone out of her.

adultery Mt 19.9; 10.11
alone 6.31; 9.2
amaze 6.2; 10.26
beg [2] 6.56; 8.22
body 6.29; 12.8
command [2] 4.39; 9.25
commit 3.29; 10.11
cup Mt 26.27; 10.38
curse Mt 25.41; 11.21
death (3) (to death) Mt 27.1; 8.31
deceive Mt 24.4; 13.5
declare Mt 12.37; Lk 12.8
demon [3] 6.13; 9.38
disciple [3] 6.1; 8.1
evil [3] 3.28; 9.39
excuse Ezek 8.12; Lk 14.18
fit (1) Mt 10.37; Lk 15.19
Gentile Mt 20.19; 10.33
greed Zeph 3.3; Lk 12.15
groan Mic 4.10; 8.12
heart [3] 6.34; 11.23
heaven 6.41; 10.21
help [2] 3.4; 9.22
honour Mt 15.6; Lk 1.50
hypocrite Mt 24.51; Lk 6.42
idea Mt 15.19; Acts 28.22
immoral Mt 15.19; Acts 15.20
intelligent Mt 15.16; Lk 2.47
jealous Mt 27.18; 15.10
Jew Mt 28.15; 12.12
law [2] 3.4; 10.2
man-made Mt 15.9; Acts 17.24
notice (1) Mt 23.5; 9.25
obey 4.41; 9.10
Pharisees [4] 3.6; 8.11
proper [2] Mt 24.45; Lk 12.42
prophecy Mt 26.68; Jn 11.51
proud Mal 4.1; Lk 1.51
reject 6.3; 8.31
respect 6.4; 10.19
right (1) [2] 6.18; 11.13
rob Mt 15.19; 12.40
saying Mt 15.15; Jn 4.35
slander Mt 15.19; 1 Cor 5.11
speech Mt 12.19; Acts 12.21
spirit (2) 6.7; 9.17
teach [7] 6.2; 8.31
teacher of the Law [2] 3.22; 8.31
trouble 5.29; 13.7
unclean [7] Mt 15.11; Acts 10.14
understand [2] 6.52; 8.17
word (1) [2] Mt 27.14; 10.24
worship (1) (of God) Mt 28.9; Lk 2.36

[l] anything that comes from the market unless they wash it first; *or* anything after they come from the market unless they wash themselves first. [m] *Some manuscripts do not have* and beds.
[n] *Some manuscripts add verse 16:* Listen, then, if you have ears! *(see 4.23).*

7.6–7: Is 29.13 (LXX) **7.10:** Ex 20.12, 21.17; Lev 20.9; Deut 5.16

Jesus Heals a Deaf-Mute

31 Jesus then left the neighbourhood of Tyre and went on through Sidon to Lake Galilee, going by way of the territory of the Ten Towns. 32 Some people brought him a man who was deaf and could hardly speak, and they **begged** Jesus to place his hands on him. 33 So Jesus took him off **alone**, away from the crowd, put his fingers in the man's ears, spat, and touched the man's tongue. 34 Then Jesus looked up to **heaven**, gave a deep **groan**, and said to the man, "*Ephphatha*," which means, "Open up!"

35 At once the man was able to hear, his **speech** impediment was removed, and he began to talk without any **trouble**. 36 Then Jesus ordered the people not to speak of it to anyone; but the more he ordered them not to, the more they spoke. 37 And all who heard were completely **amazed**. "How well he does everything!" they exclaimed. "He even causes the deaf to hear and the dumb to speak!"

Jesus Feeds Four Thousand People
(Matt. 15.32–39)

8 Not long afterwards another large crowd came together. When the people had nothing left to eat, Jesus called the **disciples** to him and said, 2 "I feel **sorry** for these people, because they have been with me for three days and now have nothing to eat. 3 If I send them home without feeding them, they will faint as they go, because some of them have come a long way."

4 His **disciples** asked him, "Where in this desert can anyone find **enough** food to feed all these people?"

5 "How much **bread** have you got?" Jesus asked.

"Seven loaves," they answered.

6 He ordered the crowd to sit down on the ground. Then he took the seven loaves, gave **thanks** to God, broke them, and gave them to his **disciples** to distribute to the crowd; and the **disciples** did so. 7 They also had a few small fish. Jesus gave **thanks** for these and told the **disciples** to distribute them too. 8-9 Everybody ate and had **enough**—there were about four thousand people. Then the **disciples** took up seven baskets full of pieces left over. Jesus sent the people away 10 and at once got into a boat with his **disciples** and went to the district of Dalmanutha.

The Pharisees Ask for a Miracle
(Matt. 16.1–4)

11 Some **Pharisees** came to Jesus and started to **argue** with him. They wanted to **trap** him, so they asked him to perform a **miracle** to show that God **approved** of him. 12 But Jesus gave a deep **groan** and said, "Why do the people of this day ask for a **miracle**? No, I tell you! No such **proof** will be given to these people!"

13 He left them, got back into the boat, and started across to the other side of the lake.

The Yeast of the Pharisees and of Herod
(Matt. 16.5–12)

14 The **disciples** had **forgotten** to bring **enough bread** and had only one loaf with them in the boat. 15 "Take **care**," Jesus **warned** them, "and be on your guard against the yeast of the **Pharisees** and the **yeast** of Herod."

16 They started **discussing** among themselves: "He says this because we haven't any **bread**."

17 Jesus knew what they were saying, so he asked them, "Why are you **discussing** about not having any **bread**? Don't you know or **understand** yet? Are your **minds** so dull? 18 You have eyes—can't you see? You have ears—can't you hear? Don't you **remember** 19 when I broke the five loaves for the five thousand people? How many baskets full of leftover pieces did you take up?"

"Twelve," they answered.

20 "And when I broke the seven loaves for the four thousand people," asked Jesus, "how many baskets full of leftover pieces did you take up?"

"Seven," they answered.

21 "And you still don't **understand**?" he asked them.

Jesus Heals a Blind Man at Bethsaida

22 They came to Bethsaida, where some people brought a **blind** man to Jesus and **begged** him to touch him. 23 Jesus took the **blind** man by the hand and led him out of the village. After spitting on the man's eyes, Jesus placed his hands on him and asked him, "Can you see anything?"

24 The man looked up and said, "Yes, I can see people, but they look like trees walking about."

25 Jesus again placed his hands on the man's eyes. This time the man looked intently, his **eyesight** returned, and he saw everything **clearly**. 26 Jesus then sent him

8.11: Mt 12.38; Lk 11.16 **8.12:** Mt 12.39; Lk 11.29 **8.15:** Lk 12.1 **8.18:** Jer 5.21; Ezek 12.2; Mk 4.12

angel 1.13; 12.25
approve Mt 16.1; Lk 11.16
argue Mt 21.25; 9.14
ashamed [2] Zeph 3.5; Lk 9.26
beg 7.26; Lk 5.12
blind [2] Mt 23.16; 10.46
bread [4] 6.8; 14.20
care 5.14; Lk 2.8
chief priests Mt 28.11; 10.33
clear [2] 1.2; Lk 6.42
cross (1) Mt 27.32; 15.21
death (3) (to death) 7.10; 13.12
disciple [12] 7.2; 9.4
discuss [2] Mt 16.7; 9.10
elder (2) Mt 28.12; 11.27
enough [3] 6.42; 9.24
eyesight *see* **sight**
Father (2) (God) Mt 28.19; 11.25
forget [2] Mt 16.5; Lk 9.23
get away Mt 16.23; Lk 13.27
glory Mt 24.30; 10.37
godless Mt 16.4; 1 Tim 1.9
gospel Mt 26.13; 10.29
groan 7.34; Acts 7.34
holy 6.20; Lk 1.35
life (1) [4] 6.14; 9.43
life (2) (to life) Mt 27.52; 9.31
Messiah Mt 27.17; 12.35
mind (1) 6.52; 12.30
miracle [2] 6.2; 9.39
Pharisees [2] 7.1; 10.2
prophet 6.4; 11.32

prove 2.10; 16.20
rebuke [2] Mt 16.22; Lk 9.55
reject 7.9; 9.12
remember Mt 28.7; 11.21
rise Mt 27.53; 9.9
Satan 4.15; Lk 10.18
save [2] 3.4; 10.26
self Mt 16.24; Lk 9.23
sight Mt 21.42; 12.11
Son of Man [2] 2.10; 9.9
sorry 3.5; 2 Cor 7.7
suffer 5.25; 9.12
teach [2] 7.3; 9.31
teacher of the Law 7.1; 9.11
thank [2] 6.41; 14.22
trap Mt 22.15; 10.2
turn 6.12; 11.17
understand [2] 7.14; 9.32
warn 6.11; Lk 9.5
who Mt 16.15; Lk 9.20
wicked Mt 7.23; Lk 6.35
win Mt 23.15; Lk 9.25
world 4.31; 9.3
yeast Mt 16.6; Lk 12.1

home with the order, "Don't go back into the village."

Peter's Declaration about Jesus
(Matt. 16.13-20; Luke 9.18-21)

27 Then Jesus and his disciples went away to the villages near Caesarea Philippi. On the way he asked them, "Tell me, who do people say I am?"

28 "Some say that you are John the Baptist," they answered; "others say that you are Elijah, while others say that you are one of the prophets."

29 "What about you?" he asked them. "Who do you say I am?"

Peter answered, "You are the Messiah."

30 Then Jesus ordered them, "Do not tell anyone about me."

Jesus Speaks about His Suffering and Death
(Matt. 16.21-28; Luke 9.22-27)

31 Then Jesus began to teach his disciples: "The Son of Man must suffer much and be rejected by the elders, the chief priests, and the teachers of the Law. He will be put to death, but three days later he will rise to life." 32 He made this very clear to them. So Peter took him aside and began to rebuke him. 33 But Jesus turned round, looked at his disciples, and rebuked Peter. "Get away from me, Satan," he said. "Your thoughts don't come from God but from man!"

34 Then Jesus called the crowd and his disciples to him. "If anyone wants to come with me," he told them, "he must forget self, carry his cross, and follow me. 35 For whoever wants to save his own life will lose it; but whoever loses his life for me and for the gospel will save it. 36 Does a person gain anything if he wins the whole world but loses his life? Of course not! 37 There is nothing he can give to regain his life. 38 If a person is ashamed of me and of my teaching in this godless and wicked day, then the Son of Man will be ashamed of him when he comes in the glory of his Father with the holy angels."

9 And he went on to say, "I tell you, there are some here who will not die until they have seen the Kingdom of God come with power."

The Transfiguration
(Matt. 17.1-13; Luke 9.28-36)

2 Six days later Jesus took with him Peter, James, and John, and led them up a high mountain, where they were alone. As they looked on, a change came over Jesus, 3 and his clothes became shining white—whiter than anyone in the world could wash them. 4 Then the three disciples saw Elijah and Moses talking with Jesus. 5 Peter spoke up and said to Jesus, "Teacher, how good it is that we are here! We will make three tents, one for you, one for Moses, and one for Elijah." 6 He and the others were so frightened that he did not know what to say.

7 Then a cloud appeared and covered them with its shadow, and a voice came from the cloud, "This is my own dear Son—listen to him!" 8 They took a quick look round but did not see anyone else; only Jesus was with them.

9 As they came down the mountain, Jesus ordered them, "Don't tell anyone what you have seen, until the Son of Man has risen from death."

10 They obeyed his order, but among themselves they started discussing the matter, "What does this 'rising from death' mean?" 11 And they asked Jesus, "Why do the teachers of the Law say that Elijah has to come first?"

12 His answer was, "Elijah is indeed coming first in order to get everything ready. Yet why do the Scriptures say that the Son of Man will suffer much and be rejected? 13 I tell you, however, that Elijah has already come and that people treated him just as they pleased, as the Scriptures say about him."

Jesus Heals a Boy with an Evil Spirit
(Matt. 17.14-21; Luke 9.37-43a)

14 When they joined the rest of the disciples, they saw a large crowd round them and some teachers of the Law arguing with them. 15 When the people saw Jesus, they were greatly surprised, and ran to him and greeted him. 16 Jesus asked his disciples, "What are you arguing with them about?"

17 A man in the crowd answered, "Teacher, I brought my son to you, because he has an evil spirit in him and cannot talk. 18 Whenever the spirit attacks him, it throws him to the ground, and he foams at the mouth, grits his teeth, and becomes stiff all over. I asked your disciples to drive the spirit out, but they could not."

19 Jesus said to them, "How unbelieving you people are! How long must I stay with you? How long do I have to put up with you? Bring the boy to me!" 20 They brought him to Jesus.

As soon as the spirit saw Jesus, it

8.28: Mk 6.14-15; Lk 9.7-8 8.29: Jn 6.68-69 8.34: Mt 10.38; Lk 14.27 8.35: Mt 10.39; Lk 17.33; Jn 12.25
9.2-7: 2 Pet 1.17-18 9.7: Mt 3.17; Mk 1.11; Lk 3.22 9.11: Mal 4.5; Mt 11.14

afraid 6.20; 10.32
alone 7.33; 10.18
argue [4] 8.11; 11.31
assure 3.28; 10.15
bad Mt 25.26; Lk 6.43
change Mt 21.29; Lk 3.18
cloud [2] Mt 26.64; 13.26
command 7.8; Lk 1.6
dead 5.39; 11.20
dear 1.11; 12.6

death (2) (from death) [2] Mt 28.7; 12.18
demon 7.26; 16.9
disciple [9] 8.1; 10.10
discuss 8.16; 12.28
enough 8.4; 14.41
evil 7.21; Lk 3.19
faith [6] 6.6; 10.52
friend Mt 26.50; 16.9
fright 4.40; Acts 22.29
hell [3] Mt 23.15; Lk 10.15
help [3] 7.11; 14.7
Kingdom (1) (of God) [2] 4.11; 10.14
last (2) Mt 27.19; 10.31
life (1) [2] 8.35; 10.17
life (2) (to life) 8.31; 10.34
miracle 8.11; 13.22
name (2) (name of God, of Jesus) [3] Mt 28.19; 11.9
notice (1) 7.2; 10.14
obey 7.8; 10.20
one another 4.41; 10.26
peace 5.34; Lk 1.28
pity 6.34; 10.47
please 6.22; 14.11
power 6.14; 10.42
prayer Mt 26.26; 11.17
pure [2] Mt 5.8; 14.3
put out Mt 12.20; Jn 1.5
reject 8.31; 12.10
reward Mt 16.27; Lk 6.23
rise [4] 8.31; 10.34
sacrifice 1.44; 12.33
scripture [2] Mt 26.24; 10.6
servant Mt 26.69; 10.43
Son of God 5.7; 13.32
Son of Man [3] 8.31; 10.33
spirit (2) [9] 7.25; 14.38
suffer 8.31; 10.38
teach [2] 8.31; 10.1
teacher [3] 5.35; 10.17
teacher of the Law [2] 8.31; 10.33
unbeliever Mt 17.17; Lk 9.41
understand 8.17; 13.14
welcome [2] 6.10; Lk 4.24
world 8.36; 13.19

threw the boy into a fit, so that he fell on
the ground and rolled round, foaming at
the mouth. 21 "How long has he been like
this?" Jesus asked the father.
"Ever since he was a child," he replied. 22 "Many times the **evil spirit** has
tried to kill him by throwing him in the
fire and into water. Have **pity** on us and
help us, if you possibly can!"
23 "Yes," said Jesus, "if you yourself
can! Everything is possible for the person who has **faith**."
24 The father at once cried out, "I do
have **faith**, but not **enough**. **Help** me to
have more!"
25 Jesus **noticed** that the crowd was
closing in on them, so he gave a **command** to the **evil spirit**. "Deaf and dumb
spirit," he said, "I order you to come out
of the boy and never go into him again!"
26 The **spirit** screamed, threw the boy
into a **bad** fit, and came out. The boy
looked like a corpse, and everyone said,
"He is **dead**!" 27 But Jesus took the boy by
the hand and **helped** him to **rise**, and he
stood up.
28 After Jesus had gone indoors, his
disciples asked him privately, "Why
couldn't we drive the **spirit** out?"
29 "Only **prayer** can drive this kind
out," answered Jesus; "nothing else can."

Jesus Speaks Again about His Death
(Matt. 17.22–23; Luke 9.43b–45)

30 Jesus and his **disciples** left that
place and went on through Galilee. Jesus
did not want anyone to know where he
was, 31 because he was **teaching** his **disciples**: "The **Son of Man** will be handed
over to men who will kill him. Three
days later, however, he will **rise to life**."
32 But they did not **understand** what
this **teaching** meant, and they were
afraid to ask him.

Who Is the Greatest?
(Matt. 18.1–5; Luke 9.46–48)

33 They came to Capernaum, and
after going indoors Jesus asked his **disciples**, "What were you **arguing** about on
the road?"
34 But they would not answer him, because on the road they had been **arguing**
among themselves about who was the
greatest. 35 Jesus sat down, called the
twelve **disciples**, and said to them, "Whoever wants to be first must place himself
last of all and be the **servant** of all."
36 Then he took a child and made him
stand in front of them. He put his arms
round him and said to them, 37 "Whoever
welcomes in my name one of these children, **welcomes** me; and whoever **welcomes** me, **welcomes** not only me but
also the one who sent me."

Whoever Is Not against Us Is for Us
(Luke 9.49–50)

38 John said to him, "**Teacher**, we saw
a man who was driving out **demons in
your name**, and we told him to stop, because he doesn't belong to our group."
39 "Do not try to stop him," Jesus told
them, "because no one who performs a
miracle in my name will be able soon
afterwards to say **evil** things about me.
40 For whoever is not against us is for us.
41 I **assure** you that anyone who gives you
a drink of water because you belong to
me will certainly receive his **reward**.

Temptations to Sin
(Matt. 18.6–9; Luke 17.1–2)

42 "If anyone should cause one of
these little ones to lose his **faith** in me, it
would be better for that person to have a
large millstone tied round his neck and
be thrown into the sea. 43 So if your hand
makes you lose your **faith**, cut it off! It is
better for you to enter **life** without a hand
than to keep both hands and go off to
hell, to the fire that never goes out.[o]
45 And if your foot makes you lose your
faith, cut it off! It is better for you to enter **life** without a foot than to keep both
feet and be thrown into **hell**.[p] 47 And if
your eye makes you lose your **faith**, take
it out! It is better for you to enter the
Kingdom of God with only one eye than
to keep both eyes and be thrown into
hell. 48 There 'the worms that eat them
never die, and the fire that burns them is
never **put out**.'
49 "Everyone will be **purified** by fire
as a **sacrifice** is **purified** by salt.
50 "Salt is good; but if it loses its saltiness, how can you make it salty again?
"Have the salt of **friendship** among
yourselves, and live in **peace** with **one
another**."

Jesus Teaches about Divorce
(Matt. 19.1–12; Luke 16.18)

10 Then Jesus left that place, went
to the province of Judaea, and

accuse 3.2; 14.60
adultery [3] 7.22; Lk 16.18

[o] *Some manuscripts add verse 44:* There 'the worms that eat them never die, and the fire that burns them is never put out' *(see verse 48).*
[p] *Some manuscripts add verse 46:* There 'the worms that eat them never die, and the fire that burns them is never put out' *(see verse 48).*

9.34: Lk 22.24 **9.35:** Mt 20.26–27, 23.11; Mk 10.43–44; Lk 22.26 **9.37:** Mt 10.40; Lk 10.16; Jn 13.20
9.40: Mt 12.30; Lk 11.23 **9.41:** Mt 10.42 **9.43:** Mt 5.30 **9.47:** Mt 5.29 **9.48:** Is 66.24
9.50: Mt 5.13; Lk 14.34–35

crossed the River Jordan. Crowds came flocking to him again, and he taught them, as he always did.

2 Some Pharisees came to him and tried to trap him. "Tell us," they asked, "does our Law allow a man to divorce his wife?"

3 Jesus answered with a question, "What law did Moses give you?"

4 Their answer was, "Moses gave permission for a man to write a divorce notice and send his wife away."

5 Jesus said to them, "Moses wrote this law for you because you are so hard to teach. 6 But in the beginning, at the time of creation, 'God made them male and female,' as the scripture says. 7 'And for this reason a man will leave his father and mother and unite with his wife,[q] 8 and the two will become one.' So they are no longer two, but one. 9 Man must not separate, then, what God has joined together."

10 When they went back into the house, the disciples asked Jesus about this matter. 11 He said to them, "A man who divorces his wife and marries another woman commits adultery against his wife. 12 In the same way, a woman who divorces her husband and marries another man commits adultery."

Jesus Blesses Little Children
(Matt. 19.13–15; Luke 18.15–17)

13 Some people brought children to Jesus for him to place his hands on them, but the disciples scolded the people. 14 When Jesus noticed this, he was angry and said to his disciples, "Let the children come to me, and do not stop them, because the Kingdom of God belongs to such as these. 15 I assure you that whoever does not receive the Kingdom of God like a child will never enter it." 16 Then he took the children in his arms, placed his hands on each of them, and blessed them.

The Rich Man
(Matt. 19.16–30; Luke 18.18–30)

17 As Jesus was starting on his way again, a man ran up, knelt before him, and asked him, "Good Teacher, what must I do to receive eternal life?"

18 "Why do you call me good?" Jesus asked him. "No one is good except God alone. 19 You know the commandments: 'Do not commit murder; do not commit adultery; do not steal; do not accuse anyone falsely; do not cheat; respect your father and your mother.'"

20 "Teacher," the man said, "ever since I was young, I have obeyed all these commandments."

21 Jesus looked straight at him with love and said, "You need only one thing. Go and sell all you have and give the money to the poor, and you will have riches in heaven; then come and follow me." 22 When the man heard this, gloom spread over his face, and he went away sad, because he was very rich.

23 Jesus looked round at his disciples and said to them, "How hard it will be for rich people to enter the Kingdom of God!"

24 The disciples were shocked at these words, but Jesus went on to say, "My children, how hard it is to enter the Kingdom of God! 25 It is much harder for a rich person to enter the Kingdom of God than for a camel to go through the eye of a needle."

26 At this the disciples were completely amazed and asked one another, "Who, then, can be saved?"

27 Jesus looked straight at them and answered, "This is impossible for man, but not for God; everything is possible for God."

28 Then Peter spoke up, "Look, we have left everything and followed you."

29 "Yes," Jesus said to them, "and I tell you that anyone who leaves home or brothers or sisters or mother or father or children or fields for me and for the gospel, 30 will receive much more in this present age. He will receive a hundred times more houses, brothers, sisters, mothers, children and fields—and persecutions as well; and in the age to come he will receive eternal life. 31 But many who now are first will be last, and many who now are last will be first."

Jesus Speaks a Third Time about His Death
(Matt. 20.17–19; Luke 18.31–34)

32 Jesus and his disciples were now on the road going up to Jerusalem. Jesus was going ahead of the disciples, who were filled with alarm; the people who followed behind were afraid. Once again Jesus took the twelve disciples aside and spoke of the things that were going to happen to him. 33 "Listen," he told them, "we are going up to Jerusalem where the Son of Man will be handed over to the chief priests and the teachers of the Law.

[q] *Some manuscripts do not have* and unite with his wife.

10.4: Deut 24.1–4; Mt 5.31 **10.6:** Gen 1.27, 5.2 **10.7–8:** Gen 2.24 **10.11–12:** Mt 5.32; 1 Cor 7.10–11 **10.15:** Mt 18.3 **10.19:** Ex 20.12–16; Deut 5.16–20 **10.31:** Mt 20.16; Lk 13.30

They will **condemn** him to death and
then hand him over to the **Gentiles**,
34 who will **mock** him, spit on him, whip
him, and kill him; but three days later he
will **rise to life**."

The Request of James and John
(Matt. 20.20–28)

35 Then James and John, the sons of
Zebedee, came to Jesus. "**Teacher**," they
said, "there is something we want you to
do for us."
36 "What is it?" Jesus asked them.
37 They answered, "When you sit on
your **throne** in your **glorious Kingdom**,
we want you to let us sit with you, one at
your **right** and one at your left."
38 Jesus said to them, "You don't
know what you are asking for. Can you
drink the **cup of suffering** that I must
drink? Can you be **baptized** in the way I
must be baptized?"
39 "We can," they answered.
Jesus said to them, "You will indeed
drink the **cup** I must drink and be **baptized** in the way I must be baptized. 40 But
I do not have the **right** to **choose** who will
sit at my **right** and my left. It is God who
will give these places to those for whom
he has prepared them."
41 When the other ten **disciples** heard
about it, they became **angry** with James
and John. 42 So Jesus called them all together to him and said, "You know that
the men who are **considered** rulers of the
heathen have **power** over them, and the
leaders have **complete authority**. 43 This,
however, is not the way it is among you.
If one of you wants to be great, he must
be the **servant** of the rest; 44 and if one of
you wants to be first, he must be the
slave of all. 45 For even the **Son of Man**
did not come to be **served**; he came to
serve and to give his **life** to **redeem** many
people."

Jesus Heals Blind Bartimaeus
(Matt. 20.29–34; Luke 18.35–43)

46 They came to Jericho, and as Jesus
was leaving with his **disciples** and a large
crowd, a **blind** beggar named Bartimaeus
son of Timaeus was sitting by the road.
47 When he heard that it was Jesus of
Nazareth, he began to shout, "Jesus! **Son
of David**! Take **pity** on me!"
48 Many of the people scolded him
and told him to be quiet. But he shouted
even more loudly, "**Son of David**, take
pity on me!"
49 Jesus stopped and said, "Call him."
So they called the **blind** man. "**Cheer**
up!" they said. "Get up, he is calling
you."
50 He threw off his cloak, jumped up,
and came to Jesus.
51 "What do you want me to do for
you?" Jesus asked him.
"**Teacher**," the **blind** man answered, "I
want to see again."
52 "Go," Jesus told him, "your **faith**
has made you well."
At once he was able to see and followed Jesus on the road.

The Triumphant Entry into Jerusalem
(Matt. 21.1–11; Luke 19.28–40;
John 12.12–19)

11 As they approached Jerusalem,
near the towns of Bethphage and
Bethany, they came to the Mount of
Olives. Jesus sent two of his **disciples** on
ahead 2 with these instructions: "Go to
the village there **ahead of you**. As soon as
you get there, you will find a colt tied up
that has never been ridden. Untie it and
bring it here. 3 And if someone asks you
why you are doing that, tell him that the
Master[r] **needs** it and will send it back at
once."
4 So they went and found a colt out in
the street, tied to the door of a house. As
they were untying it, 5 some of the bystanders asked them, "What are you doing, untying that colt?"
6 They answered just as Jesus had told
them, and the men let them go. 7 They
brought the colt to Jesus, threw their
cloaks over the animal, and Jesus got on.
8 Many people spread their cloaks on the
road, while others cut branches in the
fields and spread them on the road. 9 The
people who were in front and those who
followed behind began to shout, "**Praise
God**! God **bless** him who comes **in the
name of** the Lord! 10 God **bless** the
coming **kingdom** of King David, our
father! **Praise** God!"
11 Jesus entered Jerusalem, went into
the **Temple**, and looked round at everything. But since it was already late in the
day, he went out to Bethany with the
twelve **disciples**.

Jesus Curses the Fig-Tree
(Matt. 21.18–19)

12 The next day, as they were coming
back from Bethany, Jesus was **hungry**.
13 He saw in the distance a fig-tree
covered with leaves, so he went to see if
he could find any figs on it. But when he
came to it, he found only leaves, because
it was not the **right** time for figs. 14 Jesus

[r] the Master; *or* its owner.
10.38: Lk 12.50 **10.42–43:** Lk 22.25–26 **10.43–44:** Mt 23.11; Mk 9.35; Lk 22.26 **11.9:** Ps 118.25–26

said to the fig-tree, "No one shall ever
eat figs from you again!"
And his disciples heard him.

Jesus Goes to the Temple
(Matt. 21.12–17; Luke 19.45–48;
John 2.13–22)

15 When they arrived in Jerusalem,
Jesus went to the Temple and began to
drive out all those who were buying and
selling. He overturned the tables of the
money-changers and the stools of those
who sold pigeons, 16 and he would not let
anyone carry anything through the
temple courtyards. 17 He then taught the
people: "It is written in the Scriptures
that God said, 'My Temple will be called
a house of prayer for the people of all
nations.' But you have turned it into a
hideout for thieves!"
18 The chief priests and the teachers
of the Law heard of this, so they began
looking for some way to kill Jesus. They
were afraid of him, because the whole
crowd was amazed at his teaching.
19 When evening came, Jesus and his
disciples left the city.

The Lesson from the Fig-Tree
(Matt. 21.20–22)

20 Early next morning, as they walked
along the road, they saw the fig-tree. It
was dead all the way down to its roots.
21 Peter remembered what had happened
and said to Jesus, "Look, Teacher, the
fig-tree you cursed has died!"
22 Jesus answered them, "Have faith
in God. 23 I assure you that whoever tells
this hill to get up and throw itself in the
sea and does not doubt in his heart, but
believes that what he says will happen, it
will be done for him. 24 For this reason I
tell you: When you pray and ask for
something, believe that you have received it, and you will be given whatever
you ask for. 25 And when you stand and
pray, forgive anything you may have
against anyone, so that your Father in
heaven will forgive the wrongs you have
done."[s]

The Question about Jesus' Authority
(Matt. 21.23–27; Luke 20.1–8)

27 They arrived once again in Jerusalem. As Jesus was walking in the
Temple, the chief priests, the teachers of
the Law, and the elders came to him
28 and asked him, "What right have you to
do these things? Who gave you this
right?"
29 Jesus answered them, "I will ask
you just one question, and if you give me
an answer, I will tell you what right I
have to do these things. 30 Tell me, where
did John's right to baptize come from:
was it from God or from man?"
31 They started to argue among themselves: "What shall we say? If we
answer, 'From God,' he will say, 'Why,
then, did you not believe John?' 32 But if
we say, 'From man...'" (They were
afraid of the people, because everyone
was convinced that John had been a prophet.) 33 So their answer to Jesus was,
"We don't know."
Jesus said to them, "Neither will I tell
you, then, by what right I do these
things."

The Parable of the Tenants in the Vineyard
(Matt. 21.33–46; Luke 20.9–19)

12 Then Jesus spoke to them in
parables: "Once there was a
man who planted a vineyard, put a fence
round it, dug a hole for the winepress,
and built a watch-tower. Then he let out
the vineyard to tenants and left home on
a journey. 2 When the time came to
gather the grapes, he sent a slave to the
tenants to receive from them his share of
the harvest. 3 The tenants seized the
slave, beat him, and sent him back
without a thing. 4 Then the owner sent
another slave; the tenants beat him over
the head and treated him shamefully.
5 The owner sent another slave, and they
killed him; and they treated many others
the same way, beating some and killing
others. 6 The only one left to send was the
man's own dear son. Last of all, then, he
sent his son to the tenants. 'I am sure
they will respect my son,' he said. 7 But
those tenants said to one another, 'This is
the owner's son. Come on, let's kill him,
and his property will be ours!' 8 So they
seized the son and killed him and threw
his body out of the vineyard.
9 "What, then, will the owner of the
vineyard do?" asked Jesus. "He will
come and kill those men and hand the
vineyard over to other tenants. 10 Surely
you have read this scripture?
'The stone which the builders rejected
as worthless
turned out to be the most important
of all.
11 This was done by the Lord;
what a wonderful sight it is!'"

advantage Mal 3.5; Lk 20.47
afraid 11.18; 16.8
amaze 11.18; 15.5
angel 8.38; 13.27
arrest 6.17; 13.9
best Mt 23.6; Lk 1.1
body 7.19; 14.8
choose 10.40; 13.20
commandment [4] 10.19; Lk 18.20
consider 10.42; Lk 7.7
dare 2.7; Lk 20.40
dead [5] 11.20; 15.44
dear 9.7; Lk 1.1
death (2) (from death) 9.9; 16.9
disciple 11.1; 13.1
discuss 9.10; Lk 6.11
enemy Mt 22.44; Lk 1.71
feast 6.21; Lk 5.29
glad 4.16; Lk 1.14
harvest 4.29; Lk 10.2
heart [2] 11.23; 14.34
heaven 11.25; 13.25
I am Mt 22.32; Jn 5.45
important [6] Mt 25.40; Lk 12.23
inspire Mt 22.43; 1 Cor 13.2
Jew 7.3; 15.2
Kingdom (1) (of God) 11.10; 14.25
last (2) [2] 10.31; 16.14
law [2] 10.2; Lk 1.6
life (2) (to life) [2] 10.34; 14.28
love [4] 10.21; Lk 6.27
Messiah [2] 8.29; 13.21
mind (1) [2] 8.17; Lk 8.35
neighbour [2] Mt 22.39; Lk 1.58
notice (1) 10.14; Lk 11.38
obey 10.20; Lk 1.6
offer 2.26; Lk 2.24
one another 10.26; 13.8
parable [2] 4.2; Lk 5.36

[s] *Some manuscripts add verse 26:* If you do not forgive others, your Father in heaven will not forgive the wrongs you have done *(see Mt 6.15).*

11.17: Is 56.7; Jer 7.11 **11.23:** Mt 17.20; 1 Cor 13.2 **11.25-26:** Mt 6.14–15 **12.1:** Is 5.1–2
12.10-11: Ps 118.22–23

12 The Jewish leaders tried to arrest
Jesus, because they knew that he had
told this parable against them. But they
were afraid of the crowd, so they left him
and went away.

The Question about Paying Taxes
(Matt. 22.15–22; Luke 20.20–26)

13 Some Pharisees and some members of Herod's party were sent to Jesus
to trap him with questions. 14 They came
to him and said, "Teacher, we know that
you tell the truth, without worrying about
what people think. You pay no attention
to a man's status, but teach the truth
about God's will for man. Tell us, is it
against our Law to pay taxes to the
Roman Emperor? Should we pay them
or not?"
15 But Jesus saw through their trick
and answered, "Why are you trying to
trap me? Bring a silver coin, and let me
see it."
16 They brought him one, and he
asked, "Whose face and name are
these?"
"The Emperor's," they answered.
17 So Jesus said, "Well, then, pay the
Emperor what belongs to the Emperor,
and pay God what belongs to God."
And they were amazed at Jesus.

The Question about Rising from Death
(Matt. 22.23–33; Luke 20.27–40)

18 Then some Sadducees, who say that
people will not rise from death, came to
Jesus and said, 19 "Teacher, Moses wrote
this law for us: 'If a man dies and leaves
a wife but no children, that man's
brother must marry the widow so that
they can have children who will be considered the dead man's children.' 20 Once
there were seven brothers; the eldest got
married and died without having children. 21 Then the second one married the
woman, and he also died without having
children. The same thing happened to
the third brother, 22 and then to the rest:
all seven brothers married the woman
and died without having children. Last of
all, the woman died. 23 Now, when all the
dead rise to life on the day of resurrection, whose wife will she be? All seven of
them had married her."
24 Jesus answered them, "How wrong
you are! And do you know why? It is because you don't know the Scriptures or
God's power. 25 For when the dead rise to
life, they will be like the angels in heaven
and will not marry. 26 Now, as for the
dead being raised: haven't you ever read
in the Book of Moses the passage about
the burning bush? There it is written
that God said to Moses, 'I am the God of
Abraham, the God of Isaac, and the God
of Jacob.' 27 He is the God of the living,
not of the dead. You are completely
wrong!"

The Great Commandment
(Matt. 22.34–40; Luke 10.25–28)

28 A teacher of the Law was there
who heard the discussion. He saw that
Jesus had given the Sadducees a good answer, so he came to him with a question:
"Which commandment is the most
important of all?"
29 Jesus replied, "The most important
one is this: 'Listen, Israel! The Lord our
God is the only Lord.[t] 30 Love the Lord
your God with all your heart, with all
your soul, with all your mind, and with all
your strength.' 31 The second most important commandment is this: 'Love
your neighbour as you love yourself.'
There is no other commandment more
important than these two."
32 The teacher of the Law said to
Jesus, "Well done, Teacher! It is true, as
you say, that only the Lord is God and
that there is no other god but he. 33 And
man must love God with all his heart and
with all his mind and with all his
strength; and he must love his neighbour
as he loves himself. It is more important
to obey these two commandments than
to offer animals and other sacrifices to
God."
34 Jesus noticed how wise his answer
was, and so he told him, "You are not far
from the Kingdom of God."
After this nobody dared to ask Jesus
any more questions.

The Question about the Messiah
(Matt. 22.41–46; Luke 20.41–44)

35 As Jesus was teaching in the
Temple, he asked the question, "How can
the teachers of the Law say that the
Messiah will be the descendant of
David? 36 The Holy Spirit inspired David
to say:
'The Lord said to my Lord:
Sit here on my right
until I put your enemies under your
feet.'
37 David himself called him 'Lord'; so
how can the Messiah be David's descendant?"

[t] The Lord our God is the only Lord; *or* The Lord is our God, the Lord alone.

12.18: Acts 23.8 **12.19:** Deut 25.5 **12.26:** Ex 3.6 **12.28–34:** Lk 10.25–28 **12.29–30:** Deut 6.4–5
12.31: Lev 19.18 **12.32:** Deut 4.35 **12.33:** Hos 6.6 **12.36:** Ps 110.1

Pharisees 10.2; Lk 5.17
poor [3] 10.21; 14.5
power 10.42; 13.25
prayer 11.17; 14.22
punish 5.7; 14.71
question [4] 11.29; 14.60
raise Mt 28.6; 14.28
reject 9.12; Lk 6.22
respect [2] 10.19; 15.42
resurrection Jn 11.25
rich 10.22; Lk 1.53
riches 10.21; Lk 8.14
right (2) 10.37; 14.62
rise [3] 10.34; 16.9
rob 7.21; Lk 10.30
sacrifice 9.49; Lk 2.24
Sadducees [2] Mt 22.23; Lk 20.27
scripture [2] 11.17; 14.21
shame Zeph 3.19; Lk 20.11
share Mt 25.21; Lk 3.11
sight 8.25; Lk 1.6
slave [4] 10.44; 14.47
soul Mt 22.37; Lk 1.47
spare Jon 1.6; Lk 21.4
Spirit (1) (God's Spirit) 3.29; 13.11
strength [2] Zech 12.5; Lk 10.27
sure Mt 24.15; 13.14
synagogue 6.2; 13.9
tax Mt 22.17; Lk 20.22
teach [3] 11.17; 13.28
teacher [3] 11.21; 13.1
teacher of the Law [4] 11.18; 14.1
Temple (1) (of God) [2] 11.11; 13.1
trap [2] 10.2; Lk 10.25
trick Mt 2.16; Lk 20.23
true Mt 27.9; 14.49
truth [2] 5.33; 14.71
turn 11.17; 13.12
vineyard [5] Mt 21.28; Lk 13.6
watch [3] 3.2; 13.33
widow [4] Mt 22.24; Lk 2.36
will (1) Mt 26.42; Lk 2.32
wise Mt 25.2; Lk 10.21
wonder (1) Mt 24.24; 13.1
worry 4.19; 13.11
worse 5.26; 13.19
worth Mt 17.27; Lk 12.7
worthless Mt 21.42; Lk 16.15
wrong [2] 11.25; Lk 6.7

Jesus Warns against the Teachers of the Law

(Matt. 23.1–36; Luke 20.45–47)

A large crowd was listening to Jesus **gladly**. 38 As he **taught** them, he said, "**Watch** out for the **teachers of the Law**, who like to walk around in their long robes and be greeted with **respect** in the market-place, 39 who **choose** the reserved seats in the **synagogues** and the **best places** at **feasts**. 40 They take **advantage** of **widows** and **rob** them of their homes, and then make a show of saying long **prayers**. Their **punishment** will be all the **worse**!"

The Widow's Offering

(Luke 21.1–4)

41 As Jesus sat near the **temple** treasury, he **watched** the people as they dropped in their money. Many **rich** men dropped in a lot of money; 42 then a **poor widow** came along and dropped in two little copper coins, **worth** about a penny. 43 He called his **disciples** together and said to them, "I tell you that this **poor widow** put more in the offering box than all the others. 44 For the others put in what they had to **spare** of their **riches**; but she, **poor** as she is, put in all she had—she gave all she had to live on."

Jesus Speaks of the Destruction of the Temple

(Matt. 24.1–2; Luke 21.5–6)

13 As Jesus was leaving the **Temple**, one of his **disciples** said, "Look, **Teacher**! What **wonderful** stones and buildings!"

2 Jesus answered, "You see these great buildings? Not a single stone here will be left in its place; every one of them will be thrown down."

Troubles and Persecutions

(Matt. 24.3–14; Luke 21.7–19)

3 Jesus was sitting on the Mount of Olives, across from the **Temple**, when Peter, James, John, and Andrew came to him in private. 4 "Tell us when this will be," they said, "and tell us what will happen to show that the time has come for all these things to take place."

5 Jesus said to them, "Be on guard, and don't let anyone **deceive** you. 6 Many men, **claiming** to speak for me, will come and say, 'I am he!' and they will **deceive** many people. 7 And don't be **troubled** when you hear the noise of battles close by and news of battles far away. Such things must happen, but they do not mean that the end has come. 8 Countries will fight **each other**; kingdoms will attack **one another**. There will be earthquakes everywhere, and there will be **famines**. These things are like the first **pains** of childbirth.

9 "You yourselves must be on guard. You will be **arrested** and taken to **court**. You will be beaten in the **synagogues**; you will stand before rulers and kings for my **sake** to tell them the **Good News**. 10 But before the end comes, the **gospel** must be **preached** to all peoples. 11 And when you are **arrested** and taken to **court**, do not **worry** beforehand about what you are going to say; when the time comes, say whatever is then given to you. For the **words** you speak will not be yours; they will come from the **Holy Spirit**. 12 Men will hand over their own brothers to be put **to death**, and fathers will do the same to their children. Children will **turn** against their parents and have them put **to death**. 13 Everyone will **hate** you because of me. But whoever holds out to the end will be **saved**.

The Awful Horror

(Matt. 24.15–28; Luke 21.20–24)

14 "You will see '**The Awful Horror**' standing in the place where he should not be." (Note to the reader: be **sure** to **understand** what this means!) "Then those who are in Judaea must run away to the hills. 15 A man who is on the roof of his house must not lose time by going down into the house to get anything to take with him. 16 A man who is in the field must not go back to the house for his cloak. 17 How **terrible** it will be in those days for women who are pregnant and for mothers with little babies! 18 **Pray** to God that these things will not happen in the winter! 19 For the **trouble** of those days will be far **worse** than any the **world** has ever known from the very beginning when God **created** the **world** until the present time. Nor will there ever be anything like it again. 20 But the Lord has reduced the number of those days; if he had not, nobody would survive. For the **sake** of his **chosen people**, however, he has reduced those days.

21 "Then, if anyone says to you, 'Look, here is the **Messiah**!' or, 'Look, there he is!'—do not **believe** him. 22 For false **Messiahs** and **false prophets** will appear. They will perform **miracles** and **wonders** in order to **deceive** even God's **chosen people**, if possible. 23 Be on your guard! I

13.9–11: Mt 10.17–20; Lk 12.11–12 **13.13:** Mt 10.22 **13.14:** Dan 9.27, 11.31, 12.11 **13.15–16:** Lk 17.31 **13.19:** Dan 12.1; Rev 7.14

alert Dan 4.13; Lk 21.36
angel [2] 12.25; Lk 1.11
arrest [2] 12.12; 14.1
Awful Horror Mt 24.15
believe 11.23; 15.32
choose [3] 12.39; Lk 1.9
claim Mt 27.43; Lk 21.8
cloud 9.7; 14.62
court (1) [2] Mt 10.17; Lk 8.3
create 10.6; Lk 11.50
dark Mt 27.45; 15.33
death (3) (to death) [2] 8.31; 14.1
deceive [3] 7.22; Lk 21.8
disciple 12.43; 14.10
each other 3.24; 15.31
false 10.19; Lk 3.14
famine Mt 24.7; Lk 4.25
Father (2) (God) 11.25; 14.36
glory 10.37; Lk 2.9
God's people [3] Mt 27.52; Lk 1.68
Good News 1.1; Lk 1.19
gospel 10.29; 14.9
hate Mt 24.9; Lk 1.71
heaven [3] 12.25; 14.62
lesson Mt 24.32; Heb 5.12
master 11.3; Lk 5.5
Messiah [2] 12.35; 14.61
miracle 9.39; 16.17
one another 12.7; 14.4
pain Mt 24.8; Lk 16.23
power [2] 12.24; 14.41
pray 11.24; 14.32
preach 6.12; 14.9
prophet 11.32; Lk 1.17
remember 11.21; 14.72
sake [2] 5.7; Lk 9.24
save 10.26; 15.30
servant 10.43; 14.66
Son of God 9.7; 14.61
Son of Man 10.33; 14.21
Spirit (1) (God's Spirit) 12.36; Lk 1.15
sure 12.6; Lk 4.23
synagogue 12.39; Lk 4.15
teach 12.14; 14.49
teacher 12.14; 14.14
Temple (1) (of God) [2] 12.35; 14.49
terrible 5.25; 14.21
trouble [3] 7.35; Lk 1.29
turn 12.10; Lk 1.8
understand 9.32; 14.68
watch [3] 12.1; 14.34
wonder (1) [2] 12.11; Lk 1.58
word (1) [2] 10.24; 14.39
world [3] 9.3; 14.9
worry 12.14; Lk 2.48
worse 12.40; Lk 3.20

have told you everything before the time comes.

The Coming of the Son of Man
(Matt. 24.29–31; Luke 21.25–28)

24 "In the days after that time of **trouble** the sun will grow **dark**, the moon will no longer shine, 25 the stars will fall from **heaven**, and the **powers in space** will be driven from their courses. 26 Then the **Son of Man** will appear, coming in the **clouds** with great **power** and **glory**. 27 He will send the **angels** out to the four corners of the earth to gather God's **chosen people** from one end of the **world** to the other.

The Lesson of the Fig-Tree
(Matt. 24.32–35; Luke 21.29–33)

28 "Let the fig-tree **teach** you a **lesson**. When its branches become green and tender and it starts putting out leaves, you know that summer is near. 29 In the same way, when you see these things happening, you will know that the time is near, ready to begin.[u] 30 **Remember** that all these things will happen before the people now living have all died. 31 **Heaven and earth** will pass away, but my **words** will never pass away.

No One Knows the Day or Hour
(Matt. 24.36–44)

32 "No one knows, however, when that day or hour will come—neither the **angels** in **heaven**, nor the **Son**; only the **Father** knows. 33 Be on **watch**, be **alert**, for you do not know when the time will come. 34 It will be like a man who goes away from home on a journey and leaves his **servants** in charge, after giving to each one his own work to do and after telling the doorkeeper to keep **watch**. 35 Be on guard, then, because you do not know when the **master** of the house is coming—it might be in the evening or at midnight or before dawn or at sunrise. 36 If he comes suddenly, he must not find you asleep. 37 What I say to you, then, I say to all: **Watch**!"

The Plot against Jesus
(Matt. 26.1–5; Luke 22.1–2; John 11.45–53)

14 It was now two days before the **Festival** of **Passover** and **Unleavened Bread**. The **chief priests** and the **teachers of the Law** were looking for a way to **arrest** Jesus **secretly** and put him **to death**. 2 "We must not do it during the **festival**," they said, "or the people might riot."

Jesus Is Anointed at Bethany
(Matt. 26.6–13; John 12.1–8)

3 Jesus was in Bethany at the house of Simon, a man who had **suffered** from a dreaded **skin-disease**. While Jesus was eating, a woman came in with an alabaster jar full of a very expensive perfume made of **pure** nard. She broke the jar and poured the perfume on Jesus' head. 4 Some of the people there became **angry** and said to **one another**, "What was the use of wasting the perfume? 5 It could have been sold for more than three hundred silver coins[v] and the money given to the **poor**!" And they **criticized** her harshly.

6 But Jesus said, "Leave her **alone**! Why are you bothering her? She has done a fine and beautiful thing for me. 7 You will always have **poor** people with you, and any time you want to, you can **help** them. But you will not always have me. 8 She did what she could; she poured perfume on my **body** to prepare it ahead of time for burial. 9 Now, I **assure** you that wherever the **gospel** is **preached** all over the **world**, what she has done will be told in memory of her."

Judas Agrees to Betray Jesus
(Matt. 26.14–16; Luke 22.3–6)

10 Then Judas Iscariot, one of the twelve **disciples**, went off to the **chief priests** in order to **betray** Jesus to them. 11 They were **pleased** to hear what he had to say, and **promised** to give him money. So Judas started looking for a good chance to hand Jesus over to them.

Jesus Eats the Passover Meal with His Disciples
(Matt. 26.17–25; Luke 22.7–14, 21–23; John 13.21–30)

12 On the first day of the **Festival** of **Unleavened Bread**, the day the **lambs** for the **Passover** meal were killed, Jesus' **disciples** asked him, "Where do you want us to go and get the **Passover** meal ready for you?"

13 Then Jesus sent two of them with these instructions: "Go into the city, and a man carrying a jar of water will meet you. Follow him 14 to the house he enters, and say to the owner of the house: 'The **Teacher** says, Where is the room where my **disciples** and I will eat the **Passover** meal?' 15 Then he will show you a large

[u] the time is near, ready to begin; *or* he is near, ready to come. [v] SILVER COINS: *See 6.37.*

13.24: Is 13.10; Ezek 32.7; Joel 2.10, 31, 3.15; Rev 6.12 **13.25:** Is 34.4; Joel 2.10; Rev 6.13
13.26: Dan 7.13; Rev 1.7 **13.32:** Mt 24.36 **13.34:** Lk 12.36–38 **14.1:** Ex 12.1–27 **14.3:** Lk 7.37–38
14.7: Deut 15.11

accuse [2] 10.19; 15.3
agree [2] Mt 27.7; Lk 22.6
ahead of you 11.2; 16.7
Almighty Mt 26.64; Lk 22.69
alone 10.18; Lk 4.4
anger 10.14; Lk 4.28

anguish Mt 26.37; Lk 22.44
arrest [5] 13.9; Lk 20.19
assure 11.23; Lk 2.26
betray [4] 3.19; Lk 22.4
blasphemy 2.7; Lk 5.21
bless 11.9; Lk 1.28
blood [2] Mt 27.6; Lk 22.20
body [2] 12.8; 15.42
bread [2] 8.5; Lk 4.3
chief priests [5] 11.18; 15.1
cloud 13.26; Lk 9.34
Council Mt 26.59; 15.1
covenant Mt 26.28; Lk 1.72
criticize Ecc 10.20; Lk 11.53
cup [2] 10.38; Lk 11.39
death (3) (to death) [3] 13.12; Lk 9.22
deny [3] Mt 26.70; Lk 8.45
disciple [13] 13.1; 16.7
disease 1.34; Lk 4.27
distress Zeph 1.15; 16.8
elder (2) [2] 11.27; 15.1
enough 9.24; Lk 3.16
evidence Mt 26.59; Acts 14.17
Father (2) (God) 13.32; Lk 2.49
festival [3] Mt 27.15; 15.6
flesh Mt 26.41; Lk 24.39
gospel 13.10; 16.15
guilty Mt 26.66; Lk 23.14
heart 12.30; Lk 1.46
heaven 13.25; 16.19
help 9.22; 15.41
High Priest [7] 2.26; Lk 3.2
hymn Mt 26.30; Acts 16.25
Kingdom (1) (of God) 12.34; 15.42
kiss [2] Mt 26.48; Lk 7.38
lamb Amos 6.4; Lk 10.3
lie (2) Mt 27.63; Jn 8.44
life (2) (to life) 12.23; Lk 7.22
Messiah 13.21; 15.32
naked Mt 25.36; Rev 3.17
need 11.3; Lk 5.31
new 2.21; Lk 5.36
one another 13.8; 16.3
Passover [5] Mt 27.15; 15.6
please 9.13; 15.15
poor [2] 12.42; Lk 4.18
power 13.25; 16.17
pray [5] 13.18; Lk 1.10
prayer 12.40; Lk 1.13
preach 13.10; 16.15
promise Mt 20.21; Lk 1.20
punish 12.40; Lk 3.7
pure 9.49; Lk 2.22
question [2] 12.13; 15.2

raise 12.26; 16.6
remember 13.30; Lk 1.36
rest (1) 6.31; Lk 9.58
right (2) 12.36; 15.27
scatter 4.4; Lk 1.51
scripture [3] 12.10; Lk 4.4
seal Mt 27.66; Lk 22.20
secret 4.11; Lk 2.35
servant [2] 13.34; Lk 1.38
sheep 6.34; Lk 15.4
shepherd 6.34; Lk 2.8
slave 12.2; Lk 7.8
Son of God 13.32; 15.39
Son of Man [4] 13.26; Lk 5.24
sorrow Mt 26.38; Lk 2.35
spirit (2) 9.17; Lk 1.80
strike Mt 26.51; Lk 22.50
strong 5.4; Lk 1.15
suffer [3] 10.38; Lk 4.27
swear 6.23; Jas 5.12
teach 13.28; Lk 1.4
teacher [2] 13.1; Lk 2.46
teacher of the Law [3] 12.28; 15.1
Temple (1) (of God) [2] 13.1; 15.29
tempt 1.13; Lk 4.2
terrible 13.17; Lk 2.9
thank [2] 8.6; Lk 2.28
traitor Mt 27.3; Lk 6.16
true 12.32; 16.20
truth 12.14; Lk 1.4
understand 13.14; Lk 2.50
unleavened [2] Mt 26.17; Lk 22.1
upset Mt 26.22; Lk 10.40
watch [2] 13.33; 15.47
weak Mt 26.41; Acts 20.35
witness [2] Mt 26.65; Lk 22.71
word (1) [2] 13.11; 15.5
world 13.19; 16.15

upstairs room, prepared and furnished, where you will get everything ready for us."

16 The **disciples** left, went to the city, and found everything just as Jesus had told them; and they prepared the **Passover** meal.

17 When it was evening, Jesus came with the twelve **disciples**. 18 While they were at the table eating, Jesus said, "I tell you that one of you will **betray** me—one who is eating with me."

19 The **disciples** were **upset** and began to ask him, one after the other, "Surely you don't mean me, do you?"

20 Jesus answered, "It will be one of you twelve, one who dips his **bread** in the dish with me. 21 The **Son of Man** will die as the **Scriptures** say he will; but how **terrible** for that man who **betrays** the **Son of Man**! It would have been better for that man if he had never been born!"

The Lord's Supper

(Matt. 26.26–30; Luke 22.14–20; 1 Cor. 11.23–25)

22 While they were eating, Jesus took a piece of **bread**, gave a **prayer** of **thanks**, broke it, and gave it to his **disciples**. "Take it," he said, "this is my **body**."

23 Then he took a **cup**, gave **thanks** to God, and handed it to them; and they all drank from it. 24 Jesus said, "This is my **blood** which is poured out for many, my **blood** which **seals** God's **covenant**. 25 I tell you, I will never again drink this wine until the day I drink the **new** wine in the **Kingdom of God**."

26 Then they sang a **hymn** and went out to the Mount of Olives.

Jesus Predicts Peter's Denial

(Matt. 26.31–35; Luke 22.31–34; John 13.36–38)

27 Jesus said to them, "All of you will run away and leave me, for the **scripture** says, 'God will kill the **shepherd**, and the **sheep** will all be **scattered**.' 28 But after I am **raised to life**, I will go to Galilee **ahead of you**."

29 Peter answered, "I will never leave you, even though all the rest do!"

30 Jesus said to Peter, "I tell you that before the cock crows twice tonight, you will say three times that you do not know me."

31 Peter answered even more **strongly**, "I will never say that, even if I have to die with you!"

And all the other **disciples** said the same thing.

Jesus Prays in Gethsemane

(Matt. 26.36–46; Luke 22.39–46)

32 They came to a place called Gethsemane, and Jesus said to his **disciples**, "Sit here while I **pray**." 33 He took Peter, James, and John with him. **Distress** and **anguish** came over him, 34 and he said to them, "The **sorrow** in my **heart** is so great that it almost crushes me. Stay here and keep **watch**."

35 He went a little farther on, threw himself on the ground, and **prayed** that, if possible, he might not have to go through that time of **suffering**. 36 "Father," he **prayed**, "**my Father**! All things are possible for you. Take this **cup of suffering** away from me. Yet not what I want, but what you want."

37 Then he returned and found the three **disciples** asleep. He said to Peter, "Simon, are you asleep? Weren't you able to stay awake even for one hour?" 38 And he said to them, "Keep **watch**, and **pray** that you will not fall into **temptation**. The **spirit** is willing, but the **flesh** is **weak**."

39 He went away once more and **prayed**, saying the same **words**. 40 Then he came back to the **disciples** and found them asleep; they could not keep their eyes open. And they did not know what to say to him.

41 When he came back the third time, he said to them, "Are you still sleeping and **resting**? **Enough**! The hour has come! Look, the **Son of Man** is now being handed over to the **power** of sinful men. 42 Get up, let us go. Look, here is the man who is **betraying** me!"

The Arrest of Jesus

(Matt. 26.47–56; Luke 22.47–53; John 18.3–12)

43 Jesus was still speaking when Judas, one of the twelve **disciples**, arrived. With him was a crowd armed with swords and clubs, and sent by the **chief priests**, the **teachers of the Law**, and the **elders**. 44 The **traitor** had given the crowd a signal: "The man I **kiss** is the one you want. **Arrest** him and take him away under guard."

45 As soon as Judas arrived, he went up to Jesus and said, "**Teacher**!" and **kissed** him. 46 So they **arrested** Jesus and held him tight. 47 But one of those standing there drew his sword and **struck** at the **High Priest's slave**, cutting off his ear. 48 Then Jesus spoke up and said to them, "Did you have to come with swords and clubs to capture me, as

14.18: Ps 41.9 **14.24:** Ex 24.8; Jer 31.31–34 **14.27:** Zech 13.7 **14.28:** Mt 28.16

though I were an outlaw? 49 Day after
day I was with you **teaching** in the
Temple, and you did not **arrest** me. But
the **Scriptures** must come **true**."

50 Then all the **disciples** left him and
ran away.

51 A certain young man, dressed only
in a linen cloth, was following Jesus.
They tried to **arrest** him, 52 but he ran
away **naked**, leaving the cloth behind.

Jesus before the Council
(Matt. 26.57–68; Luke 22.54–55, 63–71;
John 18.13–14, 19–24)

53 Then Jesus was taken to the **High
Priest's** house, where all the **chief
priests**, the **elders**, and the **teachers of
the Law** were gathering. 54 Peter followed from a distance and went into the
courtyard of the **High Priest's** house.
There he sat down with the guards, keeping himself warm by the fire. 55 The **chief
priests** and the whole **Council** tried to
find some **evidence** against Jesus in
order to put him **to death**, but they could
not find any. 56 Many **witnesses** told **lies**
against Jesus, but their stories did not
agree.

57 Then some men stood up and told
this lie against Jesus: 58 "We heard him
say, 'I will tear down this **Temple** which
men have made, and after three days I
will build one that is not made by men.' "
59 Not even they, however, could make
their stories **agree**.

60 The **High Priest** stood up in front of
them all and **questioned** Jesus, "Have you
no answer to the **accusation** they bring
against you?"

61 But Jesus kept quiet and would not
say a **word**. Again the **High Priest** **questioned** him, "Are you the **Messiah**, the
Son of the Blessed God?"

62 "I am," answered Jesus, "and you
will all see the **Son of Man** seated on the
right of the **Almighty** and coming with
the **clouds of heaven**!"

63 The **High Priest** tore his robes and
said, "We don't **need** any more **witnesses**! 64 You heard his **blasphemy**.
What is your decision?"

They all voted against him: he was
guilty and should be put **to death**.

65 Some of them began to spit on
Jesus, and they blindfolded him and hit
him. "Guess who hit you!" they said. And
the guards took him and slapped him.

Peter Denies Jesus
(Matt. 26.69–75; Luke 22.56–62;
John 18.15–18, 25–27)

66 Peter was still down in the courtyard when one of the **High Priest's servant-girls** came by. 67 When she saw
Peter warming himself, she looked
straight at him and said, "You, too, were
with Jesus of Nazareth."

68 But he **denied** it. "I don't know... I
don't **understand** what you are talking
about," he answered, and went out into
the passage. Just then a cock crowed.[w]

69 The **servant-girl** saw him there and
began to repeat to the bystanders, "He is
one of them!" 70 But Peter **denied** it
again.

A little while later the bystanders **accused** Peter again, "You can't **deny** that
you are one of them, because you, too,
are from Galilee."

71 Then Peter said, "I **swear** that I am
telling the **truth**! May God **punish** me if I
am not! I do not know the man you are
talking about!"

72 Just then a cock crowed a second
time, and Peter **remembered** how Jesus
had said to him, "Before the cock crows
twice, you will say three times that you
do not know me." And he broke down
and cried.

Jesus Is Brought before Pilate
(Matt. 27.1–2, 11–14; Luke 23.1–5;
John 18.28–38)

15

Early in the morning the **chief
priests** met hurriedly with the
elders, the **teachers of the Law**, and the
whole **Council**, and made their **plans**.
They put Jesus in chains, led him away,
and handed him over to Pilate. 2 Pilate
questioned him, "Are you the **king of the
Jews**?"

Jesus answered, "So you say."

3 The **chief priests** were **accusing**
Jesus of many things, 4 so Pilate **questioned** him again, "Aren't you going to
answer? Listen to all their **accusations**!"

5 Again Jesus **refused** to say a **word**,
and Pilate was **amazed**.

Jesus Is Sentenced to Death
(Matt. 27.15–26; Luke 23.13–25;
John 18.39—19.16)

6 At every **Passover Festival** Pilate
was in the habit of **setting free** any one
prisoner the people asked for. 7 At that
time a man named Barabbas was in
prison with the **rebels** who had **committed murder** in the riot. 8 When the
crowd gathered and began to ask Pilate

abandon Mt 27.46; Lk 13.35
accuse [3] 14.60; Lk 3.14
amaze 12.17; Lk 2.18
believe 13.21; 16.11
body [4] 14.8; 16.1
bold Dan 11.25; Acts 4.13
bow (2) Mt 20.20; Lk 24.5
chief priests [5] 14.1 Lk 9.22
commit [2] 10.11; Lk 16.18
Council [2] 14.55; Lk 22.66
crime Mt 27.23; Lk 22.37
cross (1) [5] 8.34; Lk 9.23
crown Mt 27.29; Jn 19.2
crucify [8] Mt 28.5; 16.6
dark 13.24; Lk 1.79
dead [2] 12.19; Lk 7.12
each other 13.8; Lk 11.17
elder (2) 14.43; Lk 7.3
favour Mt 20.20; Lk 2.52
festival 14.1; Lk 2.41
force (1) Mt 27.32; Lk 3.14

[w] *Some manuscripts do not have* Just then a cock crowed.

14.49: Lk 19.47, 21.37 **14.58:** Jn 2.19 **14.62:** Dan 7.13 **14.64:** Lev 24.16

free [4] Mt 27.15; Lk 1.68
help 14.7; Lk 1.25
insult [2] Mt 27.39; Lk 6.22
jealous 7.22; Acts 5.17
jeer Mt 27.41; Lk 23.35
Jew [5] 12.12; Lk 2.46
Kingdom (1) (of God) 14.25; Lk 1.33
knee 5.6; Lk 5.8
last (1) 4.17; Lk 11.17
Messiah 14.61; Lk 2.26
mock 10.34; Lk 18.32
Passover 14.1; Lk 2.41
plan 3.6; Lk 1.51
please 14.11; Lk 2.14
presence Mt 27.58; Lk 1.19
prison [2] 6.17; Lk 3.20
question [2] 14.60; Lk 2.46
rebel Zeph 3.1; Jn 19.12
refuse (1) 6.26; Lk 7.30
respect 12.6; Lk 5.32
right (2) 14.62; 16.5
Sabbath 6.2; 16.1
save [2] 13.13; 16.16
Son of God 14.61; Lk 1.32
teacher of the Law [2] 14.1; Lk 5.17
Temple (1) (of God) [2] 14.49; Lk 1.8
tomb [2] 5.3; 16.2
watch 14.34; Lk 6.7
word (1) 14.39; Lk 1.22

for the usual **favour**, 9 he asked them, "Do you want me to **set free** for you the **king of the Jews**?" 10 He knew very well that the **chief priests** had handed Jesus over to him because they were **jealous**.

11 But the **chief priests** stirred up the crowd to ask, instead, for Pilate to **set Barabbas free** for them. 12 Pilate spoke again to the crowd, "What, then, do you want me to do with the one you call the **king of the Jews**?"

13 They shouted back, "**Crucify** him!"

14 "But what **crime** has he **committed**?" Pilate asked.

They shouted all the louder, "**Crucify** him!"

15 Pilate wanted to **please** the crowd, so he **set Barabbas free** for them. Then he had Jesus whipped and handed him over to be **crucified**.

The Soldiers Mock Jesus
(Matt. 27.27–31; John 19.2–3)

16 The soldiers took Jesus inside to the courtyard of the governor's palace and called together the rest of the company. 17 They put a purple robe on Jesus, made a **crown** out of thorny branches, and put it on his head. 18 Then they began to salute him: "Long live the **King of the Jews**!" 19 They beat him over the head with a stick, spat on him, fell on their **knees**, and **bowed down** to him. 20 When they had finished **mocking** him, they took off the purple robe and put his own clothes back on him. Then they led him out to **crucify** him.

Jesus Is Crucified
(Matt. 27.32–44; Luke 23.26–43; John 19.17–27)

21 On the way they met a man named Simon, who was coming into the city from the country, and the soldiers **forced** him to carry Jesus' **cross**. (Simon was from Cyrene and was the father of Alexander and Rufus.) 22 They took Jesus to a place called Golgotha, which means "The Place of the Skull." 23 There they tried to give him wine mixed with a drug called myrrh, but Jesus would not drink it. 24 Then they **crucified** him and divided his clothes among themselves, throwing dice to see who would get which piece of clothing. 25 It was nine o'clock in the morning when they **crucified** him. 26 The notice of the **accusation** against him said: "The **King of the Jews**." 27 They also **crucified** two bandits with Jesus, one on his **right** and the other on his left.[x]

29 People passing by shook their heads and hurled **insults** at Jesus: "Aha! You were going to tear down the **Temple** and build it up again in three days! 30 Now come down from the **cross** and **save** yourself!"

31 In the same way the **chief priests** and the **teachers of the Law jeered** at Jesus, saying to **each other**, "He **saved** others, but he cannot save himself! 32 Let us see the **Messiah**, the king of Israel, come down from the **cross** now, and we will **believe** in him!"

And the two who were **crucified** with Jesus **insulted** him also.

The Death of Jesus
(Matt. 27.45–56; Luke 23.44–49; John 19.28–30)

33 At noon the whole country was covered with **darkness**, which **lasted** for three hours. 34 At three o'clock Jesus cried out with a loud shout, *"Eloi, Eloi, lema sabachthani?"* which means, "My God, my God, why did you **abandon** me?"

35 Some of the people there heard him and said, "Listen, he is calling for Elijah!" 36 One of them ran up with a sponge, soaked it in cheap wine, and put it on the end of a stick. Then he held it up to Jesus' lips and said, "Wait! Let us see if Elijah is coming to bring him down from the **cross**!"

37 With a loud cry Jesus died.

38 The curtain hanging in the **Temple** was torn in two, from top to bottom. 39 The army officer who was standing there in front of the **cross** saw how Jesus had died.[y] "This man was really the **Son of God**!" he said.

40 Some women were there, looking on from a distance. Among them were Mary Magdalene, Mary the mother of the younger James and of Joseph, and Salome. 41 They had followed Jesus while he was in Galilee and had **helped** him. Many other women who had come to Jerusalem with him were there also.

The Burial of Jesus
(Matt. 27.57–61; Luke 23.50–56; John 19.38–42)

42–43 It was towards evening when Joseph of Arimathea arrived. He was a **respected** member of the **Council**, who

[x] *Some manuscripts add verse 28:* In this way the scripture came true which says, "He shared the fate of criminals" *(see Lk 22.37).* [y] had died; *some manuscripts have* had cried out and died.

15.21: Rom 16.13 **15.24:** Ps 22.18 **15.28:** Is 53.12 **15.29:** Ps 22.7, 109.25; Mk 14.58; Jn 2.19
15.34: Ps 22.1 **15.36:** Ps 69.21 **15.38:** Ex 26.31–33 **15.40–41:** Lk 8.2–3

was waiting for the coming of the **King-**
dom of God. It was Preparation day (that
is, the day before the **Sabbath**), so Joseph
went **boldly** into the **presence** of Pilate
and asked him for the **body** of Jesus.
44 Pilate was surprised to hear that Jesus
was already **dead**. He called the army
officer and asked him if Jesus had been
dead a long time. 45 After hearing the officer's report, Pilate told Joseph he could
have the **body**. 46 Joseph bought a linen
sheet, took the **body** down, wrapped it in
the sheet, and placed it in a **tomb** which
had been dug out of solid rock. Then he
rolled a large stone across the entrance
to the **tomb**. 47 Mary Magdalene and
Mary the mother of Joseph were **watch-**
ing and saw where the **body** of Jesus was
placed.

The Resurrection
(Matt. 28.1–8; Luke 24.1–12; John 20.1–10)

afraid 12.12; Lk 1.12
ahead of you 14.28; Lk 7.27
alive [2] Mt 27.63; Lk 12.22
anoint Zech 4.14
baptize 11.30; Lk 3.3
believe [5] 15.32; Lk 1.20
believer Acts 1.15
body 15.42; Lk 1.80
condemn 10.33; Lk 6.37
crucify 15.13; Lk 23.21
death (2) (from death) 12.18; Lk 14.14
demon [2] 9.38; Lk 4.33
disciple [4] 14.10; Lk 5.30
distress 14.33; Lk 12.50
eternal 10.17; Lk 10.25
faith 11.22; Lk 5.20
friend 9.50; Lk 2.44
gospel 14.9; Acts 10.42
harm 3.4; Lk 4.35
heaven 14.62; Lk 1.79
last (2) 12.6; Lk 1.25
mankind Mt 24.9; Lk 3.6
message [2] 4.14; Lk 1.2
miracle [2] 13.22; Lk 10.13
mourn Mt 5.4; Lk 6.25
name (2) (name of God, of Jesus) 11.9; Lk 1.31
one another 14.4; Lk 2.15
power 14.41; Lk 1.35
preach [3] 14.9; Lk 3.3
prove 8.12; Lk 2.12
raise 14.28; Lk 7.22

16 After the **Sabbath** was over,
Mary Magdalene, Mary the
mother of James, and Salome bought
spices to go and **anoint** the **body** of Jesus.
2 Very early on Sunday morning, at sunrise, they went to the **tomb**. 3-4 On the
way they said to **one another**, "Who will
roll away the stone for us from the entrance to the **tomb**?" (It was a very
large stone.) Then they looked up and
saw that the stone had already been
rolled back. 5 So they entered the **tomb**,
where they saw a young man sitting on
the **right**, wearing a white robe—and
they were alarmed.
6 "Don't be alarmed," he said. "I know
you are looking for Jesus of Nazareth,
who was **crucified**. He is not here—he
has been **raised**! Look, here is the place
where they put him. 7 Now go and give
this **message** to his **disciples**, including
Peter: 'He is going to Galilee **ahead of**
you; there you will see him, just as he
told you.' "
8 So they went out and ran from the
tomb, **distressed** and **terrified**. They said
nothing to anyone, because they were
afraid.

AN OLD ENDING TO THE GOSPEL[z]

Jesus Appears to Mary Magdalene
(Matt. 28.9–10; John 20.11–18)

[9 After Jesus **rose from death** early on
Sunday, he appeared first to Mary
Magdalene, from whom he had driven
out seven **demons**. 10 She went and told
his companions. They were **mourning**
and crying; 11 and when they heard her
say that Jesus was **alive** and that she had
seen him, they did not **believe** her.

Jesus Appears to Two Followers
(Luke 24.13–35)

12 After this, Jesus appeared in a different manner to two of them while they
were on their way to the country. 13 They
returned and told the others, but they
would not **believe** it.

Jesus Appears to the Eleven
(Matt. 28.16–20; Luke 24.36–49;
John 20.19–23; Acts 1.6–8)

14 **Last** of all, Jesus appeared to the
eleven **disciples** as they were eating. He
scolded them, because they did not have
faith and because they were too **stubborn**
to **believe** those who had seen him **alive**.
15 He said to them, "Go throughout the
whole **world** and **preach** the **gospel** to all
mankind. 16 Whoever **believes** and is **bap-**
tized will be **saved**; whoever does not **be-**
lieve will be **condemned**. 17 **Believers** will
be given the **power** to perform **miracles**:
they will drive out **demons in my name**;
they will speak in **strange tongues**; 18 if
they pick up snakes or drink any poison,
they will not be **harmed**; they will place
their hands on sick people, who will get
well."

Jesus Is Taken up to Heaven
(Luke 24.50–53; Acts 1.9–11)

19 After the Lord Jesus had talked
with them, he was taken up to **heaven**
and sat at the **right side of God**. 20 The **dis-**
ciples went and **preached** everywhere,
and the Lord worked with them and
proved that their **preaching** was **true** by
the **miracles** that were performed.]

ANOTHER OLD ENDING[a]

[9 The women went to Peter and his
friends and gave them a brief account of
all they had been told. 10 After this, Jesus
himself sent out through his **disciples**
from the east to the west the **sacred** and
ever-living **message** of **eternal salva-**
tion.]

right (2) [2] 15.27; Lk 1.11
rise 12.18; Lk 1.78
Sabbath 15.42; Lk 4.16
sacred Zech 14.20; Lk 1.72
salvation Jon 2.9; Lk 1.78
save 15.30; Lk 1.71
strange Hos 8.12; Lk 21.11
stubborn 3.5; Acts 7.51
terrify 6.50; Lk 21.11
tomb [4] 15.46; Lk 11.47
true 14.49; Lk 1.20
world 14.9; Lk 4.5

[z] *Some manuscripts and ancient translations do not have this ending to the Gospel (verses 9–20).*
[a] *Some manuscripts and ancient translations have this shorter ending to the Gospel in addition to the longer ending (verses 9–20).*

16.7: Mt 26.32; Mk 14.28 **16.15:** Acts 1.8 **16.19:** Acts 1.9–11

THE GOSPEL ACCORDING TO
LUKE

INTRODUCTION

The Gospel according to Luke presents Jesus as both the promised Saviour of Israel and as the Saviour of all mankind. *Luke* records that Jesus was called by the Spirit of the Lord to "preach the Good News to the poor," and this Gospel is filled with a concern for people with all kinds of need. The note of joy is also prominent in *Luke*, especially in the opening chapters that announce the coming of Jesus, and again at the conclusion, when Jesus ascends to heaven. The story of the growth and spread of the Christian faith after the ascension of Jesus is told by the same writer in the book of *Acts*.

Parts 2 and 6 (see the outline below) contain much material that is found only in this Gospel, such as the stories about the song of the angels and the shepherds' visit at the birth of Jesus, Jesus in the Temple as a boy, and the parables of the Good Samaritan and the Lost Son. Throughout the Gospel great emphasis is placed on prayer, the Holy Spirit, the role of women in the ministry of Jesus, and God's forgiveness of sins.

Outline of Contents

---

afraid [3] Mk 16.8; 2.9
altar [2] Mt 23.18; 11.51
angel [11] Mk 13.27; 2.9
believe [3] Mk 16.11; 8.12
best Mk 12.39; 12.58
birth [3] Mt 1.12; 2.7
bless [3] Mk 14.61; 2.34
body Mk 16.1; 2.52
choose Mk 13.20; 2.34
circumcise Ezek 44.7; 2.21
command Mk 9.25; 2.22
covenant Mk 14.24; 22.20
custom Zeph 1.8; Jn 18.39
dark Mk 15.33; 11.34
dear Mk 12.6; 3.22
death (1) Mt 27.4; 23.15
disgrace Mt 1.19; Acts 5.41
disobey Mt 15.2; 12.46
enemy [2] Mk 12.36; 6.27
fear [2] Mk 5.33; 5.26
forgive Mk 11.25; 3.3
free Mk 15.6; 2.38
glad [3] Mk 12.37; 6.23
God's people [2] Mk 13.20; 4.19
Good News Mk 13.9; 2.10

1 Dear Theophilus:
Many people have done their **best** to
write a report of the things that have
taken place among us. 2 They wrote what
we have been told by those who saw
these things from the beginning and who
proclaimed the **message**. 3 And so, your
Excellency, because I have carefully
studied all these matters from their
beginning, I thought it would be good to
write an orderly account for you. 4 I do
this so that you will know the full **truth**
about everything which you have been
taught.

The Birth of John the Baptist Is Announced

5 During the time when Herod was
king of Judaea,[a] there was a **priest**
named Zechariah, who belonged to the
priestly order of Abijah. His wife's name
was Elizabeth; she also belonged to a
priestly family. 6 They both lived good
lives in God's **sight** and **obeyed** fully all
the Lord's **laws** and **commands**. 7 They
had no children because Elizabeth could
not have any, and she and Zechariah
were both very old.

8 One day Zechariah was doing his
work as a **priest** in the **Temple**, taking his
turn in the daily **service**. 9 According to
the **custom** followed by the **priests**, he
was **chosen** by **lot** to burn **incense** on the
altar. So he went into the **Temple** of the
Lord, 10 while the crowd of people outside
prayed during the hour when the **incense**
was burnt.

11 An **angel of the Lord** appeared to
him, standing on the **right** of the **altar**
where the **incense** was burnt. 12 When
Zechariah saw him, he was alarmed and
felt **afraid**. 13 But the **angel** said to him,
"Don't be **afraid**, Zechariah! God has
heard your **prayer**, and your wife Elizabeth will bear you a son. You are to
name him John. 14 How **glad** and **happy**
you will be, and how **happy** many others
will be when he is born! 15 He will be a
great man in the Lord's **sight**. He must
not drink any wine or **strong** drink. From
his very **birth** he will be filled with the
Holy Spirit, 16 and he will bring back
many of the people of Israel to the Lord
their God. 17 He will go ahead of the Lord,

grace Song 7.7; Jn 1.14
guide Mt 23.16; Acts 1.16
happy [4] Mt 25.21; 6.20
hate Mk 13.13; 6.22
heart Mk 14.34; 2.35
heaven Mk 16.19; 2.13
help [3] Mk 15.41; 5.7
holy [4] Mk 8.38; 4.34
honour Mk 7.6; 11.2
hunger Mk 11.12; 4.2
incense [3] Mal 1.11; 2 Cor 2.15
Kingdom (1) (of God) Mk 15.42; 4.43
last (2) Mk 16.14; 12.59
law Mk 12.14; 2.22
life (1) [2] Mk 10.17; 6.9
lot (1) Jon 1.7; Acts 1.26
mercy [4] Mt 23.23; 6.36
message [6] Mk 16.7; 8.12
might [5] Mal 1.5; 9.43
Most High [2] Mk 5.7; 6.35
name (2) (name of God, of Jesus) [2] Mk 16.17; 2.21
neighbour [2] Mk 12.31; 10.27
oath Mt 26.63; Jas 5.12
obey Mk 12.33; 2.51

[a] JUDAEA: *The term here refers to the whole land of Palestine.*

1.5: 1 Chr 24.10 **1.15:** Num 6.3 **1.17:** Mal 4.5-6

peace [2] Mk 9.50; 2.14
plain (1) Mt 16.21; Jn 10.24
plan Mk 15.1; 14.28
power [3] Mk 16.17; 4.6
praise [3] Mk 11.9; 2.13
pray Mk 14.32; 2.36
prayer Mk 14.22; 5.33
presence Mk 15.42; 2.31
priest [5] Mk 2.26; 5.14
proclaim Mal 3.1; 4.18
promise [5] Mk 14.11; 2.5
prophet [3] Mk 13.22; 2.36
proud Mk 7.22; Rom 1.30
provide Mt 6.33; 7.46
reason Mk 11.24; 6.7
rejoice Zech 9.9; 13.17
remember [4] Mk 14.72; 2.19
rescue Zech 10.6; Acts 12.11
rich Mk 12.41; 6.24
right (1) Mk 11.13; 7.43
right (2) Mk 16.5; 6.6
righteous [2] Mt 25.33; 7.29
rise Mk 16.9; 3.15
sacred Mk 16.10; Acts 6.13
salvation Mk 16.10; 2.30
save [2] Mk 16.16; 2.25
Saviour [2] Hab 3.18; 2.11
scatter Mk 14.27; 8.5
servant [4] Mk 14.66; 2.29
serve Mk 10.45; 4.8
service [2] Ezek 46.17; Acts 1.20
sight [2] Mk 12.11; 4.18
sign (1) [2] Mt 24.30; 2.34
solemn Nah 1.15; Acts 20.21
Son of God [2] Mk 15.39; 3.22
soul Mk 12.30; 10.27
Spirit (1) (God's Spirit) [4] Mk 13.11; 2.25
spirit (2) Mk 14.38; 4.33
strong [2] Mk 14.31; 2.40
study Mt 2.1; Jn 5.39
tablet Hab 2.2; 2 Cor 3.3
teach Mk 14.49; 4.15
Temple (1) (of God) [5] Mk 15.29; 2.27
throne Mk 10.37; 22.30
trouble Mk 13.7; 6.18
true [3] Mk 16.20; 4.21
truth Mk 14.71; 20.21
turn [2] Mk 13.12; 3.3
virgin Mt 1.23; 1 Cor 7.34
vision Mt 17.9; 24.23
wonder (1) Mk 13.1; 13.17
word (1) [2] Mk 15.5; 3.2

strong and **mighty** like the **prophet** Elijah. He will bring fathers and children together again; he will **turn disobedient**
people back to the way of thinking of the
righteous; he will get the Lord's people
ready for him."

18 Zechariah said to the **angel**, "How
shall I know if this is so? I am an old
man, and my wife is old also."

19 "I am Gabriel," the **angel**
answered. "I stand in the **presence** of
God, who sent me to speak to you and tell
you this **good news**. 20 But you have not
believed my **message**, which will come
true at the **right** time. Because you have
not **believed**, you will be unable to speak;
you will remain silent until the day my
promise to you comes **true**."

21 In the meantime the people were
waiting for Zechariah and wondering
why he was spending such a long time in
the **Temple**. 22 When he came out, he
could not speak to them, and so they
knew that he had seen a **vision** in the
Temple. Unable to say a **word**, he made
signs to them with his hands.

23 When his period of **service** in the
Temple was over, Zechariah went back
home. 24 Some time later his wife Elizabeth became pregnant and did not leave
the house for five months. 25 "Now at last
the Lord has **helped** me," she said. "He
has taken away my public **disgrace**!"

The Birth of Jesus Is Announced

26 In the sixth month of Elizabeth's
pregnancy God sent the **angel** Gabriel to
a town in Galilee named Nazareth. 27 He
had a **message** for a girl **promised** in
marriage to a man named Joseph, who
was a descendant of King David. The
girl's name was Mary. 28 The **angel** came
to her and said, "**Peace** be with you! The
Lord is with you and has greatly **blessed**
you!"

29 Mary was deeply **troubled** by the
angel's message, and she wondered what
his **words** meant. 30 The **angel** said to her,
"Don't be **afraid**, Mary; God has been
gracious to you. 31 You will become pregnant and give **birth** to a son, and you will
name him Jesus. 32 He will be great and
will be called the **Son of the Most High**
God. The Lord God will make him a king,
as his ancestor David was, 33 and he will
be the king of the descendants of Jacob
for ever; his **kingdom** will never end!"

34 Mary said to the **angel**, "I am a **virgin**. How, then, can this be?"

35 The **angel** answered, "The **Holy
Spirit** will come on you, and **God's power**
will rest upon you. For this **reason** the
holy child will be called the **Son of God**.
36 **Remember** your relative Elizabeth. It
is said that she cannot have children, but
she herself is now six months pregnant,
even though she is very old. 37 For there
is nothing that God cannot do."

38 "I am the Lord's **servant**," said
Mary; "may it happen to me as you have
said." And the **angel** left her.

Mary Visits Elizabeth

39 Soon afterwards Mary got ready
and hurried off to a town in the hill-
country of Judaea. 40 She went into
Zechariah's house and greeted Elizabeth.
41 When Elizabeth heard Mary's greeting,
the baby moved within her. Elizabeth
was filled with the **Holy Spirit** 42 and said
in a loud voice, "You are the most
blessed of all women, and **blessed** is the
child you will bear! 43 Why should this
great thing happen to me, that my Lord's
mother comes to visit me? 44 For as soon
as I heard your greeting, the baby within
me jumped with **gladness**. 45 How **happy**
you are to **believe** that the Lord's **message** to you will come **true**!"

Mary's Song of Praise

46 Mary said,
"My **heart praises** the Lord;
47 my **soul** is **glad** because of God my
Saviour,
48 for he has **remembered** me, his
lowly **servant**!
From now on all people will call me
happy,
49 because of the great things the
Mighty God has done for me.
His **name** is **holy**;
50 from one generation to another
he shows **mercy** to those who
honour him.
51 He has stretched out his **mighty** arm
and **scattered** the **proud** with all
their **plans**.
52 He has brought down **mighty** kings
from their **thrones**,
and lifted up the lowly.
53 He has filled the **hungry** with good
things,
and sent the **rich** away with empty
hands.
54 He has kept the **promise** he made to
our ancestors,
and has come to the **help** of his
servant Israel.
55 He has **remembered** to show **mercy** to
Abraham
and to all his descendants for ever!"

1.19: Dan 8.16, 9.21 **1.27:** Mt 1.18 **1.31:** Mt 1.21 **1.32–33:** 2 Sam 7.12, 13, 16; Is 9.7 **1.37:** Gen 18.14
1.46–55: 1 Sam 2.1–10 **1.48:** 1 Sam 1.11 **1.52:** Job 5.11, 12.19 **1.55:** Gen 17.7

56 Mary stayed about three months
with Elizabeth and then went back home.

The Birth of John the Baptist

57 The time came for Elizabeth to
have her baby, and she gave **birth** to a
son. 58 Her **neighbours** and relatives
heard how **wonderfully** good the Lord
had been to her, and they all **rejoiced**
with her.

59 When the baby was a week old,
they came to **circumcise** him, and they
were going to name him Zechariah, after
his father. 60 But his mother said, "No!
His name is to be John."

61 They said to her, "But you have no
relatives with that name!" 62 Then they
made **signs** to his father, asking him
what name he would like the boy to have.

63 Zechariah asked for a writing
tablet and wrote, "His name is John."
How surprised they all were! 64 At that
moment Zechariah was able to speak
again, and he started **praising** God. 65 The
neighbours were all filled with **fear**, and
the news about these things spread
through all the hill-country of Judaea.
66 Everyone who heard of it thought
about it and asked, "What is this child
going to be?" For it was **plain** that the
Lord's power was upon him.

Zechariah's Prophecy

67 John's father Zechariah was filled
with the **Holy Spirit**, and he spoke God's
message:

68 "Let us **praise** the Lord, the God of
Israel!
He has come to the **help of his**
people and has **set them free**.
69 He has **provided** for us a **mighty**
Saviour,
a descendant of his **servant** David.
70 He **promised** through his **holy prophets**
long ago
71 that he would **save** us from our
enemies,
from the **power** of all those who **hate**
us.
72 He said he would show **mercy** to our
ancestors
and **remember** his **sacred covenant**.
73–74 With a **solemn oath** to our ancestor
Abraham
he **promised** to **rescue** us from our
enemies
and allow us to **serve** him without
fear,
75 so that we might be **holy** and **righteous**
before him
all the days of our **life**.

76 "You, my child, will be called a
prophet of the **Most High God**.
You will go ahead of the Lord
to prepare his road for him,
77 to tell **his people** that they will be
saved
by having their sins **forgiven**.
78 Our God is **merciful** and tender.
He will cause the bright dawn of
salvation to **rise** on us
79 and to shine from **heaven** on all
those who live in the **dark** shadow
of **death**,
to **guide** our steps into the path of
peace."

80 The child grew and developed in
body and **spirit**. He lived in the desert
until the day when he appeared publicly
to the people of Israel.

The Birth of Jesus
(Matt. 1.18–25)

2 At that time the Emperor Augustus
ordered a census to be taken
throughout the Roman Empire. 2 When
this first census took place, Quirinius was
the governor of Syria. 3 Everyone, then,
went to register himself, each to his own
town.

4 Joseph went from the town of
Nazareth in Galilee to the town of Bethlehem in Judaea, the birthplace of King
David. Joseph went there because he
was a descendant of David. 5 He went to
register with Mary, who was **promised** in
marriage to him. She was pregnant, 6 and
while they were in Bethlehem, the time
came for her to have her baby. 7 She
gave **birth** to her first son, wrapped him
in strips of cloth and laid him in a
manger—there was no room for them to
stay in the inn.

The Shepherds and the Angels

8 There were some **shepherds** in that
part of the country who were spending
the night in the fields, taking **care** of
their **flocks**. 9 An **angel of the Lord**
appeared to them, and the **glory** of the
Lord shone over them. They were
terribly afraid, 10 but the **angel** said to
them, "Don't be **afraid**! I am here with
good news for you, which will bring great
joy to all the people. 11 This very day in
David's town your **Saviour** was born—
Christ the Lord! 12 And this is what will
prove it to you: you will find a baby
wrapped in strips of cloth and lying in a
manger."

13 Suddenly a great army of **heaven's**
angels appeared with the **angel**, singing
praises to God:

afraid [2] 1.12; 5.10
amaze [3] Mk 15.5; 4.32
angel [7] 1.11; 4.10
assure Mk 14.9; 9.27
birth 1.15; Jn 16.21
bless [2] 1.28; 6.28
body 1.80; 3.22
care Mk 8.15; 4.10
ceremony Neh 12.45; Acts 7.8
choose 1.9; 4.6
Christ Mt 11.2; Jn 1.41
circumcise 1.59; Jn 7.22
command 1.6; 8.56
dedicate Zech 14.20; Jn 17.17
destroy Mk 3.4; 4.34
dove Mk 1.10; 3.22
fast (2) Mk 2.18; 5.33
Father (2) (God) Mk 14.36; 6.36
favour Mk 15.8; 18.7
festival [3] Mk 15.6; 22.1
first-born Zech 12.10; Col 1.15
flock Mk 10.1; 12.32
free 1.68; 4.18
friend Mk 16.9; 4.40
Gentile Mk 10.33; 18.32
glory [3] Mk 13.26; 9.26
God-fearing Neh 7.2
Good News 1.19; 3.18
heart [2] 1.46; 6.45
heaven [3] 1.79; 3.21
intelligent Mk 7.18; Acts 13.7
Jew Mk 15.2; 7.3
joy Mt 28.8; 6.23
law [5] 1.6; 6.2
light (1) Mt 6.22; 8.16
Messiah Mk 15.32; 3.15
name (2) (name of God, of Jesus) 1.31; 9.48
obey 1.6; 6.47
offer Mk 12.33; 5.14
one another Mk 16.3; 4.36
Passover Mk 15.6; 22.1
peace [2] 1.28; 7.50
please Mk 15.15; 3.22

1.59: Lev 12.3 **1.76:** Mal 3.1 **1.79:** Is 9.2

praise [2] 1.46; 4.15
pray 1.10; 3.21
presence 1.19; 14.10
present (1) Mt 2.11; Acts 6.6
promise [3] 1.20; 23.43
prophet 1.17; 3.4
prove Mk 16.20; 5.14
pure Mk 14.3; Jn 8.15
question Mk 15.2; 11.53
remember 1.36; 10.11
require [3] Mt 6.33; 12.48
reveal [2] Mt 11.27; 10.22
sacrifice Mk 12.33; 5.14
salvation [2] 1.78; 3.6
save 1.71; 4.19
Saviour 1.47; Jn 3.17
secret Mk 14.1; 8.10
servant 1.38; 7.2
shepherd [5] Mk 14.27; Jn 10.2
sign (1) 1.22; 11.30
sorrow Mk 14.34; 23.48
Spirit (1) (God's Spirit) [2] 1.15; 3.16
strong 1.15; 8.23
teacher Mk 14.14; 3.12
Temple (1) (of God) [4] 1.8; 4.9
terrible [2] Mk 14.21; 6.24
thank [2] Mk 14.22; 9.16
understand Mk 14.68; 8.10
widow Mk 12.19; 4.25
will (1) Mk 12.14; 20.21
wisdom [2] Mk 6.2; 7.35
worry Mk 13.11; 8.14
worship (1) (of God) Mk 7.7; 4.8

14 "**Glory** to God in the highest **heaven**,
and **peace** on earth to those with
whom he is **pleased**!"
15 When the **angels** went away from
them back into **heaven**, the **shepherds**
said to **one another**, "Let's go to
Bethlehem and see this thing that has
happened, which the Lord has told us."
16 So they hurried off and found Mary
and Joseph and saw the baby lying in the
manger. 17 When the **shepherds** saw him,
they told them what the **angel** had said
about the child. 18 All who heard it were
amazed at what the **shepherds** said.
19 Mary **remembered** all these things and
thought deeply about them. 20 The **shepherds** went back, singing **praises** to God
for all they had heard and seen; it had
been just as the **angel** had told them.

Jesus Is Named

21 A week later, when the time came
for the baby to be **circumcised**, he was
named Jesus, the **name** which the **angel**
had given him before he had been conceived.

Jesus Is Presented in the Temple

22 The time came for Joseph and
Mary to perform the **ceremony** of
purification, as the **Law of Moses commanded**. So they took the child to Jerusalem to **present** him to the Lord, 23 as it is
written in the **law** of the Lord: "Every
first-born male is to be **dedicated** to the
Lord." 24 They also went to **offer a sacrifice** of a pair of **doves** or two young
pigeons, as **required** by the **law** of the
Lord.
25 At that time there was a man
named Simeon living in Jerusalem. He
was a good, **God-fearing** man and was
waiting for Israel to be **saved**. The **Holy
Spirit** was with him 26 and had **assured**
him that he would not die before he had
seen the Lord's **promised Messiah**. 27 Led
by the **Spirit**, Simeon went into the
Temple. When the parents brought the
child Jesus into the **Temple** to do for him
what the **Law required**, 28 Simeon took
the child in his arms and gave **thanks** to
God:
29 "Now, Lord, you have kept your
promise,
and you may let your **servant** go in
peace.
30 With my own eyes I have seen your
salvation,
31 which you have prepared in the
presence of all peoples:
32 A **light** to **reveal** your **will** to the
Gentiles
and bring **glory** to your people
Israel."
33 The child's father and mother were
amazed at the things Simeon said about
him. 34 Simeon **blessed** them and said to
Mary, his mother, "This child is **chosen**
by God for the **destruction** and the
salvation of many in Israel. He will be a
sign from God which many people will
speak against 35 and so **reveal** their
secret thoughts. And **sorrow**, like a sharp
sword, will break your own **heart**."
36–37 There was a very old
prophetess, a **widow** named Anna,
daughter of Phanuel of the tribe of
Asher. She had been married for only
seven years and was now eighty-four
years old.[b] She never left the **Temple**;
day and night she **worshipped** God, **fasting** and **praying**. 38 That very same hour
she arrived and gave **thanks** to God and
spoke about the child to all who were
waiting for God to **set Jerusalem free**.

The Return to Nazareth

39 When Joseph and Mary had
finished doing all that was **required** by
the **law** of the Lord, they returned to
their home town of Nazareth in Galilee.
40 The child grew and became **strong**; he
was full of **wisdom**, and God's **blessings**
were upon him.

The Boy Jesus in the Temple

41 Every year the parents of Jesus
went to Jerusalem for the **Passover
Festival**. 42 When Jesus was twelve years
old, they went to the **festival** as usual.
43 When the **festival** was over, they
started back home, but the boy Jesus
stayed in Jerusalem. His parents did not
know this; 44 they thought that he was
with the group, so they travelled a whole
day and then started looking for him
among their relatives and **friends**. 45 They
did not find him, so they went back to
Jerusalem looking for him. 46 On the third
day they found him in the **Temple**, sitting
with the **Jewish teachers**, listening to
them and asking **questions**. 47 All who
heard him were **amazed** at his **intelligent**
answers. 48 His parents were astonished
when they saw him, and his mother said
to him, "My son, why have you done this
to us? Your father and I have been
terribly worried trying to find you."
49 He answered them, "Why did you
have to look for me? Didn't you know

[b] was now eighty-four years old; *or* had been a widow eighty-four years.

2.21: Lev 12.3; Lk 1.31 **2.22–24:** Lev 12.6–8 **2.23:** Ex 13.2, 12 **2.32:** Is 42.6, 49.6, 52.10 **2.39:** Mt 2.23
2.41: Ex 12.1–27; Deut 16.1–8

that I had to be in my **Father's** house?" 50 But they did not **understand** his answer.

51 So Jesus went back with them to Nazareth, where he was **obedient** to them. His mother treasured all these things in her **heart**. 52 Jesus grew both in **body** and in **wisdom**, gaining **favour** with God and men.

The Preaching of John the Baptist
(Matt. 3.1–12; Mark 1.1–8; John 1.19–28)

3 It was the fifteenth year of the rule of the Emperor Tiberius; Pontius Pilate was governor of Judaea, Herod was ruler of Galilee, and his brother Philip was ruler of the territory of Iturea and Trachonitis; Lysanias was ruler of Abilene, 2 and Annas and Caiaphas were **high priests**. At that time the **word of God** came to John son of Zechariah in the desert. 3 So John went throughout the whole territory of the River Jordan, **preaching**, "**Turn away from your sins** and be **baptized**, and God will **forgive** your sins." 4 As it is written in the book of the **prophet** Isaiah:

"Someone is shouting in the desert:
'Get the road ready for the Lord;
make a straight path for him to travel!
5 Every valley must be filled up,
every hill and mountain levelled off.
The winding roads must be made straight,
and the rough paths made smooth.
6 All **mankind** will see God's **salvation**!'"

7 Crowds of people came out to John to be **baptized** by him. "You snakes!" he said to them. "Who told you that you could **escape** from the **punishment** God is about to send? 8 Do those things that will show that you have **turned from your sins**. And don't start saying among yourselves that Abraham is your ancestor. I tell you that God can take these stones and make descendants for Abraham! 9 The axe is ready to cut down the trees at the roots; every tree that does not bear good fruit will be cut down and thrown in the fire."

10 The people asked him, "What are we to do, then?"

11 He answered, "Whoever has two shirts must give one to the man who has none, and whoever has food must **share** it."

12 Some **tax collectors** came to be **baptized**, and they asked him, "**Teacher**, what are we to do?"

13 "Don't collect more than is legal," he told them.

14 Some soldiers also asked him, "What about us? What are we to do?"

He said to them, "Don't take money from anyone by **force** or **accuse** anyone **falsely**. Be content with your pay."

15 People's **hopes** began to **rise**, and they began to wonder whether John perhaps might be the **Messiah**. 16 So John said to all of them, "I **baptize** you with water, but someone is coming who is much greater than I am. I am not good **enough** even to untie his sandals. He will **baptize** you with the **Holy Spirit** and fire. 17 He has his winnowing shovel with him, to thresh out all the grain and gather the wheat into his barn; but he will burn the chaff in a fire that never goes out."

18 In many different ways John **preached** the **Good News** to the people and **urged** them to **change** their **ways**. 19 But John **reprimanded** Herod, the governor, because he had married Herodias, his brother's wife, and had done many other **evil** things. 20 Then Herod did an even **worse** thing by putting John in **prison**.

The Baptism of Jesus
(Matt. 3.13–17; Mark 1.9–11)

21 After all the people had been **baptized**, Jesus also was **baptized**. While he was **praying**, **heaven** was opened, 22 and the **Holy Spirit** came down upon him in **bodily** form like a **dove**. And a voice came from **heaven**, "You are my own **dear Son**. I am **pleased** with you."

The Ancestors of Jesus
(Matt. 1.1–17)

23 When Jesus began his work, he was about thirty years old. He was the son, so people thought, of Joseph, who was the son of Heli, 24 the son of Matthat, the son of Levi, the son of Melchi, the son of Jannai, the son of Joseph, 25 the son of Mattathias, the son of Amos, the son of Nahum, the son of Esli, the son of Naggai, 26 the son of Maath, the son of Mattathias, the son of Semein, the son of Josech, the son of Joda, 27 the son of Joanan, the son of Rhesa, the son of Zerubbabel, the son of Shealtiel, the son of Neri, 28 the son of Melchi, the son of Addi, the son of Cosam, the son of Elmadam, the son of Er, 29 the son of Joshua, the son of Eliezer, the son of Jorim, the son of Matthat, the son of Levi, 30 the son of Simeon, the son of Judah, the son of Joseph, the son of Jonam, the son of Eliakim, 31 the son of

accuse Mk 15.3; 6.7
baptize [7] Mk 16.16; 7.29
body 2.52; 11.34
change Mk 9.2; 9.29
dear 1.1; 7.2
dove 2.24; Jn 1.32
enough Mk 14.41; 9.17
escape Mt 23.33; Acts 16.27
evil Mk 9.39; 4.33
false Mk 13.22; 6.26
force (1) Mk 15.21; 16.16
forgive 1.77; 5.20
Good News 2.10; 4.18
heaven [2] 2.13; 6.23
High Priest Mk 14.47; 22.50
hope Mt 12.21; 6.34
mankind Mk 16.15; Jn 1.4
Messiah 2.26; 4.41
please 2.14; 6.42
pray 2.36; 5.16
preach [2] Mk 16.15; 4.43
prison Mk 15.6; 8.29
prophet 2.36; 4.17
punish Mk 14.71; 8.28
reprimand Hos 4.4
rise 1.78; 4.29
salvation 2.30; 19.9
share Mk 12.2; 12.42
Son of God 1.32; 4.3
Spirit (1) (God's Spirit) [2] 2.25; 4.1
tax collector Mk 2.14; 5.27
teacher 2.46; 6.40
turn [2] 1.8; 4.3
urge Jer 17.16; Acts 2.40
way (3) Hos 14.9; Jn 7.7
word (1) 1.22; 4.22
worse Mk 13.19; 11.26

2.52: 1 Sam 2.26; Prov 3.4 **3.4–6:** Is 40.3–5 (LXX) **3.7:** Mt 12.34, 23.33 **3.8:** Jn 8.33 **3.9:** Mt 7.19 **3.12:** Lk 7.29 **3.19–20:** Mt 14.3–4; Mk 6.17–18 **3.22:** Gen 22.2; Ps 2.7; Is 42.1; Mt 3.17; Mk 1.11; Lk 9.35

Melea, the son of Menna, the son of Matt-
atha, the son of Nathan, the son of David,
32 the son of Jesse, the son of Obed, the
son of Boaz, the son of Salmon, the son of
Nahshon, 33 the son of Amminadab, the
son of Admin, the son of Arni, the son of
Hezron, the son of Perez, the son of
Judah, 34 the son of Jacob, the son of
Isaac, the son of Abraham, the son of
Terah, the son of Nahor, 35 the son of
Serug, the son of Reu, the son of Peleg,
the son of Eber, the son of Shelah, 36 the
son of Cainan, the son of Arphaxad, the
son of Shem, the son of Noah, the son of
Lamech, 37 the son of Methuselah, the son
of Enoch, the son of Jared, the son of
Mahalaleel, the son of Kenan, 38 the son
of Enosh, the son of Seth, the son of
Adam, the son of God.

The Temptation of Jesus
(Matt. 4.1-11; Mark 1.12-13)

4 Jesus returned from the Jordan full
of the **Holy Spirit** and was led by the
Spirit into the desert, 2 where he was
tempted by the **Devil** for forty days. In all
that time he ate nothing, so that he was
hungry when it was over.
3 The **Devil** said to him, "If you are
God's Son, order this stone to **turn** into
bread."
4 But Jesus answered, "The **scripture**
says, 'Man cannot live on **bread alone**.' "
5 Then the **Devil** took him up and
showed him in a second all the kingdoms
of the **world**. 6 "I will give you all this
power and all this wealth," the **Devil** told
him. "It has all been handed over to me,
and I can give it to anyone I **choose**. 7 All
this will be yours, then, if you **worship**
me."
8 Jesus answered, "The **scripture** says,
'**Worship** the Lord your God and **serve**
only him!' "
9 Then the **Devil** took him to
Jerusalem and set him on the highest
point of the **Temple**, and said to him, "If
you are **God's Son**, throw yourself down
from here. 10 For the **scripture** says, 'God
will order his **angels** to take good **care** of
you.' 11 It also says, 'They will hold you up
with their hands so that not even your
feet will be **hurt** on the stones.' "
12 But Jesus answered, "The **scripture**
says, 'Do not put the Lord your God to
the test.' "
13 When the **Devil** finished **tempting**
Jesus in every way, he left him for a
while.

Jesus Begins His Work in Galilee
(Matt. 4.12-17; Mark 1.14-15)

14 Then Jesus returned to Galilee, and
the **power of the Holy Spirit** was with
him. The news about him spread
throughout all that territory. 15 He **taught**
in the **synagogues** and was **praised** by
everyone.

Jesus Is Rejected at Nazareth
(Matt. 13.53-58; Mark 6.1-6)

16 Then Jesus went to Nazareth,
where he had been brought up, and on
the **Sabbath** he went as usual to the **synagogue**. He stood up to read the **Scriptures**
17 and was handed the book of the **prophet** Isaiah. He unrolled the **scroll** and
found the place where it is written,
18 "The **Spirit of the Lord** is upon me,
because he has **chosen** me to bring
good news to the **poor**.
He has sent me to **proclaim** liberty to
the **captives**
and recovery of **sight** to the **blind**;
to **set free** the **oppressed**
19 and **announce** that the time has
come
when the Lord will **save his people**."
20 Jesus rolled up the **scroll**, gave it
back to the attendant, and sat down. All
the people in the **synagogue** had their
eyes fixed on him, 21 as he said to them,
"This passage of **scripture** has come **true**
today, as you heard it being read."
22 They were all well impressed with
him and marvelled at the eloquent **words**
that he spoke. They said, "Isn't he the son
of Joseph?"
23 He said to them, "I am **sure** that
you will quote this **proverb** to me,
'Doctor, **heal** yourself.' You will also tell
me to do here in my home town the
same things you heard were done in
Capernaum. 24 I tell you this," Jesus
added, "a **prophet** is never **welcomed** in
his home town.
25 "Listen to me: it is **true** that there
were many **widows** in Israel during the
time of Elijah, when there was no rain
for three and a half years and a severe
famine spread throughout the whole
land. 26 Yet Elijah was not sent to anyone
in Israel, but only to a **widow** living in
Zarephath in the territory of Sidon. 27 And
there were many people **suffering** from a
dreaded **skin-disease** who lived in Israel
during the time of the **prophet** Elisha;
yet not one of them was **healed**, but only
Naaman the Syrian."
28 When the people in the **synagogue**
heard this, they were filled with **anger**.

alone Mk 14.6; 9.18
amaze [2] 2.18; 5.9
angel 2.9; 9.26
anger Mk 14.4; 13.14
announce Mk 1.7; Acts 3.18
authority [2] Mk 10.42; 5.24
blind Mk 10.46; 6.39
bread [2] Mk 14.20; 6.4
captive Hab 1.9; 2 Cor 10.5
care 2.8; 8.34
choose [2] 2.34; 6.13
demon [4] Mk 16.9; 7.33
destroy 2.34; 6.9
Devil [6] Mt 25.41; 8.12
disease [2] Mk 14.3; 5.12
evil 3.19; 6.22
famine Mk 13.8; 15.14
free 2.38; 13.12
friend 2.44; 5.20
God's people 1.68; 7.16
Good News [2] 3.18; 7.22
harm Mk 16.18; 6.9
heal [3] Mk 6.5; 5.15
holy 1.35; 9.26
hunger 1.53; 6.3
hurt Mt 15.12; 9.39
keep from Ezek 44.19; 8.12
Kingdom (1) (of God) 1.33; 6.20
lonely Mk 6.32; 5.16
Messiah 3.15; 9.20
one another 2.15; 8.25
oppress Zech 9.8; 2 Cor 5.4
poor Mk 14.5; 6.20
power [3] 1.35; 5.17
praise 2.13; 5.25
preach [2] 3.3; 7.22
proclaim 1.2; 9.60
prophet [3] 3.4; 6.23
proverb Hos 4.14; 2 Pet 2.22
rise 3.15; 13.21
Sabbath [2] Mk 16.1; 6.1

save 2.25; 6.9
scripture [6] Mk 14.21; 7.27
scroll [2] Zech 5.1; Rev 5.1
serve 1.73; 16.13
sight 1.6; 7.21
Son of God [3] 3.22; 8.28
Spirit (1) (God's Spirit) [4] 3.16; 10.21
spirit (2) [3] 1.80; 6.18
suffer Mk 14.3; 5.12
sure Mk 13.14; 12.28
synagogue [7] Mk 13.9; 6.6
teach [3] 1.4; 5.3
Temple (1) (of God) 2.27; 13.35
tempt [2] Mk 14.38; 22.40
test Mt 6.13; 8.13
true [2] 1.20; 5.10
turn 3.3; 7.9
welcome Mk 9.37; 7.45
widow [2] 2.36; 7.12
word (1) [2] 3.2; 5.1
world Mk 16.15; 9.25
worship (1) (of God) 2.36; 24.52
worship (2) (of other gods) Mt 4.9; Acts 7.42

4.4: Deut 8.3 **4.8:** Deut 6.13 **4.10:** Ps 91.11 **4.11:** Ps 91.12 **4.12:** Deut 6.16 **4.18-19:** Is 61.1-2 (LXX)
4.24: Jn 4.44 **4.25:** 1 Kgs 17.1 **4.26:** 1 Kgs 17.8-16 **4.27:** 2 Kgs 5.1-14

29 They **rose** up, dragged Jesus out of the
town, and took him to the top of the hill
on which their town was built. They
meant to throw him over the cliff, 30 but
he walked through the middle of the
crowd and went his way.

A Man with an Evil Spirit
(Mark 1.21–28)

31 Then Jesus went to Capernaum, a
town in Galilee, where he **taught** the
people on the **Sabbath**. 32 They were all
amazed at the way he **taught**, because he
spoke with **authority**. 33 In the **synagogue**
was a man who had the **spirit** of an **evil**
demon in him; he screamed out in a loud
voice, 34 "Ah! What do you want with us,
Jesus of Nazareth? Are you here to **de-**
stroy us? I know who you are: you are
God's **holy** messenger!"

35 Jesus ordered the **spirit**, "Be quiet
and come out of the man!" The **demon**
threw the man down in front of them and
went out of him without doing him any
harm.

36 The people were all **amazed** and
said to **one another**, "What kind of **words**
are these? With **authority** and **power** this
man gives orders to the **evil spirits**, and
they come out!" 37 And the report about
Jesus spread everywhere in that region.

Jesus Heals Many People
(Matt. 8.14–17; Mark 1.29–34)

38 Jesus left the **synagogue** and went
to Simon's house. Simon's mother-in-law
was sick with a high fever, and they
spoke to Jesus about her. 39 He went and
stood at her bedside and ordered the
fever to leave her. The fever left her, and
she got up at once and began to wait on
them.

40 After sunset all who had **friends**
who were sick with various **diseases**
brought them to Jesus; he placed his
hands on every one of them and **healed**
them all. 41 **Demons** also went out from
many people, screaming, "You are the
Son of God!"

Jesus gave the **demons** an order and
would not let them speak, because they
knew that he was the **Messiah**.

Jesus Preaches in the Synagogues
(Mark 1.35–39)

42 At daybreak Jesus left the town and
went off to a **lonely** place. The people
started looking for him, and when they
found him, they tried to **keep him from**
leaving. 43 But he said to them, "I must
preach the **Good News** about the **King-**
dom of God in other towns also, because
that is what God sent me to do."

44 So he **preached** in the **synagogues**
throughout the country.

Jesus Calls the First Disciples
(Matt. 4.18–22; Mark 1.16–20)

5 One day Jesus was standing on the
shore of Lake Gennesaret while the
people pushed their way up to him to
listen to the **word of God**. 2 He saw two
boats pulled up on the beach; the fishermen had left them and were washing the
nets. 3 Jesus got into one of the boats—it
belonged to Simon—and asked him to
push off a little from the shore. Jesus sat
in the boat and **taught** the crowd.

4 When he finished speaking, he said
to Simon, "Push the boat out further to
the deep water, and you and your partners let down your nets for a catch."

5 "**Master**," Simon answered, "we
worked **hard** all night long and caught
nothing. But if you say so, I will let down
the nets." 6 They let them down and
caught such a large number of fish that
the nets were about to break. 7 So they
motioned to their partners in the other
boat to come and **help** them. They came
and filled both boats so full of fish that
the boats were about to sink. 8 When
Simon Peter saw what had happened, he
fell on his **knees** before Jesus and said,
"Go away from me, Lord! I am a sinful
man!"

9 He and the others with him were all
amazed at the large number of fish they
had caught. 10 The same was **true** of
Simon's partners, James and John, the
sons of Zebedee. Jesus said to Simon,
"Don't be **afraid**; from now on you will be
catching men."

11 They pulled the boats up on the
beach, left everything, and followed
Jesus.

Jesus Heals a Man
(Matt. 8.1–4; Mark 1.40–45)

12 Once Jesus was in a town where
there was a man who was **suffering** from
a dreaded **skin-disease**. When he saw
Jesus, he threw himself down and **begged**
him, "Sir, if you want to, you can make
me **clean**!"[c]

13 Jesus stretched out his hand and
touched him. "I do want to," he answered. "Be **clean**!" At once the **disease**
left the man. 14 Jesus ordered him, "Don't
tell anyone, but go straight to the **priest**
and let him examine you; then to **prove**

afraid 2.9; 8.25
amaze [2] 4.32; 8.25
authority 4.32; 7.8
beg Mk 8.22; 7.4
blasphemy Mk 14.64; Jn 10.33
bridegroom [2] Mk 2.19; Jn 2.9
clean [2] Mk 1.40; 7.22
complain Hab 2.1; Acts 25.24
cure Mk 1.44; 7.21
disciple [4] Mk 16.7; 6.1
disease [3] 4.27; 6.18
faith Mk 16.14; 7.9
fast (2) [2] 2.36; 7.33
fear 1.65; 7.16
feast Mk 12.39; 12.36
forgive [4] 3.3; 6.37
friend 4.40; 7.6
hard Mk 10.5; 11.4
heal [2] 4.23; 6.7
help 1.25; 6.9
knee Mk 15.19; Eph 3.14
lonely 4.42; 9.12
master Mk 13.35; 8.24
need Mk 14.63; 9.11
new [7] Mk 14.25; 22.20
offer [2] 2.24; 6.4
outcast [2] Mk 2.15; 7.34
parable Mk 12.1; 6.39
paralyse [2] Mk 3.1; 6.6
Pharisees [4] Mk 12.13; 6.2
power 4.6; 6.19
praise [2] 4.15; 7.16
pray 3.21; 6.12
prayer 1.13; 19.46
priest 1.5; 6.4
prove [2] 2.12; 7.47
repent Mt 27.3; 15.7
respect Mk 15.42; 11.43
ruin Mk 2.22; Acts 15.16
sacrifice 2.24; 13.1
Son of Man Mk 14.21; 6.5
suffer 4.27; 7.22
tax collector [3] 3.12; 7.29
teach [2] 4.15; 6.6
teacher of the Law [3] Mk 15.1; 6.7
true 4.21; 7.35
wedding Mk 2.19; 7.32
word (1) 4.22; 6.47

[c] MAKE ME CLEAN: *This disease was considered to make a person ritually unclean.*

4.32: Mt 7.28–29 **5.1–3:** Mt 13.1–2; Mk 3.9–10, 4.1 **5.5:** Jn 21.3 **5.6:** Jn 21.6 **5.14:** Lev 14.1–32

to everyone that you are **cured**, **offer the sacrifice** as Moses ordered."

15 But the news about Jesus spread all the more widely, and crowds of people came to hear him and be **healed** from their **diseases**. [16]But he would go away to **lonely** places, where he **prayed**.

Jesus Heals a Paralysed Man
(Matt. 9.1–8; Mark 2.1–12)

17 One day when Jesus was **teaching**, some **Pharisees** and **teachers of the Law** were sitting there who had come from every town in Galilee and Judaea and from Jerusalem. The **power of the Lord** was present for Jesus to **heal** the sick. [18]Some men came carrying a **paralysed** man on a bed, and they tried to take him into the house and put him in front of Jesus. [19]Because of the crowd, however, they could find no way to take him in. So they carried him up on the roof, made an opening in the tiles, and let him down on his bed into the middle of the group in front of Jesus. [20]When Jesus saw how much **faith** they had, he said to the man, "Your sins are **forgiven**, my **friend**."

21 The **teachers of the Law** and the **Pharisees** began to say to themselves, "Who is this man who speaks such **blasphemy**! God is the only one who can **forgive** sins!"

22 Jesus knew their thoughts and said to them, "Why do you think such things? [23]Is it easier to say, 'Your sins are **forgiven** you,' or to say, 'Get up and walk'? [24]I will **prove** to you, then, that the **Son of Man** has **authority** on earth to **forgive** sins." So he said to the **paralysed** man, "I tell you, get up, pick up your bed, and go home!"

25 At once the man got up in front of them all, took the bed he had been lying on, and went home, **praising** God. [26]They were all completely **amazed**! Full of **fear**, they **praised** God, saying, "What marvellous things we have seen today!"

Jesus Calls Levi
(Matt. 9.9–13; Mark 2.13–17)

27 After this, Jesus went out and saw a **tax collector** named Levi, sitting in his office. Jesus said to him, "Follow me." [28]Levi got up, left everything, and followed him.

29 Then Levi had a big **feast** in his house for Jesus, and among the guests was a large number of **tax collectors** and other people. [30]Some **Pharisees** and some **teachers of the Law** who belonged to their group **complained** to Jesus' **disciples**. "Why do you eat and drink with **tax collectors** and other **outcasts**?" they asked.

31 Jesus answered them, "People who are well do not **need** a doctor, but only those who are sick. [32]I have not come to call **respectable** people to **repent**, but **outcasts**."

The Question about Fasting
(Matt. 9.14–17; Mark 2.18–22)

33 Some people said to Jesus, "The **disciples** of John **fast** frequently and **offer prayers**, and the **disciples** of the **Pharisees** do the same; but your **disciples** eat and drink."

34 Jesus answered, "Do you think you can make the guests at a **wedding party** go without food as long as the **bridegroom** is with them? Of course not! [35]But the day will come when the **bridegroom** will be taken away from them, and then they will **fast**."

36 Jesus also told them this **parable**: "No one tears a piece off a **new** coat to patch up an old coat. If he does, he will have torn the **new** coat, and the piece of **new** cloth will not match the old. [37]Nor does anyone pour **new** wine into used wineskins, because the **new** wine will burst the skins, the wine will pour out, and the skins will be **ruined**. [38]Instead, **new** wine must be poured into fresh wineskins! [39]And no one wants **new** wine after drinking old wine. 'The old is better,' he says."

The Question about the Sabbath
(Matt. 12.1–8; Mark 2.23–28)

6 Jesus was walking through some cornfields on the **Sabbath**. His **disciples** began to pick the ears of corn, rub them in their hands, and eat the grain. [2]Some **Pharisees** asked, "Why are you doing what our **Law** says you cannot do on the **Sabbath**?"

3 Jesus answered them, "Haven't you read what David did when he and his men were **hungry**? [4]He went into the house of God, took the **bread offered** to God, ate it, and gave it also to his men. Yet it is against our **Law** for anyone except the **priests** to eat that **bread**."

5 And Jesus concluded, "The **Son of Man** is Lord of the **Sabbath**."

The Man with a Paralysed Hand
(Matt. 12.9–14; Mark 3.1–6)

6 On another **Sabbath** Jesus went into a **synagogue** and **taught**. A man was there whose **right hand** was **paralysed**. [7]Some **teachers of the Law** and some **Pharisees** wanted a **reason** to **accuse**

accuse 3.14; 11.31
apostle [2] Mk 6.30; 9.10
bad [2] Mk 9.26; 11.13
bless [4] 2.34; 13.35
blind 4.18; 7.21
bread [2] 4.3; 11.5
child of God Mt 5.9; 20.36
choose 4.6; 9.35
clear Mk 8.25; 9.53
complete Mk 10.42; 16.2
condemn Mk 16.16; 19.22
curse Mk 11.21; Jn 7.49
destroy 4.34; 9.54
disciple [4] 5.30; 7.11
discuss Mk 12.28; 24.15
disease 5.12; 7.21
enemy [2] 1.71; 10.19
evil 4.33; 11.29
false 3.14; 18.20
Father (2) (God) 2.49; 9.26
flood Mt 24.38; 17.27
forgive 5.20; 7.43
generous Mt 20.15; Rom 12.8
glad 1.14; 8.13
grateful Ecc 11.8; Acts 24.3
happy [4] 1.14; 7.23

5.30: Lk 15.1–2 **6.1:** Deut 23.25 **6.3–4:** 1 Sam 21.1–6 **6.4:** Lev 24.9

harm 4.35; Acts 16.28
hate [2] 1.71; 16.13
heal [4] 5.15; 7.3
heart [2] 2.35; 7.13
heaven 3.21; 9.16
help [2] 5.7; 7.4
hope 3.15; 16.21
hunger [3] 4.2; Jn 6.35
hypocrite Mk 7.6; 12.1
ill-treat Mt 17.12; Acts 7.24
insult Mk 15.29; 11.45
joy 2.10; 10.17
judge Mk 4.24; 12.14
Kingdom (1) (of God) 4.43; 7.28
law [3] 2.22; 14.3
life (1) [2] 1.6; 7.37
love [4] Mk 12.30; 7.5
mercy 1.50; 10.12
Most High 1.32; 8.28
mourn Mk 16.10; 8.52
obey [2] 2.51; 7.29
offer 5.14; 10.7
parable 5.36; 8.4
paralyse 5.18; Jn 5.3
Pharisees [2] 5.17; 7.30
please 3.22; 12.32
poor [2] 4.18; 7.22
power 5.17; 8.46
pray [3] 5.16; 9.18
priest 5.14; 10.31
prophet [2] 4.17; 7.16
rage Amos 1.14; 21.25
reason 1.35; 11.49
reject Mk 12.10; 7.30
reward [2] Mk 9.41; Rom 2.6
rich 1.53; 12.15
right (2) 1.11; 20.42
Sabbath [6] 4.16; 13.10
save 4.19; 7.16
Son of Man [2] 5.24; 7.34
son *see* **child of God**
spirit (2) 4.33; 7.21
synagogue 4.15; 7.5
teach 5.3; 9.26
teacher [2] 3.12; 7.40
teacher of the Law 5.17; 7.30
terrible [5] 2.9; 8.37
traitor Mk 14.44; Jn 18.2
trouble 1.29; 7.6
watch Mk 15.47; 12.15
weep [2] Mt 26.75; 19.41
wicked Mk 8.38; 13.27
word (1) [2] 5.1; 8.11
wrong Mk 12.24; 9.41

Jesus of doing **wrong**, so they **watched** him closely to see if he would **heal** on the **Sabbath**. 8 But Jesus knew their thoughts and said to the man, "Stand up and come here to the front." The man got up and stood there. 9 Then Jesus said to them, "I ask you: What does our **Law** allow us to do on the **Sabbath**? To **help** or to **harm**? To **save** a man's **life** or **destroy** it?" 10 He looked around at them all; then he said[d] to the man, "Stretch out your hand." He did so, and his hand became well again.

11 They were filled with **rage** and began to **discuss** among themselves what they could do to Jesus.

Jesus Chooses the Twelve Apostles
(Matt. 10.1–4; Mark 3.13–19)

12 At that time Jesus went up a hill to **pray** and spent the whole night there **praying** to God. 13 When day came, he called his **disciples** to him and **chose** twelve of them, whom he named **apostles**: 14 Simon (whom he named Peter) and his brother Andrew; James and John, Philip and Bartholomew, 15 Matthew and Thomas, James son of Alphaeus, and Simon (who was called the Patriot), 16 Judas son of James, and Judas Iscariot, who became the **traitor**.

Jesus Teaches and Heals
(Matt. 4.23–25)

17 When Jesus had come down from the hill with the **apostles**, he stood on a level place with a large number of his **disciples**. A large crowd of people was there from all over Judaea and from Jerusalem and from the coastal cities of Tyre and Sidon; 18 they had come to hear him and to be **healed** of their **diseases**. Those who were **troubled** by **evil spirits** also came and were **healed**. 19 All the people tried to touch him, for **power** was going out from him and **healing** them all.

Happiness and Sorrow
(Matt. 5.1–12)

20 Jesus looked at his **disciples** and said,

"**Happy** are you **poor**;
the **Kingdom of God** is yours!
21 "**Happy** are you who are **hungry** now;
you will be filled!
"**Happy** are you who **weep** now;
you will laugh!

22 "**Happy** are you when people **hate** you, **reject** you, **insult** you, and say that you are **evil**, all because of the **Son of Man**! 23 Be **glad** when that happens, and dance for **joy**, because a great **reward** is kept for you in **heaven**. For their ancestors did the very same things to the **prophets**.

24 "But how **terrible** for you who are **rich** now;
you have had your easy **life**!
25 "How **terrible** for you who are full now;
you will go **hungry**!
"How **terrible** for you who laugh now;
you will **mourn** and **weep**!

26 "How **terrible** when all people speak well of you; their ancestors said the very same things about the **false prophets**.

Love for Enemies
(Matt. 5.38–48; 7.12a)

27 "But I tell you who hear me: **Love** your **enemies**, do good to those who **hate** you, 28 **bless** those who **curse** you, and **pray** for those who **ill-treat** you. 29 If anyone hits you on one cheek, let him hit the other one too; if someone takes your coat, let him have your shirt as well. 30 Give to everyone who asks you for something, and when someone takes what is yours, do not ask for it back. 31 Do for others just what you want them to do for you.

32 "If you **love** only the people who love you, why should you receive a **blessing**? Even sinners **love** those who love them! 33 And if you do good only to those who do good to you, why should you receive a **blessing**? Even sinners do that! 34 And if you lend only to those from whom you **hope** to get it back, why should you receive a **blessing**? Even sinners lend to sinners, to get back the same amount! 35 No! **Love** your **enemies** and do good to them; lend and expect nothing back. You will then have a great **reward**, and you will be **sons** of the **Most High God**. For he is good to the **ungrateful** and the **wicked**. 36 Be **merciful** just as your **Father** is merciful.

Judging Others
(Matt. 7.1–5)

37 "Do not **judge** others, and God will not judge you; do not **condemn** others, and God will not condemn you; **forgive** others, and God will forgive you. 38 Give to others, and God will give to you. Indeed, you will receive a full measure, a **generous helping**, poured into your hands—all that you can hold. The measure you use for others is the one that God will use for you."

39 And Jesus told them this **parable**:

[d] said; *some manuscripts have* said angrily.

6.22: 1 Pet 4.14 **6.23:** 2 Chr 36.16; Acts 7.52 **6.31:** Mt 7.12 **6.39:** Mt 15.14

"One blind man cannot lead another one;
if he does, both will fall into a ditch. 40 No
pupil is greater than his teacher; but
every pupil, when he has completed his
training, will be like his teacher.
41 "Why do you look at the speck in
your brother's eye, but pay no attention
to the log in your own eye? 42 How can
you say to your brother, 'Please, brother,
let me take that speck out of your eye,'
yet cannot even see the log in your own
eye? You hypocrite! First take the log
out of your own eye, and then you will be
able to see clearly to take the speck out
of your brother's eye.

A Tree and Its Fruit
(Matt. 7.16–20; 12.33–35)

43 "A healthy tree does not bear bad
fruit, nor does a poor tree bear good
fruit. 44 Every tree is known by the fruit it
bears; you do not pick figs from thorn
bushes or gather grapes from bramble
bushes. 45 A good person brings good out
of the treasure of good things in his
heart; a bad person brings bad out of his
treasure of bad things. For the mouth
speaks what the heart is full of.

The Two House Builders
(Matt. 7.24–27)

46 "Why do you call me, 'Lord, Lord,'
and yet don't do what I tell you? 47 Anyone who comes to me and listens to my
words and obeys them—I will show you
what he is like. 48 He is like a man who, in
building his house, dug deep and laid the
foundation on rock. The river overflowed
and hit that house but could not shake it,
because it was well built. 49 But anyone
who hears my words and does not obey
them is like a man who built his house
without laying a foundation; when the
flood hit that house it fell at once—and
what a terrible crash that was!"

Jesus Heals a Roman Officer's Servant
(Matt. 8.5–13)

7 When Jesus had finished saying all
these things to the people, he went
to Capernaum. 2 A Roman officer there
had a servant who was very dear to him;
the man was sick and about to die.
3 When the officer heard about Jesus, he
sent some Jewish elders to ask him to
come and heal his servant. 4 They came
to Jesus and begged him earnestly, "This
man really deserves your help. 5 He loves
our people and he himself built a synagogue for us."
6 So Jesus went with them. He was not
far from the house when the officer sent
friends to tell him, "Sir, don't trouble
yourself. I do not deserve to have you
come into my house, 7 neither do I consider myself worthy to come to you in
person. Just give the order, and my servant will get well. 8 I, too, am a man
placed under the authority of superior
officers, and I have soldiers under me. I
order this one, 'Go!' and he goes; I order
that one, 'Come!' and he comes; and I
order my slave, 'Do this!' and he does it."
9 Jesus was surprised when he heard
this; he turned round and said to the
crowd following him, "I tell you, I have
never found faith like this, not even in
Israel!"
10 The messengers went back to the
officer's house and found his servant
well.

Jesus Raises a Widow's Son

11 Soon afterwards[e] Jesus went to a
town called Nain, accompanied by his
disciples and a large crowd. 12 Just as he
arrived at the gate of the town, a funeral
procession was coming out. The dead
man was the only son of a woman who
was a widow, and a large crowd from the
town was with her. 13 When the Lord saw
her, his heart was filled with pity for her,
and he said to her, "Don't cry." 14 Then he
walked over and touched the coffin, and
the men carrying it stopped. Jesus said,
"Young man! Get up, I tell you!" 15 The
dead man sat up and began to talk, and
Jesus gave him back to his mother.
16 They all were filled with fear and
praised God. "A great prophet has
appeared among us!" they said; "God
has come to save his people!"
17 This news about Jesus went out
through all the country and the surrounding territory.

The Messengers from John the Baptist
(Matt. 11.2–19)

18 When John's disciples told him
about all these things, he called two of
them 19 and sent them to the Lord to ask
him, "Are you the one John said was going to come, or should we expect someone else?"
20 When they came to Jesus, they
said, "John the Baptist sent us to ask if
you are the one he said was going to
come, or if we should expect someone
else."
21 At that very time Jesus cured many
people of their sicknesses, diseases, and
evil spirits, and gave sight to many blind

[e] Soon afterwards; *some manuscripts have* The next day.

6.40: Mt 10.24–25; Jn 13.16, 15.20 **6.44:** Mt 12.33 **6.45:** Mt 12.34

accept Mk 4.20; 14.18
ahead of you Mk 16.7; 19.30
authority 5.24; 9.1
baptize [2] 3.3; 12.50
beg 5.12; 8.28
blind [2] 6.39; 14.13
clean 5.12; 11.25
compare Mt 11.16; 13.18
consider Mk 12.19; 16.15
cure 5.14; 8.36
dead [3] Mk 15.44; 8.52
dear 3.22; 20.13
debt Mt 18.25; 16.5
demand Mk 6.25; Rom 8.4
demon 4.33; 8.2
deserve [2] Mt 23.15; 12.48
disciple [2] 6.1; 8.1
disease [2] 6.18; 8.2
doubt Mk 11.23; 22.59
earnest Mk 5.23; Acts 12.5
elder (2) Mk 15.1; 9.22
faith [2] 5.20; 8.25
fast (2) 5.33; 18.12
fear 5.26; 12.5
forgive [5] 6.37; 11.4
friend [2] 5.20; 11.5
God's people 4.19; 18.7
Good News 4.18; 8.1
happy 6.20; 11.27
heal 6.7; 8.2
heart 6.45; 8.12
help 6.9; 8.3
Jew 2.46; 18.18
Kingdom (1) (of God) 6.20; 8.1
kiss [3] Mk 14.44; 15.20
least Mt 25.40; 9.48
life (1) [2] 6.9; 8.14
life (2) (to life) Mk 14.28; 9.22
love [4] 6.27; 10.27
luxury Amos 6.4; 16.19
obey 6.47; 8.15
outcast 5.30; 15.1
owe [3] Mt 18.24; 16.5
peace 2.14; 8.48
Pharisees [4] 6.2; 11.37
pity Mk 10.47; 10.33
poor 6.20; 11.41
praise 5.25; 13.13
preach 4.43; 8.1
prophet [4] 6.23; 9.8
prove 5.14; 11.19
provide 1.69; 12.31
purpose Mal 2.15; 9.31
raise Mk 16.6; 9.22
refuse (1) Mk 15.5; 18.4
reject 6.22; 9.22
right (1) 1.20; 8.35
righteous 1.17; Jn 17.25
save [2] 6.9; 8.12
scripture 4.4; 10.26
servant [4] 2.29; 12.36
sight 4.18; 12.21
slave Mk 14.47; 15.29
Son of Man 6.5; 9.22
spirit (2) 6.18; 8.2
suffer 5.12; 8.43
synagogue 6.6; 8.41
tax collector [2] 5.27; 15.1
teacher 6.40; 8.49
teacher of the Law 6.7; 9.22
tear (2) [2] Mal 2.13; Acts 20.19
trouble 6.18; 10.41
true 5.10; 12.15
turn [2] 4.3; 9.55
wedding 5.34; 12.36
welcome 4.24; 8.40
widow 4.25; 18.3
wisdom 2.40; 11.49
worthy Prov 22.29; 20.35

people. 22 He answered John's messengers, "Go back and tell John what you
have seen and heard: the **blind** can see,
the lame can walk, those who **suffer** from
dreaded **skin-diseases** are made **clean**,[f]
the deaf can hear, the **dead** are **raised to**
life, and the **Good News** is **preached** to
the **poor**. 23 How **happy** are those who
have no **doubts** about me!"

24 After John's messengers had left,
Jesus began to speak about him to the
crowds: "When you went out to John in
the desert, what did you expect to see? A
blade of grass bending in the wind?
25 What did you go out to see? A man
dressed up in fancy clothes? People who
dress like that and live in **luxury** are
found in palaces! 26 Tell me, what did you
go out to see? A **prophet**? Yes indeed,
but you saw much more than a **prophet**.
27 For John is the one of whom the **scrip-**
ture says: 'God said, I will send my
messenger **ahead of you** to open the way
for you.' 28 I tell you," Jesus added, "John
is greater than any man who has ever
lived. But he who is **least** in the **Kingdom**
of God is greater than John."

29 All the people heard him; they and
especially the **tax collectors** were the
ones who had **obeyed** God's **righteous de-**
mands and had been **baptized** by John.
30 But the **Pharisees** and the **teachers of**
the Law rejected God's **purpose** for themselves and **refused** to be **baptized** by
John.

31 Jesus continued, "Now to what can
I **compare** the people of this day? What
are they like? 32 They are like children
sitting in the market-place. One group
shouts to the other, 'We played **wedding**
music for you, but you wouldn't dance!
We sang funeral songs, but you wouldn't
cry!' 33 John the Baptist came, and he
fasted and drank no wine, and you said,
'He has a **demon** in him!' 34 The **Son of**
Man came, and he ate and drank, and
you said, 'Look at this man! He is a glutton and a drinker, a **friend** of **tax col-**
lectors and other **outcasts**!' 35 God's **wis-**
dom, however, is shown to be **true** by all
who **accept** it."

Jesus at the Home of Simon the Pharisee

36 A **Pharisee** invited Jesus to have
dinner with him, and Jesus went to his
house and sat down to eat. 37 In that town
was a woman who lived a sinful **life**. She
heard that Jesus was eating in the **Phari-**
see's house, so she brought an alabaster
jar full of perfume 38 and stood behind
Jesus, by his feet, crying and wetting his
feet with her **tears**. Then she dried his
feet with her hair, **kissed** them, and
poured the perfume on them. 39 When the
Pharisee saw this, he said to himself, "If
this man really were a **prophet**, he would
know who this woman is who is touching
him; he would know what kind of sinful
life she lives!"

40 Jesus spoke up and said to him,
"Simon, I have something to tell you."

"Yes, **Teacher**," he said, "tell me."

41 "There were two men who **owed**
money to a money-lender," Jesus began.
"One **owed** him five hundred silver coins,
and the other **owed** him fifty. 42 Neither
of them could pay him back, so he cancelled the **debts** of both. Which one, then,
will **love** him more?"

43 "I suppose," answered Simon, "that
it would be the one who was **forgiven**
more."

"You are **right**," said Jesus. 44 Then he
turned to the woman and said to Simon,
"Do you see this woman? I came into
your home, and you gave me no water
for my feet, but she has washed my feet
with her **tears** and dried them with her
hair. 45 You did not **welcome** me with a
kiss, but she has not stopped **kissing** my
feet since I came. 46 You **provided** no
olive-oil for my head, but she has
covered my feet with perfume. 47 I tell
you, then, the great **love** she has shown
proves that her many sins have been **for-**
given. But whoever has been **forgiven**
little shows only a little **love**."

48 Then Jesus said to the woman,
"Your sins are **forgiven**."

49 The others sitting at the table began to say to themselves, "Who is this,
who even **forgives** sins?"

50 But Jesus said to the woman, "Your
faith has **saved** you; go in **peace**."

Women Who Accompanied Jesus

8 Some time later Jesus travelled
through towns and villages, **preach-**
ing the **Good News** about the **Kingdom of**
God. The twelve **disciples** went with him,
2 and so did some women who had been
healed of evil spirits and **diseases**: Mary
(who was called Magdalene), from whom
seven **demons** had been driven out;
3 Joanna, whose husband Chuza was an
officer in Herod's **court**; and Susanna,
and many other women who used their
own resources to **help** Jesus and his **dis-**
ciples.

afraid [4] 5.10; 9.34
amaze 5.9; 9.43
beg [5] 7.4; 9.38
believe [3] 1.20; 12.5
calm Mk 4.39; Acts 19.35
care 4.10; 10.34
command 2.22; 9.42
court (1) Mk 13.9; 12.58
cure [2] 7.21; 9.1
danger Mt 8.24; Acts 19.27
dead [2] 7.12; 9.60
demon [8] 7.33; 9.1
deny Mk 14.68; 22.57
Devil 4.2; Jn 6.70
disciple [7] 7.11; 9.1
disease 7.21; 9.1

[f] MADE CLEAN: *See 5.12.*

7.22: Is 35.5-6, 61.1 **7.27:** Mal 3.1 **7.29-30:** Mt 21.32; Lk 3.12 **7.37-38:** Mt 26.7; Mk 14.3; Jn 12.3
8.2-3: Mt 27.55-56; Mk 15.40-41; Lk 23.49

faith [2] 7.9; 12.28
glad 6.23; 10.20
Good News 7.22; 9.6
heal [2] 7.3; 9.2
heart [2] 7.13; 10.27
help 7.4; 10.40
keep from 4.42; Jn 18.36
Kingdom (1) (of God) [2] 7.28; 9.2
knowledge Mt 13.11; 11.52
life (1) [2] 7.37; 9.7
light (1) [2] 2.32; 11.33
master [2] 5.5; 9.33
means Mk 4.11; 11.20
message [3] 1.2; 24.47
mind (1) Mk 12.30; 9.51
Most High 6.35; Acts 7.48
mourn 6.25; Acts 8.2
obey [3] 7.29; 10.17
one another 4.36; 20.14
parable [4] 6.39; 12.16
peace 7.50; 10.5
pleasure Mic 7.18; Eph 1.5
power 6.19; 9.1
preach 7.22; 9.2
prison 3.20; 21.12
punish 3.7; 11.50
riches Mk 12.44; 12.21
right (1) 7.43; 10.28
ripe Mk 4.29; Jn 4.35
save 7.16; 9.24
scatter 1.51; 11.23
secret 2.35; 12.2
seed [8] Mk 4.4; 12.24
Son of God 4.3; 9.35
sow Mk 4.3; 12.24
spirit (2) [2] 7.21; 9.39
stand for [4] Mt 13.20; 1 Cor 8.4
strong 2.40; 11.21
suffer 7.22; 9.22
synagogue 7.5; 11.43
teacher 7.40; 9.38
terrible 6.24; 10.13
test 4.12; 11.4
tremble Mk 5.33; Acts 7.32
understand 2.50; 9.45
welcome 7.45; 9.4
word (1) [2] 6.47; 11.28
worry 2.48; 10.41

The Parable of the Sower
(Matt. 13.1–9; Mark 4.1–9)

4 People kept coming to Jesus from one town after another; and when a great crowd gathered, Jesus told this **parable**:

5 "Once there was a man who went out to **sow** corn. As he **scattered** the **seed** in the field, some of it fell along the path, where it was stepped on, and the birds
ate it up. 6 Some of it fell on rocky
ground, and when the plants sprouted, they dried up because the soil had no
moisture. 7 Some of the **seed** fell among
thorn bushes, which grew up with the
plants and choked them. 8 And some
seeds fell in good soil; the plants grew and produced corn, a hundred grains each."

And Jesus concluded, "Listen, then, if you have ears!"

The Purpose of the Parables
(Matt. 13.10–17; Mark 4.10–12)

9 His **disciples** asked Jesus what this
parable meant, 10 and he answered, "The
knowledge of the **secrets** of the **Kingdom of God** has been given to you, but to the rest it comes **by means of parables**, so that they may look but not see, and listen but not **understand**.

Jesus Explains the Parable of the Sower
(Matt. 13.18–23; Mark 4.13–20)

11 "This is what the **parable** means:
the **seed** is the **word of God**. 12 The **seeds**
that fell along the path **stand for** those who hear; but the **Devil** comes and takes the **message** away from their **hearts** in order to **keep them from believing** and
being **saved**. 13 The **seeds** that fell on
rocky ground **stand for** those who hear the **message** and receive it **gladly**. But it does not sink deep into them; they **believe** only for a while but when the time
of **testing** comes, they fall away. 14 The
seeds that fell among thorn bushes **stand for** those who hear; but the **worries** and **riches** and **pleasures** of this **life** crowd in and choke them, and their fruit never
ripens. 15 The **seeds** that fell in good soil
stand for those who hear the **message** and retain it in a good and **obedient heart**, and they persist until they bear fruit.

A Lamp under a Bowl
(Mark 4.21–25)

16 "No one lights a lamp and covers it with a bowl or puts it under a bed. Instead, he puts it on the lampstand, so that people will see the **light** as they come in.

17 "Whatever is hidden away will be brought out into the open, and whatever is covered up will be found and brought to **light**.

18 "Be careful, then, how you listen; because whoever has something will be given more, but whoever has nothing will have taken away from him even the little he thinks he has."

Jesus' Mother and Brothers
(Matt. 12.46–50; Mark 3.31–35)

19 Jesus' mother and brothers came to him, but were unable to join him because
of the crowd. 20 Someone said to Jesus,
"Your mother and brothers are standing outside and want to see you."

21 Jesus said to them all, "My mother and brothers are those who hear the **word of God** and **obey** it."

Jesus Calms a Storm
(Matt. 8.23–27; Mark 4.35–41)

22 One day Jesus got into a boat with his **disciples** and said to them, "Let us go across to the other side of the lake." So
they started out. 23 As they were sailing,
Jesus fell asleep. Suddenly a **strong** wind blew down on the lake, and the boat began to fill with water, so that they were
all in great **danger**. 24 The **disciples** went
to Jesus and woke him up, saying, "**Master, Master**! We are about to die!"

Jesus got up and gave an order to the wind and the stormy water; they died down, and there was a great **calm**.
25 Then he said to the **disciples**, "Where is
your **faith**?"

But they were **amazed** and **afraid**, and said to **one another**, "Who is this man? He gives orders to the winds and waves, and they **obey** him!"

Jesus Heals a Man with Demons
(Matt. 8.28–34; Mark 5.1–20)

26 Jesus and his **disciples** sailed on
over to the territory of Gerasa,[g] which is
across the lake from Galilee. 27 As Jesus
stepped ashore, he was met by a man from the town who had **demons** in him. For a long time this man had gone without clothes and would not stay at home, but spent his time in the burial caves.
28 When he saw Jesus, he gave a loud cry,
threw himself down at his feet, and shouted, "Jesus, **Son of the Most High God**! What do you want with me? I **beg**
you, don't **punish** me!" 29 He said this be-
cause Jesus had ordered the **evil spirit** to

[g] Gerasa; *some manuscripts have* Gadara (*see Mt 8.28*); *others have* Gergesa.

8.10: Is 6.9–10 (LXX) **8.16:** Mt 5.15; Lk 11.33 **8.17:** Mt 10.26; Lk 12.2 **8.18:** Mt 25.29; Lk 19.26

go out of him. Many times it had seized
him, and even though he was kept a
prisoner, his hands and feet fastened
with chains, he would break the chains
and be driven by the **demon** out into the
desert.
30 Jesus asked him, "What is your
name?"
"My name is 'Mob,'" he answered—
because many **demons** had gone into
him. 31 The **demons begged** Jesus not to
send them into the abyss.[h]
32 There was a large herd of pigs near
by, feeding on a hillside. So the **demons**
begged Jesus to let them go into the pigs,
and he let them. 33 They went out of the
man and into the pigs. The whole herd
rushed down the side of the cliff into the
lake and was drowned.
34 The men who had been taking **care**
of the pigs saw what happened, so they
ran off and spread the news in the town
and among the farms. 35 People went out
to see what had happened, and when
they came to Jesus, they found the man
from whom the **demons** had gone out sitting at the feet of Jesus, clothed and in
his **right mind**; and they were all **afraid**.
36 Those who had seen it told the people
how the man had been **cured**. 37 Then all
the people from that territory asked
Jesus to go away, because they were
terribly afraid. So Jesus got into the boat
and left. 38 The man from whom the
demons had gone out **begged** Jesus, "Let
me go with you."
But Jesus sent him away, saying, 39 "Go
back home and tell what God has done
for you."
The man went through the town, telling what Jesus had done for him.

Jairus' Daughter and the Woman Who Touched Jesus' Cloak
(Matt. 9.18–26; Mark 5.21–43)

40 When Jesus returned to the other
side of the lake, the people **welcomed**
him, because they had all been waiting
for him. 41 Then a man named Jairus
arrived; he was an official in the local
synagogue. He threw himself down at
Jesus' feet and **begged** him to go to his
home, 42 because his only daughter, who
was twelve years old, was dying.
As Jesus went along, the people were
crowding him from every side. 43 Among
them was a woman who had **suffered**
from severe bleeding for twelve years;
she had spent all she had on doctors,[i] but
no one had been able to **cure** her. 44 She
came up in the crowd behind Jesus and
touched the edge of his cloak, and her
bleeding stopped at once. 45 Jesus asked,
"Who touched me?"
Everyone **denied** it, and Peter said,
"**Master**, the people are all round you
and crowding in on you."
46 But Jesus said, "Someone touched
me, for I knew it when **power** went out of
me." 47 The woman saw that she had
been found out, so she came **trembling**
and threw herself at Jesus' feet. There in
front of everybody, she told him why she
had touched him and how she had been
healed at once. 48 Jesus said to her, "My
daughter, your **faith** has made you well.
Go in **peace**."
49 While Jesus was saying this, a
messenger came from the official's
house. "Your daughter has died," he told
Jairus; "don't bother the **Teacher** any
longer."
50 But Jesus heard it and said to
Jairus, "Don't be **afraid**; only **believe**,
and she will be well."
51 When he arrived at the house, he
would not let anyone go in with him except Peter, John, and James, and the
child's father and mother. 52 Everyone
there was crying and **mourning** for the
child. Jesus said, "Don't cry; the child is
not **dead**—she is only sleeping!"
53 They all laughed at him, because
they knew that she was **dead**. 54 But Jesus
took her by the hand and called out, "Get
up, my child!" 55 Her **life** returned, and
she got up at once, and Jesus ordered
them to give her something to eat. 56 Her
parents were astounded, but Jesus **com-**
manded them not to tell anyone what
had happened.

Jesus Sends Out the Twelve Disciples
(Matt. 10.5–15; Mark 6.7–13)

9 Jesus called the twelve **disciples** together and gave them **power** and
authority to drive out all **demons** and to
cure diseases. 2 Then he sent them out to
preach the **Kingdom of God** and to **heal**
the sick, 3 after saying to them, "Take
nothing with you for the journey: no
stick, no beggar's bag, no food, no
money, not even an extra shirt.
4 Wherever you are **welcomed**, stay in
the same house until you leave that
town; 5 wherever people don't **welcome**
you, leave that town and shake the dust
off your feet as a **warning** to them."
6 The **disciples** left and travelled
through all the villages, **preaching** the

afraid [2] 8.25; 12.4
alone [2] 4.4; 13.8
amaze 8.25; 11.14
angel 4.10; 12.8
apostle 6.13; 17.5
appearance Mt 28.3; 2 Cor 5.12
argue Mk 11.31; 20.5
ashamed [2] Mk 8.38; 11.8
assure 2.26; 10.12
authority 7.8; 10.19
beg [2] 8.28; 15.28
change 3.18; Acts 6.14
chief priests Mk 15.1; 19.47
choose 6.13; 10.1
clear 6.42; 20.37
cloud [3] Mk 14.62; 12.54
command 8.56; 10.17
cross (1) Mk 15.21; 14.27

[h] ABYSS: *It was thought that the demons were to be imprisoned in the depths of the earth until their final punishment.* [i] *Some manuscripts do not have* she had spent all she had on doctors.

9.3–5: Lk 10.4–11; Acts 13.51

cure 8.36; 13.32
dazzling Mt 17.2; 2 Thes 2.8
dead 8.52; 10.30
death (3) (to death) Mk 14.1; 21.16
demon [3] 8.2; 10.17
destroy 6.9; 12.33
disciple [18] 8.1; 10.16
disease 8.2; 17.12
elder (2) 7.3; 20.1
enough 3.16; 14.28
Father (2) (God) 6.36; 10.21
forget [2] Mk 8.14; 12.6
fulfil Jer 33.14; Rom 13.6
glory [4] 2.9; 19.38
Good News 8.1; 16.16
heal [4] 8.2; 10.9
heaven [4] 6.23; 10.15
holy 4.34; 11.2
hurt 4.11; 10.19
Kingdom (1) (of God) [5] 8.1; 10.9
least 7.28; 1 Cor 15.9
life (1) [5] 8.14; 10.25
life (2) (to life) 7.22; 18.33
lonely 5.16
master [2] 8.24; 12.36
Messiah 4.41; 20.41
might 1.17; Eph 1.19
mind (1) 8.35; 10.27
name (2) (name of God, of Jesus) [2] 2.21; 10.17
need 5.31; 10.42
power [3] 8.46; 10.19
pray [3] 6.12; 10.2
preach [2] 8.1; 11.32
proclaim 4.18; Acts 2.17
prophet [2] 7.16; 10.24
purpose 7.30; Jn 2.6
raise 7.22; 18.13
rebuke Mk 8.32; 17.3
reject 7.30; 10.16
rest (1) Mk 14.41; 11.24
sake Mk 13.9; 18.29
save [2] 8.12; 12.33
self Mk 8.34; Rom 6.6
Son of God 8.28; 10.22
Son of Man [4] 7.34; 11.30
sound (2) Mt 6.22; 11.34
spirit (2) [2] 8.2; 10.20
suffer 8.43; 17.12
teach 6.6; 10.39
teacher 8.49; 10.25
teacher of the Law 7.30; 10.25
thank 2.28; 10.21
turn 7.9; 10.13
unbeliever Mk 9.19; Rom 11.23
understand 8.10; 18.34
warn Mk 8.15; 16.28
welcome [5] 8.40; 10.8
who Mk 8.29; Jn 1.19
win Mk 8.36; Jn 4.1
world 4.5; 11.50
wrong 6.7; 11.4

Good News and **healing** people everywhere.

Herod's Confusion
(Matt. 14.1–12; Mark 6.14–29)

7 When Herod, the ruler of Galilee,
heard about all the things that were
happening, he was very confused, because some people were saying that John
the Baptist had come back to **life**.
8 Others were saying that Elijah had
appeared, and still others that one of the
prophets of long ago had come back to
life. 9 Herod said, "I had John's head cut
off; but who is this man I hear these
things about?" And he kept trying to see
Jesus.

Jesus Feeds Five Thousand Men
(Matt. 14.13–21; Mark 6.30–44;
John 6.1–14)

10 The **apostles** came back and told
Jesus everything they had done. He took
them with him, and they went off by
themselves to a town called Bethsaida.
11 When the crowds heard about it, they
followed him. He **welcomed** them, spoke
to them about the **Kingdom of God**, and
healed those who **needed** it.

12 When the sun was beginning to set,
the twelve **disciples** came to him and
said, "Send the people away so that they
can go to the villages and farms round
here and find food and lodging, because
this is a **lonely** place."

13 But Jesus said to them, "You yourselves give them something to eat."

They answered, "All we have are five
loaves and two fish. Do you want us to go
and buy food for this whole crowd?"
14 (There were about five thousand men
there.)

Jesus said to his **disciples**, "Make the
people sit down in groups of about fifty
each."

15 After the **disciples** had done so,
16 Jesus took the five loaves and two fish,
looked up to **heaven**, **thanked** God for
them, broke them, and gave them to the
disciples to distribute to the people.
17 They all ate and had **enough**, and the
disciples took up twelve baskets of what
was left over.

Peter's Declaration about Jesus
(Matt. 16.13–19; Mark 8.27–29)

18 One day when Jesus was **praying**
alone, the **disciples** came to him. "Who
do the crowds say I am?" he asked them.

19 "Some say that you are John the
Baptist," they answered. "Others say that
you are Elijah, while others say that one
of the **prophets** of long ago has come
back to **life**."

20 "What about you?" he asked them.
"**Who** do you say I am?"

Peter answered, "You are God's
Messiah."

Jesus Speaks about His Suffering and Death
(Matt. 16.20–28; Mark 8.30—9.1)

21 Then Jesus gave them strict orders
not to tell this to anyone. 22 He also said to
them, "The **Son of Man** must **suffer** much
and be **rejected** by the **elders**, the **chief**
priests, and the **teachers of the Law**. He
will be put **to death**, but three days later
he will be **raised to life**."

23 And he said to them all, "If anyone
wants to come with me, he must **forget**
self, take up his **cross** every day, and follow me. 24 For whoever wants to **save** his
own **life** will lose it, but whoever loses his
life for my **sake** will **save** it. 25 Will a person gain anything if he **wins** the whole
world but is himself lost or defeated? Of
course not! 26 If a person is **ashamed** of
me and of my **teaching**, then the **Son of**
Man will be **ashamed** of him when he
comes in his **glory** and in the **glory** of the
Father and of the **holy angels**. 27 I **assure**
you that there are some here who will
not die until they have seen the **Kingdom**
of God."

The Transfiguration
(Matt. 17.1–8; Mark 9.2–8)

28 About a week after he had said
these things, Jesus took Peter, John, and
James with him and went up a hill to
pray. 29 While he was **praying**, his face
changed its **appearance**, and his clothes
became **dazzling** white. 30 Suddenly two
men were there talking with him. They
were Moses and Elijah, 31 who appeared
in **heavenly glory** and talked with Jesus
about the way in which he would soon
fulfil God's **purpose** by dying in
Jerusalem. 32 Peter and his companions
were **sound asleep**, but they woke up and
saw Jesus' **glory** and the two men who
were standing with him. 33 As the men
were leaving Jesus, Peter said to him,
"**Master**, how good it is that we are here!
We will make three tents, one for you,
one for Moses, and one for Elijah." (He
did not really know what he was saying.)

34 While he was still speaking, a **cloud**
appeared and covered them with its
shadow; and the **disciples** were **afraid** as
the **cloud** came over them. 35 A voice said

9.7-8: Mt 16.14; Mk 8.28; Lk 9.19 **9.19:** Mt 14.1-2; Mk 6.14-15; Lk 9.7-8 **9.20:** Jn 6.68-69
9.23: Mt 10.38; Lk 14.27 **9.24:** Mt 10.39; Lk 17.33; Jn 12.25 **9.28-35:** 2 Pet 1.17-18
9.35: Is 42.1; Mt 3.17, 12.18; Mk 1.11; Lk 3.22

from the **cloud**, "This is my **Son**, whom I have **chosen**—listen to him!"

36 When the voice stopped, there was Jesus all **alone**. The **disciples** kept quiet about all this, and told no one at that time anything they had seen.

Jesus Heals a Boy with an Evil Spirit
(Matt. 17.14–18; Mark 9.14–27)

37 The next day Jesus and the three **disciples** went down from the hill, and a large crowd met Jesus. 38 A man shouted from the crowd, "**Teacher**! I **beg** you, look at my son—my only son! 39 A **spirit** attacks him with a sudden shout and throws him into a fit, so that he foams at the mouth; it keeps on **hurting** him and will hardly let him go! 40 I **begged** your **disciples** to drive it out, but they couldn't."

41 Jesus answered, "How **unbelieving** and **wrong** you people are! How long must I stay with you? How long do I have to put up with you?" Then he said to the man, "Bring your son here."

42 As the boy was coming, the **demon** knocked him to the ground and threw him into a fit. Jesus gave a **command** to the **evil spirit**, **healed** the boy, and gave him back to his father. 43 All the people were **amazed** at the **mighty power of God**.

Jesus Speaks Again about His Death
(Matt. 17.22–23; Mark 9.30–32)

The people were still marvelling at everything Jesus was doing, when he said to his **disciples**, 44 "Don't **forget** what I am about to tell you! The **Son of Man** is going to be handed over to the **power** of men." 45 But the **disciples** did not know what this meant. It had been hidden from them so that they could not **understand** it, and they were **afraid** to ask him about the matter.

Who Is the Greatest?
(Matt. 18.1–5; Mark 9.33–37)

46 An **argument** broke out among the **disciples** as to which one of them was the greatest. 47 Jesus knew what they were thinking, so he took a child, stood him by his side, 48 and said to them, "Whoever **welcomes** this child **in my name**, **welcomes** me; and whoever **welcomes** me, also **welcomes** the one who sent me. For he who is **least** among you all is the greatest."

Whoever Is Not against You Is for You
(Mark 9.38–40)

49 John spoke up, "**Master**, we saw a man driving out **demons in your name**, and we told him to stop, because he doesn't belong to our group."

50 "Do not try to stop him," Jesus said to him and to the other **disciples**, "because whoever is not against you is for you."

A Samaritan Village Refuses to Receive Jesus

51 As the time drew near when Jesus would be taken up to **heaven**, he made up his **mind** and set out on his way to Jerusalem. 52 He sent messengers ahead of him, who went into a village in Samaria to get everything ready for him. 53 But the people there would not receive him, because it was **clear** that he was on his way to Jerusalem. 54 When the **disciples** James and John saw this, they said, "Lord, do you want us to call fire down from **heaven** to **destroy** them?"[j]

55 Jesus **turned** and **rebuked** them.[k] 56 Then Jesus and his **disciples** went on to another village.

The Would-be Followers of Jesus
(Matt. 8.19–22)

57 As they went on their way, a man said to Jesus, "I will follow you wherever you go."

58 Jesus said to him, "Foxes have holes, and birds have nests, but the **Son of Man** has nowhere to lie down and **rest**."

59 He said to another man, "Follow me."

But that man said, "Sir, first let me go back and bury my father."

60 Jesus answered, "Let the **dead** bury their own dead. You go and **proclaim** the **Kingdom of God**."

61 Another man said, "I will follow you, sir; but first let me go and say goodbye to my family."

62 Jesus said to him, "Anyone who starts to plough and then keeps looking back is of no use to the **Kingdom of God**."

Jesus Sends Out the Seventy-Two

10 After this the Lord **chose** another seventy-two[l] men and sent them out two by two, to go ahead of him to every town and place where he himself was about to go. 2 He said to them, "There is a large **harvest**, but few workers to gather it in. **Pray** to the

act Mal 4.3; 18.4
ash Mt 11.21; Heb 9.13
assure 9.27; 11.32
authority 9.1; 12.5
care [3] 8.34; 15.15
choose [3] 9.35; 14.7
command 9.42; 19.39
Day of Judgement [2] Mt 12.36; 11.31

[j] *Some manuscripts add* as Elijah did.
[k] *Some manuscripts add* and said, "You don't know what kind of a Spirit you belong to; for the Son of Man did not come to destroy men's lives, but to save them."
[l] seventy-two; *some manuscripts have* seventy.

9.46: Lk 22.24 **9.48:** Mt 10.40; Lk 10.16; Jn 13.20 **9.54:** 2 Kgs 1.9–16 **9.61:** 1 Kgs 19.20 **10.2:** Mt 9.37–38

dead 9.60; 15.24
demon 9.1; 11.14
disciple [3] 9.1; 11.1
enemy 6.27; 13.17
eternal Mk 16.10; 16.9
Father (2) (God) [5] 9.26; 11.2
fortune Mt 13.16; Acts 26.2
glad [2] 8.13; Jn 3.29
harvest [3] Mk 12.2; 12.24
heal 9.2; 13.14
heart [2] 8.12; 12.34
heaven [4] 9.16; 11.13
hell Mk 9.43; 12.5
help 8.3; 11.23
hurt 9.39; Acts 26.14
interpret Mt 16.3
joy [2] 6.23; 15.7
kind Mk 5.19; Acts 24.4
Kingdom (1) (of God) [2] 9.2; 11.2
lamb Mk 14.12; 22.7
learn [2] Mt 27.3; 23.7
Levites Ezek 48.12; Jn 1.19
life (1) 9.7; 12.15
love [2] 7.5; 11.42
mercy [2] 6.36; Rom 9.15
mind (1) 9.51; 21.14
miracle Mk 16.17; 11.16
name (2) (name of God, of Jesus) 9.48; 11.2
need 9.11; 11.3
neighbour [3] 1.58; 14.12
obey [2] 8.15; 11.28
offer 6.4; 13.1
peace [4] 8.48; 12.51
pity 7.13; 15.20
power 9.1; 11.15
pray 9.18; 11.1
priest 6.4; 17.14
prophet 9.8; 11.30
reject [2] 9.22; 12.9
remember 2.19; 16.25
reveal 2.32; 17.30
right (1) [2] 8.35; 12.57
rob [2] Mk 12.40; 20.47
sackcloth Mt 11.21; Rev 11.3
Satan Mk 8.33; 11.18
scripture 7.27; 19.46
Son of God [3] 9.35; 22.70
soul 1.47; 2 Cor 7.1
Spirit (1) (God's Spirit) 4.1; 11.13
spirit (2) 9.39; 11.24
sprinkle Mt 11.21; Heb 9.13
strength Mk 12.30; 21.36
strip (1) Mt 27.28
teach 9.26; 11.1
teacher 9.38; 11.45
teacher of the Law [3] 9.22; 11.45
terrible [2] 8.37; 11.42
thank 9.16; 17.9
trap Mk 12.13; 11.16
trouble 7.6; 18.5
turn [2] 9.55; 11.32
upset Mk 14.19; 12.29
welcome [3] 9.4; 15.2

owner of the **harvest** that he will send out
workers to gather in his **harvest**. [3]Go! I
am sending you like **lambs** among
wolves. [4]Don't take a purse or a beggar's
bag or shoes; don't stop to greet anyone
on the road. [5]Whenever you go into a
house, first say, '**Peace** be with this
house.' [6]If a **peace-loving** man lives
there, let your greeting of **peace** remain
on him; if not, take back your greeting of
peace. [7]Stay in that same house, eating
and drinking whatever they **offer** you, for
a worker should be given his pay. Don't
move round from one house to another.
[8]Whenever you go into a town and are
made **welcome**, eat what is set before
you, [9]**heal** the sick in that town, and say
to the people there, 'The **Kingdom of God**
has come near you.' [10]But whenever you
go into a town and are not **welcomed**, go
out in the streets and say, [11]'Even the
dust from your town that sticks to our
feet we wipe off against you. But **remember** that the **Kingdom of God** has
come near you!' [12]I **assure** you that on
Judgement Day God will show more
mercy to Sodom than to that town!

The Unbelieving Towns
(Matt. 11.20–24)

13 "How **terrible** it will be for you,
Chorazin! How **terrible** for you too,
Bethsaida! If the **miracles** which were
performed in you had been performed in
Tyre and Sidon, the people there would
long ago have sat down, put on **sackcloth**,
and **sprinkled ashes** on themselves, to
show that they had **turned from their
sins**! [14]God will show more **mercy** on
Judgement Day to Tyre and Sidon than
to you. [15]And as for you, Capernaum! Did
you want to lift yourself up to **heaven**?
You will be thrown down to **hell**!"

16 Jesus said to his **disciples**, "Whoever listens to you listens to me; whoever
rejects you **rejects** me; and whoever rejects me rejects the one who sent me."

The Return of the Seventy-Two

17 The seventy-two[m] men came back
in great **joy**. "Lord," they said, "even the
demons obeyed us when we gave them a
command in your name!"

18 Jesus answered them, "I saw **Satan**
fall like lightning from **heaven**. [19]Listen!
I have given you **authority**, so that you
can walk on snakes and scorpions and
overcome all the **power** of the **Enemy**,
and nothing will **hurt** you. [20]But don't be
glad because the **evil spirits obey** you;
rather be **glad** because your names are
written in **heaven**."

Jesus Rejoices
(Matt. 11.25–27; 13.16–17)

21 At that time Jesus was filled with
joy by the **Holy Spirit**[n] and said, "**Father**,
Lord of **heaven and earth**! I **thank** you
because you have shown to the **un-
learned** what you have hidden from the
wise and **learned**. Yes, **Father**, this was
how you wanted it to happen.

22 "**My Father** has given me all things.
No one knows who the **Son** is except the
Father, and no one knows who the
Father is except the **Son** and those to
whom the **Son chooses** to **reveal** him."

23 Then Jesus **turned** to the **disciples**
and said to them privately, "How **fortunate** you are to see the things you see!
[24]I tell you that many **prophets** and kings
wanted to see what you see, but they
could not, and to hear what you hear, but
they did not."

The Parable of the Good Samaritan

25 A **teacher of the Law** came up and
tried to **trap** Jesus. "**Teacher**," he asked,
"what must I do to receive **eternal life**?"

26 Jesus answered him, "What do the
Scriptures say? How do you **interpret**
them?"

27 The man answered, "'**Love** the
Lord your God **with all your heart**, with
all your **soul**, with all your **strength**, and
with all your **mind**'; and '**Love** your
neighbour as you love yourself.'"

28 "You are **right**," Jesus replied; "do
this and you will live."

29 But the **teacher of the Law** wanted
to justify himself, so he asked Jesus,
"Who is my **neighbour**?"

30 Jesus answered, "There was once a
man who was going down from
Jerusalem to Jericho when **robbers**
attacked him, **stripped** him, and beat him
up, leaving him half **dead**. [31]It so happened that a **priest** was going down that
road; but when he saw the man, he
walked on by, on the other side. [32]In the
same way a **Levite** also came along,
went over and looked at the man, and
then walked on by, on the other side.
[33]But a Samaritan who was travelling

wise Mk 12.34; 11.31
worry 8.14; 12.11

[m] seventy-two; *some manuscripts have* seventy *(see verse 1).*
[n] by the Holy Spirit; *some manuscripts have* by the Spirit; *others have* in his spirit.

10.3: Mt 10.16 **10.4–11:** Mt 10.7–14; Mk 6.8–11; Lk 9.3–5 **10.7:** 1 Cor 9.14; 1 Tim 5.18
10.10–11: Acts 13.51 **10.12:** Gen 19.24–28; Mt 11.24, 10.15
10.13: Is 23.1–18; Ezek 26.1–28.26; Joel 3.4–8; Amos 1.9–10; Zech 9.2–4 **10.15:** Is 14.13–15
10.16: Mt 10.40; Mk 9.37; Lk 9.48; Jn 13.20 **10.19:** Ps 91.13 **10.22:** Jn 3.35, 10.15
10.25–28: Mt 22.35–40; Mk 12.28–34 **10.27:** Lev 19.18; Deut 6.5 **10.28:** Lev 18.5 **10.33–34:** 2 Chr 28.15

that way came upon the man, and when
he saw him, his **heart** was filled with **pity**.
34 He went over to him, poured oil and
wine on his wounds and bandaged them;
then he put the man on his own animal
and took him to an inn, where he took
care of him. 35 The next day he took out
two silver coins and gave them to the
innkeeper. 'Take **care** of him,' he told the
innkeeper, 'and when I come back this
way, I will pay you whatever else you
spend on him.' "

36 And Jesus concluded, "In your
opinion, which one of these three **acted**
like a **neighbour** towards the man
attacked by the **robbers**?"

37 The **teacher of the Law** answered,
"The one who was **kind** to him."

Jesus replied, "You go, then, and do
the same."

Jesus Visits Martha and Mary

38 As Jesus and his **disciples** went on
their way, he came to a village where a
woman named Martha **welcomed** him in
her home. 39 She had a sister named
Mary, who sat down at the feet of the
Lord and listened to his **teaching**.
40 Martha was **upset** over all the work she
had to do, so she came and said, "Lord,
don't you **care** that my sister has left me
to do all the work by myself? Tell her to
come and **help** me!"

41 The Lord answered her, "Martha,
Martha! You are **worried** and **troubled**
over so many things, 42 but just one is
needed. Mary has **chosen** the **right** thing,
and it will not be taken away from her."

Jesus' Teaching on Prayer
(Matt. 6.9–13; 7.7–11)

11 One day Jesus was **praying** in a
certain place. When he had fin-
ished, one of his **disciples** said to him,
"Lord, teach us to **pray**, just as John
taught his **disciples**."

2 Jesus said to them, "When you **pray**,
say this:

'Father:
May your **holy name** be **honoured**;
may your **Kingdom** come.
3 Give us day by day the food we
need. *o*
4 Forgive us our sins,
for we **forgive** everyone who does us
wrong.
And do not bring us to **hard**
testing.' "

5 And Jesus said to his **disciples**,
"Suppose one of you should go to a
friend's house at midnight and say to
him, '**Friend**, let me borrow three loaves
of **bread**. 6 A **friend** of mine who is on a
journey has just come to my house, and I
haven't got any food for him!' 7 And suppose your **friend** should answer from inside, 'Don't bother me! The door is already locked, and my children and I are
in bed. I can't get up and give you anything.' 8 Well, what then? I tell you that
even if he will not get up and give you
the **bread** because you are his **friend**, yet
he will get up and give you everything
you **need** because you are not **ashamed**
to keep on asking.

9 "And so I say to you: Ask, and you
will receive; **seek**, and you will find;
knock, and the door will be opened to
you. 10 For everyone who asks will receive, and he who **seeks** will find, and the
door will be opened to anyone who
knocks. 11 Would any of you who are
fathers give your son a snake when he
asks for fish? 12 Or would you give him a
scorpion when he asks for an egg? 13 **Bad**
as you are, you know how to give good
things to your children. How much more,
then, will the **Father** in **heaven** give the
Holy Spirit to those who ask him!"

Jesus and Beelzebul
(Matt. 12.22–30; Mark 3.20–27)

14 Jesus was driving out a **demon** that
could not talk; and when the **demon** went
out, the man began to talk. The crowds
were **amazed**, 15 but some of the people
said, "It is Beelzebul, the chief of the
demons, who gives him the **power** to
drive them out."

16 Others wanted to **trap** Jesus, so
they asked him to perform a **miracle** to
show that God **approved** of him. 17 But
Jesus knew what they were thinking, so
he said to them, "Any country that
divides itself into groups which fight
each other will not **last** very long; a
family divided against itself falls **apart**.
18 So if **Satan's** kingdom has groups fighting **each other**, how can it **last**? You say
that I drive out **demons** because
Beelzebul gives me the **power** to do so.
19 If this is how I drive them out, how do
your **followers** drive them out? Your
own **followers prove** that you are **wrong**!
20 No, it is rather **by means of God's**
power that I drive out **demons**, and this
proves that the **Kingdom of God** has already come to you.

21 "When a **strong** man, with all his
weapons ready, guards his own house, all
his belongings are **safe**. 22 But when a
stronger man attacks him and defeats

o the food we need; *or* food for the next day.

10.38–39: Jn 11.1 **11.15:** Mt 9.34, 10.25 **11.16:** Mt 12.38, 16.1; Mk 8.11

accuse [2] 6.7; 18.20
admit (1) Mt 23.31; Acts 19.18
altar 1.9; Acts 17.23
amaze 9.43; 20.26
apart Mk 3.24; 18.11
approve [2] Mk 8.11; Jn 6.27
ashamed 9.26; 13.17
assure 10.12; 12.8
bad 6.43; 16.25
bitter Mt 27.34; 22.62
body [4] 3.22; 12.4
bread [2] 6.4; 22.19
certain (1) Mt 6.1; Jn 8.52
clean [3] 7.22; 17.14
create Mk 13.19; Jn 1.1
criticize Mk 14.5; Acts 11.2
cup [2] Mk 14.23; 22.17
dark [3] 1.79; 12.3
Day of Judgement [2] 10.12; Acts 24.25
demon [5] 10.17; 13.32
depend Mt 22.40; Rom 2.17

disciple [3] 10.16; 12.1
each other [2] Mk 15.31; 12.1
evil [2] 6.22; 12.10
Father (2) (God) [2] 10.21; 12.30
follower [2] Mk 2.18; 24.13
fool Mt 25.2; 12.20
forgive 7.43; 12.10
friend [5] 7.6; 12.4
grave Mt 27.52; Jn 5.29
happy [2] 7.23; 12.37
hard [2] 5.5; 18.24
heaven 10.15; 12.33
help [2] 10.40; 18.3
holy 9.26; Jn 6.69
Holy Place Mt 24.15; Acts 21.28
honour 1.50; 14.10
insult 6.22; 18.32
justice Mt 23.23; Acts 8.33
Kingdom (1) (of God) [2] 10.9; 12.31
knowledge 8.10; Acts 18.24
last (1) [2] Mk 15.33; Jn 6.27
light (1) [4] 8.16; 16.8
love [2] 10.27; 14.26
mark (1) Ezek 39.15; Jn 6.27
means 8.10; Jn 1.13
miracle [3] 10.13; 23.8
name (2) (name of God, of Jesus) 10.17; 13.35
need [2] 10.42; 12.19
neglect [2] Mt 23.23; Acts 6.1
notice (1) Mk 12.34; 14.7
obey 10.17; 17.6
persecute Mk 10.30; 21.12
Pharisees [6] 7.30; 12.1
poor 7.22; 12.33
power [3] 10.19; 20.20
practice Mt 23.3; Jn 13.17
pray [3] 10.2; 18.1
preach 9.2; 20.1
prophet [6] 10.24; 13.28
prove [2] 7.47; 13.2
punish [2] 8.28; 12.47
question 2.46; 20.3
reason 6.7; 14.20
respect 5.32; 15.7
rest (1) 9.58; 23.56
safe Mk 6.20; 15.27
Satan 10.18; 13.16
scatter 8.5; Jn 2.15
seek [2] Mt 7.7; 19.10
sign (1) [2] 2.34; Acts 7.8
Son of Man 9.22; 12.8
sound (2) 9.32; 15.27
Spirit (1) (God's Spirit) 10.21; 12.10
spirit (2) [2] 10.20; 13.11
steal Mk 10.19; 18.20
strong [2] 8.23; 14.31
synagogue 8.41; 12.11
teach [2] 10.39; 12.12
teacher 10.25; 12.13
teacher of the Law [4] 10.25; 14.3
terrible [6] 10.13; 17.1
test 8.13; 22.31
tomb [2] Mk 16.2; 23.53

trap [2] 10.25; 20.20
turn 10.13; 13.3
violent Mt 28.2; Acts 9.1
wisdom 7.35; 21.15
wise 10.21; 12.42
word (1) 8.11; 12.10
world 9.25; 12.30
worse [2] 3.20; 12.4
wrong [3] 9.41; 23.41

him, he carries away all the weapons the owner was **depending** on and divides up what he **stole**.

23 “Anyone who is not for me is really against me; anyone who does not **help** me gather is really **scattering**.

The Return of the Evil Spirit
(Matt. 12.43–45)

24 “When an **evil spirit** goes out of a person, it travels over dry country looking for a place to **rest**. If it can’t find one, it says to itself, ‘I will go back to my house.’ 25 So it goes back and finds the house **clean** and tidy. 26 Then it goes out and brings seven other **spirits** even **worse** than itself, and they come and live there. So when it is all over, that person is in a **worse** state than he was at the beginning.”

True Happiness

27 When Jesus had said this, a woman spoke up from the crowd and said to him, “How **happy** is the woman who bore you and nursed you!”

28 But Jesus answered, “Rather, how **happy** are those who hear the **word of God** and **obey** it!”

The Demand for a Miracle
(Matt. 12.38–42)

29 As the people crowded round Jesus, he went on to say, “How **evil** are the people of this day! They ask for a **miracle**, but none will be given them except the **miracle** of Jonah. 30 In the same way that the **prophet** Jonah was a **sign** for the people of Nineveh, so the **Son of Man** will be a **sign** for the people of this day. 31 On **Judgement Day** the Queen of Sheba will stand up and **accuse** the people of today, because she travelled all the way from her country to listen to King Solomon’s **wise teaching**; and I tell you there is something here greater than Solomon. 32 On **Judgement Day** the people of Nineveh will stand up and **accuse** you, because they **turned from their sins** when they heard Jonah **preach**; and I assure you that there is something here greater than Jonah!

The Light of the Body
(Matt. 5.15; 6.22–23)

33 “No one lights a lamp and then hides it or puts it under a bowl;[p] instead, he puts it on the lampstand, so that people may see the **light** as they come in. 34 Your eyes are like a lamp for the **body**. When your eyes are **sound**, your whole **body** is full of **light**; but when your eyes are no good, your whole **body** will be in **darkness**. 35 Make **certain**, then, that the **light** in you is not **darkness**. 36 If your whole **body** is full of **light**, with no part of it in **darkness**, it will be bright all over, as when a lamp shines on you with its brightness.”

Jesus Accuses the Pharisees and the Teachers of the Law
(Matt. 23.1–36; Mark 12.38–40)

37 When Jesus finished speaking, a **Pharisee** invited him to eat with him; so he went in and sat down to eat. 38 The **Pharisee** was surprised when he **noticed** that Jesus had not washed before eating. 39 So the Lord said to him, “Now then, you **Pharisees clean** the outside of your **cup** and plate, but inside you are full of **violence** and **evil**. 40 **Fools**! Did not God, who made the outside, also make the inside? 41 But give what is in your **cups** and plates to the **poor**, and everything will be ritually **clean** for you.

42 “How **terrible** for you **Pharisees**! You give God a tenth of the seasoning herbs, such as mint and rue and all the other herbs, but you **neglect justice** and **love** for God. These you should **practise**, without **neglecting** the others.

43 “How **terrible** for you **Pharisees**! You **love** the reserved seats in the **synagogues** and to be greeted with **respect** in the market-places. 44 How **terrible** for you! You are like **unmarked graves** which people walk on without knowing it.”

45 One of the **teachers of the Law** said to him, “**Teacher**, when you say this, you **insult** us too!”

46 Jesus answered, “How **terrible** also for you **teachers of the Law**! You put loads on people’s backs which are **hard** to carry, but you yourselves will not stretch out a finger to **help** them carry those loads. 47 How **terrible** for you! You make fine **tombs** for the **prophets**—the very **prophets** your ancestors murdered. 48 You yourselves **admit**, then, that you **approve** of what your ancestors did; they murdered the **prophets**, and you build their **tombs**. 49 For this **reason** the **Wisdom** of God said, ‘I will send them **prophets** and messengers; they will kill some of them and **persecute** others.’ 50 So the people of this time will be **punished** for the murder of all the **prophets** killed since the **creation** of the **world**, 51 from

[p] *Some manuscripts do not have* or puts it under a bowl.

11.23: Mk 9.40 **11.29:** Mt 16.4; Mk 8.12 **11.30:** Jon 3.4 **11.31:** 1 Kgs 10.1–10; 2 Chr 9.1–12
11.32: Jon 3.5 **11.33:** Mt 5.15; Mk 4.21; Lk 8.16 **11.42:** Lev 27.30 **11.51:** Gen 4.8; 2 Chr 24.20–21

the murder of Abel to the murder of
Zechariah, who was killed between the
altar and the **Holy Place**. Yes, I tell you,
the people of this time will be **punished**
for them all!

52 "How **terrible** for you **teachers of**
the Law! You have kept the key that
opens the door to the house of **know-**
ledge; you yourselves will not go in, and
you stop those who are trying to go in!"

53 When Jesus left that place, the
teachers of the Law and the **Pharisees**
began to **criticize** him **bitterly** and ask
him **questions** about many things, 54 trying to lay **traps** for him and catch him
saying something **wrong**.

A Warning against Hypocrisy
(Matt. 10.26–27)

12 As thousands of people crowded
together, so that they were step-
ping on **each other**, Jesus said first to his
disciples, "Be on guard against the **yeast**
of the **Pharisees**—I mean their **hypo-**
crisy. 2 Whatever is covered up will be
uncovered, and every **secret** will be
made known. 3 So then, whatever you
have said in the **dark** will be heard in
broad daylight, and whatever you have
whispered in private in a closed room
will be shouted from the housetops.

Whom to Fear
(Matt. 10.28–31)

4 "I tell you, my **friends**, do not be
afraid of those who kill the **body** but cannot afterwards do anything **worse**. 5 I will
show you whom to **fear**: **fear** God, who,
after killing, has the **authority** to throw
into **hell**. **Believe** me, he is the one you
must **fear**!

6 "Aren't five sparrows sold for two
pennies? Yet not one sparrow is **for-**
gotten by God. 7 Even the hairs of your
head have all been counted. So do not be
afraid; you are **worth** much more than
many sparrows!

Confessing and Rejecting Christ
(Matt. 10.32–33; 12.32; 10.19–20)

8 "I **assure** you that whoever **declares**
publicly that he belongs to me, the **Son of**
Man will do the same for him before the
angels of God. 9 But whoever **rejects** me
publicly, the **Son of Man** will also **reject**
him before the **angels of God**.

10 "Anyone who says a **word** against
the **Son of Man** can be **forgiven**; but whoever says **evil** things against the **Holy**
Spirit will not be **forgiven**.

11 "When they bring you to be **tried** in
the **synagogues** or before governors or
rulers, do not be **worried** about how you
will **defend** yourself or what you will say.
12 For the **Holy Spirit** will **teach** you at
that time what you should say."

The Parable of the Rich Fool

13 A man in the crowd said to Jesus,
"**Teacher**, tell my brother to divide with
me the property our father left us."

14 Jesus answered him, "My **friend**,
who gave me the **right** to **judge** or to
divide the property between you two?"
15 And he went on to say to them all,
"**Watch** out and guard yourselves from
every kind of **greed**; because a person's
true life is not made up of the things he
owns, no matter how **rich** he may be."

16 Then Jesus told them this **parable**:
"There was once a **rich** man who had
land which bore good crops. 17 He began
to think to himself, 'I haven't anywhere
to keep all my crops. What can I do?
18 This is what I will do,' he told himself;
'I will tear down my barns and build bigger ones, where I will store my corn and
all my other goods. 19 Then I will say to
myself, Lucky man! You have all the
good things you **need** for many years.
Take **life** easy, eat, drink, and **enjoy** yourself!' 20 But God said to him, 'You **fool**!
This very night you will have to **give up**
your **life**; then who will get all these
things you have kept for yourself?' "

21 And Jesus concluded, "This is how
it is with those who pile up **riches** for
themselves but are not **rich** in God's
sight."

Trust in God
(Matt. 6.25–34)

22 Then Jesus said to the **disciples**,
"And so I tell you not to **worry** about the
food you **need** to stay **alive** or about the
clothes you **need** for your **body**. 23 **Life** is
much more **important** than food, and the
body much more **important** than clothes.
24 Look at the crows: they don't **sow seeds**
or gather a **harvest**; they don't have
store-rooms or barns; God feeds them!
You are **worth** so much more than birds!
25 Can any of you live a bit longer[q] by
worrying about it? 26 If you can't manage
even such a small thing, why **worry**
about the other things? 27 Look how the
wild flowers grow: they don't work or
make clothes for themselves. But I tell
you that not even King Solomon with all
his wealth had clothes as beautiful as one

action Mt 23.3; 23.50
afraid [3] 9.34; 19.21
alive Mk 16.11; 15.24
angel [2] 9.26; 15.10
assure 11.32; 13.35
authority 10.19; 20.20
baptize 7.29; 20.4
believe 8.12; 20.5
best 1.1; 13.24
body [3] 11.34; 17.37
cloud 9.34; 21.27
concern [3] Mt 6.32; Rom 12.16
court (1) [2] 8.3; Acts 18.12
dark 11.34; 22.53
declare Mk 7.19; Jn 13.8
defend Zech 14.14; 21.14
deserve 7.4; 17.9
destroy 9.54; 19.44
disciple [2] 11.1; 14.26
disobey 1.17; 15.29
dispute Mt 5.25; Acts 9.29
distress Mk 16.8; 21.23
each other 11.17; 21.10
enjoy Zech 3.10; 16.25
evil 11.29; Jn 3.19
faith 8.25; 17.5
faithful Mt 25.21; 16.10
fate Mt 24.51; 22.37
Father (2) (God) [2] 11.2; 22.29
fear [3] 7.16; 18.2
feast 5.29; 13.29
flock 2.8; Jn 4.12
fool 11.40; 24.25
forget 9.23; Jn 16.21
forgive [2] 11.4; 17.3
friend [2] 11.5; 14.10
give up Mk 4.17; 14.33
greed Mk 7.22; 18.11
happy [3] 11.27; 14.15
harvest 10.2; 20.10
heart 10.27; 15.20
heaven 11.13; 15.7
hell 10.15; Acts 8.20
hypocrite [2] 6.42; 13.15
important [2] Mk 12.10; 14.8
jail Mt 18.30; Acts 4.3

judge [3] 6.37; 18.2
Kingdom (1) (of God) [2] 11.2; 13.18
last (2) 1.25; 13.30
life (1) [4] 10.25; 17.33
master [10] 9.33; 13.25
need [4] 11.3; 15.7
pagan Mt 18.17; 22.25
parable [2] 8.4; 13.6
peace [2] 10.5; 14.32
Pharisees 11.37; 13.31
please 6.42; 14.18
poor 11.41; 14.13
predict Mt 16.3; Acts 1.16
proper Mk 7.3; Rom 13.13
provide [2] 7.46; Jn 4.14
punish [2] 11.50; 20.47
reject [2] 10.16; 17.25
require [2] 2.24; Acts 15.1
rich [3] 6.24; 14.12
riches [3] 8.14; 18.22
right (1) 10.28; 13.33
right (3) Mk 11.28; 18.3
save 9.24; 13.23
secret 8.10; 22.2
seed 8.5; 13.19
servant [11] 7.2; 14.17
settle (2) Mt 25.19; Acts 18.15
share [2] 3.11; 15.12
sight 7.21; 16.15
Son of Man [4] 11.30; 17.22
sow 8.5; 13.19
Spirit (1) (God's Spirit) [2] 11.13; Jn 1.32
sure [2] 4.23; 18.9
synagogue 11.43; 13.10
teach 11.1; 13.10
teacher 11.45; 18.18
thief [3] Mk 11.17; 19.46
true 7.35; 16.11
try (2) Mt 10.18; 14.19
upset 10.40; Jn 14.1
watch 6.7; 14.1
wedding 7.32; 14.8
wise 11.31; Acts 24.2
wish Mt 20.15; 15.16
word (1) 11.28; 18.34
world [2] 11.50; 16.8
worry [4] 10.41; 21.14
worse 11.26; 13.2
worth [2] Mk 12.42; 1 Cor 12.23
yeast Mk 8.15; 13.21

[q] live a bit longer; *or* grow a bit taller.

12.1: Mt 16.6; Mk 8.15 **12.2:** Mk 4.22; Lk 8.17 **12.10:** Mt 12.32; Mk 3.29
12.11–12: Mt 10.19–20; Mk 13.11; Lk 21.14–15 **12.27:** 1 Kgs 10.4–7; 2 Chr 9.3–6

of these flowers. 28 It is God who clothes
the wild grass—grass that is here today
and gone tomorrow, burnt up in the oven.
Won't he be all the more **sure** to clothe
you? How little **faith** you have!
29 "So don't be all **upset**, always **con-**
cerned about what you will eat and
drink. 30 (For the **pagans** of **this world** are
always **concerned** about all these things.)
Your **Father** knows that you **need** these
things. 31 Instead, be **concerned** with his
Kingdom, and he will **provide** you with
these things.

Riches in Heaven
(Matt. 6.19–21)

32 "Do not be **afraid**, little **flock**, for
your **Father** is **pleased** to give you the
Kingdom. 33 Sell all your belongings and
give the money to the **poor**. **Provide** for
yourselves purses that don't wear out,
and **save** your **riches** in **heaven**, where
they will never decrease, because no
thief can get to them, and no moth can
destroy them. 34 For your **heart** will always be where your **riches** are.

Watchful Servants

35 "Be ready for whatever comes,
dressed for **action** and with your lamps
lit, 36 like **servants** who are waiting for
their **master** to come back from a **wed-**
ding feast. When he comes and knocks,
they will open the door for him at once.
37 How **happy** are those **servants** whose
master finds them awake and ready
when he returns! I tell you, he will take
off his coat, ask them to sit down, and
will wait on them. 38 How **happy** they are
if he finds them ready, even if he should
come at midnight or even later! 39 And
you can be **sure** that if the owner of a
house knew the time when the **thief**
would come, he would not let the **thief**
break into his house. 40 And you, too, must
be ready, because the **Son of Man** will
come at an hour when you are not
expecting him."

The Faithful or the Unfaithful Servant
(Matt. 24.45–51)

41 Peter said, "Lord, does this **parable**
apply to us, or do you mean it for everyone?"
42 The Lord answered, "Who, then, is
the **faithful** and **wise servant**? He is the
one that his **master** will put in charge, to
run the household and give the other **ser-**
vants their **share** of the food at the **pro-**
per time. 43 How **happy** that **servant** is if
his **master** finds him doing this when he
comes home! 44 Indeed, I tell you, the
master will put that **servant** in charge of
all his property. 45 But if that **servant** says
to himself that his **master** is taking a long
time to come back and if he begins to
beat the other **servants**, both the men
and the women, and eats and drinks and
gets drunk, 46 then the **master** will come
back one day when the **servant** does not
expect him and at a time he does not
know. The **master** will cut him in pieces[r]
and make him **share** the **fate** of the **dis-**
obedient.
47 "The **servant** who knows what his
master wants him to do, but does not get
himself ready and do it, will be **punished**
with a heavy whipping. 48 But the **servant**
who does not know what his **master**
wants, and yet does something for which
he **deserves** a whipping, will be **punished**
with a light whipping. Much is **required**
from the person to whom much is given;
much more is **required** from the person
to whom much more is given.

Jesus the Cause of Division
(Matt. 10.34–36)

49 "I came to set the earth on fire, and
how I **wish** it were already kindled! 50 I
have a **baptism** to receive, and how **dis-**
tressed I am until it is over! 51 Do you
suppose that I came to bring **peace** to the
world? No, not **peace**, but division.
52 From now on a family of five will be
divided, three against two and two
against three. 53 Fathers will be against
their sons, and sons against their fathers;
mothers will be against their daughters,
and daughters against their mothers;
mothers-in-law will be against their
daughters-in-law, and daughters-in-law
against their mothers-in-law."

Understanding the Time
(Matt. 16.2–3)

54 Jesus said also to the people,
"When you see a **cloud** coming up in the
west, at once you say that it is going to
rain—and it does. 55 And when you feel
the south wind blowing, you say that it is
going to get hot—and it does. 56 **Hypo-**
crites! You can look at the earth and the
sky and **predict** the weather; why, then,
don't you know the meaning of this present time?

Settle with Your Opponent
(Matt. 5.25–26)

57 "Why do you not **judge** for yourselves the **right** thing to do? 58 If someone brings a lawsuit against you and

[r] cut him in pieces; *or* throw him out.

12.35: Mt 25.1-13 **12.36:** Mk 13.34-36 **12.39-40:** Mt 24.43-44 **12.50:** Mk 10.38 **12.53:** Mic 7.6

takes you to **court**, do your **best** to **settle** the **dispute** with him before you get to **court**. If you don't, he will drag you before the **judge**, who will hand you over to the police, and you will be put in **jail**. 59 There you will stay, I tell you, until you pay the **last** penny of your fine."

Turn from Your Sins or Die

13 At that time some people were there who told Jesus about the Galileans whom Pilate had killed while they were **offering sacrifices** to God. 2 Jesus answered them, "Because those Galileans were killed in that way, do you think it **proves** that they were **worse** sinners than all the other Galileans? 3 No indeed! And I tell you that if you do not **turn from your sins**, you will all die as they did. 4 What about those eighteen people in Siloam who were killed when the tower fell on them? Do you suppose this **proves** that they were **worse** than all the other people living in Jerusalem? 5 No indeed! And I tell you that if you do not **turn from your sins**, you will all die as they did."

The Parable of the Unfruitful Fig-Tree

6 Then Jesus told them this **parable**: "There was once a man who had a fig-tree growing in his **vineyard**. He went looking for figs on it but found none. 7 So he said to his gardener, 'Look, for three years I have been coming here looking for figs on this fig-tree, and I haven't found any. Cut it down! Why should it go on using up the soil?' 8 But the gardener answered, 'Leave it **alone**, sir, just one more year; I will dig round it and put in some manure. 9 Then if the tree bears figs next year, so much the better; if not, then you can have it cut down.' "

Jesus Heals a Crippled Woman on the Sabbath

10 One **Sabbath** Jesus was **teaching** in a **synagogue**. 11 A woman there had an **evil spirit** that had made her ill for eighteen years; she was bent over and could not straighten up at all. 12 When Jesus saw her, he called out to her, "Woman, you are **free** from your illness!" 13 He placed his hands on her, and at once she straightened herself up and **praised** God.

14 The official of the **synagogue** was **angry** that Jesus had **healed** on the **Sabbath**, so he spoke up and said to the people, "There are six days in which we should work; so come during those days and be **healed**, but not on the **Sabbath**!"

15 The Lord answered him, "You **hypocrites**! Any one of you would untie his ox or his donkey from the stall and take it out to give it water on the **Sabbath**. 16 Now here is this descendant of Abraham whom **Satan** has kept **bound** up for eighteen years; should she not be released on the **Sabbath**?" 17 His answer made his **enemies ashamed** of themselves, while the people **rejoiced** over all the **wonderful** things that he did.

The Parable of the Mustard Seed

(Matt. 13.31–32; Mark 4.30–32)

18 Jesus asked, "What is the **Kingdom of God** like? What shall I **compare** it with? 19 It is like this. A man takes a mustard **seed** and **sows** it in his field. The plant grows and becomes a tree, and the birds make their nests in its branches."

The Parable of the Yeast

(Matt. 13.33)

20 Again Jesus asked, "What shall I **compare** the **Kingdom of God** with? 21 It is like this. A woman takes some **yeast** and mixes it with forty litres of flour until the whole batch of dough **rises**."

The Narrow Door

(Matt. 7.13–14, 21–23)

22 Jesus went through towns and villages, **teaching** the people and making his way towards Jerusalem. 23 Someone asked him, "Sir, will just a few people be **saved**?"

Jesus answered them, 24 "Do your **best** to go in through the narrow door; because many people will surely try to go in but will not be able. 25 The **master** of the house will get up and close the door; then when you stand outside and begin to knock on the door and say, 'Open the door for us, sir!' he will answer you, 'I don't know where you come from!' 26 Then you will answer, 'We ate and drank with you; you **taught** in our town!' 27 But he will say again, 'I don't know where you come from. **Get away** from me, all you **wicked** people!' 28 How you will cry and grind your teeth when you see Abraham, Isaac, and Jacob, and all the **prophets** in the **Kingdom of God**, while you are thrown out! 29 People will come from the east and the west, from the north and the south, and sit down at the **feast** in the **Kingdom of God**. 30 Then those who are now **last** will be first, and those who are now first will be **last**."

abandon Mk 15.34; Acts 2.27
alone 9.18; 18.19
anger 4.28; 15.28
ashamed 11.8; 16.3
assure 12.8; 18.29
best 12.58; 14.7
bind Mt 23.16; Jn 18.12
bless 6.28; 14.14
compare [2] 7.31; Rom 8.18
cure 9.1; Jn 9.14
demon 11.14; Jn 7.20
enemy 10.19; 19.27
feast 12.36; 14.8
free 4.18; 23.18
get away Mk 8.33
heal [2] 10.9; 14.3
hypocrite 12.1; Jas 3.17
Kingdom (1) (of God) [4] 12.31; 14.15
last (2) [2] 12.59; 15.17
master 12.36; 14.21
name (2) (name of God, of Jesus) 11.2; 19.38
offer 10.7; 21.4
parable 12.16; 14.7
Pharisees 12.1; 14.1
praise 7.16; 16.8
prophet [3] 11.30; 16.16
prove [2] 11.19; 20.37
rejoice 1.58; 15.10
right (1) 12.57; 16.15
rise 4.29; 14.14
Sabbath [5] 6.1; 14.1
sacrifice 5.14; Acts 7.41
Satan 11.18; 22.3
save 12.33; 17.33
seed 12.24; 17.6
sow 12.24; 19.21
spirit (2) 11.24; 23.46
synagogue [2] 12.11; 20.46
teach [3] 12.12; 18.1
Temple (1) (of God) 4.9; 18.10
turn [2] 11.32; 14.25
vineyard Mk 12.1; 20.9
wicked 6.35; Acts 2.40
wonder (1) 1.58; 24.41
worse [2] 12.4; 20.47
yeast 12.1; 1 Cor 5.6

13.14: Ex 20.9–10; Deut 5.13–14 **13.27:** Ps 6.8 **13.28:** Mt 22.13, 25.30 **13.28–29:** Mt 8.11–12
13.30: Mt 19.30, 20.16; Mk 10.31

Jesus' Love for Jerusalem
(Matt. 23.37-39)

31 At that same time some **Pharisees** came to Jesus and said to him, "You must get out of here and go somewhere else, because Herod wants to kill you."

32 Jesus answered them, "Go and tell that fox: 'I am driving out **demons** and performing **cures** today and tomorrow, and on the third day I shall finish my work.' 33 Yet I must be on my way today, tomorrow, and the next day; it is not **right** for a **prophet** to be killed anywhere except in Jerusalem.

34 "Jerusalem, Jerusalem! You kill the **prophets**, you stone the messengers God has sent you! How many times have I wanted to put my arms round all your people, just as a hen gathers her chicks under her wings, but you would not let me! 35 And so your **Temple** will be **abandoned**. I **assure** you that you will not see me until the time comes when you say, 'God **bless** him who comes **in the name of** the Lord.' "

Jesus Heals a Sick Man

14 One **Sabbath** Jesus went to eat a meal at the home of one of the **leading Pharisees**; and people were **watching** Jesus closely. 2 A man whose legs and arms were swollen came to Jesus, 3 and Jesus asked the **teachers of the Law** and the **Pharisees**, "Does our **Law** allow **healing** on the **Sabbath** or not?"

4 But they would not say anything. Jesus took the man, **healed** him, and sent him away. 5 Then he said to them, "If any one of you had a son or an ox that happened to fall in a well on a **Sabbath**, would you not pull him out at once on the **Sabbath** itself?"

6 But they were not able to answer him about this.

Humility and Hospitality

7 Jesus **noticed** how some of the guests were **choosing** the **best places**, so he told this **parable** to all of them: 8 "When someone invites you to a **wedding feast**, do not sit down in the **best place**. It could happen that someone more **important** than you has been invited, 9 and your host, who invited both of you, would have to come and say to you, 'Let him have this place.' Then you would be embarrassed and have to sit in the lowest place. 10 Instead, when you are invited, go and sit in the lowest place, so that your host will come to you and say, 'Come on up, my **friend**, to a better place.' This will bring you **honour** in the **presence** of all the other guests. 11 For everyone who makes himself great will be **humbled**, and everyone who **humbles** himself will be made great."

12 Then Jesus said to his host, "When you give a lunch or a dinner, do not invite your **friends** or your brothers or your relatives or your **rich neighbours**—for they will invite you back, and in this way you will be paid for what you did. 13 When you give a **feast**, invite the **poor**, the **crippled**, the lame, and the **blind**; 14 and you will be **blessed**, because they are not able to pay you back. God will **repay** you on the day the good people **rise from death**."

The Parable of the Great Feast
(Matt. 22.1-10)

15 When one of the men sitting at table heard this, he said to Jesus, "How **happy** are those who will sit down at the **feast** in the **Kingdom of God**!"

16 Jesus said to him, "There was once a man who was giving a great **feast** to which he invited many people. 17 When it was time for the **feast**, he sent his **servant** to tell his guests, 'Come, everything is ready!' 18 But they all began, one after another, to make **excuses**. The first one told the **servant**, 'I have bought a field and must go and look at it; **please accept** my apologies.' 19 Another one said, 'I have bought five pairs of oxen and am on my way to **try** them out; **please accept** my apologies.' 20 Another one said, 'I have just got married, and for that **reason** I cannot come.'

21 "The **servant** went back and told all this to his **master**. The **master** was **furious** and said to his **servant**, 'Hurry out to the streets and alleys of the town, and bring back the **poor**, the **crippled**, the **blind**, and the lame.' 22 Soon the **servant** said, 'Your order has been carried out, sir, but there is room for more.' 23 So the **master** said to the **servant**, 'Go out to the country roads and lanes and make people come in, so that my house will be full. 24 I tell you all that none of those men who were invited will taste my dinner!' "

The Cost of Being a Disciple
(Matt. 10.37-38)

25 Once when large crowds of people were going along with Jesus, he **turned** and said to them, 26 "Whoever comes to me cannot be my **disciple** unless he **loves** me more than he **loves** his father and his

accept [2] 7.35; Jn 3.11
best [2] 13.24; 15.22
bless 13.35; 19.38
blind [2] 7.21; 18.35
choose 10.1; 20.46
cripple [2] Mt 21.14
cross (1) 9.23; 23.26
death (2) (from death) Mk 16.9; 16.30
disciple [3] 12.1; 16.1
enough [2] 9.17; 16.3
excuse Mk 7.12; Jn 15.22
feast [5] 13.29; 15.23
friend [2] 12.4; 15.6
fury Mt 2.16; Acts 4.25
give up 12.20; Jn 6.61
happy 12.37; 15.5
heal [2] 13.14; 17.15
honour 11.2; 23.50
humble [2] Mt 23.12; 18.14
important 12.23; 20.17
Kingdom (1) (of God) 13.18; 16.16
law 6.2; 16.16
leading Mk 6.21
love [2] 11.42; 16.13
master [3] 13.25; 16.1
neighbour 10.27; 15.6
notice (1) 11.38; 22.58
parable 13.6; 15.3
peace 12.51; 19.38
Pharisees [2] 13.31; 15.2
plan 1.51; 19.12
please [2] 12.32; 22.5
poor [2] 12.33; 16.20
presence 2.31; 19.27
reason 11.49; 23.4
repay Zech 9.12; Rom 12.17
rich 12.15; 16.1
rise 13.21; 16.30
Sabbath [4] 13.10; 23.54
servant [6] 12.36; 15.22
strong 11.21; 16.3
teacher of the Law 11.45; 15.2
try (2) 12.11; 21.12
turn 13.3; 16.30
watch 12.15; 17.3
wedding 12.36; Jn 2.1

13.35: Ps 118.26; Jer 22.5 **14.5:** Mt 12.11 **14.8-10:** Prov 25.6-7 **14.11:** Mt 23.12; Lk 18.14
14.26: Mt 10.37

mother, his wife and his children, his
brothers and his sisters, and himself as
well. 27 Whoever does not carry his own
cross and come after me cannot be my
disciple.

28 "If one of you is **planning** to build a
tower, he sits down first and works out
what it will cost, to see if he has **enough**
money to finish the job. 29 If he doesn't, he
will not be able to finish the tower after
laying the foundation; and all who see
what happened will laugh at him. 30 'This
man began to build but can't finish the
job!' they will say.

31 "If a king goes out with ten
thousand men to fight another king who
comes against him with twenty thousand
men, he will sit down first and decide if
he is **strong enough** to face that other
king. 32 If he isn't, he will send messengers to meet the other king, to ask for
terms of **peace** while he is still a long
way off. 33 In the same way," concluded
Jesus, "none of you can be my **disciple**
unless he **gives up** everything he has.

Worthless Salt
(Matt. 5.13; Mark 9.50)

34 "Salt is good, but if it loses its saltiness, there is no way to make it salty
again. 35 It is no good for the soil or for
the manure heap; it is thrown away.
Listen, then, if you have ears!"

The Lost Sheep
(Matt. 18.12–14)

15 One day when many **tax collectors** and other **outcasts** came to
listen to Jesus, 2 the **Pharisees** and the
teachers of the Law started grumbling,
"This man **welcomes outcasts** and even
eats with them!" 3 So Jesus told them this
parable:

4 "Suppose one of you has a hundred
sheep and loses one of them—what does
he do? He leaves the other ninety-nine
sheep in the pasture and goes looking for
the one that got lost until he finds it.
5 When he finds it, he is so **happy** that he
puts it on his shoulders 6 and carries it
back home. Then he calls his **friends** and
neighbours together and says to them, 'I
am so **happy** I found my lost **sheep**. Let
us **celebrate**!' 7 In the same way, I tell
you, there will be more **joy** in **heaven**
over one sinner who **repents** than over
ninety-nine **respectable** people who do
not **need** to **repent**.

The Lost Coin

8 "Or suppose a woman who has ten
silver coins loses one of them—what does
she do? She lights a lamp, sweeps her
house, and looks carefully everywhere
until she finds it. 9 When she finds it, she
calls her **friends** and **neighbours** together, and says to them, 'I am so **happy**
I found the coin I lost. Let us **celebrate**!'
10 In the same way, I tell you, the **angels**
of God **rejoice** over one sinner who **repents**."

The Lost Son

11 Jesus went on to say, "There was
once a man who had two sons. 12 The
younger one said to him, 'Father, give
me my **share** of the property now.' So the
man divided his property between his
two sons. 13 After a few days the younger
son sold his part of the property and left
home with the money. He went to a
country far away, where he wasted his
money in reckless living. 14 He spent
everything he had. Then a severe **famine**
spread over that country, and he was left
without a thing. 15 So he went to work for
one of the citizens of that country, who
sent him out to his farm to take **care** of
the pigs. 16 He **wished** he could fill himself
with the bean pods the pigs ate, but no
one gave him anything to eat. 17 At **last**
he came to his **senses** and said, 'All my
father's hired workers have more than
they can eat, and here I am about to
starve! 18 I will get up and go to my
father and say, Father, I have sinned
against God and against you. 19 I am no
longer **fit** to be called your son; treat me
as one of your hired workers.' 20 So he got
up and started back to his father.

"He was still a long way from home
when his father saw him; his **heart** was
filled with **pity**, and he ran, threw his
arms round his son, and **kissed** him.
21 'Father,' the son said, 'I have sinned
against God and against you. I am no
longer **fit** to be called your son.' 22 But the
father called his **servants**. 'Hurry!' he
said. 'Bring the **best** robe and put it on
him. Put a ring on his finger and shoes on
his feet. 23 Then go and get the **prize** calf
and kill it, and let us **celebrate** with a
feast! 24 For this son of mine was **dead**,
but now he is **alive**; he was lost, but now
he has been found.' And so the **feasting**
began.

25 "In the meantime the elder son was
out in the field. On his way back, when he
came close to the house, he heard the
music and dancing. 26 So he called one of
the **servants** and asked him, 'What's going on?' 27 'Your brother has come back
home,' the **servant** answered, 'and your

alive [2] 12.22; 20.38
angel 12.8; 16.22
anger 13.14; Jn 6.52
beg 9.38; 16.3
best 14.7; 20.46
care 10.34; Jn 10.13
celebrate [4] Mt 26.18; Jn 10.22
dead [2] 10.30; 17.37
disobey 12.46; Jn 3.36
famine 4.25; 21.11
feast [3] 14.8; 16.22
fit (1) [2] Mk 7.19; Acts 22.22
friend [3] 14.10; 16.4
happy [4] 14.15; Jn 3.29
heart 12.34; 16.15
heaven 12.33; 16.17
joy 10.17; 19.6
kiss 7.38; 22.47
last (2) 13.30; 18.4
need 12.19; 18.22
neighbour [2] 14.12; Jn 9.8
outcast [2] 7.34
parable 14.7; 18.1
Pharisees 14.1; 16.14
pity 10.33; 16.24
prize [3] Mt 22.4; 1 Cor 9.24
prostitute Mt 21.31; 1 Cor 6.15
rejoice 13.17; Jn 8.56
repent [3] 5.32; 17.3
respect 11.43; 18.2
safe 11.21; 21.36
sense Zeph 2.1; 1 Cor 10.15
servant [3] 14.17; 16.1
share 12.42; 20.10
sheep [3] Mk 14.27; 17.7
slave 7.8; 16.13
sound (2) 11.34; Acts 20.9
tax collector 7.29; 18.10
teacher of the Law 14.3; 19.47
welcome 10.8; 16.4
wish 12.49; 17.22

14.27: Mt 10.38, 16.24; Mk 8.34; Lk 9.23 **15.1-2:** Lk 5.29–30

father has killed the **prize** calf, because he got him back **safe and sound**.'

28 "The elder brother was so **angry** that he would not go into the house; so his father came out and **begged** him to come in. 29 But he answered his father, 'Look, all these years I have worked for you like a **slave**, and I have never **disobeyed** your orders. What have you given me? Not even a goat for me to have a **feast** with my **friends**! 30 But this son of yours wasted all your property on **prostitutes**, and when he comes back home, you kill the **prize** calf for him!' 31 'My son,' the father answered, 'you are always here with me, and everything I have is yours. 32 But we had to **celebrate** and be **happy**, because your brother was **dead**, but now he is **alive**; he was lost, but now he has been found.' "

The Shrewd Manager

16 Jesus said to his **disciples**, "There was once a **rich** man who had a **servant** who managed his property. The **rich** man was told that the manager was wasting his **master's** money, 2 so he called him in and said, 'What is this I hear about you? Hand in a **complete** account of your handling of my property, because you cannot be my manager any longer.' 3 The **servant** said to himself, 'My **master** is going to dismiss me from my job. What shall I do? I am not **strong enough** to dig ditches, and I am **ashamed** to **beg**. 4 Now I know what I will do! Then when my job is gone, I shall have **friends** who will **welcome** me in their homes.'

5 "So he called in all the people who were in **debt** to his **master**. He asked the first one, 'How much do you **owe** my **master**?' 6 'One hundred barrels of olive-oil,' he answered. 'Here is your account,' the manager told him; 'sit down and write fifty.' 7 Then he asked another one, 'And you—how much do you **owe**?' 'A thousand sacks of wheat,' he answered. 'Here is your account,' the manager told him; 'write eight hundred.'

8 "As a **result** the **master** of this **dishonest** manager **praised** him for doing such a shrewd thing; because the people of **this world** are much more shrewd in handling their affairs than the people who belong to the **light**."

9 And Jesus went on to say, "And so I tell you: make **friends** for yourselves with **worldly** wealth, so that when it gives out, you will be **welcomed** in the **eternal** home. 10 Whoever is **faithful** in small matters will be faithful in large ones; whoever is **dishonest** in small matters will be **dishonest** in large ones. 11 If, then, you have not been **faithful** in handling **worldly** wealth, how can you be **trusted** with **true** wealth? 12 And if you have not been **faithful** with what belongs to someone else, who will give you what belongs to you?

13 "No **servant** can be the **slave** of two **masters**; he will **hate** one and **love** the other; he will be **loyal** to one and **despise** the other. You cannot **serve** both God and money."

Some Sayings of Jesus

(Matt. 11.12–13; 5.31–32; Mark 10.11–12)

14 When the **Pharisees** heard all this, they **sneered** at Jesus, because they **loved** money. 15 Jesus said to them, "You are the ones who make yourselves look **right** in other people's **sight**, but God knows your **hearts**. For the things that are **considered** of great **value** by man are **worth nothing** in God's **sight**.

16 "The **Law of Moses** and the writings of the **prophets** were in effect up to the time of John the Baptist; since then the **Good News** about the **Kingdom of God** is being told, and everyone **forces** his way in. 17 But it is easier for **heaven and earth** to disappear than for the smallest detail of the **Law** to be done away with.

18 "Any man who **divorces** his wife and marries another woman **commits** adultery; and the man who marries a **divorced** woman **commits adultery**.

The Rich Man and Lazarus

19 "There was once a **rich** man who dressed in the most expensive clothes and lived in great **luxury** every day. 20 There was also a **poor** man named Lazarus, covered with sores, who used to be brought to the **rich** man's door, 21 **hoping** to eat the bits of food that fell from the **rich** man's table. Even the dogs would come and lick his sores.

22 "The **poor** man died and was carried by the **angels** to sit beside Abraham at the **feast in heaven**. The **rich** man died and was buried, 23 and in Hades,[s] where he was in great **pain**, he looked up and saw Abraham, far away, with Lazarus at his side. 24 So he called out, 'Father Abraham! Take **pity** on me, and send Lazarus to dip his finger in some water and cool my tongue, because I am in great **pain** in this fire!'

25 "But Abraham said, '**Remember**, my son, that in your lifetime you were

[s] HADES: *The world of the dead.*

16.13: Mt 6.24 **16.16:** Mt 11.12–13 **16.17:** Mt 5.18 **16.18:** Mt 5.32; 1 Cor 7.10–11

adultery [2] Mk 10.11; 18.11
angel 15.10; 20.36
ashamed 13.17; Rom 6.21
bad 11.13; 19.22
beg [2] 15.28; 18.35
commit [2] Mk 15.7; 18.20
complete 6.40; Jn 3.29
consider 7.7; 20.28
convince Mk 11.32; 20.6
death (2) (from death) [2] 14.14; 20.27
debt 7.42; Col 2.14
despise Mt 18.10; 18.9
disciple 14.26; 17.1
dishonest [3] Mic 6.10; 18.11
divorce [2] Mk 10.2; 1 Cor 7.11
enjoy 12.19; Jn 5.35
enough [2] 14.28; 22.38
eternal 10.25; 18.18
faithful [3] 12.42; 19.17
feast 15.23; 20.46
force (1) 3.14; Jn 6.15
friend [2] 15.6; 21.16
Good News 9.6; 20.1
hate 6.22; 19.14
heart 15.20; Jn 2.25
heaven [2] 15.7; 17.29
hope 6.34; 23.8
Kingdom (1) (of God) 14.15; 17.20
law [2] 14.3; 20.22
light (1) 11.33; 17.24
love [2] 14.26; 20.46
loyal Mt 6.24; Rom 16.10
luxury 7.25; Jas 5.5
master [6] 14.21; 17.13
owe [2] 7.41; Rom 13.7
pain [4] Mk 13.8; Rom 2.9
Pharisees 15.2; 17.20
pity 15.20; 17.13
poor [2] 14.13; 18.22
praise 13.13; 17.15
prophet [3] 13.28; 18.31

remember 10.11; 17.32
result Mt 27.14; Jn 11.4
rich [8] 14.12; 18.23
right (1) 13.33; 20.21
rise [2] 14.14; 18.33
servant [3] 15.22; 17.7
serve 4.8; 22.27
sight [2] 12.21; 24.31
slave 15.29; 20.10
sneer Ezek 36.15
strong 14.31; 22.59
true 12.15; 18.31
trust Mt 27.43; Jn 2.24
turn 14.25; 19.46
value Hos 13.15; Rom 2.25
warn [2] 9.5; Acts 4.17
welcome [2] 15.2; 19.6
world 12.30; Jn 1.1
worldly [2] 1 Cor 3.4
worthless Mk 12.10; 20.17

given all the good things, while Lazarus got all the **bad** things. But now he is **enjoying** himself here, while you are in **pain**. 26 Besides all that, there is a deep pit lying between us, so that those who want to cross over from here to you cannot do so, nor can anyone cross over to us from where you are.' 27 The **rich** man said, 'Then I **beg** you, father Abraham, send Lazarus to my father's house, 28 where I have five brothers. Let him go and **warn** them so that they, at least, will not come to this place of **pain**.'

29 "Abraham said, 'Your brothers have Moses and the **prophets** to **warn** them; your brothers should listen to what they say.' 30 The **rich** man answered, 'That is not **enough**, father Abraham! But if someone were to **rise from death** and go to them, then they would **turn from their sins**.' 31 But Abraham said, 'If they will not listen to Moses and the **prophets**, they will not be **convinced** even if someone were to **rise from death**.' "

Sin
(Matt. 18.6–7, 21–22; Mark 9.42)

17 Jesus said to his **disciples**, "Things that make people fall into sin are bound to happen, but how **terrible** for the one who makes them happen! 2 It would be better for him if a large millstone were tied round his neck and he were thrown into the sea than for him to cause one of these little ones to sin. 3 So **watch** what you do!

"If your brother sins, **rebuke** him, and if he **repents**, **forgive** him. 4 If he sins against you seven times in one day, and each time he comes to you saying, '**I repent**,' you must **forgive** him."

Faith

5 The **apostles** said to the Lord, "Make our **faith** greater."

6 The Lord answered, "If you had **faith** as big as a mustard **seed**, you could say to this mulberry tree, 'Pull yourself up by the roots and plant yourself in the sea!' and it would **obey** you.

A Servant's Duty

7 "Suppose one of you has a **servant** who is ploughing or looking after the **sheep**. When he comes in from the field, do you tell him to hurry and eat his meal? 8 Of course not! Instead, you say to him, 'Get my supper ready, then put on your apron and wait on me while I eat and drink; after that you may have your meal.' 9 The **servant** does not **deserve** **thanks** for **obeying** orders, does he? 10 It is the same with you; when you have done all you have been told to do, say, 'We are ordinary **servants**; we have only done our **duty**.' "

Jesus Heals Ten Men

11 As Jesus made his way to Jerusalem, he went along the border between Samaria and Galilee. 12 He was going into a village when he was met by ten men **suffering** from a dreaded **skin-disease**. They stood at a distance 13 and shouted, "Jesus! **Master**! Take **pity** on us!"

14 Jesus saw them and said to them, "Go and let the **priests** examine you."

On the way they were made **clean**.[t] 15 When one of them saw that he was **healed**, he came back, **praising** God in a loud voice. 16 He threw himself to the ground at Jesus' feet and **thanked** him. The man was a Samaritan. 17 Jesus said, "There were ten men who were **healed**; where are the other nine? 18 Why is this foreigner the only one who came back to give **thanks** to God?" 19 And Jesus said to him, "Get up and go; your **faith** has made you well."

The Coming of the Kingdom
(Matt. 24.23–28, 37–41)

20 Some **Pharisees** asked Jesus when the **Kingdom of God** would come. His answer was, "The **Kingdom of God** does not come in such a way as to be seen. 21 No one will say, 'Look, here it is!' or, 'There it is!'; because the **Kingdom of God** is within you."[u]

22 Then he said to the **disciples**, "The time will come when you will **wish** you could see one of the days of the **Son of Man**, but you will not see it. 23 There will be those who will say to you, 'Look, over there!' or, 'Look, over here!' But don't go out looking for it. 24 As the lightning flashes across the sky and **lights** it up from one side to the other, so will the **Son of Man** be in his day. 25 But first he must **suffer** much and be **rejected** by the people of this day. 26 As it was in the time of Noah so shall it be in the days of the **Son of Man**. 27 Everybody kept on eating and drinking, and men and women married, up to the very day Noah went into the boat and the **flood** came and killed them all. 28 It will be as it was in the time of Lot. Everybody kept on eating and drinking, buying and selling, planting and building. 29 On the day Lot left Sodom, fire and sulphur rained down

[t] MADE CLEAN: *See 5.12.* [u] is within you; *or* is among you, *or* will suddenly appear among you.

17.3: Mt 18.15 **17.14:** Lev 14.1–32 **17.26:** Gen 6.5–8 **17.27:** Gen 7.6–24 **17.28-29:** Gen 18.20—19.25

from **heaven** and killed them all. [30]That is how it will be on the day the **Son of Man** is **revealed**.

31 "On that day the man who is on the roof of his house must not go down into the house to get his belongings; in the same way the man who is out in the field must not go back to the house. [32]**Remember** Lot's wife! [33]Whoever tries to **save** his own **life** will lose it; whoever loses his **life** will **save** it. [34]On that night, I tell you, there will be two people sleeping in the same bed: one will be taken away, the other will be left behind. [35]Two women will be grinding corn together: one will be taken away, the other will be left behind."[v]

37 The **disciples** asked him, "Where, Lord?"

Jesus answered, "Wherever there is a **dead body**, the vultures will gather."

The Parable of the Widow and the Judge

18 Then Jesus told his **disciples** a **parable** to **teach** them that they should always **pray** and never become **discouraged**. [2]"In a certain town there was a **judge** who neither **feared** God nor **respected** man. [3]And there was a **widow** in that same town who kept coming to him and **pleading** for her **rights**, saying, '**Help** me against my opponent!' [4]For a long time the **judge refused** to **act**, but at **last** he said to himself, 'Even though I don't **fear** God or **respect** man, [5]yet because of all the **trouble** this **widow** is giving me, I will see to it that she gets her **rights**. If I don't, she will keep on coming and finally wear me out!'"

6 And the Lord continued, "Listen to what that **corrupt judge** said. [7]Now, will God not **judge** in **favour** of his **own people** who cry to him day and night for **help**? Will he be slow to **help** them? [8]I tell you, he will **judge** in their **favour** and do it quickly. But will the **Son of Man** find **faith** on earth when he comes?"

The Parable of the Pharisee and the Tax Collector

9 Jesus also told this **parable** to people who were **sure** of their own goodness and **despised** everybody else. [10]"Once there were two men who went up to the **Temple** to **pray**: one was a **Pharisee**, the other a **tax collector**.

11 "The **Pharisee** stood **apart** by himself and **prayed**,[w] 'I **thank** you, God, that I am not **greedy**, **dishonest**, or an **adulterer**, like everybody else. I **thank** you that I am not like that **tax collector** over there. [12]I **fast** two days a week, and I give you a tenth of all my income.'

13 "But the **tax collector** stood at a distance and would not even **raise** his face to **heaven**, but beat on his breast and said, 'God, have **pity** on me, a sinner!' [14]I tell you," said Jesus, "the **tax collector**, and not the **Pharisee**, was in the **right with God** when he went home. For everyone who makes himself great will be **humbled**, and everyone who **humbles** himself will be made great."

Jesus Blesses Little Children
(Matt. 19.13–15; Mark 10.13–16)

15 Some people brought their babies to Jesus for him to place his hands on them. The **disciples** saw them and scolded them for doing so, [16]but Jesus called the children to him and said, "Let the children come to me and do not stop them, because the **Kingdom of God** belongs to such as these. [17]**Remember** this! Whoever does not receive the **Kingdom of God** like a child will never enter it."

The Rich Man
(Matt. 19.16–30; Mark 10.17–31)

18 A **Jewish** leader asked Jesus, "Good **Teacher**, what must I do to receive **eternal life**?"

19 "Why do you call me good?" Jesus asked him. "No one is good except God **alone**. [20]You know the **commandments**: 'Do not **commit adultery**; do not **commit** murder; do not **steal**; do not **accuse** anyone **falsely**; **respect** your father and your mother.'"

21 The man replied, "Ever since I was young, I have **obeyed** all these **commandments**."

22 When Jesus heard this, he said to him, "There is still one more thing you **need** to do. Sell all you have and give the money to the **poor**, and you will have **riches** in **heaven**; then come and follow me." [23]But when the man heard this, he became very **sad**, because he was very **rich**.

24 Jesus saw that he was **sad** and said, "How **hard** it is for **rich** people to enter the **Kingdom of God**! [25]It is much **harder** for a **rich** person to enter the **Kingdom of** God than for a camel to go through the eye of a needle."

26 The people who heard him asked, "Who, then, can be **saved**?"

accuse 11.31; 23.2
act 10.36; 22.53
adultery [2] 16.18; Jn 8.3
age (1) [2] Mk 10.30; 20.34
alone 13.8; Jn 5.44
apart 11.17; Acts 13.2
assure 13.35; Acts 2.26
beg 16.3; Jn 4.31
blind [2] 14.13; Jn 5.3
commandment [2] Mk 12.28; Jn 13.34
commit [2] 16.18; 23.22
corrupt Zeph 3.1; Rom 1.28
despise 16.13; Acts 4.11
disciple [4] 17.1; 19.29
discourage Hag 2.4; 2 Cor 4.1
dishonest 16.8
eternal [2] 16.9; Jn 3.15
faith [2] 17.5; 22.32
false 6.26; Jn 1.47
fast (2) 7.33; Acts 13.2
favour [2] 2.52; Jn 8.50
fear [2] 12.5; 21.26
Gentile 2.32; Acts 2.11
God's people 7.16; Jn 1.11
greed 12.15; Rom 1.29
hard [2] 11.4; 19.21
heaven [2] 17.29; 19.38
help [3] 11.23; 19.35
humble [2] 14.11; Acts 2.46
impossible Mk 10.27; Acts 2.24
insult 11.45; 22.65
Jew 7.3; 23.3
judge [5] 12.14; Jn 3.17

Kingdom (1) (of God) [5] 17.20; 19.11
last (2) 15.17; 20.32
life (1) [2] 17.33; 21.34
life (2) (to life) 9.22; 20.33
mock Mk 15.20; 22.63
need 15.7; 19.31
obey 17.6; Jn 3.21
parable [2] 15.3; 19.11
Pharisees [3] 17.20; 19.39
pity [3] 17.13; Rom 1.31
plead Hos 2.2; Rom 8.26
poor 16.20; 19.8
praise 17.15; 19.37
pray [3] 11.1; 21.36
prophet 16.16; 20.6
raise 9.22; 20.37
refuse (1) 7.30; Jn 1.20
remember 17.32; 21.32
respect [3] 15.7; 20.13
rich [3] 16.1; 19.2
riches 12.21; 21.4
right (3) [2] 12.14; 20.2
right with God Job 15.14; Rom 1.17
rise 16.30; 20.27
sad [2] Mk 10.22; 24.17
sake 9.24; 21.12
save 17.33; 19.10
Son of David [2] Mk 10.47
Son of Man [2] 17.22; 19.10
steal 11.22; Jn 10.10
sure 12.28; Acts 2.36
tax collector [4] 15.1; 19.2
teach 13.10; 19.47
teacher 12.13; 19.39
Temple (1) (of God) 13.35; 19.45
thank [3] 17.9; 19.37
trouble 10.41; Jn 12.27
true 16.11; 21.22
understand 9.45; 24.45
widow [2] 7.12; 20.28
word (1) 12.10; 19.22

[v] *Some manuscripts add verse* 36: Two men will be working in a field: one will be taken away, the other will be left behind *(see Mt 24.40).*
[w] stood apart by himself and prayed; *some manuscripts have* stood up and prayed to himself.

17.31: Mt 24.17–18; Mk 13.15–16 **17.32:** Gen 19.26 **17.33:** Mt 10.39, 16.25; Mk 8.35; Lk 9.24; Jn 12.25 **18.14:** Mt 23.12; Lk 14.11 **18.20:** Ex 20.12–16; Deut 5.16–20

27 Jesus answered, "What is **impossible** for man is possible for God."
28 Then Peter said, "Look! We have
left our homes to follow you."
29 "Yes," Jesus said to them, "and I **assure** you that anyone who leaves home
or wife or brothers or parents or children
for the **sake** of the **Kingdom of God** 30 will
receive much more in this present **age**
and **eternal life** in the **age** to come."

Jesus Speaks a Third Time about His Death
(Matt. 20.17–19; Mark 10.32–34)

31 Jesus took the twelve **disciples**
aside and said to them, "Listen! We are
going to Jerusalem where everything the
prophets wrote about the **Son of Man** will
come **true**. 32 He will be handed over to
the **Gentiles**, who will **mock** him, **insult**
him, and spit on him. 33 They will whip
him and kill him, but three days later he
will **rise to life**."
34 But the **disciples** did not **understand**
any of these things; the meaning of the
words was hidden from them, and they
did not know what Jesus was talking
about.

Jesus Heals a Blind Beggar
(Matt. 20.29–34; Mark 10.46–52)

35 As Jesus was coming near Jericho,
there was a **blind** man sitting by the
road, **begging**. 36 When he heard the
crowd passing by, he asked, "What is
this?"
37 "Jesus of Nazareth is passing by,"
they told him.
38 He cried out, "Jesus! **Son of David**!
Take **pity** on me!"
39 The people in front scolded him
and told him to be quiet. But he shouted
even more loudly, "**Son of David**! Take
pity on me!"
40 So Jesus stopped and ordered the
blind man to be brought to him. When he
came near, Jesus asked him, 41 "What do
you want me to do for you?"
"Sir," he answered, "I want to see
again."
42 Jesus said to him, "Then see! Your
faith has made you well."
43 At once he was able to see, and he
followed Jesus, giving **thanks** to God.
When the crowd saw it, they all **praised**
God.

Jesus and Zacchaeus

19 Jesus went on into Jericho and
was passing through. 2 There was
a chief **tax collector** there named
Zacchaeus, who was **rich**. 3 He was trying
to see who Jesus was, but he was a little
man and could not see Jesus because of
the crowd. 4 So he ran ahead of the crowd
and climbed a sycomore tree to see
Jesus, who was going to pass that way.
5 When Jesus came to that place, he
looked up and said to Zacchaeus, "Hurry
down, Zacchaeus, because I must stay in
your house today."
6 Zacchaeus hurried down and **welcomed** him with great **joy**. 7 All the
people who saw it started grumbling,
"This man has gone as a guest to the
home of a sinner!"
8 Zacchaeus stood up and said to the
Lord, "Listen, sir! I will give half my
belongings to the **poor**, and if I have
cheated anyone, I will pay him back four
times as much."
9 Jesus said to him, "**Salvation** has
come to this house today, for this man,
also, is a descendant of Abraham. 10 The
Son of Man came to **seek** and to **save** the
lost."

The Parable of the Gold Coins
(Matt. 25.14–30)

11 While the people were listening to
this, Jesus continued and told them a
parable. He was now almost at
Jerusalem, and they supposed that the
Kingdom of God was just about to
appear. 12 So he said, "There was once a
man of high rank who was going to a
country far away to be made king, after
which he **planned** to come back home.
13 Before he left, he called his ten **servants** and gave them each a gold coin
and told them, 'See what you can earn
with this while I am gone.' 14 Now, his
countrymen **hated** him, and so they sent
messengers after him to say, 'We don't
want this man to be our king.'
15 "The man was made king and
came back. At once he ordered his **servants** to appear before him, in order to
find out how much they had earned.
16 The first one came and said, 'Sir, I have
earned ten gold coins with the one you
gave me.' 17 'Well done,' he said; 'you are
a good **servant**! Since you were **faithful**
in small matters, I will put you in charge
of ten cities.' 18 The second **servant** came
and said, 'Sir, I have earned five gold
coins with the one you gave me.' 19 To
this one he said, 'You will be in charge of
five cities.'
20 "Another **servant** came and said,
'Sir, here is your gold coin; I kept it hidden in a handkerchief. 21 I was **afraid** of
you, because you are a **hard** man. You
take what is not yours and **reap** what you

19.10: Mt 18.11 **19.11–27:** Mt 25.14–30

afraid 12.4; 20.19
ahead of you 7.27
bad 16.25; 22.31
bless 14.14; 24.30
cheat Mk 10.19
chief priests 9.22; 20.1
command 10.17; 23.56
condemn 6.37; 23.4
destroy 12.33; 21.20
disciple [3] 18.1; 20.45
enemy [2] 13.17; 20.43
faithful 16.10; Acts 2.27
glory 9.26; 21.27
hard [2] 18.24; Jn 6.60
hate 16.13; 21.17
heaven 18.13; 21.33
help 18.3; Jn 12.2
joy 15.7; 24.41
Kingdom (1) (of God) 18.16; 21.31
master [2] 17.13; Jn 13.16
name (2) (name of God, of Jesus) 13.35; 24.47
need [3] 18.22; 22.71
parable 18.1; 20.9
peace [2] 14.32; 24.36
Pharisees 18.10; Jn 1.24
plan 14.28; Jn 11.8
poor 18.22; 21.2
praise 18.43; 23.47
prayer 5.33; 20.47
presence 14.10; 23.14
reap [2] Mt 25.24; Jn 4.36
rich 18.23; 21.1
salvation 3.6; 21.28
save [2] 18.26; 21.19
scripture 10.26; 20.17
seek 11.9; Jn 8.50
servant [7] 17.7; 22.26
Son of Man 18.8; 21.27
sow [2] 13.19; Jn 4.36
tax collector 18.10
teach 18.1; 20.1
teacher 18.18; 20.21
teacher of the Law 15.2; 20.1
Temple (1) (of God) [3] 18.10; 20.1
thank 18.11; 22.17
thief 12.33; Jn 10.1
turn 16.30; 20.17
weep 6.21; 22.62
welcome 16.4; Jn 4.45
word (1) [2] 18.34; 21.15

did not **sow**.' 22 He said to him, 'You **bad**
servant! I will use your own **words** to
condemn you! You know that I am a
hard man, taking what is not mine and
reaping what I have not **sown**. 23 Well,
then, why didn't you put my money in the
bank? Then I would have received it
back with interest when I returned.'
24 "Then he said to those who were
standing there, 'Take the gold coin away
from him and give it to the **servant** who
has ten coins.' 25 But they said to him, 'Sir,
he already has ten coins!' 26 'I tell you,'
he replied, 'that to every person who has
something, even more will be given; but
the person who has nothing, even the
little that he has will be taken away from
him. 27 Now, as for those **enemies** of mine
who did not want me to be their king,
bring them here and kill them in my **pre-**
sence!' "

The Triumphant Approach to Jerusalem
(Matt. 21.1–11; Mark 11.1–11; John 12.12–19)

28 Jesus said this and then went on to
Jerusalem ahead of them. 29 As he came
near Bethphage and Bethany at the
Mount of Olives, he sent two **disciples**
ahead 30 with these instructions: "Go to
the village there **ahead of you**; as you go
in, you will find a colt tied up that has
never been ridden. Untie it and bring it
here. 31 If someone asks you why you are
untying it, tell him that the **Master**[x]
needs it."
32 They went on their way and found
everything just as Jesus had told them.
33 As they were untying the colt, its
owners said to them, "Why are you untying it?"
34 "The **Master**[x] **needs** it," they answered, 35 and they took the colt to Jesus.
Then they threw their cloaks over the
animal and **helped** Jesus get on. 36 As he
rode on, people spread their cloaks on
the road.
37 When he came near Jerusalem, at
the place where the road went down the
Mount of Olives, the large crowd of his
disciples began to **thank** God and **praise**
him in loud voices for all the great things
that they had seen: 38 "God **bless** the king
who comes **in the name of** the Lord!
Peace in **heaven** and **glory** to God!"
39 Then some of the **Pharisees** in the
crowd spoke to Jesus. "**Teacher**," they
said, "**command** your **disciples** to be
quiet!"
40 Jesus answered, "I tell you that if
they keep quiet, the stones themselves
will start shouting."

Jesus Weeps over Jerusalem

41 He came closer to the city, and
when he saw it, he **wept** over it, 42 saying,
"If you only knew today what is **needed**
for **peace**! But now you cannot see it!
43 The time will come when your **enemies**
will surround you with barricades,
blockade you, and close in on you from
every side. 44 They will completely **des-**
troy you and the people within your
walls; not a single stone will they leave
in its place, because you did not recognize the time when God came to **save**
you!"

Jesus Goes to the Temple
(Matt. 21.12–17; Mark 11.15–19; John 2.13–22)

45 Then Jesus went into the **Temple**
and began to drive out the merchants,
46 saying to them, "It is written in the
Scriptures that God said, 'My **Temple** will
be called a house of **prayer**.' But you
have **turned** it into a hideout for
thieves!"
47 Every day Jesus **taught** in the
Temple. The **chief priests**, the **teachers**
of the Law, and the leaders of the people
wanted to kill him, 48 but they could not
find a way to do it, because all the people
kept listening to him, not wanting to miss
a single **word**.

The Question about Jesus' Authority
(Matt. 21.23–27; Mark 11.27–33)

20 One day when Jesus was in the
Temple **teaching** the people and
preaching the **Good News**, the **chief**
priests and the **teachers of the Law**, together with the **elders**, came 2 and said to
him, "Tell us, what **right** have you to do
these things? Who gave you this **right**?"
3 Jesus answered them, "Now let me
ask you a **question**. Tell me, 4 did John's
right to **baptize** come from God or from
man?"
5 They started to **argue** among themselves, "What shall we say? If we say,
'From God,' he will say, 'Why, then, did
you not **believe** John?' 6 But if we say
'From man,' this whole crowd here will
stone us, because they are **convinced**
that John was a **prophet**." 7 So they answered, "We don't know where it came
from."
8 And Jesus said to them, "Neither will
I tell you, then, by what **right** I do these
things."

advantage Mk 12.40; Rom 3.1
afraid 19.21; 21.9
age (1) [2] 18.30; Rom 16.25
alive 15.24; 24.5
amaze 11.14; 24.12
angel 16.22; 22.43
argue 9.46; 22.24
arrest Mk 14.1; 21.12
authority 12.5; Jn 5.30
baptize 12.50; Jn 1.25
believe 12.5; 22.67
best 15.22; Jn 2.10
bribe Mic 7.3; Acts 6.11
chief priests [2] 19.47; 22.2
child of God 6.35; Jn 1.12
choose 14.7; 23.35
clear 9.53; Jn 1.20
consider 16.15; 24.19
convince 16.31; Acts 9.22
dare Mk 12.34; Jn 18.22
dead [4] 17.37; 24.5
dear 7.2; Jn 11.3
death (2) (from death) [3] 16.30; 24.46
disciple 19.29; 21.5
elder (2) 9.22; 22.52

[x] the Master; *or* its owner.

19.26: Mt 13.12; Mk 4.25; Lk 8.18 **19.38:** Ps 118.26 **19.46:** Is 56.7; Jer 7.11 **19.47:** Lk 21.37

enemy 19.27; 21.15
feast 16.22; 21.34
footstool Is 66.1; Acts 2.35
Good News 16.16; 21.13
harvest 12.24; Jn 4.35
important 14.8; Jn 3.30
last (2) 18.4; 24.18
law [2] 16.16; 23.56
life (2) (to life) [2] 18.33; 24.7
love 16.13; Jn 3.16
Messiah [2] 9.20; 22.67
one another 8.25; 21.10
parable [2] 19.11; 21.29
power 11.15; 21.26
prayer 19.46; 22.45
preach 11.32; 24.47
prophet 18.31; 24.19
prove 13.2; Jn 5.31
psalm 24.44
punish 12.47; 21.22
question [3] 11.53; 22.68
raise 18.13; 21.28
reject 17.25; Jn 12.11
respect [2] 18.2; Jn 4.44
right (1) 16.15; 23.41
right (2) 6.6; 22.50
right (3) [4] 18.3; 22.29
rise [4] 18.33; 22.45
rob 10.30; Jn 10.1
Sadducees Mk 12.18; Acts 4.1
scripture 19.46; 21.22
shame Mk 12.4; Rom 1.24
share 15.12; 22.17
sincere Joel 2.12; Rom 12.9
slave [4] 16.13; 22.50
son *see* **child of God**
synagogue 13.10; 21.12
tax Mk 12.14; 23.2
teach [3] 19.47; 21.37
teacher [3] 19.39; 21.7
teacher of the Law [4] 19.47; 22.2
Temple (1) (of God) 19.45; 21.1
trap 11.16; 21.35
trick Mk 12.15; Acts 7.19
truth 1.4; Jn 1.14
turn 19.46; 22.32
vineyard [5] 13.6; 1 Cor 9.7
widow [2] 18.3; 21.2
will (1) 2.32; 22.42
worse 13.2; Jn 5.14
worthless 16.15; Jn 8.54
worthy 7.7; Acts 5.41

The Parable of the Tenants in the Vineyard
(Matt. 21.33–46; Mark 12.1–12)

9 Then Jesus told the people this
parable: "There was once a man who
planted a **vineyard**, let it out to tenants,
and then left home for a long time.
10 When the time came to gather the
grapes, he sent a **slave** to the tenants to
receive from them his **share** of the **harvest**.
But the tenants beat the **slave** and
sent him back without a thing. 11 So he
sent another **slave**; but the tenants beat
him also, treated him **shamefully**, and
sent him back without a thing. 12 Then he
sent a third **slave**; the tenants wounded
him, too, and threw him out. 13 Then the
owner of the **vineyard** said, 'What shall I
do? I will send my own **dear** son; surely
they will **respect** him!' 14 But when the
tenants saw him, they said to **one
another**, 'This is the owner's son. Let's
kill him, and his property will be ours!'
15 So they threw him out of the **vineyard**
and killed him.

"What, then, will the owner of the **vineyard**
do to the tenants?" Jesus asked.
16 "He will come and kill those men, and
hand the **vineyard** over to other tenants."

When the people heard this, they said,
"Surely not!"

17 Jesus looked at them and asked,
"What, then, does this **scripture** mean?

'The stone which the builders **rejected**
as **worthless**
turned out to be the most **important**
of all.'

18 Everyone who falls on that stone will
be cut to pieces; and if that stone falls on
someone, it will crush him to dust."

The Question about Paying Taxes
(Matt. 22.15–22; Mark 12.13–17)

19 The **teachers of the Law** and the
chief priests tried to **arrest** Jesus on the
spot, because they knew that he had told
this **parable** against them; but they were
afraid of the people. 20 So they looked for
an opportunity. They **bribed** some men to
pretend they were **sincere**, and they sent
them to **trap** Jesus with **questions**, so that
they could hand him over to the
authority and **power** of the Roman
Governor. 21 These spies said to Jesus,
"**Teacher**, we know that what you say
and **teach** is **right**. We know that you pay
no attention to a man's status, but **teach**
the **truth** about **God's will** for man. 22 Tell
us, is it against our **Law** for us to pay
taxes to the Roman Emperor, or not?"

23 But Jesus saw through their **trick**
and said to them, 24 "Show me a silver
coin. Whose face and name are these on
it?"

"The Emperor's," they answered.

25 So Jesus said, "Well, then, pay the
Emperor what belongs to the Emperor,
and pay God what belongs to God."

26 There before the people they could
not catch him out in anything, so they
kept quiet, **amazed** at his answer.

The Question about Rising from Death
(Matt. 22.23–33; Mark 12.18–27)

27 Then some **Sadducees**, who say that
people will not **rise from death**, came to
Jesus and said, 28 "**Teacher**, Moses wrote
this **law** for us: 'If a man dies and leaves
a wife but no children, that man's
brother must marry the **widow** so that
they can have children who will be **considered**
the **dead** man's children.' 29 Once
there were seven brothers; the eldest got
married and died without having children.
30 Then the second one married the
woman, 31 and then the third. The same
thing happened to all seven—they died
without having children. 32 **Last** of all, the
woman died. 33 Now, on the day when the
dead rise to life, whose wife will she be?
All seven of them had married her."

34 Jesus answered them, "The men
and women of this **age** marry, 35 but the
men and women who are **worthy** to **rise
from death** and live in the **age** to come
will not then marry. 36 They will be like
angels and cannot die. They are the **sons
of God**, because they have **risen from
death**. 37 And Moses **clearly proves** that
the **dead** are **raised to life**. In the passage
about the burning bush he speaks of the
Lord as 'the God of Abraham, the God of
Isaac, and the God of Jacob.' 38 He is the
God of the living, not of the **dead**, for to
him all are **alive**."

39 Some of the **teachers of the Law**
spoke up, "A good answer, **Teacher**!"
40 For they did not **dare** ask him any
more **questions**.

The Question about the Messiah
(Matt. 22.41–46; Mark 12.35–37)

41 Jesus asked them, "How can it be
said that the **Messiah** will be the descendant
of David? 42 For David himself says
in the book of **Psalms**,

'The Lord said to my Lord:
Sit here on my **right**
43 until I put your **enemies** as a
footstool under your feet.'

44 David called him 'Lord'; how, then, can
the **Messiah** be David's descendant?"

20.9: Is 5.1 **20.17:** Ps 118.22 **20.27:** Acts 23.8 **20.28:** Deut 25.5 **20.37:** Ex 3.6 **20.42–43:** Ps 110.1

Jesus Warns against the Teachers of the Law
(Matt. 23.1–36; Mark 12.38–40)

45 As all the people listened to him, Jesus said to his **disciples**, 46 "Be on your guard against the **teachers of the Law**, who like to walk about in their long robes and **love** to be greeted with **respect** in the market-place; who **choose** the reserved seats in the **synagogues** and the **best places** at **feasts**; 47 who take **advantage** of **widows** and **rob** them of their homes, and then make a show of saying long **prayers**! Their **punishment** will be all the **worse**!"

The Widow's Offering
(Mark 12.41–44)

21 Jesus looked round and saw **rich** men dropping their **gifts** in the **temple** treasury, 2 and he also saw a very **poor widow** dropping in two little copper coins. 3 He said, "I tell you that this **poor widow** put in more than all the others. 4 For the others **offered** their **gifts** from what they had to **spare** of their **riches**; but she, **poor** as she is, gave all she had to live on."

Jesus Speaks of the Destruction of the Temple
(Matt. 24.1–2; Mark 13.1–2)

5 Some of the **disciples** were talking about the **Temple**, how beautiful it looked with its fine stones and the **gifts offered** to God. Jesus said, 6 "All this you see—the time will come when not a single stone here will be left in its place; every one will be thrown down."

Troubles and Persecutions
(Matt. 24.3–14; Mark 13.3–13)

7 "**Teacher**," they asked, "when will this be? And what will happen in order to show that the time has come for it to take place?"

8 Jesus said, "Be on guard; don't be **deceived**. Many men, **claiming** to speak for me, will come and say, 'I am he!' and, 'The time has come!' But don't follow them. 9 Don't be **afraid** when you hear of wars and revolutions; such things must happen first, but they do not mean that the end is near."

10 He went on to say, "Countries will fight **each other**; kingdoms will attack **one another**. 11 There will be **terrible** earthquakes, **famines**, and **plagues** everywhere; there will be **strange** and **terrifying** things coming from the sky. 12 Before all these things take place, however, you will be **arrested** and **persecuted**; you will be handed over to be **tried** in **synagogues** and be put in **prison**; you will be brought before kings and rulers for my **sake**. 13 This will be your chance to tell the **Good News**. 14 Make up your **minds** beforehand not to **worry** about how you will **defend** yourselves, 15 because I will give you such **words** and **wisdom** that none of your **enemies** will be able to refute or contradict what you say. 16 You will be handed over by your parents, your brothers, your relatives, and your **friends**; and some of you will be put **to death**. 17 Everyone will **hate** you because of me. 18 But not a single hair from your heads will be lost. 19 Stand firm, and you will **save** yourselves.

Jesus Speaks of the Destruction of Jerusalem
(Matt. 24.15–21; Mark 13.14–19)

20 "When you see Jerusalem surrounded by armies, then you will know that she will soon be **destroyed**. 21 Then those who are in Judaea must run away to the hills; those who are in the city must leave, and those who are out in the country must not go into the city. 22 For those will be 'The Days of **Punishment**,' to make all that the **Scriptures** say come **true**. 23 How **terrible** it will be in those days for women who are pregnant and for mothers with little babies! **Terrible distress** will come upon this land, and God's **punishment** will fall on this people. 24 Some will be killed by the sword, and others will be taken as **prisoners** to all countries; and the **heathen** will trample over Jerusalem until their time is up.

The Coming of the Son of Man
(Matt. 24.29–31; Mark 13.24–27)

25 "There will be **strange** things happening to the sun, the moon, and the stars. On earth whole countries will be in **despair**, **afraid** of the roar of the sea and the **raging** tides. 26 People will faint from **fear** as they wait for what is coming over the whole earth, for the **powers in space** will be driven from their courses. 27 Then the **Son of Man** will appear, coming in a **cloud** with great **power** and **glory**. 28 When these things begin to happen, stand up and **raise** your heads, because your **salvation** is near."

The Lesson of the Fig-Tree
(Matt. 24.32–35; Mark 13.28–31)

29 Then Jesus told them this **parable**: "Think of the fig-tree and all the other

21.14–15: Lk 12.11–12 **21.22:** Hos 9.7 **21.25:** Is 13.10; Ezek 32.7; Joel 2.31; Rev 6.12–13
21.27: Dan 7.13; Rev 1.7

afraid [2] 20.19; 22.2
alert Mk 13.33; 1 Cor 16.13
arrest 20.19; 22.53
claim Mk 13.6; 22.25
cloud 12.54; Acts 1.9
Day of the Lord Mal 4.5; Acts 2.20
death (3) (to death) 9.22; 22.2
deceive Mk 13.5; Rom 1.29
defend 12.11; Acts 19.33
despair Zeph 1.14; 2 Cor 4.8
destroy 19.44; Jn 10.10
disciple 20.45; 22.3
distress 12.50; 1 Cor 7.26
each other 12.1; 24.14
enemy 20.43; 23.12
famine 15.14; Acts 7.11
fear 18.2; 23.40
feast 20.46; Jn 2.8
friend 16.4; 22.25
gift [3] Mt 23.18; Acts 1.4
glory 19.38; 24.26
Good News 20.1; Acts 5.42
hate 19.14; Jn 3.20
heathen Mk 10.42; Acts 7.51
heaven 19.38; 22.43
Kingdom (1) (of God) 19.11; 22.16
life (1) 18.18; Jn 1.4
mind (1) 10.27; 24.38
offer [2] 13.1; 22.5
one another 20.14; Jn 5.44
parable 20.9; Jn 10.6
persecute 11.49; Jn 5.16
plague Amos 4.10; Rev 9.18
poor [3] 19.8; Jn 12.5
power [2] 20.20; 22.25
pray 18.1; 22.32
prison [2] 8.29; 22.33
punish [2] 20.47; Jn 3.36
rage 6.11; Rev 11.18
raise 20.37; 24.6
remember 18.17; 22.61
rich 19.2; Acts 4.33
riches 18.22; Rom 11.33
safe 15.27; Jn 17.11

sake 18.29; Jn 11.15
salvation 19.9; Jn 4.22
save 19.10; 23.35
scripture 20.17; 22.37
Son of Man [2] 19.10; 22.22
spare Mk 12.44; Acts 20.29
strange [2] Mk 16.17; Jn 9.30
strength 10.27; 22.32
synagogue 20.46; Jn 6.59
teach 20.1; 23.5
teacher 20.21; 22.11
Temple (1) (of God) [4] 20.1; 22.53
terrible [3] 17.1; 22.22
terrify Mk 16.8; 24.37
trap 20.20; Jn 8.6
true 18.31; 22.37
try (2) 14.19; 22.28
widow [2] 20.28; Acts 6.1
wisdom 11.49; Acts 6.3
word (1) [2] 19.22; 23.38
worry [2] 12.11; Jn 14.1

trees. 30 When you see their leaves beginning to appear, you know that summer is near. 31 In the same way, when you see these things happening, you will know that the **Kingdom of God** is about to come.

32 "**Remember** that all these things will take place before the people now living have all died. 33 **Heaven and earth** will pass away, but my **words** will never pass away.

The Need to Watch

34 "Be on your guard! Don't let yourselves become occupied with too much **feasting** and drinking and with the **worries** of this **life**, or that **Day** may suddenly catch you 35 like a **trap**. For it will come upon all people everywhere on earth. 36 Be on the **alert** and **pray** always that you will have the **strength** to go **safely** through all those things that will happen and to stand before the **Son of Man**."

37 Jesus spent those days **teaching** in the **Temple**, and when evening came, he would go out and spend the night on the Mount of Olives. 38 Early each morning all the people went to the **Temple** to listen to him.

The Plot against Jesus
(Matt. 26.1–5; Mark 14.1–2; John 11.45–53)

22 The time was near for the **Festival of Unleavened Bread**, which is called the **Passover**. 2 The **chief priests** and the **teachers of the Law** were **afraid** of the people, and so they were trying to find a way of putting Jesus **to death secretly**.

Judas Agrees to Betray Jesus
(Matt. 26.14–16; Mark 14.10–11)

3 Then **Satan** entered Judas, called Iscariot, who was one of the twelve **disciples**. 4 So Judas went off and spoke with the **chief priests** and the officers of the temple guard about how he could **betray** Jesus to them. 5 They were **pleased** and **offered** to pay him money. 6 Judas **agreed** to it and started looking for a good chance to hand Jesus over to them without the people knowing about it.

Jesus Prepares to Eat the Passover Meal
(Matt. 26.17–25; Mark 14.12–21; John 13.21–30)

7 The day came during the **Festival** of **Unleavened Bread** when the **lambs** for the **Passover** meal were to be killed. 8 Jesus sent off Peter and John with these instructions: "Go and get the **Passover** meal ready for us to eat."

9 "Where do you want us to get it ready?" they asked him.

10 He answered, "As you go into the city, a man carrying a jar of water will meet you. Follow him into the house that he enters, 11 and say to the owner of the house: 'The **Teacher** says to you, Where is the room where my **disciples** and I will eat the **Passover** meal?' 12 He will show you a large furnished room upstairs, where you will get everything ready."

13 They went off and found everything just as Jesus had told them, and they prepared the **Passover** meal.

The Lord's Supper
(Matt. 26.26–30; Mark 14.22–26; 1 Cor. 11.23–25)

14 When the hour came, Jesus took his place at the table with the **apostles**. 15 He said to them, "I have wanted so much to eat this **Passover** meal with you before I **suffer**! 16 For I tell you, I will never eat it until it is given its full meaning in the **Kingdom of God**."

17 Then Jesus took a **cup**, gave **thanks** to God, and said, "Take this and **share** it among yourselves. 18 I tell you that from now on I will not drink this wine until the **Kingdom of God** comes."

19 Then he took a piece of **bread**, gave **thanks** to God, broke it, and gave it to them, saying, "This is my **body**, which is given for you. Do this in memory of me." 20 In the same way, he gave them the **cup** after the supper, saying, "This **cup** is God's **new covenant sealed** with my **blood**, which is poured out for you.[y]

21 "But, look! The one who **betrays** me is here at the table with me! 22 The **Son of Man** will die as God has decided, but how **terrible** for that man who betrays him!"

23 Then they began to ask among themselves which one of them it could be who was going to do this.

The Argument about Greatness

24 An **argument** broke out among the **disciples** as to which one of them should be thought of as the greatest. 25 Jesus said to them, "The kings of the **pagans** have **power** over their people, and the rulers **claim** the title '**Friends** of the People.' 26 But this is not the way it is with you;

[y] *Some manuscripts do not have the words of Jesus after* This is my body *in verse 19, and all of verse 20.*

21.37: Lk 19.47 **22.1:** Ex 12.1–27 **22.20:** Jer 31.31–34 **22.21:** Ps 41.9 **22.24:** Mt 18.1; Mk 9.34; Lk 9.46 **22.25–26:** Mt 20.25–27; Mk 10.42–44 **22.26:** Mt 23.11; Mk 9.35

act 18.4; 24.28
afraid 21.9; Jn 6.20
agree Mk 14.56; 23.50
Almighty Mk 14.62; Rom 9.29
angel 20.36; 24.23
anguish Mk 14.33
apostle 17.5; 24.10
argue 20.5; Jn 3.25
arrest [2] 21.12; Jn 7.32
bad 19.22; Jn 6.27
believe 20.5; 24.11
betray [4] Mk 14.10; Jn 6.64
bitter 11.53; Acts 8.23
blood [2] Mk 14.24; Jn 6.53
body 17.37; 23.52
bread 11.5; 24.30
chief priests [4] 20.1; 23.4
claim 21.8; 23.2
Council Mk 15.1; 23.50
covenant 1.72; Acts 3.25
crime Mk 15.14; 23.14
cup [4] 11.39; Jn 4.9
dark 12.3; 23.44
death (3) (to death) 21.16; 23.32
deny 8.45; Jn 18.25
disciple [9] 21.5; 24.9
doubt 7.23; 24.38
elder (2) [2] 20.1; Acts 4.5

enough [2] 16.3; Jn 1.27
fail Mal 1.7; Rom 9.6
faith 18.8; Jn 16.1
fate 12.46; Acts 28.4
Father (2) (God) [2] 12.30; 23.34
festival [2] 2.41; Jn 2.13
friend 21.16; 23.12
grief Mt 26.37; Rev 18.7
heal 17.15; Jn 4.47
heaven 21.33; 24.51
High Priest [2] 3.2; Jn 11.49
insult 18.32; 23.39
Kingdom (1) (of God) [3] 21.31; 23.50
kiss [2] 15.20; Acts 20.37
kneel Mk 10.17; Jn 9.38
lamb 10.3; Jn 1.29
Messiah 20.41; 23.2
mock 18.32; 23.11
need 19.31; Jn 2.25
new 5.36; Jn 13.34
notice (1) 14.7; Acts 4.29
offer 21.4; 23.36
pagan 12.30; 1 Cor 5.10
Passover [6] 2.41; Jn 2.13
permit Mk 10.4; Acts 21.40
please 14.18; 23.8
power [2] 21.26; 24.19
pray [5] 21.36; Jn 17.9
prayer 20.47; Jn 18.1
prison 21.12; 23.19
question 20.3; 23.9
remember 21.32; 23.42
right (2) [2] 20.42; 23.33
right (3) [2] 20.2; Jn 1.12
rise 20.27; 23.1
Satan [2] 13.16; Jn 13.27
scripture 21.22; 24.27
seal Mk 14.24; 1 Cor 11.25
secret 12.2; Jn 7.10
separate [2] Mk 10.9; Acts 3.23
servant [2] 19.13; Jn 2.5
serve [2] 16.13; Jn 2.10
share [2] 20.10; Jn 13.18
slave 20.10; Jn 8.33
Son of God 10.22; Jn 1.14
Son of Man [3] 21.27; 24.7
strength [2] 21.36; Acts 3.16
strike Mk 14.47; Jn 18.10
strong 16.3; 23.5
suffer [2] 17.12; 24.26
teacher 21.7; Jn 1.38
teacher of the Law [2] 20.1; 23.10
Temple (1) (of God) 21.1; 23.45
tempt [2] 4.2; 1 Cor 7.5
terrible 21.11; Acts 9.13
test 11.4; Jn 6.6
thank [2] 19.37; 24.53
throne 1.52; Acts 7.49
true [2] 21.22; 24.44

try (2) 21.12; Jn 18.31
turn [2] 20.17; 23.28
unleavened [2]
Mk 14.1; Acts 12.3
weep 19.41; 23.27
will (1) 20.21; Jn 4.34
witness Mk 14.56;
24.48

rather, the greatest one among you must
be like the youngest, and the leader must
be like the **servant**. 27 Who is greater, the
one who sits down to eat or the one who
serves him? The one who sits down, of
course. But I am among you as one who
serves.

28 "You have stayed with me all
through my **trials**; 29 and just as **my**
Father has given me the **right** to rule, so
I will give you the same **right**. 30 You will
eat and drink at my table in my **King-**
dom, and you will sit on **thrones** to rule
over the twelve tribes of Israel.

Jesus Predicts Peter's Denial
(Matt. 26.31–35; Mark 14.27–31;
John 13.36–38)

31 "Simon, Simon! Listen! **Satan** has
received **permission** to **test** all of you, to
separate the good from the **bad**, as a
farmer **separates** the wheat from the
chaff. 32 But I have **prayed** for you, Simon,
that your **faith** will not **fail**. And when you
turn back to me, you must **strengthen**
your brothers."

33 Peter answered, "Lord, I am ready
to go to **prison** with you and to die with
you!"

34 "I tell you, Peter," Jesus said, "the
cock will not crow tonight until you have
said three times that you do not know
me."

Purse, Bag, and Sword

35 Then Jesus asked his **disciples**,
"When I sent you out that time without
purse, bag, or shoes, did you lack anything?"

"Not a thing," they answered.

36 "But now," Jesus said, "whoever
has a purse or a bag must take it; and
whoever has no sword must sell his coat
and buy one. 37 For I tell you that the
scripture which says, 'He **shared** the **fate**
of **criminals**,' must come **true** about me,
because what was written about me is
coming **true**."

38 The **disciples** said, "Look! Here are
two swords, Lord!"

"That is **enough**!"[z] he replied.

Jesus Prays on the Mount of Olives
(Matt. 26.36–46; Mark 14.32–42)

39 Jesus left the city and went, as he
usually did, to the Mount of Olives; and
the **disciples** went with him. 40 When he
arrived at the place, he said to them,
"**Pray** that you will not fall into **tempta-**
tion."

41 Then he went off from them about
the distance of a stone's throw and **knelt**
down and **prayed**. 42 "**Father**," he said, "if
you will, take this **cup of suffering** away
from me. Not my **will**, however, but your
will be done." 43 An **angel** from **heaven**
appeared to him and **strengthened** him.
44 In great **anguish** he **prayed** even more
fervently; his sweat was like drops of
blood falling to the ground.[a]

45 **Rising** from his **prayer**, he went
back to the **disciples** and found them
asleep, worn out by their **grief**. 46 He said
to them, "Why are you sleeping? Get up
and **pray** that you will not fall into
temptation."

The Arrest of Jesus
(Matt. 26.47–56; Mark 14.43–50;
John 18.3–11)

47 Jesus was still speaking when a
crowd arrived, led by Judas, one of the
twelve **disciples**. He came up to Jesus to
kiss him. 48 But Jesus said, "Judas, is it
with a **kiss** that you **betray** the **Son of**
Man?"

49 When the **disciples** who were with
Jesus saw what was going to happen,
they asked, "Shall we use our swords,
Lord?" 50 And one of them **struck** the
High Priest's slave and cut off his **right**
ear.

51 But Jesus said, "**Enough** of this!"
He touched the man's ear and **healed**
him.

52 Then Jesus said to the **chief priests**
and the officers of the temple guard and
the **elders** who had come there to get
him, "Did you have to come with swords
and clubs, as though I were an outlaw?
53 I was with you in the **Temple** every
day, and you did not try to **arrest** me. But
this is your hour to **act**, when the **power**
of **darkness** rules."

Peter Denies Jesus
(Matt. 26.57–58, 69–75; Mark 14.53–54,
66–72; John 18.12–18, 25–27)

54 They **arrested** Jesus and took him
away into the house of the **High Priest**;
and Peter followed at a distance. 55 A fire
had been lit in the centre of the courtyard, and Peter joined those who were
sitting round it. 56 When one of the **ser-**
vant-girls saw him sitting there at the
fire, she looked straight at him and said,
"This man too was with Jesus!"

57 But Peter **denied** it, "Woman, I
don't even know him!"

[z] That is enough; *or* Enough of this. [a] *Some manuscripts do not have verses 43–44.*

22.27: Jn 13.12–15 **22.30:** Mt 19.28 **22.35:** Mt 10.9–10; Mk 6.8-9; Lk 9.3, 10.4 **22.37:** Is 53.12
22.53: Lk 19.47, 21.37

58 After a little while a man **noticed** Peter and said, "You are one of them, too!"

But Peter answered, "Man, I am not!"

59 And about an hour later another man insisted **strongly**, "There isn't any **doubt** that this man was with Jesus, because he also is a Galilean!"

60 But Peter answered, "Man, I don't know what you are talking about!"

At once, while he was still speaking, a cock crowed. 61 The Lord **turned round** and looked straight at Peter, and Peter **remembered** that the Lord had said to him, "Before the cock crows tonight, you will say three times that you do not know me." 62 Peter went out and **wept bitterly**.

Jesus Is Mocked and Beaten
(Matt. 26.67–68; Mark 14.65)

63 The men who were guarding Jesus **mocked** him and beat him. 64 They blindfolded him and asked him, "Who hit you? Guess!" 65 And they said many other **insulting** things to him.

Jesus Is Brought Before the Council
(Matt. 26.59–66; Mark 14.55–64; John 18.19–24)

66 When day came, the **elders**, the **chief priests**, and the **teachers of the Law** met together, and Jesus was brought before the **Council**. 67 "Tell us," they said, "are you the **Messiah**?"

He answered, "If I tell you, you will not **believe** me; 68 and if I ask you a **question**, you will not answer. 69 But from now on the **Son of Man** will be seated on the **right** of **Almighty** God."

70 They all said, "Are you, then, the **Son of God**?"

He answered them, "You say that I am."

71 And they said, "We don't **need** any **witnesses**! We ourselves have heard what he said!"

Jesus Is Brought Before Pilate
(Matt. 27.1–2, 11–14; Mark 15.1–5; John 18.28–38)

23 The whole group **rose** up and took Jesus before Pilate, 2 where they began to **accuse** him: "We caught this man **misleading** our people, telling them not to pay **taxes** to the Emperor and **claiming** that he himself is the **Messiah**, a king."

3 Pilate asked him, "Are you the **king of the Jews**?"

"So you say," answered Jesus.

4 Then Pilate said to the **chief priests** and the crowds, "I find no **reason** to **condemn** this man."

5 But they insisted even more **strongly**, "With his **teaching** he is starting a riot among the people all through Judaea. He began in Galilee and now has come here."

Jesus Is Sent to Herod

6 When Pilate heard this, he asked, "Is this man a Galilean?" 7 When he **learnt** that Jesus was from the region ruled by Herod, he sent him to Herod, who was also in Jerusalem at that time. 8 Herod was very **pleased** when he saw Jesus, because he had heard about him and had been wanting to see him for a long time. He was **hoping** to see Jesus perform some **miracle**. 9 So Herod asked Jesus many **questions**, but Jesus made no answer. 10 The **chief priests** and the **teachers of the Law** stepped forward and made **strong accusations** against Jesus. 11 Herod and his soldiers **mocked** Jesus and treated him with **contempt**; then they put a fine robe on him and sent him back to Pilate. 12 On that very day Herod and Pilate became **friends**; before this they had been **enemies**.

Jesus Is Sentenced to Death
(Matt. 27.15–26; Mark 15.6–15; John 18.39—19.16)

13 Pilate called together the **chief priests**, the leaders, and the people, 14 and said to them, "You brought this man to me and said that he was **misleading** the people. Now, I have examined him here in your **presence**, and I have not found him **guilty** of any of the **crimes** you **accuse** him of. 15 Nor did Herod find him **guilty**, for he sent him back to us. There is nothing this man has done to **deserve death**. 16 So I will have him whipped and let him go."[b]

18 The whole crowd cried out, "Kill him! **Set Barabbas free** for us!" 19 (Barabbas had been put in **prison** for a riot that had taken place in the city, and for murder.)

20 Pilate wanted to **set Jesus free**, so he appealed to the crowd again. 21 But they shouted back, "**Crucify** him! **Crucify** him!"

22 Pilate said to them the third time, "But what **crime** has he **committed**? I cannot find anything he has done to **deserve death**! I will have him whipped and **set him free**."

23 But they kept on shouting at the top

accuse [3] 18.20; Jn 5.45
action 12.35; Jn 11.48
agree 22.6; Jn 8.17
body [4] 22.19; 24.3
chief priests [3] 22.2; 24.20
choose 20.46; Jn 6.70
claim 22.25; Jn 4.12
command 19.39; Jn 8.5
commit 18.20; Jn 8.3
condemn 19.22; Jn 5.29
contempt Mal 1.7

Council 22.66; Jn 11.47
crime [5] 22.37; Jn 18.30
cross (1) 14.27; Jn 19.17
crucify [4] Mk 16.6; 24.7
dark 22.53; 24.29
death (1) [2] 1.79; Jn 11.4
death (3) (to death) 22.2; Jn 8.5
deserve [3] 17.9; Acts 23.29
enemy 21.15; Acts 2.35
Father (2) (God) [2] 22.29; 24.49
fear 21.26; 24.5
forgive 17.3; 24.47
free [4] 13.12; 24.21
friend 22.25; Jn 3.29
guilty [2] Mk 14.64; Jn 8.46
hang (2) Mt 27.5; Gal 3.13
honour 14.10; Jn 5.23
hope 16.21; 24.21
insult 22.65; Acts 13.45
jeer Mk 15.31
Jew [4] 18.18; Jn 1.19
Kingdom (1) (of God) 22.16; Jn 3.3
law 20.22; 24.44
learn 10.21; Jn 6.45
Messiah [3] 22.67; 24.26
miracle 11.16; Jn 2.11
mislead [2] Zech 10.2; Jn 7.12
mock [2] 22.63; Heb 11.36
offer 22.5; Jn 4.23
Paradise 2 Cor 12.3
pass (5) Jn 8.15
please 22.5; Jn 8.29
praise 19.37; Jn 5.41
presence [2] 19.27; 24.43
prison [2] 22.33; Jn 3.24
promise 2.5; 24.49
question 22.68; Jn 2.18
reason 14.20; Jn 6.65
rebuke 17.3; 1 Tim 5.1
remember 22.61; 24.6
rest (1) 11.24; 2 Cor 7.5
right (1) 20.21; Jn 4.17
right (2) 22.50; Jn 18.10
rise 22.45; 24.7
Sabbath [2] 14.1; Jn 5.9
save [4] 21.19; Jn 5.34
sentence [2] Zeph 2.5; 24.20
sorrow 2.35; Rom 9.2
spirit (2) 13.11; Acts 5.16
strong [2] 22.59; Jn 6.18
succeed (1) Mt 23.15; Jn 12.19
tax 20.22; Rom 13.6
teach 21.37; Jn 6.45
teacher of the Law 22.2; Jn 8.3
Temple (1) (of God) 22.53; 24.53
tomb [2] 11.47; 24.1
turn 22.32; Jn 1.38
wail Mk 5.38; Jas 5.1

[b] *Some manuscripts add verse 17:* At every Passover Festival Pilate had to set free one prisoner for them *(see Mk 15.6).*

watch [3] 17.3; Acts 1.9
weep 22.62; Jn 11.31
wish 17.22; Jn 3.8
word (1) 21.15; 24.8
wrong 11.4; Jn 16.8

of their voices that Jesus should be **cruci-**
fied, and finally their shouting **suc-**
ceeded. 24 So Pilate **passed** the **sentence**
on Jesus that they were asking for. 25 He
set free the man they wanted, the one
who had been put in **prison** for riot and
murder, and he handed Jesus over for
them to do as they **wished**.

Jesus Is Crucified
(Matt. 27.32–44; Mark 15.21–32;
John 19.17–27)

26 The soldiers led Jesus away, and as
they were going, they met a man from
Cyrene named Simon who was coming
into the city from the country. They
seized him, put the **cross** on him, and
made him carry it behind Jesus.

27 A large crowd of people followed
him; among them were some women
who were **weeping** and **wailing** for him.
28 Jesus **turned** to them and said, "Women
of Jerusalem! Don't cry for me, but for
yourselves and your children. 29 For the
days are coming when people will say,
'How lucky are the women who never
had children, who never bore babies,
who never nursed them!' 30 That will be
the time when people will say to the
mountains, 'Fall on us!' and to the hills,
'Hide us!' 31 For if such things as these
are done when the wood is green, what
will happen when it is dry?"

32 Two other men, both of them **crimi-**
nals, were also led out to be put **to death**
with Jesus. 33 When they came to the
place called "The Skull," they **crucified**
Jesus there, and the two **criminals**, one
on his **right** and the other on his left.
34 Jesus said, "**Forgive** them, **Father**!
They don't know what they are doing."[c]

They divided his clothes among themselves by throwing dice. 35 The people
stood there **watching** while the **Jewish**
leaders **jeered** at him: "He **saved** others;
let him **save** himself if he is the **Messiah**
whom God has **chosen**!"

36 The soldiers also **mocked** him: they
came up to him and **offered** him cheap
wine, 37 and said, "**Save** yourself if you
are the **king of the Jews**!"

38 Above him were written these
words: "This is the **King of the Jews**."

39 One of the **criminals hanging** there
hurled **insults** at him: "Aren't you the
Messiah? **Save** yourself and us!"

40 The other one, however, **rebuked**
him, saying, "Don't you **fear** God? You
received the same **sentence** he did.
41 Ours, however, is only **right**, because
we are getting what we **deserve** for what
we did; but he has done no **wrong**." 42 And
he said to Jesus, "**Remember** me, Jesus,
when you come as King!"

43 Jesus said to him, "I **promise** you
that today you will be in **Paradise** with
me."

The Death of Jesus
(Matt. 27.45–56; Mark 15.33–41;
John 19.28–30)

44 It was about twelve o'clock when
the sun stopped shining and **darkness**
covered the whole country until three
o'clock; 45 and the curtain hanging in the
Temple was torn in two. 46 Jesus cried out
in a loud voice, "**Father**! In your hands I
place my **spirit**!" He said this and died.

47 The army officer saw what had
happened, and he **praised** God, saying,
"Certainly he was a good man!"

48 When the people who had gathered
there to **watch** the spectacle saw what
happened, they all went back home,
beating their breasts in **sorrow**. 49 All
those who knew Jesus personally, including the women who had followed him
from Galilee, stood at a distance to
watch.

The Burial of Jesus
(Matt. 27.57–61; Mark 15.42–47;
John 19.38–42)

50–51 There was a man named Joseph
from Arimathea, a town in Judaea. He
was a good and **honourable** man, who
was waiting for the coming of the **King-**
dom of God. Although he was a member
of the **Council**, he had not **agreed** with
their decision and **action**. 52 He went into
the **presence** of Pilate and asked for the
body of Jesus. 53 Then he took the **body**
down, wrapped it in a linen sheet, and
placed it in a **tomb** which had been dug
out of solid rock and which had never
been used. 54 It was Friday, and the
Sabbath was about to begin.

55 The women who had followed Jesus
from Galilee went with Joseph and saw
the **tomb** and how Jesus' **body** was placed
in it. 56 Then they went back home and
prepared the spices and perfumes for the
body.

On the **Sabbath** they **rested**, as the **Law**
commanded.

[c] *Some manuscripts do not have* Jesus said, "Forgive them, Father! They don't know what they are doing."

23.30: Hos 10.8; Rev 6.16 **23.34:** Ps 22.18 **23.35:** Ps 22.7 **23.36:** Ps 69.21 **23.45:** Ex 26.31–33
23.46: Ps 31.5 **23.49:** Lk 8.2–3 **23.56:** Ex 20.10; Deut 5.14

above Ezek 3.12; Jn 3.31
act 22.53; Jn 8.4
alive [2] 20.38; Acts 1.3
amaze 20.26; Jn 5.20
angel 22.43; Jn 1.51
apostle [2] 22.14; Acts 1.2
believe [3] 22.67; Jn 1.7
bless [3] 19.38; Jn 1.16
body [2] 23.52; Jn 2.21
bow (2) Mk 15.19; Jn 19.30
bread [3] 22.19; Jn 6.7
chief priests 23.4; Jn 7.32
consider 20.28; Acts 5.41
crucify [2] 23.21; Jn 19.6
dark 23.44; Jn 1.5
dead 20.28; Jn 5.21
death (2) (from death) 20.27; Jn 2.22
disciple [2] 22.3; Jn 1.35
discuss 6.11; Acts 4.15
doubt 22.59; Jn 20.27
each other [3] 21.10; Acts 2.12
Father (2) (God) 23.34; Jn 1.13
fear 23.40; Acts 7.32
flesh Mk 14.38; Jn 6.51
follower 11.19; Jn 6.60
fool 12.20; Jn 7.47
forgive 23.34; Jn 20.23
free 23.18; Jn 8.32
ghost [2] Mk 6.49
glory 21.27; Jn 1.14
heaven 22.43; Jn 1.32
hope 23.8; Jn 5.45
joy [2] 19.6; Jn 15.11
last (2) 20.32; Jn 6.39
law 23.56; Jn 1.17
life (2) (to life) 20.33; Jn 5.24
message 8.12; Jn 1.7
Messiah [2] 23.2; Jn 1.20
mind (1) [2] 21.14; Jn 12.40
name (2) (name of God, of Jesus) 19.38; Jn 12.13
peace 19.38; Jn 14.27
power [2] 22.25; Jn 3.35
preach 20.1; Acts 1.21
presence 23.14; Jn 10.32
promise 23.43; Jn 9.24
prophet [4] 20.6; Jn 1.21
psalm 20.42; Acts 1.20
raise [2] 21.28; Jn 2.22
remember [2] 23.42; Jn 2.17
repent 17.3; Acts 3.19
rise [3] 23.1; Jn 5.29
sad 18.23; Jn 16.6
scripture [3] 22.37; Jn 2.17

The Resurrection
(Matt. 28.1–10; Mark 16.1–8; John 20.1–10)

24 Very early on Sunday morning the women went to the **tomb**, carrying the spices they had prepared. 2 They found the stone rolled away from the entrance to the **tomb**, 3 so they went in; but they did not find the **body** of the Lord Jesus. 4 They stood there puzzled about this, when suddenly two men in bright shining clothes stood by them. 5 Full of **fear**, the women **bowed down** to the ground, as the men said to them, "Why are you looking among the **dead** for one who is **alive**? 6 He is not here; he has been **raised**. **Remember** what he said to you while he was in Galilee: 7 'The **Son of Man** must be handed over to sinful men, be **crucified**, and three days later **rise to life**.' "

8 Then the women **remembered** his **words**, 9 returned from the **tomb**, and told all these things to the eleven **disciples** and all the rest. 10 The women were Mary Magdalene, Joanna, and Mary the mother of James; they and the other women with them told these things to the **apostles**. 11 But the **apostles** thought that what the women said was nonsense, and they did not **believe** them. 12 But Peter got up and ran to the **tomb**; he bent down and saw the linen wrappings but nothing else. Then he went back home **amazed** at what had happened.[d]

The Walk to Emmaus
(Mark 16.12–13)

13 On that same day two of Jesus' **followers** were going to a village named Emmaus, about eleven kilometres from Jerusalem, 14 and they were talking to **each other** about all the things that had happened. 15 As they talked and **discussed**, Jesus himself drew near and walked along with them; 16 they saw him, but somehow did not recognize him. 17 Jesus said to them, "What are you talking about to **each other**, as you walk along?"

They stood still, with **sad** faces. 18 One of them, named Cleopas, asked him, "Are you the only visitor in Jerusalem who doesn't know the things that have been happening there these **last** few days?"

19 "What things?" he asked.

"The things that happened to Jesus of Nazareth," they answered. "This man was a **prophet** and was **considered** by God and by all the people to be **powerful** in everything he said and did. 20 Our **chief priests** and rulers handed him over to be **sentenced** to death, and he was **crucified**. 21 And we had **hoped** that he would be the one who was going to **set Israel free**! Besides all that, this is now the third day since it happened. 22 Some of the women of our group surprised us; they went at dawn to the **tomb**, 23 but could not find his **body**. They came back saying they had seen a **vision** of **angels** who told them that he is **alive**. 24 Some of our group went to the **tomb** and found it exactly as the women had said, but they did not see him."

25 Then Jesus said to them, "How **foolish** you are, how slow you are to **believe** everything the **prophets** said! 26 Was it not necessary for the **Messiah** to **suffer** these things and then to enter his **glory**?" 27 And Jesus explained to them what was said about himself in all the **Scriptures**, beginning with the books of Moses and the writings of all the **prophets**.

28 As they came near the village to which they were going, Jesus **acted** as if he were going farther; 29 but they held him back, saying, "Stay with us; the day is almost over and it is getting **dark**." So he went in to stay with them. 30 He sat down to eat with them, took the **bread**, and said the **blessing**; then he broke the **bread** and gave it to them. 31 Then their eyes were opened and they recognized him, but he disappeared from their **sight**. 32 They said to **each other**, "Wasn't it like a fire burning in us when he talked to us on the road and explained the **Scriptures** to us?"

33 They got up at once and went back to Jerusalem, where they found the eleven **disciples** gathered together with the others 34 and saying, "The Lord is **risen** indeed! He has appeared to Simon!"

35 The two then explained to them what had happened on the road, and how they had recognized the Lord when he broke the **bread**.

Jesus Appears to His Disciples
(Matt. 28.16–20; Mark 16.14–18; John 20.19–23; Acts 1.6–8)

36 While the two were telling them this, suddenly the Lord himself stood among them and said to them, "**Peace** be with you."[e]

37 They were **terrified**, thinking that they were seeing a **ghost**. 38 But he said to them, "Why are you alarmed? Why are

sentence 23.24; Acts 13.28
sight 16.15; Jn 9.15
Son of Man 22.22; Jn 1.51
suffer [2] 22.15; Jn 12.27
Temple (1) (of God) 23.45; Jn 2.14
terrify 21.11; Jn 6.19
thank 22.17; Jn 6.11
tomb [6] 23.53; Jn 11.38
true 22.37; Jn 3.21
understand 18.34; Jn 6.26
vision 1.22; Acts 2.17
witness 22.71; Jn 3.28
wonder (1) 13.17; Jn 4.48
word (1) 23.38; Jn 1.38
worship (1) (of God) 4.8; Jn 4.20

[d] *Some manuscripts do not have verse 12.*
[e] *Some manuscripts do not have* and said to them, "Peace be with you."

24.6–7: Mt 16.21, 17.22–23, 20.18–19; Mk 8.31, 9.31, 10.33–34; Lk 9.22, 18.31–33

these **doubts** coming up in your **minds**?
39 Look at my hands and my feet, and see
that it is I myself. Feel me, and you will
know, for a **ghost** doesn't have **flesh** and
bones, as you can see I have."
40 He said this and showed them his
hands and his feet.[f] 41 They still could not
believe, they were so full of **joy** and **wonder**; so he asked them, "Have you anything here to eat?" 42 They gave him a
piece of cooked fish, 43 which he took and
ate in their **presence**.
44 Then he said to them, "These are
the very things I told you about while I
was still with you: everything written
about me in the **Law of Moses**, the
writings of the **prophets**, and the **Psalms**
had to come **true**."
45 Then he opened their **minds** to
understand the **Scriptures**, 46 and said to
them, "This is what is written: the
Messiah must **suffer** and must **rise from
death** three days later, 47 and **in his name**
the **message** about **repentance** and the
forgiveness of sins must be **preached** to
all nations, beginning in Jerusalem.
48 You are **witnesses** of these things.
49 And I myself will send upon you what
my Father has **promised**. But you must
wait in the city until the **power** from
above comes down upon you."

Jesus Is Taken up to Heaven
(Mark 16.19-20; Acts 1.9-11)

50 Then he led them out of the city as
far as Bethany, where he **raised** his
hands and **blessed** them. 51 As he was
blessing them, he departed from them
and was taken up into **heaven**.[g] 52 They
worshipped him and went back into
Jerusalem, filled with great **joy**, 53 and
spent all their time in the **Temple** giving
thanks to God.

[f] *Some manuscripts do not have verse 40.*
[g] *Some manuscripts do not have* and was taken up into heaven.
24.49: Acts 1.4 **24.50-51:** Acts 1.9-11

THE GOSPEL ACCORDING TO
JOHN

INTRODUCTION

The Gospel according to John presents Jesus as the eternal Word of God, who "became a human being and lived among us." As the book itself says, this Gospel was written so that its readers might believe that Jesus is the promised Saviour, the Son of God, and that through their faith in him they might have life (20.31).

After an introduction that identifies the eternal Word of God with Jesus, the first part of the Gospel presents various miracles which show that Jesus is the promised Saviour, the Son of God. These are followed by discourses that explain what is revealed by the miracles. This part of the book tells how some people believed in Jesus and became his followers, while others opposed him and refused to believe. Chapters 13–17 record at length the close fellowship of Jesus with his disciples on the night of his arrest, and his words of preparation and encouragement to them on the eve of his crucifixion. The closing chapters tell of Jesus' arrest and trial, his crucifixion and resurrection, and his appearances to his disciples after the resurrection.

The story of the woman caught in adultery (8.1–11) is placed in brackets because many manuscripts and early translations omit it, while others include it in other places.

John emphasizes the gift of eternal life through Christ, a gift which begins now and which comes to those who respond to Jesus as the way, the truth, and the life. A striking feature of *John* is the symbolic use of common things from everyday life to point to spiritual realities, such as water, bread, light, the shepherd and his sheep, and the grapevine and its fruit.

Outline of Contents

---

after me [3] Mk 1.7; Acts 13.25
angel Lk 24.23; 12.29
authorities Mt 27.18; 2.18
baptize [6] Lk 20.4; 3.22
being Mt 16.17; Acts 14.15
believe [3] Lk 24.11; 2.11
bless Lk 24.30; 12.13
child of God [2] Lk 20.36; Acts 17.28
Christ Lk 2.11; Rom 1.5
clear Lk 20.37; Acts 2.22
create [2] Lk 11.50; Acts 17.26
dark [2] Lk 24.29; 3.19
disciple [2] Lk 24.9; 2.2
dove Lk 3.22
enough Lk 22.38; 2.6
exist [3] Mt 11.23; Acts 14.17
false Lk 18.20; 7.18
Father (2) (God) [3] Lk 24.49; 2.16
glory Lk 24.26; 2.11

The Word of Life

1 Before the **world** was **created**, the
Word already **existed**; he was with
God, and he was the same as God. 2 From
the very beginning the **Word** was with
God. 3 Through him God made all things;
not one thing in all **creation** was made
without him. 4 The **Word** was the **source**
of **life**,[a] and this **life** brought **light** to **man-**
kind. 5 The **light** shines in the **darkness**,
and the **darkness** has never **put it out**.
6 God sent his messenger, a man
named John, 7 who came to tell people
about the **light**, so that all should hear the
message and **believe**. 8 He himself was
not the **light**; he came to tell about the
light. 9 This was the **real light**—the light
that comes into the **world** and shines on
all **mankind**.
10 The **Word** was in the **world**, and
though God made the **world** through him,
yet the **world** did not recognize him. 11 He
came to his own country, but his **own**
people did not receive him. 12 Some, however, did receive him and **believed** in
him; so he gave them the **right** to
become **God's children**. 13 They did not
become **God's children by natural**
means, that is, by being born as the children of a **human** father; God himself was
their **Father**.
14 The **Word** became a **human being**
and, full of **grace** and **truth**, lived among
us. We saw his **glory**, the glory which he
received as the **Father's** only **Son**.
15 John spoke about him. He cried out,
"This is the one I was talking about when
I said, 'He comes **after me**, but he is
greater than I am, because he **existed**
before I was born.' "
16 Out of the fullness of his **grace** he
has blessed us all, giving us one **blessing**
after another. 17 God gave the **Law**
through Moses, but **grace** and **truth** came
through Jesus Christ. 18 No one has ever
seen God. The only **Son**, who is the same

God's people Lk 18.7; 11.52
grace [3] Lk 1.30; Acts 13.43
heaven [2] Lk 24.51; 3.12
human [2] Mt 16.17; 3.6
Jew Lk 23.3; 2.6
lamb [2] Lk 22.7; 21.15
law [2] Lk 24.44; 5.10
Levites Lk 10.32; Acts 4.36
life (1) [2] Lk 21.34; 3.15
light (1) [6] Lk 17.24; 3.19
mankind [2] Lk 3.6; 17.2
means Lk 11.20; 11.4
message Lk 24.47; 3.11
Messiah [3] Lk 24.26; 3.28
natural Ezek 44.31; 8.44
Pharisees Lk 19.39; 3.1
priest Lk 17.14; Acts 4.1
prophet [4] Lk 24.19; 4.19
put out Mk 9.48; Eph 6.16

[a] The Word was the source of life; *or* What was made had life in union with the Word.

1.6: Mt 3.1; Mk 1.4; Lk 3.1–2

real [2] Mk 6.52; 5.31
refuse (1) Lk 18.4; Acts 7.39
right (3) Lk 22.29; 2.18
Son of God [4] Lk 22.70; 3.16
Son of Man Lk 24.7; 3.13
source Hos 14.8; 5.26
Spirit (1) (God's Spirit) [3] Lk 12.10; 3.5
take away (sin) Zech 3.4; Rom 11.27
teacher [2] Lk 22.11; 3.2
testimony Mt 18.16; Acts 8.25
truth [3] Lk 20.21; 3.3
turn Lk 23.28; 2.9
who [2] Lk 9.20; 6.14
word (1) [2] Lk 24.8; 3.34
Word (2) [5] 1 Jn 1.1
world [6] Lk 16.8; 3.12

as God and is at the **Father's** side, he has
made him known.

John the Baptist's Message

(Matt. 3.1–12; Mark 1.1–8; Luke 3.1–18)

19 The **Jewish authorities** in Jerusalem sent some **priests** and **Levites** to
John, to ask him, "**Who are you**?"

20 John did not **refuse** to answer, but
spoke out openly and **clearly**, saying: "I
am not the **Messiah**."

21 "**Who are you**, then?" they asked.
"Are you Elijah?"

"No, I am not," John answered.

"Are you the **Prophet**?"[b] they asked.

"No," he replied.

22 "Then tell us who you are," they
said. "We have to take an answer back to
those who sent us. What do you say about
yourself?"

23 John answered by quoting the **prophet** Isaiah:

"I am 'the voice of someone shouting
in the desert:
Make a straight path for the Lord to
travel!' "

24 The messengers, who had been
sent by the **Pharisees**, 25 then[c] asked
John, "If you are not the **Messiah** nor Elijah nor the **Prophet**, why do you **baptize**?"

26 John answered, "I **baptize** with
water, but among you stands the one you
do not know. 27 He is coming **after me**,
but I am not good **enough** even to untie
his sandals."

28 All this happened in Bethany on the
east side of the River Jordan, where
John was **baptizing**.

The Lamb of God

29 The next day John saw Jesus
coming to him, and said, "There is the
Lamb of God, who **takes away** the sin of
the **world**! 30 This is the one I was talking
about when I said, 'A man is coming **after
me**, but he is greater than I am, because
he **existed** before I was born.' 31 I did not
know who he would be, but I came **baptizing** with water in order to make him
known to the people of Israel."

32 And John gave this **testimony**: "I
saw the **Spirit** come down like a **dove**
from **heaven** and stay on him. 33 I still did
not know that he was the one, but God,
who sent me to **baptize** with water, had
said to me, 'You will see the **Spirit** come
down and stay on a man; he is the one
who **baptizes** with the **Holy Spirit**.' 34 I
have seen it," said John, "and I tell you
that he is the **Son of God**."

The First Disciples of Jesus

35 The next day John was standing
there again with two of his **disciples**,
36 when he saw Jesus walking by. "There
is the **Lamb of God**!" he said.

37 The two **disciples** heard him say
this and went with Jesus. 38 Jesus **turned**,
saw them following him, and asked,
"What are you looking for?"

They answered, "Where do you live,
Rabbi?" (This **word** means "**Teacher**.")

39 "Come and see," he answered. (It
was then about four o'clock in the afternoon.) So they went with him and saw
where he lived, and spent the rest of that
day with him.

40 One of them was Andrew, Simon
Peter's brother. 41 At once he found his
brother Simon and told him, "We have
found the **Messiah**." (This **word** means
"**Christ**.") 42 Then he took Simon to Jesus.

Jesus looked at him and said, "Your
name is Simon son of John, but you will
be called Cephas." (This is the same as
Peter and means "a rock.")

Jesus Calls Philip and Nathanael

43 The next day Jesus decided to go to
Galilee. He found Philip and said to him,
"Come with me!" 44 (Philip was from
Bethsaida, the town where Andrew and
Peter lived.) 45 Philip found Nathanael
and told him, "We have found the one
whom Moses wrote about in the book of
the **Law** and whom the **prophets** also
wrote about. He is Jesus son of Joseph,
from Nazareth."

46 "Can anything good come from
Nazareth?" Nathanael asked.

"Come and see," answered Philip.

47 When Jesus saw Nathanael coming
to him, he said about him, "Here is a **real**
Israelite; there is nothing **false** in him!"

48 Nathanael asked him, "How do you
know me?"

Jesus answered, "I saw you when you
were under the fig-tree before Philip
called you."

49 "**Teacher**," answered Nathanael,
"you are the **Son of God**! You are the
King of Israel!"

50 Jesus said, "Do you **believe** just
because I told you I saw you when you
were under the fig-tree? You will see
much greater things than this!" 51 And he
said to them, "I am telling you the **truth**:

[b] THE PROPHET: *The one who was expected to appear and announce the coming of the Messiah.*
[c] The messengers, who had been sent by the Pharisees, then; *or* Those who had been sent were Pharisees; they.

1.21: Deut 18.15, 18; Mal 4.5 **1.23:** Is 40.3 (LXX) **1.51:** Gen 28.12

you will see **heaven** open and **God's angels** going up and coming down on the **Son of Man**."

The Wedding in Cana

2 Two days later there was a **wedding** in the town of Cana in Galilee. Jesus' mother was there, 2 and Jesus and his **disciples** had also been invited to the **wedding**. 3 When the wine had given out, Jesus' mother said to him, "They have no wine left."

4 "You must not tell me what to do," Jesus replied. "My time has not yet come."

5 Jesus' mother then told the **servants**, "Do whatever he tells you."

6 The **Jews** have rules about **ritual** washing, and for this **purpose** six stone water jars were there, each one large **enough** to hold about a hundred litres. 7 Jesus said to the **servants**, "Fill these jars with water." They filled them to the brim, 8 and then he told them, "Now draw some water out and take it to the man in charge of the **feast**." They took him the water, 9 which now had **turned** into wine, and he tasted it. He did not know where this wine had come from (but, of course, the **servants** who had drawn out the water knew); so he called the **bridegroom** 10 and said to him, "Everyone else **serves** the **best** wine first, and after the guests have had **plenty** to drink, he **serves** the ordinary wine. But you have kept the **best** wine until now!"

11 Jesus performed this first **miracle** in Cana in Galilee; there he **revealed** his **glory**, and his **disciples believed** in him.

12 After this, Jesus and his mother, brothers, and **disciples** went to Capernaum and stayed there a few days.

Jesus Goes to the Temple
(Matt. 21.12–13; Mark 11.15–17; Luke 19.45–46)

13 It was almost time for the **Passover Festival**, so Jesus went to Jerusalem. 14 There in the **Temple** he found men selling cattle, **sheep**, and pigeons, and also the money-changers sitting at their tables. 15 So he made a whip from cords and drove all the animals out of the **Temple**, both the **sheep** and the cattle; he overturned the tables of the money-changers and **scattered** their coins; 16 and he ordered the men who sold the pigeons, "Take them out of here! Stop making **my Father's** house a market-place!" 17 His **disciples remembered** that the **scripture** says, "My **devotion** to your house, O God, burns in me like a fire."

18 The **Jewish authorities** replied with a **question**, "What **miracle** can you perform to show us that you have the **right** to do this?"

19 Jesus answered, "Tear down this **Temple**, and in three days I will build it again."

20 "Are you going to build it again in three days?" they asked him. "It has taken forty-six years to build this **Temple**!"

21 But the **temple** Jesus was speaking about was his **body**. 22 So when he was **raised from death**, his **disciples remembered** that he had said this, and they **believed** the **scripture** and what Jesus had said.

Jesus' Knowledge of Human Nature

23 While Jesus was in Jerusalem during the **Passover Festival**, many **believed** in him as they saw the **miracles** he performed. 24 But Jesus did not **trust** himself to them, because he knew them all. 25 There was no **need** for anyone to tell him about them, because he himself knew what was in their **hearts**.

Jesus and Nicodemus

3 There was a **Jewish** leader named Nicodemus, who belonged to the party of the **Pharisees**. 2 One night he went to Jesus and said to him, "Rabbi, we know that you are a **teacher** sent by God. No one could perform the **miracles** you are doing unless God were with him."

3 Jesus answered, "I am telling you the **truth**: no one can see the **Kingdom of God** unless he is born again."[d]

4 "How can a grown man be born again?" Nicodemus asked. "He certainly cannot enter his mother's **womb** and be born a second time!"

5 "I am telling you the **truth**," replied Jesus. "No one can enter the **Kingdom of God** unless he is born of water and the **Spirit**. 6 A person is born **physically** of **human** parents, but he is born **spiritually** of the **Spirit**. 7 Do not be surprised because I tell you that you must all be born again.[d] 8 The wind blows wherever it **wishes**; you hear the sound it makes, but you do not know where it comes from or where it is going. It is like that with everyone who is born of the **Spirit**."

9 "How can this be?" asked Nicodemus.

10 Jesus answered, "You are a great **teacher** in Israel, and you don't know

authorities 1.19; 5.10
believe [3] 1.7; 3.12
best [2] Lk 20.46; Acts 15.29
body Lk 24.3; 11.52
bridegroom Lk 5.34; 3.29
death (2) (from death) Lk 24.46; 5.24
devote Hos 10.12; Acts 13.35
disciple [5] 1.35; 3.22
enough 1.27; 6.5
Father (2) (God) 1.13; 3.35
feast Lk 21.34; Acts 7.41
festival [2] Lk 22.1; 4.45
glory 1.14; 7.18
heart Lk 16.15; 5.38
Jew [2] 1.19; 3.1
miracle [3] Lk 23.8; 3.2
need Lk 22.71; 13.29
Passover [2] Lk 22.1; 4.45
plenty Mal 3.10; 3.23
purpose Lk 9.31; 18.37
question Lk 23.9; 8.7
raise Lk 24.6; 5.21
remember [2] Lk 24.6; 3.26
reveal Lk 17.30; 12.38
right (3) 1.12; 5.22
ritual Ezek 44.8; 3.25
scatter Lk 11.23; 10.12
scripture [2] Lk 24.27; 5.39
servant [3] Lk 22.26; 4.51
serve [2] Lk 22.27; 12.2
sheep [2] Lk 17.7; 10.2
Temple (1) (of God) [5] Lk 24.53; 5.14
trust Lk 16.11; Acts 14.23
turn 1.38; 4.46
wedding [2] Lk 14.8; Rev 19.7

above Lk 24.49; 8.23
accept [3] Lk 14.18; 5.31
argue Lk 22.24; 6.52
baptize [4] 1.25; 4.1
believe [8] 2.11; 4.21
bride Jer 2.32; Rev 18.23
bridegroom [3] 2.9; Rev 18.23
complete Lk 16.2; 13.3
dark 1.5; 8.12
deed (2) [2] Mt 16.27; 5.36
disciple [2] 2.2; 4.1
disobey Lk 15.29; Acts 26.19
eternal [3] Lk 18.18; 4.14
evil [3] Lk 12.10; 5.29
Father (2) (God) 2.16; 4.21
friend Lk 23.12; 11.3
glad Lk 10.20; 4.36
happy Lk 15.5; 13.17
hate Lk 21.17; 7.7
heaven [4] 1.32; 6.31
human 1.13; 5.41
important Lk 20.17; 7.37
Jew [2] 2.6; 4.9
judge [4] Lk 18.2; 5.22
Kingdom (1) (of God) [2] Lk 23.50; 18.36
life (1) [4] 1.4; 4.10
light (1) [6] 1.4; 5.35
love [3] Lk 20.46; 5.20
message [3] 1.7; 4.41
Messiah 1.20; 4.25
miracle 2.11; 4.48
obey Lk 18.21; 4.34
Pharisees 1.24; 4.1

[d] again; *or* from above.

2.12: Mt 4.13 **2.13:** Ex 12.1–27 **2.17:** Ps 69.9 **2.19:** Mt 26.61, 27.40; Mk 14.58, 15.29

physical Dan 1.4; Rom 2.27
plenty 2.10; 2 Cor 8.13
power Lk 24.19; 4.23
prison Lk 23.19; 18.39
punish Lk 21.22; Acts 2.40
remember 2.17; 4.53
ritual 2.6; 11.55
Saviour Lk 2.11; 4.42
Son of God [7] 1.14; 5.19
Son of Man [2] 1.51; 5.27
Spirit (1) (God's Spirit) [4] 1.32; 4.23
spiritual Mt 5.3; Acts 3.20
teacher [3] 1.38; 4.31
true Lk 24.44; 4.23
truth [4] 1.14; 4.18
wish Lk 23.25; 15.7
witness Lk 24.48; 5.34
womb Hos 13.13
word (1) 1.38; 4.50
world [4] 1.1; 4.42

this? 11 I am telling you the truth: we speak of what we know and report what we have seen, yet none of you is willing to accept our message. 12 You do not believe me when I tell you about the things of this world; how will you ever believe me, then, when I tell you about the things of heaven? 13 And no one has ever gone up to heaven except the Son of Man, who came down from heaven."[x]

14 As Moses lifted up the bronze snake on a pole in the desert, in the same way the Son of Man must be lifted up, 15 so that everyone who believes in him may have eternal life. 16 For God loved the world so much that he gave his only Son, so that everyone who believes in him may not die but have eternal life. 17 For God did not send his Son into the world to be its judge, but to be its saviour.

18 Whoever believes in the Son is not judged; but whoever does not believe has already been judged, because he has not believed in God's only Son. 19 This is how the judgement works: the light has come into the world, but people love the darkness rather than the light, because their deeds are evil. 20 Anyone who does evil things hates the light and will not come to the light, because he does not want his evil deeds to be shown up. 21 But whoever does what is true comes to the light in order that the light may show that what he did was in obedience to God.

Jesus and John

22 After this, Jesus and his disciples went to the province of Judaea, where he spent some time with them and baptized. 23 John also was baptizing in Aenon, not far from Salim, because there was plenty of water in that place. People were going to him, and he was baptizing them. 24 (This was before John had been put in prison.)

25 Some of John's disciples began arguing with a Jew[f] about the matter of ritual washing. 26 So they went to John and said, "Teacher, you remember the man who was with you on the east side of the Jordan, the one you spoke about? Well, he is baptizing now, and everyone is going to him!"

27 John answered, "No one can have anything unless God gives it to him. 28 You yourselves are my witnesses that I said, 'I am not the Messiah, but I have been sent ahead of him.' 29 The bridegroom is the one to whom the bride belongs; but the bridegroom's friend, who stands by and listens, is glad when he hears the bridegroom's voice. This is how my own happiness is made complete. 30 He must become more important while I become less important."

He Who Comes from Heaven

31 He who comes from above is greater than all. He who is from the earth belongs to the earth and speaks about earthly matters, but he who comes from heaven is above all. 32 He tells what he has seen and heard, yet no one accepts his message. 33 But whoever accepts his message confirms by this that God is truthful. 34 The one whom God has sent speaks God's words, because God gives him the fullness of his Spirit. 35 The Father loves his Son and has put everything in his power. 36 Whoever believes in the Son has eternal life; whoever disobeys the Son will not have life, but will remain under God's punishment.

Jesus and the Samaritan Woman

4 The Pharisees heard that Jesus was winning and baptizing more disciples than John. 2 (Actually, Jesus himself did not baptize anyone; only his disciples did.) 3 So when Jesus heard what was being said, he left Judaea and went back to Galilee; 4 on his way there he had to go through Samaria.

5 In Samaria he came to a town named Sychar, which was not far from the field that Jacob had given to his son Joseph. 6 Jacob's well was there, and Jesus, tired out by the journey, sat down by the well. It was about noon.

7 A Samaritan woman came to draw some water, and Jesus said to her, "Give me a drink of water." 8 (His disciples had gone into town to buy food.)

9 The woman answered, "You are a Jew, and I am a Samaritan—so how can you ask me for a drink?" (Jews will not use the same cups and bowls that Samaritans use.)[g]

10 Jesus answered, "If only you knew what God gives and who it is that is asking you for a drink, you would ask him, and he would give you life-giving water."

11 "Sir," the woman said, "you haven't got a bucket, and the well is deep. Where would you get that life-giving water? 12 It was our ancestor Jacob who gave us this well; he and his sons and his flocks all

baptize [2] 3.22; 10.40
beg [2] Lk 18.35; 9.8
believe [7] 3.12; 5.24
claim Lk 23.2; 8.53
cup Lk 22.17; 18.11
disciple [6] 3.22; 6.3
eternal [2] 3.15; 5.24
Father (2) (God) [2] 3.35; 5.17
festival [2] 2.13; 5.1
flock Lk 12.32; 10.16
glad 3.29; 8.56
harvest [4] Lk 20.10; 2 Cor 9.10
heal Lk 22.51; 5.10
Jew [5] 3.1; 5.10
life (1) [5] 3.15; 5.21
message 3.11; 5.38
Messiah [2] 3.28; 7.26
miracle [2] 3.2; 6.2
obey 3.21; 7.19
offer Lk 23.36; Acts 7.41
Passover 2.13; 6.4
Pharisees 3.1; 7.32
power [2] 3.35; 6.63
prophet [2] 1.21; 6.14
provide Lk 12.31; Acts 7.46
reap [4] Lk 19.21; 1 Cor 9.10
remember 3.26; 12.16
respect Lk 20.13; 9.31
right (1) Lk 23.41; 5.30
ripe Lk 8.14; Rev 6.13
salvation Lk 21.28; Acts 4.12
Saviour 3.17; Acts 5.31
saying [2] Mk 7.17; 5.18
servant 2.5; 12.26
sow [2] Lk 19.21; 1 Cor 3.6

[x] *The quotation may continue through verse 21.* [f] a Jew; *some manuscripts have* some Jews.
[g] Jews will not use the same cups and bowls that Samaritans use; *or* Jews will have nothing to do with Samaritans.

3.14: Num 21.9 **3.24:** Mt 14.3; Mk 6.17; Lk 3.19–20 **3.28:** Jn 1.20 **3.35:** Mt 11.27; Lk 10.22
4.5: Gen 33.19; Josh 24.32 **4.9:** Ezra 4.1–5; Neh 4.1–2

Spirit (1) (God's Spirit) [2] 3.5; 6.63
teacher 3.2; 6.25
true [2] 3.21; 5.32
truth 3.3; 5.19
turn 2.9; 6.37
welcome Lk 19.6; Acts 15.4
will (1) Lk 22.42; 6.38
win Lk 9.25; 5.44
wonder (1) Lk 24.41; Acts 2.7
word (1) 3.34; 5.24
world 3.12; 6.14
worship (1) (of God) [8] Lk 24.52; 12.20

drank from it. You don't **claim** to be
greater than Jacob, do you?"
13 Jesus answered, "Whoever drinks
this water will be thirsty again, [14]but
whoever drinks the water that I will give
him will never be thirsty again. The
water that I will give him will become in
him a spring which will **provide** him with
life-giving water and give him **eternal**
life."
15 "Sir," the woman said, "give me
that water! Then I will never be thirsty
again, nor will I have to come here to
draw water."
16 "Go and call your husband," Jesus
told her, "and come back."
17 "I haven't got a husband," she
answered.
Jesus replied, "You are **right** when you
say you haven't got a husband. [18]You
have been married to five men, and the
man you live with now is not really your
husband. You have told me the **truth**."
19 "I see you are a **prophet**, sir," the
woman said. [20]"My Samaritan ancestors
worshipped God on this mountain, but
you **Jews** say that Jerusalem is the place
where we should **worship** God."
21 Jesus said to her, "**Believe** me,
woman, the time will come when people
will not **worship** the **Father** either on this
mountain or in Jerusalem. [22]You Samaritans do not really know whom you **worship**; but we **Jews** know whom we **worship**, because it is from the **Jews** that
salvation comes. [23]But the time is coming and is already here, when by the
power of God's Spirit people will **worship**
the **Father** as he really is, **offering** him
the **true worship** that he wants. [24]God is
Spirit, and only by the **power** of his Spirit
can people **worship** him as he really is."
25 The woman said to him, "I know
that the **Messiah** will come, and when he
comes, he will tell us everything."
26 Jesus answered, "I am he, I who am
talking with you."
27 At that moment Jesus' **disciples**
returned, and they were greatly surprised to find him talking with a woman.
But none of them said to her, "What do
you want?" or asked him, "Why are you
talking with her?"
28 Then the woman left her water jar,
went back to the town, and said to the
people there, [29]"Come and see the man
who told me everything I have ever
done. Could he be the **Messiah**?" [30]So
they left the town and went to Jesus.
31 In the meantime the **disciples** were
begging Jesus, "**Teacher**, have something to eat!"
32 But he answered, "I have food to
eat that you know nothing about."
33 So the **disciples** started asking
among themselves, "Could somebody
have brought him food?"
34 "My food," Jesus said to them, "is to
obey the **will** of the one who sent me and
to finish the work he gave me to do.
[35]You have a **saying**, 'Four more months
and then the **harvest**.' But I tell you, take
a good look at the fields; the crops are
now **ripe** and ready to be **harvested**!
[36]The man who **reaps** the **harvest** is
being paid and gathers the crops for
eternal life; so the man who **sows** and
the man who **reaps** will be **glad** together.
[37]The **saying** is **true**, 'One man **sows**,
another man **reaps**.' [38]I have sent you to
reap a **harvest** in a field where you did
not work; others worked there, and you
profit from their work."
39 Many of the Samaritans in that
town **believed** in Jesus because the
woman had said, "He told me everything
I have ever done." [40]So when the
Samaritans came to him, they **begged**
him to stay with them, and Jesus stayed
there two days.
41 Many more **believed** because of his
message, [42]and they said to the woman,
"We **believe** now, not because of what
you said, but because we ourselves have
heard him, and we know that he really is
the **Saviour** of the **world**."

Jesus Heals an Official's Son

43 After spending two days there,
Jesus left and went to Galilee. [44]For he
himself had said, "A **prophet** is not **respected** in his own country." [45]When he
arrived in Galilee, the people there **welcomed** him, because they had gone to the
Passover Festival in Jerusalem and had
seen everything that he had done during
the **festival**.
46 Then Jesus went back to Cana in
Galilee, where he had **turned** the water
into wine. A government official was
there whose son was ill in Capernaum.
[47]When he heard that Jesus had come
from Judaea to Galilee, he went to him
and asked him to go to Capernaum and
heal his son, who was about to die.
[48]Jesus said to him, "None of you will
ever **believe** unless you see **miracles** and
wonders."
49 "Sir," replied the official, "come
with me before my child dies."
50 Jesus said to him, "Go, your son will
live!"
The man **believed** Jesus' **words** and
went. [51]On his way home his **servants**

4.44: Mt 13.57; Mk 6.4; Lk 4.24 **4.45:** Jn 2.23 **4.46:** Jn 2.1–11

met him with the news, "Your boy is
going to live!"
52 He asked them what time it was
when his son got better, and they
answered, "It was one o'clock yesterday
afternoon when the fever left him."
53 Then the father **remembered** that it
was at that very hour when Jesus had
told him, "Your son will live." So he and
all his family **believed**.
54 This was the second **miracle** that
Jesus performed after coming from
Judaea to Galilee.

The Healing at the Pool

5 After this, Jesus went to Jerusalem
for a **religious festival**. 2 Near the
Sheep Gate in Jerusalem there is a pool[h]
with five porches; in **Hebrew** it is called
Bethzatha.[i] 3 A large crowd of sick people
were lying in the porches—the **blind**, the
lame, and the **paralysed**.[j] 5 A man was
there who had been ill for thirty-eight
years. 6 Jesus saw him lying there, and he
knew that the man had been ill for such a
long time; so he asked him, "Do you
want to get well?"
7 The sick man answered, "Sir, I have
no one here to put me in the pool when
the water is stirred up; while I am trying
to get in, somebody else gets there first."
8 Jesus said to him, "Get up, pick up
your mat, and walk." 9 Immediately the
man got well; he picked up his mat and
started walking.
The day this happened was a **Sabbath**,
10 so the **Jewish authorities** told the man
who had been **healed**, "This is a **Sabbath**,
and it is against our **Law** for you to carry
your mat."
11 He answered, "The man who made
me well told me to pick up my mat and
walk."
12 They asked him, "Who is the man
who told you to do this?"
13 But the man who had been **healed**
did not know who Jesus was, for there
was a crowd in that place, and Jesus had
slipped away.
14 Afterwards, Jesus found him in the
Temple and said, "Listen, you are well
now; so stop sinning or something **worse**
may happen to you."
15 Then the man left and told the
Jewish authorities that it was Jesus who
had **healed** him. 16 So they began to **persecute** Jesus, because he had done this
healing on a **Sabbath**. 17 Jesus answered
them, "**My Father** is always working, and
I too must work."
18 This **saying** made the **Jewish
authorities** all the more **determined** to
kill him; not only had he broken the **Sabbath law**, but he had said that God was
his own **Father** and in this way had made
himself equal with God.

The Authority of the Son

19 So Jesus answered them, "I am telling you the **truth**: the **Son** can do nothing
on his own; he does only what he sees his
Father doing. What the **Father** does, the
Son also does. 20 For the **Father loves** the
Son and shows him all that he himself is
doing. He will show him even greater
things to do than this, and you will all be
amazed. 21 Just as the **Father raises** the
dead and gives them **life**, in the same
way the **Son** gives **life** to those he wants
to. 22 Nor does the **Father** himself **judge**
anyone. He has given **his Son** the full
right to **judge**, 23 so that all will honour
the **Son** in the same way as they **honour**
the **Father**. Whoever does not **honour** the
Son does not honour the **Father** who sent
him.
24 "I am telling you the **truth**: whoever hears my **words** and **believes** in him
who sent me has **eternal life**. He will not
be **judged**, but has already passed **from
death to life**. 25 I am telling you the **truth**:
the time is coming—the time has already
come—when the **dead** will hear the voice
of the **Son of God**, and those who hear it
will come to **life**. 26 Just as the **Father** is
himself the **source** of **life**, in the same
way he has made **his Son** to be the **source
of life**. 27 And he has given the **Son** the
right to **judge**, because he is the **Son of
Man**. 28 Do not be surprised at this; the
time is coming when all the **dead** will
hear his voice 29 and come out of their
graves: those who have done good will
rise and live, and those who have done
evil will **rise** and be **condemned**.

Witnesses to Jesus

30 "I can do nothing on my own
authority; I **judge** only as God tells me, so
my **judgement** is **right**, because I am not
trying to do what I want, but only what
he who sent me wants.
31 "If I **testify** on my own behalf, what
I say is not to be **accepted** as **real proof**.
32 But there is someone else who **testifies**
on my behalf, and I know that what he

accept 3.11; 8.37
accuse [2] Lk 23.2; 8.6
alone Lk 18.19; 8.9
amaze Lk 24.12; Acts 2.7
authorities [3] 2.18; 7.1
authority [3] Lk 20.20; 7.17
believe [7] 4.21; 6.29
blind Lk 18.35; 9.1
condemn Lk 23.4; 7.51
dead [3] Lk 24.5; 11.14
death (2) (from death) 2.22; 12.1
deed (2) 3.19; 10.32
determine Zech 1.6; Acts 22.10
enjoy Lk 16.25; Acts 2.47
eternal [2] 4.14; 6.27
evil 3.19; Acts 1.18
Father (2) (God) [15] 4.21; 6.27
festival 4.45; 6.4
grave Lk 11.44; 11.31
heal [4] 4.47; 6.2
heart [2] 2.25; 7.38
Hebrew Jon 1.9; 19.13
honour [2] Lk 23.50; 8.49
hope Lk 24.21; Acts 2.26
human 3.6; 8.15
I am Mk 12.26; 6.35
Jew [3] 4.9; 7.1
judge [6] 3.17; 7.24
law [2] 1.17; 7.19
life (1) [9] 4.10; 6.27
life (2) (to life) Lk 24.7; 6.39
light (1) 3.19; 8.12
love [2] 3.16; 8.42
message 4.41; 8.43
one another Lk 21.10; 11.56
paralyse Lk 6.6; Acts 8.7
persecute Lk 21.12; 15.20
praise [3] Lk 23.47; 12.13
prove Lk 20.37; 8.13
raise 2.22; 6.39
real 1.9; 6.32
religion Mt 6.1; Acts 2.5
right (1) 4.17; 7.6
right (3) [2] 2.18; 10.18

rise [2] Lk 24.7; 11.23
Sabbath [4] Lk 23.54; 7.22
save Lk 23.35; 10.9
saying 4.35; 1 Cor 4.6
scripture [2] 2.17; 6.31
Son of God [10] 3.16; 6.40
Son of Man 3.13; 6.27
source [2] 1.4; Rom 15.5
study Lk 1.3; 7.52
Temple (1) (of God) 2.14; 7.14
testify [3] Mal 3.5; 8.13
true 4.23; 7.24
truth [4] 4.18; 6.26
win 4.1; Acts 7.46
witness [3] 3.28; 8.17
word (1) 4.50; 6.63
worse Lk 20.47; 19.11

[h] Near the Sheep Gate...a pool; *or* Near the Sheep Pool...a place.
[i] Bethzatha; *some manuscripts have* Bethesda.
[j] *Some manuscripts add verses 3b–4:* They were waiting for the water to move, 4 because every now and then an angel of the Lord went down into the pool and stirred up the water. The first sick person to go into the pool after the water was stirred up was healed from whatever disease he had.

5.10: Neh 13.19; Jer 17.21 **5.29:** Dan 12.2

says about me is **true**. 33 John is the one to whom you sent your messengers, and he spoke on behalf of the **truth**. 34 It is not that I must have a man's **witness**; I say this only in order that you may be **saved**. 35 John was like a lamp, burning and shining, and you were willing for a while to **enjoy** his **light**. 36 But I have a **witness** on my behalf which is even greater than the **witness** that John gave: what I do, that is, the **deeds my Father** gave me to do, these speak on my behalf and show that the **Father** has sent me. 37 And the **Father**, who sent me, also **testifies** on my behalf. You have never heard his voice or seen his face, 38 and you do not keep his **message** in your **hearts**, for you do not **believe** in the one whom he sent. 39 You **study** the **Scriptures**, because you think that in them you will find **eternal life**. And these very **Scriptures** speak about me! 40 Yet you are not willing to come to me in order to have **life**.

41 "I am not looking for **human praise**. 42 But I know what kind of people you are, and I know that you have no **love** for God in your **hearts**. 43 I have come with **my Father's authority**, but you have not received me; when, however, someone comes with his own **authority**, you will receive him. 44 You like to receive **praise** from **one another**, but you do not try to **win praise** from the one who **alone** is God; how, then, can you **believe** me? 45 Do not think, however, that **I am** the one who will **accuse** you to **my Father**. Moses, in whom you have put your **hope**, is the very one who will **accuse** you. 46 If you had really **believed** Moses, you would have **believed** me, because he wrote about me. 47 But since you do not **believe** what he wrote, how can you **believe** what I say?"

Jesus Feeds Five Thousand Men
(Matt. 14.13–21; Mark 6.30–44; Luke 9.10–17)

6 After this, Jesus went across Lake Galilee (or, Lake Tiberias, as it is also called). 2 A large crowd followed him, because they had seen his **miracles** of **healing** those who were ill. 3 Jesus went up a hill and sat down with his **disciples**. 4 The time for the **Passover Festival** was near. 5 Jesus looked round and saw that a large crowd was coming to him, so he asked Philip, "Where can we buy **enough** food to feed all these people?" 6 (He said this to **test** Philip; actually he already knew what he would do.)

7 Philip answered, "For everyone to have even a little, it would take more than two hundred silver coins[k] to buy **enough bread**."

8 Another of his **disciples**, Andrew, who was Simon Peter's brother, said, 9 "There is a boy here who has five loaves of barley **bread** and two fish. But they will certainly not be **enough** for all these people."

10 "Make the people sit down," Jesus told them. (There was a lot of grass there.) So all the people sat down; there were about five thousand men. 11 Jesus took the **bread**, gave **thanks** to God, and distributed it to the people who were sitting there. He did the same with the fish, and they all had as much as they wanted. 12 When they were all full, he said to his **disciples**, "Gather the pieces left over; let us not waste any." 13 So they gathered them all up and filled twelve baskets with the pieces left over from the five barley loaves which the people had eaten.

14 Seeing this **miracle** that Jesus had performed, the people there said, "Surely this is the **Prophet**[l] **who was to come** into the **world**!" 15 Jesus knew that they were about to come and seize him in order to make him king by **force**; so he went off again to the hills by himself.

Jesus Walks on the Water
(Matt. 14.22–33; Mark 6.45–52)

16 When evening came, Jesus' **disciples** went down to the lake, 17 got into a boat, and went back across the lake towards Capernaum. Night came on, and Jesus still had not come to them. 18 By then a **strong** wind was blowing and stirring up the water. 19 The **disciples** had rowed about five or six kilometres when they saw Jesus walking on the water, coming near the boat, and they were **terrified**. 20 "Don't be **afraid**," Jesus told them, "it is I!" 21 Then they willingly took him into the boat, and immediately the boat reached land at the place they were heading for.

The People Seek Jesus

22 Next day the crowd which had stayed on the other side of the lake realized that there had been only one boat there. They knew that Jesus had not gone in it with his **disciples**, but that they had left without him. 23 Other boats,

[k] SILVER COINS: *A silver coin was the daily wage of a rural worker (see Mt 20.2).*
[l] THE PROPHET: *See 1.21.*

5.33: Jn 1.19–27, 3.27–30 **5.37:** Mt 3.17; Mk 1.11; Lk 3.22

afraid Lk 22.2; 7.13
anger Lk 15.28; 7.23
approve Lk 11.16; 12.43
argue 3.25; Acts 6.9
bad Lk 22.31; 7.7
believe [9] 5.24; 7.5
betray [2] Lk 22.4; 12.4
blood [4] Lk 22.20; 19.34
bread [20] Lk 24.30; 13.26
choose Lk 23.35; 10.36
Devil Lk 8.12; 8.44
disciple [9] 4.1; 8.31
enough [3] 2.6; 9.21

eternal [5] 5.24; 10.28
Father (2) (God) [10] 5.17; 8.16
festival 5.1; 7.2
flesh [6] Lk 24.39; Rom 9.3
follower [2] Lk 24.13; 7.3
force (1) Lk 16.16; Acts 5.26
give up Lk 14.33; 10.17
hard Lk 19.21; Acts 20.19
heal 5.10; 12.40
heaven [10] 3.12; 12.28
holy Lk 11.2; 17.11
hunger Lk 6.3; Acts 10.10
I am [4] 5.45; 8.12
last (1) Lk 11.17; Rom 11.25
last (2) [4] Lk 24.18; 7.37
learn Lk 23.7; 7.52
life (1) [12] 5.21; 7.38
life (2) (to life) [4] 5.24; 11.23
manna [2] Ps 78.24; Heb 9.4
mark (1) Lk 11.44; 1 Cor 7.18
miracle [4] 4.48; 7.21
Passover 4.45; 11.55
power 4.23; 9.3
prophet [2] 4.19; 7.40
raise [4] 5.21; 7.39
real [3] 5.31; 15.1
reason Lk 23.4; 15.25
scripture 5.39; 7.38
Son of God 5.19; 8.36
Son of Man [3] 5.27; 8.28
Spirit (1) (God's Spirit) [2] 4.23; 7.39
strong Lk 23.5; Acts 2.2
synagogue Lk 21.12; 9.22
teach [3] Lk 23.5; 7.14
teacher 4.31; 8.4
terrify Lk 24.37; Acts 5.5
test Lk 22.31; Acts 5.9
thank [2] Lk 24.53; 11.41
truth [4] 5.19; 7.28
turn [2] 4.46; 12.40
understand Lk 24.45; 8.27
who 1.19; 8.25
will (1) [3] 4.34; 10.18
word (1) [2] 5.24; 8.47
world [3] 4.42; 7.4

which were from Tiberias, came to shore
near the place where the crowd had
eaten the **bread** after the Lord had given
thanks. 24 When the crowd saw that Jesus
was not there, nor his **disciples**, they got
into those boats and went to Capernaum,
looking for him.

Jesus the Bread of Life

25 When the people found Jesus on the
other side of the lake, they said to him,
"**Teacher**, when did you get here?"
26 Jesus answered, "I am telling you
the **truth**: you are looking for me
because you ate the **bread** and had all
you wanted, not because you **understood**
my **miracles.** 27 Do not work for food that
goes **bad**; instead, work for the food that
lasts for **eternal life**. This is the food
which the **Son of Man** will give you,
because God, the **Father**, has put his
mark of approval on him."
28 So they asked him, "What can we
do in order to do what God wants us to
do?"
29 Jesus answered, "What God wants
you to do is to **believe** in the one he sent."
30 They replied, "What **miracle** will
you perform so that we may see it and
believe you? What will you do? 31 Our
ancestors ate **manna** in the desert, just as
the **scripture** says, 'He gave them **bread**
from **heaven** to eat.' "
32 "I am telling you the **truth**," Jesus
said. "What Moses gave you was not[m]
the **bread** from **heaven**; it is **my Father**
who gives you the **real bread** from
heaven. 33 For the **bread** that God gives is
he who comes down from **heaven** and
gives **life** to the **world**."
34 "Sir," they asked him, "give us this
bread always."
35 "**I am** the **bread** of **life**," Jesus told
them. "He who comes to me will never
be **hungry**; he who **believes** in me will
never be thirsty. 36 Now, I told you that
you have seen me but will not **believe**.
37 Everyone whom **my Father** gives me
will come to me. I will never **turn away**
anyone who comes to me, 38 because I
have come down from **heaven** to do not
my own **will** but the **will** of him who sent
me. 39 And it is the **will** of him who sent
me that I should not lose any of all those
he has given me, but that I should **raise**
them all **to life** on the **last day.** 40 For
what **my Father** wants is that all who see
the **Son** and **believe** in him should have
eternal life. And I will **raise** them **to life**
on the **last day.**"
41 The people started grumbling
about him, because he said, "**I am** the
bread that came down from **heaven**."
42 So they said, "This man is Jesus son of
Joseph, isn't he? We know his father and
mother. How, then, does he now say he
came down from **heaven**?"
43 Jesus answered, "Stop grumbling
among yourselves. 44 No one can come to
me unless the **Father** who sent me draws
him to me; and I will **raise** him **to life** on
the **last day.** 45 The **prophets** wrote,
'Everyone will be **taught** by God.' Anyone
who hears the **Father** and **learns** from
him comes to me. 46 This does not mean
that anyone has seen the **Father**; he who
is from God is the only one who has seen
the **Father.** 47 I am telling you the **truth**:
he who **believes** has **eternal life.** 48 **I am**
the **bread of life.** 49 Your ancestors ate
manna in the desert, but they died. 50 But
the **bread** that comes down from **heaven**
is of such a kind that whoever eats it will
not die. 51 **I am** the living **bread** that came
down from **heaven.** If anyone eats this
bread, he will live for ever. The **bread**
that I will give him is my **flesh**, which I
give so that the **world** may live."
52 This started an **angry argument**
among them. "How can this man give us
his **flesh** to eat?" they asked.
53 Jesus said to them, "I am telling
you the **truth**: if you do not eat the **flesh**
of the **Son of Man** and drink his **blood**,
you will not have **life** in yourselves.
54 Whoever eats my **flesh** and drinks my
blood has **eternal life**, and I will **raise**
him **to life** on the **last day.** 55 For my **flesh**
is the **real** food; my **blood** is the **real**
drink. 56 Whoever eats my **flesh** and
drinks my **blood** lives in me, and I live in
him. 57 The living **Father** sent me, and
because of him I live also. In the same
way whoever eats me will live because of
me. 58 This, then, is the **bread** that came
down from **heaven**; it is not like the
bread that your ancestors ate, but then
later died. The one who eats this **bread**
will live for ever."
59 Jesus said this as he **taught** in the
synagogue in Capernaum.

The Words of Eternal Life

60 Many of his **followers** heard this
and said, "This **teaching** is too **hard.** Who
can listen to it?"
61 Without being told, Jesus knew that
they were grumbling about this, so he
said to them, "Does this make you want
to **give up**? 62 Suppose, then, that you
should see the **Son of Man** go back up to
the place where he was before? 63 What

[m] What Moses gave you was not; *or* It was not Moses who gave you.

6.31: Ex 16.4, 15; Ps 78.24 **6.45:** Is 54.13

gives **life** is **God's Spirit**; man's **power** is
of no use at all. The **words** I have spoken
to you bring God's **life-giving Spirit**. 64 Yet
some of you do not **believe**." (Jesus knew
from the very beginning who were the
ones that would not **believe** and which
one would **betray** him.) 65 And he added,
"This is the very **reason** I told you that no
one can come to me unless the **Father**
makes it possible for him to do so."

66 Because of this, many of Jesus'
followers turned back and would not go
with him any more. 67 So he asked the
twelve **disciples**, "And you—would you
also like to leave?"

68 Simon Peter answered him, "Lord,
to whom would we go? You have the
words that give **eternal life**. 69 And now
we **believe** and know that you are the
Holy One who has come from God."

70 Jesus replied, "I **chose** the twelve of
you, didn't I? Yet one of you is a **devil**!"
71 He was talking about Judas, the son of
Simon Iscariot. For Judas, even though
he was one of the twelve **disciples**, was
going to **betray** him.

Jesus and His Brothers

7 After this, Jesus travelled in Galilee;
he did not want to travel in Judaea,
because the **Jewish authorities** there
were wanting to kill him. 2 The time for
the **Festival of Shelters** was near, 3 so
Jesus' brothers said to him, "Leave this
place and go to Judaea, so that your
followers will see the things that you are
doing. 4 No one hides what he is doing if
he wants to be well known. Since you are
doing these things, let the whole **world**
know about you!" 5 (Not even his brothers **believed** in him.)

6 Jesus said to them, "The **right** time
for me has not yet come. Any time is
right for you. 7 The **world** cannot **hate**
you, but it hates me, because I keep telling it that its **ways** are **bad**. 8 You go on to
the **festival**. I am not going[n] to this **festival**, because the **right** time has not come
for me." 9 He said this, and then stayed on
in Galilee.

Jesus at the Festival of Shelters

10 After his brothers had gone to the
festival, Jesus also went; however, he did
not go openly, but **secretly**. 11 The **Jewish
authorities** were looking for him at the
festival. "Where is he?" they asked.

12 There was much whispering about
him in the crowd. "He is a good man,"
some people said. "No," others said, "he
is **misleading** the people." 13 But no one
talked about him openly, because they
were **afraid** of the **Jewish authorities**.

14 The **festival** was nearly half over
when Jesus went to the **Temple** and
began **teaching**. 15 The **Jewish authorities**
were greatly surprised and said, "How
does this man know so much when he
has never had any training?"

16 Jesus answered, "What I **teach** is
not my own **teaching**, but it comes from
God, who sent me. 17 Whoever is willing
to do what God wants will know whether
what I teach comes from God or whether
I speak on my own **authority**. 18 A person
who speaks on his own **authority** is trying
to gain **glory** for himself. But he who
wants **glory** for the one who sent him is
honest, and there is nothing **false** in him.
19 Moses gave you the **Law**, didn't he?
But not one of you **obeys** the **Law**. Why
are you trying to kill me?"

20 "You have a **demon** in you!" the
crowd answered. "Who is trying to kill
you?"

21 Jesus answered, "I performed one
miracle, and you were all surprised.
22 Moses ordered you to **circumcise** your
sons (although it was not Moses but your
ancestors who started it), and so you
circumcise a boy on the **Sabbath**. 23 If a
boy is **circumcised** on the **Sabbath** so that
Moses' Law is not broken, why are you
angry with me because I made a man
completely well on the **Sabbath**? 24 Stop
judging by external standards, and **judge**
by **true** standards."

Is He the Messiah?

25 Some of the people of Jerusalem
said, "Isn't this the man the **authorities**
are trying to kill? 26 Look! He is talking
in public, and they say nothing against
him! Can it be that they really know that
he is the **Messiah**? 27 But when the **Messiah** comes, no one will know where he is
from. And we all know where this man
comes from."

28 As Jesus **taught** in the **Temple**, he
said in a loud voice, "Do you really know
me and know where I am from? I have
not come on my own **authority**. He who
sent me, however, is **truthful**. You do not
know him, 29 but I know him, because I
come from him and he sent me."

30 Then they tried to seize him, but no
one laid a hand on him, because his hour
had not yet come. 31 But many in the
crowd **believed** in him and said, "When
the **Messiah** comes, will he perform
more **miracles** than this man has?"

afraid 6.20; 9.22
anger 6.52; Acts 7.54
arrest Lk 22.53; 8.20
authorities [7] 5.10; 8.22
authority [3] 5.30; 8.28
bad 6.27; 11.39
believe [5] 6.29; 8.24
chief priests [2] Lk 24.20; 11.47
circumcise [3] Lk 2.21; Acts 7.8
condemn 5.29; 8.10
curse Lk 6.28; 9.28
demon Lk 13.32; 8.48
false 1.47; Acts 24.14
festival [7] 6.4; 10.22
follower 6.60; 18.36
fool Lk 24.25; 11.49
glory [3] 2.11; 11.4
hate 3.20; 12.25
heart 5.38; 11.33
honest Mt 23.23; Eph 4.28
important 3.30; Acts 4.11
Jew [5] 5.10; 8.22
judge [2] 5.22; 8.15
last (2) 6.39; 11.24
law [5] 5.10; 8.3
learn 6.45; Acts 2.42
life (1) 6.27; 8.12
Messiah [6] 4.25; 9.22
miracle [2] 6.2; 9.16
mislead Lk 23.2; Rev 2.20
obey 4.34; 8.31
Pharisees [5] 4.1; 8.3
prophet [2] 6.14; 8.52
raise 6.39; 12.1
right (1) [3] 5.30; 8.48
Sabbath [3] 5.9; 9.14
scripture [3] 6.31; 10.35
secret Lk 22.2; 18.20
shelter Zech 14.16; Acts 27.4

Spirit (1) (God's Spirit) [2] 6.63; 14.17
study 5.39; Acts 17.11
teach [5] 6.45; 8.2
Temple (1) (of God) [2] 5.14; 8.2
true 5.32; 8.14
truth 6.26; 8.26
way (3) Lk 3.18; Acts 3.26
world [2] 6.14; 8.12

[n] I am not going; *some manuscripts have* I am not yet going.

6.68–69: Mt 16.16; Mk 8.29; Lk 9.20 **7.2:** Lev 23.34; Deut 16.13 **7.22:** Gen 17.10; Lev 12.3 **7.23:** Jn 5.9

Guards Are Sent to Arrest Jesus

32 The **Pharisees** heard the crowd
whispering these things about Jesus, so
they and the **chief priests** sent some
guards to **arrest** him. 33 Jesus said, "I
shall be with you a little while longer,
and then I shall go away to him who sent
me. 34 You will look for me, but you will
not find me, because you cannot go
where I will be."

35 The **Jewish authorities** said among
themselves, "Where is he about to go so
that we shall not find him? Will he go to
the Greek cities where our people live,
and **teach** the Greeks? 36 He says that we
will look for him but will not find him,
and that we cannot go where he will be.
What does he mean?"

Streams of Life-Giving Water

37 On the **last** and most **important** day
of the **festival** Jesus stood up and said in
a loud voice, "Whoever is thirsty should
come to me and drink. 38 As the **scripture**
says, 'Whoever **believes** in me, streams
of **life-giving** water will pour out from his
heart.' "[o] 39 Jesus said this about the
Spirit, which those who **believed** in him
were going to receive. At that time the
Spirit had not yet been given, because
Jesus had not been **raised** to **glory**.

Division among the People

40 Some of the people in the crowd
heard him say this and said, "This man is
really the **Prophet**!"[p]

41 Others said, "He is the **Messiah**!"

But others said, "The **Messiah** will not
come from Galilee! 42 The **scripture** says
that the **Messiah** will be a descendant of
King David and will be born in Bethlehem, the town where David lived." 43 So
there was a division in the crowd
because of Jesus. 44 Some wanted to seize
him, but no one laid a hand on him.

The Unbelief of the Jewish Authorities

45 When the guards went back, the
chief priests and **Pharisees** asked them,
"Why did you not bring him?"

46 The guards answered, "Nobody has
ever talked like this man!"

47 "Did he **fool** you, too?" the **Pharisees** asked them. 48 "Have you ever
known one of the **authorities** or one
Pharisee to **believe** in him? 49 This crowd
does not know the **Law of Moses**, so they
are under God's **curse**!"

50 One of the **Pharisees** there was
Nicodemus, the man who had gone to see
Jesus before. He said to the others,
51 "According to our **Law** we cannot **condemn** a man before hearing him and
finding out what he has done."

52 "Well," they answered, "are you
also from Galilee? **Study** the **Scriptures**
and you will **learn** that no **prophet** ever
comes[q] from Galilee."

The Woman Caught in Adultery

8 [Then everyone went home, but
Jesus went to the Mount of Olives.
2 Early the next morning he went back to
the **Temple**. All the people gathered
round him, and he sat down and began to
teach them. 3 The **teachers of the Law**
and the **Pharisees** brought in a woman
who had been caught **committing adultery**, and they made her stand before
them all. 4 "**Teacher**," they said to Jesus,
"this woman was caught in the very **act**
of **committing adultery**. 5 In our **Law**
Moses **commanded** that such a woman
must be stoned **to death**. Now, what do
you say?" 6 They said this to **trap** Jesus,
so that they could **accuse** him. But he
bent over and wrote on the ground with
his finger.

7 As they stood there asking him **questions**, he straightened himself up and said
to them, "Whichever one of you has **committed** no sin may throw the first stone at
her." 8 Then he bent over again and
wrote on the ground. 9 When they heard
this, they all left, one by one, the older
ones first. Jesus was left **alone**, with the
woman still standing there. 10 He straightened himself up and said to her, "Where
are they? Is there no one left to **condemn** you?"

11 "No one, sir," she answered.

"Well, then," Jesus said, "I do not **condemn** you either. Go, but do not sin
again."][r]

Jesus the Light of the World

12 Jesus spoke to the **Pharisees** again.
"**I am** the **light** of the **world**," he said.
"Whoever follows me will have the **light
of life** and will never walk in **darkness**."

13 The **Pharisees** said to him, "Now
you are **testifying** on your own behalf;
what you say **proves** nothing."

[o] *Jesus' words in verses 37–38 may be translated:* "Whoever is thirsty should come to me, and whoever believes in me should drink. [38] As the scripture says, 'Streams of life-giving water will pour out from his heart.' " [p] THE PROPHET: *See 1.21.*

[q] no prophet ever comes; *one manuscript has* the Prophet will not come.

[r] *Many manuscripts and early translations do not have this passage (8.1-11); others have it after Jn 21.24; others have it after Lk 21.38; one manuscript has it after Jn 7.36.*

7.37: Lev 23.36 **7.38:** Ezek 47.1; Zech 14.8 **7.42:** 2 Sam 7.12; Mic 5.2 **7.50:** Jn 3.1–2
8.5: Lev 20.10; Deut 22.22–24 **8.12:** Mt 5.14; Jn 9.5 **8.13:** Jn 5.31

pure Lk 2.22; 11.55
question 2.18; 16.19
rejoice Lk 15.10; Rom 5.11
right (1) 7.6; 13.13
seek [2] Lk 19.10; Rom 2.7
slave [3] Lk 22.50; 13.16
Son of God 6.40; 10.36
Son of Man 6.27; 9.35
teach [6] 7.14; 9.34
teacher 6.25; 9.2
teacher of the Law Lk 23.10; Acts 4.5
Temple (1) (of God) [3] 7.14; 10.22
testify [4] 5.31; Acts 10.42
trap Lk 21.35; Rom 11.9
true [4] 7.24; 10.35
truth [9] 7.28; 9.24
understand [2] 6.26; 10.6
who 6.14; 11.27
witness 5.34; Acts 1.8
word (1) [2] 6.63; 10.19
world [4] 7.4; 9.5
worthless Lk 20.17; Acts 14.15

14 "No," Jesus answered, "even
though I do testify on my own behalf,
what I say is true, because I know where
I came from and where I am going. You
do not know where I came from or
where I am going.
15 You make judge-
ments in a purely human way; I pass
judgement on no one.
16 But if I were to
do so, my judgement would be true,
because I am not alone in this; the
Father who sent me is with me.
17 It is
written in your Law that when two witnesses agree, what they say is true.
18 I
testify on my own behalf, and the Father
who sent me also testifies on my behalf."
19 "Where is your father?" they asked
him.
"You know neither me nor my
Father," Jesus answered. "If you knew
me, you would know my Father also."
20 Jesus said all this as he taught in
the Temple, in the room where the offering boxes were placed. And no one
arrested him, because his hour had not
come.

You Cannot Go Where I Am Going

21 Again Jesus said to them, "I will go
away; you will look for me, but you will
die in your sins. You cannot go where I
am going."
22 So the Jewish authorities said, "He
says that we cannot go where he is going.
Does this mean that he will kill himself?"
23 Jesus answered, "You belong to this
world here below, but I come from
above. You are from this world, but I am
not from this world.
24 That is why I told
you that you will die in your sins. And you
will die in your sins if you do not believe
that 'I Am Who I Am'."
25 "Who are you?" they asked him.
Jesus answered, "What I have told you
from the very beginning.[s]
26 I have much
to say about you, much to condemn you
for. The one who sent me, however, is
truthful, and I tell the world only what I
have heard from him."
27 They did not understand that Jesus
was talking to them about the Father.
28 So he said to them, "When you lift up
the Son of Man, you will know that 'I Am
Who I Am'; then you will know that I do
nothing on my own authority, but I say
only what the Father has instructed me
to say.
29 And he who sent me is with me;
he has not left me alone, because I
always do what pleases him."
30 Many who heard Jesus say these
things believed in him.

Free Men and Slaves

31 So Jesus said to those who believed
in him, "If you obey my teaching, you are
really my disciples;
32 you will know the
truth, and the truth will set you free."
33 "We are the descendants of Abraham," they answered, "and we have
never been anybody's slaves. What do
you mean, then, by saying, 'You will be
free'?"
34 Jesus said to them, "I am telling
you the truth: everyone who sins is a
slave of sin.
35 A slave does not belong to
a family permanently, but a son belongs
there for ever.
36 If the Son sets you free,
then you will be really free.
37 I know you
are Abraham's descendants. Yet you are
trying to kill me, because you will not
accept my teaching.
38 I talk about what
my Father has shown me, but you do
what your father has told you."
39 They answered him, "Our father is
Abraham."
"If you really were Abraham's children," Jesus replied, "you would do[t] the
same things that he did.
40 All I have ever
done is to tell you the truth I heard from
God, yet you are trying to kill me. Abraham did nothing like this!
41 You are
doing what your father did."
"God himself is the only Father we
have," they answered, "and we are his
true sons."
42 Jesus said to them, "If God really
were your Father, you would love me,
because I came from God and now I am
here. I did not come on my own authority, but he sent me.
43 Why do you not
understand what I say? It is because you
cannot bear to listen to my message.
44 You are the children of your father, the
Devil, and you want to follow your
father's desires. From the very beginning he was a murderer and has never
been on the side of truth, because there
is no truth in him. When he tells a lie, he
is only doing what is natural to him,
because he is a liar and the father of all
lies.
45 But I tell the truth, and that is why
you do not believe me.
46 Which one of
you can prove that I am guilty of sin? If I
tell the truth, then why do you not
believe me?
47 He who comes from God
listens to God's words. You, however, are
not from God, and that is why you will
not listen."

[s] What I have told you from the very beginning; *or* Why should I speak to you at all?
[t] If you really were...you would do; *some manuscripts have* If you are...do.

8.17: Deut 19.15 **8.33:** Mt 3.9; Lk 3.8

Jesus and Abraham

48 They asked Jesus, "Were we not **right** in saying that you are a Samaritan and have a **demon** in you?"

49 "I have no **demon**," Jesus answered. "I **honour my Father**, but you **dishonour** me. 50 I am not **seeking honour** for myself. But there is one who is **seeking** it and who **judges** in my **favour**. 51 I am telling you the **truth**: whoever **obeys** my **teaching** will never die."

52 They said to him, "Now we are **certain** that you have a **demon**! Abraham died, and the **prophets** died, yet you say that whoever **obeys** your **teaching** will never die. 53 Our father Abraham died; you do not **claim** to be greater than Abraham, do you? And the **prophets** also died. Who do you think you are?"

54 Jesus answered, "If I were to **honour** myself, that honour would be **worth nothing**. The one who **honours** me is **my Father**—the very one you say is your God. 55 You have never known him, but I know him. If I were to say that I do not know him, I would be a **liar** like you. But I do know him, and I **obey** his **word**. 56 Your father Abraham **rejoiced** that he was to see the time of my coming; he saw it and was **glad**."

57 They said to him, "You are not even fifty years old—and you have seen Abraham?"[u]

58 "I am telling you the **truth**," Jesus replied. "Before Abraham was born, 'I Am'."

59 Then they picked up stones to throw at him, but Jesus hid himself and left the **Temple**.

Jesus Heals a Man Born Blind

9 As Jesus was walking along, he saw a man who had been born **blind**. 2 His **disciples** asked him, "**Teacher**, whose sin caused him to be born **blind**? Was it his own or his parents' sin?"

3 Jesus answered, "His **blindness** has nothing to do with his sins or his parents' sins. He is **blind** so that **God's power** might be seen at work in him. 4 As long as it is day, we must keep on doing the work of him who sent me; night is coming when no one can work. 5 While I am in the world, I am the **light** for the **world**."

6 After he said this, Jesus spat on the ground and made some mud with the spittle; he rubbed the mud on the man's eyes 7 and said, "Go and wash your face in the Pool of Siloam." (This name means "Sent.") So the man went, washed his face, and came back seeing.

8 His **neighbours**, then, and the people who had seen him **begging** before this, asked, "Isn't this the man who used to sit and **beg**?"

9 Some said, "He is the one," but others said, "No he isn't; he just looks like him."

So the man himself said, "I am the man."

10 "How is it that you can now see?" they asked him.

11 He answered, "The man called Jesus made some mud, rubbed it on my eyes, and told me to go to Siloam and wash my face. So I went, and as soon as I washed, I could see."

12 "Where is he?" they asked.

"I don't know," he answered.

The Pharisees Investigate the Healing

13 Then they took to the **Pharisees** the man who had been **blind**. 14 The day that Jesus made the mud and **cured** him of his **blindness** was a **Sabbath**. 15 The **Pharisees**, then, asked the man again how he had received his **sight**. He told them, "He put some mud on my eyes; I washed my face, and now I can see."

16 Some of the **Pharisees** said, "The man who did this cannot be from God, for he does not **obey** the **Sabbath law**."

Others, however, said, "How could a man who is a sinner perform such **miracles** as these?" And there was a division among them.

17 So the **Pharisees** asked the man once more, "You say he **cured** you of your **blindness**—well, what do you say about him?"

"He is a **prophet**," the man answered.

18 The **Jewish authorities**, however, were not willing to **believe** that he had been **blind** and could now see, until they called his parents 19 and asked them, "Is this your son? You say that he was born **blind**; how is it, then, that he can now see?"

20 His parents answered, "We know that he is our son, and we know that he was born **blind**. 21 But we do not know how it is that he is now able to see, nor do we know who **cured** him of his **blindness**. Ask him; he is old **enough**, and he can answer for himself!" 22 His parents said this because they were **afraid** of the **Jewish authorities**, who had already **agreed** that anyone who said he **believed** that Jesus was the **Messiah** would be expelled from the **synagogue**. 23 That is why

power 6.63; 12.38
promise Lk 24.49; Acts 1.4
prophet 8.52; 12.38
respect 4.44; Acts 5.34
Sabbath [2] 7.22; 19.31
sight [2] Lk 24.31; 10.21
Son of Man 8.28; 12.23
strange Lk 21.11; Acts 10.46
synagogue [2] 6.59; 12.42
teach 8.2; 14.23
teacher 8.4; 11.8
truth 8.26; 10.1
world [3] 8.12; 10.36

afraid 7.13; 12.15
agree 8.17; Acts 5.2
authorities [2] 8.22; 11.48
beg [2] 4.31; Acts 3.2
believe [5] 8.24; 10.25
blind [19] 5.3; 10.21
claim 8.53; 19.7
cure [6] Lk 13.32
curse 7.49; Rom 3.14
disciple [4] 8.31; 11.7
enough [2] 6.5; Acts 10.33
guilty [2] 8.46; 15.22
I am 8.12; 10.7
Jew [2] 8.22; 11.51
judge 8.15; 12.31
kneel Lk 22.41; Acts 7.60
law 8.3; 10.34
light (1) 8.12; 11.9
Messiah 7.26; 10.24
miracle 7.21; 10.41
neighbour Lk 15.6; Rom 13.9
obey 8.31; 12.47
Pharisees [5] 8.3; 11.46

[u] you have seen Abraham?; *some manuscripts have* has Abraham seen you?

9.5: Mt 5.14; Jn 8.12

his parents said, "He is old **enough**; ask him!"

24 A second time they called back the man who had been born **blind**, and said to him, "**Promise** before God that you will tell the **truth**! We know that this man who **cured** you is a sinner."

25 "I do not know if he is a sinner or not," the man replied. "One thing I do know: I was **blind**, and now I see."

26 "What did he do to you?" they asked. "How did he **cure** you of your **blindness**?"

27 "I have already told you," he answered, "and you would not listen. Why do you want to hear it again? Maybe you, too, would like to be his **disciples**?"

28 They **cursed** him and said, "You are that fellow's **disciple**; but we are Moses' **disciples**. 29 We know that God spoke to Moses; as for that fellow, however, we do not even know where he comes from!"

30 The man answered, "What a **strange** thing that is! You do not know where he comes from, but he **cured** me of my **blindness**! 31 We know that God does not listen to sinners; he does listen to people who **respect** him and do what he wants them to do. 32 Since the beginning of the **world** nobody has ever heard of anyone giving **sight** to a person born **blind**. 33 Unless this man came from God, he would not be able to do a thing."

34 They answered, "You were born and brought up in sin—and you are trying to **teach** us?" And they expelled him from the **synagogue**.

Spiritual Blindness

35 When Jesus heard what had happened, he found the man and asked him, "Do you **believe** in the **Son of Man**?"

36 The man answered, "Tell me who he is, sir, so that I can **believe** in him!"

37 Jesus said to him, "You have already seen him, and he is the one who is talking with you now."

38 "I **believe**, Lord!" the man said, and **knelt** down before Jesus.

39 Jesus said, "I came to **this world** to **judge**, so that the **blind** should see and those who see should become blind."

40 Some **Pharisees** who were there with him heard him say this and asked him, "Surely you don't mean that we are **blind**, too?"

41 Jesus answered, "If you were **blind**, then you would not be **guilty**; but since you **claim** that you can see, this means that you are still **guilty**."

The Parable of the Shepherd

10 Jesus said, "I am telling you the **truth**: the man who does not enter the sheepfold by the gate, but climbs in some other way, is a **thief** and a **robber**. 2 The man who goes in through the gate is the **shepherd** of the **sheep**. 3 The gatekeeper opens the gate for him; the **sheep** hear his voice as he calls his own **sheep** by name, and he leads them out. 4 When he has brought them out, he goes ahead of them, and the **sheep** follow him, because they know his voice. 5 They will not follow someone else; instead, they will run away from such a person, because they do not know his voice."

6 Jesus told them this **parable**, but they did not **understand** what he meant.

Jesus the Good Shepherd

7 So Jesus said again, "I am telling you the **truth**: **I am** the gate for the **sheep**. 8 All others who came before me are **thieves** and **robbers**, but the **sheep** did not listen to them. 9 **I am** the gate. Whoever comes in by me will be **saved**; he will come in and go out and find pasture. 10 The **thief** comes only in order to **steal**, kill, and **destroy**. I have come in order that you might have **life**—life in all its fullness.

11 "**I am** the good **shepherd**, who is willing to die for the **sheep**. 12 When the hired man, who is not a **shepherd** and does not own the **sheep**, sees a wolf coming, he leaves the **sheep** and runs away; so the wolf snatches the **sheep** and **scatters** them. 13 The hired man runs away because he is only a hired man and does not **care** about the **sheep**. 14-15 **I am** the good **shepherd**. As the **Father** knows me and I know the Father, in the same way I know my **sheep** and they know me. And I am willing to die for them. 16 There are other **sheep** which belong to me that are not in this sheepfold. I must bring them, too; they will listen to my voice, and they will become[v] one **flock** with one **shepherd**.

17 "The **Father loves** me because I am willing to **give up** my **life**, in order that I may receive it back again. 18 No one takes my **life** away from me. I **give it up** of my own **free will**. I have the **right** to **give it up**, and I have the **right** to take it back. This is what **my Father** has **commanded** me to do."

19 Again there was a division among

authority 8.28; 12.49
baptize 4.1; Acts 1.5
believe [6] 9.18; 11.15
blasphemy [2] Lk 5.21; 1 Tim 1.20
blind 9.1; 11.37
care [2] Lk 15.15; 12.6
celebrate Lk 15.6; 1 Cor 5.8
choose 6.70; 13.18
command 8.5; 12.49
deed (2) [3] 5.36; Acts 4.9
demon [3] 8.48; 1 Cor 10.20
destroy Lk 21.20; 11.48
eternal 6.27; 12.25
Father (2) (God) [11] 8.16; 11.41
festival 7.2; 11.55
flock 4.12; Acts 20.28
free 8.32; 18.39
give up [3] 6.61; 16.1
god (2) (other gods) [2] Mt 6.7; Acts 7.40
I am [5] 9.5; 11.25
law 9.16; 12.34
life (1) [4] 8.12; 11.25
love 8.42; 11.5
mad Mk 3.21; Acts 12.15
message 8.43; 11.3
Messiah 9.22; 11.27
miracle 9.16; 11.47
parable Lk 21.29
plain (1) Lk 1.66; 11.14
presence Lk 24.43; 12.37
right (3) [2] 5.22; Rom 9.21
rob [2] Lk 20.47; Acts 19.37
save 5.34; 12.47
scatter 2.15; 11.52
scripture 7.38; 12.14
sheep [15] 2.14; 21.16
shepherd [5] Lk 2.8; Acts 20.28
sight 9.15; 11.37
Son of God 8.36; 11.4
steal Lk 18.20; Rom 2.21
Temple (1) (of God) [2] 8.2; 11.48
thief [3] Lk 19.46; 12.6
true [2] 8.14; 12.38
truth [3] 9.24; 12.24
understand 8.27; 12.16
will (1) 6.38; Acts 2.47
word (1) 8.47; 12.48
world 9.5; 11.9

[v] they will become; *some manuscripts have* there will be.

10.15: Mt 11.27; Lk 10.22

the people because of these **words**. 20 Many of them were saying, "He has a **demon**! He is **mad**! Why do you listen to him?"

21 But others were saying, "A man with a **demon** could not talk like this! How could a **demon** give **sight** to **blind** people?"

Jesus Is Rejected

22 It was winter, and the **Festival** of the Dedication of the **Temple** was being **celebrated** in Jerusalem. 23 Jesus was walking in Solomon's Porch in the **Temple**, 24 when the people gathered round him and asked, "How long are you going to keep us in suspense? Tell us the **plain truth**: are you the **Messiah**?"

25 Jesus answered, "I have already told you, but you would not **believe** me. The things I do by **my Father's authority** speak on my behalf; 26 but you will not **believe**, for you are not my **sheep**. 27 My **sheep** listen to my voice; I know them, and they follow me. 28 I give them **eternal life**, and they shall never die. No one can snatch them away from me. 29 What **my Father** has given me is greater[w] than everything, and no one can snatch them away from the **Father's care**. 30 The **Father** and I are one."

31 Then the people again picked up stones to throw at him. 32 Jesus said to them, "I have done many good **deeds** in your **presence** which the **Father** gave me to do; for which one of these do you want to stone me?"

33 They replied, "We do not want to stone you because of any good **deeds**, but because of your **blasphemy**! You are only a man, but you are trying to make yourself God!"

34 Jesus answered, "It is written in your own **Law** that God said, 'You are **gods**.' 35 We know that what the **scripture** says is **true** for ever; and God called those people **gods**, the people to whom his **message** was given. 36 As for me, the **Father chose** me and sent me into the **world**. How, then, can you say that I **blaspheme** because I said that **I am** the **Son of God**? 37 Do not **believe** me, then, if I am not doing the things **my Father** wants me to do. 38 But if I do them, even though you do not **believe** me, you should at least **believe** my **deeds**, in order that you may know once and for all that the **Father** is in me and that I am in the Father."

39 Once more they tried to seize Jesus, but he slipped out of their hands.

40 Jesus then went back again across the River Jordan to the place where John had been **baptizing**, and he stayed there. 41 Many people came to him. "John performed no **miracles**," they said, "but everything he said about this man was **true**." 42 And many people there **believed** in him.

The Death of Lazarus

11 A man named Lazarus, who lived in Bethany, was ill. Bethany was the town where Mary and her sister Martha lived. 2 (This Mary was the one who poured the perfume on the Lord's feet and wiped them with her hair; it was her brother Lazarus who was ill.) 3 The sisters sent Jesus a **message**: "Lord, your **dear friend** is ill."

4 When Jesus heard it, he said, "The **final result** of this illness will not be the **death** of Lazarus; this has happened in order to bring **glory** to God, and it will be the **means** by which the **Son of God** will receive **glory**."

5 Jesus **loved** Martha and her sister and Lazarus. 6 Yet when he received the news that Lazarus was ill, he stayed where he was for two more days. 7 Then he said to the **disciples**, "Let us go back to Judaea."

8 "**Teacher**," the **disciples** answered, "just a short time ago the people there wanted to stone you; and are you **planning** to go back?"

9 Jesus said, "A day has twelve hours, hasn't it? So whoever walks in broad daylight does not **stumble**, for he sees the **light of this world**. 10 But if he walks during the night he **stumbles**, because he has no **light**." 11 Jesus said this and then added, "Our **friend** Lazarus has fallen asleep, but I will go and wake him up."

12 The **disciples** answered, "If he is asleep, Lord, he will get well."

13 Jesus meant that Lazarus had died, but they thought he meant **natural** sleep. 14 So Jesus told them **plainly**, "Lazarus is **dead**, 15 but for your **sake** I am **glad** that I was not with him, so that you will **believe**. Let us go to him."

16 Thomas (called the Twin) said to his **fellow-disciples**, "Let us all go with the **Teacher**, so that we may die with him!"

Jesus the Resurrection and the Life

17 When Jesus arrived, he found that Lazarus had been buried four days before. 18 Bethany was less than three

action Lk 23.50; Acts 5.17
arrest 8.20; 18.12
authorities [2] 9.18; 12.42
bad 7.7; Acts 7.6
believe [9] 10.25; 12.11
blind 10.21; 12.40
body 2.21; 19.31
chief priests [2] 7.32; 12.10
comfort [2] Mt 5.4; Acts 20.12
Council Lk 23.50; Acts 4.13
dead [2] 5.21; 19.33
dear Lk 20.13; Acts 1.1
death (1) [2] Lk 23.15; 12.33
destroy [2] 10.10; Acts 3.23
disciple [5] 9.2; 12.4
Father (2) (God) 10.14; 12.26
festival [3] 10.22; 12.12
final Dan 11.40; 1 Cor 4.5
fool 7.47; Rom 1.22
friend [2] 3.29; 15.13
glad 8.56; 14.28
glory [3] 7.18; 12.16
God's people 1.11; Acts 3.23
grave [2] 5.29; 12.17
heart 7.38; 12.27
High Priest [2] Lk 22.50; 18.10
I am 10.7; 13.19
Jew [2] 9.18; 12.11
last (2) 7.37; 12.48
life (1) 10.10; 12.25
life (2) (to life) [2] 6.39; Acts 4.2
light (1) [2] 9.5; 12.35
love [2] 10.17; 12.25
means 1.13; 17.17
message 10.35; 12.38
Messiah 10.24; 12.34
miracle 10.41; 12.18
natural 8.44; Rom 1.26
one another 5.44; 12.19
Passover 6.4; 12.1
Pharisees [3] 9.13; 12.19
plain (1) 10.24; 16.25
plan [2] Lk 19.12; 12.10
prophecy Mk 7.6; 2 Thes 2.2
pure 8.15; 12.3
result Lk 16.8; Acts 5.15
resurrection Mk 12.23; Acts 1.21
rise [2] 5.29; 13.4
ritual 3.25; Heb 9.13
sake [2] Lk 21.12; 12.30
scatter 10.12; 16.32
sight 10.21; Acts 1.9

[w] What my Father has given me is greater; *some manuscripts have* My Father, who gave them to me, is greater.

10.33: Lev 24.16 **10.34:** Ps 82.6 **10.40:** Jn 1.28 **11.1:** Lk 10.38–39 **11.2:** Jn 12.3

Son of God [2] 10.36; 14.13
stumble [2] Hab 3.16; Rom 9.32
teacher [3] 9.2; 13.13
Temple (1) (of God) [2] 10.22; 18.20
thank 6.11; Acts 27.35
tomb Lk 24.1; 19.41
weep [4] Lk 23.27; 16.20
who 8.25; 21.12
world [2] 10.36; 12.19

kilometres from Jerusalem, 19 and many
Judaeans had come to see Martha and
Mary to **comfort** them over their
brother's **death**.

20 When Martha heard that Jesus was
coming, she went out to meet him, but
Mary stayed in the house. 21 Martha said
to Jesus, "If you had been here, Lord, my
brother would not have died! 22 But I
know that even now God will give you
whatever you ask him for."

23 "Your brother will **rise to life**,"
Jesus told her.

24 "I know," she replied, "that he will
rise to life on the **last day**."

25 Jesus said to her, "**I am** the **resurrection** and the **life**. Whoever **believes** in
me will live, even though he dies; 26 and
whoever lives and **believes** in me will
never die. Do you **believe** this?"

27 "Yes, Lord!" she answered. "I do
believe that you are the **Messiah**, the **Son
of God**, **who was to come** into the **world**."

Jesus Weeps

28 After Martha said this, she went
back and called her sister Mary privately. "The **Teacher** is here," she told
her, "and is asking for you." 29 When
Mary heard this, she got up and hurried
out to meet him. 30 (Jesus had not yet
arrived in the village, but was still in the
place where Martha had met him.) 31 The
people who were in the house with Mary,
comforting her, followed her when they
saw her get up and hurry out. They
thought that she was going to the **grave**
to **weep** there.

32 Mary arrived where Jesus was, and
as soon as she saw him, she fell at his
feet. "Lord," she said, "if you had been
here, my brother would not have died!"

33 Jesus saw her **weeping**, and he saw
how the people who were with her were
weeping also; his **heart** was touched, and
he was deeply moved. 34 "Where have
you buried him?" he asked them.

"Come and see, Lord," they answered.

35 Jesus **wept**. 36 "See how much he
loved him!" the people said.

37 But some of them said, "He gave
sight to the **blind** man, didn't he? Could
he not have kept Lazarus from dying?"

Lazarus Is Brought to Life

38 Deeply moved once more, Jesus
went to the **tomb**, which was a cave with
a stone placed at the entrance. 39 "Take
the stone away!" Jesus ordered.

Martha, the **dead** man's sister,
answered, "There will be a **bad** smell,
Lord. He has been buried four days!"

40 Jesus said to her, "Didn't I tell you
that you would see God's **glory** if you
believed?" 41 They took the stone away.
Jesus looked up and said, "I **thank** you,
Father, that you listen to me. 42 I know
that you always listen to me, but I say
this for the **sake** of the people here, so
that they will **believe** that you sent me."
43 After he had said this, he called out in a
loud voice, "Lazarus, come out!" 44 He
came out, his hands and feet wrapped in
grave clothes, and with a cloth round his
face. "Untie him," Jesus told them, "and
let him go."

The Plot against Jesus

(Matt. 26.1–5; Mark 14.1–2; Luke 22.1–2)

45 Many of the people who had come
to visit Mary saw what Jesus did, and
they **believed** in him. 46 But some of them
returned to the **Pharisees** and told them
what Jesus had done. 47 So the **Pharisees**
and the **chief priests** met with the
Council and said, "What shall we do?
Look at all the **miracles** this man is performing! 48 If we let him go on in this
way, everyone will **believe** in him, and
the Roman **authorities** will take **action**
and **destroy** our **Temple** and our nation!"

49 One of them, named Caiaphas, who
was **High Priest** that year, said, "What
fools you are! 50 Don't you realize that it
is better for you to let one man die for
the people, instead of having the whole
nation **destroyed**?" 51 Actually, he did not
say this of his own accord; rather, as he
was **High Priest** that year, he was **prophesying** that Jesus was going to die for
the **Jewish** people, 52 and not only for
them, but also to bring together into one
body all the **scattered people of God**.

53 From that day on the **Jewish authorities** made **plans** to kill Jesus. 54 So
Jesus did not travel openly in Judaea, but
left and went to a place near the desert,
to a town named Ephraim, where he
stayed with the **disciples**.

55 The time for the **Passover Festival**
was near, and many people went up from
the country to Jerusalem to perform the
ritual of **purification** before the **festival**.
56 They were looking for Jesus, and as
they gathered in the **Temple**, they asked
one another, "What do you think? Surely
he will not come to the **festival**, will he?"
57 The **chief priests** and the **Pharisees** had
given orders that if anyone knew where
Jesus was, he must report it, so that they
could **arrest** him.

Jesus Is Anointed at Bethany

(Matt. 26.6–13; Mark 14.3–9)

12 Six days before the **Passover**,
Jesus went to Bethany, the home

accept 8.37; 13.30
afraid 9.22; 14.27
alone 8.9; 14.18

angel 1.51; 20.12
approve 6.27; Acts 8.1
authorities 11.48; 13.33
authority 10.25; 16.13
believe [8] 11.15; 13.19
betray 6.64; 13.2
bless [2] 1.16; Acts 3.25
blind 11.37; Acts 13.11
care 10.13; 21.15
chief priests 11.47; 18.3
command [2] 10.18; 14.31
dark [3] 8.12; 20.1
death (1) 11.4; 18.32
death (2) (from death) [3] 5.24; 20.9
disciple [2] 11.7; 13.2
eternal [2] 10.28; 17.2
Father (2) (God) [5] 11.41; 13.1
festival [2] 11.55; 13.1
glory [5] 11.4; 13.31
grave 11.31; Acts 2.27
hate 7.7; 15.18
heal 6.2; Acts 4.9
heart 11.33; 13.2
heaven 6.31; 17.1
help [2] Lk 19.35; Acts 2.21
honour 8.49; Acts 7.41
Jew [2] 11.51; 13.33
judge [5] 9.39; 16.8
last (2) 11.24; Acts 2.17
law 10.34; 15.25
life (1) [4] 11.25; 14.6
light (1) [5] 11.9; Acts 9.3
love [2] 11.5; 13.1
message [3] 11.3; 17.8
Messiah 11.27; 20.31
mind (1) [2] Lk 24.38; Acts 4.32
miracle [2] 11.47; 20.30
name (2) (name of God, of Jesus) [2] Lk 24.47; 14.13
obey 9.16; 14.15
one another 11.56; 13.14
overthrow Zech 1.21
Passover [2] 11.55; 13.1
Pharisees [2] 11.46; 18.3
plan 11.8; Acts 2.23
poor [3] Lk 21.2; 13.29
power 9.3; 13.3
praise 5.41; Acts 2.47
presence 10.32; 17.5
prophet 9.17; Acts 2.16
pure 11.55; Acts 21.24
raise [4] 7.39; 21.14
reject [2] Lk 20.17; Acts 3.13
remember 4.53; 14.26
reveal 2.11; 13.31
sake 11.15; 17.19
save 10.9; Acts 2.21
scripture [2] 10.35; 13.18
servant 4.51; 15.15
serve [3] 2.10; 16.2

of Lazarus, the man he had **raised from**
death. 2 They prepared a dinner for him
there, which Martha **helped** to **serve**;
Lazarus was one of those who were sitting at the table with Jesus. 3 Then Mary
took half a litre of a very expensive perfume made of **pure** nard, poured it on
Jesus' feet, and wiped them with her
hair. The sweet smell of the perfume
filled the whole house. 4 One of Jesus'
disciples, Judas Iscariot—the one who
was going to **betray** him—said, 5 "Why
wasn't this perfume sold for three hundred silver coins[x] and the money given
to the **poor**?" 6 He said this, not because
he **cared** about the **poor**, but because he
was a **thief**. He carried the money bag
and would **help** himself from it.
7 But Jesus said, "Leave her **alone**!
Let her keep what she has for the day of
my burial. 8 You will always have **poor**
people with you, but you will not always
have me."

The Plot against Lazarus

9 A large number of people heard that
Jesus was in Bethany, so they went there,
not only because of Jesus but also to see
Lazarus, whom Jesus had **raised from**
death. 10 So the **chief priests** made **plans**
to kill Lazarus too, 11 because on his account many **Jews** were **rejecting** them
and **believing** in Jesus.

The Triumphant Entry into Jerusalem
(Matt. 21.1-11; Mark 11.1-11;
Luke 19.28-40)

12 The next day the large crowd that
had come to the **Passover Festival** heard
that Jesus was coming to Jerusalem. 13 So
they took branches of palm-trees and
went out to meet him, shouting, "**Praise**
God! God **bless** him who comes **in the**
name of the Lord! God **bless** the King of
Israel!"
14 Jesus found a donkey and rode on
it, just as the **scripture** says,
15 "Do not be **afraid**, city of Zion!
Here comes your king,
riding on a young donkey."
16 His **disciples** did not **understand**
this at the time; but when Jesus had been
raised to **glory**, they **remembered** that
the **scripture** said this about him and that
they had done this for him.
17 The people who had been with
Jesus when he called Lazarus out of the
grave and **raised** him **from death** had reported what had happened. 18 That was
why the crowd met him—because they
heard that he had performed this
miracle. 19 The **Pharisees** then said to **one**
another, "You see, we are not **succeeding**
at all! Look, the whole **world** is following
him!"

Some Greeks Seek Jesus

20 Some Greeks were among those
who had gone to Jerusalem to **worship**
during the **festival**. 21 They went to Philip
(he was from Bethsaida in Galilee) and
said, "Sir, we want to see Jesus."
22 Philip went and told Andrew, and
the two of them went and told Jesus.
23 Jesus answered them, "The hour has
now come for the **Son of Man** to receive
great **glory**. 24 I am telling you the **truth**:
a grain of wheat remains no more than a
single grain unless it is dropped into the
ground and dies. If it does die, then it produces many grains. 25 Whoever **loves** his
own **life** will lose it; whoever **hates** his
own **life** in **this world** will keep it for **life**
eternal. 26 Whoever wants to **serve** me
must follow me, so that my **servant** will
be with me where I am. And **my Father**
will **honour** anyone who **serves** me.

Jesus Speaks about His Death

27 "Now my **heart** is **troubled**—and
what shall I say? Shall I say, '**Father**, do
not let this hour come upon me'? But
that is why I came—so that I might go
through this hour of **suffering**. 28 **Father**,
bring **glory** to your **name**!"
Then a voice spoke from **heaven**, "I
have brought **glory** to it, and I will do so
again."
29 The crowd standing there heard
the voice, and some of them said it was
thunder, while others said, "An **angel**
spoke to him!"
30 But Jesus said to them, "It was not
for my **sake** that this voice spoke, but for
yours. 31 Now is the time for **this world** to
be **judged**; now the ruler of **this world**
will be **overthrown**. 32 When I am lifted
up from the earth, I will draw everyone
to me." 33 (In saying this he indicated the
kind of **death** he was going to **suffer**.)
34 The crowd answered, "Our **Law**
tells us that the **Messiah** will live for
ever. How, then, can you say that the **Son**
of Man must be lifted up? Who is this **Son**
of Man?"
35 Jesus answered, "The **light** will be
among you a little longer. Continue on
your way while you have the **light**, so
that the **darkness** will not come upon
you; for the one who walks in the **dark**

Son of Man [3] 9.35; 13.31
succeed (1) Lk 23.23; Acts 19.26
suffer [2] Lk 24.26; 16.21
synagogue 9.22; 16.2
thief 10.1; 1 Cor 5.10
trouble Lk 18.5; 13.21
true [2] 10.35; 13.18
truth 10.1; 13.16
turn 6.37; 13.18
understand [2] 10.6; 13.7
word (1) 10.19; 14.10
world [6] 11.9; 13.1
worship (1) (of God) 4.20; Acts 7.7

[x] SILVER COINS: *See 6.7.*

12.3: Lk 7.37-38 **12.8:** Deut 15.11 **12.13:** Ps 118.25, 26 **12.15:** Zech 9.9
12.25: Mt 10.39, 16.25; Mk 8.35; Lk 9.24, 17.33 **12.34:** Ps 110.4; Is 9.7; Ezek 37.25; Dan 7.14

does not know where he is going. 36 **Believe** in the **light**, then, while you have it,
so that you will be the people of the
light."

The Unbelief of the People

After Jesus said this, he went off and
hid himself from them. 37 Even though he
had performed all these **miracles** in their
presence, they did not **believe** in him,
38 so that what the **prophet** Isaiah had
said might come **true**:

"Lord, who **believed** the **message** we
told?
To whom did the Lord **reveal** his
power?"

39 And so they were not able to **believe**, because Isaiah also said,

40 "God has **blinded** their eyes
and closed their **minds**,
so that their eyes would not see,
and their **minds** would not
understand,
and they would not **turn to me**, says
God,
for me to **heal** them."

41 Isaiah said this because he saw
Jesus' **glory** and spoke about him.
42 Even then, many of the **Jewish
authorities believed** in Jesus; but because
of the **Pharisees** they did not talk about it
openly, so as not to be expelled from the
synagogue. 43 They **loved** the **approval** of
men rather than the approval of God.

Judgement by Jesus' Words

44 Jesus said in a loud voice, "Whoever **believes** in me believes not only in
me but also in him who sent me. 45 Whoever sees me sees also him who sent me.
46 I have come into the **world** as **light**, so
that everyone who **believes** in me should
not remain in the **darkness**. 47 If anyone
hears my **message** and does not **obey** it, I
will not **judge** him. I came, not to **judge**
the **world**, but to **save** it. 48 Whoever **rejects** me and does not **accept** my **message** has one who will **judge** him. The
words I have spoken will be his **judge** on
the **last day**! 49 This is **true**, because I
have not spoken on my own **authority**,
but the **Father** who sent me has **commanded** me what I must say and speak.
50 And I know that his **command** brings
eternal life. What I say, then, is what the
Father has told me to say."

Jesus Washes His Disciples' Feet

13 It was now the day before the
Passover Festival. Jesus knew
that the hour had come for him to leave
this world and go to the **Father**. He had
always **loved** those in the **world** who
were his own, and he **loved** them to the
very end.

2 Jesus and his **disciples** were at
supper. The **Devil** had already put into
the **heart** of Judas, the son of Simon
Iscariot, the thought of **betraying** Jesus.[y]
3 Jesus knew that the **Father** had given
him **complete power**; he knew that he
had come from God and was going to
God. 4 So he **rose** from the table, took off
his outer garment, and tied a towel round
his waist. 5 Then he poured some water
into a basin and began to wash the **disciples'** feet and dry them with the towel
round his waist. 6 He came to Simon
Peter, who said to him, "Are you going to
wash my feet, Lord?"

7 Jesus answered him, "You do not
understand now what I am doing, but you
will **understand** later."

8 Peter **declared**, "Never at any time
will you wash my feet!"

"If I do not wash your feet," Jesus answered, "you will no longer be my **disciple**."

9 Simon Peter answered, "Lord, do not
wash only my feet, then! Wash my hands
and head, too!"

10 Jesus said, "Anyone who has had a
bath is completely **clean** and does not
have to wash himself, except for his
feet.[z] All of you are **clean**—all except
one." 11 (Jesus already knew who was going to **betray** him; that is why he said,
"All of you, except one, are **clean**.")

12 After Jesus had washed their feet,
he put his outer garment back on and returned to his place at the table. "Do you
understand what I have just done to
you?" he asked. 13 "You call me **Teacher**
and Lord, and it is **right** that you do so,
because that is what I am. 14 I, your Lord
and **Teacher**, have just washed your feet.
You, then, should wash **one another's**
feet. 15 I have set an **example** for you, so
that you will do just what I have done for
you. 16 I am telling you the **truth**: no **slave**
is greater than his **master**, and no
messenger is greater than the one who
sent him. 17 Now that you know this **truth**,
how **happy** you will be if you put it into
practice!

18 "I am not talking about all of you; I
know those I have **chosen**. But the **scripture** must come **true** that says, 'The man
who **shared** my food **turned** against me.'

accept 12.48; 14.21
authorities 12.42; 18.14

believe 12.11; 14.1
betray [3] 12.4; 21.20
bread [4] 6.7; 21.9
choose 10.36; 15.16
clean [3] Lk 17.14; 15.2
commandment Lk 18.20; 14.15
complete 3.29; 15.11
declare [2] Lk 12.8; Acts 10.15
Devil 8.44; Acts 10.38
disciple [8] 12.4; 14.10
example Mic 2.4; Rom 7.2
Father (2) (God) [2] 12.26; 14.2
festival [2] 12.12; Acts 12.3
glory [4] 12.16; 14.13
happy 3.29; 16.21
heart 12.27; 16.6
I am 11.25; 14.6
Jew 12.11; 18.12
love [6] 12.25; 14.15
master Lk 19.31; 15.15
need 2.25; 14.8
new Lk 22.20; 19.41
one another [5] 12.19; 15.12
Passover 12.1; 18.28
poor 12.5; Acts 9.36
power 12.38; 14.30
practice Lk 11.42; Acts 16.21
reveal [4] 12.38; 14.17
right (1) 8.48; 16.8
rise 11.23; 20.9
Satan Lk 22.3; Acts 5.3
scripture 12.14; 17.12
share Lk 22.17; Acts 2.42
slave 8.33; 15.20
Son of Man [2] 12.23; Acts 7.56
teacher [2] 11.8; 20.16
trouble 12.27; Acts 2.25
true 12.38; 15.25
truth [5] 12.24; 14.6
turn 12.40; 16.20
understand [4] 12.16; 20.9
world [2] 12.19; 14.17

[y] The Devil...betraying Jesus; *or* The Devil had already decided that Judas, the son of Simon Iscariot, would betray Jesus. [z] *Some manuscripts do not have* except for his feet.

12.38: Is 53.1 (LXX) **12.40:** Is 6.10 (LXX) **13.12–15:** Lk 22.27 **13.16:** Mt 10.24; Lk 6.40; Jn 15.20 **13.18:** Ps 41.9

19 I tell you this now before it happens, so
that when it does happen, you will **believe** that **'I Am Who I Am.'** 20 I am telling
you the **truth**: whoever receives anyone I
send receives me also; and whoever receives me receives him who sent me."

Jesus Predicts His Betrayal
(Matt. 26.20–25; Mark 14.17–21;
Luke 22.21–23)

21 After Jesus had said this, he was
deeply **troubled** and **declared** openly, "I
am telling you the **truth**: one of you is going to **betray** me."
22 The **disciples** looked at **one
another**, completely puzzled about whom
he meant. 23 One of the **disciples**, the one
whom Jesus **loved**, was sitting next to
Jesus. 24 Simon Peter motioned to him
and said, "Ask him whom he is talking
about."
25 So that **disciple** moved closer to
Jesus' side and asked, "Who is it, Lord?"
26 Jesus answered, "I will dip some
bread in the sauce and give it to him; he
is the man." So he took a piece of **bread**,
dipped it, and gave it to Judas, the son of
Simon Iscariot. 27 As soon as Judas took
the **bread**, **Satan** entered him. Jesus said
to him, "Be quick about what you are doing!" 28 None of the others at the table
understood why Jesus said this to him.
29 Since Judas was in charge of the
money bag, some of the **disciples** thought
that Jesus had told him to go and buy
what they **needed** for the **festival**, or to
give something to the **poor**.
30 Judas **accepted** the **bread** and went
out at once. It was night.

The New Commandment

31 After Judas had left, Jesus said,
"Now the **Son of Man's glory** is **revealed**;
now God's **glory** is **revealed** through him.
32 And if God's **glory** is **revealed** through
him, then God will **reveal** the **glory** of the
Son of Man in himself, and he will do so
at once. 33 My children, I shall not be with
you very much longer. You will look for
me; but I tell you now what I told the
Jewish authorities, 'You cannot go where
I am going.' 34 And now I give you a **new
commandment**: **love one another**. As I
have loved you, so you must **love one
another**. 35 If you have **love** for **one
another**, then everyone will know that
you are my **disciples**."

Jesus Predicts Peter's Denial
(Matt. 26.31–35; Mark 14.27–31;
Luke 22.31–34)

36 "Where are you going, Lord?"
Simon Peter asked him.
"You cannot follow me now where I
am going," answered Jesus; "but later
you will follow me."
37 "Lord, why can't I follow you
now?" asked Peter. "I am ready to die
for you!"
38 Jesus answered, "Are you really
ready to die for me? I am telling you the
truth: before the cock crows you will say
three times that you do not know me.

Jesus the Way to the Father

14 "Do not be **worried** and **upset**,"
Jesus told them. "**Believe**[a] in
God and believe also in me. 2 There are
many rooms in **my Father's** house, and **I
am** going to prepare a place for you. I
would not tell you this if it were not so.[b]
3 And after I go and prepare a place for
you, I will come back and take you to myself, so that you will be where I am. 4 You
know the way that leads to the place
where I am going."
5 Thomas said to him, "Lord, we do
not know where you are going; so how
can we know the way to get there?"
6 Jesus answered him, "I am the way,
the **truth**, and the **life**; no one goes to the
Father except by me. 7 Now that you
have known me," he said to them, "you
will know[c] **my Father** also, and from
now on you do know him and you have
seen him."
8 Philip said to him, "Lord, show us
the **Father**; that is all we **need**."
9 Jesus answered, "For a long time I
have been with you all; yet you do not
know me, Philip? Whoever has seen me
has seen the **Father**. Why, then, do you
say, 'Show us the **Father**'? 10 Do you not
believe, Philip, that I am in the **Father**
and the Father is in me? The **words** that
I have spoken to you," Jesus said to his
disciples, "do not come from me. The
Father, who remains in me, does his own
work. 11 **Believe** me when I say that I am
in the **Father** and the Father is in me. If
not, **believe** because of the things I do. 12 I
am telling you the **truth**: whoever **believes** in me will do what I do—yes, he
will do even greater things, because I am
going to the **Father**. 13 And I will do whatever you ask for **in my name**, so that the

accept 13.30; Acts 6.7
afraid 12.15; 19.8
alone 12.7; 16.32
believe [6] 13.19; 16.9
command 12.49; 15.10
commandment [2] 13.34; 15.12
disciple 13.2; 15.8
Father (2) (God) [19] 13.1; 15.1
glad 11.15; 16.20
glory 13.31; 15.8
Helper (2) [2] 15.26
I am 13.19; 15.1
life (1) 12.25; 15.13
love [9] 13.1; 15.9
name (2) (name of God, of Jesus) [3] 12.13; 15.16
need 13.29; 16.30
obey [4] 12.47; 15.10
peace [2] Lk 24.36; 16.33
power 13.3; 17.11
remember 12.16; 15.18
reveal [3] 13.31; 15.26
Son of God 11.4; 17.1
Spirit (1) (God's Spirit) [2] 7.39; 15.26
teach [4] 9.34; 15.3
truth [3] 13.16; 15.26
upset [2] Lk 12.29; Acts 15.24
word (1) 12.48; 15.7
world [6] 13.1; 15.18
worry [2] Lk 21.14; Acts 20.10

[a] Believe; *or* You believe.
[b] There are...were not so; *or* There are many rooms in my Father's house; if it were not so, would I tell you that I am going to prepare a place for you?
[c] Now that you have known me...you will know; *some manuscripts have* If you had known me...you would know.

13.20: Mt 10.40; Mk 9.37; Lk 9.48, 10.16 **13.33:** Jn 7.34 **13.34:** Jn 15.12, 17; 1 Jn 3.23; 2 Jn 5

Father's glory will be shown through the Son. 14 If you ask me[d] for anything **in my name**, I will do it.

The Promise of the Holy Spirit

15 "If you **love** me, you will **obey** my **commandments.** 16 I will ask the **Father**, and he will give you another **Helper**, who will stay with you for ever. 17 He is the **Spirit** who **reveals** the **truth** about God. The **world** cannot receive him, because it cannot see him or know him. But you know him, because he remains with you and is[e] in you.

18 "When I go, you will not be left all **alone**; I will come back to you. 19 In a little while the **world** will see me no more, but you will see me; and because I live, you also will live. 20 When that day comes, you will know that I am in **my Father** and that you are in me, just as I am in you.

21 "Whoever **accepts** my **commandments** and **obeys** them is the one who **loves** me. **My Father** will **love** whoever loves me; I too will **love** him and **reveal** myself to him."

22 Judas (not Judas Iscariot) said, "Lord, how can it be that you will **reveal** yourself to us and not to the **world**?"

23 Jesus answered him, "Whoever **loves** me will **obey** my **teaching. My Father** will **love** him, and my Father and I will come to him and live with him. 24 Whoever does not **love** me does not **obey** my **teaching**. And the **teaching** you have heard is not mine, but comes from the **Father**, who sent me.

25 "I have told you this while I am still with you. 26 The **Helper**, the **Holy Spirit**, whom the **Father** will send **in my name**, will **teach** you everything and make you **remember** all that I have told you.

27 "**Peace** is what I leave with you; it is my own **peace** that I give you. I do not give it as the **world** does. Do not be **worried** and **upset**; do not be **afraid**. 28 You heard me say to you, 'I am leaving, but I will come back to you.' If you **loved** me, you would be **glad** that I am going to the **Father**; for he is greater than I. 29 I have told you this now before it all happens, so that when it does happen, you will **believe**. 30 I cannot talk with you much longer, because the ruler of **this world** is coming. He has no **power** over me, 31 but the **world** must know that I **love** the **Father**; that is why I do everything as he **commands** me.

"Come, let us go from this place.

Jesus the Real Vine

15 "I **am** the **real vine**, and **my Father** is the gardener. 2 He breaks off every branch in me that does not bear fruit, and he prunes every branch that does bear fruit, so that it will be **clean** and bear more fruit. 3 You have been made **clean** already by the **teaching** I have given you. 4 Remain **united** to me, and I will remain united to you. A branch cannot bear fruit by itself; it can do so only if it remains in the **vine**. In the same way you cannot bear fruit unless you remain in me.

5 "**I am** the **vine**, and you are the branches. Whoever remains in me, and I in him, will bear much fruit; for you can do nothing without me. 6 Whoever does not remain in me is thrown out like a branch and dries up; such branches are gathered up and thrown into the fire, where they are burnt. 7 If you remain in me and my **words** remain in you, then you will ask for anything you **wish**, and you shall have it. 8 **My Father's glory** is shown by your bearing much fruit; and in this way you become my **disciples.** 9 I **love** you just as the **Father** loves me; remain in my **love.** 10 If you **obey** my **commands**, you will remain in my **love**, just as I have **obeyed my Father's commands** and remain in his **love**.

11 "I have told you this so that my **joy** may be in you and that your **joy** may be **complete.** 12 My **commandment** is this: **love one another**, just as I **love** you. 13 The greatest love a person can have for his **friends** is to give his **life** for them. 14 And you are my **friends** if you do what I **command** you. 15 I do not call you **servants** any longer, because a **servant** does not know what his **master** is doing. Instead, I call you **friends**, because I have told you everything I have heard from **my Father**. 16 You did not **choose** me; I **chose** you and appointed you to go and bear much fruit, the kind of fruit that **endures**. And so the **Father** will give you whatever you ask of him **in my name.** 17 This, then, is what I **command** you: **love one another**.

The World's Hatred

18 "If the **world** hates you, just **remember** that it has **hated** me first. 19 If you belonged to the **world**, then the **world** would **love** you as its own. But I **chose** you from **this world**, and you do not belong to it; that is why the **world hates** you. 20 **Remember** what I told you: 'No **slave** is greater than his **master**.' If

[d] *Some manuscripts do not have* me. [e] is; *some manuscripts have* will be

15.12: Jn 13.34, 15.17; 1 Jn 3.23; 2 Jn 5 **15.20:** Mt 10.24; Lk 6.40; Jn 13.16

they persecuted me, they will **persecute**
you too; if they obeyed my **teaching**, they
will **obey** yours too. 21 But they will do all
this to you because you are mine; for
they do not know the one who sent me.
22 They would not have been **guilty** of sin
if I had not come and spoken to them; as
it is, they no longer have any **excuse** for
their sin. 23 Whoever **hates** me hates **my**
Father also. 24 They would not have been
guilty of sin if I had not done among
them the things that no one else ever
did; as it is, they have seen what I did,
and they **hate** both me and **my Father**.
25 This, however, was bound to happen so
that what is written in their **Law** may
come **true**: 'They **hated** me for no **reason**
at all.'

26 "The **Helper** will come—the **Spirit**,
who **reveals** the **truth** about God and who
comes from the **Father**. I will send him
to you from the **Father**, and he will speak
about me. 27 And you, too, will speak
about me, because you have been with
me from the very beginning.

16 "I have told you this, so that you
will not **give up** your **faith**. 2 You
will be expelled from the **synagogues**,
and the time will come when anyone
who kills you will think that by doing this
he is **serving** God. 3 People will do these
things to you because they have not
known either the **Father** or me. 4 But I
have told you this, so that when the time
comes for them to do these things, you
will **remember** that I told you.

The Work of the Holy Spirit

"I did not tell you these things at the
beginning, for I was with you. 5 But now I
am going to him who sent me, yet none
of you asks me where I am going. 6 And
now that I have told you, your **hearts** are
full of **sadness**. 7 But I am telling you the
truth: it is better for you that I go away,
because if I do not go, the **Helper** will not
come to you. But if I do go away, then I
will send him to you. 8 And when he
comes, he will **prove** to the people of the
world that they are **wrong** about sin and
about what is **right** and about God's
judgement. 9 They are **wrong** about sin,
because they do not **believe** in me; 10 they
are **wrong** about what is **right**, because I
am going to the **Father** and you will not
see me any more; 11 and they are **wrong**
about **judgement**, because the ruler of
this world has already been **judged**.

12 "I have much more to tell you, but
now it would be too much for you to bear.
13 When, however, the **Spirit** comes, who
reveals the **truth** about God, he will lead
you into all the **truth**. He will not speak
on his own **authority**, but he will speak of
what he hears, and will tell you of things
to come. 14 He will give me **glory**, because he will take what I say and tell it to
you. 15 All that **my Father** has is mine;
that is why I said that the **Spirit** will take
what I give him and tell it to you.

Sadness and Gladness

16 "In a little while you will not see
me any more, and then a little while
later you will see me."

17 Some of his **disciples** asked among
themselves, "What does this mean? He
tells us that in a little while we will not
see him, and then a little while later we
will see him; and he also says, 'It is because I am going to the **Father**.' 18 What
does this 'a little while' mean? We don't
know what he is talking about!"

19 Jesus knew that they wanted to
question him, so he said to them, "I said,
'In a little while you will not see me, and
then a little while later you will see me.'
Is this what you are asking about among
yourselves? 20 I am telling you the **truth**:
you will cry and **weep**, but the **world** will
be **glad**; you will be **sad**, but your sadness
will **turn** into **gladness**. 21 When a woman
is about to give **birth**, she is **sad** because
her hour of **suffering** has come; but when
the baby is born, she **forgets** her **suffer-**
ing, because she is **happy** that a baby has
been born into the **world**. 22 That is how it
is with you: now you are **sad**, but I will
see you again, and your **hearts** will be
filled with **gladness**, the kind of **gladness**
that no one can take away from you.

23 "When that day comes, you will not
ask me for anything. I am telling you the
truth: the **Father** will give you whatever
you ask him for **in my name**. [f] 24 Until now
you have not asked for anything **in my**
name; ask and you will receive, so that
your **happiness** may be **complete**.

Victory over the World

25 "I have used figures of speech to
tell you these things. But the time will
come when I will not use figures of
speech, but will speak to you **plainly**
about the **Father**. 26 When that day
comes, you will ask him **in my name**; and
I do not say that I will ask him on your
behalf, 27 for the **Father** himself **loves**
you. He loves you because you **love** me
and have **believed** that I came from God.

alone [2] 14.18; Acts 4.12
authority 12.49; 17.2
believe [4] 14.1; 17.8
birth Lk 2.7; Acts 14.8
complete 15.11; 19.28
disciple [2] 15.8; 18.1
faith Lk 22.32; 20.31
Father (2) (God) [10] 15.1; 17.1
forget Lk 12.6; 1 Cor 2.2
give up 10.17; Acts 18.9
glad [4] 14.28; Acts 2.26
glory 15.8; 17.1
happy [2] 13.17; 20.29
heart [2] 13.2; 17.13
Helper (2) 15.26
judge [3] 12.31; 19.13
love [2] 15.9; 17.23
name (2) (name of God, of Jesus) [3] 15.16; 17.11
need 14.8; Acts 2.45
peace 14.27; 20.19
plain (1) [2] 11.14; Acts 2.29
prove 8.13; Acts 1.3
question [2] 8.7; 18.19
remember 15.18; 19.10
reveal 15.26; Acts 19.18
right (1) [2] 13.13; 18.23
sad [4] Lk 24.17; 21.17
scatter 11.52; Acts 5.36
serve 12.2; Acts 1.25
Spirit (1) (God's Spirit) [2] 15.26; 20.22
suffer [3] 12.27; 18.11
synagogue 12.42; 18.20
truth [5] 15.26; 17.17
turn 13.18; 20.14
unite 15.4; 1 Cor 1.10

weep 11.31; Rom 12.15
world [8] 15.18; 17.5
wrong [4] Lk 23.41; 18.23

[f] the Father will give you whatever you ask him for in my name; *some manuscripts have* if you ask the Father for anything, he will give it to you in my name.

15.25: Ps 35.19, 69.4

28 I did come from the Father, and I came
into the world; and now I am leaving the
world and going to the Father."
29 Then his disciples said to him,
"Now you are speaking plainly, without
using figures of speech. 30 We know now
that you know everything; you do not
need someone to ask you questions. This
makes us believe that you came from
God."
31 Jesus answered them, "Do you believe now? 32 The time is coming, and is
already here, when all of you will be
scattered, each one to his own home, and
I will be left all alone. But I am not really
alone, because the Father is with me. 33 I
have told you this so that you will have
peace by being united to me. The world
will make you suffer. But be brave! I
have defeated the world!"

Jesus Prays for His Disciples

17 After Jesus finished saying this,
he looked up to heaven and said,
"Father, the hour has come. Give glory
to your Son, so that the Son may give
glory to you. 2 For you gave him
authority over all mankind, so that he
might give eternal life to all those you
gave him. 3 And eternal life means knowing you, the only true God, and knowing
Jesus Christ, whom you sent. 4 I have
shown your glory on earth; I have finished the work you gave me to do.
5 Father! Give me glory in your presence
now, the same glory I had with you before the world was made.
6 "I have made you known to those
you gave me out of the world. They belonged to you, and you gave them to me.
They have obeyed your word, 7 and now
they know that everything you gave me
comes from you. 8 I gave them the message that you gave me, and they received it; they know that it is true that I
came from you, and they believe that
you sent me.
9 "I pray for them. I do not pray for
the world but for those you gave me, for
they belong to you. 10 All I have is yours,
and all you have is mine; and my glory is
shown through them. 11 And now I am
coming to you; I am no longer in the
world, but they are in the world. Holy
Father! Keep them safe by the power of
your name, the name you gave me,[g] so
that they may be one just as you and I
are one. 12 While I was with them, I kept
them safe by the power of your name,
the name you gave me.[h] I protected
them, and not one of them was lost, except the man who was bound to be lost—
so that the scripture might come true.
13 And now I am coming to you, and I say
these things in the world so that they
might have my joy in their hearts in all
its fullness. 14 I gave them your message,
and the world hated them, because they
do not belong to the world, just as I do
not belong to the world. 15 I do not ask
you to take them out of the world, but I
do ask you to keep them safe from the
Evil One. 16 Just as I do not belong to the
world, they do not belong to the world.
17 Dedicate them to yourself by means of
the truth; your word is truth. 18 I sent
them into the world, just as you sent me
into the world. 19 And for their sake I
dedicate myself to you, in order that
they, too, may be truly dedicated to you.
20 "I pray not only for them, but also
for those who believe in me because of
their message. 21 I pray that they may all
be one. Father! May they be in us, just as
you are in me and I am in you. May they
be one, so that the world will believe that
you sent me. 22 I gave them the same
glory you gave me, so that they may be
one, just as you and I are one: 23 I in them
and you in me, so that they may be completely one, in order that the world may
know that you sent me and that you love
them as you love me.
24 "Father! You have given them to
me, and I want them to be with me
where I am, so that they may see my
glory, the glory you gave me; for you
loved me before the world was made.
25 Righteous Father! The world does not
know you, but I know you, and these
know that you sent me. 26 I made you
known to them, and I will continue to do
so, in order that the love you have for me
may be in them, and so that I also may
be in them."

authority 16.13; 19.10
believe [3] 16.9; 19.35
dedicate [3] Lk 2.23; Acts 22.3
eternal [2] 12.25; Acts 13.46
Evil One Mt 13.19; Eph 6.16
Father (2) (God) [6] 16.3; 18.9
glory [8] 16.14; 21.19
hate 15.18; Rom 1.30
heart 16.6; Acts 2.46
heaven 12.28; Acts 1.2
holy 6.69; 19.31
joy 15.11; 20.20
life (1) [2] 15.13; 20.31
love [3] 16.27; 19.26
mankind 1.4; Acts 15.17
means 11.4; Acts 3.12
message [3] 12.38; Acts 1.21
name (2) (name of God, of Jesus) [2] 16.23; Acts 2.38
obey 15.10; Acts 3.22
power [2] 14.30; Acts 1.2
pray [4] Lk 22.32; Acts 1.14
presence 12.37; 20.30
protect Zech 12.8; 1 Cor 10.1
righteous Lk 7.29; Acts 7.52
safe [3] Lk 21.36; Acts 7.10
sake 12.30; Acts 5.41
scripture 13.18; 19.24
Son of God [2] 14.13; 19.7
true [4] 15.25; 18.9
truth [2] 16.7; 18.37
word (1) [2] 15.7; 18.32
world [15] 16.8; 18.36

The Arrest of Jesus
(Matt. 26.47–56; Mark 14.43–50;
Luke 22.47–53)

18 After Jesus had said this prayer,
he left with his disciples and
went across the brook called Kidron.
There was a garden in that place, and
Jesus and his disciples went in. 2 Judas,
the traitor, knew where it was, because
many times Jesus had met there with his
disciples. 3 So Judas went to the garden,

accuse 8.6; Acts 19.38
advice Hos 10.6; Acts 5.39
arrest 11.57; Acts 1.16
authorities [3] 13.33; 19.31
bind [2] Lk 13.16; 21.18
chief priests [2] 12.10; 19.6

[g] Keep them safe by the power of your name, the name you gave me; *some manuscripts have* By the power of your name keep safe those you have given me.
[h] I kept them safe by the power of your name, the name you gave me; *some manuscripts have* By the power of your name I kept safe those you have given me.

17.12: Ps 41.9; Jn 13.18

clean 15.2; Acts 10.15
commit 8.3; Acts 18.14
condemn 8.10; 19.4
crime Lk 23.14; Acts 16.37
cup 4.9; 1 Cor 10.16
custom Lk 1.9; 19.40
dare Lk 20.40; 21.12
death (1) 12.33; Acts 1.3
death (3) (to death) 8.5; 19.41
deny Lk 22.57; Acts 4.16
disciple [9] 16.17; 19.26
Father (2) (God) [2] 17.1; 20.17
follower 7.3; 19.38
free [2] 10.18; 19.10
High Priest [8] 11.49; Acts 4.6
Jew [7] 13.33; 19.3
keep from Lk 8.12; Acts 4.17
Kingdom (1) (of God) [3] 3.3; Acts 1.3
law 15.25; 19.7
Passover [2] 13.1; 19.14
Pharisees 12.19; Acts 5.34
prayer Lk 22.45; Acts 2.42
prison 3.24; Acts 2.24
purpose 2.6; Acts 9.21
question [4] 16.19; Acts 4.9
reason 15.25; 19.4
right (1) 16.8; Acts 4.19
right (2) Lk 23.33; 21.6
secret 7.10; 19.38
servant 15.15; Acts 2.18
slave [3] 15.20; Acts 7.6
strike Lk 22.50; Acts 12.23
suffer 16.21; Acts 3.18
synagogue 16.2; Acts 6.9
teach [2] 15.3; Acts 1.1
Temple (1) (of God) 11.48; Acts 2.46
traitor [2] Lk 6.16; Rev 21.8
true [2] 17.3; 19.24
truth [3] 17.17; 19.35
try (2) Lk 22.28; Acts 12.4
word (1) [2] 17.6; 19.13
world [3] 17.5; 21.25
wrong 16.8; Acts 18.14

taking with him a group of Roman soldiers, and some temple guards sent by the **chief priests** and the **Pharisees**; they were armed and carried lanterns and torches. 4 Jesus knew everything that was going to happen to him, so he stepped forward and asked them, "Who is it you are looking for?"

5 "Jesus of Nazareth," they answered.

"I am he," he said.

Judas, the **traitor**, was standing there with them. 6 When Jesus said to them, "I am he," they moved back and fell to the ground. 7 Again Jesus asked them, "Who is it you are looking for?"

"Jesus of Nazareth," they said.

8 "I have already told you that I am he," Jesus said. "If, then, you are looking for me, let these others go." 9 (He said this so that what he had said might come **true**: "**Father**, I have not lost even one of those you gave me.")

10 Simon Peter, who had a sword, drew it and **struck** the **High Priest's slave**, cutting off his **right** ear. The name of the **slave** was Malchus. 11 Jesus said to Peter, "Put your sword back in its place! Do you think that I will not drink the **cup of suffering** which **my Father** has given me?"

Jesus before Annas

12 Then the Roman soldiers with their commanding officer and the **Jewish** guards **arrested** Jesus, **bound** him, 13 and took him first to Annas. He was the father-in-law of Caiaphas, who was **High Priest** that year. 14 It was Caiaphas who had **advised** the **Jewish authorities** that it was better that one man should die for all the people.

Peter Denies Jesus

(Matt. 26.69–70; Mark 14.66–68; Luke 22.55–57)

15 Simon Peter and another **disciple** followed Jesus. That other **disciple** was well known to the **High Priest**, so he went with Jesus into the courtyard of the **High Priest's** house, 16 while Peter stayed outside by the gate. Then the other **disciple** went back out, spoke to the girl at the gate, and brought Peter inside. 17 The girl at the gate said to Peter, "Aren't you also one of the **disciples** of that man?"

"No, I am not," answered Peter.

18 It was cold, so the **servants** and guards had built a charcoal fire and were standing round it, warming themselves. So Peter went over and stood with them, warming himself.

The High Priest Questions Jesus

(Matt. 26.59–66; Mark 14.55–64; Luke 22.66–71)

19 The **High Priest questioned** Jesus about his **disciples** and about his **teaching**. 20 Jesus answered, "I have always spoken publicly to everyone; all my **teaching** was done in the **synagogues** and in the **Temple**, where all the people come together. I have never said anything in **secret**. 21 Why, then, do you **question** me? **Question** the people who heard me. Ask them what I told them—they know what I said."

22 When Jesus said this, one of the guards there slapped him and said, "How **dare** you talk like that to the **High Priest**!"

23 Jesus answered him, "If I have said anything **wrong**, tell everyone here what it was. But if I am **right** in what I have said, why do you hit me?"

24 Then Annas sent him, still **bound**, to Caiaphas the **High Priest**.

Peter Denies Jesus Again

(Matt. 26.71–75; Mark 14.69–72; Luke 22.58–62)

25 Peter was still standing there keeping himself warm. So the others said to him, "Aren't you also one of the **disciples** of that man?"

But Peter **denied** it. "No, I am not," he said.

26 One of the **High Priest's slaves**, a relative of the man whose ear Peter had cut off, spoke up. "Didn't I see you with him in the garden?" he asked.

27 Again Peter said "No"—and at once a cock crowed.

Jesus is Brought Before Pilate

(Matt. 27.1–2, 11–14; Mark 15.1–5; Luke 23.1–5)

28 Early in the morning Jesus was taken from Caiaphas' house to the governor's palace. The **Jewish authorities** did not go inside the palace, for they wanted to keep themselves ritually **clean**, in order to be able to eat the **Passover** meal. 29 So Pilate went outside to them and asked, "What do you **accuse** this man of?"

30 Their answer was, "We would not have brought him to you if he had not **committed** a **crime**."

31 Pilate said to them, "Then you yourselves take him and **try** him according to your own **law**."

They replied, "We are not allowed to put anyone **to death**." 32 (This happened in order to make the **words** of Jesus

18.11: Mt 26.39; Mk 14.36; Lk 22.42 **18.14:** Jn 11.49–50 **18.32:** Jn 3.14, 12.32

come **true**, the **words** he used when he indicated the kind of **death** he would die.)
33 Pilate went back into the palace
and called Jesus. "Are you the **King of**
the Jews?" he asked him.
34 Jesus answered, "Does this **ques-**
tion come from you or have others told
you about me?"
35 Pilate replied, "Do you think I am a
Jew? It was your own people and the
chief priests who handed you over to me.
What have you done?"
36 Jesus said, "My **kingdom** does not
belong to **this world**; if my **kingdom** belonged to **this world**, my **followers** would
fight to **keep me from** being handed over
to the **Jewish authorities**. No, my **king-**
dom does not belong here!"
37 So Pilate asked him, "Are you a
king, then?"
Jesus answered, "You say that I am a
king. I was born and came into the **world**
for this one **purpose**, to speak about the
truth. Whoever belongs to the **truth** listens to me."
38 "And what is **truth**?" Pilate asked.

Jesus Is Sentenced to Death
(Matt. 27.15–31; Mark 15.6–20;
Luke 23.13–25)

Then Pilate went back outside to the
people and said to them, "I cannot find
any **reason** to **condemn** him. 39 But according to the **custom** you have, I always
set free a **prisoner** for you during the
Passover. Do you want me to **set free** for
you the **King of the Jews**?"
40 They answered him with a shout,
"No, not him! We want Barabbas!"
(Barabbas was a bandit.)

19 Then Pilate took Jesus and had
him whipped. 2 The soldiers
made a **crown** out of thorny branches
and put it on his head; then they put a
purple robe on him 3 and came to him
and said, "Long live the **King of the**
Jews!" And they went up and slapped
him.
4 Pilate went out once more and said
to the crowd, "Look, I will bring him out
here to you to let you see that I cannot
find any **reason** to **condemn** him." 5 So
Jesus came out, wearing the **crown** of
thorns and the purple robe. Pilate said to
them, "Look! Here is the man!"
6 When the **chief priests** and the
temple guards saw him, they shouted,
"**Crucify** him! **Crucify** him!"
Pilate said to them, "You take him,
then, and **crucify** him. I find no **reason** to
condemn him."
7 The crowd answered back, "We
have a **law** that says he ought to die, because he **claimed** to be the **Son of God**."
8 When Pilate heard this, he was even
more **afraid**. 9 He went back into the
palace and asked Jesus, "Where do you
come from?"
But Jesus did not answer. 10 Pilate said
to him, "You will not speak to me? **Re-**
member, I have the **authority** to **set you**
free and also to have you **crucified**."
11 Jesus answered, "You have **author-**
ity over me only because it was given to
you by God. So the man who handed me
over to you is **guilty** of a **worse** sin."
12 When Pilate heard this, he tried to
find a way to **set Jesus free**. But the
crowd shouted back, "If you **set him free**,
that means that you are not the Emperor's **friend**! Anyone who **claims** to be
a king is a **rebel** against the Emperor!"
13 When Pilate heard these **words**, he
took Jesus outside and sat down on the
judge's seat in the place called "The
Stone Pavement." (In **Hebrew** the name
is "Gabbatha.") 14 It was then almost
noon of the day before the **Passover**.
Pilate said to the people, "Here is your
king!"
15 They shouted back, "Kill him! Kill
him! **Crucify** him!"
Pilate asked them, "Do you want me to
crucify your king?"
The **chief priests** answered, "The only
king we have is the Emperor!"
16 Then Pilate handed Jesus over to
them to be **crucified**.

Jesus Is Crucified
(Matt. 27.32–44; Mark 15.21–32;
Luke 23.26–43)

So they took charge of Jesus. 17 He
went out, carrying his **cross**, and came to
"The Place of the Skull," as it is called.
(In **Hebrew** it is called "Golgotha.")
18 There they **crucified** him; and they also
crucified two other men, one on each
side, with Jesus between them. 19 Pilate
wrote a notice and had it put on the
cross. "Jesus of Nazareth, the **King of the**
Jews," is what he wrote. 20 Many people
read it, because the place where Jesus
was **crucified** was not far from the city.
The notice was written in **Hebrew**, Latin,
and Greek. 21 The **chief priests** said to
Pilate, "Do not write 'The **King of the**
Jews,' but rather, 'This man said, **I am**
the King of the Jews.' "
22 Pilate answered, "What I have
written stays written."
23 After the soldiers had **crucified**
Jesus, they took his clothes and divided
them into four parts, one part for each
soldier. They also took the robe, which

afraid [2] 14.27; 20.19
authorities [2] 18.14; 20.19
authority [2] 17.2; Acts 1.7
believe 17.8; 20.8
blood 6.53; Acts 1.19
body [7] 11.52; 20.12
bow (2) Lk 24.5; Acts 10.25
chief priests [3] 18.3; Acts 4.23
claim [2] 9.41; Acts 5.36
complete 16.24; Acts 11.4
condemn [2] 18.38; Acts 13.27
cross (1) [5] Lk 23.26; Acts 5.30
crown [2] Mk 15.17; 1 Cor 9.25
crucify [13] Lk 24.7; Acts 2.23
custom 18.39; Acts 6.14
dead 11.14; Acts 2.27
death (3) (to death) 18.31; Acts 5.33
disciple [3] 18.1; 20.2
follower 18.36; 21.23
free [3] 18.39; Acts 2.24

friend 15.13; Acts 10.24
guilty 15.22; Acts 16.37
Hebrew [3] 5.2; 20.16
holy 17.11; Acts 3.14
hyssop 1 Kgs 4.33; Heb 9.19
I am 15.1; Acts 7.32
Jew [7] 18.12; 20.19
judge 16.8; Acts 4.19
law 18.31; Acts 6.13
love 17.23; 20.2
new 13.34; Acts 3.21
one another 15.12; Acts 2.44
Passover 18.28; Acts 12.4
reason [2] 18.38; Acts 13.28
rebel Mk 15.7; Rom 10.21
remember 16.4; Acts 5.36
request Dan 6.7; 2 Cor 8.17
Sabbath [3] 9.14; Acts 13.14
scripture [4] 17.12; 20.9
secret 18.20; Acts 16.37
Son of God 17.1; 20.31
tomb [2] 11.38; 20.1
true [4] 18.9; 21.24
truth 18.37; 21.18
word (1) 18.32; Acts 2.22
worse 5.14; 2 Cor 12.13

was made of one piece of woven cloth
without any seams in it. 24 The soldiers
said to **one another**, "Let's not tear it;
let's throw dice to see who will get it."
This happened in order to make the
scripture come **true**:

"They divided my clothes among
themselves
and gambled for my robe."

And this is what the soldiers did.
25 Standing close to Jesus' **cross** were
his mother, his mother's sister, Mary the
wife of Clopas, and Mary Magdalene.
26 Jesus saw his mother and the **disciple**
he **loved** standing there; so he said to his
mother, "He is your son."
27 Then he said to the **disciple**, "She is
your mother." From that time the **disciple** took her to live in his home.

The Death of Jesus
(Matt. 27.45–56; Mark 15.33–41;
Luke 23.44–49)

28 Jesus knew that by now everything
had been **completed**; and in order to
make the **scripture** come **true**, he said, "I
am thirsty."
29 A bowl was there, full of cheap
wine; so a sponge was soaked in the
wine, put on a stalk of **hyssop**, and lifted
up to his lips. 30 Jesus drank the wine and
said, "It is finished!"
Then he **bowed** his head and died.

Jesus' Side Is Pierced

31 Then the **Jewish authorities** asked
Pilate to allow them to break the legs of
the men who had been **crucified**, and to
take the **bodies** down from the **crosses**.
They **requested** this because it was Friday, and they did not want the **bodies** to
stay on the **crosses** on the **Sabbath**, since
the coming **Sabbath** was especially **holy**.
32 So the soldiers went and broke the legs
of the first man and then of the other
man who had been **crucified** with Jesus.
33 But when they came to Jesus, they saw
that he was already **dead**, so they did not
break his legs. 34 One of the soldiers, however, plunged his spear into Jesus' side,
and at once **blood** and water poured out.
35 (The one who saw this happen has
spoken of it, so that you also may **believe**.[i] What he said is **true**, and he knows
that he speaks the **truth**.) 36 This was
done to make the **scripture** come **true**:
"Not one of his bones will be broken."
37 And there is another **scripture** that
says, "People will look at him whom they
pierced."

The Burial of Jesus
(Matt. 27.57–61; Mark 15.42–47;
Luke 23.50–56)

38 After this, Joseph, who was from
the town of Arimathea, asked Pilate if he
could take Jesus' **body**. (Joseph was a **follower** of Jesus, but in **secret**, because he
was **afraid** of the **Jewish authorities**.)
Pilate told him he could have the **body**,
so Joseph went and took it away.
39 Nicodemus, who at first had gone to
see Jesus at night, went with Joseph,
taking with him about thirty kilogrammes of spices, a mixture of myrrh
and aloes. 40 The two men took Jesus'
body and wrapped it in linen with the
spices according to the **Jewish custom** of
preparing a **body** for burial. 41 There was
a garden in the place where Jesus had
been put **to death**, and in it there was a
new tomb where no one had ever been
buried. 42 Since it was the day before the
Sabbath and because the **tomb** was close
by, they placed Jesus' **body** there.

The Empty Tomb
(Matt. 28.1–8; Mark 16.1–8; Luke 24.1–12)

20 Early on Sunday morning,
while it was still **dark**, Mary
Magdalene went to the **tomb** and saw
that the stone had been taken away from
the entrance. 2 She went running to
Simon Peter and the other **disciple**,
whom Jesus **loved**, and told them, "They
have taken the Lord from the **tomb**, and
we don't know where they have put
him!"
3 Then Peter and the other **disciple**
went to the **tomb**. 4 The two of them were
running, but the other **disciple** ran faster
than Peter and reached the **tomb** first.
5 He bent over and saw the linen wrappings, but he did not go in. 6 Behind him
came Simon Peter, and he went straight
into the **tomb**. He saw the linen wrappings lying there 7 and the cloth which
had been round Jesus' head. It was not lying with the linen wrappings but was
rolled up by itself. 8 Then the other **disciple**, who had reached the **tomb** first,
also went in; he saw and **believed**.
9 (They still did not **understand** the **scripture** which said that he must **rise from
death**.) 10 Then the **disciples** went back
home.

Jesus Appears to Mary Magdalene
(Matt. 28.9–10; Mark 16.9–11)

11 Mary stood crying outside the
tomb. While she was still crying, she bent

afraid 19.8; Acts 5.26
angel 12.29; Acts 5.19
authorities 19.31; Acts 3.13
believe [6] 19.35; Acts 2.41
body 19.31; Acts 2.31
dark 12.35; Acts 2.20
death (2) (from death) 12.1; 21.14
disciple [12] 19.26; 21.1
doubt Lk 24.38; Acts 1.3
faith 16.1; Acts 3.16
Father (2) (God) [3] 18.9; Acts 1.4
forgive [2] Lk 24.47; Acts 2.38
happy 16.21; Acts 5.41
Hebrew 19.13; Acts 21.40
Jew 19.3; Acts 2.5
joy 17.13; Acts 2.26
life (1) 17.2; Acts 2.28
love 19.26; 21.7
Messiah 12.34; Acts 2.31
miracle 12.18; Acts 2.19
peace [3] 16.33; Acts 7.26
presence 17.5; Acts 2.28
rise 13.4; 21.4
scripture 19.24; Acts 1.16
Son of God 19.7; Acts 9.20
Spirit (1) (God's Spirit) 16.13; Acts 1.2
teacher 13.13; Acts 13.1
tomb [8] 19.41; Acts 13.29
turn [2] 16.20; 21.20
understand 13.7; Acts 7.25

[i] believe; *some manuscripts have* continue to believe.

19.24: Ps 22.18 **19.28:** Ps 69.21, 22.15 **19.36:** Ex 12.46; Num 9.12; Ps 34.20 **19.37:** Zech 12.10; Rev 1.7
19.39: Jn 3.1–2

over and looked in the **tomb** 12 and saw
two **angels** there dressed in white, sitting
where the **body** of Jesus had been, one at
the head and the other at the feet.
13 "Woman, why are you crying?" they
asked her.

She answered, "They have taken my
Lord away, and I do not know where
they have put him!"

14 Then she **turned round** and saw
Jesus standing there; but she did not
know that it was Jesus. 15 "Woman, why
are you crying?" Jesus asked her. "Who
is it that you are looking for?"

She thought he was the gardener, so
she said to him, "If you took him away,
sir, tell me where you have put him, and
I will go and get him."

16 Jesus said to her, "Mary!"

She **turned** towards him and said in
Hebrew, "Rabboni!" (This means
"**Teacher**.")

17 "Do not hold on to me," Jesus told
her, "because I have not yet gone back
up to the **Father**. But go to my brothers
and tell them that I am returning to him
who is my **Father** and their Father, my
God and their God."

18 So Mary Magdalene went and told
the **disciples** that she had seen the Lord
and related to them what he had told
her.

Jesus Appears to His Disciples
(Matt. 28.16–20; Mark 16.14–18;
Luke 24.36–49)

19 It was late that Sunday evening,
and the **disciples** were gathered together
behind locked doors, because they were
afraid of the **Jewish authorities**. Then
Jesus came and stood among them.
"**Peace** be with you," he said. 20 After saying this, he showed them his hands and
his side. The **disciples** were filled with **joy**
at seeing the Lord. 21 Jesus said to them
again, "**Peace** be with you. As the **Father**
sent me, so I send you." 22 Then he
breathed on them and said, "Receive the
Holy Spirit. 23 If you **forgive** people's sins,
they are forgiven; if you do not **forgive**
them, they are not forgiven."

Jesus and Thomas

24 One of the twelve **disciples**, Thomas
(called the Twin), was not with them
when Jesus came. 25 So the other **disciples** told him, "We have seen the
Lord!"

Thomas said to them, "Unless I see the
scars of the nails in his hands and put my
finger on those scars and my hand in his
side, I will not **believe**."

26 A week later the **disciples** were together again indoors, and Thomas was
with them. The doors were locked, but
Jesus came and stood among them and
said, "**Peace** be with you." 27 Then he said
to Thomas, "Put your finger here, and
look at my hands; then stretch out your
hand and put it in my side. Stop your
doubting, and **believe**!"

28 Thomas answered him, "My Lord
and my God!"

29 Jesus said to him, "Do you **believe**
because you see me? How **happy** are
those who **believe** without seeing me!"

The Purpose of This Book

30 In his **disciples' presence** Jesus performed many other **miracles** which are
not written down in this book. 31 But these
have been written in order that you may
believe[j] that Jesus is the **Messiah**, the
Son of God, and that through your **faith** in
him you may have **life**.

Jesus Appears to Seven Disciples

21 After this, Jesus appeared once
more to his **disciples** at Lake
Tiberias. This is how it happened. 2 Simon
Peter, Thomas (called the Twin),
Nathanael (the one from Cana in
Galilee), the sons of Zebedee, and two
other **disciples** of Jesus were all together.
3 Simon Peter said to the others, "I am
going fishing."

"We will come with you," they told
him. So they went out in a boat, but all
that night they did not catch a thing. 4 As
the sun was **rising**, Jesus stood at the
water's edge, but the **disciples** did not
know that it was Jesus. 5 Then he asked
them, "Young men, haven't you caught
anything?"

"Not a thing," they answered.

6 He said to them, "Throw your net
out on the **right side** of the boat, and you
will catch some." So they threw the net
out and could not pull it back in, because
they had caught so many fish.

7 The **disciple** whom Jesus **loved** said
to Peter, "It is the Lord!" When Peter
heard that it was the Lord, he wrapped
his outer garment round him (for he had
taken his clothes off) and jumped into the
water. 8 The other **disciples** came to
shore in the boat, pulling the net full of
fish. They were not very far from land,
about a hundred metres away. 9 When
they stepped ashore, they saw a charcoal
fire there with fish on it and some **bread**.

betray 13.2; Acts 7.52
bind 18.12; Acts 21.33
bread [2] 13.26; Acts 20.11
care [3] 12.6; Acts 7.20
dare 18.22; Acts 5.13
death (2) (from death) 20.9; Acts 2.24
disciple [10] 20.2; Acts 6.1
follower 19.38; Acts 5.36
glory 17.1; Acts 2.20
lamb 1.29; Acts 8.32
love [9] 20.2; Rom 1.7
raise 12.1; Acts 2.24
right (2) 18.10; Acts 2.33
rise 20.9; Acts 4.2
sad 16.6; Acts 20.38
sheep [2] 10.2; Acts 8.32
true 19.24; Acts 1.16
truth 19.35; Acts 13.10
turn 20.14; Acts 2.20
who 11.27; Acts 9.5
world 18.36; Acts 2.5

[j] believe; *some manuscripts have* continue to believe.

20.23: Mt 16.19, 18.18 **21.3:** Lk 5.5 **21.6:** Lk 5.6

10 Then Jesus said to them, "Bring some
of the fish you have just caught."
11 Simon Peter went aboard and
dragged the net ashore full of big fish, a
hundred and fifty-three in all; even
though there were so many, still the net
did not tear. 12 Jesus said to them, "Come
and eat." None of the **disciples dared** ask
him, "**Who are you**?" because they knew
it was the Lord. 13 So Jesus went over,
took the **bread**, and gave it to them; he
did the same with the fish.
14 This, then, was the third time Jesus
appeared to the **disciples** after he was
raised from death.

Jesus and Peter

15 After they had eaten, Jesus said to
Simon Peter, "Simon son of John, do you
love me more than these others do?"
"Yes, Lord," he answered, "you know
that I **love** you."
Jesus said to him, "Take **care** of my
lambs." 16 A second time Jesus said to
him, "Simon son of John, do you **love**
me?"
"Yes, Lord," he answered, "you know
that I **love** you."
Jesus said to him, "Take **care** of my
sheep." 17 A third time Jesus said, "Simon
son of John, do you **love me**?"
Peter was **sad** because Jesus asked
him the third time, "Do you **love me**?" so
he said to him, "Lord, you know everything; you know that I **love** you!"
Jesus said to him, "Take **care** of my
sheep. 18 I am telling you the **truth**: when
you were young, you used to get ready
and go anywhere you wanted to; but
when you are old, you will stretch out
your hands and someone else will **bind**
you and take you where you don't want
to go." 19 (In saying this, Jesus was indicating the way in which Peter would
die and bring **glory** to God.) Then Jesus
said to him, "Follow me!"

Jesus and the Other Disciple

20 Peter **turned round** and saw behind
him that other **disciple**, whom Jesus
loved—the one who had leaned close to
Jesus at the meal and had asked, "Lord,
who is going to **betray** you?" 21 When
Peter saw him, he asked Jesus, "Lord,
what about this man?"
22 Jesus answered him, "If I want him
to live until I come, what is that to you?
Follow me!"
23 So a report spread among the **followers** of Jesus that this **disciple** would
not die. But Jesus did not say that he
would not die; he said, "If I want him to
live until I come, what is that to you?"
24 He is the **disciple** who spoke of
these things, the one who also wrote
them down; and we know that what he
said is **true**.

Conclusion

25 Now, there are many other things
that Jesus did. If they were all written
down one by one, I suppose that the
whole **world** could not hold the books
that would be written.

21.20: Jn 13.25

THE ACTS
OF THE APOSTLES

INTRODUCTION

The Acts of the Apostles is a continuation of *The Gospel according to Luke.* Its chief purpose is to tell how Jesus' early followers, led by the Holy Spirit, spread the Good News about him "in Jerusalem, in all Judaea and Samaria, and to the ends of the earth" (1.8). It is the story of the Christian movement as it began among the Jewish people and went on to become a faith for the whole world. The writer was also concerned to reassure his readers that the Christians were not a subversive political threat to the Roman Empire, and that the Christian faith was the fulfilment of the Jewish religion.

Acts may be divided into three principal parts, reflecting the ever widening area in which the Good News about Jesus was proclaimed and the church established: (1) the beginning of the Christian movement in Jerusalem following the ascension of Jesus; (2) expansion into other parts of Palestine; and (3) further expansion, into the Mediterranean world as far as Rome.

An important feature of *Acts* is the activity of the Holy Spirit, who comes with power upon the believers in Jerusalem on the day of Pentecost and continues to guide and strengthen the church and its leaders throughout the events reported in the book. The early Christian message is summarized in a number of sermons, and the events recorded in *Acts* show the power of this message in the lives of the believers and in the fellowship of the church.

Outline of Contents

---

act Jn 8.4; Rom 1.26
alive Lk 24.5; 9.39
apostle [5] Lk 24.10; 2.14
arrest Jn 18.12; 4.3
authority Jn 19.10; 2.22
baptize [3] Jn 10.40; 2.38
believer Mk 16.17; 2.1
blood Jn 19.34; 2.19
choose [5] Jn 15.16; 3.20
cloud Lk 21.27; 1 Cor 10.1
dear Jn 11.3; 15.25
death (1) [2] Jn 18.32; 2.24
doubt Jn 20.27; Rom 4.20
evil Jn 5.29; 8.22
Father (2) (God) [2] Jn 20.17; 2.33
gift [2] Lk 21.1; 2.33
guide Lk 1.79; Rom 2.19
heaven [5] Jn 17.1; 2.34

1 **Dear** Theophilus:
In my first book I wrote about all
the things that Jesus did and **taught** from
the time he began his work 2 until the day
he was taken up to **heaven**. Before he
was taken up, he gave instructions by the
power of the Holy Spirit to the men he
had **chosen** as his **apostles**. 3 For forty
days after his **death** he appeared to them
many times in ways that **proved** beyond
doubt that he was **alive**. They saw him,
and he talked with them about the **Kingdom of God**. 4 And when they came together,[a] he gave them this order: "Do
not leave Jerusalem, but wait for the **gift**
I told you about, the **gift my Father promised**. 5 John **baptized** with water, but in
a few days you will be **baptized** with the
Holy Spirit."

Jesus Is Taken up to Heaven

6 When the **apostles** met together with
Jesus, they asked him, "Lord, will you at
this time give the **Kingdom** back to
Israel?"
7 Jesus said to them, "The times and
occasions are set by **my Father's** own
authority, and it is not for you to know
when they will be. 8 But when the **Holy
Spirit** comes upon you, you will be filled
with **power**, and you will be **witnesses** for
me in Jerusalem, in all Judaea and
Samaria, and to the ends of the earth."
9 After saying this, he was taken up to
heaven as they **watched** him, and a **cloud**
hid him from their **sight**.
10 They still had their eyes fixed on
the sky as he went away, when two men
dressed in white suddenly stood beside

Kingdom (1) (of God) [2] Jn 18.36; 8.12
lot (1) Lk 1.9
message Jn 17.8; 2.17
power [2] Jn 17.11; 2.24
pray [2] Jn 17.9; 4.31
preach Lk 24.47; 5.42
predict Lk 12.56; 11.28
promise Jn 9.24; 2.30
prove Jn 16.8; 2.22
psalm Lk 24.44; 13.32
resurrection Jn 11.25; 2.31
scripture Jn 20.9; 4.11
serve Jn 16.2; 7.7
service Lk 1.8; 15.26
sight Jn 11.37; 4.19
Spirit (1) (God's Spirit) [4] Jn 20.22; 2.4
teach Jn 18.19; 4.2
true Jn 21.24; 3.18

[a] when they came together; *or* while he was staying with them; *or* while he was eating with them.

1.1: Lk 1.1-4 **1.4:** Lk 24.49 **1.5:** Mt 3.11; Mk 1.8; Lk 3.16; Jn 1.33 **1.8:** Mt 28.19; Mk 16.15; Lk 24.47-48 **1.9:** Mk 16.19; Lk 24.50-51

watch Lk 23.35; 5.23
witness [2] Jn 8.17; 2.32

them 11 and said, "Galileans, why are you standing there looking up at the sky? This Jesus, who was taken from you into **heaven**, will come back in the same way that you saw him go to **heaven**."

Judas' Successor

12 Then the **apostles** went back to Jerusalem from the Mount of Olives, which is about a kilometre away from the city. 13 They entered the city and went up to the room where they were staying: Peter, John, James and Andrew, Philip and Thomas, Bartholomew and Matthew, James son of Alphaeus, Simon the Patriot, and Judas son of James. 14 They gathered frequently to **pray** as a group, together with the women and with Mary the mother of Jesus and with his brothers.

15 A few days later there was a meeting of the **believers**, about a hundred and twenty in all, and Peter stood up to speak. 16 "My brothers," he said, "the **scripture** had to come **true** in which the **Holy Spirit**, speaking through David, made a **prediction** about Judas, who was the **guide** for those who **arrested** Jesus. 17 Judas was a member of our group, for he had been **chosen** to have a part in our work."

18 (With the money that Judas got for his **evil act** he bought a field, where he fell to his **death**; he burst open and all his bowels spilt out. 19 All the people living in Jerusalem heard about it, and so in their own language they call that field Akeldama, which means **"Field of Blood."**)

20 "For it is written in the book of **Psalms**,

'May his house become empty;
may no one live in it.'

It is also written,

'May someone else take his place of
service.'

21–22 "So then, someone must join us as a **witness** to the **resurrection** of the Lord Jesus. He must be one of the men who were in our group during the whole time that the Lord Jesus travelled about with us, beginning from the time John **preached** his **message** of **baptism**[b] until the day Jesus was taken up from us to **heaven**."

23 So they proposed two men: Joseph, who was called Barsabbas (also known as Justus), and Matthias. 24 Then they **prayed**, "Lord, you know the thoughts of everyone, so show us which of these two you have **chosen** 25 to **serve** as an **apostle** in the place of Judas, who left to go to the place where he belongs." 26 Then they drew **lots** to **choose** between the two men, and the one **chosen** was Matthias, who was added to the group of eleven **apostles**.

The Coming of the Holy Spirit

2 When the day of **Pentecost** came, all the **believers** were gathered together in one place. 2 Suddenly there was a noise from the sky which sounded like a **strong** wind blowing, and it filled the whole house where they were sitting. 3 Then they saw what looked like tongues of fire which spread out and touched each person there. 4 They were all filled with the **Holy Spirit** and began to talk in other languages, as the **Spirit** enabled them to speak.

5 There were **Jews** living in Jerusalem, **religious** men who had come from every country in the **world**. 6 When they heard this noise, a large crowd gathered. They were all excited, because each one of them heard the **believers** speaking in his own language. 7 In **amazement** and **wonder** they exclaimed, "These people who are talking like this are Galileans! 8 How is it, then, that all of us hear them speaking in our own native languages? 9 We are from Parthia, Media, and Elam; from Mesopotamia, Judaea, and Cappadocia; from Pontus and Asia, 10 from Phrygia and Pamphylia, from Egypt and the regions of Libya near Cyrene. Some of us are from Rome, 11 both **Jews** and **Gentiles** converted to **Judaism**, and some of us are from Crete and Arabia—yet all of us hear them speaking in our own languages about the great things that God has done!" 12 **Amazed** and confused, they kept asking **each other**, "What does this mean?"

13 But others made fun of the **believers**, saying, "These people are drunk!"

Peter's Message

14 Then Peter stood up with the other eleven **apostles** and in a loud voice began to speak to the crowd: **"Fellow-Jews** and all of you who live in Jerusalem, listen to me and let me tell you what this means. 15 These people are not drunk, as you suppose; it is only nine o'clock in the morning. 16 Instead, this is what the **prophet** Joel spoke about:

abandon [2] Lk 13.35; 21.21
amaze [2] Jn 5.20; 3.10
apostle [4] 1.2; 4.2
assure Lk 18.29; Rom 9.1
authority 1.7; 9.14
awe Hab 3.2; 2 Cor 7.1
baptize [2] 1.5; 8.12
believe Jn 20.8; 4.4
believer [4] 1.15; 4.24
blood [2] 1.19; 15.20
body Jn 20.12; 5.6
clear Jn 1.20; 10.3
crucify [2] Jn 19.6; 4.10
dark Jn 20.1; 13.11
Day of the Lord Lk 21.34; Rom 2.5
dead [2] Jn 19.33; 4.2
death (1) 1.3; 5.28
death (2) (from death) [2] Jn 21.14; 3.15
divine Ezek 28.2; 3.13
dream Mt 27.19
each other Lk 24.14; 26.31
enemy Lk 23.12; 13.10
enjoy Jn 5.35; Rom 15.24
faithful Lk 19.17; 11.23
Father (2) (God) 1.4; 13.32
fellowship [2] Mic 6.8; Rom 6.10
fellowship meal 20.7
footstool Lk 20.43; 7.49
forgive Jn 20.23; 3.19
free Jn 19.10; 3.13
Gentile Lk 18.32; 4.25
gift [2] 1.4; 5.32
glad [2] Jn 16.20; 11.23
glory Jn 21.19; 3.13
grave [3] Jn 12.17; 7.16
heart Jn 17.13; 4.32
heaven 1.2; 3.21
help Jn 12.2; 3.7
hope Jn 5.45; 23.6
humble Lk 18.14; 20.19
impossible Lk 18.27; 4.21
Jew [3] Jn 20.19; 4.5
joy [2] Jn 20.20; 8.8
Judaism 6.5
last (2) Jn 12.48; 7.18
learn Jn 7.52; 4.13
life (1) Jn 20.31; 3.2
message [3] 1.21; 3.24
Messiah [2] Jn 20.31; 3.18
miracle [3] Jn 20.30; 4.16
mortal Dan 8.17; Rom 1.23

[b] John preached his message of baptism; *or* John baptized him.

1.13: Mt 10.2–4; Mk 3.16–19; Lk 6.14–16 **1.18–19:** Mt 27.3–8 **1.20:** Ps 69.25, 109.8
1.22: Mt 3.16; Mk 1.9, 16.19; Lk 3.21, 24.51 **2.1:** Lev 23.15–21; Deut 16.9–11

name (2) (name of God, of Jesus) Jn 17.11; 3.6
need Jn 16.30; 4.34
one another Jn 19.24; 4.32
Pentecost 20.16
plain (1) Jn 16.25; Rom 1.19
plan Jn 12.10; 5.38
possess Mt 25.34; Rom 8.17
power 1.2; 3.12
praise Jn 12.13; 3.8
prayer Jn 18.1; 3.1
presence Jn 20.30; 3.13
prison Jn 18.39; 5.19
proclaim [2] Lk 9.60; 4.31
promise [3] 1.4; 3.25
prophet [2] Jn 12.38; 3.18
prove 1.3; 4.2
punish Jn 3.36; 4.21
raise [3] Jn 21.14; 3.15
religion Jn 5.1; 10.2
resurrection 1.21; 4.33
right (2) [2] Jn 21.6; 3.7
save [3] Jn 12.47; 4.12
servant [2] Jn 18.18; 3.13
share [2] Jn 13.18; 3.25
Spirit (1) (God's Spirit) [6] 1.2; 4.8
strong Jn 6.18; 3.7
sure Lk 18.9; 13.34
Temple (1) (of God) Jn 18.20; 3.1
trouble [2] Jn 13.21; 7.10
turn [2] Jn 21.20; 3.14
urge Lk 3.18; 11.23
vision Lk 24.23; 9.10
vow Mk 6.23; 18.18
wicked Lk 13.27; 3.26
will (1) Jn 10.18; 4.28
witness 1.8; 3.15
wonder (1) [4] Jn 4.48; 4.30
word (1) [3] Jn 19.13; 6.2
world Jn 21.25; 4.12
world of the dead [2] Jon 2.2; Rom 8.39

17 'This is what I will do in the **last days**,
God says:
I will pour out my **Spirit** on
everyone.
Your sons and daughters will **proclaim**
my **message**;
your young men will see **visions**,
and your old men will have **dreams**.
18 Yes, even on my **servants**, both men
and women,
I will pour out my **Spirit** in those
days,
and they will **proclaim** my **message**.
19 I will perform **miracles** in the sky
above
and **wonders** on the earth below.
There will be **blood**, fire, and thick
smoke;
20 the sun will be **darkened**,
and the moon will **turn** red as **blood**,
before the great and **glorious Day of
the Lord** comes.
21 And then, whoever calls out to the
Lord for **help** will be **saved**.'

22 "Listen to these **words**, fellow-
Israelites! Jesus of Nazareth was a man
whose **divine authority** was **clearly
proven** to you by all the **miracles** and
wonders which God performed through
him. You yourselves know this, for it happened here among you. 23 In accordance
with his own **plan** God had already decided that Jesus would be handed over to
you; and you killed him by letting sinful
men **crucify** him. 24 But God **raised** him
from death, **setting him free** from its
power, because it was **impossible** that
death should hold him **prisoner**. 25 For
David said about him,

'I saw the Lord before me at all times;
he is near me, and I will not be
troubled.
26 And so I am filled with **gladness**,
and my **words** are full of **joy**.
And I, **mortal** though I am,
will rest **assured in hope**,
27 because you will not **abandon** me in
the **world of the dead**;
you will not allow your **faithful
servant** to rot in the **grave**.
28 You have shown me the paths that
lead to **life**,
and your **presence** will fill me with
joy.'

29 "My brothers, I must speak to you
plainly about our famous ancestor King
David. He died and was buried, and his
grave is here with us to this very day.
30 He was a **prophet**, and he knew what
God had **promised** him: God had made a
vow that he would make one of David's
descendants a king, just as David was.
31 David saw what God was going to do in
the future, and so he spoke about the
resurrection of the **Messiah** when he
said,

'He was not **abandoned** in the **world of
the dead**;
his **body** did not rot in the **grave**.'

32 God has **raised** this very Jesus **from
death**, and we are all **witnesses** to this
fact. 33 He has been **raised** to the **right-
hand side of God**, his **Father**, and has received from him the **Holy Spirit**, as he
had **promised**. What you now see and
hear is his **gift** that he has poured out on
us. 34 For it was not David who went up
into **heaven**; rather he said,

'The Lord said to my Lord:
Sit here at my **right**
35 until I put your **enemies** as a **footstool**
under your feet.'

36 "All the people of Israel, then, are
to know for **sure** that this Jesus, whom
you **crucified**, is the one that God has
made Lord and **Messiah**!"

37 When the people heard this, they
were deeply **troubled** and said to Peter
and the other **apostles**, "What shall we
do, brothers?"

38 Peter said to them, "Each one of
you must **turn away from his sins** and be
baptized in the name of Jesus Christ, so
that your sins will be **forgiven**; and you
will receive God's **gift**, the **Holy Spirit**.
39 For God's **promise** was made to you
and your children, and to all who are far
away—all whom the Lord our God calls
to himself."

40 Peter made his appeal to them and
with many other **words** he **urged** them,
saying, "**Save** yourselves from the
punishment coming on this **wicked**
people!" 41 Many of them **believed** his
message and were **baptized**, and about
three thousand people were added to the
group that day. 42 They spent their time
in **learning** from the **apostles**, taking part
in the **fellowship**, and **sharing** in the
fellowship meals and the **prayers**.

Life among the Believers

43 Many **miracles** and **wonders** were
being done through the **apostles**, and
everyone was filled with **awe**. 44 All the
believers continued together in close
fellowship and **shared** their belongings
with **one another**. 45 They would sell their
property and **possessions**, and distribute
the money among all, according to what

2.17–21: Joel 2.28–32 (LXX) **2.23:** Mt 27.35; Mk 15.24; Lk 23.33; Jn 19.18
2.24: Mt 28.5–6; Mk 16.6; Lk 24.5 **2.25–28:** Ps 16.8–11 (LXX) **2.30:** Ps 132.11; 2 Sam 7.12–13
2.34–35: Ps 110.1 **2.44:** Acts 4.32–35

each one **needed**. 46 Day after day they met as a group in the **Temple**, and they had their meals together in their homes, eating with **glad** and **humble hearts**, 47 **praising** God, and **enjoying** the **good will** of all the people. And every day the Lord added to their group those who were being **saved**.

A Lame Man Is Healed

3 One day Peter and John went to the **Temple** at three o'clock in the afternoon, the hour for **prayer**. 2 There at the Beautiful Gate, as it was called, was a man who had been lame all his **life**. Every day he was carried to the gate to **beg** for money from the people who were going into the **Temple**. 3 When he saw Peter and John going in, he **begged** them to give him something. 4 They looked straight at him, and Peter said, "Look at us!" 5 So he looked at them, expecting to get something from them. 6 But Peter said to him, "I have no money at all, but I give you what I have: **in the name of** Jesus Christ of Nazareth I order you to get up and walk!" 7 Then he took him by his **right hand** and **helped** him up. At once the man's feet and ankles became **strong**; 8 he jumped up, stood on his feet, and started walking around. Then he went into the **Temple** with them, walking and jumping and **praising** God. 9 The people there saw him walking and **praising** God, 10 and when they recognized him as the beggar who had sat at the Beautiful Gate, they were all surprised and **amazed** at what had happened to him.

Peter's Message in the Temple

11 As the man held on to Peter and John in Solomon's Porch, as it was called, the people were **amazed** and ran to them. 12 When Peter saw the people, he said to them, "Fellow-Israelites, why are you surprised at this, and why do you stare at us? Do you think that it was **by means of** our own **power** or **godliness** that we made this man walk? 13 The God of Abraham, Isaac, and Jacob, the God of our ancestors, has given **divine glory** to his **Servant** Jesus. But you handed him over to the **authorities**, and you **rejected** him in Pilate's **presence**, even after Pilate had decided to **set him free**. 14 He was **holy** and good, but you **rejected** him, and instead you asked Pilate to do you the **favour** of **turning** loose a murderer. 15 You killed the one who leads to **life**, but God **raised him from death**—and we are **witnesses** to this. 16 It was the **power** of his **name** that gave **strength** to this lame man. What you see and know was done by **faith in his name**; it was **faith** in Jesus that has made him well, as you can all see.

17 "And now, my brothers, I know that what you and your leaders did to Jesus was due to your **ignorance**. 18 God **announced** long ago through all the **prophets** that his **Messiah** had to **suffer**; and he made it come **true** in this way. 19 **Repent**, then, and **turn to God**, so that he will **forgive** your sins. If you do, 20 times of **spiritual strength** will come from the Lord, and he will send Jesus, who is the **Messiah** he has already **chosen** for you. 21 He must remain in **heaven** until the time comes for all things to be made **new**, as God **announced** through his **holy prophets** who lived long ago. 22 For Moses said, 'The Lord your God will send you a **prophet**, just as he sent me,[d] and he will be one of your own people. You are to **obey** everything that he tells you to do. 23 Anyone who does not **obey** that **prophet** shall be **separated** from **God's people** and **destroyed**.' 24 And all the **prophets** who had a **message**, including Samuel and those who came after him, also **announced** what has been happening these days. 25 The **promises** of God through his **prophets** are for you, and you **share** in the **covenant** which God made with your ancestors. As he said to Abraham, 'Through your descendants I will **bless** all the people on earth.' 26 And so God **chose** his **Servant** and sent him first to you, to **bless** you by making every one of you **turn away from his wicked ways**."

Peter and John before the Council

4 Peter and John were still speaking to the people when some **priests**,[e] the officer in charge of the temple guards, and some **Sadducees** arrived. 2 They were annoyed because the two **apostles** were **teaching** the people that Jesus had **risen from death**, which **proved** that the **dead** will **rise to life**. 3 So they **arrested** them and put them in **jail** until the next day, since it was already late. 4 But many who heard the **message believed**; and the number of men grew to about five thousand.

5 The next day the **Jewish** leaders, the **elders**, and the **teachers of the Law** gathered in Jerusalem. 6 They met with the **High Priest** Annas and with Caiaphas, John, Alexander, and the

[d] just as he sent me; *or* like me. [e] priests; *some manuscripts have* chief priests.

3.13: Ex 3.15 **3.14:** Mt 27.15–23; Mk 15.6–14; Lk 23.13–23; Jn 19.12–15 **3.22:** Deut 18.15, 18 (LXX) **3.23:** Deut 18.19 **3.25:** Gen 22.18

elder (2) [3] Lk 22.52; 5.21
encourage Is 62.1; 13.15
free [2] 3.13; 5.40
fury Lk 14.21; 5.33
Gentile [2] 2.11; 6.5
grant Mt 14.9; 2 Tim 1.18
heal [4] Jn 12.40; 5.16
heart 2.46; 7.51
heaven 3.21; 7.42
High Priest [2] Jn 18.10; 5.17
holy [2] 3.14; 7.33
important Jn 7.37; 8.27
impossible 2.24; 26.8
jail Lk 12.58; 5.18
Jew 2.5; 5.21
judge Jn 19.13; 7.27
keep from Jn 18.36; 8.36
learn 2.42; 10.17
Levites Jn 1.19; Heb 7.11
life (2) (to life) Jn 11.23; 13.32
master Jn 15.15; Rom 6.14
means 3.12; 17.31
message [3] 3.24; 7.14
Messiah [2] 3.18; 5.42
mind (1) Jn 12.40; 16.14
miracle [3] 2.19; 5.12
name (2) (name of God, of Jesus) [4] 3.6; 5.28
need [2] 2.45; 17.25
notice (1) Lk 22.58; 10.31
obey 3.22; 5.21
one another 2.44; 21.6
plot (1) Mt 12.15; 20.3
power [4] 3.12; 6.8
praise 3.8; 10.46
pray 1.14; 6.6
prayer 3.1; 6.4
priest Jn 1.19; 6.7
proclaim 2.17; 8.25
prove 2.22; 9.22
punish 2.40; 22.5
question Jn 18.19; 5.27
raise 3.15; 5.30
resurrection 2.31; 17.18
rich Lk 21.1; 6.8
right (1) Jn 18.23; 6.2
rise [2] Jn 21.4; 10.26
Sadducees Lk 20.27; 5.17
salvation Jn 4.22; 13.26
save 2.21; 11.14
scripture 1.16; 8.32
servant [4] 3.13; 7.52
share 3.25; 8.21
sight 1.9; 8.21
Spirit (1) (God's Spirit) [3] 2.4; 5.3
strong 3.7; 15.16
teach [2] 1.1; 5.21
teacher of the Law Jn 8.3; 5.34
threat Zech 14.11; 9.1
turn 3.14; 7.42
useless Mt 25.30; 1 Cor 15.58
warn [2] Lk 16.28; 20.21
will (1) 2.47; 18.21
witness 3.15; 5.32
wonder (1) 2.7; 5.12
world 2.5; 13.47

others who belonged to the **High Priest's**
family. 7 They made the **apostles** stand
before them and asked them, "How did
you do this? What **power** have you got or
whose name did you use?"
8 Peter, full of the **Holy Spirit**, answered them, "Leaders of the people and
elders: 9 if we are being **questioned** today
about the good **deed** done to the lame
man and how he was **healed**, 10 then you
should all know, and all the people of
Israel should know, that this man stands
here before you completely well through
the **power** of the **name of Jesus** Christ of
Nazareth—whom you **crucified** and
whom God **raised from death**. 11 Jesus is
the one of whom the **scripture** says,

'The stone that you the builders
despised
turned out to be the most **important**
of all.'

12 **Salvation** is to be found through him
alone; in all the **world** there is no one
else whom God has given who can **save**
us."
13 The members of the **Council** were
amazed to see how **bold** Peter and John
were and to **learn** that they were ordinary men of no education. They realized
then that they had been companions of
Jesus. 14 But there was nothing that they
could say, because they saw the man
who had been **healed** standing there with
Peter and John. 15 So they told them to
leave the **Council** room, and then they
started **discussing** among themselves.
16 "What shall we do with these men?"
they asked. "Everyone in Jerusalem
knows that this extraordinary **miracle**
has been performed by them, and we
cannot **deny** it. 17 But to **keep this matter**
from spreading any further among the
people, let us **warn** these men never
again to speak to anyone **in the name of**
Jesus."
18 So they called them back in and
told them that on no condition were they
to speak or to **teach in the name of** Jesus.
19 But Peter and John answered them,
"You yourselves **judge** which is **right** in
God's **sight**—to **obey** you or to obey God.
20 For we cannot stop speaking of what
we ourselves have seen and heard." 21 So
the **Council warned** them even more
strongly and then **set them free**. They
saw that it was **impossible** to **punish**
them, because the people were all **prais-**
ing God for what had happened. 22 The
man on whom this **miracle** of **healing**
had been performed was over forty
years old.

The Believers Pray for Boldness

23 As soon as Peter and John were **set**
free, they returned to their group and
told them what the **chief priests** and the
elders had said. 24 When the **believers**
heard it, they all joined together in
prayer to God: "**Master** and **Creator** of
heaven, earth, and sea, and all that is in
them! 25 **By means of** the **Holy Spirit** you
spoke through our ancestor David, your
servant, when he said,

'Why were the **Gentiles furious**;
why did people make their **useless**
plots?
26 The kings of the earth prepared
themselves,
and the rulers met together
against the Lord and his **Messiah**.'

27 For indeed Herod and Pontius Pilate
met together in this city with the **Gen-**
tiles and the people of Israel against
Jesus, your **holy Servant**, whom you
made **Messiah**. 28 They gathered to do
everything that you by your **power** and
will had already decided would happen.
29 And now, Lord, take **notice** of the
threats they have made, and allow us,
your **servants**, to speak your **message**
with all **boldness**. 30 Stretch out your hand
to **heal**, and **grant** that **wonders** and **mir-**
acles may be performed through the
name of your **holy Servant** Jesus."
31 When they finished **praying**, the
place where they were meeting was
shaken. They were all filled with the
Holy Spirit and began to **proclaim** God's
message with **boldness**.

The Believers Share Their Possessions

32 The group of **believers** was one in
mind and **heart**. No one said that any of
his belongings was his own, but they all
shared with **one another** everything they
had. 33 With great **power** the **apostles**
gave **witness** to the **resurrection** of the
Lord Jesus, and God poured **rich bless-**
ings on them all. 34 There was no one in
the group who was in **need**. Those who
owned fields or houses would sell them,
bring the money received from the sale,
35 and hand it over to the **apostles**; and
the money was distributed to each one
according to his **need**.
36 And so it was that Joseph, a **Levite**
born in Cyprus, whom the **apostles** called
Barnabas (which means "One who **En-**
courages"), 37 sold a field he owned,
brought the money, and handed it over to
the **apostles**.

4.11: Ps 118.22 **4.24:** Ex 20.11; Neh 9.6; Ps 146.6 **4.25–26:** Ps 2.1–2 (LXX)
4.27: Mt 27.1–2; Mk 15.1; Lk 23.1, 7–11; Jn 18.28–29 **4.32:** Acts 2.44–45

action [2] Jn 11.48; Rom 8.13
advice Jn 18.14; 27.9
afraid Jn 20.19; 9.26
agree Jn 9.22; 15.15
alone 4.12; Rom 4.23
angel Jn 20.12; 6.15
apostle [17] 4.2; 6.2
arrest 4.3; 9.2
believe 4.4; 8.12
believer 4.24; 6.2
body 2.31; 7.16
chief priests 4.23; 9.14
church Mt 18.17; 8.1
claim Jn 19.7; 6.1
consider Lk 24.19; 10.15
control Mk 5.4; Rom 8.5
Council [8] 4.13; 6.12
cross (1) Jn 19.17; 10.39
dare Jn 21.12; 7.32
dead [2] 4.2; 10.42
death (1) 2.24; 13.28
death (2) (from death) 4.2; 10.40
death (3) (to death) Jn 19.41; 10.39
disgrace Lk 1.25; 1 Cor 11.4
elder (2) 4.5; 6.12
follower [2] Jn 21.23; 9.1
force (1) Jn 6.15; 7.19
forgive 3.19; 8.22
free 4.21; 7.25
fury 4.25; 7.54
gift 2.33; 8.20
Good News Lk 21.13; 8.12
happy Jn 20.29; 12.14
heal 4.9; 8.7
High Priest [3] 4.6; 7.1
human Jn 8.15; 14.15
jail [2] 4.3; 8.3
jealous Mk 15.10; 7.9
Jew 4.5; 6.1
lie (2) [2] Jn 8.44; 6.13
life (1) 3.2; 8.33
Messiah 4.26; 8.5
miracle 4.16; 6.8
name (2) (name of God, of Jesus) [2] 4.10; 8.16
new 3.21; 17.19
obey [3] 4.19; 7.39
Pharisees Jn 18.3; 15.5
plan 2.23; 8.22
preach 1.21; 6.2
prison [4] 2.24; 8.23
question 4.9; 12.19
raise [2] 4.10; 10.40
remember Jn 19.10; 7.60
repent 3.19; 8.22
respect Jn 9.31; 10.22
result Jn 11.4; Rom 1.27
right (2) 3.7; 7.55
Sadducees 4.1; 23.6
sake Jn 17.19; 9.16
Satan Jn 13.27; 26.18
Saviour Jn 4.42; 13.23
scatter [2] Jn 16.32; 8.1
Spirit (1) (God's Spirit) [3] 4.8; 6.3
spirit (2) Lk 23.46; 7.59
suffer 3.18; 7.11
teach [5] 4.2; 7.22
teacher of the Law 4.5; 6.12
Temple (1) (of God) [4] 3.1; 6.13

Ananias and Sapphira

5 But there was a man named
Ananias, who with his wife Sapphira
sold some property that belonged to
them. 2 But with his wife's agreement he
kept part of the money for himself and
handed the rest over to the apostles.
3 Peter said to him, "Ananias, why did
you let Satan take control of you and
make you lie to the Holy Spirit by keeping part of the money you received for
the property? 4 Before you sold the property, it belonged to you; and after you
sold it, the money was yours. Why, then,
did you decide to do such a thing? You
have not lied to men—you have lied to
God!" 5 As soon as Ananias heard this, he
fell down dead; and all who heard about
it were terrified. 6 The young men came
in, wrapped up his body, carried him out,
and buried him.
7 About three hours later his wife, not
knowing what had happened, came in.
8 Peter asked her, "Tell me, was this the
full amount you and your husband received for your property?"
"Yes," she answered, "the full
amount."
9 So Peter said to her, "Why did you
and your husband decide to put the
Lord's Spirit to the test? The men who
buried your husband are now at the door,
and they will carry you out too!" 10 At
once she fell down at his feet and died.
The young men came in and saw that she
was dead, so they carried her out and
buried her beside her husband. 11 The
whole church and all the others who
heard of this were terrified.

Miracles and Wonders

12 Many miracles and wonders were
being performed among the people by
the apostles. All the believers met together in Solomon's Porch. 13 Nobody outside the group dared to join them, even
though the people spoke highly of them.
14 But more and more people were added
to the group—a crowd of men and
women who believed in the Lord. 15 As a
result of what the apostles were doing,
sick people were carried out into the
streets and placed on beds and mats so
that at least Peter's shadow might fall on
some of them as he passed by. 16 And
crowds of people came in from the towns
around Jerusalem, bringing those who
were ill or who had evil spirits in them;
and they were all healed.

The Apostles Are Persecuted

17 Then the High Priest and all his
companions, members of the local party
of the Sadducees, became extremely
jealous of the apostles; so they decided to
take action. 18 They arrested the apostles
and put them in the public jail. 19 But that
night an angel of the Lord opened the
prison gates, led the apostles out, and
said to them, 20 "Go and stand in the
Temple, and tell the people all about this
new life." 21 The apostles obeyed, and at
dawn they entered the Temple and
started teaching.
The High Priest and his companions
called together all the Jewish elders for a
full meeting of the Council; then they
sent orders to the prison to have the
apostles brought before them. 22 But
when the officials arrived, they did not
find the apostles in prison, so they returned to the Council and reported,
23 "When we arrived at the jail, we found
it locked up tight and all the guards on
watch at the gates; but when we opened
the gates, we found no one inside!"
24 When the chief priests and the officer
in charge of the temple guards heard
this, they wondered what had happened
to the apostles. 25 Then a man came in
and said to them, "Listen! The men you
put in prison are in the Temple teaching
the people!" 26 So the officer went off
with his men and brought the apostles
back. They did not use force, however,
because they were afraid that the people
might stone them.
27 They brought the apostles in, made
them stand before the Council, and the
High Priest questioned them. 28 "We gave
you strict orders not to teach in the name
of this man," he said; "but see what you
have done! You have spread your teaching all over Jerusalem, and you want to
make us responsible for his death!"
29 Peter and the other apostles replied, "We must obey God, not men.
30 The God of our ancestors raised Jesus
from death, after you had killed him by
nailing him to a cross. 31 God raised him
to his right-hand side as Leader and
Saviour, to give the people of Israel the
opportunity to repent and have their sins
forgiven. 32 We are witnesses to these
things—we and the Holy Spirit, who is
God's gift to those who obey him."
33 When the members of the Council
heard this, they were so furious that they
wanted to have the apostles put to death.
34 But one of them, a Pharisee named
Gamaliel, who was a teacher of the Law
and was highly respected by all the
people, stood up in the Council. He
ordered the apostles to be taken out for a

terrify [2] Jn 6.19; Heb 10.31
test Jn 6.6; 15.10
watch 1.9; 9.24
witness 4.33; 7.58
wonder (1) 4.30; 6.8
worthy Lk 20.35; 13.46

5.28: Mt 27.25

teacher of the Law 5.34; 23.9
Temple (1) (of God) [2] 5.20; 21.26
widow Lk 21.2; 9.39
wisdom [2] Lk 21.15; 7.10
wonder (1) 5.12; 7.36
word (1) [2] 2.22; 7.22

while, 35 and then he said to the **Council**, "Fellow-Israelites, be careful what you do to these men. 36 You **remember** that Theudas appeared some time ago, **claiming** to be somebody great, and about four hundred men joined him. But he was killed, all his **followers** were **scattered**, and his movement died out. 37 After that, Judas the Galilean appeared during the time of the census; he drew a crowd after him, but he also was killed, and all his **followers** were **scattered**. 38 And so in this case, I tell you, do not take any **action** against these men. Leave them **alone**! If what they have **planned** and done is of **human** origin, it will disappear, 39 but if it comes from God, you cannot possibly defeat them. You could find yourselves fighting against God!"

The **Council** followed Gamaliel's **advice**. 40 They called the **apostles** in, had them whipped, and ordered them never again to speak **in the name of** Jesus; and then they **set them free**. 41 As the **apostles** left the **Council**, they were **happy**, because God had **considered** them **worthy** to **suffer disgrace** for the **sake** of Jesus. 42 And every day in the **Temple** and in people's homes they continued to **teach** and **preach** the **Good News** about Jesus the **Messiah**.

The Seven Helpers

6 Some time later, as the number of **disciples** kept growing, there was a **quarrel** between the Greek-speaking **Jews** and the native **Jews**. The Greek-speaking Jews **claimed** that their **widows** were being **neglected** in the daily distribution of funds. 2 So the twelve **apostles** called the whole group of **believers** together and said, "It is not **right** for us to **neglect** the **preaching** of **God's word** in order to handle finances. 3 So then, brothers, **choose** seven men among you who are known to be full of the **Holy Spirit** and **wisdom**, and we will put them in charge of this matter. 4 We ourselves, then, will give our full time to **prayer** and the work of **preaching**."

5 The whole group was **pleased** with the **apostles'** proposal, so they **chose** Stephen, a man full of **faith** and the **Holy Spirit**, and Philip, Prochorus, Nicanor, Timon, Parmenas, and Nicolaus, a **Gentile** from Antioch who had earlier been converted to **Judaism**. 6 The group **presented** them to the **apostles**, who **prayed** and placed their hands on them.

7 And so the **word of God** continued to spread. The number of **disciples** in Jerusalem grew larger and larger, and a great number of **priests accepted** the **faith**.

The Arrest of Stephen

8 Stephen, a man **richly blessed** by God and full of **power**, performed great **miracles** and **wonders** among the people. 9 But he was opposed by some men who were members of the **synagogue** of the Freedmen[f] (as it was called), which included **Jews** from Cyrene and Alexandria. They and other **Jews** from the provinces of Cilicia and Asia started **arguing** with Stephen. 10 But the **Spirit** gave Stephen such **wisdom** that when he spoke, they could not refute him. 11 So they **bribed** some men to say, "We heard him speaking against Moses and against God!" 12 In this way they stirred up the people, the **elders**, and the **teachers of the Law**. They seized Stephen and took him before the **Council**. 13 Then they brought in some men to tell **lies** about him. "This man," they said, "is always talking against our **sacred Temple** and the **Law of Moses**. 14 We heard him say that this Jesus of Nazareth will tear down the **Temple** and **change** all the **customs** which have come down to us from Moses!" 15 All those sitting in the **Council** fixed their eyes on Stephen and saw that his face looked like the face of an **angel**.

Stephen's Speech

7 The **High Priest** asked Stephen, "Is this **true**?"

2 Stephen answered, "Brothers and fathers, listen to me! Before our ancestor Abraham had gone to live in Haran, the God of **glory** appeared to him in Mesopotamia 3 and said to him, 'Leave your family and country and go to the land that I will show you.' 4 And so he left his country and went to live in Haran. After Abraham's father died, God made him move to this land where you now live. 5 God did not then give Abraham any part of it as his own, not even a square metre of ground, but God **promised** to give it to him, and that it would belong to him and to his descendants. At the time God made this **promise**, Abraham had no children. 6 This is what God said to him: 'Your descendants will live in a foreign country, where they will be **slaves** and will be **badly** treated for four hundred years. 7 But I will **pass judgement** on the people that they will **serve**, and afterwards they will come out of that country and will **worship** me in

accept Jn 14.21; 10.35
angel 5.19; 7.30
apostle [3] 5.2; 8.1
argue Jn 6.52; 15.2
believer 5.12; 8.1
bless 4.33; 11.23
bribe Lk 20.20
change Lk 9.29; 28.6
choose [2] 3.20; 9.15
claim 5.36; 8.9
Council [2] 5.21; 7.54
custom Jn 19.40; 16.21
disciple [2] Jn 21.1; 9.26
elder (2) 5.21; 11.30
faith [2] 3.16; 11.24
Gentile 4.25; 9.15
Jew [4] 5.21; 9.22
Judaism 2.11; 13.43
law Jn 19.7; 7.53
lie (2) 5.3; 13.10
miracle 5.12; 7.36
neglect [2] Lk 11.42; Phil 4.11
please Jn 8.29; 7.10
power 4.7; 8.10
pray 4.31; 8.15
prayer 4.24; 10.4
preach [2] 5.42; 8.4
present (1) Lk 2.22; 9.41
priest 4.1; 14.13
quarrel Hab 1.3; 23.7
rich 4.33; Rom 10.12
right (1) 4.19; 8.21
sacred Lk 1.72; 13.34
Spirit (1) (God's Spirit) [3] 5.3; 7.51
synagogue Jn 18.20; 9.2

amaze 4.13; 9.21
angel [4] 6.15; 8.26
anger Jn 7.23; 12.20
announce 3.18; 12.14
bad Jn 11.39; 19.27
betray Jn 21.20; 1 Cor 11.23
body 5.6; 9.37
care [2] Jn 21.15; 13.40
ceremony Lk 2.22; 21.24
circumcise [4] Jn 7.22; 11.2
Council [2] 6.12; 17.19
covenant 3.25; Rom 9.4
cruel [2] Mal 2.16; 8.1
dare 5.13; Rom 5.7
deed (2) 4.9; Rom 4.5
exile Mt 1.6
famine Lk 21.11; 11.28
favour 3.14; 11.2
fear Lk 24.5; 10.4
feast Jn 2.8; Rom 11.9
flee Zech 14.5; 14.6
footstool 2.35; Heb 1.13
force (1) 5.26; 28.19
free [3] 5.40; 13.38
fury 5.33; 19.28
glory [2] 3.13; Rom 2.7
god (2) (other gods) [2] Jn 10.34; 12.22

[f] FREEDMEN: *These were Jews who had been slaves, but had bought or been given their freedom.*

7.2–3: Gen 12.1 **7.4:** Gen 11.31, 12.4 **7.5:** Gen 12.7, 13.15, 15.18, 17.8 **7.6–7:** Gen 15.13–14 **7.7:** Ex 3.12

God's people 3.23; 9.32
grave 2.27; 13.34
groan Mk 8.12; Rom 8.22
heart 4.32; 8.21
heathen Lk 21.24; 1 Cor 5.1
heaven [4] 4.24; 10.11
help [2] 3.7; 9.27
High Priest 5.17; 9.1
holy 4.27; Rom 1.2
honour Jn 12.26; 12.23
I am Jn 19.21; 10.21
idol [2] Zech 13.1; 15.20
ill-treat [2] Lk 6.28; 14.5
image Mic 5.14; 17.29
jealous 5.17; 13.45
judge [2] 4.19; 10.42
kneel Jn 9.38; 9.40
last (2) 2.17; 12.10
law 6.13; 13.15
message [3] 4.4; 8.4
miracle 6.8; 8.6
Most High Lk 8.28; 16.17
obey [2] 5.21; 15.5
offer Jn 4.23; 8.18
pass (5) Jn 8.15; 13.28
peace Jn 20.19; 9.31
persecute Jn 15.20; 8.1
please 6.5; 8.24
promise [3] 3.25; 13.23
prophet [4] 3.18; 8.27
provide Jn 4.14; 20.34
race (1) Zech 9.6; 10.35
refuse (1) Jn 1.20; Rom 1.28
reject 3.13; 13.46
remember 5.36; 11.16
resist Dan 8.7; Rom 9.19
revenge Mt 5.39; Rom 12.19
right (2) [2] 5.31; Rom 8.34
righteous Jn 17.25; 22.14
sacrifice [2] Lk 13.1; 14.13
safe Jn 17.11; 23.24
servant 4.25; 10.7
serve 1.25; 9.15
sign (1) Lk 11.30; Rom 4.11
slaughter Zeph 1.8; 8.32
slave [2] Jn 18.10; 16.16
Son of Man Jn 13.31
Spirit (1) (God's Spirit) [2] 6.3; 8.15
spirit (2) 5.16; 8.7
stubborn Mk 16.14; 19.9
suffer [2] 5.41; 8.1
teach 5.21; 11.26
Tent (2) (of the Lord's presence) [2] Ps 78.60; Heb 8.5
throne Lk 22.30; 12.21
tremble Lk 8.47; 16.29
trick Lk 20.23; 13.10
trouble 2.25; 14.22

this place.' 8 Then God gave Abraham the
ceremony of **circumcision** as a **sign** of
the **covenant**. So Abraham **circumcised**
Isaac a week after he was born; Isaac
circumcised his son Jacob, and Jacob
circumcised his twelve sons, the famous
ancestors of our **race**.
9 "Jacob's sons became **jealous** of
their brother Joseph and sold him to be a
slave in Egypt. But God was with him
10 and brought him **safely** through all his
troubles. When Joseph appeared before
the king of Egypt, God gave him a
pleasing manner and **wisdom**, and the
king made Joseph governor over the
country and the royal household. 11 Then
there was a **famine** all over Egypt and
Canaan, which caused much **suffering**.
Our ancestors could not find any food,
12 and when Jacob heard that there was
corn in Egypt, he sent his sons, our
ancestors, on their first visit there. 13 On
the second visit Joseph made himself
known to his brothers, and the king of
Egypt came to know about Joseph's
family. 14 So Joseph sent a **message** to his
father Jacob, telling him and the whole
family, seventy-five people in all, to
come to Egypt. 15 Then Jacob went to
Egypt, where he and his sons died.
16 Their **bodies** were taken to Shechem,
where they were buried in the **grave**
which Abraham had bought from the
clan of Hamor for a sum of money.
17 "When the time drew near for God
to keep the **promise** he had made to
Abraham, the number of our people in
Egypt had grown much larger. 18 At **last** a
king who did not know about Joseph began to rule in Egypt. 19 He **tricked** our
ancestors and was **cruel** to them, **forcing**
them to put their babies out of their
homes, so that they would die. 20 It was at
this time that Moses was born, a very
beautiful child. He was **cared** for at home
for three months, 21 and when he was put
out of his home, the king's daughter
adopted him and brought him up as her
own son. 22 He was **taught** all the **wisdom**
of the Egyptians and became a great
man in **words and deeds**.
23 "When Moses was forty years old,
he decided to find out how his fellow-
Israelites were being treated. 24 He saw
one of them being **ill-treated** by an
Egyptian, so he went to his **help** and took
revenge on the Egyptian by killing him.
25 (He thought that his own people would
understand that God was going to use
him to **set them free**, but they did not
understand.) 26 The next day he saw two
Israelites fighting, and he tried to make
peace between them. 'Listen, men,' he
said, 'you are fellow-Israelites; why are
you fighting like this?' 27 But the one who
was **ill-treating** the other pushed Moses
aside. 'Who made you ruler and **judge**
over us?' he asked. 28 'Do you want to kill
me, just as you killed that Egyptian
yesterday?' 29 When Moses heard this, he
fled from Egypt and went to live in the
land of Midian. There he had two sons.
30 "After forty years had passed, an
angel appeared to Moses in the flames of
a burning bush in the desert near Mount
Sinai. 31 Moses was **amazed** by what he
saw, and went near the bush to get a
better look. But he heard the Lord's
voice: 32 '**I am** the God of your ancestors,
the God of Abraham, Isaac, and Jacob.'
Moses **trembled** with **fear** and **dared** not
look. 33 The Lord said to him, 'Take your
sandals off, for the place where you are
standing is **holy** ground. 34 I have seen the
cruel suffering of **my people** in Egypt. I
have heard their **groans**, and I have
come down to **set them free**. Come now;
I will send you to Egypt.'
35 "Moses is the one who was **rejected**
by the people of Israel. 'Who made you
ruler and **judge** over us?' they asked. He
is the one whom God sent to rule the
people and **set them free** with the **help** of
the **angel** who appeared to him in the
burning bush. 36 He led the people out of
Egypt, performing **miracles** and **wonders**
in Egypt and at the Red Sea and for forty
years in the desert. 37 Moses is the one
who said to the people of Israel, 'God will
send you a **prophet**, just as he sent me,[g]
and he will be one of your own people.'
38 He is the one who was with the people
of Israel assembled in the desert; he was
there with our ancestors and with the
angel who spoke to him on Mount Sinai,
and he received God's living **messages** to
pass on to us.
39 "But our ancestors **refused** to **obey**
him; they pushed him aside and **wished**
that they could go back to Egypt. 40 So
they said to Aaron, 'Make us some **gods**
who will lead us. We do not know what
has happened to that man Moses, who
brought us out of Egypt.' 41 It was then

true 3.18; 10.34
turn 4.11; 9.35
understand [2] Jn 20.9; 8.30
win Jn 5.44; 14.19
wisdom [2] 6.3; Rom 11.33
wish Jn 15.7; 15.29
witness 5.32; 10.39
wonder (1) 6.8; 8.13
word (1) 6.2; 8.14
worship (1) (of God) Jn 12.20; 8.27
worship (2) (of other gods) [2] Lk 4.7; 17.23

[g] just as he sent me; *or* like me.

7.8: Gen 17.10–14, 21.2–4, 25.26, 29.31–35.18 **7.9:** Gen 37.11, 28, 39.2, 21 **7.10:** Gen 41.39–41
7.11: Gen 42.1–2 **7.13:** Gen 45.1, 16 **7.14:** Gen 45.9–10, 17–18, 46.27 **7.15:** Gen 46.1–7, 49.33
7.16: Gen 23.3–16, 33.19, 50.7–13; Josh 24.32 **7.17–18:** Ex 1.7–8 **7.19:** Ex 1.10–11, 22 **7.20:** Ex 2.2
7.21: Ex 2.3–10 **7.23–29:** Ex 2.11–15 **7.29:** Ex 18.3–4 **7.30–34:** Ex 3.1–10 **7.35:** Ex 2.14
7.36: Ex 7.5, 14.21; Num 14.33 **7.37:** Deut 18.15, 18 **7.38:** Ex 19.1–20.17; Deut 5.1–33 **7.40:** Ex 32.1
7.41: Ex 32.2–6

that they made an **idol** in the shape of a
bull, **offered sacrifice** to it, and had a
feast in **honour** of what they themselves
had made. 42 So God **turned away** from
them and gave them over to **worship the
stars** of **heaven**, as it is written in the
book of the **prophets**:

'People of Israel! It was not to me
that you **slaughtered** and **sacrificed**
animals
for forty years in the desert.
43 It was the tent of the **god Molech** that
you carried,
and the **image** of Rephan, your star
god;
they were **idols** that you had made
to **worship**.
And so I will send you into **exile**
beyond Babylon.'

44 "Our ancestors had the **Tent** of
God's presence with them in the desert.
It had been made as God had told Moses
to make it, according to the pattern that
Moses had been shown. 45 Later on, our
ancestors who received the **tent** from
their fathers carried it with them when
they went with Joshua and took over the
land from the nations that God drove out
as they advanced. And it stayed there until the time of David. 46 He **won** God's
favour and asked God to allow him to
provide a dwelling place for the God of
Jacob.[h] 47 But it was Solomon who built
him a house.

48 "But the **Most High God** does not
live in houses built by men; as the **prophet** says,

49 '**Heaven** is my **throne**, says the Lord,
and the earth is my **footstool**.
What kind of house would you build for
me?
Where is the place for me to live in?
50 Did not I myself make all these
things?'

51 "How **stubborn** you are!" Stephen
went on to say. "How **heathen** your
hearts, how deaf you are to God's **message**! You are just like your ancestors:
you too have always **resisted** the **Holy
Spirit**! 52 Was there any **prophet** that your
ancestors did not **persecute**? They killed
God's messengers, who long ago **announced** the coming of his **righteous Servant**. And now you have **betrayed** and
murdered him. 53 You are the ones who
received God's **law**, that was handed
down by **angels**—yet you have not
obeyed it!"

The Stoning of Stephen

54 As the members of the **Council** listened to Stephen, they became **furious**
and ground their teeth at him in **anger**.
55 But Stephen, full of the **Holy Spirit**,
looked up to **heaven** and saw God's **glory**
and Jesus standing at the **right-hand side**
of God. 56 "Look!" he said. "I see **heaven**
opened and the **Son of Man** standing at
the **right-hand side** of God!"

57 With a loud cry the members of the
Council covered their ears with their
hands. Then they all rushed at him at
once, 58 threw him out of the city, and
stoned him. The **witnesses** left their
cloaks in the **care** of a young man named
Saul. 59 They kept on stoning Stephen as
he called out to the Lord, "Lord Jesus, receive my **spirit**!" 60 He **knelt** down and
cried out in a loud voice, "Lord! Do not
remember this sin against them!" He
8 said this and died.
And Saul **approved** of his murder.

Saul Persecutes the Church

That very day the **church** in Jerusalem
began to **suffer cruel persecution**. All the
believers, except the **apostles**, were **scattered** throughout the provinces of Judaea
and Samaria. 2 Some devout men buried
Stephen, **mourning** for him with loud
cries.

3 But Saul tried to **destroy** the **church**;
going from house to house, he dragged
out the **believers**, both men and women,
and threw them into **jail**.

The Gospel Is Preached in Samaria

4 The **believers** who were **scattered**
went everywhere, **preaching** the **message**. 5 Philip went to the principal city[i] in
Samaria and **preached** the **Messiah** to
the people there. 6 The crowds paid close
attention to what Philip said, as they listened to him and saw the **miracles** that
he performed. 7 **Evil spirits** came out
from many people with a loud cry, and
many **paralysed** and lame people were
healed. 8 So there was great **joy** in that
city.

9 A man named Simon lived there,
who for some time had astounded the
Samaritans with his **magic**. He **claimed**
that he was someone great, 10 and everyone in the city, from all classes of
society, paid close attention to him. "He
is that **power of God** known as 'The
Great Power'," they said. 11 They paid

angel 7.30; 10.3
apostle [3] 6.2; 9.27
approve Jn 12.43; 15.8
baptize [5] 2.38; 9.18
believe [2] 5.14; 9.26
believer [5] 6.2; 9.19
bitter Lk 22.62; Rom 3.14
church [2] 5.11; 9.31
claim 6.1; 13.6
cruel 7.19
deny 4.16; 19.36
destroy 3.23; 13.19
envy Ezek 31.9; Gal 5.21
evil 1.18; 13.10
forgive 5.31; 10.43
gift 5.32; 10.45
Good News [4] 5.42; 10.36
heal 5.16; 10.38
heart 7.51; 11.23
hell Lk 12.5; Gal 1.8
humiliate Hab 2.15; 2 Cor 12.21
important 4.11; 21.39
jail 5.18; 12.4
joy [2] 2.26; 13.52
justice Lk 11.42; 17.31
keep from 4.17; 14.18
Kingdom (1) (of God) 1.3; 14.22
lamb Jn 21.15; 1 Cor 5.7
life (1) 5.20; 13.46
magic [2] Mal 3.5; 13.6
message [3] 7.14; 9.38
Messiah 5.42; 9.22
miracle [2] 7.36; 14.3
mourn Lk 8.52; Rev 1.7
name (2) (name of God, of Jesus) 5.28; 9.15
offer 7.41; 14.13
paralyse Jn 5.3; 9.33
persecute 7.52; 9.4
plan 5.38; 9.23
please 7.10; 9.38
power [2] 6.8; 9.22
pray [3] 6.6; 9.11

[h] the God of Jacob; *some manuscripts have* the people of Israel.
[i] the principal city; *some manuscripts have* a city.

7.42–43: Amos 5.25–27 (LXX) **7.44:** Ex 25.9, 40 **7.45:** Josh 3.14–17 **7.46:** 2 Sam 7.1–16; 1 Chr 17.1–14
7.47: 1 Kgs 6.1–38; 2 Chr 3.1–17 **7.49–50:** Is 66.1–2 **7.51:** Is 63.10 **8.3:** Acts 22.4–5, 26.9–11

preach [4] 6.2; 9.20
prison 5.19; 12.6
proclaim 4.31; 10.36
prophet [3] 7.37; 10.43
repent 5.31; 11.18
right (1) 6.2; 10.35
scatter [2] 5.36; 11.19
scripture [2] 4.11; 13.29
share 4.32; Rom 1.11
sheep Jn 21.16; Rom 8.36
sight 4.19; Rom 3.20
slaughter 7.42; Rom 8.36
Spirit (1) (God's Spirit) [7] 7.51; 9.17
spirit (2) 7.59; 16.16
suffer 7.11; 9.16
testimony Jn 1.32; 1 Tim 1.10
understand [2] 7.25; 10.19
wonder (1) 7.36; 14.3
word (1) [2] 7.22; 9.7
worship (1) (of God) 7.7; 9.14

this attention to him because for such a long time he had astonished them with his **magic**. 12 But when they **believed** Philip's **message** about the **good news** of the **Kingdom of God** and about Jesus Christ, they were **baptized**, both men and women. 13 Simon himself also **believed**; and after being **baptized**, he stayed close to Philip and was astounded when he saw the great **wonders** and **miracles** that were being performed.

14 The **apostles** in Jerusalem heard that the people of Samaria had received the **word of God**, so they sent Peter and John to them. 15 When they arrived, they **prayed** for the **believers** that they might receive the **Holy Spirit**. 16 For the **Holy Spirit** had not yet come down on any of them; they had only been **baptized in the name of** the Lord Jesus. 17 Then Peter and John placed their hands on them, and they received the **Holy Spirit**.

18 Simon saw that the **Spirit** had been given to the **believers** when the **apostles** placed their hands on them. So he **offered** money to Peter and John, 19 and said, "Give this **power** to me too, so that anyone I place my hands on will receive the **Holy Spirit**."

20 But Peter answered him, "May you and your money go to **hell**, for thinking that you can buy God's **gift** with money! 21 You have no part or **share** in our work, because your **heart** is not **right** in God's **sight**. 22 **Repent**, then, of this **evil plan** of yours, and **pray** to the Lord that he will **forgive** you for thinking such a thing as this. 23 For I see that you are full of **bitter envy** and are a **prisoner** of sin."

24 Simon said to Peter and John, "**Please pray** to the Lord for me, so that none of these things you spoke of will happen to me."

25 After they had given their **testimony** and **proclaimed** the Lord's **message**, Peter and John went back to Jerusalem. On their way they **preached** the **Good News** in many villages of Samaria.

Philip and the Ethiopian Official

26 An **angel of the Lord** said to Philip, "Get ready and go south[j] to the road that goes from Jerusalem to Gaza." (This road is not used nowadays.)[k] 27-28 So Philip got ready and went. Now an Ethiopian eunuch, who was an **important** official in charge of the treasury of the queen of Ethiopia, was on his way home. He had been to Jerusalem to **worship** God and was going back home in his carriage. As he rode along, he was reading from the book of the **prophet** Isaiah. 29 The **Holy Spirit** said to Philip, "Go over to that carriage and stay close to it." 30 Philip ran over and heard him reading from the book of the **prophet** Isaiah. He asked him, "Do you **understand** what you are reading?"

31 The official replied, "How can I **understand** unless someone explains it to me?" And he invited Philip to climb up and sit in the carriage with him. 32 The passage of **scripture** which he was reading was this:

"Like a **sheep** that is taken to be
slaughtered,
like a **lamb** that makes no sound
when its wool is cut off,
he did not say a **word**.
33 He was **humiliated**, and **justice** was
denied him.
No one will be able to tell about his
descendants,
because his **life** on earth has come
to an end."

34 The official asked Philip, "Tell me, of whom is the **prophet** saying this? Of himself or of someone else?" 35 Then Philip began to speak; starting from this passage of **scripture**, he told him the **Good News** about Jesus. 36 As they travelled down the road, they came to a place where there was some water, and the official said, "Here is some water. What is to **keep me from** being **baptized**?"[l]

38 The official ordered the carriage to stop, and both Philip and the official went down into the water, and Philip **baptized** him. 39 When they came up out of the water, the **Spirit of the Lord** took Philip away. The official did not see him again, but continued on his way, full of **joy**. 40 Philip found himself in Azotus; he went on to Caesarea, and on the way he **preached** the **Good News** in every town.

The Conversion of Saul
(Acts 22.6-16; 26.12-18)

9 In the meantime Saul kept up his **violent threats** of murder against the **followers** of the Lord. He went to the **High Priest** 2 and asked for **letters** of introduction to the **synagogues** in Damascus, so that if he should find there any **followers** of the **Way of the Lord**, he would be able to **arrest** them, both men

afraid 5.26; 16.38
alive [2] 1.3; 20.10
amaze 7.31; 10.45
apostle 8.1; 11.1
arrest [3] 5.18; 12.3
authority 2.22; 26.10
baptize 8.12; 10.37
believe [2] 8.12; 10.43
believer [5] 8.1; 10.23
body [2] 7.16; 13.36
bold [2] 4.13; 13.46

[j] south; *or* at midday. [k] This road is not used nowadays; *or* This is the desert road.
[l] *Some manuscripts add verse 37:* Philip said to him, "You may be baptized if you believe with all your heart." "I do," he answered; "I believe that Jesus Christ is the Son of God."

8.32-33: Is 53.7-8 (LXX)

chief priests [2] 5.24; 22.30
choose 6.3; 10.41
Christian 11.26
church 8.1; 11.22
convince Lk 20.6; 12.20
disciple [2] 6.1; 11.29
dispute Lk 12.58; 13.45
follower [3] 5.36; 1 Cor 10.2
Gentile 6.5; 10.28
God's people 7.34; 13.19
help [4] 7.24; 10.2
High Priest 7.1; 19.14
Jew [3] 6.1; 10.2
kneel 7.60; 20.36
letter (2) Jer 29.1; 15.20
light (1) Jn 12.35; 12.7
message 8.4; 10.36
Messiah 8.5; 17.3
name (2) (name of God, of Jesus) [3] 8.16; 10.43
paralyse 8.7
peace 7.26; 10.36
persecute [2] 8.1; 11.19
plan [2] 8.22; 12.4
please 8.24; 10.4
poor Jn 13.29; 10.2
power 8.10; 10.38
pray [2] 8.15; 10.2
preach [4] 8.4; 10.37
present (1) 6.6; Eph 5.27
prove 4.2; 14.3
purpose Jn 18.37; 13.36
reverence Zeph 3.7; Rom 3.18
sake 5.41; 21.13
serve 7.7; 13.2
Son of God Jn 20.31; 13.32
Spirit (1) (God's Spirit) [2] 8.15; 10.19
strength [2] 3.16; 14.22
suffer 8.1; 17.3
synagogue [2] 6.9; 13.5
terrible Lk 22.22; Rom 7.13
threat 4.29; Rom 3.13
turn [2] 7.42; 11.21
violent Lk 11.39; 16.26
vision [2] 2.17; 10.3
watch 5.23; 20.28
Way (2) 18.25
who Jn 21.12; 19.15
widow [2] 6.1; 1 Cor 7.8
word (1) 8.14; 11.1
worship (1) (of God) [2] 8.27; 10.2

and women, and bring them back to
Jerusalem.
3 As Saul was coming near the city of
Damascus, suddenly a light from the sky
flashed round him. 4 He fell to the ground
and heard a voice saying to him, "Saul,
Saul! Why do you persecute me?"
5 "Who are you, Lord?" he asked.
"I am Jesus, whom you persecute," the
voice said. 6 "But get up and go into the
city, where you will be told what you
must do."
7 The men who were travelling with
Saul had stopped, not saying a word; they
heard the voice but could not see anyone.
8 Saul got up from the ground and opened
his eyes, but could not see a thing. So
they took him by the hand and led him
into Damascus. 9 For three days he was
not able to see, and during that time he
did not eat or drink anything.
10 There was a Christian in Damascus
named Ananias. He had a vision, in
which the Lord said to him, "Ananias!"
"Here I am, Lord," he answered.
11 The Lord said to him, "Get ready
and go to Straight Street, and at the
house of Judas ask for a man from
Tarsus named Saul. He is praying, 12 and
in a vision he has seen a man named
Ananias come in and place his hands on
him so that he might see again."
13 Ananias answered, "Lord, many
people have told me about this man and
about all the terrible things he has done
to your people in Jerusalem. 14 And he
has come to Damascus with authority
from the chief priests to arrest all who
worship you."
15 The Lord said to him, "Go, because
I have chosen him to serve me, to make
my name known to Gentiles and kings
and to the people of Israel. 16 And I myself will show him all that he must suffer
for my sake."
17 So Ananias went, entered the house
where Saul was, and placed his hands on
him. "Brother Saul," he said, "the Lord
has sent me—Jesus himself, who
appeared to you on the road as you were
coming here. He sent me so that you
might see again and be filled with the
Holy Spirit." 18 At once something like
fish scales fell from Saul's eyes, and he
was able to see again. He stood up and
was baptized; 19 and after he had eaten,
his strength came back.

Saul Preaches in Damascus

Saul stayed for a few days with the believers in Damascus. 20 He went straight
to the synagogues and began to preach
that Jesus was the Son of God.
21 All who heard him were amazed
and asked, "Isn't he the one who in
Jerusalem was killing those who worship
that man Jesus? And didn't he come
here for the very purpose of arresting
those people and taking them back to the
chief priests?"
22 But Saul's preaching became even
more powerful, and his proofs that Jesus
was the Messiah were so convincing that
the Jews who lived in Damascus could
not answer him.
23 After many days had gone by, the
Jews met together and made plans to kill
Saul, 24 but he was told of their plan. Day
and night they watched the city gates in
order to kill him. 25 But one night Saul's
followers took him and let him down
through an opening in the wall, lowering
him in a basket.

Saul in Jerusalem

26 Saul went to Jerusalem and tried to
join the disciples. But they would not believe that he was a disciple, and they
were all afraid of him. 27 Then Barnabas
came to his help and took him to the
apostles. He explained to them how Saul
had seen the Lord on the road and that
the Lord had spoken to him. He also told
them how boldly Saul had preached in
the name of Jesus in Damascus. 28 And so
Saul stayed with them and went all over
Jerusalem, preaching boldly in the name
of the Lord. 29 He also talked and disputed
with the Greek-speaking Jews, but they
tried to kill him. 30 When the believers
found out about this, they took Saul to
Caesarea and sent him away to Tarsus.
31 And so it was that the church
throughout Judaea, Galilee, and Samaria
had a time of peace. Through the help of
the Holy Spirit it was strengthened and
grew in numbers, as it lived in reverence
for the Lord.

Peter in Lydda and Joppa

32 Peter travelled everywhere, and on
one occasion he went to visit God's
people who lived in Lydda. 33 There he
met a man named Aeneas, who was
paralysed and had not been able to get
out of bed for eight years. 34 "Aeneas,"
Peter said to him, "Jesus Christ makes
you well. Get up and make your bed." At
once Aeneas got up. 35 All the people
living in Lydda and Sharon saw him, and
they turned to the Lord.
36 In Joppa there was a woman
named Tabitha, who was a believer. (Her

9.23–25: 2 Cor 11.32–33

name in Greek is Dorcas, meaning "a
deer.") She spent all her time doing good
and **helping** the **poor**. 37 At that time she
became ill and died. Her **body** was
washed and laid in a room upstairs.
38 Joppa was not very far from Lydda,
and when the **believers** in Joppa heard
that Peter was in Lydda, they sent two
men to him with the **message**, "**Please**
hurry and come to us." 39 So Peter got
ready and went with them. When he
arrived, he was taken to the room upstairs, where all the **widows** crowded
round him, crying and showing him all
the shirts and coats that Dorcas had
made while she was **alive**. 40 Peter put
them all out of the room, and **knelt** down
and **prayed**; then he **turned** to the **body**
and said, "Tabitha, get up!" She opened
her eyes, and when she saw Peter, she
sat up. 41 Peter reached over and **helped**
her get up. Then he called all the **be-**
lievers, including the **widows**, and **pre-**
sented her **alive** to them. 42 The news
about this spread all over Joppa, and
many people **believed** in the Lord.
43 Peter stayed on in Joppa for many days
with a tanner of leather named Simon.

Peter and Cornelius

10 There was a man in Caesarea
named Cornelius, who was a captain in the Roman regiment called "The
Italian Regiment." 2 He was a **religious**
man; he and his whole family **wor-**
shipped God. He also did much to **help**
the **Jewish poor** people and was **con-**
stantly praying to God. 3 It was about
three o'clock one afternoon when he had
a **vision**, in which he **clearly** saw an
angel of God come in and say to him,
"Cornelius!"
4 He stared at the **angel** in **fear** and
said, "What is it, sir?"
The **angel** answered, "God is **pleased**
with your **prayers** and works of charity,
and is ready to answer you. 5 And now
send some men to Joppa for a certain
man whose full name is Simon Peter. 6 He
is a guest in the home of a tanner of
leather named Simon, who lives by the
sea." 7 Then the **angel** went away, and
Cornelius called two of his house **ser-**
vants and a soldier, a **religious** man who
was one of his personal attendants. 8 He
told them what had happened and sent
them off to Joppa.
9 The next day, as they were on their
way and coming near Joppa, Peter went
up on the roof of the house about noon in
order to **pray**. 10 He became **hungry** and
wanted something to eat; while the food
was being prepared, he had a **vision**.
11 He saw **heaven** opened and something
coming down that looked like a large
sheet being lowered by its four corners to
the earth. 12 In it were all kinds of animals, reptiles, and wild birds. 13 A voice
said to him, "Get up, Peter; kill and eat!"
14 But Peter said, "Certainly not,
Lord! I have never eaten anything ritually **unclean** or **defiled**."
15 The voice spoke to him again, "Do
not **consider** anything **unclean** that God
has **declared clean**." 16 This happened
three times, and then the thing was
taken back up into **heaven**.
17 While Peter was wondering about
the meaning of this **vision**, the men sent
by Cornelius had **learnt** where Simon's
house was, and they were now standing
in front of the gate. 18 They called out and
asked, "Is there a guest here by the
name of Simon Peter?"
19 Peter was still trying to **understand**
what the **vision** meant, when the **Spirit**
said, "Listen! Three[m] men are here looking for you. 20 So get ready and go down,
and do not hesitate to go with them, for I
have sent them." 21 So Peter went down
and said to the men, "**I am** the man you
are looking for. Why have you come?"
22 "Captain Cornelius sent us," they
answered. "He is a good man who **wor-**
ships God and is highly **respected** by all
the **Jewish** people. An **angel of God** told
him to invite you to his house, so that he
could hear what you have to say."
23 Peter invited the men in and **persuaded**
them to spend the night there.
The next day he got ready and went
with them; and some of the **believers**
from Joppa went along with him. 24 The
following day he arrived in Caesarea,
where Cornelius was waiting for him, together with relatives and close **friends**
that he had invited. 25 As Peter was about
to go in, Cornelius met him, fell at his
feet, and **bowed down** before him. 26 But
Peter made him **rise**. "Stand up," he said;
"I myself am only a man." 27 Peter kept
on talking to Cornelius as he went into
the house, where he found many people
gathered. 28 He said to them, "You yourselves know very well that a **Jew** is not
allowed by his **religion** to visit or associate with **Gentiles**. But God has shown me
that I must not **consider** any person ritually **unclean** or **defiled**. 29 And so when
you sent for me, I came without any
objection. I ask you, then, why did you
send for me?"
30 Cornelius said, "It was about this
time three days ago that I was **praying**[n]

accept 6.7; 16.21
amaze 9.21; 12.16
angel [5] 8.26; 11.13
baptize [3] 9.18; 11.16
basis Rom 3.30
believe 9.26; 11.17
believer [2] 9.19; 11.1
bow (2) Jn 19.30; 1 Cor 14.25
choose 9.15; 12.21
clean Jn 18.28; 11.9
clear 2.22; 11.17
command Jn 15.10; 17.30
consider [2] 5.41; 11.9
constant Mic 7.18; Col 3.10
cross (1) 5.30; 13.29
dead 5.5; 14.19
death (2) (from death) [2] 5.30; 13.30
death (3) (to death) 5.33; 12.2
declare Jn 13.8; 11.9
defile [2] Mal 2.11; 11.8
Devil Jn 13.2; 13.10
enough Jn 9.21; 13.25
fear 7.32; 19.17
forgive 8.22; 13.38
friend Jn 19.12; 13.7
Gentile [2] 9.15; 11.1
gift 8.20; 11.17
Good News 8.12; 11.20
gospel Mk 16.15; Rom 1.16
heal 8.7; 14.9
heaven [2] 7.42; 11.5
help 9.27; 11.29
hunger Jn 6.35; Rom 8.35
I am 7.32; Rom 14.11
Jew [4] 9.22; 11.19
judge 7.27; 13.20
learn 4.13; 14.6

message [3] 9.38; 11.19
name (2) (name of God, of Jesus) [2] 9.15; 16.18
notice (1) 4.29; 17.16
peace 9.31; 12.20
persuade Mt 27.20; 16.15
please 9.38; 12.3
poor 9.36; Rom 8.35
power [3] 9.22; 11.21
praise 4.21; 11.18
pray [3] 9.11; 11.5
prayer [2] 6.4; 14.23
preach [2] 9.20; 13.5
presence 3.13; Rom 3.23
proclaim 8.25; 11.20
prophet 8.27; 11.27
race (1) 7.8; 17.26
raise 5.30; 13.30
religion [3] 2.5; 17.22
respect 5.34; 15.22
right (1) 8.21; 14.17
rise [2] 4.2; 17.3
servant 7.52; 12.13
Spirit (1) (God's Spirit) [5] 9.17; 11.12
strange Jn 9.30; 17.20
testify Jn 8.13; 18.5
true 7.1; 11.23
unclean [3] Mk 7.2; 11.8
understand 8.30; 13.27
vision [4] 9.10; 11.5
witness [2] 7.58; 13.31
worship (1) (of God) [3] 9.14; 13.16

[m] Three; *some manuscripts have* Some; *one manuscript has* Two.
[n] praying; *some manuscripts have* fasting and praying.

in my house at three o'clock in the afternoon. Suddenly a man dressed in shining
clothes stood in front of me 31 and said:
'Cornelius! God has heard your **prayer**
and has taken **notice** of your works of
charity. 32 Send someone to Joppa for a
man whose full name is Simon Peter. He
is a guest in the home of Simon the
tanner of leather, who lives by the sea.'
33 And so I sent for you at once, and you
have been good **enough** to come. Now we
are all here in the **presence** of God, waiting to hear anything that the Lord has
instructed you to say."

Peter's Speech

34 Peter began to speak: "I now
realize that it is **true** that God treats
everyone on the same **basis**. 35 Whoever
worships him and does what is **right** is
acceptable to him, no matter what **race**
he belongs to. 36 You know the **message**
he sent to the people of Israel, **proclaiming** the **Good News** of **peace** through
Jesus Christ, who is Lord of all. 37 You
know of the great event that took place
throughout the land of Israel, beginning
in Galilee after John **preached** his **message** of **baptism**. 38 You know about Jesus
of Nazareth and how God poured out on
him the **Holy Spirit** and **power**. He went
everywhere, doing good and **healing** all
who were under the **power** of the **Devil**,
for God was with him. 39 We are **witnesses** of everything that he did in the
land of Israel and in Jerusalem. Then
they put him **to death** by nailing him to a
cross. 40 But God **raised** him **from death**
three days later and caused him to
appear, 41 not to everyone, but only to the
witnesses that God had already **chosen**,
that is, to us who ate and drank with him
after he **rose from death**. 42 And he **commanded** us to **preach** the **gospel** to the
people and to **testify** that he is the one
whom God has appointed **judge** of the
living and the **dead**. 43 All the **prophets**
spoke about him, saying that everyone
who **believes** in him will have his sins **forgiven** through the **power** of his **name**."

The Gentiles Receive the Holy Spirit

44 While Peter was still speaking, the
Holy Spirit came down on all those who
were listening to his **message**. 45 The
Jewish believers who had come from
Joppa with Peter were **amazed** that God
had poured out his **gift** of the **Holy Spirit**
on the **Gentiles** also. 46 For they heard
them speaking in **strange tongues** and
praising God's greatness. Peter spoke
up: 47 "These people have received the
Holy Spirit, just as we also did. Can anyone, then, stop them from being **baptized**
with water?" 48 So he ordered them to be
baptized in the name of Jesus Christ.
Then they asked him to stay with them
for a few days.

Peter's Report to the Church at Jerusalem

11 The **apostles** and the other **believers** throughout Judaea heard
that the **Gentiles** also had received the
word of God. 2 When Peter went to
Jerusalem, those who were in **favour** of
circumcising Gentiles criticized him, saying, 3 "You were a guest in the home of
uncircumcised Gentiles, and you even
ate with them!" 4 So Peter gave them a
complete account of what had happened
from the very beginning:
5 "While I was **praying** in the city of
Joppa, I had a **vision**. I saw something
coming down that looked like a large
sheet being lowered by its four corners
from **heaven**, and it stopped next to me.
6 I looked closely inside and saw domesti-
cated and wild animals, reptiles, and wild
birds. 7 Then I heard a voice saying to
me, 'Get up, Peter; kill and eat!' 8 But I
said, 'Certainly not, Lord! No ritually **unclean** or **defiled** food has ever entered
my mouth.' 9 The voice spoke again from
heaven, 'Do not **consider** anything **unclean** that God has **declared clean**.'
10 This happened three times, and finally
the whole thing was drawn back up into
heaven. 11 At that very moment three
men who had been sent to me from
Caesarea arrived at the house where I
was[o] staying. 12 The **Spirit** told me to go
with them without hesitation. These six
fellow-believers from Joppa accompanied me to Caesarea, and we all went
into the house of Cornelius. 13 He told us
how he had seen an **angel** standing in his
house, who said to him, 'Send someone to
Joppa for a man whose full name is
Simon Peter. 14 He will speak **words** to
you by which you and all your family will
be **saved**.' 15 And when I began to speak,
the **Holy Spirit** came down on them just
as on us at the beginning. 16 Then I
remembered what the Lord had said:
'John **baptized** with water, but you will be
baptized with the **Holy Spirit**.' 17 It is **clear**
that God gave those **Gentiles** the same
gift that he gave us when we **believed** in
the Lord Jesus Christ; who was I, then, to
try to stop God!"
18 When they heard this, they stopped

[o] I was; *some manuscripts have* we were.

10.34: Deut 10.17 **11.16:** Acts 1.5

angel 10.3; 12.7
apostle 9.27; 13.43
baptize [2] 10.37; 13.24
believe [2] 10.43; 13.12
believer [6] 10.23; 12.17
bless 6.8; 13.34
Christian 9.10; 16.1
church [3] 9.31; 12.1
circumcise [2] 7.8; 15.1
clean 10.15; Eph 5.26
clear 10.3; 23.1
complete Jn 19.28; 14.26
consider 10.15; 13.46
criticize [2] Lk 11.53; 1 Cor 9.3
declare 10.15; 20.24
defile 10.14; 21.28
disciple 9.26; 14.21
elder (2) 6.12; 14.23
faith 6.5; 13.8
faithful 2.27; Rom 3.3
famine 7.11; Rev 6.8
favour 7.46; 24.27
Gentile [6] 10.28; 13.16
gift 10.45; 28.10
glad 2.26; 13.48
Good News 10.36; 13.32
heart 8.21; 14.17
heaven [3] 10.11; 14.15
help 10.2; 12.20
Jew 10.2; 12.3
message [2] 10.36; 13.15
persecute 9.4; 12.1
power [2] 10.38; 12.11
praise 10.46; 13.48
pray 10.2; 12.5
predict 1.16; 16.16
proclaim 10.36; 17.23
prophet 10.43; 13.1
remember 7.60; 20.31
repent 8.22; 26.20
save 4.12; 13.47
scatter 8.1; 1 Cor 10.5
Spirit (1) (God's Spirit) [5] 10.19; 13.2
teach 7.22; 13.12
true 10.34; 12.11
turn 9.35; 13.8
unclean [2] 10.14; 15.20
urge 2.40; 18.27
vision 10.3; 12.9
word (1) [2] 9.7; 12.24

their **criticism** and **praised** God, saying, "Then God has given to the **Gentiles** also the opportunity to **repent** and live!"

The Church at Antioch

19 Some of the **believers** who were **scattered** by the **persecution** which took place when Stephen was killed went as far as Phoenicia, Cyprus, and Antioch, telling the **message** to **Jews** only. 20 But other **believers**, men from Cyprus and Cyrene, went to Antioch and **proclaimed** the **message** to **Gentiles**[p] also, telling them the **Good News** about the Lord Jesus. 21 The **Lord's power** was with them, and a great number of people **believed** and **turned to the Lord**.

22 The news about this reached the **church** in Jerusalem, so they sent Barnabas to Antioch. 23 When he arrived and saw how God had **blessed** the people, he was **glad** and **urged** them all to be **faithful** and **true** to the Lord **with all their hearts**. 24 Barnabas was a good man, full of the **Holy Spirit** and **faith**, and many people were brought to the Lord.

25 Then Barnabas went to Tarsus to look for Saul. 26 When he found him, he took him to Antioch, and for a whole year the two met with the people of the **church** and **taught** a large group. It was at Antioch that the **believers** were first called **Christians**.

27 About that time some **prophets** went from Jerusalem to Antioch. 28 One of them, named Agabus, stood up and by the **power of the Spirit predicted** that a severe **famine** was about to come over all the earth. (It came when Claudius was emperor.) 29 The **disciples** decided that each of them would send as much as he could to **help** their **fellow-believers** who lived in Judaea. 30 They did this, then, and sent the money to the **church elders** by Barnabas and Saul.

More Persecution

12 About this time King Herod[q] began to **persecute** some members of the **church**. 2 He had James, the brother of John, put **to death** by the sword. 3 When he saw that this **pleased** the **Jews**, he went on to **arrest** Peter. (This happened during the time of the **Festival of Unleavened Bread**.) 4 After his **arrest** Peter was put in **jail**, where he was handed over to be guarded by four groups of four soldiers each. Herod **planned** to put him on **trial** in public after **Passover**. 5 So Peter was kept in **jail**, but the people of the **church** were **praying earnestly** to God for him.

Peter Is Set Free from Prison

6 The night before Herod was going to bring him out to the people, Peter was sleeping between two guards. He was tied with two chains, and there were guards on **duty** at the **prison** gate. 7 Suddenly an **angel of the Lord** stood there, and a **light** shone in the cell. The **angel** shook Peter by the shoulder, woke him up, and said, "Hurry! Get up!" At once the chains fell off Peter's **hands**. 8 Then the **angel** said, "Fasten your belt and put on your sandals." Peter did so, and the **angel** said, "Put your cloak round you and come with me." 9 Peter followed him out of the **prison**, not knowing, however, if what the **angel** was doing was **real**; he thought he was seeing a **vision**. 10 They passed by the first guard post and then the second, and came at **last** to the iron gate leading into the city. The gate opened for them by itself, and they went out. They walked down a street, and suddenly the **angel** left Peter.

11 Then Peter realized what had happened to him, and said, "Now I know that it is really **true**! The Lord sent his **angel** to **rescue** me from Herod's **power** and from everything the **Jewish** people expected to happen."

12 Aware of his situation, he went to the home of Mary, the mother of John Mark, where many people had gathered and were **praying**. 13 Peter knocked at the outside door, and a **servant-girl** named Rhoda came to answer it. 14 She recognized Peter's voice and was so **happy** that she ran back in without opening the door, and **announced** that Peter was standing outside. 15 "You are **mad**!" they told her. But she insisted that it was **true**. So they answered, "It is his **angel**."

16 Meanwhile Peter kept on knocking. At **last** they opened the door, and when they saw him, they were **amazed**. 17 He motioned with his hand for them to be quiet, and he explained to them how the Lord had brought him out of **prison**. "Tell this to James and the rest of the **believers**," he said; then he left and went somewhere else.

18 When morning came, there was a tremendous confusion among the guards—what had happened to Peter? 19 Herod gave orders to search for him, but they could not find him. So he had the

amaze 10.45; 13.12
angel [9] 11.13; 23.8
anger 7.54; Rom 1.18
announce 7.52; 14.15
arrest [2] 9.2; 21.33
believer 11.1; 13.48
choose 10.41; 13.17
church [2] 11.22; 13.1
convince 9.22; 17.4
death (3) (to death) [2] 10.39; 13.28
duty (1) Lk 17.10; Rom 12.16
earnest Lk 7.4; 2 Cor 7.11
festival Jn 13.1; 20.6
god (2) (other gods) 7.40; 14.11
happy 5.41; 14.17

help 11.29; 13.5
honour 7.41; 19.17
jail [2] 8.3; 16.23
Jew [2] 11.19; 13.6
last (2) [2] 7.18; 19.35
light (1) 9.3; 13.11
mad Jn 10.20; 26.24
Passover Jn 19.14; 1 Cor 5.7
peace 10.36; 15.33
persecute 11.19; 13.50
plan 9.23; 23.12
please 10.4; 21.39
power 11.21; 13.17
pray [2] 11.5; 13.3
prison [3] 8.23; 16.25
question 5.27; 15.6
real Jn 15.1; Rom 2.28
rescue Lk 1.73; 23.27
servant 10.7; 13.35
speech Mk 7.35; 19.33
strike Jn 18.10; 23.2
throne 7.49; Col 3.1
true [2] 11.23; 13.27
try (2) Jn 18.31; 22.25
unleavened Lk 22.1; 20.6
vision 11.5; 16.9
word (1) 11.1; 13.5

[p] Gentiles; *some manuscripts have* Greek-speaking Jews *or* Greek-speaking people.
[q] KING HEROD: *Herod Agrippa I, ruler of all Palestine.*

11.19: Acts 8.1–4 **11.28:** Acts 21.10 **12.4:** Ex 12.1–27

guards **questioned** and ordered them to
be put **to death**.
After this, Herod left Judaea and spent
some time in Caesarea.

The Death of Herod

20 Herod was very **angry** with the
people of Tyre and Sidon, so they went in
a group to see him. First they **convinced**
Blastus, the man in charge of the palace,
that he should **help** them. Then they
went to Herod and asked him for **peace**,
because their country got its food supplies from the king's country.
21 On a **chosen** day Herod put on his
royal robes, sat on his **throne**, and made
a **speech** to the people. 22 "It isn't a man
speaking, but a **god**!" they shouted. 23 At
once the **angel of the Lord struck** Herod
down, because he did not give **honour** to
God. He was eaten by worms and died.
24 Meanwhile the **word of God** continued to spread and grow.
25 Barnabas and Saul finished their
mission and returned from[r] Jerusalem,
taking John Mark with them.

Barnabas and Saul Are Chosen and Sent

13 In the **church** at Antioch there
were some **prophets** and
teachers: Barnabas, Simeon (called the
Black), Lucius (from Cyrene), Manaen
(who had been brought up with Herod[s]
the governor), and Saul. 2 While they
were **serving** the Lord and **fasting**, the
Holy Spirit said to them, "Set **apart** for
me Barnabas and Saul, to do the work to
which I have called them."
3 They **fasted** and **prayed**, placed their
hands on them, and sent them off.

In Cyprus

4 Having been sent by the **Holy Spirit**,
Barnabas and Saul went to Seleucia and
sailed from there to the island of Cyprus.
5 When they arrived at Salamis, they
preached the **word of God** in the **synagogues**. They had John Mark with them
to **help** in the work.
6 They went all the way across the
island to Paphos, where they met a certain **magician** named Bar-Jesus, a **Jew**
who **claimed** to be a **prophet**. 7 He was a
friend of the governor of the island,
Sergius Paulus, who was an **intelligent**
man. The governor called Barnabas and
Saul before him because he wanted to
hear the **word of God**. 8 But they were opposed by the **magician** Elymas (that is
his name in Greek), who tried to **turn** the
governor away from the **faith**. 9 Then
Saul—also known as Paul—was filled
with the **Holy Spirit**; he looked straight at
the **magician** 10 and said, "You son of the
Devil! You are the **enemy** of everything
that is good. You are full of all kinds of
evil tricks, and you always keep trying to
turn the Lord's **truths** into **lies**! 11 The
Lord's hand will come down on you now;
you will be **blind** and will not see the **light**
of day for a time."
At once Elymas felt a **dark** mist cover
his eyes, and he walked about trying to
find someone to lead him by the hand.
12 When the governor saw what had happened, he **believed**; for he was greatly
amazed at the **teaching** about the Lord.

In Antioch in Pisidia

13 Paul and his companions sailed
from Paphos and came to Perga, a city
in Pamphylia, where John Mark left
them and went back to Jerusalem.
14 They went on from Perga and arrived
in Antioch in Pisidia, and on the **Sabbath**
they went into the **synagogue** and sat
down. 15 After the reading from the **Law
of Moses** and from the writings of the
prophets, the officials of the **synagogue**
sent them a **message**: "Brothers, we
want you to speak to the people if you
have a **message** of **encouragement** for
them." 16 Paul stood up, motioned with
his hand, and began to speak:
"Fellow-Israelites and all **Gentiles**
here who **worship** God: hear me! 17 The
God of the people of Israel **chose** our
ancestors and made the people a great
nation during the time they lived as
foreigners in Egypt. God brought them
out of Egypt by his great **power**, 18 and
for forty years he **endured**[t] them in the
desert. 19 He **destroyed** seven nations in
the land of Canaan and made **his people**
the owners of the land. 20 All this took
about four hundred and fifty years.
"After this[u] he gave them **judges** until
the time of the **prophet** Samuel. 21 And
when they asked for a king, God gave
them Saul son of Kish from the tribe of
Benjamin, to be their king for forty
years. 22 After removing him, God made
David their king. This is what God said
about him: 'I have found that David son
of Jesse is the kind of man I like, a man
who will do all I want him to do.' 23 It was

after me Jn 1.15
amaze 12.16; Rev 13.3
apart Lk 18.11; Rom 2.12
apostle [2] 11.1; 14.3
baptize 11.16; 16.15
believe [3] 11.17; 14.2
believer [2] 12.17; 14.1
bless 11.23; 20.32
blind Jn 12.40; 22.11
body 9.37; Rom 4.19
bold 9.27; 14.3
care 7.20; 14.26
choose [2] 12.21; 15.7
church 12.1; 14.23
claim 8.9; 25.19
commandment Jn 15.12; Rom 7.8
condemn Jn 19.4; 25.15
consider 11.9; 15.6
cross (1) 10.39; Rom 6.6
dark 2.20; 26.18
death (1) 5.28; 20.28
death (2) (from death) [3] 10.40; 17.3
death (3) (to death) 12.2; 22.20
destroy 8.3; 19.27
Devil 10.38; 2 Cor 6.15
devote Jn 2.17; 21.20
dispute 9.29; 26.3
encourage [2] 4.36; 14.22
endure Jn 15.16; Rom 5.4
enemy 2.35; Rom 5.10
enough 10.33; 27 38
eternal [2] Jn 17.2; Rom 1.20

evil 8.22; 17.30
faith 11.24; 14.22
fast (2) [2] Lk 18.12; 14.23
Father (2) (God) 2.33; Rom 1.7
forgive 10.43; 15.9
free [2] 7.25; 24.23
friend 10.24; 15.25
Gentile [7] 11.1; 14.1
glad 11.23; 2 Cor 2.3
God's people 9.32; 18.10
Good News 11.20; 14.7
grace Jn 1.14; 14.3
grave [3] 7.16
help 12.20; 16.9
insult Lk 23.39; 23.4
intelligent Lk 2.47; Rev 13.18
jealous 7.9; 17.5
Jew [4] 12.3; 14.1
joy 8.8; 15.3
Judaism 6.5; Tit 1.10
judge 10.42; 17.31
law [2] 7.53; 15.1
lie (2) 6.13; 20.30
life (1) [2] 8.33; 15.26
life (2) (to life) 4.2; 23.6
light (1) [2] 12.7; 16.29
magic [3] 8.9; 19.19
message [5] 11.19; 14.3
pass (5) 7.7; Rom 2.1
persecute 12.1; 22.4
power 12.11; 14.3
praise 11.18; 21.20
pray 12.5; 16.25
preach [3] 10.37; 14.7
promise [3] 7.5; 26.6
prophet [7] 11.27; 15.15
psalm 1.20; Eph 5.19
purpose 9.21; 20.27
raise [4] 10.40; 17.31
reason Jn 19.4; 18.14
reject 7.35; Rom 2.8
Sabbath [4] Jn 19.31; 15.21
sacred 6.13; 19.35
salvation 4.12; 26.23
save 11.14; 15.1
Saviour [2] 5.31; Rom 11.26
scripture 8.32; 15.15
sentence Lk 24.20; 25.25
servant 12.13; 16.17
serve [2] 9.15; Rom 1.9
Son of God 9.20; 20.28
Spirit (1) (God's Spirit) [4] 11.12; 15.8
sure 2.36; 21.22
synagogue [4] 9.2; 14.1
teach 11.26; 14.22
teacher Jn 20.16; 17.18
tomb Jn 20.1
trick 7.19; Eph 4.14
true 12.11; 14.3
truth Jn 21.18; 21.24
turn [3] 11.21; 14.2
understand 10.19; 28.26
witness 10.39; 22.15
word (1) [7] 12.24; 14.9
world 4.12; 17.24
worship (1) (of God) [3] 10.2; 16.14

[r] from; *some manuscripts have* to. [s] HEROD: *Herod Antipas, ruler of Galilee (see Lk 3.1).*
[t] he endured; *some manuscripts have* he took care of.
[u] All this took about four hundred and fifty years. After this; *or* Some four hundred and fifty years later.

13.17: Ex 1.7, 12.51 **13.18:** Num 14.34; Deut 1.31 **13.19:** Deut 7.1; Josh 14.1
13.20: Judg 2.16; 1 Sam 3.20 **13.21:** 1 Sam 8.5, 10.21 **13.22:** 1 Sam 13.14, 16.12; Ps 89.20

worthy 5.41;
1 Cor 7.25

Jesus, a descendant of David, whom God
made the **Saviour** of the people of Israel,
as he had **promised.** 24 Before Jesus began his work, John **preached** to all the
people of Israel that they should **turn
from their sins** and be **baptized.** 25 And as
John was about to finish his mission, he
said to the people, 'Who do you think I
am? I am not the one you are waiting
for. But listen! He is coming **after me,**
and I am not good **enough** to take his sandals off his feet.'

26 "My fellow-Israelites, descendants
of Abraham, and all **Gentiles** here who
worship God: it is to us that this **message**
of **salvation** has been sent! 27 For the
people who live in Jerusalem and their
leaders did not know that he is the
Saviour, nor did they **understand** the
words of the **prophets** that are read
every **Sabbath**. Yet they made the **prophets' words** come **true** by **condemning**
Jesus. 28 And even though they could find
no **reason** to **pass** the **death sentence** on
him, they asked Pilate to have him put to
death. 29 And after they had done everything that the **Scriptures** say about him,
they took him down from the **cross** and
placed him in a **tomb.** 30 But God **raised**
him **from death,** 31 and for many days he
appeared to those who had travelled with
him from Galilee to Jerusalem. They are
now **witnesses** for him to the people of
Israel. 32-33 And we are here to bring the
Good News to you: what God **promised**
our ancestors he would do, he has now
done for us, who are their descendants,
by **raising** Jesus **to life**. As it is written in
the second **Psalm,**

'You are my **Son**;
today I have become your **Father**.'

34 And this is what God said about **raising**
him **from death,** never to rot away in the
grave:

'I will give you the **sacred** and **sure
blessings**
that I **promised** to David.'

35 As indeed he says in another passage,

'You will not allow your **devoted
servant** to rot in the **grave**.'

36 For David **served** God's **purposes** in his
own time, and then he died, was buried
with his ancestors, and his **body** rotted in
the **grave.** 37 But this did not happen to
the one whom God **raised from death.**
38-39 We want you to know, my fellow-
Israelites, that it is through Jesus that the
message about **forgiveness** of sins is
preached to you; and that everyone who
believes in him is **set free** from all the
sins from which the **Law of Moses** could
not **set you free.** 40 Take **care**, then, so
that what the **prophets** said may not happen to you:[v]

41 'Look, you scoffers! Be astonished and
die!
For what I am doing today
is something that you will not
believe,
even when someone explains it to
you!' "

42 As Paul and Barnabas were leaving
the **synagogue**, the people invited them
to come back the next **Sabbath** and tell
them more about these things. 43 After
the people had left the meeting, Paul and
Barnabas were followed by many **Jews**
and by many **Gentiles** who had been converted to **Judaism**. The **apostles** spoke to
them and **encouraged** them to keep on
living in the **grace** of God.

44 The next **Sabbath** nearly everyone
in the town came to hear the **word of the
Lord.** 45 When the **Jews** saw the crowds,
they were filled with **jealousy**; they **disputed** what Paul was saying and **insulted**
him. 46 But Paul and Barnabas spoke out
even more **boldly**: "It was necessary that
the **word of God** should be spoken first to
you. But since you **reject** it and do not
consider yourselves **worthy** of **eternal
life**, we will leave you and go to the **Gentiles.** 47 For this is the **commandment** that
the Lord has given us:

'I have made you a **light** for the
Gentiles,
so that all the **world** may be
saved.' "

48 When the **Gentiles** heard this, they
were **glad** and **praised** the Lord's **message**; and those who had been **chosen** for
eternal life became **believers.**

49 The **word of the Lord** spread everywhere in that region. 50 But the **Jews**
stirred up the leading men of the city and
the **Gentile** women of high social standing who **worshipped** God. They started a
persecution against Paul and Barnabas
and threw them out of their region. 51 The
apostles shook the dust off their feet in
protest against them and went on to
Iconium. 52 The **believers** in Antioch were
full of **joy** and the **Holy Spirit.**

[v] *Some manuscripts do not have* to you.

13.24: Mk 1.4; Lk 3.3 **13.25:** Mt 3.11; Mk 1.7; Lk 3.16; Jn 1.20, 27
13.28: Mt 27.22–23; Mk 15.13–14; Lk 23.21–23; Jn 19.15
13.29: Mt 27.57–61; Mk 15.42–47; Lk 23.50–56; Jn 19.38–42 **13.31:** Acts 1.3 **13.33:** Ps 2.7
13.34: Is 55.3 (LXX) **13.35:** Ps 16.10 **13.41:** Hab 1.5 (LXX) **13.47:** Is 42.6, 49.6
13.51: Mt 10.14; Mk 6.11; Lk 9.5, 10.11

announce 12.14; 16.17
apostle [6] 13.43; 15.2
being Jn 1.14; Rom 4.17
believe [3] 13.12; 15.7
believer [5] 13.48; 15.1
birth Jn 16.21; 15.23
bold 13.46; 18.26
care 13.40; 15.14
church [2] 13.1; 15.3
complete 11.4; 20.24
dead 10.42; 20.9
disciple 11.29; 19.1
elder (2) 11.30; 15.2
encourage 13.15; 15.31
evidence Mk 14.55; 2 Cor 13.1
exist Jn 1.1; 17.28
faith 13.8; 16.5
fast (2) 13.2
flee 7.29; Rev 9.6
Gentile [4] 13.16; 15.3
god (2) (other gods) [2] 12.22; 17.18
Good News [3] 13.32; 15.7
grace [2] 13.43; 15.11
happy 12.14; 20.35
heal 10.38; 28.8
heart 11.23; 21.13
heaven [2] 11.5; 17.24
human 5.38; Rom 1.3
ill-treat 7.24; 1 Thes 2.2
Jew [5] 13.6; 16.1
keep from 8.36; 15.20
Kingdom (1) (of God) 8.12; 19.8
learn 10.17; 23.27
message [2] 13.15; 15.31
miracle 8.6; 15.12
offer [2] 8.18; 15.20
power 13.17; 19.20
prayer 10.4; 16.13
preach [3] 13.5; 15.7
priest 6.7; Rom 15.16
prove 9.22; 17.3
right (1) 10.35; 15.38
sacrifice [2] 7.41; 20.28
strength 9.19; 15.32
synagogue 13.5; 15.21
teach 13.12; 15.1
temple (2) (of other gods) Zech 5.11; 17.24
trouble 7.10; 15.19
true [2] 13.27; 16.15
trust Jn 2.24; 27.25
turn [2] 13.8; 15.3
win [2] 7.46; Rom 1.13
wonder (1) 8.13; 15.12
word (1) [2] 13.5; 15.15
worthless Jn 8.54; 17.5

In Iconium

14 The same thing happened in
Iconium: Paul and Barnabas
went to the synagogue and spoke in such
a way that a great number of Jews and
Gentiles became believers. 2 But the Jews
who would not believe stirred up the
Gentiles and turned them against the believers. 3 The apostles stayed there for a
long time, speaking boldly about the
Lord, who proved that their message
about his grace was true by giving them
the power to perform miracles and wonders. 4 The people of the city were
divided: some were for the Jews, others
for the apostles.
5 Then some Gentiles and Jews, together with their leaders, decided to ill-
treat the apostles and stone them. 6 When
the apostles learnt about it, they fled to
the cities of Lystra and Derbe in
Lycaonia and to the surrounding territory. 7 There they preached the Good
News.

In Lystra and Derbe

8 In Lystra there was a man who had
been lame from birth and had never
been able to walk. 9 He sat there and
listened to Paul's words. Paul saw that he
believed and could be healed, so he
looked straight at him 10 and said in a
loud voice, "Stand up straight on your
feet!" The man jumped up and started
walking around. 11 When the crowds saw
what Paul had done, they started shouting in their own Lycaonian language,
"The gods have become like men and
have come down to us!" 12 They gave
Barnabas the name Zeus, and Paul the
name Hermes, because he was the chief
speaker. 13 The priest of the god Zeus,
whose temple stood just outside the town,
brought bulls and flowers to the gate, for
he and the crowds wanted to offer sacrifice to the apostles.
14 When Barnabas and Paul heard
what they were about to do, they tore
their clothes and ran into the middle of
the crowd, shouting, 15 "Why are you doing this? We ourselves are only human
beings like you! We are here to announce the Good News, to turn you away
from these worthless things to the living
God, who made heaven, earth, sea, and
all that is in them. 16 In the past he
allowed all people to go their own way.
17 But he has always given evidence of his
existence by the good things he does: he
gives you rain from heaven and crops at
the right times; he gives you food and
fills your hearts with happiness." 18 Even
with these words the apostles could
hardly keep the crowd from offering a
sacrifice to them.
19 Some Jews came from Antioch in
Pisidia and from Iconium; they won the
crowd over to their side, stoned Paul and
dragged him out of the town, thinking
that he was dead. 20 But when the believers gathered round him, he got up
and went back into the town. The next
day he and Barnabas went to Derbe.

The Return to Antioch in Syria

21 Paul and Barnabas preached the
Good News in Derbe and won many disciples. Then they went back to Lystra, to
Iconium, and on to Antioch in Pisidia.
22 They strengthened the believers and
encouraged them to remain true to the
faith. "We must pass through many
troubles to enter the Kingdom of God,"
they taught. 23 In each church they appointed elders, and with prayers and fasting they commended them to the Lord,
in whom they had put their trust.
24 After going through the territory of
Pisidia, they came to Pamphylia. 25 There
they preached the message in Perga and
then went to Attalia, 26 and from there
they sailed back to Antioch, the place
where they had been commended to the
care of God's grace for the work they
had now completed.
27 When they arrived in Antioch, they
gathered the people of the church together and told them about all that God
had done with them and how he had
opened the way for the Gentiles to believe. 28 And they stayed a long time
there with the believers.

The Meeting at Jerusalem

15 Some men came from Judaea to
Antioch and started teaching the
believers, "You cannot be saved unless
you are circumcised as the Law of Moses
requires." 2 Paul and Barnabas got into a
fierce argument with them about this, so
it was decided that Paul and Barnabas
and some of the others in Antioch should
go to Jerusalem and see the apostles and
elders about this matter.
3 They were sent on their way by the
church; and as they went through
Phoenicia and Samaria, they reported
how the Gentiles had turned to God; this
news brought great joy to all the
believers. 4 When they arrived in
Jerusalem, they were welcomed by the
church, the apostles, and the elders, to
whom they told all that God had done

agree [3] 5.2; 23.20
apostle [5] 14.3; 16.4
approve 8.1; 22.20
argue [2] 6.9; 18.15
believe [3] 14.2; 16.31
believer [8] 14.1; 16.2
best Jn 2.10; 24.16
birth 14.8; 22.28
blood [2] 2.19; 21.25
burden Mic 6.3; Rom 15.1
care [3] 14.26; 20.28
choose [5] 13.17; 17.31
church [4] 14.23; 16.5
circumcise [2] 11.2; 16.3
consider 13.46; 26.2
courage Mk 6.50; 2 Cor 5.6
dear 1.1; Rom 16.5
elder (2) [5] 14.23; 16.4
encourage 14.22; 16.40
forgive 13.38; 26.18
friend 13.7; 19.31
Gentile [9] 14.1; 17.17

14.15: Ex 20.11; Ps 146.6 **15.1:** Lev 12.3

Good News 14.7; 16.10
grace [2] 14.3; 18.27
idol [2] 7.41; 17.16
immoral [2] Mk 7.21; 21.25
joy [2] 13.52; 16.34
keep from [2] 14.18; 21.25
law [3] 13.15; 16.21
letter (2) [3] 9.2; 21.25
life (1) 13.46; 17.25
mankind Jn 17.2; 17.26
message 14.3; 16.6
miracle 14.3; 19.11
obey 7.39; 16.4
offer [2] 14.13; 21.25
peace 12.20; 16.36
Pharisees 5.34; 23.6
preach [4] 14.7; 16.6
prophet [2] 13.1; 21.10
question 12.19; 22.29
require Lk 12.48; 17.9
respect 10.22; 22.12
restore Mt 9.30; Jas 5.15
right (1) 14.17; Rom 2.2
ruin Lk 5.37; Rom 3.16
Sabbath 13.14; 16.13
save [2] 13.47; 16.17
scripture 13.29; 17.3
separate 3.23; Rom 8.35
service 1.20; Rom 7.4
sex [2] Mt 1.25; 21.25
Spirit (1) (God's Spirit) [2] 13.2; 16.6
strength [2] 14.22; 18.23
strong 4.21; 16.5
synagogue 14.1; 17.1
teach [2] 14.22; 16.21
test 5.9; 1 Cor 3.13
trouble [2] 14.22; 16.20
turn [3] 14.2; 16.18
unclean 11.8; Rom 14.14
upset Jn 14.1; 16.18
welcome Jn 4.45; 18.27
wish 7.39; Rom 9.3
wonder (1) 14.3; Rom 10.15
word (1) [4] 14.9; 16.32

through them. 5 But some of the believers
who belonged to the party of the Pharisees stood up and said, "The Gentiles
must be circumcised and told to obey the
Law of Moses."

6 The apostles and the elders met together to consider this question. 7 After a
long debate Peter stood up and said, "My
brothers, you know that a long time ago
God chose me from among you to preach
the Good News to the Gentiles, so that
they could hear and believe. 8 And God,
who knows the thoughts of everyone,
showed his approval of the Gentiles by
giving the Holy Spirit to them, just as he
had to us. 9 He made no difference between us and them; he forgave their sins
because they believed. 10 So then, why do
you now want to put God to the test by
laying a load on the backs of the believers which neither our ancestors nor
we ourselves were able to carry? 11 No!
We believe and are saved by the grace of
the Lord Jesus, just as they are."

12 The whole group was silent as they
heard Barnabas and Paul report all the
miracles and wonders that God had performed through them among the Gentiles. 13 When they had finished speaking,
James spoke up: "Listen to me, my
brothers! 14 Simon has just explained how
God first showed his care for the Gentiles
by taking from among them a people to
belong to him. 15 The words of the prophets agree completely with this. As the
scripture says,

16 'After this I will return, says the Lord,
and restore the kingdom of David.
I will rebuild its ruins
and make it strong again.
17 And so all the rest of mankind will
come to me,
all the Gentiles whom I have called
to be my own.
18 So says the Lord, who made this known
long ago.'

19 "It is my opinion," James went on,
"that we should not trouble the Gentiles
who are turning to God. 20 Instead, we
should write a letter telling them not to
eat any food that is ritually unclean because it has been offered to idols; to keep
themselves from sexual immorality; and
not to eat any animal that has been
strangled, or any blood. 21 For the Law of
Moses has been read for a very long time
in the synagogues every Sabbath, and his
words are preached in every town."

The Letter to the Gentile Believers

22 Then the apostles and the elders,
together with the whole church, decided
to choose some men from the group and
send them to Antioch with Paul and
Barnabas. They chose two men who
were highly respected by the believers,
Judas, called Barsabbas, and Silas, 23 and
they sent the following letter by them:

"We, the apostles and the elders,
your brothers, send greetings to all
our brothers of Gentile birth who
live in Antioch, Syria, and Cilicia.
24 We have heard that some men
who went from our group have
troubled and upset you by what they
said; they had not, however, received any instruction from us.
25 And so we have met together and
have all agreed to choose some
messengers and send them to you.
They will go with our dear friends
Barnabas and Paul, 26 who have
risked their lives in the service of
our Lord Jesus Christ. 27 We send
you, then, Judas and Silas, who will
tell you in person the same things
we are writing. 28 The Holy Spirit
and we have agreed not to put any
other burden on you besides these
necessary rules: 29 eat no food that
has been offered to idols; eat no
blood; eat no animal that has been
strangled; and keep yourselves from
sexual immorality. You will do well
if you take care not to do these
things. With our best wishes."

30 The messengers were sent off and
went to Antioch, where they gathered
the whole group of believers and gave
them the letter. 31 When the people read
it, they were filled with joy by the message of encouragement. 32 Judas and Silas,
who were themselves prophets, spoke a
long time with them, giving them
courage and strength. 33 After spending
some time there, they were sent off in
peace by the believers and went back to
those who had sent them. [w]

35 Paul and Barnabas spent some
time in Antioch, and together with many
others they taught and preached the
word of the Lord.

Paul and Barnabas Separate

36 Some time later Paul said to
Barnabas, "Let us go back and visit our
brothers in every town where we
preached the word of the Lord, and let us
find out how they are getting on."

[w] *Some manuscripts add verse 34:* But Silas decided to stay there.

15.7: Acts 10.1–43 **15.8:** Acts 2.4, 10.44 **15.16–18:** Amos 9.11–12 (LXX)
15.20: Ex 34.15–17; Lev 17.10–16, 18.6–23

37 Barnabas wanted to take John Mark with them, 38 but Paul did not think it was **right** to take him, because he had not stayed with them to the end of their mission, but had **turned back** and left them in Pamphylia. 39 There was a sharp **argument**, and they **separated**: Barnabas took Mark and sailed off for Cyprus, 40 while Paul **chose** Silas and left, commended by the **believers** to the **care** of the Lord's **grace**. 41 He went through Syria and Cilicia, **strengthening** the **churches**.

Timothy Goes with Paul and Silas

16 Paul travelled on to Derbe and Lystra, where a **Christian** named Timothy lived. His mother, who was also a **Christian**, was **Jewish**, but his father was a Greek. 2 All the **believers** in Lystra and Iconium spoke well of Timothy. 3 Paul wanted to take Timothy along with him, so he **circumcised** him. He did so because all the **Jews** who lived in those places knew that Timothy's father was Greek. 4 As they went through the towns, they delivered to the **believers** the rules decided upon by the **apostles** and **elders** in Jerusalem, and told them to **obey** those rules. 5 So the **churches** were made **stronger** in the **faith** and grew in numbers every day.

In Troas: Paul's Vision

6 They travelled through the region of Phrygia and Galatia because the **Holy Spirit** did not let them **preach** the **message** in the province of Asia. 7 When they reached the border of Mysia, they tried to go into the province of Bithynia, but the **Spirit** of Jesus did not allow them. 8 So they travelled right on through[x] Mysia and went to Troas. 9 That night Paul had a **vision** in which he saw a Macedonian standing and **begging** him, "Come over to Macedonia and **help** us!" 10 As soon as Paul had this **vision**, we got ready to leave for Macedonia, because we decided that God had called us to **preach** the **Good News** to the people there.

In Philippi: the Conversion of Lydia

11 We left by ship from Troas and sailed straight across to Samothrace, and the next day to Neapolis. 12 From there we went inland to Philippi, a city of the first district of Macedonia;[y] it is also a Roman colony. We spent several days there. 13 On the **Sabbath** we went out of the city to the river-side, where we thought there would be a place where **Jews** gathered for **prayer**. We sat down and talked to the women who gathered there. 14 One of those who heard us was Lydia from Thyatira, who was a dealer in purple cloth. She was a woman who **worshipped** God, and the Lord opened her **mind** to pay attention to what Paul was saying. 15 After she and the people of her house had been **baptized**, she invited us, "Come and stay in my house if you have decided that I am a **true believer** in the Lord." And she **persuaded** us to go.

In Prison at Philippi

16 One day as we were going to the place of **prayer**, we were met by a **slave-girl** who had an **evil spirit** that enabled her to **predict** the future. She earned a lot of money for her owners by telling **fortunes**. 17 She followed Paul and us, shouting, "These men are **servants** of the **Most High God**! They **announce** to you how you can be **saved**!" 18 She did this for many days, until Paul became so **upset** that he **turned round** and said to the **spirit**, "**In the name of** Jesus Christ I order you to come out of her!" The **spirit** went out of her that very moment.

19 When her owners realized that their chance of making money was gone, they seized Paul and Silas and dragged them to the **authorities** in the public square. 20 They brought them before the Roman officials and said, "These men are **Jews**, and they are causing **trouble** in our city. 21 They are **teaching customs** that are against our **law**; we are Roman citizens, and we cannot **accept** these **customs** or **practise** them." 22 And the crowd joined in the attack against Paul and Silas.

Then the officials tore the clothes off Paul and Silas and ordered them to be whipped. 23 After a severe beating, they were thrown into jail, and the **jailer** was ordered to lock them up tight. 24 Upon receiving this order, the **jailer** threw them into the inner cell and fastened their feet between heavy blocks of wood.

25 About midnight Paul and Silas were **praying** and singing **hymns** to God, and the other **prisoners** were listening to them. 26 Suddenly there was a **violent** earthquake, which shook the **prison** to its foundations. At once all the doors opened, and the chains fell off all the **prisoners**. 27 The **jailer** woke up, and when he saw the **prison** doors open, he

accept 10.35; 22.18
afraid 9.26; 18.9
announce 14.15; 17.3
apostle 15.2; Rom 1.1
authorities [2] 3.13; 17.6
baptize [2] 13.24; 18.8
beg 3.2; 19.31
believe [2] 15.7; 17.12
believer [4] 15.1; 17.6
Christian [2] 11.26; 26.28
church 15.3; 18.22
circumcise 15.1; 21.21
crime Jn 18.30; 18.14
custom [2] 6.14; 21.21
elder (2) 15.2; 20.17
encourage 15.31; 20.1
escape Lk 3.7; 25.11
faith 14.22; 24.24
fortune-teller Zech 10.2
Good News 15.7; 20.24
guilty Jn 19.11; 24.20
harm Lk 6.9; 18.10
help 13.5; 18.27
hymn Mk 14.26; 1 Cor 14.26
jail [6] 12.4
Jew [4] 14.1; 17.5
joy 15.3; Rom 12.12
law 15.1; 17.7
light (1) 13.11; 22.6
message 15.31; 17.11
mind (1) 4.32; 19.21
Most High 7.48; Heb 7.1
name (2) (name of God, of Jesus) 10.43; 17.7
obey 15.5; 20.22
peace 15.33; 24.2
persuade 10.23; 18.13
practice Jn 13.17; 19.19
pray 13.3; 20.36
prayer [2] 14.23; 26.29
preach [3] 15.7; 17.13
predict 11.28; Gal 3.8
prison [8] 12.6; 20.23
Sabbath 15.21; 17.2
save [3] 15.1; 27.20
secret Jn 19.38; Rom 2.16
servant 13.35; 20.19
slave 7.6; Rom 6.6
Spirit (1) (God's Spirit) [2] 15.8; 19.2
spirit (2) [3] 8.7; 19.12
strong 15.16; 18.28
teach 15.1; 17.19

tremble 7.32; 1 Cor 2.3
trouble 15.19; 17.6
true 14.3; 17.11
turn 15.3; 17.30
upset 15.24; 17.16
violent 9.1; 19.16
vision [2] 12.9; 18.9
word (1) [3] 15.15; 17.8
worship (1) (of God) 13.16; 17.4

[x] travelled right on through; *or* passed by.
[y] a city of the first district of Macedonia; *some manuscripts have* a leading city of the district of Macedonia; *or* a leading city of that district in Macedonia.

15.38: Acts 13.13

thought that the **prisoners** had **escaped**;
so he pulled out his sword and was about
to kill himself. 28 But Paul shouted at the
top of his voice, "Don't **harm** yourself!
We are all here!"

29 The **jailer** called for a **light**, rushed
in, and fell **trembling** at the feet of Paul
and Silas. 30 Then he led them out and
asked, "Sirs, what must I do to be
saved?"

31 They answered, "**Believe** in the
Lord Jesus, and you will be **saved**—you
and your family." 32 Then they **preached**
the **word of the Lord** to him and to all the
others in his house. 33 At that very hour of
the night the **jailer** took them and
washed their wounds; and he and all his
family were **baptized** at once. 34 Then he
took Paul and Silas up into his house and
gave them some food to eat. He and his
family were filled with **joy**, because they
now **believed** in God.

35 The next morning the Roman
authorities sent police officers with the
order, "Let those men go."

36 So the **jailer** told Paul, "The officials have sent an order for you and Silas
to be released. You may leave, then, and
go in **peace**."

37 But Paul said to the police officers,
"We were not found **guilty** of any **crime**,
yet they whipped us in public—and we
are Roman citizens! Then they threw us
in **prison**. And now they want to send us
away **secretly**. Not likely! The Roman
officials themselves must come here and
let us out."

38 The police officers reported these
words to the Roman officials; and when
they heard that Paul and Silas were
Roman citizens, they were **afraid**. 39 So
they went and apologized to them; then
they led them out of the **prison** and asked
them to leave the city. 40 Paul and Silas
left the **prison** and went to Lydia's house.
There they met the **believers**, spoke
words of **encouragement** to them, and
left.

In Thessalonica

17 Paul and Silas travelled
on through Amphipolis and
Apollonia and came to Thessalonica,
where there was a **synagogue**. 2 According to his usual habit Paul went to the
synagogue. There during three **Sabbaths**
he held **discussions** with the people,
quoting 3 and explaining the **Scriptures**
and **proving** from them that the **Messiah**
had to **suffer** and **rise from death**. "This
Jesus whom I **announce** to you," Paul
said, "is the **Messiah**." 4 Some of them
were **convinced** and joined Paul and
Silas; so did many of the leading women
and a large group of Greeks who **worshipped** God.

5 But the **Jews** were **jealous** and
gathered some of the **worthless** loafers
from the streets and formed a mob. They
set the whole city in an uproar and
attacked the home of a man called
Jason, in an attempt to find Paul and
Silas and bring them out to the people.
6 But when they did not find them, they
dragged Jason and some other **believers**
before the city **authorities** and shouted,
"These men have caused **trouble** everywhere! Now they have come to our city,
7 and Jason has kept them in his house.
They are all breaking the **laws** of the
Emperor, saying that there is another
king, whose **name** is Jesus." 8 With these
words they threw the crowd and the city
authorities into an uproar. 9 The **authorities** made Jason and the others pay the
required amount of money to be released, and then let them go.

In Berea

10 As soon as night came, the **believers** sent Paul and Silas to Berea.
When they arrived, they went to the
synagogue. 11 The people there were
more open-minded than the people in
Thessalonica. They listened to the **message** with great **eagerness**, and every day
they **studied** the **Scriptures** to see if what
Paul said was really **true**. 12 Many of
them **believed**; and many Greek women
of high social standing and many Greek
men also **believed**. 13 But when the **Jews**
in Thessalonica heard that Paul had
preached the **word of God** in Berea also,
they came there and started exciting and
stirring up the mob. 14 At once the **believers** sent Paul away to the coast; but
both Silas and Timothy stayed in Berea.
15 The men who were taking Paul went
with him as far as Athens and then returned to Berea with instructions from
Paul that Silas and Timothy should join
him as soon as possible.

In Athens

16 While Paul was waiting in Athens
for Silas and Timothy, he was greatly **upset** when he **noticed** how full of **idols** the
city was. 17 So he held **discussions** in the
synagogue with the **Jews** and with the
Gentiles who **worshipped** God, and also
in the public square every day with the
people who happened to pass by. 18 Certain Epicurean and Stoic **teachers** also
debated with him. Some of them asked,
"What is this **ignorant** show-off trying to
say?"

Others answered, "He seems to be
talking about foreign **gods**." They said
this because Paul was **preaching** about
Jesus and the **resurrection**.[z] 19 So they
took Paul, brought him before the city
council, the Areopagus, and said, "We
would like to know what this **new teaching** is that you are talking about. 20 Some
of the things we hear you say sound
strange to us, and we would like to know
what they mean." 21 (For all the citizens
of Athens and the foreigners who lived
there liked to spend all their time telling
and hearing the latest **new** thing.)
22 Paul stood up in front of the city
council and said, "I see that in every way
you Athenians are very **religious**. 23 For
as I walked through your city and looked
at the **places** where you **worship**, I found
an **altar** on which is written, 'To an Unknown God'. That which you **worship**,
then, even though you do not know it, is
what I now **proclaim** to you. 24 God, who
made the **world** and everything in it, is
Lord of **heaven and earth** and does not
live in **man-made temples**. 25 Nor does he
need anything that we can supply by
working for him, since it is he himself
who gives **life** and breath and everything
else to everyone. 26 From one man he
created all **races** of **mankind** and made
them live throughout the whole earth. He
himself fixed beforehand the exact times
and the limits of the places where they
would live. 27 He did this so that they
would look for him, and perhaps find him
as they felt about for him. Yet God is
actually not far from any one of us; 28 as
someone has said,

'In him we live and move and **exist**.'

It is as some of your poets have said,

'We too are **his children**.'

29 Since we are **God's children**, we should
not suppose that his **nature** is anything
like an **image** of gold or silver or stone,
shaped by the art and skill of man. 30 God
has overlooked the times when people
did not know him, but now he **commands**
all of them everywhere to **turn away
from their evil ways**. 31 For he has fixed a
day in which he will **judge** the whole
world with **justice by means of** a man he
has **chosen**. He has given **proof** of this to
everyone by **raising** that man **from
death**!"
32 When they heard Paul speak about
a **raising from death**, some of them made
fun of him, but others said, "We want to
hear you speak about this again." 33 And
so Paul left the meeting. 34 Some men
joined him and **believed**, among whom
was Dionysius, a member of the **council**;
there was also a woman named Damaris,
and some other people.

In Corinth

18 After this, Paul left Athens and
went on to Corinth. 2 There he
met a **Jew** named Aquila, born in Pontus,
who had recently come from Italy with
his wife Priscilla, for the Emperor
Claudius had ordered all the **Jews** to
leave Rome. Paul went to see them, 3 and
stayed and worked with them, because
he earned his living by making tents, just
as they did. 4 He held **discussions** in the
synagogue every **Sabbath**, trying to **convince** both **Jews** and Greeks.
5 When Silas and Timothy arrived
from Macedonia, Paul gave his whole
time to **preaching** the **message**, **testifying**
to the **Jews** that Jesus is the **Messiah**.
6 When they opposed him and said **evil**
things about him, he protested by
shaking the dust from his clothes and
saying to them, "If you are lost, you yourselves must take the **blame** for it! I am
not responsible. From now on I will go to
the **Gentiles**." 7 So he left them and went
to live in the house of a **Gentile** named
Titius Justus, who **worshipped** God; his
house was next to the **synagogue**.
8 Crispus, who was the leader of the **synagogue**, **believed** in the Lord, together
with all his family; and many other
people in Corinth heard the **message**, **believed**, and were **baptized**.
9 One night Paul had a **vision** in which
the Lord said to him, "Do not be **afraid**,
but keep on speaking and do not **give up**,
10 for I am with you. No one will be able
to **harm** you, for many in this city are **my
people**." 11 So Paul stayed there for a year
and a half, **teaching** the people the **word
of God**.
12 When Gallio was made the Roman
governor of Achaia, the **Jews** got together, seized Paul, and took him into
court. 13 "This man," they said, "is trying
to **persuade** people to **worship** God in a
way that is against the **law**!"
14 Paul was about to speak when
Gallio said to the **Jews**, "If this were a
matter of some **evil crime** or **wrong** that
has been **committed**, it would be **reason-
able** for me to be **patient** with you **Jews**.
15 But since it is an **argument** about **words**
and names and your own **law**, you yourselves must **settle** it. I will not be the
judge of such things!" 16 And he drove

afraid 16.38; 23.10
argue [2] 15.2; 23.10
baptize [2] 16.15; 19.3
believe [2] 17.12; 19.4
believer [5] 17.6; 19.2
blame Mic 1.5; Phil 1.10
bold 14.3; 19.8
church 16.5; 20.17
commit Jn 18.30; Rom 2.22
convince 17.4; 19.8
correct [2] Jer 10.24; 2 Tim 2.15
court (1) [3] Lk 12.58; 19.38
crime 16.37; 22.25
discuss [2] 17.2; 19.8
evil [2] 17.30; 19.9
Gentile [2] 17.17; 19.10
give up Jn 16.1; 21.14
God's people 13.19; 20.32
grace 15.11; 20.24
harm 16.28; 28.5
help [2] 16.9; 19.22
Jew [10] 17.5; 19.10
judge 17.31; 23.3
knowledge Lk 11.52; Rom 1.28
law [2] 17.7; 21.20
message [2] 17.11; 19.6
Messiah [2] 17.3; 26.23
patient Mt 18.26; 26.3
persuade 16.15; 2 Cor 5.11
preach 17.13; 19.13
proclaim 17.23; 19.6
prove 17.3; 22.5
reason 13.28; 19.40
Sabbath 17.2; Col 2.16
scripture [2] 17.3; 23.5
settle (2) Lk 12.58; 19.39
shave Amos 8.10; 21.24
strength 15.32; Rom 14.19
strong 16.5; 19.20
synagogue [6] 17.1; 19.8
teach [2] 17.19; 20.20
testify 10.42; 26.5
urge 11.23; Rom 15.30
vision 16.9; 22.17
vow 2.30; 21.23
Way (2) [2] 9.2; 19.9
welcome 15.4; 21.17
will (1) 4.28; 22.14
word (1) [2] 17.8; 19.10
worship (1) (of God) [2] 17.4; 24.11
wrong Jn 18.23; 23.9

[z] JESUS AND THE RESURRECTION: *In Greek, the feminine noun "resurrection" could be understood to be the name of a goddess.*

17.24-25: 1 Kgs 8.27; Is 42.5; Acts 7.48

them out of the **court**. 17 They all seized Sosthenes, the leader of the **synagogue**, and beat him in front of the **court**. But that did not bother Gallio a bit.

The Return to Antioch

18 Paul stayed on with the **believers** in Corinth for many days, then left them and sailed off with Priscilla and Aquila for Syria. Before sailing from Cenchreae he had his head **shaved** because of a **vow** he had taken.[a] 19 They arrived in Ephesus, where Paul left Priscilla and Aquila. He went into the **synagogue** and held **discussions** with the **Jews**. 20 The people asked him to stay longer, but he would not consent. 21 Instead, he told them as he left, "If it is the **will of God**, I will come back to you." And so he sailed from Ephesus.

22 When he arrived at Caesarea, he went to Jerusalem and greeted the **church**, and then went to Antioch. 23 After spending some time there, he left and went through the region of Galatia and Phrygia, **strengthening** all the **believers**.

Apollos in Ephesus and Corinth

24 At that time a **Jew** named Apollos, who had been born in Alexandria, came to Ephesus. He was an eloquent speaker and had a thorough **knowledge** of the **Scriptures**. 25 He had been instructed in the **Way of the Lord**, and with great enthusiasm he **proclaimed** and **taught correctly** the facts about Jesus. However, he knew only the **baptism** of John. 26 He began to speak **boldly** in the **synagogue**. When Priscilla and Aquila heard him, they took him home with them and explained to him more **correctly** the **Way of God**. 27 Apollos then decided to go to Achaia, so the **believers** in Ephesus **helped** him by writing to the **believers** in Achaia, **urging** them to **welcome** him. When he arrived, he was a great **help** to those who through God's **grace** had become **believers**. 28 For with his **strong arguments** he defeated the **Jews** in public debates by **proving** from the **Scriptures** that Jesus is the **Messiah**.

Paul in Ephesus

19 While Apollos was in Corinth, Paul travelled through the interior of the province and arrived in Ephesus. There he found some **disciples** 2 and asked them, "Did you receive the **Holy Spirit** when you became **believers**?"

"We have not even heard that there is a **Holy Spirit**," they answered.

3 "Well, then, what kind of **baptism** did you receive?" Paul asked.

"The **baptism** of John," they answered.

4 Paul said, "The **baptism** of John was for those who **turned from their sins**; and he told the people of Israel to **believe** in the one who was coming after him—that is, in Jesus."

5 When they heard this, they were **baptized in the name of** the Lord Jesus. 6 Paul placed his hands on them, and the **Holy Spirit** came upon them; they spoke in **strange tongues** and also **proclaimed** God's **message**. 7 They were about twelve men in all.

8 Paul went into the **synagogue** and during three months spoke **boldly** with the people, holding **discussions** with them and trying to **convince** them about the **Kingdom of God**. 9 But some of them were **stubborn** and would not **believe**, and before the whole group they said **evil** things about the **Way of the Lord**. So Paul left them and took the **believers** with him, and every day[b] he held **discussions** in the lecture hall of Tyrannus. 10 This went on for two years, so that all the people who lived in the province of Asia, both **Jews** and **Gentiles**, heard the **word of the Lord**.

The Sons of Sceva

11 God was performing unusual **miracles** through Paul. 12 Even handkerchiefs and aprons he had used were taken to those who were ill, and their **diseases** were driven away, and the **evil spirits** would go out of them. 13 Some **Jews** who travelled round and drove out **evil spirits** also tried to use the **name of the** Lord Jesus to do this. They said to the **evil spirits**, "I **command** you **in the name** of Jesus, whom Paul **preaches**." 14 Seven brothers, who were the sons of a **Jewish High Priest** named Sceva, were doing this.

15 But the **evil spirit** said to them, "I know Jesus, and I know about Paul; but you—**who are you**?"

16 The man who had the **evil spirit** in him attacked them with such **violence** that he overpowered them all. They ran away from his house, wounded and with their clothes torn off. 17 All the **Jews** and **Gentiles** who lived in Ephesus heard about this; they were all filled with **fear**, and the **name of the Lord** Jesus was

[a] A VOW HE HAD TAKEN: *This refers to the Jewish custom of shaving the head as a sign that a vow has been kept.* [b] *Some manuscripts add* from 11a.m. until 4p.m.

18.18: Num 6.18 **19.4:** Mt 3.11; Mk 1.4, 7–8; Lk 3.4, 16; Jn 1.26–27

accuse [2] Jn 18.29; 22.30
admit (1) Lk 11.48; 24.14
authorities [2] 17.6; 23.20
bad 7.6; 24.15
baptize [4] 18.8; 22.16
beg 16.9; 21.12
believe [2] 18.8; 20.21
believer [4] 18.18; 20.1
bold 18.26; 26.26
calm [2] Lk 8.24
charge (3) Ezek 23.45; 23.30
command 17.30; Rom 2.13
convince [2] 18.4; 21.14
court (1) 18.12; 25.6
danger [3] Lk 8.23; 24.5
defend Lk 21.14; 22.1
deny 8.33; 26.11
destroy 13.19; Rom 3.16
disciple 14.21; 21.16
discuss [2] 18.4; 24.25
disease Lk 17.12; 1 Cor 12.30
evil [2] 18.6; 23.5
excuse Jn 15.22; Rom 1.20
fear 10.4; Rom 13.3
friend 15.25; 24.23
fury 7.54; 26.11
Gentile [2] 18.6; 20.21
god (2) (other gods) 17.18; 28.6
goddess [4] Mic 5.14
heaven 17.24; 26.19
help 18.27; 20.20
High Priest 9.1; 22.5
honour 12.23; Rom 1.21
Jew [6] 18.2; 20.3
Kingdom (1) (of God) 14.22; 20.25
last (2) 12.10; 27.23
magic 13.6; Rev 9.21
man-made 17.24; Col 2.22
message [2] 18.5; 20.2
mind (1) 16.14; 28.6
miracle 15.12; Rom 15.19
name (2) (name of God, of Jesus) [4] 17.7; Rom 16.2
power 14.3; 21.4
practice 16.21; Gal 1.14
preach 18.5; 20.20
proclaim 18.25; 21.9
prosper Mal 3.15
reason 18.14; 24.26
reveal Jn 16.13; Rom 1.17
rob Jn 10.1; Rom 2.22
sacred 13.34; Eph 2.21
serious Mal 2.2; 25.7
settle (2) 18.15; Rom 9.28
speech 12.21; Rom 3.14
Spirit (1) (God's Spirit) [3] 16.6; 20.22
spirit (2) [5] 16.16; 23.8
strange 17.20; 1 Cor 12.10
strong 18.28; 23.9
stubborn 7.51; Rom 2.5
succeed (1) Jn 12.19; Rom 14.4
synagogue 18.4; 22.19
temple (2) (of other gods) [4] 17.24; Rom 2.22
trouble 17.6; 20.23
turn 17.30; 20.21
violent 16.26; 23.10
Way (2) [2] 18.25; 22.4
who 9.5; 22.8

word (1) [3] 18.11; 20.1
world 17.24; 24.5
worship (2) (of other gods) 17.23; Rom 1.23

given greater **honour**. [18] Many of the **believers** came, publicly **admitting** and **revealing** what they had done. [19] Many of those who had **practised magic** brought their books together and burnt them in public. They added up the price of the books, and the total came to fifty thousand silver coins.[c] [20] In this **powerful** way the **word of the Lord**[d] kept spreading and growing **stronger**.

The Riot in Ephesus

21 After these things had happened, Paul made up his **mind**[e] to travel through Macedonia and Achaia and go on to Jerusalem. "After I go there," he said, "I must also see Rome." [22] So he sent Timothy and Erastus, two of his **helpers**, to Macedonia, while he spent more time in the province of Asia.

23 It was at this time that there was **serious trouble** in Ephesus because of the **Way of the Lord**. [24] A certain silversmith named Demetrius made silver models of the **temple** of the **goddess** Artemis, and his business brought a great deal of profit to the workers. [25] So he called them all together with others whose work was like theirs and said to them, "Men, you know that our **prosperity** comes from this work. [26] Now, you can see and hear for yourselves what this fellow Paul is doing. He says that **man-made gods** are not gods at all, and he has **succeeded** in **convincing** many people, both here in Ephesus and in nearly the whole province of Asia. [27] There is the **danger**, then, that this business of ours will get a **bad** name. Not only that, but there is also the **danger** that the **temple** of the great **goddess** Artemis will come to mean nothing and that her greatness will be **destroyed**—the **goddess worshipped** by everyone in Asia and in all the **world**!"

28 As the crowd heard these **words**, they became **furious** and started shouting, "Great is Artemis of Ephesus!" [29] The uproar spread throughout the whole city. The mob seized Gaius and Aristarchus, two Macedonians who were travelling with Paul, and rushed with them to the theatre. [30] Paul himself wanted to go before the crowd, but the **believers** would not let him. [31] Some of the provincial **authorities**, who were his **friends**, also sent him a **message begging** him not to show himself in the theatre. [32] Meanwhile the whole meeting was in an uproar: some people were shouting one thing, others were shouting something else, because most of them did not even know why they had come together. [33] Some of the people concluded that Alexander was responsible, since the **Jews** made him go up to the front. Then Alexander motioned with his hand for the people to be silent, and he tried to make a **speech** of **defence**. [34] But when they recognized that he was a **Jew**, they all shouted together the same thing for two hours: "Great is Artemis of Ephesus!"

35 At **last** the town clerk was able to **calm** the crowd. "Fellow-Ephesians!" he said. "Everyone knows that the city of Ephesus is the keeper of the **temple** of the great Artemis and of the **sacred** stone that fell down from **heaven**. [36] Nobody can **deny** these things. So then, you must **calm** down and not do anything reckless. [37] You have brought these men here even though they have not **robbed temples** or said **evil** things about our **goddess**. [38] If Demetrius and his workers have an **accusation** against anyone, we have the **authorities** and the regular days for **court**; **charges** can be made there. [39] But if there is something more that you want, it will have to be **settled** in a legal meeting of citizens. [40] For after what has happened today, there is the **danger** that we will be **accused** of a riot. There is no **excuse** for all this uproar, and we would not be able to give a good **reason** for it." [41] After saying this, he dismissed the meeting.

To Macedonia and Achaia

20 After the uproar died down, Paul called together the **believers** and with **words** of **encouragement** said goodbye to them. Then he left and went on to Macedonia. [2] He went through those regions and **encouraged** the people with many **messages**. Then he came to Achaia, [3] where he stayed three months. He was getting ready to go to Syria when he discovered that the **Jews** were **plotting** against him; so he decided to go back through Macedonia. [4] Sopater son of Pyrrhus, from Berea, went with him; so did Aristarchus and Secundus, from Thessalonica; Gaius, from Derbe; Tychicus and Trophimus, from the province of Asia; and Timothy. [5] They went ahead and waited for us in Troas. [6] We sailed from Philippi after the **Festival** of **Unleavened Bread**, and five days later we joined them in Troas, where we spent a week.

alive [2] 9.39; 25.19
announce 17.3; 26.23
believe 19.4; 22.19
believer [2] 19.2; 21.4
bless 13.34; Rom 1.11
bread Jn 21.9; 27.35
care [2] 15.14; 22.20
church [2] 18.22; 21.18
comfort Jn 11.19; 1 Cor 14.3
complete 14.26; 21.19
dead 14.19; 23.6
death (1) 13.28; 22.4
declare [2] 11.9; Rom 4.5
elder (2) 16.4; 21.18
encourage [2] 16.40; 28.15
fellowship meal 2.42; Jude 1.12
festival 12.3; 1 Cor 5.7
flock [2] Jn 10.16; 1 Pet 5.2
Gentile 19.10; 21.11
God's people 18.10; 26.10
Good News 16.10; Rom 1.1
grace [2] 18.27; Rom 1.7

[c] SILVER COINS: *A silver coin was the daily wage of a rural worker (see Mt 20.2).*
[d] In this...Lord; *or* And so, by the power of the Lord, the message.
[e] Paul made up his mind; *or* Paul, led by the Spirit, decided.

happy 14.17; 24.10
hard [2] Jn 6.60; 27.20
help [2] 19.22; 21.28
humble 2.46;
Rom 12.16
Jew [3] 19.10; 21.11
Kingdom (1) (of God) 19.8; 28.23
kiss Lk 22.47;
Rom 16.16
kneel 9.40; 21.5
lie (2) 13.10;
Rom 1.25
life (1) 17.25; 26.4
message [3] 19.6;
21.9
need 17.25; 24.23
obey 16.4; 22.12
Pentecost 2.1;
1 Cor 16.8
plot (1) [2] 4.25; 23.16
pray 16.25; 21.5
preach [2] 19.13;
26.20
prison 16.25; 22.4
provide 7.46; 23.24
purpose 13.36; 26.12
remember [2] 11.16;
Rom 1.9
sacrifice 14.13; 21.26
sad Jn 21.17;
1 Cor 5.2
servant 16.17; 22.14
shepherd Jn 10.2;
1 Cor 9.7
solemn [2] Lk 1.73;
23.14
Son of God 13.32;
Rom 1.3
sound (2) Lk 15.27;
1 Tim 1.10
spare Lk 21.4; 27.24
Spirit (1) (God's Spirit) [3] 19.2; 21.4
teach [2] 18.11; 21.21
tear (2) [2] Lk 7.38;
2 Cor 2.4
trouble 19.23;
Rom 5.3
turn 19.4; 26.18
unleavened 12.3
warn [2] 4.17;
1 Cor 10.6
watch [2] 9.24;
Rom 16.17
weak Mk 14.38;
Rom 4.19
word (1) [2] 19.10;
23.15
worry Jn 14.1;
1 Cor 7.32
worthless 17.5;
Rom 4.14

Paul's Last Visit to Troas

7 On Saturday[f] evening we gathered
together for the **fellowship meal**. Paul
spoke to the people and kept on speaking
until midnight, since he was going to
leave the next day. 8 Many lamps were
burning in the upstairs room where we
were meeting. 9 A young man named
Eutychus was sitting in the window, and
as Paul kept on talking, Eutychus got
sleepier and sleepier, until he finally
went **sound asleep** and fell from the third
storey to the ground. When they picked
him up, he was **dead**. 10 But Paul went
down and threw himself on him and
hugged him. "Don't **worry**," he said, "he
is still **alive**!" 11 Then he went back upstairs, broke **bread**, and ate. After talking
with them for a long time, even until sunrise, Paul left. 12 They took the young
man home **alive** and were greatly **comforted**.

From Troas to Miletus

13 We went on ahead to the ship and
sailed off to Assos, where we were going
to take Paul aboard. He had told us to do
this, because he was going there by land.
14 When he met us in Assos, we took him
aboard and went on to Mitylene. 15 We
sailed from there and arrived off Chios
the next day. A day later we came to
Samos, and the following day we reached
Miletus. 16 Paul had decided to sail on
past Ephesus, so as not to lose any time
in the province of Asia. He was in a hurry
to arrive in Jerusalem by the day of
Pentecost, if at all possible.

Paul's Farewell Speech to the Elders of Ephesus

17 From Miletus Paul sent a **message**
to Ephesus, asking the **elders** of the
church to meet him. 18 When they
arrived, he said to them, "You know how
I spent the whole time I was with you,
from the first day I arrived in the province of Asia. 19 With all **humility** and
many **tears** I did my work as the Lord's
servant during the **hard** times that came
to me because of the **plots** of the **Jews**.
20 You know that I did not hold back anything that would be of **help** to you as I
preached and **taught** in public and in
your homes. 21 To **Jews** and **Gentiles** alike
I gave **solemn warning** that they should
turn from their sins to God and **believe** in
our Lord Jesus. 22 And now, in **obedience**
to the **Holy Spirit** I am going to
Jerusalem, not knowing what will happen to me there. 23 I only know that in
every city the **Holy Spirit** has **warned** me
that **prison** and **troubles** wait for me.
24 But I reckon my own **life** to be **worth
nothing** to me; I only want to **complete**
my mission and finish the work that the
Lord Jesus gave me to do, which is to **declare** the **Good News** about the **grace** of
God.

25 "I have gone about among all of
you, **preaching** the **Kingdom of God**. And
now I know that none of you will ever see
me again. 26 So I **solemnly declare** to you
this very day: if any of you should be lost,
I am not responsible. 27 For I have not
held back from **announcing** to you the
whole **purpose** of God. 28 So keep **watch**
over yourselves and over all the **flock**
which the **Holy Spirit** has placed in your
care. Be **shepherds** of the **church** of
God,[g] which he made his own through
the **sacrificial death of his Son**.[h] 29 I know
that after I leave, fierce wolves will
come among you, and they will not **spare**
the **flock**. 30 The time will come when
some men from your own group will tell
lies to lead the **believers** away after
them. 31 **Watch**, then, and **remember** that
with many **tears**, day and night, I **taught**
every one of you for three years.

32 "And now I commend you to the
care of God and to the **message** of his
grace, which is able to build you up and
give you the **blessings** God has for all **his
people**. 33 I have not wanted anyone's
silver or gold or clothing. 34 You yourselves know that I have worked with
these hands of mine to **provide** everything that my companions and I have
needed. 35 I have shown you in all things
that by working **hard** in this way we must
help the **weak**, **remembering** the **words**
that the Lord Jesus himself said, 'There
is more **happiness** in giving than in receiving.' "

36 When Paul finished, he **knelt** down
with them and **prayed**. 37 They were all
crying as they hugged him and **kissed**
him good-bye. 38 They were especially
sad because he had said that they would
never see him again. And so they went
with him to the ship.

Paul Goes to Jerusalem

21 We said good-bye to them and
left. After sailing straight across,
we came to Cos; the next day we
reached Rhodes, and from there we went
on to Patara. 2 There we found a ship that
was going to Phoenicia, so we went

abandon 2.27;
Rom 11.23
arrest 12.3; 22.4
beg 19.31; 24.4
believer [6] 20.1;
28.14
bind Jn 21.18; 28.20
blood 15.20; Rom 9.3

[f] Saturday; *or* Sunday. [g] God; *some manuscripts have* the Lord.
[h] the sacrificial death of his Son; *or* his own death.

20.24: 2 Tim 4.7

ceremony [2] 7.8; 24.18
choose 17.31; 22.14
church 20.17; Rom 15.26
circumcise 16.3; Rom 2.25
complete 20.24; 24.18
convince 19.8; 27.11
custom 16.21; 26.3
defile 11.8; 24.6
devote 13.35; Rom 10.2
disciple 19.1; 1 Cor 1.13
elder (2) 20.17; 23.14
Gentile [5] 20.21; 22.21
give up 18.9; 27.15
heart 14.17; 27.22
Hebrew Jn 20.16; 22.2
help 20.20; 26.22
helper (1) Phil 1.1
Holy Place Lk 11.51; Heb 8.2
idol 17.16; Rom 2.22
immoral 15.20; Rom 13.13
important 8.27; Rom 14.5
Jew [6] 20.3; 22.3
keep from 15.20; 27.42
kneel 20.36; Rom 14.11
law [4] 18.13; 22.3
letter (2) 15.20; 22.5
message 20.2; 28.23
offer [2] 15.20; 24.17
one another 4.32; 28.4
permit Lk 22.31; 26.1
please 12.3; Rom 8.8
power 19.20; 26.18
praise 13.48; Rom 1.25
pray 20.36; 22.16
proclaim 19.6; Rom 10.14
prophet 15.15; 24.14
pure [3] Jn 12.3; 24.18
sacrifice 20.28; 24.17
sake 9.16; 28.20
sex 15.20; Rom 1.26
shave 18.18; 1 Cor 11.5
Spirit (1) (God's Spirit) [2] 20.22; 28.25
sure 13.34; 26.26
teach [2] 20.20; 28.31
Temple (1) (of God) [7] 6.13; 22.17
truth 13.10; 22.5
unmarried Ezek 44.25; 1 Cor 7.8
vow 18.18; 23.12
welcome 18.27; 24.3

aboard and sailed away. 3 We came to where we could see Cyprus, and then sailed south of it on to Syria. We went ashore at Tyre, where the ship was going to unload its cargo. 4 There we found some **believers** and stayed with them a week. By the **power of the Spirit** they told Paul not to go to Jerusalem. 5 But when our time with them was over, we left and went on our way. All of them, together with their wives and children, went with us out of the city to the beach, where we all **knelt** and **prayed.** 6 Then we said goodbye to **one another**, and we went on board the ship while they went back home.

7 We continued our voyage, sailing from Tyre to Ptolemais, where we greeted the **believers** and stayed with them for a day. 8 On the following day we left and arrived in Caesarea. There we stayed at the house of Philip the evangelist, one of the seven men who had been **chosen** as **helpers** in Jerusalem. 9 He had four **unmarried** daughters who **proclaimed** God's **message.** 10 We had been there for several days when a **prophet** named Agabus arrived from Judaea. 11 He came to us, took Paul's belt, tied up his own feet and hands with it, and said, "This is what the **Holy Spirit** says: The owner of this belt will be tied up in this way by the **Jews** in Jerusalem, and they will hand him over to the **Gentiles.**"

12 When we heard this, we and the others there **begged** Paul not to go to Jerusalem. 13 But he answered, "What are you doing, crying like this and breaking my **heart**? I am ready not only to be tied up in Jerusalem but even to die there for the **sake** of the Lord Jesus."

14 We could not **convince** him, so we **gave up** and said, "May the Lord's will be done."

15 After spending some time there, we got our things ready and left for Jerusalem. 16 Some of the **disciples** from Caesarea also went with us and took us to the house of the man we were going to stay with[i] —Mnason, from Cyprus, who had been a **believer** since the early days.

Paul Visits James

17 When we arrived in Jerusalem, the **believers welcomed** us warmly. 18 The next day Paul went with us to see James; and all the **church elders** were present. 19 Paul greeted them and gave a **complete** report of everything that God had done among the **Gentiles** through his work. 20 After hearing him, they all **praised** God. Then they said, "Brother Paul, you can see how many thousands of **Jews** have become **believers**, and how **devoted** they all are to the **Law.** 21 They have been told that you have been **teaching** all the **Jews** who live in **Gentile** countries to **abandon** the **Law of Moses**, telling them not to **circumcise** their children or follow the **Jewish customs.** 22 They are **sure** to hear that you have arrived. What should be done, then? 23 This is what we want you to do. There are four men here who have taken a **vow.** 24 Go along with them and join them in the **ceremony** of **purification** and pay their expenses; then they will be able to **shave** their heads.[j] In this way everyone will know that there is no **truth** in any of the things that they have been told about you, but that you yourself live in accordance with the **Law of Moses.** 25 But as for the **Gentiles** who have become **believers,** we have sent them a **letter** telling them we decided that they must not eat any food that has been **offered** to **idols**, or any **blood**, or any animal that has been strangled, and that they must **keep themselves from sexual immorality.**"

26 So Paul took the men and the next day performed the **ceremony** of **purification** with them. Then he went into the **Temple** and gave notice of how many days it would be until the end of the period of **purification**, when a **sacrifice** would be **offered** for each one of them.

Paul Is Arrested in the Temple

27 But just when the seven days were about to come to an end, some **Jews** from the province of Asia saw Paul in the **Temple.** They stirred up the whole crowd and seized Paul. 28 "Men of Israel!" they shouted. "**Help**! This is the man who goes everywhere **teaching** everyone against the people of Israel, the **Law of Moses,** and this **Temple.** And now he has even brought some **Gentiles** into the **Temple** and **defiled** this **holy place**!" 29 (They said this because they had seen Trophimus from Ephesus with Paul in the city, and they thought that Paul had taken him into the **Temple.**)

30 Confusion spread through the whole city, and the people all ran together, seized Paul, and dragged him out of the **Temple.** At once the **Temple** doors were closed. 31 The mob was trying to kill Paul, when a report was sent up to the

[i] and took us to the house of the man we were going to stay with; *or* bringing with them the man at whose house we were going to stay. [j] SHAVE THEIR HEADS: *See 18.18.*

21.8: Acts 6.5, 8.5 **21.10:** Acts 11.28 **21.23–24:** Num 6.13–21 **21.25:** Acts 15.29 **21.29:** Acts 20.4

commander of the Roman troops that all
Jerusalem was rioting. 32 At once the
commander took some officers and soldiers and rushed down to the crowd.
When the people saw him with the soldiers, they stopped beating Paul. 33 The
commander went over to Paul, arrested
him, and ordered him to be bound with
two chains. Then he asked, "Who is this
man, and what has he done?" 34 Some in
the crowd shouted one thing, others
something else. There was such confusion that the commander could not find
out exactly what had happened, so he
ordered his men to take Paul up into the
fort. 35 They got as far as the steps with
him, and then the soldiers had to carry
him because the mob was so wild. 36 They
were all coming after him and screaming, "Kill him!"

Paul Defends Himself

37 As the soldiers were about to take
Paul into the fort, he spoke to the commander: "May I say something to you?"

"You speak Greek, do you?" the commander asked. 38 "Then you are not that
Egyptian fellow who some time ago
started a revolution and led four
thousand armed terrorists out into the
desert?"

39 Paul answered, "I am a Jew, born
in Tarsus in Cilicia, a citizen of an important city. Please let me speak to the
people."

40 The commander gave him permission, so Paul stood on the steps and
motioned with his hand for the people to
be silent. When they were quiet, Paul
spoke to them in Hebrew:

22 "My fellow-Israelites, listen to
me as I make my defence before
you!" 2 When they heard him speaking to
them in Hebrew, they became even
quieter; and Paul went on:

3 "I am a Jew, born in Tarsus in
Cilicia, but brought up here in Jerusalem
as a student of Gamaliel. I received strict
instruction in the Law of our ancestors
and was just as dedicated to God as are
all of you who are here today. 4 I persecuted to the death the people who followed this Way. I arrested men and
women and threw them into prison. 5 The
High Priest and the whole Council can
prove that I am telling the truth. I received from them letters written to
fellow-Jews in Damascus, so I went there
to arrest these people and bring them
back in chains to Jerusalem to be punished.

Paul Tells of His Conversion
(Acts 9.1–19; 26.12–18)

6 "As I was travelling and coming
near Damascus, about midday a bright
light from the sky flashed suddenly round
me. 7 I fell to the ground and heard a
voice saying to me, 'Saul, Saul! Why do
you persecute me?' 8 'Who are you,
Lord?' I asked. 'I am Jesus of Nazareth,
whom you persecute,' he said to me.
9 The men with me saw the light, but did
not hear the voice of the one who was
speaking to me. 10 I asked, 'What shall I
do, Lord?' and the Lord said to me, 'Get
up and go into Damascus, and there you
will be told everything that God has
determined for you to do.' 11 I was blind
because of the bright light, and so my
companions took me by the hand and led
me into Damascus.

12 "In that city was a man named
Ananias, a religious man who obeyed our
Law and was highly respected by all the
Jews living there. 13 He came to me,
stood by me, and said, 'Brother Saul, see
again!' At that very moment I saw again
and looked at him. 14 He said, 'The God of
our ancestors has chosen you to know his
will, to see his righteous Servant, and to
hear him speaking with his own voice.
15 For you will be a witness for him to tell
everyone what you have seen and heard.
16 And now, why wait any longer? Get up
and be baptized and have your sins
washed away by praying to him.'

Paul's Call to Preach to the Gentiles

17 "I went back to Jerusalem, and
while I was praying in the Temple, I had
a vision, 18 in which I saw the Lord, as he
said to me, 'Hurry and leave Jerusalem
quickly, because the people here will not
accept your witness about me.' 19 'Lord,' I
answered, 'they know very well that I
went to the synagogues and arrested and
beat those who believe in you. 20 And
when your witness Stephen was put to
death, I myself was there, approving of
his murder and taking care of the cloaks
of his murderers.' 21 'Go,' the Lord said to
me, 'for I will send you far away to the
Gentiles.'"

22 The people listened to Paul until he
said this; but then they started shouting
at the top of their voices, "Away with
him! Kill him! He's not fit to live!"
23 They were screaming, waving their
clothes, and throwing dust up in the air.
24 The Roman commander ordered his
men to take Paul into the fort, and he
told them to whip him in order to find out

fit (1) Lk 15.19; Eph 5.4
fright Mk 9.6; 2 Cor 10.9
Gentile 21.11; 26.17
Hebrew 21.40; 26.14
High Priest 19.14; 23.2
Jew [5] 21.11; 23.12
law [2] 21.20; 23.3
letter (2) 21.25; 23.25
light (1) [3] 16.29; 26.13
obey 20.22; Rom 1.5
persecute [3] 13.50; 26.11
pray [2] 21.5; 27.29
prison 20.23; 23.18
prove 18.28; 24.13
punish 4.21; 26.11
question 15.6; 23.29
religion 17.22; 25.19
respect 15.22; Rom 12.10
righteous 7.52; Rom 2.5
servant 20.19; 26.16
study 17.11
synagogue 19.8; 24.12
Temple (1) (of God) 21.26; 24.6
truth 21.24; 25.11
try (2) 12.4; 23.6
vision 18.9; 26.19
Way (2) 19.9; 24.14
who 19.15; 26.15
will (1) 18.21; Rom 1.10
witness [3] 13.31; 23.11

accept 16.21; Rom 4.3
accuse 19.38; 23.28
approve 15.8; Rom 1.32
arrest [3] 21.33; 24.6
baptize 19.3; Rom 6.3
believe 20.21; 23.8
birth 15.23; 1 Cor 15.8
blind 13.11; Rom 2.19
care 20.28; 1 Cor 12.23
certain (1) Jn 8.52; Rom 2.20
chief priests 9.14; 23.14
choose 21.8; 26.18
Council [2] 17.19; 23.1
crime 18.14; 24.20
death (1) 20.28; 25.11
death (3) (to death) 13.28; Rom 6.6
dedicate Jn 17.17; Rom 6.22
defend 19.33; 24.10
determine Jn 5.18; Heb 12.1

22.3: Acts 5.34–39 **22.4–5:** Acts 8.3, 26.9–11 **22.20:** Acts 7.58

why the **Jews** were screaming like this
against him. [25]But when they had tied
him up to be whipped, Paul said to the
officer standing there, "Is it lawful for
you to whip a Roman citizen who hasn't
even been **tried** for any **crime**?"
26 When the officer heard this, he
went to the commander and asked him,
"What are you doing? That man is a
Roman citizen!"
27 So the commander went to Paul
and asked him, "Tell me, are you a
Roman citizen?"
"Yes," answered Paul.
28 The commander said, "I became
one by paying a large amount of money."
"But I am one by **birth**," Paul answered.
29 At once the men who were going to
question Paul drew back from him; and
the commander was **frightened** when he
realized that Paul was a Roman citizen
and that he had put him in chains.

Paul before the Council

30 The commander wanted to find out
for **certain** what the **Jews** were **accusing**
Paul of; so the next day he had Paul's
chains taken off and ordered the **chief**
priests and the whole **Council** to meet.
Then he took Paul and made him stand
before them.

23 Paul looked straight at the
Council and said, "My fellow-
Israelites! My **conscience** is **perfectly**
clear about the way in which I have lived
before God to this very day." [2]The **High**
Priest Ananias ordered those who were
standing close to Paul to **strike** him on
the mouth. [3]Paul said to him, "God will
certainly **strike** you—you whitewashed
wall! You sit there to **judge** me according to the **Law**, yet you break the **Law** by
ordering them to **strike** me!"
4 The men close to Paul said to him,
"You are **insulting** God's **High Priest**!"
5 Paul answered, "My fellow-
Israelites, I did not know that he was the
High Priest. The **scripture** says, 'You
must not speak **evil** of the ruler of your
people.' "
6 When Paul saw that some of the
group were **Sadducees** and the others
were **Pharisees**, he called out in the
Council, "Fellow-Israelites! I am a **Phari-**
see, the son of Pharisees. I am on **trial**
here because of the **hope** I have that the
dead will **rise to life**!"
7 As soon as he said this, the **Pharisees**
and **Sadducees** started to **quarrel**, and the
group was divided. [8](For the **Sadducees**
say that people will not **rise from death**
and that there are no **angels** or **spirits**;
but the **Pharisees believe** in all three.)
[9]The shouting became louder, and some
of the **teachers of the Law** who belonged
to the party of the **Pharisees** stood up
and protested **strongly**: "We cannot find
anything **wrong** with this man! Perhaps
a **spirit** or an **angel** really did speak to
him!"
10 The **argument** became so **violent**
that the commander was **afraid** that Paul
would be torn to pieces. So he ordered his
soldiers to go down into the group, get
Paul away from them, and take him into
the fort.
11 That night the Lord stood by Paul
and said, "Don't be **afraid**! You have
given your **witness** for me here in
Jerusalem, and you must also do the
same in Rome."

The Plot against Paul's Life

12 The next morning some **Jews** met
together and made a **plan**. They took a
vow that they would not eat or drink anything until they had killed Paul. [13]There
were more than forty who **planned** this
together. [14]Then they went to the **chief**
priests and **elders** and said, "We have
taken a **solemn vow** together not to eat a
thing until we have killed Paul. [15]Now
then, you and the **Council** send **word** to
the Roman commander to bring Paul
down to you, pretending that you want to
get more accurate information about
him. But we will be ready to kill him before he ever gets here."
16 But the son of Paul's sister heard
about the **plot**; so he went to the fort and
told Paul. [17]Then Paul called one of the
officers and said to him, "Take this
young man to the commander; he has
something to tell him." [18]The officer took
him, led him to the commander, and
said, "The **prisoner** Paul called me and
asked me to bring this young man to you,
because he has something to say to you."
19 The commander took him by the
hand, led him off by himself, and asked
him, "What have you got to tell me?"
20 He said, "The **Jewish authorities**
have **agreed** to ask you tomorrow to take
Paul down to the **Council**, pretending
that the **Council** wants to get more
accurate information about him. [21]But
don't listen to them, because there are
more than forty men who will be hiding
and waiting for him. They have taken a
vow not to eat or drink until they have
killed him. They are now ready to do it
and are waiting for your decision."
22 The commander said, "Don't tell

accuse [4] 22.30; 24.2
afraid [2] 18.9; 24.25
agree 15.15; 28.25
angel [2] 12.7; 27.23
argue 18.15; 24.12
authorities 19.31; Rom 13.1
believe 22.19; 24.14
charge (3) 19.38; 24.1
chief priests 22.30; 25.2
clear 11.17; 24.16
conscience Prov 20.9; 24.16
Council [6] 22.5; 24.20
dead 20.9; 24.21
death (2) (from death) 17.3; 24.15
deserve Lk 23.15; 25.11
elder (2) 21.18; 24.1
evil 19.9; 25.18
High Priest [3] 22.5; 24.1
hope 2.26; 24.15
insult 13.45; Rom 3.8
Jew [3] 22.3; 24.5
judge 18.15; 24.10
law [3] 22.3; 24.14
learn 14.6; 24.8
letter (2) [3] 22.5; 28.21
life (2) (to life) 13.32; 24.21
perfect Mt 21.16; Rom 12.2
Pharisees [5] !5.5; 26.5
plan [2] 12.4; 27.13
plot (1) [2] 20.3; 25.3
prison [2] 22.4; 24.27
provide 20.34; 24.23
quarrel 6.1; 1 Cor 1.11
question 22.29; 24.8

rescue 12.11; 26.17
rise [2] 17.3; 24.15
Sadducees [3] 5.17
safe 7.10; 27.44
scripture 18.24; Rom 1.2
solemn 20.21; 1 Tim 5.21
spirit (2) [2] 19.12; Rom 8.16
strike [3] 12.23; Rev 8.12
strong 19.20; 27.14
teacher of the Law 6.12; 1 Tim 1.7
try (2) 22.25; 24.21
violent 19.16; 27.18
vow [3] 21.23; Heb 6.13
witness 22.15; 26.22
word (1) 20.1; 28.24
wrong 18.14; 25.5

23.3: Mt 23.27–28 **23.5:** Ex 22.28 **23.6:** Acts 26.5; Phil 3.5 **23.8:** Mt 22.23; Mk 12.18; Lk 20.27

anyone that you have reported this to me." And he sent the young man away.

Paul Is Sent to Governor Felix

23 Then the commander called two of his officers and said, "Get two hundred soldiers ready to go to Caesarea, together with seventy horsemen and two hundred spearmen, and be ready to leave by nine o'clock tonight. 24 **Provide** some horses for Paul to ride and get him **safely** through to the governor Felix." 25 Then the commander wrote a **letter** that went like this:

> 26 "Claudius Lysias to His Excellency, the governor Felix: Greetings. 27 The **Jews** seized this man and were about to kill him. I **learnt** that he was a Roman citizen, so I went with my soldiers and **rescued** him. 28 I wanted to know what they were **accusing** him of, so I took him down to their **Council**. 29 I found out that he had not done anything for which he **deserved** to die or be put in **prison**; the **accusation** against him had to do with **questions** about their own **law**. 30 And when I was informed that there was a **plot** against him, at once I decided to send him to you. I have told his **accusers** to make their **charges** against him before you."

31 The soldiers carried out their orders. They got Paul and took him that night as far as Antipatris. 32 The next day the foot-soldiers returned to the fort and left the horsemen to go on with him. 33 They took him to Caesarea, delivered the **letter** to the governor, and handed Paul over to him. 34 The governor read the **letter** and asked Paul what province he was from. When he found out that he was from Cilicia, 35 he said, "I will hear you when your **accusers** arrive." Then he gave orders for Paul to be kept under guard in the governor's headquarters.

Paul Is Accused by the Jews

24 Five days later the **High Priest** Ananias went to Caesarea with some **elders** and a lawyer named Tertullus. They appeared before Felix and made their **charges** against Paul. 2 Then Paul was called in, and Tertullus began to make his **accusation**, as follows:

"Your Excellency! Your **wise** leadership has brought us a long period of **peace**, and many necessary reforms are being made for the good of our country. 3 We **welcome** this everywhere and at all times, and we are deeply **grateful** to you. 4 I do not want to take up too much of your time, however, so I **beg** you to be **kind** and listen to our brief account. 5 We found this man to be a **dangerous** nuisance; he starts riots among the **Jews** all over the **world** and is a leader of the party of the Nazarenes. 6 He also tried to **defile** the **Temple**, and we **arrested** him.[k] 8 If you **question** this man, you yourself will be able to **learn** from him all the things that we are **accusing** him of." 9 The **Jews** joined in the **accusation** and said that all this was **true**.

Paul's Defence before Felix

10 The governor then motioned to Paul to speak, and Paul said,

"I know that you have been a **judge** over this nation for many years, and so I am **happy** to **defend** myself before you. 11 As you can find out for yourself, it was no more than twelve days ago that I went to Jerusalem to **worship**. 12 The **Jews** did not find me **arguing** with anyone in the **Temple**, nor did they find me stirring up the people, either in the **synagogues** or anywhere else in the city. 13 Nor can they give you **proof** of the **accusations** they now bring against me. 14 I do **admit** this to you: I **worship** the God of our ancestors by following that **Way** which they say is **false**. But I also **believe** in everything written in the **Law of Moses** and the books of the **prophets**. 15 I have the same **hope** in God that these themselves have, namely, that all people, both the good and the **bad**, will **rise from death**. 16 And so I do my **best** always to have a **clear conscience** before God and man.

17 "After being away from Jerusalem for several years, I went there to take some money to my own people and to **offer sacrifices**. 18 It was while I was doing this that they found me in the **Temple** after I had **completed** the **ceremony** of **purification**. There was no crowd with me and no disorder. 19 But some **Jews** from the province of Asia were there; they themselves ought to come before you and make their **accusations** if they have anything against me. 20 Or let these men here tell what **crime** they found me **guilty** of when I stood before the **Council**—21 except for the one thing I called

[k] *Some manuscripts add verses 6b–8a:* We planned to judge him according to our own Law, 7 but Lysias the commander came, and with great violence took him from us. 8 Then Lysias gave orders that his accusers should come before you.

24.17–18: Acts 21.17–28 **24.21:** Acts 23.6

accuse [5] 23.28; 25.5
admit (1) 19.18; 2 Cor 11.21
afraid 23.10; 27.17
argue 23.10; 25.19
arrest 22.4; 2 Cor 11.32
bad 19.27; 28.21
beg 21.12; 25.2
believe [2] 23.8; 26.8
best 15.29; 1 Cor 12.31
case (2) Mic 6.1; 25.21
ceremony 21.24; 25.23

charge (3) 23.30; 25.7
clear 23.1; 25.27
complete 21.19; Rom 1.16
conscience 23.1; Rom 1.31
Council 23.1
crime 22.25; 25.16
danger 19.27; 27.9
Day of Judgement Lk 11.31; 2 Pet 2.4
dead 23.6; 26.8
death (2) (from death) 23.8; 26.23
defend 22.1; 25.8
defile 21.28; 1 Cor 8.7
discuss 19.8; 1 Tim 1.6
elder (2) 23.14; 25.15
faith 16.5; 26.11
false Jn 7.18; Rom 11.4
favour 11.2; 25.3
free 13.38; 28.31
friend 19.31; 27.3
grateful Lk 6.35; Rom 16.4
guilty 16.37; Rom 4.5
happy 20.35; Rom 4.6
High Priest 23.2; Heb 2.17
hope [2] 23.6; 26.6
Jew [6] 23.12; 25.2
judge 23.3; 25.6
kind Lk 10.37; 27.3
law 23.3; 25.8
learn 23.27; 26.24
life (2) (to life) 23.6; Rom 4.17
need 20.34; 27.3
offer 21.25; Rom 3.25
peace 16.36; Rom 1.7
prison 23.18; 25.4
prophet 21.10; 26.22
prove 22.5; 25.7
provide 23.24; 1 Cor 6.13
pure 21.24; 1 Cor 5.7
question 23.29; 28.18
reason 19.40; 26.21
rise [2] 23.6; 26.23
sacrifice 21.26; Rom 3.25
self-control Prov 5.23; 1 Cor 7.5
synagogue 22.19; 26.11
Temple (1) (of God) [3] 22.17; 25.8
true 17.11; Rom 1.9
try (2) 23.6; 25.9
Way (2) [2] 22.4; 2 Pet 2.2
welcome 21.17; 25.13
wise Lk 12.42; Rom 1.22
world 19.27; Rom 1.8
worship (1) (of God) [2] 18.7; 26.7

out when I stood before them: 'I am being **tried** by you today for **believing** that the **dead** will **rise to life**.' "

22 Then Felix, who was well informed about the **Way**, brought the hearing to a close. "When Lysias the commander arrives," he told them, "I will decide your **case**." 23 He ordered the officer in charge of Paul to keep him under guard, but to give him some **freedom** and allow his **friends** to **provide** for his **needs**.

Paul before Felix and Drusilla

24 After some days Felix came with his wife Drusilla, who was **Jewish**. He sent for Paul and listened to him as he talked about **faith** in Christ Jesus. 25 But as Paul went on **discussing** about goodness, **self-control**, and the coming **Day of Judgement**, Felix was **afraid** and said, "You may leave now. I will call you again when I get the chance." 26 At the same time he was **hoping** that Paul would give him some money; and for this **reason** he would often send for him and talk with him.

27 After two years had passed, Porcius Festus succeeded Felix as governor. Felix wanted to gain **favour** with the **Jews** so he left Paul in **prison**.

Paul Appeals to the Emperor

25 Three days after Festus arrived in the province, he went from Caesarea to Jerusalem, 2 where the **chief priests** and the **Jewish** leaders brought their **charges** against Paul. They **begged** Festus 3 to do them the **favour** of bringing Paul to Jerusalem, for they had made a **plot** to kill him on the way. 4 Festus answered, "Paul is being kept a **prisoner** in Caesarea, and I myself will be going back there soon. 5 Let your leaders go to Caesarea with me and **accuse** the man if he has done anything **wrong**."

6 Festus spent another eight or ten days with them and then went to Caesarea. On the next day he sat down in the **court of judgement** and ordered Paul to be brought in. 7 When Paul arrived, the **Jews** who had come from Jerusalem stood round him and started making many **serious charges** against him, which they were not able to **prove**. 8 But Paul **defended** himself: "I have done nothing **wrong** against the **Law** of the **Jews** or against the **Temple** or against the Roman Emperor."

9 But Festus wanted to gain **favour** with the **Jews**, so he asked Paul, "Would you be willing to go to Jerusalem and be **tried** on these **charges** before me there?"

10 Paul said, "I am standing before the Emperor's own **court of judgement**, where I should be **tried**. I have done no **wrong** to the **Jews**, as you yourself well know. 11 If I have broken the **law** and done something for which I **deserve** the **death** penalty, I do not ask to **escape** it. But if there is no **truth** in the **charges** they bring against me, no one can hand me over to them. I appeal to the Emperor."

12 Then Festus, after conferring with his advisers, answered, "You have appealed to the Emperor, so to the Emperor you will go."

Paul before Agrippa and Bernice

13 Some time later King Agrippa and Bernice came to Caesarea to pay a visit of **welcome** to Festus. 14 After they had been there several days, Festus explained Paul's situation to the king: "There is a man here who was left a **prisoner** by Felix; 15 and when I went to Jerusalem, the **Jewish chief priests** and **elders** brought **charges** against him and asked me to **condemn** him. 16 But I told them that we Romans are not in the habit of handing over any man **accused** of a **crime** before he has met his **accusers** face to face and has had the chance of **defending** himself against the **accusation**. 17 When they came here, then, I lost no time, but on the very next day I sat in the **court** and ordered the man to be brought in. 18 His opponents stood up, but they did not **accuse** him of any of the **evil crimes** that I thought they would. 19 All they had were some **arguments** with him about their own **religion** and about a man named Jesus, who has died; but Paul **claims** that he is **alive**. 20 I was undecided about how I could get information on these matters, so I asked Paul if he would be willing to go to Jerusalem and be **tried** there on these **charges**. 21 But Paul appealed; he asked to be kept under guard and to let the Emperor decide his **case**. So I gave orders for him to be kept under guard until I could send him to the Emperor."

22 Agrippa said to Festus, "I would like to hear this man myself."

"You will hear him tomorrow," Festus answered.

23 The next day Agrippa and Bernice came with great pomp and **ceremony** and entered the audience hall with the military chiefs and the leading men of the city. Festus gave the order, and Paul was brought in. 24 Festus said, "King Agrippa and all who are here with us: You see this man against whom all the

Temple (1) (of God) 24.6; 26.21
truth 22.5; 26.25
try (2) [3] 24.21; 26.6
welcome 24.3; 28.2
wrong [3] 23.9; Rom 1.27

accuse [5] 24.2; 26.2
alive 20.10; Rom 7.3
argue 24.12; Rom 14.1
beg 24.4; 27.22
case (2) [2] 24.22; Rom 3.4
ceremony 24.18; Gal 6.13
charge (3) [7] 24.1
chief priests [2] 23.14; 26.10
claim 13.6; 1 Cor 9.15
clear 24.16; Rom 1.20
complain Lk 5.30; 1 Cor 10.10
condemn 13.27; Rom 2.1
court (1) [3] 19.38; 1 Cor 6.6
crime [2] 24.20; 1 Tim 1.9
death (1) [2] 22.4; Rom 1.32
defend [2] 24.10; 26.1
deserve [2] 23.29; 28.18
elder (2) 24.1; 1 Tim 4.14
escape 16.27; 27.30
evil 23.5; Rom 1.18
favour [2] 24.27; 27.12
Jew [7] 24.5; 26.2
judge [2] 24.10; Rom 2.1
law [2] 24.14; 28.23
plot (1) 23.16
prison [3] 24.27; 26.10
prove 24.13; Rom 16.10
religion 22.12; 26.5
sentence 13.28; 26.10
serious 19.23; Tit 2.7

Jewish people, both here and in
Jerusalem, have brought **complaints** to
me. They scream that he should not live
any longer. 25 But I could not find that he
had done anything for which he **deserved**
the **death sentence**. And since he himself
made an appeal to the Emperor, I have
decided to send him. 26 But I have nothing
definite about him to write to the Emperor. So I have brought him here before
you—and especially before you, King
Agrippa!—so that, after investigating his
case, I may have something to write.
27 For it seems unreasonable to me to
send a **prisoner** without **clearly** indicating the **charges** against him."

Paul Defends Himself before Agrippa

26 Agrippa said to Paul, "You have
permission to speak on your own
behalf." Paul stretched out his hand and
defended himself as follows:

2 "King Agrippa! I **consider** myself
fortunate that today I am to **defend** myself before you from all the things the
Jews accuse me of, 3 particularly since
you know so well all the **Jewish customs**
and **disputes**. I ask you, then, to listen to
me with **patience**.

4 "All the **Jews** know how I have lived
ever since I was young. They know how I
have spent my whole **life**, at first in my
own country and then in Jerusalem.
5 They have always known, if they are
willing to **testify**, that from the very first
I have lived as a member of the strictest
party of our **religion**, the **Pharisees**. 6 And
now I stand here to be **tried** because of
the **hope** I have in the **promise** that God
made to our ancestors—7 the very thing
that the twelve tribes of our people **hope**
to receive, as they **worship** God day and
night. And it is because of this **hope**, Your
Majesty, that I am being **accused** by the
Jews! 8 Why do you who are here find it
impossible to **believe** that God **raises** the
dead?

9 "I myself thought that I should do
everything I could against the **cause** of
Jesus of Nazareth. 10 That is what I did in
Jerusalem. I received **authority** from the
chief priests and put many of **God's
people** in **prison**; and when they were
sentenced to death, I also voted against
them. 11 Many times I had them **punished**
in the **synagogues** and tried to make
them **deny** their **faith**. I was so **furious**
with them that I even went to foreign
cities to **persecute** them.

Paul Tells of His Conversion
(Acts 9.1-19; 22.6-16)

12 "It was for this **purpose** that I went
to Damascus with **authority** and orders
from the **chief priests**. 13 It was on the
road at midday, Your **Majesty**, that I saw
a **light** much brighter than the sun,
coming from the sky and shining round
me and the men travelling with me. 14 All
of us fell to the ground, and I heard a
voice say to me in **Hebrew**, 'Saul, Saul!
Why are you **persecuting** me? You are
hurting yourself by hitting back, like an
ox kicking against its owner's stick.'
15 '**Who are you**, Lord?' I asked. And the
Lord answered, 'I am Jesus, whom you
persecute. 16 But get up and stand on your
feet. I have appeared to you to appoint
you as my **servant**. You are to tell others
what you have seen of me[l] today and
what I will show you in the future. 17 I will
rescue you from the people of Israel and
from the **Gentiles** to whom I will send
you. 18 You are to open their eyes and
turn them from the **darkness** to the **light**
and from the **power** of **Satan** to God, so
that through their **faith** in me they will
have their sins **forgiven** and receive their
place among God's **chosen people**.'

Paul Tells of His Work

19 "And so, King Agrippa, I did not **disobey** the **vision** I had from **heaven**.
20 First in Damascus and in Jerusalem
and then in all Judaea and among the
Gentiles, I **preached** that they must **repent** of their sins and **turn to God** and do
the things that would show they had **repented**. 21 It was for this **reason** that the
Jews seized me while I was in the
Temple, and they tried to kill me. 22 But
to this very day I have been **helped** by
God, and so I stand here giving my **witness** to all, to small and great alike. What
I say is the very same thing which the
prophets and Moses said was going to
happen: 23 that the **Messiah** must **suffer**
and be the first one to **rise from death**, to
announce the **light** of **salvation** to the
Jews and to the **Gentiles**."

24 As Paul **defended** himself in this
way, Festus shouted at him, "You are
mad, Paul! Your great **learning** is
driving you **mad**!"

25 Paul answered, "I am not **mad**,
Your Excellency! I am speaking the
sober **truth**. 26 King Agrippa! I can speak
to you with all **boldness**, because you
know about these things. I am **sure** that
you have taken **notice** of every one of

[l] *Some manuscripts do not have* of me.

26.5: Acts 23.6; Phil 3.5 **26.9-11:** Acts 8.3, 22.4-5 **26.20:** Acts 9.20, 28-29
26.23: Is 42.6, 49.6; 1 Cor 15.20

accuse [2] 25.5; 28.19
announce 20.27; Gal 3.8
authority [2] 9.14; Rom 12.8
believe [2] 24.14; 28.24
bold 19.8; 28.31
cause (2) Jer 51.36; 2 Cor 9.8
chief priests [2] 25.2
choose 22.14; Rom 1.1
Christian 16.1; Rom 12.10
consider 15.6; Rom 8.18
custom 21.21; 28.17
dark 13.11; Rom 1.21
dead 24.21; 28.6
death (2) (from death) 24.15; Rom 1.4
defend [3] 25.8; Rom 2.15
deny 19.36; 1 Cor 7.5
disobey Jn 3.36; Rom 1.30
dispute 13.45; 1 Cor 6.1
each other 2.12; Rom 1.24
faith [2] 24.24; Rom 1.8
forgive 15.9; Rom 3.25
fortune Lk 10.23; Jas 1.2
fury 19.28; Rom 2.8
Gentile [3] 22.21; 28.28
God's people [2] 20.32; Rom 1.7
heaven 19.35; Rom 1.18
Hebrew 22.2; Rom 9.5
help 21.28; Rom 1.12
hope [3] 24.15; 27.20
hurt Lk 10.19; Rom 3.15
impossible 4.21; 27.15
Jew [6] 25.2; 28.17
learn 24.8; 28.1
life (1) 20.24; 27.10
light (1) [3] 22.6; Rom 2.19
mad [3] 12.15; 2 Cor 11.23
Majesty [2] Mic 5.4; Heb 8.1

Messiah 18.5; Heb 11.26
notice (1) 17.16; 27.39
patient 18.14; Rom 2.4
permit 21.40; Rom 13.1
persecute [3] 22.4; Rom 8.35
Pharisees 23.6; Phil 3.5
power 21.4; Rom 1.4
prayer 16.13; 1 Cor 7.5
preach 20.20; 28.31
prison [2] 25.4; 27.1
promise 13.23; Rom 1.2
prophet [2] 24.14; 28.23
punish 22.5; Rom 1.19
purpose 20.27; Rom 6.13
raise 17.31; 27.40
reason 24.26; Rom 3.27
religion 25.19; Gal 1.13
repent [2] 11.18; Rom 2.4
rescue 23.27; Rom 7.24
rise 24.15; Rom 14.9
salvation 13.26; 28.28
Satan 5.3; Rom 16.20
sentence 25.25; 2 Cor 1.9
servant 22.14; Rom 1.1
suffer 17.3; Rom 2.9
sure 21.22; Rom 2.19
synagogue 24.12
Temple (1) (of God) 25.8; 1 Cor 3.16
testify 18.5; Col 4.13
truth 25.11; Rom 1.18
try (2) 25.9; Rom 3.4
turn [2] 20.21; 28.27
vision 22.17; 2 Cor 12.1
who 22.8; Rom 5.14
witness 23.11; Rom 1.9
worship (1) (of God) 24.11; 27.23

trust 14.23; Rom 3.2
violent [2] 23.10;
1 Tim 3.3
worship (1) (of God)
26.7; Rom 1.23

them, for this thing has not happened
hidden away in a corner. 27 King Agrippa,
do you **believe** the **prophets**? I know that
you do!"
28 Agrippa said to Paul, "In this short
time do you think you will make me a
Christian?"
29 "Whether a short time or a long
time," Paul answered, "my **prayer** to
God is that you and all the rest of you
who are listening to me today might become what I am—except, of course, for
these chains!"
30 Then the king, the governor,
Bernice, and all the others got up, 31 and
after leaving they said to **each other**,
"This man has not done anything for
which he should die or be put in **prison**."
32 And Agrippa said to Festus, "This man
could have been released if he had not
appealed to the Emperor."

Paul Sails for Rome

27 When it was decided that we
should sail to Italy, they handed
Paul and some other **prisoners** over to
Julius, an officer in the Roman regiment
called "The Emperor's Regiment." 2 We
went aboard a ship from Adramyttium,
which was ready to leave for the sea-
ports of the province of Asia, and we
sailed away. Aristarchus, a Macedonian
from Thessalonica, was with us. 3 The
next day we arrived at Sidon. Julius was
kind to Paul and allowed him to go and
see his **friends**, to be given what he
needed. 4 We went on from there, and because the winds were blowing against us,
we sailed on the **sheltered side** of the
island of Cyprus. 5 We crossed over the
sea off Cilicia and Pamphylia and came
to Myra in Lycia. 6 There the officer
found a ship from Alexandria that was
going to sail for Italy, so he put us
aboard.
7 We sailed slowly for several days
and with great **difficulty** finally arrived
off the town of Cnidus. The wind would
not let us go any further in that direction,
so we sailed down the **sheltered side** of
the island of Crete, passing by Cape
Salmone. 8 We kept close to the coast and
with great **difficulty** came to a place
called Safe Harbours, not far from the
town of Lasea.
9 We spent a long time there, until it
became **dangerous** to continue the
voyage, for by now the Day of
Atonement[m] was already past. So Paul
gave them this **advice**: 10 "Men, I see that
our voyage from here on will be
dangerous; there will be great damage to
the cargo and to the ship, and **loss of life**
as well." 11 But the army officer was **convinced** by what the captain and the
owner of the ship said, and not by what
Paul said. 12 The harbour was not a good
one to spend the winter in; so most of the
men were in **favour** of putting out to sea
and trying to reach Phoenix, if possible,
in order to spend the winter there.
Phoenix is a harbour in Crete that faces
south-west and north-west.[n]

The Storm at Sea

13 A soft wind from the south began to
blow, and the men thought that they
could carry out their **plan**, so they pulled
up the anchor and sailed as close as possible along the coast of Crete. 14 But soon a
very **strong** wind—the one called "North-
easter"—blew down from the island. 15 It
hit the ship, and since it was **impossible**
to keep the ship headed into the wind, we
gave up trying and let it be carried along
by the wind. 16 We got some **shelter** when
we passed to the south of the little island
of Cauda. There, with some **difficulty**, we
managed to make the ship's boat **secure**.
17 They pulled it aboard and then
fastened some ropes tight round the ship.
They were **afraid** that they might run
into the sandbanks off the coast of Libya,
so they lowered the sail and let the ship
be carried by the wind. 18 The **violent**
storm continued, so on the next day they
began to throw some of the ship's cargo
overboard, 19 and on the following day
they threw part of the ship's equipment
overboard. 20 For many days we could
not see the sun or the stars, and the wind
kept on blowing very **hard**. We finally
gave up all **hope** of being **saved**.
21 After the men had gone a long time
without food, Paul stood before them and
said, "Men, you should have listened to
me and not have sailed from Crete; then
we would have avoided all this damage
and **loss**. 22 But now I **beg** you, take **heart**!
Not one of you will lose his **life**; only the
ship will be lost. 23 For **last** night an **angel**
of the God to whom I belong and whom I
worship came to me 24 and said, 'Don't be
afraid, Paul! You must stand before the
Emperor. And God in his goodness to you
has **spared** the **lives** of all those who are
sailing with you.' 25 So take **heart**, men!
For I **trust** in God that it will be just as I
was told. 26 But we will be driven ashore
on some island."

advice 5.39;
Rom 11.34
afraid [3] 24.25;
Rom 8.15
angel 23.8; Rom 8.38
Atonement Lev 25.9
beg [3] 25.2;
1 Cor 4.16
bread 20.11;
Rom 11.16
convince 21.14; 28.23
danger [2] 24.5;
Rom 3.13
difficult [3]
Dan 2.11; Rom 5.7
enough 13.25;
2 Cor 2.6
escape [2] 25.11; 28.4
favour 25.3; 2 Cor 6.2
friend 24.23; 28.2
give up [2] 21.14;
Rom 1.27
hard 20.19; Rom 2.5
heart [3] 21.13;
Rom 1.9
hope [2] 26.6; 28.20
impossible 26.8;
1 Cor 1.21
keep from 21.25;
Rom 1.13
kind 24.4; 28.7
last (2) 19.35;
Rom 1.10
life (1) [3] 26.4;
Rom 2.7
loss [2] Hos 10.5;
Phil 3.7
need [2] 24.23; 28.10
notice (1) 26.26;
1 Cor 16.18
plan [2] 23.12;
Rom 1.13
pray 22.16; 28.8
prison [2] 26.10; 28.17
raise 26.8; Rom 1.4
safe 23.24; 28.1
save [3] 16.17;
Rom 1.16
secure Mt 27.65
shelter [3] Jn 7.2;
2 Cor 11.27
spare 20.29;
Rom 11.21
strong 23.9;
Rom 1.11
thank Jn 11.41; 28.15

[m] DAY OF ATONEMENT: *This was celebrated towards the end of September or beginning of October, at which time bad weather made sailing dangerous.*
[n] south-west and north-west; *or* north-east and south-east.

27 It was the fourteenth night, and we
were being driven about in the
Mediterranean by the storm. About midnight the sailors suspected that we were
getting close to land. 28 So they dropped a
line with a weight tied to it and found
that the water was forty metres deep; a
little later they did the same and found
that it was thirty metres deep. 29 They
were **afraid** that the ship would go on the
rocks, so they lowered four anchors from
the back of the ship and **prayed** for daylight. 30 Then the sailors tried to **escape**
from the ship; they lowered the boat into
the water and pretended that they were
going to put out some anchors from the
front of the ship. 31 But Paul said to the
army officer and soldiers, "If the sailors
don't stay on board, you have no **hope** of
being **saved**." 32 So the soldiers cut the
ropes that held the boat and let it go.

33 Just before dawn, Paul **begged**
them all to eat some food: "You have
been waiting for fourteen days now, and
all this time you have not eaten anything.
34 I **beg** you, then, eat some food; you
need it in order to survive. Not even a
hair of your heads will be lost." 35 After
saying this, Paul took some **bread**, gave
thanks to God before them all, broke it,
and began to eat. 36 They took **heart**, and
every one of them also ate some food.
37 There was a total of 276[p] of us on
board. 38 After everyone had eaten
enough, they lightened the ship by throwing all the wheat into the sea.

The Shipwreck

39 When day came, the sailors did not
recognize the coast, but they **noticed** a
bay with a beach and decided that, if
possible, they would run the ship aground
there. 40 So they cut off the anchors and
let them sink in the sea, and at the same
time they untied the ropes that held the
steering oars. Then they **raised** the sail
at the front of the ship so that the wind
would blow the ship forward, and we
headed for shore. 41 But the ship hit a
sandbank and went aground; the front
part of the ship got stuck and could not
move, while the back part was being
broken to pieces by the **violence** of the
waves.

42 The soldiers made a **plan** to kill all
the **prisoners**, in order to **keep them**
from swimming ashore and **escaping**.
43 But the army officer wanted to **save**
Paul, so he stopped them from doing this.
Instead, he ordered all the men who
could swim to jump overboard first and
swim ashore; 44 the rest were to follow,
holding on to the planks or to some
broken pieces of the ship. And this was
how we all got **safely** ashore.

In Malta

28 When we were **safely** ashore, we
learnt that the island was called
Malta. 2 The natives there were very
friendly to us. It had started to rain and
was cold, so they lit a fire and made us
all **welcome**. 3 Paul gathered up a bundle
of sticks and was putting them on the fire
when a snake came out on account of the
heat and fastened itself to his hand. 4 The
natives saw the snake hanging on Paul's
hand and said to **one another**, "This man
must be a murderer, but **Fate** will not let
him live, even though he **escaped** from
the sea." 5 But Paul shook the snake off
into the fire without being **harmed** at all.
6 They were waiting for him to swell up
or suddenly fall down **dead**. But after
waiting for a long time and not seeing
anything unusual happening to him, they
changed their **minds** and said, "He is a
god!"

7 Not far from that place were some
fields that belonged to Publius, the chief
official of the island. He **welcomed** us
kindly and for three days we were his
guests. 8 Publius' father was in bed, sick
with fever and dysentery. Paul went into
his room, **prayed**, placed his hands on
him, and **healed** him. 9 When this happened, all the other sick people on the
island came and were **healed**. 10 They
gave us many **gifts**, and when we sailed,
they put on board what we **needed** for
the voyage.

From Malta to Rome

11 After three months we sailed away
on a ship from Alexandria, called "The
Twin Gods," which had spent the winter
in the island. 12 We arrived in the city of
Syracuse and stayed there for three days.
13 From there we sailed on and arrived in
the city of Rhegium. The next day a wind
began to blow from the south, and in two
days we came to the town of Puteoli.
14 We found some **believers** there who
asked us to stay with them a week. And
so we came to Rome. 15 The **believers** in
Rome heard about us and came as far as
the towns of Market of Appius and Three
Inns to meet us. When Paul saw them, he
thanked God and was greatly **encouraged**.

In Rome

16 When we arrived in Rome, Paul

[p] 276; *some manuscripts have* 275; *others have* about 76.

accuse 26.2; Rom 2.15
agree 23.20; Rom 7.16
bad 24.15; Rom 9.11
believe 26.8; Rom 1.5
believer [2] 21.4; 1 Cor 7.15
bind 21.33; Rom 7.2
bold 26.26; Rom 10.20
change 6.14; Rom 11.15
convince [2] 27.11; 1 Cor 2.4
custom 26.3; 1 Cor 11.16
dead 26.8; Rom 4.17
deserve 25.11; Rom 1.27
encourage 20.1; Rom 12.8
escape 27.30; Rom 2.3
fate Lk 22.37
force (1) 7.19; 1 Cor 7.37
free 24.23; Rom 3.24
friend 27.3; Rom 2.1
Gentile 26.17; Rom 1.13
gift 11.17; Rom 3.24
god (2) (other gods) 19.26; Rom 11.4
harm 18.10; 1 Cor 11.17
heal [3] 14.9; 1 Cor 12.9
hope 27.20; Rom 4.18
idea Mk 7.21
Jew [2] 26.2; Rom 1.16
kind 27.3; Rom 1.31
Kingdom (1) (of God) [2] 20.25; Rom 14.17
law 25.8; Rom 1.32
learn 26.24; Rom 2.18
letter (2) 23.25; Rom 15.15
message [2] 21.9; Rom 3.2
mind (1) [3] 19.21; Rom 1.21
need 27.3; Rom 12.13
one another 21.6; Rom 1.30
pray 27.29; Rom 1.10
preach 26.20; Rom 1.1
prison 27.1; Rom 7.6
prophet [2] 26.22; Rom 1.2
question 24.8; Rom 3.5
safe 27.44; Rom 15.31
sake 21.13; Rom 1.5
salvation 26.23; Rom 11.11
Spirit (1) (God's Spirit) 21.4; Rom 2.29
teach 21.21; Rom 2.21
thank 27.35; Rom 1.8
turn 26.18; Rom 3.12
understand [2] 13.27; Rom 7.1
welcome [3] 25.13; Rom 10.21
word (1) 23.15; Rom 3.13

was allowed to live by himself with a soldier guarding him.
17 After three days Paul called the
local **Jewish** leaders to a meeting. When
they had gathered, he said to them, "My
fellow-Israelites, even though I did
nothing against our people or the **cus-**
toms that we received from our ancestors, I was made a **prisoner** in Jerusalem
and handed over to the Romans. 18 After
questioning me, the Romans wanted to
release me, because they found that I
had done nothing for which I **deserved** to
die. 19 But when the **Jews** opposed this, I
was **forced** to appeal to the Emperor,
even though I had no **accusation** to make
against my own people. 20 That is why I
asked to see you and talk with you. As a
matter of fact, I am **bound** in chains like
this for the **sake** of him for whom the
people of Israel **hope**."
21 They said to him, "We have not received any **letters** from Judaea about
you, nor have any of our people come
from there with any news or anything
bad to say about you. 22 But we would like
to hear your **ideas**, because we know that
everywhere people speak against this
party to which you belong."
23 So they fixed a date with Paul, and
a large number of them came that day to
the place where Paul was staying. From
morning till night he explained to them
his **message** about the **Kingdom of God**,
and he tried to **convince** them about
Jesus by quoting from the **Law of Moses**
and the writings of the **prophets**. 24 Some
of them were **convinced** by his **words**, but
others would not **believe**. 25 So they left,
disagreeing among themselves, after
Paul had said this one thing: "How well
the **Holy Spirit** spoke through the **prophet**
Isaiah to your ancestors! 26 For he said,

'Go and say to this people:
You will listen and listen, but not
  understand;
  you will look and look, but not see,
27 because this people's **minds** are dull,
  and they have stopped up their ears
  and closed their eyes.
Otherwise, their eyes would see,
  their ears would hear,
  their **minds** would **understand**,
and they would **turn to me**, says God,
  and I would **heal** them.' "

28 And Paul concluded: "You are to
know, then, that God's **message of salva-**
tion has been sent to the **Gentiles**. They
will listen!"[q]
30 For two years Paul lived in a place
he rented for himself, and there he **wel-**
comed all who came to see him. 31 He
preached about the **Kingdom of God** and
taught about the Lord Jesus Christ,
speaking with all **boldness** and **freedom**.

[q] *Some manuscripts add verse 29:* After Paul said this, the Jews left, arguing violently among themselves.

28.19: Acts 25.11 **28.26–27:** Is 6.9–10 (LXX)

PAUL'S LETTER TO THE
ROMANS

INTRODUCTION

Paul's Letter to the Romans was written to prepare the way for a visit Paul planned to make to the church at Rome. His plan was to work among the Christians there for a while and then, with their support, to go on to Spain. He wrote to explain his understanding of the Christian faith and its practical implications for the lives of Christians. The book contains Paul's most complete statement of his message.

After greeting the people of the church at Rome and telling them of his prayers for them, Paul states the theme of the letter: "The gospel reveals how God puts people right with himself: it is through faith from beginning to end" (1.17).

Paul then develops this theme. All mankind, both Jews and Gentiles, needs to be put right with God, for all alike are under the power of sin. People are put right with God through faith in Jesus Christ. Next Paul describes the new life in union with Christ that results from this new relation with God. The believer has peace with God and is set free by God's Spirit from the power of sin and death. In chapters 5—8 Paul also discusses the purpose of the Law of God and the power of God's Spirit in the believer's life. Then the apostle wrestles with the question of how Jews and Gentiles fit into the plan of God for mankind. He concludes that the Jewish rejection of Jesus is part of God's plan for bringing all mankind within the reach of God's grace in Jesus Christ, and he believes that the Jews will not always reject Jesus. Finally Paul writes about how the Christian life should be lived, especially about the way of love in relations with others. He takes up such themes as service to God, the duty of Christians to the state and to one another, and questions of conscience. He ends the letter with personal messages and with words of praise to God.

Outline of Contents

---

act Acts 1.18; 5.18
anger Acts 12.20; 2.5
apostle [2] Acts 16.4; 11.13
approve Acts 22.20; 5.4
believe [2] Acts 28.24; 3.22
bless Acts 20.32; 8.17
boast Zeph 2.8; 2.17
choose Acts 26.18; 2.18
Christ Jn 1.41; 3.22
clear Acts 25.27; 3.5
complete [2] Acts 24.18; 8.37
confident Zeph 1.12; 2 Cor 3.4
conscience Acts 24.16; 2.15
corrupt Lk 18.6; 2 Cor 11.3
create [2] Acts 17.26; 5.4
Creator Acts 4.24; 1 Cor 8.6
dark Acts 26.18; 2.19
death (1) Acts 25.11; 3.25
death (2) (from death) Acts 26.23; 4.24
deceive Lk 21.8; 3.13
deserve [2] Acts 28.18; 5.16

1 From Paul, a **servant** of Christ Jesus
and an **apostle chosen** and called by
God to **preach** his **Good News**.
2 The **Good News** was **promised** long
ago by God through his **prophets**, as
written in the **Holy Scriptures**. 3 It is
about **his Son**, our Lord Jesus Christ: as
to his **humanity**, he was born a descendant of David; 4 as to his **divine holiness**,
he was shown with great **power** to be the
Son of God by being **raised from death**.
5 Through him God gave me the **privilege**
of being an **apostle** for the **sake** of **Christ**,
in order to lead people of all nations to
believe and **obey**. 6 This also includes you
who are in Rome, whom God has called
to belong to Jesus Christ.
7 And so I write to all of you in Rome
whom God **loves** and has called to be his
own people:
May God **our Father** and the Lord
Jesus Christ give you **grace** and **peace**.

1.13: Acts 19.21

Prayer of Thanksgiving

8 First, I **thank** my God through Jesus
Christ for all of you, because the whole
world is hearing about your **faith**. 9 God is
my **witness** that what I say is **true**—the
God whom I **serve with all my heart** by
preaching the **Good News** about **his Son**.
God knows that I **remember** you 10 every
time I **pray**. I ask that God in his **good**
will may at **last** make it possible for me
to visit you now. 11 For I want very much
to see you, in order to **share** a **spiritual**
blessing with you to make you **strong**.
12 What I mean is that both you and I will
be **helped** at the same time, you by my
faith and I by yours.
13 You must **remember**, my brothers,
that many times I have **planned** to visit
you, but something has always **kept me**
from doing so. I want to **win** converts
among you also, as I have among other
Gentiles. 14 For I have an **obligation** to all

desire Jn 8.44; 6.12
disobey Acts 26.19; 2.25
divine [2] Acts 3.13; Col 2.9
each other [3] Acts 26.31; 12.5
eager Acts 17.11; 8.19
eternal Acts 13.46; 2.7
evil [5] Acts 25.18; 2.
excuse Acts 19.40; 2.1
faith [4] Acts 26.11; 3.22
Father (2) (God) Acts 13.32; 6.4
filthy Zech 3.3; Gal 5.19
fool Jn 11.49; 2.20
Gentile [2] Acts 28.28; 2.9
give up Acts 27.15; 1 Cor 13.3
God's people Acts 26.10; 8.17
Good News [4] Acts 20.24; 2.16
gospel [2] Acts 10.42 16.19
grace Acts 20.24; 3.24
greed Lk 18.11; 1 Cor 5.10

peoples, to the civilized and to the
savage, to the educated and to the **ignorant.** 15 So then, I am **eager** to **preach** the
Good News to you also who live in Rome.

The Power of the Gospel

16 I have **complete confidence** in the
gospel; it is **God's power** to **save** all who
believe, first the **Jews** and also the **Gentiles.** 17 For the **gospel reveals** how God
puts people **right with himself**: it is
through **faith** from beginning to end. As
the **scripture** says, "The person who is
put **right with God** through **faith** shall
live."[a]

The Guilt of Mankind

18 **God's anger** is **revealed** from
heaven against all the sin and **evil** of the
people whose **evil ways prevent** the **truth**
from being known. 19 God **punishes** them,
because what can be known about God is
plain to them, for God himself made it
plain. 20 Ever since God **created** the
world, his invisible qualities, both his
eternal power and his **divine nature**,
have been **clearly** seen; they are perceived in the things that God has made.
So those people have no **excuse** at all!
21 They know God, but they do not give
him the **honour** that belongs to him, nor
do they **thank** him. Instead, their
thoughts have become **complete** nonsense, and their empty **minds** are filled
with **darkness.** 22 They say they are **wise**,
but they are **fools**; 23 instead of **worshipping** the **immortal** God, they **worship**
images made to look like **mortal** man or
birds or animals or reptiles.
24 And so God has given those people
over to do the **filthy** things their **hearts**
desire, and they do **shameful** things with
each other. 25 They exchange the **truth**
about God for a **lie**; they **worship** and
serve what God has **created** instead of
the **Creator** himself, who is to be **praised**
for ever! Amen.
26 Because they do this, God has given
them over to **shameful passions.** Even
the women **pervert** the **natural** use of
their **sex** by unnatural **acts.** 27 In the same
way the men **give up natural sexual
relations** with women and burn with
passion for **each other.** Men do **shameful**
things with **each other**, and as a **result**
they bring upon themselves the **punishment** they **deserve** for their **wrongdoing.**
28 Because those people **refuse** to
keep in **mind** the **true knowledge** about
God, he has given them over to **corrupted minds**, so that they do the things that
they should not do. 29 They are filled with
all kinds of **wickedness, evil, greed**, and
vice; they are full of **jealousy**, murder,
fighting, **deceit**, and malice. They gossip
30 and speak **evil** of **one another**; they are
hateful to God, insolent,[b] **proud**, and
boastful; they think of more ways to do
evil; they **disobey** their parents; 31 they
have no **conscience**; they do not keep
their **promises**, and they show no **kindness** or **pity** for others. 32 They know that
God's **law** says that people who live in
this way **deserve death.** Yet, not only do
they continue to do these very things, but
they even **approve** of others who do
them.

God's Judgement

2 Do you, my **friend, pass judgement**
on others? You have no **excuse** at
all, whoever you are. For when you **judge**
others and then do the same things
which they do, you **condemn** yourself.
2 We know that God is **right** when he
judges the people who do such things as
these. 3 But you, my **friend**, do those very
things for which you **pass judgement** on
others! Do you think you will **escape**
God's **judgement**? 4 Or perhaps you **despise** his great **kindness, tolerance**, and
patience. Surely you know that God is
kind, because he is trying to lead you to
repent. 5 But you have a **hard** and **stubborn heart**, and so you are making your
own **punishment** even greater on the **Day**
when **God's anger** and **righteous judgements** will be **revealed.** 6 For God will
reward every person according to what
he has done. 7 Some people keep on doing
good, and **seek glory, honour**, and **immortal life**; to them God will give **eternal
life.** 8 Other people are **selfish** and **reject**
what is **right**, in order to follow what is
wrong; on them God will pour out his
anger and **fury.** 9 There will be **suffering**
and **pain** for all those who do what is **evil**,
for the **Jews** first and also for the **Gentiles.** 10 But God will give **glory, honour**,
and **peace** to all who do what is good, to
the **Jews** first and also to the **Gentiles.**
11 For God **judges** everyone by the same
standard.
12 The **Gentiles** do not have the **Law**
of **Moses**; they sin and are lost **apart
from** the **Law.** The **Jews** have the **Law**;
they sin and are **judged** by the **Law.**
13 For it is not by hearing the **Law** that

[a] put right with God through faith shall live; *or* put right with God shall live through faith.
[b] are hateful to God, insolent; *or* hate God, and are insolent.

1.16: Mk 8.38 **1.17:** Hab 2.4 **1.21:** Eph 4.17–18 **1.23:** Deut 4.16–18 **2.1:** Mt 7.1; Lk 6.37
2.6: Ps 62.12; Prov 24.12 **2.11:** Deut 10.17

life (1) [2] Acts 27.10; 4.12
light (1) Acts 26.13; 13.12
obey [3] 1.5; 3.27
pain Lk 16.23; 8.22
pass (5) [2] Acts 13.28; 14.3
patient Acts 26.3; 3.25
peace 1.7; 3.17
physical [2] Jn 3.6; 1 Cor 6.16
praise 1.25; 4.20
preach [2] 1.1; 10.8
punish 1.19; 3.5
real [2] Acts 12.9; 11.6
reject Acts 13.46; 11.1
repent Acts 26.20; 2 Cor 12.21
reveal 1.17; 3.21
reward Lk 6.23; 1 Cor 3.8
right (1) [3] Acts 15.38; 3.4
right with God 1.17; 3.20
righteous Acts 22.14; 3.10
rob Acts 19.37; 1 Cor 1.17
scripture 1.2; 3.4
secret Acts 16.37; 11.25
seek Jn 8.50; 9.31
selfish Mt 23.25; 7.8
shame 1.24; 12.20
Spirit (1) (God's Spirit) Acts 28.25; 5.5
steal Jn 10.10; 13.9
stubborn Acts 19.9; 9.18
suffer Acts 26.23; 8.17
sure Acts 26.26; 4.21
teach Acts 28.31; 6.17
teacher Acts 17.18; 1 Cor 12.28
temple (2) (of other gods) Acts 19.24; 1 Cor 8.10
tolerate Nah 1.2; 2 Cor 11.1
true [2] 1.9; 3.4
truth 1.18; 3.7
value Lk 16.15; 3.1
wrong 1.27; 3.5

people are put right with God, but by
doing what the Law commands. 14 The
Gentiles do not have the Law; but whenever they do by instinct what the Law
commands, they are their own law, even
though they do not have the Law. 15 Their
conduct shows that what the Law commands is written in their hearts. Their
consciences also show that this is true,
since their thoughts sometimes accuse
them and sometimes defend them. 16 And
so, according to the Good News I preach,
this is how it will be on that Day when
God through Jesus Christ will judge the
secret thoughts of all.

The Jews and the Law

17 What about you? You call yourself
a Jew; you depend on the Law and boast
about God; 18 you know what God wants
you to do, and you have learnt from the
Law to choose what is right; 19 you are
sure that you are a guide for the blind, a
light for those who are in darkness, 20 an
instructor for the foolish, and a teacher
for the ignorant. You are certain that in
the Law you have the full content of
knowledge and of truth. 21 You teach
others—why don't you teach yourself?
You preach, "Do not steal"—but do you
yourself steal? 22 You say, "Do not commit adultery"—but do you commit adultery? You detest idols—but do you rob
temples? 23 You boast about having
God's law—but do you bring shame on
God by breaking his law? 24 The scripture says, "Because of you Jews, the Gentiles speak evil of God."

25 If you obey the Law, your circumcision is of value; but if you disobey the
Law, you might as well never have been
circumcised. 26 If the Gentile, who is not
circumcised, obeys the commands of the
Law, will God not regard him as though
he were circumcised? 27 And so you Jews
will be condemned by the Gentiles because you break the Law, even though
you have it written down and are circumcised; but they obey the Law, even
though they are not physically circumcised. 28 After all, who is a real Jew, truly
circumcised? It is not the man who is a
Jew on the outside, whose circumcision
is a physical thing. 29 Rather, the real Jew
is the person who is a Jew on the inside,
that is, whose heart has been circumcised, and this is the work of God's Spirit,
not of the written Law. Such a person receives his praise from God, not from
man.

3 Have the Jews then any advantage
over the Gentiles? Or is there any
value in being circumcised? 2 Much,
indeed, in every way! In the first place,
God trusted his message to the Jews.
3 But what if some of them were not faithful? Does this mean that God will not be
faithful? 4 Certainly not! God must be
true, even though every man is a liar. As
the scripture says,

"You must be shown to be right when
you speak;
you must win your case when you
are being tried."

5 But what if our doing wrong serves
to show up more clearly God's doing
right? Can we say that God does wrong
when he punishes us? (This would be the
natural question to ask.) 6 By no means!
If God is not just, how can he judge the
world?

7 But what if my untruth serves God's
glory by making his truth stand out more
clearly? Why should I still be condemned as a sinner? 8 Why not say, then,
"Let us do evil so that good may come"?
Some people, indeed, have insulted me
by accusing me of saying this very thing!
They will be condemned, as they should
be.

No One Is Righteous

9 Well then, are we Jews in any better
condition than the Gentiles? Not at all! [c]
I have already shown that Jews and Gentiles alike are all under the power of sin.
10 As the Scriptures say:

"There is no one who is righteous,
11 no one who is wise
or who worships God.
12 All have turned away from God;
they have all gone wrong;
no one does what is right, not even
one.
13 Their words are full of deadly deceit;
wicked lies roll off their tongues,
and dangerous threats, like snake's
poison, from their lips;
14 their speech is filled with bitter
curses.
15 They are quick to hurt and kill;
16 they leave ruin and destruction
wherever they go.
17 They have not known the path of
peace,
18 nor have they learnt reverence for
God."

accuse 2.15; 8.33
advantage Lk 20.4' 2 Cor 7.2
basis Acts 10.34; 4.
believe [3] 1.5; 4.3
bitter Acts 8.23; Eph 4.31
boast 2.17; 4.2
case (2) Acts 25.21; 1 Cor 6.6
Christ 1.5; 5.6
circumcise 2.25; 4.
clear [2] 1.20; 1 Cor 4.4
command 2.13; 4.1
condemn [2] 2.1; 5.
curse Jn 9.28; 9.3
danger Acts 27.9; 8.35
deadly Nah 3.4; 2 Cor 2.16
death (1) 1.32; 5.9
deceive 1.29; 7.11
destroy Acts 19.27; 6.6
evil 2.9; 7.19
excuse 2.1; Gal 5.13
faith [6] 1.8; 4.3
faithful [2] Acts 11.23; 15.8
forgive Acts 26.18; 4.7
free [2] Acts 28.31; 4.16
Gentile [5] 2.9; 9.24
gift Acts 28.10; 4.4
glory 2.7; 5.2
grace 1.7; 5.2
human 1.3; 5.12
hurt Acts 26.14; 14.
insult Acts 23.4; 15.
Jew [6] 2.9; 9.24
judge [2] 2.1; 5.16
justice Acts 17.31; Col 4.1
law [10] 2.12; 4.13
learn 2.18; 1 Cor 2.1
lie (2) [2] 1.25; 9.1
means Acts 17.31; 5.5
message Acts 28.23 10.8
natural 1.26; 6.12
obey 2.25; 4.13
offer Acts 24.17; 8.3
patient 2.4; 8.25
peace 2.10; 5.1
power 1.4; 4.20
presence Acts 10.3 8.11
prophet 1.2; 11.3
punish 2.5; 11.9
question Acts 28.18 1 Cor 10.25
reason Acts 26.21; 4.18
require Acts 17.9; 1 Cor 4.2
reveal 2.5; 7.13
reverence Acts 9.31 Eph 5.21
right (1) [3] 2.2; 7.12
right with God [8] 2.13; 4.2
righteous [4] 2.5; 4.3
ruin Acts 15.16; 11.1
sacrifice Acts 24.17 5.9
save 1.16; 5.9
scripture [2] 2.24; 4.
serve [2] 1.9; 7.6
sight Acts 8.21; 4.2
speech Acts 19.33; 16.18
threat Acts 9.1; Eph 6.9

[c] any better condition than the Gentiles? Not at all!; *or* any worse condition than the Gentiles? Not altogether.

2.24: Is 52.5 (LXX) **2.29:** Deut 30.6 **3.4:** Ps 51.4 (LXX) **3.10-12:** Ps 14.1-3 (LXX), 53.1-3 (LXX) **3.13:** Ps 5.9 (LXX), 140.3 **3.14:** Ps 10.7 (LXX) **3.15-17:** Is 59.7-8 **3.18:** Ps 36.1

true 2.15; 5.15
trust Acts 27.25; 1 Cor 1.9
truth 2.20; 6.17
try (2) Acts 26.6; Gal 4.14
turn Acts 28.27; 1 Cor 9.15
value 2.25; 1 Cor 2.14
wicked 1.29; 5.6
win 1.13; 1 Cor 9.19
wise 1.22; 11.25
witness 1.9; 2 Cor 1.23
word (1) Acts 28.24; 4.23
world [2] 1.8; 4.13
worship (1) (of God) 1.23; 9.4
wrong [3] 2.8; 4.7

19 Now we know that everything in the **Law** applies to those who live under the **Law**, in order to stop all **human excuses** and bring the whole **world** under God's **judgement**. 20 For no one is put **right** in God's **sight** by doing what the **Law requires**; what the **Law** does is to make man know that he has sinned.

How God Puts Us Right with Him

21 But now God's way of putting people **right with himself** has been **revealed**. It has nothing to do with **law**, even though the **Law of Moses** and the **prophets** gave their **witness** to it. 22 God puts people **right** through their **faith** in Jesus Christ. God does this to all who **believe** in **Christ**, because there is no difference at all: 23 everyone has sinned and is far away from God's **saving presence**. 24 But by the **free gift** of God's **grace** all are put **right with him** through Christ Jesus, who **sets them free**. 25-26 God **offered** him, so that by his **sacrificial death** he should become the **means** by which people's sins are **forgiven** through their **faith** in him. God did this in order to demonstrate that he is **righteous**. In the past he was **patient** and overlooked people's sins; but in the present time he deals with their sins, in order to demonstrate his **righteousness**. In this way God shows that he himself is **righteous** and that he puts **right** everyone who **believes** in Jesus.

27 What, then, can we **boast** about? Nothing! And what is the **reason** for this? Is it that we **obey** the **Law**? No, but that we **believe**. 28 For we conclude that a person is put **right with God** only through **faith**, and not by doing what the **Law commands**. 29 Or is God the God of the **Jews** only? Is he not the God of the **Gentiles** also? Of course he is. 30 God is one, and he will put the **Jews right with himself** on the **basis** of their **faith**, and will put the **Gentiles right** through their **faith**. 31 Does this mean that by this **faith** we do away with the **Law**? No, not at all; instead, we uphold the **Law**.

The Example of Abraham

4 What shall we say, then, of Abraham, the father of our **race**? What was his **experience**? 2 If he was put **right with God** by the things he did, he would have something to **boast** about—but not in God's **sight**. 3 The **scripture** says, "Abraham **believed** God, and because of his **faith** God **accepted** him as **righteous**." 4 A person who works is paid his **wages**, but they are not regarded as a **gift**; they are something that he has earned. 5 But the person who **depends** on his **faith**, not on his **deeds**, and who **believes** in the God who **declares** the **guilty** to be **innocent**, it is his **faith** that God takes into account in order to put him **right with himself**. 6 This is what David meant when he spoke of the **happiness** of the person whom God **accepts** as **righteous**, **apart from** anything that person does:

7 "**Happy** are those whose **wrongs** are
 forgiven,
 whose sins are pardoned!
8 **Happy** is the person whose sins the
 Lord will not keep account of!"

9 Does this **happiness** that David spoke of belong only to those who are **circumcised**? No indeed! It belongs also to those who are not **circumcised**. For we have quoted the **scripture**, "Abraham **believed** God, and because of his **faith** God **accepted** him as **righteous**." 10 When did this take place? Was it before or after Abraham was **circumcised**? It was before, not after. 11 He was **circumcised** later, and his circumcision was a **sign** to show that because of his **faith** God had **accepted** him as **righteous** before he had been **circumcised**. And so Abraham is the **spiritual** father of all who **believe** in God and are **accepted** as **righteous** by him, even though they are not **circumcised**. 12 He is also the father of those who are **circumcised**, that is, of those who, in addition to being **circumcised**, also live the same **life** of **faith** that our father Abraham lived before he was **circumcised**.

God's Promise Is Received through Faith

13 When God **promised** Abraham and his descendants that the **world** would belong to him, he did so, not because Abraham **obeyed** the **Law**, but because he **believed** and was **accepted** as **righteous** by God. 14 For if what God **promises** is to be given to those who **obey** the **Law**, then man's **faith** means nothing and God's **promise** is **worthless**. 15 The **Law** brings down **God's anger**; but where there is no law, there is no **disobeying** of the **law**.

16 And so the **promise** was **based on faith**, in order that the **promise** should be **guaranteed** as God's **free gift** to all of Abraham's descendants—not just to those who **obey** the **Law**, but also to those who **believe** as Abraham did. For

accept [9] Acts 22.18; 10.16
alone Acts 5.38; 8.23
anger 2.5; 5.9
apart 2.12; 7.8
basis 3.30; 9.11
being Acts 14.15; 6.6
believe [9] 3.22; 6.8
boast 3.27; 5.2
body Acts 13.36; 6.12
circumcise [9] 3.1; 1 Cor 7.18
command 3.28; 5.14

dead [2] Acts 28.6; 6.11
death (2) (from death) 1.4; 6.4
declare Acts 20.24; 8.16
deed (2) Acts 7.22; 15.18
depend 2.17; 9.16
disobey 2.25; 5.14
doubt Acts 1.3; 14.23
exist Acts 17.28; 11.36
experience Mic 2.4; 5.2
faith [12] 3.22; 5.1
forgive 3.25; 2 Cor 2.7
free 3.24; 5.15
gift [2] 3.24; 5.5
guarantee Ezek 37.26; 1 Cor 15.20
guilty Acts 24.20; 5.16
happy [4] Acts 24.10; 7.24
hope [2] Acts 28.20; 5.2
innocent Mt 28.14; 16.18
law [5] 3.19; 5.13
life (1) 2.7; 5.10
life (2) (to life) [2] Acts 24.21; 6.5
obey [3] 3.27; 5.19
power 3.9; 6.4
praise 2.29; 9.5
promise [8] 1.2; 9.4
race (1) Acts 17.26; 5.12
raise [2] 1.4; 6.4
reason 3.27; 13.5
right with God [3] 3.20; 5.1
righteous [9] 3.10; 5.7
scripture [4] 3.4; 8.36
sight [2] 3.20; 1 Cor 3.19
sign (1) Acts 7.8; Gal 2.9
spiritual [2] 1.11; 7.14
sure 2.19; 15.14
wage Mt 20.2; 6.23
weak Acts 20.35; 6.19
word (1) 3.13; 8.26
world 3.6; 5.12
worthless Acts 20.24; 1 Cor 3.20
wrong 3.5; 5.20

3.20: Ps 143.2; Gal 2.16 **3.22:** Gal 2.16 **3.30:** Deut 6.4; Gal 3.20 **4.3:** Gen 15.6; Gal 3.6 **4.7-8:** Ps 32.1-2 **4.11:** Gen 17.10 **4.13:** Gen 17.4-6, 22.17-18; Gal 3.29 **4.14:** Gal 3.18 **4.16:** Gal 3.7

Abraham is the spiritual father of us all; 17 as the scripture says, "I have made you father of many nations." So the promise is good in the sight of God, in whom Abraham believed—the God who brings the dead to life and whose command brings into being what did not exist. 18 Abraham believed and hoped, even when there was no reason for hoping, and so became "the father of many nations." Just as the scripture says, "Your descendants will be as many as the stars." 19 He was then almost one hundred years old; but his faith did not weaken when he thought of his body, which was already practically dead, or of the fact that Sarah could not have children. 20 His faith did not leave him, and he did not doubt God's promise; his faith filled him with power, and he gave praise to God. 21 He was absolutely sure that God would be able to do what he had promised. 22 That is why Abraham, through faith, "was accepted as righteous by God." 23 The words "he was accepted as righteous" were not written for him alone. 24 They were written also for us who are to be accepted as righteous, who believe in him who raised Jesus our Lord from death. 25 Because of our sins he was handed over to die, and he was raised to life in order to put us right with God.

Right with God

5 Now that we have been put right with God through faith, we have[d] peace with God through our Lord Jesus Christ. 2 He has brought us by faith into this experience of God's grace, in which we now live. And so we boast[e] of the hope we have of sharing God's glory! 3 We also boast[f] of our troubles, because we know that trouble produces endurance, 4 endurance brings God's approval, and his approval creates hope. 5 This hope does not disappoint us, for God has poured out his love into our hearts by means of the Holy Spirit, who is God's gift to us.

6 For when we were still helpless, Christ died for the wicked at the time that God chose. 7 It is a difficult thing for someone to die for a righteous person. It may even be that someone might dare to die for a good person. 8 But God has shown us how much he loves us—it was while we were still sinners that Christ died for us! 9 By his sacrificial death we are now put right with God; how much more, then, will we be saved by him from God's anger! 10 We were God's enemies, but he made us his friends through the death of his Son. Now that we are God's friends, how much more will we be saved by Christ's life! 11 But that is not all; we rejoice because of what God has done through our Lord Jesus Christ, who has now made us God's friends.

abundant Mal 3.10; 9.23
act 1.26; 14.15
anger 4.15; 9.22
approve 1.32; 7.23
boast [2] 4.2; 1 Cor 1.29
choose 2.18; 7.21
Christ [4] 3.22; 6.4
command 4.17; 10.5
condemn 3.7; 8.1
create 1.20; 8.19
dare Acts 7.32; 1 Cor 6.1
death (1) [7] 3.25; 6.3
deserve 1.27; 1 Cor 4.5
difficult Acts 27.7; 2 Cor 6.4
disappoint Zech 4.10; 9.33
disobey [2] 4.15; 10.21
endure Acts 13.18; 9.22
enemy Acts 13.10; 8.7
eternal 2.7; 6.22
experience 4.1; 1 Cor 10.13
faith [2] 4.3; 9.30
free [4] 4.16; 6.7
friend [3] 2.1; 9.20
gift [5] 4.4; 6.23
glory 3.7; 6.4
grace [6] 3.24; 6.1
guilty [2] 4.5; 8.33
heart 2.5; 6.17
helpless Mt 9.36

Adam and Christ

12 Sin came into the world through one man, and his sin brought death with it. As a result, death has spread to the whole human race because everyone has sinned. 13 There was sin in the world before the Law was given; but where there is no law, no account is kept of sins. 14 But from the time of Adam to the time of Moses death ruled over all mankind, even over those who did not sin in the same way that Adam did when he disobeyed God's command.

Adam was a figure of the one who was to come. 15 But the two are not the same, because God's free gift is not like Adam's sin. It is true that many people died because of the sin of that one man. But God's grace is much greater, and so is his free gift to so many people through the grace of the one man, Jesus Christ. 16 And there is a difference between God's gift and the sin of one man. After the one sin, came the judgement of "Guilty"; but after so many sins, comes the undeserved gift of "Not guilty!" 17 It is true that through the sin of one man death began to rule because of that one man. But how much greater is the result of what was done by the one man, Jesus Christ! All who receive God's abundant grace and are freely put right with him will rule in life through Christ.

18 So then, as the one sin condemned all mankind, in the same way the one righteous act sets all mankind free and gives them life. 19 And just as all people were made sinners as the result of the disobedience of one man, in the same way they will all be put right with God as the result of the obedience of the one man.

20 Law was introduced in order to increase wrongdoing; but where sin increased, God's grace increased much more. 21 So then, just as sin ruled by means of death, so also God's grace rules by means of righteousness, leading us to eternal life through Jesus Christ our Lord.

hope [3] 4.18; 8.20
human 3.19; 7.5
judge 3.6; 12.3
law [3] 4.13; 6.14
life (1) [4] 4.12; 6.4
love [2] 1.7; 8.28
mankind [3] Acts 17.26; 11.15
means [3] 3.25; 7.8
obey 4.13; 6.12
peace 3.17; 8.6
race (1) 4.1; 9.5
rejoice Jn 8.56; 15.10
result [4] 1.27; 6.16
right with God [4] 4.2; 6.16
righteous [3] 4.3; 6.13
sacrifice 3.25; 12.1
save [2] 3.23; 8.24
share 1.11; 6.4
Son of God 1.3; 8.3
Spirit (1) (God's Spirit) 2.29; 7.6
trouble [2] Acts 20.23; 8.35
true [2] 3.4; 7.13
who Acts 26.15; 9.20
wicked 3.13; 6.13
world [2] 4.13; 9.17
wrong 4.7; 12.17

[d] we have; *some manuscripts have* let us have. [e] we boast; *or* let us boast.
[f] We also boast; *or* Let us also boast.

4.17: Gen 17.5 **4.18:** Gen 15.5 **4.19:** Gen 17.17 **4.25:** Is 53.4–5 **5.12:** Gen 3.6

ashamed Lk 16.3; 1 Cor 4.14
baptize [3] Acts 22.16; 1 Cor 1.13
being [2] 4.17; 7.22
believe 4.3; 9.33
body 4.19; 7.4
Christ [4] 5.6; 7.4
cross (1) Acts 13.29; 1 Cor 1.13
dead 4.17; 7.8
death (1) [6] 5.9; 7.5
death (2) (from death) [3] 4.24; 7.4
death (3) (to death) Acts 22.20; 8.13
dedicate Acts 22.3; 12.1
desire 1.24; 7.5
destroy 3.16; 9.22
eternal [2] 5.21; 16.26
Father (2) (God) 1.7; 8.15
fellowship [2] Acts 2.42; 16.8
free [5] 5.15; 7.2
gift 5.5; 8.23
glory 5.2; 8.17
grace [3] 5.2; 11.5
heart 5.5; 8.27
holy 1.2; 7.12
impure Is 1.25; Phil 1.10
law [2] 5.13; 7.1
life (1) [5] 5.10; 7.9
life (2) (to life) [2] 4.17; 8.34
master [2] Acts 4.24; 14.4
mortal 1.23; 7.14
natural [2] 3.5; 11.21
new Acts 17.19; 7.6
obey [5] 5.19; 8.7
power [4] 4.20; 8.15
purpose [4] Acts 26.12; 8.20
raise [3] 4.24; 7.4
result [4] 5.12; 8.6
right with God 5.1; 8.10
righteous [4] 5.7; 8.4
self [3] Lk 9.23; Eph 3.16
share 5.2; 8.17
slave [9] Acts 16.16; 7.14
teach 2.21; 12.7
thank 1.8; 7.25
truth 3.7; 9.1
union [3] 8.1
wage 4.4; Jas 5.4
weak 4.19; 8.3
wicked [2] 5.6; 11.26

Dead to Sin but Alive in Union with Christ

6 What shall we say, then? Should we continue to live in sin so that God's **grace** will increase? [2] Certainly not! We have died to sin—how then can we go on living in it? [3] For surely you know that when we were **baptized** into **union with** Christ Jesus, we were **baptized** into **union with** his **death**. [4] By our **baptism**, then, we were buried with him and **shared** his **death**, in order that, just as **Christ** was **raised from death** by the **glorious power** of the **Father**, so also we might live a **new life**.

5 For since we have become one with him in dying as he did, in the same way we shall be one with him by being **raised to life** as he was. [6] And we know that our old **being** has been put **to death** with **Christ** on his **cross**, in order that the **power** of the sinful **self** might be **destroyed**, so that we should no longer be the **slaves** of sin. [7] For when a person dies, he is **set free** from the **power** of sin. [8] Since we have died with **Christ**, we **believe** that we will also live with him. [9] For we know that **Christ** has been **raised from death** and will never die again—**death** will no longer rule over him. [10] And so, because he died, sin has no **power** over him; and now he lives his **life** in **fellowship** with God. [11] In the same way you are to think of yourselves as **dead**, so far as sin is concerned, but living in **fellowship** with God through Christ Jesus.

12 Sin must no longer rule in your **mortal bodies**, so that you **obey** the **desires** of your **natural self**. [13] Nor must you surrender any part of yourselves to sin to be used for **wicked purposes**. Instead, give yourselves to God, as those who have been brought **from death to life**, and surrender your whole **being** to him to be used for **righteous purposes**. [14] Sin must not be your **master**; for you do not live under **law** but under God's **grace**.

Slaves of Righteousness

15 What, then? Shall we sin, because we are not under **law** but under God's **grace**? By no means! [16] Surely you know that when you surrender yourselves as **slaves** to **obey** someone, you are in fact the **slaves** of the **master** you **obey**—either of sin, which **results** in **death**, or of **obedience**, which **results** in being put **right with God**. [17] But **thanks** be to God! For though at one time you were **slaves** to sin, you have **obeyed with all your heart** the **truths** found in the **teaching** you received. [18] You were **set free** from sin and became the **slaves of righteousness**. [19] (I use everyday language because of the **weakness** of your **natural selves**.) At one time you surrendered yourselves entirely as **slaves** to **impurity** and **wickedness** for wicked **purposes**. In the same way you must now surrender yourselves entirely as **slaves of righteousness** for **holy purposes**.

20 When you were the **slaves** of sin, you were **free** from **righteousness**. [21] What did you gain from doing the things that you are now **ashamed** of? The **result** of those things is **death**! [22] But now you have been **set free** from sin and are the **slaves** of God. Your gain is a **life** fully **dedicated** to him, and the **result** is **eternal life**. [23] For sin pays its **wage**—**death**; but God's **free gift** is **eternal life** in **union with** Christ Jesus our Lord.

An Illustration from Marriage

7 Certainly you will **understand** what I am about to say, my brothers, because all of you know about **law**. The **law** rules over people only as long as they live. [2] A married woman, for **example**, is **bound** by the **law** to her husband as long as he lives; but if he dies, then she is **free** from the **law** that **bound** her to him. [3] So then, if she lives with another man while her husband is **alive**, she will be called an **adulteress**; but if her husband dies, she is legally a **free** woman and does not **commit adultery** if she marries another man. [4] That is how it is with you, my brothers. As far as the **Law** is concerned, you also have died because you are part of the **body** of **Christ**; and now you belong to him who was **raised from death** in order that we might be useful in the **service** of God. [5] For when we lived according to our **human nature**, the sinful **desires** stirred up by the **Law** were at work in our **bodies**, and all we did ended in **death**. [6] Now, however, we are **free** from the **Law**, because we died to that which once held us **prisoners**. No longer do we **serve** in the old way of a written **law**, but in the **new** way of the **Spirit**.

Law and Sin

7 Shall we say, then, that the **Law** itself is sinful? Of course not! But it was the **Law** that made me know what sin is. If the **Law** had not said, "Do not **desire** what belongs to someone else," I would not have known such a **desire**. [8] But **by means** of that **commandment** sin found its chance to stir up all kinds of **selfish desires** in me. **Apart from law**, sin is a

adultery [2] 2.22; 13.9
agree Acts 28.25; 1 Cor 1.10
alive [2] Acts 25.19; 1 Cor 15.6
apart [2] 4.6; 8.29
approve 5.4; 14.18
being 6.6; 8.23
bind [2] Acts 28.20; Eph 4.3
body [5] 6.12; 8.10
choose 5.6; 8.29
Christ 6.4; 8.9
commandment [6] Acts 13.47; 13.9
commit 2.22; 13.9
dead 6.11; 11.15
death (1) [5] 6.3; 8.2
death (2) (from death) 6.4; 8.11
deceive 3.13; 16.18
delight Zeph 3.17
desire [5] 6.12; 13.9
evil [2] 3.8; 12.9
example Jn 13.15; 15.5
free [3] 6.7; 8.2
happy 4.6; 12.15
hate 1.30; 9.13
holy [2] 6.19; 1 Cor 3.17
human [3] 5.12; 8.3
law [23] 6.14; 8.2
life (1) [2] 6.4; 8.2
means [3] 5.5; 10.19
mind (1) [2] 1.21; 8.5
mortal 6.12; 8.11
nature [4] 1.20; 8.3
new 6.4; 1 Cor 4.17
prison [2] Acts 28.17; 11.32
raise 6.4; 8.11
rescue Acts 26.17; Col 1.13
reveal 3.21; 8.18
right (1) [2] 3.4; 9.9
selfish 2.8; 1 Cor 13.5
serve [3] 3.5; 9.11
service Acts 15.26; 12.1
slave 6.6; 8.15
Spirit (1) (God's Spirit) 5.5; 8.2
spiritual 4.11; 11.12
terrible Acts 9.13; 1 Cor 5.1
thank 6.17; 14.6
true 5.15; 9.4

6.4: Col 2.12 **7.7:** Ex 20.17; Deut 5.21

understand [2] Acts 28.26; 10.19

dead thing. 9 I myself was once **alive apart from law**; but when the **commandment** came, sin sprang to **life**, 10 and I died. And the **commandment** which was meant to bring **life**, in my case brought **death**. 11 Sin found its chance, and **by means of** the **commandment** it **deceived** me and killed me.

12 So then, the **Law** itself is **holy**, and the **commandment** is **holy**, **right**, and good. 13 But does this mean that what is good caused my **death**? By no means! It was sin that did it; by using what is good, sin brought **death** to me, in order that its **true nature** as sin might be **revealed**. And so, **by means of** the **commandment** sin is shown to be even more **terribly** sinful.

The Conflict in Man

14 We know that the **Law** is **spiritual**; but I am a **mortal** man, sold as a **slave** to sin. 15 I do not **understand** what I do; for I don't do what I would like to do, but instead I do what I **hate**. 16 Since what I do is what I don't want to do, this shows that I **agree** that the **Law** is **right**. 17 So I am not really the one who does this thing; rather it is the sin that lives in me. 18 I know that good does not live in me—that is, in my **human nature**. For even though the **desire** to do good is in me, I am not able to do it. 19 I don't do the good I want to do; instead, I do the **evil** that I do not want to do. 20 If I do what I don't want to do, this means that I am no longer the one who does it; instead, it is the sin that lives in me.

21 So I find that this **law** is at work: when I want to do what is good, what is **evil** is the only **choice** I have. 22 My inner **being delights** in the **law** of God. 23 But I see a different **law** at work in my **body**—a **law** that fights against the law which my **mind approves** of. It makes me a **prisoner** to the **law** of sin which is at work in my **body**. 24 What an **unhappy** man I am! Who will **rescue** me from this **body** that is taking me to **death**? 25 **Thanks** be to God, who does this through our Lord Jesus Christ!

This, then, is my condition: on my own I can **serve** God's **law** only with my **mind**, while my **human nature serves** the **law** of sin.

Life in the Spirit

above Jn 8.23; Phil 2.9
accuse 3.8; 2 Cor 13.1
action Acts 5.17; 14.23

8 There is no **condemnation** now for those who live in **union with** Christ Jesus. 2 For the **law** of the **Spirit**, which brings us **life** in **union with** Christ Jesus, has **set me**[g] free from the **law** of sin and **death**. 3 What the **Law** could not do, because **human nature** was **weak**, God did. He **condemned** sin in **human nature** by sending his own **Son**, who came with a **nature** like man's sinful nature, to do away with sin. 4 God did this so that the **righteous demands** of the **Law** might be fully **satisfied** in us who live according to the **Spirit**, and not according to **human** nature. 5 Those who live as their **human nature** tells them to, have their **minds controlled** by what **human nature** wants. Those who live as the **Spirit** tells them to, have their **minds controlled** by what the **Spirit** wants. 6 To be **controlled** by **human nature results** in **death**; to be **controlled** by the **Spirit results** in **life** and **peace**. 7 And so a person becomes an **enemy** of God when he is **controlled** by his **human nature**; for he does not obey God's **law**, and in fact he cannot **obey** it. 8 Those who **obey** their **human nature** cannot **please** God.

9 But you do not live as your **human nature** tells you to; instead, you live as the **Spirit** tells you to—if, in fact, **God's Spirit** lives in you. Whoever does not have the **Spirit** of **Christ** does not belong to him. 10 But if **Christ** lives in you, the **Spirit** is **life** for you[h] because you have been put **right with God**, even though your **bodies** are going to die because of sin. 11 If the **Spirit of God**, who **raised** Jesus **from death**, lives in you, then he who **raised Christ from death** will also give **life** to your **mortal bodies** by the **presence** of his **Spirit** in you.

12 So then, my brothers, we have an **obligation**, but it is not to live as our **human nature** wants us to. 13 For if you live according to your **human nature**, you are going to die; but if by the **Spirit** you put **to death** your sinful **actions**, you will live. 14 Those who are led by **God's Spirit** are **God's sons**. 15 For the **Spirit** that God has given you does not make you **slaves** and cause you to be **afraid**; instead, the **Spirit** makes you **God's children**, and by the **Spirit's power** we cry out to God, "Father! my Father!" 16 **God's Spirit** joins himself to our **spirits** to **declare** that we are **God's children**. 17 Since we are **his** children, we will **possess** the **blessings** he keeps for **his people**, and we will also **possess** with **Christ** what God has kept for him; for if we **share Christ's suffering**, we will also **share** his **glory**.

The Future Glory

18 I **consider** that what we **suffer** at this present time cannot be **compared** at

afraid Acts 27.17; 11.20
alone 4.23; 16.27
angel Acts 27.23; 1 Cor 4.9
apart [2] 7.8; 2 Cor 1.21
being 7.22; 9.5
bless 1.11; 10.12
body [2] 7.4; 12.4
certain (1) 2.20; 14.14
child of God [7] Acts 17.28; 9.4
choose [2] 7.21; 9.11
Christ [6] 7.4; 9.1
compare Lk 13.18; 2 Cor 10.12
complete 1.16; 11.12
condemn [4] 5.18; 14.23
consider Acts 26.2; 12.17
control [5] Acts 5.3; 1 Cor 7.37
create [6] 5.4; 11.36
danger [2] 3.13; 1 Cor 15.30
death (1) [5] 7.5; 1 Cor 1.17
death (2) (from death) [2] 7.4; 10.7
death (3) (to death) 6.6; 2 Cor 13.4
declare [2] 4.5; 1 Cor 15.31
demand Lk 7.29; 2 Cor 12.14
eager 1.15; 12.10
enemy 5.10; 11.15
Father (2) (God) [2] 6.4; 15.6
free [5] 7.2; 15.26
gift 6.23; 12.3
glory [4] 6.4; 9.4
God's people [3] 1.7; 9.4
groan [4] Acts 7.34; 2 Cor 5.4
guilty 5.16; 14.22
heart 6.17; 9.2
heaven 1.18; 10.6
help 1.12; 10.13
hope [6] 5.2; 12.12
human [11] 7.5; 9.5
hunger Acts 10.10; 12.20
law [5] 7.1; 9.4
life (1) [5] 7.9; 11.15
life (2) (to life) 6.5; 14.9
long (2) Mal 3.1; Heb 11.16
love [5] 5.5; 9.13
mind (1) [2] 7.23; 11.8
mortal 7.14; 1 Cor 15.42
nature [12] 7.5; 11.24
obey [2] 6.12; 10.5
obligation 1.14; 13.8
offer 3.25; 11.16
pain 2.9; 9.2
patient 3.25; 9.22
peace 5.1; 12.18
persecute Acts 26.11; 12.14
plead [3] Lk 18.3; 11.2
please Acts 21.39; 12.1
poor Acts 10.2; 11.12
possess [2] Acts 2.45; 1 Cor 6.9
poverty *see* **poor**
power [2] 6.4; 9.17
pray 1.10; 10.1
presence 3.23; 1 Cor 1.29
purpose [2] 6.13; 9.11
raise [3] 7.4; 10.9

[g] me; *some manuscripts have* you; *others have* us.
[h] the Spirit is life for you; *or* your spirit is alive.

7.11: Gen 3.13 **7.15:** Gal 5.17 **8.11:** 1 Cor 3.16 **8.15:** Mk 14.36; Gal 4.6 **8.15–17:** Gal 4.5–7

result [2] 6.16; 9.8
reveal [2] 7.13; 9.4
right (2) Acts 7.55; Eph 1.20
right with God [2] 6.16; 9.30
righteous 6.13; 14.17
sake 1.5; 9.3
satisfy Mt 10.25; 13.14
save 5.9; 9.27
scripture 4.3; 9.13
separate [3] Acts 15.39; 9.3
share [4] 6.4; 11.17
sheep Acts 8.32; 1 Cor 9.7
slaughter Acts 8.32; Jas 5.5
slave [2] 7.14; 1 Cor 6.12
son *see* **child of God**
Son of God [5] 5.10; 1 Cor 1.9
Spirit (1) (God's Spirit) [22] 7.6; 9.1
spirit (2) Acts 23.8; 1 Cor 2.11
suffer [2] 2.9; 1 Cor 12.26
trouble 5.3; 11.10
union [2] 6.3; 12.5
victory Zech 12.7; 1 Cor 15.54
weak [2] 6.19; 14.1
will (1) [3] 1.10; 9.19
word (1) 4.23; 9.9
world above Eph 1.3
world of the dead (world below) Acts 2.27; 10.7

all with the **glory** that is going to be **re-**
vealed to us. 19 All of **creation** waits with
eager longing for God to **reveal** his **sons.**
20 For **creation** was **condemned** to lose its
purpose, not of its own **will**, but because
God **willed** it to be so. Yet there was the
hope 21 that **creation** itself would one day
be **set free** from its **slavery** to decay and
would **share** the **glorious freedom** of the
children of God. 22 For we know that up
to the present time all of **creation groans**
with **pain**, like the pain of childbirth.
23 But it is not just **creation alone** which
groans; we who have the **Spirit** as the
first of God's **gifts** also **groan** within ourselves, as we wait for God to make us his
sons and[i] **set our whole being free.** 24 For
it was by **hope** that we were **saved**; but if
we see what we **hope** for, then it is not
really **hope**. For who **hopes** for something he sees? 25 But if we **hope** for what
we do not see, we wait for it with
patience.

26 In the same way the **Spirit** also
comes to **help** us, **weak** as we are. For we
do not know how we ought to **pray**; the
Spirit himself **pleads** with God for us in
groans that **words** cannot express. 27 And
God, who sees into our **hearts**, knows
what the thought of the **Spirit** is; because
the **Spirit pleads** with God on behalf of
his people and in accordance with his
will.

28 We know that in all things God
works for good with those who **love him,**[j]
those whom he has called according to
his **purpose.** 29 Those whom God had already **chosen** he also set **apart** to become
like **his Son**, so that the **Son** would be the
first among many brothers. 30 And so
those whom God set **apart**, he called; and
those he called, he put **right with himself**,
and he **shared** his **glory** with them.

God's Love in Christ Jesus

31 In view of all this, what can we
say? If God is for us, who can be against
us? 32 Certainly not God, who did not
even keep back his own **Son**, but **offered**
him for us all! He gave us **his Son**—will
he not also **freely** give us all things?
33 Who will **accuse** God's **chosen people**?
God himself **declares** them not **guilty**!
34 Who, then, will **condemn** them? Not
Christ Jesus, who died, or rather, who
was **raised to life** and is at the **right-hand**
side of God, **pleading** with him for us!
35 Who, then, can **separate** us from the
love of Christ? Can **trouble** do it, or hardship or **persecution** or **hunger** or **poverty**
or **danger** or **death**? 36 As the **scripture**
says,

"For your **sake** we are in **danger** of
death at all times;
we are treated like **sheep** that are
going to be **slaughtered**."

37 No, in all these things we have **com-**
plete victory through him who **loved** us!
38 For I am **certain** that nothing can
separate us from his **love**: neither **death**
nor **life**, neither **angels** nor other
heavenly rulers or **powers**, neither the
present nor the future, 39 neither the
world above nor the **world below**—there
is nothing in all **creation** that will ever be
able to **separate** us from the **love** of God
which is ours through Christ Jesus our
Lord.

God and His People

9 I am speaking the **truth**; I belong to
Christ and I do not **lie**. My **con-**
science, ruled by the **Holy Spirit**, also **as-**
sures me that I am not **lying** 2 when I say
how great is my **sorrow**, how endless the
pain in my **heart** 3 for my people, my own
flesh and blood! For their **sake** I could
wish that I myself were under God's
curse and **separated** from **Christ.** 4 They
are **God's people**; he made them his **sons**
and **revealed** his **glory** to them; he made
his **covenants**[k] with them and gave them
the **Law**; they have the **true worship**;
they have received God's **promises**;
5 they are descended from the famous
Hebrew ancestors; and **Christ**, as a
human being, belongs to their **race**. May
God, who rules over all, be **praised** for
ever![l] Amen.

6 I am not saying that the **promise** of
God has **failed**; for not all the people of
Israel are the **people of God.** 7 Nor are all
Abraham's descendants the **children of**
God. God said to Abraham, "It is through
Isaac that you will have the descendants
I **promised** you." 8 This means that the
children born in the usual way[m] are not
the **children of God**; instead, the children
born as a **result** of God's **promise** are re-
garded as the **true** descendants. 9 For
God's **promise** was made in these **words**:
"At the **right** time[n] I will come back, and
Sarah will have a son."

10 And this is not all. For Rebecca's

abundant 5.17; Eph 2.4
Almighty Lk 22.69; 2 Cor 6.18
anger [2] 5.9; 10.19
assure Acts 2.26; 10.2
bad Acts 28.21; 14.16
basis 4.16; 10.2
being 8.23; 1 Cor 15.39
believe 6.8; 10.4
Beloved *see* **love**
blood Acts 21.25; 1 Cor 10.16
child of God [4] 8.14; 2 Cor 6.18
choose [2] 8.29; 11.2
Christ [3] 8.9; 10.4
conscience 2.15; 13.5
covenant Acts 7.8; 11.27
curse 3.14; 12.14
depend [2] 4.5; 2 Cor 7.16
destroy 6.6; 14.20
disappoint 5.5; 10.11
doom Zech 11.17
endure 5.4; 1 Cor 4.12
fail Lk 22.32; 14.4
faith [2] 5.1; 10.6
fault Mt 18.15; 1 Cor 1.8
flesh Jn 6.51; 1 Cor 15.39
friend 5.10; 11.15
Gentile [2] 3.1; 10.12
glory [3] 8.17; 11.36
God's people [5] 8.17; 10.19
hate 7.15; 12.9
heart 8.27; 10.1
Hebrew Acts 26.14; 2 Cor 11.22
human 8.3; 1 Cor 1.17
Jew 3.1; 10.12
law [2] 8.2; 10.4
lie (2) [2] 3.4; 1 Cor 15.15

[i] *Some manuscripts do not have* make us his sons and.
[j] in all things God works for good with those who love him; *some manuscripts have* all things work for good for those who love God. [k] covenants; *some manuscripts have* covenant.
[l] May God, who rules over all, be praised for ever!; *or* And may he, who is God ruling over all, be praised for ever!
[m] CHILDREN BORN IN THE USUAL WAY: *This refers to the descendants Abraham had through Ishmael, his son by Hagar (see Gal 4.22–23).* [n] At the right time; *or* At this time next year.

8.20: Gen 3.17–19 **8.23:** 2 Cor 5.2–4 **8.36:** Ps 44.22 **9.4:** Ex 4.22 **9.7:** Gen 21.12 **9.9:** Gen 18.10

love [3] 8.28; 12.9
mercy [4] Lk 10.12; 11.30
pain 8.22; 2 Cor 12.7
patient 8.25; 12.12
pity 1.31; 1 Cor 15.19
power [2] 8.15; 13.4
praise 4.20; 13.3
promise [5] 4.13; 15.8
purpose 8.20; 1 Cor 1.10
race (1) 5.12; 11.14
resist Acts 7.51; Eph 6.13
result [2] 8.6; 1 Cor 9.1
reveal [2] 8.18; 16.25
right (1) 7.12; 14.21
right (3) Jn 10.18; 1 Cor 9.4
right with God [3] 8.10; 10.3
sake 8.36; 11.28
save 8.24; 10.1
scripture [3] 8.36; 10.6
seek 2.7; Heb 11.6
separate 8.35; 2 Cor 6.17
serve 7.6; 12.7
settle (2) Acts 19.39; 1 Cor 6.1
son *see* **child of God**
sorrow Lk 23.48; Phil 2.27
special Zech 2.12; 1 Cor 7.7
Spirit (1) (God's Spirit) 8.2; 14.17
stubborn 2.5; 11.25
stumble [2] Jn 11.9; 11.11
true [3] 7.13; 10.2
truth 6.17; 11.25
unjust Dan 9.26
who 5.14; 14.4
will (1) 8.20; 12.2
wish [6] Acts 15.29; 10.1
word (1) 8.26; 10.18
world [2] 5.12; 10.18
worship (1) (of God) 3.11; 12.1

two sons had the same father, our ancestor Isaac. 11–12 But in order that the **choice** of one son might be completely the **result** of God's own **purpose**, God said to her, "The elder will **serve** the younger." He said this before they were born, before they had done anything either good or **bad**; so God's **choice** was **based on** his call, and not on anything they had done. 13 As the **scripture** says, "I **loved** Jacob, but I **hated** Esau."

14 Shall we say, then, that God is **unjust**? Not at all. 15 For he said to Moses, "I will have **mercy** on anyone I **wish**; I will take **pity** on anyone I **wish**." 16 So then, everything **depends**, not on what man wants or does, but only on God's **mercy**. 17 For the **scripture** says to the king of Egypt, "I made you king in order to use you to show my **power** and to spread my fame over the whole **world**." 18 So then, God has **mercy** on anyone he **wishes**, and he makes **stubborn** anyone he **wishes**.

God's Anger and Mercy

19 But one of you will say to me, "If this is so, how can God find **fault** with anyone? Who can **resist God's will**?" 20 But **who are you**, my **friend**, to answer God back? A clay pot does not ask the man who made it, "Why did you make me like this?" 21 After all, the man who makes the pots has the **right** to use the clay as he **wishes**, and to make two pots from the same lump of clay, one for **special** occasions and the other for ordinary use.

22 And the same is **true** of what God has done. He wanted to show his **anger** and to make his **power** known. But he was very **patient** in **enduring** those who were the objects of his **anger**, who were **doomed** to **destruction**. 23 And he also wanted to **reveal** his **abundant glory**, which was poured out on us who are the objects of his **mercy**, those of us whom he has prepared to receive his **glory**. 24 For we are the people he called, not only from among the **Jews** but also from among the **Gentiles**. 25 This is what he says in the book of Hosea:

"The people who were not mine
I will call '**My People**.'
The nation that I did not **love**
I will call '**My Beloved**.'
26 And in the very place where they were
told, 'You are not **my people**,'
there they will be called the **sons** of
the living God."

27 And Isaiah exclaims about Israel: "Even if the people of Israel are as many as the grains of sand by the sea, yet only a few of them will be **saved**; 28 for the Lord will quickly **settle** his full account with the **world**." 29 It is as Isaiah had said before, "If the Lord **Almighty** had not left us some descendants, we would have become like Sodom, we would have been like Gomorrah."

Paul's Prayer for Israel

30 So we say that the **Gentiles**, who were not trying to put themselves **right with God**, were put **right with him** through **faith**; 31 while **God's people**, who were **seeking** a **law** that would put them **right with God**, did not find it. 32 And why not? Because they did not **depend** on **faith** but on what they did. And so they stumbled over the "**stumbling stone**" 33 that the **scripture** speaks of:

"Look, I place in Zion a stone
that will make people **stumble**,
a rock that will make them fall.
But whoever **believes** in him will not
be **disappointed**."

10 My brothers, how I **wish with all** my **heart** that my own people might be **saved**! How I **pray** to God for them! 2 I can **assure** you that they are deeply **devoted** to God; but their **devotion** is not **based on true knowledge**. 3 They have not known the way in which God puts people **right with himself**, and instead, they have tried to set up their own way; and so they did not **submit** themselves to God's way of putting people **right**. 4 For **Christ** has brought the **Law** to an end, so that everyone who **believes** is put **right with God**.

Salvation Is for All

5 Moses wrote this about being put **right with God** by **obeying** the **Law**: "Whoever **obeys** the **commands** of the **Law** will live." 6 But what the **scripture** says about being put **right with God** through **faith** is this: "You are not to ask yourself, Who will go up into **heaven**?" (that is, to bring **Christ** down). 7 "Nor are you to ask, Who will go down into the **world below**?" (that is, to bring **Christ** up **from death**). 8 What it says is this: "God's **message** is near you, on your lips and in your **heart**"—that is, the **message of faith** that we **preach**. 9 If you **confess** that Jesus is Lord and **believe** that God **raised** him **from death**, you will be **saved**. 10 For it is by our **faith** that we are put **right with** God; it is by our **confession** that we are

accept 4.3; 11.15
anger 9.22; 12.19
assure 9.1; 2 Cor 1.12
basis 9.11; 11.6
believe [6] 9.33; 11.20
bless 8.17; 11.12
bold Acts 28.31; 15.15
Christ [4] 9.1; 12.5
command 5.14; 13.9
confess [2] Mk 1.5; 14.11
death (2) (from death) [2] 8.11; 1 Cor 6.14
devote [2] Acts 21.20; 12.11
disappoint 9.33; 2 Cor 7.14
disobey 5.14; 11.30
faith [4] 9.30; 12.3
fool 2.20; 1 Cor 1.20
Gentile 9.24; 11.11
God's people [2] 9.4; 11.1
Good News [2] 2.16; 11.28
heart [2] 9.2; 11.8
heaven 8.38; 1 Cor 8.5
help [2] 8.26; 14.19
jealous 1.29; 11.11
Jew 9.24; 11.11
knowledge 2.20; 11.33
law [3] 9.4; 13.8
means 7.8; 15.13
message [9] 3.2; 12.6
obey [2] 8.7; 13.1
pray 8.26; 12.12
preach [2] 2.16; 15.16
proclaim [2] Acts 21.9; 15.19
raise 8.11; 15.28
rebel Jn 19.12; 2 Thes 2.3
rich Acts 6.8; 11.12
right with God [6] 9.30; 1 Cor 1.30
save [4] 9.27; 11.14
scripture [5] 9.13; 11.2

9.12: Gen 25.23 **9.13:** Mal 1.2–3 **9.15:** Ex 33.19 **9.17:** Ex 9.16 (LXX) **9.20:** Is 29.16, 45.9
9.25: Hos 2.23 **9.26:** Hos 1.10 **9.27–28:** Is 10.22–23 (LXX) **9.29:** Is 1.9 (LXX) **9.33:** Is 28.16 (LXX)
10.5: Lev 18.5 **10.6–8:** Deut 30.12–14

saved. 11 The scripture says, "Whoever believes in him will not be disappointed." 12 This includes everyone, because there is no difference between Jews and Gentiles; God is the same Lord of all and richly blesses all who call to him. 13 As the scripture says, "Everyone who calls out to the Lord for help will be saved."

14 But how can they call to him for help if they have not believed? And how can they believe if they have not heard the message? And how can they hear if the message is not proclaimed? 15 And how can the message be proclaimed if the messengers are not sent out? As the scripture says, "How wonderful is the coming of messengers who bring good news!" 16 But not all have accepted the Good News. Isaiah himself said, "Lord, who believed our message?" 17 So then, faith comes from hearing the message, and the message comes through preaching Christ.

18 But I ask: Is it true that they did not hear the message? Of course they did—for as the scripture says:

"The sound of their voice went out to
all the world;
their words reached the ends of the
earth."

19 Again I ask: Did the people of Israel not understand? Moses himself is the first one to answer:

"I will use a so-called nation
to make my people jealous;
and by means of a nation of fools
I will make my people angry."

20 And Isaiah is even bolder when he says,

"I was found by those who were not
looking for me;
I appeared to those who were not
asking for me."

21 But concerning Israel he says, "All day long I held out my hands to welcome a disobedient and rebellious people."

God's Mercy on Israel

11 I ask, then: Did God reject his own people? Certainly not! I myself am an Israelite, a descendant of Abraham, a member of the tribe of Benjamin. 2 God has not rejected his people, whom he chose from the beginning. You know what the scripture says in the passage where Elijah pleads with God against Israel: 3 "Lord, they have killed your prophets and torn down your altars; I am the only one left, and they are trying to kill me." 4 What answer did God give him? "I have kept for myself seven thousand men who have not worshipped the false god Baal." 5 It is the same way now: there is a small number left of those whom God has chosen because of his grace. 6 His choice is based on his grace, not on what they have done. For if God's choice were based on what people do, then his grace would not be real grace.

7 What then? The people of Israel did not find what they were looking for. It was only the small group that God chose who found it; the rest grew deaf to God's call. 8 As the scripture says, "God made their minds and hearts dull; to this very day they cannot see or hear." 9 And David says,

"May they be caught and trapped at
their feasts;
may they fall, may they be
punished!
10 May their eyes be blinded so that they
cannot see;
and make them bend under their
troubles at all times."

11 I ask, then: When the Jews stumbled, did they fall to their ruin? By no means! Because they sinned, salvation has come to the Gentiles, to make the Jews jealous of them. 12 The sin of the Jews brought rich blessings to the world, and their spiritual poverty brought rich blessings to the Gentiles. Then, how much greater the blessings will be when the complete number of Jews is included!

The Salvation of the Gentiles

13 I am speaking now to you Gentiles: As long as I am an apostle to the Gentiles, I will take pride in my work. 14 Perhaps I can make the people of my own race jealous, and so be able to save some of them. 15 For when they were rejected, mankind was changed from God's enemies into his friends. What will it be, then, when they are accepted? It will be life for the dead!

16 If the first piece of bread is given to God, then the whole loaf is his also; and if the roots of a tree are offered to God, the branches are his also. 17 Some of the branches of the cultivated olive-tree have been broken off, and a branch of a wild olive-tree has been joined to it. You Gentiles are like that wild olive-tree, and now you share the strong spiritual life of the Jews. 18 So then, you must not despise those who were broken off like branches. How can you be proud? You are just a

submit Lam 5.11; 1 Cor 9.25
true [2] 9.4; 11.20
understand 7.1; 11.33
welcome Acts 28.2; 14.1
wish 9.3; 1 Cor 4.8
wonder (1) Acts 15.12; 15.19
word (1) 9.9; 15.18
world 9.17; 11.12
world of the dead (world below) 8.39; Phil 2.10

abandon Acts 21.21; 2 Cor 11.3
accept 10.16; 12.16
advice Acts 27.9; 1 Cor 2.16
afraid 8.15; 13.3
altar Acts 17.23; 1 Cor 9.13
apostle 1.1; 16.7
basis [2] 10.2; 14.23
believe [2] 10.4; 13.11
bless [4] 10.12; 12.14
blind 2.19; 1 Jn 2.11
bread Acts 27.35; 1 Cor 5.8
change [2] Acts 28.6; 12.2
choose [7] 9.11; 1 Cor 1.27

complete [2] 8.37; 12.2
covenant 9.4; 1 Cor 11.25
create 8.19; 1 Cor 8.6
dead 7.8; 14.9
despise 2.4; 14.3
disobey [4] 10.21; Eph 2.1
enemy [2] 8.7; 12.20
exist 4.17; 13.1
false Acts 24.14; 2 Cor 4.2
feast Acts 7.41; 1 Cor 10.7
friend [2] 9.20; 12.19
Gentile [9] 10.12; 15.9
glory 9.4; 15.7
god (2) (other gods) Acts 28.6; 1 Cor 8.5
God's people [2] 10.19; 15.10
Good News 10.15; 15.16
grace [3] 6.1; 12.3
heart 10.1; 12.11
jealous [2] 10.19; 13.13
Jew [11] 10.12; 15.8
keep from 1.13; 14.21
kind [3] 2.4; 12.8
knowledge 10.2; 15.14
last (1) Jn 6.27; 1 Cor 7.31
life (1) [2] 8.2; 15.8
mankind 5.14; 1 Cor 2.7
mercy [4] 9.15; 12.1
mind (1) [3] 8.5; 12.2
natural 6.12; Gal 6.8
nature 8.3; 13.14
offer 8.32; 12.1
plead 8.26; 2 Cor 5.20
poor 8.35; 15.26
poverty *see* **poor**
prison 7.6; 16.7
prophet 3.21; 16.26
proud [3] 1.30; 12.16
punish 3.5; 13.4
race (1) 9.5; Eph 2.15
real 2.28; 13.4
reject [4] 2.8; Gal 2.21
rich [2] 10.12; 1 Cor 1.5
riches Lk 21.4; Eph 3.8
ruin 3.16; 14.15
sake 9.3; 1 Cor 4.6
salvation Acts 28.28; 2 Cor 1.6
save [2] 10.1; 13.11
Saviour Acts 13.23; Eph 5.23
scripture [4] 10.6; 12.19
secret 2.16; 16.25
share 8.17; 12.8
spare [2] Acts 27.24; 1 Cor 7.28
spiritual [2] 7.14; 15.27
strong 1.11; 15.1
stubborn 9.18; Eph 4.18
stumble 9.32; 14.13
take away (sin) Jn 1.29; Heb 9.13
trap Jn 8.6; 1 Cor 3.19
trouble 8.35; 12.12
true 10.2; 12.1
truth 9.1; 16.25
unbeliever Lk 9.41; 15.31
understand 10.19; 15.21
way (3) 1.18; 1 Cor 13.11

10.11: Is 28.16 (LXX) **10.13:** Joel 2.32 **10.15:** Is 52.7 **10.16:** Is 53.1 (LXX) **10.18:** Ps 19.4 (LXX) **10.19:** Deut 32.21 **10.20:** Is 65.1 (LXX) **10.21:** Is 65.2 (LXX) **11.1:** Phil 3.5 **11.3:** 1 Kgs 19.10, 14 **11.4:** 1 Kgs 19.18 **11.8:** Deut 29.4; Is 29.10 **11.9-10:** Ps 69.22-23 (LXX)

wicked 6.13;
1 Cor 5.8
wisdom Acts 7.10;
1 Cor 1.17
wise 3.11; 12.16
world 10.18; 12.2
worship (2) (of other gods) 1.23;
1 Cor 5.10

branch; you don't support the roots—the
roots support you.
19 But you will say, "Yes, but the
branches were broken off to make room
for me." 20 That is **true**. They were
broken off because they did not **believe**,
while you remain in place because you
do **believe**. But do not be **proud** of it; instead, be **afraid**. 21 God did not **spare** the
Jews, who are like **natural** branches; do
you think he will **spare** you? 22 Here we
see how **kind** and how severe God is. He
is severe towards those who have fallen,
but **kind** to you—if you continue in his
kindness. But if you do not, you too will
be broken off. 23 And if the **Jews abandon**
their **unbelief**, they will be put back in
the place where they were; for God is
able to do that. 24 You **Gentiles** are like
the branch of a wild olive-tree that is
broken off and then, contrary to **nature**,
is joined to a cultivated olive-tree. The
Jews are like this cultivated tree; and it
will be much easier for God to join these
broken-off branches to their own tree
again.

God's Mercy on All

25 There is a **secret truth**, my
brothers, which I want you to know, for it
will **keep you from** thinking how **wise**
you are. It is that the **stubbornness** of the
people of Israel is not permanent, but
will **last** only until the **complete** number
of **Gentiles** comes to God. 26 And this is
how all Israel will be **saved**. As the **scripture** says,

"The **Saviour** will come from Zion
and remove all **wickedness** from the
descendants of Jacob.
27 I will make this **covenant** with them
when I **take away** their sins."

28 Because they **reject** the **Good News**,
the **Jews** are God's **enemies** for the **sake**
of you **Gentiles**. But because of God's
choice, they are his **friends** because of
their ancestors. 29 For God does not
change his **mind** about whom he **chooses**
and **blesses**. 30 As for you **Gentiles**, you
disobeyed God in the past; but now you
have received God's **mercy** because the
Jews were **disobedient**. 31 In the same
way, because of the **mercy** that you have
received, the **Jews** now **disobey** God, in
order that they also may now[o] receive
God's **mercy**. 32 For God has made all
people **prisoners of disobedience**, so that
he might show **mercy** to them all.

Praise to God

33 How great are God's **riches**! How
deep are his **wisdom** and **knowledge**!
Who can explain his decisions? Who can
understand his ways? 34 As the **scripture**
says,

"Who knows the **mind** of the Lord?
Who is able to give him **advice**?
35 Who has ever given him anything,
so that he had to pay it back?"

36 For all things were **created** by him, and
all things **exist** through him and for him.
To God be the **glory** for ever! Amen.

Life in God's Service

12 So then, my brothers, because of
God's great **mercy** to us I appeal
to you: **Offer** yourselves as a living **sacrifice** to God, **dedicated** to his **service** and
pleasing to him. This is the **true worship**
that you should **offer**. 2 Do not conform
yourselves to the standards of **this world**,
but let God transform you inwardly by a
complete change of your **mind**. Then you
will be able to know the **will of God**—
what is good and is pleasing to him and is
perfect.
3 And because of God's **gracious gift** to
me I say to every one of you: Do not
think of yourself more highly than you
should. Instead, be modest in your thinking, and **judge** yourself according to the
amount of **faith** that God has given you.
4 We have many parts in the one **body**,
and all these parts have different func-
tions. 5 In the same way, though we are
many, we are one **body** in **union with
Christ**, and we are all joined to **each
other** as different parts of one **body**. 6 So
we are to use our different **gifts** in
accordance with the **grace** that God has
given us. If our **gift** is to speak God's
message, we should do it according to
the **faith** that we have; 7 if it is to **serve**,
we should serve; if it is to **teach**, we
should teach; 8 if it is to **encourage**
others, we should do so. Whoever **shares**
with others should do it **generously**; whoever has **authority** should work **hard**;
whoever shows **kindness** to others should
do it **cheerfully**.
9 **Love** must be completely **sincere**.
Hate what is **evil**, hold on to what is good.
10 **Love one another** warmly as **Christian**
brothers, and be **eager** to show **respect**
for **one another**. 11 Work **hard** and do not
be lazy. **Serve** the Lord with a **heart** full
of **devotion**. 12 Let your **hope** keep you
joyful, be **patient** in your **troubles**, and

accept 11.15; 14.3
anger 10.19; Gal 5.20
authority Acts 26.10;
13.1
bless [2] 11.12; 15.27
body [3] 8.10;
1 Cor 5.3
change 11.15;
1 Cor 15.51
cheer (1) Mk 10.49;
1 Cor 16.18
Christ 10.4; 14.9
Christian [2]
Acts 26.28; 16.7
complete 11.12;
1 Cor 7.37
concern Lk 12.29;
1 Cor 4.3
conquer Hab 2.5;
2 Pet 2.19
consider 8.18;
1 Cor 1.27
curse 9.3; 1 Cor 4.12
dedicate 6.22; 15.16
devote 10.2;
2 Cor 7.11
duty (1) Acts 12.6;
13.6
each other 1.24;
1 Cor 7.3
eager 8.19;
1 Cor 14.12
encourage
Acts 28.15; 15.4
enemy 11.15;
1 Cor 15.25
evil [3] 7.19; 13.3
faith [2] 10.6; 14.1
friend 11.15; 16.2
generous Lk 6.38;
2 Cor 8.2
gift [3] 8.23;
1 Cor 2.14
grace [2] 11.5; 16.20
happy 7.24; 14.22
hard [2] 2.5; 16.6
hate 9.13; Eph 4.31
heart 11.8;
1 Cor 12.31
hope 8.20; 15.4
humble Acts 20.19;
2 Cor 11.7
hunger 8.35;
1 Cor 4.11
joy Acts 16.34; 14.17
judge 5.16; 13.2
kind 11.22; 1 Cor 4.13
love [2] 9.13; 13.8
mercy 11.30; 15.9
message 10.8;
1 Cor 1.6
mind (1) 11.8; 14.5
need Acts 28.10; 16.2
offer [2] 11.16; 15.16
one another [2] 1.30;
13.8
patient 9.22; 15.4
peace 8.6; 14.17
perfect Acts 23.1;
1 Cor 13.10

[o] *Some manuscripts do not have* now.

11.26: Is 59.20 (LXX) **11.27:** Jer 31.33–34 **11.33:** Is 55.8 **11.34:** Is 40.13 (LXX) **11.35:** Job 41.11
11.36: 1 Cor 8.6 **12.4–5:** 1 Cor 12.12 **12.6–8:** 1 Cor 12.4–11

persecute 8.35; 1 Cor 4.12
please [2] 8.8; 14.18
pray 10.1; 15.30
proud 11.13; 15.17
repay Lk 14.14; Col 3.25
respect Acts 22.12; 13.7
revenge [2] Acts 7.24; Heb 10.30
sacrifice 5.9; 1 Cor 5.7
scripture [2] 11.2; 14.11
serve [2] 9.11; 14.18
service 7.4; 15.8
shame 2.23; 1 Cor 1.27
share [2] 11.17; 15.27
sincere Lk 20.20; 2 Cor 1.12
stranger Mt 25.35; Eph 2.19
teach 6.17; 15.4
trouble 11.10; 1 Cor 7.28
true 11.20; 15.8
union 8.1; 14.14
weep Jn 16.20; 1 Cor 7.30
will (1) 9.19; 15.32
wise 11.25; 16.19
world 11.12; 1 Cor 1.20
worship (1) (of God) 9.4; 1 Cor 1.2
wrong 5.20; 13.10

adultery 7.3; 1 Cor 6.9
afraid [2] 11.20; 2 Cor 11.3
authorities [4] Acts 23.20; 1 Cor 15.24
authority [3] 12.8; 1 Cor 1.10
believe 11.20; 14.14
command 10.5; 16.26
commandment 7.8; 1 Cor 7.19
commit [2] 7.3; 1 Cor 6.18
conduct 2.15; Gal 6.4
conscience 9.1; 1 Cor 4.4
dark 2.19; 1 Cor 4.5
desire [2] 7.5; 1 Cor 7.9
duty (1) 12.16; 1 Cor 7.3
evil [3] 12.9; 16.19
exist [3] 11.36; 1 Cor 8.4
fear Acts 19.17; 1 Cor 2.3
fulfil Lk 9.31; 1 Cor 7.3
honour 2.7; 14.6
immoral Acts 21.25; 1 Cor 5.1
jealous 11.11; 1 Cor 3.3
judge 12.3; 14.4
law [2] 10.4; 1 Cor 9.8
light (1) [2] 2.19; 1 Cor 4.5
love [4] 12.9; 14.15
nature 11.24; 1 Cor 11.14
neighbour Jn 9.8; Gal 5.14
obey [4] 10.5; 15.18
obligation [2] 8.12; 15.27
one another 12.10; 14.13

pray at all times. 13 **Share** your belongings with your **needy fellow-Christians**, and open your homes to **strangers**.

14 Ask God to **bless** those who **persecute** you—yes, ask him to **bless**, not to **curse**. 15 Be **happy** with those who are happy, **weep** with those who weep. 16 Have the same **concern** for everyone. Do not be **proud**, but **accept humble duties**.[p] Do not think of yourselves as **wise**.

17 If someone has done you wrong, do not **repay** him with a **wrong**. Try to do what everyone **considers** to be good. 18 Do everything possible on your part to live in **peace** with everybody. 19 Never take **revenge**, my **friends**, but instead let **God's anger** do it. For the **scripture** says, "I will take **revenge**, I will pay back, says the Lord." 20 Instead, as the **scripture** says: "If your **enemy** is **hungry**, feed him; if he is thirsty, give him a drink; for by doing this you will make him burn with **shame**." 21 Do not let **evil** defeat you; instead, **conquer evil** with good.

Duties towards the State Authorities

13 Everyone must **obey** the state **authorities**, because no **authority exists** without God's **permission**, and the **existing authorities** have been put there by God. 2 Whoever opposes the **existing authority** opposes what God has ordered; and anyone who does so will bring **judgement** on himself. 3 For rulers are not to be **feared** by those who do good, but by those who do **evil**. Would you like to be **unafraid** of the man in **authority**? Then do what is good, and he will **praise** you, 4 because he is God's **servant** working for your own good. But if you do **evil**, then be **afraid** of him, because his **power** to **punish** is **real**. He is God's **servant** and carries out God's **punishment** on those who do **evil**. 5 For this **reason** you must **obey** the **authorities**—not just because of God's **punishment**, but also as a matter of **conscience**.

6 That is also why you pay **taxes**, because the **authorities** are working for God when they **fulfil** their **duties**. 7 Pay, then, what you **owe** them; pay them your personal and property **taxes**, and show **respect** and **honour** for them all.

Duties towards One Another

8 Be under **obligation** to no one—the only **obligation** you have is to **love one another**. Whoever does this has **obeyed** the **Law**. 9 The **commandments**, "Do not **commit adultery**; do not **commit murder**; do not **steal**; do not **desire** what belongs to someone else"—all these, and any others besides, are summed up in the one **command**, "Love your **neighbour** as you **love** yourself." 10 If you love someone, you will never do him **wrong**; to **love**, then, is to **obey** the whole **Law**.

11 You must do this, because you know that the time has come for you to wake up from your sleep. For the moment when we will be **saved** is closer now than it was when we first **believed**. 12 The night is nearly over, day is almost here. Let us stop doing the things that belong to the **dark**, and let us take up weapons for fighting in the **light**. 13 Let us **conduct** ourselves **properly**, as people who live in the **light** of day—no orgies or drunkenness, no **immorality** or indecency, no fighting or **jealousy**. 14 But take up the weapons of the Lord Jesus Christ, and stop paying attention to your sinful **nature** and **satisfying** its **desires**.

Do Not Judge Your Brother

14 **Welcome** the person who is **weak** in **faith**, but do not **argue** with him about his personal opinions. 2 One person's **faith** allows him to eat anything, but the person who is **weak** in the **faith** eats only vegetables. 3 The person who will eat anything is not to **despise** the one who doesn't; while the one who eats only vegetables is not to **pass judgement** on the one who will eat anything; for God has **accepted** him. 4 **Who are you to judge** the **servant** of someone else? It is his own **Master** who will decide whether he **succeeds** or **fails**. And he will **succeed**, because the Lord is able to make him succeed.

5 One person thinks that a certain day is more **important** than other days, while someone else thinks that all days are the same. Each one should firmly make up his own **mind**. 6 Whoever thinks highly of a certain day does so in **honour** of the Lord; whoever will eat anything does so in **honour** of the Lord, because he gives **thanks** to God for the food. Whoever **refuses** to eat certain things does so in **honour** of the Lord, and he gives **thanks** to God. 7 None of us lives for himself only, none of us dies for himself only. 8 If we live, it is for the Lord that we live, and if we die, it is for the Lord that we die. So whether we live or die, we belong to the Lord. 9 For **Christ** died and **rose to life** in order to be the Lord of the living and of

owe Lk 16.5; Phlm 18
permit Acts 26.1; Rev 13.5
power 9.17; 15.13
praise 9.5; 15.6
proper Lk 12.42; 1 Cor 4.6
punish [3] 11.9; 1 Cor 11.32
real 11.6; 1 Cor 3.13
reason 4.18; 16.19
respect 12.10; 2 Cor 8.18
satisfy 8.4; 1 Cor 7.3
save 11.14; 1 Cor 1.18
servant [2] 1.1; 14.4
steal 2.21; 1 Cor 6.10
tax [2] Lk 23.2
wrong 12.17; 14.20

accept 12.16; 15.7
act 5.18; 1 Cor 3.4
action 8.13; 1 Cor 8.9
approve 7.23; 1 Cor 16.3
argue Acts 25.19; 1 Cor 11.16
bad 9.11; 1 Cor 15.33
basis [2] 11.6; 1 Cor 2.14
believe [2] 13.11; 16.5
certain (1) 8.38; 1 Tim 6.17
Christ [3] 12.5; 15.3
condemn 8.1; 1 Cor 4.9
confess 10.9; 1 Cor 12.3
dead 11.15; 1 Cor 10.5
despise [2] 11.18; 1 Cor 1.28
destroy 9.22; 1 Cor 1.19
doubt 4.20; 1 Cor 11.19
fail 9.6; 1 Cor 1.7
faith [5] 12.3; 15.1
guilty 8.33; 1 Cor 5.1
happy 12.15; 16.19
help 10.13; 15.1
honour [3] 13.7; 1 Cor 4.10
hurt 3.15; 1 Cor 15.55
I am Acts 10.21; Rev 1.8
important Acts 21.39; 1 Cor 1.28
joy 12.12; 15.13
judge [4] 13.2; 1 Cor 2.14
keep from 11.25; 16.17
Kingdom (1) (of God) Acts 28.23; 1 Cor 4.20
kneel Acts 21.5
life (2) (to life) 8.34; 1 Cor 15.4
love 13.8; 15.30

[p] accept humble duties; *or* make friends with humble people.

12.14: Mt 5.44; Lk 6.28 **12.16:** Prov 3.7 **12.19:** Deut 32.35 **12.20:** Prov 25.21–22 (LXX)
13.6–7: Mt 22.21; Mk 12.17; Lk 20.25 **13.9:** Ex 20.13–15, 17; Deut 5.17–19, 21; Lev 19.18 **14.1–6:** Col 2.16

master 6.14; 1 Cor 4.2
mind (1) 12.2; 1 Cor 2.2
one another [2] 13.8; 15.7
pass (5) [2] 2.1; 1 Cor 4.3
peace [2] 12.18; 15.13
please 12.1; 15.1
refuse (1) 1.28; Gal 2.21
right (1) [2] 9.9; 1 Cor 4.5
righteous 8.4; 2 Cor 5.21
rise Acts 26.23; 1 Cor 5.6
ruin 11.11; 1 Cor 15.33
scripture 12.19; 15.3
servant 13.4; 15.16
serve 12.7; 15.16
Spirit (1) (God's Spirit) 9.1; 15.13
strength Acts 18.23; 1 Cor 1.25
stumble 11.11; 1 Pet 2.8
succeed (1) [2] Acts 19.26; 2 Cor 13.7
thank [2] 7.25; 1 Cor 1.4
unclean [3] Acts 15.20; 2 Cor 6.17
union 12.5; 15.17
weak [2] 8.3; 15.1
welcome 10.21; 1 Cor 16.10
who 9.20; Rev 1.4
wrong 13.10; 1 Cor 6.7

the dead. 10 You then, who eat only vegetables—why do you pass judgement on
your brother? And you who eat anything—why do you despise your brother?
All of us will stand before God to be
judged by him. 11 For the scripture says,

"As surely as I am the living God, says
the Lord,
everyone will kneel before me,
and everyone will confess that I am
God."

12 Every one of us, then, will have to give
an account of himself to God.

Do Not Make Your Brother Fall

13 So then, let us stop judging one
another. Instead, you should decide
never to do anything that would make
your brother stumble or fall into sin.
14 My union with the Lord Jesus makes
me certain that no food is of itself ritually
unclean; but if a person believes that
some food is unclean, then it becomes unclean for him. 15 If you hurt your brother
because of something you eat, then you
are no longer acting from love. Do not let
the food that you eat ruin the person for
whom Christ died! 16 Do not let what you
regard as good get a bad name. 17 For
God's Kingdom is not a matter of eating
and drinking, but of the righteousness,
peace, and joy which the Holy Spirit
gives. 18 And when someone serves Christ
in this way, he pleases God and is
approved by others.
19 So then, we must always aim[q] at
those things that bring peace and that
help to strengthen one another. 20 Do not,
because of food, destroy what God has
done. All foods may be eaten, but it is
wrong to eat anything that will cause
someone else to fall into sin. 21 The right
thing to do is to keep from eating meat,
drinking wine, or doing anything else
that will make your brother fall. 22 Keep
what you believe about this matter, then,
between yourself and God. Happy is the
person who does not feel guilty when he
does something he judges is right! 23 But
if he has doubts about what he eats, God
condemns him when he eats it, because
his action is not based on faith. And anything that is not based on faith is sin.

Please Others, Not Yourselves

accept [4] 14.3; 1 Cor 7.14
bless [3] 12.14; 1 Cor 1.7
bold [3] 10.20; 2 Cor 3.12

15 We who are strong in the faith
ought to help the weak to carry
their burdens. We should not please ourselves. 2 Instead, we should all please our
brothers for their own good, in order to
build them up in the faith. 3 For Christ did
not please himself. Instead, as the scripture says, "The insults which are hurled
at you have fallen on me." 4 Everything
written in the Scriptures was written
to teach us, in order that we might
have hope through the patience and
encouragement which the Scriptures
give us. 5 And may God, the source of
patience and encouragement, enable you
to have the same point of view among
yourselves by following the example of
Christ Jesus, 6 so that all of you together
may praise with one voice the God and
Father of our Lord Jesus Christ.

Good News for the Gentiles

7 Accept one another, then, for the
glory of God, as Christ has accepted you.
8 For I tell you that Christ's life of service
was on behalf of the Jews, to show that
God is faithful, to make his promises to
their ancestors come true, 9 and to enable
even the Gentiles to praise God for his
mercy. As the scripture says,

"And so I will praise you among the
Gentiles;
I will sing praises to you."

10 Again it says,

"Rejoice, Gentiles, with God's people!"

11 And again,

"Praise the Lord, all Gentiles;
praise him, all peoples!"

12 And again, Isaiah says,

"A descendant of Jesse will appear;
he will come to rule the Gentiles,
and they will put their hope in him."

13 May God, the source of hope, fill
you with all joy and peace by means of
your faith in him, so that your hope will
continue to grow by the power of the
Holy Spirit.

Paul's Reason for Writing So Boldly

14 My brothers: I myself feel sure that
you are full of goodness, that you have all
knowledge, and that you are able to
teach one another. 15 But in this letter I
have been quite bold about certain subjects of which I have reminded you. I
have been bold because of the privilege
God has given me 16 of being a servant of
Christ Jesus to work for the Gentiles. I
serve like a priest in preaching the Good
News from God, in order that the Gentiles may be an offering acceptable to
God, dedicated to him by the Holy Spirit.
17 In union with Christ Jesus, then, I can
be proud of my service for God. 18 I will
be bold and speak only about what Christ

burden Acts 15.28; 2 Cor 1.8
Christ [7] 14.9; 16.5
church Acts 21.18; 16.1
dedicate 12.1; 1 Cor 6.11
deed (2) 4.5; 2 Cor 4.2
encourage [2] 12.8; 1 Cor 8.10
enjoy [2] Acts 2.47; 1 Tim 6.17
example 7.2; 1 Cor 4.6
faith [3] 14.1; 16.17
faithful 3.3; 1 Cor 4.2
Father (2) (God) 8.15; 1 Cor 1.3
free 8.2; 1 Cor 1.30
Gentile [10] 11.11; 16.4
glory 11.36; 16.25
God's people [4] 11.1; 16.2
Good News [3] 11.28; 16.25
help [5] 14.19; 16.2
hope [5] 12.12; 1 Cor 9.10
insult 3.8; 1 Cor 4.13
Jew [3] 11.11; 16.7
joy [2] 14.17; 2 Cor 7.4
knowledge 11.33; 1 Cor 1.5
letter (2) Acts 28.21; 16.22
life (1) 11.15; 16.4
love 14.15; 1 Cor 2.9
material (2) 1 Cor 7.31
means [2] 10.19; 1 Cor 1.21
mercy 12.1; 1 Cor 7.25
miracle Acts 19.11; 1 Cor 1.22
obey 13.1; 16.26
obligation 13.8; Gal 5.3
offer [2] 12.1; 1 Cor 8.1
one another [2] 14.13; 16.16
patient [2] 12.12; 1 Cor 13.4
peace [2] 14.17; 16.20
please [3] 14.18; 1 Cor 7.32
poor 11.12; 2 Cor 6.10
power [3] 13.4; 1 Cor 1.17
praise [6] 13.3; 1 Cor 4.5
pray [2] 12.12; 1 Cor 11.4
preach 10.8; 16.25
prevent 1.18
priest Acts 14.13; Heb 5.6
privilege 1.5; 1 Cor 9.18
proclaim [2] 10.14; 1 Cor 1.23
promise 9.4; 1 Cor 10.13
proud 12.16; 1 Cor 4.6
raise 10.9; 1 Cor 6.14
rejoice 5.11; Phil 3.3
remind Ezek 29.16; 1 Cor 4.17
safe Acts 28.1; 1 Cor 10.1
scripture [5] 14.11; 1 Cor 1.19
servant 14.4; 1 Cor 3.5
serve 14.18; 16.1

q we must always aim; *some manuscripts have* we always aim.

14.10: 2 Cor 5.10 14.11: Is 45.23 (LXX) 15.3: Ps 69.9 15.9: 2 Sam 22.50; Ps 18.49 15.10: Deut 32.43
15.11: Ps 117.1 15.12: Is 11.10 (LXX)

service [4] 12.1; 16.3
share 12.8; 1 Cor 9.10
source [3] Jn 5.26; 16.20
Spirit (1) (God's Spirit) [4] 14.17; 1 Cor 2.4
spiritual 11.12; 1 Cor 2.6
strong 11.17; 1 Cor 1.25
sure 4.21; 1 Cor 1.17
task Is 52.13; 1 Cor 9.17
teach [2] 12.7; 16.17
true 12.1; 1 Cor 8.1
unbeliever 11.23; 1 Cor 6.6
understand 11.33; 1 Cor 1.19
union 14.14; 1 Cor 1.2
urge Acts 18.27; 16.17
weak 14.1; 1 Cor 1.25
will (1) 12.2; 1 Cor 1.1
wonder (1) 10.15; 2 Cor 12.7
word (1) 10.18; 16.18

has done through me to lead the Gentiles
to obey God. He has done this by means
of words and deeds, [19] by the power of
miracles and wonders, and by the power
of the Spirit of God. And so, in travelling
all the way from Jerusalem to Illyricum,
I have proclaimed fully the Good News
about Christ. [20] My ambition has always
been to proclaim the Good News in
places where Christ has not been heard
of, so as not to build on a foundation laid
by someone else. [21] As the scripture says,

"Those who were not told about him
will see,
and those who have not heard will
understand."

Paul's Plan to Visit Rome

22 And so I have been prevented
many times from coming to you. [23] But
now that I have finished my work in
these regions and since I have been
wanting for so many years to come to
see you, [24] I hope to do so now. I would
like to see you on my way to Spain, and
be helped by you to go there, after I have
enjoyed visiting you for a while. [25] Just
now, however, I am going to Jerusalem
in the service of God's people there.
[26] For the churches in Macedonia and
Achaia have freely decided to give an
offering to help the poor among God's
people in Jerusalem. [27] That decision was
their own; but, as a matter of fact, they
have an obligation to help them. Since
the Jews shared their spiritual blessings
with the Gentiles, the Gentiles ought to
use their material blessings to help the
Jews. [28] When I have finished this task
and have handed over to them all the
money that has been raised for them, I
shall leave for Spain and visit you on my
way there. [29] When I come to you, I know
that I shall come with a full measure of
the blessing of Christ.

30 I urge you, brothers, by our Lord
Jesus Christ and by the love that the
Spirit gives: join me in praying fervently
to God for me. [31] Pray that I may be kept
safe from the unbelievers in Judaea and
that my service in Jerusalem may be
acceptable to God's people there. [32] And
so I will come to you full of joy, if it is
God's will, and enjoy a refreshing visit to
you. [33] May God, our source of peace, be
with all of you. Amen.

Personal Greetings

age (1) Lk 20.34; Gal 1.4
alone 8.23; 1 Cor 7.8

16 I recommend to you our sister
Phoebe, who serves the church
at Cenchreae. [2] Receive her in the Lord's
name, as God's people should, and give
her any help she may need from you; for
she herself has been a good friend to
many people and also to me.

3 I send greetings to Priscilla and
Aquila, my fellow-workers in the service
of Christ Jesus; [4] they risked their lives
for me. I am grateful to them—not only I,
but all the Gentile churches as well.
[5] Greetings also to the church that meets
in their house.

Greetings to my dear friend Epae-
netus, who was the first man in the
province of Asia to believe in Christ.
[6] Greetings to Mary, who has worked so
hard for you. [7] Greetings also to
Andronicus and Junias,[r] fellow-Jews who
were in prison with me; they are well
known among the apostles, and they became Christians before I did.

8 My greetings to Ampliatus, my dear
friend in the fellowship of the Lord.
[9] Greetings also to Urbanus, our fellow-
worker in Christ's service, and to
Stachys, my dear friend. [10] Greetings to
Apelles, whose loyalty to Christ has been
proved. Greetings to those who belong to
the family of Aristobulus. [11] Greetings to
Herodion, a fellow-Jew, and to the
Christian brothers in the family of
Narcissus.

12 My greetings to Tryphaena and
Tryphosa, who work in the Lord's service, and to my dear friend Persis, who
has done so much work for the Lord. [13] I
send greetings to Rufus, that outstanding
worker in the Lord's service, and to his
mother, who has always treated me like
a son. [14] My greetings to Asyncritus,
Phlegon, Hermes, Patrobas, Hermas, and
all the other Christian brothers with
them. [15] Greetings to Philologus and
Julia, to Nereus and his sister, to
Olympas and to all of God's people who
are with them.

16 Greet one another with a brotherly
kiss. All the churches of Christ send you
their greetings.

Final Instructions

17 I urge you, my brothers: watch out
for those who cause divisions and upset
people's faith and go against the teaching which you have received. Keep away
from them! [18] For those who do such
things are not serving Christ our Lord,
but their own appetites. By their fine
words and flattering speech they deceive
innocent people. [19] Everyone has heard

apostle 11.13; 1 Cor 1.1
believe [2] 14.14; 1 Cor 1.21
Christ [5] 15.3; 1 Cor 1.5
Christian [4] 12.10; 1 Cor 3.1
church [5] 15.26; 1 Cor 1.2
command 13.9; 1 Cor 7.10
dear [4] Acts 15.25; 1 Cor 4.14
deceive 7.11; 2 Cor 4.2
eternal 6.22; 1 Cor 13.8
evil 13.3; 1 Cor 5.12
faith [2] 15.1; 1 Cor 2.5
fellowship 6.10; 1 Cor 1.9
friend [5] 12.19; 1 Cor 10.14
Gentile 15.9; 1 Cor 1.23
glory [2] 15.7; 1 Cor 2.7
God's people [2] 15.10; 1 Cor 1.2
Good News 15.16; 1 Cor 1.17
gospel 1.16; 1 Cor 9.14
grace 12.3; 1 Cor 1.3
grateful Acts 24.3; 2 Cor 9.12
happy 14.22; 1 Cor 7.30
hard 12.8; 1 Cor 4.12
help 15.1; 1 Cor 7.35
innocent [2] 4.5; 1 Cor 4.4
Jew [3] 15.8; 1 Cor 1.22
keep from 14.21; 1 Cor 7.5
kiss Acts 20.37; 1 Cor 16.20
letter (2) 15.15; 1 Cor 5.9
life (1) 15.8; 1 Cor 3.22
loyal [2] Lk 16.13; 2 Cor 9.13
name (2) (name of God, of Jesus) Acts 19.5; 1 Cor 5.3
need 12.13; 1 Cor 4.8
obey 15.18; 1 Cor 7.19
one another 15.7; 1 Cor 3.3
peace 15.13; 1 Cor 1.3
preach 15.16; 1 Cor 1.21
prison 11.32; 2 Cor 2.14
prophet 11.3; 1 Cor 12.28
prove Acts 25.7; 1 Cor 1.22
reason 13.5; 2 Cor 4.16
reveal 9.4; 1 Cor 1.7
Satan Acts 26.18; 1 Cor 5.5
secret 11.25; 1 Cor 2.1
serve [2] 15.16; 1 Cor 6.13
service [4] 15.8; 1 Cor 7.35
source 15.5; Col 1.18
speech 3.14; 1 Cor 1.5
teach 15.4; 1 Cor 2.4
truth [2] 11.25; 1 Cor 2.1

[r] Junias; *or* June; *some manuscripts have* Julia.

15.21: Is 52.15 (LXX) **15.22:** Rom 1.13 **15.25-26:** 1 Cor 16.1-4 **15.27:** 1 Cor 9.11 **16.3:** Acts 18.2
16.13: Mk 15.21

upset Acts 17.16; Gal 1.7
urge 15.30; 2 Cor 8.6
watch Acts 20.28; Gal 5.15
wise [2] 12.16; 1 Cor 1.19
word (1) 15.18; 1 Cor 2.1

of your **loyalty** to the **gospel**, and for this
reason I am **happy** about you. I want you
to be **wise** about what is good, but **inno-**
cent in what is **evil**. 20 And God, our
source of peace, will soon crush **Satan**
under your feet.

The **grace** of our Lord Jesus be with
you.[s]

21 Timothy, my fellow-worker, sends
you his greetings; and so do Lucius,
Jason, and Sosipater, **fellow-Jews**.

22 I, Tertius, the writer of this **letter**,
send you **Christian** greetings.

23 My host Gaius, in whose house the
church meets, sends you his greetings;
Erastus, the city treasurer, and our
brother Quartus send you their greetings.[t]

Concluding Prayer of Praise

25 Let us give **glory** to God! He is able
to make you stand firm in your **faith**,
according to the **Good News I preach**
about Jesus Christ and according to the
revelation of the **secret truth** which was
hidden for long **ages** in the past. 26 Now,
however, that **truth** has been brought out
into the open through the writings of the
prophets; and by the **command** of the
eternal God it is made known to all
nations, so that all may **believe and obey**.

27 To the only God, who **alone** is **all-**
wise, be **glory** through Jesus Christ for
ever! Amen.[u]

[s] *Some manuscripts omit this sentence.*
[t] *Some manuscripts add verse 24:* The grace of our Lord Jesus Christ be with you all. Amen; *others add this after verse 27.*
[u] *Some manuscripts have verses 25–27 here and after 14.23; others have them only after 14.23; one has them after 15.33.*

16.21: Acts 16.1 **16.23:** Acts 19.29; 1 Cor 1.14; 2 Tim 4.20

PAUL'S FIRST LETTER TO THE CORINTHIANS

INTRODUCTION

Paul's First Letter to the Corinthians was written to deal with problems of Christian life and faith that had arisen in the church which Paul had established at Corinth. At that time Corinth was a great cosmopolitan Greek city, the capital of the Roman province of Achaia. It was noted for its thriving commerce, proud culture, widespread immorality, and variety of religions.

The apostle's chief concerns are with problems such as divisions and immorality in the church, and with questions about sex and marriage, matters of conscience, church order, gifts of the Holy Spirit, and the resurrection. With deep insight he shows how the Good News speaks to these questions.

Chapter 13, which presents love as the best of God's gifts to his people, is probably the most widely known passage in the book.

Outline of Contents

agree Rom 7.16; 7.5
apostle Rom 16.7; 4.9
authority Rom 13.1; 11.10
baptize [6] Rom 6.3; 10.2
believe Rom 16.5; 3.5
bless Rom 15.27; 4.12
boast [2] Rom 5.2; 3.21
choose [3] Rom 11.2; 2.7
Christ [10] Rom 16.5; 2.16
church Rom 16.1; 4.17
consider [2] Rom 12.17; 3.19
cross (1) [3] Rom 6.6; 2.2
crucify Acts 4.10; 2.8
Day of the Lord Rom 2.5; 3.13
death (1) [2] Rom 8.2; 2.2
despise Rom 14.3; 4.6
destroy [2] Rom 14.20; 3.17
disciple [2] Acts 21.16
establish Hos 2.23; Phil 1.7
fail Rom 14.4; 6.7
Father (2) (God) Rom 15.6; 8.6
fault Rom 9.19; 2 Cor 6.3
fellowship Rom 16.8; 5.2

1 From Paul, who was called by the
will of God to be an **apostle** of Christ
Jesus, and from our brother Sosthenes—
2 To the **church** of God which is in
Corinth, to all who are called to be God's
holy people, who belong to him in **union**
with Christ Jesus, together with all
people everywhere who **worship** our
Lord Jesus Christ, their Lord and ours:
3 May God **our Father** and the Lord
Jesus Christ give you **grace** and **peace**.

Blessings in Christ

4 I always give **thanks** to my God for
you because of the **grace** he has given
you through Christ Jesus. [5]For in **union**
with Christ you have become **rich** in all
things, including all **speech** and all **know-**
ledge. [6]The **message** about **Christ** has become so firmly **established** in you [7]that
you have not **failed** to receive a single
blessing, as you wait for our Lord Jesus
Christ to be **revealed**. [8]He will also keep
you firm to the end, so that you will be
faultless on the **Day of our Lord** Jesus
Christ. [9]God is to be **trusted**, the God who
called you to have **fellowship** with **his Son**
Jesus Christ, our Lord.

Divisions in the Church

10 By the **authority** of our Lord Jesus
Christ I appeal to all of you, my brothers,
to **agree** in what you say, so that there
will be no divisions among you. Be completely **united**, with only one thought and
one **purpose**. [11]For some people from
Chloe's family have told me quite **plainly**,
my brothers, that there are **quarrels**
among you. [12]Let me put it this way:
each one of you says something different.
One says, "I follow Paul"; another, "I follow Apollos"; another, "I follow Peter";
and another, "I follow **Christ**." [13]**Christ**
has been divided[a] into groups! Was it
Paul who died on the **cross** for you?
Were you **baptized** as Paul's **disciples**?
14 I **thank** God that I did not **baptize**
any of you except Crispus and Gaius.
[15]No one can say, then, that you were
baptized as my **disciples**. [16](Oh yes, I also
baptized Stephanas and his family; but I
can't **remember** whether I **baptized** anyone else.) [17]**Christ** did not send me to
baptize. He sent me to tell the **Good**
News, and to tell it without using the
language of **human wisdom**, in order to
make **sure** that **Christ's death** on the
cross is not **robbed** of its **power**.

fool [3] Rom 10.19; 3.18
free Rom 15.26; 7.15
Gentile [2] Rom 16.4; 9.21
God's people [2] Rom 16.2; 6.1
Good News Rom 16.25; 4.15
grace [2] Rom 16.20; 15.10
human [4] Rom 9.5; 2.4
important Rom 14.5; 12.31
impossible Acts 27.15; 6.15
Jew [3] Rom 16.7; 9.20
knowledge Rom 15.14; 8.1
look down on Dan 9.16; 16.11
means [2] Rom 15.13; 2.10
message [5] Rom 12.6; 2.4
miracle Rom 15.19; 12.10
peace Rom 16.20; 7.15
plain (1) Rom 1.19; 6.16
power [5] Rom 15.13; 2.4
preach Rom 16.25; 2.1
presence Rom 8.11; 12.7
proclaim Rom 15.19; 2.6
prove Rom 16.10; 2.4

[a] Christ has been divided; *some manuscripts have* Christ cannot be divided.

1.2: Acts 18.1 **1.12:** Acts 18.24 **1.14:** Acts 18.8, 19.29; Rom 16.23 **1.16:** 1 Cor 16.15

purpose [2] Rom 9.11; 2.10
quarrel Acts 23.7; 3.3
remember [2] Rom 1.9; 10.1
reveal Rom 16.25; 3.13
rich Rom 11.12; 4.8
right with God Rom 10.3; 6.11
rob Rom 2.22; 6.7
save [2] Rom 13.11; 3.15
scholar [2] Is 19.11
scripture [2] Rom 15.3; 2.9
shame [2] Rom 12.20; 6.5
Son of God Rom 8.3; 15.28
speech Rom 16.18; 13.1
strength Rom 14.19; 10.13
strong Rom 15.1; 4.10
sure Rom 15.14; 7.16
thank [2] Rom 14.6; 10.16
trust Rom 3.2; 7.25
understand Rom 15.21; 2.14
union [3] Rom 15.17; 4.10
unite Jn 16.33; 7.14
weak [2] Rom 15.1; 2.3
will (1) Rom 15.32; 7.37
wisdom [9] Rom 11.33; 2.4
wise [5] Rom 16.19; 3.18
world [6] Rom 12.2; 2.6
worship (1) (of God) Rom 12.1; 11.4

Christ the Power and the Wisdom of God

18 For the message about Christ's
death on the cross is nonsense to those
who are being lost; but for us who are being saved it is God's power. 19 The scripture says,

"I will destroy the wisdom of the wise
and set aside the understanding of
the scholars."

20 So then, where does that leave the
wise? or the scholars? or the skilful de-
baters of this world? God has shown that
this world's wisdom is foolishness!

21 For God in his wisdom made it impossible for people to know him by
means of their own wisdom. Instead, by
means of the so-called "foolish" message
we preach, God decided to save those
who believe. 22 Jews want miracles for
proof, and Greeks look for wisdom. 23 As
for us, we proclaim the crucified Christ, a
message that is offensive to the Jews and
nonsense to the Gentiles; 24 but for those
whom God has called, both Jews and
Gentiles, this message is Christ, who is
the power of God and the wisdom of God.
25 For what seems to be God's foolishness
is wiser than human wisdom, and what
seems to be God's weakness is stronger
than human strength.

26 Now remember what you were, my
brothers, when God called you. From the
human point of view few of you were
wise or powerful or of high social standing. 27 God purposely chose what the
world considers nonsense in order to
shame the wise, and he chose what the
world considers weak in order to shame
the powerful. 28 He chose what the world
looks down on and despises, and thinks is
nothing, in order to destroy what the
world thinks is important. 29 This means
that no one can boast in God's presence.
30 But God has brought you into union
with Christ Jesus, and God has made
Christ to be our wisdom. By him we are
put right with God; we become God's
holy people and are set free. 31 So then, as
the scripture says, "Whoever wants to
boast must boast of what the Lord has
done."

The Message about the Crucified Christ

2 When I came to you, my brothers, to
preach God's secret truth,[b] I did not
use big words and great learning. 2 For
while I was with you, I made up my mind
to forget everything except Jesus Christ
and especially his death on the cross. 3 So
when I came to you, I was weak and
trembled all over with fear, 4 and my
teaching and message were not delivered with skilful words of human wisdom, but with convincing proof of the
power of God's Spirit. 5 Your faith, then,
does not rest on human wisdom but on
God's power.

God's Wisdom

6 Yet I do proclaim a message of
wisdom to those who are spiritually
mature. But it is not the wisdom that belongs to this world or to the powers that
rule this world—powers that are losing
their power. 7 The wisdom I proclaim is
God's secret wisdom, which is hidden
from mankind, but which he had already
chosen for our glory even before the
world was made. 8 None of the rulers of
this world knew this wisdom. If they had
known it, they would not have crucified
the Lord of glory. 9 However, as the scripture says,

"What no one ever saw or heard,
what no one ever thought could
happen,
is the very thing God prepared for
those who love him."

10 But[c] it was to us that God made known
his secret by means of his Spirit. The
Spirit searches everything, even the hidden depths of God's purposes. 11 It is only
a person's own spirit within him that
knows all about him; in the same way,
only God's Spirit knows all about God.
12 We have not received this world's
spirit; instead, we have received the
Spirit sent by God, so that we may know
all that God has given us.

13 So then, we do not speak in words
taught by human wisdom, but in words
taught by the Spirit, as we explain
spiritual truths to those who have the
Spirit.[d] 14 Whoever does not have the
Spirit cannot receive the gifts that come
from God's Spirit. Such a person really
does not understand them; they are nonsense to him, because their value can be
judged only on a spiritual basis. 15 Whoever has the Spirit, however, is able to
judge the value of everything, but no one
is able to judge him. 16 As the scripture
says,

"Who knows the mind of the Lord?
Who is able to give him advice?"

We, however, have the mind of Christ.

convince Acts 28.23; 14.24
cross (1) 1.13; 2 Cor 13.4
crucify 1.23; Heb 6.6
death (1) 1.17; 3.22
faith Rom 16.17; 3.1
fear Rom 13.3; 2 Cor 5.11
forget Jn 16.21; Phil 3.13
gift Rom 12.3; 3.10
glory [2] Rom 16.25; 6.20
human [3] 1.17; 4.3
judge [3] Rom 14.4; 4.3
learn Rom 3.18; 4.6
love Rom 15.30; 4.21
mankind Rom 11.15; 4.9
mature Prov 16.21; Gal 4.3
means 1.21; 9.22
message [2] 1.6; 11.4
mind (1) [3] Rom 14.5; 4.5
power [4] 1.17; 4.19
preach 1.21; 9.14
proclaim [2] 1.23; 11.4
prove 1.22; 3.3
purpose 1.10; 4.5
scripture [2] 1.19; 3.19
secret [3] Rom 16.25; 4.1
Spirit (1) (God's Spirit) [10] Rom 15.13; 3.1
spirit (2) [2] Rom 8.16; 4.21
spiritual [3] Rom 15.27; 6.17
teach [3] Rom 16.17; 4.17
tremble Acts 16.29; 2 Cor 7.15
truth [2] Rom 16.25; 4.1
understand 1.19; 11.3
value [2] Rom 3.1; 14.5
weak 1.25; 4.10
wisdom [7] 1.17; 3.19
word (1) [4] Rom 16.18; 4.13
world [5] 1.20; 3.1

advice Rom 11.34; Gal 1.16
basis Rom 14.23; 2 Cor 8.12
choose 1.27; 9.17
Christ 1.5; 3.23

[b] God's secret truth; *some manuscripts have* the testimony about God.
[c] But; *some manuscripts have* For.
[d] to those who have the Spirit; *or* with words given by the Spirit.

1.19: Is 29.14 (LXX) **1.20:** Job 12.17; Is 19.12, 33.18, 44.25 **1.31:** Jer 9.24 **2.3:** Acts 18.9 **2.9:** Is 64.4
2.16: Is 40.13 (LXX)

act Rom 14.15; 7.15
believe 1.21; 11.18
boast 1.29; 4.7
Christ 2.16; 4.1
Christian Rom 16.7; 4.15
consider 1.27; 7.26
Day of the Lord [2] 1.8; 5.5
death (1) 2.2; 10.10
destroy 1.19; 5.5
escape Rom 2.3; 2 Cor 11.33
faith 2.5; 8.9
fool [2] 1.20; 4.10
gift 2.14; 4.7
holy Rom 7.12; 2 Cor 7.1
jealous Rom 13.13; 10.22
life (1) Rom 16.4; 4.15
matter [2] Ps 10.4; 7.19
one another Rom 16.16; 6.8
prove 2.4; 4.4
quarrel 1.11; 2 Cor 7.5
real Rom 13.4; 16.9
reveal 1.7; 14.6
reward [2] Rom 2.6; Eph 6.8
save 1.18; 5.5
scripture [2] 2.9; 5.12
seed Lk 17.6; 9.11
servant Rom 15.16; 4.1
sight Rom 4.2; 2 Cor 4.2
sow [3] Jn 4.36; 9.11
Spirit (1) (God's Spirit) [2] 2.4; 6.11
Temple (1) (of God) [3] Acts 26.21; 6.19
test Acts 15.10; 10.9
trap Rom 11.9; 2 Cor 11.20
wisdom 2.4; 12.8
wise [4] 1.19; 4.10
world [6] 2.6; 4.9
worldly Lk 16.9; 7.33
worthless Rom 4.14; Eph 4.17

Servants of God

3 As a matter of fact, my brothers, I
could not talk to you as I talk to
people who have the Spirit; I had to talk
to you as though you belonged to this
world, as children in the Christian faith.
2 I had to feed you with milk, not solid
food, because you were not ready for it.
And even now you are not ready for it,
3 because you still live as the people of
this world live. When there is jealousy
among you and you quarrel with one
another, doesn't this prove that you belong to this world, living by its standards? 4 When one of you says, "I follow
Paul," and another, "I follow Apollos"—
aren't you acting like worldly people?

5 After all, who is Apollos? And who is
Paul? We are simply God's servants, by
whom you were led to believe. Each one
of us does the work which the Lord gave
him to do: 6 I sowed the seed, Apollos
watered the plant, but it was God who
made the plant grow. 7 The one who sows
and the one who waters really do not
matter. It is God who matters, because
he makes the plant grow. 8 There is no
difference between the man who sows
and the man who waters; God will reward each one according to the work he
has done. 9 For we are partners working
together for God, and you are God's field.

You are also God's building. 10 Using
the gift that God gave me, I did the work
of an expert builder and laid the foundation, and another man is building on it.
But each one must be careful how he
builds. 11 For God has already placed
Jesus Christ as the one and only foundation, and no other foundation can be laid.
12 Some will use gold or silver or precious
stones in building on the foundation;
others will use wood or grass or straw.
13 And the quality of each person's work
will be seen when the Day of Christ ex-
poses it. For on that Day fire will reveal
everyone's work; the fire will test it and
show its real quality. 14 If what was built
on the foundation survives the fire, the
builder will receive a reward. 15 But if
anyone's work is burnt up, then he will
lose it; but he himself will be saved, as if
he had escaped through the fire.

16 Surely you know that you are God's
temple and that God's Spirit lives in you!
17 So if anyone destroys God's temple,
God will destroy him. For God's temple is
holy, and you yourselves are his temple.

18 No one should fool himself. If anyone among you thinks that he is wise by
this world's standards, he should become
a fool, in order to be really wise. 19 For
what this world considers to be wisdom is
nonsense in God's sight. As the scripture
says, "God traps the wise in their cleverness"; 20 and another scripture says, "The
Lord knows that the thoughts of the wise
are worthless." 21 No one, then, should
boast about what men can do. Actually
everything belongs to you: 22 Paul,
Apollos, and Peter; this world, life and
death, the present and the future—all
these are yours, 23 and you belong to
Christ, and Christ belongs to God.

Apostles of Christ

4 You should think of us as Christ's
servants, who have been put in
charge of God's secret truths. 2 The one
thing required of such a servant is that
he be faithful to his master. 3 Now, I am
not at all concerned about being judged
by you or by any human standard; I don't
even pass judgement on myself. 4 My conscience is clear, but that does not prove
that I am really innocent. The Lord is the
one who passes judgement on me. 5 So
you should not pass judgement on anyone
before the right time comes. Final judgement must wait until the Lord comes; he
will bring to light the dark secrets and
expose the hidden purposes of people's
minds. And then everyone will receive
from God the praise he deserves.

6 For your sake, my brothers, I have
applied all this to Apollos and me, using
the two of us as an example, so that you
may learn what the saying means, "Observe the proper rules." None of you
should be proud of one person and despise another. 7 Who made you superior to
others? Didn't God give you everything
you have? Well, then, how can you boast,
as if what you have were not a gift?

8 Do you already have everything you
need? Are you already rich? Have you
become kings, even though we are not?
Well, I wish you really were kings, so
that we could be kings together with you.
9 For it seems to me that God has given
the very last place to us apostles, like
men condemned to die in public as a
spectacle for the whole world of angels
and of mankind. 10 For Christ's sake we
are fools; but you are wise in union with
Christ! We are weak, but you are strong!
We are despised, but you are honoured!
11 To this very moment we go hungry and
thirsty; we are clothed in rags; we are
beaten; we wander from place to place;
12 we wear ourselves out with hard work.
When we are cursed, we bless; when we

angel Rom 8.38; 6.3
apostle 1.1; 9.1
ashamed Rom 6.21; 2 Cor 9.4
beg Acts 27.22; 16.15
bless 1.7; 9.23
boast 3.21; 9.15
Christ [3] 3.23; 5.7
Christian [2] 3.1; 6.1
church 1.2; 6.4
clear Rom 3.5; 11.19
concern Rom 12.16; 7.32
condemn Rom 14.23; 11.32
conscience Rom 13.5; 8.7
curse Rom 12.14; 12.3
dark Rom 13.12; 2 Cor 4.4
dear [2] Rom 16.5; 10.14
deserve Rom 5.16; 15.9
despise [2] 1.28; 11.22
endure Rom 9.22; 9.12
example [2] Rom 15.5; 9.5
faithful [2] Rom 15.8; Gal 5.22
final Jn 11.4; 2 Thes 2.3
fool 3.18; 6.9
gentle Mt 11.29; 2 Cor 10.1
gift 3.10; 7.7
Good News 1.17; 9.12
hard Rom 16.6; 9.27
honour Rom 14.6; 12.24
human 2.4; 15.32
hunger Rom 12.20; 11.21
innocent Rom 16.18; 2 Cor 7.11
insult Rom 15.3; 2 Cor 6.8
judge [2] 2.14; 5.12
kind Rom 12.8; 13.4
Kingdom (1) (of God) Rom 14.17; 6.9
last (2) Rom 1.10; 15.8
learn 2.1; 14.31
life (1) [4] 3.22; 6.3
light (1) Rom 13.12; 2 Cor 4.2
love 2.9; 8.1
mankind 2.7; 2 Cor 5.19
master Rom 14.4; 7.4
mind (1) 2.2; 7.37
need Rom 16.2; 7.3
new Rom 7.6; 5.7
observe Dan 6.11; 2 Tim 3.10

3.2: Heb 5.12–13 **3.4:** 1 Cor 1.12 **3.6:** Acts 18.4–11, 24–28 **3.16:** 1 Cor 6.19; 2 Cor 6.16 **3.19:** Job 5.13 **3.20:** Ps 94.11 **4.12:** Acts 18.3

pass (5) [3] Rom 14.3; 5.3
persecute Rom 12.14; 15.9
power [2] 2.4; 5.3
praise Rom 15.6; 11.2
proper Rom 13.13; 7.35
proud [3] Rom 15.17; 5.2
prove 3.3; 9.2
purpose [2] 2.10; 2 Cor 2.4
remind Rom 15.15; 15.1
require Rom 3.20; Gal 2.16
rich 1.5; 2 Cor 6.10
right (1) Rom 14.21; 5.6
sake [2] Rom 11.28; 9.23
saying Jn 5.18; 5.6
secret [2] 2.1; 13.2
servant [2] 3.5; 2 Cor 2.17
spirit (2) 2.11; 5.3
strong 1.25; 7.36
teach 2.4; 7.17
truth 2.1; 5.8
union [3] 1.2; 9.2
weak 2.3; 8.7
wise 3.18; 6.5
wish Rom 10.1; 7.15
word (1) [2] 2.1; 9.15
world [2] 3.1; 5.10

are persecuted, we endure; 13 when we are insulted, we answer with kind words. We are no more than this world's refuse; we are the scum of the earth to this very moment!

14 I write this to you, not because I want to make you feel ashamed, but to instruct you as my own dear children. 15 For even if you have ten thousand guardians in your Christian life, you have only one father. For in your life in union with Christ Jesus I have become your father by bringing the Good News to you. 16 I beg you, then, to follow my example. 17 For this purpose I am sending to you Timothy, who is my own dear and faithful son in the Christian life. He will remind you of the principles which I follow in the new life in union with Christ Jesus and which I teach in all the churches everywhere.

18 Some of you have become proud because you have thought that I would not be coming to visit you. 19 If the Lord is willing, however, I will come to you soon, and then I will find out for myself the power which these proud people have, and not just what they say. 20 For the Kingdom of God is not a matter of words but of power. 21 Which do you prefer? Shall I come to you with a whip, or in a spirit of love and gentleness?

body [2] Rom 12.4; 6.13
bread [3] Rom 11.16; 10.3
celebrate Jn 10.22; Rev 11.10
Christ 4.1; 6.15
Day of the Lord 3.13; 2 Cor 1.13
destroy 3.17; 10.10
evil Rom 16.19; 10.6
fellowship [2] 1.9; 6.5
festival Acts 20.6; Col 2.16
greed [2] Rom 1.29; 6.10
guilty Rom 14.22; 6.18
heathen Acts 7.51; 6.1
idol [2] Rom 2.22; 6.9
immoral [4] Rom 13.13; 6.9
judge [3] 4.3; 6.1
lamb Acts 8.32; 1 Pet 1.19
letter (2) Rom 16.22; 16.3
name (2) (name of God, of Jesus) Rom 16.2; 2 Cor 11.31
new 4.17; 11.25
pagan Lk 22.25; 7.14
pass (5) 4.3; 2 Cor 1.9
Passover [3] Acts 12.4; Heb 11.28
power 4.19; 6.14
proud [2] 4.6; 8.1
pure [2] Acts 24.18; 6.11

right (1) 4.5; 7.35
rise Rom 14.9; 15.21
sacrifice Rom 12.1; 9.13
sad Acts 20.38; 7.30
Satan Rom 16.20; 7.
save 3.15; 7.16
saying 4.6; 15.32
scripture 3.19; 6.16
sex Rom 1.26; 6.13
slander Mk 7.22; 6.1
spirit (2) [3] 4.21; 7.34
terrible [2] Rom 7.13; 9.16
thief [2] Jn 12.6; 6.10
truth 4.1; 8.7
wicked Rom 11.26; 6.9
world 4.9; 6.2
worship (2) (of other gods) [2] Rom 11.4; 6.9
yeast [5] Lk 13.21; Gal 5.9

Immorality in the Church

5 Now, it is actually being said that there is sexual immorality among you so terrible that not even the heathen would be guilty of it. I am told that a man is sleeping with his stepmother! 2 How, then, can you be proud? On the contrary, you should be filled with sadness, and the man who has done such a thing should be expelled from your fellowship. 3-4 And even though I am far away from you in body, still I am there with you in spirit; and as though I were there with you, I have in the name of our Lord Jesus already passed judgement on the man who has done this terrible thing. As you meet together, and I meet with you in my spirit, by the power of our Lord Jesus present with us, 5 you are to hand this man over to Satan for his body to be destroyed, so that his spirit may be saved in the Day of the Lord.

6 It is not right for you to be proud! You know the saying, "A little bit of yeast makes the whole batch of dough rise." 7 You must remove the old yeast of sin so that you will be entirely pure. Then you will be like a new batch of dough without any yeast, as indeed I know you actually are. For our Passover Festival is ready, now that Christ, our Passover lamb, has been sacrificed. 8 Let us celebrate our Passover, then, not with bread having the old yeast of sin and wickedness, but with the bread that has no yeast, the bread of purity and truth.

9 In the letter that I wrote you I told you not to associate with immoral people. 10 Now I did not mean pagans who are immoral or greedy or are thieves or who worship idols. To avoid them you would have to get out of the world completely. 11 What I meant was that you should not associate with a person who calls himself a brother but is immoral or greedy or worships idols or is a slanderer or a drunkard or a thief. Don't even sit down to eat with such a person.

12-13 After all, it is none of my business to judge outsiders. God will judge them. But should you not judge the members of your own fellowship? As the scripture says, "Remove the evil man from your group."

adultery Rom 13.9; Heb 13.4
angel 4.9; 10.10
body [11] 5.3; 7.4
case (2) Rom 3.4
Christ [2] 5.7; 7.22
Christian [3] 4.15; 7.12
church 4.17; 7.17
commit Rom 13.9; 7.28
court (1) Acts 25.6
dare Rom 5.7; 2 Cor 10.12
death (2) (from death) Rom 10.7; 15.12
dedicate Rom 15.16; 7.34
dispute [3] Acts 26.3 1 Tim 6.4
fail 1.7; 13.7
fellowship 5.2; 7.24
fool 4.10; 15.33
glory 2.7; 10.31
God's people [2] 1.2; 14.21
greed 5.10; Eph 5.3
guilty 5.1; 10.8
heathen 5.1; 12.2
idol 5.10; 8.1
immoral [4] 5.1; 7.2
impossible 1.21; Heb 6.6
judge [6] 5.12; 10.15
Kingdom (1) (of God) [2] 4.20; 15.24
life (1) 4.15; 9.2
one another [2] 3.3; 11.33
pervert Rom 1.26; 1 Tim 1.10
physical Rom 2.27; 15.44
plain (1) 1.11; 2 Cor 7.12
possess [2] Rom 8.17; 15.50
power 5.3; 10.13

Lawsuits against Fellow-Christians

6 If one of you has a dispute with a fellow-Christian, how dare he go before heathen judges instead of letting God's people settle the matter? 2 Don't you know that God's people will judge the world? Well, then, if you are to judge the world, aren't you capable of judging small matters? 3 Do you not know that we shall judge the angels? How much more, then, the things of this life! 4 If such matters come up, are you going to take them to be settled by people who have no standing in the church? 5 Shame on you! Surely there is at least one wise person in your fellowship who can settle a dispute between fellow-Christians. 6 Instead, one Christian goes to court against another and lets unbelievers judge the case!

7 The very fact that you have legal disputes among yourselves shows that you have failed completely. Would it not be better for you to be wronged? Would it not be better for you to be robbed? 8 Instead, you yourselves wrong one another and rob one another, even your own brothers! 9 Surely you know that the wicked will not possess God's Kingdom. Do not fool yourselves; people who are immoral or who worship idols or are adulterers or homosexual perverts 10 or who steal or are greedy or are drunkards

4.16: 1 Cor 11.1; Phil 3.17 **5.1:** Deut 22.30 **5.6:** Gal 5.9 **5.7:** Ex 12.5 **5.8:** Ex 13.7; Deut 16.3 **5.13:** Deut 13.5, 17.7 (LXX)

prostitute [2]
Lk 15.30; Heb 11.31
provide Acts 24.23;
10.13
pure 5.7; 2 Cor 6.6
raise [2] Rom 15.28;
15.4
right with God 1.30;
Gal 2.16
rob [2] 1.17;
2 Cor 11.8
scripture 5.12; 10.7
serve Rom 16.1;
11.15
settle (2) [3]
Rom 9.28; 11.34
sex [2] 5.1; 10.7
shame 1.27; 11.6
slander 5.11;
2 Tim 3.3
slave Rom 8.15; 7.21
Spirit (1) (God's
Spirit) [2] 3.1; 7.40
spiritual 2.6; 9.11
steal Rom 13.9;
Tit 2.10
Temple (1) (of God)
3.16; 9.13
thief 5.10; 1 Thes 5.2
unbeliever
Rom 15.31; 7.12
wicked 5.8; Eph 6.12
wise 4.10; 2 Cor 11.19
world [2] 5.10; 7.31
worship (2) (of
other gods) 5.10; 10.7
wrong [2] Rom 14.20;
13.5

or who **slander** others or are **thieves**—
none of these will **possess God's Kingdom**. 11 Some of you were like that. But
you have been **purified** from sin; you
have been **dedicated** to God; you have
been put **right with God** by the Lord
Jesus Christ and by the **Spirit of our God**.

Use Your Bodies for God's Glory

12 Someone will say, "I am allowed to
do anything." Yes; but not everything is
good for you. I could say that I am
allowed to do anything, but I am not going to let anything make me its **slave**.
13 Someone else will say, "Food is for the
stomach, and the stomach is for food."
Yes; but God will put an end to both. The
body is not to be used for **sexual immorality**, but to **serve** the Lord; and the
Lord **provides** for the **body**. 14 God **raised**
the Lord **from death**, and he will also
raise us by his **power**.

15 You know that your bodies are
parts of the **body** of **Christ**. Shall I take a
part of **Christ's body** and make it part of
the **body** of a **prostitute**? **Impossible**!
16 Or perhaps you don't know that the
man who joins his **body** to a **prostitute** becomes **physically** one with her? The
scripture says quite **plainly**, "The two
will become one **body**." 17 But he who
joins himself to the Lord becomes **spiritually** one with him.

18 Avoid **immorality**. Any other sin a
man **commits** does not affect his **body**;
but the man who is **guilty** of **sexual immorality** sins against his own **body**.
19 Don't you know that your **body** is the
temple of the **Holy Spirit**, who lives in
you and who was given to you by God?
You do not belong to yourselves but to
God; 20 he bought you for a price. So use
your **bodies** for God's **glory**.

Questions about Marriage

accept [6] Rom 15.7;
9.2
act [2] 3.4; 10.29
agree [3] 1.10;
2 Cor 6.15
alone Rom 16.27;
Col 1.18
believer Acts 28.14;
14.22
body [3] 6.13; 9.27
Christ 6.15; 8.11
Christian [8] 6.1; 8.12
church 6.4; 10.32
circumcise [5]
Rom 4.9; Gal 2.3
command [2]
Rom 16.26; 14.37
commandment
Rom 13.9; Gal 5.14
commit [2] 6.18;
1 Thes 2.16

7 Now, to deal with the matters you
wrote about.
A man does well not to marry.[e] 2 But
because there is so much **immorality**,
every man should have his own wife, and
every woman should have her own hus-
band. 3 A man should **fulfil** his **duty** as a
husband, and a woman should **fulfil** her
duty as a wife, and **each** should **satisfy**
the other's **needs**. 4 A wife is not the
master of her own **body**, but her husband
is; in the same way a husband is not the
master of his own **body**, but his wife is.
5 Do not **deny** yourselves to **each other**,
unless you first **agree** to do so for a while
in order to spend your time in **prayer**;
but then resume normal marital **relations**. In this way you will be **kept from**
giving in to **Satan's temptation** because
of your lack of **self-control**.

6 I tell you this not as an order, but
simply as a concession. 7 Actually I would
prefer that all of you were as I am; but
each one has a **special gift** from God, one
person this **gift**, another one that gift.

8 Now, to the **unmarried** and to the
widows I say that it would be better for
you to continue to live **alone** as I do. 9 But
if you cannot restrain your **desires**, go
ahead and marry—it is better to marry
than to burn with **passion**.

10 For married people I have a **command** which is not my own but the
Lord's: a wife must not leave her husband; 11 but if she does, she must remain
single or else be reconciled to her husband; and a husband must not **divorce**
his wife.

12 To the others I say (I, myself, not
the Lord): if a **Christian** man has a wife
who is an **unbeliever** and she **agrees** to
go on living with him, he must not
divorce her. 13 And if a **Christian** woman
is married to a man who is an **unbeliever**
and he **agrees** to go on living with her,
she must not **divorce** him. 14 For the **unbelieving** husband is made **acceptable** to
God by being **united** to his wife, and the
unbelieving wife is made **acceptable** to
God by being **united** to her **Christian husband**. If this were not so, their children
would be like **pagan** children; but as it is,
they are **acceptable** to God. 15 However,
if the one who is not a **believer wishes** to
leave the **Christian** partner, let it be so.
In such cases the **Christian** partner,
whether husband or wife, is **free** to **act**.
God has called you to live in **peace**.
16 How can you be **sure**, **Christian wife**,
that you will not **save**[f] your husband? Or
how can you be **sure**, **Christian husband**,
that you will not **save**[f] your wife?

Live as God Called You

17 Each one should go on living
according to the Lord's **gift** to him, and
as he was when God called him. This is
the rule I **teach** in all the **churches**. 18 If a
circumcised man has **accepted** God's
call, he should not try to remove the
marks of **circumcision**; if an **uncircumcised** man has **accepted** God's call, he
should not get **circumcised**. 19 For

complete Rom 12.2;
9.27
concern [4] 4.3; 9.9
consider 3.19; 10.18
control Rom 8.5;
9.27
dedicate 6.11;
Eph 2.21
deny Acts 26.11;
1 Tim 3.16
desire Rom 13.9;
10.6
distress Lk 21.23;
2 Cor 2.4
divorce [3] Lk 16.18
duty (1) [2]
Rom 13.6; 9.17
each other [2]
Rom 12.5; Gal 5.15
fellowship 6.5;
2 Cor 13.13
force (1) Acts 28.19;
2 Cor 10.2
free [7] 1.30; 8.9
fulfil [2] Rom 13.6;
2 Thes 1.11
gift [3] 4.7; 12.1
happy [2] Rom 16.19;
12.26
help Rom 16.2; 10.23
immoral 6.9; 10.8
keep from
Rom 16.17; 9.27
last (1) Rom 11.25;
9.25
mark (1) Jn 6.27;
2 Cor 1.22
master [2] 4.2;
Eph 6.5
material (2)
Rom 15.27; 9.11
matter 3.7; Gal 5.6
mercy Rom 15.9;
2 Cor 1.3
mind (1) [2] 4.5; 14.14
need 4.8; 11.7
obey Rom 16.26; 9.21
pagan 5.10; 10.20
passion [2]
Rom 1.26; Gal 5.24
peace 1.3; 14.33
please [3] Rom 15.1;
10.5
prayer Acts 26.29;
14.16
proper [2] 4.6; 11.13
relations Rom 1.27;
8.8
rid Zech 13.2;
2 Cor 5.4
right (1) 5.6; 11.19
sad 5.2; 2 Cor 2.1
Satan 5.5; 2 Cor 2.11
satisfy Rom 13.14;
Gal 5.16
save [2] 5.5; 9.22
self-control
Acts 24.25; Gal 5.23
service Rom 16.3;
10.18
slave [4] 6.12; 9.19
spare Rom 11.21;
2 Cor 1.23
special Rom 9.21;
12.23
Spirit (1) (God's
Spirit) 6.11; 12.1
spirit (2) 5.3; 14.14
strong 4.10; 10.22
sure [2] 1.17; 16.10
teach 4.17; 11.2
tempt Lk 22.40;
Gal 6.1
trouble Rom 12.12;
10.32
trust 1.9; 2 Cor 13.6
unbeliever [4] 6.6;
10.27

[e] A man does well not to marry; *or* You say that a man does well not to marry.
[f] How can you be sure...that you will not save; *or* How do you know...that you will save.

6.12: 1 Cor 10.23 **6.16:** Gen 2.24 **6.19:** 1 Cor 3.16; 2 Cor 6.16
7.10-11: Mt 5.32, 19.9; Mk 10.11-12; Lk 16.18

unite [2] 1.10; Eph 2.16
unmarried [6] Acts 21.9
virgin Lk 1.34; 2 Cor 11.2
weep Rom 12.15; 2 Cor 12.21
widow Acts 9.39; 1 Tim 5.3
will (1) 1.1; 2 Cor 1.1
wish [2] 4.8; 12.11
world 6.2; 11.32
worldly [2] 3.4; 2 Cor 10.2
worry Acts 20.10; 2 Cor 2.13
worthy Acts 13.46; 1 Thes 2.4

whether or not a man is **circumcised**
means nothing; what **matters** is to **obey**
God's **commandments**. 20 Everyone
should remain as he was when he
accepted God's call. 21 Were you a **slave**
when God called you? Well, never mind;
but if you have a chance to become a
free man, use it.[g] 22 For a **slave** who has
been called by the Lord is the Lord's **free**
man; in the same way a **free** man who
has been called by **Christ** is his **slave**.
23 God bought you for a price; so do not
become **slaves** of men. 24 My brothers,
each one should remain in **fellowship**
with God in the same condition as he was
when he was called.

Questions about the Unmarried and the Widows

25 Now, concerning what you wrote
about **unmarried** people: I do not have a
command from the Lord, but I give my
opinion as one who by the Lord's **mercy**
is **worthy** of **trust**.

26 **Considering** the present **distress**, I
think it is better for a man to stay as he
is. 27 Have you got a wife? Then don't try
to get **rid** of her. Are you **unmarried**?
Then don't look for a wife. 28 But if you do
marry, you haven't **committed** a sin; and
if an **unmarried** woman marries, she
hasn't **committed** a sin. But I would
rather **spare** you the everyday **troubles**
that married people will have.

29 What I mean, my brothers, is this:
there is not much time left, and from
now on married men should live as
though they were not married; 30 those
who **weep**, as though they were not **sad**;
those who laugh, as though they were not
happy; those who buy, as though they did
not own what they bought; 31 those who
deal in **material** goods, as though they
were not fully occupied with them. For
this world, as it is now, will not **last** much
longer.

32 I would like you to be **free** from
worry. An **unmarried** man **concerns** himself with the Lord's work, because he is
trying to **please** the Lord. 33 But a
married man **concerns** himself with
worldly matters, because he wants to
please his wife; 34 and so he is pulled in
two directions. An **unmarried** woman or
a **virgin** **concerns** herself with the Lord's
work, because she wants to be **dedicated**
both in **body** and **spirit**; but a married
woman **concerns** herself with **worldly**
matters, because she wants to **please** her
husband.

35 I am saying this because I want to
help you. I am not trying to put restric-
tions on you. Instead, I want you to do
what is **right** and **proper**, and to give
yourselves completely to the Lord's service without any reservation.

36 In the case of an engaged couple
who have decided not to marry: if the
man feels that he is not **acting properly**
towards the girl and if his **passions** are
too **strong** and he feels that they ought to
marry, then they should get married, as
he wants to.[h] There is no sin in this. 37 But
if a man, without being **forced** to do so,
has firmly made up his **mind** not to
marry,[i] and if he has his **will** under **com-**
plete control and has already decided in
his own **mind** what to do—then he does
well not to marry the girl.[j] 38 So the man
who marries[k] does well, but the one who
doesn't marry[l] does even better.

39 A married woman is not **free** as
long as her husband lives; but if her husband dies, then she is **free** to be married
to any man she **wishes**, but only if he is a
Christian. 40 She will be **happier**, however,
if she stays as she is. That is my opinion,
and I think that I too have **God's Spirit**.

The Question about Food Offered to Idols

8 Now, concerning what you wrote
about food **offered** to **idols**.

It is **true**, of course, that "all of us have
knowledge," as they say. Such **know-**
ledge, however, puffs a person up with
pride; but **love** builds up. 2 Whoever
thinks he knows something really doesn't
know as he ought to know. 3 But the person who **loves** God is known by him.

4 So then, about eating the food
offered to **idols**: we know that an **idol**
stands for something that does not really
exist; we know that there is only the one
God. 5 Even if there are so-called "**gods**,"
whether in **heaven** or on earth, and even
though there are many of these "**gods**"
and "lords," 6 yet there is for us only one
God, the **Father**, who is the **Creator** of all
things and for whom we live; and there
is only one Lord, Jesus Christ, through
whom all things were **created** and
through whom we live.

7 But not everyone knows this **truth**.
Some people have been so used to **idols**
that to this day when they eat such food

action Rom 14.23; 2 Cor 11.15
Christ [2] 7.22; 9.12
Christian 7.12; 9.5
conscience [3] 4.4; 10.25
create Rom 11.36; 11.8
Creator Rom 1.25; Eph 3.9
defile Acts 24.6; Tit 1.15
encourage Rom 15.4; 14.3
exist Rom 13.1; 11.12
faith 3.1; 9.22
Father (2) (God) 1.3; 15.24
free 7.15; 9.1
god (2) (other gods) [2] Rom 11.4; 2 Cor 4.4
heaven Rom 10.6; 15.40
idol [7] 6.9; 10.7
knowledge [4] 1.5; 12.8
love [2] 4.21; 13.1
offer [3] Rom 15.16; 9.13
perish Ps 73.27; 2 Thes 2.10
proud 5.2; 13.4
relations 7.5; 2 Cor 1.12
stand for Lk 8.12; Gal 4.25

[g] but if you have a chance to become a free man, use it; *or* but even if you have a chance to become a free man, choose rather to make the best of your condition as a slave.
[h] an engaged couple...as he wants to; *or* a man and his unmarried daughter: if he feels that he is not acting properly towards her, and if she is at the right age to marry, then he should do as he wishes and let her get married. [i] not to marry; *or* not to let his daughter get married.
[j] marry the girl; *or* let her get married. [k] marries; *or* lets his daughter get married.
[l] doesn't marry; *or* doesn't let her get married.

temple (2) (of other gods) Rom 2.22
true Rom 15.8; 10.23
truth 5.8; 12.1
weak [5] 4.10; 9.22

they still think of it as food that belongs
to an idol; their conscience is weak, and
they feel they are defiled by the food.
8 Food, however, will not improve our
relations with God; we shall not lose anything if we do not eat, nor shall we gain
anything if we do eat.
9 Be careful, however, not to let your
freedom of action make those who are
weak in the faith fall into sin. 10 Suppose a
person whose conscience is weak in this
matter sees you, who have so-called
"knowledge," eating in the temple of an
idol; will not this encourage him to eat
food offered to idols? 11 And so this weak
person, your brother for whom Christ
died, will perish because of your "knowledge"! 12 And in this way you will be sinning against Christ by sinning against
your Christian brothers and wounding
their weak conscience. 13 So then, if food
makes my brother sin, I will never eat
meat again, so as not to make my
brother fall into sin.

Rights and Duties of an Apostle

accept 7.14; 2 Cor 6.17
altar Rom 11.3; 10.18
apostle [4] 4.9; 12.28
benefit Ezek 13.18; Eph 3.13
bless 4.12; 2 Cor 1.11
boast [2] 4.7; 2 Cor 3.1
body 7.4; 10.5
choose 2.7; 2 Cor 8.19
Christ [2] 8.11; 10.4
Christian 8.12; 16.15
claim [2] Acts 25.19; 15.29
complete 7.37; 13.12
concern 7.32; 12.25
control 7.37; 14.32
criticize Acts 11.2; 10.30
crown Jn 19.2; Heb 2.7
defend Rom 2.15; 2 Cor 6.7
discipline Zeph 3.2; Eph 6.4
duty (1) 7.3; 2 Cor 9.7
endure 4.12; 10.13
entrust Jer 13.20; 1 Thes 2.4
example [2] 4.6; 10.6
faith 8.9; 12.9
free [3] 8.9; 10.25
Gentile [2] 1.23; 10.32
Good News [2] 4.15; 15.1
gospel [5] Rom 16.19; 15.2
hard 4.12; 15.10
hope Rom 15.4; 13.7
Jew [2] 1.22; 10.32
keep from 7.5; 10.14
last (1) [2] 7.31; 2 Cor 3.11
law [6] Rom 13.8; 14.34
life (1) 6.3; 11.11
material (2) 7.31
means 2.10; 14.21
obey 7.19; 2 Cor 2.9
offer 8.1; 10.18
preach [4] 2.1; 13.2
privilege Rom 15.15; 2 Cor 8.4

9 Am I not a free man? Am I not an
apostle? Haven't I seen Jesus our
Lord? And aren't you the result of my
work for the Lord? 2 Even if others do
not accept me as an apostle, surely you
do! Because of your life in union with the
Lord you yourselves are proof of the fact
that I am an apostle.
3 When people criticize me, this is
how I defend myself: 4 Haven't I the right
to be given food and drink for my work?
5 Haven't I the right to follow the example of the other apostles and the
Lord's brothers and Peter, by taking a
Christian wife with me on my travels?
6 Or are Barnabas and I the only ones
who have to work for our living? 7 What
soldier ever has to pay his own expenses
in the army? What farmer does not eat
the grapes from his own vineyard? What
shepherd does not use the milk from his
own sheep?
8 I don't have to limit myself to these
everyday examples, because the Law
says the same thing. 9 We read in the
Law of Moses, "Do not muzzle an ox
when you are using it to thresh corn."
Now, is God concerned about oxen?
10 Didn't he really mean us when he said
that? Of course that was written for us.
The man who ploughs and the man who
reaps should do their work in the hope of
getting a share of the crop. 11 We have
sown spiritual seed among you. Is it too
much if we reap material benefits from
you? 12 If others have the right to expect
this from you, haven't we an even
greater right?
But we haven't made use of this right.
Instead, we have endured everything in
order not to put any obstacle in the way
of the Good News about Christ. 13 Surely
you know that the men who work in the
Temple get their food from the Temple
and that those who offer the sacrifices on
the altar get a share of the sacrifices.
14 In the same way, the Lord has ordered
that those who preach the gospel should
get their living from it.
15 But I haven't made use of any of
these rights, nor am I writing this now in
order to claim such rights for myself. I
would rather die first! Nobody is going to
turn my rightful boast into empty words!
16 I have no right to boast just because I
preach the gospel. After all, I am under
orders to do so. And how terrible it would
be for me if I did not preach the gospel!
17 If I did my work as a matter of free
choice, then I could expect to be paid;
but I do it as a matter of duty, because
God has entrusted me with this task.
18 What pay do I get, then? It is the
privilege of preaching the Good News
without charging for it, without claiming
my rights in my work for the gospel.
19 I am a free man, nobody's slave;
but I make myself everybody's slave in
order to win as many people as possible.
20 While working with the Jews, I live like
a Jew in order to win them; and even
though I myself am not subject to the
Law of Moses, I live as though I were
when working with those who are, in
order to win them. 21 In the same way,
when working with Gentiles, I live like a
Gentile, outside the Jewish Law, in order
to win Gentiles. This does not mean that
I don't obey God's law; I am really under
Christ's law. 22 Among the weak in faith I
become weak like one of them, in order
to win them. So I become all things to all
men, that I may save some of them by
whatever means are possible.
23 All this I do for the gospel's sake, in
order to share in its blessings. 24 Surely
you know that many runners take part in
a race, but only one of them wins the
prize. Run, then, in such a way as to win
the prize. 25 Every athlete in training submits to strict discipline, in order to be
crowned with a wreath that will not last;
but we do it for one that will last for ever.
26 That is why I run straight for the
finishing-line; that is why I am like a
boxer who does not waste his punches.
27 I harden my body with blows and bring
it under complete control, to keep myself

prize [2] Lk 15.23; Phil 3.12
prove 4.4; 14.22
race (2) Jer 12.5; 1 Tim 6.12
reap [2] Jn 4.36; Gal 6.7
result Rom 9.8; 2 Cor 12.6
right (3) [10] Rom 9.21; 2 Thes 3.9
sacrifice [2] 5.7; 10.18
sake 4.6; 10.28
save 7.16; 10.33
seed 3.6; 15.36
share [3] Rom 15.27; 10.16
sheep Rom 8.36; Heb 11.37
shepherd Acts 20.28; Heb 13.20
slave [2] 7.21; 12.13
sow 3.6; 15.36
spiritual 6.17; 10.4
subject (1) Jer 34.1; Gal 4.21
submit Rom 10.3; Gal 6.13
task Rom 15.28; 2 Cor 2.16
Temple (1) (of God) 6.19; 2 Cor 6.16
terrible 5.1; 2 Cor 1.10
turn Rom 3.12; 10.7
union 4.10; 15.22
vineyard Lk 20.9; Rev 6.6
weak 8.7; 11.30
win [7] Rom 3.4; Gal 1.10
word (1) 4.13; 14.9

9.9: Deut 25.4; 1 Tim 5.18 **9.11:** Rom 15.27 **9.13:** Deut 18.1 **9.14:** Mt 10.10; Lk 10.7

from being disqualified after having
called others to the contest.

Warnings against Idols

10 I want you to **remember**, my
brothers, what happened to our
ancestors who followed Moses. They
were all under the **protection** of the
cloud, and all passed **safely** through the
Red Sea. [2]In the **cloud** and in the sea
they were all **baptized** as **followers** of
Moses. [3]All ate the same spiritual **bread**
[4]and drank the same **spiritual** drink.
They drank from the **spiritual** rock that
went with them; and that rock was
Christ himself. [5]But even then God was
not **pleased** with most of them, and so
their **dead bodies** were **scattered** over
the desert.

6 Now, all this is an **example** for us, to
warn us not to **desire evil** things, as they
did, [7]nor to **worship idols**, as some of
them did. As the **scripture** says, "The
people sat down to a **feast** which **turned**
into an orgy of drinking and **sex**." [8]We
must not be **guilty** of **sexual immorality**,
as some of them were—and in one day
twenty-three thousand of them fell **dead**.
[9]We must not put the Lord[m] **to the test**,
as some of them did—and they were
killed by snakes. [10]We must not **complain**, as some of them did—and they
were **destroyed** by the **Angel of Death**.

11 All these things happened to them
as **examples** for others, and they were
written down as a **warning** for us. For we
live at a time when the end is about to
come.

12 Whoever thinks he is standing firm
had better be careful that he does not
fall. [13]Every **test** that you have **experienced** is the kind that normally
comes to people. But God keeps his **promise**, and he will not allow you to be
tested beyond your **power** to remain
firm; at the time you are put **to the test**,
he will give you the **strength** to **endure** it,
and so **provide** you with a way out.

14 So then, my **dear friends**, **keep
away from** the **worship of idols**. [15]I speak
to you as **sensible** people; **judge** for yourselves what I say. [16]The **cup** we use in
the Lord's Supper and for which we give
thanks to God: when we drink from it,
we are **sharing** in the **blood** of **Christ**. And
the **bread** we break: when we eat it, we
are **sharing** in the **body** of **Christ**. [17]Be-
cause there is the one loaf of **bread**, all of
us, though many, are one **body**, for we all
share the same loaf.

18 **Consider** the people of Israel; those
who eat what is **offered in sacrifice share**
in the **altar's service** to God. [19]Do I
imply, then, that an **idol** or the food
offered to it really amounts to anything?
[20]No! What I am saying is that what is
sacrificed on **pagan altars** is **offered** to
demons, not to God. And I do not want
you to be partners with **demons**. [21]You
cannot drink from the Lord's **cup** and
also from the **cup** of **demons**; you cannot
eat at the Lord's table and also at the
table of **demons**. [22]Or do we want to
make the Lord **jealous**? Do we think that
we are **stronger** than he?

23 "We are allowed to do anything," so
they say. That is **true**, but not everything
is good. "We are allowed to do anything"—but not everything is **helpful**.
[24]No one should be looking to his own
interests, but to the interests of others.

25 You are **free** to eat anything sold in
the meat-market, without asking any
questions because of your **conscience**.
[26]For, as the **scripture** says, "The earth
and everything in it belong to the Lord."

27 If an **unbeliever** invites you to a
meal and you decide to go, eat what is
set before you, without asking any **questions** because of your **conscience**. [28]But if
someone says to you, "This food was
offered to **idols**," then do not eat that
food, for the **sake** of the one who told you
and for **conscience' sake**—[29]that is, not
your own **conscience**, but the other person's conscience.

"Well, then," someone asks, "why
should my **freedom** to **act** be limited by
another person's **conscience**? [30]If I
thank God for my food, why should anyone **criticize** me about food for which I
give **thanks**?"

31 Well, whatever you do, whether you
eat or drink, do it all for God's **glory**.
[32]Live in such a way as to cause no
trouble either to **Jews** or **Gentiles** or to
the **church** of God. [33]Just do as I do; I try
to **please** everyone in all that I do, not
thinking of my own good, but of the good
of all, so that they might be **saved**.

11 Imitate me, then, just as I imitate
Christ.

Covering the Head in Worship

2 I **praise** you because you always
remember me and follow the **teachings**
that I have handed on to you. [3]But I want

act 7.15; 2 Cor 4.2
altar [2] 9.13; Heb 9.4
angel 6.3; 11.10
baptize 1.13; 12.13
blood Rom 9.3; 11.25
body [3] 9.27; 11.24
bread [3] 5.8; 11.23
Christ [3] 9.12; 11.1
church 7.17; 11.16
cloud [2] Acts 1.9; 1 Thes 4.17
complain Acts 25.24; 2 Cor 8.20
conscience [5] 8.7; 2 Cor 1.12
consider 7.26; Gal 3.6
criticize 9.3; Tit 2.8
cup [3] Jn 18.11; 11.25
dead [2] Rom 14.9; 15.12
dear 4.14; 15.58
death (1) 3.22; 11.26
demon [4] Jn 10.20; 1 Tim 4.1
desire 7.9; 2 Cor 5.2
destroy 5.5; 15.54
endure 9.12; 2 Cor 1.6
evil 5.12; 13.6
example [2] 9.5; Gal 3.15
experience Rom 5.2; Gal 3.4
feast Rom 11.9; Rev 19.9
follower Acts 9.1; 15.6
free [2] 9.1; 12.13
friend Rom 16.2; 2 Cor 4.9
Gentile 9.21; 12.13
glory 6.20; 11.7
guilty 6.18; 11.27
help 7.35; 12.28
idol [4] 8.1; 12.2
immoral 7.2; 2 Cor 12.21
interest (1) Dan 6.2; Gal 4.17
jealous 3.3; 13.4
Jew 9.20; 12.13
judge 6.1; 11.13
keep from 9.27; 12.15
offer [4] 9.13; 2 Cor 2.15
pagan 7.14; 2 Cor 6.16
please [2] 7.32; 2 Cor 5.9
power 6.14; 12.9
promise Rom 15.8; 2 Cor 1.18
protect Jn 17.12; 2 Cor 12.9
provide 6.13; 15.38
question [2] Rom 3.5
remember 1.16; 11.2
sacrifice [2] 9.13; Eph 1.7
safe Rom 15.31; Gal 2.5
sake [2] 9.23; 11.9
save 9.22; 15.2
scatter Acts 11.19; Jas 1.1
scripture [2] 6.16; 14.21
sense Lk 15.17; 15.34
service 7.35; 12.6
sex [2] 6.13; 2 Cor 12.21

share [4] 9.10; 12.26
spiritual [2] 9.11; 12.4
strength 1.25; 2 Cor 1.6
strong 7.36; 15.43
test [4] 3.13; 2 Cor 2.9
thank [3] 1.4; 11.24
trouble 7.28; 2 Cor 1.4
true 8.1; 11.18
turn 9.15; 2 Cor 3.16
unbeliever 7.12; 14.22
warn [2] Acts 20.21; Gal 5.3
worship (2) (of other gods) [2] 6.9; 12.2

angel 10.10; 13.1
argue Rom 14.1; 2 Cor 10.4
authority 1.10; 2 Cor 10.8
believe 3.5; 15.2
betray Acts 7.52
blood [2] 10.16; 15.50
body [3] 10.5; 12.12

[m] the Lord; *some manuscripts have* Christ.

10.1: Ex 13.21–22, 14.22–29 **10.3:** Ex 16.35 **10.4:** Ex 17.6; Num 20.11 **10.5:** Num 14.29–30
10.6: Num 11.4 **10.7:** Ex 32.6 **10.8:** Num 25.1–18 **10.9:** Num 21.5–6 **10.10:** Num 16.41–49
10.16: Mt 26.26–28; Mk 14.22–24; Lk 22.19–20 **10.18:** Lev 7.6 **10.20:** Deut 32.17 (LXX)
10.22: Deut 32.21 **10.23:** 1 Cor 6.12 **10.26:** Ps 24.1 **11.1:** 1 Cor 4.16; Phil 3.17

bread [5] 10.3; 2 Cor 9.10
Christ [4] 10.4; 12.12
church [2] 10.32; 12.28
clear 4.4; 14.8
condemn 4.9; 2 Cor 3.9
covenant Rom 11.27; 2 Cor 3.6
create [3] 8.6; 15.45
cup [5] 10.16; Rev 14.10
custom Acts 28.17
death (1) 10.10; 15.20
despise 4.6; Gal 4.14
disgrace [3] Acts 5.41; 14.35
dishonour Jn 8.49; Jas 2.6
doubt Rom 14.23; 2 Cor 4.8
exist 8.4; Col 1.17
glory [2] 10.31; 2 Cor 1.20
guilty 10.8; 1 Tim 5.12
harm Acts 28.5; 2 Cor 7.9
hunger [2] 4.11; 2 Cor 11.27
image Rom 1.23; 13.12
judge [5] 10.15; 14.24
life (1) 9.2; 15.19
message [2] 2.4; 12.8
nature Rom 13.14; Gal 4.19
need [2] 7.3; 12.21
new 5.7; 2 Cor 3.6
one another 6.8; 12.25
praise [3] 4.5; 12.26
pray [3] Rom 15.30; 14.13
proclaim [3] 2.6; 14.1
proper 7.35; 14.40
punish Rom 13.4; 2 Cor 2.6
remember 10.1; 2 Cor 7.15
right (1) 7.35; 15.34
sake 10.28; 2 Cor 4.5
seal Lk 22.20; Heb 9.20
serve 6.13; 12.5
settle (2) 6.1; Heb 6.16
shame [2] 6.5; 15.34
shave [2] Acts 21.24
supreme [3] Dan 11.36; 2 Cor 4.7
teach [3] 7.17; 14.6
thank 10.16; 14.16
true 10.23; 14.25
understand 2.14; 13.2
weak 9.22; 12.22
world 7.31; 14.10
worship (1) (of God) [5] 1.2; 14.19

you to **understand** that **Christ** is **supreme**
over every man, the husband is **supreme**
over his wife, and God is **supreme** over
Christ. 4 So a man who **prays** or **pro-**
claims God's **message** in public **worship**
with his head covered **disgraces Christ**.
5 And any woman who **prays** or **pro-**
claims God's **message** in public **worship**
with nothing on her head **disgraces** her
husband; there is no difference between
her and a woman whose head has been
shaved. 6 If the woman does not cover
her head, she might as well cut her hair.
And since it is a **shameful** thing for a
woman to **shave** her head or cut her hair,
she should cover her head. 7 A man has
no **need** to cover his head, because he reflects the **image** and **glory** of God. But
woman reflects the **glory** of man; 8 for
man was not **created** from woman, but
woman from man. 9 Nor was man
created for woman's sake, but woman
was **created** for man's **sake**. 10 On account
of the **angels**, then, a woman should have
a covering over her head to show that
she is under her husband's **authority**. 11 In
our **life** in the Lord, however, woman is
not independent of man, nor is man
independent of woman. 12 For as woman
was made from man, in the same way
man is born of woman; and it is God who
brings everything into **existence**.
13 **Judge** for yourselves whether it is
proper for a woman to **pray** to God in
public **worship** with nothing on her head.
14 Why, **nature** itself **teaches** you that long
hair on a man is a **disgrace**, 15 but on a
woman it is a thing of beauty. Her long
hair has been given her to **serve** as a
covering. 16 But if anyone wants to **argue**
about it, all I have to say is that neither
we nor the **churches** of God have any
other **custom** in **worship**.

The Lord's Supper
(Matt. 26.26–29; Mark 14.22–25;
Luke 22.14–20)

17 In the following instructions, however, I do not **praise** you, because your
meetings for **worship** actually do more
harm than good. 18 In the first place, I
have been told that there are opposing
groups in your meetings; and this I **be-**
lieve is partly **true**. 19 (No **doubt** there
must be divisions among you so that the
ones who are in the **right** may be **clearly**
seen.) 20 When you meet together as a
group, it is not the Lord's Supper that you
eat. 21 For as you eat, each one goes
ahead with his own meal, so that some
are **hungry** while others get drunk.
22 Haven't you got your own homes in
which to eat and drink? Or would you
rather **despise** the **church** of God and put
to **shame** the people who are in **need**?
What do you expect me to say to you
about this? Shall I **praise** you? Of course
I don't!
23 For I received from the Lord the
teaching that I passed on to you: that the
Lord Jesus, on the night he was **betrayed**,
took a piece of **bread**, 24 gave **thanks** to
God, broke it, and said, "This is my **body**,
which is for you. Do this in memory of
me." 25 In the same way, after the supper
he took the **cup** and said, "This cup is
God's **new covenant**, **sealed** with my
blood. Whenever you drink it, do so in
memory of me."
26 This means that every time you eat
this **bread** and drink from this **cup** you
proclaim the Lord's **death** until he
comes. 27 It follows that if anyone eats the
Lord's **bread** or drinks from his **cup** in a
way that **dishonours** him, he is **guilty** of
sin against the Lord's **body** and **blood**.
28 So then, everyone should examine himself first, and then eat the **bread** and
drink from the **cup**. 29 For if he does not
recognize the meaning of the Lord's **body**
when he eats the **bread** and drinks from
the **cup**, he brings **judgement** on himself
as he eats and drinks. 30 That is why
many of you are **weak** and ill, and
several have died. 31 If we would examine
ourselves first, we would not come under
God's **judgement**. 32 But we are **judged**
and **punished** by the Lord, so that we
shall not be **condemned** together with
the **world**.
33 So then, my brothers, when you
gather together to eat the Lord's Supper,
wait for **one another**. 34 And if anyone is
hungry, he should eat at home, so that
you will not come under God's **judgement**
as you meet together. As for the other
matters, I will **settle** them when I come.

Gifts from the Holy Spirit

12 Now, concerning what you wrote
about the **gifts** from the **Holy**
Spirit.
I want you to know the **truth** about
them, my brothers. 2 You know that while
you were still **heathen**, you were led
astray in many ways to the **worship of**
lifeless idols. 3 I want you to know that no
one who is led by **God's Spirit** can say "A
curse on Jesus!" and no one can **confess**
"Jesus is Lord," unless he is **guided** by
the **Holy Spirit**.
4 There are different kinds of **spiritual**
gifts, but the same **Spirit** gives them.
5 There are different ways of **serving**, but

apostle [2] 9.1; 15.5
baptize 10.2; 15.29
best Acts 24.16; Gal 1.13
body [18] 11.24; 13.3
care Acts 22.20; 2 Cor 8.20
Christ [2] 11.1; 15.3
church 11.16; 14.4
concern 9.9; 2 Cor 11.28
confess Rom 14.11; 14.25
curse 4.12; 16.22
direct Hab 1.14; Gal 5.16
disease Acts 19.12; Rev 6.8
faith 9.22; 13.2
free 10.25; 2 Cor 3.17
Gentile 10.32; 2 Cor 11.26

11.7: Gen 1.26–27 **11.8–9:** Gen 2.18–23 **11.25:** Ex 24.6–8; Jer 31.31–34 **12.4–11:** Rom 12.6–8

gift [6] 7.7; 13.2
guide Rom 2.19; Col 3.15
happy 7.30; 13.6
heal [3] Acts 28.8; Heb 12.13
heart Rom 12.11; 14.1
heathen 6.1; Eph 4.17
help 10.23; 14.3
honour 4.10; 2 Cor 6.8
idol 10.7; 2 Cor 6.16
important 1.28; 15.3
Jew 10.32; 2 Cor 11.24
keep from [2] 10.14; 2 Cor 2.7
knowledge 8.1; 13.2
message [3] 11.4; 13.8
miracle [3] 1.22; 2 Cor 12.12
need [4] 11.7; 13.2
one another 11.33; 16.20
power [4] 10.13; 14.2
praise 11.2; 2 Cor 6.8
presence 1.29; 2 Cor 2.10
prophet [2] Rom 16.26; Eph 2.20
serve 11.15; 16.16
service [2] 10.18; 15.58
share 10.16; 15.50
slave 9.19; Gal 2.4
special 7.7; 2 Cor 8.6
Spirit (1) (God's Spirit) [13] 7.40; 14.2
spiritual 10.4; 14.1
strange [3] Acts 19.6; 13.8
suffer Rom 8.17; 2 Cor 1.5
teacher [2] Rom 2.20; Gal 6.6
truth 8.7; 13.6
weak 11.30; 15.43
wisdom 3.19; 2 Cor 1.12
wish 7.15; 15.38
worship (2) (of other gods) 10.7; Gal 5.20
worth Lk 12.7; Phil 2.22

the same Lord is served. 6 There are different abilities to perform service, but the same God gives ability to all for their particular service. 7 The Spirit's presence is shown in some way in each person for the good of all. 8 The Spirit gives one person a message full of wisdom, while to another person the same Spirit gives a message full of knowledge. 9 One and the same Spirit gives faith to one person, while to another person he gives the power to heal. 10 The Spirit gives one person the power to work miracles; to another, the gift of speaking God's message; and to yet another, the ability to tell the difference between gifts that come from the Spirit and those that do not. To one person he gives the ability to speak in strange tongues, and to another he gives the ability to explain what is said. 11 But it is one and the same Spirit who does all this; as he wishes, he gives a different gift to each person.

One Body with Many Parts

12 Christ is like a single body, which has many parts; it is still one body, even though it is made up of different parts. 13 In the same way, all of us, whether Jews or Gentiles, whether slaves or free, have been baptized into the one body by the same Spirit, and we have all been given the one Spirit to drink.

14 For the body itself is not made up of only one part, but of many parts. 15 If the foot were to say, "Because I am not a hand, I don't belong to the body," that would not keep it from being a part of the body. 16 And if the ear were to say, "Because I am not an eye, I don't belong to the body," that would not keep it from being a part of the body. 17 If the whole body were just an eye, how could it hear? And if it were only an ear, how could it smell? 18 As it is, however, God put every different part in the body just as he wanted it to be. 19 There would not be a body if it were all only one part! 20 As it is, there are many parts but one body.

21 So then, the eye cannot say to the hand, "I don't need you!" Nor can the head say to the feet, "Well, I don't need you!" 22 On the contrary, we cannot do without the parts of the body that seem to be weaker; 23 and those parts that we think aren't worth very much are the ones which we treat with greater care; while the parts of the body which don't look very nice are treated with special modesty, 24 which the more beautiful parts do not need. God himself has put the body together in such a way as to give greater honour to those parts that need it. 25 And so there is no division in the body, but all its different parts have the same concern for one another. 26 If one part of the body suffers, all the other parts suffer with it; if one part is praised, all the other parts share its happiness.

27 All of you are Christ's body, and each one is a part of it. 28 In the church God has put all in place: in the first place apostles, in the second place prophets, and in the third place teachers; then those who perform miracles, followed by those who are given the power to heal or to help others or to direct them or to speak in strange tongues. 29 They are not all apostles or prophets or teachers. Not everyone has the power to work miracles 30 or to heal diseases or to speak in strange tongues or to explain what is said. 31 Set your hearts, then, on the more important gifts.

Best of all, however, is the following way.

Love

13 I may be able to speak the languages of men and even of angels, but if I have no love, my speech is no more than a noisy gong or a clanging bell. 2 I may have the gift of inspired preaching; I may have all knowledge and understand all secrets; I may have all the faith needed to move mountains—but if I have no love, I am nothing. 3 I may give away everything I have, and even give up my body to be burnt[n] —but if I have no love, this does me no good.

4 Love is patient and kind; it is not jealous or conceited or proud; 5 love is not ill-mannered or selfish or irritable; love does not keep a record of wrongs; 6 love is not happy with evil, but is happy with the truth. 7 Love never gives up; and its faith, hope, and patience never fail.

8 Love is eternal. There are inspired messages, but they are temporary; there are gifts of speaking in strange tongues, but they will cease; there is knowledge, but it will pass. 9 For our gifts of knowledge and of inspired messages are only partial; 10 but when what is perfect comes, then what is partial will disappear.

11 When I was a child, my speech, feelings, and thinking were all those of a child; now that I am a man, I have no more use for childish ways. 12 What we see now is like a dim image in a mirror;

angel 11.10; 2 Cor 11.14
body 12.12; 15.35
complete 9.27; 15.54
conceited Jer 48.29; 2 Tim 3.2
eternal Rom 16.26; 2 Cor 4.17
evil 10.6; 14.20
fail 6.7; 2 Cor 13.5
faith [3] 12.9; 15.1
gift [3] 12.1; 14.1
give up [2] Rom 1.27; 2 Cor 1.8
happy 12.26; 16.17
hope [2] 9.10; 15.19
image 11.7; Col 3.10
inspire [3] Mk 12.36; 14.6
jealous 10.22; 2 Cor 11.2
kind 4.13; 2 Cor 6.6
knowledge [4] 12.8; 14.6
love [11] 8.1; 14.1
message [2] 12.8; 14.1
need 12.21; 16.2
patient [2] Rom 15.4; 2 Cor 1.6
perfect Rom 12.2; 2 Cor 13.9
preach 9.14; 15.1
proud 8.1; 15.31
secret 4.1; 14.2
selfish Rom 7.8; 2 Cor 1.17
speech [2] 1.5; 2 Cor 8.7
strange 12.10; 14.2
truth 12.1; 14.2
understand 11.3; 14.2
way (3) Rom 11.33; 15.34
wrong 6.7; 2 Cor 6.14

[n] to be burnt; *some manuscripts have* in order to boast.

12.12: Rom 12.4–5 **12.28:** Eph 4.11 **13.2:** Mt 17.20, 21.21; Mk 11.23

then we shall see face to face. What I
know now is only partial; then it will be
complete—as complete as God's **knowledge** of me.
13 Meanwhile these three remain:
faith, **hope**, and **love**; and the greatest of
these is **love**.

More about Gifts from the Spirit

14 It is **love**, then, that you should
strive for. Set your **hearts** on
spiritual gifts, especially the **gift** of **proclaiming** God's **message**. 2 The one who
speaks in **strange tongues** does not speak
to others but to God, because no one
understands him. He is speaking **secret
truths** by the **power of the Spirit**. 3 But the
one who **proclaims** God's **message**
speaks to people and gives them **help**, **encouragement**, and **comfort**. 4 The one
who speaks in **strange tongues helps** only
himself, but the one who **proclaims** God's
message helps the whole **church**.
5 I would like all of you to speak in
strange tongues; but I would rather that
you had the **gift** of **proclaiming** God's
message. For the person who **proclaims**
God's **message** is of greater **value** than
the one who speaks in **strange tongues**—
**unless there is someone present who can
explain what he says, so that the whole
church** may be **helped**. 6 So when I come
to you, my brothers, what use will I be to
you if I speak in **strange tongues**? Not a
bit, unless I bring you some **revelation**
from God or some **knowledge** or some **inspired message**, or some **teaching**.
7 Take such lifeless musical instruments as the flute or the harp—how will
anyone know the tune that is being
played unless the notes are sounded dis-
tinctly? 8 And if the man who plays the
bugle does not sound a **clear** call, who
will prepare for battle? 9 In the same
way, how will anyone **understand** what
you are talking about if your **message**
given in **strange tongues** is not **clear**?
Your **words** will **vanish** in the air!
10 There are many different languages in
the **world**, yet none of them is without
meaning. 11 But if I do not know the
language being spoken, the person who
uses it will be a foreigner to me and I will
be a foreigner to him. 12 Since you are
eager to have the **gifts** of the **Spirit**, you
must try above everything else to make
greater use of those which **help** to build
up the **church**.
13 The person who speaks in **strange
tongues**, then, must **pray** for the **gift** to
explain what he says. 14 For if I **pray** in
this way, my **spirit** prays indeed, but my
mind has no part in it. 15 What should I
do, then? I will **pray** with my **spirit**, but I
will **pray** also with my **mind**; I will sing
with my **spirit**, but I will sing also with
my **mind**. 16 When you give **thanks** to God
in **spirit** only, how can an ordinary person taking part in the meeting say
"Amen" to your **prayer** of **thanksgiving**?
He has no way of knowing what you are
saying. 17 Even if your **prayer of thanks** to
God is quite good, the other person is not
helped at all.
18 I **thank** God that I speak in **strange
tongues** much more than any of you.
19 But in **church worship** I would rather
speak five **words** that can be **understood**,
in order to **teach** others, than speak
thousands of **words** in **strange tongues**.
20 Do not be like children in your
thinking, my brothers; be children so far
as **evil** is concerned, but be grown-up in
your thinking. 21 In the **Scriptures** it is
written,

"**By means of** men speaking **strange**
languages
I will speak to **my people**, says the
Lord.
I will speak through lips of foreigners,
but even then **my people** will not
listen to me."

22 So then, the **gift** of speaking in **strange**
tongues is **proof** for **unbelievers**, not for
believers, while the **gift** of **proclaiming**
God's **message** is **proof** for **believers**, not
for **unbelievers**.
23 If, then, the whole **church** meets together and everyone starts speaking in
strange tongues—and if some ordinary
people or **unbelievers** come in, won't
they say that you are all crazy? 24 But if
everyone is **proclaiming** God's **message**
when some **unbeliever** or ordinary person comes in, he will be **convinced** of his
sin by what he hears. He will be **judged**
by all he hears, 25 his **secret** thoughts will
be brought into the open, and he will **bow
down** and **worship** God, **confessing**,
"**Truly God is here among you!**"

Order in the Church

26 This is what I mean, my brothers.
When you meet for **worship**, one person
has a **hymn**, another a **teaching**, another
a **revelation** from God, another a **message in strange tongues**, and still another
the explanation of what is said. Everything must be of **help** to the **church**. 27 If
someone is going to speak in **strange**
tongues, two or three at the most should
speak, one after the other, and someone
else must explain what is being said.
28 But if no one is there who can explain,

14.21: Is 28.11–12

believer [2] 7.15; 15.18
bow (2) Acts 10.25; Rev 3.9
church [8] 12.28; 15.9
clear [2] 11.19; 15.27
comfort Acts 20.12; Phil 2.1
command 7.10; Phil 3.6
confess 12.3; Heb 13.15
control 9.27; Gal 5.13
convince 2.4; 16.12
disgrace 11.4; 2 Cor 6.8
eager Rom 12.10; 2 Cor 7.11
encourage [2] 8.10; 16.12
evil 13.6; 2 Cor 4.4
forbid Mt 16.22
gift [9] 13.2; 16.3
God's people [3] 6.1; 16.1
heart [2] 12.31; 2 Cor 1.22
help [7] 12.28; 16.1
hymn Acts 16.25; Eph 5.19
inspire 13.2; 1 Thes 5.20
judge [2] 11.13; 2 Cor 5.10
knowledge 13.2; 2 Cor 2.14
law 9.8; 15.56
learn 4.6; Eph 3.4
love 13.1; 16.14
means 9.22; 15.21
message [15] 13.8; 15.2
mind (1) [3] 7.37; 2 Cor 2.1
peace 7.15; 16.11
power 12.9; 15.24
pray [4] 11.4; 2 Cor 9.14
prayer [2] 7.5; 2 Cor 1.11
proclaim [10] 11.4; Phil 1.17
proper 11.13; 15.23
prove [2] 9.2; 2 Cor 7.11
reveal [2] 3.13; 2 Cor 12.1
scripture 10.7; 15.3
secret [2] 13.2; 15.51
Spirit (1) (God's Spirit) [2] 12.1; 15.45
spirit (2) [4] 7.34; 2 Cor 4.13
spiritual [2] 12.4; 15.24
strange [16] 13.8; Heb 13.9
teach [3] 11.2; Gal 1.12
thank [4] 11.24; 15.57
true 11.18; 15.13
truth 13.6; 15.20
unbeliever [4] 10.27; 2 Cor 6.14
understand [3] 13.2; 2 Cor 1.13
value 2.14; Phil 3.8
vanish Obad 16; 2 Pet 3.10

word (1) [4] 9.15; 15.27
world 11.32; 15.19
worship (1) (of God) [3] 11.4; Phil 3.3

then the one who speaks in **strange**
tongues must be quiet and speak only to
himself and to God. 29 Two or three who
are given God's **message** should speak,
while the others are to **judge** what they
say. 30 But if someone sitting in the meeting receives a **message** from God, the
one who is speaking should stop. 31 All of
you may **proclaim** God's **message**, one by
one, so that everyone will **learn** and be
encouraged. 32 The **gift** of **proclaiming**
God's **message** should be under the
speaker's **control**, 33 because God does
not want us to be in disorder but in
harmony and **peace**.

As in all the **churches** of **God's people**,
34 the women should keep quiet in the
meetings. They are not allowed to speak;
as the Jewish **Law** says, they must not be
in charge. 35 If they want to find out about
something, they should ask their husbands at home. It is a **disgraceful** thing
for a woman to speak in **church**.

36 Or could it be that the **word of God**
came from you? Or are you the only
ones to whom it came? 37 If anyone
supposes he is God's messenger or has a
spiritual gift, he must realize that what I
am writing to you is the Lord's **com-**
mand. 38 But if he does not pay attention
to this, pay no attention to him.

39 So then, my brothers, set your **heart**
on **proclaiming** God's **message**, but do
not **forbid** the speaking in **strange**
tongues. 40 Everything must be done in a
proper and orderly way.

The Resurrection of Christ

15 And now I want to **remind** you,
my brothers, of the **Good News**
which I **preached** to you, which you received, and on which your **faith** stands
firm. 2 That is the **gospel**, the **message**
that I **preached** to you. You are **saved** by
the **gospel** if you hold firmly to it—unless
it was for nothing that you **believed**.

3 I passed on to you what I received,
which is of the greatest **importance**: that
Christ died for our sins, as written in the
Scriptures; 4 that he was buried and that
he was **raised to life** three days later, as
written in the **Scriptures**; 5 that he
appeared to Peter and then to all twelve
apostles. 6 Then he appeared to more
than five hundred of his **followers** at
once, most of whom are still **alive**,
although some have died. 7 Then he
appeared to James, and afterwards to all
the **apostles**.

8 **Last** of all he appeared also to me—
even though I am like someone whose
birth was abnormal.[o] 9 For I am the **least**
of all the **apostles**—I do not even **deserve**
to be called an **apostle**, because I **per-**
secuted God's **church**. 10 But by God's
grace I am what I am, and the **grace** that
he gave me was not without effect. On
the contrary, I have worked **harder** than
any of the other **apostles**, although it was
not really my own doing, but God's **grace**
working with me. 11 So then, whether it
came from me or from them, this is what
we all **preach**, and this is what you **be-**
lieve.

Our Resurrection

12 Now, since our **message** is that
Christ has been **raised from death**, how
can some of you say that the **dead** will
not be **raised to life**? 13 If that is **true**, it
means that **Christ** was not **raised**; 14 and
if **Christ** has not been **raised from death**,
then we have nothing to **preach** and you
have nothing to **believe**. 15 More than
that, we are shown to be **lying** about God,
because we said that he **raised Christ**
from death—but if it is **true** that the **dead**
are not **raised to life**, then he did not
raise Christ. 16 For if the **dead** are not
raised, neither has **Christ** been **raised**.
17 And if **Christ** has not been **raised**, then
your **faith** is a delusion and you are still
lost in your sins. 18 It would also mean
that the **believers** in **Christ** who have
died are lost. 19 If our **hope** in **Christ** is
good for this **life** only and no more,[p] then
we **deserve** more **pity** than anyone else
in all the **world**.

20 But the **truth** is that **Christ** has been
raised from death, as the **guarantee** that
those who sleep in **death** will also be
raised. 21 For just as **death** came **by**
means of a man, in the same way the
rising from death comes **by means of** a
man. 22 For just as all people die because
of their **union with** Adam, in the same
way all will be **raised to life** because of
their **union with Christ**. 23 But each one
will be **raised** in his **proper** order: **Christ**,
first of all; then, at the time of his
coming, those who belong to him. 24 Then
the end will come; **Christ** will overcome
all **spiritual** rulers, **authorities**, and
powers, and will hand over the **Kingdom**
to God the **Father**. 25 For **Christ** must rule
until God defeats all **enemies** and puts
them under his feet. 26 The **last enemy** to

[o] whose birth was abnormal; *or* who was born at the wrong time.
[p] If our hope in Christ is good for this life only and no more; *or* If all we have in this life is our hope in Christ.

15.3: Is 53.5–12 **15.4:** Ps 16.8–10; Mt 12.40; Acts 2.24–32
15.5: Mt 28.16–17; Mk 16.14; Lk 24.34, 36; Jn 20.19 **15.8:** Acts 9.3–6 **15.9:** Acts 8.3 **15.25:** Ps 110.1

alive Rom 7.3; 2 Cor 1.8
apostle [5] 12.28; 2 Cor 1.1
authorities Rom 13.1; Eph 1.21
bad Rom 14.16; 2 Cor 4.9
baptize [2] 12.13; Gal 3.27
beast (1) Dan 7.3; Tit 1.12
being [3] Rom 9.5; 2 Cor 4.16
believe [3] 11.18; 2 Cor 1.24
believer 14.22; 2 Cor 6.15
birth Acts 22.28; Gal 2.15
blood 11.25; Phil 2.17
body [12] 13.3; 2 Cor 4.10
change [5] Rom 12.2; 2 Cor 5.5
Christ [17] 12.12; 2 Cor 1.5
church 14.4; 16.1
claim 9.15; 2 Cor 3.5
clear 14.8; 2 Cor 3.3

complete 13.12; 2 Cor 8.6
create 11.8; Eph 1.10
danger Rom 8.35; 2 Cor 1.10
dead [10] 10.5; 2 Cor 1.9
dear 10.14; 2 Cor 6.11
death (1) [8] 11.26; 2 Cor 1.9
death (2) (from death) [5] 6.14; Gal 1.1
declare [2] Rom 8.16; Heb 5.10
deserve [2] 4.5; 16.18
destroy 10.10; 2 Cor 4.9
enemy [2] Rom 12.20; 2 Cor 4.9
faith [2] 13.2; 16.13
Father (2) (God) 8.6; 2 Cor 1.2
flesh [3] Rom 9.3; 2 Tim 2.17
follower 10.2; Eph 4.21
fool [2] 6.9; 2 Cor 11.1
Good News 9.12; 2 Cor 2.12
gospel [2] 9.14; 2 Cor 4.3
grace [3] 1.3; 16.23
guarantee Rom 4.16; 2 Cor 1.22
hard 9.27; 2 Cor 2.5
heaven [6] 8.5; 2 Cor 5.1
hope [2] 13.7; 16.7
human [2] 4.3; 2 Cor 1.12
hurt [2] Rom 14.15; 2 Cor 4.9
immortal [4] Rom 2.7; 1 Tim 1.17
important 12.31; 2 Cor 11.7
Kingdom (1) (of God) [2] 6.9; Gal 5.21
last (2) [4] 4.9; 2 Cor 8.10
law 14.34; 2 Cor 3.6
least Lk 9.48; 2 Cor 11.5
lie (2) Rom 9.1; 2 Cor 6.8
life (1) [4] 11.11; 2 Cor 1.12
life (2) (to life) [8] Rom 14.9; 2 Cor 4.14
means [2] 14.21; 2 Cor 1.11
message [2] 14.1; 2 Cor 2.17
mortal [4] Rom 8.11; 2 Cor 4.10
motive Dan 11.27; 2 Cor 1.17
persecute 4.12; 2 Cor 12.10
physical [3] 6.16; 2 Cor 4.16
pity Rom 9.15; Phil 2.27
possess 6.9; 2 Cor 6.10
power [4] 14.2; 2 Cor 1.12
preach [4] 13.2; 2 Cor 1.19
proper [2] 14.40; Col 1.17
proud 13.4; 2 Cor 1.12
provide 10.13; 2 Cor 12.14
raise [22] 6.14; 16.1

remind 4.17; 2 Cor 1.8
right (1) 11.19; 2 Cor 6.14
rise 5.6; Gal 5.9
ruin Rom 14.15; 2 Cor 7.2
save 10.33; 16.2
saying 5.6; 1 Tim 1.15
scripture [5] 14.21; 2 Cor 3.16
secret 14.2; 2 Cor 4.2
seed [4] 9.11; 2 Cor 9.6
sense 10.15; 2 Cor 9.7
service 12.6; 16.15
shame 11.6; 2 Cor 4.2
share 12.26; 2 Cor 1.5
Son of God 1.9; 2 Cor 1.19
sow [2] 9.11; 2 Cor 9.6
Spirit (1) (God's Spirit) 14.2; 2 Cor 1.22
spiritual [5] 14.1; 2 Cor 4.7
strong 10.22; 16.13
thank 14.16; 2 Cor 1.3
true [4] 14.25; 2 Cor 6.6
truth [2] 14.2; 2 Cor 1.18
union [3] 9.2; 2 Cor 1.21
useless Acts 4.25; Col 2.22
victory [3] Rom 8.37; 2 Cor 2.14
way (3) 13.11; 2 Cor 7.9
weak 12.22; 2 Cor 10.10
wish 12.11; 2 Cor 11.1
word (1) 14.9; 2 Cor 4.2
world 14.10; 2 Cor 1.12

be defeated will be **death**. 27 For the **scrip-**
ture says, "God put *all* things under his
feet." It is **clear**, of course, that the **words**
"all things" do not include God himself,
who puts all things under **Christ**. 28 But
when all things have been placed under
Christ's rule, then he himself, the **Son**,
will place himself under God, who placed
all things under him; and God will rule
completely over all.
29 Now, what about those people who
are **baptized** for the **dead**? What do they
hope to accomplish? If it is **true**, as some
claim, that the **dead** are not **raised to life**,
why are those people being **baptized** for
the **dead**? 30 And as for us—why would
we run the risk of **danger** every hour?
31 My brothers, I face **death** every day!
The **pride** I have in you, in our **life** in
union with Christ Jesus our Lord, makes
me **declare** this. 32 If I have, as it were,
fought "wild **beasts**" here in Ephesus
simply from **human motives**, what have I
gained? But if the **dead** are not **raised to**
life, then, as the **saying** goes, "Let us eat
and drink, for tomorrow we will die."
33 Do not be **fooled**. "**Bad** companions
ruin good character." 34 Come back to
your **right senses** and stop your sinful
ways. I **declare** to your **shame** that some
of you do not know God.

The Resurrection Body

35 Someone will ask, "How can the
dead be **raised to life**? What kind of **body**
will they have?" 36 You **fool**! When you
sow a **seed** in the ground, it does not
sprout to **life** unless it dies. 37 And what
you **sow** is a bare **seed**, perhaps a grain
of wheat or some other grain, not the
full-bodied plant that will later grow up.
38 God **provides** that **seed** with the **body**
he **wishes**; he gives each **seed** its own
proper body.
39 And the flesh of living **beings** is not
all the same kind of **flesh**; **human beings**
have one kind of **flesh**, animals another,
birds another, and fish another.
40 And there are **heavenly bodies** and
earthly bodies; the beauty that belongs
to **heavenly bodies** is different from the
beauty that belongs to earthly **bodies**.
41 The sun has its own beauty, the moon
another beauty, and the stars a different
beauty; and even among stars there are
different kinds of beauty.
42 This is how it will be when the **dead**
are **raised to life**. When the **body** is
buried, it is **mortal**; when **raised**, it will
be **immortal**. 43 When buried, it is ugly
and **weak**; when **raised**, it will be beautiful and **strong**. 44 When buried, it is a
physical body; when **raised**, it will be a
spiritual body. There is, of course, a
physical body, so there has to be a
spiritual body. 45 For the **scripture** says,
"The first man, Adam, was **created** a
living **being**"; but the **last Adam** is the
life-giving Spirit. 46 It is not the **spiritual**
that comes first, but the **physical**, and
then the **spiritual**. 47 The first Adam,
made of earth, came from the earth; the
second Adam came from **heaven**.
48 Those who belong to the earth are like
the one who was made of earth; those
who are of **heaven** are like the one who
came from **heaven**. 49 Just as we wear the
likeness of the man made of earth, so we
will wear[q] the likeness of the Man from
heaven.
50 What I mean, brothers, is that what
is made of **flesh and blood** cannot **share**
in **God's Kingdom**, and what is **mortal**
cannot **possess immortality**.
51–52 Listen to this **secret truth**: we
shall not all die, but when the **last** trumpet sounds, we shall all be **changed** in an
instant, as quickly as the blinking of an
eye. For when the trumpet sounds, the
dead will be **raised**, never to die again,
and we shall all be **changed**. 53 For what
is **mortal** must be **changed** into what is
immortal; what will die must be **changed**
into what cannot die. 54 So when this
takes place, and the **mortal** has been
changed into the **immortal**, then the
scripture will come **true**: "**Death** is **des-**
troyed; **victory** is **complete**!"
55 "Where, **Death**, is your **victory**?
Where, **Death**, is your **power** to **hurt**?"
56 **Death** gets its **power** to **hurt** from sin,
and sin gets its **power** from the **Law**.
57 But **thanks** be to God who gives us the
victory through our Lord Jesus Christ!
58 So then, my **dear** brothers, stand
firm and steady. Keep busy always in
your work for the Lord, since you know
that nothing you do in the Lord's **service**
is ever **useless**.

The Offering for Fellow-Believers

16 Now, concerning what you wrote
about the money to be **raised** to
help God's people in Judaea. You must
do what I told the **churches** in Galatia to
do. 2 Every Sunday each of you must put
aside some money, in proportion to what
he has earned, and **save** it up, so that
there will be no **need** to collect money
when I come. 3 After I come, I shall give

alert Lk 21.36; Eph 6.18
approve Rom 14.18; 2 Cor 10.18
beg 4.16; 2 Cor 2.8
cheer (1) [2] Rom 12.8; 2 Cor 2.2
Christian [2] 9.5; 2 Cor 12.2
church [3] 15.9; 2 Cor 1.1
convince 14.24; 2 Cor 2.3

[q] we will wear; *some manuscripts have* let us wear.

15.27: Ps 8.6 **15.32:** Is 22.13 **15.45:** Gen 2.7 **15.51–52:** 1 Thes 4.15–17 **15.54:** Is 25.8
15.55: Hos 13.14 (LXX) **16.1:** Rom 15.25–26

curse 12.3; Gal 3.10
deserve 15.9; 2 Cor 5.10
encourage 14.3; 2 Cor 2.7
faith 15.1; 2 Cor 1.24
gift 14.1; 2 Cor 8.12
God's people [2] 14.21; 2 Cor 1.1
grace 15.10; 2 Cor 1.2
happy 13.6; 2 Cor 1.24
help [3] 14.3; 2 Cor 1.3
hope 15.19; 2 Cor 1.7
kiss Rom 16.16; 2 Cor 13.12
letter (2) 5.9; 2 Cor 2.3
look down on 1.28; 2 Cor 11.20
love [3] 14.1; 2 Cor 2.4
need 13.2; 2 Cor 2.10
notice (1) Acts 27.39
one another 12.25; 2 Cor 13.11
peace 14.33; 2 Cor 1.2
Pentecost Acts 20.16
raise 15.4; 2 Cor 1.9
real 3.13; 2 Cor 8.8
save 15.2; 2 Cor 1.10
serve 12.5; 2 Cor 3.6
service 15.58; 2 Cor 8.6
strong 15.43; 2 Cor 3.7
sure 7.16; 2 Cor 1.15
welcome Rom 14.1; 2 Cor 7.15

letters of introduction to the men you have **approved**, and send them to take your **gift** to Jerusalem. [4]If it seems worth while for me to go, then they can go along with me.

Paul's Plans

5 I shall come to you after I have gone through Macedonia—for I have to go through Macedonia. [6]I shall probably spend some time with you, perhaps the whole winter, and then you can **help** me to continue my journey, wherever it is I shall go next. [7]I want to see you more than just briefly in passing; I **hope** to spend quite a long time with you, if the Lord allows.

8 I will stay here in Ephesus until the day of **Pentecost**. [9]There is a **real** opportunity here for great and worthwhile work, even though there are many opponents.

10 If Timothy comes your way, be **sure** to make him feel **welcome** among you, because he is working for the Lord, just as I am. [11]No one should **look down on** him, but you must **help** him to continue his trip in **peace**, so that he will come back to me; for I am expecting him back with the brothers.

12 Now, about brother Apollos. I have often **encouraged** him to visit you with the other brothers, but he is not completely **convinced**[r] that he should go at this time. When he gets the chance, however, he will go.

Final Words

13 Be **alert**, stand firm in the **faith**, be brave, be **strong**. [14]Do all your work in **love**.

15 You know about Stephanas and his family; they are the first **Christian** converts in Achaia and have given themselves to the **service** of **God's people**. I **beg** you, my brothers, [16]to follow the leadership of such people as these, and of anyone else who works and **serves** with them.

17 I am **happy** about the coming of Stephanas, Fortunatus, and Achaicus; they have made up for your absence [18]and have **cheered** me up, just as they **cheered** you up. Such men as these **deserve notice**.

19 The **churches** in the province of Asia send you their greetings; Aquila and Priscilla and the **church** that meets in their house send warm **Christian** greetings. [20]All the brothers here send greetings.

Greet **one another** with a brotherly **kiss**.

21 With my own hand I write this: *Greetings from Paul.*

22 Whoever does not **love** the Lord—a **curse** on him!

Marana tha—Our Lord, come!

23 The **grace** of the Lord Jesus be with you.

24 My **love** be with you all in Christ Jesus.

[r]he is not completely convinced; *or* it is not at all God's will.

16.5: Acts 19.21 **16.8:** Lev 23.15–21; Deut 16.9–11 **16.8–9:** Acts 19.8–10 **16.10:** 1 Cor 4.17 **16.15:** 1 Cor 1.16 **16.19:** Acts 18.2

PAUL'S SECOND LETTER TO THE CORINTHIANS

INTRODUCTION

Paul's Second Letter to the Corinthians was written during a difficult period in his relations with the church at Corinth. Some members of the church had evidently made strong attacks against Paul, but he shows his deep longing for reconciliation and expresses his great joy when this is brought about.

In the first part of the letter Paul discusses his relationship with the church at Corinth, explaining why he had responded with severity to insult and opposition in the church and expressing his joy that this severity had resulted in repentance and reconciliation. Then he appeals to the church for a generous offering to help the needy Christians in Judaea. In the final chapters Paul defends his apostleship against a few people at Corinth who had set themselves up as true apostles, while accusing Paul of being a false one.

Outline of Contents

---

alive 1 Cor 15.6; Phil 1.24
apart Rom 8.29; Eph 2.12
apostle 1 Cor 15.5; 11.5
assure Rom 10.2; 8.3
believe 1 Cor 15.2; 4.4
bless [2] 1 Cor 9.23; 11.31
burden Rom 15.1; 8.13
Christ [3] 1 Cor 15.3; 2.10
church 1 Cor 16.1; 8.1
conscience 1 Cor 10.25; 4.2
danger 1 Cor 15.30; 4.11
Day of the Lord 1 Cor 5.5; Eph 4.30
dead 1 Cor 15.12; 6.9
death (1) [2] 1 Cor 15.20; 3.6
endure 1 Cor 10.13; 6.4
faith 1 Cor 16.13; 4.13
Father (2) (God) [3] 1 Cor 15.24; 6.18
give up 1 Cor 13.3; 2.7
glory 1 Cor 11.7; 3.7
God's people 1 Cor 16.1; 6.16
grace [2] 1 Cor 16.23; 4.15
guarantee 1 Cor 15.20; 5.5
happy 1 Cor 16.17; 2.3
heart [2] 1 Cor 14.1; 2.4
help [10] 1 Cor 16.1; 6.2
hope [4] 1 Cor 16.7; 3.12

1 From Paul, an apostle of Christ Jesus by God's will, and from our brother Timothy—

To the church of God in Corinth, and to all God's people throughout Achaia:

2 May God our Father and the Lord Jesus Christ give you grace and peace.

Paul Gives Thanks to God

3 Let us give thanks to the God and Father of our Lord Jesus Christ, the merciful Father, the God from whom all
help comes! 4 He helps us in all our
troubles, so that we are able to help others who have all kinds of troubles, using the same help that we ourselves
have received from God. 5 Just as we
have a share in Christ's many sufferings, so also through Christ we share in God's
great help. 6 If we suffer, it is for your
help and salvation; if we are helped, then you too are helped and given the strength to endure with patience the
same sufferings that we also endure. 7 So
our hope in you is never shaken; we know that just as you share in our sufferings, you also share in the help we receive.

8 We want to remind you, brothers, of the trouble we had in the province of Asia. The burdens laid upon us were so great and so heavy that we gave up all
hope of staying alive. 9 We felt that the
death sentence had been passed on us. But this happened so that we should rely, not on ourselves, but only on God, who
raises the dead. 10 From such terrible
dangers of death[a] he saved us, and will save us; and we have placed our hope in
him that he will save us again, 11 as you
help us by means of your prayers for us. So it will be that the many prayers for us will be answered, and God will bless us; and many will raise their voices to him in thanksgiving for us.

The Change in Paul's Plans

12 We are proud that our conscience assures us that our lives in this world, and especially our relations with you, have been ruled by God-given frankness[b] and sincerity, by the power of God's
grace, and not by human wisdom. 13–14 We
write to you only what you can read and understand. But even though you now understand us only in part, I hope that you will come to understand us completely, so that in the Day of our Lord Jesus you can be as proud of us as we shall be of you.

15 I was so sure of all this that I made plans at first to visit you, in order that
you might be blessed twice. 16 For I
planned to visit you on my way to Macedonia and again on my way back, in

human 1 Cor 15.32; 3.3
life (1) [2] 1 Cor 15.19; 2.16
mark (1) 1 Cor 7.18; Eph 4.30
means 1 Cor 15.21; 8.9
mercy 1 Cor 7.25; 4.1
motive 1 Cor 15.32; 10.2
pass (5) 1 Cor 5.3
patient 1 Cor 13.4; 6.4
peace 1 Cor 16.11; 13.11
plan [4] Rom 1.13; 2.11
power 1 Cor 15.24; 4.7
prayer [2] 1 Cor 14.16; 4.15
preach 1 Cor 15.1; 2.12
promise [2] 1 Cor 10.13; 7.1
proud [2] 1 Cor 15.31; 5.12
raise [2] 1 Cor 16.1; 4.14
relations 1 Cor 8.8; 13.4
rely Hos 7.8; 2 Tim 2.2
remind 1 Cor 15.1; 2 Tim 1.6
salvation Rom 11.11; 3.9
save [2] 1 Cor 16.2; 2.15
selfish 1 Cor 13.5; 12.20
sentence Acts 26.10; 2 Tim 4.17
share [4] 1 Cor 15.50; 5.14
sincere Rom 12.9; 2.17

[a] terrible dangers of death; *some manuscripts have* terrible death.
[b] frankness; *some manuscripts have* holiness.

1.1: Acts 18.1 **1.8:** 1 Cor 15.32 **1.16:** Acts 19.21

Son of God
1 Cor 15.28; Gal 1.16
spare 1 Cor 7.28;
Phil 2.27
**Spirit (1) (God's
Spirit)** 1 Cor 15.45;
3.3
strength 1 Cor 10.13;
Eph 1.19
suffer [4] 1 Cor 12.26;
4.17
sure [2] 1 Cor 16.10;
7.4
terrible 1 Cor 9.16;
2 Tim 3.11
thank [2] 1 Cor 15.57;
2.14
trouble [3]
1 Cor 10.32; 2.4
truth 1 Cor 15.20; 4.2
understand [3]
1 Cor 14.2; 10.11
union 1 Cor 15.22;
2.14
will (1) 1 Cor 7.37;
8.3
wisdom 1 Cor 12.8;
Eph 1.8
witness Rom 3.21;
13.1
world 1 Cor 15.19;
4.4

order to get **help** from you for my journey to Judaea. 17 In **planning** this, did I
appear fickle? When I make my **plans**,
do I make them from **selfish motives**,
ready to say "Yes, yes" and "No, no" at
the same time? 18 As surely as God
speaks the **truth**, my **promise** to you was
not a "Yes" and a "No." 19 For Jesus
Christ, the **Son of God**, who was **preached**
among you by Silas, Timothy, and myself,
is not one who is "Yes" and "No." On the
contrary, he is God's "Yes"; 20 for it is he
who is the "Yes" to all God's **promises**.
This is why through Jesus Christ our
"Amen" is said to the **glory** of God. 21 It is
God himself who makes us, together with
you, **sure** of our **life** in **union with Christ**;
it is God himself who has set us **apart**,
22 who has placed his **mark** of ownership
upon us, and who has given us the **Holy
Spirit** in our **hearts** as the **guarantee** of
all that he has in store for us.

23 I call God as my **witness**—he knows
my **heart**! It was in order to **spare** you
that I decided not to go to Corinth. 24 We
are not trying to dictate to you what you
must **believe**; we know that you stand
firm in the **faith**. Instead, we are working
with you for your own **happiness**.

beg 1 Cor 16.15; 6.1
cheer (1)
1 Cor 16.18; 7.7
Christ [7] 1.5; 3.3
convince
1 Cor 16.12; Col 4.12
deadly Rom 3.13;
Jas 3.8
distress 1 Cor 7.26;
11.29
encourage
1 Cor 16.12; 7.6
enough Acts 27.38;
9.8
forgive [3] Rom 4.7;
12.13
give up 1.8; Gal 6.9
glad Acts 13.48; 6.10
Good News
1 Cor 15.1; 4.4
happy [2] 1.24; 7.7
hard 1 Cor 15.10;
11.23
heart 1.22; 3.2
incense Lk 1.9;
Heb 9.4
keep from [2]
1 Cor 12.15; 4.4
knowledge
1 Cor 14.6; 4.6
letter (2) [2]
1 Cor 16.3; 3.1
life (1) 1.12; 3.6
love [2] 1 Cor 16.14;
5.14
message 1 Cor 15.2;
5.19
mind (1) 1 Cor 14.14;
3.14
need 1 Cor 16.2; 3.1
obey 1 Cor 9.21; 7.15
offer 1 Cor 10.18;
4.15
plan 1.15; 8.11
preach 1.19; 4.3
presence [2]
1 Cor 12.7; 4.14
prison Rom 16.7; 6.5

2 So I made up my **mind** not to come
to you again to make you **sad**. 2 For
if I were to make you **sad**, who would be
left to **cheer** me up? Only the very persons I had made **sad**. 3 That is why I
wrote that **letter** to you—I did not want
to come to you and be made **sad** by the
very people who should make me **glad**.
For I am **convinced** that when I am
happy, then all of you are **happy** too. 4 I
wrote to you with a greatly **troubled** and
distressed heart and with many **tears**;
my **purpose** was not to make you **sad**, but
to make you realize how much I **love** you
all.

Forgiveness for the Offender

5 Now, if anyone has made somebody
sad, he has not done it to me but to all of
you—in part at least. (I say this because I
do not want to be too **hard** on him.) 6 It is
enough that this person has been **punished** in this way by most of you. 7 Now,
however, you should **forgive** him and **encourage** him, in order to **keep him from**
becoming so **sad** as to **give up** completely. 8 And so I **beg** you to let him
know that you really do **love** him. 9 I
wrote you that **letter** because I wanted to
find out how well you had stood the **test**
and whether you are always ready to
obey my instructions. 10 When you **forgive**
someone for what he has done, I **forgive**
him too. For when I forgive—if, indeed, I
need to forgive anything—I do it in
Christ's presence because of you, 11 in
order to **keep Satan from** getting the
upper hand of us; for we know what his
plans are.

Paul's Anxiety in Troas

12 When I arrived in Troas to **preach**
the **Good News** about **Christ**, I found that
the Lord had opened the way for the
work there. 13 But I was deeply **worried**,
because I could not find our brother
Titus. So I said good-bye to the people
there and went on to Macedonia.

Victory through Christ

14 But **thanks** be to God! For in **union
with Christ** we are always led by God as
prisoners in **Christ's victory procession**.
God uses us to make the **knowledge**
about **Christ** spread everywhere like a
sweet fragrance. 15 For we are like a
sweet-smelling **incense offered** by **Christ**
to God, which spreads among those who
are being **saved** and those who are being
lost. 16 For those who are being lost, it is a
deadly stench that kills; but for those
who are being **saved**, it is a fragrance
that brings **life**. Who, then, is capable of
such a **task**? 17 We are not like so many
others, who handle God's **message** as if it
were cheap merchandise; but because
God has sent us, we speak with **sincerity**
in his **presence**, as **servants of Christ**.

punish 1 Cor 11.32;
6.9
purpose 1 Cor 4.5;
8.21
sad [7] 1 Cor 7.30;
6.10
Satan 1 Cor 7.5; 11.1
save [2] 1.10; 6.2
servant 1 Cor 4.1; 4.
sincere 1.12; Eph 6.
task 1 Cor 9.17; 5.18
tear (2) Acts 20.19;
Phil 3.18
test 1 Cor 10.9; 8.2
thank 1.3; 4.15
trouble 1.4; 4.8
union 1.21; 5.21
victory 1 Cor 15.54;
Phil 1.28
worry 1 Cor 7.32;
Gal 4.11

Servants of the New Covenant

3 Does this sound as if we were again
boasting about ourselves? Could it
be that, like some other people, we **need**
letters of recommendation to you or
from you? 2 You yourselves are the **letter**
we have, written on our **hearts** for everyone to know and read. 3 It is **clear** that
Christ himself wrote this **letter** and sent
it by us. It is written, not with ink but
with the **Spirit of the living God**, and not
on stone **tablets** but on **human hearts**.

4 We say this because we have **confidence** in God through **Christ**. 5 There is
nothing in us that allows us to **claim** that
we are capable of doing this work. The
capacity we have comes from God; 6 it is
he who made us capable of **serving** the
new covenant, which consists not of a
written **law** but of the **Spirit**. The written
law brings **death**, but the **Spirit** gives **life**.

7 The **Law** was carved in letters on
stone **tablets**, and God's **glory** appeared
when it was given. Even though the

boast 1 Cor 9.15; 5.12
bold Rom 15.15;
Eph 3.12
Christ [3] 2.10; 4.4
claim 1 Cor 15.29;
Phil 3.12
clear 1 Cor 15.27;
11.6
condemn
1 Cor 11.32; 7.3
confident Rom 1.16;
8.22
covenant [2]
1 Cor 11.25; Gal 3.17
death (1) [2] 1.9; 4.10
free 1 Cor 12.13; 8.3
glory [11] 1.20; 4.4
heart [2] 2.4; 4.6
hope 1.7; 5.11
human 1.12; 5.16
last (1) [2] 1 Cor 9.25;
4.18
law [5] 1 Cor 15.56;
Gal 2.16
letter (2) [3] 2.3; 7.8
life (1) 2.16; 4.10
mind (1) [3] 2.1; 4.4
need 2.10; 8.13
new 1 Cor 11.25; 5.17
salvation 1.6; 7.10
scripture 1 Cor 15.3;
4.13
serve 1 Cor 16.16;
Gal 1.15

1.19: Acts 18.5 **2.12-13:** Acts 20.1 **3.3:** Ex 24.12; Jer 31.33; Ezek 11.19, 36.26 **3.6:** Jer 31.31
3.7: Ex 34.29

Spirit (1) (God's Spirit) [7] 1.22; 5.5
strong 1 Cor 16.13; 7.15
tablet [2] Lk 1.63; Heb 9.4
turn 1 Cor 10.7; 9.3

brightness on Moses' face was fading, it
was so **strong** that the people of Israel
could not keep their eyes fixed on him. If
the **Law**, which brings **death** when it is in
force, came with such **glory**, 8 how much
greater is the glory that belongs to the
activity of the **Spirit**! 9 The system which
brings **condemnation** was **glorious**; how
much more **glorious** is the activity which
brings **salvation**! 10 We may say that because of the far brighter **glory** now the
glory that was so bright in the past is
gone. 11 For if there was **glory** in that
which **lasted** for a while, how much more
glory is there in that which **lasts** for
ever!

12 Because we have this **hope**, we are
very **bold**. 13 We are not like Moses, who
had to put a veil over his face so that the
people of Israel would not see the brightness fade and disappear. 14 Their **minds**,
indeed, were closed; and to this very day
their **minds** are covered with the same
veil as they read the books of the old
covenant. The veil is removed only when
a person is joined to **Christ**. 15 Even today,
whenever they read the **Law of Moses**,
the veil still covers their **minds**. 16 But it
can be removed, as the **scripture** says
about Moses: "His veil was removed
when he **turned to the Lord**."[c] 17 Now,
"the Lord" in this passage is the **Spirit**;
and where the **Spirit of the Lord** is present, there is **freedom**. 18 All of us, then,
reflect the **glory** of the Lord with uncovered faces; and that same **glory**,
coming from the Lord, who is the **Spirit**,
transforms us into his likeness in an ever
greater degree of **glory**.

Spiritual Treasure in Clay Pots

4 God in his **mercy** has given us this
work to do, and so we are not **discouraged**. 2 We put aside all **secret** and
shameful deeds; we do not **act** with **deceit**, nor do we **falsify** the **word of God**. In
the full **light** of **truth** we live in God's
sight and try to commend ourselves to
everyone's good **conscience**. 3 For if the
gospel we **preach** is hidden, it is hidden
only from those who are being lost.
4 They do not **believe**, because their
minds have been kept in the **dark** by the
evil god of this world. He **keeps them
from** seeing the **light** shining on them,
the **light** that comes from the **Good News**
about the **glory** of **Christ**, who is the exact likeness of God. 5 For it is not ourselves that we **preach**; we **preach** Jesus
Christ as Lord, and ourselves as your **servants** for Jesus' **sake**. 6 The God who said,
"Out of **darkness** the **light** shall shine!" is
the same God who made his **light** shine
in our **hearts**, to bring us the **knowledge**
of God's **glory** shining in the face of
Christ.

7 Yet we who have this **spiritual**
treasure are like common clay pots, in
order to show that the **supreme power**
belongs to God, not to us. 8 We are often
troubled, but not crushed; sometimes in
doubt, but never in **despair**; 9 there are
many **enemies**, but we are never without
a **friend**; and though **badly hurt** at times,
we are not **destroyed**. 10 At all times we
carry in our **mortal bodies** the **death** of
Jesus, so that his **life** also may be seen in
our **bodies**. 11 Throughout our **lives** we are
always in **danger** of **death** for Jesus' **sake**,
in order that his **life** may be seen in this
mortal body of ours. 12 This means that
death is at work in us, but **life** is at work
in you.

13 The **scripture** says, "I spoke because I **believed**." In the same **spirit** of
faith, we also speak because we **believe**.
14 We know that God, who **raised** the Lord
Jesus **to life**, will also **raise** us up with
Jesus and take us, together with you, into
his **presence**. 15 All this is for your **sake**;
and as God's **grace** reaches more and
more people, they will **offer** to the **glory**
of God more **prayers** of **thanksgiving**.

Living by Faith

16 For this **reason** we never become
discouraged. Even though our **physical
being** is gradually decaying, yet our
spiritual being is renewed day after day.
17 And this small and temporary **trouble**
we **suffer** will bring us a tremendous and
eternal glory, much greater than the
trouble. 18 For we fix our attention, not on
things that are seen, but on things that
are unseen. What can be seen **lasts** only
for a time, but what cannot be seen **lasts**
for ever.

5 For we know that when this tent we
live in—our **body** here on earth—is
torn down, God will have a house in
heaven for us to live in, a home he himself has made, which will **last** for ever.
2 And now we sigh, so great is our **desire**
that our home which comes from **heaven**
should be put on over us; 3 by being
clothed with it we shall not be without a
body. 4 While we live in this earthly tent,
we **groan** with a feeling of **oppression**; it
is not that we want to get **rid** of our
earthly **body**, but that we want to have
the **heavenly** one put on over us, so that
what is **mortal** will be transformed by

act 1 Cor 10.29; 8.10
bad 1 Cor 15.33; 5.10
being [2] 1 Cor 15.39; 5.17
believe [3] 1.24; Gal 2.16
body [3] 1 Cor 15.35; 5.1
Christ [2] 3.3; 5.10
conscience 1.12; 1 Tim 1.5
danger 1.10; 11.26
dark [2] 1 Cor 4.5; 6.14
death (1) [3] 3.6; 5.14
deceive Rom 16.18; 11.3
deed (2) Rom 15.18; Eph 2.10
despair Lk 21.25
destroy 1 Cor 15.54; 10.4
discourage [2] Lk 18.1; Eph 3.13
doubt 1 Cor 11.19; Heb 7.7
enemy 1 Cor 15.25; 5.18
eternal 1 Cor 13.8; Gal 6.8

evil 1 Cor 14.20; Gal 1.4
faith 1.24; 5.7
false Rom 11.4; 10.4
friend 1 Cor 10.14; 5.18
glory [4] 3.7; 8.19
god (2) (other gods) 1 Cor 8.5; Gal 4.8
Good News 2.12; 10.14
gospel 1 Cor 15.2; 8.18
grace 1.2; 6.1
heart 3.2; 5.11
hurt 1 Cor 15.55; Gal 5.15
keep from 2.7; 11.12
knowledge 2.14; 6.6
last (1) [2] 3.11; 5.1
life (1) [4] 3.6; 5.4
life (2) (to life) 1 Cor 15.4; 5.15
light (1) [5] 1 Cor 4.5; 6.14
mercy 1.3; Gal 1.13
mind (1) 3.14; 11.3
mortal [2] 1 Cor 15.42; 5.4
offer 2.15; Eph 5.2
physical 1 Cor 15.44; 12.7
power 1.12; 6.7
prayer 1.11; Eph 1.16
preach [3] 2.12; 8.18
presence 2.10; 12.19
raise [2] 1.9; 5.15
reason Rom 16.19; 5.12
sake [3] 1 Cor 11.9; 5.13
scripture 3.16; 8.15
secret 1 Cor 15.51; Eph 1.9
servant 2.17; 6.4
shame 1 Cor 15.34; 9.4
sight 1 Cor 3.19; 5.7
spirit (2) 1 Cor 14.14; 11.4
spiritual [2] 1 Cor 15.24; Gal 4.3
suffer 1.5; Eph 2.3
supreme 1 Cor 11.3; Eph 1.22
thank 2.14; 8.16
trouble [3] 2.4; 6.4
truth 1.18; 6.7
word (1) 1 Cor 15.27; 9.3
world 1.12; 10.3

appearance Lk 9.29; 10.7
bad 4.9; 2 Tim 3.13
being 4.16; Gal 4.8
boast 3.1; 7.14
body [6] 4.10; 7.1
change [3] 1 Cor 15.51; 7.9
Christ [9] 4.4; 6.15
courage [2] Acts 15.32; 7.4
death (1) 4.10; 7.10
deserve 1 Cor 16.18; 11.15
desire 1 Cor 10.6; Gal 5.13
enemy [2] 4.9; Gal 4.16
faith 4.13; 8.7
fear 1 Cor 2.3; 7.5
friend [5] 4.9; 6.11
groan Rom 8.22

[c] *Verse 16 may be translated:* But the veil is removed whenever someone turns to the Lord.

3.13: Ex 34.33 **3.16:** Ex 34.34 **4.6:** Gen 1.3 **4.13:** Ps 116.10 (LXX)

- guarantee 1.22; Eph 1.14
- heart 4.6; 6.11
- heaven [3] 1 Cor 15.40; 12.2
- hope 3.12; 8.5
- human [2] 3.3; 7.10
- judge [3] 1 Cor 14.24; 10.12
- last (1) 4.18; 9.9
- life (1) [3] 4.10; 13.4
- life (2) (to life) 4.14; Eph 2.5
- love 2.4; 6.6
- mankind 1 Cor 4.9; Gal 3.8
- message [2] 2.17; 6.7
- mortal 4.10; Phil 3.21
- new [2] 3.6; Gal 2.6
- oppress Lk 4.18; Jas 2.6
- persuade Acts 18.13; Gal 5.7
- plead Rom 11.2; 8.4
- please 1 Cor 10.5; 11.1
- proud 1.12; 7.4
- raise 4.14; 10.5
- reason 4.16; 11.12
- rid 1 Cor 7.27; Eph 4.22
- righteous Rom 14.17; 6.7
- sake [4] 4.5; 8.9
- share [3] 1.5; 9.13
- sight 4.2; 7.12
- Spirit (1) (God's Spirit) 3.3; 6.6
- task 2.16; Gal 2.7
- union 2.14; 13.4

life. 5 God is the one who has prepared us
for this change, and he gave us his Spirit
as the guarantee of all that he has in
store for us.
6 So we are always full of courage. We
know that as long as we are at home in
the body we are away from the Lord's
home. 7 For our life is a matter of faith,
not of sight. 8 We are full of courage and
would much prefer to leave our home in
the body and be at home with the Lord.
9 More than anything else, however, we
want to please him, whether in our home
here or there. 10 For all of us must appear
before Christ, to be judged by him. Each
one will receive what he deserves,
according to everything he has done,
good or bad, in his bodily life.

Friendship with God through Christ

11 We know what it means to fear the
Lord, and so we try to persuade others.
God knows us completely, and I hope
that in your hearts you know me as well.
12 We are not trying again to recommend
ourselves to you; rather, we are trying to
give you a good reason to be proud of us,
so that you will be able to answer those
who boast about a man's appearance and
not about his character. 13 Are we really
insane? It is for God's sake. Or are we
sane? Then it is for your sake. 14 We are
ruled by the love of Christ, now that we
recognize that one man died for everyone, which means that all share in his
death. 15 He died for all, so that those who
live should no longer live for themselves,
but only for him who died and was raised
to life for their sake.
16 No longer, then, do we judge anyone by human standards. Even if at one
time we judged Christ according to
human standards, we no longer do so.
17 When anyone is joined to Christ, he is a
new being; the old is gone, the new has
come. 18 All this is done by God, who
through Christ changed us from enemies
into his friends and gave us the task of
making others his friends also. 19 Our
message is that God was making all mankind his friends through Christ.[d] God did
not keep an account of their sins, and he
has given us the message which tells how
he makes them his friends.
20 Here we are, then, speaking for
Christ, as though God himself were
making his appeal through us. We plead
on Christ's behalf: let God change you
from enemies into his friends! 21 Christ
was without sin, but for our sake God
made him share our sin in order that in
union with him we might share the
righteousness of God.

6 In our work together with God, then,
we beg you who have received
God's grace not to let it be wasted. 2 Hear
what God says:

"When the time came for me to show
you favour
I heard you;
when the day arrived for me to save
you,
I helped you."

Listen! This is the hour to receive God's
favour; today is the day to be saved!
3 We do not want anyone to find fault
with our work, so we try not to put obstacles in anyone's way. 4 Instead, in
everything we do we show that we are
God's servants by patiently enduring
troubles, hardships, and difficulties. 5 We
have been beaten, imprisoned, and
mobbed; we have been overworked and
have gone without sleep or food. 6 By our
purity, knowledge, patience, and kindness we have shown ourselves to be
God's servants—by the Holy Spirit, by
our true love, 7 by our message of truth,
and by the power of God. We have
righteousness as our weapon, both to
attack and to defend ourselves. 8 We are
honoured and disgraced; we are insulted
and praised. We are treated as liars, yet
we speak the truth; 9 as unknown, yet we
are known by all; as though we were
dead, but, as you see, we live on. Although punished, we are not killed;
10 although saddened, we are always
glad; we seem poor, but we make many
people rich; we seem to have nothing,
yet we really possess everything.
11 Dear friends in Corinth! We have
spoken frankly to you; we have opened
our hearts wide. 12 It is not we who have
closed our hearts to you; it is you who
have closed your hearts to us. 13 I speak
now as though you were my children:
show us the same feelings that we have
for you. Open your hearts wide!

Warning against Pagan Influences

14 Do not try to work together as
equals with unbelievers, for it cannot be
done. How can right and wrong be partners? How can light and darkness live
together? 15 How can Christ and the
Devil agree? What does a believer have
in common with an unbeliever? 16 How
can God's temple come to terms with

- accept 1 Cor 9.2; 8.12
- agree 1 Cor 7.5; 12.16
- Almighty Rom 9.29; Jas 5.4
- beg 2.8; 8.4
- believer 1 Cor 15.18; Gal 2.4
- child of God Rom 9.4; Gal 3.26
- Christ 5.10; 8.23
- dark 4.4; Eph 4.18
- dead 1.9; Gal 2.19
- dear 1 Cor 15.58; 7.1
- defend 1 Cor 9.3; 7.7
- Devil Acts 13.10; Eph 4.27
- difficult Rom 5.7; 12.10
- disgrace 1 Cor 14.35; 1 Tim 3.7
- endure 1.6; Col 1.11
- Father (2) (God) 1.2; 11.31
- fault 1 Cor 1.8; 7.11
- favour [2] Acts 27.12; Gal 2.12
- friend 5.18; 7.1
- glad 2.3; 9.7
- God's people [2] 1.1; 8.4
- grace 4.15; 8.1
- heart [4] 5.11; 7.2
- help 1.3; 7.13
- honour 1 Cor 12.24; Phil 1.20
- idol 1 Cor 12.2; Gal 5.20
- insult 1 Cor 4.13; 12.10
- kind 1 Cor 13.4; 9.9
- knowledge 4.6; 8.7
- lie (2) 1 Cor 15.15; 11.3
- light (1) 4.2; 11.14
- love 5.14; 7.15
- message 5.19; Gal 2.2
- pagan 1 Cor 10.20
- patient [2] 1.6; 12.12
- poor Rom 15.26; 8.2
- possess 1 Cor 15.50; Gal 5.21
- power 4.7; 10.4
- praise 1 Cor 12.26; Gal 1.24
- prison 2.14; 11.23
- punish 2.6; 7.11
- pure 1 Cor 6.11; 7.1
- rich 1 Cor 4.8; 8.7
- right (1) 1 Cor 15.34; 8.21
- righteous 5.21; 11.15
- sad 2.1; 7.8
- save [2] 2.15; Eph 2.5
- separate Rom 9.3; Gal 4.17
- servant [2] 4.5; 11.15
- son *see* child of God
- Spirit (1) (God's Spirit) 5.5; 11.4
- Temple (1) (of God) [2] 1 Cor 9.13; Eph 2.21
- trouble 4.8; 7.4
- true 1 Cor 15.13; 7.14
- truth [2] 4.2; 7.14
- unbeliever [2] 1 Cor 14.22; 1 Tim 5.8
- unclean Rom 14.14; 7.1
- wrong 1 Cor 13.5; 7.2

[d] God was making all mankind his friends through Christ; *or* God was in Christ making all mankind his friends.

5.10: Rom 14.10 **6.2:** Is 49.8 **6.5:** Acts 16.23 **6.16:** Lev 26.12; Ezek 37.27; 1 Cor 3.16, 6.19

pagan idols? For we are the temple of
the living God! As God himself has said,
"I will make my home with my people
and live among them;
I will be their God,
and they shall be my people."
17 And so the Lord says,
"You must leave them
and separate yourselves from them.
Have nothing to do with what is
unclean,
and I will accept you.
18 I will be your father,
and you shall be my sons and
daughters,
says the Lord Almighty."

7 All these promises are made to us,
my dear friends. So then, let us
purify ourselves from everything that
makes body or soul unclean, and let us be
completely holy by living in awe of God.

Paul's Joy

2 Make room for us in your hearts. We
have wronged no one; we have ruined no
one, nor tried to take advantage of anyone. 3 I do not say this to condemn you;
for, as I have said before, you are so dear
to us that we are always together,
whether we live or die. 4 I am so sure of
you; I take such pride in you! In all our
troubles I am still full of courage; I am
running over with joy.
5 Even after we arrived in Macedonia,
we had no rest. There were troubles
everywhere, quarrels with others, fears
in our hearts. 6 But God, who encourages
the downhearted, encouraged us with the
coming of Titus. 7 It was not only his coming that cheered us, but also his report of
how you encouraged him. He told us how
much you want to see me, how sorry you
are, how ready you are to defend me;
and so I am even happier now.
8 For even if that letter of mine made
you sad, I am not sorry I wrote it. I could
have been sorry when I saw that it made
you sad for a while. 9 But now I am
happy—not because I made you sad, but
because your sadness made you change
your ways. That sadness was used by
God, and so we caused you no harm.
10 For the sadness that is used by God
brings a change of heart that leads to
salvation—and there is no regret in that!
But sadness that is merely human causes
death. 11 See what God did with this sadness of yours: how earnest it has made
you, how eager to prove your innocence!
Such indignation, such alarm, such feelings, such devotion, such readiness to
punish wrongdoing! You have shown
yourselves to be without fault in the
whole matter.
12 So, even though I wrote that letter,
it was not because of the one who did
wrong or the one who was wronged. Instead, I wrote it to make plain to you, in
God's sight, how deep your devotion to us
really is. 13 That is why we were
encouraged.
Not only were we encouraged; how
happy Titus made us with his happiness
over the way in which all of you helped
to cheer him up! 14 I did boast of you to
him, and you have not disappointed me.
We have always spoken the truth to you,
and in the same way the boast we made
to Titus has proved true. 15 And so his
love for you grows stronger, as he
remembers how all of you were ready to
obey his instructions, how you welcomed
him with fear and trembling. 16 How
happy I am that I can depend on you
completely!

Christian Giving

8 Our brothers, we want you to know
what God's grace has accomplished
in the churches in Macedonia. 2 They
have been severely tested by the troubles
they went through; but their joy was so
great that they were extremely generous
in their giving, even though they are
very poor. 3 I can assure you that they
gave as much as they could, and even
more than they could. Of their own free
will 4 they begged us and pleaded for the
privilege of having a part in helping
God's people in Judaea. 5 It was more
than we could have hoped for! First they
gave themselves to the Lord; and then,
by God's will they gave themselves to us
as well. 6 So we urged Titus, who began
this work, to continue it and help you
complete this special service of love.
7 You are so rich in all you have: in faith,
speech, and knowledge, in your eagerness to help and in your love for us.[e] And
so we want you to be generous also in
this service of love.
8 I am not laying down any rules. But
by showing how eager others are to help,
I am trying to find out how real your own
love is. 9 You know the grace of our Lord
Jesus Christ; rich as he was, he made
himself poor for your sake, in order to
make you rich by means of his poverty.
10 My opinion is that it is better for
you to finish now what you began last
year. You were the first, not only to act,
but also to be willing to act. 11 On with it,

advantage Rom 3.1; 11.20
awe Acts 2.43; Heb 12.28
boast [2] 5.12; 8.24
body 5.1; Gal 6.17
change [2] 5.5; Gal 1.7
cheer (1) [2] 2.2; Eph 6.7
condemn 3.9; Gal 1.8
courage 5.6; Phil 1.20
dear [2] 6.11; 12.19
death (1) 5.14; 11.23
defend 6.7; 12.19
depend Rom 9.16; Gal 3.10
devote [2] Rom 12.11; 11.3
disappoint Rom 10.11; 1 Pet 2.6
eager 1 Cor 14.12; 8.7
earnest Acts 12.5; Heb 13.19
encourage [5] 2.7; Eph 6.22
fault 6.3; Eph 1.4
fear [2] 5.11; Eph 6.5
friend 6.11; 11.26
happy [4] 2.3; 12.9
harm 1 Cor 11.17; Gal 5.15
heart [3] 6.11; Gal 4.6
help 6.2; 8.4
holy 1 Cor 3.17; Eph 1.4
human 5.16; 11.18
innocent 1 Cor 4.4; Phil 2.15
joy Rom 15.13; 8.2
letter (2) [2] 3.1; 10.9
love 6.6; 8.6
obey 2.9; 10.5
plain (1) 1 Cor 6.16; Gal 5.19
promise 1.18; 9.5
proud 5.12; 10.5
prove [2] 1 Cor 14.22; 9.13
punish 6.9; 10.6
pure 6.6; 11.2
quarrel 1 Cor 3.3; 12.20
remember 1 Cor 11.2; 9.6
rest (1) Lk 23.56; Heb 3.11
ruin 1 Cor 15.33; Eph 5.18
sad [8] 6.10; Eph 4.30
salvation 3.9; Eph 1.13
sight 5.7; 8.21
sorry [3] Mk 8.2
soul Lk 10.27; Phil 2.2

strong 3.7; 10.10
sure 1.15; 8.24
tremble 1 Cor 2.3; Eph 6.5
trouble [2] 6.4; 8.2
true 6.6; 10.3
truth 6.7; 11.10
unclean 6.17; Heb 9.13
way (3) 1 Cor 15.34; 2 Pet 2.2
welcome 1 Cor 16.10; 8.17
wrong [3] 6.14; 11.7

accept 6.17; 11.4
act 4.2; 10.2
assure 1.12; Eph 1.14
basis 1 Cor 2.14; Gal 3.22
beg 6.1; 10.1
boast 7.14; 9.2
burden 1.8; 11.9
care 1 Cor 12.23; Gal 4.2
choose 1 Cor 9.17; Gal 1.15
Christ 6.15; 9.13
church [5] 1.1; 11.8
complain 1 Cor 10.10; Phil 2.14
complete 1 Cor 15.54; 10.6
confident 3.4; Gal 5.10
eager [8] 7.11; 9.2
faith 5.7; 10.15
free [2] 3.17; Gal 1.4
generous [3] Rom 12.8; 9.9
gift [2] 1 Cor 16.3; 9.5
glory [2] 4.4; 9.13
God's people 6.16; 9.1
gospel 4.3; 9.13
grace [2] 6.1; 9.14
help [12] 7.13; 9.1
hope 5.11; 10.15
joy 7.4; Gal 4.27
knowledge 6.6; 10.5
last (2) 1 Cor 15.8; 9.2
love [6] 7.15; 9.7
means 1.11; Gal 1.1
need [2] 3.1; 9.1
plan 2.11; Eph 1.9
plead 5.20; Heb 7.25
plenty [2] Jn 3.23
poor [3] 6.10; Eph 4.28
poverty *see* **poor**
preach 4.3; 10.16
privilege 1 Cor 9.18; Eph 3.8
purpose 2.4; Gal 3.19
real 1 Cor 16.9; 11.13

[e] your love for us; *some manuscripts have* our love for you.

6.17: Is 52.11 **6.18:** 2 Sam 7.14; 1 Chr 17.13; Is 43.6; Jer 31.9 **7.5:** 2 Cor 2.13 **8.1-4:** Rom 15.26

relieve (1) Mic 1.12; 2 Thes 1.7
represent Zech 5.8; Gal 4.24
request Jn 19.31; 1 Tim 2.1
respect Rom 13.7; Eph 5.33
rich [3] 6.10; 9.10
right (1) [2] 6.14; 13.7
sake [2] 5.13; 12.10
scripture 4.13; 9.9
service [3] 1 Cor 16.15; 9.12
sight [2] 7.12; 2 Tim 2.15
special 1 Cor 12.23; 11.5
speech 1 Cor 13.1; Col 4.6
sure 7.4; 9.4
test [2] 2.9; 13.5
thank 4.15; 9.11
trouble 7.4; Gal 5.11
urge Rom 16.17; 9.5
welcome 7.15; Col 4.10
will (1) [3] 1.1; Gal 1.4

then, and finish the job! Be as **eager** to finish it as you were to **plan** it, and do it with what you now have. 12 If you are **eager** to give, God will **accept** your **gift** on the **basis** of what you have to give, not on what you haven't.

13–14 I am not trying to **relieve** others by putting a **burden** on you; but since you have **plenty** at this time, it is only fair that you should **help** those who are in **need**. Then, when you are in **need** and they have **plenty**, they will **help** you. In this way both are treated equally. 15 As the **scripture** says, "The one who gathered much did not have too much, and the one who gathered little did not have too little."

Titus and His Companions

16 How we **thank** God for making Titus as **eager** as we are to **help** you! 17 Not only did he **welcome** our **request**; he was so **eager** to **help** that of his own **free will** he decided to go to you. 18 With him we are sending the brother who is highly **respected** in all the **churches** for his work in **preaching** the **gospel**. 19 And besides that, he has been **chosen** and appointed by the **churches** to travel with us as we carry out this **service** of **love** for the **sake** of the Lord's **glory**, and in order to show that we want to **help**.

20 We are taking **care** not to stir up any **complaints** about the way we handle this **generous gift**. 21 Our **purpose** is to do what is **right**, not only in the **sight** of the Lord, but also in the **sight** of man.

22 So we are sending our brother with them; we have **tested** him many times and found him always very **eager** to **help**. And now that he has so much **confidence** in you, he is all the more **eager** to **help**. 23 As for Titus, he is my partner and works with me to **help** you; as for the other brothers who are going with him, they **represent** the **churches** and bring **glory** to **Christ**. 24 Show your **love** to them, so that all the **churches** will be **sure** of it and know that we are **right** in **boasting** about you.

affection Hos 11.4; 2 Pet 1.7
ashamed 1 Cor 4.14; 10.8
boast [2] 8.24; 10.8
bread 1 Cor 11.23; Heb 9.2
cause (2) Acts 26.9; Gal 2.17
Christ 8.23; 10.1
duty (1) 1 Cor 9.17; Eph 6.1
eager 8.7; Gal 2.10
enough [2] 2.6; 11.27

Help for Fellow-Christians

9 There is really no **need** for me to write to you about the **help** being sent to **God's people** in Judaea. 2 I know that you are willing to **help**, and I have **boasted** of you to the people in Macedonia. "The brothers in Achaia," I said, "have been ready to **help** since **last** year." Your **eagerness** has stirred up most of them. 3 Now I am sending these brothers, so that our **boasting** about you in this matter may not **turn** out to be empty **words**. But, just as I said, you will be ready with your **help**. 4 However, if the people from Macedonia should come with me and find out that you are not ready, how **ashamed** we would be—not to speak of your **shame**—for feeling so **sure** of you! 5 So I thought it was necessary to **urge** these brothers to go to you ahead of me and get ready in advance the **gift** you **promised** to make. Then it will be ready when I arrive, and it will show that you give because you want to, not because you have to.

6 **Remember** that the person who **sows** few **seeds** will have a small crop; the one who **sows** many **seeds** will have a large crop. 7 Each one should give, then, as he has decided, not with regret or out of a **sense** of **duty**; for God **loves** the one who gives **gladly**. 8 And God is able to give you more than you **need**, so that you will always have all you **need** for yourselves and more than **enough** for every good **cause**. 9 As the **scripture** says,

"He gives **generously** to the **needy**;
his **kindness lasts** for ever."

10 And God, who supplies **seed** to **sow** and **bread** to eat, will also supply you with all the **seed** you **need** and will make it grow and produce a **rich harvest** from your **generosity**. 11 He will always make you **rich enough** to be **generous** at all times, so that many will **thank** God for your **gifts** which they receive from us. 12 For this **service** you perform not only meets the **needs** of **God's people**, but also produces an outpouring of **gratitude** to God. 13 And because of the **proof** which this **service** of yours brings, many will give **glory** to God for your **loyalty** to the **gospel** of **Christ**, which you profess, and for your **generosity** in **sharing** with them and everyone else. 14 And so with deep **affection** they will **pray** for you because of the extraordinary **grace** God has shown you. 15 Let us **thank** God for his priceless **gift**!

generous [4] 8.2; 1 Tim 6.17
gift [3] 8.12; Gal 3.18
glad 6.10; 11.4
glory 8.19; Gal 1.5
God's people [2] 8.4; 13.12
gospel 8.18; 11.4
grace 8.1; 12.9
grateful Rom 16.4; 2 Tim 3.2
harvest Jn 4.35; Gal 6.8
help [4] 8.4; 11.8
kind 6.6; 10.1
last (1) 5.1; Gal 3.19
last (2) 8.10; 1 Thes 2.16
love 8.6; 11.11
loyal Rom 16.10; 10.(
need [6] 8.13; 11.9
pray 1 Cor 14.13; 12.
promise 7.1; 11.2
prove 7.11; 10.6
remember 7.15; Gal 2.10
rich [2] 8.7; Eph 1.18
scripture 8.15; 10.17
seed [4] 1 Cor 15.36; Jas 3.18
sense 1 Cor 15.34; 1 Tim 2.9
service [2] 8.6; Eph 4.12
shame 4.2; Eph 4.19
share 5.14; 13.4
sow [3] 1 Cor 15.36; Gal 6.7
sure 8.24; 10.2
thank [2] 8.16; Eph 1.3
turn 3.16; Gal 4.9
urge 8.6; Eph 4.1
word (1) 4.2; 10.10

Paul Defends His Ministry

10 I, Paul, make a personal appeal to you—I who am said to be meek and mild when I am with you, but harsh with you when I am away. By the **gentleness** and **kindness** of **Christ** I **beg** you 2 not to **force** me to be harsh when I come; for I am **sure** I can deal harshly with those who say that we **act** from **worldly motives**. 3 It is **true** that we live in the **world**, but we do not fight from **worldly motives**. 4 The weapons we use in our fight are not the **world's** weapons but

act [2] 8.10; 12.7
appearance 5.12; Gal 2.6
approve 1 Cor 16.3; 12.11
argue 1 Cor 11.16; Phil 2.14
ashamed 9.4; 11.21
authority [2] 1 Cor 11.10; 13.10
beg 8.4; 12.18
boast [5] 9.2; 11.10
captive Lk 4.18; Eph 4.8
Christ [5] 9.13; 11.2
compare Rom 8.18; Gal 6.4

8.15: Ex 16.18 **8.21:** Prov 3.4 (LXX) **9.9:** Ps 112.9 **9.10:** Is 55.10

complete 8.6; Eph 1.9
dare 1 Cor 6.1; 11.21
destroy [2] 4.9; Gal 1.13
faith 8.7; 13.5
false 4.2; 11.13
force (1) 1 Cor 7.37; Gal 2.3
fright Acts 22.29
gentle 1 Cor 4.21; Gal 6.1
Good News [2] 4.4; 11.7
hope 8.5; Gal 5.5
judge 5.10; 13.5
kind 9.9; Gal 5.22
knowledge 8.7; 11.6
letter (2) [3] 7.8; Col 4.16
loyal 9.13; 2 Tim 2.3
motive [2] 1.17; 12.18
obey 7.15; Gal 1.4
power 6.7; 12.9
preach 8.18; 11.4
proud 7.4; 12.7
prove 9.13; 12.12
punish 7.11; 13.2
raise 5.15; Gal 1.1
scripture 9.9; 13.1
strong 7.15; 12.10
stupid Jer 51.17; 2 Tim 3.9
sure 9.4; Eph 5.5
true 7.14; 11.13
understand 1.13; Gal 4.24
weak 1 Cor 15.43; 11.29
word (1) 9.3; 12.3
world [2] 4.4; Gal 3.22
worldly [2] 1 Cor 7.33; Tit 2.12

God's **powerful** weapons, which we use to **destroy** strongholds. We **destroy false arguments**; 5 we pull down every **proud** obstacle that is **raised** against the **knowledge** of God; we take every thought **captive** and make it **obey Christ**. 6 And after you have **proved** your **complete loyalty**, we will be ready to **punish** any **act** of disloyalty.

7 You are looking at the outward **appearance** of things. Is there someone there who reckons himself to belong to **Christ**? Well, let him think again about himself, because we belong to **Christ** just as much as he does. 8 For I am not **ashamed**, even if I have **boasted** somewhat too much about the **authority** that the Lord has given us—**authority** to build you up, not to tear you down. 9 I do not want it to appear that I am trying to **frighten** you with my **letters**. 10 Someone will say, "Paul's **letters** are severe and **strong**, but when he is with us in person, he is **weak**, and his **words** are nothing!" 11 Such a person must **understand** that there is no difference between what we write in our **letters** when we are away and what we will do when we are there with you.

12 Of course we would not **dare** to classify ourselves or **compare** ourselves with those who rate themselves so highly. How **stupid** they are! They make up their own standards to measure themselves by, and they **judge** themselves by their own standards! 13 As for us, however, our **boasting** will not go beyond certain limits; it will stay within the limits of the work which God has set for us, and this includes our work among you. 14 And since you are within those limits, we were not going beyond them when we came to you, bringing the **Good News** about **Christ**. 15 So we do not **boast** about the work that others have done beyond the limits God set for us. Instead, we **hope** that your **faith** may grow and that we may be able to do a much greater work among you, always within the limits that God has set. 16 Then we can **preach** the **Good News** in other countries beyond you and shall not have to **boast** about work already done in another man's field.

17 But as the **scripture** says, "Whoever wants to **boast** must boast about what the Lord has done." 18 For it is when the Lord thinks well of a person that he is really **approved**, and not when he thinks well of himself.

Paul and the False Apostles

11 I wish you would **tolerate** me, even when I am a bit **foolish**. **Please** do! 2 I am **jealous** for you, just as God is; you are like a **pure virgin** whom I have **promised** in marriage to one man only, **Christ** himself. 3 I am **afraid** that your **minds** will be **corrupted** and that you will **abandon** your full and **pure devotion** to **Christ**—in the same way that Eve was **deceived** by the snake's clever **lies**. 4 For you **gladly tolerate** anyone who comes to you and **preaches** a different Jesus, not the one we **preached**; and you **accept** a **spirit** and a **gospel** completely different from the **Spirit** and the **gospel** you received from us!

5 I do not think that I am the **least** bit inferior to those very **special** so-called "**apostles**" of yours! 6 Perhaps I am an amateur in speaking, but certainly not in **knowledge**; we have made this **clear** to you at all times and in all conditions.

7 I did not charge you a thing when I **preached** the **Good News** of God to you; I **humbled** myself in order to make you **important**. Was that **wrong** of me? 8 While I was working among you, I was paid by other **churches**. I was **robbing** them, so to speak, in order to **help** you. 9 And during the time I was with you I did not bother you for **help** when I **needed** money; the brothers who came from Macedonia brought me everything I **needed**. As in the past, so in the future: I will never be a **burden** to you! 10 By **Christ's truth** in me, I **promise** that this **boast** of mine will not be silenced anywhere in all Achaia. 11 Do I say this because I don't **love** you? God knows I **love** you!

12 I will go on doing what I am doing now, in order to **keep** those other "**apostles**" from having any **reason** for **boasting** and saying that they work in the same way that we do. 13 Those men are not **true apostles**—they are **false apostles**, who **lie** about their work and disguise themselves to look like **real apostles** of **Christ**. 14 Well, no wonder! Even **Satan** can disguise himself to look like an **angel of light**! 15 So it is no great thing if his **servants** disguise themselves to look like servants of **righteousness**. In the end they will get exactly what their **actions deserve**.

Paul's Sufferings as an Apostle

16 I repeat: no one should think that I am a **fool**. But if you do, at least **accept** me as a **fool**, so that I will have a little to

abandon Rom 11.23; 1 Tim 4.1
accept [2] 8.12; Gal 1.6
action 1 Cor 8.9; Gal 2.13
admit (1) Acts 24.14; Heb 11.13
advantage 7.2; 12.17
afraid Rom 13.3; 12.20
angel 1 Cor 13.1; Gal 1.8
apostle [5] 1.1; 12.11
arrest Acts 24.6
ashamed 10.8; Phil 3.19
bless 1.11; Gal 3.8
boast [8] 10.8; 12.1
burden 8.13; 12.16
Christ [5] 10.1; 12.9
church [2] 8.1; 12.13
clear 3.3; Gal 2.11
concern 1 Cor 12.25; Phil 2.21
corrupt Rom 1.28; Phil 2.15
danger [4] 4.11; Heb 6.8
dare [2] 10.12; Jude 9
death (1) 7.10; Gal 3.1
deceive 4.2; Gal 6.3
deserve 5.10; Phil 4.8
devote 7.11; Gal 1.13
distress 2.4; 2 Pet 2.7
enough 9.8; Phil 4.12
escape 1 Cor 3.15; 13.2
false [2] 10.4; Col 2.4
Father (2) (God) 6.18; Gal 1.1
flood Lk 17.27; 2 Pet 2.5
fool [6] 1 Cor 15.33; 12.6
friend 7.1; 12.19
Gentile 1 Cor 12.13; Gal 1.16
glad [2] 9.7; 12.15
Good News 10.14; Gal 1.16
gospel [2] 9.13; Gal 1.6
hard 2.5; Phil 4.3
Hebrew Rom 9.5; Phil 3.5
help [2] 9.1; 12.13
human 7.10; 12.3
humble Rom 12.16; Gal 5.23
hunger 1 Cor 11.21; Phil 4.12
important 1 Cor 15.3; Phil 1.24
jealous 1 Cor 13.4; 12.20
Jew [2] 1 Cor 12.13; Gal 1.13
keep from 4.4; 12.7
knowledge 10.5; Eph 4.13
least 1 Cor 15.9; Eph 3.8
lie (2) [3] 6.8; 12.16
light (1) 6.14; Eph 1.18
look down on 1 Cor 16.11; 1 Tim 4.12
love [2] 9.7; 12.15
mad Acts 26.24
mind (1) 4.4; Eph 1.18
name (2) (name of God, of Jesus) 1 Cor 5.3; Eph 4.17
need [2] 9.1; 12.9

10.17: Jer 9.24 **11.3:** Gen 3.1-5, 13 **11.9:** Phil 4.15-18

please 5.9; 12.13
preach [3] 10.16; Gal 1.8
prison 6.5; Gal 3.23
promise [2] 9.5; Gal 3.14
pure [2] 7.1; Eph 5.27
real 8.8; Gal 3.7
reason [2] 5.12; Eph 1.15
righteous 6.7; Gal 3.6
rob [2] 1 Cor 6.7; Eph 4.28
Satan 2.11; 12.7
servant [3] 6.4; Gal 1.10
shelter Acts 27.4
special 8.6; 12.11
Spirit (1) (God's Spirit) 6.6; 13.13
spirit (2) 4.13; Gal 4.3
tolerate [4] Rom 2.4; Eph 4.2
trap 1 Cor 3.19; 12.16
true 10.3; Gal 1.20
truth 7.14; 12.6
virgin 1 Cor 7.34; Rev 14.4
weak [2] 10.10; 12.5
wise 1 Cor 6.5; Eph 1.17
wish 1 Cor 15.38; 12.19
wrong 7.2; 13.7

boast of. 17 Of course what I am saying now is not what the Lord would like me to say; in this matter of **boasting** I am really talking like a **fool**. 18 But since there are so many who **boast** for merely **human reasons**, I will do the same. 19 You yourselves are so **wise**, and so you **gladly tolerate fools**! 20 You **tolerate** anyone who orders you about or takes **advantage** of you or **traps** you or **looks down on** you or slaps you in the face. 21 I am **ashamed** to **admit** that we were too timid to do those things!

But if anyone **dares** to **boast** about something—I am talking like a **fool**—I will be just as **daring**. 22 Are they **Hebrews**? So am I. Are they Israelites? So am I. Are they Abraham's descendants? So am I. 23 Are they **Christ's servants**? I sound like a **madman**—but I am a better **servant** than they are! I have worked much **harder**, I have been in **prison** more times, I have been whipped much more, and I have been near **death** more often. 24 Five times I was given the thirty-nine lashes by the **Jews**; 25 three times I was whipped by the Romans; and once I was stoned. I have been in three shipwrecks, and once I spent twenty-four hours in the water. 26 In my many travels I have been in **danger** from **floods** and from **robbers**, in **danger** from **fellow-Jews** and from **Gentiles**; there have been **dangers** in the cities, **dangers** in the wilds, dangers on the high seas, and dangers from **false friends**. 27 There has been work and toil; often I have gone without sleep; I have been **hungry** and thirsty; I have often been without **enough** food, **shelter**, or clothing. 28 And not to mention other things, every day I am under the pressure of my **concern** for all the **churches**. 29 When someone is **weak**, then I feel weak too; when someone is led into sin, I am filled with **distress**.

30 If I must **boast**, I will **boast** about things that show how **weak** I am. 31 The God and **Father** of the Lord Jesus—**blessed** be his **name** for ever!—knows that I am not **lying**. 32 When I was in Damascus, the governor under King Aretas placed guards at the city gates to **arrest** me. 33 But I was let down in a basket through an opening in the wall and **escaped** from him.

Paul's Visions and Revelations

12 I have to **boast**, even though it doesn't do any good. But I will now talk about **visions** and **revelations** given me by the Lord. 2 I know a certain **Christian** man who fourteen years ago was snatched up to the highest **heaven** (I do not know whether this actually happened or whether he had a **vision**—only God knows). 3-4 I repeat, I know that this man was snatched to **Paradise** (again, I do not know whether this actually happened or whether it was a **vision**—only God knows), and there he heard things which cannot be put into **words**, things that **human** lips may not speak. 5 So I will **boast** about this man—but I will not **boast** about myself, except the things that show how **weak** I am. 6 If I wanted to **boast**, I would not be a **fool**, because I would be telling the **truth**. But I will not **boast**, because I do not want anyone to have a higher opinion of me than he has as a **result** of what he has seen me do and heard me say.

7 But to **keep me from** being puffed up with **pride** because of the many **wonderful** things I saw, I was given a **painful physical** ailment, which **acts** as **Satan's** messenger to beat me and **keep me from** being **proud**. 8 Three times I **prayed** to the Lord about this and asked him to take it away. 9 But his answer was: "My **grace** is all you **need**, for my **power** is greatest when you are **weak**." I am most **happy**, then, to be **proud** of my **weaknesses**, in order to feel the **protection** of **Christ's power** over me. 10 I am content with **weaknesses**, **insults**, hardships, **persecutions**, and **difficulties** for **Christ's sake**. For when I am **weak**, then I am **strong**.

Paul's Concern for the Corinthians

11 I am **acting** like a **fool**—but you have made me do it. You are the ones who ought to show your **approval** of me. For even if I am nothing, I am in no way inferior to those very **special "apostles"** of yours. 12 The many **miracles** and **wonders** that **prove** that I am an **apostle** were performed among you with much **patience**. 13 How were you treated any **worse** than the other **churches**, except that I did not bother you for financial **help**? **Please forgive** me for being so unfair!

14 This is now the third time that I am ready to come to visit you—and I will not make any **demands** on you. It is you I want, not your money. After all, children should not have to **provide** for their parents, but parents should **provide** for their children. 15 I will be **glad** to spend all I have, and myself as well, in order to

act [3] 10.2; Gal 2.13
advantage [2] 11.20; 1 Thes 4.6
afraid [3] 11.3; Gal 2.12
agree 6.15; 13.11

apostle [2] 11.5; Gal 1.1
approve 10.18; Gal 1.10
beg 10.1; Gal 4.12
boast [5] 11.10; Gal 6.12
burden 11.9; Gal 6.2
Christ [3] 11.2; 13.3
Christian [2] 1 Cor 16.15; Gal 6.6
church 11.8; Gal 1.2
dear 7.1; Gal 4.19
defend 7.7; Phil 1.7
demand Rom 8.4; 1 Thes 2.7
difficult 6.4; 2 Tim 3.1
fool [2] 11.1; Gal 3.1
forgive 2.7; Eph 1.7
friend 11.26; Phil 2.12
glad 11.4; 13.9
grace 9.14; 13.13
happy 7.7; Gal 4.15
heaven 5.1; Gal 1.8
help [3] 11.8; Gal 6.2
human 11.18; Gal 1.11
humiliate Acts 8.33
immoral 1 Cor 10.8; Gal 5.19
insult [2] 6.8; Eph 4.31
jealous 11.2; Gal 5.20
keep from [2] 11.12; 2 Thes 2.6
lie (2) 11.3; Gal 1.20
love 11.11; 13.11
lust Ezek 23.5; Col 3.5
miracle 1 Cor 12.10; Gal 3.5
motive 10.2; Phil 1.18
need 11.9; Gal 2.10
pain Rom 9.2; Gal 4.19
Paradise Lk 23.43
patient 6.4; Gal 5.22
persecute 1 Cor 15.9; Gal 1.13
physical 4.16; Gal 4.14
please 11.1; Eph 5.2
power [2] 10.4; 13.3
pray 9.14; 13.7
presence [2] 4.14; Eph 2.18
protect 1 Cor 10.1; Jude 1
proud [4] 10.5; Gal 5.26
prove 10.6; 13.3
provide [2] 1 Cor 15.38; Eph 4.16
quarrel 5.7; Phil 1.15
repent Rom 2.4; 2 Tim 2.25
result 1 Cor 9.1; Gal 4.23
reveal 1 Cor 14.6; Gal 1.12
sake 8.9; Eph 3.1
Satan 11.14; 1 Thes 2.18
selfish 1.17; Phil 1.17
sex 1 Cor 10.7; Eph 5.3
special 11.5; Gal 2.9
strong 10.10; 13.9
trap 11.20; 1 Tim 3.7
truth 11.10; 13.8
vision [3] Acts 26.19; Col 2.18
weak [5] 11.29; 13.3
weep 1 Cor 7.30; Jas 4.9
wish 11.1; Gal 4.20
wonder (1) [2] Rom 15.19; Eph 1.18

11.23: Acts 16.23 **11.24:** Deut 25.3 **11.25:** Acts 16.22, 14.19 **11.26:** Acts 9.23, 14.15
11.32-33: Acts 9.23-25

word (1) 10.10; Eph 4.29
worse Jn 19.11; 1 Tim 5.8

help you. Will you **love** me less because I
love you so much?
16 You will **agree**, then, that I was not
a **burden** to you. But someone will say
that I was crafty, and **trapped** you with
lies. 17 How? Did I take **advantage** of you
through any of the messengers I sent?
18 I **begged** Titus to go, and I sent the
other **Christian brother** with him. Would
you say that Titus took **advantage** of
you? Do he and I not **act** from the very
same **motives** and behave in the same
way?
19 Perhaps you think that all along we
have been trying to **defend** ourselves
before you. No! We speak as **Christ**
would **wish** us to speak in the **presence** of
God, and everything we do, **dear friends,**
is done to **help** you. 20 I am **afraid** that
when I get there I will find you different
from what I would like you to be and you
will find me different from what you
would like me to be. I am **afraid** that I
will find **quarrelling** and **jealousy**, hot
tempers and **selfishness**, **insults** and gossip, **pride** and disorder. 21 I am **afraid** that
the next time I come my God will **humiliate** me in your **presence**, and I shall
weep over many who sinned in the past
and have not **repented** of the **immoral**
things they have done—their **lust** and
their **sexual** sins.

Final Warnings and Greetings

accuse Rom 8.33; 1 Tim 5.19
agree 12.16; Gal 2.9
authority [2] 10.8; Eph 1.21
Christ 12.9; Gal 1.4
cross (1) 1 Cor 2.2; Gal 2.19
death (3) (to death) Rom 8.13; Gal 2.19
escape 11.33; 1 Thes 5.3
evidence Acts 14.17; Heb 10.28

13 This is now the third time that I
am coming to visit you. "Any
accusation must be upheld by the **evidence** of two or more **witnesses**"—as the
scripture says. 2 I want to say to those of
you who have sinned in the past, and to
all the others; I said it before during my
second visit to you, but I will say it again
now that I am away: the next time I
come nobody will **escape punishment.**
3 You will have all the **proof** you want
that **Christ** speaks through me. When he
deals with you, he is not **weak**; instead,
he shows his **power** among you. 4 For
even though it was in **weakness** that he
was put **to death** on the **cross**, it is by
God's power that he lives. In **union with**
him we also are **weak**; but in our **relations** with you we shall **share God's
power** in his **life.**
5 Put yourselves **to the test** and **judge**
yourselves, to find out whether you are
living in **faith.** Surely you know that
Christ Jesus is in you?—unless you have
completely **failed.** 6 I **trust** you will know
that we are not **failures.** 7 We **pray** to God
that you will do no **wrong**—not in order
to show that we are a **success**, but so that
you may do what is **right**, even though
we may seem to be **failures.** 8 For we cannot do a thing against the **truth**, but only
for it. 9 We are **glad** when we are **weak**
but you are **strong.** And so we also **pray**
that you will become **perfect.** 10 That is
why I write this while I am away from
you; it is so that when I arrive I will not
have to deal harshly with you in using
the **authority** that the Lord has given
me—**authority** to build you up, not to tear
you down.
11 And now, my brothers, good-bye!
Strive for **perfection**; listen to my
appeals; **agree** with **one another**; live in
peace. And the God of **love** and **peace**
will be with you.
12 Greet **one another** with a brotherly
kiss.
All **God's people** send you their
greetings.
13 The **grace** of the Lord Jesus Christ,
the **love** of God, and the **fellowship** of the
Holy Spirit be with you all.

13.1: Deut 17.6, 19.15

fail [3] 1 Cor 13.7; Gal 2.2
faith 10.15; Gal 1.23
fellowship 1 Cor 7.24; Phil 2.1
glad 12.15; Phil 2.17
God's people 9.1; Gal 6.16
grace 12.9; Gal 1.3
judge 10.12; Gal 2.6
kiss 1 Cor 16.20; 1 Thes 5.26
life (1) 5.4; Gal 2.20
love [2] 12.15; Gal 2.20
one another [2] 1 Cor 16.20; Gal 5.13
peace [2] 1.2; Gal 1.3
perfect [2] 1 Cor 13.10; Phil 1.9
power [3] 12.9; Gal 2.8
pray [2] 12.8; Eph 3.1
prove 12.12; Phil 1.28
punish 10.6; Gal 5.10
relations 1.12; Rev 14.4
right (1) 8.21; Gal 4.4
scripture 10.17; Gal 3.6
share 9.13; Gal 6.6
Spirit (1) (God's Spirit) 11.4; Gal 3.2
strong 12.10; Eph 3.16
succeed (1) Rom 14.4; Phil 3.12
test 8.2; 1 Thes 2.4
trust 1 Cor 7.25; Phil 2.24
truth 12.6; Gal 2.5
union 5.21; Gal 2.4
weak [4] 12.5; Gal 4.9
witness 1.23; Phil 1.8
wrong 11.7; Gal 2.11

PAUL'S LETTER TO THE GALATIANS

INTRODUCTION

As the good news about Jesus began to be preached and welcomed among people who were not Jews, the question arose as to whether a person must obey the Law of Moses in order to be a true Christian. Paul had argued that this was not necessary—that in fact, the only sound basis for life in Christ was faith, by which all are put right with God. But among the churches of Galatia, a Roman province in Asia Minor, there had come people who opposed Paul and claimed that one must also observe the Law of Moses in order to be right with God.

Paul's Letter to the Galatians was written in order to bring back to true faith and practice those people who were being misled by this false teaching. Paul begins by defending his right to be called an apostle of Jesus Christ. He insists that his call to be an apostle came from God, not from any human authority, and that his mission was especially to the non-Jews. Then he develops the argument that it is by faith alone that people are put right with God. In the concluding chapters Paul shows that Christian conduct flows naturally from the love that results from faith in Christ.

Outline of Contents

---

accept [2] 2 Cor 11.4; 3.6
advice 1 Cor 2.16; Rev 3.18
age (1) Rom 16.25; Eph 3.9
angel 2 Cor 11.14; 3.19
apostle [3] 2 Cor 12.11; 2.8
approve [2] 2 Cor 12.11; Eph 6.6
best 1 Cor 12.31; Eph 4.3
change 2 Cor 7.9; Phil 3.21
choose 2 Cor 8.19; Eph 1.4
Christ [4] 2 Cor 13.3; 2.16
church [3] 2 Cor 12.13; Eph 1.22
condemn [2] 2 Cor 7.3; Col 2.18
death (2) (from death) 1 Cor 15.12; Eph 1.20
destroy [2] 2 Cor 10.4; 5.15
devote [2] 2 Cor 11.3; 1 Tim 4.15
evil 2 Cor 4.4; Eph 2.2
faith 2 Cor 13.5; 2.16
Father (2) (God) [3] 2 Cor 11.31; 4.6
free 2 Cor 8.3; 2.4
Gentile 2 Cor 11.26; 2.2
glory 2 Cor 9.13; Eph 1.6
Good News 2 Cor 11.7; 3.8

1 From Paul, whose call to be an
apostle did not come from man or
by means of man, but from Jesus Christ
and God the **Father**, who **raised** him
from death. 2 All the brothers who are
here join me in sending greetings to the
churches of Galatia:
3 May God **our Father** and the Lord
Jesus Christ give you **grace** and **peace**.
4 In order to **set us free** from this
present **evil age**, **Christ** gave himself for
our sins, in **obedience** to the **will of our**
God and Father. 5 To God be the **glory** for
ever and ever! Amen.

The One Gospel

6 I am surprised at you! In no time at
all you are deserting the one who called
you by the **grace of Christ**,[a] and are
accepting another **gospel**. 7 Actually,
there is no "other **gospel**," but I say this
because there are some people who are
upsetting you and trying to **change** the
gospel of Christ. 8 But even if we or an
angel from **heaven** should **preach** to you
a **gospel** that is different from the one we
preached to you, may he be **condemned**
to **hell**! 9 We have said it before, and now
I say it again: if anyone **preaches** to you
a **gospel** that is different from the one
you **accepted**, may he be **condemned** to
hell!
10 Does this sound as if I am trying to
win man's **approval**? No indeed! What I
want is God's **approval**! Am I trying to
be popular with men? If I were still trying to do so, I would not be a **servant** of
Christ.

How Paul Became an Apostle

11 Let me tell you, my brothers, that
the **gospel** I **preach** is not of **human**
origin. 12 I did not receive it from any
man, nor did anyone **teach** it to me. It
was Jesus Christ himself who **revealed** it
to me.
13 You have been told how I used to
live when I was **devoted** to the **Jewish**
religion, how I **persecuted** without **mercy**
the **church** of God and did my **best** to **des-**
troy it. 14 I was ahead of most **fellow-Jews**
of my age in my **practice** of the **Jewish**
religion, and was much more **devoted** to
the traditions of our ancestors.
15 But God in his **grace chose** me even
before I was born, and called me to **serve**
him. And when he decided 16 to **reveal his**
Son to me, so that I might **preach** the

gospel [6] 2 Cor 11.4; 2.2
grace [3] 2 Cor 13.13; 2.21
heaven 2 Cor 12.2; 4.14
hell [2] Acts 8.20; Phil 3.19
human 2 Cor 12.3; 4.4
Jew [3] 2 Cor 11.24; 2.7
lie (2) 2 Cor 12.16; Eph 4.25
means 2 Cor 8.9; 3.11
mercy 2 Cor 4.1; 6.16
obey 2 Cor 10.5; 3.10
peace 2 Cor 13.11; 5.22
persecute [2] 2 Cor 12.10; 4.29
practice Acts 19.19; 6.13
praise 2 Cor 6.8; Eph 1.6
preach [6] 2 Cor 11.4; 2.2
raise 2 Cor 10.5; Eph 1.20
religion [2] Acts 26.5; 1 Tim 1.9
reveal [2] 2 Cor 12.1; 2.2
servant 2 Cor 11.15; Eph 3.7
serve 2 Cor 3.6; 2.17
Son of God 2 Cor 1.19; 2.20
teach 1 Cor 14.6; 6.6
true 2 Cor 11.13; 4.18
upset Rom 16.17; 5.10
will (1) 2 Cor 8.3; Eph 1.1

[a] by the grace of Christ; *some manuscripts have* by his grace.

1.13: Acts 8.3, 22.4-5, 26.9-11 **1.14:** Acts 22.3 **1.15-16:** Acts 9.3-6, 22.6-10, 26.13-18

win 1 Cor 9.19; Phil 1.28

Good News about him to the Gentiles, I did not go to anyone for advice, 17 nor did I go to Jerusalem to see those who were apostles before me. Instead, I went at once to Arabia, and then I returned to Damascus. 18 It was three years later that I went to Jerusalem to obtain information from Peter, and I stayed with him for two weeks. 19 I did not see any other apostle except James,[b] the Lord's brother.

20 What I write is true. God knows that I am not lying!

21 Afterwards I went to places in Syria and Cilicia. 22 At that time the members of the churches in Judaea did not know me personally. 23 They knew only what others were saying: "The man who used to persecute us is now preaching the faith that he once tried to destroy!" 24 And so they praised God because of me.

Paul and the Other Apostles

2 Fourteen years later I went back to Jerusalem with Barnabas, taking Titus along with me. 2 I went because God revealed to me that I should go. In a private meeting with the leaders I explained the gospel message that I preach to the Gentiles. I did not want my work in the past or in the present to be a failure. 3 My companion Titus, even though he is Greek, was not forced to be circumcised, 4 although some wanted it done. Pretending to be fellow-believers, these men slipped into our group as spies, in order to find out about the freedom we have through our union with Christ Jesus. They wanted to make slaves of us, 5 but in order to keep the truth of the gospel safe for you, we did not give in to them for a minute.

6 But those who seemed to be the leaders—I say this because it makes no difference to me what they were; God does not judge by outward appearances—those leaders, I say, made no new suggestions to me. 7 On the contrary, they saw that God had given me the task of preaching the gospel to the Gentiles, just as he had given Peter the task of preaching the gospel to the Jews. 8 For by God's power I was made an apostle to the Gentiles, just as Peter was made an apostle to the Jews. 9 James, Peter, and John, who seemed to be the leaders, recognized that God had given me this special task; so they shook hands with Barnabas and me, as a sign that we were all partners. We agreed that Barnabas and I would work among the Gentiles and they among the Jews. 10 All they asked was that we should remember the needy in their group, which is the very thing I have[c] been eager to do.

Paul Rebukes Peter at Antioch

11 But when Peter came to Antioch, I opposed him in public, because he was clearly wrong. 12 Before some men who had been sent by James arrived there, Peter had been eating with the Gentile brothers. But after these men arrived, he drew back and would not eat with the Gentiles, because he was afraid of those who were in favour of circumcising them. 13 The other Jewish brothers also started acting like cowards along with Peter; and even Barnabas was swept along by their cowardly action. 14 When I saw that they were not walking a straight path in line with the truth of the gospel, I said to Peter in front of them all, "You are a Jew, yet you have been living like a Gentile, not like a Jew. How, then, can you try to force Gentiles to live like Jews?"

Jews and Gentiles Are Saved by Faith

15 Indeed, we are Jews by birth and not "Gentile sinners," as they are called. 16 Yet we know that a person is put right with God only through faith in Jesus Christ, never by doing what the Law requires. We, too, have believed in Christ Jesus in order to be put right with God through our faith in Christ, and not by doing what the Law requires. For no one is put right with God by doing what the Law requires. 17 If, then, as we try to be put right with God by our union with Christ, we are found to be sinners as much as the Gentiles are—does this mean that Christ is serving the cause of sin? By no means! 18 If I start to rebuild the system of Law that I tore down, then I show myself to be someone who breaks the Law. 19 So far as the Law is concerned, however, I am dead—killed by the Law itself—in order that I might live for God. I have been put to death with Christ on his cross, 20 so that it is no longer I who live, but it is Christ who lives in me. This life that I live now, I live by faith in the Son of God, who loved me and gave his life for me. 21 I refuse to reject the grace of God. But if a person is put right with God through the Law, it means that Christ died for nothing!

[b] any other apostle except James; *or* any other apostle; the only other person I saw was James.
[c] have; *or* had.

1.18: Acts 9.26–30 **2.1:** Acts 11.30, 15.2 **2.6:** Deut 10.17 **2.16:** Ps 143.2; Rom 3.20, 22

act 2 Cor 12.7; 3.19
action 2 Cor 11.15; 5.19
afraid 2 Cor 12.20; Phil 1.28
agree 2 Cor 13.11; 3.15
apostle [2] 1.1; Eph 1.1
appearance 2 Cor 10.7; Jas 2.1
believe 2 Cor 4.4; 3.2
believer 2 Cor 6.15; Eph 4.25
birth 1 Cor 15.8; Eph 2.11
cause (2) 2 Cor 9.8; Phil 2.21
Christ [6] 1.4; 3.13
circumcise [2] 1 Cor 7.18; 5.2
clear 2 Cor 11.6; 3.1
cross (1) 2 Cor 13.4; 3.1
dead 2 Cor 6.9; 6.14
death (3) (to death) 2 Cor 13.4; 5.24
eager 2 Cor 9.2; Phil 2.28
fail 2 Cor 13.5; Phil 1.20
faith [3] 1.23; 3.6
favour 2 Cor 6.2; 1 Tim 5.21
force (1) [2] 2 Cor 10.2; 6.12
free 1.4; 3.28
Gentile [10] 1.16; 3.8
gospel [5] 1.6; 3.2
grace 1.3; 5.4
Jew [8] 1.13; 3.28
judge 2 Cor 13.5; 6.4
law [8] 2 Cor 3.6; 3.2
life (1) [2] 2 Cor 13.4; 3.21
love 2 Cor 13.11; 5.6
message 2 Cor 6.7; 6.6
need 2 Cor 12.9; 3.20
new 2 Cor 5.17; 6.15
power 2 Cor 13.3; 3.3
preach [3] 1.8; 4.13
refuse (1) Rom 14.6; 2 Thes 3.10

reject Rom 11.1; 4.14
remember 2 Cor 9.6; 4.13
require [3] 1 Cor 4.2; 3.2
reveal 1.12; 3.23
right with God [5] 1 Cor 6.11; 3.8
safe 1 Cor 10.1; Phil 3.1
serve 1.15; 5.13
sign (1) Rom 4.11
slave 1 Cor 12.13; 3.28
Son of God 1.16; 4.4
special 2 Cor 12.11; 4.10
task [3] 2 Cor 5.18; Col 1.25
truth [2] 2 Cor 13.8; 4.16
union [2] 2 Cor 13.4; 3.26
wrong 2 Cor 13.7; 3.19

accept 1.6; Eph 6.17
act 2.13; 5.15
agree 2.9; Phil 4.2
angel 1.8; 4.14
announce Acts 26.23; Eph 6.15
baptize 1 Cor 15.29; Eph 4.5
basis 2 Cor 8.12; Eph 1.11
believe [6] 2.16; Eph 1.13
bless [4] 2 Cor 11.31; Eph 1.3
child of God 2 Cor 6.18; 4.5
Christ [6] 2.16; 4.19
clear [2] 2.11; Eph 5.13
consider 1 Cor 10.18; Phil 2.3
covenant [2] 2 Cor 3.6; 4.24
cross (1) 2.19; 5.11
curse [5] 1 Cor 16.22; Heb 6.8
death (1) 2 Cor 11.23; 6.8
depend [3] 2 Cor 7.16; 1 Thes 4.12
example 1 Cor 10.6; Phil 3.17
experience [2] 1 Cor 10.13; Phil 3.10
faith [12] 2.16; 5.5
fool [2] 2 Cor 12.6; 6.7
free 2.4; 4.22
Gentile [3] 2.2; Eph 2.11
gift [3] 2 Cor 9.5; Eph 1.6
Good News 1.16; Eph 1.13
gospel [2] 2.2; 4.13
hang (2) Lk 23.39
Jew 2.7; Eph 2.11
last (1) 2 Cor 9.9; Heb 1.8
law [17] 2.16; 4.4
life (1) [2] 2.20; 5.10
mankind [2] 2 Cor 5.19; Eph 3.5
means [2] 1.1; 6.14
miracle 2 Cor 12.12; 2 Thes 2.9
need 2.10; Eph 4.29
obey [3] 1.4; 5.3
power [2] 2.8; 5.5
predict Acts 16.16; 1 Pet 1.11
prison 2 Cor 11.23; Eph 3.1
promise [11] 2 Cor 11.2; 4.23
purpose 2 Cor 8.21; 4.18
real 2 Cor 11.13; Col 2.17
redeem Mk 10.45; 4.5
require [3] 2.16; Phil 1.27
reveal 2.2; Eph 1.17
right with God [5] 2.16; 5.4
righteous 2 Cor 11.15; Eph 5.9
scripture [9] 2 Cor 13.1; 4.27
slave 2.4; 4.1
son *see* **child of God**
Spirit (1) (God's Spirit) [4] 2 Cor 13.13; 4.6
union [3] 2.4; 5.6
world 2 Cor 10.3; 6.14
wrong 2.11; 4.12

Law or Faith

3 You foolish Galatians! Who put a spell on you? Before your very eyes you had a clear description of the death of Jesus Christ on the cross! 2 Tell me this one thing: did you receive God's Spirit by doing what the Law requires or by hearing the gospel and believing it? 3 How can you be so foolish! You began by God's Spirit; do you now want to finish by your own power? 4 Did all your experience mean nothing at all? Surely it meant something! 5 Does God give you the Spirit and work miracles among you because you do what the Law requires or because you hear the gospel and believe it?

6 Consider the experience of Abraham; as the scripture says, "He believed God, and because of his faith God accepted him as righteous." 7 You should realize then, that the real descendants of Abraham are the people who have faith. 8 The scripture predicted that God would put the Gentiles right with himself through faith. And so the scripture announced the Good News to Abraham: "Through you God will bless all mankind." 9 Abraham believed and was blessed; so all who believe are blessed as he was.

10 Those who depend on obeying the Law live under a curse. For the scripture says, "Whoever does not always obey everything that is written in the book of the Law is under God's curse!" 11 Now, it is clear that no one is put right with God by means of the Law, because the scripture says, "Only the person who is put right with God through faith shall live."[d] 12 But the Law has nothing to do with faith. Instead, as the scripture says, "Whoever *does* everything the Law requires will live."

13 But by becoming a curse for us Christ has redeemed us from the curse that the Law brings; for the scripture says, "Anyone who is hanged on a tree is under God's curse." 14 Christ did this in order that the blessing which God promised to Abraham might be given to the Gentiles by means of Christ Jesus, so that through faith we might receive the Spirit promised by God.

The Law and the Promise

15 My brothers, I am going to use an everyday example: when two people agree on a matter and sign an agreement, no one can break it or add anything to it. 16 Now, God made his promises to Abraham and to his descendant. The scripture does not use the plural "descendants," meaning many people, but the singular "descendant," meaning one person only, namely, Christ. 17 What I mean is that God made a covenant with Abraham and promised to keep it. The Law, which was given four hundred and thirty years later, cannot break that covenant and cancel God's promise. 18 For if God's gift depends on the Law, then it no longer depends on his promise. However, it was because of his promise that God gave that gift to Abraham.

19 What, then, was the purpose of the Law? It was added in order to show what wrongdoing is, and it was meant to last until the coming of Abraham's descendant, to whom the promise was made. The Law was handed down by angels, with a man acting as a go-between. 20 But a go-between is not needed when only one person is involved; and God is one.[e]

The Purpose of the Law

21 Does this mean that the Law is against God's promises? No, not at all! For if mankind had received a law that could bring life, then everyone could be put right with God by obeying it. 22 But the scripture says that the whole world is under the power of sin; and so the gift which is promised on the basis of faith in Jesus Christ is given to those who believe.

23 But before the time for faith came, the Law kept us all locked up as prisoners until this coming faith should be revealed. 24 And so the Law was in charge of us until Christ came, in order that we might then be put right with God through faith. 25 Now that the time for faith is here, the Law is no longer in charge of us.

26 It is through faith that all of you are God's sons in union with Christ Jesus. 27 You were baptized into union with Christ, and now you are clothed, so to speak, with the life of Christ himself. 28 So there is no difference between Jews and Gentiles, between slaves and free men, between men and women; you are all one in union with Christ Jesus. 29 If you

[d] put right with God through faith shall live; *or* put right with God shall live through faith.
[e] and God is one; *or* and God acts alone.

3.6: Gen 15.6; Rom 4.3 **3.7:** Rom 4.16 **3.8:** Gen 12.3 **3.10:** Deut 27.26 (LXX) **3.11:** Hab 2.4 **3.12:** Lev 18.5 **3.13:** Deut 21.23 **3.16:** Gen 12.7 **3.17:** Ex 12.40 **3.18:** Rom 4.14 **3.29:** Rom 4.13

angel 3.19; Eph 3.10
beg 2 Cor 12.18; Eph 3.13
being 2 Cor 5.17; Eph 6.12
care 2 Cor 8.20; Eph 5.29
child of God [6] 3.26; Eph 1.5
Christ 3.13; 5.1
covenant [2] 3.17; Eph 2.12
dear 2 Cor 12.19; Eph 1.6
despise 1 Cor 11.22; 1 Thes 5.20
enemy 2 Cor 5.18; 5.17
Father (2) (God) 1.1; Eph 1.2
free [5] 3.28; 5.1
god (2) (other gods) 2 Cor 4.4; Phil 3.19
gospel 3.2; Eph 3.6
happy [2] 2 Cor 12.9; Phil 1.18
heart 2 Cor 7.2; Eph 3.17
heaven [2] 1.8; Eph 1.3
human 1.11; 5.16
intend Ezek 38.13
interest (1) [3] 1 Cor 10.24; Phil 2.4
joy 2 Cor 8.2; 5.22
law [4] 3.2; 5.3
mature 1 Cor 2.6; Eph 4.13
nature 1 Cor 11.14; 5.16
pain [2] 2 Cor 12.7; 1 Thes 5.3
persecute 1.13; 5.11
physical 2 Cor 12.7; 5.13
preach 2.2; 5.11
promise [2] 3.14; Eph 1.13
purpose 3.19; Eph 1.5
redeem 3.13; 1 Tim 2.6
reject 2.21; 1 Thes 4.8
remember 2.10; Eph 1.16
represent [2] 2 Cor 8.23; Heb 9.5
result [2] 2 Cor 12.6; Eph 2.8
right (1) 2 Cor 13.7; 6.1
scripture [2] 3.6; Eph 4.8
separate 2 Cor 6.17; 5.20
slave [12] 3.28; 5.1
son *see* child of God
Son of God [2] 2.20; Eph 1.6
special 2.9; Eph 3.7
Spirit (1) (God's Spirit) [3] 3.2; 5.5
spirit (2) [2] 2 Cor 11.4; Eph 2.2
spiritual 2 Cor 4.7; 6.1
stand for 1 Cor 8.4; Rev 13.17
subject (1) 1 Cor 9.20; 5.18
true 1.20; 5.11
truth 2.5; 5.7
try (2) Rom 3.4; Heb 3.9

belong to Christ, then you are the descendants of Abraham and will receive
what God has promised.

4 But now to continue—the son who
will receive his father's property is
treated just like a slave while he is
young, even though he really owns everything. 2 While he is young, there are men
who take care of him and manage his
affairs until the time set by his father. 3 In
the same way, we too were slaves of the
ruling spirits of the universe before we
reached spiritual maturity. 4 But when
the right time finally came, God sent his
own Son. He came as the son of a human
mother and lived under the Jewish Law,
5 to redeem those who were under the
Law, so that we might become God's
sons.

6 To show that you are[f] his sons, God
sent the Spirit of his Son into our hearts,
the Spirit who cries out, "Father, my
Father." 7 So then, you are no longer a
slave but a son. And since you are his
son, God will give you all that he has for
his sons.

Paul's Concern for the Galatians

8 In the past you did not know God,
and so you were slaves of beings who are
not gods. 9 But now that you know God—
or, I should say, now that God knows
you—how is it that you want to turn back
to those weak and pitiful ruling spirits?
Why do you want to become their slaves
all over again? 10 You pay special attention to certain days, months, seasons, and
years. 11 I am worried about you! Can it
be that all my work for you has been for
nothing?

12 I beg you, my brothers, be like me.
After all, I am like you. You have not
done me any wrong. 13 You remember
why I preached the gospel to you the first
time; it was because I was ill. 14 But even
though my physical condition was a
great trial to you, you did not despise or
reject me. Instead, you received me as
you would an angel from heaven; you received me as you would Christ Jesus.
15 You were so happy! What has
happened? I myself can say that you
would have taken out your own eyes, if
you could, and given them to me. 16 Have
I now become your enemy by telling you
the truth?

17 Those other people show a deep
interest in you, but their intentions are
not good. All they want is to separate you
from me, so that you will have the same
interest in them as they have in you.
18 Now, it is good to have such a deep
interest if the purpose is good—this is
true always, and not merely when I am
with you. 19 My dear children! Once
again, just like a mother in childbirth, I
feel the same kind of pain for you until
Christ's nature is formed in you. 20 How I
wish I were with you now, so that I could
take a different attitude towards you. I
am so worried about you!

The Example of Hagar and Sarah

21 Let me ask those of you who want
to be subject to the Law: do you not hear
what the Law says? 22 It says that Abraham had two sons, one by a slave-
woman, the other by a free woman. 23 His
son by the slave-woman was born in the
usual way, but his son by the free woman
was born as a result of God's promise.
24 These things can be understood as a
figure: the two women represent two
covenants. The one whose children are
born in slavery is Hagar, and she represents the covenant made at Mount Sinai.
25 Hagar, who stands for Mount Sinai in
Arabia, is[g] a figure of the present city of
Jerusalem, in slavery with all its people.
26 But the heavenly Jerusalem is free, and
she is our mother. 27 For the scripture
says,

"Be happy, you childless woman!
Shout and cry with joy, you who
never felt the pains of childbirth!
For the woman who was deserted will
have more children
than the woman whose husband
never left her."

28 Now, you, my brothers, are God's
children as a result of his promise, just as
Isaac was. 29 At that time the son who
was born in the usual way persecuted the
one who was born because of God's
Spirit; and it is the same now. 30 But what
does the scripture say? It says, "Send the
slave-woman and her son away; for the
son of the slave-woman will not have a
part of the father's property along with
the son of the free woman." 31 So then,
my brothers, we are not the children of a
slave-woman but of a free woman.

Preserve Your Freedom

5 Freedom is what we have—Christ
has set us free! Stand, then, as free
people, and do not allow yourselves to become slaves again.

2 Listen! I, Paul, tell you that if you
allow yourselves to be circumcised, it

turn 2 Cor 9.3; Phil 2.23
understand 2 Cor 10.11; Eph 3.4
universe Is 66.2; Eph 4.10
weak 2 Cor 13.3; Phil 3.21
wish 2 Cor 12.19; 5.12
worry [2] 2 Cor 2.13; Phil 4.6
wrong 3.19; 6.1

act 3.19; Col 4.5
action 2.13; Phil 4.9
anger Rom 12.19; Eph 2.3
Christ [4] 4.19; 6.2
circumcise [4] 2.3; 6.12
commandment 1 Cor 7.19; Eph 2.15

[f] To show that you are; *or* Because you are.
[g] Hagar...is; *some manuscripts have* Sinai is a mountain in Arabia, and it is.

4.5-7: Rom 8.15-17 4.22: Gen 16.15, 21.2 4.27: Is 54.1 4.29: Gen 21.9 4.30: Gen 21.10

means that Christ is of no use to you at
all. 3 Once more I warn any man who
allows himself to be circumcised that he
is obliged to obey the whole Law. 4 Those
of you who try to be put right with God
by obeying the Law have cut yourselves
off from Christ. You are outside God's
grace. 5 As for us, our hope is that God
will put us right with him; and this is
what we wait for by the power of God's
Spirit working through our faith. 6 For
when we are in union with Christ Jesus,
neither circumcision nor the lack of it
makes any difference at all; what matters is faith that works through love.
7 You were doing so well! Who made
you stop obeying the truth? How did he
persuade you? 8 It was not done by God,
who calls you. 9 "It takes only a little
yeast to make the whole batch of dough
rise," as they say. 10 But I still feel confident about you. Our life in union with the
Lord makes me confident that you will
not take a different view and that the
man who is upsetting you, whoever he is,
will be punished by God.
11 But as for me, my brothers, if I continue to preach that circumcision is
necessary, why am I still being persecuted? If that were true, then my
preaching about the cross of Christ
would cause no trouble. 12 I wish that the
people who are upsetting you would go
all the way; let them go on and castrate
themselves!
13 As for you, my brothers, you were
called to be free. But do not let this freedom become an excuse for letting your
physical desires control you. Instead, let
love make you serve one another. 14 For
the whole Law is summed up in one commandment: "Love your neighbour as you
love yourself." 15 But if you act like wild
animals, hurting and harming each
other, then watch out, or you will completely destroy one another.

The Spirit and Human Nature

16 What I say is this: let the Spirit
direct your lives, and you will not satisfy
the desires of the human nature. 17 For
what our human nature wants is opposed
to what the Spirit wants, and what the
Spirit wants is opposed to what our
human nature wants. These two are enemies, and this means that you cannot do
what you want to do. 18 If the Spirit leads
you, then you are not subject to the Law.
19 What human nature does is quite
plain. It shows itself in immoral, filthy,
and indecent actions; 20 in worship of
idols and witchcraft. People become
enemies and they fight; they become
jealous, angry, and ambitious. They
separate into parties and groups; 21 they
are envious, get drunk, have orgies, and
do other things like these. I warn you
now as I have before: those who do these
things will not possess the Kingdom of
God.
22 But the Spirit produces love, joy,
peace, patience, kindness, goodness,
faithfulness, 23 humility, and self-control.
There is no law against such things as
these. 24 And those who belong to Christ
Jesus have put to death their human
nature with all its passions and desires.
25 The Spirit has given us life; he must
also control our lives. 26 We must not be
proud or irritate one another or be
jealous of one another.

Bear One Another's Burdens

6 My brothers, if someone is caught in
any kind of wrongdoing, those of
you who are spiritual should set him
right; but you must do it in a gentle way.
And keep an eye on yourselves, so that
you will not be tempted, too. 2 Help to
carry one another's burdens, and in this
way you will obey[h] the law of Christ. 3 If
someone thinks he is somebody when
really he is nobody, he is only deceiving
himself. 4 Each one should judge his own
conduct. If it is good, then he can be
proud of what he himself has done, without having to compare it with what someone else has done. 5 For everyone has to
carry his own load.
6 The man who is being taught the
Christian message should share all the
good things he has with his teacher.
7 Do not deceive yourselves; no one
makes a fool of God. A person will reap
exactly what he sows. 8 If he sows in the
field of his natural desires, from it he will
gather the harvest of death; if he sows in
the field of the Spirit, from the Spirit he
will gather the harvest of eternal life. 9 So
let us not become tired of doing good; for
if we do not give up, the time will come
when we will reap the harvest. 10 So then,
as often as we have the chance, we
should do good to everyone, and especially to those who belong to our family in
the faith.

Final Warning and Greeting

11 See what big letters I make as I
write to you now with my own hand!
12 The people who are trying to force you
to be circumcised are the ones who want

[h] you will obey; *some manuscripts have* obey.

5.9: 1 Cor 5.6 **5.14:** Lev 19.18 **5.17:** Rom 7.15–23

confident [2] 2 Cor 8.22; Eph 3.12
control [2] 1 Cor 14.32; Eph 2.2
cross (1) 3.1; 6.12
death (3) (to death) 2.19; Col 3.5
desire [3] 2 Cor 5.2; 6.8
destroy 1.13; Eph 2.16
direct 1 Cor 12.28
each other 1 Cor 7.3; Col 3.16
enemy [2] 4.16; Eph 2.14
envy Acts 8.23; Tit 3.3
excuse Rom 3.19; Jude 4
faith [2] 3.6; 6.10
faithful 1 Cor 4.2; Eph 1.1
filthy Rom 1.24; Jas 1.21
free [5] 4.22; Eph 1.6
grace 2.21; 6.18
harm 2 Cor 7.9; Eph 4.29
hope 2 Cor 10.15; Eph 1.12
human [5] 4.4; Eph 6.5
humble 2 Cor 11.7; Eph 4.2
hurt 2 Cor 4.9; Rev 2.11
idol 2 Cor 6.16; Eph 5.5
immoral 2 Cor 12.21; Eph 5.3
jealous [2] 2 Cor 12.20; Phil 1.15
joy 4.27; Phil 1.4
kind 2 Cor 10.1; Eph 4.32
Kingdom (1) (of God) 1 Cor 15.24; Eph 5.5
law [5] 4.4; 6.2
life (1) [4] 3.21; 6.8
love [4] 2.20; Eph 1.4
matter 1 Cor 7.19; 6.15
nature [5] 4.19; Eph 3.19
neighbour Rom 13.9; Jas 2.8
obey [3] 3.10; 6.2
obligation Rom 15.27
one another [4] 2 Cor 13.11; 6.2
passion 1 Cor 7.9; Eph 4.31
patient 2 Cor 12.12; Eph 4.2
peace 1.3; 6.16
persecute 4.29; 6.12
persuade 2 Cor 5.11; Rev 2.14
physical 4.14; 6.13
plain (1) 2 Cor 7.12; 1 Tim 5.24
possess 2 Cor 6.10; 1 Thes 5.9
power 3.3; Eph 1.19
preach [2] 4.13; Eph 2.17
proud 2 Cor 12.7; 6.4
punish 2 Cor 13.2; 1 Thes 4.6
right with God [2] 3.8; 2 Tim 4.8
rise 1 Cor 15.21; Eph 5.14
satisfy 1 Cor 7.3; Phil 4.11
self-control 1 Cor 7.5; 1 Tim 3.2

separate 4.17; Eph 2.14
serve 2.17; Eph 4.1
slave 4.1; 6.17
Spirit (1) (God's Spirit) [7] 4.6; 6.8
subject (1) 4.21
trouble 2 Cor 8.2; 6.17
true 4.18; Eph 1.13
truth 4.16; Eph 4.15
union [2] 3.26; Eph 1.1
upset [2] 1.7; Phil 2.26
warn [2] 1 Cor 10.6; Eph 4.17
watch Rom 16.17; Eph 6.6
wish 4.20; Eph 2.3
worship (2) (of other gods) 1 Cor 12.2; Col 2.18
yeast 1 Cor 5.6

boast [3] 2 Cor 12.1; Eph 2.8
body 2 Cor 7.1; Eph 1.23
burden 2 Cor 12.16; 1 Tim 5.16
ceremony Acts 25.23; Phil 3.3
Christ [2] 5.1; Eph 1.3
Christian 2 Cor 12.2; Eph 4.12
circumcise [4] 5.2; Eph 2.11
compare 2 Cor 10.12
conduct Rom 13.13; 1 Thes 2.10
creature Ezek 41.18; Heb 9.5
cross (1) [3] 5.11; Eph 2.16
dead 2.19; Eph 2.1
death (1) 3.1; Eph 1.7
deceive [2] 2 Cor 11.3; Eph 4.14
desire 5.13; Eph 2.3
eternal 2 Cor 4.17; Eph 3.11
faith 5.5; Eph 1.15
fool 3.1; Eph 5.6
force (1) 2.3; Phil 2.6
gentle 2 Cor 10.1; Eph 4.2
give up 2 Cor 2.7; Eph 6.18
God's people 2 Cor 13.12; Eph 1.1
grace 5.4; Eph 1.2
harvest [3] 2 Cor 9.10; Eph 5.9
help 2 Cor 12.13; Eph 4.28
judge 2.6; Eph 6.9
law [2] 5.3; Eph 2.15
life (1) [2] 5.10; Eph 1.1
matter [2] 5.6; Phil 1.18
means 3.11; Eph 1.9
mercy 1.13; Eph 2.4
message 2.2; Eph 1.13
natural Rom 11.21; Eph 2.3
new 2.6; Eph 2.15
obey [2] 5.3; Eph 2.2
one another 5.13; Eph 4.2

peace 5.22; Eph 1.2
persecute 5.11; Phil 3.6
physical 5.13; Col 1.22
practice 1.14; Phil 4.9
proud 5.26; Phil 1.26
reap [2] 1 Cor 9.10; Heb 12.11
right (1) 4.4; Eph 1.10
share 2 Cor 13.4; Eph 3.6
slave 5.1; Eph 6.5
sow [3] 2 Cor 9.6
Spirit (1) (God's Spirit) [2] 5.5; Eph 1.13

to show off and **boast** about external matters. They do it, however, only so that
they may not be **persecuted** for the **cross**
of **Christ**. 13 Even those who **practise cir-**
cumcision do not **obey** the **Law**; they
want you to be **circumcised** so that they
can **boast** that you **submitted** to this
physical ceremony. 14 As for me, however, I will **boast** only about the **cross** of
our Lord Jesus Christ; for **by means of**
his **cross** the world is **dead** to me, and I
am dead to the **world**. 15 It does not **mat-**
ter at all whether or not one is **circum-**
cised; what does **matter** is being a **new**
creature. 16 As for those who follow this
rule in their **lives**, may **peace** and **mercy**
be with them—with them and with all
God's people!

17 To conclude: let no one give me
any more **trouble**, because the scars I
have on my **body** show that I am the
slave of Jesus.

18 May the **grace** of our Lord Jesus
Christ be with you all, my brothers.
Amen.

spiritual 4.3; Eph 1.3
submit 1 Cor 9.25; Eph 5.21
teach 1.12; Eph 4.14
teacher 1 Cor 12.28; Eph 4.11
tempt 1 Cor 7.5; 1 Thes 3.5
trouble 5.11; Phil 1.17
world 3.22; Eph 1.3
wrong 4.12; Phil 1.18

PAUL'S LETTER TO THE EPHESIANS

INTRODUCTION

Paul's Letter to the Ephesians is concerned first of all with "God's plan...to bring all creation together, everything in heaven and on earth, with Christ as head" (1.10). It is also an appeal to God's people to live out the meaning of this great plan for the unity of mankind through oneness with Jesus Christ.

In the first part of *Ephesians* the writer develops the theme of unity by speaking of the way in which God the Father has chosen his people, how they are forgiven and set free from their sins through Jesus Christ the Son, and how God's great promise is guaranteed by the Holy Spirit. In the second part he appeals to the readers to live in such a way that their oneness in Christ may become real in their life together.

Several figures of speech are used to show the oneness of God's people in union with Christ: the church is like a body, with Christ as the head; or like a building, with Christ as the cornerstone; or like a wife, with Christ as the husband. This letter rises to great heights of expression as the writer is moved by the thought of God's grace in Christ. Everything is seen in the light of Christ's love, sacrifice, forgiveness, grace, and purity.

Outline of Contents

Introduction 1.1-2
Christ and the church 1.3—3.21
The new life in Christ 4.1—6.20
Conclusion 6.21-24

---

apostle Gal 2.8; 2.20
assure 2 Cor 8.3; Col 2.2
authorities 1 Cor 15.24; 6.12
authority 2 Cor 13.10; 5.23
basis Gal 3.22; 2.12
believe [2] Gal 3.2; Phil 1.29
bless [3] Gal 3.8; 3.6
body Gal 6.17; 2.3
child of God Gal 4.5; 5.1
choose [2] Gal 1.15; 2.12
Christ [12] Gal 6.2; 2.5
church [2] Gal 1.2; 3.10
complete [5] 2 Cor 10.6; Phil 2.12
create 1 Cor 15.45; 2.10
dear Gal 4.19; 5.1
death (1) Gal 6.8; 2.13
death (2) (from death) Gal 1.1; 5.14
faith Gal 6.10; 2.8
faithful Gal 5.22; 6.21
Father (2) (God) [3] Gal 4.6; 2.18
fault 2 Cor 7.11; 5.27
forgive 2 Cor 12.13; 4.32
free [3] Gal 5.1; 4.30
gift Gal 3.18; 2.8
glory [4] Gal 1.5; 3.16
God's people [6] Gal 6.16; 2.12
Good News Gal 3.8; 2.17

1 From Paul, who by God's will is an
apostle of Christ Jesus—
To God's people in Ephesus,[a] who are
faithful in their life in union with Christ
Jesus:
2 May God our Father and the Lord
Jesus Christ give you grace and peace.

Spiritual Blessings in Christ

3 Let us give thanks to the God and
Father of our Lord Jesus Christ! For in
our union with Christ he has blessed us
by giving us every spiritual blessing in
the heavenly world. 4 Even before the
world was made, God had already
chosen us to be his through our union
with Christ, so that we would be holy and
without fault before him.
Because of his love 5 God[b] had already
decided that through Jesus Christ he
would make us his sons—this was his
pleasure and purpose. 6 Let us praise God
for his glorious grace, for the free gift he
gave us in his dear Son! 7 For by the
sacrificial death of Christ we are set free,
that is, our sins are forgiven. How great
is the grace of God, 8 which he gave to us
in such large measure!
In all his wisdom and insight 9 God did
what he had purposed, and made known
to us the secret plan he had already
decided to complete by means of Christ.
10 This plan, which God will complete
when the time is right, is to bring all
creation together, everything in heaven
and on earth, with Christ as head.
11 All things are done according to
God's plan and decision; and God chose
us to be his own people in union with
Christ because of his own purpose, based
on what he had decided from the very
beginning. 12 Let us, then, who were the
first to hope in Christ, praise God's glory!
13 And you also became God's people
when you heard the true message, the
Good News that brought you salvation.
You believed in Christ, and God put his
stamp of ownership on you by giving you
the Holy Spirit he had promised. 14 The
Spirit is the guarantee that we shall
receive what God has promised his
people, and this assures us that God will
give complete freedom to those who are
his. Let us praise his glory!

Paul's Prayer

15 For this reason, ever since I heard
of your faith in the Lord Jesus and your
love for all God's people, 16 I have not
stopped giving thanks to God for you. I

grace [3] Gal 6.18; 2.5
guarantee 2 Cor 5.5; 4.30
heaven [4] Gal 4.14; 2.6
holy 2 Cor 7.1; 3.5
hope [2] Gal 5.5; 2.12
insight Prov 28.11
life (1) Gal 6.8; 2.10
light (1) 2 Cor 11.14; 5.8
love [2] Gal 5.6; 2.4
means Gal 6.14; 2.16
message Gal 6.6; 6.19
might Lk 9.43; 6.10
mind (1) 2 Cor 11.3; 2.3
peace Gal 6.16; 2.14
plan [3] 2 Cor 8.11; 3.3
pleasure Lk 8.14; 2 Thes 2.12
power [3] Gal 5.5; 2.2
praise [3] Gal 1.24; 5.19
prayer 2 Cor 4.15; 6.18
promise [3] Gal 4.23; 2.12
purpose [3] Gal 4.18; 3.11
raise Gal 1.1; 2.6
reason 2 Cor 11.12; 3.1
remember Gal 4.13; 2.11
reveal Gal 3.23; 3.3
rich 2 Cor 9.10; 5.9
right (1) Gal 6.1; 5.3
right (2) Rom 8.34; Col 3.1
sacrifice 1 Cor 10.18; 2.13

[a] *Some manuscripts do not have* in Ephesus.
[b] before him. Because of his love God; *or* before him, and to live in love. God.

1.1: Acts 18.19-21, 19.1 **1.7:** Col 1.14

salvation 2 Cor 7.10; 6.17
secret 2 Cor 4.2; 3.3
son *see* child of God
Son of God Gal 4.4; 4.13
Spirit (1) (God's Spirit) [3] Gal 6.8; 2.18
spiritual Gal 6.1; 2.1
strength 2 Cor 1.6; 6.10
supreme 2 Cor 4.7; Col 2.10
thank [2] 2 Cor 9.11; 5.4
true Gal 5.11; 3.15
union [4] Gal 5.6; 2.6
will (1) Gal 1.4; Phil 2.7
wisdom 2 Cor 1.12; 3.10
wise 2 Cor 11.19; 5.15
wonder (1) 2 Cor 12.7; 2 Thes 2.9
world [4] Gal 6.14; 2.2
world above [2] Rom 8.39; 2.6

remember you in my prayers 17 and ask
the God of our Lord Jesus Christ, the
glorious Father, to give you the Spirit,
who will make you wise and reveal God
to you, so that you will know him. 18 I ask
that your minds may be opened to see his
light, so that you will know what is the
hope to which he has called you, how
rich are the wonderful blessings he
promises his people, 19 and how very
great is his power at work in us who
believe. This power working in us is the
same as the mighty strength 20 which he
used when he raised Christ from death
and seated him at his right side in the
heavenly world. 21 Christ rules there
above all heavenly rulers, authorities,
powers, and lords; he has a title superior
to all titles of authority in this world and
in the next. 22 God put all things under
Christ's feet and gave him to the church
as supreme Lord over all things. 23 The
church is Christ's body, the completion of
him who himself completes all things
everywhere.[c]

From Death to Life

abundant Rom 9.23; Phil 4.19
anger Gal 5.20; 4.26
apart 2 Cor 1.21; Heb 7.26
apostle 1.1; 3.5
basis 1.11; Phil 3.9
birth Gal 2.15; Phil 3.5
boast Gal 6.12; Phil 2.3
body [4] 1.23; 3.6
choose 1.4; Phil 1.10
Christ [7] 1.3; 3.4
circumcise [2] Gal 6.12; Phil 3.3
commandment Gal 5.14; 6.2
control Gal 5.13; 4.16
covenant Gal 4.24; Heb 7.22
create [2] 1.10; 4.24
cross (1) [2] Gal 6.12; Phil 2.8
dead [2] Gal 6.14; Col 2.13
death (1) [2] 1.7; Phil 1.21
dedicate 1 Cor 7.34; 5.26
deed (2) 2 Cor 4.2; Col 1.10
desire Gal 6.8; 4.22
destroy Gal 5.15; 4.22
disobey [3] Rom 11.30; 2 Tim 3.2
enemy Gal 5.17; 6.13
evil Gal 1.4; 5.16
faith 1.15; 3.12
Father (2) (God) 1.2; 3.14
Gentile [5] Gal 3.8; 3.1
gift 1.6; 3.7

2 In the past you were spiritually dead
because of your disobedience and
sins. 2 At that time you followed the
world's evil way; you obeyed the ruler of
the spiritual powers in space, the spirit
who now controls the people who disobey
God. 3 Actually all of us were like them
and lived according to our natural
desires, doing whatever suited the wishes
of our own bodies and minds. In our
natural condition we, like everyone else,
were destined to suffer God's anger.
4 But God's mercy is so abundant, and
his love for us is so great, 5 that while we
were spiritually dead in our disobedience
he brought us to life with Christ. It is by
God's grace that you have been saved.
6 In our union with Christ Jesus he raised
us up with him to rule with him in the
heavenly world. 7 He did this to demonstrate for all time to come the extraordinary greatness of his grace in the
love he showed us in Christ Jesus. 8-9 For
it is by God's grace that you have been
saved through faith. It is not the result of
your own efforts, but God's gift, so that
no one can boast about it. 10 God has
made us what we are, and in our union
with Christ Jesus he has created us for a
life of good deeds, which he has already
prepared for us to do.

One in Christ

11 You Gentiles by birth—called "the
uncircumcised" by the Jews, who call
themselves "the circumcised" (which
refers to what men do to their bodies)—
remember what you were in the past.
12 At that time you were apart from
Christ. You were foreigners and did not
belong to God's chosen people. You had
no part in the covenants, which were
based on God's promises to his people,
and you lived in this world without hope
and without God. 13 But now, in union
with Christ Jesus, you who used to be far
away have been brought near by the
sacrificial death of Christ. 14 For Christ
himself has brought us peace by making
Jews and Gentiles one people. With his
own body he broke down the wall that
separated them and kept them enemies.
15 He abolished the Jewish Law with its
commandments and rules, in order to
create out of the two races one new
people in union with himself, in this way
making peace. 16 By his death on the
cross Christ destroyed their enmity; by
means of the cross he united both races
into one body and brought them back to
God. 17 So Christ came and preached the
Good News of peace to all—to you Gentiles, who were far away from God, and
to the Jews, who were near to him. 18 It is
through Christ that all of us, Jews and
Gentiles, are able to come in the one
Spirit into the presence of the Father.
19 So then, you Gentiles are not
foreigners or strangers any longer; you
are now fellow-citizens with God's people
and members of the family of God.
20 You, too, are built upon the foundation
laid by the apostles and prophets,[d] the
cornerstone being Christ Jesus himself.
21 He is the one who holds the whole
building together and makes it grow into
a sacred temple dedicated to the Lord.
22 In union with him you too are being
built together with all the others into a
place where God lives through his Spirit.

Paul's Work for the Gentiles

3 For this reason I, Paul, the prisoner
of Christ Jesus for the sake of you
Gentiles, pray to God. 2 Surely you have
heard that God in his grace has given me
this work to do for your good. 3 God revealed his secret plan and made it
known to me. (I have written briefly
about this, 4 and if you will read what I

God's people [3] 1.1; 3.8
Good News 1.13; 3.8
grace [3] 1.2; 3.2
heaven 1.3; 3.10
hope 1.12; 4.4
Jew [4] Gal 3.28; 3.6
law Gal 6.2; Phil 3.5
life (1) 1.1; 4.1
life (2) (to life) 2 Cor 5.15; Phil 3.11
love [2] 1.4; 3.17
means 1.9; 3.6
mercy Gal 6.16; 1 Tim 1.2
mind (1) 1.18; 4.18
natural [2] Gal 6.8; Jude 19
new Gal 6.15; 4.23
obey Gal 6.2; 5.6
peace [3] 1.2; 4.3
power 1.19; 3.7
preach Gal 5.11; Phil 1.14
presence 2 Cor 12.19; 3.12
promise 1.13; 3.6
prophet 1 Cor 12.28; 3.5
race (1) [2] Rom 11.14; 1 Pet 2.9
raise 1.20; Phil 2.9
remember 1.16; 6.8
result Gal 4.23; Phil 1.13
sacred Acts 19.35; 5.19
sacrifice 1.7; 5.2
save [2] 2 Cor 6.2; 2 Thes 2.10
separate Gal 5.20; 4.16
Spirit (1) (God's Spirit) [2] 1.13; 3.5
spirit (2) Gal 4.3; 4.15
spiritual [3] 1.3; 6.12
stranger Rom 12.13; 1 Tim 3.2
suffer 2 Cor 4.17; 3.13
Temple (1) (of God) 2 Cor 6.16; 2 Thes 2.4
union [5] 1.1; 3.12
unite 1 Cor 7.14; 4.3
wish Gal 5.12; Col 4.15
world [3] 1.3; 3.10
world above 1.3; 3.10

age (1) Gal 1.4; 6.12
angel Gal 4.14; Col 2.18
apostle 2.20; 4.11
beg Gal 4.12; Phil 4.2
benefit 1 Cor 9.11; 1 Tim 6.2
bless 1.3; Col 1.6
body 2.3; 4.4
bold 2 Cor 3.12; 6.19
Christ [5] 2.5; 4.7
church [2] 1.22; 5.23

[c] who himself completes all things everywhere; *or* who is himself completely filled with God's fullness.
[d] the foundation laid by the apostles and prophets; *or* the foundation, that is, the apostles and prophets.

1.20: Ps 110.1 **1.22:** Ps 8.6 **1.22-23:** Col 1.18 **2.1-5:** Col 2.13 **2.15:** Col 2.14 **2.16:** Col 1.20 **2.17:** Is 57.19 **3.4-6:** Col 1.26-27

confident Gal 5.10; Phil 1.14
Creator 1 Cor 8.6; Col 3.10
discourage 2 Cor 4.1; Col 3.21
eternal Gal 6.8; 2 Thes 1.9
faith [2] 2.8; 4.5
Father (2) (God) 2.18; 4.6
Gentile [3] 2.11; Col 2.13
gift 2.8; 4.7
glory [2] 1.6; Phil 1.11
God's people [2] 2.12; 4.12
Good News 2.17; 6.15
gospel [2] Gal 4.13; 6.19
grace 2.5; 6.24
heart Gal 4.6; 4.23
heaven [2] 2.6; 4.10
holy 1.4; 4.24
Jew 2.11; Col 3.11
knee Lk 5.8; Phil 2.10
learn [2] 1 Cor 14.31; 4.20
least 2 Cor 11.5; Heb 8.11
love [3] 2.4; 4.2
mankind Gal 3.8; 4.6
means [3] 2.16; 4.3
nature Gal 5.16; 5.13
plan [2] 1.9; Col 1.27
power [5] 2.2; 6.10
pray [3] 2 Cor 13.7; 6.18
presence 2.18; 4.10
prison Gal 3.23; 4.1
privilege 2 Cor 8.4; Phil 1.7
promise 2.12; 6.2
prophet 2.20; 4.11
purpose 1.5; Phil 1.27
reason [2] 1.15; 5.31
reveal [2] 1.17; 4.24
riches Rom 11.33; 1 Tim 6.17
sake 2 Cor 12.10; 6.20
secret [6] 1.9; 5.12
self Rom 6.6; 4.22
servant Gal 1.10; 6.21
share Gal 6.6; 5.5
special Gal 4.10; 4.7
Spirit (1) (God's Spirit) [2] 2.18; 4.3
strong 2 Cor 13.9; Phil 2.1
suffer 2.3; Phil 1.29
true 1.13; 4.24
understand [2] Gal 4.24; 5.32
union 2.6; 6.10
wisdom 1.8; Col 1.9
world 2.2; 6.12
world above 2.6; 6.12

have written, you can learn about my
understanding of the secret of Christ.)
5 In past times mankind was not told this
secret, but God has revealed it now by
the Spirit to his holy apostles and prophets. 6 The secret is that by means of the
gospel the Gentiles have a part with the
Jews in God's blessings; they are members of the same body and share in the
promise that God made through Christ
Jesus.

7 I was made a servant of the gospel
by God's special gift, which he gave me
through the working of his power. 8 I am
less than the least of all God's people; yet
God gave me this privilege of taking to
the Gentiles the Good News about the
infinite riches of Christ, 9 and of making
all people see how God's secret plan is to
be put into effect. God, who is the
Creator of all things, kept his secret hidden through all the past ages, 10 in order
that at the present time, by means of the
church, the angelic rulers and powers in
the heavenly world might learn of his
wisdom in all its different forms. 11 God
did this according to his eternal purpose,
which he achieved through Christ Jesus
our Lord. 12 In union with Christ and
through our faith in him we have the
boldness to go into God's presence with
all confidence. 13 I beg you, then, not to be
discouraged because I am suffering for
you; it is all for your benefit.

The Love of Christ

14 For this reason I fall on my knees
before the Father, 15 from whom every
family in heaven and on earth receives
its true name. 16 I ask God from the
wealth of his glory to give you power
through his Spirit to be strong in your
inner selves, 17 and I pray that Christ will
make his home in your hearts through
faith. I pray that you may have your
roots and foundation in love, 18 so that
you, together with all God's people, may
have the power to understand how broad
and long, how high and deep, is Christ's
love. 19 Yes, may you come to know his
love—although it can never be fully
known—and so be completely filled with
the very nature of God.

20 To him who by means of his power
working in us is able to do so much more
than we can ever ask for, or even think
of: 21 to God be the glory in the church
and in Christ Jesus for all time, for ever
and ever! Amen.

The Unity of the Body

4 I urge you, then—I who am a
prisoner because I serve the Lord:
live a life that measures up to the
standard God set when he called you.
2 Be always humble, gentle, and patient.
Show your love by being tolerant with
one another. 3 Do your best to preserve
the unity which the Spirit gives by means
of the peace that binds you together.
4 There is one body and one Spirit, just as
there is one hope to which God has
called you. 5 There is one Lord, one faith,
one baptism; 6 there is one God and
Father of all mankind, who is Lord of all,
works through all, and is in all.

7 Each one of us has received a
special gift in proportion to what Christ
has given. 8 As the scripture says,

"When he went up to the very heights,
he took many captives with him;
he gave gifts to mankind."

9 Now, what does "he went up" mean? It
means that first he came down to the
lowest depths of the earth.[e] 10 So the one
who came down is the same one who
went up, above and beyond the heavens,
to fill the whole universe with his
presence. 11 It was he who "gave gifts to
mankind"; he appointed some to be
apostles, others to be prophets, others to
be evangelists, others to be pastors and
teachers. 12 He did this to prepare all
God's people for the work of Christian
service, in order to build up the body of
Christ. 13 And so we shall all come together to that oneness in our faith and in
our knowledge of the Son of God; we
shall become mature people, reaching to
the very height of Christ's full stature.
14 Then we shall no longer be children,
carried by the waves and blown about by
every shifting wind of the teaching of
deceitful men, who lead others into error
by the tricks they invent. 15 Instead, by
speaking the truth in a spirit of love, we
must grow up in every way to Christ, who
is the head. 16 Under his control all the
different parts of the body fit together,
and the whole body is held together by
every joint with which it is provided. So
when each separate part works as it
should, the whole body grows and builds
itself up through love.

The New Life in Christ

17 In the Lord's name, then, I warn
you: do not continue to live like the
heathen, whose thoughts are worthless
18 and whose minds are in the dark. They

anger [4] 2.3; 5.6
apostle 3.5; Col 1.1
baptize Gal 3.27; Col 2.12
believer Gal 2.4; Col 4.5
best Gal 1.13; Phil 1.10
bind Rom 7.2; Col 2.14
bitter Rom 3.14; Heb 12.15
body [6] 3.6; 5.23
captive 2 Cor 10.5; Col 2.15
Christ [7] 3.4; 5.2
Christian Gal 6.6; 6.
control 2.2; 5.2
create 2.10; Col 1.15
dark 2 Cor 6.14; 5.8
Day of the Lord 2 Cor 1.13; Phil 1.6
deceive [2] Gal 6.3; 5.6
desire 2.3; Phil 1.20
destroy 2.16; 1 Thes 5.3
Devil 2 Cor 6.15; 6.1
error Ps 25.7; 1 Thes 2.3
faith [2] 3.12; 6.16
Father (2) (God) 3.14; 5.20
follower 1 Cor 15.6; 1 Pet 3.16
forgive 1.7; Col 1.14
free 1.6; 6.8
gentle Gal 6.1; Phil 4.5
gift [3] 3.7; Phil 4.17
God's people 3.8; 5.3
guarantee 1.14; Heb 7.22
harm Gal 5.15; 1 Tim 6.9
hate Rom 12.9; 5.29
heart 3.17; 5.19
heathen 1 Cor 12.2; 1 Thes 4.5
heaven 3.10; 6.9
help [2] Gal 6.2; 6.18
holy 3.5; Col 1.22
honest Jn 7.18; 1 Tim 3.11
hope 2.12; Phil 1.20
humble Gal 5.23; Phil 2.3
ignorant Rom 2.20; 5.15
insult 2 Cor 12.10; Col 3.8
kind Gal 5.22; Phil 2.1
knowledge 2 Cor 11.6; Phil 1.9
learn 3.4; 5.10
lie (2) Gal 1.20; Col 3.9
life (1) [3] 2.10; 5.2
love [3] 3.17; 5.2
mankind [3] 3.5; Col 1.26
mark (1) 2 Cor 1.22; Rev 7.3
mature Gal 4.3; Phil 3.15
means 3.6; 6.10
mind (1) [2] 2.3; Phil 2.2
name (2) (name of God, of Jesus) 2 Cor 11.31; 5.20
need Gal 3.20; Phil 4.6
new [2] 2.15; Col 3.10
one another [3] Gal 6.2; 5.19
passion Gal 5.24; Col 2.23

[e] the lowest depths of the earth; *or* the lower depths, the earth itself.

4.2: Col 3.12–13 **4.8:** Ps 68.18 **4.16:** Col 2.19

patient Gal 5.22; Col 1.11
peace 2.14; 6.15
poor 2 Cor 8.2; Heb 11.37
presence 3.12; Col 1.22
preserve Jer 32.14; Heb 2.10
prison 3.1; 6.20
prophet 3.5; 1 Thes 2.15
provide [2] 2 Cor 12.14; Tit 3.14
reveal 3.3; 5.13
rid [2] 2 Cor 5.4; Col 3.8
rob 2 Cor 11.8; Rev 3.11
sad 2 Cor 7.8; 1 Thes 4.13
scripture Gal 4.27; 5.31
self [3] 3.16; Col 2.11
separate 2.14; 1 Thes 2.17
serve Gal 5.13; 6.5
service 2 Cor 9.12; Col 4.17
shame 2 Cor 9.4; 5.12
Son of God 1.6; Col 1.13
special 3.7; Col 2.18
Spirit (1) (God's Spirit) [4] 3.5; 5.18
spirit (2) 2.2; Phil 1.17
stubborn Rom 11.25; Heb 3.8
teach [2] Gal 6.6; Col 1.28
teacher Gal 6.6; 1 Tim 2.7
tolerate 2 Cor 11.1; Col 3.13
trick Acts 13.10; 6.11
true 3.15; 5.13
truth [3] Gal 5.7; 5.9
unite 2.16; 5.31
universe Gal 4.3; Col 1.16
urge 2 Cor 9.5; Phil 2.2
warn Gal 5.3; Col 1.28
word (1) 2 Cor 12.3; 5.6
worthless 1 Cor 3.20; 5.11

anger 4.26; 6.4
authority [2] 1.21; Col 2.10
body [4] 4.4; Phil 3.2
care Gal 4.2; Phil 2.20
child of God 1.5; Phil 2.15
Christ [10] 4.7; 6.5
church [8] 3.10; Phil 1.1
clean Acts 11.9; 2 Tim 2.21
clear [2] Gal 3.1; Phil 3.15
control 4.16; Col 2.19
dark [2] 4.18; 6.12
dear 1.6; 6.21
death (2) (from death) 1.20; Phil 3.11
deceive 4.14; Col 2.4

have no part in the **life** that God gives,
for they are completely **ignorant** and
stubborn. 19 They have lost all feeling of
shame; they give themselves over to vice
and do all sorts of indecent things without restraint.

20 That was not what you **learnt** about
Christ! 21 You certainly heard about him,
and as his **followers** you were **taught** the
truth that is in Jesus. 22 So get **rid** of your
old **self**, which made you live as you used
to—the old **self** that was being **destroyed**
by its **deceitful desires**. 23 Your **hearts** and
minds must be made completely **new**,
24 and you must put on the **new self**,
which is **created** in God's likeness and
reveals itself in the **true life** that is upright and **holy**.

25 No more **lying**, then! Everyone
must tell the **truth** to his **fellow-believer**,
because we are all members together in
the **body** of **Christ**. 26 If you become
angry, do not let your **anger** lead you into
sin, and do not stay **angry** all day. 27 Don't
give the **Devil** a chance. 28 The man who
used to **rob** must stop robbing and start
working, in order to earn an **honest**
living for himself and to be able to **help**
the **poor**. 29 Do not use **harmful words**, but
only **helpful** words, the kind that build up
and **provide** what is **needed**, so that what
you say will do good to those who hear
you. 30 And do not make God's **Holy Spirit**
sad; for the **Spirit** is God's **mark** of
ownership on you, a **guarantee** that the
Day will come when God will **set you**
free. 31 Get **rid** of all **bitterness**, **passion**,
and **anger**. No more shouting or **insults**,
no more **hateful** feelings of any sort.
32 Instead, be **kind** and tender-hearted to
one another, and forgive **one another**, as
God has **forgiven** you through **Christ**.

Living in the Light

5 Since you are **God's dear children**,
you must try to be like him. 2 Your
life must be **controlled** by **love**, just as
Christ loved us and gave his **life** for us as
a sweet-smelling **offering** and **sacrifice**
that **pleases** God.

3 Since you are **God's people**, it is not
right that any matters of **sexual im-**
morality or indecency or **greed** should
even be mentioned among you. 4 Nor is it
fitting for you to use language which is
obscene, **profane**, or vulgar. Rather you
should give **thanks** to God. 5 You may be
sure that no one who is **immoral**, indecent, or greedy (for **greed** is a form of
idolatry) will ever receive a **share** in the
Kingdom of **Christ** and of God.

6 Do not let anyone **deceive** you with
foolish words; it is because of these very
things that **God's anger** will come upon
those who do not **obey** him. 7 So have
nothing at all to do with such people.
8 You yourselves used to be in the **dark-**
ness, but since you have become the
Lord's people, you are in the **light**. So you
must live like people who belong to the
light, 9 for it is the **light**[f] that brings a **rich**
harvest of every kind of goodness,
righteousness, and **truth**. 10 Try to **learn**
what **pleases** the Lord. 11 Have nothing to
do with the **worthless** things that people
do, things that belong to the **darkness**.
Instead, bring them out to the **light**. 12 (It
is really too **shameful** even to talk about
the things they do in **secret**.) 13 And when
all things are brought out to the **light**,
then their **true nature** is **clearly**
revealed; 14 for anything that is **clearly**
revealed becomes **light**.[g] That is why it is
said,

"Wake up, sleeper,
and **rise from death**,
and **Christ** will shine on you."

15 So be careful how you live. Don't
live like **ignorant** people, but like **wise**
people. 16 Make good use of every opportunity you have, because these are **evil**
days. 17 Don't be **fools**, then, but try to find
out what the Lord wants you to do.

18 Do not get drunk with wine, which
will only **ruin** you; instead, be filled with
the **Spirit**. 19 Speak to **one another** with
the **words** of **psalms**, **hymns**, and **sacred**
songs; sing **hymns** and **psalms** to the
Lord with **praise** in your **hearts**. 20 In the
name of our Lord Jesus Christ, always
give **thanks** for everything to God the
Father.

Wives and Husbands

21 **Submit** yourselves to **one another**
because of your **reverence** for **Christ**.

22 Wives, **submit** to your husbands as
to the Lord. 23 For a husband has
authority over his wife just as **Christ** has
authority over the **church**; and **Christ** is
himself the **Saviour** of the **church**, his
body. 24 And so wives must **submit** completely to their husbands just as the
church submits itself to **Christ**.

25 Husbands, **love** your wives just as
Christ loved the **church** and gave his **life**
for it. 26 He did this to **dedicate** the **church**
to God by his **word**, after making it **clean**

dedicate 2.21; 1 Tim 2.8
evil 2.2; 6.11
Father (2) (God) 4.6; 6.23
fault 1.4; Phil 3.6
fit (1) Acts 22.22; Col 1.11
fool [2] Gal 6.7; 1 Tim 1.6
God's people 4.12; 6.18
greed [2] 1 Cor 6.10; Col 3.5
harvest Gal 6.8; 2 Tim 2.6
hate 4.31; Col 3.8
heart 4.23; 6.5
hymn [2] 1 Cor 14.26; Col 3.16
idol Gal 5.20; Col 3.5
ignorant 4.18; 2 Tim 2.23
immoral [2] Gal 5.19; Col 3.5
Kingdom (1) (of God) Gal 5.21; Col 1.11
learn 4.20; Phil 4.9
life (1) [3] 4.1; Phil 1.11
light (1) [6] 1.18; Phil 2.15
love [5] 4.2; 6.23
name (2) (name of God, of Jesus) 4.17; Phil 2.9
nature 3.19; Phil 2.6
obey 2.2; 6.1
offer 2 Cor 4.15; Phil 2.16
one another [2] 4.2; Phil 2.1
please [2] 2 Cor 12.13; Phil 4.2
praise 1.6; Phil 1.11
present (1) Acts 9.41; Heb 8.3
profane Amos 2.7; 1 Tim 6.20
psalm [2] Acts 13.32; Col 3.16
pure 2 Cor 11.2; Phil 2.15
reason 3.1; 6.18
respect 2 Cor 8.18; 6.2
reveal [3] 4.24; Col 1.26
reverence Rom 3.18; Col 3.22
rich 1.18; Col 1.27
right (1) 1.10; 6.1
righteous Gal 3.6; 6.14
rise Gal 5.9; 1 Thes 4.14
ruin 2 Cor 7.2; 1 Tim 1.19
sacred 2.21; Col 3.16
sacrifice 2.13; Phil 2.17
Saviour Rom 11.26; Phil 3.20
scripture [2] 4.8; 1 Tim 4.13
secret [2] 3.3; 6.19
sex 2 Cor 12.21; Col 3.5
shame 4.19; Tit 1.11
share 3.6; Phil 1.7
Spirit (1) (God's Spirit) 4.3; 6.17
submit [4] Gal 6.13; Col 3.18
sure 2 Cor 10.2; Phil 1.6
thank [2] 1.3; Phil 1.3

[f] the light; *some manuscripts have* the Spirit.
[g] anything that is clearly revealed becomes light; *or* it is light that clearly reveals everything.

4.22: Col 3.9 **4.24:** Gen 1.26; Col 3.10 **4.25:** Zech 8.16 **4.26:** Ps 4.4 (LXX) **4.32:** Col 3.13
5.2: Ex 29.18; Ps 40.6 **5.16:** Col 4.5 **5.19–20:** Col 3.16–17 **5.22:** Col 3.18; 1 Pet 3.1
5.25: Col 3.19; 1 Pet 3.7

true 4.24; Phil 1.9
truth [2] 4.15; 6.14
understand 3.4; Phil 4.7
unite 4.3; Phil 3.9
wise 1.17; Col 4.5
word (1) [3] 4.29; 6.17
worthless 4.17; Col 2.8

by washing it in water, 27 in order to
present the church to himself in all its
beauty—pure and faultless, without spot
or wrinkle or any other imperfection.
28 Men ought to love their wives just as
they love their own bodies. A man who
loves his wife loves himself. 29 (No one
ever hates his own body. Instead, he
feeds it and takes care of it, just as Christ
does the church; 30 for we are members
of his body.) 31 As the scripture says, "For
this reason a man will leave his father
and mother and unite with his wife, and
the two will become one." 32 There is a
deep secret truth revealed in this scripture, which I understand as applying to
Christ and the church. 33 But it also
applies to you: every husband must love
his wife as himself, and every wife must
respect her husband.

Children and Parents

6 Children, it is your Christian duty
to[h] obey your parents, for this is the
right thing to do. 2 "Respect your father
and mother" is the first commandment
that has a promise added: 3 "so that all
may go well with you, and you may live a
long time in the land."
4 Parents, do not treat your children
in such a way as to make them angry.
Instead, bring them up with Christian
discipline and instruction.

Slaves and Masters

5 Slaves, obey your human masters
with fear and trembling; and do it with a
sincere heart, as though you were serving Christ. 6 Do this not only when they
are watching you, because you want to
gain their approval; but with all your
heart do what God wants, as slaves of
Christ. 7 Do your work as slaves cheerfully, as though you served the Lord, and
not merely men. 8 Remember that the
Lord will reward everyone, whether
slave or free, for the good work he does.
9 Masters, behave in the same way
towards your slaves and stop using
threats. Remember that you and your
slaves belong to the same Master in
heaven, who judges everyone by the
same standard.

The Whole Armour of God

10 Finally, build up your strength in
union with the Lord and by means of his
mighty power. 11 Put on all the armour
that God gives you, so that you will be
able to stand up against the Devil's evil
tricks. 12 For we are not fighting against
human beings but against the wicked
spiritual forces in the heavenly world,
the rulers, authorities, and cosmic
powers of this dark age. 13 So put on God's
armour now! Then when the evil day
comes, you will be able to resist the
enemy's attacks; and after fighting to the
end, you will still hold your ground.
14 So stand ready, with truth as a belt
tight round your waist, with righteousness as your breastplate, 15 and as your
shoes the readiness to announce the
Good News of peace. 16 At all times carry
faith as a shield; for with it you will be
able to put out all the burning arrows
shot by the Evil One. 17 And accept salvation as a helmet, and the word of God as
the sword which the Spirit gives you.
18 Do all this in prayer, asking for God's
help. Pray on every occasion, as the
Spirit leads. For this reason keep alert
and never give up; pray always for all
God's people. 19 And pray also for me,
that God will give me a message when I
am ready to speak, so that I may speak
boldly and make known the gospel's
secret. 20 For the sake of this gospel I am
an ambassador, though now I am in
prison. Pray that I may be bold in speaking about the gospel as I should.

Final Greetings

21 Tychicus, our dear brother and
faithful servant in the Lord's work, will
give you all the news about me, so that
you may know how I am getting on.
22 That is why I am sending him to you—
to tell you how all of us are getting on,
and to encourage you.
23 May God the Father and the Lord
Jesus Christ give to all Christian brothers
peace and love with faith. 24 May God's
grace be with all those who love our Lord
Jesus Christ with undying love.

accept Gal 3.6; Phil 4.18
age (1) 3.9; Col 1.26
alert 1 Cor 16.13; Col 4.2
anger 5.6; Col 3.6
announce Gal 3.8; 1 Tim 1.11
approve Gal 1.10; Col 3.22
authorities 1.21; Col 1.16
being Gal 4.8; Phil 1.20
bold [2] 3.12; Phil 1.14
cheer (1) 2 Cor 7.7; Col 4.8
Christ [2] 5.2; Phil 1.13
Christian [3] 4.12; Col 3.18
commandment 2.15; Tit 1.14
dark 5.8; Col 1.13
dear 5.1; Phil 2.12
Devil 4.27; 1 Thes 3.5
discipline 1 Cor 9.25; Tit 1.8
duty (1) 2 Cor 9.7; Phil 1.20
encourage 2 Cor 7.6; Phil 2.19
enemy 2.14; Phil 1.28
evil [2] 5.16; Phil 3.2
Evil One Jn 17.15; 2 Thes 3.3
faith [2] 4.5; Phil 1.25
faithful 1.1; Phil 4.3
Father (2) (God) 5.20; Phil 1.2
fear 2 Cor 7.5; Phil 1.14
free 4.30; Phil 1.7
give up Gal 6.9; Phil 2.7

God's people 5.3; Phil 1.1
Good News 3.8; Phil 4.15
gospel [3] 3.6; Phil 1.5
grace 3.2; Phil 1.2
heart [2] 5.19; Phil 1.7
heaven [2] 4.10; Phil 2.10
help 4.28; Phil 1.5
human [2] Gal 5.16; Phil 2.7
judge Gal 6.4; Phil 1.9
love [2] 5.2; Phil 1.9
master [3] 1 Cor 7.4; Col 3.22
means 4.3; Phil 1.19
message 1.13; Phil 1.14
might 1.19; Col 1.29
obey [2] 5.6; Phil 2.8
peace [2] 4.3; Phil 1.2
power [2] 3.7; Phil 3.10
pray [4] 3.1; Phil 1.4
prayer 1.16; Phil 1.19
prison 4.1; Phil 1.7
promise 3.6; 1 Tim 4.8
put out Jn 1.5; Heb 11.34
reason 5.31; Phil 1.2
remember [2] 2.11; Col 3.24
resist Rom 9.19; Heb 12.4
respect 5.33; Phil 2.29
reward 1 Cor 3.8; Col 3.24
right (1) 5.3; Phil 1.7
righteous 5.9; Phil 3.6
sake 3.1; Phil 1.24
salvation 1.13; Phil 2.12
secret 5.12; Phil 4.12
servant 3.7; Phil 1.1
serve [2] 4.1; Phil 1.29
sincere 2 Cor 2.17; Phil 1.17
slave [6] Gal 6.17; Col 2.8
Spirit (1) (God's Spirit) [2] 5.18; Phil 1.19
spiritual 2.1; Phil 3.15
strength 1.19; Phil 4.13
threat Rom 3.13; 1 Pet 2.23
tremble 2 Cor 7.15; Phil 2.12
trick 4.14; 1 Thes 2.3
truth 5.9; Phil 1.8
union 3.12; Phil 1.1
watch Gal 5.15; Phil 3.2
wicked 1 Cor 6.9; 2 Thes 2.3
word (1) 5.6; Phil 4.9
world 3.10; Phil 2.15
world above 3.10

[h] *Some manuscripts do not have* it is your Christian duty to.

5.31: Gen 2.24 **6.1:** Col 3.20 **6.2-3:** Ex 20.12; Deut 5.16 **6.4:** Col 3.21 **6.5-8:** Col 3.22-25
6.9: Deut 10.17; Col 3.25, 4.1 **6.14:** Is 11.5, 59.17 **6.15:** Is 52.7 **6.17:** Is 59.17 **6.21:** Acts 20.4; 2 Tim 4.12
6.21-22: Col 4.7-8

PAUL'S LETTER TO THE
PHILIPPIANS

INTRODUCTION

Paul's Letter to the Philippians was written to the first church that Paul established on European soil, in the Roman province of Macedonia. It was written while the apostle was in prison, and at a time when he was troubled by the opposition of other Christian workers towards himself and was distressed by false teaching in the church at Philippi. Yet this letter breathes a joy and confidence that can be explained only by Paul's deep faith in Jesus Christ.

The immediate reason for writing the letter was to thank the Philippian Christians for the gift which they had sent to help him in his time of need. He uses this opportunity to reassure them, so that they may have courage and confidence in spite of all his troubles and their own as well. He pleads with them to have the humble attitude of Jesus, rather than to be controlled by selfish ambition and pride. He reminds them that their life in union with Christ is a gift of God's grace which they have received through faith, not through obedience to the ceremonies of the Jewish Law. He writes of the joy and peace that God gives to those who live in union with Christ.

This letter is marked by its emphasis on joy, confidence, unity, and perseverance in the Christian faith and life. It also reveals the deep affection Paul had for the church at Philippi.

Outline of Contents

afraid Gal 2.12; 1 Tim 5.20
alive 2 Cor 1.8; 1 Thes 4.15
being Eph 6.12; 2.10
believe Eph 1.13; 1 Thes 2.10
best Eph 4.3; 3.13
blame Acts 18.6; Tit 1.6
bold Eph 6.19; 1 Tim 3.13
choose [2] Eph 2.12; Col 3.12
Christ [9] Eph 6.5; 2.1
church Eph 5.23; 3.6
confident Eph 3.12; 2 Thes 3.4
courage [2] 2 Cor 7.4; Col 2.2
Day of the Lord [2] Eph 4.30; 2.16
death (1) Eph 2.13; 2.8
defend [2] 2 Cor 12.19; 2 Tim 4.16
desire [2] Eph 4.22; 2.3
duty (1) Eph 6.1; Col 3.20
enemy Eph 6.13; 3.18
establish 1 Cor 1.6; Heb 9.10
fail Gal 2.2; 1 Thes 2.1

1 From Paul and Timothy, **servants** of
Christ Jesus—
To all **God's people** in Philippi who are
in **union with** Christ Jesus, including the
church leaders and **helpers**:
2 May God our **Father** and the Lord
Jesus Christ give you **grace** and **peace**.

Paul's Prayer for His Readers

3 I **thank** my God for you every time I
think of you; 4 and every time I **pray** for
you all, I pray with **joy** 5 because of the
way in which you have **helped** me in the
work of the **gospel** from the very first
day until now. 6 And so I am **sure** that
God, who began this good work in you,
will carry it on until it is finished on the
Day of Christ Jesus. 7 You are always in
my **heart**! And so it is only **right** for me
to feel as I do about you. For you have all
shared with me in this **privilege** that God
has given me, both now that I am in
prison and also while I was **free** to
defend the **gospel** and **establish** it firmly.
8 God is my **witness** that I am telling the
truth when I say that my deep feeling for
you all comes from the **heart** of Christ
Jesus himself.
9 I **pray** that your **love** will keep on
growing more and more, together with
true knowledge and **perfect judgement**,
10 so that you will be able to **choose** what
is **best**. Then you will be **free** from all **impurity** and **blame** on the **Day of Christ**.
11 Your **lives** will be filled with the **truly**
good qualities which only Jesus Christ
can produce, for the **glory** and **praise** of
God.

To Live Is Christ

12 I want you to know, my brothers,
that the things that have happened to me
have really **helped** the progress of the
gospel. 13 As a **result**, the whole palace
guard and all the others here know that I
am in **prison** because I am a **servant** of
Christ. 14 And my being in **prison** has
given most of the brothers more **confidence** in the Lord, so that they grow
bolder all the time to **preach** the **message**[a] **fearlessly**.
15 Of course some of them **preach**

faith [2] Eph 6.16; 2.17
Father (2) (God) Eph 6.23; 2.11
fear Eph 6.5; 2.12
free [3] Eph 6.8; 2.7
glory Eph 3.16; 2.11
God's people Eph 6.18; 4.21
gospel [6] Eph 6.19; 2.22
grace Eph 6.24; 4.23
happy [2] Gal 4.15; 2.2
heart [2] Eph 6.5; 4.6
help [3] Eph 6.18; 2.25
helper (1) Acts 21.8; 1 Tim 3.8
honour 2 Cor 6.8; 2.10
hope Eph 4.4; 2.19
important [2] 2 Cor 11.7; 2.12
impure Rom 6.19; 1 Thes 2.3
jealous Gal 5.20; 1 Tim 6.4
joy [2] Gal 5.22; 2.17
judge Eph 6.9; Col 3.25
knowledge Eph 4.13; 3.8
life (1) [5] Eph 5.2; 2.1
love [2] Eph 6.23; 2.1
matter Gal 6.15
means Eph 6.10; 3.3

[a] the message; *some manuscripts have* God's message.

1.1: Acts 16.12 **1.13:** Acts 28.30

message Eph 6.19; 2.16
motive 2 Cor 12.18; 1 Thes 2.3
peace Eph 6.15; 4.7
perfect 2 Cor 13.9; 2.15
praise Eph 5.19; 4.8
pray [2] Eph 6.18; Col 1.3
prayer Eph 6.18; 4.6
preach [3] Eph 2.17; 4.15
prison [4] Eph 6.20; Col 4.3
privilege [2] Eph 3.8
proclaim 1 Cor 14.1; 2.11
proud Gal 6.4; 2.16
prove 2 Cor 13.3; 2.22
purpose Eph 3.11; 2.13
quarrel 2 Cor 12.20; 1 Tim 6.4
reason Eph 6.18; 2.9
require Gal 3.2; Heb 8.4
result Eph 2.8; Col 3.11
right (1) [2] Eph 6.1; 3.17
sake Eph 6.20; 2.22
selfish 2 Cor 12.20; 2.3
servant [2] Eph 6.21; 2.7
serve Eph 6.5; 2.25
share Eph 5.5; 2.2
sincere Eph 6.5; Col 3.22
Spirit (1) (God's Spirit) Eph 6.17; 2.1
spirit (2) Eph 4.15; Col 2.5
suffer Eph 3.13; 3.10
sure [3] Eph 5.5; Col 1.23
thank Eph 5.4; 4.6
trouble Gal 6.17; 4.14
true [2] Eph 5.13; 3.3
truth Eph 6.14; 1 Thes 1.5
union [2] Eph 6.10; 3.1
victory 2 Cor 2.14; Col 2.15
win Gal 1.10; 3.12
witness 2 Cor 13.1; 1 Thes 2.5
wrong Gal 6.1; Col 3.25

Christ because they are **jealous** and
quarrelsome, but others from genuine
goodwill. 16 These do so from **love**, because they know that God has given me
the work of **defending** the **gospel**. 17 The
others do not **proclaim Christ sincerely**,
but from a **spirit** of **selfish** ambition; they
think that they will make more **trouble**
for me while I am in **prison**.

18 It does not **matter**! I am **happy**
about it—so long as **Christ** is **preached** in
every way possible, whether from **wrong**
or **right motives**. And I will continue to
be **happy**, 19 because I know that **by
means of** your **prayers** and the **help**
which comes from the **Spirit** of Jesus
Christ I shall be **set free**. 20 My deep
desire and **hope** is that I shall never **fail**
in my **duty**, but that at all times, and
especially just now, I shall be full of
courage, so that with my whole **being** I
shall bring **honour** to **Christ**, whether I
live or die. 21 For what is **life**? To me, it is
Christ. **Death**, then, will bring more.
22 But if by continuing to live I can do
more worthwhile work, then I am not
sure which I should **choose**. 23 I am pulled
in two directions. I want very much to
leave this **life** and be with **Christ**, which
is a far better thing; 24 but for your **sake** it
is much more **important** that I remain
alive. 25 I am **sure** of this, and so I know
that I will stay. I will stay on with you all,
to add to your progress and **joy** in the
faith, 26 so that when I am with you again,
you will have even more **reason** to be
proud of me in your **life** in **union with**
Christ Jesus.

27 Now, the **important** thing is that
your way of **life** should be as the **gospel**
of **Christ requires**, so that, whether or not
I am able to go and see you, I will hear
that you are standing firm with one common **purpose** and that with only one
desire you are fighting together for the
faith of the **gospel**. 28 Don't be **afraid** of
your **enemies**; always be **courageous**,
and this will **prove** to them that they will
lose and that you will **win**, because it is
God who gives you the **victory**. 29 For you
have been given the **privilege** of **serving**
Christ, not only by **believing** in him, but
also by **suffering** for him. 30 Now you can
take part with me in the battle. It is the
same battle you saw me fighting in the
past, and as you hear, the one I am fighting still.

Christ's Humility and Greatness

2 Your **life** in **Christ** makes you
strong, and his **love comforts** you.
You have **fellowship** with the **Spirit**,[b] and
you have **kindness** and **compassion** for
one another. 2 I **urge** you, then, to make
me completely **happy** by having the
same thoughts, **sharing** the same **love**,
and being one in **soul** and **mind**. 3 Don't
do anything from **selfish** ambition or
from a cheap **desire** to **boast**, but be
humble towards **one another**, always
considering others better than yourselves. 4 And look out for **one another's**
interests, not just for your own. 5 The attitude you should have is the one that
Christ Jesus had:

6 He always had the **nature** of God,
but he did not think that by **force** he
should try to become[c] equal with
God.
7 Instead of this, of his own **free will** he
gave up all he had,
and took the **nature** of a **servant**.
He became like man
and appeared in **human** likeness.
8 He was **humble** and walked the path of
obedience all the way to **death**—
his death on the **cross**.
9 For this **reason** God **raised** him to the
highest place **above**
and gave him the **name** that is
greater than any other name.
10 And so, in **honour** of the **name of Jesus**
all **beings** in **heaven**, on earth, and in
the **world below**[d]
will fall on their **knees**,
11 and all will openly **proclaim** that Jesus
Christ is Lord,
to the **glory** of God the **Father**.

Shining as Lights in the World

12 So then, **dear friends**, as you always
obeyed me when I was with you, it is
even more **important** that you **obey** me
now while I am away from you. Keep on
working with **fear** and **trembling** to **complete** your **salvation**, 13 because God is
always at work in you to make you willing and able to **obey** his own **purpose**.

14 Do everything without **complaining**
or **arguing**, 15 so that you may be **innocent**
and **pure** as **God's perfect children**, who
live in a **world** of **corrupt** and sinful
people. You must shine among them like
stars **lighting** up the sky, 16 as you **offer**
them the **message** of **life**. If you do so, I
shall have **reason** to be **proud** of you on
the **Day of Christ**, because it will show

above Rom 8.39; 3.14
anxious Mic 1.12
argue 2 Cor 10.4; Col 2.4
being 1.20; Col 3.10
blood 1 Cor 15.50; Heb 2.14
boast Eph 2.8; 1 Thes 2.19
care Eph 5.29; 4.10
cause (2) Gal 2.17
child of God [2] Eph 5.1; Heb 12.5
Christ [2] 1.13; 3.7
comfort 1 Cor 14.3; 1 Thes 2.12
compassion Zech 10.6; Col 3.12
complain 2 Cor 8.20; Col 3.13
complete Eph 1.9; 3.8
concern 2 Cor 11.28; Tit 3.8
consider Gal 3.6; 3.8
corrupt 2 Cor 11.3; Tit 3.11
cross (1) Eph 2.16; 3.18
Day of the Lord 1.6; 1 Thes 5.2
dear Eph 6.21; 4.1
death (1) 1.21; 3.10
desire 1.20; 3.19
eager Gal 2.10; 3.20
encourage Eph 6.22; 1 Thes 2.12
faith 1.25; 3.9
Father (2) (God) 1.2; 4.20
fear 1.14; Heb 2.15
fellowship 2 Cor 13.13; Phlm 6
force (1) Gal 6.12; Col 2.23
free 1.7; Col 1.14
friend 2 Cor 12.19; Col 1.22
give up Eph 6.18; 1 Tim 1.4
glad [3] 2 Cor 13.9; Col 2.5
glory 1.11; 3.21
gospel 1.5; 4.3
happy 1.18; 4.1
heaven Eph 6.9; 3.20
help [2] 1.5; 4.3
honour 1.20; 4.8
hope [2] 1.20; 3.11
human Eph 6.5; 4.7
humble [2] Eph 4.2; Col 2.18
important 1.24; 1 Pet 2.7
innocent 2 Cor 7.11; Jas 5.6
interest (1) Gal 4.17; Col 4.6
joy [3] 1.4; 3.1
kind Eph 4.32; Col 3.12
knee Eph 3.14; Heb 12.12
life (1) [4] 1.11; 3.3
light (1) Eph 5.8; Col 1.11
love [2] 1.9; Col 1.4
message 1.14; Col 1.5
mind (1) Eph 4.18; 4.7
name (2) (name of God, of Jesus) [2] Eph 5.20; Col 3.17
nature [2] Eph 5.13; Col 1.19
obey [4] Eph 6.1; 3.6
offer [3] Eph 5.2; 4.18

[b] You have fellowship with the Spirit; *or* The Spirit has brought you into fellowship with one another. [c] become; *or* remain.
[d] WORLD BELOW: *It was thought that the dead continued to exist in a dark world under the ground.*

1.30: Acts 16.19–40 **2.10–11:** Is 45.23 (LXX) **2.15:** Deut 32.5

one another [3] Eph 5.19; Col 3.9
perfect 1.9; 3.12
pity 1 Cor 15.19
proclaim 1.17; Col 1.25
proud 1.26; 3.19
prove 1.28; 2 Thes 1.5
pure Eph 5.27; 3.5
purpose 1.27; 1 Tim 1.5
raise Eph 2.6; 3.11
reason [2] 1.26; 3.4
respect Eph 6.2; 1 Thes 4.12
sacrifice Eph 5.2; 4.18
sake [2] 1.24; 3.7
salvation Eph 6.17; 1 Thes 2.16
selfish 1.17; 2 Tim 3.2
servant 1.1; Col 1.7
serve 1.29; Col 3.24
share [4] 1.7; 3.10
sorrow [2] Rom 9.2; 1 Tim 6.10
soul 2 Cor 7.1; 1 Thes 5.23
spare 2 Cor 1.23; 2 Pet 2.4
Spirit (1) (God's Spirit) 1.19; 3.3
strong Eph 3.16; Col 1.11
tremble Eph 6.5; Heb 12.12
trust 2 Cor 13.6; 3.3
turn Gal 4.9; 1 Thes 1.9
upset Gal 5.10; 2 Thes 2.2
urge Eph 4.1; 1 Thes 2.12
will (1) [2] Eph 1.1; Col 1.1
world Eph 6.12; 3.19
world of the dead (world below) Rom 10.7; Rev 1.18
worth 1 Cor 12.23; Heb 11.26

that all my effort and work have not
been wasted.
17 Perhaps my **life's blood** is to be
poured out like an **offering** on the **sacrifice** that your **faith offers** to God. If that
is so, I am **glad** and **share** my **joy** with
you all. 18 In the same way, you too must
be **glad** and **share** your **joy** with me.

Timothy and Epaphroditus

19 If it is the **Lord's will**, I **hope** that I
will be able to send Timothy to you soon,
so that I may be **encouraged** by news
about you. 20 He is the only one who
shares my feelings and who really **cares**
about you. 21 Everyone else is **concerned**
only with his own affairs, not with the
cause of Jesus Christ. 22 And you yourselves know how he has **proved** his
worth, how he and I, like a son and his
father, have worked together for the
sake of the **gospel**. 23 So I **hope** to send
him to you as soon as I know how things
are going to **turn** out for me. 24 And I **trust**
in the Lord that I myself will be able to
come to you soon.
25 I have thought it necessary to send
you our brother Epaphroditus, who has
worked and fought by my side and who
has **served** as your messenger in **helping**
me. 26 He is **anxious** to see you all and is
very **upset** because you had heard that
he was ill. 27 Indeed he was ill and almost
died. But God had **pity** on him, and not
only on him but on me, too, and **spared**
me an even greater **sorrow**. 28 I am all
the more **eager**, then, to send him to you,
so that you will be **glad** again when you
see him, and my own **sorrow** will disappear. 29 Receive him, then, with **joy**, as
a brother in the Lord. Show **respect** to all
such people as he, 30 because he risked
his **life** and nearly died for the **sake** of
the work of **Christ**, in order to give me
the **help** that you yourselves could not
give.

The True Righteousness

above 2.9; Jas 3.17
ashamed 2 Cor 11.21; 2 Thes 3.14
basis Eph 2.12; Col 1.5
best 1.10; Col 4.15
birth Eph 2.11; Tit 3.5
body [4] Eph 5.23; Col 1.18
ceremony [2] Gal 6.13; Heb 9.10
change Gal 1.7; Heb 1.12
Christ [5] 2.1; 4.13
church 1.1; 4.15
circumcise [2] Eph 2.11; Col 2.11

3 In conclusion, my brothers, be **joyful**
in your **union with** the Lord. I don't
mind repeating what I have written
before, and you will be **safer** if I do so.
2 **Watch** out for those who do **evil** things,
those dogs, those men who insist on cutting the **body**. 3 It is we, not they, who
have received the **true circumcision**, for
we **worship** God **by means of** his **Spirit**
and **rejoice** in our **life** in **union with**
Christ Jesus. We do not put any **trust** in
external **ceremonies**. 4 I could, of course,
put my **trust** in such things. If anyone
thinks he can **trust** in external **ceremonies**, I have even more **reason** to feel
that way. 5 I was **circumcised** when I was
a week old. I am an Israelite by **birth**, of
the tribe of Benjamin, a **pure-blooded
Hebrew**. As far as keeping the Jewish
Law is concerned, I was a **Pharisee**, 6 and
I was so zealous that I **persecuted** the
church. As far as a person can be
righteous by **obeying** the **commands** of
the **Law**, I was without **fault**. 7 But all
those things that I might count as profit I
now reckon as **loss** for **Christ's sake**. 8 Not
only those things; I reckon everything as
complete loss for the **sake** of what is so
much more **valuable**, the **knowledge** of
Christ Jesus my Lord. For his **sake** I have
thrown everything away; I **consider** it all
as mere refuse, so that I may gain **Christ**
9 and be completely **united** with him. I no
longer have a **righteousness** of my own,
the kind that is gained by **obeying** the
Law. I now have the **righteousness** that is
given through **faith** in **Christ**, the
righteousness that comes from God and
is **based on faith**. 10 All I want is to know
Christ and to **experience** the **power** of his
resurrection, to **share** in his **sufferings**
and become like him in his **death**, 11 in
the **hope** that I myself will be **raised from
death to life**.

Running towards the Goal

12 I do not **claim** that I have already
succeeded or have already become **perfect**. I keep striving to **win** the **prize** for
which Christ Jesus has already **won** me
to himself. 13 Of course, my brothers, I
really do not[e] think that I have already
won it; the one thing I do, however, is to
forget what is behind me and do my **best**
to reach what is ahead. 14 So I run
straight towards the goal in order to **win**
the **prize**, which is God's call through
Christ Jesus to the **life above**.
15 All of us who are **spiritually mature**
should have this same attitude. But if
some of you have a different attitude,
God will make this **clear** to you. 16 However that may be, let us go forward
according to the same rules we have
followed until now.
17 Keep on imitating me, my brothers.
Pay attention to those who follow the
right example that we have set for you.
18 I have told you this many times before,
and now I repeat it with **tears**: there are
many whose **lives** make them **enemies** of
Christ's death on the **cross**. 19 They are
going to end up in **hell**, because their **god**
is their **bodily desires**. They are **proud** of

claim 2 Cor 3.5; Col 2.18
clear Eph 5.13; Col 4.4
command 1 Cor 14.37; 1 Thes 4.16
complete 2.12; Col 1.24
consider 2.3; 1 Tim 1.12
cross (1) 2.8; Col 1.20
death (1) [2] 2.8; Col 1.20
death (2) (from death) Eph 5.14; Col 1.18
desire 2.3; Col 3.5
eager 2.28; 1 Tim 3.1
enemy 1.28; Col 1.21
evil Eph 6.11; Col 1.21
example Gal 3.15; 1 Thes 1.7
experience Gal 3.4; 2 Thes 1.4
faith [2] 2.17; Col 1.4
fault Eph 5.27; Col 1.22
forget 1 Cor 2.2; Col 4.18
glory 2.11; 4.20
god (2) (other gods) Gal 4.8; 2 Thes 2.4
heaven [2] 2.10; Col 1.5
Hebrew 2 Cor 11.22; Rev 9.11
hell Gal 1.8; 2 Thes 2.3
hope 2.19; Col 1.5
joy 2.17; 4.4
knowledge 1.9; Col 1.9
law [3] Eph 2.15; Col 2.13
life (1) [3] 2.1; 4.1
life (2) (to life) Eph 2.5; Col 2.13
loss [2] Acts 27.10; 4.15
mature Eph 4.13; Col 1.28
means 1.19; Col 1.22
mortal 2 Cor 5.4; 1 Pet 1.23
obey [2] 2.8; Col 2.20
perfect 2.15; Col 3.14
persecute Gal 6.12; 1 Thes 2.14
Pharisees Acts 26.5
power [2] Eph 6.10; 4.13
prize [2] 1 Cor 9.24; 2 Tim 2.5
proud 2.16; 4.1
pure 2.15; 4.8
raise 2.9; Col 1.18
reason 2.9; Col 1.9
rejoice Rom 15.10; 4.4
resurrection Acts 17.18; 2 Tim 2.18
right (1) 1.7; 4.8
righteous [4] Eph 6.14; 1 Tim 6.11
safe Gal 2.5; 4.7
sake [3] 2.22; 2 Tim 1.8
Saviour Eph 5.23; 1 Tim 1.1
share 2.2; 4.15
Spirit (1) (God's Spirit) 2.1; Col 1.8
spiritual Eph 6.12; Col 1.16
succeed (1) 2 Cor 13.7; Jas 1.3
suffer 1.29; Col 1.24
tear (2) 2 Cor 2.4; 2 Tim 1.4

[e] not; *some manuscripts have* not yet.

3.5: Acts 23.6, 26.5; Rom 11.1 **3.6:** Acts 8.3, 22.4, 26.9–11 **3.17:** 1 Cor 4.16, 11.1

true 1.9; 4.8
trust [3] 2.24;
2 Tim 1.12
union [2] 1.1; 4.4
unite Eph 5.31;
Col 3.14
value 1 Cor 14.5;
Col 2.23
watch Eph 6.6;
Col 3.22
weak Gal 4.9;
1 Thes 5.14
win [4] 1.28;
1 Thes 4.12
world 2.15; Col 1.6
worship (1) (of God)
1 Cor 14.19; Heb 1.6

abundant Eph 2.4;
1 Tim 1.14
accept Eph 6.17;
Col 2.6
action Gal 5.19;
Tit 1.16
agree Gal 3.15;
1 Tim 6.3
beg Eph 3.13;
1 Thes 4.1
care [2] 2.20;
1 Thes 2.7
Christ 3.7; Col 1.2
church 3.6; Col 1.18
dear [2] 2.12; Col 1.7
deserve 2 Cor 11.15;
Heb 2.2
enough [2]
2 Cor 11.27; 1 Tim 6.8
faithful Eph 6.21;
Col 1.2
Father (2) (God)
2.11; Col 1.2
gentle Eph 4.2;
Col 3.12
gift [2] Eph 4.7;
1 Tim 4.14
glory 3.21; Col 1.11
God's people [2] 1.1;
Col 1.2
Good News
Eph 6.15; Col 1.5
gospel 2.22; Col 1.6
grace 1.2; Col 1.2
happy 2.2; Col 1.24
hard 2 Cor 11.23;
Col 2.1
heart [2] 1.7; Col 3.1
help [4] 2.25; Col 1.24
honour 2.10;
1 Thes 4.4
human 2.7; Col 2.8
hunger 2 Cor 11.27;
Rev 7.16
joy [2] 3.1; Col 1.11
learn [3] Eph 5.10;
Col 1.7
life (1) [2] 3.3;
Col 1.10
loss 3.7; Heb 10.34
mind (1) [2] 2.2;
Col 3.2
need [5] Eph 4.29;
1 Thes 1.8

what they should be **ashamed** of, and
they think only of things that belong to
this world. 20 We, however, are citizens of
heaven, and we **eagerly** wait for our
Saviour, the Lord Jesus Christ, to come
from **heaven.** 21 He will **change** our **weak**
mortal bodies and make them like his
own **glorious body**, using that **power** by
which he is able to bring all things under
his rule.

Instructions

4 So then, my brothers, how **dear** you
are to me and how I miss you! How
happy you make me, and how **proud** I am
of you! This then, **dear** brothers, is how
you should stand firm in your **life** in the
Lord.

2 Euodia and Syntyche, **please**, I **beg**
you, try to **agree** as sisters in the Lord.
3 And you too, my **faithful** partner, I want
you to **help** these women; for they have
worked **hard** with me to spread the
gospel, together with Clement and all my
other fellow-workers, whose names are
in God's book of the living.

4 May you always be **joyful** in your
union with the Lord. I say it again:
rejoice!

5 Show a **gentle** attitude towards
everyone. The Lord is coming soon.
6 Don't **worry** about anything, but in all
your **prayers** ask God for what you **need**,
always asking him with a **thankful heart**.
7 And God's **peace**, which is far beyond
human understanding, will keep your
hearts and **minds safe** in **union with**
Christ Jesus.

8 In conclusion, my brothers, fill your
minds with those things that are good
and that **deserve praise**: things that are
true, noble, **right**, **pure**, lovely, and
honourable. 9 Put into **practice** what you
learnt and received from me, both from
my **words** and from my **actions**. And the
God who gives us **peace** will be with you.

Thanks for the Gift

10 In my **life in union with** the Lord it
is a great **joy** to me that after so long a
time you once more had the chance of
showing that you **care** for me. I don't
mean that you had stopped **caring** for
me—you just had no chance to show it.
11 And I am not saying this because I feel
neglected, for I have **learnt** to be **satisfied** with what I have. 12 I know what it is
to be in **need** and what it is to have more
than **enough**. I have **learnt** this **secret**, so
that anywhere, at any time, I am content,
whether I am full or **hungry**, whether I
have too much or too little. 13 I have the
strength to face all conditions by the
power that **Christ** gives me.

14 But it was very good of you to **help**
me in my **troubles**. 15 You Philippians
know very well that when I left Macedonia in the early days of **preaching** the
Good News, you were the only **church** to
help me; you were the only ones who
shared my profits and **losses**. 16 More
than once when I **needed help** in Thessalonica, you sent it to me. 17 It is not that I
just want to receive **gifts**; rather, I want
to see profit added to your account.
18 Here, then, is my receipt for everything
you have given me—and it has been
more than **enough**! I have all I **need** now
that Epaphroditus has brought me all
your **gifts**. They are like a sweet-smelling
offering to God, a **sacrifice** which is
acceptable and **pleasing** to him. 19 And
with all his **abundant** wealth through
Christ Jesus, my God will supply all your
needs. 20 To our God and **Father** be the
glory for ever and ever! Amen.

Final Greetings

21 Greetings to each one of **God's**
people who belong to Christ Jesus. The
brothers here with me send you their
greetings. 22 All **God's people** here send
greetings, especially those who belong to
the Emperor's palace.

23 May the **grace** of the Lord Jesus
Christ be with you all.

4.15-16: 2 Cor 11.9 **4.16:** Acts 17.1 **4.18:** Ex 29.18

neglect Acts 6.1;
1 Tim 4.14
offer 2.16; Col 1.5
peace [2] 1.2; Col 1.2
please [2] Eph 5.2;
Col 1.10
power 3.10; Col 1.11
practice Gal 6.13;
1 Thes 1.3
praise 1.11;
1 Thes 2.6
prayer 1.19; Col 4.2
preach 1.14; Col 1.23
proud 3.19;
1 Thes 2.20
pure 3.5; Col 1.22
rejoice 3.3; 1 Pet 1.8
right (1) 3.17; Col 4.6
sacrifice 2.17;
Col 1.20
safe 3.1; Col 1.5
satisfy Gal 5.16;
1 Tim 6.6
secret Eph 6.19;
Col 1.26
share 3.10; Col 1.11
strength Eph 6.10;
Col 1.11
thank 1.3; Col 1.3
trouble 1.17;
1 Thes 2.9
true 3.3; Col 1.5
understand
Eph 5.32; Col 1.9
union [3] 3.1; Col 1.2
word (1) Eph 6.17;
1 Thes 1.5
worry Gal 4.11;
1 Pet 3.14

PAUL'S LETTER TO THE COLOSSIANS

INTRODUCTION

Paul's Letter to the Colossians was written to the church at Colossae, a town in Asia Minor east of Ephesus. This church had not been established by Paul, but was in an area for which Paul felt responsible, as he sent out workers from Ephesus, the capital of the Roman province of Asia. Paul had learnt that there were false teachers in the church at Colossae who insisted that in order to know God and have full salvation one must worship certain "spiritual rulers and authorities." In addition, these teachers said, one must submit to special rites such as circumcision and must observe strict rules about foods and other matters.

Paul writes to oppose these teachings with the true Christian message. The heart of his reply is that Jesus Christ is able to give full salvation and that these other beliefs and practices actually lead away from him. Through Christ, God created the world and through him he is bringing it back to himself. Only in union with Christ is there hope of salvation for the world. Paul then spells out the implications of this great teaching for the lives of believers.

It is noteworthy that Tychicus, who took this letter to Colossae for Paul, was accompanied by Onesimus, the slave on whose behalf Paul wrote *Philemon.*

Outline of Contents

---

1 From Paul, who by **God's will** is an **apostle** of Christ Jesus, and from our brother Timothy—

2 To **God's people** in Colossae, who are our **faithful** brothers in **union with Christ**:

May God **our Father** give you **grace** and **peace.**

Prayer of Thanksgiving

3 We always give **thanks** to God, the **Father** of our Lord Jesus Christ, when we **pray** for you. 4 For we have heard of your **faith** in Christ Jesus and of your **love** for all **God's people.** 5 When the **true message**, the **Good News**, first came to you, you heard about the **hope** it **offers**. So your **faith** and **love** are **based on** what you **hope** for, which is kept **safe** for you in **heaven.** 6 The **gospel** keeps bringing **blessings** and is spreading throughout the **world**, just as it has among you ever since the day you first heard about the **grace** of God and came to know it as it really is. 7 You **learnt** of God's **grace** from Epaphras, our **dear fellow-servant**, who is **Christ's faithful** worker on our[a] behalf. 8 He has told us of the **love** that the **Spirit** has given you.

9 For this **reason** we have always **prayed** for you, ever since we heard about you. We ask God to fill you with the **knowledge** of his **will**, with all the **wisdom** and **understanding** that his **Spirit** gives. 10 Then you will be able to live as the Lord wants and will always do what **pleases** him. Your **lives** will produce all kinds of good **deeds**, and you will grow in your **knowledge** of God. 11-12 May you be made **strong** with all the **strength** which comes from his **glorious power**, so that you may be able to **endure** everything with **patience**. And with **joy** give **thanks** to[b] the Father, who has made you **fit** to have your **share** of what God has reserved for **his people** in the **kingdom** of **light.** 13 He **rescued** us from the **power** of **darkness** and brought us **safe** into the **kingdom** of his **dear Son**, 14 by whom we are **set free**, that is, our sins are **forgiven.**

The Person and Work of Christ

15 **Christ** is the visible likeness of the invisible God. He is the **first-born Son**, superior to all **created** things. 16 For through him God **created** everything in **heaven and on earth**, the seen and the unseen things, including **spiritual powers**,

[a] our; *some manuscripts have* your.
[b] with patience. And with joy give thanks to; *or* with patience and joy. And give thanks to.

1.7: Col 4.12; Phlm 23 **1.14:** Eph 1.7

age (1) Eph 6.12; Heb 6.5
alone 1 Cor 7.8; 1 Thes 3.1
apostle Eph 4.11; 1 Thes 2.7
authorities Eph 6.12; 2.15
basis Phil 3.9; 2.23
bless Eph 3.6; 1 Tim 1.11
body [3] Phil 3.2; 2.5
Christ [9] Phil 4.13; 2.2
church [3] Phil 4.15; 4.15
complete Phil 3.8; 4.12
create [3] Eph 4.24; 1 Tim 2.13
cross (1) Phil 3.18; 2.14
dark Eph 6.12; 1 Thes 5.4
dear [2] Phil 4.1; 4.7
death (1) [2] Phil 3.10; 2 Tim 1.10
death (2) (from death) Phil 3.11; 2.12
deed (2) Eph 2.10; 1 Tim 2.10
endure 2 Cor 6.4; 2 Thes 1.4
enemy Phil 3.18; 2 Thes 3.15
evil Phil 3.2; 3.5
exist 1 Cor 11.12; Heb 11.6
faith [2] Phil 3.9; 2.5
faithful [3] Phil 4.3; 4.7
Father (2) (God) [3] Phil 4.20; 3.17

fault Phil 3.6; 1 Thes 2.10
first-born [2] Lk 2.23; Heb 1.6
fit (1) Eph 5.4; Tit 1.16
forgive Eph 4.32; 2.13
free Phil 2.7; 2.11
friend Phil 2.12; Tit 3.2
glory [3] Phil 4.20; 3.4
God's people [5] Phil 4.21; 3.12
Good News Phil 4.15; 1 Thes 1.5
gospel [4] Phil 4.3; 1 Tim 1.11
grace [3] Phil 4.23; 4.18
happy Phil 4.1; Jas 1.12
heaven [3] Phil 3.20; 3.1
help Phil 4.3; 4.11
holy Eph 4.24; 2.16
hope [3] Phil 3.11; 1 Thes 1.3
joy Phil 4.4; 1 Thes 1.6
Kingdom (1) (of God) [2] Eph 5.5; 4.11
knowledge [2] Phil 3.8; 2.3
learn Phil 4.9; 1 Thes 4.1
life (1) [2] Phil 4.1; 2.7
light (1) Phil 2.15; 1 Thes 5.5
love [3] Phil 2.1; 2.2

mankind Eph 4.6; 1 Tim 2.5
mature Phil 3.15; 4.12
means [2] Phil 3.3; 2.8
message [2] Phil 2.16; 3.16
might Eph 6.10; 2 Thes 1.7
nature Phil 2.6; 2.9
offer Phil 4.18; 1 Tim 2.1
patient Eph 4.2; 3.12
peace [2] Phil 4.7; 3.15
physical [2] Gal 6.13; 2.23
plan Eph 3.3; 1 Tim 1.4
please Phil 4.2; 3.20
power [3] Phil 4.13; 2.11
pray [2] Phil 1.4; 4.2
preach [2] Phil 4.15; 4.3
presence [2] Eph 4.10; 1 Thes 2.19
proclaim Phil 2.11; 1 Tim 2.7
proper 1 Cor 15.23; 1 Thes 5.12
pure Phil 4.8; 1 Thes 2.10
raise Phil 3.11; 2.12
reason Phil 3.4; 2.18
rescue Rom 7.24; 1 Thes 1.10
reveal Eph 5.13; 2 Thes 2.8
rich Eph 5.9; 3.16
sacrifice Phil 4.18; 2 Tim 4.6
safe [2] Phil 4.7; 1 Thes 5.3
secret [4] Phil 4.12; 2.2
servant [3] Phil 2.7; 4.7
share [2] Phil 4.15; 3.4
Son of God [7] Eph 4.13; 1 Thes 1.10
source Rom 16.20; 2 Thes 3.16
Spirit (1) (God's Spirit) [2] Phil 3.3; 1 Thes 1.5
spiritual Phil 3.15; 2.10
strength [2] Phil 4.13; 1 Thes 3.2
strong Phil 2.1; 2.7
struggle Hos 12.3; 1 Tim 4.10
suffer [3] Phil 3.10; 1 Thes 1.6
sure Phil 1.6; 4.16
task [2] Gal 2.7; 4.17
teach Eph 4.14; 2.7
thank [2] Phil 4.6; 2.7
true Phil 4.8; 2.2
understand Phil 4.7; 2.2
union [3] Phil 4.4; 2.6
universe [2] Eph 4.10; 2.8
warn Eph 4.17; 1 Thes 4.6
will (1) [2] Phil 2.7; 4.12
wisdom [2] Eph 3.10; 2.3
world [2] Phil 3.19; 2.20

lords, rulers, and **authorities**. God **created** the whole **universe** through him and for him. 17 **Christ existed** before all things, and in **union with** him all things have their **proper** place. 18 He is the head of his **body**, the **church**; he is the **source** of the **body's life**. He is the **first-born Son**, who was **raised from death**, in order that he **alone** might have the first place in all things. 19 For it was by God's own decision that the **Son** has in himself the full **nature** of God. 20 Through the **Son**, then, God decided to bring the whole **universe** back to himself. God made **peace** through **his Son's sacrificial death** on the **cross** and so brought back to himself all things, both on earth and in **heaven**.

21 At one time you were far away from God and were his **enemies** because of the **evil** things you did and thought. 22 But now, **by means of** the **physical death of his Son**, God has made you his **friends**, in order to bring you, **holy**, **pure**, and **faultless**, into his **presence**. 23 You must, of course, continue **faithful** on a firm and **sure** foundation, and must not allow yourselves to be shaken from the **hope** you gained when you heard the **gospel**. It is of this **gospel** that I, Paul, became a **servant**—this **gospel** which has been **preached** to everybody in the **world**.

Paul's Work as a Servant of the Church

24 And now I am **happy** about my **sufferings** for you, for **by means of** my **physical sufferings** I am **helping** to complete what still remains of **Christ's sufferings** on behalf of his **body**, the **church**. 25 And I have been made a **servant** of the **church** by God, who gave me this **task** to perform for your good. It is the **task** of fully **proclaiming** his **message**, 26 which is the **secret** he hid through all past **ages** from all **mankind** but has now **revealed** to **his people**. 27 God's **plan** is to make known his **secret** to **his people**, this **rich** and **glorious secret** which he has for all peoples. And the **secret** is that **Christ** is in you, which means that you will **share** in the **glory** of God. 28 So we **preach Christ** to everyone. With all possible **wisdom** we **warn** and **teach** them in order to bring each one into God's **presence** as a **mature** individual **in union with Christ**. 29 To get this done I toil and **struggle**, using the **mighty strength** which **Christ** supplies and which is at work in me.

2 Let me tell you how **hard** I have worked for you and for the people in Laodicea and for all others who do not know me personally. 2 I do this in order that they may be filled with **courage** and may be drawn together in **love**, and so have the full wealth of **assurance** which **true understanding** brings. In this way they will know God's **secret**, which is **Christ** himself.[c] 3 He is the key that opens all the hidden treasures of God's **wisdom** and **knowledge**.

4 I tell you, then, do not let anyone **deceive** you with **false arguments**, no matter how good they seem to be. 5 For even though I am absent in **body**, yet I am with you in **spirit**, and I am **glad** as I see the resolute firmness with which you stand together in your **faith in Christ**.

Fullness of Life in Christ

6 Since you have **accepted** Christ Jesus as Lord, live in **union with** him. 7 Keep your roots deep in him, build your **lives** on him, and become **stronger** in your **faith**, as you were **taught**. And be filled with **thanksgiving**.

8 See to it, then, that no one **enslaves** you **by means of** the **worthless deceit** of **human wisdom**, which comes from the **teachings** handed down by men and from the ruling **spirits** of the **universe**, and not from **Christ**. 9 For the full content of **divine nature** lives in **Christ**, in his **humanity**, 10 and you have been given full **life** in **union with** him. He is **supreme** over every **spiritual** ruler and **authority**.

11 In **union with Christ** you were **circumcised**, not with the **circumcision** that is made by men, but with the **circumcision** made by **Christ**, which consists of being **freed** from the **power** of this sinful **self**. 12 For when you were **baptized**, you were buried with **Christ**, and in **baptism** you were also **raised** with **Christ** through your **faith** in the active **power of God**, who **raised** him **from death**. 13 You were at one time **spiritually dead** because of your sins and because you were **Gentiles** without the **Law**. But God has now brought you **to life** with **Christ**. God **forgave** us all our sins; 14 he cancelled the unfavourable record of our **debts** with its **binding** rules and did away with it completely by nailing it to the **cross**. 15 And on that **cross Christ freed** himself from the **power** of the **spiritual** rulers and **authorities**;[d] he made a public spectacle

accept Phil 4.18; 1 Thes 2.13
angel [2] Eph 3.10; 1 Thes 4.16
argue Phil 2.14; 1 Tim 1.4
assure Eph 1.14
authorities 1.16; Tit 3.1
authority Eph 5.23; 1 Thes 4.2
baptize [2] Eph 4.5; Heb 6.2
basis 1.5; 1 Thes 2.3
bind Eph 4.3; 3.14
body [4] 1.18; 3.15
captive Eph 4.8
Christ [14] 1.2; 3.1
circumcise [3] Phil 3.3; 3.11
claim Phil 3.12; 2 Thes 2.2
condemn Gal 1.8; 2 Thes 2.12
control [2] Eph 5.2; 2 Tim 3.6
courage Phil 1.20; 1 Thes 2.2
cross (1) [2] 1.20; Heb 12.2
dead Eph 2.1; 1 Thes 5.10
death (2) (from death) 1.18; 1 Thes 1.10
debt Lk 16.5
deceive [2] Eph 5.6; 2 Thes 2.3
divine Rom 1.4; Heb 8.1
faith [3] 1.4; 1 Thes 1.3
false [3] 2 Cor 11.13; 2 Thes 2.9
festival 1 Cor 5.7
force (1) Phil 2.6; Phlm 14
forgive 1.14; 3.13
free [3] 1.14; 3.11
Gentile Eph 3.1; 3.11
glad Phil 2.17; Heb 10.34
hard Phil 4.3; 4.13
holy 1.22; 1 Thes 3.1
human [3] Phil 4.7; 3.22
humble [2] Phil 2.3; 3.12
knowledge 1.9; 3.10
law Phil 3.5; 1 Tim 1.8
life (1) [2] 1.10; 3.3
life (2) (to life) Phil 3.11; 3.1
love 1.4; 3.12
man-made Acts 19.26; Heb 9.1
means 1.22; 2 Tim 1.9
nature 1.19; Heb 2.1
New Moon Festival Ezek 46.1
obey Phil 3.6; 3.6
passion Eph 4.31; 3.5
physical 1.22; 1 Tim 4.8
power [3] 1.11; 1 Thes 1.5
raise [2] 1.18; 3.1
real [2] Gal 3.7; 3.4
reason 1.9; 1 Thes 2.13
Sabbath Acts 18.4
secret 1.26; 4.3
self Eph 4.22; 3.9
slave Eph 6.5; 3.11
special Eph 4.7; 2 Tim 2.20

[c] God's secret, which is Christ himself; *some manuscripts have* God's secret; *others have* the secret of God the Father of Christ; *others have* the secret of the God and Father, and of Christ.
[d] Christ freed himself from the power of the spiritual rulers and authorities; *or* Christ stripped the spiritual rulers and authorities of their power.

1.18: Eph 1.22–23 **1.20:** Eph 2.16 **2.12:** Rom 6.4 **2.13:** Eph 2.1–5 **2.14:** Eph 2.15

of them by leading them as **captives** in his **victory procession**.

16 So let no one make rules about what you eat or drink or about **holy** days or the **New Moon Festival** or the **Sabbath**. 17 All such things are only a shadow of things in the future; the **reality** is **Christ**. 18 Do not allow yourselves to be **condemned** by anyone who **claims** to be superior because of **special visions** and who insists on **false humility** and the **worship of angels**. For no **reason** at all, such a person is all puffed up by his **human** way of thinking 19 and has stopped holding on to **Christ**, who is the head of the **body**. Under **Christ's control** the whole **body** is nourished and held together by its joints and ligaments, and it grows as God wants it to grow.

Dying and Living with Christ

20 You have died with **Christ** and are **set free** from the ruling **spirits** of the **universe**. Why, then, do you live as though you belonged to **this world**? Why do you **obey** such rules as 21 "Don't handle this," "Don't taste that," "Don't touch the other"? 22 All these refer to things which become **useless** once they are used; they are only **man-made** rules and **teachings**. 23 Of course such rules appear to be **based on wisdom** in their **forced worship of angels**, and **false humility**, and severe treatment of the **body**; but they have no **real value** in **controlling physical passions**.

3 You have been **raised to life** with **Christ**, so set your **hearts** on the things that are in **heaven**, where **Christ** sits on his **throne** at the **right-hand side** of God. 2 Keep your **minds** fixed on things there, not on things here on earth. 3 For you have died, and your **life** is hidden with **Christ** in God. 4 Your **real life** is **Christ** and when he appears, then you too will appear with him and **share** his **glory**!

The Old Life and the New

5 You must put **to death**, then, the earthly **desires** at work in you, such as **sexual immorality**, indecency, **lust**, **evil passions**, and **greed** (for greed is a form of **idolatry**). 6 Because of such things **God's anger** will come upon those who do not **obey** him.[e] 7 At one time you yourselves used to live according to such **desires**, when your **life** was dominated by them.

8 But now you must get **rid** of all these things: **anger**, **passion**, and **hateful** feelings. No **insults** or obscene talk must ever come from your lips. 9 Do not **lie** to **one another**, for you have taken off the old **self** with its habits 10 and have put on the **new self**. This is the **new being** which God, its **Creator**, is **constantly** renewing in his own **image**, in order to bring you to a full **knowledge** of himself. 11 As a **result**, there is no longer any **distinction** between **Gentiles** and **Jews**, **circumcised** and uncircumcised, barbarians, savages, **slaves**, and **free** men, but **Christ** is all, Christ is in all.

12 You are the **people of God**; he **loved** you and **chose** you for his own. So then, you must clothe yourselves with **compassion**, **kindness**, **humility**, **gentleness**, and **patience**. 13 Be **tolerant** with **one another** and **forgive** one another whenever any of you has a **complaint** against someone else. You must **forgive one another** just as the Lord has forgiven you. 14 And to all these qualities add **love**, which **binds** all things together in **perfect unity**. 15 The **peace** that **Christ** gives is to **guide** you in the decisions you make; for it is to this **peace** that God has called you together in the one **body**. And be **thankful**. 16 **Christ's message** in all its **richness** must live in your **hearts**. **Teach** and instruct **each other** with all **wisdom**. Sing **psalms**, **hymns**, and **sacred** songs; sing to God with **thanksgiving** in your **hearts**. 17 Everything you do or say, then, should be done **in the name of** the Lord Jesus, as you give **thanks** through him to God the **Father**.

Personal Relations in the New Life

18 Wives, **submit** to your husbands, for that is what you should do as **Christians**.

19 Husbands, **love** your wives and do not be harsh with them.

20 Children, it is your **Christian duty** to **obey** your parents always, for that is what **pleases** God.

21 Parents, do not irritate your children, or they will become **discouraged**.

22 **Slaves**, **obey** your **human masters** in all things, not only when they are **watching** you because you want to gain their **approval**; but do it with a **sincere heart** because of your **reverence** for the Lord. 23 Whatever you do, work at it **with all your heart**, as though you were working for the Lord and not for men. 24 **Remember** that the Lord will give you

[e] *Some manuscripts do not have* upon those who do not obey him.

2.16: Rom 14.1–6 **2.19:** Eph 4.16 **3.1:** Ps 110.1 **3.9:** Eph 4.22 **3.10:** Gen 1.26; Eph 4.24
3.12–13: Eph 4.2 **3.13:** Eph 4.32 **3.16–17:** Eph 5.19–20 **3.18:** Eph 5.22; 1 Pet 3.1
3.19: Eph 5.25; 1 Pet 3.7 **3.20:** Eph 6.1 **3.21:** Eph 6.4 **3.22–25:** Eph 6.5–8

self [2] 2.11; Phlm 19
serve Phil 2.25; 1 Thes 1.9
sex Eph 5.3; 1 Thes 4.3
share 1.11; 1 Thes 2.8
sincere Phil 1.17; 1 Tim 3.8
slave [2] 2.8; 4.1
submit Eph 5.21; Tit 2.5
teach 2.7; 1 Thes 4.8
thank [3] 2.7; 4.2
throne Acts 12.21; Heb 4.16
tolerate Eph 4.2; Rev 2.2
unite Phil 3.9
watch Phil 3.2; 1 Tim 4.16
wisdom 2.3; 2 Tim 3.15
wrong Phil 1.18; 1 Thes 4.6

Chapter 4
act Gal 5.15; Jas 2.12
alert Eph 6.18; 1 Pet 1.13
believer [2] Eph 4.25; 1 Thes 1.7
best Phil 3.13; 1 Tim 6.12
cheer (1) Eph 6.7; 2 Tim 1.16
Christ 3.1; 1 Thes 2.7
Christian 3.18; 1 Thes 4.6
church [2] 1.18; 1 Thes 1.1
clear Phil 3.15; 1 Tim 1.5
complete 1.24; 1 Thes 1.5
convince 2 Cor 2.3; 1 Thes 1.5
dear [3] 1.7; 1 Thes 2.8
faithful [2] 1.2; 1 Thes 5.24
forget Phil 3.13; Heb 6.10
grace 1.2; 1 Thes 1.1

as a **reward** what he has kept for **his people**. For **Christ** is the **real Master** you **serve**. 25 And every **wrongdoer** will be **repaid** for the wrong things he does, because God **judges** everyone by the same standard.

4 **Masters**, be fair and **just** in the way you treat your **slaves**. **Remember** that you too have a **Master in heaven**.

Instructions

2 Be persistent in **prayer**, and keep **alert** as you **pray**, giving **thanks** to God. 3 At the same time **pray** also for us, so that God will give us a good opportunity to **preach** his **message** about the **secret** of **Christ**. For that is why I am now in **prison**. 4 **Pray**, then, that I may speak, as I should, in such a way as to make it **clear**.

5 Be **wise** in the way you **act** towards those who are not **believers**, making good use of every opportunity you have. 6 Your **speech** should always be pleasant and **interesting**, and you should know how to give the **right** answer to everyone.

Final Greetings

7 Our **dear** brother Tychicus, who is a **faithful** worker and **fellow-servant** in the Lord's work, will give you all the news about me. 8 That is why I am sending him to you, in order to **cheer** you up by telling you how all of us are getting on. 9 With him goes Onesimus, that **dear** and **faithful** brother, who belongs to your group. They will tell you everything that is happening here.

10 Aristarchus, who is in **prison** with me, sends you greetings, and so does Mark, the cousin of Barnabas. (You have already received instructions to **welcome** Mark if he comes your way.) 11 Joshua, also called Justus, sends greetings too. These three are the only **Jewish believers** who work with me for the **Kingdom of God**, and they have been a great **help** to me.

12 Greetings from Epaphras, another member of your group and a **servant** of Christ Jesus. He always **prays** fervently for you, asking God to make you stand firm, as **mature** and fully **convinced Christians**, in **complete obedience** to **God's will**. 13 I can personally **testify** to his **hard work** for you and for the people in Laodicea and Hierapolis. 14 Luke, our **dear** doctor, and Demas send you their greetings.

15 Give our **best wishes** to the brothers in Laodicea and to Nympha and the **church** that meets in her house.[f] 16 After you read this **letter**, make **sure** that it is read also in the **church** at Laodicea. At the same time, you are to read the **letter** that the brothers in Laodicea will send you. 17 And say to Archippus, "Be **sure** to finish the **task** you were given in the Lord's **service**."

18 With my own hand I write this: *Greetings from Paul.* Do not **forget** my chains!

May God's **grace** be with you.

[f]Nympha...her house; *some manuscripts have* Nymphas...his house.

3.25: Deut 10.17; Eph 6.9 **4.1:** Eph 6.9 **4.5:** Eph 5.16 **4.7:** Acts 20.4; 2 Tim 4.12 **4.7–8:** Eph 6.21–22 **4.9:** Phlm 10–12 **4.10:** Acts 19.29, 27.2; Phlm 24; Acts 12.12, 25, 13.13, 15.37–39 **4.12:** Col 1.7; Phlm 23 **4.14:** 2 Tim 4.10, 11; Phlm 24 **4.17:** Phlm 2

hard 2.1; 1 Thes 1.3
heaven 3.1; 1 Thes 1.10
help 1.24; 1 Thes 3.2
interest (1) Phil 2.4
Jew 3.11; 1 Thes 2.14
justice Rom 3.6; 2 Thes 1.5
Kingdom (1) (of God) 1.11; 1 Thes 2.12
letter (2) [2] 2 Cor 10.9; 1 Thes 5.27
master [2] 3.22; 1 Tim 6.1
mature 1.28; 1 Tim 3.6
message 3.16; 1 Thes 1.6
obey 3.6; 2 Thes 1.8
pray [4] 1.3; 1 Thes 5.17
prayer Phil 4.6; 1 Thes 1.2
preach 1.23; 1 Thes 2.9
prison [2] Phil 1.7; 2 Tim 1.8
remember 3.24; 1 Thes 1.3
right (1) Phil 4.8; 1 Thes 2.10
secret 2.2; 1 Tim 3.16
servant [2] 1.7; 1 Tim 4.6
service Eph 4.12; 1 Tim 2.8
slave 3.11; 1 Tim 6.1
speech 2 Cor 8.7; 1 Tim 4.12
sure [2] 1.23; 2 Thes 3.4
task 1.25
testify Acts 26.5; 1 Jn 5.6
thank 3.15; 1 Thes 1.2
welcome 2 Cor 8.17; 1 Thes 3.6
will (1) 1.1; 1 Thes 3.3
wise Eph 5.15; Jas 3.13
wish Eph 2.3; 1 Pet 3.10

PAUL'S FIRST LETTER TO THE THESSALONIANS

INTRODUCTION

Thessalonica was the capital city of the Roman province of Macedonia. Paul established a church there after he left Philippi. Soon, however, there was opposition from Jews who were jealous of Paul's success in preaching the Christian message among the non-Jews who had become interested in Judaism. Paul was forced to leave Thessalonica and go on to Berea. Later on, after he reached Corinth, Paul received a personal report from his companion and fellow-worker Timothy about the situation in the church at Thessalonica.

Paul's First Letter to the Thessalonians was then written to encourage and reassure the Christians there. He gives thanks for the news about their faith and love; he reminds them of the kind of life he had lived while he was with them, and then answers questions that had arisen in the church about the return of Christ: Could a believer who died before Christ's return still share in the eternal life that his return will bring? And when will Christ come again? Paul takes this occasion to tell them to go on working quietly while waiting in hope for Christ's return.

Outline of Contents

---

anger Col 3.6; 2.16
believer Col 4.5; 4.9
choose Col 3.12; 5.9
church Col 4.15; 2.14
complete Col 4.12; 2.16
convince Col 4.12; 2 Tim 4.2
death (2) (from death) Col 2.12; 2 Tim 2.8
example Phil 3.17; 2 Thes 3.9
faith [2] Col 2.5; 3.2
Father (2) (God) [2] Col 3.17; 3.11
Good News Col 1.5; 2.2
grace Col 4.18; 5.28
hard Col 4.13; 2.17
heaven Col 4.1; 4.16
hope Col 1.5; 2.19
idol Col 3.5; 1 Pet 4.3
joy Col 1.11; 2.19
love [2] Col 3.12; 2.8
message [2] Col 4.3; 2.13
need Phil 4.6; 3.10
peace Col 3.15; 5.13
power Col 2.11; 2 Thes 1.11
practice Phil 4.9; 1 Tim 4.15
prayer Col 4.2; 1 Tim 2.1
raise Col 3.1; 2 Tim 2.8
remember Col 4.1; 2.9
rescue Col 1.13; 2 Thes 3.2
serve Col 3.24; 1 Tim 1.4

1 From Paul, Silas, and Timothy—
To the people of the **church** in
Thessalonica, who belong to God the
Father and the Lord Jesus Christ:
May **grace** and **peace** be yours.

The Life and Faith of the Thessalonians

2 We always **thank** God for you all and
always mention you in our **prayers**. 3 For
we **remember** before our God and
Father how you put your **faith** into
practice, how your **love** made you work
so **hard**, and how your **hope** in our Lord
Jesus Christ is firm. 4 Our brothers, we
know that God **loves** you and has **chosen**
you to be his own. 5 For we brought the
Good News to you, not with **words** only,
but also with **power** and the **Holy Spirit**,
and with **complete conviction** of its **truth**.
You know how we lived when we were
with you; it was for your own good. 6 You
imitated us and the Lord; and even
though you **suffered** much, you received
the **message** with the **joy** that comes
from the **Holy Spirit**. 7 So you became an
example to all **believers** in Macedonia
and Achaia. 8 For not only did the **message**
about the Lord go out from you
throughout Macedonia and Achaia, but
the news about your **faith** in God has
gone everywhere. There is nothing, then,
that we **need** to say. 9 All those people
speak about how you received us when
we visited you, and how you **turned away**
from idols to God, to **serve** the **true** and
living God 10 and to wait for **his Son** to
come from **heaven**—**his Son** Jesus, whom
he **raised from death** and who **rescues** us
from **God's anger** that is coming.

Son of God [2] Col 1.13; Heb 1.2
Spirit (1) (God's Spirit) [2] Col 1.8; 4.8
suffer Col 1.24; 2.14
thank Col 4.2; 2.13
true Col 2.2; 1 Tim 1.2
truth Phil 1.8; 4.13
turn Phil 2.23; 3.3
word (1) Phil 4.9; 2.5

Paul's Work in Thessalonica

2 Our brothers, you yourselves know
that our visit to you was not a
failure. 2 You know how we had already
been **ill-treated** and **insulted** in Philippi
before we came to you in Thessalonica.
And even though there was much opposition,
our God gave us **courage** to tell you
the **Good News** that comes from him.
3 Our appeal to you is not **based on error**
or **impure motives**, nor do we try to **trick**
anyone. 4 Instead, we always speak as
God wants us to, because he has **judged**
us **worthy** to be **entrusted** with the **Good
News**. We do not try to **please** men, but
to please God, who **tests** our **motives**.
5 You know very well that we did not
come to you with flattering talk, nor did

accept Col 2.6; 2 Thes 3.8
anger 1.10; 5.9
apostle Col 1.1; 1 Tim 1.1
basis Col 2.23; Tit 1.2
believe [2] Phil 1.29; 4.14
boast Phil 2.3; 2 Thes 1.4
body Col 3.15; 5.23
care Phil 4.10; 1 Tim 3.5
Christ Col 4.3; 3.2
church 1.1; 2 Thes 1.1
comfort Phil 2.1
commit 1 Cor 7.28; 1 Tim 5.20
complete 1.5; 2 Thes 1.11
conduct Gal 6.4; 1 Tim 2.2
courage Col 2.2; 2 Thes 2.16

1.1: Acts 17.1 **1.6:** Acts 17.5-9 **2.2:** Acts 16.19-24, 17.1-9

dear Col 4.7; 2 Tim 1.2
demand 2 Cor 12.14; 2 Thes 3.9
displease Jer 32.30
encourage Phil 2.19; 3.7
entrust 1 Cor 9.17; 1 Tim 1.11
error Eph 4.14; 2 Thes 2.11
fail Phil 1.20; 2 Tim 3.8
fault Col 1.22; 5.23
Gentile Col 3.11; 1 Tim 2.7
gentle Col 3.12; 1 Tim 3.3
glory Col 3.4; 2 Thes 1.9
Good News [4] 1.5; 3.2
greed Col 3.5; 1 Tim 3.8
hard 1.3; 1 Tim 4.10
hope 1.3; 4.13
ill-treat Acts 14.5; Heb 10.33
impure Phil 1.10; Heb 9.13
insult Col 3.8; 1 Tim 1.13
Jew Col 4.11; Tit 1.14
joy [2] 1.6; 3.9
judge Col 3.25; 2 Thes 1.5
Kingdom (1) (of God) Col 4.11; 2 Thes 1.5
last (2) 2 Cor 9.2; 2 Tim 3.1
life (1) [2] Col 3.3; 3.8
love 1.3; 3.6
message [3] 1.6; 5.20
motive [2] Phil 1.18; Jas 2.4
persecute [2] Phil 3.6; 3.3
please [2] Col 3.20; 4.1
praise Phil 4.8; Heb 2.12
preach [2] Col 4.3; 3.2
presence Col 1.22; 3.9
prophet Eph 4.11; 1 Tim 4.14
proud Phil 4.1; 1 Tim 3.6
pure Col 1.22; 1 Tim 1.5
reason [2] Col 2.18; 2 Tim 1.6
remember 1.3; 2 Thes 2.5
right (1) Col 4.6; 2 Thes 1.3
salvation Phil 2.12; 5.8
Satan 2 Cor 12.7; 2 Thes 2.9
separate Eph 4.16; 2 Thes 1.9
share [2] Col 3.4; 2 Thes 2.14
suffer [2] 1.6; 3.7
test 2 Cor 13.5; 5.21
thank 1.2; 3.9
trick Eph 6.11
trouble Phil 4.14; 3.7
urge Phil 2.2; 4.1
victory Col 2.15; 2 Tim 4.8
witness [2] Phil 1.8; 1 Tim 5.19
word (1) 1.5; 4.18
worthy 1 Cor 7.25; 2 Thes 1.5

we use **words** to cover up **greed**—God is our **witness**! 6 We did not try to get **praise** from anyone, either from you or from others, 7 even though as **apostles of Christ** we could have made **demands** on you. But we were **gentle** when we were with you, like a mother[a] taking **care** of her children. 8 Because of our **love** for you we were ready to **share** with you not only the **Good News** from God but even our own **lives**. You were so **dear** to us! 9 Surely you **remember**, our brothers, how we worked and toiled! We worked day and night so that we would not be any **trouble** to you as we **preached** to you the **Good News** from God.

10 You are our **witnesses**, and so is God, that our **conduct** towards you who **believe** was **pure**, **right**, and without **fault**. 11 You know that we treated each one of you just as a father treats his own children. 12 We **encouraged** you, we **comforted** you, and we kept **urging** you to live the kind of **life** that **pleases** God, who calls you to **share** in his own **Kingdom** and **glory**.

13 And there is another **reason** why we always give **thanks** to God. When we brought you God's **message**, you heard it and **accepted** it, not as man's **message** but as God's message, which indeed it is. For God is at work in you who **believe**. 14 Our brothers, the same things happened to you that happened to the **churches** of God in Judaea, to the people there who belong to Christ Jesus. You **suffered** the same **persecutions** from your own countrymen that they **suffered** from the **Jews**, 15 who killed the Lord Jesus and the **prophets**, and **persecuted** us. How **displeasing** they are to God! How hostile they are to everyone! 16 They even tried to stop us from **preaching** to the **Gentiles** the **message** that would bring them **salvation**. In this way they have brought to **completion** all the sins they have always **committed**. And now **God's anger** has at **last** come down on them!

Paul's Desire to Visit Them Again

17 As for us, brothers, when we were **separated** from you for a little while—not in our thoughts, of course, but only in **body**—how we missed you and how **hard** we tried to see you again! 18 We wanted to return to you. I myself tried to go back more than once, but **Satan** would not let us. 19 After all, it is you—you, no less than others!—who are our **hope**, our **joy**, and our **reason** for **boasting** of our **victory** in the **presence** of our Lord Jesus when he comes. 20 Indeed, you are our **pride** and our **joy**!

3 Finally, we could not bear it any longer. So we decided to stay on **alone** in Athens 2 while we sent Timothy, our brother who works with us for God in **preaching** the **Good News** about **Christ**. We sent him to **strengthen** you and **help** your **faith**, 3 so that none of you should **turn back** because of these **persecutions**. You yourselves know that such **persecutions** are part of **God's will** for us. 4 For while we were still with you, we told you beforehand that we were going to be **persecuted**; and as you well know, that is exactly what happened. 5 That is why I had to send Timothy. I could not bear it any longer, so I sent him to find out about your **faith**. Surely it could not be that the **Devil** had **tempted** you and all our work had been for nothing!

6 Now Timothy has come back, and he has brought us the **welcome** news about your **faith** and **love**. He has told us that you always think well of us and that you want to see us just as much as we want to see you. 7 So, in all our **trouble** and **suffering** we have been **encouraged** about you, brothers. It was your **faith** that **encouraged** us, 8 because now we really live if you stand firm in your **life** in **union** with the Lord. 9 Now we can give **thanks** to our God for you. We **thank** him for the **joy** we have in his **presence** because of you. 10 Day and night we ask him **with all our heart** to let us see you personally and supply what is **needed** in your **faith**.

11 May our God and **Father** himself and our Lord Jesus prepare the way for us to come to you! 12 May the Lord make your **love** for **one another** and for all people grow more and more and become as great as our **love** for you. 13 In this way he will **strengthen** you, and you will be **perfect** and **holy** in the **presence** of our God and **Father** when our Lord Jesus comes with all who belong to him.[b]

alone Col 1.18; 1 Tim 5.3
Christ 2.7; 4.16
Devil Eph 6.11; 1 Tim 3.6
encourage [2] 2.12; 4.18
faith [5] 1.3; 5.8
Father (2) (God) [2] 1.1; 2 Thes 1.1
Good News 2.2; 2 Thes 1.8
heart Col 3.1; 1 Tim 1.5
help Col 4.11; 5.11
holy Col 2.16; 4.3
joy 2.19; 5.16
life (1) 2.8; 4.11
love [3] 2.8; 4.9
need 1.8; 4.9
one another Col 3.9; 4.9
perfect Col 3.14; Heb 2.10
persecute [3] 2.14; 2 Thes 1.4
preach 2.9; 2 Thes 2.2
presence [2] 2.19; 2 Thes 1.9
strength [2] Col 1.11; 2 Thes 2.17
suffer 2.14; 5.9
tempt Gal 6.1; 1 Tim 6.9
thank [2] 2.13; 5.18
trouble 2.9; 1 Tim 5.10
turn 1.9; 1 Tim 1.6
union Col 2.6; 5.18
welcome Col 4.10; 2 Thes 2.10
will (1) Col 4.12; 2 Tim 1.1

A Life that Pleases God

4 Finally, our brothers, you **learnt** from us how you should live in order to **please** God. This is, of course, how you have been living. And now we **beg** and **urge** you **in the name of** the Lord Jesus to do even more. 2 For you know the instructions we gave you by the **authority**

advantage 2 Cor 12.17
alive Phil 1.24; 5.10
angel Col 2.18; 2 Thes 1.7
archangel *see* **angel**
authority Col 2.10; 5.27
beg [2] Phil 4.2; 5.12

[a] we were gentle when we were with you, like a mother; *some manuscripts have* we were like children when we were with you; we were like a mother.
[b] all who belong to him; *or* all his angels.

2.14: Acts 17.5 **2.15:** Acts 9.23, 29, 13.45, 50, 14.2, 5, 19, 17.5, 13, 18.12 **3.1:** Acts 17.15 **3.6:** Acts 18.5

believe [4] 2.10; 2 Thes 1.4
believer [2] 1.7; 5.26
Christ 3.2; 2 Thes 3.5
Christian Col 4.12; 5.12
cloud 1 Cor 10.1; 2 Pet 2.17
command Phil 3.6; 2 Thes 3.6
depend Gal 3.10; Heb 12.2
desire Col 3.5; 2 Thes 1.11
encourage 3.7; 5.11
free Col 3.11; 5.23
heathen Eph 4.17; 1 Pet 2.12
heaven 1.10; 2 Thes 1.7
holy [3] 3.13; 5.23
honour Phil 4.8; 2 Thes 1.10
hope 2.19; 5.8
immoral [2] Col 3.5; 1 Tim 1.10
learn Col 1.7; 1 Tim 2.11
life (1) 3.8; 5.12
life (2) (to life) Col 3.1; Heb 11.35
love [2] 3.6; 5.8
lust Col 3.5; 1 Pet 4.3
name (2) (name of God, of Jesus) Col 3.17; 2 Thes 1.12
need [2] 3.10; 5.1
one another [2] 3.12; 5.11
please 2.4; 1 Tim 2.3
punish Gal 5.10; 2 Thes 1.8
reject Gal 4.14; 2 Thes 1.8
respect Phil 2.29; 5.12
rise [2] Eph 5.14; Jas 1.11
sad Eph 4.30; Heb 12.11
sex Col 3.5; 1 Tim 1.10
Spirit (1) (God's Spirit) 1.5; 5.19
strong Col 2.7; 2 Tim 2.1
teach [3] Col 3.16; 2 Thes 2.15
truth 1.5; 2 Thes 2.10
urge 2.12; 5.14
warn Col 1.28; 5.14
win Phil 3.12; 1 Tim 3.13
word (1) 2.5; 1 Tim 1.7
wrong Col 3.25; 5.15

of the Lord Jesus. [3]God wants you to be
holy and completely **free** from **sexual im-**
morality. [4]Each of you men should know
how to live with his wife[c] in a **holy** and
honourable way, [5]not with a **lustful**
desire, like the **heathen** who do not know
God. [6]In this matter, then, no man should
do **wrong** to his **fellow-Christian** or take
advantage of him. We have told you this
before, and we **strongly warned** you that
the Lord will **punish** those who do that.
[7]God did not call us to live in **immorality**,
but in **holiness**. [8]So then, whoever **rejects**
this **teaching** is not rejecting man, but
God, who gives you his **Holy Spirit**.

9 There is no **need** to write to you
about **love** for your **fellow-believers**. You
yourselves have been **taught** by God how
you should **love one another**. [10]And you
have, in fact, behaved like this towards
all the brothers in all Macedonia. So we
beg you, our brothers, to do even more.
[11]Make it your aim to live a quiet **life**, to
mind your own business, and to earn
your own living, just as we told you
before. [12]In this way you will **win** the **res-**
pect of those who are not **believers**, and
you will not have to **depend** on anyone
for what you **need**.

The Lord's Coming

13 Our brothers, we want you to know
the **truth** about those who have died, so
that you will not be **sad**, as are those who
have no **hope**. [14]We **believe** that Jesus
died and **rose** again, and so we **believe**
that God will take back with Jesus those
who have died **believing** in him.

15 What we are **teaching** you now is
the Lord's teaching: we who are **alive** on
the day the Lord comes will not go ahead
of those who have died. [16]There will be
the shout of **command**, the **archangel's**
voice, the sound of God's trumpet, and
the Lord himself will come down from
heaven. Those who have died **believing**
in **Christ** will **rise to life** first; [17]then we
who are living at that time will be
gathered up along with them in the
clouds to meet the Lord in the air. And so
we will always be with the Lord. [18]So
then, **encourage one another** with these
words.

Be Ready for the Lord's Coming

alive 4.15; 2 Tim 1.6
anger 2.16; 1 Tim 2.8
authority 4.2; 1 Tim 2.2
beg 4.1; 2 Thes 2.1

5 There is no **need** to write to you,
brothers, about the times and
occasions when these things will happen.
[2]For you yourselves know very well that
the **Day of the Lord** will come as a **thief**
comes at night. [3]When people say,
"Everything is quiet and **safe**," then suddenly **destruction** will hit them! It will
come as suddenly as the **pains** that come
upon a woman in labour, and people will
not **escape**. [4]But you, brothers, are not in
the **darkness**, and the **Day** should not
take you by surprise like a **thief**. [5]All of
you are people who belong to the **light**,
who belong to the day. We do not belong
to the night or to the **darkness**. [6]So then,
we should not be sleeping like the others;
we should be awake and sober. [7]It is at
night that people sleep; it is at night that
they get drunk. [8]But we belong to the
day, and we should be sober. We must
wear **faith** and **love** as a breastplate, and
our **hope** of **salvation** as a helmet. [9]God
did not **choose** us to **suffer** his **anger**, but
to **possess salvation** through our Lord
Jesus Christ, [10]who died for us in order
that we might live together with him,
whether we are **alive** or **dead** when he
comes. [11]And so **encourage one another**
and **help** one another, just as you are now
doing.

Final Instructions and Greetings

12 We **beg** you, our brothers, to pay
proper respect to those who work among
you, who **guide** and instruct you in the
Christian life. [13]Treat them with the
greatest **respect** and **love** because of the
work they do. Be at **peace** among
yourselves.

14 We **urge** you, our brothers, to **warn**
the idle, **encourage** the timid, **help** the
weak, be **patient** with everyone. [15]See
that no one pays back **wrong** for wrong,
but at all times make it your aim to do
good to **one another** and to all people.

16 Be **joyful** always, [17]**pray** at all
times, [18]be **thankful** in all circumstances.
This is what God wants from you in your
life in union with Christ Jesus.

19 Do not restrain the **Holy Spirit**; [20]do
not **despise inspired messages**. [21]Put all
things **to the test**: keep what is good
[22]and avoid every kind of **evil**.

23 May the God who gives us **peace**
make you **holy** in every way and keep
your whole **being—spirit**, **soul**, and
body—free from every **fault** at the
coming of our Lord Jesus Christ. [24]He
who calls you will do it, because he is
faithful.

25 **Pray** also for us, brothers.

26 Greet all the **believers** with a
brotherly **kiss**.

being Col 3.10; Heb 1.3
believer [2] 4.9; 1 Tim 4.3
body 2.17; Heb 7.10
choose 1.4; 2 Thes 2.13
Christian 4.6; 1 Tim 5.10
dark [2] Col 1.13; Heb 12.18
Day of the Lord [2] Phil 2.16; 2 Thes 1.10
dead Col 2.13; 1 Tim 4.2
despise Gal 4.14; 1 Tim 6.2
destroy Eph 4.22; 2 Thes 1.9
encourage [2] 4.18; 2 Thes 2.17
escape 2 Cor 13.2; 2 Tim 2.26
evil Col 3.5; 2 Thes 3.2
faith 3.2; 2 Thes 1.3
faithful Col 4.7; 2 Thes 3.3
fault 2.10; 1 Tim 3.2
free 4.3; Phlm 14
grace 1.1; 2 Thes 1.2
guide Col 3.15; Rev 7.17
help [2] 3.2; 1 Tim 5.5
holy 4.3; 1 Tim 2.15
hope 4.13; 2 Thes 2.16
inspire 1 Cor 14.6; 2 Tim 3.16
joy 3.9; 2 Tim 1.4
kiss 2 Cor 13.12; 1 Pet 5.14
letter (2) Col 4.16; 2 Thes 2.2
life (1) [2] 4.11; 2 Thes 1.11
light (1) Col 1.11; 1 Tim 6.16
love [2] 4.9; 2 Thes 1.3
message 2.13; 2 Thes 1.10
need 4.9; Tit 1.5
one another [2] 4.9; Heb 3.13
pain Gal 4.19; 1 Pet 2.19
patient Col 3.12; 1 Tim 1.16
peace [2] 1.1; 2 Thes 1.2
possess Gal 5.21; 2 Thes 2.14
pray [2] Col 4.2; 2 Thes 1.11
proper Col 1.17; 2 Thes 2.6
respect [2] 4.12; 1 Tim 3.4
safe Col 1.5; 2 Thes 3.3
salvation [2] 2.16; 2 Tim 2.10
soul Phil 2.2; Heb 4.12
Spirit (1) (God's Spirit) 4.8; 2 Thes 2.13
spirit (2) Col 2.5; 1 Tim 4.1
suffer 3.7; 2 Thes 1.4
test 2.4; 1 Tim 3.10
thank 3.9; 2 Thes 1.3
thief [2] 1 Cor 6.10; 1 Pet 4.15
union 3.8; 1 Tim 1.14
urge [2] 4.1; 1 Tim 1.3
warn 4.6; 2 Thes 3.12
weak Phil 3.21; 2 Tim 3.6
wrong 4.6; 1 Tim 4.3

[c] live with his wife; *or* control his body.

4.15-17: 1 Cor 15.51-52 **5.2:** Mt 24.43; Lk 12.39; 2 Pet 3.10 **5.8:** Is 59.17; Eph 6.13-17

27 I urge you by the authority of the Lord to read this letter to all the believers.

28 The grace of our Lord Jesus Christ be with you.

PAUL'S SECOND LETTER TO THE THESSALONIANS

INTRODUCTION

Confusion over the expected return of Christ continued to cause disturbances in the church at Thessalonica. *Paul's Second Letter to the Thessalonians* deals with the belief that the day of the Lord's coming had already arrived. Paul corrects this idea, pointing out that before Christ returns, evil and wickedness will reach a climax under the leadership of a mysterious figure called "the Wicked One," who would be opposed to Christ.

The apostle emphasizes the need for his readers to remain steady in their faith in spite of trouble and suffering, to work for a living as did Paul and his fellow-workers, and to persevere in doing good.

Outline of Contents

---

1 From Paul, Silas, and Timothy—
To the people of the church in
Thessalonica, who belong to God our
Father and the Lord Jesus Christ:
2 May God our Father and the Lord
Jesus Christ give you grace and peace.

The Judgement at Christ's Coming

3 Our brothers, we must thank God at
all times for you. It is right for us to do so,
because your faith is growing so much
and the love each of you has for the
others is becoming greater. 4 That is why
we ourselves boast about you in the
churches of God. We boast about the way
you continue to endure and believe
through all the persecutions and sufferings you are experiencing.
5 All of this proves that God's judgement is just and as a result you will
become worthy of his Kingdom, for
which you are suffering. 6 God will do
what is right: he will bring suffering on
those who make you suffer, 7 and he will
give relief to you who suffer and to us as
well. He will do this when the Lord Jesus
appears from heaven with his mighty
angels, 8 with a flaming fire, to punish
those who reject God and who do not
obey the Good News about our Lord
Jesus. 9 They will suffer the punishment
of eternal destruction, separated from
the presence of the Lord and from his
glorious might, 10 when he comes on that
Day to receive glory from all his people
and honour from all who believe. You too
will be among them, because you have
believed the message that we told you.
11 That is why we always pray for
you. We ask our God to make you worthy
of the life he has called you to live. May
he fulfil by his power all your desire for
goodness and complete your work of
faith. 12 In this way the name of our Lord
Jesus will receive glory from you, and
you from him, by the grace of our God
and of the Lord[a] Jesus Christ.

The Wicked One

2 Concerning the coming of our Lord
Jesus Christ and our being gathered
together to be with him: I beg you, my
brothers, 2 not to be so easily confused in
your thinking or upset by the claim that
the Day of the Lord has come. Perhaps it
is thought that we said this while prophesying or preaching, or that we wrote
it in a letter. 3 Do not let anyone deceive
you in any way. For the Day will not
come until the final Rebellion takes
place and the Wicked One appears, who
is destined for hell. 4 He will oppose every
so-called god or object of worship and
will put himself above them all. He will
even go in and sit down in God's Temple
and claim to be God.
5 Don't you remember? I told you all
this while I was with you. 6 Yet there is

[a] our God and of the Lord; *or* our God and Lord.

1.1: Acts 17.1 **1.9:** Is 2.10 **2.1:** 1 Thes 4.15–17 **2.4:** Dan 11.36; Ezek 28.2

angel 1 Thes 4.16; 1 Tim 3.16
believe [3] 1 Thes 4.14; 2.11
boast [2] 1 Thes 2.19; 2 Tim 3.2
church [2] 1 Thes 2.14; 1 Tim 2.8
complete 1 Thes 2.16; Heb 10.19
Day of the Lord 1 Thes 5.2; 2.2
desire 1 Thes 4.5; 1 Tim 3.1
destroy 1 Thes 5.3; 2.8
endure Col 1.11; 3.5
eternal Eph 3.11; 1 Tim 1.16
experience Phil 3.10; Heb 5.13
faith [2] 1 Thes 5.8; 2.13
Father (2) (God) [2] 1 Thes 3.11; 2.16
fulfil 1 Cor 7.3
glory [3] 1 Thes 2.12; 2.14
God's people Col 3.12; 2.13
Good News 1 Thes 3.2; 2.14
grace [2] 1 Thes 5.28; 2.16
heaven 1 Thes 4.16; 1 Tim 3.16
honour 1 Thes 4.4; 3.1
judge 1 Thes 2.4; 1 Tim 5.24
justice Col 4.1; Heb 1.8
Kingdom (1) (of God) 1 Thes 2.12; 2 Tim 4.18
life (1) 1 Thes 5.12; 3.6
love 1 Thes 5.8; 2.10
message 1 Thes 5.20; 3.1
might [2] Col 1.29; Heb 11.34
name (2) (name of God, of Jesus) 1 Thes 4.1; 3.6
obey Col 4.12; 3.14
peace 1 Thes 5.13; 3.16
persecute 1 Thes 3.3; 1 Tim 1.13
power 1 Thes 1.5; 2.9
pray 1 Thes 5.17; 3.1
presence 1 Thes 3.9; 2.8
prove Phil 2.22; 1 Tim 2.6
punish [2] 1 Thes 4.6; 1 Tim 1.20
reject 1 Thes 4.8; 1 Tim 4.4
relieve (1) 2 Cor 8.13; Rev 14.11
result Col 3.11; 2.12
right (1) [2] 1 Thes 2.10; 1 Tim 2.6
separate 1 Thes 2.17
suffer [5] 1 Thes 5.9; 2 Tim 1.8
thank 1 Thes 5.18; 2.13
worthy [2] 1 Thes 2.4; 1 Tim 1.12

Chapter 2
beg 1 Thes 5.12; Heb 12.19
believe [2] 1.4; 3.2
choose 1 Thes 5.9; 2 Tim 2.10
claim [2] Col 2.18; 1 Tim 2.10
condemn Col 2.18; 1 Tim 3.6
courage 1 Thes 2.2; Heb 3.6
Day of the Lord [2] 1.10; 1 Tim 6.14
dazzling Lk 9.29
deceive [2] Col 2.4; 1 Tim 2.14
destroy 1.9; 1 Tim 6.9

encourage 1 Thes 5.11; 2 Tim 4.2
error 1 Thes 2.3; 2 Tim 3.16
faith 1.3; 1 Tim 1.2
false [2] Col 2.4; 1 Tim 1.3
Father (2) (God) 1.1; 1 Tim 1.2
final 1 Cor 4.5; Rev 15.1
glory 1.9; 1 Tim 1.11
god (2) (other gods) Phil 3.19; 1 Jn 5.21
God's people 1.10; 2 Tim 1.9
Good News 1.8; 1 Tim 1.11
grace 1.2; 3.18
hell Phil 3.19; Jas 3.6
hope 1 Thes 5.8; 1 Tim 1.1
keep from 2 Cor 12.7; 3.6
letter (2) [2] 1 Thes 5.27; 3.14
love [3] 1.3; 3.5
miracle Gal 3.5; Heb 2.4
mystery Dan 5.12; Rev 12.1
perish [2] 1 Cor 8.11
pleasure Eph 1.5; 1 Tim 5.6
possess 1 Thes 5.9; 1 Tim 6.21
power [3] 1.11; 1 Tim 1.20
preach [3] 1 Thes 3.2; 1 Tim 3.16
presence 1.9; 1 Tim 5.21
proper 1 Thes 5.12; 1 Tim 2.2
prophecy Jn 11.51; 1 Tim 1.18
rebel Rom 10.21; Tit 1.10
remember 1 Thes 2.9; 1 Tim 1.9
result 1.5; 1 Tim 6.21
reveal Col 1.26; 1 Tim 3.9
Satan 1 Thes 2.18; 1 Tim 1.20
save [2] Eph 2.5; 1 Tim 1.15
share 1 Thes 2.8; 1 Tim 6.18
Spirit (1) (God's Spirit) 1 Thes 5.19; 1 Tim 3.16
strength 1 Thes 3.2; 3.3
teach 1 Thes 4.8; 1 Tim 1.3
Temple (1) (of God) Eph 2.21; Heb 6.19
thank 1.3; 1 Tim 1.12
truth [4] 1 Thes 4.13; 1 Tim 2.4
upset Phil 2.26; 2 Tim 2.18
welcome 1 Thes 3.6; 1 Tim 3.2
wicked [6] Eph 6.12; 3.2
wonder (1) Eph 1.18; Heb 2.4

something that **keeps this from** happening now, and you know what it is. At the
proper time, then, the **Wicked One** will
appear. 7 The **Mysterious Wickedness** is
already at work, but what is going to
happen will not happen until the one who
holds it back is taken out of the way.
8 Then the **Wicked One** will be **revealed**,
but when the Lord Jesus comes, he will
kill him with the breath from his mouth
and **destroy** him with his **dazzling
presence**. 9 The **Wicked One** will come
with the **power** of **Satan** and perform all
kinds of **false miracles** and **wonders**,
10 and use every kind of **wicked deceit** on
those who will **perish**. They will **perish**
because they did not **welcome** and **love**
the **truth** so as to be **saved**. 11 And so God
sends the **power of error** to work in them
so that they **believe** what is **false**. 12 The
result is that all who have not **believed**
the **truth**, but have taken **pleasure** in sin,
will be **condemned**.

You Are Chosen for Salvation

13 We must **thank** God at all times for
you, brothers, you whom the Lord **loves**.
For God **chose** you as the first[b] to be
saved by the **Spirit's power** to make you
his **holy people** and by your **faith** in the
truth. 14 God called you to this through
the **Good News** we **preached** to you; he
called you to **possess** your **share** of the
glory of our Lord Jesus Christ. 15 So then,
our brothers, stand firm and hold on to
those **truths** which we **taught** you, both in
our **preaching** and in our **letter**.
16 May our Lord Jesus Christ himself
and God **our Father**, who **loved** us and in
his **grace** gave us unfailing **courage** and
a firm **hope**, 17 **encourage** you and
strengthen you to always do and say
what is good.

Pray for Us

3 Finally, our brothers, **pray** for us,
that the Lord's **message** may continue to spread rapidly and be received
with **honour**, just as it was among you.
2 **Pray** also that God will **rescue** us from
wicked and **evil** people; for not everyone
believes the **message**.
3 But the Lord is **faithful**, and he will
strengthen you and keep you **safe** from
the **Evil One**. 4 And the Lord gives us
confidence in you, and we are **sure** that
you are doing and will continue to do
what we tell you.
5 May the Lord lead you into a greater
understanding of God's **love** and the **endurance** that is given by **Christ**.

The Obligation to Work

6 Our brothers, we **command** you **in
the name of** our Lord Jesus Christ to
keep away from all brothers who are
living a lazy **life** and who do not follow
the instructions that we gave them. 7 You
yourselves know very well that you
should do just what we did. We were not
lazy when we were with you. 8 We did not
accept anyone's support without paying
for it. Instead, we worked and toiled; we
kept working day and night so as not to
be an expense to any of you. 9 We did this,
not because we have no **right** to **demand**
our support; we did it to be an **example**
for you to follow. 10 While we were with
you, we used to say to you, "Whoever
refuses to work is not allowed to eat."
11 We say this because we hear that
there are some people among you who
live lazy **lives** and who do nothing except
meddle in other people's business. 12 **In
the name of** the Lord Jesus Christ we
command these people and **warn** them
to lead orderly **lives** and work to earn
their own living.
13 But you, brothers, must not get
tired of doing good. 14 It may be that
someone there will not **obey** the **message**
we send you in this **letter**. If so, take note
of him and have nothing to do with him,
so that he will be **ashamed**. 15 But do not
treat him as an **enemy**; instead, **warn**
him as a brother.

Final Words

16 May the Lord himself, who is our
source of **peace**, give you peace at all
times and in every way. The Lord be
with you all.
17 With my own hand I write this:
Greetings from Paul. This is the way I
sign every **letter**; this is how I write.
18 May the **grace** of our Lord Jesus
Christ be with you all.

worship (2) (of other gods) Col 2.18; 1 Pet 4.3

Chapter 3
accept 1 Thes 2.13; 1 Tim 1.15
ashamed Phil 3.19; 2 Tim 1.8
believe 2.11; 1 Tim 1.15
Christ 1 Thes 4.16; 1 Tim 5.11
command [2] 1 Thes 4.16; 1 Tim 1.18
confident Phil 1.14; 1 Tim 1.7
demand 1 Thes 2.7
endure 1.4; 1 Tim 6.11
enemy Col 1.21; 1 Tim 5.14
evil 1 Thes 5.22; 1 Tim 1.13
Evil One Eph 6.16; 1 Jn 2.13
example 1 Thes 1.7; 1 Tim 1.16
faithful 1 Thes 5.24; 1 Tim 6.14
grace 2.16; 1 Tim 1.2
honour 1.10; 1 Tim 1.17
keep from 2.6; 1 Tim 4.7
letter (2) [2] 2.2; 1 Tim 3.14
life (1) [3] 1.11; 1 Tim 1.16
love 2.10; 1 Tim 1.5
message [3] 1.10; 1 Tim 2.7
name (2) (name of God, of Jesus) [2] 1.12; 1 Tim 6.1
obey 1.8; 1 Tim 3.4
peace 1.2; 1 Tim 1.2
pray [2] 1.11; 1 Tim 2.8
refuse (1) Gal 2.21; Heb 3.10
rescue 1 Thes 1.10; 2 Tim 3.11
right (3) 1 Cor 9.4; Heb 12.16
safe 1 Thes 5.3; 1 Tim 6.20
source Col 1.18; 1 Tim 6.10
strength 2.17; 1 Tim 1.12
sure Col 4.16; 2 Tim 1.5
understand Col 2.2; 1 Tim 1.7
warn [2] 1 Thes 5.14; 2 Tim 2.14
wicked 2.3; Tit 1.12

[b] as the first; *some manuscripts have* from the beginning.

2.8: Is 11.4 **2.9:** Mt 24.24

PAUL'S FIRST LETTER TO TIMOTHY

INTRODUCTION

Timothy, a young Christian from Asia Minor, was the son of a Jewish mother and a Greek father. He became a companion and assistant to Paul in his missionary work. *Paul's First Letter to Timothy* deals with three main concerns.

The letter is first of all a warning against false teaching in the church. This teaching, a mixture of Jewish and non-Jewish ideas, was based on the belief that the physical world is evil and that one can attain salvation only by special secret knowledge and by practices such as avoiding certain foods and not marrying. The letter also contains instructions about church administration and worship, with a description of the kind of character that church leaders and helpers should have. Finally, Timothy is advised how to be a good servant of Jesus Christ and about the responsibilities that he has towards various groups of believers.

Outline of Contents

Introduction 1.1-2
Instructions concerning the church and its officers 1.3—3.16
Instructions to Timothy about his work 4.1—6.21

---

abundant Phil 4.19; Tit 3.6
accept 2 Thes 3.8; 4.5
announce Eph 6.15; Heb 2.3
apostle 1 Thes 2.7; 2.7
argue Col 2.4; 2.8
believe [2] 2 Thes 3.2; 3.16
blasphemy Jn 10.33
bless Col 1.6; 6.15
clear [2] Col 4.4; 3.9
command 2 Thes 3.6; 6.13
confident 2 Thes 3.4; 2 Tim 1.12
conscience [3] 2 Cor 4.2; 3.9
consider Phil 3.8; 5.17
crime Acts 25.16; 2 Tim 2.9
discuss Acts 24.25; 2 Tim 2.16
doctrine [2] 6.3
entrust [2] 1 Thes 2.4; 6.20
eternal [2] 2 Thes 1.9; 6.12
evil 2 Thes 3.2; 5.14
example 2 Thes 3.9; 4.12
faith [7] 2 Thes 2.13; 2.7
false [2] 2 Thes 2.9; 2 Tim 2.13
Father (2) (God) 2 Thes 2.16; 2 Tim 1.2
fool Eph 5.6; 6.9
give up Phil 2.7; Tit 2.12
glory [2] 2 Thes 2.14; 2 Tim 2.10
godless Mk 8.38; 4.7
Good News 2 Thes 2.14; 2 Tim 1.8
gospel Col 1.6; 2 Tim 1.10
grace [2] 2 Thes 3.18; 6.21
heart 1 Thes 3.10; 6.10
honour 2 Thes 3.1; 6.16

1 From Paul, an **apostle** of Christ Jesus by order of God our **Saviour** and Christ Jesus our **hope**—

2 To Timothy, my **true** son in the **faith**:

May God the **Father** and Christ Jesus our Lord give you **grace**, **mercy**, and **peace**.

Warnings against False Teaching

3 I want you to stay in Ephesus, just as I **urged** you when I was on my way to Macedonia. Some people there are **teaching false doctrines**, and you must order them to stop. 4 Tell them to **give up** those legends and those long lists of ancestors, which only produce **arguments**; they do not **serve** God's **plan**, which is known by **faith**. 5 The **purpose** of this order is to arouse the **love** that comes from a **pure heart**, a **clear conscience**, and a genuine **faith**. 6 Some people have **turned away** from these and have lost their way in **foolish discussions**. 7 They want to be **teachers of God's law**, but they do not **understand** their own **words** or the matters about which they speak with so much **confidence**.

8 We know that the **Law** is good if it is used as it should be used. 9 It must be **remembered**, of course, that **laws** are made, not for good people, but for lawbreakers and **criminals**, for the **godless** and sinful, for those who are not **religious** or **spiritual**, for those who kill their fathers or mothers, for murderers, 10 for the **immoral**, for **sexual perverts**, for kidnappers, for those who **lie** and give **false testimony** or who do anything else contrary to **sound doctrine**. 11 That **teaching** is found in the **gospel** that was **entrusted** to me to **announce**, the **Good News** from the **glorious** and **blessed** God.

Gratitude for God's Mercy

12 I give **thanks** to Christ Jesus our Lord, who has given me **strength** for my work. I **thank** him for **considering** me **worthy** and appointing me to **serve** him, 13 even though in the past I spoke **evil** of him and **persecuted** and **insulted** him. But God was **merciful** to me because I did not yet have **faith** and so did not know what I was doing. 14 And our Lord poured out his **abundant grace** on me and gave me the **faith** and **love** which are ours in **union with** Christ Jesus. 15 This is a **true saying**, to be completely **accepted** and **believed**: Christ Jesus came into the **world** to **save** sinners. I am the **worst** of them, 16 but God was **merciful** to me in order that Christ Jesus might show his full **patience** in dealing with me, the **worst** of sinners, as an **example** for all those who would later **believe** in him and receive **eternal life**. 17 To the **eternal** King, **immortal** and invisible, the only God—to him be **honour** and **glory** for ever and ever! Amen.

18 Timothy, my child, I **entrust** to you this **command**, which is in accordance with the **words** of **prophecy** spoken in the

1.2: Acts 16.1 **1.13:** Acts 8.3, 9.4-5

hope 2 Thes 2.16; 3.14
immoral 1 Thes 4.3; Heb 12.16
immortal 1 Cor 15.42; 6.16
insult 1 Thes 2.2; 6.4
law [2] Col 2.13; 2.14
lie (2) Col 3.9; 2.7
life (1) 2 Thes 3.6; 2.2
love [2] 2 Thes 3.5; 2.15
mercy [3] Eph 2.4; 2 Tim 1.2
patient 1 Thes 5.14; 2 Tim 2.24
peace 2 Thes 3.16; 2.2
persecute 2 Thes 1.4; 2 Tim 3.11
pervert 1 Cor 6.9; Jude 7
plan Col 1.27; Heb 11.40
power 2 Thes 2.9; 2 Tim 1.7
prophecy 2 Thes 2.2; 1 Pet 1.10
punish 2 Thes 1.8; Heb 2.2
pure 1 Thes 2.10; 4.12
purpose Phil 2.13; 2 Tim 1.9
religion Gal 1.13; 2.10
remember 2 Thes 2.5; 2 Tim 1.3
ruin Eph 5.18; 6.9
Satan 2 Thes 2.9; 5.15
save 2 Thes 2.10; 2.4
Saviour Phil 3.20; 2.3
saying 1 Cor 15.32; 3.1
serve [2] 1 Thes 1.9; 3.10
sex 1 Thes 4.3; 1 Pet 3.7
sound (2) Acts 20.9; 2 Tim 4.3
spiritual Col 2.10; 4.6
strength 2 Thes 3.3; 2 Tim 1.8

teach [3] 2 Thes 2.15; 2.12
teacher of the Law Acts 23.9
testimony Acts 8.25; 1 Pet 5.12
thank [2] 2 Thes 2.13; 2.1
true [2] 1 Thes 1.9; 3.1
turn 1 Thes 3.3; 5.11
understand 2 Thes 3.5; 2 Tim 2.7
union 1 Thes 5.18; 2 Tim 1.1
urge 1 Thes 5.14; 2.1
word (1) [3] 1 Thes 4.18; 4.5
world Col 2.20; 3.16
worst [2] Mt 10.36; Rev 16.18
worthy 2 Thes 1.5; 5.17

Chapter 2
anger 1 Thes 5.9; Heb 3.10
apostle 1.1; 2 Tim 1.1
argue 1.4; 6.4
authority [2] 1 Thes 5.27; Tit 2.15
church 2 Thes 1.1; 3.1
claim 2 Thes 2.2; 6.21
conduct 1 Thes 2.10; 3.15
create Col 1.15; 4.3
deceive [2] 2 Thes 2.3; 4.2
dedicate Eph 5.26; 5.22
deed (2) Col 1.10; 5.10
faith [2] 1.2; 3.6
Gentile 1 Thes 2.16; 2 Tim 4.17
holy 1 Thes 5.23; 5.21
humble Col 3.12; 5.10
law 1.8; Tit 3.9
learn 1 Thes 4.1; 5.4
lie (2) 1.10; 4.1
life (1) 1.16; 4.7
love 1.5; 3.3
mankind [2] Col 1.26; Tit 2.11
message 2 Thes 3.1; 2 Tim 2.15
offer Col 1.5; Heb 4.1
peace 1.2; 3.3
please 1 Thes 4.1; 5.4
pray 2 Thes 3.1; 5.5
prayer [2] 1 Thes 1.2; 4.3
proclaim Col 1.25; 2 Tim 1.1
proper [3] 2 Thes 2.6; 1 Pet 3.7
prove 2 Thes 1.5; Tit 3.11
redeem Gal 4.5; 2 Pet 2.1
religion 1.9; 3.16
request 2 Cor 8.17; Phlm 9
reverence Col 3.22; Heb 12.28
right (1) 2 Thes 1.3; 3.16
save [3] 1.15; 4.16
Saviour 1.1; 4.10
sense 2 Cor 9.7; 2 Tim 2.26
service Col 4.17; 5.22
teach 1.3; 3.2
teacher Eph 4.11; 2 Tim 1.11
thank 1.12; 4.3
truth [3] 2 Thes 2.10; 3.9
urge 1.3; 2 Tim 4.1

past about you. Use those **words** as weapons in order to fight well, 19 and keep your **faith** and a **clear conscience**. Some men have not listened to their **conscience** and have made a **ruin** of their **faith**. 20 Among them are Hymenaeus and Alexander, whom I have **punished** by handing them over to the **power** of **Satan**; this will **teach** them to stop their **blasphemy**.

Church Worship

2 First of all, then, I **urge** that petitions, **prayers**, **requests**, and **thanksgivings** be **offered** to God for all people; 2 for kings and all others who are in **authority**, that we may live a quiet and **peaceful life** with all **reverence** towards God and with **proper conduct**. 3 This is good and it **pleases** God our **Saviour**, 4 who wants everyone to be **saved** and to come to know the **truth**. 5 For there is one God, and there is one who brings God and **mankind** together, the man Christ Jesus, 6 who gave himself to **redeem** all **mankind**. That was the **proof** at the **right** time that God wants everyone to be **saved**, 7 and that is why I was sent as an **apostle** and **teacher** of the **Gentiles**, to **proclaim** the **message** of **faith** and **truth**. I am not **lying**; I am telling the **truth**!

8 In every **church service** I want the men to **pray**, men who are **dedicated** to God and can lift up their hands in **prayer** without **anger** or **argument**. 9 I also want the women to be modest and **sensible** about their clothes and to dress **properly**; not with fancy hair styles or with gold ornaments or pearls or expensive dresses, 10 but with good **deeds**, as is **proper** for women who **claim** to be **religious**. 11 Women should **learn** in silence and all **humility**. 12 I do not allow them to **teach** or to have **authority** over men; they must keep quiet. 13 For Adam was **created** first, and then Eve. 14 And it was not Adam who was **deceived**; it was the woman who was **deceived** and broke God's **law**. 15 But a woman will be **saved** through having children,[a] if she perseveres[b] in **faith** and **love** and **holiness**, with modesty.

Leaders in the Church

3 This is a **true saying**: If a man is **eager** to be a **church** leader, he **desires** an excellent work. 2 A **church** leader must be without **fault**; he must have only one wife,[c] be sober, **self-controlled**, and orderly; he must **welcome strangers** in his home; he must be able to **teach**; 3 he must not be a drunkard or a **violent** man, but **gentle** and **peaceful**; he must not **love** money; 4 he must be able to manage his own family well and make his children **obey** him with all **respect**. 5 For if a man does not know how to manage his own family, how can he take **care** of the **church** of God? 6 He must be **mature** in the **faith**, so that he will not swell up with **pride** and be **condemned**, as the **Devil** was. 7 He should be a man who is **respected** by the people outside the **church**, so that he will not be **disgraced** and fall into the **Devil's** trap.

Helpers in the Church

8 **Church helpers** must also have a good character and be **sincere**; they must not drink too much wine or be **greedy** for money; 9 they should hold to the **revealed truth** of the **faith** with a **clear conscience**. 10 They should be **tested** first, and then, if they pass the **test**, they are to **serve**. 11 Their wives[d] also must be of good character and must not gossip; they must be sober and **honest** in everything. 12 A **church helper** must have only one wife,[e] and be able to manage his children and family well. 13 Those **helpers** who do their work well **win** for themselves a good standing and are able to speak **boldly** about their **faith** in Christ Jesus.

The Great Secret

14 As I write this **letter** to you, I **hope** to come and see you soon. 15 But if I am delayed, this **letter** will let you know how we should **conduct** ourselves in God's household, which is the **church** of the living God, the pillar and support of the **truth**. 16 No one can **deny** how great is the **secret** of our **religion**:

He appeared in **human** form,
was shown to be **right** by the **Spirit**,[f]
and was seen by **angels**.
He was **preached** among the nations,
was **believed** in throughout the
world,
and was taken up to **heaven**.

False Teachers

4 The **Spirit** says **clearly** that some people will **abandon** the **faith** in later times; they will **obey lying spirits** and follow the **teachings** of **demons**.

Chapter 3
angel 2 Thes 1.7; 5.2
believe 1.15; 4.9
bold Phil 1.14; Phlm 8
care 1 Thes 2.7; 5.5
church [7] 2.8; 5.16
clear 1.5; 4.1
condemn 2 Thes 2.12; Heb 11.7
conduct 2.2; 4.12
conscience 1.5; 4.2
deny 1 Cor 7.5; 5.8
desire 2 Thes 1.11; 5.11
Devil [2] 1 Thes 3.5; 2 Tim 2.26
disgrace 2 Cor 6.8; Heb 12.2
eager Phil 3.20; 6.10
faith [3] 2.7; 4.1
fault 1 Thes 5.23; 5.7
gentle 1 Thes 2.7; 6.11
greed 1 Thes 2.5; 2 Tim 3.2
heaven 2 Thes 1.7; 2 Tim 4.18
helper (1) [3] Phil 1.
honest Eph 4.28
hope 1.1; 4.10
human Col 3.22; Tit 1.14
letter (2) [2] 2 Thes 3.14; Heb 13.22
love 2.15; 4.12
mature Col 4.12; Heb 6.1
obey 2 Thes 3.14; 4.1
peace 2.2; 2 Tim 1.2
preach 2 Thes 2.2; 4.13
proud 1 Thes 2.20; 6.4
religion 2.10; 5.4
respect [2] 1 Thes 5.12; 5.3
reveal 2 Thes 2.8; 2 Tim 1.10
right (1) 2.6; 6.15
saying 1.15; 4.9
secret Col 4.3; Rev 1.20
self-control Gal 5.23; 2 Tim 1.7
serve 1.4; 6.2
sincere Col 3.22; 2 Tim 1.5
Spirit (1) (God's Spirit) 2 Thes 2.13; 4.1
stranger Eph 2.19; 5.10
teach 2.12; 4.1
test [2] 1 Thes 5.21; Heb 3.8
trap 2 Cor 12.16; 6.9
true 1.2; 4.6
truth [2] 2.4; 4.3
violent Acts 27.18; 2 Tim 3.3
welcome 2 Thes 2.10; Phlm 17
win 1 Thes 4.12; 6.12
world 1.15; 6.7

abandon 2 Cor 11.3; Heb 6.4
accept [2] 1.15; Heb 4.2
believe [2] 3.16; 2 Tim 3.14
believer [2] 1 Thes 5.26; 6.2
clear 3.9; 2 Tim 1.3
conduct 3.15; 2 Tim 3.10

[a] will be saved through having children; *or* will be kept safe through childbirth.
[b] if she perseveres; *or* if they persevere. [c] have only one wife; *or* be married only once.
[d] Their wives; *or* Women helpers. [e] have only one wife; *or* be married only once.
[f] was shown to be right by the Spirit; *or* and, in spiritual form, was shown to be right.

2.7: 2 Tim 1.11 **2.9:** 1 Pet 3.3 **2.13:** Gen 2.7, 21–22 **2.14:** Gen 3.1–6 **3.2–7:** Tit 1.6–9

conscience 3.9; 2 Tim 1.3
create [2] 2.13; Heb 1.2
dead 1 Thes 5.10; 2 Tim 4.1
deceive 2.14; 2 Tim 3.13
demon 1 Cor 10.20; Jas 2.19
devote Gal 1.13; 5.10
elder (2) Acts 25.15; 5.17
example 1.16; 2 Tim 1.13
faith [3] 3.6; 5.8
gift Phil 4.17; 2 Tim 1.6
godless 1.9; 1 Pet 4.18
godly Acts 3.12; 6.11
hard 1 Thes 2.17; 5.17
hope 3.14; 5.5
keep from 2 Thes 3.6; 2 Tim 2.16
lie (2) [2] 2.7; Tit 1.2
life (1) [2] 2.2; 6.12
look down on 2 Cor 11.20; Tit 2.15
love 3.3; 6.2
neglect Phil 4.11
obey 3.4; 5.21
physical Col 2.23; 1 Pet 3.18
practice 1 Thes 1.3; Heb 5.14
prayer [3] 2.1; 2 Tim 1.3
preach 3.16; 5.17
promise Eph 6.2; 5.12
prophet 1 Thes 2.15; Tit 1.12
pure 1.5; 5.2
reject 2 Thes 1.8; 2 Tim 3.5
save 2.4; 2 Tim 1.9
Saviour 2.3; 2 Tim 1.10
saying 3.1; 2 Tim 2.11
scripture Eph 5.31; 5.18
servant Col 4.7; 2 Tim 2.24
speech Col 4.6
Spirit (1) (God's Spirit) 3.16; 2 Tim 1.7
spirit (2) 1 Thes 5.23; 2 Tim 4.22
spiritual [3] 1.9; Phlm 10
struggle Col 1.29; Heb 10.32
teach [7] 3.2; 5.17
thank [2] 2.1; 2 Tim 1.3
true [2] 3.1; 6.3
truth 3.9; 6.5
value [2] Col 2.23; 1 Pet 2.4
watch Col 3.22; Heb 13.17
word (1) [2] 1.7; 6.3
worthless Col 2.8; Tit 3.9
wrong 1 Thes 5.15; 6.20

Chapter 5
accuse 2 Cor 13.1; 1 Pet 2.12
afraid Phil 1.28; Heb 11.23
alone [3] 1 Thes 3.1; 6.16
angel 3.16; Heb 1.4
burden Gal 6.2; 2 Tim 3.6

2 Such **teachings** are spread by **deceitful**
liars, whose **consciences** are **dead**, as if
burnt with a hot iron. 3 Such people **teach**
that it is **wrong** to marry and to eat certain foods. But God **created** those foods to
be eaten, after a **prayer** of **thanks**, by
those who are **believers** and have come
to know the **truth**. 4 Everything that God
has **created** is good; nothing is to be **rejected**, but everything is to be received
with a **prayer** of **thanks**, 5 because the
word of God and the **prayer** make it
acceptable to God.

A Good Servant of Christ Jesus

6 If you give these instructions to the
brothers, you will be a good **servant** of
Christ Jesus, as you feed yourself **spiritually** on the **words** of **faith** and of the **true
teaching** which you have followed. 7 But
keep away from those **godless** legends,
which are **not worth** telling. Keep yourself in training for a **godly life**. 8 **Physical**
exercise has some **value**, but **spiritual**
exercise is **valuable** in every way, because it **promises life** both for the
present and for the future. 9 This is a **true
saying**, to be completely **accepted** and
believed. 10 We **struggle**[g] and work **hard**,
because we have placed our **hope** in the
living God, who is the **Saviour** of all and
especially of those who **believe**.
11 Give them these instructions and
these **teachings**. 12 Do not let anyone **look
down on** you because you are young, but
be an **example** for the **believers** in your
speech, your **conduct**, your **love**, **faith**,
and **purity**. 13 Until I come, give your time
and effort to the public reading of the
Scriptures and to **preaching** and **teaching**. 14 Do not **neglect** the **spiritual gift**
that is in you, which was given to you
when the **prophets** spoke and the **elders**
laid their hands on you. 15 **Practise** these
things and **devote** yourself to them, in
order that your progress may be seen by
all. 16 **Watch** yourself and watch your
teaching. Keep on doing these things, because if you do, you will **save** both yourself and those who hear you.

Responsibilities towards Believers

5 Do not **rebuke** an older man, but
appeal to him as if he were your
father. Treat the younger men as your
brothers, 2 the older women as mothers,
and the younger women as sisters, with
all **purity**.
3 Show **respect** for **widows** who really
are all **alone**. 4 But if a **widow** has children or grandchildren, they should **learn**
first to carry out their **religious duties**
towards their own family and in this way
repay their parents and grandparents,
because that is what **pleases** God. 5 A
widow who is all **alone**, with no one to
take **care** of her, has placed her **hope** in
God and continues to **pray** and ask him
for his **help** night and day. 6 But a **widow**
who gives herself to **pleasure** has already
died, even though she lives. 7 Give them
these instructions, so that no one will find
fault with them. 8 But if anyone does not
take **care** of his relatives, especially the
members of his own family, he has
denied the **faith** and is **worse** than an
unbeliever.
9 Do not add any **widow** to the list of
widows unless she is over sixty years of
age. In addition, she must have been
married only once[h] 10 and have a **reputation** for good **deeds**: a woman who
brought up her children well, received
strangers in her home, performed
humble duties for **fellow-Christians**,
helped people in **trouble**, and **devoted**
herself to doing good.
11 But do not include younger **widows**
in the list; because when their **desires**
make them want to marry, they **turn
away** from **Christ**, 12 and so become **guilty**
of breaking their earlier **promise** to him.
13 They also **learn** to waste their time in
going round from house to house; but
even **worse**, they **learn** to be gossips and
busybodies, talking of things they should
not. 14 So I would prefer that the younger
widows get married, have children, and
take **care** of their homes, so as to give
our **enemies** no chance of speaking **evil**
of us. 15 For some **widows** have already
turned away to follow **Satan**. 16 But if any
Christian woman has **widows** in her
family, she must take **care** of them and
not put the **burden** on the **church**, so that
it may take **care** of the **widows** who are
all **alone**.
17 The **elders** who do good work as
leaders should be **considered worthy** of
receiving double pay, especially those
who work **hard** at **preaching** and **teaching**. 18 For the **scripture** says, "Do not
muzzle an ox when you are using it to
thresh corn" and "A worker should be
given his pay." 19 Do not listen to an
accusation against an **elder** unless it is
brought by two or more **witnesses**.
20 **Rebuke** publicly all those who **commit**
sins, so that the rest may be **afraid**.
21 In the **presence** of God and of
Christ Jesus and of the **holy angels** I
solemnly call upon you to **obey** these

care [5] 3.5; 6.20
Christ 2 Thes 3.5; 2 Tim 1.8
Christian [2] 1 Thes 5.12; 6.2
church 3.1; Tit 1.5
commit 1 Thes 2.16; Heb 9.7
consider 1.12; 6.1
dedicate 2.8; 2 Tim 2.21
deed (2) [2] 2.10; 2 Tim 2.21
deny 3.16; 2 Tim 2.12
desire 3.1; 6.4
devote 4.15; Heb 5.7
duty (1) [2] Col 3.20; 2 Tim 4.5
elder (2) [2] 4.14; Tit 1.5
enemy 2 Thes 3.15; Tit 2.8
evil 1.13; 6.1
faith 4.1; 6.10
fault 3.2; 2 Tim 3.16
favour Gal 2.12; Phlm 20
guilty 1 Cor 11.27; 2 Tim 3.6
hard 4.10; 2 Tim 2.6
help [3] 1 Thes 5.11; 2 Tim 2.22
holy 2.15; 2 Tim 3.15
hope 4.10; 6.17
humble 2.11; Heb 5.7
judge 2 Thes 1.5; 2 Tim 4.1
learn [3] 2.11; 2 Tim 3.7
obey 4.1; 6.14
plain (1) [3] Gal 5.19; Heb 7.15
please 2.3; 2 Tim 2.4
pleasure 2 Thes 2.12; 2 Tim 3.4
pray 2.8; Phlm 4
preach 4.13; 6.2
presence 2 Thes 2.8; 2 Tim 2.2
promise 4.8; 2 Tim 1.1
pure [2] 4.12; 2 Tim 2.22
rebuke [2] Lk 23.40; 2 Tim 3.16
religion 3.16; 6.3
repay Col 3.25; Heb 10.30
reputation Mk 6.14; Tit 1.6
respect 3.4; 6.1
Satan 1.20; Rev 2.9
scripture 4.13; 2 Tim 3.15
service 2.8; 2 Tim 2.4
solemn Acts 23.14; 2 Tim 2.14
stranger 3.2; Heb 13.2
teach 4.1; 6.1
trouble 1 Thes 3.7; Heb 12.15
turn [2] 1.6; 2 Tim 2.19
unbeliever 2 Cor 6.14; Tit 1.15
widow [11] 1 Cor 7.8; Jas 1.27
witness 1 Thes 2.5; 6.12
worse [2] 2 Cor 12.13; 2 Tim 3.13
worthy 1.12; 6.1

[g] struggle; *some manuscripts have* are reviled. [h] married only once; *or* faithful to her husband.

5.18: Deut 25.4; Mt 10.10; Lk 10.7 **5.19:** Deut 17.6, 19.15

instructions without showing any prejudice or favour to anyone in anything you
do. 22 Be in no hurry to lay hands on
someone to dedicate him to the Lord's
service. Take no part in the sins of
others; keep yourself pure.
23 Do not drink water only, but take a
little wine to help your digestion, since
you are ill so often.
24 The sins of some people are plain
to see, and their sins go ahead of them to
judgement; but the sins of others are
seen only later. 25 In the same way good
deeds are plainly seen, and even those
that are not so plain cannot be hidden.

6 Those who are slaves must consider
their masters worthy of all respect,
so that no one will speak evil of the name
of God and of our teaching. 2 Slaves belonging to Christian masters must not
despise them, for they are their brothers.
Instead, they are to serve them even better, because those who benefit from their
work are believers whom they love.

False Teaching and True Riches

You must teach and preach these
things. 3 Whoever teaches a different doctrine and does not agree with the true
words of our Lord Jesus Christ and with
the teaching of our religion 4 is swollen
with pride and knows nothing. He has an
unhealthy desire to argue and quarrel
about words, and this brings on jealousy,
disputes, insults, evil suspicions, 5 and
constant arguments from people whose
minds do not function and who no longer
have the truth. They think that religion is
a way to become rich.
6 Well, religion does make a person
very rich, if he is satisfied with what he
has. 7 What did we bring into the world?
Nothing! What can we take out of the
world? Nothing! 8 So then, if we have
food and clothes, that should be enough
for us. 9 But those who want to get rich
fall into temptation and are caught in the
trap of many foolish and harmful desires,
which pull them down to ruin and
destruction. 10 For the love of money is a
source of all kinds of evil. Some have
been so eager to have it that they have
wandered away from the faith and have
broken their hearts with many sorrows.

Personal Instructions

11 But you, man of God, avoid all these
things. Strive for righteousness, godliness, faith, love, endurance, and gentleness. 12 Run your best in the race of faith,
and win eternal life for yourself; for it
was to this life that God called you when
you firmly professed your faith before
many witnesses. 13 Before God, who gives
life to all things, and before Christ Jesus,
who firmly professed his faith before
Pontius Pilate, I command you 14 to obey
your orders and keep them faithfully
until the Day when our Lord Jesus Christ
will appear. 15 His appearing will be
brought about at the right time by God,
the blessed and only Ruler, the King of
kings and the Lord of lords. 16 He alone is
immortal; he lives in the light that no
one can approach. No one has ever seen
him; no one can ever see him. To him be
honour and eternal dominion! Amen.
17 Command those who are rich in the
things of this life not to be proud, but to
place their hope, not in such an uncertain thing as riches, but in God, who
generously gives us everything for our
enjoyment. 18 Command them to do good,
to be rich in good works, to be generous
and ready to share with others. 19 In this
way they will store up for themselves a
treasure which will be a solid foundation
for the future. And then they will be able
to win the life which is true life.
20 Timothy, keep safe what has been
entrusted to your care. Avoid the profane
talk and foolish arguments of what some
people wrongly call "Knowledge." 21 For
some have claimed to possess it, and as a
result they have lost the way of faith.
God's grace be with you all.

6.13: Jn 18.37

agree Phil 4.2; Tit 1.9
alone 5.3; Tit 2.14
argue [3] 2.8; 2 Tim 2.23
believer 4.3; 2 Tim 2.18
benefit Eph 3.13; 1 Pet 1.12
best Col 4.15; 2 Tim 2.15
bless 1.11; Tit 2.13
care 5.5; Heb 2.6
certain (1) Rom 14.14; Heb 11.1
Christian 5.10; 2 Tim 4.21
claim 2.10; Tit 1.16
command [3] 1.18; Heb 3.10
consider 5.17; Jas 1.2
constant Col 3.10; Jas 4.1
Day of the Lord 2 Thes 2.2; 2 Tim 1.12
desire [2] 5.11; 2 Tim 3.6
despise 1 Thes 5.20; Heb 10.29
destroy 2 Thes 2.8; Heb 2.14
dispute 1 Cor 6.1
doctrine 1.3; 2 Tim 4.3
eager 3.1; Tit 2.14
endure 2 Thes 3.5; 2 Tim 2.10
enjoy Rom 15.24; Heb 11.25
enough Phil 4.12; Phlm 8
entrust 1.11; 2 Tim 1.12
eternal [2] 1.16; 2 Tim 2.10
evil [3] 5.14; 2 Tim 2.21
faith [6] 5.8; 2 Tim 1.5
faithful 2 Thes 3.3; 2 Tim 2.13
fool [2] 1.6; 2 Tim 2.16
generous [2] 2 Cor 9.9; Jas 1.5
gentle 3.3; 2 Tim 2.25
godly 4.7; 2 Tim 3.12
grace 1.2; 2 Tim 1.2
harm Eph 4.29; 2 Tim 4.14

heart 1.5; 2 Tim 2.22
honour 1.17; Heb 1.9
hope 5.5; Tit 1.2
immortal 1.17; 2 Tim 1.10
insult 1.13; 2 Tim 3.2
jealous Phil 1.15; Jas 3.14
knowledge Col 3.10; 2 Pet 1.2
life (1)-[5] 4.7; 2 Tim 1.1
light (1) 1 Thes 5.5; Heb 6.4
love [3] 4.12; 2 Tim 1.7
master [2] Col 4.1; 2 Tim 2.21
mind (1) Col 3.2; 2 Tim 3.8
name (2) (name of God, of Jesus) 2 Thes 3.6; Heb 1.4
obey 5.21; 2 Tim 2.5
possess 2 Thes 2.14; Tit 3.7
preach 5.17; 2 Tim 2.8
profane Eph 5.4; 2 Tim 2.16
proud [2] 3.6; 2 Tim 3.4
quarrel Phil 1.15; 2 Tim 2.23
race (2) 1 Cor 9.24; 2 Tim 2.5
religion [3] 5.4; 2 Tim 3.5
respect 5.3; Heb 12.9
result 2 Thes 2.12; Heb 11.7
rich [5] Col 3.16; Jas 1.10
riches Eph 3.8; Jas 5.2
right (1) 3.16; 2 Tim 3.16
righteous Phil 3.6; 2 Tim 2.22
ruin 1.19; 2 Tim 2.14
safe 2 Thes 3.3; 2 Tim 1.12
satisfy Phil 4.11; Heb 13.5
serve 3.10; 2 Tim 1.3
share 2 Thes 2.14; 2 Tim 2.6
slave [2] Col 4.1; Tit 2.3
sorrow Phil 2.27; Jas 4.9
source 2 Thes 3.16; Heb 5.9
teach [4] 5.17; 2 Tim 1.13
tempt 1 Thes 3.5; Heb 2.18
trap 3.7; 2 Tim 2.26
true [2] 4.6; 2 Tim 1.13
truth 4.3; 2 Tim 2.15
win [2] 3.13; 2 Tim 2.5
witness 5.19; 2 Tim 1.8
word (1) [2] 4.5; 2 Tim 1.13
world [2] 3.16; 2 Tim 4.10
worthy 5.17; Heb 3.3
wrong 4.3; 2 Tim 2.19

PAUL'S SECOND LETTER TO
TIMOTHY

INTRODUCTION

Paul's Second Letter to Timothy consists largely of personal advice to Timothy, as a younger colleague and assistant. The main theme is endurance. Timothy is advised and encouraged to keep on witnessing faithfully to Jesus Christ, to hold to the true teaching of the Good News and the Old Testament, and to do his duty as teacher and evangelist, all in the face of suffering and opposition.

Timothy is especially warned about the dangers of becoming involved in "foolish and ignorant arguments" that do no good, but only ruin the people who listen to them.

In all this, Timothy is reminded of the example of the writer's own life and purpose—his faith, patience, love, endurance, and suffering in persecution.

Outline of Contents

---

1 From Paul, an **apostle** of Christ
Jesus by **God's will**, sent to **proclaim**
the **promised life** which we have in **union**
with Christ Jesus—
2 To Timothy, my **dear** son:
May God the **Father** and Christ Jesus
our Lord give you **grace**, **mercy**, and
peace.

Thanksgiving and Encouragement

3 I give **thanks** to God, whom I **serve**
with a **clear conscience**, as my ancestors
did. I **thank** him as I **remember** you always in my **prayers** night and day. 4 I
remember your **tears**, and I want to see
you very much, so that I may be filled
with **joy**. 5 I **remember** the **sincere faith**
you have, the kind of **faith** that your
grandmother Lois and your mother
Eunice also had. I am **sure** that you have
it also. 6 For this **reason** I **remind** you to
keep **alive** the **gift** that God gave you
when I laid my hands on you. 7 For the
Spirit that God has given us does not
make us timid; instead, his **Spirit** fills us
with **power**, **love**, and **self-control**.
8 Do not be **ashamed**, then, of **witness-**
ing for our Lord; nor be **ashamed** of me,
a **prisoner** for **Christ's sake**. Instead, take
your part in **suffering** for the **Good News**,
as God gives you the **strength** to do it.
9 He **saved** us and called us to be his **own**
people, not because of what we have
done, but because of his own **purpose** and
grace. He gave us this **grace by means of**
Christ Jesus before the beginning of time,
10 but now it has been **revealed** to us
through the coming of our **Saviour**, Christ
Jesus. He has ended the **power** of **death**
and through the **gospel** has **revealed im-**
mortal life.
11 God has appointed me as an
apostle and **teacher** to **proclaim** the
Good News, 12 and it is for this **reason**
that I **suffer** these things. But I am still
full of **confidence**, because I know whom
I have **trusted**, and I am **sure** that he is
able to keep **safe** until that **Day** what he
has **entrusted** to me.[a] 13 Hold firmly to
the **true words** that I **taught** you, as the
example for you to follow, and remain in
the **faith** and **love** that are ours in **union**
with Christ Jesus. 14 Through the **power of**
the Holy Spirit, who lives in us, keep the
good things that have been **entrusted** to
you.
15 You know that everyone in the province of Asia, including Phygelus and
Hermogenes, has deserted me. 16 May the
Lord show **mercy** to the family of Onesiphorus, because he **cheered** me up many
times. He was not **ashamed** that I am in
prison, 17 but as soon as he arrived in
Rome, he started looking for me until he
found me. 18 May the Lord **grant** him his

[a] what he has entrusted to me; *or* what I have entrusted to him.

1.2: Acts 16.1 **1.5:** Acts 16.1 **1.11:** 1 Tim 2.7

alive 1 Thes 5.10; Heb 4.12
apostle [2] 1 Tim 2.7; Tit 1.1
ashamed [3] 2 Thes 3.14; 2.15
cheer (1) Col 4.8; Phlm 7
Christ 1 Tim 5.11; Phlm 6
clear 1 Tim 4.1; Heb 2.8
confident 1 Tim 1.7; Heb 3.6
conscience 1 Tim 4.2; Tit 1.15
Day of the Lord [2] 1 Tim 6.14; 4.8
dear 1 Thes 2.8; Phlm 7
death (1) Col 1.20; Heb 2.9
entrust [2] 1 Tim 6.20; 2.2
example 1 Tim 4.12; Tit 2.7
faith [3] 1 Tim 6.10; 2.18
Father (2) (God) 1 Tim 1.2; Tit 1.4
gift 1 Tim 4.14; Heb 2.4
God's people 2 Thes 2.13; 2.10
Good News [2] 1 Tim 1.11; 2.8
gospel 1 Tim 1.11; Phlm 13
grace [3] 1 Tim 6.21; 2.1
grant Acts 4.30
immortal 1 Tim 6.16; 1 Pet 1.23
joy 1 Thes 5.16; Phlm 7
life (1) [2] 1 Tim 6.12; 2.4
love [2] 1 Tim 6.2; 2.22
means Col 2.8; Heb 7.21
mercy [3] 1 Tim 1.2; 3.3

peace 1 Tim 3.3; 2.22
power [3] 1 Tim 1.20; 3.5
prayer 1 Tim 4.3; Phlm 6
prison [2] Col 4.3; Phlm 1
proclaim [2] 1 Tim 2.7; 2.2
promise 1 Tim 5.12; Tit 1.2
purpose 1 Tim 1.5; 2.21
reason [2] 1 Thes 2.13; Tit 1.12
remember [3] 1 Tim 1.9; 2.8
remind 2 Cor 1.8; 2.14
reveal [2] 1 Tim 3.9; Tit 1.3
safe 1 Tim 6.20; 4.18
sake Phil 3.7; 2.10
save 1 Tim 4.16; Tit 3.5
Saviour 1 Tim 4.10; Tit 1.3
self-control 1 Tim 3.2; Tit 1.8
serve 1 Tim 6.2; 3.17
sincere 1 Tim 3.8; Tit 2.7
Spirit (1) (God's Spirit) [3] 1 Tim 4.1; Tit 3.5
strength 1 Tim 1.12; 4.17
suffer [2] 2 Thes 1.4; 2.3
sure [2] 2 Thes 3.4; Phlm 21
teach 1 Tim 6.1; 2.2
teacher 1 Tim 2.7; 2.24
tear (2) Phil 3.18; Heb 5.7
thank [2] 1 Tim 4.3; Phlm 4
true 1 Tim 6.3; 2.11
trust Phil 3.3; Tit 1.9
union [2] 1 Tim 1.14; 2.1

will (1) 1 Thes 3.3; 2.26
witness 1 Tim 6.12; 2.2
word (1) 1 Tim 6.3; 2.9

Chapter 2
approve Col 3.22; Heb 11.2
argue 1 Tim 6.4; Tit 3.9
ashamed 1.8; Heb 2.11
believer 1 Tim 6.2; Tit 1.6
best 1 Tim 6.12; 4.7
choose 2 Thes 2.13; Tit 1.1
clean Eph 5.26; Heb 10.22
correct [2] Acts 18.25; 3.16
crime 1 Tim 1.9; 1 Pet 4.15
death (2) (from death) 1 Thes 1.10; Heb 5.7
dedicate 1 Tim 5.22; 2 Pet 3.11
deed (2) 1 Tim 5.10; 3.17
deny 1 Tim 5.8; Tit 1.16
Devil 1 Tim 3.6; Heb 2.14
discuss 1 Tim 1.6
endure [2] 1 Tim 6.11; 3.10
entrust 1.12; Tit 1.3
escape 1 Thes 5.3; Heb 2.3
eternal 1 Tim 6.12; Tit 1.2
evil 1 Tim 6.1; 3.13
faith [2] 1.5; 3.8
faithful 1 Tim 6.14; Tit 2.10
false 1 Tim 1.3; 2 Pet 2.1
flesh 1 Cor 15.39; Heb 2.14
fool [2] 1 Tim 6.9; Tit 3.3
gentle 1 Tim 6.11; Tit 3.2
glory 1 Tim 1.11; 4.18
God's people 1.9; Tit 1.1
Good News [2] 1.8; 4.5
grace 1.2; 4.22
hard 1 Tim 5.17; Heb 5.11
harvest Eph 5.9; Jas 3.17
heart 1 Tim 6.10; Phlm 7
help 1 Tim 5.5; 4.11
ignorant Eph 5.15; Heb 5.2
keep from [2] 1 Tim 4.7; 3.5
kind Col 3.12; Tit 3.4
life (1) 1.1; 3.10
love 1.7; 3.4
loyal 2 Cor 10.6; Rev 17.6
master 1 Tim 6.1; Tit 2.9
message 1 Tim 2.7; 4.2
obey [2] 1 Tim 6.14; Tit 3.1
passion Col 3.5; Tit 2.12
patient 1 Tim 1.16; 3.10
peace 1.2; Tit 1.4
please 1 Tim 5.4; Tit 2.9
preach [2] 1 Tim 6.2; 4.2

mercy on that Day! And you know very
well how much he did for me in Ephesus.

A Loyal Soldier of Christ Jesus

2 As for you, my son, be strong
through the grace that is ours in
union with Christ Jesus. 2 Take the teachings that you heard me proclaim in the
presence of many witnesses, and entrust
them to reliable people, who will be able
to teach others also.
3 Take your part in suffering, as a
loyal soldier of Christ Jesus. 4 A soldier on
active service wants to please his commanding officer and so does not get
mixed up in the affairs of civilian life.
5 An athlete who runs in a race cannot
win the prize unless he obeys the rules.
6 The farmer who has done the hard
work should have the first share of the
harvest. 7 Think about what I am saying,
because the Lord will enable you to
understand it all.
8 Remember Jesus Christ, who was
raised from death, who was a descendant
of David, as is taught in the Good News I
preach. 9 Because I preach the Good
News, I suffer and I am even chained like
a criminal. But the word of God is not in
chains, 10 and so I endure everything for
the sake of God's chosen people, in order
that they too may obtain the salvation
that comes through Christ Jesus and
brings eternal glory. 11 This is a true
saying:

"If we have died with him,
we shall also live with him.
12 If we continue to endure,
we shall also rule with him.
If we deny him,
he also will deny us.
13 If we are not faithful,
he remains faithful,
because he cannot be false to
himself."

An Approved Worker

14 Remind your people of this, and
give them a solemn warning in God's
presence not to fight over words. It does
no good, but only ruins the people who
listen. 15 Do your best to win full approval
in God's sight, as a worker who is not
ashamed of his work, one who correctly
teaches the message of God's truth.
16 Keep away from profane and foolish
discussions, which only drive people
further away from God. 17 Such teaching
is like an open sore that eats away the
flesh. Two men who have taught such
things are Hymenaeus and Philetus.
18 They have left the way of truth and are
upsetting the faith of some believers by
saying that our resurrection has already
taken place. 19 But the solid foundation
that God has laid cannot be shaken; and
on it are written these words: "The Lord
knows those who are his" and "Whoever
says that he belongs to the Lord must
turn away from wrongdoing."
20 In a large house there are dishes
and bowls of all kinds: some are made of
silver and gold, others of wood and clay;
some are for special occasions, others
for ordinary use. 21 If anyone makes himself clean from all those evil things, he
will be used for special purposes, because he is dedicated and useful to his
Master, ready to be used for every good
deed. 22 Avoid the passions of youth, and
strive for righteousness, faith, love, and
peace, together with those who with a
pure heart call out to the Lord for help.
23 But keep away from foolish and ignorant arguments; you know that they end
up in quarrels. 24 The Lord's servant must
not quarrel. He must be kind towards all,
a good and patient teacher, 25 who is
gentle as he corrects his opponents, for it
may be that God will give them the
opportunity to repent and come to know
the truth. 26 And then they will come to
their senses and escape from the trap of
the Devil, who had caught them and
made them obey his will.

The Last Days

3 Remember that there will be
difficult times in the last days.
2 People will be selfish, greedy, boastful,
and conceited; they will be insulting, disobedient to their parents, ungrateful, and
irreligious; 3 they will be unkind, merciless, slanderers, violent, and fierce; they
will hate the good; 4 they will be
treacherous, reckless, and swollen with
pride; they will love pleasure rather than
God; 5 they will hold to the outward form
of our religion, but reject its real power.
Keep away from such people. 6 Some of
them go into people's houses and gain
control over weak women who are burdened by the guilt of their sins and
driven by all kinds of desires, 7 women
who are always trying to learn but who
can never come to know the truth. 8 As
Jannes and Jambres were opposed to
Moses, so also these people are opposed
to the truth—people whose minds do not
function and who are failures in the faith.
9 But they will not get very far, because
everyone will see how stupid they are.
That is just what happened to Jannes and
Jambres.

2.12: Mt 10.33; Lk 12.9 **2.19:** Num 16.5 **3.8:** Ex 7.11

presence [2] 1 Tim 5.21; 4.1
prize Phil 3.12; 4.8
proclaim 1.1; 4.2
profane 1 Tim 6.20
pure 1 Tim 5.2; Tit 1.15
purpose 1.9; 3.10
quarrel [2] 1 Tim 6.4; Tit 3.9
race (2) 1 Tim 6.12; 4.7
raise 1 Thes 1.10; Heb 7.26
rely 2 Cor 1.9
remember 1.3; 3.1
remind 1.6; Tit 3.1
repent 2 Cor 12.21; Heb 6.4
resurrection Phil 3.10; Heb 6.2
righteous 1 Tim 6.11; 4.8
ruin 1 Tim 6.9
sake 1.8; Phlm 1
salvation 1 Thes 5.8; 3.15
saying 1 Tim 4.9; Tit 3.8
sense 1 Tim 2.9; Tit 2.2
servant 1 Tim 4.6; 4.5
service 1 Tim 5.22; Heb 2.17
share 1 Tim 6.18; Heb 2.10
sight 2 Cor 8.21; Heb 12.21
solemn 1 Tim 5.21; 4.1
special [2] Col 2.18; Tit 3.8
strong 1 Thes 4.6; Heb 11.34
suffer [2] 1.8; 3.11
teach [6] 1.13; 3.10
teacher 1.11; 3.14
trap 1 Tim 6.9; Jas 1.14
true 1.13; Tit 1.4
truth [3] 1 Tim 6.5; 3.7
turn 1 Tim 5.11; 4.4
understand 1 Tim 1.7; Phlm 6
union 1.1; 3.12
upset 2 Thes 2.2; Tit 1.11
warn 2 Thes 3.12; Tit 3.10
will (1) 1.1; Phlm 14
win [2] 1 Tim 6.12; Heb 11.2
witness 1.8; Heb 2.4
word (1) [3] 1.13; Tit 2.8
wrong 1 Tim 6.20; Tit 3.3

Chapter 3
bad 2 Cor 5.10; Tit 2.8
believe 1 Tim 4.9; Tit 3.8
boast 2 Thes 1.4; Jas 3.5
burden 1 Tim 5.16; Rev 2.24
conceited 1 Cor 13.4
conduct 1 Tim 4.12; Jas 1.21
control Col 2.19; 4.5
correct 2.15; Heb 12.5
deceive 1 Tim 4.2; Tit 1.10
deed (2) 2.21; Tit 3.5
desire 1 Tim 6.4; 4.3
difficult 2 Cor 12.10; 1 Pet 4.18

disobey Eph 2.1; Tit 1.6
endure [2] 2.10; 4.5
error 2 Thes 2.11; Tit 1.9
evil 2.21; 4.18
fail 1 Thes 2.1; Heb 4.1
faith [3] 2.18; 4.7
fault 1 Tim 5.7; Heb 7.26
godly 1 Tim 6.11; Tit 2.12
grateful 2 Cor 9.12; Heb 12.28
greed 1 Tim 3.8; Tit 1.7
guilty 1 Tim 5.12; Heb 10.2
hate Col 3.8; Tit 1.16
holy 1 Tim 5.21; Tit 1.8
inspire 1 Thes 5.20; Rev 19.10
insult 1 Tim 6.4; Heb 10.29
keep from 2.16; Heb 11.5
last (2) 1 Thes 2.16; Heb 1.2
learn 1 Tim 5.4; Tit 3.14
life (1) [2] 2.4; 4.6
love [2] 2.22; 4.8
mercy 1.2; Tit 3.5
mind (1) 1 Tim 6.5; Tit 1.15
observe 1 Cor 4.6
patient 2.24; 4.2
persecute [3] 1 Tim 1.13; Heb 11.37
pleasure 1 Tim 5.6; Tit 3.3
power 1.7; Heb 1.3
proud 1 Tim 6.4; Jas 4.6
purpose 2.21; Tit 1.11
real Col 3.4; Tit 3.14
rebuke 1 Tim 5.1; Tit 1.12
reject 1 Tim 4.4; Tit 1.14
religion 1 Tim 6.3; Tit 1.1
remember [2] 2.8; Tit 1.5
rescue 2 Thes 3.2; 4.17
right (1) 1 Tim 6.15; 4.2
salvation 2.10; Tit 2.11
scripture [2] 1 Tim 5.18; Heb 2.6
selfish Phil 2.3; Jas 3.14
serve 1.3; Heb 1.14
slander 1 Cor 6.10; Tit 2.3
stupid 2 Cor 10.12; Tit 3.9
suffer 2.3; 4.5
teach [3] 2.2; 4.2
teacher 2.24; 4.3
terrible 2 Cor 1.10; 3 Jn 1.10
truth [4] 2.15; 4.4
union 2.1; Phlm 6
violent 1 Tim 3.3; 4.15
weak 1 Thes 5.14; Heb 4.15
wisdom Col 3.16; Jas 1.5
worse 1 Tim 5.8; Heb 10.29

Last Instructions

10 But you have followed my **teaching**,
my **conduct**, and my **purpose** in **life**; you
have **observed** my **faith**, my **patience**, my
love, my **endurance**, 11 my **persecutions**,
and my **sufferings**. You know all that
happened to me in Antioch, Iconium, and
Lystra, the **terrible persecutions** I endured! But the Lord **rescued** me from
them all. 12 Everyone who wants to live a
godly life in **union with** Christ Jesus will
be **persecuted**; 13 and **evil** persons and
impostors will keep on going from **bad** to
worse, deceiving others and being
deceived themselves. 14 But as for you,
continue in the **truths** that you were
taught and firmly **believe**. You know who
your **teachers** were, 15 and you **remember**
that ever since you were a child, you
have known the **Holy Scriptures**, which
are able to give you the **wisdom** that
leads to **salvation** through **faith** in Christ
Jesus. 16 All **Scripture** is **inspired** by God
and is useful[b] for **teaching** the **truth**, **rebuking error**, **correcting faults**, and
giving instruction for **right** living, 17 so
that the person who **serves** God may be
fully qualified and equipped to do every
kind of good **deed**.

4 In the **presence** of God and of Christ
Jesus, who will **judge** the living and
the **dead**, and because he is coming to
rule as King, I **solemnly urge** you 2 to
preach the **message**, to insist upon **proclaiming** it (whether the time is **right** or
not), to **convince**, reproach, and **encourage**, as you **teach** with all **patience**.
3 The time will come when people will
not listen to **sound doctrine**, but will
follow their own **desires** and will collect
for themselves more and more **teachers**
who will tell them what they are itching
to hear. 4 They will **turn away** from listening to the **truth** and give their attention
to legends. 5 But you must keep **control** of
yourself in all circumstances; **endure
suffering**, do the work of a **preacher** of
the **Good News**, and perform your whole
duty as a **servant** of God.
6 As for me, the hour has come for me
to be **sacrificed**; the time is here for me
to leave this **life**. 7 I have done my **best** in
the **race**, I have run the full distance, and
I have kept the **faith**.[c] 8 And now there is
waiting for me the **victory prize** of being
put **right with God**, which the Lord, the
righteous Judge, will give me on that
Day—and not only to me, but to all those
who wait with **love** for him to appear.

Personal Words

9 Do your **best** to come to me soon.
10 Demas fell in **love** with this present
world and has deserted me, going off to
Thessalonica. Crescens went to Galatia,
and Titus to Dalmatia. 11 Only Luke is
with me. Get Mark and bring him with
you, because he can **help** me in the work.
12 I sent Tychicus to Ephesus. 13 When you
come, bring my coat that I left in Troas
with Carpus; bring the books too, and
especially the ones made of parchment.
14 Alexander the metal-worker did me
much **harm**; the Lord will **reward** him
according to what he has done. 15 Be on
your guard against him yourself, because
he was **violently** opposed to our **message**.
16 No one stood by me the first time I
defended myself; all deserted me. May
God not count it against them! 17 But the
Lord stayed with me and gave me
strength, so that I was able to **proclaim**
the full **message** for all the **Gentiles** to
hear; and I was **rescued** from being **sentenced** to death. 18 And the Lord will **rescue** me from all **evil** and take me **safely**
into his **heavenly Kingdom**. To him be
the **glory** for ever and ever! Amen.

Final Greetings

19 I send greetings to Priscilla and
Aquila and to the family of Onesiphorus.
20 Erastus stayed in Corinth, and I left
Trophimus in Miletus, because he was ill.
21 Do your **best** to come before winter.
Eubulus, Pudens, Linus, and Claudia
send their greetings, and so do all the
other **Christian brothers**.
22 The Lord be with your **spirit**.
God's **grace** be with you all.

[b] All Scripture is inspired by God and is useful; *or* Every scripture inspired by God is also useful.
[c] kept the faith; *or* been true to my promise.

3.11: Acts 13.14–52, 14.1–7, 8–20 **4.10:** Col 4.14; Phlm 24; 2 Cor 8.23; Gal 2.3; Tit 1.4
4.11: Col 4.14; Phlm 24; Acts 12.12, 25, 13.13, 15.37–39; Col 4.10 **4.12:** Acts 20.4; Eph 6.21–22; Col 4.7–8
4.13: Acts 20.6 **4.14:** 1 Tim 1.20; Ps 62.12; Rom 2.6 **4.19:** Acts 18.2; 2 Tim 1.16–17
4.20: Acts 19.22; Rom 16.23; Acts 20.4, 21.29

Chapter 4
best [3] 2.15; Tit 3.12
Christian 1 Tim 6.2; Heb 3.1
control 3.6; Jas 1.26
convince 1 Thes 1.5
Day of the Lord 1.12; Tit 2.13
dead 1 Tim 4.2; Heb 3.17
defend Phil 1.7
desire 3.6; Heb 4.12
doctrine 1 Tim 6.3; Tit 1.9
duty (1) 1 Tim 5.4; Heb 9.6
encourage 2 Thes 2.17; Tit 1.9
endure 3.10; Tit 2.2
evil 3.13; Tit 2.5
faith 3.8; Tit 1.1
Gentile 1 Tim 2.7
glory 2.10; Tit 2.13
Good News 2.8; Heb 4.2
grace 2.1; Tit 1.4
harm 1 Tim 6.9; 1 Pet 3.13
heaven 1 Tim 3.16; Heb 1.3
help 2.22; Tit 1.1
judge [2] 1 Tim 5.24; Heb 4.12
Kingdom (1) (of God) 2 Thes 1.5; Heb 1.8
life (1) 3.10; Tit 1.2
love [2] 3.4; Tit 1.8
message [3] 2.15; Tit 1.3
patient 3.10; Heb 6.12
preach [2] 2.8; 1 Pet 3.19
presence 2.2; Heb 4.14
prize 2.5; Rev 2.10
proclaim [2] 2.2; Tit 1.3
race (2) 2.5; Heb 12.1
rescue [2] 3.11; Tit 2.14
reward Col 3.24; Heb 10.35
right (1) 3.16; Tit 1.3
right with God Gal 5.4; Tit 3.7
righteous 2.22; Heb 7.2
sacrifice Col 1.20; Heb 5.1
safe 1.12; Heb 6.18
sentence 2 Cor 1.9
servant 2.24; Tit 1.1
solemn 2.14; Heb 3.11
sound (2) 1 Tim 1.10; Tit 2.1
spirit (2) 1 Tim 4.1; Heb 1.14
strength 1.8; Heb 12.12
suffer 3.11; Heb 2.9
teach 3.10; Tit 1.1
teacher 3.14; Heb 5.12
truth 3.7; Tit 1.1
turn 2.19; Heb 3.12
urge 1 Tim 2.1; Tit 2.6
victory 1 Thes 2.19; 1 Jn 5.4
violent 3.3; Tit 1.7
world 1 Tim 6.7; Tit 2.12

PAUL'S LETTER TO
TITUS

INTRODUCTION

Titus was a Gentile convert to Christianity who became a fellow-worker and assistant to Paul in his missionary work. *Paul's Letter to Titus* is addressed to his young helper in Crete, who had been left there to supervise the work of the church. The letter expresses three main concerns.

First, Titus is reminded of the kind of character that church leaders should have, especially in view of the bad character of many Cretans. Next, Titus is advised how to teach the various groups in the church, the older men, the older women (who are, in turn, to teach the younger women), the young men, and the slaves. Finally, the writer gives Titus advice regarding Christian conduct, especially the need to be peaceful and friendly, and to avoid hatred, argument, and division in the church.

Outline of Contents

Introduction 1.1–4
Church officers 1.5–16
Duties of various groups in the church 2.1–15
Exhortations and warning 3.1–11
Conclusion 3.12–15

---

1 From Paul, a **servant** of God and an **apostle** of Jesus Christ.

I was **chosen** and sent to **help** the **faith** of God's **chosen people** and to lead them to the **truth taught** by our **religion**, 2 which is **based on** the **hope** for **eternal** life. God, who does not **lie**, **promised** us this **life** before the beginning of time, 3 and at the **right** time he **revealed** it in his **message**. This was **entrusted** to me, and I **proclaim** it by order of God our **Saviour**.

4 I write to Titus, my **true** son in the **faith** that we have in common.

May God the **Father** and Christ Jesus our **Saviour** give you **grace** and **peace**.

Titus' Work in Crete

5 I left you in Crete, so that you could put in order the things that still **needed** doing and appoint **church elders** in every town. **Remember** my instructions: 6 an **elder** must be **blameless**; he must have only one wife,[a] and his children must be **believers** and not have the **reputation** of being wild or **disobedient**. 7 For since a **church** leader is in charge of God's work, he should be **blameless**. He must not be **arrogant** or quick-tempered, or a drunkard or **violent** or **greedy** for money. 8 He must be hospitable and **love** what is good. He must be **self-controlled**, upright, **holy**, and **disciplined**. 9 He must hold firmly to the **message** which can be **trusted** and which **agrees** with the **doctrine**. In this way he will be able to **encourage** others with the **true teaching** and also to show the **error** of those who are opposed to it.

10 For there are many, especially converts from **Judaism**, who **rebel** and **deceive** others with their nonsense. 11 It is necessary to stop their talk, because they are **upsetting** whole families by **teaching** what they should not, and all for the **shameful purpose** of making money. 12–13 It was a Cretan himself, one of their own **prophets**, who spoke the **truth** when he said, "Cretans are always **liars**, **wicked beasts**, and lazy gluttons." For this **reason** you must **rebuke** them sharply, so that they may have a healthy **faith** 14 and no longer hold on to **Jewish** legends and to **human commandments** which come from people who have **rejected** the **truth**. 15 Everything is **pure** to those who are themselves **pure**; but nothing is pure to those who are **defiled** and **unbelieving**, for their **minds** and **consciences** have been **defiled**. 16 They **claim** that they know God, but their **actions deny** it. They are **hateful** and **disobedient**, not **fit** to do anything good.

Sound Doctrine

2 But you must **teach** what **agrees** with **sound doctrine**. 2 Instruct the

[a] have only one wife; *or* be married only once.

1.4: 2 Cor 8.23; Gal 2.3; 2 Tim 4.10 **1.6–9:** 1 Tim 3.2–7

action Phil 4.9; Jas 2.14
agree 1 Tim 6.3; 2.1
apostle 2 Tim 1.1; 1 Pet 1.1
arrogant Zeph 3.11; 2 Pet 2.10
basis 1 Thes 2.3; Heb 7.11
beast (1) 1 Cor 15.32
believer 2 Tim 2.18; Phlm 6
blame [2] Phil 1.10; Jude 16
choose [2] 2 Tim 2.10; Heb 1.2
church [2] 1 Tim 5.16; Phlm 2
claim 1 Tim 6.21; 1 Jn 3.17
commandment Eph 6.2; Heb 9.4
conscience 2 Tim 1.3; Heb 9.14
deceive 2 Tim 3.13; Heb 3.13
defile [2] 1 Cor 8.7
deny 2 Tim 2.12; 2 Pet 2.1
discipline Eph 6.4; Heb 12.11
disobey [2] 2 Tim 3.2; 3.3
doctrine 2 Tim 4.3; 2.1
elder (2) [2] 1 Tim 5.17; Jas 5.14
encourage 2 Tim 4.2; 2.15
entrust 2 Tim 2.2
error 2 Tim 3.16; 2 Pet 2.18
eternal 2 Tim 2.10; 3.7
faith [3] 2 Tim 4.7; 2.2
Father (2) (God) 2 Tim 1.2; Phlm 3
fit (1) Col 1.11
God's people 2 Tim 2.10; Phlm 5
grace 2 Tim 4.22; 2.11
greed 2 Tim 3.2; 2 Pet 2.3
hate 2 Tim 3.3; 3.3
help 2 Tim 4.11; 3.13
holy 2 Tim 3.15; 2.3
hope 1 Tim 6.17; 2.13
human 1 Tim 3.16; Heb 2.14
Jew 1 Thes 2.14; Heb 9.25
Judaism Acts 13.43

lie (2) [2] 1 Tim 4.1; Heb 6.18
life (1) [2] 2 Tim 4.6; 2.3
love 2 Tim 4.8; 2.2
message [2] 2 Tim 4.2; 2.5
mind (1) 2 Tim 3.8; Heb 8.10
need 1 Thes 5.1; 3.13
peace 2 Tim 2.22; 3.2
proclaim 2 Tim 4.2; Heb 9.19
promise 2 Tim 1.1; Heb 3.11
prophet 1 Tim 4.14; Heb 1.1
pure [2] 2 Tim 2.22; 2.5
purpose 2 Tim 3.10; Heb 6.17
reason 2 Tim 1.6; Phlm 8
rebel 2 Thes 2.3; Heb 3.8
rebuke 2 Tim 3.16; 2.15
reject 2 Tim 3.5; 1 Pet 2.4
religion 2 Tim 3.5; Jas 1.26
remember 2 Tim 3.1; Heb 8.12
reputation 1 Tim 5.10; Rev 3.1
reveal 2 Tim 1.10; 2.11
right (1) 2 Tim 4.2; Heb 1.9
Saviour [2] 2 Tim 1.10; 2.10
self-control 2 Tim 1.7; 2.2
servant 2 Tim 4.5; Heb 1.7
shame Eph 5.12; 2.8
teach [3] 2 Tim 4.2; 2.1
true [2] 2 Tim 2.11; 3.8
trust 2 Tim 1.12; Heb 2.13
truth [3] 2 Tim 4.4; Heb 2.1
unbeliever 1 Tim 5.8; Heb 3.12
upset 2 Tim 2.18
violent 2 Tim 4.15; Rev 6.12
wicked 2 Thes 3.2; 2.14

Chapter 2
agree 1.9; Phlm 14

alone 1 Tim 6.16; Jas 2.17
authority 1 Tim 2.2; 1 Pet 2.13
bad 2 Tim 3.13; Jas 4.3
bless 1 Tim 6.15; Phlm 6
criticize 1 Cor 10.30; Jas 4.11
Day of the Lord 2 Tim 4.8; Heb 10.25
doctrine 1.9; 2 Pet 2.1
eager 1 Tim 6.10; Heb 6.11
encourage 1.9; Phlm 7
endure 2 Tim 4.5; Heb 10.34
enemy 1 Tim 5.14; Heb 1.13
evil 2 Tim 4.18; 3.2
example 2 Tim 1.13; Jas 5.10
faith 1.1; 3.15
faithful 2 Tim 2.13; Heb 2.17
give up 1 Tim 1.4; Heb 10.25
glory 2 Tim 4.18; Heb 1.3
godly 2 Tim 3.12; 2 Pet 1.6
grace [2] 1.4; 3.7
holy 1.8; Heb 7.26
hope 1.2; 3.7
life (1) [2] 1.2; 3.3
look down on 1 Tim 4.12
love [2] 1.8; 3.4
mankind 1 Tim 2.5; Heb 1.3
master 2 Tim 2.21; 1 Pet 2.18
message 1.3; Heb 2.2
passion 2 Tim 2.22; 3.3
please 2 Tim 2.4; Phlm 20
pure [2] 1.15; Heb 2.11
rebuke 1.12; Heb 12.5
rescue 2 Tim 4.17; 2 Pet 2.7
reveal 1.3; 3.4
salvation 2 Tim 3.15; Heb 1.14
Saviour [2] 1.3; 3.4
self-control [4] 1.8; 1 Pet 4.7
sense 2 Tim 2.26
serious Acts 25.7
shame 1.11; Heb 6.6
sincere 2 Tim 1.5; Heb 10.22
slander 2 Tim 3.3
slave [2] 1 Tim 6.1; 3.3
sound (2) [3] 2 Tim 4.3
steal 1 Cor 6.10; Rev 9.21
submit [2] Col 3.18; 3.1
teach [5] 1.1; Heb 5.12
ungodly Ezek 32.19
urge 2 Tim 4.1
wicked 1.12; Jas 1.21
word (1) 2 Tim 2.9; Heb 1.3
world 2 Tim 4.10; Heb 1.6
worldly 2 Cor 10.2

Chapter 3
abundant 1 Tim 1.14; 2 Pet 1.8

older men to be sober, **sensible**, and **self-**
controlled; to be **sound** in their **faith**,
love, and **endurance**. 3 In the same way
instruct the older women to behave as
women should who live a **holy life**. They
must not be **slanderers** or **slaves** to wine.
They must **teach** what is good, 4 in order
to train the younger women to **love** their
husbands and children, 5 to be **self-**
controlled and **pure**, and to be good
housewives who **submit** to their husbands, so that no one will speak **evil** of
the **message** that comes from God.

6 In the same way **urge** the young
men to be **self-controlled**. 7 In all things
you yourself must be an **example** of good
behaviour. Be **sincere** and **serious** in your
teaching. 8 Use **sound words** that cannot
be **criticized**, so that your **enemies** may
be put to **shame** by not having anything
bad to say about us.

9 **Slaves** are to **submit** to their **masters**
and **please** them in all things. They must
not answer them back 10 or **steal** from
them. Instead, they must show that they
are always good and **faithful**, so as to
bring credit to the **teaching** about God
our **Saviour** in all they do.

11 For God has **revealed** his **grace** for
the **salvation** of all **mankind**. 12 That
grace instructs us to **give up ungodly**
living and **worldly passions**, and to live
self-controlled, upright, and **godly lives** in
this world, 13 as we wait for the **blessed**
Day we **hope** for, when the **glory** of our
great God and **Saviour** Jesus Christ[b] will
appear. 14 He gave himself for us, to **res-**
cue us from all **wickedness** and to make
us a **pure** people who belong to him **alone**
and are **eager** to do good.

15 **Teach** these things and use your
full **authority** as you **encourage** and **re-**
buke your hearers. Let none of them **look**
down on you.

Christian Conduct

3 **Remind** your people to **submit** to
rulers and **authorities**, to **obey** them,
and to be ready to do good in every way.
2 Tell them not to speak **evil** of anyone,
but to be **peaceful** and **friendly**, and
always to show a **gentle** attitude towards
everyone. 3 For we ourselves were once
foolish, **disobedient**, and **wrong**. We were
slaves to **passions** and **pleasures** of all
kinds. We spent our **lives** in malice and
envy; others **hated** us and we hated
them. 4 But when the **kindness** and **love** of
God our **Saviour** was **revealed**, 5 he **saved**
us. It was not because of any good **deeds**
that we ourselves had done, but because
of his own **mercy** that he **saved** us,
through the **Holy Spirit**, who gives us new
birth and **new life** by washing us. 6 God
poured out the **Holy Spirit abundantly** on
us through Jesus Christ our **Saviour**, 7 so
that by his **grace** we might be put **right**
with God and come into **possession** of the
eternal life we **hope** for. 8 This is a **true**
saying.

I want you to give **special** emphasis to
these matters, so that those who **believe**
in God may be **concerned** with giving
their time to doing good **deeds**, which are
good and useful for everyone. 9 But avoid
stupid arguments, long lists of ancestors,
quarrels, and fights about the **Law**. They
are **useless** and **worthless**. 10 Give at least
two **warnings** to the person who causes
divisions, and then have nothing more to
do with him. 11 You know that such a
person is **corrupt**, and his sins **prove** that
he is **wrong**.

Final Instructions

12 When I send Artemas or Tychicus
to you, do your **best** to come to me in
Nicopolis, because I have decided to
spend the winter there. 13 Do your **best** to
help Zenas the lawyer and Apollos to get
started on their travels, and see to it that
they have everything they **need**. 14 Our
people must **learn** to spend their time
doing good, in order to **provide** for **real**
needs; they should not live **useless lives**.

15 All who are with me send you
greetings. Give our greetings to our
friends in the **faith**.

God's **grace** be with you all.

[b] our great God and Saviour Jesus Christ; *or* the great God and our Saviour Jesus Christ.

2.14: Ps 130.8; Ex 19.5; Deut 4.20, 7.6, 14.2; 1 Pet 2.9 **3.12:** Acts 20.4; Eph 6.21–22; Col 4.7–8; 2 Tim 4.12
3.13: Acts 18.24; 1 Cor 16.12

argue 2 Tim 2.23; Heb 6.16
authorities Col 2.15; 1 Pet 3.22
believe 2 Tim 3.14; Heb 3.19
best [2] 2 Tim 4.7; Heb 4.11
birth Phil 3.5; Heb 7.3
concern Phil 2.21; Heb 10.24
corrupt Phil 2.15; Jas 1.27
deed (2) [2] 2 Tim 3.17; Heb 10.17
disobey 1.6; Heb 10.28
envy Gal 5.21
eternal 1.2; Heb 5.9
evil 2.5; Heb 3.12
faith 2.2; Phlm 5
fool 2 Tim 2.16; Jas 2.20
friend [2] Col 1.22; Phlm 1
gentle 2 Tim 2.25; Heb 5.2
grace [2] 2.11; Phlm 3
hate 1.16; Heb 1.9
help 1.1; Phlm 13
hope 2.13; Phlm 22
kind 2 Tim 2.24; 1 Pet 2.3
law 1 Tim 2.14; Heb 7.5
learn 2 Tim 3.7; Heb 5.8
life (1) [4] 2.3; Phlm 6
love 2.2; Phlm 5
mercy 2 Tim 3.3; Heb 2.17
need [2] 1.5; Heb 4.16
new Col 3.10; Heb 2.5
obey 2 Tim 2.5; Heb 2.2
passion 2.12; 1 Pet 2.11
peace 1.4; Phlm 3
pleasure 2 Tim 3.4; Jas 4.1
possess 1 Tim 6.21; Heb 1.2
prove 1 Tim 2.6; Heb 2.3
provide Eph 4.16; Heb 7.19
quarrel 2 Tim 2.23; Jas 4.1
real 2 Tim 3.5; Heb 8.2
remind 2 Tim 2.14; Phlm 19
reveal 2.11; 1 Pet 1.5
right with God 2 Tim 4.8; Jas 2.21
save [2] 2 Tim 1.9; Heb 5.7
Saviour [2] 2.10; 2 Pet 1.1
saying 2 Tim 2.11
slave 2.3; Phlm 16
special 2 Tim 2.20; 1 Pet 4.10
Spirit (1) (God's Spirit) [2] 2 Tim 1.7; Heb 2.4
stupid 2 Tim 3.9; 2 Pet 2.18
submit 2.5; Heb 12.9
true 1.4; Heb 2.2
useless [2] Col 2.22; Heb 6.1
warn 2 Tim 2.14; Heb 11.7
worthless 1 Tim 4.7; Heb 6.8
wrong [2] 2 Tim 2.19; Phlm 18

PAUL'S LETTER TO PHILEMON

INTRODUCTION

Philemon was a prominent Christian, probably a member of the church at Colossae and the owner of a slave named Onesimus. This slave had run away from his master, and then somehow he had come in contact with Paul, who was then in prison. Through Paul, Onesimus became a Christian. *Paul's Letter to Philemon* is an appeal to Philemon to be reconciled to his slave, whom Paul is sending back to him, and to welcome him not only as a forgiven slave but as a Christian brother.

Outline of Contents

Introduction 1–3
Praise for Philemon 4–7
Appeal for Onesimus 8–22
Conclusion 23–25

---

agree Tit 2.1
believer Tit 1.6; Heb 3.12
bless Tit 2.13; Heb 6.7
bold 1 Tim 3.13; Heb 13.6
cheer (1) [2] 2 Tim 1.16
Christ [5] 2 Tim 1.8; Heb 3.6
church Tit 1.5; Jas 5.14
dear [2] 2 Tim 1.2; Heb 6.9
encourage Tit 2.15; Heb 6.18
enough 1 Tim 6.8; Heb 5.12
faith Tit 3.15; Heb 3.1
Father (2) (God) Tit 1.4; Heb 1.5
favour 1 Tim 5.21; 1 Pet 5.5
fellowship Phil 2.1; 1 Jn 1.3
force (1) Col 2.23; Rev 13.12
free 1 Thes 5.23; Heb 2.15
friend Tit 3.2; Heb 6.9
God's people [2] Tit 1.1; Heb 4.9
gospel 2 Tim 1.10
grace [2] Tit 3.7; Heb 2.9
heart [2] 2 Tim 2.22; Heb 3.12
help [2] Tit 3.13; Heb 1.14
hope Tit 3.7; Heb 3.6
joy 2 Tim 1.4; Heb 1.9
life (1) Tit 3.3; Heb 1.12
love [3] Tit 3.4; Heb 1.9
owe [2] Rom 13.7
peace Tit 3.2; Heb 7.2
please Tit 2.9; Heb 10.6

1 From Paul, a **prisoner** for the **sake** of
Christ Jesus, and from our brother
Timothy—
To our **friend** and fellow-worker
Philemon, 2 and the **church** that meets in
your house, and our sister Apphia, and
our fellow-soldier Archippus:
3 May God **our Father** and the Lord
Jesus Christ give you **grace** and **peace**.

Philemon's Love and Faith

4 Brother Philemon, every time I
pray, I mention you and give **thanks** to
my God. 5 For I hear of your **love** for all
God's people and the **faith** you have in
the Lord Jesus. 6 My **prayer** is that our
fellowship with you as **believers** will
bring about a deeper **understanding** of
every **blessing** which we have in our **life**
in **union with Christ**. 7 Your **love**, **dear**
brother, has brought me great **joy** and
much **encouragement**! You have
cheered the **hearts** of all **God's people**.

A Request for Onesimus

8 For this **reason** I could be **bold**
enough, as your brother in **Christ**, to
order you to do what should be done.
9 But because I **love** you, I make a **request**
instead. I do this even though I am Paul,
the ambassador of Christ Jesus, and at
present also a **prisoner** for his **sake**.[a] 10 So
I make a **request** to you on behalf of
Onesimus, who is my own son in **Christ**;
for while in **prison** I have become his
spiritual father. 11 At one time he was of
no use to you, but now he is useful[b] both
to you and to me.
12 I am sending him back to you now,
and with him goes my **heart**. 13 I would
like to keep him here with me, while I
am in **prison** for the **gospel's sake**, so that
he could **help** me in your place. 14 However, I do not want to **force** you to **help**
me; rather, I would like you to do it of
your own **free will**. So I will not do anything unless you **agree**.
15 It may be that Onesimus was away
from you for a short time so that you
might have him back for all time. 16 And
now he is not just a **slave**, but much more
than a slave: he is a **dear** brother in
Christ. How much he means to me! And
how much more he will mean to you,
both as a **slave** and as a brother in the
Lord!
17 So, if you think of me as your partner, **welcome** him back just as you would
welcome me. 18 If he has done you any
wrong or **owes** you anything, charge it to
my account. 19 Here, I will write this with
my own hand: *I, Paul, will pay you back.*
(I should not have to **remind** you, of
course, that you **owe** your very **self** to
me.) 20 So, my brother, **please** do me this
favour for the Lord's **sake**; as a brother
in **Christ**, **cheer** me up!
21 I am **sure**, as I write this, that you
will do what I ask—in fact I know that
you will do even more. 22 At the same
time, get a room ready for me, because I
hope that God will answer the **prayers** of
all of you and give me back to you.

pray 1 Tim 5.5; Heb 13.18
prayer [2] 2 Tim 1.3; Heb 5.7
prison [5] 2 Tim 1.8; Heb 10.34
reason Tit 1.12; Heb 9.15
remind Tit 3.1; Heb 10.3
request [2] 1 Tim 2.1; Heb 5.7
sake [5] 2 Tim 2.10; 1 Pet 1.20
self Col 3.9; 1 Pet 3.4
slave [2] Tit 3.3; Heb 2.15
spiritual 1 Tim 4.6; Heb 12.9
sure 2 Tim 1.5; Heb 6.9
thank 2 Tim 1.3; Heb 12.28
understand 2 Tim 2.7; Heb 5.11
union 2 Tim 3.12; 1 Pet 5.10
welcome 1 Tim 3.2; Heb 11.13
will (1) 2 Tim 2.26; Heb 2.4
wrong Tit 3.3; Heb 1.9

[a] the ambassador of Christ Jesus, and at present also a prisoner for his sake; *or* an old man, and at present a prisoner for the sake of Christ Jesus. [b] *The Greek name Onesimus means "useful".*

2: Col 4.17 **10:** Col 4.9

Final Greetings

23 Epaphras, who is in **prison** with me
for the **sake** of Christ Jesus, sends you his
greetings, 24 and so do my fellow-workers
Mark, Aristarchus, Demas, and Luke.
25 May the **grace** of the Lord Jesus
Christ be with you all.

23: Col 1.7, 4.12 **24:** Acts 12.12, 25, 13.13, 15.37–39, 19.29, 27.2; Col 4.10, 14; 2 Tim 4.10, 11

THE LETTER TO THE
HEBREWS

INTRODUCTION

The Letter to the Hebrews was written to a group of Christians who, faced with increasing opposition, were in danger of abandoning the Christian faith. The writer encourages them in their faith primarily by showing that Jesus Christ is the true and final revelation of God. In doing this he emphasizes three truths: (1) Jesus is the eternal Son of God, who learnt true obedience to the Father through the suffering that he endured. As the Son of God, Jesus is superior to the prophets of the Old Testament, to the angels, and to Moses himself. (2) Jesus has been declared by God to be an eternal priest, superior to the priests of the Old Testament. (3) Through Jesus the believer is saved from sin, fear, and death; and Jesus, as High Priest, provides the true salvation, which was only foreshadowed by the rituals and animal sacrifices of the Hebrew religion.

By citing the example of the faith of some famous persons in Israel's history (chapter 11), the writer appeals to his readers to remain faithful, and in chapter 12 he urges his readers to continue faithful to the end, with eyes fixed on Jesus, and to endure whatever suffering and persecution may come to them. The book closes with words of advice and warning.

Outline of Contents

---

angel [7] 1 Tim 5.21; 2.2
being 1 Thes 5.23; Jas 1.18
change Phil 3.21; 6.17
choose [2] Tit 1.1; 3.2
create [2] 1 Tim 4.3; 2.10
enemy Tit 2.8; 10.13
Father (2) (God) [2] Phlm 3; 2.11
first-born Col 1.15; 11.28
footstool Acts 7.49; 10.13
forgive Col 3.13; 2.17
glory Tit 2.13; 2.7
hate Tit 3.3; 12.3
heaven [2] 2 Tim 4.18; 6.4
help Phlm 13; 2.16
honour 1 Tim 6.16; 2.7
joy Phlm 7; 12.2
justice 2 Thes 1.5; Rev 15.4
Kingdom (1) (of God) 2 Tim 4.18; 12.28
last (1) Gal 3.19; 10.34

God's Word through His Son

1 In the past, God spoke to our ancestors many times and in many
ways through the **prophets**, 2 but in these
last days he has spoken to us through **his Son**. He is the one through whom God **created** the **universe**, the one whom God has **chosen** to **possess** all things at the
end. 3 He reflects the brightness of God's **glory** and is the exact likeness of God's own **being**, sustaining the **universe** with his **powerful word**. After achieving **forgiveness** for the sins of **mankind**, he sat down in **heaven** at the **right-hand side** of God, the **Supreme Power**.

The Greatness of God's Son

4 The **Son** was made greater than the **angels**, just as the **name** that God gave
him is greater than theirs. 5 For God never said to any of his **angels**,
"You are my **Son**;
today I have become your **Father**."
Nor did God say about any **angel**,
"I will be his **Father**,
and he will be my **Son**."
6 But when God was about to send his **first-born Son** into the **world**, he said,
"All **God's angels** must **worship** him."
7 But about the **angels** God said,
"God makes his angels winds,
and his **servants** flames of fire."
8 About the **Son**, however, God said:
"Your **kingdom**, O God, will **last**[a] for
ever and ever!
You rule over your[b] people with
justice.
9 You **love** what is **right** and **hate** what is
wrong.
That is why God, your God, has **chosen**
you
and has given you the **joy** of an
honour far greater
than he gave to your companions."
10 He also said,

last (2) 2 Tim 3.1; Jas 5.3
life (1) Phlm 6; 2.15
love Phlm 5; 6.10
mankind Tit 2.11; 12.23
name (2) (name of God, of Jesus) 1 Tim 6.1; Jas 5.10
possess Tit 3.7; 10.34
power [2] 2 Tim 3.5; 2.14
prophet Tit 1.12; 11.32
right (1) Tit 1.3; 2.10
right (2) [2] Col 3.1; 8.1
salvation Tit 2.11; 2.3
servant Tit 1.1; 3.5
serve 2 Tim 3.17; 5.1
Son of God [6] 1 Thes 1.10; 3.6
spirit (2) 2 Tim 4.22; 4.12
supreme Col 2.10; 1 Pet 2.13
universe [2] Col 2.8; 11.3
word (1) Tit 2.8; 3.13
world Tit 2.12; 2.5

[a] Your kingdom, O God, will last; *or* God is your kingdom. [b] your; *some manuscripts have* his.

1.5: Ps 2.7; 2 Sam 7.14; 1 Chr 17.13 **1.6:** Deut 32.43 (LXX) **1.7:** Ps 104.4 (LXX) **1.8–9:** Ps 45.6–7
1.10–12: Ps 102.25–27 (LXX)

worship (1) (of God) Phil 3.3; 9.1
wrong Phlm 18; 5.13

"You, Lord, in the beginning **created**
the earth,
and with your own hands you made
the **heavens**.
11 They will disappear, but you will
remain;
they will all wear out like clothes.
12 You will fold them up like a coat,
and they will be **changed** like
clothes.
But you are always the same,
and your **life** never ends."
13 God never said to any of his **angels**:
"Sit here on my **right**
until I put your **enemies**
as a **footstool** under your feet."
14 What are the **angels**, then? They
are **spirits** who **serve** God and are sent
by him to **help** those who are to receive
salvation.

The Great Salvation

angel [5] 1.4; 11.28
announce 1 Tim 1.11; 1 Pet 1.12
ashamed 2 Tim 2.15; 11.16
blood Phil 2.17; 9.7
care 1 Tim 6.20; 4.1
clear [2] 2 Tim 1.3; 6.17
create 1.2; 4.3
crown [2] 1 Cor 9.25; 1 Pet 5.4
death (1) [4] 2 Tim 1.10; 5.7
deserve Phil 4.8; 10.29
destroy 1 Tim 6.9; 6.8
Devil 2 Tim 2.26; Jas 4.7
escape 2 Tim 2.26; 11.34
faithful Tit 2.10; 3.2
Father (2) (God) 1.5; 5.5
fear Phil 2.12; 10.27
flesh 2 Tim 2.17; Jas 5.3
forgive 1.3; 8.12
free Phlm 14; 9.15
gift 2 Tim 1.6; 6.4
glory [3] 1.3; 13.20
grace Phlm 3; 4.16
help [3] 1.14; 3.13
High Priest Acts 24.1; 3.1
honour [2] 1.9; 3.3
human Tit 1.14; 7.16
life (1) 1.12; 5.7
mercy Tit 3.5; 4.16
message Tit 2.5; 4.2
miracle 2 Thes 2.9; Rev 13.13
nature Col 2.9; 2 Pet 1.4
new Tit 3.5; 8.8
obey Tit 3.1; 3.10
perfect 1 Thes 3.13; 5.9
power 1.3; 6.5
praise 1 Thes 2.6; 13.15
preserve Eph 4.3; 2 Pet 3.7
prove Tit 3.11; 9.16
punish 1 Tim 1.20; 10.29
pure [2] Tit 2.5; 9.10

2 That is why we must hold on all the
more firmly to the **truths** we have
heard, so that we will not be carried
away. 2 The **message** given to our
ancestors by the **angels** was shown to be
true, and anyone who did not follow it or
obey it received the **punishment** he
deserved. 3 How, then, shall we **escape** if
we pay no attention to such a great
salvation? The Lord himself first **announced** this **salvation**, and those who
heard him **proved** to us that it is **true**. 4 At
the same time God added his **witness** to
theirs by performing all kinds of
miracles and **wonders** and by distributing the **gifts** of the **Holy Spirit** according
to his **will**.

The One Who Leads Us to Salvation

5 God has not placed the **angels** as
rulers over the **new world to come**—the
world of which we speak. 6 Instead, as it
is said somewhere in the **Scriptures**:
"What is man, O God, that you should
think of him;
mere man, that you should **care** for
him?
7 You made him for a little while lower
than the **angels**;
you **crowned** him with **glory** and
honour,[c]
8 and made him ruler over all things."
It says that God made man "ruler over
all things"; this **clearly** includes everything. We do not, however, see man
ruling over all things now. 9 But we do see
Jesus, who for a little while was made
lower than the **angels**, so that through
God's **grace** he should die for everyone.
We see him now **crowned** with **glory** and
honour because of the **death** he **suffered**.
10 It was only **right** that God, who **creates**
and **preserves** all things, should make
Jesus **perfect** through **suffering**, in order
to bring many sons to **share** his **glory**.
For Jesus is the one who leads them to
salvation.
11 He **purifies** people from their sins,
and both he and those who are made
pure all have the same **Father**. That is
why Jesus is not **ashamed** to call them
his brothers. 12 He says to God,
"I will tell my brothers what you have
done;
I will **praise** you in their meeting."
13 He also says, "I will put my **trust** in
God." And he also says, "Here I am with
the children that God has given me."
14 Since the children, as he calls them,
are people of **flesh and blood**, Jesus himself became like them and **shared** their
human nature. He did this so that
through his **death** he might **destroy** the
Devil, who has the **power** over **death**,
15 and in this way **set free** those who were
slaves all their **lives** because of their **fear**
of death. 16 For it is **clear** that it is not the
angels that he **helps**. Instead, as the
scripture says, "He **helps** the descendants of Abraham." 17 This means that he
had to become like his brothers in every
way, in order to be their **faithful** and
merciful High Priest in his **service** to
God, so that the people's sins would be
forgiven. 18 And now he can **help** those
who are **tempted**, because he himself
was tempted and **suffered**.

right (1) 1.9; 5.13
salvation [3] 1.14; 5.9
scripture [2] 2 Tim 3.15; 3.13
service 2 Tim 2.4; 10.11
share [2] 2 Tim 2.6; 6.4
slave Phlm 16; 1 Pet 2.16
Spirit (1) (God's Spirit) Tit 3.5; 3.7
suffer [3] 2 Tim 4.5; 5.8
tempt 1 Tim 6.9; 4.15
true [2] Tit 3.8; 6.11
trust Tit 1.9; 10.23
truth Tit 1.1; 10.26
will (1) Phlm 14; 10.7
witness 2 Tim 2.2; 10.15
wonder (1) 2 Thes 2.9; 1 Pet 2.9
world [2] 1.6; 4.3

Jesus Is Greater than Moses

3 My **Christian brothers**, who also
have been called by God! Think of
Jesus, whom God sent to be the **High
Priest** of the **faith** we profess. 2 He was
faithful to God, who **chose** him to do this
work, just as Moses was **faithful** in his
work in God's house. 3 A man who builds
a house receives more **honour** than the
house itself. In the same way Jesus is
worthy of much greater **honour** than
Moses. 4 Every house, of course, is built
by someone—and God is the one who has
built all things. 5 Moses was **faithful** in
God's house as a **servant**, and he spoke of
the things that God would say in the
future. 6 But **Christ** is **faithful** as the **Son** in
charge of God's house. We are his house
if we keep up our **courage** and our **confidence** in what we **hope** for.

anger [3] 1 Tim 2.8; 4.3
believe Tit 3.8; 4.3
believer Phlm 6; Jas 2.1
choose 1.2; 5.1
Christ [2] Phlm 6; 5.5
Christian 2 Tim 4.21; 6.1
command 1 Tim 6.13; 7.5
confident [2] 2 Tim 1.12; 4.16
courage 2 Thes 2.16; 10.35
dead 2 Tim 4.1; 6.2
deceive Tit 1.10; Jas 1.16
evil Tit 3.2; 5.14
faith Phlm 5; 4.2
faithful [4] 2.17; 8.9
heart Phlm 7; 4.12
help 2.16; 4.16
High Priest 2.17; 4.14
honour [2] 2.7; 5.4
hope Phlm 22; 6.11
obey 2.2; 5.8

[c] *Many manuscripts add:* You made him ruler over everything you made *(see Ps 8.6)*.

1.13: Ps 110.1 **2.6–8:** Ps 8.4–6 (LXX) **2.12:** Ps 22.22 **2.13:** Is 8.17, 18 **2.16:** Is 41.8–9 **3.2:** Num 12.7

one another 1 Thes 5.11; 10.24
promise [2] Tit 1.2; 4.1
rebel [4] Tit 1.10; Jude 11
refuse (1) 2 Thes 3.10; 11.24
rest (1) [2] 2 Cor 7.5; 4.1
scripture [2] 2.6; 4.4
servant 1.7; Jas 1.1
solemn [2] 2 Tim 4.1; 4.3
Son of God 1.2; 4.14
Spirit (1) (God's Spirit) 2.4; 6.4
stubborn [3] Eph 4.18; 4.7
test [2] 1 Tim 3.10; 11.17
try (2) Gal 4.14; Jas 1.2
turn 2 Tim 4.4; 6.1
unbeliever Tit 1.15; 3 Jn 7
word (1) 1.3; 4.12
worthy 1 Tim 6.1; Rev 3.4

A Rest for God's People

7 So then, as the Holy Spirit says,
"If you hear God's voice today,
8 do not be stubborn, as your
ancestors were when they
rebelled against God,
as they were that day in the desert
when they put him to the test.
9 There they put me to the test and tried
me, says God,
although they had seen what I did
for forty years.
10 And so I was angry with those people
and said,
'They are always disloyal
and refuse to obey my commands.'
11 I was angry and made a solemn
promise:
'They will never enter the land
where I would have given them
rest!' "

12 My fellow-believers, be careful that
no one among you has a heart so evil and
unbelieving that he will turn away from
the living God. 13 Instead, in order that
none of you be deceived by sin and become stubborn, you must help one
another every day, as long as the word
"Today" in the scripture applies to us.
14 For we are all partners with Christ if
we hold firmly to the end the confidence
we had at the beginning.

15 This is what the scripture says:
"If you hear God's voice today,
do not be stubborn, as your
ancestors were
when they rebelled against God."

16 Who were the people who heard
God's voice and rebelled against him?
All those who were led out of Egypt by
Moses. 17 With whom was God angry for
forty years? With the people who sinned,
who fell down dead in the desert. 18 When
God made his solemn promise, "They
will never enter the land where I would
have given them rest"—of whom was he
speaking? Of those who rebelled. 19 We
see, then, that they were not able to
enter the land, because they did not
believe.

accept 1 Tim 4.5; 11.35
alive 2 Tim 1.6; 9.17
anger 3.10; 11.27
believe [2] 3.19; 6.1
best Tit 3.12; Jas 2.3
care 2.6; Jas 1.27
confident 3.6; 2 Pet 1.19
create [2] 2.10; 9.11
desire 2 Tim 4.3; 6.11
fail [2] 2 Tim 3.8; Jas 1.4
faith [3] 3.1; 6.4

4 Now, God has offered us the
promise that we may receive that
rest he spoke about. Let us take care,
then, that none of you will be found to
have failed to receive that promised rest.
2 For we have heard the Good News, just
as they did. They heard the message, but
it did them no good, because when they
heard it, they did not accept it with faith.
3 We who believe, then, do receive that
rest which God promised. It is just as he
said,
"I was angry and made a solemn
promise:
'They will never enter the land
where I would have given them
rest!' "
He said this even though his work had
been finished from the time he created
the world. 4 For somewhere in the Scriptures this is said about the seventh day:
"God rested on the seventh day from all
his work." 5 This same matter is spoken
of again: "They will never enter that
land where I would have given them
rest." 6 Those who first heard the Good
News did not receive that rest, because
they did not believe. There are, then,
others who are allowed to receive it.
7 This is shown by the fact that God sets
another day, which is called "Today."
Many years later he spoke of it through
David in the scripture already quoted:
"If you hear God's voice today,
do not be stubborn."

8 If Joshua had given the people the
rest that God had promised, God would
not have spoken later about another day.
9 As it is, however, there still remains for
God's people a rest like God's resting on
the seventh day. 10 For whoever receives
that rest which God promised will rest
from his own work, just as God rested
from his. 11 Let us, then, do our best to receive that rest, so that no one of us will
fail as they did because of their lack of
faith.

12 The word of God is alive and active,
sharper than any double-edged sword. It
cuts all the way through, to where soul
and spirit meet, to where joints and mar-
row come together. It judges the desires
and thoughts of man's heart. 13 There is
nothing that can be hidden from God;
everything in all creation is exposed and
lies open before his eyes. And it is to him
that we must all give an account of
ourselves.

Jesus the Great High Priest

14 Let us, then, hold firmly to the faith
we profess. For we have a great High
Priest who has gone into the very presence of God—Jesus, the Son of God.
15 Our High Priest is not one who cannot
feel sympathy for our weaknesses. On
the contrary, we have a High Priest who
was tempted in every way that we are,
but did not sin. 16 Let us have confidence,
then, and approach God's throne, where
there is grace. There we will receive

God's people Phlm 5; 8.6
Good News [2] 2 Tim 4.5; 1 Pet 1.12
grace [2] 2.9; 10.29
heart 3.12; 8.10
help 3.13; 6.10
High Priest [3] 3.1; 5.1
judge 2 Tim 4.1; 6.2
mercy 2.17; 10.28
message 2.2; 5.12
need Tit 3.13; 5.12
offer 1 Tim 2.1; 5.1
presence 2 Tim 4.1; 9.5
promise [6] 3.11; 6.1
rest (1) [13] 3.11; 13.17
scripture [2] 3.13; 7.
solemn 3.11; 7.21
Son of God 3.6; 5.5
soul 1 Thes 5.23; 13.17
spirit (2) 1.14; 12.23
stubborn 3.8
sympathy Nah 3.7
tempt 2.18; Jas 1.13
throne Col 3.1; 8.1
weak 2 Tim 3.6; 5.2
word (1) 3.13; 6.5
world 2.5; 9.11

3.7-11: Ps 95.7-11 (LXX) **3.15:** Ps 95.7-8 (LXX) **3.16-18:** Num 14.1-35 **4.3:** Ps 95.11 **4.4:** Gen 2.2
4.5: Ps 95.11 **4.7:** Ps 95.7-8 (LXX) **4.8:** Deut 31.7; Josh 22.4 **4.10:** Gen 2.2

mercy and find **grace** to **help** us just
when we **need** it.
5 Every **high priest** is **chosen** from his
fellow-men and appointed to **serve**
God on their behalf, to offer **sacrifices**
and **offerings** for sins. 2 Since he himself
is **weak** in many ways, he is able to be
gentle with those who are **ignorant** and
make **mistakes**. 3 And because he is himself **weak**, he must **offer sacrifices** not
only for the sins of the people but also for
his own sins. 4 No one **chooses** for himself
the **honour** of being a **high priest**. It is
only by God's call that a man is made a
high priest—just as Aaron was.
5 In the same way, **Christ** did not take
upon himself the **honour** of being a **high**
priest. Instead, God said to him,
"You are my **Son**;
today I have become your **Father**."
6 He also said in another place,
"You will be a **priest** for ever,
in the **priestly order** of
Melchizedek."[c]
7 In his **life** on earth Jesus made his
prayers and **requests** with loud cries and
tears to God, who could **save** him **from**
death. Because he was **humble** and
devoted, God heard him. 8 But even
though he was **God's Son**, he **learnt**
through his **sufferings** to be **obedient**.
9 When he was made **perfect**, he became
the **source** of **eternal salvation** for all
those who **obey** him, 10 and God **declared**
him to be **high priest**, in the **priestly**
order of Melchizedek.[c]

Warning against Abandoning the Faith

11 There is much we have to say
about this matter, but it is **hard** to explain
to you, because you are so slow to **under-**
stand. 12 There has been **enough** time for
you to be **teachers**—yet you still **need**
someone to **teach** you the first **lessons** of
God's **message**. Instead of eating solid
food, you still have to drink milk. 13 Anyone who has to drink milk is still a child,
without any **experience** in the matter of
right and **wrong**. 14 Solid food, on the
other hand, is for adults, who through
practice are able to **distinguish** between
good and **evil**.
6 Let us go forward, then, to **mature**
teaching and leave behind us the
first **lessons** of the **Christian message**. We
should not lay again the foundation of
turning away from **useless** works and
believing in God; 2 of the **teaching** about
baptisms[d] and the laying on of hands; of
the **resurrection** of the **dead** and the **eter-**
nal judgement. 3 Let us go forward! And
this is what we will do, if God allows.
4 For how can those who **abandon**
their **faith** be brought back to **repent**
again? They were once in God's **light**;
they tasted **heaven's gift** and received
their **share** of the **Holy Spirit**; 5 they knew
from **experience** that **God's word** is good,
and they had felt the **powers** of the
coming **age**. 6 And then they **abandoned**
their **faith**! It is **impossible** to bring them
back to **repent** again, because they are
again **crucifying** the **Son of God** and exposing him to public **shame**.
7 God **blesses** the soil which drinks in
the rain that often falls on it and which
grows plants that are useful to those for
whom it is cultivated. 8 But if it grows
thorns and **weeds**, it is **worth nothing**; it
is in **danger** of being **cursed** by God and
will be **destroyed** by fire.
9 But even if we speak like this, **dear**
friends, we feel **sure** about you. We know
that you have the better **blessings** that
belong to your **salvation**. 10 God is not unfair. He will not **forget** the work you did
or the **love** you showed for him in the
help you gave and are still giving to your
fellow-Christians. 11 Our great **desire** is
that each one of you keep up his **eager-**
ness to the end, so that the things you
hope for will come **true**. 12 We do not
want you to become lazy, but to be like
those who **believe** and are **patient**, and so
receive what God has **promised**.

God's Sure Promise

13 When God made his **promise** to
Abraham, he made a **vow** to do what he
had **promised**. Since there was no one
greater than himself, he used his own
name when he made his **vow**. 14 He said,
"**I promise** you that I will **bless** you and
give you many descendants." 15 Abraham
was **patient**, and so he received what
God had **promised**. 16 When a person
makes a **vow**, he uses the name of someone greater than himself, and the **vow**
settles all **arguments**. 17 To those who
were to receive what he **promised**, God
wanted to make it very **clear** that he
would never **change** his **purpose**; so he
added his **vow** to the **promise**. 18 There
are these two things, then, that cannot
change and about which God cannot **lie**.
So we who have found **safety** with him
are greatly **encouraged** to hold firmly to
the **hope** placed before us. 19 We have this

[c] in...Melchizedek; *or* like Melchizedek; *or* in the line of succession to Melchizedek.
[d] baptisms; *or* purification ceremonies.

5.3: Lev 9.7 **5.4:** Ex 28.1 **5.5:** Ps 2.7 **5.6:** Ps 110.4 **5.7:** Mt 26.36–46; Mk 14.32–42; Lk 22.39–46
5.12–13: 1 Cor 3.2 **6.8:** Gen 3.17–18 **6.14:** Gen 22.16–17 **6.19:** Lev 16.2

hope as an anchor for our **lives**. It is **safe** and **sure**, and goes through the curtain of the **heavenly temple** into the inner **sanctuary**. 20 On our behalf Jesus has gone in there before us, and has become a **high priest** for ever, in the **priestly order** of Melchizedek.[e]

The Priest Melchizedek

7 This Melchizedek was king of Salem and a **priest** of the **Most High God**. As Abraham was coming back from the battle in which he defeated the four kings, Melchizedek met him and **blessed** him, 2 and Abraham gave him a tenth of all he had taken. (The first meaning of Melchizedek's name is "King of **Righteousness**"; and because he was king of Salem, his name also means "King of **Peace**.") 3 There is no record of Melchizedek's father or mother or of any of his ancestors; no record of his **birth** or of his **death**. He is like the **Son of God**; he remains a **priest** for ever.

4 You see, then, how great he was. Abraham, our famous ancestor, gave him a tenth of all he got in the battle. 5 And those descendants of Levi who are **priests** are **commanded** by the **Law** to collect a tenth from the people of Israel, that is, from their own countrymen, even though their countrymen are also descendants of Abraham. 6 Melchizedek was not descended from Levi, but he collected a tenth from Abraham and **blessed** him, the man who received God's **promises**. 7 There is no **doubt** that the one who blesses is greater than the one who is **blessed**. 8 In the case of the **priests** the tenth is collected by men who die; but as for Melchizedek the tenth was collected by one who lives, as the **scripture** says. 9 And, so to speak, when Abraham paid the tenth, Levi (whose descendants collect the tenth) also paid it. 10 For Levi had not yet been born, but was, so to speak, in the **body** of his ancestor Abraham when Melchizedek met him.

11 It was on the **basis** of the **levitical priesthood** that the **Law** was given to the people of Israel. Now, if the work of the **levitical priests** had been **perfect**, there would have been no **need** for a different kind of **priest** to appear, one who is in the **priestly order** of Melchizedek,[e] not of Aaron. 12 For when the **priesthood** is **changed**, there also has to be a **change** in the **law**. 13 And our Lord, of whom these things are said, belonged to a different tribe, and no member of his tribe ever **served** as a **priest**. 14 It is well known that he was born a member of the tribe of Judah; and Moses did not mention this tribe when he spoke of **priests**.

Another Priest, like Melchizedek

15 The matter becomes even **plainer**; a different **priest** has appeared, who is like Melchizedek. 16 He was made a **priest**, not by **human** rules and **regulations**, but through the **power** of a **life** which has no end. 17 For the **scripture** says, "You will be a **priest** for ever, in the **priestly order** of Melchizedek."[e] 18 The old rule, then, is set aside, because it was **weak** and **useless**. 19 For the **Law of Moses** could not make anything **perfect**. And now a better **hope** has been **provided** through which we come near to God.

20 In addition, there is also God's **vow**. There was no such **vow** when the others were made **priests**. 21 But Jesus became a **priest by means of a vow** when God said to him,

"The Lord has made a **solemn promise**
and will not take it back:
'You will be a **priest** for ever.' "

22 This difference, then, also makes Jesus the **guarantee** of a better **covenant**.

23 There is another difference: there were many of those other **priests**, because they died and could not continue their work. 24 But Jesus lives on for ever, and his work as **priest** does not pass on to someone else. 25 And so he is able, now and always, to **save** those who come to God through him, because he lives for ever to **plead** with God for them.

26 Jesus, then, is the **High Priest** that meets our **needs**. He is **holy**; he has no **fault** or sin in him; he has been set **apart** from sinners and **raised** above the **heavens**. 27 He is not like other **high priests**; he does not **need** to **offer sacrifices** every day for his own sins first and then for the sins of the people. He **offered one sacrifice**, once and for all, when he offered himself. 28 The **Law of Moses** appoints men who are imperfect to be **high priests**; but God's **promise** made with the **vow**, which came later than the **Law**, appoints the **Son**, who has been made **perfect** for ever.

Jesus Our High Priest

8 The whole point of what we are saying is that we have such a **High Priest**, who sits at the **right** of the **throne** of the **Divine Majesty** in **heaven**. 2 He

[e] in...Melchizedek (*see 5.6*).

6.20: Ps 110.4 **7.1-2:** Gen 14.17-20 **7.5:** Num 18.21 **7.17:** Ps 110.4 **7.21:** Ps 110.4 **7.27:** Lev 9.7 **8.1:** Ps 110.1

apart Eph 2.12
basis Tit 1.2; 8.6
birth Tit 3.5; Jas 1.15
bless [3] 6.7; 9.15
body 1 Thes 5.23; 10.5
change [2] 6.17; 12.17
command 3.10; 9.20
covenant Eph 2.12; 8.5
death (1) 5.7; 9.15
doubt 2 Cor 4.8; Jas 1.6
fault 2 Tim 3.16; 8.8
guarantee Eph 4.30
heaven 6.4; 8.1
High Priest [3] 6.20; 8.1
holy Tit 2.3; 12.10
hope 6.11; 10.23
human 2.14; 12.9
law [6] Tit 3.9; 8.4
Levites [2] Acts 4.36
life (1) 6.19; 11.35
means 2 Tim 1.9; 10.1
Most High Acts 16.17
need [3] 5.12; 8.7
offer [2] 5.1; 8.3
peace Phlm 3; 12.11
perfect [3] 5.9; 9.9
plain (1) 1 Tim 5.24; 12.27
plead 2 Cor 8.4; 1 Jn 2.1
power 6.5; Jas 5.16
priest [20] 6.20; 8.4
promise [3] 6.12; 8.6
provide Tit 3.14; 13.20
raise 2 Tim 2.8; 11.19
regulation Ezek 44.5
righteous 2 Tim 4.8; 10.38
sacrifice [2] 5.1; 8.3
save 5.7; 9.28
scripture [2] 4.4; 10.37
serve 5.1; 8.2
solemn 4.3; Rev 22.18
Son of God [2] 6.6; 10.29
useless 6.1; 9.14
vow [4] 6.13; Rev 10.6
weak 5.2; 11.34

basis 7.11; Jas 2.4
covenant [8] 7.22; 9.1
divine Col 2.9; 12.25
faithful 3.2; 10.1
fault 7.26; 2 Pet 3.14
forgive 2.17; 9.5

gift 6.4; 11.4
God's people [3] 4.9; 10.30
heart 4.12; 9.9
heaven [2] 7.26; 9.23
High Priest [4] 7.26; 9.7
Holy Place Acts 21.28; 9.2
law [2] 7.5; 9.19
least Eph 3.8
Majesty Acts 26.7; Jude 25
mind (1) Tit 1.15; 10.16
need 7.11; 10.18
new [2] 2.5; 9.10
offer [3] 7.27; 9.2
present (1) Eph 5.27; 9.9
priest [4] 7.1; 9.6
promise 7.6; 9.15
real Tit 3.14; 9.24
remember Tit 1.5; 10.17
require Phil 1.27; 9.23
right (2) 1.3; 10.12
sacrifice 7.27; 9.9
serve 7.13; 9.11
sure 6.9; 10.22
teach 6.1; 9.8
Tent (2) (of the Lord's presence) Acts 7.44; 9.2
throne 4.16; 12.2
wrong [2] 5.13; 9.15

serves as **High Priest** in the **Most Holy Place**, that is, in the **real** tent which was put up by the Lord, not by man.

3 Every **High Priest** is appointed to **present offerings** and animal **sacrifices** to God, and so our **High Priest** must also have something to **offer**. 4 If he were on earth, he would not be a **priest** at all, since there are **priests** who **offer** the **gifts required** by the Jewish **Law**. 5 The work they do as **priests** is really only a copy and a shadow of what is in **heaven**. It is the same as it was with Moses. When he was about to build the **Covenant Tent**, God said to him, "Be **sure** to make everything according to the pattern you were shown on the mountain." 6 But now, Jesus has been given **priestly** work which is superior to theirs, just as the **covenant** which he arranged between God and **his people** is a better one, because it is **based on promises** of better things.

7 If there had been nothing **wrong** with the first **covenant**, there would have been no **need** for a second one. 8 But God finds **fault** with **his people** when he says,

"The days are coming, says the Lord,
when I will draw up a **new covenant**
with the people of Israel and with
the people of Judah.
9 It will not be like the **covenant** that I
made with their ancestors
on the day I took them by the hand
and led them out of Egypt.
They were not **faithful** to the **covenant**
I made with them,
and so I paid no attention to them.
10 Now, this is the **covenant** that I will
make with the people of Israel
in the days to come, says the Lord:
I will put my **laws** in their **minds**
and write them on their **hearts**.
I will be their God,
and they will be **my people**.
11 None of them will have to **teach** his
fellow-citizen
or say to his fellow-countryman,
'Know the Lord.'
For they will all know me,
from the **least** to the greatest.
12 I will **forgive** their sins
and will no longer **remember** their
wrongs."

13 By speaking of a **new covenant**, God has made the first one old; and anything that becomes old and worn out will soon disappear.

Earthly and Heavenly Worship

9 The first **covenant** had rules for **worship** and a **man-made** place for **worship** as well. 2 A **Tent** was put up, the outer one, which was called the **Holy Place**. In it were the lampstand and the table with the **bread offered** to God. 3 Behind the second curtain was the **Tent** called the **Most Holy Place**. 4 In it were the gold **altar** for the burning of **incense** and the **Covenant Box** all covered with gold and containing the gold jar with the **manna** in it, Aaron's stick that had sprouted leaves, and the two stone **tablets** with the **commandments** written on them. 5 Above the **Box** were the winged **creatures representing** God's **presence**, with their wings spread over the place where sins were **forgiven**. But now is not the time to explain everything in detail.

6 This is how those things have been arranged. The **priests** go into the outer **Tent** every day to perform their **duties**, 7 but only the **High Priest** goes into the inner **Tent**, and he does so only once a year. He takes with him **blood** which he **offers** to God on behalf of himself and for the sins which the people have **committed** without knowing they were sinning. 8 The **Holy Spirit clearly teaches** from all these arrangements that the way into the **Most Holy Place** has not yet been opened as long as the outer **Tent** still stands. 9 This is an illustration which points to the present time. It means that the **offerings** and animal **sacrifices presented** to God cannot make the **worshipper's heart perfect**, 10 since they have to do only with food, drink, and various **purification ceremonies**. These are all outward rules, which apply only until the time when God will **establish** the **new** order.

11 But **Christ** has already come as the **High Priest** of the good things that are already here.[e] The **tent** in which he **serves** is greater and more **perfect**; it is not a **man-made tent**, that is, it is not a part of this **created world**. 12 When **Christ** went through the **tent** and entered once and for all into the **Most Holy Place**, he did not take the **blood** of goats and bulls to **offer as a sacrifice**; rather, he took his own **blood** and obtained **eternal salvation** for us. 13 The **blood** of goats and bulls and the **ashes** of a burnt calf are **sprinkled** on the people who are ritually **unclean**, and this **purifies** them by **taking away** their **ritual impurity**. 14 Since this is **true**, how

age (1) 6.5; Jude 25
alive 4.12; 1 Pet 3.18
altar 1 Cor 10.18; 10.6
ash Lk 10.13
bless 7.1; 11.20
blood [13] 2.14; 10.4
box *see* **Covenant Box**
bread 2 Cor 9.10
ceremony Phil 3.3
Christ [7] 5.5; 10.5
clear 6.17; 11.14
command 7.5; 2 Pet 2.21
commandment [2] Tit 1.14; Jas 2.10
commit 1 Tim 5.20; 13.4
conscience Tit 1.15; 10.22
covenant [6] 8.5; 10.16
Covenant Box [2] Jer 3.16; Rev 11.19
create [2] 4.3; 11.3
creature Gal 6.15; Jas 1.18
death (1) [2] 7.3; 10.19
duty (1) 2 Tim 4.5
establish Phil 1.7; 11.28
eternal [3] 6.2; 13.20
forgive [2] 8.12; 10.18
free 2.15; 10.19
heart 8.10; 10.16
heaven [3] 8.1; 11.16
High Priest [3] 8.1; 13.11
Holy Place [6] 8.2; 10.19
hyssop Jn 19.29
impure 1 Thes 2.3; Rev 21.27
incense 2 Cor 2.15; Rev 5.8
Jew Tit 1.14; 10.11
judge 6.2; 10.27
law [3] 8.4; 10.1
man-made [3] Col 2.22
manna Jn 6.31; Rev 2.17
new [2] 8.8; 10.20
obey 5.8; 11.7
offer [7] 8.3; 10.1
perfect [3] 7.11; 10.1
presence [2] 4.14; 2 Pet 2.11
present (1) 8.3; 13.15
priest 8.4; 10.11
proclaim Tit 1.3; 1 Pet 1.25
promise 8.6; 10.23
prove 2.3; Jas 2.14
pure [5] 2.11; 10.2
real 8.2; 10.1
reason Phlm 8; 10.5
represent Gal 4.24; Rev 15.2
require 8.4
ritual [2] Jn 11.55
sacrifice [6] 8.3; 10.1
salvation 6.9; 1 Pet 1.5
save 7.25; 10.39
seal 1 Cor 11.25; 13.20
serve [2] 8.2; 10.3
Spirit (1) (God's Spirit) [2] 6.4; 10.15
sprinkle [3] Lk 10.13; 11.28
suffer 5.8; 10.32
tablet 2 Cor 3.3

[e] already here; *some manuscripts have* coming.

8.5: Ex 25.40 **8.8-12:** Jer 31.31-34 (LXX) **9.2:** Ex 26.1-30, 25.31-40, 23-30 **9.3:** Ex 26.31-33 **9.4:** Ex 30.1-6, 25.10-16, 16.33; Num 17.8-10; Ex 25.16; Deut 10.3-5 **9.5:** Ex 25.18-22 **9.6:** Num 18.2-6 **9.7:** Lev 16.2-34 **9.13:** Lev 16.15-16; Num 19.9, 17-19

take away (sin) [2] Rom 11.27; 10.4
teach 8.11; 13.9
Tent (2) (of the Lord's presence) [9] 8.5; Rev 15.5
true 6.11; Jas 2.23
unclean 2 Cor 7.1; Rev 16.13
useless 7.18; Jas 2.20
world [2] 4.3; 10.5
worship (1) (of God) [4] 1.6; 10.2
wrong 8.7; Jas 3.6

much more is accomplished by the **blood** of **Christ**! Through the **eternal Spirit** he **offered** himself as a **perfect sacrifice** to God. His **blood** will **purify** our **consciences** from **useless rituals**, so that we may **serve** the living God.

15 For this **reason Christ** is the one who arranges a **new covenant**, so that those who have been called by God may receive the **eternal blessings** that God has **promised**. This can be done because there has been a **death** which **sets people free** from the **wrongs** they did while the first **covenant** was in force.

16 In the case of a will it is necessary to **prove** that the person who made it has died, 17 for a will means nothing while the person who made it is **alive**; it comes into effect only after his **death**. 18 That is why even the first **covenant**[f] came into effect only with the use of **blood**. 19 First, Moses **proclaimed** to the people all the **commandments** as set forth in the **Law**. Then he took the **blood** of bulls and goats, mixed it with water, and **sprinkled** it on the book of the **Law** and all the people, using a sprig of **hyssop** and some red wool. 20 He said, "This is the **blood** which **seals** the **covenant** that God has **commanded** you to **obey**." 21 In the same way Moses also **sprinkled** the **blood** on the **Covenant Tent** and over all the things used in **worship**. 22 Indeed, according to the **Law** almost everything is **purified** by **blood**, and sins are **forgiven** only if **blood** is poured out.

Christ's Sacrifice Takes Away Sins

23 Those things, which are copies of the **heavenly** originals, had to be **purified** in that way. But the **heavenly** things themselves **require** much better **sacrifices**. 24 For **Christ** did not go into a **man-made Holy Place**, which was a copy of the **real** one. He went into **heaven** itself, where he now appears on our behalf in the **presence** of God. 25 The **Jewish High Priest** goes into the **Most Holy Place** every year with the **blood** of an animal. But **Christ** did not go in to **offer** himself many times, 26 for then he would have had to **suffer** many times ever since the **creation** of the **world**. Instead, now when all **ages** of time are nearing the end, he has appeared once and for all, to remove sin through the **sacrifice** of himself. 27 Everyone must die once, and after that be **judged** by God. 28 In the same manner **Christ** also was **offered in sacrifice** once to **take away** the sins of many. He will appear a second time, not to deal with sin, but to **save** those who are waiting for him.

10 The Jewish **Law** is not a full and **faithful** model of the **real** things; it is only a faint outline of the good things to come. The same **sacrifices** are **offered** for ever, year after year. How can the **Law**, then, **by means of** these **sacrifices** make **perfect** the people who come to God? 2 If the people **worshipping** God had really been **purified** from their sins, they would not feel **guilty** of sin any more, and all **sacrifices** would stop. 3 As it is, however, the **sacrifices serve** year after year to **remind** people of their sins. 4 For the **blood** of bulls and goats can never **take away** sins.

5 For this **reason**, when **Christ** was about to come into the **world**, he said to God:

"You do not want **sacrifices** and
offerings,
but you have prepared a **body** for
me.
6 You are not **pleased** with animals
burnt whole on the **altar**
or with **sacrifices** to **take away** sins.
7 Then I said, 'Here I am,
to do your **will**, O God,
just as it is written of me in the book
of the **Law**.' "

8 First he said, "You neither want nor are you **pleased** with **sacrifices** and **offerings** or with animals burnt on the **altar** and the **sacrifices** to **take away** sins." He said this even though all these **sacrifices** are **offered** according to the **Law**. 9 Then he said, "Here I am, O God, to do your **will**." So God does away with all the old sacrifices and puts the **sacrifice** of **Christ** in their place. 10 Because Jesus Christ did what God wanted him to do, we are all **purified** from sin by the **offering** that he made of his own **body** once and for all.

11 Every **Jewish priest** performs his **services** every day and **offers** the same **sacrifices** many times; but these **sacrifices** can never **take away** sins. 12 **Christ**, however, **offered one sacrifice** for sins, an **offering** that is effective for ever, and then he sat down at the **right-hand side** of God. 13 There he now waits until God puts his **enemies** as a **footstool** under his feet. 14 With one **sacrifice**, then, he has made **perfect** for ever those who are **purified** from sin.

15 And the **Holy Spirit** also gives us his **witness**. First he says,

altar [2] 9.4; 13.10
believe 6.1; Jas 1.6
blood [2] 9.7; 11.28
body [4] 7.10; 11.22
Christ [3] 9.11; 13.20
clean 2 Tim 2.21; Rev 3.4
complete 2 Thes 1.11; Jas 1.4
concern Tit 3.8
conscience 9.14; 13.18
courage 3.6; 1 Jn 2.28
covenant [2] 9.1; 12.24
Day of the Lord Tit 2.13; 1 Pet 1.7
death (1) 9.15; 11.28
death (3) (to death) Col 3.5; 12.20
deed (2) Tit 3.5; Jas 3.13
deserve 2.2; 1 Pet 2.19
despise 1 Tim 6.2; 2 Pet 2.10
destroy 6.8; 12.29
disobey Tit 3.3; 11.23
encourage 6.18; 12.5
endure Tit 2.2; 12.7
enemy 1.13; Jas 4.4
evidence 2 Cor 13.1
evil 5.14; Jas 1.13
faith [2] 6.4; 11.1
faithful 8.9; 13.4
fear 2.15; Jas 2.19
footstool 1.13
forgive 9.5; Jas 5.15
free 9.15; 11.35
give up Tit 2.12; 12.2
glad Col 2.5; 12.11
God's people 8.6; 11.25
grace 4.16; 12.15
guilty [3] 2 Tim 3.6; Jas 2.4
heart [3] 9.9; Jas 1.21
help 6.10; 13.6
Holy Place 9.2; 13.11
hope 7.19; 11.1
ill-treat 1 Thes 2.2; 11.37
insult [2] 2 Tim 3.2; 1 Pet 2.1
Jew 9.25; 13.10
judge [3] 9.27; 12.23
last (1) 1.8; Rev 2.10
law [6] 9.19; Jas 1.25
light (1) 6.4; Jas 1.17
loss Phil 4.15
love 6.10; 12.6
means [2] 7.21; 11.4
mercy 4.16; Jas 2.13
mind (1) 8.10; Jas 1.7
need [2] 8.7; 13.20
new 9.10; 12.24
offer [9] 9.2; 11.4
one another [3] 3.13; 13.1
patient 6.12; 13.22
perfect [2] 9.9; 11.40
please [3] Phlm 20; 11.5
possess 1.2; Jas 2.5
priest [2] 9.6; 13.10
prison Phlm 1; 11.36
promise [2] 9.15; 11.8
punish 2.2; 12.6
pure [5] 9.10; 13.12
purpose 6.17; 11.40
real 9.24; 12.8
reason 9.15; 13.12
remember [2] 8.12; 13.2

[f] COVENANT: *In Greek the same word means "will" and "covenant."*

9.19-20: Ex 24.6-8 **9.21:** Lev 8.15 **9.22:** Lev 17.11 **9.28:** Is 53.12 **10.5-7:** Ps 40.6-8 (LXX) **10.11:** Ex 29.38 **10.12-13:** Ps 110.1

remind Phlm 19; 2 Pet 1.12
repay 1 Tim 5.4; Rev 2.23
revenge Rom 12.19
reward 2 Tim 4.14; 11.6
right (2) 8.1; 12.2
righteous 7.2; 11.4
sacrifice [15] 9.9; 11.4
save 9.28; 11.7
scripture 7.8; 11.5
serve 9.11; 13.10
service 2.17; 13.17
share 6.4; 12.10
sincere Tit 2.7; 1 Pet 1.22
Son of God 7.3; 2 Pet 1.17
Spirit (1) (God's Spirit) [2] 9.8; 1 Pet 1.2
struggle 1 Tim 4.10; 12.4
suffer [2] 9.26; 11.25
sure 8.5; 11.1
take away (sin) [6] 9.13; 1 Jn 3.5
terrify Acts 5.5; 12.21
trust 2.13; 11.11
truth 2.1; Jas 1.18
turn [2] 6.1; 11.27
will (1) [3] 2.4; 13.20
witness [2] 2.4; 12.1
world 9.11; 11.7
worse 2 Tim 3.13; 2 Pet 2.20
worship (1) (of God) 9.1; 11.21

16 "This is the covenant that I will make
with them
in the days to come, says the Lord:
I will put my laws in their hearts
and write them on their minds."
17 And then he says, "I will not remember
their sins and evil deeds any longer."
18 So when these have been forgiven, an
offering to take away sins is no longer
needed.

Let Us Come Near to God

19 We have, then, my brothers,
complete freedom to go into the Most
Holy Place by means of the death of
Jesus. 20 He opened for us a new way, a
living way, through the curtain—that is,
through his own body. 21 We have a great
priest in charge of the house of God. 22 So
let us come near to God with a sincere
heart and a sure faith, with hearts that
have been purified from a guilty conscience and with bodies washed with
clean water. 23 Let us hold on firmly to
the hope we profess, because we can
trust God to keep his promise. 24 Let us be
concerned for one another, to help one
another to show love and to do good.
25 Let us not give up the habit of meeting
together, as some are doing. Instead, let
us encourage one another all the more,
since you see that the Day of the Lord is
coming nearer.

26 For there is no longer any sacrifice
that will take away sins if we purposely
go on sinning after the truth has been
made known to us. 27 Instead, all that is
left is to wait in fear for the coming
Judgement and the fierce fire which will
destroy those who oppose God! 28 Anyone
who disobeys the Law of Moses is put to
death without any mercy when judged
guilty on the evidence of two or more
witnesses. 29 What, then, of the person
who despises the Son of God? who treats
as a cheap thing the blood of God's
covenant which purified him from sin?
who insults the Spirit of grace? Just
think how much worse is the punishment
he will deserve! 30 For we know who
said, "I will take revenge, I will repay";
and who also said, "The Lord will judge
his people." 31 It is a terrifying thing to
fall into the hands of the living God!

32 Remember how it was with you in
the past. In those days, after God's light
had shone on you, you suffered many
things, yet were not defeated by the
struggle. 33 You were at times publicly insulted and ill-treated, and at other times
you were ready to join those who were
being treated in this way. 34 You shared
the sufferings of prisoners, and when all
your belongings were seized, you endured your loss gladly, because you knew
that you still possessed something much
better, which would last for ever. 35 Do
not lose your courage, then, because it
brings with it a great reward. 36 You need
to be patient, in order to do the will of
God and receive what he promises.
37 For, as the scripture says,
"Just a little while longer,
and he who is coming will come;
he will not delay.
38 My righteous people, however, will
believe and live;
but if any of them turns back,
I will not be pleased with him."
39 We are not people who turn back and
are lost. Instead, we have faith and are
saved.

Faith

11 To have faith is to be sure of the
things we hope for, to be certain
of the things we cannot see. 2 It was by
their faith that people of ancient times
won God's approval.

3 It is by faith that we understand that
the universe was created by God's word,
so that what can be seen was made out of
what cannot be seen.

4 It was faith that made Abel offer to
God a better sacrifice than Cain's.
Through his faith he won God's approval
as a righteous man, because God himself
approved of his gifts. By means of his
faith Abel still speaks, even though he is
dead.

5 It was faith that kept Enoch from
dying. Instead, he was taken up to God,
and nobody could find him, because God
had taken him up. The scripture says
that before Enoch was taken up, he had
pleased God. 6 No one can please God
without faith, for whoever comes to God
must have faith that God exists and
rewards those who seek him.

7 It was faith that made Noah hear
God's warnings about things in the future
that he could not see. He obeyed God and
built a boat in which he and his family
were saved. As a result, the world was
condemned, and Noah received from
God the righteousness that comes by
faith.

8 It was faith that made Abraham
obey when God called him to go out to a
country which God had promised to give

accept 4.2; 12.6
admit (1) 2 Cor 11.21
afraid [2] 1 Tim 5.20; 12.21
ancient Hab 3.6; 2 Pet 2.5
angel 2.2; 12.22
anger 4.3; Jas 1.19
approve [3] 2 Tim 2.15
ashamed 2.11; 1 Pet 3.16
bless [2] 9.15; 12.17
blood 10.4; 12.24
body 10.5; 13.11
certain (1) 1 Tim 6.17
clear 9.8; 13.18
condemn 1 Tim 3.6; Jas 2.9
create 9.11; 12.27
dead [3] 6.2; Jas 2.17
death (1) 10.19; 13.20
death (2) (from death) [2] 5.7; 13.20
disobey [2] 10.28
enjoy 1 Tim 6.17; 1 Pet 3.10
enough [2] 5.12; 13.23
escape 2.3; 12.25
establish 9.10
exist Col 1.17; Jas 3.6
faith [29] 10.22; 12.2
first-born 1.6; 12.23
free 10.19; 13.5
friend 6.9; Jas 2.23
gift 8.4; Jas 1.17
God's people 10.30; 13.24
heaven 9.23; 12.22
hope 10.23; Jas 5.8
ill-treat 10.33
keep from 2 Tim 3.5; Jas 1.27
life (1) 7.16; 12.11
life (2) (to life) 1 Thes 4.16; Rev 20.4
long (2) Rom 8.19; Rev 18.14
means 10.1; 2 Pet 1.4
Messiah Acts 26.23; 1 Jn 2.22
might 2 Thes 1.7; 1 Pet 5.6

10.16: Jer 31.33 10.17: Jer 31.34 10.22: Lev 8.30; Ezek 36.25 10.27: Is 26.11 (LXX)
10.28: Deut 17.6, 19.15 10.29: Ex 24.8 10.30: Deut 32.35, 36 10.37-38: Hab 2.3-4 (LXX)
11.3: Gen 1.1; Ps 33.6, 9; Jn 1.3 11.4: Gen 4.3-10 11.5: Gen 5.21-24 (LXX) 11.7: Gen 6.13-22
11.8: Gen 12.1-5

mock Lk 23.11; 2 Pet 3.3
obey [2] 9.20; 13.9
offer [3] 10.1; 13.11
Passover 1 Cor 5.7
perfect 10.1; 12.23
persecute 2 Tim 3.11; Rev 7.14
plan 1 Tim 1.4; Rev 10.7
please [2] 10.6; 12.28
poor Eph 4.28; Jas 1.9
prison 10.34; 13.3
promise [10] 10.23; 12.24
prophet 1.1; Jas 5.10
prostitute 1 Cor 6.15; Jas 2.25
purpose 10.26; Jas 1.20
put out Eph 6.16
raise [3] 7.26; 13.20
refugee [2] Ezek 29.12; 1 Pet 1.1
refuse (1) [3] 3.10; 12.25
result 1 Tim 6.21; 13.20
reward [2] 10.35; 12.11
right (1) 5.13; 12.10
righteous [2] 10.38; 12.11
sacrifice [3] 10.1; 13.10
save 10.39; Jas 1.21
scorn Hab 2.6
scripture 10.37; Jas 2.8
seek Rom 9.31; Rev 9.6
sheep 1 Cor 9.7; 13.20
sprinkle 9.13; 12.24
strong 2 Tim 2.1; Jas 3.4
suffer [2] 10.32; 12.7
sure 10.22; 13.18
test 3.8; Jas 1.12
trust 10.23; 1 Pet 4.19
turn 10.38; 12.15
understand 5.11; Jas 3.13
universe 1.2; Rev 5.13
warn Tit 3.10; Jude 7
weak 7.18; 1 Pet 3.7
welcome [2] Phlm 17; 13.2
win [4] 2 Tim 2.5; 1 Pet 3.1
word (1) 6.5; 12.5
world [2] 10.5; Jas 1.1
worship (1) (of God) 10.2; 12.28
worth Phil 2.22

him. He left his own country without
knowing where he was going. 9 By **faith**
he lived as a foreigner in the country
that God had **promised** him. He lived in
tents, as did Isaac and Jacob, who
received the same **promise** from God.
10 For Abraham was waiting for the city
which God has designed and built, the
city with permanent foundations.

11 It was **faith** that made Abraham
able to become a father, even though he
was too old and Sarah herself could not
have children. He[g] **trusted** God to keep
his **promise**. 12 Though Abraham was
practically **dead**, from this one man
came as many descendants as there are
stars in the sky, as many as the number-
less grains of sand on the sea-shore.

13 It was in **faith** that all these persons
died. They did not receive the things God
had **promised**, but from a long way off
they saw them and **welcomed** them, and
admitted openly that they were
foreigners and **refugees** on earth.
14 Those who say such things make it
clear that they are looking for a country
of their own. 15 They did not keep thinking about the country they had left; if
they had, they would have had the
chance to return. 16 Instead, it was a better country they **longed** for, the **heavenly**
country. And so God is not **ashamed** for
them to call him their God, because he
has prepared a city for them.

17 It was **faith** that made Abraham
offer his son Isaac as a **sacrifice** when
God put Abraham **to the test**. Abraham
was the one to whom God had made the
promise, yet he was ready to **offer** his
only son as a **sacrifice**. 18 God had said to
him, "It is through Isaac that you will
have the descendants I **promised**."
19 Abraham reckoned that God was able
to **raise** Isaac **from death**—and, so to
speak, Abraham did receive Isaac back
from death.

20 It was **faith** that made Isaac **promise blessings** for the future to Jacob and
Esau.

21 It was **faith** that made Jacob **bless**
each of the sons of Joseph just before he
died. He leaned on the top of his walking-
stick and **worshipped** God.

22 It was **faith** that made Joseph,
when he was about to die, speak of the
departure of the Israelites from Egypt,
and leave instructions about what should
be done with his **body**.

23 It was **faith** that made the parents
of Moses hide him for three months after
he was born. They saw that he was a
beautiful child, and they were not **afraid**
to **disobey** the king's order.

24 It was **faith** that made Moses, when
he had grown up, **refuse** to be called the
son of the king's daughter. 25 He preferred to **suffer** with **God's people** rather
than to **enjoy** sin for a little while. 26 He
reckoned that to **suffer scorn** for the
Messiah was **worth** far more than all the
treasures of Egypt, for he kept his eyes
on the future **reward**.

27 It was **faith** that made Moses leave
Egypt without being **afraid** of the king's
anger. As though he saw the invisible
God, he **refused** to **turn back**. 28 It was
faith that made him **establish** the **Passover** and order the **blood** to be **sprinkled**
on the doors, so that the **Angel of Death**
would not kill the **first-born** sons of the
Israelites.

29 It was **faith** that made the Israelites
able to cross the Red Sea as if on dry
land; when the Egyptians tried to do it,
the water swallowed them up.

30 It was **faith** that made the walls of
Jericho fall down after the Israelites had
marched round them for seven days. 31 It
was **faith** that kept the **prostitute** Rahab
from being killed with those who **disobeyed** God, for she gave the Israelite
spies a **friendly welcome**.

32 Should I go on? There isn't **enough**
time for me to speak of Gideon, Barak,
Samson, Jephthah, David, Samuel, and
the **prophets**. 33 Through **faith** they fought
whole countries and **won**. They did what
was **right** and received what God had
promised. They shut the mouths of lions,
34 **put out** fierce fires, **escaped** being
killed by the sword. They were **weak**, but
became **strong**; they were **mighty** in
battle and defeated the armies of
foreigners. 35 Through **faith** women
received their **dead** relatives **raised** back
to life.

Others, **refusing** to **accept freedom**,
died under torture in order to be **raised**
to a better **life**. 36 Some were **mocked** and
whipped, and others were put in chains
and taken off to **prison**. 37 They were
stoned, they were sawn in two, they were

[g] It was faith...children. He; *some manuscripts have* It was faith that made Sarah herself able to conceive, even though she was too old to have children. She.

11.9: Gen 35.27 **11.11:** Gen 18.11–14, 21.2 **11.12:** Gen 15.5, 22.17, 32.12
11.13: Gen 23.4; 1 Chr 29.15; Ps 39.12 **11.17:** Gen 22.1–14 **11.18:** Gen 21.12 **11.20:** Gen 27.27–29, 39–40
11.21: Gen 47.31 (LXX), 48.1–20 **11.22:** Gen 50.24–25; Ex 13.19 **11.23:** Ex 2.2, 1.22 **11.24:** Ex 2.10–12
11.28: Ex 12.21–30 **11.29:** Ex 14.21–31 **11.30:** Josh 6.12–21 **11.31:** Josh 2.1–21, 6.22–25
11.32: Judg 6.11–8.32, 4.6–5.31, 13.2–16.31, 11.1–12.7; 1 Sam 16.1–1 Kgs 2.11; 1 Sam 1.1–25.1
11.33: Dan 6.1–27 **11.34:** Dan 3.1–30 **11.35:** 1 Kgs 17.17–24; 2 Kgs 4.25–37
11.36: 1 Kgs 22.26–27; 2 Chr 18.25–26; Jer 20.2, 37.15, 38.6 **11.37:** 2 Chr 24.21

killed by the sword. They went round
clothed in skins of sheep or goats—poor,
persecuted, and ill-treated. 38 The world
was not good enough for them! They
wandered like refugees in the deserts
and hills, living in caves and holes in the
ground.
39 What a record all of these have
won by their faith! Yet they did not
receive what God had promised,
40 because God had decided on an even
better plan for us. His purpose was that
only in company with us would they be
made perfect.

God Our Father

12 As for us, we have this large
crowd of witnesses round us. So
then, let us rid ourselves of everything
that gets in the way, and of the sin which
holds on to us so tightly, and let us run
with determination the race that lies
before us. 2 Let us keep our eyes fixed on
Jesus, on whom our faith depends from
beginning to end. He did not give up
because of the cross! On the contrary,
because of the joy that was waiting for
him, he thought nothing of the disgrace
of dying on the cross, and he is now
seated at the right-hand side of God's
throne.
3 Think of what he went through; how
he put up with so much hatred from sinners! So do not let yourselves become
discouraged and give up. 4 For in your
struggle against sin you have not yet had
to resist to the point of being killed.
5 Have you forgotten the encouraging
words which God speaks to you as his
sons?

"My son, pay attention when the Lord
corrects you,
and do not be discouraged when he
rebukes you.
6 Because the Lord corrects everyone
he loves,
and punishes everyone he accepts
as a son."

7 Endure what you suffer as being a
father's punishment; your suffering
shows that God is treating you as his
sons. Was there ever a son who was not
punished by his father? 8 If you are not
punished, as all his sons are, it means you
are not real sons, but bastards. 9 In the
case of our human fathers, they punished
us and we respected them. How much
more, then, should we submit to our
spiritual Father and live! 10 Our human
fathers punished us for a short time, as it
seemed right to them; but God does it for
our own good, so that we may share his
holiness. 11 When we are punished, it
seems to us at the time something to
make us sad, not glad. Later, however,
those who have been disciplined by such
punishment reap the peaceful reward of
a righteous life.

Instructions and Warnings

12 Lift up your tired hands, then, and
strengthen your trembling knees!
13 Keep walking on straight paths, so that
the lame foot may not be disabled, but instead be healed.
14 Try to be at peace with everyone,
and try to live a holy life, because no one
will see the Lord without it. 15 Guard
against turning back from the grace of
God. Let no one become like a bitter
plant that grows up and causes many
troubles with its poison. 16 Let no one become immoral or unspiritual like Esau,
who for a single meal sold his rights as
the elder son. 17 Afterwards, you know, he
wanted to receive his father's blessing;
but he was turned away, because he
could not find any way to change what
he had done, even though in tears he
looked for it.[h]
18 You have not come, as the people
of Israel came, to what you can feel, to
Mount Sinai with its blazing fire, the
darkness and the gloom, the storm, 19 the
blast of a trumpet, and the sound of a
voice. When the people heard the voice,
they begged not to hear another word,
20 because they could not bear the order
which said, "If even an animal touches
the mountain, it must be stoned to
death." 21 The sight was so terrifying that
Moses said, "I am trembling and afraid!"
22 Instead, you have come to Mount
Zion and to the city of the living God, the
heavenly Jerusalem, with its thousands
of angels. 23 You have come to the joyful
gathering of God's first-born sons, whose
names are written in heaven. You have
come to God, who is the judge of all
mankind, and to the spirits of good
people made perfect. 24 You have come
to Jesus, who arranged the new covenant, and to the sprinkled blood that
promises much better things than does
the blood of Abel.
25 Be careful, then, and do not refuse
to hear him who speaks. Those who
refused to hear the one who gave the

[h] he looked for it; *or* he tried to get the blessing.

12.5–6: Job 5.17; Prov 3.11–12 (LXX) **12.12:** Is 35.3 **12.13:** Prov 4.26 (LXX) **12.15:** Deut 29.18 (LXX) **12.16:** Gen 25.29–34 **12.17:** Gen 27.30–40 **12.18–19:** Ex 19.16–22, 20.18–21; Deut 4.11–12, 5.22–27 **12.20:** Ex 19.12–13 **12.21:** Deut 9.19 **12.24:** Gen 4.10 **12.25:** Ex 20.22

accept 11.35; Jas 1.21
afraid 11.23; 13.6
angel 11.28; 13.2
awe 2 Cor 7.1; Rev 15.4
beg 2 Thes 2.1; 13.19
bitter Eph 4.31; Jas 3.11
bless 11.20; Jas 1.25
blood [2] 11.28; 13.11
change 7.12; Jas 1.17
child of God [6] Phil 2.15; 1 Jn 2.29
correct [2] 2 Tim 3.16
covenant 10.16; 13.20
create 11.3; Jas 2.4
cross (1) [2] Col 2.14; 1 Pet 2.24
dark 1 Thes 5.4; Jas 1.17
death (3) (to death) 10.28; 1 Pet 3.18
depend 1 Thes 4.12; 2 Pet 1.16
destroy 10.27; Jas 1.11
determine Acts 22.10
discipline Tit 1.8
discourage [2] Col 3.21
disgrace 1 Tim 3.7; 2 Pet 2.13
divine 8.1; 2 Pet 1.3
encourage 10.25; 13.22
endure 10.34; Jas 1.3
escape [2] 11.34; Jas 2.25
faith 11.1; 13.7
Father (2) (God) 5.5; Jas 1.27
first-born 11.28
forget 6.10; 13.16
give up [2] 10.25; Rev 2.3
glad 10.34; 13.17
gloom Mk 10.22; Jas 4.9
grace 10.29; 13.9
grateful 2 Tim 3.2
hate 1.9; 1 Jn 2.9
heal 1 Cor 12.9; Jas 5.15
heaven [4] 11.16; Jas 1.17
holy [2] 7.26; 1 Pet 1.2
human [2] 7.16; 1 Pet 2.13
immoral 1 Tim 1.10; 13.4
joy [2] 1.9; Jas 4.9
judge 10.27; 13.4

Kingdom (1) (of God) 1.8; Jas 2.5
knee Phil 2.10
life (1) [2] 11.35; 13.5
love 10.24; 13.1
mankind 1.3; 1 Pet 1.24
message 6.1; 13.7
new 10.20; 1 Pet 1.3
peace [2] 7.2; 13.20
perfect 11.40; Jas 1.4
plain (1) 7.15; 2 Pet 1.14
please 11.5; 13.16
promise [2] 11.8; Jas 1.12
punish [8] 10.29; 1 Pet 2.14
race (2) 2 Tim 4.7
real 10.1; 1 Pet 5.2
reap Gal 6.7; Rev 14.15
rebuke Tit 2.15; 2 Pet 2.16
refuse (1) [2] 11.24; Rev 15.4
resist Eph 6.13; Jas 4.6
respect 1 Tim 6.1; Jas 2.3
reverence 1 Tim 2.2; 1 Pet 1.17
reward 11.6; Jas 1.12
rid Col 3.8; Jas 1.21
right (1) 11.33; 13.9
right (2) 10.12; 1 Pet 3.22
right (3) 2 Thes 3.9; 13.10
righteous 11.4; Jas 1.20
sad 1 Thes 4.13; 13.17
share 10.34; 13.13
sight 2 Tim 2.15; 1 Pet 3.4
son *see* **child of God**
spirit (2) 4.12; Jas 2.26
spiritual [2] Phlm 10; Jas 3.15
sprinkle 11.28
strength 2 Tim 4.17; 13.9
struggle 10.32
submit Tit 3.1; Jas 1.21
suffer [2] 11.25; 13.3
tear (2) 5.7; Rev 7.17
terrify 10.31; Rev 11.11
thank Phlm 4; Jas 3.9
throne 8.1; Rev 1.4
tremble [2] Phil 2.12; Jas 2.19
trouble 1 Tim 5.10; Jas 5.13
turn [3] 11.27; Jas 1.17
witness 10.15; Jas 5.3
word (1) [3] 11.3; Jas 1.18
worship (1) (of God) 11.21; 13.10

divine message on earth did not **escape.**
How much less shall we **escape**, then, if
we **turn away** from the one who speaks
from **heaven**! 26 His voice shook the
earth at that time, but now he has
promised, "I will once more shake not
only the earth but **heaven** as well." 27 The
words "once more" **plainly** show that the
created things will be shaken and
removed, so that the things that cannot
be shaken will remain.
28 Let us be **thankful**, then, because
we receive a **kingdom** that cannot be
shaken. Let us be **grateful** and **worship**
God in a way that will **please** him, with
reverence and **awe**; 29 because our God is
indeed a **destroying** fire.

How to Please God

13 Keep on **loving one another** as
Christian brothers. 2 **Remember**
to **welcome strangers** in your homes.
There were some who did that and **welcomed angels** without knowing it.
3 **Remember** those who are in **prison**, as
though you were in **prison** with them.
Remember those who are **suffering**, as
though you were suffering as they are.
4 Marriage is to be **honoured** by all,
and husbands and wives must be **faithful**
to **each other**. God will **judge** those who
are **immoral** and those who **commit
adultery**.
5 Keep your **lives free** from the **love** of
money, and be **satisfied** with what you
have. For God has said, "I will never
leave you; I will never **abandon** you."
6 Let us be **bold**, then, and say,

"The Lord is my **helper**,
I will not be **afraid**.
What can anyone do to me?"

7 **Remember** your former leaders,
who spoke God's **message** to you. Think
back on how they lived and died, and imitate their **faith**. 8 Jesus Christ is the same
yesterday, today, and for ever. 9 Do not
let all kinds of **strange teachings** lead you
from the **right** way. It is good to receive
inner **strength** from God's **grace**, and not
by **obeying** rules about foods; those who
obey these rules have not been **helped** by
them.
10 The **priests** who **serve** in the **Jewish
place of worship** have no **right** to eat any
of the **sacrifice** on our **altar**. 11 The **Jewish
High Priest** brings the **blood** of the animals into the **Most Holy Place** to **offer it**
as a **sacrifice** for sins; but the **bodies** of
the animals are burnt outside the camp.
12 For this **reason** Jesus also died outside
the city, in order to **purify** the people
from sin with his own **blood**. 13 Let us,
then, go to him outside the camp and
share his **shame**. 14 For there is no
permanent city for us here on earth; we
are looking for the city which is to come.
15 Let us, then, always **offer praise** to God
as our **sacrifice** through Jesus, which is
the **offering presented** by lips that **confess** him as Lord. 16 Do not **forget** to do
good and to **help one another**, because
these are the **sacrifices** that **please** God.
17 **Obey** your leaders and follow their
orders. They **watch** over your **souls** without **resting**, since they must give God an
account of their **service**. If you **obey**
them, they will do their work **gladly**; if
not, they will do it with **sadness**, and that
would be of no **help** to you.
18 Keep on **praying** for us. We are
sure we have a **clear conscience**, because we want to do the **right** thing at all
times. 19 And I **beg** you even more
earnestly to **pray** that God will send me
back to you soon.

Closing Prayer

20–21 God has **raised from death** our
Lord Jesus, who is the Great **Shepherd** of
the **sheep** as the **result** of his **sacrificial**
death, by which the **eternal covenant** is
sealed. May the God of **peace provide**
you with every good thing you **need** in
order to do his **will**, and may he, through
Jesus Christ, do in us what **pleases** him.
And to **Christ** be the **glory** for ever and
ever! Amen.

Final Words

22 I **beg** you, my brothers, to listen
patiently to this **message** of **encouragement**; for this **letter** I have written to you
is not very long. 23 I want you to know
that our brother Timothy has been let
out of **prison**. If he comes soon **enough**, I
will have him with me when I see you.
24 Give our greetings to all your
leaders and to all **God's people**. The
brothers from Italy send you their
greetings.
25 May God's **grace** be with you all.

12.26: Hag 2.6 (LXX) **12.29:** Deut 4.24 **13.2:** Gen 18.1–8, 19.1–3 **13.5:** Deut 31.6, 8; Josh 1.5
13.6: Ps 118.6 (LXX) **13.11:** Lev 16.27

abandon 6.4; 2 Pet 1.10
adultery 1 Cor 6.9; Jas 2.11
afraid 12.21; 1 Pet 3.6
altar 10.6; Jas 2.21
angel 12.22; 1 Pet 1.12
beg [2] 12.19
blood [2] 12.24; 1 Pet 1.2
body 11.22; Jas 2.26
bold Phlm 8; 2 Pet 2.10
Christ 10.5; 1 Pet 1.11
Christian 6.1; Jas 1.9
clear 11.14; 1 Pet 3.16
commit 9.7; Jas 2.11
confess 1 Cor 14.25; Jas 5.16
conscience 10.22; 1 Pet 3.16
covenant 12.24
death (1) 11.28; Jas 1.15
death (2) (from death) 11.19; Jas 5.20
each other Col 3.16; 1 Pet 4.9
earnest 2 Cor 7.11; Jas 5.17
encourage 12.5; 1 Pet 5.12
enough 11.32; Jas 2.15
eternal 9.12; 1 Pet 1.23
faith 12.2; Jas 1.3
faithful 10.1; Jas 1.12
forget 12.5; Jas 1.24
free 11.35; Jas 1.25
glad 12.11; Jas 1.9
glory 2.7; Jas 2.1
God's people 11.25; Jas 1.1
grace [2] 12.15; Jas 1.5
help [4] 10.24; Jas 2.25
High Priest 9.7
Holy Place 10.19
honour 5.4; 1 Pet 1.7

immoral 12.16; 2 Pet 2.2
Jew [2] 10.11; Rev 2.9
judge 12.23; Jas 2.4
letter (2) 1 Tim 3.14; 1 Pet 5.12
life (1) 12.11; Jas 1.12
love [2] 12.6; Jas 1.12
message [2] 12.25; 1 Pet 4.11
need 10.18; Jas 2.15
obey [4] 11.7; Jas 2.8
offer [3] 11.4; Jas 2.21
one another [2] 10.24; Jas 4.11
patient 10.36; Jas 5.7
peace 12.11; Jas 3.17
place of worship Acts 17.23
please [2] 12.28; 2 Pet 1.17
praise 2.12; Jas 5.13
pray [2] Phlm 4; Jas 1.5
present (1) 9.9
priest 10.11; 1 Pet 2.5
prison [3] 11.36; 1 Pet 3.19
provide 7.19; Jas 5.11
pure 10.2; Jas 1.27
raise 11.19; 1 Pet 1.3
reason 10.5; 2 Pet 1.5
remember [4] 10.17; Jas 1.19
rest (1) 4.1; Rev 6.11
result 11.7; Jas 1.3
right (1) [2] 12.10; Jas 2.8
right (3) 12.16; 2 Pet 1.11
sacrifice [5] 11.4; 1 Pet 1.19
sad 12.11; 1 Pet 1.6
satisfy 1 Tim 6.6; 2 Pet 2.13
seal 9.20; Rev 5.1
serve 10.3; 1 Pet 2.5
service 10.11; 3 Jn 7
shame 6.6; 2 Pet 2.13
share 12.10; 1 Pet 4.13
sheep 11.37; 1 Pet 2.25
shepherd 1 Cor 9.7; 1 Pet 2.25
soul 4.12; Jas 5.20
strange 1 Cor 14.2
stranger 1 Tim 5.10; 1 Pet 2.11
strength 12.12; 1 Pet 4.1
suffer 12.7; Jas 1.27
sure 11.1; Jas 1.4
teach 9.8; 1 Jn 2.27
watch 1 Tim 4.16; 1 Pet 3.12
welcome [2] 11.13; Jas 2.25
will (1) 10.7; Jas 1.18
worship (1) (of God) 12.28; Rev 4.10

THE LETTER FROM JAMES

INTRODUCTION

The Letter from James is a collection of practical instructions, written to "all God's people scattered over the whole world." The writer uses many vivid figures of speech to present instructions regarding practical wisdom and guidance for Christian attitudes and conduct. From the Christian perspective he deals with a variety of topics such as riches and poverty, temptation, good conduct, prejudice, faith and actions, the use of the tongue, wisdom, quarrelling, pride and humility, judging others, boasting, patience, and prayer.

The letter emphasizes the importance of actions along with faith, in the practice of the Christian religion.

Outline of Contents

---

accept Heb 12.6; 2.23
anger [2] Heb 11.27; Rev 6.16
being Heb 1.3; 3.2
believe Heb 10.38; 2.19
birth [2] Heb 7.3; Rev 12.2
bless Heb 12.17; 2.16
care Heb 4.1; 1 Pet 5.2
change Heb 12.17; 4.9
Christian [2] Heb 13.1; 4.11
complete Heb 10.19; 1 Pet 2.18
conduct 2 Tim 3.10; 1 Pet 2.12
consider [2] 1 Tim 6.1
control 2 Tim 4.5; 3.2
corrupt Tit 3.11; 2 Pet 2.20
Creator Col 3.10; 1 Pet 4.19
creature Heb 9.5; 3.7
dark Heb 12.18; 1 Pet 2.9
dear [2] Heb 6.9; 2.5
death (1) Heb 13.20; 2 Pet 1.15
deceive [3] Heb 3.13; 2 Pet 2.13
desire [2] Heb 6.11; 4.1
destroy [2] Heb 12.29; 4.12
doubt [2] Heb 7.7; Jude 22
endure [2] Heb 12.7; 5.10
evil [3] Heb 10.17; 2.4
fail Heb 4.1
faith Heb 13.7; 2.5

1 From James, a **servant** of God and
of the Lord Jesus Christ:
Greetings to all **God's people scattered**
over the whole **world**.

Faith and Wisdom

2 My brothers, **consider** yourselves
fortunate when all kinds of **trials** come
your way, 3 for you know that when your
faith succeeds in facing such **trials**, the
result is the ability to **endure**. 4 Make **sure**
that your **endurance** carries you all the
way without **failing**, so that you may be
perfect and **complete**, lacking nothing.
5 But if any of you lacks **wisdom**, he
should **pray** to God, who will give it to
him; because God gives **generously** and
graciously to all. 6 But when you **pray**,
you must **believe** and not **doubt** at all.
Whoever **doubts** is like a wave in the sea
that is driven and blown about by the
wind. 7-8 A person like that, unable to
make up his **mind** and undecided in all
he does, must not think that he will
receive anything from the Lord.

Poverty and Riches

9 The **Christian** who is **poor** must be
glad when God lifts him up, 10 and the
rich Christian must be **glad** when God
brings him down. For the **rich** will pass
away like the flower of a wild plant.
11 The sun **rises** with its blazing heat and
burns the plant; its flower falls off, and
its beauty is **destroyed**. In the same way
the **rich** man will be **destroyed** while he
goes about his business.

Testing and Tempting

12 **Happy** is the person who remains
faithful under **trials**, because when he
succeeds in passing such a **test**, he will
receive as his **reward** the **life** which God
has **promised** to those who **love** him. 13 If
a person is **tempted** by such **trials**, he
must not say, "This **temptation** comes
from God." For God cannot be tempted
by **evil**, and he himself **tempts** no one.
14 But a person is **tempted** when he is
drawn away and **trapped** by his own **evil**
desire. 15 Then his **evil desire** conceives
and gives **birth** to sin; and sin, when it is
full-grown, gives **birth** to **death**.
16 Do not be **deceived**, my **dear**
brothers! 17 Every good **gift** and every
perfect present comes from **heaven**; it
comes down from God, the **Creator** of the
heavenly lights, who does not **change** or
cause **darkness** by **turning**. 18 By his own
will he brought us into **being** through the

faithful Heb 13.4; 1 Pet 5.12
Father (2) (God) Heb 12.9; 3.9
filthy Gal 5.19; 2 Pet 2.10
forget [2] Heb 13.16; 2 Pet 1.9
fortune Acts 26.2
free Heb 13.5; 2.12
generous 1 Tim 6.17
gift Heb 11.4; 1 Pet 1.10
glad [2] Heb 13.17; 1 Pet 1.6
God's people Heb 13.24; 1 Pet 1.1
grace Heb 13.9; 4.6
happy Col 1.24; 5.11
heart Heb 10.16; 3.14
heaven [2] Heb 12.22; 3.15
keep from Heb 11.5; 1 Pet 3.10
law Heb 10.1; 2.8
life (1) Heb 13.5; 2.16
light (1) Heb 10.32; 1 Pet 2.9
love Heb 13.1; 2.5
mind (1) Heb 10.16; 1 Pet 1.13
orphan Mal 3.5
perfect [3] Heb 12.23; 2.22
poor Heb 11.37; 2.2
practice [3] Heb 5.14; Rev 2.14
pray [2] Heb 13.18; 5.13
promise Heb 12.24; 2.5
pure Heb 13.12; 3.17
purpose Heb 11.40; 1 Pet 1.2

1.1: Mt 13.55; Mk 6.3; Acts 15.13; Gal 1.19 **1.10–11:** Is 40.6–7 (LXX)

religion [3] Tit 1.1; 2 Pet 1.3
remember Heb 13.2; 5.10
result Heb 13.20; Rev 14.13
reward Heb 12.11; 2 Jn 8
rich [3] 1 Tim 6.5; 2.2
rid Heb 12.1; 1 Pet 2.1
righteous Heb 12.11; 2.23
rise 1 Thes 4.14
save Heb 11.7; 2.14
scatter 1 Cor 10.5; 1 Pet 1.1
servant Heb 3.5; 1 Pet 2.18
submit Heb 12.9; 4.7
succeed (1) [2] Phil 3.12
suffer Heb 13.3; 5.10
sure Heb 13.18; 1 Pet 5.10
tempt [4] Heb 4.15
test Heb 11.17; 1 Pet 1.7
trap 2 Tim 2.26; 2 Pet 2.14
truth Heb 10.26; 3.14
try (2) [4] Heb 3.9; 1 Pet 1.6
turn Heb 12.15; 5.20
wicked Tit 2.14; 2 Pet 2.9
widow 1 Tim 5.3; Rev 18.7
will (1) Heb 13.20; 1 Pet 2.8
wisdom 2 Tim 3.15; 3.13
word (1) [4] Heb 12.5; 3.10
world [2] Heb 11.7; 2.5
worthless Heb 6.8; 1 Pet 1.18

word of **truth**, so that we should have first place among all his **creatures**.

Hearing and Doing

19 **Remember** this, my **dear** brothers! Everyone must be quick to listen, but slow to speak and slow to become **angry**. 20 Man's **anger** does not achieve God's **righteous purpose**. 21 So get **rid** of every **filthy** habit and all **wicked conduct**. **Submit** to God and **accept** the **word** that he plants in your **hearts**, which is able to **save** you.

22 Do not **deceive** yourselves by just listening to his **word**; instead, put it into **practice**. 23 Whoever listens to the **word** but does not put it into **practice** is like a man who looks in a mirror and sees himself as he is. 24 He takes a good look at himself and then goes away and at once **forgets** what he looks like. 25 But whoever looks closely into the **perfect law** that **sets people free**, who keeps on paying attention to it and does not simply listen and then **forget** it, but puts it into **practice**—that person will be **blessed** by God in what he does.

26 Does anyone think he is **religious**? If he does not **control** his tongue, his **religion** is **worthless** and he **deceives** himself. 27 What God the **Father** considers to be **pure** and genuine **religion** is this: to take **care** of **orphans** and **widows** in their **suffering** and to **keep oneself** from being **corrupted** by the **world**.

Warning against Prejudice

accept 1.21; 1 Pet 2.5
act Col 4.5; 1 Pet 2.9
action [12] Tit 1.16; 1 Pet 1.13
adultery [2] Heb 13.4; Rev 2.22
alone [2] Tit 2.14; 4.12
altar Heb 13.10; Rev 6.9
appearance [2] Gal 2.6
basis Heb 8.6
believe [3] 1.6; 1 Pet 1.8
believer Heb 3.12; 1 Pet 1.22
best Heb 4.11; 2 Pet 1.5
bless 1.25; 1 Pet 1.4
body Heb 13.11; 3.6
choose Heb 5.1; 1 Pet 1.1
commandment Heb 9.4; Rev 12.17
commit [4] Heb 13.4; 5.15
condemn Heb 11.7; 5.6
create Heb 12.27; 3.9
dead [3] Heb 11.4; 1 Pet 4.5
dear 1.16; 1 Pet 4.12

2 My brothers, as **believers** in our Lord Jesus Christ, the Lord of **glory**, you must never treat people in different ways according to their outward **appearance**. 2 Suppose a **rich** man wearing a gold ring and fine clothes comes to your meeting, and a **poor** man in ragged clothes also comes. 3 If you show more **respect** to the well-dressed man and say to him, "Have this **best seat** here," but say to the **poor** man, "Stand over there, or sit here on the floor by my feet," 4 then you are **guilty of creating distinctions** among yourselves and of making **judgements based on evil motives**.

5 Listen, my **dear** brothers! God **chose** the **poor** people of **this world** to be **rich** in **faith** and to **possess** the **kingdom** which he **promised** to those who **love** him. 6 But you **dishonour** the **poor**! Who are the ones who **oppress** you and drag you before the **judges**? The **rich**! 7 They are the ones who speak **evil** of that good name which has been given to you.

8 You will be doing the **right** thing if you **obey** the **law** of the **Kingdom**, which is found in the **scripture**, "**Love** your **neighbour** as you love yourself." 9 But if you treat people according to their outward **appearance**, you are **guilty** of sin, and the **Law condemns** you as a lawbreaker. 10 Whoever breaks one **commandment** is **guilty** of breaking them all. 11 For the same one who said, "Do not **commit adultery**," also said, "Do not **commit murder**." Even if you do not **commit adultery**, you have become a law-breaker if you **commit murder**. 12 Speak and **act** as people who will be **judged** by the **law** that **sets us free**. 13 For God will not show **mercy** when he **judges** the person who has not been **merciful**; but **mercy triumphs** over **judgement**.

Faith and Actions

14 My brothers, what good is it for someone to say that he has **faith** if his **actions** do not **prove** it? Can that **faith save** him? 15 Suppose there are brothers or sisters who **need** clothes and don't have **enough** to eat. 16 What good is there in your saying to them, "God **bless** you! Keep warm and eat well!"—if you don't give them the necessities of **life**? 17 So it is with **faith**: if it is **alone** and includes no **actions**, then it is **dead**.

18 But someone will say, "One person has **faith**, another has **actions**." My answer is, "Show me how anyone can have **faith** without **actions**. I will show you my **faith** by my **actions**." 19 Do you **believe** that there is only one God? Good! The **demons** also **believe**—and **tremble** with **fear**. 20 You **fool**! Do you want to be shown that **faith** without **actions** is **useless**? [a] 21 How was our ancestor Abraham put **right with God**? It was through his **actions**, when he **offered** his son Isaac on the **altar**. 22 Can't you see? His **faith** and his **actions** worked together; his **faith** was made **perfect** through his **actions**. 23 And the **scripture** came **true** that said, "Abraham **believed** God, and because of his **faith** God **accepted** him as **righteous**." And so Abraham was called God's **friend**. 24 You see, then, that it is by his **actions** that a person is put **right with God**, and not by his **faith alone**.

25 It was the same with the **prostitute** Rahab. She was put **right with God** through her **actions**, by **welcoming** the

demon 1 Tim 4.1; 3.15
dishonour 1 Cor 11.27
distinguish Heb 5.14
enough Heb 13.23; 1 Pet 4.3
escape Heb 12.25; 2 Pet 1.4
evil [2] 1.13; 3.6
faith [13] 1.3; 5.15
fear Heb 10.27; 1 Jn 4.18
fool Tit 3.3; 1 Pet 2.15
free 1.25; 3.17
friend Heb 11.31; 3.17
glory Heb 13.20; 1 Pet 1.7
guilty [3] Heb 10.2; 4.17
help Heb 13.6; 1 Pet 5.12
judge [5] Heb 13.4; 3.1
Kingdom (1) (of God) [2] Heb 12.28; 2 Pet 1.11
law [3] 1.25; 4.11
life (1) 1.12; 3.13
love [2] 1.12; 1 Pet 1.8
mercy [3] Heb 10.28; 5.11
motive 1 Thes 2.3; 4.3
need Heb 13.20; 2 Pet 1.3
neighbour Gal 5.14
obey Heb 13.9; 3.3
offer Heb 13.11; 1 Pet 2.5
oppress 2 Cor 5.4
perfect 1.4; 3.2
poor [4] 1.9; Rev 2.9
possess Heb 10.34; 1 Pet 1.4
promise 1.12; 5.12
prostitute Heb 11.31; Rev 17.1
prove Heb 9.16; 3.13
respect Heb 12.9; 1 Pet 2.17
rich [3] 1.10; 5.1
right (1) Heb 13.9; 1 Pet 2.20
right with God [3] Tit 3.7
righteous 1.20; 1 Pet 2.23
save 1.21; 4.12
scripture [2] Heb 11.5; 4.5
spirit (2) Heb 12.23; 4.5
tremble Heb 12.12
triumph Mt 12.20
true Heb 9.14; 1 Pet 3.4
useless Heb 9.14
welcome Heb 13.2; 2 Jn 10
world 1.1; 3.6

[a] useless; *some manuscripts have* dead.

2.8: Lev 19.18 **2.11:** Ex 20.13, 14; Deut 5.17, 18 **2.21:** Gen 22.1–14 **2.23:** Gen 15.6; 2 Chr 20.7; Is 41.8 **2.25:** Josh 2.1–21

Israelite spies and **helping** them to **escape** by a different road.

26 So then, as the **body** without the **spirit** is **dead**, so also **faith** without **actions** is **dead**.

The Tongue

3 My brothers, not many of you should become **teachers**. As you know, we **teachers** will be **judged** with greater strictness than others. 2 All of us often make **mistakes**. But if a person never makes a **mistake** in what he says, he is **perfect** and is also able to **control** his whole **being**. 3 We put a bit into the mouth of a horse to make it **obey** us, and we are able to make it go where we want. 4 Or think of a ship: big as it is and driven by such **strong** winds, it can be steered by a very small rudder, and it goes wherever the pilot wants it to go. 5 So it is with the tongue: small as it is, it can **boast** about great things.

Just think how large a forest can be set on fire by a tiny flame! 6 And the tongue is like a fire. It is a **world** of **wrong**, occupying its place in our **bodies** and spreading **evil** through our whole **being**. It sets on fire the entire course of our **existence** with the fire that comes to it from **hell** itself. 7 Man is able to tame and has tamed all other **creatures**—wild animals and birds, reptiles and fish. 8 But no one has ever been able to tame the tongue. It is **evil** and **uncontrollable**, full of **deadly** poison. 9 We use it to give **thanks** to our Lord and **Father** and also to **curse** our fellow-man, who is **created** in the likeness of God. 10 **Words** of **thanksgiving** and **cursing** pour out from the same mouth. My brothers, this should not happen! 11 No spring of water pours out sweet water and **bitter** water from the same opening. 12 A fig-tree, my brothers, cannot bear olives; a **grapevine** cannot bear figs, nor can a salty spring produce sweet water.

The Wisdom from Above

13 Is there anyone among you who is **wise** and **understanding**? He is to **prove** it by his good **life**, by his good **deeds** performed with **humility** and **wisdom**. 14 But if in your **heart** you are **jealous**, **bitter**, and **selfish**, don't sin against the **truth** by **boasting** of your **wisdom**. 15 Such **wisdom** does not come down from **heaven**; it belongs to the **world**, it is **unspiritual** and **demonic**. 16 Where there is **jealousy** and **selfishness**, there is also disorder and every kind of **evil**. 17 But the **wisdom** from **above** is **pure** first of all; it is also **peaceful**, **gentle**, and **friendly**; it is full of **compassion** and produces a **harvest** of good **deeds**; it is **free** from prejudice and **hypocrisy**. 18 And goodness is the **harvest** that is produced from the **seeds** the **peace**makers plant in peace.

Friendship with the World

4 Where do all the fights and **quarrels** among you come from? They come from your **desires** for **pleasure**, which are **constantly** fighting within you. 2 You want things, but you cannot have them, so you are ready to kill; you **strongly desire** things, but you cannot get them, so you **quarrel** and fight. You do not have what you want because you do not ask God for it. 3 And when you ask, you do not receive it, because your **motives** are **bad**; you ask for things to use for your own **pleasures**. 4 **Unfaithful** people! Don't you know that to be the **world's friend** means to be God's **enemy**? Whoever wants to be the **world's friend** makes himself God's **enemy**. 5 Don't think that there is no **truth** in the **scripture** that says, "The **spirit** that God placed in us is filled with fierce **desires**."[b] 6 But the **grace** that God gives is even **stronger**. As the **scripture** says, "God **resists** the **proud**, but gives **grace** to the **humble**."

7 So then, **submit** to God. **Resist** the **Devil**, and he will run away from you. 8 Come near to God, and he will come near to you. Wash your hands, you sinners! **Purify** your **hearts**, you **hypocrites**! 9 Be **sorrowful**, cry, and **weep**; **change** your laughter into crying, your **joy** into **gloom**! 10 **Humble** yourselves before the Lord, and he will lift you up.

Warning against Judging a Christian Brother

11 Do not **criticize one another**, my brothers. Whoever **criticizes** a **Christian brother** or **judges** him, **criticizes** the **Law** and **judges** it. If you **judge** the **Law**, then you are no longer one who **obeys** the **Law**, but one who **judges** it. 12 God is the only lawgiver and **judge**. He **alone** can **save** and **destroy**. Who do you think you are, to **judge** your fellow-man?

Warning against Boasting

13 Now listen to me, you that say, "Today or tomorrow we will travel to a certain city, where we will stay a year and go into business and make a lot of money." 14 You don't even know what your **life** tomorrow will be! You are like

[b] The spirit...fierce desires; *or* God yearns jealously over the spirit that he placed in us.

3.9: Gen 1.26 **4.6:** Prov 3.34 (LXX) **4.13-14:** Prov 27.1

above Phil 3.14; 2 Pet 2.10
being [2] 1.18; 2 Pet 2.10
bitter [2] Heb 12.15; Rev 5.4
boast [2] 2 Tim 3.2; 4.16
body 2.26; 1 Pet 2.11
compassion Col 3.12; 5.11
control [2] 1.26; 1 Pet 4.2
create 2.4; 1 Pet 1.20
creature 1.18; Rev 4.6
curse [2] Heb 6.8; 1 Pet 3.9
deadly 2 Cor 2.16
deed (2) [2] Heb 10.17; 1 Pet 2.12
demon 2.19; Rev 9.20
evil [3] 2.4; 1 Pet 2.1
exist Heb 11.6; 1 Pet 3.19
Father (2) (God) 1.27; 1 Pet 1.2
free 2.12; 1 Pet 1.18
friend 2.23; 4.4
gentle Heb 5.2; 1 Pet 3.4
grapevine *see* **vine**
harvest [2] 2 Tim 2.6; Rev 14.15
heart 1.21; 4.8
heaven 1.17; 5.12
hell 2 Thes 2.3; 2 Pet 2.4
humble Heb 5.7; 4.6
hypocrite Lk 13.15; 4.8
jealous [2] 1 Tim 6.4; 1 Pet 2.1
judge 2.4; 4.11
life (1) 2.16; 4.14
mistake [2] Heb 5.2
obey 2.8; 4.11
peace [2] Heb 13.20; 1 Pet 1.2
perfect 2.22; 1 Pet 5.10
prove 2.14; 1 Pet 1.7
pure 1.27; 4.8
seed 2 Cor 9.6
selfish [2] 2 Tim 3.2
spiritual Heb 12.9; 1 Pet 2.2
strong Heb 11.34; 4.2
teacher [2] Heb 5.12; 2 Pet 2.1
thank [2] Heb 12.28; 1 Pet 1.3
truth 1.18; 4.5
understand Heb 11.3; 1 Pet 1.12
vine Jn 15.1; Rev 14.19
wisdom [4] 1.5; 2 Pet 3.15
wise Col 4.5
word (1) 1.18; 1 Pet 1.8
world [2] 2.5; 4.4
wrong Heb 9.15; 4.16

alone 2.17; Rev 15.4
bad Tit 2.8; 3 Jn 11
boast [2] 3.5; Jude 16
change 1.17
Christian 1.9; 1 Pet 4.16
constant 1 Tim 6.5
criticize [3] Tit 2.8
desire [3] 1.14; 1 Pet 1.14
destroy 1.11; 1 Pet 1.7
Devil Heb 2.14; 1 Pet 5.8
enemy [2] Heb 10.13; 1 Pet 5.8
friend [2] 3.17; 1 Pet 2.11
gloom Heb 12.18
grace [2] 1.5; 1 Pet 1.2
guilty 2.4; 1 Jn 3.4
heart 3.14; 1 Pet 1.22
humble [2] 3.13; 1 Pet 3.8
hypocrite 3.17; 1 Pet 2.1
joy Heb 12.2; 1 Pet 1.8
judge [6] 3.1; 5.9
law [3] 2.8; 1 Jn 3.4
life (1) 3.13; 5.5
motive 2.4
obey 3.3; 1 Pet 1.2
one another Heb 13.1; 5.9
pleasure [2] Tit 3.3; 5.5
proud [2] 2 Tim 3.4; 1 Pet 5.5
pure 3.17; 1 Pet 1.2
quarrel [2] Tit 3.9; Jude 9
resist [2] Heb 12.4; 5.6
save 2.14; 5.20
scripture [2] 2.8; 1 Pet 1.16
sorrow 1 Tim 6.10
spirit (2) 2.26; 1 Pet 3.4
strong [2] 3.4; 2 Pet 2.11
submit 1.21; 1 Pet 2.13
truth 3.14; 5.19
unfaithful Mt 19.9
weep 2 Cor 12.21; 5.1
world [2] 3.6; 1 Pet 1.20
wrong 3.6; 5.20

a puff of smoke, which appears for a moment and then disappears. [15] What you should say is this: "If the Lord is willing, we will live and do this or that." [16] But now you are proud, and you boast; all such boasting is wrong.

17 So then, the person who does not do the good he knows he should do is guilty of sin.

Warning to the Rich

5 And now, you rich people, listen to me! Weep and wail over the miseries that are coming upon you! [2] Your riches have rotted away, and your clothes have been eaten by moths. [3] Your gold and silver are covered with rust, and this rust will be a witness against you and will eat up your flesh like fire. You have piled up riches in these last days. [4] You have not paid any wages to the men who work in your fields. Listen to their complaints! The cries of those who gather in your crops have reached the ears of God, the Lord Almighty. [5] Your life here on earth has been full of luxury and pleasure. You have made yourselves fat for the day of slaughter. [6] You have condemned and murdered innocent people, and they do not resist you. [c]

Patience and Prayer

7 Be patient, then, my brothers, until the Lord comes. See how patient a farmer is as he waits for his land to produce precious crops. He waits patiently for the autumn and spring rains. [8] You also must be patient. Keep your hopes high, for the day of the Lord's coming is near.

9 Do not complain against one another, my brothers, so that God will not judge you. The Judge is near, ready to appear. [10] My brothers, remember the prophets who spoke in the name of the Lord. Take them as examples of patient endurance under suffering. [11] We call them happy because they endured. You have heard of Job's patience, and you know how the Lord provided for him in the end. For the Lord is full of mercy and compassion.

12 Above all, my brothers, do not use an oath when you make a promise. Do not swear by heaven or by earth or by anything else. Say only "Yes" when you mean yes, and "No" when you mean no, and then you will not come under God's judgement.

13 Is anyone among you in trouble? He should pray. Is anyone happy? He should sing praises. [14] Is there anyone who is ill? He should send for the church elders, who will pray for him and rub olive-oil on him in the name of the Lord. [15] This prayer made in faith will heal the sick person; the Lord will restore him to health, and the sins he has committed will be forgiven. [16] So then, confess your sins to one another and pray for one another, so that you will be healed. The prayer of a good person has a powerful effect. [17] Elijah was the same kind of person as we are. He prayed earnestly that there would be no rain, and no rain fell on the land for three and a half years. [18] Once again he prayed, and the sky poured out its rain and the earth produced its crops.

19 My brothers, if one of you wanders away from the truth and another one brings him back again, [20] remember this: whoever turns a sinner back from his wrong way will save that sinner's soul [d] from death and bring about the forgiveness of many sins.

[c] people, and they do not resist you; *or* people. Will God not resist you?
[d] that sinner's soul; *or* his own soul.

5.2-3: Mt 6.19 **5.4:** Deut 24.14-15 **5.11:** Job 1.21-22, 2.10; Ps 103.8 **5.12:** Mt 5.34-37 **5.14:** Mk 6.13
5.17: 1 Kgs 17.1, 18.1 **5.18:** 1 Kgs 18.42-45 **5.20:** Prov 10.12; 1 Pet 4.8

Almighty 2 Cor 6.18; Rev 1.8
church Phlm 2; 1 Pet 5.1
commit 2.11; 1 Pet 2.22
compassion 3.17
complain [2] Col 3.13; 1 Pet 4.9
condemn 2.9; 2 Pet 2.6
confess Heb 13.15; 1 Jn 1.9
death (2) (from death) Heb 13.20; 1 Pet 1.3
earnest Heb 13.19; 1 Pet 1.22
elder (2) Tit 1.5; 1 Pet 5.1
endure [2] 1.3; 1 Pet 1.7
example Tit 2.7; 1 Pet 2.21
faith 2.5; 1 Pet 1.5
flesh Heb 2.14; Rev 17.16
forgive [2] Heb 10.18; 1 Jn 1.9
happy [2] 1.12; 1 Pet 3.14
heal [2] Heb 12.13; 1 Pet 2.24
heaven 3.15; 1 Pet 1.4
hope Heb 11.1; 1 Pet 1.3
innocent Phil 2.15
judge [3] 4.11; 1 Pet 1.17
last (2) Heb 1.2; 1 Pet 1.20
life (1) 4.14; 1 Pet 1.3
luxury Lk 16.19; Rev 18.7
mercy 2.13; 1 Pet 1.3

misery Ezek 23.33; Rev 3.17
name (2) (name of God, of Jesus) [2] Heb 1.4; 1 Pet 4.16
oath Lk 1.73
one another [2] 4.11; 1 Pet 1.22
patient [6] Heb 13.22; 1 Pet 3.20
pleasure 4.1; 2 Pet 2.13
power Heb 7.16; 1 Pet 1.5
praise Heb 13.15; 1 Pet 1.7
pray [5] 1.5; 1 Pet 1.17
prayer [2] Heb 5.7; 1 Pet 3.7
promise 2.5; 1 Pet 3.9
prophet Heb 11.32; 1 Pet 1.10
provide Heb 13.20; 2 Pet 1.15
remember [2] 1.19; 2 Pet 1.15
resist 4.6; 1 Pet 5.5
restore Acts 15.16
rich 2.2; 1 Pet 1.4
riches [2] 1 Tim 6.17
save 4.12; 1 Pet 2.2
slaughter Rom 8.36
soul Heb 13.17; 1 Pet 1.9
suffer 1.27; 1 Pet 1.6
swear Mk 14.71
trouble Heb 12.15; Rev 2.9
truth 4.5; 1 Pet 1.22
turn 1.17; 1 Pet 2.7
wage Rom 6.23; Rev 6.6
wail Lk 23.27
weep 4.9; Rev 18.9
witness Heb 12.1; 1 Pet 5.1
wrong 4.16; 1 Pet 2.20

THE FIRST LETTER FROM PETER

INTRODUCTION

The First Letter from Peter was addressed to Christians, here called "God's chosen people," who were scattered throughout the northern part of Asia Minor. The main purpose of the letter is to encourage the readers, who were facing persecution and suffering for their faith. The writer does this by reminding his readers of the Good News about Jesus Christ, whose death, resurrection, and promised coming give them hope. In the light of this they are to accept and endure their suffering, confident that it is a test of the genuineness of their faith and that they will be rewarded on "the Day when Jesus Christ is revealed."

Along with his encouragement in time of trouble, the writer also urges his readers to live as people who belong to Christ.

Outline of Contents

Introduction 1.1-2
Reminder of God's salvation 1.3-12
Exhortation to holy living 1.13—2.10
The Christian's responsibilities in time of suffering 2.11—4.19
Christian humility and service 5.1-11
Conclusion 5.12-14

---

action Jas 2.14; 4.19
alert Col 4.2; 4.7
angel Heb 13.2; 3.22
announce Heb 2.3; 1 Jn 1.3
apostle Tit 1.1; 2 Pet 1.1
believe [2] Jas 2.19; 2.6
believer Jas 2.1; 2.17
benefit 1 Tim 6.2
bless [2] Jas 2.16; 2.19
blood Heb 13.11; 1 Jn 1.7
choose [3] Jas 2.5; 2.4
Christ [3] Heb 13.20; 2.21
create Jas 3.9; 2 Pet 3.4
Day of the Lord Heb 10.25; 2.12
death (2) (from death) [2] Jas 5.20; Rev 1.5
desire Jas 4.1; 4.2
destroy [2] Jas 4.12; 2 Pet 1.4
earnest Jas 5.17; 4.8
endure [2] Jas 5.10; 2.19
eternal Heb 13.20; 5.10
faith [5] Jas 5.15; 5.9
Father (2) (God) [3] Jas 3.9; 2 Pet 1.17
free Jas 3.17; 2.16
gift Jas 1.17; 3.7
glad Jas 1.9; 4.13
glory [5] Jas 2.1; 4.11
God's people [2] Jas 1.1; 2.9
Good News [2] Heb 4.2; 4.6
grace Jas 4.6; 5.10
heart Jas 4.8; 3.11
heaven [2] Jas 5.12; 3.22

1 From Peter, **apostle** of Jesus
Christ—
To God's **chosen people** who live as
refugees scattered throughout the provinces of Pontus, Galatia, Cappadocia,
Asia, and Bithynia. 2 You were **chosen**
according to the **purpose** of God the
Father and were made a **holy** people by
his **Spirit**, to **obey** Jesus Christ and be
purified by his **blood**.
May **grace** and **peace** be yours in full
measure.

A Living Hope

3 Let us give **thanks** to the God and
Father of our Lord Jesus **Christ**! Because
of his great **mercy** he gave us **new life** by
raising Jesus Christ **from death**. This fills
us with a living **hope**, 4 and so we look forward to **possessing** the **rich blessings** that
God keeps for **his people**. He keeps them
for you in **heaven**, where they cannot
decay or spoil or fade away. 5 They are
for you, who through **faith** are kept **safe**
by **God's power** for the **salvation** which is
ready to be **revealed** at the end of time.
6 Be **glad** about this, even though it
may now be necessary for you to be **sad**
for a while because of the many kinds of
trials you **suffer**. 7 Their **purpose** is to
prove that your **faith** is genuine. Even
gold, which can be **destroyed**, is **tested** by
fire; and so your **faith**, which is much
more precious than gold, must also be
tested, so that it may **endure**. Then you
will receive **praise** and **glory** and **honour**
on the **Day** when Jesus Christ is **revealed**.
8 You **love** him, although you have not
seen him, and you **believe** in him, although you do not now see him. So you
rejoice with a great and **glorious joy**
which **words** cannot express, 9 because
you are receiving the **salvation** of your
souls, which is the **purpose** of your **faith**
in him.
10 It was concerning this **salvation**
that the **prophets** made careful search
and investigation, and they **prophesied**
about this **gift** which God would give you.
11 They tried to find out when the time
would be and how it would come.[a] This
was the time to which **Christ's Spirit** in
them was pointing, in **predicting** the
sufferings that **Christ** would have to **endure** and the **glory** that would follow.
12 God **revealed** to these **prophets** that
their work was not for their own **benefit**,
but for yours, as they spoke about those
things which you have now heard from
the messengers who **announced** the **Good
News** by the **power of the Holy Spirit** sent
from **heaven**. These are things which
even the **angels** would like to **understand**.

A Call to Holy Living

13 So then, have your **minds** ready for

holy [4] Heb 12.10; 2.5
honour Heb 13.4; 2.17
hope [3] Jas 5.8; 2.23
ignorant Heb 5.2; 2.15
immortal 2 Tim 1.10
joy Jas 4.9; 4.13
judge Jas 5.9; 2.23
lamb 1 Cor 5.7; Rev 5.6
last (2) Jas 5.3; 2 Pet 3.3
life (1) [4] Jas 5.5; 3.7
love [3] Jas 2.5; 2.17
mankind Heb 12.23; Rev 9.15
mercy Jas 5.11; 2.10
mind (1) Jas 1.7; 2 Pet 3.1
mortal Phil 3.21; 2 Pet 1.14
new Heb 12.24; 2 Pet 3.13
obey [3] Jas 4.11; 3.6
one another Jas 5.9; 3.8
peace Jas 3.17; 3.11
possess Jas 2.5
power [2] Jas 5.16; 3.22
praise Jas 5.13; 2.12
pray Jas 5.13; 4.7
predict Gal 3.8; Jude 1.4
proclaim Heb 9.19; 2.9
prophecy 1 Tim 1.18; 2 Pet 1.20
prophet [2] Jas 5.10; 2 Pet 1.19
prove Jas 3.13
pure [2] Jas 4.8; 2.2
purpose [3] Jas 1.20; 2 Pet 3.5
raise [2] Heb 13.20; Rev 1.5

[a] when the time would be and how it would come; *or* who the person would be and when he would come.

action. Keep **alert** and set your **hope**
completely on the **blessing** which will be
given you when Jesus Christ is **revealed**.
14 Be **obedient** to God, and do not allow
your **lives** to be shaped by those **desires**
you had when you were still **ignorant**.
15 Instead, be **holy** in all that you do, just
as God who called you is **holy**. 16 The
scripture says, "Be **holy** because I am
holy."
17 You call him **Father**, when you
pray to God, who **judges** all people by the
same standard, according to what each
one has done; so then, spend the rest of
your **lives** here on earth in **reverence** for
him. 18 For you know what was paid to **set
you free** from the **worthless** manner of
life handed down by your ancestors. It
was not something that can be **destroyed**,
such as silver or gold; 19 it was the costly
sacrifice of Christ, who was like a **lamb**
without defect or flaw. 20 He had been
chosen by God before the **creation** of the
world and was **revealed** in these **last
days** for your **sake**. 21 Through him you
believe in God, who **raised** him **from
death** and gave him **glory**; and so your
faith and **hope** are fixed on God.
22 Now that by your **obedience** to the
truth you have **purified** yourselves and
have come to have a **sincere love** for
your **fellow-believers**, **love one another
earnestly with all your heart**.[b] 23 For
through the living and **eternal word of**
God you have been born again as the
children of a parent who is **immortal**, not
mortal. 24 As the **scripture** says,
"All **mankind** are like grass,
and all their **glory** is like wild
flowers.
The grass withers, and the flowers fall,
25 but the **word of the Lord** remains for
ever."
This **word** is the **Good News** that was
proclaimed to you.

The Living Stone and the Holy Nation

2 Rid yourselves, then, of all **evil**; no
more **lying** or **hypocrisy** or **jealousy**
or **insulting** language. 2 Be like new-born
babies, always thirsty for the **pure spiritual** milk, so that by drinking it you may
grow up and be **saved**. 3 As the **scripture**
says, "You have found out for yourselves
how **kind** the Lord is."
4 Come to the Lord, the living stone
rejected by man as **worthless** but **chosen**
by God as **valuable**. 5 Come as living
stones, and let yourselves be used in
building the **spiritual temple**, where you
will **serve** as **holy priests** to **offer spiritual**
and **acceptable sacrifices** to God through
Jesus Christ. 6 For the **scripture** says,
"I **chose** a **valuable** stone,
which I am placing as the
cornerstone in Zion;
and whoever **believes** in him will
never be **disappointed**."
7 This stone is of great **value** for you that
believe; but for those who do not **believe**:
"The stone which the builders **rejected**
as **worthless**
turned out to be the most **important**
of all."
8 And another **scripture** says,
"This is the stone that will make
people **stumble**,
the rock that will make them fall."
They **stumbled** because they did not
believe in the **word**; such was **God's will**
for them.
9 But you are the **chosen race**, the
King's **priests**, the **holy** nation, **God's own
people**, **chosen** to **proclaim** the **wonderful
acts** of God, who called you out of **darkness** into his own marvellous **light**. 10 At
one time you were not God's people, but
now you are **his people**; at one time you
did not know God's **mercy**, but now you
have received his mercy.

Slaves of God

11 I appeal to you, my **friends**, as
strangers and **refugees in this world**! Do
not give in to **bodily passions**, which are
always at war against the **soul**. 12 Your
conduct among the **heathen** should be so
good that when they **accuse** you of being
evildoers, they will have to recognize
your good **deeds** and so **praise** God on the
Day of his coming.
13 For the **sake** of the Lord **submit** to
every **human authority**: to the Emperor,
who is the **supreme authority**, 14 and to
the governors, who have been appointed
by him to **punish** the **evildoers** and to
praise those who do good. 15 For God
wants you to silence the **ignorant** talk of
foolish people by the good things you do.
16 Live as **free** people; do not, however,
use your **freedom** to cover up any **evil**,
but live as God's **slaves**. 17 **Respect** everyone, **love** your **fellow-believers**, **honour**
God, and **respect** the Emperor.

The Example of Christ's Suffering

18 You servants must **submit** to your
masters and show them **complete respect**, not only to those who are **kind** and
considerate, but also to those who are

[b] with all your heart; *some manuscripts have* with a pure heart.

1.16: Lev 11.44–45, 19.2 **1.24–25:** Is 40.6–8 (LXX) **2.3:** Ps 34.8 **2.6:** Is 28.16 (LXX) **2.7:** Ps 118.22
2.8: Is 8.14–15 **2.9:** Ex 19.5–6; Is 43.20, 21 (LXX); Deut 4.20, 7.6, 14.2; Tit 2.14; Is 9.2 **2.10:** Hos 2.23

stumble [2] Rom 14.13
submit [2] Jas 4.7; 3.1
suffer [4] 1.6; 3.14
supreme Heb 1.3; 2 Pet 1.17
Temple (1) (of God) Heb 6.19; Rev 3.12
threat Eph 6.9
turn Jas 5.20; 3.11
value [3] 1 Tim 4.8; 3.4
will (1) [2] Jas 1.18; 3.17
wonder (1) Heb 2.4; Rev 15.3
word (1) 1.8; 3.1
world 1.20; 5.9
worthless [2] 1.18
wrong Jas 5.20; 2 Pet 2.15

harsh. [19]God will **bless** you for this, if you **endure** the **pain** of **undeserved suffering** because you are conscious of his **will**. [20]For what credit is there if you **endure** the beatings you **deserve** for having done **wrong**? But if you **endure suffering** even when you have done **right**, God will **bless** you for it. [21]It was to this that God called you, for **Christ** himself **suffered** for you and left you an **example**, so that you would follow in his steps. [22]He **committed** no sin, and no one ever heard a **lie** come from his lips. [23]When he was insulted, he did not answer back with an **insult**; when he **suffered**, he did not **threaten**, but placed his **hopes** in God, the **righteous Judge**. [24]**Christ** himself carried our sins in his **body** to the **cross**, so that we might die to sin and live for **righteousness**. It is by his wounds that you have been **healed**. [25]You were like **sheep** that had lost their way, but now you have been brought back to follow the **Shepherd** and Keeper of your **souls**.

Wives and Husbands

3 In the same way you wives must **submit** to your husbands, so that if any of them do not **believe God's word**, your **conduct** will **win** them over to **believe**. It will not be necessary for you to say a **word**, [2]because they will see how **pure** and **reverent** your **conduct** is. [3]You should not use outward aids to make yourselves beautiful, such as the way you do your hair, or the jewellery you put on, or the dresses you wear. [4]Instead, your beauty should consist of your **true** inner **self**, the ageless beauty of a **gentle** and quiet **spirit**, which is of the greatest **value** in God's **sight**. [5]For the devout women of the past who placed their **hope** in God used to make themselves beautiful by **submitting** to their husbands. [6]Sarah was like that; she **obeyed** Abraham and called him her **master**. You are now her daughters if you do good and are not **afraid** of anything.

7 In the same way you husbands must live with your wives with the **proper understanding** that they are the **weaker sex**. Treat them with **respect**, because they also will receive, together with you, God's **gift** of **life**. Do this so that nothing will interfere with your **prayers**.

Suffering for Doing Right

8 To conclude: you must all have the same attitude and the same feelings; **love one another** as brothers, and be **kind** and **humble** with **one another**. [9]Do not pay back **evil** with evil or **cursing** with cursing; instead, pay back with a **blessing**, because a **blessing** is what God **promised** to give you when he called you. [10]As the **scripture** says,

"Whoever wants to **enjoy life**
and **wishes** to see good times,
must **keep from** speaking **evil**
and stop telling **lies**.
[11]He must **turn away from evil** and do good;
he must strive for **peace with all his heart**.
[12]For the Lord **watches** over the **righteous**
and listens to their **prayers**;
but he opposes those who do **evil**."

13 Who will **harm** you if you are **eager** to do what is good? [14]But even if you should **suffer** for doing what is **right**, how **happy** you are! Do not be **afraid** of anyone, and do not **worry**. [15]But have **reverence** for **Christ** in your **hearts**, and **honour** him as Lord. Be ready at all times to answer anyone who asks you to explain the **hope** you have in you, [16]but do it with **gentleness** and **respect**. Keep your **conscience clear**, so that when you are **insulted**, those who speak **evil** of your good **conduct** as **followers of Christ** will be **ashamed** of what they say. [17]For it is better to **suffer** for doing good, if this should be **God's will**, than for doing **evil**. [18]For **Christ** died[c] for sins once and for all, a good man on behalf of sinners, in order to lead you to God. He was put **to death physically**, but made **alive spiritually**, [19]and in his **spiritual existence** he went and **preached** to the **imprisoned spirits**. [20]These were the **spirits** of those who had not **obeyed** God when he waited **patiently** during the days that Noah was building his boat. The few people in the boat—eight in all—were **saved** by the water, [21]which was a **symbol** pointing to **baptism**, which now **saves** you. It is not the washing away of **bodily** dirt, but the **promise** made to God from a good **conscience**. It **saves** you through the **resurrection** of Jesus Christ, [22]who has gone to **heaven** and is at the **right-hand side** of God, ruling over all **angels** and **heavenly authorities** and **powers**.

afraid [2] Heb 13.6; 1 Jn 4.18
alive Heb 9.17; 2 Pet 1.13
angel 1.12; 2 Pet 2.4
ashamed Heb 11.16; 4.16
authorities Tit 3.1
baptize Heb 6.2; 1 Jn 5.6
believe [2] 2.6; 4.17
bless [2] 2.19; Rev 20.6
body 2.11; 2 Pet 1.14
Christ [3] 2.21; 4.1
clear Heb 13.18; 1 Jn 2.19
conduct [3] 2.12; 2 Pet 2.7
conscience [2] Heb 13.18; 1 Jn 3.20
curse Jas 3.9; 2 Pet 2.14
death (3) (to death) Heb 12.20; Rev 13.15
eager Heb 6.11
enjoy Heb 11.25; 2 Pet 2.13
evil [6] 2.1; 2 Pet 2.2
exist Jas 3.6; 4.6
follower Eph 4.21; 4.14
gentle [2] Jas 3.17
gift 1.10; 4.10
happy Jas 5.11; 4.14
harm 2 Tim 4.14; 1 Jn 5.18
heart [2] 1.22; 2 Pet 1.19
heaven [2] 1.4; 2 Pet 1.18
honour 2.17; 2 Pet 1.17
hope [2] 2.23; 1 Jn 3.3
humble Jas 4.6; 5.5
insult 2.1; 4.4
keep from Jas 1.27; Jude 24
kind 2.3

lie (2) 2.1; 1 Jn 1.6
life (1) [2] 1.3; 4.2
love 2.17; 4.8
master 2.18; 2 Pet 2.1
obey [2] 1.2; 1 Jn 2.3
one another [2] 1.22; 4.8
patient Jas 5.7; 2 Pet 3.9
peace 1.2; 5.14
physical 1 Tim 4.8; 4.1
power 1.5; 4.11
prayer [2] Jas 5.15; Rev 5.8
preach 2 Tim 4.2; 4.6
prison Heb 13.3; Rev 2.10
promise [2] Jas 5.12; 4.19
proper 1 Tim 2.2; Jude 6
pure 2.2; 2 Pet 1.9
respect [2] 2.17; 2 Pet 2.10
resurrection Heb 6.2
reverence [2] 1.17; Rev 11.18
right (1) 2.20; 2 Pet 1.13
right (2) Heb 12.2; Rev 1.16
righteous 2.23; 2 Pet 1.1
save [3] 2.2; 4.18
scripture 2.3; 4.18
self Phlm 19; 1 Jn 2.16
sex 1 Tim 1.10; Jude 7
sight Heb 12.21; 2 Pet 1.9
spirit (2) [3] Jas 4.5; 1 Jn 4.1
spiritual [2] 2.2; 4.6
submit [2] 2.13; 5.5
suffer [2] 2.19; 4.1
symbol Jer 17.2; Rev 11.8
true Jas 2.23; 5.12
turn 2.7; 2 Pet 2.21
understand 1.12; 2 Pet 2.12
value 2.4
watch Heb 13.17; 5.8
weak Heb 11.34; 2 Pet 2.14
will (1) 2.8; 4.2
win Heb 11.2; 1 Jn 5.4
wish Col 4.15; 2 Jn 11
word (1) [2] 2.8; 2 Pet 3.2
worry Phil 4.6; 5.7

[c] died; *many manuscripts have* suffered.

2.22: Is 53.9 **2.23:** Is 53.7 **2.24:** Is 53.5 **2.25:** Is 53.6 **3.1:** Eph 5.22; Col 3.18 **3.3:** 1 Tim 2.9 **3.6:** Gen 18.12 **3.7:** Eph 5.25; Col 3.19 **3.10–12:** Ps 34.12–16 (LXX) **3.14–15:** Mt 5.10; Is 8.12–13 **3.20:** Gen 6.1—7.24

Changed Lives

4 Since **Christ suffered physically**, you
too must **strengthen** yourselves with
the same way of thinking that he had;
because whoever **suffers physically** is no
longer involved with sin. 2 From now on,
then, you must live the rest of your
earthly **lives controlled** by **God's will** and
not by **human desires**. 3 You have spent
enough time in the past doing what the
heathen like to do. Your **lives** were spent
in indecency, **lust**, drunkenness, orgies,
drinking parties, and the **disgusting wor-**
ship of idols. 4 And now the **heathen** are
surprised when you do not join them in
the same wild and reckless living, and so
they **insult** you. 5 But they will have to
give an account of themselves to God,
who is ready to **judge** the living and the
dead. 6 That is why the **Good News** was
preached also to the **dead**, to those who
had been **judged** in their **physical exist-**
ence as everyone is **judged**; it was
preached to them so that in their
spiritual existence they may live as God
lives.

Good Managers of God's Gifts

7 The end of all things is near. You
must be **self-controlled** and **alert**, to be
able to **pray**. 8 Above everything, **love one**
another earnestly, because love covers
over many sins. 9 Open your homes to
each other without **complaining**. 10 Each
one, as a good manager of God's different **gifts**, must use for the good of others
the **special gift** he has received from
God. 11 Whoever **preaches** must preach
God's **messages**; whoever serves must
serve with the **strength** that God gives
him, so that in all things **praise** may be
given to God through Jesus Christ, to
whom belong **glory** and **power** for ever
and ever. Amen.

Suffering as a Christian

12 My **dear friends**, do not be surprised at the **painful test** you are **suffer-**
ing, as though something unusual were
happening to you. 13 Rather be **glad** that
you are **sharing Christ's sufferings**, so
that you may be full of **joy** when his **glory**
is **revealed**. 14 **Happy** are you if you are
insulted because you are **Christ's**
followers; this means that the **glorious**
Spirit, the **Spirit of God**, is resting on you.
15 If any of you **suffers**, it must not be
because he is a murderer or a **thief** or a
criminal or a meddler in other people's
affairs. 16 However, if you **suffer** because
you are a **Christian**, don't be **ashamed** of
it, but **thank** God that you bear **Christ's**
name.
17 The time has come for **judgement**
to begin, and **God's own people** are the
first to be **judged**. If it starts with us, how
will it end with those who do not **believe**
the **Good News** from God? 18 As the
scripture says,

"It is **difficult** for good people to be
saved;
what, then, will become of **godless**
sinners?"

19 So then, those who **suffer** because it is
God's will for them, should by their good
actions trust themselves completely to
their **Creator**, who always keeps his
promise.

The Flock of God

5 I, who am an elder myself, appeal to
the **church elders** among you. I am
a **witness** of **Christ's sufferings**, and I will
share in the **glory** that will be **revealed**. I
appeal to you 2 to be **shepherds** of the
flock that God gave you and to take **care**
of it willingly, as God wants you to, and
not unwillingly. Do your work, not for
mere pay, but from a **real desire** to
serve. 3 Do not try to rule over those who
have been put in your **care**, but be
examples to the **flock**. 4 And when the
Chief **Shepherd** appears, you will receive
the **glorious crown** which will never lose
its brightness.
5 In the same way you younger men
must **submit** to the older men. And all of
you must put on the apron of **humility**, to
serve one another; for the **scripture** says,
"God **resists** the **proud**, but shows **favour**
to the **humble**." 6 **Humble** yourselves,
then, under God's **mighty** hand, so that
he will lift you up in his own good time.
7 Leave all your **worries** with him,
because he **cares** for you.
8 Be **alert**, be on the **watch**! Your
enemy, the **Devil**, roams round like a
roaring lion, looking for someone to
devour. 9 Be firm in your **faith** and **resist**
him, because you know that your **fellow-**
believers in all the **world** are going
through the same kind of **sufferings**.
10 But after you have **suffered** for a little
while, the God of all **grace**, who calls you
to **share** his **eternal glory** in **union with**
Christ, will himself **perfect** you and give
you firmness, **strength**, and a **sure** foundation. 11 To him be the **power** for ever!
Amen.

Final Greetings

12 I write you this brief **letter** with the

4.8: Prov 10.12 **4.18:** Prov 11.31 (LXX) **5.2:** Jn 21.15–17 **5.5:** Prov 3.34 (LXX) **5.6:** Mt 23.12; Lk 14.11, 18.14 **5.12:** Acts 15.22, 40

action 1.13; 2 Pet 2.8
alert 1.13; 5.8
ashamed 3.16; Rev 16.15
believe 3.1; 1 Jn 3.23
Christ [4] 3.15; 5.1
Christian Jas 4.11; 5.12
complain Jas 5.4
control Jas 3.2; 2 Pet 1.21
Creator Jas 1.17
crime 2 Tim 2.9
dead [2] Jas 2.17; Jude 12
dear Jas 2.5; 2 Pet 1.17
desire 1.14; 5.2
difficult 2 Tim 3.1; 2 Pet 3.16
disgust Hos 9.10
each other Heb 13.4; Rev 6.4
earnest 1.22; Rev 3.19
enough Jas 2.15; 3 Jn 10
exist [2] 3.19; 2 Pet 3.7
follower 3.16; Rev 1.9
friend 2.11; 2 Pet 3.1
gift [2] 3.7; 2 Pet 1.4
glad 1.6; Rev 12.12
glory [3] 1.7; 5.1
God's people 2.9; Jude 3
godless 1 Tim 4.7; 2 Pet 2.5
Good News [2] 1.12; Rev 14.6
happy 3.14; 2 Jn 4
heathen [2] 2.12; Rev 11.2
human 2.13; 2 Pet 2.16
idol 1 Thes 1.9; Rev 2.14
insult [2] 3.16; 2 Pet 2.10
joy 1.8; 1 Jn 1.4
judge [5] 2.23; 2 Pet 2.3
life (1) [2] 3.7; 2 Pet 1.3
love 3.8; 5.14
lust 1 Thes 4.5; 2 Pet 1.4
message Heb 13.7; 2 Pet 1.19
name (2) (name of God, of Jesus) Jas 5.10; Rev 3.12
one another 3.8; 5.5
pain 2.19; Rev 9.5
physical [3] 3.18
power 3.22; 5.11
praise 2.12; Rev 5.12
pray 1.17; 1 Jn 5.16
preach [3] 3.19; 2 Pet 2.5
promise 3.9; 2 Pet 1.4
reveal 1.5; 5.1
save 3.20; 2 Pet 2.5
scripture 3.10; 5.5
self-control Tit 2.2; 2 Pet 1.6
serve 2.5; 5.2
share Heb 13.13; 5.1
special Tit 3.8
Spirit (1) (God's Spirit) 1.2; 2 Pet 1.21
spiritual 3.18
strength [2] Heb 13.9; 5.10
suffer [7] 3.14; 5.1
test 1.7; 1 Jn 4.1
thank 1.3; Rev 4.9
thief 1 Thes 5.2; 2 Pet 3.10
trust Heb 11.11; Rev 21.5
will (1) [2] 3.17; 1 Jn 5.14
worship (2) (of other gods) 2 Thes 2.4; Rev 9.20

alert 4.7
believer 2.17
care [3] Jas 1.27; Jude 12
choose 2.4; 2 Pet 1.10
Christ [2] 4.1; 1 Jn 2.2
Christian [2] 4.16; 3 Jn 3
church [2] Jas 5.14; 3 Jn 6
crown Heb 2.7; Rev 4.4
desire 4.2; 1 Jn 2.16
Devil Jas 4.7; 1 Jn 3.8
devour Joel 1.4
elder (2) Jas 5.14; Rev 4.4
encourage Heb 13.22; Jude 3
enemy Jas 4.4; 1 Jn 2.18
eternal 1.23; 2 Pet 1.11
example 2.21; 2 Pet 2.6
faith 1.5; 2 Pet 1.1
faithful Jas 1.12; 3 Jn 3
favour Phlm 20; Rev 2.6
flock [2] Acts 20.28
glory [3] 4.11; 2 Pet 1.3
grace [2] 1.2; 2 Pet 1.2
help Jas 2.25; 3 Jn 6
humble [3] 3.8
kiss 1 Thes 5.26
letter (2) Heb 13.22; 2 Pet 3.1
love 4.8; 2 Pet 1.7
might Heb 11.34; 2 Pet 1.16
one another [2] 4.8; 1 Jn 1.7
peace 3.11; 2 Pet 1.2
perfect Jas 3.2; 1 Jn 2.5
power 4.11; 2 Pet 1.3
proud Jas 4.6; 2 Pet 2.18
real Heb 12.8; 1 Jn 2.8
resist [2] Jas 5.6
reveal 4.13; Rev 1.1
scripture 4.18; 2 Pet 1.20
serve [2] 4.11; Rev 1.6
share [2] 4.13; 2 Pet 1.3

shepherd [2] 2.25; Rev 7.17
strength 4.1; Rev 3.2
submit 3.1
suffer [3] 4.1; 2 Pet 2.8
sure Jas 1.4; 1 Jn 2.3
testimony 1 Tim 1.10; 1 Jn 5.8

help of Silas, whom I regard as a **faithful**
Christian brother. I want to **encourage**
you and give my **testimony** that this is
the **true grace** of God. Stand firm in it.
13 Your sister **church** in Babylon,[d]
also **chosen** by God, sends you greetings,
and so does my son Mark. 14 Greet **one**
another with the **kiss** of **Christian love**.

May **peace** be with all of you who belong to Christ.

[d] BABYLON: *As in the book of Revelation, this probably refers to Rome.*

5.13: Acts 12.12, 25, 13.13, 15.37–39; Col 4.10; Phlm 24

true 3.4; 2 Pet 1.3
union Phlm 6; 1 Jn 2.5
watch 3.12; Rev 11.12
witness Jas 5.3; 1 Jn 5.7
world 2.11; 2 Pet 1.4
worry 3.14

THE SECOND LETTER FROM PETER

INTRODUCTION

The Second Letter from Peter is addressed to a wide circle of early Christians. Its main concern is to combat the work of false teachers and the immorality which results from such teaching. The answer to these problems is found in holding to the true knowledge of God and of the Lord Jesus Christ, knowledge which has been conveyed by persons who themselves have seen Jesus and have heard him teach. The writer is especially concerned with the teaching of those who claim that Christ will not return again. He says that the apparent delay in Christ's return is due to the fact that God "does not want anyone to be destroyed, but wants all to turn away from their sins."

Outline of Contents

---

abandon Heb 13.5; Jude 6
abundant Tit 3.6
affection [2] 2 Cor 9.14
alive 1 Pet 3.18; Rev 1.18
apostle 1 Pet 1.1; 3.2
best [2] Jas 2.3; 3.12
body 1 Pet 3.21; 2.10
choose 1 Pet 5.13; Rev 17.14
confident Heb 4.16; 1 Jn 3.19
control 1 Pet 4.2; 3.3
dark 1 Pet 2.9; 2.4
Day of the Lord 1 Pet 2.12; 3.10
dear 1 Pet 4.12; 3.1
death (1) Jas 1.15; 1 Jn 3.14
depend Heb 12.2
destroy 1 Pet 1.7; 2.1
divine [2] Heb 12.25
endure [2] 1 Pet 2.19; Rev 1.9
escape Jas 2.25; 2.18
eternal 1 Pet 5.10; 1 Jn 1.2
experience Heb 6.5
faith [3] 1 Pet 5.9; 1 Jn 5.4
Father (2) (God) 1 Pet 1.2; 1 Jn 1.2
forget Jas 1.24; 3.8
gift [2] 1 Pet 4.10; Rev 22.17
glory [3] 1 Pet 5.1; 2.10
godly [2] Tit 2.12; 2.9
grace 1 Pet 5.10; 3.18
hard Heb 5.11; 1 Jn 5.3
heart 1 Pet 3.11; 2.14
heaven 1 Pet 3.22; 3.5
holy 1 Pet 2.5; 3.2
honour 1 Pet 3.15; Rev 4.9
Kingdom (1) (of God) Jas 2.5; Rev 1.6

1 From Simon Peter, a **servant** and
apostle of Jesus Christ—
To those who through the **righteousness** of our God and **Saviour** Jesus Christ
have been given a **faith** as precious as
ours:
2 May **grace** and **peace** be yours in full
measure through your **knowledge** of God
and of Jesus our Lord.

God's Call and Choice

3 **God's divine power** has given us
everything we **need** to live a **truly
religious life** through our **knowledge** of
the one who called us to **share** in his
own[a] **glory** and goodness. 4 In this way he
has given us the very great and precious
gifts he **promised**, so that **by means of**
these **gifts** you may **escape** from the **destructive lust** that is in the **world**, and may
come to **share** the **divine nature**. 5 For
this very **reason** do your **best** to add
goodness to your **faith**; to your goodness
add **knowledge**; 6 to your **knowledge** add
self-control; to your **self-control** add **endurance**; to your **endurance** add **godliness**; 7 to your **godliness** add brotherly
affection; and to your brotherly **affection**
add **love**. 8 These are the qualities you
need, and if you have them in **abundance**, they will make you active and
effective in your **knowledge** of our Lord
Jesus Christ. 9 But whoever does not have
them is so **short-sighted** that he cannot
see and has **forgotten** that he has been
purified from his past sins.
10 So then, my brothers, try even
harder to make God's call and his **choice**
of you a permanent **experience**; if you do
so, you will never **abandon** your **faith**.[b]
11 In this way you will be given the full
right to enter the **eternal Kingdom** of our
Lord and **Saviour** Jesus Christ.
12 And so I will always **remind** you of
these matters, even though you already
know them and are firmly grounded in
the **truth** you have received. 13 I think it
only **right** for me to stir up your memory
of these matters as long as I am still
alive. 14 I know that I shall soon put off
this **mortal body**, as our Lord Jesus Christ
plainly told me. 15 I will do my **best**, then,
to **provide** a way for you to **remember**
these matters at all times after my
death.

Eye-Witnesses of Christ's Glory

16 We have not **depended** on made-up
stories in making known to you the
mighty coming of our Lord Jesus Christ.
With our own eyes we saw his greatness.
17 We were there when he was given
honour and **glory** by God the **Father**,
when the voice came to him from the
Supreme Glory, saying, "This is my own
dear Son, with whom I am **pleased**!"
18 We ourselves heard this voice coming
from **heaven**, when we were with him on
the **holy** mountain.

knowledge [5] 1 Tim 6.20; 2.20
life (1) 1 Pet 4.2; 3.3
light (1) 1 Pet 2.9; 1 Jn 1.5
love 1 Pet 5.14; 2.15
lust 1 Pet 4.3; 2.10
means Heb 11.4; 1 Jn 2.2
message [3] 1 Pet 4.11; 1 Jn 1.5
might 1 Pet 5.6; 2.11
mortal 1 Pet 1.23
nature Heb 2.14; 1 Jn 3.9
need [2] Jas 2.15; 1 Jn 2.27
peace 1 Pet 5.14; 3.14
plain (1) Heb 12.27; Jude 7
please Heb 13.16; 1 Jn 3.22
power 1 Pet 5.11; 1 Jn 3.14
proclaim 1 Pet 2.9; Rev 1.9
promise 1 Pet 4.19; 2.19
prophecy 1 Pet 1.10; Jude 14
prophet [2] 1 Pet 1.10; 2.1
provide Jas 5.11; Rev 16.12
pure 1 Pet 3.2; 3.1
reason Heb 13.12; 1 Jn 3.8
religion Jas 1.26
remember [2] Jas 5.10; 3.2
remind Heb 10.3; 3.1
right (1) 1 Pet 3.14; 1 Jn 1.9
right (3) Heb 13.10; Rev 2.7
righteous 1 Pet 3.12; 2.5
Saviour [2] Tit 3.4; 2.20
scripture 1 Pet 5.5; 3.16

[a] to share in his own; *some manuscripts have* through his. [b] abandon your faith; *or* fall into sin.

1.17–18: Mt 17.1–5; Mk 9.2–7; Lk 9.28–35

19 So we are even more **confident** of
the **message proclaimed** by the **prophets**.
You will do well to pay attention to it,
because it is like a lamp shining in a **dark**
place until the **Day** dawns and the **light**
of the morning star shines in your **hearts**.
[20] Above all else, however, **remember**
that no one can explain by himself a **pro-**
phecy in the **Scriptures**. [21] For no **pro-**
phetic message ever came just from the
will of man, but men were under the **con-**
trol of the **Holy Spirit** as they spoke the
message that came from God.

False Teachers

2 **False prophets** appeared in the past
among the people, and in the same
way **false teachers** will appear among
you. They will bring in **destructive**, untrue **doctrines**, and will **deny** the **Master**
who **redeemed** them, and so they will
bring upon themselves sudden **destruc-**
tion. [2] Even so, many will follow their **im-**
moral ways; and because of what they
do, others will speak **evil** of the **Way** of
truth. [3] In their **greed** these **false teachers**
will make a profit out of telling you
made-up stories. For a long time now
their **Judge** has been ready, and their
Destroyer has been wide awake!
4 God did not **spare** the **angels** who
sinned, but threw them into **hell**, where
they are kept chained in **darkness**,[c] waiting for the **Day of Judgement**. [5] God did
not **spare** the **ancient world**, but brought
the **flood** on the **world** of **godless** people;
the only ones he **saved** were Noah, who
preached righteousness, and seven other
people. [6] God **condemned** the cities of
Sodom and Gomorrah, **destroying** them
with fire, and made them an **example** of
what will happen to the **godless**. [7] He
rescued Lot, a good man, who was **dis-**
tressed by the **immoral conduct** of lawless people. [8] That good man lived among
them, and day after day he **suffered**
agony as he saw and heard their **evil**
actions. [9] And so the Lord knows how to
rescue godly people from their **trials** and
how to keep the **wicked** under **punish-**
ment for the **Day of Judgement**, [10] especially those who follow their **filthy**
bodily lusts and **despise** God's **authority**.
These **false teachers** are **bold** and
arrogant, and show no **respect** for the
glorious beings above; instead, they **in-**
sult them. [11] Even the **angels**, who are so
much **stronger** and **mightier** than these
false teachers, do not **accuse** them with
insults in the **presence** of the Lord. [12] But
these men **act** by instinct, like wild animals born to be captured and killed; they
attack with **insults** anything they do not
understand. They will be **destroyed** like
wild animals, [13] and they will be paid with
suffering for the suffering they have
caused. **Pleasure** for them is to do anything in broad daylight that will **satisfy**
their **bodily** appetites; they are a **shame**
and a **disgrace** as they join you in your
meals, all the while **enjoying** their **deceit-**
ful ways! [14] They want to look at nothing
but **immoral** women; their appetite for
sin is never **satisfied**. They lead **weak**
people into a **trap**. Their **hearts** are
trained to be **greedy**. They are under
God's **curse**! [15] They have left the
straight path and have lost their way;
they have followed the path taken by
Balaam son of Beor, who **loved** the
money he would get for doing **wrong**
[16] and was **rebuked** for his sin. His donkey
spoke with a **human** voice and stopped
the **prophet's** insane **action**.
17 These men are like dried-up
springs, like **clouds** blown along by a
storm; God has reserved a place for
them in the deepest **darkness**. [18] They
make **proud** and **stupid** statements, and
use **immoral bodily lusts** to **trap** those
who are just beginning to **escape** from
among people who live in **error**. [19] They
promise them **freedom** while they themselves are **slaves** of **destructive** habits—
for a person is a **slave** of anything that
has **conquered** him. [20] If people have **es-**
caped from the **corrupting** forces of the
world through their **knowledge** of our
Lord and **Saviour** Jesus Christ, and then
are again caught and **conquered** by
them, such people are in a **worse** state at
the end than they were at the beginning.
[21] It would have been much better for
them never to have known the way of
righteousness than to know it and then
turn away from the **sacred command**
that was given them. [22] What happened to
them shows that the **proverbs** are **true**:
"A dog goes back to what it has vomited"
and "A pig that has been washed goes
back to roll in the mud."

The Promise of the Lord's Coming

3 My **dear friends**, this is now the
second **letter** I have written to you.
In both **letters** I have tried to arouse **pure**
thoughts in your **minds** by **reminding** you
of these things. [2] I want you to **remember**
the **words** that were spoken long ago by
the **holy prophets**, and the **command**
from the Lord and **Saviour** which was
given you by your **apostles**. [3] First of all,

[c] chained in darkness; *some manuscripts have* in dark pits.

2.5: Gen 6.1—7.24 **2.6:** Gen 19.24 **2.7:** Gen 19.1-16 **2.15-16:** Num 22.4-35 **2.22:** Prov 26:11
3.3: Jude 18

self-control [2] 1 Pet 4.7
servant 1 Pet 2.18; Jude 1
share [2] 1 Pet 5.1; 3 Jn 8
short-sighted *see* **sight**
sight 1 Pet 3.4; 3.8
Son of God Heb 10.29; 1 Jn 1.3
Spirit (1) (God's Spirit) 1 Pet 4.14; 1 Jn 2.20
supreme 1 Pet 2.13
true 1 Pet 5.12; 2.22
truth 1 Pet 1.22; 2.2
world 1 Pet 5.9; 2.5

above Jas 3.17; Jude 8
accuse 1 Pet 2.12; Rev 12.10
act 1 Pet 2.9; Jude 7
action [2] 1 Pet 4.19; 1 Jn 1.6
ancient Heb 11.2; Rev 12.9
angel [2] 1 Pet 3.22; Jude 6
arrogant Tit 1.7
authority 1 Pet 2.13; Jude 6
being Jas 3.2; 1 Jn 4.2
body [3] 1.14; 3.10
bold Heb 13.6
cloud 1 Thes 4.17; Jude 12
command Heb 9.20; 3.2
condemn Jas 5.6; 1 Jn 3.20
conduct 1 Pet 3.1
conquer [2] Rom 12.21; Rev 6.2
corrupt Jas 1.27; Rev 19.2
curse 1 Pet 3.9; Rev 13.6
dark [2] 1.19; 1 Jn 1.5
Day of Judgement [2] Acts 24.25; 1 Jn 4.17
deceive Jas 1.16; 1 Jn 1.8
deny Tit 1.16; 1 Jn 4.3
despise Heb 10.29; Jude 8
destroy [5] 1.4; 3.6
Destroyer Rev 9.11
disgrace Heb 12.2
distress 2 Cor 11.29
doctrine Tit 2.1
enjoy 1 Pet 3.10; Rev 14.13
error Tit 1.9; 3.17
escape [2] 1.4
evil [2] 1 Pet 3.9; 2 Jn 11
example 1 Pet 5.3
false [5] 2 Tim 2.13; 3.16
filthy Jas 1.21; Rev 17.4
flood 2 Cor 11.26; 3.6
free 1 Pet 2.16; Rev 1.5
glory 1.3; 3.18
godless [2] 1 Pet 4.18; 3.7
godly 1.6
greed [2] Tit 1.7
heart 1.19; 1 Jn 2.24
hell Jas 3.6

human 1 Pet 4.2; 1 Jn 4.2
immoral [4] Heb 13.4; Jude 4
insult [3] 1 Pet 4.4; Jude 8
judge 1 Pet 4.5; 3.7
knowledge 1.2; 3.18
love 1.7; 1 Jn 2.5
lust [2] 1.4; 3.3
master 1 Pet 3.6; Jude 4
might 1.16; Jude 25
pleasure Jas 5.5
preach 1 Pet 4.6
presence Heb 9.5; 1 Jn 3.19
promise 1.4; 3.4
prophet [2] 1.19; 3.2
proud 1 Pet 5.5; 1 Jn 2.16
proverb Lk 4.23
punish 1 Pet 2.14; 1 Jn 4.18
rebuke Heb 12.5; Jude 9
redeem 1 Tim 2.6; Rev 14.3
rescue [2] Tit 2.14; Jude 5
respect 1 Pet 3.7
righteous [2] 1.1; 3.13
sacred Col 3.16; Jude 20
satisfy [2] Heb 13.5
save 1 Pet 4.18; 3.15
Saviour 1.1; 3.2
shame Heb 13.13; 1 Jn 2.28
slave [2] 1 Pet 2.16; Rev 6.15
spare [2] Phil 2.27
strong Jas 4.2; 1 Jn 2.14
stupid Tit 3.9
suffer [2] 1 Pet 5.1; Jude 7
teacher [4] Jas 3.1
trap [2] Jas 1.14
true 1.3; 1 Jn 2.27
truth 1.12; 1 Jn 1.8
try (2) 1 Pet 1.6
turn 1 Pet 3.11; 3.9
understand 1 Pet 3.7; 3.3
Way (2) Acts 24.14
way (3) [2] 2 Cor 7.9; Jude 4
weak 1 Pet 3.7
wicked Jas 1.21; Rev 2.22
world [3] 1.4; 3.4
worse Heb 10.29
wrong 1 Pet 2.20; 1 Jn 1.9

apostle 1.1; Jude 17
best [2] 1.5; Jude 3
body [2] 2.10; Jude 8
command [3] 2.21; 1 Jn 2.3
control 1.21; Jude 19
create [2] 1 Pet 1.20; Rev 3.14
Day of the Lord [5] 1.19; 1 Jn 2.28
dear [3] 1.17; 1 Jn 2.7

dedicate 2 Tim 2.21
destroy [8] 2.1; 1 Jn 3.8
difficult 1 Pet 4.18
error 2.18; 1 Jn 4.6
exist 1 Pet 4.6; 1 Jn 1.1
false 2.1; 1 Jn 2.27
fault Heb 8.8; Jude 24
flood 2.5; Rev 12.15
forget 1.9
friend [4] 1 Pet 4.12; 1 Jn 2.7
glory 2.10; Jude 8
godless 2.5; Jude 4
grace 1.2; 2 Jn 3
heaven [7] 1.18; Rev 3.12
holy [2] 1.18; Jude 14
ignorant 1 Pet 2.15
ignore Hos 14.9
judge 2.3; Jude 15
knowledge 2.20
last (2) 1 Pet 1.20; Jude 18
letter (2) [4] 1 Pet 5.12; 3 Jn 9
life (1) [2] 1.3; 1 Jn 1.1
lust 2.10; Jude 23
mind (1) 1 Pet 1.13
mock Heb 11.36; Jude 18
new 1 Pet 1.3; 1 Jn 2.7
patient [2] 1 Pet 3.20; Rev 1.9
peace 1.2; 2 Jn 3
preserve Heb 2.10
promise [3] 2.19; 1 Jn 1.9
prophet 2.1; 1 Jn 4.1
pure [2] 1.9; 1 Jn 1.7
purpose 1 Pet 1.2; Rev 17.13
remember 1.15; Jude 6
remind 1.12; Jude 5

you must **understand** that in these **last**
days some people will appear whose
lives are **controlled** by their own **lusts**.
They will **mock** you 4 and will ask, "He
promised to come, didn't he? Where is
he? Our fathers have already died, but
everything is still the same as it was
since the **creation** of the **world**!" 5 They
purposely ignore the fact that long ago
God gave a **command**, and the **heavens**
and earth were **created**. The earth was
formed out of water and by water, 6 and it
was also by water, the water of the **flood**,
that the old **world** was **destroyed**. 7 But
the **heavens** and the earth that now **exist**
are being **preserved** by the same **com-**
mand of God, in order to be **destroyed** by
fire. They are being kept for the day
when **godless** people will be **judged** and
destroyed.

8 But do not **forget** one thing, my **dear**
friends! There is no difference in the
Lord's **sight** between one day and a
thousand years; to him the two are the
same. 9 The Lord is not slow to do what
he has **promised**, as some think. Instead,
he is **patient** with you, because he does
not want anyone to be **destroyed**, but
wants all to **turn away from their sins**.

10 But the **Day of the Lord** will come
like a **thief**. On that **Day** the **heavens** will
disappear with a shrill noise, the
heavenly bodies will burn up and be **de-**
stroyed, and the earth with everything in
it will **vanish**.[d] 11 Since all these things
will be **destroyed** in this way, what kind
of people should you be? Your **lives**
should be **holy** and **dedicated** to God, 12 as
you wait for the **Day of God** and do your
best to make it come soon—the **Day**
when the **heavens** will burn up and be
destroyed, and the **heavenly bodies** will
be melted by the heat. 13 But we wait for
what God has **promised**: **new heavens**
and a new earth, where **righteousness**
will be at home.

14 And so, my **friends**, as you wait for
that **Day**, do your **best** to be **pure** and
faultless in God's **sight** and to be at **peace**
with him. 15 Look on our Lord's **patience**
as the opportunity he is giving you to be
saved, just as our **dear** brother Paul
wrote to you, using the **wisdom** that God
gave him. 16 This is what he says in all his
letters when he writes on the subject.
There are some **difficult** things in his
letters which **ignorant** and unstable
people explain **falsely**, as they do with
other passages of the **Scriptures**. So they
bring on their own **destruction**.

17 But you, my **friends**, already know
this. Be on your guard, then, so that you
will not be led away by the **errors** of lawless people and fall from your **safe**
position. 18 But continue to grow in the
grace and **knowledge** of our Lord and
Saviour Jesus Christ. To him be the **glory**,
now and for ever! Amen.

righteous 2.5; 1 Jn 2.1
safe 1 Pet 1.5; 1 Jn 5.18
save 2.5; Jude 23
Saviour [2] 2.20; 1 Jn 4.14
scripture 1.20; Jude 4
sight [2] 1.9; Rev 3.2
thief 1 Pet 4.15; Rev 3.3
turn 2.21; Rev 1.12
understand 2.12; 1 Jn 5.20
vanish 1 Cor 14.9; Rev 16.20
wisdom Jas 3.13; Rev 5.12
word (1) 1 Pet 3.1; 1 Jn 1.6
world [2] 2.5; 1 Jn 2.15

[d] vanish; *some manuscripts have* be found; *others have* be burnt up; *one has* be found destroyed.

3.5: Gen 1.6–9 **3.6:** Gen 7.11 **3.8:** Ps 90.4 **3.10:** Mt 24.43; Lk 12.39; 1 Thes 5.2; Rev 16.15
3.13: Is 65.17, 66.22; Rev 21.1

THE FIRST LETTER OF JOHN

INTRODUCTION

The First Letter of John has two main purposes: to encourage its readers to live in fellowship with God and with his Son, Jesus Christ, and to warn them against following false teaching that would destroy this fellowship. This teaching was based on the belief that evil results from contact with the physical world, and so Jesus, the Son of God, could not really have been a human being. Those teachers claimed that to be saved was to be set free from concern with life in this world; and they also taught that salvation had nothing to do with matters of morality or of love for one's fellow-man.

In opposition to this teaching the writer clearly states that Jesus Christ was a real human being, and he emphasizes that all who believe in Jesus and love God must also love one another.

Outline of Contents

The Word of Life

1 We write to you about the **Word of life**, which has **existed** from the very beginning. We have heard it, and we have seen it with our eyes; yes, we have seen it, and our hands have touched it. 2 When this **life** became visible, we saw it; so we speak of it and tell you about the **eternal life** which was with the **Father** and was made known to us. 3 What we have seen and heard we **announce** to you also, so that you will join with us in the **fellowship** that we have with the **Father** and with **his Son** Jesus Christ. 4 We write this in order that our[a] **joy** may be **complete**.

God Is Light

5 Now the **message** that we have heard from **his Son** and **announce** is this: God is **light**, and there is no **darkness** at all in him. 6 If, then, we say that we have **fellowship** with him, yet at the same time live in the **darkness**, we are **lying** both in our **words** and in our **actions**. 7 But if we live in the **light**—just as he is in the **light**—then we have **fellowship** with **one another**, and the **blood** of Jesus, **his Son**, **purifies** us from every sin.

8 If we say that we have no sin, we **deceive** ourselves, and there is no **truth** in us. 9 But if we **confess** our sins to God, he will keep his **promise** and do what is **right**: he will **forgive** us our sins and **purify** us from all our **wrongdoing**. 10 If we say that we have not sinned, we make God out to be a **liar**, and his **word** is not in us.

action 2 Pet 2.8; 3.18
announce [2] 1 Pet 1.12; Rev 5.2
blood 1 Pet 1.2; 5.6
complete 1 Pet 2.18; Rev 6.11
confess Jas 5.16
dark [2] 2 Pet 2.4; 2.8
deceive 2 Pet 2.13; 2.26
eternal 2 Pet 1.11; 2.25
exist 2 Pet 3.7; 2.13
Father (2) (God) [2] 2 Pet 1.17; 2.1
fellowship [3] Phlm 6; 2.19
forgive Jas 5.15; 2.2
joy 1 Pet 4.13; Jude 24
lie (2) [2] 1 Pet 3.10; 2.4
life (1) [3] 2 Pet 3.3; 2.25
light (1) [3] 2 Pet 1.19; 2.8
message 2 Pet 1.19; 2.7
one another 1 Pet 5.5; 3.11
promise 2 Pet 3.4; 2.25
pure [2] 2 Pet 3.1; 3.3
right (1) 2 Pet 1.13; 2.29
Son of God [3] 2 Pet 1.17; 2.22
truth 2 Pet 2.2; 2.4
word (1) [2] 2 Pet 3.2; 2.5
Word (2) Jn 1.1; Rev 19.13
wrong 2 Pet 2.15; 3.12

Christ Our Helper

2 I am writing this to you, my children, so that you will not sin; but if anyone does sin, we have someone who **pleads** with the **Father** on our behalf—Jesus Christ, the **righteous** one. 2 And **Christ** himself is the **means** by which our sins are **forgiven**, and not our sins only, but also the sins of everyone.

3 If we **obey** God's **commands**, then we are **sure** that we know him. 4 If someone says that he knows him, but does not **obey** his **commands**, such a person is a **liar** and there is no **truth** in him. 5 But whoever **obeys** his **word** is the one whose **love** for God has really been made **perfect**. This is how we can be **sure** that we are in **union with** God: 6 whoever says that he remains in **union with** God should live just as Jesus Christ did.

The New Command

7 My **dear friends**, this **command** I am writing to you is not **new**; it is the old **command**, the one you have had from

accept 1 Pet 2.5; 3 Jn 7
blind Rom 11.10; Rev 3.17
child of God Heb 12.5; 3.1
Christ [11] 1 Pet 5.1; 3.2
clear 1 Pet 3.16; 3.2
command [6] 2 Pet 3.2; 3.22
courage Heb 10.35; 3.21
dark [4] 1.5; Jude 6
Day of the Lord 2 Pet 3.10; Jude 6
dear 2 Pet 3.1; 3.2
deceive 1.8; 3.7
desire [2] 1 Pet 5.2; Jude 16
enemy [3] 1 Pet 5.8; 4.3
eternal 1.2; 3.15
Evil One [2] 2 Thes 3.3; 3.12
exist [2] 1.1; Rev 4.11
false 2 Pet 3.16; 4.1
Father (2) (God) [8] 1.2; 3.1
fellowship [2] 1.3
forgive [2] 1.9; 4.10
friend 2 Pet 3.1; 3.2
hate [2] Heb 12.3; 3.13
heart 2 Pet 2.14; 3.17
lie (2) [3] 1.6; 4.20

[a] our; *some manuscripts have* your.

1.1: Jn 1.1 **1.2:** Jn 1.14 **2.7:** Jn 13.34

life (1) 1.1; 3.14
light (1) [3] 1.5; Rev 8.12
love [4] 2 Pet 2.15; 3.1
means 2 Pet 1.4; 4.10
message [3] 1.5; 3.11
Messiah Heb 11.26; 5.1
need [2] 2 Pet 1.3; 3.17
new [2] 2 Pet 3.13; 2 Jn 5
obey [4] 1 Pet 3.6; 3.22
perfect 1 Pet 5.10; 4.12
plead Heb 7.25
promise 1.9
proud 2 Pet 2.18; Rev 13.5
real 1 Pet 5.2
reject [2] 1 Pet 2.4; Jude 4
right (1) 1.9; 3.7
righteous [2] 2 Pet 3.13; 3.7
sake 1 Pet 2.13; Jude 11
self 1 Pet 3.4
shame 2 Pet 2.13; Jude 12
Son of God [4] 1.3; 3.8
Spirit (1) (God's Spirit) [5] 2 Pet 1.21; 3.24
strong 2 Pet 2.11; 5.9
sure [3] 1 Pet 5.10; 4.13
teach [4] Heb 13.9; 2 Jn 9
true 2 Pet 2.22; 3.18
truth [5] 1.8; 3.19
union [5] 1 Pet 5.10; 3.6
word (1) [2] 1.6; 3.18
world [6] 2 Pet 3.4; 3.1

the very beginning. The old **command** is the **message** you have already heard. 8 However, the **command** I am now writing to you is **new**, because its **truth** is seen in **Christ** and also in you. For the **darkness** is passing away, and the **real light** is already shining.

9 Whoever says that he is in the **light**, yet **hates** his brother, is in the **darkness** to this very hour. 10 Whoever **loves** his brother lives in the **light**, and so there is nothing in him that will cause someone else[b] to sin. 11 But whoever **hates** his brother is in the **darkness**; he walks in it and does not know where he is going, because the **darkness** has made him **blind**.

12 I am writing to you, my children, because your sins are **forgiven** for the **sake** of **Christ**. 13 I am writing to you, fathers, because you know him who has **existed** from the beginning. I am writing to you, young men, because you have defeated the **Evil One**.

14 I am writing to you, my children, because you know the **Father**. I am writing to you, fathers, because you know him who has **existed** from the beginning. I am writing to you, young men, because you are **strong**; the **word of God** lives in you, and you have defeated the **Evil One**.

15 Do not **love** the **world** or anything that belongs to the world. If you **love** the **world**, you do not love the **Father**. 16 Everything that belongs to the **world**—what the sinful **self desires**, what people see and want, and everything in **this world** that people are so **proud** of—none of this comes from the **Father**; it all comes from the **world**. 17 The **world** and everything in it that people **desire** is passing away; but he who does the will of God lives for ever.

The Enemy of Christ

18 My children, the end is near! You were told that the **Enemy of Christ** would come; and now many **enemies** of **Christ** have already appeared, and so we know that the end is near. 19 These people really did not belong to our **fellowship**, and that is why they left us; if they had belonged to our **fellowship**, they would have stayed with us. But they left so that it might be **clear** that none of them really belonged to us.

20 But you have had the **Holy Spirit** poured out on you by **Christ**, and so all of you know the **truth**. 21 I am writing to you, then, not because you do not know the **truth**; instead, it is because you do know it, and you also know that no **lie** ever comes from the **truth**.

22 Who, then, is the **liar**? It is anyone who says that Jesus is not the **Messiah**. Such a person is the **Enemy of Christ**—he **rejects** both the **Father** and the **Son**. 23 For whoever **rejects** the **Son** also rejects the **Father**; whoever **accepts** the **Son** has the **Father** also.

24 Be **sure**, then, to keep in your **hearts** the **message** you heard from the beginning. If you keep that **message**, then you will always live in **union with** the **Son** and the **Father**. 25 And this is what **Christ** himself **promised** to give us—**eternal life**.

26 I am writing this to you about those who are trying to **deceive** you. 27 But as for you, **Christ** has poured out his **Spirit** on you. As long as his **Spirit** remains in you, you do not **need** anyone to **teach** you. For his **Spirit teaches** you about everything, and what he **teaches** is **true**, not **false**. **Obey** the **Spirit's teaching**, then, and remain in **union with Christ**.

28 Yes, my children, remain in **union with** him, so that when he appears we may be full of **courage** and **need** not hide in **shame** from him on the **Day** he comes. 29 You know that **Christ** is **righteous**; you should know, then, that everyone who does what is **right** is **God's child**.

Children of God

3 See how much the **Father** has **loved** us! His **love** is so great that we are called **God's children**—and so, in fact, we are. This is why the **world** does not know us: it has not known God. 2 My **dear friends**, we are now **God's children**, but it is not yet **clear** what we shall become. But we know that when **Christ** appears, we shall be like him, because we shall see him as he really is. 3 Everyone who has this **hope** in **Christ** keeps himself **pure**, just as **Christ** is pure.

4 Whoever sins is **guilty** of breaking God's **law**, because sin is a breaking of the **law**. 5 You know that **Christ** appeared in order to **take away** sins,[c] and that there is no sin in him. 6 So everyone who lives in **union with Christ** does not continue to sin; but whoever continues to sin has never seen him or known him.

7 Let no one **deceive** you, my children! Whoever does what is **right** is **righteous**, just as **Christ** is **righteous**. 8 Whoever continues to sin belongs to the **Devil**, because the **Devil** has sinned from the very beginning. The **Son of God**

action 1.6; Rev 15.4
believe 1 Pet 4.17; 4.1
child of God [5] 2.29; 4.7
Christ [8] 2.2; 4.3
claim Tit 1.16; 4.1
clear [2] 2.19; Rev 4.6
command [4] 2.3; 4.21
condemn [2] 2 Pet 2.6; Jude 4
confident 2 Pet 1.19
conscience [3] 1 Pet 3.16
courage 2.28; 4.17
dear [2] 2.7; 4.1
death (1) [2] 2 Pet 1.15; 5.6
deceive 2.26; 2 Jn 7
destroy 2 Pet 3.6; Jude 5
Devil [4] 1 Pet 5.8; Jude 9
eternal 2.25; 5.11
Evil One 2.13; 5.18
Father (2) (God) [2] 2.1; 4.14
friend [2] 2.7; 4.1
guilty Jas 4.17
hate [2] 2.9; 4.20
heart 2.24; 5.10
hope 1 Pet 3.5; 2 Jn 12
law [2] Jas 4.11
life (1) [4] 2.25; 4.9
love [11] 2.5; 4.7

[b] someone else; *or* him. [c] sins; *some manuscripts have* our sins.

3.1: Jn 1.12 **3.5:** Jn 1.29

message 2.7; Jude 4
nature 2 Pet 1.4
need 2.27; Jude 3
obey [2] 2.3; 5.2
one another [2] 1.7; 4.7
please 2 Pet 1.17; 3 Jn 6
power 2 Pet 1.3; 4.4
presence [2] 2 Pet 2.11; 5.14
pure 1.7; Rev 3.18
reason 2 Pet 1.5
rich 1 Pet 1.4; Rev 2.9
right (1) [3] 2.29; Rev 15.3
righteous [2] 2.1
Son of God [2] 2.22; 4.9
Spirit (1) (God's Spirit) 2.20; 4.1
take away (sin) Heb 10.4
true 2.27; 5.6
truth 2.4; 4.6
union [4] 2.5; 4.12
word (1) 2.5; Jude 9
world [2] 2.15; 4.3
wrong 1.9; 5.17

appeared for this very reason, to destroy
what the Devil had done.
9 Whoever is a child of God does not
continue to sin, for God's very nature is
in him; and because God is his Father, he
cannot continue to sin. [10] This is the clear
difference between God's children and
the Devil's children: anyone who does
not do what is right or does not love his
brother is not God's child.

Love One Another

11 The message you heard from the
very beginning is this: we must love one
another. [12] We must not be like Cain; he
belonged to the Evil One and murdered
his own brother Abel. Why did Cain murder
him? Because the things he himself
did were wrong, but the things his
brother did were right.
13 So do not be surprised, my brothers,
if the people of the world hate you. [14] We
know that we have left death and come
over into life; we know it because we
love our brothers. Whoever does not love
is still under the power of death. [15] Whoever
hates his brother is a murderer, and
you know that a murderer has not got
eternal life in him. [16] This is how we
know what love is: Christ gave his life for
us. We too, then, ought to give our lives
for our brothers! [17] If a rich person sees
his brother in need, yet closes his heart
against his brother, how can he claim
that he loves God? [18] My children, our
love should not be just words and talk; it
must be true love, which shows itself in
action.

Courage before God

19 This, then, is how we will know that
we belong to the truth; this is how we
will be confident in God's presence. [20] If
our conscience condemns us, we know
that God is greater than our conscience
and that he knows everything. [21] And so,
my dear friends, if our conscience does
not condemn us, we have courage in
God's presence. [22] We receive from him
whatever we ask, because we obey his
commands and do what pleases him.
[23] What he commands is that we believe
in his Son Jesus Christ and love one
another, just as Christ commanded us.
[24] Whoever obeys God's commands lives
in union with God and God lives in union
with him. And because of the Spirit that
God has given us we know that God lives
in union with us.

The True Spirit and the False

4 My dear friends, do not believe all
who claim to have the Spirit, but test
them to find out if the spirit they have
comes from God. For many false prophets
have gone out everywhere. [2] This is
how you will be able to know whether it
is God's Spirit: anyone who acknowledges
that Jesus Christ came as a
human being has the Spirit who comes
from God. [3] But anyone who denies this
about Jesus does not have the Spirit from
God. The spirit that he has is from the
Enemy of Christ; you heard that it would
come, and now it is here in the world
already.
4 But you belong to God, my children,
and have defeated the false prophets,
because the Spirit who is in you is more
powerful than the spirit in those who
belong to the world. [5] Those false prophets
speak about matters of the world,
and the world listens to them because
they belong to the world. [6] But we belong
to God. Whoever knows God listens to us;
whoever does not belong to God does not
listen to us. This, then, is how we can tell
the difference between the Spirit of truth
and the spirit of error.

God Is Love

7 Dear friends, let us love one another,
because love comes from God. Whoever
loves is a child of God and knows God.
[8] Whoever does not love does not know
God, for God is love. [9] And God showed
his love for us by sending his only Son
into the world, so that we might have life
through him. [10] This is what love is: it is
not that we have loved God, but that he
loved us and sent his Son to be the means
by which our sins are forgiven.
11 Dear friends, if this is how God
loved us, then we should love one
another. [12] No one has ever seen God, but
if we love one another, God lives in union
with us, and his love is made perfect in
us.
13 We are sure that we live in union
with God and that he lives in union with
us, because he has given us his Spirit.
[14] And we have seen and tell others that
the Father sent his Son to be the Saviour
of the world. [15] If anyone declares that
Jesus is the Son of God, he lives in union
with God and God lives in union with
him. [16] And we ourselves know and
believe the love which God has for us.
God is love, and whoever lives in love
lives in union with God and God lives in
union with him. [17] Love is made perfect in

acknowledge Zech 1.6; 2 Jn 7
afraid 1 Pet 3.6; Rev 1.17
being 2 Pet 2.10; 2 Jn 7
believe [2] 3.23; 5.1
child of God 3.1; 5.1
Christ [3] 3.2; 2 Jn 7
claim 3.17; Rev 2.9
command 3.22; 5.2
courage 3.21; 5.14
Day of Judgement 2 Pet 2.4
dear [3] 3.2; 2 Jn 1
declare Heb 5.10; Rev 3.5
deny 2 Pet 2.1
enemy 2.18; 2 Jn 7
error 2 Pet 3.17; Jude 11
false [3] 2.27; 5.21
Father (2) (God) 3.1; 2 Jn 3
fear [3] Jas 2.19; Jude 23
forgive 2.2
friend [3] 3.2; 3 Jn 2
hate 3.13; Jude 23
human 2 Pet 2.16; 2 Jn 7
lie (2) 2.4; 5.10
life (1) [2] 3.14; 5.11
love [23] 3.1; 5.1
means 2.2; 5.4
one another [3] 3.11; 2 Jn 5
perfect [4] 2.5; Rev 3.2
power 3.14; Jude 20
prophet [3] 2 Pet 3.2; Rev 1.3
punish 2 Pet 2.9; Jude 7
Saviour 2 Pet 3.2; Jude 25
Son of God [4] 3.8; 5.5
Spirit (1) (God's Spirit) [7] 3.24; 5.6
spirit (2) [4] 1 Pet 3.4; 3 Jn 2
sure 2.3; 5.14
test 1 Pet 4.12; Rev 2.2
truth 3.19; 5.6
union [7] 3.6; 5.20
world [8] 3.1; 5.4

3.11: Jn 13.34 **3.12:** Gen 4.8 **3.14:** Jn 5.24 **3.23:** Jn 13.34, 15.12, 17 **4.12:** Jn 1.18

us in order that we may have courage on
Judgement Day; and we will have it
because our life in this world is the same
as Christ's. 18 There is no fear in love;
perfect love drives out all fear. So then,
love has not been made perfect in anyone who is afraid, because fear has to do
with punishment.
19 We love because God first loved us.
20 If someone says he loves God, but hates
his brother, he is a liar. For he cannot
love God, whom he has not seen, if he
does not love his brother, whom he has
seen. 21 The command that Christ has
given us is this: whoever loves God must
love his brother also.

Our Victory over the World

5 Whoever believes that Jesus is the
Messiah is a child of God; and whoever loves a father loves his child also.
2 This is how we know that we love God's
children: it is by loving God and obeying
his commands. 3 For our love for God
means that we obey his commands. And
his commands are not too hard for us,
4 because every child of God is able to
defeat the world. And we win the victory
over the world by means of our faith.
5 Who can defeat the world? Only the
person who believes that Jesus is the Son
of God.

The Witness about Jesus Christ

6 Jesus Christ is the one who came
with the water of his baptism and the
blood of his death. He came not only with
the water, but with both the water and
the blood. And the Spirit himself testifies
that this is true, because the Spirit is
truth. 7 There are three witnesses: 8 the
Spirit, the water, and the blood; and all
three give the same testimony. 9 We
believe man's testimony; but God's testimony is much stronger, and he has given
this testimony about his Son. 10 So whoever believes in the Son of God has this
testimony in his own heart; but whoever
does not believe God, has made him out
to be a liar, because he has not believed
what God has said about his Son. 11 The
testimony is this: God has given us eternal life, and this life has its source in his
Son. 12 Whoever has the Son has this life;
whoever does not have the Son of God
does not have life.

Eternal Life

13 I am writing this to you so that you
may know that you have eternal life—
you that believe in the Son of God. 14 We
have courage in God's presence, because
we are sure that he hears us if we ask
him for anything that is according to his
will. 15 He hears us whenever we ask
him; and since we know this is true, we
know also that he gives us what we ask
from him.
16 If you see your brother commit a
sin that does not lead to death, you
should pray to God, who will give him
life. This applies to those whose sins do
not lead to death. But there is sin which
leads to death, and I do not say that you
should pray to God about that. 17 All
wrongdoing is sin, but there is sin which
does not lead to death.
18 We know that no child of God keeps
on sinning, for the Son of God keeps him
safe, and the Evil One cannot harm him.
19 We know that we belong to God
even though the whole world is under the
rule of the Evil One.
20 We know that the Son of God has
come and has given us understanding, so
that we know the true God. We live in
union with the true God—in union with
his Son Jesus Christ. This is the true God,
and this is eternal life.
21 My children, keep yourselves safe
from false gods!

5.3: Jn 14.15 5.11: Jn 3.36

baptize 1 Pet 3.21
believe [7] 4.1; Jude 5
blood [3] 1.7; Rev 6.12
child of God [4] 4.7; Rev 21.7
command [3] 4.21; 2 Jn 4
commit 1 Pet 2.22; Jude 11
courage 4.17
death (1) [5] 3.14; Rev 1.5
eternal [3] 3.15; Jude 6
Evil One [2] 3.12
faith 2 Pet 1.1; Jude 3
false 4.1; Rev 16.13
god (2) (other gods) 2 Thes 2.4
hard 2 Pet 1.10; Rev 2.2
harm 1 Pet 3.13; Rev 7.3
heart 3.17; Rev 17.17
lie (2) 4.20; 3 Jn 10
life (1) [7] 4.9; Jude 21
love [4] 4.7; 2 Jn 1
means 4.10; Rev 6.8
Messiah 2.22; Rev 11.15
obey [2] 3.22; 2 Jn 6
pray [2] 1 Pet 4.7; 3 Jn 2
presence 3.19; Jude 24
safe [2] 2 Pet 3.17; Rev 3.10

Son of God [11] 4.9; 2 Jn 3
source Heb 5.9
Spirit (1) (God's Spirit) [3] 4.1; Jude 19
strong 2.14; Rev 6.13
sure 4.13
testify Col 4.13
testimony [6] 1 Pet 5.12; 3 Jn 12
true [5] 3.18; 2 Jn 1
truth 4.6; 2 Jn 1
understand 2 Pet 3.3; Jude 10
union [2] 4.12
victory 2 Tim 4.8; Rev 2.7
will (1) 1 Pet 4.2; Rev 17.17
win 1 Pet 3.1; Rev 2.7
witness 1 Pet 5.1; Rev 1.5
world [4] 4.3; 2 Jn 7
wrong 3.12

THE SECOND LETTER OF JOHN

INTRODUCTION

The Second Letter of John was written by "the Elder" to "the dear Lady and to her children," probably meaning a local church and its members. The brief message is an appeal to love one another and a warning against false teachers and their teachings.

Outline of Contents

Introduction 1–3
The primacy of love 4–6
Warning against false doctrine 7–11
Conclusion 12–13

---

1 From the **Elder**—
To the **dear** Lady and to her children,[a]
whom I **truly love**. And I am not the only
one, but all who know the **truth love** you,
2 because the **truth** remains in us and will
be with us for ever.
3 May God the **Father** and Jesus
Christ, the Father's **Son**, give us **grace**,
mercy, and **peace**; may they be ours in
truth and **love**.

Truth and Love

4 How **happy** I was to find that some
of your children live in the **truth**, just as
the **Father commanded** us. 5 And so I ask
you, **dear** Lady: let us all **love one
another**. This is no **new command** I am
writing to you; it is the **command** which
we have had from the beginning. 6 This
love I speak of means that we must live
in **obedience** to God's **commands**. The
command, as you have all heard from
the beginning, is that you must all live in
love.
7 Many **deceivers** have gone out all
over the **world**, people who do not
acknowledge that Jesus Christ came as a
human being. Such a person is a **deceiver**
and the **Enemy of Christ**. 8 Be on your
guard, then, so that you will not lose what
we[b] have worked for, but will receive
your **reward** in full.
9 Anyone who does not stay with the
teaching of **Christ**, but goes beyond it,
does not have God. Whoever does stay
with the **teaching** has both the **Father**
and the **Son**. 10 So then, if someone comes
to you who does not bring this **teaching**,
do not **welcome** him in your homes; do
not even say, "**Peace** be with you." 11 For
anyone who **wishes** him **peace** becomes
his partner in the **evil** things he does.

Final Words

12 I have so much to tell you, but I
would rather not do it with paper and
ink; instead, I **hope** to visit you and talk
with you personally, so that we shall be
completely **happy**.
13 The children of your **dear** Sister[c]
send you their greetings.

[a] LADY AND...HER CHILDREN: *This probably refers to a church and its members (also in verses 4–5).*
[b] we; *some manuscripts have* you. [c] CHILDREN OF YOUR DEAR SISTER: *This probably refers to the members of the church to which the writer belonged.*

5: Jn 13.34, 15.12, 17

acknowledge 1 Jn 4.2
being 1 Jn 4.2; Jude 8
Christ [2] 1 Jn 4.3; 3 Jn 7
command [5] 1 Jn 5.2; Rev 3.10
dear [3] 1 Jn 4.1; 3 Jn 1
deceive [2] 1 Jn 3.7; Rev 12.9
Elder (3) 3 Jn 1
enemy 1 Jn 4.3; Rev 11.5
evil 2 Pet 2.2; Jude 16
Father (2) (God) [3] 1 Jn 4.14; Jude 1
grace 2 Pet 3.18; Jude 4
happy [2] 1 Pet 4.14; 3 Jn 3
hope 1 Jn 3.3; 3 Jn 14
human 1 Jn 4.2; Rev 1.13
love [6] 1 Jn 5.1; 3 Jn 1
mercy 1 Pet 2.10; Jude 2
new 1 Jn 2.7; Rev 2.17
obey 1 Jn 5.2; Rev 1.3
one another 1 Jn 4.7
peace [3] 2 Pet 3.14; 3 Jn 15
reward Jas 1.12; Rev 11.18
Son of God [2] 1 Jn 5.5; Rev 2.18
teach [3] 1 Jn 2.27; Rev 2.14
true 1 Jn 5.6; 3 Jn 1
truth [4] 1 Jn 5.6; 3 Jn 3
welcome Jas 2.25
wish 1 Pet 3.10; Rev 2.23
world 1 Jn 5.4; Rev 1.5

THE THIRD LETTER OF
JOHN

INTRODUCTION

The Third Letter of John was written by "the Elder" to a church leader named Gaius. The writer praises Gaius because of his help to other Christians, and warns against a man named Diotrephes.

Outline of Contents

---

accept 1 Jn 2.23; Rev 22.17
bad [2] Jas 4.3
Christ 2 Jn 7; Rev 1.1
Christian [4] 1 Pet 5.12
church [3] 1 Pet 5.1; Rev 1.4
dear [4] 2 Jn 1; Jude 3
Elder (3) 2 Jn 1
enough 1 Pet 4.3
faithful [2] 1 Pet 5.12; Rev 1.5
friend [5] 1 Jn 4.1; Jude 3
happy [2] 2 Jn 4; Rev 1.3
help [3] 1 Pet 5.12; Rev 12.16
hope 2 Jn 12
letter (2) 2 Pet 3.1
lie (2) 1 Jn 5.10; Rev 2.2
love [2] 2 Jn 1; Jude 1
peace 2 Jn 3; Jude 2
please [2] 1 Jn 3.22
pray 1 Jn 5.16; Jude 20
service Heb 13.17; Rev 2.19
share 2 Pet 1.3; Jude 3
spirit (2) 1 Jn 4.1; Rev 1.4
stranger 1 Pet 2.11
terrible 2 Tim 3.11; Jude 11

1 From the **Elder**—
To my **dear** Gaius, whom I **truly love**.
2 My **dear friend**, I **pray** that everything may go well with you and that you
may be in good health—as I know you
are well in **spirit**. [3]I was so **happy** when
some **Christian brothers** arrived and told
me how **faithful** you are to the **truth**—just
as you always live in the **truth**. [4]Nothing
makes me **happier** than to hear that my
children live in the **truth**.

Gaius Is Praised

5 My **dear friend**, you are so **faithful** in
the work you do for your **fellow-
Christians**, even when they are
strangers. [6]They have spoken to the
church here about your **love**. **Please help**
them to continue their journey in a way
that will **please** God. [7]For they set out on
their journey in the **service** of **Christ**
without **accepting** any **help** from **unbelievers**. [8]We **Christians**, then, must
help these people, so that we may **share**
in their work for the **truth**.

Diotrephes and Demetrius

9 I wrote a short **letter** to the **church**;
but Diotrephes, who likes to be their
leader, will not pay any attention to what
I say. [10]When I come, then, I will call
attention to everything he has done: the
terrible things he says about us and the
lies he tells! But that is not **enough** for
him; he will not receive the **Christian
brothers** when they come, and even stops
those who want to receive them and tries
to drive them out of the **church**!
11 My **dear friend**, do not imitate what
is **bad**, but imitate what is good. Whoever
does good belongs to God; whoever does
what is **bad** has not seen God
12 Everyone speaks well of Demetrius; **truth** itself speaks well of
him. And we add our **testimony**, and you
know that what we say is **true**.

Final Greetings

13 I have so much to tell you, but I do
not want to do it with pen and ink. [14]I
hope to see you soon, and then we will
talk personally.
15 **Peace** be with you.
All your **friends** send greetings. Greet
all our **friends** personally.

1: Acts 19.29; Rom 16.23; 1 Cor 1.14

testimony 1 Jn 5.8; Rev 22.20
true [2] 2 Jn 1; Rev 2.13
truth [5] 2 Jn 1; Rev 1.2
unbeliever Heb 3.1

THE LETTER FROM JUDE

INTRODUCTION

The Letter from Jude was written to warn against false teachers who claimed to be believers. In this brief letter, which is similar in content to *2 Peter,* the writer encourages his readers "to fight on for the faith which once and for all God has given to his people."

Outline of Contents

Introduction 1–2
Character, teaching, and doom of the false teachers 3–16
Admonition to keep the faith 17–23
Benediction 24–25

---

abandon 2 Pet 1.10; Rev 2.13
above 2 Pet 2.10
act 2 Pet 2.12; Rev 17.17
age (1) Heb 9.26
angel [4] 2 Pet 2.4; Rev 1.1
apostle 2 Pet 3.2; Rev 2.2
argue Heb 6.16
authority [3] 2 Pet 2.10; Rev 1.18
being 2 Jn 7; Rev 1.13
believe 1 Jn 5.1
best 2 Pet 3.12
bind Col 3.14; Rev 9.14
blame Tit 1.6
boast Jas 4.16
body [2] 2 Pet 3.10; Rev 11.8
care 1 Pet 5.2; Rev 12.6
cloud 2 Pet 2.17; Rev 1.7
commit 1 Jn 5.16; Rev 2.22
condemn [4] 1 Jn 3.20; Rev 18.20
control 2 Pet 3.3; Rev 1.10
dare 2 Cor 11.21
dark [2] 1 Jn 2.8; Rev 9.2
Day of the Lord 1 Jn 2.28; Rev 16.14
dead 1 Pet 4.5; Rev 1.17
dear 3 Jn 1
deed (2) [2] 1 Pet 2.12; Rev 15.3
desire [3] 1 Jn 2.16
despise 2 Pet 2.10
destroy [3] 1 Jn 3.8; Rev 8.9
Devil [2] 1 Jn 3.8; Rev 2.10
doubt Jas 1.6
encourage 1 Pet 5.12
error 1 Jn 4.6
eternal [3] 1 Jn 5.11; Rev 14.6
evil 2 Jn 1.11; Rev 2.2
excuse Gal 5.13
faith [2] 1 Jn 5.4; Rev 2.13

1 From Jude, **servant** of Jesus Christ,
and brother of James—
To those who have been called by God,
who live in the **love** of God the **Father**
and the **protection** of Jesus Christ:
2 May **mercy**, **peace**, and **love** be
yours in full measure.

False Teachers

3 My **dear friends**, I was doing my **best**
to write to you about the **salvation** we
share in common, when I felt the **need** of
writing at once to **encourage** you to fight
on for the **faith** which once and for all
God has given to **his people**. 4 For some
godless people have slipped in unnoticed
among us, persons who distort the **mess-**
age about the **grace** of our God in order
to **excuse** their **immoral ways**, and who
reject Jesus Christ, our only **Master** and
Lord. Long ago the **Scriptures predicted**
the **condemnation** they have received.
5 For even though you know all this, I
want to **remind** you of how the Lord[a]
once **rescued** the people of Israel from
Egypt, but afterwards **destroyed** those
who did not **believe**. 6 **Remember** the
angels who did not stay within the limits
of their **proper authority**, but **abandoned**
their own dwelling place: they are **bound**
with **eternal** chains in the **darkness**
below, where God is keeping them for
that great **Day** on which they will be **con-**
demned. 7 **Remember** Sodom and Gomorrah, and the nearby towns, whose people
acted as those **angels** did and indulged in
sexual immorality and **perversion**: they
suffer the **punishment** of **eternal** fire as a
plain warning to all.
8 In the same way also, these people
have **visions** which make them sin
against their own **bodies**; they **despise**
God's **authority** and **insult** the **glorious**
beings above. 9 Not even the **chief angel**
Michael did this. In his **quarrel** with the
Devil, when they **argued** about who
would have the **body** of Moses, Michael
did not **dare** to **condemn** the **Devil** with
insulting words, but said, "The Lord **re-**
buke you!" 10 But these people attack
with **insults** anything they do not **under-**
stand; and those things that they know
by instinct, like wild animals, are the
very things that **destroy** them. 11 How
terrible for them! They have followed
the way that Cain took. For the **sake** of
money they have given themselves over
to the **error** that Balaam **committed**.
They have **rebelled** as Korah rebelled,
and like him they are **destroyed**. 12 With
their **shameless** carousing they are like
dirty spots in your **fellowship meals**.
They take **care** only of themselves. They
are like **clouds** carried along by the wind,
but bringing no rain. They are like trees
that bear no fruit, even in autumn, trees
that have been pulled up by the roots and
are completely **dead**. 13 They are like
wild waves of the sea, with their **shame-**
ful deeds showing up like foam. They are
like wandering stars, for whom God has
reserved a place for ever in the deepest
darkness.
14 It was Enoch, the sixth direct descendant from Adam, who long ago
prophesied this about them: "The Lord
will come with many thousands of his
holy angels 15 to bring **judgement** on all,

Father (2) (God) 2 Jn 3; Rev 1.6
fault 2 Pet 3.14; Rev 14.5
fear 1 Jn 4.18
fellowship meal Acts 20.7
friend [3] 3 Jn 2
glory [3] 2 Pet 3.18; Rev 1.6
God's people 1 Pet 4.17; Rev 5.8
godless [4] 2 Pet 3.7
grace 2 Jn 3; Rev 1.4
hate 1 Jn 4.20; Rev 2.6
holy 2 Pet 3.2; Rev 3.7
immoral [2] 2 Pet 2.2; Rev 2.14
insult [3] 2 Pet 2.10; Rev 13.1
joy 1 Jn 1.4
judge 2 Pet 3.7; Rev 6.10
keep from 1 Pet 3.10
last (2) 2 Pet 3.3; Rev 1.8
life (1) 1 Jn 5.11; Rev 2.7
love [3] 3 Jn 1; Rev 1.5
lust 2 Pet 3.3; Rev 14.8
Majesty Heb 8.1
master 2 Pet 2.1
mercy [4] 2 Jn 3
message 1 Jn 3.11; Rev 1.2
might 2 Pet 2.11; Rev 5.2
mock 2 Pet 3.3
natural Eph 2.3
need 1 Jn 3.17; Rev 3.17
peace 3 Jn 15; Rev 1.4
pervert 1 Tim 1.10; Rev 17.5
plain (1) 2 Pet 1.14
power 1 Jn 4.4; Rev 1.6
pray 3 Jn 2
predict 1 Pet 1.11
presence 1 Jn 5.14; Rev 3.5
proper 1 Pet 3.7

[a] the Lord; *some manuscripts have* Jesus, *which in Greek is the same as* Joshua.

1: Mt 13.55; Mk 6.3 **5:** Ex 12.51 **5:** Num 14.29–30 **7:** Gen 19.1–24 **9:** Dan 10.13, 21, 12.1 **9:** Rev 12.7 **9:** Deut 34.6 **9:** Zech 3.2 **11:** Gen 4.3–8 **11:** Num 22.1–35, 16.1–35 **14:** Gen 5.18, 21–24

prophecy 2 Pet 1.20
protect 2 Cor 12.9; Rev 7.15
punish 1 Jn 4.18; Rev 3.19
quarrel Jas 4.1
rebel Heb 3.8
rebuke 2 Pet 2.16; Rev 3.19
reject 1 Jn 2.22
remember [3] 2 Pet 3.2; Rev 3.3
remind 2 Pet 3.1
rescue 2 Pet 2.7
sacred 2 Pet 2.21
sake 1 Jn 2.12; Rev 2.3
salvation 1 Pet 1.5; Rev 7.10
save 2 Pet 3.15
Saviour 1 Jn 4.14
scripture 2 Pet 3.16
servant 2 Pet 1.1; Rev 1.1
sex 1 Pet 3.7; Rev 2.14
shame [2] 1 Jn 2.28; Rev 3.18
share 3 Jn 8; Rev 18.4

to **condemn** them all for the **godless**
deeds they have performed and for all
the **terrible words** that **godless** sinners
have spoken against him!"
16 These people are always grumbling
and **blaming** others; they follow their
own **evil desires**; they **boast** about themselves and flatter others in order to get
their own way.

Warnings and Instructions

17 But **remember**, my **friends**, what
you were told in the past by the **apostles**
of our Lord Jesus Christ. 18 They said to
you, "When the **last days** come, people
will appear who will **mock** you, people
who follow their own **godless desires**."
19 These are the people who cause
divisions, who are **controlled** by their
natural desires, who do not have the
Spirit. 20 But you, my **friends**, keep on
building yourselves up on your most
sacred faith. **Pray** in the **power of the**
Holy Spirit, 21 and keep yourselves in the
love of God, as you wait for our Lord
Jesus Christ in his **mercy** to give you
eternal life.
22 Show **mercy** towards those who
have **doubts**; 23 **save** others by snatching
them out of the fire; and to others show
mercy mixed with **fear**, but **hate** their
very clothes, stained by their sinful **lusts**.

Prayer of Praise

24 To him who is able to **keep you**
from falling, and to bring you **faultless**
and **joyful** before his **glorious presence**—
25 to the only God our **Saviour**, through
Jesus Christ our Lord, be **glory**, **majesty**,
might, and **authority**, from all **ages** past,
and now, and for ever and ever! Amen.

18: 2 Pet 3.3

Spirit (1) (God's Spirit) [2] 1 Jn 5.6; Rev 1.10
suffer 2 Pet 2.8; Rev 1.9
terrible [2] 3 Jn 10; Rev 2.22
understand 1 Jn 5.20; Rev 17.9
vision Col 2.18; Rev 4.1
warn Heb 11.7; Rev 22.18
way (3) 2 Pet 2.2; Rev 15.3
word (1) [2] 1 Jn 3.18; Rev 1.3

THE REVELATION
TO JOHN

INTRODUCTION

The Revelation to John was written at a time when Christians were being persecuted because of their faith in Jesus Christ as Lord. The writer's main concern is to give his readers hope and encouragement, and to urge them to remain faithful during times of suffering and persecution.

For the most part the book consists of several series of revelations and visions presented in symbolic language that would have been understood by Christians of that day, but would have remained a mystery to all others. As with the themes of a symphony, the themes of this book are repeated again and again in different ways through the various series of visions. Although there are differences of opinion regarding the details of interpretation of the book, the central theme is clear: through Christ the Lord, God will finally and totally defeat all his enemies, including Satan, and will reward his faithful people with the blessings of a new heaven and a new earth when this victory is complete.

Outline of Contents

---

1 This book is the record of the events
that Jesus Christ **revealed**. God gave
him this **revelation** in order to show his
servants what must happen very soon.
Christ made these things known to his
servant John by sending his **angel** to him,
2 and John has told all that he has seen.
This is his report concerning the **message** from God and the **truth revealed** by
Jesus Christ. 3 **Happy** is the one who
reads this book, and **happy** are those who
listen to the **words** of this **prophetic message** and **obey** what is written in this
book! For the time is near when all these
things will happen.

Greetings to the Seven Churches

4 From John to the seven **churches** in
the province of Asia:

Grace and **peace** be yours from God,
who is, who was, and **who is to come**, and
from the seven **spirits** in front of his
throne, 5 and from Jesus Christ, the **faithful witness**, the first to be **raised from**
death and who is also the ruler of the
kings of the **world**.

He **loves** us, and by his **sacrificial**
death he has **freed** us from our sins 6 and
made us a **kingdom of priests** to **serve** his
God and **Father**. To Jesus Christ be the
glory and **power** for ever and ever!
Amen.

7 Look, he is coming on the **clouds**!
Everyone will see him, including those
who pierced him. All peoples on earth
will **mourn** over him. So shall it be!

8 "**I am** the first and the **last**," says the
Lord God **Almighty, who is, who was, and
who is to come.**

A Vision of Christ

9 I am John, your brother, and as a **follower** of Jesus I am your partner in
patiently enduring the **suffering** that
comes to those who belong to his **Kingdom**. I was put on the island of Patmos
because I had **proclaimed God's word**
and the **truth** that Jesus **revealed**. 10 On

1.4: Ex 3.14; Rev 4.5 **1.5:** Is 55.4; Ps 89.27 **1.6:** Ex 19.6; Rev 5.10
1.7: Dan 7.13; Mt 24.30; Mk 13.26; Lk 21.27; 1 Thes 4.17; Zech 12.10; Jn 19.34, 37 **1.8:** Rev 22.13; Ex 3.14

afraid 1 Jn 4.18; 2.10
alive 2 Pet 1.13; 3.1
Almighty Jas 5.4; 4.8
angel [2] Jude 6; 2.1
authority Jude 6; 2.26
being Jude 8; 5.13
Christ 3 Jn 7; 20.4
church [4] 3 Jn 6; 2.1
cloud Jude 12; 10.1
control Jude 19; 4.2
dead [3] Jude 12; 3.1
death (1) [2] 1 Jn 5.6; 2.10
death (2) (from death) 1 Pet 1.3
endure 2 Pet 1.6; 3.10
faithful 3 Jn 3; 2.10
Father (2) (God) Jude 1; 2.26
follower 1 Pet 4.14; 2.23
free 2 Pet 2.19; 6.15
glory Jude 8; 4.9
grace Jude 4; 22.21
happy [2] 3 Jn 3; 11.10
human 2 Jn 7; 14.14
I am [3] Rom 14.11; 2.23
Kingdom (1) (of God) [2] 2 Pet 1.11; 5.10

last (2) [2] Jude 18; 2.8
love Jude 1; 2.4
message [2] Jude 4; 2.1
mourn Acts 8.2; 18.11
obey 2 Jn 6; 3.3
patient 2 Pet 3.9; 2.2
peace Jude 2
power Jude 20; 3.8
priest 1 Pet 2.5; 5.10
proclaim 2 Pet 1.19; 6.9
prophet 1 Jn 4.1; 10.7
raise 1 Pet 1.3; 10.5
refine Mal 3.2
reveal [4] 1 Pet 5.1; 12.17
right (2) [3] 1 Pet 3.22; 2.1
sacrifice 1 Pet 2.5; 5.9
secret 1 Tim 3.16; 2.24
servant [2] Jude 1; 2.20
serve 1 Pet 5.2; 5.10
Spirit (1) (God's Spirit) Jude 19; 2.7
spirit (2) 3 Jn 2; 3.1
suffer Jude 7; 2.3
throne Heb 12.2; 2.13
truth [2] 3 Jn 3; 12.11
turn 2 Pet 3.9; 2.5

who [2] Rom 14.4; 4.8
witness 1 Jn 5.7; 2.13
word (1) [2] Jude 9; 6.9
world 2 Jn 7; 3.10
world of the dead Phil 2.10; 5.3

the Lord's day the **Spirit** took **control** of me, and I heard a loud voice, that sounded like a trumpet, speaking behind me. [11] It said, "Write down what you see, and send the book to the **churches** in these seven cities: Ephesus, Smyrna, Pergamum, Thyatira, Sardis, Philadelphia, and Laodicea."

12 I **turned round** to see who was talking to me, and I saw seven gold lamp-stands, [13] and among them there was what looked like a **human being**, wearing a robe that reached to his feet, and a gold belt round his chest. [14] His hair was white as wool, or as snow, and his eyes blazed like fire; [15] his feet shone like brass that has been **refined** and polished, and his voice sounded like a roaring waterfall. [16] He held seven stars in his **right hand**, and a sharp two-edged sword came out of his mouth. His face was as bright as the midday sun. [17] When I saw him, I fell down at his feet like a **dead** man. He placed his **right hand** on me and said, "Don't be **afraid**! **I am** the first and the **last**. [18] **I am** the living one! I was **dead**, but now I am **alive** for ever and ever. I have **authority** over **death** and the **world of the dead**. [19] Write, then, the things you see, both the things that are now and the things that will happen afterwards. [20] This is the **secret** meaning of the seven stars that you see in my **right hand**, and of the seven gold lamp-stands: the seven stars are the **angels** of the seven **churches**, and the seven lamp-stands are the seven **churches**.

abandon Jude 6
adultery Jas 2.11
afraid 1.17; 18.10
angel [4] 1.1; 3.1
apostle Jude 17; 18.20
authority [2] 1.18; 6.8
burden 2 Tim 3.6
church [9] 1.4; 3.1
claim 1 Jn 4.1; 3.9
commit Jude 11
death (1) [2] 1.5; 5.9
Devil Jude 9; 12.9
evil [3] Jude 16; 16.11
faith Jude 3; 13.10
faithful [3] 1.5; 3.8
Father (2) (God) 1.6; 3.5
favour 1 Pet 5.5
follower 1.9; 17.14
give up Heb 12.2; 12.11
hard 1 Jn 5.3; 14.13
hate Jude 23; 17.16
hurt Gal 5.15; 9.10
I am 1.8; 3.11
idol [2] 1 Pet 4.3; 9.20
immoral [3] Jude 4; 9.21
Jew Heb 13.10; 3.9

The Message to Ephesus

2 "To the **angel** of the **church** in Ephesus write:

"This is the **message** from the one who holds the seven stars in his **right hand** and who walks among the seven gold lamp-stands. [2] I know what you have done; I know how **hard** you have worked and how **patient** you have been. I know that you cannot **tolerate evil** men and that you have **tested** those who say they are **apostles** but are not, and have found out that they are **liars**. [3] You are **patient**, you have **suffered** for my **sake**, and you have not **given up**. [4] But this is what I have against you: you do not **love** me now as you did at first. [5] Think how far you have fallen! **Turn from your sins** and do what you did at first. If you don't **turn from your sins**, I will come to you and take your lamp-stand from its place. [6] But this is what you have in your **favour**: you **hate** what the Nicolaitans do, as much as I do.

7 "If you have ears, then, listen to what the **Spirit** says to the **churches**!

"To those who **win** the **victory** I will give the **right** to eat the fruit of the tree of **life** that grows in the Garden of God.

The Message to Smyrna

8 "To the **angel** of the **church** in Smyrna write:

"This is the **message** from the one who is the first and the **last**, who died and lived again. [9] I know your **troubles**; I know that you are **poor**—but really you are **rich**! I know the **evil** things said against you by those who **claim** to be **Jews** but are not; they are a group that belongs to **Satan**! [10] Don't be **afraid** of anything you are about to **suffer**. Listen! The **Devil** will put you **to the test** by having some of you thrown into **prison**, and your **troubles** will **last** ten days. Be **faithful** to me, even if it means **death**, and I will give you **life** as your **prize** of **victory**.

11 "If you have ears, then, listen to what the **Spirit** says to the **churches**!

"Those who **win** the **victory** will not be **hurt** by the second **death**.

The Message to Pergamum

12 "To the **angel** of the **church** in Pergamum write:

"This is the **message** from the one who has the sharp two-edged sword. [13] I know where you live, there where **Satan** has his **throne**. You are **true** to me, and you did not **abandon** your **faith** in me even during the time when Antipas, my **faithful witness**, was killed there where **Satan** lives. [14] But there are a few things I have against you: there are some among you who follow the **teaching** of Balaam, who taught Balak how to lead the people of Israel into sin by **persuading** them to eat food that had been **offered** to **idols** and to **practise sexual immorality**. [15] In the same way you have people among you who follow the **teaching** of the Nicolaitans. [16] Now **turn from your sins**! If you don't, I will come to you soon and fight against those people with the sword that comes out of my mouth.

17 "If you have ears, then, listen to what the **Spirit** says to the **churches**!

"To those who **win** the **victory** I will give some of the hidden **manna**. I will also give each of them a white stone on

last (1) Heb 10.34
last (2) 1.8; 15.1
learn Heb 5.8; 14.3
lie (2) 3 Jn 10; 3.9
life (1) [2] Jude 21; 4.11
love [2] 1.5; 3.9
manna Heb 9.4
message [4] 1.2; 3.1
mislead Jn 7.12
new 2 Jn 5; 3.12
offer [2] 1 Pet 2.5; 8.
patient [3] 1.9
persuade Gal 5.7
poor Jas 2.2; 3.17
practice [2] Jas 1.22; 17.2
prison 1 Pet 3.19; 19.20
prize 2 Tim 4.8; 3.11
repay Heb 10.30
repent [2] Heb 6.4; 9.21
rich 1 Jn 3.17; 3.17
right (2) 1.16; 5.1
right (3) 2 Pet 1.11; 3.21
sake Jude 11
Satan [4] 1 Tim 5.15; 3.9
secret 1.20; 10.4
servant 1.1; 6.11
service 3 Jn 7; 14.13
sex [2] Jude 7; 9.21
Son of God 2 Jn 3
Spirit (1) (God's Spirit) [4] 1.10; 3.6
suffer [3] 1.9; 11.10
teach [4] 2 Jn 9; 3.3
terrible Jude 11; 6.17
test [2] 1 Jn 4.1; 3.10
throne 1.4; 3.21
tolerate [2] Col 3.13
trouble [2] Jas 5.13; 3.10
true 3 Jn 1; 3.7
turn [4] 1.12; 3.3
victory [5] 1 Jn 5.4; 3.5
wicked 2 Pet 2.9; 18.5
win [4] 1 Jn 5.4; 3.5
wish 2 Jn 11; 3.15
witness 1.5; 3.14

1.13: Dan 7.13, 10.5 **1.14–15:** Dan 7:9, 10.6 **1.15:** Ezek 1.24, 43.2 **1.17:** Is 44.6, 48.12; Rev 2.8, 22.13
2.7: Gen 2.9; Rev 22.2; Ezek 28.13, 31.8 (LXX) **2.8:** Is 44.6, 48.12; Rev 1.17, 22.13 **2.11:** Rev 20.14, 21.8
2.14: Num 22.5, 7, 31.16; Deut 23.4; Num 25.1–3 **2.17:** Ex 16.14–15, 16.33–34; Jn 6.48–50; Is 62.2, 65.15

which is written a new name that no one
knows except the one who receives it.

The Message to Thyatira

18 "To the angel of the church in
Thyatira write:
"This is the message from the Son of
God, whose eyes blaze like fire, whose
feet shine like polished brass. [19]I know
what you do. I know your love, your
faithfulness, your service, and your
patience. I know that you are doing more
now than you did at first. [20]But this is
what I have against you: you tolerate
that woman Jezebel, who calls herself a
messenger of God. By her teaching she
misleads my servants into practising
sexual immorality and eating food that
has been offered to idols. [21]I have given
her time to repent of her sins, but she
does not want to turn from her immorality. [22]And so I will throw her on to
a bed where she and those who committed adultery with her will suffer
terribly. I will do this now unless they repent of the wicked things they did with
her. [23]I will also kill her followers, and
then all the churches will know that I am
the one who knows everyone's thoughts
and wishes. I will repay each one of you
according to what he has done.
24 "But the rest of you in Thyatira
have not followed this evil teaching; you
have not learnt what the others call 'the
deep secrets of Satan.' I say to you that I
will not put any other burden on you.
[25]But until I come, you must hold firmly
to what you have. [26-28]To those who win
the victory, who continue to the end to do
what I want, I will give the same
authority that I received from my
Father: I will give them authority over
the nations, to rule them with an iron rod
and to break them to pieces like clay
pots. I will also give them the morning
star.
29 "If you have ears, then, listen to
what the Spirit says to the churches!

The Message to Sardis

3 "To the angel of the church in
Sardis write:
"This is the message from the one who
has the seven spirits of God and the
seven stars. I know what you are doing; I
know that you have the reputation of being alive, even though you are dead! [2]So
wake up, and strengthen what you still
have before it dies completely. For I find
that what you have done is not yet perfect in the sight of my God. [3]Remember,
then, what you were taught and what you
heard; obey it and turn from your sins. If
you do not wake up, I will come upon you
like a thief, and you will not even know
the time when I will come. [4]But a few of
you there in Sardis have kept your
clothes clean. You will walk with me,
clothed in white, because you are worthy
to do so. [5]Those who win the victory will
be clothed like this in white, and I will
not remove their names from the book of
the living. In the presence of my Father
and of his angels I will declare openly
that they belong to me.
6 "If you have ears, then, listen to
what the Spirit says to the churches!

The Message to Philadelphia

7 "To the angel of the church in
Philadelphia write:
"This is the message from the one who
is holy and true. He has the key that belonged to David, and when he opens a
door, no one can close it, and when he
closes it, no one can open it. [8]I know
what you do; I know that you have a little
power; you have followed my teaching
and have been faithful to me. I have
opened a door in front of you, which no
one can close. [9]Listen! As for that group
that belongs to Satan, those liars who
claim that they are Jews but are not, I
will make them come and bow down at
your feet. They will all know that I love
you. [10]Because you have kept my command to endure, I will also keep you safe
from the time of trouble which is coming
upon the world to test all the people on
earth. [11]I am coming soon. Keep safe
what you have, so that no one will rob
you of your victory prize. [12]I will make
him who is victorious a pillar in the
temple of my God, and he will never
leave it. I will write on him the name of
my God and the name of the city of my
God, the new Jerusalem, which will
come down out of heaven from my God. I
will also write on him my new name.
13 "If you have ears, then, listen to
what the Spirit says to the churches!

The Message to Laodicea

14 "To the angel of the church in
Laodicea write:
"This is the message from the Amen,
the faithful and true witness, who is the
origin[b] of all that God has created. [15]I

advice Gal 1.16
alive 1.18; 17.8
angel [4] 2.1; 5.2
blind 1 Jn 2.11
bow (2) 1 Cor 14.25
church [6] 2.1; 22.16
claim 2.9; 13.5
clean Heb 10.22; 15.6
command 2 Jn 4
create 2 Pet 3.4; 4.11
dead 1.17; 11.18
declare 1 Jn 4.15; 15.4

earnest 1 Pet 4.8
endure 1.9; 13.10
faithful [2] 2.10; 6.9
Father (2) (God) [2] 2.26; 14.1
heaven 2 Pet 3.5; 4.1
holy Jude 14; 4.8
I am 2.23; 21.6
Jew 2.9
lie (2) 2.2; 14.5
love [2] 2.4; 20.9
message [3] 2.1; 10.11
misery Jas 5.1
naked [2] Mk 14.52; 16.15
name (2) (name of God, of Jesus) [2] 1 Pet 4.16; 10.6
need Jude 3; 21.23
new [2] 2.17; 5.9
obey 1.3; 12.17
perfect 1 Jn 4.12; 21.16
poor 2.9; 13.16
power 1.6; 4.11
presence Jude 24; 7.15
prize 2.10
punish Jude 7; 6.10
pure 1 Jn 3.3; 14.4
rebuke Jude 9
remember Jude 6; 16.19
reputation Tit 1.6
rich [2] 2.9; 6.15
right (3) 2.7; 21.6
rob Eph 4.28
safe [2] 1 Jn 5.18; 7.14
Satan 2.9; 12.9
shame Jude 12; 21.27
sight 2 Pet 3.8; 12.1
Spirit (1) (God's Spirit) [3] 2.7; 4.2
spirit (2) 1.4; 4.5
strength 1 Pet 5.10; 5.12
teach [2] 2.14
Temple (1) (of God) 1 Pet 2.5; 7.15
test 2.2
thief 2 Pet 3.10; 16.15
throne [2] 2.13; 4.2
trouble 2.9
true [2] 2.13; 6.10
turn [2] 2.5; 6.12
victory [5] 2.7; 5.5
win [2] 2.7; 5.5
wish 2.23; 11.6
witness 2.13; 6.9
world 1.5; 11.15
worthy Heb 3.3; 4.11

[b]origin; *or* ruler.

2.20: 1 Kgs 16.31; 2 Kgs 9.22, 30 **2.23:** Ps 7.9; Jer 17.10; Ps 62.12 **2.26–27:** Ps 2.8–9 (LXX)
3.3: Mt 24.43–44; Lk 12.39–40; Rev 16.15 **3.5:** Ex 32.32–33; Ps 69.28; Rev 20.12; Mt 10.32; Lk 12.8
3.7: Is 22.22; Job 12.14 **3.9:** Is 49.23, 60.14, 43.4 **3.12:** Rev 21.2; Is 62.2, 65.15 **3.14:** Prov 8.22

know what you have done; I know that
you are neither cold nor hot. How I **wish**
you were either one or the other! 16 But
because you are lukewarm, neither hot
nor cold, I am going to spit you out of my
mouth! 17 You say, 'I am **rich** and well
off; I have all I **need**.' But you do not
know how **miserable** and pitiful you are!
You are **poor, naked**, and **blind**. 18 I **advise** you, then, to buy gold from me, **pure**
gold, in order to be **rich**. Buy also white
clothing to dress yourself and cover up
your **shameful nakedness**. Buy also some
ointment to put on your eyes, so that you
may see. 19 I **rebuke** and **punish** all whom
I **love**. Be in **earnest**, then, and **turn from
your sins**. 20 Listen! I stand at the door
and knock; if anyone hears my voice and
opens the door, I will come into his house
and eat with him, and he will eat with
me. 21 To those who **win** the **victory** I will
give the **right** to sit beside me on my
throne, just as I have been **victorious** and
now sit by **my Father** on his **throne**.
22 "If you have ears, then, listen to
what the **Spirit** says to the **churches**!"

Worship in Heaven

4 At this point I had another **vision**
and saw an open door in **heaven**.
And the voice that sounded like a trumpet, which I had heard speaking to me
before, said, "Come up here, and I will
show you what must happen after this."
2 At once the **Spirit** took **control** of me.
There in **heaven** was a **throne** with someone sitting on it. 3 His face gleamed like
such precious stones as jasper and carnelian, and all round the **throne** there
was a rainbow the colour of an emerald.
4 In a circle round the **throne** were
twenty-four other thrones, on which were
seated twenty-four **elders** dressed in
white and wearing **crowns** of gold.
5 From the **throne** came flashes of lightning, rumblings, and peals of thunder. In
front of the **throne** seven lighted torches
were burning, which are the seven **spirits**
of God. 6 Also in front of the **throne** there
was what looked like a sea of glass, **clear**
as crystal.
Surrounding the **throne** on each of its
sides, were four living **creatures** covered
with eyes in front and behind. 7 The first
one looked like a lion; the second looked
like a bull; the third had a face like a
man's face; and the fourth looked like an
eagle in flight. 8 Each one of the four
living **creatures** had six wings, and they
were covered with eyes, inside and out.
Day and night they never stop singing:

"**Holy, holy, holy**, is the Lord God
Almighty,
who was, who is, and who is to
come."

9 The four living **creatures** sing songs
of **glory** and **honour** and **thanks** to the
one who sits on the **throne**, who lives for
ever and ever. When they do so, 10 the
twenty-four **elders** fall down before the
one who sits on the **throne**, and **worship**
him who lives for ever and ever. They
throw their **crowns** down in front of the
throne and say,

11 "Our Lord and God! You are **worthy**
to receive **glory, honour**, and **power**.
For you **created** all things,
and by your will they were given
existence and **life**."

Almighty 1.8; 6.10
clear 1 Jn 3.2; 21.11
control 1.10; 17.3
create 3.14; 10.6
creature [3] Jas 3.7; 5.6
crown [2] 1 Pet 5.4; 6.2
elder (2) [2] 1 Pet 5.1; 5.5
exist 1 Jn 2.13
glory [2] 1.6; 5.12
heaven [2] 3.12; 5.3
holy 3.7; 6.10
honour [2] 2 Pet 1.17; 5.12
life (1) 2.7; 7.17
power 3.8; 5.12
Spirit (1) (God's Spirit) 3.6; 14.13
spirit (2) 3.1; 5.6
thank 1 Pet 4.16; 7.12
throne [10] 3.21; 5.1
vision Jude 8; 9.17
who 1.4
worship (1) (of God) Heb 13.10; 5.14
worthy 3.4; 5.2

The Scroll and the Lamb

5 I saw a **scroll** in the **right hand** of
the one who sits on the **throne**; it
was covered with writing on both sides
and was **sealed** with seven seals. 2 And I
saw a **mighty angel**, who **announced** in a
loud voice, "Who is **worthy** to break the
seals and open the **scroll**?" 3 But there
was no one in **heaven** or on earth or in
the **world below**[c] who could open the
scroll and look inside it. 4 I cried **bitterly**
because no one could be found who was
worthy to open the **scroll** or look inside
it. 5 Then one of the **elders** said to me,
"Don't cry. Look! The Lion from Judah's
tribe, the great descendant of David, has
won the **victory**, and he can break the
seven **seals** and open the **scroll**."
6 Then I saw a **Lamb** standing in the
centre of the **throne**, surrounded by the
four living **creatures** and the **elders**. The
Lamb appeared to have been killed. It
had seven horns and seven eyes, which
are the seven **spirits** of God that have
been sent throughout the whole earth.
7 The **Lamb** went and took the **scroll** from
the **right hand** of the one who sits on the
throne. 8 As he did so, the four living
creatures and the twenty-four **elders** fell
down before the **Lamb**. Each had a harp
and gold bowls filled with **incense**, which
are the **prayers** of **God's people**. 9 They
sang a **new** song:

"You are **worthy** to take the **scroll**
and to break open its **seals**.
For you were killed, and by your
sacrificial death you bought for
God

angel [2] 3.1; 7.1
announce 1 Jn 1.3; 10.7
being 1.13; 14.14
bitter Jas 3.11; 8.11
creature [5] 4.6; 6.1
death (1) 2.10; 6.8
elder (2) [5] 4.4; 7.11
glory [2] 4.9; 7.12
God's people Jude 3; 8.3
heaven [2] 4.1; 8.1
honour [2] 4.9; 7.12
incense Heb 9.4; 8.3
Kingdom (1) (of God) 1.6
lamb [6] 1 Pet 1.19; 6.1
might [2] Jude 25; 7.12
new 3.12; 14.3
power 4.11; 6.4
praise [2] 1 Pet 4.11; 7.12
prayer 1 Pet 3.7; 8.3
priest 1.6; 20.6
race (1) 1 Pet 2.9; 7.9
right (2) [2] 2.1; 10.2
sacrifice 1.5
scroll [7] Lk 4.17; 6.14
seal [4] Heb 13.20; 6.1
serve 1.6; 7.15
spirit (2) 4.5; 16.13
strength 3.2; 14.10
throne [5] 4.2; 6.16
universe Heb 11.3
victory 3.5; 12.11
win 3.5; 12.11
wisdom 2 Pet 3.15; 7.12
world of the dead (world below) [2] 1.18; 20.13
worship (1) (of God) 4.10; 7.11
worthy [4] 4.11

[c] WORLD BELOW: *The world of the dead (see 1.18).*

3.19: Prov 3.12; Heb 12.6 **4.2–3:** Ezek 1.26–28, 10.1
4.5: Ex 19.16; Rev 8.5, 11.19, 16.18; Ezek 1.13; Rev 1.4; Zech 4.2 **4.6–7:** Ezek 1.22, 5–10, 10.14
4.8: Ezek 1.18, 10.12; Is 6.2–3 **5.1:** Ezek 2.9–10; Is 29.11 **5.5:** Gen 49.9; Is 11.1, 10 **5.6:** Is 53.7; Zech 4.10
5.8: Ps 141.2 **5.9:** Ps 33.3, 98.1; Is 42.10

people from every tribe, language,
nation, and race.
10 You have made them a kingdom of
priests to serve our God,
and they shall rule on earth."
11 Again I looked, and I heard angels,
thousands and millions of them! They
stood round the throne, the four living
creatures, and the elders, 12 and sang in a
loud voice:
"The Lamb who was killed is worthy
to receive power, wealth, wisdom,
and strength,
honour, glory, and praise!"
13 And I heard every creature in heaven,
on earth, in the world below, and in the
sea—all living beings in the universe—
and they were singing:
"To him who sits on the throne and to
the Lamb,
be praise and honour, glory and
might,
for ever and ever!"
14 The four living creatures answered,
"Amen!" And the elders fell down and
worshipped.

The Seals

6 Then I saw the Lamb break open
the first of the seven seals, and I
heard one of the four living creatures say
in a voice that sounded like thunder,
"Come!" 2 I looked, and there was a
white horse. Its rider held a bow, and he
was given a crown. He rode out as a conqueror to conquer.
3 Then the Lamb broke open the
second seal; and I heard the second
living creature say, "Come!" 4 Another
horse came out, a red one. Its rider was
given the power to bring war on the
earth, so that men should kill each other.
He was given a large sword.
5 Then the Lamb broke open the third
seal; and I heard the third living
creature say, "Come!" I looked, and
there was a black horse. Its rider held a
pair of scales in his hand. 6 I heard what
sounded like a voice coming from among
the four living creatures, which said, "A
litre of wheat for a day's wages, and
three litres of barley for a day's wages.
But do not damage the olive-trees and
the vineyards!"
7 Then the Lamb broke open the
fourth seal; and I heard the fourth living
creature say, "Come!" 8 I looked, and
there was a pale-coloured horse. Its rider
was named Death, and Hades[d] followed
close behind. They were given authority
over a quarter of the earth, to kill by
means of war, famine, disease, and wild
animals.
9 Then the Lamb broke open the fifth
seal. I saw underneath the altar the souls
of those who had been killed because
they had proclaimed God's word and had
been faithful in their witnessing. 10 They
shouted in a loud voice, "Almighty Lord,
holy and true! How long will it be until
you judge the people on earth and punish
them for killing us?" 11 Each of them was
given a white robe, and they were told to
rest a little while longer, until the complete number of their fellow-servants and
brothers had been killed, as they had
been.
12 And I saw the Lamb break open the
sixth seal. There was a violent earthquake, and the sun became black like
coarse black cloth, and the moon turned
completely red like blood. 13 The stars fell
down to the earth, like unripe figs falling
from the tree when a strong wind shakes
it. 14 The sky disappeared like a scroll being rolled up, and every mountain and island was moved from its place. 15 Then
the kings of the earth, the rulers and the
military chiefs, the rich and the powerful, and all other men, slave and free, hid
themselves in caves and under rocks on
the mountains. 16 They called out to the
mountains and to the rocks, "Fall on us
and hide us from the eyes of the one who
sits on the throne and from the anger of
the Lamb! 17 The terrible day of their
anger is here, and who can stand against
it?"

The 144,000 People of Israel

7 After this I saw four angels standing
at the four corners of the earth,
holding back the four winds so that no
wind should blow on the earth or the sea
or against any tree. 2 And I saw another
angel coming up from the east with the
seal of the living God. He called out in a
loud voice to the four angels to whom
God had given the power to damage the
earth and the sea. 3 The angel said, "Do
not harm the earth, the sea, or the trees,
until we mark the servants of our God
with a seal on their foreheads." 4 And I
was told that the number of those who
were marked with God's seal on their
foreheads was 144,000. They were from
the twelve tribes of Israel, 5-8 twelve
thousand from each tribe: Judah,

witness 3.14; 11.3
word (1) 1.3; 17.17

Almighty 4.8; 11.17
altar Jas 2.21; 8.3
anger [2] Jas 1.19; 11.18
authority 2.26; 11.6
blood 1 Jn 5.6; 7.14
complete 1 Jn 1.4
conquer 2 Pet 2.19
creature [5] 5.6; 7.11
crown 4.4; 9.7
death (1) 5.9; 9.6
disease 1 Cor 12.30; 18.8
each other 1 Pet 4.9; 11.10
faithful 3.8; 12.17
famine Acts 11.28; 18.8
free 1.5; 13.16
holy 4.8; 11.2
judge Jude 15; 11.18
lamb [7] 5.6; 7.9
means 1 Jn 5.4; 13.14
power [2] 5.12; 7.2
proclaim 1.9; 10.11
punish 3.19; 17.1
rest (1) Heb 13.17; 14.13
rich 3.17; 13.16
ripe Jn 4.35; 14.15
scroll 5.1; 10.2
seal [6] 5.1; 7.2
servant 2.20; 7.3
slave 2 Pet 2.19; 13.16
soul 1 Pet 2.11; 20.4
strong 1 Jn 5.9; 14.8
terrible 2.22; 7.14
throne 5.1; 7.9
true 3.7; 15.3
turn 3.3; 8.8
vineyard 1 Cor 9.7; 14.18
violent Tit 1.7; 11.13
wage [2] Jas 5.4

angel [5] 5.2; 8.2
blood 6.12; 8.7
creature 6.1; 8.9
elder (2) [2] 5.5; 11.16
forehead [2] Mt 23.5; 9.4
glory 5.12; 15.8
guide 1 Thes 5.12
harm 1 Jn 5.18; 9.4
honour 5.12; 13.14
hunger Phil 4.12
lamb [4] 6.1; 8.1
life (1) 4.11; 11.11
mark (1) [2] Eph 4.30; 9.4
might 5.2; 10.1
persecute Heb 11.37
power [2] 6.4; 9.3
praise 5.12; 11.13
presence 3.5; 13.12
protect Jude 1
race (1) 5.9; 10.11
safe 3.10; 12.14
salvation Jude 3; 12.10
seal [3] 6.1; 8.1

[d]HADES: *The world of the dead (see 1.18).*

5.10: Ex 19.6; Rev 1.6 **5.11:** Dan 7.10 **6.2:** Zech 1.8, 6.3, 6 **6.4:** Zech 1.8, 6.2 **6.5:** Zech 6.2, 6
6.8: Ezek 14.21 **6.12:** Rev 11.13, 16.18; Is 13.10; Joel 2.10, 31, 3.15; Mt 24.29; Mk13.24–25; Lk 21.25
6.13–14: Is 34.4 **6.14:** Rev 16.20 **6.15:** Is 2.19, 21 **6.16:** Hos 10.8; Lk 23.30 **6.17:** Joel 2.11; Mal 3.2
7.1: Jer 49.36; Dan 7.2; Zech 6.5 **7.3:** Ezek 9.4, 6

servant 6.11; 10.7
serve 5.10
shepherd 1 Pet 5.2
tear (2) Heb 12.17; 21.4
Temple (1) (of God) 3.12; 11.1
terrible 6.17; 12.12
thank 4.9; 11.17
throne [7] 6.16; 8.3
wisdom 5.12; 13.18
worship (1) (of God) 5.14; 11.1

Reuben, Gad, Asher, Naphtali, Manasseh, Simeon, Levi, Issachar, Zebulun, Joseph, and Benjamin.

The Enormous Crowd

9 After this I looked, and there was an enormous crowd—no one could count all the people! They were from every **race**, tribe, nation, and language, and they stood in front of the **throne** and of the **Lamb**, dressed in white robes and holding palm branches in their hands. 10 They called out in a loud voice: "**Salvation** comes from our God, who sits on the **throne**, and from the **Lamb**!" 11 All the **angels** stood round the **throne**, the **elders**, and the four living **creatures**. Then they threw themselves face downwards in front of the **throne** and **worshipped** God, 12 saying, "Amen! **Praise**, **glory**, **wisdom**, **thanksgiving**, **honour**, **power**, and **might** belong to our God for ever and ever! Amen!"

13 One of the **elders** asked me, "Who are these people dressed in white robes, and where do they come from?"

14 "I don't know, sir. You do," I answered.

He said to me, "These are the people who have come **safely** through the **terrible persecution**. They have washed their robes and made them white with the **blood** of the **Lamb**. 15 That is why they stand before God's **throne** and **serve** him day and night in his **temple**. He who sits on the **throne** will **protect** them with his **presence**. 16 Never again will they **hunger** or thirst; neither sun nor any scorching heat will burn them, 17 because the **Lamb**, who is in the centre of the **throne**, will be their **shepherd**, and he will **guide** them to springs of **life-giving** water. And God will wipe away every **tear** from their eyes."

The Seventh Seal

altar [3] 6.9; 9.13
angel [10] 7.1; 9.1
bitter [3] 5.4
blood [2] 7.14; 11.6
creature 7.11; 14.3
destroy Jude 5; 11.5
God's people [2] 5.8; 13.7
heaven 5.3; 10.1
horror [3] Mal 2.11; 9.12
incense [4] 5.8; 18.13
lamb 7.9; 12.11
light (1) [2] 1 Jn 2.8; 18.23
offer 2.14; 14.4
prayer [2] 5.8
seal 7.2; 9.4

8 When the **Lamb** broke open the seventh **seal**, there was silence in **heaven** for about half an hour. 2 Then I saw the seven **angels** who stand before God, and they were given seven trumpets.

3 Another **angel**, who had a gold **incense-burner**, came and stood at the **altar**. He was given a lot of **incense** to add to the **prayers** of all **God's people** and to **offer** it on the gold **altar** that stands before the **throne**. 4 The smoke of the burning **incense** went up with the **prayers** of **God's people** from the hands of the **angel** standing before God. 5 Then the **angel** took the **incense-burner**, filled it with fire from the **altar**, and threw it on the earth. There were rumblings and peals of thunder, flashes of lightning, and an earthquake.

strike Acts 23.2; 11.
throne 7.9; 11.16
turn [3] 6.12; 9.20

The Trumpets

6 Then the seven **angels** with the seven trumpets prepared to blow them.

7 The first **angel** blew his trumpet. Hail and fire, mixed with **blood**, came pouring down on the earth. A third of the earth was burnt up, a third of the trees, and every blade of green grass.

8 Then the second **angel** blew his trumpet. Something that looked like a huge mountain on fire was thrown into the sea. A third of the sea was **turned** into **blood**, 9 a third of the living **creatures** in the sea died, and a third of the ships were **destroyed**.

10 Then the third **angel** blew his trumpet. A large star, burning like a torch, dropped from the sky and fell on a third of the rivers and on the springs of water. 11 (The name of the star is "**Bitterness**.") A third of the water **turned bitter**, and many people died from drinking the water, because it had **turned bitter**.

12 Then the fourth **angel** blew his trumpet. A third of the sun was **struck**, and a third of the moon, and a third of the stars, so that their **light** lost a third of its brightness; there was no **light** during a third of the day and a third of the night.

13 Then I looked, and I heard an eagle that was flying high in the air say in a loud voice, "O **horror**! **horror**! How **horrible** it will be for all who live on earth when the sound comes from the trumpets that the other three **angels** must blow!"

9 Then the fifth **angel** blew his trumpet. I saw a star which had fallen down to the earth, and it was given the key to the abyss.[e] 2 The star opened the abyss, and smoke poured out of it, like the smoke from a large furnace; the sunlight and the air were **darkened** by the smoke from the abyss. 3 Locusts came down out of the smoke upon the earth, and they were given the same kind of **power** that scorpions have. 4 They were told not to **harm** the grass or the trees or any other plant; they could **harm** only the people who did not have the **mark** of

altar 8.3; 11.1
angel [5] 8.2; 10.1
bind Jude 6
crown 6.2; 12.1
dark Jude 6; 16.10
death (1) [2] 6.8; 11.10
demon Jas 3.15; 16.14
Destroyer 2 Pet 2.3
flee Acts 14.6; 12.6
forehead 7.3; 13.16
harm [2] 7.3; 11.5
Hebrew Phil 3.5; 16.16
horror [2] 8.13; 11.14
hurt [2] 2.11
idol 2.14; 21.8
immoral 2.14; 14.8
magic Acts 19.19; 18.23

[e] ABYSS: *The place in the depths of the earth where the demons were imprisoned until their final punishment.*

7.14: Dan 12.1; Mt 24.21; Mk 13.19 **7.16:** Is 49.10 **7.17:** Ps 23.1; Ezek 34.23; Ps 23.2; Is 49.10, 25.8
8.3: Amos 9.1; Ex 30.1, 3 **8.5:** Lev 16.12; Ezek 10.2; Ex 19.16; Rev 11.19, 16.18
8.7: Ex 9.23–25; Ezek 38.22 **8.10:** Is 14.12 **8.11:** Jer 9.15 **8.12:** Is 13.10; Ezek 32.7; Joel 2.10, 31, 3.15
9.2: Gen 19.28 **9.3:** Ex 10.12–15 **9.4:** Ezek 9.4

mankind [3] 1 Pet 1.24; 11.10
mark (1) 7.3; 13.16
pain [2] 1 Pet 4.12; 12.2
plague [2] Lk 21.11; 11.6
power [3] 7.2; 11.15
repent 2.21
seal 8.1; 20.3
seek Heb 11.6
sex 2.14; 14.4
steal Tit 2.10
turn 8.8; 10.9
vision 4.1
worship (2) (of other gods) 1 Pet 4.3; 13.4

God's **seal** on their **foreheads.** 5 The locusts were not allowed to kill these people, but only to torture them for five months. The **pain** caused by the torture is like the **pain** caused by a scorpion's sting. 6 During those five months they will **seek death**, but will not find it; they will want to die, but **death** will **flee** from them.

7 The locusts looked like horses ready for battle; on their heads they had what seemed to be **crowns** of gold, and their faces were like men's faces. 8 Their hair was like women's hair, their teeth were like lions' teeth. 9 Their chests were covered with what looked like iron breastplates, and the sound made by their wings was like the noise of many horse-drawn chariots rushing into battle. 10 They have tails and stings like those of a scorpion, and it is with their tails that they have the **power** to **hurt** people for five months. 11 They have a king ruling over them, who is the **angel** in charge of the abyss. His name in **Hebrew** is Abaddon; in Greek the name is Apollyon (meaning "The **Destroyer**").

12 The first **horror** is over; after this there are still two more **horrors** to come.

13 Then the sixth **angel** blew his trumpet. I heard a voice coming from the four corners of the gold **altar** standing before God. 14 The voice said to the sixth **angel**, "Release the four angels who are **bound** at the great river Euphrates!" 15 The four **angels** were released; for this very hour of this very day of this very month and year they had been kept ready to kill a third of all **mankind**. 16 I was told the number of the mounted troops: it was two hundred million. 17 And in my **vision** I saw the horses and their riders: they had breastplates red as fire, blue as sapphire, and yellow as sulphur. The horses' heads were like lions' heads, and from their mouths came out fire, smoke, and sulphur. 18 A third of **mankind** was killed by those three **plagues**: the fire, the smoke, and the sulphur coming out of the horses' mouths. 19 For the **power** of the horses is in their mouths and also in their tails. Their tails are like snakes with heads, and they use them to **hurt** people.

20 The rest of **mankind**, all those who had not been killed by these **plagues**, did not **turn away** from what they themselves had made. They did not stop **worshipping demons**, nor the **idols** of gold, silver, bronze, stone, and wood, which cannot see, hear, or walk. 21 Nor did they **repent** of their murders, their **magic**, their **sexual immorality**, or their **stealing**.

The Angel and the Little Scroll

10 Then I saw another **mighty angel** coming down out of **heaven**. He was wrapped in a **cloud** and had a rainbow round his head; his face was like the sun, and his legs were like pillars of fire. 2 He had a small **scroll** open in his hand. He put his **right** foot on the sea and his left foot on the land, 3 and called out in a loud voice that sounded like the roar of lions. After he had called out, the seven thunders answered with a roar. 4 As soon as they spoke, I was about to write. But I heard a voice speak from **heaven**, "Keep **secret** what the seven thunders have said; do not write it down!"

5 Then the **angel** that I saw standing on the sea and on the land **raised** his **right hand** to **heaven** 6 and took a **vow in the name of** God, who lives for ever and ever, who **created heaven**, earth, and the sea, and everything in them. The **angel** said, "There will be no more delay! 7 But when the seventh **angel** blows his trumpet, then God will accomplish his **secret plan**, as he **announced** to his **servants**, the **prophets**."

8 Then the voice that I had heard speaking from **heaven** spoke to me again, saying, "Go and take the open **scroll** which is in the hand of the **angel** standing on the sea and on the land."

9 I went to the **angel** and asked him to give me the little **scroll**. He said to me, "Take it and eat it; it will **turn** sour in your stomach, but in your mouth it will be sweet as honey."

10 I took the little **scroll** from his hand and ate it, and it tasted sweet as honey in my mouth. But after I swallowed it, it **turned** sour in my stomach. 11 Then I was told, "Once again you must **proclaim** God's **message** about many nations, **races**, languages, and kings."

angel [6] 9.1; 11.15
announce 5.2; 14.6
cloud 1.7; 11.12
create 4.11; 13.8
heaven [5] 8.1; 11.12
message 3.1; 11.3
might 7.12; 18.8
name (2) (name of God, of Jesus) 3.12; 13.6
plan Heb 11.40
proclaim 6.9; 11.3
prophet 1.3; 11.10
race (1) 7.9; 11.9
raise 1.5; 20.5
right (2) [2] 5.1; 13.16
scroll [4] 6.14
secret [2] 2.24; 17.5
servant 7.3; 11.18
turn [2] 9.20; 11.6
vow Heb 7.20

The Two Witnesses

11 I was then given a stick that looked like a measuring-rod, and was told, "Go and measure the **temple** of God and the **altar**, and count those who are **worshipping** in the **temple**. 2 But do not measure the outer courts, because they have been given to the **heathen**, who will trample on the **Holy City** for forty-two months. 3 I will send my two **witnesses** dressed in **sackcloth**, and they

Almighty 6.10; 15.3
altar 9.13; 14.18
angel 10.1; 12.7
anger 6.16; 14.10
authority [3] 6.8; 12.10
beast (2) 13.1
blood 8.7; 12.11
body [2] Jude 8
celebrate 1 Cor 5.8
cloud 10.1; 14.14
Covenant Box Heb 9.4
crucify Heb 6.6
dead 3.1; 16.3

9.6: Job 3.21; Jer 8.3 **9.7:** Joel 2.4 **9.8:** Joel 1.6 **9.9:** Joel 2.5 **9.13:** Ex 30.1–3
9.20: Ps 115.4–7, 135.15–17; Dan 5.23 **10.5–7:** Ex 20.11; Deut 32.40; Dan 12.7; Amos 3.7
10.8–10: Ezek 2.8–3.3 **11.1:** Ezek 40.3; Zech 2.1–2 **11.2:** Lk 21.24

death (1) 9.6; 20.6
destroy [3] 8.9; 16.19
each other 6.4
elder (2) 7.11; 14.3
enemy [2] 2 Jn 7
happy 1.3; 14.13
harm [2] 9.4
heathen [2] 1 Pet 4.3
heaven [5] 10.1; 12.7
holy 6.10; 14.10
horror 9.12
judge 6.10; 14.7
life (1) 7.17; 12.11
mankind 9.15; 14.3
message [3] 10.11; 14.6
Messiah 1 Jn 5.1; 12.10
plague 9.18; 15.1
power [2] 9.3; 12.10
praise 7.12; 14.7
proclaim [3] 10.11; 12.11
prophet [3] 10.7; 16.6
race (1) 10.11; 13.7
rage Lk 21.25; 12.12
reverence 1 Pet 3.2; 19.5
reward 2 Jn 8; 22.12
sackcloth Lk 10.13
servant 10.7; 15.3
strike 8.12; 18.8
suffer 2.3; 12.2
symbol 1 Pet 3.21
Temple (1) (of God) [3] 7.15; 14.15
terrify [2] Heb 12.21
thank 7.12
throne 8.3; 12.5
turn 10.9; 16.4
violent 6.12; 18.21
watch 1 Pet 5.8
wish 3.15
witness [2] 6.9
world 3.10; 12.9
worship (1) (of God) [2] 7.11; 14.7

will **proclaim** God's **message** during
those 1,260 days."
4 The two **witnesses** are the two olive-
trees and the two lamps that stand before the Lord of the earth. 5 If anyone
tries to **harm** them, fire comes out of
their mouths and **destroys** their **enemies**;
and in this way, whoever tries to **harm**
them will be killed. 6 They have **authority**
to shut up the sky so that there will be no
rain during the time they **proclaim** God's
message. They have **authority** also over
the springs of water, to **turn** them into
blood; they have **authority** also to **strike**
the earth with every kind of **plague** as
often as they **wish**.
7 When they finish **proclaiming** their
message, the **beast** that comes up out of
the abyss will fight against them. He will
defeat them and kill them, 8 and their
bodies will lie in the street of the great
city, where their Lord was **crucified**. The
symbolic name of that city is Sodom, or
Egypt. 9 People from all nations, tribes,
languages, and **races** will look at their
bodies for three and a half days and will
not allow them to be buried. 10 The people
of the earth will be **happy** because of the
death of these two. They will **celebrate**
and send presents to **each other**, because
those two **prophets** brought much **suffering** upon **mankind**. 11 After three and a
half days a **life-giving** breath came from
God and entered them, and they stood
up; and all who saw them were **terrified**.
12 Then the two **prophets** heard a loud
voice say to them from **heaven**, "Come
up here!" As their **enemies watched**,
they went up into **heaven** in a **cloud**. 13 At
that very moment there was a **violent**
earthquake; a tenth of the city was **destroyed**, and seven thousand people were
killed. The rest of the people were **terrified** and **praised** the greatness of the God
of **heaven**.
14 The second **horror** is over, but the
third horror will come soon!

The Seventh Trumpet

15 Then the seventh **angel** blew his
trumpet, and there were loud voices in
heaven, saying, "The **power** to rule over
the **world** belongs now to our Lord and
his **Messiah**, and he will rule for ever and
ever!" 16 Then the twenty-four **elders**
who sit on their **thrones** in front of God
threw themselves face downwards and
worshipped God, 17 saying:

"Lord God **Almighty**, the one who is
and who was!
We **thank** you that you have taken
your great **power**
and have begun to rule!
18 The **heathen** were filled with **rage**,
because the time for your **anger** has
come,
the time for the **dead** to be **judged**.
The time has come to **reward** your
servants, the **prophets**,
and all your people, all who have
reverence for you,
great and small alike.
The time has come to **destroy** those
who destroy the earth!"
19 God's **temple** in **heaven** was
opened, and the **Covenant Box** was seen
there. Then there were flashes of lightning, rumblings and peals of thunder, an
earthquake, and heavy hail.

The Woman and the Dragon

12 Then a great and **mysterious**
sight appeared in the sky. There
was a woman, whose dress was the sun
and who had the moon under her feet
and a **crown** of twelve stars on her head.
2 She was soon to give **birth**, and the **pains**
and **suffering** of childbirth made her cry
out.
3 Another **mysterious sight** appeared
in the sky. There was a huge red **dragon**
with seven heads and ten horns and a
crown on each of his heads. 4 With his tail
he dragged a third of the stars out of the
sky and threw them down to the earth.
He stood in front of the woman, in order
to eat her child as soon as it was born.
5 Then she gave **birth** to a son, who will
rule over all nations with an iron rod. But
the child was snatched away and taken
to God and his **throne**. 6 The woman **fled**
to the desert, to a place God had prepared for her, where she will be taken
care of for 1,260 days.
7 Then war broke out in **heaven**.
Michael and his **angels** fought against the
dragon, who fought back with his **angels**;
8 but the **dragon** was defeated, and he
and his **angels** were not allowed to stay
in **heaven** any longer. 9 The huge **dragon**
was thrown out—that **ancient** serpent,
called the **Devil**, or **Satan**, that **deceived**
the whole **world**. He was thrown down to
earth, and all his **angels** with him.
10 Then I heard a loud voice in
heaven saying, "Now God's **salvation** has
come! Now God has shown his **power** as

accuse 2 Pet 2.11
ancient 2 Pet 2.5; 20.2
angel [4] 11.15; 14.6
authority 11.6; 13.2
birth [3] Jas 1.15
blood 11.6; 14.20
care [2] Jude 12
commandment Jas 2.10; 14.12
crown [2] 9.7; 13.1
deceive 2 Jn 7; 13.14
Devil [2] 2.10; 20.2
dragon [10] Is 30.6; 13.2
faithful 6.9; 14.12
flee 9.6; 20.11
flood 2 Pet 3.6; 14.20
fury Rom 2.8; 14.10
give up 2.3
glad 1 Pet 4.13; 18.20
heaven [5] 11.12; 13.6
help 3 Jn 6
lamb 8.1; 13.8
life (1) 11.11; 13.15
Messiah 11.15
mystery [2] 2 Thes 2.7; 15.1
obey 3.3; 14.12
pain 9.5; 16.2
power 11.15; 13.2
proclaim 11.3; 20.4
rage 11.18
reveal 1.1; 19.10
safe 7.14
salvation 7.10; 19.1
Satan 3.9; 20.2
sight [2] 3.2; 13.13
suffer 11.10; 18.7
terrible 7.14; 16.2
throne 11.16; 13.2
truth [2] 1.2; 19.10
victory 5.5; 15.2
win 5.5; 15.2
world 11.15; 13.8

11.4: Zech 4.3, 11–14 **11.6:** 1 Kgs 17.1; Ex 7.17–19; 1 Sam 4.8 **11.7:** Dan 7.7, 21; Rev 13.5–7, 17.8
11.8: Is 1.9–10 **11.11:** Ezek 37.10 **11.12:** 2 Kgs 2.11 **11.13:** Rev 6.12, 16.18
11.15: Ex 15.18; Dan 2.44, 7.14, 27 **11.18:** Ps 2.5, 110.5, 115.13 **11.19:** Rev 8.5, 16.18, 21 **12.3:** Dan 7.7
12.4: Dan 8.10 **12.5:** Is 66.7; Ps 2.9 **12.7:** Dan 10.13, 21, 12.1; Jude 9 **12.9:** Gen 3.1; Lk 10.18
12.10: Job 1.9–11; Zech 3.1

King! Now his Messiah has shown his authority! For the one who stood before our God and accused our brothers day and night has been thrown out of heaven. 11 Our brothers won the victory over him by the blood of the Lamb and by the truth which they proclaimed; and they were willing to give up their lives and die. 12 And so be glad, you heavens, and all you that live there! But how terrible for the earth and the sea! For the Devil has come down to you, and he is filled with rage, because he knows that he has only a little time left."

13 When the dragon realized that he had been thrown down to the earth, he began to pursue the woman who had given birth to the boy. 14 She was given the two wings of a large eagle in order to fly to her place in the desert, where she will be taken care of for three and a half years, safe from the dragon's attack. 15 And then from his mouth the dragon poured out a flood of water after the woman, so that it would carry her away. 16 But the earth helped the woman; it opened its mouth and swallowed the water that had come from the dragon's mouth. 17 The dragon was furious with the woman and went off to fight against the rest of her descendants, all those who obey God's commandments and are faithful to the truth revealed by Jesus. 18 And the dragon stood[f] on the sea-shore.

The Two Beasts

13 Then I saw a beast coming up out of the sea. It had ten horns and seven heads; on each of its horns there was a crown, and on each of its heads there was a name that was insulting to God. 2 The beast looked like a leopard, with feet like a bear's feet and a mouth like a lion's mouth. The dragon gave the beast his own power, his throne, and his vast authority. 3 One of the heads of the beast seemed to have been fatally wounded, but the wound had healed. The whole earth was amazed and followed the beast. 4 Everyone worshipped the dragon because he had given his authority to the beast. They worshipped the beast also, saying, "Who is like the beast? Who can fight against it?"

5 The beast was allowed to make proud claims which were insulting to God, and it was permitted to have authority for forty-two months. 6 It began to curse God, his name, the place where he lives, and all those who live in heaven. 7 It was allowed to fight against God's people and to defeat them, and it was given authority over every tribe, nation, language, and race. 8 All people living on earth will worship it, except those whose names were written before the creation of the world in the book of the living which belongs to the Lamb that was killed.

9 "Listen, then, if you have ears! 10 Whoever is meant to be captured will surely be captured; whoever is meant to be killed by the sword will surely be killed by the sword. This calls for endurance and faith on the part of God's people."

11 Then I saw another beast, which came up out of the earth. It had two horns like a lamb's horns, and it spoke like a dragon. 12 It used the vast authority of the first beast in its presence. It forced the earth and all who live on it to worship the first beast, whose wound had healed. 13 This second beast performed great miracles; it made fire come down out of heaven to earth in the sight of everyone. 14 And it deceived all the people living on earth by means of the miracles which it was allowed to perform in the presence of the first beast. The beast told them to build an image in honour of the beast that had been wounded by the sword and yet lived. 15 The second beast was allowed to breathe life into the image of the first beast, so that the image could talk and put to death all those who would not worship it. 16 The beast forced all the people, small and great, rich and poor, slave and free, to have a mark placed on their right hands or on their foreheads. 17 No one could buy or sell unless he had this mark, that is, the beast's name or the number that stands for the name.

18 This calls for wisdom. Whoever is intelligent can work out the meaning of the number of the beast, because the number stands for a man's name. Its number is 666.

The Lamb and His People

14 Then I looked, and there was the Lamb standing on Mount Zion; with him were 144,000 people who have his name and his Father's name written on their foreheads. 2 And I heard a voice from heaven that sounded like a roaring waterfall, like a loud peal of thunder. It

amaze Acts 13.12; 15.1
authority [5] 12.10; 16.9
beast (2) [21] 11.7; 14.9
claim 3.9
create 10.6; 16.18
crown 12.1; 14.14
curse 2 Pet 2.14; 16.9
death (3) (to death) 1 Pet 3.18
deceive 12.9; 18.23
dragon [3] 12.3; 16.13
endure 3.10; 14.12
faith 2.13
force (1) [2] Phlm 14
forehead 9.4; 14.1
free 6.15; 19.18
God's people [2] 8.3; 14.12
heal [2] 1 Pet 2.24; 22.2
heaven [2] 12.7; 14.2
honour 7.12; 14.7
image [3] Col 3.10; 14.9
insult [2] Jude 8; 17.3
intelligent Acts 13.7
lamb [2] 12.11; 14.1
life (1) 12.11; 18.13
mark (1) [2] 9.4; 14.9

means 6.8
miracle [2] Heb 2.4; 16.14
name (2) (name of God, of Jesus) 10.6; 14.1
permit Rom 13.1
poor 3.17
power 12.10; 15.8
presence [2] 7.15; 19.20
proud 1 Jn 2.16
race (1) 11.9; 14.6
rich 6.15; 18.3
right (2) 10.2
sight 12.1; 15.1
slave 6.15; 18.13
stand for [2] Gal 4.25
throne 12.5; 14.3
wisdom 7.12; 17.9
world 12.9; 16.14
worship (2) (of other gods) [5] 9.20; 14.9

altar 11.1; 16.7
angel [9] 12.7; 15.1
anger [2] 11.18; 15.1
announce 10.7; 22.16
beast (2) [2] 13.1; 15.2
being 5.13
blood 12.11; 16.3
cloud [4] 11.12
commandment 12.17

[f] And the dragon stood; *some manuscripts have* And I stood, *connecting this verse with what follows.*

12.14: Dan 7.25, 12.7 **13.1:** Dan 7.3; Rev 17.3, 7–12 **13.2:** Dan 7.4–6 **13.5–6:** Dan 7.8, 25, 11.36 **13.7:** Dan 7.21 **13.8:** Ps 69.28 **13.10:** Jer 15.2, 43.11 **14.1:** Ezek 9.4; Rev 7.3

sounded like the music made by musicians playing their harps. 3 The 144,000
people stood before the throne, the four
living creatures, and the elders; they
were singing a new song, which only
they could learn. Of all mankind they are
the only ones who have been redeemed.
4 They are the men who have kept themselves pure by not having sexual relations with women; they are virgins. They
follow the Lamb wherever he goes. They
have been redeemed from the rest of
mankind and are the first ones to be
offered to God and to the Lamb. 5 They
have never been known to tell lies; they
are faultless.

The Three Angels

6 Then I saw another angel flying high
in the air, with an eternal message of
Good News to announce to the peoples of
the earth, to every race, tribe, language,
and nation. 7 He said in a loud voice,
"Honour God and praise his greatness!
For the time has come for him to judge
mankind. Worship him who made
heaven, earth, sea, and the springs of
water!"

8 A second angel followed the first
one, saying, "She has fallen! Great
Babylon has fallen! She made all peoples
drink her wine—the strong wine of her
immoral lust!"

9 A third angel followed the first two,
saying in a loud voice, "Whoever worships the beast and its image and receives the mark on his forehead or on his
hand 10 will himself drink God's wine, the
wine of his fury, which he has poured at
full strength into the cup of his anger! All
who do this will be tormented in fire and
sulphur before the holy angels and the
Lamb. 11 The smoke of the fire that tor-
ments them goes up for ever and ever.
There is no relief day or night for those
who worship the beast and its image, for
anyone who has the mark of its name."

12 This calls for endurance on the part
of God's people, those who obey God's
commandments and are faithful to Jesus.

13 Then I heard a voice from heaven
saying, "Write this: Happy are those who
from now on die in the service of the
Lord!"

"Yes indeed!" answers the Spirit.
"They will enjoy rest from their hard
work, because the results of their service
go with them."

The Harvest of the Earth

14 Then I looked, and there was a
white cloud, and sitting on the cloud was
what looked like a human being, with a
crown of gold on his head and a sharp
sickle in his hand. 15 Then another angel
came out from the temple and cried out
in a loud voice to the one who was sitting
on the cloud, "Use your sickle and reap
the harvest, because the time has come;
the earth is ripe for the harvest!" 16 Then
the one who sat on the cloud swung his
sickle on the earth, and the earth's harvest was reaped.

17 Then I saw another angel come out
of the temple in heaven, and he also had
a sharp sickle.

18 Then another angel, who is in
charge of the fire, came from the altar.
He shouted in a loud voice to the angel
who had the sharp sickle, "Use your
sickle, and cut the grapes from the vineyard of the earth, because the grapes are
ripe!" 19 So the angel swung his sickle on
the earth, cut the grapes from the vine,
and threw them into the winepress of
God's furious anger. 20 The grapes were
squeezed out in the winepress outside the
city, and blood came out of the winepress
in a flood three hundred kilometres long
and nearly two metres deep.

The Angels with the Last Plagues

15 Then I saw in the sky another
mysterious sight, great and amazing. There were seven angels with
seven plagues, which are the last ones,
because they are the final expression of
God's anger.

2 Then I saw what looked like a sea of
glass mixed with fire. I also saw those
who had won the victory over the beast
and its image and over the one whose
name is represented by a number. They
were standing by the sea of glass, holding
harps that God had given them 3 and
singing the song of Moses, the servant of
God, and the song of the Lamb:

"Lord God Almighty,
how great and wonderful are your
deeds!
King of the nations,[g]
how right and true are your ways!
4 Who will not stand in awe of you,
Lord?
Who will refuse to declare your
greatness?
You alone are holy.
All the nations will come
and worship you,
because your just actions are seen
by all."

5 After this I saw the temple in heaven

[g] nations; *some manuscripts have* ages.

14.5: Zeph 3.13 **14.8:** Is 21.9; Jer 51.8; Rev 18.2 **14.10:** Is 51.17; Gen 19.24; Ezek 38.22 **14.11:** Is 34.10 **14.14:** Dan 7.13 **14.15:** Joel 3.13 **14.20:** Is 63.3; Lam 1.15; Rev 19.15 **15.3:** Ex 15.1 **15.4:** Jer 10.7; Ps 86.9 **15.5:** Ex 38.21

open, with the **Tent** of God's presence in
it. 6 The seven **angels** who had the seven
plagues came out of the **temple**, dressed
in **clean** shining linen and with gold belts
tied around their chests. 7 Then one of the
four living **creatures** gave the seven
angels seven gold bowls full of the **anger**
of God, who lives for ever and ever. 8 The
temple was filled with smoke from the
glory and **power of God**, and no one
could go into the **temple** until the seven
plagues brought by the seven **angels** had
come to an end.

The Bowls of God's Anger

16 Then I heard a loud voice speaking from the **temple** to the seven
angels: "Go and pour out the seven bowls
of **God's anger** on the earth!"
2 The first **angel** went and poured out
his bowl on the earth. **Terrible** and **pain-**
ful sores appeared on those who had the
mark of the **beast** and on those who had
worshipped its image.
3 Then the second **angel** poured out
his bowl on the sea. The water became
like the **blood** of a **dead** person, and
every living **creature** in the sea died.
4 Then the third **angel** poured out his
bowl on the rivers and the springs of
water, and they **turned** into **blood**. 5 I
heard the **angel** in charge of the waters
say, "The **judgements** you have made are
just, O **Holy One**, you who are and who
were! 6 They poured out the **blood** of
God's people and of the **prophets**, and so
you have given them **blood** to drink.
They are getting what they **deserve**!"
7 Then I heard a voice from the **altar** saying, "Lord God **Almighty**! **True** and **just**
indeed are your **judgements**!"
8 Then the fourth **angel** poured out his
bowl on the sun, and it was allowed to
burn people with its fiery heat. 9 They
were burnt by the fierce heat, and they
cursed the **name of God**, who has
authority over these **plagues**. But they
would not **turn from their sins** and **praise**
his greatness.
10 Then the fifth **angel** poured out his
bowl on the **throne** of the **beast**. **Dark-**
ness fell over the **beast's** kingdom, and
people bit their tongues because of their
pain, 11 and they **cursed** the God of
heaven for their **pains** and sores. But
they did not **turn from their evil ways**.
12 Then the sixth **angel** poured out his
bowl on the great river Euphrates. The
river dried up, to **provide** a way for the
kings who come from the east. 13 Then I
saw three **unclean spirits** that looked like
frogs. They were coming out of the
mouth of the **dragon**, the mouth of the
beast, and the mouth of the **false prophet**.
14 They are the **spirits of demons** that perform **miracles**. These three **spirits** go out
to all the kings of the **world**, to bring
them together for the battle on the great
Day of Almighty God.
15 "Listen! I am coming like a **thief**!
Happy is he who stays awake and guards
his clothes, so that he will not walk
around **naked** and be **ashamed** in
public!"
16 Then the **spirits** brought the kings
together in the place that in **Hebrew** is
called Armageddon.
17 Then the seventh **angel** poured out
his bowl in the air. A loud voice came
from the **throne** in the **temple**, saying, "It
is done!" 18 There were flashes of lightning, rumblings and peals of thunder,
and a **terrible** earthquake. There has
never been such an earthquake since the
creation of man; this was the **worst**
earthquake of all! 19 The great city was
split into three parts, and the cities of all
countries were **destroyed**. God **remem-**
bered great Babylon and made her drink
the wine from his **cup**—the wine of his
furious anger. 20 All the islands disappeared, all the mountains **vanished**.
21 Huge hailstones, each weighing as
much as fifty kilogrammes, fell from the
sky on people, who **cursed** God on account of the **plague** of hail, because it
was such a **terrible plague**.

The Famous Prostitute

17 Then one of the seven **angels**
who had the seven bowls came
to me and said, "Come, and I will show
you how the famous **prostitute** is to be
punished, that great city that is built near
many rivers. 2 The kings of the earth
practised sexual immorality with her,
and the people of the **world** became
drunk from drinking the wine of her **im-**
morality."
3 The **Spirit** took **control** of me, and
the **angel** carried me to a desert. There I
saw a woman sitting on a red **beast** that
had names **insulting** to God written all
over it; the **beast** had seven heads and
ten horns. 4 The woman was dressed in
purple and scarlet, and covered with
gold ornaments, precious stones, and
pearls. In her hand she held a gold **cup**
full of obscene and **filthy** things, the **re-**
sult of her **immorality**. 5 On her **forehead**

Almighty [2] 15.3; 19.6
altar 14.18
angel [9] 15.1; 17.1
anger [2] 15.1; 19.15
ashamed 1 Pet 4.16
authority 13.2; 17.12
beast (2) [4] 15.2; 17.3
blood [4] 14.20; 17.6
create 13.8; 17.8
creature 15.7; 19.4
cup 14.10; 17.4
curse [3] 13.6; 22.3
dark 9.2
Day of the Lord Jude 6
dead 11.18; 20.5
demon 9.20; 18.2
deserve 1 Pet 2.19
destroy 11.5; 17.8
dragon 13.2; 20.2
evil 2.2; 22.11
false 1 Jn 5.21; 18.23
fury 14.10; 19.15
God's people 14.12; 17.6
happy 14.13; 19.9
heaven 15.5; 18.1
Hebrew 9.11
holy 15.4; 21.2
image 15.2; 19.20
judge [2] 14.7; 18.8
justice [2] 15.4; 19.2
mark (1) 14.9; 19.20
miracle 13.13; 19.20
naked 3.17; 17.16
name (2) (name of God, of Jesus) 14.1; 22.4
pain [3] 12.2; 21.4
plague [3] 15.1; 18.8
praise 14.7; 19.1
prophet [2] 11.10; 18.20
provide 2 Pet 1.15
remember 3.3; 18.5
spirit (2) [4] 5.6; 18.2
Temple (1) (of God) [2] 15.5; 21.22
terrible [3] 12.12; 18.10
thief 3.3
throne [2] 14.3; 19.4
true 15.3; 17.17
turn [3] 11.6
unclean Heb 9.13; 18.2
vanish 2 Pet 3.10; 21.1
way (3) 15.3; 18.5
world 13.8; 17.2
worship (2) (of other gods) 14.9; 19.10
worst 1 Tim 1.15

act Jude 7
alive [3] 3.1; 19.20
amaze [3] 15.1
angel [4] 16.1; 18.1
authority [2] 16.9; 18.1
beast (2) [11] 16.2; 19.19
blood [2] 16.3; 18.24
choose 2 Pet 1.10
control 4.2; 21.10
create 16.18
cup 16.19; 18.6
destroy [3] 16.19; 18.20
faithful 14.12; 19.11
filthy 2 Pet 2.10; 18.2
flesh Jas 5.3; 19.18
follower 2.23
forehead 14.1; 20.4
God's people 16.6; 18.4
hate 2.6; 18.2
heart 1 Jn 5.10
immoral [3] 14.8; 18.3
insult 13.1
lamb [2] 15.3; 19.7
loyal 2 Tim 2.3
naked 16.15

15.8: Ex 40.34; 1 Kgs 8.10–11; 2 Chr 5.13–14; Is 6.4 **16.2:** Ex 9.10 **16.4:** Ex 7.17–21; Ps 78.44
16.10: Ex 10.21 **16.12:** Is 11.15 **16.15:** Mt 24.43–44; Lk 12.39–40; Rev 3.3 **16.16:** 2 Kgs 23.29; Zech 12.11
16.18: Rev 8.5, 11.13, 19 **16.19:** Is 51.17 **16.20:** Rev 6.14 **16.21:** Ex 9.23; Rev 11.19 **17.1:** Jer 51.13
17.2: Is 23.17; Jer 51.7 **17.3:** Rev 13.1 **17.4:** Jer 51.7

pervert Jude 7; 21.8
power [2] 15.8; 18.23
practice 2.14; 18.3
prostitute [4] Jas 2.25; 19.2
punish 6.10; 18.4
purpose [2] 2 Pet 3.5
race (1) 14.6
result 14.13
secret [2] 10.4; 22.10
sex 14.4; 18.3
Spirit (1) (God's Spirit) 14.13; 21.10
true 16.7; 19.2
understand Jude 10
will (1) 1 Jn 5.14
wisdom 13.18
word (1) 6.9; 19.9
world [3] 16.14; 18.3

was written a name that has a secret
meaning: "Great Babylon, the mother of
all the prostitutes and perverts in the
world." 6 And I saw that the woman was
drunk with the blood of God's people and
the blood of those who were killed because they had been loyal to Jesus.

When I saw her, I was completely
amazed. 7 "Why are you amazed?" the
angel asked me. "I will tell you the secret
meaning of the woman and of the beast
that carries her, the beast with seven
heads and ten horns. 8 That beast was
once alive, but lives no longer; it is about
to come up from the abyss and will go off
to be destroyed. The people living on
earth whose names have not been written before the creation of the world in
the book of the living, will all be amazed
as they look at the beast. It was once
alive; now it no longer lives, but it will re-
appear.

9 "This calls for wisdom and understanding. The seven heads are seven
hills, on which the woman sits. They are
also seven kings: 10 five of them have
fallen, one still rules, and the other one
has not yet come; when he comes, he
must rule only a little while. 11 And the
beast that was once alive, but lives no
longer, is itself an eighth king who is one
of the seven and is going off to be destroyed.

12 "The ten horns you saw are ten
kings who have not yet begun to rule, but
who will be given authority to rule as
kings for one hour with the beast.
13 These ten all have the same purpose,
and they give their power and authority
to the beast. 14 They will fight against the
Lamb; but the Lamb, together with his
called, chosen, and faithful followers, will
defeat them, because he is Lord of lords
and King of kings."

15 The angel also said to me, "The
waters you saw, on which the prostitute
is sitting, are nations, peoples, races, and
languages. 16 The ten horns you saw, and
the beast, will hate the prostitute; they
will take away everything she has and
leave her naked; they will eat her flesh
and destroy her with fire. 17 For God has
placed in their hearts the will to carry
out his purpose by acting together and
giving the beast their power to rule until
God's words come true.

18 "The woman you saw is the great
city that rules over the kings of the
earth."

The Fall of Babylon

18 After this I saw another angel
coming down out of heaven. He
had great authority, and his splendour
brightened the whole earth. 2 He cried
out in a loud voice: "She has fallen!
Great Babylon has fallen! She is now
haunted by demons and unclean spirits;
all kinds of filthy and hateful birds live in
her. 3 For all the nations have drunk her
wine—the strong wine of her immoral
lust. The kings of the earth practised
sexual immorality with her, and the
businessmen of the world grew rich from
her unrestrained lust."

4 Then I heard another voice from
heaven, saying,

"Come out, my people! Come out from
her!
You must not take part in her sins;
you must not share in her
punishment!
5 For her sins are piled up as high as
heaven,
and God remembers her wicked
ways.
6 Treat her exactly as she has treated
you;
pay her back double for all she has
done.
Fill her cup with a drink twice as
strong
as the drink she prepared for you.
7 Give her as much suffering and grief
as the glory and luxury she gave
herself.
For she keeps telling herself:
'Here I sit, a queen!
I am no widow,
I will never know grief!'
8 Because of this, in one day she will be
struck with plagues—
disease, grief, and famine.
And she will be burnt with fire,
because the Lord God, who judges
her, is mighty."

9 The kings of the earth who took part
in her immorality and lust will cry and
weep over the city when they see the
smoke from the flames that consume
her. 10 They stand a long way off, because
they are afraid of sharing in her suffering. They say, "How terrible! How awful! This great and mighty city Babylon!
In just one hour you have been punished!"

11 The businessmen of the earth also
cry and mourn for her, because no one
buys their goods any longer; 12 no one

afraid [2] 2.10
angel [2] 17.1; 19.9
apostle 2.2; 21.14
authority 17.12
blood [2] 17.6; 19.13
bride Jn 3.29; 19.7
bridegroom Jn 3.29
condemn Jude 4; 19.2
cup 17.4
deceive 13.14; 19.20
demon 16.14
destroy 17.8; 20.9
disease 6.8
false 16.13; 19.20
famine 6.8
filthy 17.4; 22.11
glad [2] 12.12; 19.7
glory 15.8; 19.1
God's people [3] 17.6; 19.8
grief [3] Lk 22.45; 21.4
groom *see* **bridegroom**
hate 17.16
heaven [4] 16.11; 19.1
human [2] 14.14
immoral [3] 17.2; 19.2
incense 8.3
judge 16.5; 19.2
life (1) 13.15; 21.6
light (1) 8.12; 21.24
long (2) Heb 11.16
lust [3] 14.8
luxury Jas 5.5
magic 9.21; 21.8
might [3] 10.1
mourn [3] 1.7
plague 16.9; 21.9
power 17.13; 19.1
practice 17.2; 21.8
prophet [2] 16.6; 19.10
punish [3] 17.1; 19.2
remember 16.19
rich [3] 13.16
sex 17.2
share [3] Jude 3; 22.19
sheep 1 Pet 2.25
slave 13.16; 19.18
spirit (2) 16.13
splendour Hag 2.3
strike 11.6
strong [2] 14.8
suffer [3] 12.2
terrible [3] 16.2
unclean 16.13
violent 11.13
way (3) 16.11
weep Jas 5.1
wicked 2.22
widow Jas 1.27
world [3] 17.2; 20.8

17.8: Dan 7.7; Rev 11.7; Ps 69.28 **17.12:** Dan 7.24 **18.2:** Is 13.21, 21.9; Jer 50.39, 51.8; Rev 14.8
18.3: Is 23.17; Jer 51.7 **18.4:** Is 48.20; Jer 50.8, 51.6, 45 **18.5:** Gen 18.20–21; Jer 51.9
18.6: Ps 137.8; Jer 50.29 **18.7–8:** Is 47.7–9 **18.9–10:** Ezek 26.16–17 **18.11:** Ezek 27.31, 36
18.12–13: Ezek 27.12, 13, 22

buys their gold, silver, precious stones, and pearls; their goods of linen, purple cloth, silk, and scarlet cloth; all kinds of rare woods and all kinds of objects made of ivory and of expensive wood, of bronze, iron, and marble; 13 and cinnamon, spice, **incense**, myrrh, and frankincense; wine and oil, flour and wheat, cattle and **sheep**, horses and carriages, **slaves**, and even **human lives**. 14 The businessmen say to her, "All the good things you **longed** to own have disappeared, and all your wealth and glamour are gone, and you will never find them again!" 15 The businessmen, who became **rich** from doing business in that city, will stand a long way off, because they are **afraid** of **sharing** in her **suffering**. They will cry and **mourn**, 16 and say, "How **terrible**! How awful for the great city! She used to dress herself in linen, purple, and scarlet, and cover herself with gold ornaments, precious stones, and pearls! 17 And in one hour she has lost all this wealth!"

All the ships' captains and passengers, the sailors and all others who earn their living on the sea, stood a long way off, 18 and cried out as they saw the smoke from the flames that consumed her: "There never has been another city like this great city!" 19 They threw dust on their heads, they cried and **mourned**, saying, "How **terrible**! How awful for the great city! She is the city where all who have ships sailing the seas became **rich** on her wealth! And in one hour she has lost everything!"

20 Be **glad**, **heaven**, because of her **destruction**! Be **glad**, **God's people** and the **apostles** and **prophets**! For God has **condemned** her for what she did to you!

21 Then a **mighty angel** picked up a stone the size of a large millstone and threw it into the sea, saying, "This is how the great city Babylon will be **violently** thrown down and will never be seen again. 22 The music of harps and of **human** voices, of players of the flute and the trumpet, will never be heard in you again! No workman in any trade will ever be found in you again; and the sound of the millstone will be heard no more! 23 Never again will the **light** of a lamp be seen in you; no more will the voices of **brides** and **grooms** be heard in you. Your businessmen were the most **powerful** in all the **world**, and with your **false magic** you **deceived** all the peoples of the **world**!"

24 Babylon was **punished** because the **blood** of **prophets** and of **God's people** was found in the city; yes, the **blood** of all those who have been killed on earth.

19 After this I heard what sounded like the roar of a large crowd of people in **heaven**, saying, "**Praise** God! **Salvation**, **glory**, and **power** belong to our God! 2 **True** and **just** are his **judgements**! He has **condemned** the **prostitute** who was **corrupting** the earth with her **immorality**. God has **punished** her because she killed his **servants**." 3 Again they shouted, "**Praise** God! The smoke from the flames that consume the great city goes up for ever and ever!" 4 The twenty-four **elders** and the four living **creatures** fell down and **worshipped** God, who was seated on the **throne**. They said, "Amen! **Praise** God!"

The Wedding-Feast of the Lamb

5 Then there came from the **throne** the sound of a voice, saying, "**Praise** our God, all his **servants** and all people, both great and small, who have **reverence** for him!" 6 Then I heard what sounded like a large crowd, like the sound of a roaring waterfall, like loud peals of thunder. I heard them say, "**Praise** God! For the Lord, our **Almighty** God, is King! 7 Let us **rejoice** and be **glad**; let us **praise** his greatness! For the time has come for the **wedding** of the **Lamb**, and his **bride** has prepared herself for it. 8 She has been given **clean** shining linen to wear." (The linen is the good **deeds** of **God's people**.)

9 Then the **angel** said to me, "Write this: **Happy** are those who have been invited to the **wedding-feast** of the **Lamb**." And the **angel** added, "These are the **true words of God**."

10 I fell down at his feet to **worship** him, but he said to me, "Don't do it! I am a **fellow-servant** of yours and of your brothers, all those who hold to the **truth** that Jesus **revealed**. **Worship** God!"

For the **truth** that Jesus **revealed** is what **inspires** the **prophets**.

The Rider on the White Horse

11 Then I saw **heaven** open, and there was a white horse. Its rider is called **Faithful** and **True**; it is with **justice** that he **judges** and fights his battles. 12 His eyes were like a flame of fire, and he wore many **crowns** on his head. He had a name written on him, but no one except himself knows what it is. 13 The robe he wore was covered with **blood**. His name

alive 17.8
Almighty [2] 16.7; 21.22
angel [3] 18.1; 20.1
anger 16.1
beast (2) [5] 17.3; 20.4
blood 18.24
bride 18.23; 21.2
clean [2] 15.6; 22.14
condemn 18.20
corrupt 2 Pet 2.20
creature 16.3
crown 14.14
deceive 18.23; 20.3
deed (2) 15.3; 22.15
elder (2) 14.3
faithful 17.14
false [2] 18.23; 20.10
feast [2] 1 Cor 10.7
flesh [4] 17.16
free 13.16
fury 16.19
glad 18.20
glory 18.7; 21.11
God's people 18.4; 20.9
happy 16.15; 20.6
heaven [3] 18.1; 20.1
image 16.2; 20.4
immoral 18.3; 21.8
inspire 2 Tim 3.16
judge [2] 18.8; 20.4
justice [2] 16.5
lamb [2] 17.14; 21.9
mark (1) 16.2; 20.4
miracle [2] 16.14
power 18.23; 20.4
praise [6] 16.9
presence 13.12; 20.11
prison 2.10; 20.7
prophet [3] 18.20; 20.10
prostitute 17.1
punish 18.4; 22.18
rejoice 1 Pet 1.8
reveal [2] 12.17; 20.4
reverence 11.18
salvation 12.10
servant [3] 15.3; 22.3
slave 18.13
throne [2] 16.10; 20.4
true [3] 17.17; 21.5
truth [2] 12.11; 20.4
wedding [2] Jn 2.1
word (1) 17.17; 20.4
Word (2) 1 Jn 1.1
worship (1) (of God) [2] 15.4; 22.3
worship (2) (of other gods) [2] 16.2; 20.4

18.15: Ezek 27.31, 36 **18.17:** Is 23.14; Ezek 27.26–30 **18.18:** Ezek 27.32 **18.19:** Ezek 27.30–34
18.20: Deut 32.43; Jer 51.48 **18.21:** Jer 51.63–64; Ezek 26.21 **18.22:** Ezek 26.13; Is 24.8
18.22–23: Jer 7.34, 25.10 **18.24:** Jer 51.49 **19.2:** Deut 32.43; 2 Kgs 9.7 **19.3:** Is 34.10 **19.5:** Ps 115.13
19.6: Ezek 1.24; Ps 93.1, 97.1, 99.1 **19.9:** Mt 22.2–3 **19.11:** Ezek 1.1; Ps 96.13; Is 11.4 **19.12:** Dan 10.6

is "The **Word of God**." 14 The armies of
heaven followed him, riding on white
horses and dressed in **clean** white linen.
15 Out of his mouth came a sharp sword,
with which he will defeat the nations. He
will rule over them with a rod of iron,
and he will trample out the wine in the
winepress of the **furious anger of the Almighty God**. 16 On his robe and on his
thigh was written the name: "King of
kings and Lord of lords."

17 Then I saw an **angel** standing on
the sun. He shouted in a loud voice to all
the birds flying in midair: "Come and
gather together for God's great **feast**!
18 Come and eat the **flesh** of kings,
generals, and soldiers, the **flesh** of horses
and their riders, the **flesh** of all people,
slave and **free**, great and small!"

19 Then I saw the **beast** and the kings
of the earth and their armies gathered to
fight against the one who was riding the
horse and against his army. 20 The **beast**
was taken **prisoner**, together with the
false prophet who had performed
miracles in his **presence**. (It was by those
miracles that he had **deceived** those who
had the **mark** of the **beast** and those who
had **worshipped the image** of the **beast**.)
The **beast** and the **false prophet** were
both thrown **alive** into the lake of fire
that burns with sulphur. 21 Their armies
were killed by the sword that comes out
of the mouth of the one who was riding
the horse; and all the birds ate all they
could of their **flesh**.

The Thousand Years

20 Then I saw an **angel** coming
down from **heaven**, holding in his
hand the key of the abyss and a heavy
chain. 2 He seized the **dragon**, that **ancient** serpent—that is, the **Devil**, or
Satan—and chained him up for a
thousand years. 3 The **angel** threw him
into the abyss, locked it, and **sealed** it, so
that he could not **deceive** the nations any
more until the thousand years were over.
After that he must be let loose for a little
while.

4 Then I saw **thrones**, and those who
sat on them were given the **power** to
judge. I also saw the **souls** of those who
had been **executed** because they had **proclaimed** the **truth** that Jesus **revealed**
and the **word of God**. They had not **worshipped the beast** or its **image**, nor had
they received the **mark** of the **beast** on
their **foreheads** or their hands. They
came **to life** and ruled as kings with
Christ for a thousand years. 5 (The rest of
the **dead** did not come **to life** until the
thousand years were over.) This is the
first **raising** of the **dead**. 6 **Happy** and
greatly **blessed** are those who are included in this first **raising** of the **dead**.
The second **death** has no **power** over
them; they shall be **priests** of God and of
Christ, and they will rule with him for a
thousand years.

ancient 12.9
angel [2] 19.9; 21.9
beast (2) [3] 19.19
bless 1 Pet 3.9
Christ [2] 1.1
dead [8] 16.3
death (1) [4] 11.10; 21.4
deceive [3] 19.20
destroy 18.20
Devil [2] 12.9
dragon 16.13
execute Dan 2.12
false 19.20
flee 12.6
forehead 17.5; 22.4
God's people 19.8; 21.3
happy 19.9; 22.7
heaven [3] 19.1; 21.1
image 19.20
judge [3] 19.2
life (2) (to life) [2] Heb 11.35
love 3.9
mark (1) 19.20
power [2] 19.1
presence 19.20
priest 5.10; Neh 10.2
prison 19.20
proclaim 12.11
prophet 19.10; 22.6
raise [2] 10.5

reveal 19.10
Satan [3] 12.9
scatter 1 Pet 1.1
seal 9.4
soul 6.9
throne [3] 19.4; 21.3
torment 14.10
truth 19.10
word (1) 19.9; 21.5
world 18.3; 21.24
world of the dead [2] 5.3
worship (2) (of other gods) 19.10; 21.8

The Defeat of Satan

7 After the thousand years are over,
Satan will be let loose from his **prison**,
8 and he will go out to **deceive** the nations
scattered over the whole **world**, that is,
Gog and Magog. **Satan** will bring them all
together for battle, as many as the grains
of sand on the sea-shore. 9 They spread
out over the earth and surrounded the
camp of **God's people** and the city that he
loves. But fire came down from **heaven**
and **destroyed** them. 10 Then the **Devil**,
who **deceived** them, was thrown into the
lake of fire and sulphur, where the **beast**
and the **false prophet** had already been
thrown; and they will be **tormented** day
and night for ever and ever.

The Final Judgement

11 Then I saw a great white **throne**
and the one who sits on it. Earth and
heaven fled from his **presence** and were
seen no more. 12 And I saw the **dead**,
great and small alike, standing before
the **throne**. Books were opened, and then
another book was opened, the book of
the living. The **dead** were **judged** according to what they had done, as recorded in
the books. 13 Then the sea gave up its
dead. **Death** and the **world of the dead**
also gave up the **dead** they held. And all
were **judged** according to what they had
done. 14 Then **death** and the **world of the
dead** were thrown into the lake of fire.
(This lake of fire is the second **death**.)
15 Whoever did not have his name written
in the book of the living was thrown into
the lake of fire.

The New Heaven and the New Earth

21 Then I saw a **new heaven** and a
new earth. The first **heaven** and
the first earth disappeared, and the sea
vanished. 2 And I saw the **Holy City**, the
new Jerusalem, coming down out of
heaven from God, prepared and ready,
like a **bride** dressed to meet her husband.
3 I heard a loud voice speaking from the
throne: "Now God's home is with **mankind**! He will live with them, and they

Almighty 19.6
angel [6] 20.1; 22.1
apostle 18.20
bride [2] 19.7; 22.17
child of God 1 Jn 5.1
clear [2] 4.6
control 17.3
death (1) [2] 20.6
glory [2] 19.1
God's people 20.9
grief 18.7
heaven [4] 20.1
holy [2] 16.5; 22.11
I am 3.11; 22.7

19.15: Ps 2.9; Is 63.3; Joel 3.13; Rev 14.20 **19.17-18:** Ezek 39.17-20 **19.20:** Rev 13.1-18 **20.2:** Gen 3.1
20.4: Dan 7.9, 22 **20.8:** Ezek 7.2, 38.2, 9, 15 **20.11-12:** Dan 7.9-10 **21.1:** Is 65.17, 66.22; 2 Pet 3.13
21.2: Is 52.1, 61.10; Rev 3.12 **21.3:** Ezek 37.27; Lev 26.11, 12

idol 9.20; 22.15
immoral 19.2; 22.15
impure Heb 9.13
lamb [5] 19.7; 22.1
last (2) [2] 15.1; 22.13
lie (2) [2] 14.5; 22.15
life (1) 18.13; 22.1
light (1) 18.23; 22.5
magic 18.23; 22.15
mankind 14.3
need 3.17; 22.5
new [3] 14.3
pain 16.2
perfect 3.2
pervert 17.5; 22.15
plague 18.8; 22.18
practice 18.3; 22.15
pure [2] 14.4
right (3) 3.21; 22.14
shame 3.18
son *see* child of God
Spirit (1) (God's Spirit) 17.3; 22.6
tear (2) 7.17
Temple (1) (of God) [2] 16.1
throne [2] 20.4; 22.1
traitor Jn 18.2
true 19.2; 22.6
trust 1 Pet 4.19; 22.6
vanish 16.20
victory 15.2
win 15.2
word (1) 20.4; 22.6
world 20.8
worship (2) (of other gods) 20.4; 22.8

shall be **his people**. God himself will be
with them, and he will be their God. 4 He
will wipe away all **tears** from their eyes.
There will be no more **death**, no more
grief or crying or **pain**. The old things
have disappeared."
5 Then the one who sits on the **throne**
said, "And now I make all things **new**!"
He also said to me, "Write this, because
these **words** are **true** and can be **trusted**."
6 And he said, "It is done! **I am** the first
and the **last**, the beginning and the end.
To anyone who is thirsty I will give the
right to drink from the spring of the
water of **life** without paying for it. 7 Whoever **wins** the **victory** will receive this
from me: I will be his God, and he will be
my **son**. 8 But cowards, **traitors**, **perverts**,
murderers, the **immoral**, those who **practise magic**, those who **worship idols**, and
all **liars**—the place for them is the lake
burning with fire and sulphur, which is
the second **death**."

The New Jerusalem

9 One of the seven **angels** who had the
seven bowls full of the seven **last plagues**
came to me and said, "Come, and I will
show you the **Bride**, the wife of the
Lamb." 10 The **Spirit** took **control** of me,
and the **angel** carried me to the top of a
very high mountain. He showed me
Jerusalem, the **Holy City**, coming down
out of **heaven** from God 11 and shining
with the **glory** of God. The city shone like
a precious stone, like a jasper, **clear** as
crystal. 12 It had a great, high wall with
twelve gates and with twelve **angels** in
charge of the gates. On the gates were
written the names of the twelve tribes of
the people of Israel. 13 There were three
gates on each side: three on the east,
three on the south, three on the north,
and three on the west. 14 The city's wall
was built on twelve foundation-stones, on
which were written the names of the
twelve **apostles** of the **Lamb**. 15 The **angel**
who spoke to me had a gold measuring-
rod to measure the city, its gates, and its
wall. 16 The city was **perfectly** square, as
wide as it was long. The **angel** measured
the city with his measuring-rod: it was
2,400 kilometres long and was as wide
and as high as it was long. 17 The **angel**
also measured the wall, and it was sixty
metres high,[h] according to the standard
unit of measure which he was using.[i]
18 The wall was made of jasper, and the
city itself was made of **pure** gold, as **clear**
as glass. 19 The foundation-stones of the
city wall were adorned with all kinds of
precious stones. The first foundation-
stone was jasper, the second sapphire,
the third agate, the fourth emerald, 20 the
fifth onyx, the sixth carnelian, the
seventh yellow quartz, the eighth beryl,
the ninth topaz, the tenth chalcedony, the
eleventh turquoise, the twelfth amethyst.
21 The twelve gates were twelve pearls;
each gate was made from a single pearl.
The street of the city was of **pure** gold,
transparent as glass.
22 I did not see a **temple** in the city,
because its **temple** is the Lord God
Almighty and the **Lamb**. 23 The city has
no **need** of the sun or the moon to shine
on it, because the **glory** of God shines on
it, and the **Lamb** is its lamp. 24 The
peoples of the **world** will walk by its **light**,
and the kings of the earth will bring their
wealth into it. 25 The gates of the city will
stand open all day; they will never be
closed, because there will be no night
there. 26 The greatness and the wealth of
the nations will be brought into the city.
27 But nothing that is **impure** will enter
the city, nor anyone who does **shameful**
things or tells **lies**. Only those whose
names are written in the **Lamb's** book of
the living will enter the city.

22 The **angel** also showed me the
river of the water of **life**,
sparkling like crystal, and coming from
the **throne** of God and of the **Lamb** 2 and
flowing down the middle of the city's
street. On each side of the river was the
tree of **life**, which bears fruit twelve
times a year, once each month; and its
leaves are for the **healing** of the nations.
3 Nothing that is under God's **curse** will
be found in the city.
The **throne** of God and of the **Lamb**
will be in the city, and his **servants** will
worship him. 4 They will see his face, and
his **name** will be written on their **foreheads**. 5 There shall be no more night,
and they will not **need** lamps or sun**light**,
because the Lord God will be their light,
and they will rule as kings for ever and
ever.

The Coming of Jesus

6 Then the **angel** said to me, "These
words are **true** and can be **trusted**. And

accept 3 Jn 7
angel [5] 21.9
announce 14.6
bride 21.2
church 3.1
clean 19.8
curse 16.9
deed (2) 19.8
evil 16.11
filthy 18.2
forehead 20.4
gift 2 Pet 1.4
grace 1.4
happy [2] 20.6
heal 13.3
holy [2] 21.2
I am [5] 21.6
idol 21.8
immoral 21.8
lamb [2] 21.9
last (2) 21.6
lie (2) 21.8
life (1) [5] 21.6
light (1) 21.24
magic 21.8
name (2) (name of God, of Jesus) 16.9
need 21.23
obey [2] 14.12
pervert 21.8
plague 21.9
practice 21.8
prophet [6] 20.10
punish 19.2
reward 11.18
right (3) 21.6

[h] high; *or* thick.
[i] *In verses 16 and 17 the Greek text speaks of "12,000 furlongs" and "144 cubits" which may have symbolic significance.*

21.4: Is 25.8, 35.10, 65.19 **21.6:** Is 55.1 **21.7:** 2 Sam 7.14; Ps 89.26–27 **21.10:** Ezek 40.2 **21.12–13:** Ezek 48.30–35 **21.15:** Ezek 40.3 **21.18–21:** Is 54.11–12 **21.23:** Is 60.19–20 **21.24:** Is 60.3 **21.25–26:** Is 60.11 **21.27:** Is 52.1; Ezek 44.9 **22.1:** Ezek 47.1; Zech 14.8 **22.2:** Gen 2.9; Ezek 47.12 **22.3:** Zech 14.11 **22.5:** Is 60.19; Dan 7.18

secret 17.5
servant [3] 19.2
share 18.4
solemn Heb 7.21
Spirit (1) (God's Spirit) [2] 21.10
testimony 3 Jn 1.12
throne [2] 21.3
true 21.5
trust 21.5
warn Jude 7
word (1) [7] 21.5
worship (1) (of God) [2] 19.4
worship (2) (of other gods) [2] 21.8

the Lord God, who gives his **Spirit** to the
prophets, has sent his **angel** to show his
servants what must happen very soon."
7 "Listen!" says Jesus. "**I am coming**
soon! **Happy** are those who **obey** the **pro-**
phetic words in this book!"
8 I, John, have heard and seen all
these things. And when I finished hearing
and seeing them, I fell down at the feet of
the **angel** who had shown me these
things, and I was about to **worship** him.
9 But he said to me, "Don't do it! I am a
fellow-servant of yours and of your
brothers the **prophets** and of all those
who **obey** the **words** in this book. **Worship**
God!" 10 And he said to me, "Do not keep
the **prophetic words** of this book a **secret**,
because the time is near when all this
will happen. 11 Whoever is **evil** must go on
doing evil, and whoever is **filthy** must go
on being filthy; whoever is good must go
on doing good, and whoever is **holy** must
go on being holy."
12 "Listen!" says Jesus. "**I am coming**
soon! I will bring my **rewards** with me,
to give to each one according to what he
has done. 13 **I am** the first and the **last**, the
beginning and the end."
14 **Happy** are those who wash their
robes **clean** and so have the **right** to eat
the fruit from the tree of **life** and to go
through the gates into the city. 15 But outside the city are the **perverts** and those
who **practise magic**, the **immoral** and the
murderers, those who **worship idols** and
those who are **liars** both in **words** and
deeds.
16 "I, Jesus, have sent my **angel** to **an-**
nounce these things to you in the
churches. **I am** descended from the
family of David; I am the bright morning
star."
17 The **Spirit** and the **Bride** say,
"Come!"
Everyone who hears this must also
say, "Come!"
Come, whoever is thirsty; **accept** the
water of **life** as a **gift**, whoever wants it.

Conclusion

18 I, John, **solemnly warn** everyone
who hears the **prophetic words** of this
book: if anyone adds anything to them,
God will add to his **punishment** the
plagues described in this book. 19 And if
anyone takes anything away from the
prophetic words of this book, God will
take away from him his **share** of the fruit
of the tree of **life** and of the **Holy City**,
which are described in this book.
20 He who gives his **testimony** to all
this says, "Yes indeed! **I am coming**
soon!"
So be it. Come, Lord Jesus!
21 May the **grace** of the Lord Jesus be
with everyone.[j]

[j] everyone; *some manuscripts have* God's people; *others have* all God's people.

22.11: Dan 12.10 **22.12:** Is 40.10, 62.11; Ps 28.4; Jer 17.10 **22.13:** Rev 1.8, 17, 2.8; Is 44.6, 48.12
22.14: Gen 2.9, 3.22 **22.16:** Is 11.1, 10 **22.17:** Is 55.1 **22.18-19:** Deut 4.2, 12.32

Word List

This word list identifies many objects or cultural features whose meaning may not be known to all readers.

A

Abib The first month of the Hebrew calendar. It runs from about mid-March to about mid-April. This month is also called Nisan.

Abyss The place in the depths of the earth where, according to ancient Jewish teaching, the demons were imprisoned until their final punishment.

Acacia A flowering tree with hard and durable wood.

Adar The twelfth month of the Hebrew calendar. It runs from about mid-February to about mid-March.

Agate A semi-precious stone of different colours, but usually white and brown.

Alabaster A soft stone, usually of light creamy colour, from which vases and jars were made.

Aloes A sweet-smelling liquid, produced from a plant. It was used as medicine and as a perfume.

Amen A Hebrew word which means "it is so" or "may it be so". It can also be translated "certainly", "truly", or "surely". In Revelation 3.14 it is used as a name for Christ.

Amethyst A semi-precious stone, usually purple or violet in colour.

Anoint To pour or rub olive-oil on someone in order to honour him or to appoint him to some special work. The Israelite kings were anointed when they took office, and so the king could be called "the anointed one". Christ, the Greek word for "The Anointed One", is the title of the one whom God chose and appointed as Saviour and Lord.

Apostle Usually one of the group of twelve men whom Jesus chose to be his special followers and helpers. It is also used in the New Testament to refer to Paul and other Christian workers. The word means "messenger".

Areopagus A hill in Athens where the city council used to meet. For this reason the council itself was called Areopagus, even after it no longer met on the hill.

Artemis The Greek name of an ancient goddess of fertility, worshipped especially in Asia Minor.

Asherah A goddess of fertility worshipped by the Canaanites; her male counterpart was Baal. After the Hebrews invaded Canaan, many of them began worshipping these two gods.

Astarte A goddess of fertility and war who was widely worshipped in the ancient Near East.

Atonement, Day of The most important of Israel's holy days, when the High Priest would offer sacrifice for the sins of the people of Israel (Leviticus 16). It was held on the 10th day of the seventh month of the Hebrew calendar (about October 1st). The Jewish name for this day is Yom Kippur.

B

Baal The god of fertility worshipped by the Canaanites; his female counterpart was Asherah. After the Hebrews invaded Canaan, many of them began worshipping these two gods.

Baal-of-the-Covenant A name by which the god Baal was known by the people of Shechem.

Balsam A tree from which sweet-smelling resin was obtained; the resin was used for perfume and medicine.

Barley A cultivated grain similar to wheat, grown as a food crop.

Bear: Great Bear and **Little Bear** Two groups of stars which can be seen north of the equator in the northern sky. The star at the end of the "tail" of the Little Bear is Polaris, the Pole Star.

Beelzebul A New Testament name given to the Devil as the chief of the evil spirits.

Beryl A semi-precious stone, usually green or bluish green in colour.

Breastplate Part of a soldier's armour, made of leather or metal; it covered the chest and sometimes the back, to protect him against arrows and the blows of a sword.

Bul The eighth month of the Hebrew calendar. It runs from about mid-October to about mid-November.

Burnt-offering A kind of sacrifice in which all the parts of the animal were completely burnt on the altar; in other sacrifices only certain parts of the animal were burnt.

C

Calamus A sweet-smelling plant, like a reed.

Capital The top part of a pillar holding up a roof.

Carnelian A semi-precious stone, usually red in colour.

Cassia A spice made from the bark of a tree; it is very like cinnamon.

Chalcedony A semi-precious stone, usually milky or grey in colour.

Christ At first it was a title, the Greek word for the Hebrew "Messiah". It means "the anointed one". Jesus was called the Christ because he was the one whom God chose and sent as Saviour and Lord.

Circumcise To cut off the foreskin of the penis. As a sign of God's covenant with his people Israelite boys were circumcised eight days after they were born (Genesis 17.9-14).

Concubine A servant-woman who, although not a wife, had sexual relations with her master. She had important legal rights, and her master was referred to as her husband.

Coral A brightly-coloured stony substance found in the sea; it was used as jewellery.

Council The highest religious court of the Jews. It was made up of seventy leaders of the Jewish people. Its president was the High Priest.

Covenant An agreement, either between people, or between God and a person or a group of people. God made a covenant with Noah (Genesis 9.8-17) and with Abraham (Genesis 17.1-8), but in the Old Testament the term usually refers to the covenant made between God and the people of Israel at the time of Moses (Exodus 24.4-8).

Covenant Box A wooden chest covered with gold. The two stone tablets with the Ten Commandments written on them were kept in it. It is often called "the Ark of the Covenant".

Cumin A small plant whose seeds are crushed and used for seasoning foods.

Cymbals A pair of thin pieces of metal held in the hands and struck together to make a loud sound in time with the music.

D

David's city In the Old Testament it usually refers to the part of Jerusalem which was captured from the Jebusites by King David. In the New Testament Bethlehem, David's boyhood home where Jesus was born, is referred to as David's town.

Dedication, Festival of A Jewish festival in which people remembered how Judas Maccabeus rededicated the altar in the temple in 165 B.C. The festival began on the 25th day of the month of Kislev (about December 10th) and lasted eight days. The Jewish name for this festival is Hanukkah.

Defile To make a person unfit to worship God. Some foods and actions were forbidden by the Law of Moses. If people broke these laws they were not allowed into the place where they worshipped God. Such people could not take part in worship until they had gone through certain rituals.

Demon An evil spirit with the power to harm people; it was regarded as a messenger and servant of the Devil.

Dill A small plant whose stems, leaves, and seeds are used for seasoning food.

Disciple A person who follows and learns from someone else. In the New Testament the word is used of the followers of John the Baptist and especially of the followers of Jesus, particularly the twelve apostles.

Divination The attempt to discover a message from God or the gods by examining such things as marked stones or the liver of a sacrificed animal.

Dragon A beast in old legends, thought to be like a huge lizard. It is also called a serpent and appears as a picture of the Devil (Revelation 12.3-13.4; 20.2-3).

E

Elders In the Old Testament this is a name given to certain respected leaders of a tribe, nation, or city. In the New Testament three different groups are called elders: (1) in the Gospels the elders are important Jewish religious leaders, some of whom were members of their highest Council; (2) in Acts 11-21 and the Letters, the elders are Christian church officers who were responsible for the work of the church; (3) in Revelation the twenty-four elders are part of God's court in heaven, perhaps as representatives of God's people.

Elul The sixth month of the Hebrew calendar. It runs from about mid-August to about mid-September.

Ephod A Hebrew word. Its meaning is not clear in a number of places. It usually refers to the piece of cloth worn over the shoulders by the High Priest which had the Urim and the Thummim attached to it. In some places, however, it refers to something the people worshipped. In some other passages it seems to refer to an object used to foretell future events.

Epicureans Those who followed the teaching of Epicurus (died 270 B.C.), a Greek philosopher who taught that happiness is the highest good in life.

Epileptic A person who suffers from a nervous disease which causes fits and fainting.

Ethanim The seventh month of the Hebrew calendar. It runs from about mid-September to about mid-October; it was later called Tishri.

Eunuch A man who has had an operation which prevents him from having normal sexual relations. Eunuchs were often important officials in the courts of ancient kings, and the word may have come to be used of such officials, even if they had not had the operation.

F

Fast To go without food for a while as a religious duty.

Feldspar A colourful, rather hard rock, often glassy in appearance.

Fellowship-offerings A sacrifice offered to restore or keep a right relationship with God. Only a part of the animal was burnt on the altar; the rest was eaten by the worshippers or the priests.

Flax A small cultivated plant; the fibres of its stem are spun into thread used in making linen cloth.

Frankincense A valuable substance made from the sap of a certain tree, probably brought from Arabia. It was burnt to give a pleasant smell.

G

Garnet A semi-precious stone, usually red in colour.

Gazelle A kind of deer, known for its beauty and gracefulness.

Gentile A person who is not a Jew.

H

Hades The Greek name used in the New Testament to refer to the world of the dead.

Harrow A metal frame used to break up the ground and level it after it has been ploughed.

Harvest Festival The Israelite festival celebrating the wheat harvest, held in the latter part of May, fifty days after Passover. The Jewish name for this festival is Shavuoth (the Feast of Weeks). It has also been called Pentecost.

Hermes The name of a Greek god who served as messenger of the gods.

Herod's Party A political party in New Testament times made up of Jews who wanted to be ruled by one of the family of Herod the Great rather than by the Roman governor.

High Priest The chief Jewish priest and president of their supreme Council. Once a year (on the Day of Atonement) he would enter the Most Holy Place in the Temple and offer a sacrifice for himself and for the sins of the people of Israel.

Hyssop A small bushy plant used in religious ceremonies to sprinkle liquids.

I

Incense Material which is burnt in order to produce a pleasant smell. The Israelites used it in their worship.

J

Jackal A small wild animal like a fox.

Jasper A semi-precious stone of various colours. The jasper mentioned in the Bible was probably green, or else clear.

Javelin A short, light spear used by soldiers in ancient times.

K

Kislev The ninth month of the Hebrew calendar. It runs from about mid-November to about mid-December.

L

Law The name which the Jews applied to the first five books of the Old Testament, also called "The Books of Moses". Sometimes, however, the name is used in a more general way for the entire Old Testament.

Leviathan An animal in old legends that lived in water. Scholars think it was the crocodile. It is used to represent the chaos that existed before God created the world (Isaiah 27.1; Psalm 74.14).

Levite (1) A member of the tribe of Levi; (2) a man who helped the priest to perform religious duties.

Levitical Priest A Hebrew priest descended from the tribe of Levi. All priests were supposed to be members of the tribe of Levi, but in later times not all members of the tribe of Levi were priests.

Living Creatures (also called "winged creatures"). Symbols of God's majesty and his presence. For a description of them, see Exodus 25.18-20; Ezekiel 1.5-13; 10; Revelation 4.6-9. Older translations call them cherubim.

LORD In this translation " LORD " stands for the Hebrew name **Yahweh** (some translations use **Jehovah**). Sometimes it refers to the name itself, sometimes to a pronoun standing for the name.

Lyre A kind of harp.

M

Mandrake A small plant; it was believed that eating its root or fruit would help a woman to have children.

Manna A food eaten by the Israelites during their travels in the wilderness. It was white and flaky, and looked like small seeds (Exodus 16.14-21; Numbers 11.7-9).

Medium A person who believes that he or she can communicate with the dead.

Messiah A Hebrew title (meaning "the anointed one") given to the Saviour whose coming was promised by the Hebrew prophets; the Greek word "the Christ" has the same meaning.

Mildew A fungus that appears on various objects, especially in damp weather.

Millet A cultivated grain that is grown as a food crop.

Molech One of the gods of the ancient people of Canaan.

Most Holy Place The innermost room of the Tent of the LORD's presence or the Temple. The Covenant Box was kept there. Only the High Priest could enter the Most Holy Place, and he did so only once a year, on the Day of Atonement.

Mustard A large plant which grows from a very small seed. The seeds are ground into powder and used as spice on food.

Myrrh A sweet-smelling resin that was very valuable. It served as a medicine (Mark 15.23) and was used by the Jews in preparing bodies for burial (John 19.39).

Myrtle A kind of evergreen shrub or tree.

N

Nard An expensive perfume made from a plant.

Nazarene Someone from the town of Nazareth. The name was used as a title for Jesus and also as a name for the early Christians (Acts 24.5).

Nazirite A person who took a special vow to serve God. Such a person was not to drink beer or wine, cut his hair, or touch a dead body (Numbers 6.1-21). The vow could be taken for a certain period of time, but some persons were dedicated to God as Nazirites from their birth.

New Moon Festival A religious ceremony held by the Israelites on the day of each new moon.

New Year Festival The Jewish name for this festival is "Rosh Hashanah".

Nisan The first month of the Hebrew calendar. It runs from about mid-March to about mid-April. The month is also called Abib.

O

Onyx A semi-precious stone of various colours.

Orion A group of bright stars that can be seen during winter evenings.

Outcasts In other Bibles this word is translated "sinners". In the Gospels it refers to Jews who were not allowed to attend synagogue worship because they had broken rules about foods that should not be eaten, and about being friendly with people who were not Jews. Such outcasts were looked down on by many of their fellow-Jews, and Jesus was criticized for being friendly with them (Mark 2.15-17; Luke7.34; 15.1-2).

P

Parable A story which teaches spiritual truth. It was often used by Jesus.

Paradise A name for heaven (Luke 23.43; 2 Corinthians 12.3).

Paralytic Someone who suffers from a disease that prevents him from moving part or all of his body.

Passover The Israelite festival, on the 14th day of the month Nisan (about April 1st), which celebrated the freeing of the Hebrews from their captivity in Egypt. The Angel of Death killed the first-born in the Egyptian homes but passed over the Hebrew homes (Exodus 12.23-27). The Jewish name for this festival is Pesach.

Pentecost, Day of The Greek name for the Israelite festival of wheat harvest (see Harvest Festival). The name Pentecost (meaning "fiftieth") comes from the fact that the feast was held fifty days after Passover.

Pervert One who commits unnatural sexual acts.

Pharisees A Jewish religious party during the time of Jesus. They were strict in obeying the Law of Moses and other regulations which had been added to it through the centuries.

Pistachio nut A small greenish nut.

Pleiades A small group of stars visible during winter evenings.

Pomegranate A reddish fruit about the size of a large apple. It has a hard rind and is full of tasty seeds.

Preparation, Day of The sixth day of the week (Friday), on which the Jews got ready to keep the Sabbath (Saturday).

Prophet A person who proclaims a message from God. The word usually refers to certain men in the Old Testament, but the New Testament speaks of prophets in the early church. John the Baptist is also called a prophet.

Purim The Jewish religious holiday held on the 14th day of the month Adar (about March 1st), celebrating the deliverance of the Jews from Haman by Esther and Mordecai. The story is told in the book of Esther.

Q

Quartz A semi-precious stone of various colours, but usually clear.

R

Rabbi A Hebrew word which means "my teacher".

Red Sea (in Hebrew literally "Sea of Reeds"). Referred at first to (1) a series of lakes and marshes between the head of the Gulf of Suez and the Mediterranean, where the events described in Exodus 13 are thought to have taken place. It was also used for (2) the Gulf of Suez, and (3) the Gulf of Aqaba.

Rephan The name of an ancient god who was worshipped as the ruler of the planet Saturn.

Resin A fragrant, gummy substance produced from the sap of certain trees and shrubs.

Restoration, Year of The year, coming every fifty years, when the ancient Israelites returned to the original owner any property they were holding. They also freed their Israelite slaves, and did not cultivate their fields.

S

Sabbath The seventh day of the week (from sunset on Friday to sunset on Saturday), a holy day on which no work was permitted.

Sackcloth A coarse cloth made of goats' hair, which was worn as a sign of mourning or distress.

Sadducees A small Jewish religious party in New Testament times. Most of them were priests. They based their beliefs mainly on the first five books of the Old Testament. They had several beliefs and practices which were different from those of the larger party of the Pharisees.

Samaritan A name used to refer to a native of Samaria, the region between Judaea and Galilee. Because of differences in politics, race, customs, and religion (including especially the central place of worship), there was much bad feeling between the Jews and the Samaritans.

Sanctuary A building dedicated to the worship of God. Sometimes the word refers to the central place of worship and not to the whole building.

Sapphire A very valuable stone, usually blue in colour.

Sceptre A short rod held by kings as a sign of their authority.

Scorpion A small creature which has eight legs and a long tail with a poisonous sting. It can inflict a very painful, and sometimes fatal, wound.

Scribe A person who wrote documents for others or copied written material. Some scribes were employed by ancient kings to prepare official documents, and so became important officials.

Scriptures In the New Testament the word refers to the Hebrew sacred writings, known to Christians as the Old Testament. Various names are used: the Law (or the Law of Moses) and the prophets (Matthew 5.17; 7.12; Luke 2.22; 24.44; Acts 13.15; 28.23); the Holy Scriptures (Romans 1.2; 2 Timothy 3.15); the old covenant (2 Corinthians 3.14). The singular "scripture" refers to a single passage of the Old Testament.

Serpent A name given to the dragon, which appears in the New Testament as a picture of the Devil (Revelation 12.3-17; 20.2-3).

Seventh Year The year, coming every seventh year, when the Israelites did not cultivate their fields and when debts were cancelled.

Shebat The eleventh month of the Hebrew calendar. It runs from about mid-January to about mid-February.

Shelters, Festival of A happy festival celebrated by the Israelites in the autumn after the harvest was complete. In order to help them remember the years when their ancestors wandered through the wilderness, the Israelites built rough shelters to live in during the festival. The Jewish name for this festival is Sukkoth. It is also called the Feast of Tabernacles or the Feast of Booths.

Sickle A tool consisting of a curved metal blade and a wooden handle, used for cutting wheat and other crops.

Sivan The third month of the Hebrew calendar. It runs from about mid-May to about mid-June.

Snuffer An instrument used to trim the oil lamps used in the Tent of the LORD's presence or the Temple.

Sorcerer A person who works magic for evil purposes.

Stoics Those who followed the teachings of the Greek philosopher Zeno (died 265 B.C.), who taught that happiness is to be found in being free from pleasure and pain.

Sulphur In the Bible this refers to a chemical which burns with great heat and produces an unpleasant smell.

T

Tambourine A small drum with pieces of metal in the rim, held in the hand and shaken. In biblical times it was generally used by women.

Tassel A group of threads or chords, fastened together at one end and loose at the other. The Israelites were ordered to wear these on their clothes (Numbers 15.37-41).

Teachers of the Law Men who in New Testament times taught and explained the teachings of the Old Testament, especially the first five books.

Tebeth The tenth month of the Hebrew calendar. It runs from about mid-December to about mid-January.

Tenant In Bible times, a man who grows crops on land owned by someone else, and hands over a part of the harvest to the owner to pay for the use of his land.

Tent of the LORD's Presence The large tent described in detail in Exodus 26, where the Israelites worshipped God until Solomon built the Temple. It is also called the Tabernacle or Tent of Meeting.

Tithe A tenth part of a person's crops or income, given to God.

Topaz A semi-precious stone, usually yellow in colour.

Turban A kind of hat made of cloth wrapped round the head.

Turquoise A semi-precious stone, blue or bluish green in colour.

U

Unleavened Bread, Festival of The Israelite festival, lasting seven days after Passover; it also celebrated the deliverance of the ancient Hebrews from Egypt. The name came from the practice of not using leaven (yeast) in making bread during that week (Exodus 12.14-20). It was held from the 15th to the 22nd day of the month Nisan (about the first week of April).

Urim and Thummim Two small objects used by Israelite priests to find out God's will.

V

Vow A strong statement or promise, often made by calling upon God to punish the speaker if the statement should prove to be untrue or if the promise was not kept.

W

Winged Creatures See "Living Creatures".

Winnowing Shovel A tool like a shovel or a large fork, used to separate the grains from the husks.

Wreath Flowers or leaves arranged in a circle, to be placed on a person's head. In ancient times a wreath of leaves was the prize given to winners in athletic games.

Y

Yeast A substance, also called leaven, which is added to dough made from flour of wheat or barley to make it rise before being baked into bread.

Yoke A heavy bar of wood which is fitted over the necks of two oxen to make it possible for them to pull a plough or a cart. The word is used to describe the rules for living that a teacher passes on to his pupils.

Z

Zeus The name of the supreme god of the Greeks.

Zion Originally a name for "David's City", the Jebusite stronghold captured by King David's men. The word "Zion" was later used to refer to the hill on which the Temple stood.

Ziv The second month of the Hebrew calendar. It runs from about mid-April to about mid-May.

Maps

1 **The World of Genesis**
Included here are many of the places visited by Abraham and his immediate descendants. Their travels are described in Genesis 11-50.

2 **Liberation from Egypt—the Route of the Exodus**
God led his people out of Egypt (Exodus 12), across the sea (Exodus 14), through the desert to Mount Sinai where they received the Ten Commandments (Exodus 20), and on to the edge of the "Promised Land" (Numbers 33 and Deuteronomy 34).

3 **Canaan Settled by the Israelites**
The land of Canaan was divided between the twelve tribes of Israel (Exodus 34-35 and Joshua 13-21). Shown on this map are many of the places featured in the stories of three of Israel's Judges—Deborah, Gideon and Samson (Judges 4-8, 13-16).

4 **The United Israelite Kingdom**
and
5 **The Divided Israelite Kingdom**
These two maps relate to the books of Samuel, Kings and Chronicles. At the height of its power, the influence of the united Israelite kingdom spread beyond the region shown. The dividing line following the split described in 1 Kings 12 and 2 Chronicles 10 is shown on The Divided Israelite Kingdom.

6 **Palestine in the Time of Jesus**
Under Roman rule, Palestine was divided into regions for government. Many of the places visited by Jesus can be found on this map.

7 **Jerusalem in New Testament Times**
Shown here are the Temple and other places which featured in the last week of Jesus' life.

8 **Paul's First Missionary Journey**
The Acts of the Apostles tells how the Gospel began to spread. Paul's first missionary journey is described in Acts 13-14.

9 **Paul's Second and Third Missionary Journeys**
These two journeys can be found in Acts 15-20.

10 **Paul's Journey to Rome**
This journey is described in Acts 27-28.

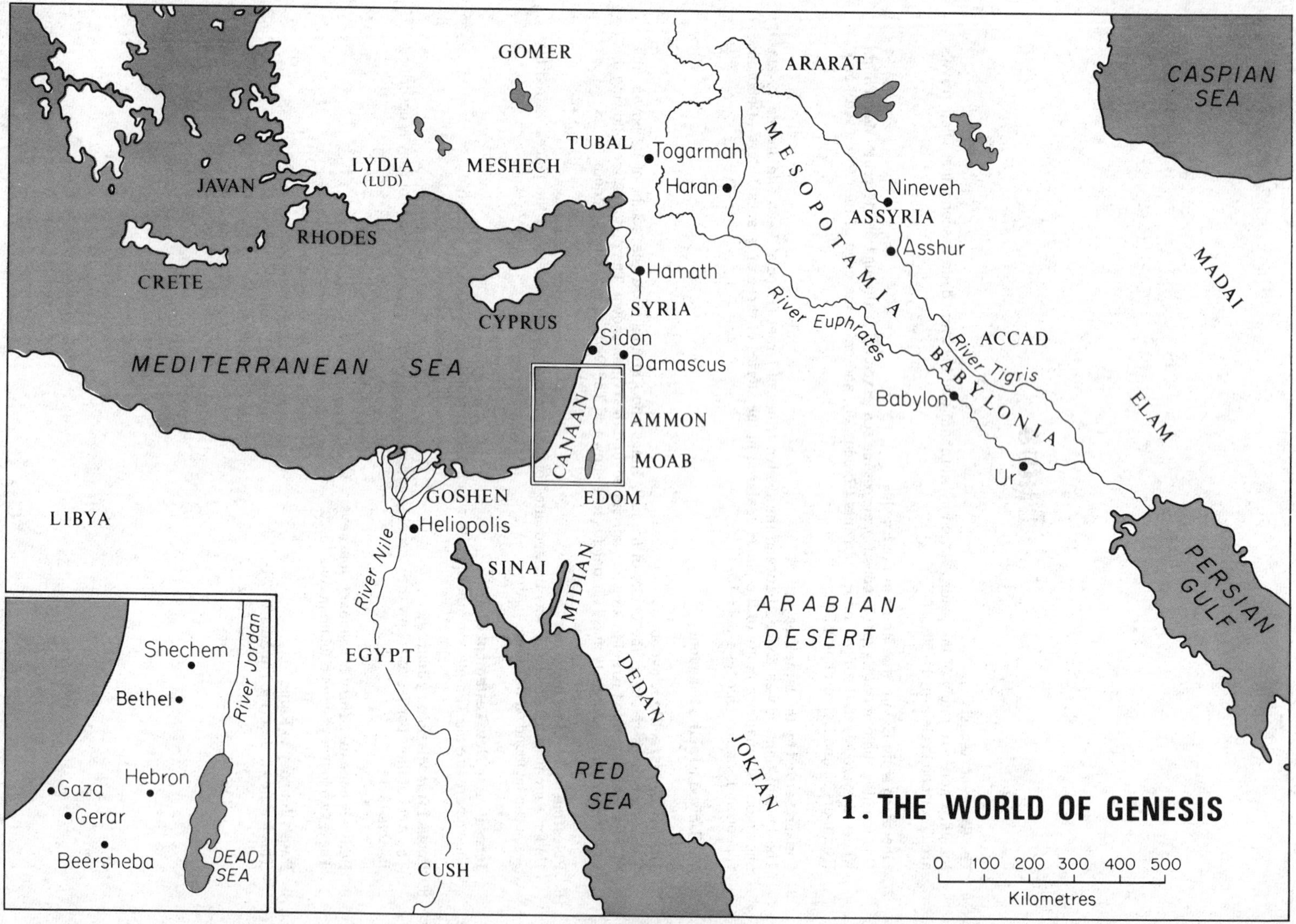
1. THE WORLD OF GENESIS
CASPIAN SEA
GOMER
ARARAT
TUBAL
Togarmah
MESOPOTAMIA
LYDIA (LUD)
MESHECH
JAVAN
Haran
Nineveh
ASSYRIA
RHODES
Asshur
MADAI
CRETE
Hamath
SYRIA
CYPRUS
River Euphrates
Sidon
ACCAD
MEDITERRANEAN SEA
Damascus
River Tigris
BABYLONIA
Babylon
CANAAN
AMMON
ELAM
MOAB
Ur
GOSHEN
EDOM
LIBYA
Heliopolis
River Nile
SINAI
MIDIAN
PERSIAN GULF
ARABIAN DESERT
EGYPT
DEDAN
JOKTAN
RED SEA
CUSH
Shechem
Bethel
River Jordan
Gaza
Hebron
Gerar
Beersheba
DEAD SEA
0 100 200 300 400 500
Kilometres

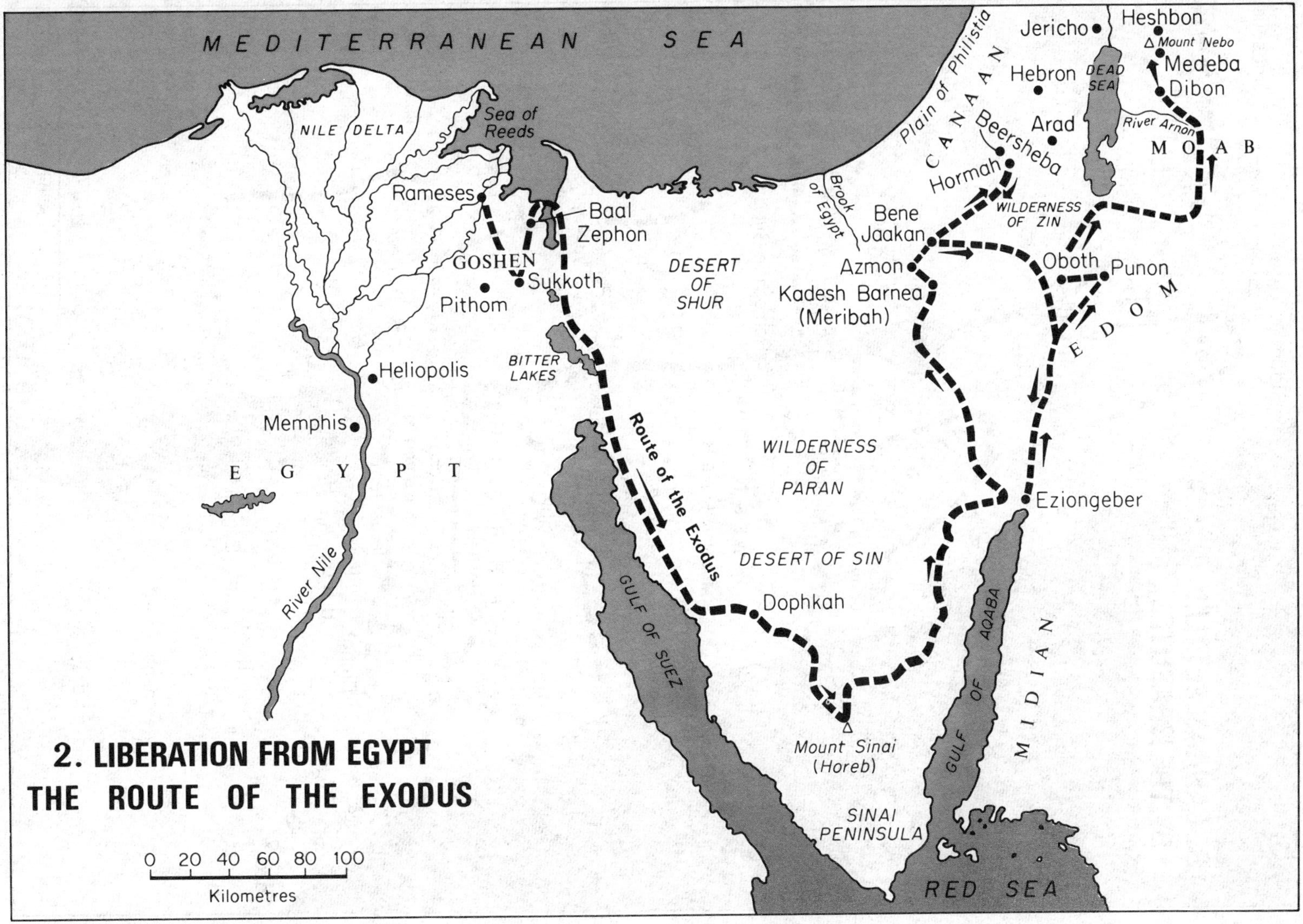

2. LIBERATION FROM EGYPT THE ROUTE OF THE EXODUS

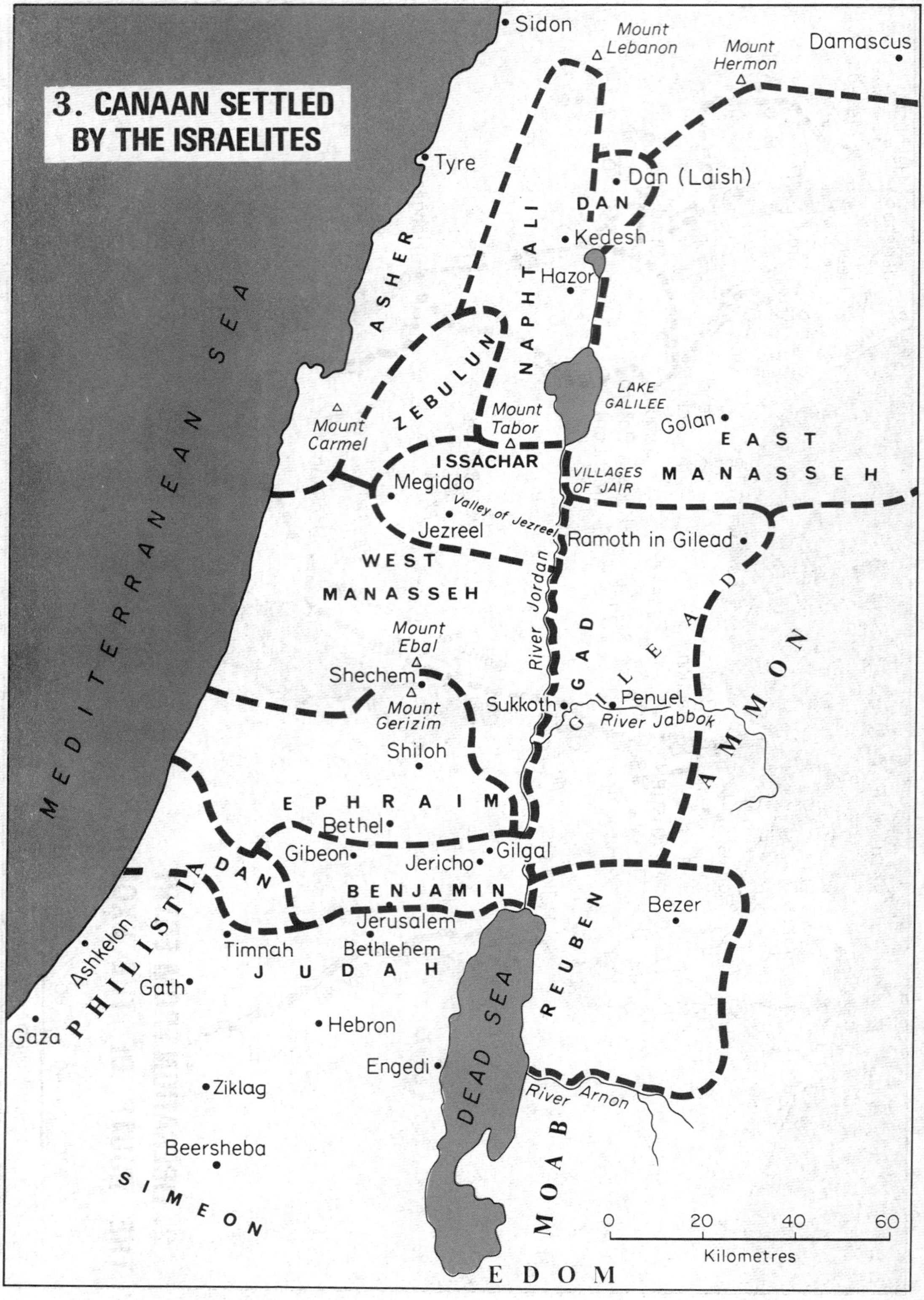
3. CANAAN SETTLED BY THE ISRAELITES
Sidon
Mount Lebanon
Mount Hermon
Damascus
Tyre
Dan (Laish)
DAN
Kedesh
Hazor
ASHER
NAPHTALI
ZEBULUN
MEDITERRANEAN SEA
LAKE GALILEE
Mount Carmel
Mount Tabor
Golan
EAST MANASSEH
ISSACHAR
Megiddo
VILLAGES OF JAIR
Valley of Jezreel
Jezreel
Ramoth in Gilead
WEST MANASSEH
River Jordan
GAD
GILEAD
AMMON
Mount Ebal
Shechem
Mount Gerizim
Sukkoth
Penuel
River Jabbok
Shiloh
EPHRAIM
Bethel
Gibeon
Gilgal
Jericho
DAN
BENJAMIN
Jerusalem
Bezer
REUBEN
PHILISTIA
Ashkelon
Timnah
Bethlehem
JUDAH
Gath
Gaza
Hebron
DEAD SEA
Engedi
River Arnon
Ziklag
MOAB
Beersheba
SIMEON
0
20
40
60
Kilometres
EDOM

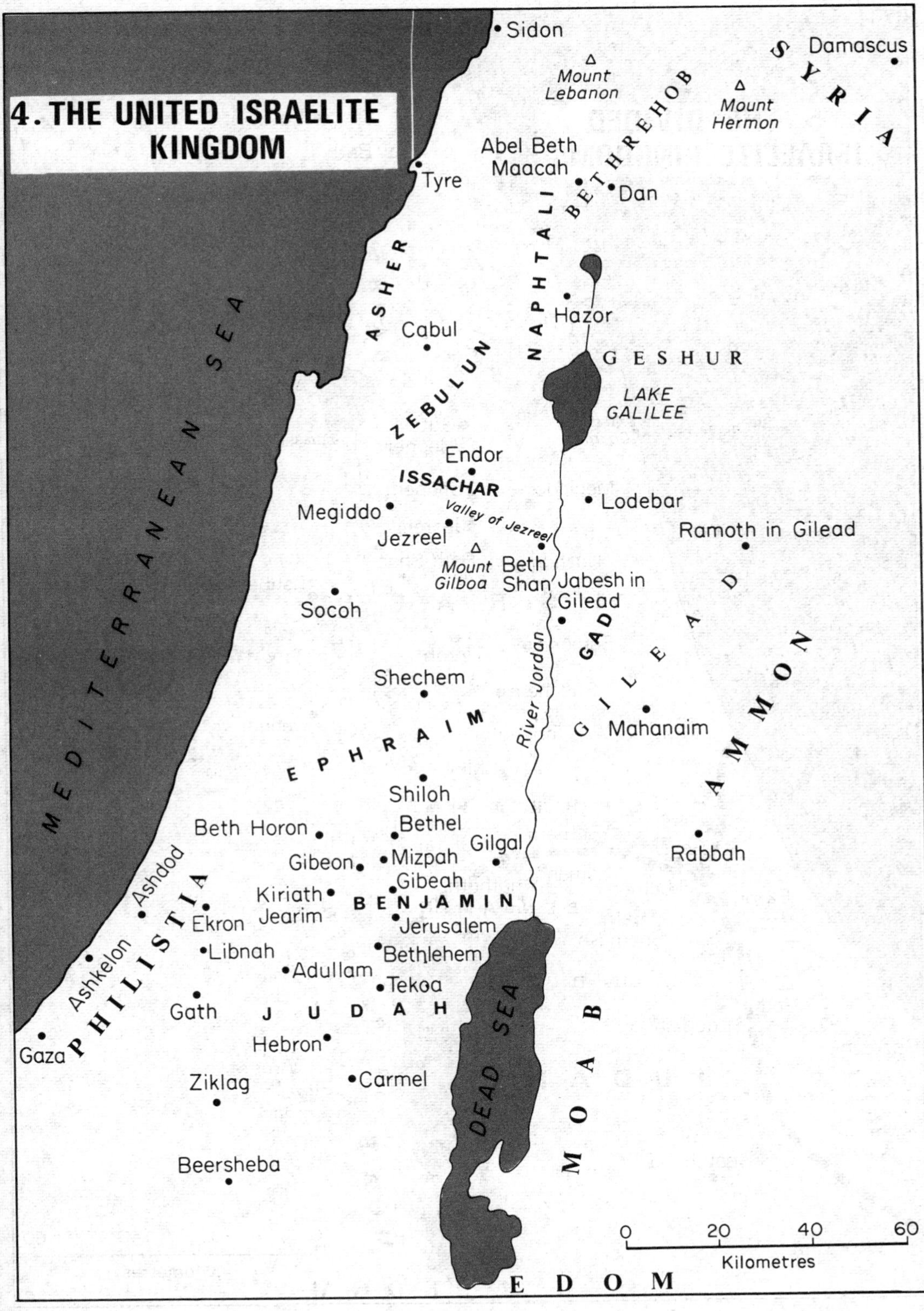
4. THE UNITED ISRAELITE KINGDOM
Sidon
Damascus
Mount Lebanon
Mount Hermon
SYRIA
BETHREHOB
Abel Beth Maacah
Tyre
Dan
NAPHTALI
ASHER
Hazor
Cabul
GESHUR
LAKE GALILEE
ZEBULUN
MEDITERRANEAN SEA
Endor
ISSACHAR
Megiddo
Lodebar
Valley of Jezreel
Jezreel
Ramoth in Gilead
Mount Gilboa
Beth Shan
Jabesh in Gilead
Socoh
GAD
GILEAD
AMMON
River Jordan
Shechem
Mahanaim
EPHRAIM
Shiloh
Beth Horon
Bethel
Gilgal
Rabbah
Gibeon
Mizpah
Gibeah
Ashdod
Kiriath Jearim
BENJAMIN
Ekron
Jerusalem
Libnah
Bethlehem
Ashkelon
Adullam
Tekoa
PHILISTIA
Gath
JUDAH
DEAD SEA
MOAB
Gaza
Hebron
Ziklag
Carmel
Beersheba
0
20
40
60
Kilometres
EDOM

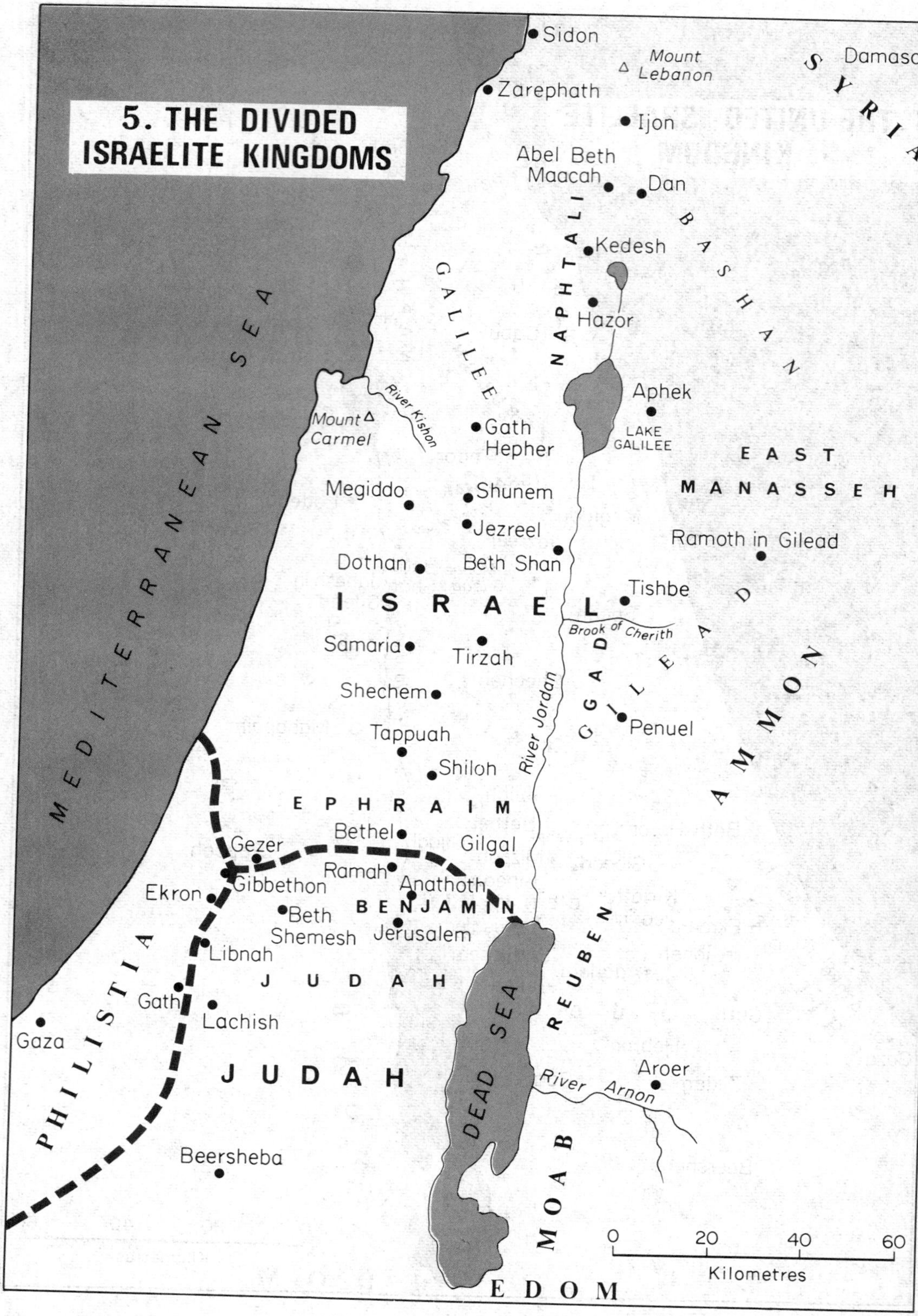

5. THE DIVIDED ISRAELITE KINGDOMS
MEDITERRANEAN SEA
Sidon
Mount Lebanon
Damascus
SYRIA
Zarephath
Ijon
Abel Beth Maacah
Dan
NAPHTALI
BASHAN
Kedesh
GALILEE
Hazor
Aphek
LAKE GALILEE
Mount Carmel
River Kishon
Gath Hepher
EAST MANASSEH
Megiddo
Shunem
Jezreel
Ramoth in Gilead
Dothan
Beth Shan
Tishbe
ISRAEL
Brook of Cherith
Samaria
Tirzah
GILEAD
GAD
Shechem
Penuel
AMMON
Tappuah
River Jordan
Shiloh
EPHRAIM
Bethel
Gilgal
Gezer
Ramah
Gibbethon
Anathoth
Ekron
BENJAMIN
Beth Shemesh
Jerusalem
Libnah
PHILISTIA
JUDAH
Gath
Lachish
DEAD SEA
REUBEN
Gaza
JUDAH
Aroer
River Arnon
MOAB
Beersheba
EDOM
0 20 40 60
Kilometres

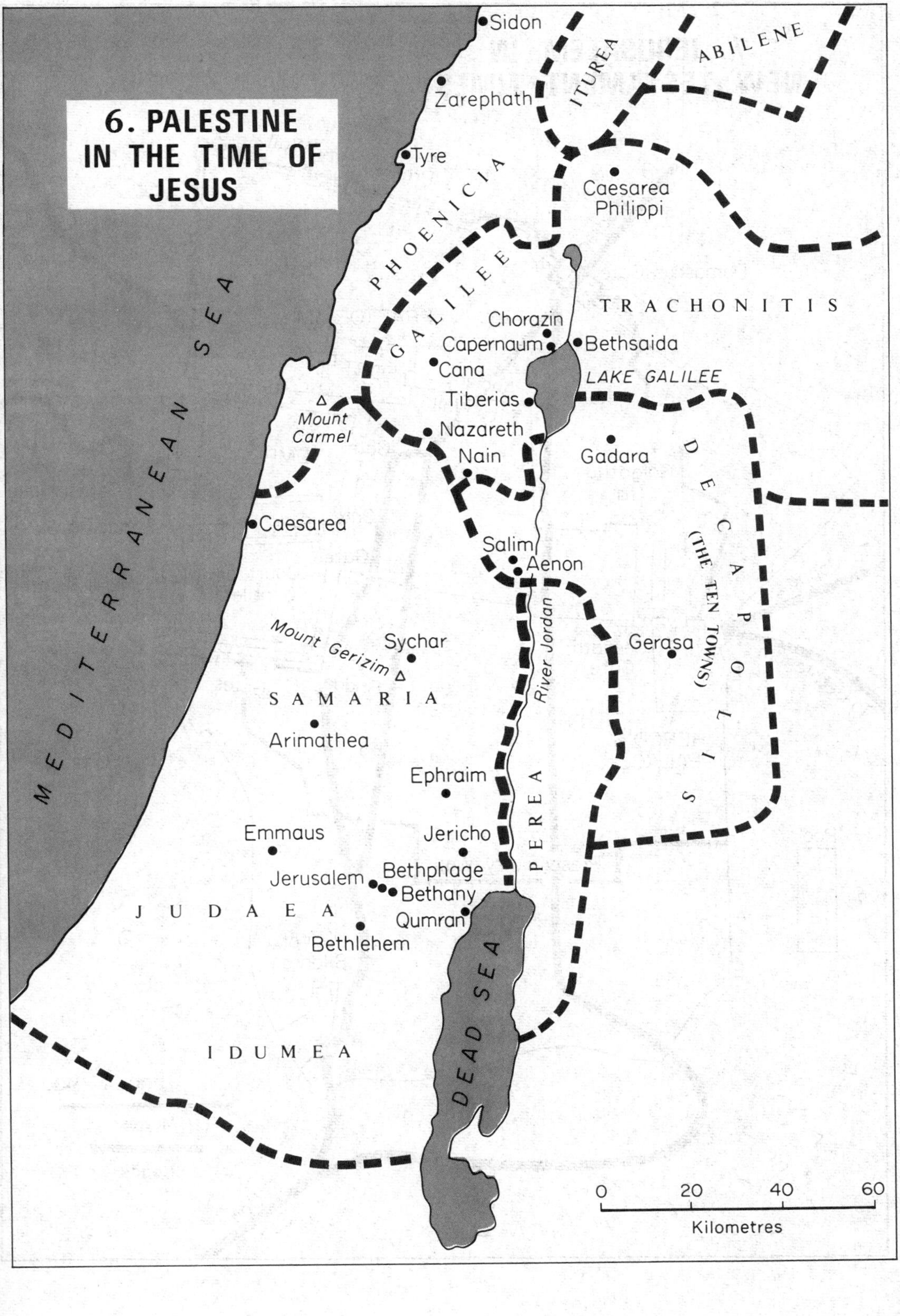

6. PALESTINE IN THE TIME OF JESUS
Sidon
Zarephath
Tyre
ITUREA
ABILENE
PHOENICIA
Caesarea Philippi
GALILEE
TRACHONITIS
Chorazin
Capernaum
Bethsaida
Cana
LAKE GALILEE
Tiberias
Mount Carmel
Nazareth
Nain
Gadara
MEDITERRANEAN SEA
Caesarea
DECAPOLIS
(THE TEN TOWNS)
Salim
Aenon
Mount Gerizim
Sychar
Gerasa
River Jordan
SAMARIA
Arimathea
Ephraim
PEREA
Emmaus
Jericho
Jerusalem
Bethphage
Bethany
JUDAEA
Qumran
Bethlehem
DEAD SEA
IDUMEA
0
20
40
60
Kilometres

7. JERUSALEM IN NEW TESTAMENT TIMES

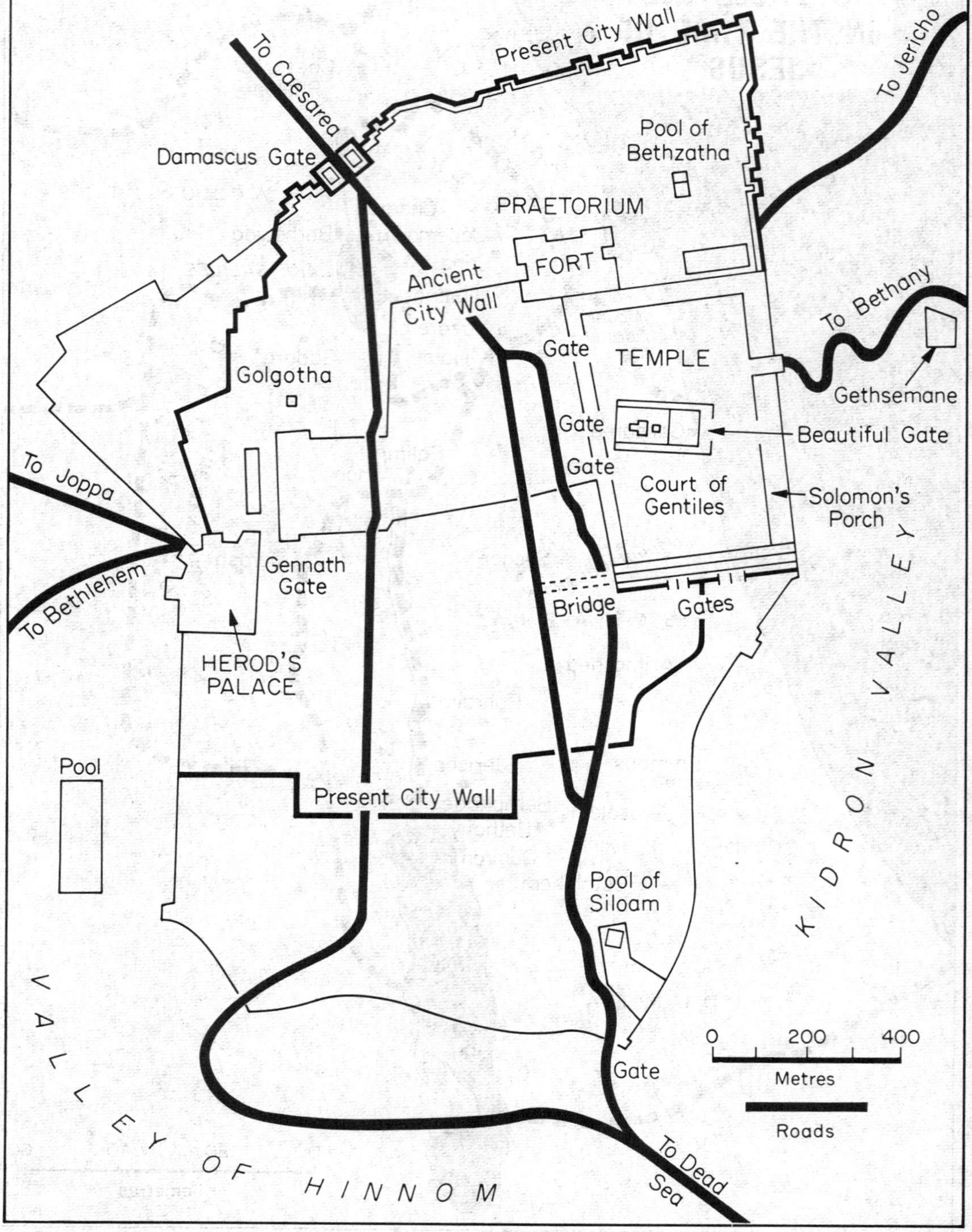

Present City Wall
To Caesarea
To Jericho
Pool of Bethzatha
Damascus Gate
PRAETORIUM
FORT
Ancient City Wall
To Bethany
Gate
TEMPLE
Golgotha
Gethsemane
Gate
Beautiful Gate
To Joppa
Gate
Court of Gentiles
Solomon's Porch
Gennath Gate
To Bethlehem
Bridge
Gates
HEROD'S PALACE
KIDRON VALLEY
Pool
Present City Wall
Pool of Siloam
VALLEY OF HINNOM
0
200
400
Metres
Gate
Roads
To Dead Sea

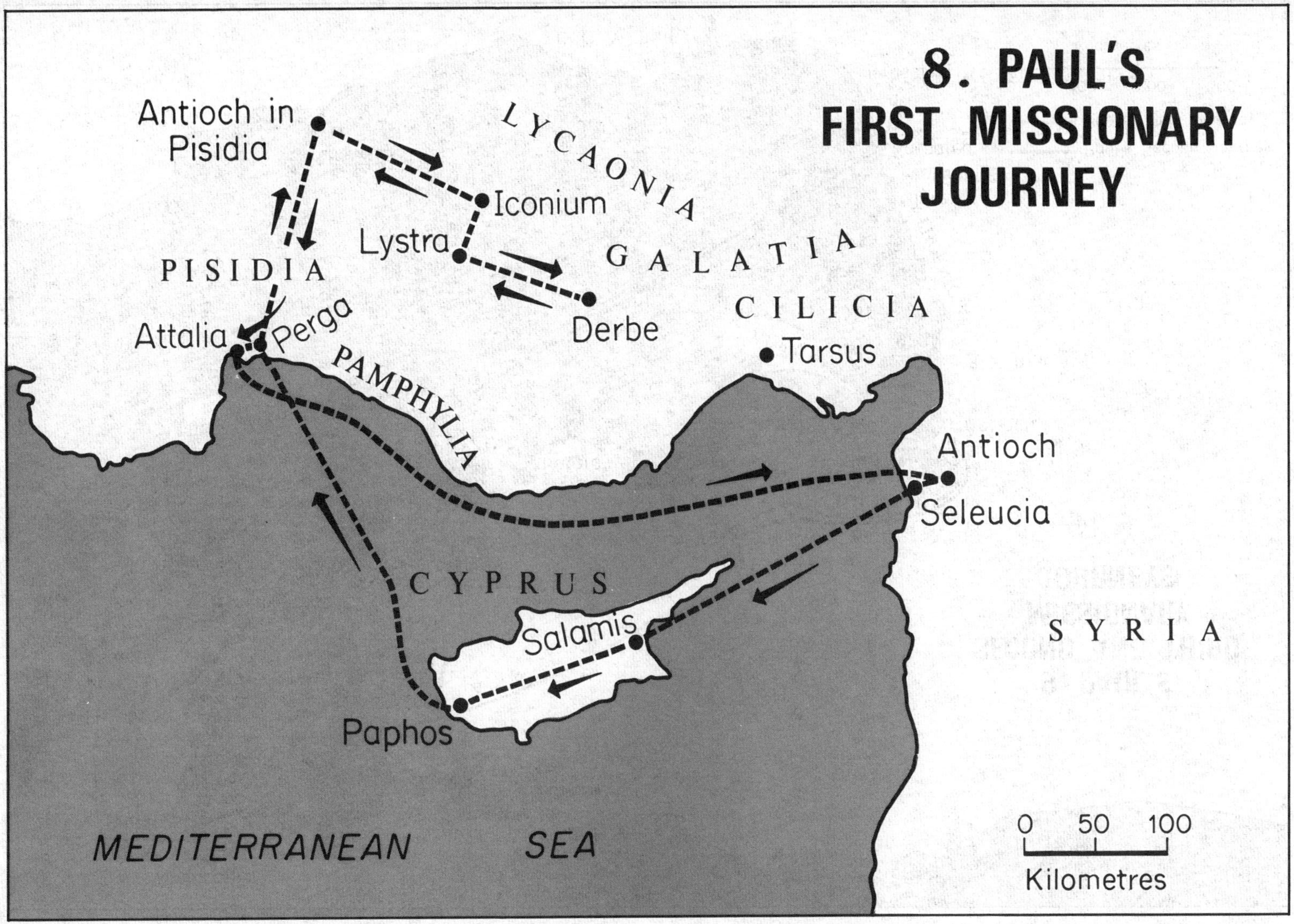
8. PAUL'S
FIRST MISSIONARY
JOURNEY
Antioch in
Pisidia
LYCAONIA
Iconium
Lystra
GALATIA
PISIDIA
Derbe
CILICIA
Attalia
Perga
Tarsus
PAMPHYLIA
Antioch
Seleucia
CYPRUS
Salamis
SYRIA
Paphos
0 50 100
Kilometres
MEDITERRANEAN SEA

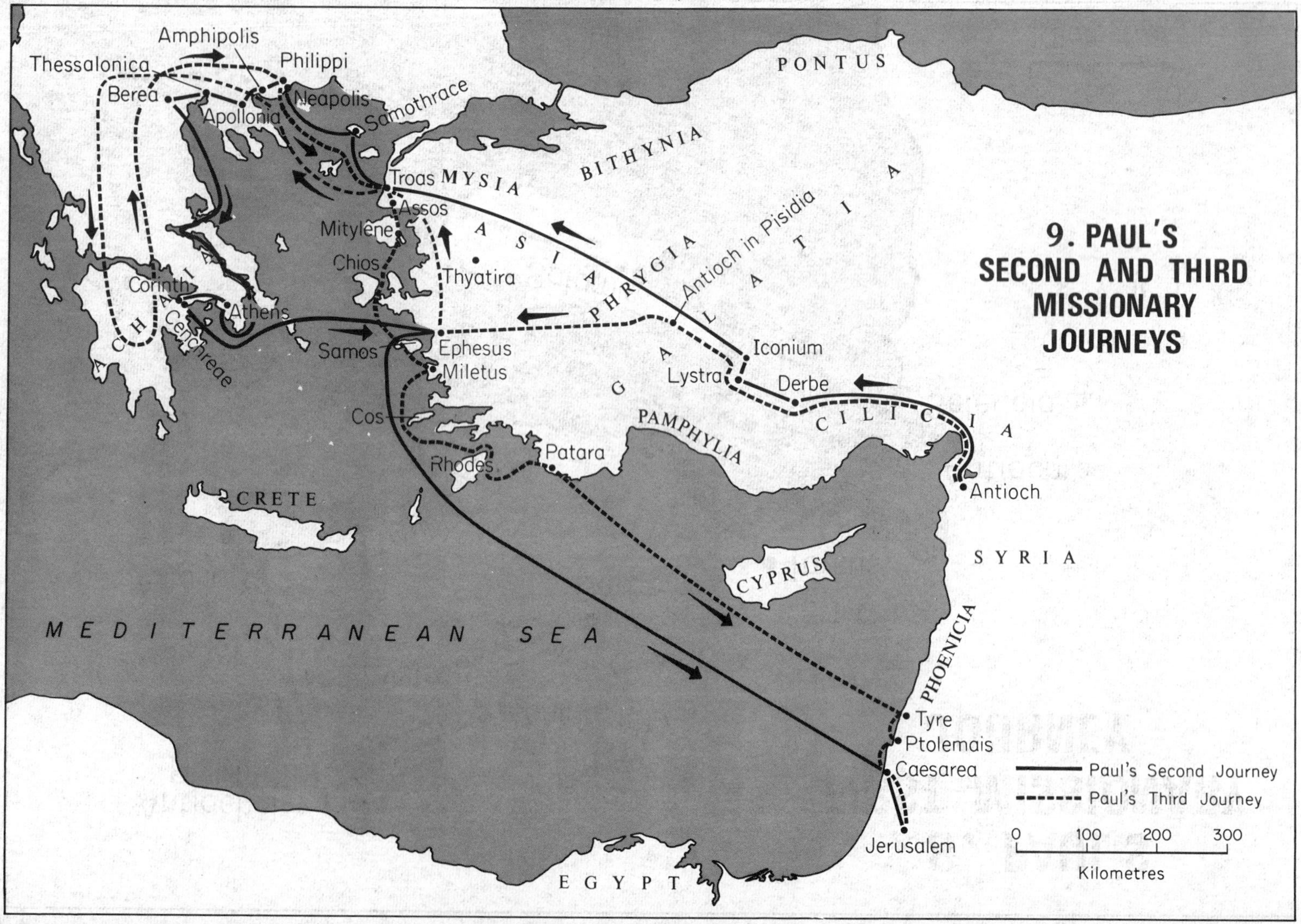
9. PAUL'S SECOND AND THIRD MISSIONARY JOURNEYS
Thessalonica
Amphipolis
Philippi
Berea
Apollonia
Neapolis
Samothrace
Troas
MYSIA
BITHYNIA
PONTUS
Assos
Mitylene
Chios
Thyatira
ASIA
PHRYGIA
GALATIA
Antioch in Pisidia
Iconium
Lystra
Derbe
CILICIA
Antioch
SYRIA
Corinth
Cenchreae
ACHAIA
Athens
Samos
Ephesus
Miletus
Cos
Rhodes
Patara
PAMPHYLIA
CRETE
CYPRUS
PHOENICIA
Tyre
Ptolemais
Caesarea
Jerusalem
MEDITERRANEAN SEA
EGYPT
Paul's Second Journey
Paul's Third Journey
0
100
200
300
Kilometres

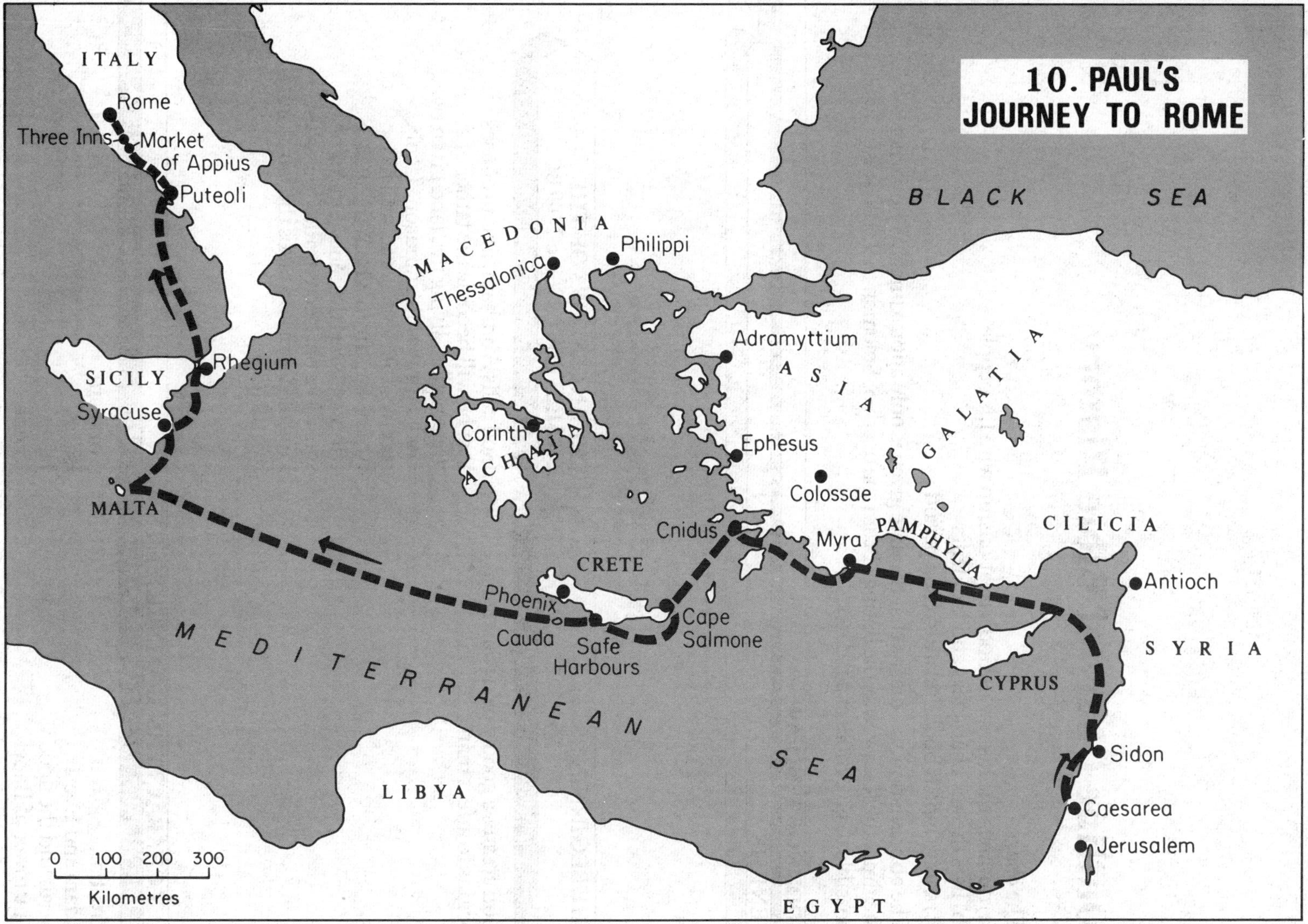
10. PAUL'S JOURNEY TO ROME
ITALY
Rome
Three Inns
Market of Appius
Puteoli
SICILY
Rhegium
Syracuse
MALTA
MACEDONIA
Thessalonica
Philippi
Corinth
ACHAIA
CRETE
Phoenix
Cauda
Safe Harbours
Cape Salmone
Cnidus
Adramyttium
ASIA
Ephesus
Colossae
GALATIA
BLACK SEA
Myra
PAMPHYLIA
CILICIA
Antioch
SYRIA
CYPRUS
Sidon
Caesarea
Jerusalem
MEDITERRANEAN SEA
LIBYA
EGYPT
0 100 200 300
Kilometres

Outline Chart of Bible History

The chart
(a) outlines the history of God's relationship with his people
(b) lists the key characters and incidents
(c) shows which books relate to each period

The abbreviation "c." means that the date given is only approximate. The earlier the time, the less precise the dating. From the death of Solomon in 931 BC it is possible to give more exact dates.

BOOKS OF THE LAW

GENESIS

THE BEGINNINGS

God creates a good world, but evil begins to affect man.

THE ANCESTORS OF THE ISRAELITES c.2000-c.1700 BC

God calls Abraham, and promises that he will become the father of a great nation, living in a land given by God. Abraham's grandson, Jacob, receives the name Israel and has twelve sons from whom the twelve tribes of Israel descend. One of his sons, Joseph, becomes adviser to the king of Egypt and takes the family to live there.

KEY CHARACTERS AND INCIDENTS

Creation
Adam and Eve
Noah and the flood
The tower of Babel

Abraham
Isaac
Jacob
Joseph

Books are placed on the chart, as far as possible, according to the period of history to which they relate, rather than according to when they may have been written. The letters of the New Testament cannot be put into strict chronological order, so this chart lists them in the order in which they appear in the Bible.

EXODUS
LEVITICUS
NUMBERS
DEUTERONOMY

THE ISRAELITES IN EGYPT: SLAVERY AND LIBERATION c.1700-c.1250 BC

The descendants of Israel become slaves in Egypt for about four hundred and fifty years, but the promise to Abraham is renewed when God calls Moses to lead them out of Egypt. For about forty years the people wander in the desert. God gives them the Law on Mount Sinai, and makes a covenant with them – this is an agreement of special relationship between the Israelites and God.

Moses
The Ten Commandments

HISTORICAL BOOKS

JOSHUA
JUDGES
1 SAMUEL
RUTH

CONQUEST AND SETTLEMENT OF CANAAN c.1250-1030 BC

God's promise begins to take shape as the Israelites conquer and settle the land of Canaan. However, they are not yet one nation, but a loose confederation of tribes led by various heroic figures known as Judges.

Joshua
Gideon
Samson
Ruth
Samuel

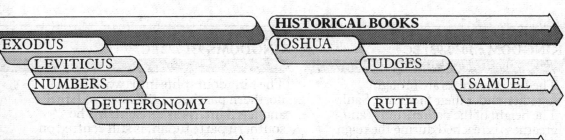

HISTORICAL BOOKS

1 SAMUEL — 2 SAMUEL — 1 KINGS — 2 KINGS

1 CHRONICLES — 2 CHRONICLES

POETRY AND WISDOM

The books of JOB, PSALMS, PROVERBS, ECCLESIASTES, and SONG OF SONGS developed over the years from c.1000 BC within the united Israelite kingdom, to c.350 BC during the

THE UNITED ISRAELITE KINGDOM c.1030-931 BC

The Israelite tribes are brought together under their first king, Saul. The height of the nation's unity and greatness is reached during the reign of David, who leads the nation in obedience to God and honour of the covenant. David makes Jerusalem his capital city and God promises that his descendants will be a continuous royal line. Solomon, David's son, builds the Temple in Jerusalem, which becomes central to the life of Israel.

THE TWO ISRAELITE KINGDOMS 931-722 BC

The kingdom splits into two. The northern part keeps the name of Israel and has Samaria as its capital. The southern part, Judah, is still centred on Jerusalem and ruled by David's descendants. During this period prophets call the kings and the people to remember God's covenant, and declare that they must keep his laws or face judgement.

KINGS OF ISRAEL AND JUDAH

THE UNITED ISRAELITE KINGDOM

Saul c.1030-c.1010
David c.1010-c.970
Solomon c.970-931

ISRAEL

Jeroboam	931-910	Ahaziah	853-852
Nadab	910-909	Joram	852-841
Baasha	909-886	Jehu	841-814
Elah	886-885	Jehoahaz	814-798
Zimri	7 days	Jehoash	798-783
Omri	885-874		
Ahab	874-853		

JUDAH

Rehoboam	931-913	Jehoram	848-841
Abijah	913-911	Ahaziah	841
Asa	911-870	Athaliah	841-835
Jehoshaphat	870-848	Joash	835-796
		Amaziah	796-781

NEHEMIAH

EZRA

ESTHER

period between the two Testaments.

THE PROPHETS

JONAH cannot be placed accurately on this time scale.

DANIEL — JOEL

AMOS — JEREMIAH — OBADIAH — HAGGAI

HOSEA — ZEPHANIAH — LAMENTATIONS — ZECHARIAH

ISAIAH

MICAH — NAHUM — HABAKKUK — EZEKIEL — MALACHI

In 722 the northern kingdom, Israel, falls to the Assyrians and many of the people are deported as foretold by the prophets. The prominent prophets are Elijah and Elisha, followed by Amos and Hosea in Israel, and Isaiah and Micah in Judah.

THE LAST YEARS OF THE KINGDOM OF JUDAH 722-587/6 BC

Judah continues for another century. From 605 onwards the Jews (the people of Judah) are taken into exile by the Babylonians. In 587 or 586 Jerusalem is captured and the Temple destroyed, but a new covenant relationship is promised under a king descended from David.

EXILE AND RETURN 587/6-c.400 BC

The exile lasts around seventy years. The Persian king Cyrus allows Jews to return to Jerusalem in 538. The foundations of the new Temple are laid and over the years more exiles return, and Jerusalem is gradually rebuilt. But the long-term hopes and visions of the prophets are not yet fulfilled.

Jeroboam II	783-743
Zechariah	6 mths
Shallum	1 mth
Menahem	743-738
Pekahiah	738-737
Pekah	737-732
Hoshea	732-723

Uzziah	781-740
Jotham	740-736
Ahaz	736-716
Hezekiah	716-

JUDAH

Hezekiah	-687
Manasseh	687-642
Amon	642-640
Josiah	640-609
Joahaz	3 mths
Jehoiakim	609-598
Jehoiachin	3 mths
Zedekiah	598-587

NEW TESTAMENT HISTORY

MATTHEW

MARK

LUKE

JOHN

THE TIME BETWEEN THE TESTAMENTS c.400-c.6 BC*

333 Alexander the Great establishes Greek rule in Palestine.

323-166 Palestine ruled by the Ptolemies and then the Seleucids, descendants of Alexander's generals.

166-63 Jewish revolt under Judas Maccabaeus re-establishes Jewish independence. Palestine is ruled by Judas' family, the Hasmoneans.

The Roman general Pompey takes Jerusalem in 63 BC. Palestine is ruled by puppet kings appointed by Rome, one of whom is Herod the Great, who rules from 37-4 BC.

*6 BC is an approximate date for the birth of Jesus Christ. The calculations for the transition from BC to AD (meaning Anno Domini "in the year of our Lord") were later found to have "lost" some years.

THE LIFE OF JESUS c.6 BC-c.AD 30

During the Roman occupation Jesus, a descendant of David, is born. When about thirty years old he begins teaching about God's kingdom and demonstrating its character by healing people. He has a unique relationship with God, but the religious authorities resent this, and organize Jesus' crucifixion. At the "last supper" Jesus introduces the new covenant, and promises his followers a gift from God which will establish that special relationship with God which was always intended. Jesus dies on the cross, but returns to life. He is seen by his disciples and many others before being taken into heaven.

KEY CHARACTERS AND INCIDENTS

John the Baptist
Jesus' birth, life, miracles, teaching, crucifixion, resurrection and ascension.

ROMAN EMPERORS

Augustus
30 BC-AD 14

Tiberius
AD 14-37

THE ACTS OF THE APOSTLES

LETTERS

ROMANS	COLOSSIANS	TITUS	1 JOHN
1 CORINTHIANS	1 THESSALONIANS	PHILEMON	2 JOHN
2 CORINTHIANS	2 THESSALONIANS	HEBREWS	3 JOHN
GALATIANS	1 TIMOTHY	JAMES	JUDE
EPHESIANS	2 TIMOTHY	1 PETER	
PHILIPPIANS		2 PETER	

A PROPHETIC BOOK

REVELATION

THE YOUNG CHURCH
c. AD 30-c. AD 100

The followers of Jesus receive God's gift, the Holy Spirit, and find that they have a new experience of God's presence and power. Christian communities develop and grow. They become not a Jewish sect but the Christian Church, made up of people of many nationalities and backgrounds believing in Jesus as the Saviour who has made possible a new relationship between man and God. The letters and prophecy of the New Testament are written by Church leaders, helping people to work out how their faith affects everyday living and their hopes for the future.

The beginnings of the Church
The conversion of Saul of Tarsus (Paul) c. AD 37
The travels and ministry of Paul c. AD 41-c. AD 65
The letters (or epistles) to the young churches

Caligula
AD 37-41

Claudius
AD 41-54

Nero
AD 54-68

Septuagint Readings

NEW TESTAMENT PASSAGES
QUOTED OR PARAPHRASED FROM THE SEPTUAGINT

The writers of the New Testament generally quoted or paraphrased the ancient Greek translation of the Old Testament, commonly known as the Septuagint Version (LXX), made some two hundred years before the time of Christ. In a number of instances this version differs significantly in meaning from the Masoretic Hebrew text, and as a special help to the reader such occurrences of LXX quotations, paraphrases, or evident allusions are listed here. The following translations of the LXX passages reflect in general the wording of Today's English Version of the New Testament. When, however, a LXX quotation occurs several times in the New Testament, the TEV wording of the translation may vary because of evident differences in meaning or emphasis reflected in the different contexts. Chapter and verse numbers are those of the English Bible.

Matthew 1.23 (Isaiah 7.14) A virgin will become pregnant and have a son.

Matthew 3.3 (Isaiah 40.3) Someone is shouting in the desert, "Prepare a road for the Lord; make a straight path for our God to travel!"

Matthew 12.21 (Isaiah 42.4) And on him all peoples will put their hope.

Matthew 13.14-15 (Isaiah 6.9-10) This people will listen and listen, but not understand; they will look and look, but not see, because their minds are dull, and they have stopped up their ears, and have closed their eyes. Otherwise, their eyes would see, their ears would hear, their minds would understand, and they would turn to me, says God, and I would heal them.

Matthew 15.8-9 (Isaiah 29.13) These people, says God...honour me with their words, but their heart is really far away from me. It is no use for them to worship me, because they teach man-made rules and laws.

Matthew 21.16 (Psalm 8.2) You have trained children and babies to offer perfect praise.

Mark 1.3 (Isaiah 40.3) Someone is shouting in the desert, "Get the road ready for the Lord; make a straight path for our God to travel!"

Mark 4.12 (Isaiah 6.9-10) This people will listen and listen, but not understand; they will look and look, but not see...; for if they did...they would turn to me, says God, and I would heal them.

Mark 7.6-7 (Isaiah 29.13) These people, says God......honour me with their words, but their heart is really far away from me. It is no use for them to worship me, because they teach man-made rules and laws.

Luke 3.4-6 (Isaiah 40.3-5) Someone is shouting in the desert: "Get the road ready for the Lord, make a straight path for our God to travel! Every valley must be filled up, every hill and mountain levelled off. All the winding roads must be made straight, and the rough paths made smooth... All mankind will see God's salvation!"

Luke 4.18 (Isaiah 61.1) The Spirit of the Lord is upon me, because he has chosen me to bring good news to the poor. He has sent me...to proclaim liberty to the captives and recovery of sight to the blind.

Luke 8.10 (Isaiah 6.9) You will listen and listen, but not understand; you will look and look, but not see.

John 1.23 (Isaiah 40.3) The voice of someone shouting in the desert... "Make a straight path for our God to travel!"

John 12.38 (Isaiah 53.1) Lord, who believed the message we told ?

John 12.40 (Isaiah 6.10) This people's minds are dull, and they have stopped up their ears and have closed their eyes. Otherwise, their eyes would see, and their ears would hear, their minds would understand, and they would turn to me, says God, for me to heal them.

Acts 2.19-20 (Joel 2.30-31) There will be blood, fire, and thick smoke; the sun will be darkened, and the moon will turn red as blood, before the great and glorious Day of the Lord comes.

Acts 2.25-28 (Psalm 16.8-11) I saw the Lord before me at all times. He is near me, and I will not be troubled. And so I am filled with gladness, and my words are full of joy. And I, mortal though I am, will rest assured in hope, because you will not abandon me in the world of the dead; you will not allow your faithful servant to rot in the grave. You have shown me the paths that lead to life, and by your presence you will fill me with joy.

Acts 3.22 (Deuteronomy 18.15) You are to obey him in all things.

Acts 4.25-26 (Psalm 2.1-2) Why were the Gentiles furious; why did the people plot in vain ? The kings of the earth prepared themselves, and the rulers met together.

Acts 7.14 (Genesis 46.27) Seventy-five people.

Acts 7.42-43 (Amos 5.25-27) People of Israel! It was not to me that you slaughtered and sacrificed animals for forty years in the desert. It was the tent of the god Molech that you carried, and the image of Rephan, your star god; they were idols that you had made for yourselves. And so I will send you into exile beyond Damascus.

Acts 8.33 (Isaiah 53.8) He was humiliated, and justice was denied him. No one will be able to tell about his descendants, because his life on earth has come to an end.

Acts 13.34 (Isaiah 55.3) I will make an everlasting covenant with you, the sacred and sure blessings that I promised to David.

Acts 13.41 (Habakkuk 1.5) Look, you scoffers! Be astonished and die!

Acts 15.16-17 (Amos 9.11-12) In that day, says the Lord, I will restore the kingdom of David. I will rebuild its ruins, and make it strong again... And so all the rest of mankind will come to me, all the Gentiles whom I have called to be my own.

Acts 28.26-27 (Isaiah 6.9-10) Go and say to this people: You will listen and listen, but not understand; you will look and look, but not see, because this people's minds are dull, and they have stopped up their ears and closed their eyes. Otherwise, their eyes would see, their ears would hear, their minds would understand, and they would turn to me, says God, and I would heal them.

Romans 2.24 (Isaiah 52.5) Because of you Jews, the Gentiles continually speak evil of God.

Romans 3.4 (Psalm 51.4) You must be shown to be right when you speak; you must win your case when you are being tried.

Romans 3.12 (Psalms 14.3, 53.3) All have turned away from God; they have all gone wrong.

Romans 3.13 (Psalm 5.9) Wicked lies roll off their tongues.

Romans 3.14 (Psalm 10.7) Their speech is filled with bitter curses and guile.

Romans 9.17 (Exodus 9.16) To use you to show my power.

Romans 9.27-28 (Isaiah 10.22-23) Even if the people of Israel are as many as the grains of sand by the sea, yet only a few of them will be saved; for God will quickly and justly settle his full account with all the world.

Romans 9.29 (Isaiah 1.9) If the Lord Almighty had not left us some descendants.

Romans 9.33 (Isaiah 28.16) Whoever believes in him will not be disappointed.

Romans 10.11 (Isaiah 28.16) Whoever believes in him will not be disappointed.

Romans 10.16 (Isaiah 53.1) Lord, who believed our message?

Romans 10.18 (Psalm 19.4) The sound of their voice went out to all the world; their words reached the ends of the earth.

Romans 10.20 (Isaiah 65.1) I appeared to those who were not looking for me; I was found by those who were not asking for me.

Romans 10.21 (Isaiah 65.2) All day long I held out my hands to welcome a disobedient and rebellious people.

Romans 11.9-10 (Psalm 69.22-23) May they fall, may they be punished!... Make them bend under their troubles at all times.

Romans 11.26-27 (Isaiah 59.20-21) The Saviour will come for the sake of Zion, and remove all wickedness from the descendants of Jacob. I will make this covenant with them, (Isaiah 27.9) when I take away their sins.

Romans 11.34 (Isaiah 40.13) Who knows the mind of the Lord ?

Romans 12.20 (Proverbs 25.21-22) If your enemy is hungry, feed him; if he is thirsty, give him a drink; for by doing this you will make him burn with shame.

Romans 14.11 (Isaiah 45.23) Everyone will kneel before me, and everyone will confess that I am God.

Romans 15.12 (Isaiah 11.10) A descendant of Jesse will appear; he will come to rule the Gentiles, and they will put their hope in him.

Romans 15.21 (Isaiah 52.15) Those who were not told about him will see, and those who have not heard will understand.

1 Corinthians 1.19 (Isaiah 29.14) I will destroy the wisdom of the wise, and hide the understanding of the scholars.

1 Corinthians 2.16 (Isaiah 40.13) Who knows the mind of the Lord ?

1 Corinthians 5.13 (Deuteronomy 17.7) Take the evil man out of your group.

1 Corinthians 10.20 (Deuteronomy 32.17) What is sacrificed on pagan altars is offered to demons, not to God.

1 Corinthians 15.55 (Hosea 13.14) Where, Death, is your punishment? Where, Hades, is your power to hurt?

2 Corinthians 4.13 (Psalm 116.10) I spoke because I believed.

2 Corinthians 8.21 (Proverbs 3.4) Make it your purpose to do what is right, not only in the sight of the Lord, but also in the sight of men.

Galatians 3.10 (Deuteronomy 27.26) Whoever does not always obey everything that is written in this Law is under God's curse.

Ephesians 4.26 (Psalm 4.4) If you become angry, do not let your anger lead you into sin.

Philippians 2.11 (Isaiah 45.23) And all will openly proclaim God.

Hebrews 1.6 (Deuteronomy 32.43) All God's sons must worship him.

Hebrews 1.7 (Psalm 104.4) God makes his angels winds, and his servants a flaming fire.

Hebrews 1.10-12 (Psalm 102.25-27) You, Lord, in the beginning created the earth... You will fold them up like a coat, and they will be changed.

Hebrews 2.7 (Psalm 8.5) You made him for a little while lower than the angels.

Hebrews 3.7-9 (Psalm 95.7-9) If you hear God's voice today, do not be stubborn, as your ancestors were when they rebelled against God, as they were that day in the desert when they put him to the test.There they put me to the test and tried me, says God, although they saw what I did.

Hebrews 3.15 (Psalm 95.7-8) If you hear God's voice today, do not be stubborn as your ancestors were when they rebelled against God.

Hebrews 4.7 (Psalm 95.7-8) If you hear God's voice today, do not be stubborn.

Hebrews 8.9 (Jeremiah 31.32) They were not faithful to the covenant I made with them, and so I paid no attention to them.

Hebrews 10.5 (Psalm 40.6) You do not want sacrifices and offerings, but you have prepared a body for me.

Hebrews 10.27 (Isaiah 26.11) The fierceness...and now fire will destroy those who oppose God.

Hebrews 10.38b (Habakkuk 2.4a) If he turns back, I will not be pleased with him.

Hebrews 11.5 (Genesis 5.24) Enoch pleased God, and nobody could find him, because God had taken him up.

Hebrews 11.21 (Genesis 47.31) Jacob worshipped, leaning on the top of his walking-stick.

Hebrews 12.5-6 (Proverbs 3.11-12) My son, pay attention when the Lord corrects you, and do not be discouraged when he rebukes you. Because the Lord corrects everyone he loves, and punishes everyone he accepts as a son.

Hebrews 12.13 (Proverbs 4.26) Keep walking on straight paths.

Hebrews 12.15 (Deuteronomy 29.18) A bitter plant that grows up.

Hebrews 12.26 (Haggai 2.6) I will once more shake the heavens and the earth.

Hebrews 13.6 (Psalm 118.6) The Lord is my helper; I will not fear what anyone may do to me.

James 1.10-11 (Isaiah 40.6-7) Like the flower of a wild plant... Its flower falls off.

James 4.6 (Proverbs 3.34) The Lord resists the proud, but gives grace to the humble.

1 Peter 1.24 (Isaiah 40.6-7) All mankind are like grass and all their glory is like wild flowers. The grass withers, and the flowers fall.

1 Peter 2.6 (Isaiah 28.16) I chose a valuâble and costly stone, which now I am placing as the corner-stone in the foundations of Zion, and whoever believes in him will never be disappointed.

1 Peter 2.9 (Isaiah 43.20) the chosen race, (Exodus 19.5-6) the king's priests, the holy nation, (Isaiah 43.21) my own people, chosen to proclaim my wonderful acts.

1 Peter 3.10 (Psalm 34.12) Whoever wishes life and wants to see good times.

1 Peter 4.18 (Proverbs 11.31) It is difficult for good people to be saved; what, then, will become of godless sinners ?

1 Peter 5.5 (Proverbs 3.34) The Lord resists the proud, but shows favour to the humble.

Revelation 2.7 (Ezekiel 28.13, 31.8,9) the Garden of God.

Revelation 2.27 (Psalm 2.9) You will rule them with an iron rod.

Well-known Passages of the Bible

OLD TESTAMENT STORIES AND EVENTS

Creation Gen 1
The Garden of Eden Gen 2
Man's disobedience Gen 3
Cain and Abel Gen 4
Noah and the flood Gen 6—8
The tower of Babel (Babylon) Gen 11
God's call to Abraham Gen 12
Abraham and Melchizedek Gen 14
Hagar and Ishmael Gen 16
Destruction of Sodom and Gomorrah Gen 19
Birth of Isaac Gen 21
"Sacrifice" of Isaac Gen 22
Jacob and Esau Gen 25—27
Jacob's dream Gen 28
Joseph's special coat Gen 37
Joseph in prison Gen 39—40
Pharaoh's dream Gen 41
Joseph and the missing cup Gen 44
Moses and the princess of Egypt Ex 2
Moses and the burning bush Ex 3
Plagues of Egypt Ex 7—12
Crossing of the Red Sea Ex 14
Water from the rock Ex 17; Num 20
The Ten Commandments Ex 20
Aaron and the gold bull Ex 32
The spies Num 13
Balaam and his donkey Num 22—24
Death of Moses Deut 34
Rahab and the spies Josh 2
Crossing of the Jordan Josh 3
Fall of Jericho Josh 6
Joshua's farewell Josh 23—24
Deborah and Barak Judg 4
Gideon's fleece Judg 6
Gideon's army Judg 7—8
Birth of Samson Judg 13
Samson and Delilah Judg 16
Samson's last victory Judg 16
Ruth and Naomi Ruth
Birth of Samuel 1 Sam 1
Samuel and Eli 1 Sam 3
David anointed king 1 Sam 16
David and Goliath 1 Sam 17
David and Jonathan 1 Sam 18—20
David and Abigail 1 Sam 25
Saul and the "witch" at Endor 1 Sam 28
David and Bathsheba 2 Sam 11
Nathan's story 2 Sam 12
Solomon the wise judge 1 Kgs 3
Building the Temple 1 Kgs 6
Solomon and the queen of Sheba 1 Kgs 10; 2 Chr 9
Elijah and the drought 1 Kgs 17
Elijah and the widow's last meal 1 Kgs 17
Elijah and the prophets of Baal 1 Kgs 18
Elijah and the voice of God 1 Kgs 19
Naboth's vineyard 1 Kgs 21
Elijah and the chariot of fire 2 Kgs 2
Elisha and the woman from Shunem 2 Kgs 4
Naaman's cure 2 Kgs 5
Siege of Samaria 2 Kgs 6—7
Joash the boy king 2 Kgs 12; 2 Chr 24
Fall of Samaria 2 Kgs 17
Siege of Jerusalem by the Assyrians 2 Kgs 18; 2 Chr 32; Is 36—37
Fall of Jerusalem to Babylon 2 Kgs 25
Jerusalem's walls rebuilt Neh 3—6
Ezra reads the Law Neh 8
Call of Isaiah Is 6
Isaiah's message to the king Is 37
Jeremiah at the potter's house Jer 18
Jeremiah buys a field Jer 32
Jeremiah's scroll Jer 36
Jeremiah's escape from the well Jer 38
Ezekiel's vision of God Ezek 1
Ezekiel and the valley of dry bones Ezek 37
Ezekiel's vision of the Temple Ezek 40—44; Ezek 47
Nebuchadnezzar's dream Dan 2
The blazing furnace Dan 3
Nebuchadnezzar's golden statue Dan 3
Belshazzar's banquet Dan 5
Daniel in the pit of lions Dan 6
Jonah's mission Jon 1—4

WELL-KNOWN BIBLE POEMS AND PROPHECIES

Jacob's last words Gen 49
Song of Moses after crossing the Red Sea Ex 15
Song of Moses Deut 32
Moses blesses the tribes Deut 33
Song of Deborah and Barak Judg 5
David's lament for Saul and Jonathan 2 Sam 1
David's song of victory 2 Sam 22; Ps 18
David's last words 2 Sam 23
Job rests his case with God Job 19
In praise of wisdom Job 28
The power of God Job 36—37
God speaks out of the storm Job 38—41
True happiness Ps 1
"What is man?" Ps 8
God's glory in creation Ps 19
"The Lord is my shepherd" Ps 23
The great King - "Fling wide the gates" Ps 24
"Where is your God?" Ps 42
"I will put my hope in God" Ps 43
A royal wedding song Ps 45
"God is with us" Ps 46
A prayer for forgiveness - "Create a pure heart in me, O God" Ps 51
"O God, you are my God" Ps 63
"God, be merciful to us" (Deus Misereatur) Ps 67
In old age Ps 71
"The Lord your defender" Ps 91
"The Lord is king" Ps 93
"The Lord is a mighty God" (Venite) Ps 95
A new song (Cantate Domino) Ps 98
"We are his people" (Jubilate) Ps 100
"Praise the Lord, my soul" Ps 103
In praise of the Creator Ps 104
"In their trouble they called to the Lord" Ps 107
The Law of the Lord Ps 119
Help from the Lord Ps 121
In praise of Jerusalem Ps 122
"If the Lord does not build the house" Ps 127
"Give thanks to the Lord, because he is good; his love is eternal" Ps 136
"By the rivers of Babylon" Ps 137
"Lord... you know me" Ps 139
"Praise God in his Temple!" Ps 150
In praise of wisdom Prov 8

A time for everything Ecc 3
Songs of love Song
Everlasting peace Is 2
Song of the vineyard Is 5
The future king: "The people who walked in darkness" Is 9
The peaceful kingdom: "Calves and lion cubs will feed together" Is 11
"The desert will rejoice" Is 35
"The glory of the Lord will be revealed" Is 40
The Lord's servant Is 42
The clay and the potter Is 45
"A light to the nations" Is 49
The suffering servant Is 52.13—53.12
"Come, everyone who is thirsty" Is 55
Jerusalem, city of God Is 60
"Good news to the poor" Is 61
Jeremiah's sorrow Jer 8—9
Trust in God Jer 17
Laments for the fall of Jerusalem Lam
The sword of God Ezek 21
Funeral song for Tyre Ezek 27
A song of joy Zeph 3
"Your king is coming" Zech 9
Mary's song of praise (Magnificat) Lk 1.46-55
Zechariah's prophecy (Benedictus) Lk 1.68-79
Simeon's thanksgiving (Nunc Dimittis) Lk 2.29-32
An early Christian hymn
hymn Phil 2.6-11

NEW TESTAMENT STORIES AND EVENTS

(For Jesus' parable stories and his miracles see Section 5)

Birth of John the Baptist Lk 1
Birth of Jesus Mt 1; Lk 2
Wise men from the East Mt 2
The escape to Egypt Mt 2.13-15
Slaughter at Bethlehem Mt 2.16-18
The boy Jesus in the Temple Lk 2.41-51
Preaching of John the Baptist
Mt 3; Mk 1; Lk 3; Jn 1
Baptism of Jesus Mt 3; Mk1; Lk 3
Temptation of Jesus Mt 4; Mk 1; Lk 4
Jesus calls out the twelve Mt 10; Mk 3; Lk 6
Death of John the Baptist Mt 14; Mk 6; Lk 9
Peter's declaration Mt 16; Mk 8; Lk 9
The transfiguration Mt 17; Mk 9; Lk 9
Jesus and the rich young man Mt 19; Mk 10; Lk 18
Anointing of Jesus Mt 26; Mk 14; Jn 12
Jesus visits Martha and Mary Lk 10.38-41
Jesus and Zacchaeus Lk 19
The widow's offering Mt 12.41-44; Lk 21.1-4
The Word of life Jn 1
The Lamb of God Jn 1.29-34
The wedding in Cana Jn 2
Jesus and Nicodemus (the new birth) Jn 3
Jesus and the Samaritan woman (the woman at the well) Jn 4
Death of Lazarus Jn 11
Entry into Jerusalem Mt 21; Mk 11; Lk 19; Jn 12
Jesus and the moneychangers Mt 21; Mk 11; Lk 19; Jn 2
The last supper Mt 26; Mk 14; Lk 22; Jn 13
Jesus in Gethsemane Mt 26; Mk 14; Lk 22
The arrest of Jesus Mt 26; Mk 14; Lk 22; Jn 18
Jesus before Pilate Mt 27; Mk 15; Lk 23; Jn 18
Death of Jesus Mt 27; Mk 15; Lk 23; Jn 19
Jesus' resurrection Mt 28; Mk 16; Lk 24; Jn 20
The walk to Emmaus Lk 24
Jesus and Thomas Jn 20.24-29
Jesus and Peter Jn 21
"Go, then, to all peoples" - the "great commission" Mt 28.16-20
The "ascension" Acts 1
The coming of the Holy Spirit - birth of the church Acts 2
Peter's message Acts 2—3
Ananias and Sapphira Acts 5
The story of Stephen Acts 6—7
Philip and the Ethiopian Acts 8
Conversion of Saul (Paul) Acts 9
Peter and Cornelius Acts 10
Peter's rescue from prison Acts 12
Paul and Barnabas commissioned Acts 13
Jerusalem council Acts 15
Paul at Athens Acts 17
Paul's arrest and defence Acts 21—26
Paul's shipwreck Acts 27
Paul in Rome Acts 28.16—31

WELL-KNOWN PASSAGES IN THE LETTERS AND REVELATION

Peace with God Rom 5
Life in God's service Rom 12
Love 1 Cor 13
Resurrection 1 Cor 15
The one gospel Gal 1
Christian unity Eph 4
The whole armour of God Eph 6
Faith Heb 11
God is light 1 Jn 1
God is love 1 Jn 4
The throne of God Rev 4
The final judgement Rev 20
The new heaven and the new earth Rev 21

WELL-KNOWN WORDS OF JESUS

"The scripture says 'Man cannot live on bread alone' " Mt 4.4
The Sermon on the Mount Mt 5—7
"Beatitudes" - "happy are those..." Mt 5.3-12
"You are like salt" Mt 5.13
"You are like light"; "your light must shine" Mt 5.14-16
"If anyone slaps you on the right cheek" Mt 5.39; Lk 6.29
"Love your enemies" Mt 5.44; Lk 6.27-38
The Lord's prayer Mt 6.5-15; Lk 11.1-4
Riches in heaven Mt 6.19; Lk 12.32-34
God and money Mt 6.24; Lk 16.13
Why worry? "Look how the wild flowers grow" Mt 6.25-34; Lk 12.22-31
Judging others Mt 7.1-5
Ask, seek, knock Mt 7.7-11; Lk 11.9-13
The "golden rule" Mt 7.12
The narrow gate Mt 7.13-14
"I never knew you" Mt 7.21-23
The house on the rock Mt 7.24-27; Lk 6.46-49
"Foxes have holes, and birds have nests..." Mt 8.20; Lk 9.58
"Let the dead bury their own dead" Mt 8.22; Lk 9.60
New wine, fresh wineskins Mt 9.17; Mk 2.22; Lk 5.37-38
No pupil is greater than his teacher Mt 10.24
Sparrows two a penny Mt 10.29; Lk 12.6-7
"I did not come to bring peace but a sword" Mt 10.34
"Whoever tries to gain his own life will lose it" Mt 10.39; Mt 16.24-28; Mk 8.35-36; Lk 9.24
"Come to me... Take my yoke... and you will find rest" Mt 11.28-30
"The Son of Man is Lord of the Sabbath" Mt 12.8; Lk 6.5
"The mouth speaks what the heart is full of" Mt 12.34; Mt 15.17-20
"Who is my mother? Who are my brothers?" Mt 12.48-50; Mk 3.33-35
"A man went out to sow" Mt 13.3

"Blind leaders of the blind"
Mt 15.14; Lk 6.39
"Peter: you are a rock, and on this rock foundation I will build my church" Mt 16.18
"The keys of the Kingdom"
Mt 16.19
"Faith as big as a mustard seed" Mt 17.20
Who is the greatest? Mt 18.1-5
"Where two or three come together in my name, I am there with them" Mt 18.20
"Let the children come to me"
Mt 19.14; Mk 10.14; Lk 19.15-17
"First will be last" Mt 19.30; Mt 20.1-16
The Son of Man who came to serve Mt 20.27
"Many are invited, but few are chosen" Mt 22.14
"Pay the Emperor what belongs to the Emperor, and pay God what belongs to God" Mt 22.21; Mk 12.17; Lk 20.25
"Love your neighbour"
Mt 22.36-40; Mk 12.28-34
"Jerusalem! Jerusalem!"
Mt 23.37; Lk 13.34-35
"This is my body... this is my blood" Mt 26.26-29; Mk 14.22-25
"I was hungry and you fed me" Mt 25.35-36
"I will be with you always"
Mt 28.20
"People who are well do not need a doctor" Mk 2.17; Lk 5.31
"The Sabbath was made for the good of man" Mk 2.27
"Anyone who is not for me is really against me" Lk 11.23
"God loved the world so much that he gave his only Son"
Jn 3.16
"I am the bread of life" Jn 6.35
"I am the light of the world"
Jn 8.12
"If the Son sets you free, then you will be really free"
Jn 8.36
"I am the gate. Whoever comes in by me will be saved"
Jn 10.9
"I am the good shepherd"
Jn 10.11
"I am the resurrection and the life" Jn 11.25
"Love one another"
Jn 13.34; Jn 15.12-17
"In my Father's house" Jn 14.2
"I am the way, the truth, and the life" Jn 14.6
"Peace is what I leave with you" Jn 14.27
"I am the vine, and you are the branches" Jn 15.1,5

Jesus' words from the cross:
"My God, my God, why did you abandon me?" Mt 27.46; Mk 15.34
"Forgive them, Father!"
Lk 23.34
"Today you will be in Paradise with me" Lk 23.43
"Father! In your hands I place my spirit!" Lk 23.46
"He is your son... she is your mother" Jn 19.26-27
"I am thirsty" Jn 19.28
"It is finished" Jn 19.30

Jesus' Teaching about...

Any attempt to classify Jesus' teaching in this way is bound to be inadequate. The subjects and passages listed here may serve as an introduction. The Indexes supply wider Bible references for further study of many of these subjects.

Anger Mt 5.21-26
Discipleship Mt 10.34-39, 16.24-28; Mk 1.14-20; Lk 9.21-27, 57-62, 10.1-12, 14.25-33; Jn 14—17
Divorce Mt 5.31-32, 19.1-12; Lk 16.18
Eternal life Mt 19.16-30; Lk 10.25-37, 18.18-30; Jn 3.1-21, 4.1-41, 5.19-47, 10.7-30, 12.44-50
Faith Mt 18.6-9, 21.18-22; Mk 11.20-25; Lk 17.5-6
Faithfulness Mt 24.45-51; Lk 12.41-48, 16.1-13, 19.11-27
Fasting Mt 6.16-18, 9.14-17; Mk 2.18-22; Lk 5.33-39
Fear and worry Mt 10.26-31; Lk 12.4-7; Jn 14.1-14
Freedom Jn 8.31-47
Future events Mt 24; Mk 13; Lk 17.20-37, 21.5-38; Jn 14—17
Giving Mt 6.1-4; Lk 21.1-4
God Jn 3.1-21, 5.19-47, 6.25-71, 8.12-30, 10.7-42, 14—17
Greatest commandment Mt 22.34-40; Mk 12.28-34; Lk 10.25-28
Greatness Mt 18.1-5; Mk 9.33-37; Lk 9.46-48, 22.24-30
Happiness Mt 5.3-12; Lk 6.20-26, 11.27-28
Hearing and obeying Mt 7.24-27; Lk 8.11-18; Jn 14.15—15.17
Himself Mt 16.13-21, 20.17-19, 26.26-35; Mk 8.31-38, 10.32-34; Lk 4.16-30, 9.21-27, 43-45, 18.31-34, 20.1-8, 24.13-49; Jn 2.13-22, 3.1-21, 5.19-47, 6.25-71, 7.16-31, 37-38, 8.12-59, 9.3-5, 35-41, 10, 11.17-27, 12.27-36, 14—17
Judgement Mt 11.20-24, 12.33-42, 25.31-46; Jn 12.44-50
Judging others Mt 7.1-5; Lk 6.37-42
Keeping a promise Mt 5.33-37
Kingdom of God (heaven) Mt 5—7, 13, 18.1-5, 19.13-15, 16-30, 20, 21.33—22.14, 24, 25; Mk 1.14-15, 4; Lk 13.18-30, 14.15-24, 17.20-37, 18.18-30, 19.11-27, 22.24-30; Jn 3.1-21
Law (the) Mt 5.17-20, 15.1-9; Lk 16.14-18; Jn 7.10-24, 8.1-11
Love Jn 13.20-35, 14—17
Love for enemies Mt 5.38-48, 7.12a; Lk 6.27-36
Love for neighbours Lk 10.25-37
Messiah Mt 16.13-20, 22.41-46, 24; Mk 12.35-37
New birth Jn 3.1-21
Paying taxes Mt 22.15-22; Mk 12.13-17; Lk 20.19-26
Peace Jn 14.27-31
Persecution Mt 10.16-25; Jn 15.18-27
Prayer Mt 6.5-15, 21.18-22; Mk 11.20-25; Lk 11.1-13, 18.1-8
Repentance Mk 1.14-15; Lk 15
Resurrection Mt 22.23-33; Mk 12.18-27; Lk 20.27-39
Revenge Mt 5.38-42
Rewards Mt 10.40-42
Sabbath Mt 12.1-8; Mk 2.23-28; Lk 6.1-5, 13.10-17, 14.1-6; Jn 5.1-18
Serving others Mt 20.20-28; Mk 10.35-45; Jn 13.1-20
Sin and forgiveness Mt 18.21-35, 26.26-29; Mk 1.14-15; Lk 7.36-50, 17.1-4, 18.9-13; Jn 8.1-11
Temptation Mk 9.42-48
Trust in God Mt 6.25-34; Lk 12.22-31
Wealth and possessions Mt 6.19-21, 24; Lk 12.13-21, 12.32-34, 16.1-13, 18.18-30
Worship Jn 4.1-26

Prayers of the Bible

Abraham's prayer for Sodom
Genesis 18.22-33

Abraham's servant prays for guidance   Genesis 24.12-14

Isaac's blessing   Genesis 27

Jacob's vow at Bethel
Genesis 28

Jacob's desperate prayer at Penuel   Genesis 32

Jacob blesses his sons
Genesis 48—49

Moses' song of thanksgiving for deliverance from Egypt
Exodus 15

Moses' plea for Israel when they had worshipped the golden calf
Exodus 32; Deuteronomy 9

Moses asks to see God's glory
Exodus 33

Aaron's blessing   Numbers 6

Moses pleads with God to forgive his rebellious people
Numbers 14

Balaam, on God's instruction, blesses Israel   Numbers 22—24

Moses' song: God and his people
Deuteronomy 32

Moses blesses the people of Israel   Deuteronomy 33

Joshua's prayer after defeat at Ai   Joshua 7

Joshua prays for time to complete his victory   Joshua 10

Deborah's song of thanksgiving for victory   Judges 5

Gideon's prayer for signs
Judges 6

Hannah's prayer for a son
1 Samuel 1; her thanksgiving
1 Samuel 2

Samuel's prayer for the nation
1 Samuel 7

David's prayer following God's promise of a lasting succession
2 Samuel 7;   1 Chronicles 17

David's song of thanksgiving for deliverance   2 Samuel 22;
Psalm 18

Solomon's prayer for wisdom
1 Kings 3;   2 Chronicles 1

Solomon's prayer at the dedication of the Temple
1 Kings 8;   2 Chronicles 6

Elijah's prayer on Mt Carmel
1 Kings 18

Elijah and the "still, small voice"
1 Kings 19

Hezekiah's prayer at the time of Sennacherib's siege   2 Kings 19;
Isaiah 37

Thanksgiving as the ark is brought to Jerusalem
1 Chronicles 16

David's prayer for Solomon
1 Chronicles 29

Ezra's confession of the nation's sin   Ezra 9

Nehemiah's prayer for his people   Nehemiah 1

The public confession led by Ezra   Nehemiah 9

Job seeks the reason for his suffering   Job 10

Job pleads his case   Job 13—14

Job's confession   Job 42

The Psalms include an enormous number of prayers: some are listed here, under themes:
Evening prayer   4
Morning prayer   5
The shepherd psalm   23
Praise and worship   24, 67, 92, 95—98, 100, 113, 145, 148, 150
Guidance   25
Trust   37, 62
Deliverance   40, 116
Longing for God   27, 42, 63, 84
Forgiveness   51, 130
Thanksgiving   65, 111, 136
Help in trouble   66, 69, 86, 88, 102, 140, 143
God's constant love and care   89, 103,107, 146
God's majesty and glory   8, 29, 93, 104
God's knowledge and presence   139
God's word   19, 119
God's protection   46, 91, 125

Prayers of Isaiah   Isaiah 25, 33, 63—64

Hezekiah's prayer in his illness
Isaiah 38

Jeremiah's prayers
Jeremiah 11, 14, 20, 32

Laments for the fall of Jerusalem   Lamentations 1—4

Prayer for restoration
Lamentations 5

The king's dream; Daniel's prayer   Daniel 2

Nebuchadnezzar praises God
Daniel 4

Daniel's prayer at the end of the exile   Daniel 9

Jonah's prayer   Jonah 2

Habakkuk questions God
Habakkuk 1

Habakkuk's prayer
Habakkuk 3

Prayers of Jesus:
The Lord's Prayer
Matthew 6.9-13; Luke 11.2-4
Praise that God reveals himself to simple people
Matthew 11.25-26; Luke 10.21
In the Garden of Gethsemane
Matthew 26.36-44; Mark 14.32-39; Luke 22.46
From the cross   Matthew 27.46; Mark 15.34; Luke 23.34,46
At the raising of Lazarus
John 11.41-42
Facing death   John 12.27-28
For his followers   John 17

Mary's thanksgiving (Magnificat)   Luke 1.46-55

Zechariah's prayer (Benedictus)   Luke 1.68-79

Simeon's prayer (Nunc Dimittis)
Luke 2.29-35

Prayers of the Pharisee and the tax-collector   Luke 18.10-13

The church's prayer in the face of threats   Acts 4.24-30

Stephen's prayer at his death
Acts 7.59-60

Prayers of Paul:
For the Christians at Rome
Romans 1.8-10
For Israel Romans 10.1
For the church at Corinth
1 Corinthians 1.4-9;
2 Corinthians 13.7-9
Thanksgiving for God's comfort in trouble 2 Corinthians 1.3-4
Thanksgiving for spiritual riches in Christ
Ephesians 1.8-14
For the Ephesian Christians
Ephesians 1.16-23, 3.14-19
For the Philippian Christians Philippians 1.8-11
For the church at Colossae
Colossians 1.3-14
For the Thessalonian Christians
1 Thessalonians 1.2-3, 2.13, 3.9-13, 5.23; 2 Thessalonians 1.3, 2.13, 16-17, 3.16
For Timothy 2 Timothy 1.3-4
For Philemon Philemon 4-6

Doxologies – praise to God – and benedictions Romans 16.25-27; Ephesians 3.20-21; Philippians 4.20; 1 Thessalonians 3.11-13; Hebrews 13.20-21; 1 Peter 5.10-11; 2 Peter 3.18; Jude 24-25

Peter's thanksgiving
1 Peter 1.3-5

John's prayer for Gaius
3 John 2

Topical Keywords

This index contains many important and theologically ignificant words. The references to each word are listed n order of their frequency of occurrence in any one hapter.

The first reference in each chapter is given, and the umber of times the word occurs in that chapter. Chapters n which the word occurs only once have not been ncluded.

The entries under each word begin with the chapter in which the word occurs most frequently. For example, FAITH occurs 29 times in Hebrews 11, the first occurrence being in verse 1 (Heb. 11.1), so that is the first ntry in the **FAITH** listing.

The symbol < indicates that the word also appears in the preceding chapter of that book, and the symbol > indicates that it appears in the following chapter. If the word occurs more than once in those chapters, you will find the reference further down the list. For example, the word **FAITH** also occurs twice in Hebrews 10, the first occurrence being in verse 22 (Heb. 10.22).

When there are several chapters in which the word occurs the same number of times, the chapters are listed in Bible order.

This index enables you to find the areas of the text where a word is most significant, so that you can start your reading and study from there. It will be particularly useful for those wanting to use a word or topic as the basis for a study, talk or discussion.

ABANDON

Deut	31.6		4	>
Ps	27.9		3	
	37.25		3	>
	71.9		3	
	88.5		3	
Lev	26.34		2	
Deut	32.15	<	2	
1 Sam	28.15		2	
1 Kgs	9.7	<	2	
2 Kgs	7.7		2	
	17.13		2	
1 Chr	28.9		2	
2 Chr	7.20		2	
	12.1	<	2	>
	13.10	<	2	
	24.20		2	
Ps	74.1	<	2	
	119.8		2	
Jer	2.15	<	2	
	14.5		2	
	17.13	<	2	
Ezek	39.9		2	
Dan	11.30		2	
Acts	2.27		2	
Heb	6.4		2	

ACCEPT

Rom	4.3		9	
Lev	22.19		7	>
2 Kgs	5.15		6	
1 Cor	7.14		6	
Rom	15.7	<	4	
Gen	33.10		3	>
Mal	1.10		3	>
Jn	3.11		3	
Lev	1.3		2	
	19.5		2	
	27.9	<	2	

ACCEPT (cont.)

Num	18.15		2	
1 Sam	25.27		2	
2 Chr	30.9		2	
Prov	15.5		2	
Amos	5.22		2	
Zeph	3.2		2	
Mal	2.13	<	2	
Lk	14.18		2	
2 Cor	11.4		2	
Gal	1.6		2	
1 Tim	4.5		2	

ACCUSE

Acts	24.2	<	5	>
	25.5	<	5	>
	23.28	<	4	>
Num	35.12		3	
Deut	19.16		3	
Dan	6.5		3	
Mt	12.10		3	
	27.12	<	3	
Mk	15.3	<	3	
Lk	23.2		3	
Gen	18.20		2	>
1 Sam	12.3		2	
1 Kgs	21.10		2	
Ps	35.11		2	
Is	50.8		2	
Hos	4.1		2	
	12.2		2	
Mk	14.60		2	>
Lk	11.31		2	
Jn	5.45		2	
Acts	19.38		2	
	26.2	<	2	

ACKNOWLEDGE

Hos	4.1		4	>
Deut	26.3		2	
Dan	4.26		2	
Hos	2.8		2	

ACT

Ps	106.7	<	3	>
	145.4		3	
Hos	12.1		3	
2 Cor	12.7		3	
Judg	20.6		2	
2 Chr	19.6		2	
Neh	5.7		2	
Job	12.12		2	
Prov	14.16	<	2	
Is	32.4	<	2	>
Jer	3.2		2	
Ezek	16.51		2	
	24.14	<	2	
	36.17		2	
Dan	9.8		2	
Zech	11.4		2	
1 Cor	7.15		2	
2 Cor	10.2		2	

ACTION

Jas	2.14		12	
Ps	106.29		2	
Ecc	9.1		2	
Ezek	16.27		2	
Acts	5.17		2	
2 Pet	2.8		2	

ADULTERY

Ezek	23.37	<	5	
Num	5.19		4	
Mt	5.27		4	
Ezek	16.17		3	

ADULTERY (cont.)

Mk	10.11		3	
Prov	6.26		2	
Hos	3.1	<	2	>
	4.2	<	2	
Mt	19.9		2	
Lk	16.18		2	
	18.11		2	
Jn	8.3		2	
Rom	7.3		2	
Jas	2.11		2	

ADVICE

2 Sam	17.4	<	9	
1 Kgs	12.6		5	
2 Chr	10.6		5	
Prov	1.2		4	
Esth	2.4	<	3	
Is	19.3		3	
Ex	18.19		2	
2 Sam	15.31		2	>
	16.20	<	2	>
2 Chr	22.2		2	
	25.16		2	
Prov	13.10	<	2	
	15.12		2	

AFRAID

Deut	1.17		4	>
Mt	10.26		4	
	28.4		4	
Lk	8.25		4	>
Deut	20.1	<	3	>
1 Sam	18.12	<	3	
1 Kgs	1.43		3	>
Ps	56.3		3	
Is	8.9		3	
	41.10	<	3	
Jer	1.8		3	

AFRAID (cont.)

Zeph	3.13		3	
Mt	14.5		3	
Lk	1.12		3	>
	12.4		3	
Acts	27.17		3	
2 Cor	12.20	<	3	
Gen	26.7		2	
	42.4		2	>
	43.18	<	2	
Ex	20.19		2	
Num	14.9		2	
Deut	2.4	<	2	>
	3.2	<	2	
	7.18		2	
	31.6		2	
Josh	10.8		2	>
Judg	6.23		2	>
	7.3	<	2	
1 Sam	12.18	<	2	
	23.3	<	2	
2 Kgs	25.24		2	
2 Chr	20.15		2	
Esth	9.2	<	2	
Ps	27.1		2	
	31.11	<	2	
	64.1		2	
	112.7		2	
Is	43.1		2	>
	44.2	<	2	
Jer	30.10		2	
	46.27		2	
Ezek	2.6		2	>
Joel	2.21		2	
Amos	3.6		2	
Zech	8.13		2	>
Mt	21.26		2	
Mk	5.15	<	2	>
	6.20	<	2	
	11.18	<	2	>
Lk	2.9	<	2	
	9.34	<	2	
	21.9	<	2	>
Jn	19.8		2	>
Acts	23.10		2	>
Rom	13.3		2	
Heb	11.23		2	>
1 Pet	3.6		2	
Rev	18.10		2	

AGE (1) [TIME]

Mt	13.39		3	
Is	34.10		2	
Mk	10.30		2	
Lk	18.30		2	
	20.34		2	

AGREE

Gen	34.9		6	
1 Kgs	20.4		5	
2 Sam	3.12		3	
Jer	34.8		3	
Acts	15.15		3	
1 Cor	7.5		3	
Gen	17.9	<	2	
	21.27		2	
	30.31	<	2	>
	31.44	<	2	
Ex	22.7		2	>
Num	5.19		2	
2 Kgs	12.8	<	2	
Job	34.32		2	
Is	28.15		2	
Mt	20.2		2	
	27.7		2	
Mk	14.56		2	

ALIVE

Gen	45.3	<	3	>
Josh	10.28		3	>
	11.8	<	3	
2 Kgs	10.11		3	
Rev	17.8		3	
Gen	43.27		2	>
Num	16.30		2	
	31.15		2	
1 Sam	20.14		2	
2 Sam	12.21		2	
	18.14		2	>
1 Kgs	20.18	<	2	
2 Chr	24.2		2	
Ps	119.93		2	
Lam	1.11		2	
Jon	4.3		2	
Mk	16.11		2	
Lk	15.24		2	
	24.5		2	
Acts	9.39		2	
	20.10		2	
Rom	7.3		2	

ALMIGHTY

Is	19.4	<	7	
Zech	8.1	<	7	>
Jer	51.5	<	6	
Is	10.16		5	
	14.14	<	5	
	22.5	<	5	>
Jer	25.8		5	>
	29.4	<	5	>
	50.18	<	5	>
Zech	1.2		5	>
Ps	80.4		4	
	84.1		4	
Is	5.7		4	>
Jer	35.12		4	

ALMIGHTY (cont.)

Jer	44.2	<	4	
	46.10		4	
Zech	14.16	<	4	
Mal	2.1	<	4	>
	3.1	<	4	>
2 Sam	7.8	<	3	
Job	27.1		3	
	31.2		3	>
Is	9.7	<	3	
	28.5		3	>
Jer	9.7	<	3	
	11.17	<	3	
	19.3		3	>
	23.15		3	
	27.4	<	3	>
	32.14	<	3	>
	49.7	<	3	>
Amos	5.14	<	3	>
Hag	2.9	<	3	
Num	24.4		2	
Ruth	1.20		2	
1 Sam	1.3		2	
2 Sam	6.2	<	2	>
1 Kgs	19.10		2	
1 Chr	17.7		2	
Job	34.10		2	>
Ps	46.7		2	
	50.1		2	
	78.35		2	
Is	1.9		2	>
	3.1	<	2	
	6.3	<	2	
	8.13		2	>
	13.6		2	>
	18.7	<	2	>
	31.4		2	
	37.16		2	
Jer	6.6	<	2	>
	28.2	<	2	>
	31.23	<	2	>
	33.11	<	2	
	48.1		2	>
Amos	6.8	<	2	
Zeph	2.8		2	
Hag	1.2		2	>
Zech	2.8	<	2	>
	6.12	<	2	>
	13.1	<	2	>
Mal	1.6		2	>
Rev	16.7	<	2	
	19.6		2	

ALONE

Ps	62.1		4	
2 Sam	18.24		3	
Ecc	4.8		3	
Jn	8.9		3	
1 Tim	5.3		3	>

ALONE (cont.)

Ex	18.14		2	>
Num	18.5		2	
	23.3		2	
Deut	1.9		2	
	6.4		2	
	32.12		2	
Judg	3.19		2	
Ruth	1.3		2	
2 Sam	22.32		2	
1 Kgs	8.39		2	
	19.10	<	2	
2 Kgs	4.27		2	
Ps	18.31		2	
	115.1		2	
Is	2.11	<	2	
	37.16		2	>
Lam	3.28		2	
Dan	10.8		2	
Mk	4.10		2	
	6.31		2	>
Lk	9.18		2	
Jn	16.32		2	
Jas	2.17		2	

ALTAR

Lev	4.7	<	18	>
2 Kgs	23.5		15	
Lev	9.7	<	13	
Ex	29.12	<	12	>
Ezek	43.13		12	>
Lev	1.5		11	>
Josh	22.10		10	
Ex	30.1	<	9	>
	38.1	<	9	>
	40.5	<	9	
Lev	8.11	<	9	>
	6.9	<	8	>
Num	16.5	<	8	
Judg	6.24		8	
1 Kgs	13.1	<	8	
2 Kgs	16.10		8	>
Lev	16.12		7	>
1 Chr	21.18		7	>
Ex	27.1		6	>
Lev	3.2	<	6	>
	7.2	<	6	>
Num	23.1		6	
1 Kgs	18.26		6	>
Num	7.1		5	
	18.3		5	
2 Chr	29.18	<	5	>
	33.3	<	5	>
	34.4	<	5	>
Ezek	6.4		5	
Mt	23.18		5	
Lev	2.2	<	4	>
Num	4.11	<	4	>
	5.16	<	4	

ALTAR (cont.)

Deut	12.3		4	
2 Sam	24.18		4	
1 Kgs	8.22	<	4	>
Is	29.1		4	
Mal	1.7		4	>
Gen	35.1		3	
Ex	20.24		3	>
Lev	5.9	<	3	>
1 Kgs	1.50		3	>
	2.28	<	3	>
	3.2	<	3	
2 Kgs	21.3		3	
Hos	10.1		3	
Rev	8.3		3	>
Gen	8.20		2	
	12.7		2	>
	13.4	<	2	
	22.9		2	
Ex	24.4		2	
	31.8	<	2	>
	35.15	<	2	
	39.38	<	2	>
Lev	17.6	<	2	
	22.3	<	2	
Num	3.26		2	>
Deut	27.5	<	2	
Josh	8.30		2	>
Judg	13.19		2	
1 Sam	2.28		2	
	10.5		2	
1 Kgs	6.20		2	>
	12.32		2	>
	19.10	<	2	
2 Kgs	11.18		2	>
	18.22	<	2	
2 Chr	1.5		2	
	4.1		2	>
	6.12	<	2	>
	7.7	<	2	>
	14.3		2	>
	23.17		2	
	26.16		2	
	30.14	<	2	>
	32.12	<	2	>
	35.11	<	2	
Ezra	3.2		2	
Is	17.8		2	
	27.9		2	
	36.7		2	
Jer	7.21		2	
	17.1		2	
Ezek	8.5		2	>
	40.46		2	>
Amos	3.14		2	
Mt	5.23		2	
Lk	1.9		2	
1 Cor	10.18		2	
Heb	10.6		2	

AMAZE

Lk	2.18		3	
Rev	17.6		3	
Job	37.5		2	
Mt	22.22		2	
Mk	1.22		2	>
	5.20		2	>
	6.2	<	2	>
Lk	4.32		2	>
	5.9	<	2	
Acts	2.7		2	>
	3.10	<	2	>

ANGEL

Lk	1.11		11	>
Judg	13.3		10	
1 Chr	21.12		10	
Rev	8.2	<	10	>
Num	22.22		9	
Acts	12.7	<	9	
Rev	14.6		9	>
	16.1	<	9	>
Judg	6.11	<	8	
Dan	10.11		7	>
Zech	1.8		7	>
Lk	2.9	<	7	
Heb	1.4		7	>
Zech	3.1	<	6	>
Rev	10.1		6	>
	21.9	<	6	>
Dan	4.13	<	5	
Acts	10.3		5	>
Heb	2.2	<	5	
Rev	7.1		5	>
	9.1	<	5	
	22.1	<	5	
2 Sam	24.16		4	
Dan	12.1	<	4	
Zech	4.1	<	4	>
	5.2	<	4	>
Acts	7.30	<	4	>
Jude	6		4	
Rev	2.1	<	4	>
	3.1	<	4	
	12.7	<	4	
	15.1	<	4	>
	17.1	<	4	>
Gen	19.1		3	
Job	33.23		3	
Zech	6.4	<	3	
Mt	13.39		3	
Rev	19.9	<	3	>
Gen	22.11	<	2	
	24.7		2	
Ex	23.20		2	
Judg	2.1		2	
2 Sam	14.17		2	
1 Kgs	19.5		2	
	22.19		2	

ANGEL (cont.)

2 Kgs	1.3		2	
2 Chr	18.18		2	
Ps	35.5	<	2	
Ezek	28.14		2	
Dan	3.25		2	>
	8.13		2	
	11.2	<	2	>
Zech	2.3	<	2	>
Mt	1.20		2	>
	2.13	<	2	
	4.6		2	
	24.31		2	>
	25.31	<	2	>
	28.2		2	
Mk	13.27	<	2	
Lk	12.8		2	
Acts	23.8		2	
Col	2.18		2	
2 Pet	2.4		2	
Rev	1.1		2	>
	5.2		2	
	18.1	<	2	>
	20.1	<	2	>

ANGER

Ps	78.21	<	9	>
Deut	9.7		6	
	29.20		6	
Lam	2.1	<	6	>
Ezek	20.8	<	6	>
	22.20	<	6	>
Deut	32.16	<	5	
1 Kgs	16.2	<	5	
Jer	25.6		5	
Ezek	16.26		5	
Ex	32.10		4	
Num	25.3	<	4	
2 Chr	28.9		4	>
Ps	90.7	<	4	
	106.23		4	
Is	9.12	<	4	
	13.3	<	4	>
Jer	10.10		4	>
	32.29		4	>
Ezek	7.3	<	4	>
Jon	4.1	<	4	
Nah	1.2		4	
Zech	1.2		4	
Eph	4.26		4	>
Num	11.1		3	>
	16.15		3	
	32.10	<	3	
1 Kgs	14.9		3	>
2 Kgs	17.11		3	
	22.13	<	3	>
2 Chr	34.21	<	3	
Job	32.2		3	
Ps	79.5	<	3	>

ANGER (cont.)

Ps	85.3		3	
	89.9	<	3	>
Is	2.10		3	
	10.4		3	
	51.17		3	
	63.3		3	>
	64.5	<	3	>
Jer	3.5	<	3	>
	4.4	<	3	
	7.20	<	3	>
	15.6		3	
	44.3		3	
Ezek	23.22	<	3	>
	36.5	<	3	
Hab	3.2		3	
Heb	3.10		3	>
Gen	4.5		2	
	18.30		2	
	31.35	<	2	
	49.6		2	
Lev	10.6		2	
Deut	1.34		2	
	4.21	<	2	
	31.17		2	>
1 Sam	20.7		2	
2 Sam	6.7		2	
	22.8		2	
1 Kgs	21.4		2	>
2 Kgs	13.3		2	
	21.6		2	>
	23.19	<	2	>
1 Chr	13.10		2	
2 Chr	12.7		2	
	19.2		2	
	25.10	<	2	>
	29.8	<	2	>
Job	9.5		2	
	15.12	<	2	>
	18.4		2	>
	20.23	<	2	>
	21.17	<	2	
Ps	2.5		2	
	6.1		2	>
	18.7		2	
	38.1	<	2	
	74.1		2	>
	76.7	<	2	>
	80.4	<	2	
	88.7		2	>
	103.8	<	2	
	119.53		2	
Prov	6.34		2	
	20.2	<	2	>
	25.23		2	
Ecc	5.6		2	
Is	5.25		2	
	12.1		2	>
	30.27		2	

ANGER (cont.)

Is	42.25	<	2	
	54.8		2	
	57.16		2	
	65.3	<	2	>
	66.14	<	2	
Jer	6.11		2	>
	18.20	<	2	
	21.5		2	
	50.13	<	2	>
Ezek	5.13		2	>
	8.17	<	2	>
	13.13		2	>
	21.17	<	2	>
	24.8	<	2	>
	25.14	<	2	
Dan	8.7		2	>
Hos	7.6		2	
	11.9		2	>
Mic	7.9		2	
Zeph	2.2	<	2	>
Zech	8.2	<	2	
Mk	10.14		2	
Rom	2.5	<	2	
	9.22		2	
Col	3.6		2	
Jas	1.19		2	
Rev	6.16		2	
	14.10		2	>
	15.1	<	2	>
	16.1	<	2	

ANOINT

Ex	40.9	<	5	
	29.7	<	4	>
	30.25	<	4	>
Lev	8.2		4	
Ex	35.8		3	
1 Sam	16.3	<	3	
1 Kgs	1.34		3	
	19.15		3	
2 Kgs	9.3		3	
1 Sam	15.1		2	>
2 Sam	2.4		2	

APART

Mk	3.24		3	
Lev	20.24		2	>
1 Kgs	13.3		2	
Ezek	48.8		2	
Mt	12.25		2	
Rom	7.8		2	>
	8.29	<	2	

APOSTLE

Acts	5.2	<	17	>
	4.2		6	>
	14.3	<	6	>
	1.2		5	>

APOSTLE (cont.)

Acts	15.2	<	5	>
1 Cor	15.5		5	
2 Cor	11.5		5	>
Acts	2.14	<	4	
1 Cor	9.1		4	
Acts	6.2	<	3	
	8.1		3	>
Gal	1.1		3	>
Lk	6.13		2	
	24.10		2	
Acts	13.43		2	>
Rom	1.1		2	
1 Cor	12.28		2	
2 Cor	12.11	<	2	
Gal	2.8	<	2	
2 Tim	1.1		2	

ARGUE

Mk	9.14	<	4	
Job	13.3		3	
1 Tim	6.4		3	
Prov	22.10		2	>
	26.17		2	
Ecc	6.10		2	
Acts	15.2		2	
	18.15		2	

ARREST

Mt	26.4		5	
Mk	14.1	<	5	
Acts	9.2		3	
	22.4	<	3	
Dan	6.16		2	
Mk	13.9	<	2	>
Lk	22.53	<	2	
Acts	12.3		2	

ARROGANT

Prov	16.5	<	3	
	13.1		2	
	21.4		2	
Is	2.11		2	
Jer	48.29		2	
Dan	8.4		2	
	11.18		2	
Hos	7.10		2	

ASH

Num	19.9		3	
Ex	9.8		2	
Lev	6.10		2	
1 Kgs	13.3		2	
2 Kgs	23.4		2	
Esth	4.1		2	
Jer	52.18	<	2	

ASHAMED

Ezek	16.54		3	
2 Tim	1.8		3	>
Ps	119.46		2	
Prov	29.15		2	
Jer	6.15		2	
	8.12		2	
Ezek	43.10		2	
Zeph	3.5		2	
Mk	8.38		2	
Lk	9.26		2	

AUTHORITIES

Jn	7.1		7	>
Rom	13.1		4	
Jn	5.10		3	
	18.14		3	>
Acts	17.6	<	3	
Jn	9.18	<	2	
	11.48		2	>
	19.31	<	2	>
Acts	16.19		2	>
	19.31		2	

AUTHORITY

Rev	13.2	<	5	
2 Chr	19.6		4	
Dan	7.6		3	
Jn	5.30		3	
	7.17		3	>
Rom	13.1	<	3	
Jude	6		3	
Rev	11.6		3	>
Gen	41.35		2	
Is	22.21		2	
Mt	9.6	<	2	
Mk	1.22		2	>
Lk	4.32		2	>
Jn	8.28	<	2	
	19.10		2	
Acts	26.10		2	
2 Cor	10.8		2	
	13.10		2	
Eph	5.23		2	
1 Tim	2.2		2	
1 Pet	2.13		2	
Rev	2.26	<	2	
	17.12	<	2	>

B

BAD

Jer	24.2	<	3	
Mt	7.11		3	
	12.33		3	
Gen	2.9		2	>
	3.5	<	2	
Lev	27.12		2	

BAD (cont.)

1 Kgs	22.8		2	
2 Chr	18.7		2	
Prov	28.12		2	
Ecc	9.2		2	
Jer	14.17		2	
Ezek	34.17		2	
Lk	6.43		2	
3 Jn	11		2	

BANQUET

Esth	5.4		6	>
	1.3		4	>
Is	25.6		2	
Dan	5.1		2	

BAPTIZE

Mt	3.6		7	
Lk	3.3		7	
Mk	1.4		6	
Jn	1.25		6	
1 Cor	1.13		6	
Acts	8.12		5	>
Jn	3.22		4	>
Acts	19.3	<	4	
	1.5		3	>
	10.37		3	>
Rom	6.3		3	
Mk	10.38		2	>
Lk	7.29		2	
Jn	4.1	<	2	
Acts	2.38	<	2	
	11.16	<	2	
	16.15		2	
	18.8		2	>
1 Cor	15.29		2	
Col	2.12		2	

BEAST (1) [ANIMAL]

Dan	7.3		12	

BEAST (2) [DEVIL]

Rev	13.1		21	>
	17.3	<	11	
	19.19		5	>
	16.2	<	4	>
	20.4	<	3	
	14.9	<	2	>

BEG

Mk	5.7		5	>
Lk	8.28	<	5	>
Mt	8.5		3	
Acts	27.22		3	
1 Sam	20.6		2	
Esth	7.7		2	>
Jer	38.20	<	2	
Mt	18.26		2	
Mk	7.26	<	2	>

BEG (cont.)

Lk	9.38	<	2	
	16.3	<	2	
Jn	4.31		2	
	9.8		2	
Acts	3.2		2	
1 Thes	4.1		2	>
Heb	13.19	<	2	

BEING

Gen	9.10	<	6	
	7.4	<	5	>
	1.20		3	
	6.2	<	3	>
1 Cor	15.39		3	
Lev	27.28		2	
Ps	56.4		2	
Rom	6.6		2	>
2 Cor	4.16		2	>
Jas	3.2		2	

BELIEVE

Jn	6.29	<	9	>
	11.15	<	9	>
Rom	4.3	<	9	
Jn	3.12	<	8	>
	12.11	<	8	>
	4.21	<	7	>
	5.24	<	7	>
1 Jn	5.1	<	7	
Mt	21.21		6	
Jn	10.25		6	>
	14.1	<	6	
	20.8	<	6	
Rom	10.4		6	>
Gal	3.2	<	6	
Mk	16.11	<	5	
Jn	7.5	<	5	>
	8.24	<	5	>
	9.18	<	5	
Ex	4.1		4	
Jn	16.9		4	>
1 Thes	4.14		4	
1 Pet	2.6	<	4	>
Mk	11.23		3	
Lk	1.20		3	
	8.12		3	
	24.11		3	
Jn	1.7		3	>
	2.11	<	3	>
	17.8	<	3	
Acts	13.12		3	>
	14.2	<	3	>
	15.7	<	3	>
	17.12	<	3	>
Rom	3.22		3	>
1 Cor	15.2		3	
2 Cor	4.4		3	
2 Thes	1.4		3	>

BELIEVE (cont.)

Jas	2.19	<	3	
Ps	106.12		2	
Mt	9.28	<	2	
	24.23		2	
Acts	8.12		2	>
	9.26	<	2	
	11.17	<	2	
	16.31	<	2	>
	18.8	<	2	>
	19.4	<	2	>
	24.14	<	2	
	26.8		2	
Rom	1.5		2	
	11.20	<	2	
	14.14	<	2	
	16.5		2	
Eph	1.13		2	
1 Thes	2.10		2	
2 Thes	2.11	<	2	>
1 Tim	1.15		2	
	4.9	<	2	
Heb	4.3	<	2	
	6.1		2	
1 Pet	1.8		2	>
	3.1	<	2	>
1 Jn	4.1	<	2	>

BELIEVER

Acts	15.1	<	8	>
	11.1	<	6	>
	21.4	<	6	
	8.1		5	>
	9.19	<	5	
	14.1	<	5	>
	18.18	<	5	>
	2.1	<	4	
	16.2	<	4	>
	19.2	<	4	>
	17.6	<	3	>
	4.24		2	>
	10.23		2	>
	13.48	<	2	>
	20.1	<	2	>
	28.14		2	
1 Cor	14.22		2	>
Col	4.5		2	
1 Thes	4.9		2	>
	5.26	<	2	
1 Tim	4.3		2	

BEST

Num	18.12		5	
1 Sam	15.9	<	5	
Gen	45.18		3	
Ex	29.2		3	
Lev	3.4		3	>
2 Kgs	7.1		3	
Ezek	16.10		3	>

BEST (cont.)

2 Tim	4.7		3	
Gen	47.6		2	
Lev	8.16	<	2	>
Deut	33.14	<	2	
1 Sam	8.14		2	
	14.36		2	>
2 Kgs	10.3		2	
2 Chr	11.1		2	
Esth	2.4		2	>
Ecc	2.3		2	>
	3.12	<	2	
Lam	3.26		2	
Lk	14.7	<	2	>
Jn	2.10		2	
Tit	3.12		2	
2 Pet	1.5		2	
	3.12		2	

BETRAY

Mt	26.15		5	>
Mk	14.10		4	
Lk	22.4		4	
Jn	13.2	<	3	
1 Chr	12.17		2	
Is	33.1		2	
Jn	6.64		2	

BIND

Mt	23.16		4	
Jn	18.12		2	
Rom	7.2		2	

BIRTH

Gen	29.32		4	>
Mt	1.12		4	
Gen	4.2	<	3	
	25.13		3	
Lev	12.2		3	
Lk	1.15		3	>
Rev	12.2		3	
Gen	30.23	<	2	
Ex	1.16		2	
Deut	28.54		2	
Judg	13.5		2	
1 Kgs	3.17		2	
Job	39.1		2	
Is	66.7		2	
Jas	1.15		2	

BITTER

Num	5.17		5	
Is	38.3		3	
Rev	8.11		3	
Lam	3.15		2	
Ezek	27.30		2	
Obad	16		2	
Jas	3.11		2	

BLESS

Gen	27.4	<	20	>
Deut	28.2	<	9	
Gen	48.3	<	8	>
Deut	33.1		7	
Gen	26.3	<	6	>
	28.3	<	5	
Num	23.9	<	5	>
Deut	7.13		5	>
	15.4	<	5	>
Zech	8.12	<	5	>
Gen	12.2		4	
	24.1		4	>
	49.25	<	4	
Num	6.23		4	
Ps	115.12		4	
Lk	6.28		4	
Rom	11.12	<	4	>
Gal	3.8		4	
Gen	17.16		3	>
Num	24.1	<	3	
Deut	11.26	<	3	>
	16.10	<	3	
	30.1		3	
Ruth	2.4	<	3	>
1 Sam	2.20		3	
2 Sam	6.11		3	>
1 Kgs	8.14		3	
Ps	67.1		3	
Prov	10.6		3	>
Is	19.24		3	
	65.9		3	
Lk	1.28		3	>
	24.30		3	
Rom	15.27		3	
Eph	1.3		3	
Heb	6.7		3	>
	7.1	<	3	
Gen	1.22		2	>
	14.19		2	
	22.16	<	2	
	30.27		2	
	32.26		2	
	39.5		2	
	47.7		2	>
Ex	20.11		2	
Lev	9.22		2	
Num	22.6		2	>
Deut	14.24		2	>
	23.5		2	>
	26.15		2	>
Josh	8.33		2	
2 Sam	7.29	<	2	
1 Chr	17.27	<	2	
2 Chr	6.3		2	>
	26.5		2	
Job	42.12		2	
Ps	21.3		2	
	37.22		2	

BLESS (cont.)

Ps	72.15		2	
	84.9		2	
	109.17		2	
	118.26		2	>
	128.4	<	2	>
	129.8	<	2	
Is	56.2	<	2	
Jer	30.19		2	>
Ezek	34.26		2	
Hos	10.12		2	
Mk	11.9	<	2	
Lk	2.34	<	2	
Jn	12.13		2	
Acts	3.25		2	>
Rom	12.14	<	2	
2 Cor	1.11		2	
Heb	11.20		2	>
1 Pet	1.4		2	>
	2.19	<	2	>
	3.9	<	2	

BLIND

Jn	9.1		19	
Mt	23.16		5	
Is	42.7		4	>
Mt	15.14		4	
2 Sam	5.6		3	
Mk	10.46		3	
Deut	28.28	<	2	
2 Kgs	6.18		2	
Is	29.9		2	
Mt	9.27		2	
Mk	8.22		2	
Lk	7.21	<	2	
	14.13		2	
	18.35		2	

BLOOD

Heb	9.7		13	
Lev	17.3	<	10	
	4.5	<	9	>
	14.6		8	>
	8.15	<	7	>
Ex	29.12		6	>
Lev	16.14	<	6	>
Ex	7.17		5	
	12.7		5	
Deut	12.16		5	
Lev	3.2		4	>
	7.2	<	4	>
Is	34.3		4	
Ezek	16.6		4	
Zech	9.7		4	
Jn	6.53		4	
Rev	16.3		4	>
Ex	24.6		3	
Lev	1.5		3	
	9.9	<	3	

BLOOD (cont.)

1 Sam	14.32		3	
Ps	79.3	<	3	
Ezek	39.17	<	3	
	43.18		3	>
1 Jn	5.6		3	
Gen	4.10		2	
	9.4		2	
	37.27		2	
	49.11		2	
Ex	4.9		2	
Lev	5.9	<	2	>
	6.27	<	2	>
	12.4		2	
Num	19.4	<	2	
Deut	22.15		2	
1 Kgs	22.35	<	2	
2 Kgs	3.22		2	
	16.13		2	
1 Chr	11.1		2	
2 Chr	29.22		2	>
Is	1.11		2	
	15.9		2	
	63.3		2	
Jer	2.34		2	
	52.18		2	
Ezek	24.7	<	2	
	44.7	<	2	>
Joel	2.30		2	
Mt	26.28		2	>
	27.6	<	2	
Mk	14.24		2	
Lk	22.20		2	
Acts	2.19	<	2	
	15.20		2	
1 Cor	11.25	<	2	
Heb	10.4		2	>
	12.24	<	2	>
	13.11	<	2	
Rev	8.7	<	2	
	17.6	<	2	>
	18.24	<	2	>

BOAST

2 Cor	11.10	<	8	>
	10.8		5	>
	12.1	<	5	
2 Kgs	19.23		3	
Is	10.8		3	
	37.24		3	
Jer	9.23		3	
Dan	7.8		3	
Gal	6.12		3	
Amos	6.13		2	
Rom	2.17	<	2	>
	5.2	<	2	
1 Cor	1.29		2	
	9.15		2	
2 Cor	7.14		2	>

BOAST (cont.)

2 Cor	9.2	<	2	
2 Thes	1.4		2	
Jas	3.5		2	>
	4.16	<	2	

BODY

1 Cor	12.12	<	18	>
	15.35		12	
	6.13	<	11	>
Lev	11.8	<	10	
1 Kgs	13.22		7	
Jn	19.31		7	>
2 Kgs	9.10		6	
2 Cor	5.1	<	6	
Eph	4.4	<	6	>
Deut	21.2		5	
Mt	6.22	<	5	
Rom	7.4	<	5	>
Gen	50.2		4	
2 Sam	20.11		4	>
Mk	15.42	<	4	>
Lk	11.34		4	>
	23.52	<	4	>
Eph	2.3	<	4	>
	5.23	<	4	
Phil	3.2		4	
Col	2.5	<	4	>
Heb	10.5		4	>
Judg	20.1	<	3	
1 Sam	31.8		3	
Job	33.19		3	
Jer	41.7		3	
Ezek	1.9		3	
	37.8		3	
	39.4		3	
Mt	5.29		3	>
	27.58	<	3	>
Lk	12.4	<	3	
Rom	12.4		3	
1 Cor	7.4	<	3	
	10.5		3	>
	11.24	<	3	>
2 Cor	4.10		3	>
Col	1.18		3	>
2 Pet	2.10	<	3	>
Ex	13.19		2	
Deut	28.26		2	
Josh	8.29		2	
	10.26		2	
Judg	14.8		2	
	19.28		2	>
1 Sam	17.44		2	
1 Chr	10.8		2	
Esth	9.13		2	
Job	2.5		2	
	6.4		2	>
	7.5	<	2	
	20.11	<	2	>

BODY (cont.)

Job	21.23	<	2	
Ps	79.2		2	
Jer	14.16		2	>
	16.4	<	2	
Lam	2.10		2	>
Mt	10.28		2	
	26.12		2	>
Mk	14.8		2	>
Lk	24.3	<	2	
Acts	9.37		2	
Rom	8.10	<	2	
1 Cor	5.3		2	>
1 Pet	2.11		2	>
2 Pet	3.10	<	2	
Jude	8		2	
Rev	11.8		2	

BOLD

Acts	4.13		3	
Rom	15.15		3	
Gen	18.27		2	
Acts	9.27		2	
Eph	6.19		2	

BOW (2) [WORSHIP]

Dan	3.5	<	10	
1 Kgs	1.16		5	>
Gen	33.3		3	
	37.7		3	
Esth	3.2		3	
Gen	17.3		2	>
	23.7		2	>
	27.29		2	
	43.26	<	2	>
	49.8	<	2	>
Num	16.22		2	
2 Sam	9.6		2	
	14.4		2	>
1 Kgs	18.7		2	>
2 Kgs	17.35		2	
1 Chr	21.16		2	
2 Chr	20.18		2	
Ps	22.29		2	
	72.9		2	
Is	44.17		2	>
	49.7		2	

BREAD

Jn	6.7		20	
Ex	12.8		6	>
Lev	23.6		6	>
Ezek	4.9		6	
1 Sam	21.3		5	
Mt	16.5	<	5	
1 Cor	11.23	<	5	
Ex	13.3	<	4	
	29.2		4	
Lev	8.2	<	4	

BREAD (cont.)

Lev	24.5	<	4	
Deut	16.3		4	
Judg	6.19		4	>
Mk	6.8		4	
	8.5		4	
Jn	13.26		4	
Ex	23.15		3	
	34.18		3	>
Lev	2.4		3	
	7.12	<	3	>
Num	6.15		3	
1 Kgs	17.6		3	
Lk	24.30		3	
1 Cor	5.8		3	
	10.3		3	>
Ex	16.8		2	
Num	4.7		2	
	15.20		2	
Josh	9.5		2	
1 Sam	25.11		2	
2 Sam	16.1		2	
2 Chr	30.13	<	2	
Is	44.15		2	
Jer	37.21		2	
Mt	4.3		2	
	12.4		2	
	26.23		2	
Mk	2.26		2	
	14.20		2	
Lk	4.3		2	
	6.4		2	
	11.5		2	
Jn	21.9		2	

BRIDE

Song	4.8		4	>
Ex	22.16		2	
Is	62.5	<	2	
Rev	21.2		2	>

BRIDEGROOM

Mt	25.1		5	
Jn	3.29	<	3	
Mt	9.15		2	
Mk	2.19		2	
Lk	5.34		2	

BULL-CALF

Ex	32.4		6	
1 Kgs	12.28		3	
Deut	9.16		2	

BURDEN

1 Kgs	12.4		5	
2 Chr	10.4		5	
Jer	23.33		5	
Neh	5.15	<	2	
Is	43.23		2	

BURNT-OFFERING

Num	28.3		11	>
Lev	9.2	<	8	
Num	29.2	<	8	
2 Chr	29.7	<	7	>
Lev	4.10	<	4	>
	6.9	<	4	>
	14.13		4	>
	16.3	<	4	>
Num	15.3		4	
	23.3		4	
Lev	7.2	<	3	>
	8.18	<	3	>
	23.12	<	3	
Num	6.11		3	>
2 Kgs	16.3		3	>
Ex	29.25		2	
Lev	1.3		2	
	5.7	<	2	>
	12.6		2	
	15.15	<	2	>
Num	7.12	<	2	>
1 Sam	6.14		2	
	13.9		2	
1 Kgs	3.4		2	
2 Kgs	17.17	<	2	
2 Chr	31.2	<	2	
	35.12		2	
Ps	51.16	<	2	

C

CARE

Ezek	34.2		7	
1 Tim	5.5		5	>
Gen	37.2	<	4	
Esth	2.3		4	
Gen	30.29		3	
1 Sam	17.15	<	3	
1 Kgs	1.2		3	>
Prov	27.5		3	
Is	46.3		3	
Jer	23.2		3	
	30.13		3	>
Lk	10.34		3	
Jn	21.15		3	
Acts	15.14	<	3	
1 Pet	5.2		3	
Gen	13.7		2	
	46.32	<	2	
	50.21		2	
Num	18.21		2	
Ruth	4.14	<	2	
1 Sam	16.11		2	>
1 Chr	23.28		2	
Ps	10.4		2	
	31.5		2	
Is	40.11		2	

CARE (cont.)

Jer	12.2		2	>
	31.28	<	2	
	39.12		2	>
Hos	12.12	<	2	>
Mt	25.36		2	
Jn	10.13		2	
Acts	7.20		2	
	20.28		2	
Phil	4.10		2	
Rev	12.6		2	

CASE (2) [LEGAL]

Deut	17.8		5	
Job	13.3		5	
2 Chr	19.8		4	
Mic	6.1		4	
Ex	18.22		2	
Deut	19.18		2	
Is	41.1		2	
Acts	25.21	<	2	

CELEBRATE

2 Chr	30.1		8	
Ex	12.14		6	>
2 Chr	35.1		5	
Ex	23.14		4	
Deut	16.1		4	
Lk	15.6		4	
Lev	23.5		3	
2 Kgs	23.21		3	
Zech	14.16		3	
Gen	29.27		2	
Ex	13.5	<	2	
2 Chr	7.8		2	
	23.13		2	
Ezra	6.19		2	
Neh	12.27		2	
Is	22.1		2	

CHALLENGE

1 Sam	17.4		6	

CHANGE

1 Cor	15.51		5	
Jer	26.3		4	
Lev	13.23		3	
2 Kgs	5.5		3	
Jer	7.1		3	>
	34.11		3	
Dan	6.8		3	>
Amos	7.3		3	>
2 Cor	5.5		3	
Gen	31.7		2	
	45.22		2	
Ex	32.12		2	
1 Sam	15.29	<	2	
Joel	2.7		2	
Amos	8.1	<	2	

CHANGE (cont.)

Jon	3.9		2	>
Mt	21.29		2	
Rom	11.15		2	>
2 Cor	7.9		2	
Heb	6.17		2	>
	7.12	<	2	

CHARGE (3) [LEGAL]

Acts	25.2	<	7	
Deut	22.14		3	
Job	13.23		2	

CHEAT

Mal	3.5		4	
Ezek	18.7		3	
Lev	19.11		2	
Deut	25.13	<	2	
1 Sam	12.3		2	
Ezek	22.7		2	

CHIEF PRIESTS

Mt	27.1	<	7	>
Mk	14.1		5	>
	15.1	<	5	
Mt	26.3		4	>
Lk	22.2		4	>
Mt	21.15	<	3	
Lk	23.4	<	3	>
Jn	19.6	<	3	
Mt	28.11	<	2	
Mk	11.18	<	2	
Lk	20.1	<	2	
Jn	7.32		2	
	11.47		2	>
	18.3		2	>
Acts	9.14		2	
	25.2		2	>
	26.10	<	2	

CHILD OF GOD

Rom	8.14		7	>
Gal	4.5	<	6	
Heb	12.5		6	
1 Jn	3.1	<	5	>
Rom	9.4	<	4	
1 Jn	5.1	<	4	
Mt	5.9		2	
Jn	1.12		2	
Acts	17.28		2	
Phil	2.15		2	

CHOOSE

1 Kgs	8.12		7	
1 Chr	15.2		7	>
2 Chr	6.1		7	>
Rom	11.2		7	
Deut	30.1		6	
1 Sam	16.1		6	>

CHOOSE (cont.)

1 Chr	28.4		6	>
Gen	24.3		5	
Deut	12.5	<	5	
Ps	89.3		5	
Acts	1.2		5	
	15.7		5	
Num	16.1		4	>
1 Sam	2.10		4	
	12.3		4	
Ps	105.5		4	>
1 Pet	2.4	<	4	
Ex	12.3		3	
Lev	16.9		3	
Deut	17.8		3	>
Josh	20.2		3	
Judg	20.9		3	>
1 Sam	24.6		3	
2 Sam	24.11	<	3	
1 Kgs	11.32		3	>
1 Chr	16.12	<	3	>
Ps	132.10		3	
Is	41.8	<	3	>
	44.1	<	3	>
	65.9		3	>
Jer	12.7		3	
	33.15		3	
Dan	4.17		3	>
Mt	24.22		3	
Mk	3.14		3	
	13.20	<	3	
Lk	10.1		3	
Jn	15.16		3	
1 Cor	1.27		3	>
1 Pet	1.1		3	>
Gen	13.9		2	
Ex	18.21		2	>
	33.13		2	
Num	35.11	<	2	
Deut	1.13		2	
	7.6		2	
	10.15		2	>
	14.2		2	
	20.9		2	>
Josh	4.2	<	2	
1 Sam	10.1		2	
2 Sam	1.14		2	
1 Kgs	14.7	<	2	
2 Kgs	23.27		2	
1 Chr	21.10		2	
	25.1		2	>
Neh	9.7		2	
Ps	78.68		2	
	106.23	<	2	
Prov	8.10		2	
	22.1		2	
Is	43.10	<	2	>
	45.1	<	2	
	49.1	<	2	

CHOOSE (cont.)

Ezek	20.5		2	>
Dan	9.25		2	
Lk	4.6		2	
Acts	3.20		2	
	6.3		2	
	13.17	<	2	
Rom	8.29	<	2	>
	9.11	<	2	
Eph	1.4		2	>
Phil	1.10		2	
Tit	1.1		2	
Heb	1.2		2	
	5.1		2	

CHRIST

1 Cor	15.3		17	
Col	2.2	<	14	>
Eph	1.3		12	>
1 Jn	2.2		11	>
1 Cor	1.5		10	>
Eph	5.2	<	10	>
2 Cor	5.10	<	9	>
Phil	1.13		9	>
Col	1.2		9	>
	3.1	<	8	>
1 Jn	3.2	<	8	>
Rom	15.3	<	7	>
2 Cor	2.10	<	7	>
Eph	2.5	<	7	>
	4.7	<	7	>
Heb	9.11		7	
Rom	8.9	<	6	>
Gal	2.16	<	6	>
	3.13	<	6	>
Rom	16.5	<	5	
2 Cor	10.1		5	>
	11.2	<	5	>
Eph	3.4	<	5	>
Phil	3.7	<	5	>
Phlm	6		5	
Rom	5.6		4	>
	6.4	<	4	>
	10.4		4	
1 Cor	11.1	<	4	>
Gal	1.4		4	>
	5.1	<	4	>
1 Pet	4.1	<	4	>
Rom	9.1	<	3	
	14.9		3	>
1 Cor	4.1	<	3	>
	10.4		3	>
2 Cor	1.5		3	>
	3.3	<	3	>
	12.9	<	3	>
Heb	10.5		3	
1 Pet	1.11		3	>
	3.15	<	3	>
1 Jn	4.3	<	3	

CHRIST (cont.)

1 Cor	6.15	<	2	>
	8.11	<	2	>
	9.12	<	2	
	12.12	<	2	
2 Cor	4.4	<	2	>
Gal	6.2	<	2	
Eph	6.5	<	2	
Phil	2.1	<	2	>
Heb	3.6		2	
1 Pet	2.21	<	2	>
	5.1	<	2	
2 Jn	7		2	
Rev	20.4		2	

CHRISTIAN

1 Cor	7.12	<	8	>
Rom	16.7		4	
3 Jn	3		4	
1 Cor	6.1		3	>
Eph	6.1		3	
Acts	16.1		2	
Rom	12.10		2	
1 Cor	4.15	<	2	
	16.15		2	
2 Cor	12.2		2	
Col	3.18		2	>
1 Tim	5.10		2	>
Heb	6.1		2	
Jas	1.9		2	
1 Pet	5.12	<	2	

CHURCH

Rev	2.1	<	9	>
1 Cor	14.4		8	>
Eph	5.23		8	
1 Tim	3.1	<	7	
Rev	3.1	<	6	
Rom	16.1	<	5	
2 Cor	8.1		5	
Acts	15.3	<	4	>
Rev	1.4		4	>
Acts	11.22		3	>
1 Cor	16.1	<	3	
Gal	1.2		3	
Col	1.18		3	
3 Jn	6		3	
Mt	18.17		2	
Acts	8.1		2	>
	12.1	<	2	>
	14.23	<	2	>
	20.17		2	>
1 Cor	11.16	<	2	>
2 Cor	11.8		2	>
Eph	1.22		2	
	3.10		2	
Col	4.15		2	
2 Thes	1.1		2	
Tit	1.5		2	

CHURCH (cont.)

1 Pet	5.1		2	

CIRCUMCISE

Rom	2.25		9	>
	4.9	<	9	
Gen	17.10		7	
Josh	5.2		7	
Ezek	32.24		7	
Gen	34.14		6	
1 Cor	7.18		5	
Acts	7.8		4	
Gal	5.2		4	>
	6.12	<	4	
Ex	12.44		3	
Jn	7.22		3	
Col	2.11		3	>
Ezek	44.7		2	
Acts	11.2		2	
	15.1		2	>
Gal	2.3		2	
Eph	2.11		2	
Phil	3.3		2	

CLAIM

Is	48.1	<	3	
Num	3.40		2	
Josh	22.4		2	
2 Sam	19.43		2	
Neh	5.10		2	
Job	11.4		2	
	17.8		2	
	21.16		2	
Jer	23.25		2	
Ezek	28.2		2	
Zech	13.2		2	
Jn	19.7		2	
1 Cor	9.15		2	
2 Thes	2.2		2	

CLEAN

Lev	13.6	<	15	>
	14.2	<	11	>
Num	19.9	<	8	
2 Chr	29.15		5	>
Lev	12.4	<	4	>
2 Chr	30.1	<	4	
Lev	11.36	<	3	>
	15.8	<	3	>
Is	1.6		3	
Ezek	36.25		3	
	39.12		3	
Mt	23.25		3	
Mk	1.40		3	
Lk	11.25		3	
Jn	13.10		3	
Gen	7.2		2	>
Lev	7.19	<	2	
	10.10		2	>

CLEAN (cont.)

Lev	17.13	<	2	
	22.4		2	
Num	18.11		2	>
Deut	12.15		2	
	14.11		2	>
2 Kgs	21.13		2	
Ps	51.2		2	
Jer	43.12		2	
Ezek	44.23		2	
Mt	8.2		2	
Lk	5.12		2	
Jn	15.2		2	
Rev	19.8		2	

CLOUD

Num	9.15		11	
Ex	24.15		4	
	40.34		4	
Rev	14.14		4	
Gen	9.13		3	
Ex	14.19	<	3	
	33.9		3	>
Num	10.11		3	>
Job	37.11	<	3	>
	38.9	<	3	
Ps	18.9		3	
Ezek	31.3	<	3	>
Lk	9.34		3	
Ex	13.21		2	>
	19.9		2	>
Num	12.5	<	2	
	14.14		2	
Judg	20.38		2	
2 Sam	22.10		2	>
1 Kgs	8.10		2	
	18.44		2	
Neh	9.12		2	
Job	22.13		2	
	26.8		2	
	36.28	<	2	>
Is	14.14		2	
	25.5		2	
Ezek	10.3		2	
	30.3		2	>
Joel	2.2		2	
Hab	3.8		2	
Mt	17.5		2	
Mk	9.7		2	
1 Cor	10.1		2	

COMFORT

Lam	1.2		4	>
Ps	119.50		3	
Gen	37.35		2	
Job	16.1	<	2	
	21.1		2	
	29.18		2	
Is	40.1		2	

COMFORT (cont.)

Jer	31.13		2	
Jn	11.19		2	

COMMAND

Ps	119.2		39	
Num	10.13		13	
Lev	8.4	<	12	>
Ex	39.1	<	10	>
	40.16	<	8	
1 Kgs	13.1	<	8	>
Gen	1.3		7	
Num	31.6		7	>
	32.21	<	7	>
Ezek	20.11		7	
Ex	16.16	<	6	>
Num	15.23		6	>
Deut	5.12	<	6	>
	26.13		6	
Josh	11.9	<	6	
1 Kgs	11.2		6	>
2 Kgs	17.12	<	6	>
Ezra	6.3		6	>
Jer	35.7		6	
1 Jn	2.3		6	>
Ex	24.3	<	5	
Lev	4.1		5	>
	9.5	<	5	
	10.1		5	
	26.3	<	5	>
Num	9.5	<	5	
	27.11		5	>
Deut	1.3		5	>
	6.1	<	5	>
	11.13	<	5	>
	12.11	<	5	>
Josh	22.2	<	5	>
1 Sam	15.11		5	
1 Kgs	20.14		5	>
1 Chr	12.3		5	>
Ps	105.7	<	5	>
2 Jn	4		5	
Ex	7.2	<	4	>
	35.1	<	4	>
Num	36.2		4	
Deut	28.1		4	>
	30.2	<	4	>
Josh	4.3		4	>
2 Sam	18.1	<	4	
2 Kgs	18.6	<	4	
1 Chr	28.1	<	4	>
Job	37.5	<	4	>
Jer	7.22		4	
Jn	15.10	<	4	
Rom	2.13		4	>
1 Jn	3.22	<	4	>
Gen	7.5	<	3	
Ex	18.16	<	3	>
	31.6		3	>

COMMAND (cont.)

Ex	34.4	<	3	>
	36.1	<	3	
Lev	17.1	<	3	>
	18.4	<	3	>
	19.3	<	3	>
	22.1	<	3	
	25.1	<	3	>
Num	4.34	<	3	>
	20.9	<	3	
Deut	4.2		3	>
	13.4	<	3	
	15.5		3	>
	17.3	<	3	>
	33.3	<	3	>
Josh	21.2	<	3	>
1 Kgs	2.3		3	>
	8.44		3	>
	17.4		3	>
1 Chr	21.6		3	>
2 Chr	17.4		3	
	33.8	<	3	>
	34.16	<	3	>
Ezra	7.11	<	3	
Neh	1.5		3	
Esth	1.12		3	
Ps	106.3	<	3	>
	107.11	<	3	
	148.5	<	3	>
Jer	22.3		3	>
Ezek	5.6		3	
Dan	9.4		3	
Amos	9.1		3	
Mal	2.1		3	
1 Tim	6.13		3	
2 Pet	3.2	<	3	
1 Jn	5.2	<	3	
Ex	12.28		2	
	17.1	<	2	>
	19.7	<	2	>
	23.15		2	>
	27.20		2	
	32.8	<	2	>
Lev	6.8	<	2	>
	7.36	<	2	>
	21.1	<	2	>
Num	1.19		2	>
	2.33	<	2	>
	3.14	<	2	>
	5.2	<	2	>
	6.1	<	2	
	8.20		2	>
	33.2	<	2	
Deut	2.1	<	2	
	7.9	<	2	>
	8.2	<	2	>
	9.12	<	2	
	10.5		2	>
	18.18	<	2	>

COMMAND (cont.)

Deut	24.18		2	
Josh	8.8	<	2	>
	14.2	<	2	>
	17.4		2	
	24.24	<	2	
Judg	2.17	<	2	>
1 Sam	12.14		2	>
2 Sam	10.10		2	>
	12.9	<	2	
1 Kgs	9.4	<	2	
	18.18	<	2	
2 Kgs	1.3		2	
	21.8		2	
	24.3	<	2	>
1 Chr	15.15	<	2	>
	19.11		2	
	22.6	<	2	
	29.19	<	2	
2 Chr	7.17	<	2	>
	8.14	<	2	
	14.4	<	2	
	25.4	<	2	>
	29.15	<	2	>
	30.6	<	2	
	35.10	<	2	>
	36.22	<	2	
Ezra	1.1		2	
	4.3		2	
Neh	9.16		2	
Esth	3.3		2	
	9.31	<	2	
Job	38.12	<	2	>
	39.25	<	2	
Ps	19.7	<	2	
	33.6		2	
	103.18		2	>
	111.7		2	>
	147.15		2	>
Jer	1.7		2	>
	3.13	<	2	>
	11.4	<	2	
	17.22		2	
	26.2	<	2	>
	32.23		2	
	42.5		2	>
	43.4	<	2	>
	51.11	<	2	>
Ezek	11.12	<	2	
	18.9		2	
	36.27		2	>
Dan	3.20	<	2	
Mt	15.3		2	
Mk	7.8		2	
Jn	12.49		2	
1 Cor	7.10		2	
2 Thes	3.6		2	

COMMANDMENT

Ps	119.10		10	
Rom	7.8		6	
Mt	22.36		4	
Mk	12.28		4	
Ps	78.5		3	
Mt	19.17		3	
Ex	32.15	<	2	
	34.28		2	
Deut	5.22	<	2	
Mk	10.19		2	
Lk	18.20		2	
Jn	14.15	<	2	>
Heb	9.4		2	

COMMIT

Mt	5.21		5	
Num	5.19		4	
Mk	10.11		4	
Jas	2.11		4	
Ezek	22.6		3	>
Mt	19.9		3	
Jn	8.3		3	
Ex	20.13		2	
Deut	5.17		2	
Ezek	16.17		2	
	23.37	<	2	
	33.25		2	
Hos	3.1		2	>
	4.2	<	2	
Mk	15.7		2	
Lk	16.18		2	
	18.20		2	
Rom	13.9		2	
1 Cor	7.28	<	2	

COMMUNITY

Num	16.1	<	9	
	15.23	<	7	>
	27.2	<	7	
	20.1	<	6	
	31.12		5	>
Ex	16.1		4	>
Lev	4.13		4	
	20.2	<	4	
Josh	22.12		4	
Ex	12.3		3	
Lev	16.5		3	>
	17.8	<	3	
Num	1.5		3	
Lev	8.3		2	>
	10.6		2	
	24.14	<	2	
Num	10.3		2	
	26.2	<	2	>
	35.24		2	
Ezek	14.7		2	

COMPLAIN

Ex	16.2	<	6	>
Num	14.2	<	5	
Ex	17.2	<	4	
Num	11.1		4	
	16.11		2	>
	17.5	<	2	
	20.3		2	>
1 Sam	8.18		2	
Neh	5.1		2	
Jas	5.4		2	

COMPLETE

Eph	1.9		5	
Gen	2.1		2	
Lev	12.4		2	
1 Kgs	7.22		2	
2 Chr	8.16		2	
Ezra	4.13		2	
Rom	1.16		2	
	11.12		2	>

CONCERN

1 Cor	7.32		4	
Prov	29.4		3	
Lk	12.29		3	
Gen	39.6		2	
Mt	6.32		2	

CONCUBINE

Judg	19.1		8	>
Gen	33.1	<	3	
Judg	20.4	<	3	
2 Sam	16.21	<	2	
1 Chr	2.46	<	2	>
2 Chr	11.21		2	
Song	6.8		2	
Dan	5.2		2	

CONDEMN

Josh	7.11		4	
Rom	8.1		4	
Jude	4		4	
Ezek	20.35		3	>
Jn	8.10	<	3	
Job	15.6		2	
	34.17		2	
Is	34.2		2	
Zech	3.2		2	
Jn	19.4	<	2	
Rom	2.1		2	>
	3.7	<	2	
Gal	1.8		2	
1 Jn	3.20		2	

CONFESS

Ps	32.3		3	
Ezra	10.1		2	
Neh	9.1		2	

CONFESS (cont.)

Dan	9.4		2	
Rom	10.9		2	

CONFIDENT

Josh	1.6		4	
Deut	31.6		3	
2 Chr	32.7		2	
Prov	11.7		2	
Gal	5.10		2	
Heb	3.6		2	>

CONQUER

Neh	9.22		7	
Hab	2.5	<	4	
Josh	10.13		3	>
Num	21.2		2	
	24.18		2	
2 Kgs	14.22		2	
Is	10.9		2	>
	14.6		2	
Lam	1.7		2	
Ezek	25.4		2	>
Dan	11.18		2	
Obad	7		2	
Mic	5.6		2	
Hab	1.6		2	>
2 Pet	2.19		2	

CONSCIENCE

1 Cor	10.25		5	
	8.7		3	
1 Tim	1.5		3	
1 Jn	3.20		3	
Gen	20.5		2	
Prov	20.9		2	
1 Pet	3.16		2	

CONSECRATE

Num	6.8		4	
2 Chr	7.7		3	
1 Kgs	9.3	<	2	
Ezek	43.20		2	
Hag	2.12		2	

CONSTANT

Ps	107.8		5	>
	119.64		5	
	33.5	<	3	
Deut	7.9		2	
	28.33		2	
Ps	25.6		2	>
	31.7		2	>
	36.5		2	
	57.3		2	
	86.5	<	2	
Mic	7.18	<	2	

CONSULT

2 Kgs	1.2		5	
Ezek	14.1		4	
Josh	18.6		3	>
2 Kgs	3.11		3	
Lev	20.6	<	2	
1 Sam	14.19		2	
	22.13		2	>
	28.7		2	
1 Kgs	22.5		2	
2 Kgs	22.13	<	2	
1 Chr	10.13		2	
2 Chr	18.4		2	
	34.21	<	2	

CONTRIBUTE

Num	18.8		8	
Lev	7.14		3	
Num	15.19		3	
	31.29		3	
2 Chr	35.7		3	
Neh	10.32		2	
	12.44		2	

CONTROL

Rom	8.5		5	
1 Sam	19.9	<	3	
Deut	15.6		2	
1 Sam	10.6		2	>
2 Sam	8.1		2	
1 Chr	18.1		2	
2 Chr	1.1		2	
	11.1		2	
Prov	21.1		2	
Ezek	13.20		2	
Dan	4.25		2	>
	5.21	<	2	
Gal	5.13		2	
Col	2.19		2	
Jas	3.2		2	

CORRECT

Prov	15.5		5	
	9.7		3	
	13.1	<	3	
	29.1	<	3	
	1.25		2	
	3.11		2	
Acts	18.25		2	
2 Tim	2.15		2	>
Heb	12.5		2	

COUNCIL

Acts	5.21	<	8	>
	23.1	<	6	>
	4.13		3	>
	17.19		3	
Mk	15.1	<	2	
Acts	6.12	<	2	>

COUNCIL (cont.)

Acts	7.54	<	2	
	22.5		2	>

COURT (1) [LAW]

Dan	1.4		6	>
Jer	36.10		5	>
Amos	5.10		3	
Mt	5.25		3	
Acts	18.12		3	>
	25.6		3	
1 Kgs	1.33		2	
2 Kgs	22.3		2	
Job	9.19		2	
Prov	18.17		2	>
	19.5	<	2	
	25.1		2	
Is	41.1		2	
	43.8		2	
Dan	7.10		2	
Mk	13.9		2	
Lk	12.58		2	

COVENANT

Gen	17.2		10	
Heb	8.5	<	8	>
Deut	29.1		7	
Jer	33.20	<	7	>
Lev	26.9		6	
Jer	11.2		6	
Ezek	16.8		6	
Heb	9.1	<	6	
Gen	9.9		5	
2 Kgs	23.2		5	
2 Chr	34.30		5	
Ps	89.3		4	
Jer	31.31		4	>
	34.13	<	4	
Mal	2.4		4	>
Ex	34.10		3	
Deut	4.13		3	>
	9.9	<	3	
Judg	2.1		3	
1 Kgs	8.9		3	
2 Kgs	17.15		3	>
1 Chr	16.15		3	
2 Chr	15.12		3	
Ex	6.4		2	
	24.7		2	
Deut	7.9		2	>
	31.16		2	
1 Kgs	19.10		2	
2 Kgs	11.17		2	
2 Chr	6.11	<	2	
	23.3		2	
Neh	9.8		2	
Ps	25.10		2	
	50.5		2	
	78.10		2	

COVENANT (cont.)

Ps	105.8		2	>
	111.5		2	
Is	56.4	<	2	
Jer	9.25		2	
Ezek	20.20		2	
Zech	11.10		2	
2 Cor	3.6		2	
Gal	3.17		2	>
	4.24	<	2	
Heb	10.16		2	

COVENANT BOX

1 Sam	4.3	<	12	>
1 Chr	15.1		12	>
1 Sam	6.1	<	11	>
2 Sam	6.2		10	>
Josh	3.3		8	>
1 Sam	5.1	<	8	>
1 Kgs	8.1		7	
1 Chr	13.3		7	
Ex	40.3	<	6	
Josh	6.4		6	>
2 Chr	5.2		6	>
Ex	25.10		5	>
Deut	10.1		5	
Josh	4.5	<	5	
Lev	16.2		4	
1 Chr	16.1	<	4	>
Ex	30.6		3	
Num	17.4		3	
Deut	31.9		3	
2 Sam	15.24		3	
Ex	26.33	<	2	>
	37.1		2	
Num	10.33		2	
1 Sam	7.1	<	2	
1 Chr	28.2		2	
2 Chr	1.4		2	
	6.11	<	2	
Ps	132.6		2	
Heb	9.4		2	

CREATE

Rom	8.19		6	
Gen	1.1		4	>
Is	43.1	<	3	>
	44.2	<	3	>
	45.7	<	3	
1 Cor	11.8		3	
Col	1.15		3	
Gen	2.3	<	2	
	5.1		2	>
Ps	33.6		2	
	89.12		2	>
	104.19		2	
Is	40.26		2	
	54.16		2	
Ezek	28.13		2	

CREATE (cont.)

Jn	1.1		2	
Rom	1.20		2	
Eph	2.10	<	2	
1 Tim	4.3		2	
Heb	1.2		2	>
	4.3		2	
	9.11		2	
2 Pet	3.4		2	

CREATURE

Ezek	10.1		19	>
	1.5		17	
1 Kgs	6.23		6	>
Rev	5.6	<	5	>
	6.1	<	5	>
Ezek	41.18		4	
Ex	25.18		3	>
2 Chr	3.7		3	
Is	6.2		3	
Rev	4.6		3	>
Gen	1.21		2	
Ex	26.1	<	2	
	36.8		2	>
	37.7	<	2	
1 Kgs	7.29	<	2	>
Job	12.8		2	
Ps	104.24	<	2	
	145.10		2	
Is	34.16		2	

CRIME

Lk	23.14	<	5	
Deut	24.16		3	>
2 Kgs	14.6		3	
2 Chr	25.4		3	
Ecc	8.11		3	
Deut	19.15		2	
Judg	9.24		2	
	20.3		2	
2 Sam	3.34		2	
Ps	94.4		2	
Is	59.12		2	
Amos	3.9		2	
Acts	25.16	<	2	

CRIPPLE

2 Sam	5.6	<	3	
Josh	11.6		2	
2 Sam	9.3	<	2	
Mt	15.30		2	
Lk	14.13		2	

CROSS (1) [OF JESUS]

Mk	15.21		5	
Jn	19.17		5	
Mt	27.32		3	
1 Cor	1.13		3	>
Gal	6.12	<	3	

CROSS (1)(cont.)

Eph	2.16		2	
Col	2.14	<	2	
Heb	12.2		2	

CRUCIFY

Jn	19.6		13	
Mk	15.13		8	>
Mt	27.22	<	7	>
Lk	23.21		4	>
	24.7	<	2	
Acts	2.23		2	

CRUEL

Is	25.3		3	
Ex	3.7		2	>
Is	13.9		2	>
Ezek	25.12		2	
Acts	7.19		2	>

CUP

Gen	44.2		6	
1 Cor	11.25	<	5	
Jer	25.15		4	
Ezek	23.31		4	
Lk	22.17		4	
Gen	40.11		3	
Dan	5.2		3	
Mt	26.27		3	
1 Cor	10.16		3	>
1 Kgs	7.26		2	
Is	51.17		2	
Jer	49.12		2	
Obad	16		2	
Mt	20.22		2	
	23.25		2	
Mk	10.38		2	
	14.23		2	
Lk	11.39		2	

CURE

2 Kgs	5.3		8	
Jn	9.14		6	
Lk	8.36	<	2	>

CURSE

Deut	27.13		13	>
2 Sam	16.5		7	
Num	22.6		6	>
	23.7	<	6	>
	5.18		5	
Job	3.1	<	5	
Gal	3.10		5	
Lev	24.10		4	
Deut	28.16	<	4	>
1 Sam	14.24		4	
Ps	109.17		4	
Gen	27.12		3	
Deut	11.26		3	

CURSE (cont.)

Deut	30.1	<	3	
Neh	13.2		3	
Jer	44.8		3	
Mal	2.2	<	3	>
Rev	16.9		3	
Gen	3.14		2	>
Num	24.9	<	2	
Deut	7.26		2	
	23.4		2	
Judg	5.23		2	
	17.2		2	
1 Kgs	21.10		2	
Job	2.5	<	2	>
Ps	10.3		2	
Prov	30.10	<	2	
Jer	15.10		2	
	20.14		2	
	29.18		2	
	48.10		2	>
Zech	5.3		2	
Jas	3.9		2	

CUSTOM

2 Kgs	17.8		7	
Acts	16.21		2	

D

DANGER

2 Cor	11.26		4	
Ps	18.4		3	
Jon	1.4		3	
Acts	19.27		3	
Lev	26.6		2	
2 Sam	22.6		2	
Ps	91.3		2	
	116.3		2	
Jer	2.6		2	
Acts	27.9		2	
Rom	8.35		2	

DARK

Gen	1.2		4	
Ps	18.9		4	
Joel	2.2		4	>
1 Jn	2.8	<	4	
2 Sam	22.10		3	
Job	15.22		3	
	38.9		3	
Ps	88.6		3	
	139.11		3	
Is	5.20		3	
Ezek	12.6		3	
Amos	5.8		3	
Lk	11.34		3	>
Jn	12.35		3	
Ex	10.21		2	

DARK (cont.)

Job	3.4		2	
	10.21		2	>
	12.22	<	2	
	17.12		2	>
	18.6	<	2	>
	23.16	<	2	>
	28.3		2	>
	30.26	<	2	
	34.22		2	>
Ps	107.10		2	
Song	1.5		2	>
Is	8.22		2	>
	42.7		2	
	45.3		2	
	50.3	<	2	
	59.9	<	2	>
Jer	13.16		2	
Lam	3.2	<	2	
Mt	4.16		2	
	6.23		2	
Jn	1.5		2	
2 Cor	4.4		2	
Eph	5.8	<	2	>
1 Thes	5.4		2	
2 Pet	2.4	<	2	
1 Jn	1.5		2	>
Jude	6		2	

DAY OF JUDGEMENT

Mt	12.36	<	3	
	11.22	<	2	>
Lk	10.12		2	>
	11.31	<	2	
2 Pet	2.4		2	

DAY OF THE LORD

2 Pet	3.10		5	
Joel	2.1	<	3	>
Is	13.6		2	
Amos	5.18		2	
Rom	2.5		2	
1 Cor	3.13		2	
Phil	1.6		2	>
1 Thes	5.2		2	
2 Thes	2.2	<	2	
2 Tim	1.12		2	

DAZZLING

Ezek	10.4		3	>
	43.2		3	>
Ex	16.7		2	
	33.18		2	
Lev	9.6		2	
Num	14.10		2	
	16.19		2	
2 Chr	7.1		2	
Ezek	1.22		2	
	11.22	<	2	

DEAD

1 Cor	15.12		10	
Lev	11.8		9	
Rev	20.5		8	
Num	35.12		6	
1 Kgs	3.20	<	5	
Mt	22.24		5	
Mk	12.19	<	5	
Lk	20.28		4	
Gen	42.13		3	
Ex	21.34		3	
Deut	25.5		3	>
2 Sam	1.5		3	>
	2.7	<	3	>
	12.18		3	>
Jon	4.3		3	
Lk	7.12		3	>
Jn	5.21		3	
Heb	11.4		3	
Jas	2.17		3	
Rev	1.17		3	
Ex	12.30		2	
Lev	19.28		2	>
	20.6	<	2	>
Deut	14.1		2	
Judg	14.8		2	
Ruth	4.5		2	
1 Sam	25.22	<	2	
2 Sam	3.9	<	2	
	13.32	<	2	>
	14.5	<	2	
	19.6	<	2	
1 Kgs	1.5		2	>
	11.15		2	
	19.2		2	>
1 Chr	10.5		2	
Ps	88.5		2	
Ecc	9.4		2	
Is	26.14		2	
Ezek	32.24		2	
	39.4		2	
Nah	3.3		2	
Zeph	1.11		2	
Mt	2.18		2	
Mk	15.44		2	
Lk	8.52	<	2	>
	15.24		2	
Jn	11.14		2	
Acts	2.27		2	
	5.5	<	2	
Rom	4.17		2	
1 Cor	10.5		2	
Eph	2.1		2	
1 Pet	4.5		2	

DEAR

Rom	16.5		4	
3 Jn	1		4	
Col	4.7		3	

DEAR (cont.)

2 Pet	3.1		3	
1 Jn	4.1	<	3	
2 Jn	1		3	
2 Sam	1.23		2	
1 Cor	4.14		2	
2 Cor	7.1	<	2	
Phil	4.1		2	
Col	1.7		2	
Phlm	7		2	
Jas	1.16		2	>
1 Jn	3.2	<	2	>

DEATH (1)

1 Cor	15.20		8	
Rom	5.9		7	>
Lev	20.9		6	>
Rom	6.3	<	6	>
Num	35.24		5	
Jer	50.35		5	>
Rom	7.5	<	5	>
	8.2	<	5	
1 Jn	5.6		5	
Ezek	33.4		4	
Heb	2.9		4	
Rev	20.6		4	>
Job	31.11	<	3	
Ps	49.14		3	
Ecc	7.2		3	>
Jer	51.49	<	3	
Lam	4.8	<	3	
Mt	27.4		3	
2 Cor	4.10	<	3	>
Gen	26.11	<	2	>
	42.2		2	>
Num	19.14	<	2	
Deut	28.51		2	
	30.15		2	>
	31.16	<	2	>
Judg	2.7	<	2	
2 Sam	1.1		2	
	4.4		2	
	22.5		2	
1 Kgs	2.5		2	>
	17.12		2	
2 Kgs	14.17	<	2	>
	15.18	<	2	
2 Chr	32.26		2	
Ps	18.4		2	
	88.3		2	
Prov	5.5		2	
	7.26		2	>
	14.12		2	>
	17.11	<	2	
	21.6		2	
Song	8.6		2	
Is	28.15		2	
Jer	22.10	<	2	
Lam	3.6	<	2	>

DEATH (1)(cont.)

Ezek	3.18		2	>
	13.18		2	
Hos	13.14	<	2	
Lk	23.15		2	
Jn	11.4		2	>
Acts	1.3		2	>
	25.11		2	
1 Cor	1.17		2	>
2 Cor	1.9		2	
	3.6		2	>
Eph	2.13	<	2	
Phil	3.10	<	2	
Col	1.20		2	
Heb	9.15		2	
1 Jn	3.14		2	
Rev	1.5		2	>
	2.10	<	2	
	9.6		2	
	21.4	<	2	

DEATH (2) (FROM DEATH)

1 Cor	15.12		5	
Lk	20.27		3	
Jn	12.1		3	
Acts	13.30		3	
	17.3		3	
Rom	6.4		3	>
Job	5.15		2	
Ps	49.12		2	
	116.8		2	
Mt	27.53		2	>
Mk	9.9		2	
Lk	16.30		2	
Acts	2.24		2	>
	4.2	<	2	>
	10.40		2	
Rom	8.11	<	2	
	10.7		2	
Heb	11.19		2	
1 Pet	1.3		2	

DEATH (3) (TO DEATH)

Lev	20.2	<	11	>
Ex	21.12		9	>
Num	35.12		7	
Lev	24.14	<	6	
Num	15.30	<	4	>
Deut	17.5		4	
	22.21	<	4	
	24.7		4	
Josh	10.28		4	>
	11.11	<	4	
1 Sam	14.39		4	
2 Sam	19.21		4	
Jer	38.4		4	>
Ex	22.18	<	3	>
Num	18.3		3	
Deut	13.5		3	

DEATH (3)(cont.)

1 Kgs	21.10		3	
2 Kgs	7.4	<	3	>
	10.11		3	
	14.6		3	
2 Chr	25.4		3	
Jer	26.11	<	3	
Mk	14.1	<	3	
Gen	42.2		2	>
Ex	19.12		2	
	31.14		2	
Num	3.10		2	
Deut	19.10		2	
	21.21		2	>
2 Sam	21.1		2	
1 Kgs	2.9	<	2	
	19.1	<	2	
2 Kgs	25.7		2	
Is	13.15		2	
Jer	39.6	<	2	
	52.10		2	
Nah	3.10		2	
Zech	13.3	<	2	
Mt	10.21		2	
	26.4		2	>
	27.1	<	2	
Mk	13.12		2	>
Acts	12.2		2	>

DEBT

Deut	15.1		4	
Mt	18.25		4	
2 Kgs	4.1		2	
Neh	5.11		2	
Job	24.3		2	
Amos	2.6		2	
Hab	2.6		2	

DECEIVE

Mt	24.4		4	
Gen	31.20		3	
1 Kgs	22.20		3	
2 Chr	18.19		3	
Dan	11.23		3	
Mk	13.5		3	
Jas	1.16		3	
Rev	20.3	<	3	
Gen	27.12		2	
Josh	9.4		2	
2 Chr	32.11		2	
Ps	5.6		2	
Jer	7.4		2	
	9.4		2	
	27.10		2	
Ezek	14.9		2	
Dan	8.23		2	
Obad	3		2	
Gal	6.3		2	
Eph	4.14		2	>

DECEIVE (cont.)

Col	2.4		2	
2 Thes	2.3		2	
1 Tim	2.14		2	
2 Jn	7		2	

DEDICATE

Lev	27.14		10	
Ex	29.1	<	7	>
Lev	8.9		6	
Num	8.11	<	5	
Ex	28.3		4	>
Num	6.2	<	4	>
	7.1	<	4	>
1 Chr	26.20		4	
Ex	30.10	<	3	>
	40.9	<	3	
Jn	17.17		3	
Ex	16.23		2	
	35.2		2	
	38.24		2	>
	39.30	<	2	>
Lev	19.8		2	
	22.2	<	2	
Num	3.45		2	
	18.6		2	
Deut	20.5		2	
Judg	13.5		2	
1 Sam	1.11		2	>
1 Kgs	15.15		2	
2 Kgs	23.8		2	
2 Chr	7.5		2	
	15.18		2	
	30.15	<	2	>
Ezra	6.16		2	
Neh	3.1		2	
	10.36		2	
	12.27		2	
Ezek	48.9		2	
Dan	3.2		2	

DEED (2) [ACTION]

Jn	10.32		3	
	3.19		2	
1 Tim	5.10		2	
Tit	3.5		2	
Jas	3.13		2	
Jude	13		2	

DEFEND

Ps	18.1		5	
2 Sam	22.3		4	>
Judg	6.31		3	
Ps	28.1		3	
	91.2		3	
Is	1.8		3	
Acts	26.1	<	3	
Deut	33.27	<	2	
1 Sam	2.25		2	

DEFEND (cont.)

2 Chr	32.5		2	
Ps	31.2		2	
	62.2	<	2	
	71.3		2	
	119.114		2	
	140.7		2	
Is	17.3		2	
Ezek	30.6		2	
Dan	9.16		2	
	11.1		2	
Mic	5.5		2	
Nah	3.8	<	2	
Acts	25.8	<	2	>
Phil	1.7		2	

DEFILE

Ezek	20.18		4	
	36.17		4	>
Num	6.6	<	3	
	35.33		3	
Jer	3.1	<	3	
Ezek	23.7	<	3	>
Hag	2.13		3	
Num	5.3		2	>
	19.13		2	
Jer	2.7		2	>
Lam	4.7		2	
Ezek	7.21		2	
	22.3		2	>
	24.13	<	2	
Acts	10.14		2	>
Tit	1.15		2	

DEMAND

1 Kgs	20.2		4	
2 Kgs	23.3		2	

DEMON

Lk	8.2	<	8	>
	11.14	<	5	
Mt	8.16	<	4	>
	9.32	<	4	
	12.22	<	4	
Mk	1.32		4	
Lk	4.33		4	
1 Cor	10.20		4	
Mk	5.15		3	>
	7.26	<	3	
Lk	9.1	<	3	
Jn	8.48	<	3	
	10.20		3	
Mt	17.18		2	
Mk	3.15		2	
	16.9		2	

DEPEND

Ps	62.1		4	
Gal	3.10		3	

DEPEND (cont.)

Num	32.16		2	
Ps	118.8		2	
	123.2		2	
Is	28.15		2	
Rom	9.16		2	

DESERVE

Lk	23.15		3	
Deut	9.4		2	
2 Sam	19.28		2	
1 Kgs	8.32		2	
2 Chr	6.23		2	
Prov	14.14		2	
Jer	51.6		2	
Ezek	13.19		2	>
Lk	7.4		2	
Acts	25.11		2	
Rom	1.27		2	
1 Cor	15.9		2	>
1 Pet	2.19		2	

DESIRE

Rom	7.5	<	5	
Ezra	7.13		3	
Gal	5.13		3	>
Jas	4.1		3	
Jude	16		3	
Ex	20.17		2	
Deut	5.21		2	
Ps	119.36		2	
Rom	13.9		2	
Phil	1.20		2	>
Col	3.5		2	
1 Tim	6.4	<	2	
Jas	1.14		2	
1 Jn	2.16		2	

DESOLATE

Ezek	35.3		6	
Is	6.11		2	
	45.18		2	
Ezek	30.7	<	2	

DESPAIR

Deut	28.53		4	
Ps	69.20		2	
Ezek	21.6		2	

DESPISE

Joel	2.17		4	
Gen	16.4		3	
Deut	23.7		2	
Mal	1.6		2	>
	2.9	<	2	
Rom	14.3		2	
1 Cor	4.6		2	

DESTROY

Jer	51.1	<	18	
	48.1	<	14	>
	49.3	<	9	>
Zeph	1.2		9	>
Is	10.7		8	
Jer	50.21	<	8	>
2 Pet	3.6	<	8	
Gen	18.23		7	>
	19.13	<	7	>
Deut	7.4	<	7	>
	28.20		7	>
Jer	44.2	<	7	
Lam	2.2	<	7	>
Lev	26.22		6	
Deut	2.12		6	>
	9.3	<	6	
Josh	7.1	<	6	
Jer	46.8		6	>
Joel	1.5		6	>
Mic	5.9	<	6	>
Zech	11.2		6	>
Jer	4.6		5	>
	6.1	<	5	>
Nah	1.8		5	>
2 Pet	2.1	<	5	>
Num	21.2		4	>
Deut	31.3	<	4	>
1 Sam	15.3		4	
2 Kgs	18.4		4	>
2 Chr	20.10		4	>
Is	23.1		4	
Jer	5.10	<	4	>
	25.9		4	>
Ezek	30.6		4	
	32.7		4	
Dan	8.24	<	4	>
Hos	10.2		4	>
Amos	3.11		4	>
Gen	9.11	<	3	
Num	16.21		3	
	25.8	<	3	>
Deut	4.3	<	3	>
	8.19	<	3	>
	12.2		3	>
	20.8	<	3	
	29.19	<	3	>
Josh	6.17		3	>
	11.20	<	3	
Judg	20.34		3	
2 Sam	22.5	<	3	
2 Kgs	15.4	<	3	
	19.11	<	3	
Neh	2.3		3	
Ps	18.4		3	
	73.18		3	>
	106.23	<	3	
	118.10		3	
Is	1.9		3	>

DESTROY (cont.)

Is	2.11	<	3	
	9.5		3	
	16.4	<	3	
	25.2		3	>
	36.7		3	>
	37.11	<	3	
Jer	10.11		3	>
	12.10	<	3	>
	26.3	<	3	>
Ezek	6.3	<	3	
	14.13	<	3	
	21.28	<	3	>
	25.7	<	3	>
	26.4	<	3	
Dan	9.17	<	3	
	11.17		3	
Hos	11.6	<	3	>
Amos	9.4	<	3	
Obad	8		3	
Hab	1.3		3	>
Zeph	2.5	<	3	>
Jude	5		3	
Rev	11.5		3	
	17.8	<	3	>
Gen	6.13		2	>
	7.4	<	2	>
Ex	23.23		2	
	32.10		2	>
	33.3	<	2	>
Num	33.52	<	2	
Deut	13.15	<	2	
Josh	10.1		2	>
	24.8		2	
2 Sam	20.19		2	>
	21.2	<	2	>
1 Kgs	20.10		2	
2 Kgs	13.7	<	2	>
1 Chr	21.15	<	2	
2 Chr	12.7		2	
	21.7	<	2	>
	34.3	<	2	>
Esth	8.5	<	2	>
Job	9.5		2	
	15.28	<	2	
	20.26	<	2	
	24.20	<	2	
	31.8	<	2	
Ps	5.6		2	
	9.5		2	
	35.8		2	
	37.13		2	
	46.5		2	
	59.13		2	>
	64.4		2	
	78.38		2	
	88.11		2	
	94.23		2	
Prov	10.15		2	>

DESTROY (cont.)

Prov	14.1	<	2	>
	16.4	<	2	
	18.9		2	>
Is	13.6		2	>
	14.17	<	2	>
	26.5	<	2	
	28.17		2	>
	29.20	<	2	>
	31.3	<	2	>
	34.2	<	2	
	43.17	<	2	
	48.9		2	>
	60.12	<	2	
	65.8	<	2	
Jer	1.10		2	
	11.11	<	2	>
	20.8	<	2	>
	27.8	<	2	
	30.11		2	>
	31.28	<	2	>
	32.23	<	2	
	36.3	<	2	
	47.4	<	2	>
Ezek	22.30	<	2	
	43.3		2	
Dan	7.11	<	2	>
Hos	2.12	<	2	
	5.7	<	2	>
	13.9	<	2	
Amos	7.9		2	>
Mic	1.7		2	>
	6.13	<	2	
Nah	3.13	<	2	
Zeph	3.6	<	2	
Zech	9.10		2	
	12.6	<	2	
Mt	6.19		2	
Jn	11.48	<	2	
1 Cor	1.19		2	
2 Cor	10.4		2	
Gal	1.13		2	
Jas	1.11		2	
1 Pet	1.7		2	

DETERMINE

Josh	1.6		4	
Deut	31.6		3	>
1 Sam	20.7		3	
Is	14.13		3	
Ex	28.15		2	
Lev	5.15		2	>
1 Chr	28.10		2	
Ecc	1.13		2	
	7.23	<	2	
Jer	42.13		2	

DEVIL

Mt	4.1		6	
Lk	4.2		6	
1 Jn	3.8		4	
1 Tim	3.6		2	
Jude	9		2	
Rev	12.9		2	
	20.2		2	

DIFFICULT

Acts	27.7		3	
Ex	18.22		2	
1 Kgs	10.1		2	
2 Chr	9.1		2	
Jer	32.17		2	
Ezek	3.5		2	

DISASTER

Deut	29.20	<	4	
	28.20		3	>
	31.17		3	>
1 Kgs	21.21		3	>
Prov	24.16		3	
Jer	11.15		3	
	25.13	<	3	>
Ezek	7.5		3	
Ex	32.12		2	
Job	21.9		2	
	31.3		2	
Is	28.15		2	>
Jer	4.6		2	
	17.16		2	>
	23.12		2	>
	26.19	<	2	
Lam	4.10	<	2	
Mic	2.3	<	2	
Zech	8.13		2	

DISCIPLE

Lk	9.1	<	18	
Mt	26.1		16	>
Mk	14.10	<	13	
	6.1	<	12	>
	8.1	<	12	>
Jn	20.2	<	12	>
Mk	10.10		11	>
Jn	21.1	<	10	
Mt	17.3	<	9	>
Mk	9.4	<	9	
Lk	22.3	<	9	
Jn	6.3		9	
	18.1		9	>
Mt	14.12	<	8	>
	15.2	<	8	>
Jn	13.2	<	8	>
Lk	8.1	<	7	>
Mt	16.5	<	6	>
Mk	2.15	<	6	>
	4.10	<	6	>

DISCIPLE (cont.)

Jn	4.1	<	6	
Mt	9.10	<	5	
	28.7	<	5	
Jn	2.2	<	5	>
	11.7		5	>
Mt	8.18		4	>
	10.1		4	>
	19.10	<	4	>
	21.1	<	4	>
Mk	11.1	<	4	>
	16.7		4	
Lk	5.30		4	>
	6.1	<	4	>
	18.1	<	4	>
Jn	9.2	<	4	
Mt	11.1	<	3	>
	12.1	<	3	>
	13.10	<	3	>
	20.17	<	3	>
Mk	3.7	<	3	>
	5.1	<	3	>
	7.2	<	3	>
Lk	10.16		3	>
	11.1	<	3	>
	14.26		3	
	17.1	<	3	>
	19.29	<	3	>
Jn	19.26	<	3	>
Mt	24.1	<	2	
	27.57	<	2	>
Mk	1.21		2	>
Lk	7.11	<	2	>
	12.1	<	2	
	24.9		2	
Jn	1.35		2	>
	3.22	<	2	>
	12.4	<	2	>
	16.17	<	2	
Acts	6.1		2	
	9.26		2	
1 Cor	1.13		2	

DISEASE

Lev	13.2		17	>
2 Kgs	5.1		7	
Lev	14.2	<	5	
Deut	28.21		5	
2 Chr	26.19		3	
Jer	21.6		3	
Zech	14.12		3	
Mt	8.2		3	>
Mk	1.34		3	
Lk	5.12	<	3	>
Ex	9.3		2	
Lev	26.16		2	
Num	12.10		2	
2 Chr	21.15		2	
Ps	106.15		2	

DISEASE (cont.)

Jer	27.8		2	>
	29.17	<	2	
	32.24		2	
	42.17		2	>
	44.13	<	2	
Mt	4.23		2	
	10.1		2	>
Lk	4.27		2	>
	7.21	<	2	>

DISGRACE

Lev	20.3	<	6	>
Ezek	36.20		6	
Lev	18.7		5	>
Gen	34.5		4	
Ezek	32.24		4	
Is	45.16	<	3	
Jer	2.26		3	>
	20.11		3	
1 Cor	11.4		3	
Lev	19.12	<	2	>
	21.6	<	2	>
	22.2	<	2	
Deut	22.19		2	
Ps	31.17		2	
	35.4		2	
	69.6		2	>
	71.13	<	2	
Prov	11.2	<	2	
	13.5		2	>
	19.22		2	
Is	44.9		2	>
Jer	48.20		2	
Ezek	16.52		2	
	39.7		2	
	43.7		2	
Hos	4.7		2	
Hab	2.15		2	

DISGUST

Ezek	16.2		8	
	7.3	<	5	>
	8.6	<	5	>
	20.4		4	
	23.17	<	4	
1 Kgs	11.5		3	
Is	66.3		3	
Ezek	18.12		3	
	44.6	<	3	
Lev	18.26		2	
	20.13		2	
Deut	18.9		2	
2 Kgs	21.2		2	
Ezra	9.1		2	
Ezek	5.11		2	>
	6.9	<	2	>
	11.18		2	>

DISHONEST

Prov	20.10		3	>
	28.6		3	
Lk	16.8		3	
Prov	10.2		2	>
	11.1	<	2	
Jer	8.8		2	>
Hos	12.7		2	

DISOBEY

Ps	119.10		5	
Rom	11.30	<	4	
Eph	2.1		3	
Deut	17.12		2	
	28.14		2	
1 Sam	15.11		2	
2 Sam	12.9		2	
1 Kgs	11.11		2	
	13.21		2	
2 Kgs	17.12		2	>
	18.6	<	2	
Jer	42.13		2	>
Dan	3.12		2	
Mt	15.2		2	
Rom	5.14	<	2	
Tit	1.6		2	
Heb	11.23	<	2	

DISPUTE

Ex	18.13		6	
Deut	1.12		3	
1 Cor	6.1		3	
1 Sam	7.6		2	
2 Sam	15.2		2	

DISTRESS

Ps	107.6	<	4	
Judg	10.9		2	
Obad	12		2	

DIVORCE

Mt	19.3		4	
Mk	10.2		4	
1 Cor	7.11		3	
Lev	21.7		2	>
Deut	22.19		2	
	24.1		2	
Ezra	10.19		2	
Is	50.1		2	
Jer	3.1		2	
Mt	5.31		2	
Lk	16.18		2	

DOME

Ezek	1.22		4	
Gen	1.6		3	

DOOM
Is 5.8 6 >
Hab 2.6 5
Jer 15.2 4
Is 3.8 3
29.1 < 3 >
Jer 4.13 3
43.11 3
Is 1.4 2
Jer 22.13 2
Ezek 13.3 2
16.23 2
24.6 2
31.14 2
Amos 5.5 2
Zeph 3.1 < 2

DOVE
Gen 8.8 4
Song 5.2 3 >
Lev 5.7 2
12.6 2
14.22 2 >
15.14 < 2
Song 2.12 2

DRAGON
Rev 12.3 10 >
13.2 < 3
Is 30.6 2

DREAM
Dan 2.1 < 19
Gen 41.1 < 13 >
37.5 9
40.5 8 >
Dan 4.5 8 >
Jer 23.25 6
Mt 2.12 < 4
Gen 31.10 3
Judg 7.13 3
Is 29.7 3
Gen 20.3 2
Deut 13.1 2
1 Sam 28.6 2
1 Kgs 3.5 2
Ecc 5.3 2
Dan 7.1 2

DUTY (1) [OBLIGATION]
1 Chr 26.12 < 6 >
2 Chr 23.4 6
Num 3.7 4 >
2 Kgs 11.5 4 >
2 Chr 31.2 4
Num 8.24 3
1 Chr 9.25 3
23.5 3 >
Ezek 44.11 3 >

DUTY (1)(cont.)
Num 18.3 2
Deut 24.5 2 >
25.5 < 2
1 Chr 6.32 2
24.3 < 2 >
25.8 < 2 >
28.13 < 2
2 Chr 19.9 2
1 Cor 7.3 2
1 Tim 5.4 2

E

EACH OTHER
1 Sam 20.16 4
Lk 24.14 3
Rom 1.24 3
1 Sam 17.21 2
1 Kgs 15.16 < 2
Mt 12.25 2
Mk 3.24 2
Lk 11.17 2 >
1 Cor 7.3 2

EAGER
2 Cor 8.7 < 8 >
Is 42.4 3
Ps 130.5 2

ELDER (2) [CHURCH]
Mt 27.1 < 5 >
Acts 15.2 < 5 >
Rev 5.5 < 5
Mt 26.3 3 >
Acts 4.5 3 >
2 Kgs 6.32 2
Mk 14.43 2 >
Lk 22.52 2
1 Tim 5.17 < 2
Tit 1.5 2
Rev 4.4 2 >
7.11 2

ENCOURAGE
2 Cor 7.6 5
Deut 13.6 2
Is 41.6 < 2
Acts 13.15 2 >
20.1 2
Rom 15.4 2
1 Cor 14.3 2
1 Thes 3.7 < 2 >
5.11 < 2

ENDURE
Is 53.3 3
1 Pet 2.19 < 3

ENDURE (cont.)
Is 40.7 2
51.8 < 2
66.22 2
Jer 10.10 2
2 Tim 2.10 2 >
3.10 < 2 >
Jas 1.3 2
5.10 2
1 Pet 1.7 2 >
2 Pet 1.6 2

ENEMY
Lev 26.7 11
2 Sam 22.1 11
Ps 18.3 < 10
Lam 1.3 9 >
2.3 < 8 >
Deut 28.7 7
Esth 9.1 < 7
Deut 32.27 6 >
Ps 74.3 6
1 Kgs 8.33 5
Neh 4.11 5 >
Ps 31.8 < 5
55.3 < 5 >
78.42 5
109.6 < 5 >
Ex 23.4 4
Deut 20.1 < 4
33.7 < 4
1 Sam 14.24 4
2 Chr 6.24 4
Ps 27.3 4
44.5 < 4 >
69.4 < 4
89.10 4
106.10 < 4 >
119.98 < 4
Jer 15.9 4
51.25 < 4
Ezek 33.3 4 >
Mic 7.6 4
Ex 15.6 3
Num 10.9 3
24.8 < 3
Deut 19.4 3 >
Josh 7.8 3 >
10.13 3 >
Judg 2.3 3 >
7.11 3 >
1 Sam 25.26 < 3 >
2 Sam 7.1 3
10.6 3 >
11.16 < 3
18.3 3 >
1 Kgs 5.3 3
2 Chr 20.24 3
Ps 3.1 3

ENEMY (cont.)
Ps 7.3 < 3 >
9.3 < 3
17.7 3 >
41.2 3 >
56.1 < 3 >
59.1 3 >
68.1 3 >
110.1 < 3
143.3 < 3 >
Is 30.16 3
63.4 < 3 >
Jer 4.13 3 >
20.4 < 3 >
30.14 3 >
46.10 3
Lam 3.46 < 3 >
Ezek 26.3 < 3
39.1 < 3
Obad 5 3
Mic 1.7 3 >
Nah 2.2 < 3 >
Mt 13.25 3
1 Jn 2.18 3
Gen 14.15 2
49.8 2
Deut 1.39 2 >
7.15 < 2
Josh 21.44 2 >
Judg 8.4 < 2
16.23 2
20.35 2
1 Sam 2.1 2
12.10 < 2
18.25 2 >
24.4 2 >
2 Sam 1.6 2
1 Kgs 11.21 2
2 Kgs 3.23 2
17.20 2
1 Chr 5.21 2
17.8 2
19.6 2
2 Chr 25.8 < 2 >
Ezra 4.1 2
8.22 2
Neh 6.1 < 2
9.27 2
Esth 8.1 < 2 >
Ps 5.8 2 >
6.7 < 2 >
13.2 2
22.12 < 2 >
25.2 2
35.19 2
37.20 2 >
38.16 < 2
42.3 < 2 >
54.5 < 2 >

ENEMY (cont.)

Ps	57.4	<	2	
	60.11	<	2	>
	66.3		2	
	80.6		2	>
	92.9		2	
	108.12	<	2	>
	118.7		2	>
	124.2		2	
	129.1		2	
	142.3		2	>
	144.6	<	2	
Is	10.28		2	>
	25.2		2	>
	27.5	<	2	
	33.1		2	>
	66.6		2	
Jer	8.16		2	
	17.3		2	>
	18.17	<	2	>
	19.7	<	2	>
	44.30		2	
	49.22	<	2	>
Ezek	21.3		2	
	28.7		2	>
	29.3	<	2	>
	30.22	<	2	
	35.3	<	2	>
Dan	11.10		2	
Hos	8.1		2	>
Mic	4.10		2	>
	5.3	<	2	
Nah	3.11	<	2	
Zech	8.2		2	>
	9.15	<	2	
	10.5		2	
Mt	5.43		2	
Lk	1.71		2	
	6.27		2	
	19.27		2	>
Rom	11.15		2	>
1 Cor	15.25		2	
2 Cor	5.18	<	2	
Gal	5.17	<	2	
Jas	4.4		2	
Rev	11.5		2	

ENJOY

Ecc	2.1		3	>
	5.18		3	>
	6.2	<	3	
Lev	26.34		2	
Judg	19.6		2	
Job	20.12		2	
Ecc	3.13	<	2	
	8.15		2	>
	9.9	<	2	
	11.7		2	>
Is	65.21		2	>

ENJOY (cont.)

Rom	15.24		2	

ENOUGH

Lev	25.21		5	
Num	11.13		4	
Hag	1.6		4	
Ex	16.4		3	
Num	13.30		3	>
Deut	9.8		3	
Is	30.14		3	
Mk	8.4		3	>
Jn	6.5		3	
Gen	33.5		2	>
1 Kgs	8.27		2	
	17.15	<	2	>
	18.5	<	2	>
2 Kgs	4.7		2	
2 Chr	6.18		2	
	28.13		2	>
Neh	8.2		2	>
Ecc	1.8		2	
Is	7.13		2	>
	40.2		2	
Ezek	16.5		2	
Dan	4.12		2	
Mt	13.6		2	>
	15.33	<	2	
	17.20		2	>
	25.9		2	
Lk	14.28		2	
	16.3		2	
	22.38		2	
Jn	9.21		2	
2 Cor	9.8		2	
Phil	4.12		2	
Heb	11.32		2	

EPHOD (1)

Ex	28.4		10	>
	39.2		10	
	35.9		2	
Judg	18.14	<	2	
1 Sam	14.3		2	
	23.6	<	2	

ESCAPE

Num	35.6		6	
1 Kgs	20.20	<	6	
1 Sam	19.10		5	
Job	1.15		4	
Ex	14.5		3	
Deut	19.2		3	
Is	2.10		3	
Jer	38.2		3	>
	39.4	<	3	
Gen	14.10		2	
Deut	4.42		2	
Judg	3.26		2	

ESCAPE (cont.)

Judg	12.5		2	
	20.42		2	
1 Sam	23.6	<	2	
1 Kgs	11.17		2	>
	12.2	<	2	
	19.17		2	>
2 Kgs	10.24		2	>
	19.11		2	
2 Chr	10.2		2	
Job	15.22		2	
Prov	19.5		2	
Is	9.1		2	
	15.5		2	
	23.6		2	>
	24.18	<	2	
	30.16		2	
	37.11		2	
Jer	44.14		2	>
	46.6	<	2	
	48.8		2	
	50.28		2	>
Ezek	33.5		2	
Joel	2.3		2	
Amos	2.14		2	
Obad	14		2	
Nah	3.11		2	
Mt	3.7	<	2	
Acts	27.30		2	>
Heb	12.25	<	2	
2 Pet	2.18	<	2	

ETERNAL

Ps	118.1	<	5	>
Jn	6.27	<	5	
Ps	119.89	<	3	
Dan	12.2		3	
Mt	25.41		3	
Jn	3.15		3	>
Heb	9.12		3	
1 Jn	5.11		3	
Jude	6		3	
1 Chr	16.34		2	
2 Chr	7.3		2	
Ps	111.3		2	
Is	60.19		2	>
Mt	19.16	<	2	
Mk	10.17		2	
Lk	18.18		2	
Jn	4.14	<	2	>
	5.24	<	2	>
	12.25		2	
	17.2		2	
Acts	13.46		2	
Rom	6.22	<	2	
1 Tim	1.16		2	
	6.12		2	

EVIL

Ezek	18.8		12	
	33.8		7	
Prov	16.6	<	6	>
1 Pet	3.9	<	6	
1 Sam	16.14		5	
Prov	15.3	<	5	>
Jer	18.8		5	
Mt	12.31		5	>
Rom	1.18		5	>
Gen	6.5		4	
Deut	13.5		4	
Job	34.8		4	>
Ps	34.13		4	>
	51.2	<	4	>
	101.3		4	
	109.3		4	
	141.4	<	4	
Prov	14.11	<	4	>
	17.4	<	4	
Is	1.4		4	
Jer	23.2	<	4	
	44.3		4	
Hos	7.1	<	4	
1 Pet	2.1		4	>
Deut	17.4		3	
	22.21	<	3	
Job	8.16		3	
	15.16		3	>
	22.5	<	3	
	36.10	<	3	
Ps	1.1		3	
	7.9	<	3	
	10.3		3	
	36.4	<	3	>
	64.2		3	
	73.7		3	
	140.1	<	3	>
Prov	4.14	<	3	
	12.2	<	3	>
	21.10	<	3	
	24.1		3	>
Is	53.5		3	
	59.5	<	3	
	65.7		3	>
Jer	4.4	<	3	>
	11.8		3	>
Ezek	3.18		3	
	16.23		3	
Dan	9.5		3	
Hos	9.9		3	
Amos	5.13		3	
Hab	1.4		3	>
Mk	7.21		3	
Jn	3.19		3	
Rom	12.9		3	>
	13.3	<	3	
1 Tim	6.1	<	3	
Jas	1.13		3	>

EVIL (cont.)

Jas	3.6	<	3	
Rev	2.2		3	
Ex	34.7		2	
Deut	19.19		2	
	28.15		2	>
Judg	20.6	<	2	
1 Sam	25.28	<	2	
2 Kgs	13.2		2	
Job	1.1		2	>
	4.8	<	2	>
	11.11		2	
	20.12		2	>
	21.7	<	2	>
Ps	14.4		2	
	17.3		2	
	26.5		2	>
	28.3	<	2	
	35.11	<	2	>
	37.7	<	2	>
	52.1	<	2	>
	58.2		2	>
	59.2	<	2	
	119.101		2	
	139.20		2	>
Prov	6.14		2	
	8.13		2	>
	11.20	<	2	>
	25.5	<	2	>
	28.5		2	>
	29.6	<	2	>
Ecc	9.3	<	2	
Is	11.4		2	
	14.5		2	
	30.8		2	>
	32.6	<	2	>
Jer	3.5	<	2	>
	5.26	<	2	>
	6.7	<	2	>
	7.24	<	2	>
	9.3	<	2	
	13.10	<	2	
	36.3	<	2	
	51.24	<	2	
Ezek	6.9	<	2	>
	7.13	<	2	>
	20.43		2	>
	21.3	<	2	>
	28.15		2	
Dan	11.21		2	
Hos	6.8	<	2	>
	10.13		2	
Mic	2.1		2	>
	3.2	<	2	
	6.10		2	>
Mal	2.6	<	2	>
	3.15	<	2	>
Mt	5.11		2	
	13.41	<	2	

EVIL (cont.)

Mk	3.28		2	
Lk	11.29		2	>
Acts	18.6	<	2	>
	19.9	<	2	
Rom	2.9	<	2	>
	7.19		2	
Eph	6.11	<	2	
Jas	2.4	<	2	>
2 Pet	2.2		2	

EXAMPLE

2 Kgs	15.3	<	6	>
2 Chr	21.6		3	>
1 Sam	8.3		2	
2 Kgs	16.2	<	2	
	23.32	<	2	>
2 Chr	28.1		2	>
1 Cor	4.6		2	
	9.5		2	
	10.6		2	

EXILE

Ezra	2.1	<	10	>
Neh	7.6		9	
Ezek	11.15		5	>
Lev	26.34		4	
Ezra	6.16	<	3	>
	10.6		3	
Jer	29.2	<	3	
Mt	1.6		3	
2 Sam	14.13		2	
2 Kgs	17.23		2	
	25.21		2	
Ezra	1.4		2	>
	3.3	<	2	>
	8.1	<	2	>
Is	27.8		2	
	49.20		2	
Jer	22.26		2	
	48.7		2	>
	52.27		2	
Ezek	1.1		2	
	3.11		2	
	8.1		2	
	12.4	<	2	
	29.1		2	>
	32.1	<	2	>
Amos	1.9		2	
	5.5		2	>
	7.11	<	2	
Obad	20		2	
Mic	1.11		2	>
Hag	1.12		2	
Zech	6.10		2	
	9.11		2	

F

FAIL

Job	32.12		3	
2 Cor	13.5		3	
Lev	5.15		2	
Num	15.22	<	2	
Deut	31.6		2	>
Ps	112.6		2	
Heb	4.1		2	

FAITH

Heb	11.1	<	29	>
Jas	2.5	<	13	
Rom	4.3	<	12	>
Gal	3.6	<	12	
1 Tim	1.2		7	>
Mk	9.23		6	
Rom	3.22		6	>
1 Tim	6.10	<	6	
Rom	14.1		5	>
1 Thes	3.2		5	
1 Pet	1.5		5	
Mt	18.6	<	4	
Rom	1.8		4	
	10.6		4	
Lk	17.5		3	>
Rom	15.1	<	3	>
1 Cor	13.2	<	3	
Gal	2.16	<	3	>
Col	2.5	<	3	
1 Tim	3.6	<	3	>
	4.1	<	3	>
2 Tim	1.5		3	>
	3.8	<	3	>
Tit	1.1		3	>
Heb	4.2	<	3	
2 Pet	1.1		3	
Mt	8.10		2	>
	9.2	<	2	
	17.20	<	2	>
Lk	7.9		2	>
	8.25	<	2	
	18.8	<	2	
Acts	3.16		2	
	6.5		2	
	26.11		2	
Rom	5.1	<	2	
	9.30		2	
	12.3		2	
	16.17	<	2	
1 Cor	15.1		2	>
Gal	5.5		2	>
Eph	3.12	<	2	>
	4.5	<	2	
	6.16		2	
Phil	1.25		2	>
	3.9	<	2	
Col	1.4		2	>

FAITH (cont.)

1 Thes	1.3		2	
2 Thes	1.3		2	>
1 Tim	2.7	<	2	>
2 Tim	2.18	<	2	>
Heb	6.4		2	
	10.22		2	>
Jude	3		2	

FAITHFUL

Ps	89.1	<	7	
Deut	28.1		4	>
Neh	9.8		4	
Ps	119.4		4	
Mt	25.21	<	4	
Heb	3.2	<	4	
Job	2.3	<	3	
Ps	31.5	<	3	
Is	38.3		3	
Lk	16.10		3	
Col	1.2		3	
Rev	2.10	<	3	>
Deut	4.4		2	
	7.9	<	2	>
	8.1	<	2	
	11.22	<	2	>
	32.4	<	2	>
	33.8	<	2	
Josh	14.8		2	
1 Sam	2.9		2	
2 Sam	15.20		2	
Job	1.1		2	>
Ps	16.3		2	
	57.3		2	
	78.8		2	
	86.11	<	2	
Is	1.21		2	
	56.4		2	
	65.16		2	>
Jer	3.20	<	2	>
	5.1	<	2	
Dan	12.12		2	
Zech	8.3		2	
Mal	2.14		2	
Rom	3.3		2	
1 Cor	4.2		2	
Col	4.7		2	
3 Jn	3		2	
Rev	3.8	<	2	

FALSE

Ezek	13.6	<	5	>
2 Pet	2.1		5	>
Ex	23.1		3	
Col	2.4		3	
1 Jn	4.1		3	>
Deut	19.16		2	
	22.14		2	
Prov	8.8		2	

FALSE (cont.)

Jer	16.18		2	
Mic	6.10		2	
Mt	7.15		2	
	24.11		2	
2 Cor	11.13	<	2	
2 Thes	2.9		2	
1 Tim	1.3		2	
Rev	19.20	<	2	>

FAMINE

Gen	41.27		10	>
	47.4		3	
	45.6		2	
Ezek	14.13		2	
	36.29		2	

FAST (2) [NOT EAT]

Is	58.3		7	
Jer	36.6		3	
Mt	6.16		3	
Mk	2.18		3	
Lev	16.29		2	
2 Sam	12.22		2	
1 Kgs	21.9		2	
Ezra	8.21		2	
Esth	4.3		2	>
Joel	2.12	<	2	
Zech	7.3		2	>
Mt	9.14		2	
Lk	5.33		2	
Acts	13.2		2	>

FATE

Job	18.20		3	
	20.29		2	
Ecc	2.14	<	2	>
	9.2		2	
Is	53.8		2	
	65.11		2	
Ezek	27.35	<	2	>
	28.12	<	2	>

FATHER (2) (GOD)

Jn	14.2	<	19	>
	5.17	<	15	>
Mt	6.1	<	12	>
Jn	8.16		11	
	10.14		11	>
	6.27	<	10	
	15.1	<	10	>
	16.3	<	10	>
1 Jn	2.1	<	8	>
Jn	17.1	<	6	>
Mt	11.25	<	5	>
Lk	10.21		5	>
Jn	12.26	<	5	>
Mt	10.20		4	>
	18.10		4	

FATHER (2)(cont.)

Mt	26.29	<	4	
	5.16		3	>
Jn	1.13		3	>
	20.17		3	
2 Cor	1.2		3	
Gal	1.1		3	
Eph	1.2		3	>
Col	1.2		3	
1 Pet	1.2		3	
2 Jn	3		3	
Is	63.16		2	>
Jer	3.4		2	
Mt	7.11	<	2	
	16.17	<	2	
Lk	11.2	<	2	>
	12.30	<	2	
	22.29		2	>
	23.34	<	2	>
Jn	4.21	<	2	>
	13.1	<	2	>
	18.9	<	2	
Acts	1.4		2	>
Rom	8.15		2	
1 Thes	1.1		2	
	3.11		2	
2 Thes	1.1		2	>
Heb	1.5		2	>
1 Jn	1.2		2	>
	3.1	<	2	>
Rev	3.5	<	2	

FAVOUR

Prov	19.6	<	4	
Gen	33.8	<	3	>
Num	35.24		2	
1 Kgs	16.21		2	
Esth	2.9		2	
Prov	16.13		2	
Zech	11.7		2	
Lk	18.7		2	
Acts	25.3	<	2	
2 Cor	6.2		2	

FEAR

Ex	1.12		3	
Job	31.23		3	
	41.24		3	
Is	8.9		3	
Lk	12.5		3	
1 Jn	4.18		3	
Ex	15.14		2	
Deut	7.19		2	
	28.66		2	
Ps	55.5		2	
	76.7		2	
	102.15		2	
	119.39		2	
Is	18.2		2	

FEAR (cont.)

Is	41.5		2	
	51.12		2	
	64.1		2	
	66.2		2	
Ezek	12.18		2	
	38.8		2	
Mal	3.16	<	2	
Lk	1.65		2	
	18.2		2	
2 Cor	7.5		2	

FEAST

Mt	22.2		6	>
Lk	14.8	<	5	>
1 Kgs	1.9		4	
Job	1.4		4	
Esth	9.17	<	3	
Lk	15.23	<	3	>
Judg	14.12		2	
1 Sam	25.8		2	
Ecc	10.16		2	
Jer	16.8		2	
Amos	6.4		2	
Rev	19.9		2	

FELLOWSHIP

1 Jn	1.3		3	>
Gen	5.22		2	>
Acts	2.42		2	
Rom	6.10		2	
1 Cor	5.2		2	>
1 Jn	2.19	<	2	

FELLOWSHIP-OFFERING

Lev	7.11	<	5	
	4.10	<	4	
Num	6.14		3	>
Lev	3.1		2	>
	9.4		2	
Num	7.12	<	2	
Josh	22.23		2	
1 Kgs	8.63		2	>
2 Chr	7.5		2	
Ezek	45.13		2	>
	46.2	<	2	

FESTIVAL

Lev	23.2		9	
Ex	23.14		7	
Jn	7.2	<	7	
Ex	12.11		6	>
	34.18		5	
1 Sam	20.5		5	
Ezek	45.17	<	5	>
	46.1	<	5	
Ex	13.5	<	4	
Num	28.16		4	>
Deut	16.10		4	

FESTIVAL (cont.)

2 Chr	35.1		4	
1 Kgs	12.32		3	
2 Chr	8.13	<	3	
	30.1		3	>
	31.1	<	3	
Zech	14.16		3	
Mt	26.2		3	>
Mk	14.1		3	>
Lk	2.41		3	
Jn	11.55	<	3	>
Num	10.10		2	
	29.12	<	2	
Judg	21.19		2	
1 Kgs	8.2		2	
2 Chr	7.8		2	>
Ezra	3.4		2	
Is	1.13		2	
Hos	9.1		2	
Lk	22.1		2	
Jn	2.13		2	
	4.45		2	>
	12.12	<	2	>
	13.1	<	2	

FIRST-BORN

Ex	13.2	<	10	
Num	3.12		10	
	8.16		4	
	18.15		4	
Ex	12.12	<	3	>
	22.29		3	
	34.19		3	
Gen	25.31		2	
Ex	4.22		2	
	11.5		2	>
Lev	27.26		2	
Deut	12.6		2	
Col	1.15		2	

FLEE

1 Kgs	2.7		5	
1 Sam	31.1		3	
2 Sam	13.29		3	
2 Kgs	9.10		3	
2 Sam	4.3		2	>
	10.13		2	
	19.8	<	2	
1 Kgs	20.20	<	2	
2 Kgs	7.7		2	
	14.12		2	
1 Chr	10.1		2	
	19.14		2	
2 Chr	25.22		2	

FLESH

Jn	6.51		6	
Rev	19.18		4	
1 Cor	15.39		3	

FLESH (cont.)

Gen	2.21		2	

FLOCK

Gen	29.2		9	>
	30.29	<	9	>
	31.4	<	8	
Zech	11.4		5	
Gen	37.12		4	>
Song	6.2		4	
	1.7		3	>
Ezek	34.17		3	
Gen	47.1	<	2	
Ps	78.48		2	>
Jer	31.10		2	
Zeph	2.7		2	
Acts	20.28		2	
1 Pet	5.2		2	

FLOOD

Gen	7.6	<	4	
	9.11		4	
	10.1		2	>
Job	22.11		2	
Is	8.7		2	
	28.2		2	
Jer	46.7		2	>
Dan	11.10		2	
Mt	24.38		2	

FOLLOWER

Num	16.5		5	
Acts	9.1		3	
Num	26.9		2	>
2 Sam	15.12		2	>
Mt	12.27		2	
Lk	11.19		2	
Jn	6.60		2	>
Acts	5.36		2	

FOOD-OFFERING

Lev	23.8	<	7	>
Num	28.2		7	>
Lev	3.3	<	6	>
	21.6		5	>
Num	15.3		4	
Ex	29.18		3	>
Lev	1.9		3	>
	2.2	<	3	>
	7.5	<	3	>
	22.22	<	3	>
Num	29.6	<	3	
Lev	6.16	<	2	>
	8.20	<	2	

FOOL

Prov	14.1		10	>
	17.7		8	>
	26.1		8	>

FOOL (cont.)

Ecc	2.2	<	8	
	7.4	<	6	
2 Cor	11.1		6	>
Prov	10.1		5	>
	15.5	<	4	
Ecc	10.2		4	
Mt	25.2		4	
Judg	16.10		3	
Job	5.2		3	
Prov	18.2	<	3	>
	19.1	<	3	>
	29.3	<	3	>
Ecc	5.1	<	3	>
Is	44.20		3	
1 Cor	1.20		3	
Deut	32.6		2	
Job	12.17		2	>
Prov	1.22		2	
	9.4	<	2	
	11.12	<	2	>
	20.1	<	2	
	27.22	<	2	>
	30.22	<	2	
Ecc	4.5		2	>
Is	19.11		2	
	29.14		2	
	32.5		2	
Jer	5.4	<	2	
	50.36		2	
1 Cor	3.18		2	>
	15.33		2	
2 Cor	12.6	<	2	
Gal	3.1		2	
Eph	5.6		2	
1 Tim	6.9		2	
2 Tim	2.16		2	

FORCE (1) [COMPEL]

Judg	1.28		5	
1 Kgs	9.15		4	
2 Chr	8.7		3	
Ezek	20.8		3	
Ex	6.1	<	2	
Judg	11.2		2	
1 Sam	28.3		2	
Job	9.19		2	
Is	30.30		2	
Jer	34.11		2	
Lam	5.11	<	2	
Hab	2.6		2	
Gal	2.3		2	
Rev	13.12		2	

FORGET

Deut	4.9		4	
Ps	119.16		4	
Is	49.14		4	
Gen	41.30	<	3	

FORGET (cont.)

Deut	8.11	<	3	>
Ps	78.7	<	3	
	106.7		3	
Jer	20.9		3	
Deut	6.6		2	>
2 Sam	19.19		2	
Neh	9.17		2	
Ps	9.6		2	
	44.17		2	>
	74.19		2	
	88.5		2	>
	109.13		2	
	111.4		2	
Prov	2.1		2	>
	4.4	<	2	>
	31.5		2	
Is	23.15		2	
	65.16		2	
Jer	2.32		2	>
	23.27		2	
	44.9		2	
Mt	16.5		2	
Mk	8.14		2	
Lk	9.23		2	
Jas	1.24		2	

FORGIVE

1 Kgs	8.30		6	
2 Chr	6.21		6	>
Mt	6.12		6	
Lk	7.43	<	5	
Lev	4.20		4	>
	5.10	<	4	>
Num	14.18		4	>
Mt	12.31		4	
	18.21		4	
Mk	2.5	<	4	>
Lk	5.20		4	>
Num	15.25	<	3	
	30.5		3	
Ps	25.7		3	
Is	53.10		3	
Dan	9.9		3	
Mt	9.2		3	
2 Cor	2.7		3	
Gen	18.27		2	
	50.17		2	
Ex	29.33		2	
	32.30		2	
	34.7		2	
Deut	21.8		2	
2 Kgs	5.18		2	
2 Chr	30.19		2	
Ps	32.1		2	
Jer	5.1		2	
Mk	3.28	<	2	>
	11.25		2	
Lk	12.10	<	2	

FORGIVE (cont.)

Lk	17.3		2	
Jn	20.23		2	
Col	3.13	<	2	
Heb	9.5	<	2	
Jas	5.15		2	
1 Jn	2.2	<	2	

FREE

Jer	34.8		10	
1 Cor	7.15		7	>
Ex	21.2		6	
Deut	15.10		5	
Mt	27.15		5	
Rom	6.7	<	5	>
	8.2	<	5	
Gal	4.22	<	5	>
	5.1	<	5	
Lev	25.10		4	
Mk	15.6		4	
Lk	23.18		4	>
Rom	5.15	<	4	>
Gen	24.8		3	
Ex	6.6		3	
Ps	119.22	<	3	
Is	32.9		3	
	52.2	<	3	
Jn	8.32		3	
	19.10	<	3	
Acts	7.25		3	
Rom	7.2	<	3	>
1 Cor	9.1	<	3	
Eph	1.6		3	
Phil	1.7		3	>
Col	2.11	<	3	>
Gen	26.22		2	
	34.10		2	
	44.10		2	
Deut	7.8	<	2	
Judg	3.9		2	
Job	3.18		2	
	33.9		2	
Is	5.18		2	
	14.17		2	
	45.8		2	
	49.9	<	2	
	51.11		2	>
Jer	40.1		2	
Jn	18.39		2	>
Acts	4.21	<	2	>
	13.38		2	
Rom	3.24		2	>
1 Cor	10.25		2	
2 Cor	8.3		2	
1 Pet	2.16	<	2	

FRIEND

Jer	9.4		5	
Lk	11.5		5	>

FRIEND (cont.)

Rom	16.2		5	
2 Cor	5.18	<	5	>
3 Jn	2		5	
2 Pet	3.1		4	
Job	6.14		3	
	19.14		3	
	42.7		3	
Prov	16.7	<	3	>
	19.4	<	3	
	27.6		3	>
Is	5.1		3	
Jer	20.4		3	
Lk	15.6	<	3	>
Jn	15.13		3	
Rom	5.10		3	
1 Jn	4.1	<	3	
Jude	3		3	
Gen	26.27		2	
	31.2		2	
	38.12	<	2	
Judg	7.13		2	
	11.37		2	
	15.2	<	2	
1 Sam	25.6		2	
2 Sam	15.32		2	>
	16.16	<	2	
2 Kgs	9.17		2	
Esth	5.10		2	>
	6.13	<	2	
Job	16.20		2	>
	17.5	<	2	
Ps	35.14	<	2	
	55.13		2	
	88.8		2	
Prov	17.9	<	2	>
	18.24	<	2	>
	22.11		2	
	24.1		2	
Jer	38.22		2	
Dan	2.13	<	2	
Mt	5.43		2	>
Lk	7.6		2	
	12.4	<	2	
	14.10		2	>
	16.4	<	2	
Jn	11.3		2	
Rom	2.1		2	
	11.15		2	>
Tit	3.2		2	
Jas	4.4	<	2	
1 Jn	3.2	<	2	>

FRIGHT

Neh	6.9		4	
2 Kgs	19.6		2	
Is	37.6		2	
Dan	11.30	<	2	

FULFIL

Num	18.3		4	
	30.5	<	4	
Lev	22.18		3	>
Num	15.3		2	
1 Cor	7.3		2	

G

GENEROUS

2 Cor	9.9	<	4	
Deut	15.8		3	
2 Cor	8.2		3	>
Ps	112.5		2	
1 Tim	6.17		2	

GENTILE

Rom	15.9		10	>
Gal	2.2	<	10	>
Acts	15.3	<	9	
Rom	11.11	<	9	
Acts	13.16		7	>
Rom	2.9	<	7	>
Acts	11.1	<	6	
	21.11	<	5	>
Rom	3.1	<	5	
Eph	2.11		5	>
Acts	14.1	<	4	>
	26.17		3	
Gal	3.8	<	3	
Eph	3.1	<	3	
Mt	10.5		2	
Acts	4.25		2	
	10.28		2	>
	18.6	<	2	>
	19.10	<	2	>
Rom	1.13		2	>
	9.24		2	
1 Cor	1.23		2	
	9.21		2	

GIFT

1 Cor	14.1	<	9	
2 Chr	31.5		7	>
1 Cor	12.1		6	>
1 Sam	6.3		5	
Rom	5.5	<	5	>
Ex	29.24		4	
Num	8.11	<	4	
	18.6		4	
Deut	12.6		4	
Gen	43.15		3	
Lev	7.29		3	>
	14.12		3	
	23.17		3	
Num	7.5	<	3	>
Judg	3.15		3	
1 Kgs	10.10		3	

GIFT (cont.)

2 Kgs	5.15		3	
1 Chr	26.20		3	
2 Chr	9.9		3	
Ezek	20.31		3	
Mt	5.23		3	
	23.18		3	
Lk	21.1		3	
Rom	12.3		3	
1 Cor	7.7		3	
	13.2	<	3	>
2 Cor	9.5	<	3	
Gal	3.18		3	
Eph	4.7	<	3	
Gen	32.20		2	>
	33.10	<	2	
Lev	8.27	<	2	>
Deut	16.16		2	
2 Kgs	12.4		2	
2 Chr	17.5		2	
Esth	9.19		2	
Ps	68.18		2	
Jer	31.12		2	
Dan	2.6		2	
Acts	1.4		2	>
	2.33	<	2	
Rom	4.4	<	2	>
2 Cor	8.12		2	>
Phil	4.17		2	
1 Pet	4.10	<	2	
2 Pet	1.4		2	

GLAD

Ps	97.1	<	4	
Jn	16.20		4	
1 Chr	16.10		3	
Lk	1.14		3	
Phil	2.17		3	
Judg	5.2		2	
Ps	34.2	<	2	>
	35.9	<	2	
	51.8		2	
	68.3	<	2	>
	94.3		2	
	96.11		2	>
	105.3	<	2	>
	107.30	<	2	
Is	51.3		2	
	66.10	<	2	
Joel	2.21		2	
Lk	10.20		2	
Acts	2.26		2	
2 Cor	11.4		2	>
Jas	1.9		2	
Rev	18.20		2	>

GLORY

2 Cor	3.7		11	>
Jn	17.1	<	8	

GLORY (cont.)

Jn	12.16	<	5	>
1 Pet	1.7		5	
1 Chr	16.24		4	
Ps	29.1		4	
	96.3		4	>
Is	60.1		4	
Dan	4.30		4	
Lk	9.26		4	
Jn	13.31	<	4	>
Rom	8.17		4	>
2 Cor	4.4	<	4	
Eph	1.6		4	
1 Chr	29.11		3	
Ps	145.5		3	
Is	2.10		3	
	28.1		3	
Lk	2.9		3	
Jn	7.18		3	
	11.4		3	>
Rom	9.4	<	3	
Col	1.11		3	
2 Thes	1.9		3	>
Heb	2.7	<	3	
1 Pet	4.11		3	>
	5.1	<	3	
2 Pet	1.3		3	>
Jude	8		3	
Ex	15.1		2	
1 Sam	4.21		2	
Ps	57.5		2	
	66.2		2	
	72.19	<	2	
	104.1		2	
Is	4.5		2	
	42.8		2	>
Ezek	3.12		2	
Zech	11.2		2	
Acts	7.2		2	
Rom	2.7		2	>
	16.25	<	2	
1 Cor	2.7		2	
	11.7	<	2	
2 Cor	8.19		2	>
Eph	3.16		2	
1 Tim	1.11		2	
Rev	4.9		2	>
	5.12	<	2	
	21.11		2	

GOD (2) (OTHER GODS)

2 Kgs	17.7		11	>
1 Kgs	11.2		10	>
Deut	32.8	<	9	>
Is	44.6	<	9	>
Dan	11.8		9	
Jer	2.11	<	8	>
Gen	31.19		7	
Josh	24.2	<	7	

GOD (2)(cont.)

2 Kgs	1.2		7	
Deut	4.7	<	6	>
2 Chr	32.13		6	>
Is	57.5		6	
Jer	16.11		6	
Dan	3.12	<	6	>
	5.4	<	6	>
Ex	23.13	<	5	
	32.1		5	
	34.14		5	
Deut	12.2	<	5	>
	13.2	<	5	
Is	45.5	<	5	>
Jer	11.10	<	5	
	44.3	<	5	
Ezek	28.2		5	
Deut	28.14		4	>
Judg	2.3		4	>
	10.6		4	>
2 Kgs	18.33	<	4	>
	23.10	<	4	
Is	36.18		4	>
	41.21		4	>
	43.9	<	4	>
Jer	48.7		4	>
Dan	4.8	<	4	>
Num	25.2		3	
Deut	6.14	<	3	>
	29.18	<	3	>
	31.16	<	3	>
Josh	23.7		3	>
Judg	9.9	<	3	
	16.23		3	
1 Sam	4.7		3	>
	5.2	<	3	>
1 Kgs	18.24		3	>
	20.10	<	3	
2 Kgs	5.15		3	
	19.12	<	3	
Is	37.12	<	3	
	46.1	<	3	
Jer	7.6		3	>
	13.10		3	
	43.12		3	>
	46.15		3	
Hos	4.10	<	3	
Gen	35.2		2	
Ex	20.3		2	
Lev	19.4	<	2	>
Deut	7.4	<	2	>
	11.16	<	2	>
Judg	6.10	<	2	
1 Kgs	9.6	<	2	
1 Chr	16.25		2	
2 Chr	7.19	<	2	
	13.8		2	
Ps	16.4		2	
	82.1	<	2	
Ps	96.4	<	2	>
	97.7	<	2	
	135.5		2	>
Is	42.8	<	2	>
Jer	3.13	<	2	
	5.7		2	
	10.11		2	>
	19.4		2	
	32.29		2	
	51.17	<	2	
Ezek	20.7		2	
	43.7		2	
Dan	2.11	<	2	>
	6.7	<	2	
Hos	9.1	<	2	
Amos	8.14		2	
Jon	1.5		2	
Jn	10.34		2	
Acts	7.40		2	
	14.11		2	
1 Cor	8.5		2	

GOD'S PEOPLE

Jer	23.1		13	>
Ps	78.20		10	
Jer	8.4	<	10	>
Deut	32.3	<	9	>
Is	56.1	<	9	>
Jer	9.1	<	8	
Ezek	13.9		8	>
1 Kgs	8.16		7	>
Ps	106.9	<	7	>
Is	63.4	<	7	
Jer	5.7	<	7	>
	12.8	<	7	>
	30.3	<	7	>
Zech	9.7	<	7	
Ps	105.12		6	>
Is	49.5	<	6	>
	65.1		6	>
Jer	6.14	<	6	>
	31.1	<	6	>
Ezek	37.12	<	6	>
Hos	2.1	<	6	
Eph	1.1		6	>
Ex	3.7		5	
1 Chr	17.7	<	5	
Is	3.12	<	5	
	43.6	<	5	>
	44.1	<	5	>
Jer	7.12	<	5	>
Ezek	21.10		5	
Rom	9.4	<	5	
Col	1.2		5	
Ex	8.1	<	4	>
Lev	7.20		4	
	17.3		4	>
Deut	23.1		4	

GOD'S PEOPLE (cont.)

2 Sam	7.8	<	4	
Is	61.2	<	4	>
Jer	2.9	<	4	
Dan	7.21		4	>
Hos	11.2		4	>
Mic	3.2	<	4	>
Zech	10.3		4	
Rom	15.10		4	>
Ex	9.1	<	3	
	12.15	<	3	
Lev	20.3	<	3	>
	26.12		3	
Deut	29.13	<	3	
	33.2	<	3	
1 Sam	9.16		3	
	10.1		3	
2 Kgs	21.2	<	3	
2 Chr	6.5		3	>
	36.15	<	3	
Ps	81.8		3	
	111.1		3	
	136.14	<	3	
	149.4	<	3	
Is	14.1		3	
	27.5	<	3	>
	30.26	<	3	
	42.14	<	3	>
	52.3	<	3	
	57.14	<	3	>
Jer	25.30	<	3	
	51.10	<	3	
Lam	4.3	<	3	
Ezek	34.27	<	3	>
	36.8	<	3	>
	39.7	<	3	
Dan	11.28		3	>
Hos	1.2		3	>
	4.6		3	>
	8.1	<	3	>
Joel	2.18		3	>
Amos	7.4		3	>
	9.10	<	3	
Mic	2.5	<	3	>
	5.3	<	3	>
	6.2	<	3	
Nah	1.7		3	
Zeph	3.5	<	3	
Zech	2.6	<	3	
Mt	24.22		3	
Mk	13.20		3	
Rom	8.17		3	>
1 Cor	14.21		3	
Eph	2.12	<	3	>
Heb	8.6		3	
Rev	18.4	<	3	>
Ex	6.1	<	2	>
	7.3	<	2	>
	19.5	<	2	
Ex	22.25		2	
	28.12		2	>
	29.28	<	2	>
	30.33	<	2	>
Num	19.13		2	
Deut	14.2		2	
	26.18		2	
	28.9		2	>
Judg	5.11		2	
1 Sam	2.29		2	
2 Sam	5.2		2	>
	14.13		2	
1 Kgs	16.2		2	
2 Chr	7.10	<	2	
	31.8		2	>
	33.2	<	2	
Ezra	1.3		2	
Ps	34.9		2	
	50.4		2	
	53.4		2	
	68.26		2	>
	69.33	<	2	
	107.38	<	2	>
	116.14		2	
	135.12		2	>
Is	5.16		2	>
	10.1		2	>
	11.11	<	2	>
	12.3	<	2	
	19.25		2	
	32.13		2	>
	45.15	<	2	>
	50.1	<	2	>
	51.4	<	2	>
	60.9	<	2	>
Jer	4.12		2	>
	13.11	<	2	>
	14.7	<	2	>
	15.7	<	2	>
	18.15		2	
	33.24	<	2	
Lam	1.15		2	>
Ezek	14.8	<	2	
	38.14	<	2	>
	44.7		2	>
Dan	9.4	<	2	
Hos	6.6	<	2	>
	9.8	<	2	
Joel	3.2	<	2	
Obad	13		2	
Mic	4.2	<	2	>
Zeph	2.8	<	2	>
Zech	1.15		2	>
	7.9		2	>
	8.7	<	2	>
	13.7	<	2	
Mal	2.9	<	2	>
	3.17	<	2	

GOD'S PEOPLE (cont.)

Mt	13.17		2	
Lk	1.68		2	
Acts	26.10		2	
Rom	10.19		2	>
	11.1	<	2	
	16.2	<	2	
1 Cor	1.2		2	
	6.1		2	
	16.1		2	
2 Cor	6.16		2	
	9.1	<	2	
Eph	3.8	<	2	>
Phil	4.21		2	
Col	3.12		2	
Phlm	5		2	
1 Pet	1.1		2	>
	2.9	<	2	
Rev	8.3		2	
	13.7		2	>

GODDESS

2 Kgs	23.4		4	
Acts	19.24		4	
1 Kgs	11.5		2	
2 Kgs	17.10		2	>
	21.3		2	
2 Chr	33.3		2	>

GODLESS

Jude	4		4	
Ps	74.18		2	
2 Pet	2.5		2	>

GOOD NEWS

2 Sam	18.19		6	
Acts	8.12		4	
Rom	1.1		4	>
1 Thes	2.2	<	4	>
Mk	1.1		3	
Acts	14.7	<	3	>
Rom	15.16		3	>
2 Sam	4.10		2	
Is	40.9		2	
Lk	4.18	<	2	
Rom	10.15		2	>
1 Cor	9.12		2	
2 Cor	10.14		2	>
2 Tim	1.8		2	>
	2.8	<	2	
Heb	4.2		2	
1 Pet	1.12		2	
	4.6		2	

GOSPEL

Gal	1.6		6	>
Phil	1.5		6	>
1 Cor	9.14		5	
Gal	2.2	<	5	>

GOSPEL (cont.)

Col	1.6		4	
Eph	6.19		3	
Rom	1.16		2	
1 Cor	15.2		2	
2 Cor	11.4		2	
Gal	3.2	<	2	>
Eph	3.6		2	

GRACE

Rom	5.2		6	>
Jn	1.14		3	
Rom	6.1	<	3	
	11.5		3	>
1 Cor	15.10		3	>
Gal	1.3		3	>
Eph	1.2		3	>
	2.5	<	3	>
Col	1.2		3	
2 Tim	1.2		3	>
Neh	9.17		2	
Acts	14.3	<	2	>
	15.11	<	2	
	20.24		2	
Rom	12.3	<	2	
1 Cor	1.3		2	
2 Cor	1.2		2	
	8.1		2	>
2 Thes	1.2		2	>
1 Tim	1.2		2	
Tit	2.11	<	2	>
	3.7	<	2	
Phlm	3		2	
Heb	4.16		2	
	13.9	<	2	
Jas	4.6		2	
1 Pet	5.10		2	

GRAIN-OFFERING

Num	29.3	<	8	
	28.5		6	>
Lev	6.14	<	5	>
Num	15.4		4	
Ezek	46.5	<	4	
Lev	2.3		3	
	7.9	<	3	
	14.20		3	
2 Kgs	16.13		3	
Ezek	45.13	<	3	>
Lev	5.11		2	>
	9.4		2	
	23.18		2	
Num	7.12		2	>
Josh	22.23		2	
Is	66.3		2	

GRAVE

Ezek	32.22		6	
1 Kgs	13.22		3	

GRAVE (cont.)

Ps	49.9		3	
Acts	2.27		3	
	13.34		3	
Gen	23.6		2	
Num	19.16		2	
Job	3.17		2	
	17.1		2	
Ps	30.3		2	
	88.5		2	>
Ezek	37.12		2	
Mt	27.52		2	
Jn	11.31		2	>

GRIEF

Judg	11.37		3	
2 Sam	1.2		3	
Ezra	9.3		3	
Is	15.2		3	>
	23.1		3	
Rev	18.7		3	
Job	3.10	<	2	
Jer	16.5	<	2	
	31.18		2	
Lam	2.11		2	>
	3.33	<	2	

GROAN

Lam	1.4		5	
Rom	8.22		4	
Ezek	21.6		3	
Ex	2.23		2	
Ps	38.8		2	
	102.5		2	

GUILTY

Num	35.16		6	
Lev	5.2	<	5	>
	4.3		4	>
Job	9.20		4	
Gen	18.23		3	
Ex	22.2		3	>
Num	5.8		3	
Ezek	4.4		3	
Mt	12.5		3	
Heb	10.2		3	
Jas	2.4		3	
Lev	22.9		2	
Num	18.1		2	
Deut	19.10		2	
	25.1	<	2	
1 Sam	14.39		2	
2 Chr	19.10		2	
Job	16.8		2	
Prov	24.24		2	
Lam	4.13		2	
Mt	5.28		2	
Lk	23.14		2	
Jn	9.41	<	2	

GUILTY (cont.)

Jn	15.22		2	
Rom	5.16	<	2	

H

HANG (2) [KILL]

2 Sam	21.6		4	
Esth	7.9	<	3	>
Deut	21.22		2	
Esth	9.13	<	2	

HAPPY

Mt	5.3		10	
Ps	119.1	<	7	
Prov	15.13	<	5	>
1 Chr	29.9		4	
Lk	1.14		4	
	6.20		4	>
	15.5	<	4	
Rom	4.6		4	
2 Cor	7.7		4	
Job	21.21		3	
Ps	84.4		3	
Prov	3.13		3	
	8.31	<	3	
	23.15		3	
	29.2	<	3	
Is	24.7	<	3	>
	30.18	<	3	
Lk	12.37	<	3	
Gen	30.13		2	
Judg	9.13		2	
Esth	5.9		2	
	8.16		2	>
Ps	19.5		2	
	32.1		2	>
	33.12	<	2	>
	34.8	<	2	>
	40.4	<	2	>
	41.1	<	2	>
	68.3		2	
	89.15		2	>
	104.15		2	
	106.3		2	
	112.1		2	>
	128.1	<	2	
	144.15		2	
Prov	5.18		2	
	11.1		2	>
	12.20	<	2	
	14.13		2	>
	16.14	<	2	
	27.9		2	>
	28.14	<	2	>
Ecc	2.1		2	>
	7.4	<	2	
	9.7		2	

HAPPY (cont.)

Is	32.13		2	
	65.13		2	
Jer	15.10		2	>
Mal	3.12		2	>
Mt	25.21	<	2	
Lk	11.27		2	>
Jn	16.21		2	
1 Cor	7.30		2	
2 Cor	2.3	<	2	
Gal	4.15		2	
Phil	1.18		2	>
Jas	5.11		2	
2 Jn	4		2	
3 Jn	3		2	
Rev	1.3		2	
	22.7		2	

HARD

Mk	10.5		4	
Lev	26.19		3	
Job	41.15		3	
Prov	12.11		3	>
Ecc	4.4		3	
Mt	7.14	<	3	
	19.8		3	
Gen	3.17		2	>
Deut	28.23		2	
2 Sam	17.8		2	
Ezra	10.9		2	
Prov	10.4		2	
	13.4	<	2	
	31.10		2	
Ecc	2.11		2	
	9.1	<	2	
Lk	11.4		2	
	18.24		2	>
	19.21	<	2	
Acts	20.19		2	
Rom	12.8		2	

HARM

1 Sam	24.6	<	8	>
	26.9	<	5	
	20.7		3	
	25.7	<	3	>
Gen	26.29		2	
	31.7		2	
Lev	6.18		2	
Num	5.19		2	
2 Sam	18.5		2	
Is	11.8		2	
Rev	9.4		2	
	11.5		2	

HARVEST

Ex	23.11		4	
	34.21		4	
Lev	23.9		4	

HARVEST (cont.)

Lev	25.5		4	>
Deut	16.9		4	
Mt	13.30		4	
Jn	4.35		4	
Lev	26.5	<	3	
Ruth	2.2	<	3	
2 Kgs	4.18		3	
Hag	1.6		3	
Mt	9.37		3	
Lk	10.2		3	
Gal	6.8		3	
Rev	14.15		3	
Gen	47.24		2	
Lev	2.12		2	
Deut	26.2		2	
Judg	15.1		2	
Ruth	1.6		2	>
2 Sam	21.9		2	
Neh	10.35		2	
Job	24.6		2	
Ps	126.5		2	
Is	17.5	<	2	>
Jer	8.13		2	
Ezek	45.13	<	2	
Mt	21.34		2	
	25.24		2	
Jas	3.17		2	

HATE

Ezek	16.27		5	
Jn	15.18		5	
Ps	119.104		4	>
Prov	8.7		4	>
	15.8		4	>
	26.24	<	4	
Gen	37.4		3	
Deut	7.10		3	
2 Sam	13.15		3	
Amos	5.10		3	>
Num	35.20		2	
2 Sam	22.18		2	
Job	16.9		2	
Ps	18.17		2	
	35.16	<	2	
	44.7		2	>
	55.3		2	
	109.5		2	
	139.21		2	
Prov	10.12		2	>
	11.1	<	2	>
	12.1	<	2	>
	20.10		2	>
	24.9		2	>
	28.9		2	>
	29.10	<	2	>
Ecc	9.1		2	
Jer	7.10		2	
Lam	3.52	<	2	

HATE (cont.)

Ezek	23.28		2	
Hos	9.7	<	2	
Mic	3.2		2	
Mal	2.16	<	2	
Mt	24.9		2	
Lk	6.22		2	
1 Jn	2.9		2	>
	3.13	<	2	>

HEAL

Lk	6.7	<	4	>
	9.2	<	4	
Jn	5.10	<	4	>
Acts	4.9		4	>
Lev	13.16		3	>
Jer	8.15		3	
	30.12		3	
Mt	8.3		3	>
	10.1		3	
	12.10		3	>
Lk	4.23		3	>
Acts	28.8		3	
1 Cor	12.9		3	
Gen	20.17		2	
Num	21.8		2	
1 Kgs	13.6		2	
2 Kgs	20.5		2	
Is	19.22		2	
	38.16		2	
	57.18		2	>
Jer	14.19		2	>
	17.9		2	
Ezek	34.4		2	
Mt	4.23		2	
	9.28	<	2	
	15.28	<	2	
	17.16		2	
Mk	3.2		2	
	5.29		2	>
	6.5	<	2	
Lk	5.15	<	2	>
	8.2	<	2	>
	13.14		2	>
	14.3	<	2	
	17.15		2	
Jas	5.15		2	
Rev	13.3		2	

HEART

Ps	119.2		13	
Col	3.1		5	
Deut	30.2		4	
Jer	4.14	<	4	
2 Cor	6.11	<	4	>
1 Kgs	8.23		3	
1 Chr	29.17	<	3	
2 Chr	6.14		3	
Prov	7.3	<	3	

HEART (cont.)

Jer	17.1		3	
Ezek	11.19		3	
	36.26		3	
Mt	15.8	<	3	
Mk	7.6	<	3	
Acts	27.22		3	
Rom	2.5	<	3	
2 Cor	7.2	<	3	
Heb	10.16		3	
Deut	28.47		2	
1 Sam	12.20		2	
2 Kgs	23.3		2	
2 Chr	15.12		2	>
Ps	37.4	<	2	>
	38.8	<	2	
	42.4		2	
	51.10		2	
	55.15		2	
	73.1		2	
Prov	3.3		2	>
Jer	8.18	<	2	
	15.9	<	2	
	31.20		2	>
	48.10		2	
Lam	1.20		2	>
	3.41	<	2	
Ezek	14.3		2	
	21.6		2	
Hos	14.4		2	
Mt	5.8		2	>
Mk	12.30	<	2	
Lk	2.35	<	2	
	6.45		2	>
	8.12	<	2	
	10.27		2	
Jn	5.38		2	
	16.6		2	>
Rom	1.9		2	>
	10.1		2	>
1 Cor	14.1		2	
2 Cor	1.22		2	>
	3.2	<	2	>
Eph	6.5	<	2	
Phil	1.7		2	
	4.6		2	
Phlm	7		2	
1 Pet	3.11		2	

HEATHEN

Ps	9.5		3	
	106.27		3	
1 Sam	17.26		2	
Ps	59.5		2	
1 Pet	4.3		2	
Rev	11.2		2	

HEAVEN

2 Chr	6.13		11	>
1 Kgs	8.23		10	
Jn	6.31		10	
Mt	6.1	<	7	>
	18.10		7	>
2 Pet	3.5		7	
Neh	9.6		6	
Mt	5.12		6	>
1 Cor	15.40		6	
Dan	2.18		5	
	4.13		5	>
Acts	1.2		5	>
Rev	10.1		5	>
	11.12	<	5	>
	12.7	<	5	>
Ps	89.5		4	
	148.1		4	
Is	51.6		4	
Jer	44.17		4	
Mt	24.29	<	4	
Lk	9.16		4	
	10.15		4	>
Jn	3.12		4	
Acts	7.42		4	
Eph	1.3		4	>
Heb	12.22	<	4	
Rev	14.2	<	4	>
	18.1		4	>
	21.1	<	4	
Deut	4.26	<	3	>
2 Kgs	1.10		3	>
2 Chr	7.1	<	3	
Ezra	7.12	<	3	
Ps	115.3		3	
Dan	8.10	<	3	
Mt	16.17	<	3	
Mk	13.25	<	3	>
Lk	2.13	<	3	>
Acts	11.5	<	3	
2 Cor	5.1		3	
Col	1.5		3	
Heb	9.23	<	3	
Rev	19.1	<	3	>
	20.1	<	3	>
Gen	6.2		2	
	14.19		2	
	22.11	<	2	
	24.3		2	
	27.28		2	>
	28.12	<	2	
Ex	20.4		2	
2 Kgs	2.1	<	2	
2 Chr	2.6		2	
Ezra	5.11		2	>
	6.9	<	2	>
Neh	2.4	<	2	
Ps	33.6		2	
	50.4		2	

HEAVEN (cont.)

Ps	57.3		2	
	73.9		2	
	78.24		2	
	102.19		2	>
	103.19	<	2	>
	113.4		2	
	136.5	<	2	
Is	14.12	<	2	
	44.23		2	>
	45.12	<	2	
	66.1	<	2	
Lam	3.41	<	2	
Amos	9.2		2	
Hag	2.6		2	
Mt	3.16		2	
	7.11	<	2	
	10.32		2	>
	11.23	<	2	>
	23.9	<	2	>
	28.2		2	
Mk	1.10		2	
Lk	3.21	<	2	
	16.17	<	2	>
	18.13	<	2	>
Jn	1.32		2	
Acts	10.11		2	>
	14.15		2	
Gal	4.14		2	
Eph	3.10	<	2	>
	6.9		2	
Phil	3.20	<	2	
Heb	1.3		2	
	6.4		2	>
	8.1	<	2	>
Jas	1.17		2	
1 Pet	1.4		2	
	3.22		2	
Rev	4.1	<	2	>
	5.3	<	2	
	13.6	<	2	>

HEBREW

Ex	2.6	<	6	>
	1.15		4	>
1 Sam	4.6		3	
Jn	19.13		3	>
Gen	39.14		2	>
Ex	9.1		2	
1 Sam	13.3		2	>
	14.11	<	2	
2 Kgs	18.26		2	
Is	36.11		2	
Jer	34.9		2	

HELP

2 Cor	8.4	<	12	>
Ps	119.27	<	10	
2 Cor	1.3		10	

HELP (cont.)

1 Cor	14.3		7	
Is	30.2		6	>
2 Sam	22.7	<	5	
2 Chr	28.16		5	>
Jer	14.2		5	>
Rom	15.1	<	5	>
1 Sam	7.2		4	
1 Chr	12.17	<	4	
	19.9	<	4	
Ps	18.6	<	4	
	22.1	<	4	
	142.1	<	4	
Ecc	4.1		4	
Is	41.6	<	4	
Acts	9.27		4	
2 Cor	9.1	<	4	
Phil	4.3		4	
Heb	13.6		4	
Num	11.2	<	3	
Deut	22.4		3	>
	32.12	<	3	>
	33.7	<	3	
1 Sam	12.8	<	3	
2 Sam	10.11		3	
2 Kgs	18.20	<	3	
Ezra	1.4		3	>
Job	8.6		3	>
	29.12		3	>
	35.7	<	3	>
	36.13	<	3	>
Ps	28.2	<	3	
	30.2		3	>
	37.5		3	>
	40.1		3	>
	41.1	<	3	
	88.2		3	>
	115.9		3	
Is	19.3		3	
	31.1	<	3	
	36.5		3	
	44.2		3	>
	57.12		3	>
Jer	11.11		3	
Lam	1.7		3	>
Dan	11.1	<	3	
Mt	25.44		3	>
Mk	1.13		3	
	9.22		3	
Lk	1.25		3	
	18.3		3	>
1 Cor	16.1		3	
2 Cor	12.13	<	3	
Phil	1.5		3	>
1 Tim	5.5		3	
Heb	2.16	<	3	>
3 Jn	6		3	
Gen	2.18		2	
Ex	1.15		2	>

HELP (cont.)

Ex	4.12		2	>
	14.10		2	
	22.23	<	2	>
	23.1	<	2	>
Num	1.4		2	
	10.9		2	>
	32.3		2	
Deut	1.38		2	
	3.18		2	>
	28.29		2	
Josh	1.1		2	
	10.4		2	
Judg	1.18		2	>
	6.7	<	2	
1 Sam	2.1		2	
	14.6		2	
	19.4		2	
2 Sam	15.33	<	2	
1 Kgs	8.39		2	
2 Kgs	6.26		2	
2 Chr	14.11	<	2	
	26.7		2	
	29.34	<	2	
	32.8		2	>
Ezra	5.2	<	2	>
Neh	9.9		2	
Job	9.8	<	2	
	22.3		2	
	30.1	<	2	>
Ps	3.2		2	>
	6.3	<	2	>
	10.14		2	
	51.15		2	
	60.11		2	
	69.3		2	>
	86.6	<	2	
	108.12	<	2	>
	109.21	<	2	
	118.7		2	>
	121.1		2	
	130.2		2	
	146.5	<	2	
Prov	8.15		2	
	21.13		2	
	27.10		2	
Is	14.2		2	
	49.8		2	>
	51.1	<	2	
	59.1	<	2	
	63.3		2	>
	65.1	<	2	>
Jer	3.23		2	
	23.14		2	
	47.2		2	
Lam	4.17	<	2	
Dan	10.13		2	>
Hos	5.11		2	
	7.7		2	>

HELP (cont.)

Jon	1.5		2	>
Zeph	3.2		2	
Mt	12.12		2	
	15.5		2	
Mk	7.11		2	
Lk	6.9	<	2	>
	11.23	<	2	
Jn	12.2		2	
Acts	7.24		2	
	18.27		2	>
	20.20	<	2	>
Rom	10.13		2	
2 Cor	11.8		2	>
Eph	4.28		2	
Phil	2.25	<	2	
1 Thes	5.11		2	
Phlm	13		2	

HIGH PRIEST

Mt	26.3		8	
Jn	18.10		8	
Mk	14.47		7	
Heb	5.1	<	5	>
	8.1	<	4	>
Lev	4.3		3	
Num	35.25		3	
Neh	12.1	<	3	>
Acts	5.17	<	3	
	23.2	<	3	>
Heb	4.14	<	3	>
	7.26	<	3	>
	9.7	<	3	
Lev	21.10		2	
2 Kgs	23.4	<	2	
2 Chr	31.10		2	
Neh	3.1		2	
Hag	1.1		2	>
Zech	3.1		2	
Lk	22.50		2	
Jn	11.49		2	
Acts	4.6		2	>

HOLY

Lev	21.6	<	9	>
Ex	30.10	<	8	
Lev	6.16		8	>
Ex	29.11	<	7	>
Lev	22.2	<	6	>
Ezek	20.12		6	
	42.13		6	>
	45.1	<	6	>
	48.10		6	
Lev	10.1		5	>
	20.3	<	5	>
Ps	89.5		5	
Ezek	36.20		5	
	44.3	<	5	>
	28.14		4	

HOLY (cont.)

Ezek	39.7	<	4	
Lk	1.35		4	
1 Pet	1.2		4	>
Lev	16.19		3	
Neh	8.9		3	>
Ps	99.3	<	3	
Is	5.16	<	3	>
	30.11	<	3	>
	41.14	<	3	
	43.3		3	
	52.1		3	
	63.10	<	3	
Ezek	22.8		3	
	43.7	<	3	>
Dan	4.8		3	>
	9.20		3	
1 Thes	4.3	<	3	>
Ex	3.1		2	>
	20.8		2	
	40.9		2	
Lev	2.3		2	
	7.1	<	2	
	11.44	<	2	>
	24.9	<	2	
Num	16.37		2	
	18.10		2	
	20.12		2	
1 Sam	9.6		2	
1 Chr	16.29		2	
2 Chr	2.4		2	
	8.11		2	
Ezra	9.2		2	
Neh	11.1	<	2	
Ps	78.41	<	2	>
	106.16		2	
Is	1.4		2	
	6.3	<	2	
	8.13		2	
	10.17		2	
	29.19		2	>
	48.2	<	2	>
	49.7	<	2	
	57.15		2	>
	60.9		2	
Jer	51.5	<	2	
Lam	2.6	<	2	
Ezek	38.16		2	>
	46.19	<	2	
Dan	5.11	<	2	
Hos	11.9		2	
Amos	4.2		2	
Jon	2.4		2	
Hab	1.12		2	>
Mt	23.17		2	
Acts	3.14		2	>
	4.27	<	2	
Rom	1.2		2	
	7.12	<	2	

HOLY (cont.)

Heb	12.10		2	
1 Pet	2.5	<	2	
2 Pet	3.2		2	
Rev	21.2		2	>
	22.11	<	2	

HOLY PLACE

Lev	16.2		11	
Ezek	41.1		9	
1 Kgs	6.16		6	>
Heb	9.2	<	6	
Num	3.31		4	>
2 Chr	3.8		4	>
Ex	26.33		3	
	28.29		3	>
Num	18.3		3	
Ex	39.1		2	
1 Kgs	7.49	<	2	>
	8.6	<	2	
2 Chr	4.20	<	2	>
	5.7	<	2	

HONEST

Prov	11.1	<	6	>
Gen	42.11		5	
Prov	28.1		5	>
	10.2		4	>
	20.7	<	3	>
	24.15		3	
Lev	19.15		2	
Judg	9.16		2	
Job	17.3		2	
Prov	12.5	<	2	>
	16.8	<	2	
	29.6	<	2	
Ecc	12.9		2	
Is	32.5		2	
	59.14		2	
Ezek	18.5		2	
Mic	7.2		2	

HONOUR

Esth	6.3		6	
Dan	5.7	<	6	
Lev	23.5		4	
Deut	16.1		4	>
2 Sam	6.5		4	
Dan	4.34		4	>
Mal	1.6		4	>
Jn	8.49		4	
Ex	12.11		3	>
Deut	6.2	<	3	
1 Sam	2.8		3	
2 Chr	32.23		3	
Ps	34.7	<	3	
	103.11		3	
	111.3		3	>
Prov	3.9		3	>

HONOUR (cont.)

Is	43.4	<	3	
	49.5		3	>
Dan	2.6		3	
Rom	14.6	<	3	
Ex	14.4	<	2	
Lev	19.30		2	
Josh	4.14	<	2	
1 Kgs	21.9		2	
1 Chr	29.16	<	2	
2 Chr	2.4		2	
Ps	62.4	<	2	
	119.74		2	
Prov	8.13		2	
	25.2	<	2	
Is	9.1		2	
	23.8	<	2	
	32.5		2	
	58.13	<	2	
	60.9		2	
Jer	10.7		2	
	13.11		2	
Lam	1.1		2	
Dan	11.38		2	
Hos	4.7		2	
Hab	2.16		2	
Zech	6.13		2	>
Mt	15.6		2	
Jn	5.23		2	
Rom	2.7	<	2	
Heb	2.7	<	2	>
	3.3	<	2	
	5.4		2	
Rev	4.9		2	>
	5.12	<	2	

HOPE

Ps	119.5		6	
Rom	8.20		6	
Lam	3.7	<	5	
Rom	15.4		5	
Job	17.11		4	
2 Cor	1.7		4	
Jer	14.8	<	3	
Acts	26.6		3	>
Rom	5.2	<	3	
Col	1.5		3	
Heb	6.11		3	>
1 Pet	1.3		3	>
2 Sam	14.7		2	
Job	6.11	<	2	>
	11.18		2	
	14.7	<	2	>
Ps	33.20		2	>
	39.7		2	
	42.5		2	>
	62.5		2	
	71.5		2	
Jer	28.6		2	>

HOPE (cont.)

Zech	9.5		2	
Acts	24.15	<	2	
	27.20	<	2	>
Rom	4.18		2	>
1 Cor	13.7		2	
	15.19		2	>
Eph	1.12		2	>
Phil	2.19	<	2	>
1 Pet	3.5	<	2	

HORROR

Jer	44.6		3	
	51.37	<	3	
Rev	8.13		3	>
2 Kgs	8.11		2	
Jer	49.13		2	>
Rev	9.12	<	2	

HUMAN

Rom	8.3	<	11	>
Dan	4.16		7	>
Gal	5.16	<	5	
1 Cor	1.17		4	>
Ezek	1.5		3	
	10.8		3	
Dan	5.5	<	3	
	7.4		3	>
Rom	7.5		3	>
1 Cor	2.4	<	3	
Col	2.8		3	>
Gen	1.26		2	
	9.5		2	
Lev	27.28		2	
Num	19.16		2	
2 Kgs	23.14		2	
2 Chr	32.8		2	
Ps	56.4		2	
	146.3		2	
Is	2.11		2	
	31.3		2	
	44.11		2	
Jn	1.13		2	
1 Cor	15.32		2	
2 Cor	5.16		2	
Eph	6.5		2	
Heb	12.9		2	
Rev	18.13		2	

HUMBLE

1 Pet	5.5		3	
2 Sam	22.28		2	
1 Kgs	8.33		2	
2 Chr	6.24		2	
	33.12	<	2	>
Job	22.23		2	
Ps	18.27		2	
	51.17		2	
Zeph	2.3		2	>

HUMBLE (cont.)

Zech	9.6		2	
Mt	23.12		2	
Lk	14.11		2	
	18.14		2	
Phil	2.3		2	
Col	2.18		2	>
Jas	4.6	<	2	

HUNGER

Mt	25.35		4	
1 Sam	14.24		3	
Ps	107.5		3	
Ezek	5.12		3	
Lk	6.3		3	
Lev	26.26		2	
Deut	8.3		2	
Job	5.5		2	
	38.39		2	
Prov	13.2	<	2	
Is	8.21		2	>
	58.7		2	
Jer	42.13		2	
Ezek	7.15		2	
	18.7		2	
Amos	8.11		2	
Mt	12.1		2	
1 Cor	11.21		2	

HURT

Prov	26.2		3	>
Jer	7.18		3	
Gen	37.22		2	
Ex	21.22		2	
2 Kgs	4.19		2	
Ecc	10.9		2	
Jer	14.17		2	
	38.4		2	
Ezek	34.4		2	
Dan	6.22		2	
1 Cor	15.55		2	
Rev	9.10		2	

HYPOCRITE

Mt	23.13	<	7	>
	6.2		3	>
Lk	12.1		2	>

HYSSOP

Lev	14.4		5	
Num	19.6		2	

I

I AM

Jn	10.7		5	>
Rev	22.7	<	5	
Jn	6.35	<	4	

I AM (cont.)

Jn	8.12		3	>
Rev	1.8		3	>
Ex	3.14		2	
Jn	15.1	<	2	

IDOL

2 Kgs	17.12	<	9	
Ezek	20.7		9	>
	16.19		8	
Is	44.9		7	>
Ezek	14.3		7	
	23.7	<	7	
1 Cor	8.1		7	
Judg	18.14	<	6	
Ezek	6.3		6	>
Deut	7.5		5	
2 Chr	15.8		4	
	34.3	<	4	
Is	57.8		4	
Jer	10.5		4	
1 Cor	10.7		4	
Deut	4.16		3	>
Judg	17.3		3	>
1 Kgs	15.12	<	3	>
2 Kgs	21.11		3	
Ps	106.19		3	
Is	2.8		3	
	10.10		3	
Jer	51.17	<	3	
Ezek	18.6		3	
	22.3	<	3	>
Hos	8.4		3	
	10.5		3	>
Zech	13.1		3	
Lev	26.1		2	
Deut	9.12		2	
	27.15		2	
	32.16		2	
Judg	8.27		2	
1 Sam	19.13		2	
1 Kgs	14.9		2	>
	16.13	<	2	
2 Kgs	23.13		2	
2 Chr	25.14	<	2	
	33.19	<	2	>
Is	19.1		2	
	30.22		2	>
	41.7	<	2	>
	42.8	<	2	
	45.16	<	2	>
Jer	2.5	<	2	
	8.5	<	2	>
	16.18		2	
	25.6		2	
	50.2		2	>
Ezek	8.3	<	2	
	11.18		2	
	36.18		2	>

IDOL (cont.)

Ezek	44.10		2	
Hos	3.1		2	>
	13.2	<	2	>
	14.3	<	2	
Mic	1.5		2	
Hab	2.18		2	
Acts	7.41		2	
	15.20		2	
1 Cor	5.10		2	>
Rev	2.14		2	

IMAGE

2 Chr	33.3		3	>
Rev	13.14		3	>
2 Kgs	17.10		2	>
Ezek	16.17		2	
Amos	5.26		2	
Rev	14.9	<	2	>

IMMORAL

Ezek	23.13		6	>
1 Cor	5.1		4	>
	6.9	<	4	>
2 Pet	2.2		4	
Rev	2.14		3	
	17.2		3	>
	18.3	<	3	>
Judg	20.6	<	2	
Ezek	16.27		2	
Acts	15.20		2	
Eph	5.3		2	
1 Thes	4.3		2	
Jude	4		2	

IMPORTANT

Mk	12.10		6	
2 Kgs	25.9	<	3	
Jer	52.13		3	
Mt	23.17	<	3	
Prov	24.5	<	2	>
	25.6	<	2	
Mt	22.38	<	2	>
	25.40		2	
Lk	12.23		2	
Phil	1.24		2	>

INCENSE

Ex	30.1		8	>
Num	16.6		7	
Ex	35.8		4	
Lev	2.1		4	
2 Chr	26.16	<	4	>
Rev	8.3		4	
Lev	16.12		3	
2 Chr	28.3	<	3	>
Lk	1.9		3	
Ex	31.8	<	2	
	37.25		2	

INCENSE (cont.)

Ex	40.5	<	2	
Lev	4.7		2	>
Num	4.7		2	>
	7.12		2	
2 Kgs	15.4	<	2	>
2 Chr	2.4		2	
	29.7	<	2	>
	34.4		2	
Neh	13.5		2	
Song	3.6		2	>
	4.6	<	2	
Is	43.23		2	
	65.3		2	>
Jer	34.5		2	
	52.18		2	
Ezek	6.4		2	
	8.11		2	

INHERIT

Num	27.7		5	
Gen	15.3		2	
Num	36.8		2	

INNOCENT

Gen	18.23		7	
Job	9.15		5	
1 Kgs	2.5		3	
Gen	20.4		2	
Ex	23.7		2	
Deut	19.6		2	
2 Sam	22.21		2	
1 Kgs	8.31		2	
2 Chr	6.22		2	
Job	22.19		2	>
Ps	18.20		2	
	26.1		2	
Prov	17.15		2	>
Jer	2.34		2	
	22.3		2	
Ezek	16.51		2	
Mt	23.35		2	
	27.4		2	>
Rom	16.18		2	

INSULT

Ps	69.7		5	
2 Kgs	19.4		4	
Is	37.4		4	
Ps	89.50		3	
	119.22		3	
Lam	3.30		3	
2 Pet	2.10		3	
Jude	8		3	
Gen	39.14		2	
1 Sam	25.14		2	
Neh	9.18		2	
Ps	79.4		2	>
Ecc	7.21		2	

INSULT (cont.)

Is	50.6		2	>
Ezek	36.3		2	
Zeph	2.8		2	
Mt	27.39		2	
Mk	15.29		2	
2 Cor	12.10		2	
Heb	10.29		2	
1 Pet	2.1		2	>
	4.4	<	2	
Rev	13.1		2	

INTEND

Lev	4.2		4	
Deut	9.5	<	2	
2 Chr	2.5		2	

J

JAIL

Acts	16.23		6	
Gen	39.21		2	
Mt	18.30		2	
Acts	5.18	<	2	
	12.4		2	

JEW

Esth	9.1	<	25	
	8.1		16	>
Rom	11.11	<	11	
Acts	18.2	<	10	>
Rom	2.9	<	10	>
Gal	2.7	<	8	>
Jn	18.12		7	>
	19.3	<	7	>
Acts	25.2	<	7	>
Esth	4.3	<	6	>
Acts	19.10	<	6	>
	21.11	<	6	>
	24.5	<	6	>
	26.2	<	6	
Rom	3.1	<	6	
Neh	5.1	<	5	>
Esth	3.4	<	5	>
Mk	15.2		5	
Jn	4.9	<	5	>
	7.1		5	>
Acts	14.1	<	5	
	22.3	<	5	>
Mt	27.11		4	>
Lk	23.3		4	
Acts	6.1	<	4	
	10.2		4	>
	13.6	<	4	>
	16.1		4	>
Eph	2.11		4	>
Ezra	4.4		3	>
Neh	4.1		3	>

JEW (cont.)

Neh	6.6	<	3	>
Esth	2.5		3	>
Jn	5.10	<	3	
Acts	2.5		3	
	9.22		3	
	17.5	<	3	>
	20.3	<	3	>
	23.12	<	3	>
Rom	15.8		3	>
	16.7	<	3	
1 Cor	1.22		3	
Gal	1.13		3	>
Ezra	5.1	<	2	>
	6.7	<	2	
Neh	13.17		2	
Esth	6.10	<	2	
	10.3		2	
Dan	3.8	<	2	
Jn	2.6	<	2	>
	3.1	<	2	>
	9.18	<	2	
	11.51		2	>
	12.11	<	2	>
Acts	12.3	<	2	>
	28.17		2	
1 Cor	9.20		2	
2 Cor	11.24		2	
Heb	13.10		2	

JOY

Ps	98.4		4	
Jer	31.4	<	4	
1 Chr	15.16		3	>
2 Chr	30.21	<	3	
Ezra	6.16		3	
Esth	8.15		3	>
	9.17	<	3	
Ps	30.5		3	
	65.8		3	>
	119.92		3	
	126.2		3	
Is	35.2		3	
	65.14	<	3	
Lam	2.4		3	
Zeph	3.14		3	
Phil	2.17	<	3	>
Deut	16.11		2	
1 Sam	2.1		2	
1 Kgs	1.40		2	
1 Chr	16.27	<	2	
Ezra	3.12		2	
Neh	8.10		2	
Job	33.26		2	
Ps	33.1	<	2	
	47.1	<	2	>
	48.2	<	2	
	51.8		2	
	95.1		2	>

JOY (cont.)

Ps	132.9		2	
Is	24.8	<	2	>
	44.23		2	
	51.3		2	>
	52.8	<	2	>
	55.12	<	2	>
	60.5		2	>
	61.3	<	2	
Jer	33.9		2	
	48.33		2	
Joel	1.12		2	>
Lk	10.17		2	
	24.41		2	
Jn	15.11		2	
Acts	2.26		2	
	8.8		2	
	15.3		2	>
Rom	15.13	<	2	
Phil	1.4		2	>
	4.4	<	2	
1 Thes	2.19	<	2	>
Heb	12.2		2	

JUDGE

Ps	119.7		11	
Rom	2.1		7	>
Jn	5.22		6	
1 Cor	6.1	<	6	
Jas	4.11	<	6	>
Ps	9.4		5	
Joel	3.2		5	
Lk	18.2		5	
Jn	12.31		5	
1 Cor	11.13	<	5	
Jas	2.4		5	>
1 Pet	4.5		5	
Ps	7.8		4	
	75.2		4	>
Jn	3.17		4	
Rom	14.4	<	4	
Deut	16.18		3	>
	17.8	<	3	
	19.17		3	
2 Chr	19.5		3	
Job	9.15		3	
Prov	24.12		3	
Is	3.2		3	>
Ezek	7.3		3	
	34.17	<	3	
Mt	7.1		3	
Lk	12.14		3	
Jn	8.15	<	3	>
	16.8		3	
1 Cor	2.14		3	
	5.12	<	3	>
2 Cor	5.10		3	
Heb	10.27		3	
Jas	5.9	<	3	

JUDGE (cont.)

Rev	20.4	<	3	
Gen	31.42	<	2	
Ex	18.22		2	
Deut	1.16		2	
1 Sam	2.3		2	
	8.1	<	2	
	24.12		2	
1 Kgs	7.7		2	>
Ps	10.5		2	
	50.4		2	>
	58.1		2	
	72.1		2	
	76.8	<	2	
	94.2		2	
Is	5.3	<	2	
	11.3		2	
Jer	48.21		2	>
Ezek	23.24	<	2	
Dan	7.22		2	
Hos	5.1		2	>
Mal	3.3		2	
Mt	12.18		2	
Mk	4.24		2	
Jn	7.24		2	>
Acts	7.27		2	
	25.6	<	2	
Rom	3.6	<	2	
1 Cor	4.3		2	>
	14.24		2	
2 Tim	4.1		2	
Rev	16.5		2	
	19.2	<	2	>

JUSTICE

Ps	119.106		4	
Is	42.1		4	
	59.4	<	4	>
Amos	5.7		4	>
Mic	3.1		3	
Gen	18.19		2	
Ex	23.2		2	
Deut	32.4		2	
2 Sam	15.4		2	
1 Kgs	3.9		2	
Job	34.5		2	
	36.3		2	>
Ps	7.6		2	
	19.8		2	
	45.4		2	
	72.1		2	
	96.10		2	>
Prov	17.23	<	2	>
	29.4	<	2	
Is	5.7		2	
	28.6		2	>
	32.1		2	>
Jer	22.3	<	2	>
Hab	1.4		2	

JUSTICE (cont.)

Zech	8.8	<	2	
Rev	16.5	<	2	

K

KEEP FROM

1 Sam	25.26	<	4	
Ps	119.10		4	
2 Sam	22.24		2	
Ps	18.23		2	
	30.1		2	
Acts	15.20	<	2	
1 Cor	12.15		2	
2 Cor	2.7		2	
	12.7	<	2	
2 Tim	2.16		2	>

KIND

2 Sam	9.1		3	
Ps	103.2		3	
Rom	11.22		3	>
Ruth	2.10		2	
1 Kgs	2.7		2	
2 Kgs	25.27		2	
Ps	4.1		2	
	109.12		2	
	112.4	<	2	
Prov	14.21		2	>
Jer	52.31		2	
Rom	2.4	<	2	
1 Pet	2.3		2	>

KINGDOM (1) (OF GOD)

Mt	13.11	<	12	
Mk	10.14		6	>
Mt	5.3	<	5	>
Lk	9.2	<	5	
	18.16	<	5	>
Mt	18.1		4	>
	19.12	<	4	>
Lk	13.18	<	4	>
Mt	11.11	<	3	>
	25.1	<	3	>
Mk	4.11		3	
Lk	17.20	<	3	>
	22.16	<	3	>
Jn	18.36		3	
Mt	4.17	<	2	>
	6.10	<	2	>
	8.11	<	2	>
	21.31	<	2	>
Mk	9.1		2	
Lk	8.1	<	2	>
	10.9		2	>
	11.2	<	2	>
	12.31	<	2	>
Jn	3.3		2	

KINGDOM (1)(cont.)

Acts	1.3		2	
	28.23		2	
1 Cor	6.9		2	
	15.24		2	
Col	1.11		2	
Jas	2.5		2	
Rev	1.6		2	

KISS

Lk	7.38		3	
Gen	27.26		2	
	29.11		2	
	31.28		2	
Ruth	1.9		2	
1 Kgs	19.18		2	
Mt	26.48		2	
Mk	14.44		2	
Lk	22.47		2	

KNOWLEDGE

Prov	1.5		5	>
2 Pet	1.2		5	>
1 Cor	8.1		4	
	13.2	<	4	>
2 Chr	1.10		3	
Prov	2.3	<	3	>
Gen	2.9		2	>
Ezra	7.6		2	
Prov	8.10		2	>
	9.6	<	2	
	15.2	<	2	>
	24.4		2	
Ecc	1.16		2	>
	2.21	<	2	
	7.12		2	
Is	11.2		2	
Dan	5.11		2	
Col	1.9		2	>

L

LAMB

Num	29.2	<	13	
	28.3		12	>
Lev	14.10		8	
Ezek	46.4		7	
Rev	6.1	<	7	>
	5.6		6	>
2 Chr	35.6		5	
Rev	21.9		5	>
Ex	29.38		4	
Lev	23.12	<	4	
Num	7.12	<	4	
Rev	7.9	<	4	>
	14.1	<	4	>
Num	6.12		3	>
2 Sam	12.3		3	

LAMB (cont.)

2 Chr	29.21		3	>
	30.15	<	3	
Gen	21.28		2	>
Ex	12.3		2	>
Lev	12.6		2	
	22.26		2	>
1 Sam	17.34		2	
Ezra	6.9		2	>
Ps	114.4		2	
Jn	1.29		2	
Rev	13.8	<	2	>
	17.14		2	
	19.7		2	
	22.1	<	2	

LAST (1) [ENDURE]

Ps	119.89		3	
1 Chr	16.15		2	
Ps	72.7		2	
	89.2		2	>
	90.5	<	2	
Is	45.17		2	
	51.6		2	
	55.3		2	
Ezek	4.4		2	
Lk	11.17		2	
1 Cor	9.25		2	
2 Cor	3.11		2	>
	4.18	<	2	>

LAST (2) [FINAL]

Mt	20.8	<	5	>
Jn	6.39		4	>
1 Cor	15.8		4	
Mt	27.19		3	
Ex	26.5		2	
	36.12		2	
Num	2.17		2	
2 Sam	19.11		2	
Mt	19.30		2	>
Mk	10.31		2	
	12.6		2	
Lk	13.30	<	2	
Acts	12.10		2	
Rev	1.8		2	>
	21.6		2	>

LAW

Ps	119.1		52	
Rom	7.1	<	23	>
	2.12	<	21	>
Gal	3.2	<	17	>
Neh	8.1		13	>
Ezra	7.6		10	
Rom	3.19	<	10	>
Deut	4.1		8	>
Ezek	20.11		8	
Gal	2.16		8	>

LAW (cont.)

2 Kgs	17.13		7	>
Neh	9.3	<	7	
Mt	12.2	<	6	
1 Cor	9.8		6	
Heb	7.5		6	>
	10.1		6	
Deut	6.1	<	5	>
Neh	10.28		5	
Lk	2.22	<	5	
Jn	7.19		5	>
Rom	4.13	<	5	>
	8.2	<	5	>
2 Cor	3.6		5	
Gal	5.3	<	5	>
Lev	26.3	<	4	
Deut	5.1	<	4	>
	11.1	<	4	>
	27.3	<	4	>
	31.9	<	4	
Josh	8.31		4	
2 Chr	34.2	<	4	>
Ezek	18.9		4	
Dan	9.10		4	
Acts	21.20		4	>
Gal	4.4	<	4	>
Lev	14.32	<	3	
	18.4	<	3	>
Deut	8.1	<	3	
	26.16		3	>
	28.15	<	3	>
	33.4		3	
1 Kgs	11.33	<	3	
2 Kgs	23.3	<	3	
2 Chr	31.3	<	3	
Neh	13.1	<	3	
Esth	1.13		3	
	4.11	<	3	
Ps	78.5		3	
Prov	28.4		3	>
Jer	8.7		3	
Ezek	11.12		3	
Dan	6.8		3	>
Mt	5.17		3	
	22.17		3	>
Mk	10.2		3	
Lk	6.2		3	
Jn	8.3	<	3	>
Acts	15.1		3	>
	23.3	<	3	>
Rom	5.13	<	3	>
	10.4		3	
Phil	3.5		3	
Heb	9.19	<	3	
Jas	2.8	<	3	
	4.11		3	
Gen	47.26		2	
Ex	34.11		2	
Lev	10.9		2	>

LAW (cont.)

Lev	20.8	<	2	
Deut	30.10	<	2	>
Josh	1.7		2	
	24.25	<	2	
2 Sam	22.22		2	
1 Kgs	2.3		2	>
	8.58		2	>
	9.4	<	2	
2 Kgs	22.2	<	2	>
1 Chr	22.12		2	
2 Chr	7.17	<	2	>
	19.8		2	
	23.11		2	
	30.5	<	2	>
	35.12	<	2	
Neh	12.26		2	>
Ps	18.21		2	>
	19.7	<	2	
	147.19		2	
Is	58.2		2	
Ezek	5.6	<	2	
Hab	1.4		2	
Mt	19.3		2	
Mk	2.24		2	>
	7.7		2	
	12.14		2	
Lk	16.16		2	
	20.22		2	
Jn	1.17		2	
	5.10		2	
Acts	13.15		2	
	18.13	<	2	
	22.3	<	2	>
	25.8	<	2	
Rom	6.14	<	2	>
	9.4	<	2	
	13.8		2	
Gal	6.2	<	2	
1 Tim	1.8		2	>
Heb	8.4	<	2	>
1 Jn	3.4		2	

LEADING

2 Kgs	10.1		3	
Josh	22.14		2	
1 Kgs	21.8		2	
2 Kgs	24.14		2	
1 Chr	11.15		2	>
Neh	11.3		2	

LEARN

Prov	19.8	<	7	
Ps	119.7		5	
Mt	11.25		3	
Phil	4.9		3	
1 Tim	5.4		3	
Gen	28.6		2	
Deut	31.12		2	

LEARN (cont.)

Josh	9.16		2	
Job	15.10		2	
	28.12		2	
Prov	1.7		2	>
	2.1	<	2	
	8.5		2	
	15.14	<	2	>
	17.10	<	2	>
	21.11		2	>
	23.12	<	2	>
Ecc	7.25		2	>
Is	23.1		2	
	26.9		2	
Jer	2.19		2	
Lk	10.21		2	
Eph	3.4		2	>

LETTER (2) [MESSAGE]

Ezra	4.7		6	
2 Kgs	10.1		5	
Esth	9.20	<	5	
Jer	29.1		5	
2 Kgs	5.5		4	
Esth	8.9		4	>
2 Pet	3.1		4	
2 Kgs	19.9		3	>
Neh	2.7		3	
Is	37.9		3	
Acts	15.20		3	
	23.25	<	3	
2 Cor	3.1	<	3	
	10.9		3	
1 Kgs	21.8		2	
Neh	6.5		2	
2 Cor	2.3		2	>
	7.8		2	
Col	4.16		2	
2 Thes	2.2		2	>
	3.14	<	2	
1 Tim	3.14		2	

LEVITES

Num	8.6	<	18	
1 Chr	15.2		15	>
Neh	12.1	<	12	>
Num	3.9	<	11	>
2 Chr	35.3	<	11	
	29.4		10	>
	31.2	<	10	
Josh	21.1		8	
1 Chr	9.2		8	
	23.2		8	>
2 Chr	30.15	<	7	>
Neh	10.9		7	>
	11.3	<	7	>
	13.5	<	7	
Num	18.1		6	
Judg	19.1	<	6	>

LEVITES (cont.)

2 Chr	23.2		6	>
Ezra	3.8	<	6	
	8.15	<	6	>
2 Chr	24.5	<	5	
	34.9		5	>
Lev	25.32		4	
Num	1.47		4	>
	4.2	<	4	
	16.1		4	
	35.2		4	
Deut	12.12		4	
Judg	17.7		4	>
1 Chr	24.6	<	4	>
2 Chr	5.4		4	
Ezra	6.16		4	>
Neh	8.7	<	4	>
Ex	32.26		3	
Deut	26.11		3	>
1 Chr	6.48		3	
	16.4	<	3	
	25.1	<	3	>
	26.1	<	3	
2 Chr	11.13		3	
Ezra	7.6	<	3	>
	10.5		3	
Neh	7.1		3	>
	9.4	<	3	
Ezek	48.12		3	
Num	2.17	<	2	>
	7.5		2	>
	31.30		2	
Deut	14.27		2	
	16.11		2	>
	17.9	<	2	>
	18.6	<	2	
	27.9	<	2	
	31.9		2	
Judg	18.3	<	2	>
1 Chr	28.13		2	>
2 Chr	8.14	<	2	
	13.9		2	
	17.8		2	
	19.8		2	>
	20.14	<	2	
Ezra	2.40	<	2	>
Heb	7.11		2	

LIE (2) [DECEIVE]

Jer	23.14		5	
Ezek	13.6		5	
Prov	19.1		4	
Jer	29.9	<	4	
Job	13.4		3	
Ps	119.69		3	>
Prov	6.12		3	
	12.17		3	>
Is	59.3		3	
Jer	9.3		3	

LIE (2)(cont.)

Jer	27.15		3	>
2 Cor	11.3		3	>
1 Jn	2.4	<	3	
Lev	19.11		2	
1 Kgs	22.22		2	
2 Chr	18.21		2	
Job	6.28		2	
Ps	35.19	<	2	>
	52.2		2	
	109.2		2	
	120.2	<	2	
	144.8		2	
Prov	14.5	<	2	
	17.4		2	
	30.6	<	2	
Is	28.15		2	>
	57.4		2	
Zech	5.3		2	
Mt	27.63	<	2	
Jn	8.44		2	
Acts	5.3		2	>
Rom	3.4		2	
	9.1		2	
1 Tim	4.1		2	
Tit	1.2		2	
1 Pet	2.1		2	>
1 Jn	1.6		2	>
Rev	21.8		2	>

LIFE (1)

Jn	6.27	<	12	>
	5.21	<	9	>
Ps	119.1		8	
1 Jn	5.11	<	7	
Is	38.10		6	
Ezek	33.8	<	6	
Prov	3.2	<	5	>
Jer	38.2		5	>
Ezek	14.14	<	5	
Lk	9.7	<	5	
Jn	4.10	<	5	>
Rom	6.4	<	5	>
	8.2	<	5	
Phil	1.11		5	>
1 Tim	6.12		5	
Rev	22.1	<	5	
1 Kgs	20.31	<	4	
Job	14.1	<	4	
Ps	90.9	<	4	>
	102.3	<	4	>
Prov	4.10	<	4	>
	13.3	<	4	>
	15.4	<	4	>
	16.15	<	4	
	22.4	<	4	>
Ecc	6.5	<	4	>
Jer	51.6	<	4	>
Ezek	13.18		4	>

LIFE (1)(cont.)

Ezek	20.11		4	
Mt	16.25		4	
Mk	8.35		4	>
Lk	12.15		4	
Jn	3.15		4	>
	10.10		4	>
	12.25	<	4	
Rom	5.10	<	4	>
1 Cor	4.15	<	4	
	15.19		4	
2 Cor	4.10	<	4	>
Gal	5.10		4	>
Phil	2.1	<	4	>
Tit	3.3	<	4	
1 Pet	1.3		4	
1 Jn	3.14	<	4	>
Gen	3.17	<	3	>
	9.4		3	
	19.15		3	
	44.30	<	3	>
Ex	21.6		3	
	30.12		3	
Lev	17.11		3	>
Deut	30.15	<	3	
	32.18		3	
2 Sam	19.5		3	>
1 Kgs	3.11	<	3	>
Job	7.1		3	>
	10.5		3	>
	21.13		3	
Prov	2.13	<	3	>
	10.2		3	>
	11.4	<	3	>
	23.14	<	3	
Ecc	2.3	<	3	>
	5.17	<	3	>
	8.13	<	3	>
Is	32.9		3	
	53.10		3	
Ezek	3.18		3	
	18.4		3	
	32.10		3	>
Mt	19.16	<	3	>
Mk	10.17		3	
Acts	27.10	<	3	
2 Cor	5.4	<	3	
Eph	4.1		3	>
	5.2	<	3	
Phil	3.3	<	3	>
Col	3.3	<	3	
2 Thes	3.6		3	
1 Jn	1.1		3	>
Gen	2.7	<	2	>
	4.15	<	2	>
	47.9	<	2	
Deut	12.23		2	>
1 Sam	1.11		2	>
	26.21		2	>

LIFE (1)(cont.)

1 Kgs	19.3		2	>
2 Kgs	7.4		2	
Neh	9.6		2	
Esth	7.7		2	
Job	9.18	<	2	
	11.17	<	2	>
	12.10	<	2	>
	27.1		2	
	29.2		2	
	33.4		2	>
	36.11		2	
Ps	27.4		2	
	34.12		2	>
	39.4		2	
	49.8		2	
	61.4		2	
	71.6		2	>
	72.13	<	2	
	78.33		2	
	103.5	<	2	>
	104.30	<	2	
Prov	12.19	<	2	>
	14.25	<	2	>
	20.20	<	2	>
	28.13		2	>
Ecc	1.2		2	>
	7.15	<	2	>
	9.9	<	2	
	12.1	<	2	
Is	55.3		2	
	57.2		2	
	65.20		2	
Jer	17.11		2	>
	21.8	<	2	
	22.15	<	2	>
	23.10	<	2	
Lam	5.9	<	2	
Amos	2.14		2	
Jon	1.6		2	>
Mt	10.39		2	
	18.8		2	>
Mk	6.14		2	
	9.43	<	2	
Lk	1.6		2	
	6.9		2	>
	7.37	<	2	>
	8.14	<	2	>
	17.33		2	>
	18.18	<	2	
Jn	1.4		2	
	17.2		2	
Acts	3.2	<	2	
	13.46		2	
Rom	2.7		2	
	7.9	<	2	>
	11.15		2	
2 Cor	1.12		2	>
Gal	2.20		2	>

LIFE (1)(cont.)

Gal	3.21	<	2	
	6.8	<	2	
Phil	4.1	<	2	
Col	1.10		2	>
	2.7	<	2	>
1 Thes	2.8		2	>
	5.12	<	2	
1 Tim	4.7		2	
2 Tim	1.1		2	>
	3.10	<	2	>
Tit	1.2		2	>
	2.3	<	2	>
Heb	12.11	<	2	>
1 Pet	3.7		2	>
	4.2	<	2	
2 Pet	3.3		2	
1 Jn	4.9	<	2	>
Rev	2.7		2	

LIFE (2) (TO LIFE)

1 Cor	15.4		8	
Ezek	37.3		6	
Jn	6.39	<	4	
2 Kgs	8.1		3	
Mt	22.28		3	
Job	14.7		2	
Mt	27.52	<	2	
Mk	12.23		2	
Lk	20.33		2	
Jn	11.23		2	
Rom	4.17		2	
	6.5		2	
Rev	20.4		2	

LIGHT (1)

Gen	1.3		8	
Is	60.2	<	7	
Jn	1.4		6	
	3.19		6	
Eph	5.8		6	
Jn	12.35	<	5	
2 Cor	4.2		5	
Ezek	10.4		4	>
Lk	11.33		4	
Lev	13.21		3	
2 Chr	7.1		3	
Job	24.13		3	>
Ezek	43.2		3	>
Mt	5.14	<	3	>
Acts	22.6		3	
	26.13		3	
1 Jn	1.5		3	>
	2.8	<	3	
Ex	16.7		2	
	24.16		2	
	33.18		2	
	35.3		2	
Lev	9.6		2	

LIGHT (1)(cont.)

Num	14.10		2	
	16.19		2	
Job	3.4		2	
	18.5	<	2	
	38.15	<	2	
Ps	72.5		2	
	97.4		2	
	119.105		2	
	139.11		2	
Is	5.20		2	
	9.2		2	
	42.6		2	
	49.6		2	
Ezek	1.27		2	
	11.22	<	2	
	32.7		2	
Amos	5.18		2	
Mic	7.8		2	
Mt	4.16		2	>
	6.22	<	2	
Lk	8.16		2	
Jn	8.12		2	>
	11.9		2	>
Acts	13.11	<	2	
Rom	13.12		2	
Rev	8.12		2	

LOSS

Ex	22.5	<	3	
	21.21		2	>
Lev	12.4		2	
Acts	27.10		2	
Phil	3.7		2	>

LOVE

1 Jn	4.7	<	23	>
Ps	119.41	<	19	
1 Cor	13.1		11	>
1 Jn	3.1	<	11	>
Jn	14.15	<	9	>
	21.7	<	9	
Song	1.2		8	>
Jn	15.9	<	8	>
Ps	89.1	<	7	>
Gen	29.18		6	
Deut	7.7	<	6	
Ps	107.1	<	6	>
Song	8.2	<	6	
Jn	13.1	<	6	>
2 Cor	8.6	<	6	>
2 Jn	1		6	
Ps	103.4	<	5	
	109.4	<	5	
	118.1	<	5	>
Song	2.3	<	5	>
	4.1	<	5	>
Rom	8.28		5	>
Eph	5.2	<	5	>

LOVE (cont.)

Deut	10.12		4	>
1 Sam	18.1		4	
2 Sam	13.1	<	4	
1 Kgs	3.3		4	
Ps	31.7		4	>
	33.5	<	4	
Song	3.1	<	4	>
Is	54.7		4	
	63.7	<	4	>
Jer	31.3		4	>
Ezek	16.5		4	
Mk	12.30		4	
Lk	6.27		4	>
	7.5	<	4	
Rom	13.8	<	4	>
Gal	5.6		4	
1 Jn	2.5		4	>
	5.1	<	4	
Gen	34.3		3	
Deut	11.1	<	3	
	30.6		3	
Ps	5.7	<	3	
	25.6		3	>
	36.5		3	>
	40.8	<	3	
	52.3	<	3	
	59.10		3	>
	69.13	<	3	
	86.5	<	3	>
	106.1		3	>
	145.8		3	>
Prov	5.15	<	3	
	8.17	<	3	
Ecc	3.5		3	
	9.1		3	
Song	6.4	<	3	>
Lam	2.13		3	>
Hos	2.14	<	3	>
	9.1		3	
	11.1		3	>
Zech	8.2		3	
Mal	1.2		3	>
Mt	5.43		3	>
Jn	3.16		3	
	17.23	<	3	
Rom	9.13	<	3	
1 Cor	16.14		3	
Eph	3.17	<	3	>
	4.2	<	3	>
Col	1.4		3	>
	3.12	<	3	
1 Thes	3.6	<	3	>
2 Thes	2.10	<	3	>
1 Tim	6.2		3	
Phlm	5		3	
1 Pet	1.8		3	>
Jude	1		3	
Gen	37.3		2	

LOVE (cont.)

Ex	20.6		2	>
Lev	19.18		2	
Num	14.18		2	
Deut	5.10	<	2	>
	13.3		2	
	28.54		2	
	33.3		2	
Judg	16.4		2	
1 Sam	20.17		2	
2 Sam	1.26		2	
	12.24	<	2	>
1 Chr	16.34		2	
2 Chr	6.14	<	2	>
	7.3	<	2	
Neh	13.22		2	
Ps	18.1	<	2	
	26.3	<	2	
	44.3		2	>
	57.3		2	
	85.7	<	2	>
	108.4	<	2	>
	138.2		2	
	143.8		2	
Prov	4.6	<	2	>
	13.24	<	2	
	15.9		2	
	22.5		2	
Song	7.6	<	2	>
Is	49.10		2	
	56.6		2	
	66.10		2	
Jer	2.2		2	>
	3.4	<	2	
	12.3	<	2	
	16.5		2	>
Lam	3.22	<	2	>
Ezek	33.31		2	
Dan	9.4		2	
	10.11		2	>
Hos	1.6		2	>
	3.1	<	2	>
	6.4		2	
Mic	7.18	<	2	
Mt	6.5	<	2	
	10.37		2	
	22.37		2	>
	23.6	<	2	>
Lk	10.27		2	>
	11.42	<	2	
	14.26		2	
	16.13		2	
Jn	5.20		2	
	11.5	<	2	>
	12.25	<	2	>
	16.27	<	2	>
Rom	5.5		2	
	12.9		2	>
1 Cor	8.1		2	

LOVE (cont.)

2 Cor	2.4		2	
	11.11		2	>
	13.11	<	2	
Eph	1.4		2	>
	2.4	<	2	>
	6.23	<	2	
Phil	1.9		2	>
	2.1	<	2	
1 Thes	1.3		2	>
	4.9	<	2	>
	5.8	<	2	
1 Tim	1.5		2	>
2 Tim	1.7		2	>
	3.4	<	2	>
	4.8	<	2	
Tit	2.2	<	2	>
Heb	13.1	<	2	
Jas	2.5	<	2	
3 Jn	1		2	
Rev	2.4	<	2	>
	3.9	<	2	

LOYAL

1 Kgs	12.4	<	3	
2 Kgs	2.2		3	
Gen	21.23	<	2	
Num	32.11		2	
1 Sam	20.14		2	
	29.6		2	
2 Sam	2.5		2	>
	3.6	<	2	
	15.6		2	>
	20.2	<	2	
1 Chr	12.23		2	
2 Chr	10.4		2	
Ps	40.10		2	
Dan	6.16		2	
Rom	16.10		2	

LUST

Ezek	23.5	<	9	
Rev	18.3		3	
2 Pet	2.10	<	2	>

M

MAGIC

Ex	7.11		4	>
	8.7	<	3	>
Is	47.9		3	
Dan	2.2	<	3	
	5.7	<	3	
Acts	13.6		3	
Gen	41.8		2	
Is	3.3	<	2	
Acts	8.9		2	

MAJESTY

Dan	2.4		13	>
2 Sam	19.19	<	11	
	14.4	<	9	>
1 Kgs	1.2		9	>
Dan	6.6	<	9	
	4.19	<	7	>
	3.9	<	6	>
2 Sam	24.3		4	
Ezra	4.12		4	>
1 Sam	17.32		3	
	26.17		3	
2 Sam	16.2	<	3	
Dan	5.10	<	3	>
2 Sam	13.24		2	>
	15.15	<	2	>
	18.28		2	>
1 Kgs	3.17	<	2	
2 Kgs	6.12		2	
1 Chr	21.3		2	
Ezra	5.8	<	2	
Neh	2.3		2	
Esth	1.4		2	
	5.4		2	
	7.3		2	>
Ps	45.3		2	
	145.5		2	
Acts	26.7		2	

MAN OF GOD

2 Kgs	1.9		5	
Judg	13.6		2	
1 Kgs	17.18		2	
Neh	12.24		2	

MANKIND

Rom	5.14		3	
Eph	4.6	<	3	
Rev	9.15		3	
	14.3		3	
Gen	6.1	<	2	
Is	40.5		2	
Zeph	1.3		2	
Mt	24.9		2	
Jn	1.4		2	
Gal	3.8		2	
1 Tim	2.5		2	

MANNA

Ex	16.31		4	
Num	11.6		2	
Deut	8.3		2	
Jn	6.31		2	

MASTER

Gen	24.9		23	
Lk	12.36		10	>
Ex	21.4		6	
Mt	24.45		6	>

MASTER (cont.)

Lk	16.1		6	>
Gen	39.2		5	
Mt	25.18	<	5	
Gen	32.4		3	
1 Sam	26.15	<	3	
	30.13	<	3	
2 Kgs	2.3		3	
	5.3		3	
Lk	14.21	<	3	
Eph	6.5		3	
Gen	44.5		2	
Judg	19.10		2	
1 Sam	25.14	<	2	>
	29.4		2	>
2 Sam	9.9		2	
	16.3		2	
Prov	30.4		2	
Mal	1.6		2	
Mt	10.24		2	
Lk	8.24		2	>
	9.33	<	2	
	19.31		2	
Jn	15.15		2	
Rom	6.14		2	
1 Cor	7.4		2	
Col	3.22		2	>
	4.1	<	2	
1 Tim	6.1		2	

MEANS

Rom	5.5		3	
	7.8		3	
Eph	3.6	<	3	>
Rom	15.13		2	
1 Cor	1.21		2	>
	15.21	<	2	
Gal	3.11		2	
Col	1.22		2	>
Heb	10.1		2	>

MERCY

Neh	9.17		6	
Ps	119.58		5	
Lam	2.2	<	4	>
	3.3	<	4	
Lk	1.50		4	
Rom	9.15		4	
	11.30		4	>
Jude	2		4	
Deut	13.8		3	
Ps	80.3	<	3	
	86.3	<	3	
	145.8		3	
1 Tim	1.2		3	
2 Tim	1.2		3	
Jas	2.13		3	
Deut	7.2		2	
	19.13		2	

MERCY (cont.)

1 Kgs	8.49		2	
2 Kgs	1.13		2	
	3.10		2	
Ps	41.4	<	2	
	51.1		2	
	103.4	<	2	
	123.2		2	
Jer	16.5	<	2	
	31.2	<	2	
	42.12		2	
Ezek	7.4		2	>
Dan	9.9		2	
Hos	2.4		2	
Joel	2.13		2	
Zech	1.12		2	
Mal	3.17		2	
Mt	5.7		2	
	11.22	<	2	
	18.33	<	2	
Lk	10.12		2	

MESSAGE

1 Cor	14.1	<	15	>
Jer	23.18		9	
Rom	10.8		9	
Mk	4.14	<	8	
Mt	13.19		6	
Lk	1.2		6	
Acts	13.15		5	>
1 Cor	1.6		5	>
1 Kgs	5.2		4	
Is	8.16	<	4	
Rev	2.1	<	4	>
Gen	50.4		3	
Num	22.5		3	>
Deut	18.20		3	
2 Kgs	19.3	<	3	>
1 Chr	25.1		3	
Neh	6.2		3	
Is	21.1		3	>
	37.3		3	
Jer	29.19		3	
Hag	1.1		3	>
Zech	1.1		3	>
	7.1	<	3	>
Lk	8.12		3	
Jn	3.11		3	>
	12.38	<	3	
	17.8		3	
Acts	2.17	<	3	>
	4.4	<	3	
	7.14		3	>
	8.4	<	3	>
	10.36		3	>
	20.2	<	3	>
1 Cor	12.8	<	3	>
1 Thes	2.13	<	3	
2 Thes	3.1		3	

MESSAGE (cont.)

2 Tim	4.2		3	
2 Pet	1.19		3	
1 Jn	2.7	<	3	>
Rev	3.1	<	3	
	11.3	<	3	
Num	23.5	<	2	>
	24.3	<	2	
Judg	3.19		2	
2 Sam	11.5		2	
1 Kgs	16.1	<	2	
	20.7	<	2	>
	21.14	<	2	
2 Kgs	22.16		2	
2 Chr	25.17		2	
	34.24	<	2	>
Esth	4.10		2	
Is	28.9		2	
	40.6	<	2	
Jer	2.2		2	
	11.6	<	2	
	18.2	<	2	>
	19.2	<	2	>
	20.8	<	2	>
	27.3		2	
	37.2	<	2	>
Ezek	12.10	<	2	>
	36.1		2	
Dan	4.1		2	
	10.1		2	
Amos	3.1	<	2	
	8.11		2	
Jon	3.2		2	
Zech	4.6		2	
	8.1	<	2	>
Mt	11.12		2	
Mk	16.7		2	
Acts	11.19	<	2	
	14.3	<	2	>
	18.5	<	2	>
	19.6	<	2	>
	28.23		2	
1 Cor	2.4	<	2	
	11.4		2	>
	13.8	<	2	>
	15.2	<	2	
2 Cor	5.19		2	>
Col	1.5		2	
1 Thes	1.6		2	>
Tit	1.3		2	>
Heb	13.7	<	2	
Rev	1.2		2	>

MESSIAH

Jn	7.26		6	
Mt	24.5	<	3	
Lk	23.2	<	3	>
Jn	1.20		3	
Mt	1.12		2	>

MESSIAH (cont.)

Mt	16.16		2	
	22.42		2	>
	26.63		2	>
	27.17	<	2	
Mk	12.35		2	>
	13.21	<	2	>
Lk	20.41		2	
	24.26	<	2	
Jn	4.25	<	2	
Acts	2.31		2	>
	3.18	<	2	>
	4.26	<	2	>
	17.3		2	>
	18.5	<	2	

MIGHT

Deut	32.4		6	
Ps	68.15		5	
Lk	1.17		5	
Ps	145.4		4	
Jer	32.17	<	3	
	48.1		3	
Rev	18.8		3	
Ex	15.11		2	
Deut	2.10		2	>
Josh	22.22		2	
2 Sam	6.5		2	
1 Chr	16.24		2	
Ps	77.12		2	>
	89.8		2	>
	90.16	<	2	
	96.3	<	2	
	99.2		2	
	103.7		2	
	118.15		2	
	132.2		2	
Jer	51.9	<	2	
2 Thes	1.7		2	
Rev	5.2		2	

MIND (1) [THINK]

Jer	26.3	<	3	
	34.11		3	
Amos	7.3		3	>
Acts	28.6		3	
Rom	1.21		3	
	11.8		3	>
1 Cor	2.2		3	
	14.14		3	
2 Cor	3.14	<	3	>
Ex	32.12		2	
Deut	28.28		2	
1 Sam	15.29		2	
1 Chr	28.9		2	
Ps	73.7		2	
Prov	6.14		2	
Dan	2.5	<	2	
Jon	3.9		2	>

MIND (1)(cont.)

Mt	13.15		2	
	21.29		2	>
Mk	12.30		2	
Lk	24.38		2	
Jn	12.40		2	
Rom	7.23		2	>
	8.5	<	2	
1 Cor	7.37		2	
Eph	4.18		2	
Phil	4.7		2	

MIRACLE

Ex	4.8		6	
Ps	78.11	<	4	
Mt	12.38	<	4	>
Jn	6.2		4	>
Mt	11.20		3	>
	16.1		3	
Mk	6.2		3	
Lk	11.16	<	3	
Jn	2.11		3	>
Acts	2.19		3	
	4.16		3	>
1 Cor	12.10		3	
Ex	10.1		2	>
	11.9	<	2	
Num	14.11		2	
Neh	9.10		2	
Ps	88.10		2	
	105.5		2	
Jer	32.20		2	
Dan	4.2		2	
Mt	13.54	<	2	>
Mk	8.11		2	>
	16.17		2	
Jn	4.48	<	2	
	7.21	<	2	
	12.18	<	2	
Acts	8.6	<	2	
Rev	13.13		2	
	19.20		2	

MORTAL

Ezek	21.2	<	7	>
	3.1	<	6	>
	8.5	<	6	
	12.2	<	6	>
	33.2	<	6	>
	2.1		4	>
	20.3		4	>
	37.3	<	4	>
1 Cor	15.42		4	
Ezek	11.2		3	>
	22.2	<	3	>
	24.2	<	3	>
	28.2	<	3	>
	43.7		3	>
	4.1	<	2	>

MORTAL (cont.)

Ezek	13.2	<	2	>
	14.3	<	2	>
	23.2	<	2	>
	29.2	<	2	>
	30.2	<	2	>
	32.2	<	2	>
	36.1	<	2	>
	39.1	<	2	>
2 Cor	4.10		2	>

MOST HIGH

Gen	14.18		4	
Lk	1.32		2	

MOURN

Zech	12.10		7	
Gen	50.3		6	
Ezek	24.17		4	
Joel	1.8		4	>
Gen	37.34		3	>
2 Sam	14.2	<	3	
Ps	35.13		3	
Jer	9.10	<	3	
	16.4		3	
	48.17	<	3	>
Mic	1.8		3	
Rev	18.11		3	
Lev	10.6		2	
	21.5		2	
Judg	20.22		2	>
2 Sam	1.12		2	
	11.26		2	
	19.1		2	
1 Kgs	13.29		2	>
	14.13	<	2	
2 Chr	35.24		2	
Is	61.2		2	
Jer	22.10		2	>
	25.33		2	
	49.3	<	2	
	51.8		2	
Ezek	32.16	<	2	
Amos	8.3		2	>
Zech	7.3		2	

MYSTERY

Dan	2.18		7	
	5.12	<	2	
Rev	12.1		2	

N

NAKED

Ezek	16.7		5	
Is	20.2		4	
Mt	25.36		4	
Gen	3.7	<	3	

NAKED (cont.)

Gen	9.21		3	
Ezek	18.7		2	
	23.10		2	
Hos	2.3		2	
Mic	1.8		2	
Rev	3.17		2	

NAME (2) [GOD OR JESUS

Is	48.1	<	4	
Ezek	20.9		4	
	36.20		4	
Acts	4.10	<	4	>
	19.5		4	
Deut	18.19		3	
1 Kgs	2.8	<	3	
1 Chr	16.2		3	
	29.13		3	
Ps	113.1		3	
	148.5		3	>
Jer	26.9		3	>
	29.9		3	
	44.16		3	
Ezek	39.7		3	
Mk	9.37		3	
Jn	14.13		3	>
	16.23	<	3	>
Acts	3.6	<	3	>
	9.15	<	3	
Ex	3.13		2	
	20.7		2	
Lev	19.12	<	2	>
	22.2	<	2	
Deut	5.11		2	>
	10.8		2	
Josh	9.18		2	
2 Sam	6.2		2	
1 Kgs	1.17		2	>
Ps	66.2		2	
	68.4		2	
	135.1		2	
	138.2		2	>
Jer	10.6		2	
	14.14	<	2	
	23.21		2	
Ezek	43.7		2	
Dan	9.6		2	
Amos	5.8	<	2	>
Mt	7.22	<	2	
	18.5		2	
Lk	1.31		2	>
	9.48		2	
Jn	12.13		2	
	17.11	<	2	
Acts	5.28	<	2	
	10.43		2	
Phil	2.9		2	
2 Thes	3.6		2	
Jas	5.10		2	

NAME (2)(cont.)

Rev	3.12		2	

NATURE

Rom	8.3	<	12	
Gal	5.16	<	5	
Rom	7.5		4	>
Prov	10.6		2	
Phil	2.6		2	

NAZIRITE

Num	6.2		12	
Judg	13.5		2	
Amos	2.11		2	

NEED

Mt	6.2		7	
2 Cor	9.1	<	6	
Phil	4.6		5	
1 Kgs	4.22	<	4	
Prov	30.8		4	>
	31.5	<	4	
Lk	12.19	<	4	
1 Cor	12.21	<	4	>
Ex	16.16		3	
	22.11		3	
Deut	15.7	<	3	
2 Kgs	4.13		3	
Ps	72.4		3	>
	145.15		3	
Lk	19.31	<	3	
Heb	7.11		3	>
Gen	33.11		2	
Ex	36.1	<	2	
Lev	13.11		2	
Deut	24.14	<	2	
2 Kgs	12.5		2	
	25.24		2	
Job	34.23		2	>
Ps	109.16		2	
Jer	31.12		2	
Mk	2.17		2	
Lk	11.3	<	2	>
Acts	4.34		2	
	27.3		2	>
1 Cor	11.7		2	>
2 Cor	8.13		2	>
	11.9		2	>
1 Thes	4.9	<	2	>
Tit	3.13		2	
Heb	10.18		2	
2 Pet	1.3		2	
1 Jn	2.27		2	>

NEGLECT

Ps	119.87		6	
Mt	23.23		2	
Lk	11.42		2	
Acts	6.1		2	

NEIGHBOUR

Jer	25.9		3	
Lk	10.27		3	
1 Kgs	4.24		2	
Ezra	1.4		2	
Prov	3.28		2	
	25.9		2	
Ezek	16.26		2	
	36.3		2	
Mk	12.31		2	
Lk	1.58		2	
	15.6	<	2	

NEVER AGAIN

Gen	9.11	<	3	
	8.21		2	>
Job	3.4		2	
Jer	22.10		2	
Ezek	29.15		2	
	34.10		2	

NEW

Lk	5.36		7	
Judg	16.7	<	4	
Mt	9.16		4	
Mk	2.21	<	4	
Is	11.1		3	
	65.15		3	>
Jer	31.22		3	
Rev	21.1		3	
Lev	23.14		2	
Num	32.14		2	
2 Kgs	16.14		2	
Ecc	1.9		2	
Is	42.9	<	2	>
	62.2		2	
Zech	3.4		2	
Acts	17.19		2	
2 Cor	5.17		2	
Eph	4.23		2	
Col	3.10		2	
Heb	8.8		2	>
	9.10	<	2	
1 Jn	2.7		2	
Rev	3.12	<	2	

NEW MOON FESTIVAL

1 Sam	20.5		5	
Ezek	46.1	<	3	
Is	1.13		2	

O

OBEY

Ps	119.2		39	
Deut	4.1		10	>
	30.2	<	10	>
2 Kgs	17.13		9	>

OBEY (cont.)

Jer	35.8		8	
Deut	6.1	<	7	>
	28.1	<	7	>
Lev	26.3	<	6	
Deut	5.1	<	6	>
	11.1	<	6	>
1 Kgs	8.23		6	>
Jer	11.3		6	>
Ezek	20.11		6	
Deut	8.1	<	5	>
	26.14		5	>
	33.3	<	5	>
Josh	22.2		5	>
1 Sam	15.13		5	
Rom	6.12	<	5	
Lev	19.14	<	4	>
	25.17		4	>
Deut	7.9	<	4	>
	32.17	<	4	>
1 Kgs	2.3		4	>
2 Chr	6.14		4	>
	34.2	<	4	>
Neh	9.16		4	
Prov	28.4		4	
Jn	8.31	<	4	>
	14.15		4	>
Rom	13.1		4	
Phil	2.8		4	>
Heb	13.9		4	
1 Jn	2.3		4	>
Deut	10.13		3	>
	12.1	<	3	>
	27.1	<	3	>
Josh	1.7		3	
1 Kgs	11.9		3	>
1 Chr	21.4		3	>
Ps	78.7		3	
Ecc	8.5		3	
Is	66.2	<	3	
Jer	3.13	<	3	
	7.23	<	3	
	17.23	<	3	
	26.4	<	3	
	42.5		3	>
Lk	8.15	<	3	
Jn	15.10	<	3	
Acts	5.21	<	3	
Rom	2.25	<	3	>
	4.13	<	3	>
Gal	3.10		3	
	5.3		3	>
Col	3.6	<	3	>
1 Pet	1.2		3	
Gen	17.1		2	>
	22.12		2	
	24.37		2	
Ex	12.24		2	
	20.6	<	2	

OBEY (cont.)

Ex	23.21		2	>
Lev	18.4		2	>
Num	3.42		2	
	9.19	<	2	
Deut	13.4	<	2	
	18.15	<	2	
	21.18		2	
	29.9	<	2	>
	31.12	<	2	>
Josh	14.8		2	
Judg	2.17		2	>
1 Sam	12.14		2	>
	13.13	<	2	
2 Sam	22.22		2	>
	24.4	<	2	
2 Kgs	18.12	<	2	
	21.8		2	>
	23.3	<	2	
1 Chr	28.7		2	>
	29.19	<	2	
2 Chr	30.8	<	2	
Neh	10.28		2	
Esth	2.20	<	2	>
Ps	15.2	<	2	
	18.21	<	2	>
	19.8	<	2	
	25.10		2	
	33.1	<	2	>
	34.9	<	2	
	37.18		2	
	81.11		2	
	103.18		2	
	105.28		2	>
	128.1		2	
Is	11.3		2	
	59.21	<	2	
	65.13		2	>
Jer	13.10	<	2	
	16.11	<	2	>
	22.5		2	
Ezek	11.19		2	
	18.9		2	
Mic	4.5		2	>
Mal	4.2		2	
Mt	7.24		2	>
	23.3		2	
Lk	6.47		2	>
	10.17		2	>
	17.6		2	>
Acts	3.22		2	>
	7.39		2	
Rom	8.7		2	
	10.5		2	
Gal	6.2	<	2	
Eph	6.1	<	2	
Phil	3.6	<	2	
2 Tim	2.5		2	
Heb	5.8		2	

OBEY (cont.)

Heb	11.7		2	
1 Pet	3.6		2	
1 Jn	3.22	<	2	
	5.2		2	
Rev	22.7		2	

OBSERVE

Esth	9.19		7	
Num	9.2		6	
Lev	23.14	<	5	>
Ex	13.9		3	
Lev	16.29		3	
Num	15.2		3	
Is	56.2		3	
Jer	17.22		3	
Deut	5.12		2	

OFFER

Num	29.3	<	27	
	28.4		21	>
Lev	7.2	<	20	>
	22.2	<	19	>
Ezek	46.2	<	18	
Lev	2.1	<	16	>
	23.8	<	15	>
Ex	29.3	<	13	>
Deut	12.6		13	>
Lev	5.6		11	>
	6.2	<	10	>
Num	15.3		10	>
	6.11	<	9	>
Heb	10.1		9	>
Lev	4.21	<	8	>
Ezek	45.13	<	8	>
Ex	35.5	<	7	>
Lev	9.2	<	7	
Num	5.9	<	7	>
	18.9		7	
1 Sam	2.13	<	7	>
2 Chr	29.7	<	7	>
Jer	44.3		7	
Heb	9.2	<	7	
Lev	14.11		6	>
2 Chr	7.1	<	6	>
Neh	10.33		6	
Ezek	20.26		6	
	43.19	<	6	>
	44.7	<	6	>
Ex	30.8	<	5	
Lev	1.2		5	>
Num	7.3	<	5	>
2 Sam	24.22	<	5	
1 Kgs	3.2		5	
2 Kgs	12.3		5	
1 Chr	21.23		5	>
	23.29	<	5	
Ezra	6.3		5	>
Mal	1.7		5	>

OFFER (cont.)

Gen	4.3		4	
Ex	25.2		4	
	34.15		4	>
Lev	10.12		4	
	16.1	<	4	>
Num	23.2		4	
Josh	22.26		4	
2 Chr	31.2	<	4	>
	35.9	<	4	
Ezra	1.4		4	>
	3.4	<	4	>
	8.28	<	4	>
Neh	13.5	<	4	
Is	57.5	<	4	
Ezek	16.18		4	
1 Cor	10.18		4	
Ex	5.3		3	
	8.8		3	
	22.20		3	>
	40.6	<	3	
Lev	3.1	<	3	>
	17.3	<	3	
	19.5		3	
	21.6		3	>
	27.9		3	
Judg	13.15		3	
1 Sam	1.3		3	>
	10.3		3	>
	15.15		3	>
	16.2	<	3	
2 Sam	6.13		3	
1 Kgs	1.9		3	
	8.62	<	3	>
	12.26	<	3	>
	13.1	<	3	
	22.43	<	3	
2 Kgs	10.19		3	
	17.32	<	3	
	23.5	<	3	
1 Chr	16.1		3	
	29.5	<	3	
2 Chr	30.14	<	3	>
Ezra	7.15	<	3	>
Ps	66.2		3	
Jer	11.12		3	
Ezek	18.6		3	
	40.39		3	
	42.13		3	>
Dan	8.11		3	>
Joel	1.9		3	>
Mal	3.3	<	3	
1 Cor	8.1		3	>
Phil	2.16		3	
Heb	8.3	<	3	>
	11.4	<	3	
	13.11		3	
Gen	22.2		2	
Ex	13.12		2	

OFFER (cont.)

Ex	18.12		2	
	23.15	<	2	
	28.38		2	>
	36.3	<	2	
Lev	8.28	<	2	>
	15.15	<	2	>
Num	4.7	<	2	>
	9.7	<	2	
Deut	33.10	<	2	
Judg	6.18		2	
	11.31		2	
	21.4	<	2	
1 Sam	6.14		2	>
	7.6	<	2	
	13.9		2	
2 Kgs	5.17		2	
	15.4	<	2	>
2 Chr	2.4	<	2	
	8.12	<	2	>
	13.11		2	
	28.4		2	>
	33.17	<	2	>
Ezra	2.63	<	2	>
Neh	12.43		2	>
Ps	56.12		2	
	69.21	<	2	
	72.10		2	
	106.28		2	
	116.12		2	
Prov	3.9		2	
Is	1.11		2	
	19.15	<	2	
	65.3		2	>
	66.3	<	2	
Jer	19.4		2	
Dan	9.21	<	2	
	11.17		2	
Hos	4.13	<	2	>
	9.4	<	2	
Amos	4.5		2	>
	5.22	<	2	
Mic	6.6		2	
Mal	2.12	<	2	>
Mt	5.23		2	
Lk	5.14		2	>
	21.4		2	>
Acts	14.13		2	>
	15.20	<	2	
	21.25		2	
Rom	12.1	<	2	
	15.16		2	
Heb	5.1	<	2	
	7.27		2	>
Rev	2.14		2	

ONE ANOTHER

Jn	13.14	<	5	
Gal	5.13		4	>

ONE ANOTHER (cont.)

Eph	4.2		3	>
Phil	2.1		3	
Col	3.9		3	
Heb	10.24		3	
1 Jn	4.7	<	3	
Mt	24.7	<	2	
Jn	15.12		2	
Rom	12.10		2	>
	14.13	<	2	>
	15.7	<	2	>
1 Cor	6.8		2	
2 Cor	13.11		2	
Eph	5.19	<	2	
1 Thes	4.9	<	2	>
	5.11	<	2	
Heb	13.1		2	
Jas	5.9	<	2	
1 Pet	3.8		2	>
	5.5	<	2	
1 Jn	3.11		2	>

OPPRESS

Is	58.3		4	>
	59.9	<	4	>
Deut	28.29		3	
1 Sam	12.3		3	
Ps	72.2		3	>
	119.122		3	
Is	14.2		3	
Judg	10.8		2	
2 Kgs	13.4		2	
Neh	5.7		2	
	9.10		2	
Ps	34.2		2	>
	55.3		2	
	106.42	<	2	>
	107.39	<	2	
Prov	22.8		2	
Ecc	4.1		2	>
Is	10.1		2	
	51.13		2	
	60.14	<	2	>
Jer	22.3		2	
	30.16		2	
Ezek	45.8		2	>
Zeph	3.1		2	

ORDAIN

Ex	29.9	<	7	>
Lev	8.12	<	6	>
	6.20		2	>
	7.35	<	2	>

ORPHAN

Deut	24.17		4	
	16.11		2	
	26.12		2	>
Job	31.17		2	

ORPHAN (cont.)

Ps	109.9		2	
Is	1.17		2	

OWE

Mt	18.24		4	
Deut	15.1		3	
Lk	7.41		3	
	16.5		2	

P

PAGAN

2 Kgs	23.5		5	
	17.9	<	4	>
2 Chr	33.3		4	>
Is	65.3		4	>
Lev	18.24		3	
2 Chr	34.3	<	3	
Ex	34.15		2	
1 Kgs	15.12	<	2	
	22.43		2	
2 Kgs	15.4	<	2	>
	21.3		2	
2 Chr	14.3		2	>
	28.4		2	
Hos	4.14		2	
Zeph	1.4		2	
Mt	6.7	<	2	

PAIN

Lam	1.12		4	
Lk	16.23		4	
Ps	38.3		3	
Rev	16.2		3	
Num	5.24		2	
1 Chr	4.9		2	
2 Chr	21.15		2	
Job	30.17		2	
Is	13.6		2	>
	26.17		2	
	53.3		2	
Jer	4.19		2	
	22.23		2	
Lam	3.19		2	
Gal	4.19		2	
Rev	9.5		2	

PARABLE

Mt	13.3		12	
Mk	4.2	<	8	
Lk	8.4		4	
Ezek	17.2		2	
Mt	21.33		2	>
Mk	12.1		2	
Lk	12.16		2	>
	18.1		2	>
	20.9	<	2	>

PARALYSE

Mk	2.3		4	>
Mt	9.2		3	
	12.10		2	
Lk	5.18		2	>

PASSOVER

2 Chr	35.1		10	
Ex	12.11		8	
Num	9.2		7	
2 Chr	30.1		6	
Lk	22.1		6	
Mk	14.1		5	>
Deut	16.1		4	
Mt	26.2		4	>
2 Kgs	23.21		3	
1 Cor	5.7		3	
Ezra	6.19		2	
Jn	2.13		2	
	12.1	<	2	>
	18.28		2	>

PATIENT

Jas	5.7		6	
Lam	3.26		3	
Rev	2.2	<	3	
Mt	18.26		2	
Rom	15.4		2	
1 Cor	13.4		2	
2 Cor	6.4		2	
Heb	6.12		2	
2 Pet	3.9		2	

PEACE

1 Chr	22.9		4	>
Mt	10.12		4	
Lk	10.5		4	
1 Kgs	22.1		3	
2 Chr	14.1		3	>
Ps	122.6		3	
Zech	8.12		3	>
Jn	20.19		3	
Eph	2.14	<	3	
2 Jn	3		3	
Deut	12.9		2	
Josh	10.1		2	>
Judg	3.11		2	>
	6.23	<	2	
	18.7		2	
2 Sam	15.9		2	
1 Kgs	5.4	<	2	
2 Kgs	9.22		2	
Job	3.18		2	
Ps	37.11		2	
	85.8		2	
	120.6		2	
Is	9.6		2	
	11.6		2	
	27.5	<	2	

PEACE (cont.)

Is	32.17		2	>
	54.10		2	>
	57.2		2	
Jer	14.13		2	
	30.5		2	
Mt	5.9		2	
Lk	1.28		2	>
	2.14	<	2	
	12.51		2	
	19.38		2	
Jn	14.27		2	
Rom	14.17		2	>
	15.13	<	2	>
2 Cor	13.11		2	
Eph	6.15		2	
Phil	4.7		2	
Col	1.2		2	
	3.15		2	
1 Thes	5.13		2	
Heb	12.11		2	>
Jas	3.17		2	

PERFECT

Ps	119.45		4	
1 Jn	4.12		4	
Heb	7.11		3	
	9.9		3	
Jas	1.4		3	>
2 Sam	22.26		2	
Ps	18.25		2	>
	19.7	<	2	
Song	4.2		2	
Ezek	28.12	<	2	
2 Cor	13.9		2	
Heb	10.1		2	>

PERSECUTE

Mt	5.10		4	
Ps	119.84		3	
Acts	22.4		3	
	26.11		3	
1 Thes	3.3	<	3	
2 Tim	3.11		3	
Ps	109.16		2	
	129.1		2	
Acts	9.4	<	2	
Gal	1.13		2	
1 Thes	2.14		2	>

PHARISEES

Mt	23.2	<	8	
Lk	11.37		6	>
Jn	7.32		5	>
	9.13	<	5	
Acts	23.6		5	
Mt	12.2		4	
	16.1	<	4	
Mk	2.16		4	>

PHARISEES (cont.)

Mk	7.1		4	>
Lk	5.17		4	>
	7.30	<	4	
Mt	9.11		3	
	22.15	<	3	>
Lk	18.10	<	3	>
Jn	8.3	<	3	>
	11.46		3	>
Mt	15.1		2	>
	19.3		2	
Mk	8.11	<	2	
Lk	6.2	<	2	>
	14.1	<	2	>
Jn	12.19	<	2	

PHYSICAL

Lev	21.17		4	
1 Cor	15.44		3	
1 Pet	4.1	<	3	
Rom	2.27		2	
Col	1.22		2	>

PITY

Mt	20.30		3	
Lk	18.13	<	3	
Ps	102.13		2	
Jer	48.1		2	
Zech	11.5		2	
Mt	9.27		2	
Mk	10.47		2	

PLACE OF WORSHIP

Deut	16.2	<	6	>
Ex	22.8	<	3	
Deut	12.18		3	
1 Sam	9.14		3	
2 Kgs	23.10		3	
2 Chr	33.3		3	>
Lev	26.30		2	
Deut	14.24		2	>
Judg	20.18		2	
1 Kgs	12.31	<	2	>
	14.23	<	2	>
	15.12	<	2	
2 Kgs	15.4	<	2	>
	17.9	<	2	>
1 Chr	6.31		2	
2 Chr	1.3		2	
	14.3		2	>
	28.4		2	

PLAGUE

Num	16.47		3	
Rev	15.1		3	>
	16.9	<	3	
1 Sam	6.4		2	
Rev	9.18		2	

PLAN

1 Chr	28.11		4	
Dan	11.17		4	
Zech	8.14	<	4	
2 Cor	1.15		4	>
1 Sam	23.9		3	
Ps	64.5		3	
Prov	16.1		3	
Is	23.8	<	3	
	30.1	<	3	
Jer	29.11		3	
Mic	2.1		3	
Eph	1.9		3	
Gen	27.42		2	
Ex	25.9		2	>
2 Sam	20.21		2	
Ezra	10.15		2	
Neh	4.12		2	
Esth	9.24		2	
Job	10.13		2	
	15.8		2	
	23.14		2	
Ps	2.1		2	
	33.10		2	
	83.3		2	
Prov	6.14		2	>
	12.2		2	
	24.6		2	
Is	14.24		2	
	19.3		2	
	33.11		2	
	44.26		2	
	46.10		2	
	59.4		2	
Ezek	11.2		2	
	43.10		2	
Mt	22.15		2	
Jn	11.8		2	>
Acts	9.23	<	2	
	23.12		2	
	27.13		2	
Eph	3.3		2	

PLEAD

Dan	9.3		4	
Rom	8.26		3	
Job	16.21		2	
Jer	15.1		2	
Hos	2.2		2	

PLEASE

Gen	1.4		7	
Num	15.3	<	6	
	28.2		6	>
	29.2	<	5	
Ex	33.12		4	>
	29.18		3	
Lev	1.9		3	>
Deut	12.8		3	

PLEASE (cont.)

1 Sam	18.5		3	
Dan	11.16		3	
Rom	15.1	<	3	
1 Cor	7.32		3	
Heb	10.6		3	>
Gen	39.4		2	
Lev	2.2	<	2	>
	3.5	<	2	>
	6.15		2	
	8.20		2	
	23.13		2	
2 Sam	3.36		2	
	15.25	<	2	>
1 Kgs	15.5	<	2	
2 Kgs	15.3	<	2	>
	16.2	<	2	
2 Chr	24.2		2	>
Neh	9.24		2	
Ps	51.16		2	
Prov	8.31		2	
	12.2		2	
	15.8	<	2	>
Ecc	2.26		2	
Is	56.4		2	>
	62.4		2	
	66.2		2	
Jer	14.10		2	
Ezek	20.39		2	
Mal	1.8		2	
Mt	17.5		2	
Lk	14.18		2	
Rom	12.1		2	
1 Cor	10.5		2	
Eph	5.2		2	
Phil	4.2		2	
1 Thes	2.4		2	
Heb	11.5	<	2	>
	13.16	<	2	
3 Jn	6		2	

PLEASURE

Ps	119.16		5	
	16.3		2	
	147.10		2	
Prov	2.10		2	
Ecc	2.2		2	
Jas	4.1		2	>

PLENTY

Gen	41.29		5	
Lev	26.5		2	
1 Chr	4.40		2	
Joel	2.22		2	>
2 Cor	8.13		2	

PLOT (1) [PLAN]

1 Sam	22.8		3	
Ps	140.2		3	

PLOT (1)(cont.)

Hos	7.3		3	
2 Sam	15.11		2	
1 Kgs	16.9	<	2	
2 Kgs	15.25	<	2	
2 Chr	24.25		2	>
	25.17	<	2	
Neh	4.8		2	
Esth	6.2		2	
	8.3		2	
Ps	2.1		2	
	31.13		2	
	64.2		2	
Is	50.11		2	
	59.5		2	
Jer	11.9		2	
Lam	3.60		2	
Nah	1.9		2	
Acts	20.3		2	
	23.16		2	

POOR

Prov	28.3		9	>
Job	24.4		5	
Prov	14.20	<	5	>
	19.1	<	5	>
	22.2	<	5	>
Lev	25.25		4	
Prov	13.7		4	>
	31.7	<	4	
Jas	2.2	<	4	
Ex	23.3	<	3	
2 Sam	12.1		3	
Ps	72.4		3	
	109.16		3	
Prov	29.7	<	3	>
	30.8	<	3	>
Amos	2.6		3	
Mk	12.42		3	
Lk	21.2		3	
Jn	12.5		3	>
2 Cor	8.2		3	
Ex	6.12		2	
Lev	19.10		2	
	27.8		2	
Deut	15.4		2	
	24.12		2	
1 Sam	2.7		2	
2 Kgs	25.12	<	2	
Esth	1.5		2	
Job	5.15		2	
	20.10		2	
	29.12		2	>
	31.16	<	2	
	34.19		2	
Ps	10.2		2	
	22.24		2	
Prov	10.4		2	>
	15.15	<	2	>

POOR (cont.)

Ecc	4.13		2	>
	9.15		2	
Is	3.14		2	
Amos	5.11	<	2	
	8.4		2	
Mt	7.17		2	
	26.9		2	
Mk	14.5		2	
Lk	6.20		2	>
	14.13		2	
	16.20		2	

POSSESS

Josh	13.7	<	8	>
	19.8	<	6	
	17.4	<	4	>
Ps	37.9		4	
Num	16.14		3	
	32.18		3	
Josh	18.4	<	3	>
	21.12		3	
1 Kgs	21.15		3	
Gen	14.12		2	
Num	18.24		2	
Deut	9.4	<	2	
Josh	7.13		2	
	12.6		2	>
	14.9	<	2	>
	16.4	<	2	>
2 Chr	21.3		2	
Ezek	35.10		2	>
	47.14		2	>
Obad	17		2	
Rom	8.17		2	
1 Cor	6.9		2	

POWER

Dan	7.7	<	9	>
	4.3	<	7	>
	11.2		7	
Deut	7.1	<	6	>
Job	12.10	<	6	>
Ps	118.10		6	>
Dan	8.4	<	6	>
2 Chr	32.7		5	
1 Cor	1.17		5	>
Eph	3.7	<	5	
Ex	13.3		4	>
Deut	9.1	<	4	
Ps	78.4	<	4	>
Is	2.10	<	4	
	59.16		4	>
	63.1	<	4	>
Ezek	13.18		4	
	32.18	<	4	>
Dan	5.7	<	4	>
Mt	12.24		4	
Acts	4.7	<	4	

POWER (cont.)

Rom	6.4		4	
1 Cor	2.4	<	4	
	12.9		4	
	15.24	<	4	
Num	14.12	<	3	
Deut	4.34	<	3	>
1 Sam	24.4	<	3	
1 Chr	29.11		3	
2 Chr	25.3		3	>
Neh	9.6		3	
Esth	9.1		3	
Ps	18.17		3	
	44.3		3	
	68.28		3	
	71.4		3	
	89.9		3	>
Prov	28.12		3	>
Is	33.10		3	
	40.10		3	>
	66.18		3	
Jer	27.5	<	3	>
	28.2	<	3	>
	32.17		3	
Ezek	3.14		3	
	33.22	<	3	
Dan	2.10		3	>
	9.15	<	3	
Zech	11.6	<	3	
Lk	1.35		3	
	4.6		3	>
	9.1	<	3	
	11.15	<	3	
Acts	10.38		3	>
Rom	1.4		3	
	15.13		3	
2 Cor	13.3	<	3	
Eph	1.19		3	>
Col	1.11		3	>
	2.11	<	3	
2 Thes	2.9	<	3	
2 Tim	1.7		3	
Rev	9.3		3	
Gen	1.2		2	
Lev	6.18		2	
	26.13		2	
Num	13.28		2	>
	20.12		2	
	22.28		2	
Deut	2.24		2	>
	8.17	<	2	>
	11.2	<	2	
	26.5		2	
Judg	14.6	<	2	>
1 Sam	17.46		2	
	26.8		2	
2 Sam	22.18		2	
1 Kgs	15.16		2	
2 Kgs	2.9		2	>

POWER (cont.)

2 Kgs	19.25		2	
2 Chr	6.32		2	
	13.20	<	2	>
	26.8	<	2	>
Ezra	4.10		2	>
Job	27.11	<	2	>
Ps	20.6		2	>
	75.10		2	
	77.10		2	>
	98.1	<	2	
	106.8	<	2	
	112.2	<	2	
	136.12	<	2	
	144.7		2	>
Is	1.24		2	>
	9.7	<	2	
	14.5		2	
	18.2	<	2	>
	30.3		2	>
	37.26		2	
	42.6	<	2	>
	45.1	<	2	
	47.6		2	>
Jer	5.5		2	
	10.6		2	
	20.4		2	
	48.17		2	>
	49.4	<	2	
Ezek	20.33		2	>
	30.12		2	>
Nah	1.3		2	>
Hab	1.6		2	
Zeph	2.13		2	>
Zech	10.3		2	>
Mt	24.29		2	
Mk	13.25	<	2	>
Lk	21.26	<	2	>
	22.25	<	2	
	24.19		2	
Jn	4.23	<	2	
	17.11		2	
Acts	1.2		2	>
	3.12	<	2	>
	8.10		2	>
	11.21	<	2	>
Rom	8.15		2	>
	9.17	<	2	
1 Cor	4.19		2	>
2 Cor	12.9		2	>
Gal	3.3	<	2	
Eph	6.10		2	
Phil	3.10		2	>
Heb	1.3		2	>
1 Pet	1.5		2	
Rev	6.4	<	2	>
	7.2	<	2	
	11.15		2	>
	17.13		2	>

POWER (cont.)

Rev	20.4	<	2	

PRACTICE

Lev	18.3		3	>
Deut	18.9		3	
Jas	1.22		3	
2 Kgs	17.11	<	2	
	21.2		2	
2 Chr	33.2		2	>
Jer	44.5		2	
Ezek	16.24		2	
Mt	23.3		2	
Rev	2.14		2	

PRAISE

Ps	148.1	<	13	>
	150.1	<	13	
1 Chr	16.4		12	
Ps	135.1	<	10	
	66.1	<	7	>
	103.1	<	7	>
	106.1	<	7	>
	147.1	<	7	>
Is	42.8	<	7	>
Ps	68.4	<	6	>
	71.6		6	>
	145.2	<	6	>
	149.1	<	6	>
Rom	15.6		6	
Rev	19.1		6	
1 Chr	29.10		5	
Ps	22.3	<	5	
	96.2	<	5	
	113.1	<	5	
	119.7	<	5	
2 Sam	22.4		4	
Neh	9.5	<	4	
Ps	9.1	<	4	
	18.3		4	
	30.1	<	4	>
	47.1		4	>
	67.3	<	4	>
	104.1	<	4	>
	146.1	<	4	>
Is	38.9		4	
Mt	21.9		4	
1 Kgs	8.15		3	
2 Chr	20.19		3	
	30.21	<	3	>
Ezra	3.10		3	
Ps	29.1	<	3	>
	34.1	<	3	>
	42.4	<	3	>
	63.3		3	>
	99.3	<	3	
	117.1	<	3	>
	138.1		3	>
Is	24.15		3	>

PRAISE (cont.)

Is	61.3	<	3	>
Dan	2.19		3	>
Lk	1.46		3	>
Jn	5.41		3	
1 Cor	11.2		3	>
Eph	1.6		3	
Gen	24.27		2	
Ex	18.10		2	
Deut	32.3		2	>
Judg	5.2		2	
1 Sam	25.32		2	
1 Chr	23.5		2	
2 Chr	5.11		2	>
	7.3	<	2	
	29.27		2	>
	31.2	<	2	
Neh	12.24	<	2	
Job	29.13		2	
	36.24		2	
Ps	21.13	<	2	>
	28.6	<	2	>
	35.18	<	2	
	41.13	<	2	>
	43.4	<	2	>
	48.1	<	2	>
	56.4		2	>
	57.7	<	2	
	69.30	<	2	
	72.18	<	2	
	86.9	<	2	
	89.16	<	2	
	95.1		2	>
	98.4		2	>
	100.4		2	
	102.18		2	>
	105.2	<	2	>
	107.2	<	2	>
	108.1	<	2	>
	109.1	<	2	
	111.1		2	>
	115.17		2	>
	134.1		2	>
Prov	26.1	<	2	>
	31.28		2	
Song	6.9		2	
Is	25.1	<	2	
	43.20	<	2	
	62.7	<	2	>
Dan	4.34	<	2	>
	5.4	<	2	
Mk	11.9		2	
Lk	2.13	<	2	
	5.25	<	2	
Acts	3.8	<	2	>
1 Pet	2.12	<	2	
Rev	5.12		2	

PRAY

1 Kgs	8.12		12	
2 Chr	6.1		10	>
Ex	8.8		8	>
1 Kgs	18.24	<	7	>
1 Sam	1.9		6	>
Jer	42.2		6	
Mt	6.5	<	6	
Dan	9.3		5	
Mt	26.36		5	
Mk	14.32	<	5	
Lk	22.32	<	5	
Jas	5.13		5	
1 Sam	12.17		4	
Jn	17.9		4	
1 Cor	14.13		4	
Eph	6.18		4	
Col	4.2		4	
Gen	24.12		3	>
1 Sam	7.5		3	>
2 Kgs	6.17	<	3	
2 Chr	20.3		3	
Is	65.1		3	>
Dan	6.10		3	
Hos	7.7		3	
Lk	6.12	<	3	
	9.18		3	
	11.1	<	3	
	18.1		3	
Acts	8.15		3	>
	10.2		3	>
1 Cor	11.4		3	
Eph	3.1		3	
Gen	20.7		2	
	32.9		2	
Ex	10.17		2	
Num	14.17		2	
	21.7		2	
	27.15		2	
Deut	9.20		2	
2 Sam	7.18		2	
1 Kgs	13.6		2	
	17.20		2	>
2 Kgs	19.4		2	>
	20.2	<	2	
1 Chr	4.10		2	>
	17.16		2	
	21.17		2	
2 Chr	32.20		2	
Neh	1.4		2	>
	4.4		2	>
	6.9	<	2	
	9.4		2	
Job	42.8		2	
Ps	4.1		2	>
	14.4		2	
	35.13	<	2	
	53.4		2	
	86.3		2	

PRAY (cont.)

Ps	122.6		2	
Prov	15.8		2	
Is	37.4		2	>
Jer	7.16		2	
	11.14		2	
	29.7		2	
Jon	1.6		2	>
	2.1	<	2	>
Zech	7.2		2	>
	8.21	<	2	
Mk	11.24		2	
Acts	1.14		2	
	9.11	<	2	
	12.5	<	2	>
	22.16	<	2	
Rom	15.30		2	
2 Cor	13.7	<	2	
Phil	1.4		2	
Col	1.3		2	
1 Thes	5.17		2	
2 Thes	3.1		2	
Heb	13.18		2	
Jas	1.5		2	
1 Jn	5.16		2	

PRAYER

1 Kgs	8.28		12	>
2 Chr	6.12		12	>
Gen	30.6		3	
2 Kgs	6.17		3	
2 Chr	7.1	<	3	
	30.18		3	
	33.13		3	>
Neh	1.6		3	
Ps	86.4		3	
	143.1		3	
Hos	14.2		3	
1 Tim	4.3		3	
Ex	9.29		2	
Job	42.8		2	
Ps	66.19	<	2	
	72.15		2	
	88.2		2	
	102.1		2	
	116.1		2	
	119.108		2	
Is	56.7		2	
	65.1	<	2	
Dan	10.12		2	
Zech	3.7		2	
Mt	21.13		2	
Acts	10.4		2	
	16.13		2	
1 Cor	14.16		2	
2 Cor	1.11		2	
1 Tim	2.1		2	
Phlm	6		2	
Jas	5.15		2	

PRAYER (cont.)

1 Pet	3.7		2	
Rev	8.3		2	

PREACH

Gal	1.8		6	>
Mk	1.4		4	>
Acts	8.4		4	>
	9.20	<	4	
	15.7	<	4	>
1 Cor	9.14		4	
	15.1		4	
Mt	11.1	<	3	>
Mk	16.15		3	
Acts	13.5		3	>
	14.7	<	3	>
	16.6	<	3	>
Rom	1.1		3	>
2 Cor	4.3		3	
	11.4	<	3	
Gal	2.2	<	3	
Phil	1.14		3	
2 Thes	2.2		3	
1 Pet	4.6	<	3	
Mic	2.6		2	
Mt	4.17	<	2	
Lk	3.3		2	>
	4.43	<	2	
	9.2	<	2	
Acts	6.2	<	2	
	10.37		2	
	17.13	<	2	>
	20.20	<	2	
Rom	2.16	<	2	
	10.8		2	
Gal	5.11	<	2	
Col	1.23		2	
1 Thes	2.9		2	>
2 Tim	2.8		2	
	4.2		2	

PREDICT

Is	44.7	<	5	>
Ezek	13.6	<	5	
Is	48.3		4	
2 Kgs	23.16		3	
Jer	28.8	<	3	>
Is	41.22		2	>
	43.9	<	2	>
Ezek	12.22		2	>
	21.23		2	>
Mic	3.6		2	

PRESENCE

Ex	33.16		4	>
Lev	24.3		4	
Deut	12.5		4	
Judg	20.1		4	>
Ex	29.11	<	3	

PRESENCE (cont.)

Ex	40.25		3	
Num	14.10		3	
Ps	68.2		3	
Jer	28.1		3	
Ezek	44.3	<	3	
Gen	4.14		2	
	23.9		2	
	43.3		2	>
	44.23	<	2	
Ex	16.7		2	>
	28.30	<	2	>
Lev	9.6		2	
	14.16		2	
Num	16.19		2	
	19.3		2	>
Deut	9.18		2	
	14.23		2	>
	26.5	<	2	>
	29.10		2	
	32.51	<	2	
Judg	21.2	<	2	
1 Kgs	8.11		2	
Ezra	9.6		2	
Ps	5.4		2	
	16.8		2	>
	31.20		2	
Jer	32.12		2	
Ezek	10.4		2	>
	40.1		2	>
	43.2	<	2	>
Lk	23.14		2	>
2 Cor	2.10		2	
	12.19		2	
Col	1.22		2	
1 Thes	3.9	<	2	
2 Tim	2.2		2	
Heb	9.5		2	
1 Jn	3.19		2	
Rev	13.12		2	

PRESENT (1) [GIFT]

Lev	23.11	<	16	
Num	18.9		10	
	15.3		7	>
Lev	10.1		5	
	1.3		4	>
	2.1	<	4	>
	7.11	<	4	>
	9.7	<	4	
Num	6.14	<	4	>
	7.3	<	4	
	28.2	<	4	>
Lev	3.3	<	3	>
	6.14		3	>
	21.8		3	>
Num	5.9		3	>
	16.17	<	3	
Gen	43.15		2	

PRESENT (1)(cont.)

Gen	47.2		2	
Lev	8.27	<	2	>
	14.12		2	
	16.10		2	
	22.18	<	2	>
Num	9.7		2	
1 Kgs	18.1		2	
2 Chr	29.27		2	
Is	41.1		2	
	45.20		2	

PRIEST

Lev	13.2	<	43	>
	14.2	<	22	>
Heb	7.1	<	20	>
Ezek	44.13	<	14	>
Lev	7.5	<	13	>
	22.4	<	13	>
1 Sam	2.11	<	13	
Ex	29.1	<	11	>
Lev	6.6	<	11	
Num	5.8	<	11	>
Judg	18.4	<	11	
Neh	12.1	<	11	>
Josh	6.4		10	
2 Chr	29.4		10	>
Lev	5.6	<	9	>
Ex	28.1		8	>
Lev	21.1		8	>
	27.8		8	
2 Kgs	12.2	<	8	
	23.2	<	8	
2 Chr	35.2	<	8	>
Ezra	7.6	<	8	>
Neh	7.39		8	>
Lev	1.5		7	>
	2.2	<	7	>
	4.10	<	7	>
Num	3.3		7	>
	6.10	<	7	
Josh	3.3		7	>
1 Sam	22.11	<	7	>
2 Chr	23.1	<	7	>
	30.1	<	7	>
	31.2	<	7	
Ezra	2.36	<	7	>
	8.15	<	7	>
Lev	3.2	<	6	>
Deut	18.1	<	6	>
Josh	4.3	<	6	
1 Kgs	1.7		6	>
2 Chr	13.9		6	
Neh	10.28		6	>
	13.4	<	6	
1 Sam	14.3		5	
1 Kgs	2.22	<	5	
1 Chr	24.2	<	5	
2 Chr	5.5	<	5	>

PRIEST (cont.)

2 Chr	26.17		5	
Ezra	6.9		5	>
Lk	1.5		5	
Ex	39.1	<	4	>
	40.13	<	4	
Lev	15.14	<	4	>
	16.4	<	4	>
	23.9	<	4	>
Num	4.16	<	4	>
	18.1		4	>
	27.2		4	
Josh	21.1		4	>
Judg	17.5		4	>
1 Kgs	8.3		4	
1 Chr	9.2		4	
2 Chr	24.2	<	4	
Ezra	3.2	<	4	
	10.5		4	
Neh	3.1	<	4	
Ezek	43.19	<	4	>
	48.10		4	
Hos	4.4		4	
Mal	2.1	<	4	>
Heb	8.4	<	4	>
Ex	19.6	<	3	
	35.19		3	
Lev	12.6		3	>
Num	16.10	<	3	
	31.6		3	
Deut	10.6		3	
	17.9		3	>
Josh	22.13	<	3	
1 Sam	21.1		3	>
2 Sam	15.24		3	
1 Kgs	4.2		3	
	13.2	<	3	
2 Kgs	10.11		3	>
	11.4	<	3	>
	17.27	<	3	
1 Chr	15.11		3	>
	23.2		3	>
2 Chr	7.2	<	3	>
	8.14	<	3	
	11.13		3	
Neh	8.1	<	3	>
	9.32	<	3	
Jer	2.8	<	3	
	23.11		3	
	26.7		3	>
	29.1	<	3	
	33.18	<	3	
Ezek	40.45		3	>
	42.13	<	3	>
	46.2	<	3	
Hag	2.11		3	
Heb	5.6		3	>
Gen	47.22	<	2	
Ex	30.30	<	2	>

PRIEST (cont.)

Ex	31.10	<	2	>
Lev	8.2	<	2	>
	17.5	<	2	
Num	15.25		2	>
	19.3	<	2	>
	20.26	<	2	
	25.7		2	
Deut	26.3		2	>
	31.9		2	
1 Sam	1.3		2	>
2 Sam	8.17		2	
	20.25	<	2	
1 Kgs	12.31		2	>
2 Kgs	22.4		2	>
1 Chr	16.6	<	2	
	28.13	<	2	>
2 Chr	4.6		2	>
	17.8		2	
	34.5		2	>
Ezra	9.1	<	2	
Neh	11.3	<	2	>
Ps	115.10		2	
	132.9		2	
Is	28.7		2	
Jer	1.1		2	>
	8.1		2	
	28.1	<	2	>
Lam	1.4		2	>
	2.6	<	2	
	4.13		2	
Ezek	45.4	<	2	>
Joel	1.9		2	>
Zech	7.3	<	2	
Mal	1.6		2	>
Mt	12.4		2	
Heb	10.11		2	
1 Pet	2.5		2	
Neh	12.2	<	2	

PRISON

2 Chr	28.5		9	>
Acts	16.25		8	
Jer	29.1	<	7	>
	52.11		6	
Gen	40.3	<	5	>
Num	31.11		5	
Phlm	1		5	
Gen	39.20		4	>
2 Kgs	25.18	<	4	
Jer	37.4		4	>
	41.10	<	4	
Mt	25.36		4	
Acts	5.19		4	
Phil	1.7		4	
2 Kgs	17.4	<	3	>
	24.12	<	3	>
Is	49.9		3	
Lam	3.5		3	

PRISON (cont.)

Acts	12.6		3	
	25.4	<	3	>
Heb	13.3		3	
Gen	41.10	<	2	>
	42.17	<	2	
Judg	16.21	<	2	
2 Chr	36.3		2	
Job	12.14		2	
Is	24.22		2	
	42.7		2	
Jer	30.10	<	2	
	38.23	<	2	>
	39.9	<	2	>
	46.19		2	
Ezek	30.17		2	
Mt	14.3		2	
	27.15		2	
Mk	6.17		2	
	15.6		2	
Lk	21.12		2	>
	23.19	<	2	
Acts	23.18	<	2	>
	26.10	<	2	>
	27.1	<	2	>
Rom	7.6		2	
Col	4.3		2	
2 Tim	1.8		2	

PROCLAIM

1 Cor	14.1		10	
Esth	3.10	<	4	>
	8.5		4	>
Is	40.6		4	
2 Kgs	9.3		3	
1 Chr	16.8		3	
	25.1		3	
Esth	2.1	<	3	>
Ps	71.8		3	
	145.1		3	
Jer	23.22		3	
Jon	3.2		3	
1 Cor	11.4		3	
Rev	11.3	<	3	>
Num	27.19		2	
1 Sam	11.14		2	
1 Kgs	21.9		2	
2 Kgs	10.20		2	>
Esth	1.19		2	>
	4.3	<	2	
	9.1	<	2	
Ps	96.2		2	>
	118.17		2	
Jer	11.6		2	
	19.2	<	2	>
	20.1	<	2	
	26.2	<	2	
Zech	1.14		2	
Acts	2.17		2	

PROCLAIM (cont.)

Rom	10.14		2	
	15.19		2	
1 Cor	2.6	<	2	
2 Tim	1.1		2	>
	4.2		2	

PROFANE

Ezek	20.13		4	
	7.22		2	
	23.38		2	>

PROMISE

Ps	119.25		28	
Gal	3.14		11	>
Num	30.2		10	
Heb	11.8	<	10	>
Mal	2.5	<	8	
Rom	4.13		8	
1 Kgs	8.15		7	>
Ezek	20.5		7	
Heb	6.12		7	>
Gen	24.7		6	
Deut	6.3		6	>
1 Sam	20.8		6	
2 Sam	7.10		6	
1 Kgs	2.4	<	6	
2 Chr	6.4		6	>
Ps	89.3		6	
Heb	4.1	<	6	
Num	14.16		5	
Deut	12.6	<	5	>
	26.3		5	>
Josh	23.5	<	5	
Neh	9.8		5	
Ecc	5.2		5	
Jer	44.24		5	
Lk	1.20		5	>
Rom	9.4		5	
Gen	21.1		4	>
	26.3		4	
	50.5		4	
Num	32.10		4	
Deut	31.7	<	4	
Josh	2.13	<	4	
	9.15		4	
Judg	11.30		4	
1 Sam	1.11		4	>
1 Kgs	1.13		4	>
1 Chr	17.9	<	4	
Gen	9.11		3	
Ex	13.5	<	3	
Deut	1.8		3	
	7.8	<	3	>
	9.3	<	3	
	10.9		3	>
	11.9	<	3	>
	13.1	<	3	
Josh	14.9		3	

PROMISE (cont.)

Josh	21.43		3	>
Judg	21.1		3	
2 Sam	21.2		3	
1 Chr	11.2		3	>
Neh	5.12		3	
Ps	56.4	<	3	
	105.8		3	>
	106.8	<	3	
	132.2		3	>
Is	54.9		3	>
Jer	14.7		3	
Mt	5.5		3	
Lk	2.5	<	3	
Acts	2.30	<	3	>
	7.5		3	
	13.23		3	
Eph	1.13		3	>
Heb	7.6	<	3	>
2 Pet	3.4	<	3	
Gen	17.4		2	>
Ex	6.4		2	
	32.13		2	>
Num	6.21		2	
	20.12		2	
Deut	28.9	<	2	>
1 Sam	14.39		2	
	24.21	<	2	>
2 Sam	3.9		2	
	14.11		2	>
	15.7	<	2	
1 Kgs	5.5		2	>
2 Kgs	9.26	<	2	
	10.10		2	
	20.6	<	2	
1 Chr	22.9		2	
Ezra	10.3		2	
Ps	61.5		2	
	116.14		2	
	138.4		2	
Prov	6.1		2	
	20.16		2	
Song	5.8		2	
Is	19.21		2	
	45.23		2	
	62.6		2	
Jer	11.5		2	
	32.22	<	2	>
	33.14	<	2	
	35.17		2	
	38.16		2	
Ezek	16.8		2	
	36.7		2	>
Dan	11.16		2	>
Hos	4.2		2	
Mt	14.7		2	
Rom	1.2		2	
2 Cor	1.18		2	
	11.2		2	

PROMISE (cont.)

Gal	4.23	<	2	
Heb	3.11		2	>
	10.23		2	>
	12.24	<	2	
1 Pet	3.9		2	>

PROPER

Num	28.14		3	>
	29.3	<	3	
1 Tim	2.2		3	
Lev	16.2		2	
Esth	9.27		2	
Mk	7.3		2	
1 Cor	7.35		2	
	15.23	<	2	

PROPHECY

Num	24.3	<	5	
Ezek	37.4	<	5	
1 Kgs	22.8		4	
2 Chr	18.7		4	
Amos	7.13		4	
Ezek	21.9	<	3	
Num	23.7		2	>
Ezek	12.24	<	2	>
	36.3		2	>
Dan	9.22		2	
Zech	13.3		2	

PROPHET

1 Kgs	13.1	<	26	>
Jer	23.11		17	
1 Kgs	18.4	<	13	>
	20.13	<	13	>
	22.6	<	8	
2 Chr	18.5		8	>
Ezek	13.2		8	>
Deut	18.15		7	
Jer	29.1	<	7	
Acts	13.1		7	
2 Chr	25.7	<	6	>
Lk	11.30	<	6	
Acts	3.18	<	6	
Rev	22.6		6	
1 Sam	10.5		5	
1 Kgs	19.1	<	5	>
2 Kgs	2.3	<	5	>
	4.1	<	5	>
	5.3	<	5	>
	9.1	<	5	
	23.2	<	5	>
2 Chr	36.12	<	5	
Jer	26.5	<	5	>
	27.9	<	5	>
	28.1	<	5	>
Mic	3.5	<	5	
Zech	13.2		5	
Mt	23.29	<	5	>

PROPHET (cont.)

Jer	14.13	<	4	>
Ezek	14.4	<	4	
Zech	1.1		4	
Mt	2.5	<	4	>
	21.4		4	>
Lk	7.16	<	4	
	24.19		4	
Jn	1.21		4	
Acts	7.37		4	>
Num	11.25		3	>
Deut	34.10		3	
1 Kgs	1.8		3	
	16.1	<	3	>
2 Kgs	3.11	<	3	>
	13.14		3	>
	17.13		3	
2 Chr	12.5	<	3	>
	29.25	<	3	
	35.15	<	3	>
Neh	9.26		3	
Jer	2.8	<	3	
	5.13	<	3	>
Lam	2.9		3	
Dan	9.2		3	
Hos	9.7		3	
	12.10		3	
Hag	1.1		3	>
Zech	7.3		3	>
Mt	7.12		3	>
	11.9		3	>
	13.17	<	3	>
	24.11	<	3	
Lk	1.17		3	>
	4.17	<	3	
	13.28		3	
	16.16		3	
Acts	8.27	<	3	
1 Jn	4.1		3	
Rev	11.10	<	3	
	19.10	<	3	>
Deut	13.1		2	
1 Sam	19.20		2	
	28.6		2	
2 Sam	12.1		2	
1 Kgs	12.15	<	2	>
	14.2	<	2	>
	21.17	<	2	>
2 Kgs	6.1	<	2	
	10.10		2	
	20.1	<	2	>
2 Chr	9.29		2	
	16.7		2	
	32.20		2	>
	33.18	<	2	>
Ezra	5.1		2	>
Neh	6.7		2	
Is	28.7		2	>
	29.10	<	2	>

PROPHET (cont.)

Jer	8.1	<	2	
	35.4		2	
Amos	2.11		2	>
	7.12		2	
Hag	2.1	<	2	
Mt	5.12	<	2	
	12.17	<	2	>
Mk	6.4		2	
Lk	6.23		2	>
	9.8		2	
Jn	4.19		2	
	6.14		2	>
	7.40	<	2	>
	8.52	<	2	>
Acts	2.16		2	>
	15.15		2	
	26.22		2	
	28.23		2	
1 Cor	12.28		2	
1 Pet	1.10		2	
2 Pet	1.19		2	>
	2.1	<	2	>
Rev	16.6		2	
	18.20		2	>

PROSPER

Deut	30.3		6	
Jer	33.7		4	
Deut	28.13		3	
Ezek	16.53		3	
Gen	26.13		2	
Num	10.29		2	
Deut	6.10		2	
1 Kgs	1.37		2	>
Ps	37.7		2	
	72.3		2	
	85.1		2	
	122.6		2	
	128.2		2	
Prov	11.25		2	
Is	66.11		2	
Jer	12.1		2	
	22.15		2	
	29.7		2	
	44.17		2	
	49.6	<	2	
Dan	4.4		2	
Zeph	3.13	<	2	

PROSTITUTE

Ezek	16.16		15	
	23.3		13	
Jer	3.2		6	
Gen	38.15		4	
Hos	4.12	<	4	
Rev	17.1		4	
Lev	21.7		3	
Josh	6.17		3	

PROSTITUTE (cont.)

Deut	23.17		2	
1 Kgs	22.38		2	
Hos	2.2		2	>
Mic	1.7		2	
Mt	21.31		2	
1 Cor	6.15		2	

PROTECT

2 Sam	22.2	<	8	>
Ps	18.2	<	7	
	91.1		6	>
	37.17	<	5	
	121.3		5	
	31.1	<	4	>
Is	31.2	<	4	
Deut	33.3	<	3	
Ezra	8.21		3	
Ps	62.2	<	3	
	71.1		3	
	115.9		3	>
Prov	2.7		3	
Is	33.2		3	
Ezek	11.3		3	
Gen	28.15		2	
Num	31.50		2	
Deut	19.2		2	
	23.14		2	
	32.10		2	>
Josh	20.5		2	
1 Sam	2.2		2	
	25.16		2	>
	26.15	<	2	
2 Sam	21.2		2	>
2 Kgs	11.7		2	
Ps	5.11		2	
	7.1		2	
	16.1		2	>
	28.7	<	2	
	32.7	<	2	>
	59.1		2	
	61.3		2	>
	89.18		2	
	140.4	<	2	>
	141.8	<	2	>
	142.4	<	2	>
	144.1	<	2	>
Prov	10.15		2	>
	13.3		2	>
	14.3	<	2	>
	18.11		2	
	31.8	<	2	
Ecc	5.8		2	
Is	16.3		2	>
	30.2		2	>
	49.2		2	
Jer	1.8		2	
Hos	14.3		2	

PROUD

Ps	119.21		5	
Is	13.2		4	
2 Cor	12.7		4	
Neh	9.16		3	
Ps	10.2		3	
	73.3		3	
Prov	23.16		3	
Is	2.11		3	>
	28.1		3	
Jer	13.9		3	
	50.29	<	3	
Ezek	16.49		3	
	28.2		3	
Rom	11.13		3	>
1 Cor	4.6		3	>
Job	31.25		2	
	40.10		2	>
Ps	31.18		2	
	94.2		2	
Prov	17.6	<	2	
	29.3		2	
Is	3.16	<	2	>
	10.12		2	
Jer	48.29		2	>
Ezek	7.10		2	
	24.21		2	
	30.6		2	>
Dan	7.8		2	>
Zeph	2.10		2	>
1 Cor	5.2	<	2	
2 Cor	1.12		2	
1 Tim	6.4		2	
Jas	4.6		2	

PROVE

Deut	22.15		3	
Ezra	2.59		3	
Neh	7.61		3	
Gen	42.19		2	
2 Kgs	20.8		2	
Is	38.7		2	
	43.9		2	
	50.8		2	
Mt	12.27		2	
Lk	5.14		2	
	11.19		2	
	13.2		2	
Jn	8.13		2	
Acts	17.3		2	>
1 Cor	14.22		2	
2 Cor	7.11		2	

PROVERB

Prov	1.1		4	
Job	17.5		2	
Ecc	12.9		2	
Ezek	12.22		2	
	18.2		2	

PROVIDE

Gen	22.8		3	
Ps	104.11		3	
Gen	1.29		2	
Ex	28.2		2	
Lev	25.6		2	
Judg	21.7	<	2	
1 Kgs	5.8	<	2	
	8.21		2	>
2 Kgs	6.23		2	
Ezra	7.21		2	
Neh	10.33		2	
Ps	65.9		2	
	132.5		2	
Ezek	45.17		2	
	47.12		2	
Lk	12.31		2	
2 Cor	12.14		2	
Eph	4.16		2	

PUNISH

Lev	26.14		8	
Is	10.3		8	>
Heb	12.6		8	
Ex	21.18	<	6	
1 Sam	5.6		6	>
Is	9.12		6	
Jer	25.6		6	
Amos	1.3		6	>
Job	21.17	<	5	>
Is	26.11		5	>
	53.4		5	>
Jer	30.11	<	5	>
Ezek	7.4	<	5	
Deut	32.34		4	
Josh	22.17		4	>
2 Sam	24.14		4	
1 Kgs	2.9		4	
1 Chr	21.7		4	
Ps	119.67	<	4	>
Is	66.6	<	4	
Jer	6.6	<	4	>
	23.2		4	
	46.10		4	
	49.8		4	>
	50.18	<	4	>
	51.6	<	4	
Ezek	21.10	<	4	>
Zeph	1.4		4	>
Ex	9.3	<	3	
2 Kgs	22.16	<	3	
2 Chr	34.24		3	
Job	31.11		3	>
Ps	10.12		3	>
	28.4		3	
	94.1		3	
Prov	19.5		3	>
Is	13.3		3	>
	27.1	<	3	

PUNISH (cont.)

Is	65.6		3	>
Jer	2.19	<	3	
	44.13		3	
Lam	3.1		3	>
Ezek	5.9	<	3	>
	11.11		3	
	14.10	<	3	>
	16.27	<	3	>
	17.15	<	3	
	25.11	<	3	
	44.10		3	
Dan	9.12	<	3	
Hos	4.9		3	>
	5.2	<	3	>
Amos	2.1	<	3	>
Obad	8		3	
Mic	4.6		3	
Rom	13.4		3	
Rev	18.4	<	3	>
Gen	9.5		2	
	15.14		2	
Ex	8.2	<	2	>
	12.12	<	2	
	19.22		2	>
	20.5	<	2	>
Num	31.2		2	>
Deut	5.9		2	
	19.19	<	2	
1 Sam	3.13		2	
	6.3	<	2	
	25.26	<	2	>
2 Sam	3.29		2	
	7.14	<	2	
2 Kgs	9.7		2	
	19.3		2	
2 Chr	20.9		2	>
	24.22		2	
	28.11		2	
Ezra	9.13	<	2	
Job	27.7		2	
	36.13	<	2	>
Ps	39.10	<	2	
	79.8		2	
	125.5		2	
	149.7		2	
Prov	11.21	<	2	
	17.5	<	2	
	24.18		2	
Ecc	8.11		2	
Is	5.25		2	
	14.26	<	2	
	19.16		2	
	24.21		2	
	37.3		2	
	59.17		2	>
Jer	5.9		2	>
	9.9	<	2	
	11.8	<	2	

PUNISH (cont.)

Lam	4.6	<	2	
Ezek	4.4		2	>
	15.7	<	2	>
	23.31	<	2	>
	28.22		2	>
	30.14	<	2	
	33.12		2	
	35.5		2	
Hos	8.10	<	2	>
	9.7	<	2	
	10.10		2	>
	12.2	<	2	>
Amos	3.2	<	2	>
	7.4		2	>
Nah	1.2		2	
	3.4		2	
Zeph	2.3	<	2	>
	3.15	<	2	
Mt	3.7		2	
	23.35		2	>
Lk	11.50		2	>
	12.47	<	2	
	21.22	<	2	
Rom	1.19		2	>
2 Thes	1.8		2	

PURE

Lev	14.2		13	>
Ex	37.2		10	
Lev	16.16	<	9	
Num	19.12		9	
Ex	25.11		8	
Num	8.6		6	
	31.19		5	
Heb	9.10		5	
	10.2		5	
Ex	30.3	<	4	>
	39.15		4	
Lev	24.2		4	
2 Chr	29.5		4	>
Ex	28.14		3	>
Num	15.25		3	>
Neh	13.9	<	3	
Ezek	24.11		3	
Zech	13.1		3	
Acts	21.24		3	
Ex	19.10		2	
	29.36	<	2	>
Lev	12.4		2	
	15.15	<	2	>
Num	16.46	<	2	
	28.22		2	>
	29.5	<	2	
1 Sam	16.5		2	
2 Kgs	2.21		2	
1 Chr	15.12		2	
	28.17		2	>
2 Chr	9.17		2	

PURE (cont.)

2 Chr	30.18	<	2	
Neh	12.30		2	>
Job	15.14		2	
	25.4		2	
Ps	73.1		2	
	119.7		2	
Ezek	43.20		2	>
Mal	3.3		2	
Mk	9.49		2	
1 Cor	5.7		2	>
2 Cor	11.2		2	
1 Tim	5.2	<	2	
Tit	1.15		2	>
	2.5	<	2	
Heb	2.11		2	
1 Pet	1.2		2	>
2 Pet	3.1		2	
1 Jn	1.7		2	
Rev	21.18		2	

PURPOSE

Rom	6.13		4	
Eph	1.5		3	
1 Pet	1.2		3	
Ps	33.10		2	
Is	45.13		2	
Rom	8.20		2	>
1 Cor	1.10		2	>
	4.5		2	
Rev	17.13		2	

Q

QUARREL

Gen	26.20		3	
	13.7		2	
Lev	24.10		2	
2 Tim	2.23		2	
Jas	4.1		2	

QUESTION

Mk	12.13	<	4	
Jn	18.19		4	
Mt	22.15	<	3	
Lk	20.3		3	
1 Sam	9.9		2	
	17.29		2	
2 Sam	14.18		2	
1 Kgs	10.1		2	
2 Chr	9.1		2	
Job	38.2		2	
	42.3		2	
Prov	26.4		2	
Ecc	7.10		2	
Jer	38.14		2	
Hag	2.11		2	
Mk	14.60		2	>

QUESTION (cont.)

Mk	15.2	<	2	
Jn	16.19		2	

R

RAISE

1 Cor	15.4		22	>
Ex	10.12		4	
Num	30.4		4	
Jn	6.39	<	4	>
	12.1		4	
Acts	13.30		4	
Ex	9.15		3	
Mt	27.52	<	3	>
Acts	2.24		3	>
Rom	6.4		3	>
	8.11	<	3	
Heb	11.19		3	
Ex	7.5	<	2	
2 Chr	6.12		2	
Ps	93.3		2	
Is	13.2		2	
Mt	17.9	<	2	
	28.6	<	2	
Lk	24.6		2	
Acts	5.30	<	2	
	17.31		2	
Rom	4.24		2	
1 Cor	6.14		2	
2 Cor	1.9		2	
	4.14		2	>
Col	2.12	<	2	>
1 Pet	1.3		2	
Rev	20.5		2	

REAL

Jn	6.32	<	3	
Deut	32.17		2	
1 Kgs	3.26		2	
Jn	1.9		2	
Rom	2.28		2	
Col	2.17		2	>
	3.4	<	2	

REAP

Jn	4.36		4	
Hos	10.12		2	
Mt	25.24		2	
Lk	19.21		2	
1 Cor	9.10		2	
Gal	6.7		2	
Rev	14.15		2	

REASON

Mt	19.3		3	
Ps	35.7		2	
Jn	19.4	<	2	

REASON (cont.)

2 Cor	11.12		2	
Eph	3.1		2	
Phil	2.9	<	2	>
1 Thes	2.13		2	
2 Tim	1.6		2	

REBEL

Josh	22.16		7	
Ezek	2.3		6	>
Ps	78.8		5	
Ezek	12.2		5	
Is	1.2		4	
Heb	3.8		4	
Num	16.1		3	>
Deut	9.7		3	
	31.27		3	>
2 Sam	18.28		3	
Ezra	4.12		3	
Ezek	3.9	<	3	
Zeph	3.1		3	
Ex	23.21		2	
Lev	26.40		2	
Num	14.9		2	
	20.10		2	
	27.3	<	2	
Deut	1.26		2	>
	21.18		2	
1 Kgs	12.16		2	
2 Kgs	3.5		2	
	18.7		2	
2 Chr	10.16		2	
Ps	68.6		2	
	106.7		2	>
Is	30.1		2	
Jer	2.8		2	>
	48.26		2	
Ezek	17.12		2	
Dan	11.14		2	
Hos	7.13		2	>
Mic	1.5		2	

REFUGE

Num	35.6		7	
Josh	21.13		5	
Ps	59.9		3	
Josh	20.2		2	
1 Chr	6.57		2	
Ps	31.2		2	
	46.7		2	

REFUSE (1) [DENY]

Lev	26.15		4	
1 Kgs	2.16		4	
Num	14.11		3	
Deut	15.7		3	
	25.7		3	
Neh	9.16		3	
Esth	1.12		3	

REFUSE (1)(cont.)

Job	22.7		3	
Prov	21.7		3	
Zech	14.17		3	
Heb	11.24		3	>
Ex	4.9		2	
	7.14		2	>
	8.2	<	2	>
	9.2	<	2	
	10.3		2	>
Num	20.18		2	
	22.13		2	>
Josh	22.18		2	
2 Sam	12.16		2	
1 Kgs	21.15	<	2	>
Prov	1.7		2	
	13.13		2	
Is	30.9		2	
Jer	5.3		2	>
	11.8		2	
	25.7		2	
Ezek	18.8		2	
Mt	25.45		2	
Heb	12.25	<	2	

REGULATION

Lev	7.1	<	7	
	23.2	<	6	>
Num	15.2		6	
Lev	6.1	<	5	>
	16.29	<	3	>
	22.9		3	>
Num	9.2	<	3	
Ex	12.43		2	
Lev	5.10		2	>
	14.2	<	2	>
	15.1	<	2	>
	17.2	<	2	>
	20.9	<	2	
Num	19.2		2	
Ezek	44.5	<	2	

REIGN

2 Kgs	15.1	<	8	>
1 Kgs	16.8	<	6	
2 Kgs	18.1	<	6	
Ezra	4.5		6	>
1 Kgs	15.1	<	5	>
2 Kgs	13.1	<	4	>
1 Kgs	6.1		3	
2 Kgs	8.16		3	
1 Kgs	1.37		2	
	22.41		2	
2 Kgs	12.1		2	>
	14.1	<	2	>
	17.1	<	2	>
	23.23	<	2	>
	24.10	<	2	>
2 Chr	9.27		2	

REIGN (cont.)

2 Chr	13.1	<	2	
	16.1	<	2	>
Ezra	6.3	<	2	>
	7.6	<	2	
Dan	6.28		2	

REJECT

Rom	11.1		4	
Lev	18.25		3	
Num	14.11		3	>
1 Sam	15.23		3	>
Ezek	20.13		3	
Deut	31.20		2	>
	32.15	<	2	
1 Sam	8.7		2	
	16.1	<	2	
Ps	36.1		2	
	44.9		2	
	60.1		2	
	78.59	<	2	
Jer	2.20		2	
	6.19	<	2	>
Hos	4.6		2	
	8.3		2	>
Mt	10.33		2	
Lk	10.16		2	
	12.9		2	
Jn	12.11		2	
Acts	3.13		2	
1 Pet	2.4		2	
1 Jn	2.22		2	

REJOICE

Is	66.5	<	3	
Ps	97.1		2	
	149.2		2	
Is	9.3		2	
Ezek	35.14		2	

RELIGION

Lev	23.2		4	
Dan	11.28		4	
Acts	10.2		3	
1 Tim	6.3	<	3	
Jas	1.26		3	
1 Sam	10.6		2	
1 Chr	26.30		2	
Gal	1.13		2	

RELY

2 Kgs	18.21		3	
2 Chr	16.7		3	
Is	36.6		3	
Hos	7.8		3	
1 Chr	12.1		2	
Ps	22.8		2	
Prov	14.5	<	2	
	25.13		2	

RELY (cont.)

Is	30.5		2	>
	31.1	<	2	
Ezek	29.6		2	

REMEMBER

Ps	74.2		5	
Neh	13.14		4	
Ps	137.1		4	
Prov	4.2	<	4	
Lk	1.36		4	>
Heb	13.2		4	
Ex	32.13		3	>
Deut	7.9	<	3	>
	8.2	<	3	>
Ps	106.4	<	3	
	119.49		3	
Ezek	16.22		3	
Mic	6.5		3	
2 Tim	1.3		3	>
Jude	6		3	
Gen	9.15		2	
Ex	28.12		2	
Deut	9.14	<	2	
	11.2		2	>
	24.9		2	>
	25.17	<	2	
	32.26		2	
Josh	1.9		2	
	22.17		2	
Judg	9.2	<	2	
1 Sam	1.11		2	
1 Kgs	2.5		2	
Neh	6.14	<	2	
Ps	9.5		2	
	25.6		2	
	77.5		2	>
	78.35	<	2	
	89.47		2	
	105.5		2	>
	109.14		2	
Prov	3.1		2	>
	22.6	<	2	>
Ecc	1.11		2	>
	11.8		2	>
Is	44.21		2	
	46.8		2	
Jer	14.10		2	>
	15.15	<	2	
Lam	5.1		2	
Ezek	3.10	<	2	
Zech	10.7		2	
Mt	5.18		2	
Lk	24.6	<	2	
Jn	2.17		2	>
	15.18	<	2	>
Acts	20.31		2	
Rom	1.9		2	
1 Cor	1.16		2	

REMEMBER (cont.)

Eph	6.8		2	
2 Tim	3.1	<	2	
Heb	10.17		2	
Jas	5.10		2	
2 Pet	1.15		2	

REMIND

Ex	13.9	<	4	
Gen	31.44		3	
Ezek	20.4		3	>
Num	15.39		2	
Josh	4.6		2	

REPAY

Ex	22.7		4	
Lev	6.4		2	

REPAYMENT-OFFERING

Lev	7.1	<	4	
	5.15		3	>
	14.12		3	
	6.6	<	2	>

REPENT

1 Kgs	8.35		3	
2 Chr	6.26		3	>
Lk	15.7		3	
	17.3		2	
Acts	26.20		2	
Heb	6.4		2	
Rev	2.21		2	

REPRESENT

Ezek	4.1		3	
Dan	8.20		3	
Ex	28.12		2	
	39.7		2	
Num	17.3		2	
Ezek	23.4		2	
	37.19		2	
Gal	4.24		2	

REQUIRE

Num	29.15	<	8	>
	30.5	<	3	
2 Chr	31.3		3	
Neh	10.29		3	
Mt	5.6		3	>
Lk	2.24		3	
Gal	2.16		3	>
	3.2	<	3	
Num	6.15	<	2	
2 Chr	34.32		2	
Neh	8.9		2	
	12.44		2	
Jer	5.4		2	
Lk	12.48		2	

RESCUE

Judg	6.9		5	>
Dan	6.14		4	
1 Chr	17.5	<	3	
Ps	71.2		3	>
	144.7	<	3	
Ex	2.17		2	>
	3.7	<	2	
Deut	5.6	<	2	>
	6.12	<	2	
	13.5		2	
	32.36		2	
Judg	10.13		2	
1 Sam	10.18		2	>
	11.9	<	2	>
	12.10	<	2	
	30.8		2	
2 Sam	7.6		2	
2 Kgs	11.2		2	
	17.7	<	2	>
Neh	9.27		2	
Ps	22.19		2	
	34.7		2	>
	35.2	<	2	
	72.12	<	2	
	106.10		2	>
	107.2	<	2	>
	143.9		2	>
Is	29.6		2	
	35.4	<	2	>
	38.6	<	2	
	49.24		2	
	63.9	<	2	
Ezek	34.10		2	
Dan	3.28		2	
Zech	10.6		2	
2 Tim	4.17	<	2	
2 Pet	2.7		2	

RESPECT

Ezek	22.8		3	
Lk	18.2		3	
1 Pet	2.17		3	>
Lev	19.3		2	
2 Sam	14.4		2	
Esth	1.18		2	
Ps	119.48		2	
Prov	11.16		2	
	13.15		2	>
	31.25		2	
Is	3.5		2	
	49.7		2	
Dan	6.13		2	
Mal	1.6		2	>
	2.5	<	2	>
	3.5	<	2	
Mk	12.6		2	
Lk	20.13		2	
1 Thes	5.12	<	2	

RESPECT (cont.)

1 Tim	3.4		2	
1 Pet	3.7	<	2	

REST (1) [RELAX]

Heb	4.1	<	13	
Ex	16.23		4	
	31.13		4	
Lev	23.3		4	
	26.34	<	3	
Job	3.13		3	
Ex	20.10		2	
	23.11		2	
Lev	25.4		2	>
Deut	5.14		2	>
1 Kgs	7.2		2	
Prov	6.4		2	
Is	57.2		2	
Jer	47.6		2	
Ezek	32.30	<	2	
Dan	4.12		2	
Mt	11.28		2	>
Heb	3.11		2	>

RESTORATION

Lev	25.15		9	
	27.17		5	

RESTORE

Jer	30.3	<	4	>
Dan	9.17	<	3	
Gen	40.13		2	>
Lev	25.10		2	
Ps	41.3		2	
Amos	9.11		2	

RESULT

Rom	5.12		4	>
	6.16	<	4	
	8.6		2	>
	9.8	<	2	
Gal	4.23		2	

REVEAL

Dan	2.19		6	
1 Pet	1.5		5	
Jn	13.31	<	4	>
Rev	1.1		4	
Jn	14.17	<	3	>
Eph	5.13	<	3	
2 Sam	7.17		2	
1 Chr	17.15		2	
Dan	10.1		2	
Hab	2.2	<	2	
Lk	2.32		2	
Rom	1.17		2	>
	8.18	<	2	>
	9.4	<	2	
1 Cor	14.6		2	

REVEAL (cont.)

Gal	1.12		2	>
Eph	3.3		2	>
2 Tim	1.10		2	
Rev	19.10		2	>

REVENGE

Ezek	25.12	<	6	
1 Sam	25.26		4	
Num	35.12		3	
Deut	32.35		3	
Josh	20.3		3	
Jer	50.15		3	>
Gen	4.10		2	
Deut	19.6		2	
2 Sam	4.8	<	2	
Jer	5.9		2	
	20.10		2	
	51.6	<	2	
Rom	12.19		2	

REWARD

Mt	6.1	<	4	
Esth	6.3		3	
Prov	14.14	<	3	
Mt	10.41		3	
Gen	15.1		2	
Num	22.17		2	
	24.11		2	
Ruth	2.12		2	
2 Sam	22.21		2	
Ps	18.20		2	>
Prov	11.18	<	2	>
	13.2	<	2	>
Mt	5.12		2	>
Lk	6.23		2	
1 Cor	3.8		2	
Heb	11.6	<	2	>

RICH

Lk	16.1		8	
2 Sam	12.1		5	
Prov	28.6		5	
1 Tim	6.5		5	
Prov	22.2	<	4	>
Ecc	5.10		4	
Deut	33.14	<	3	
Prov	10.4		3	>
Mt	19.22		3	
Mk	10.22		3	
Lk	12.15		3	
	18.23		3	>
2 Cor	8.7		3	>
Jas	1.10		3	>
	2.2	<	3	
Rev	18.3		3	
Ex	3.8		2	
Deut	26.9		2	>
	28.12	<	2	

ICH (cont.)

Esth	1.5		2	
Ps	49.2		2	
	65.9		2	
	119.36		2	
Prov	11.16	<	2	
	13.7		2	>
	18.11		2	>
	23.4	<	2	
Ecc	10.6		2	
Ezek	20.6		2	
	22.12		2	
Dan	11.2	<	2	
Hos	12.8		2	
Hab	2.6		2	
Rom	11.12	<	2	
2 Cor	9.10	<	2	
Rev	3.17	<	2	

ICHES

Mt	6.19		3	
Lk	12.21		3	
Ps	49.6		2	
Prov	11.4		2	
Jas	5.2		2	

ID

Deut	22.21	<	3	
Ex	8.9		2	
Lev	26.6		2	
Deut	19.13		2	
Josh	24.14		2	
1 Sam	7.3		2	
Esth	9.16		2	
Eph	4.22		2	

IGHT (1) [CORRECT]

Ezek	18.19		10	
	33.14		6	>
Prov	21.2	<	4	>
Dan	9.5		4	
Ex	18.16		3	
Job	33.26	<	3	
Prov	4.11	<	3	
	11.18		3	>
	15.9	<	3	>
	16.2	<	3	>
	18.1	<	3	
	20.4		3	>
Is	30.10		3	
Mal	2.6		3	>
Jn	7.6		3	>
Rom	2.2		3	>
	3.4	<	3	
1 Jn	3.7	<	3	
Deut	32.4		2	>
2 Sam	22.21		2	
1 Kgs	8.18		2	
2 Chr	6.8		2	

RIGHT (1)(cont.)

2 Chr	19.2		2	>
Job	6.29		2	
	10.3		2	>
	11.1	<	2	
	22.3		2	
	27.5		2	
Ps	14.1		2	>
	18.20	<	2	>
	26.1	<	2	
	37.14		2	>
	53.1		2	
	119.121		2	
Ecc	3.11	<	2	
	5.1		2	
Is	5.7		2	
	26.2		2	
	32.8		2	>
	41.1		2	
	43.9		2	
	45.13		2	
	59.14		2	>
	60.21	<	2	>
Jer	33.10		2	
Dan	4.27		2	
Amos	5.14		2	>
Mal	3.3	<	2	
Mt	15.7	<	2	
	21.32		2	
Mk	7.6	<	2	
Lk	10.28		2	
Jn	16.8		2	
Rom	7.12		2	
	14.21		2	
2 Cor	8.21		2	
Phil	1.7		2	
2 Thes	1.3		2	
Heb	13.9	<	2	

RIGHT (2) [HAND]

Lev	14.14		14	
	8.23	<	8	>
Gen	48.13		4	
Ex	29.20		4	
Mt	5.29		3	
Rev	1.16		3	>
Ex	15.6		2	
Lev	7.32		2	>
Judg	3.16		2	
Ps	110.1		2	
Ezek	21.16		2	
Mt	20.21		2	
	25.33		2	>
	27.29	<	2	
Mk	10.37		2	
	16.5	<	2	
Lk	22.50		2	>
Acts	2.33		2	>
	7.55		2	

RIGHT (2)(cont.)

Heb	1.3		2	
Rev	5.1		2	
	10.2		2	

RIGHT (3) [CLAIM]

1 Cor	9.4		10	
Lev	25.24		6	
Gen	25.31		5	
Mt	21.23	<	5	
Mk	11.28	<	5	
Lk	20.2		4	
2 Sam	19.28		3	
Prov	31.5		3	
Jon	4.4		3	
Ruth	4.4		2	
1 Chr	5.1		2	
Prov	29.7		2	
Mt	20.15		2	>
Lk	18.3		2	
	22.29		2	
Jn	5.22		2	
	10.18		2	

RIGHT WITH GOD

Rom	3.20	<	8	>
	10.3		6	
Gal	2.16		5	>
	3.8	<	5	
Rom	5.1	<	4	>
	4.2	<	3	>
	9.30	<	3	
Jas	2.21		3	
Rom	1.17		2	>
	8.10		2	>
Gal	5.4		2	

RIGHTEOUS

Rom	4.3	<	9	>
Ps	119.7	<	8	
Prov	11.6	<	7	>
	12.3	<	7	>
	13.6	<	5	>
Ps	37.6	<	4	
	72.1	<	4	
	97.2		4	
Prov	2.7		4	>
	10.24		4	>
	29.2	<	4	
Ezek	18.5		4	
Rom	3.10	<	4	>
	6.13	<	4	
Phil	3.6		4	
Ps	34.15	<	3	>
	71.2		3	>
	85.10		3	
Prov	21.12		3	
Is	1.21		3	
Mt	25.33		3	

RIGHTEOUS (cont.)

Rom	5.7	<	3	>
Job	4.7		2	
Ps	7.9		2	
	9.8		2	
	31.1		2	>
	33.1	<	2	>
	35.24	<	2	>
	36.6	<	2	>
	58.10		2	
	111.3		2	
	125.3		2	
Prov	3.32	<	2	>
	14.19	<	2	>
Ecc	8.14		2	>
	9.1	<	2	
Hab	1.4		2	>
Lk	1.17		2	
Heb	11.4	<	2	>
1 Pet	2.23		2	>
2 Pet	2.5	<	2	>
1 Jn	2.1		2	>
	3.7	<	2	

RISE

Mt	22.23		4	
Mk	9.9	<	4	
Lk	20.27		4	
Jer	46.7		3	>
Mk	12.18		3	
Lk	24.7	<	3	
Gen	19.23		2	
Deut	33.2		2	
Job	41.18		2	
Ezek	1.19		2	
	8.11		2	>
	10.4		2	
Amos	8.8		2	>
Lk	16.30		2	
Jn	5.29		2	
	11.23		2	
Acts	4.2		2	
	10.26		2	
	23.6		2	>
	24.15	<	2	
1 Thes	4.14		2	

RITUAL

Lev	16.16	<	8	
	14.2		7	>
Ex	12.25		2	
	29.4		2	>
Lev	12.7		2	
	15.15	<	2	>
	23.26		2	
Num	5.8		2	>
	6.11	<	2	
	8.12		2	
	15.25		2	>

RITUAL (cont.)

Num	16.46	<	2	
	19.9		2	
	28.22		2	>
	29.5	<	2	
2 Chr	30.18	<	2	
Neh	12.30		2	
Heb	9.13		2	

ROB

Ezek	18.7		5	
Is	33.1		4	
Ezek	36.13		3	
Prov	24.15	<	2	
Ezek	7.21		2	
	22.13		2	>
Hos	7.1	<	2	
Mt	6.19		2	
Lk	10.30		2	
Jn	10.1		2	
1 Cor	6.7		2	
2 Cor	11.8		2	

RUIN

Jer	48.8		6	>
Ezek	36.4	<	6	
Jer	25.9		4	>
Lam	2.1	<	4	>
Jer	4.7		3	
	44.2		3	
Ezek	26.10		3	
Zeph	2.9	<	3	>
Ex	9.31	<	2	
Lev	26.31		2	
Num	21.11		2	
2 Sam	20.19		2	
Neh	2.3		2	
Ps	52.2		2	
	79.1	<	2	
	102.6		2	
Prov	11.9	<	2	
	13.15		2	
	18.7		2	>
	19.3	<	2	
Is	5.9		2	>
	14.20	<	2	
	17.1		2	
	23.1		2	>
	24.3	<	2	>
	32.7		2	
	49.19		2	
	58.12		2	>
	64.10		2	
Jer	2.7		2	
	9.11		2	
	10.20		2	
	49.2	<	2	>
	51.26	<	2	
Ezek	21.27		2	

RUIN (cont.)

Ezek	30.4	<	2	
	33.24		2	
Hos	5.9	<	2	
Amos	9.11		2	
Mic	6.13		2	
Hag	1.4		2	>

S

SABBATH

Neh	13.15		10	
Mt	12.1		8	
Lev	23.3		6	>
Jer	17.21		6	
Ezek	20.12		6	
Lk	6.1		6	
Mk	2.23	<	5	>
Lk	13.10		5	>
Ezek	46.1	<	4	
Lk	14.1	<	4	
Jn	5.9		4	
Acts	13.14		4	
2 Kgs	11.5		3	
Is	56.2		3	
Jn	7.22		3	
	19.31		3	
Ex	20.8		2	
Lev	19.3		2	
Num	28.9		2	
Deut	5.12		2	
2 Chr	23.4		2	
Neh	10.31		2	
Ezek	22.8		2	>
Mk	3.2	<	2	
Lk	4.16		2	
	23.54		2	
Jn	9.14		2	

SACKCLOTH

Esth	4.1		4	
Jon	3.5		3	
1 Kgs	20.31		2	>
	21.27	<	2	
2 Kgs	19.1		2	
Is	37.1		2	

SACRED

Lev	22.2	<	10	
Num	18.3		5	
	4.15		4	
Ex	29.6		3	>
	36.1	<	3	>
Lev	10.4		3	
1 Sam	20.8		3	>
	21.4	<	3	
2 Kgs	10.22		3	
Neh	10.33		3	

SACRED (cont.)

Is	65.3	<	3	>
Jer	17.22		3	
Ex	25.8		2	>
	33.7		2	>
	35.2	<	2	>
	38.24	<	2	>
	39.30	<	2	>
Lev	21.11	<	2	>
Judg	18.18		2	
1 Chr	9.29		2	
	23.13	<	2	
2 Chr	35.3		2	
Is	64.10		2	>
	66.17	<	2	
Jer	31.23		2	
Ezek	44.8	<	2	
Dan	9.2		2	
Hos	10.1		2	
Joel	2.1		2	>
	3.17	<	2	
Obad	16		2	
Zeph	3.4		2	

SACRIFICE

Heb	10.1		15	>
Jer	44.3		10	
Deut	12.6		9	
2 Chr	29.21	<	9	>
Ex	8.8		7	
Lev	4.3		7	>
1 Sam	2.13	<	7	>
Ezek	43.15	<	7	>
	20.26		6	>
	40.38	<	6	
	45.18	<	6	>
Heb	9.9	<	6	
Ex	29.3		5	>
Lev	1.2		5	
	5.6	<	5	>
Josh	22.23		5	
1 Sam	16.2	<	5	
2 Kgs	17.17	<	5	
2 Chr	7.1		5	>
	30.14	<	5	
	35.6	<	5	
Ezra	3.2		5	>
	6.3		5	
Dan	8.11		5	>
Heb	13.10		5	
Gen	22.2		4	
Lev	7.7	<	4	
Num	15.3		4	
1 Sam	1.3		4	>
	15.15		4	>
1 Kgs	1.9		4	
	8.5		4	
2 Kgs	16.3	<	4	>
	23.5	<	4	

SACRIFICE (cont.)

2 Chr	28.3		4	>
Ps	50.5		4	>
	51.16	<	4	
Jer	7.9	<	4	
	11.12		4	
Ezek	16.19		4	
	44.7	<	4	>
	46.2	<	4	
Hos	4.10	<	4	>
Ex	5.3		3	
Lev	6.7	<	3	>
	16.6		3	>
Deut	18.1	<	3	
2 Sam	6.13		3	
1 Kgs	3.2		3	
	12.26	<	3	>
2 Kgs	12.3		3	
1 Chr	16.1	<	3	
	21.26		3	
2 Chr	33.6		3	>
Ezek	18.6		3	
Mal	1.8		3	>
Heb	11.4	<	3	
Gen	8.20		2	
Ex	10.25		2	
	23.18	<	2	>
	24.5	<	2	
	32.6		2	
	34.15		2	
Lev	9.4		2	
	17.7	<	2	
	22.28		2	>
	23.12	<	2	
Num	18.8		2	
Deut	27.6		2	
	32.17		2	>
	33.10	<	2	
Judg	20.26		2	>
	21.4	<	2	
1 Sam	7.9	<	2	
	9.12		2	
	20.6		2	
1 Kgs	13.1	<	2	
	18.36		2	
2 Kgs	3.20		2	
	10.19		2	
	15.4	<	2	>
1 Chr	6.49		2	
	29.21		2	
2 Chr	34.4	<	2	>
Ezra	8.35		2	>
	9.4	<	2	
Neh	10.33		2	
Ps	40.6		2	
	106.28		2	>
Prov	21.3		2	
Is	1.11		2	
	34.6		2	

SACRIFICE (cont.)

Is	57.5	<	2	
	65.3		2	>
	66.3	<	2	
Jer	19.4		2	
	52.18		2	
Ezek	23.37	<	2	
	39.17		2	>
Dan	9.21	<	2	
Zech	9.11		2	
	14.21		2	
Acts	7.41		2	
	14.13		2	
1 Cor	9.13		2	
	10.18		2	
Heb	5.1		2	
	7.27		2	>

SAD

2 Cor	7.8	<	8	
	2.1		7	
Jn	16.6		4	
Neh	2.1		3	
1 Sam	1.8		2	
2 Sam	13.4		2	
Neh	8.10		2	
Ps	42.5		2	>
Lk	18.23		2	

SADDUCEES

Mt	16.1		4	
Acts	23.6		3	
Mt	22.23		2	
Mk	12.18		2	

SAFE

Ps	18.2	<	5	>
2 Sam	22.3		4	
Ezek	34.14		4	
1 Sam	20.7		3	
2 Sam	3.21		3	
Ps	31.4		3	
	91.1		3	
Prov	3.17		3	>
Mic	2.2		3	
Jn	17.11		3	
Gen	19.20		2	
Ex	21.13		2	
Lev	25.18		2	>
	26.5	<	2	
Deut	19.4		2	
Josh	10.20		2	
2 Sam	7.1		2	
	18.29	<	2	>
1 Kgs	22.27		2	
2 Chr	18.26		2	>
Ezra	9.8		2	
Job	5.4		2	
Ps	22.9		2	

SAFE (cont.)

Ps	27.5	<	2	
	40.2		2	
	48.3		2	
	61.2		2	
	119.73		2	
	140.1		2	
Prov	10.9		2	
	28.18		2	>
Is	14.30		2	
	32.18		2	>
	33.16	<	2	
	59.8		2	
Jer	7.4	<	2	
	17.14		2	
	39.14		2	
Col	1.5		2	
Heb	6.18		2	
1 Jn	5.18		2	
Rev	3.10		2	

SAKE

1 Kgs	11.12		6	
Phlm	1		5	
2 Cor	5.13	<	4	
Ezek	36.22		3	
2 Cor	4.5		3	>
Phil	3.7	<	3	
2 Sam	9.1		2	
	18.5		2	
Ps	122.8		2	
Is	63.17		2	
Mt	10.18		2	
	19.12		2	
Mk	13.9		2	
Jn	11.15		2	>
1 Cor	4.6		2	
	10.28		2	>
2 Cor	8.9		2	
Phil	2.22	<	2	>

SALVATION

Heb	2.3	<	3	
1 Pet	1.5		3	
Ps	40.10		2	
Lk	2.30	<	2	>
1 Thes	5.8		2	

SATAN

Job	1.6		5	>
	2.1	<	5	
Rev	2.9		4	>
	20.2		3	
Zech	3.1		2	
Mk	3.23		2	>
Lk	22.3		2	

SATISFY

Ezek	16.28		3	
Josh	22.30		2	
Ps	49.13		2	
	78.29		2	
Is	58.10	<	2	
Jer	31.14		2	
Joel	2.19		2	
2 Pet	2.13		2	

SAVE

Ps	119.39	<	15	>
2 Sam	22.1		10	
2 Chr	32.11		8	
Ps	18.3	<	8	
Ezek	14.14	<	7	
2 Kgs	18.29		6	>
Ps	31.1	<	6	>
	69.1	<	6	>
	80.2	<	6	>
	107.2	<	6	>
Is	36.14		6	>
	43.1	<	6	>
Ps	22.4		5	
	25.2	<	5	>
	106.4		5	>
	116.4		5	
Is	45.15	<	5	>
	51.1	<	5	>
	59.1	<	5	>
	63.1	<	5	
Ex	18.4		4	
Job	5.15		4	>
Ps	34.6	<	4	>
	86.2	<	4	
Mt	27.40		4	
Lk	23.35		4	
Rom	10.1		4	>
1 Sam	14.23		3	
	17.37		3	
Job	33.17		3	
Ps	7.1	<	3	
	17.7		3	>
	35.3	<	3	
	44.6		3	
	49.12		3	>
	50.15	<	3	>
	62.1		3	
	85.7		3	>
	109.26	<	3	
Is	44.17	<	3	>
	46.2	<	3	>
	47.13	<	3	>
	49.6	<	3	>
	62.1	<	3	>
Ezek	33.8		3	
Dan	6.20		3	
Mic	6.5	<	3	>
Acts	2.21		3	

SAVE (cont.)

Acts	16.17	<	3	
	27.20		3	
1 Tim	2.4	<	3	
1 Pet	3.20	<	3	>
Gen	37.21		2	
Ex	14.13		2	>
	16.20	<	2	
Judg	2.16		2	
	8.22		2	>
	10.12		2	
1 Sam	4.3		2	
	12.7		2	
	23.2		2	>
2 Sam	19.5	<	2	
2 Kgs	19.6	<	2	
1 Chr	16.23		2	
Job	6.13	<	2	
Ps	28.8		2	
	33.17	<	2	>
	37.39		2	
	40.9	<	2	
	59.1		2	>
	68.19		2	>
	71.2	<	2	>
	78.22	<	2	>
	91.14		2	
	118.14		2	>
	130.7		2	
	144.7	<	2	>
Prov	11.4	<	2	
Is	37.6	<	2	>
	41.10		2	>
	48.17	<	2	>
	50.2	<	2	>
	54.5		2	
	60.16	<	2	>
	61.2	<	2	>
Jer	2.27		2	
	31.7	<	2	
Lam	3.26		2	
Dan	3.15		2	
Hos	13.10		2	>
Mic	7.7	<	2	
Hab	3.13		2	
Zech	9.16	<	2	
Mk	8.35		2	
	15.30		2	>
Lk	1.71		2	>
	7.16	<	2	>
	9.24	<	2	
	17.33		2	>
	19.10	<	2	
Acts	15.1		2	>
Rom	5.9		2	
	11.14	<	2	
1 Cor	1.18		2	
	7.16		2	
2 Cor	1.10		2	>

SAVE (cont.)

2 Cor	2.15	<	2	
	6.2		2	
Eph	2.5		2	
2 Thes	2.10		2	
Tit	3.5		2	

SCATTER

Ezek	6.5	<	5	
Jer	23.1		4	>
Ezek	34.5		4	
Gen	11.4		3	
Deut	30.1		3	
Ps	68.1		3	
Ezek	5.2	<	3	>
	20.23		3	
Deut	28.37		2	
Neh	1.8		2	
Is	41.2		2	
Jer	9.16	<	2	
	29.14		2	>
	40.12		2	
	49.32		2	>
Lam	4.1		2	
Ezek	11.16	<	2	>
	12.14	<	2	
	30.23	<	2	>
Zeph	3.10		2	
Zech	1.19		2	>
Mt	25.24		2	>
Mk	4.4		2	
Acts	5.36		2	
	8.1		2	

SCHOLAR

Ezra	7.6		4	
Neh	8.1		2	
	12.26		2	>
1 Cor	1.19		2	

SCRIPTURE

Gal	3.6		9	>
Lk	4.4		6	
Rom	10.6		5	>
	15.3	<	5	
1 Cor	15.3	<	5	
Mt	4.4		4	
	26.24		4	
Jn	19.24		4	>
Rom	4.3	<	4	
	11.2	<	4	>
Mt	21.13		3	>
Mk	14.21		3	
Lk	24.27		3	
Jn	7.38	<	3	
Rom	9.13	<	3	
1 Pet	2.3	<	3	>
Mk	9.12		2	
	12.10	<	2	

SCRIPTURE (cont.)

Jn	2.17		2	
	5.39		2	>
	12.14		2	>
Acts	8.32		2	
	17.3		2	>
	18.24	<	2	
Rom	1.2		2	>
	3.4	<	2	>
	12.19	<	2	
1 Cor	1.19		2	>
	2.9	<	2	>
	3.19	<	2	
	10.7		2	
Gal	4.27	<	2	
Eph	5.31	<	2	
2 Tim	3.15		2	
Heb	2.6		2	>
	3.13	<	2	>
	4.4	<	2	
	7.8		2	
Jas	2.8		2	
	4.5		2	
1 Pet	1.16		2	>

SCROLL

Jer	36.2		18	
Rev	5.1		7	>
	10.2		4	
Ezek	3.1	<	3	
Zech	5.1		3	
Ezek	2.9		2	>
Lk	4.17		2	

SEAL

Rev	6.1	<	6	>
Esth	8.2		4	
Jer	32.10		4	
Rev	5.1		4	>
	7.2	<	3	>
Gen	38.18		2	
Is	29.11		2	
Dan	6.17		2	

SECRET

Eph	3.3		6	
Col	1.26		4	>
1 Cor	2.1		3	
Deut	27.15		2	>
Prov	25.9		2	
Is	45.3		2	
Jer	23.18		2	
1 Cor	4.1		2	
	14.2	<	2	>
Eph	5.12		2	>
Rev	10.4		2	
	17.5		2	

SECURE

Deut	24.6		3	
Ezek	18.7		3	
Deut	33.25		2	
Prov	10.9		2	>
Ezek	38.11	<	2	
Mt	27.65		2	

SEED

Mt	13.4		14	
Mk	4.4		11	
Lk	8.5		8	
1 Cor	15.36		4	
2 Cor	9.6		4	
Gen	47.19		3	
Lev	11.37		3	
Ps	126.5		2	
Is	28.25		2	
Mt	25.24		2	

SELF-CONTROL

Tit	2.2	<	4	
2 Pet	1.6		2	

SENSE

Prov	10.5		3	>
Deut	32.6		2	
Job	34.34		2	
Prov	12.16	<	2	>
	17.16		2	
	19.11		2	
	23.9	<	2	
	28.2	<	2	>
Is	44.19		2	
Hos	4.11		2	

SEPARATE

Gen	1.4		5	
Rom	8.35		3	>
Num	8.6		2	
Judg	7.4		2	
Ezek	34.17		2	
Lk	22.31		2	

SERVANT

Gen	24.2		18	
Mt	25.14	<	12	>
Lk	12.36		11	
1 Sam	25.8		9	>
2 Kgs	4.12		9	>
Ps	119.17		9	
Mt	18.23		9	
1 Sam	9.3	<	8	
Mt	24.45	<	8	>
Gen	26.14		7	>
2 Kgs	5.2	<	7	>
Job	1.3		7	>
Lk	19.13		7	
Gen	32.4		6	

SERVANT (cont.)

Gen	43.16		6	>
1 Kgs	8.26		6	
	11.13	<	6	
Is	49.1	<	6	>
Mt	22.3		6	>
Lk	14.17		6	>
Josh	1.1		5	
Judg	19.3		5	
2 Sam	9.2		5	
	13.17		5	>
2 Chr	6.17		5	
Ps	89.3		5	>
	105.5	<	5	>
Is	44.1	<	5	>
Gen	44.1	<	4	>
2 Sam	7.5	<	4	
1 Kgs	18.36		4	>
1 Chr	17.4	<	4	
Neh	1.6		4	>
Esth	1.8		4	
Lk	1.38		4	>
	7.2		4	
Acts	4.25	<	4	
Gen	22.3	<	3	
	39.4		3	>
1 Sam	2.13	<	3	>
2 Sam	19.17		3	
2 Kgs	8.4		3	>
Ezra	2.55		3	
Neh	7.57	<	3	
Esth	4.4		3	
Is	42.1	<	3	>
Jer	33.21		3	
Ezek	37.24		3	>
Dan	9.6		3	
Mt	8.6		3	
Lk	15.22	<	3	>
	16.1	<	3	>
	17.7	<	3	
Jn	2.5		3	
2 Cor	11.15		3	
Col	1.7		3	
Rev	19.2		3	
	22.3		3	
Num	12.7		2	
Deut	12.12	<	2	
	16.11	<	2	
Josh	8.31		2	>
	11.12		2	>
	22.2		2	
Judg	3.19	<	2	
	7.10	<	2	
1 Sam	3.9	<	2	
	10.10		2	
2 Sam	14.30	<	2	
	16.1		2	>
1 Kgs	10.5		2	>
	14.8		2	>

SERVANT (cont.)

1 Kgs	19.3	<	2	>
2 Kgs	6.15	<	2	
	9.7	<	2	
	17.13	<	2	>
	21.8	<	2	>
1 Chr	16.12		2	>
2 Chr	24.6		2	
Esth	6.3		2	
Job	19.15		2	
	31.13		2	
Ps	69.17		2	
	79.2	<	2	
	86.2		2	
	90.13	<	2	
	106.16	<	2	
	135.1	<	2	>
	143.2		2	>
Prov	27.18		2	
	29.19		2	>
	30.10	<	2	>
Is	37.24		2	
	41.8		2	>
	53.2	<	2	>
Jer	25.4		2	>
Ezek	34.23		2	
Mt	26.69	<	2	
Mk	14.66	<	2	
Lk	22.26		2	
Jn	15.15		2	
Acts	2.18		2	>
	3.13	<	2	>
Rom	13.4		2	>
1 Cor	4.1	<	2	
2 Cor	6.4		2	
Phil	1.1		2	>
Col	4.7		2	
Rev	1.1		2	>

SERVE

Josh	24.14	<	13	
Ezek	44.11	<	7	>
1 Sam	2.11		6	>
Jer	27.6		6	>
Gen	43.31		5	
Ex	28.1		5	>
Deut	28.14		5	>
Judg	2.7		4	
1 Kgs	12.6		4	>
2 Chr	17.4		4	
Gen	18.3		3	>
Ex	29.9	<	3	
Deut	18.5	<	3	
Judg	9.28	<	3	
	18.4		3	
1 Sam	12.14		3	
2 Sam	13.5	<	3	
1 Kgs	9.4		3	
2 Kgs	17.16		3	

SERVE (cont.)

2 Kgs	23.9		3	
Ezek	40.45		3	
Dan	7.10	<	3	
Mal	3.14		3	
Jn	12.2		3	
Rom	7.6		3	
Ex	18.22		2	>
	40.13	<	2	
Lev	25.40		2	
Num	3.4		2	>
	18.1		2	
Deut	4.19		2	
	10.8		2	>
	11.13	<	2	
	15.12		2	
2 Sam	16.19	<	2	
1 Kgs	13.2	<	2	>
	19.10	<	2	
	22.46		2	
2 Kgs	10.18		2	
	20.3		2	
1 Chr	28.9		2	
2 Chr	9.4	<	2	
	10.6		2	>
	11.14	<	2	>
	34.13		2	>
Ps	86.11		2	
	119.10		2	
Prov	23.3		2	
Is	60.10		2	>
	65.8		2	
Jer	5.19		2	
	15.11		2	>
	16.11	<	2	>
	25.6		2	
	28.14	<	2	
	33.18		2	>
	35.15	<	2	
Ezek	20.24		2	
	42.14		2	>
Dan	3.17		2	
	6.16		2	>
Mk	10.45		2	
Lk	22.27		2	
Jn	2.10		2	
Acts	13.2		2	
Rom	1.9		2	
	3.5		2	
	12.7		2	
	16.1	<	2	
Eph	6.5		2	
1 Tim	1.4		2	
Heb	9.11	<	2	
1 Pet	5.2	<	2	

SERVICE

1 Chr	7.4		6	
Num	3.26		4	>

SERVICE (cont.)

Num	18.1		4	
Rom	15.8		4	>
	16.3	<	4	
Num	1.3		3	
	4.4	<	3	
2 Cor	8.6		3	>
Ex	30.30	<	2	
Josh	9.8		2	
1 Sam	16.21		2	
2 Sam	9.2		2	
1 Chr	25.1		2	
2 Chr	24.16		2	
Esth	3.2		2	
Lk	1.8		2	
1 Cor	12.6		2	
2 Cor	9.12	<	2	
Rev	14.13		2	

SEX

Lev	15.18		3	
	18.6		3	>
	20.13	<	3	
Judg	19.22		2	
Is	57.5		2	
Ezek	23.17		2	
Acts	15.20		2	
Rom	1.26		2	
1 Cor	6.13	<	2	
	10.7		2	
Rev	2.14		2	

SHAME

Ps	119.6		3	
Jer	3.3	<	3	
Rom	1.24		3	>
Ps	69.6		2	
Prov	25.10		2	
Jer	46.12		2	
Ezek	16.30		2	
Hab	2.10		2	
1 Cor	1.27		2	
	11.6		2	
Jude	12		2	

SHARE

Rom	8.17		4	
1 Cor	10.16		4	
2 Cor	1.5		4	
Phil	2.2	<	4	>
Num	31.36		3	>
Deut	18.1		3	
	21.16		3	
Josh	18.2	<	3	
1 Sam	1.4		3	>
Ezek	47.22		3	
1 Cor	9.10		3	
2 Cor	5.14		3	
Rev	18.4		3	

SHARE (cont.)

Num	10.29		2	
	32.19	<	2	
Josh	13.14		2	
	17.5		2	>
1 Sam	30.24		2	
Neh	8.10		2	
Prov	1.14		2	
Is	42.8		2	
Ezek	32.25		2	
	45.1	<	2	
Mt	10.41		2	
	21.34		2	
	25.21	<	2	
Lk	12.42		2	
	22.17		2	
Acts	2.42		2	>
Rom	12.8	<	2	
Col	1.11		2	
1 Thes	2.8		2	
Heb	2.10		2	
1 Pet	5.1	<	2	
2 Pet	1.3		2	

SHEEP

Ezek	34.2		20	
Jn	10.2		15	
Ex	22.1		6	>
1 Sam	15.3	<	6	>
Zech	11.4	<	6	
Num	31.28		5	>
Lev	5.6	<	4	>
Deut	28.4		4	
1 Sam	17.15	<	4	
	25.2	<	4	
2 Chr	29.21		4	>
Gen	30.33	<	3	>
	31.19	<	3	>
	32.5	<	3	>
Ex	12.5		3	
Num	15.3		3	
	32.16	<	3	
Deut	12.6		3	
	14.4		3	>
	15.14	<	3	>
1 Kgs	1.9		3	
Jer	50.6		3	
Mt	18.12		3	
Lk	15.4		3	
Gen	13.2	<	2	
	29.2		2	>
	38.12	<	2	
Ex	10.9		2	
	34.3		2	
Lev	1.2		2	
	3.6		2	>
	4.32	<	2	>
1 Sam	14.32		2	>
	16.11	<	2	>

SHEEP (cont.)

2 Sam	13.23	<	2	
1 Kgs	8.5		2	
2 Kgs	3.4		2	
1 Chr	4.39		2	>
2 Chr	18.2	<	2	
	30.24	<	2	>
	32.28	<	2	
Ezra	6.9		2	
Job	1.3		2	
Ps	44.11		2	
Prov	27.23		2	
Is	1.11		2	
	53.6		2	
Jer	33.12		2	
Ezek	36.37		2	
	45.13		2	
Mic	2.12		2	
Mt	10.6		2	
	12.11		2	
Jn	2.14		2	
	21.16		2	

SHELTER

Neh	8.14		4	
Lev	23.33		3	
Zech	14.16		3	
Acts	27.4		3	
Ex	9.19		2	
Deut	16.13		2	
1 Kgs	8.2		2	
Ps	31.4		2	

SHEPHERD

Ezek	34.2		11	
Zech	11.4		8	
Lk	2.8		5	
Jn	10.2		5	
Gen	29.3		2	
	46.32		2	>
Ex	2.17		2	
Ps	23.1		2	
	78.52	<	2	
Ecc	12.11		2	
Song	1.7		2	
Is	13.14		2	>
Jer	31.10		2	
	33.12		2	
1 Pet	5.2		2	

SIGHT

2 Kgs	17.17		4	
Jer	51.17		4	>
	25.9		3	
	44.6		3	
Deut	34.7		2	
1 Kgs	21.20		2	>
2 Kgs	24.3	<	2	
Jer	10.2		2	

SIGHT (cont.)

Lk	1.6		2	
	16.15		2	
Jn	9.15		2	
Rom	4.2	<	2	
2 Cor	8.21	<	2	
2 Pet	3.8		2	
Rev	12.1		2	>

SIGN (1) [INDICATION]

Gen	9.12		3	
Ex	31.13		3	
Is	7.11		3	
Ezek	24.17		3	
Josh	22.27		2	
2 Kgs	20.8	<	2	
Is	38.7	<	2	
Ezek	20.12		2	
Lk	1.22		2	>
	11.30		2	

SIN-OFFERING

Lev	16.3	<	7	
	5.1	<	5	>
	9.2	<	5	
	14.13		5	>
	10.16		4	
	4.14		3	>
	6.16	<	3	>
Num	6.11		3	>
	15.24		3	
	28.15		3	>
	29.5	<	3	
Ezek	45.17	<	3	
Lev	7.7	<	2	>
	8.2	<	2	>
	12.6		2	
	15.15	<	2	>
Num	7.12	<	2	>
	8.8	<	2	

SLAUGHTER

1 Sam	14.14		4	
Jer	51.23	<	3	
Deut	16.2		2	
Josh	10.10		2	
1 Sam	4.8		2	
Esth	8.11	<	2	>
	9.5	<	2	
Ps	44.11		2	

SLAVE

Ex	21.2	<	17	>
Gal	4.1	<	12	>
Lev	25.6		9	>
Rom	6.6		9	>
Jer	34.9		8	
Deut	15.12		6	>
Eph	6.5		6	

SLAVE (cont.)

Gen	16.1	<	5	>
	44.9	<	5	
Deut	5.6		5	>
2 Sam	18.21		5	
Gen	15.3		4	>
	30.3	<	4	>
Ex	6.5	<	4	
Deut	24.7	<	4	
Ezra	9.8		4	
Mk	12.2		4	
Lk	20.10		4	
1 Cor	7.21	<	4	
Gen	9.25		3	
	17.11	<	3	
	21.10	<	3	
	47.19	<	3	
Ex	2.5	<	3	
	14.5	<	3	>
	20.2		3	>
1 Sam	17.8		3	
Mt	21.34	<	3	
Jn	8.33		3	
	18.10		3	
Gen	12.5		2	
	20.14		2	>
	27.37		2	
	29.24		2	>
	35.25		2	
	46.18		2	>
Ex	9.20		2	
	13.3	<	2	>
Lev	19.20		2	
Deut	6.12	<	2	>
	13.5		2	
	28.32		2	
Josh	9.23		2	
1 Kgs	2.39		2	
	9.20		2	
Neh	5.5		2	
	9.17		2	
Prov	22.7		2	
Jer	2.14		2	
Lam	1.1		2	
	5.8		2	
Amos	2.6	<	2	
Mt	10.24		2	
	18.25		2	
Acts	7.6		2	
Rom	8.15	<	2	
1 Cor	9.19		2	
Col	3.11	<	2	>
1 Tim	6.1		2	
Tit	2.3		2	>
Phlm	16		2	
2 Pet	2.19		2	

SOLEMN

Ex	13.5		3	
Josh	9.15		3	
Judg	21.1		3	
Gen	50.11		2	
1 Kgs	1.13		2	>
	2.8	<	2	
Ezek	32.2		2	
Acts	20.21		2	
Heb	3.11		2	>

SON OF GOD

1 Jn	5.5	<	11	
Jn	5.19		10	>
	3.16		7	
Col	1.13		7	
Heb	1.2		6	
Rom	8.3		5	
Jn	1.14		4	
1 Jn	2.22	<	4	>
	4.9	<	4	>
Mt	11.27		3	
	27.40	<	3	>
Lk	4.3	<	3	
	10.22		3	
Rom	1.3		3	
1 Jn	1.3		3	>
Mt	4.3	<	2	
Mk	1.1		2	
Lk	1.32		2	
Jn	11.4	<	2	
	17.1		2	
Gal	4.4		2	
1 Thes	1.10		2	
Heb	5.5	<	2	>
	7.3	<	2	
1 Jn	3.8	<	2	>
2 Jn	3		2	

SON OF MAN

Mt	24.27		6	>
	26.2	<	5	
Mk	14.21	<	4	
Lk	9.22		4	
	12.8	<	4	
	17.22		4	>
Mt	12.8	<	3	>
	16.13		3	>
	17.9	<	3	
Mk	9.9	<	3	
Lk	22.22	<	3	
Jn	6.27	<	3	
	12.23		3	>
Mt	13.37	<	2	
	20.18	<	2	
Mk	2.10		2	
	8.31		2	>
	10.33		2	
Lk	6.5	<	2	>

SON OF MAN (cont.)

Lk 18.8 < 2 >
21.27 2 >
Jn 3.13 2
13.31 < 2

SORROW

Gen 44.13 3
37.29 2
Jer 14.2 2
Ezek 19.1 2
Phil 2.27 2

SOUL

Ps 103.1 3 >
63.1 2
104.1 < 2
Mt 10.28 2
1 Pet 2.11 < 2

SOVEREIGN

Ezek 36.2 < 14 >
16.3 < 11 >
20.3 11 >
14.4 < 9 >
39.1 < 9
34.2 < 8 >
13.3 < 7 >
23.22 < 7 >
26.3 < 7 >
28.2 < 7 >
2 Sam 7.18 6
Ezek 12.10 < 6 >
24.3 < 6 >
25.3 < 6 >
29.3 < 6 >
32.8 < 6 >
37.3 < 6 >
38.3 < 6 >
Is 22.5 5
Ezek 17.3 < 5 >
18.3 < 5
22.3 < 5 >
30.2 < 5 >
44.6 < 5 >
5.5 < 4 >
11.7 4 >
21.7 < 4 >
35.3 < 4 >
45.9 < 4 >
Amos 7.1 < 4 >
Is 50.4 < 3
Ezek 31.10 < 3 >
33.11 < 3 >
43.18 3 >
Amos 3.7 3 >
8.1 < 3 >
Gen 15.2 2
Ps 71.5 2

SOVEREIGN (cont.)

Is 10.23 2
61.1 2
Jer 2.19 < 2
32.17 2
50.25 2
Ezek 3.11 < 2 >
6.3 < 2 >
7.2 < 2 >
15.6 < 2 >
46.1 < 2 >
47.13 < 2 >
Amos 4.2 < 2 >
5.3 < 2 >
9.5 < 2

SOW

Mt 13.3 10
Lev 25.3 6 >
Is 28.24 4
Mk 4.3 4
Ecc 11.4 3
1 Cor 3.6 3
2 Cor 9.6 3
Gal 6.7 3
Gen 26.12 2
47.19 2
Lev 26.5 < 2 >
Mt 25.24 2
Lk 19.21 2
Jn 4.36 2
1 Cor 15.36 2

SPARE

Josh 10.30 3
Jer 38.17 3
Gen 18.24 2
Deut 32.25 2
Josh 6.17 2
1 Sam 26.21 2
Jer 21.7 2
Ezek 3.19 2
7.4 < 2 >
33.9 2
Rom 11.21 2
2 Pet 2.4 2

SPECIAL

Num 18.8 9
Lev 7.14 6 >
23.11 6
Ezek 48.8 6
Num 15.19 4
Ex 29.24 3
Lev 14.12 3
Num 8.11 3
Lev 8.27 < 2 >
Num 6.2 < 2
31.29 2

SPECIAL (cont.)

Judg 20.15 2
Esth 2.9 2
2 Tim 2.20 2

SPIRIT (1)
(GOD'S SPIRIT)

Rom 8.2 < 22 >
1 Cor 12.1 13
2.4 10 >
Acts 8.15 < 7 >
2 Cor 3.3 7
Gal 5.5 < 7 >
1 Jn 4.1 < 7 >
Acts 2.4 < 6
Num 11.17 5
Acts 10.19 5 >
11.12 < 5
1 Jn 2.20 5 >
Mt 12.18 < 4
Lk 1.15 4 >
4.1 < 4
Jn 3.5 4 >
Acts 1.2 4 >
13.2 4
Rom 15.13 < 4
Gal 3.2 4 >
Eph 4.3 < 4 >
Rev 2.7 < 4 >
Ezek 3.12 < 3
11.1 3
Mk 1.8 3
Jn 1.32 3
Acts 4.8 3 >
5.3 < 3 >
6.3 < 3 >
19.2 3 >
20.22 < 3 >
Gal 4.6 < 3 >
Eph 1.13 3 >
2 Tim 1.7 3
1 Pet 1.2 3
1 Jn 5.6 < 3
Rev 3.6 < 3 >
1 Sam 10.6 2 >
16.13 2
19.20 2
Is 63.10 2
Joel 2.28 2
Mt 1.18 2
3.11 2 >
Lk 2.25 < 2 >
3.16 < 2 >
12.10 < 2
Jn 4.23 < 2
6.63 2 >
7.39 < 2
14.17 2 >
16.13 < 2

SPIRIT (1)(cont.)

Acts 7.51 < 2 >
9.17 < 2
15.8 2 >
16.6 < 2
21.4 < 2
1 Cor 3.1 < 2
6.11 2 >
14.2 2 >
Gal 6.8 < 2
Eph 2.18 < 2 >
3.5 < 2 >
6.17 < 2
Col 1.8 2
1 Thes 1.5 2
Tit 3.5 2
Heb 9.8 2
10.15 2
Jude 19 2
Rev 22.6 < 2

SPIRIT (2)
[OTHER SPIRITS]

Mk 9.17 9
1 Sam 16.14 5
Mk 5.2 5 >
Acts 19.12 5
Mk 1.23 4
1 Cor 14.14 4
1 Jn 4.1 4
Rev 16.13 4
1 Sam 28.8 3
Dan 4.8 3 >
Mk 3.11 3
Lk 4.33 3
Acts 16.16 3
1 Cor 5.3 < 3
Col 2.5 3
1 Pet 3.4 3
Lev 20.6 < 2
1 Kgs 22.21 2
2 Chr 18.20 2
Ps 51.10 2
Ecc 3.21 2
Lam 3.20 2
Dan 5.11 < 2
Mt 12.43 2
Lk 8.2 < 2 >
9.39 < 2
11.24 < 2
Acts 23.8 2
1 Cor 2.11 2
Gal 4.3 2

SPIRITUAL

1 Cor 15.24 < 5
2.6 3
Eph 2.1 < 3
Col 2.10 < 3

SPIRITUAL (cont.)

1 Tim	4.6		3	
1 Pet	2.2		3	>
Rom	4.11		2	
	11.12		2	
1 Cor	10.4		2	
	14.1		2	>
2 Cor	4.7		2	
Heb	12.9		2	
1 Pet	3.18	<	2	>

SPRINKLE

Num	19.4		5	
Lev	14.7		4	
	16.14		4	
Heb	9.13		3	
Lev	4.6		2	>
	8.11		2	
Ezek	43.18		2	

STAND FOR

Lk	8.12		4	
Mt	13.20		3	
Rev	13.17		2	

STEAL

Ex	22.1		9	
Gen	31.19	<	4	
1 Sam	25.7		3	
Gen	44.5		2	
Job	20.10		2	
	24.2		2	
Prov	9.17		2	
Mt	6.19		2	

STRANGE

1 Cor	14.2	<	16	
	12.10		3	>
Is	28.11		2	
Lk	21.11		2	

STRANGER

Mt	25.35		4	
Job	19.13		3	
Prov	5.10		2	
	27.2		2	

STRENGTH

Judg	16.9		4	
Ps	59.9		3	
	89.10	<	3	
Ex	15.13		2	
2 Sam	22.30		2	
Job	6.11		2	
	12.6		2	
	39.11		2	>
Ps	18.29		2	>
	21.1		2	>
	33.16	<	2	

STRENGTH (cont.)

Ps	119.28		2	
Is	40.29		2	>
	45.5		2	
	49.4		2	>
Ezek	22.6		2	
	30.18		2	
Dan	2.23		2	
	10.8		2	>
Mk	12.30		2	
Lk	22.32	<	2	
Acts	3.16		2	
	9.19		2	
	15.32	<	2	
Col	1.11		2	
1 Thes	3.2		2	
1 Pet	4.1		2	>

STRIKE

Ex	7.17		3	>
	9.15	<	3	
2 Kgs	2.8		3	
	6.18		3	
	13.18		3	
Acts	23.2		3	
Gen	32.25		2	
Ex	8.16	<	2	>
	17.5		2	
Deut	28.22		2	
1 Sam	25.22		2	>
2 Sam	1.15		2	>
	3.9	<	2	
Ps	35.6		2	
	91.6		2	
Dan	2.34		2	
Zech	14.5		2	

STRONG

2 Sam	22.2		5	
Judg	14.6		4	>
Ps	18.2		4	
Is	7.8		4	
Ex	1.7		3	
Num	13.18		3	
Judg	16.5	<	3	
2 Sam	11.16	<	3	
Job	40.9	<	3	>
Prov	18.10		3	
Dan	8.10		3	>
	11.5	<	3	
Zech	10.6		3	
Gen	49.3		2	
Josh	14.11		2	
	17.13		2	
1 Chr	11.9		2	
	29.12		2	
2 Chr	26.16	<	2	
Job	12.16		2	
	39.4		2	>

STRONG (cont.)

Job	41.12	<	2	
Ps	62.3	<	2	
	71.3		2	
	78.31		2	
	80.15		2	
	92.10		2	
	103.5		2	
	105.24		2	
	147.10		2	>
	148.8	<	2	
Prov	30.26	<	2	>
	31.17	<	2	
Is	18.2		2	
	26.1		2	
	28.2		2	
	59.17	<	2	
Jer	20.7		2	
	50.9		2	>
Ezek	13.11		2	
	19.11		2	>
	30.21	<	2	
	34.16		2	
Dan	2.40	<	2	>
	10.18		2	>
Amos	2.9		2	
Mt	12.29		2	
Mk	3.27		2	>
Lk	1.15		2	>
	11.21		2	
	23.5	<	2	
Jas	4.2	<	2	
Rev	18.3		2	

STUBBORN

Ex	7.3		4	>
	8.15	<	3	>
	9.7	<	3	
	10.1		3	>
	14.4	<	3	
Deut	9.6		3	
Heb	3.8		3	>
Ex	33.3	<	2	>
Deut	21.18		2	
Neh	9.16		2	
Jer	5.3		2	>
	6.10	<	2	>
	7.24	<	2	
Ezek	3.7	<	2	

STUPID

Prov	12.1		5	>
Ecc	10.1		4	
Prov	13.16	<	3	>
	14.8	<	3	>
	15.2	<	3	>
	26.8		3	>
Jer	10.8		3	
Prov	1.7		2	

STUPID (cont.)

Prov	10.13		2	
	19.3	<	2	>
	20.1	<	2	>
	24.7		2	
	27.3	<	2	
	29.11		2	
Ecc	7.5		2	

SUBJECT (1) [ALLEGIANCE]

2 Sam	8.2		3	
1 Chr	18.2		3	>
2 Sam	10.19		2	
1 Kgs	4.21		2	
1 Chr	19.19	<	2	

SUBMIT

Jer	27.8		6	
Eph	5.21		4	
Tit	2.5		2	>
1 Pet	2.13		2	>
	3.1	<	2	

SUCCEED (1) [ACCOMPLISH]

Gen	24.12		5	
1 Sam	18.5		5	
Gen	39.2		3	
Dan	8.12		3	
Josh	1.7		2	
1 Kgs	22.13		2	
1 Chr	22.11		2	
2 Chr	18.12		2	
Ps	140.8		2	
Prov	16.3	<	2	
Dan	11.17		2	
Rom	14.4		2	
Jas	1.3		2	

SUFFER

Is	53.3		7	>
1 Pet	4.1	<	7	>
2 Thes	1.4		5	
Neh	9.9		4	
Ps	119.50		4	
2 Cor	1.5		4	
1 Pet	2.19	<	4	>
Job	2.10		3	
	36.8	<	3	>
Ps	73.4		3	
	107.10		3	
Lam	1.4		3	>
Ezek	18.19		3	
Hos	5.11	<	3	
Zech	9.5		3	
Mt	26.6		3	>
Mk	14.3		3	
Jn	16.21		3	

SUFFER (cont.)
Col 1.24 3
Heb 2.9 3
1 Pet 5.1 < 3
Rev 2.3 < 3
18.7 3
Gen 42.21 < 2
Lev 20.17 2
Num 14.33 2
18.1 2
Deut 16.3 2
Job 30.16 2 >
Ps 9.12 2
10.12 2
39.2 2
88.9 2 >
Is 14.3 2
26.11 < 2
40.2 2
48.10 < 2 >
Jer 15.8 2
Lam 3.15 < 2
Ezek 4.4 2
Mic 4.6 2
Zech 1.6 2
Mt 8.2 2 >
11.5 < 2
Lk 17.12 2
22.15 2
24.26 2
Jn 12.27 2
Acts 7.11 2 >
Rom 8.17 2
1 Thes 2.14 < 2 >
2 Tim 1.8 2 >
2.3 < 2 >
Heb 10.32 2 >
11.25 < 2 >
12.7 < 2 >
1 Pet 1.6 2 >
3.14 < 2 >
2 Pet 2.8 2

SUPREME
Dan 4.2 < 6 >
7.18 4
1 Cor 11.3 3
Dan 5.18 < 2

SURE
Num 14.21 < 3
Deut 5.1 3 >
Josh 1.7 3 >
1 Sam 23.20 < 3 >
Ezek 14.16 3
17.14 < 3 >
20.3 3
Hos 6.1 < 3
Phil 1.6 3

SURE (cont.)
1 Jn 2.3 3
Deut 12.19 < 2
29.18 2
32.40 2
Judg 13.13 2
1 Sam 20.23 2
Neh 13.19 2
Prov 11.21 2
24.14 2 >
Lam 3.23 < 2
Ezek 33.11 2 >
35.6 < 2 >
Mal 2.15 2
Mt 24.15 2
Lk 12.28 2
1 Cor 7.16 2
2 Cor 1.15 2
Col 4.16 2
2 Tim 1.5 2
Heb 6.9 2

SWEAR
Mt 23.16 10
2 Kgs 2.2 3 >
Num 14.28 2
1 Sam 20.3 2
25.26 2 >
2 Sam 12.5 < 2
1 Kgs 18.10 < 2
Job 31.5 2
Jer 12.16 2
16.14 2
23.7 < 2
Ezek 17.13 2
Amos 8.7 2
Mt 5.34 2
26.72 2

SYMBOL
Judg 6.25 4
2 Kgs 23.6 2
2 Chr 34.3 < 2

SYNAGOGUE
Lk 4.15 7
Acts 18.4 < 6 >
Mk 1.21 4
Acts 13.5 4 >
17.1 4 >
Mt 23.6 2
Mk 3.1 2
Lk 13.10 < 2
Jn 9.22 2
Acts 9.2 2

T

TABLET
Deut 10.1 6
9.9 5
Ex 34.1 4
32.15 < 3
25.16 < 2 >
1 Kgs 8.9 2
2 Cor 3.3 2

TAKE AWAY (SIN)
Heb 10.4 6
Lev 16.6 3 >
4.21 2 >
5.9 < 2 >
9.7 < 2
12.7 2
17.11 < 2
23.26 2
2 Chr 29.21 2
Zech 3.4 2
Heb 9.13 2

TAX
Num 31.28 6
Mt 17.24 5
2 Chr 24.6 3
2 Sam 8.2 2
1 Chr 18.2 2
Ezra 4.13 2
Mt 22.17 2
Rom 13.6 2

TAX COLLECTOR
Lk 18.10 4 >
Mk 2.14 3
Lk 5.27 3
Mt 9.9 2
21.31 2
Lk 7.29 2

TEACH
Ps 119.12 20
Mk 7.3 < 7 >
1 Tim 4.1 < 7 >
Deut 4.1 6 >
Jn 8.2 < 6 >
2 Tim 2.2 < 6 >
Deut 32.2 < 5 >
Prov 22.6 < 5
Is 28.9 5 >
Mt 5.2 < 5
15.2 5 >
Mk 1.17 5 >
Jn 7.14 < 5 >
Acts 5.21 < 5
Tit 2.1 < 5
Deut 31.12 < 4 >

TEACH (cont.)
Ps 25.4 4
Prov 4.1 < 4
Jer 9.5 4
Mal 2.6 4
Mk 6.2 4 >
Jn 14.23 4 >
1 Tim 6.1 < 4
1 Jn 2.27 4
Rev 2.14 4 >
Neh 9.13 < 3
Prov 1.3 3 >
6.20 3 >
Is 42.4 3
51.4 < 3
Mt 7.12 3
19.8 3
22.16 < 3 >
23.16 < 3 >
Mk 12.14 < 3 >
Lk 4.15 3 >
13.10 < 3
20.1 < 3 >
Jn 6.45 3 >
1 Cor 2.4 3
11.2 3
14.6 3
Col 2.7 < 3 >
1 Thes 4.8 3
1 Tim 1.3 3 >
2 Tim 3.10 < 3 >
Tit 1.1 3 >
2 Jn 9 3
Deut 6.1 < 2 >
27.3 2 >
28.58 < 2 >
29.6 < 2 >
2 Kgs 17.27 2
2 Chr 17.7 2
Ezra 7.10 2
Ps 40.3 2
78.1 2
86.11 2
Prov 3.1 < 2 >
7.2 < 2 >
Is 2.3 < 2
30.9 < 2
50.4 2 >
59.21 2
Jer 31.18 2 >
32.23 < 2
Hos 8.1 2
Mic 4.2 2
Mt 4.19 2 >
13.1 < 2
26.1 2
Mk 4.1 2
8.31 < 2 >
9.31 < 2

TEACH (cont.)

Mk	10.1	2 >
	11.17	< 2 >
Lk	5.3	< 2 >
	11.1	< 2 >
Jn	15.3	< 2
	18.19	2
Acts	4.2	2 >
	15.1	< 2 >
	18.11	< 2
	20.20	2 >
	21.21	< 2
Rom	15.4	2 >
Eph	4.14	2
Heb	6.1	< 2
Rev	3.3	< 2

TEACHER

Mt	23.7	< 4
Mk	10.17	4 >
2 Pet	2.1	4
Mt	22.16	3 >
	26.18	3
Mk	9.5	3
	12.14	< 3 >
Lk	20.21	< 3 >
Jn	3.2	3 >
	11.8	3
Ps	119.99	2
Mt	10.24	2
Mk	14.14	< 2
Lk	6.40	2 >
Jn	1.38	2
	13.13	2
1 Cor	12.28	2
Jas	3.1	2

TEACHER OF THE LAW

Mt	23.2	< 7
Mk	12.28	< 4
Lk	11.45	< 4
	20.1	< 4
Mk	14.1	3 >
Lk	5.17	3 >
	10.25	3 >
Mk	2.6	< 2 >
	7.1	2 >
	9.11	< 2
	11.18	< 2 >
	15.1	< 2
Lk	22.2	2 >

TEMPLE (1) (OF GOD)

1 Kgs	8.16	20 >
2 Chr	6.2	< 19 >
	23.3	< 14 >
Ezra	5.2	< 14 >
	6.3	< 13 >
2 Chr	24.4	< 12 >

TEMPLE (1)(cont.)

2 Kgs	11.2	11 >
	23.2	< 11 >
2 Chr	7.1	< 11 >
Neh	10.28	11 >
1 Chr	22.1	10 >
Neh	13.4	< 10
1 Chr	9.2	9
2 Chr	34.8	< 9 >
	36.7	< 9
Ezra	7.6	< 9 >
1 Kgs	9.1	< 8
2 Kgs	12.4	< 8
Ezra	3.6	< 8 >
	8.17	< 8 >
Jer	7.1	8
2 Chr	2.1	7
	31.2	< 7
Neh	11.3	< 7 >
Jer	26.2	7 >
Acts	21.26	7 >
2 Kgs	22.3	< 6 >
1 Chr	23.4	< 6 >
	26.12	< 6
2 Chr	33.4	6 >
	35.2	< 6 >
Ezra	1.2	6 >
	2.40	< 6 >
Neh	12.25	< 6 >
Hag	1.2	6 >
Mt	23.16	6 >
1 Kgs	5.3	5
2 Kgs	16.8	< 5
	25.9	< 5
2 Chr	20.5	5
Neh	7.43	< 5 >
Jer	52.13	< 5
Ezek	9.2	< 5
	10.3	5 >
Dan	9.17	< 5
Hag	2.3	< 5
Mt	21.12	5
Mk	11.11	5
Lk	1.8	5
Jn	2.14	5
2 Sam	7.5	4
2 Kgs	21.4	< 4 >
1 Chr	17.4	< 4 >
2 Chr	26.16	< 4 >
	30.1	4 >
Ezra	4.1	< 4 >
Neh	3.25	< 4
Ps	84.1	4
Jer	27.16	< 4 >
	28.1	< 4 >
	36.5	< 4
Lam	2.1	< 4
Ezek	8.3	< 4 >
Joel	1.9	4 >

TEMPLE (1)(cont.)

Mt	27.5	< 4
Lk	2.27	< 4
	21.1	< 4 >
Acts	5.20	4 >
Rev	15.5	4 >
2 Chr	8.1	< 3 >
	28.21	< 3
Ezra	10.1	3
Ps	74.3	< 3
Is	6.1	3
Jer	35.2	3 >
Dan	8.11	3 >
Zech	4.7	< 3
	6.12	3 >
Mt	17.24	3
Lk	19.45	< 3 >
Jn	8.2	< 3
Acts	3.1	< 3
	24.6	3 >
1 Cor	3.16	3
Rev	11.1	3
1 Kgs	3.1	2
	10.5	2
	14.26	2 >
	15.15	< 2
2 Kgs	18.15	2 >
	19.1	< 2 >
	20.5	< 2 >
	24.13	< 2 >
1 Chr	6.10	2
	16.27	2 >
	24.5	< 2 >
	29.16	2
2 Chr	9.4	< 2
	12.9	2
	15.8	2 >
	25.24	< 2 >
	27.2	< 2 >
Neh	6.10	2 >
Ps	27.5	2 >
	68.5	2 >
	96.6	2
	118.19	2
	134.1	2 >
Is	2.2	< 2
	37.1	2 >
	38.20	< 2
	56.5	2 >
	60.7	2
	66.6	2
Jer	17.12	2
	20.1	< 2
	51.11	< 2 >
Lam	1.4	2 >
Ezek	23.38	2 >
	24.21	< 2 >
	37.26	2
Dan	5.2	2

TEMPLE (1)(cont.)

Dan	11.31	2
Hos	9.4	2
Jon	2.4	2
Mic	4.1	< 2
Zech	7.2	< 2 >
	11.13	2
	14.20	2
Mal	3.1	< 2
Mt	12.5	2
	26.55	2 >
Mk	12.35	< 2 >
	13.1	< 2 >
	14.49	< 2 >
	15.29	< 2
Jn	7.14	2 >
	10.22	2 >
	11.48	< 2
Acts	6.13	< 2
2 Cor	6.16	2
Rev	14.15	2 >
	16.1	< 2
	21.22	2

TEMPLE (2) (OF OTHER GODS)

2 Kgs	10.21	6 >
Acts	19.24	4
Judg	9.4	3
1 Kgs	16.32	2
1 Chr	10.10	2
Jer	43.12	2
Dan	1.2	2
Zech	5.11	2

TEMPT

Jas	1.13	4
Lk	4.2	2
	22.40	2

TENT (2) (OF THE LORD'S PRESENCE)

Ex	40.2	< 20
Num	4.3	< 15 >
Ex	26.1	< 14 >
	36.1	< 11
Num	3.7	< 9 >
	18.1	< 9 >
Heb	9.2	< 9
Ex	38.8	8 >
Lev	4.4	< 8
Ex	29.4	< 7 >
Num	16.9	7 >
Lev	16.7	< 6 >
Num	8.9	< 6 >
Ex	30.16	< 5 >
	33.7	5 >
	39.32	< 5 >
Lev	8.2	5 >

TENT (2)(cont.)

Num	1.1		5	>
	9.15	<	5	
2 Chr	1.3		5	
Ex	27.9	<	4	>
	35.11	<	4	>
Lev	10.4		4	
	17.3	<	4	
Num	7.1	<	4	>
	10.3		4	>
	17.4	<	4	>
1 Kgs	2.28	<	4	
Lev	1.1		3	
	3.2		3	>
	6.16		3	
	15.14	<	3	>
Num	6.10	<	3	>
	11.16	<	3	>
	12.4	<	3	
	19.4	<	3	>
	31.30		3	
Deut	31.14		3	
Josh	22.19		3	
2 Sam	7.2	<	3	
Ex	31.7	<	2	
Lev	9.5	<	2	
	12.4		2	
	14.11		2	>
Num	2.2	<	2	>
	20.3	<	2	
1 Kgs	1.39		2	>
1 Chr	9.19		2	
	17.1	<	2	
	23.26		2	
Acts	7.44		2	

TERRIBLE

Mt	23.13		7	>
Lk	11.42	<	6	
	6.24		5	
Ex	32.21		3	
Lk	21.11		3	>
Rev	16.2		3	
	18.10		3	
Deut	31.17		2	>
1 Sam	3.11		2	>
Ps	106.15		2	
Jer	19.8	<	2	
	25.9		2	>
Lam	1.8		2	
Joel	2.11		2	
Amos	5.12		2	>
	6.1	<	2	
Zech	14.12		2	
Mt	11.21		2	
	18.7	<	2	
	24.19	<	2	
Lk	2.9		2	
	10.13		2	>

TERRIBLE (cont.)

1 Cor	5.1		2	
Jude	11		2	

TERRIFY

Ezek	26.15		4	>
1 Sam	28.5		3	
Is	7.2		3	>
Ezek	32.23		3	
Dan	7.7		3	>
Lev	26.17		2	
Josh	2.9		2	
Job	41.14		2	
Ps	55.3		2	
	83.15		2	
Jer	50.36	<	2	>
Ezek	27.35	<	2	>
	28.14	<	2	
	30.9		2	
Jon	1.5		2	
Acts	5.5		2	
Rev	11.11		2	

TERROR

Jer	20.3		3	
	49.5	<	3	
Ezek	32.24		3	
Ex	15.14		2	
Job	13.11		2	
Is	21.3		2	
	24.17		2	
Jer	17.17		2	>
	48.43		2	>

TEST

1 Cor	10.9		4	
Ps	78.18		3	
Gen	42.15		2	
Ex	17.2	<	2	
Deut	8.2		2	
Judg	3.1		2	
Ps	66.10		2	
Prov	17.3		2	
	27.21		2	
Zech	13.9		2	
Mal	3.10		2	
2 Cor	8.2		2	
1 Tim	3.10		2	
Heb	3.8		2	
1 Pet	1.7		2	
Rev	2.2		2	>

TESTIFY

Jn	8.13		4	
	5.31		3	

TESTIMONY

1 Jn	5.8		6	

THANK

Neh	12.8	<	7	
Ps	107.1	<	6	>
	118.1		4	>
	136.1		4	
1 Cor	14.16		4	>
1 Chr	16.8		3	
Ps	145.1		3	
Lk	17.9		3	>
	18.11	<	3	>
1 Cor	10.16		3	>
Col	3.15	<	3	>
Ps	30.4		2	
	50.14		2	
	100.4		2	
	106.1	<	2	>
	116.13	<	2	
	119.108	<	2	
Mt	26.26		2	
Mk	8.6		2	
	14.22		2	
Lk	2.28		2	
	22.17		2	
Jn	6.11		2	
Rom	1.8		2	
	14.6		2	
1 Cor	1.4		2	
2 Cor	1.3		2	>
	9.11	<	2	
Eph	1.3		2	
	5.4		2	
Col	1.3		2	>
1 Thes	3.9	<	2	
1 Tim	1.12		2	>
	4.3		2	
2 Tim	1.3		2	
Jas	3.9		2	

THIEF

Ex	22.2		3	
Lk	12.33		3	
Jn	10.1		3	
Zech	5.3		2	
Mt	24.43		2	
1 Cor	5.10		2	>
1 Thes	5.2		2	

THRONE

Rev	4.2	<	10	>
	7.9	<	7	>
	5.1	<	5	>
1 Kgs	2.19	<	4	
	10.18		4	
2 Chr	9.17		4	
Dan	7.9		3	
Rev	20.4	<	3	>
1 Kgs	22.10		2	
2 Chr	18.9		2	
Esth	5.1		2	

THRONE (cont.)

Ps	47.5		2	
	89.19		2	
	99.1		2	
Song	3.7		2	
Is	14.9		2	
Ezek	1.26		2	
Mt	19.28		2	
Rev	3.21	<	2	>
	16.10		2	
	19.4		2	>
	21.3	<	2	>
	22.1	<	2	

TITHE

Num	18.21		4	
Deut	14.22		4	
	26.12		4	
Neh	10.37		4	
Deut	12.6		3	
2 Chr	31.5		3	
Neh	13.5	<	2	
Mal	3.8		2	

TOLERATE

2 Cor	11.1		4	
Num	25.11		2	
Esth	3.4		2	
Ps	101.3		2	
Rev	2.2		2	

TOMB

Jn	20.1	<	8	
Mt	27.60		6	>
Lk	24.1	<	6	
2 Kgs	23.16		5	
Mk	16.2	<	4	
2 Kgs	14.16	<	3	>
Mt	28.1	<	3	
2 Kgs	13.13	<	2	>
2 Chr	21.1		2	
	24.16		2	>
Mt	23.27		2	
Mk	5.3		2	
	15.46		2	>
Lk	11.47		2	
	23.53		2	>
Jn	19.41		2	>

TRAP

Ps	119.61		3	
Prov	6.2	<	3	>
Mt	22.15		3	
Job	18.9		2	>
Ps	9.15		2	
	10.2		2	
	35.7		2	
	124.7		2	
	140.5		2	>

TRAP (cont.)

Ps	141.9	<	2	>
Prov	1.18		2	
	22.5		2	>
	29.5	<	2	
Ecc	9.12		2	
Is	8.14		2	
	24.17		2	
Jer	48.43		2	
Ezek	19.4		2	
Amos	3.5		2	
Mk	12.13		2	
Lk	11.16	<	2	
2 Pet	2.14		2	

TREMBLE

Hab	3.6	<	4	
Ezek	26.16		3	
Dan	10.10		3	
Ex	15.14		2	
	19.16		2	>
2 Sam	22.8		2	
Job	26.5		2	
Ps	18.7		2	
	77.16		2	
Is	19.1		2	
	64.2		2	
Ezek	12.18		2	
Joel	2.1		2	>
Heb	12.12		2	

TROUBLE

Prov	17.1	<	5	
Josh	7.24	<	4	
Ps	107.6	<	4	
Prov	13.10	<	4	>
	15.16	<	4	>
	27.3	<	4	>
2 Chr	15.4		3	
	28.19		3	
Ps	10.1		3	
	31.7		3	>
	34.6		3	>
	55.3	<	3	>
Prov	10.10		3	>
	11.8	<	3	>
Jer	2.24		3	
Mt	24.6		3	
Mk	13.7		3	
2 Cor	1.4		3	>
	4.8		3	
Gen	21.11		2	
	42.21	<	2	>
Deut	2.9		2	
Judg	10.14		2	>
1 Sam	1.11		2	>
2 Sam	22.7		2	
	24.1		2	
1 Kgs	18.17		2	

TROUBLE (cont.)

2 Kgs	6.28		2	
Ezra	4.15		2	
Job	3.10	<	2	>
	5.6	<	2	>
	6.1	<	2	
	14.1		2	>
	30.25	<	2	
Ps	18.6		2	
	25.17		2	
	32.6	<	2	
	37.8		2	>
	40.12	<	2	>
	42.5	<	2	>
	56.5	<	2	
Prov	1.26		2	>
	6.14		2	
	12.13	<	2	>
	19.2		2	
	24.2	<	2	
	26.6		2	>
Ecc	7.14		2	
Is	65.10		2	
Jer	17.16	<	2	
Dan	9.18		2	
Zech	10.2		2	
Mk	5.29	<	2	
Acts	2.25		2	
	15.19	<	2	>
Rom	5.3		2	
2 Cor	7.4	<	2	>
Rev	2.9		2	>

TRUE

1 Jn	5.6		5	
Jn	8.14	<	4	
	17.3		4	>
	19.24	<	4	
1 Cor	15.13	<	4	
Jer	28.6		3	
Dan	8.12		3	>
Mt	2.15	<	3	
Lk	1.20		3	
Rom	9.4		3	
Rev	19.2		3	
Deut	13.2		2	
Judg	13.12		2	
1 Kgs	8.26		2	
2 Chr	6.17		2	
Jer	44.28		2	
Dan	9.7	<	2	
Hab	2.3		2	
Mal	2.7		2	
Mt	26.54		2	>
Lk	4.21		2	>
	22.37	<	2	
Jn	4.23	<	2	>
	10.35		2	
	12.38		2	>

TRUE (cont.)

Jn	18.9	<	2	>
Acts	12.11	<	2	>
	14.3	<	2	
Rom	1.9		2	>
	2.15	<	2	>
	5.15		2	
	10.2		2	>
Phil	1.9		2	
1 Tim	1.2		2	
	4.6	<	2	
	6.3		2	
Tit	1.4		2	
Heb	2.2		2	
3 Jn	1		2	
Rev	3.7	<	2	

TRUST

Ps	119.42	<	5	
	25.2		4	>
	115.8		4	>
Prov	11.3		4	
Is	30.2		4	
Ps	22.4	<	3	
	27.3	<	3	>
	31.6		3	>
	37.3		3	>
	56.3	<	3	
	78.7		3	
Phil	3.3	<	3	
Job	4.18		2	
	15.15		2	
Ps	20.7	<	2	>
	33.18	<	2	
	40.3		2	>
	49.6		2	
	52.7		2	
	62.8		2	
	118.8		2	>
	130.5		2	>
Prov	3.5	<	2	
	13.15		2	>
Is	25.9		2	>
	26.3	<	2	
Jer	7.8		2	
	17.5		2	
	48.7		2	>

TRUTH

Jn	8.26	<	9	>
Judg	16.10		5	
Jn	13.16	<	5	>
	16.7	<	5	>
1 Jn	2.4	<	5	>
3 Jn	3		5	
Jn	3.3		4	>
	5.19	<	4	>
	6.26	<	4	>
2 Thes	2.10		4	

TRUTH (cont.)

2 Tim	3.7	<	4	>
2 Jn	1		4	
Ps	119.18		3	
Jn	1.14		3	
	10.1		3	
	14.6	<	3	>
	18.37	<	3	>
Eph	4.15		3	>
1 Tim	2.4		3	>
2 Tim	2.15		3	>
Tit	1.1		3	
Gen	42.16		2	
Job	42.7		2	
Ps	144.8		2	
Prov	12.17		2	
	14.5		2	
	22.12		2	>
Jer	9.3	<	2	
	38.14		2	
Zech	8.16		2	
Mt	22.16		2	
Mk	12.14		2	
Jn	17.17	<	2	>
Rom	1.18		2	>
	16.25		2	
1 Cor	2.1		2	
	15.20	<	2	
2 Cor	6.7		2	>
Gal	2.5		2	
Eph	5.9	<	2	>
1 Tim	3.9	<	2	>
Rev	1.2		2	
	12.11		2	
	19.10		2	>

TRY (2) [LEGAL]

Jas	1.2		4	
Acts	25.9	<	3	>
Josh	20.6		2	
Ps	109.6		2	
Is	43.2		2	>
Mt	5.21		2	
	10.18		2	

TURN

Lev	13.3		9	
Jer	2.5		8	>
Ex	7.9		7	>
Lev	26.11		6	
Josh	19.13	<	6	
1 Kgs	11.3		5	
Jer	3.6	<	5	>
Josh	15.3		4	
Judg	20.39	<	4	
Jer	5.3	<	4	>
Ezek	39.2	<	4	
Rev	2.5	<	4	>
Lev	20.3	<	3	

TURN (cont.)

Num	34.4	<	3	
Deut	30.2	<	3	>
Josh	8.5		3	
Judg	18.21		3	>
2 Chr	18.31		3	>
Neh	9.26		3	
Job	36.10	<	3	>
Ps	78.6		3	>
Is	50.2		3	
Jer	4.1	<	3	>
	8.4		3	
	18.4	<	3	
	36.3		3	
Ezek	14.5		3	
Dan	11.18		3	
Mal	3.7	<	3	
Acts	3.14	<	3	>
	13.8		3	>
	15.3	<	3	>
Heb	12.15	<	3	
Rev	8.8		3	>
Ex	4.3		2	>
	14.2		2	
Num	22.23	<	2	
	24.1		2	
Deut	2.1	<	2	
	9.12	<	2	
	23.5		2	
Josh	18.14		2	>
Ruth	3.8		2	
1 Sam	12.10		2	
	15.11		2	
	17.30		2	
1 Kgs	8.14		2	
	22.32		2	
2 Chr	6.3		2	>
	15.2		2	>
	20.23		2	
	33.12		2	
Esth	2.12	<	2	
Job	5.1	<	2	>
	20.11	<	2	
	30.11	<	2	>
	35.10	<	2	>
	39.5	<	2	
Ps	17.6		2	>
	22.24	<	2	
	40.4		2	>
	80.14	<	2	
Is	3.12		2	
	5.20		2	>
	14.17		2	
	19.2		2	
	29.14		2	
	34.9		2	
	38.2	<	2	
	42.15	<	2	>
	55.6	<	2	

TURN (cont.)

Is	59.13	<	2	
Jer	10.22		2	
	12.8		2	>
	15.6	<	2	>
	25.5		2	
	31.13		2	>
	32.33	<	2	>
	46.5		2	>
Lam	3.9	<	2	>
Ezek	1.9		2	>
	4.6		2	
	10.11		2	
	18.30	<	2	
	21.16		2	>
	38.4		2	>
	41.19		2	
Dan	9.5		2	
Hos	3.1	<	2	>
	4.7	<	2	
	11.2	<	2	
Joel	2.6	<	2	
Nah	1.4		2	>
Hab	2.16		2	
Mal	2.8	<	2	>
Mt	3.2		2	>
	4.3	<	2	
	11.20	<	2	>
Mk	1.4		2	
Lk	1.8		2	
	3.3		2	>
	7.9		2	
	10.13		2	>
	13.3		2	>
	22.32		2	>
Jn	6.37		2	
	20.14		2	>
Acts	2.20		2	>
	9.35		2	
	14.2	<	2	>
	26.18		2	
1 Tim	5.11		2	
Heb	10.38		2	>
Rev	3.3	<	2	
	10.9		2	>

U

UNBELIEVER

1 Cor	7.12	<	4	
	14.22		4	
2 Cor	6.14		2	

UNCLEAN

Lev	15.2	<	24	>
	11.4	<	22	>
	13.3	<	20	>
Num	19.7	<	16	

UNCLEAN (cont.)

Lev	18.19		8	>
	14.36	<	7	>
Mk	7.2		7	
Lev	20.3	<	5	>
	22.3	<	5	
Deut	14.3		5	>
Mt	15.11		5	
Lev	21.1	<	4	>
	5.2		3	
	7.18		3	
	19.7	<	3	>
Num	9.6		3	
Acts	10.14		3	>
Rom	14.14		3	
Gen	7.2		2	
Lev	12.2	<	2	>
	16.16	<	2	
	27.11		2	
Num	5.2		2	
Deut	12.15		2	
	23.9		2	
Acts	11.8	<	2	

UNDERSTAND

Ps	119.27		8	
Mt	13.13		6	
Dan	12.4		4	
Mk	4.12		4	
Jn	13.7	<	4	
Neh	8.2		3	
Job	28.12		3	
Prov	2.2	<	3	>
Dan	8.15		3	>
	10.1		3	
Mt	16.9	<	3	>
1 Cor	14.2	<	3	
2 Cor	1.13		3	
Ps	73.17		2	
	139.2		2	
Prov	1.2		2	>
	4.1	<	2	
	24.3		2	
	29.7	<	2	>
Ecc	7.3		2	>
	11.5		2	
Is	6.9	<	2	
	40.14	<	2	>
Jer	9.12		2	
	23.18		2	
Dan	2.21		2	
	9.22	<	2	
Mt	15.10		2	>
Mk	7.14	<	2	>
	8.17	<	2	>
Jn	8.27		2	
	12.16		2	>
Acts	7.25		2	>
	8.30	<	2	

UNDERSTAND (cont.)

Acts	28.26		2	
Rom	7.1		2	
Eph	3.4		2	

UNFAITHFUL

Jer	3.6		8	
Num	5.6		3	
Deut	32.5	<	3	
2 Chr	21.13		2	
	29.6		2	>
Hos	1.2		2	
	5.3	<	2	

UNINTENTIONAL

Lev	5.2		5	
Num	15.22		4	

UNION

1 Jn	4.12	<	7	>
Eph	2.6	<	5	>
1 Jn	2.5		5	>
Eph	1.1		4	>
1 Jn	3.6	<	4	>
Rom	6.3		3	
1 Cor	1.2		3	
	4.10		3	
	15.22		3	
Gal	3.26	<	3	
Phil	4.4	<	3	
Col	1.2		3	>
	2.6	<	3	
Rom	8.1		2	
Gal	2.4		2	>
	5.6		2	
Phil	1.1		2	
	3.1		2	>
2 Tim	1.1		2	>
1 Jn	5.20	<	2	

UNLEAVENED

Ex	12.8		4	>
	34.18		2	
Lev	2.4		2	
	7.12	<	2	>
	8.2	<	2	
Deut	16.3		2	
2 Chr	30.13		2	
Mk	14.1		2	
Lk	22.1		2	

UNMARRIED

1 Cor	7.8		6	
Num	30.6		2	
2 Sam	13.1		2	

USELESS

Ecc	2.1	<	6	
	4.4		4	>

USELESS (cont.)
Ecc 6.2 < 4 >
Ps 127.1 3
Ecc 1.2 3 >
Job 35.13 2
Ps 119.83 2
Ecc 5.7 < 2 >
8.10 < 2 >
9.9 < 2
12.8 2
Is 33.11 2
Ezek 15.5 2
Tit 3.9 2

V

VALUE
Job 28.13 4
1 Pet 2.4 3 >
Lev 5.15 2 >
27.18 2
1 Cor 2.14 2
1 Tim 4.8 2

VICTORY
1 Sam 14.6 7
Josh 10.8 5 >
Judg 7.2 5
11.9 5 >
Rev 2.7 5 >
3.5 < 5
Judg 4.7 < 4 >
2 Sam 22.40 4 >
Ps 18.39 4
20.5 4 >
118.15 4
2 Sam 8.6 3
23.5 < 3
1 Kgs 22.6 3
1 Chr 18.6 3
2 Chr 18.5 3
Ps 89.17 3
98.1 3
Is 45.8 3 >
51.5 3 >
1 Cor 15.54 3
Gen 14.17 2
Ex 14.4 2 >
15.1 < 2
Josh 11.1 < 2
24.8 2
Judg 3.10 < 2 >
16.23 < 2
20.27 2
2 Sam 5.19 2
18.28 2 >
19.2 < 2
1 Kgs 20.13 2

VICTORY (cont.)
2 Kgs 13.17 2
1 Chr 14.10 2
Ps 3.3 2
45.4 < 2
149.4 2
Is 46.12 < 2
62.1 < 2 >
63.1 < 2
Lam 2.7 2
Dan 11.12 2
Zech 10.5 2

VINE
Ezek 17.6 6
Is 5.2 4
Ezek 19.10 4
Ps 80.8 3
Ezek 15.2 3
Jn 15.1 3
Gen 49.11 2
Judg 9.12 2
Is 16.8 2
24.7 2
Jer 2.21 2
Joel 1.7 2

VINEYARD
1 Kgs 21.1 9
Mt 21.28 < 6
Is 5.1 5
Mk 12.1 5
Lk 20.9 5
Neh 5.3 4
Mt 20.1 4 >
Lev 25.3 3
Ex 22.5 2 >
23.11 < 2
Deut 28.30 2
Judg 21.20 2
Job 24.6 2
Song 1.6 2 >
8.11 2
Is 16.8 2
27.2 2
Jer 31.5 2 >
35.7 2
Hos 2.12 2
Amos 5.11 < 2

VIOLENT
Ps 140.1 < 3
Ezek 7.10 3 >
Hab 1.2 3 >
2.8 < 3
Gen 6.11 2
2 Sam 22.3 2
Ps 7.3 2
Prov 10.6 2 >

VIOLENT (cont.)
Jer 51.35 2
Jon 1.4 2
Mt 11.12 2
Acts 27.18 2

VIRGIN
Deut 22.14 5
Num 31.18 4
Lev 21.7 3
Ezek 23.3 3
Ex 22.16 2
Judg 11.37 2
21.11 2

VISION
Dan 8.1 < 8 >
Ezek 13.3 < 6
Dan 10.1 5 >
Num 24.4 4
Amos 7.1 4 >
Acts 10.3 4 >
Is 21.2 3 >
Dan 2.19 < 3
4.5 3
7.1 3 >
9.21 < 3
2 Cor 12.1 3
1 Sam 3.1 2
Is 22.1 < 2
Ezek 8.2 2
11.24 < 2 >
12.24 < 2 >
Zech 1.7 2 >
Acts 9.10 2
16.9 2

VOW
Num 30.2 < 19
Gen 24.2 5 >
Lev 27.2 5
Num 6.2 5
Heb 6.13 5 >
Deut 23.18 4
Heb 7.20 < 4
Gen 47.29 3
Lev 22.18 3 >
Jer 44.24 3
Acts 23.12 3
Gen 21.23 2 >
25.33 < 2 >
26.31 < 2
31.13 2
Num 15.3 2
Mt 5.33 2
23.16 2
Mk 6.23 2

W

WAGE
Gen 30.28 4 >
31.7 < 4
Mt 20.2 3
Zech 11.12 2
Rev 6.6 2

WARN
Ezek 33.3 < 7
3.17 6
Neh 9.26 4
2 Kgs 17.13 3 >
Jer 6.8 3
11.7 3
Ezek 20.18 3 >
21.2 < 3
Num 16.38 2 >
2 Kgs 6.9 2
Neh 13.15 2
Ps 2.5 2
Ezek 12.6 2
32.2 2 >
Lk 16.28 2
Acts 4.17 2
20.21 2
1 Cor 10.6 2
Gal 5.3 2
2 Thes 3.12 2

WATCH
Ezek 12.4 4
33.2 4
Dan 7.4 4 >
2 Sam 18.24 3
Dan 4.13 3
Mt 26.38 3 >
27.36 < 3
Mk 12.1 3 >
13.33 < 3 >
Lk 23.35 3
Ex 12.42 2
1 Sam 6.9 2
2 Kgs 9.17 2
2 Chr 7.15 < 2
Job 39.1 2
Ps 119.82 2
Prov 16.17 < 2
Song 6.13 < 2
Ezek 10.2 2
Dan 8.4 < 2
Mic 7.4 2
Mk 14.34 < 2 >
Acts 20.28 2

WAY (3) [ACTION]
Ps 119.3 4
Judg 2.19 3

WAY (3)(cont.)

Is	55.8		2	
Jer	18.11		2	
	36.3	<	2	
Ezek	33.8		2	
2 Pet	2.2		2	

WEAK

1 Cor	8.7		5	>
2 Cor	12.5	<	5	>
Judg	16.7		4	
2 Cor	13.3	<	4	
1 Sam	14.24		3	
Is	40.29		3	>
Ezek	29.6		3	>
Gen	30.42		2	
	42.9		2	
2 Sam	3.1		2	
Job	30.2		2	
Is	41.14	<	2	
Jer	49.15		2	>
Lam	1.6		2	
Ezek	34.4		2	
Amos	4.1		2	
	7.2		2	
Rom	8.3		2	
	14.1		2	>
1 Cor	1.25		2	>
2 Cor	11.29	<	2	>
Heb	5.2	<	2	

WEDDING

Mt	22.2		6	
Deut	22.15		2	
Judg	14.12		2	
Jn	2.1		2	
Rev	19.7		2	

WEED

Mt	13.25		11	
Job	8.16		2	
Ps	58.7		2	
Hos	10.4		2	

WEEP

Jn	11.31		4	
Ps	6.6		3	
Is	16.7	<	3	
Jer	22.10		3	
2 Sam	3.32		2	
	12.21		2	>
	15.30		2	
Ezra	10.1		2	
Job	30.25		2	
Ps	126.5		2	
Is	15.2		2	>
	22.4		2	
Jer	31.9		2	
	48.20		2	

WEEP (cont.)

Lam	2.11		2	
Joel	1.5		2	>
	2.12	<	2	
Zech	11.2		2	
Lk	6.21		2	

WELCOME

Mt	10.11		8	
Lk	9.4	<	5	
	10.8		3	
Acts	28.2		3	
Judg	19.3		2	
1 Chr	12.17		2	
Job	29.23		2	
Mt	25.38		2	
Mk	6.10		2	
	9.37		2	
Lk	16.4	<	2	
Heb	11.13		2	
	13.2		2	

WICKED

Ps	37.1	<	15	
Prov	10.3		11	>
	12.3	<	10	>
Ps	10.2		8	>
Prov	11.5	<	8	>
	21.4		8	>
Ps	119.53		6	
2 Thes	2.3		6	>
Job	21.14	<	5	>
2 Kgs	15.9	<	4	
Job	24.6		4	
	27.7		4	
Ps	73.3		4	
	94.3		4	
Prov	4.14	<	4	>
	13.5	<	4	>
	29.2	<	4	
Ecc	8.10	<	4	>
Deut	9.4		3	
Job	4.8	<	3	>
	20.5		3	>
	22.18	<	3	
Ps	7.9		3	
	9.5		3	
	11.2	<	3	>
	36.1		3	>
	75.4		3	
	92.7	<	3	
Prov	24.15		3	
	28.1		3	>
Jer	12.1		3	>
	23.10		3	
	30.14		3	
Num	14.27		2	
Job	15.5		2	
	31.5		2	

WICKED (cont.)

Job	38.13		2	
Ps	17.9		2	>
	106.6		2	>
	107.34	<	2	
	125.3		2	
	139.19		2	>
	140.4	<	2	>
	141.4	<	2	
Prov	3.25	<	2	>
	6.12	<	2	
	15.6	<	2	>
	16.4	<	2	>
	17.11	<	2	
Ecc	7.17		2	>
Is	9.17		2	
Jer	25.5		2	>
	44.9		2	
Ezek	21.25	<	2	
Dan	12.10		2	
Jon	3.8		2	
Nah	1.11		2	
Rom	6.13	<	2	

WIDOW

1 Tim	5.3		11	
Gen	38.8		5	
1 Kgs	17.9		5	
Deut	24.17		4	>
Mk	12.19		4	
Ex	22.22		2	
Deut	16.11		2	
	25.5	<	2	>
	26.12	<	2	>
Ruth	4.5		2	
Job	24.3		2	
Is	1.17		2	
Ezek	22.7		2	
Mt	22.24		2	
Lk	4.25		2	
	18.3		2	
	20.28		2	>
	21.2	<	2	
Acts	9.39		2	

WILL (1) [INTEND]

Ezek	20.1		3	
Jn	6.38		3	
Rom	8.20		3	>
2 Cor	8.3		3	
Heb	10.7		3	
Ex	28.15		2	
1 Kgs	12.15		2	
2 Chr	14.4	<	2	
Is	53.2	<	2	
Mal	2.7		2	
Phil	2.7		2	
Col	1.1		2	
1 Pet	2.8		2	>

WILL (1)(cont.)

1 Pet	4.2	<	2	

WIN

1 Cor	9.19		7	
Phil	3.12		4	
Heb	11.2		4	
Rev	2.7		4	>
Gen	32.20	<	3	
Ex	15.1		2	
	17.11		2	
1 Sam	17.9		2	
2 Sam	3.12		2	
	23.10		2	
1 Kgs	11.19		2	
	22.12		2	
2 Kgs	13.17		2	
2 Chr	18.11		2	
Esth	2.9		2	
Ps	45.4	<	2	
Ecc	9.11		2	
Is	59.4		2	
	63.5		2	
Acts	14.19		2	
1 Tim	6.12		2	
2 Tim	2.5		2	
Rev	3.5	<	2	

WINE-OFFERING

Num	28.7		8	>
	29.6	<	5	
Jer	44.17		4	
Lev	23.18		2	
2 Kgs	16.13		2	

WISDOM

1 Cor	1.17		9	>
Job	28.12		8	
Prov	3.15	<	7	>
1 Cor	2.4	<	7	>
Ecc	2.3	<	6	
Job	12.1	<	5	
Prov	1.2		5	>
	4.5	<	5	>
1 Kgs	3.9		4	>
	10.4		4	>
2 Chr	9.3		4	
Ps	119.66		4	
Ecc	7.12		4	>
	9.10	<	4	
Jas	3.13		4	
2 Chr	1.10		3	
Job	32.7		3	
Prov	8.1	<	3	>
	9.1	<	3	
	14.1		3	
	24.3	<	3	
Col	2.3	<	3	>
Gen	41.33		2	

WISDOM (cont.)

1 Kgs	4.29	<	2	>
Job	15.8		2	
Prov	10.23		2	>
	16.16		2	
	23.16		2	>
Ecc	1.16		2	>
Jer	51.15	<	2	
Ezek	28.4		2	
Dan	2.21		2	
	5.11		2	
Lk	2.40		2	
Acts	6.3		2	>
	7.10	<	2	
Col	1.9		2	>

WISE

Prov	15.2	<	9	>
	14.3	<	7	>
Ecc	2.12	<	6	
	7.4	<	6	>
1 Cor	1.19		5	
1 Kgs	4.30		4	>
Job	34.1	<	4	>
Prov	3.7	<	4	>
	13.1	<	4	>
	23.4	<	4	>
Ecc	8.1	<	4	>
	9.1	<	4	
Mt	25.2	<	4	
1 Cor	3.18		4	>
2 Chr	9.6		3	
Prov	9.8	<	3	
	10.1		3	>
	16.14	<	3	>
	24.5	<	3	
Ezek	28.3		3	
Deut	1.13		2	
1 Kgs	10.8		2	
2 Chr	2.12		2	
Job	15.3		2	>
	32.9		2	>
Prov	1.5		2	>
	2.2	<	2	>
	11.2	<	2	>
	12.15	<	2	>
	17.24	<	2	
	19.20		2	>
	21.11	<	2	>
	26.9		2	>
	28.11	<	2	>
Ecc	1.16		2	>
	10.2		2	
	12.9		2	
Jer	8.8		2	>
	9.12	<	2	
Dan	2.20		2	
	11.33		2	>
	12.3	<	2	

WISE (cont.)

Rom	16.19		2	

WISH

Rom	9.3		6	
Lev	27.13		4	
Esth	6.6		3	>
Ps	81.8		3	
Gen	34.10		2	
Ex	35.5		2	
Num	11.18		2	
Deut	12.20		2	
	28.67		2	
2 Sam	15.4		2	
Ps	139.19		2	
Jer	9.1		2	
Ezek	1.12		2	
1 Cor	7.15		2	

WITNESS

Josh	24.22		4	
Jer	32.10		4	
Deut	17.6		3	
Ruth	4.9		3	
Is	43.9		3	>
Jn	5.34		3	
Acts	22.15		3	>
Num	35.30		2	
Deut	19.15		2	
	31.26	<	2	
Josh	22.34		2	
1 Sam	12.5		2	
1 Chr	24.6		2	
Prov	14.5		2	
Mk	14.56		2	
Acts	1.8		2	>
	10.39		2	
1 Thes	2.5		2	
Heb	10.15		2	
Rev	11.3		2	

WONDER (1) [AMAZE]

Ps	107.8	<	5	
	119.18	<	4	
Acts	2.7		4	
Judg	13.18		2	
2 Sam	1.23		2	
	7.23		2	
1 Chr	17.21	<	2	
Job	37.5		2	
Ps	31.19		2	
	66.3	<	2	
	106.7	<	2	>
	111.2		2	
Jer	32.20		2	>
Dan	4.2		2	
Mt	21.15		2	
Mk	13.1	<	2	
2 Cor	12.7		2	

WORD (1)

Prov	12.6	<	7	>
Jer	23.9		7	
Acts	13.5	<	7	>
Rev	22.6	<	7	
Job	15.1		6	>
Ps	119.42		6	
Prov	10.6		5	>
Ex	34.1		4	
Prov	16.1	<	4	
Ezek	13.2		4	
	33.30		4	
Acts	15.15	<	4	>
1 Cor	2.1		4	
	14.9		4	>
Jas	1.18		4	
1 Pet	1.8		4	>
Deut	32.1		3	
2 Sam	19.14		3	
Job	6.3		3	
	16.1	<	3	>
	19.1		3	
Prov	6.2	<	3	>
	15.4	<	3	>
	18.4		3	
Is	48.1		3	>
Jer	7.4	<	3	>
Ezek	37.4		3	
Acts	2.22		3	
	16.32	<	3	>
	19.10	<	3	>
Eph	5.6	<	3	>
1 Tim	1.7		3	
2 Tim	2.9	<	3	
Heb	12.5	<	3	
Num	24.3		2	
Deut	27.8	<	2	
Josh	11.1	<	2	
	24.9		2	
Judg	13.12		2	
1 Kgs	13.20		2	
	20.5		2	
2 Kgs	18.20		2	>
2 Chr	36.12		2	
Job	9.14		2	
	31.35		2	>
	32.15	<	2	>
Ps	5.1		2	
	19.3	<	2	
	33.4		2	
	39.2		2	
	55.21	<	2	
	64.3		2	
Prov	4.20		2	>
	8.6	<	2	
Ecc	1.1		2	
	12.10		2	
Is	6.5		2	>
	36.5		2	>

WORD (1)(cont.)

Is	44.25	<	2	
	53.7		2	
	55.10		2	
Jer	1.9		2	
	9.8	<	2	
	15.16	<	2	
	36.8		2	
Ezek	22.14		2	
Dan	4.31		2	>
Mt	7.24	<	2	>
	12.36		2	
	15.8		2	
Mk	7.6		2	
	13.11		2	>
	14.39	<	2	>
Lk	1.22		2	
	4.22	<	2	>
	6.47	<	2	
	8.11		2	
	19.22	<	2	
	21.15		2	
Jn	1.38		2	
	6.63	<	2	
	8.47		2	
	17.6		2	>
	18.32	<	2	>
Acts	6.2		2	>
	8.14	<	2	>
	11.1		2	>
	14.9	<	2	>
	17.8	<	2	>
	18.11	<	2	>
	20.1	<	2	
1 Cor	4.13		2	
1 Tim	4.5		2	
	6.3		2	
1 Pet	3.1	<	2	
1 Jn	1.6		2	>
	2.5	<	2	>
Jude	9		2	
Rev	1.3		2	

WORD (2) [JESUS]

Jn	1.1		5	

WORLD

Jn	17.5	<	15	>
	16.8	<	8	>
1 Jn	4.3	<	8	>
Dan	4.1		7	
Ecc	9.3	<	6	
Jn	1.1		6	
	12.19	<	6	>
	14.17	<	6	>
1 Cor	1.20		6	>
	3.1	<	6	>
1 Jn	2.15		6	>
Jer	51.7	<	5	

WORLD (cont.)

Jn	15.18	<	5	>
1 Cor	2.6	<	5	>
Job	38.4	<	4	>
Ecc	1.4		4	>
	8.9		4	>
Is	24.4	<	4	>
Jn	3.12		4	>
	8.12	<	4	>
Eph	1.3		4	>
1 Jn	5.4	<	4	
Gen	6.1		3	>
Ecc	4.1	<	3	>
Is	14.7		3	
Ezek	30.7	<	3	>
Zech	1.11		3	
Mt	24.14		3	>
Mk	13.19		3	>
Jn	6.14		3	>
	9.5	<	3	
	18.36	<	3	
Eph	2.2	<	3	>
2 Pet	2.5	<	3	>
Rev	17.2	<	3	>
	18.3	<	3	
Gen	10.8		2	>
Ex	9.14		2	
1 Sam	2.8		2	
2 Sam	7.9		2	
1 Kgs	8.43		2	
2 Kgs	19.15		2	
1 Chr	1.10		2	
	16.14		2	>
	17.8	<	2	
Ps	8.1		2	>
	33.8		2	
	46.9		2	>
	47.2	<	2	>
	65.5		2	
	82.5		2	
	96.1		2	>
Prov	8.23		2	
Ecc	3.1	<	2	>
	5.13	<	2	>
	6.1	<	2	
Is	18.2		2	>
	25.6	<	2	
	37.16		2	>
	40.21		2	
	45.6		2	
Jer	10.10		2	
	15.4		2	
Ezek	32.4	<	2	
Hab	2.8	<	2	
Zeph	3.19	<	2	
Mt	13.35		2	
Lk	12.30	<	2	
Jn	7.4	<	2	>
	11.9	<	2	>
	13.1	<	2	>
Acts	17.24		2	
Rom	1.8		2	
	3.6		2	>
	5.12	<	2	
	9.17		2	
1 Cor	4.9	<	2	>
	6.2	<	2	>
2 Cor	10.3		2	
Col	1.6		2	>
1 Tim	6.7		2	
Heb	2.5	<	2	
	9.11		2	
	11.7	<	2	
Jas	1.1		2	>
	3.6	<	2	>
	4.4	<	2	
2 Pet	3.4	<	2	
1 Jn	3.1	<	2	>

WORLD OF THE DEAD

Ezek	32.18	<	8	
	31.14		6	>
Job	33.22		3	
Is	14.9		3	
Num	16.30		2	
Job	17.13		2	
Is	28.15		2	
	38.10		2	
Ezek	26.20		2	
Hos	13.14		2	
Acts	2.27		2	
Rev	5.3		2	
	20.13		2	

WORRY

Mt	6.25		6	
Ecc	5.3		4	
Lk	12.11		4	
Ps	37.1		3	
Is	32.9		3	
1 Sam	9.5		2	
Ecc	2.22	<	2	
Dan	2.1		2	
Lk	21.14		2	
Jn	14.1		2	
Gal	4.11		2	

WORSHIP (1) (OF GOD)

Lev	23.2		11	
Jn	4.20		8	
2 Chr	29.11		7	>
Ex	10.3		6	
1 Kgs	8.16		6	>
2 Kgs	17.25		6	>
2 Chr	6.5	<	6	>
Deut	12.4		5	>
1 Chr	16.4	<	5	

WORSHIP (1)(cont.)

1 Chr	23.13	<	5	
Ezek	46.2		5	
1 Cor	11.4		5	
Num	29.1		4	
1 Kgs	18.3		4	
2 Chr	33.4	<	4	>
Zech	14.9		4	
Heb	9.1		4	
Gen	24.26		3	
Ex	12.16		3	
	23.15		3	>
Num	28.18		3	>
Josh	22.19		3	
1 Sam	1.3		3	
	15.25		3	
1 Chr	25.1		3	
2 Chr	7.3	<	3	
	15.12		3	
	20.9		3	
	30.8	<	3	>
Neh	9.3	<	3	
Job	1.1		3	>
Ps	22.23		3	
Mt	2.2		3	
Acts	10.2		3	
	13.16		3	
	17.4	<	3	>
1 Cor	14.19		3	
Ex	4.23	<	2	
	8.1	<	2	>
	9.1	<	2	
	19.10	<	2	>
	20.3	<	2	
	34.8		2	>
Deut	10.12		2	
	16.8		2	
Judg	2.12		2	
	10.6		2	
1 Sam	7.3		2	
1 Kgs	5.3		2	
	9.3	<	2	
2 Kgs	21.4		2	
2 Chr	1.5		2	>
	2.1	<	2	
Ezra	6.12		2	
Ps	69.6		2	
	99.5		2	
	105.3		2	
Is	19.21	<	2	
	58.2	<	2	>
	65.10		2	>
Jer	7.1		2	
Lam	2.6	<	2	
Zech	8.21		2	
Mt	6.2		2	
	28.9		2	
Acts	9.14	<	2	
	18.7	<	2	
	24.11		2	
Rev	11.1		2	
	19.4		2	
	22.3		2	

WORSHIP (2) (OF OTHER GODS)

Dan	3.5		10	
2 Kgs	10.19		8	
	17.7		8	
Deut	12.2	<	7	>
1 Kgs	11.4		6	>
2 Kgs	23.4		6	
Deut	13.2	<	5	
2 Chr	33.3		5	>
Is	44.9		5	
Rev	13.4		5	>
Ex	34.14		4	
Num	25.2		4	
Judg	2.3		4	>
2 Kgs	21.3		4	
Is	57.5		4	
Jer	2.5	<	4	>
Ex	20.3		3	
Deut	4.3		3	>
	31.16	<	3	
Josh	24.2	<	3	
Judg	10.6		3	
1 Kgs	14.9		3	
2 Chr	25.14	<	3	
	34.4	<	3	
Ps	106.19		3	
Jer	3.9	<	3	
Ezek	8.10		3	
	16.24		3	
	18.6		3	
	20.16		3	>
Zeph	1.4		3	
Ex	23.24		2	
	32.8		2	
Lev	19.4	<	2	>
	20.2	<	2	
Deut	5.7	<	2	>
	6.14	<	2	>
	7.4	<	2	>
	11.16		2	>
	28.14	<	2	>
	29.18	<	2	>
Josh	23.7		2	>
Judg	3.6	<	2	
	8.27		2	
1 Kgs	9.6		2	
	18.18		2	
2 Chr	7.19		2	
	24.7		2	>
	28.4		2	
Is	10.10		2	
	46.1		2	

WORSHIP (2)(cont.)

Is	66.3	<	2	
Jer	7.6		2	>
	8.2	<	2	>
	25.6		2	
Ezek	23.7	<	2	
	43.7		2	>
	44.10	<	2	
Hos	4.10		2	
	8.5		2	>
	10.1		2	
	12.11		2	>
	13.1	<	2	
Acts	7.42		2	
Rom	1.23		2	
1 Cor	5.10		2	>
	10.7		2	
Col	2.18		2	
Rev	14.9	<	2	
	19.10		2	>
	22.8	<	2	

WORTHLESS

Mal	1.7		3	
Job	30.1		2	
Jer	2.5		2	
	10.3		2	
Zech	11.15		2	
Mt	5.13		2	
1 Pet	2.4	<	2	

WORTHY

Rev	5.2	<	4	
2 Thes	1.5		2	

WRONG

1 Sam	24.11		5	>
Ps	119.3		4	
Mt	6.12	<	4	
Jn	16.8		4	
Gen	20.5		3	
1 Sam	19.4		3	>
Ps	32.1		3	
Prov	10.17		3	>
	28.21		3	

WRONG (cont.)

Dan	6.4		3	
Zeph	3.5		3	
Lk	11.4		3	
Acts	25.5		3	
Rom	3.5	<	3	>
2 Cor	7.2	<	3	
Gen	50.17		2	
Num	5.6		2	
Judg	11.27		2	
1 Sam	25.28	<	2	>
1 Kgs	21.20		2	
Job	33.9	<	2	>
	34.6	<	2	>
Ps	92.7		2	
Prov	2.12		2	>
	17.9		2	
	20.22	<	2	
Ecc	10.2		2	
Is	59.11		2	
Dan	9.5		2	
Hab	1.3		2	
Mal	2.6	<	2	

WRONG (cont.)

Mt	12.10		2	
Mk	3.2		2	
	12.24	<	2	
1 Cor	6.7		2	
Tit	3.3		2	
Heb	8.7		2	>

Y

YEAST

Ex	12.8		7	>
1 Cor	5.6		5	
Lev	2.4		4	
Deut	16.3		4	
Mt	16.6		3	
Ex	13.7	<	2	
	23.15		2	
Lev	7.12	<	2	
	23.6		2	

Word Index

This index lists words which appear too frequently or infrequently to make a useful chain through the Bible. It also lists some of the most significant words included in the chains but excluded from the index of *Topical Keywords* (because they never appear frequently in any chapter). These words are printed in **bold**. For each word in the index, each occurrence in the *Good News Bible* is listed by book, chapter and verse. When words occur frequently in a chapter, the number of occurrences in the chapter is given alongside the first reference, rather than including a full list, e.g. **CHARGE** (1) Gen 24.2 x 2.

If the word has more than one meaning (e.g. **BARK**) you will find a different list for each meaning. These are marked with numbers after the word e.g. **BARK** (1), **BARK** (2). Sometimes you may find a (1) but no (2), or vice versa. This is because the numbering links directly with the *Concordance to the Good News Bible*, so that readers can cross-refer, but not all the meanings of that word have been included in this, much smaller, index.

There are some words whose references it was not useful to include either because of their frequency of occurrence (LORD occurs over 6,000 times) or because they were not thought to be useful for study and reference (e.g. "go", "come"). Such words, listed at the end of the *Theme Index* can be found in the *Concordance to the Good News Bible*.

NAG (cont.)
Prov 27.15

NAIL (2) [BODY]
Deut 21.12
Dan 4.33

NAMELY
Acts 24.15
Gal 3.16

NAP
2 Sam 11.2
Prov 6.10
24.33

NARD
Song 4.13
Mk 14.3
Jn 12.3

NARROW
Num 22.24
22.26
1 Kgs 6.4
Is 28.20
Ezek 42.5
Mt 7.13
7.14
Lk 13.24

NATURAL
Lev 7.24
17.15
22.8
Num 16.29
19.16
Deut 14.21
1 Sam 26.10
1 Kgs 2.6
Ps 109.18
Prov 22.15
Ecc 10.2
Jer 31.36
Ezek 4.14
44.31
Jn 1.13
8.44
11.13
Rom 1.26
1.27
3.5
6.12
6.19
11.21
Gal 6.8
Eph 2.3
Jude 19

NECKLACE
Ex 35.22
Num 31.50
Judg 8.26
Ps 73.6
Prov 1.9
Song 4.4
4.9
Ezek 16.11

NEEDLE
Mt 19.24
Mk 10.25
Lk 18.25

NEIGH
Jer 8.16
50.11

NEIGHBOURHOOD
Ruth 4.17
Mt 2.16
Mk 7.31

NEPHEW
Gen 12.5
14.12
14.14
14.16
29.13
2 Chr 22.8

NERVE
Deut 20.8

NEW-BORN
Ex 1.22
Deut 28.56
Jer 14.5
1 Pet 2.2

NEXT-DOOR
Ex 12.4

NICE
1 Sam 17.42
Is 44.16
1 Cor 12.23

NIGHTMARE
Job 4.13
7.14

NOD
Mt 25.5

NORMAL
Gen 50.3
Ex 14.27

NORMAL (cont.)
Lev 11.34
14.32
1 Cor 7.5
10.13

NORTH-EAST
Deut 2.8
Josh 17.10
Neh 3.31

NORTH-EASTER
Acts 27.14

NORTH-WEST
Num 34.4
Josh 17.10
Ezek 47.19
48.28
Acts 27.12

NOSTRILS
Gen 2.7
2 Sam 22.9
Ps 18.8
Amos 4.10

NOTE (1) [NOTICE]
2 Sam 3.36
Lam 1.14
Ezek 44.5
47.6
Dan 9.25
2 Thes 3.14

NOTE (2) [MUSIC]
Josh 6.5
1 Cor 14.7

NOTICE (1) [PERCEIVE]
Gen 31.5
Ex 2.5
Judg 14.1
19.17
Ruth 3.4
1 Sam 18.15
20.6
20.18
20.19
2 Sam 12.19
13.28
16.12
17.19
1 Kgs 11.28
21.29
Job 1.8

NOTICE (1) (cont.)
Job 2.3
Ps 10.14
28.5
37.37
48.13
94.7
106.44
144.3
Prov 7.7
Ecc 3.16
4.7
6.1
Is 53.2
58.3
Jer 33.24
Ezek 12.3
Mt 8.18
14.30
23.5
Mk 7.2
9.25
10.14
12.34
Lk 11.38
14.7
22.58
Acts 4.29
10.31
17.16
26.26
27.39
1 Cor 16.18

NOTICE (2) [WRITTEN]
Mt 5.31
19.7
27.37
Mk 10.4
15.26
Jn 19.19
19.20
Acts 21.26

NOURISH
Job 21.23
Col 2.19

NOWADAYS
1 Sam 25.10
Acts 8.26

NUISANCE
Acts 24.5

NUT
Gen 43.11

Name Index

This index includes references to all biblical names as they appear in the *Good News Bible*.

For some people who appear very frequently, the index begins with references to incidents in the person's life, based on the sections in the GNB. Other references to that person follow, listed in biblical order in the normal way.

Rather than listing several references in one chapter, the number of times the name occurs in that chapter is given after the first reference, e.g. **Aaron** Lev 6.14 x 4. This helps you to see clearly where important people appear frequently in the biblical text.

Some important people and places also have a brief description in their index entry. Where the same name is used for two or more different people or places, they are distinguished by numbers in round brackets following the name.

If the name of a place features in the *Maps* in this book, the number of the map is also listed.

ANAKIM (cont.)
Josh 14.12 ×2
15.13 ×2
21.11
Judg 1.20

ANAM
Gen 10.13
1 Chr 1.11

ANAMMELECH
2 Kgs 17.31

ANAN
Neh 10.14

ANANI
1 Chr 3.24

ANANIAH (1)
Neh 3.23

ANANIAH (2)
Neh 11.32

ANANIAS (1)
Early Christian who kept part of the money obtained by selling his property.
Acts 5. 1 ×3

ANANIAS (2)
Christian in Damascus who supported Paul at the time of his conversion.
Acts 9.10 ×5
22.12

ANANIAS (3)
High Priest.
Acts 23. 2
24. 1

ANATH
Judg 3.31
5. 6

ANATHOTH (1) Map 5
Josh 21.18
2 Sam 23.24
1 Kgs 2.26
1 Chr 6.60
11.26
12. 3
27. 2
Ezra 2.21
Neh 7.26
11.32
Is 10.30
Jer 1. 1
11.21 ×2
29.27
32. 7

ANATHOTH (2)
1 Chr 7. 8

ANATHOTH (3)
Neh 10.14

ANDREW
One of Jesus' first disciples, and Simon Peter's brother.
Mt 4.18
10. 2
Mk 1.16 ×2
3.18
13. 3
Lk 6.14
Jn 1.40 ×2
6. 8
12.22
Acts 1.13

ANDRONICUS
Rom 16. 7

ANEM
1 Chr 6.73

ANER (1)
Gen 14.13 ×2

ANER (2)
1 Chr 6.70

ANIAM
1 Chr 7.19

ANIM
Josh 15.50

ANNA
Lk 2.36

ANNAS
Lk 3. 2
Jn 18.13 ×2
Acts 4. 6

ANTHOTHIJAH
1 Chr 8.24

ANTIOCH IN PISIDIA
Map 8,9
A city in Asia Minor.
Acts 13.14 ×2
14.19 ×2
2 Tim 3.11

ANTIOCH IN SYRIA
Map 8,9,10
Large city in Syria and an early stronghold of Christianity, the starting point of Paul's missionary journeys.
Acts 6. 5
11.19 ×6
13. 1
14.26 ×2
15. 1 ×6
18.22
Gal 2.11

ANTIPAS
Rev 2.13

ANTIPATRIS
Acts 23.31

ANUB
1 Chr 4. 8

APELLES
Rom 16.10

APHEK (1)
Josh 12.18
1 Sam 4. 1
29. 1

APHEK (2) Map 5
1 Kgs 20.26 ×2
2 Kgs 13.17

APHEK (3)
Josh 13. 4
19.30
Judg 1.31

APHEKAH
Josh 15.53

APHIAH
1 Sam 9. 1

APIS
Jer 46.15

APOLLONIA Map 9
Acts 17. 1

APOLLOS
Jew who was a native of Alexandria and who preached in Ephesus and Corinth.
Acts 18.24 ×2
19. 1
1 Cor 1.12
3. 4 ×4
4. 6
16.12
Tit 3.13

APOLLYON
Rev 9.11

APPAIM
1 Chr 2.30 ×2

APPHIA
Phlm 2

APPIUS
Acts 28.15

AQABA Map 2
A northward extension of what is now known as the Red Sea.
Ex 23.31
Num 14.25
21. 4
Deut 1.40
2. 1
Judg 11.16
1 Kgs 9.26
2 Chr 8.17
Jer 49.21

AQUILA
Acts 18. 2 ×4
Rom 16. 3
1 Cor 16.19
2 Tim 4.19

AR
Num 21.15 ×2
22.36
Deut 2. 9 ×4
Is 15. 1

ARA
1 Chr 7.38

ARAB (1) Map 1
Inhabitant of Arabia or desert area of Palestine.
1 Kgs 10.15
2 Chr 9.14
17.11
21.16
22. 1
26. 7
Neh 2.19
4. 7
Is 13.20
21.13 ×2
Jer 3. 2
25.19
Ezek 27.21
30. 5
Acts 2.11
Gal 1.17
4.25

ARAB (2)
Josh 15.52
2 Sam 23.24

ARABAH
see also Beth Arabah, (Jordan) Valley

ARABAH (1)
2 Sam 23.24

ARABAH (2)
Amos 6.14

ARAD (1) Map 2
1 Chr 8.15

ARAD (2)
Num 21. 1
33.40
Josh 12.14
Judg 1.16

ARAH (1)
1 Chr 7.39

ARAH (2)
Ezra 2. 3
Neh 7. 8

ARAH (3)
Neh 6.18

SIMEON (1) (cont.)
1 Chr 27.16
2 Chr 15. 9
34. 6
Ezek 48.23 ×2
Rev 7. 5

SIMEON (2)
An ancestor of Jesus.
Lk 3.30

SIMEON (3)
An old man who greeted the baby Jesus in the Temple.
Lk 2.25 ×5

SIMEON (4)
Simeon the Black, a leader of the church in Antioch.
Acts 13. 1

SIMON (1)
see Peter

SIMON (2)
Simon the Patriot, one of the twelve apostles.
Mt 10. 4
Mk 3.18
Lk 6.15
Acts 1.13

SIMON (3)
Jesus' brother.
Mt 13.55
Mk 6. 3

SIMON (4)
Simon of Cyrene.
Mt 27.32
Mk 15.21 ×2
Lk 23.26

SIMON (5)
Simon Iscariot, Judas' father.
Jn 6.71
13. 2 ×2

SIMON (6)
Simon of Bethany.
Mt 26. 6
Mk 14. 3

SIMON (7)
Simon the Pharisee.
Lk 7.40 ×3

SIMON (8)
Simon the tanner.
Acts 9.43
10. 6 ×2

SIMON (9)
Simon the magician.
Acts 8. 9 ×4

SIMON PETER
see Peter

SIN (2) Map 2
see also Pelusium
Ex 16. 1
17. 1
Num 33.11

SINAI Map 1,2
Mountain between Egypt and Palestine where Moses received the Law.
Ex 3. 1
16. 1
17. 6
19. 1 ×5
24.15
31.18
33. 6
34. 2 ×4
Lev 7.38
25. 1
26.46
27.34
Num 1. 1 ×2
3. 1 ×3
9. 1 ×2
10.12 ×2
26.64
28. 6
33.15
Deut 1. 2 ×4
4.10 ×2
5. 2
9. 8
18.16
29. 1
33. 2
Judg 5. 5
1 Kgs 8. 9
19. 8
2 Chr 5.10
Neh 9.13
Ps 68. 8 ×2
106.19
Ezek 20.36
Mal 4. 4
Acts 7.30 ×2
Gal 4.24 ×2
Heb 12.18

SINITES
Gen 10.17
1 Chr 1.15

SIPHMOTH
1 Sam 30.28

SIPPAI
1 Chr 20. 4

SIRAH
2 Sam 3.26

SIRION
see also (Mount) Hermon, Senir
Deut 3. 9

SIRION (cont.)
Deut 4.48

SISERA (1)
Canaanite military leader defeated by Israel.
Judg 4. 2 ×13
5.20 ×5
1 Sam 12. 9
Ps 83. 9

SISERA (2)
Ezra 2.43
Neh 7.46

SISMAI
1 Chr 2.40

SITHRI
Ex 6.22

SIVAN
Third month of the Hebrew calendar.
Esth 8. 9

SMYRNA
Rev 1.11
2. 8

SO
2 Kgs 17. 4

SOCO (1)
2 Chr 11. 7
28.18

SOCO (2)
1 Chr 4.17

SOCOH (1) Map 4
Josh 15.35
1 Sam 17. 1 ×2
1 Kgs 4.10

SOCOH (2)
Josh 15.48

SODI
Num 13. 3

SODOM
City near the Dead Sea destroyed by fire in Abraham's time.
Gen 10.19
13.10 ×2
14. 2 ×7
18.16 ×4
19. 1 ×6
Deut 29.23
32.32
Is 1. 9 ×2
3. 9
13.19
Jer 23.14
49.18
50.40
Lam 4. 6
Ezek 16.46 ×4

SODOM (cont.)
Amos 4.11
Zeph 2. 9
Mt 10.15
11.23 ×2
Lk 10.12
17.29
Rom 9.29
2 Pet 2. 6
Jude 7
Rev 11. 8

SOLOMON
David's son, who succeeded him as king of Israel and built the Temple.
2 Sam 5.1-16
12.24-25
1 Kgs 1.5-10
11-53
2.1-9
10-12
13-25
26-35
36-46
3.1-15
16-28
4.1-19
20-34
5.1-18
6.1-14
6.15-38
7.1-12
13-14
40-51
8.1-13
14-21
22-53
54-61
62-66
9.1-9
10-14
15-28
10.1-13
14-29
11.1-13
14-25
26-40
41-43
1 Chr 3.1-9
10-16
6.1-15
14.1-7
18.1-17
22.2—23.1
28.1-21
29.1-9
10-25
26-30
2 Chr 1.1-12
13-17
2.1-16
2.17—3.14
4.1—5.1
5.2-10
6.1-11
12-42

ZEDEKIAH (2)
1 Kgs 22.11 ×2
2 Chr 18.10 ×2

ZEDEKIAH (3)
Jer 29.21 ×2

ZEDEKIAH (4)
Jer 36.12

ZEDEKIAH (5)
Neh 10. 1

ZEDEKIAH (6)
1 Chr 3.16

ZEEB
Judg 7.25 ×2
8. 3
Ps 83.11

ZELA
Josh 18.28
2 Sam 21.14

ZELEK
2 Sam 23.24
1 Chr 11.26

ZELOPHEHAD
Num 26.33
27. 1 ×2
36. 2 ×4
Josh 17. 3
1 Chr 7.15

ZELZAH
1 Sam 10. 2

ZEMARAIM (1)
Josh 18.22

ZEMARAIM (2)
2 Chr 13. 4

ZEMARITES
Gen 10.18
1 Chr 1.16

ZEMIRAH
1 Chr 7. 8

ZENAN
Josh 15.37

ZENAS
Tit 3.13

ZEPHANIAH (1)
2 Kgs 25.18
Jer 21. 1
29.24 ×3
37. 3
52.24

ZEPHANIAH (2)
Zeph 1. 1 ×2

ZEPHANIAH (3)
Zech 6.10

ZEPHANIAH (4)
1 Chr 6.36

ZEPHATH
Judg 1.17

ZEPHATHAH
2 Chr 14.10

ZEPHI
1 Chr 1.36

ZEPHO
Gen 36.10 ×2

ZEPHON
see also Baal Zephon
Gen 46.16
Num 26.15

ZER
Josh 19.35

ZERAH (1)
Judah's son and the clan descended from him.
Gen 38.30
46.12
Num 26.19
Josh 7. 1 ×3
22.20
1 Chr 2. 4 ×3
9. 4
27. 2 ×2
Neh 11.24
Mt 1. 2

ZERAH (2)
Gen 36.10 ×2
1 Chr 1.37

ZERAH (3)
Gen 36.31
1 Chr 1.43

ZERAH (4)
Num 26.13
1 Chr 4.24

ZERAH (5)
1 Chr 6.21

ZERAH (6)
1 Chr 6.41

ZERAH (7)
2 Chr 14. 9

ZERAHIAH (1)
1 Chr 6. 6 ×2
Ezra 7. 4

ZERAHIAH (2)
Ezra 8. 2

ZERED
Num 21.12
Deut 2.13

ZEREDAH (1)
Perhaps the same as (2).
1 Kgs 11.26

ZEREDAH (2)
see also Zarethan
2 Chr 4.17

ZERESH
Esth 5.10

ZERETH
1 Chr 4. 7

ZERETH-SHAHAR
Josh 13.19

ZERI
1 Chr 25. 3 ×2

ZEROR
1 Sam 9. 1

ZERUAH
1 Kgs 11.26

ZERUBBABEL
One of the leaders of those who returned from exile (to Jerusalem).
1 Chr 3.19 ×2
Ezra 2. 2
3. 2 ×2
4. 2 ×2
5. 2
Neh 7. 7
12. 1 ×2
Hag 1. 1 ×3
2. 2 ×3
Zech 4. 6 ×3
Mt 1.12
Lk 3.27

ZERUIAH
Mother of Abishai, Joab and Asahel.
1 Sam 26. 6
2 Sam 2.13 ×2
3.39
8.16
16. 9
17.25
19.21
21.17
23.18
1 Kgs 1. 7
1 Chr 2.16 ×2
11. 6
18.12
26.28
27.24

ZETHAM
1 Chr 23. 8
26.22

ZETHAN
1 Chr 7.10

ZETHAR
Esth 1.10

ZEUS
Acts 14.12 ×2

ZIA
1 Chr 5.13

ZIBA
Saul's servant, later Mephibosheth's.
2 Sam 9. 2 ×8
16. 1 ×5
19.17 ×3

ZIBEON
Gen 36. 2 ×5
1 Chr 1.38

ZIBIA
1 Chr 8. 8

ZIBIAH
2 Kgs 12. 1
2 Chr 24. 1

ZICHRI (1)
1 Chr 27.16

ZICHRI (2)
2 Chr 17.16

ZICHRI (3)
Ex 6.21

ZICHRI (4)
1 Chr 26.25

ZICHRI (5)
see also Zabdi (4)
1 Chr 9.14

ZICHRI (6)
Neh 12.12

ZICHRI (7)
1 Chr 8.19

ZICHRI (8)
1 Chr 8.23

ZICHRI (9)
1 Chr 8.27

ZICHRI (10)
Neh 11. 9

ZICHRI (11)
2 Chr 23. 1

ZICHRI (12)
2 Chr 28. 7

ZIDDIM
Josh 19.35

ZIHA
Ezra 2.43
Neh 7.46
11.21

Theme Index

This index is a complete list of all the words referenced in this book, in the *Chain References*, in the *Topical Keywords* and in the *Word Index*. It is therefore a key to the whole book. At the end of this index is a list of words which are in the *Concordance to the Good News Bible* but are not included in the *Chain Reference Bible*.

Words in capitals are theme headings, and grouped below each is a list of words related to that heading.

If the word you look up is not a theme heading, you will be directed to one or more theme headings under which this word appears.

If the word is included in the *Chain References* in the Bible margins the reference for its first occurrence in the Old Testament and New Testament is given.

Words with more than one meaning are marked with numbers after the word, e.g. **BARK** (1), **BARK** (2). Sometimes you may find a (1) but no (2), or vice versa. This is because the numbering links directly with the *Concordance to the Good News Bible*, so that readers can cross-refer, but not all the meanings of that word have been included in this, much smaller, index.

W alongside a word means that it also appears in the *Word Index*.

T alongside a word means that it also appears in the index of *Topical Keywords*.

The number of times each word occurs in the *Good News Bible* is given in square brackets (omitting duplicate references when the word is repeated in the same phrase).

The titles of well-known *Bible passages, parables and miracles* with their references are included in this index.

If you wish to make a full study of a theme, you can look up references to the most appropriate words listed under the theme heading.

L

Labour (2) *see* BIRTH

LACK
abstain W [6]
drought W [8]
EMPTY
famine T [56]
Gen 12.10; Mt 24.7
fast (2) T [55]
Lev 16.29; Mt 6.16
FOOD
go without W [7]
hunger T [102]
Gen 25.29; Mt 4.2
need T [254]
Gen 33.11; Mt 4.4
POOR

Lady *see* PERSON
Lamb *see* ANIMAL
see JESUS
see MEAT

LAMENT
gloom W [13]
1 Kgs 21.27; Mk 10.22
grief T [70]
Josh 7.6; Mt 26.37
lament W [5]
misery W [31]
Gen 26.35; Jas 5.1
mourn T [145]
Gen 23.2; Mt 5.4
PAIN
remorse W [1]
REPENT
sad T [63]
1 Sam 1.8; Mt 6.16
sigh W [3]
sob W [3]
sorrow T [60]
Gen 37.29; Mt 26.38
sorry W [25]
Gen 6.6; Mt 15.32
tear (2) W [40]
Judg 14.16; Lk 7.38
wail W [22]
Ezra 3.12; Mk 5.38
weep T [86]
Gen 35.8; Mt 2.18
whining W [2]
WORRY

Lance *see* WEAPON
Landowner *see* MASTER
Landslide *see* DISASTER
Lane *see* ROAD

LANGUAGE
Aramaic W [4]

LANGUAGE (cont.)
COMMUNICATE
Eli (2) W [1]
Eloi W [1]
Ephphatha W [1]
Hebrew T [55]
Gen 10.21; Jn 5.2
interpret W [14]
Gen 40.8; Mt 16.3
language W [49]
Latin W [1]
Marana tha W [1]
Talitha koum W [1]
tongue W [51]
translate W [4]

Lantern *see* LIGHT
Lap (1) *see* BODY
Lap (2) *see* DRINK
Lash *see* PUNISH
see TIE
Last (1) *see* CONSTANT
Last (2) *see* END
Late (2) *see* DIE
Latest *see* NEW
Latin *see* LANGUAGE
Latrine *see* DEFILE
Lattice *see* BUILDING
Launch *see* WAR
Laurel-tree *see* TREE

LAW
COMMAND
commandment T [69]
Ex 25.16; Mt 5.19
decree W [8]
JUDAISM
JUDGEMENT
law T [589]
Gen 26.5; Mt 5.17
lawful W [1]
lawgiver W [1]
lawyer W [2]
ordinance W [1]
regulation T [73]
Ex 12.43; Heb 7.16

Law-breaker *see* CRIMINAL
Lawful *see* CORRECT
see LAW
Lawgiver *see* LAW
Lawless *see* CRIMINAL
Lawsuit *see* JUDGEMENT
Lawyer *see* LAW
Lay (2) *see* BIRD
see BREED
Layer *see* BUILDING
see PIECE
Laymen *see* PERSON
Lead (2) *see* METAL
Leading *see* STATUS
Leak *see* HOLE

Leak *see* WATER
Lean *see* HELP
Leap *see* MOVE
Learn *see* KNOW
see PERCEIVE

LEARNING
CLEVER
disciple T [347]
Is 8.16; Mt 5.1
educate W [8]
Epicurean W [1]
expert W [10]
follower T [47]
Num 16.5; Mt 5.11
IGNORANT
insight W [20]
Gen 41.33; Eph 1.8
intelligent W [28]
1 Sam 25.2; Mt 15.16
KNOW
knowledge T [101]
Gen 2.9; Mt 13.11
lesson W [13]
Ps 2.10; Mt 24.32
philosopher W [8]
pupil W [4]
scholar T [13]
1 Chr 27.32; 1 Cor 1.19
scribes W [1]
Stoic W [1]
study W [22]
Ex 13.9; Mt 2.1
teach T [417]
Ex 18.20; Mt 4.19
understand T [209]
Gen 3.7; Mt 13.13
wisdom T [193]
Gen 41.33; Mt 11.19
wise T [211]
Gen 3.6; Mt 7.24
WRITE

Least *see* SIZE
see USELESS
Leaven *see* BREAD
Lecture hall *see* BUILDING
Ledge *see* BUILDING
Leech *see* ANIMAL
see SELFISH
Leeks *see* VEGETABLES
Legend *see* DECEIVE
Leopard *see* ANIMAL
Lesson *see* LEARNING
Let *see* LOAN
Letter (1) *see* GRAMMAR
Letter (2) *see* WRITE

LEVEL
calm W [26]
Neh 8.11; Mt 8.26
even W [5]

THEME INDEX

Listed below are words which are in the *Concordance to the Good News Bible* but are not included in the *Chain Reference Bible*, either because of their frequency of occurrence (LORD occurs over 6,000 times) or because they were not thought to be useful for study and reference (e.g. "go", "come").

ABLE
ACACIA-WOOD
ACCIDENT
ACCOMPANY
ACCOUNT
ADD
ADMINISTER
ADVANCE
ADVISER
AGAINST
AGE (2)
AID
AIR
ALARM
ALL
ALLOW
ALLY
ALOUD
ALWAYS
AMOUNT
ANCESTOR
ANIMAL
ANSWER
APPEAL
APPEAR
APPLY
APPOINT
APPROACH
AREA
ARM (1)
ARM (2)
ARMY
AROUSE
ARRANGE
ARRIVE
ARROW
ARTICLE
ASHORE
ASK
ASLEEP
ASSASSIN
ASSEMBLE
ASSIGN
ASSIST
ASSOCIATE
AT ONCE
ATTACH
ATTACK
ATTENTION
AUTUMN
AVOID
AWAKE
BABY
BACK
BAG
BAKE
BANK (1)
BANNER
BAR (2)
BARE
BARLEY
BARN
BASE
BASIN
BASKET
BATH (1)
BATTER
BATTLE
BEAM
BEARD
BEAT
BEAUTY
BED (1)
BEGIN
BEHALF
BELONG
BELOW
BELT
BEND
BESIEGE
BETTER
BIG
BIRD
BITE
BLACK
BLAST
BLAZE
BLOSSOM
BLOW (1)
BLUE
BOAT
BODYGUARD
BOIL (1)
BOIL (2)
BONE
BORDER
BORN
BORROW
BOTHER
BOTTOM
BOUNDARY
BOW (1)
BOWL
BOX
BOY
BRANCH
BRAVE
BREAK
BREAK OUT
BREAST
BREAST-PIECE
BRICK
BRIGHT
BRING
BRING UP
BRONZE
BROOK
BROTHER
BUD
BUILD
BUILDING
BULL
BURN
BURY
BUSH
BUY
CAKE
CALF
CALL
CAMEL
CAMP
CANCEL
CAPABLE
CAPITAL (1)
CAPITAL (2)
CAPTAIN
CAPTURE
CAREFUL
CARPENTER
CARRY
CART
CARVE
CATAPULT
CATCH
CATTLE
CAUSE (1)
CAVALRY
CAVE
CEDAR
CENTIMETRE
CENTRE
CERTAIN (2)
CHAIN
CHARIOT
CHASE
CHEW
CHIEF
CHILD
CHILDLESS
CITIZEN
CITY
CLAN
CLAY
CLIFF
CLIMB
CLOAK
CLOSE (2)
CLOTH
CLOTHE
CLUB
COAL
COAST
COAT
COCK
COIN
COLD
COLLAPSE
COLLECT
COLOUR
COLT
COLUMN
COME
COMMANDER
COMMON
COMPANION
CONFUSE
CONTINUE
COOK
COPY
CORD
CORN
CORNER
CORPSE
COST
COUNT
COUNTRY
COUNTRYMAN
COUNTRYSIDE
COURT (2)
COURTYARD
COVER
COW
CRAFTSMAN
CROP (1)
CROSS (2)
CROW (2)
CROWD
CRUMBLE
CRUSH
CRY
CUB
CURTAIN
CUT
CYMBALS
DAILY
DAUGHTER
DAUGHTER-IN-LAW
DAY
DAYLIGHT
DEAL (2)
DECIDE
DECORATE
DEEP
DEER
DEFEAT
DEFECT
DELAY
DESCENDANT
DESCRIBE
DESERT (1)
DESERT (2)
DESIGN
DEW
DICTATE
DIE
DIFFERENT
DIG
DIP
DIRECTION
DISAPPEAR
DISCOVER
DISGUISE
DISH
DISTANCE
DISTRIBUTE
DISTRICT
DISTURB
DIVIDE
DO
DOG
DONKEY
DOOR
DOUBLE
DOUGH
DRAG
DRAW
DRESS
DRINK
DRIVE
DROP
DROWN
DRUNK
DRY
DYNASTY
EAGLE
EAR
EAR OF CORN
EARN
EARRINGS
EARTH
EAST
EASY
EDGE
EFFECT
EGG
EIGHT
ELDER (1)
ELEVEN
EMBROIDER
EMPEROR
EMPIRE
EMPTY
ENCLOSURE
END
ENGAGED
ENGRAVE
ENTER